1994

INDONESIA MALAYSIA & SINGAPORE HANDBOOK

SECOND EDITION

Editors **Joshua Eliot, Jane Bickersteth, Jonathan Miller and Georgina Matthews**
Cartographer **Sebastian Ballard**

"....where the gorgeous east with richest hand
show'rs on her kings barbaric pearl and gold"
Milton *Paradise lost: a poem in twelve books*

TRADE & TRAVEL

Trade & Travel Publications Limited
6 Riverside Court, Lower Bristol Road, Bath BA2 3DZ, England
Telephone 0225 469141 Fax 0225 469461

©Trade & Travel Publications Ltd., September 1993

ISBN 0 900751 49 5   ISSN 0968-0942

CIP DATA: A catalogue record for this book is available from the British Library

In North America, published by

PASSPORT BOOKS
a division of NTC *Publishing Group*

4255 West Touhy Avenue
Lincolnwood (Chicago), Illinois 60646-1975, USA

ISBN 0-8442-9976-6

Library of Congress Catalog Card Number   93-84184

Passport Books and colophon are registered trademarks of NTC Publishing Group

**WARNING: While every endeavour is made to ensure that the facts
printed in this book are correct at the time of going to press, travellers
are cautioned to obtain authoritative advice from consulates, airlines,
etc, concerning current travel and visa requirements and conditions
before embarking. The publishers cannot accept legal responsibility for
errors, however caused, that are printed in this book.**

Cover illustration by Suzanne Evans

Printed and bound in Great Britain by Clays Ltd., Bungay, Suffolk

CONTENTS

PREFACE 5

HOW TO USE THIS HANDBOOK 7

INTRODUCTION AND HINTS 11

Travel to and within island
  Southeast Asia 11
Documentation and security 13
Etiquette and language 16
Accommodation, food and
  drink 16
Internal travel 18
General advice 19
Health information 21

SOUTHEAST ASIA: INTRODUCTION 28

Mainland & island
  Southeast Asia 28
Land & life 29
Southeast Asian history:
  pre-colonial 36
Colonial history 44
Modern Southeast Asia 47
Southeast Asia:
  suggested reading 49

MALAYSIA 51

Kuala Lumpur 91
North to Penang & Thailand 115
South from Kuala Lumpur 157
The Peninsula's East Coast 181
Borneo 222
Sarawak 230
Sabah 293
Information for visitors 344

SINGAPORE 367

Singapore places of interest 393
Around Singapore island 411
Services 421
Information for visitors 436

BRUNEI 457

Bandar Seri Begawan 475
Around Bandar Seri Begawan 481
Information for visitors 484

INDONESIA 490

Java 513
Jakarta 537
West Java 557
Central Java & Yogyakarta 587
East Java 638
Bali 666
Sumatra 731
Northern Sumatra 738
Southern Sumatra 772
Kalimantan 821
Sulawesi 857
West Nusa Tenggara, Lombok &
  Sumbawa 903
Lombok 904
Sumbawa 922
East Nusa Tenggara &
  East Timor 929
Komodo 931
Flores 933
Alor 948
Sumba 949
Timor 956
West Timor 957
Roti 961
Savu 962
East Timor 963
Maluku 971
Irian Jaya 989
Information for visitors 1003

INDEXES 1032

Glossary **1032**
Index **1038**
Index to maps **1048**
Index to tinted boxes **1050**
Index to advertisers **1055**

PREFACE

For this, the second edition of the *Indonesia, Malaysia and Singapore Handbook* we have extensively expanded and updated the section on the east coast of Peninsular Malaysia. In addition, the Singapore section has been considerably re-worked and revised. In Malaysia, the confrontation between the Sultans and the government over their immunity from prosecution, and more generally over their lavish lifestyles, resulted – in most people's view – in a victory for Prime Minister Mahathir Mohamad. Mahathir has become a figurehead among leaders in the developing world, daring to confront the West over such issues as environmentalism ('Green imperialism') and human rights (a 'luxury' which is 'not universal'). Regarding the Malaysia section, we would particularly like to thank Mr Hafiz Abdul Majid of Tourism Malaysia in Kuala Lumpur who helped beyond the call of duty, and Adrian Finn who gallantly assisted with the updating of the east coast section.

In Indonesia, an earthquake struck East Nusa Tenggara in December 1992 devastating the towns of Maumere and Ende on the island of Flores and literally submerging some smaller off-shore islands and their fishing communities. Although reconstruction is well underway, the after-effects are likely to persist for at least the next year. At the beginning of 1993, Suharto was elected for his fifth consecutive term as President of Indonesia and will need to deal with continuing rumblings over the East Timor issue – which remains closed to tourists – and calls for a switch in economic strategy. Although we have received assistance from many quarters, we are particularly grateful to Maria Hooper in Maumere for helping us with the updating of the Flores section in the wake of the earthquake.

We would also like to thank the following for their help in revising this edition: Frances B. Affandy of the Bandung Society for Heritage Conservation for information on Bandung's Art Deco architecture; Robert Welsh for his helpful faxes from Jakarta; Janet Krengel of Lloyds Bank for information on exchange rates; Jenny Barry for reading and commenting in detail on the Indonesia section; Mr Johari of Hertz Rent-a-Car in Johor Bahru; Paul Hewlett in Singapore; and Paul Blount for keeping us on our toes vis a vis the region's natural history. Other people who have provided information and assistance are acknowledged at the end of the relevant country sections.

The Editors
London

ABOUT THE EDITORS

Joshua Eliot has had a long-standing interest in Asia. He was born in Calcutta, grew up in Hong Kong, gained his PhD in Thai agricultural geography from the School of Oriental & African Studies, and now lectures on Southeast Asia at the University of Durham. He is the author of a book on the geography of the region and has also written well over 30 papers and articles on Southeast Asia. He has lived and conducted research in Thailand, Sumatra and Laos and has travelled extensively in the region over a period of more than 10 years. He speaks Thai, Lao and Indonesian.

Jane Bickersteth is an artist by training and has travelled widely in the region – particularly in Thailand and Indonesia – over a period of more than ten years. She spent a year in the region with her young son researching the first edition of this guide and has held exhibitions of work inspired by her travels in Southeast Asia.

Georgina Matthews is a professional guidebook editor. She has published books for Nicholson and Dorling Kindersley and has a particular interest in Burma, Laos and Cambodia. She has travelled to the region regularly and spent a year in the field researching the first edition of this guide.

Jonathan Miller is a journalist with the BBC World Service in London working on Dateline East Asia – an Asian current affairs programme. He was raised in Malaysia and Singapore and before joining the BBC was a foreign correspondent in the region contributing pieces for such newspapers and magazines as *The Economist*, the *Asian Wall Street Journal*, *South*, and the *Daily Telegraph*. He speaks Malay, knows Malaysia and Singapore intimately, and returns regularly to the region on assignment.

HOW TO USE THIS HANDBOOK

The *Indonesia, Malaysia & Singapore Handbook* encompasses the predominantly Muslim countries of Indonesia, Malaysia and Brunei, and the city-state of Singapore. The guide is the most up-to-date source of information for independent travellers to peninsular and island Southeast Asia, and provides detailed background sections to each of the countries. Like the other books in this series, the *Indonesia, Malaysia & Singapore Handbook* will be thoroughly updated each year.

Editorial logic This book is one of a pair of publications covering nine countries of Southeast Asia. These nine countries have been divided into an 'Island' volume (four countries) and a 'Mainland' volume (five countries), reflecting the cultural, natural and historical distinctiveness of the mainland vis à vis the islands.

The book begins with a short practical introduction, including a section on health care, followed by an overview of the Southeast Asian region. Thereafter, it is arranged according to country. Each country section opens with a substantial introduction to its geography, history, culture, politics and economics. Where aspects of, for example, religion or art apply to another country, these are cross-referenced. Following the country introduction, the capital city is covered, before continuing to cover the various regions. Generally, entries are town-focused, although in some cases national parks or prominent archaeological sights may have a separate entry to themselves. Throughout the region, road is the main mode of transport. However, where appropriate, information on air, rail and sea/river connections is also provided. At the end of each country entry is a section entitled 'Information for Visitors' covering such things as visa formalities, conduct, food and drink, and transport. Also in this section, for some countries, is a short list of useful words and phrases.

Cross-referencing, boxes, index and glossary With a book of over 1,000 pages, getting around the guide, let alone the countries, is important. To help link related themes, the book makes use of extensive cross-referencing. For example, a mention of shifting cultivation might be cross-referenced to a longer description of this type of agriculture. There are also 'boxes' scattered through the text which aim to provide more information on a particular subject – for example, the krisses of the Malay world, the ikat blankets of Sumba, or profiles of prominent people (like Sir Stamford Raffles).

There is also a full index, listing the town entries and major individual sights. The glossary at the back of the book provides short explanations of local terms (e.g. *pura*) and unusual terms (e.g. laterite). Where there is a fuller explanation of a term in the text, like for example the Buddhist mudras, this will be cross-referenced back from the glossary.

Maps and diagrams All the maps have been specially drawn for this book, using a wide range of sources. Where possible, accurate, scale maps have been used; in the few cases where these have been unavailable the map is marked 'not to scale'.

Map Symbols

International Border		State, Regional Capitals	□
State / Province Border		Other Towns	o
Main Roads (National Highways)	Rt 15	Bus Stations	B
Other Roads		Hospitals	H
Jeepable Roads, Tracks, Treks, Paths, Ferries		Key Numbers	27
Railways, Station		Airport	✈
Contours (approx)		Bridges	⨝
		Mountains	⛰
Rivers	Rokan River	Waterfall	⊓
Fortified Walls	▲ ▲ ▲	National Parks, Wildlife Parks, Bird Sanctuaries	◆
Built Up Areas		Church / Cathedral	✝
Lakes, Reservoirs		Hindu Temple	🛕
Sand Banks, Beaches		Buddhist monastery	⛩
National Parks, Gardens, Stadiums		Chinese temple	🛕
		Mosque	🕌

IMS

Types of maps
Relief maps The centre pages of the book have coloured relief maps of each country. These provide a good idea of terrain and overall geography.
Country maps Mark the main towns, routes and geographical features.
Regional maps More detailed maps showing all the town entries and road and rail links between destinations.
Town maps Detailed maps of towns and cities marking roads, sights, hotels and restaurants, post offices and other useful information.
Special sight maps These include plans of historical or archaeological sights, maps of national parks, and mountain trails.

Health information Dr David Snashall, of St. Thomas' Medical School, London and Chief Adviser to the British Foreign and Commonwealth Office, has specially written a section on health. This provides an authoritative summary of health risks in Southeast Asia and advice on how best to combat them (**see page 21**).

Country sections Each country section is arranged according to approximately the same format, as follows:
❑ List of contents
❑ Introduction

Environment	History
Art and architecture	Culture and life
Politics	Economy

❑ Capital city entry

❏ Regions, arranged by town/city
❏ Information for visitors

Town and city entries Information on each town is presented in a set sequence.
But not all entries are provided for every town – only capital cities and important
regional centres are likely to have information under every heading. Towns are
linked together on 'routes' which are summarized at the beginning of the route
in short 'gobbets'. Town information is presented in the following sequence:

❏ General introduction
❏ Places of interest
❏ Excursions
❏ Tours
❏ Festivals
❏ Services

Accommodation	Restaurants
Bars	Entertainment
Sports	Shopping
Local transport	Banks & money changers
Embassies and consulates	Useful addresses
Airline offices	Travel agents
Tourist offices	Transport to & from ...

Information for visitors The final part of each country section is an entry
entitled Information for Visitors. This aims to summarize practical information on
such aspects as visa formalities, food, postal services and conduct. The sequence
of information here is:

❏ Documents
❏ Transport to and from ...
❏ Customs
❏ Internal transport
❏ Accommodation, food and drink
❏ Public holidays and national festivals
❏ Other essential information

Conduct	Tipping
Shopping	Safety
Health	Best time to visit
Clothing	Official time
Hours of business	Money
Cost of living	Weights and measures
Voltage	Postal services
Telephone services	Media
Language	Tourist information
Suggested reading	Acknowledgements

Hotels All hotels and restaurants are graded by cost. What a particular grade
might mean in terms of hotel facilities is summarized under *Accommodation* in
each country's *Information for visitors* sections.

Hotel categories

L	US$200+	**A+**	US$100-200	**A**	US$40-100
B	US$20-40	**C**	US$12-20	**D**	US$6-12
E	US$3-6	**F**	under US$3		

Restaurant categories

♦♦♦♦	US$15+	♦♦♦	US$5-15
♦♦	US$2-5	♦	under US$2

Usually these US$ prices are converted into the national currency.

INTRODUCTION AND HINTS

	Page		Page
Travel to and within the region	11	Accommodation, food and drink	16
Documentation and security	13	Internal travel	18
Etiquette and language	16	General advice	19

General note: the advice given below represents a regional summary of more detailed information provided in the *Information for visitors* sections of each country entry.

TRAVEL TO AND WITHIN ISLAND SOUTHEAST ASIA

Air travel It is possible to fly direct to several island Southeast Asian destinations from Europe and Australasia, the west coast of North America, as well as from the Gulf, South Asia, Japan and Hong Kong. The major destination is Singapore, followed by Kuala Lumpur and Jakarta. Many airlines offer non-stop flights from European cities. The scheduled flying time from London to Singapore is 13 hrs on direct flights, but may be up to 20 hrs on flights with more than one stop. Many of the world's top airlines fly the Southeast Asian routes and standards are therefore high. Onward reservations should be reconfirmed at every stage. Within Southeast Asia there is a wide range of flight connections on internal airlines.

Discounts It is possible to obtain significant discounts, especially outside European holiday times, most notably in London, even on non-stop flights. Shop around and book early. It is also possible to get discounts from Australasia, South Asia and Japan. Mid-July to mid-August is the peak season and most expensive although 'peak season' varies from airline to airline.

Air passes **Visit Indonesia Air Pass** Three types of pass are available: 4 cities – US$350 (maximum stay 20 days), 8 cities – US$500 (maximum stay 30 days), 12 cities – US$600 (maximum stay 60 days). Travel cannot finish at the point of starting and routing cannot be changed once booked. **Discover Malaysia Air Pass** This is a 21 day pass for up to 5 sectors on internal flights for US$115. It is valid within (a) Peninsular Malaysia or (b) Sabah or (c) Sarawak. For travel between these places there is a 40% discount on normal fares. The pass must be in conjunction with at least one international sector on Malaysia Airlines. As air passes on offer change frequently, check with a good travel agent before booking flights. Be particularly careful to check any restrictions on either international or internal flights.

Non-stop flights to Singapore, and to a lesser extent, Jakarta and Kuala Lumpur, are readily available from Europe, Australasia, South Asia and from Dubai. From North America's west coast there are direct flights from Los Angeles and Vancouver. From Japan, Hong Kong, Bangkok and the Philippines, there are frequent flights.

Stop-overs and round the world tickets It is possible to arrange several stop-overs in Southeast Asia on round the world and other longer distance tickets. RTW tickets allow you to fly in to Singapore and out from another international airport such as Jakarta or Kuala Lumpur. Different travel agents organize different deals. Trailfinders of London, one of the world's biggest agencies, has a range of discounted deals. Contact at 194 Kensington High St, London W8 7RG, T 071 938 3939. Tickets can be purchased locally and paid for in local currency, but this is not a particularly cheap option.

Airline security International airlines vary in their arrangements and requirements for security, in particular, the carrying of equipment like radios, tape-recorders and lap top computers. It is advisable to ring the airline in advance to confirm their current regulations. **Note that internal airlines often have different rules from the international carriers.**

In this Handbook, further details on air links to and from each country, arrival and departure regulations, airport taxes, customs regulations and security arrangements for air travel are outlined in the relevant country sections as they vary from country to country. Further details of air links to and from each country covered is contained at the beginning of the relevant *Information for visitors* sections.

Sea travel Few people arrive in island Southeast Asia by sea, despite the fact every country is a maritime nation. There are few regular oceanic passenger ships to Indonesia, Malaysia, Brunei or Singapore. However, there are international ferry links between Singapore and Indonesia (via Batam Island, Sumatra), between Peninsular Malaysia and Indonesia (Sumatra), between Singapore and Peninsular Malaysia, and between Brunei and East Malaysia. There are also a number of domestic ferry services, in particular, those linking the myriad islands of Indonesia. For those interested in booking a passage on a cargo ship travelling to the region, contact the Strand Cruise Centre, Charing Cross Shopping Concourse, The Strand, London WC2N 4HZ, T 071-836-6363, F 071-497-0078.

Overland travel There are road links between Thailand and Peninsular Malaysia, and Peninsular Malaysia and Singapore (the latter via a 1.2 km causeway). There are also overland links between the Borneo states of East Malaysia and Brunei and Kalimantan. The border separating the Indonesian province of Irian Jaya and Papua New Guinea is not open to tourists. The most commonly used border crossings are those separating Malaysia from Thailand to the north, and Singapore to the south. Regular buses and trains ply these routes.

ISIC Anyone in full-time education is entitled to an International Student Identity Card (ISIC). These are issued by student travel offices and travel agencies across the world and offer special rates on all forms of transport and other concessions and services. The ISIC head office is: ISIC Association, Box 9048, 1000 Copenhagen, Denmark, T (45) 33 93 93 03.

When to visit Malaysia recently announced that it no longer has an 'off-season' for tourism. This attempt to even-out arrivals through the year has not, however, changed the pattern of the seasons. In general, the dry season in the archipelago extends from May/Jun to Aug/Sept, and the wet season from Nov/Dec to Feb/Mar. Nearer the equator – on the Malay peninsula and in Sumatra and Borneo – this division is far less distinct. In eastern Indonesia (Maluku and Nusa Tenggara), the seasons are rather different: the dry season runs from May to Sept, and the wet season from Dec to Mar (see rainfall chart, **page 31**). Note that in many areas it is possible to travel throughout the year, and the low season for visitors has the advantage of discounted hotel rates.

DOCUMENTATION AND SECURITY

Documents Passports should be valid for at least 6 months from the day of entry. Visitors intending to stay for an extended period or those visiting a number of countries should ensure their passports are valid for even longer than this. Also ensure there is sufficient space for entry and exit stamps. Details of visa formalities are given in the relevant *Information for Visitors* sections. Passports should be carefully looked after. Those travelling overland on a low budget, should keep their passport and other valuables in a money-belt, hidden beneath clothing. In hotels, keep valuables in a safe deposit box. In case of theft, keep a photocopy of your passport and other important documents in a separate place.

Money Travellers cheques denominated in most major currencies can be easily exchanged in Malaysia, Singapore and Brunei. In Indonesia the same is true in major tourist destinations, but in more remote areas US$ travellers cheques are easiest to change. Because transaction charges are often calculated per travellers cheque, it is best to take mostly high-value cheques (US$100). A small amount of cash (in US$) can also be useful in an emergency. Keep it separate from your travellers cheques.

Exchange rates (June 1993)					
	US$	£	Ffr	DM	Nlg
Brunei (dollar)	1.6	2.5	.3	1.0	.9
Indonesia (rupiah)	2,082	3,211	386	1,302	1,161
Malaysia (ringgit)	2.6	3.9	0.5	1.6	1.4
Singapore (dollar)	1.6	2.5	.3	1.1	.9

Sensitive areas in island Southeast Asia In Indonesia, visitors should be careful travelling to Aceh (north Sumatra), East Timor and Irian Jaya. Note that in some areas of Irian Jaya visitors require a *surat jalan* – literally a 'letter to travel'; other areas in Irian Jaya are entirely closed to visitors. Following the events of late 1991 in East Timor (**see page 967**), visitors may also be barred from visiting that province. In East Malaysia, visitors should take care travelling through logging areas because of the Malaysian government's sensitivity over the timber industry. Elsewhere in island Southeast Asia travel is not restricted. The Communist insurgency along the Malaysia-Thailand border has ended.

Travelling with children & babies in Southeast Asia

Many people are daunted by the prospect of taking a child to Southeast Asia. Naturally, it is not something which is taken on lightly; travelling is slower and more expensive and there are additional health risks for the child or baby. But it can be a most rewarding experience, and with sufficient care and planning, it can also be safe. Children are excellent passports into a local culture. You will also receive the best service, and help from officials and members of the public when in difficulty.

Children in Southeast Asia are given 24-hour attention by parents, grandparents and siblings. They are rarely left to cry and are carried for most of the first 8 months of their lives – crawling is considered animal-like. A non-Asian child is still something of a novelty and parents will find their child frequently taken off their hands, even mobbed in more remote areas. This can be a great relief (at mealtimes, for instance) or most alarming. Some children love the attention, others react against it; it is best simply to gauge your own child's reactions.

Accommodation At the hottest time of year, air-conditioning may be essential for a baby or young child's comfort. This rules out many of the cheaper hotels, but a/c accommodation is available in all but the most out-of-the-way spots. When the child is bathing, be aware that the water could carry parasites, so avoid letting him or her drink it.

Transport Public transport may be a problem; trains are fine but long bus journeys are restrictive and uncomfortable. It is best to travel by short hops. Hiring a car is undoubtedly the most convenient way to see a country with a small child. Back-seatbelts are rarely fitted but it is possible to buy child-seats in capital cities.

Food & drink The advice given in the health section on food and drink (**see page 23**) should be applied even more stringently where young children are concerned. Be aware that expensive hotels may have squalid cooking conditions; the cheapest street stall is often more hygienic. Where possible, try to watch food being prepared. Stir-fried vegetables and rice or noodles are the best bet; meat and fish may be pre-cooked and then left out before being re-heated. Fruit can be bought cheaply right across Southeast Asia: papaya, banana and avocado are all excellent sources of nutrition, and can be self-peeled ensuring cleanliness. Powdered milk is also available throughout the region, although some brands have added sugar. But if taking a baby, breast-feeding is strongly recommended. Powdered food can be bought in most towns – the quality may not be the same as equivalent foods bought in the West, but it is perfectly adequate for short periods. Bottled water and fizzy drinks are sold widely. If your child is at the 'grab everything and put it in mouth' stage, a damp cloth and some *dettol* (or equivalent) are useful. Frequent wiping of hands and tabletops can help to minimize the chance of infection.

Sunburn NEVER allow your child to be exposed to the harsh tropical sun without protection. A child can burn in less than 5 minutes. Loose cotton-clothing, with long sleeves and legs and a sun-hat are best. High-factor sun-protection cream is essential.

Disposable nappies These can be bought in Indonesia, Malaysia, Singapore and Brunei, but are often expensive. If you are staying any length of time in one place, it may be worth taking Terry's (cloth) nappies. All you need is a bucket and some double-strength nappy cleanse (simply soak and rinse). Cotton nappies dry quickly in the heat and are generally more comfortable for the baby or child. They also reduce rubbish – many countries are not geared to the disposal of nappies. Of course, the best way for a child to be is nappy-free – like the local children.

Baby products Many Western baby products are now available in Southeast Asia: shampoo, talcum powder, soap and lotion. Baby wipes can be difficult to find.

Emergencies Babies and small children deteriorate very rapidly when ill. A travel insurance policy which has an air ambulance provision is strongly recommended. When planning a route, try to stay within 24 hours' travel of a hospital with good care and facilities. Many expatriats fly to Singapore for medical care, which has the best doctors and facilities in the region.

Check-list:
Baby wipes
Calpol
Dettol (or other disinfectant)
Dioralyte
First aid kit
Flannel
Immersion element for boiling water
Kalvol and/or *Snuffle Babe* or equivalent for colds
Milupa for under-one-year-olds
Mug/bottle/bowl/spoons
Nappy cleanse, double-strength
Portable baby chair, to hook onto tables; this is not essential but can be very useful
Sarung or backpack for carrying child (and/or light weight collapsible buggy)
Sterilising tablets (and an old baby-wipes container for sterilising bottles, teats, utensils)
Sudocreme, or equivalent, for nappy rash and other skin complaints
Sunblock, factor 15 or higher
Sunhat
Terry's (cloth) nappies, liners, pins and plastic pants
Thermometer (the easy-to-use unbreakable strip kind)
Zip-lock bags (not widely available in the UK) for carrying snacks, powdered food, wet flannel are invaluable.

Suggested reading: Pentes, Tina and Truelove, Adrienne (1984) *Travelling with children to Indonesia and South-East Asia*, Hale & Iremonger: Sydney. Wheeler, Maureen *Travel with children*, Lonely Planet: Hawthorne, Australia.

Personal safety So far as visitors are concerned, violence against the person is rare in Southeast Asia (but note above). If attacked, do not try to resist – firearms are widespread.

Theft is far more common than violence. Thieves favour public transport; confidence tricksters frequent popular tourist destinations. Personal valuables – money, travellers cheques, passports, jewellery – should be kept safe. Do not leave valuables in hotel rooms; place them in a safe deposit box if possible, or keep them with you. A money-belt, concealed beneath clothing, is the safest way to carry valuables. Generally, the cheaper the mode or class of transport or hotel, the more likely thieves will be at work. Drugging of tourists on buses and trains by offering doped food does occur, particularly in Indonesia. Simple common sense is the best defence.

Confidence tricksters Most common of all are confidence tricksters: people selling fake gems and antiques, informal currency exchange services offering surprisingly good rates, and card sharps. Confidence tricksters are, by definition, extremely convincing and persuasive. Time is cheap in Southeast Asia, and people are willing to invest long hours lulling tourists into a false sense of security.

Be suspicious of any offer than seems too good to be true. That is probably what it is.

Women travelling alone Women travelling alone face greater difficulties than men or couples. The general advice given above should be observed even more carefully. Young Southeast Asian women rarely travel without a partner, so it is believed to be strange for a Western woman to do so. Western women are often believed to be of easy virtue – a view perpetuated by Hollywood and in local films, for example. To minimize the pestering that will occur, dress modestly – particularly in staunchly Muslim areas such as the east coast of Peninsular Malaysia, South Kalimantan (Indonesia) and Aceh (north Sumatra, Indonesia). Comments, sometimes derogatory, will be made however carefully you dress and act; simply ignore them. Toiletries such as tampons are widely available in the main towns and cities of the region.

Drugs Drugs (narcotics) are available in Southeast Asia. However, penalties are harsh; in Malaysia and Singapore the death penalty applies for trafficking in even modest quantities. In Indonesia there are scores of former tourists overstaying their visas in prisons across the country.

Police Report any incident that involves you or your possessions. In general, police will act promptly and properly. Local people throughout the region are proud of their country's reputation and are often all too willing to help a foreigner in trouble.

ETIQUETTE AND LANGUAGE

Appearance Southeast Asians admire neatness and cleanliness. They find it difficult to understand how some Westerners – by definition wealthy – can dress so poorly and untidily. By dressing well, you will be accorded more respect and face fewer day-to-day difficulties. Women, particularly, should also dress modestly. Short skirts and bare shoulders are regarded as unacceptable except in beach resorts and one or two, more cosmopolitan, cities like Singapore. Both men and women should be particularly sure to dress appropriately if visiting a religous site – a Buddhist temple or mosque for example.

Etiquette As a general rule, Southeast Asians admire a calm and considered approach to all aspects of life. Open anger or shows of temper should be avoided. Causing another person to 'lose face' is not recommended, and status – particularly in terms of age – should be accorded due respect.

Language English is widely spoken in Singapore and Malaysia and in popular tourist areas in Indonesia. Off the tourist track, it is useful to be able to speak a few words of the local language.

ACCOMMODATION, FOOD AND DRINK

The main towns and tourist destinations in Indonesia, Malaysia and Singapore offer a wide range of accommodation. Some of the finest hotels in the world are to be found in these countries and are moderately priced by Western standards. Mid-range and budget accommodation are also generally of a relatively good standard. However, outside the main towns and tourist areas, accommodation can be surprisingly limited – restricted to one or two 'Chinese' hotels with neither budget places for backpackers, nor more expensive establishments. Paradoxically therefore, it can become more expensive the further one ventures off the tourist 'trail'. In Brunei, budget accommodation is not available, and rates are high.

The price categories of accommodation (in US$) used in this book are listed

Distinctive fruits of Southeast Asia

Custard apple (or sugar apple) Scaly green skin, squeeze the skin to open the fruit and scoop out the flesh with a spoon.

Durian (*Durio zibethinus*) A large prickly fruit, with yellow flesh, about the size of a football. Infamous for its pungent smell. While it is today regarded by many visitors as simply revolting, early Europeans (16th-18th centuries) raved about it, possibly because it was similar in taste to Western delicacies of the period. Borri (1744) thought that "God himself, who had produc'd that fruit". But by 1880 Burbridge was writing: "Its odour - one scarcely feels justified in using the word 'perfume' - is so potent, so vague, but withal so insinuating, that it can scarcely be tolerated inside the house". Banned from public transport in Singapore and hotel rooms throughout the region, and beloved by most Southeast Asians (where prize specimens can cost a week's salary), it has an alluring taste if the odour can be overcome (it has been described as like eating blancmange on the toilet). Some maintain it is an addiction. Durian-flavoured chewing gum, ice cream and jams are all available.

Jackfruit Similar in appearance to durian but not so spiky. Yellow flesh, tasting slightly like custard.

Mango (*Mangifera indica*) A rainforest fruit which is now cultivated. Widely available in the West; in Southeast Asia there are hundreds of different varieties with subtle variations in flavour. Delicious eaten with sticky rice and a sweet sauce (in Thailand). The best mangoes in the region are considered to be those from South Thailand.

Mangosteen (*Garcinia mangostana*) An aubergine-coloured hard shell covers this small fruit which is about the size of a tennis ball. Cut or squeeze the purple shell to reach its sweet white flesh which is prized by many visitors above all others. In 1898, an American resident of Java wrote, erotically and in obvious ecstasy: "The five white segments separate easily, and they melt on the tongue with a touch of tart and a touch of sweet; one moment a memory of the juiciest, most fragrant apple, at another a remembrance of the smoothest cream ice, the most exquisite and delicately flavoured fruit-acid known - all of the delights of nature's laboratory condensed in that ball of *neige parfumée*". Southeast Asians believe it should be eaten as a chaser to durian.

Papaya (*Carica papaya*) A New World Fruit that was not introduced into Southeast Asia until the 16th century. Large, round or oval in shape, yellow or green-skinned, with bright orange flesh and a mass of round, black seeds in the middle. The flesh, in texture and taste, is somewhere between a mango and a melon. Some maintain that it tastes 'soapy'.

Pomelo A large round fruit the size of anything from an ostrich egg to a football, with thick, green skin, thick pith, and flesh not unlike that of the grapefruit, but less acidic.

Rambutan (*Nephelium lappaceum*) The bright red and hairy rambutan - *rambut* is the Malay word for 'hair' - with its slightly rubbery but sweet flesh is a close relative of the lychee of southern China and tastes similar. The Thai word for rambutan is *ngoh*, which is the nickname given by Thais to the fuzzy-haired Negrito aboriginals in the southern jungles.

Salak (*Salacca edulis*) A small pear-shaped fruit about the size of a large plum with a rough, brown, scaly skin (somewhat like a miniature pangolin) and yellow-white, crisp flesh. It is related to the sago and rattan trees.

Tamarind (*Tamarindus indicus*) Brown seedpods with dry brittle skins and a brown tart-sweet fruit which grow on a tree introduced into Southeast Asia from India. The name is Arabic for 'Indian date'. The flesh has a high tartaric acid content and is used to flavour curries, jams, jellies and chutneys as well as for cleaning brass and copper. Elephants have a predilection for tamarind balls.

above. They are also listed in the local currency in the relevant *Information for visitors* sections, together with a brief summary of the facilities to be expected.

Camping Camping is becoming increasingly popular in Malaysia and Singapore. Most national parks offer camping facilities. In Malaysia they are generally good; in Indonesia rather less so. Outside national parks however, there are very few dedicated camping grounds. Southeast Asians find it strange that anyone should want to camp out when it is possible to stay in a hotel.

Food Food in Indonesia, Malaysia and Singapore is generally good, and excellent value for money. Although care regarding what you eat and where you eat it is obviously recommended, levels of hygiene are reasonable – particularly in Singapore. The incidence of tourists suffering from serious stomach upsets is far less than, say, in South Asia. All towns have local restaurants and stalls serving cheap, tasty and nourishing dishes. Most towns will also have their requisite Chinese restaurant, so it is usually possible to order food that is not spicy-hot. Details on local cuisines are contained in each *Information for visitors* section.

In tourist areas and more expensive hotels Western food is also widely available. This ranges from fast food outlets like McDonalds, Pizza Hut and Kentucky Fried Chicken, to top class French and Italian restaurants. In areas popular with backpackers, so-called travellers' food is also available: dishes such as chocolate fudge cake, pancakes, fruit shakes (or 'smoothies'), and garlic toast.

Across the region, fruit can be a life-saver. It is varied, cheap, exotic, safe to eat (if peeled oneself) and delicious. A list of the more exotic Southeast Asian fruits is given below. More details on food and restaurants in each country are contained in the relevant *Information for visitors* sections.

Drinks Alcoholic drinks, soft drinks such as Coca-cola and 7-Up, and tea and coffee are available in all the countries of island Southeast Asia except Brunei, where alcohol is banned. Locally brewed beers (light lagers) are comparatively expensive. Bottled water is also easily obtainable in these countries. It is only advisable to drink water straight from the tap in Singapore.

Tipping Tipping is not customary in Southeast Asia except in more expensive hotels and restaurants. It is also common for a 10% service charge and government tax (usually of 10%-11%) to be added on to bills in more expensive hotels and restaurants.

INTERNAL TRAVEL

Road
Road is the main mode of transport in the region. **Buses** link nearly all towns, however small. In much of Malaysia (except the Borneo states of Sabah and Sarawak), Brunei and Singapore roads are good, and air-conditioned 'VIP' buses are available on the more popular routes. These are considerably cheaper than travelling by air. Non a/c buses and other vicarious forms of transport are cheaper still, but usually slower and more uncomfortable. In Indonesia, main highways are good, particularly in Java and Bali. In the Outer Islands of Indonesia roads can be poor, and during the wet season sometimes impassable. Again, buses are the main mode of transport in Indonesia and both a/c and non a/c buses regularly ply the main routes. In the East Malaysian states of Sabah and Sarawak, the road network is limited and air or river transport sometimes the only options. **NB**: security can be a problem on long-distance bus journeys.

Cars for self-drive hire are available in Indonesia, Malaysia, Singapore and Brunei (in all four countries, motorists drive on the left). But road 'courtesy' is not a feature of the region, and larger vehicles expect smaller ones to give way, even where the latter may have right of way. More common than self-drive, is for visitors to hire a car and driver. This is possible in all the countries covered in this book.

Hitchhiking is not common in Southeast Asia, although it is easy in Malaysia and Brunei. However there are small but increasing numbers of visitors who tour Indonesia and Malaysia by **bicycle**. It is strongly recommended that bicyclists arrange their route on minor roads; drivers use the hard shoulder.

Rail
All the countries covered in this book, with the exception of Brunei, have passenger railways but the networks are limited. Travelling third class is often the cheapest way to get from A to B, while first class (a/c) is more comfortable (and safer) than travelling by bus (although usually slower). **NB**: theft can be a problem on long-distance train journeys.

Boat
Boats and ferries are important modes of transport in island Southeast Asia. In Indonesia, particularly, a network of ferries and ships link both the major and minor islands. For visitors with the time, these can be a relaxing and interesting alternative to flying around the archipelago. In Malaysia, Singapore and Brunei there are regular ferries to off-shore islands and Malaysian passenger ferries link the main port towns of the Peninsula with Singapore, Sabah and Sarawak. In Kalimantan and East Malaysia, river-craft are a more usual mode of transport than road.

Air
Domestic airlines link major towns and cities in Malaysia and Indonesia. Services are efficient and safe, although considerably more expensive, than the overland alternatives. In Indonesia, flights to more remote towns tend to suffer from delays and overbooking.

GENERAL ADVICE

What to take Travellers usually tend to take too much. Almost everything is available in the region's towns and cities – and often at a lower price than in the West. Remoter areas of Indonesia and Malaysia are less well supplied.

Suitcases are not appropriate if you are intending to travel overland by bus. A backpack, or even better a travelpack (where the straps can be zipped out of sight), is recommended. Travelpacks have the advantage of being hybrid backpacks-suitcases; they can be carried on the back for easy porterage, but they can also be taken into hotels without the owner being labelled a 'hippy'. Note however, that for serious hikers, a backpack with an internal frame is still by far the better option for longer treks.

In terms of clothing, dress in Southeast Asia is relatively casual – even at formal functions. Suits are not necessary except in a very few of the most expensive

Short wave radio guide (KHz)
British Broadcasting Corporation (BBC, London) *Southeast Asian service* 3915, 6195, 9570, 9740, 11750, 11955, 15360; *Singapore service* 88.9MHz; *East Asian service* 5995, 6195, 7180, 9740, 11715, 11750, 11945, 11955, 15140, 15280, 15360, 17830, 21715.
Voice of America (VoA, Washington) *Southeast Asian service* 1143, 1575, 7120, 9760, 9770, 15185, 15425; *Indonesian service* 6110, 11760, 15425.
Radio Beijing *Southeast Asian service (English)* 11600, 11660.
Radio Japan (Tokyo) *Southeast Asian service (English)* 11815, 17810, 21610.

restaurants. There is a tendency, rather than to take inappropriate articles of clothing, to take too many of the same article. Laundry services are cheap, and the turn-around rapid.

Checklist:

Earplugs	Sun protection
First aid kit	Sunglasses
Insect repellent and/or electric mosquito mats, coils	Swiss Army knife
	Torch
International driving licence	Umbrella
Photocopies of essential documents	Wipes (*Damp Ones*, *Baby Wipes*
Short wave radio	or equivalent)
Spare passport photographs	Zip-lock bags

Those intending to stay in budget accommodation might also include:

Padlock (for hotel room and pack)	Soap
Cotton sheet sleeping bag	Student card
Money belt	Towel

Maps of mainland Southeast Asia

A decent map is an indispensable aid to travelling. Although maps are usually available locally, it is sometimes useful to buy a map prior to departure to plan routes and itineraries. Below is a select list of maps. Scale is provided in brackets.

Regional maps: Bartholomew Southeast Asia (1:5,800,000); Nelles Southeast Asia (1:4,000,000); Hildebrand Thailand, Burma, Malaysia and Singapore (1:2,800,000).

Country maps: Bartholomew Thailand (1:1,500,000); Bartholomew Vietnam, Laos and Cambodia (1:2,000,000); Nelles Burma (1:1,500,000); Nelles Thailand (1:1,500,000); Nelles Vietnam, Laos and Cambodia (1:1,500,000).

City maps: Nelles Bangkok.

Other maps: Tactical Pilotage Charts (TPC, US Airforce) (1:500,000); Operational Navigational Charts (ONC, US Airforce) (1:500,000). Both of these are particularly good at showing relief features (useful for planning treks); less good on roads, towns and facilities.

Locally available maps: maps are widely available in Thailand and many are given out free, although the quality of information is sometimes poor. In Vietnam, Laos and Cambodia maps are cheap although not always available beyond the capital cities; again, quality may be poor.

Map shops: in London, the best selection is available from Stanfords, 12-14 Long Acre WC2E 9LP, T (071) 836-1321; also recommended is McCarta, 15 Highbury Place, London N15 1QP, T (071) 354-1616.

HEALTH INFORMATION

The following information has been very kindly compiled by Dr David Snashall, Senior Lecturer in Occupational Health, United Medical Schools of Guy's and St Thomas' Hospitals and Chief Medical Adviser, Foreign and Commonwealth Office, London. The publishers have every confidence that the following information is correct but cannot assume any direct responsibility in this connection.

The traveller to Southeast Asia is inevitably exposed to health risks not encountered in North America, Western Europe or Australasia. All of the countries have a tropical climate; nevertheless the acquisition of true tropical disease by the visitor is probably conditioned as much by the rural nature and standard of hygiene of the countries concerned than by the climate. There is an obvious difference in health risks between the business traveller who tends to stay in international class hotels in large cities and the backpacker trekking through rural areas. There are no hard and fast rules to follow; you will often have to make your own judgements on the healthiness or otherwise of your surroundings.

In Singapore, medical care is first class and health care in Malaysia and Brunei is of a high standard. In the former colonial countries or protectorates – Malaysia, Singapore and Brunei – most doctors speak English, but the likelihood of finding this and a good standard of care diminishes very rapidly as you move away from the big cities. In some of the countries – and especially in rural areas – there are systems and traditions of medicine wholly different from the Western model and you may be confronted with less orthodox forms of treatment such as herbal medicine and acupuncture. At least you can be sure that local practitioners have a lot of experience with the particular diseases of their region. If you are in a city it may be worthwhile calling on your embassy to provide a list of recommended doctors.

If you are a long way away from medical help, a certain amount of self administered medication may be necessary and you will find many of the drugs available have familiar names. However, always check the date stamping (sell-by date) and buy from reputable pharmacists because the shelf life of some items, especially vaccines and antibiotics, is markedly reduced in hot conditions. Unfortunately, many locally produced drugs are not subjected to quality control procedures and so can be unreliable. There have, in addition, been cases of substitution of inert materials for active drugs. With the following precautions and advice you should keep as healthy as usual. Make local enquiries about health risks if you are apprehensive and take the general advice of European or North American families who have lived or are living in the area.

Before you go

Take out medical insurance. You should also have a dental check-up, obtain a spare glasses prescription and, if you suffer from a long-standing condition, such as diabetes, high blood pressure, heart/lung disease or a nervous disorder, arrange for a check-up with your doctor who can at the same time provide you with a letter explaining details of your medical disorder. Check the current practice for malaria prophylaxis (prevention) for the countries you intend to visit.

Inoculations Smallpox vaccination is no longer required. Neither is cholera vaccination, despite the fact that the disease occurs – but not at present in epidemic form – in some of these countries. Yellow fever vaccination is not required either, although you may be asked for a certificate if you have been in a country affected by yellow fever immediately before travelling to Southeast Asia. The following vaccinations are recommended:

Typhoid (monovalent): one dose followed by a booster one month later. Immunity from this course lasts 2-3 years. An oral preparation is also available.
Poliomyelitis: this is a live vaccine generally given orally but a full course consists of three doses with a booster in tropical regions every 3-5 years.
Tetanus: one dose should be given, with a booster at 6 weeks and another at 6 months. Ten yearly boosters thereafter are recommended.
Meningitis and Japanese B encephalitis (JVE): there is an extremely small risk of these rather serious diseases; both are seasonal and vary according to region. Meningitis can occur in epidemic form; JVE is a viral disease transmitted from pigs to man by mosquitos. For details of the vaccinations, consult a travel clinic.
Children: should, in addition to the above, be properly protected against diphtheria, whooping cough, mumps and measles. Teenage girls, if they have not had the disease, should be given a rubella (German measles) vaccination. Consult your doctor for advice on BCG inoculation against tuberculosis: the disease is still common in the region.

Infectious hepatitis (jaundice) is common throughout Southeast Asia. It seems to be frequently caught by travellers. The main symptoms are stomach pains, lack of appetite, nausea, lassitude and yellowness of the eyes and skin. Medically speaking there are two types: the less serious but more common is *hepatitis A* for which the best protection is careful preparation of food, the avoidance of contaminated drinking water and scrupulous attention to toilet hygiene. Human normal immunoglobulin (gammaglobulin) confers considerable protection against the disease and is particularly useful in epidemics. It should be obtained from a reputable source and is certainly recommended for travellers who intend to travel and live rough. The injection should be given as close as possible to your departure and as the dose depends on the likely time you are to spend in potentially infected areas, the manufacturers' instructions should be followed. A vaccination against hepatitis A has recently become generally available and seems to be safe and effective. Three shots are given over six months and confer excellent protection against the disease for up to ten years. Eventually this vaccine is likely to supersede the use of gammaglobulin.

The other, more serious, version is *hepatitis B* which is acquired as a sexually transmitted disease, from a blood transfusion or an injection with an unclean needle, or possibly by insect bites. The symptoms are the same as hepatitis A but the incubation period is much longer.

You may have had jaundice before or you may have had hepatitis of either type before without becoming jaundiced, in which case it is possible that you could be immune to either hepatitis A or B (or C or a number of other letters). This immunity can be tested for before you travel. If you are not immune to hepatitis B already, a vaccine is available (3 shots over 6 months) and if you are not immune to hepatitis A already, then you should consider having gammaglobulin or a vaccination.

AIDS in Southeast Asia is increasingly prevalent. Thus, it is not wholly confined to the well known high risk sections of the population i.e. homosexual men, intravenous drug abusers, prostitutes and the children of infected mothers. Heterosexual transmission is probably now the dominant mode of infection and so the main risk to travellers is from casual sex. The same precautions should be taken as when encountering any sexually transmitted disease. In some Southeast Asian countries, Thailand is an example, almost the entire population of female prostitutes is HIV positive and in other parts intravenous drug abuse is common.

The AIDS virus (HIV) can be passed via unsterile needles which have been previously used to inject an HIV positive patient, but the risk of this is very small indeed. It would, however, be sensible to check that needles have been properly sterilized or disposable needles used. The chance of picking up hepatitis B in this way is much more of a danger. Be wary of carrying disposable needles. Customs officials may find them suspicious. The risk of receiving a blood transfusion with blood infected with the HIV virus is greater than from dirty needles because of the amount of fluid exchanged. Supplies of blood for transfusion are supposed to be screened for HIV in all reputable hospitals so the risk should be small. Catching the virus which causes AIDS does not necessarily produce an illness in itself; the only way to be sure if you feel you have been put at risk is to have a blood test for HIV antibodies on your return to a place where there are reliable laboratory facilities. However, the test does not become positive for many weeks.

Common problems

Heat and cold

Full acclimatization to tropical temperatures takes about two weeks and during this period it is normal to feel relatively apathetic, especially if the humidity is high. Drink plenty of water (up to 15 litres a day are required when working physically hard in the tropics). Use salt on your food and avoid extreme exertion. Tepid showers are more cooling than hot or cold ones. Large hats do not cool you down but do prevent sunburn. Remember that, especially in highland areas, there can be a large and sudden drop in temperature between sun and shade and between night and day so dress accordingly. Loose-fitting cotton clothes are best for hot weather. Warm jackets and woollens are often necessary after dark at high altitude.

Intestinal upsets

Practically nobody escapes tummy upsets, so be prepared for them. Most of the time intestinal upsets are due to the insanitary preparation of food. Do not eat uncooked fish, vegetables or meat (especially pork), fruit without the skin (always peel fruit yourself), or food that is exposed to flies (particularly salads). Tap water may be unsafe, especially in the monsoon seasons and the same goes for stream water or well water. Filtered or bottled water is usually available and safe but you cannot rely on it. If your hotel has a central hot water supply, this is safe to drink after cooling. Ice should be made from boiled water but rarely is, so stand your glass on the ice cubes instead of putting them in the drink. Dirty water should first be strained through a filter bag (available from camping shops) and then boiled or treated. Bringing the water to a rolling boil at sea level is sufficient. In the highlands, you have to boil the water a bit longer to ensure that all the microbes are killed. Various sterilizing methods can be used and there are proprietary preparations containing chlorine or iodine compounds. Pasteurized or heat-treated milk is now fairly widely available as is ice cream and yoghurt produced by the same methods. Unpasteurized milk products, including cheese, are sources of tuberculosis, brucellosis, listeria and food poisoning germs. You can render fresh milk safe by heating it to 62°C for 30 mins followed by rapid cooling or by boiling. Matured or processed cheeses are safer than fresh varieties.

Fish and shellfish are popular foods throughout island Southeast Asia but can be the source of health problems. Shellfish which are eaten raw will transmit food poisoning or hepatitis if they have been living in contaminated water. Certain fish accumulate toxins in their bodies at certain times of the year, which give rise to illness when they are eaten. The phenomenon known as 'red tide' can also affect fish and shellfish which eat large quantities of tiny sea creatures and thereby become poisonous. The only way to guard against this is to keep as well informed as possible about fish and shellfish quality in the area you are visiting. Most countries impose a ban on fishing in periods when red tide is prevalent, although this is often flouted.

Diarrhoea is usually the result of food poisoning, but can occasionally result from contaminated water. There are various causes — viruses, bacteria, protozoa (like amoeba), salmonella and cholera organisms. It may take one of several forms coming on suddenly or rather slowly. It may be accompanied by vomiting or severe abdominal pain, and the passage of blood or mucus (when it is called dysentery). The different types of diarrhoea and the best ways to treat them are listed in the box below.

Diarrhoea – diagnosis and treatment

All kinds of diarrhoea, whether or not accompanied by vomiting, respond favourably to the replacement of water and salts taken as frequent small sips of some kind of rehydration solution. There are proprietary preparations consisting of sachets of oral rehydration electrolyte powder which are dissolved in water, or make up your own by adding half a teaspoonful of salt (3.5 grams) and 4 tablespoons of sugar (40 grams) to a litre of boiled water. If it is possible to time the onset of diarrhoea to the minute, then it is probably viral or bacterial and/or the onset of dysentery. The treatment in addition to rehydration is Ciprofloxacin (500 mgs every 12 hours). The drug is now widely available as are various similar ones.

If the diarrhoea has come on slowly or intermittently, then it is more likely to be protozoal, i.e. caused by amoeba or giardia, and antibiotics will have no effect. These cases are best treated by a doctor as should any diarrhoea continuing for more than 3 days. If there are severe stomach cramps, the following drugs may help: Loperamide (*Imodium, Arret*) and Diphenoxylate with Atropine (*Lomotil*). The drug usually used for giardia or amoeba is Metronidazole (*Flagyl*).

The lynchpins of treatment for diarrhoea are rest, fluid and salt replacement, antibiotics such as Ciprofloxacin for the bacterial types, and special diagnostic tests and medical treatment for amoeba and giardia infections. Salmonella infections and cholera can be devastating diseases and it would be wise to get to a hospital as soon as possible if these were suspected. Fasting, peculiar diets and the consumption of large quantities of yoghurt have not been found useful in calming travellers' diarrhoea or in rehabilitating inflamed bowels. Oral rehydration has, especially in children, been a lifesaving technique and as there is some evidence that alcohol and milk might prolong diarrhoea they should probably be avoided during, and immediately after, an attack. There are ways of preventing travellers' diarrhoea for short periods of time when visiting these countries by taking antibiotics but these are ineffective against viruses and, to some extent, against protozoa. This technique should not be used other than in exceptional circumstances. Some preventatives such as Enterovioform can have serious side effects if taken for long periods.

Insects

These can be a great nuisance. Some, of course, are carriers of serious diseases such as malaria, dengue fever or filariasis and various worm infections. The best way of keeping mosquitos away at night is to sleep off the ground with a mosquito net and to burn mosquito coils containing Pyrethrum. Aerosol sprays or a 'flit gun' may be effective as are insecticidal tablets which are heated on a mat which is plugged into the wall socket (if taking your own, check the voltage of the area you are visiting so that you can take an appliance that will work; similarly, check that your electrical adaptor is suitable for the repellent plug; note that they are widely available in the region).

You can, in addition, use personal insect repellent of which the best contain a high concentration of diethyltoluamide (DET). Liquid is best for arms and face (take care around eyes and make sure you do not dissolve the plastic of your spectacles). Aerosol spray on clothes and ankles deter mites and ticks. Liquid DET suspended in water can be used to impregnate cotton clothes and mosquito nets. The latter are now available in wide mesh form which are lighter to carry and less claustrophobic to sleep under.

If you are bitten, itching may be relieved by cool baths and antihistamine tables (take care with alcohol or when driving), corticosteroid creams (great care – never use if any hint of septic poisoning) or by judicious scratching. Calamine lotion and cream have limited effectiveness and antihistamine creams have a tendency to cause skin allergies and are therefore not generally recommended. Bites which become infected (a common problem in the tropics) should be treated with a local antiseptic or antibiotic cream such as Cetrimide, as should infected scratches. Skin infestations with body lice, crabs and scabies are unfortunately easy to pick up. Use gamma benzene hexachloride for lice and benzyl benzoate for scabies. Crotamiton cream alleviates itching and also kills a number of skin parasites. Malathion lotion is good for lice but avoid the highly toxic full strength Malathion which is used as an agricultural insecticide.

Malaria is prevalent in Southeast Asia

Malaria remains a serious disease and you are advised to protect yourself against mosquito bites as above and to take prophylactic (preventative) drugs. Start taking the tablets a few days before exposure and continue to take them six weeks after leaving the malarial zone. Remember to give the drugs to babies and children, pregnant women also.

The subject of malaria prevention is becoming more complex as the malaria parasite becomes immune to some of the older drugs. In particular, there has been an increase in the proportion of cases of falciparum malaria which are resistant to the normally used drugs. It would not be an exaggeration to say that we are near to the situation where some cases of malaria will be untreatable with presently available drugs.

Some of the prophylactic drugs can cause side effects, especially if taken for long periods of time, so before you travel you must check with a reputable agency the likelihood and type of malaria in the countries which you intend to visit. Take their advice on prophylaxis but be prepared to receive conflicting advice. Because of the rapidly changing situation in the Southeast Asian region, the names and dosage of the drugs have not been included. But Chloroquine and Proguanil may still be recommended for the countries where malaria is still fully sensitive; while Doxycycline, Halofantrine and Quinghaosu are presently being used in resistant areas. Quinine and tetracycline drugs remain the mainstay of treatment.

It is still possible to catch malaria even when taking prophylactic drugs, although this is unlikely. If you do develop symptoms (high fever, shivering, severe headache, and sometimes diarrhoea) seek medical advice immediately. The risk of the disease is obviously greater the further you move from the cities into rural areas, with primitive facilities and standing water.

Sunburn & heat stroke

The burning power of the tropical sun is phenomenal, especially in highland areas. Always wear a wide-brimmed hat, and use some form of sun cream or lotion on untanned skin. Normal temperate zone suntan lotions (protection factors up to 7) are not much good. You need to use the types designed specifically for the tropics or for mountaineers or skiers, with a protection factor between 7 and 15 or higher. Glare from the sun can cause conjunctivitis so wear sunglasses, particularly on beaches.

There are several varieties of heat stroke. The most common cause is severe dehydration. Avoid this by drinking lots of non-alcoholic fluid, and adding salt to your food.

Children & babies

Younger travellers seem to be more prone to illness abroad, but that should not put you off taking them. More preparation is necessary than for an adult and perhaps a little more care should be taken when travelling to remote areas where health services are primitive. This is because children can become more rapidly ill than adults (they often recover more quickly however). For more practical advice on travelling with children and babies **see page 14**.

·Diarrhoea and vomiting are the most common problems so take the usual precautions, but more intensively. Make sure all basic childhood **vaccinations** are up to date as well as the more exotic ones. Children should be properly protected against diphtheria, whooping cough, mumps and measles. If they have not had the disease, teenage girls should be given rubella (german measles) vaccination. Consult your doctor for advice on BCG inoculation against tuberculosis: the disease is still common in the region. Protection against mosquitos and drug prophylaxis against malaria is essential. Many children take to "foreign" food quite happily. Milk in Southeast Asia may be unavailable outside big cities. Powdered milk may be the answer; breast feeding for babies even better.

Upper respiratory infections such as colds, catarrh and middle ear infections are common – antibiotics could be carried against the possibility. **Outer ear infections** after swimming are also common – antibiotic ear drops will help. The treatment of **diarrhoea** is the same as for adults except that it should start earlier and be continued with more persistence. Children get dehydrated very quickly in the tropics and can become drowsy and uncooperative unless cajoled to drink water or juice plus salts. Oral rehydration has been a lifesaving technique in children.

Protect children against the sun with a hat and high factor tanning lotion. Severe sunburn at this age may well lead to serious skin cancer in the future.

Snake and other bites & stings

If you are unlucky enough to be bitten by a venomous snake, spider, scorpion, centipede or sea creature, try (within limits) to catch or kill the animal for identification. Reactions to be expected are shock, swelling, pain and bruising around the bite, soreness of the regional lymph glands, nausea, vomiting and fever. If in addition any of the following symptoms should follow closely, get the victim to a doctor without delay: numbness, tingling of the face, muscular spasms, convulsions, shortness of breath or haemorrhage. Commercial snake-bite or scorpion-sting kits may be available but these are only useful against the specific type of snake or scorpion for which they are designed. The serum has to be given intravenously so is not much good unless you have had some practice in making injections into veins. If the bite is on a limb, immobilize it and apply a tight bandage between the bite and the body, releasing it for 90 seconds every 15 minutes. Reassurance of the victim is very important because death from snake bite is very rare. Do not slash the bite area and try to suck out the poison because this sort of heroism does more harm than good. Hospitals usually hold stocks of snake-bite serum. The best precaution is not walk in long grass with bare feet, sandals or in shorts.

When swimming in an area where there are poisonous fish such as stone or scorpion fish (also called by a variety of local names) or sea urchins on rocky coasts, tread carefully or wear plimsolls/trainers. The sting of such fish is intensely painful. This can be relieved by immersing the injured part of the body in water as hot as you can bear for as long as it remains painful. This is not always very practical and you must take care not to scald yourself, but it does work. Avoid spiders and scorpions by keeping your bed away from the wall, look under lavatory seats and inside your shoes in the morning. In the rare event of being bitten, consult a doctor.

Other afflictions
Remember that **rabies** is endemic in many Southeast Asian countries. If bitten by a domestic animal, try to have it captured for observation and see a doctor at once. Treatment with human diploid vaccine is now extremely effective and worth seeking out if the likelihood of having contracted rabies is high. A course of anti-rabies vaccine before leaving might be a good idea.

Dengue fever is present in most of the countries of Southeast Asia. It is a viral disease transmitted by mosquito and causes severe headaches and body pains. Complicated types of dengue known as haemorrhagic fevers occur throughout Asia but usually in persons who have caught the disease a second time. Thus, although it is a very serious type it is rarely caught by visitors. There is no treatment, you must just avoid mosquito bites.

Intestinal worms are common and the more serious ones, such as hook worm can be contracted by walking barefoot on infested earth or beaches.

Influenza and **respiratory diseases** are common, perhaps made worse by polluted cities and rapid temperature and climatic changes – accentuated by air-conditioning.

Prickly heat is a very common itchy rash, best avoided by frequent washing and by wearing loose clothing. It can be helped by the use of talcum powder, allowing the skin to dry thoroughly after washing.

Athlete's foot and other **fungal infections** are best treated by sunshine and a proprietary preparation such as Tolnaftate.

Hangovers can be bad in the tropics as alcohol accentuates dehydration. The best way to avoid them is by drinking several litres of water if you have been drinking.

On returning home
On returning home, remember to take anti-malarial tablets for 6 weeks. If you have had attacks of diarrhoea, it is worth having a stool specimen tested in case you have picked up amoebic dysentery. If you have been living rough, a blood test may also be worthwhile to detect worms and other parasites.

Basic supplies You may find the following items useful to take with you from home: suntan cream, insect repellent, flea powder, mosquito net, coils or tablets, tampons, condoms, contraceptives, water sterilizing tablets, anti-malaria tablets, anti-infective ointment, dusting powder for feet, travel sickness pills, antiacid tablets, anti-diarrhoea tablets, sachets of rehydration salts, a first aid kit and disposable needles (also **see page 23**).

Further health information Information regarding country-by-country malaria risk can be obtained from the World Health Organization (WHO) or in Britain from the Ross Institute, London School of Hygiene and Tropical Medicine, Keppel Street, London WC1E 7HT which also publishes a highly recommended book: *The preservation of personal health in warm climates*. The Centres for Disease Control (CDC) in Atlanta, Georgia, USA will provide equivalent information. The organization MASTA (Medical Advisory Service for Travellers Abroad) also based at the London School of Hygiene and Tropical Medicine (T 071 631-4408) will provide up-to-date country-by-country information on health risks. Further information on medical problems overseas can be obtained from the new edition of *Travellers health, how to stay healthy abroad*, edited by Richard Dawood (Oxford University Press, 1992). This revised and updated edition is highly recommended, especially to the intrepid traveller. A more general publication, with hints on health and much more besides, is John Hatt's new edition of *The tropical traveller* (Penguin, 1993).

THE SOUTHEAST ASIAN REALM

	Page		Page
Regional introduction	28	Colonial history	44
Land and life	29	Modern Southeast Asia	47
Pre-colonial history	36	Suggested reading	49

MAINLAND AND ISLAND SOUTHEAST ASIA

This book, along with its sister publication which deals with Thailand, Burma, Vietnam, Cambodia and Laos, cover 9 countries of 'mainland' and 'island' Southeast Asia. The logic of the division into mainland and island sections is based on cultural, historical and geographical grounds. The dominant religion of mainland Southeast Asia is Theravada Buddhism; in the islands of the Malay world it is Islam. The flora and fauna of the mainland is almost exclusively 'Asian' in origin; in the islands, there is a significant Australasian element. On the mainland, the wet season extends from May/Jun to Oct; in the archipelago, it runs from Nov/Dec to Feb/Mar. But although there may be a logic to dividing Southeast Asia into 2 in this way, there are also common threads that bind all the 9 countries together. This introductory section is intended to provide an overview of history, culture and geography for both books, complementing the country introductions that precede each section.

Southeast Asia: a name to conjure with

Since the end of the Second World War, the term 'Southeast Asia' has come to be widely used to describe that portion of the world that lies between India, China and Australasia. Early Chinese and Japanese traders and mariners referred to the area as *Nanyang* or *Nangyo* (both meaning the 'Southern Seas'), while Indian texts talked of a *Suvarnabhumi* ('Land of Gold') or *Suvarnadvipa* ('Island of Gold'), and Persian and Arab accounts of *Zir-e Bad* (the lands 'Below the Wind(s)'). However all the terms employed are loose and indistinct. In the first 2 cases, the terms merely describe Southeast Asia with respect to its geographical position vis à vis China and Japan. *Suvarnabhumi* and *Suvarnadvipa* – the El Dorados of the East – meanwhile probably only related to the Malay Peninsula, Sumatra, and possibly Java and parts of Burma. *Zir-e Bad* just made reference to the lands sailors arrived at by sailing E on the monsoon winds.

During the colonial period, Southeast Asia graduated to the status of a region – albeit still loose and ill-defined – virtually by default. To the Western colonial powers, it was that area which lay between the 2 cultural superpowers of China and India. The terms used to describe it indicate that it was viewed very much as a residual region: Further India, Chin-India, Little China, Indochina, the Indian Archipelago, the Far Eastern Tropics, and the Tropical Far East. In this way, Southeast Asia became defined either as an appendage of India, or as a tropical extension of China and Japan. The terms also indicate the extent to which the region has been overshadowed by its more illustrious neighbours, India and China.

The first use in English of the term 'Southeast Asia' may have been when the Reverend Howard Malcolm, an American from Boston, published a book with the title *Travels in South-Eastern Asia* in 1839. He describes the area covered by his book as including 'all the region between China and the Bay of Bengal, southward of the Thibet Mountains'. Although Malcolm, as well as a handful of anthropologists and other scholars, began to write about 'Southeast Asia' towards the middle of the 19th century, the colonial period prevented the further evolution of a Southeast Asian 'identity'. As Portugal, Britain, France, Holland and Spain (and later the United States) divided the region between themselves, leaving only Thailand with its independence, so the countries of the region became orientated toward one or other of the colonial powers. Economically, politically and to an extent, culturally, the countries' concerns and interests were focused outwards, beyond the region, postponing, for nearly a century, the development of a Southeast Asian regional identity.

It was not until the 1940s that the term Southeast Asia began to be more widely used again in English. In response to the Japanese invasion of Southeast Asia, wartime British and American leaders Churchill and Roosevelt created the South-East Asia Command (SEAC) in 1943, placing it under the leadership of Lord Louis Mountbatten. The creation of SEAC brought the term Southeast Asia into widespread and general usage. This was greatly accentuated by the onset of the Second Indochinese War in Vietnam in 1965, and growing US involvement in that war. The media coverage of the 'War in Southeast Asia', and particularly television coverage, brought the region to the attention of the public across the globe.

LAND AND LIFE

A region that has lost its heart to the sea

It is not so much the land, but the sea, which dominates Southeast Asia. At the heart of the region are the shallow waters of the South China Sea. During the last Ice Age, 15,000 years ago (when sea levels were considerably lower than they are today), much of this would have been exposed, linking the islands of Sumatra, Java and Borneo, and forming a Southeast Asian continent. In a quite literal sense therefore, Southeast Asia lost its heart to the sea. But the drowning of the once sprawling land mass has had one important side-effect: it has made the region uniquely accessible by sea. The region has a longer coastline than any other area of comparable size. It is no accident therefore that Southeast Asia's early history is one based upon maritime empires and trade.

The geological evolution of Southeast Asia

Originally, the world consisted of just 2 supercontinents: Gondwanaland to the S, and Laurasia to the N. Through a process of 'continental drift' whereby the earth's continental plates slide over and under each other, sections of Gondwanaland and Laurasia have broken away and ploughed across the oceans to take up their present positions. In the case of Southeast Asia this 'rifting' has been particularly complex. Over a period of 350 million years, successive fragments of Gondwanaland have detached themselves and drifted northwards eventually to collide with the other supercontinent, Laurasia. This process explains the peculiar spider-like shape of the Indonesian island of Sulawesi which consists of 2 halves that did not collide until the Miocene (15 million years ago).

Each fragment of Southeast Asia became a 'Noah's Ark' of plants and animals isolated from outside disturbance. The effect of this isolation can be seen reflected in the remarkable change in the fauna of the region from the Indo-Malayan zoological realm in the N, to the Austro-Malayan in the S. The point of change from one to the other is known as Wallace's Line. This runs approximately N to S between the Indonesian islands of Bali and Lombok and then through the Makassar Strait, and is named after one of Victorian England's greatest naturalists, Alfred Russel Wallace. It was Wallace, working in the former Dutch East Indies, who encouraged Charles Darwin to publish his seminal *Origin of species by means of natural selection*. For, independently of Darwin, Wallace too arrived at a theory of natural selection and coincidentally sent the paper outlining his ideas to Darwin in England. Darwin was appalled that his work might be eclipsed, but nevertheless acted entirely properly. Papers by both men were presented to a meeting of the Linnean Society in London in 1858, where they provoked surprisingly little reaction. One year later, in 1859, the *Origin of species* was published.

Despite Southeast Asia's complex geological origins, it is clearly demarcated from the regions that surround it. To the N are the highlands of Burma, Thailand, Laos and Vietnam which form a natural barrier with China and India. Running from western Burma southwards through Sumatra and Java and finally northwards to Sulawesi and the Philippines, the region is bounded by a series of deep-sea trenches. These mark the point at which the earth's plates plunge one beneath the other and are zones of intense volcanic activity. Indonesia alone has about 300 volcanoes, of which 200 have been active in historical times, and 127 are active today. The volcanic activity of the area was most dramatically displayed when Krakatau (Krakatoa), located in the Sunda Straits between Java and Sumatra, erupted in 1883. Today, Anak Krakatoa (Child of Krakatoa) and the other remaining islands, are a reserve where scientists have been able to record the recolonization by plants and animals of an island that had effectively died.

Climate

At sea level, **temperatures** are fairly uniform, both across the region and through the year. With the exception of the NE corner of Vietnam, annual average sea-level temperatures are close to 26°C. Travelling N and S from the equator, seasonal variations do become more pronounced. Therefore, while Singapore, virtually on the equator, has a monthly average temperature which varies by a mere 1.5°C, Sittwe (Akyab) in Burma which is 2,600 km to the N – has a monthly average which ranges across 7°C. The sea can also have a significant moderating effect. For example, Mandalay, on the same latitude as Sittwe but over 400 km inland, has a monthly average which spans 10°C. But these figures are monthly averages: before the onset of the SW monsoon in Apr or May, temperatures during the day in the Dry Zone of Burma and in Northeastern Thailand can reach a debilitating 40°C or more. At times like this nothing moves; even the farmers remain in the shade.

Heat & lust: colonial impressions

Many colonial visitors were tempted to see a link between the hot climate and the Southeast Asian character. In 1811, John Joseph Stockdale, a British publisher, ascribed what he saw as the "wantonness" of Javanese women to the warm temperatures. The British administrator William Marsden wrote in the same year that the Sumatran tradition of polygamy was based on the "influence of a warm atmosphere upon the passions of men" and the "cravings of other disordered appetites". Nor were the judgemental links between climate and activity restricted purely to people: Robert Mac Micking a British traveller who visited the Philippines in the mid 19th century wrote that because of the heat the Filipino dog did not have the same "strength or swiftness, nor is he of equal courage, sincerity and gentleness of character" to those faithful hounds back home.

Altitude has the greatest effect on temperature, and in the highlands of the region it can become distinctly cool. It is not surprising that the colonial powers built hill retreats in these areas: in the Cameron Highlands and at Fraser's Hill on the Malay Peninsula, at Brastagi in Sumatra (Indonesia), at Mymyo in Burma, and Dalat in southern Vietnam. In the Cameron Highlands, with its rose gardens, afternoon teas and half-timbered houses and log fires, it is easy to believe you are in rural England.

Patterns of **rainfall** in the region are more complex. They vary considerably both across the region and through the year, and seasonality – both for the farmer and the visitor – is linked to rainfall, not to temperature. The pattern of rainfall is intimately related to the monsoons, a term which is taken from the Arabic word *mawsim*, meaning 'season'.

Much of island Southeast Asia experiences what is termed an 'equatorial monsoon' climate. Annual rainfall usually exceeds 2,000 mm and can be as high as 5,000 mm. Close to the equator rainfall *tends* to be distributed evenly through the year, and there is no marked dry season. However, travelling N and S from the equator, the dry season becomes more pronounced, and rainfall concentrated in one or 2 seasonal peaks. This pattern of rainfall is determined by 2 monsoons: the NE and the SW monsoons. The NE monsoon, prevails from Nov/Dec to Feb/Mar and forms the wet season. While the SW monsoon, extends from Jun to Aug/Sept and brings dry conditions to the area.

Rainy seasons and monthly temperatures

	Jan	Feb	Mar	Apr	May	Jun	Jul	Aug	Sep	Oct	Nov	Dec
Bangkok	28	28	31	31	31	31	28	28	28	28	27	27
Phuket	28	28	28	28	28	28	28	28	28	28	28	28
Kuala Lumpur	27	27	28	28	28	28	28	28	28	28	27	27
Singapore	27	27	27	27	28	28	27	27	27	27	26	26
Jakarta	27	27	28	28	29	29	28	28	28	28	27	27
Denpasar (Bali)	27	27	27	27	28	28	28	28	27	27	27	27

☐ denotes wet season

Temperatures are in degrees celcius. Note that near the equator the distinction between 'wet' and 'dry' seasons is less pronounced.

In mainland Southeast Asia, rainfall tends to be less than in the archipelago (less than 1,500 mm), and more seasonally concentrated with the dry season in many places extending over 5 or 6 months. In comparison with island Southeast Asia, the seasons on the mainland are generally reversed. The NE monsoon from Nov to Mar brings cool, dry air to Thailand, Burma and much of Indochina. During this period rainfall may be very low indeed. Just before the SW monsoon arrives in Jun, the heating of the land can lead to torrential thunderstorms – referred to in Burma and Thailand as 'mango rains'. The SW monsoon corresponds with the period of heaviest rainfall, and over much of the mainland 80%-97% of the year's rain falls between the months of May and Oct.

It should be emphasized that local wind systems and the shadowing effects of mountains often distort this generalized pattern of rainfall. Nonetheless, like the English, Southeast Asians talk endlessly about the weather. The seasons – and this means rain – determine the very pattern of life in the region. Rice cultivation, and its associated festivals, is dependent in most areas on the arrival of the rains,

Fields in the forest – shifting cultivation

Shifting cultivation, also known as slash-and-burn agriculture or swiddening, as well as by a variety of local terms, is one of the characteristic farming systems of Southeast Asia. It is a low-intensity form of agriculture, in which land is cleared from the forest through burning, cultivated for a few years, and then left to regenerate over 10-30 years. It takes many forms, but an important distinction can be made between shifting field systems where fields are rotated but the settlement remains permanently sited, and migratory systems where the shifting cultivators shift both field (swidden) and settlement. The land is usually only rudimentarily cleared, tree stumps being left in the ground, and seeds sown in holes made by punching the soil with a dibble stick.

For many years, shifting cultivators were regarded as 'primitives' who follow an essentially primitive form of agriculture and their methods were contrasted unfavourably with 'advanced' settled rice farmers. There are still many government officials in Southeast Asia who continue to adhere to this mistaken belief, arguing that shifting cultivators are the principal cause of forest loss and soil erosion. They are, therefore, painted as the villains in the region's environmental crisis, neatly sidestepping the considerably more detrimental impact that commercial logging has had on Southeast Asia's forest resources.

Shifting cultivators have an intimate knowledge of the land, plants and animals on which they depend. One study of a Dayak tribe, the Kantu' of Kalimantan (Borneo), discovered that households were cultivating an average of 17 rice varieties and 21 other food crops each year in a highly complex system. Even more remarkably, Harold Conklin's classic 1957 study of the Hanunóo of the Philippines – a study which is a benchmark for such work even today – found that they identified 40 types and subtypes of rocks and minerals when classifying different soils. The shifting agricultural systems are usually also highly productive in labour terms, allowing far more leisure time than farmers using permanent field systems.

But shifting cultivation contains the seeds of its own extinction. Extensive, and geared to low population densities and abundant land, it is coming under pressure in a region where land is becoming an increasingly scarce resource, where patterns of life are dictated by an urban-based elite, and where populations are pressing on the means of subsistence.

and religious ceremonies are timed to coincide with the seasons. Kampoon Boontawee in his novel *Luuk Isan* (Child of the Northeast) about village life in the Northeastern region of Thailand writes: "When Koon and Jundi and their fathers arrived at the *phuyaiban*'s [headman's] house, the men were talking about what they always talked about – the lack of rain and the lack of food in the village".

The Southeast Asian landscape

In island Southeast Asia there are few favourable areas for human settlement. Much of the lowland in places such as eastern Sumatra and southern Borneo is swamp, and rivers are short, offering only limited scope for rice cultivation. The highland areas are cloaked in forest, and their traditional inhabitants such as the Dayaks of the island of Borneo and the tribes of Irian Jaya practise shifting cultivation like their brothers on the mainland. But, the islands are not entirely devoid of areas with significant agricultural potential. The fertile volcanic soils of central Java for example have supported a large population for hundreds of years. Today Java's population is nearly 110 million, and agricultural population densities in some areas exceed 2,000 people/sq km. Taking advantage of the abundance of rain and the rich soils, farmers grow up to 3 crops of rice each year.

On the mainland, mountains, valleys and rivers run N-S. The great rivers of the region are found here: the Irrawaddy, Sittang, Salween, Chao Phraya, Mekong and the Red rivers. It is along these river valleys that people have settled in the greatest numbers, exploiting the rich alluvial soils and the abundance of water by cultivating wet rice. Except for narrow bands of lowland – for example, along the Vietnamese coast – much of the remainder of the mainland is mountainous. Here, tribal peoples such as the Hmong of N Thailand and Laos, and the Karen of Burma support themselves through shifting cultivation. One of the challenges facing the region is how to protect these people and their way of life – and the forests themselves – when population pressure is growing and commercialization spreading.

Tropical forests
Across Southeast Asia from N Burma through the arc of the Indonesian islands eastwards to Irian Jaya, tropical rainforest – of which there are 13 different types – predominates. Southeast Asia supports the largest area of tropical rainforest in the world outside Latin America. The core areas, located on the islands of Borneo and New Guinea and in Peninsular Malaysia, are possibly the most diverse of all the world's terrestrial ecosystems. In a single hectare of Malayan rainforest there may be as many as 176 species of tree with a diameter of 10 cm or more, and island Southeast Asia as a whole contains 25,000 species of flowering plant – 10% of the world's flora. It is because of this bewildering diversity that environmentalists claim the forest resource must be preserved. And not just because mankind has a moral duty, but also because the forests are an invaluable genetic and pharmaceutical warehouse. Currently over 10% of all prescription drugs are derived from tropical forests, products, and the great majority of species have yet to be named and recorded, let alone chemically investigated.

Water for life: wet rice cultivation
Rice probably spread into Southeast Asia from a core area which spanned the highlands from Assam (India) to N Vietnam. Some of the earliest evidence of agriculture in the world has been uncovered in and around the village of Ban Chiang in Northeastern Thailand, and also from Bac-son in N Vietnam. However archaeologists are far from agreed about the dating and significance of the evidence. Some believe that rice may have been cultivated as early as 7000 BC; others say it dates back no further than 3000-2000 BC.

By the time the first Europeans arrived in the 15th century the crop was well-established as the staple for the region. Only on the dry islands of Timor and N Maluku (in Indonesia) did the environment preclude its cultivation. Today other staples such as taro (a root crop) and sago (produced from the sago palm) are frowned upon, being widely regarded as 'poor man's food'. The importance of rice can be seen reflected in the degree to which culture and crop have become intermeshed, and in the mythology and ceremony associated with its cultivation. The American anthropologist DeYoung, who worked in a village in Central Thailand in the late 1950s, writes that the farmer:

> "...reverences the crop he grows as a sentient being; he marks its stages of growth by ceremonies; and he propitiates the spirit of the soil in which it grows and the good or evil spirits that may help or harm it. He considers rice to possess a life spirit (*kwan*) and to grow much as a human being grows; when it bears grain, it has become 'pregnant' like a mother, and the rice is the seed or child of the Rice Goddess".

Wet rice, more than any other staple crop, is dependent on an ample and constant supply of water. The links between rice and water, wealth and poverty, and abundance and famine are clear. Throughout the region, there are numerous rituals and songs which honour the 'gift of water' and dwell upon the vagaries of the monsoon. Water-throwing festivals, designed to induce abundant rainfall, are widespread, and if they do not have the desired effect villagers will often resort to magic. The struggle to ensure a constant supply of water can also be seen reflected in the sophisticated irrigation systems of Northern Thailand, Bali and

The cycle of wet rice cultivation

There are an estimated 120,000 rice varieties. Rice seed – either selected from the previous harvest or, more commonly, purchased from a dealer or agricultural extension office – is soaked overnight before being sown into a carefully prepared nursery bed. Today farmers are likely to plant one of the Modern Varieties or MVs bred for their high yields.

The nursery bed into which the seeds are broadcast (scattered) is often a farmer's best land, with the most stable water supply. After a month the seedlings are up-rooted and taken out to the paddy fields. These will also have been ploughed, puddled and harrowed, turning the heavy clay soil into a saturated slime. Traditionally buffalo and cattle would have performed the task; today rotavators, and even tractors are becoming more common. The seedlings are transplanted into the mud in clumps. Before transplanting the tops of the seedlings are twisted off (this helps to increase yield) and then they are pushed in to the soil in neat rows. The work is back-breaking and it is not unusual to find labourers – both men and women – receiving a premium – either a bonus on top of the usual daily wage or a free meal at midday, to which marijuana is sometimes added to ease the pain.

After transplanting, it is essential that the water supply is carefully controlled. The key to high yields is a constant flow of water, regulated to take account of the growth of the rice plant. In 'rain-fed' systems where the farmer relies on rainfall to water the crop, he has to hope that it will be neither too much nor too little. Elaborate ceremonies are performed to appease the rice goddess and to ensure bountiful rainfall.

In areas where rice is grown in irrigated conditions, farmers need not concern themselves with the day-to-day pattern of rainfall, and in such areas 2 or even 3 crops can be grown each year. But such systems need to be carefully managed, and it is usual for one man to be in charge of irrigation. In Bali he is known as the *kliang subak*, in North Thailand as the *hua naa muang fai*. He decides when water should be released, organizes labour to repair dykes and dams and to clear channels, and decides which fields should receive the water first.

Traditionally, while waiting for the rice to mature, a farmer would do little except weed the crop from time to time. He and his family might move out of the village and live in a field hut to keep a close eye on the maturing rice. Today, farmers also apply chemical fertilisers and pesticides to protect the crop and ensure maximum yield. After 90-130 days, the crop should be ready for harvesting.

Harvesting also demands intensive labour. Traditionally, farmers in a village would secure their harvesters through systems of reciprocal labour exchange; now it is more likely for a harvester to be paid in cash. After harvesting, the rice is threshed, sometimes out in the field, and then brought back to the village to be stored in a rice barn or sold. It is only at the end of the harvest, with the rice safely stored in the barn, that the festivals begin. As Thai farmers say, having rice in the barn is like having money in the bank.

Java. Less obvious, but no less ingenious and complex, farmers without the benefits of irrigation have also developed sophisticated cultivation strategies designed to maintain production through flood and drought.

People and land

An Indian king is reported to have said to a man boasting about the extent of the lands ruled by the King of Siam: "It is true, I admit, that they are greater in extent than mine, but then the King of Golconda is a king of men, while your king is only king of forests and mosquitoes". Southeast Asia has always been relatively land-rich when compared with India and China. In 1600 the population of the region was probably about 20 million, and even by 1800 this had only increased to 30 million. Except for a few areas such as the island of Java and the Red River Delta of Vietnam, the region was sparsely populated. Forests and wildlife abounded, and the inhabitants at times had great trouble maintaining their small areas of 'civilized space'. Even today local words for 'forest' also often imply 'wild' and 'uncivilized'.

The wealth of forest resources has meant that most buildings – even those of the richest nobles and merchants – have always been constructed of wood, bamboo and other forest products. The only exception to this rule was in the construction of religious edifices. In these, stone and brick were used, no doubt signifying the permanence of faith, and the impermanence of men. Today the building skills of the early civilizations of Southeast Asia can be seen reflected in the temples of Prambanan and Borobudur (Java), Angkor (Cambodia), Champa (Vietnam), Sukhothai and Ayutthaya (Thailand), and Pagan (Burma). In most cases the temples stand stark and isolated, which accentuates their visual impact. However, when they were built they would have been surrounded by wooden houses, shops and the bustle and infrastructure of an ancient ceremonial city. These have now rotted away in the region's humid climate.

The abundance of land in Southeast Asia during historical times meant that people were very highly valued. A king's wealth was not measured in terms of the size of his kingdom, but the number of people that came under his control. Land was not 'owned' in the usual sense; ownership was transitory and related to utilization. When a farmer stopped cultivating a piece of land it would revert to the ownership of the sultan or king, but ultimately to God. The value of people becomes clear in the art of warfare in the region. In general, the objective was not to gain land, but to capture prisoners who could then be carried off to become slaves on the victorious king's land. This principle held true for the great kingdoms of Burma, Siam and Cambodia and the remotest tribes of Borneo. At times entire villages would be transported into captivity. Battles rarely led to many casualties. There was much noise, but little action, and the French envoy Simon de la Loubère in his 17th century account of Siam wrote: "Kill not is the order, which the King of Siam gives his troops, when he sends them into the field".

The universal stimulant – the betel nut

Throughout the countryside in Southeast Asia, and in more remote towns, it is common to meet men and women whose teeth are stained black, and gums red, by continuous chewing of the 'betel nut'. This, though, is a misnomer. The betel 'nut' is not chewed at all: the 3 crucial ingredients that make up a betel 'wad' are the nut of the areca palm (*Areca catechu*), the leaf or catkin of the betel vine (*Piper betle*), and lime. When these 3 ingredients are combined with saliva they act as a mild stimulant. Other ingredients (people have their own recipes) are tobacco, gambier, various spices and the gum of *Acacia catechu*. The habit, though also common in South Asia and parts of China, seems to have evolved in Southeast Asia and it is mentioned in the very earliest chronicles. The lacquer betel boxes of Burma and Thailand, and the brass and silver ones of Indonesia, illustrate the importance of chewing betel in social intercourse. Galvao in his journal of 1544 noted: "They use it so continuously that they never take it from their mouths; therefore these people can be said to go around always ruminating". Among Westernized Southeast Asians the habit is frowned upon: the disfigurement and ageing that it causes, and the stained walls and floors that result from the constant spitting, are regarded as distasteful products of an earlier age. But beyond the elite it is still widely practised.

In Siddhartha's footsteps: a short history of Buddhism

Buddhism was founded by Siddhartha Gautama, a prince of the Sakya tribe of Nepal, who probably lived between 563 and 483BC. He achieved enlightenment and the word *buddha* means 'fully enlightened one', or 'one who has woken up'. Siddhartha Gautama is known by a number of titles. In the W, he is usually referred to as *The Buddha*, i.e. the historic Buddha (but not just Buddha); more common in Southeast Asia is the title *Sakyamuni*, or Sage of the Sakyas (referring to his tribal origins).

Over the centuries, the life of the Buddha has become part legend, and the Jataka tales which recount his various lives are colourful and convoluted. But, central to any Buddhist's belief is that he was born under a *sal* tree (*Shorea robusta*), that he achieved enlightenment under a bodhi tree (*Ficus religiosa*) in the Bodh Gaya Gardens, that he preached the First Sermon at Sarnath, and that he died at Kusinagara (all in India or Nepal).

The Buddda was born at Lumbini (in present-day Nepal), as Queen Maya was on her way to her parents' home. She had had a very auspicious dream before the child's birth of being impregnated by an elephant, whereupon a sage prophesied that Siddhartha would become either a great king or a great spiritual leader. His father, being keen that the first option of the prophesy be fulfilled, brought him up in all the princely skills (at which Siddhartha excelled) and ensured that he only saw beautiful things, not the harsher elements of life.

Despite his father's efforts Siddhartha saw 4 things while travelling between palaces – a helpless old man, a very sick man, a corpse being carried by lamenting relatives, and an ascetic, calm and serene as he begged for food. These episodes made an enormous impact on the young prince, and he renounced his princely origins and left home to study under a series of spiritual teachers. He finally discovered the path to enlightenment at the Bodh Gaya Gardens in India. He then proclaimed his thoughts to a small group of disciples at Sarnath, near Benares, and continued to preach and attract followers until he died at the age of 81 at Kusinagara.

PRE-COLONIAL HISTORY

Prehistory

Histories are never simple, cut and dried affairs, and Southeast Asia's prehistory must rank among the most confused. Not only is the evidence available to archaeologists fragmentary and highly dispersed (partly because the humid conditions promote rapid decay), but it has also been subject to multiple interpretations. At the core of the debate, is the question as to whether Southeast Asia was a cultural 'receptacle'or a 'hearth' of civilization in itself. In other words, have people, technologies and cultures diffused into the region from the outside, or has Southeast Asia evolved a 'personality' independent of such influences? Ultimately the answer must be one of degree, not of kind.

Racial groups and migrations

The bulk of Southeast Asia's population are Southern Mongoloid. However, there are small numbers of Negritos and Melanesians still living in the region; the Semang and Sakais of Malaysia, for example. However, these true indigenous inhabitants of Southeast Asia have been overwhelmed and marginalized by more recent arrivals. First, from around 5000 BC, there began a gradual southerly migration of Southern Mongoloids from southern China and eastern Tibet. This did not occur in a great wave, as at one time postulated, but as a slow process of displacement and replacement. Later, during the early centuries of the Christian

In the First Sermon at the deer park in Sarnath, the Buddha preached the Four Truths, which are still considered the root of Buddhist belief and practical experience. These are the 'Noble Truth' that suffering exists, the 'Noble Truth' that there is a cause of suffering, the 'Noble Truth' that suffering can be ended, and the 'Noble Truth' that to end suffering it is necessary to follow the 'Noble Eightfold Path' – namely, right speech, livelihood, action, effort, mindfulness, concentration, opinion and intention.

Soon after the Buddha began preaching, a monastic order – the *Sangha* – was established. As the monkhood evolved in India, it also began to fragment as different sects developed different interpretations of the life of the Buddha. An important change was the belief that the Buddha was transcendent: he had never been born, nor had he died; he had always existed and his life on earth had been mere illusion. The emergence of these new concepts helped to turn what up until then was an ethical code of conduct, into a religion. It eventually led to the appearance of a new Buddhist movement, Mahayana Buddhism which split from the more traditional Theravada 'sect'.

Despite the division of Buddhism into 2 sects, the central tenets of the religion are common to both. Specifically, the principles pertaining to the Four Noble Truths, the Noble Eightfold Path, the Dependent Origination, the Law of Karma and nirvana. In addition, the principles of non-violence and tolerance are also embraced by both sects. In essence, the differences between the 2 are of emphasis and interpretation. Theravada Buddhism is strictly based on the original Pali Canon, while the Mahayana tradition stems from later Sanskrit texts. Mahayana Buddhism also allows a broader and more varied interpretation of the doctrine. Other important differences are that while the Thervada tradition is more 'intellectual' and self-obsessed, with an emphasis upon the attaining of wisdom and insight for oneself, Mahayana Buddhism stresses devotion and compassion towards others.

era, the political consolidation of the Chinese empire displaced increasing numbers of Deutero-Malays, as well as Tais, Khmers, Mons, Burmans, Viets and the various hill tribes of the mainland. These groups, the ancestors of the present populations of Thailand, Burma, Indochina, Malaysia and Indonesia, used the great river valleys of the region – the Mekong, Irrawaddy, Salween and Chao Phraya – as their routes S.

Southeast Asia has therefore represented a fragmented land bridge between Asia and Australasia into and through which successive racial groups have filtered. The original inhabitants of the region have all but disappeared. Most have been absorbed into the racial fabric of more recent arrivals; many others have been displaced into the highlands or out of the region altogether. The Melanesians for example now inhabit islands in the Pacific including New Guinea, while remnant Proto-Malays include the forest-dwelling Dayaks of Borneo and the Bataks of Sumatra.

Not only did these more recent migrants physically displace the earlier inhabitants, they also displaced them culturally. They brought with them knowledge of metallurgy, rice cultivation, the domestication of livestock, and new religious beliefs. But these cultural elements were not incorporated wholesale and unchanged. The nature of the Southeast Asian environment, the abundance of land and food, and the passage of time, have all served to allow the development of a distinctly Southeast Asian cultural heritage.

The historic period: water for communication

Southeast Asia's fragmented geography has made the region remarkably accessible. Winds tend to be moderate and the abundance of wood close to the shoreline has enabled ship-building to flourish. This has had 2 effects: on the one hand, it has meant that Southeast Asia has felt the effects of successive seaborne invasions, and on the other that different parts of the region have been in surprisingly close contact with one another. This is reflected in commonalities of language, particularly in the archipelago, and in the universality of cultural traits such as the chewing of betel nut. During the historic period there have been 5 major infusions of culture and technology into Southeast Asia – all of which have left their imprint on the region: Indianization, Chinese influences, Buddhism, Islam and Westernization.

1. The Indianization of Southeast Asia

From the beginning of the 1st century AD, the allure of gold and spices brought Indian traders to the region. Although they were not on a proselytizing mission – they came to make money – this resulted in the introduction of Hindu-Buddhist culture and the so-called 'Indianization' of Southeast Asia. 'Indianization' was the result not of the immigration of large numbers of Indians; rather the gradual infusion of an Indian cultural tradition introduced by small numbers of traders and priest-scholars. Given the nature of the contact, it is not surprising that the Indian influence was geographically uneven. Northern Vietnam – then under Chinese suzerainty – was never affected. Elsewhere however, kings quickly adopted and adapted elements of the Indian cultural tradition. For example, the cult of the *deva raja* – or 'god king'- in which the ruler claimed to be a reincarnation of Siva or Vishnu (or to be a Bodhisattva – a future Buddha) was used to legitimate kingship. Pagan (Burma) and Angkor (Cambodia), 2 of the greatest archaeological sites in the world, bear testament to the power and influence of these 'Indianized' empires.

2. Chinese influences

At the same time as this 'Indianization' was underway, Imperial China was also beginning to intensify its links with the region. This was prompted in the 5th century AD by the Jin Dynasty's loss of access to the central Asian caravan routes which brought luxury goods from the West. In response, maritime trading routes through the Southeast Asian archipelago were developed by the Chinese. Tribute-bearing missions from the states of Southeast Asia to the Chinese court became more common and the settlement of Chinese in the region increased as the area grew in commercial importance. In turn, the cultural impact of China also became more pronounced. Chinese medical theory, technology, cloth, games, music, and calligraphy were all assimilated to a greater or lesser degree. The Chinese diplomat Chou Ta-kuan who visited the city of Angkor in 1296 notes in his journal the large number of his countrymen who had arrived in the city and were gradually being absorbed into the social fabric of the kingdom:

> "The Chinese who follow the sea as a profession take advantage of their being in this country to dispense with wearing clothes. Rice is easy to obtain, women are easy to find, the houses are easy to run, personal property is easy to come by, commerce is easy to engage in. Thus there are constantly those who direct themselves towards this country."

3. Buddhism

By the early part of the second millennium the elitist cult of the god king had become corrupt and degenerate, and was in decline on the mainland. At the same time a third infusion of culture was underway. During the early part of the 12th century, Burmese Buddhist monks travelled to Ceylon and came in contact with Theravada Buddhism (the 'Way of the Elders'). They returned to Burma with news of this populist faith and aggressively spread the word. Unlike the deva raja cult it was an inclusive, rather than an exclusive religion, and it found a willing and receptive audience among the common people. By the 15th century Theravada Buddhism was the dominant religion across much of the mainland – in Burma, Thailand, Laos, and Cambodia.

The practice of Islam: living by the Prophet

Islam is an Arabic word meaning 'submission to God'. As Muslims often point out, it is not just a religion but a total way of life. The main Islamic scripture is the Koran or Quran, the name being taken from the Arabic *al-qur'an* or 'the recitation'. The Koran is divided into 114 *sura*, or 'units'. Most scholars are agreed that the Koran was partially written by the Prophet Mohammad. In addition to the Koran there are the hadiths, from the Arabic word *hadith* meaning 'story', which tell of the Prophet's life and works. These represent the second most important body of scriptures.

The practice of Islam is based upon 5 central tenets, known as the Pillars of Islam: Shahada (profession of faith), Salat (worship), Zakat (charity), *saum* (fasting) and Haj (pilgrimage). The mosque is the centre of religious activity. The 2 most important mosque officials are the *imam* – or leader – and the *khatib* or preacher – who delivers the Friday sermon.

The **Shahada** is the confession, and lies at the core of any Muslim's faith. It involves reciting, sincerely, 2 statements: 'There is no god, but God', and 'Mohammad is the Messenger [Prophet] of God'. A Muslim will do this at every **Salat**. This is the daily prayer ritual which is performed 3 times a day, at sunrise, midday and sunset. There is also the important Friday noon worship. The Salat is performed by a Muslim bowing and then prostrating himself in the direction of Mecca (in Indonesian *kiblat*, in Arabic *qibla*). In hotel rooms throughout Indonesia, Malaysia and Brunei, there is nearly always a little arrow, painted on the ceiling – or sometimes inside a wardrobe – indicating the direction of Mecca and labelled kiblat. The faithful are called to worship by a mosque official. Beforehand, a worshipper must wash to ensure ritual purity. The Friday midday service is performed in the mosque and includes a sermon given by the *khatib*.

A third essential element of Islam is **Zakat** – charity or alms-giving. A Muslim is supposed to give up his 'surplus' (according to the Koran); through time this took on the form of a tax levied according to the wealth of the family. In Indonesia there is no official Zakat as there is in Saudi Arabia, but good Muslims are expected to contribute a tithe to the Muslim community. In Bahasa Indonesia, *zakat* is translated as 'obligatory alms'.

The fourth pillar of Islam is **saum** or fasting. The daytime month-long fast of Ramadan is a time of contemplation, worship and piety – the Islamic equivalent of lent. Muslims are expected to read one-thirtieth of the Koran each night. Muslims who are ill or on a journey have dispensation from fasting, but otherwise they are only permitted to eat during the night until "so much of the dawn appears that a white thread can be distinguished from a black one".

The **Haj** or Pilgrimmage to the holy city of Mecca in Saudi Arabia is required of all Muslims once in their lifetime if they can afford to make the journey and are physically able to. It is restricted to a certain time of the year, beginning on the 8th day of the Muslim month of Dhu-l-Hijja. Men who have been on the Haj are given the title *Haji*, and women *hajjah*. The Koran also advises on a number of other practices and customs, in particular the prohibitions on usury, the eating of pork, the taking of alcohol, and gambling. In Indonesia, these are not strictly interpreted. Islamic banking laws have not been introduced, drinking is fairly widespread – although not in all areas – and the national lottery might be interpreted as a form of gambling. There is quite a powerful Islamic revival in Indonesia – as well as in Brunei and Malaysia – which is attempting to change what is perceived as the rather lax approach to Islamic prohibitions. For example, there is an effort to have the national lottery abolished. The use of the veil in its most extreme form is not common in Indonesia but is becoming *de rigeur* in Brunei and in areas of Malaysia. The Koran says nothing about the need for women to veil, although it does stress the necessity of women dressing modestly.

Buddhism shares the belief, in common with Hinduism, in rebirth. A person goes through countless lives and the experience of one life is conditioned by the acts in a previous one. This is the Law of Karma (act or deed, from Pali *kamma*), the law of cause and effect. But, it is not, as commonly thought in the West, equivalent to fate.

For most people, nirvana is a distant goal, and they merely aim to accumulate merit by living good lives and performing good deeds such as giving alms to monks. In this way the layman embarks on the Path to Heaven. It is also common for a layman to become ordained, at some point in his life (usually as a young man), for a 3 month period during the Buddhist Rains Retreat.

Monks should endeavour to lead stringently ascetic lives. They must refrain from murder, theft, sexual intercourse, untruths, eating after noon, alcohol, entertainment, ornament, comfortable beds and wealth. They are allowed to own only a begging bowl, 3 pieces of clothing, a razor, needle, belt and water filter. They can only eat food that they have received through begging. Anyone who is male, over 20, and not a criminal can become a monk.

Theravada Buddhism (Hinayana) The 'Way of the Elders', is believed to be closest to Buddhism as it originally developed in India. It is often referred to by the term 'Hinayana' (Lesser Vehicle), a disparaging name foisted onto Theravadans by Mahayanists. This form of Buddhism is the dominant contemporary religion in the mainland Southeast Asian countries of Thailand, Cambodia, Laos and Burma.

In Theravadan Buddhism, the historic Buddha, Sakyamuni, is revered above all else and most images of the Buddha are of Sakyamuni. Importantly, and unlike Mahayana Buddhism, the Buddha image is only meant to serve as a meditation aid. In theory, it does not embody supernatural powers, and it is not supposed to be worshipped. But, the popular need for objects of veneration has meant that most images *are* worshipped. Pilgrims bring flowers and incense, and prostrate themselves in front of the image. This is a Mahayanist influence which has been embraced by Theravadans.

Mahayana Buddhism In the 1st century AD a new movement evolved in South India. Initially the differences between this and the 'original' Theravada tradition were not great. But in time the 2 diverged, with the 'new' tradition gaining converts at the expense of its rival. Eventually, a new term was coined – Mahayana Buddhism or the Greater Vehicle. Although the schism is usually presented as a revolutionary development, a gradual evolution is more accurate. The most important difference between Mahayana and Theravada Buddhism is that the principal aim of Mahayana Buddhism should not be to attain enlightenment only for oneself, but to reach Bodhisattvahood (someone who embodies the essence of enlightenment) and then to remain on earth to assist others in their quest for nirvana.

Mahayana Buddhism was a response to a popular appeal for a more approachable and accessible religion – in India, at the time, the Hindu gods Siva and Vishnu were attracting substantial numbers of followers and Buddhism had to respond in some way. Monks were no longer required to retire from everyday life in their ultimately selfish quest for nirvana; they were to lead active lives in the community. And, no longer was there just one distant historic Buddha to look up to; there was a pantheon of Buddhas and Bodhisattvas, all objects of veneration, worship and prayer. Now, Buddhas and Bodhisattvas such as the Buddhas Amitabha, Vajrapani, Vairocana and Avalokitsvara (all various reincarnations of the Buddha) could actively intervene in the world for the betterment of mankind. Within Mahayana Buddhism there was a vast growth in doctrine (contained in the *sutras*) which accompanied this dramatic growth in the numbers of Buddhas and Bodhisattvas.

Mahayana Buddhism became the dominant form of Buddhism practiced in

Penis balls and sexual roles in historical Southeast Asia

One notable feature of Southeast Asian society is the relative autonomy of women. This is most clearly illustrated in sexual relations. As the historian Anthony Reid writes in his book *Southeast Asia in the age of commerce 1450-1680*: "Southeast Asian literature of the period leaves us in little doubt that women took a very active part in courtship and lovemaking, and demanded as much as they gave by way of sexual and emotional gratification". He then goes on to describe the various ways – often involving painful surgery – that men would try to satisfy their partners. Metal pins, for example, were inserted into the penis, and wheels, studs and spurs attached as accessories to increase the female's pleasure. Alternatively, metal balls or bells, sometimes made of gold or ivory, would be inserted beneath the skin of the penis. Numerous early European visitors expressed their astonishment at the practice. Tomé Pires, the 16th century Portuguese apothecary observed that Pegu lords in Burma "wear as many as 9 gold ones [penis bells], with beautiful treble, contralto and tenor tones, the size of the Alvares plums in our country; and those who are too poor...have them in lead...Malay women rejoice greatly when the Pegu men come to their country... [because of] their sweet harmony". Whereas in Africa, genital surgery was, and is, often intended to suppress pleasure for women or increase it for men, in Southeast Asia the reverse was the case. The surgery described above was also widely practiced – in Burma, Siam, Makassar, among the Torajans of Sulawesi, and Java.

Northern Asia (China and Japan), and also in ancient Cambodia and Indonesia. Today, in Southeast Asia, it is most widely practiced in Vietnam where it has, in most instances, fused with the Chinese 'religions', Taoism and Confucianism.

4. Islam

In island Southeast Asia, a similar displacement of an elitist Hindu-Buddhist religion by a popular religion was underway. In this case however it was Arab and Indian traders who introduced Islam to the area, and this religion has always had strong links with coastal locations and maritime trading routes. Like Theravada Buddhism on the mainland, Islam spread rapidly and by the time the Spanish had begun to colonize the Philippines during the mid- to late-16th century it had diffused northwards as far as the Philippine island of Mindanao.

5. Western cultural influences

The fifth cultural infusion, and one that continues, was that associated with the colonization of Southeast Asia by Portugal, Spain, Holland, Great Britain, France and the United States. Their activities also created the conditions that would promote the immigration of large numbers of Chinese (and to a lesser extent Indians) from the end of the 19th century and into the 20th. In the 1890s for example, up to 150,000 Chinese were arriving annually in Singapore alone. Today the Chinese in Peninsular Malaysia make up a third of the total population. Much of Southeast Asia has been so integrated into the world economy that it comes as a genuine surprise to many first-time visitors. Words like Coca-Cola, Pepsi, Marlboro and Levi's all enter a Southeast Asian's vocabulary at an early age. Many Thais believe that 'supermarket' is a word of Thai origin; while everywhere advertisements entice Southeast Asians to buy Western consumer goods. Even in isolated Indochina and Burma, Western products are highly prized and a mark of success: Johnny Walker Red Label whisky and 555 cigarettes in Burma, jeans in Vietnam, cassette recorders and Western music in Cambodia.

Local genius

Because of these successive cultural infusions over the past 2,000 years, there has been a tendency to emphasize the degree to which the inhabitants of Southeast Asia have been moulded by external cultural influences. They have; but foreign cultural elements have also been adapted and tailored to meet the needs and preferences of the people. Islam in Central Java, for example, includes many elements of Buddhism, Hinduism and Sufi mysticism – religious precursors to Islam on the island. The same is true of Theravada Buddhism in Thailand, which incorporates a large number of essentially animist and Brahmanical elements. The important role of women in Southeast Asian society for example, reflects a tradition which has survived the diffusion of different religions – where women are accorded lesser roles – into the region. Historically at least, this was most clearly reflected in the role of women in sexual relations (see box).

The major empires

Southeast Asia has witnessed the development of dozens of states since the turn of the Christian era. In several cases their power and artistic accomplishments can still be seen reflected in the magnificence of the buildings that have survived. There can be few regions in the world offering the visitor such varied and glorious reminders of past civilisations. The Victorian naturalist Joseph Jukes on seeing the Hindu temples at Malang in East Java, and in a characteristically long Victorian sentence, records:

> "The imagination became busy in restoring their fallen glories, in picturing large cities, adorned with temples and palaces, seated on the plain, and in recalling the departed power, wealth and state of the native kingdom that once flourished in a land so noble, so beautiful, and so well-adapted for its growth and security" (1847).

A broad – although rather simplistic – distinction can be drawn between those Southeast Asian empires which drew their power and their wealth from maritime trade, and those which were founded on agricultural production.

Maritime empires

Southeast Asia straddles the trade route between East and West. From the early years of the Christian era through to the colonial period, a succession of indigenous empires exploited these trade links with Europe, the Middle East, China and Japan, deriving wealth, power and prestige from their ability to control maritime trade. Foremost among them were Funan (Cambodia, 1st-6th century), and Srivijaya (Sumatra, 7th-13th century).

With its capital near Palembang in SE Sumatra, Srivijaya was in a strategic location to control trade through the 2 most important straits in Southeast Asia: the Strait of Melaka between the Malay peninsula and Sumatra, and the Sunda Strait between Sumatra and Java. Palembang offered seafarers an excellent harbour and repair facilities. The kings also used their wealth to build an impressive fleet with which they suppressed piracy in the Strait of Melaka. Srivijaya's empire expanded so fast that by the 9th century it included much of Sumatra, western Java, the Malay peninsula and the eastern portion of Borneo. In total, Srivijaya was the dominant power in the area for 350 years, from 670 AD to 1025.

Trade not only brought wealth to these maritime states. It also resulted in a fusion of Indian and Southeast Asian cultural traditions, a fact reflected in the legend of Funan's origins. Local legend records that a great Indian Brahmin with the name Kaundinya, acting on the instructions of a dream, sailed to the coast of Vietnam carrying with him a bow and arrow. On arriving, he shot the arrow and where it landed, he established the future capital of Funan. Following this act, Kaundinya married the princess Soma, daughter of the local King of the Nagas. The legend symbolizes the union between Indian and local cultural traditions – the *naga* representing indigenous fertility rites and customs, and the arrow, the potency of Hinduism.

Land-based empires
In addition to Funan and Srivijaya, Southeast Asia also witnessed the development of empires whose wealth was based upon the exploitation of the land, and in particular the cultivation of wet rice. Angkor (Cambodia, 9th-15th century), and the Sailendra Dynasty (Java, mid 8th-10th century) are both examples of such empires.

Angkor's power was derived from a coincidence of environmental wealth, human genius, and religious belief. The location of Angkor, close to the Tonle Sap or Great Lake meant that it had access to sufficient water to grow a surplus of rice large enough to support an extensive court, army and religious hierarchy. At the same time, it is also usually claimed that the kings of Angkor built an irrigation network of immense complexity – able to irrigate over 5 million hectares of land, and producing 3 to 4 crops of rice each year. This is now subject to dispute, with scholars arguing that the tanks at Angkor were not for agricultural, but for urban use. The third element contributing to Angkor's success was the legitimacy provided to its kings by the deva raja cult. As long as the king was accepted as divine, as a *chakravartin* or ruler of the universe, by all his subjects and the vassal states and princes under his control, then the empire would remain stable. This was the case from the 9th to the 15th centuries: for over 600 years Angkor lay at the centre of the grandest empire in Southeast Asia. King Jayavarman VII (1181-1219) for example, built the famous Bayon, as well as around 200 hospitals and rest houses, and 20,000 shrines. There were an estimated 300,000 priests and monks. It is said that Ta Phrom – just one of the temples in the complex at Angkor – required 79,365 people from 3,140 villages to build it. In 1864 the French explorer Henri Mouhot declared Angkor to be "grander than anything of Greece or Rome".

Like the rulers of Angkor, the kings of the Sailendra dynasty in island Southeast Asia, derived their wealth and power from agriculture. Exploiting the year-long rains, warmth, and fertile volcanic soil of Java, a substantial surplus of rice was produced. This fed a large court and a series of impressive monuments were built. The Sailendras were patrons of Buddhism, and they attracted Buddhist scholars from all over Asia to their court. It also seems that the kings were linked through marriage with the rulers of Srivijaya.

Of all the monuments of the Sailendra period none is more imposing the Borobudur built between 778 AD and 824 – to many the single greatest temple in all of Southeast Asia. This colossal monument, located on the Kedu Plain, represented the cosmological and spiritual centre of Sailendra power. Along its terraces, in row upon row of superbly executed reliefs (some 2,000 of them), the Sailendra world order is depicted: the 9 previous lives of the Gautama Buddha, princes and carpenters, dancers and fishermen. Borobudur was a religious justification for Sailendra rule, and at the same time gave the kings religious authority over Srivijaya. Johann Scheltema, a German traveller, on seeing Java's monuments wrote at the beginning of this century that they were: "...eloquent evidence of that innate conciousness which moves men to propitiate the principle of life by sacrifice in temples as gloriously divine as mortal hand can raise".

COLONIAL HISTORY

Early European contact: the allure of spices (16th-18th century)

During the course of the 15th century, the 2 great European maritime powers of the time, Spain and Portugal, were exploring sea routes to the E. Two forces were driving this search: the desire for profits, and the drive to evangelize. At the time, even the wealthy in Europe had to exist on pickled and salted fish and meat during the winter months (fodder crops for winter feed were not grown until the 18th century). Spices to flavour what would otherwise be a very monotonous diet were greatly sought after and commanded a high price. This was not just a passing European fad. An Indian Hindu wrote that: "When the palate revolts against the insipidness of rice boiled with no other ingredients, we dream of fat, salt and spices".

Of the spices, cloves and nutmeg originated from just one location, the Moluccas (Maluku) – the Spice Islands of eastern Indonesia. Perhaps because of their value, spices and their places of origin were accorded mythical status in Europe. The 14th century French friar Catalani Jordanus claimed for example that the clove flowers of Java produced an odour so strong it killed "every man who cometh among them, unless he shut his mouth and nostrils".

It was in order to break the monopoly on the spice trade held by Venetian and Muslim Arab traders that the Portuguese began to extend their possessions eastwards. This finally culminated in the capture of the port of Melaka by the Portuguese seafarer Alfonso de Albuquerque in Jun 1511. The additional desire to spread the Word of God is clear in the speech that Albuquerque made before the battle with the Muslim sultan of Melaka, when he exorted his men, stressing:

> "...the great service which we shall perform to our Lord in casting the Moors out of this country and of quenching the fire of the sect of Mohammet so that it may never burst out again hereafter".

From their base in Melaka, the Portuguese established trading relations with the Moluccas, and built a series of forts across the region: at Bantam (Banten), Flores, Ternate, Tidore, Timor and Ambon (Amboyna).

As the Portuguese were sailing E to Southeast Asia, the Spanish, from their possessions in South America, were sailing W. It was in order to prevent clashes between the 2 powers that a Papal Bull of 1493 divided the world along a line just W of the Azores: everywhere to the W of this line was left for the Spanish, and everything to the E of it for the Portuguese. Unfortunately, the Pope remained convinced that the earth was flat and never envisaged the 2 powers meeting in Southeast Asia. This occurred when Ferdinand Magellan arrived in the Philippines in 1521 having crossed the Pacific – in a remarkable feat of seamanship. After a short period of conflict, the 2 protagonists settled their differences, the Portuguese leaving the Philippines to the Spanish, and the Spanish agreeing not to interfere in the Moluccas.

By the late 16th century, Portuguese influence in Southeast Asia was waning. Their empire was over-extended, and the claim that Portuguese seafarers were helping to introduce Christianity to the infidels of the region sat uneasily next to the barbaric methods they employed. Francis Xavier, the canonised Catholic missionary, is said to have been so appalled by the debauchery and vice of Melaka that when he left he shook the sand from his shoes, vowing never to return to the cursed city again. The Portuguese were supplanted by the Dutch in the region who, by 1616, had established 15 trading posts and gained control of the spice trade.

But despite these advances, in many respects the European presence was peripheral. The motivation was to secure spices and to make money, not to extend territorially. The stupendous lost city of Angkor in Cambodia for example, was not extensively reported upon until the French naturalist Henri Mouhot published the diary of his 1861 visit 3 years later.

The intensification of the European presence (19th-20th century)

At the beginning of the 19th century, a number of developments markedly increased European interest in the colonization of Southeast Asia. Most important, was the region's new-found economic potential. Europe's industrial revolution led to increased demand for industrial raw materials, while at the same time companies were looking for markets for their manufactured goods. Southeast Asia was in a position to provide the first of these at the beginning, and as the region's development proceeded, the second too. Allied to these developments, there were also a number of technological advances which considerably shortened the journey to Southeast Asia. The opening of the Suez canal in 1869 precluded the dangerous trip around Cape Horn, while the development of the steam ship slashed days off the journey. The active spread of Christianity was once again firmly on the agenda, and European governments found it hard not to interfere when zealous missionaries and their converts were persecuted by local leaders. This was especially true in Vietnam where missionaries had been periodically persecuted from the early 17th century. This reached its height during the reigns of the Vietnamese emperors Minh Mang (1820-41), Thieu Tri (1841-47) and Tu Duc (1847-83). Minh Mang, for example, issued a decree in 1833 ordering churches to be destroyed and made profession of the Catholic faith a capital offence. French ecclesiastical magazines contained vivid accounts of the torture and murder of French missionaries, and the clamour raised by the French public ultimately led to the invasion and colonization of Vietnam by France.

The effect of these developments was that over a relatively short space of time – about 45 years, between 1825 and 1870 – all of Southeast Asia with the exception of Siam (the old name for Thailand) fell under European control. More detailed discussion about the final subjugation of the region is contained in the introductory sections dealing with the individual countries. In essence however, there were 2 set of rivalries: between the French and the British on the mainland, and between the Dutch and the British in the archipelago. The local empires had neither the economic power, military might nor, in many cases, the political skills to withstand the Europeans.

The impact of the colonial period in Southeast Asia

The impact of the colonial period extended far beyond mere political domination. Southeast Asia was irreparably affected economically, socially, culturally, even physically. More to the point, these effects are still visible today in the region's economic and social fabric.

The principal effect of the colonial period was to alter the economic basis of life in Southeast Asia. In brief, a process of commercialization was set in train. Huge areas of land were cleared in the river deltas of the region and planted to rice. Along the Irrawaddy in Burma for example, the area under rice cultivation increased from 400,000 hectares in 1855, to 4 million hectares by 1930. This process was pioneered by large numbers of individual peasants responding to the new economic opportunities provided by the presence of the colonial powers. This was even the case in independent Thailand, where the king could do little to constrain the economic influence of the West.

Even more dramatically, Western-financed estates growing plantation crops such as rubber and coffee were widely established. In Malaysia, the area planted to rubber – a crop which was only introduced to the region in the late 19th century – increased from a paltry 137 hectares in 1897, to 1.4 million hectares by 1939. These estates used immigrant labour, imported machinery, they were managed

peans, financed by foreign capital, and exported all their production. They
d 'enclaves', completely separate from the local, traditional, economy.
or did the economic effects of the colonial period merely affect agriculture.
The Western powers also needed minerals and timber to fuel their industrial
revolutions. Most spectacularly, tin-mining expanded. The introduction of the
steam chain-bucket dredge, steam pumps, and new drilling methods
revolutionized the tin industry. By the later 1930s, Indonesia, Thailand and Malaya
were supplying 60% of the world's tin.

Not surprisingly, this process of commercialization deeply affected the
inhabitants of the region. Farmers were inexorably drawn into the cash economy.
Seeds and fertilisers were purchased in increasing quantities, money was
borrowed, labour hired, land rented and surplus production sold. The process of
commercialization not only undermined the traditional self-sufficiency of the
Southeast Asian village, it also affected the social fabric of the village. People
became dependent on economic developments in the international economy.
This was thrown into stark perspective during the Great Depression of the early
1930s when the price of rubber halved, and then halved again, between 1929
and 1932. Rice farmers had their land repossessed as money lenders foreclosed
on their loans. Riots broke out across the region as dispossessed peasants
demonstrated their anger and frustration.

The exploitation of Southeast Asia's natural resources entailed the
improvement of communications and transport infrastructure. As a result, a
network of roads and railways were built. However these did not serve all areas
equally. Mainly they linked areas of export commodity production with the outside
world. In the same way, although the colonial presence led to a dramatic growth
in the number and size of urban settlements, these occupied different locations
and had different *raisons d'être* from their indigenous precursors. The great port
cities of Singapore, Georgetown (Penang), Batavia (Jakarta), Rangoon, Saigon,
even Bangkok developed in order to funnel export commodities out of the region,
and manufactured imports in. Likewise, many inland towns owed their existence
to the export commodities that were produced in the surrounding areas such as
Taiping and Sungei Ujong (now Seremban), both Malayan towns that grew on
the back of the tin trade.

Another feature of modern Southeast Asia, which has its roots in the colonial
period, is their multi-racial make-up. These groups, although they lived (and
continued to live) in close proximity to one another, rarely mixed. The most striking
example of a plural society is Malaysia where 32% of the population of Peninsular
Malaysia are Chinese, 8% Indian, and nearly 60% Malay. The explanation for this
heterogeneous population lies in the demand for labour during the colonial
period. For the colonial authorities found it extremely hard to recruit sufficient
local labour to work on the plantations, in the tin mines, and in the other export
industries. The logical solution was to import labour from abroad. From the end
of the 19th century, hundreds of thousands of Chinese and Indians arrived in
Malaya. It was usually these immigrants' intention to return to their mother
countries, but many stayed on – sometimes because they were too poor to leave,
sometimes because they wished to keep an eye on the wealth that they had
accumulated. The immigration of 'indentured' labourers was greatest in British
Malaya: between 1909 and 1940 some 16 million Indians and Chinese arrived in
Malaya. Today Malaysia's total population is only 18 million.

The Second World War and the Japanese interregnum

Prior to the outbreak of the Second World War, the strains of commercialization,
domination by foreign powers, and the often heavy-handed and insensitive
behaviour of colonial officials had engendered only a limited reaction from the
local populations. Nationalist movements lacked focus, and charismatic leaders

were needed to add coherence and direction to nascent independence movements. Rather ironically, this was provided by a Western-educated Southeast Asian elite. Men such as Sukarno of Indonesia and Ho Chi Minh of Vietnam, travelled abroad for their further education, were introduced to notions of self-government and nationhood, and read works by Marx, Lenin, Locke and Rousseau. But even with the establishment of a handful of nationalist parties prior to the outbreak of the Second World War, they were regarded as only a minor irritation by the colonial powers. Few would have dreamt that within so short a space of time – less than a decade in most cases – the countries of Southeast Asia would have achieved independence.

The war changed the nature of the relationship between the colonial powers and the people that they ruled. In the space of less than 6 months, virtually the entire region was over-run by Japanese forces. In Dec 1941, the Japanese landed in Northern Malaya, having already taken control of French Indochina; on 11th Jan, Kuala Lumpur fell; on 15th Feb, Singapore capitulated; on 7th Mar, Rangoon was abandoned; and on 8th Mar, the Dutch surrendered in Indonesia. This was the darkest period of the entire war for the Allies. However, not only did the Japanese demonstrate the military fallibility of the colonial powers in a style that could not have been more compelling; they were also Asian. The war made independence inevitable – and sooner rather than later. The colonial powers were drained and exhausted; they had lost much of their credibility; and they returned to find that the fragmented nationalist parties of the pre-war years had grown in size, influence and authority. Burma was granted independence in 1948, Indonesia in 1949, Cambodia in 1953, North Vietnam and Laos in 1954, South Vietnam in 1955, Malaya in 1957, and Singapore in 1963. Brunei only attained full independence in 1984.

MODERN SOUTHEAST ASIA

Southeast Asia's recent history has effectively divided the region into 2 groups of countries. On the one hand there are the market economies of the Association of Southeast Asian Nations (ASEAN). These include Thailand, Malaysia, Indonesia, Singapore and Brunei, as well as the Philippines. And on the other there are the Communist/socialist countries of Indochina – Vietnam, Laos and Cambodia – and Burma. These 2 sets of countries have embraced economic and political ideologies which, until very recently, were diametrically opposed to one another. The countries of ASEAN have followed – simplistically-speaking – the Western, capitalist, consumer-orientated path to economic success, although many have begun to look to Japan, rather than to Europe or America, as their role model. At the same time they have tended to side with the West politically. In contrast, the countries of Indochina and Burma have embraced a socialist or Communist vision of reconstruction and development. They also supported the former Soviet Union or China in the East-West conflict, except Burma which followed a policy of non-alignment and self-sufficiency. Since the late 1980s, the countries of ASEAN and Indochina have grown together politically and economically, and for the first time in recent history there is the possibility that the region might become a 'united' area of 400 million people – former Thai Prime Minister Chatichai's *Suwannaphume* or Golden Land.

The market economies: rapid growth and change

The countries of ASEAN, which include Thailand, Malaysia, Singapore, Brunei and Indonesia (as well as the Philippines), are among the fastest-growing economies in the world. Since 1965 they have achieved average annual rates of growth of over 6%, and they are seen by many analysts to represent a second tier of or 'tigers': countries which are basing their success on aggressive, orientated, industrial growth in the way Japan, South Korea and Taiwan ore them. Undoubtedly the most successful country in this group – in economic terms – has been Singapore. When the island-state achieved self government in 1959, it was in a woeful condition with high unemployment, a decaying urban core, political unrest and no manufacturing base to speak of. Today Singapore is one of the wealthiest countries in the world. Average incomes exceed US$12,000 – higher than Spain and Ireland – and far-sighted planning has given the city a futuristic feel. The oil-rich Sultanate of Brunei has an even higher average income – over US$20,000.

Thailand, Indonesia and Malaysia have had to support sizeable poor rural populations and have enjoyed rather less stratospheric rates of economic growth. Nonetheless, they have still progressed at a speed which would be the envy of many Latin American and African countries. The proportion of the population living in absolute poverty has decreased from 60% to 15% between 1970 and 1990 in Indonesia, and from 26% to 16% over the same period in the case of Thailand.

Politically, these market economies have also moved gradually – but often haltingly – towards more representative government. Thailand experienced a coup at the beginning of 1991 and popular demonstrations in early 1992, while Indonesia's system of government is still a far cry from Western democracy. Nonetheless, there is a growing recognition that governments must reflect the will of the people.

The city and countryside

Development in the West has been evolutionary rather than revolutionary. In Southeast Asia the reverse has been the case. Progress has been bewilderingly fast and has resulted in the uneven distribution of wealth. The contrast between city and countryside provides tangible evidence of this. For the visitor, the capital cities of the region can be thoroughly exhausting, with hot and humid climates, noise and bustle, and often appalling traffic conditions. Away from the cities in the countryside, landscape and life tend to be much more in keeping with the popular view of Southeast Asia – rice, buffaloes, tropical forests, traditional festivals and ceremonies. Superficially, rural life seems to reflect traditional patterns and processes. But, in the same way that the modern cities embody many traditional elements, so the traditional countryside is rapidly modernizing. Beneath the surface, the technology of agriculture and the aspirations and outlook of farmers have changed dramatically. Improving communications in the form of better roads and transport, and radio and television, have meant that farmers are aware of developments in the wider world. Today they wish to provide for their families the benefits of modern health care and education, and this has necessitated that they embrace the cash economy.

But, the process of development has not always been devoid of tensions and frictions. In the forested areas of Southeast Asia, tribal groups such as the Hmong of Thailand and the upriver Dayak tribes of Sarawak have suffered both economically and culturally as a dominant, Western-style consumer culture has impinged on their lives. Some groups have tried to fight the process of commercialization, often in league with foreign environmentalist groups. A large segment of the population has also become economically marginalized – despite the rapid economic growth. In the cities, there are millions of slum dwellers and squatters, living without clean water, medical care and education and subsisting in the informal sector. In rural areas, farmers have been pushed off their land as population has begun to press upon the land resource, and as the commercialization of producton has led to the accumulation of land in the hands of a small number of wealthy landowners. The resulting army of landless peasants have been forced to work for wages of perhaps a dollar a day on other people's fields.

Indochina and Burma: stagnation and reform

The countries of Indochina and Burma, like the other former Communist states of the world, are having to contend with an entirely new global landscape. They have responded to economic stagnation and the general failure of their socialist programmes of development by introducing increasingly reformist economic policies. In Laos, the government talks of *chin thanakan mai* or 'new thinking', while in Vietnam there is *doi moi* or 'renovation' – both Southeast Asian equivalents to the former Soviet Union's *perestroika*. This new outlook embraces the market, foreign investment, material incentives and private ownership. As the *Economist* recently put it:-

> "The reality that can be seen, touched, heard and on occasion sniffed is that the average Vietnamese, Lao, Cambodian or Burmese is dirt-poor. Bangkok's street vendors peddle fake designer watches to foreign tourists; Hanoi's mend odd bits of ancient machinery for other townsfolk, or give them shaves and haircuts in front of cracked pieces of mirror."

But although market-orientated reform may be at the top of the agenda among the Communist and Socialist parties of Indochina and Burma, there has not be – a concomitant process of *glasnost* in the political system. With the exception of Cambodia, the ruling parties have retained tight control of the reins of power. They appear unwilling to allow greater plurality of political expression, and outspoken critics are quickly silenced. Whether these countries will be able to maintain the delicate balancing act of allowing greater economic freedom while denying their people any significant political freedom is a moot point.

SOUTHEAST ASIA: SUGGESTED READING

Magazines

Asiaweek (weekly). A lightweight *Far Eastern Economic Review*; rather like a regional *Time* magazine in style.

The Far Eastern Economic Review (weekly). Authoritative Hong Kong-based regional magazine; their correspondents based in each country provide knowledgeable, in-depth analysis particularly on economics and politics, sometimes in rather a turgid style (although a recent change of editor has meant some lightening of style).

Books

Buruma, Ian (1989) *God's dust*, Jonathan Cape: London. Enjoyable journey through Burma, Thailand, Malaysia and Singapore along with the Philippines, Taiwan, South Korea and Japan; journalist Buruma questions how far culture in this region has survived the intrusion of the West.

Caufield, C. (1985) *In the rainforest*, Heinemann: London. This readable and well-researched analysis of rainforest ecology and the pressures on tropical forests is part-based in the region.

Clad, James (1989) *Behind the myth: business, money and power in Southeast Asia*, Unwin Hyman: London. Clad, formerly a journalist with the *Far Eastern Economic Review*, distilled his experiences in this book; as it turned out, rather disappointingly – it is a hotch-potch of journalistic snippets.

Conrad, Joseph (1900) *Lord Jim*, Penguin: London. The tale of Jim, who abandons his ship and seeks refuge from his guilt in Malaya, earning the sobriquet Lord.

Conrad, Joseph (1902) *Heart of darkness*, Penguin: London. In probably Conrad's most famous book, Kurtz travels to the 'heart of darkness'.

Conrad, Joseph (1915) *Victory: an island tale*, Penguin: London. Arguably Conrad's finest novel, based in the Malay Archipelago.

Conrad, Joseph (1920) *The rescue*, Penguin: London. Set in the Malay Archipelago in the 1860s; the hero, Captain Lingard, is forced to choose between his Southeast Asian friend and his countrymen.

Dumarçay, Jacques (1991) *The palaces of South-East Asia: architecture and customs*, OUP: Singapore. A broad summary of palace art and architecture in both mainland and island Southeast Asia.

Fenton, James (1988) *All the wrong places: adrift in the politics of Asia*, Penguin: London.

nalist James Fenton skilfully and entertainingly recounts his experiences in Vietnam, , the Philippines and Korea.

-Lu, Sylvia (1988) *Handwoven textiles of South-East Asia*, OUP: Singapore. Wei-... .trated, large-format book with informative text.

Higham, Charles (1989) *The archaeology of mainland Southeast Asia from 10,000 BC to the fall of Angkor*, Cambridge University Press: Cambridge. Best summary of changing views of the archaeology of the mainland.

Keyes, Charles F. (1977) *The golden peninsula: culture and adaptation in mainland Southeast Asia*, Macmillan: New York. Academic, yet readable summary of the threads of continuity and change in Southeast Asia's culture.

King, Ben F. and Dickinson, E.C. (1975) *A field guide to the birds of South-East Asia*, Collins: London. Best regional guide to the birds of the region.

Miettinen, Jukko O. (1992) *Classical dance and theatre in South-East Asia*, OUP, Singapore. Expensive, but accessible survey of dance and theatre, mostly focusing on Indonesia, Thailand and Burma.

Osborne, Milton (1979) *Southeast Asia: an introductory history*, Allen & Unwin: Sydney. Good introductory history, clearly written, published in a portable paperback edition.

Rawson, Philip (1967) *The art of Southeast Asia*, Thames & Hudson: London. Portable general art history of Cambodia, Vietnam, Thailand, Laos, Burma, Java and Bali; by necessity, rather superficial.

Reid, Anthony (1988) *Southeast Asia in the age of commerce 1450-1680*, Yale University Press: New Haven. Perhaps the best history of everyday life in Southeast Asia, looking at such themes as physical well-being, material culture and social organization.

Rigg, Jonathan (1991) *Southeast Asia: a region in transition*, Unwin Hyman: London. A thematic geography of the ASEAN region, providing an insight into some of the major issues affecting the region today.

SarDesai, D.R. (1989) *Southeast Asia: past and present*, Macmillan: London. Skilful but at times frustratingly thin history of the region from the 1st century to the withdrawal of US forces from Vietnam.

Savage, Victor R. (1984) *Western impressions of nature and landscape in Southeast Asia*, Singapore University Press: Singapore. Based on a geography PhD thesis, the book is a mine of quotations and observations from Western travellers.

Steinberg, D.J. *et al.* (1987) *In search of Southeast Asia: a modern history*, University of Hawaii Press: Honolulu. The best standard history of the region; it skilfully examines and assesses general processes of change and their impacts from the arrival of the Europeans in the region.

Wallace, Alfred Russel (1869) *The Malay Archipelago: the land of the orang-utan and the bird of paradise; a narrative of travel with studies of man and nature*, MacMillan: London. A classic of natural history writing, recounting Wallace's 8 years in the archipelago and now re-printed.

Young, Gavin (1991) *In search of Conrad*, Hutchinson: London. This well-known travel writer retraces the steps of Conrad; part travel-book, part fantasy, it is worth reading but not up to the standard of his other books.

MALAYSIA

	Page		Page
Introduction	51	**Borneo Introduction**	222
Kuala Lumpur	91	**Sarawak**	230
Northern Peninsula Malaysia	115	**Sabah**	293
Southern Peninsula Malaysia	157	**Information for Visitors**	344
The Peninsula's East Coast	181		

INTRODUCTION

Malaysia is sometimes called 'the lucky country of Asia' because it is so richly endowed with natural resources. It has the world's largest tin deposits, extensive oil and gas reserves and is cloaked in rainforest containing valuable tropical hardwoods. Until very recently, the economy was heavily dependent on these resources and plantation crops such as palm oil, natural rubber, timber, pepper and cocoa. But in the late 1980s and early 1990s, a sudden explosion of industrial growth, spearheaded by a surge in manufacturing, changed the complexion of Malaysia's economy beyond recognition. In 1992, Michael Vatikiotis, Kuala Lumpur correspondent for *The Far Eastern Economic Review*, wrote: "Malaysia in many ways forms the leading edge of social change in Southeast Asia... Prime Minister Dr Mahathir Mohamad has captivated his people with a vision of a developed Malaysia by 2020. Deploying this distant vision of the future has allowed Malaysians to think of themselves as becoming a nation of airline pilots and nuclear physicists by 2020."

Malaysia is a young country – until the end of the last century there was just a collection of divided coastal sultanates around the peninsula and three colonial trading settlements. The British grouped the different states into a federation, but Malaysia did not emerge in its present form until 1965, 8 years after independence from the British. Today the Federation of Malaysia includes the 11 peninsular states together with Sabah and Sarawak on the island of Borneo (East Malaysia). Singapore left the federation in 1965 after an unsuccessful two-year experiment. The politically dominant Malays of the peninsula had felt uncomfortable with the destabilizing effect of Singapore's mainly Chinese population on the country's racial equation.

A favourite Malaysian dish is *rojak* – a tossed salad with many different ingredients. It is not uncommon to hear the rojak analogy applied to Malaysia's exotic ethnic mix of Malays, Chinese, Indians and indigenous tribes. The country's cultural blend makes Malaysia interesting, but it is also a potentially volatile

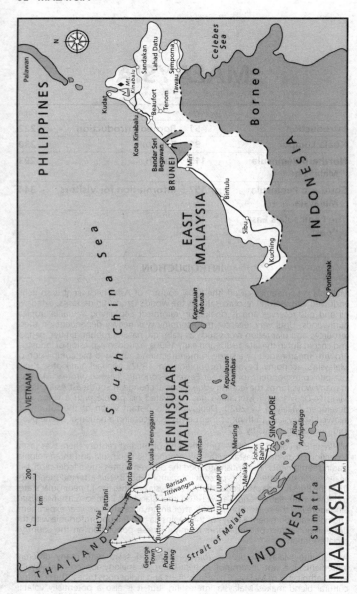

mixture. Yet only once since independence in 1957 has the communal melting pot boiled over. Today, most Malaysians are too young to remember the 1969 race riots, although they have lived with their consequences for more than 2 decades. The government's affirmative action policies have attempted to lessen the economic disparities between the races (**see page 86**) and have given the Malays – the economic underdogs – a helping hand. Over the years, non-Malays have complained bitterly about discrimination against them by the Malay-led government, but somehow, tensions have been kept below boiling point. Today, there is much more inter-mixing between Malaysians from all ethnic backgrounds; many of them are more interested in cashing in on the economic boom than worrying about race. When Malaysia celebrated 35 years of nationhood in August 1992, Dr Mahathir said that on independence, many had predicted that its multiracial, multicultural and multireligious society would collapse. "Malaysia has proven to the world", he said, "that its multiracial nature has not prevented it from achieving progress and success. We must continue to cooperate and be united."

The government of Dr Mahathir has ushered in an era of undreamt of economic growth. He has capitalized on the boom his policies helped create by promoting his coalition government as the one and only hope for a stable and prosperous Malaysia. He is widely regarded as the architect of Malaysia's success. In 1990 the electorate resoundingly voted for more of the same and the foreign investors on whom the Malaysian economy increasingly relies continued to vote with their feet. Today Malaysians are bristling with self-confidence in their new-found prosperity, which is a key ingredient of the social glue that binds the country's plural society.

The tourism industry plays a crucial role in Malaysia's economy. The country is endowed with good beaches, coral reefs, ancient jungle, mountains and hill resorts, islands and, these days, hundreds of golf courses. It also has a handful of

Putting Malaya on the map

The names of most of Malaysia's states are older than the name Malaya – until the 1870s the scattered coastal sultanates were independent of each other. Many of the Malay areas were colonized by Sumatrans long ago and it is possible that the word 'Melayu' – or 'Malay' – derives from the Sungei Melayu (Melayu River) in Sumatra. The name in turn is derived from the Dravidian (Tamil) word *malai*, or 'hill'. As the Malays are coastal people, the paradox is explained by their pre-Islamic religion, which is thought to have been based on a cult in which a sacred mountain took pride of place.

The Graeco-Roman geographer Ptolemy called the Malay peninsula *Aurea Chersonesus* – 'The Golden Chersonese': it was the fabled land of gold. By the early 1500s, European maps were already marking Melaka and Pulau Tioman, which were well known to Chinese mariners. During the Portuguese and Dutch colonial periods, the whole peninsula was simply labelled 'Malacca', and the town was the only significant European outpost until the British took possession of Penang in 1786. There was very little mapping of the peninsula until the early 19th century, and the names of states only gradually appeared on maps over the course of the 17th and 18th centuries.

According to cartographic historian R T Fell, the first maps of the interior of the peninsula, beyond the bounds of the British Straits Settlements, did not appear until the late 19th century. In 1885 the Survey Department was founded and charged with mapping the interior – one of the tasks William Cameron was undertaking when he stumbled across the highland plateau named after him that same year. But right into the 20th century, large tracts of mountainous jungle were still unexplored.

urban attractions: notably Penang's beautifully preserved Chinatown and Melaka's architectural heritage. As the world's largest exporter of sawn timber Malaysia's logging industry has earned the country notoriety among environmentalists. The industry is riddled with corruption and the Malaysian government admits to problems enforcing its surprisingly stringent forestry policies. But well over half Malaysia's land area is forested and the government has been enthusiastically promoting ecotourism; there are several magnificent national parks, both on the peninsula and in the East Malaysian states of Sarawak and Sabah. In Sarawak there are also many jungle tribes, whose culture has remained remarkably intact.

For an historical introduction to Sarawak **see page 232**, and for Sabah **see page 293**.

ENVIRONMENT

Land

Malaysia covers a total land area of 329,054 sq km and includes Peninsular Malaysia (131,587 sq km) and the Borneo states of Sarawak (124,967 sq km) and Sabah (72,500 sq km). Geologically, both the peninsula and Borneo are part of the Sunda shelf, although the mountains of the peninsula were formed longer ago than those in Borneo. This 'shelf' was inundated as glaciers retreated at the end of the Pleistocene ice-age.

The Malay peninsula is about 800 km N-S, has a long narrow neck, a tapered tail and a bulging, mountainous, middle. The neck is called the **Kra Isthmus**, which links the peninsula to the Southeast Asian mainland. The isthmus itself is in southern Thailand – Peninsular Malaysia comprises only the lower portion of the peninsula and covers an area larger than England and a little smaller than Florida. Nestled into the southernmost end of the peninsula is the island of Singapore, separated from the peninsula by the narrow Strait of Johor. The thin western coastal plain drains into the Strait of Melaka, which separates the peninsula from Sumatra (Indonesia) and is one of the oldest shipping lanes in the world. The eastern coastal lowlands drain into the South China Sea.

The **Barisan Titiwangsa** (Main Range) comprises the curved jungle-clad spine of Peninsular Malaysia. It is the most prominent of several, roughly parallel ranges running longitudinally down the peninsula. These subsidiary ranges include the **Kedah-Singgora Range** in the north-west; the **Bintang Range** (stretching north-east from Taiping), the **Tahan Range** (which includes the peninsula's highest mountain, Gunung Tahan, 2,187m). In the northern half of the peninsula, the mountainous belt is very wide, leaving only a narrow coastal strip on either side.

The Main Range – or Barisan Titiwangsa – runs S from the Thai border for nearly 500 km, gradually fizzling out on the coastal plain, near Melaka. The average elevation is about 1,000m and there are several peaks of more than 2,000m. The southern end of the range is much narrower and the mountains, lower; the most prominent southern 'outlier' is Gunung Ledang (Mount Ophir) in Johor. Until just over a century ago, when William Cameron first ventured into the mountains of the Main Range, this was uncharted territory – British colonial Malaya was, in fact, little more than the W coastal strip. Not only was the W coast adjacent to the important trade routes (and therefore had most of the big towns), its alluvial deposits were also rich in tin. Because roads and railways were built along this western side of the peninsula during the colonial period, it also became the heart of the plantation economy.

In addition to the mountain ranges, the Malay peninsula also has many spectacular limestone outcrops. These distinctive outcrops are mainly in the Kuala

Lumpur area (such as Batu Caves and those in and around Templer Park) and in the Kampar Valley near Ipoh, to the north. The erosion of the limestone has produced intricate solution-cave systems, some with dramatic formations. The vegetation on these hills is completely different to the surrounding lowland rainforest.

Malaysia's year-round rainfall has resulted in a dense network of rivers. The peninsula's longest river is the Sungei Pahang, which runs for just over 400 km. Most rivers flood regularly – particularly during the NE monsoon season – and during the heavy rain the volume of water can more than double in the space of a few hours. The flooding of Malaysian rivers has become more pronounced due to logging and mining. Waterfalls are very common features in Peninsular Malaysia; these occur where rivers, with their headwaters in the hills, encounter resistant (usually igneous) rocks as they cut their valleys.

Climate

The Malay peninsula has an equatorial monsoon climate (for more details on the climatic features of Sabah and Sarawak, see page 223). Temperatures are uniformly high throughout the year – as is humidity – and rainfall is abundant and well distributed, although it peaks during the NE monsoon period from Nov to Feb.

Mean annual temperature on the coastal lowlands is around 26°C. The mean

Climatic variations: yes, we have no monsoons

One of the problems frustrating Peninsular Malaysia's E coast states in their efforts to promote tourism is the weather. Although coconut palms sway gently over sun-splashed sandy beaches most of the year round, the NE monsoon starts to blow just as the northern hemisphere's Christmas holidays get underway and antipodeans start thinking about their summer getaways. State authorities contend that the Nov to Mar monsoon is blown out of all proportion in the minds of Western tourists (and most Malaysians for that matter).

Tourism Malaysia says too much is made of the word 'monsoon' and points the finger at Club Med – which owns an idyllic private beach at Cerating in Pahang – for reinforcing the problem by shutting down during the NE monsoon season. The tourism committee in NE Terengganu state has gone as far as to ban the use of the word altogether because they believe it has created a stigma among tourists and investors. They say 'rainy weather' is a perfectly adequate description. Others might consider this an understatement: more than 600 mm of rain has fallen on parts of the E coast within a single day.

On the other side of the peninsula, however, states occasionally suffer from too little rain. In 1991, for example, there was a water-crisis in Melaka – the worst for 30 years – and on behalf of the state government, the Chief Minister contracted an American company, TJC-Atmos Engineers, to help resolve the problem. The company was promised more than M$3 if it created enough rain to fill the local reservoir. But after claiming to have produced rain on 30 separate occasions over a two-month period, Kuala Lumpur's Meteorological Services Department (MSD) dismissed the company's techniques as 'unscientific' and said any rain was a natural consequence of the SW monsoon.

The director of TJC-Atmos claimed to use 'etheric engineering techniques' to attract clouds, by "manipulating the *qi* [or subtle life-force] in the atmosphere". He had developed the techniques while investigating Unidentified Flying Objects in the 1950s and described himself as 'a hi-tech *bomoh*' (Malay witch doctor). The director of the MSD took a dim view of his 'metaphysical' techniques however and TJC-Atmos Engineering left Malaysia empty-handed.

daily minima in the lowlands is between 21.7°C and 24.4°C; the mean daily maxima is between 29.4°C and 32.8°C. The maxima are higher and the minima, lower, towards the interior. In the Cameron Highlands, the mean annual temperature is 18°C. Temperatures dip slightly during the north-east monsoon period. The highest recorded temperature, 39.4°C, was recorded on Pulau Langkawi in March 1931. The lowest absolute minimum temperature ever recorded on the peninsula was in the Cameron Highlands in Jan 1937 when the temperature fell to 2.2°C. The Cameron Highlands also claims the most extreme range in temperature – the absolute maximum recorded there is 26.7°C.

The developed W coast of the peninsula is sheltered from the NE monsoon which strikes the E coast with full force between Nov and Feb. The east coast's climatic vagaries have reinforced its remoteness: it is particularly wet and the area N of Kuantan receives between 3,300 mm and 4,300 mm a year. About half of this falls in the NE monsoon period. The NW coast of the peninsula is also wet and parts receive more than 3,000 mm of rain a year. Bukit Larut (Maxwell Hill), next to Taiping has an annual rainfall of more than 5,000 mm. The W coast receives its heaviest rainfall in Mar and Apr. Oct and Apr are the transitional months between the SW and NE monsoons.

Thunderstorms provide most of Malaysia's rainfall. In the most torrential downpour ever recorded in Kuala Lumpur 51 mm of rain fell in 15 minutes. Heavy rain like this causes serious soil erosion in areas which have been cleared of vegetation.

In the more heavily populated coastal districts of the peninsula, the temperature is ameliorated by sea breezes which set in about 1000 and gather force until early afternoon. In the evenings, a land breeze picks up. These winds are only felt for distances up to 15 km inland. Another typical weather feature on the Malay peninsula is the squall – a sudden, violent storm characterized by sharp gusts of wind. These can be very localized in their effect, very unpredictable and, from time to time, very hazardous to light fishing vessels. Squalls are caused by cool air (either from sea breezes in the late morning or land breezes in the evening) undercutting warmer air; squall lines are marked by stacks of cumulo-nimbus clouds. Most squalls occur between May and Aug; the ones that develop along the W coast between Port Klang and Singapore during this period are called 'Sumatras' and produce particularly violent cloudbursts. Most Sumatras occur at night or in the early morning, while squalls between Nov and Feb usually occur in the afternoon.

Flora and fauna

Originally 97% of Malaysia's land area was covered in closed-canopy forest. According to the government, about 56% of Malaysia is still forested – although it is difficult to ascertain exactly how much of this is primary rainforest. Only 5% of the remaining jungle is under conservation restrictions. The Malaysian jungle, which, at about 130 million years old, is believed to be among the oldest forest in the world, supports more than 145,000 species of flowering plant (well over 1,000 of which are already known to have pharmaceutical value), 200 mammal species, 600 bird species and countless thousands of insect species. The rainforest is modified by underlying rock-type (impervious rocks and soils result in swamp forest) and by altitude (lowland rainforest gives way to thinner montane forest on higher slopes). All the main forest types are represented on the peninsula; these include mangrove swamp forest, peat swamp forest, heath forest, lowland and hill mixed *Dipterocarp* forest and montane forest. Where primary forest has been logged, burned or cleared by shifting cultivators or miners, secondary forest grows up quickly. In Malaysia, this is known as *belukar*. It can take up to 250 years before climax rainforest is re-established. The pioneer plant species colonizing abandoned *ladang* (sites cleared by shifting cultivators) is called *lalang* (elephant grass).

Mammals

Malaysia has a varied mammal population, although the continual development of forested areas has destroyed many habitats in recent years. Malaysia's, and Asia's, biggest mammal is the Asiatic elephant. Adult elephants weigh up to 3-4 tonnes; they are rarely seen, although the carnage caused by a passing herd can sometimes be seen in Taman Negara (the National Park). For more detail on elephants, **see page 225**. One of the strangest Malayan mammals is the tapir, with its curled snout – or trunk – and white bottom. The starkly contrasting black and white is good camouflage in the jungle, where it is effectively concealed by light and shade. Young tapirs are dark brown with light brown spots, simulating the effect of sun-dappled leaf-litter.

Other large mammals include the common wild pig and the bearded pig, and the *seladang* (or gaur) wild cattle; the latter live in herds in deep jungle. There are two species of deer on the Malay peninsula: the *sambar* (or *rusa*) and the *kijang* (barking deer); the latter gets its name from its dog-like call. The mouse deer (*kanchil* and *napoh*) are not really deer; they are hoofed animals, standing just 20 cm high. The mouse deer has legendary status in Malay lore – for example, the Malay Annals tell of Prince Parameswara's decision to found Melaka on the spot where he saw a mouse deer beat off one of his hunting dogs (**see page 161**). Despite their reputation for cunning, they are also a favoured source of protein.

Malaysia's most famous carnivore is the tiger – *harimau* in Malay. Tigers still roam the jungle in the centre of the peninsula, and on several occasions have made appearances in the Cameron Highlands, particularly during the dry season, when they move into the mountains to find food. Other members of the cat family include the clouded leopard and 4 species of wild cat: the leopard cat, the golden cat, the flat-headed cat and the marbled cat. Other jungle animals include the Malayan sun bear (which have a penchant for honey), the *serigala* (wild dog), civet cats (of which there are many different varieties), mongooses, weasels and otters.

The ape family includes the white-handed gibbon (known locally as *wak-wak*), the dark-handed gibbon (which is rarer) and *siamang*, which are found in more mountainous areas. The 5 species of monkeys are the long-tailed macaque, pig-tailed macaque, and 3 species of leaf monkey (langur) – the banded, dusky

---

Nepenthes – the jungle's poisoned chalice

There are about 30 species of insectivorous pitcher plants in Malaysia; they come in all shapes and sizes – some are bulbous and squat, some are small and elegant, others are huge and fat. All are killers, and are among the handful of insect-eating plants in the world. Pitcher plants grow on poor soils, either in the mountains or in heath (*kerangas*) forest. The Malay name for the *Nepenthes* family is *periuk kera* – or 'monkey cups'. The Chinese call them after the tall wicker baskets used to take pigs to market – *shu long cao*. The plants remain sealed until they have begun to secrete the fluids which help them supplement their meagre diet. One of these liquids is sweet and sticky and attracts insects; the other, which builds up at the bottom, digests each victim which ventures in. The 'lid' opens invitingly when the plant is ready for business and it is virtually impossible for insects to escape – the pitcher plant's waxed interior offers little traction for the uphill climb and the upper lips, past the overhanging ridge, are serated and very slippery. This plant amazed the first Europeans to visit the Malay archipelago. George Rumphius, the German naturalist, thought it one of nature's freaks when he travelled through the region at the end of the 17th century. Two centuries later, the British naturalist, Frederick Burbridge, wrote that seeing the plants "was a sensation I shall never forget – one of those which we experience but rarely in a whole lifetime".

and silvered varieties. Malaysia's cutest animal is the little slow loris, with its huge sad eyes and lethargic manner; among the most exotic is the flying lemur, whose legs and tail are joined together by a skin membrane. It parachutes and glides from tree to tree, climbing each one to find a new launch-pad.

Malaysia has several species of fruit bats and insect-eating bats, but the best-known insect-eater is the pangolin (scaly anteater), the animal world's answer to the armoured car. Its scales are formed of matted hair (like rhinoceros horn) and it has a long thin tongue which it flicks into termite nests. More common jungle mammals include rodents, including 5 varieties of giant flying squirrels. Like the flying lemur, these glide spectacularly from tree to tree and can cover up to about 500m in one 'flight'.

Birds

In ornithological circles, Malaysia is famed for its varied bird-life. The country is visited by many migratory water birds, and there are several wetland areas where the Malayan Nature Society has set up bird-watching hides; the most accessible to Kuala Lumpur is the Kuala Selangor Nature Park (see page 103). Migratory birds winter on Selangor's mangrove-fringed mudflats from Sept to May. There are also spectacular birds of prey, the most common of which are the hawk eagles and brahminy kites. Among the most fascinating and beautiful jungle species are the crested firebacks, a kind of pheasant; the kingfisher family, with their brilliantly coloured plumage; the hornbills (see page 227), greater racquet-tailed drongos – dark blue with long, sweeping tails – and black-naped orioles, saffron-coloured lowland residents. There are also wagtails, mynas, sunbirds, humming birds (flower-peckers), bulbuls, barbets, woodpeckers and weaver-birds. The latter makes incredible, finely woven, hanging tubular nests from strips of grass.

Reptiles

The kings of Malaysia's reptile population are the giant leatherback turtles (see page 203), hawksbill and green turtles (see page 336); there are several other species of turtle and 3 species of land tortoise. The most notorious reptile is the estuarine crocodile (*Crocodilus porosus*) – which can grow up to 8m long. The Malayan gharial (*Tomistoma schlegeli*) is a fish-eating, freshwater crocodile which grows to just under 3m. Lizards include common house geckos (*Hemidactylus frenatus* – or cikcak in Malay), green crested lizards (*Calotes cristatellus*), which change colour like chameleons, and flying lizards (*Draco*), which have an extendable undercarriage allowing the lizard to glide from tree to tree. Monitors are the largest of Malaysian lizards, the most widespread of which is the common water monitor (*Varanus salvator*), which can grow to about 2.5m.

The Malaysian jungles also have 140 species of frogs and toads, which are more often heard than seen. Some are dramatically coloured, such as the appropriately named green-backed frog (*Rana erythraea*) and others have particular skills, such as Wallace's flying frog (*Rana migropalmatus*) which parachutes around on its webbed feet.

Of Malaysia's 100-odd land snakes, only 16 are poisonous; all 20 species of sea snake are poisonous. There are two species of python, the reticulated python (*Python reticulatus*) – which can grow to nearly 10m in length and has iridescent black and yellow scales – and the short python (*Python curtus*), which rarely grows more than 2.5m and has a very thick, rusty-brown body. Among the most common non-poisonous snakes is the dark brown house snake (*Lycodon aulicus*) which likes to eat geckos and the common Malayan racer (*Elaphe flavolineata*), which grows to about 2m and is black with a pale underbelly. The most beautiful non-poisonous snakes are the paradise tree snake (*Chrysopelea paradisi*), which is black with an iridescent green spot on every scale and the mangrove snake (*Boiga dendrophilia*) which grows to about 2m long and is black with yellow

stripes. The former is famed for its gliding skills: it can leap from tree-to-tree in a controlled glide by hollowing its underbelly, trapping a cushion of air below it. In the jungle it is quite common to see the dull brown river snake which goes by the unfortunate name of the dog-faced water snake (*Cerberus rhynchops*); it has a healthy appetite for fish and frogs.

The most feared venomous snake is the king cobra (*Naja hannah*) which grows to well over 4m long and is olive-green with an orange throat-patch. They are often confused with non-poisonous rat snakes and racers. The king cobra eats snakes and lizards – including monitor lizards. Its reputation as an aggressive snake is unfounded but its venom is deadly. Both the king cobra and the common cobra (*Naja naja*) are hooded; the hood is formed by loose skin around the neck and is pushed outwards on elongated ribs when the snake rears to its strike posture.

Other poisonous snakes are: the banded krait (*Bungarus fasciatus*) with its distinctive black and yellow stripes and the Malayan krait (*Bungarus candidus*) with black and white stripes. Kraits are not fast movers and are said to bite only under extreme provocation. Coral snakes (of the genus *Maticora*) have extremely poisonous venom, but because the snake virtually has to chew its victim before the venom can enter the bite (its poison glands are located at the very back of its mouth), there have been no recorded fatalities. Pit vipers have a thermo-sensitive groove between the eye and the nostril which can detect warm-blooded prey even in complete darkness. The bite of the common, bright green Wagler's pit viper (*Trimeresurus wagleri*) is said to be extremely painful, but is never fatal. They have broad, flattened heads; adults have yellow bars and a bright red tip to the tail.

Insects

Malaysia has a literally countless population of insect species; new ones are constantly being discovered and named. There are 120 species of butterfly in Malaysia. The king of them is the male Rajah Brooke's birdwing (*Troides brookiana*) – the national butterfly – with its iridescent, emerald zig-zag markings on jet-black velvety wings. It was named by Victorian naturalist Alfred Russel Wallace after his friend James Brooke, the first White Rajah of Sarawak (see page 234). The males can be found along rivers while the much rarer females (which are less-spectacularly coloured), remain out of sight among the treetops.

There are more than 100 other magnificently coloured butterflies, including the black and yellow common birdwing, the swallowtails and swordtails, the leaf butterflies (which are camouflaged as leaves when their wings are folded) such as the blue and brown saturn and the rust, white and brown tawny rajah. Among the most beautiful of all is the delicately patterned Malayan lacewing (*Cethosia hypsea*) with its jagged markings of red, orange, brown and white. There are several butterfly farms around the country, including one in Kuala Lumpur (see page 104), Penang (see page 147) and the butterfly capital of Malaysia, the Cameron Highlands (see page 122).

The most spectacular moths are the huge atlas moth (*Attacus atlas*) and the swallow-tailed moth (*Nyctalemon patroclus*); these can often be found on exterior walls illuminated by strip-lights late at night, particularly in remoter parts of the country.

The Malaysian beetle population is among the most varied in the world. The best known is the rhinoceros beetle (*Oryctes rhinoceros*), which can grow to nearly 6 cm in length and is characterized by its dramatic horns. The empress cicada (*Pomponia imperatoria*) is the biggest species in Malaysia and can have a wingspan of more than 20 cm. The male cicada is the noisiest jungle resident. The incredible droning and whining noises are created by the vibration of membranes in the body, the sound of which is amplified in the body cavity.

One of the most famous insects is the praying mantis. In *Malayan animal life*, M W F Tweedie writes: "They owe their name to the deceptively devotional

Fireflies – flashers in the forest

There are plenty of fireflies (*Lampyridae*) in Malaysia. But the ones which sit in the trees along the Selangor River, to the west of Kuala Lumpur, are special. They flash in synch – thousands of them go on and off like Christmas-tree lights. Although there are a few reported instances of this happening elsewhere in Southeast Asia, Kampung Kuantan, near Kuala Selangor (**see page 103**), is the best place to witness the phenomenon, which many visitors suspect is a clever electric hoax. The Lampyrid beetle which exhibits the synchrony is the *Pteroptyx malaccae*, which grows to about 9 mm in length and emits flashes at the rate of just over one per second. In the days before batteries, villagers used to put the fireflies in bottles to serve as torches. Because they stick to the same trees – which are chosen because they are always free of *keringga* weaving ants (see below) – local fishermen are said to use them as navigational beacons. Only the males are synchronous flashers, and scientists have yet to come up with an explanation for their behaviour. The females, which are the first to settle in the trees, shortly after sunset, emit dimmer light, and the males, which fly around the water level as it gets dark, join the females which respond to their flashes. The light is produced by cells on the firefly's lower abdomen.

appearance of their characteristic pose, with the fore legs held up as if in prayer. In reality the mantis is, of course, waiting for some unwary insect to stray within reach; if it does, the deadly spined fore limbs will strike and grasp and the mantis will eat its victim alive, daintily, as a lady eats a sandwich." There are several other species of mantis, and the most intriguing is the flower mantis (*Hymenopus coronatus*) which is bright pink and can twist and extend itself to resemble a four-petalled flower, a camouflage which protects it from predators, while attracting meals such as bees.

Of the less attractive insect life, it is advisable to be wary of certain species of wasps and hornets. The most dangerous is the slender banded hornet (*Polistes sagittarius*) which is big (3 cm long) and has a black and orange striped abdomen. Its nests are paper-like, and hang from trees and the eaves of houses by a short stalk. They are extremely aggressive and do not need to be provoked before they attack. The golden wasp (*Vespa auraria*) is found in montane jungle – notably the Cameron Highlands, and, like the hornet above, will attack anything coming near its nest. The wasp is a honey-gold colour, it nests in trees and shrubs and its sting is vicious. There are several other wasp species which attack ferociously, and stings can be extremely painful. One of the worst is the night wasp (*Provespa anomala*), which is an orangy-brick colour and commonly flies into houses at night, attracted by lights. Bee stings can also be very serious, and none more so than that of the giant honey bee, which builds pendulous combs on overhanging eaves and trees. It is black with a yellow mark at the front end of the abdomen; multiple stings can be fatal.

Another insect species to be particularly wary of is the fire ant (*Tetraponera rufonigra*). It has a red body and a big black head; it will enthusiastically sting anything it comes into contact with, and the pain is acute. Weaver ants (*Oecophylla smaragdina*) are common but do not sting. Instead, their powerful jaws can be used as jungle sutures to stitch up open wounds. The bites alone are very painful, and the ant (which is also known as the *kerengga*) adds insult to injury by spitting an acidic fluid on the bite. It is difficult to extract the pincers from the skin, and once attached, the ant will not let go. The biggest of all ants, the giant ant (*Camponotus gigas*), can be nearly 3 cm in length; (it is also variously known as the elephant ant and the 'big-bum ant'). They are largely nocturnal, however, so tend to cause less trouble in the jungle.

Other jungle residents worth avoiding are the huge, black and hairy *Mygalomorph*

spiders, whose bodies alone can be about 5 cm long. Their painful bites cause localized swelling. Scorpions are dangerous but not fatal. The biggest scorpion, the wood scorpion (*Hormurus australasiae*) can grow to about 16 cm long; it is black, lives under old logs and is mainly nocturnal. In rural areas, the particularly paranoid might shake their shoes for the spotted house-scorpion (*Isometrus maculatus*), which is quite common. Centipedes (*Chilopoda*) have a poisonous bite and can grow up to about 25 cm in length. The Malaysian peninsula is malaria-free, although the *Aedes*, tiger mosquito, with its black and white striped body and legs, is a daytime mosquito that carries dengue fever (**see page 27**).

HISTORY

With the arrival of successive waves of Malay immigrants about 5 millennia ago, the earliest settlers – the *Orang Asli* aboriginals (**see page 75**) – moved into the interior. The Malays established agricultural settlements on the coastal lowlands and in riverine areas and from very early on, were in contact with foreign traders, thanks to the peninsula's strategic location on the sea route between India and China. Malay culture on the peninsula reflected these contacts, embracing Indian cultural traditions, Hinduism among them. In the late 14th century, the centre of power shifted from Sumatra's Srivijayan Empire (**see page 733**) across the strait to Melaka (**see page 161**). In 1430, the third ruler of Melaka embraced Islam, and became the first sultan; the city quickly grew into a flourishing trading port. By the early 1500s, it was the most important entrepôt in the region and its fame brought it to the attention of the Portuguese, who, in 1511, ushered in the colonial epoch. They sacked the town and sent the sultan fleeing to Johor, where a new sultanate was established (**see page 175**). But because of internal rivalries and continued conflict with the Acehnese and the Portuguese, Johor never gained the prominence of Melaka, and was forced to alternate its capital between Johor and the Riau archipelago (**see page 175**).

The Portuguese were the first of three European colonial powers to arrive on the Malay peninsula. They were followed by the Dutch, who took Melaka in 1641. When Holland was occupied by Napoleon's troops at the end of the 18th century, Britain filled the vacuum, and the British colonial era began. Historian John M Gullick writes: "The main effects of European control were, firstly, to break the sequence of indigenous kingdoms and to disrupt the trade system upon which they had been based; secondly to delimit colonial spheres of influence and thereby to fix the subsequent boundaries of the national states which are heirs to colonial rule; and lastly to promote economic development and establish the infrastructure of government and other services which that development required; mass immigration from India and China was an incidental consequence of economic development."

During the 17th century, the Dutch came into frequent conflict with the Bugis – the fiercesome master-seafarers who the Dutch had displaced from their original homeland in south Sulawesi (**see page 864**). In 1784, in league with the Minangkabau, the Bugis nearly succeeded in storming Melaka and were only stymied by the arrival of Dutch warships. The Bugis eventually established the Sultanate of Selangor on the W coast of the peninsula and, in the S, exerted increasing influence on the Johor-Riau sultans, until they had reduced them to puppet-rulers. By then however, offshoots of the Johor royal family had established the sultanates of Pahang and Perak. The Minangkabau-dominated states between Melaka and Selangor formed a confederacy of 9 states – or Negeri Sembilan (**see page 158**). To the NE, the states of Kelantan and Terengganu came under the Siamese sphere of influence.

Malaysia's monarchs – the public swings against the sultans

Malaysia's nine hereditary rulers, who take it in turn to be king, represent the greatest concentration of monarchs in the world. In 1993 they were at the forefront of the most heated political controversy that Malaysia has seen in years. The battle royal ended in mid-March with the virtually unprecedented decision of the opposition Democratic Action Party voting with the government to remove the sultans' personal immunity from prosecution. For Prime Minister Dr Mahathir Mohamad, the 1993 Constitutional Amendment Bill was a personal victory. He had long made it known that he regarded the country's nine traditional rulers as a residual anachronism in modern Malaysia.

Malaysia's sultans emerged in the 14th and 15th centuries as the rulers of the small rivermouth states – or *negeri* – that grew up around the peninsula's coasts. The word 'sultan' is a Turkish term for the Malay *Yang di-Pertuan* – literally, 'He who is made Lord'. Sultans wielded more than temporal authority (*kuasa*); they were vested with an aura of sanctity and magical authority, or *dualat*. Malaya's sultans came through the British colonial period and the Japanese interregnum with their status and powers surprisingly intact. The post-war British government was forced by Malay lobbyists to adhere to the principle set by colonial administrator Sir Hugh Clifford in 1927: "The States were, when the British government was invited by their rulers and chiefs to set their troubled houses in order, Muhammadan monarchies: such they are today, and such they must continue to be".

On independence in 1957, Malaysia became a constitutional monarchy, with the king elected for a 5-year term from among the ranks of the sultans. In 1969, following race riots, the government amended the Sedition Act to make it an offence to question the position or prerogatives of traditional rulers. But in 1983, Prime Minister Mahathir provoked a constitutional crisis when he curtailed the power of the king by removing the monarch's right to veto legislation. Mahathir made it clear that henceforth real power would lie with the elected government.

Most of Malaysia's rulers have expensive tastes and some live jet-setting playboy lifestyles. Many have used their position to amass prodigious wealth and their hedonistic instincts have been channelled into the consumer-culture which has come to characterize urban Malaysia in the 1990s. Several sultans and their wayward offspring fitted snugly into the polo-set and the golfing and yachting elites, frequenting glitzy nightclubs, attended by retinues of security men. Traditional Malays considered such behaviour unacceptable in light of the sultans' traditional position as the upholders of Islamic values.

Hedonism is not a crime. But one or two sultans added to their unsavoury reputation by committing acts of violence and murder, safe in the knowledge that they would not be prosecuted. Resentment over such acts could never be articulated without falling foul of the Sedition Act. The activities of some contemporary rulers are not without precedent. In the 17th century, Sultan Mahmud of Johor was notorious for his cruelty, which included shooting men at random to test a new gun. On one occasion he ordered a pregnant woman to be ripped apart because she had eaten a jackfruit from his garden. In the end the woman's husband ran the sultan through with a *kris* with the full support of palace officials.

Until this year it has not been possible to print the alleged crimes of Sultan Mahmud's modern successors in the house of Johor. But in early 1993 a government MP referred in parliament to 23 incidents since 1972 involving today's Sultan Mahmood of Johor and his son, the Rajah Muda Abdul Majid Idris. The most notorious of these concerned the death of a caddie on the Cameron Highlands golf course. Sultan Mahmood allegedly killed him by smashing his head with a club after the caddie sniggered at a duffed shot. On another occasion a man was shot and killed after an argument with the prince in a Johor Bahru nightclub. Abdul Majid was convicted for this but was pardoned by his father. The event which brought the sultans to the forefront of the national agenda in 1993, was an assault on a state hockey coach by the former King, Sultan Mahmood.

Other sultans' disregard for various facets of the law of the land was highlighted by His Royal Highness Tuanku Ismail Petra Ibni Al-Marhum Sultan Tahya Petra of Kelantan. He managed to import 30 luxury cars duty-free. In March 1992, he eluded customs officials by claiming he was taking his new Lamborghine Diablo for a test-drive. Following that incident, the government took full advantage of its ownership of most national newspapers by devoting pages and pages to exposés of the sultans' flamboyant lifestyles. The M$200 million it cost Malaysian tax-payers each year to maintain them was broken down in detail. It emerged that entire hospital wards were reserved for their exclusive use. More than M$9 million was spent on new cutlery and bedsheets for the King – a sum which the *New Straits Times* said would have built two new hospitals or 46 rural clinics or 46 primary schools.

Dr Mahathir gambled that the unveiling of these royal scams would swing public opinion in favour of constitutional amendments. The Prime Minister had long lost patience with the sultans over their interference in politics and business. He was particularly angered by the Sultan of Kelantan who backed the state's Islamic opposition's campaign against his government in the 1990 general election. In July 1992 his government agreed a 'code of conduct' with the sultans in which they said they would stay out of politics and business, but they refused to accept constitutional amendments undermining their powers. Mahathir responded by withdrawing royal privileges such as their generous financial stipends, preferential share allocations and timber concessions. In Jan 1993, parliament passed amendments removing their legal immunity which had earlier been rejected by the rulers themselves. Deadlock ensued as Malaysian law said the sultans had to approve legislation affecting their position. Finally, after a tense stand-off, the government and the sultans agreed to a compromise. The sultans secured an undertaking that no ruler would be taken to court without the Attorney General's approval.

Malaysia's Deputy Prime Minister, Ghafar Baba said the government had achieved its objective of subjecting the rulers to the law and protecting commoners from being oppressed by the rulers. Mahathir emerged from the fray with his executive powers strengthened and his no-nonsense reputation enhanced. The sultans' reputation, by contrast, has been severely dented. As one commentator noted, "the palace doors have been thrown open", adding that public prying into royal affairs is unlikely to cease.

The British occupied Dutch colonies during the Napoleonic Wars, following France's invasion of the Netherlands in 1794. Dutch King William of Orange, who fled to London, instructed Dutch governors overseas to end their rivalry with the British and to permit the entry of British troops to their colonies in a bid to keep the French out. Historian William R Roff writes: "From being an Indian power interested primarily... in the free passage of trade through the Malacca Straits and beyond to China, the East India Company suddenly found itself possessor not merely of a proposed naval station on Penang island but of numerous other territorial dominions and responsibilities. Nor were some of the company's servants at all reluctant to assume these responsibilities and, indeed to extend them."

The British had their own colonial designs, having already established a foothold on Penang where Captain Francis Light had set up a trading post in 1786 (**see page 132**). The Anglo-Dutch Treaty of London, which was signed in 1824, effectively divided insular Southeast Asia into British and Dutch spheres of influence. Britain retained Penang, Melaka (which it swapped for the Sumatran port of Bengkulu) and Singapore – which had been founded by Stamford Raffles in 1819 (**see page 372**) – and these formed the Straits Settlements. The Dutch regained control of their colonial territories in the Indonesian archipelago. Britain promised to stay out of Sumatra and the Dutch promised not to meddle in the affairs of the peninsula, thus separating two parts of the Malay world whose histories had been intertwined for centuries.

The British did very little to interfere with the Malay sultanates and chiefdoms on the peninsula, but the Straits Settlements grew in importance – particularly Singapore, which soon superceded Penang, which in turn, had eclipsed Melaka. Chinese immigrants arrived in all three ports and from there expanded into tin mining which rapidly emerged as the main source of wealth on the peninsula. The extent of the tin-rush in the mid-19th century is exemplified in the town of Larut in north-western Perak. Around 25,000 Chinese speculators arrived in Larut between 1848 and 1872. The Chinese fought over the rights to mine the most lucrative deposits and organized into secret societies and *kongsis*, which by the 1860s, were engaged in open warfare. At the same time, the Malay rulers in the states on the peninsula were busily taxing the tin traders while in the Straits Settlements, British investors in the mining industry put increasing pressure on the Colonial Office to intervene in order to stabilize the situation. In late-1873 Britain decided it could not rule the increasingly lawless and anarchic states by remote control any longer and the western-central states were declared a British protectorate. In his account of British intervention, William R Roff quotes a Malay proverb: 'Once the needle is in, the thread is sure to follow'.

In 1874, the Treaty of Pangkor established the Residential system whereby British officers were posted to key districts; it became their job to determine all administrative and policy matters other than those governing Islam and Malay custom. This immediately provoked resentment and sparked uprisings in Perak, Selangor and Negeri Sembilan, as well as a Malay revolt in 1875. The revolts were put down and the system was institutionalized; in 1876 these three states plus Pahang became the Federated Malay States. By 1909 the N states of Kedah, Perlis, Kelantan and Terengganu – which previously came under Siamese suzerainty – finally agreed to accept British advisers and became known as the Unfederated Malay States. Johor remained independent until 1914 (**see page 176**). The British system of government relied on the political power of the sultans and the Malay aristocracy: residents conferred with the rulers of each state and employed the aristocrats as civil servants. Local headmen (known as *penghulu*) were used as administrators in rural areas.

Meanwhile, the British continued to encourage the immigration of Chinese, who formed a majority of the population in Perak and Selangor by the early 1920s. Apart from the wealthy traders based in the Straits Settlements, the Chinese immigrants were organized (and exploited) by their secret societies, which provided welfare services, organized work gangs and ran local government. In 1889 the societies were officially banned, and while this broke their hold on political power, they simply re-emerged as a criminal underworld. In the Federated Malay States, there was an eight-fold population increase to 1.7 million between 1891 and 1931. Even by 1891 the proportion of Malays had declined to a fraction over a third of the population, with the Chinese making up 41.5% and Indians – imported as indentured labourers by the British (**see page 74**) – comprising 22%. To the S, Johor, which in the late 1800s was not even a member of the federation, had a similar ethnic balance.

For the most part, the Malay population remained in the countryside and were only gradually drawn into the modern economy. But by the 1920s Malay nationalism was on the rise, partly prompted by the Islamic reform movement and partly by intellectuals in secular circles who looked to the creation of a Greater Malaysia (or Greater Indonesia), under the influence of left-wing Indonesian nationalists. These Malay nationalists were as critical of the Malay elite as they were of the British colonialists. The elite itself was becoming increasingly outspoken for different reasons – it felt threatened by the growing demands of Straits-born Chinese and second-generation Indians for equal rights.

The first semi-political nationalist movement was the *Kesatuan Melayu Singapura* (Singapore Malay Union), formed in 1926 (**see page 382**). The Union found early support in the Straits Settlements where Malays were outnumbered and there was no sultan. They gradually spread across the peninsula and held a pan-Malayan conference in 1939. These associations were the forerunners of the post-war Malay nationalist movement. In the run-up to World War II the left-wing split off to form the *Kesatuan Melayu Muda* – the Union of Young Malays, which was strongly anti-British and whose leaders were arrested by the colonial authorities in 1940. The Chinese were more interested in business than politics and any political interests were focused on China. The middle class supported the Chinese nationalist Kuomintang (KMT), although it was eventually banned by the British, as it was becoming an obvious focus of anti-colonial sentiment. The KMT allowed Communists to join the movement until 1927, but in 1930 they split off to form the Malayan Communist Party (MCP) which drew its support from the working class.

The Japanese occupation

Under cover of darkness on the night of 8 Dec 1941, the Japanese army invaded Malaya, landing in S Thailand and pushing into Kedah, and at Kota Bahru in Kelantan (**see page 217**). The invasion – which took place an hour before the attack on Pearl Harbour – took the Allies in Malaya and 'Fortress' Singapore completely by surprise. The Japanese forces had air, land and sea superiority and quickly overwhelmed the Commonwealth troops on the peninsula. Militarily, it was a brilliant campaign, made speedier by the fact that the Japanese troops stole bicycles in every town they took, thus making it possible for them to outpace all Allied estimates of their likely rate of advance.

By 28 Dec they had taken Ipoh and all of northern Malaya. Kuantan fell on the 31st, the Japanese having sunk the British warships *Prince of Wales* and *Repulse* (**see page 195**) and Kuala Lumpur on 11 Jan 1942. They advanced down the east coast, centre and west coast simultaneously and by the end of the month had taken Johor Bahru and were massed across the strait from Singapore. By 15 Feb they had forced the capitulation of the Allies in Singapore (**see page 375**). This was a crushing blow, and, according to Malaysian historian Zainal Abidin bin Abudul Wahid, "the speed with which the Japanese managed to achieve victory, however temporary that might have been, shattered the image of the British, and generally the 'whiteman', as a superior people". Right up until the beginning of World War II, the British had managed to placate the aristocratic leaders of the Malay community and the wealthy Chinese merchants and there was little real threat to the status quo. The Japanese defeat of the British changed all that by altering the balance between conservatism and change. Because Britain had failed so miserably to defend Malaya, its credentials as a protector were irrevocably tarnished.

For administrative purposes, the Japanese linked the peninsula with Sumatra as part of the Greater East Asia Co-prosperity Sphere. All British officials were interned and the legislative and municipal councils swept aside. But because the Japanese had lost their command of the seas by the end of 1942, nothing could be imported and there was a shortage of food supplies. The 'banana' currency introduced by the Japanese became worthless as inflation soared. Japan merely regarded Malaya as a source of raw materials, yet the rubber and tin industries stagnated and nothing was done to develop the economy.

After initially severing sultans' pensions and reducing their powers, the Japanese realized that their cooperation was necessary if the Malay bureaucracy was to be put to work for the occupation government (see page 62). The Indians were treated well – they were seen as a key to fighting the British colonial regime in India. But Malaya's Chinese – while they were not rounded up and executed as they were in Singapore (see page 376) – were not trusted. The Japanese, however, came to recognize the importance of the Chinese community in oiling the wheels of the economy. The Chinese Dalforce militia (set up by the Allies as the Japanese advanced southwards) joined the Communists and other minor underground dissident groups in forming the Malayan People's Anti-Japanese Army. British army officers and arms were parachuted into the jungle to support the guerrillas. It was during this period that the Malayan Communist Party (MCP) broadened its membership and appeal, under the guise of a nationwide anti-Japanese alliance.

The brutality of the Japanese regime eased with time; as the war began to go against them, they increasingly courted the different communities, giving them more say in the run of things in an effort to undermine any return to colonial rule. But the Japanese's favourable treatment of Malays and their general mistrust of the Chinese did not exactly foster good race relations between the two. A Malay paramilitary police force was put to work to root out Chinese who were anti-Japanese, which exacerbated inter-communal hostility. The Japanese never offered Malaya independence but allowed Malay nationalist sentiments to develop in an effort to deflect attention from the fact they had ceded the N Malay states of Kedah, Perlis, Kelantan and Terengganu to Thailand.

The British return

During the war, the British drew up secret plans for a revised administrative structure in Malaya. The plan was to create a Malayan Union by combining the federated and unfederated states as well as Melaka and Penang, leaving Singapore as a crown colony. Plans were also drawn up to buy North Borneo from the Chartered Company (see page 296) and to replace the anachronous White Rajahs of Sarawak (see page 234) with a view to eventually grouping all the territories together as a federation. As soon as the Japanese surrendered in September 1945, the plan was put into action. Historian Mary Turnbull notes that "Malaya was unique [among Western colonies] because the returning British were initially welcomed with enthusiasm and were themselves unwilling to put the clock back. But they were soon overwhelmed by the reaction against their schemes for streamlining the administration and assimilating the different immigrant communities."

A unitary state was formed on the peninsula and everyone, regardless of race or origin, who called Malaya 'home', was accorded equal status. But the resentment caused by British high-handedness was the catalyst which triggered the foundation of the United Malays National Organization (UNMO) which provided a focus for opposition to the colonial regime and, following independence, formed the ruling party. Opposition to UMNO – led by the Malay ruling class – forced the British to withdraw the Union proposal – the sultans refused to attend the installation of the governor and the Malays boycotted advisory councils. Mary Turnbull notes that the Malayan Union scheme was "conceived as a civil servant's dream but was born to be a politician's nightmare". Vehement Malay opposition prompted negotiations with Malay leaders which hammered out the basis of a Federation of Malaya which was established in

February 1948. It was essentially the same as the Union in structure, except that it recognized the sovereignty of the sultans in the 11 states and the so-called 'special position' of the Malays as the indigenous people of Malaya. The federation had a strong central government (headed by a High Commissioner) and a federal executive council.

In this federal system, introduced in 1948, non-Malays could only become Malaysian citizens if they had been resident in Malaya for a minimum of 15 out of the previous 25 years, were prepared to sign a declaration of permanent settlement and were able to speak either Malay or English. This meant only 3 million of Malaya's 5 million population qualified as citizens, of whom 78% were Malay, 12% Chinese and 7% Indian. Historian Mary Turnbull says that while the British believed they had achieved their objective of common citizenship (even on more restricted terms), they had, in reality "accepted UMNO's concept of a Malay nation into which immigrant groups would have to be integrated, and many difficulties were to develop from this premise".

The rise of Communism

The Chinese and Indian communities were not consulted in these Anglo-Malay negotiations and ethnic and religious tensions between the 3 main communities were running high, unleashing the forces of racialism which had been lying dormant for years. Because their part in the political process had been ignored, many more Chinese began to identify with the Malaysian Communist Party (MCP) which was still legal. It was not until the Communist victory in China in 1949 that the Chinese began to think of Malaya as home. During the war the MCP had gained legitimacy and prestige as a patriotic resistance movement. The MCP's *de facto* military wing, the MPAJA, had left arms dumps in the jungle, but the Communist leadership was split as to whether negotiation or confrontation was the way forward. Then in 1947 the MCP suffered what many considered to be a disastrous blow: its Vietnamese-born secretary-general, Lai Teck, absconded with all the party's funds having worked as a double agent for both the Japanese and the British. He was suspected of having betrayed the entire MCP central committee to the Japanese in 1942. The new 26-year-old MCP leader, former schoolmaster Chin Peng, immediately abandoned Lai's soft approach.

In June 1948 he opted for armed rebellion, and the Malayan Communist Emergency commenced with the murder of three European planters. According to John Gullick, the historian and former member of the Malayan civil service, it was called an 'Emergency' because the Malayan economy was covered by the London insurance market for everything other than war. Premiums covered loss of stock, property and equipment through riot and civil commotion, but not through civil war, so the misnomer continued throughout the 12-year insurrection. Others say it got its name from the Emergency Regulations that were passed in June 1948 which were designed to deny food supplies and weapons to the Communists.

The Emergency was characterized by armed Communist raids on indiscriminate economic targets – often rubber estates and tin mines – and violent ambushes which were aimed at loosening and undermining central government control. Chinese 'squatters' in areas fringing the jungle (many of whom had fled from the cities during the Japanese occupation) provided an information and supply network for the Communists. In 1950 the British administration moved these people into 500 'New Villages', where they could be controlled and protected. This policy – known as 'The Briggs Plan' after the Director of Operations, Lt-Gen. Sir Harold Briggs – was later adopted (rather less successfully) by the Americans in South Vietnam.

In much the same way as they had been caught unprepared by the Japanese invasion in 1941, the British were taken by surprise and in the first few years the MCP (whose guerrillas were labelled 'CTs' – or Communist Terrorists) gained the upper hand. In 1951 British morale all but crumbled when the High Commissioner,

Sir Henry Gurney, was ambushed and assassinated on the road to Fraser's Hill (**see page 116**). His successor General Sir Gerald Templer took the initiative, however, with his campaign to 'win the hearts and minds of the people'. Templer's biographer, John Cloake, gave him Japanese General Tomoyuki Yamashita's old sobriquet 'Tiger of Malaya' (**see page 375**), and there is little doubt that his tough policies won the war. In his book *Emergency Years*, former mine-manager Leonard Rayner says the chain-smoking Templer "exuded nervous energy like an overcharged human battery". Within 2 years the Communists were on the retreat. They had also begun to lose popular support due to the climate of fear they introduced – although the Emergency did not officially end until 1960.

Historians believe the Communist rebellion failed because it was too slow to take advantage of the economic hardships in the immediate aftermath of World War II and because it was almost exclusively Chinese. It also only really appealed to the Chinese working class and alienated and shunned the Chinese merchant community and Straits-born Chinese.

The road to merdeka

The British had countered the MCP's claim to be a multi-racial nationalist movement by accelerating moves towards Malayan independence – which Britain promised, once the Emergency was over. The only nationalist party with any political credibility was UMNO. Its founder, Dato' Onn bin Jaafar, wanted to allow non-Malays to become members, and when his proposal was rejected, he resigned to form the Independence of Malaya Party. The brother of the Sultan of Kedah, Tunku Abdul Rahman, took over as head of UMNO and to counter Onn's new party, he made an electoral pact with the Malayan Chinese Association (MCA) and the Malayan Indian Congress (MIC). With the MCP out of the picture, the Chinese community had hesitantly grouped itself around the MCA. The Alliance (which trounced Onn's party in the election) is still in place today, in the form of the ruling *Barisan Nasional* (National Front). After sweeping the polls in 1955, the Alliance called immediately for *merdeka* – independence – which the British guaranteed within two years.

With independence promised by non-violent means, Tunku Abdul Rahman offered an amnesty to the Communists. Together with Singapore's Chief Minister, David Marshall (**see page 377**) and Straits-Chinese leader Tan Cheng Lock (**see page 169**), he met Chin Peng in 1956. But they failed to reach agreement and the MCP fled through the jungle into the mountains in southern Thailand around Betong. While the Emergency was declared 'over' in 1960, the MCP only finally agreed to lay down its arms in 1989, in a peace agreement brokered by Thailand. The party had been riven by factionalism and its membership had dwindled to under 1,000. In 1991, the legendary Chin Peng struck a deal with the Malaysian government allowing the former guerrillas to return home.

Historian Mary Turnbull writes: "When Malaya attained independence in 1957 it was a prosperous country with stable political institutions, a sound administrative system and a good infrastructure of education and communications – a country with excellent resources and a thriving economy based on export agriculture and mining". Under the new constitution, a king was to be chosen from one of the nine sultans, and the monarchy was to be rotated every 5 years. A 2-tier parliament was set up, with a *Dewan Rakyat* (People's House) of elected representatives and a *Dewan Negara* (Senate) to represent the state assemblies. Each of the 11 states had its own elected government and a sultan or governor.

Politicians in Singapore made it clear that they also wanted to be part of an independent Malaya, but in Kuala Lumpur, UMNO leaders were opposed to a merger because the island had a Chinese majority. (A straight merger would have resulted in a small Chinese majority in Malaya.) Increasing nationalist militancy in

Singapore was of particular concern to UMNO and the radical wing of the People's Action Party, which was swept to power with Lee Kuan Yew at its head in 1959 (**see page 377**), was dominated by Communists. Fearing the emergence of 'a second Cuba' on Malaysia's doorstep, Tunku Abdul Rahman proposed that Singapore join a greater Malaysian Federation, in which a racial balance would be maintained by the inclusion of Sarawak, Brunei and British North Borneo (Sabah). Britain supported the move, as did all the states involved. Kuala Lumpur was particularly keen on Brunei joining the Federation on two scores: it had Malays and it had oil. But at the eleventh hour, Brunei's Sultan Omar backed out, mistrustful of Kuala Lumpur's obvious designs on his sultanate's oil revenues and unhappy at the prospect of becoming just another sultan in Malaya's collection of 9 monarchs (**see page 62**).

Prime Minister Tunku Abdul Rahman was disheartened, but the Malaysia Agreement was signed in Jul 1963 with Singapore, Sarawak and Sabah. Without Brunei, there was a small Chinese majority in the new Malaysia. The Tunku did not have time to dwell on racial arithmetic, however, because almost immediately the new federation was plunged into an undeclared war with Indonesia – which became known as *Konfrontasi*, or Confrontation (**see page 237**) – due to President Sukarno's objection to the participation of Sabah and Sarawak. Indonesian saboteurs were landed on the peninsula and in Singapore and there were Indonesian military incursions along the borders of Sabah and Sarawak with Kalimantan. Konfrontasi was finally ended in 1966 when Sukarno fell from power. But relations with Singapore – which had been granted a greater measure of autonomy than other states – were far from smooth. Communal riots in Singapore in 1964 and Lee Kuan Yew's efforts to forge a nation-wide opposition alliance which called for 'a democratic Malaysian Malaysia' further opened the rift with Kuala Lumpur. Feeling unnerved by calls for racial equality while the Malays did not form a majority of the population, Tunku Abdul Rahman expelled Singapore from the federation in August 1965 against Lee Kuan Yew's wishes (**see page 378**).

Racial politics in the 1960s

The expulsion of Singapore did not solve the racial problem on the peninsula, however. Because the Malay and Chinese communities felt threatened by each other – one wielded political power, the other economic power – racial tensions built up. Resentment focused on the enforcement of Malay as the medium of instruction in all schools and as the national language and on the privileged educational and employment opportunities afforded to Malays. The tensions finally exploded on 13 May 1969, in the wake of the general election.

The UMNO-led Alliance faced opposition from the Democratic Action Party (DAP) which was built from the ashes of Lee Kuan Yew's People's Action Party. The DAP was a radical Chinese-dominated party and called for racial equality. Also in opposition was *Gerakan* (the People's Movement), supported by Chinese and Indians, and the Pan-Malayan Islamic Party, which was exclusively Malay and very conservative. In the election, the opposition parties – which were not in alliance – deprived the Alliance of its $2/3$ majority in parliament; it required this margin to amend the constitution unimpeded. Gerakan and DAP celebrations provoked counter-demonstrations from Malays and in the ensuing mayhem hundreds were killed in Kuala Lumpur.

The government suspended the constitution for over a year and declared a state of emergency. A new national ideology was drawn up – the controversial New Economic Policy (**see page 86**) – which was an ambitious experiment in social engineering aimed at ironing out discrepancies between ethnic communities. The *Rukunegara*, a written national ideology aimed at fostering nation-building, was introduced in August 1970. It demanded loyalty to the king and the constitution, respect for Islam and observance of the law and morally acceptable behaviour. All discussion of the Malays' 'special position' was banned as was discussion about the national language and the sovereignty of the sultans. In the words of historian John Gullick, "Tunku Abdul Rahman, whose anguish at the disaster had impeded his ability to deal with it effectively," resigned the following month and handed over to Tun Abdul Razak. Tun Razak was an able administrator, but lacked the dynamism of his predecessor. He did however unify UMNO and patched up the old Alliance, breathing new life into the coalition by incorporating every political party except the DAP and one or two other small parties into the newly named *Barisan Nasional* (BN), or National Front. In 1974 the Barisan won a landslide majority.

Tun Razak shifted Malaysia's foreign policy from a pro-Western stance to non-alignment and established diplomatic relations with both Moscow and Beijing. But within Malaysia, Communist paranoia was rife: as Indochina fell to Communists in the mid-1970s, many Malaysians became increasingly convinced that Malaysia was just another 'domino' waiting to topple. There were even several arrests of prominent Malays (including two newspaper editors and five top UMNO politicians). But when Chin Peng's revolutionaries joined forces with secessionist Muslims in south Thailand, the Thai and Malaysian governments launched a joint clean-out operation in the jungle along the frontier. By the late 1970s the North Kalimantan Communist Party had also been beaten into virtual submission too (**see page 238**). In 1976 Tun Razak died and was succeeded by his brother-in-law, Dato' Hussein Onn (the son of Umno's founding father). He inherited an economy which was in good shape, thanks to strong commodity prices, and in the general election of 1978, the BN won another comfortable parliamentary majority. 3 years later he handed over to Dr Mahathir Mohamad (see profile, **page 84**).

ART AND ARCHITECTURE

In his book *The Malay House*, architect Lim Jee Yuan writes that traditional houses, which are built without architects, "reflect good housing solutions, as manifested by the display of a good fit to the culture, lifestyle and socio-economic needs of the users; the honest and efficient use of materials; and appropriate climatic design". Classic Malay houses are built of timber and raised on stilts with wooden or bamboo walls and an *atap* roof – made from the leaves of the nipah palm. It should have plenty of windows and good ventilation – the interior is usually airy and bright. It is also built on a prefabricated system and can be expanded to fit the needs of a growing family. Malay houses are usually simple, functional and unostentatious, and even those embellished by woodcarvings blend into their environment. Lim Jee Yuan says "the Malay house cannot be fully appreciated without its setting – the house compound and the kampung". Kampung folk, he says, prefer "community intimacy over personal privacy" which means villages are closely knit communities.

Most Malays on the peninsula traditionally lived in pile-houses built on stilts along the rivers. The basic design is called the *bumbung panjang* ('long roof'), although there are many variations and hybrids; these are influenced both by Minangkabau house-forms and by Thai-Khmer designs. The differences in house-styles between regions is mainly in the shape of the roof. The bumbung panjang is the oldest, commonest, simplest and most graceful, with a long gable roof, thatched with atap. There are ventilation grills at either end, allowing a throughflow of air. From the high apex, the eaves slope down steeply, then, towards the bottom, the angle lessens, extending out over the walls. Bumbung panjang are most commonly found in

Melaka, but the design is used widely throughout the peninsula.

These days it is more usual to find the atap replaced with corrugated zinc roofs which require less maintenance and are a measure of status in the community. But zinc turns houses into ovens during the day, makes them cold at night and makes a deafening noise in rainstorms. On the E coast of the peninsula, the use of tiled roofs is more common. Towards the N, Thai and Khmer influences are more pronounced in roof style. As in Thai houses, walls are panelled; there are also fewer windows and elaborate carving is more common. Because Islam proscribes the use of the human figure in art, ornamental woodcarvings depict floral and geometric designs as well as Koranic calligraphy. Most are relief-carvings on wood panels or grilles. In Melaka, colourful ceramic tiles are also commonly used as exterior decoration.

The oldest surviving Malay houses date from the 19th century. The traditional design is the *rumah berpanggung*, which is built high off the ground on stilts with an A-shaped roof. The basic features include:

❏ *Anjung*: covered porch at the top of entranceway stairs where formal visitors are entertained.
❏ *Serambi gantung*: verandah, where most guests are entertained.
❏ *Rumah ibu* ('the domain of the mother of the house'): private central core of the house, with raised floor level, where the family talks, sleeps, prays, studies and eats (particularly during festivals).
❏ *Dapur*: kitchen, always at the back, and below the level of the rest of the house; most meals are taken here. The dapur is connected to the rumah ibu by the *selang*, a closed walkway. Near the dapur, there is usually a *pelantar*, with a washing area for clothes, a mandi and a toilet.

The best places to see traditional Malay houses are Melaka and Negri Sembilan, on

The Malay Istana – royals on the riverside

The Malay word *istana* derives from the Sanskrit for 'sleeping place' – but the Malay sultans adopted it as the term for their royal palaces. Because Malay sultanates were usually focused on the mouths of rivers, the istanas were normally sited on a prominent point on the riverbank, along which the sultan's powerbase extended. This meant they were prone to flooding, however, and over the centuries, a number slipped into the river – notably in Perak. The 16th century *Sejarah Melayu* (Malay Annals) provide a description of Sultan Mansur Shah's palace in Melaka (see page 167). The building has been reconstructed from notes and historical data and now serves as Melaka's *Muzium Budaya* (Cultural Museum). The original palace was said to have had a 7-tiered roof and 12 halls; it was razed to the ground by the invading Portuguese in 1511.

Traditionally, istanas included everything from the sultan's private quarters (at the rear) to the state administrative and cultural centre. They also doubled as forts in time of war. The sultan's concubines lived in outhouses, dotted around the compound, which also included the mosque and the *rumah wakaf* – the lodging house for commoners (such as the Istana Jahar in Kota Bahru, which is now the Kelantan State Museum). There are several other istanas in Kelantan and Terengganu states, all dating from the 19th century. The most impressive of the surviving istanas are the Istana Lama Sri Menanti and the Istana Ampang Tinggi in Negri Sembilan (see page 159), the Istana Balai Besar in Kedah – one of the grandest and best-preserved on the peninsula, and now the state museum – and the Istana Kenangan at Kuala Kangsar in Perak, which is now the Royal Museum (see page 127). There are only 11 wooden palaces remaining in Malaysia, and none of them houses a royal family any longer.

the W coast, and TeIangganu and Kelantan states to the NE. Minangkabau influence is most pronounced in Negri Sembilan state, between Kuala Lumpur and Melaka. There, houses have a distinctive, elegant, curved roofline, where the gable sweeps up into 'wings' at each end – the so-called Minangkabau 'buffalo horns'.

Today the traditional Malay house has lost its status in the kampung – now everyone wants to build in concrete and brick. Many planned modern kampungs have been built throughout Malaysia, with little regard for traditional building materials or for the traditional houseforms. Lim Jee Yuan writes that: "Unless there are positive steps taken to uplift the status of the traditional Malay house... it is bound for extinction in the near future despite its superior design principles and suitability to our environmental, economic and socio-cultural needs". Many like-minded architects despair of the 'vulgarization' of the Malay houseform, which has been used as an inspiration for many modern buildings (notably in Kuala Lumpur, **see page 95**). The curved Minangabau roof, for example, which has been borrowed for everything from modern bank buildings to toll-booths, has merely become a cultural symbol, and has been deprived of its deeper significance.

Peranakan
The Straits Chinese (Peranakan) communities of Melaka, Penang and Singapore developed their own architectural style to match their unique cultural traditions (**see page 168**). The finest Peranakan houses can be seen along Jalan Tun Tan Cheng Lock in Melaka (**see page 167**), notably the Baba-Nonya Heritage Museum. Typical Peranakan houses were long and narrow, and built around a central courtyard. Their interiors are characterized by dark, heavy wood and marble-topped furniture, often highly decorated, and made by Chinese craftsmen who were brought over from China.

Immigrant Chinese
For background on Chinese temple architecture and the basic principles of geomancy (*feng shui*), **see page 379**.

CULTURE AND LIFE

People
Visitors sometimes get confused over the different races that make up Malaysia's population. All citizens of Malaysia are 'Malaysians'; they are comprised of Malays, Chinese and Indians as well as other tribal groups, most of whom live in the East Malaysian states of Sabah and Sarawak (**see page 228**).

Malaysia has a total population of about 18 million, of which 83% lives on the peninsula, 8% in Sabah and 9% in Sarawak. Statistics on the ethnic breakdown of Malaysia's multi-racial population tend to differ because politics is divided along racial lines, they are sensitive figures. For Malaysia as a whole, Malays make up roughly 48%, Chinese 34%, Indians 9% and indigenous tribes, 9%. The Malays and indigenous groups are usually grouped together under the umbrella term *bumiputra* – literally, 'sons of the soil'. On the peninsula, bumiputras comprise 58% of the population while the Chinese make up 31% and Indians 9%.

Malaysia's population is growing by about 2.5% per annum. Since 1970, the Bumiputra population has grown fastest, and, on the peninsula, their proportion of the total population has increased from 53%. In the same period, the proportion of the Chinese population has declined from 36% while the proportion of Indians has remained roughly the same. Mahatir announced recently that for Malaysia to become an industrialized country, it would need a strong domestic market, so he encouraged Malaysians to procreate – his once suggested target was a population of 70 million by 2010, up from 17 million in 1990. The target date has subsequently been revised to 2095.

Malays

The Malay people probably first migrated to the peninsula from Sumatra. Anthropologists speculate that the race originally evolved from the blending of a Mongoloid people from Central Asia with an island race living between the Indian and Pacific oceans. They are lowland people and originally settled around the coasts. These 'Coastal Malays' are also known as 'Deutero-Malays'. They are ethnically similar to the Malays of Indonesia and are the result of intermarriage with many other racial groups, including Indians, Chinese, Arabs and Thais. They are a very relaxed, warm-hearted people who had the good fortune to settle in a land where growing food was easy. For centuries they have been renowned for their hospitality and generosity as well as their well-honed sense of humour. When Malays converted to Islam in the early 15th century, the language was written in Sanskrit script which evolved into the Arabic-looking *Jawi*.

Because Malays were traditionally farmers and were tied to rural kampungs, they remain insulated from the expansion of colonial Malaya's export economy. Few of them worked as wage labourers and only the aristocracy, which had been educated in English, were intimately involved in the British system of government, as administrators. "...In return for the right to develop a modern extractive economy within the *negeri* [states] by means of alien immigrant labor," writes historian William R Roff, "the British undertook to maintain intact the position and prestige of the ruling class and to refrain from catapulting the Malay people into the modern world". Rural Malays only began to enter the cash economy when they started to take up rubber cultivation on their smallholdings – but this was not until after 1910. In 1921, less than 5% of Malays lived in towns.

On attaining independence in 1957, the new constitution allowed Malays to be given special rights for 10 years. The idea was that this would allow the Malay community to become as prosperous as the Chinese 'immigrants'. To this end, they were afforded extra help in education and in securing jobs. The first economic development plan focused on the rural economy, with the aim of improving the lot of the rural Malays. It was the Malay community's sense of its own weakness in comparison with the commercial might of the Chinese that led to ethnic tensions erupting onto the streets in May 1969. Following the race riots, the Malays were extended special privileges in an effort to increase their participation in the modern economy (**see page 86**). Along with indigenous groups, they were classed as bumiputras, usually shortened to 'bumis' – a label many were able to use a a passport to a better life.

Chinese

The Chinese community accounts for about a third of Malaysia's population. In 1794, just 8 years after he had founded Georgetown in Penang, Sir Francis Light wrote: "The Chinese constitute the most valuable part of our inhabitants: ...they possess the different trades of carpenters, masons, smiths, traders, shopkeepers and planters; they employ small vessels. They are the only people from whom a revenue may be raised without expense and extraordinary effort by the government. They are a valuable acquisition..." Chinese immigrants went on to become invaluable members of the British Straits Settlements – from the early 1820s they began to flood into Singapore from China's southern provinces (**see page 374**). At the same time they arrived in droves on the Malay peninsula, most of them working as tin prospectors, shopkeepers and small traders.

In Melaka, however, there had been a settled community of Chinese since the 15th century. Many had arrived as members of the retinue of the Chinese princess

Li Poh who married Melaka's Sultan Mansur Shah in 1460 (**see page 170**). Over the centuries their descendants evolved into a wealthy and influential community with its own unique, sophisticated culture (**see page 168**). These Straits Chinese became known as *Peranakans* (which means 'born here'); men were called Babas and women, Nonyas (sometimes spelt Nyonyas). But the vast majority of modern Malaysia's prosperous Chinese population arrived from China as penniless immigrants; they left China because of poverty, over-population, religious persecution and the lure of gold. In the mid-19th century, these newly arrived immigrants came under the jurisdiction of secret societies and *kongsis* – or clan associations. Some of the most striking examples of the latter are in Penang (see, for example the Khoo Kongsi, **see page 139**). The secret societies sometimes engaged in open warfare with each other as rival groups fought over rights to tin mining areas.

The overseas Chinese have been described as possessing these common traits: the ability to smell profits and make quick business decisions; a penchant for good food (they prefer to sit at round tables to facilitate quicker exchange of information); and a general avoidance of politics in favour of money-making pursuits. These pointers hold true for Malaysia's Chinese. They felt little loyalty to their host society, however, until the 1949 Communist take-over in China, which effectively barred their return. Despite the community's political and economic gripes and traumas in the intervening years (**see page 86**), Chinese culture has survived intact and the community enjoys religious freedom; Chinese cuisine is enthusiastically devoured by all races and the mahjong tiles are still clacking in upstairs rooms. Today about 80% of Chinese schoolchildren attend private Chinese primary schools – all secondary and tertiary education is in Malay.

Indians

Indian traders first arrived on the shores of the Malay peninsula more than 2,000 years ago in search of Suvarnadvipa, the fabled land of gold. There was a well established community of Indian traders in Melaka when the first sultanate grew up in the 1400s – there was even Tamil blood in the royal lineage. But most of the 1.5 million Indians in modern Malaysia – who make up nearly 9% of the population – are descendants of indentured Tamil labourers shipped to Malaya from south India by the British in the 19th century. They were nicknamed 'Klings' – a name which today has a deeply derogatory connotation. Most were put to work as coolies on the roads and railways or as rubber tappers.

A hundred years on, 4 out of 5 Indians are still manual labourers on plantations or in the cities. This has long been explained as a colonial legacy, but as modern Malaysia has grown more prosperous, the Tamils have remained at the bottom of the heap. Other Indian groups – the Keralans (Malayalis), Gujeratis, Bengalis, Sikhs and other N Indians, who came to colonial Malaya under their own volition, are now well represented in the professional classes. The S Indian Chettiar money-lending caste, which was once far more numerous than it is today, left the country in droves in the 1930s. Their confidence in British colonial rule was shaken by events in Burma, where anti-Indian riots prompted tens of thousands of Chettiars to return to India. While most of Malaysia's Indian community are Hindus, there are also Indian Muslims, Christians and Sikhs. In Melaka there is a small group of Indians with Portuguese names – known as Chitties.

Today the chanted names of the Hindu pantheon echo around the cool interior of the Sri Mariamman Temple in the heart of Kuala Lumpur as they have since its construction in 1873. But large numbers of Tamils still live in the countryside, where they still make up more than half the plantation workforce. Because the estates are on private land, they fall outside the ambit of national development policies and Malaysia's economic boom has passed them by. The controversial New Economic Policy – or NEP (**see page 86**) – gave Malays a helping hand, and although it was aimed at irradicating poverty generally, it did not help Indians much.

The new policy document which replaced the NEP in 1991 officially recognizes that Indians have lagged behind in the development stakes. Education is seen as the key to broadening the entrepreneurial horizons of Tamils, getting them off the plantations, out of the urban squatter settlements and into decent jobs. But in the privately-run Tamil shanty schools on the estates, the drop-out rate is double the national average. Critics accuse the Malaysian Indian Congress (MIC), which is part of the ruling coalition, of perpetuating this system in an effort to garner support. Because Indians are spread throughout the country and do not form the majority in any constituency, the plantations have been the MIC's traditional support base. It is not in the MIC's interests to see them move off the estates.

But things are beginning to change on the plantations – an unprecedented national strike in 1990 guaranteed plantation workers a minimum wage for the first time. Workers are becoming more assertive and aware of their individual and political rights. A new party, the Indian Progressive Front, has drawn its support from working class Indians. It seems that these stirrings of new assertiveness represent rising aspirations on the estates – which will have to continue to rise if the Tamils are ever going to escape from their plantation poverty trap, which one prominent Indian leader refers to as 'the green ghetto'.

Orang Asli (Aboriginals)

While the Malay population originally settled on the coasts of the peninsula, the mountainous, jungled interior was the domain of the oldest indigenous groups – the aboriginals, known variously as the Negrito, Semang or Pangan. They are a sinewy, dark-skinned race, characterized by their curly hair and are probably of Melanesian origin – possibly related to Australian aborigines. During the Pleistocene ice age, when a land-bridge linked the Philippines to Borneo and mainland Southeast Asia, these people spread throughout the continent. Today they are confined to the mountains of the Malay peninsula, NE India, N Sumatra, the Andaman Islands and the Philippines. The Negrito aboriginals – who in Malay are known as *Orang Asli*, or 'Indigenous People' – are mainly hunter-gatherers. As the Malays spread inland, the Orang Asli were pushed further and further into the mountainous interior; they are timid, gentle and shy. Traditionally, the Negritos did not build permanent houses – preferring makeshift shelters – and depend on the jungle and the rivers for their food.

A second group of Orang Asli, the *Senoi* – who are also known as the *Sakai* – arrived later than the Negritos. They practiced shifting cultivation to supplement their hunting and gathering and built sturdier houses. The third aboriginal group to come to the peninsula were the Jakuns – or proto-Malays – who were mainly of Mongoloid stock. They were comprised of several subgroups, the main ones being the Mantera and Biduanda of Negri Sembilan and Melaka and the Orang Ulu, Orang Kanak and Orang Laut ('Sea People') of Johor. Their culture and language became closely linked to that of the coastal Malays and over the centuries, many of them assimilated into Malay society. Most practised shifting cultivation; the Orang Laut were fishermen.

Malaysia's aborigines have increasingly been drawn into the modern economy. Along with the Malays, they are classified as *bumiputras* – literally, 'sons of the soil' – and as such, became eligible, as with other tribal groups in East Malaysia, for the privileges extended to all bumiputras following the introduction of the New Economic Policy (NEP) in 1970 (**see page 86**). In reality, however, the NEP offered few tangible benefits to the Orang Asli, and while the government has sought to integrate them – there is a Department of Aboriginal Affairs in Kuala Lumpur – there is no separate mechanism to encourage entrepreneurism among the group.

Religion

Islam

Malays are invariably Muslims and there is also a small population of Indian Muslims in Malaysia. (For a detailed background on Islam, **see page 39**). The earliest recorded evidence of Islam on the Malay peninsula is an inscription in Terengganu dating from 1303, which prescribed penalties for those who did not observe *adat* – the moral codes of the faith. Islam did not really gain a foothold on the peninsula, however, until Sri Maharaja of Melaka – the third ruler – converted in 1430 and changed his name to Mohamed Shah (**see page 162**). He retained many of the ingrained Hindu traditions of the royal court and did not attempt to enforce Islam as the state religion. The Arab merchant ships which made regular calls at Melaka probably brought Muslim missionaries to the city. Many of them were Sufis – belonging to a mystical order of Islam which was tolerant of local customs and readily synthesized with existing animist and Hindu beliefs. The adoption of this form of Islam is one reason why animism and the Muslim faith still go hand in hand in Malaysia (see below). Mohamad Shah's son, Rajah Kasim was the first ruler to adopt the title 'Sultan', and he became Sultan Muzaffar; all subsequent rulers have continued to preserve and uphold the Islamic faith. The Portuguese and Dutch colonialists, while making a few local converts to Christianity, were more interested in trade than religion.

The British colonial system of government was more 'progressive' than most colonial regimes in that it barred the British Residents from interfering in 'Malay religion and custom'. So-called Councils of Muslim Religion and Malay Custom were set up in each state answerable to the sultans. These emerged as bastions of Malay conservatism and served to make Islam the rallying point of nascent nationalism. The Islamic reform movement was imported from the Middle East at the turn of the 19th century and Malays determined that the unity afforded by Islam transcended any colonial authority and the economic dominance of immigrant groups. The ideas spread as increasing numbers of Malays made the Haj to Mecca, made possible by the advent of regular steamer services. But gradually the sultans and the Malay aristocracy – who had done well out of British rule – began to see the Islamic renaissance as a threat.

On Fridays, the Muslim day of prayer, Malaysian Muslims congregate at mosques in their 'Friday best'. The 'lunch hour' starts at 1130 and runs through to about 1430 to allow Muslims to attend the mosque; in big towns and cities, Friday lunchtimes are marked by traffic jams. In the fervently Islamic E coast states, Friday is the start of the weekend. Men traditionally wear *songkoks* – black velvet hats – to the mosque and often wear their best sarung (sometimes *songket*) over their trousers. Those who have performed the Haj pilgrimage to Mecca wear a white skullcap.

Buddhism

While Buddhism is the formal religion of most of Malaysia's Chinese population, many are Taoists, who follow the teachings of the three sages – Confucius, Mencius and Lao Tse. Taoism is characterized by ancestor worship and a plethora of deities. As with Islam, this has been mixed with animist beliefs and spirit worship forms a central part of the faith.

Hinduism

Hindu (and Buddhist) religions were established on the Malay peninsula long before Islam arrived. Remains of ancient Hindu-Buddhist temples dating from the Kingdom of Langkasuka in the early years of the first millennium have been found in the Bujang Valley, at the foot of Gunung Jerai (Kedah Peak) in Kedah (**see page 149**). The majority of Malaysia's Indian population is Hindu, although there are also many Indian Muslims.

Malay magic and the spirits behind the prophet

Despite the fact that all Malays are Muslims, some traditional, pre-Islamic beliefs are still practiced by Malays – particularly in the NE of the peninsula, the conservative Islamic heartland. The *bomoh* – witch doctor and magic-man – is alive and well in modern Malaysia. The use of *ilmu* (the malay name for magic), which is akin to voodoo, is still widely practiced and bomohs are highly respected and important members of kampung communities. Consulting bomohs is a commonplace event; they are often called in to perform their ancient rituals – sometimes they are contracted to bring rain or to determine the site of a new house; on other occasions to make fields (or married couples) fertile or to heal sickness. The healing ceremony is called the *main puteri*: there are certain illnesses which are believed to be caused by spirits – or *hantu* – who have been offended and must be placated.

The bomoh's job is to get the protective, friendly spirits on his side, in the belief that they can influence the evil ones. He knows many different spirits by name; some are the spirits of nature, others are spirits of ancestors. Many bomohs are specialists in particular fields. Some, known as *pewangs*, traditionally concentrated on performing spells to ensure fruitful harvests or safe fishing expeditions. Bomohs are still consulted and contracted to formulate herbal remedies, charms, love potions and perform traditional massage (*urut*). The *belian* – or sharman – specializes in more extreme forms of magic conducting exorcisms and spirit-raising seances, or *berhantu*. In Kelantan, a bomoh who acts as a spirit medium is known as a *Tok Peteri* and once a spirit has entered him, during a seance, his assistant, called the *Tok Mindok*, is required to question the spirit, present offerings and address the spirit in a secret language of magic formulae. Seances are always held in public – in front of the whole village – and are held after evening prayers.

Manipulation of the weather is one area where the magic is still widely used. The government has been known to employ a pewang to perform rituals designed to keep rain from falling during large public events. In 1991 actors from Kuala Lumpur's Instant Café Theatre Company called on a bomoh to ensure their open-air production of *A Midsummer Night's Dream* was not washed out. The only occasion on which rain interupted the play was during an extra performance, not covered in the bomoh's contract.

All natural and inanimate objects are also capable of having spirits and Malays often refer to them using the respectful title *Datuk*. Other spirits, like the *pontianak* (the vampire ghost of a woman who dies in childbirth) are greatly feared. Any suspicion of the presence of a pontianak calls for the immediate intervention of a belian, who is believed to inherit his powers from a *hantu raya* – great spirit – which attaches itself to a bloodline and is subsequently passed from generation to generation.

Language and literature

Bahasa Melayu (literally, 'Malay Language') – or to give the language its official title, *Bahasa Kebangsaan* ('National Language') – is an Austronesian language which has been the language of trade and commerce throughout the archipelago for centuries. It is the parent language of – and is closely related to – modern Indonesian. In 1972, Indonesia and Malaysia came to an agreement to standardize spelling – although many differences still remain.

Modern Malay has been affected by a succession of external influences – Sanskrit from the 7th century, Arabic from the 14th and English from the 19th century. These influences are reflected in a number of words, most of them of a religious or technical nature. All scientific terminology is directly borrowed from the English or Latin. However, there are many common everyday words borrowed from Arabic or English: *pasar*, for example, comes from the Arabic *bazaar* (market) and there are countless examples of English words used in Malay – particularly when it comes to modern modes of transport – *teksi*, *bas* and *tren*. Where a Malay term has been devised for a 20th century phenomenon, it is usually a fairly straightforward description. An alternative word for train, for example is *keretapi* (literally 'fire car') and the word for aeroplane is *kapalterbang* (flying ship).

From the 7th century, the Indian Pallava script was in restricted use, although few examples survive. The *Jawi* script, adapted from Arabic, was adopted in the 14th century, with the arrival of Muslim traders and Sufi missionaries in Melaka. To account for sounds in the Malay language which have no equivalent in Arabic, five additional letters had to be invented, giving 33 letters in all. Jawi script was used for almost all Malay writings until the 19th century, and romanized script only began to supplant Jawi after World War II. Many older Malays still read and write the script and it is not uncommon to see it along the streets. Some Chinese-owned banks, for example, have transliterated their names into Jawi script so as to make Malays feel a little more at home in them.

Malay literature is thought to date from the 14th century – although surviving manuscripts written in Jawi only date from the beginning of the 15th century. The first printed books in Malay were produced by European missionaries in the 17th century. The best known of Malay literary works are the 16th century *Sejara Melayu* or Malay Annals; others include the romantic *Hikayat Hang Tuah* and the 19th century *Tuhfat al-Nafis*.

The first of Malaysia's 'modern' authors was the 19th century writer Munshi Abdullah – who has lent his name to a few streets around the country. Although he kept to many of the classical strictures, Abdullah articulated a personal view and challenged many of the traditional assumptions underlying Malay society. His best known work was his autobiography, *Hikayat Abdullah*. However, it was not until the 1920s that Malayan authors began to write modern novels and short stories. Among the best known writers are Ahmad bin Mohd. Rashid Talu, Ishak Hj. Muhammad and Harun Aminurrashid. Their work laid the foundations for a expansion of Malaysian literature from the 1950s and today there is a prodigious Malay-language publishing industry.

Dance, drama and music

Wayang Kulit Shadow puppet plays, were the traditional form of entertainment in Malay kampungs. Shadow plays are still performed in some rural parts of the peninsula's east coast and are regular fixtures at cultural events. The art form was originally imported from Java, probably during the days of the Majapahit Empire in the 14th century (**see page 517**). Puppets are made from buffalo hide and mounted on bamboo sticks. Oil lamps traditionally cast their shadows onto a white screen. The plays are based on adaptations of the Indian epics, the *Mahabharata* and the *Ramayana* (**see page 505**), and the plots are fairly predictable: good always triumphs over evil. The puppet-master is known as the *to' dalang*; he narrates each story in lyrical classical Malay – with a great sense of melodrama – and is accompanied by a traditional orchestra of gongs, drums, *rebab* (violins) and woodwind instruments. He slips in and out of different characters, using many different voices throughout the performances, which lasts as long as 3-4 hrs. Shows usually begin at about 2000.

Chinese classical street operas (wayang) date back to the 7th century. They are performed in Malaysia by troupes of roving actors during Chinese festivals, particularly during the seventh lunar month, following the Festival of the Hungry Ghosts. For more details on the wayang, **see page 383**.

Dance

Silat (or, more properly, *bersilat*) is a traditional Malay martial art, but is so highly stylized that it has become a dance form and is often demonstrated with the backing of a percussion orchestra. *Pencak silat* is the more formal martial art of self-defence; *seni silat* is the graceful aesthetic equivalent. A variety of the latter is commonly performed at ceremonial occasions – such as Malay weddings – it is called *silat pulut*. Silat comprises a fluid combination of movements and is designed to be as much a comprehensive and disciplined form of physical exercise as it is a martial art. It promotes good blood circulation and deep-breathing, which are considered essential for strength and stamina. The fluidity of the body movements require great suppleness, flexibility and poise. Malaysia's best known silat gurus live along the east coast.

The *Mak Yong* was traditionally a Kelantanese court dance-drama, performed only in the presence of the sultan and territorial chiefs. The dance is performed mainly by women (the mak yong being the 'queen' and lead dancer), and is accompanied by an orchestra of gongs, drums and the *rebab* (violin). There are only ever two or three male dancers who provide the comic interludes. The dance is traditionally performed during the Sultan of Kelantan's birthday celebrations. Unlike the wayang kulit shadow puppet theatre (above), the stories are not connected to the Hindu epics; they are thought to be of Malay origin. Other Kelantanese court dances include: the *garong*, a lively up-tempo dance by 5 pairs of men and women, in a round (a *garong* is a bamboo cow bell). The *payang*, a folk dance, is named after the distinctive east coast fishing boats; traditionally it was danced on the beach while waiting for the kampung fishing fleet to return.

The *joget* dance is another Malay art form which is the result of foreign cultural influence – in this case, Portuguese. It has gone by a variety of other names, notably the *ronggeng* and the *branyo*. It is traditionally accompanied by the gamelan orchestra. In 1878, Frank Swettenham (the first British Resident at Kuala Lumpur, but then, a young colonial officer) witnessed a performance of the joget, which he described in his book *Malay Sketches*. "Gradually raising themselves from a sitting to a kneeling posture, acting in perfect accord in every motion, then rising to their feet, they began a series of figures hardly to be exceeded in grace and difficulty, considering that the movements are essentially slow, the arms, hands and body being the performers, whilst the feet are scarcely noticed and half the time not visible..."

Arab traders were responsible for importing the *zapin* dance and Indonesians introduced the *inang*. Immigrants from Banjarmasin (South Kalimantan), who arrived in Johor in the early 1900s, brought with them the so-called Hobbyhorse Dance – the *Kuda Kepang* – which is performed at weddings and on ceremonial occasions in Johor. The hobbyhorses are made of goat or buffalo skin, stretched over a rotan frame. There are countless other local folk dances around Malaysia, usually associated with festivals – such as the *wau bulan* kite dance in Kelantan.

The **Lion Dance** is performed in Chinese communities, particularly around Chinese New Year, and the dances are accompanied by loud drums and cymbals, so are hard to miss. The lion dance actually originated in India, where tame lions were led around public fairs and festivals to provide entertainment along with jugglers. But because lions were in short supply, dancers with lion masks took their place. The dance was introduced to China during the Tang Dynasty. The lion changed its image from that of a clown to a symbol of the Buddha and is now regarded as 'the protector of Buddhism'. The lion dance developed into a ceremony in which demons and evil spirits are expelled (hence the deafening cymbals and drums).

Bharata Natyam (Indian classical dance) is performed by Malaysia's Indian community and is accompanied by Indian instruments such as the *tambura* (which has 4 strings), the *talam* (cymbals), *mridanga* (double-headed drum), *vina* (single stringed instrument) and flute. In Malaysia, the Temple of Fine Arts in Kuala Lumpur is an Indian cultural organization which promotes Indian dance forms. The Temple organizes an annual Festival of Arts (**see page 110**).

Music and musical instruments

Traditional Malay music, which accompanies the various traditional dances, offers a taste of all the peninsula's different cultural influences. The most prominent of these were Indian, Arab, Portuguese, Chinese, Siamese and Javanese – and finally, Western musical influence which gave birth to the all-pervasive genre 'Pop Melayu' – typically melancholic heavy rock. Traditional musical instruments reflect similar cultural influences, notably the *gambus* or lute (which has Middle Eastern origins and is used to accompany the *zapin* dance), the Indian harmonium, the Chinese *serunai* (clarinet) and gongs, the *rebana* drums, also of Middle Eastern origin, and the Javanese *gamelan* orchestra (**see page 534**). Because Malays have traditionally been so willing to absorb new cultural elements, some of their traditional art forms have been in danger of extinction. Most traditional Malay instruments are percussion instruments; there are very few stringed or wind instruments. There are 6 main Malay drums, the most common of which is the cylindrical, double-headed *gendang*, which is used to accompany wayang kulit performances and silat. Other drums include the *geduk* and the *gedombak*; all 3 of these are played in orchestras.

Rebana, another traditional Malay drum, is used on ceremonial occasions as well as being a musical instrument. Traditionally, drumming competitions would be held following the rice-harvesting season (in May) and judges award points for timing, tone and rhythm. The best place to see the rebana in action is during Kelantan's giant drum festivals at the end of June. The drums are made from metre-long hollowed-out logs and are brightly painted. In competitions, drummers from different kampungs compete against each other in teams of up to 12 men. Traditionally the rebana was used as a means of communication between villages, and different rhythms were devised as a sort of morse code to invite distant kampungs to weddings or as warnings of war. *Kertok* are drums made from coconuts whose tops are sliced off and replaced with a block of *nibong* wood (from the sago palm) as a sounding board; these are then struck with padded drumsticks.

There are three main **gongs**; the biggest and most common, the *tawak* or *tetawak* is used to accompany wayang kulit shadow puppet theatre and Mak Yong dance dramas. The other smaller gongs are called *canang* and also accompany wayang kulit performances. The only Malay stringed instrument is the *rebab*, a violin-type instrument found throughout the region. The main wind instrument is the *serunai*, or oboe, which is of Persian origin and traditionally accompanies wayang kulit and dance performances. Its reed is cut from a palm leaf.

The *Nobat* is the ancient royal orchestra which traditionally plays at the installation of sultans in Kedah, Perak, Selangor, Terangganu and Brunei. It is thought to have been introduced at the royal court of Melaka in the 15th century. The instruments include two types of drums (*negara* and *gendang*), a trumpet (*nafiri*), a flute (*serunai*) and a gong. The Nobat also plays at the coronation of each new king, every five years.

Crafts

The Malay heartland, on the east coast of Peninsular Malaysia, is the centre of the handicraft industry – particularly Kelantan. An extensive variety of traditional handicrafts, as well as batiks, are widely available in this area, although they are also sold throughout the country, notably in Kuala Lumpur and other main towns (see individual town entries). In East Malaysia, Sarawak has an especially active handicraft industry (**see page 245**).

Kites Malaysia's most famous kite is the crescent-shaped Kelantanese *wau bulan* (moon kite) which has a wingspan of up to 3m and a length of more than 3m; they can reach altitudes of nearly 500m. Bow-shaped pieces of bamboo are often secured underneath, which make a melodious humming noise (*dengung*) in the wind. Wau come in all shapes and sizes however, and scaled-down versions of wau bulan and other kites can be bought. It is even possible to find batik-covered *wau cantik* or *wau sobek*, which are popular wall-hangings but make for awkward hand-luggage. There are often kite-flying competitions on the E coast, where competitors gain points for height and manoeuvering skills. Kites are also judged for their physical attributes, their ability to stay in the air and their sound. Most kite-flying competitions take place after the rice harvest in May, when kampungs compete against each other. On the E coast, all kites are known as **wau**. Perhaps the most recognizable one is Terangganu's *wau kucing* (cat kite), which Malaysia Airlines adopted as its logo. There are also *wau daun* (leaf kites) and *wau jala budi* (which literally means 'the net of good deeds kite'). Elsewhere in Malaysia, kites are known as *layang-layang* (literally, 'floating objects').

Tops Top spinning (*gasing*) is another traditional form of entertainment, still popular in rural Malay kampungs – particularly on the E coast of the peninsula. The biggest tops have diameters as big as frisbees and can weigh more than 5 kg; the skill required in launching a top is considerable. To launch the larger tops requires wrapping them in a tightly coiled 4m long rope which is smeared with resin. Once spinning, the top is scooped up on a wooden batton and left to spin on top of a small wooden post – sometimes for as long as 2 hours. Some tops have added metal or lead, and these are used in top-fighting events. Top-making is a precision-craft, and each one can take up to 3 days to make; they are carved from the upper roots and stem-bases of merbau and afzelia trees.

Woodcarving Originally craftsmen were commissioned by sultans and the Malay nobility to decorate the interiors, railings, doorways, shutters and stilts of palaces and public buildings. In Malay woodcarving, only floral and animal motifs are used as Islam prohibits depiction of the human form. But most widely acclaimed are the carved statues of malevolent spirits of the Mah Meris, an Orang Asli tribe.

Batik (*Batek*) Although batik-technology was actually imported from their Indonesia several centuries ago, this coloured and patterned cloth is now a mainstay of Malaysian cultural identity. Malaysian batik are very different from their Indonesian counterparts, which are, on the whole, much darker; the best Malaysian batiks come from the east coast states, particularly Kelantan. Patterns are usually stamped onto cotton using a batik 'iron' or *jap* – which looks something like a domestic iron, except that it has an artistically patterned bottom, usually made from twisted copper and strips of soldered tin. Dripping with molten wax, the jap stamps the same pattern across the length and breadth of the cloth, which is then put into a vat of dye. The waxed areas resist the dye and after drying, the process is repeated several times for the different colours. The cracking effect is produced by crumpling the waxed material, which allows the dye to penetrate the cracks. The cloth is traditionally printed in 12m lengths. (For a more detailed description of the batik printing process, **see page 535**.)

In recent years there has been a revival of hand-painted batiks (*batik tulis*), particularly on silk. Price depends on the type of material, design, number of colours used and method employed: factory-printed materials are cheaper than those made by hand. Batik is sold by the *sarung*-length or made up into shirts – and other items of clothing.

Kain songket is Malaysia's 'cloth of gold', although it is also woven in other parts of the region (**see page 810**). Originally it was richly woven with gold or silver thread – today imitation thread is used. The songket evolved when the Malay sultanates first began trading with China (where the silk came from) and India (where the gold and silver thread derived). Designs are reproduced from Islamic motifs and Arabic calligraphy. It was once exclusive to royalty, but is used today during formal occasions and ceremonies (such as weddings). In Kelantan,

Terengganu and Pahang, the cloth can be purchased directly from workshops. Prices increase with the intricacy of the design and the number of threads used. Each piece is woven by hand and different weavers specialize in particular patterns – one length of cloth may be the work of several weavers.

Pewterware   Pewter-making was introduced from China in the mid-19th century; it was the perfect alloy for Malaysia, which until very recently, was the world's largest tin-producer: pewter is 95% tin. Straits tin is alloyed with antimony and copper. The high proportion of tin lends to the fineness of the surface. Malaysia's best pewter is made by Selangor Pewter, which has factories in KL and Singapore. It is made mainly into vases, tankards, water jugs, trays and dressing table ornaments. The Selangor Pewter factory on the outskirts of KL (**see page 104**) employs about 400 craftsmen and has a good showroom. Selangor pewter was started in 1885 by Yong Koon, a Chinese immigrant from Swatow province who came to Malaya by junk. Using the ample supply of tin, he started making items for ancestral worship, such as incense burners and joss-stick holders. The third generation of the Yong family now runs the operation. The dimpling effect is made by tapping the surface with a small hammer. Selangor Pewter is the world's biggest pewter manufacturer.

Wayang kulit (shadow puppets – see above) are crafted from buffalo-hide and represent figures from the Indian epic tales. They are popular handicrafts as they are light and portable.

Silverware   Silverwork is a traditional craft and is now a thriving cottage industry in Kelantan. It is crafted into brooches, pendants, belts, bowls and rings. Design patterns incorporate traditional motifs such as *wayang kulit* (see above) and hibiscus flowers (the national flower). The Iban of Sarawak also use silver for ceremonial headdresses and girdles, and some Iban silvercraft can be found for sale on the peninsula.

MODERN MALAYSIA

Politics

Malaysia's economy has boomed in recent years, but with every year, Prime Minister Dr Mahathir Mohamad has concentrated more and more power in his government. With the creation of a *nouveau riche* middle class, there were hopes that a more open political system might evolve. But the government does not readily tolerate dissent and Dr Mahathir is aware that his political dominance hinges largely on economic recess.

Dr Mahathir, as leader of the United Malays National Organization (UMNO), heads the *Barisan Nasional* (BN), or National Front coalition, has won every election since coming to power in 1981. In 1987, however, just a year after securing another landslide victory, he narrowly retained his premiership following a challenge from then trade and industry minister Tunku Razaleigh Hamzah. The same year, Mahathir became embroiled in an education controversy after non-Chinese administrators were appointed to Chinese schools. In an atmosphere of rising political tension, the government used the draconian Internal Security Act (a legislative hang-over from the British administration which allows for unlimited detention without trial), to arrest more than 100 opponents. The clampdown was known as Operation Lalang. The Prime Minister dealt with his opponents within UMNO by excluding them when he formed a new party – UMNO Baru (or New UMNO) – which is still just known as UMNO. Since then, Mahathir has consolidated his position and the strength of the economy has enabled him to promote himself as the architect of Malaysia's new-found prosperity.

Drugs trafficking – stiff punishment

Malaysia is well known around the world for its stringent laws against drugs. As they fill in their immigration forms, visitors cannot fail to notice the bold block capitals reading: "BE FOREWARNED – DEATH FOR DRUG TRAFFICKERS UNDER MALAYSIAN LAW". At entry points to Malaysia there are prominent posters repeating this warning, the words emblazoned over an ominous picture of a noose. World attention focuses on Malaysia whenever Westerners go to the gallows, but they represent a tiny fraction of those hanged for drug trafficking offences. Since 1983 about 150 prisoners have been hanged and about 4,000 arrested under Section 39(B) of the Dangerous Drugs Act; about a quarter of those face execution within the next few years. Malaysia's biggest-ever mass-hanging of traffickers took place at Taiping jail in May 1990. Eight Hong Kong people were executed – including one woman – despite many pleas for clemency from around the world.

The Dadah Act – *dadah* is the Malay word for drugs – stipulates a mandatory death sentence upon conviction for anyone in possession of 15 or more grams of heroin or morphine, 200 g of cannabis or hashish or 40 g of cocaine. Those caught with more than 10 g of heroin or 100 g of cannibis are deemed to be traffickers and face lengthy jail sentences and flogging with a rotan cane. Following the execution of two Australians in 1986, the then Australian Prime Minister, Bob Hawke, branded the Malaysian government 'barbaric'. A similar outcry resulted from the hanging of a Briton in 1987 – the British opposition even called for a trade embargo of Malaysia. But Malaysian Prime Minister Dr Mahathir Mohamad – who is a medical doctor and as such has taken the Hypocratic Oath – has consistently refused to bow to international pleas for clemency. He has personally sat on the pardons board when it has upheld the death sentence.

In the UN General Assembly in 1986 Mahathir said: "Why should we be any less tough? The death penalty is... a just punishment for such criminals for only death will stop these purveyors of misery and death." He took the same line when interviewed for a British television documentary in 1991, saying that drug traffickers were murderers. In the film, *The Prime Minister, the junkie and the boys on death row*, he said: "We have to carry out this death penalty because it would not be fair to those who had already been hanged and their families."

In 1990, for the first time in the 33 years since Malaysian independence, the BN coalition faced a credible multi-racial opposition. The opposition alliance was led by Tunku Razaleigh Hamzah, a former UMNO cabinet minister (and member of the Kelantan royal family) who had challenged Mahathir for the UMNO leadership in 1987, and lost. His faction broke away from UMNO and called itself Semangat '46 – or 'Spirit of '46', the year in which UMNO had been founded. In the run-up to the election, Semangat struck electoral pacts with the predominantly Chinese Democratic Action Party (DAP) and, separately, the conservative Parti Islam, whose powerbase was in the NE Malay heartland of Terengganu and Kelantan states. Despite much speculation that the opposition would unseat the ruling BN coalition – or at least, deprive it of its crucial two-thirds majority in parliament – Dr Mahathir won a landslide victory, securing 127 seats in the 180-seat parliament. A two-thirds majority allows the government to amend the constitution and has been Mahathir's measuring stick for electoral success.

Semangat and the DAP both lost several seats in the election, although Dr Mahathir lost his control of Kelantan and Sabah states. In the former, Parti Islam (PAS) now forms the state government (see page 214), having regained control of the state legislature which it had controlled from independence until 1978. In Sabah, the defection of the ruling Christian-led party from BN, a few days before

Mahathir Mohamad – the doctor's prescription

During Malaysia's race riots of May 1969, a young radical called Dr Mahathir Mohamad gained notoriety as a rabble-rouser and outspoken critic of Tunku Abdul Rahman, independent Malaysia's first Prime Minister. He outlined his extreme pro-Malay views in a controversial book, *The Malay dilemma*, which was promptly banned. Ironically, Mahathir himself is not fully Malay: his father was an Indian Muslim. But through the early 1970s, Mahathir fought his way into the upper echelons of the Malay political hierarchy. He became education minister and then, in 1976, he rose to become deputy prime minister under Tun Hussein Onn. Over the next five years, he gained a reputation as a no-nonsense, dynamic Malay leader with a sense of purpose. In 1981 Mahathir became Prime Minister having been elected president of the politically dominant United Malays National Organization (UMNO). He was the first Malaysian leader not to have been educated in the West – he trained as a medical doctor at the University of Singapore – and he sold himself as a home-grown, made-in-Malaysia product who, unlike his predecessors, had climbed the political ladder without the help of aristocratic connections.

Mahathir had humble origins, having been born in a small, typically Malay kampung house, next door to an ice factory, on the outskirts of Alor Setar in Kedah state. In 1992, the Culture, Arts and Tourism minister announced that the delapidated house would be restored as a national monument. It was good, the minister said, to depict the Prime Minister's modest background. In his school days, during the Japanese occupation, Mahathir worked as a stallholder at Pekan Rabu market, where he sold ginger drinks and bananas. His first stall was torn down by Japanese soldiers. He revealed all this in 1991, while attempting to convince stallholders in the same market of the wisdom of turning it into a modern shopping complex.

From his first day in office, Mahathir gained respect for his determination to root out corruption. All politicians and civil servants were required to wear a name tag so they could be identified and held accountable. Ever since, he has worn one himself, although these days nobody needs reminding of who he is. The rise of money politics in the 1980s – largely as a result of his policy to promote the Malay role in business, undermined this government's anti-corruption drive however. The new premier won his first landslide election victory for the 11-party *Barisan Nasional* (BN – or National Front) coalition in 1982, having campaigned under the slogan 'clean, efficient and trustworthy'.

the election, was described by Dr Mahathir as 'a stab in the back'. The rebel states have suffered for their 'disloyalty' and frequently accuse the federal government of failing to promote them to foreign investors. Sabah's Chief Minister was arrested on corruption charges and his influential brother was arrested for his supposed role in a Sabahan secessionist conspiracy (**see page 302**). Their trials were still in progress when this book went to press. Meanwhile, back in Kuala Lumpur, the battle has been hotting-up in the succession stakes. Dr Mahathir is getting on and this is likely to be his final term in office. The ruling party appears split between the older generation who support the current deputy prime minister, Abdul Ghafar Baba and the younger former Islamic firebrand, turned finance minister, Anwar Ibrahim.

In foreign affairs Malaysia follows a non-aligned stance and is fiercely anti-Communist. This, however, has not stopped its enthusiastic investment in Indochina and Burma. Malaysia is a leading light in Asean, and Mahathir has made his mark as an outspoken champion of the developing world. As such, he has frequently clashed with the West. Malaysia needs continued foreign investment from industrialized countries, but Dr Mahathir remains deeply suspicious of Western motives and intentions.

One of his first actions was to loosen Malaysia's ties with the Commonwealth, and, particularly, with Britain. He instructed Malaysians to "Buy British Last" and "Look East" instead, whereby the country's role models became the booming economies of Japan, South Korea and Taiwan. (The "Buy British Last" policy was finally buried when Mahathir and the then British Prime Minister Margaret Thatcher exchanged smiles and handshakes in London a few years later.) He stressed the importance of self-reliance, and at home, this strong economic-nationalist stance won him increasing support from Malaysia's pro-business Chinese community as well as from the Malays. One of Mahathir's enduring legacies will be the Proton Saga, the national car (**see page 104**), which survived teething problems in the mid-1980s to become a symbol of the new high-tech "Made-in-Malaysia" image the Prime Minister has been so keen to promote.

Mahathir has won a string of impressive election victories and has weathered both economic recession and criticism of his sometimes abrasive and often autocratic style. Foreign investors like the stability Mahathir offers, and thanks to them, he has generated the prosperity which has kept most Malaysians happy. His detractors say he never listens; his admirers talk of his strength of conviction. In July 1991, at the age of 65, he celebrated a decade in power. He is tough on his opponents, and is renowned for his tremendous energy – despite a heart attack in 1989 and subsequent multiple bypass surgery.

Mahathir has many dislikes; at the top of the list are journalists and environmentalists, both of whom stand accused of projecting an unbalanced and inaccurate image of Malaysia. On the world stage he has made a name for himself defending Malaysia's environmental record – notably at the Earth Summit in Rio de Janeiro in June 1992 (**see page 88**). He has also emerged as a champion of 'the South' – the developing countries – who, Mahathir maintains, have suffered too long at the hands of Western imperialists and neo-colonialists. In his view, the value of industrialization and economic development is its promise to free the South from the over-dependence that has forced countries to compromise their independence and sovereignty. Since Singapore's Lee Kuan Yew stepped down as Prime Minister in 1990, Mahathir has assumed a more prominent role in regional affairs too, and his lengthy tenure in office has added to his stature and credibility.

Economy

Malaysia has an abundance of natural resources. Today, though, tin-mining, rubber and palm oil are declining in importance, and while the country's oil, gas and timber wealth are valuable sources of revenue, the manufacturing sector has become the powerhouse of the economy. At the same time, the services sector is booming, and tourism is now the third largest foreign exchange earner. Malaysia has one of the fastest-growing economies in the world. The World Bank defines Malaysia as an upper-middle-income country. In 1990 GNP per capita was US$2,277. There is a Malay saying which goes: *ada gula, ada semut* ('where there's sugar, there's ants') – and from the late 1980s foreign investors swarmed to Malaysia thanks to its sugar-coated investment incentives as well as its cheap land and labour, its good infrastructure and political stability.

In the late 1800s, as the British colonial government developed the infrastructure of the Federated Malay States, they built a network of roads, railways, telephones and telegraphs which served as the backbone of the export economy. In the 50 years following 1880, export earnings rose 30-fold. Most of the tin mines and plantations were in the hands of British-owned companies and remained foreign-owned until the Malaysian government restructured foreign equity holdings in the 1970s.

On independence in 1957, resource-rich Malaysia's future looked bright and

The New Economic Policy – Malaysia's recipe for racial harmony

Just over 2 decades ago Malaysia's Malay-led government woke up to the fact that Malays and indigenous groups – collectively called *bumiputras*, or 'sons of the soil' – made up more than half the country's population but owned just 2% of corporate equity. Their average income was also less than half that of non-Malays. The Malay elite worked in the civil service, but most Malays were poor farmers. Economic power was concentrated in the hands of foreigners and urban Chinese while rural Malays lived on, or under, the breadline. The Chinese virtually ran the economy – they were the bankers, brokers and businessmen. In 1970, in the wake of the bloody race riots in which hundreds died (see page 69), the controversial New Economic Policy, or NEP, was introduced; it was a radical experiment in social engineering. The NEP aimed to wipe out poverty irrespective of race and completely restructure society by putting the Malay, Chinese and Indian communities on an equal footing. The idea was to abolish racial stereotyping, making it more difficult to associate a person's job with the colour of his skin.

The NEP was designed to prevent a recurrence of the bloodletting by keeping multiracial Malaysia intact. It offered Malays, the economic underdogs, a chance to catch up and encouraged them to move to the cities. Racial quotas were introduced to raise their stake in the economy to at least 30%. They were granted scholarships and directorships, they were pushed into managerial jobs, subsidized, goaded and given a ticket to get rich quick – which many did. But because the NEP favoured the Malays, it antagonized almost everyone else. For 20 years, the NEP was denounced as racist by its critics and flagrantly abused by many of those it tried to help. The policy was an invitation to bribery and corruption and the hijacking and exploitation of the NEP by wealthy bumiputras alienated non-Malays and fanned resentment.

But the NEP's targets were not met. Although poverty has been markedly reduced since 1970, the bumiputras' stake in the economy is today around 20% instead of the targeted 30%. While the jump from 2% to 20% is enormous, only 7% of that is in the hands of individuals – most is owned by big bumiputra investment companies, institutions and government trust agencies. A sizeable chunk of the remainder is concentrated in the hands of a stratum of bumiputra

foreign investment was encouraged, the capitalist system maintained and there was no threat to nationalize industry. The first national development plan aimed to expand the agricultural sector and begin to reduce dependence on rubber, which, even then, was beginning to encounter competition from synthetic alternatives. But rubber and tin remained the main economic props. In 1963, when the Federation of Malaysia was formed, only 6% of the workforce was employed in industry.

The structure of Malaysia's economy has been radically altered since independence, and particularly, since the 1980s. Commodity exports such as rubber and palm oil, which were the mainstay of the post-colonial economy, having declined in significance and, within 30 years, this sector is unlikely to contribute more than 6% of Malaysia's export earnings. 1987 was the turning point, when agriculture was overtaken by the manufacturing sector in terms of contribution to Gross Domestic Product. Manufacturing output has almost tripled in 25 years – thanks mainly to the fact that Malaysia has been the darling of foreign investors. By 1995, the government wants industry to account for a third of the country's GDP. The value of manufactured exports is growing even faster; today they comprise more than 60% of Malaysia's export earnings and by 1995 they should account for three quarters. The country that used to be the world's biggest producer of rubber and tin is now the world's leading producer of semi-conductors and air-conditioning units. In May 1993, another landmark was fat cats who act as 'sleeping partners' in big firms. Today, the government admits that the biggest income disparities in Malaysia are within the bumiputra community itself. There are still relatively few high-calibre Malays with relevant management qualifications and experience to fill the posts available.

In the months before the NEP expired in 1990, many Malays were arguing for the continuation of the policy; they must still be given special treatment, they said, to enable them to catch up. However much the Chinese have been disadvantaged by the policy, their robust business acumen has meant that they are far from being a downtrodden minority. Even the NEP's most outspoken critics accept the need to rectify Malaysia's socio-economic imbalances, but they say the solution does not lie in a programme discriminating along racial lines. Yet despite the simmering ethnic tensions, Malaysia has enjoyed two decades of peace and stability.

The spectre of a repeat of the 1969 race riots has been constantly raised by the government in an effort to promote racial harmony – but today Malaysians look to the Los Angeles riots of 1992 as an example of unwanted mayhem, rather than 1969. There is little doubt that despite the abuses of political patronage, the bumiputras are now in a better position to compete. A fairly large number of bumiputras have become leading lights in Kuala Lumpur's business and financial community. As a group, Malays are more self-confident and more competitive than they were in 1970; they are also less prone to cast themselves as a disenfranchised majority.

In 1991, the old policy was replaced with the New Development Policy (NDP), which formalized a more liberal strategy. The NDP sets no deadline for the achievement of the 30% bumiputra ownership target – although it is still there. The new policy uses incentives instead of quotas – in the words of one commentator, it uses 'more carrot and less stick'. The emphasis now is on ensuring that bumiputras retain and build on the wealth they have accumulated. The government now wants to wean Malays off government hand-outs and patronage but it appears to believe that until the dependency syndrome has completely disappeared, bumiputras should be protected. Most Malaysians have welcomed the change in emphasis, but critics still maintain the NDP is just old wine in a new bottle.

created in Malaysia's economic history: the Malaysia Mining Corporation, one of the country's biggest remaining tin producers, pulled out of tin mining. Tin production costs have increased while the price of tin has slumped. In 1990 there were still 141 tin mines in Malaysia; by 1993 there were only 50.

But the type of products Malaysia manufactures is also undergoing rapid change. The New Development Policy (NDP), unveiled in 1991 (see above) promotes hi-tech industries, higher value-added production, skills development and increased productivity. One of the main reasons for this is Malaysia's labour squeeze. The main industrial boom zones (the Klang Valley around Kuala Lumpur, Johor and Penang) are already suffering shortages, and while infrastructural developments have just about kept pace with the flood of foreign manufacturing investment, the labour pool is drying up. Already the government has been forced to recruit blue-collar migrant labourers from Thailand and Indonesia; most still work in the plantation sector, although it is likely that more and more will be brought in to man the production lines. There are also hundreds of thousands of illegal immigrants; in July 1992 the government forced illegals to register or face deportation, realizing it could no longer turn a blind eye to the labour-smuggling racket. The rate at which wages have risen in recent years has also meant that more labour-intensive industries now find it considerably cheaper to locate in Thailand or Indonesia.

Environment – mud-slinging in the greenhouse

In recent years, environmental protest groups around the world have stepped up pressure on timber-rich Malaysia over its logging practices. They say the industry is not sustainably managed, that tribal people are suffering and that the government's conservation strategies have not been implemented. In the face of calls in the West to ban all imports of unsustainably managed tropical hardwoods and fears that Malaysia's jungle is about to disappear, the government has begun to fight back.

Malaysia is the world's biggest exporter of tropical hardwoods and earns US$3 billion a year from the trade. More than half the country is still swathed in jungle, but environmentalists are now very concerned about the rate of logging and its effect on forest tribes (see page 282). Malaysia says it is being victimized by ill-informed hypocrites. The government maintains that the people who created the greenhouse effect should not be throwing stones and that the West has double standards when it comes to environmental issues. Western countries have already cleared their forests in the name of development, the government says, so why shouldn't Malaysia be free to do so to? If the West argues that Malaysia's forests are a global resource, then they should pay to keep them intact. Industrialized countries have also been reluctant to set targets for the reduction of carbon dioxide emission and other 'greenhouse gases', yet they draw attention to the effects of Malaysian logging on global warming.

At the Earth Summit in Rio de Janeiro in June 1992, Prime Minister Dr Mahathir Mohamad attacked developed countries for their hypocrisy. In addition to concerns over the supposed climatic effects of deforestation, Mahathir noted that poor countries have been told to preserve their forests and other genetic resources for research purposes. He said: "This is the same as telling these countries that they must continue to be poor because their forests and other resources are more precious than [the people] themselves". He added that "when biodiversity refers to the gene-rich banks of the tropical countries, it is only fair that they have a share in whatever happens to the genes". At Rio, it became clear that the United States did not ratify the convention on biodiversity because it wanted to protect its lucrative bio-technology industries.

While the double standards are not lost on Malaysian environmental groups, they say the government is too busy deflecting criticism and is ignoring the mess in its own back yard. Environmental groups at Rio blacklisted Malaysia for indiscriminate logging practices and while Malaysian forestry policy looks tough on paper, it has not been adequately enforced. Groups like the Environmental Protection Society of Malaysia, which for years has been pressing for greater public accountability and a crackdown on corruption, found that being in the international limelight gave them more political leverage at home. Meanwhile, Western environmental protests contributed to a slump in Malaysia's timber sales to Europe. Malaysia alleges that these campaigns are bankrolled by European softwood producers. It says such campaigns are forcing Malaysia to fell more trees in order to earn the same amount of money.

Environmental groups rubbish such claims – more trees are cut down when timber prices are high they say. But Malaysia says it would not be so stupid or greedy as to kill the goose that lays the golden egg; it maintains that sustained-yield harvesting means its forests will be there in perpetuity. To convince the world of this, Malaysia has declared war on the green lobby and has announced plans to launch a counter-offensive. Slick public relations campaigns will be expensive, but they will be cheaper than stopping logging.

But Malaysia does not want to be seen as a cheap-labour country any more. The government has become increasingly selective with the sorts of industries it allows to locate in the country, and prefers capital-intensive, hi-tech manufacturers. The NDP is more liberal than its predecessor, the New Economic Policy, when it comes to foreign investors. Through it, the government tacitly concedes that without continued inflows of foreign capital, Malaysia's ambitious targets will not be realized. The NDP envisages a fourfold increase in the value of private-sector investment by 2000 and the private sector – both local and foreign – has been charged with spearheading economic growth and enhancing the country's industrial profile. The Ministry of International Trade and Industry has energetically promoted the concept of 'Malaysia Incorporated' in its effort to foster consultation and dialogue with the private sector and the all-important foreign investors. This has helped cut the red tape. Since Mahathir adopted his 'Look East' policy in the 1980s (instead of relying solely on trade links with the West), most of Malaysia's foreign investment has come from Japan, Taiwan and South Korea.

Tourism has grown to assume a critical role in Malaysia's economy in the past few years. In 1990, Malaysia launched itself into big league tourism with a bang, joining the swelling ranks of Southeast Asian countries to host 'tourism years'. Visit Malaysia Year (VMY) was a big success: 7.4 million tourists arrived – half as many again as in 1989 and receipts rose 61% to US$1.5 billion. This made tourism Malaysia's third biggest earner after manufacturing and oil – up from sixth position the previous year. Now Prime Minister Dr Mahathir Mohamad calls tourism "Malaysia's goldmine"; he says there should be "no saturation point" and wants

Malaysia: fact file

Geographic		Social	
Land area	330,000 sq km	Population	18.4 million
Arable land as % of total	13%	Population growth rate (1960-91)	2.6%
Average annual rate of deforestation	1.2%	Adult literacy rate	78%
		Mean years of schooling	5.3 years
Highest mountain, Gunung Kinabalu	4,101 m	Tertiary graduate as % of age group	1.4%
Average rainfall in Kuala Lumpur	2,250 mm	Population in absolute poverty (1977-89)	32%
Average temperature in Kuala Lumpur	26°C	Rural population as % of total	57%
		Growth of urban population (1960-91)	4.5%/year
Economic		Urban population in largest city (%)	27%
GNP/person (1990)	US$2,330	Televisions per 1,000 people	148
GDP/person (PPP*, 1990)	US$6,140	**Health**	
GNP growth (/capita, 1980-1990)	2.5%	Life expectancy at birth	70 years
GDP growth 1992	8.0%	Population with access to clean water	78%
GDP growth 1993	7.6% (est.)	Calorie intake as % of requirements	120%
% labour force in agriculture	42%	Malnourished children under 5 years	n.a.
Total debt (% GNP)	48%	Contraceptive prevalence rate†	51%
Debt service ratio (% exports)	12%		
Military expenditure (% GNP)	3.6%		

* PPP = Purchasing Power Parity (based on what it costs to buy a similar basket of goods and services in different countries)
† % of women of childbearing age using a form of modern contraception
Source: World Bank (1993) *Human Development Report 1993*, OUP: New York; and other sources.

a three-fold increase in tourist arrivals by the end of the 1990s.

While the vast majority of tourists still come from neighbouring Singapore and Thailand, the government is targeting the big spenders – the 'high-yield markets' like the Japanese, who spend 70% more than the average tourist. Smart new hotel and resort complexes are springing up around the country and scores of golf courses are being carved out of the jungle. Until fairly recently, the government paid scant regard to the lower-middle end of the tourism market, favouring sparkling new 5-star complexes instead. 1990's VMY was such a success that the government has now decided to have another VMY in 1994. It says that the more cultural events it stages, the more visitors come to Malaysia.

The NDP is a ten-year policy which forms part of Mahathir's 30-year economic blueprint. His appropriately labelled 'Vision 2020' aims to quadruple per-capita income, double the size of the economy and make Malaysia a fully developed industrialized country within 30 years. Between now and then, the economy must average 7% growth a year in order to meet the target. Analysts say this is ambitious but not impossible. Since the late 1980s, however, the economy has grown so fast that it has been in danger of overheating – inflation has been rising steadily and the trade balance is deep in the red. It's been growing faster than any other economy in Asean and many analysts have been privately hoping for a slow-down, to enable the government to catch up and the spending public to cool out. As Malaysians have grown richer, they have developed refined tastes for imported luxury items – a trend which the government wants to curb. The flashy imported cars on the streets of Kuala Lumpur say it all. The expectations of many Malaysians have become so geared to high growth, however, that to them, economic expansion below 7% a year smacks of recession.

Malaysia may soon be a 'Newly Industrialized Economy' (NIE) – the level of development which bridges the grey area between the Third World and the industrialized countries. Many nations would give anything to be dubbed an NIE – it signifies the fact they they have 'made it'. But the Malaysian government is in no rush to acquire the label, suspecting that NIE status would be used as a pretext for Western trading partners to withdraw special trade privileges. Some analysts believe Malaysia has already reached NIE status.

KUALA LUMPUR

INTRODUCTION

Just over a century ago, Kuala Lumpur was nothing more than a collection of attap-roofed huts in a jungle clearing. Its history therefore starts in the British colonial period: the city's most imposing Moorish-style buildings date from the end of the 19th and the beginning of the 20th centuries. The route around the capital first covers these historical sights, museums and galleries, before moving out to the parliament area with the lake gardens and national monument. The main excursions outside KL are the Batu Caves and Templer Park to the N and Klang, the old royal capital of Selangor, to the W.

Kuala Lumpur highlights

Museums & historical sights the centre of colonial Kuala Lumpur includes several *Moorish-style buildings* (page 96); *National Art Gallery* (page 96); *Muzium Negara* (the national museum) (page 99).

Mosques and temples *Masjid Jame*, the old Moghul-style mosque (page 96); the modern *Masjid Negara* (the National Mosque) (page 99); *Sri Mahamariamman Hindu Temple* (page 97); *Chan See Shu Yuen Temple* (page 98); *Sze Ya Temple* (page 98).

Other sights *Chinatown*, which retains much of its original turn-of-the-century architecture and comes alive each night with its *pasar malam* (night market) (page 97); *Batu Caves*, high on the cliff-face of a limestone massif, and focus of Hindu pilgrimage (page 101); *Templer Park*, a 1,200 ha tract of jungle (page 101).

Shopping Kuala Lumpur's Art Deco-style *central market* has been converted into a lively focus for the local artistic community and contains shops and stalls selling art and handicrafts (page 97); the *Chinatown street market* (*pasar malam*) sells everything from ten-cent trinkets and cheap T-shirts to bargain-basement leather goods and copy watches (page 97).

Sport *Royal Selangor Club* for golf (page 110); a superb watersports centre at *Sungei Besi* (page 111).

Nightlife Kuala Lumpur is very lively after dark, with scores of excellent bars, nightclubs and discos (page 109).

HISTORY

Kuala Lumpur means 'muddy confluence' in Malay – as apt a description today as it was in the pioneer days of the 1870s. This romantic name refers to the Klang and Gombak rivers that converge in the middle of the city – there is also some evidence that the *kopi-susu*-coloured Gombak was once known as the *Sungei Lumpur*. Kuala Lumpur, which nearly everyone knows as **KL**, has grown up around the Y-shaped junction of these rivers in the area called *Ulu Klang* – the upper reaches of the Klang River.

In the space of a century, KL grew from a trading post and tin mining shanty into a colonial capital. Today it is a modern, cosmopolitan business hub and the centre of government. But it may not entirely have outgrown its pioneering tin-town mentality: rumour has it that the speculators were still looking for tin

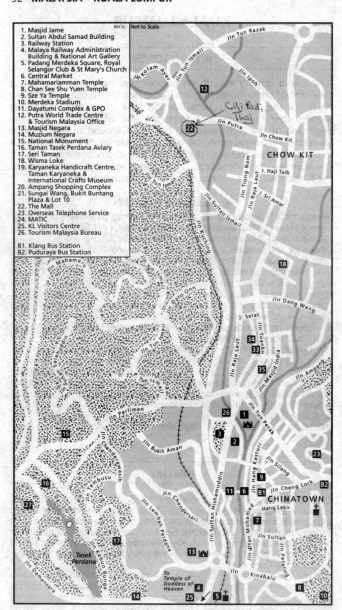

IMS 2L Not to Scale

1. Masjid Jame
2. Sultan Abdul Samad Building
3. Railway Station
4. Malaya Railway Administration
   Building & National Art Gallery
5. Padang Merdeka Square, Royal
   Selangor Club & St Mary's Church
6. Central Market
7. Mahamariamman Temple
8. Chan See Shu Yuen Temple
9. Sze Ya Temple
10. Merdeka Stadium
11. Dayatumi Complex & GPO
12. Putra World Trade Centre
    & Tourism Malaysia Office
13. Masjid Negara
14. Muzium Negara
15. National Monument
16. Taman Tasek Perdana Aviary
17. Seri Taman
18. Wisma Loke
19. Karyaneka Handicraft Centre,
    Taman Karyaneka &
    International Crafts Museum
20. Ampang Shopping Complex
21. Sungai Wang, Bukit Buntang
    Plaza & Lot 10
22. The Mall
23. Overseas Telephone Service
24. MATIC
25. KL Visitors Centre
26. Tourism Malaysia Bureau

B1. Klang Bus Station
B2. Puduraya Bus Station

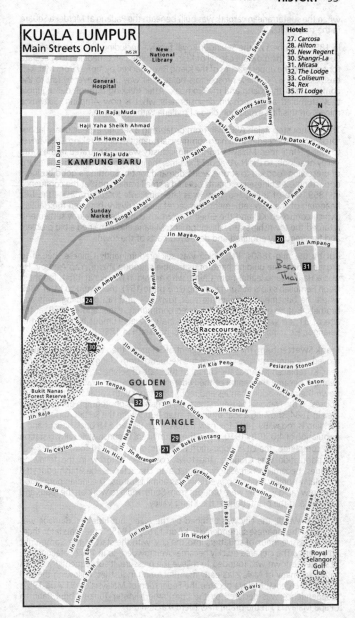

KUALA LUMPUR
Main Streets Only

IMS 2R

Hotels:
27. *Carcosa*
28. *Hilton*
29. *New Regent*
30. *Shangri-La*
31. *Micasa*
32. *The Lodge*
33. *Coliseum*
34. *Rex*
35. *Ti Lodge*

New National Library

General Hospital

Jln Tun Razak

Jln Raja Muda

Haji Yaha Sheikh Ahmad

Jln Hamzah

Jln Raja Uda

KAMPUNG BARU

Jln Dang Jln

Jln Raja Muda Musa

Sunday Market

Jln Sungai Baharu

Jln Saleh

Pesiaran Gurney

Jln Gurney Satu Gurney

Jln Semarak

Jln Perumahan Gurney

N

Jln Datok Keramat

Jln Tun Razak

Jln Aman

Jln Yap Kwan Seng

Jln Mayang

Jln Ampang

Jln Ampang

20

Jln Ampang

Basn Thai

31

Jln Ampang

Jln P. Ramlee

Jln Lumba Ruda

24

Jln Sultan Ismail

Jln Pinang

Racecourse

30

Jln Perak

Jln Kia Peng

Pesiaran Stonor

Bukit Nanas Forest Reserve

Jln Tengah

GOLDEN

28

32

Jln Raja Chulan

Jln Conlay

Jln Stonor

Jln Kia Peng

Jln Eaton

Jln Raja

TRIANGLE

29

21

Jln Bukit Bintang

19

Jln Nagasari

Jln Berangan

Jln Ceylon

Jln Hicks

Jln W. Grenier

Jln Imbi

Jln Kampong

Jln Inai

Jln Pudu

Jln Kamuning

Jln Barat

Jln Delima

Jln Tun Razak

Jln Galloway

Jln Hang Tuah

Jln Eberwein

Jln Imbi

Jln Horley

Jln Davis

Royal Selangor Golf Club

when the subterranean carpark was built beneath the Padang at Merdeka Square in the mid-1980s.

In 1857, members of the Selangor Royal family – including Rajah Abdullah, the Bugis chief of the old state capital of Klang – mounted an expedition to speculate for tin along the upper reaches of the Klang River. Backed by money from Melakan businessmen, 87 Chinese prospectors poled their way up the river by raft to the confluence of the Klang and the Gombak. After trekking through dense jungle they stumbled across rich tin deposits near what is now Ampang. Sixty-nine miners on this first expedition died of malaria within a month.

This did not stop Rajah Abdullah from organizing a second expeditionary labour force, which succeeded in mining commercial quantities of tin, taking it downriver to Klang. Until then Malaya's tin-mining industry was concentrated in the Kinta Valley near Ipoh, to the N. At about this time, the invention of canning as a means of preserving food led to strong world demand for tin. Spotting a good business opportunity, 2 Chinese merchants opened a small trading post at the confluence in 1859. One of them, Hiu Siew, was later appointed *Kapitan Cina* – the first headman of the new settlement. But secret society rivalry, between the Hai San (which controlled KL) and the Ghee Hin (which controlled a nearby settlement) retarded the township's early development. Malaria also remained a big problem and fires regularly engulfed and destroyed parts of the town.

But by the mid-1860s, KL, which was still predominantly Chinese, began to prosper under the guiding hand of its trouble-shooting sheriff, **Yap Ah Loy**. He was a Hakka gang leader from China, who arrived in Melaka in 1854, fought in Negri Sembilan's riots at Sungei Ujong (**see page 157**), then went to KL in 1862 where he became a tin magnate – or *towkay* – and ran gambling dens and brothels. But he emerged as a respected community leader and in 1868, at the age of 31, he was appointed *Kapitan Cina* of Kuala Lumpur by the Sultan of Selangor. He remained the headman until his death in 1885.

Frank Swettenham, the British Resident of Selangor, then took the reins, having moved the administrative centre of the Residency from Klang in 1880. The same year, KL replaced Klang as the capital of the state of Selangor; shortly after Yap's death, it became the capital of the Federated Malay States. Swettenham pulled down the ramshackle shanties and rebuilt the town with wider streets and brick houses. In the National Museum there is a remarkable photograph of the Padang area in 1884, showing a shabby line of attap huts where the Sultan Abdul Samad Building is today. By 1887 the new national capital had 518 brick houses and a population of 4,050. By 1910, when the magnificent Moorish-style railway station was completed, the city's population had risen more than 10-fold; nearly ⁴/₅ of the population was Chinese. The town continued to grow in the following decades, becoming increasingly multiracial in character, as the British educated the Malay nobility then employed them as administrators. The Indian population also grew rapidly; many were brought from South India to work on the roads and railways and the plantations in the Klang Valley.

In World War II, the city was bombed by the Allies, but little real damage was incurred. The Japanese surrendered in KL on 13 Sept 1945. Three years later, there was a massive influx of squatters into the city, with the start of the Communist Emergency. The city area quickly became overcrowded, so in 1952 Petaling Jaya, KL's satellite town was founded to relieve the pressure. It subsequently went on to attract many of Malaysia's early manufacturing industries. Following the end of the Emergency, Malaya became the Federation of Malaysia on 31 Aug 1957. Independence was declared by the late Prime Minister Tunku Abdul Rahman ('Papa Malaysia') in the brand new Merdeka Stadium.

In 1974, the 243 sq km area immediately surrounding the city was formerly declared the Federal Territory of Kuala Lumpur, with a separate administration from its mother-state of Selangor. Today KL's population is approaching 1.5 million, and although one of the smallest capitals in Southeast Asia, it is a rapidly growing business centre, its industrial satellites gaining the lion's share of the country's manufacturing investment. The economic boom that started in the late 1980s caused a building boom that rivals Singapore's. In downtown KL, old and new are juxtaposed. The jungled backdrop of the copper-topped clock tower of the Supreme Court of a century ago has been replaced by scores of stylish high-rise office blocks, dominated by the soaring, angular-roofed Maybank headquarters. The Victorian Moorish and Moghul-style buildings, the Art Deco central market and cinemas and the Chinese shophouses stand in marked contrast to these impressive skyscrapers which have sprouted over the past decade.

There have been efforts to create a 'new Malaysian architecture', to lend the city a more integrated look and a national identity. Such buildings include the modern-Islamic National Mosque, the National Museum and the Putra World Trade Centre (the latter two have *Minangkabau*-style roofs) and the 34-storey Dayabumi complex, by the river, with its modern Islamic latticed arches. At the same time, KL has also been trying to cultivate a 'garden city' image like neighbouring Singapore. From the top of its sky-scrapers, KL looks green and spacious.

Modern Kuala Lumpur

For years, KL enjoyed a reputation as the least-congested capital in Southeast Asia. But this has changed of late. The Kuala Lumpur basin is geologically unsuited to an underground railway, so in the early 1980s it was proposed that KL should have a monorail service around the city. The proposal has been scuppered and then refloated several times, and it now looks to be going ahead ... maybe. The plan is to link the main bus terminals of Pudu Raya, Putra Centre, Jalan Tun Razak and Sri Jaya over an 8 km route. The project's optimistic shareholders hope it will be ready within 2 years – once construction starts.

The streets to the N and NW of the Padang – the cricket pitch in front of the old Selangor Club, next to the new Merdeka Square – are central shopping streets with modern department stores and smaller shops.

The colonial core is around the Padang and down Jalan Raja and Jalan Tun Perak. West of the Padang, straight over the bridge on Lebuh Pasar Besar is the main commercial area, occupied by banks and finance companies. To the SE of Merdeka Square is KL's vibrant Chinatown. To find a distinctively Malay area, it is necessary to venture further out, along Jalan Raja Muda Musa to Kampung Baru, to the NE.

To the S of Kampung Baru, on the opposite side of the Klang River, is Jalan Ampang, once KL's 'millionaires' row' – where tin towkays and sultans first built their homes. The road is now mainly occupied by embassies and high commissions. To the SE of Jalan Ampang, on the far side of the racecourse is KL's so-called Golden Triangle, to which the modern central business district has migrated and where property prices have shot up. In recent years the city's residential districts have been expanding out towards the jungled hills surrounding the KL basin, at the far end of Ampang, past the zoo to the north, and to Bangsar, to the SW. KL has become a city of condominiums, which have sprung up everywhere from the centre of town to these outlying suburbs. Greater Kuala Lumpur sprawls out into the Klang Valley, once plantation country and now home to the industrial satellites of Petaling Jaya and Shah Alam.

PLACES OF INTEREST

The Colonial core

KL's sights are spread out and although the central area is easy to walk around, taxis or buses might be a better way of seeing the capital.

At the muddy confluence of the Klang and Gombak rivers where KL's founders stepped ashore, stands the **Masjid Jame**, formerly the National Mosque (main entrance on Jalan Tun Perak). Built in 1909, English architect, A B Hubbock's design was based on that of a Moghul mosque in N India. The mosque has a walled courtyard – or *sahn* – and a 3-domed prayer hall. It is striking with its striped white and salmon-coloured brickwork and domed minarets, cupolas and arches. Surrounded by coconut palms, the mosque is an oasis of peace in the middle of modern KL, as is testified by the number of Malays who sleep through the heat of the lunchtime rush-hour on the prayer hall's cool marbled floors.

Behind the mosque, from the corner of Jalan Tunku Abdul Rahman and Jalan Raya, are the colonial-built public buildings, distinguished by their grand, Moorish architecture. All were the creation of A C Norman, a colleague of Hubbock's, and were built between 1894 and 1897. The photogenic former State Secretariat, now called the **Sultan Abdul Samad – or SAS – Building**, with its distinctive clock tower and bulbous copper domes, houses the City Hall, Supreme Court and Infokraf – the Handicrafts Information Centre (open: 0900-1800 Sat-Thur). At the far end of the complex is the Moorish-style old General Post Office.

Not to be outdone by Norman, Hubbock designed the fairy-tale Moorish-style **Railway Station** in 1910 and the **Malaya Railway Administration Building**, opposite, in 1917. Beneath the Islamic exterior of the former, the building is similar to the glass and iron railway stations constructed in England during the Victorian era – except this one was built by convict labour. It is said that the station's construction was delayed because the original roof design did not meet British railway specifications – it had to be able to support 1m of snow.

Also opposite the station on Jalan Sultan Hishamuddin is the former *Majestic Hotel*, built in 1932. Saved from demolition in 1983, it has been converted into the **National Art Gallery**, housing a permanent collection of about 2,000 works by Malaysian artists and touring exhibitions. For a chronological tour start at the top of the building and work down. It is a diverse collection but refreshing to see that most of the work retains a distinctively Malay spirit, some of it exciting and very original. Open: 1000-1800 Mon-Sun. Closed: 1200-1500 Fri.

Central to the old city is the **Padang**, next to **Merdeka Square**. The old Selangor Club cricket pitch is the venue for Independence Day celebrations. The centispiece of Merdeka Square is the tallest flagpole in the world (100m high) and the huge Malaysian flag that flies from the top can be seen across half the city, particularly at night when it is floodlit. The Padang was trimmed to make way for the square, which is also the venue for impromptu rock concerts and is a popular meeting place. A huge shopping complex was built underneath the square but in 1992 it closed due to flooding problems. It is scheduled to re-open as a bowling alley.

The very British mock-Tudor **Royal Selangor Club** fronts the Padang and was the centre of colonial society after its construction in 1890. Some of the building was damaged by a fire in the late 1960s and the N wing was built in 1970. The Selangor Club is still a gathering place for KL's VIPs. It has one of the finest colonial saloons, filled with trophies and pictures of cricket teams. Non-members can only visit if accompanied by a member and the famous Long Bar – which contains a fascinating collection of old photographs of KL – is still an exclusively male preserve. (Those venturing into the Long Bar should observe a formal dress code.) On the other side of the Padang is **St Mary's Church**, one of the oldest Anglican churches built in 1894.

Jalan Ampang became the home of KL's early tin millionaires and an important leafy adjunct to the colonial capital. The styles of its stately mansions ranged from Art Deco and mock-Palladian to Islamic. Today many of these buildings have become embassies and consulates – KL's Embassy Row. One of the lovelier Art Deco-style buildings now houses the Rubber Research Institute. Another of Jalan Ampang's fine old buildings is the old Coq D'Or restaurant, formerly the residence of a Chinese tin mogul, and still a great place for dinner and 'stengahs' on the terrace (*setengah* is Malay for 'half', and became the colonial term for shots of whisky and water). Further into town, yet another house has been refurbished and is now the Malaysian Tourist Information Centre (Matic). It was the headquarters of the Japanese Imperial Army during World War II. The intersection of Jalan Ampang and the old circular road, Jalan Tun Razak, has become a booming shopping area with Ampang Park and City Square shopping centres. Jalan Ampang itself is now rather congested as its outer end, known as Ulu Klang, which has been the focus of much modern residential development.

Back in the old part of town, just downriver from the Masjid Jame and on the opposite bank to the Dayabumi complex, is the pastel pink and blue **Central Market**, a former wet market built in 1928 in Art Deco-style, tempered with 'local Baroque' trimmings. In the early 1980s it was revamped to become a focus for KL's artist community and a handicraft centre – KL's version of London's Covent Garden or San Francisco's Fisherman's Wharf. It is a warren of boutiques, handicraft and souvenir stalls – some with their wares laid out on the wet market's original marble slabs – and is now a bit of a tourist trap, although it is definitely worth visiting. On the second level of the market are several restaurants and a small hawker centre on the top floor.

Chinatown

South-east of the Central Market, lies Chinatown, roughly bounded by Jalan Bandar, Jalan Petaling and Jalan Sultan. It was the core of Yap Ah Loy's KL (**see page 94**) and is a mixture of crumbling shophouses, market stalls, coffee shops and restaurants. This quarter wakes up during late afternoon and evening, when its streets become the centre of frenetic trading and haggling. Jalan Petaling (and parts of Jalan Sultan) are transformed into an open air night market (*pasar malam*) and food stalls, fruit stalls, copy watch stalls, leather bag stalls and all manner of impromptu boutiques line the streets. Jalan Hang Lekir, which straddles the gap between Jalan Sultan and Jalan Petaling, is full of popular Chinese restaurants and coffee shops.

On Jalan Tun H S Lee (Jalan Bandar) is the extravagantly decorated **Sri Mahamariamman Temple**, incorporating gold, precious stones and Spanish and Italian tiles. It was founded in 1873 by Tamils who had come to Malaya as contract labourers to work in the rubber plantations or on the roads and railways. Its construction was funded by the wealthy Chettiar money-lending caste, and it was rebuilt on its present site in 1885. It has a silver chariot dedicated to Lord Murugan (Subramaniam), which is taken in procession to the Batu Caves (**see page 101**) during the Thaipusam festival, when Hindu devotees converge on the temple. The best time to visit is on Friday lunchtimes, from 1230, when Muslims head off to the mosques. Large numbers flock to the temple to participate in the ritual; this is usually preceded by about half an hour's chanting, accompanied by music. In testament to Malaysia's sometimes muddled ethnic and religious mix, it is not uncommon to find Chinese devotees joining in the ceremony.

The only legal hash in Malaysia

Around the turn of the century, the annual dare in colonial KL involved swimming from the Royal Selangor Club terrace to the State Secretariat and back when the Klang River flooded the Padang. But the *Spotted Dog*, as the club was affectionately known, was also home to another eccentric sporting event which caught on around the world. The **Hash**, a cross-country chase – which is invariably followed by a drinking bout – was started in 1938, when the Selangor Club was the preferred watering hole for colonial bachelors. A Mr G S Gisbert, having drunk too much at the Long Bar, went for a jog around the Padang to sober up. In no time, Mr Gilbert's Hash had a band of disciples who took to the new sport with varying degrees of seriousness.

The run, named after the Club's dining room, the Hash House, ventured into the countryside surrounding KL where 'hounds' chased 'hares' – along a paper trail. The KL hash, known as the 'mother hash' to **Hash House Harriers** around the world (there are now 300 clubs in more than 60 countries) normally involves runs of 3-8 km, which are usually fairly jovial affairs. Most big Malaysian towns have a Hash and there are several branches in KL – men-only, women-only and mixed. Although popular among expatriates, many locals participate these days and visitors are welcome. (For details, contact Kuala Lumpur Hash House Harriers, PO Box 10182, KL; T 2484846.)

There are 2 prominent Chinese temples in the Chinatown area. The elaborate **Chan See Shu Yuen Temple**, at the southernmost end of Jalan Petaling was built in 1906 and has a typical open courtyard and symmetrically laid-out pavilions. Paintings, woodcarvings and ceramic sculptures decorate the façade. It serves both as a place of worship and as a community centre. The older **Sze Ya Temple**, close to the central market on Lebuh Pudu, off Jalan Cheng Lock, was built in the 1880s on land donated by Yap Ah Loy. He also funded the temple's construction and a photograph of him sits on the altar. Ancestor worship is more usually confined to the numerous ornate clan houses (*kongsis*); a typical one is the **Chan Kongsi** on Jalan Maharajalela, near the Chan See Shu Yuen Temple.

Off Jalan Stadium is the 50,000-capacity **Merdeka Stadium**, the site of Malaysia's declaration of independence on 31 Aug 1957 (merdeka means 'freedom' in Malay). National and international sports events are held at the stadium (the famous Mohammad Ali vs. Joe Bugner fight was staged here in 1975) as well as the annual international Koran reading competition, held during Ramadan.

Modern Kuala Lumpur

The 35-storey, marble **Dayabumi Complex**, on Jalan Raya, is one of KL's most striking modern landmarks. It was designed by local architect Datuk Nik Mohamed, and introduces contemporary Islamic achitecture to the skyscraper era. The government office-cum-shopping centre houses Petronas, the secretive national oil company. Petronas occasionally permits tourists to admire the view from the 30th floor helipad where a superb, but fading pictorial map of all the city's sights has been painted on the rooftop. Next door to the Dayabumi Complex is the new and imposing General Post Office.

The other notable modern building is the US$150 million **Putra World Trade Centre**, on Jalan Tun Ismail. It took nearly 15 years to materialise, but when it opened in 1985, Malaysia proudly announced that it was finally on the international convention and trade fair circuit. The luxurious complex of buildings includes the *Pan-Pacific Hotel*, a sleek 41-storey office block and a splendid exhibition centre, adorned with a traditional *Minangkabau* roof. The headquarters of Prime Minister Dr Mahathir Mohamad's ruling United Malays

National Organisation occupies the top floors and there is a tourist information centre on the 2nd floor.

The modern spiritual centre of KL's Malay population and the symbol of Islam for the whole country is the **Masjid Negara** (National Mosque), near the railway station. Abstract, geometric shapes have been used in the roofing and grillwork, while the Grand Hall is decorated with verses from the Koran. Completed in 1965, it occupies a 5-ha site at the end of Jalan Hishamuddin. The prayer hall has a star-shaped dome with 18 points, representing Malaysia's 13 states and the 5 pillars of Islam. The 48 smaller domes emulate the great mosque in Mecca. The single minaret is 73m tall and the grand hall can accommodate 8,000 people. An annex contains the mausoleum of Tun Abdul Razak, independent Malaysia's second Prime Minister. Open: Sat-Thur 0900-1800, 1445-1800 Fri. Muslims can visit the mosque from 0630-2200. Women must use a separate entrance.

Parliament Area

Overlooking Jalan Travers, near the S tip of the Lake Gardens, is the **Muzium Negara** (National Museum), with its traditional *Minangkabau*-style roof, and 2 large murals of Italian glass mosaic either side of the main entrance. They depict the main historical episodes and cultural activities of Malaysia. The museum's displays of photographs, models, artefacts and dioramas (with English-language texts) are excellent introductions to Malaysia's history, geography, natural history and culture. A Straits Chinese house from Melaka has been reconstructed in one gallery and the possessions and collections of various sultans are on show in another. Over the next few years, the present museum building will become the Museum of Culture while a new Museum of National History will be set up at Merdeka Square in KL and a Museum of Natural Science will open near Titiwangsa Lake Gardens, on the city's N outskirts. Open: 0900-1800 Mon-Sun. Closed: 1200-1500 Fri. **Getting there** Buses 47, 30 & 238 from Jalan Sultan Mohammed and minibuses 22, 23 & 38 from Lebuh Besar.

Close to the museum is the S entrance to the man-made **Lake Gardens**, a 70-ha park, a joggers' paradise and popular city escape. Pedal boats can be hired on the main lake (Tasek Perdana) for M$4 per hour. The gardens become crowded on weekends and holidays. Nearby is the orchid garden with over 800 species, a bird park and a deer park. The **National Monument** is at the N end of the Lake Gardens, on the other side of Jalan Parlimen. The memorial, with its dramatically-posed sculpted figures, is dedicated to the heroes of Malaya's 12-year Communist Emergency (**see page 67**). The state of emergency was lifted in 1960, but members of the banned Communist Party managed to put a bomb under the memorial in 1975. Near the monument is a sculpture garden with exhibits from all over ASEAN – the Association of Southeast Asian Nations.

Taman Tasek Perdana Walk-in Aviary, at the Lake Gardens, near the *Carcosa Hotel*, opened in 1991. In an effort to out-do neighbouring Singapore's famous Jurong Bird Park, this aviary is twice the size of Jurong, and encloses 4,000 birds of 120 species, from ducks to hornbills. Reference centre, refreshment kiosk and binoculars for hire. Admission: M$3. T 2742042. Open: 0900-1800 Mon-Sun.

On the SE edge of the park is **Seri Taman**, the former residence of Malaysia's revered second prime minister, the late Tun Abdul Razak, whose great, great, great, great, great grandfather, Sultan Abdullah of Kedah, ceded Penang to the British (**see page 134**). In recognition of his services – he is popularly known as the father of Malaysia's development – his old home has been turned into a memorial with the aim of preserving his documents, speeches, books and awards, including his collection of walking sticks and pipes. Open: 0900-1800 Tue-Sun. Closed: 1200-1500 Fri. **Getting there**: Buses 19, 244 & 250 from Jalan Sultan

Kuala Lumpur's Golden Triangle

High-rise development came late to KL but has rapidly gained a foothold; the city's offices, hotels and new shopping complexes are mostly concentrated in the 'Golden Triangle', on the E side of the city, S of the race course. Jalan Bukit Bintang and Jalan Sultan Ismail was where the first modern hotels and shopping complexes went up – the *Concorde* (formerly the *Merlin*), the *Regent*, *Hilton*, *Equatorial*, *Holiday Inn* and *Shangri-La*. More recently the area around Jalan Ampang and Jalan Tun Razak has been transformed into a commercial centre; several towers have sprung up in the area in recent years, including the MBf building and the extraordinary hour-glass-shaped Pilgrims' Building, which coordinates the annual Haj and looks after the pilgrims' funds.

Mohammed and minibus 18 from Jalan Tun Perak.

The modern 18-storey **Parliament House** and its *Toblerone*-shaped House of Representatives is on the W fringe of the gardens. When parliament is in session, visitors may observe parliamentary proceedings (permission must be formally obtained beforehand), and must be smartly dressed. In years gone by, many of the administrative arms of government were housed in the State Secretariat (now renamed the Sultan Abdul Samad Building) on the Padang. Most of the main government ministries are now situated in scruffy 1960s suburban office blocks off Jalan Duta, to the W.

Around the city area

Wisma Loke (or the Artiquarium) on Jalan Medan Tunku Abdul Rahman (off the N end of Jalan Tunku Abdul Rahman near the junction with Jalan Sultan Ismail), was built in a mixture of Eastern and Western styles by a wealthy Chinese businessman. It was the first private house in KL to have electricity. One of the mansion's prominent features is its ancient Chinese-style circular 'moon gate', rarely found in more modern houses. Wisma Loke was recently restored to its former glory by self-made millionaire Datuk Lim Kok Wing, to house antiques and artifacts from around Southeast Asia. All the items on display are for sale (do not expect any bargains), including artistic work on the top floor (the exhibition changes every fortnight). In reality, it is more of a shop than a gallery, but has a big selection of (rather over-priced) handicrafts from around the region. T 2921222. Open: 1000-1830 Mon-Fri, 1000-1700 Sat. Closed Sun.

The **Karyaneka Handicraft Centre** is at the junction of Jalan Bukit Bintang and Jalan Raja Chulan, to the E of the city. It contains 14 typical Malay-style houses, 13 of which represent each of the Malaysian states and the other, a large exhibition room. Each house displays the crafts of that particular state. Demonstrations from 0930-1730. There is a good selection of crafts for sale. Part of the grounds make up the **Taman Karyaneka**, an ethno-botanical garden where one can see the trees and plants used by Malaysians for making handicrafts, woodcarvings, foods and medicines. In the same compound is the **International Crafts Museum**. Open: 0900-1800 Mon-Sun.

Thean Hou Temple or the **Temple of the Goddess of Heaven** is situated at Jalan Klang Lama (off Jalan Tun Sambathan, to the SW of the city). Perched on a hill, it has a panoramic view over KL. A contemporary Buddhist pagoda and Buddha images are enshrined in the octagonal hall. It stands between a sacred Bodhi tree and a Buddhist shrine, built by Sinhalese Buddhists in 1894. **Getting there**: minibus 27 from Klang Bus Station to Jalan Syed Putra.

KUALA LUMPUR
Environs

(Map labels:)

To Ipoh

To Tapah, Ipoh & Cameron Highlands

Bentong

To Telok Intan

To Kuantan

Sungei Selangor

North-South Hwy.

Genting Highlands

Kuala Selangor

Batang Berjuntai

Orang Asli Museum

Rawang

N

Kuala Selangor N.P.

Templer Park

Batu Caves

Sungai Buloh

National Zoo & Aquarium

KULAL LUMPUR

Subang International Airport

Ampang

Shah Alam

Ulu Langat

Petaling Jaya

Pulau Ketam

Klang

Serdang Bahru

Kajang-Sungai Chua

Port Swettenham

Semenyih

Pulau Pintu Gedong

Bangi

Jenjarom

Kampong Dengkil

Mantin

Telok Datok

Salak

To Seremban & Melaka

Banting

Merib

0   15
km

EXCURSIONS

North

Batu Caves are a system of caverns set high in a massive limestone outcrop 13 km N of KL – they were 'discovered' by American naturalist William Hornaby in the 1880s. In 1891 Hindu priests set up a shrine in the main cave dedicated to Lord Subramaniam and it has now become the biggest Indian pilgrimage centre in Malaysia during the annual Thaipusam festival (**see page 354**) when over 100,000 Hindus congregate here.

The main cave is reached by a steep flight of 272 steps. Coloured lights provide illumination for the disappointing fantasy features and formations of the karst limestone cavern. There are a number of other less spectacular caves in the outcrop, including the Museum Cave (at ground level) displaying elaborate sculptures of Hindu mythology. During World War II, the Japanese Imperial Army used some of the caves as factories for the manufacture of ammunition and as arms dumps. The concrete foundations for the machinery can be seen at the foot of the cliffs. It is one of the main sights outside KL, but makes for a rather dull outing if Thaipusam is not going on (the festival takes place in late Jan or early Feb; **see page 354**). **Getting there**: buses Len 68, 69 and 70 from Lebuh Pudu or minibus 11 from Pertama Shopping Centre (M\$0.50). Special trains run from the Railway Station to Batu Caves during Thaipusam.

Templer Park is about 10 km further on up the main road from the turn-off to the Batu Caves. Covering 500 ha, it serves as Kuala Lumpur's nearest jungle playground, apart from the tiny Bukit Nanas Forest Reserve in the middle of the city. It opened as a park in 1954 and is named after the last British High Commissioner of Malaya, Sir Gerald Templer, 'the Tiger of Malaya', who oversaw the tactical defeat of the Communist insurgents during the Emergency (**see page 67**). The park is dominated by several impressive 350m-high limestone hills and outcrops, the biggest being **Bukit Takun** and **Bukit Anak Takun** (similar to the Batu Caves outcrop).

There are extensive networks of underground passages and cave systems within the hills, thought to have formed 400 million years ago. Unfortunately a huge new floodlit golf course has impinged on the N boundaries of the park making access to some of these massifs more difficult – and another 180 ha golf resort is being developed. The park has a wide variety of jungle flora and fauna. Other features include a waterfall, reservoir and swimming pool on a 5 km trail loop. Templer Park is a popular venue for boy scout and youth camps and tends to attract swarms of day-trippers at weekends – although most of them do not venture much beyond the car park and picnic area. **Getting there**: buses Len 66, 78, 83 or 81 from Pudu Raya bus terminal (M$1.20).

The **Orang Asli Museum** is 25 km N of KL on the old Gombak Road, past the Mimaland amusement park. It preserves the traditions of Malaysia's indigenous Orang Asli aboriginals – there are about 60,000 living on the peninsula. Displays give the background on the 18 different tribes and their geographical dispersal. There are also models of Orang Asli village houses and a souvenir shop attached to the museum selling Orang Asli crafts. Open: 0930-1730 Sat-Thur. **Getting there**: Long Seng bus 174 from Lebuh Ampang terminus (M$1.50).

West and South-west
Petaling Jaya, 15 km SW of KL, is a thriving industrial satellite and middle-class dormitory town for the capital and is known as PJ. It was initially built to provide low-cost housing for squatter resettlement but is now a city in its own right, with shopping and administration centres. The whole town, with its streets running in semi-circles, was planned on a drawing board, but despite its unimaginative street names (or rather, numbers), is not as sterile as it might sound. In recent years it has become quite lively, with its own nightlife scene and several gourmet restaurants, many of which cater for PJ's expatriate and wealthy Malaysian population. **Accommodation**: these hotels are mainly used by businessmen, as the airport is easily accessible from here. **A+** *Hyatt Saujana Hotel & Country Club*, Subang International Airport Highway, Petaling Jaya, T 7461188, F 7462789, 5 mins from the airport and 2 mins from the golf course (it has two 18-hole championship courses), the *Saujana* is a low-rise hotel set in landscaped gardens, it is a particularly convenient stop-over for early-morning flights, but is 25 mins drive from *KL Hotel* provides shuttle service to and from airport; **A+** *Petaling Jaya Hilton*, 2 Jln Barat, T 7559122, a/c, restaurant, pool; **A** *Holiday Villa*, 9 Jln SS 12/1, Subang Jaya, T 7338788, a/c, restaurant, pool; **A** *Merlin Subang*, Jln 12/1, Subang Jaya, T 7335211, a/c, restaurant, pool; **A** *Subang Airport Hotel*, Kompleks Airtel Fima, T 7462122, F 7461097, a/c, restaurant, pool; **B** *Shah's Village*, 3 & 5 Lorong Sultan, T 7569702, F 7557715, a/c, restaurant. **Getting there**: buses to most parts of Petaling Jaya can be boarded at Bangkok Bank stop and Klang Bus Terminal (M$0.50).

Shah Alam, the new state capital of Selangor, is situated between KL and Port Klang. It has the reputation as Malaysia's best planned city and is an ultra-modern showpiece town. The skyline is dominated by the Sultan Salahuddin Abdul Aziz Shah Mosque, which those landing at KL's Subang Aiport usually get a good aerial view of. Completed in 1988, it is the largest mosque in Southeast Asia and can accommodate up to 16,000. **Getting there**: minibuses 1, 9 from PKNS complex for Shah Alam, or buses 338, 337 and 222 (M$1.30).

Klang, 30 km SW of KL, is a royal town with a magnificent mosque and royal palace, the **Istana Alam Shah**, and had been the capital of Selangor for centuries before the tin mining town of Kuala Lumpur assumed the mantle in 1880. Klang was the name for the whole state of Selangor at the time when it was one of the *Negri Sembilan* – the 9 states of the Malay Federation. The town is also known as Kelang; it is thought to derive from an old Sumatran word for tin. Today **Port Klang** (which used to be known as Port Swettenham, after former British Resident Frank Swettenham) is KL's seaport and is a busy container terminal. Klang is also an important service centre for nearby rubber and palm oil plantations, which in the early decades of the 20th century, spread the length of the Klang Valley to KL.

The **Gedung Rajah Abdullah** warehouse, built in 1857, is one of the oldest buildings in the town. (Rajah Abdullah was the Bugis Chief who first dispatched the expedition to the upper reaches of the Klang River, which resulted in the founding of KL.) In 1991 it was turned from an historical museum into Malaysia's first tin-mining museum. Open: 0900-1600 Mon-Sun. Closed: 1200-1445 Fri. There is also a fort in Klang, built by Rajah Mahdi (a rival of Raja Abdullah), which guarded the entrance to the Klang valley from its strategic position overlooking the river.

The town is well known for its seafood; most of the restaurants are close to the bus terminal. Ferries leave from Klang for offshore islands such as Pulau Ketam (see below), Pulau Morib (golf course, **see page 110**) and Pulau Angsa. **Getting there**: buses 51, 58, 225 (Klang Bus Co) from Klang Bus Terminal (M$1.70).

Pulau Ketam (Crab Island), off Port Klang is like a downmarket Venice, Malaysian-style, with the whole village on stilts over the fetid water. Good spot for seafood. **Getting there**: bus to Port Klang (M$1.70), ferry from Port Klang (M$2.20).

Kuala Selangor is on the banks of the Sungei Selangor, about 60 km N of Klang on the coast road. In the last century, it was a focal point of the Sultanate of Selangor. The Dutch built 2 fortresses there in 1784 which they used to blockade the river, Sungei Selangor, in retaliation for Sultan Ibrahim of Selangor's attacks on Melaka. Nearly a century later, in 1871, British gunboats blasted the forts – then occupied by Malays – for several hours, marking the first British intervention in the Selangor Civil War, over the possession of the tin-rich Klang Valley. The 2 fortresses are on the hills overlooking the Sungei Selangor estuary. The larger of the 2, **Fort Altingberg**, on Bukit Melawati, serves as a royal mausoleum and museum. Open: daylight hours Mon-Sun.

The fort overlooks the **Kuala Selangor Nature Park**, 250 ha of coastal mangrove swamp and wetland. It has several observation hides and more than 130 bird species – including bee eaters, kingfishers and sea eagles – have been recorded. There are also leaf monkeys. It is one of the best places to see Malaysia's famous synchronized fireflies – the only fireflies in Southeast Asia which manage to co-ordinate their flashing (**see page 60**). The fireflies are best observed from about one hour after sunset and are particularly impressive when there is no moon. The actual riverside site is about 8 km from Kuala Selangor, near a village called Kampung Kuantan. **Getting there**: regular direct buses from KL's Puduraya bus terminal (Platform 24) to Kuala Selangor (M$3). Taxis can be chartered from there to Kampung Kuantan (wait and return M$25-30; whole car). The *Malayan Nature Society*, which operates the Nature Park will also arrange private transport to Kampung Kuantan and back for about the same price. This must be pre-arranged by booking with their KL Office (T 8892294 before 1700; T 8892403 after 1700). **Accommodation**: the Society runs chalets in the Park (which is a short walk from the last bus stop). 'A'-frames $15 (accommodates 2); chalets $25-30 (accommodates 4). These must also be booked in advance on the above numbers – a few days in advance for weekend visitors.

Proton Saga: driving the flag

Shah Alam is the production centre for Malaysia's home-made car, the Proton Saga. The huge manufacturing plant, located just off the highway from Kuala Lumpur, makes the only car designed and built in Southeast Asia. Around 65,000 are sold in Malaysia each year – 2 out of every 3 new cars sold – and they have made an impact abroad too – Protons are now being sold in 12 countries. In Britain it was the only car to increase sales during the recession in the early 1990s and leading car magazines named it 'the best value car you can buy' and the 'rising star in the east'. One newspaper even labelled it one of the greatest marketing sensations of the 1990s.

Recent profits at home and the car's success abroad have vindicated Prime Minister Dr Mahathir Mohamad's determination to launch the National Car Project in 1984. He wanted Proton to be the flagship of Malaysia's drive for industrialization but his brainchild coincided with a recession and was nearly written-off by inept management. The car itself is a locally-customized and updated version of the 1982 Mitsubishi Mirage. "They say it's a boring car," the Prime Minister says. "On the other hand, it doesn't break down either." The Japanese company has a 17% stake in Proton and the company is currently under Japanese management. In reality it is not as home-grown as Malaysians would like it to be, but the proportion of locally made components has been rising rapidly – by 1995, 80% of Proton's parts should be sourced in Malaysia. A racey new model is to be unveiled in 1993, and by 1995, output should top 180,000 cars a year.

In common with Malaysia's bumiputra Malay majority, the car enjoys certain privileges and advantages in the marketplace that other makes do not. It is exempt from the hefty duty other car assemblers pay on imported kits. The government has also set a compulsory profit margin on all car sales, which means no price wars and, for Proton, no competition. But Dr Mahathir now wants to make an even cheaper 660cc Made-in-Malaysia saloon in conjunction with the Daihatsu Company of Japan, giving more Malaysians the chance to own a car. Production of the car, which will be modelled on the Daihatsu *Mira*, is scheduled to get underway in mid-1994.

East

Malaysian Armed Forces Museum, on Jalan Gurney, exhibits pictures, paintings, weapons – including those captured from the so-called Communists Terrorists (CTs) during the emergency. Open: 1000-1800 Mon-Thur & Sat. **Getting there**: minibus 19 (M$0.50).

Selangor Pewter Factory on Jalan Pahang, in Setapak Jaya, to the N of the city, is one of the biggest pewter factories in the world, employing over 400 craftsmen. Selangor Pewter was founded in 1885, using Straits tin (95%) which is alloyed with antimony and copper. Visitors can watch demonstrations of hand-casting and pewter working, as well as the crafting of silverware and batik-making. As well as the Setapak Jaya factory, there are showrooms on Jalan Genting, Jalan Klang Lama and Jalan Tunku Abdul Rahman. Open: 0830-1645 Mon-Sat, 0900-1600 Sun. **Getting there**: Len Seng bus W12 or 10 (M$0.70).

National Zoo & Aquarium is 13 km from the centre of KL, down Jalan Ampang to Ulu Klang. The zoo encompasses a forest and a lake and houses 1,000 different species of Malaysian flora and fauna in addition to collections from elsewhere in the world. Admission: M$4. Open: 0900-1700 Mon-Sun. **Getting there**: Len Seng bus 170, Len Chee 177, Sri Jaya 270 or minibus 17 from Jalan Ampang (M$0.50).

Tours Many companies offer city tours, usually of around 3 hours, which include visits to Chinatown, Muzium Negara (the National Museum), the Railway Station, Thean Hou Temple,

Masjid Negara (the National Mosque), the Padang area and Masjid Jame – most of which cost in the region of M$22. City night tours take in Chinatown, the Sri Mahmariamman Temple and a cultural show (M$55). Other tours on offer visit sights close to the city such as Batu Caves, a batik factory and pewter factory (M$22) as well as day trips to Melaka, Port Dickson, Fraser's Hill, Genting Highlands and Pulau Ketam (M$40-80). Most of these tour companies offer endless combinations of tours to destinations around the peninsula.

SERVICES

Accommodation Room rates in KL's top hotels have escalated as the economy has boomed – in the early 1990s prices in some hotels doubled within a matter of months. By international standards they are still excellent value for money, but because of the city's growing traffic problems, the location of a hotel has become an increasingly important consideration. Most top hotels are between Jln Sultan Ismail and Jln P Ramlee, in KL's so-called 'Golden Triangle'. South of Jln Raja Chulan, in the Bukit Bintang area, there is another concentration of big hotels. Corporate discounts of 10-15% are usually on offer; even if you are just on holiday, you are likely to qualify for the reduced rates by simply giving your company's name. Many of the cheaper hotels are around Jln Tunku Abdul Rahman, Jln Masjid India and Jln Raja Laut, all of which are within easy walking distance of the colonial core of KL. There are also cheap hotels in the Chinatown area.

L *Carcosa Seri Negara*, Taman Tasek Perdana, T 2306766, F 2306959, a/c, restaurant, pool. Former residence of the British High Commissioner, it is now a luxury hotel, where Queen Elizabeth II stayed when she visited Malaysia during the Commonwealth Conference in 1989 and where other important dignitaries, presidents and prime ministers are pampered on state visits, 13 suites served by over 100 staff, rec.

A+ *Crown Princess*, City Square Shopping Mall, Jln Tun Razak, T 2421566, F 2621494, opened in 1992, pitching itself to compete with the crème de la crème; **A+** *Grand Continental*, Jln Belia/Jln Raja Laut, T 2939333, a/c, restaurant, pool, not really in the big league, but reasonable facilities, similar to nearby *Plaza Hotel*; **A+** *Hilton*, Jln Sultan Ismail, T 3433333, F 2438069, a/c, restaurant, pool, magnificent aspect overlooking the racecourse – which is up for redevelopment, take great care when returning to the hotel by taxi, unless you specify 'KL Hilton', you are liable to end up in the PJ Hilton (in Petaling Jaya), the latter largely caters for businesspeople visiting outlying industrial zones, rec; **A+** *Istana*, 73 Jln Raja Chulan, T/F 2441445, a/c, restaurant, pool. This striking, luxuriously appointed hotel in the heart of KL's business district, the Golden Triangle, opened in September 1992. It is aiming to compete with the *Shangri-La*, *Hilton* and *Regent*. **A+** *Melia*, 16 Jln Imbi, T 2428333, F 2426623, not up to the standard of many of the other big hotels which charge the same prices; **A+** *Ming Court*, Jln Ampang, T 2619066, F 2612393, a/c, restaurant, pool, way over-priced; **A+** *New Regent*, 160 Jln Bukit Bintang, T 2418000, F 2421441, a/c, restaurant, pool, the ultimate hotel in KL – it won the "Best Hotel in Malaysia" award the year it opened in 1990, all suites have butler service and the rooms and bathrooms are lavishly appointed, rec; **A+** *Pan Pacific*, Jln Chow Kit Baru, T 4425555, F 4417236, a/c, restaurant, pool, attached to the huge Putra World Trade Centre, so favoured by convention delegates, good views over the city, excellent dim sum restaurant and located opposite The Mall shopping centre; **A+** *Parkroyal*, Jln Sultan Ismail, T 2425588, a/c, restaurant, pool, formerly called *The Regent*, the hotel underwent major cosmetic surgery in 1989, allowing it to charge more for its good range of facilities; **A+** *Plaza*, Jln Raja Laut, T 2982255, a/c, restaurant, cheaper rooms are good value for money; **A+** *Shangri-La*, 11 Jln Sultan Ismail, T 2322388, F 2301414, a/c, restaurant, pool, KL's ritziest hotel until the *New Regent* appeared, the *Shang* has big bright rooms and an excellent bar, styled as an English pub, rec.

A *Concorde*, 2 Jln Sultan Ismail, T 2242200, a/c, restaurant, pool, opened in late 1991 – it is the old *Merlin* (the first big modern hotel in KL) masquerading behind a face-lift and new interior decor, it has 4 good restaurants and a coffee shop and has the added advantage of having the *Hard Rock Café* attached to it; **A** *Equatorial*, Jln Sultan Ismail (opposite MAS building), 50250, T 2617777, a/c, restaurant, pool, one of KL's earlier international hotels, the *Equatorial* has had several revamps over the years, most recently in 1990, its 1960s-style coffee shop has metamorphosed into one the best hotel coffee shops in town, open 24 hrs (see below), with an international news agency in the basement, the hotel is the favoured repose of visiting journalists; **A** *Federal*, 35 Jln Bukit Bintang, T 2489168, F 2438381, a/c, restaurant, pool, when it first opened in the early 1960s, it was the pride of KL: it was air-conditioned and its *Mandarin Palace* restaurant was rated as the most elegant restaurant in the Far East, It is still reasonable value for money, but does not compare with the world-class glitz that KL has attracted of late, the Merdeka wing has been renovated, close to good shopping centres; **A** *Fortuna*, 87 Jln Berangan, T 2419111, F 2418237, located just off Bukit Bintang, near the big international hotels and shopping centres, good value for money; **A** *Grand Central*, Jln Putra/Jln Raja Laut, T 4410318, a/c, near the Putra World Trade Centre, clean but drab middle-market hotel; **A** *Holiday Inn City Centre*, Jln Raja Laut, T 2939233, F 2939634, a/c, restaurant, pool, big enough hotel, but inside everything is rather bijou – the lobby is squashed, the swimming pool tiny and the fitness and business centres on the miniature side; **A** *Holiday Inn on the Park*, Jln Pinang, T 2481066, a/c, restaurant, pool, large pool and garden area, located across the road from a string of lively bars; **A** *Mandarin*, 2-8 Jln Sultan, T 2303000, F 2304363, a/c, restaurant, in Chinatown, used by businessmen, not as plush as its name suggests (it is not a part of the Mandarin group), but is clean, with an interesting location and is reasonable value for money; **A** *MiCasa Hotel Apartments*, 368b Jln Tun Razak (near junction with Jln Ampang), T 2618833, F 2611186, a/c, restaurant, pool. First rate, especially for longer stays, KL's only apartment hotel with suites which include kitchen area and sitting room, excellent restaurants and bar, rec; **A** *Wisma Belia*, 40 Jln Syed Putra, T 2746262, a/c, restaurant.

B *Apollo*, 106-110 Jln Bukit Bintang, T 2428133, F 2427815, a/c, popular restaurant, one of the more reasonable hotels in area increasingly dominated by international class hotels; **B** *Chamtan*, 62 Jln Masjid India, T 2930144, a/c, restaurant, clean and reasonable value; **B** *City*, 366 Jln Raja Laut, T 2924466, a/c, restaurant, reasonably priced for the upper end of the market; **B** *Emerald*, 166 Jln Pudu, T 2429233, a/c, noisy location, within walking distance of large shopping area; **B** *Grand Pacific*, Jln Ipoh/Jln Sultan Ismail, T 4422177, a/c, restaurant, not very grand, but delightful views of the highway, drivers have delightful views into hotel bedrooms; **B** *Imperial*, 76-80 Jln Changkat Bukit Bintang (Jln Hicks), T 2922377, a/c, restaurant, reasonable modern Chinese hotel in an otherwise pricey part of town, well located for shopping centres; **B** *Kowloon*, 142-146 Jln Tunku Abdul Rahman, T 2934246, F 2926548, a/c, clean, value for money, rec.; **B** *Lock Ann*, 118A Jln Petaling, T 2389544, a/c, clean, large rooms, centrally located in Chinatown; **B** *The Lodge*, Jln Sultan Ismail, T 2420122, F 2416819/5503913, a/c, restaurant, pool, small pre-war style hotel in Golden Triangle area, annexe rooms are cheaper, restaurant, rec.; **B** *Palace*, 46-1 Jln Masjid India, T 2986122, a/c, good lively location, but very average hotel; **B** *Park*, 80 Jln Bukit Bintang, T 2427284, a/c, reasonable value for this more expensive area of town, popular restaurant; **B** *Pudu Raya*, 4th Floor, Pudu Raya Bus Station, Jln Pudu, T 2321000, a/c, restaurant, pool, clean, but nothing to recommend it other than its convenience for early morning departures and late night arrivals; **B** *South East Asia*, 69 Jln Haji Hussein, T 2926077, a/c, restaurant, has its own cinema, good value for money; **B** *Shiraz*, 1-3 Jln Medan Tuanku, T 2922625, a/c, restaurant, good value for money; **B** *Station Hotel*, Banguanan Stesen Keretapi, Jln Sultan Hishamuddin, T 2741433, restaurant, large, noisy rooms with balconies – which all need a lick of paint, part of the magnificent Moorish-style railway station and may well get a face-lift in the near future, plans are also afoot to redevelop the Malayan Railway Administration Building (opposite) – into a colonial-style 5-star hotel, elegant grill room has not changed for decades; **C** *Paradise*, 319 Jln Tunku Abdul Rahman, T 2922872, some a/c, restaurant, well run bed and breakfast, rec by travellers; **C** *Starlight*, 90-92 Jln Hang Kasturi, T 2321744, a/c, well situated for Central Market and Chinatown; **C** *Tai Ichi*, 78 Jln Bukit Bintang, T 2427669, a/c, dark rooms, but one of the more reasonable hotels along this road.

D *Backpackers' Travellers' Inn*, 2nd Flr, 60 Jln Sultan, T 2382473, some a/c, rooms and dorms, located in Chinatown next to excellent stalls/restaurants, offers guests free transfer to and from bus and railway stations (but must book in advance); **D** *Chinatown Guesthouse*, 2nd Flr, Wisma BWT, Jln Petaling (in the centre of the *pasar malam*), T 2320417, right in the middle of Chinatown, travel bulletin board, clean budget guest house and price includes bed and breakfast, dorm (**E**); **D** *Coliseum*, 100 Jln Tunku Abdul Rahman, T 2926270, some a/c, restaurant, colonial hotel, large, simply furnished, clean rooms and a famous bar and restaurant (see below) and incredibly noisy a/c, but no attached bathrooms and incredibly noisy a/c, attracts a number of longer-term visitors, so rooms often in heavy demand, with small queues forming outside before it opens at 1000, rec; **D** *Colonial*, 39-45 Jln Sultan, T 2380336, some a/c, noisy, as rooms are partitioned, but in a central location in Chinatown, complimentary Chinese tea at any time; **D** *Rex*, 132 Jln Tunku Abdul Rahman, T 2983895, fan only, restaurant, lower floors noisy due to bar downstairs, value for money, rec; **D** *Travellers' Moon Lodge*, 36c Jln Silang, T 2306601, some a/c, conveniently located for Chinatown Central Market and Pudu Raya bus station, popular with budget travellers, breakfast and bed bugs included in price, rooms and dorm; **D** *Tivoli*, 134 Jln Tunku Abdul Rahman, T 2924108, fan only, restaurant, not as good as the *Rex* or the *Coliseum* on the same stretch of road; **D-E** *Sunrise Travellers' Lodge*, 89B Jln Pudu Lama, T 2308878, some a/c, located near bus terminal round the corner from Maybank HQ; **D** *Ti Lodge*, 20 Lorong Bunus Enam (off Jln Masjid India,

T 2930261, a/c, bed and breakfast, rooms and dorms, rec.

E *Malaysia Guides Tourist Centre Bed & Breakfast*, 68-A Jln Putra, T 20522, a/c, dormitory-style accommodation, rec by travellers.

Youth hostels C-D *YWCA*, 12 Jln Hang Jebat (to the E of Chinatown and S of Jln Pudu), T 283225, a/c, restaurant, also caters for couples; **D** *Meridien International Youth Hostel*, 38 Jln Hang Kasturi, T 2321428, some a/c, good location near Central Market and Chinatown, rec by travellers; **D** *Wisma Belia*, 40 Jln Syed Putra, T 2744833, on the SW side of town – a bit of a hike, but good value; **E** *Kuala Lumpur City Hostel*, 21 Jln Kampung Attap, a/c, on the S edge of KL, near the railway station and tucked in behind some big bank buildings, good hawker stalls nearby to serve office staff; **E** *YMCA*, 95 Jln Padang Belia/Jln Kandang Kerbau, T 2741439, a/c, restaurant, excellent facilities – sports facilities, language courses, shop – neutralized by inconvenient location in Brickfields district on the SW outskirts, off Jln Tun Sambathan, it is, however, within sniffing distance of Raju's tandoori ovens (see Sri Vani's Corner, *Restaurants*), dormitory for men only (D) also private rooms, getting there: minibus 12.

Homes Away From Home Run by the *Asian Overland Service*, the Homes Away from Home programme gives visitors first-hand experience of Malaysian life by staying in fishing kampungs, rubber plantations, tin mines or pensioners' homes. M$45/day including pick-up service, accommodation and 2 meals. Contact *Asian Overland Services*, 33M Jln Dewan Sultan Sulaiman Satu, T 2925622/2925637, F 2925209; *Village Home Stay*, 178 Jln Tunku Abdul Rahman, T 2920319.

Restaurants Many of KL's big hotels in the Jln Sultan Ismail/Bukit Bintang areas serve buffet lunches for M$15-25, which are excellent value and offer a selection of local and international dishes.

Malay: ♦♦♦*Bunga Raya*, Level 2, Putra World Trade Centre; ♦♦*Jamal Bersaudara*, Jln Raja Abdullah, Kampung Baru; ♦♦♦*Nelayan Floating Restaurant*, Titiwangsa Lake Gardens, good but expensive; ♦♦*Rasa Utara*, Bukit Bintang Plaza, Jln Bukit Bintang; ♦*Satay Anika*, Grd Flr, Bukit Bintang Plaza, Jln Bukit Bintang, fast food satay, rec; ♦♦*Satay Express*, Grd Flr, Central Sq (next to Central Market), Jln Hang Kasturi, also serves other Malay dishes, outdoor terrace; ♦*Sate Ria*, 9 Jln Tunku Abdul Rahman, fast food; ♦♦*Wan Kembang* (Cik Siti), 24 Jln 14/22, Petaling Jaya (in front of the mosque), specializing in Kelantanese food; ♦♦♦♦*Yazmin*, 6 Jln Kia Peng, old colonial bungalow, cultural shows come with the buffets downstairs.

Chinese: ♦♦♦*Cha Yuan Teahouse*, 5B Jln SS2/67, Petaling Jaya. Traditional Chinese teahouse offers light meals and tea prepared by tea-master Paul Lim, rec; ♦♦*Ampang Yong Tau Foo*, 53 Jln SS2/30, Petaling Jaya, T 7753686, *yong tau foo* (stuffed beancurd dishes) in a coffee shop, rec, closed Mon; ♦♦*Balakon*, half way to Kajang, near Sungei Besi (take Seremban highway, exit to left at Taman Sri Petaling – before toll gates, right at T-junction, over railway line and past Shell and Esso stations, turn left towards Sungei Besi tin mine, then branch right to Balakong, the restaurant is signposted), it is little more than a tin shed (with a fruit stall outside) but is famed among KL's epicurians for its deep-fried paper-wrapped chicken, wild boar curry and vinegar pork shank, rec; ♦♦*Cameleon Vegetarian Restaurant*, 1 Jln Thamboosamy (off Jln Putra, near The Mall and Pan Pacific), Thai & Chinese, good *kway teow*, but vegetarians with carnivorous instincts rate the soyabean roast duck and various other ersatz meat and fish dishes whose presentation (and sometimes taste) is convincing; ♦♦♦♦*Dynasty Garden Chinese Restaurant*, Lot M72-75, Mezzanine Flr, Plaza Yow Chuan, Jln Tun Razak; ♦♦♦*Hai Tien Lo*, Pan Pacific Hotel, Jln Chow Kit Baru, excellent dim sum buffet every lunchtime, rec; ♦*Nam Heong*, 54 Jln Sultan, Hainanese chicken rice; ♦♦♦*Oversea*, G2, Central Market, Jln Hang Kasturi; Cantonese restaurant, very popular with locals. Good range of dishes (dim sum particularly rec, 0700-1500) and pleasant location with outdoor terrace overlooking the river; *Seng Nam*, Lebuh Pasar Besar, Hainanese; *Shang Palace*, Shangri-La Hotel, Jln Sultan Ismail, T 2322388; ♦♦*Sin Kiew Yee*, Jln Hang Lekir (Jln Cecil, between Jln Petaling and Jln Sultan, Chinatown), mouthwatering dishes, good value for money, tables on pavement, rec; ♦♦♦*Tsui Yuen*, 5th Flr, Hilton Hotel, Jln Sultan Ismail, main attraction is the lunchtime dim sum; ♦♦*Westlake*, Jln Petalin, highly rated for its Hokkien mee and mee hun, mixed with raw egg; ♦♦*Yook Woo Hin*, 100 Jln Petaling, cheap dim sum in the middle of Chinatown – until 1400.

Nonya: ♦♦♦*Dondang Sayang*, 12, Lwr Grd Flr, The Weld, Jln Raja Chulan, T 2613831; also branch at 28 Jln Telawi Lima, Bangsar Baru, T 2549388. Popular and reasonably priced restaurant with big Nonya menu; ♦♦*Nonya Heritage*, 44-4 Jln Sultan/Jln Bukit Bintang (next to Hong Kong Shanghai Bank), Straits Chinese cuisine; ♦♦*Sri Penang*, Lwr Grd Flr, Menara Aik Hua, Changkat Raja Chulan (Jln Hicks), variety of Nonya and N Malaysian dishes.

Indian & Pakistani: ♦*Alhmdoolilla*, 12 Jln Dang Wangi, rated for its rotis; ♦♦*Annalakshmi*, 46 Lorong Maarof, Bangsar Baru, T 2823799. Excellent Indian vegetarian restaurants run by the Temple of Fine Arts, dedicated to the preservation of Indian cultural heritage in Malaysia, the buffet is particularly recommended; ♦♦♦♦*Baluchi's*, 3 Jln SS21/60, Petaling Jaya, T 7190879 (advisable to take taxi; ask for Damansara Utama Shophouse Complex). North Indian cuisine; modest decor but excellent food; chicken tika, tandoori chicken, prawn *masala* and *palak paneer* particularly recommended; freshly baked naan, rec; ♦♦♦*Bangles*, 60A Jln Tunku Abdul Rahman, T 2986770, reckoned to be among the best N Indian restaurants in KL, often necessary to book in the evenings, rec; ♦♦*Kampung Pandan*, 1st Flr, Central Market, specialist in fish-head curry; ♦*Lay Sin Coffee Shop*, 248 Jln Tun Sambathan, banana leaf; ♦♦*Sri Vani's Corner* (Raju's), Jln Tun Sambathan 4 (next to YMCA tennis courts), overgrown hawker stall rated among its dedicated clientele as the best place for tandoori and oven-baked naan in KL, rec.

Seafood: ♦♦*Bangsar Seafood Village*, Jln Telawi Empat, Bangsar Baru, large restaurant complex with reasonably priced seafood (and a good satay stall); ♦♦♦*Eden Village*, 260 Jln Raja Chulan, wide-ranging menu, but probably best known for seafood, resembles a glitzy Minangkabau palace with garden behind, cultural Malay, Chinese and Indian dances every night; ♦♦*Hai Peng Seafood Restaurant*, Taman Evergreen, Batu Empat, Jln Klang Lama (Old Klang Rd), the smallest and least assuming restaurant in a row of Chinese shophouses (red neon sign), but one of the very best seafood restaurants in Malaysia, where the Chinese community's seafood connoisseurs come to eat (the other seafood restaurants in the cluster include *Chian Kee*, *Pacific Sea Foods* and *Yee Kee* – most of which are good, but not as good as *Hai Peng*), its specialities include butter crab (in clove and coconut), belacan crab, sweet & sour chilli crab and bamboo clams, the *siu yit kum* (small gold-leaf tea) is a delicious, fragrant Chinese tea, which is perfect with seafood, open until 0100, rec; ♦♦*MASs*, 228 Jln Dua A, Subang, Selangor, T 7461200, well out of town, past Subang airport's Terminal 2, and strung out along the road running beside Runway One are about 10 seafood restaurants, they all do a brisk turnover, and there is not much between them; they all serve seafood and each has its own speciality, *MASs* is the one with the front end of an MAS jumbo jet on the roof, rec; ♦♦*New Ocean*, 29B Medan Imbi (off Jln Imbi and Jln Hoo Teik Ee), good seafood restaurant just round the corner from the Sungei Wang and Lot 10 shopping complexes; ♦♦♦*Restoran 123*, 159 Jln Ampang, good choice of seafood; ♦♦*Unicorn Sharkfin & Seafood*, 1st Flr, Annex Block, Lot 10 Shopping Centre, Jln Sultan Ismail, big, smart Chinese seafood restaurant in the new Lot 10 complex, just by the footbridge to Sungei Wang, good stop for shoppers. **NB**: for additional seafood entries, see also Port Klang and Pulau Ketam (**see page 103**).

Thai: ♦♦*Cili Padi Thai Restaurant*, 2nd Flr, The Mall, Jln Putra, soups and seafood are excellent, recommended speciality: King Solomon's Treasure (chicken wrapped in pandan leaves), closes 2200 sharp, rec; ♦♦♦*Sawasdee Thai Restaurant*, *Holiday Inn on the Park*, Jln Pinang; ♦♦♦*Barn Thai*, 370B Jln Tun Razak (opposite *Micasa Hotel*), T 2446699, very tastefully decorated Thai style 'Jazzaurant' with excellent live music, extensive Thai menu, rec.

Japanese: ♦♦*Chikuyo-Tei Basement*, Plaza See Hoy Chuan, Jln Raja Chulan, good value for money; ♦♦♦♦*Keyaki*, Pan Pacific Hotel, Jln Putra, robat ayaki grill, highly rated, but extremely expensive; ♦♦♦*Munakata Japanese Restaurant*, 2nd Flr, Menara Promet, Jln Sultan Ismail; ♦♦♦♦*Nanadaman*, Shangri-La Hotel, 11 Jln Sultan Ismail, Shang quality and Shang prices; ♦♦♦*Tykoh Inagiku*, Grd Flr, Kompleks Antarabangsa, Jln Sultan Ismail (between *Equatorial* and *Hilton* hotels), T 2482133.

Korean: ♦♦♦*Koryo-Won*, Kompleks Antarabangsa, Jln Sultan Ismail (between *Hilton* and *Equatorial* hotels), excellent barbecues – particularly when washed down with Jung Jong rice wine, rec.

French: ♦♦♦♦*Lafite*, Shangri-La Hotel, Jln Sultan Ismail, best French restaurant in Malaysia, but very expensive.

Italian: ♦♦♦♦*Ciao Caffé Ristorante*, 428 Jln Tun Razak, T 9854827, authentic tasty Italian food served in a beautifully renovated bungalow, rec. ♦♦*Caleos*, 1 Jln Pinang, pastas and pizzas, Napoli-style seafood, upstairs bar and karaoke lounge.

International: ♦♦♦♦*Carcosa Seri Negara*, Persiaran Mahameru, Taman Tasek Perdana (Lake Gdns), T 2306766 (reservations), built in 1896 to house the British Administrator for the Federated Malay States, Carcosa offers English-style high tea in a sumptuous, colonial setting, expensive continental lunches and dinners are also served in the Mahsuri dining hall on fine china plates with solid silver cutlery, Continental and Malay cuisine, high tea (rec) M$25 (1530-1800, Mon-Sun); ♦♦♦*Bon Ton*, 7 Jln Kia Peng, European and Asian food, in a 1930s colonial bungalow, just S of the racecourse, closed Sun, rec; ♦♦*Coliseum Café*, 100 Jln Tunku Abdul Rahman (Batu Rd), next door to the old Coliseum Theatre, long-famed for its sizzling steaks, served by frantic waiters in buttoned-up white suits, rec; ♦♦♦*D'Ribeye*, Grd Flr, Central Market, Jln Hang Kasturi, recommended by correspondent as having good atmosphere, good steak and offering good value; ♦♦*Equatorial Coffee Shop*, Basement, Equatorial Hotel, Jln Sultan Ismail, recommended Malay curry buffets 1230-1400, Mon-Sat,

(♦♦♦) Sam's Curry Lunch (Indian buffet, Sunday 1230-1400), excellent à la carte selection of Malaysian dishes, including *nasi lemak* and *rendang*, open 24 hrs, rec; ♦♦*Federal Hotel Revolving Restaurant*, Jln Bukit Bintang, was once one of KL's tallest buildings, now rather dwarfed but still a good spot for icecream sundaes with a view; ♦♦♦*Hard Rock Café*, Grd Flr, Wisma Concorde, 2 Jln Sultan Ismail, opened in 1991, one of the best places for top-quality American burgers, steaks and salads, rec; ♦♦♦*Jake's Charbroil Steaks*, 21 Jln Setiapuspa, Medan Damansara, off Jln Damansara, towards PJ, Jake's steaks are highly rated in KL, served by cowboys and cowgirls, rec; ♦♦♦*Le Coq D'Or*, 121 Jln Ampang, European/Malay, former residence of a rich mining towkay with a porticoed veranda and Italian marble. Western, Chinese and Malay cooking, great atmosphere of crumbling grandeur, rec; ♦♦*Lodge Coffee Shop*, Jln Sultan Ismail, excellent value for money – particularly local dishes: *nasi goreng* and curries; rec; ♦♦♦♦*Melaka Grill*, Hilton Hotel, Jln Sultan Ismail; ♦♦♦♦*Sakura Café & Cuisine*, 165-169 Jln Imbi, excellent variety of Malay, Chinese and Indian dishes including fish-head curry; located in an area with many other good cheap restaurants, rec. ♦♦♦*The Ship*, 40 Jln Sultan Ismail (next to Bukit Bintang), loud music downstairs and good steaks upstairs.

Foodstalls: *Brickfields* (Jln Tun Sambathan), string of small outdoor restaurants; *Central Market*, (Top Flr), Jln Hang Kasturi, excellent, but small centre with good *nasi campur* (lunchtimes); *Ampang Park Shopping Complex*, Food Court (along Jln Tun Razak), popular, but small centre, with good variety of stalls; *Imbi Foodfest 28*, Lwr Grd Flr, Imbi Plaza, Jln Imbi (next door to Sungei Wang Plaza, opposite *Parkroyal Hotel*), hawker-style stalls in air-conditioned complex; *Jln Raja Alang* and *Jln Raja Bot* stalls, off Jln Tunku Abdul Rahman (Chow Kit area), mostly Malay stalls, stalls set up along Jln Haji Hussein when the market closes at 1800 and stays open until 0200; *Kia Peng*, Jln Kia Peng/Jln Perak, hawker centre and gallery, open from 1000-1800 (gallery), 1000-2300 (hawker centre), the hawker centre is locally dubbed "the Hilton drive-in", and is behind the big hotels on Jln Sultan Ismail, particularly popular at lunchtimes; *Lorong Raja Muda Food Centre*, off Jln Raja Muda, on the edge of Kampung Baru, mainly Malay food; *Medan Hang Tuah*, The Mall (Top Flr), Jln Putra (opposite the *Pan Pacific Hotel*); *Medan Pasar Car Park*, across the river from Masjid Jame, Jln Tun Perak; *Merdeka Square Stalls*, the car park behind St Mary's Church becomes a hawker centre after dark; *Munshi Abdullah Food Complex*, off Lorong Tunku Abdul Rahman (near *Coliseum*), good satay; *Pudu Raya Bus Station*, Jln Pudu, good variety of stalls, open at all hours; *Sunday Market*, Kampung Baru (main market actually takes place on Sat night), many Malay hawker stalls.

Bars There is no shortage of good watering holes in KL; many have live Filipino and local cover bands, and others have discotheques attached. *Barn Thai*, 370B Jln Tun Razak, self-styled 'Jazzaurant', Bangkok-type wooden bar with panelled interior and tasteful Thai decor, some of KL's best live acts with excellent jazz, drinks are expensive, also serves good Thai food, rec; *Betelnut*, Jln Pinang, located in the ruins of a former colonial bungalow in a strip of bars and clubs which are not as good, disco in main house, but relaxed outdoor bar, rec; *Bull's Head*, on the corner of Central Market facing the Dayabumi Complex, off Jln Hang Kasturi, large bar with the darkened atmosphere of a London pub inside and with tables on the terrace outside; *Centrepoint*, Jln Setiapuspa, Medan Damansara, off Jln Damansara, lively bar with live music every night; *Coliseum*, 100 Jln Tunku Abdul Rahman, the bar, which has a number of long-term residents who never seem to move, is the haunt of Malaysia's star cartoonist, Lat (his Coliseum sizzling steak cartoon hangs on the wall along with his caricatures of regulars). The so-called Planters' Bar used to be the gathering point for colonial rubber planters and tin miners then became the hangout of war correspondents during the Malayan Emergency. The bar is frequented by everyone from diplomats and businessmen to backpackers, it is a pleasant old-time bar which opens for business before lunch and shuts at 2200 sharp, rec; *English Pub*, Shangri-La Hotel, not as naff as it sounds, and popular with visiting business people; *Hard Rock Café*, Basement & Grd Flr Wisma Concorde, 2 Jln Sultan Ismail, T 2444152, The *Hard Rock*, with its Harley Davidson chopper posing on the rooftop, opened in 1991 and quickly became one of the most popular and lively bars in town, good atmosphere and even a small disco floor, rec; *London Pub*, Lorong Hampshire, off Jln Ampang (behind *Ming Court Hotel*), continuing KL's obsession with recreating English pubs, this one, part-owned by a London Cockney is not a mock-Tudor half-timbered mess. It has a good atmosphere and a regular darts competition; *MiCasa Hotel Bar*, 368b Jln Tun Razak (near junction with Jln Ampang), serves what are arguably the best margaritas in KL (there is also a pretty average Mexican restaurant across the road), rec; *Traffic Lights*, 42 Jln Sultan Ismail (near Bukit Bintang junction), music (sometimes live) and attached grill.

Entertainment Nightclubs and discos: since the mid-1980s, with the rise of the local yuppy, KL has shaken off its early-to-bed image and now has a lively club scene. Several old colonial buildings have been converted into night spots. The *Metro* section in *The Star* is devoted to what's on where. Most nightclubs and discos in KL are open until 0300 during the week and until 0400 on Friday nights and weekends. In the past few years, Jln Pinang, once a backstreet of crumbling bungalows, has emerged as a late-night strip of bars. There are also hundreds of karaoke lounges around KL. *11-L A*, 11 Lebuh Ampang, off Jln Gereja, usually heaving by the weekend, disco plays up-to-the-minute tracks, busy upstairs bar with live music, M$10 cover, rec; *Betelnut*, Jln Pinang, very popular bar/disco complex, behind the disco clubhouse is a spacious outdoor bar area, *Betelnut* is the best in a strip of bars just down from the *Holiday Inn on the Park*, rec; *Cee Jay's*, Grd Flr, Menara SMI, 6 Lorong P Ramlee (behind *Shangri-La Hotel*), *Cee Jay's* has a good bar and a restaurant, but is best known for its live music, with classy local acts playing covers; *Club Syabas*, 1 Lorong Sultan, Petaling Jaya, the club's renowned *DV8* disco is very popular with KL ravers, rec, cover charge: M$12-15. *Club Oz*, *Shangri-La Hotel*, Jln Sultan Ismail – expensive; *Faces*, 103 Jln Ampang, also in an old colonial house, cover: M$16; *Hippodrome Worldwide Nite Club*, Rooftop, Ampang Park Shopping Centre, Jln Ampang, huge hostess bar ("every inch of the way we will make you feel like an Emperor"), Chinese bands (imported from Hong Kong and Taiwan) perform every night; *Legends*, 1 Jln Kia Peng, particularly popular with local KL crowd and again, in an old converted bungalow; *Tin Mine*, Basement, *KL Hilton*, Jln Sultan Ismail, one of the few old nightclubs still going strong, small dance floor and backgammon for the less energetic, has a reputation as a hostess hangout, rec, cover charge: M$25.

Cultural shows: *City Hall Auditorium*, Jln Raja Laut, T 2916011, traditional Malaysian songs and plays, call for current programme; *Dayang Hotel*, Jln Barat, Petaling Jaya, T 7555011; *Eden Village*, 260 Jln Raja Chulan, Malay, Indian and Chinese dancing every night; *Karyaneka Handicraft Centre*, Jln Raja Chulan/Jln Imbi, shows every Saturday evening; *Malaysian Tourist Information Complex* (Matic), 109 Jln Ampang, T 2434929, cultural shows every evening; *Putra World Trade Centre*, Jln Tun Ismail, T 4422999, cultural shows at 2045 Mon-Sat; *Temple of Fine Arts*, 116 Jln Berhala, Brickfields, T 2743709, this organization, set up in Malaysia to preserve and promote Indian culture, stages cultural shows every month with dinner, music and dancing, the *Temple* organizes an annual Festival of Arts (call for details), which involves a week-long stage production featuring traditional and modern Indian dance (free – "...the Temple believes art has no price"), it also runs classes in classical and folk dancing and teaches traditional musical instruments; *Yazmin Restaurant*, 6 Jln Kia Peng, T 2415655, nightly cultural entertainment with Malay buffet.

Art Galleries: Malays are a naturally artistic people and KL is a growing centre for the arts. Some of the main galleries include: *Anak Alam Art Gallery*, 905 Pesiaran Tun Ismail off Jln Parliamen; *A P Art Gallery*, Grd Flr, Central Market, off Jln Hang Kasturi; *Art House*, 2nd Flr, Wisma Stephens, Jln Raja Chulan; *Balai Seni*, Menara Maybank, Jln Tun Perak; *Galeri APS*, Pusat Kreatif, Jln Tun Razak; *Galericitra*, 1st Flr, Shopping Arcade, *Shangri-La Hotel*, Jln Sultan Ismail; *Impression Arts*, Wisma Stephens, Jln Raja Chulan; *National Art Gallery*, Jln Sultan Hishamuddin; *Rupa Gallery*, Lot 158 Menara Dayabumi, Jln Sultan Hishamuddin; *10 Kia Peng*, Jln Kia Peng, cultural, arts and crafts centre, needs a facelift. Also see *Wisma Loke* (see page 100).

Cinemas: open daily from 1100. The first showing is usually a 1300 matinee with the last show at 2115 (midnight show Sat). Tickets range from M$2-4. Screenings listed in *The New Straits Times*, *Star* of *Malay Mail*. Main cinemas: *Cathay*, Jln Bukit Bintang, T 2429942; *Coliseum*, Jln Tunku Abdul Rahman, T 2925995; *Federal*, Jln Raja Laut, T 4425041; *Odeon*, Jln Tunku Abdul Rahman, T 2920084; *President*, Sungei Wang Plaza, Jln Sultan Ismail, T 2480084.

Sports Badminton: *Bangsar Sports Complex*, Jln Terasek Tiga, Bangsar Baru; *YMCA*, 95 Jln Padang Belia, off Jln Tun Sambathan, Brickfields. **Bowling:** *Federal Bowl*, Federal Hotel, Jln Bukit Bintang; *Miramar Bowling Centre*, Wisma Miramar, Jln Wisma Putra; *Pekeliling Bowl*, Yow Chuan Plaza, Jln Tun Razak. **Golf:** *Kelab Golf Negara*, Subang (near Subang International Airport). Green fees: M$50-80 weekdays, M$100 weekends; *Morib Island Golf Course*, off Port Klang. Green fees: M$15; *Royal Selangor Golf Club*, Jln Kelab Golf, off Jln Tun Razak. Exclusive championship course (includes two 18-hole courses and one 9-hole), one of the oldest in the country. Non-members can only play on weekdays. Green fees M$150 per day (without membership introduction); *Saujana Golf & Country Resort*, Subang (near Subang International Airport). Two 18-hole championship courses. Green fees: M$100; *Sentul Golf Club*, 84 Jln Strachan, Sentul. Green fees: M$30 weekdays, M$50 weekends; *Templer Park Country Club*, 21 km N of KL. Fully floodlit course for 24-hour golf; golfers use electric cars on tarmac paths to get around. Mainly frequented by Japanese golf package tourists, and developed and part-owned by Japanese company. The more environmentally-minded have complained that the course has ruined the N end of Templer Park; jungled limestone outcrops now divide the fairways. Green fees: M$100.

Health Centres: *Fitness International*, Parkroyal Hotel, Jln Sultan Ismail; *Good Friend Health Centre*, 33 Jln Tun Sambathan 5; *Recreation Health Centre*, 4th Flr, *Furama Hotel*,

Komleks Selangor, Jln Sultan Ismail. **Roller Skating**: *Fun World Roller Disco*, 1st Flr Asiajaya Shopping Complex, Petaling Jaya. **Squash**: *Bangsar Sports Complex*, Jln Terasek Tiga, Bangsar Baru. **Snooker**: *Jade Snooker Centre*, GBC Plaza, Jln Ampang, T 4570345; *Snooker Paradise*, Kompleks Kotaraya. **Swimming**: All international-class hotels in KL have their own pools for guests. Public pools charge a nominal fee. *Bangsar Sports Complex*, Jln Terasek Tiga, Bangsar Baru; *Mimaland*, Jln Gombak, 17 km N of KL. Long water slide; *Weld Swimming Pool*, Jln Raja Chulan. **Tennis**: *Kelana Jaya Sports Complex*, Lot 1772, Taman Tasek Subang, Kelana Jaya; *YMCA*, 95 Jln Padan Belia, Brickfields. **Water sports**: *Water World*, Sungei Besi Tin Mine (mobile phone: T 01-331687). 20 min drive from KL, before the toll booths on highway to Seremban, exit on left (at Taman Sri Petaling), turn right at T-junction, over the railway line and past Shell and Esso stations towards Serdang and Kajang. Signposted to the left. Located in what was the biggest tin mine in the world, in clean, turquoise water and beneath dramatic rocky cliffs you can hire power boats, waterskis, jetskis, waterskis and canoes. For half-hour's waterskiing, M$50/boat. Now in the hands of a developer with big ideas.

Spectator sports: Cricket, rugby and hockey are played on the Padang, in the centre of KL, most weekends. Horse race meetings are held at the *Selangor Turf Club Race Course*, Jln Ampang. The race course, which occupies what is now KL's prime real estate, is to be redeveloped in the course of the next decade into a park, surrounded by new hotels and shopping complexes. A new race course will be operating at Sungei Besi, SE of KL, by late 1993. Football and badminton are Malaysia's most popular sports. Inter-state Malaysia Cup football matches are played at the *Merdeka Stadium* and the Stadium on Jln Stadium, off Jln Maharajalela.

Shopping As recently as the early 1980s Malaysians and KL's expatriates used to go on shopping expeditions to neighbouring Singapore – KL just was not up to it. These days however, the city has more or less everything; it is generally a cheaper place to shop than Singapore – electrical and electronic goods are duty-free – and new shopping complexes are springing up every year. They are not concentrated in any particular area – and ordinary shopping streets and markets are also dotted all around the city. The duty free shops at Subang International Airport are reasonably priced by world standards and include handicraft, art and batik shops for last-minute purchases. **Books**: *Bookazine*, 8 Jln Batai, Damansara Heights; *Berita Book Centre* and *MPH Bookstores*, Bukit Bintang Plaza, Jln Bukit Bintang; *Times Books*, Yow Chuan Plaza, Jln Tun Razak; *Minerva Book Store*, 114 Jln Tunku Abdul Rahman.

Batik: *Aran Novabatika Malaysia*, 174 Grd Flr, Ampang Park Shopping Centre, Jln Ampang; *Batik Bintang*, Lobby Arcade, *Federal Hotel*, Jln Bukit Bintang; *Batik Malaysia*, 114 Jln Bukit Bintang, Mun Loong, 113 Jln Tunku Abdul Rahman; *Batik Permai*, Lobby Arcade, *Hilton Hotel*, Jln Sultan Ismail; *Central Market*, Jln Hang Kasturi. Hand-painted silk batik scarves downstairs; many shops sell batik in sarong lengths; *Heritage*, 38 1st Flr, has a big selection of very original Kelantanese batiks (M$15-90/m). Most ordinary batiks cost about M$7/m; *Evolution*, Lot 117, Citypoint, Dayabumi Complex; fashionable range of readymades and other batik gift ideas by designer Peter Hoe; *Faruzzi Weld Shopping Centre*, Jln Raja Chulan (also at 42B Jln Nirwana, just off Jln Tun Ismail) exclusive and original batiks, rec; *Globe Silk Store*, 185 Jln Tunku Abdul Rahman; *Infrokraf*, Jln Raja (Sultan Abdul Samad Building), has a good selection of batik from all parts of Malaysia; *Khalid Batik*, 48, Grd Flr, Ampang Park Shopping Centre, Jln Ampang.

Pewter: 1st Floor, The Mall, 100 Jln Putra (opposite *Pan Pacific Hotel*), 231 Jln Tunku Abdul Rahman; *Dai-Ichi Arts and Crafts*, 122 Mezanine Flr, *Parkroyal Hotel*, Jln Sultan Ismail/Jln Imbi; *KL Arts & Crafts*, 18 Grd Flr, Central Market, Jln Hang Kasturi; *Selangor Pewter*, Jln Pahang, Setapak Jaya and showroom on Jln Tunku Abdul Rahman.

Handicrafts: *Aked Ibu Kota*, Jln Tunku Abdul Rahman. Shopping centre with wide variety of goods including local handicrafts; *Amazing Grace*, G-3P Yow Chuan Plaza, Jln Tun Razak; *Andida Handicraft Centre*, 10 Jln Melayu; *Central Market*, Jln Hang Kasturi. The old wet market is now full of handicrafts stalls, not always the cheapest but big selection; tourist orientated; *Eastern Dreams*, 101A Jln Ampang; *Infrokraf*, Jln Raja (located at one end of the Sultan Abdul Samad Building) is one of the country's official craft centres, there is a permanent exhibition of handicrafts for sale, open: 0900-1800 Sat-Thur; *Karyaneka Handicraft Village*, Jln Raja Chulan, government-run, exhibiting and selling Malaysian handicrafts, daily demonstrations, open: 0900-1800 Mon-Sun (in the same compound is the International Craft Museum and a small ethno-botanical garden); *Lavanya Arts*, 116A Jln Berhala Brickfields, run by the Temple of Fine Arts of Annalakshmi vegetarian restaurant fame, which aims to preserve Malaysia's Indian heritage. The shop sells Indian crafts: jewellery, bronzes, wood carvings, furniture, paintings and textiles; *Lum Trading*, 123 Jln SS2/24 SEA Park, Petaling Jaya, baskets and bambooware, 64 Jln Tun Perak; *Malaysian Arts*, 23 Jln Bukit Bintang; *South China Seas*, Level 4 Metro Jaya, Jln Bukit Bintang.

Film processing: there are plenty of colour print processing houses around KL, but slide processing is a risky business. Singapore is much better for this, but there are 2 recommended places in KL: *E6 Quick Colour Slide*, 44 Jln Landak, off Jln Pudu, T 2411505; *Translide*, 47A, Jln SS2/75, Petaling Jaya.

Markets and shopping streets: *Chow Kit* (Jln Haji Hussein), just off Jln Tunku Abdul Rahman, is a cheap place to buy almost anything – it doubles as a red light district. Jln Haji Hussein market closes at 1800, when it becomes a hawker centre until 0200; *Jalan Melayu* is another interesting area for browsing – Indian shops filled with silk saris, brass pots and Malay shops specializing in Islamic paraphernalia such as *songkok* (velvet Malay hats) and prayer rugs as well as herbal medicines and oils; *Jalan Tunku Abdul Rahman* (Batu Rd) was KL's best shopping street for decades and is transformed into a pedestrian mall and night market every Saturday after 1730. KL's original department store, Globe Silk Store, is on Jln Tunku Abdul Rahman; *Kampung Baru Sunday Market* (Pasar Minggu), off Jln Raja Muda Musa (a large Malay enclave at the N end of KL) is an open air market which comes alive on Saturday nights. Malays know it as the Sunday market as their Sunday starts at dusk on Saturday – so don't go on the wrong night). A variety of stalls selling batik sarongs, bamboo birdcages and traditional handicrafts compete with dozens of food stalls. The Pasar Minggu has largely been superceded by Central Market as a place to buy handicrafts however; *Lebuh Ampang*, off Jln Gereja was the first area to be settled by Indian immigrants and today remains KL's "Little India", selling everything from samosas to silk saris; *Pasar Malam*, Jln Petaling, Chinatown is a night market full of copy watches, pirate cassettes and cheap clothes; *Pudu market*, bordered by Jln Yew, Jln Pasar and Jln Pudu, is a traditional wet market selling food and produce – mainly patronized by Chinese.

Shopping complexes: *Ampang Park Shopping Centre* (good computer shops on level 2), with Yow Chuan and City Square opposite, on Jln Ampang/Jln Tun Razak; *Sungei Wang, KL and Bukit Bintang Plazas* and *Lot 10* on Jln Bukit Bintang/Jln Sultan Ismail; *Imbi Plaza*, Jln Imbi is KL's best computer centre; *The Mall*, Jln Putra, opposite the *Pan Pacific Hotel* is a huge modern shopping complex; *The Weld*, Jln Raja Chulan.

Local transport Bus: buses charge M$0.20 for the first km and M$0.05 for each additional km. The city's bus service is supplemented by minibuses (*bas mini*) which charge a flat fare of M$0.50. **Taxi**: KL is one of the cheapest cities in Southeast Asia for taxis; there are taxi stands all over town. Most are air-conditioned and metered: M$0.70 for the first 1.6 km. Extra charges between 2400 and 0600 (50% surcharge), and for each extra passenger in excess of 2 and luggage. **NB**: a coupon system operates at Subang Airport and railway station. For 24-hour taxi service: Comfort Radio Taxi Service, T 7330507; Telecab, T 211011; Koteksi, T 7815352; Sakti Radio Teksi, T 4420848; Selangor Radio Teksi, T 2936211.

Car hire: **Apex**, 6th Flr, Imbi Plaza, Jln Imbi, T 2438934; **Avis**, 40 Jln Sultan Ismail, T 2423500 (also desk at *Hilton Hotel* and Subang Airport); **Budget**, 20 Jln Telawi, Bangsar Baru, T 2420240 or Grd Flr, Wisma MCA, 163 Jln Ampang, T 2611122 (also desk at Subang Airport); **Express**, 2nd Flr, Bangunan Sateras, 152 Jln Ampang, T 2424113; **Hertz**, Lot 11, *Kuala Lumpur Hilton*, Jln Sultan Ismail, T 2433014 and 214A Kompleks Antarabangsa, Jln Sultan Ismail, T 2421014 (also desk at Subang Airport); **Mayflower Acme**, Angkasa Raya Building, 123 Jln Ampang, T 2611136 and at *Ming Court Hotel*, Jln Ampang, T 261136 (also desk at Subang Airport); **National Car Rental**, Grd Flr, Wisma HLA, Jln Raja Chulan, T 2480522 (also desk at Subang Airport and *Shangri-La Hotel*); **Orix**, 42 Jln Sultan Ismail, T 2423009; **Sintat**, Lobby Floor, *Holiday Inn on the Park*, Jln Pinang, T 2482388; **SMAS**, 3rd Floor, Menara Tun Razak, Jln Raja Laut, T 2936233 (also desk at Subang Airport); **Thrifty**, *Holiday Inn City Centre*, Jln Raja Laut, T 2932388 (also desk at Subang Airport); **Tomo Express**, 3rd Flr Podium, Kompleks Nagaria, 12 Jln Imbi, T 2417312 (also desk at Subang Airport); **Toyota Rent a Car**, Grd Flr, *Federal Hotel*, Jln Bukit Bintang, T 2481567 (also desk at Subang Airport); **Trans Rent-a-Car**, Lot 1.28, 1st Flr, 12 Jln Imbi Podium Kompleks Nagaria, T 2439127; **U-Drive**, GF4, Cahaya Suria Bldg, Jln Silang, T 2308158 (also desk at Subang Airport).

Banks & money changers There are money changers in all the big shopping centres and along the main shopping streets. Most branches of the leading Malaysian and foreign banks have foreign exchange desks, although some (eg Bank Bumiputra) impose limits on charge card cash advances. The following addresses are for bank headquarters; **Bank Bumiputra**, Menara Bumiputra, Jln Melaka; **Bank of America**, 1st Flr, Wisma Stephens, Jln Raja Chulan; **Chase Manhattan**, 1st Flr, Bangunan Pernas International, Jln Sultan Ismail; **Hongkong Bank**, 2 Lebuh Ampang (off Jln Gereja); **Maybank**, 100 Jln Tun Perak; **Public Bank**, Bangunan Public Bank, 6 Jln Sultan Sulaiman (off Jln Syed Putra); **Standard Chartered Bank**, 2 Jln Ampang; **United Malayan Banking Corporation**, Bangunan UMBC, Jln Sultan Sulaiman (off Jln Syed Putra).

Embassies & consulates Australia, 6 Jln Yap Kwan Sweng, T 2423122; Austria, 7th Flr, MUI Plaza, Jln P Ramlee, T 2484277; Belgium, 4th Flr, Wisma DNP, 12 Lorong Yap Kwan Seng,

T 2485733; **Brunei Darussalam**, 16th Flr, Plaza MBF, Jln Ampang, T 2612800; **Burma (Myanmar)**, 5 Jln Taman U Thant Satu, T 2423863; **Canada**, 7th Flr, Plaza MBS, 172 Jln Ampang, T 2612000; **China**, 229 Jln Ampang, T 2428495; **Czechoslovakia**, 32 Jln Mesra (off Jln Damai), T 2427185; **Denmark**, 22nd Flr, Bangunan Angkasa Raya, 123 Jln Ampang, T 2303895; **Finland**, 15th Flr, MBF Plaza, Jln Ampang, T 2611088; **France**, 196 Jln Ampang, T 2484318; **Germany**, 3 Jln U Thant, T 2429666; **India**, 20th Flr, West Block, Wisma Selangor Dredgin, 142 Jln Ampang, T 2617000; **Indonesia**, 233 Jln Tun Razak, T 9842011; **Italy**, 99 Jln U Thant, T 4565122; **Japan**, 11 Persiaran Stonor, off Jln Tun Razak, T 2438044.

Netherlands, 4 Jln Mesra (off Jln Damai), T 2431143; **New Zealand**, 193 Jln Tun Razak, T 2486422; **Norway**, 11th Flr, Bangunan Angkasa Raya, Jln Ampang, T 2430144; **Papua New Guinea High Commission**, 1 Lorong Ru Kedua (off Jln Ampang), T 4574203; **Philippines**, 1 Chnagkat Kia Peng, T 2484233; **Poland**, 495, 4½ mile, Jln Ampang, T 4576733; **Romania**, 114 Jln Damai, T 2423172; **Singapore**, 209 Jln Tun Razak, T 2616277; **Spain**, 200 Jln Ampang, T 2484868; **Sweden**, 6th Flr, Angkasa Raya Building, 123 Jln Ampang, T 2485981; **Switzerland**, 16 Persiaran Madge, T 2480622; **Thailand**, 206 Jln Ampang, T 2488222; **Turkey**, Bangunan Citi 1, Jln Perumahan Gurney, T 2986455; **UK**, 185 Jln Ampang, T 2487122; **USSR**, 263 Jln Ampang, T 4560009; **USA**, 376 Jln Tun Razak, T 2489011; **Vietnam**, Vietnam House, 4 Persiaran Stonor, T 2484036; **Yugoslavia**, Batu 4 1/2, Jln Ampang, T 4564561.

Useful addresses **General Post Office**: Dayabumi Complex, Jln Sultan Hishamuddin (*Poste Restante*). **Overseas Telephone Service**: Kedai Telekom at the airport; Kaunter Telegraf STM, Wisma Jothi, Jln Gereja; Grd Flr, Syarikat Telekom Malaysia, Bukit Mahkamah. **Kuala Lumpur area code**: 03. **Immigration**: Jln Pantai Bahru, T 7578155. **Hospitals**: *Assunta Hospital*, Petaling Jaya, T 7923433; *Lourdes Medical Centre*, T 4425335; Pantai Medical Centre, T 7575077; *Pudu Specialist Centre*, T 2431146; *Tung Shin Hospital*, T 2388900. All have casualty wards open 24 hrs. **National Library**: Jln Tun Razak, T 2923144.

Churches (times of English-language Sunday services): *St Andrews International Church*, 31 Jln Raja Chulan, 0900, 1100; *Wesley Methodist Church*, 2 Jln Wesley, 0815, 1030, 1800; *Baptist Church*, 70 Cangkat Bukit Bintang, 0830, 0945; *St Mary's (Anglican) Church*, Jln Raja, 0700, 0800, 1800; *St John's Cathedral (Roman Catholic)*, 5 Jln Bukit Nanas, 0800, 1030, 1800.

Airline offices **Aeroflot**, Grd Flr, Wisma Tong Ah, 1 Jln Perak, T 2613231; **Air India**, Bangunan Ankasa Raya, 123 Jln Ampang, T 2420166; **Air Lanka**, UG4 Bangunan Perangasang Segemai, Jln Kampung Attap, T 2740211; **Alitalia**, Plaza See Hoy Chan, Jln Raja Chulan, T 2387057; **America West Airlines**, UBN Tower, 10 Jln P Ramlee, T 2387057; **American Airlines**, Bangunan Angkasa Raya, 123 Jln Ampang, T 2480644; **Bangladesh Biman**, Subang International Airport, T 7461118; **British Airways**, Mezz. Flr., See Hoy Chan Plaza, Jln Raja Chulan, T 2325824; **Cathay Pacific**, UBN Tower, 10 Jln P Ramlee, T 2383377; **China Airlines**, Level 3, Bangunan Amoda, 22 Jln Imbi, T 2422383; **Czechoslavak Airlines**, 12th Flr, Plaza Atrium, 10 Lorong P Ramlee, T 2380176; **Delta Airlines**, UBN Tower, Jln P Ramlee, T 2324700; **Garuda**, 1st Flr, Angkasa Raya Building, 123 Jln Ampang, T 2482524/2410811; **Japan Airlines**, 1st Flr, Pernas International, Lot 1157, Jln Sultan Ismail, T 2611733/2611711; **KLM**, Shop 7, Grd Flr, President House, Jln Sultan Ismail, T 2427011; **Korean Air**, 17th Flr, MUI Plaza, Jln P Ramlee, T 2428311; **Lufthansa**, 3rd Flr, Pernas International Bldg, Jln Sultan Ismail, T 2614646/2614666; **MAS**, UMBC Building, Jln Sulaiman, T 2305115; MAS Building, Jln Sultan Ismail, T 2610555; Dayabumi Complex, T 2748734; **Northwest Orient Airlines**, UBN Tower, Jln P Ramlee, T 2384355; **Philippine Airlines**, 104-107 Wisma Stephens, Jln Raja Chulan, T 429041; **PIA**, Grd Flr, Angkasa Raya Building, 123 Jln Ampang, T 2425444; **Qantas**, UBN Tower, 10 Jln P Ramlee, T 2389133; **Royal Brunei**, 1st Floor, Wisma Merlin, Jln Sultan Ismail, T 2426511; **Royal Jordanian**, 8th Flr, Mui Plaza, Jln P Ramlee, T 2487500; **Sabena**, 1st Flr, Wisma Stephens, Jln Raja Chulan, T 2425244; **Scandanavian Airlines**, Bangunan Angkasa Raya, 123 Jln Ampang, T 2426044; **Saudi**, c/o Safuan Travel & Tours, 7 Jln Raja Abdullah, T 2984566; **Singapore Airlines**, Wisma SIA, 2 Jln Sang Wangi, T 2987033; **Thai International**, Kuwasa Building, 5 Jln Raja Laut, T 2937100; **Turkish**, *Hotel Equatorial*, 20 Jln Sultan Ismail, T 2614055; **UTA**, Plaza See Hoy Chan, Jln Raja Chulan, T 2326952; **United Airlines**, Bangunan MAS, Jln Sultan Ismail, T 2611433.

Tour companies & travel agents Most of the big hotels have their own in-house travel agents and ticketing agencies. For domestic flights it can be cheaper to buy tickets though ticketing agencies rather than going to MAS headquarters on Jalan Sultan Ismail. The Malaysian Tourist Information Centre (Matic), 109 Jln Ampang, T 2423929 (see below) provides free consultation to tourists and offers a tour, hotel and travel reservation service.

Angkasa Travel Services 1st Flr, Bangunan Angkasaraya, Jln Ampang, T 2486066; *Asian Overland Services*, 33, 33M, Jln Dewan Sultan Sulaiman 1, T 2925622; *Babin Tours*, 105E, Jln Ampang, T 243888, F 2415808; *Boustead Travel*, 13th Flr Menara Boustead, 69, Jln Raja

Chulan, T 2417022, F 2437530; *Harpers Tours*, 20th Flr, Plaza Atrium, Lorong P Ramlee, T 2322200, F 2321728; *Inter-Pacific Travel & Tours*, Tingkat Bawah, Wisma Golden City, 75, Jln Bukit Bintang, T 2480011, F 2413004; *Vacasia Tours & Travel*, 279, Jln Perkasa Satu, Taman Maluri, Cheras, T 9844005, F 9859611; *Reliance Travel Agencies*, 3rd Flr, Sungei Wang Plaza, Jln Sultan Ismail, T 2480111, F 2418480. Tourism Malaysia has a comprehensive list of tour companies offering standard and tailored packages; visitors are recommended to consult staff there. It also has a list, published each month, of agents offering discounted deals.

Around Malaysia: *Adventures Malaysia*, 1 Bangunan Bakti, Jln Dang Wangi, T 2924403. Diving trips around Malaysia; *Asia Overland Services*, 35M Jln Dewan Sultan Sulaiman Satu (off Jln Tuanku Abdul Rahman), T 2925622, tours around Malaysia, also run the *Homes Away from Home* programme; *Hamsa-vahini*, 84 Lorong Maarof, Bangsar Park, T 2255695, run by the Temple of Fine Arts, the organization set up by His Holiness Swami Shantanand Saraswati. Ticket agent and tailored package tours around Malaysia at very reasonable prices. Hamsa-vahini's motto: "Everywhere and everywhen with love we serve"; *Harper*, 20th Flr, Plaza Atrium, Jln P Ramlee, T 2322200; *Kingfisher Tours*, Rm 1107, 11th Flr, Bangunan Yayasan Selangor, Jln Bukit Bintang, T 2421454, F 2422801, specializes in nature-oriented tours; *Masmara Travel & Tours*, Grd Flr, Medan Mara, Jln Raja Laut, T 2936677; *MSL Travel*, *1st Asia Hotel*, 69 Jln Haji Hussein, T 2989722, discounted student and youth travel (also branch in Penang); *Overland Discovery Tours*, Unit 5, 1st Podium Floor, *Shangri-La Hotel*, 11 Jln Ismail, T 2302942; *Reliance Travel Agencies*, 3rd Floor Sungei Wang Plaza, Jln Sultan Ismail, T 2486022; *Semestra Travel*, 52 Jln Bulan, off Jln Bukit Bintang, T 2434802; *Sharita Travel Mart*, 96B Jln Masjid India, T 293371; *Student Travel Association*, UBN Tower, 6th Flr, Jln P Ramlee, T 2305720; *Tina Travel*, Arcade 2, 1st Floor, Holiday Inn, Jln Raja Laut, T 4578877; *Tour East*, Suite 2405, 24th Floor, Plaza See Hoy Chan, Jln Raja Chulan, T 2382200, F 2305014; *Vacasia Tours & Travel*, 279 Jln Perkasa Satu, Taman Maluri, Cheras, T 9540455.

Tourist offices Malaysian Tourist Information Centre (Matic), 109 Jln Ampang, T 2423929. Located in an opulent mansion formerly belonging to a Malaysian planter and tin miner. Information on all 13 states. Cultural performances and demonstrations of traditional handicrafts. It also has a tour, hotel and transport reservation offices as well as money-changing facilities; K L Visitor Centre, 3 Jln Sultan Hishamuddin, T 2301369; **Tourism Malaysia Bureau**, corner of Jln Raja/Jln Parlimen (the *Minangkabau*-styled building in the gardens at the end of the Padang). Open: 0800-1615 Mon-Fri, 0800-1245 Sat. **Tourism Malaysia**, Information Centre, Level 2, Putra World Trade Centre, Jln Tun Ismail, T 4411295. Also runs the KL Tourist Information Centre, Jln Parlimen, T 2936664 and Tourist Information Desks, Terminals 1 & 2, Subang International Airport as well as the information counter at the Railway Station.

Transport to & from KL Butterworth 383 km, Cameron Highlands 219 km, Ipoh 217 km, Melaka 148 km, Johor Bahru 365 km, Singapore 393 km, Kuantan 274 km, Kuala Terengganu 491 km, Kota Bahru 657 km. **By air**: Subang International Airport 24 km from KL. Buses 47 and 343 connect the airport with central KL. Connections to most other capitals in Southeast Asia (see Transport to & from Malaysia, **page 345**). MAS flights to other Malaysian destinations. Regular connections with Alor Setar (M$161), Ipoh (M$66), Johor Bahru (M$92), Kota Bahru (M$103), Kota Kinabalu (M$437), Kuala Terengganu (M$103), Kuantan (M$84), Kuching (M$266), Langkawi (M$134), Penang (M$96).

By train: Central Railway Station, Jln Hishamuddin, T 2747435. Left luggage office on Platform 4 and tourist information desk. KL is on the main line from Singapore to the S and Butterworth (Penang) to the N, some of these trains go on through to Bangkok (**see page 347**). To get on the East Coast line you have to go to Gemas, the junction S of KL or to Kuala Lipis or Mentakab 150 km to the W of KL. Regular connections with Alor Setar (M$32), Butterworth (M$28), Taiping (M$23), Ipoh (M$21), Tapah Road (for Cameron Highlands) (M$15), Tampin (M$13), Gemas (M$16), Johor Bahru (M$27).

By bus: buses heading N and S leave from Puduraya bus station, Jln Pudu. Most large bus companies have their offices here, including the biggest, Mara Ekspres. Buses to Pahang leave from Central Pahang bus station, Jln Tun Razak. Express buses to the East Coast depart from Hentian Bas Putra, Dewan Bandaraya, near the Putra World Trade Centre (or from Pekeliling and Puduraya bus stations). Southbound buses leave from Medan Mara. Regular connections to Singapore (M$17), Johor Bahru (M$15.30), Melaka (M$6.50), Butterworth (M$16), Ipoh (M$8.50), Kuantan (M$11.10), Kota Bahru (M$25.10). (Approximate prices only, as they vary slightly between bus companies.) **Outstation taxis**: leave from Jln Pudu, outside Puduraya bus station. Approximate prices to the following: Kuantan M$30, Butterworth M$40, Ipoh M$20, Taiping M$20, Melaka M$16, JB M$40, Singapore M$45, Kota Bahru M$60, Terrangganu M$50, Cameron Highlands M$30.

NORTH TO PENANG AND THAILAND

Introduction, 115; Barisan Titiwangsa and the hill stations, 115; Ipoh, 125; Taiping, 130; Penang (Pulau Pinang), 132; Alor Setar, 149; Kangar, 151; Langkawi, 152.

Maps North of Kuala Lumpur, 117; Cameron Highlands, 119; Pulau Pankgor, 129; Pulau Pinang, 133; Georgetown, 136-137; Langkawi, 153.

INTRODUCTION

The main road N from Kuala Lumpur is a straightforward journey up Malaysia's heavily populated W coast. The trip will be even easier once the much-vaunted North-South Highway is completed. Until then, the congested single-lane trunk road through Tanjung Malim, Tapah, Ipoh, Kuala Kangsar and Taiping is the only way to Penang. The trunk road – and the new highway – cut inland, avoiding the coast which is skirted by mangrove swamps and mudflats. Rubber and oil palm plantations line the route and open-cast tin mines and dredges are a common sight, particularly in the Kinta Valley, S of Ipoh.

BARISAN TITIWANGSA AND THE HILL STATIONS

On the road N, Peninsular Malaysia's mountainous jungled backbone lies to the E. It is called the **Barisan Titiwangsa** – or Main Range. It is largely unsettled – apart from the old British hill stations (Fraser's Hill, Cameron Highlands and Maxwell Hill) and scattered Orang Asli aboriginal villages. During the Malayan Emergency in the late 1940s and early 1950s, the Communist guerrillas operated from jungle camps in the mountains and later used the network of aboriginal trails to infiltrate the peninsula from their bases in southern Thailand. From Butterworth, the road leaves the plantations behind and enters the ricebowl states of Kedah and Perlis. The latter produces over half Malaysia's rice output, with the help of the Muda irrigation scheme.

Genting Highlands

A resort and recreation centre built like an airport terminal, Genting Highlands is best known for its gambling. Genting is Malaysia's answer to Las Vegas: *Casino de Genting* is the only place in Malaysia where gambling is legal. Genting also has a 4-ha 'funland' with a bowling alley, disco, cable car, mini-train, picnic pavilion, golf course and swimming pools. It is modern, brash and commercial, designed to cater for KL's affluent and nouveau riche. For fresher air and a better atmosphere, the old colonial hill stations of Fraser's Hill and the much larger Cameron Highlands are a better bet.

Accommodation Most of the hotels are pricey and have recreational facilities such as tennis, squash, snooker and health centres. There is no accommodation for budget travellers. **A+-A** *Awana Golf Club & Country Club*, T 2113015, F 211355, a/c, restaurant, pool, also have apartments to let; **A** *Genting*, T 2111118, F 811118, a/c, restaurant, pool, *Casino de Genting*; **A-B** *Highlands*, T 812812, a/c, restaurant, pool; **A-B** *Ria Apartments*, T 2613833, a/c, restaurant; **B** *Pelangi*, T 2112812, a/c, restaurant.

Restaurants The only restaurants are in the hotels, there are no hawker stalls or cheap places to eat.

Entertainment Casinos: *Casino de Genting*, *Genting Hotel*: Blackjack, baccarat, roulette, Tai Sai. **Discos**: Most of the big hotels have discos and nightclubs.

Sport Golf: *Awana Golf & Country Club*, Km 13. Green fees: M$40 weekdays, M$80 weekend. Riding: *Awana Horse Ranch*.

Banks & money changers Maybank, *Genting Hotel*.

Transport To & from Genting Highlands 48 km from KL, 131 km from Kuantan. **By bus**: buses leave from the *Genting Hotel*. Genting operates its own air-conditioned coaches with regular connections with Puduraya bus terminal, KL (M$5). **By taxi**: share taxis leave from the *Genting Hotel*. KL (M$5.00).

Fraser's Hill (Bukit Fraser)

Fraser's Hill is named after Englishman Louis James Fraser, who ran a gambling den, traded in tin and opium and operated a mule train in these hills at the end of the 19th century. He went on to manage a transport service between Kuala Kubu and Raub. Before Mr Fraser lent his name to it, the 7 hills were known as Ulu Tras. The development of the hill station began in the early 1920s.

It was along the road from Kuala Bubu Bahru that Sir Henry Gurney, the British High Commissioner, was ambushed and killed by Communist insurgents during the Malayan Emergency in 1951 (**see page 67**). A few years earlier British soldiers were involved in the massacre of suspected Communist sympathizers near Kuala Kubu. They shot dead a number of rubber tappers from a local village. There are a number of Orang Asli villages along rivers and tracks leading from the twisting road up the hill.

Fraser's Hill, 1524m above sea-level, is close enough to KL to be a favoured weekend resort. And because it was easily accessible by train from Kuala Kubu Road, it was a popular weekend retreat long before the Cameron Highlands. Most of colonial Malaya's big companies – such as Sime Darby, Guthries' and Harrisons & Crosfield – built holiday bungalows among the hills. More and more luxury bungalows are now being built here to cater for wealthy Malaysians, but it is still more tranquil and attractive than Genting. Although it is not as varied as the Cameron Highlands by way of attractions, there are jungle walks, swimming at Jerian waterfalls, a golf course, tennis courts and gardens.

Accommodation Many of the hotels have recreation facilities such as tennis, squash, riding, snooker. **A** *Fraser's Pine Resort*, Fraser's Condominium, Jln Kuari Bukit, T 7832810/7815510, restaurant, apartments; **A-B** *Merlin Inn Resort*, Jln Lady Guilemard, T 382300, a/c, restaurant, pool; **B** *Puncak Inn*, T 382055, restaurant; **B-C** *Fraser's Hill Development Corporation Bungalows*: Temerloh Bungalow, Raub Bungalow, Pekan Bungalow, Jelai Bungalow, Rompin Bungalow, *Puncak Inn*, T 382201/382248/382044 (bookings through the district office), restaurant, pool; **C** *Seri Berkat Rest House*, T 382213/8041026 (book through district office); **E** *Corona Nursery Youth Hostel*, T 382225.

Restaurants Chinese: ♦♦♦*Kheng Yuen Lee Eating Shop*, sports club. **International**: ♦♦♦*Restoran Puncak*, below *Puncak Inn*; ♦♦♦*Temerloh Steak House*, Temerloh Bungalow.

Bars Ye Olde Tavern, above the *Puncak Inn*. Fraser's answer to an English inn; with log fire.

Sport Golf: *Royal Fraser Hill Golf Club*. Green fees: M$15 weekdays, M$25 weekends.

Banks & money changers It is possible to change money at the *Merlin Hotel*, but there are no banks.

Tourist office between golf club and the *Merlin Hotel*.

Transport To & from Fraser's Hill 104 km from KL. **By bus**: bus station at Kuala Bubu Bahru. Regular connections with KL (M$3), change here to Fraser's Hill (M$1.50). Bus only runs at 0800 and 1200 from Kuala Bubu Bahru to Fraser's Hill and returns at 1000 and 1400. **By taxi**: share taxis go direct to Fraser's Hill. KL (M$15). **By car**: one way traffic system operates 8 km from Fraser's Hill: uphill traffic gets right-of-way on the odd hours, downhill traffic on the even hours.

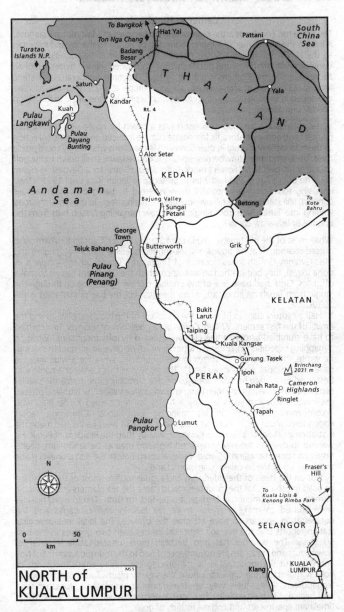

NORTH of KUALA LUMPUR

Cameron Highlands

The Cameron Highlands is the biggest and best known of Malaysia's hill stations. It lies on the NW corner of Pahang, bounded by Perak, to the W, and Kelantan to the N. On the jungly 1,500m plateau the weather is reassuringly British – unpredictable, often wet and decidedly cool – but when the sun blazes out of an azure-blue sky, the Camerons is hard to beat. Daytime temperatures average around 23°C, and in the evening, when it drops to 10°C and the hills are enveloped in swirling cloud – 'the white witch' – pine log fires are lit in the hilltop holiday bungalows.

In the colonial era the mountain resort was a haven for home-sick, over-heated planters and administrators. Its temperate climate induced an eccentric collection of them to settle and retire in their Surrey-style mansions where they could prune their roses, tend their strawberries, sip G & Ts on the lawn, stroll down to the golf course or nip over to Mr Foster's mock-Tudor Smokehouse for a Devonshire cream tea. The British Army also had a large presence in Tanah Rata until 1971 – their imposing former military hospital (now reverted to being a Roman Catholic convent) still stands on the hill overlooking the main street. To the left of the road leading into Tanah Rata from Ringlet are a few remaining Nissen huts from the original British army camp.

While most of the old timers – the likes of Stanley Foster, Captain Bloxham (who nursed racehorses at his bougainvillaea-fringed 'spelling station' at Ringlet) and Miss Gwenny Griffith-Jones (founder of Singapore's Tanglin School) – have now gone to rest, they bequeathed an ambience which the Camerons has yet to shake off. Miss 'Griff' had been one of the original pioneers, trudging up through the jungle from Tapah on an oxcart, when they first cut the hair-pinned road in the 1930s.

Half a century elapsed between the discovery of the highland plateau and the arrival of the first settlers. William Cameron, a government surveyor, first claimed to have stumbled across "a fine plateau... shut in by lofty mountains" while on a mapping expedition in 1885. In a letter in which he gave an account of this trip, he wrote: "[I saw] a sort of vortex in the mountains, while for a wide area we have gentle slopes and plateau land". The irony was that Cameron's name was bestowed on a place he never set eyes on. He probably came across the smaller plateau area farthest from Tanah Rata, known as Blue Valley. The highland plateau itself was discovered years later by a Malay warrior named Kulop Riau who accompanied Cameron on his mapping expeditions. Cameron's report engendered much excitement. Sir Hugh Low, who 34 years earlier had made the first attempt at Sabah's Gunung Kinabalu, was by then the Resident of Perak. He wanted to develop the newly reported highland area as "a sanitorium, health resort and open farmland". Two decades elapsed before the first pioneers made their way up to the so-called 'Cameron's Land'.

Hot on the heels of the elderly gin and Jaguar settlers (most of them insisted on solid British cars for the mountain roads) came the tea planters and vegetable farmers. The cool mountain climate was perfect for both. The forested hillsides were shaved to make way for more tea bushes and cabbages and the deforestation appears to have affected the climate. The local meteorological station reports that the average temperature has risen two degrees in the past 50 years. The weather has also become more unpredictable – torrential downpours and landslides are no longer confined to the monsoon months of Nov and Dec. But the mountain air is still bracing enough to entice thousands of holiday makers to the Camerons from the steamy plains. Today coach-loads of Singaporeans wind their way up the mountain roads and, together with well-heeled KL businessfolk, fork out extortionate sums for weekends in timeshare apartments and endless rounds of golf.

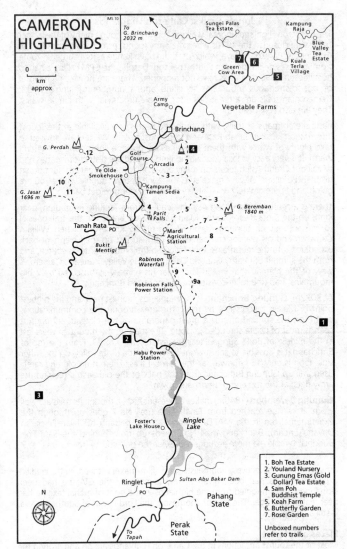

CAMERON HIGHLANDS

IMS 10

0   1
km
approx

To
G. Brinchang
2032 m

Sungei Palas
Tea Estate

Kampung
Raja

Blue
Valley
Tea
Estate

Green
Cow Area

Kuala
Terla
Village

7

6

5

Army
Camp

Vegetable Farms

Brinchang

G. Perdah

12

Golf
Course

4

Arcadia

Ye Olde
Smokehouse

3

2

G. Jasar
1696 m

10

11

Kampung
Taman Sedia

3

G. Bereman
1840 m

4

Parit
Falls

5

Tanah Rata   PO

Mardi
Agricultural
Station

7

8

Bukit
Mentigi

Robinson
Waterfall

9

9a

Robinson Falls
Power Station

1

2

Habu Power
Station

3

Foster's
Lake House

Ringlet
Lake

N

Ringlet   PO

Sultan Abu Bakar Dam

Pahang
State

To
Tapah

Perak
State

1. Boh Tea Estate
2. Youland Nursery
3. Gunung Emas (Gold Dollar) Tea Estate
4. Sam Poh Buddhist Temple
5. Keah Farm
6. Butterfly Garden
7. Rose Garden

Unboxed numbers refer to trails

The Camerons' most talked-about visitor arrived in Mar 1967 for a quiet sojourn in Moonlight bungalow, perched on a hilltop above the golf course. The disappearance of the US-born Thai silk emperor, art collector and military intelligence agent Jim Thompson from a lonely Cameronian backroad, propelled the hill resort into the headlines. Teams of Orang Asli trackers combed the jungle

Jungle walks: Cameron Highlands

The Cameron Highlands is great walking country – although many of the longer trails were closed in the 1970s when the army found secret food dumps for the Communist Party of Malaya, which used the Main Range as its insurgency route from its bases near Betong in South Thailand. Despite the CPM calling a halt to hostilities in 1990, the trails have not reopened. There are however a handful of not-so-strenuous mountains to climb and a number of jungle walks. Cameronian trails are a great place for people unfamiliar with jungle walks. They are also very beautiful.

Basic sketch maps of trails, with numbered routes, are available at the Tourist Information kiosk in Tanah Rata and from most hotels. Walkers are advised to take plenty of water with them as well as a whistle, a lighter and something warm. It is very easy to lose your way in jungle – and the district officer has had to call out Orang Asli trackers on many occasions over the years to hunt down disoriented hikers. Always make sure someone knows roughly where you are going and approximately what time you are expecting to get back.

There is a centuries-old Orang Asli trail leading from Tanjung Rambutan, near Ipoh, up the Kinta River into the Main Range. One branch of this trail goes N to the summit of Gunung Korbu (2,183m), 16 km away. When William Cameron and his warrior companion Kulop Riau left on their elephant-back expedition into the mountains, they followed the Kinta River to its source, and from the summit of nearby Gunung Calli, saw Blue Valley 'plateau'. Cameron's view of the plateau that would later bear his name was obscured by 2 big mountains, Irau (the roller-coaster-shaped one) and Brinchang.

At 2032m, **Gunung Brinchang** is the Highlands' highest peak and the highest point in Malaysia accessible by road. The area around the communications centre on the summit affords a great panorama of the plateau, although it spends most of its life shrouded in cloud. The road up the mountain veers left in the middle of Boh's Sungei Palas tea estate past Km 73. From the top of Brinchang it is possible to see straight down into the Kinta valley, on the other side. Ipoh is only 15 km away, as the hornbill flies. There is an old and rarely used trail up Gunung Brinchang from the back of the old airstrip (behind the army flats) at the top end of Brinchang town.

Gunung Beremban (1840m) makes a pleasant hike, although its trails are well worn. It can be reached from Tanah Rata (trail No.7 goes up through the experimental tea in the MARDI station past the padang off Jalan Persiaran Dayang Endah), Brinchang (trail No.2 leads up from behind the Sam Poh Buddhist temple – a more arduous route), or the golf course (follow trail No.3

in vain while detectives, journalists and film-makers toyed with credible explanations: he had been given a new identity by the CIA; he had been kidnapped and smuggled from the highlands in the boot of a Thai taxi; he had been eaten by a tiger. The fate of Thompson, the Lord Lucan of Southeast Asia, is still a mystery.

Places of interest

Most of the tourist attractions in the Cameron Highlands are on and around the plateau but there are a handful of sights on the road from Tapah. These are listed in order from the bottom of the mountain up. There are 3 main townships in the Highlands: Ringlet, Tanah Rata – literally 'flat land' – and Brinchang (in order as you go up). The latter 2 are in the plateau area, either side of the golf course.

Kuala Woh, a jungle park with a swimming pool, fishing and natural hot pools, is only 13 past the Arcadia bungalow where the road stops) – this is the easiest. Allow about 4 hours to get up and down. There is a good view down Tanah Rata's main street from the top. It is also possible to climb Gunung Beremban from Robinson Falls (trail No.8 leads off trail No.9). The trail heading for the latter is from the very bottom of the road leading past MARDI from Tanah Rata.

The trail to **Bukit Mentigi** (the Malay for Rhododendron Hill) cuts up to the right behind the veterinary centre, about 500 m down Jalan Persiaran Dayang Endah past the padang. Virtually no one goes up here now, and the trail is hard to find in places – just head straight up. It is a very short walk to the top, but very rewarding, for on the crest of the hill there is a spiked observation tower, about 10 m high, built by the Japanese during the war. From the top of the swaying pole, there is a fantastic view of the whole plateau, with Gunung Brinchang and Gunung Irau to the N, Gunung Beremban to the E and Gunung Jasar to the W. It is possible to look down through the valleys, past Robinson Falls, deep into the seemingly endless jungles of Pahang. For the more adventurous, it is also possible to follow the trail from the top of Mintigi down the mountain towards Ringlet. Beware of Second World War-vintage rusty barbed wire in places. It comes out in vegetable gardens, near the main road to Tanah Rata, opposite Gold Dollar tea estate.

Gunung Jasar (1696m), between the golf course and Tanah Rata, is a pleasant – but gentler – walk of about 3 hrs (trail No.10). The trail goes from half way along the old back road to Tanah Rata near the meteorological station (the road – Jalan Titiwangsa – leaves Tanah Rata next to the Police Station and emerges at the golf course, on the corner next to the Golf Course Hotel). The Jasar trail also forks off to **Bukit Perdah** (trail No.12, which branches off the Jasar trail) 2 hrs to the top and back. The path down from the summit comes out on a road leading back into the top end of Tanah Rata.

The trails to **Robinson Falls** (trail No. 9) and **Parit Falls** (trail No. 4) are more frequently trampled. The trail branches off to No.9a which leads down to the Boh tea estate road near Ringlet Lake. The short trail to Parit Falls starts behind the *Garden Hotel* and mosque on the far side of Tanah Rata's padang and ends up below the Slim army camp. Parit Falls is a small waterfall in between the two, with what was once a beautiful jungle pool before it became cluttered with day-trippers and their rubbish.

There are hundreds of other trails through the Camerons, traversing ridges and leading up almost every hill and mountain. Most are *Orang Asli* paths, some date from the Japanese occupation in World War II (these are marked by barbed wire) and some aren't really trails at all – beware.

km from Tapah, on the road to the Camerons.

14th Mile Waterfall (22½ km from Tapah) is a beautiful jungle waterfall, right by the roadside, which has been ruined by commercial ventures capitalizing on the picnic spot. The **19th Mile**, further up the hill, is a pleasanter spot for a stop-off. To the right of the little shop, a path leads along the side of the river, up into the jungle, past Orang Asli villages, waterfalls and jungle pools. Good for birdwatching and butterflies.

The first township on the road to the Cameron Highlands is **Ringlet**, just inside Pahang state. It was relocated to its present site in the 1960s when the original village was flooded to make way for the Sultan Abu Bakar hydro-electric scheme. *Ringlet* is the Semai aboriginal word for a jungle tree. When the water level is high, Ringlet Lake is very picturesque.

There are several large tea estates in the Cameron Highlands but **Boh Tea Estate** is the biggest and probably the best known. Tea grows very well in this climate and was first planted here in the early 1920s: Boh's Fairley estate (off to the right at Habu power station, between Ringlet and Tanah Rata, just after the lake) offers free guided tours of the factory (1100 Tues-Sun,

T 996032). The tea estates all use Tamil tea-pickers (and a few Orang Asli), who pluck more than 40 kg of green-leaf a day (only the tenderest top most shoots are selected). The green tea leaves are artificially withered in the factory, to reduce their water content, they are then crushed and fermented before sifting and packing. The dusty factories exude a rich aroma of tea.

The workers live in self-contained quarters on the estates, normally centred on the weighing-in stations. Most of them were shipped in as indentured labourers from South India by the British in the late 19th century – many are now 3rd or 4th generation. Blue Valley tea estate, at 'the top of the mountain', near Kampung Rajah, is a particularly beautiful area. It is possible to visit Blue Valley Estate (T 947847 to arrange) or Gold Dollar (Gunung Emas) Estate (near Ringlet) (T 946107).

Youland Nursery is on the road to Gold Dollar tea estate, left off the main road to Tanah Rata from Ringlet (milestone 32). At the same turn-off there is a racehorse spelling station, formerly owned by Cameronian pioneer Captain Bloxham.

Tanah Rata is another 15 km up the mountain, at 1,440m, and is the biggest of three Cameronian towns. In recent years **Brinchang**, 7 km beyond Tanah Rata, on the far side of the golf course, has grown fast: since the mid-1980s several new hotels have sprung up, mainly catering for mass-market Malaysian Chinese and Singaporean package tourists. It is not a very beautiful little town.

A popular sight with Chinese visitors – who arrive by the coach load – is the **Sam Poh Buddhist Temple**, just outside Brinchang (on the way in, turn right at the foot of the hill along Jalan Pecah Batu), overlooking the golf course extension. It is backed by Gunung Beremban. The temple (and monastery), built in 1971, are vast, gaudy and unattractive.

Further expansion of Tanah Rata and Brinchang can be expected in the next few years – particularly if Prime Minister Dr Mahathir's plan to build a road connecting the Cameron Highlands with Ipoh and Fraser's Hill ever sees the light of day. At present the road to Tapah is the only way up and down; this road runs through Perak until it reaches Ringlet, and the Perak state authorities are unlikely to spend much money upgrading it as Pahang state accrues all the financial returns of Cameron Highlands tourism.

Up the hill from Brinchang the Cameron Highlands becomes one big market garden. 4 km up the road from Brinchang, there is a large market selling local produce to eager customers from the plains below.

The Cameronian climate is particularly suited to the cultivation of vegetables more usually associated with temperate climates. Cabbages, cauliflowers, carrots and tomatoes – as well as fruit such as strawberries and passion fruit – are taken by truck from the Camerons to the supermarkets of Kuala Lumpur and Singapore. **Keah Farm**, with its neatly terraced hillsides, is on the far side of Brinchang (at Milestone 43).

Butterfly garden is past Keah Farm (framed dead ones are also on sale). Admission: M$2.50. Open: 0800-1700 Mon-Sun. There is a large shop attached to the garden, where everything from flowers to Cameronian souvenirs (beetles embedded in key rings) is on sale. Outside there are fruit and vegetable stalls – all very popular with Chinese visitors.

The **rose garden** is 2 km further up the mountain, past Keah Farm towards Sungei Palas tea estate (take a left turn at the Green Cow area – a village there was burned to the ground by the Communists during the insurgency). There are many vegetable farms in the area.

Accommodation During school and public holidays the Cameron Highlands gets very booked up and prices rise by 30-50%. If you are travelling in a group, hiring a bungalow is much the best bet; most have gardens, log fires and are away from the towns. The cheaper hotels in Brinchang and Tanah Rata are not good value for money. If you plan to stay for a few days it is worth finding a hotel/bungalow out of town where you can enjoy the peace and quiet. The top hotels, the government resthouse, the bungalows and Bala's place all have gardens.

Condominiums: A+-A *Country Lodge*, Lot 47, Section 3, T 901811, good for families as it has suites, not rooms, opened in 1991, on hillside overlooking Brinchang, as the town's first condo-style hotel; **A** *Strawberry Park Motel*, PO Box 81, above golf course, turn left after *Merlin Hotel*, T 901166, restaurant, huge complex, mostly made up of time-share apartments, and the number-one destination for holidaying Singaporeans, unfortunately it can be seen from just about everywhere on the plateau, some apartments to let out.

Bungalows: (rates for whole bungalow per night unless stated; most prices include resident cook. Rates may vary according to season – request discounts). **A+** *Fair Haven*, Tanah

Rata; **A+** *Golf View Villa*, Tanah Rata, T 901624, 6 rooms, residential cook available; **A** *Beautiful House*, Brinchang; **A** *Highlands Villa*, near Tanah Rata, T 901405; **A** *Mount Regalis*, Brinchang, T 901324; **A** *Rose Cottage* (I and II), T 901173; **B** *Gunder Singh*, near trailhead to Gunung Jasar, Jln Titiwangsa (back road to golf course from Tanah Rata police station); **B** *Lutheran Bungalow*, Jln Kamunting (between Tanah Rata and Brinchang), T 901584, friendly, cosy rooms with fireplace, it is possible to book individual rooms or the whole bungalow, guests also have the option of eating breakfast, lunch and supper at the bungalow – all at set times, tennis court and interesting local jungle trails nearby – including one to an *Orang Asli* graveyard, rec; **D** *Rumah Tetamu Sri Pahang*, next to *Merlin Hotel*, T 901544.

Hotels before Tanah Rata **A** *Foster's Lake House*, Lubok Taman, Ringlet, T 996152, restaurant, exclusive mock-Tudor black and white, the final brainchild of the late Mr Foster.

Tanah Rata **A+-A** *Merlin Inn Resort*, by the golf course, T 901205, restaurant, overlooking the golf course on the road between Tanah Rata and Brinchang, on the site of the old *Cameron Highlands Hotel* which burned down in 1970, great view but not worth the money; **A+-A** *Ye Olde Smokehouse*, by the golf course, T 901214/5, restaurant, beautifully done up in 'ye olde English' style, by old-time resident Stanley Foster, it is now well run by local management who have taken care to preserve its home counties ethos, the rooms are first class, and there is an original red British telephone box in the private garden, rec; **A-B** *Garden Inn* (off the padang in Tanah Rata), T 901911, restaurant, formerly 'Dalat School' – used by children of US forces in Vietnam; **B-D** *Balas Holiday Chalets*, 1 km out of Tanah Rata towards Brinchang, signposted to left, T 901660, not chalets at all, but a rambling colonial house (formerly a British school) with plenty of character and a pleasant garden; Bala also has plenty of character too and knows the Camerons well, there is a pinboard with information on jungle walks and the latest gen from travellers, common sitting rooms, log fires, restaurant rec – good breakfast and vegetarian dinners, accommodation to suit all budgets, dorm (F, basic: rotan bed). **B** *Federal*, 44 Main Rd, T 941777, restaurant, hot baths, large comfortable rooms, travel agent; ; **B** *Golf Course Inn*, by the golf course, T 901411, restaurant, concrete monstrosity with a great view; **B-C** *Town House*, 41 Main Rd, T 901666, restaurant, tourist information, national express booking office, rec.

C *Cameron*, 29 Jln Besar, T 901160, above saloon-doored bar; **C** *Orient*, 38A Main Rd, restaurant, rec; **C** *Rumah Rehat* (Rest House), Jalan Persiaran Dayang Endah, T 901254, exceptionally nice little resthouse, just up the hill, opposite the padang, tends to get rather over-booked by government people so it pays to book in advance, tennis court, rec; **C** *Seah Meng*, 39 Main Rd, T 901618; **C-D** *Cameron Highlands Resthouse*, T 901066, restaurant, must book first, well run, rec; **C-E** *Twin Pines Chalet*, 2 Jln Mentigi, T 902169, very popular guesthouse at top end of town, off the main street on road behind Esso garage, hot showers, clean and friendly, rooms and dorm, recommended by correspondents.

E *Highlands Lodge*, near the hospital, noisy, dorm (F); **F** *Father's Place*, Jln Gereja, convent end of Tanah Rata, up a long flight of steps, basic, dorm.

Brinchang **B** *Brinchang*, 36 Jln Besar, T 901755/901122, F 901246, restaurant (speciality: steamboat), very clean; **B** *Hill Garden Lodge*, 15-16 Jln Besar, T 902308, very clean; **B** *Plastro*, 19 Main Rd, T 901009, reasonably nice; **B-C** *Kowloon*, 34-35 Jln Besar, T 901366, F 901803, restaurant, best value for money in Brinchang, with excellent restaurant downstairs; **C** *Sri Sentosa*, 38 Jln Besar, T 901907, restaurant; **D** *Chua Gin*, 11 Jln Besar, T 901801, shared bathrooms only; **D** *Hong Kong*, 4 Jln Besar, T 901722, restaurant, triple (C); **D** *Hong Kong*, 5 Jln Besar, T 901722, restaurant (good Chinese menu). **F** *Wong Villa Hostel*, behind the post office, T 901145, organizes bus tickets, basic – but it has hot water, dorm slightly cheaper.

Restaurants The Cameron Highlands is about the only place in Malaysia where you can have roast beef and Yorkshire pudding and Devonshire cream teas (see *Bala's*, the *Lakehouse* and *The Smokehouse* below).

Tanah Rata Chinese: ♦♦*Diamond*, Federal Hotel, 44 Main Rd; ♦♦♦*Mayflower*, Main Rd, rec by locals; ♦♦♦*Orient*, 38A Main Rd, excellent steamboat; ♦♦♦*Garden Hotel*, opposite the padang, good steamboat. Nonya: ♦♦*Excellent Nonya*, 44 Rain Rd, (opposite Esso garage), rec. Indian (both opposite the stalls): ♦*Kumar*, good banana leaf;♦ *Thanam*, Indian Muslim food, including murtabak and excellent breakfast rotis. International: ♦♦*Bala's*, 1 km from Tanah Rata towards Brinchang, good breakfasts and vegetarian dinners, also a popular stop for cream teas; ♦♦♦♦*Lakehouse*, Ringlet, similar menu to *The Smokehouse* – very English; ♦♦♦*Merlin*, by the golf course, international menu, over-priced; ♦♦*Rose Lane*, Main Rd, Chinese and Western, popular; ♦♦♦♦*The Smokehouse*, by the golf course, expensive restaurant serving English favourites: beef Wellington, roast beef, Yorkshire pudding and steak and kidney pies, also serves Devonshire cream teas. **Stalls** on the other side of the road to the shops, next to the bus station, serve excellent food, Malay, Indian and Chinese. Budget.

Brinchang Malay ♦♦*Sri Sentosa*, choice of other cuisines. **Chinese**: ♦♦*Kowloon Hotel*, lemon chicken and steamboat rec, good Western selection too; ♦♦*Kwan Kee*, Main Rd, next door to *Lido Hotel*, steamboat speciality – better than *Silverstar Restaurant* on the other side of the *Lido*; ♦♦*You Ho*, Main Rd (past *Hong Kong Hotel*), seafood and good vegetables; ♦♦*Brinchang*, Main Rd, large Chinese menu, some European. **International** ♦♦♦*Parkland*, Jln Besar, international menu, steaks rec, breakfast menu♦♦. **Stalls** Hawker stalls in the centre of Brinchang, only open after 1600. Roti and satay.

Entertainment Not much – most visitors prefer to sit around log fires in the evenings. Such nightlife as there is is in the bars and discos of the big hotels. There is a run-down cinema in Tanah Rata, behind the bus station.

Sport Golf: *Cameron Highlands Golf Club*, Tanah Rata. Magnificent 18-hole golf course, occupying pride of place in the centre of the plateau, and surrounded by jungled hills. It is a favourite haunt of Malaysian royalty. Green fees: M$40/day; M$20 for 9 holes. Club hired M$10 (half-set). It is also possible to play tennis on the courts across the road from the clubhouse: M$4 an hour (racquets and balls for hire from shop in clubhouse).

Local transport Bus/taxis: nearly all the buses from Tapah go through Ringlet, Tanah Rata and on to Brinchang. Rex buses go from Tanah Rata to the farthest outpost on the mountain. Taxis are always available in the main towns and should cost around M$10/hr. It is also possible just to take a seat in a taxi going from Tanah Rata to Brinchang, for example – costs about M$1.50. Taxi and local bus station on either side of the Shell station in Tanah Rata. To order a taxi: T 901234/901555. **Car hire**: because visitors pose a serious insurance problem on the mountain roads, the car rental business is not well developed in the Camerons. The only one available is semi-official: contact Ravi at *Rainbow Garden Centre* (between *The Smokehouse* and Tanah Rata), T 901782.

Banks & money changers Tanah Rata: Sampanian National, Arab-Malaysian Finance, Visa Finance Berhad, Hong Kong Shanghai Bank, Maybank all on Main Rd. C S Tour Agency, next to Federal Diamond Restaurant, changes money. **Brinchang**: Public Bank, Main Rd, next to *Hill Garden Lodge*, has foreign exchange facilities.

Useful addresses General Post Office: opposite Esso station at the convent end of Tanah Rata; opposite Petronas station in Brinchang. **Hospital**: opposite gardens, Tanah Rata. **Police**: opposite gardens, Tanah Rata, T 901222. **District office**: T 901066 (alert the office if someone you know is long-overdue after a jungle walk). **All Souls' Church** (Anglican): between Kampung Taman Sedia and golf course. Converted army Nissen hut with lych-gate in memory of Miss Griffeths Jones. Services: 1030 Sun.

Travel agents *C S Travel Agents* and *Town House Hotel*, useful for bus tickets.

Tourist office Tourist Information Centre, on the right as you come into Tanah Rata. Small museum in the centre. The *Orang Asli* exhibit is worth a browse. Open: 0900-1700 Mon-Sat.

Transport to & from the Cameron Highlands 214 km from KL, 121 km from Ipoh. **NB**: those who suffer from travel sickness are advised to take some anti-nausea medication before setting out on the mountain road. **By train**: the nearest station to the Camerons is Tapah Road in Tapah, 67 km from Tanah Rata. Regular connections with Ipoh (M$11.50), KL (M$22), Butterworth (M$20). Regular bus or taxi connections to the Cameron Highlands from nearby Tapah. Bus 153 leaves for Tapah every hour until 1600, 2 hrs (M$3). **By bus**: most buses leave from Tapah, 67 km from Tanah Rata. Regular connections with Brinchang and Tanah Rata (M$4). Tickets can be booked at travel agents (see below) or at the bus station in Tanah Rata. Regular connections with Ipoh (M$6), KL (M$15), Butterworth (M$9), Kuantan (M$22), Melaka (M$22), Singapore (M$28). Can reserve tickets for the MARA bus at the *Town House Hotel* or *C S Travel*, Tanah Rata. Bus leaves once a day to KL (M$7.50). **By taxi**: regular connections from Tapah to Brinchang/Tanah Rata (M$8).

IPOH TO BUTTERWORTH

Ipoh

The northern state of Perak is known for its tin ore (mainly in the Kinta Valley) and Ipoh, its capital, is Malaysia's third city with a population of about 250,000. The city is situated in the Kinta Valley, between the Main Range and the Keledang Mountains, to the W. Ipoh is named after the abundance of the huge, elusive Ipoh (or upas) trees that once grew there; the Orang Asli tribes procured the poison for their blowpipe darts from its fabled lethal sap. It was known as the deadliest poison in the world. The city also has an abundance of imposing limestone outcrops. These jungle-topped hills, with their precipitous white cliffs, are riddled with passages and caves, many of which have been made into cave temples.

In its early days, Ipoh's citizens became wealthy on the back of the tin mining industry. In 1884 the Kinta Valley tin rush brought an influx of Chinese immigrants to Ipoh; many made their fortunes and built opulent town houses. Chinese immigrants have bequeathed what is now one of Malaysia's best-preserved Chinatowns (the 'Old Town'). In the 1880s Ipoh vied with Kuala Lumpur to be the capital of the Federated States of Malaya, and long after KL took the title, Ipoh remained the commercial 'hub of Malaya'. The city has long had an active 'flesh trade': there are frequent round-ups of Thai and Burmese prostitutes who are smuggled across Malaysia's N border.

Few tourists spend long in Ipoh – most are en route to Penang, KL or Pulau Pangkor. Those who do stay rarely regret it: there are excellent Chinese restaurants (a speciality is the rice noodle dish, *hor he fun*), Buddhist temples and examples of Straits Chinese architecture.

Places of interest

The Kinta River separates the old and new parts of town. The **Old Town** is centred along the river between Jalan Sultan Idris Shah and Jalan Sultan Iskander Shah and is known for its old Chinese and British colonial architecture particularly on Jalan Sultan Yusof, Jalan Leech and Jalan Treacher.

Prominent landmarks include the **Birch Memorial**, a clock tower erected in memory of the first British resident of Perak, J W W Birch. His murder, in 1875, was one of colonial Malaya's first anti-British incidents. The Moorish-style **railway station** (off Jalan Kelab), built in 1917, bears close resemblance to its Kuala Lumpur counterpart, and is known as "the Taj Mahal" of Ipoh. **Ipoh Town Hall**, with its Palladian façade, stands opposite. A solitary Ipoh (or upas) tree, after which the city is named, stands in the centre of **Taman D R Seenivasagam Park.** There are also Japanese Gardens nearby on Jalan Tambun. Open: 1600-2000 Mon-Fri, 0900-2000 Sat & Sun. The **Geological Museum**, on Lorong Hariman (out of town centre), was set up in 1957. It is known for its exhibition of tin ore and collection of fossils and precious stones. Open: 0800-1645 Mon-Fri, 0800-1245 Sat.

Excursions

Kellie's Castle, down the road to Batu Gajah, just to the S of Ipoh, is the eccentric edifice of Scotsman William Kellie Smith, a rubber tycoon in the late 19th century. He shipped in Tamil workers from South India to build his fanciful Moorish-style mansion, and after an outbreak of fever, he allowed them to build a Hindu temple in the grounds. An image of Smith is among the sculpted Hindu pantheon on the temple roof. The castle was never completed as Smith left in the middle of its construction and died in Portugal on a business trip.

Sam Poh Tong at Gunung Rapat, 5 km S of Ipoh, is the largest of the cave temples in the area. There are Buddha statues among the stalactites and stalagmites. The

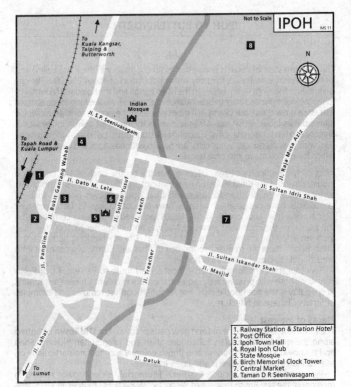

Map legend:
1. Railway Station & Station Hotel
2. Post Office
3. Ipoh Town Hall
4. Royal Ipoh Club
5. State Mosque
6. Birch Memorial Clock Tower
7. Central Market
8. Taman D R Seenivasagam

temple was founded 100 years ago by a monk who lived and meditated in the cave for 20 years; and it has been inhabited by monks ever since. The only break was during the Japanese occupation when the cave was turned into a Japanese ammunition and fuel dump. There is a pond at the entrance where locals release tortoises to earn merit. Open: 0900-1600 Mon-Sun. **Getting there**: Kampar bus (M$1).

Perak Tong 6½ km N of Ipoh at Gunung Tasek, is one of the largest Chinese temples in Malaysia. Built in 1926 by a Buddhist priest from China, the temple houses over 40 Buddha statues and mystical traditional Chinese-style murals depicting legends. It is visited by thousands of pilgrims every year and is the most ornately decorated of the many cave temples at the base of the 122m limestone hill. A path beyond the altar leads into the cave's interior and up a brick stairway to an opening 100m above ground with a view of the surrounding countryside. Another climb leads to a painting of Kuan Yin, Goddess of Mercy, who looks out from the face of the limestone cliff. A 15m-high reinforced concrete statue of the Buddha stands in the compound. Open: 0900-1600 Mon-Sun. **Getting there**: Kuala Kangsar bus (90¢).

Gua Tambun (Tambun Cave) is 3 km from Ipoh, near Tambun. Traces of a 10,000 year-old civilization were discovered here in the 1930s. The drawings on the cave

Perak: the silver state that grew rich on tin

Perak is nicknamed the 'Silver State' because *perak* is the Malay for silver. This was, according to one account, a misnomer, as the locals mistook their plentiful tin ore for silver. All the way through the Kinta and Perak river valleys, huge areas of sand lie bleached and desolate, after the tin dredges have passed over them. A more likely derivation of Perak's name is from the word *bharat*, meaning 'west'. In maps prior to 1561 the area is marked as 'Perat' – historians speculate this may be a corruption of Bharat. The state became "the senior state of the federation" in colonial Malaya – before its governmental role passed to Kuala Lumpur at the end of the 19th century.

Perak's ancient name was Gangga-Negara, a Sanskrit word, meaning 'City on the Ganges'... in this case referring to an ancient kingdom centred on the estuary of the Perak River, where the village of Bruas is today. Gangga-Negara was the capital of this powerful kingkom, referred to by an Arab chronicler as far back as 644AD. It is said that many Buddha statues have been found in the area. Gangga-Negara was the site chosen by the Bendahara rulers of old Melaka who founded the Perak dynasty. The settlement was finally sacked by Rajendra Chola, the son of the first Hindu ruler of Kedah – who also destroyed Temasek, which in later life re-emerged as Singapore.

walls depict the life of prehistoric man, especially interesting is the 'Degong' fish, a drawing of a large fish which feeds on meat, rather like a piranha. **Tambun Hot Springs** nestle at the foot of the hill. The Japanese were responsible for their initial development during the occupation. Two swimming pools have been built – one filled with luke warm water and one with hot. **Getting there**: Tambun bus (90¢).

Kuala Kangsar, half way between Ipoh and Taiping, is a royal town. It lies on the Kangsar River, a tributary of the Perak River. Just off the main road is the home of the Sultan of Perak. The beautiful **Istana Iskandariah**, was built in 1930 on Bukit Chandan, a hill overlooking the Perak River. It is a massive marble structure with a golden dome set among trees and rolling lawns. The former palace, Istana Kenangan (next door to the current Istana), is now the **Museum di Raja** and exhibits royal regalia. It is a fine example of Malay architecture and was built by Sultan Idris of Perak between 1913 and 1917 without recourse to any architectural plans or a single nail. Open: 0900-1800 Mon-Sun. In the vicinity of the palace are several traditional wooden Malay homes, which used to house court officials.

On Bukit Chandan the **Ubudiah Mosque**, completed in 1917, is one of the most beautiful mosques in the country with its golden domes and elegant minarets. Next to it are the graves of the Perak royal family. The Istana and mosque can be reached by walking along the river out of town. Besides these grand buildings, in the grounds of the district office near the Agricultural Department, are 2 of the first three rubber trees planted in Malaysia. Kuala Kangsar could easily be visited in a day from Ipoh or Taiping. **Getting there**: trains every 2 hrs from Ipoh. Bus every half hour (M$2.40).

Accommodation A *Excelsior*, 43 Clarke St, T 536666, a/c, restaurant; **A** *Royal Casuarina*, 18 Jln Gopeng, T 505555, F 508177, a/c, restaurant, pool, Ipoh's finest; **B** *Eastern*, 118 Jln Sultan Idris Shah, T 543936, a/c, restaurant; **B** *French*, 60-62 Jln Dato Onn Jaafar, T 513455, a/c, restaurant; **B** *Mikado*, Jln Yang Kalsom, T 505855, a/c, restaurant; **B** *Station Hotel*, 3rd Flr, Railway Station, off Jln Kelab, a/c, restaurant, like KL's station hotel, this is a colonial classic, albeit in a state of disrepair, the rooms are really suites, complete with sitting rooms, rec; **C** *Central*, 26 Jln Ali Pitchay, T 500142, a/c, restaurant, friendly, rec; **C** *Fairmont*, 10-12 Kampar Rd, T 511004, a/c, restaurant; **C** *Golden Inn*, 17 Jln Che Tak, T 530866, a/c, efficiently run, rec; **C** *Hollywood*, 72-76 Jln Chamberlain, T 515322, fan only; **C** *Lotte*, 97 Jln Dato Onn Jaafar, T 542215, a/c; **C** *Merlin*, 92-98 Jln Clare, T 541351, a/c, restaurant, tourist information; **C** *Robin*, 106-110 Jln Clare, T 513408, a/c, rec; **D** *New Kowloon*, 92 Jln Yang

Kalsom, T 515264, a/c; **D** *New Perak*, 20-26 Jln Ali Pitchay, T 515011, a/c (some rooms); **D** *Shangai*, Jln Clare, fan only, restaurant, clean and central, rec; **D** *YMCA*, 211 Jln Raja Musa Aziz, T 540809, fan only, dorm (F); **E** *Ipoh*, 163 Jln Sultan Idris Shah, T 548663, fan only; **E** *Kuo Ming*, 48-50 Jln Dato Onn Jaafar, T 512087, fan only, restaurant, no hot water.

Restaurants Ipoh is well known for its Chinese food, especially Ipoh chicken rice and *kway teow* – liquid and fried versions. Malay: ♦♦♦*Perwira*, Medan Gopeng; ♦♦♦*Semenanjung*, Jln Sultan Idris Shah; ♦♦♦*Sabar Menanti*, Jln Raja Musa Aziz. Chinese: ♦♦♦*Central*, 51-53 Cowan Street; ♦*Chuan Fong*, 175 Jln Sultan Iskandar, speciality: curry laksa; ♦♦*Foh San*, Jln Osbourne, dim sum; ♦♦*Kawan*, Jln Sultan Iskandar Shah, also Malay and Indian dishes; ♦♦*Kok Kee*, 272 Jln Sultan Iskandar Shah; ♦♦*Ming Court*, 36 Jln Leong Sin Nam, dim sum; ♦♦*Mung Cheong*, 511 Jln Pasir Putih, Cantonese. Indian: ♦♦♦*Comfy Corner*, 61 Jln Pasar; ♦♦♦*Gopal Corner*, Buntong; ♦♦♦*Guru's Chapati*, Cheong Seng Restaurant Complex, Lebuh Raya Ipoh, Punjabi, rec; ♦♦♦*Krishna Bhawan*, 8 Jln Lahat; ♦♦*Majeedia*, Jln Dendahara/Jln Leong Boon Swee; ♦*Mohamad Ibrahim*, 786 Jln Yang Kalsom, speciality: *mee rebus*.

Vegetarian: ♦♦*Nam Thim Tong*, Mile 3.5 Gopeng Rd. Chinese, serve ersatz meat dishes made of soya bean. International: ♦♦♦♦*Royal Casurina Coffee House*, 18 Jln Gopeng; ♦♦*Excelsior Hotel Coffee House*, 43 Clarke St; ♦♦♦*Panorama Hotel Coffee House*, 61-79 Jln Kota; ♦♦♦*Station Hotel Coffee House*, Jln Kelab.

Stalls: *Jln Dewan, Ipoh Garden*, Jln Sultan Idris Shah. Mainly Chinese stalls. *Railway Station*, Jln Kelab, rec; *Wooley Food Centre*, Canning Gardens.

Sport Golf: *Royal Perak Golf Club*, Jln Sultan Azlan Shah. Green fees: M$60 weekdays, M$100 weekends. Racing: races held every Sat and Sun at *Perak Turf Club*. Swimming: *DBI Swimming Complex*, Perak Sports Centre, Lebuh Raya Thivy. Admission: M$1 weekdays, M$2 weekends. Open: 0900-2100 Mon-Sun.

Local transport Car hire: Avis, Sultan Azian Shah Airport, T 206586; Hertz, *Royal Casuarina Hotel*, 18 Jln Gopeng, T 505533.

Banks & money changers Bank Bumiputra Malaysia Berhad and Maybank are both on Jln Sultan Idris Shah; **Standard Chartered**, 21-27 Jln Stetser; UMBC, 86 Jln Yang Kalsom.

Useful addresses General Post Office: next to the railway station on Jln Kelab. **Area code**: 05.

Airline offices MAS, Lot 108 Bangunan Seri Kinta, Jln Sultan Idris Shah, T 51455.

Tourist offices Perak Tourist Information Centre, State Economic Planning Unit, Jln Dewan, T 532800, crafts shop and exhibition centre. Tourist Information, *Royal Casurina Hotel*, 18 Jln Gopeng, T 532008.

Transport to & from Ipoh 205 km from KL, 161 km from Butterworth. **By air**: regular connections with Penang (M$53) and KL (M$55). **By train**: Ipoh is on the main north-south line. Regular connections with Butterworth (M$5.30), KL (M$16.50) and Singapore (M$37.80). **By bus**: Ipoh is on the main north-south road and is well connected. The bus terminal is at the intersection of Jln Kelab, Kidd and Silbin. Buses to Taiping and Kuala Kangsar leave from the local bus terminal. Regular connections with Butterworth (M$7), KL (M$8.50), Alor Setar (M$13), Kuantan (M$20), Taiping (M$3), Lumut (M$2.90). **By taxi**: share taxis leave from beside the bus station. KL (M$15), Butterworth (M$15), Taiping (M$7), Kuantan (M$30).

Lumut

Lumut is little more than a transit point for Pulau Pangkor and a base for the Royal Malaysian Navy. This small town does, however, come alive for the *Pesta Laut* or sea festival in July/August with boat races, competitions, cultural shows and funfairs. A few kilometres S there are beaches at Teluk Tubiah, Teluk Muruk and Teluk Batik (often used by the naval base). There are now a few hotels in town if you get stuck here.

Transport to & from Lumut 183 km from KL, 170 km from Butterworth, 83 km from Ipoh. **By air**: connections on Tue, Fri & Sun on Pelangi Air from KL to Sitiawan, 15 mins drive from Lumut (M$63). Also flights from Singapore every Tue, Thur, Sat & Sun (M$195). **By bus**: regular connections from Ipoh (M$4), KL (M$12) and Butterworth (M$8.50). **By taxi**: KL (M$12), Butterworth (M$21), Ipoh (M$6). **By boat**: regular connections to Pulau Pangkor, see below.

Pulau Pangkor

Pangkor is one of the most easily accessible islands in Malaysia. It was on board a British ship anchored off the island that the historic Treaty of Pangkor was signed in 1874, granting the British entry into the Malay states for the first time.

There is old Pangkor with its fishing villages – Sungei Pinang Kecil, Sungei Pinang Besar and Pangkor (main village), and modern Pangkor to the N with a modern luxury hotel. To the SW is the tiny island of Pankgor Laut. The main island is pretty but gets very busy, particularly at weekends and during school holidays, as it is one of the few places on the W coast with good beaches. It is disappointing compared to some of the peninsula's East Coast islands however, and could open up even more to tourists with the new airport at Teluk Dalam beach.

Some of the best beaches and coral can be found on nearby islands – such as **Emerald Bay** on Pangkor Laut. Pangkor Laut has now been taken over by the *Pulau Pangkor Laut Resort* and visitors are charged M$10 each to use the island's facilities. There are some hidden beaches on the main island: N of Pasir Bagak, turtles lay their eggs right on **Teluk Ketapang** beach (mainly during May, June and July); N of this are two of the nicest beaches, **Coral Bay** and **Golden Sands** (Teluk Belanga); others include Marina and Royal bays. Visitors have to pay M$30/day to use the resort beach. Away from Pasir Bogak, the most popular resort, beaches improve considerably. Visitors can also take boats to Pulau Mentagor and Pulau Sembilan.

There are good walks round the island; it takes nearly a day to walk all the way round. There is a South Indian temple, **Sri Pathirakaliaman**, at Sungei Pinang Kecil and the **Foo Lin Kong Temple** at the foot of Sungai Pinang Besar, with a miniature Great Wall of China in the garden. To the S at Teluk Gedan there are ruins of a Dutch fort, **Kota Belanda**. It was built by the Dutch East India Company in 1680 to protect Dutch interests, especially the rich tin traders, from attack by Malay pirates. It was heavily fortified and apparently its cannon could protect the whole Strait of Dinding. The Dutch were forced to leave the fort after an assault by the Malays although they reoccupied it from 1745-1748.

PULAU PANGKOR

IMS 12

0   300
metres

Teluk
Dalam

To
Lumut

Golden
Sands

Coral Bay

Pulau Glani

Sungei Pinang Kecil
Sungei Pinang Besar

To
Lumut

Pulau
Mentagor

Teluk
Ketapang

PANGKOR

Pasir
Bogak

Kota
Belanda

Teluk
Gedong

Emerald
Bay

Pulau
Pangkor
Laut

N

1. Sri Pathirakaliaman Temple
2. Foo Lun Kong Temple

Accommodation

Most accommodation is in Pasir Bogak and can be reached from Kelang Pangkor by taxi. **A+-A** *Pan Pacific Resort*, T 951091, a/c, restaurant, pool, golf course. **Pulau Pangkor Laut: A** *Pangkor Laut Resorts*, T (05) 951973/951375, F (05) 951320 (also bookable through KL office, T (03) 2423300, F (03) 2418562 or through British rep office (Maidenhead, Berks), T (0628) 773300, F (0628) 21033), a/c, restaurant, pool, Malay-style pile houses, magnificent setting offering luxurious accommodation in private villas, either built on stilts out over the sea, set on a jungled hillside overlooking the beach or on the beach itself – similar facilities at *Royal Bay* (newly opened Jul 1993) and at *Coral Bay* (closed indefinitely for refurbishing in Jun 1993), watersports and full range of facilities at both resorts, rec. **Pasir Bogak: B-C** *Beach Hotel*, T 939159; **B** *Beach Huts*, T 951159, a/c, restaurant, watersports; **B** *Seaview*,

T 951605, a/c, restaurant, watersports. **Golden Sands (Teluk Belanga): D-E** *Government Resthouse*, T 951236; **D** *Khoo's Minicamp*, T 951164, restaurant, chalet and dorm both E; **F** *Pangkor Anchor*, T 951363, restaurant, clean and well run, rec; **E** *Pangkor New Rest House*, friendly, rec.

Restaurants Most hotels have their own restaurants. Seafood is always on the menu. **Chinese:** ♦♦*Guan Guan*, Pangkor town; ♦♦*Fook Heng*, Pangkor town; ♦♦*Wah Mooi*, Sungei Pinang Kecil, steamed carp rec by locals. **Seafood:** ♦♦♦*Pansea*, Pangkor Laut, Malay-style wooden restaurant on the beach, local and western. **Stalls:** beach side stalls at Pasir Bogak.

Local transport Buses/taxis: there are taxis from Pangkor town to accommodation at Pasir Bogak (M$3) as well as island buses every half hour. **Motorbikes/bicycles:** it is possible to hire motorbikes from Pangkor village for M$20/day. There is only one road around the island, of which some stretches are only suitable for motorbikes. **Boats:** there are inter-island ferries or it is possible to hire fishing boats from the main villages. Large hotels will organize trips to the islands.

Sports Golf: *Pangkor Island Country Club*, Golden Sands. 9-hole, on the coast; green fees: M$20.

Banks & money changers Large hotels will change money and there's a bank in Pangkor village.

Transport to & from Pulau Pangkor 90 km SW of Ipoh. **By air:** in 1991 work started on the construction of a small airport at Kampung Teluk Dalam; direct flights between KL, Penang, Johor Bahru and Singapore will be operating by 1993. **By boat:** ferries leave from Lumut jetty. Connections every 15 minutes to Pangkor jetty (M$1), and regular connections with *Pan Pacific Resort* jetty close to Golden Sands (M$4 return), and Pangkor Laut (M$6 return). The first boat to Pangkor is at 0645 and the last at 1930. From Pangkor, the first boat leaves at 0645 and the last 1830.

Taiping

Taiping, with a backdrop of the Bintang Mountains, is the capital of Perak and one of the oldest towns in Malaysia. Around 1840, Chinese immigrants started mining tin in the area, and the town, as its name suggests, is predominantly Chinese. In the 1860s and 70s the Larut district of Taiping – then known as Kelian Pauh – was the scene of the 'Perak War', caused by bloody feuding between two rival Chinese secret societies – the Hai San and Ghee Hin – over rights to the rich tin deposits. The fighting between these Hakka and Hokkien groups resulted in British armed intervention and when it subsided, the town was renamed *thai-peng* – or 'everlasting peace'. It is the only big Malaysian town with a Chinese name.

In the *Straits Times* in 1933, colonial administrator G L Peet wrote: "What a pleasant town Taiping is! I first saw it some years ago on a rainy, cool evening, when the air was laden with the scent of flowering angsana trees and golden light bathed the slopes of the *ijau* [green] range. Taiping... has the feeling of being lived in for a long time. It was a thriving and well-appointed town when Ipoh was still a Chinese village, when Seremban was in the same state and when Kuala Lumpur was just beginning to take on some semblance of permanence and solidity."

The Japanese built a prison in Taiping during the war (next to the Lake Garden), which was then converted into a rehabilitation centre for captured Communist Terrorists during the Emergency. Some of the executions carried out under Malaysia's draconian drugs legislation now take place in Taiping jail (**see page 83**).

Places of interest

As early as 1890 the **Lake Garden** was set up on the site of an abandoned tin mine. It is very lush due to the high rainfall and is the pride of the town (boating facilities and zoo). Built in 1883, the lovely **Perak Museum** (on the Butterworth Road, opposite the prison) is the oldest museum in Malaysia. It contains a collection of ancient weapons, aboriginal implements and archaeological finds. Open: 0930-1700 (Sat-Thur), 0930-1215, 1445-1700 Fri. Near the museum is **All Saints' Church**. Built of wood in 1889, it is the oldest Anglican church in Malaysia. The graveyard contains graves of early settlers and those who died in the Japanese prisoner-of-war camp nearby. The **Ling Nam Temple** on Station Street is worth a visit for the Chinese antiques inside.

Accommodation B *Panarama*, 61-79 Jln Kota, T 834129, a/c, restaurant; **C** *Meridien*, 2 Simpang Rd, T 831133, a/c, restaurant; **C** *Pelangi Inn*, 14 Barrack Rd, T 839335, a/c, restaurant, rec; **C** *Taiping New Rest House*, Taman Tasek, T 822044, a/c, restaurant, rec; **C** *Furama*, 30 Jln Peng Loong, T 821077, a/c, restaurant, rec; **D** *Ann Chuan*, 25 Jln Kota, T 825322, a/c, restaurant; **D** *Lake View*, opposite Lake Gardens Circular Rd, T 822911, a/c, very noisy but cheap and clean; **D** *Nanyung*, 129-131 Jln Market, T 824488, a/c; **D** *Town*, 320 Jln Kota, T 821166, basic; **E** *Merlin*, 73 Jln Pesar, T 825033, restaurant; **E** *Government Rest House*, Jln Residensi (opposite King Edwards School), T 822044, restaurant, rec.

Restaurants Chinese: ♦♦*Government Resthouse Restaurant*, Jln Residensi. **Stalls:** large night market. Satay is one of the city's specialities.

Sport Golf: *The New Club*, Taiping. Green fees: M$20 weekdays, M$40 weekends.

Banks & money changers Bank Bumiputra and UMBC on Jln Kota.

Transport to & from Taiping 304 km N of KL, 88 km from Butterworth. **By train:** station is on Station St. Regular connections with Ipoh (M$7.10), KL (M$23) and Butterworth (M$12). **By bus:** regular connections with Butterworth (M$3), Ipoh (M$3) and KL. For other connections, go to Ipoh and change.

Bukit Larut (Maxwell Hill)

Bukit Larut, formerly known as Maxwell Hill, 12 km from Taiping, is Malaysia's oldest hill station. At an elevation of 1034m it is the wettest place in Malaysia – it receives an average of 5,029 mm of rain a year – and was once a tea plantation. Bukit Larut is a small resort with limited facilities compared to the peninsula's other hill stations. The road up was built by prisoners of war during the Japanese occupation in World War II. It is in such bad repair that it is virtually inaccessible in anything other than a 4-wheel-drive vehicle. On clear days, it is possible to see for miles along the coast.

Accommodation For bungalows it is essential to book in advance, T 886241: **C** *Bukit Larut, Gunung Hijau, Cempaka, Beringin, Cendana, Tempinis* all between the 6th and 7th milestones.

Restaurants Food available at ♦♦♦*Gunung Hijau* or *Bukit Larut guesthouses*. At the bungalows meals can be arranged with the caretaker.

Transport to & from Bukit Larut Land Rovers, from the foot of the hill just above the Lake Gardens in Taiping, operate every hour from 0800-1800 (M$2.50).

Butterworth

An industrial and harbour town and base for the Royal Australian Air Force which is billeted here under the terms of the Five Powers Pact. It is the main port for ferries to Penang Island.

Accommodation Butterworth is not a recommended stopping point – most tourists head straight for Penang. **B** *Travel Lodge*, 1 Lorong Bagan Luar, T 348899, a/c, restaurant; **B** *Berlin*, 4802 Jln Bagan Luar, T 321701, a/c, restaurant; **C** *Ambassadress*, 4425 Jln Bagan Luar, T 342788, a/c, restaurant; **D** *City*, 4591 Jln Chain Ferry, T 340705; **D** *Federal*, 4293-4294 Kampung Bengali, T 341911, restaurant; **D** *Paris*, 4382, 2nd Flr, Jln Bagan Luar, T 346863, a/c.

Banks & money changers UMBC and Maybank on Jln Bagan Luar.

Transport to & from Butterworth 369 km from KL, 386 km from Kota Bahru. Butterworth is the main transport hub for Penang and buses and trains operate into Thailand and down to KL and Singapore. **By train:** the railway station is beside the Penang ferry terminal. Regular connections with Alor Setar (M$12), Taiping (M$12), Ipoh (M$17), KL (M$28) and JB (M$48). **By bus:** bus station next to the ferry terminal. Regular connections with KL (M$15), Taiping (M$3), Melaka (M$26), JB (M$28), Kota Bahru (M$18), Kuala Terengganu (M$22) and Kuantan (M$25). Buses leave every half hour from Butterworth for Kuala Perlis (M$3) (Langkawi ferry). There are also buses to Keroh, on the border with Thailand, from where it is possible to get Thai taxis to Betong. **By taxi:** taxis leave from next to the ferry terminal. If you take a taxi across to Penang you must pay the taxi fare plus M$7 each way for the toll bridge (M$25 total). KL (M$27), Kota Bahru (M$27) and Alor Setar (M$10). **By ferry:** ferry (pedestrian and car) costs M$0.40 return to Georgetown and leaves every 15-20 minutes.

International connections To Singapore By train: M$47. **To Thailand** By train: M$65.70 to Bangkok.

PENANG (Pulau Pinang)

Penang – or more properly, Pulau Pinang – is the northern gateway to Malaysia and is the country's oldest British settlement. It has been sold to generations of tourists as 'the Pearl of the Orient' but in plan Penang looks more like a frog than a pearl. Penang state also includes a strip of land on the mainland opposite, Province Wellesley – named after Colonel Arthur Wellesley, later to become the Duke of Wellington, who went on to defeat Napoleon at Waterloo. (The 738 sq km Province Wellesley is also known by its Malay name, Seberang Perai.) Colonel Wellesley stopped off in Georgetown in 1797. Georgetown's founder, Captain Francis Light, originally christened Penang 'Prince of Wales Island'. In Malay, *pinang* is the word for the areca nut palm, an essential ingredient of betel nut (see page 35). The palm was incorporated into the state crest in the days of the Straits Settlements during the 19th century. Today Pulau Pinang is translated as "betel nut island". Light called Georgetown after George, the Prince of Wales, who later became King George IV as it was acquired on his birthday; most Malaysians know the town by its nickname: *Tanjung*, as it is situated on a sandy headland called Tanjung Penaga.

Penang highlights

Museums and historical sights Fort Cornwallis, on the site of Francis Light's original stockade (see page 137); Penang Museum & Art Gallery, located in Penang's former English public school, founded in 1816 (see page 138); Khoo Kongsi, a magnificent and well-preserved Chinese clan association house (see page 139).

Temples and mosques Goddess of Mercy Temple (Kuan Yin Teng), built by Chinese settlers at the beginning of the 19th century (see page 138); Kek Lok Si (Monastery of Supreme Bliss) which took 20 years to build and is modelled on a monastery in China (see page 141); Snake Temple (Temple of the Azure Cloud), built in 1850 and populated by Pit Vipers (see page 142); Sri Mariamann (Hindu) Temple, built by Georgetown's South Indian community in 1883 (see page 138); Kapitan Kling Mosque, built in 1800 (see page 139); Wat Chayamangkalaram (Wat Buppharam) Thai Buddhist temple with Burmese temple opposite (see page 139).

Other sights Chinatown, one of the liveliest and best-preserved in the region; Clan Piers, a Chinese water village, linked to Pengkalan Weld (Weld Quay) by jetties named after different clans (see page 139); Penang Hill, overlooking Georgetown, with a funicular railway to the top (see page 140); Butterfly Farm, claiming to be the largest tropical butterfly farm in the world, with more than 120 Malaysian species (see page 147).

Beaches Batu Feringghi, the most famous beach in Malaysia, now a hotel strip (see page 146); Muka Head, on the NW tip of the island, with a series of secluded coves around a rocky headland (see page 147).

Shopping Antiques, basketware, handicrafts and batik (see page 148).

Sports Golf, swimming, watersports and sailing – including yacht cruises around the islands of the Langkawi group (see page 148).

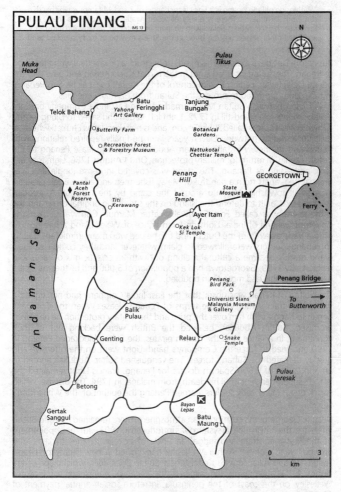

Before the arrival of Francis Light, who captained a ship for a British trading company, in 1786, Penang was ruled by the Sultan of Kedah. The sultanate had suffered repeated invasions by the Thais from the N and *Orang Bugis* pirates from the sea. Sultan Muhammad Jawa Mu'Azzam Shah II was also beset by a seccession crisis and when this turned into a civil war he requested help from Francis Light, then based at Acheen in Sumatra, whom he met in 1771. Light was in search of a trading base on the N shore of the Strait of Melaka which could be used by his firm, Jordain, Sulivan and De Souza, and the British East India Company. In 1771, Light sent a letter to one of his bosses, De Souza, in which he first described Penang's advantages:

> *"Withinside of Pulo Pinang is a fine clear channel of 7 and 14 fathoms which a ship can work anytime. ... There is plenty of wood, water and provisions there, (the European ships) may be supplied with tin, pepper, beetelnut, rattans and birdsnests, and ... all other vessels passing through the Straits may be as easily supplied as at Malacca."*

But before De Souza made up his mind, Light struck a private deal with the Sultan of Kedah. The Sultan installed Light in the fort at Kuala Kedah and gave him the title of Deva Rajah, ceding to him control of the Kedah coast as far S as Penang. In turn, Light promised to protect the Sultan from his many enemies.

A frisson between Sultan Muhammad and the East India Company brought developments to a standstill in 1772. Light left Kedah and sailed to Ujung Salang (which English sailors called Junk Ceylon, and is now known as Phuket) where he built up a trading network. Eleven years later he finally repaired relations with Kedah and the newly installed Sultan Abdullah agreed to lease Penang to the British – again, in return for military protection. On 11 August 1786, Light formally took possession of Penang. The island was covered in dense jungle and was uninhabited, apart from a handful of Malay fishermen and a few Bugis pirates.

A small township grew up around the camp by the harbour. A wooden stockade was built to defend the island on the site of the original camp and the cantonment was called Fort Cornwallis, after Marquis Cornwallis, then the Governor-General of India. Light declared Prince of Wales Island a free port to attract trade away from the Dutch, and this helped woo many immigrant traders to Penang. Settlers were allowed to claim whatever land they could clear. The island quickly became a cultural melting pot with an eclectic mix of races and religions. By 1789, Georgetown had a population of 5,000 and by the end of the next decade, this had more than doubled.

The Sultan of Kedah was upset that the East India Company had not signed a written contract setting out the terms of Penang's lease. When the Company began to haggle with him over the price and the military protection he had been promised, Sultan Abdullah believed the British were backing out of their agreement. In alliance with the Illanun pirates, the Sultan blockaded Penang in 1790 and tried to force the Company's hand. Light went on the offensive and quickly defeated the Sultan's forces. The vanquished Sultan Abdullah agreed to an annual fee of 6,000 Spanish dollars for Penang. Francis Light remained the island's superintendent until his death, from malaria, in 1794. The disease, which struck down many early settlers, earned Penang the epithet of 'the White Man's Grave'.

Despite Georgetown's cosmopolitan atmosphere, there remained a strong British influence: the British judicial system was introduced in 1801 with the appointment of the first magistrate and judge, an uncle of novelist Charles Dickens. The previous year, Colonel Arthur Wellesley had signed a new Treaty of Peace, Friendship and Alliance with Kedah's new Sultan Diyauddin, which superceded Light's 1791 agreement and allowed for Penang's annexation of Province Wellesley, on the coast of the peninsula, in return for an annual payment of 10,000 Spanish dollars.

In 1805 Penang's colonial status was raised to that of a Residency. A young administrative secretary, Stamford Raffles, arrived to work for the governor. Georgetown became the capital of the newly established Straits Settlements, which included Melaka and Singapore (**see page 64**). But the glory was shortlived. With the rise of Singapore, following Raffles' founding of the settlement in 1819, Georgetown was quickly eclipsed by the upstart at the southern tip of the peninsula and by the 1830s had been reduced to a colonial backwater. From an architectural perspective, this proved a saving grace: unlike Singapore, Penang retains many of its original colonial buildings and its rich cultural heritage.

In the early 19th century Penang was used as a staging post for the opium trade between India and China. The East India Company auctioned off licences to gambling dens, brothels and opium traders – the latter accounted for about 60% of colonial Penang's revenue. Vice gangs carved out territories for themselves in Georgetown and secret society feuds finally erupted on the streets in the Penang Riots of 1876. The nine days of fighting started when a member of the White Flag society (a Malay gang) threw a rambutan skin at a Toh-Peh-Kong society member whom he caught peering through his front door. Open warfare ensued and bullet holes can still be seen in the walls of the shophouses in Cannon Square. The riots were finally put down when troop reinforcements arrived from Singapore. The societies were fined M$5,000 each, which funded the construction of four new police stations in the different parts of town where the societies operated.

Colonial Penang prospered, through tin booms and rubber booms, until the outbreak of World War II. When the Japanese raced down the peninsula on stolen bicycles, Penang was cut off, without being formally taken. The British residents were evacuated to Singapore within days, leaving the undefended island in the hands of a "State Committee", which, after three days, put down the riots which followed the British withdrawal. The Japanese administration lasted from December 1941 to July 1945; remarkably, Georgetown's buildings were virtually unscathed, despite Allied bombing attacks.

Penang now has a population of 1.2 million, 53% of which is Chinese, 35% Malay and 11% Indian.

Georgetown, the capital of Penang state, is on the NE point of the island, nearest the mainland; Bayan Lepas Airport is on the SE tip. The 13 km-long Penang Bridge, linking the island to Butterworth, is half way down the E coast, just S of Georgetown. Batu Ferringghi, now a strip of luxury hotels, is Penang's most famous beach and is on the N coast. A handful of small secluded coves with good beaches remain on the NW tip. The W of the island is a mixture of jungled hills, rubber plantations and a few fishing kampungs. There are more beaches and fishing villages on the S coast. A short steep mountain range forms a central spine, which includes Penang Hill, overlooking Georgetown, at 850m above sea level.

Georgetown

The first 4 streets of Georgetown – Beach (now known as Lebuh Pantai), Lebuh Light, Jalan Kapitan Kling Mosque (previously Jalan Pitt) and Lubuh Chulia – still form the main thoroughfares of modern Georgetown. Lebuh Chulia was formerly the Cantonese heartland of the Ghee Hin triad, one of the secret societies involved in the 1867 Penang Riots. The older part of town to the W of Weld Quay, in the shadow of Kapitan Kling Mosque, is predominantly Indian.

Georgetown is, however, mainly Chinese; the main Chinatown area is contained by Jalan Kapitan Kling Mosque, Lebuh Chulia, Jalan Penang and Jalan Magazine. The shophouses were built by craftsmen from China: the rituals, burial customs, clan associations, temples and restaurants make up a self-contained Chinese community. Despite the traffic and a skyline pierced by the KOMTAR (Kompleks Tun Abdul Razak) skyscraper, the crowded streets still have plenty of charm. Penang's Chinatown is one of the liveliest in Malaysia; its atmosphere and most of its original architecture remain intact.

The same cannot be said for the rest of the island, pollution and litter have spoiled parts of Penang in recent years. Beaches have became dirtier, the sea filthier and monsoon drains in Georgetown, clogged with stinking rubbish. In Apr 1991 Prime Minister Dr Mahathir Mohamad referred to Penang as "the dustbin of the Orient". This embarrassed the state government into pulling their socks up in an effort to

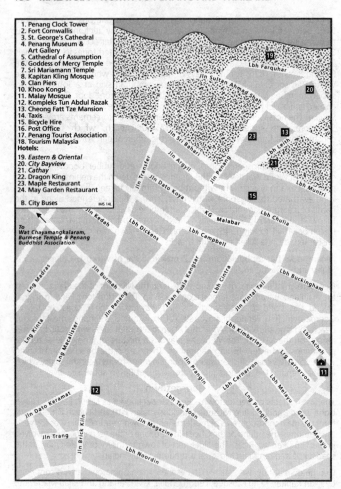

1. Penang Clock Tower
2. Fort Cornwallis
3. St. George's Cathedral
4. Penang Museum & Art Gallery
5. Cathedral of Assumption
6. Goddess of Mercy Temple
7. Sri Mariamann Temple
8. Kapitan Kling Mosque
9. Clan Piers
10. Khoo Kongsi
11. Malay Mosque
12. Kompleks Tun Abdul Razak
13. Cheong Fatt Tze Mansion
14. Taxis
15. Bicycle Hire
16. Post Office
17. Penang Tourist Association
18. Tourism Malaysia

Hotels:

19. Eastern & Oriental
20. City Bayview
21. Cathay
22. Dragon King
23. Maple Restaurant
24. May Garden Restaurant

B. City Buses

IMS 14L

To
Wat Chayamangkalaram,
Burmese Temple & Penang
Buddhist Association

clean the place up. The effect in Georgetown has been noticeable, and on Batu Feringghi, many beach-front hotels have gone to great lengths to keep the beach in pristine condition. The coral which used to line the shore at Batu Feringghi has all gone, mainly due to the silt washed around the headland during the construction of the Penang Bridge. But the sea is not as dirty as in some of the region's other big resorts, as testified by the presence of otters on the beach at Batu Feringghi in the early morning.

Places of interest

NB: street names in Georgetown are confusing as many are now being rechristened with Malay names; streets are known by both their Malay and

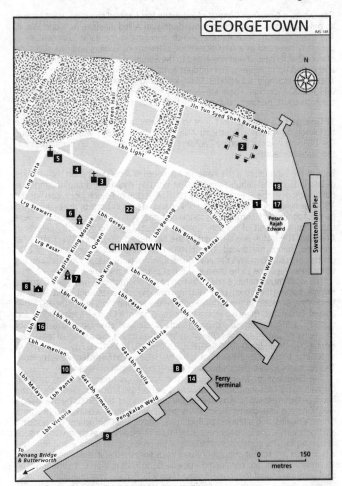

English names (eg Jalan Penang/Penang Road – not to be muddled with Lebuh Penang/Penang Street). Of particular note: Lebuh Pitt (Pitt Street) has been renamed Jalan Kapitan Kling Mosque; Beach Street is now Lebuh Pantai.

The **Penang Clock Tower**, at the junction of Lebuh Light and Lebuh Pantai, was presented to Georgetown by a Chinese millionaire, Chen Eok, in 1897 during Queen Victoria's Diamond Jubilee celebrations. The tower is 60 ft (20m) tall – one foot for every year she had been on the throne.

Fort Cornwallis is opposite the clock tower, on the N tip of the island. It stands on the site of Francis Light's wooden stockade and was built by convict labour between 1808 and 1810; only its outer walls remain. Named after Marquis

Cornwallis, a Governor-General of India, the fort has had an insignificant history. Its only taste of military action came during an Allied air-strike in World War II. The main cannon, *Serai Rambai*, which was cast in the early 17th century, is popularly regarded as a fertility symbol; offerings of flowers and joss sticks are often left at its base. It was presented to the Sultan of Johor by the Dutch in 1606 and ended up in Penang. The modern amphitheatre hosts concerts and shows. There is an example of a wooden Malay kampung house near the entrance. Open: 0830-1800 Mon-Sun. There are many colonial buildings on Lebuh Farquhar like the high court, mariners' club and the town hall.

St George's Cathedral, next door to the museum on Lebuh Farquhar, was the first Anglican church in Southeast Asia. It was built in 1817 with convict labour. The building was designed by Captain Robert Smith (some of his paintings are in the State Museum).

Behind the high court is the **Penang Museum & Art Gallery**, on the junction of Lebuh Light and Lebuh Farquhar. The building was the first English language public school in the E, established in 1816. A statue of Francis Light, cast for the 150th anniversary of the founding of Penang, stands in front of the building. As no photograph of Georgetown's founding father was available, his features were cast from a portrait of his son, Colonel William Light, founder of Adelaide in Australia. The statue was removed by the Japanese during World War II and later returned, minus the sword. The museum contains another sculpture: a 19th century bust of Germany's Kaiser Wilhelm II, which turned up in Wellesley primary school. How it came to be there in the first place is a mystery.

The small museum has a fine collection of old photographs, maps and historical records charting the growth of Penang from the days of Francis Light. There are some fascinating accounts in the History Room of the Penang Riots in August 1876 (see above). Downstairs there is a replica of the main hall of a Chinese trader's home and upstairs, a Straits Chinese exhibition with a marriage chamber and a room of traditional ornamental gowns. The art gallery, also upstairs, has a series of temporary exhibitions. Open: 0900-1700 Sat-Thur, 0900-1215, 1445-1700 Fri.

Nearby, also on Lebuh Farquhar, is the twin-spired **Cathedral of Assumption**. This Roman Catholic church houses the only pipe-organ in Penang.

The **Goddess of Mercy Temple** (also known as Kuan Yin Teng) on Jalan Captain Kling Mosque/Lorong Steward is a short walk from St George's, in the heart of Georgetown. It was built at the beginning of the 1800s by the island's early Chinese immigrants. Kuan Yin is probably the most-worshipped of all the Chinese deities, and is revered by Buddhists, Taoists and Confucians. The goddess is a Bodhisattva, one who rejected entry into nirvana as long as there was injustice in the world. The goddess is associated with peace, good fortune and fertility – which accounts for her popularity. Kuan Yin is portrayed as a serene goddess with 18 arms – 2 arms are considered inadequate to rid the world of suffering. The roof-tops are carved to represent waves, on which stand two guardian dragons. Shops in the area sell temple-related goods: lanterns, provisions for the after life (such as paper Mercedes'), joss sticks and figurines.

Although Georgetown is mainly Chinese, it has always had a large population of Indians, living in the city centre. The Hindu **Sri Mariamann Temple**, on Lebuh Queen/Lebuh Chulia, was built in 1883. It is richly decorated and dedicated to the Hindu god Lord Subramaniam. The main statue is strung with gold, silver, diamond and emerald jewellery. It is normally used to lead a chariot procession to the Waterfall Temple during Thaipusam (see page 354). The symbols of the 9 planets and the signs of the zodiac are carved into the ceiling. The surrounding area is largely Indian, with money changers and jewellery shops, as well as restaurants and tea-stalls.

There is also a Muslim community in Georgetown and the Indo-Moorish **Kapitan Kling Mosque** (on Jalan Kapitan Kling Mosque) was built by the island's first Indian Muslim settlers around 1800. It was named after the 'kapitan' or headman of the Kling – the South Indian community. As a sight it is rather disappointing.

Straight down Lebuh Chulia is the Chinese water village off Pengkalan Weld. The entrance is through the temple on the quayside. It is known as the **Clan Piers**, as each of the jetties is named after a different Chinese clan. None of the families pays tax as they are not living on land. Rows of junks belonging to the resident traders are moored at the end of the piers.

Khoo Kongsi (on Jalan Aceh, off Lebuh Pitt), is approached through an archway to Cannon Square, and is one of the most interesting sights in Georgetown. A *kongsi* is a Chinese clan house which doubles as a temple and a meeting place. Clan institutions originated in China as associations for people with the same surname. Today they are benevolent organizations which look after the welfare of clan members and safeguard ancestral shrines. Most of the kongsis in Penang were established in the 19th century when clashes between rival clans were commonplace.

The Khoo Kongsi is the most lavishly decorated of the kongsis in Penang, with its ornate Dragon Mountain Hall. It was built at the end of the 19th century by the descendents of Hokkien-born Khoo Chian Eng. A fire broke out in it the day it was completed in 1898, destroying its roof. It was rebuilt by craftsmen from China and was renovated in the 1950s; the present tiled roof is said to weigh 25 tonnes. The kongsi contains many fine pieces of Chinese art and sculpture, including 2 huge carved stone guardians which ensure the wealth, longevity and happiness of all who came under the protection of the kongsi. The interior hall houses an image of Tua Sai Yeah, the Khoo clan's patron saint, who was a general during the Ch'in Dynasty in the 2nd century BC. Admission: pass from adjoining office. Open: 0900-1700 Mon-Fri, 0900-1300 Sat.

There are other kongsis in Georgetown, although none is as impressive as the Khoo Kongsi. The Chung Keng Kwee Kongsi is on Lebuh Gereja and the Tua Peh Kong Kongsi on Lebuh Armenian. The Khaw Kongsi and the modern Lee Kongsi are both on Jalan Burmah; Yap Kongsi on Lebuh Armenian and the combined kongsi of the Chuah, Sin and Quah clans at the junction of Jalan Burmah and Codrington Avenue. Every kongsi has ancestral tablets as well as a hall of fame to honour its 'sons' or clansmen who have achieved fame in various spheres of life. Today women are honoured in these halls of fame too.

Near the Khoo Kongsi, on Jalan Aceh, is the **Malay Mosque**. Its most noteworthy feature is the Egyptian-style minaret – most in Malaysia are Moorish. In the past it was better known as the meeting place for the notorious White Flag Malays, who sided with the Hokkien Chinese in street battles against the Cantonese (Red Flags) in the Penang Riots of 1867. The hole halfway up the minaret is said to have been made by a cannonball fired from Khoo Kongsi during the clan riots. The mosque is one of the oldest buildings in Georgetown, built in 1808.

Apart from the M\$850 million **Penang Bridge** (which, at 13.5 km is the longest bridge in Asia and the third longest in the world) and several new hotels, one of the few visible architectural monuments of the 20th century is **Kompleks Tun Abdul Razak** (KOMTAR) on Jalan Penang. This cylindrical skyscraper, which houses the state government offices and a shopping centre, dominates Georgetown. There are spectacular views of the island and across the straits to the mainland from the 59th floor.

Outside the town centre on Jalan Burmah is **Wat Chayamangkalaram** (also known as Wat Buppharam), the largest Thai temple in Penang. It houses a

32m-long reclining Buddha, Pra Chaiya Mongkol. There is a 9-storey pagoda behind the temple. The Thais and the Burmese practice Theravada Buddhism as opposed to the Mahayana school of the Chinese. Queen Victoria gave this site to Penang's Thai community in 1845. Opposite Wat Chayamangkalaram is Penang's only **Burmese temple**. It has ornate carvings and two huge white stone elephants at its gates. The original 1805 pagoda (to the right of the entrance) has been enshrined in a more modern structure. **Getting there**: city bus 2 (M$0.50) from Lebuh Victoria terminal.

The **Penang Buddhist Association**, Jalan Burmah (near the Shell garage), is more like an Art-Deco mansion than a typical Malaysian Chinese temple. The Buddha statues are carved from Carrara marble from Italy, the glass chandeliers were made in what was Czechoslovakia and there are paintings depicting the many stages of the Buddha's path to enlightenment. **Getting there**: city bus 2 (M$0.50) from Lebuh Victoria terminal.

Other places of interest in and around Georgetown

Cheong Fatt Tze Mansion, on Lebuh Leith, is now a state monument – albeit in a dilapidated condition. Built by Thio Thiaw Siat, a Kwangtung (Guandong) businessman who imported craftsmen from China, this stately home is one of only three surviving Chinese mansions in this style – the others are in Manila and Medan. It is privately owned and is not open to the public but still worth marvelling at from the outside.

Jalan Sultan Ahmed Shah (previously North Road Mansions) became known as millionaires' row as it was home to many wealthy rubber planters in the wake of the boom of 1911-20. Many of the palatial mansions were built by Straits Chinese in a sort of colonial baroque style, complete with turrets and castellations. Many of them have now gone to seed as they are too expensive to keep up; a few have been lavishly done up by today's generation of rich Chinese businessmen. The largest houses, are the Yeap family mansion, known as the White House, and the Sultan of Kedah's palace.

Excursions

Around the Island

From Georgetown, the round-the-island trip is a 70 km circuit. It is recommended as a day-trip as there is little or no accommodation available outside Georgetown apart from the N coast beaches.

Batu Feringghi and **Teluk Bahang**: see page 146.

The **Nattukotai Chettiar Temple**, on Waterfall Road, was built by members of the Indian Chettiar money-lending fraternity, and is the biggest Hindu temple on the island. It is a centre of pilgrimage during the Thaipusam festival (see page 354). **Getting there**: city bus 7 from Lebuh Victoria terminal; get off at the stop before the Botanical Gardens (M$0.60).

The **Botanical Gardens**, also on Waterfall Road, are situated in a valley surrounded by hills. The gardens are well landscaped and contain many indigenous and exotic plant species. They were established in 1844. The more interesting plants are kept under lock and key and are open to visitors 0900-1700 Mon-Fri. A path leads from the Gardens' Moon Gate up Penang Hill; the 8 km hike takes about 1½ hrs. Open: daylight hours Mon-Sun. **Getting there**: city bus 7 from Lebuh Victoria terminal (M$0.60).

Penang Hill A short distance from Kek Lok Si is the funicular railway, which started operating in 1922. It climbs 850m up Penang Hill (M$3 return); leaves every half hour 0630-2330. (A vintage steam engine is on display at the Penang

Museum.) The railway was originally completed in 1899, but on its inauguration by the governor, it didn't work and had to be dismantled. Penang Hill is about 5°C cooler than Georgetown and was a favoured expatriate refuge before the advent of air-conditioning. The ridge on top of Penang Hill is known as Strawberry Hill after Francis Light's strawberry patch. On a clear day it is possible to see the mountains of Langkawi and N Kedah from the top.

Bel Retiro, designed as a get-away for the governor, was the first bungalow to be built on the hill. There is a small hotel, some pleasant gardens, a temple, a mosque and a post office and police station on the top. There are also a few restaurants and a small hawker centre. The hill gets very crowded on weekends and public holidays. A well marked 8 km path leads down to the Moon Gate at the Botanical Gardens (about an hour's walk) from behind the post office. **Getting there**: city bus 1 (from Lebuh Victoria terminal) then change to 8 to the railway (M$1).

State Mosque, Jalan Air Itam/Jalan Masjid Negeri, is the largest and newest mosque in Penang and can accommodate 5,000. It was designed by a Filipino architect. Good views from the top of the 57m-high minaret. **Getting there**: city bus 1 from Lebuh Victoria terminal (M$0.60).

Bat Temple at Ayer Itam, is a sanctuary for fruit bats, which hang from the cave roof. The sacred bats are protected by Buddhist monks who guard them zealously. About 60 years ago the wealthy Madam Lim Chooi Yuen, built the bat temple to protect the bats. **Getting there**: city bus 1 from Lebuh Victoria terminal (M$0.60).

Ayer Itam Dam is a pleasant place to relax just above the town. There are several trails around the lake, originally shortcuts to other parts of the island. **Getting there**: city bus 1 (from Lebuh Victoria terminal) then change to 8 (M$1).

Kek Lok Si Temple (or Monastery of Supreme Bliss), S of Ayer Itam, can be seen from some distance away. It took Burmese, Chinese and Thai artisans, who were shipped in specially, 2 decades to build it. The abbot of the Goddess of Mercy Temple on Lebuh Pitt came from China in 1885 and the landscape around Ayer Itam reminded him of his homeland. He collected money from rich Chinese merchants to fund the construction of the huge temple, modelled on Fok San Monastery in Fuchow, China. On the way up the 'ascending plane' is a turtle pond (turtles are a symbol of eternity).

The temple sprawls across 12 ha and is divided into 3 main sections: the Hall of Bodhisattvas, the Hall of Devas and the sacred Hall of the Buddha. The 7-tier pagoda – or Ban Po, the Pagoda of a Thousand Buddhas – is built in three different styles: the lower follows a Chinese design honouring the Goddess of Mercy, Kuan Yin; the middle is Thai-Buddhist and commemorates to Bee Lay Hood (the Laughing Buddha) and the upper Burmese levels are dedicated to the Gautama or historic Buddha with thousands of gilded statues. The topmost tier contains a relic of the Buddha, a statue of pure gold and other treasures, but it is closed to visitors. Admission: voluntary contribution to climb the 30m-high tower. **Getting there**: city bus 1 (from Lebuh Victoria terminal), then change to 8 (M$0.60).

Penang Bird Park, on Jalan Todak, Seberang Jaya (near the Penang Bridge), includes a huge walk-in aviary. Admission: M$3. Open: 1000-1900 Mon-Wed & Thur, 0900-1900 Fri-Sun. **Getting there**: yellow bus 66 from Pengkalan Weld (Weld Quay) (M$0.60).

Universiti Sians Malaysia Museum and Gallery is at Minden (near the Penang Bridge interchange). It has a large ethnographic and performing arts sections with a special exhibition on *wayang kulit* (shadow puppets – **see page 78**). There is also an art gallery with works by Malaysian artists and visiting temporary exhibitions. Open: 0900-1700 Mon-Sun. **Getting there**: yellow bus 66 from Pengkalan Weld (Weld Quay) (M$0.60).

Snake Temple (also known as Temple of the Azure Cloud), was built in 1850 at Bayan Lepas. Snakes were kept in the temple as they were believed to be the disciples of the deity Chor Soo Kong, to whom the temple is dedicated. Nowadays the reptilian disciples (almost exclusively Wagler's pit vipers) are a bit thin on the ground. The number of snakes in the temple varies from day to day – there are usually more around during festivals. The incense smoke keeps them in a drugged stupor, and most of them have had their fangs extracted. **Getting there**: yellow bus 66 from Pengkalan Weld (Weld Quay) (M$0.90).

Batu Maung A Chinese fishing village, near Bayan Lepas, is known for its 'floating' seafood restaurant, built out over the water. **Getting there**: yellow bus 69 (M$0.90). Around the S coast, there are a few beaches and a couple of unremarkable fishing kampungs. The southern beaches are more secluded than the ones along the N coast; the drawbacks are the absence of accommodation and the litter. Veering N towards the centre of the island, however, beyond Barat, is **Balik Pulau**, a good *makan* stop with a number of restaurants and cafés. Around the town, which is known as the "Durian capital" of Penang, there are a number of picturesque Malay kampungs. Further up the W side of the island is the **Pantai Aceh Forest Reserve**, which also has well marked trails into the jungle and to the bays further round, eg Pantai Keracut (1 hr). After the Pantai Aceh junction, and on up a twisting, forested section of road, there is a waterfall with a pleasant pool, suitable for swimming, just off the road (20th milestone) called **Titi Kerawang**. **Getting there**: yellow buses 11 or 66 go from Pengkalan Weld (Weld Quay) or Jalan Maxwell in Georgetown to the S of the island. Change at Balik Pulau to bus 76 for Teluk Bahang. From there blue bus 93 to Georgetown. Longer fare stages are M$0.60-M$1.50. As the island buses are infrequent, it is advisable to check departure times at each place to avoid being stranded. It is much easier to explore the kampungs and beaches around the S and W coasts – most of which are off the main road – if you have private transport. Most of them are off the main road.

Tours The three main tours offered by companies are: the city tour, the Penang Hill and temple tour and the round-the-island tour. All cost M$20-30 and most run every hour.

Festivals May: *Penang Bridge Run*; open to all visitors (end of May). *Penang International Dragon Boat Race*, near Penang Bridge; teams compete from around the region and beyond. June (end): *International Beach Volleyball Championship*; held on Kital Beach, Bath Feringghi, next to *Bayview Beach Hotel*. July: *Penang on Parade*, with three major annual events; details from Tourist Information Centre. *Equestrian*: Royal Malayan Polo Association international championship; competing for Sultan Ahmad Shah Trophy; also race meeting at Penang Turf Club and dressage and showjumping events. *Floral Festival* at Komtar Hall. *City parades* by Malays (at Fort Cornwallis), Chinese (at Khoo Kongsi) and Indians (at Market Street).

Accommodation In Georgetown, most upmarket hotels are concentrated in the Jln Penang area. Most of the cheaper hotels are around Lebuh Chulia and Lebuh Leith. **A+-A** *Eastern & Oriental (E&O)*, 10 Farquhar St, T 375322, a/c, restaurant, pool, built in 1885 by the Armenian Sarkies brothers, who operated Singapore's *Raffles Hotel* (**see page 397**) and the *Strand Hotel* in Rangoon. Noel Coward and Somerset Maugham figured on former guest lists. The swimming pool terrace, on the sea wall, decorated with old cannons, makes for a cool and pleasant evening 'stenggah'. Suites are furnished and decorated with the opulent trappings of empire... but today the hotel lacks charisma and character; **A** *City Bay View Hotel*, 25a Lebuh Farquhar, T 633161, a/c, restaurant, pool, revolving restaurant and bar on 15th Flr; **A** *Equatorial International*, 1 Bukit Jambal, T 838111, a/c, restaurant, between the airport and town, on a hill with a view over the Penang Bridge, mostly used by visiting business people as it is conveniently located for Penang's duty-free industrial zone, which lies between it and the airport; **A** *Merlin Penang*, 3 Jln Larut, T 376166, a/c, restaurant, pool, good central location; **A** *Shangri-La*, Jln Magazine, T 622622, a/c, restaurant, pool, mostly used by business people rather than tourists, next to KOMTAR; **A-B** *Malaysia*, 7 Jln Penang, T 363311, a/c, restaurant, high-rise hotel, plush decor with good range of facilities; **A-B** *Merchant*, 55 Jln Penang, T 632828, F 625511, a/c, restaurant, handsomely decorated; **B** *Ambassador*, 55 Jln Penang, T 364101, a/c, restaurant; **B** *Bellevue*, Penang Hill, T 699500, a/c, restaurant, colonial-style house, cool retreat up on the hill; **B** *Central*, 404 Jln Penang, T 366411, a/c, restaurant; **B** *Continental*, 5 Jln Penang, T 636388, F 04638718, a/c, restaurant, not great value for money; **B** *Garden Inn*, 42 Jln Anson, T 363655, a/c, restaurant, good hawker centre on the doorstep; **B** *Ming Court Penang*, 202a Lorong Macalister, T 368588, a/c, restaurant, pool; **B** *Mingood*, 164 Argyle Rd, T 373375, a/c, restaurant, not good value for money; **B** *Oriental*, 105 Jln Penang, T 634211/6, a/c, restaurant, smartly decorated, big rooms and good value, rec; **B** *Town House Hotel*, 70 Jln Penang, T 368722, a/c, restaurant.

B-C *Embassy*, 12 Jln Burmah, T 23145, a/c, restaurant, rec by travellers; **C** *Cathay*, 15 Lebuh Leith, T 626273, a/c, restaurant, large old Chinese house, great atmosphere, scrupulously maintained and friendly management, organizes minibuses to Hat Yai and Phuket (Thailand), rec; **C** *Federal*, Jln Penang, T 634170, good location, near some excellent restaurants, recently revamped; **C** *Joyplanet*, 26 Kuala Kangsar Rd, T 619043, clean and friendly, front rooms are noisy, dorm (F); **C** *Metropole*, 46 Jln Sultan Ahmad Shah, T 364471, a/c, away from the centre of town in an eccentric building; **C** *Paramount*, 48F Jln Sultan Ahmad Shah, T 363649, a/c, restaurant, big rooms in run-down colonial house, right on the sea, but not central; **C** *YMCA*, 211 Lorong Macalister, T 372211, a/c; **D** *Eung Aun*, 380 Lebuh Chulia, T 612333, fan, restaurant, old house set back from the road, basic but popular; **D** *Lum Thean*, 422 Lebuh Chulia, T 614117, restaurant, a/c, Chinese nationalist General Chiang Kai Shek once took refuge here, average Chinese-run hotel; **D** *New Asia*, 111 Rope Walk, a/c, bar, family run, rec; **D** *New China*, 22 Lebuh Leith, T 631601, large old house set back from the road, one of the nicer budget hotels, management helpful for those having trouble procuring Thai visas; **D** *Singapore*, 495h Jln Penang, T 620323, a/c, basic, next to KOMTAR; **D** *Tiong Wah*, 23 Love Lane, T 622057, reasonable value – better than most on Lebuh Chulia in a less frenetic corner of town, shared bathrooms; **D-E** *Plaza Hostel*, 32 Ah Quee St, T 630560, very popular, cheap hotel, recommended by correspondent as clean and friendly (rooms and dorm), ticketing service; **E** *Chung King*, 398 Lebuh Chulia, T 617607, basic; **E** *Hang Cheow*, Lebuh Chulia, T 610810, restaurant, rec by travellers; **E** *Swiss*, 431F Lebuh Chulia, T 720133, a better bet than some of the others in this area, but unhelpful management; **E** *Tye Ann*, 282 Lebuh Chulia, T 614875, clean but small rooms, hotel staff will help organize Thai visas; **E** *Wan Hai*, 35 Love Lane, T 616853, restaurant, run-of-the-mill budget hotel, motorcycles for hire, visa applications for Thailand and bus tickets to Thailand organized, dorm (F); **E** *Yeng Keng*, 362 Lebuh Chulia, T 610610, central but basic, good-sized rooms but hotel is very run down. **Bayan Lepas A** *Samad's Guest House*, Glugor, Balik Pulau, Bayan Lepas, restaurant, vehicle hire.

Restaurants Penang's specialities include *assam laksa* (a hot-and-sour fish soup), *nasi kandar* (a curry), *mee yoke* (prawns in chilli-noodle soup) and *inche kabin* (chicken marinated in spices and then fried).

Malay Best Malay food is from the stalls: ♦♦*Minah*, Gelugar (on the way to the airport), home-style cooking; ♦♦♦*Eliza*, 14th Flr, *City Bayview Hotel*, 25a Gurong Farquhar, sumptuous Malay menu eaten in traditional style, seated on pandan mats. Good views over the town and coast. ♦*Spice Café*, 55 Jln Penang (next to *Merchant Hotel*), excellent choice of local food, with Malay, Chinese, Thai and some international.

Chinese: ♦♦*Ang Hoay Loh*, 60 Jln Brick Kiln, Hokkien food: specialities include glass noodles and pork and prawn soups; ♦♦♦*Goh Huat Seng*, 59A Lebuh Kimberley, Teochew cuisine, best known for its steamboats; ♦♦*Holoman*, L43 Jln Anson, possibly the best dim sum restaurant on the island, brunches only (open 0730-1130); ♦*Loke Thye Kee*, 2B Jln Burmah, Hainanese cuisine, good place to try *inche kabin* – stewed marinated chicken; ♦♦*Sin Kheng Hooi Hong*, 350 Lebuh Pantai, Hainanese cuisine, *lor bak* (crispy deep-fried seafood rolls, with sweet-and-sour plum sauce) rec.

Nonya: Penang and Melaka are the culinary centres of Nonya cuisine – a mixture of Malay and Chinese cooking, with a number of specialities (**see page 353**). Nonya food is spicy and uses plenty of coconut milk. ♦♦*Dragon King*, 99 Lebuh Bishop, family-run business, probably the best Nonya food in any of the old Straits Settlements, specializes in fish-head curry, good satay, *otak-otak*, curry Kapitan and *kiam chye boey* – a meat casserole, rec; ♦♦*Nonya Corner*, 1 Pesara Mahsuri Lima/Jln Bukit Jambul, excellent otak-otak (fish marinated in lime and wrapped in banana leaf).

Indian: Penang's "Little India" is bounded by Lebuh Bishop, Lebuh Pasar and Lebuh King, close to the quay. There is a string of good Indian restaurants along Lebuh Penang, in this area, notably: *Veloo Vilas*, *Murugan Vilas*, *Nava India* and *Susila*. They are renowned for their banana-leaf curries; ♦♦*Dawood*, 63 Lebuh Queen (across from Sri Mariamman Temple), Indian Muslim restaurant known for its curries; ♦*Hameediyah*, 164A Lebuh Campbell, Indian Muslim food, murtabak, rotis; ♦♦*Kaliaman's*, 43 Lebuh Penang, one of Penang's best Indian restaurants, N and S Indian cuisine, banana-leafs rec; ♦*Kassim Nasi Kandar*, 2-1 Jln Brick Kiln, hot Indian Muslim food, open 24 hrs, rec by locals; ♦♦*Kashmir*, base of *Oriental Hotel*, 105 Jln Penang (**NB**: not Lubuh Penang), North Indian food – usually very busy, rec; ♦*Kedai Kopi Yasmeen*, 117 Jln Penang, simple open-fronted Indian coffeeshop, murtabak, roti etc, rec; ♦♦*The Tandoor*, Lorong Hutton, nicer decor than *Kashmir* (above), but food not as good.

Indonesian: ♦*Nasi Padang*, 511 Jalan Chulia.

Japanese: *The City Bayview*, *Rasa Sayang* and *Mutiara Beach* hotels all have Japanese restaurants; ♦♦♦*Miyabi*, Lorong Macalister, old converted mansion; ♦♦♦*Shin Miyako*, 105 Jln Penang (next to the *Oriental Hotel*), smart-looking restaurant, and reasonably priced for Japanese food.

Thai: ♦♦*Thai Food Restaurant*, below *New Pathe Hotel*, Lebuh Light; ♦♦*Café D'Chiangmai*, 11 Burmah Cross, serves an interesting mixture of Thai and local dishes, renowned for its fish-head curry popular in the evenings.

Seafood: ♦♦♦♦*Eden*, 11B Lorong Hutton, popular chain of restaurants, seafood and grills; ♦♦♦*Grand Garden Seafood*, 164 Jln Penang, seafood market restaurant, outside eating; ♦♦*Lam Kee Seafood*, next to stalls on Esplanade (Padang Kota Lama); ♦♦*Maple*, 106 Jln Penang (near *Oriental Hotel*), same management as *May Garden* and food is in the same league; ♦♦*May Garden*, 70 Penang Rd, reckoned to be among the best seafood restaurants in Georgetown, with an aquarium full of fish and shellfish to choose from, the crab is excellent and *May Garden's* speciality is frogs' legs, fried with chilli and ginger or just crispy, rec; ♦♦*Ocean-Green*, 48F Jln Sultan Ahmad Shah, T 374530 (in quiet alleyway in front of *Paramount Hotel*), specialities include lobster and crab thermidor, drunken prawns and fresh frogs' legs ("paddy chicken"), lovely location, overlooking fishing boats, rec; ♦♦*Sea Palace*, 7 Jln Penang (next to *Malaysia Hotel*), huge menu, popular.

International: *Tye Ann Hotel*, Lebuh Chulia, rec for breakfast; *English Thai Café*, 417b Lebuh Chulia; *Magnolia Snack Bar*, Jln Penang; ♦♦*Eden Steak House*, Jln Hutton; *The Ship Steakhouse*; *OG Bakery*, Jln Penang.

Coffee shops: most Chinese coffee shops along Jln Burmah and Jln Penang, also some in the financial district along Lebuh Bishop, Lebuh Cina and Lebuh Union. *Khuan Kew* and *Sin Kuan Hwa*, both in Love Lane are particularly popular – the latter is well known for its Hainan chicken rice; The *Maxim Cakehouse and Bakery* on Penang Road is also a popular stop. The oldest in Georgetown is the *Kek Seng* (382 Jln Penang), founded in 1906 and still serving *kway teow* soup and colourful *ais-kacangs*.

Stalls: Penang's hawker stalls are renowned in Malaysia, and serve some of the best food on the island. *Datuk Keramat Hawker Centre* (also called *Padang Brown*), junction of Anson and Perak roads, this is one of the venues for Georgetown's roving night market – possible to check if it's on by calling tourist information centre (T 614461), rec; *Food Court*, base of KOMTAR; *Kota Selera Hawker Centre*, next to Fort Cornwallis, off Lebuh Light, rec; *Padang Kota Lama/Jln Tun Syed Sheh Barakbah* (Esplanade), busy in the evenings, rec; *Lebuh Keng Kwee*, famed locally for its *cendol* stalls – cocktails of shaved ice, palm sugar and jelly topped with *gula melaka* and coconut milk; *Lebuh Kimberley* (called noodle-maker street by the Chinese), good variety of hawker food at night; *Lorong Selamat Hawker Stalls*, highly recommended by locals; *Pesiaran Gurney Seawall* (Gurney Drive), long row of hawkers opposite the coffeeshops. There are also popular stalls along Jln Burmah, Love Lane and at Ayer Itam.

Bars *Anchor bar & poolside bar*, *E & O Hotel*, 10 Farquhar St; *Revolving bar*, 15th Flr, *City Bayview Hotel*, 25a Farquhar St, views over the town and coast, starts turning 1900; *20 Lieth St* (opposite *Cathay Hotel*), pleasant bar with outside tables, but not well patronized.

Entertainment **Discos**: most of the big hotels, have in-house nightclubs and discos. Expect to pay cover charges if you are not a guest. *Hotlips Disco*, next to *Continental Hotel*; *Xanadu Disco*, next to *Malaysia Hotel*; *Penny Lane*, bottom of *City Bayview Hotel*; *Celebrity*, 48H Jln Sultan Ahmad Shah. **Cinemas**: *Cathay Cinema* on Jln Penang (between Jln Hutton and Jln Dato Koyah; *Rex Cinema*, junction of Jln Burmah and Transfer.

Sports **Golf**: *Airforce Golf Club*, Butterworth. Green fees: M$10; *Bukit Jambul Golf & Country Club*, Jln Bukit Jambul. Tough, hilly course. 18-hole. Green fees: M$50 weekdays, M$100 weekends; *Penang Turf Club* Golf Section, Jln Batu Gantong. 18-hole. M$30 weekdays, M$50 weekends. **Swimming**: *Chinese Swimming Club*, between Tanung Bunga and Georgetown (about 8 km from the city). Admission: M$2. Open: 0900-2045 Mon-Sun.

Shopping Shopping in Georgetown requires a lot of wandering around the narrow streets and alleyways off Jln Penang. Main areas are Jln Penang, Jln Burmah and Lebuh Campbell. **Antiques**: shops on and around Jln Penang with the best ones at the top end behind the *City*

Bayview Hotel. Also antique shops along Rope Walk (Jln Pintal Tali). Most stock antiques from Burma, Thailand, Indonesia, Malaysia, Sabah and Sarawak, as well as a few local bargains. *Penang Antique House*, 27 Jln Patani, showcase of Peranakan (Straits Chinese) artefacts – porcelain, rosewood with mother-of-pearl inlay, Chinese embroideries and antique jewellery; *Saw Joo Aun*, 139 Rope Walk (Jln Pintal Tali). The best in a row of similar shops; *Eastern Curios*, 35 Lebuh Bishop; *Kuan Antique*, 7A Aboo Sitee Lane. Handicrafts: Jln Penang is a good place to start; also Karyaneka centre, Cawangan Pulau Pinang, Pantai Mas, Batu Feringghi. *Lucky Handicraft Centre*, 167 Batu Feringghi; *See Koon Hoe*, 315 Lebuh Chulia sells Chinese opera masks, jade seals and paper umbrellas; *The Mah Jong Factory* in Love Lane sells high-quality Mah Jong sets; *Selangor Pewter*, E & O Shopping Arcade, Lebuh Farquhar. Shop and demonstrations. Batik: *Maphilindo Baru*, 217 Penang Rd, excellent range of batiks and sarongs (including songket) from Malaysia, Sumatra and Java; *Asia Co.*, 314 Jln Penang. *Craft Batik*, 651, Mukim 2, Teluk Bahang; *Sam's Batik House*, 159 Jln Penang. *Yuyi Batik House*, Level 3, Kompleks Tun Abdul Razak (KOMTAR), Jln Penang. Basketry: several shops along Jln Penang, around junction with Jln Burmah. Curios and unusual bargains: *Lebuh Chulia*, Bishop and Rope Walk. Books: bookshops in *E & O Hotel*, several in Lebon Chulia near *Swiss Hotel* and second hand bookshops on Lorong Macalister. *United Books*, 213 Jln Penang, good English-language bookshop. Cassettes, electrical and photographic equipment: Jln Campbell, Jln Penang. Camping gear: *Tye Yee Seng Canvas*, 162 Chulia St, good stock of tents, rucksacks, sleeping bags and beach umbrellas.

Markets Penang's night market (1900-2300) changes locations every fortnight. To check venue, call Tourist Information Centre (T614461) or refer to the Penang Diary column in the daily newspapers.

Local transport Bus: city buses leave from Lebuh Victoria near the Butterworth ferry terminal and serve Georgetown and the surrounding districts. Green, yellow and blue buses leave from Pengkalan Weld (Weld Quay) – next to the ferry terminal or Jln Maxwell. These buses go to various points around the island. **Blue buses** go W along the N coast to Tanjung Bungah, Batu Feringghi and Teluk Bahang. **Green buses** head towards the centre of the island to Ayer Itam area. **Yellow buses** go S (including Snake Temple and Bayan Lepas Airport), and then up the W side to Teluk Bahang. Prices from M$0.60 to M$0.90. **Taxi**: taxi stands on Jln Dr Lim Chwee Leong, Pengkalan Weld and Jln Magazine. Fares can be calculated on the basis of M$0.70 for the first mile and M$0.30 for each additional half mile. A trip to the airport costs M$10-12. Taxis often have no meters, so settle price in advance. Radio taxis: T 6177098, 6177933. **Trishaw**: bicycle rickshaws are one of the most practical and enjoyable ways to explore Georgetown. Cost: M$0.40-M$0.50/half mile; if taking an hour's trip around town, agree on the route first, bargain and set the price in advance. **Bicycle hire**: rental from the *Eng Ann Hotel* or *Swiss Hotel*, both on Lebuh Chulia, M$20/day. **Motorcycle hire**: in Georgetown there are several motorbike rental shops, many of them along Lebuh Chulia. Cost: from about M$20/day depending on size; most are Honda 70s. **Car hire**: Avis, branches at *E & O Hotel*, 10 Lebuh Farquhar, T 361685, Bayan Lepas Airport; **Budget**, 28 Jln Penang, T 635800 and Bayan Lepas Airport; **Hertz**, 38 Lebuh Farquhar, T 638602 and Bayan Lepas Airport; **Mayflower**, Tan Chong Building, 23 Pengkalan Weld, T 628196; **National Car Rental**, 17 Lebuh Leith, T 629404; Orix, *City Bayview Hotel*, 25A Lebuh Farquhar, T 2423009; **Pernas Sime Darby Rent-a-Car**, 38/7 Lebuh Farquhar, T 375914; **Sistem Sewa Kereta Malaysia**, Lobby *E&O Hotel*, Lebuh Farquhar, T 361684; **SMAS**, Grd Flr Komplek Mutiara, 125 Jln Anson, T 361308; **Thrifty**, Lobby Floor, Ming Court, 202A Jln Macalister, T 363688; **Tomo**, 386A, 1st Flr Wayton Court, Jln Burmah, T 365636.

Banks & money changers Most banks in Georgetown are around the GPO area and Lebuh Pantai. Most money changers are in banking area and Jln Captain Kling Mosque. **Bank Bumiputra**, 37 Lebuh Pantai; **Citibank**, 42 Jln Sultan Ahmad Shah; **Hongkong Bank**, Lebuh Pantai; **Maybank**, 9 Lebuh Union; **Standard Chartered**, 2 Lebuh Pantai.

Embassies & consulates Denmark, Bernam Agencies, Hong Kong Bank Chambers, Lebuh Downing, T 624886; **France**, 82 Bishop St, Wisma Rajab, T 629707; **Germany**, Bayan Lepas Free Trade Zone, T 838340; **Indonesia**, 467 Jln Burmah, T 25162; **Japan**, 2 Jln Biggs, T 368222; **Netherlands**, Algemen Bank Nederland, 9 Lebuh Pantai, T 622144; **Thailand**, 1 Jln Ayer Raja, T 23352; **UK**, Birch House, 73 Jln Datuk Keramat, T 27166.

Useful addresses General Post Office: Lebuh Pitt. Efficient poste restante. Also provides a parcel-wrapping service. Hospitals: *General Hospital*, Jln Residensi, T 373333; *Penang Medical Centre*, 1 Jln Pangkor, T 20731. Immigration Office: on the corner of Lebuh Light and Lebuh Pantai, T 365122. St George's Church: Lebuh Farquhar. Services in English 0830 & 1830 every Sunday. Penang Public Library: Dewan Sri Pinang, Lebuh Light. Telecoms office: (international calls; fax and telex facilities) Jln Burmah. Area Code: 04.

Airline offices Cathay Pacific, AIA Building, Lebuh Farquhar, T 6204111; **Garuda**, 41 Aboo Sitee Lane, T 365257; **MAS**, Kompleks Tun Abdul Razak (KOMTAR), Jln Penang, T 620011; **Singapore Airlines**, Wisma Penang Gardens, 42 Jln Sultan Ahmad Shah, T 363201; **Thai International**, Wisma Central, 202 Jln Macalister, T 23484.

Tour companies and travel agents Most of the budget travel agents are along Lebuh Chulia. *MSL Travel*, Ming Court Inn Lobby, Jln Macalister, T 372655 or 340 Lebuh Chulia, T 616154, student and youth travel bureau; *Georgetown Tourist Service*, 18 Pengkalan Weld, T 613853, city island tours; *Everrise Tours & Travel*, Lot 323, 2nd Floor, Wisma Central, 202 Jln, *Macalister*, T 20453; *Tour East*, 18th Flr, The Merlin Penang, 4 Jln Larut, T 362315, F 375557, offers the best selection of tours, including round-the-island tours (individual or group), rec.

Tourist offices Penang Tourist Association, Penang Port Commission Building, Jln Tun Syed Sheikh Barakbah (off Victoria Clocktower roundabout, opposite Fort Cornwallis), T 616663. **Tourist Information Centre**, 3rd Floor, Komplex Tun Abdul Razak (KOMTAR), Jln Penang, T 614461, also branch at Batu Feringghi, outside Eden Seafood Village and at Bayan Lepas Airport (T 831501). The information centre has a list of tour companies in Georgetown. **Tourism Malaysia Northern Regional Office**, 10 Jln Tun Syed Sheh Barakbah, round the corner from the Penang Tourist Association (above), T 619067.

Transport to & from Georgetown NB: Butterworth is the railway stop for Georgetown and Penang; taxis also tend to terminate there, with local taxis making the run across the bridge to the island; long-distance taxis will however cross the bridge for an extra charge. **By Air**: Bayan Lepas Airport is 18 km S of Georgetown and 36 km from Batu Feringghi. Taxis operate on a coupon system from the airport (M$16 to town and M$23 to Batu Feringghi) or take yellow bus 83 (M$0.90) for either Teluk Bahang (up the west coast) or Georgetown (up the east coast). Direct international connections with Singapore (M$230), Bangkok (M$730), Hong Kong (M$1,727) and Medan. Regular domestic connections with KL (M$96), Kota Bahru (M$86), Kuala Terengganu (M$96), Langkawi (M$50) and Ipoh (M$49).

By train: station is by the Butterworth Ferry Terminal. Advance bookings for onward rail journeys can be made at the station or at the Ferry Terminal, Pengkalan Weld, Georgetown. From Butterworth: regular connections with Alor Setar (M$12), Taiping (M$12), Ipoh (M$17), KL (M$28), Johor Bahru (M$48).

By bus: terminal is beside the ferry terminal at Butterworth. Booking offices along Lebuh Chulia. Some coaches operate from Pengkalan Weld direct to major towns on the peninsula (see Butterworth section). *Masa Mara Travel* (54/4 Jln Burmah) is an agent for direct express buses from Penang to Kota Bahru (M$18), KL (M$15).

By taxi: long-distance taxis to all destinations on peninsula operate from the depot beside the Butterworth ferry on Pengkalan Weld (Kota Bahru M$30, KL M$30).

By boat: boats from Georgetown for Langkawi on Sat-Mon, Wed, 3 hrs, (M$30 economy). Tickets from Kuala Perlis ferry service, Ground Floor, PPC Shipping Arcades, Pesara Rajah Edward. Boats leave from Swettenham Pier. Possible to take motor cycle (M$20) or bicycle (M$10). Departs 0800. There is also a weekly overnight service to Langkawi (fortnightly during the monsoon season) from Swettenham Pier. Leaves Georgetown at 2300 and arrives Langkawi at 0700 the next morning. For schedules contact Sanren Delta Marine at E & O Shopping Complex, 10 Lebuh Farquhar.

By car: M$7 toll to drive across the Penang Bridge. **By ferry**: passenger and car ferries operate from adjacent terminals, Pengkalan Raja Tun Uda. 24-hour ferry service between Georgetown and Butterworth. Ferries leave every 20 minutes 0600-2400. M$0.40 return.

International connections to Thailand **By train**: see Butterworth section. **By bus**: express bus services are along Lebuh Chulia. Regular connections to Bangkok (M$60); also connections to Phuket (M$40), Hat Yai (M$20), Surat Thani (M$40). Also some hotels eg New Asia & Cathay organize minibuses to destinations in Thailand. Bus and ferry to Koh Samui (M$32), Krabi (M$32), Phuket (M$32). **By taxi**: direct taxis from Penang to Thailand: overnight to Hat Yai (M$22); Surat Thani for Koh Samui (M$40), Krabi (for Phuket) M$40. **By boat**: there is now a regular ferry service from Georgetown to Langkawi and on to Phuket; check details at Kuala Perlis Ferry service (see below). **To Singapore By bus**: overnight to Singapore (M$32). **To Sumatra**: two companies run ferry services to Medan, Sumatra; boats leave Mon & Wed-Sat (M$80). Ticket offices – Express Bahagia T 631943 and Kuala Perlis Ferry Service – on Grd Flr, PPC Shopping Arcades, Pesara Rajah Edward. Boats leave from Swettenham Pier.

Batu Feringghi & Teluk Bahang

The main beach **Batu Feringghi**, whose hot white sands were once the nirvana of Western hippies, has been transformed into an upmarket tropical version of the Costa Brava. There are now 10 hotels along the beach strip and graffiti are splashed across the famous Foreigner's Rock. *Feringghi* – which is related to the Thai word *farang*, or foreigner – actually means "Portuguese" in Malay. Portuguese Admiral Albuquerque, who captured Melaka in 1511, stopped off at Batu Feringghi for fresh water on his way down the Straits. And St Francis Xavier is said to have visited Batu Feringghi in 1545. Towards the end of the 16th century, Captain James Lancaster, who later founded the East India Company in 1600, also came ashore at the beach.

To the majority of today's tourists, Batu Feringghi *is* Penang. The beach is just over 3 km long but it has been extended to the fishing village of Teluk Bahang at the W end. Most holiday-makers and honeymooners prefer to stick to their hotel swimming pools rather than risk bathing in the sea. Pollution and siltation in recent years have seriously effected water quality, but of late, the hotels have taken much more care of the beach itself. Despite the explosion of development, Batu Feringghi still meets most visitors' expectations. With its palms and casuarina trees and its (almost) turquoise water, it retains at least some of its picture-postcard beauty. The hotels offer many different activities: windsurfing, water skiing, diving, sailing and fishing as well as jungle walks and sightseeing tours of the island.

Apart from the string of plush modern hotels, the Batu Feringghi area also has many excellent restaurants, hawker stalls and handicraft shops. The **Yahong Art Gallery** is on Batu Feringghi, which displays batik paintings by the Teng family (the elder Teng is regarded as the father of Malaysian batik painting).

Teluk Bahang is a small fishing kampung at the W end of this N stretch of beach. It is where the Malabar fishermen used to live and has now been dramatically changed by the *Penang Mutiara Beach Resort*. Beyond Teluk Bahang, around **Muka Head**, the coast is broken into a series of small secluded coves separated by rocky headlands; there are several tiny secluded beaches. Some of these are only accessible by boat, which can be hired either from the beach hotels, or from fishermen in Teluk Bahang (much cheaper). Trails also lead over the headland from the fishing kampung. One goes along the coast past the Universiti Malaya Marine Research Station to Mermaid Beach and Muka Head lighthouse (1½ hrs); another leads straight over the headland to Pantai Keracut (2 hrs).

The **Teluk Bahang Recreation Forest** has several well marked trails and a **Forestry Museum**. Open: 0900-1300, 1400-1700 Tue-Thur, Sat & Sun; 0900-1200, 1445-1700 Fri.

The Butterfly Farm, a kilometre up the road from the Teluk Bahang junction, claims to be the largest tropical butterfly farm in the world. It has around 4,000 butterflies at any one time, representing over 120 species of Malaysian butterflies. The best time to visit the farm is in the late morning or early afternoon when the butterflies are most active. There is an insect museum next door. The farm is also an important research centre and breeding station. Admission: M$3. Open: 0900-1700 Mon-Fri, 0900-1800 Sat & Sun. There are two **batik factories** along the road near the butterfly farm; visitors welcome. Demonstrations of batik block designing, stamp waxing and dyeing.

Accommodation The big international hotels all have excellent facilities – including tennis, watersports, sailing and sightseeing tours. A room glut in the early 1990s – due mainly to the knock-on from recession in the West – has meant several hotels have been offering very competitive deals. With fewer European customers, many turned their attention to the incentive travel business and the Asian market, targeting Singaporeans in particular. Hotels are still going up though. While middle-to-upmarket tourists are spoilt for choice, budget travellers' options on the N coast are rather more limited. **Batu Feringghi**: **A+** *Golden Sands*, T 811911, a/c, restaurant, pool, popular and central on the beach, arguably the best swimming pool; **A+** *Rasa Sayang*, T 811311, a/c, restaurant, pool, probably the most popular along the beach strip, modern interpretation of Minangkabau-style, horse-shoe design around central pool and garden area, rec; **A** *Bayview Beach Hotel*, T 812123, a/c, restaurant, pool, pleasant location, away from others on the strip; **A** *Casuarina Beach*, T 811711, a/c, restaurant, pool, named after the trees which line Batu Feringghi's beach, particularly nice grounds; **A** *Feringghi Beach*, T 805999, a/c, restaurant, pool, caters mainly for tour groups; **A** *Holiday Inn Penang*, T 8116011, a/c, restaurant, pool, good pool and beach area; **A** *Lone Pine*, T 811511, a/c, restaurant, one of the oldest hotels along Batu Feringghi, reasonably priced for the area, but not up to the standards of its neighbours. Built in the days when the sea was the obvious place for a swim, the Lone Pine does not have its own pool. It does, however, serve tiffin curry on the lawn, rec; **A** *Palm Beach*, T 811621, a/c, restaurant, pool.

Teluk Bahang: **A+** *Penang Mutiara Beach Resort*, Jln Teluk Bahang, T 812828, a/c, restaurant, pool, the last outpost of luxury along the beach, and a member of the 'Leading Hotels of the World' group, the Mutiara (Malay for 'pearl') has landscaped garden, great pool with a bar and every conceivable facility. A drink at the Mutiara bar costs the same as a huge meal in some nearby restaurants, rec; **A** *Novotel*, T 803333, F 803303, a/c, restaurant, pool; **B** *Motel Sri Pantai*, T 895566, a/c, restaurant; **E** *Loke Thean*, T 894231; **E** *Madame Loh*, near the mosque (left at the roundabout), clean, good atmosphere; **E-F** *Rama's*, 365 Mukim 2, T 811179, homestay-type accommodation, dorm or rooms.

Restaurants Many of the big Batu Feringghi hotels have excellent restaurants – they have to be good as there is plenty of competition from roadside restaurants. Virtually every cuisine is represented along this stretch. Malay: ♦♦*Papa Din Bamboo*, 124-B Batu Feringghi (turn left after police station and *Eden Restaurant*, 200 m up the kampung road by *Happy Garden Restaurant*), home-cooked Malay fish curries made by loveable bumoh who prides himself on being able to say 'thank you' in 30 languages, Papa Din Salat is also a renowned masseur. Seafood: ♦♦♦*Eden Seafood Village*, if it swims, Eden cooks it – but it is over-priced, nightly cultural shows, Eden has now expanded to include two other big, clean red restaurants, adjacent and opposite the original; ♦♦*End of the World*, end of Mutiara Beach, at Teluk Bahang, huge quantities of fresh seafood, its chilli crabs are superb and its lobster is the best value for money on the island (about M$25 each), rec; ♦♦*Happy Garden*, Batu Feringghi (round the corner from Bayview, left after police station and Eden restaurant), pretty garden, Chinese and Western dishes; ♦♦*Hollywood*, Tanjung Bungah, Batu Feringghi, great views over the beach, serves *inche kabin* chicken stews and good selection of seafood; ♦♦♦*Pearl Garden*, Batu Feringghi; ♦♦*Sin Hai Keng*, 551 Jln Tanjung Tokong, overlooks the sea and serves everything from noodles to pork chops, excellent satay; ♦♦♦*The Catch*, Tanjung Bungah, next to *Mutiara Hotel*, Malay, Chinese, Thai and international seafood dishes, huge fish tanks for fresh fish, prawns, crabs, lobster etc, hour-long cultural show daily, pleasant setting, one of the best seafood restaurants on the island, rec.

Entertainment Cultural shows: *The Catch Restaurant*, next door to the *Mutiara*, Tanjung Bungah: hour-long Malay cultural show 0830 Mon-Sun. *Eden Seafood Village*, Batu Feringghi. **Traditional massage**: *Papa Din*, 124B Batu Feringghi (see directions under Malay restaurants, above). Most big Batu Feringghi hotels have discos, but apart from them, most other places close around 2330.

Sport Sailing: the most popular route is to sail N towards the islands around Langkawi and Turatao. *Pelangi Cruises*, Mutiara Beach Resort, Jln Teluk Bahang, T 812828/811305, F 812829/811498. 12 yachts, with or without skipper; M$50/person for 3 hours, M$100/person for 6 hrs. Also run overnight cruises, buying fresh fish from fishermen en route. It takes 8-10 hrs to Langkawi.

Shopping Batik: the factories at Mukim 2, Teluk Bahang will sell sarong lengths to visitors, but few ready-mades. *Sim Seng Lee Batik and Handicrafts*, 391 Batu Feringghi. *Deepee's Silk Shop*, offering reasonable tailoring service.

Local transport Car hire: Avis, *Rasa Sayang Hotel*, Batu Ferringghi; **Hertz**, *Casuarina Beach Hotel*, Batu Feringghi; **Mayflower**, *Casuarina Beach Hotel*, Batu Feringghi; **Ruhanmas**, 157B Batu Feringghi, T 811576; **Sintat Rent-a-Car**, *Lone Pine Hotel*, Batu Feringghi; **Kasina Baru**, 651 Mukim 2, Teluk Bahang (opposite *Mutiara Beach Resort*), T 811988. **Motorbike hire**: there are also quite a few places along Batu Feringghi with bikes for hire, all of them clearly signposted on the road. **Boats**: boat trips can be arranged through fishermen at Teluk Bahang. Negotiate the price in advance.

Transport to & from Batu Feringghi/Teluk Bahang By bus: blue bus 93 goes to Batu Feringghi/Teluk Bahang from Pengkalan Weld (Weld Quay) or Jln Maxwell in Georgetown (M$0.60). By taxi: stands on Batu Feringghi (eg opposite *Golden Sands Hotel*). The big hotels along the strip are well served by taxis.

ALOR SETAR & LANGKAWI

Alor Setar is the capital of Kedah state on the road N to the Thai border. It is the home town of Prime Minister Dr Mahathir Mohamad and is the commercial centre for NW Malaysia. Its name, which is often corrupted to Alor Star, means 'grove of setar trees' (which produce a sour fruit). Kedah is now Malaysia's most important rice-growing state; together with neighbouring Perlis it produces 44% of the country's rice, and is known as *jelapang padi* – 'rice barn country'. Kedah is the site of some of the oldest settlements on the peninsula and the state's royal family can trace its line back several centuries. The ancient Indian names for the state are Kadaram and Kathah, and archaeologists believe the site of the 5th century Kingdom of Langkasuka was just to the SE of Kedah Peak (Gunung Jerai), in the Bujang River valley, half-way between Butterworth and Alor Setar (see below).

Alor Setar has some interesting buildings, most of which are clustered round the central Padang Besar (Jalan Pekan Melayu/Jalan Raja); apart from them, the town is unremarkable. The most interesting is the state mosque, the Moorish-style **Masjid Zahir**, completed in 1912. Almost directly opposite is the Thai-inspired **Balai Besar**, or audience hall, built in 1898, which is still used by the Sultan of Kedah on ceremonial occasions – it houses the royal throne. It is not open to the public. Close to the mosque is the **Balai Seni Negeri**, or State Art Gallery, which contains a collection of historical paintings and antiques. Further down Jalan Raja is the 400-year-old **Balai Nobat**, an octagonal building topped by an onion dome. This building houses Kedah's royal percussion orchestra or *nobat*; it is said to date back to the 15th century. Again, it is not open to the public.

The **State Museum**, styled on the Balai Besar and built in 1936, is on Jalan Bakar Bata. The museum houses exhibits on local farming and fishing practices, a collection of early Sung Dynasty porcelain and some finds from the archaeological excavations in the Bujang Valley (see below). Open: 0900-1700 Mon-Wed, Sat & Sun, 0900-1200 Thur. Next to the museum is the royal boathouse and the **Pekan Rabu**, or Wednesday market (which is now held all week long) and is a good place to buy local handicrafts.

Excursions

Bujang Valley near the small town of Sungei Petani, to the SE of Kedah Peak (Gunung Jerai), is the site of some of Malaysia's most exciting archaeological discoveries: finds there have prompted the establishment of the Bajung Valley Historical Park (under the management of the National Museum). The name 'Bujang' is derived from a Sanskrit word, *bhujanga* meaning serpent. It is thought to be the site of the capital of the 5th century Hindu kingdom of Langkasuka, the hearthstone of Malay fairytale romance. While the architectural remains are a far cry from those of Cambodia's Angkor Wat, they are of enormous historical significance.

The city is thought to represent one of the very earliest Hindu settlements in Southeast Asia, several centuries before Angkor, and at least 200 years before the founding of the first Hindu city in Java. The capital of Langkasuka is thought to have been abandoned in the 6th century, probably following a pirate raid. There have been some remarkable finds at the site, including brick and marble temple and palace complexes – of both Hindu and Buddhist origin – coins, statues, Sanskrit inscriptions, weapons and jewellery. In 1925 archaeologists stumbled across "a magnificent little granite temple near a beautiful waterfall" on a hillside above the ancient city. One of them, Dr Quarith Wales, the director of the Greater-India Research Committee wrote of the temple: "It had never been robbed, except of images, although the bronze trident of Shiva was found. In each of the stone post-holes were silver caskets containing rubies and sapphires." More than 50 temples have now been unearthed in the Bujang area, most of them buried in soft mud along the river bank.

For several centuries, Indian traders used the city as an entrepôt in their dealings with China. Rather than sail through the pirate-infested Melaka Strait, the traders stopped at the natural harbour at Kuala Merbok and had their goods portered across the isthmus to be collected by ships on the E side. There is speculation that the area of the Sungei Bujang was later used as a major port of the Srivijaya Empire (see page 733), whose capital was at Palembang, Sumatra. But recent findings by Malaysian archaeologists have begun to contradict some of the earlier theories that Hinduism was the earliest of the great religions to be established on the Malay peninsula. Recently excavated artifacts suggest that Buddhism was introduced to the area before Hinduism. The local archaeologists maintain the Buddhist and Hindu phases of Bujang Valley's history are distinct, with the Hindu period following on much later, in the 10th-14th centuries. This is at odds with previous assertions by archaeologists that the remains of the temples' "laterite sanctuary towers are of the earliest type and... not yet suggestive of pre-Angkorian architecture".

Many of the finds can be seen in the museum at Bukit Batu Pahat near Bedong; alongside the museum is a reconstruction of the most significant temple unearthed so far, **Candi Bukit Batu Pahat**, Temple of the Hill of Chiselled Stone. Eight sanctuaries have been restored and a museum displays statues and other finds. Open: 0900-1700. **Getting there**: change buses at Bedong; easier to take a taxi from Alor Setar (M$2.50).

Kedah Peak (Gunung Jerai) is the highest mountain (1206m) in the NW and part of the **Sungei Teroi Forest Recreation Park**. The peak has been used as a navigational aid for ships heading down the Strait of Melaka for centuries. It is between the main road and the coast, N of Sungei Petani. In 1884, the remains of a 6th century Hindu shrine were discovered on the summit. It had been hidden under a metre-thick layer of peat, which caught fire, revealing the brick and stone construction, thought to be linked with the Kingdom of Langkasuka (above). Archaeologists speculate that the remains may originally have been a series of fire altars. But they are destined to remain a mystery as a radio station has now been built on top. About 3 km N of Gurun, between Sungei Petani and Alor Setar, a narrow road goes off to the left and leads to the top of the mountain (11 km). There is even a small hotel just below the summit and the Museum of Forestry on top. There are good views out over Kedah's paddy fields and the coast. **Accommodation**: **B** *Gunung Jerai Resort*, T 414311, 1920s resthouse, rooms and chalets, garden, chalets M$99; **B** *Peranginan Gunung Jerai*, Sungai Teroi Forest Recreation Park, T 729786, a/c, restaurant. **Getting there**: jeeps from Gurun run 900-1600, 33 km S of Alor Star (M$5).

Accommodation A *Kedah Merlin Inn*, 134-141 Jln Sultan Badlishah, T 735917, a/c, restaurant; **A-B** *Grand Continental*, 134-141 Jln Sultan Badlishah, T 735917, a/c, restaurant, bar; **B** *Samila*, 27 Jln Kancut, T 722344, a/c, restaurant, not as good as the brochure makes out; **B-D** *Mahawangsa*, 449 Jln Raja, T 721433, a/c, restaurant, clean, but *Regent* (below) is better value for money; **C** *Regent*, 1536 Jln Sultan Badlishah, T 721291, friendly and helpful, rec; **C** *Rumah Rehat* (*Government Rest House*), 75 Pumpong, T 722422, some a/c, book beforehand as it tends to fill up with government people; **C-D** *Miramar*, 246 Jln Putra, T 738144, a/c; **D** *Federal*, 429 Jln Kancut, T 730055, a/c; **D** *Station*, 2nd Flr, Jln Stesyen, T 733786, fan only, laundry, very noisy; **E** *Lim Kung*, 36A Jln Langgar, T 722459, fan only.

Restaurants Chinese: ♦♦♦*Samila Hotel*, 27 Jln Kancut, rec; ♦♦*Sri Pumpong*, Jln Pumpong, speciality: barbecued fish; *Kway Teow Jonid*, Jln Stadium (next to the police station), fried *kway teow*, washed down with *teh tarik*. Indian: ♦♦*Bunga Tanjong*, Jln Seberang, Indian Muslim food, seafood curries. Thai: ♦♦*Café de Siam*, Jln Kota, lashings of Thai-style seafood. **Stalls**: *Old Market* (Pekan Rabu hawker centre), Jln Tunku Ibrahim; "*Garden*" *Hawker Centre*, Jln Stadium, good range of cuisines, leafy setting.

Sport Golf: *Royal Kedah Club*. Green fees: M$15 weekdays, M$30 weekends.

Banks & money changers Bank Bumiputra, Jln Tunku Ibrahim; **Chartered Bank, UMBC** and **Overseas Union Bank** are all on Jln Raja.

Useful addresses General Post Office: Jln Tunku Ibrahim, near Jln Raja intersection.

Airline offices MAS, 180 Kompleks Alor Setar, Lebuhraya Darulaman, T 711106.

Tourist offices Tourist Office, Wisma Negeri, Jln Raja (opposite mosque); there is also a tourist information booth on Jln Raja.

Transport to & from Alor Setar 93 km N of Butterworth, 462 km from KL, 409 km from Kota Bahru. **By air**: connections with Kota Bahru (M\$101) and Kuala Lumpur. **By train**: station is off Jln Langgar. Regular connections with KL (M\$32), Butterworth (M\$12). **By bus**: the northern section of the new N-S Highway runs to the Malaysian border crossing at Bukit Kayu Hitam, from where it is easy to cross to Sadao, the nearest Thai town on the other side of the border. North-bound buses from the station next to the istana off Jln Raja; southbound buses from the station in front of the Railway Station, Jln Stesyen. Regular connections with KL (M\$19.50), JB (M\$34.00), Kota Bahru (M\$26), Kuala Terengganu (M\$26). **By taxi**: Penang (M\$24), Kuala Kedah (for Langkawi) (M\$4), Kangar (Perlis).

International connections to Thailand **By train**: there is no longer a through-train from Alor Setar to Hat Yai. The international express from Singapore goes through Alor Setar but does not stop to pick up passengers. (See Butterworth section for trains to Thailand.) **By bus**: most of the buses leave from Penang/Butterworth to Bangkok and other destinations on the Kra Isthmus. It is possible to get to Changlun, the Malay border post for Thailand by bus or taxi but it is then difficult to cross from Bukit Kayu Hitam to Sadao, the Thai town, several kilometres N of the border. The new N-S highway follows this route. If you go to Padang Besar (accessible from Kangar in Perlis), where the railway line crosses the border, you can easily walk across and take a bus or train from there to Hat Yai. The other option is to take a taxi from Sungei Petani to Keroh and cross the border into Thailand's red-light outpost at Betong.

Kuala Kedah

Historically the town has been an important port for trade with India and there are the ruins of an old fort, built between 1771 and 1780. The fort was built for defence of the state capital from pirate attacks. It fell into the hands of the Siamese army, under the leadership of Raja Ligor in 1821 and was occupied by Siam until 1842, after which it was abandoned. Kuala Kedah is renowned for its seafood stalls. It is also a departure point for Langkawi (see below).

Transport to & from Kuala Kedah 12 km W of Alor Setar. **By bus**: buses leave every ½ hr from Alor Setar to Kuala Kedah, M\$0.75. **By taxi**: Alor Setar (M\$4). **By boat**: regular connections with Langkawi (M\$12). Langkawi ferry leaves 0800, 0930, 1130, 1200, 1330, 1430 and 1600.

Kangar

The state of Perlis is the smallest in Malaysia and Kangar is the capital. **Arau**, near Kangar is the royal capital of Perlis, where the state mosque and the istana are located. The area is very picturesque, with limestone outcrops surrounded by paddy fields.

Accommodation The new luxury *Pens Hotel* will be opening in 1993. **B-C** *Sri Perlis Inn*, 135 Jlan Besar, T 767266, a/c, restaurant; **C** *Federal*, 104A Jln Kangar, T 766288, a/c.

Transport to & from Kangar 45 km from Alor Setar, 138 km from Butterworth. **By bus**: regular connections with Alor Setar (M\$2), KL (M\$22) and Butterworth (M\$6). **By taxi**: Alor Setar (M\$3), Kuala Perlis (M\$1), Padang Besar (M\$3).

Kuala Perlis

Small port at the delta of the Sungei Perlis. Mainly a jumping-off point for Pulau Langkawi. Food stalls by the jetty. If you miss the boat to Langkawi, the **E** *Soon Hin Hotel* is across from the taxi rank.

Transport to & from Kuala Perlis 14 km from Kangar. **By bus**: regular connections with Butterworth (M\$3) and local buses to Kangar. **By taxi**: Alor Setar (M\$3), Padang Besar (M\$4). **By boat**: Langkawi ferry leaves nearly every hour (M\$10). Also hovercraft crossings: 0930, 1200, 1415, 1615.

Padang Besar

The town is on the border with Thailand. The railway station platform is very long as half is managed by Thai officials and half by Malaysians. Pekan Siam, opposite the railway station, is full of Thai goods and a popular shopping spot for Malaysians.

Transport to & from Padang Besar 35 km from Kangar. **By bus**: regular connections from Kuala Perlis and Kangar (M$2). **By taxi**: from Kuala Perlis and Kangar (M$4).

Pulau Langkawi

The name Langkawi is the last surviving namesake of the ancient Kingdom of Langkasuka, known as *negari alang-kah suka* – 'the land of all one's wishes'. The Langkawi group is an archipelago of 99 islands, and Pulau Langkawi itself is a mountainous, palm-fringed island with scattered fishing kampungs, paddy fields and sandy coves. Some of the islands are nothing more than deserted limestone outcrops rearing out of the turquoise sea, cloaked in jungle, and ringed by coral.

Langkasuka, whose capital is thought to have stood at the base of Kedah Peak, S of Alor Setar (**see page 150**) is mentioned in Chinese accounts as far back as 500 AD. According to a Chinese Liang Dynasty record, the kingdom of 'Langgasu' was founded in the first century and its Hindu king, Bhagadatta, paid tribute to the Chinese Emperor. The names of its kings – known as *daprenta-hyangs* – resurface in Malay legends and fairytales.

In Jan 1987 the Malaysian government conferred duty-free status on Langkawi to promote tourism on the island. The little airport was upgraded, as befitting a world-class resort island with one of the plushest hotels in Asia (*Pelangi*) and the ferry service from Penang was instructed to run regularly. These efforts to turn Langkawi into one of Malaysia's big tourism moneyspinners are beginning to bear fruit as the island is attracting increasing numbers of visitors. Its status grew when Prime Minister Dr Mahathir Mohamad entertained Commonwealth leaders at the *Pelangi* resort during the Heads of Government meeting in 1989. The promotion campaign and improved transport links to the mainland means the islands can no longer be touted as 'Malaysia's best kept secret'. But development has been concentrated in a handful of places, so much of the island remains unspoilt. Nearby islands are only just starting to develop as investors begin building small resorts on them.

Every so often, Langkawi's beautiful beaches are threatened by oil spills in the nearby Strait of Melaka. Langkawi had a close call in Jan 1993 when the *Maersk Navigator*, a Danish-owned supertanker carrying 2-million barrels of crude oil to Japan, was in collision with another vessel. One of its tanks was ruptured, the ship burst into flames and oil began gushing into the sea just north of Sumatra. The slick fortunately drifted off into the Indian Ocean where it was broken down with chemical dispersants. But Malaysia's environment minister, Law Hieng Ding, predicted that unless there was more rigid policing of the busy waterway, and adequate pollution-prevention measures were enforced, it would only be a matter of time before Malaysia was struck by a pollution disaster.

Kuah, the main town, is strung out along the seafront, and is the landing point for ferries from Satun (Thailand), Kuala Perlis and Kuala Kedah. The town is growing fast and developers are reclaiming land along the shoreline to cope with the expansion. Kuah has several restaurants, a few grotty hotels, plenty of coffee shops and a string of duty free shops, which do a roaring trade in cheap liquor, cigarettes and electronics. The town goes by the glorious name of 'Gravy' (Kuah), which is said to derive from a legend about a fight that broke out between two families which fell out over the breaking of a betrothal. Kitchen pots and pans were thrown around and a cooking pot smashed onto Belgana Pecah ('broken pot'); its contents splashed all over Kuah. A saucepan of boiling water landed at Telaga Air Panas (the motley hot springs on the N of the island).

It is easy to get round the island at a fairly leisurely pace within a day. The road W to the golf course goes to **Makam Mahsuri**, the tomb of the legendary Princess Mahsuri, in the village of Mawat (12 km from Kuah). The beautiful Mahsuri was condemned to death for alleged adultery in 1355. She protested her innocence

LANGKAWI

and several attempts to execute her failed. According to the legend, the sentence was finally carried out using her own *tombak* (lance) and her severed head bled white blood, thus confirming her innocence. Before Mahsuri died she cursed the island, saying it would remain barren for 7 generations. Shortly afterwards, the Thais attacked, killing, plundering, looting and razing all the settlements to the ground. At the time of the Thai attacks, villagers buried their entire rice harvest on Padang Matsirat in **Kampung Raja**, but the Thais found it and set fire to it too, giving rise to the name **Beras Terbakar –** the 'field of burnt rice', nearby. The legend is more interesting than the field.

SE of Mahsuri's tomb, past some beautiful paddy fields and coconut groves, are the 2 main beaches, **Pantai Cenang** and **Pantai Tengah**. At the former, a sandbar appears at low tide between Nov and Jan, and it is possible to walk across to the nearby **Pulau Rebak Kecil**. It is also possible to hire boats to the other islands off Pantai Cenang from the beach. Most of the new beach chalet development is along the 3 km stretch of coast from Pantai Cenang to Pantai Tengah, which is at the far end, around a small promontory. The beaches can get crowded at weekends and during school and public holidays. Pantai Cenang, with the *Pelangi Beach Resort* at the top end, is still one of the nicest beaches on the island and there is accommodation to suit all budgets.

The road W leads, past the airport, to the magnificent bay of **Pantai Kok**, with its dramatic backdrop of the forested and poetically named Gunung Macincang.

There are several isolated beaches along the bay, accessible by boat from either Pantai Kok itself, Pantai Cenang (12 km away) or Kampung Kuala Teriang, a small fishing village en route. On the W headland, a 2 km walk from Pantai Kok, are the **Telaga Tujuh** waterfalls. The water cascades down a steep hillside, between huge rocks and through a series of seven (tujuh) pools (telaga) – particularly impressive when it has been raining. They are a great place for a swim.

Right on the NW tip of Langkawi is **Pantai Datai**, which is disappointing apart from its beautifully landscaped golf course. It is accessible via a new road, which cuts up through the hills to the coast from the Pantai Kok-Pasir Hitam road. The latter is at the centre of the N coast, past the Kedah Cement Plant (the island's only industrial monster). As its name suggests, **Pasir Hitam** is streaked with black sand; but that is about the only thing worth noting about it.

Pantai Rhu (also known as Casuarina Beach) is a beautiful white-sand cove, enclosed by a jungled promontory with **Gua Cerita**, or the 'Cave of Legends', at the end of it. Beneath the sheer limestone cliff faces, there are a couple of small beaches accessible by boat. The Thai island Koh Turatao is just 4 km away. Past the *Mutiara*, there is a collection of food stalls and small shops next to the beach. It is possible to hire boats and canoes from the beach, which is backed by a small lagoon. On the road back to Kuah, at the 9th milestone, a 3 km-long path branches off to the **Durian Perangin** waterfall, on the slopes of Gunung Raya.

Excursions to neighbouring islands

Pulau Dayang or 'Island of the Pregnant Maiden', is the second largest island in the archipelago, and lies just S of Langkawi. Separated from the sea by only a few metres of limestone, is a freshwater lake renowned for its powers to enhance the fertility of women; unfortunately it is also said to be inhabited by a big white crocodile. To the N of the lake, is the intriguingly named **Gua Langsir** – the 'Cave of the Banshee'. The cave is high on a limestone cliff and is home to a large population of bats. Other nearby islands include **Pulau Bumbon**, **Pulau Beras Basah** and **Pulau Singa Besar** – there is some coral between the last two. Pulau Singa Besar is now a wildlife sanctuary, with about 90 resident bird species, wild boar and a huge population of mouse deer. A network of paths and trails will be built around the island.

Pulau Paya, a tiny island about an hour SE of Langkawi, is part of a marine park (the other islands are **Segantang**, **Kala** and **Lembu**). Just to the S of Paya there is a good coral reef – reckoned to be the best off Malaysia's W coast. There are basic facilities on the island for day visitors, but those intending to camp on the island require the permission of the Fisheries Management and Protection Office, Wisma Tani, Jalan Mahameru, KL, T 2982011 or Wisma Persekutuan, Jalan Kampung Baru, Alor Setar, T 725573. **Getting there**: trips to the islands can be arranged through many of the hotels or tour companies listed below. Several hotels and companies run day-trips to Pulau Paya for M$130-200/head. These islands are also within reach of Kuala Kedah, on the mainland.

Tours Organized tours around Langkawi and neighbouring islands can be booked through the two main hotels *Pelangi Beach Resort* and *Langkawi Island Resort*. *Sala Travel and Tours*, 2 Pokok Asam, Kuah, T 789521 also run tours around the island (and to offshore islands). Round-the-island coach tours M$15 (9-12 in minibus). Many hotels run boat trips and fishing trips round the islands. *Island Motel*, 18 Dundong, Kuah, T 789143, arranges snorkeling, fishing and island tours. *Langkawi Island Resort* runs fishing trips (M$39-180, depending on duration) and diving trips to Pulau Paya (M$220). At the cheaper end of the market, Mr Chen Kim Kee of the *Island Motel*, 18 Dundong Kuah (T 789143) organizes boat trips to neighbouring islands (about M$35/head) and day-long trips to Pulau Paya (M$130 with minimum of six people).

Accommodation Kuah: Most of the hotels in Kuah itself tend to be rather seedy and poor value for money. Tourists are advised to head straight for the beach resorts. **A-B** *Langkasuka*,

Pokok Asam, T 789828, F 788882, a/c, the best Kuah can offer; **C** *Asia*, 1 Jln Persiaran Putra, T 788216, a/c, reasonable, ¼ hrs walk from the jetty; **C** *Fairwinds*, 13 Jln Persiaran Putra, T 789359, clean boxes without windows or bathrooms; **D** *Gaya*, between Kuah and the jetty, T 788704, fan only, family run, basic but well kept; **D** *Langkawi*, 6 & 7 Pekan Kuah, T 788248, fan, bathroom outside, basic; **D** *Sri Pulau Montel*, Jln Pejabat Pos, T 789185; **E** *Island Motel*, 18 Dundong, T 789143, a/c & fan, small rooms, bathroom outside (see Tours), hires cars and motorcycles; **E** *Malaysia Hotel & Restaurant*, 66 Pokok Assam, T 788298, fan, no attached bathrooms, basic but good value for money.

Outside Kuah: **A** *Beringin Beach Resort*, round the corner from the *Langkawi Island Resort* (below), T 789966, F 789970, a/c, restaurant, own private beach, rec; **A** *Langkawi Island Resort*, Jln Pantai Dato' Syed Omar, T 788209, a/c, restaurant, pool, mainly used by tour groups, has its own private beach with watersports facilities, rents out bicycles (M\$6.60/day), motorbikes (M\$22/day) and cars (M\$90-160/day), quite a sophisticated little resort for the price; **C** *Lam Wit Village*, Batu 3, Bukit Tekoh, T 788669, rooms & dorm; **C-D** *Captain Resort*, Jln Penarak, T 789100, fan, restaurant, comfortable enough; **D** *Langkawi Chalet*, 1 Kampung Penarak, T 789993; **E** *Mahsuri Motel*, Bukit Tekoh, Jln Pantai Km6, T 788762; **F** *Countryside Motel*, Kampung Yu, Mukim Padang Matsirat, T 789268.

Pantai Cenang: the most popular of the three main beaches, with plenty of hotels and chalets to choose from; some are cramped a little too closely together. Despite the development, it is a picturesque beach. On Pulau Rebak Besar (dubbed Fantasy Island), opposite Pantai Cenang, there is a small resort with chalets. **A+** *Pelangi Beach Resort* T(04)911001/(03)2613306, F 911122, a/c, restaurant, pool, magnificent chalet-styled 5-star resort – regal enough even for Margaret Thatcher and her husband Denis, who stayed here along with other heads of state during the 1989 Commonwealth Conference, guests and their baggage are whisked around in electric cars, beach-side pool and atap-roofed bar on the sand, rec; **A** *Beach Garden Resort*, T 911363, F 911221, a/c, restaurant, pool, apart from the *Pelangi* this is the nicest hotel along this stretch, with thatched roofs, a tiny swimming pool and a wonderful restaurant on the beach, rec; **A-B** *Semarak Langkawi Beach Resort* T(04)911377/(03)7173651, a/c, restaurant, rooms & bungalows, well appointed rooms; **B-D** *Sandy Beach*, T 911308, a/c & fan, restaurant, simple A-frame chalets with more upmarket a/c rooms, good restaurant and friendly staff; **D** *Budget Travel Lodge*, T 911186; **D** *Inapan Sri Inai*, T 911269; **D-E** *Suria Beach Motel*, T 911232, you get what you pay for.

Pantai Tengah: next beach adjoining Pantai Cenang but not as nice. **B-C** *Sunset Beach Resort*, T 411109, a/c, restaurant, some time-share apartments and 8 rooms, rec; **C-D** *Charlie's*, T 911200/911316, a/c & fan, restaurant, chalets, at the end of Pantai Tengah, so has a more private stretch of beach, often booked up, rec; **D** *Delta Motel*, T 911307, restaurant, right on the end of the beach, well positioned chalets; **D** *Green Hill Beach Motel*, T 911935, fan, restaurant; **D** *Tanjung Malie Beach Motel*, T 911891, a/c, restaurant, pretty standard but organizes vacuum-packed island tours by what its brochure calls 'hoover craft'.

Pantai Kok: smaller, but more secluded beach, mainly cheaper chalet-style accommodation. **B** *Burau Bay*, T 911061, F 911172, a/c, restaurant, at the far end of Pantai Kok, with Gunung Macincang behind it, away from other chalets, twinned with *Pelangi*, so offers same facilities, excellent value for money, rec; **B-D** *Idaman Bay Resort*, T 911066, a/c & fan, restaurant, more upmarket than some of the others along this stretch; **C** *Mila Beach Motel*, T 911049, fan, restaurant, nice chalets, manager arranges fishing trips, rec; **C-D** *Last Resort*, T 911406, fan, restaurant, name refers to its location rather than its accommodation, the more expensive chalets right on the beach are a good bet; **C-D** *Pantai Kok Motel & Restaurant*, T 911048, some a/c, restaurant, wide range of accommodation at different prices, top end not bad; **D** *Coral Beach*, T 911000, fan, restaurant, chalets, bog standard; **D** *Dayang Beach Resort*, T 911058, fan, restaurant; **D** *Koh Bay Motel*, fan, very ordinary chalets; **D** *Tropica Beach Motel*, T 911049, fan, restaurant, on the other side of the road from the beach but the rooms are good value; **D-E** *Country Beach*, T 911212, a/c & fan, restaurant, chalets, friendly. Boats, bicycles and motorbikes for hire.

Pantai Rhu: the bay has a great view of Thailand's Koh Turatao and other islands. Only two hotels and not as popular as the other beaches. **A+** *Mutiara Court*, T 2484899, F 2482902, a/c, restaurant, pool, tastefully decorated but badly designed apartments with only most expensive look onto the bay, plans to build a swimming pool; **A** *Mutiara Beach Resort* T(04)788488/(03)2986779, a/c, restaurant, pool, large rooms, private beach, watersports.

Restaurants   *Mee Gulong* is Langkawi's speciality: fried noodles cooked with shredded prawns, slices of beef, chicken, carrots, cauliflower are rolled into a pancake, served with a thick potato gravy. **Kuah**: there are several Chinese seafood restaurants along the main street in Kuah, all quite good and reasonable value for money. **♦♦*Fortuna*, 19 Dundong Kuah, rec by locals; **♦♦*Golden Beach Seafood Restaurant*, Jln Persiaran Putra (near *Asia Hotel*), not much beach but good seafood; **♦♦*Orchid*, 3 Dundong Kuah, Chinese; **♦♦*Restoran Ria*, 71 Pokok Asam, seafood; **♦♦*Sari Restaurant*, Kompleks Pasar Lama, built out on stilts over the sea – which is now being reclaimed, vast selection of seafood. **Foodstalls**: roadside foodstalls in Kuah, down from *Langkasuka Hotel*, rec.

Outside Kuah: virtually all of the beach hotels have their own restaurants, some of which are excellent; seafood is an obvious choice on Langkawi. Of particular note are the ♦♦♦♦*Pelangi Beach Resort's* 2 first class international restaurants and the ♦♦♦*Beach Garden Restaurant* next door, which offers a good international selection, beautifully prepared. The latter is right on the beach and is highly rec. Both are on Pantai Cenang.

Sport Golf: *Langkawi Golf Club*, Jln Bukit Malut. A new 18-hole course has been built at Datai, with magnificent fairways, overlooking the bay. **Watersports**: the big resorts and hotels all offer watersports facilities. *Langkawi Marine Sports* in the centre of Pantai Cenang.

Shopping Duty free shops line the main street in Kuah, alcohol is especially good value. **Handicrafts**: many small shops in Kuah selling textiles. The best-stocked handicraft shop is in front of the *Sari Restaurant* in Kuah, *Batik Jawa Store*, 58 Pekan Pokok Asam. **Fishing tackle**: shop opposite the *Langasuka Hotel* in Kuah.

Local transport By bus: irregular and undependable and to get to the beaches you often have to walk quite a way from the bus stop. Buses from Kuah jetty to Pantai Cenang (M$2.80) and Tanjung Rhu (M$3). **By taxi**: fares around the island are very reasonable eg jetty-Kuah M$2 (M$7 for the whole taxi), Kuah-Pantai Cenang M$12. **Car hire**: *Mayflower Acme*, *Pelangi Beach Resort*, Pantai Cenang, T 911001; *Tomo Express*, 14 Jln Pandak Maya 4, Pekan Kuah, T 789252; *Langkawi Island Resort* (see above) and *Island Motel* in Kuah (also see above). **Motorcycle**: motorbikes, usually Honda 70s, are reasonably cheap to hire (M$20-25/day) and are far-and-away the best way to scoot around the island. Rental shops in Kuah and on all the main beaches. Kuah: *Island Motel*, 18 Dundong, T 789143. Pantai Cenang: *MBO*, opposite Semarak Langkawi. Pantai Tengah: *ASK*, opposite *Green Hill Beach Motel*. Pantai Kok: *Mila Beach Motel*, T 911049. *Tropica Beach Motel*, T 911049. **Bicycles**: for hire on the main beaches, M$10-15/day. **Boats**: it is well worth hiring a boat if you can get a large group of people together, otherwise it tends to be expensive – approximately M$150/day. Many of the beach hotels run boat trips to the islands as well as one or two places in Kuah (see tours above). Trips to Fantasy Island (opposite Pantai Cenang) leave from the beach next to *Pelangi Resort* (signposted from the road). *Langkawi Marine Sports* in the middle of Pantai Cenang organizes island trips.

Banks & money changers Maybank and United Malayan Banking Corporation are just off the main street in Kuah in the modern shophouse block. Several money changers along the main street, mainly in textile shops.

Useful addresses General Post Office at the jetty end of the main street in Kuah.

Airline offices MAS, *Langkawi Island Resort*, Kuah, T 788622.

Tourist offices Situated where the ferry arrives in Kuah; also tourist information booths in main hotels.

Transport to & from Langkawi 112 km N of Penang, 30 km from Kuala Perlis. **By air**: airport is the other side of Pantai Cenang, about 30 km from Kuah. Regular connections with KL (M$134), Penang (M$50). Also flights from Singapore twice a week (M$180). Germany's LTU International Airways now operates a direct, 14-hour, once-a-week (Thurs) flight from Munich to Langkawi. **By boat**: from Kuah jetty. Timetables subject to seasonal change (few boats during the monsoon months); new services will be starting up, as Langkawi is being heavily promoted. Regular connections with Kuala Perlis 45 mins (M$10) and Kuala Kedah 1 hr (M$12). Cheaper for the slow boats. The Kuala Perlis-Langkawi Ferry Service (T 917688, ticket counter; T 917868, office) operates boats to Penang (2½-3 hrs) Thurs-Mon at 1800. **International connections to Thailand**: regular express boat connections with Pak Bara (port 8 km from Satun, Thailand); departures 0830, 1500 Mon-Sun (M$15). From late-1992 there will also be a regular Penang-Langkawi-Phuket ferry; schedules and details from Kuala Perlis-Langkawi Ferry Service (see above).

SOUTH FROM KUALA LUMPUR

Introduction, 157; Seremban and Port Dickson, 157; Melaka, 161; Johor Bahru (JB), 175.

Maps South of Kuala Lumpur, 158; Melaka, 163; Johor Bahru, 176.

INTRODUCTION

The drive south from Kuala Lumpur through Seremban to Melaka runs on the first-to-be-completed stretch of the much-vaunted North-South Highway and is an easy, pleasant drive through rubber and oil palm plantations, formerly owned by big British companies. Like the route N from KL, the towns are predominantly Chinese, while the rural kampungs are almost exclusively Malay. Negri Sembilan, a confederacy of 9 small states united under the British colonial administration as part of the Federated Malay States, is renowned for its Minangkabau-style architecture. This is characterized by buffalo-horn shaped roof peaks, reflecting the influence of the state's first inhabitants who came from Sumatra.

On the coast, SW of Seremban, off the main highway, is the seaside resort town of **Port Dickson** (PD), which serves as a popular weekend retreat from Kuala Lumpur. The drive SE from PD to Melaka (Malacca) is much more interesting along the coastal backroads which run through open countryside and Malay kampungs. **Melaka** is one of the Malaysian tourism industry's trump cards, thanks to its Portuguese, Dutch and British colonial history, its rich Peranakan (Straits Chinese) cultural heritage and its picturesque hinterland of rural Malay kampungs. The route S from Melaka is a pleasant but unremarkable drive through plantation country to **Johor Bahru** (JB), on the southernmost tip of the peninsula. It is a short hop across the causeway from JB to Singapore, and Malaysia's E coast islands and resorts are within easy reach.

SEREMBAN AND PORT DICKSON

Seremban

Seremban (formerly known as Sungei Ujong) started life as another rough and ready tin-mining centre with a large population of Chinese. Tin mining flourished in the early years of the 19th century – one of the reasons Melaka continued as a thriving trading port. The control of the river, Sungei Linggi, which was the route Sungei Ujong's tin took to the sea, became a great source of contention between the 1820s and 1860s. The *Dato Klana*, or territorial chief of the Sungei Ujong district, frequently clashed with other members of the council of chiefs over the highly profitable river taxes and port dues. All wanted a share of the river tolls and erected illegal forts along the river to levy tolls from the Chinese merchants from Melaka and the Chinese miners. In 1857 the British sent an expedition up the river to destroy these fortified toll booths, but in no time they were back in business. In 1860 the confrontation came to a head when the tin miners in Sungei Ujong rebelled against the chiefs; hundreds were killed in the subsequent riots. One of the Chinese ringleaders was a ruthless young Hakka ruffian named **Yap Ah Loy**, who went on to become headman of a new tin boomtown called Kuala Lumpur in 1862 (**see page 94**).

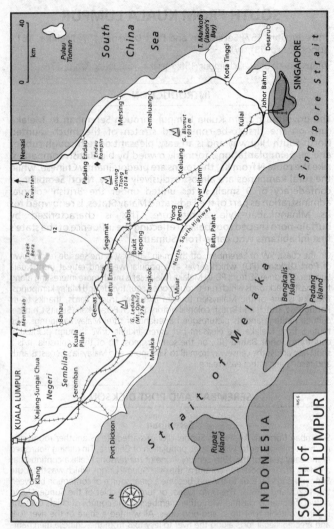

Today Seremban is the capital of the state of Negri Sembilan – which translates from Bahasa as 'nine states' and was historically a loose federation of districts, lorded over by 4 territorial chiefs. The town can easily be visited in a day from either Kuala Lumpur or Melaka.

Places of interest

Along the fringe of the outstanding **Taman Bunga** (Lake Gardens) is the **State Mosque**, with its 9 pillars representing the 9 old mini-states of Negri Sembilan. The **Teman Seni Budaya** (Cultural Complex) is on a 4-ha site at the junction of Jalan Sungai Ujong and the KL-Seremban road, 2 km from the centre of town. The main building is the **Terak Perpatih**, originally constructed as the pavilion for an international Koran-reading competition in 1984 and now a museum. On the ground floor are handicraft displays and upstairs there is an exhibition of historical artefacts. Also within the complex is a beautifully carved traditional Minangkabau wooden house, **Rumah Contoh Minangkabau**, built in 1898 (originally at Kampung Air Garam). In 1924 it was shipped to England and exhibited as an example of Malay architecture. On its return it was reassembled near the Lake Gardens in Seremban before being moved to Taman Seni Budaya. The **State Museum** is also part of the complex and is itself a good example of Minangkabau architecture; it is a reconstructed 19th century palace (Istana Ampang Tinggi), a high stilt building with an atap roof. The museum houses a small collection of ceremonial weapons and tableaux depicting a royal wedding. Complex open: 0900-1800 Sat-Wed, 0900-1200 Thur.

Excursions

Sri Menanti, the old Minangkabau capital of Negri Sembilan is 30 km E of Seremban, about 10 km before Kuala Pilah. This area is the Minangkabau heartland. *Sri* is the Minangkabau word for 'ripe paddy', and *Menanti* means 'awaiting' – although it is coloquially translated as 'beautiful resting place'. It was also common for early kings to add the Sanskrit honorific *Sri* to their titles and palaces. The former royal capital is on the upper reaches of Sungei Muar, which meanders through the valley which was known as *Londar Naga* – the tail of the dragon.

The **Istana Lama Sri Menanti** is a beautifully carved wooden palace built in Minangkabau style in 1908. It has 99 pillars depicting the 99 warriors of the various *luak-luak* (clans). It was, until 1931, the official residence of the Yang di-Pertuan Besar, the state ruler. On the fourth floor is a display of royal treasures. It is not officially a museum but is open to visitors. Open: 0900-1700 Sat-Wed, 0900-1200 Thur. This royal town also has a large mosque. **Getting there**: United Bus to Kuala Pilah every 15 mins (M$1.30).

Accommodation Seremban has a poor selection of hotels – particularly good ones – but there are several basic Chinese-run hotels. **B** *Tasik*, Jln Tetamu, T 730994, a/c, restaurant, pool, the best in town; **D** *Continental*, 45 Jln Dato Sheikh Ahmad, T 735742; **D** *Golden Hill*, 42 Jln Tuan Sheikah, T 713760, basic; **D** *International New*, 126 Jln Veloo, T 734959, fan only; **D** *Majestic*, 1 Jln Lee Hoon Yee, T 722506; **D** *Milo*, 22 & 24 Jln Wilkinson, T 723451, a/c, restaurant; **D** *Nam Yong*, 11 Jln Tuanku Munawir, T 720155, restaurant; **D** *Oriental*, 11 Jln Lemon, T 730119, restaurant; **D** *Wado*, 171 G-H Jln Tuanku Antah, T 730148, bar, parking; **D-E** *Carlton*, 47 Jln Tuan Sheikh, T 725336, a/c, restaurant; **D-E** *Century*, 25-29 Jln Tuanku Munawir, T 726261/3.

Restaurants Malay: *Flamingo Inn*, 1a Jln Zaaba; *Bilal*, 100 Jln Dato Bandar Tunggal; *Fatimah*, 419 Jln Tuanku Manawir; *Anira*, Kompleks Negeri Sembilan. Chinese: *Sunton*, 10-11 Jln Dato Sheikh Ahmad; *Regent*, 2391-2 Taman Bukit Labu; *Seafood*, 2017-8 Blossom Heights, Jln Tok Ungku; *Happy*, 1 Jln Dato Bandar Tunggal. Indian: *Sammy*, 120 Jln Yam Tuan, banana leaf, budget; *Anura*, 97 Jln Tuanku Antah. Foodstalls: *Jnl Tuanku Antah*, near the post office; *Jnl Tun Dr Ismail*, near the market; *Jnl Tuanku Munawir*.

Banks & money changers Bumiputra, Wisma Dewan Permagaa Melayu; Maybank, 10-11

Brand-name satay from the source

Kajang, about 20 km S of KL on the Seremban road, is named after the palm-leaf canopy of a bullock cart, once ubiquitous and still occasionally seen in Negri Sembilan. At hawker centres all over Malaysia, there are stalls called 'Satay Kajang': the town long ago gained the reputation for the best satay in the country. There are many satay stalls in Kajang today. *Selamat makan!*

Minangkabau – the 'buffalo-horn' people from across the water

Negri Sembilan's early inhabitants were immigrants from Minangkabau in Sumatra (see page 772). They started to settle in the hinterland of Melaka and around Sungei Ujong (modern Seremban) during the 16th and 17th centuries and were skilled irrigated paddy farmers. *Minangkabau* roughly translates as 'buffalo horns' and the traditional houses of rural Negri Sembilan and Melaka have magnificent roofs that sweep up from the centre into 2 peaks. The Minangkabau architectural style (see page 776) has been the inspiration behind many modern Malaysian buildings, notably the Muzium Negara (National Museum) and the Putra World Trade Centre in Kuala Lumpur.

The Minangkabau introduced Islam, a sophisticated legal system and their matrilineal society to the interior of the Malay peninsula. In 1773 they appealed to the Minangkabau court at Pagar Ruyong in Sumatra to appoint a ruler over them and a Sumatran prince – Raja Melewar – was installed as the first king, or *Yang di-Pertuan Besar* of the confederacy of mini-states, with his capital at Sri Menanti. But Negri Sembilan's 4 *undang* – territorial chiefs – saw to it that he wielded no real power. In all there were 4 kings from Sumatra, all of them ineffectual, and the link with Sumatra finally ended in 1824 with the establishment of an indigenous hereditary royal family.

Jln Dato Abdul Rahman; **OCBC**, 63-65 Jln Dato Bandar Tunggal; **Public Bank**, 46 Jln Dato Lee Fong Yee; **Standard & Chartered**, 128 Jln Dato Bandar Tunggal; **UMBC**, 39 Jln Tuanku Munawir.

Tourist offices State Economic Planning Unit, 5th Floor Wisma Negeri, T 06722311.

Transport to & from Seremban 62 km S of KL, 83 km N of Melaka. **By train**: connections every 2 hrs with KL. **By bus**: station on Jln Sungai Ujong. Connections with JB (M\$15.20), Melaka (M\$2.85), KL (M\$2.30), Kota Bahru (M\$26). **By taxi**: Port Dickson (M\$2.50), KL (M\$6), Melaka (M\$7).

Port Dickson

Port Dickson – typically shortened to PD – is 32 km from Seremban and is one of the most popular seaside resorts in Malaysia, as testified by all the modern condominium developments. The pace of development has given the little fishing port a pollution problem in recent years. This is a narrow point of the Melaka Strait and large ships use the deep-water channel which cuts close to the Malaysian coast. Rarely a month goes by during which the Malaysian authorities aren't giving chase to tankers which have an increasingly alarming tendency to dump thousands of tonnes of sludge, oil and effluent into the strait. Port Dickson itself is quiet and undistinguished but to the S is a long sandy beach, stretching 18 km down to the Cape Rachado lighthouse, although there are cleaner places to swim in Malaysia. Built by the British on the site of a 16th century Portuguese lighthouse, Cape Rachado has panoramic views along the coast (it is necessary to acquire permission from the Marine Department in Melaka to climb to the top). The port town, originally called Tanjung Kamuning, was renamed after Sir Frederick Dickson, British Colonial Secretary and acting Governor in 1890. At **Kota Lukut**, 7 km from Port Dickson, is Raja Jamaat fort, built in 1847 to control the tin trade in the area.

Accommodation Because PD is a favourite family getaway for KL's weekenders, beach hotels are often quite full. During the week, discounts are sometimes on offer. **A** *Ming Court Beach*, Batu 71/2 Mile, Jln Pantai, T 405244, a/c, restaurant, pool, best hotel on the strip with good range of sports and watersport facilities; **A** *Pantai Dickson Resort*, Batu 12, Jln Pantai, T 405473, a/c, restaurant, pool, beach bungalows; **A-B** *Golden Resort*, Batu 10 Jln Pantai, T 405176, a/c, restaurant, pool; **B** *Pantai Motel*, Batu 9, Jln Pantai, T 405265, a/c, restaurant, popular but run-down; **B** *Si Rusa Beach Resort*, Batu 7, Jln Pantai, T 405233, a/c, restaurant; **B** *Tanjung Tuan Beach Resort*, T 473013, a/c, restaurant, pool, good sports facilities and weekday discounts; **C** *Coastal Inn*, Batu 4, Jln Pantai, T 473388, a/c, run-down; **C** *Kong*

Ming, Batu 8, Teluk Kemang, T 405683, restaurant, on the beachfront, reasonable for the price; **C** *Lido*, Batu 8, Jln Pantai, T 405273, restaurant, quiet location, set in large grounds; **C-D** *Merlin*, 218-9 Jln Pantai T 473388, restaurant; **D** *Sea View*, 841, Batu 1, Jln Pantai, T 471811, restaurant; **E** *Happy City*, 24 Jln Raja Aman Shah, T 473103, basic.

Restaurants Malay: **♦♦***Santan Berlada*, Batu 1, Jln Pantai. **Chinese**: **♦♦***Pantai Ria*, Batu 7½, Jln Pantai, seafood. **Seafood**: **♦♦♦***Blue Lagoon*, Cape Rachado (on the way to the lighthouse). **Foodstalls**: scattered around town and along Jln Pantai.

Banks & money changers Bumiputra, 745 Jln Bahru; **Public**, 866 Jln Pantai; **Standard Chartered**, 61 Jln Bahru.

Useful addresses Hospital on the waterfront by the bus station, Jln Pantai.

Transport to & from Port Dickson 94 km from KL, 32 km from Seremban, 90 km from Melaka. **By bus**: station on Jln Pantai, just outside the main centre but buses will normally stop on request anywhere along the beach. Regular connections with KL (M$4.50) and Melaka (M$4). **By taxi**: share taxis to Melaka (M$8), KL (M$8), Seremban (M$2.50).

MELAKA

Thanks to its strategic location on the strait which bears its name, Melaka was a rich, cosmopolitan port city long before it fell victim to successive colonial invasions. Its wealth and influence are now a thing of the past, and the old city's colourful history is itself a major money-spinner for Malaysia's modern tourism industry.

The city was founded by Parameswara, a fugitive prince from Palembang in Sumatra. According to the 16th century *Sejara Melayu* (the Malay Annals), he was a descendent of the royal house of Srivijaya, whose lineage could be traced back to Alexander the Great. Historians, however, suspect that he was really a Javanese refugee who, during the 1390s, invaded and took Temasek (Singapore) before he himself was ousted by the invading Siamese. He fled up the W coast of the peninsula and, with a few followers, settled in a fishing kampung.

The Malay Annals relate how Parameswara was out hunting one day, and while resting in the shade of a tree watched a tiny mouse deer turn and kick one of his hunting dogs and drive it into the sea. He liked its style and named his nearby settlement after the *malaka* tree he was sitting under. Sadly it seems more likely that the name Melaka is derived from the Arabic word *malakat* – or market – and from its earliest days the settlement, with its sheltered harbour, was an entrepôt. Melaka was sheltered from the monsoons by the island of Sumatra, and perfectly located for merchants to take advantage of the trade winds. Because the Strait's deep-water channel lay close to the Malayan coast, Melaka had command over shipping passing through it.

In 1405 a Chinese Admiral, the eunuch Cheng Ho, arrived in Melaka bearing gifts from the Ming Emperor (including a yellow parasol, which has been the emblem of Malay royalty ever since) and the promise of protection from the Siamese. Cheng Ho made 7 voyages to the Indian Ocean over the next 3 decades and used Melaka as his supply base. The Chinese gained a vassal state and Melaka gained a sense of security: Parameswara was wary of possible Siamese encroachment. Court rituals, ceremony and etiquette were formalized and an exclusive royal court language evolved. In 1411, 3 years before his death, Parameswara sailed with Cheng Ho to China with a large retinue and was received by the third Ming Emperor, Chu Ti. Melaka's next 2 rulers continued this tradition, making at least 2 visits each to China.

But China began to withdraw its patronage in the 1430s, and to make sure Melaka retained at least one powerful friend, the third ruler, Sri Maharaja, married the daughter of the sultan of the flourishing maritime state of Samudra-Pasai in

Sumatra. Historian Mary Turnbull says "he embraced Islam and hitched Melaka's fortunes to the rising star of the Muslim trading fraternity". He adopted the name Mohamed Shah, but retained the court's long-standing Hindu rituals and ceremonies. He died without a child from his marriage to the Pasai princess and a succession crisis followed. The rightful royal heir, the young Rajah Ibrahim was murdered in a palace coup after a year on the throne and Kasim, one of Mohamed's sons by a non-royal marriage declared himself Sultan Muzaffar Shah. Melaka's first proper sultan made Islam the state religion and beat off 2 Siamese invasions during his reign. Islam was also spreading through the merchant community. In the latter half of the 15th century the faith was taken from Melaka to other states on the peninsula as well as to Brunei and Javanese port cities which were breaking away from the Hindu kingdom of Majapahit.

In the late 15th century, Malay power reached its pinnacle. Muzaffar's successor, Sultan Mansur Shah, extended Melaka's sway over Pahang, Johor and Perak, the Riau archipelago and Sumatra. Contemporary European maps label the entire peninsula 'Malacca'. According to the Malay Annals, the sultan married a Chinese princess in 1460. This marriage and the arrival of the princess and her followers marked the formal beginning of the unique and prosperous Straits Chinese *Peranakan* culture (see page 168).

Another cultural blend that had its roots in medieval Melaka was the Chitty Indian community, the result of Indian merchants inter-marrying with local women, including the Malay nobility. Because foreign traders had to wait several months before the winds changed to allow them to return home, many put down roots and Melaka, 'the city where the winds met', had hundreds of permanent foreign residents. There were no taboos concerning cross-cultural marriage: the polygamous Muslim Sultan Mansur Shah even visited the crumbling Majapahit court in E Java where he cemented relations by his second royal marriage, to the Hindu ruler's daughter.

By the beginning of the 16th century Melaka was the most important port in the region. Foreign merchants traded in Indian and Persian textiles, spices from the Moluccas (Maluku), silk and porcelain from China as well as gold, pepper, camphor, sandalwood and tin. The Malay language became the *lingua franca* throughout the region.

Tales of luxuriance and prosperity attracted the Portuguese. They came in search of trading opportunities and with the aim of breaking the Arab merchants' stranglehold on trade between Europe and Asia. Spices from the Moluccas came through the Strait and whoever controlled the waterway determined the price of cloves in Europe. The Portuguese – known to Melakans as 'the white Bengalis' – combined their quest for riches with a fervent anti-Muslim crusade, spurred by their hatred of their former Moorish overlords on the Iberian peninsula. They arrived in 1509, received a royal welcome and then fled for their lives when Gujerati (Indian) traders turned the Sultan against them. Alfonso d'Albuquerque, the viceroy of Portuguese India, returned 2 years later with 18 ships and 1,400 men. After an initial attempt at reconciliation, he too was beaten off. D'Albuquerque then stormed and conquered the city in Jul 1511, the year after he seized Goa on India's W coast. The Melakan court fled to Johor where Sultan Ahmad re-established his kingdom.

The foreign merchants quickly adapted to the new rulers and under the Portuguese the city continued to thrive. Tomé Pires, a Portuguese apothecary who arrived with d'Albuquerque's fleet and stayed 2 years, wrote in his account, *Suma Oriental*: "Whoever is lord of Melaka has his hand on the throat of Venice," adding that "the trade and commerce between different nations for a thousand leagues on every hand must come to Melaka". The port became known as the 'Babylon

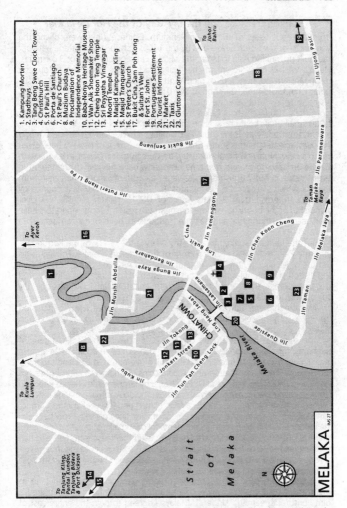

1. Kampung Morten
2. Stadthuys
3. Tang Beng Swee Clock Tower
4. Christchurch
5. St Paul's Hill
6. Porta de Santiago
7. St Paul's Church
8. Muzium Budaya
9. Proclamation of Independence Memorial
10. Baba-Nonya Heritage Museum
11. Wah Aik Shoemaker Shop
12. Cheng Hoon Teng Temple
13. Sri Poyyatha Vinayagar Moorti Temple
14. Masjid Kampung Kling
15. Masjid Tranquerah
16. St Peter's Church
17. Bukit Cina, Sam Poh Kong & Sultan's Well
18. Fort St. John
19. Portuguese Settlement
20. Tourist Information
21. Market
22. Taxis
23. Gluttons Corner

MELAKA

of the Orient'. Despite the 2-year sojourn of French Jesuit priest St Francis Xavier, Christianity had little impact on the Muslim Malays or the hedonistic merchant community. A large Eurasian population grew up, adding to Melaka's cosmopolitan character; there are still many Pereiras, D'Cruzes, de Silvas, Martinezes and Fernandezes in the Melaka phone book.

Back in Lisbon in the early 17th century, the Portuguese monarchy was on the decline, the government in serious debt and successive expeditions failed to acquire anything more than a tenuous hold over the Spice Islands, to the E. The Portuguese never managed to subdue the Sumatran pirates, the real rulers of the

Sunken treasure and the mystery of the *Flor de la Mar*

From the early years of the first millennium, Chinese junks were plying the *Nanyang* – or the South Seas – and by the 1400s a sophisticated trade network had built up, linking Asia to India, the Middle East and Europe. For 3 centuries, Melaka was at the fulcrum of the China trade route and even before the Europeans arrived, hundreds of merchants came each year from Arabia, Persia, India, China, Champa, Cambodia, Siam, Java, Sumatra and the Eastern Isles. Historian Mary Turnbull writes that "by the first decade of the 16th century, more than 100 large ships called there each year, and at any one time up to 2,000 small boats could be seen in the harbour."

But this trade was not without its casualties and the sunken wrecks littering the coastal waters of the South China Sea and the Strait of Melaka have given rise to a new, highly profitable industry: treasure hunting. Divers, in league with marine archaeologists and maritime historians, have flocked to the region in recent years. In 1987 British divers salvaged a cargo of Chinese porcelain from a vessel which sank off the Riau islands in 1752; the booty was auctioned by Christie's in Amsterdam 2 years later for US$16 million. Sensitivities over ownership of the booty have come to a head as a result. Salvage operators have been jailed in Indonesia and salvaged antiquities have been confiscated in Thailand.

But the ultimate sunken treasure trove lies in the wreck of the Portuguese ship, the *Flor de la Mar*, at the bottom of the Strait of Melaka. Following his capture of Melaka in Jul 1511, Admiral Alfonso d'Albuquerque set off for Goa and Lisbon with the plundered riches of Sultan Ahmad's palace and assorted loot from across Africa and Asia. On a stormy night in Jan 1512, just one day out of port, his flagship hit a reef and sank in 20m of water. D'Albuquerque survived the shipwreck and managed to salvage a gold sword, a jewel-encrusted crown, a ruby bracelet and a ring which today are on display in a Lisbon museum. But the rest of the loot was lost... in Indonesian waters.

The ship was believed to be carrying 20 tonnes of solid gold statues of elephants, tigers and monkeys, studded with gemstones. In addition, there were several gold-plated royal litters and chests full of diamonds, rubies and sapphires and several tonnes of Chinese and Arabic coins. Sotheby's auction house has tentatively valued the treasure at US$9 billion... by far the world's richest wreck. In 1988 an Italian specialist in underwater wrecks and an Australian marine historian claimed to have located the *Flor de la Mar*, hidden under several metres of mud, using satellite imaging. The announcement of their find sparked a row between the Indonesian and Malaysian governments following allegations that 'powerful interests linked to President Suharto' had harrassed the treasure-hunters and had privately tried to force them to disclose its location so they could mount a covert salvage operation. The Italian, Bruno de Vincentiis, began negotiations with both governments, proposing to split the booty 3 ways.

In late 1991, following reports that Indonesian Navy divers had tried to locate the wreck – to no avail – Jakarta and Kuala Lumpur finally entered a joint-venture agreement. Under it, Malaysia agreed to bear the entire cost of the operation and split the booty 50/50. The work is being carried out by the Indonesian firm Jayatama Istikacipta under a 5-year recovery licence. In Mar 1991 the company claimed to have located the wreck, 8 km off Tanjung Jambu Air in Aceh, without de Vincentiis' help. It is understood to be buried under a 10m-thick layer of mud and sand on the sea bed. In 1992, rumours surfaced that some of the gold had already been secretly salvaged. Investigations among Singapore's commercial diving community in 1993 suggested there was some truth to these rumours, but the matter is so sensitive and the stakes so high that lips are firmly sealed.

Strait of Melaka. As Dutch influence increased in Indonesia, Batavia (Jakarta) developed as the principal port of the region and Melaka declined. The Dutch entered into an alliance with the Sultanate of Johor and foreign traders began to move there. This paved the way for a Dutch blockade of Melaka and in 1641, after a 6 month seige of the city, Dutch forces, together with troops from Johor, forced the surrender of the last Portuguese governor.

Over the next 150 years the Dutch carried out an extensive building programme; some of these still stand in Dutch Square. Melaka was the collecting point for Dutch produce from Sumatra and the Malay peninsula, where the new administration attempted to enforce a monopoly on the tin trade. They built forts on Pulau Pangkor and at Kuala Selangor, N of Klang, to block Acehnese efforts to muscle in on the trade, but the Dutch, like the Portuguese before them, were more interested in trade than territory. Apart from their buildings, the Dutch impact on Melaka was minimal. Their tenure of the town was periodically threatened by the rise of the Bugis, Minangkabaus and Makassarese who migrated to the Malay peninsula having been displaced by the activities of the Dutch East India Company in Sulawesi and Sumatra. In 1784 Melaka was only saved from a joint Bugis and Minangkabau invasion by the arrival of the Dutch fleet from Europe.

By the late 18th century, the Dutch hold on the China trade route was bothering the English East India Company. In 1795 France conquered the Netherlands and the British made an agreement with the exiled Dutch government allowing them to become the caretaker of Dutch colonies. Four years later the Dutch East India Company went bankrupt, but just to make sure that they would not be tempted to make a comeback in Melaka, the British started to demolish the fortress in 1807. The timely arrival of Stamford Raffles, the founder of modern Singapore, prevented the destruction from going further, and in 1824, under the Treaty of London, Melaka was surrendered to the British in exchange for the Sumatran port of Bencoolen (Bengkulu).

In 1826 Melaka became a part of the British Straits Settlements, along with Penang and Singapore. But by then, its harbour had silted up and it was a town of little commercial importance. In 1826 it had a population of 31,000 and was the biggest of the settlements; by 1860, although its population had doubled, it was the smallest and least significant of the 3. In 1866, a correspondent for the *Illustrated London News* described Melaka (which the British spelled *Malacca*) as "a land where it is 'always afternoon' – hot still, dreamy. Existence stagnates. Trade pursues its operations invisibly... It has no politics, little crime, rarely gets even 2 lines in an English newspaper and does nothing towards making contemporary history". In 1867 the Straits Settlements were transferred to direct colonial rule and Melaka faded into obscurity. Strangely, it was the town's infertile agricultural hinterland which helped re-invigorate the local economy at the turn of the century. The first rubber estate in Malaya was started by Melakan planter Tan Chay Yan, who accepted some seedlings from 'Mad' Henry Ridley, director of Singapore's Botanic Gardens (see page 411) and planted out 1,200 ha in 1896. The idea caught on among other Chinese and European planters and Melaka soon became one of the country's leading rubber producers.

Places of interest

Arriving in Melaka by road, it is not immediately apparent that the city is Malaysia's historical treasure-trove. Jalan Munshi Abdullah, which runs through the middle of the more recent commercial district, is like any Malaysian main street. The taxi station and express bus terminal are away from the central core of old Melaka, and while the old city is quite compact, the town itself is neither as small or medieval-looking as visitors are led to suppose. The historical sights from the Portuguese and Dutch periods are interesting because they are in Malaysia – not because they are stunning architectural wonders. That said, the old red Dutch buildings on the E bank of the river and the magnificent Peranakan architecture and stuccoed shophouses on the W side, lend Melaka an atmosphere unlike any other Malaysian town. It also lays claim to many of the country's oldest Buddhist and Hindu temples, mosques and churches. Although it is possible to walk around these sights, the most leisurely way to get around is by trishaw. There are also many places around town which rent bicycles.

The most interesting parts of the old town are close to the waterfront. There are boat tours (see below) down the river through the original port area and past some of the old Dutch houses. On the W bank is **Kampung Morten**, a village of traditional Melakan houses. It was named after a man who built Melaka's wet market and donated the land to the Malays. The main attraction here is **Kassim Mahmood's hand-crafted house**.

The Dutch colonial architecture in the town square is the most striking feature of the riverfront. The buildings are painted a bright terracotta red and are characterised by their massive walls, chunky doors with wrought iron hinges and louvred windows. The most prominent of these is the **Stadthuys**. Completed in 1660, it is said to be the oldest-surviving Dutch building in the East, and served as the official residence of the Dutch governors. The recently renovated building now houses a museum. Admission: M$1.50. Open: 0900-1800 Sat-Thur 0900-1215, 1500-1800 Fri. The **Tang Beng Swee Clock Tower** looks Dutch but was built by a wealthy Straits Chinese family in 1886. **Christ Church** was built between 1741 and 1753 to replace an earlier Portuguese church, which was by then a ruin (church records date back to 1641). Its red bricks were shipped out from Zeeland in Holland. It is Malaysia's oldest Protestant church and the floor is still studded with Dutch tombstones. The original pews are intact – as are its ceiling beams, each hewn from a single tree trunk more than 15m long. On the altar there is a collection of sacramental silverware bearing the Dutch coat-of-arms. Open: Thur-Tue.

On Jalan Kota, which runs in a curve round **St Paul's Hill** from the square, is the **Porta de Santiago**, the remains of the great Portuguese fort **A Famosa**, said to have been built in 4 months flat under Admiral Alfonso d'Albequerque's supervision in 1511. What remains is largely a Dutch reconstruction, the result of repair work carried out following the siege in 1641 – it prominently displays the Dutch East India Company's coat-of-arms. The fort originally sprawled across the whole hill and housed the entire Portuguese administration, including their hospitals and 5 churches. It was flattened by the British between 1806 and 1808 when they occupied Melaka during the Napoleonic Wars. They wanted to ensure that the fort was not reclaimed by the Dutch. Stamford Raffles arrived for a holiday in Melaka just in time to forestall the destruction of its last remaining edifice.

From behind the gate, a path leads up to the ruins of **St Paul's Church**, built on the site of the last Melakan sultan's istana. The small chapel was originally built by the Portuguese in 1521 and called *Nossa Senhora da Annunciada* – Our Lady of the Anunciation. The body of St Francis Xavier (the 16th century Jesuit missionary who translated the catechism into Malay and visited the church regularly), was temporarily interred in the church vault following his death off the coast of China in 1552. His remains were later sent to Portuguese Goa on the W coast of India. An armless marble statue, erected in 1953, now commemorates Malaysia's best known missionary. The Portuguese added gun turrets and a tower to the church and it became a fortress between 1567 and 1596. During the Dutch seige of Melaka in 1641, it was badly damaged but the invaders repaired it and renamed it St Paul's. It became a Protestant church and remained so until Christ Church was completed in 1753. St Paul's ended its life as a cemetery; it was used as a special burial ground for Dutch nobles, whose tombs line the walls.

A wooden replica of Sultan Mansur Shah's 15th century istana now houses the **Muzium Budaya** (Melaka Cultural Museum) below St Paul's. The palace has been painstakingly reconstructed from a description in the 16th century *Serjarah Melayu* (Malaya Annals) and built in 1985 using traditional construction techniques and materials. Mansur – who came to the throne in 1459 – inherited what was reputed to be the finest royal palace in the world, with a roof of copper and zinc in 7 tiers, supported by wooden carved pillars. According to the Annals, his magnificent istana was destroyed by fire after being struck by lightning the year after his accession. Exhibits in the museum focus on Melakan culture including clothes, games, weapons, musical instruments, stone inscriptions and photographs. It also features a diorama of the Sultan's court. Admission: M$1.50. Open: 0900-1800 Sat-Thur, 0900-1200, 1500-1800 Fri.

The **Proclamation of Independence Memorial**, opposite the Cultural Museum, was built in 1912 and formerly housed the Malacca Club. The old Dutch colonial building was the social centre of British colonial Melaka. It now contains a collection of photographs and exhibits depicting the run-up to Malaysian independence in 1957. Open: 0900-1800 Tue-Thur, Sat & Sun, 0900-1200 Fri.

A concrete bridge from the S end of Dutch Square leads to **Chinatown**, the old trading section of Melaka. Jalan Hang Jebat, formerly known as **Jonkers Street**, is famous for its antique shops: Nonya porcelain, Melakan-style 'red and gold' carved furniture, wooden opium beds, Victorian mirrors, antique fans and Peranakan blackwood furniture inlaid with mother-of-pearl. There are some good examples of Peranakan architecture along the street – notably the renowned Jonkers Melaka Restoran. But none of these Peranakan houses compare with the picturesque **Jalan Tun Tan Cheng Lock**. Named after a leading Melakan Baba, instrumental in pre-independence politics (see box), it is lined with the Straits Chinese community's ancestral homes and is Melaka's 'Millionaires Row'. Many of the houses have intricately carved doors that were often specially built by immigrant craftsmen from China. Today huge tour buses clog the narrow one-way street, but many of its Peranakan mansions are still lived in by the same families that built them in the 19th century.

One of the most opulent of these houses has been converted into the **Baba-Nonya Heritage Museum**, 48-50 Jalan Tun Tan Cheng Lock. It is in a well preserved traditional Peranakan town house, built in 1896 by millionaire rubber planter Chan Cheng Siew. Today it is owned by William Chan and his family, who conduct tours of their ancestral home. The interior is that of a typical 19th century residence and all the rooms left as they would have been 100 years ago. The house contains family heirlooms and antiques, including Nonyaware porcelain and blackwood furniture with marble or mother-of-pearl inlay, and silverware. There is also a collection of traditional wedding costumes, photographs and kitchen utensils. The kitchen sink has the name of William Chan's great grandfather carved on it. The information-packed tours are run regularly throughout the day. Admission: M$7. Open: 1000-1230, 1400-1630 Sat-Wed, 0900-1200 Thur.

Wah Aik Shoemaker Shop, 92 Jonkers St (Jalan Hang Jebat), is Malaysia's most unusual shoe shop. For 2 generations the Yeo family have been the only cobblers catering for the country's dwindling population of ageing Chinese women with bound feet. The practice, which was considered *de rigeur* for women of noble stock during the Ch'ing Dynasty (1644-1912), was rekindled among the families of nouveau riche Chinese tin towkays during the days of the British Straits Settlements. The process involved binding the feet firmly with bandages before they were fully formed; it was supposed to add to a woman's sensuality, but in reality it just caused a lot of pain. In China, the practice was outlawed in 1912.

The Nonyas and the Babas

Chinese traders in the *Nanyang*, or South Seas, visited Melaka from its earliest days and by the early 1400s the town was one of the most important ports of call for Chinese trade missions. They arrived between Nov and Mar on the NE monsoon winds and left again in late Jun on the SW monsoon. This gave them plenty of time to settle down and start families. Melaka's early sultans made several visits to China, paying obeisance to the Ming emperors to ensure Chinese imperial protection for the sultanate. When Sultan Mansur Shah married the Ming Chinese princess Hang Li Poh in 1460, she brought with her a retinue of 500 'youths of noble birth' and handmaidens who settled around Bukit Cina – or Chinese Hill.

Subsequent generations of Straits Chinese came to be known as *Peranakans* – the term comes from the Bahasa word *anak*, or offspring and means 'born here'. Peranakan women were called Nonyas and the men, Babas. Sultan Mansur's marriage set a precedent and Peranakans combined the best of Chinese and Malay cultures. They created a unique, sophisticated and influential society and were known for their shrewd business acumen and opulent lifestyles. When the Dutch colonists moved out in the early 1800s, more Chinese moved in, continuing the tradition of intermarriage while clinging to the ancient customs brought with them from China. Jonas Vaughan, a Victorian colonial administrator wrote: "One may see in Malacca Babas who can claim no connection with China for centuries, clad in long jackets, loose drawers, and black skull caps, the very conterparts of Chinese to be seen any day at Amoy, Chusan, or under the walls of Nanking."

Peranakan culture reached its zenith in the 19th century. Although Melaka was the Peranakan hearthstone, there were also large Straits Chinese communities in Penang and Singapore too. The Nonyas adopted Malay dress – they wore Malay-style jackets and sarongs and were known for their fastidiousness when it came to clothes. The women were renowned for their intricate jewellery and glass beadwork – which are now prized antiques. The Nonyas imported colourful porcelain from China for ceremonial occasions which became known as Nonyaware and was typically emblazoned with phoenix and peony-flower motifs. They also imported craftsmen from China to make their intricate silver jewellery including elaborate belts, hairpins, and pillow end plates.

Peranakan weddings were elaborate affairs; couples were paired off by marriage-brokers, contracted by the groom's parents to consult horoscopes and judge the suitability of the match. If a match proved auspicious, there was a lengthy present-exchanging ritual for the young couple who were not permitted to see each other until they finally got to the nuptial chamber. Wedding rituals often went on for 12 days and ended in a lavish feast before the couple went upstairs and the heavily veiled bride first showed her face to her new husband. As was the custom, he would then say: "Lady, I have perforce to be rude with you", whether he liked what he saw or not, for the marriage had to be consummated immediately.

There are only a handful of women in Malaysia with bound feet, most of them in Melaka and all of them in their 80s or 90s. Mr Yeo Sing Guat makes these *san choon chin lian* (three-inch golden lotus feet) shoes – with brocade on authentic Shanghai Hang Chong silk – for them and as tourist souvenirs; he also makes the Peranakan *kasut manik* 'pearl shoes', sewn with miniature pearl beads.

The **Cheng Hoon Teng Temple**, on Jalan Tokong, was built in 1645 and is the oldest Chinese temple in Malaysia (although there were later additions in 1704 and 1804). The name literally means 'Temple of the Evergreen Clouds' and was founded by Melaka's Kapitan Cina, Lee Wi King from Amoy, a political refugee

Peranakan architecture is exemplified in the 'Chinese Palladian' townhouses – the best examples of which are in Melaka – with their open courtyards and lavish interiors, dominated by heavy dark furniture, inlaid with marble and mother-of-pearl. Aside from their magnificent homes, one of the Peranakans' most enduring endowments is their cuisine, which is the result of the melding of cultures. The food is spicy but uses lots of coconut milk and is painstakingly prepared – one reason that Nonya-Baba restaurants are difficult business propositions. Traditionally, would-be brides would have to impress their future mother-in-laws with their kitchen-competence, particularly in their fine-slicing of ingredients. Typical meals, served with rice and *sambal* (crushed chilli fried in oil), include *otak-otak* and *ayam pongteh* and deserts such as iced *chendol*, and *gula melaka* (for details on particular dishes, **see page 352**).

The cliquey Peranakan upper-class assimilated easily into British colonial society, following the formation of the Straits Settlements in 1826. The billiard-playing, brandy-swilling Babas, in their Mandarin dresses, conical hats, pigtails and thick-soled shoes successfully penetrated the commercial sector and entered public office. Many became professionals: lawyers, doctors and teachers, although they were barred from entering government above the clerical level. "Strange to say," wrote Vaughan, "that although the Babas adhere so loyally to the customs of their progenitors they despise the real Chinamen and are exclusive fellows indeed; [there is] nothing they rejoice in more than being British subjects... They have social clubs of their own to which they will admit no native of China." In Penang they were dubbed 'the Queen's Chinese'. Over the years they evolved their own Malay patois, and, in the 19th century, English was also thrown into their linguistic cocktail. They even devised a secret form of slang by speaking Baba Malay backwards.

Although they chose not to mix with immigrant Chinese, they retained a strong interest in events in China. The Straits Settlements provided a refuge for exiled reformers from the motherland – most notably Dr Sun Yat-sen, who lived in both Singapore and Penang in the early 1900s and became the first president of the Republic of China in 1911.

The Baba community's most famous son was Tan Cheng Lock, who was born into a distinguished Melakan Baba family in 1883. He lent his name to the Peranakans' architectural treasure, Jalan Tun Tan Chen Lock (formerly Heeren Street) in Melaka's Chinatown. Tan served in local government in colonial Melaka from 1912-1935 and vociferously fought British discrimination against the Straits and Malayan Chinese. He charged that the British had done nothing to "foster and strengthen their spirit of patriotism and natural love for the country of their birth and adoption". Tan was the spokesman for Malaya's Chinese community and fought for equality among the races; he founded the Overseas Chinese Association and became a prominent reformist politician in the years leading up to Malaysian independence.

who fled from China. All the materials used in the original building were imported from China as were the craftsmen who built it in typical S Chinese style. The elaborate tiled roofs are decorated with mythological figures, flowers and birds, and inside there are woodcarvings and lacquer work. The main altar houses an image of Kuan Yin, the Goddess of Mercy (cast in solid bronze and bought from India in the last century), who is associated with peace, good fortune and fertility. On her left sits Ma Cho Po, the guardian of fishermen and on her right, Kuan Ti, the god of war, literature and justice. The halls to the rear of the main temple are dedicated to Confucius and contain ancestral tablets.

Nearby, on Jalan Tukang Emas, is the **Sri Poyyatha Vinayagar Moorthi Temple**, built in 1781 and the oldest Hindu temple in use in Malaysia. It is dedicated to the elephant-headed god Vinayagar (more usually known as Ganesh). Near to this Hindu temple on Jalan Tukang Emas is the **Masjid Kampung Kling**, a mosque built in 1748 in Sumatran style, with a square base surmounted by a 3-tiered roof and pagoda-like minaret. Another 18th century mosque in the same style is the **Masjid Tranquerah**, 2 km out of town on the road to Port Dickson. Next door is an unusual free-standing octagonal minaret with Chinese-style embellishments, in marked contrast to Malaysia's traditional Moorish-style mosques. In the graveyard is the tomb of Sultan Hussein Shah of Johor who, in 1819, signed the cession of Singapore to Stamford Raffles.

St Peter's Church on Jalan Taun Sri Lanang was built in 1710 by descendants of the early Portuguese settlers when the Dutch became more tolerant of different faiths. Iberian design is incorporated in the interior where Corinthian pillars support a curved ceiling above the aisle, similar to churches in Goa and Macau. It is the centre of the Catholic church in Malaysia. Easter candlelit processions to St Peter's seem strangely out of context in Malaysia. Open: until 1900 Mon-Sun.

In 1460 when Sultan Mansur Shah married Li Poh, a Ming princess, she took up residence on Melaka's highest hill, **Bukit Cina**, which became the Chinese quarter. The Malay Annals do not record what became of the Princess's palace but the hill, off Jalan Munshi Abdullah/Jalan Laksamana Cheng Ho, remained in the possession of the Chinese community and because of its good *feng shui* – its harmony with the supernatural forces and the elements – it was made into a graveyard. The cemetery now sprawls across the adjoining hills – Bukit Gedona and Bukit Tempurong – and is the largest traditional Chinese burial ground outside China, containing more than 12,000 graves. Chinese graveyards are often built on hillsides because the hill is said to protect the graves from evil winds; this hill has the added advantage of overlooking water, and the ancestral spirits are said to enjoy the panoramic view over the city and across the Strait of Melaka. Some of the graves date back to the Ming dynasty but most of these are overgrown or disintegrating.

The hill was ceded in perpetuity to the Chinese by successive colonial governments, but in mid-1991 the city burghers, backed by the Lands and Mining Department, demanded M$10 million in rent arrears, going back 500 years, from the general manager of Cheng Hoon Teng temple, who is responsible for the upkeep of Bukit Cina. Unless the Chinese community paid up in full, the city threatened to repossess the 42 ha of prime-site real estate it sits on. An impasse ensued which was still unresolved at the time of writing.

At the foot of the hill is an old Chinese temple called **Sam Poh Kong**, built in 1795 and dedicated to the famous Chinese seafarer, Admiral Cheng Ho (**see page 161**).It was originally built to cater for those whose relatives were buried on Bukit Cina. Next to the temple is the **Sultan's Well** (Perigi Rajah), said to have been sunk in the 15th century. It is believed that drinking from this well ensures a visitor's return to Melaka – but anyone foolhardy to try this today is liable to contract dysentery.

The ruined **Fort St John**, another relic of the Dutch occupation, is to the W of Bukit Cina on Jalan Bendahara (Air Keroh road, off Jalan Munshi Abdullah at *Ramada Renaissance Hotel*). Its hilltop location affords some excellent views although its aspect has been spoiled by the water treatment plant and high rise apartment block on either side of it.

The **Portuguese Settlement** (Medan Portugis) at Ujong Pasir, about 3 km from the town centre, is where the descendants of the Portuguese occupiers settled. A Portuguese community (of sorts) has managed to survive here for nearly 5 centuries; unlike the subsequent Dutch and British colonial regimes, the Portuguese garrison was encouraged to intermarry and generally treat the Malays as social equals. The process was so successful that when the Dutch, after capturing the city in 1641, offered Portuguese settlers a choice between amnesty and deportation to their nearest colony, many chose to stay. Their descendants still speak a medieval Portuguese dialect called *Cristao* (pronounced 'Cristang'), spoken nowhere else in the world. Today there are just a few tourist-oriented restaurants and shops in the modern Portuguese Square, and cultural shows are staged on Saturday nights. **Getting there**: bus 17 (M$2).

Excursions

North-west of Melaka
Tanjung Kling is about 9 km out of Melaka. It is a pleasant drive past beachside kampungs, and Tanjung Kling is a much more relaxing place to stay than in Melaka itself. But because passing tankers have a habit of swilling out their tanks, the sea is muddy and the beach dirty. This does not seem to affect the taste of the seafood and there are several restaurants and hawker stalls along the roadside at **Pantai Kundor**, where there are a number of hotels. Kampung Kling is thought to have got its name from Tamils who originally settled there, having come from Kalingapatam, N of Madras. **Accommodation**: **B** *Shah's Beach Resort*, Batu 61/2, Tanjung Kling, T 511088, a/c, restaurant, pool, only swish resort on this stretch of beach, 1950s front with 2 lines of chalets behind, tennis court and pool can be used by non-guests for a fee; **D** *Motel Tanjung Kling*, Batu 8, Pantai Kundor, T 511652, a/c, restaurant; **D** *Westernhay*, Batu 4, Klebang Besar (between Tanjung Kling and Melaka), restaurant, an old colonial-style hotel (formerly a British Army kindergarden) with large, airy rooms and a big garden going down to the beach, rec; **D-E** *Yashika Traveller Hostel*, Batu 8, Pantai Kundor, restaurant, small but clean rooms, right on the beach; **D-F** *Melaka Beach Bungalow & Youth Hostel*, 739C Spring Gardens, just off the road to Pantai Kundor, T 512935, dormitory and rooms in modern suburbia. **Restaurants**: ♦*Roti John*, Pantai Kundor, on the seafront, Melaka's Roti John specialist; ♦♦*Yashika Traveller Hostel*, Batu 8, Pantai Kundor, beach restaurant, international. **Getting there**: Patt Hup buses 51, 18, 42 & 47 (M$1) (buses can be caught from Jalan Tengkera (at the N end of Jalan Tun Tan Cheng Lock, in Melaka); taxi (M$1-3).

Tanjung Bidara is further up the road towards Port Dickson, about 20 km NW of Melaka. It has a long beach and plenty of hawker stalls; the sea is generally rather dirty. **Accommodation**: **A+-B** *Tanjung Bidara Beach Resort*, T 542990, a/c, restaurant, pool, upmarket chalet-style. **Getting there**: Patt Hup buses 51, 18, 42 & 47 (M$1) (buses can be caught from Jalan Tengkera (at the N end of Jalan Tun Tan Cheng Lock, in Melaka); taxi (M$1-3).

North-east of Melaka
Ayer Keroh, 11 km from Melaka, has a lake, jungle, a golf course and a country club and is just off the highway to KL. It is also the site of Melaka zoo, reptile park and Mini-Malaysia Complex, where the various states of Malaysia are represented by 13 traditional houses containing works of art and culture (similar to the Karyaneka Handicraft Centre in KL) as well as an Orang Asli village. It also stages cultural shows. **Accommodation**: **A** *Air Keroh Country Resort*, T 325210, a/c, restaurant, pool; **A** *Malacca Village Resort*, Batu 6, T 323600, F 3259555, a/c, restaurant, pool, first class hotel right in the middle of a new area for recreation and culture being developed by the Melaka state government. **Camping**: only at Ayer Keroh Recreational Forest and at Durian Tunggal Recreational Lake (on the way to Selandar). Admission to Mini Malaysia Complex: M$2. Open: 0900-1800 Mon-Sun. **Getting there**: bus 19 every half hour (M$1).

South-east of Melaka

Pulau Besar, contrary to its name, is a small island, about 8 km SE of Melaka, which is a popular weekend jaunt. According to local legend, a princess became pregnant to a Melakan commoner and was banished to the island to die. There is a shrine on the island dedicated to an early Muslim missionary, who is said to have come to Melaka in the 1400s. The island has good beaches (although the sea is not clean) and there are jungle walks. A marina is under construction and a yacht club proposed. **Accommodation: A** *Tapa Nyai Resort*, 37 Jalan Chan Koon Cheng, T 456730, F 236739, a/c, restaurant, pool, deluxe beach resort designed to look like a traditional Melakan village. **Getting there**: buses 17 & 25 to Umbai (M$1). Boats operate from Umbai Jetty (M$4/person, M$35/boat).

Gunung Ledang (1276m) – or Mount Ophir – on the E side of the North-South Highway, equidistant from Melaka and Muar and just inside Johor state, is one of the peninsula's best known mountains. It is isolated from the mountains of the Main Range and is sacred to the Orang Asli of Melaka. A Straits Chinese and Malay rumour has it that the mountain is the domain of a beautiful fairy endowed with the local version of the Midas Touch: she has a habit of turning Gunung Ledang's plant-life into gold. The mountain is said to be guarded by a sacred tiger which is possessed by the fairy.

Gunung Ledang is a strenuous climb involving some very steep scrambles, particularly towards the top. In 1884 an expedition reached the summit while trying to demarcate the boundary between Johor and Melaka. Most climbers choose to camp overnight on the summit, although, at a push, it can be done in a day – dawn to dusk. The mountain is surrounded by and covered in virgin jungle, and rises through mossy forest (where there are several varieties of pitcher plant, **see page 57**) to the rocky summit. Climbers are strongly advised to stick closely to the trails: since 1987, 2 separate parties of Singaporeans have become lost for several days after straying off the trail. The trail is complex in places and the climb should be carefully planned: would-be climbers are strongly recommended to refer to the detailed trail-guide in John Briggs' *Mountains of Malaysia*, which is available in Singapore and KL bookshops. There are 2 main trails up the mountain; the best route starts 15 km from Tangkak, just beyond Sagil. Waterfalls (*Air Terjun*) are signposted off the road which leads to Air Penas, an over-popular local picnic spot. The trail begins just beyond the rubber factory. Those attempting the climb without a trail-guide can hire a local guide from Tangkak.

Sadly, the Johor state government has announced plans to build a huge resort on the S slopes to include two 300-room hotels, an 18-hole golf course, 300 holiday chalets and a 'village'. It wants the first phase completed by 1997. **Getting there**: take the Tangkak road from Melaka or the old KL-Johor Bahru trunk road from Segamat. There is a metalled road to the radio station on the lower peak, but this is not open to the public beyond the half-way stage.

Festivals Mar/Apr: *Easter Procession*, (moveable) on Good Friday and Easter Sunday, starts from St Peter's Church. **May**: *Saint Sohan Singh's Prayer Anniversary* (moveable) thousands of Sikhs from all over Malaysia and Singapore congregate at the Melaka Sikh temple, Jln Temenggong, to join in the memorial prayers. **Jun**: *Pesta San Pedro* (Feast of St Peter) (moveable) celebrated at the Portuguese Settlement by fishermen. The brightly decorated fishing boats are blessed and prayers offered for a good season. *Mandi Safar* (moveable) bathing festival at Tanjung Kling. *Kite Festival* (moveable) on the sea front.

Accommodation There's plenty of choice in Melaka but the cheaper hotels tend to be further out of town. There are several nice hotels around Tanjung Kling, like the *Westernhay* (see Excursions, above). There are several good budget hotels at Taman Melaka Raya. **A+** *Ramada Renaissance*, Jln Bendahara, T 248888, F 249269, a/c, restaurant, all the facilities one expects for the price; **A** *City Bayview*, Jln Bendahara, T 239888, F 236699, a/c, restaurant, pool; **B** *Emperor*, Jln Munshi Abdullah, T 240777, F 238989, a/c, restaurant, pool; **B** *Palace*, 201 Jln Munshi Abdullah, T 225115, a/c, restaurant; **B** *Plaza Inn*, 2 Jln Munshi Abdullah, T 240888, a/c, restaurant, high-rise, so good views over town and river, prices include breakfast; **C** *Regal*, 66 Jln Munshi Abdullah, T 235959, a/c; **C** *Melaka Sentosa*, 91 Jln Bachang, T 358288, a/c; **C** *Majestic*, 188 Jln Bunga Raya, T 222367, a/c, restaurant, in a big colonial-style house, with high-ceilinged rooms, plenty of atmosphere and good downtown location, but in a bad state of repair; **C** *Lotus Inn*, 2846 Jln Semabok, T 237211, a/c, restaurant; **C** *New Lido*, 332 Jln Kilang, T 238788, a/c, bar; **C** *Sri Kota*, 318-319 Jln Kilang, T 226794, a/c; **C** *Tropicana*, 22 Jln Munshi Abdullah, T 237558; **C** *Valiant*, 41b Jln Bendahara, T 222323, a/c; **C-D** *Ng Fook*, 154 Jln Bunga Raya, T 2280206, a/c, clean but very basic; **C-D** *Tanjong Klong*, 5 & 55c Pantai Pengkalan Perigi, T 511652, a/c, restaurant; **D** *Chong Hoe*, Jln Tukang Emas, T 226102, a/c, good location near all the central sights and temples and reasonable value; **D** *Merryland*, 49 Jln Pasar Baru, T 220371, a/c; **D** *New Chin Nam*, 151 Jln Bunga Raya, T 224962; **D** *Paradise Hostel*, 4 Jln Tengkerea, T 230821, a/c, a former hospital, many of the rooms are cubicles with no windows, dormitory, friendly management; **D** *Trilogy Hostel*, 218a Jln Parameswara Garden, T 245319, breakfast, TV, laundry, bikes for hire, also has more expensive rooms with bathrooms; **D-E** *Samudara Inn*, 250B Taman Melaka Raya, T 246364, restaurant, cooking facilities, laundry, bikes for hire; **E** *Kancil*, 177 Jln Parameswara (Bandar Hillir), cool, quiet backyard/garden, bicycles for hire; **E** *Melaka Town Holiday Lodge*, 148b Taman Melaka Raya, T 248830, restaurant, clean and well looked after, dormitory or rooms; **E** *Suan Kee*, 105-107 Jln Bunga Raya T 223040; **E** *Sunny's Inn*, 253B Taman Melaka Raya, kitchen, bikes for hire, dorm (F); **E-F** *Robins Nest Guest House*, 247B Taman Melaka Raya, clean and comfortable, helpful proprietor, dorm and rooms; **E-F** *St Paul's*, 12 Church Lane, T 320891.

Restaurants **Malay**: ♦♦*Anda*, 8b Jln Hang Tuah, popular modern coffeeshop, specialities include *ikan bakar* (grilled fish), *sayur masak lemak* (deep-fried marinated prawns) and *rendang*; ♦*Mini*, 35 Jln Merdeka, good for *ikan panggang* (grilled fish with spicy sauce), also *nasi campur*; ♦*Sederhana*, 18A Jln Hang Tuah, near the bus station, good selection of Malay dishes; ♦*Taman*, 10 Jln Merdeka, on the sea front, known for its *ikan assam pedas* – hot (chilli-hot) fish curry.

Nonya: ♦♦♦*Jonkers*, 17 Jln Hang Jebat, old Nonya house, with restaurant in the old ancestral hall, good atmosphere and excellent food – Nonya and International, set menu good value, rec; ♦♦♦*Nam Hoe Villa* (Restoran Peranakan), 317c Klebang Besar (6 km towards Port Dickson), T 354436, cultural show at 2000 (except Sat), originally the house of a Chinese rubber tycoon, now a restaurant and Peranakan showpiece, all the best known Nonya dishes are served, buffet; ♦♦*Nonya Makko*, 124 Taman Melaka Raya, located near the bottom of St Paul's Hill, good selection; ♦♦♦*Ole Sayang*, 192 Taman Melaka Raya, serves all the favourites, including chicken *pongteh* (in sweet and sour spicy sauce), rec.

Chinese: ♦*Bee Bee Hiong*, City Park, Jln Bunga Raya, for fish-ball fans; ♦♦*Chop Teo Soon Leng*, 55 Jln Hang Tuah, Teochew cuisine; ♦*Hoe Kee Chicken Rice*, Jln Hang Jebat, Hainanese chicken rice in Chinatown coffee shop; ♦♦*Keng Dom*, 148 Melaka Raya, renowned for its steamboats; ♦*Kim Swee Huat*, 38 Jln Laksamana, big menu with staple Western fillers as well as local food; ♦*Melaka Raya Hikeng*, 112 Taman Melaka Raya, on the seafront, best for *assam* steamed fish, good varied menu; ♦*New Oriental Satay and Mee*, 82 Jln Tengkera (road to Tanjung Kling), being a Chinese stall, serves pork satay and other variations such as cuttlefish (*sotong*) satay, also well known for its *yee kiow mee*; ♦*U E Teahouse*, 20 Lorong Bukit Cina, dim sum from early morning until 1200, rec.

Indian: ♦*Banana Leaf*, 42 Jln Munshi Abdullah, S Indian meat curries and vegetarian dishes, biriyani specials on Wed and Sat evenings; ♦*Kerala*, Jln Melaka Raya, good value; ♦♦*Mitchell Raaju Nivaas*, Jln Laksamana, aside from its good curries, this restaurant also offers cooking lessons, M$2, for those who want to make Indian breads and basic curries; ♦*Sri Krishan Bavan*, 4 Jln Temengong, banana leaf; ♦*Sri Lakshmi Vilas*, 2 Jln Temengong, rotis and murtabak; ♦♦*Veni*, 34 Jln Temenggong, banana leaf restaurant with good selection of meat curries and vegetarian dishes, roti canai breakfasts.

Portuguese: most restaurants in the *Medan Portugis* are expensive tourist traps but some of the spicy seafood dishes are worth trying. ♦♦♦*Restoran de Lisbon*, Portuguese Square, cultural shows Sat evenings; ♦♦♦*San Pedro*, Portuguese Settlement (just off the square), family run and probably the best at the Portuguese settlement, specialities include spicy baked fish, wrapped in banana leaf.

Seafood: *Pengkalan Pernu* (Pernu Jetty), 10 km S on the way to Muar, has several fish restaurants and stalls where you can catch your own fish and have it grilled. N of Melaka, towards Tanjung Kling there are a few Chinese seafood restaurants along the beach. **Thai**: ♦♦♦*My Place*, 357 Jln Melaka, also some Malay, Chinese and Indian dishes. **International**: ♦♦*Pandan*, Jln Merdeka (behind tourist information office), Western and local dishes, pleasant location by riverside.

Foodstalls: *Satay celup* is a Melakan variation on a Malaysian theme: an assortment of skewered meats, fishballs, quails' eggs, crab, prawns, mussels, mushrooms and yams with traditional peanut sauce. *Glutton's Corner*, along the old esplanade on Jln Merdeka/Jln Taman: excellent choice of food although the stalls now face a painted wall rather than the sea, thanks to a land reclamation project, *Prince Satay Celup* at No. 16, rec; *Klebang Beach*, off Jln Klebang Besar, Tanjung Kling – stalls, with several *ikan panggang* (grilled fish) specialists; *Jalan Bukit Baru*, just off the main road past the state mosque, mostly Chinese food; *Jalan Bendahara*, several noodle stalls and a Mamak man (Indian Muslim) who serves *sup kambing* (mutton soup) and the bits – for marrow suckers (opposite the Capitol); *Jalan Bunga Raya*, stalls (next to Rex Cinema), seafood rec; *Jalan Semabok* (after Bukit Cina on road to JB), Malay-run fish-head curry stall which is a local favourite.

Entertainment Son et Lumiere: *Melaka Light and Sound Show*, on the Padang, opposite St Paul's Hill, chronological history of Melaka, Mon-Sun, 2000 (Malay), 2100 (English) Admission: M$5. **Cultural shows**: at the Portuguese Settlement every Saturday at 2030. Songs and dances include the famous *beranyo*, an excuse for a sing-along and knees-up. *Nam Hoe Villa* (Restoran Peranakan), 317c Klebang Besar (6 km towards Port Dickson), T 354436, 2000 Sun-Fri.

Tours Tickets for the river boat can be purchased from the Tourist Office (45 mins, M$5) to see the old Dutch trading houses; predictably this area is known as Melaka's 'Little Venice', which does not live up to the description.

Sports Golf: *Ayer Keroh Golf & Country Club*, 14 km from Melaka. Longest 18-hole course in Malaysia. Green fees: M$60 weekdays; M$80 weekends.

Shopping Melaka is best known for its antique shops, which mainly sell European and Chinese items. **Antiques**: *Jalan Hang Jebat* (formerly Jonker St), is the best place for antiques. **Books**: *Boon Hoong Sports and Bookstore*, 13 Jln Bunga Raya. **Handicrafts**: *Karkaneka* (handicraft) centres at *1 Jln Laksamana* and *Mini Malaysia Complex*, Ayer Keroh. Also *Crystal D'beaute*, 18 Medan Portugis. **Shoes**: *Wah Aik Shoemaker Shop*, 92 Jln Hang Jebat. Shoes are still made here for Chinese grannies with bound feet (**see page 167**) and tourists. **General**: main shopping centres on Jln Hang Tuah and Jln Munshi Abdullah.

Local transport Buses: local buses leave from Jln Hang Tuah, right next to the long distance bus station. Less than M$1 round town. **Trishaws**: congregate at several points in town (there are usually a number near the the tourist information centre on the town square. M$2 for single destination or M$8/hr. **Car hire**: Avis, 27 Jln Laksamana, T 237126; **Thrifty**, G-5 Pasar Pelancong, Jln Tun Sri Lanang, T 249471. **Bicycle hire**: many of the cheaper hotels/hostels rent out bikes, as do one or 2 shops in town, M$8/day.

Banks & money changers Bumiputra, Jln Kota; **Hong Kong & Shanghai**, Jln Kota. Several banks on Jln Hang Tuah near the bus station and Jln Munshi Abdullah.

Useful addresses General Post Office: 3 km N of town on Jln Tan Sri Lanang (bus 19). Straits Hospital: 37 Jln Parameswara, T 235336. **Area Code**: 06.

Tour companies & travel agents AR Tours, 302a Jln Kilang, T 231977; *Annah (Melaka) Tours & Travel*, 27 Jln Laksamana, T 235626; *Sanlet Agencies*, 329 Jln Tun Ali, T 244960; *Satic Tour & Travel*, 143 Jln Bendahara, T 235712.

Tourist offices Tourism Malaysia, Jln Kota (opposite Christ Church), T 236538. Also tourist information desk at Ayer Keroh, T 325811.

Transport to & from Melaka 149 km from KL, 216 km from Johor Bahru, 90 km from Port Dickson. **By air**: airport is at Batu Berendam, 10 km out of town. Connections with Ipoh 3 times a week (M$110) Johor Bahru and Singapore (M$132), weekly service to Pekan Baru, Sumatra (Fri, 1300) (MAS, T 235722). Airport flight information, T 222648. (MAS, T 235722). **By train**: nearest station is at Tampin, 40 km N; Melaka railway enquiry office, T 223091; Tampin railway station, T 411034. **By bus**: long distance buses leave from the terminal on Jln Hang Tuah. Regular connections with KL (M$6.50), Seremban (M$2.85), Port Dickson (M$3.20), Ipoh (M$13), Butterworth (21.40), Lumut (Pulau Pangkor) (M$17), Kuantan (M$11), Kuala Terengganu ($16.70), Kota Bahru (M$20), Johor Bahru (M$10.00). Direct bus connections with Singapore (M$11). **By taxi**: station next to the bus terminal, Jln Hang Tuah. KL (M$15), Seremban (M$7), Penang (M$43), Mersing (M$20), Johor Bahru (M$17). Passengers for Singapore must change taxis at the long-distance terminal in JB. **International connections to Sumatra, Indonesia**: **NB**: it is necessary to secure a visa from the Indonesian Embassy in KL (**see page 145**) before departing for Sumatra from Melaka. **By ferry**: boats to Dumai (Sumatra), leave from the public jetty on Melaka River. Ferries leave Mon, Wed, Fri & Sat, 2 hrs, (M$80). Tickets from *Tunar Rapat Utama Express*, 17A Jln Merdeka, T 232505; *Madai Shipping*, Jln Tun Ali T 240671; *Atlas Travel Service*, Jln Hang Jebat, T 220777.

JOHOR BAHRU (JB)

Modern **Johor Bahru** – more commonly called JB – is not a pretty town. It is right on the southernmost tip of the peninsula and is the gateway to Malaysia from Singapore. During the 1980s it became an industrial adjunct to Singapore, attracting land and labour-intensive manufacturing industries (see page 390). Johor's manufacturing boom has brought a measure of prosperity to the state capital and its dingy streets have begun to get a much-needed face-lift. Foreign investors have embarked on property-buying sprees and new hotels, shopping plazas and office complexes have been springing up. The state government's intention is to emulate the development process of neighbouring Singapore.

The old causeway across the *Selat Tebrau* (Strait of Johor), built in 1924, is still the only land-link to Singapore. It is overburdened with road traffic and also carries the railway and water pipelines: Singapore relies on Johor for most of its water supply. A new bridge is finally being built from Gelang Patah, to the W of JB, to Singapore, which is scheduled for completion in 1995. JB is short on tourist attractions but has for many years served as a tacky red-light reprieve for Singaporeans. But Johor's paucity of cultural attractions belies its pivotal role in Malay history.

Following his trouncing by the Portuguese invaders in 1511, Melaka's young Sultan Ahmad fled S with what remained of the royal court eventually arriving at Bintan in the Riau Archipelago (**see page 784**). Ahmad was promptly executed by his father, Mahmud, for gross ineptitude and there then followed 15 years of attrition between the Portuguese and Mahmud before the Portuguese destroyed his capital at Bintan in 1526. Mahmud died 2 years later and his remaining son became the first Sultan of Perak while his stepson established the Sultanate of Johor near Kota Tinggi, to the E of modern JB.

At the same time, the Sultanate of Aceh, on the N tip of Sumatra, was enjoying a meteoric rise to prominence (**see page 745**). Rivalry between Johor and Aceh overshadowed either's hatred of the Portuguese and the Acehnese terrorized Johor for another 60 years, frequently sacking the capital and twice carrying the royal family back as prisoners to Sumatra.

The Johor court was re-established on the Johor River in 1641 and the sultanate grew strong and powerful again as an entrepôt until the capital was destroyed by the rival Sumatran kingdom of Jambi in 1673. The sultanate moved to Bintan, then back to Kota Tinggi in 1685. But Sultan Mahmud, was a tyrant who frightened off foreign traders; he was also a murderer and sexual pervert and was finally assassinated by his own people, thus ending the centuries-old Melaka dynasty. Switching its capitals between the Johor River and Riau, the sultanate went downhill and remained weak throughout the 18th century; the Malay rulers, wracked by in-fighting, were by then firmly under the thumb of the ascendant Buginese (**see page 864**) and constantly squabbling over trade issues with the Dutch.

In 1818, with the Dutch temporarily out of the picture due to the Napoleonic Wars, the British resident of Melaka, Colonel William Farquhar signed a trade pact with the sultan in Riau. Thomas Stamford Raffles was meanwhile looking to set up a British trading post on the S end of the peninsula and after casting around the Riau Archipelago, settled on Singapore. There, in 1819, he signed a deal with Temenggong Abdur Rahman, the sultan's minister on the island, and later with

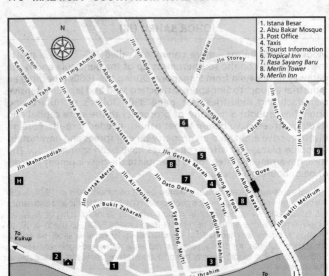

1. Istana Besar
2. Abu Bakar Mosque
3. Post Office
4. Taxis
5. Tourist Information
6. *Tropical Inn*
7. *Rasa Sayang Baru*
8. *Merlin Tower*
9. *Merlin Inn*

JOHOR BAHRU IMS 26

one of 2 blue-blooded Malays claiming to be Sultan of Johor, allowing the English East India Company to establish a trading post in Singapore.

The 1824 Treaty of London, between the British and the Dutch put an end to the Johor-Riau Empire, partitioning it between the 2 European powers. The Riau side became known as the Sultanate of Lingga, while the Temenggong was left to wield Malay power. Abu Bakar, the grandson of Singapore's Temenggong Abdur Rahman, moved his headquarters to the small settlement of Tanjong Putri in Johor, which he renamed Johor Bahru in 1866. The Anglophile Abu Bakar was known as the Maharajah of Johor until 1877, and in 1885, was recognized as Sultan by Queen Victoria. He developed the state's agricultural economy, and in the early 20th century Johor attracted many European rubber planters. Sultan Abu Bakar is known as the father of modern Johor, which became the last state to join the colonial Malay Federation, in 1914.

Places of interest
One of the most prominent buildings in JB is the recently renovated **Istana Besar**, the Sultan's former residence on Jalan Tun Dr Ismail (built by Sultan Abu Bakar in 1866), and now a royal museum. Today the Sultan lives in the Istana Bukit Serene, which is on the W outskirts of town (it is not open to the public). The Istana Besar is a slice of Victorian England set in beautiful gardens, overlooking the strait. In the N wing is the throne room and museum containing a superb collection of royal treasures, including hunting trophies, as well as Chinese and Japanese ceramics. It is one of Malaysia's best museums. Admission: US$7 (ringgit equivalent). Open: 0900-1600 Sat-Wed, 0900-1200 Thur.

Not far away, on Jalan Abu Bakar, is the **Sultan Abu Bakar Mosque**, which faces the Strait of Johor. It was finished in 1900 and can accommodate 2,500 worshippers.

Modern Johor: riding on the merlion's tail

Johor is still a predominantly agricultural state, and is Malaysia's leading producer of palm oil, rubber, cocoa and coconuts. But in recent years, Singapore's prosperity has spilled across the 1.2 km causeway linking the island republic with JB. An explosion in foreign manufacturing investment – led by Singapore – has turned Johor into an industrial oasis.

The state planners are as startled as anyone at the suddenness of the transformation: in the past few years Johor has attracted about a quarter of total foreign investment in Malaysia. The industrial estates surrounding JB produce everything from typewriters and televisions to condoms and Kentucky Fried Chickens. Almost everything is immediately exported from JB's Pasir Gudang port. Recently, big Japanese and Taiwanese petrochemicals plants have set up in the state too, one of them near Johor Lama, the site of the old royal capital.

Johor is now the northern point of the so-called 'Growth Triangle' which also incorporates Singapore and parts of Indonesia's Riau Archipelago. The state government, now facing a labour shortage, wants its industries to be increasingly hi-tech, and the Chief Minister has repeatedly stated that he aims to turn his state into a Singapore-clone by the year 2000. Tourism is big in Johor too, mainly because Singaporeans flood across the causeway to get a break from city life. Nearly three-quarters of all tourists visiting Malaysia come from Singapore: each day about 50,000 people cross the causeway to JB.

The 32m-high tower of the Istana Bukit Serene is only outdone by the 64m tower of the State Secretariat, on Bukit Timbalan, which dominates the town.

Excursions

Kukup, 40 km SW of Johor on the Straits of Melaka, is a small Chinese fishing kampung renowned throughout the country – and in Singapore – for its seafood (especially prawns and chilli crab). Most of the restaurants are built on stilts over the water. The kampung has become so popular with Singaporeans that coach tours are laid on, and some of the restaurants – notably *Restoran Kukup* – are geared to cater for big groups. Weekend visits are not recommended for this reason. **Getting there**: bus 3 to Pontian (M$2.20); from there to Kukup by taxi (M$6).

At **Lombong**, below Gunung Muntahak, a series of waterfalls have cut natural swimming pools; the falls are 56 km NE of JB and 13 km from **Kota Tinggi**, a former royal capital of Johor. Many of the mausoleums of the former sultans of Johor – including that of Mahmud Shah, the last sultan of the Melaka Dynasty – are nearby. The mausoleum of Sultan Mahmud, the feared ruler who was finally assassinated by one of his courtesans (**see page 175**) is at Kampung Makam (turn right 1 km N of Kota Tinggi, before Desaru sign). The site of the old royal capital of **Johor Lama** ('Old Johor' – as opposed to Johor Bahru, or 'New Johor') is on the E bank of the Johor River, S of Kota Tinggi. Because it was twice burned to the ground, there are no impressive ruins. The site is, however, clearly signposted off the Kota Tinggi-Desaru road (12 km). Just before Telok Sengat, turn right down a laterite track through an oil palm estate. Johor Lama, most of which lies under a rubber tappers' kampung, is 6 km down the track. There is no public transport to the site or to Telok Sengat. **Accommodation**: **C** *Waterfall Chalet*, Kota Tinggi Waterfall, T 241957 (must be booked in advance). **Getting there**: to the waterfalls, either take a taxi (M$3) or bus 8 (M$1) to the falls. **C** *Sri Bayn Resort*, near Telok Sengat (5 km up laterite track through oil palm estate opposite turn-off to Johor Lama), only accessible for those with own transport, possibly the most tranquil and certainly the most remote chalet resort on the peninsula, set on steep hillside overlooking Johor estuary among coconut palms in neat gardens, chalets have balconies and fantastic views, as of mid-1993 the resort had not received official permission to open, check with Tourism Malaysia information line in Johor Bahru, T 223591, which will be able to advise on status. Seafood restaurant and coffee shops in nearby Telok Sengat, rec.

Desaru holiday resort, set on a 20 km-long beach at Tanjung Penawar, 90 km E of JB, has been aggressively marketed in Singapore – as a result it gets invaded on weekends and public holidays. Although the beach is picturesque, the sea at Desaru can get very rough at times, and there is a strong undertow – most holiday-makers stick to their hotel swimming pools. The most popular pursuit which Desaru has to offer is its beautifully landscaped seaside golf course. There is a fast road to Desaru from Kota Tinggi, the last 4 km of which is lined with bougainvillaea, à la Singapore. **Desaru accommodation**: Desaru's hotels are designed with golf-crazed Singaporeans in mind, although on weekdays, chalet accommodation is reasonable. Budget travellers are better advised to head for Mersing and the offshore islands. **A+ *Desaru Golf Inn***, T 821106/821187, F 821408, a/c, restaurant, pool; **A *Desaru View***, (PO Box 71, Kota Tinggi) Tanjung Penawar, T 838221, a/c, restaurant, pool; **A-C *Desaru Garden Beach Resort***, PO Box 50, Tanjung Penawar, T 07-821101, F 07-821480, a/c, restaurant, pool, former *Merlin Inn* with standard four-star facilities. Fills up with golfers on weekends. Chalets next door are part of same resort (guests can use hotel pool) and offer good value-for-money during the week. **Getting there**: bus 41; regular connections via JB via Kota Tinggi (M$3.50); taxi from JB (M$50 whole car). 2 daily shuttles from most major hotels in Singapore (S$40). Regular boats connect Desaru with Changi Point, Singapore to Tanjung Pengileh (S$6), where taxis are available to Desaru (M$28).

Teluk Makhota Those taking the road north from Kota Tinggi may be tempted by countless roadside signs to *Jason's Bay Beach Resort* at Teluk Makhota (25 km off main E Coast road from turning 15 km NE of Kota Tinggi). It can be reached via bus 300 from Kota Tinggi, but, despite its privacy, is not really worth the bother. The once-lovely beach is muddy and disappointing; the resort is grimy and rooms smell musty.

Accommodation   JB's top hotels cater for visiting businesspeople and have all the 5-star facilities. Middle-market and cheaper hotels are as tacky as ever though: the 'hostess girl industry' is big business in JB. Many hotels rent out rooms by the hour. As such facilities are usually prominently advertised, patrons should know what to expect. Room rates also increase on Fridays and weekends. **A+ *Puteri Pan Pacific***, T 233333, a/c, restaurant, pool, opened in mid-1991, this is JB's latest effort to persuade visiting business people not to commute from Singapore, owned by the Johor State Economic Development Corporation, best in town; **A+-A *Holiday Inn***, Jln Dato' Sulaiman, Century Gardens, T 323800, a/c, restaurant, pool, unhelpfully located on suburban one-way system, frequented by the rich and the royal because of its Szechuan restaurant; **A *Merlin Inn***, 10 Jln Bukit Meldrum, T 228581, a/c, restaurant, comfortable hotel that looks like a truncated Toblerone, good value but cut off from centre of town by railway and flyovers; **A *Tropical Inn***, 15 Jln Gereja, T 247888, a/c, restaurant, pool; **B *Causeway Inn***, Jln Meldrum, T 248811, a/c, unlike neighbouring premises, this is a clean, quiet, well-run hotel that looks smart and does not overcharge, rec; **B *Straits View***, 1d Jln Scudai, T 241400, a/c, restaurant (next door to *Jaws 5*), not much of a Straits View from downstairs rooms but the hotel is clean and the management friendly; **B-C *Peninsular***, 6 Jln Abiad, Tebran Jaya, T 323277, a/c; **C *Fortuna***, 29a Jln Meldrum, T 233210, this hotel has gone downhill, small, smelly rooms, there are better places to stay; **C *Hawaii***, 21 Jln Meldrum, T 240633, average Chinese-run hotel – much better value on weekdays; **C *Hong Kong***, 31a Jln Meldrum, T 246407, a/c, restaurant; **C *JB Hotel***, 80a Jln Ah Fook, T 234788, a/c, clean, reasonable; **C *Le Tian***, 2, A-D Jln Sin Nam, T 248151 (just off Jln Meldrum), small rooms and chocolate decor doesn't help, but cleaner than most others in the area; **C *Rasa Sayang Baru***, 10 Jln Dato Dalam, T 224744, a/c, restaurant, on the outskirts of town, but excellent value, rec; **C *Regent Elite***, 1 Jln Siu Nam, T 243812, a/c, not a Regent and not élite; **E** *Footloose*, 4H Jln Ismail (off Jln Yahya Awal, opposite the convent school), T 242881, run by Brenda McKechnie, a Glaswegian who has lived in Malaysia for more than 10 years, rooms and dorm, breakfast included with additional M$4 for generous evening meal, popular with travellers, 10 mins' walk from bus station or buses 8, 9, 12, 46 (M$0.40).

Restaurants Malay: ♦♦♦*Dapur Rembia*, 1A-2 Jln Mohd Amin (close to *Jaws 5 restaurant*), old bungalow with tables outside; ♦♦*Sedap Corner*, 11 Jln Abdul Samad, Chinese as well as Malay dishes, a good line in fish-head curries. **Chinese**: ♦♦♦*Ming Dragon*, G12-14 Holiday Plaza, rec. **Thai**: ♦♦♦♦*Manhattan Grill*, Plaza Kotaraya, Jln Trus (opposite Pan Pac), haunt of JB's rich and relatively famous, new grill room with excellent food at half the price of the equivalents across the causeway; ♦♦♦♦*Meisan Szechuan*, Holiday Inn JB, Jln Dato' Sulaiman, Century Garden, superb but expensive spicy Szechuan restaurant; ♦♦♦♦*Selashi*, Puteri Par Pacific, The Kotaraya, top quality Malay cuisine in tastefully decorated, expensive restaurant; ♦♦♦*134 Jalan Serampang* Taman Pelangi, tables in the garden; ♦♦♦*Jaws 5 Seafood*, 1d Jln Skudai, very popular, next to *Straits View Hotel* and Machinta strip club, the food is very good, but not cheap, specialities include drunken prawns, frogs' legs and chilli crabs, diners may find flashing neons and revolving stage unsettling, rec; ♦♦♦*Newsroom Café*, Puteri Pan Pacific, The Kotaraya, in new Pan Pac hotel offering reasonably priced local/continental dishes (enclosed brasserie area called *Editor's Corner*); ♦♦*Medina*, corner of Jln Meldrum and Jln Siew Niam, cheap and delicious murtabak, rotis, fish-head curries etc., open 24 hrs.
Foodstalls: *Tepian Tebrau*, Jln Skudai (facing the sea beside the General Hospital) good for Malay food – satay and grilled fish. There is also good food at the long-distance bus terminal and outside the railway station. There is a sprawling outdoor hawker centre right in the centre of town, adjacent to the new Plaza Kotaraya. *Pantai Lido* is another well known hawker centre and there is a 'food court' in *Kompleks Tun Abdul Razak* on Jln Wong Ah Fook.

Entertainment Discos: *Millennium*, Holiday Inn, Jln Dato Suleiman; *Caesar's Palace*, Holiday Plaza; *Machinta*, next to Jaws on Jln Skudai, is JB's famous strip club, which is mainly patronized by Singaporeans.

Shopping Handicrafts: *Jaro*, Jln Sungai Chat; *Mawar*, Jln Sultanah Rogayah, Istana Besar; *Craftown Handicraft Centre*, Jln Skudai; *Karyaneka Centre* at Kompleks Mawar, 562 Jln Sungeai Chat; *Johorcraft*, Kompleks Kotaraya & Kompleks Tun Abdul Razak, Jln Trus. There is also a big new Johorcraft complex 1 km before Kota Tinggi on the road from JB selling rather downmarket arts and crafts from all over Malaysia. It is aimed at big coach tours from Singapore, has a large restaurant and provides demonstrations of pottery, batik and songkhet production. Open Mon-Sun 0800-1800. **General**: large shopping complexes include *Kompleks Tun Abdul Razak* (KOMTAR), Jln Wong Ah Fook; *Plaza Pelangi*, Jln Tebrau; *Holiday Plaza*, Jln Datuk Sulaiman, and *Sentosa Complex*, Jln Sutera.

Sport Bowling: *Holiday Bowl*, 2nd Flr Holiday Plaza, Jln Dato Suleiman. **Golf**: *Royal Johor Country Club*, Jln Larkin. Green fees: M$40 weekdays, M$60 weekends.

Local transport Local buses leave from the main bus terminal; there is no shortage of local taxis (no meters). **Car hire**: it is much cheaper to hire a car in JB than it is in neighbouring Singapore. **Avis**, 37 Jln Ibrahim, T 237970; **Budget**, Suite 216, 2nd Flr Orchid Plaza, T 243951; **Calio**, *Tropical Inn*, Jln Gereja, T 233325; **Halaju Selatan**, 4M-1 Larkin Complex, Jln Larkin; **Hertz**, 3b, Jln Ibrahim, T 237520; **National**, 50-B Grd Flr Bangunan Felda, Jln Sengget, T 230503; **Thrifty**, *Holiday Inn*, Jln Dato Sulaiman, T 332313; **Sintat**, 2nd Flr, Tun Abdul Razak Kompleks, Jln Wong Ah Fook, T 227110.

Banks & money changers Hong Kong Shanghai, Bumiputra and United Asia are on Bukit Timbalan. Other big banks are on Jln Wong Ah Fook, several money changers in the big shopping centres and on/around Jln Ibrahim/Jln Meldrum.

Useful addresses Post Office: Jln Tun Dr Ismail. **Hospital**: *Sultanah Aminah General Hospital*, Jln Sekudai. **Area Code**: 07.

Airline offices MAS, Orchid Plaza, off Jln Wong Ah Fook, T 220888.

Tourist offices Southern Region, 1, 4th Flr, Kompleks Tun Abdul Razak, Jln Wong Ah Fook, T 223591. **Tourism Malaysia Information Centre**, Grd Flr, 52 Kompleks Tun Abdul Razak (KOMTAR).

Transport to & from Johor Bahru 134 km from Mersing, 224 km from Melaka. **By air**: MAS flies into Senai, JB's airport, 20 km N of the city. Buses every hour (M$1.40), taxis (M$5). For passengers flying MAS from Singapore, there is a shuttle service from the airport to *Novotel Orchid Inn*, Singapore (M$10) with express immigration clearance. **NB**: flights within Malaysia are much cheaper from Senai than from Changi, Singapore. Regular connections with KL (M$92), Kuantan (M$92), Kuala Terengganu (M$197), KK (M$492), Kuala Terengganu (M$280), Kuching (M$240). **By train**: the station is on Jln Campbell, near the causeway, off Jln Tun Abdul Razak. Regular connections with KL (M$27) and all destinations on the West Coast. **By bus**: bus station is just off Jln Wong Ah Fook. Regular connections with KL (M$15.20), Ipoh (M$23.00), Butterworth (M$29.00), Kuantan (M$15.00), Kuala Terengganu (M$22), Kota Bahru (M$24). **By taxi**: the long-distance taxi station is just down the road from the bus station, on Jln Wong Ah Fook, KL (M$31), Kuantan (M$30), Melaka (M$17). **International connections to Singapore**: the causeway between JB and Singapore gets jammed, particularly at rush hours. Malaysian immigration has opened new booths however, which has helped speed things up. **By boat**: bumboats leave from various points along Johor's ragged coastline for Singapore; most go to Changi Point (Changi Village), on the NE of the island where there is an immigration and customs post. Although it is technically possible to take a boat across to Singapore from JB itself, there does not seem much point. The bumboat routes from Tanjung Surat and Tanjung Pengileh to Changi Point (M$5) make sense for those coming from the E coast, Teluk Makhota (Jason's Bay) or Desaru (taxis to the jetty from Desaru cost M$28). The boats run from 0700-1600 and depart when full (12 passengers). **By bus**: Singapore Bus Service bus 170 operates every 10 minutes between JB and Queen St in Singapore (S$0.90). The Johor Bahru Express goes from the main bus station in JB to Rochor Canal Rd, Singapore (M$1). **NB**: regular buses from the airport to the *Novotel* in Singapore (see **By air**, above). **By taxi**: Malaysian taxis leave for Singapore from the taxi rank on Jln Wong Ah Fook. They leave when full and go to the JB taxi rank on Rochor Canal Rd in Singapore (M$7). Drivers provide immigration forms and take care of formalities making this a painless way of crossing the causeway. Touts also hang around JB's taxi rank offering the trip to Singapore for S$9-10 in a private car. They will take you directly to your address in Singapore, although their geography of the island is not that good. This is also a fairly cost-effective way to travel, and, from experience, is reliable. **By train**: Malaysian and Singapore immigration desks are actually in the Singapore railway station, so for those wanting to avoid delays on the causeway, this is a quick way to get across the border; there are regular commuter trains across to the island (M$8).

THE PENINSULA'S EAST COAST

Introduction, 181; **Mersing and Pulau Tioman**, 184; **North to Kuantan via Endau Rompin and Pekan**, 191; **Kuantan and Taman Negara**, 193; **Kuantan to Kota Bahru**, 202; **Kuala Terengganu**, 208; **Kota Bahru**, 213; **Butterworth to Kota Bahru**, 220.

Maps East Coast, 182; Pulau Tioman, 187; Kuantan, 194; Taman Negara, 199; Kuala Terengganu, 208; Kota Bahru, 215.

INTRODUCTION

It might just be on the other side of the peninsula, but Malaysia's east coast could as well be on a different planet than the populous, hectic and industrialized west coast. The coastline of the states of Johor, Pahang, Terengganu and Kelantan is lined with coconut palms, dotted with sleepy fishing kampungs and interspersed with rubber and oil palm plantations, paddy fields, beaches and mangroves. For centuries, the narrow coastal plain between the jungled mountains and the sea, was largely bypassed by trade and commerce and its 60-odd coral-ringed (and largely uninhabited) offshore islands were known only to local fishermen. The east coast is sold by Tourism Malaysia as 'the real Malaysia'.

The mountainous interior effectively cut the E coast off from the W coast, physically, commercially and culturally. The E coast did not have the tin deposits which attracted Chinese speculators and miners to the towns on the other side of the Main Range in the 19th century; and in more recent decades it was left behind as Malaysia joined the development race. The rural parts have been buffered from Western influence; traditional kampung lifestyles have been tempered only by the arrival of the electric lightbulb, the outboard motor and the Honda 70. The E coast's fishermen and paddy farmers are Malaysia's most conservative Muslims. In the 1990 general election, the people of Kelantan voted a hard-line Islamic opposition party into power. Parti Islam now runs the state government and represents its Kelantan constituencies in federal parliament. The rural Malays of the E coast have not enjoyed much in the way of 'trickledown' from Malaysia's new-found economic prosperity. Although they are *bumiputras* – or 'sons of the soil' (**see page 86**) – few have reaped the benefits of more than 2 decades of pro-Malay policies.

During World War II, the Japanese Imperial Army landed at Kota Bahru and sped the length of the peninsula within 6 weeks on stolen bicycles (**see page 65**). The E coast did not figure prominently during the war, except in the realm of literary fiction, where it starred in Neville Shute's *A Town Like Alice*.

Before and after the war, rubber and oil palm plantations sprang up – particularly in the S state of Johor – which changed the shape of the agricultural economy. But the most dramatic change followed the discovery of large quantities of high-grade crude oil and natural gas off the NE coast in the 1970s. By the mid-1980s, huge storage depots, gas processing plants and refineries had been built in Terengganu, and the battered old coast road was upgraded to cater for Esso and Petronas tankers. The town of Kerteh, half-way between Kuantan and Kuala Terengganu is a refinery town, built along one of the best beaches on the peninsula. The construction boom and the rig work, helped boost the local

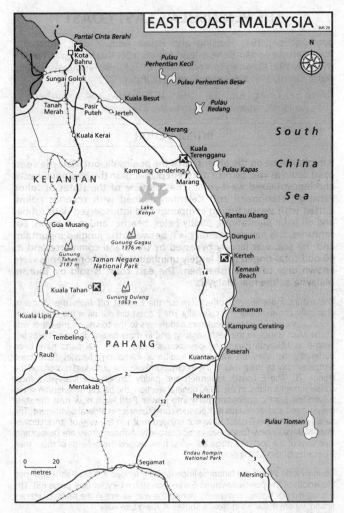

EAST COAST MALAYSIA

Pantai Cinta Berahi
Kota Bahru
Sungai Golok
Tanah Merah
Pasir Puteh
Jerteh
Kuala Kerai
Pulau Perhentian Kecil
Pulau Perhentian Besar
Kuala Besut
Pulau Redang
Merang

KELANTAN

Kuala Terengganu
Kampung Cendering
Marang
Pulau Kapas

South China Sea

Lake Kenyir
Gua Musang
Gunung Gagau 1376 m
Rantau Abang
Dungun
Kerteh
Kemasik Beach

Gunung Tahan 2187 m
Taman Negara National Park
Kuala Tahan
Gunung Dulang 1063 m

Kuala Lipis
Kemaman
Kampung Cerating

Tembeling
PAHANG
Raub
Kuantan
Beserah

Mentakab
Pekan

Pulau Tioman

0   20
metres

Segamat
Endau Rompin National Park
Mersing

economy and provide employment, but the E coast states (bar Johor, which straddles the entire S tip of the peninsula) have singularly failed to attract much industrial investment in the way their W coast neighbours have. Oil money has, however, helped transform the fortunes of Terengganu.

On the whole, the E coast has been less sullied by industrial pollution; the South China Sea is a lot cleaner than the Strait of Melaka. Despite the oil the E coast is still the rural backwater of the peninsula (95% of state revenues from oil go straight into federal coffers in KL). With its jungle, beaches and islands and its

Islam on the East Coast: fundamental pointers

Because the East coast states are a bastion of Islamic conservatism – which was reinforced by the resounding victory of Parti Islam in Kelantan in the 1990 general election – visitors should be particularly sensitive to the strictures of Islam. Those determined to get an all-over tan should not attempt to acquire it on the East coast's beaches, and women should dress 'respectfully' in public. Many Malay women choose to wear the *tudung* – the veil which signifies adherence to the puritanical lifestyle of the fervently Islamic *dakwah* movement. The East coast stands in contrast to other parts of the peninsula, where this garb is more often a fashion accessory than representative of a lifestyle. In 1988 cultural purists on the E coast began voicing concern about the 'cultural and moral pollution' that tourism brought in its wake. But any resentment that the arrival of Western tourists may have sparked seems to have evaporated in the face of the economic opportunities generated by tourism.

Malaysia's Islamic powerhouse in Kelantan and Terengganu states poses one possible occupational hazard for tourists – particularly if they travel north-to-south. In these two states, the weekend starts on Thursday lunchtime and everyone drifts back to work on Saturday. By and large, even the Chinese businesses observe the Muslim weekend. This means banks are shut – and those unfortunate to mistime their travels can find themselves arriving in Kuantan just in time for the banks there to close down too. Pahang state observes the Sat/Sun weekend. Be warned. In common with other strict Islamic states, there have also been moves in Kelantan to restrict the sale of alcohol, although at present it is still widely available in Chinese-run shops. Malay-run establishments in Terengganu and Kelantan are barred from serving alcohol. The bars and discos which contribute to a lively nightlife scene on the W coast are conspicuously absent on the E coast although life in the big resorts and hotels is largely unaffected. During Ramadan, which is strictly observed, Malay food and beverage outlets remain closed until Muslims break *puasa* (fast) after sundown. Although this means that it is impossible to find a good rendang or satay until the evening, travellers can feast on the amazing variety of colourful *kueh* – or cakes – which are sold at roadside stalls.

strong Malay cultural traditions, it holds many attractions for tourists. The only problem is that during the Western world's winter holiday period, the E coast is awash with monsoon flood water, which confines the tourist season to between Mar and Oct. Many beach resorts completely close down during the monsoon months. The best known tourist attraction on the E coast is the grimy village of Rantau Abang in Terengganu, where leatherback turtles lumber up the beach to lay their eggs between May and Oct.

Getting to the East Coast

Peninsular Malaysia's E coast can be reached from various points on the W coast. Routes from Butterworth (Penang) and Kuala Kangsar in the N, lead across to Kota Bahru on the NE coast. The highway from Kuala Lumpur goes to Kuantan (half-way down the E coast) and the railway cuts N from Gemas (S of KL) to Kota Bahru. There are also road routes from KL to the SE coast. Another common route is to follow the trunk road N from Johor Bahru which hits the E coast at Mersing, the launch-pad for Pulau Tioman and the islands of the Seribuat group.

Desaru beach resort and **Teluk Makhota** (Jason's Bay), (see *Johor Bahru, Excursions*, see page 178).

MERSING AND PULAU TIOMAN

Mersing

The small fishing port of Mersing is a pleasant but undistinguished little town. Most people are in a hurry to get to the islands and spend as little time as possible in the town, but as fishing boats can only make it out into the sea at high tide, some people will inevitably get stuck here for the night. In the past couple of years a number of good little restaurants have sprung up and Mersing is not an unpleasant place to spend a day or two. The town is evidently prospering thanks to the through flow of tourists to the islands. A big new plaza with a smart blue-tiled roof opened in 1992 and now accommodates the plethora of tour and ticketing agencies. On the mainland, 9 km N of Mersing on the road to Endau, there is a reasonably good beach, **Pantai Air Papan**, signposted off the road. Formerly, the most popular beach was **Sri Pantai**, but it is now stoney and unpleasant.

Mersing is, however, the main departure point for the islands off Pahang and Johor. The riverside jetty (just out of town to the E) is the jumping-off point for Pulau Tioman, the best known of the E coast's offshore islands. There are, however, 64 islands in total; others that can be reached from Mersing include Pulau Rawa, Pulau Sibu, Pulau Tinggi, Pulau Tengah, Pulau Aur and Pulau Pemanggil (see below).

Excursions

Endau Rompin National Park (see page 190); **Air Papan beach**, 9 km N of Mersing, passes as the best mainland beach in the area. It is 5 km off the main road N and the beach is about 2 km long, between two headlands. Pantai Air Papan is quite exposed but is backed by lines of casuarina and coconut palms. There is a liberal scattering of rubbish among the trees. There are a number of places at the end of the road offering budget accommodation within the C-E range. These include *Teluk Godek Chalet (Lani's Place)*, T 07-792569 which looks the newest and best; *Mersing Chalet and Restaurant*, T 07-794194; *Air Papan Chalets*, T 07-792993. More secluded is *Nusantara Chalet*, 1.5 km N through the kampung which stretches along the beach. There are a few beach-shelters dotted along the beach. **Getting there: by bus**: Mersing-Endau bus (No 5) to Simpang Air Papan (turn-off) (M$0.60); there is no bus service connecting with the beach, although it is possible to hitch-hike. **By taxi**: chartered taxi from Mersing costs M$12 one way. Arrangements can be made for pick-ups later in the day.

Accommodation **A** *Sutera Emas Villa*, c/o Sutera Emas Tour, No 13 Plaza R & R, Jln Abu Bakar, T 07-793155, a/c, for those wanting a bit more comfort, this small tour company has two fully furnished, self-catering apartments 3 km N of Mersing; **B** *Mersing Merlin Inn*, Batu 1, Jln Endau, T 791313, a/c, restaurant, pool, decaying concrete block on a hill out of town; **C** *Rumah Rehat* (Rest House), 490 Jln Ismail, T 792102/3, a/c, restaurant, a bit of a walk out of town towards the sea but one of the nicest in Malaysia, overlooking the golf course and the sea, big, clean rooms with views, well-kept garden and airy communal sitting area with balcony, rec; **C-D** *Country Hotel*, 11 Jln Sulaiman, T 791799, a/c/fan formerly the Mandarin Hotel, very clean and pleasant, but in noisy downtown location near the market and the bus and taxi stands; **C-D** *Embassy*, 2 Jln Ismail, T 7913545, some a/c, restaurant, very well-kept hotel – scrupulously clean, rooms without TVs considerably cheaper, *Embassy* annexe across the street above *Restoran Keluarga* (basic, cheap rooms), mountain bike hire (M$10/day, M$2/hr) and ticketing, rec; **C-D** *Kali's Guesthouse*, No 12E Kampung Sri Lalang, T 793613, fan only, restaurant, without doubt the best-kept, friendliest and most relaxed place to stay in Mersing area, rooms range from longhouse dorm to 'A'-frames and bungalows, atap-roofed bar and small Italian restaurant in garden next to beach, managed by Kali (a qualified diving instructor) and two Italians. **Getting there**: Mersing-Endau bus (M$0.40) or taxi M$3, highly rec; **C-D** *Mersing*, 1 Jln Dato' Mohammed Ali, T 791004, a/c, restaurant, spartan rooms now a bit tatty, clean enough but *Embassy* a better bet; **D** *Golden City*, 23 Jln Abu Bakar, T 791325, some a/c, near the bus station, clean but a bit run-down; **D** *Wisma Sutera Emas* (Juni Guesthouse), c/o Sutera Emas Tour, No 13 Plaza R & R, Jln Abu Bakar, T 07-793155, some a/c, 500 m down Kota Tinggi road, guesthouse inside small complex, run by tour and ticketing agency; **D-F** *Farm Guesthouse*, Kampung Tenglu Laut, chalets and dorm in relaxed kampung setting next to muddy beach, all food for extra M$10/day, run by a Malay (Ramli) and his Swiss wife (Marianne). **Getting there**: Mersing-Endau bus (No 5) 7 km N (M$0.45), walk 600 m to mosque, turn right for further 300 m, taxi M$5; **E** *East Coast*, 43a Jln Abu Bakar, T 791337; **E** *Syuan Koong*, 44A Jln Abu Bakar, T 791135, fan only, some rooms with attached bath, clean and fairly new-looking; **F** *Omar Backpackers' Dorm*, Jln Abu Bakar, clean and well looked-after but only 10 beds, excellent information on Sibu and other less-visited islands, rec; **F** *Sheikh Guest House*, 1B Jln Abu Bakar, T 793767, clean and friendly, efficient tourist agency attached with information on all the islands, dorms only, the *Sheikh Tourist Agency* downstairs offers ticketing, tours, accommodation booking and up-to-date information on Tioman and other islands; **F** *Tioman Lodging*, 2 Jln Ismail (above *Malayan Muslim Seafood Restaurant*), dorms and rooms run by young Malay couple from Tioman, clean with information about islands, ticketing.

Restaurants Malay: ♦*Malaysia*, opposite the bus stop, open all night; ♦*Sri Mersing Café*, opposite *Restoran Malaysia*; ♦*Restoran Al-Arif*, 44 Jln Ismail (opposite *Parkson* supermarket), cheap Muslim restaurant with good rotis and curries; ♦*Sofair*, 25 Jln Ismail, Indian coffee shop serving rotis and murtabak; ♦*Zam-Zam*, 51 Jln Abu Bakar, more Muslim food with dosai, prata and Mersing's best murtabaks; ♦*Malayan Muslim Seafood*, 2 Jln Ismail, very cheap and unusual Malay restaurant with coconutty seafood dishes, special Indonesian fish-head curry, rec. Chinese: ♦♦*Sin Nam Kee Seafood*, 387 Jln Jemaluang (1 km out of town on Kota Tinggi road, huge seafood menu and reckoned by locals to be the best restaurant in Mersing, also does karaoke sometimes, so can be noisy; ♦♦*Embassy Hotel Restaurant*, 2 Jln Ismail, big Chinese seafood menu, reasonably priced, chilli crabs, drunken prawns, wild boar and kang-kong belacan, rec; ♦♦*Mersing* (Grd Flr, *Mersing Hotel*), Jln Dato Mohammed Ali, excellent seafood; ♦♦*Mersing Seafood*, 56 Jln Ismail, a/c restaurant with spicy Szechuan or Cantonese seafood dishes, specials include squid with salted egg yoke, spicy coconut butter prawns, big menu, reasonable prices; ♦*Yung Chuan Seafood*, 51 Jln Ismail, big open coffee shop with vast selection, special: seafood steamboat. Indian: ♦*Taj Mahal*, vast selection. **Stalls**: there are a number of upmarket stalls and coffee shops in the new Plaza R & R next to the river.

Banks & money changers UMBC, Jln Ismail. No exchange on Sat; **Maybank**, Jln Ismail. Money changer on Jln Abu Bakar and Giamso Safari, 23 Jln Abu Bakar also changes travellers cheques.

Tour companies & travel agents There are ticketing and travel agents all over town dealing with travel to and from the islands and accommodation. They are much of a muchness and visitors are unlikely to be ripped off. Many agents are now located in the new Plaza R & R on Jln Tun Dr Ismail, next to the river. Competition is intense at peak season and tourists can be hassled for custom. Many agents also promote specific chalet resorts on the islands to which they offer package deals; sometimes these can be good value, but buying a boat ticket puts you under no obligation to stay at a particular place. Among the better agents are: *Sheikh Tourist Agency*, 1B Jln Abu Bakar, T 793767; *Dura Tourist Agency*, 7 Jln Abu Bakar, T 791002; *Island Connection*, 19 Plaza R & R (owns *Mukut Village Chalets* on Tioman); *Giamso Safari*, 23 Jln Abu Bakar, T 792253, F 791723 (owns *Paya Beach Resort* on Tioman).

Shopping *Lee Arts Souvenir*, 1, Gerai MDM, Jln Tun Dr Ismail, next to Malay restaurants on the corner after R & R Plaza. Artist Sulaiman Aziz specializes in colourful T-shirts, shorts and beachware and hand-painted batiks. There are some nick-nacky souvenir shops in the R & R Plaza.

Useful addresses Post Office: Jln Abu Bakar. Doctor: Dr Lai Chin Lai, Klinik Grace, 48 Jln Abu Bakar, T 792399. Dentist: Dr Logesh, Klinik Pergigian, 28 Jln Mohd. Ali, T 793135. .

Transport to & from Mersing 133 km N of Johor Bahru and 189 km S of Kuantan; 353 km from KL. **By bus**: long-distance buses leave from opposite *Hotel Golden City* on Jln Sulaiman. Regular connections with KL (M$18), JB (M$10.50), Terengganu (M$15), Kuantan (M$11) and Singapore (M$10). **By taxi**: taxis leave from Jln Sulaiman, next to the local bus station; KL (M$32), JB (M$12) (for Singapore, change at JB), Kuala Terengganu (M$32) and Kuantan

(M$15). **By boat**: the jetty is a 5 min walk from the bus stop. Most of the ticket offices are by the jetty but boat tickets are also sold from booths near the bus stop. (See transport to individual islands.) **NB**: the boat trip to the islands from Mersing can be extremely rough during the monsoon season; boats will sometimes leave Mersing in the late afternoon, on the high tide, but rough seas can delay the voyage considerably. It is advisable only to travel during daylight hours.

Pulau Tioman

Tioman, 56 km off Mersing, is the largest island in the volcanic Seribuat Archipelago – it is all of 20 km by 12 km. The island is dominated by several jagged peaks (notably the twin peaks of Nenek Semukut and Bau Sirau) and in Malay legend its distinctive profile is the back of a dragon whose feet got stuck in the coral. Tioman is densely forested and is fringed by white coral-sand beaches; there are a few kampungs around the coast. The highest peak is Gunung Kajang (1049m) or 'Palm Frond Mountain'. It has been used as a navigational aid for centuries and is mentioned in early Arab and Chinese sailing charts. In the mid-1970s, 12th century Sung Dynasty porcelain was unearthed on the island.

Tioman, rated as one of the world's 10 best 'desert island escapes' by *Time* magazine, is indeed very beautiful. In the 1950s it was discovered by Hollywood and selected as the location for the musical *South Pacific* where it starred as the mythical island of Bali Hai. All this attention put Tioman on the map; tourism accelerated during the 1970s and 1980s as facilities were expanded. The island now gets quite crowded at peak season. There is only one big hotel however, and the government has given a commitment not to build any more resorts; there is plenty of cheaper kampung-style beach-hut accommodation, particularly on the NW side of the panhandle. As yet, there are no nightclubs, fast-food restaurants or tourist-trinket shops.

There are very few trails around the island and only one road – a 2 km-long stretch from the airstrip at Tekek to the *Berjaya Imperial Beach Resort*. Plans are afoot, however, to build a road across to the less-developed E side of the island, presently connected by a beautiful jungle trail. Although the W side of the island – Salang, ABC (Kampung Ayer Batang) and Tekek – are now quite touristy, the E side has not yet been invaded in force. Despite the growth of tourism, Tioman retains most of its idyllic beauty.

Treks The cross-island trail, from the mosque in Kampung Tekek to Kampung Juara, on the E coast, is a 2-3 hour hike, which is quite steep in places. Three-quarters of the way up from Tekek there is a waterfall – just off the path to the right. It is a clearly marked trail and a great walk, although for those planning to stay at Juara, it is a tough climb with a full pack. There are also many easier jungle and coastal walks along the W coast: S from Tekek, past the resort to Kampungs Paya and Genting and N to Salang. Mount Kajang can be climbed from the E or W sides of the island; an unmarked trail leads from the Tioman Island golf course (advisable to take a guide). It is also possible to trek to Bukit Nenek Semukut (Twin Peaks) and Bukit Seperok. The trail up Semukut starts from Pasir Burong, the beach at Kampung Pasir. Guides available from *Berjaya Imperial Beach Resort* and *Happy Café*, *Juara* and *Zaha's Information Service* (near the jetty at Tekek) and *Kampung Tekek*. The trail from Kampung Juara, on the E coast, is longer and more arduous.

Diving Tioman's coral reefs are mainly on the NW side of the island, although large areas have been killed off. This is in part due to fishing boats dragging anchor, partly through nimble-fingered snorkellers pilfering coral stalks (this kills neighbouring corals) and partly because of the crown-of-thorns starfish (**see page 210**). Wholesale coral 'harvesting' has also been going on, to feed the increasingly lucrative trade in salt-water aquaria. Live coral specimens are loaded into water-filled bags, having been hacked off reefs with pick axes. This practice has more or less finished around Tioman now, but is still reported to be going on off other East Coast islands. Pollution is also said to be a coral-killer. Both sewerage and spillage from building sites can alter water salinity levels, killing coral and resulting in the proliferation of harmful algae. There are still some magnificent coral beds on the S side of the island, notably off Pasir Burong, and several of the nearby islands have good reefs. Pulau Rengis, just off the *Berjaya Imperial Beach Resort*, is the most easily accessible coral from the shore. The coral is a bit patchy and the resort seems to have a monopoly on snorkelling and diving there.

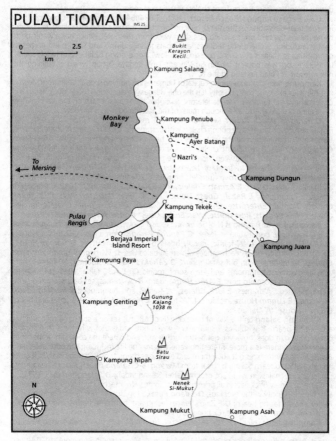

PULAU TIOMAN IMS 25

0 ——— 2.5
km

Bukit
Kerayon
Kecil

Kampung Salang

Monkey
Bay

Kampung Penuba

Kampung
Ayer Batang

Nazri's

To
Mersing

Kampung Dungun

Kampung Tekek

Pulau
Rengis

Berjaya Imperial
Island Resort

Kampung Juara

Kampung Paya

Kampung Genting

Gunung
Kajang
1038 m

Batu
Sirau

Kampung Nipah

Nenek
Si-Mukut

N

Kampung Mukut   Kampung Asah

It is also possible to dive the wreck of a Japanese warship near Mukut (on the S coast) and there are underwater caves around Pulau Cebeh (to the NW). *Berjaya Imperial Beach Resort*, *Ben's Diving Centre* at Salang, *Swiss Cottages*, at Kampung Tekek and *Paya Beach Resort* all organize dives (see *Sport*). There are also dive shops at Tekek and Genting.

Boat tours Boats leave from Kampung Tekek: to Pulau Tulai – or Coral Island – (M$20 return); Turtle Island (M$10 return); waterfall (M$26 return), around-the-island trip (M$35). All boats must be full – otherwise prices increase. Boat trips can also be arranged to other nearby islands. Boats can be booked through *Zaha's Information Service*, near the jetty, Kampung Tekek.

Accommodation The exclusive *Berjaya Imperial Beach Resort* and most of the cheaper places to stay are along the W coast (the island is virtually uninhabited on the SE and SW sides, apart from one or 2 fishing kampungs). Most of the accommodation on the island is simple: atap or tin-roofed chalets/huts (M$20-30), 'A'-frames (M$8-15) or dorms (M$5-10). Chalets with attached bathrooms are around M$30. Not all have electricity and most have communal bathrooms. Rooms are fairly spartan; expect to pay more for mosquito nets, electricity and attached bathrooms. It is sometimes possible to negotiate discounts for longer stays and during the off-season. Beach-front chalets usually cost more.

L-A+ *Berjaya Imperial Beach Resort*, Lalang, T 09445445, a/c, restaurant, pool, the only international-class hotel on the island, built on the site of the old Kampung Lalang, the beach, by no means the best on the island, is a short walk from the hotel, which has a watersports centre (including scuba diving facilities) and boats to take diving and snorkelling parties to nearby islands, there is also a golf course (see below), horse-riding facilities and tennis courts. In 1993 resort was bought by Tan Sri Vincent Tan's Berjaya Group which is building the mega-resort at Pulau Redang to the N.

Kampung Tekek is the kampung-capital of Tioman and is nothing special. Boats from Mersing first call at Tekek's large concrete jetty. It is the only village with electricity (1800-0600); hotels and chalets elsewhere run their own generators. Tekek has the longest beach on the island, where there are many places to stay, although much of the accommodation is run down.

C *Paradise Beach Resort* (left from jetty, 15 mins' walk, near Tioman Enterprises), restaurant, government-style boring chalets with bathrooms; **C-D** *Sri Tioman Chalet & Cafe*, turn right from jetty, chalets with attached bathrooms overlooking beach; **C-D** *Swiss Cottages*, T 248728, restaurant, chalets, fans, snorkelling & diving gear for hire, rec; **D** *Seroja Inn Resort*, T 794071 (between *Tioman Enterprises* and *Manggo Grove*), restaurant, 24 undistinguished chalets in front of beach, bicycles for hire; **D** *Tioman Safari Chalet*, T 791029; **D-E** *Manggo Grove* (turn left from jetty, 20 mins' walk), restaurant, 'A'-frames and chalets, near beach; **E** *Azman Chalets*, rec; **E** *Rahim House*, T 731012, chalets with attached bathrooms; **E** *Razali Guest House*, rec; **E** *Tekek Inn*, rec. Also all **E**: *Tekek Chalets*, *Tioman Enterprise Chalet & Huts*, *Manap Chalets*, *Yaha Chalets*, *Rallay's Chalets*, *Aris Chalets*, *Rest House*, *Wan Endut Guest House*, *Jumaat Guest House*.

Kampung Ayer Batang is N of Tekek and is also known as ABC. Accommodation here is, on the whole, better than at Tekek. **C** *Panuba Paradise Inn*, chalets; **D** *Johan House*, chalets; **D** *Nazri's Place*, 'A'-frame, friendly, boats to hire, spartan but rec; **D** *Tioman House*, 20 chalets backing on to each other with small balconies; **D** *Warison Tioman Heritage Chalets*, restaurant, clean but small rooms; **D** *Zahara's Place*, restaurant, 'A'-frames, huts with and without bathrooms and fans, some rooms **C**; **E** *ABC* (also called *Zul's Place*), 'A'-frames with mosquito nets; **E** *Aton House*, dorm & 'A'-frames, set back from the path; **E** *Double Ace*, 'A'-frames; **E** *Idris Chalet*, 'A'-frames and hammocks; **E** *Kartinis Place*, 'A'-frames; **E** *Lugam House*, restaurant, 'A'-frames; **E** *Nordin House*, 'A'-frames and dorm; **E** *Rinda House*, 'A'-frames.

Kampung Salang on the NW of the island (N of ABC), is set on a sheltered cove and has a beautiful beach. It is sold as a snorkellers' haven but, sadly, that is history – the coral is disappearing. It does, however, get better further out, and where the coral cliff drops off to deeper water, there is a more interesting variety of marine life including the odd reef shark. *Ben's Diving Centre* hires out equipment and organizes diving trips to nearby islands. It costs an extra M$5 to reach Salang by boat from Mersing. **B-C** *Salang Beach Resort*, restaurant, big, spacious chalets in well-kept grounds after Salang Indah; **D** *Salang Indah*, T 793155, restaurant, variety of chalets in all price brackets, some with attached bathrooms right on the sea, fans, electricity in the evenings; **D** *Salang Pusaka* (on the right from jetty before *Zaid's Place*), chalets facing beach; **D-F** *Zaid's Place*, restaurant, dorm, 'A' frames and bungalows on the hill, dorm (**F**), 'A'-frame (**E**), bungalows (**D**).

Kampung Paya is S of *Tioman Island Resort*. No regular scheduled boats go to Paya, so it is necessary to charter one from Tekek – which can be expensive (M$50) if you are not in a group. **A** *Paya Resort* (booking office 11 Jln Sulaiman, Mersing or in Singapore at 101 Upper Cross St, 01-36 People's Park Centre T 5341010), T 01762534, restaurant, small resort which is clean and well looked-after, diving can be organized from here. The resort, which is owned by director of Giamso Safari tour agency in Mersing, also has a NAUI diving school which is close to good coral, courses: M$600 for 6 days.

Kampung Genting S of Kampung Paya, is the second largest village on the island, but is not on the tourist-track. There are a handful of cheap places to stay, all with typical budget-type 'A'-frames and chalets. *Coco's Island Resort*, run by eco-entrepenneur William Thaddaeus who has dug special septic tanks to prevent effluent from running into the sea, one of the few resort-owners with any hint of environmental responsibility; **B-C** *Genting Damai Holiday Resort*, some a/c, restaurant, opened in 1991 with two rows of chalets built a little too close together, bookable through Mersing office, 4 Jln Abu Bakar or 16 Plaza R & R, T 794355; **C-D** *Dumba Beach Resort*, to the left of the jetty, chalets.

Kampung Nipah (S of Kampung Genting): **B-D** *Desa Nipah*, beachside chalets with attached bathrooms, because this is the only accommodation available, Kampung Nipah is one of the most secluded and tranquil spots on the island.

Kampung Mukut (on S side of island): **C** *Mukut Village Chalets*, restaurant, backed by coconut palms, traditional-style atap-roofed chalets with balconies, secluded, beautiful location with magnificent backdrop of the 'Twin Peaks', owned by *Island Connection* ticketing agency, 19 Plaza R & R, Mersing. Also at Mukut: *Asah Resort* and *Mukut Waterfall Backpacker Resort*.

Kampung Juara on the W coast, has beautiful long white beaches with some good breakers. Being on the seaward side, Juara has a completely different atmosphere from the W coast kampungs – it is quieter, friendlier and more laid-back, thanks mainly to its seclusion. There is a well-marked route from Kampung Tekek, through the jungle, to Juara (see *Treks*). Alternatively, it is possible to take a boat from Tekek. Accommodation is cheaper at Juara, this may all change if plans to build the road from Tekek to Juara take shape. Beer is not available on this side of the island and sandflies can be a problem. **D** *Muhara Chalet*, attached bathrooms; **D-F** *Atan's Place*, restaurant (*Turtle Cafe* – but you don't go there for the food), 'A'-frames and chalets; **D-F** *Juara Mutiara*, same management as *Atan's Place*, organizes diving trips/island tours, booking office in Mersing, 6 Jln Abu Bakar, near Plaza R & R; **E** *Butterfly's Huts*, 'A'-frames; **E** *Do Ray Me Chalet*, 'A'-frames; **F** *Rainbow Chalet*, restaurant, 'A'-frames, clean and cheap with electricity and mosquito nets, rec.

Restaurants Most restaurants are small family-run kitchens attached to groups of beach huts. All provide Western staples such as omelettes and French toast, as well as Malay dishes. On the whole, the food is of a high standard. *Berjaya Imperial Beach Resort Restaurant* is generally over-rated and expensive. *Liza Restaurant*, along the road from Tekek to the *Berjaya Imperial Beach Resort* serves delicious Malay food. It is more expensive than the beach restaurants – of which there are many at Tekek.

Sport Diving: *Ben's Diving Centre*, Salang Beach. Snorkelling and scuba; for the latter: one dive M$70; 2 dives M$90, which includes equipment and boat. *Berjaya Imperial Beach Resort* also has an energetically run 'activities' desk, which organizes snorkelling and scuba-diving. Diving trips can also be organized by a number of other small resorts, notably *Paya Beach Resort* and the *Juara Mutiara*. Golf: *Tioman Island Golf Club*, most club-members are weekend trippers from KL and Singapore. Beautiful course. Green fees: M$30. Watersports: *Berjaya Imperial Beach Resort* has jet skis, windsurfers and sailing dinghies for hire; also waterskiing.

Local transport Boat: beaches and kampungs are connected by an erratic sea-bus service, which runs roughly every hour or so from 0800 to 1800. The early-morning sea-bus goes right round the island (M$35), otherwise it is necessary to charter a boat to get to the waterfalls (on the S coast) and Kampung Juara. All the boats from Mersing take passengers to the kampungs on the W side; the first port of call is Kampung Tekek. Sea-bus fares (per person) from Kampung Tekek to: ABC (M$5), Salang (M$7-8), Lalang (*Berjaya Imperial Beach Resort*) (M$5), Genting (M$8), Mukut (M$12-15), Juara (M$12-15). The E coast is accessible by boat or by the jungle trail.

Banks & money changers No banks or money changers. Travellers' cheques can be changed at the *Berjaya Imperial Beach Resort* (large surcharge). Recently, some smaller resorts have begun to accept them.

Useful addresses Post Office: in Kampung Tekek.

Travel agent *Zaha's*, Tekek Pier. Sells boat tickets to Mersing and round-the-island excursion tickets.

Transport to & from Tioman 60 km from Mersing. **By air**: daily connections with KL (M$120), Kuantan (M$72) and Kerteh (M$96). **By boat**: the jetty is a 5 min walk out of Mersing next to the new blue-roofed Plaza R & R. It is not necessary to buy return tickets as it is easy to buy them on the island. All boats land on the W coast of Tioman, with the first port of call at Kampung Tekek. During the monsoon season (Nov through Feb) the sea can get quite rough; it is inadvisable to leave Mersing if the high tide is after 1500. (It is particularly difficult to find accommodation if you arrive in Tioman after nightfall and most restaurants close early). The timetable for launch departures is only drawn up one month in advance because it depends on tides. Fast boats leave at roughly one-hour intervals when the tide is high. A hydrofoil service to Tioman stopped running after a few months of operation but fast cruiser boats have cut down travelling times. A/c fast boats (*Seagull Express*, *Open Sea Express*, *Zahara Catamaran*, *Damai Express* and *Sri Kador*): M$25 per person (one way), 1½-2 hrs; moderate speed boats taking about 45 passengers: M$20 per person (one way), 3 hrs; fishing boats can be chartered by groups of 12 or more people for M$180, 4-5 hrs. There is a direct catamaran service (*Island Pearl*) between Singapore and Tioman; it leaves Singapore 0800 and returns 1700 4 hrs (S$120 return). Reservations at 3rd Flr, Finger Pier, Singapore, T 2226178.

International connections to Singapore By air: to Seletar Airport (on N of Singapore Island), M$90. By hydrofoil: a direct service leaves Singapore 0800 and returns 1700, 4 hrs (S$120 return). Reservations at 3rd Flr, Finger Pier, T 2226178.

Pulau Rawa

A small island, 16 km off Mersing, Pulau Rawa is owned by a nephew of the Sultan of Johor and is highly rated by lots of travellers. The island has a fantastic beach and for those in need of a desert island break, Rawa is perfect for there is absolutely nothing to do except mellow-out. Unfortunately the coral reef is disappointing, but more active visitors can windsurf, canoe, and fish. The island gets busy at weekends as it is close enough for day-visitors; it is also a popular getaway for Singaporeans.

Accommodation Rawa has no kampungs on it, and, as yet, only one resort. **B-C** *Rawa Safaris Island Resort*, Tourist Centre, Jln Abu Bakar, Mersing T 791204, some a/c, restaurant (Malay and international dishes), bungalows, chalets and 'A'-frames, watersports. Sahid mixes some mean cocktails in the bar – drink more than 2 Rawa specials and you'll be on the island for good.

Transport to & from Rawa By boat: daily connection via slow boat with Mersing, 1½ hours (M$16 return).

Other islands

There are a total of 64 islands off Mersing; many are inaccessible and uninhabited. There is accommodation available and boats to Pulau Babi Besar (Big Pig Island), Pulau Tinggi, Pulau (Babi) Tengah (which the government has declared a marine park because of its reef and the fact that Giant Leatherback turtles (**see page 203**) lay their eggs there between June and August), Pulau Sibu (the 'Island of Perilous Passage' – it used to be a pirate haunt), Pulau Aur (Bamboo Island) and Pulau Pemanggil. Pemanggil's best beaches are at Kampungs Buan and Pa Kaleh – which is fortunately where the accommodation is sited. **Pulau Babi Besar** is larger and closer to the mainland than Rawa. It is a very peaceful island and is particularly well-known for its beaches and coral. **Pulau Tinggi** is probably the most dramatic-looking island in the Seribuat group, with its 650 m volcanic peak. **Pulau Tengah** (formerly a refugee camp for Vietnamese boat people) is an hour away from Mersing. The island is a marine park, as the giant leatherback turtles (**see page 203**) come here to lay their eggs in Jul/Aug. **Pulau Sibu** has been recommended by many travellers for its beaches and watersports. Sibu is frequented more by Singaporeans and expatriates than by Western tourists. It is popular for fishing and diving.

Accommodation Most of the accommodation on these islands is run by small operators, who organize packages from Mersing. Resort bookings must be made in either Mersing or Johor Bahru. **Pulau Besar**: **A** *Radin Island Resort*, 9 Tourist Information Centre, Jln Abu Bakar, Mersing, T 793124, restaurant, (some a/c) stylish traditional chalets with jungle hillside backdrop; **A** *White Sand Beach Resort*, 98 Jln Harimau Tarum, Century Garden, Johor Bahru, T 07-334669/332358. Runs diving packages, 4 days for 2 people; **B** *Besar Marina Resort*, 10, Tourist Information Centre, Jln Abu Bakar, Mersing, T 793606. **B** *Hillside Beach Resort*, 5B Jln Abu Bakar, Mersing or book through Suite 125, 1st Flr, Johor Tower, 15 Jln Gereja, Johor Bahru, T 07-236603, F 244329, restaurant, very attractively designed Kampung-style resort, nestling on jungled slopes above beach, watersports; **C** *Besar Beach Chalet*, new resort with government-style chalets backed by Irish jungle. **Pulau Tinggi**: **A** *Smailing Island Resort*, c/o 17 Tingkat 2, Kompleks Tun Abdul Razak, Jln Wong Ah Fook, Johor Bahru, T 07-231694, also booking office in Mersing opposite Plaza R & R, Jln Abu Bakar, restaurant, pool, luxurious Malay-style wooden chalets. Also 'A'-frames (F), chalets (D) and bungalows (C) on the island; **A** *Tinggi Island Resort*, bookings from *Sheikh Tourist Agency*, 1B Jln Abu Bakar, Mersing T 793767, attractive chalets balanced precariously on steep hillside and next to beach, excellent range of indoor and outdoor facilities, boat trips arranged to nearby islands (Pulau Lima and Pulau Simbang) for diving. **Pulau (Babi) Tengah**: more accommodation is planned on the island. **B** *Pirate Bay Island Resort*, restaurant, spacious cottages built in traditional style with full selection of amenities, watersports. **Pulau Sibu Besar**: **A-D** *Sibu Island Cabanas* (c/o G105 Holiday Plaza, Century Garden JB), T 317216, restaurant, chalets and de luxe bungalows; **C** *Sibu Island Resort*, T 316201, restaurant, bungalows only, watersports; **D** *O & H Kampung Huts* (c/o 9 Tourist Information Centre, Jalan Abu Bakar, Mersing), T 793124, restaurant, chalets, some with attached bathrooms, clean and friendly, trekking & snorkelling, rec; **C-D** *Sea Gypsy Village Resort*, 9, Tourist Information Centre, Jln Abu Bakar, Mersing, T 793124, restaurant, chalets and bungalows, rec. **Pulau Sibu Tengah**: *Sibu Island Resorts*, Suite 2-10, PKEINJ Bldg, Jln Rebana, Johor Bahru, T 316201. **Pulau Aur**: **F** *Longhouse* provides basic accommodation. **Pulau Pemanggil**: Package deals for *Wira Chalets and longhouse* (also has dive shop). There is a small agent at the very front of Mersing's Plaza R & R dealing exclusively with Pemanggil travel and accommodation. **C-E** *Dagang Chalets and Longhouse*, Kampung Buau (one longhouse room sleeps 8 at M$10 per person), restaurant serving local food, *Mara Chalet* at Kampung Pa Kaleh, on southwest side. Contact *Tioman Accommodation & Boat Services*, 3 Jln Abu Bakar, Mersing, T 793048.

Restaurants All resorts have their own restaurants.

Transport to & from the Islands Boats to the islands leave daily from Mersing, usually around 1100 and return 1530 (all slow boats): Tengah (M$18 return), Besar (M$22-24 return), Sibu (M$22 return), Tinggi (M$22 return). No regular boats to Pulau Aur or Pulau Pemanggil. Also boats to Sibu from Tanjung Sedili Besar at Teluk Mahkota (23 km off the Kota Tinggi-Mersing road), S of Mersing (M$22 return).

NORTH TO KUANTAN AND TAMAN NEGARA

Endau Rompin National Park

Endau Rompin National Park straddles the border of Johor and Pahang states and is one of the biggest remaining tracts of virgin rainforest on the peninsula, about 80,000 hectares. In the late 1980s it was upgraded to the status of a National Park to protect the area from the logging companies, although transport and accommodation facilities are still skeletal. Access to the park will become easier and cheaper during the next few years and new accommodation is planned for upriver. However, because it lacks facilities the authorities have been reluctant to publicise it. Trips to Endau require careful planning – it is not like Taman Negara – and are best organized by tour agents (see below).

It is possible to hire boats from Endau, on the coast road, up the Endau River. The first 10 km to Kampung Punan is navigable by larger motor boats; from there, smaller boats head on upstream to Orang Asli villages. The junction of the Endau and Jasin rivers (9 hrs from Endau) is a good campsite and base for trekking and fishing expeditions. Boats go further upstream, but it is advisable to take a guide. They can be hired from Endau or from the Orang Asli kampungs (M$20-30/day). At present it is necessary to take all provisions and camping equipment with you. It is inadvisable to travel during the monsoon season from Nov to Mar. Following the drowning of a Singaporean student in rapids in 1992, it has become much more difficult to visit Endau Rompin independently and it is now essential to secure a permit (see below). Visitors are strongly recommended to go to Endau with a travel agency, which can obtain permits on a visitor's behalf.

Most package trips involve a 70 km jeep trip from Mersing to Kampung Peta followed by $1\frac{1}{2}$ hr longboat ride to first campsite. The rest of the trip involves trekking around the Asli trails and visiting spectacular waterfalls, the biggest of which is the Buaya Sangkut waterfall on Sungei Jasin. Fishing trips are best organized between Feb and Aug.

Permit from Johor State Security Council, 2nd Floor, Bangunan Sultan Ibrahim, Bukit Timbalan, Johor Bahru, T 237344. Applications for permits must be made at least 2 weeks in advance, in writing, with passport details, two passport photographs, and proposed length of trip. The travel agencies listed below can secure permits within 5 days – one week, but it is advisable to leave more time if possible. Permits are considered necessary because the area still falls under the Internal Security Act; in the days before the surrender of the Communist Party of Malaya in 1990, the Endau-Rompin jungle used to be part of the guerrillas' supply route through the peninsula.

Tours Organized expeditions, in which prices are inclusive of return vehicle and boat transfer, camping equipment, cooking utensils and permits, can be booked through: Giamso Travel, 23 Jalan Abu Bakar, Mersing, T 792253. Approximately M$190/person for 3 days/2 nights, M$210/person for 4 days 3 nights. The company can supply camping equipment. Shah Alam Tours, 138 Mezz. Flr, Jln Tun Sambanthan, Kuala Lumpur, T 03-2307161, F 03-2745739. (Tours are organized by Encik Majid).

Accommodation Kuala Rompin: C *Rumah Rehat* (Rest House), 122.5 Milestone, T 565245, restaurant, two-storied resthouse, all rooms with attached bathroom. There is no accommodation available in the park: camping only.

Tour companies Organized expeditions, in which prices are inclusive of return vehicle and boat transfer, camping equipment, cooking utensils and permits, can be booked through: *Giamso Travel*, 23 Jln Abu Bakar, Mersing, T 792253. Approximately M$190/person for 3 days/2 nights, M$210/person for 4 days 3 nights. The company can supply camping equipment, or through *Shah Alam Tours*, 138 Mezz. Flr, Jln Tun Sambanthan, Kuala Lumpur T 03-2307161, F 03-2745739. *Sheikh Tourist Agency*, 1B Jln Abu Bakar, Mersing T 793767. 4 day/3 night trips M$380 per person, all in M$100 deposit payable on booking. *Eureka Travel*, 277A Holland Ave, Holland Village, Singapore, T 4625077, F 4622853, offers ecologically orientated tours to Endau Rompin National Park, rec.

Transport to & from Endau Rompin National Park 130 km S of Kuantan, 37 km N of Mersing. **By bus**: connections with JB (M$6), Terengganu (M$15) and Kuantan (M$10.50). Buses from Johor Bahru and Kuantan stop on demand at Endau, or regular local buses from Mersing to Endau (M$2.50) and then into the park by boat. Speed boats to first Orang Asli village (Kampung Punan). This can cost anything from M$200-400. It is possible to charter longboats (carrying up to 6 passengers) from Kampung Punan to go further upstream. **By taxi**: (M$3 per person) from Mersing.

Pekan

Pekan is the old royal capital of Pahang. *Pekan* means 'town' in Malay – it used to be known as Pekan Pahang, the town of Pahang. Even before the Melakan sultanate was established in the late 14th century, it was known by the Sanskrit name for 'town' – *Pura*. It is divided into Old Pekan (Pekan Lama) and New Pekan (Pekan Bahru); the former was the exclusive abode of the Malay nobility for centuries. Today the town has a languid feel to it. It has a reasonably picturesque row of older wooden shop houses on the busy street along the river, but is otherwise not a particularly photogenic town. Aside from its mosques, Pekan's most distinguishing feature is its bridge, which straddles the Pahang River, the longest river on the peninsula.

There are 2 mosques in the centre of Pekan: the **Abdullah Mosque**, Jalan Sultan Ahmad (beyond the museum) and the more modern **Abu Bakar Mosque** next door. On the N outskirts of the town is the **Istana Abu Bakar** – the royal palace – just off Jalan Istana Abu Bakar. Its opulent trimmings are visible from the road, although not worth the hassle as you cannot get in. The small but interesting **Sultan Abu Bakar Museum**, on Jalan Sultan Ahmad is housed in a splendid colonial building and has a jet-fighter mounted Airfix-style in the front garden. The museum includes a collection of brass and copperware, royal regalia, porcelain from a wrecked Chinese junk and an exhibition of local arts and crafts. In the back garden there is a depressing mini-zoo which rarely gets visited. It is home to Malayan Honey Bears, a tapir, a collection of monkeys, a black panther and a fish eagle, all squeezed into tiny cages. Open: 0930-1700 Tue-Thur, Sat & Sun; 0930-1215, 1445-1700 Fri.

Festivals Oct: *Sultan's Birthday* (24th: state holiday) celebrated with processions, dancing and an international polo championship which the sultan hosts on his manicured polo ground at the istana.

Accommodation There is a poor selection of hotels in Pekan – the government rest house is the best bet. Few people will have much reason to stay in Pekan for long. **D** *Rumah Rehat* (rest house), beside the football field (*padang*), off Jln Sultan Abu Bakar, T 421240, restaurant. It is a big, low-slung colonial building – which is in need of a lick of paint – with a cool, spacious interior and big, clean rooms. It is advisable to try to book accommodation in advance if visiting

Pahang: the land of the sacred tree

A Malay legend tells of a huge, majestic Mahang (softwood) tree that once stood on the bank of the Pahang River, not far from Pekan, towering over everything else in the jungle. The tree was said to resemble the thigh of a giant and considered sacred by the Orang Asli and the Jakun tribespeople. The Malays adopted the name, which, in time, became Pahang. Perhaps not coincidentally, *pahang* also happens to be the Khmer word for 'tin' – there are ancient tin workings at Sungei Lembing near Kuantan, where traces of early human habitation have been found.

Until the end of the 19th century, Pahang, the peninsula's largest, but least populous state, had always been a vassal. It paid tribute to Siam, Melaka and then Johor. In 1607 the Dutch set up a trading post in Pahang, but the state found itself caught in the middle of protracted rivalries between Johor and Aceh, the Dutch and the Portuguese. Pekan was sacked repeatedly by Johor and Aceh in the early 17th century, before coming under the direct rule of the Sultan of Johor in 1641; it stayed that way for 2 centuries.

In 1858, the death of the chief minister of Pahang, resulted in a 5-year civil war. The dispute between his 2 sons was finally settled when the youngest, Wan Ahmad, declared himself Chief Minister and then became the Pahang's first sultan in 1863. Sultan Wan Ahmad was autocratic and unpopular, so the British entered the fray, declaring the state a protectorate in 1887. An anti-British revolt ensued, supported by the sultan, but Wan Ahmad's power was whittled away. In 1895 the state's administrative capital was moved from Pekan to Kuala Lipis, 300 km up the Pahang River and later to Kuantan. Pahang became part of the federated Malay states in 1896. It was completely cut off from the W coast states, except for a couple of jungle trails, until a road was built from Kuala Lumpur to Kuantan in 1901. Pahang remains a predominantly Malay state.

during the Sultan's birthday celebrations. **D** *Pekan*, 60 Jln Tengku Ariff Bendahara, T 71378, a/c, restaurant, badly run.

Restaurants ✦✦*Pekan Hotel Restaurant*, 60 Jln Tengku Ariff Bendahara, nothing special. There are a couple of reasonable coffee shops in the new town. The food stalls on Jln Sultan Ahmad, near the bus/taxi stands, are the best Pekan has to offer.

Banks & money changers Bumiputra, 117 Jln Engku Muda Mansur.

Transport to & from Pekan 47 km S of Kuantan. **By bus**: bus stop on Jln Sultan Ahmad. Regular connections with Kuantan (M\$2.20). **By taxi**: taxis stand between Jln Sultan Ahmad and the waterfront, opposite the indoor market. Kuantan (M\$3.50).

Kuantan

The modern capital of Pahang has a population of around 100,000 and is a bustling, largely Chinese, town at the mouth of the Kuantan River. Kuantan is the main transport and business hub for the E coast; most visitors spend at least a night here. Kuantan's short on sights, but the brand new **Sultan Ahmad Shah** mosque, in the centre of town, is worth wandering around. It is an impressive building, freshly decorated in blue and white with a cool marbled interior. It has blue and yellow stained glass windows and the morning sun projects their coloured patterns on the interior walls. Kuantan has several streets of old shophouses which date from the 1920s. Most of the oldest buildings are opposite the padang on Jln Makhota. The 300 km stretch of coast between Kuantan and Kota Bahru, is comprised of long beaches, interspersed with fishing kampungs and the occasional natural gas processing plant and oil refinery.

Excursions

Teluk Cempedak is just 4 km NE of Kuantan and marks the beginning of the beaches. It was once the site of a quiet kampung, and is now a beach strip with

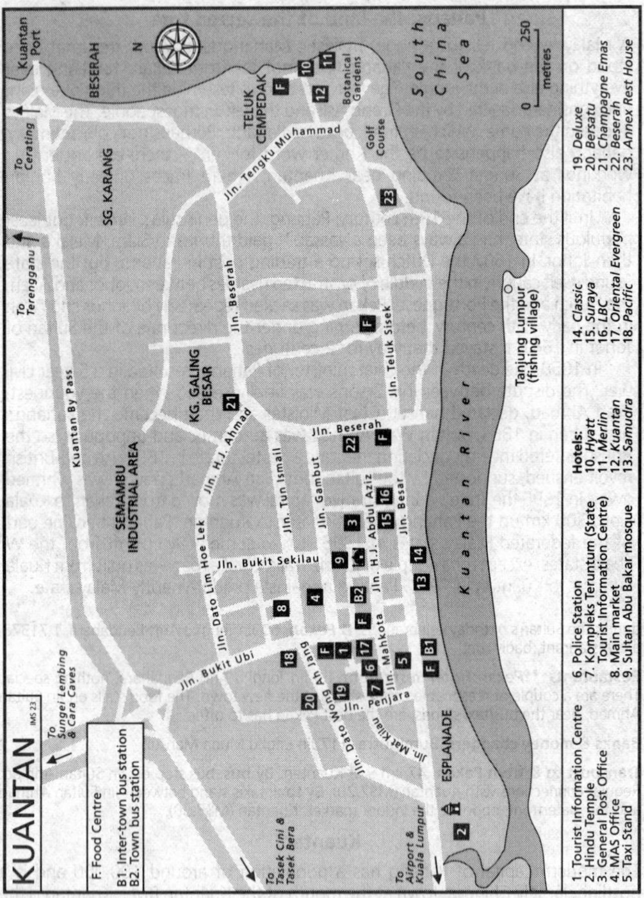

KUANTAN

Map labels: Kuantan Port · BESERAH · SG. KARANG · N · TELUK CEMPEDAK · Botanical Gardens · South China Sea · Golf Course · Jln. Tengku Muhammad · Jln. Beserah · KG. GALING BESAR · Jln. Teluk Sisek · Kuantan By Pass · SEMAMBU INDUSTRIAL AREA · Jln. H.J. Ahmad · Jln. Beserah · Jln. Tun Ismail · Jln. Gambut · Jln. Bukit Sekilau · Jln. Dato Lim Hoe Lek · Jln. H.J. Abdul Aziz · Jln. Besar · Jln. Bukit Ubi · Jln. Dato Wong Ah Jang · Jln. Mahkota · Jln. Penjara · Jln. Mat Kilau · Kuantan River · Tanjung Lumpur (fishing village) · ESPLANADE · To Cerating · To Terengganu · To Sungei Lembing & Cave Caves · B1. Inter-town bus station · B2. Town bus station · To Tasek Cini & Tasek Bera · To Airport & Kuala Lumpur · F. Food Centre · MG 23 · 0–250 metres

1. Tourist Information Centre
2. Hindu Temple
3. General Post Office
4. MAS Office
5. Taxi Stand
6. Police Station
7. Kompleks Teruntum (State Tourist Information Centre)
8. Main market
9. Sultan Abu Bakar mosque

Hotels:
10. Hyatt
11. Merlin
12. Kuantan
13. Samudra
14. Classic
15. Suraya
16. LBC
17. Oriental Evergreen
18. Pacific
19. Deluxe
20. Bersatu
21. Champagne Emas
22. Beserah
23. Annex Rest House

2 big hotels and a string of bars, karaoke pubs and restaurants. The E coast has much more to offer than Teluk Cempedak, but there is a good range of accommodation. There is a government-run handicraft shop (*Kedai Kraf*) beside the beach, specializing in batik.

The Pahang state government has reserved the 30 km stretch of coast from Teluk Cempedak beach to Chendor (on the Terengganu state border) exclusively for tourism-related projects, so there is likely to be much more development in the next few years.

Accommodation Teluk Cempedak now offers an excellent choice of hotels to suit most budgets – three of which have been recommended. The area provides a more relaxed alternative to the noisier hotels in Kuantan itself. **A** *Hyatt*, Teluk Cempedak, T 525211, a/c, restaurant (overlooking the waves), pool (with bar), low-rise hotel in landscaped gardens with

Dateline Kuantan: Churchill's Malayan nightmare

"In all the war, I never received a more direct shock," wrote former British wartime Prime Minister Winston Churchill in his memoirs. "As I turned and twisted in bed, the full horror of the news sank in upon me." On 10 Dec 1941 Churchill got the news that a Japanese air strike force operating from Saigon had destroyed and sunk 2 of the most powerful warships in the British Royal Navy. *HMS Prince of Wales*, a 35,000-ton battleship and *HMS Repulse*, a 32,000-ton battle cruiser, sank within an hour of each other, with the loss of 1,196 lives, 95 km off Kuantan.

A few days earlier the ships had arrived in Singapore, then the biggest naval operations base in the world, to underscore Britain's commitment to protecting its colonies in the East. They were soon speeding N in an effort to pre-empt and disrupt Japan's amphibious invasion of Malaya, but the flotilla, which had no air cover, was spotted by a Japanese submarine. The first wave of Japanese fighter-bombers arrived at 1100; by 1233, the *Repulse*, its thick armour-plated hull holed by 5 torpedoes, was sunk. *The Prince of Wales* went down 47 minutes later in about 60 m of water. Accompanying destroyers rescued 1,900 men from the 2 vessels before retreating to Singapore, which fell to the Japanese Imperial Army 8 weeks later. The wrecks of the 2 ships were declared war graves and in 1991, on the 50th anniversary of the Japanese attack, a team of British Navy divers laid white ensign flags on both ships to commemorate the dead.

a leafy lobby, good sports (including watersports) facilities, well-stocked craft shop, well-managed with good views, Sampan bar (formerly a Vietnamese refugee boat), the hotel is being extended to include apartments in an ugly 10-storey block, rec; **A** *Merlin Inn Resort*, Teluk Cempedak, T 522388, a/c, restaurant, pool, modern hi-rise hotel which plays second fiddle to the *Hyatt*, next door, restaurant built out on stilts over the sea, tours run from hotel; **B** *Annex Rest House*, Jln Teluk Sisek, 2 km before Teluk Cempedak, newly renovated (in great taste), modernized and smartened, spacious grassy grounds, best value on E Coast, highly rec; **B** *Samudra Beach Resort*, T 505933, a/c, restaurant, rooms look like municipal toilets from the outside, but they have big French windows overlooking spacious gardens and the bay, nice place; **B-C** *Kuantan*, opposite *Hyatt*, T 500026, a/c, restaurant, very clean, cheaper rooms fan only but all have attached bathroom, noisy television lounge, very pleasant terrace for sun-downers – although it now faces the new Hyatt extension, rec; **C** *Hill View*, T 521555, a/c, restaurant in block of karaoke lounges, bars and restaurants, not good value for money.

Restaurants ♦♦*Cempedak Seafood*, A-1122, Jln Teluk Sisek, big Chinese restaurant at the crossroads on the way to Teluk Cempedak, specialities: chilli crab and freshwater fish; ♦♦♦*Nisha's Curry House*, 13 Teluk Cempedak, N Indian cuisine plus fish-head curry; ♦♦*Pattaya*, on the beach front, good views of the beach; ♦♦*Tan's*, 29 Teluk Cempedak, Malay/Chinese, also fish head curry. **Getting there**: regular connections from Kuantan – bus 39 from local bus station. A short walk N of Teluk Cempedak are Methodist Bay and Teluk Pelindong, which are beyond the range of most picknickers.

South of Kuantan

Tasek Cini is an amalgam of 13 freshwater lakes, whose fingers reach deep into the surrounding forested hills, 100 km SW of Kuantan. The lake and the adjoining mountain are sacred to the Malays; legend has it that Lake Cini is the home of a huge white crocodile. The Jakun proto-Malay aboriginals, who live around Tasek Cini, believe a naga, or serpent, personifying the spirit of the lake, inhabits and guards its depths. Some commentators think that as tourism picks up there, Tasek Cini will acquire the status of Scotland's Loch Ness – although Lake Cini's monster has not been spotted now for twelve years. Locals call their monster 'Chinnie'. More intriguing still are tales that the lake covers a 12th-14th century Khmer walled city. The rather unlikely story maintains that a series of aquaducts were used as the city's defence and that when under attack, the city would be submerged. In late-1992, however, the Far Eastern Economic Review reported that recent archaeological expeditions had uncovered submerged stones a few metres underwater at various points around the lake. But the Orang Asli fishermen do not need archaeologists to support their convictions that the lost city exists. Between Jun and Sept the lake is carpeted with red and white lotus flowers. **Accommodation**: **C** *Lake Cini Resort*, chalets, camping (**F**), small restaurant attached to the resort. **Getting there**: difficult by public transport; by far the easiest way to visit the lake is on an organized tour (M$50). Contact **Tourist Information Centre**, 15th Flr, Kompleks Teruntum, Jalan Mahkota, T 505566. **By bus**: take the KL highway from Kuantan towards Maran (M$4); 56 km down the road, Tasek Cini is signposted to the left. Take a bus to Kampung Belimbing (0600, 0900, 1200 and 1500; M$2.50). At Belimbing it is possible to hire a boat across the Pahang River and onto the waterways of Tasek Cini (M$40-50/day). It is also possible to be dropped off at the resort and picked up at an arranged time (M$80). There are also buses leaving Kuantan and Pekan for Kampung Cini (8 km from the resort). There are a few tour companies which run package tours to the lake. The best is Malaysian Overland Adventures, Lot 1.23, 1st Flr, Bangunan Angkasaraya, Jalan Ampang, Kuala Lumpur, T 03-2413569.

Tasek Bera Temerloh is one of the best access points for Tasek Bera – 'the lake of changing colours' – the biggest natural lake in Malaysia. There are several Jakun – so-called proto-Malays – and Semelai aboriginal kampungs around the lake which was once a major centre for the export of jelutong resin, used as a sealant on boats and as jungle chewing gum. Similar to Tasek Cini (see above), Tasek Bera is a maze of shallow channels connecting smaller lakes, in all about 5 km wide and 27 km long. One of the lake's resident species is the rare fish-eating 'false' gharial crocodile (*Tomistoma schlegeli*). Asli boatmen on the lake can be hired for about M$10/day. **Getting there**: it is necessary to acquire police permission in Temerloh to visit the area, but the lake is virtually inaccessible by public transport. It is possible to take a bus or shared taxi to Triang, due S of Temerloh, and then charter a taxi to the lake; but this is expensive. Alternatively, bus from Temerloh to Triang, 2 hrs (M$1.70); bus from Kemayan to Bahau, 45 mins (M$1); bus from Bahau to Ladang Geddes, 30 mins (M$0.60); hitch or taxi (M$15-20) to Fort Iskander on the S side of the lake (where there are bungalows with cooking facilities, bookable through the Department of Aboriginal Affairs in Temerloh). Fort Iskandar is one of the best places on the peninsula to visit Orang Asli villages. **NB**: do not attempt this trip without taking adequate supplies and provisions (including basic cooking utensils).

North of Kuantan

Caras Caves lies 25 km NW of town. Take a right fork at the 24 km mark. In 1954, the Sultan of Pahang gave a Thai Buddhist monk permission to build a temple in a limestone cave at Pancing, known as the 'yawning skull' cave. A steep climb up 200 stone steps leads into the cave which contains shrines and religious icons cut into the rock. The collection is dominated by a 9m-long reclining Buddha, set among the limestone formations. There is always a monk in residence in the cave. Admission: M$2.

Beyond the caves is **Sungei Lembing**, an old tin mine and the site of some of the oldest tin workings on the peninsula. It has now opened to visitors. **Getting there**: bus, every hour (M$2.50).

Gunung Tapis Park is a new state park, offering rafting, fishing and trekking 49 km from Kuantan. Arrangements have to be made through the Tourist Information Centre or the local Outward Bound Society. **Getting there**: only accessible by jeep via Sungei Lembing, from here accessible via a 12 km track.

Beserah Once a picturesque fishing kampung, 10 km N of Kuantan. Now it sprawls and is not much more than a suburb of Kuantan. Beserah is a friendly place but aesthetically it bears little comparison with villages further N. There is, however, a local handicraft industry still; there is a batik factory to the N of the village. The village's speciality is *ikan bilis*, or anchovies, which are boiled, dried and chillied on the beach and end up on Malaysian breakfast tables, gracing *nasi lemak*. Beserah's fishermen use water buffalo to cart their catch directly from their boats to the kampung, across the middle of the shallow lagoon.

The kampung has become rather touristy in recent years, but there is a good beach, just to the N, at Batu Hitam.

Accommodation Most of the resort hotels are around Sungei Karang, 3-4 km N of Beserah. **A** *Coral Beach Resort* (formerly Ramada), 152 Sungei Karang, T 587544, a/c, restaurant, good range of facilities including tennis, squash and watersports, adjacent to fine white-sand beach, appears to attract more senior citizens than honeymooners, *Reliance tour agency* in arcade; **A-B** *Le Village Beach Resort*, Sungei Karang, Beserah, T 587900, F 587899, restaurants, pool and many recreational facilities, neatly landscaped grounds with well-spaced chalets, good atmosphere; **B** *Blue Horizon Beach Resort*, T 588119, N of Beserah on good beach, pool, very new, clean and spruce with big chalet rooms, built around central area, garden a bit of a wilderness; **B** *Gloria Maris Resort*, T 587788, a/c, restaurant, watersports, very small pool, sandwiched between road and Pasir Hitam (not such a good stretch of beach), but well-appointed chalets and friendly management; **F** *Jaffar's Place*, very rudimentary kampung accommodation.

Restaurants ✦✦✦*Beserah Seafood*, Malay/Chinese, speciality: buttered prawns; ✦✦✦*Gloria Maris*, near the chalets, Malay/Indian/Thai. **Getting there**: buses 27, 28, 30 from Kuantan every half hour (M$1.50).

Kampung Sungei Ular (Snake River Village), 31 km N of Kuantan, is a typical laid-back and very photogenic Malay fishing village. There is a small island (Pulau Ular), just offshore. Beach is deserted, is backed by coconut palms and has fine white sand. The Kampung is signposted to the right, just off the main road.

Accommodation The upmarket hotels are mostly at Teluk Cempedak (4 km N of Kuantan, see page 193). The *Hyatt* and the *Merlin* are the best. There are plenty of cheap Chinese hotels in Kuantan itself, mostly on and around Jln Teluk Sisek and Jln Besar. Several smart new hotels have sprung up in the B-C range which offer excellent value for money. **A-B** *Samudra River View*, Jln Besar, T 522688, F 500618, a/c, restaurant, next to *Kuantan Swimming Centre*, was Kuantan's best, but new mid-market hotels are smarter and better value, carpets shabby, doubles are small, twins bigger with sitting area; **B** *Classic*, 7 Bangunan LKNP (formerly *Hotel Pahang*), Jln Besar, T 554599, F 504141, a/c, scooped *Tourism Malaysia's Best Hotel of the Year Award 1992* (in budget category), extremely clean, big rooms and spacious attached bathrooms, one of the best-value-for-money hotels in the country, conveniently located next to *Kuantan Swimming Centre*, behind the *Samudra River View* next door, rec; **B** *Oriental Evergreen*, 157 Jln Haji Abdul Rahman, T 500168, a/c, restaurant (Chinese), prominently advertised hotel that's clean but rather average, nightmare decor with avocado suites, clashing bedspreads and astroturf carpets; **B** *Pacific*, 60-62 Jln Bukit Ubi, T 511979, a/c, restaurant, one step down from the *Samudra*, the 6th Flr has recently been renovated and upgraded – tasteful and recommended – good hotel in central location; **B** *Suraya*, Jln Haji Abdul Aziz, T 554268, F 526728, a/c, coffee area, another *Tourism Malaysia* award-winning hotel (1990, 1992), simple, well-appointed rooms, attached bathrooms, video, catering mainly for business people and domestic tourist market, good value; **B-C** *Bersatu*, 2-4 Jln Darat Makbar (off Jln Wong Ah Jang), T 512328, F 506822, a/c, opened 1993, very clean and new, attached bathrooms, aimed at Malaysian executives; **C** *Champagne Emas*, 3002 Jln Haji Ahmad Shah, T 528820, a/c; **C** *Chusan*, 37-39 Jln Wong Ah Jang, T 504422, clean but smallish rooms; **C** *Deluxe*, 1st Flr, 53 Jln Wong Ah Jang (next to *Chusan Hotel*), a/c, above all-night restaurant, small rooms but clean and well-kept, caters mostly for itinerant businessmen, excellent value, rec; **C** *LBC* (above *Loo Brothers Co.*), 59 Jln Haji Abdul Aziz, T 528252, a/c, big rooms and reasonably well-kept, can be noisy, attached showers but outside loos; **C** *New Embassy*, Jln Besar, T 52593, some a/c, restaurant, clean and well looked after; **C-D** *Embassy*, 60 Jln Teluk Sisek, T 527486, well looked after, all rooms have attached bathroom, good value, above *Tanjung Ria* coffee shop, some rooms rather noisy because of main road; **D** *Tong Nam Ah*, Jln Teluk Sisek, T 521204, basic, but conveniently located for bus station and hawker stalls; **E** *Min Heng Hotel & Bakery*, 22 Jln Mahkota, T 524885, restaurant, Kuantan's oldest hotel, opened 1926, basic, rooms partitioned with grills, entrance down side street, next to steakhouse and cake shop; **E** *Sin Nam Fong*, 44 Jln Teluk Sisek, T 521561, restaurant, friendly management but when the traffic is heavy you might as well be camped on the central reservation.

Restaurants ◆◆◆*Cheun Kee*, Jln Mahkota, large open-air Chinese restaurant, good selection of seafood; ◆◆*BKT* (also known as Restoran Malam), 53 Jln Wong Ah Jang, open coffee-shop/restaurant under *Hotel Deluxe*, best known for chicken rice and fish head curries and for being open until 4 am; ◆◆*Cantina*, 16 Lorong Tun Ismail 1 (off Jln Bukit Ubi), smart a/c restaurant with waiters in batik bajus, Indonesian-style seafood and curries, recommended by locals; ◆◆*Kuantan Seafood*, Jln Wong Ah Jong, opposite *BKT* (*Restoran Malam*), hawker-style stalls in big open restaurant, very popular; ◆*Kheng Hup*, 17 Jln Makhota (on corner, opposite *Taman Salera Hawker Centre*), big old coffee shop with marble-top tables, raised voices and good *nasi lemak* and *nasi daggang* in the mornings, unchanged for fifty years; ◆*Salme*, 10 Jln Besar, cheap Malay dishes – *ikan bakar* (grilled fish) and *nasi campur* (pick-your-own curries); ◆*Sri Patani*, 79 Bangunan Udarulaman, Jln Tun Ismail, excellent Malay/S Thai food, rec; ◆*Tanjung Ria Coffee Shop*, 60 Jln Teluk Sisek (below *Embassy Hotel*), good breakfasts (especially *nasi lemak*), bright and sunny and friendly; ◆*Tiki's*, Jln Mahkota (opposite Maybank), cheap Western fare and local dishes; *Zul Satay*, junction of Jln Teluk Sisek and Jln Beserah (known as Kuantan Garden, between Kuantan and Teluk Cempedak), upmarket satay joint with all the usual plus rabbit, liver and offal (M$0.20-40 per stick), rec. **Foodstalls:** Malay cafés and foodstalls along the river bank, behind the long distance bus station, busy and popular, rec. There are more hawker stalls on junction of Jln Mahkota and Jln Masjid (Taman Salera), next to local bus station. *Kuantan Garden*, junction of Jln Teluk Sisek and Jln Beserah (between Kuantan and Teluk Cempedak), large number of Chinese stalls.

Bars The best bars and nightlife are along the beachfront at Teluk Cempadek. *The Sampan Bar*, on the *Hyatt Hotel* beachfront, is in the atap-roofed shell of a junk which beached in 1978 with 162 Vietnamese refugees aboard. The bar capitalises on this slightly perverse novelty by charging more.

Sport Swimming: *Kuantan Swimming Centre* (behind *Classic* and *Samudra View* hotels on Jln Besar) is a public pool next to the river; M$5/day, restaurant next to river, very clean and good value. **Golf:** *Royal Pahang Golf Club*. Green fees: M$30 weekdays, M$40 weekends.

Shopping Several craft shops along Jln Besar, expensive and touristy.

Local transport Bus: local bus station is on junction of Jln Masjid and Jln Mahkota. Regular connections with Teluk Cempedak (M$1). **Car hire:** Avis, *Hyatt Hotel*, Teluk Cempedak, T 525211 and Grd Flr, Loo Bros. Bldg, 59 Jln Haji Abdul Aziz, T 523831; **Budget**, 59 Jln Haji Abdul Aziz, T 526370 or *Coral Beach Resort*, 152 Sungei Karang, Beserah, T 587544; **Hertz**, *Samudra River View Hotel*, Jln Besar, T 522688; **Mayflower**, *Hyatt Kuantan*, Teluk Cempedak, T 501866; **National**, 49 Jln Teluk Sisek, T 527303; **Sinat**, Lot 3, *Merlin Inn*, Teluk Cempedak, T 524716; **SMAS**, Lot 107, Kompleks Teruntum, Jln Mahkota, T 51388; **Thrifty**, *Merlin Inn*, Teluk Cempedak, T 528400.

Banks & money changers Along Jln Mahkota and Jln Besar, between GPO and bus station.

Useful addresses General Post Office: Jln Makota (E end). Hospital: Jln Mat Kilau. **Area Code:** 09.

Airline offices MAS, Wisma Persatuan Bolasepak Pahang, Jln Gambut, T 512218.

Tour companies & travel agents Tours include trips around the Kuantan area, river tours and trips to Lake Kenyir (see page 209). *Convenience Travels*, Merlin Inn Resort, Teluk Cempedak, T 256360; *East Coast Holidays*, 33 Teluk Cempedak, T 505228, helpful staff; *Kenyir Lake Tourist*, 01-83 Jln Tun Ismail, T 505687; *Mayflower Acme Tours*, Hyatt Kuantan, Teluk Cempedak, T 521469; *Morahols Travel*, 11 Teluk Cempedak, T 500851; *Reliance*, 66 Jln Teluk Sisek, T 502566; *Syarikat Perusahaan*, 38, 2nd Flr, Bangunan DPMP, Jln Wong Ah Jang, T 513528; *SMAS Travels*, 1st Flr, Kompleks Teruntum, Jln Mahkota, T 513888; *Taz Ben Travel & Tours*, 2nd Flr, Kompleks Teruntum, Jln Mahkota, T 502255.

Tourist offices Tourist Information Centre, Tingkat Bawah Bangunan, Jln Haji Abdul Aziz, T 512960. LKNP Tourist Information Centre, 15th Flr, Kompleks Teruntum, Jln Mahkota, T 505566.

Transport to & from Kuantan 219 km from Kuala Terengganu, 229 km from KL, 325 km from Johor Bahru. **By air:** airport is 20 km S of town. Regular connections with KL several flights daily (M$84), Johor Bahru and Singapore (M$156) with direct flights on Fri, Sat, Sun & Tue. It is also possible to fly direct from Kuantan to Tioman on Tue, Fri & Sun (M$72). **By bus:** long-distance bus station on Jln Besar. Regular connections with KL (M$12.20), Mersing (M$10.40), JB (M$15.40), Singapore (M$16.50), Kuala Terengganu (M$8) and Kota Bahru

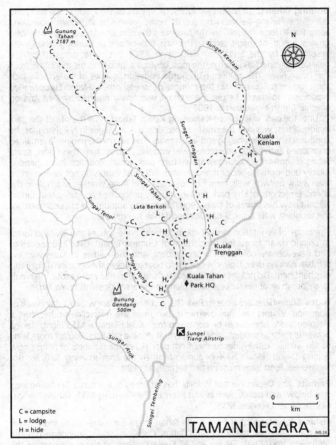

TAMAN NEGARA

C = campsite
L = lodge
H = hide

Gunung Tahan 2187 m
Sungei Keniam
Sungei Trenggan
Kuala Keniam
Sungei Tahan
Lata Berkoh
Sungai Tenor
Kuala Trenggan
Sungai Yong
Kuala Tahan Park HQ
Bunung Gendang 500m
Sungei Tiang Airstrip
Sungai Atok
Sungai Tembeling

0   5
km

(M$16). **By taxi**: taxi station next to bus station on Jln Besar. KL (M$25), Mersing (M$15) and
Kuala Terengganu (M$15). **By boat**: *Cruise Muhibbah* (Feri Malaysia) starts in Kuantan and
goes to Kota Kinabalu, Kuching, Singapore and Port Klang. To KK (M$265), Kuching (M$160),
Singapore (M$99). The well-appointed ferry leaves Kuantan Sat 1800. Schedules subject to
change: enquire at tourist information centre.

Taman Negara (National Park)

Once known as King George V Park, Taman Negara was gazetted as a national
park in 1938 when the Sultans of Pahang, Terengganu and Kelantan agreed to
set aside a 43,000 ha tract of virgin jungle where all 3 states meet. Taman Negara
is in a mountainous area (it includes Gunung Tahan, the highest mountain on the
peninsula) and lays claim to some of the oldest rainforest in the world. This area
was left untouched by successive ice ages and has been covered in jungle for
about 130 million years which makes it older than the rainforests in the Congo
or Amazon basins.

Gunung Tahan (2,187m) is the highest of 3 peaks on the E side of the park, and marks the Pahang-Kelantan border. Its name mean 'the forbidden mountain': according to local Asli folklore the summit is the domain of a giant monkey, who guards 2 pots of magic stones. The first expeditions to Gunung Tahan were despatched by the Sultan of Pahang in 1863 but were defeated by the near-vertical-sided Teku Gorge, the most obvious approach to the mountain, from the Tahan River. The 1,000m-high gorge ended in a series of waterfalls which came crashing 600m down the mountain. Several other ill-fated European-led expeditions followed, before the summit was finally reached by 4 Malays on another British expedition in 1905.

Until the park was set up, **Kampung Kuala Tahan**, now the site of the park headquarters, was one the most remote Orang Asli villages in N Pahang, at the confluence of the Tembeling and Tahan rivers. This area of the peninsula remained unmapped and mostly unexplored well into the 20th century. These days, Kuala Tahan is sometimes over-run with visitors; park accommodation has expanded rapidly under private sector management. But most visitors do not venture more than a day or two's walk from headquarters, and huge swathes of jungle in the N and E sections of the park remain virtually untouched and unvisited. Taman Negara now has scores of trails, requiring varying amounts of physical exertion; the toughest walk is the 9-day Gunung Tahan summit trek.

The range of vegetation in the park includes riverine species and lowland forest to upland dwarf forest (on the summit of Gunung Tahan). Over 250 species of bird have been recorded in Taman Negara, and the wildlife includes wild ox, sambar, barking deer, tapir, civet cat, wild boar and even the occasional tiger and elephant herd. Do not set your expectations too high: the more exotic mammals rarely put in an appearance – particularly in the areas closer to Kuala Tahan.

Hides Some hides are close to Park HQ, but nearly all are within a day's walk or boat ride. Visitors can stay overnight, but there are no facilities other than a sleeping space (sheets can be borrowed from Kuala Tahan – M$5/night). Take a powerful torch to spotlight any animals that visit the salt-licks. You are more likely to see wildlife at the hides further from park HQ as the numbers of people now visiting Taman Negara have begun to frighten the animals away. Rats are not frightened: food bags must be tied securely at night.

Permits The Department of Wildlife has a bureau at the Kuala Tembeling jetty (see below) and issues permits and licences. Park permits M$1; fishing licences M$10; camera licences M$5.

Fishing Is better further from Kuala Tahan; there are game-fishing lodges near the confluence of the Tenor and Tahan rivers, at Kuala Terenggan (up the Tembeling from Kuala Tahan) and at Kuala Kenyam, at the confluence of the Kenyam and the Tembeling. The best months to fish are Feb-Mar and Jul-Aug; during the monsoon season. Sungei Tahan, Sungei Kenyam and the more remote Sungei Sepia (all tributaries of the Tembeling) are reckoned to be the best waters. There are more than 200 species of fish in the park's rivers. (See also **Booking**, **Equipment** and **Accommodation**, below).

River trips Boat trips can be arranged from Park HQ to the Lata Berkoh rapids on Sungei Tahan (near Kuala Tahan), Kuala Terenggan (several sets of rapids to be negotiated), Kuala Keniam (from where a trail leads to the top of a limestone outcrop). Boats accommodating 3 passengers cost M$60/hr.

Treks Trails are signposted from Park HQ. Tours are conducted twice daily by park officials (about M$40/person incl lunch). Guides must be taken on all longer treks.

Gunung Tahan (2,187m), is a 9-day trek to the summit and back. It is best climbed in Feb and Mar, the driest months. **Day 1**: Kuala Tahan to Kuala Melantai (4-5 hrs). **Day 2**: Kuala

Melantai to Kuala Puteh (8 hrs). No streams en route; succession of tough climbs along the ridge, final one is Gunung Rajah; 1½ hr descent to campsite by Sungei Tahan. **Day 3**: Kuala Puteh to Kuala Teku (2½-4½ hrs). Route follows Sungei Tahan, which must be crossed several times. The campsite is at the Sungei Teku confluence and was the base camp for the first successful Gunung Tahan expedition in 1905. **Day 4**: Kuala Teku to Gunung Tangga Lima Belas (7 hrs). Long uphill slog (4½ hrs) to Wray's Camp (named after 1905 expedition member). This is a good campsite; alternatively climb through mossy forest to Gunung Tangga Lima Belas campsite, which has magnificent views, but is very exposed. **Day 5**: Gunung Tangga Lima Belas to summit, returning to Padang. After a scramble up the side of a rockface on Gunung Gedong, the trail leads to the Padang – a plateau area (3-4 hrs). Set up tents and leave equipment at campsite; route to summit follows ridge and takes 2½hrs. Essential to take raincoat; summit often shrouded in mist. Begin descent to Padang by 1600. **Days 6-9**: Padang to Kuala Tahan, following the same route. A sleeping bag and a tent are vital for those climbing Gunung Tahan. All of the camps have water and firewood. A guide is necessary for the Gunung Tahan climb (M\$400/week, M\$50 for each additional day); maximum of 12 people with one guide.

Another mountain in Taman Negara that is less frequently climbed is **Gunung Gagau** (1,377m), far to the NE of Kuala Tahan. It is a 6-7 day trek of which one day is spent travelling upriver on Sungei Sat. This area of the park is rarely visited and it is advisable to take a guide.

Equipment For trekking it is worth having canvas jungle boots or light walking boots, a thick pair of socks and long trousers. Leeches are common in the park after rain – spraying clothes and boots with insect repellent helps. (It is not necessary to use salt or cigarette tips to get leeches off – just pull/flick them). A good torch is essential equipment for those going to hides. The shop at Park HQ hires out torches, tents, water bottles, cooking equipment and fishing tackle.

Booking Visits to the national park have to be pre-arranged at *River Park Sdn Bhd*, 260 h, 2nd Mile Jln Ipoh, KL, T 2915299 or *Malaysian Tourist Information Centre* (MATIC), Jln Ampang, KL, T 2434929. Visitors are required to pay a M\$30 deposit to confirm bookings for the park boat and accommodation at Kuala Tahan (park headquarters). The boat to headquarters costs M\$15/person (one way). Admission: M\$1; camera fee: M\$5, fishing licence: M\$10. Those who risk turning up at the Kuala Tembeling jetty without booking risk being turned away if boats are full.

Best time to visit Between Mar and Sept – the park is closed during the height of the monsoon season from the beginning of Nov to the end of Dec, when the rivers are in flood.

Park Headquarters At Kuala Tahan, on the S boundary of the park, accessible by boat from Kuala Tembeling.

Tours Various companies run tours to Taman Negara. It is a more expensive way to visit the park, but permits, itineraries etc are well-organized in advance. Many visitors, particularly those unfamiliar with travelling in Malaysia, have recommended tours for their logistical advantages. Since the park has been run privately, however, it has become much more user-friendly and it is easy to visit independently. *Asia Overland Services*, 35M Jln Dewan Sultan Sulaiman Satu (off Jln Tunku Abdul Rahman), Kuala Lumpur, T 2925622. Three-day safari US\$245. *Malaysia Overland Adventures*, Lot 1.23, 1st Flr, Bangunan Angkasaraya, Jln Ampang, Kuala Lumpur, T 03-2413659. *Overland Discovery Tours*, Unit 5, 1st Podium Floor, *Shangri-La Hotel*, 11 Jln Sultan Ismail, Kuala Lumpur, T 2302942. *Scenic Holidays and Travel*, Lot SO64, 2nd Flr Sungei Wang Plaza, Jln Sultan Ismail, Kuala Lumpur, T 2424522. *SPKG Tours*, 16th Flr LKNP Bldg, Bandar Baru, Jerantut, T 262369. *Tuah Travel & Tours*, 12 Jln Lipis, Kuala Lipis, T 312144. Taman Negara and Kenong Rimba Jungle Park (**see page 221**).

Accommodation The management of *Taman Negara* was handed over to the private sector in 1990 and the newly developed Taman Negara Resort now touts its classy new accommodation in glossy brochures, styled after *National Geographic*. All accommodation should be booked in advance if possible, either direct to Taman Negara Resort, Kuala Tahan, 27000 Jerantut, Pahang T 09-263500, F 09-261500 or through the sales office: Suite 1901, 19th Flr, Pernas International, Jln Sultan Ismail, 50250 KL T 03-2610393, F 03-2610615.

Chalets and bungalows (some with self-catering facilities), a/c, M\$90-190. Two-bedroom bungalows \$400. Hostel (8 persons/dorm) M\$11/person. In addition, there are a number of fishing lodges in the park, in which beds and mattresses are provided; there is no bedding or cooking equipment however. These can be booked at Kuala Tahan HQ (M\$8/night). Visitor Lodges for hides at Kuala Terengggan and Kuala Kenyam can also be booked from Kuala Tahan HQ (M\$5). Beds and bedding provided, as are cooking utensils, stove and lanterns. There is no charge for staying in the hides themselves.

Budget travellers report that the *Nusa Camp* – an independently-run alternative to the *Taman Negara Resort* – offers good value for money. The camp is located a few minutes further upriver from Kuala Tahan, on the other side of the river: it is not in the park itself. There are very reasonably priced dorms and bungalows as well as tents for hire. There are regular longboat connections with Kuala Tahan. **Getting there**: *Nusa Camp* has its own ticketing office at the Kuala Tembeling jetty.

Camping The newly landscaped campsite can accommodate up to 200, but fortunately never does. Taman Negara Resort rents out tents (2/3/4-person) for $6-12/night. There is an additional M$1 fee for use of the campsite. Tents, once hired, can be taken with you on treks. There are communal toilet facilities and lockers available.

Restaurants The newly developed resort operates two restaurants and a bar – the rotan and bamboo Tembeling Lounge which even gets daily newspapers. It is open 1100-2400, Mon-Sun. The Tahan Restaurant and Teresek Cafeteria serve both local and Western cuisine; the former is more expensive. Both are open 0700-2300 Mon-Sun. Because of the cost of food at the resort, many tourists prefer to bring their own.

Other facilities The Taman Negara Resort includes an overpriced mini-market (selling provisions for trekking and camping, open 0800-2300), a clinic (open 0800-1615 Mon-Sun; hospital attendant on call 24 hrs, for emergencies), a mini-post office, a library and a Pelangi Air reservations and ticketing counter. There is also a jungle laundry service. In the 'Interpretative Room', there is a daily film and slide-show on the park's flora and fauna (2045 Mon-Sun).

Transport to & from Taman Negara All access to Taman Negara – other than for those who fly in – is by longboat from Kuala Tembeling. **By air**: Pelangi Air only, from KL (M$160 return; 45 mins one way). There are also regular flights from Kerteh in Terengganu (M$75 one way). The Sungei Tiang airstrip is 30 mins' boat ride from Kuala Tahan. **By train**: Jerantut and Tembeling Halt are accessible from Kuala Lumpur, Kota Bahru and Singapore. It is necessary to inform the guard/conductor if you want to alight at Tembeling Halt, as it is still an unscheduled stop. From there it is a half-hour walk to the jetty at Kuala Tembeling. From Kota Bahru: to Tembeling Halt/Jerantut; departures from Wakaf Bahru station (outside KB) at 1150 on Sun, Tue, Wed & Fri. From KL: trains to Jerantut/Tembeling Halt, via Gemas (on KL-Singapore line). The overnight sleeper departs 2200, arrives Tembeling Halt 0630. From Singapore: change at Gemas; connections to Jerantut/Tembeling Halt at 0530 Mon-Sun. **By bus/taxi**: regular connections from KL to Temerloh (M$5.50). Temerloh is a short bus/taxi ride from Jerantut (regular buses M$2.25; taxi M$5). Taxis direct to Jerantut from KL: M$15. From the E coast, there are buses from Kuantan to Jerantut; hourly bus connections (M$7.70); taxi (M$13). Jerantut is 16 km from Kuala Tembeling (blue Jelai buses M$1.10; taxi M$3). **Accommodation** in Jerantut: **C** *Rumah Rehat* (Rest House), Jalan Benta, T 262257; **E** *Hotel Piccadilly*, 312 Sungei Jan, T 62895; **D** *Hotel Jerantut*. **By boat**: it is a 59 km journey from Kuala Tembeling jetty, up Sungei Tembeling to Kuala Tahan (Park HQ), 3-4 hrs, depending on river level (M$30 return/person); departures at 0900 and 1430. The return trip takes 2½ hrs; departures at 0900 and 1430.

KUANTAN TO KOTA BAHRU

Kampung Cerating

A quiet seaside village, set among coconut palms, a short walk from the beach, Kampung Cerating has become a haven for those who want to sample kampung life or just hang out in a simple chalet-style budget resort. Cerating never was much of a kampung until the tourists arrived – there was a small charcoal 'factory', using *bakau* mangrove wood, but the local economy is now entirely dependent on sarong-clad Westerners and, more recently, growing numbers of Malaysian and Singaporean tourists. The beach at Cerating is big, but not brilliant for swimming because the sea is so shallow; it is also quite dirty. Cerating is named after the sand-crabs which are very common along the beach. They may look like heavily armoured tanks, but they are not dangerous. There are a couple of very private and beautiful little beaches tucked into the rocky headland dividing Cerating beach and the *Club Med* next door. These are more easily accessible from the sea (boats can be hired from the kampung) than from the steep trail leading over the promontory. This path goes right over to the *Club Med* Beach...

The giant leatherback turtle (*Dermochelys coriacea*)

The symbol of the old Malaysian Tourist Development Corporation, the giant leatherback turtle is so-called for its leathery carapace, or shell. It is the biggest sea turtle and one of the biggest reptiles in the world. The largest grow to 3 in length and most of the females who lumber up Rantau Abang's beach to lay their eggs are over 1.5m long. On average they weigh more than 350 kg, but are sometimes more than double that. Giant leatherbacks are also said to live for hundreds of years. They spend most of their lives in the mid-Pacific Ocean – although they have been sighted as far afield as the Atlantic – and return to this stretch of beach around Rantau Abang each year to lay their eggs, in the way salmon return to the same river. The beach shelves steeply into deeper water, allowing turtles to reach the beach easily.

They are not well-designed for the land. It requires huge effort to struggle up the beach, to above the high-tide mark. After selecting a nesting site, the turtle first digs a dummy hole before carefully scooping out the actual nest pit, in which she lays up to 150 soft white eggs between the size of a golf ball and a tennis ball. The digging and egg-laying procedure, punctuated by much groaning and heaving and several rest-stops, takes up to 2 hours, after which she covers the hole and returns to the sea. During the egg-laying period, the turtle's eyes secrete a lubricant to protect them from the sand, making it appear as if it is crying. In the course of the egg-laying season (from May to Sept) this exhausting slog up the beach might be repeated several times.

The gestation period for the eggs is 52-70 days. During this period the eggs are in danger from predators, so the Fisheries Department collects up to 50,000 eggs each season for controlled hatching in fenced-off sections of beach. The eggs are also believed to be an aphrodisiac and can be bought in wet markets along the E coast for about M$1 each (a small quota is set aside for public consumption). Young hatchlings are regularly released into the sea from the government hatchery. Many are picked off by predators, such as gulls and fish, and few reach adulthood. The turtles have been endangered by drift-net fishing and pollution. In 1990 the Malaysian government announced it would start fitting radio transmitters to leatherbacks to enable satellites to monitor their movements in international waters. French satellite information will provide a stronger database on turtle populations and movements allowing the formulation of a more effective conservation strategy.

Green turtles come ashore to lay their eggs later in the season. (For more detailed information on the green turtle, **see page 336**.)

which is private. Bathers and sun-bathers should be prepared for periodic low-level fly-pasts by the Royal Malaysian Army whose helicopters swoop low over the beaches to check out the latest swimwear fashions.

Cerating has grown explosively in recent years. Big, modern resort complexes have sprung up 3 km S of the original kampung – it is known as Cerating Bahru (New Cerating). The old roadside village (together with the string of atap-roofed chalet resorts) is called Cerating Lama. Although the old kampung atmosphere has been irreversibly tempered by the arrival of Anchor Beer and the population explosion, Cerating is still a peaceful haunt with some excellent places to stay and one or two of the best bars in Malaysia. Cerating's Malay residents have taken the boom stoically – although their obvious prosperity has helped them tolerate the 'cultural pollution'.

It is possible to hire boats to paddle through the mangroves of the Cerating River, to the S side of the kampung, where there is a good variety of birdlife as well as monkeys, monitor lizards and otters. For a price there are also demonstrations of silat (the Malay martial art), top-spinning, kite-flying and batik-printing in the village. There are some monkeys in the kampung which are trained to pluck coconuts. A couple of kilometres up the road, on Cendor Beach, green turtles come ashore to lay their eggs; they are much smaller than the leatherbacks which lay their eggs at Rantau Abang, further N.

Boat trips Organized from Checkpoint Cerating (see below) and by several beach hotels/chalets. Six people are needed to fill a boat, with a full boat approx M$8/person, depending on distance up river.

Accommodation Kampung Cerating has grown explosively in the past decade and many new bungalows and chalets have sprung up along the beach; more big developments are planned including the vast *Impiana* mega-resort which is going up about 2 km N of Cerating Lama. There is a good range of accommodation available, from simple kampung-style stilt-houses to 'A'-frame huts and upmarket chalets. Some of the accommodation in the kampung proper is family run; 'A'-frame and chalet accommodation is along the beach. The smarter, plusher hotels 3 km down the road at Cerating Lama are much closer to the sea – and have a much nicer stretch of beach – than their poorer neighbours up the road. When it comes to choosing a place to stay in Cerating, it comes down to shopping around for an interpretation of kampung paradise most in line with your own. For the genuine kampung-feel, nothing beats *Mak Long Teh's* and *Mak De's*. *Mazri's* and *Riverside* (in Cerating Bahru) are less well-kept and are unappealing. **L-B** *Cerating Holiday Villa*, Lot 1303, Mukim Sungei Karang, T 2434693, a/c, restaurant, pool, bungalows and 9 'tribal houses' – corny but nice inside, rec; **A+** *Palm Grove Beach Resort*, Lot 1290, Mukim Sungei Karang (Cerating Bahru), a/c, restaurant, huge pool, villas near the beach with smartly appointed rooms, sports centre, tennis courts, watersports facilities, disco, rooms, which overlook big garden and beach, are pleasant and bright, rec; **A** *Club Med* (round the headland from Kampung Cerating), T 591131, a/c, restaurant, totally self contained resort "where the beep of the horn, or ring of the telephone would never be allowed to disrupt the tranquillity" – private beach, watersports facilities, body-building classes and evening entertainment; minimum stay: 2 nights, closed Nov-Jan, non-guests can use facilities, 0900-1100 and 1400-1600 Mon-Sun (M$60 for half-day); **A** *Canoona Beach Resort* (just N of Holiday Villa, Cerating Bahru), pleasant hotel with chalet blocks in grounds next to beach; **B-C** *Ranting Holiday Resort* (turn left at bottom of lane from main road bridge), restaurant (Western and local dishes), fan only, two-room chalets and doubles, quite smart; **C** *Duyong Beach Resort* (left at end of lane from main road, at far end), modern chalets at the end of the beach next to jungled hillside, mainly attracts Malaysian and Singaporean tourists; **C-D** *Tanjong Inn* (turn right at bottom of lane down from main road, after *Coconut Inn*), restaurant, atap-roofed chalets in carefully tended and landscaped grounds with palms and a lake which residents say isn't mozzy-ridden, rec; **C-D** *The Moon* (the northernmost chalet resort on the loop off the main road), attractive, more rustic chalets in spacious leafy grounds, up a hillside, excellent bar (see below) and restaurant, chalets and longhouse, much more tranquil surrounds than chalet resorts along the beach, rec; **C-F** *The Kampung Inn* (right at end of lane from main road, at far end on left), nothing too special with very average chalet accommodation and not much atmosphere, but advantageously located near *Boathouse Bar* and close to beach; **D** *Mak De's House*, in the old village, next to police station, opposite bus stop, T 511316, Mak De has been offering kampung-accommodation since the late-1970s and has an equally long-standing reputation for hospitality and good food, rec; **D** *Mak Long Teh Guesthouse*, T 503290, restaurant, like *Mak De*, this family-run operation was up-and-running long before Cerating was discovered by main-stream tourists, friendly with excellent Malay home cooking; **D** *Riverside*, rec; **D-E** *Coconut Inn*, T 503299, run by Ilal – one of the kampung's best-known characters – and his Dutch wife, comfortable, spacious chalets in leafy grounds, rec; **E** *Green Leaves Inn* (right at end of lane from main road, on right), T 378242, tucked in among the riverside mangroves, *Green Leaves* looks like a Vietkong jungle camp, albeit with decent 'A'-frames, sheltered and shaded, close to sea and cheap with breakfast thrown in, very clean.

Restaurants A few new restaurants have sprung up along the main road but because most chalet hotels have attached restaurants there's not much demand for outside food outlets. ♦♦*B & R*, north end of Cerating beach road (next to Duyong), travellers' fare and some local dishes; ♦♦*Blue Lagoon* (right at end of land from main road, after *Moonlight Lagoon* restaurant), another big neon-lit establishment offering wide selection of Chinese, Malay and Western dishes, good on seafood, friendly atmosphere; ♦♦*Moonlight Lagoon* (Nancy's Place), bottom of lane coming down off main road next to bridge, big, bright restaurant with big menu to match, specializes in seafood, butter prawns with asparagus and crabmeat soup particularly good, serves beer; ♦♦*Payung Inn 'n' Cafe*, next to river, opposite *Coconut Inn*, pleasant little open coffee shop, but forget the 'inn' bit; ♦♦*The Deadly Nightshade* (part of *The Moon* chalet resort at NW end of loop off main road), also known as 'the restaurant at the end of the universe', enchantingly vague menu, mainly Western with some concessions to local tastes, great atmosphere; ◆*Coral Beach Resort*, dim sum served on Sundays; *Mimi's Restaurant, Services and Tours* (left at end of lane from main road, on left) restaurant and tours par for the course but Mimi's offers useful laundry service.

Bars *Boathouse* (turn right at the end of the lane down from main road bridge, walk through *Kampung Inn* or *Coconut Inn* and head for beach), groovy bamboo and atap-roofed bar on beach playing good music, belongs to Hilal of *Coconut Inn* (who is a Prince of the Negri Sembilan royal family), nice spot for sundowners, rec; *The Moon* (part of chalet resort of same name at NW end of loop off main road), great bar amid atap and leafy foliage, second only to the *Boathouse*, rec.

Shopping Batik: there are three batik shops in Cerating; all the artists offer classes; prices (which include tuition) T-shirt: M$20-25, sarong: M$25, singlet: M$18. *Limbong Art* (left at bottom of lane down from main road bridge), mainly shirts, T-shirts painted by *Munif. Ayu Art* (on lane down from main road bridge); *Cherating Collection* (in old village, next to main road and *Mak De's*), designs more colourful and abstract than its two local competitors.

Banks & money changers (see Checkpoint Cerating, below). Nearest bank at Kemaman, 27 km N.

Local transport (see Checkpoint Cerating, below).

Sport *Kelab Golf Desa Dungun*, Dungun. 9 holes. Green fees: M$15. *Cerating Beach Recreation Centre*, arranges water skiing and windsurfing, M$10 hire, M$15 lesson.

Useful addresses Checkpoint Cerating (about 100 m down on left from lane leading from main road bridge), ticketing (buses, taxis, minibuses), vehicle hire: car (M$90/day), motorbike (M$25/day), mountain bike (M$10/day), boats (M$10/day), foreign exchange (incl. travellers' cheques), mobile phone, book rental, newspapers and tourist info, also organizes tours to Lake Cini, Terengganu National Park and batik factories.

Transport to & from Cerating 50 km from Kuantan. **By bus**: regular buses from Kuantan (Kemaman km; M$2.20). Bus stops at both ends of the kampung. Regular connections with Rantau Abang (M$15), Kuala Terengganu (M$20), Marang (M$17), Kota Bahru (M$40). Minibuses leave Checkpoint Cerating for Kuantan at 07.30 Mon-Sun (M$7). **By taxi**: Rantau Abang (M$25), Kuantan (M$10), Kuantan airport (M$12).

Kemasik

On the road N from Cerating there are several stretches of beach, among the best of which is Kemasik. It is off the main road to the right (85 km N of Kuantan, 28 km N of Cerating), just before the oil and gas belt of Kerteh. Ask buses to stop shortly after windy stretch through hills. At Kemasik, the beach is deserted; there is a lagoon, some rocky headlands and safe bathing. No facilities.

Rantau Abang

This strung-out beachside settlement owes its existence to turtles. Every year between May and Sept, 5 different species of turtle (*penyu* in Malay) come to this long stretch of beach to lay their eggs, including the endangered giant leatherbacks. And every year, tens of thousands of tourists also make the pilgrimage. During the peak egg-laying season, in Aug (which coincides with Malaysia's school holidays), the beach gets very crowded. Up until the mid-1980s the egg-laying 'industry' was poorly controlled; tourists and locals played guitars around bonfires on the beach and scrambled onto turtles' backs for photographs as they laid. Conservationists became increasingly concerned about the declining number of giant leatherbacks that chose to nest on the beach and began to press for stricter policing and management.

Parts of the beach have now been set aside by the government, and access is prohibited; there are also sections of beach with restricted access, where a small admission charge is levied by guides. The Fisheries Department does not charge. Local guides, who trawl the beach at night for leatherbacks coming ashore, charge tourists M$2 a head for a wake-up call. Turtle-watching is free along the stretch around the Turtle Information Centre. The Fisheries Department also runs three hatcheries to protect the eggs from predators and egg-hunters: they are a local delicacy. The closest is 5 mins' walk from *Awang's*. Officers from the department patrol the beach in 3-wheeler beach buggies. Out of peak-season, Rantau Abang has the feel of a British seaside resort in winter.

NB: do not interfere with the turtles while they are laying. There is now a ban on flash photography and unruly behaviour is punishable by a M$1,000 fine or 6 months' imprisonment. Camp fires, loud music, excessive noise and littering are all illegal, although the latter is not well enforced.

Rantau Abang Turtle Information Centre, 13th Mile Jln Dungun, opposite the big new Plaza R & R, has an excellent exhibition and film presentation about sea turtles, focusing on the giant leatherback. A slide-show also opened in 1993. The Fisheries Department at the centre are very helpful and friendly. Open: 1000-1230, 1500-2300 Sat-Thur (Jun-Aug); 0800-1245, 1400-1600 Sat-Wed, 0800-1245 Thur (Sept-May).

Turtles also come ashore at nearby **Kuala Abang** (a few kilometres N of Dungun), which is much quieter than Rantau Abang, although there are fewer hotels. There are also several places to stay, although not right on the beach, at the small port of **Kuala Dungun** (famed for its *kuini*, a local mango). There is a weekly night-market (*pasar malam*) in Dungun on Thursdays. From there it is possible to hire a boat to Pulau Tenggol, 29 km out – popular with snorkellers.

Excursions from Dungun

Pulau Tenggol: small island, still unspoilt.

Accommodation Rantau Abang's accommodation is strung-out along the main road; there are many over-priced, unpleasant little hovels. New places are opening and still ones closing all the time. Security is a problem here: it is inadvisable to leave valuables in rooms. **B** *Rantau Abang Visitor's Centre*, 13th Mile, Jln Dungun, T 841533, fan only, restaurant (on beach-side of lagoon), beautiful chalets overlooking lagoon in landscaped gardens, a little noisy as next to road, but by far the nicest place to stay, all chalets have hot water showers, fridges, TVs and small kitchens and at M$60-100 split between maximum of 4 people, superb value for money; **B-E** *Ismail's*, next to *Awang's*, restaurant (only open in peak season), S of the Visitor's Centre, average beach-side set-up, similar to Awang's; **D** *Awang's*, T 842236, restaurant, some rooms are very poor, the best are only average; *Awang's* organizes trips to nearby Pulau Kapuas and to batik factories; **D** *Dahimah's*, 1 km S of Visitor's Centre, restaurant, new, clean rooms. Kuala Abang: **B-C** *Merantau Inn*, T 841131, at the S end of the turtle beach, restaurant, big, clean chalets above old fish ponds, past its prime, but three decent chalets on the beach.

Kuala Dungun: 15 km from Rantu Abang. **C-D** *Kasanya*, 225-227 Jln Tambun, T 841704, a/c; **D** *Mido*, 145-6 Jln Tambun, a/c, T 841246; **C-D** *Sri Dungun*, K135 Jln Tambun, T 841881, a/c, restaurant; **D** *Sri Gate*, 5025 Jln Sure Gete, a/c; **D** *Sun Chew*, 10 Jln Besar Sura Gate, T 841412, a/c, restaurant. Tanjung Jara: **A+-A** *Tanjung Jara Beach Hotel* (6 km N of Dungun), T 841801, F 842653, a/c, restaurant, pool, the best known 5-star beach resort on the E coast, its Malay-inspired design won it the Aga Khan award for outstanding Islamic architecture, tour excursions, windsurfing, golf and tennis facilities, also offers local tours.

Restaurants Most hotels have their own restaurants, stalls along the roadside and several coffee shops around the bus stop. ♦♦*Awang's*, right on the beach, Awang was formerly the chef at the *Tanjung Jara Beach Hotel*. *Ismail's* also has a restaurant and there are some stalls in the Plaza R & R.

Transport to & from Rantau Abang 58 km S of Kuala Terengganu and 160 km N of Kuantan. **By bus**: regular connections with Kuala Terengganu (M$3) and Kuala Dungun (M$0.90) from opposite Turtle Information Centre. From Kuala Dungun express buses leave for Kuantan (M$8), Mersing (M$16), KL (M$16.50) and JB/Singapore (M$22/25). **By taxi**: Kuala Terrenganu (M$5); Kota Bahru (M$12), Dungun (M$2), Kuantan (M$12).

Marang

Marang is a colourful Malay fishing kampung at the mouth of the Marang River, although it is not as idyllic as the tourist literature suggests. To get into the town from the main road, follow signs to LKIM Komplex from the N end of the bridge. The recent rush to put up budget accommodation has placed it firmly on the tourist map. Since then it has begun to acquire a bit of a run-down look. It is still a very lovely village though, with its shallow lagoon, full of fishing boats. The best beach is opposite Pulau Kepas at Kampung Ru Muda. It was the centre of a mini-gold-rush in 1988 when gold was found 6 km up the road at Rusila. On the road N of Marang there are a number of batik workshops, all of which welcome visitors.

Excursions

Pulau Kapas is 6 km (30 mins) off the coast, with some good coral and beaches. Those wanting a quiet beach holiday should avoid weekends and public holidays. **Accommodation**: **A** *Primula Kepas Village Beach Resort*, best on island, Malay-style chalets; pool; **B-C** *Tenggol Aqua Resort*, T 861807, the only accommodation on the island; **D** *Kepas Garden Resort*, T 971306; **D** *Mak Cik Gemok Chalet*, T 681221; **D** *Pulau Kapas Resort*, T 632989, restaurant, snorkelling (M$5/day), forest tours, fishing trips (M$150/day); **D** *Zaki Beach Resort*, restaurant, chalets; **E** *Sri Kepas Lodge*, T 09-681529. **Pulau Raja**, just off Kapas, has been declared a marine park and there is some excellent coral. **Getting there**: many hotels offer day-trips to the islands (M$15-20 return).

River and island tours Half-day river tours organized by *Ping Anchorage 2* or *Marang Inn*. The same people also offer efficiently-run tours to nearby islands; most hotels in town can arrange trips to Pulau Kapas.

Accommodation There are hotels and guesthouses in Marang itself and in Kampung Ru Muda, a couple of kilometres before the bridge over the Marang River. **B-C** *Liza Inn Marang*, Kampung Pulau Kerengga, 10 km S of Marang, T 632989, a/c, restaurant; **B-D** *Angullia Beach House*, 12¼ milestone, Kampung Ru Muda, T 681322, some a/c, restaurant, extremely friendly, family-run chalet resort on lovely stretch of beach opposite Pulau Kapas (therefore sheltered), leafy, well-kept grounds and very clean chalets (**NB**: no alcohol served), rec; **C** *Rumah Rehat Semarak* (Rest House), Taman Rehat Semarak, Km 17, Jln Kuala Terengganu (4 km S of Marang), chalets on the beach, formerly government-owned, past its prime, but pleasant rooms with balconies, the best ones facing the sea, small restaurant and stalls next door; **C-E** *Mare Nostrum Holiday Resort*, Kampung Ru Muda, T 682417, a/c, restaurant, clean and hospitable, boat trips, pleasant little resort next door to *Angullia*, well-kept compound (if a little cramped) and clean chalets, rec; **D** *Zakaria Guesthouse*, Kampung Ru Muda, T 682328, basic and further out of the village, dormitory or rooms; **E** *Island View*, 1 km out of town, opposite the lagoon, T 682006, free bicycles, chalets; **E** *Marang Guesthouse*, N of town centre, restaurant, large, spacious bungalows on the hillside, with mosquito nets and attached bath, also dormitory, the guesthouse is on the hill above the road, so not as noisy as some of the other places in Marang, food reasonably priced, friendly proprietor, rec; **E** *Marang Inn & Garden Café*, 132 Bandar Marang, T 682132, restaurant, in decorated blue-and-orange shophouse overlooking lagoon, helpful, organizes tours around Terengganu and trips to islands; **E-F** *Kamal's*, opposite the lagoon, very popular, dormitory and chalets, more upmarket than the *Inn* and the *Anchorage*, set in pleasant garden; **E-F** *Marang Inn*, Batu 22 Rhu Muda, T 682288, dorm and chalets; **F** *Ping Anchorage II*, 190A Bandar Marang, T 628093, run by same people who run the *Marang Inn* and *Ping Anchorage I* in Kuala Terengganu, they also run tours and trips to islands, rec.

Restaurants Most hotels have good restaurants serving Malay and international dishes. The *Marang Inn* restaurant is particularly good. There are cheap food stalls along the waterfront next to the market. Stalls at Taman Selera, Kampung Ru Muda (along the roadside) are well known (particularly by long-distance bus and taxi drivers) for their Malay and Thai-style seafood, (closed Friday).

Shopping Handicrafts: market in Marang has a craft market upstairs and there are several handicraft shops along the main street. *Balai Ukiran Terengganu* (Terengganu Woodcarving Centre), Kampung Ru Rendang, near Marang. Master-carver Abdul Malek Ariffin runs the east coast's best-known woodcarving workshop. Makes wide range of intricately carved furniture from cengal wood; carved with traditional floral geometric and Islamic calligraphic patterns. The varnished cengal wood is not to everyone's taste, but everything from mirrors to beds can be ordered for export. Because most pieces are made to order there is little on show in Abdul's chaotic workshop, but carvers can be seen at work during the day.

Transport to & from Marang 18 km from Terengganu. **By bus**: bus station between *Marang Inn* and *Ping Anchorage*. Regular connections with Kuala Terengganu (M$2).

KUALA TERENGGANU   IMS 22

1. Pasar Besar Kedai Payang
2. Zainal Abdin Mosque
3. Istana Mazia
4. Post Office
5. Taxi
6. Tourist Information
7. Malaysian Airlines
8. Trengganu Hotel
9. Ping Anchorage Hotel
10. Pantai Primula Hotel
11. Hotel Seri Hoover

Kuala Terengganu

The royal capital of Terengganu state was a small fishing port (the state accounts for about a quarter of all Malaysia's fishermen) until oil and gas money started pumping into development projects in the 1980s. The town has long been a centre for arts and crafts, and is known for its *kain songket* (see page 810), batik, brass and silverware.

Like neighbouring Pahang, Terengganu state was settled at least as far back as the 14th century, and over the years has paid tribute to Siam and, in the 15th century, to the sultanate of Melaka. When the Portuguese forced the Melaka royal house to flee to Johor, Terengganu became a vassal of the new sultanate. In the 18th century, Terengganu is recorded as having a thriving textile industry; it also traded in pepper and gold with Siam, Cambodia, Brunei and China. A Chinese merchant community grew up in Kuala Terengganu. In 1724, the youngest brother of a former sultan of Johor, Zainal Abidin, established Terengganu as an independent state and declared himself its first sultan. Today's sultan is a direct descendent. The state has always been known for its ultra-conservative Islamic traditions.

Places of interest

The **Pasar Besar Kedai Payang**, the main market place on Jalan Pantai, is still the busiest spot in town – particularly in the early morning, when the fishing fleet comes in. The market also sells, batik, brocade, songket, brassware, and basketware as well as fruit and vegetables. **Jalan Bandar**, leading off from the market, is a street of old Chinese shophouses and there is also a busy and colourfully painted Chinese temple. Nearby is the imposing **Zainal Abdin Mosque**. Not far from the mosque (on the other side of Jalan Kota) is the apricot-coloured **Istana Maziah**, the old home of Terengganu's royal family, built in French style. It is now only used on ceremonial occasions and is not open to the public.

Some of Kuala Terengganu's older buildings have fine examples of traditional Malay carvings. One of these has been moved from the centre of town to the southern outskirts, along the seafront on Pantai Batu Buruk, and houses the **Gelanggan Seni** (Cultural Centre), which stages cultural shows on Fridays at 1700. Another of these traditional houses was taken apart and reassembled in Kuala Lumpur in the grounds of the National Museum as an example of classical Malay architecture.

The **State Museum**, at the top of the hill on Jalan Cherong Lanjut, exhibits rare Islamic porcelain, silver jewellery, musical instruments and weaponry – including a fine selection of *parangs* and *krises*. An eclectic collection, erratically labelled. The building is in bad need of renovation and will be moving to a new location some time in 1994. Check with *Tourism Malaysia* office. Open: 0800-1600 Sat-Wed; 0800-1245, Thurs. **Bukit Besar**, a steep hill immediately behind Kuala Terengganu, has excellent views of the town.

Excursions
There is a thriving cottage industry in and around Kuala Terengganu and many of Malaysia's best-known handicrafts are made locally. Surrounding kampungs practice silverwork, batik-printing, songket-weaving and *wau* kite-building, but the best way to see these under one roof is in the Cenering handicraft centres (see below).

Pulau Duyung Besar is the largest island in the Terengganu Estuary and famed for its traditional boat-building. It now mainly survives by custom-building yachts. **Accommodation**: F *Awi's Yellow House*, built out over the river on stilts, very popular with budget travellers, dorm and atap-roofed huts, some with balconies over river, pleasant location with cool breezes, there are some stalls at the bus stop near the bridge, but most travellers bring their own food from KT and have use of kitchen facilities, *Awi's Yellow House* is not yellow and can be hard to find. **Getting there**: boat from jetty on Jalan Bandar (M$0.50) – last boat around 2200 – or by road, via the new *Sultan Mahmud* bridge (taxis M$5 from KT, bus M$0.50). The river is navigable for quite a distance upstream and it is possible to hire boats from the jetty for river trips.

Kampung Pulau Rusa, 6 km upriver, is a songket-weaving and batik centre, and is known for its traditional Petani-Terengganu wooden houses. **Getting there**: boat from the jetty on Jalan Bandar (M$2). (The village can also be reached by bus from the bus station on Jalan Masjid.)

Cendering is 7 km S of Kuala Terengganu. *Infokraf Centre*, with a beautifully displayed selection of silver, woodwork, silk, batik, brass and basketware as well as handicrafts from elsewhere in Malaysia, very classy compared with Rusila below. Open: 0830-1700 Sat-Wed, 0830-1200 Thur. Next door to *Infokraf* is the huge *Nor Arfa Batik Factory*, producing modern and traditional designs and readymades. Behind *Infokraf* is the *Suterasemai* silk factory. **Getting there**: Marang-bound buses from Jalan Masjid (M$0.50). The turning is clearly signposted off the main road.

Rusila Handicraft Centre, at Rusila, 10 km S of Kuala Terengganu on road from Marang. Showroom but rather trinkety and tacky compared with Cendering. Open: 0900-1800 Sat-Thur. **Getting there**: Marang-bound buses from Jalan Masjid (M$0.50).

Kenyir Lake 55 km S of Kuala Terengganu, is a man-made 370 km^2 lake and Kuala Terengganu's latest holiday destination. Having completed the Kenyir Dam

The Crown-of-Thorns – the terminator on the reef

The crown-of-thorns starfish (*Acanthaster planci*) – a ruthlessly efficient, cold-blooded killing machine – launched an invasion of the Pulau Redang Marine Park in the early 1990s. The destructive starfish, which did serious damage to Australia's Great Barrier Reef in the 1980s, can regenerate and multiply rapidly leading to sudden infestations on coral reefs. The crown-of-thorns grazes on staghorn coral (*Acropora*) in particular and if population explosions are left unchecked, the starfish can reduce rich coral colonies into blanched skeletal debris. One crown-of-thorns can suck the living tissues from a coral in a matter of hours and, if present in large numbers, they can eat their way across a reef, devastating it in a matter of weeks or months.

The crown-of-thorns is aptly named. It measures about 50 cm across and is covered in thousands of poisonous spines, each 3-5 cm long. The spines are extremely sharp and toxic – if they puncture human skin, they cause a severe reaction, including nausea, vomiting and swelling. These short spines grow on the starfish's legs, of which it has more than 20. But marine conservationists, concerned about the threat to the coral and fish breeding grounds, face a daunting task in ridding reefs of the unwelcome echinoderms. Because of their amoeba-like regenerative abilities, the crown-of-thorns cannot simply be chopped in half *in situ* – that would create 2 of them. Instead, each one has to be prised off the coral, taken to the surface and buried on land.

The Malaysian Fisheries Department, with private sector backing, mounted a reef-rescue expedition to Redang in 1992 to do exactly this. The department's marine biologists were unsure as to what had triggered the infestation of crown-of-thorns starfish; it could be that they invade in natural cycles – or human interference could have something to do with it. The last major infestation was in the early 1970s. Following their difficult task of picking the starfish off the reef, the divers buried them on shore, as instructed. Perhaps they should have driven wooden stakes through their hearts too: the starfish can go for as long as 9 months without food.

in 1985, the state economic development board has built a 2½ km access road, a jetty and a tourist information centre. There are facilities for fishing, canoeing and boating. Major hotel and resort developments will be going up in the course of the next few years; luxury chalets – some of them 'floating chalets', built over the lake – and the inevitable 18-hole golf course are among projects in the pipeline. (Enquire at tourist information office in Kuala Terengganu as to what stage developments have reached). The lake is surrounded by jungled hills and there are plans to use Kenyir Lake as a back-door to the remote E side of Taman Negara. The lake itself has more than 300 islands. In parts swimming can be as hazardous as navigation thanks to the millions of submerged and semi-submerged trees. It has been stocked with fish and tour operators from Kuala Terengganu, some of which have houseboats on the lake, offer fishing tackle, canoeing and water-skiing as part of the package. The **Sekayu waterfalls**, with natural water-cut pools for swimming, are also 15 km from Kuala Berang. **Accommodation**: A *Primula Lake Resort*, restaurant, Malay-style chalets (and 8 floating chalets), organizes activities on the lake; *Kenyir Lake Resort*, T 011-950609 or 09-516002, restaurant, floating chalets. **Getting there**: bus to Kuala Berang, off the inland road S at Ajil, and then taxi to the lake (M$20-25).

Beaches Batu Buruk beach, running down the NE side of KT is not safe for swimming. But there are some good beaches near Kuala Terengganu – Merang 15 km (**see page 212**) and Batu Rakit 25 km N. There is a guesthouse at the latter (M$24). **Getting there**: regular buses to both beaches from Jalan Masjid.

Islands (see page 213). **Getting there**: boats leave for the islands from Merang and from the Jalan Bandar jetty in Kuala Terengganu, from which there are now scheduled departures.

Tours A number of tour agents offer tours to the offshore islands and trekking tours to the Kenyir Lake area (see page 212).

Accommodation There are only a couple of hotels at the top-end of the market but there are several cheaper hotels scattered round town, mainly at the jetty-end of Jln Sultan Ismail and on Jln Banggol, but the selection is not great. **A** *Primula Beach Resort*, Jln Persinggahan, T 622100, a/c, restaurant (good Malay-food buffet for M$25), pool, hi-rise hotel with all mod-cons, also organizes island excursions; **B** *Kenangan*, 65 Jln Sultan Ismail, T 622342, a/c, restaurant, smart, very clean and friendly hotel; **B** *Motel Desa*, Bukit Pak Api, T 623033, a/c, restaurant, pool, set in gardens on a small hill overlooking the town; **B** *Seaview*, 18a Jln Masjid Abidin, T 621911, a/c, centrally located opposite Istana Maziah; **B-C** *Batu Burok Chalet*, 906-A, Pantai Batu Burok, T 637266, some a/c, restaurant, the only chalet-style accommodation in town, not bad, but a bit over-priced, pleasant open restaurant overlooking beach (which is dangerous for swimming); **B-C** *Bunga Raya*, 105-111 Jln Banggol, T 620527, bit run-down and noisy, on road; **B-C** *Seri Hoover*, 49 Jln Sultan Ismail, T 633655, a/c, restaurant, big, clean rooms, although slightly musty smell; **B-C** *Trengganu*, 12 Jln Sultan Ismail (opposite junction with Jln Halirah), a/c, plush new foyer, rooms could do with lick of paint but clean and reasonable value, rec; **C-D** *Meriah*, 67 Jln Sultan Ismail, T 622655, restaurant, bar and nightclub, good, clean Malay-run hotel; **C** *Warisan*, 65 Jln Sultan Ismail, T 622688, a/c, restaurant, attached to shopping arcade, cultural performances can be arranged; **C-D** *Sri Dungun Hotel*, K-135 Jln Tambun, T 841881; **D-E** *Rex*, 112 Jln Sultan Ismail, clean Chinese hotel, some rooms with attached bathroom; **E** *Nam Tan*, 8 Jln Kota Hilir, T 621481, some rooms with attached bath; **E-F** *Ping Anchorage*, 77A Jln Dato' Issac, T 620851, roof-top café, free breakfast, helpful with travel information, although rooms can be noisy, organizes trekking trips to Kenyir Lake area and offshore islands, now has sister hotel (*Ping Anchorage II*) in Marang, and the *Marang Inn* is part of the empire, rec.

Restaurants *Nasi dagang* – known as 'fishermen's breakfast' – is a speciality of the area. It is made with aromatic or glutinous rice, served with *gulai ikan tongkol* (tunafish with tamarind and coconut gravy). *Keropok* – or prawn crackers – are another Terengganu speciality. **Malay**: ♦♦*Keluarga IQ*, 74 Jln Banggol, good place for *nasi dagang* breakfast, also excellent *nasi campur* (curry buffet), open 0630-0300, closed Friday; ♦*Mali*, 77 Jln Banggol, near the bus station, popular, cheap coffee shop – *nasi lemak*, *nasi campur*, *satay* and good rotis; ♦*Nik*, 104 Jln Sultan Ismail, standard curries; *Sri Intan*, 14 Taman Sri Intan, Jln Sultan Omar, well-appointed restaurant serving standard Malay dishes; ♦*Zainuddin*, Jln Tok Lam. **Seafood**: ♦♦♦*Nil*, Jln Pantai Batu Buruk (near the *Pantai Primula Hotel*), view of the beach, good selection of seafood and renowned for its butter crabs in batter; ♦♦*Taz*, Jln Sultan Zainal Abidin (below *Asrama Seri Pantai hotel*). **Chinese**: ♦♦*Awana*, near public swimming pool, Jln Pantai Batu Buruk, rec by locals; ♦♦*One-Two-Six*, 102 Jln Kampung Tiong 2 (off Jln Sultan Ismail), big open-air restaurant with hawker stalls, good seafood menu, special: fire chicken wings (comes to table in flames), rec; ♦♦*Restaurants Good Luck, Kui Ping and Lee Kee* all along Jln Engku Sar, standard Chinese fare. **Indian**: ♦♦*Taufik*, 18 Jln Masjid (opposite Istana Maziah), N and S Indian dishes, well-known for its rotis; ♦*Kari Asha*, 1-H Jln Air Jermh, good range of curries (incl fish heads, dosai and rotis). **International**: ♦♦*Husni*, 954 Jln Negara, Thai, Malay and Western dishes, vast menu. **Foodstalls**: *Gerai Makanan* (food stalls) opposite the bus station; Malay; *Kampung Tiong* (off Jln Bandar), excellent hawker centre with Malay food on one side, Chinese and Indian on the other, open eight till late; *Jaln Batu Buruk*, near the cultural centre, some excellent Malay food and seafood stalls, rec; also *Warung Pak Maidin*, nearby on Jln Haji Busu, which is good on seafood. *Kompleks Taman Selera Tanjung* (1st Floor), huge area of stalls with good variety of dishes, open-air terrace. *Majlis Perbandaran* stalls, Jln Tok Lam; *Pasar Besar Kedai Payang* (Central Market), 1st Flr, Malay snacks, good views over the river. There are also some stalls next to *Stadium Negeri*.

Entertainment Cultural shows: *Gelanggang Seni* (Cultural Centre), Pantai Batu Buruk. Displays of *silat* (Malay art of self-defence), traditional dances, top-spinning and sometimes *wayang kulit* (shadow puppets), 1700-1830 every Fri.

Shopping Handicrafts: in town, there is a craft centre next to the post office on Jln Sultan Zainal Abidin. *Karyankeka (Handicrafts) Centre*, Cawangan Rusila, Km13, Kampung Rusila and Cendering weaving centre and shop (see excursions). **Batik**: *Wan Ismail Tembaga & Batik*, near roundabout with turtle, off Jln Sultan Zainal Abidin – a small, old-fashioned batik factory. There are a number of small craft and batik factories in Kampung Ladang – the area around Jln Sultan Zainal Abidin; *DesaCraft Silk & Souvenirs*, 73 Jln Sultan Ismail, in the centre of town, has a good selection of silk and batik readymades and sarongs.

Sport Diving: *Merlin Enterprise*, 1-E, 1st Flr, Wisma Guru, Jln Hiliran, T 636200. Manager David Chua has a reputation as one of the country's leading divers and is well known for his scuba expeditions. **Golf**: *Badariah Golf Club*, S of town. 9 holes. Requires special permission from the Sultan's private secretary's office, T 632456.

Local transport Trishaw: M\$2-3 for short trips around town. **Car hire**: **SMAS**, 60 Kompleks Permint, Bandar Baru Kerteh, T 861097.

Banks & money changers UMBC, 59 Jln Sultan Ismail. **Bumiputra**, UMNO Jln Masjid Zainal Abidin; **Maybank**, 69 Jln Paya Bunga. **Public**, 1 Jln Balas Baru; **Standard Chartered**, 31 Jln Sultan Ismail. There are virtually no money-changers in Kuala Terengganu.

Useful addresses General Post Office: Jln Sultan Zainal Abidin. **Hospital**: Jln Peranginan (just off Jln Sultan Mahmud).

Airline offices MAS, 13 Jln Sultan Omar, T 622266/621415.

Tour companies & travel agents *Hedaco Travel*, Grd Flr, Terengganu Foundation Bldg, Jln Sultan Ismail, T 631744; *The Little Traveller*, PO Box 117, Kuala Terengganu, T 673218, F 671527, trips to islands, equipped with comfortable houseboats on Lake Kenyir; *Ria Holiday*, Grd Flr, MCIS Bldg, Jln Sultan Zainal Abidin, T 861546; *Ruways Travel*, 14 Bangunan Yayasan Terengganu, Jln Sultan Ismail, T 635582; *WLO Travel & Air Cargo*, Grd Flr, *Hotel Pantai Primula*, Jln Persinggahan, T 635844.

Tourist office Tourism Malaysia, 2243 Grd Flr, Wisma MCIS, Jln Sultan Zainal Abidin, T 621433/621893.

Transport to & from Kuala Terengganu 455 km from KL, 168 km from Kota Bahru, 209 km from Kuantan. **By air**: regular connections with KL (M\$86), Penang (M\$80), Johor Bahru (M\$163), Kerteh (M\$40). **By bus**: bus station on Jln Sultan Zainal Abidin. Regular connections with KL (M\$20), JB (M\$22), Kota Bahru (M\$5.70), Kuantan (M\$8). **By taxi**: taxis operate from behind the bus station and from the waterfront. Kota Bahru (M\$12), Rantau Abang (M\$6), Kuantan (M\$15), KL (M\$35), JB (M\$40), Penang (M\$60).

Merang

Merang is another small fishing kampung with a long white sandy beach; it is also the departure point for the many offshore islands, the biggest and best-known of which is Pulau Redang. Recently, Pulau Bidong has opened to tourists (Bidong's coral is said to be superb); throughout the 1980s it served as a Vietnamese refugee camp. The only island with accommodation is Pulau Redang.

Excursions

Pulau Redang is about 27 km off Merang; the archipelago has been gazetted as a marine park and it has some of Malaysia's best reefs. In the months after the monsoon, underwater visibility increases to at least 20m. Line-fishing is permitted and squid fishing, using bright lights, is popular between Jun and Sept; the fishermen use a special hook called a *candat sotong*. The lamps light the surrounding waters, attracting the squid. Pulau Redang is to be developed into a luxury resort – the *Berjaya Inn Golf & Beach Resort* – with a hotel, 12 villas, 150 chalets. There will also be riding stables and a sports complex. Construction is scheduled for completion in 1994 – although the project sparked vehement protests from environmental groups. **Accommodation**: Resorts on Redang offer competitive and flexible package deals; check with *Tourism Malaysia*. **A** *Redang Beach Resort*, T (09) 623521 (contact office: 36E, 1st Flr, Jln Dato' Issac), full range of facilities, package deals available; **A** *Redang Bay Resort*, T (09) 636048, (011) 971261; **A** *Redang Pelangi Resort*, T (09) 635202; **D** *Pulau Redang Resort* (book in Kuala Terengganu, T 627050), bungalows, 'A'-frames slightly cheaper. **Getting there**: boats leave for the islands from Merang as well as from the jetty in Kuala Terengganu. It has, however, become very expensive to charter boats from Merang. *Tourism Malaysia* in Kuala Terengganu recommends that tourists take advantage of the package deals offered by the island's resorts; further details can be obtained from the *Tourism Malaysia* office. There are now scheduled departures to Redang from Kuala Terengganu. From Merang: M\$40 per person return for boat (takes 8 people) or slow fishing boat for M\$30 per person return (takes 12 people). A typical 2-day/2-night trip costs around M\$230/person; all food, camping and snorkelling equipment included. As always, if you value a measure of privacy and seclusion, avoid weekends and public holidays.

Other islands most of which are uninhabited, and all of which are endowed with good coral include Pulau Pinang, Pulau Lima, Pulau Lang Tengah, Pulau Tenggol and Pulau Ekor Tebu; fishing boats are usually happy to stop off on request.

Accommodation D *Mare Nostrum Beach Resort*, 1 km out of town on road to *Penarik,* restaurant, rooms and 'A'-frames on beautiful stretch of beach. **E** *Sugi Man's Homestay,* 500m beyond junction, on road to Penarik (signposted from the road), restaurant, basic kampung farm house, quite a walk from the beach, cooking lessons and kite making, includes meals.

Transport to & from Merang 38 km N of Kuala Terengganu, on the coast road. **By bus:** regular buses from Kuala Terengganu to Merang (M\$1.70); infrequent buses to Penarik. **By taxi:** taxis from Merang to Penarik (M\$5/person).

Pulau Perhentian

Two more beautiful E coast islands – Pulau Perhentian Besar (big) and Pulau Perhentian Kecil (small) are separated by a narrow sound with a strong current. The Perhentian islands have good coral, magnificent beaches and some of the best places for swimming on the E coast... but big plans for development are afoot. There is a fishing village on the small island and a turtle hatchery on the big one. There are jungle trails across Perhentian Besar; all are well marked.

Accommodation NB: All the resorts and chalets now have their own generators; all fresh water from wells. Visitors are advised to bring some food and bottled water from Kota Bahru or Kuala Terengganu as restaurants are relatively expensive. **B-E** *Cozy Chalet*, Perhentian Besar, T (09) 970090; **C** *Abdul's*, chalets; **C** *Flora Bay Chalet*, Telok Dalam, T (011) 977266; **C** *Perhentian Island Resort* (bookings c/o 25 Menara Promet, Jln Sultan Ismail, KL, T 03-2480811), T (011) 345562, a/c, restaurant, owned by the government and poorly run, some watersports facilities, dormitory, 'A'-frames and bungalows; **D** *Pasir Petani Resort*, W side, Perhentian Kecil, chalets; **D** *Rest House*, 4 chalets which can be booked through the District Office in Jerteh, each chalet can accommodate 4; **E** *Coco Hut Chalets*, T 972085, restaurant, 'A'-frames; **E** *Cottage Hut*, Pasir Panjang, Perhentian Kecil, T (011) 977252; **E** *D'Lagoon*, Perhentian Kecil, T (09) 970105; **E** *Rosali*, restaurant, 3 chalets, fishing and diving packages (2 dives M\$130), need PADI certificate.

Camping M\$5 at *Perhentian Island Resort*; camping is not restricted on the island.

Restaurants There are a couple of restaurants on Perhentian Besar serving simple food – banana pancakes etc: *Coral Cave Café* and *Isabella Coffee Shop* (next to *Rest House*). There are also coffee shops in the kampung on Perhentian Kecil.

Transport to & from Pulau Perhentian 20 km offshore. **By bus:** from Kuala Terengganu (Jln Masjid): Kota Bahru-bound bus to Jerteh (M\$4). Regular connections between Jerteh and Kuala Besut (M\$1). From Kota Bahru: Bus 3, S-bound to Pasir Puteh (36 km S) (M\$2). Regular connections between Pasir Puteh and Kuala Besut (M\$0.90). Boats leave from here to Perhentian. **By taxi:** Kuala Terengganu (M\$10); Kota Bahru (M\$5). Taxis from Pasir Puteh or Jerteh to Kuala Besut (M\$2). Boats leave from here to Perhentian. **By boat:** regular connections with Kuala Besut, 2 hrs (M\$15 one-way). Boats leave Kuala Besut between 0700 and 0900 and will stop at beaches on request. Those staying at the more remote *Pasir Petani Resort* on Perhentian Kecil should pre-arrange a pick-up time.

Kota Bahru

Kota Bahru is the royal capital of Kelantan, 'the land of lightning', and is situated near the mouth of the Kelantan River. The city is one of Malaysia's Malay strongholds, despite its proximity to the Thai border. The state's S and W regions include some of the most mountainous country on the peninsula, but the fertile alluvial soils of the Kelantan River valley and the coastal plain have supported mixed farming and a thriving peasant economy for centuries. Kelantan may have

Cementing neighbourly relations

Eighteen months after the Berlin Wall came down, Malaysia announced its intention to build a 100 km-long border wall between Kelantan and S Thailand. Malaysia and Thailand are both members of the Association of Southeast Asian Nations (ASEAN), but political analysts say that as Cold War tensions have evaporated, and the Cambodian conflict – which for years was ASEAN'S *raison d'être* – moved from being a regional problem to a world problem, old animosities are coming to the fore again. The new wall is one such example of Malaysia washing its dirty laundry. It will cost the federal government M$7 million.

The wall will be the first physical barrier along Kelantan's border; the Thai frontier with Perlis, Kedah and Perak states is already strung with barbed wire fencing, an erstwhile precaution against the now disbanded Communist Party of Malaya, which operated from jungle camps inside Thailand. Several incidents over recent years led to a build-up in tensions between Thailand and Malaysia, already locked in competition to attract foreign investors.

In mid-1991 Thai authorities arrested 11 Malaysian forestry officers for alleged illegal logging on the Thai side of the border. In Malaysia this was read as tit-for-tat retaliation for the arrest and detention of more than 1,000 S Thai fishermen by the Royal Malaysian Navy which accused them of fishing illegally in Malaysian waters. Thailand alleged that Kelantan's Islamic Party government has been providing refuge and support to Muslim secessionists in the S Thai provinces of Yala, Petani and Narathiwat. In Kuala Lumpur, the government says the wall is being built in an effort to stem the flow of smuggled drugs as well as cigarettes and other taxable merchandise which floods over the border into Kota Bahru.

been part of the 2nd century kingdom of Langkasuka (**see page 149**), but from early in the first millennium AD, it was an established agricultural state which adopted the farming practices of the kingdom of Funan on the lower Mekong River. Because it was effectively cut off from the W coast states of the peninsula, Kelantan always looked N: it traded with Funan, the Khmer Empire and the Siamese Kingdom of Ayutthaya.

By the 14th century, Kelantan was under Siamese suzerainty – although at that time it also fell under the influence of the Javanese Majapahit empire. For a while, during the 15th and 16th centuries, Kelantan joined other peninsular states in sending tribute to the Sultanate of Melaka, and its successor, Johor. By then the state had splintered into a number of small chiefdoms; one local chief, Long Mohammed, proclaimed himself Kelantan's first sultan in 1800.

When a succession dispute erupted on the death of the heirless Sultan Mohammed, Siam supported his nephew, Senik the 'Red-Mouth' who reigned for 40 peaceful years. On the next succession crisis, in 1900, Bangkok installed its own nominee as sultan. But in 1909, a treaty between Siam and Britain pushed Bangkok to cede its suzerainty over Kelantan to the British. This severed the state from its Islamic neighbour, the former sultanate of Petani, in SE Thailand. British interference caused much resentment and provoked a brief revolt in 1912. After using Kota Bahru as one of their beachheads for the invasion of Malaya in Dec 1941, the Japanese Imperial Army won support for restoring Kelantan to Thailand. In Oct 1945 however, Kelantan reluctantly joined the Malayan Union, under the British colonial administration.

Today Kelantan is Malaysia's most conservative and traditional state, and since Oct 1990, has been ruled by the hard-line Parti Islam – or *PAS*, its Malay acronym. For the purposes of forging an electoral alliance – the party joined forces with the chief opposition leader Tunku Razaleigh Hamzah, himself a member of the Kelantan royal family. Since then, Parti Islam has moved towards the establishment of an Islamic state government, based on the Koranic principles of *Syariat* law. To

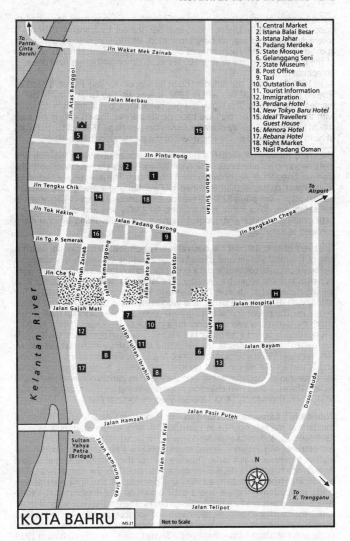

To Pantai Cinta Berahi

Jln Wakat Mek Zainab

Jalan Merbau

Jln Atas Banggol

1. Central Market
2. Istana Balai Besar
3. Istana Jahar
4. Padang Merdeka
5. State Mosque
6. Gelanggang Seni
7. State Museum
8. Post Office
9. Taxi
10. Outstation Bus
11. Tourist Information
12. Immigration
13. *Perdana Hotel*
14. *New Tokyo Baru Hotel*
15. *Ideal Travellers Guest House*
16. *Menora Hotel*
17. *Rebana Hotel*
18. Night Market
19. Nasi Padang Osman

Jln Pintu Pong

Jln Tengku Chik

Jln Tok Hakim

Jalan Padang Garong

Jln Tg. P. Semerak

Jln Che Su

Jalan Gajah Mati

Jln Sultanah Zainab

Jalan Temenggong

Jalan Dato Pati

Jalan Doktor

Jln Kebun Sultan

Jln Pengkalan Chepa

To Airport

Jalan Hospital

Jalan Sultan Ibrahim

Jalan Mahmud

Jalan Bayam

Dusun Muda

Jalan Pasir Puteh

Jalan Kuala Krai

Jalan Hamzah

Jalan Kampung Sireh

Sultan Yahya Petra (Bridge)

Kelantan River

N

To K. Trengganu

Jalan Telipot

KOTA BAHRU IMS 21   Not to Scale

the chagrin of the federal government, which is always mindful of Malaysia's
potentially volatile ethnic mix, the state government has attempted to implement
these laws (known as *hudud*) and extend them to non-Muslims – a move deeply
resented by Kelantan's mainly Chinese minority. The federal government has been
caught in a cleft stick over the emotive issue of whether or not to condone the
implementation of hudud. The Malay-led government finally opted to support it,

lest it be seen as anti-Islamic, while its Chinese coalition partner has opted to oppose it vehemently. Under hudud law, punishment for 'criminal' offences is severe. For theft, highway robbery, fornication, intoxication, false allegation and apostasy the mandatory punishments are respectively: severing of hands, severing of the hands and legs (or death), 100 lashes, 80 lashes, 40 lashes (and death, if unrepentant).

In 1991 Parti Islam attempted to drum up support for Iraqi President Saddam Hussein during the Gulf War and in 1992, it even went so far as to try to bar all women from working. This highly-charged political/religious atmosphere contrasts with the Kelantanese people's laid-back, gentle manner. Tourists visiting the state should be particularly aware of Islamic sensitivities (**see page 183**), but the trappings of Islam rarely impinge on the enjoyment of the state's rich cultural heritage.

The crafts for which Kelantan is renowned – such as silverware, weaving and metal-working – were in part the result of the state's close relations with the Siamese kingdom of Ayutthaya in the 17th century. The makyung, a traditional Malay court dance, is still performed in Kelantan and wayang kulit (shadow puppet plays – **see page 529**) still provide entertainment on special occasions in the kampungs. Kota Bahru is the centre for Malay arts and crafts, although batik-printing, woodcarving, songket-weaving and silver-working are more often confined to the villages.

The heart of Kota Bahru is the **central market** off Jalan Temenggong, which is one of the most vibrant and colourful markets in the country. It is housed in a 3-storey octagonal complex and is a good place to buy textiles and bamboo-work as well as fruit and vegetables. Nearby is the **Istana Balai Besar**, the 'palace with the big audience hall', built in Patani-style in 1844 by Sultan Mohammed II. The istana, with its decorative panels and wood-carvings is still used on ceremonial occasions. The palace contains the throne-room and the elaborate royal barge, which the sultan only ever used once for a joy ride on the Kelantan River in 1900. It is not usually open to the public but visitors can obtain permission to visit from the palace caretaker. Beside the old istana is the single-storey **Istana Jahar**, constructed in 1889 by Sultan Mohammed IV; it is now the 'centre for royal customs' and is part of the new cultural complex (see below). It exemplifies the skilled craftsmanship of the Kelantanese woodcarvers in its intricately carved beams and panels. There is a small craft collection including songket and silverware. Admission: M$1. Open: 0930-1230, 1400-1700 Sat-Wed, 0930-1200 Thur.

Kota Bahru's **Kampung Kraftangan** – or Handicraft Village – which is close to the central market, opened in mid-1992. It aims to give visitors a taste of Kelantan's arts and crafts all under one roof. The large enclosure, in which merbuk birds (doves) sing in their bamboo cages, contains 4 buildings, all wooden and built in traditional Malay style. They are part of the Kelantan Cultural Square Project which will include several museums, including the Istana Jahar. The Handicraft Museum contains exhibits and dioramas of traditional Kelantanese crafts and customs. There is also a batik workshop and demonstration centre where local artists produce hand-painted batiks. There are several stalls, stocked with handicrafts such as batik, silverware and songket, for sale. At ground level there is a pleasant restaurant serving Kelantanese delicacies. Opposite the new complex is the Istana Batu – the sky-blue Stone Palace – which was built in 1939 and was one of the first concrete buildings in the state. The former royal palace was presented to the state by the Sultan for use as a royal museum and contains many personal possessions of the royal family. Admission: Kampung Kraftangan free; Handicraft Museum M$1.

A little N of the commercial centre is **Padang Merdeka**, built after World War I as a memorial. Merdeka Square is also where the British hanged Tok Janggut –

'Father Long-beard' – who led the short-lived revolt against British land taxes in 1915. Opposite (on Jalan Sultan Zainab), is the **State Mosque** completed in 1926. Next door is the State Religious Council building, dating from 1914.

At the **Gelanggang Seni** (Cultural Centre), on Jalan Mahmud, opposite the stadium, many traditional arts are regularly performed. The centre tends to get rather touristy but it is the best place to see a variety of cultural performances in one place. For more detail on each of these traditional forms of entertainment, **see page 81**. These include:

❑ Demonstrations of *silat* (the Malay art of self-defence).
❑ Drumming competitions (Wed afternoons) using the *rebana ubi* Kelantan drums, made from hollowed-out logs.
❑ *Wayang kulit* (shadow-puppet) performances (Wed nights). (For a detailed history of *wayang kulit* in the region, **see page 529**.)
❑ Kite-flying competitions (Sat afternoons) with the famous paper-and-bamboo *wau bulan* – or Kelantan moon-kites, the symbol of MAS. This has been a Kelantanese sport for centuries; the aim is to fly your kite higher than anyone else's and, once up there, to defend your superiority by being as aggressive as possible towards other competitors' kites. Kite-flying, according to the Malay Annals, was a favourite hobby in the hey-day of the Melaka sultanate in the 15th century.
❑ **Top-spinning** competitions (Wed and Sat afternoons).

Other cultural performances include traditional dance routines such as the royal *Mak Yong* dance and the *Menora*, both of which relate local legends. A set programme of shows (available from the Tourist Promotion Board) usually starts at 1500 or in the early evening from Feb to Oct.

The **State Museum**, on Jalan Sultan Ibrahim (near the clock tower and next to the Tourism Malaysia office), whose proudest boast is its big collection of krisses.

Excursions
Pantai Cinta Berahi KB's most famous beach, 10 km N of the city, is really only famous for its name meaning the 'Beach of Passionate Love'. In comparison with some other E coast beaches, it is not very special; nor particularly romantic. In Malay, the word *berahi* is, according to one scholar, "loaded with sexual dynamite... a love madness". Local Malays, alluding to this heated innuendo, used to euphemistically call it *pantai semut api* – the beach of the fire ants. Today, young Malay lovers do not even dare to hold hands on the beach, for fear of being caught by the religious police and charged with *khalwat*, the crime of 'close proximity', under *Syariat* Islamic law. The origin of the name *cinta berahi* is lost. One theory is that it was used as a code word by Malay and British commandos during the Japanese wartime occupation: the site of the Imperial Army's invasion, in 1941, is nearby, on Pantai Dasar Sabak (**see page 217**). Despite being rather over-rated, there are several resorts along the beach. It gets crowded on weekends. **Accommodation: C** *Long House Beach Motel*, T 740090, a/c, restaurant (Thai food), good value; **B** *Pantai Cinta Berahi Resort*, T 781307, a/c, restaurant, up-market chalets, watersports, deep sea fishing; *Perdana Resort*, Jalan Kuala Pa'Amat, a/c, restaurant, pool, water sports, chalets and rooms. **Getting there**: minibus 10 every 20 mins (M$0.60) from Bazaar Buluh Kubu, off Jalan Tengku Chik or from Jalan Padang Garong.

Other beaches Pantai Dalam Rhu (40 km SE of KB): **Accommodation: E** *Dalam Rhu Homestay*, simple kampung-style accommodation, well looked-after. **Getting there**: bus 3, S bound (M$2); change at Pasir Puteh. **Pantai Irama** – the 'Beach of Melody' (25 km S of KB): the best of the nearby beaches for swimming. Bus 2A or 2B every half hour (M$1.20). **Pantai Dasar Sabak** (13 km NE of KB) is where the Japanese troops landed on 7 Dec 1941, 90 mins before they bombed Pearl Harbour. Nearby Kampung Sabak is a good place to watch fishing boats come in in the morning. **Getting there**: bus 8 or 9 (M$1.50).

Waterfalls In the area round Pasir Puteh there are several waterfalls – Jeram Pasu, Jeram Tapeh and Cherang Tuli. **Jeram Pasu** is the most popular. **Getting there**: most easily accessible by taxi or bus 3 to Padang Pak Amat (M$1.70) and taxi to the waterfalls.

Tumpat Around Tumpat, next to the border, are small Thai communities where there are a few Thai-style buildings and wats; they do not, however, compare with the Thai architecture on the other side of the border. **Wat Phothivian** at Kampung Berok (12 km E of KB, on the Malaysian side of Sungei Golok) has a 41m reclining Buddha statue, built in 1973 by chief abbot Phra Kruprasapia Chakorn, which attracts thousands of Thai pilgrims every year. **Getting there**: bus 27 or 19 to Chabang Empat (M$0.70) and taxi to Kampung Jambu (M$1).

Masjid Kampung Laut at Kampung Nilam Puri, 10 km S of KB, was built 300 years ago by Javanese Muslims as an offering of thanks for being saved from pirates. Having been damaged once too often by monsoon floods, it was dismantled and moved inland to Kampung Nilam Puri, which is an Islamic scholastic centre. It was built entirely of cengal, a prized hardwood, and constructed without the use of nails. It vies with Masjid Kampung Kling (in Melaka) for the title of Malaysia's oldest mosque. **Getting there**: bus 44 (M$0.70) or express bus 5 every half hour.

River trips From Kuala Kerai (a 1 hr bus trip S from Kota Bahru, bus 5; M$3.20), it is possible to take a boat upriver to Dabong, a small kampung nestled among the jungled foothills of the Main Range 3 hrs (M$4), where there is a resthouse and restaurant. Dabong, in the centre of Kelantan state, is on the north-south railway, so it is possible to catch the *Golden Blowpipe* back to Wakaf Bahru (across the river from KB). Alternatively, taxi (M$5).

Tours *Tourism Malaysia* organizes a number of tours – river and jungle-safari trips, staying in kampungs and learning local crafts. There are also several private local tour companies (**see page 219**).

Festivals Jun: *Bird Singing Contest* (moveable) when the prized *merbuk* (doves) or *burong ketitir* birds compete on top of 8m-high poles. Bird singing contests are also held on Friday mornings around Kota Bahru. Jul: *Sultan's birthday celebrations* (10-12).

Accommodation Budget travellers are spoilt for choice in KB; there are some very pleasant cheaper hostels and guesthouses (most of them in secluded alleyways with gardens) and they are locked in fearsome competition. The selection of top-bracket and mid-range hotels is pretty average. **A** *Murni*, Jln Datuk Pati, T 785255, a/c, restaurant; **A** *Perdana*, Jln Mahmud, T 785000, a/c, restaurant, pool, best in town, central location, but overpriced; **B** *Irama*, Jln Sultan Ibrahim, T 782722, a/c, restaurant; **B** *Kencana Inn*, Jln Padang Garong, T 747944, a/c, restaurant, up-market and reasonable value for money, car rental service; **B** *Temenggong*, Jln Tok Hakim, T 783103, a/c, restaurant, similar to Kencana, discounts on request; **B-C** *Indah*, 236a Jln Tengku Besar, T 785081, a/c, restaurant, opposite *Padang Merdeka*; **B-C** *New Tokyo Baru*, 3945 Jln Tok Hakim, a/c, well-kept, rec; **C** *Aman*, 23C/D Jln Tengku Besar, T 743049, a/c, restaurant; **C** *Suria Baru*, Jln Padan Garong, T 746567, a/c, good value for money compared to others in this category; **D** *Milton*, 5471a Jln Pengkalan Chepa, T 782744, a/c; **C-E** *Johnty's Guest House*, 822 Jln Kebun Sultan, T 748866 (off Jln Dusun Raja), some a/c, popular place opposite bird-singing contest area, rooms and dorm, offers excursions, bike-hire, traditional massage and free breakfast to keep up with the Joneses; **D-E** *Ideal Travellers' House*, 5504a Jln Padang Garong, T 742246, quiet, friendly, pleasant verandah, rooms and dormitory, rec by many travellers; **E** *Menora*, Wisma Chua Tong Boon, 3338D (1st Flr) Jln Sultanah Zainab, T 781669, well kept, facilities include TV and 'strong showers', dorm (F), rec; **E** *Mummy's Hitec Hostel*, 4398 Jln Pengkalan Chepa, set in an old house, garden, breakfast included; **E** *Rainbow*, 4423 Jln Pengkalan Chepa, helpful, garden, breakfast included; **E** *Rebana*, 1218a Jln Sultan Zainab, opposite the old istana, bicycle hire, excellent value for money, garden, rec by travellers; **E-F** *City*, 2nd Flr, 35 Jln Pintu Pong (next to *Kentucky Fried Chicken*), clean and helpful on local information, price includes breakfast, dorm, rec; **E-F** *Friendly*, 4278D Jln Kebun Sultan, T 742246, dorm and rooms, garden; **E-F** *Town*, 4959B

(1st Flr) Jln Pengkalan Chepa, T 785192, restaurant, friendly and clean, close to the bus terminal, travel services, dorm and rooms; **E-F** *Yee*, Jln Padang Garong, T 741944, everything you need: laundry, breakfast, showers, travel information, bicycles for hire, dorm and rooms, M$4-10; **F** *DE999*, 3188G Taman Sri Bayam, Jln Sultan Ibrahim, cheap and clean rooms, close to the Cultural Centre, price includes breakfast, free bicycles, dorm and rooms.

Restaurants The Kelantan speciality is *ayam percik* – roast chicken, marinated in spices and served with a coconut-milk gravy. *Nasi tumpang* is a typical Kelantanese breakfast; banana-leaf funnel of rice layers interspersed with prawn and fish curries and salad. **♦♦*Azam*,** Jln Padang Garong, N Indian tandoori, with fresh oven-baked naan, good rotis and curry; **♦♦*Malaysia*,** 2527 Jln Kebun Sultan, Chinese cuisine, speciality: steamboat, this is the place to sample turtle eggs – legally; **♦♦*Meena Curry House*,** 3377 Jln Gajah Mati, Indian curry house, rec; **♦♦*Neelavathy*,** Jln Tengku Maharani (behind *Kencana Inn*), S Indian banana-leaf curries, rec; **♦♦*Qing Liang*,** Jln Zainal Abidin, excellent Chinese vegetarian, also Malay and Western dishes, rec; **♦♦*Satay Taman Indraputra*,** Jln Pekeliling/Jln Hospital garden; **♦♦*Syam*,** Jln Hospital. Thai-influenced. **Foodstalls:** *Night market* (in car park opposite local bus station, in front of Central Market), Chinese, Malay and Indian stalls, rec; *Nasi Padang Osman Larin* (otherwise known as *Nasi Hoover* as it is outside *Hotel Hoover*) is a stall on Jln Datuk Pati (between the Tourist Information Centre and the bus station) famed locally for its curries.

Entertainment Cultural shows: Regular cultural shows at the *Gelanggang Seni* (cultural centre), Jln Mahmud (see above).

Sport Golf: *Royal Kelantan Golf Club*, Jln Hospital. Green fees: M$50.

Shopping Handicrafts: *Karyaneka (handicrafts) Centre*, Jln Sultan/Jln Post Office Lama. Housed in the building which served as the Japanese Imperial Army Headquarters during their wartime occupation of Malaya. Reasonable selection, but prices rather inflated. The central market is cheaper. There are numerous handicraft stalls, silver-workers, kite-makers and wood-carvers scattered along the road N to Pantai Cinta Berahi. At Kampung Penambang, on this road, just outside KB, there is a batik and songket centre. **Batik:** *Wisma Batik*, Jln Datuk Pati (at the end of Jln Che Su). **Antiques:** *Lam's*, Jln Post Office Lama (in contrast to the modern town walk there are several old bamboo raft houses along this street). **Silverware:** on Jln Sultanah Zainab (near *Rabana Guest House*), before junction with Jln Hamzah, there are 3 shops selling Kelantan silver. The new Kampung Kraftangan (Handicraft Village) contains many stalls with a huge range of batik sarongs and ready-mades, silverware, songket, basketry and various Kelantanese nick-nacks.

Local transport Bus: city buses and buses to outlying districts (including Thai border, see below) leave from the Central Bus Station, Jln Hilir Pasar. Trishaw: short journeys M$1-2. **Car hire:** Pelancongan Bumi Mars, Tingkat Bawah, Kompleks Yakin, Jln Gajah Mati, T 740591; or from Kencana Inn, Jln Padang Garong, T 747944.

Banks & money changers Money changers in main shopping area. **Hongkong & Shanghai,** Jln Sultan; **D & C,** Jln Gajah Mati; **Bumiputra,** Jln Maju.

Embassies & consulates Royal Thai Consulate, Jln Pengkalan Chepa, T 722545/782545.

Useful addresses General Post Office: Jln Sultan Ibrahim. **Hospital:** Jln Hospital. **Telegraph Office:** Jln Doktor. **Immigration Office:** 3rd Flr, Federal Bldg, Jln Bayan. **Area code:** 09.

Airline offices MAS, Kompleks Yakin, Jln Gajah Mati (opposite the clock tower), T 747000.

Tour companies & travel agents *Batuta Travel & Tour*, 1st Flr, Bangunan PKDK, Jln Datuk Pati, T 742652; *Boustead Travel*, 2833 Jln Temenggong, T 749952; *Kelmark Travel*, Kelmark House, 5220 Jln Telipot, T 744211; *Pelancongan Bumi Mars*, Tingkat Bawah, Kompleks Yakin, Jln Gajah Mati, T 740591.

Tourist office Tourist Information Centre, Jln Sultan Ibrahim, T 785534.

Transport to & from Kota Bahru 474 km from Kuala Lumpur, 168 km from Terengganu, 371 km from Kuantan. **By air:** airport is 8 km from town. Regular connections with Alor Setar (M$101), Penang (M$86) and KL (M$103). **By train:** Wakaf Bahru station is 5 km out of town, across the Kelantan River. Bus 19/27/43 (M$1). Daily connections at 1050 with Kuala Lipis (M$15.90); connections with KL (M$37.80) and Singapore (M$40.50) on Sun, Tue, Wed & Fri at 1150. **By bus:** long-distance express depart from bus station on Jln Hamzah. Inter-city buses belonging to the SKMK (the Kelantan state bus company) operate from the Langgar bus station on Jln Pasir Puteh. Both bus stations are at the S end of town; regular connections with Kuala Terengganu (M$6.80), Kuantan (M$16.80), KL (M$25), JB (M$28), Singapore (M$30) and Butterworth (M$18). **By taxi:** taxi station next to the Central Bus Station, Jln Hilir

Pasar. Kuala Terengganu (M$12), Kuantan (M$25) KL (M$45), JB (M$52), Butterworth (M$30). Taxis to Rantau Panjang (for Sungei Golok, Thailand) (M$3.50). **International connections to Thailand:** buses leave from the central bus station, off Jln Hilir Pasar. Bus 29 departs on the hour to the Thai border at Rantau Panjang/Sungei Golok (1½hrs). Trains leave Sungei Golok daily (all before 1100) to Bangkok and Hat Yai. Sungei Golok railway and bus stations are 1 km from the bridge over border; trishaws or motorbike taxis can be hired (M$3-4). Buses 27, 27a and 43 also go to Pengkalan Kubor (M$1.20), for the quieter and much more interesting crossing to Ta Ba (Tak Bai), Thailand. Small boats cross the river regularly (M$3) or car ferry (M$0.50). Long-tails cater for the clientele of the cross-border prostitution industry only.

COAST TO COAST

The **E-W highway**, which runs straight across the forested backbone of the peninsula was one of the biggest civil engineering projects ever undertaken in Malaysia. During its 11-year construction, contractors had to push their way through densely jungled mountains, coping with frequent landslides and even hit-and-run attacks by Communist insurgents.

To the E of Grik, the highway runs close to the former bases of the Communist Party of Malaya, who, until 1989, operated out of their jungle headquarters near Betong, just across the Thai border. The area was known as 'Target One' by the Malaysian security forces. The construction of the road opened the previously inaccessible area up to timber companies; there has been much illegal logging – and cross-border drug-smuggling – in this 'cowboy country' of N Perak and Kelantan. The 200 km-long highway opened in 1982, and for the first few years was closed to traffic after 1600 because of the security threat posed by Communist insurgents; this threat has now ended. **NB**: hire-car drivers should note that there is no petrol station along the central 116 km stretch between Grik and Jeli (on the E side of the main range).

Grik, once a remote logging town, just a few kilometres S of the Thai border, is now an important junction, and the beginning of the highway. Few people stay the night there, but it is a good staging post and *makan* stop. (The huge Temenggor and Lenering man-made reservoirs are near-by.) Grik can be reached from Kuala Kangsar in Perak (**see page 127**) or from Butterworth via either Kulim (directly E of the town) or Sungei Petani (35 km N of town) which lead first to Keroh, on the Thai border, then on to Grik. The Kuala Kangsar route is a particularly scenic drive along a 111 km road which winds its way up the Perak River valley, enclosed by the Bintang mountains to the W and the Main Range to the E. En route, the road passes Tasek Chenderoh, a beautiful reservoir, surrounded by jungled hills. At **Kota Tampan**, just N of the lake, archaeologists have unearthed the remains of a Stone Age workshop, with roughly chiselled stone tools dating back 35,000 years. The road cuts through the jungle and there are some spectacular view-points. There are often landslides along this stretch of road during the wet season.

Accommodation en route Because Grik is not on the main tourist track, accommodation is basic. **D** *Diamond*, 40A Jln Sultan Iskander, T 892388; **D** *Kong Seng*, 32 Jln Sultan Iskander, T 892180; **D** *Rumah Rehat Grik*, Jln Meor Yahaya, T 891211; **D-E** *Bee Hoon*, Jln Tan Sabah, T 892201.

To Thailand from Keroh It is possible to cross the border into Thailand from Keroh. There are regular taxis from the town to the border post (M$1) and Thai taxis and *saamlors* on the other side. A Thai taxi costs ฿15-20 a head to Betong which is 8 km from the border. A taxi to Keroh costs M$2 from Butterworth and M$10 from Sungei Petani.

Kuala Lumpur to Kota Bahru The *Golden Blowpipe* trundles along the railwayline which cuts a diagonal through the peninsula, running due N from Gemas (S of KL on the KL-Singapore line) to Kota Bahru. Much of the route is through the jungle, and the track skirts the W boundary of Taman Negara, the national park (**see page 199**). Those heading into Taman Negara must disembark at Tembeling Halt, to the SE of Kuala Lipis, or at Jerantut. The train is slow, but it is an interesting journey. From Gemas the line goes through Jeranut, Kuala Lipis, Gua Musang, Kuala Krai and on to Kota Bahru. It is possible to catch the train at Mentakab (along the Karak Highway, E of KL) or at Kuala Lipis, which can be reached by road via Fraser's Hill and Raub. It is also possible to drive from Kuala Lipis via Gua Musang to Kota Bahru. The jungle is studded with limestone outcrops, and a particularly impressive one overshadows Gua Musang. There are buses from Kuala Lipis to Gua Musang (0800 & 1300, M$5) and Kuala Krai (1430, M$11). There are plans to upgrade the stretch of road from Kuala Lipis to Gua Musang.

Kenong Rimba Park is 1½ hrs E of Kuala Lipis by boat down the Jelai River to Kampung Kuala Kenong. The park, which encompasses the Kenong river valley, is the home of the *Batik* Orang Asli tribe, who are shifting cultivators. There is a network of Asli trails around the park and several caves and waterfalls. There are 2 campsites along the river; the first, *Kesong Campsite*, has 3 atap huts which serve as basic accommodation. Organized treks into Kenong Rimba are run by *Tuah Travel & Tours*, 12 Jalan Lipis, Kuala Lipis, T 312144. There are other registered freelance guides which can be hired from Kuala Lipis. **Accommodation** in Kuala Lipis: **D** *Rumah Rehat* (Rest House), (formerly the home of the British Resident in Pahang); **D** *Hotel Seri Pahang*; **E** *Hotel Paris*. **Getting there**: the *Golden Blowpipe* train, which runs from Kuala Lumpur, passes through Kuala Lipis and there are buses from Fraser's Hill.

Kuala Lumpur To Kuantan The Karak Highway tunnels through the Genting Pass, to the NE of KL. The half-way point is **Temerloh**, on the Pahang River, which is the main *makan*-stop on the KL-Kuantan road. From Temerloh it is possible to take a river trip to **Pekan**, the old royal capital of Pahang (**see page 192**) and to **Tasek Bera** (page 196).

    Accommodation en route The accommodation in Temerloh is basic: **C** *Kam San*, C-67 Jln Datuk Ngau Ken Lock, T 295606; **C** *Rumah Rehat* (Rest House), Jln Datuk Hamzah, T 291254; **C-D** *Ban Hin*, 40 Jln Tangku, T 292331; **D** *Kwai Pan*, 66 Jln Datuk Ngau Ken Lock, T 291431; **E** *Isbis*, 12 Jln Tengku Babar, T 293126.

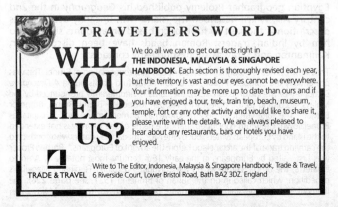

BORNEO

	Page		Page
Borneo introduction	222	**Bareo & Kelabit Highlands**	290
SARAWAK	230	**Limbang & Lawas**	291
Kuching & the Skrang River	248	**SABAH**	293
Sibu & the Rejang River	263	**Kota Kinabalu & Tunku Abdul Rahman NP**	302
Bintulu & Niah Caves	273	**South of Kota Kinabalu**	312
Niah National Park	276	**North & Gunung Kinabalu**	320
Miri & the Baram River	279	**Gunung Kinabalu NP**	322
Gunung Mulu NP	285	**The East Coast**	327

INTRODUCTION

Borneo has always held a mystical fascination for Westerners – it was a vast isolated, jungle-covered island, where head-hunters ran wild, and which, if romantic myths were to be believed, was rich in gold and diamonds. It is the third largest island in the world (after Greenland and New Guinea – Australia is considered a continent) and is divided between 3 countries: Malaysia, Brunei and Indonesia. Borneo has been known about in the Western world ever since the Egyptian geographer Ptolemy published his *Geography* in the 2nd century AD, which described the island with uncanny accuracy. His description is thought to have been based on accounts supplied to him by Indian traders. Roman beads have been discovered in Kalimantan and Sarawak suggesting early contacts.

The name Borneo is thought to be a European mispronunciation of Brunei. This was not entirely the Europeans' fault, for as John Crawfurd points out in *A Descriptive Dictionary of the Indian Isles* (1856), the name is "indifferently pronounced by the Malays, according to the dialect they happen to speak – Brune, Brunai, Burne or Burnai". The sultanate itself became known as 'Borneo Proper', and its capital as Brunei Town. Crawfurd concluded that "the name of the town was not extended to the island by European writers, but by the Mohamedan navigators who conducted the carrying trade of the archipelago before the advent of Europeans". Borneo Proper was first visited by Europeans in the early 16th century, most notably by Antonio Pigafetta, the official chronicler on the Portuguese explorer Ferdinand Magellan's expedition, which called in on the Sultan of Brunei in 1521 (**see page 226**). The Ibans of Sarawak maintain that the name Borneo derives from the Malay *buah* *nyior*, meaning 'coconut', while the Malays had another, less well-known name for the island: Kalimantan. This, according to Crawfurd, was the name of a species of wild mango "and the word... would simply mean 'Isle of Mangoes'". This was the name chosen by Indonesia for its section of the island; for some reason, it is generally translated as 'River of Diamonds' – probably because of the diamond fields near Martapura in the S (**see page 829**).

ENVIRONMENT

Three countries have territory on Borneo, but only one of them, the once all-powerful and now tiny but oil-rich sultanate of Brunei, is an independent sovereign state in itself. It is flanked to the W by the Malaysian state of Sarawak and to the E by Sabah. Sarawak severs and completely surrounds Brunei. Sabah, formerly British North Borneo, and now a Malaysian state, occupies the NE portion of Borneo. The huge area to the S is Kalimantan, Indonesian Borneo, which occupies about ¾ of the island. Kalimantan is divided into 4 provinces which have 24 regencies and five municipalities.

Land

During the Pleistocene period, about 2.5 million years ago, Borneo was joined to mainland Southeast Asia, forming a continent which geologists know as Sundaland. The land bridge to mainland Asia meant that many species – both flora and fauna – arrived in what is now Borneo before it was cut off by rising sea levels. Borneo is part of the Sunda shelf. Its interior is rugged and mountainous and is dissected by many large rivers, navigable deep into the interior. The two biggest rivers are in Kalimantan: the Kapuas flows W from the centre of the island, and the Mahakam flows E. About half of Borneo's land area however, is under 150m – particularly the swampy S coastal region. About half of Indonesia's total swampland is in Kalimantan.

Borneo's highest mountain, Gunung Kinabalu in Sabah (4,101m) is the highest mountain in Southeast Asia (**see page 302**). It is a granite mound called a pluton, which was forced up through the sandstone strata during the Pliocene period, about 15 million years ago. The highest peak in Kalimantan is Gunung Rajah (2,278m) in the Schwaner Range, to the SW. The mountain ranges in the W and centre of the island run east-to-west and curve round to the NE. Borneo's coal, oil and gas-bearing strata are Tertiary deposits which are heavily folded; most of the oil and gas is found off the NW and E coasts. The island is much more geologically stable than neighbouring Sulawesi or Java – the so-called 'ring of fire'. Borneo only experiences about 4 mild earthquakes a year compared with 40-50 on other nearby islands. But because there are no active volcanoes, Borneo's soils are not particularly rich.

Climate

Borneo has a typical equatorial monsoon climate: the weather usually follows predictable patterns, although in recent years it has been less predictable – a phenomenon some environmentalists attribute to deforestation. Temperatures are fairly uniform, averaging 23-33°C during the day and rarely dropping below 20°C at night, except in the mountains, where they can drop to below 10°C. Most rainfall occurs between November and January during the NE monsoon; this causes rivers to flood, and there are many short, sharp cloudbursts. The dry season runs from May to September. It is characterized by dry south-easterly winds and is the best time to visit. Rainfall generally increases towards the interior; most of Borneo receives about 2,000-3,000 mm a year, although some upland areas get more than 4,000 mm.

Flora and fauna

Borneo's ancient rainforests are rich in flora and fauna, including over 9,000 species of flowering plant, 200 species of mammals, 570 species of birds, 100 species of snake, 250 species of fresh water fish and 1,000 species of butterfly. The theory of natural selection enunciated by Victorian naturalist Alfred Russel Wallace (**see page 905**) – while that other great Victorian scientist Charles Darwin was coming to similar conclusions several thousand miles away – was influenced by Wallace's observations in Borneo. He travelled widely in Sarawak between 1854 and 1862.

Flora

Borneo's jungle is disappearing fast, and since the mid-1980s there has been a mounting international environmental campaign against deforestation – particularly in Sarawak (**see page 282**). But other parts of the island are also suffering rapid deforestation, notably Sabah and East Kalimantan (**see page 839**). The best known timber trees fall into three categories, all of them hardwoods. Heavy hardwoods include *selangan batu* and *resak*; medium hardwoods include *kapur, keruing* and *keruntum*; light hardwoods include *madang tabak, ramin* and *meranti*. There are both peat-swamp and hill varieties of meranti, which is one of the most valuable export logs. On average, there are about 25 commercial tree species per hectare, but because they are hard to extract, selective logging is rarely practiced.

The main types of forest include: **lowland rainforest** (mixed dipterocarp) on slopes up to 600m. Dipterocarp forest is stratified into 3 main layers, the top one rising to heights of 45m. In the top layer, trees' crowns interlock to form a closed canopy of foliage. The word 'dipterocarp' comes from the Greek and means 'two-winged fruit'. The leaf-like appendages of the mature dipterocarp fruits have 'wings' which makes them spin as they fall to the ground, like giant sycamore seeds. Some species have more than 2 wings but are all members of the dipterocarp family. **Montane forest** occurs at altitudes above 600m; above 1,200m mossy forest predominates. Many of the rainforest trees are an important resource for Dayak communities. The jelutong tree, for example, is tapped like a rubber tree for its sap ('jungle chewing gum') which is used to make tar for waterproof sealants – used in boat-building. It also hardens into a tough but brittle black plastic-like substance used for *parang* (machette) handles.

The low-lying river valleys are characterized by **peat swamp** forest – where the peat is up to 9m thick – which makes wet-rice agriculture impossible. **Heath forest** (or *kerangas* – the Iban word meaning 'land on which rice cannot grow') is found on sandy soils near the coast. Along beaches there are often stretches of **casuarina forest**; the casuarina grows up to 27m, and looks like a conifer, with needle-shaped leaves. **Mangrove** occupies tidal mud flats around sheltered bays and estuaries. The most common mangrove tree is the *bakau* (*Rhizophora*) which grows to heights of about 9m and has stilt roots to trap sediment. Bakau wood is used for pile-house stilts and for charcoal. Further upstream, but still associated with mangrove, is the *nipah* palm (*Nipa fruticans*), whose light-green leaves come from a squat stalk; it was traditionally of great importance as it provided roofing and wickerwork materials.

Mammals

Orang utan (*Pongo pygmaeus*) Walt Disney's film of Rudyard Kipling's *Jungle Book* made the orang utan a big-screen celebrity, dubbing him "the king of the swingers" and "the jungle VIP". Borneo's great red-haired ape is also known as 'the wild man of the jungle', after the translation from the Malay: orang (man), utan (jungle). The orang utan is endemic to the tropical forests of Sumatra and Borneo. It is Asia's only great ape; it has 4 hands, rather than feet, bow-legs and has no tail. The orang utan moves slowly and deliberately, sometimes swinging under branches, although it seldom travels far by arm-swinging. Males of over

15 years old stand up to 1.6m tall and their arms span 2.4m. Adult males (which make loud roars) weigh 50-100 kg – about twice that of adult females (whose call sounds like a long, unattractive belch). Orang utans are said to have the strength of 7 men but they are not aggressive. They are peaceful, gentle animals, particularly with each other. Orang utans have bluey-grey skin and their eyes are close together, giving them an almost human look. Males develop cheek pouches when they reach maturity, which they fill with several litres of air; this is exhaled noisily when they demarcate territory.

Orang utans are easily detected by their nests of bent and broken twigs, which are woven together, in much the same fashion as a sun bear's, in the fork of a tree. They always sleep alone. Orang utans have a largely vegetarian diet consisting of fruit and young leaves, supplemented by termites, bark and birds' eggs. They are usually solitary but the young remain with their mothers until they are 5 or 6 years old. Two adults will occupy an area of about 2 sq km. They can live up to 30 years and a female will have an average of 3-4 young during her lifetime. They mainly inhabit riverine swamp forests or lowland dipterocarp forests.

Proboscis monkey (*Nasalis larvatus*) The proboscis monkey is an extraordinary-looking animal, endemic to Borneo, which lives in lowland forests and mangrove swamps all around the island. Little research has been done on proboscis monkeys; they are notoriously difficult to study as they are so shy. Their fur is reddish-brown and they have white legs, arms, tail and a ruff on the neck, which gives the appearance of a pyjama-suit. Their facial skin is red and the males have grotesquely enlarged, droopy noses; females' noses are shorter and upturned. The male's nose is the subject of some debate among zoologists: what ever else it does, it apparently increases their sex-appeal. To ward off intruders, the nose is straightened out, "like a party whoopee whistle", according to one description. Recently a theory has been advanced that the nose acts as a thermostat, helping to regulate body temperature. But it also tends to get in the way: old males often have to resort to holding their noses up with one hand while stuffing leaves into their mouths with the other.

Proboscises' penises are almost as obvious as their noses – the proboscis male glories in a permanent erection, which is probably why they are rarely displayed in zoos. The other way the males attract females is by violently shaking branches and making spectacular – and sometimes near-suicidal – leaps into the water, in which they attempt to hit as many dead branches as they can on the way down, so as to make the loudest noise possible. The monkeys organize themselves into harems, with one male and several females and young – there are sometimes up to 20 in a group. Young males leave the harem they are born into when the adult male becomes aggressive towards them and they rove around in bachelor groups until they are in a position to form their own harem.

Proboscis monkeys belong to the leaf monkey family, and have large, pouched stomachs to help digest bulky food – they feed almost entirely on the leaves of one tree – the *Sonneratia*. The proboscis is a diurnal animal, but keeps to the shade during the heat of the day. The best time to see them is very early in the morning or around dusk. They can normally be heard before they are seen: they make loud honks, rather like geese; they also groan, squeal and roar. Proboscis monkeys are good swimmers; they even swim underwater for up to 20m – thanks to their partially webbed feet. Males are about twice the size and weight of females. They are known fairly ubiquitously (in both Malaysian and Indonesian Borneo) as 'Orang Belanda', or Dutchmen – which is not entirely complimentary. In Kalimantan they also have other local names including *Bekantan, Bekara, Kahau, Rasong, Pika* and *Batangan*.

Elephant Borneo's wild elephants pose a zoological mystery. They occur only at the far NE tip of the island, at the furthest possible point from their Sumatran and

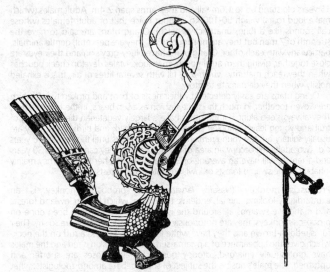

Kenyalang, hornbill image from Roth, Henry (1896) *The natives of Sarawak and British North Borneo*, Truslove & Hanson: London.

The Iban hornbill festival

One of the main Iban festivals is *Gawai Kenyalang*, or the Hornbill Festival. The *kenyalang* – a carved wooden hornbill – traditionally played an important part in the ceremony which preceded head-hunting expeditions, and the often ornate, brightly painted images also made appearances at other *gawais*, or festivals. The kenyalang is carved from green wood and the design varies from area to area. A carved hornbill can be about 2 m long and 1 m high and is stored until a few days before the festival, when it is painted, bringing the carving to life. It is carried in procession and offered *tuak* (rice wine), before being mounted on a carved base on the *tanju*, the longhouse's open verandah. As the singing gets underway, the kenyalang is adorned with specially woven *pua kumbu* (**see page 245**) and then raised off the ground to face enemy territory. Its soul is supposed to attack the village's enemies, destroying their houses and crops.

mainland Southeast Asian relatives. No elephant remains have been found in Sabah, Sarawak or Kalimantan. Zoologists speculate that they were originally introduced at the time of the Javan Majapahit Empire, in the 13th and 14th centuries. Antonio Pigafetta, an Italian historian who visited the Sultanate of Brunei as part of Portuguese explorer Ferdinand Magellan's expedition in July 1521, tells of being taken to visit the sultan on two domesticated elephants, which may have been gifts from another ruler.

It is possible, however, that elephants are native to Borneo and migrated from the Southeast Asian mainland during the Pleistocene when sea levels were lower and land-bridges would have existed between Borneo and the mainland. Their concentration in NE Borneo could be explained by the presence of numerous salt-licks between the Sandakan and Lahad Datu areas of Sabah. This would make the present population a relic of a much larger group of elephants. Borneo's male elephants are up to 2.6m tall; females are usually less than 2.2m. Males' tusks can grow up to 1.7m in length and weigh up to 15 kg each. Mature males are solitary creatures, only joining herds to mate. The most likely places to see elephants in the wild are the Danum Valley Conservation Area (**see page 338**) and the lower Kinabatangan basin (**see page 331**), both in Sabah.

Rhinoceros The two-horned Sumatran rhinoceros was once widespread throughout Sumatra and Borneo (**see page 806**). The population has been greatly reduced by excessive hunting (the horn is worth more than its weight in gold in Chinese apothecaries) and the destruction of their habitat. Most of Borneo's remaining wild population is in Sabah, where some are also being bred in captivity, for they are in serious danger of extinction (**see page 337**).

Birds
Hornbill There are nine types of hornbill on Borneo, the most striking and biggest of which is the rhinoceros hornbill (*Buceros rhinoceros*) – or *kenyalang*. They can grow up to 1.5m long and are mainly black, with a white belly. The long tail feathers are white too, crossed with a thick black bar near the end. They make a remarkable, resonant "GERONK" call in flight, which can be heard over long distances; they honk when resting. Hornbills are usually seen in pairs – they are believed to be monogamous. After mating, the female imprisons herself in a hole in a tree, building a sturdy wall with her own droppings. The male bird fortifies the wall from the outside, using a mulch of mud, grass, sticks and saliva, leaving only a vertical slit for her beak. She remains incarcerated in her cell for about 3 months, during which the male supplies her and the nestlings with food – mainly fruit, lizards, snakes and mice. Usually, only one bird is hatched and reared in the hole and when it is old enough to fly, the female breaks out of the nest hole. Both emerge looking fat and dirty.

The 'bill' itself has no known function, but the males have been seen duelling in mid-air during the courting season. They fly straight at each other and collide head-on. The double-storeyed yellow bill has a projection, called a casque, on top, which has a bright red tip. Most Dayak groups consider the hornbill to have magical powers and the feathers are worn as symbols of heroism. In tribal mythology the bird is associated with the creation of mankind, and is a symbol of the upper world. The hornbill is also the official state emblem of Sarawak. The best place to see hornbills is near wild fig trees – they love the fruit and play an important role in seed dispersal. The helmeted hornbill's bill is heavy and solid and can be carved, like ivory. These bills were highly valued by the Dayaks, and have been traded for centuries. The 3rd largest hornbill is the wreathed hornbill which makes a yelping call and a loud – almost mechanical – noise when it beats its wings. Others species on Borneo include the wrinkled, black, bushy-crested, white-crowned and pied hornbills.

HISTORY

Archaeological evidence from Sarawak shows that *Homo sapiens* was established on Borneo at least 40,000 years ago (**see page 276**). The outside world may have been trading with Borneo from Roman times, and there is evidence in Kaltim (East Kalimantan) of Indian cultural influence from as early as the 4th century. Chinese traders began to visit Borneo from about the 7th century – they traded beads and porcelain in exchange for jungle produce and birds' nests. By the 14th century, this trade appears to have been flourishing, particularly with the newly formed Sultanate of Brunei. The history of the N coast of Borneo is dominated by the Sultanate of Brunei from the 14th-19th centuries (**see page 463**). The Europeans began arriving in the East in the early 1500s, but had little impact on N Borneo until British adventurer James Brooke arrived in Sarawak in 1839. From then on, the Sultan's empire and influence shrank dramatically as he ceded more and more territory to the expansionist White Rajahs (see page 232) and to the British North Borneo Chartered Company to the N (see page 295).

To the S, in what now comprises Kalimantan, it was a similar story. A number of small coastal sultanates grew up (see respective provincial history sections), many of which were tributary states of Brunei, and most of which are thought to have been founded by members of the Brunei nobility. The upriver Dayaks were left largely to themselves. In the 16th century, following the conversion of Banjarmasin to Islam, the religion was embraced by these other sultanates. The Dutch, who first tried to muscle-in on Banjarmasin's pepper trade in the late 1500s, were unsuccessful in establishing themselves in Kalimantan until 1817 when they struck a deal with the Sultan of Banjarmasin. In return for their support in a succession dispute, he ceded to Holland the sultanates he considered under his control. Their claim was never recognized and from the very beginning of their intervention in Indonesia, the Dutch found Kalimantan a difficult proposition.

CULTURE AND LIFE

People

The vast majority of Borneo's population is concentrated in the narrow coastal belt; the more mountainous, jungled interior is sparsely populated by Dayak tribes. Kalimantan accounts for about 28% of Indonesia's land area, but has only 5% of Indonesia's population.

Whereas the word 'native' has taken on a derogatory connotation in English – it tends to smack of colonial arrogance towards indigenous people – this is not the case in Borneo, particularly in Sarawak and Sabah. Tribespeople are proud to be called natives, with a meaning equivalent to that of *bumiputra* – literally, 'sons of the soil' – on the Malaysian peninsula (see page 73). Borneo's 200-odd Dayak tribes are the indigenous people; they are generally fairly light-skinned with rounded facial features and slightly slanted eyes, although physical characteristics vary from tribe to tribe. Their diverse anthropological backgrounds have defied most attempts at neat classification. In Sabah and Sarawak, Dayaks are known by their individual tribal names – except in the case of the Orang Ulu, a collective term for upriver groups. Kalimantan's tribespeople are simply labelled Dayaks, however: few outsiders ever refer to their separate tribal identities, although there are many different groups and subgroups. Today, Dayak cultural identity is strong, and upriver tribespeople are proud of their heritage.

Dayak groups are closely-knit communities and many traditionally live in longhouses. Many Dayaks are shifting cultivators (see page 32). Most are skillful hunters but few made good traders – historically, that was the domain of the coastal Malays and, later, the Chinese. While Dayak communities are represented in all state and provincial governments in Borneo, they only have one province of their own – Kalimantan Tengah (Central Kalimantan), with its capital at Palangkaraya. The Dayaks lived in self-sufficient communities in the interior until they began to come under the influence of Malay coastal sultanates from the 14th and 15th centuries. Some turned to Islam, and more recently, many have converted to Christianity – due to the activities of both Roman Catholic and Protestant missionaries (see page 229). Few Dayaks – other than those in the remoter parts of the interior – still wear their traditional costumes. Most have abandoned them in favour of jeans and T-shirts.

Dayaks throughout Borneo have only been incorporated into the economic mainstream relatively recently. Relations with coastal groups were not always good, and there was also constant fighting between groups. Differences between the coastal peoples and inland tribes throughout Borneo were accentuated as competition for land increased. The situation was aggravated by a general movement of the population towards the coasts. There was constant rivalry between tribes, with the stronger groups taking advantage of the weaker. Today however, Dayak groups have relatively good access to education and many now work in the timber and oil and gas industries, which has caused out-migration from their traditional homelands. This has completely changed the lifestyles of most Dayak communities, who used to live in what some anthropologists term 'primitive affluence'. With a few exceptions, everything the people needed came from the jungle. There was an abundance of fish and wild game and building materials; medicine and plant foods were easily obtainable. Jungle products such as rattan, tree resins, edible birds nests were traded on the coast for steel tools, salt, brass gongs, cooking pots and rice wine jars from China. Villages are now tied to a coastal cash culture and Western subculture.

Religion

In Sabah and Sarawak, apart from the Malays, Bajaus, Illanuns and Suluks, who accepted Islam, all the inland tribes were originally animists. The religion of all the Dayak tribes in Borneo boiled down to placating spirits, and the purpose of tribal totems, images, icons and statues was to chase bad spirits away and attract good ones, which were believed to be capable of bringing fortune and prosperity. Head-hunting (**see page 243**) was central to this belief, and most Dayak tribes practiced it, in the belief that freshly severed heads would bring blessing to their longhouses. Virtually everything had a spirit, and complex rituals and ceremonies were devised to keep them happy. Motifs associated with the spirit world – such as the hornbill (**see page 226**) – dominate artwork and textiles and many of the woodcarvings for sale in art and antique shops had religious significance. Islam began to spread to the tribes of the interior from the late 15th century, but mostly it was confined to coastal districts. Christian missionaries arrived with the Europeans. Both Christianity and Islam had enormous influence on the animist tribes, and many converted en-mass to one or the other. Despite this, many of the old superstitions and ceremonial traditions, which are deeply ingrained, remain a part of Dayak culture today.

The traditional beliefs of Kalimantan's Dayaks is formalized in the *Kaharingan* faith, which, despite the in-roads made by Christianity and Islam, is still practiced by some Mahakam and Barito river groups. The religion became a focus of Dayak cultural identity when Kalteng split from Kalsel province in the late 1950s, and the Indonesian government recognizes it as an official religion, bracketing it (absurdly) with Balinese Hinduism. Kaharingan revolves around spirit and ancestor worship and is characterized by complex sets of rites and rituals, particularly those relating to death and burial. Several months after the initial funeral, a body is exhumed and cleaned and placed in a *sandung* (mausoleum), which is finely carved and decorated, alongside the remains of the deceased's ancestors. The Dayaks believe that after death, a person will join the spirit world. All the different Dayak groups have different variations on this faith.

In 1973 a fanatical Christian revival spread through longhouse communities in Sarawak. In some villages people went to church up to 3 times a day and drinking and dancing were forbidden. Priceless family heirlooms such as beads, charms, statues, totems (including the carved *tegundo* guardian spirits which traditionally stood at the entrance to villages) and old headhunting swords were thrown in the rivers or burned because of their association with magical powers. These objects are an indispensable part of animist beliefs and are considered wholly incompatible with Christian teachings.

SARAWAK

Introduction, 230; Kuching and the Skrang River, 248; Sibu and the Rejang River, 263; Bintulu and Niah caves, 273; Niah National Park, 276; Miri and the Baram River, 279; Gunung Mulu National Park, 285; Bareo and the Kelabit Highlands, 290; Limbang and Liwas, 291.

Maps Sarawak, 231; Kuching, 249; Sibu, 264; Kapit, 267; Upper Rejang, 271; Bintulu, 274; Niah Caves Park, 277; Miri, 280; Gunung Mulu National Park, 286.

INTRODUCTION

Sarawak, 'the land of the hornbill', is the largest state in Malaysia, covering an area of 124,967 sq km in NW Borneo. In the mid-19th century, the naturalist Charles Darwin described Sarawak as "one great wild, untidy, luxuriant hothouse, made by nature for herself". Despite the state's rapacious logging industry, which has drawn world attention to Sarawak in recent years, more than two-thirds of its land area (roughly equivalent to that of England and Scotland combined) is still covered in jungle. Much of it is still as the Victorian naturalist, Alfred Russel Wallace (whose theories of natural selection influenced Darwin) saw it in 1855. "For hundreds of miles in every direction," he wrote, "a magnificent forest extended over plain and mountain, rock and morass". Sarawak has swampy coastal plain, a hinterland of undulating foothills and an interior of steep-sided, jungle-covered mountains. The lowlands and plain are dissected by a network of broad rivers which are the main arteries of communication. Sarawak has a population of around 1.5 million, most of which is settled along the rivers.

About 30% of the population is made up of Iban tribespeople – who used to be known as the 'Sea Dayaks' – former headhunters, who live in longhouses on the lower reaches of the rivers. Chinese immigrants, whose forebears arrived during the 19th century, make up another 30%. A fifth of the population is Malay – most are native Sarawakians, but some came from the peninsula after the state joined the Malaysian Federation in 1963. The rest of Sarawak's inhabitants are indigenous tribal groups – of which the main ones are the Melanau, the Bidayuh and upriver Orang Ulu such as the Kenyah, Kayan and Kelabits; the Penan are among Southeast Asia's few remaining hunter-gatherers.

For over 150 years, Sarawak was under the rule of the 'White Rajahs' who tried to keep the peace between warring tribes of headhunters. The Brooke family ran Sarawak as their private country and their most obvious legacies are the public buildings in Kuching, the state capital, and the forts along the rivers. Outside Kuching, the towns have little to offer; most are predominantly Chinese, they are mainly modern, without much character. One or two are boom-towns, having grown rich on the back of the logging and oil and gas industries. From a tourist's point of view, the towns are just launching-pads for the longhouses and jungle upriver.

For information on geography, climate, flora and fauna, **see pages 223-227**).

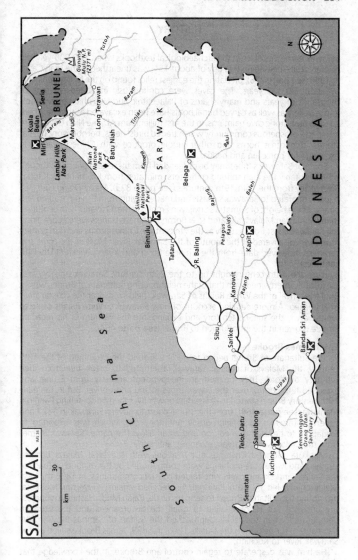

HISTORY

Sarawak earned its place in the archaeological textbooks when a 40,000-year-old human skull – belonging to a boy of about 15 – was unearthed in the Niah Caves in 1958 (**see page 276**), predating the earliest relics found on the Malay peninsula by about 30,000 years. The caves were continuously inhabited for tens of thousands of years and many shards of Palaeolithic and Neolithic pottery, tools and jewellery as well as carved burial boats have been excavated at the site. There are also prehistoric cave paintings. In the first millennium AD, the Niah Caves were home to a prosperous community, which traded birds' nests, hornbill ivory, bezoar stones, rhinoceros horns and other jungle produce with Chinese traders in exchange for porcelain and beads.

Some of Sarawak's tribes may be descended from these cave people, although others, notably the Iban shifting cultivators, migrated from Kalimantan's Kapuas River valley from the 16th-19th centuries (**see page 823**). Malay *Orang Laut,* sea people, migrated to Sarawak's coasts and made a living from fishing, trading and piracy. At the height of Sumatra's Srivijayan Empire in the 11th and 12th centuries, many Sumatran Malays migrated to N Borneo. Chinese traders were active along the Sarawak coast from as early as the 7th century: Chinese coins and Han pottery have been discovered at the mouth of the Sarawak River. Most of the coins and ceramics, however, date from the Chinese Song and Yuan periods (11th-14th centuries).

From the 14th century right up to the 20th century, Sarawak's history was inextricably intertwined with that of the neighbouring Sultanate of Brunei, which, until the arrival of the White Rajahs of Sarawak, held sway over the coastal areas of N Borneo. A more detailed account of how Sarawak's White Rajahs came to whittle away the sultan's territory and expand into the vacuum of his receding empire is given in the introduction to Brunei (**see page 464**).

Enter James Brooke

As the Sultanate of Brunei began to decline around the beginning of the 18th century, the Malays of coastal Sarawak attempted to break free from their tributary overlord. They claimed an independent ancestry from Brunei and exercised firm control over the Dayak tribes inland and upriver. But in the early 19th century Brunei started to reassert its power over them, dispatching Pangiran Mahkota (**see page 464**), from the Brunei court to govern Sarawak in 1827 and supervise the mining of high-grade antimony ore, which was exported to Singapore to be used in medicine and as an alloy. The name 'Sarawak' comes from the Malay word *serawak,* meaning 'antimony'.

Mahkota founded Kuching, but relations with the local Malays became strained and Mahkota's problems were compounded by the marauding Ibans of the Saribas and Skrang rivers who raided coastal communities. In 1836 the local Malay chiefs, led by Datu Patinggi Ali, rebelled against Governor Mahkota, prompting the Sultan of Brunei to send his uncle, Rajah Muda Hashim to suppress the uprising. But Hashim failed to quell the disturbances and the situation deteriorated when the rebels approached the Sultan of Sambas (now in NW Kalimantan) for help from the Dutch. Then, in 1839, James Brooke sailed up the Sarawak River to Kuching.

Hashim was desperate to regain control and Brooke, in the knowledge that the British would support any action that countered the threat of Dutch influence, struck a deal with him. He pressed Hashim to grant him the governorship of Sarawak in exchange for suppressing the rebellion, which he duly did. In 1842 Brooke became Rajah of Sarawak. Pangiran Mahkota – the now disenfranchised former governor of Sarawak – formed an alliance with an Iban pirate chief on the

Skrang River, while another Brunei prince, Pangiran Usop, joined Illanun pirates. Malaysian historian J Kathirithamby-Wells writes: "... piracy and politics became irrevocably linked and Brooke's battle against his political opponents became advertised as a morally justified war against the pirate communities of the coast."

The suppression of piracy in the 19th century became a full-time occupation for the rulers of Sarawak and Brunei – although the court of Brunei was well known to have derived a substantial chunk of its income from piracy. Rajah James Brooke believed that as long as pirates remained free to pillage the coasts, commerce would not pick up and his kingdom would never develop; ridding Sarawak's estuaries of pirates – both Iban ('Sea Dayaks') and Illanun – became an act of political survival. In his history of the White Rajahs, Robert Payne writes:

> "Nearly every day people came to Kuching with tales about the pirates: how they had landed in a small creek, spread out, made their way to a village, looted everything in sight, murdered everyone they could lay their hands on, and then vanished as swiftly as they came. The Sultan of Brunei was begging for help against them."

Anti-piracy missions afforded James Brooke an excuse to extend his kingdom, as he worked his way up the coasts, 'pacifying' the Sea Dayak pirates. Brooke declared war on them and with the help of Royal Naval Captain Henry Keppel (of latter-day Singapore's Keppel Shipyard fame), he led a number of punitive raids against the Iban 'Sea Dayaks' in 1833, 1834 and 1849. "The assaults", writes D J M Tate in *Rajah Brooke's Borneo*, "largely achieved their purpose, and were

Piracy: the resurgence of an ancient scourge

In Feb 1992, the International Maritime Bureau convened a conference on Piracy in the Far East Region in Kuala Lumpur. The IMB had become alarmed at the increase in piracy and by the fact that attacks were becoming more ferocious. The number of ships arriving in Singapore that had suffered pirate attacks doubled to 61 in 1991. A total of nearly 150 pirate attacks were logged throughout Southeast Asia that year, compared with 60 in 1990 and 3 in 1989. Some ships just suffer hit-and-run attacks; other pirates hijack entire vessels, whose cargo is removed and the ship resold under another name. On 2 May 1991, for example, the *Hai Hui I*, a Singapore-registered ship bound for Cambodia was attacked and relieved of its cargo in the Strait of Singapore. The pirates seized 400 tonnes of electronics, motorcycles and beer. Most attacks took place in the Strait of Melaka, in the Riau Archipelago, to the NW of Sarawak in the South China Sea, and around Sabah (**see page 337**).

Many modern pirates use high-speed boats to escape into international waters and avoid capture by racing from one country's waters into another's. Cooperative international action offers the only way to successfully patrol the shipping lanes. Following the IMB conference, a Regional Piracy Centre was set up in Kuala Lumpur.

But while modern shipping companies might consider the rise in piracy a new and dangerous threat, there is nothing new about piracy in Southeast Asian waters. For centuries, pirates have murdered and pillaged their way along the region's coasts, taking hundreds of slaves as part of their booty. As far back as the 6th century, pirates are thought to have been responsible for the destruction and abandonment of the ancient Hindu capital of Langkasuka, in the NW Malaysian state of Kedah. Piracy grew as trade flourished: the Strait of Melaka and the South China Sea were perfect haunts, being on the busy trade routes between China, India, the Middle East and Europe. Most of the pirates were the Malay Orang Laut (sea gypsies) and Bugis who lived in the Riau Archipelago, the Acehnese of N Sumatra, the Ibans of the Sarawak estuaries and – most feared of all – the Illanun and Balinini pirates of Sulu and Mindanao in the Philippines. The Illanuns were particularly ferocious pirates, sailing in huge *perahus* with up to 150 slaves as oarsmen, in as many as three tiers. The name *lanun* means pirate in Malay.

James Brooke: the white knight errant

James Brooke lived the life of a *Boy's Own* comic-book hero. To the socialites of London, who idolised him, he was the king of an exotic far-away country, on a mysterious jungled island, inhabited by roving tribes of headhunters. It was a romantic image, but while it was also a tough life, it was not far from the truth. The Brookes were a family of benevolent despots, characterized by historian Robert Payne as "tempestuous and dedicated men, who sometimes quarrelled violently among themselves, but closed ranks whenever the fortunes of their people were at stake. They were proud and possessive, but also humble." There were 3 White Rajahs, who ruled for over a century, but it was James Brooke, with his forceful personality, violent temper, vengeful instincts but compassion for his people, that set the tone and created the legend.

James was born in India in 1803, the son of a High Court judge in Benares. He joined the Indian army, and fought in the First Anglo-Burmese War as a cavalry officer, where he was mentioned in dispatches for "most conspicuous gallantry." But in 1825 he was hit in the chest by a bullet and almost left for dead on the battlefield. He was forced to return to England where any military ambitions he might have had were dashed by the severity of his injury. He recovered enough to make 2 trips to the East in the 1830s, on one of which he visited Penang and Singapore where he became an admirer of Sir Thomas Stamford Raffles, Singapore's founding father (see page 372). Back in England, he bought a schooner, *The Royalist*, and drew up plans to sail to Maurdu Bay (N Sabah), to explore the fabled lake at Kini Ballu (see page 320). His trip did not work out as planned.

The Royalist arrived in Singapore in 1839 and the governor asked Brooke to deliver a letter of thanks to Rajah Muda Hashim, the ruler in Kuching, who had rescued some shipwrecked British sailors. He called in briefly, as promised, was intrigued with what he found, but sailed on. When he returned a year later, the Rajah Mudah was still struggling to contain the rebellion of local Malay chiefs. Hashim said that if Brooke helped suppress the rebellion, he could have the Sarawak River area as his and the title of Rajah. Brooke took him up on the offer, quelled the revolt and after leaning heavily on Hashim to keep his word, became acting Rajah of Sarawak on 24 Sept 1841. His title was confirmed by the Sultan of Brunei the following year.

The style of Brooke's government – which also characterized that of his successors – is described by historian Mary Turnbull as "a paternal, informal applauded in the Straits, but the appalling loss of life incurred upset many drawing-room humanitarians in Britain." There were an estimated 25,000 pirates living along the N Borneo coast when Brooke became Rajah. He led many punitive expeditions against them, culminating in his notorious battle against the Saribas pirate fleet in 1849.

In that incident, Brooke ambushed and killed hundreds of Saribas Dayaks at Batang Maru. The barbarity of the ambush (which was reported in the *Illustrated London News*) outraged public opinion in Britain and in Singapore – a commission of inquiry in Singapore acquitted Brooke, but badly damaged his prestige. In the British parliament, he was cast as a 'mad despot' who had to be prevented from committing further massacres. But the action led the Sultan of Brunei to grant him the Saribas and Skrang districts (now Sarawak's Second Division) in 1853, marking the beginning of the Brookes' relentless expansionist drive. Eight years later, James Brooke persuaded the sultan to give him what became Sarawak's Third Division, after he drove out the Illanun pirates who had disrupted the sago trade from Mukah and Oya, around Bintulu.

In 1857, James Brooke ran into more trouble. Chinese Hakka goldminers –

government based upon consultation with local community chiefs". Brooke realized the importance of maintaining tribal laws and observing local customs; he also recognized that without his protection, the people of Sarawak would be open to exploitation by Europeans and Chinese. He determined to keep such influences out. In 1842, shortly after he was confirmed as Rajah, he wrote: "I hate the idea of a Utopian government, with laws cut and dried ready for the natives... I am going on slowly and surely basing everything on their own laws, consulting all the headmen at every stage, instilling what I think is right – separating the abuses from the customs." Like his successors, James Brooke had great respect for the Dayaks and the Malays, whom he treated as equals. In the 1840s he wrote: "Sarawak belongs to the Malays, Sea Dayaks, Land Dayaks, Kenyahs, Milanos, Muruts, Kadayans, Bisayahs, and other tribes, and not to us. It is for them we labour, not for ourselves."

Unlike most colonial adventurers of the time, Brooke was not in it for the money. He had a hopeless head for figures and his country was constantly in debt – it would have gone bankrupt if it were not for an eccentric English spinster, Angela Burdett-Coutts, who lent him large amounts of money. In his history of *The White Rajahs of Sarawak*, Robert Payne wrote that "he was incapable of drawing up a balance sheet [and] could never concentrate upon details. He had the large view always and large views incline dangerously towards absolute power, and he had seized power with all the strength and cunning that was in him. He possessed the Elizabethan love for power, believing that some Englishmen are granted a special dispensation by God to wield power to the uttermost."

By pacifying pirate-infested coastal districts, Brooke persuaded the Sultan of Brunei to cede him more and more territory, so that towards the end of his reign, Sarawak was a sizeable country. An attack of smallpox, combined with the emotional traumas of a Chinese rebellion in 1857 and the public inquiry into his punitive ambush on the Saribas pirates, seems to have broken his spirit, however. His illness aged him, although an old Malay man, who knew him well, said his eyes remained "fierce like those of a crocodile". Rajah Sir James Brooke (he was knighted by Queen Victoria) visited Sarawak for the last time in 1863 following a succession dispute in which he disinherited his heir, Brooke Johnson. He retired to Dorset in England a disillusioned and embittered man. On Christmas Eve 1867 he had a stroke, and died 6 months later. When news of his death reached Sarawak, guns sounded a thunderous salute across the Sarawak River.

who had been in Bau (further up the Sarawak River) longer than he had been in Kuching, had grown resentful of his attempts to stamp out the opium trade and their secret societies. They attacked Kuching, set the Malay kampungs ablaze and killed several European officials; Brooke escaped by swimming across the river from his *astana*. His nephew, Charles, led a group of Skrang Dayaks to chase after the Hakka invaders, who fled across the border into Dutch Borneo; about 1,000 were killed by the Ibans on the way; 2,500 survived. Historian Robert Payne writes: "The fighting lasted for more than a month. From time to time Dayaks would return with strings of heads, which they cleaned and smoked over slow fires, especially happy when they could do this in full view of the Chinese in the bazaars who sometimes recognized people they had known." Payne says Brooke was plagued by guilt over how he handled the Chinese rebellion, for so many deaths could not easily be explained away. Neither James nor Charles ever fully trusted the Chinese ever again, although the Teochew, Cantonese and Hokkien merchants in Kuching never caused them any trouble.

The second generation: Rajah Charles Brooke
Charles Johnson (who changed his name to Brooke after his elder brother, Brooke

Johnson, had been disinherited by James for insubordination) became the second Rajah of Sarawak in 1863. He ruled for nearly 50 years. Charles did not have James Brooke's forceful personality, and was much more reclusive – probably as a result of working in remote jungle outposts for 10 years in government service. Historian Robert Payne notes that "In James Brooke there was something of the knight errant at the mercy of his dream. Charles was the pure professional, a stern soldier who thought dreaming was the occupation of fools. There was no nonsense about him." He engendered great loyalty, however, in his administrators, who he worked hard for little reward.

Charles maintained his uncle's consultative system of government and formed a Council Negeri, or national council – comprised of his top government officials, Malay leaders and tribal headmen – which met every couple of years to hammer out policy changes. His frugal financial management meant that by 1877 Sarawak was out of debt and the economy gradually expanded. The country was not a wealthy one, however, and had very few natural resources – its soils proved unsuitable for agriculture. In the 1880s, Charles' faith in the Chinese community was sufficiently restored to allow Chinese immigration, and the government subsidized the new settlers. By using 'friendly' downriver Dayak groups to subdue belligerent tribes upriver, Charles managed to pacify the interior by 1880.

When Charles took over from his ailing uncle in 1863, he found himself in charge of a large country; but he proved to be even more of an expansionist. In 1868 he tried to take control of the Baram River valley, but London did not approve the cession of the territory until 1882. It became the Fourth Division; in 1884, Charles acquired the Trusan Valley from the Sultan of Brunei, and in 1890, he annexed Limbang ending a 6-year rebellion by local chiefs against the sultan. The 2 territories were united to form the Fifth Division, after which Sarawak completely surrounded Brunei. In 1905, the British North Borneo Chartered Company gave up the Lawas Valley to Sarawak too. "By 1890," writes Robert Payne, "Charles was ruling over a country as large as England and Scotland with the help of about twenty European officers." When the Second World War broke out in 1914, Charles was in England, and he ruled Sarawak from Cirencester.

The third generation: Charles Vyner Brooke
At the age of 86, Charles handed the reins to his eldest son, Charles Vyner Brooke, in 1916 and died the following year. Vyner was 42 when he became Rajah and had already served his father's government for nearly 20 years. "Vyner was a man of peace, who took no delight in bloodshed and ruled with humanity and compassion," writes Robert Payne. He was a delegator by nature, and under him the old paternalistic style of government gave way to a more professional bureaucracy. On the centenary of the Brooke administration in Sept 1941, Vyner promulgated a written constitution, and renounced his autocratic powers in favour of working in cooperation with a Supreme Council. This was vehemently opposed by his nephew and heir, Anthony Brooke, who saw it as a move to undermine his succession. To protest against this, and his uncle's decision to appoint a mentally deranged Muslim Englishman as his Chief Secretary, Anthony left for Singapore. The Rajah dismissed him summarily from the service in Sept 1941. Three months later the Japanese Imperial Army invaded; Vyner Brooke was in Australia at the time, and his younger brother, Bertram, was ill in London.

Japanese troops took Kuching on Christmas Day 1941 having captured the Miri oilfield a few days earlier. European administrators were interned and many later died. A Kuching-born Chinese, Albert Kwok, led an armed resistance against the Japanese in neighbouring British North Borneo (Sabah) – **see page 296** – but in Sarawak, there was no organized guerrilla movement. Iban tribespeople instilled fear into the occupying forces, however, by roaming the jungle taking Japanese heads, which were proudly added to much older longhouse head galleries.

Despite the Brooke regime's century-long effort to stamp out head-hunting, the practice was encouraged by Tom Harrisson (one of Sarawak's most famous 'adopted' sons) who parachuted into the Kelabit Highlands towards the end of World War II and put together an irregular army of upriver tribesmen to fight the Japanese. He offered them 'ten-bob-a-nob' for Japanese heads. Australian forces liberated Kuching on 11 Sept 1945 and Sarawak was placed under Australian Military Administration for 7 months.

After the war, the Colonial Office in London decided the time had come to bring Sarawak into the modern era, replacing the anachronous White Rajahs, introducing an education system and building a rudimentary infrastructure. The Brookes had become an embarrassment to the British government as they continued to squabble among themselves. Anthony Brooke desperately wanted to claim what he felt was his, while the Colonial Office wanted Sarawak to become a crown colony or revert to Malay rule. No one was sure whether Sarawak wanted the Brookes back or not.

Konfrontasi

The birth of the Federation of Malaysia on 31 Aug 1963 was not helped by the presence of heckling spectators. The Philippines was opposed to British North Borneo (Sabah) joining the federation because the territory had been a dependency of the Sultan of Sulu for over 170 years until he had agreed to lease it to the North Borneo Chartered Company in 1877 (**see page 295**). But Indonesia's objection to the formation of the federation was even more vociferous. In Jakarta, crowds were chanting "Crush Malaysia!" at President Sukarno's bidding. He launched an undeclared war against Malaysia, which became known as *konfrontasi* – or confrontation.

Indonesian armed forces made numerous incursions across the jungled frontier between Kalimantan and the 2 new East Malaysian states; it also landed commandos on the Malaysian peninsula and despatched 300 saboteurs who infiltrated Singapore and launched a bombing campaign. Sarawakian Communists fought alongside Indonesians in the Konfrontasi and there were countless skirmishes with Malaysian and British counter-terrorist forces in which many were killed. Sukarno even managed to secure Soviet weapons, dispatched by Moscow "to help Indonesia crush Malaysia". Konfrontasi fizzled out in 1965 following the Communist-inspired coup attempt in Indonesia (**see page 502**), which finally dislodged Sukarno from power.

The end of empire

In Feb 1946, the ageing Vyner shocked his brother Bertram and his nephew Anthony, the Rajah Muda (or heir apparent), by issuing a proclamation urging the people of Sarawak to accept the King of England as their ruler. In doing so he effectively handed the country over to Britain. Vyner thought the continued existence of Sarawak as the private domain of the Brooke family an anachronism; but Anthony thought it a betrayal. The British government sent a commission to Sarawak to ascertain what the people wanted. In May 1946, the Council Negri agreed – by a 19-16 majority – to transfer power to Britain, provoking protests and demonstrations and resulting in the assassination of the British governor by a Malay in Sibu in 1949. He and 3 other anti-cessionists were sentenced to death. Two years later, Anthony Brooke, who remained deeply resentful about the demise of the Brooke dynasty, abandoned his claim and urged his supporters to end their campaign.

As a British colony, Sarawak's economy expanded and oil and timber production increased which funded the much-needed expansion of education and health services. As with British North Borneo (Sabah), Britain was keen to give

Sarawak political independence and, following Malaysian independence in 1957, saw the best means to this end as being through the proposal of Malaysian Prime Minister Tunku Abdul Rahman, who suggested the formation of a federation to include Singapore, Sarawak, Sabah and Brunei as well as the peninsula. In the end, Brunei opted out, Singapore left after 2 years, but Sarawak and Sabah joined the federation, having accepted the recommendations of the British government. Indonesia's President Sukarno denounced the move, claiming it was all part of a neo-colonialist conspiracy. He declared a policy of confrontation – *Konfrontasi*. A United Nations commission which was sent to ensure that the people of Sabah and Sarawak wanted to be part of Malaysia reported that Indonesia's objections were unfounded.

Communists had been active in Sarawak since the 1930s. The *Konfrontasi* afforded the Sarawak Communist Organization (SCO) Jakarta's support against the Malaysian government. The SCO joined forces with the North Kalimantan Communist Party (NKCO) and were trained and equipped by Indonesia's President Sukarno. But following Jakarta's brutal suppression of the Indonesian Communists – the Perserikatan Komunis di India (PKI) – in the wake of the attempted coup in 1965 (see page 502), Sarawak's Communists fled back across the Indonesian border, along with their Kalimantan comrades. There they continued to wage guerrilla war against the Malaysian government throughout the 1970s. The Sarawak state government offered amnesties to guerrillas wanting to come out of hiding. In 1973 the NKCP leader surrendered along with 482 other guerrillas. A handful remained in the jungle, most of them in the hills around Kuching. The last of them surrendered in 1990.

CULTURE AND LIFE

People

About 30% of Sarawak's population is Iban, another 30% Chinese, 20% is Malay and the remaining fifth is divided into other tribal groups. The people of the interior are classified as Proto-Malays and Deutero-Malays and are divided into at least 14 distinct tribal groups including Iban, Murut (see page 297), Melanau, Bidayuh, Kenyah, Kayan, Kelabit and Penan. In upriver Dayak communities, both men and women traditionally distend their earlobes with brass weights – long earlobes are considered a beauty feature – and practice extensive body tattooing.

Tribal tattoos

Tattooing is practiced by many indigenous groups in Sarawak, but the most intricate designs are those of the upriver Orang Ulu tribes. Designs vary from group to group and for different parts of the body. Circular designs are mostly used for the shoulder, chest or wrists, while stylized dragon-dogs (*aso*), scorpions and dragons are used on the thigh and, for the Iban, on the throat. Tattoos can mean different things; for the man it is a symbol of bravery and for women, a good tattoo is a beauty-feature. More elaborate designs often denote high social status in Orang Ulu communities – the Kayans, for example, reserved the *aso* design for the upper classes and slaves were barred from tattooing themselves at all. In these Orang Ulu groups, the ladies have the most impressive tattoos; the headman's daughter has her hands, arms and legs completely covered in a finely patterned tattoo. Designs are first carved on a block of wood, which is then smeared with ink. The design is printed on the body and then punctured into the skin with needles dipped in ink, usually made from a mixture of sugar, water and soot. Rice is smeared over the inflamed area to prevent infection, but it usually swells up for some time.

Shifting cultivation – how to grow hill rice

As you wind your way upriver on Sarawak's express boats, the hillsides on either bank have been shaved of their jungle: evidence of shifting cultivation (**see page 32**). The Iban, who live in the middle reaches of Sarawak's big rivers, have always been shifting cultivators – the deep peat soils meant it was impossible to farm wet-rice. Any secondary forest (*belukar*) seen growing on the riverside slopes is really just fallow land, and in 8-15 years' time, it will be cut again and the *ladang* will be replanted. The Malaysian government claims there are 3 million hectares of land like this in Sarawak, left idle, through slash-and-burn cultivation. In defence of its environmental record, it says shifting cultivators are more destructive than logging firms and cause serious soil erosion.

What the government tends to overlook, however, is that the rivers were clear before the loggers arrived and that the swidden farmers managed highly productive agricultural systems. As long as the land is allowed to lie fallow for long enough, the Iban can produce rice with far less effort than lowland wet rice farmers. The Iban clear their designated hillsides in the middle of the year and burn them off in Aug. In Sept, planting starts: holes are made in the soot-blackened soil with sharp-pointed dibble-sticks called *tugal*. Women drop a few grains into each hole and the rice is interplanted with maize. Harvesting is done by the women, who use special knives called *ketap*.

For the longhouse communities, the staple diet is hill rice, which is cultivated with slash-and-burn farming techniques.

Malays About half of Sarawak's 300,000-strong Malay community lives around the state capital; most of the other half lives in the Limbang Division, near Brunei. The Malays traditionally live near the coast, although today there are small communities far upriver. There are some old wooden Malay houses, with carved facades, in the kampungs along the banks of the Sarawak river in Kuching; other traditional Malay houses still stand on Jalan Datus in Kuching. In all Malay communities, the mosque is the centre of the village, but while their faith is important to them, the strictures of Islam are generally less rigorously enforced in Sarawak than on the peninsula. Of all the Malays in Malaysia, the Sarawak Malays are probably the most easy-going. During the days of the White Rajahs, the Malays were recruited into government service, as they were on the Malay peninsula. They were renowned as good administrators and the men were mostly literate in Jawi script. Over the years there has been much intermarriage between the Malay and Melanau communities. Traditionally, the Malays were fishermen and farmers.

Chinese Hakka goldminers had already settled at Bau, upriver from Kuching, long before James Brooke arrived in 1839. Cantonese, Teochew and Hokkien merchants also set up in Kuching, but the Brookes did not warm to the Chinese community, believing the traders would exploit the Dayak communities if they were allowed to venture upriver. In the 1880s, however, Rajah Charles Brooke allowed the immigration of large numbers of Chinese – mainly Foochows – who settled in coastal towns like Sibu (**see page 263**). Many became farmers and ran rubber smallholdings. The Sarawak government subsidized the immigrants for the first year. During the Brooke era, the only government-funded schools were for Malays and few tribal people ever received a formal education. The Chinese however, set up and funded their own private schools and many attended Christian missionary schools, so they formed a relatively prosperous, educated elite. Now the Chinese comprise nearly a third of the state's population and are almost as numerous as the Iban; they are the middlemen, traders, shopkeepers, timber *towkays* (magnates) and express-boat owners.

Ibans Sarawak's best known erstwhile head-hunters make up nearly a third of the state's population and while some have moved to coastal towns for work, many remain in their traditional longhouses. But with Iban men now earning good money in the timber and oil industries, it is increasingly common to see longhouses bristling with television aerials, equipped with fridges, self-cleaning ovens and flush-toilets, and with Land Cruisers in the car park. Even modern longhouses retain the traditional features of gallery, verandah and doors. The Iban are an out-going people and usually extend a warm welcome to visitors. Iban women are skilled weavers; even today a girl is not considered eligible until she has proven her skills at the loom by weaving a ceremonial textile, the *pua kumbu* (**see page 245**). The Ibans love to party, and during the Gawai harvest festival (Jun), visitors are particularly welcome to drink copious amounts of *tuak* (rice wine) and dance through the night.

The Iban are shifting cultivators who originated in the Kapuas River basin of W Kalimantan and migrated into Sarawak's Second Division in the early 16th century, settling along the Batang Lupar, Skrang and Saribas rivers. By the early 19th century, they had begun to spill into the Rejang River valley. It was this growing pressure on land as more and more migrants settled in the river valleys that led to fighting and headhunting (**see page 243**). Probably because they were shifting cultivators, the Iban remained in closely bonded family groups and were a classless society. Historian Mary Turnbull says "they retained their pioneer social organization of nuclear family groups living together in longhouses and did not evolve more sophisticated social institutions. Long-settled families acquired prestige, but the Ibans did not merge into tribes and had neither chiefs, *rakyat* class, nor slaves."

The Ibans joined local Malay chiefs and turned to piracy – which is how Europeans first came into contact with them. They were dubbed 'Sea Dayaks' as a result – which is really a misnomer as they are an inland people. The name stuck, however, and in the eyes of Westerners, it distinguished them from 'Land Dayaks' – who were the Bidayuh people from the Sarawak River area (**see page 241**). While Rajah James Brooke only won the Ibans' loyalty after he had crushed them in battle (**see page 234**), he had great admiration of them, and they bore no bitterness towards him. He once described them as "good-looking a set of men, or devils, as one could cast eye on. Their wiry and supple limbs might have been compared to the troops of wild horses that followed Mazeppa in his perilous flight." The Iban have a very easy-going attitude to love and sex (best explained in Redmond O'Hanlon's book *Into the Heart of Borneo*). Free love is the general rule among Iban communities which have not become evangelical Christians, although once married, the Iban divorce rate is low and they are monogamous.

Melanaus The Melanau are a handsome, relaxed and humorous people. Rajah James Brooke, like generations of men before and after him, thought the Melanau girls particularly pretty. He said that they had "agreeable countenances, with the dark, rolling, open eye of the Italians, and nearly as fair as most of that race". The Melanau live along the coast between the Baram and Rejang rivers; originally they lived in magnificent communal houses built high off the ground, like the one that has been reconstructed at the Cultural Village in Kuching, but these have long since disappeared. The houses were designed to afford protection from incessant pirate raids (**see page 233**), for the Melanau were easy pickings, being coastal people. Their stilt-houses were often up to 12m off the ground. Today most Melanau live in Malay-style pile-houses facing the river. Hedda Morrison, in her classic 1957 book *Sarawak*, says: "As a result of living along the rivers in swamp country, the Melanaus are an exceptionally amphibious people. The children learn to swim almost before they can walk. Nearly all progress is by canoe, sometimes even to visit the house next door."

The traditional Melanau fishing boat is called a *barong*. Melanau fishermen employed a unique fishing technique. They would anchor palm leaves at sea as they discovered that shoals of fish would seek refuge under them. After rowing out to the leaves, one fisherman would dive off his barong and chase the fish into the nets which his colleague hung over the side. The Melanaus were also noted for their sago production – which they ate instead of rice (see page 973). At Kuching's Cultural Village there is a demonstration of traditional sago production, showing how the starch-bearing pith is removed, mashed, dried and ground into flour. Most Melanau are now Muslim and have assimilated with the Malays through intermarriage. Originally, however, they were animists (animist Melanau are called *Likaus*) and were particularly famed for their elaborately carved 'sickness images', which represented the form of spirits which caused specific illnesses (see page 246).

Bidayuh In the 19th century, Sarawak's European community called the Bidayuh 'Land Dayaks' – mainly to distinguish them from the Iban 'Sea Dayak' pirates. The Bidayuh make up 8.4% of the population and are concentrated to the W of the Kuching area, towards the Kalimantan border. There are also related groups living in West Kalimantan. They were virtually saved from extinction by the White Rajahs. Because the Bidayuh were quiet, mild-mannered people, they were at the mercy of the Iban head-hunters and the Brunei Malays who taxed and enslaved them. The Brookes afforded them protection from both groups.

Most live in modern longhouses and are dry rice farmers. Their traditional longhouses are exactly like Iban ones, but without the *tanju* verandah. The Bidayuh tribe comprises 5 sub-groups: the Jagoi, Biatah, Bukar-Sadong, Selakau and Lara, all of whom live in far W Sarawak. They are the state's best traditional plumbers, and are known for their ingenious gravity-fed bamboo water-supply systems. They are bamboo-specialists, making everything from cooking pots and utensils to finely carved musical instruments (see page 245) from it. Among other tribal groups, the Bidayuh are renowned for their rice wine and sugar cane toddy. Henry Keppel, who with Rajah James Brooke fought the Bidayuhs' dreaded enemies, the Sea Dayaks, described an evening spent with the Land Dayaks thus: "They ate and drank, and asked for everything, but stole nothing."

Orang Ulu The jungle – or upriver – people encompass a swathe of different small tribal groups. Orang Ulu longhouses are usually made of belian (ironwood) and are built to last. They are well known swordsmiths, forging lethal *parangs* from any piece of scrap metal they can lay their hands on. They are also very artistic people, are skilled carvers and painters and are famed for their beadwork

The palang - the stimulant that makes a vas diferens

One of the more exotic features of upriver sexuality is the *palang*, or penis pin, which is the versatile jungle version of the French tickler. Traditionally, women suffer heavy weights being attached to their earlobes to enhance their sex-appeal. In turn, men are expected to enhance their physical attributes and entertain their womenfolk by drilling a hole in their organs, into which they insert a range of items, aimed at heightening their partner's pleasure on the rattan mat. Tom Harrisson, a former curator of the Sarawak Museum, was intrigued by the palang; some suspect his authority on the subject stemmed from first-hand experience. He wrote: "When the device is put into use, the owner adds whatever he prefers to elaborate and accentuate its intention. A lively range of objects can so be employed – from pigs' bristles and bamboo shavings to pieces of metal, seeds, beads and broken glass. The effect, of course, is to enlarge the diameter of the male organ inside the female." It is said that many Dayak men, even today, have the tattoo man come and drill a hole in them as they stand in the river. As the practice has gone on for centuries, one can only assume that its continued popularity proves it is worth the agony, see page 41.

– taking great care decorating even simple household utensils. Most Orang Ulu are plastered with traditional tattoos (**see page 238**).

Kenyahs and Kayans These 2 closely related groups were the traditional rivals of the Ibans and were notorious for their warlike ways. Historian Robert Payne, in his history *The White Rajahs of Sarawak* described the Kayans of the upper Rejang as "a treacherous tribe, [who] like nothing better than putting out the eyes and cutting the throats of prisoners, or burning them alive". They probably originally migrated into Sarawak from the Apo Kayan district in East Kalimantan (**see page 846**). Kenyah and Kayan raids on downriver people were greatly feared, but their power was broken by Charles Brooke, just before he became the second White Rajah, in 1863. The Kayans had retreated upstream above the Pelagus Rapids on the Rejang River (**see page 267**), to an area they considered out of reach from their Iban enemies. In 1862 they killed 2 government officers at Kanowit and went on a killing spree. Charles Brooke led 15,000 Ibans past the Pelagus Rapids, beyond Belaga and attacked the Kayans in their heartland. Many hundreds were killed. In Nov 1924, Rajah Vyner Brooke presided over a peace-making ceremony between the Orang Ulu and the Iban in Kapit (there is a photograph of the ceremony on display in the Kapit Museum).

The Kenyahs and Kayans in Sarawak live in pleasant upriver valleys and are settled rice farmers. They are very different from other tribal groups, have a completely different language (which has ancient Malayo-Polynesian roots) and are class-conscious, with a well-defined social hierarchy. Traditionally their society was composed of aristocrats, noblemen, commoners and slaves (who were snatched during raids on other tribes). One of the few things the Kayan and Kenyah have in common with other Dayak groups is the fact that they live in longhouses, although even these are of a different design, and are much more carefully constructed, in ironwood. Subgroups include the Kejamans, Skapans, Berawans and Sebops. Many have now been converted to Christianity.

In contrast to their belligerent history, the Kenyahs and Kayans are much more introverted than the Ibans; they are slow and deliberate in their ways, and are very artistic and musical. They are also renowned for their parties; visitors recovering from drinking *borak* rice beer have their faces covered in soot before being thrown in the river. This is to test the strength of the newly forged friendship with visitors, who are ill-advised to lose their sense of humour on such occasions.

Penans Perhaps Southeast Asia's only remaining true hunter-gatherers live mainly in the upper Rejang area and Limbang. They are nomads and are related – linguistically at least – to the Punan, former nomadic forest-dwellers who are now settled in longhouses along the upper Rejang. The Malaysian government has long wanted the Penan to sedentarise too, but has had limited success in attracting them to expensive new longhouses. Groups of Penan hunter-gatherers still wander through the forest in groups to hunt wild pigs, birds and monkeys and search for sago palms from which they make their staple food, sago flour. The Penan are considered to be the jungle experts by all the other inland tribes. Because they live in the shade of the forest, their skin is relatively fair. They have a great affection for the coolness of the forest and until the 1960s were rarely seen by the outside world. For them sunlight is extremely unpleasant. They are broad and much more stocky than other river people and are extremely shy, having had little contact with the outside world. Most of their trade is conducted with remote Kayan, Kenyah and Kelabit longhouse communities on the edge of the forest.

In the eyes of the West, the Penan have emerged as the 'noble savages' of the late 20th century for their spirited defence of their lands against encroachment by logging companies. But it is not just recently that they have been cheated: they have long been the victims of other upriver tribes. A Penan, bringing baskets full of rotan to a Kenyah or Kayan longhouse to sell may end up exchanging his

Skulls in the longhouse: heads you win

Although head-hunting has been largely stamped out in Borneo, there is still the odd reported case, once every few years. But until the early 20th century, head-hunting was commonplace among many Dayak tribes, and the Iban were the most fearsome of all. Following a head-hunting expedition, the freshly taken heads were skinned, placed in rattan nets and smoked over a fire – or sometimes boiled. The skulls were then hung from the rafters of the longhouse and they possessed the most powerful form of magic.

The skulls were considered trophies of manhood (they increased a young bachelor's eligibility), symbols of bravery and they testified to the unity of a longhouse. The longhouse had to hold festivals – or *gawai* – to appease the spirits of the skulls. Once placated, the heads were believed to bring great blessing – they could ward off evil spirits, save villages from epidemics, produce rain and increase the yield of rice harvests. Heads that were insulted or ignored were capable of wreaking havoc in the form of bad dreams, plagues, floods and fires. To keep the spirits of the skulls happy, they would be offered food and cigarettes and made to feel welcome in their new home. Because the magical powers of a skull faded with time, fresh heads were always in demand. Tribes without heads were considered spiritually weak.

Today, young Dayak men no longer have to take heads to gain respect. They are, however, expected to go on long journeys (the equivalent of the Australian aborigines' Walkabout) – or *bejalai* in Iban. The one unspoken rule is that they should come back with plenty of good stories, and, these days, as most berjalai expeditions translate into stints at timber camps or on oil rigs, they are expected to come home bearing video recorders, TV sets and motorbikes. During the Communist Emergency on the Malay peninsula during the 1950s (**see page 67**), many Iban men went berjalai by working as jungle trackers for the elite Sarawak Rangers regiment, which was originally set up by Rajah Charles Brooke. Many Dayak tribes continue to celebrate their head-hunting ceremonies. In Kalimantan, for example, the *Adat Ngayau* ceremony uses coconut shells, wrapped in leaves, as substitutes for freshly cut heads.

produce for one bullet or shotgun cartridge. In his way of thinking, a bullet will kill one wild boar which will last his family 10 days. In turn, the buyer knows he can sell the same rotan downstream for M$50-100. Penan still use the blowpipe for small game, but shotguns for wild pig. If they buy the shotgun cartridges for themselves, they have to exchange empties first. Some of their shotguns date back to the Second World War, when the British supplied them to upriver tribespeople to fight the Japanese. During the Brooke era, a large annual market would be held which both Chinese traders and Orang Ulu (including Penan) used to attend; the district officer would have to act as judge to ensure the Penan did not get cheated.

Those wishing to learn more about the Penan should refer to Denis Lau's *The Vanishing Nomads of Borneo* (Interstate Publishing, 1987). Lau has lived among the Penan and has photographed them for many years; some of his recent photographs appear in the photographic collection entitled *Malaysia – Heart of Southeast Asia* (published by Archipelago Press, 1991).

Kelabits The Kelabits, who live in the highlands at the headwaters of the Baram River, are closely related to the Muruts (**see page 297**) and the Lun Dayeh of Kalimantan. It was into Kelabit territory that Tom Harrisson parachuted with Allied Special Forces towards the end of World War II. The Kelabit Highlands, around Bareo, were chosen because they were so remote. Of all the tribes in Sarawak, the Kelabits have the sturdiest, strongest builds, which is usually ascribed to the cool and invigorating mountain climate. They are skilled hill-rice farmers and their fragrant Bareo rice is prized throughout Sarawak. The highland climate also allows them to cultivate vegetables. Kelabit parties are also famed as boisterous occasions, and large quantities of *borak* rice beer are consumed – despite the fact that the majority of Kelabits have converted to Christianity. They are renowned as among the most hospitable people in Borneo. For information on religion, **see page 229.**

Dance, drama and music

Dance

Dayak tribes are renowned for their singing and dancing, and the most famous is the hornbill dance. In her book *Sarawak*, Hedda Morrison writes: "The Kayans are probably the originators of the stylized war dance which is now common among the Ibans but the girls are also extremely talented and graceful dancers. One of their most delightful dances is the hornbill dance, when they tie hornbill feathers to the ends of their fingers which accentuate their slow and graceful movements. For party purposes everyone in the longhouse joins in and parades up and down the communal room led by one or two musicians and a group of girls who sing." On these occasions, drink flows freely. With the Ibans, it is *tuak* (rice wine), with the Kayan and Kenyah it is *borak*, a bitter rice beer. After being entertained by dancers, a visitor is under compunction to drink a large glassful, before bursting into song and doing a dance routine themselves. The best guideline for visitors on how to handle such occasions is provided by Redmond O'Hanlon in his book *Into the Heart of Borneo*. The general rule of thumb is to be prepared to make an absolute fool of yourself, throwing all inhibition to the wind. This will immediately endear you to your hosts.

The most common dances in Sarawak are: *Kanjet Ngeleput* (Orang Ulu) dance performed in full warrior regalia, traditionally celebrating the return of a hunter or head-hunters. *Mengarang Menyak* (Melanau) dance depicting the processing of sago from the cutting of the tree to the production of the sago pearls or pellets. *Ngajat Bebunuh* (Iban) war dance, performed in full battle dress and armed with sword and shield. *Ngajat Induk* (Iban) performed as a welcome dance for those visiting longhouses. *Ngajat Lesong* (Iban) dance of the *lesong* or mortar, performed during gawai. *Tarian Kris* (Malay) dance of the *kris*, the Malay dagger, which symbolizes power, courage and strength. *Tarian Rajang Beuh* (Bidayuh) dance performed after the harvesting season as entertainment for guests to the longhouse. *Tarian Saga Lupa* (Orang Ulu) performed by women to welcome guests to the longhouse, accompanied by the *sape* (see below). *Ule Nugan* (Orang Ulu) dance to the sound of the *kerebo bulo*, or bamboo slates. The music is designed to inspire the spirit of the paddy seeds to flourish. The male dancers hold a dibbling stick used in the planting of hill rice.

Music

Gongs range from the single large gong, the **tawak**, to the **engkerumong**, a set of small gongs, arranged on a horizontal rack, with 5 players. An engkerumong ensemble usually involves between 5 and 7 drums, which include 2 suspended gongs (*tawak* and *bendai*) and 5 hour-glass drums (*ketebong*). They are used to celebrate victory in battle or to welcome home a successful head-hunting expedition. Sarawak's Bidayuh also make a bamboo gong called a **pirunchong**. The **jatang uton** is a wooden xylophone which can be rolled up like a rope ladder; the keys are struck with hardwood sticks.

The Bidayuh, Sarawak's bamboo-specialists, make 2 main stringed instruments – a 3-stringed cylindrical bamboo harp called a **tinton** and the **rabup**, a rotan-stringed fiddle with a bamboo cup. The Orang Ulu (Kenyah and Kayan tribes) play a 4-stringed guitar called a **sape**, which is also common on the Kalimantan side of the border. It is the most common and popular lute-type instrument, whose body, neck and board are cut from one piece of softwood. It is used in Orang Ulu dances and by witch doctors. It is usually played by 2 musicians, one keeping the rhythm, the other the melody. Traditional sapes had rotan strings, today they use wire guitar strings and electric pick-ups. Another stringed instrument, more usually found in Kalimantan, or deep in Sarawak's interior, is the **satang**, a bamboo tube with strings around the outside, cut from the bamboo and tightened with pegs.

One of the best known instruments in Sarawak is the **engkerurai** (or *keluri*), the bagpipes of Borneo, which is usually associated with the Kenyahs and Kayans, but is also found in Sabah (where it is called a *sompoton*). It is a hand-held organ in which 4 vertical bamboo pan-pipes of different lengths are fixed to a gourd, which acts as the wind chamber. Simple engkerurai can only manage one chord; more sophisticated ones allow the player to use 2 pipes for the melody, while the others provide an harmonic drone. The Bidayuh are specialists in bamboo instruments and make flutes of various sizes; big thick ones are called **branchi**, long ones with 5 holes are **kroto** and small ones are called **nchiyo**.

Textiles

The weaving of cotton *pua kumbu* is one of the oldest Iban traditions, and literally means 'blanket' or 'cover'. The weaving is done by the women and is a vital skill for a would-be bride to acquire. There are 2 main methods employed in making and decorating pua kumbu: the more common is the *ikat* tye-dyeing technique (**see page 721**). The other method is the *pileh*, or floating weft. The Ibans use a warp-beam loom which is tied to two posts, to which the threads are attached. There is a breast-beam at the weaving end, secured by a back strap to the weaver. A pedal, beneath the threads, lowers and raises the alternate threads which are separated by rods. The woven material is tightly packed by a beater. The material is tye-dye in the warp.

Because the pua kumbu is made by the warp-tie-dyeing method, the number of colours is limited. The most common are a rich browny-brick-red colour and black, as well as the undyed white sections; blues and greens are used in more modern materials. Traditionally, pua kumbu were hung in longhouses during ceremonies and were used to cover images during rituals. The designs and patterns are representations of deities which figure in Iban myths and are believed to protect individuals from harm; they are passed down from generation to generation. Such designs, with deep spiritual significance, can only be woven by wives and daughters of chiefs. Other designs and patterns are representations of birds and animals, including hornbills, crocodiles, monitor lizards and shrimps, which are either associated with worship or are sources of food. Symbolic representations of trees, plants and fruits are also included in the designs as well as the events of everyday life. A typical example is the zigzag pattern which represents the act of crossing a river – the zigzag course is explained by the canoe's attempts to avoid strong currents. Many of the symbolic representations are highly stylized and can be difficult to pick out.

Malay women in Sarawak are traditionally renowned for their *kain songket*, sarongs woven with silver and gold thread (**see page 721**).

Crafts

Woodcarvings Many of Sarawak's tribal groups are skilled carvers, producing everything from huge burial poles (like the Kejaman pole outside the Sarawak museum in Kuching) to small statues, masks and other decorative items and utensils. The Kenyah's traditional masks, which are used during festivals, are elaborately carved and often have large protruding eyes. Other typical items carved by tribal groups include spoons, stools, doors, walking sticks, *sapes* (guitars), ceremonial shields, tops of water containers, tattoo plaques, and the hilts of *parang ilang* (ceremonial knives). The most popular Iban motif is the hornbill, which holds an honoured place in Iban folklore (**see page 227**), being the messenger for the sacred Brahminy kite, the ancestor of the Iban. Another famous Iban carving is the sacred measuring stick called the *tuntun peti*, used to trap deer and wild boar; it is carved to represent a forest spirit. The Kayan and Kenyahs' most common motif is the *aso*, a dragon-like dog with a long snout. It also has religious and mythical significance. The Kenyah and Kayan carve huge burial structures, or *salong*, as well as small ear pendants made of hornbill ivory. The elaborately carved masks used for their harvest ceremony are unique.

Bamboo carving The Bidayuh ('Land Dayaks') are best known for their bamboo carving. The bamboo is usually carved in shallow relief and then stained with dye, which leaves a pattern in the areas which have been scraped out. The Bidayuh carve utilitarian objects as well as ceremonial shields, musical instruments and spirit images used to guard the longhouse. The Cultural Village (Kampung Budaya) in Kuching is one of the best places to see demonstrations of Bidayuh carving.

Blowpipes Blowpipes are made by several Orang Ulu tribes in Sarawak and are usually carved from hardwood – normally belian (ironwood). The first step is to make a rough cylinder about 10 cm wide and 2.5m long. This rod is tied to a platform, from which a hole is bored through the rod. The bore is skillfully chiselled by an iron rod with a pointed end. The rod is then sanded down to about 5 cm in diameter. Traditionally, the sanding was done using the rough underside of *macaranga* leaves. The darts are made from the *nibong* and wild sago palms and the poison itself is the sap of the *upas* (Ipoh) tree (*Antiaris toxicari*) into which the point is dipped.

Beadwork Among many Kenyah, Kayan, Bidayuh, and Kelabit groups, beads have long been symbols of status and wealth; necklaces, skull caps and girdles are handed down from generation to generation. Smaller glass – or plastic – beads (usually imported from Europe) are used to decorate baby carriers, baskets, headbands, jackets, hats, sheaths for knives, tobacco boxes and handbags. Beaded baby carriers are mainly used by the Kelabit, Kenyah and Kayan and often have shells and animals' teeth attached which make a rattling sound to frighten away evil spirits. Rounded patterns require more skill than geometric patterns, the quality of the pattern used to reflect the status of the owner. Only upper-classes are permitted to have beadwork depicting 'high-class' motifs such as human faces or figures. Early beads were made from clay, metal, glass, bone or shell (the earliest have been found in the Niah Caves). Later on, many of the beads that found their way upriver were from Venice, Greece, India and China – even Roman and Alexandrian beads have made their way into Borneo's jungle. Orang Ulu traded them for jungle produce. Tribes attach different values to particular types of beads.

Sickness images The coastal Melanau, who have now converted to Islam, but used to be animists, have a tradition of carving sickness images (*blum*). They are usually carved from sago or other soft woods. The image is believed to take the form of the evil spirit causing a specific illness. They are carved in different forms according to the ailment. The Melanau developed elaborate healing ceremonies; if someone was struck down by a serious illness, the spirit medium would perform the *berayun* ceremony, using the blum to extract the illness from the victim's body. Usually, the image is in a half-seated position, with the hands crossed across the part of the body which was affected. During the ceremony, the medium attempts to draw the spirit out of the sick person and into the image, after which it is set adrift on a river in a tiny purpose-made boat or it is hidden in the jungle. These images are roughly carved and can, from time to time, be found in antique shops.

Basketry A wide variety of household items are woven from rotan, bamboo, bemban reed as well as nipah and pandanus palms. Malaysia supplies 30% of the world's demand for *manau rotan* (rattan). Basketry is practised by nearly all the ethnic groups in Sarawak and they are among the most popular handicrafts in the state. A variety of baskets are made for harvesting, storing and winnowing paddy as well as for collecting and storing other items. The Penan are reputed to produce the finest rattan sleeping mats – closely plaited and pliable – as well as the *ajat* and *ambong* baskets (all-purpose jungle rucksacks, also produced by the Kayan and Kenyah). Many of the native patterns used in basketry are derived from Chinese patterns and take the form of geometrical shapes and stylized birds. The Bidayuh also make baskets from either rotan or sago bark strips. The most common Bidayuh basket is the *tambok*, which is simply patterned and has bands of colour; it also has thin wooden supports on each side.

Hats The Melanau people living around Bintulu make a big colourful conical hat from nipah leaves called a *terindak*. Orang Ulu hats are wide-brimmed and are often decorated with beadwork or cloth appliqué. Kelabit and Lun Bawan women wear skull-caps made entirely of beads, which are heavy and extremely valuable.

Pottery Malaysia's most distinctive ceramic designs are found in Sarawak where Iban potters reproduce shapes and patterns of Chinese porcelain which was originally brought to Borneo by traders centuries ago (**see page 253**). Copies of these old Chinese jars are mostly used for brewing *tuak* rice wine.

MODERN SARAWAK

Politics

In 1957 Kuala Lumpur was keen to have Sarawak and Sabah in the federation of Malaysia and offered the two states a degree of autonomy, allowing their local governments control over state finances, agriculture and forestry. Sarawak's racial mix was reflected in its chaotic state politics. The Ibans dominated the Sarawak National Party (SNAP), which provided the first Chief Minister, Datuk Stephen Kalong Ningkan. He raised a storm over Kuala Lumpur's introduction of Bahasa Malaysia in schools and complained bitterly about the federal government's policy of filling the Sarawakian civil service with Malays from the peninsula. An 'us' and 'them' mentality developed: in Sarawak, the Malay word *semenanjung* – peninsula – was used to label the newcomers. To many, semenanjung was Malaysia, Sarawak was Sarawak.

In 1966 the federal government ousted the SNAP, and a new Muslim-dominated government – led by the Sarawak Alliance – took over in Kuching. But there was still strong political opposition to federal encroachment. Throughout the 1970s, as in Sabah, Sarawak's strongly Muslim government drew the state closer and closer to the peninsula: it supported *Rukunegara* – the policy of Islamization – and promoted the use of Bahasa Malaysia. Muslims make up less than ⅓ of the population of Sarawak. The Malays, Melanaus and Chinese communities grew rich from the timber industry; the Ibans and the Orang Ulu (the upriver tribespeople) saw little in the way of development. They did not reap the benefits of the expansion of education and social services, they were unable to get public sector jobs and to make matters worse, logging firms were encroaching on their native lands and threatening their traditional lifestyles.

It has only been in more recent years that the tribespeoples' political voice has been heard at all. In 1983, Iban members of SNAP – which was a part of Prime Minister Dr Mahathir Mohamad's ruling Barisan Nasional (National Front) coalition – split to form the Party Bansa Dayak Sarawak (PBDS), which, although it initially remained in the coalition, became more outspoken on native affairs. At about the same time, international outrage was sparked over the exploitation of Sarawak's tribespeople by politicians and businessmen involved in the logging industry. The plight of the Penan hunter-gatherers came to world attention due to their blockades of logging roads (**see page 282**) and the resulting publicity highlighted the rampant corruption and greed that characterized modern Sarawak's political economy.

Today there are many in Sarawak as well as in Sabah, who wish their governments had opted out of the Federation like Brunei. Sarawak is of great economic importance to Malaysia, thanks to its oil, gas and timber. The state now accounts for more than $\frac{1}{3}$ of Malaysia's petroleum production (worth more than US$800 million/year) and more than half of its natural gas. As with neighbouring Sabah, however, 95% of Sarawak's oil and gas revenues go directly into federal coffers.

A famous cartoon in a Sarawak newspaper once depicted a cow grazing in Sarawak and being milked on the peninsula. While Sarawak has traditionally been closer to federal government than Sabah (there has never been any hint of a seccessionist movement), discontent surfaces from time to time. In late-1989, all it took was a quarrel over a football match between Sarawak and Selangor state to touch off deep-seated resentments in Kuching.

KUCHING AND THE SKRANG RIVER

From the historic capital of Sarawak, the State's first National Park, Bako, and the often-visited Skrang River longhouses are easily accessible. However, most visitors head for the up-market Damai Beach Resort and the Cultural Village.

Kuching

Shortly after dawn on 15 Aug 1839 James Brooke sailed round a bend in the Sarawak River and, from the deck of his schooner, *The Royalist*, had his first view of Kuching. According to the historian Robert Payne, he saw "...a very small town of brown huts and longhouses made of wood or the hard stems of the nipah palm, sitting in brown squalor on the edge of mudflats." The settlement, 32 km upriver from the sea, had been established less than a decade earlier by Brunei chiefs who had come to oversee the mining of antimony in the Sarawak River valley. The antimony – used as an alloy to harden other metals, particularly pewter – was exported to Singapore where the tin-plate industry was developing.

By the time James Brooke had become Rajah in 1841, the town had a population of local Malays and Dayaks and Cantonese, Hokkien and Teochew traders. Chinatown dominated the S side of the river while the Malay kampungs were strung out along the riverbanks to the W. A few Indian traders also set up in the bazaar, among the Chinese shophouses. Under Charles Brooke, the second of the White Rajahs, Kuching began to flourish; he commissioned most of the town's main public buildings. Ranee Margaret Brooke (Charle's wife) wrote: "The little town looked so neat and fresh and prosperous under the careful jurisdiction of the Rajah and his officers, that it reminded me of a box of painted toys kept scrupulously clean by a child." Because of Kuching's relative isolation, and the fact that it was not bombed during the Second World War, the town has retained much of its 19th century charm; there is only a handful of modern high-rise buildings and Chinese shophouses line the narrow streets. Covered sampans, or *perahu tambang*, still paddle back and forth across the river from the quayside bazaar to the kampungs and the Astana on the N bank.

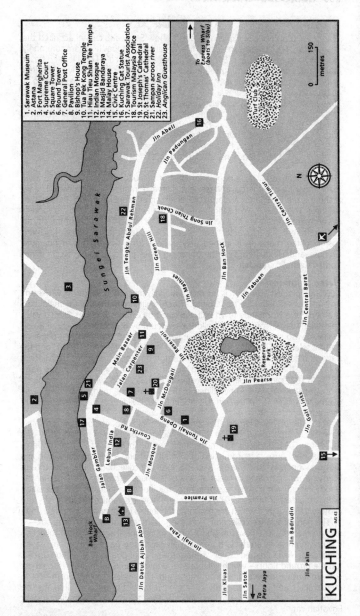

KUCHING

1. Sarawak Museum
2. Astana
3. Fort Margherita
4. Supreme Court
5. Square Tower
6. Round Tower
7. General Post Office
8. Pavilion
9. Bishop's House
10. Tua Pek Kong Temple
11. Hiau Tieu Shian Tee Temple
12. Indian Mosque
13. Masjid Bandaraya
14. Malay House
15. Civic Centre
16. Kuching Cat Statue
17. Sarawak Tourist Association
18. Tourism Malaysia Office
19. St Joseph's Cathedral
20. St Thomas' Cathedral
21. Sampan across river
22. Holiday Inn
23. Anglican Guesthouse

Sungei Sarawak

Express Wharf
(boats to Sibu)

To

Turf Club

metres
0   150

N

Jln Abell

Jln Padungan

Jln Tengku Abdul Rehman

Jln Song Thian Cheok

Jln Green Hill

Jln Ban Hock

Jln Mathies

Jln Central Timur

Jln Tabuan

Jln Central Barat

Main Bazaar

Jalan Carpenter

Jln Reservoir

Reservoir
Park

Jln McDougall

Jln Pearse

Courts' Rd

Jln Tunku Openg

Jln Golf Links

Jalan Gambier

Lebuh India

Jln Mosque

Ban Hock Wharf

Jln Framlee

Jln Datuk Ajibah Abol

Jln Haji Taha

Jln Kluas

Jln Satok

To
Petra Jaya

Jln Badrudin

Jln Palm

KUCHING IMS-43

A town called Cat

There are a number of explanations as to how Sarawak's capital acquired the name 'Cat'. (*Kuching* means 'cat' in Malay – although today it is more commonly spelt *kucing* as in modern Bahasa, 'c' is pronounced 'ch'). Local legend has it that James Brooke, pointing towards the settlement across the river, inquired what it was called. Whoever he asked, mistakenly thought he was pointing at a passing cat. If that seems a little far-fetched, the Sarawak museum offers a few more plausible alternatives. Kuching may have been named after the wild cats (*kucing hutan*) which, in the 19th century, were commonly seen along jungled banks of the Sarawak River. Another theory is that it was called after the fruit *buah mata kucing* ('cat's eyes'), which grows locally. Most likely however, is the theory that the town may originally have been known as *Cochin* – or port – a word commonly used across India and Indochina.

The city, which today has a population of about 70,000, is divided by the Sarawak River; the S is a commercial and residential area, dominated by Chinese while the N shore is predominantly Malay in character with the old kampung houses lining the river. The Astana, Fort Margherita and the Petra Jaya area, with its modern government offices, are also on the N side of the river. The 2 parts of the city are very different in character and even have separate mayors. Kuching's cosmopolitan make-up is immediately evident from its religious architecture: Chinese and Hindu temples, the imposing state mosque and Protestant and Roman Catholic churches.

Places of interest

Kuching's biggest attraction is the internationally renowned **Sarawak Museum**, on both sides of Jalan Tun Haji Openg. The old building (to the E of the main road) is a copy of a Normandy town hall, designed by Charles Brooke's French valet. The Rajah was encouraged to build the museum by the naturalist Alfred Russel Wallace, who spent over 2 years in Sarawak, where he wrote his first paper on natural selection. The museum was opened in 1891, extended in 1911, and the new wing built in 1983. Its best-known curators have been naturalist Eric Mjoberg (who made the first ascent of Gunung Murud – Sarawak's highest peak (**see page 281**) – in 1922) and ethnologist and explorer Tom Harrisson, whose archaeological work at Niah made world headlines in 1957. Across the road, and linked by an overhead bridge, is the Dewan Tun Abdul Razak building, a newer extension of the museum.

The museum has a strong ethnographic section, although some of its displays have been superceded by the Cultural Village (see below), Sarawak's 'living museum'. The old museum's ethnographic section includes a full-scale model of an Iban longhouse, a reproduction of a Penan hut and a selection of Kayan and Kenyah woodcarvings. There is also an impressive collection of Iban war totems (*kenyalang*) and carved Melanau sickness images (*blum*), used in healing ceremonies. The museum's assortment of traditional daggers (or *kris*, **see page 548**) is the best in Malaysia. The Chinese and Islamic ceramics include 17th-20th century Chinese jars, which are treasured hierlooms in Sarawak (**see page 253**).

The natural science collection – covering the flora and fauna of Sarawak – is also noteworthy. The new Tun Abdul Razak ethnological and historical collection includes prehistoric artefacts from the Niah caves (**see page 276**); there is even a replica of Niah's Painted Cave – without the smell of guano. The section on cats (on the ground floor) – which celebrates the town's unusual name – is the most comprehensive feline exhibition in the world. It includes displays on the cat in medieval art, cats and the Japanese, cats in Malay society and a small treatise on Mark Twain's cat. The museum has even managed to procure a mumified ancient Egyptian cat.

There is a library attached to the museum as well as an excellent bookshop and giftshop. Permits to visit the Niah's Painted Cave can be obtained, free of charge, from the curator's office. Open: 0900-1800 Mon-Sun. Audio-visual showings: 1015, 1215, 1430, 1445, 1530.

Apart from the Sarawak Museum, the White Rajahs bequeathed several other architectural monuments to Kuching. The **Astana** (a variant of the usual spelling *istana*, or palace) was built in 1869, 2 years after Charles Brooke took over from his uncle. It stands on the N bank of the river (almost opposite the market on Jalan Gambier). The Astana was hurriedly completed for the arrival of Charles' new bride (and cousin), Margaret. It was originally 3 colonial-style bungalows, with wooden shingle roofs, the largest being the central bungalow with the reception room, dining and drawing room. "How I delighted in those many hours spent on the broad verandah of our house, watching the life going on in the little town on the other side of the river," Ranee Margaret later reminisced in her book *My Life in Sarawak*. The crenellated tower on the E end was added in the 1880s at her request. Charles Brooke is said to have cultivated betel nut in a small plantation behind the Astana, so that he could offer fresh betel nut to visiting Dayak chiefs. Today it is the official residence of the governor (Yang Di Pertuan Negeri) of Sarawak and is only open to the public on Hari Raya Puasa, at the end of Ramadan. To the W of the Astana, in the traditionally Malay area, are many old wooden kampung houses.

Not far away (and also on the N shore) is **Fort Margherita** (now the Police Museum) on Jalan Sapi; it was also built by Rajah Charles Brooke in the 1870s and named after Ranee Margaret, although there was a fort on the site from 1841 when James Brooke became Rajah. It commanded the river approach to Kuching, but was never used defensively, although its construction was prompted by a near-disastrous river-borne attack on Kuching by the Ibans of the Rejang in 1878. Even so, until World War II a sentry was always stationed on the lookout post on top of the fort; his job was to pace up and down all night and shout "All's well" on the hour every hour until 0800. The news that nothing was awry was heard at the Astana and the government offices.

After 1946, Fort Margherita was first occupied by the Sarawak Rangers and was finally converted into a police museum in 1971; this is a lot more interesting than it sounds. There is a large collection of armour and weaponry on the ground floor, including weapons captured during the Indonesian *konfrontasi* from 1963-65 (**see page 237**). Up the spiral staircase, on the 2nd floor, there is a display of police uniforms and communications equipment used by jungle patrols. The 3rd floor houses an exhibition on drugs, conterfeit currency and documents, supplies and weapons captured from Communist insurgents in the 1960s and 70s. From the top, there are good views across the city and up and down the Sarawak River. En route to the courtyard at the bottom, former prison cells have been set up to recreate an opium den – complete with emaciated dummy – and to reinforce the dangers of *dadah*, the courtyard itself contains the old town gallows. (During the rule of the White Rajahs, however, death sentences were carried out by a slash of the *kris* through the heart). Open: 1000-1800 Tues-Sun. Closed public holidays. **Getting there**: sampan across the river from the Pangkalan Batu next to Square Tower on Main Bazaar to the Istana and Fort (M$0.60 return; the boats can be hired for around M$5 an hour).

On the S side of the river around Main Bazaar are some other important buildings dating from the Brooke era; most of them are closed to the public. The **Supreme Court** on Main Bazaar, was built in 1871 as an administrative centre. State council meetings were held here from the 1870s until 1973, when it was converted to law courts. In front of the grand entrance is a memorial to Rajah Charles Brooke

(1924) and on each corner, there is a bronze relief representing the 4 main ethnic groups in Sarawak – Iban, Orang Ulu, Malay and Chinese. The clock tower was built in 1883. The **Square Tower**, also on Main Bazaar, was built as an annex to Fort Margherita in 1879 and was used as a prison. Later in the Brooke era it was used as a ballroom and is now the cultural department of the state government. The austere-looking **Round Tower** on Jalan Tun Abang Hagi Openg, behind the Supreme Court, was built in 1886 as a dispensary, with a view to it serving as a fort in an emergency. It is now used by the judicial department.

The **General Post Office**, with its majestic Corinthian columns, stands in the centre of town, on Jalan Tun Abang Hagi Openg. It was built in 1931 and was one of the few buildings built by Vyner Brooke, the last Rajah. The **Pavilion**, opposite the post office, was built in 1907 and now houses government offices. The **Bishop's House**, off Jalan McDougall, near the Anglican cathedral, is the oldest surviving residence in Sarawak. It was built in 1849, entirely of wood, for the first Anglican Bishop of Borneo, Dr McDougall. The first mission school was started in the attic – developed into St Thomas's and St Mary's School, which is now across the road on Jalan McDougall.

Kuching's Chinese population, part of the town's community since its foundation, live in the shophouses lining the narrow streets around **Main Bazaar**. The Chinese temple, **Tua Pek Kong**, in the shadow of the *Hilton* on Jalan Tunku Abdul Rahman, was built in 1876, although it is now much modernized. **Hian Tien Shian Tee** (Hong San) temple, at the junction of Jalan Carpenter and Jalan Wayang, was built in 1897. The **Indian mosque**, on Lebuh India, originally had an atap roof; in 1876 belian-wood walls were erected. The mosque was built by S Indians and is surrounded by Indian shops and restaurants. The Moorish, gilt-domed **Masjid Bandaraya** (old state mosque) is near the market, on the E side of town; it was built in 1968 on the site of an old wooden mosque dating from 1852. Close by is one of the oldest examples of a **Malay house** in Sarawak.

Kuching's architectural heritage did not end with the White Rajahs; the town's modern buildings are often based on local styles. The new administration centre is in Petra Jaya, on the N side of the river. The **Bapak** (father) **Malaysia** building, in Petra Jaya, is named after the first Prime Minister of Malaysia and houses government offices; the **Dewan Undangan Negeri**, next door, is based on the Minangkabau style (see page 772). Kuching's latest building is the ostentatious **Masjid Jamek** at Petra Jaya.

The **Timber Museum** nearby, on Wisma Sumber Alam (next to the stadium in Petra Jaya), is meant to look like a log. It was built in the mid-1980s to try to engender a bit more understanding about Sarawak's timber industry (see page 282). The museum, which has many excellent exhibits and displays, toes the official line about forest management and presents facts and figures on the timber trade, along with a detailed history of its development in Sarawak. The exhibition provides an insight into all the different forest types. It has background information on and examples of important commercial tree species, jungle produce as well as many traditional wooden implements. The final touch is an air-conditioned forest and wildlife diorama, complete with leaf-litter; all the trees come from the Rejang River area. While the museum sidesteps the more delicate moral issues involved in the modern logging business, its detractors might do worse than to brush up on some of the less emotive aspects of Sarawak's most important industry. The museum has a research library attached to it. Open: 0800-1615 Mon-Fri, 0800-1245 Sat.

On the S side of the river the extraordinary-looking **Civic Centre** on Jalan Taman Budaya, is Kuching's stab at the avant garde. It has a viewing platform (open:

A ceramic inheritance

Family wealth and status in Sarawak was traditionally measured in ceramics. In the tribal longhouses upriver, treasured heirlooms include ancient glass beads, brass gongs and cannons and Chinese ceramic pots and beads (such as those displayed in the Sarawak Museum). They were often used as currency and dowries. Spencer St John, the British consul in Brunei, mentions using beads as currency on his 1858 expedition to Gunung Mulu. Jars (*pesaka*) had more practical applications; they were (and still are) used for storing rice, brewing *tuak* (rice wine) or for keeping medicines. Their value was dependent on their rarity: brown jars, emblazoned with dragon motifs, are more recent and quite common while olive-glazed *dusun* jars, dating from the 15th-17th centuries are rare. The Kelabit people, who live in the highlands around Bario, treasure the dragon jars in particular. Although some of the more valuable antique jars have found their way to the Sarawak Museum, many magnificent jars remain in the Iban and other tribal longhouses along the Skrang, Rejang and Baram rivers. Many are covered by decoratively carved wooden lids.

Chinese contact and trade with the N coast of Borneo has gone on for at least a millennium, possibly two. Chinese Han pottery fragments and coins have been discovered near the estuary of the Sarawak River and from the 7th century, China is known to have been importing birds' nests and jungle produce from Brunei (which then encompassed all of N Borneo), in exchange for ceramic wares. Chinese traders arrived in the *Nanyang* (South Seas) in force from the 11th century, particularly during the Sung and Yuan dynasties. Some Chinese pottery and porcelain even bore Arabic and Koranic inscriptions – the earliest such dish is thought to have been produced in the mid-14th century. In the 1500s, as China's trade with the Middle East grew, many such Islamic wares were traded and the Chinese emperors presented them as gifts to seal friendships with the Muslim world, including Malay and Indonesian kingdoms.

0800-0930, 1030-1200, 1400-1530, 1630-1800) for panoramas of Kuching. The Civic Centre complex houses an art gallery with temporary exhibits, mainly of Sarawakian art. Open: 0915-1730 Mon-Thur, 0915-1800 Sat & Sun. Malaysia's first planetarium is also within the complex: **Sultan Iskandar Planetarium**. It opened in 1989 and has a 15m dome and a 170-seat auditorium. Admission: M$2. Shows at: 1500 Mon-Sun plus 1930 Tues & Thurs. On public holidays there are afternoon and evening shows. **Getting there:** bus from Lebuh Market, S along Jalan Tun Haji Openg.

Excursions
Permits for national parks and the orang utan sanctuary are available from the Sarawak Tourist Information Centre on Main Bazaar or the National Parks office on Jalan Gartak.

South and west of Kuching
Semonggoh Orang Utan Sanctuary is 32 km from Kuching, on the road to Serian. Semonggoh became the first forest reserve in Sarawak when the 800 ha of jungle was set aside by Rajah Vyner Brooke in 1920. It was turned into a wildlife rehabilitation centre for monkeys, orang utans, honey bears and hornbills in 1975. All were either orphaned as a result of logging or were confiscated having been kept illegally as pets. The aim is to reintroduce as many of the animals as possible to their natural habitat. The feeding platform is a 5 min walk from the park office, which is about 1 km walk from the main gates along a tarmac road. Feeding times: 0830-0900 & 1500-1515 Mon-Sun. There is more to see in the morning, as the young monkeys and orang utans are put back in cages after 1500. The star attraction is the 19-year-old orang utan called Bullet, who earned his name

after being shot in the head by hunters. There are a few trails around the park and a botanical research centre, dedicated to jungle plants with medicinal applications. As an orang utan rehabilitation centre, however, it does not compare with Sepilok in Sabah (see page 336), which is an altogether more sophisticated affair; that said, Semonggoh gets few visitors and is a good place to watch orang utans close up. Visitors need a permit to visit the sanctuary, available from Sarawak Tourist Information Centre on Main Bazaar. Open: 0830-1545 Mon-Sun. **Getting there**: Sarawak Transport Co bus 6 from Ban Hock Wharf, Jawa St (M$1.60).

Jong's Crocodile Farm, Mile 18.5 Kuching, Serian Highway, has several types of crocodile – albino, saltwater, and the freshwater Malayan gharial (*Tomistoma schlegeli*) – all bred for their skins. These are 'harvested' at about 10 years of age and 2 sq cm of skin fetches about M$60; younger crocodiles are also killed for their valuable tender belly skin. In the entrance area, there is a ghoulish collection of photographs of people who have been mauled by crocodiles... and one depicting the contents of a maneater's stomach – not for the faint-hearted. There have been 8 fatal attacks from crocodiles in Sarawak since the mid-1970s; thus far none of these has been at Jong's. Admission: M$5 Mon-Fri, M$3 Sat and Sun. Open: 0900-1700 Mon-Sun. **Getting there**: bus 3, 3A and 9 from Ban Hock Wharf, Sat and Sun, Jawa St.

Gunung Penrissen (1,329m) is the highest peak in the mountain range S of Kuching running along the Kalimantan border. The mountain was visited by naturalist Alfred Wallace in 1855. Just over 100 years later, the mountain assumed a strategic role in Malaysia's *konfrontasi* with Indonesia (see page 237) – there is a Malaysian military post on the summit. Gunung Penrissen is accessible from Kampung Padawan on the road to Serian, to the SE of Kuching. It is a difficult mountain to climb (requiring 2 long days), but affords views over Kalimantan to the S and Kuching and the South China Sea to the N. Guides – most of whom were former border scouts during *konfrontasi* – can be hired through the headman at Kampung Padawan; prospective climbers are advised to consult the detailed trail-guide in John Briggs' *Mountains of Malaysia*. (The book is obtainable in the Sarawak museum bookshop.)

Gunung Gading National Park was constituted in 1983 but is little visited at the moment because there are no facilities for visitors. (Plans are afoot to build tourist accommodation: check with Tourist Promotion Board or National Parks and Wildlife Office in Kuching.) There are some marked trails and basic day-visitor facilities. The park is made up of a complex of mountains with several dominant peaks including Gunung Gading (906m). The upper Sungei Lundu flows through the park and has a series of reportedly magnificent waterfalls. The Rafflesia (see page 780) is found in the park. Gunung Gading National Park is between Lundu and Semantan – regular bus connections with Kuching (see below).

Lundu and **Sematan** are villages with beautiful, lonely beaches and there is a collection of deserted islands off Sematan. One of the islands, **Talang Talang**, is a turtle sanctuary and permission to visit it must be obtained from the local district officer. **Accommodation**: **B** *Folkland Beach Bungalow*, Sematan, T 65387. Call first for boat transfer from Siar Beach to Folkland Beach. **Getting there**: Sarawak Transport Co. bus 2B to Lundu (via Bau) (2 hrs, M$5.60) from Ban Hock Wharf, Jawa St; bus 17 from Lundu to Sematan (M$2).

Kubah National Park is 20 km W of Kuching. This is a mainly sandstone, siltstone and shale area with 3 mountains: Gunung Serapi, Gunung Selang and Gunung Sendok; again there are several waterfalls. Flora include mixed dipterocarp and *kerangas* (heath) forest; the park is also rich in palms and wild orchids. Wildlife includes bearded pig, mouse deer and hornbills. There are some jungle trails, but, as yet, no accommodation facilities for visitors.

North of Kuching

Bako National Park lies 37 km N of Kuching, and one of the most rewarding excursions from the city. Accommodation is also available for overnight visits. For more information see page 259.

Sarawak Cultural Village (Kampung Bidayu) was the brainchild of the Sarawak Development Corporation which built Sarawak's 'living museum' at a cost of M$9.5 million to promote and preserve Sarawak's cultural heritage. With increasing numbers of young tribal people being tempted from their longhouses

The Penan – museum pieces for the 21st century?

Economic progress has altered many Sarawakians' lifestyles in recent years; the oil and natural gas sector now offers many employment prospects and upriver tribespeople have been drawn into the logging industry (see page 282). But it is logging that has directly threatened the 9,000-strong Penan tribe's traditional way of life. Sarawak's nomadic hunter-gatherers have emerged as 'the noble savages' of the late 20th century, as their blockades of logging roads drew world attention to their plight. In 1990, Britain's Prince Charles' remarks about Malaysia's "collective genocide" against the Penan prompted an angry letter of protest from Prime Minister Dr. Mahathir Mohamad. He is particularly irked by Western environmentalists, notably Bruno Manser, who lived with the Penan in the late 1980s. "We don't need any more Europeans who think they have a white man's burden to shoulder," Dr Mahathir said.

Malaysia wants to integrate the Penan into mainstream society, on the grounds that it is morally wrong to condemn them to a life expectancy of 40 years, when the average Malaysian lives to well over 60. "There is nothing romantic about these helpless, half-starved, disease-ridden people," the Prime Minister said. The government has launched resettlement programmes to transform the Penan from hunters into fishermen and farmers. One of these new longhouses can be visited in Mulu (see page 285); it has failed to engender much enthusiasm from the Penan, although 4,000-5,000 Penan have now been resettled. Environmentalists countered that the Penan should be given the choice, but, the government asks, what choice do they have if they have only lived in the jungle?

The Cultural Village, opened by Dr Mahathir in 1990, offered a compromise or sorts – but the Penan had the last laugh. One tribal elder, called Apau Madang, and his grandson were paid to parade in loincloths and make blowpipes at the Penan hut while tourists took their snapshots. The arrangement did not last long as they did not like posing as artefacts in Sarawak's 'living museum'. They soon complained of boredom and within months had wandered back to the jungle where they could at least wear jeans and T-shirts. Today, the Penan hut is staffed by other Orang Ulu.

into the modern sectors of the economy, many of Sarawak's traditional crafts have begun to die out. The Cultural Village set out to teach the old arts and crafts to new generations. For the state development corporation, the concept had the added appeal of creating a money-spinning 'Instant Sarawak' for the benefit of tourists lacking the time or inclination to head into the jungle. As with any such artificial scheme, it is rather contrived, but the Cultural Village has been a resounding success; it is a hotbed of creativity and contains some superb examples of traditional architecture. It should be on the sight-seeing agenda of every visitor to Kuching, if only to provide an introduction to the cultural traditions of all the main ethnic groups in Sarawak.

Each tribal group is represented by several craftsmen and women who produce handicrafts and practice traditional skills in houses built to carefully researched design specifications. Many authentic every-day articles have been collected from longhouses all over Sarawak. In one case the Village has served to preserve a culture that is already effectively dead: today the Melinau people all live in Malay-style kampungs, but a magnificent traditional wooden Melinau house has been built at the Cultural Village and is now the only such building in Sarawak. Alongside it there is a demonstration of traditional sago processing. A resident Melanau craftsman makes sickness images (*blum*) – each representing the spirit of an illness, which were floated downriver in tiny boats as part of the healing ritual.

There are also Bidayuh, Iban and Orang Ulu longhouses, depicting the lifestyles of each group. In each there are textile or basket-weavers, wood-carvers or sword-makers. There are exhibits of beadwork, bark clothing, and *tuak* (rice wine) brewing. At the Penan hut there is a demonstration of blow-pipe making – visitors are invited to test their hunting skills. There is a Malay house and even a Chinese farmhouse with a pepper processer and demonstrations of Chinese cookery – although they concede that is not yet a dying art. The tour of all the houses is capped by an Andrew Lloyd Webber-style cultural show which is expertly choreographed – if rather ersatz.

The Cultural Village employs 140 people, including dancers, who earn around M$300 a month and take home the profits from handicraft and tuak sales. The village runs workshops in various crafts (such as wood-carving, mat-weaving, batik-painting) as well as in music, dance and cookery. These are attended by locals as well as foreigners. A month-long course at these heritage centre workshops costs M$45; also intensive day-long and 3-4 day courses, M$60-90. Restaurant (M$13.50 for buffet lunch) and craft shop, Sarakraf. Admission: M$20, including guide and cultural show. Open: 0900-1730 Mon-Sun. **Getting there**: regular buses to **Damai Beach** (M$1.50).

Beaches The best known resort in Sarawak is **Damai Beach**, 25 km N of Kuching – but facilities are only open to guests at the resort. **Accommodation**: **A** *Holiday Inn Damai Beach*, Teluk Bandung Beach, T 411777, F 428911, a/c, restaurant, pool, the hotel, formerly a *Sheraton*, has won a succession of awards for the best *Holiday Inn* in the world, it has recently undergone a big extension programme and has traditional-style chalets and watersports facilities, the resort is next door to the cultural village; in the same area, but in a lower price bracket are: **A-B** *Santin Resort*, Lot 237, Kampung Santin, Sibu Laut (28 km from Kuching), T 413252/241300, a/c, restaurant, pool, watersports, bungalows and chalets; **B** *Buntal Village Resort*, Buntal (25 km from Kuching), T 212457, a/c, restaurant, watersports and riding (see also Kampung Buntal seafood restaurants, below). **Getting there**: regular buses (M$1.50); the smaller resorts can be reached via Damai Beach.

Gunung Santubong (810m) is on the Santubong Peninsula, and its precipitous S side provides a moody backdrop to Damai Beach. The distinctive – and very steep – mountain is most accessible from the E side, where there is a clear ridge trail to the top. The last stretch towards the summit is a tough scramble. The conical peak – from which there are spectacular views – can be reached in a day, guides not necessary but take supplies of food and water. **Getting there**: bus to Damai Beach (M$1.50).

Tours Most tour companies offer city tours as well as trips around Sarawak: to Semonggoh, Bako, Niah, Lambir Hills, Miri, Mulu and Bareo. There are also competitively-priced packages to longhouses (mostly up the Skrang River – **see page 262**). It is cheaper and easier to take organized tours to Mulu, but these should be arranged in Miri (**see page 279**) as they are much more expensive if arranged from Kuching. Other areas are easy enough to get to independently.

Accommodation There is a good choice of international-standard hotels in Kuching – most of them are along Jln Tunku Abdul Rahman with views of the river and the Astana and Fort Margherita on the opposite bank. The choice at the lower end of the market is limited, except for the *Anglican Guesthouse*; the cheaper hotels and lodging houses are concentrated around Jln Green Hill, near the Tua Pek Kong temple. **A** *Hilton*, Jln Tunku Abdul Rahman, T 248200, F 428984, a/c, restaurant, pool, very smart, new and white, overlooking the river, might have spoilt Ranee Margaret Brooke's view from the Astana, well-managed, but not as competitively priced as the *Holiday Inn*; **A** *Holiday Inn*, Jln Tunku Abdul Rahman, T 423111, a/c, restaurant, pool, all mod-cons, good value for money – mainly because it plays second fiddle to its sister hotel at Damai Beach (**see page 256**), it was the first international hotel to open in Kuching and has become the focus of entertainment, excellent bookshop, regular shuttle for guests to Damai Beach, rec; **B** *Borneo*, 30 Jln Tabuan, T 244121, F 254848, a/c, restaurant, reasonable value, central location, breakfast included; **B** *Country View*, Jln Tan Sri Ong Kee

Hui, T 247111, a/c, restaurant, pool, bit out of town; **B** *Metropole Inn*, 22-23 Jln Green Hill, T 412561, a/c, poor quality but offers reasonable rates; **C** *Fata*, Jln McDougall, T 248111, a/c, restaurant, rooms in the older part of the hotel are cheaper and better value for money; **C** *Green Mountain Lodging House*, 1 Jln Green Hill, T 246952, a/c, reasonable value; **C** *Kapit*, 59 Jln Padungan, T 244179, a/c, attached bathrooms, located past the *Holiday Inn*, to the E end of town; **C** *Longhouse*, Jln Abell, T 249333, F 421563, a/c, restaurant, good value but a bit out of town (past the *Holiday Inn*); **C** *Mandarin Lodging House*, 6 Jln Green Hill, T 418269, a/c; **C** *Orchid Inn*, 2 Jln Green Hill, T 411417, F 424561, a/c; **C** *Rumah Rehat* (Rest House), Jln Crookshank, T 242042; **D** *Anglican Guesthouse*, back of St Thomas's Cathedral (path from Jln Carpenter), T 414027, fan, old building set in beautiful gardens on top of the hill, spacious, pleasantly furnished rooms, with basic facilities, far and away the best of the cheaper accommodation in town, family rooms are big with sitting room and attached bathroom, recent visitors warn, however, of a spate of thefts from the guesthouse, so take precautions, rec.

Restaurants Kuching, with all its old buildings and godowns along the river, seems made for open-air restaurants and cafes – but good ones are notably absent. However, the town is not short of hawker centres. **Malay**: ♦*Azul*, Jln Satok, buffet lunch and dinner; ♦♦♦*Malay Restaurant*, Jln Kulas, buffet lunch only (M$10). **Chinese**: ♦♦*Mei-San*, Holiday Inn, Jln Tunku Abdul Rahman, dim sum, M$12.50 set lunch; Sun eat-as-much-as-you-can dim sum special (M$13), also Sichuan cuisine, rec; *Lan Ya Keng*, Jln Carpenter, opposite old temple, specializes in pepperfish steak. **Indian**: there are several cheap Indian Muslim restaurants along Lebuh India. ♦*Duffy Banana-leaf Restaurant*, Jln Ban Hock, good and cheap. **Thai**: ♦♦*Bangkok Thai Seafood Restaurant*, Jln Pending, maybe not up to Bangkok standards, but not bad for Sarawak, rec by locals. **Japanese**: ♦♦♦*Kikyo-Tei*, Jln Crookshank (near the Civic Centre), also some Chinese dishes, rec by locals. **International**: ♦♦♦*Hilton Steak House*, Jln Tunku Abdul Rahman, New Zealand sirloin steaks; ♦♦♦*Orchid Garden*, Holiday Inn, Jln Tunku Abdul Rahman, good breakfast and evening buffets, international and local cuisine, rec; ♦♦*Trumps*, 2nd Flr, Civic Centre, Jln Taman Budaya, Malay dishes more reasonable than Western and Chinese, good view; ♦♦*Waterfront*, Hilton Hotel, Jln Tunku Abdul Rahman, reasonably priced for the venue. **Coffee Shops**: Kuching has many good Chinese coffee shops, which are known for their excellent *laksa* (breakfast of curried coconut milk soup with noodles, served with prawns, shredded omelette, chicken, bean sprouts, coriander and a side plate of *sambal belacan* (chillied prawn paste). *Chang Choon Café*, opposite City Inn, Jln Abell; *Choon Hui Caf*, Jln Ban Hock; *Green Hill Corner*, Lebuh Temple; *Tiger Garden*, opposite Rex Cinema, Lebuh Temple; *Wonderful Café*, opposite Miramar Theatre, Jln Palm. **Foodstalls**: *Batu Lintang Open-Air Market*, Jln Rock (to the S of town, past the hospital); *Capital Cinema Hawker Centre*, Jln Padungan; *Jln Palm Open-Air Market*; *King's Food Centre*, Jln Simpang Tiga; *Kubah Ria*, Jln Tunku Abdul Rahman (on the road out of town towards Damai Beach, next to Satok Suspension Bridge), very popular; *Lau Ya Keng*, Jln Carpenter; *Market Street Open-Air Market*, next to the taxi stands; ♦♦*Permata Food Centre*, Jln Padungan, behind the AIA building, purpose-built alternative to the central market, prices are higher but the choice is better, bird-singing contests (mainly Red-Whiskered Bulbuls and White-Rumped Sharmas) every Sun morning, rec; *Rex Cinema Hawker Centre*, Jln Wayang/Jln Temple, squashed down an alleyway, satay rec; *Thompson's Corner*, Jln Palm/Jln Nanas; *Tower Market*, Lebuh Market. **Outside Kuching**: *Kampung Buntal*: several seafood restaurants built on stilts over the sea, 25 km N of Kuching. (There is a reasonably priced chalet-style resort accommodation nearby.) ♦♦*Lim Hok Ann*, rec. **Getting there**: buses from Lebuh Market (M$2).

Entertainment Cultural shows: every Wed at 1900 and 2200 at *Jala Seafood Restaurant* at Buntal Village Resort (see restaurants above). *Cultural Village*, Damai Beach, cultural shows, with stylized and expertly choreographed tribal dance routines, 1130 and 1630, Mon-Sun.

Sport Golf: *Sarawak Golf and Country Club*, Petra Jaya, 18-hole and 9-hole courses, green fees: M$50 weekdays, M$60 weekends; *Holiday Inn Damai Beach*, Santubong, designed by Arnold Palmer, right on the sea, 18-hole; *Prison Golf Club*, 6th Mist Old Airport Rd, 9-hole, green fees: M$30. **Outward bound**: *Camp Permai Sarawak*, Menara SEDC, Jln Tunku Abdul Rahman, T 416777, F 243716. **Swimming**: *Kuching Municipal Swimming Pool*, next to Kuching Turf Club, Serian Rd, admission M$1, open: am only. **General**: Canoes, fishing trips (M$220 for a full day) and horse riding (M$30/hr) at *Buntal Village Resort* (see *Beaches*, above). **Spectator Sports**: Malaysia Cup football matches held in the *Stadium Negeri Sarawak*, Petra Jaya. The *Turf Club* on Serian Rd is the biggest in Borneo (see newspapers for details of meetings).

Shopping When it comes to choice, Kuching is the best place in Malaysia to buy tribal handicrafts, textiles and other artifacts, but they are not cheap. In some of Sarawak's smaller coastal and upriver towns, you are more likely to find a better bargain, although the selection is not as good. If buying several items, it is a good idea to find one shop which sells the lot, as good discounts can be negotiated. It is essential to shop around: the best-stocked handicraft and antique shops near the big hotels are usually the most expensive; it is possible to bargain everywhere. **NB**: it is illegal to export any antiquity without a licence from the curator of the museum. An antiquity is defined as any object made before 1850. Most things sold as antiquities are not: some very convincing weathering and ageing processes are employed. **Books & maps**: *H N Mohd Yahia & Son*, *Holiday Inn*, Jln Tunku Abdul Rahman, and in the basement of the Sarawak Shopping Plaza, sells a 1:500,000 map of Sarawak. It is also possible to get good maps from the State Government offices (2nd Flr) near the end of Jln Simpang Tiga. It is necessary to obtain police clearance for the purchase of more detailed sectional maps. *Berita Book Centre*, Jln Haji Taha has a good selection English-language books.

Handicrafts: most handicraft and antique shops are along Main Bazaar, Lebuh Temple and Lebuh Wayang; *The Curio Shop* is attached to the Sarawak Museum. There is a Sunday market on Jln Satok, to the SW of town, with a few handicraft stalls; *Bong & Co.*, 78 Main Bazaar; *Borneo Arts & Crafts*, 56 Main Bazaar; *Eeze Trading*, Lot 250, Section 49, Grd Flr, Jln Tunku Abdul Rahman; *Borneo Art Gallery*, Sarawak Plaza, Jln Tunku Abdul Rahman; *Karyaneka (handicrafts) Centre* at Cawangan Kuching, Lot 324 Bangunan Bina, Jln Satok; *Loo Pan Arts*, 83 Jln Ban Hock; *Native Arts*, 94 Main Bazaar; *Sarakraf*, Main Bazaar (next to Sarawak Tourist Information Centre); *Sarawak Batik Art Shop*, 1 Lebuh Temple; *Sarawak House*, 67 Main Bazaar, (more expensive); *Syarikat Pemasarah Karyaneka*, Lot 87, Jln Rubber; *Tan & Sons*, 54 Jln Padungan; *Thian Seng*, 48 Main Bazaar, (good for *pua kumbu*).

Pottery: rows of pottery stalls along Jln Airport Lama.

Markets: the *Vegetable and Wet market* are on the riverside on Jln Gambier; further up is the *Ban Hock Wharf market*, now full of cheap imported clothes. The *Sunday Market* on Jln Satok sells jungle produce, fruit and vegetables (there are a few handicraft stalls) and all sorts of intriguing merchandise; it starts on Sat night and runs through Sun morning and is well worth visiting. There is a jungle produce market, Pasar Tani, on Fri and Sat at Kampung Pinang Jawa in Petra Jaya.

Shopping complexes: Sarawak Plaza, next to the *Holiday Inn*, Jln Tunku Abdul Rahman.

Local transport **Bus**: there are 2 bus companies around town: blue Chin Lian Long buses (which leave from Lebuh Gartak, next to the state mosque) and the green Sarawak Transport Company (STC) buses, which leave from the end of Lebuh Jawa, next to Ban Hock Wharf and the market. STC buses operate on regional routes; bus 12A (M$0.80) goes to the airport. Chin Lian Long blue buses 19 or 17 go to the jetty for boats to Sibu (M$0.40). **Taxi**: local taxis congregate at the taxi stand on Jln Merket. 'Midnight' surcharge of 50% 2400-0600. **Boat**: sampans cross the Sarawak River from next to the Square Tower on Main Bazaar to Fort Margherita and the Astana on the N bank (M$0.30). Small boats and some express boats connect with outlying kampungs on the river. **Car hire**: *Avis*, Grd Flr, *Holiday Inn*, Jln Tunku Abdul Rahman, T 411370; **Mahana Rent-a-Car**, 18G, Level 1, Taman Sri Sarawak Mall, Jln Borneo (opposite *Hilton Hotel*), T 411370, F 423644.

Banks & money changers There are money changers in the main shopping complexes. **Chartered**, near *Holiday Inn*, Jln Tunku Abdul Rahman; **Overseas Union**, Jln Tun Haji Openg (Main Bazaar end); **Hongkong**, Jln Tun Haji Openg (Main Bazaar end).

Consulates Indonesian Consulate, 5a Jln Pisang, T 241734, M$10 for visa, only if travelling overland. **Getting there**: blue bus 5A or 6 from State Mosque.

Useful addresses General Post Office: Jln Tun Haji Openg. **Telekom**: (for international telephone calls) Jln Batu Lintang (Open: 0800-1800 Mon-Fri; 0800-1200 Sat & Sun). **Immigration**: 1st Flr, Bangunan Sultan Iskandar, Simpang Tiga, Jln Simpang Tiga. **Sarawak General Hospital**: Jln Tan Sri Ong Kee Hui, off Jln Tun Haji Openg. **National Parks and Wildlife Office**: Wisma Sumber Alam, Petra Jaya, T 24474. **Resident's Office**: T 243301.

Airline offices British Airways, 92 Jln Green Hill; **Hornbill Skyways**, Jln Rubber, T 411737; **MAS**, Electra House, Leboh Power, T 454255 or on Jln Song Thian, T 244144; **Merpati** ticket agent, Sin Hwa Travel Service, 8 Lebuh Temple, T 246688; **Singapore Airlines**, Jln Tunku Abdul Rahman, T 20266.

Tour companies & travel agents *Borneo Adventure*, 1st Flr, 12 Padungan Arcade, Jln Song Thian Cheok, T 245175, F 422626, rec; *Borneo Sightseeing*, Lot 173, Jln Chan Chin Ann, T 410688, F 415300; *Borneo Transverse*, 10b 1st Flr, Wayang St, T 257784, F 421419; *East-West Agencies*, 41 Jln P Ramlee, T 241401, F 424529; *Ibanika Expeditions*, Lot 4,11, 4th Flr, Wisma Saberkas, T 424021, also offers French and German-speaking guides; *Insar Tour & Travel*, 524 Jln Pisang West, T 416223, F 424206; *Inter-World Services*, 85 Jln Rambutan, T 252344, F 424515; *Journey Travel Agencies*, Lobby Flr, *Hilton Hotel*, Jln Borneo, T 240652, F 415775; *Long House Tours*, 1st Flr, 253, Jln Datok Wee Kheng Chiang, T 422215,

F 412728; *MBF Insight Travel*, Lot 260, 1st Flr, Bangunan Lai Chin Hung, Jln Chan Chin Ann, T 241305, F 241557; *Pan Asia Travel*, 2nd Flr, Unit 217-218, Sarawak Plaza, Jln Tunku Abdul Rahman, T 419754, half day excursions from Kuching; *Samasa Tours & Travel*, Lot 358, Lwr Grd Flr, Jln Rubber, T 250603, F 481588; *Sarawak Travel Agencies*, Unit UG 17, Sarawak Plaza, Jln Tunku Abdul Rahman, T 418280 or 70 Jln Padungan, T 243708, F 424587; *Vista Borneo*, Level 3, Block G, Lot 13, Taman Sri Sarawak, Jln Borneo, T 417791, F 417781; *Wah Tung Travel*, Teochew Association Building, Jln Tambunan, T 248888, river cruises.

Tourist offices The state and national tourism organizations are both well informed and helpful; they can offer advice on itineraries, travel agents and up-to-date information on facilities in national parks. **Sarawak Tourist Association Information Centre**, in the old Sarawak steamship building on Main Bazaar, T 240620. It is possible to book national park accommodation at this office. Historical exhibitions on Sarawak. (Also has an office at Kuching airport.) **Tourism Malaysia**, 2nd Flr, AIA Building, Jln Song Thian Cheok, T 246775/246575. **National Parks Office**, Jln Mosque, T 2466477 for information on national parks and advance bookings. **Sarawak Tourist Guide Association**, c/o 10-B Wayang St.

Transport to & from Kuching **By air**: the airport is 10 km S of Kuching. Green bus 12A (M$0.80) from Lebuh Jawa or taxi (M$12) from Lebuh Market. Regular connections with KL (M$186 – early morning economy), JB (M$169), KK (M$237), Bintulu (M$116), Miri (M$166), Sibu (M$72), Bandar Seri Begawan, Brunei (M$192). SIA also operates direct flights to and from Singapore (M$170).

By bus: long-distance buses are operated by the Sarawak Transport Company (green buses) and leave from Lebuh Jawa, next to Ban Hock Wharf. Regular connections with Bandar Sri Aman (M$12), Bau (M$2) and Lundu (M$5.60). It is possible to get to Sibu by bus, but until the road is upgraded, it is necessary to stop off overnight in Sarikei, on the lower Rejang. Those suffering this misfortune have a choice between the *Hoover, Ambassador* or the *Golden City hotels*. It is generally a better idea to fly or take the express boat.

By boat: express boats leave from the Marine Base, Jln Pending, 4 km E of town. **Getting there**: blue bus 19 or 17 (M$0.50) from Lubuh Jawa; taxi (M$8) from Lebuh Market. Tickets for the Kuching-Sibu express boats can be bought in advance at the *Metropole Inn Hotel*, 196 Jln Padungan. Regular connections with Sibu (involving a change to a river express boat at Sarikei); 4 hrs (M$29). There are also cargo boats going to Sibu and Miri 18 hrs (M$12): further information from Sarawak Tourist Association or Tourist Promotion Board.

International connections with Indonesia
MAS operates a once-weekly flight from Kuching to Pontianak, Kalimantan, on Mondays. Regular express buses go to Pontianak (M$55 single, M$100 return). It is necessary to have a valid Indonesian visa (see *Consulates*, above). Buses leave from Khoo Hun Yeang St. Booking office: Mile 3.5, Penrissen Rd, T 454548/454668 or through Kedai Jam Ban Poh, 130 Jln Padungan. For a more adventurous route, it is possible to take Sarawak Transport Company buses 3 or 3A to Serian, 1 hr (M$3.60); Mara Transport Company bus from Serian to Tebedu, 1½ hrs (M$3.50), and from Tebedu it is possible to trek across the border to Balai Kerangan in Kalimantan.

Bako National Park

Established in 1957, Bako was Sarawak's first national park. It is a very small park (2,728 ha) but it has an exceptional variety of flora, and contains almost every type of forest in Borneo. Bako is situated on the beautiful Muara Tebas peninsula, a former river delta which has been thrust above sea level. Its sandstone cliffs, which are patterned and streaked with iron deposits, have been eroded to produce a dramatic coastline with secluded coves and beaches and rocky headlands. Millions of years of erosion by the sea has resulted in the formation of wave-cut platforms, 'honeycomb' weathering, solution pans, arches and sea stacks. Bako's most distinctive feature is the westernmost headland – Tanjung Sapi – a 100m high sandstone plateau, which is unique in Borneo.

Flora and fauna There are 7 separate types of vegetation in Bako. These include mangroves (*bakau* is the most common stilt-rooted mangrove species), swamp forest and heath forest – known as *kerangas*, an Iban word meaning 'land on which rice cannot grow'. Pitcher plants (*Nepenthes ampullaria*) do however grow in profusion on the sandy soil (**see page 57**). There is also mixed dipterocarp rainforest (the most widespread forest type in Sarawak, characterized by its 30-40m-high canopy), beach forest, and *padang* vegetation, comprised of scrub

Visiting longhouses: house rules

There are more than 1,500 longhouses in Sarawak, and as the state's varied tribal culture is one of its biggest attractions, trips to longhouses are on most visitors' itineraries. Longhouses are usually situated along the big rivers and their tributaries... notably the Skrang (the most easily accessible to Kuching, **see page 262**), the Rejang (**see page 268**) and the Baram (**see page 281**). The **Iban**, who are characteristically extrovert and hospitable to visitors, live on the lower reaches of the rivers. The **Orang Ulu tribes** – mainly Kayan and Kenyah – live further upriver, and are generally less outgoing than the Iban. The **Bidayuh** (formerly known as the 'Land Dyaks') live mainly around Bau and Serian, near Kuching. Their longhouses are usually more modern than those of the Iban and Orang Ulu, and are less often visited for that reason. The **Kelabit** people live in the remote plateau country near the Kalimantan border around Bareo (**see page 290**).

The most important ground rule is not to visit a longhouse without an invitation... people who arrive unannounced may get an embarrassingly frosty reception. Tour companies offer the only exception to this rule, as most have tribal connections. Upriver, particularly at Kapit, on the Rejang (**see page 268**), such 'invitations' are not hard to come by; it is good to ensure that your host actually comes from the longhouse he is inviting you to. The best time to visit Iban longhouses is during the *gawai* harvest festival at the beginning of June, when communities throw an open-house and everyone is invited to join the drinking, story-telling and dancing sessions, which continue for several days.

On arrival, visitors should pay an immediate courtesy call on the headman (known as the *tuai rumah* in Iban longhouses). It is normal to bring him gifts; those staying overnight should offer the headman between M$10 and M$20/head. The money is kept in a central fund and saved for use by the whole community during festivals. Small gifts such as beer, cigarettes, batik, food and sweets go down well. It is best to arrive at a longhouse during late afternoon after people have returned from the fields. Visitors who have time to stay the night generally have a much more enjoyable experience than those who pay fleeting visits. They can share the evening meal and have time to talk... and drink. Visitors should note the following:

❑ On entering a longhouse, take off your shoes.
❑ It is usual to accept food and drink with both hands. If you do not want to eat or drink, the accepted custom is to touch the brim of the glass or the plate and then touch your lips as a symbolic gesture; sit cross-legged when eating.
❑ When washing in the river, women should wear a sarong and men, shorts.
❑ Ask permission to take photographs. It is not uncommon to be asked for a small fee.
❑ Do not enter a longhouse during *pantang* (taboo), a period of misfortune – usually following a death. There is normally a white flag hanging near the longhouse as a warning to visitors.

Trips upriver are not cheap. If you go beyond the limits of the express boats, it is necessary to charter a longboat. Petrol costs M$2-4/litre, depending on how far upriver you are. Guides charge M$40-80 a day and sometimes it is necessary to hire a boatman or front-man as well. Prices increase in the dry season when boats have to be lifted over shallow rapids. Permits are required for most upriver areas; these can be obtained at the resident's or district office in the nearest town.

and bare rock from which there are magnificent views of the coast. The rare *daun payang* (umbrella palm) is found in Bako park; it is a litter-trapping plant as its large fronds catch falling leaves from the trees above and funnel them downwards where they eventually form a thick organic mulch enabling the plant to survive on otherwise infertile soil. There are also wild durian trees in the forest – they can take up to 60 years to bear fruit.

Bako is one of the few areas in Sarawak inhabited by the proboscis monkey (*Nasalis larvatus*), known by Malays as 'Orang Belanda' – or Dutchmen – because of their long noses (**see page 225**). They are most often seen in the early morning or at dusk in the Teluk Assam and Teluk Delima areas (at the far W side of the park, closest to the headquarters) or around Teluk Paku, a 45 min walk from park HQ. The park also has resident populations of sambar deer, wild pigs, long-tailed macaques, flying lemur, silver leaf monkeys and palm civet cats. Telok Assam, in the area around park HQ, is one of the best places for birdwatching: over 150 species have been recorded in the park, including pied and black hornbills. Large numbers of migratory birds come to Bako between Sept and Nov. The blue fiddler crab – which has one big claw, and is forever challenging others to a fight, can also be seen in the park and mudskippers – evolutionary throw-backs (half-fish, half-frog) are common in mangrove areas.

Treks There are well marked trails throughout the park – over 30 km in total; all paths are colour coded, corresponding with the map available from Park HQ. The shortest trek is the steep climb to the top of Tanjung Sapi, overlooking Teluk Assam, which affords good views of Gunung Santubong, on the opposite peninsula, across Tanjung Sipang, to the W. The longest treks (about 10 km from HQ) lead to Tanjung Limau (facing Pulau Lakei) and Tanjung Kruin beach; they are about 7 hrs' walk, and pass through almost every vegetation zone in Borneo other than montane forest. It is possible to camp overnight or to arrange for a park boat to pick you up at a specified time.

Beaches The best swimming beach is at Teluk Pandan Kecil, about 1½ hrs walk, NE from Park HQ. It is also possible to swim at Teluk Assam and Teluk Paku.

Transport around the park It is possible to hire boats around the park: speed boats M$60 (can accommodate 5-6).

Permits are available from the Savanah Tourist Information Centre on Main Bazaar or the National Parks office, Forest Department, Jln Gartak, Kuching, T 24474. Day-trippers do not require permits. All accommodation should be booked in advance and a deposit paid in Kuching. Bookings can also be made at Sarawak Tourist Association information centre, Main Bazaar, T 248088/410944.

Park Information Centre is next to park HQ, with a small exhibition on geology, flora and fauna within the park. Visitors can request to see an introductory video to Bako National Park. Open: 0800-2200 Mon-Sun.

Accommodation It is possible to book accommodation at the National Parks and Wildlife Office, Jln Gartak, Kuching, T 24474. The hostels are equipped with mattresses, kerosene stoves and cutlery. Resthouses have refrigerators. Resthouses and the hostel have fans. *Deluxe resthouse*, M$60 per house, M$30 per room; *Standard resthouse*, M$40 per house, M$20 per room; *Old resthouse*, M$30 for a double; *Semi-detached lodge*, M$20; *Four door hostel*, M$12 per room, M$2 per person.

Camping For those not intending to trek to the other side of the park, it is not worth camping as monkeys steal anything left lying around. It is however necessary to camp if you go to the beaches on the NE peninsula. Tents can be hired M$3 per person; campsite M$1.

Restaurant The canteen is open 0700-2200. It serves basic local food and sells tinned foods and drinks.

Transport to & from Bako 37 km from Kuching. **By bus & boat**: Petra Jaya (blue, white and orange) bus 6 from Electra House on Lebuh Market to Kampung Bako (M$1.90) every hour; also minibuses from Lebuh Market. From Kampung Bako, charter a private boat to

Sungei Assam (30 mins) which is a short walk from Park HQ, M$25/boat (up to 8 people); M$3 per person if more than 8 in the boat. **NB**: in the monsoon season, between Nov and Feb, the sea can be rough.

Bandar Sri Aman

Bandar Sri Aman, previously called Simmanggang, lies on the Batang Lupar. The river is famous for its tidal bore and divides into several tributaries: the Skrang River is one of these (see below). The Batang Lupar provided Somerset Maugham with the inspiration for his short story *Yellow Streak* in *Borneo Tales*. It was one of the few stories he wrote from personal experience: he nearly drowned after being caught by the bore in 1929. On another of the Lupar's tributaries, Batang Ai, a section of the river has been harnessed for Sarawak's first hydro-electric plant which came into service in 1985.

Bandar Sri Aman is the administrative capital of the 2nd division. **Fort Alice** is the only building of note and was constructed in 1864. It has small turrets, a central courtyard and a medieval-looking drawbridge. Rajah Charles Brooke lived in the Batang Lupar district for about 10 years, using this fort – and another downriver at Lingga – as bases for his punitive expeditions against pirates and Ibans in the interior. The fort is the only one of its type in Sarawak and was built here on the Batang Lupar River as protection against Iban raids. Most tourists do not stop in Bandar but pass through on day trips up the Skrang River from Kuching. The route to Bandar goes through pepper plantations and many 'new' villages. During Communist guerrilla activity in the 1960s (see page 238), whole settlements were uprooted in this area and placed in guarded camps.

Excursions

Skrang longhouses The Skrang River was one of the first areas settled by Iban immigrants in the 16th-18th centuries. The slash-and-burn agriculturalists originally came from the Kapual river basin in Kalimantan. They later joined forces with Malay chiefs in the coastal areas and terrorized the Borneo coasts; the first Europeans to encounter these pirates called them 'Sea Dayaks' (see page 240). They took many heads. Blackened skulls – which local headmen say date back to those days – hang in some of the Skrang longhouses. In 1849, more than 800 Iban pirates from the Batang Lupar and Skrang River were massacred by Rajah James Brooke's forces in the notorious Battle of Beting Marau. Four years later the Sultan of Brunei agreed to cede these troublesome districts to Brooke; they became the Second Division of Sarawak.

There are many traditional Iban longhouses along the Skrang River, although those closer to Pias and Lamanak (the embarkation points on the Skrang) tend to be very touristy – they are visited by tour groups almost every day. Long Mujang, the first Iban longhouse, is an hour upriver. Pias and Lamanak are within 5 hrs drive of Kuching. **Getting there**: bus 14 and 19 to Pias (M$4) and bus 9 to Lemanak (M$6). From these points it is necessary to charter a boat, which costs around M$100 to reach the nearest longhouses. Many of the Kuching-based tour agencies offer cut-price deals for day-long or 2-day excursions to Skrang. Unless you are already part of a small group, these tours work out cheaper because of the boat costs.

Accommodation Limited selection. **B-C** *Alison*, 4 Jln Council, T 322578/9; **B-C** *Hoover*, Tiong Hua Building, 139 Jln Club, T 321985-8; **B-C** *Taiwan*, 1 Jln Council, T 322493, a/c; **C** *Sum Sun*, 62 Jln Club, T 322191, a/c.

Restaurants ✦*Alison Café & Restaurant*, 4 Jln Council, Chinese cuisine; *Chuan Hong*, 1 Jln Council, Chinese coffee shop, also serves Muslim food; *Melody*, 432 Jln Hospital, Chinese and Muslim food.

Useful addresses Resident's Office: T 322004.

Transport to & from Bandar Sri Aman 135 km from Kuching. By bus: regular connections with Kuching ($12) and Sibu (via Sarikei).

SIBU AND THE REJANG RIVER

Sibu

The Batang Rejang is an important thoroughfare and Malaysia's longest river at 563 km (it is, however, 12 times shorter than the Nile). Tours to upriver longhouses can be organized from Sibu, or more cheaply from Kapit and Belaga.

With a population of 150,000, Sibu is the 2nd largest town in Sarawak. The town is sited at the confluence of the Rejang and the Igan rivers 60 km upstream from the sea. Thanks to the discovery of the Kuala Paloh channel in 1961, Sibu is accessible to boats with a sizeable draft. It is the starting-point for trips up the Rejang to the towns of Kapit and Belaga.

Sibu is a busy Chinese trading town – the majority of the population came originally from China's Foochow Province – and is the main port on the Batang Rejang (also spelt 'Rajang'). In 1899, Rajah Charles Brooke agreed with Wong Nai Siong, a Chinese scholar from Fukien, to allow settlers to Sibu. Brooke had reportedly been impressed with the industriousness of the Chinese: he saw the women toiling in the paddy fields from dawn to dusk and commented to an aide: "If the women work like that, what on earth must the men be like?"
   The Kuching administration provided these early agricultural pioneers with temporary housing on arrival, a steamer between Sibu and Kuching, rice rations for the first year and tuition in Malay and Iban. The town grew quickly (its rapid early expansion is documented in a photographic exhibition in the Civic Centre), but was razed to the ground in 'the great fire' of 1828. The first shophouses to be constructed after the fire are the 3-storey ones still standing on Jalan Channel. In the first few years of the 20th century, Sibu became the springboard for Foochow migration to the rest of Sarawak. Today it is an industrial and trading centre for timber, pepper and rubber. It is home to some of Sarawak's wealthiest families – nearly all of them timber towkays.

The old trading port has now been graced with a pagoda, a couple of big hotels and a smart new **esplanade**, completed in 1987. The 1929 shophouses along the river are virtually all that remains of the old town. The 7 storey **pagoda**, adjacent to Tua Pek Kong Temple, cost M$1.5 million to build; there are good views over the town from the top. In the **Sibu Civic Centre**, 2.5 km out of town on Jalan Tun Abang Haji Openg, there is an exhibition of old photographs of Sibu and an unspectacular tribal display. This serves as Sibu's municipal museum. Five aerial photographs of the town, taken every 5 years or so between 1947 and 1987, chart the town's explosive growth. Open: 1500-2000 Tues-Sat, 0900-1200, 1400-2000 Sun.

Tours Most companies run city tours plus tours of longhouses, Mulu National Park and Niah Caves. It is cheaper to organize upriver trips from Kapit or Belaga (see below) than from Sibu.

Accommodation Hotels are scattered all over Sibu; cheaper ones tend to be around the nightmarket in Chinatown. A couple of the top hotels are good, but those at the lower end of the market are very mediocre. **A** *Tanahmas*, Jln Kampung Nyabor, T 333188, F 333288, a/c, restaurant, run to a very high standard, very well-appointed modern hotel, rec; **B** *Centre Point Inn*, Jing Hwa Bldg, off Central Rd, T 320222, F 320496, a/c, often offers sizeable discounts; **B** *Garden Hotel*, 1 Jln Huo Ping, T 317888, F 330999, a/c, restaurant, well-kept and efficiently run, rec; **B** *Premier*, Jln Kampung Nyabor, T 23222, a/c, restaurant, many rooms have TV, own bath, bar etc, clean, helpful staff, rec; **B-C** *Phoenix*, 1 & 3 Jln Kai Peng (off Jln Kampung Nyabor), T 313877, F 320392, a/c, reasonable; **C** *Bahagia*, 11 Central Rd, T 320303, a/c, restaurant, reasonable value for money; **C** *Capitol*, 19 Jln Wong Nai Siong, T 336444, a/c, restaurant, also reasonable value; **C** *Mandarin*, 183 Jln Kampong Nyabor, T 339177, F 333425, a/c, popular with travellers; **C** *Miramar*, 1st Flr, Channel Rd, T 338008,

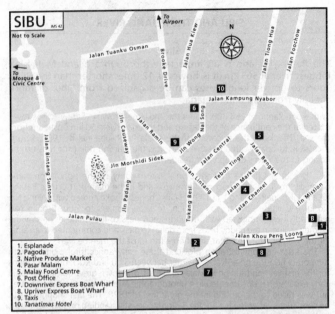

SIBU JMS 42
Not to Scale

To Airport

N

To Mosque & Civic Centre

Jalan Tuanku Osman

Brooke Drive

Jalan Hua Kiew

Jalan Tiong Hua

Jalan Foochow

Jalan Kampung Nyabor

Jln Causeway

Jalan Awang Ramli Amit

Jalan Ramin

Jln Wong Nai Song

Jalan Central

Jalan Bengkel

Jalan Bintang Suntong

Jln Morshidi Sidek

Jalan Lintang

Teboh Tinggi

Jln Padang

Tukang Besi

Jalan Market

Jalan Channel

Jalan Mission

Jalan Pulau

Jalan Khou Peng Loong

1. Esplanade
2. Pagoda
3. Native Produce Market
4. Pasar Malam
5. Malay Food Centre
6. Post Office
7. Downriver Express Boat Wharf
8. Upriver Express Boat Wharf
9. Taxis
10. *Tanatimas Hotel*

some a/c, best of a bad bunch, next to the *pasar malam* (night market); **C** *New World*, 1 Jln Wong Nai Siong, T 310311, a/c, clean rooms with attached bathrooms, good value; **C** *Rumah Rehat* (Rest House), Jln Awang Ramli Amit, T 332834 and Jln Bujang Suntong, T 330406; **C** *Wen Ya*, 1st Flr, 39 High St, T 321288/321290, big rooms, one of the better in this price bracket; **D** *Emas*, 3 Foochow Lane, T 310877, some a/c, clean; **D** *Rejang*, 40 Jln Blacksmith (opposite Standard Chartered), T 315590, some a/c, some rooms have attached bathrooms; **D-E** *Hoover House* (Methodist Guest House), Jln Pulau (next to church), some a/c, fan-cooled rooms are particularly good value for money, spotless rooms.

Restaurants Malay: ♦*Metropol*, 1st Flr, 20 Jln Morshidi Sidek, also serves Melanau curries; ♦♦*Sheraton*, Delta Estate (out of town), Malay (and some Chinese), fish head curries rec by locals. Chinese: ♦♦*Blue Splendour*, 1st Flr, 60-62 Jln Kampung Nyabor (opposite *Premier Hotel*), rec by locals; ♦♦*Golden Palace*, Tanahmas Hotel, Jln Kampung Nyabor, Cantonese and Schezuan; ♦♦*Hock Chu Leu*, 28 Jln Blacksmith, Foochow dishes only; ♦♦♦*Jhong Kuo*, 13 Jln Wong Nai Siong, Foochow. International: ♦♦♦*Peppers Café*, Tanahmas Hotel, Jln Kampung Nyabor, western and local food, curries particularly recommended, popular; ♦♦♦*Villa by the Grand*, Grand Meridien Building, 2nd Flr, 131 Jln Kampung Nyabor, run by a group of Canadian graduates. Foodstalls: there is a good hawker centre on Market Road, in the centre of town. *Rex Food Court*, 28 Cross Rd, is new and clean, one correspondent recommends it, saying it serves an excellent selection of foods.

Sport Golf: *Sibu Golf Club*, Km 17 Ulu Oya Rd, green fees: M\$15.

Shopping Handicrafts: stalls along express boat wharves at Channel Rd, mainly selling basketware. Pottery: 2 potteries at Km 7 and 12 Ulu Oya Rd. Markets: Pasar malam (night market), along High St, Market Rd and Lembangan Lane (Chinatown). Native market (Lembangan market), on Lembangan River between Mission Rd and Channel Rd, sells jungle produce.

Banks & money changers Chartered, Jln Cross; Hong Kong, 17 Jln Wong Nai Siong.

Useful addresses General Post Office: Jln Kampung Nyabor. Resident's Office: T 321963.

Airline offices MAS, 19 Raminway, T 26166.

Sarawak's river express boats – smoke on the water

Sarawak's *Ekspres* boats, powered by turbo-charged V-12 engines, are the closest most upriver tribespeople come to experiencing supersonic flight. They look like floating aircraft fuselages, are piloted from a cockpit and have aircraft-style cabins below, complete with reclining seats and head-rests. Coming downriver, these sleek Chinese-run bullet-boats reach speeds of 70 km/h, and in their wake, longhouse landing rafts are left rocking in metre-high swell. On straighter stretches of river, pilots like to race each other, while the 'front-man', perched on the bows, keeps a desperate look-out for semi-submerged logs – or 'floaters' – which mangle propellors regularly. Incapsulated in the air-conditioned cabins, passengers (everyone from Chinese businessmen to tattooed Orang Ulu) are oblivious to the hazards. Most of them remain gripped, throughout the trip, by the deafening kung-fu films which are continuously screened on video. These movies made mockery of the Malaysian government's decision to ban *The Godfather*, on the grounds that it was too violent.

Express boats are in use on most of the major rivers in Sarawak; ocean-going versions also ply the coastal waters. They have cut travelling times down from days and weeks to a matter of hours: when Ranee Margaret Brooke made the most exciting trip of her life, from Kapit to Belaga and back, in the 1880s, the journey upriver took 6 days. Today the Kapit-Belaga leg can be done in 5 hours. But navigating the coffee-coloured waters of the Rejang and Baram rivers is a dangerous occupation. Free-floating logs pose an ever-present threat. And passing log rafts – huge chevrons of timber, up to 500 m long, which are towed downstream by tugs – swing wide on meanders, leaving only narrow gaps for the express boats to power through. But a pilot can truly only claim to have cut his teeth once he has shot the Rejang's famous Pelagus Rapids, 45 mins upriver from Kapit.

Over this 2½ km-long stretch of white water, he has to dodge logs, rocks, whirlpools and cataracts while keeping a casual look-out for express boats coming in the opposite direction. He takes sharp corners with the powerful engine screaming in reverse thrust; the boat swings around the red-painted oil-drums, anchored to the river-bed, which serve as buoys, listing and rocking violently. The Pelagus is 'one of life's experiences'. When Ranee Margaret Brooke shot these rapids over a century ago, she wrote: "As I stood looking at the whirlpool, Hovering Hawk [her Iban steersman], who was standing near me, pointed with his thumb to the swirling water, all flecked with foam. 'See there,' he said, 'who knows how many eyes lie buried beneath that foam!'" Express boats have not entirely managed to tame the Pelagus: from time to time they run into difficulties. More eyes have been buried beneath the foam in recent years. In Jun 1991, one Kapit-Belaga express capsized on the rapids with the loss of 10 lives.

But accidents happen even without the rapids. In 1990, 2 express boats collided head-on in early morning fog just downriver from Kapit, with serious loss of life. One boat rolled and sank within seconds. Older boats have just one emergency exit, at the back, which is said to be impossible to open underwater as it opens outwards; windows are sealed. Newer boats have more exits, fitted under a more rigid safety code introduced in 1990. On the older boats, it is, however, possible to ride the gauntlet on the roof-top. (Tourists are strongly advised to take adequate precautions against sunburn if travelling on the roof.) Other points to bear in mind when travelling by express boat: first, given the number of express boat trips made daily in Sarawak, the actual accident rate is lower than might be expected, and second, it only costs M$56 to fly from Kapit to Belaga.

Tour companies & travel agents *Equatorial Tour & Travel Centre*, 11 Raminway, T 331599; *Golden Horse Travel*, 20B-21B Sarawak House Complex, T 323288, F 310600; *Hunda Holiday Tours*, 11 Tingkat Bawah, Lorong 1, Brooke Drive, T 326869, F 310396; *Kiew Kwong Travel*, 175B Jln Kampong Nyabor, T 315994, F 318236; *Metropolitan Travel*, 72-4 Jln Pasar, T 322251, F 310831; *R H Tours & Travel*, 32 Blacksmith Rd, T 316767, F 316185; *Sazhong Trading & Travel*, 4 Central Rd, T 336017, F 338031, very efficient and courteous, rec; *Sibu Golden Tours*, 15 1st Flr, Jln Workshop, T 316861, F 318606; *Sitt Travel*, 146 Grd Flr, Kampong Nyabor Rd, T 320168; *Travel Consortium*, 14 Central Rd, T 330720, F 330589; *WTK Travel*, Grd Flr Bangunan Hung Ann, T 326155, F 316160.

Tourist office *Sarawak Third Division Travel Agents' Tourist Association*, 4 Central Rd; *Third Division Hotel Association*, c/o *Sarawak Hotel*, 34 Jln Cross.

Transport to & from Sibu By air: the airport is 6 km N of town, bus 1 (M$1). A new airport is being built, 23 km out of town, which will begin operating during 1993. Regular connections with Kuching (M$72), Bintulu (M$64), Miri (M$90), Marudi (M$120), Kapit (M$68) and Belaga (M$91). There are also some connections with Kota Kinabalu (M$187). By bus: buses leave from Jln Khoo Peng Loong (near Jln Workshop, close to the river). Regular connections with Bintulu, 3 hrs (M$14-18) and Miri (M$36). The early morning buses to Bintulu connect with the buses direct to Batu Niah (see Bintulu).

By boat: boats leave from the wharf in front of the pagoda. Ticket agents Sibu-Kuching: 20 Jln Blacksmith and *Capital Hotel*; 1 Bank Rd and 14 Jln Khoo Peng Loong. There are 2 express boats a day between Sibu and Kuching (M$25-28). These boats also stop off at Sarekei (Sibu-Sarekei (M$6) Sarekei-Kuching (M$$25-28). It is necessary to change to an ocean-going boat at Sarekei for Sibu. Boats to Kapit leave from the Kapit wharf, a little further upriver. Regular express boats to Kapit 2-3 hrs (M$15) and in the wet season, when the river is high enough, they continue to Belaga, 5-6 hrs (M$15). If travelling from Sibu through Kapit to Belaga, take one of the early morning boats, as they connect all the way through. The last Sibu-Kapit boat departs 1300. In the dry season passengers must change on to smaller launches to get upriver to Belaga (see below).

Kapit

Kapit is the 'capital' of Sarawak's 7th division, through which flows the Batang Rejang and its main tributaries, the Batang Balleh, Batang Katibas, Batang Balui and Sungei Belaga. In a treaty with the Sultan of Brunei, Rajah James Brooke acquired the Rejang Basin for Sarawak in 1853. Kapit is the last 'big' town on the Rejang and styles itself as the gateway to 'the heart of Borneo' – after Redmond O'Hanlon's book (*Into the Heart of Borneo*) which describes his adventure up the Batang Balleh in the 1980s. Kapit is full of people who claim to be characters in this book. Like O'Hanlon and his journalist companion James Fenton, most visitors coming to Belaga, venture into the interior to explore the upper Rejang and its tributaries, where there are many Iban and Orang Ulu longhouses.

There are only 20 km of metalled road in and around Kapit, but the little town has a disproportionate number of cars. It is a trading centre for the tribespeople upriver and has grown enormously in recent years with the expansion of the logging industry upstream (**see page 282**). Logs come in 2 varieties – 'floaters' and 'sinkers'. Floaters are pulled downstream by tugs in huge chevron formations. Sinkers – like belian (ironwood) – are transported in the Chinese-owned dry bulk carriers which line up along the wharves at Kapit. When the river is high these timber ships are able to go upstream, past the Pelagus Rapids. The Batang Rejang at Kapit is normally 500m wide and in the dry season, the riverbank slopes steeply down to the water. When it floods, however, the water level rises more than 10m, as is testified by the high water marks on Fort Sylvia. The highest recorded level was in 1983 when the water reached half way up the fort's walls.

Fort Sylvia, was built of belian (ironwood) by Rajah Charles Brooke in 1880, and is now occupied by government offices – it is near the wharves. It was originally called Kapit Fort but was renamed in 1925 after Rajah Vyner Brooke's wife. Most of the forts built during this time were designed to prevent the Orang Ulu going downriver; Fort Sylvia was built to stop the beligerent Iban head-hunters from attacking Kenyah and Kayan settlements upstream.

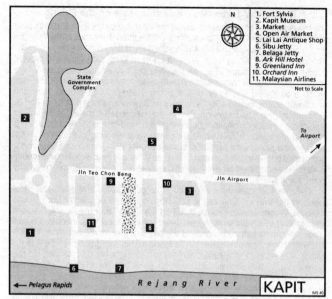

The other main sight is the **Kapit Museum** in the Dewan Suarah, Jalan Hospital. It is a small museum with exhibits on Rejang tribes and the local economy. It was set up by the Sarawak Museum in Kuching and includes a section of an Iban longhouse and several Iban artifacts including a wooden hornbill (**see page 226**). The Orang Ulu section has a reconstruction of a longhouse and mural, painted by local tribespeople. An Orang Ulu *salong* (burial hut), totem pole and other wood-carvings are also on display. The museum also has representative exhibits from the small Malay community and the Chinese. Hokkien traders settled at Kapit and Belaga and traded salt, sugar and ceramics for pepper, rotan and rubber; they were followed by Foochow traders. Appropriately, the Chinese exhibit is a shop. There are also displays on the natural history of the upper Rejang and modern industries such as mining, logging and tourism. All exhibits are labelled in English. The museum's energetic and erudite curator, Wilfred Billy Panyau, is very knowledgeable on the area. Open: 0900-1200, 1400-1600 Mon-Thur & Sat.

Kapit has a particularly colourful daily **market** in the centre of town. Tribeswomen bring in fruit, vegetables and animals to sell; it is quite normal to see everything from turtles, frogs, birds and catfish to monkeys, wild boar and even pangolin and pythons.

Excursions
The **Pelagus Rapids** are 45 mins upstream from Kapit on the Batang Rejang. The 2½ km-long series of cataracts and whirlpools are the result of a sudden drop in the riverbed, caused by a geological fault-line. Express boats can make it up the Pelagus to Belaga in the wet season, but the rapids are still regarded with some trepidation by the pilots (**see page 265**). When the water is low, the rapids can only be negotiated by the smallest longboats. There are 7 rapids in total, each with local names such as 'The Python', 'The Knife' and one, more ominously,

The Rajahs' fortresses – war and peace on the Rejang

The lower reaches of the Batang Rejang are inhabited by the Iban and the upper reaches by the Kenyah and Kayan tribes, the traditional enemies of the Iban (for details on tribes, **see page 238**). During the days of the White Rajahs, a number of forts were built along the river in an effort to keep the peace and prevent head-hunting (**see page 266**). All the forts in Sarawak had chambers where confiscated heads were stored, each with a tag detailing the name of the tribe which took it and the name of the victim. Head-hunting proved a difficult practice to stamp out. In 1904, when Vyner Brooke was based at Kapit Fort as Resident of the Third Division (before he succeeded Charles as Rajah) he reported an attack on one longhouse in which head-hunters severed the heads of 80 women and children while their men were working in the fields. Tribal head-hunting raids were regular occurrences until 1924, when wild boars were exchanged between the Iban and Orang Ulu tribes at a peace-making ceremony in Kapit, presided over by the Rajah. (There are photographs of this ceremony in the Kapit Museum.)

The river fortresses were also used as bases for punitive raids against tribal rebels in the interior. One of the first stops on the route upriver from Sibu is Kanowit, where Charles Brooke built Fort Emma. In 1859 the Rejang Resident and the fort commander were murdered there by local tribespeople. Charles Brooke swore to bathe his hands in the blood of the murderers. With 15,000 'friendly' Ibans, he went upriver in 1862, and led his expedition past the Pelagus Rapids and Belaga to the Kayan and Kenyah strongholds. Brooke then led the Ibans into a lengthy pitched battle in which hundreds died that finally broke the power of the Orang Ulu.

While the Brookes successfully forged alliances with the Rejang's Ibans, some individual groups rebelled from time to time. In her book *My Life in Sarawak*, Ranee Margaret (Charles Brooke's wife) relates the story of one Iban chief's dawn attack on the Rajah's fort at Sibu. Inside were several other 'friendly' Dayak chiefs. "...The manner in which the friendly Dyak chiefs behaved during the skirmish amused me very much," she wrote, "for they did nothing but peer through the lattice-work, and shout Dyak insults at the attacking party, most of whom they knew very well. They made unpleasant remarks about the enemy's mothers, and inquired whether the men themselves belonged to the female sex, as their efforts were so feeble."

called 'The Grave'. A developer has plans to build a resort complex overlooking the rapids; it is scheduled for completion by the mid-1990s. **Getting there**: regular express boats pass through the rapids upstream.

Longhouses around Kapit Some longhouses around Kapit are accessible by road, and several others are within an hour's longboat ride from town. In Kapit you are likely to be invited to visit one of these (some hotels will help organize trips, but it is easy to meet people – the best way is to ensconce yourself in a coffee shop). There are guides in Kapit who charge too much for very unsatisfactory tours. Visitors are strongly advised not to visit a longhouse without an invitation, ideally from someone who lives in it (**see page 260**). As a general rule, the further from town a longhouse is, the more likely it is to conform with the image of what a traditional longhouse should be like. That said, there are some beautiful traditional longhouses nearby, mainly Iban. One of the most accessible, for example is **Rumah Seligi**, about 30 mins drive from Kapit. (Cars or vans can be hired by the half-day; M$50.) Only a handful of longhouses are more than 500m from the riverbanks of the Rejang and its tributaries. Most longhouses still practice shifting cultivation (**see page 239**); rice is the main crop but under government aid programmes many are now growing cash crops such as cocoa.

The longhouse – prime-site apartments with river view

Most longhouses are built on stilts, high on the riverbank, on prime real estate. They are 'prestigious properties' with 'lots of character', and with their 'commanding views of the river', they are the condominiums of the jungle. They are long-rise rather than high-rise however, and the average longhouse has 20-25 'doors' (although there can be as many as 60). Each represents one family. The word *long* in a settlement's name – as in Long Liput or Long Terawan – means 'confluence' (the equivalent of *kuala* in Malay), and does not refer to the length of the longhouse.

Behind each of the doors – which even today, are rarely locked – is a *bilik*, or apartment, which includes the family living room and a loft, where paddy and tools are stored. In Kenyah and Kayan longhouses, paddy (which can be stored for years until it is milled) is kept in elaborate barns, built on stilts away from the longhouse, in case of fire. In traditional longhouses, the living rooms are simple atap roofed, bamboo-floored rooms; in modern longhouses – which are designed on exactly the same principles – the living rooms are commonly furnished with sofas, lino floors, a television and an en suite bathroom. All biliks face out onto the *ruai*, or gallery, which is the focus of communal life, and is where visitors are usually entertained. Attached to this there is usually a *tanju* – an open verandah, running the full length of the house – where rice and other agricultural products are dried. Long ladders – notched hardwood trunks – lead up to the tanju; these can get very slippery and do not always come with handrails.

Longhouse tours To go upriver beyond Kapit it is necessary to get a permit (no charge) from the offices in the State Government Complex. The permit is valid for travel up the Rejang as far as Belaga and for an unspecified distance up the Balleh. For upriver trips beyond Belaga another permit must be obtained there. If you are going up a long way up the Batang Rejang, it is probably cheaper to organize a tour from Belaga (see below). Those planning to visit longhouses should refer to the guidelines on visiting longhouses (**see page 260**).

The vast majority of the population in Sarawak's 7th Division is Iban (about 72%). They inhabit the Rejang up to (and a little beyond) Kapit as well as the lower reaches of the Balleh and its tributaries. The Iban people are traditionally the most hospitable to visitors, but as a result, their longhouses are the most frequently visited by tourists. Malays and Chinese account for 5% and 3% of the population respectively. The Orang Ulu live further upriver; the main tribes are the Kayan and the Kenyah (12%) and a long list of sub-groups such as the Kejaman, Beketan, Sekapan, Lahanan, Seping, and Tanjong. In addition there are the nomadic and semi-nomadic Penan, Punan and Ukit. Many tribal people are employed in the logging industry, and with their paid jobs, have brought the trappings of modernity to even the remotest longhouses.

Longhouses between Kapit and Belaga are accessible by the normal passenger boats but these boats only go as far as Sungei Mena on the Balleh River (2½ hrs). To go further upriver it is necessary to take a tour or organize your own guides and boatmen. The sort of trip taken by Redmond O'Hanlon and James Fenton (as described in O'Hanlon's book *Into the Heart of Borneo*) would cost more than M$1,500 a head. Longhouse tours along the Rejang and Balleh rivers can be organized by the following: *Ark Hill Inn*, Lot 451, Shop Lot 10, Jln Airport, T 794168, F 796337, manager David Tan can organize upriver trips and tours of longhouses around Kapit (M$100 for one night, all inclusive), if contacted in advance, they can arrange full itinerary from Kuching or Sibu; *Donald Ak Ding* (can be contacted through *Hua Hua coffee shop*, Kapit), upriver tours M$30/day plus fuel and lodging; *Dinnel Nuing*, PBDS office, Kapit, T 796494; *Rejang Hotel*, 28 New Bazaar, T 796709, rec; *Tan Seng Hi*, Jln Tan Sit Leong. The *Resident's office* also has some official tourist guides on its books.

Accommodation All hotels are within walking distance of the wharves. **B** *Meligai*, 334 Jln

Airport, T 796611, full range of accommodation from VIP suite to dingy standard rooms; **B-C Well Inn**, 40 Jln Court, T 796009/796566, a/c, variable rooms; **C Ark Hill Inn**, 451 Jln Airport, T 794168, F 796337, a/c, friendly, clean rooms, rec; **C-D Greenland Inn**, 463 Jln Teo Chow Beng, T 796388, F 796979, a/c, well kept, rec; **D Hiap Chong**, 33 New Bazaar, T 96213, some a/c, no attached bath, top floor best bet; **D Kapit Longhouse**, New Bazaar, T 796415, a/c, grubby hotel with a few dubious business sidelines; **D Orchard Inn**, 64 Jln Airport, T 796891, a/c, restaurant, clean rooms and helpful staff, deluxe rooms with a/c, TV, bath to economy rooms (cheapest rooms have no window); **D-E Rejang**, 28 New Bazaar, T 796709, some a/c, basic but clean, helpful staff.

Restaurants Kapit's cuisine is predominantly Chinese. **Chuong Hin**, opposite the Sibu wharf. Best stocked coffeeshop in town; ♦**Frosty Boy**, Jln Teo Chow Beng (below **Greenland Inn**), fast food: pizzas, burgers, ice cream; ♦**Hua Hua**, Jln Airport/Jln Court, the proprietor (who read chemistry at Imperial College, London) cooks excellent vegetarian dishes, rec; ♦**Leong Kung**, near Rejang Hotel, rec by locals; ♦**Lily Pond**, in the middle of the lily pond, off Jln Hospital, pleasant setting, plenty of mosquitoes and an unimaginative menu; ♦**Ming Hok**, above the market, only open after 1730, good selection, views over Rejang, rec; ♦♦♦**Orchard Inn**, 64 Jln Airport, T 796891, the most upmarket restaurant in Kapit, food well presented but the coffee shops taste just as good, disco from 2200-0100; ♦**S'ng Ee Ho Restaurant**, next to Metox supermarket, happy to cook anything you ask for; ♦**Ung Tong Bakery**, opposite the market, bakery and café, good continental style breakfasts – big selection of rolls and good coffee, fresh bread baked twice daily (0600 and 1100), rec. **Foodstalls**: stalls at the top end of the road opposite the market (dead end road; brightly painted on the outside). Good satay stall on Jln Hospital, next to the lily pond.

Shopping Handicrafts: **Putena Jaya**, opposite market, from the outside it looks like a café, inside antique and new handicrafts. **Lai Lai Antique shop**, next road along on the right; reasonable selection of woven rugs/sarongs. Prices seem high but they are similar to the starting prices at the longhouses.

Banks & money changers There are 2 banks which will accept travellers' cheques, one in the New Bazaar and the other on Jln Airport, but it is easier to change money in Sibu.

Useful addresses Resident's Office: 1st Flr State Government Complex (opposite the lily pond), T 796963. Permits for upriver trips. Tourists going to Baleh or upper Rejang areas must sign a form saying they fully understand they are travelling at their own risk. **Library**: on the other side of the road from the Government Complex. Good selection of books on history and natural history of Borneo. Open: 1615-2030 Mon-Sat, 0900-1115, 1400-1630 Sat, 0900-1100, 1400-1830 Sun. **Maps**: Top Flr, State Government Complex. Maps of Kapit Division and other parts of Sarawak.

Airline offices MAS, in block opposite Sibu jetty.

Transport to & from Kapit 160 km from Sibu. **By air**: regular connections with Sibu (M$58) and Belaga (M$56). Low cloud at Kapit often prevents landing and the plane goes straight to Belaga. **By boat**: all 3 wharves are close together. Regular connections with Sibu from 0600-1300, 2-3 hours (M$15). Belaga is not accessible by large express boats during the dry season. Prices for the express boats start from M$15. For the smaller boats going upriver in the dry season prices are higher and start from M$30. It is also possible to charter a longboat to Belaga but prices start from M$100.

Belaga

Belaga is the archetypal sleepy little town; most people while their time away in coffee shops. They are the best place to watch life go by, and there are always interesting visitors in town, from itinerant wild honey-collectors from Kalimantan to Orang Ulu who have brought their jungle produce downriver to the Belaga bazaar or are heading to the metropolis of Kapit for medical treatment. In the afternoons, *sepak takraw* matches are held on the court below the shops. At night, when the neon lights flicker on, Belaga's coffee shops are invaded by thousands of cicadas, beetles and moths.

A few Chinese traders set up shop in Belaga in the early 1900s, and traded with the tribespeople upriver, supplying essentials such as kerosene, cooking oil and shotgun cartridges. The Orang Ulu brought their beadwork and mats as well jungle produce such as beeswax, ebony, gutta-percha (rubbery tree-gum) and, most prized of all, bezoar stones. These are gall-stones found in certain monkeys

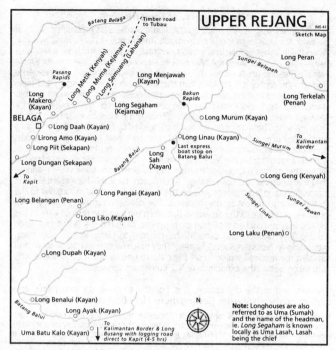

UPPER REJANG

IMS 41

Sketch Map

Batang Belaga / Timber road to Tubau

Pasang Rapids

Long Metik (Kenyah)
Long Muma (Kejaman)
Long Semuang (Lahanan)

Long Menjawah (Kayan)

Sungei Belepeh

Long Peran

Long Makero (Kayan)

BELAGA □ ○ Long Daah (Kayan)

Long Segaham (Kejaman)

Bakun Rapids

Long Terkelah (Penan)

○ Lirong Amo (Kayan)
○ Long Piit (Sekapan)

Long Murum (Kayan)

Long Linau (Kayan)

Sungei Murum

To Kalimantan Border

Long Dungan (Sekapan)

Batang Balui

Long Sah (Xayan)

Last express boat stop on Batang Balui

← To Kapit

Long Geng (Kenyah)

Long Pangai (Kayan)

Sungei Linau
Sungei Kawan

Long Belangan (Penan)

Long Liko (Kayan)

Long Laku (Penan) ○

○ Long Dupah (Kayan)

○ Long Benalui (Kayan)

N

Batang Balui

Long Ayak (Kayan)

Uma Batu Kalo (Kayan)

To Kalimantan Border & Long Busang with logging road direct to Kapit (4-5 hrs)

Note: Longhouses are also referred to as Uma (Sumah) and the name of the headman, ie. *Long Segaham* is known locally as Uma Lasah, Lasah being the chief

(the *wah-wahs*, *jelu-merahs* and *jelu-jankits*) and porcupines. To the Chinese, they have much the same properties as rhinoceros horn (mainly aphrodisiacal) and even today, they are exported from Sarawak to Singapore where they fetch S$300/kg.

Belaga serves as a small government administration centre for the remoter parts of the 7th Division. There is a very pretty **Malay kampung** (Kampung Bahru) along the esplanade downriver from the Belaga Bazaar. (The Kejaman burial pole on display outside the Sarawak Museum in Kuching was brought from the Belaga area in 1902.)

Excursions To go upriver beyond Belaga it is necessary to obtain a permit from the Resident's office and permission from the police station. When the river is high, express boats go upstream as far as **Rumah Belor** on the Batang Balui, but for the purpose of visiting longhouses in the Belaga area, it is best to hire a boat in Belaga. Many of the longhouses around Belaga are quite modern, although several of the Kenyah and Kayan settlements have beautifully carved wooden tombstones – or *salongs* – nearby. All the longhouses beyond Belaga are Orang Ulu. Even longhouses which, on the map, appear very remote (such as Long Busang), are now connected by logging roads from Kapit – only 4 hrs drive away. To get well off the beaten track, into Penan country, it is possible to organize treks from Belaga towards the Kalimantan border, staying in longhouses en route.

Pasang Rapids About 2 km up the Batang Belaga from Belaga. These spectacular rapids are certainly the biggest in Sarawak. It appears that no one has purposely tried to shoot them – they are too dangerous. Boats can get reasonably close,

The massacre at Long Nawang

One-hundred years and 3 months after James Brooke was proclaimed Rajah of Sarawak, the Japanese Imperial Army invaded the country. On Christmas Day 1941, when Rajah Vyner Brooke was visiting Australia, they took Kuching; a few days earlier they had occupied the Miri oilfields. Japanese troops, dressed for jungle warfare, headed upriver. They did not expect to encounter such stiff resistance from the tribespeople. The Allies had the brainwave of rekindling an old tribal pastime – head-hunting, which successive Brooke administrations had tried to stamp out. Iban and Orang Ulu warriors were offered 'ten-bob-a-knob' for Japanese heads, and many of the skulls still hanging in longhouses are said to date from this time. The years of occupation were marked by terrible brutality, and many people fled across the border into Dutch Borneo – now Kalimantan. The most notorious massacre in occupied Sarawak involved refugees from Kapit.

Just a month after the Japanese invasion, a forestry officer stationed on the Rejang heard that a group of women and children from Kapit were planning to escape across the Iran Range into Dutch territory. He organized the evacuation, and led the refugees up the rivers and over the mountains to the Dutch military outpost at Long Nawang. The forester returned to Kapit to help organize resistance to the Japanese. But when the invading forces heard of the escape they dispatched a raiding party upriver, captured the Dutch fort, lined up the fifty women and ordered the children to climb into nearby trees. According to historian Robert Payne: "They machine-gunned the women and amused themselves by picking off the children one by one... Of all those who had taken part in the expedition only 2 Europeans survived."

however, and in the dry season, it is possible to climb up to a picnic area, overlooking the white water. **Getting there**: hire a boat from Belaga (M$40-50).

Tours The *Belaga Hotel* will contact guides for upriver trips and the District Office can also recommend a handful of experienced guides. In this part of Sarawak, guides are particularly expensive – sometimes up to M$80 a day, mainly because there are not enough tourists to justify full-time work. It is necessary to hire experienced boatmen too, because of the numerous rapids. The best guide for longer trips (to jungle areas NE of Belaga and to Penan areas along the Kalimantan border) is reputed to be **John Bampa**, who can be contacted through Andrew Tong at the *Belaga Hotel*. Such trips require at least 5 or 6 days. Prices for trips to longhouses upriver vary according to distance and the water level, but are similar to those in Kapit. As a rough guideline, a litre of petrol costs about M$4; a 40 hp boat uses nearly 20 litres to go 10 km. English is not widely spoken upriver, basic *Bahasa* comes in handy. (See page 365.)

Accommodation **C** *Bee Lian*, 11 Belaga Bazaar, T 461416, a/c; **C-D** *Belaga*, 14 Belaga Bazaar, T 461244, some a/c, restaurant, no hot water, particularly friendly proprietor, good coffee shop downstairs, in-house video and cicadas; **D** *Sing Soon Huat*, 27 New Bazaar, T 461257, F 461346, a/c.

Restaurants Several small, cheap coffee shops along Belaga Bazaar and Main Bazaar, the menus are all pretty similar.

Shopping Handicrafts: *Chop Teck Hua*, Belaga Bazaar has an intriguing selection of tribal jewellery, old coins, beads, feathers, woodcarvings, blowpipes, parangs, tattoo boards and other curios buried under cobwebs and gekko droppings at the back of the shop, rec.

Useful addresses General Post Office: in the District Office building. District Office: (for upriver permits) on the far side of the basketball/*sepak takraw* courts.

Airline offices MAS, c/o Lau Chun Kiat, Main Bazaar.

Transport to & from Belaga **By air**: connections with Kapit (M$56) and on to Sibu (M$91). **By boat**: express boats from Kapit only when the river level is high enough to negotiate the Pelagus Rapids, 5-8 hrs (depending on season). Prices start at M$15. When the river is very low the only option is to fly to Belaga.

To Tabau & on to Bintulu It is possible to hire a boat from Belaga to Kestima Kem (logging camp) near Rumah Lahanan Laseh (M$60); from there logging trucks go to Tabau on the Kemena River. **NB**: logging trucks leave irregularly and you can get stuck in logging camps. It is 3 hrs drive to Tabau; this trip is not possible in the wet season. There are regular express boats from Tabau to Bintulu (M$14). This is the fastest and cheapest route to Bintulu, but not the most reliable. It is necessary to obtain permission from the Resident's office and the police station in Belaga to take this route.

To Kalimantan It is possible to get to Kalimantan from Belaga, although it is an expensive trip due to the cost of chartering longboats. It is necessary to get your passport stamped at the immigration department in Kapit. The longboat trip takes about 2 days, following the Batang Balui (past the last express boat stop at Rumah Belor) to the Kenyah longhouse of Long Busang on the Sungei Busang. From there, Sungei Aput flows towards the border. There is a trail from the river across the frontier to Long Nawan, where there is an Indonesian immigration post. The territory on the other side is called the Apo Kayan, and it is possible to trek through this region (see page 846).

BINTULU AND NIAH CAVES

Bintulu

The Niah Caves are just off the Miri-Bintulu road and are easily accessible from both towns. Trips to Similajau National Park and longhouses on the Kemena River (rarely visited) can be organized from Bintulu.

The word Bintulu is thought to be a corruption of *Mentu Ulau*, which translates as 'the place for gathering heads'. Bintulu, on the Kemena River, is in the heart of Melinau country and was traditionally a fishing and farming centre... until the largest natural gas reserve in Malaysia was discovered just offshore in the late 1970s, turning Bintulu into a boomtown overnight; Shell, Petronas and Mitsubishi moved to the town in force. In 1978 the town's population was 14,000; it is now over 50,000. More than M$11 billion was invested in Bintulu's development between 1980 and 1990.

The remnants of the old fishing village at Kampung Jepak are on the opposite bank of the Kemena River. During the Brooke era the town was a small administrative centre. The **clock tower** commemorates the meeting of 5 representatives from the Brooke government and sixteen local chieftains, the birth of Council Negeri, the state legislative body.

The first project to break ground in Bintulu was the M$100 million crude oil terminal at Tanjung Kidurong from which 45,000 barrels of petroleum are exported daily. A deep-water port was built and the liquefied natural gas (LNG) plant started operating in 1982. It is one of the Malaysian government's biggest investment projects. The abundant supply of natural gas also created investment in related downstream projects. The main industrial area at Tanjung Kidurong is 20 km from Bintulu. The **viewing tower** at Tanjung Kidurong gives a panoramic view of the new-look Bintulu, out to the timber ships on the horizon. They anchor 15 km offshore to avoid port duties and the timber is taken out on barges.

Bintulu has a modern **Moorish- style mosque**, completed in 1988. **Pasar Bintulu** is also an impressive new building in the centre of town, built to house the local jungle produce market, foodstalls and some handicrafts stalls. A landscaped **Wildlife Park** has been developed on the outskirts of town, on the way to Tanjung Batu. It is a local recreational area and contains a small zoo and a botanic garden (the only one in Sarawak). Admission: M$1. Open: 0800- 1900 Mon-Sun. Few tourists stay long in Bintulu, although it is the jump-off point to the Similajau National Park (which opened in 1991) and Niah Caves. The longhouses on the Kemena River are accessible, but tend not to be as interesting as those further up the Rejang and Baram rivers.

Excursions
Similajau National Park, see below.

Niah Caves & National Park, see page 276.

Upriver More than 20 Kemena River longhouses can be reached by road or river within 30 min of Bintulu. Iban longhouses are the closest; further upriver are the more traditional Kayan and Kenyah longhouses. **Getting there:** tours organized by Similajau Adventure Tours (see below) or hire a boat from the wharf.

Accommodation A *Plaza*, Dagang Commercial Centre, Jln Abang Galau, T 35111, F 32742, a/c, restaurant, pool, very smart new hotel, and, compared with other upmarket hotels in Sarawak, excellent value for money, rec; **B** *Li hua*, Berjaya Commercial Centre, Km 2, T 35000, F 35222, a/c, restaurant; **B** *Regent*, Kemena Commercial Complex (on the way to Tanjung Batu), T 35511, F 33770, a/c, restaurant; **B** *Sunlight*, 7 Pedada St, T 32577, F 34075, a/c; **C** *My House*, 2nd Flr, 161 Taman Sri Dagang, Jln Masjid, T 36399, F 32050, a/c, rec; **C** *National*, 2nd Flr, 5 Temple St, T 31279/33346, a/c, clean and well kept, rec; **D** *Kemena Lodging*, 78 Keppel Rd, T 31533, a/c, no attached bath.

Restaurants *Umai*, raw fish pickled with lime or the fruit of wild palms (*assam*) and mixed with salted vegetables, onions and chillies is a Melanau speciality. Bintulu is famed for its *belacan* – prawn paste – and in the local dialect, prawns are *urang*, not *udang*. Locals quip that they are 'man-eaters' because they *makan urang*. ◆◆*Fook Lu Shou*, Plaza Hotel, Dagang Commercial Centre, Jln Abang Galau, seafood and Chinese cuisine, including birds' nest soup, boiled in rock sugar (M$45); ◆*Kemena Coffee House*, Western, Malay and Chinese, open 24 hrs; ◆◆◆*Marco Polo*, on the waterfront, locals recommend pepper steak; ◆*Sarawak*, 160 Taman Sri Dagan (near *Plaza Hotel*), cheap Malay food. Foodstalls: ◆◆*Pantai Ria*, near Tanjung Batu, mainly seafood, only open in the

BINTULU IMS 37

Not to Scale

N

Jln. Abang Galau
Jln. Masjid
Kemena River
Jln. Pedada
Jln. Reservoir
Jln. Somerville
Jln. Temple
Jln. Main Market
Jln. Market
Jln. Lan Law Gek Soon
Lebuh Queen

To Tanjung Kiderong, Mosque & Wildlife Park, Miri

1. Clocktower
2. Pasar Bintulu
3. Jetty
4. Taxi
5. Post Office
6. Foodstalls
7. My House
8. Plaza Hotel
9. National Hotel

evenings, rec. ♦*Chinese stalls* behind the Chinese temple on Jln Temple.

Sport Golf: *Tanjung Kidurong*, new 18-hole course, N of Bintulu, by the sea, green fees: M$15.

Shopping Handicrafts: *Robin Enterprise*, 98 Taman Sri Dagang and *Dyang Enterprise*, Lobby Flr, *Plaza Hotel*, Dagang Commercial Centre, Jln Abang Galau. The latter is rather overpriced because of the Plaza's more upmarket clientele.

Banks & money changers Bank Bumiputra & Bank Utama on Jln Somerville; **Standard Chartered**, Jln Keppel.

Useful addresses General Post Office: far side of the airport near the Resident's office. **National Parks & Wildlife Department**: T 36101. **Resident's Office**: far side of the airport, T 31896.

Airline offices MAS, Jln Masjid, T 31554.

Tour companies & travel agents *Similajau Travel and Tours*, *Plaza Hotel*, Jln Abang Galau is the only tour company at the moment. It offers tours around the city, to the Niah caves, longhouses and Similajau National Park.

Transport to & from Bintulu By air: the airport is in the centre of town. Regular connections with Kuching (M$116), Miri (M$68). There are also some connections with Kota Kinabalu. **By bus**: buses leave from Jln Masjid (close to the river). Regular connections with Miri and Sibu; fares to both places are the same (M$14.80-$18). The Sibu-Miri buses stop at Niah junction (M$10) but this involves a 6 km walk to Batu Niah. There are also direct buses to Batu Niah (M$10). **By taxi**: taxis also leave from Jln Masjid. M$25 per person to Miri or Sibu. Because of the regular bus services and the poor state of the roads, most taxis are for local use only and chartering them is expensive. **By boat**: regular connections with Tabau, 2½ hrs (M$14-18). Last boat leaves 1330 (connections with Belaga, via logging road, **see page 272**; this route is popular with people in Belaga as it is much cheaper than going from Sibu).

Similajau National Park

Sarawak's most unusually shaped national park is more than 32 km long and only 1.5 km wide. Similajau was gazetted in 1976, but has only really been open to tourists since the construction of decent facilities in 1991. Lying 20 km NE of Bintulu, Similajau is a coastal park with sandy beaches, broken by rocky headlands. **Pasir Mas** – or Golden Sands – is a beautiful 3.5 km-long stretch of coarse beach, to the N of the Likau river, where green turtles (**see page 336**) come ashore to lay their eggs between Jul and Sept. A few kilometres from park headquarters at **Kuala Likau** is a small coral reef, known as Batu Mandi. The area is renowned for birdwatching. Because it is so new, and because Bintulu is not on the main tourist track, the park is very quiet. Its seclusion makes it a perfect escape.

The beaches are backed by primary rainforest: peatswamp, *kerangas* (heath forest), mixed dipterocarp and mangrove (along Sungei Likau and Sungei Sebubong). There are small rapids on the Sebulong River. The rivers (particularly the beautiful **Sungei Likau**) have sadly been polluted by indiscriminate logging activities upstream.

Flora and fauna One of the first things a visitor notices on arrival at Kual Likau is the prominent sign advising against swimming in the river, and to watch your feet in the headquarters area: Similajau is well known for its saltwater crocodiles (*Crocodylus perosus*). Similajau also has 24 resident species of mammals (including gibbons, Hose's langurs, banded langurs, long tailed macaques, civets, wild boar, porcupines, squirrels) and 185 species of birds, including many migratory species. Marine life includes dolphins, porpoises and turtles; there are some good coral reefs to the N. Pitcher plants grow in the *kerangas* forest and along the beach.

Treks A rough trail has been cut by park rangers going NE from the other side of Sungei Likau. The path follows undulating terrain, parallel to the coast. It is possible to cut to the left, through the jungle, to the coast, and walk back to Kuala Likau along the beach.

Permits are available from the Bintulu Development Authority.

Park information centre at Park Headquarters at the mouth of Sungei Likau.

Accommodation Chalets at Park Headquarters, a/c (**C**); Hostel (**F**).

Restaurant Canteen at Park Headquarters serving basic food. Picnic shelters at Park HQ.

Transport to & from Similajau By boat: at the moment the only way to get to Similajau is through *Sun Adventure Tours* in Bintulu (**see page 273**). By road: plans to build a road from Bintulu.

NIAH NATIONAL PARK

Niah's famous caves, tucked into a limestone massif called Gunung Sabis, made world headlines in 1959, when they were confirmed as the most important archaeological site in Asia. About 40,000 years ago, when the Gulf of Thailand and the Sunda Shelf were still dry ground, and a land-bridge connected the Philippines and Borneo, Niah was home to *Homo sapiens*. It was the most exciting archaeological discovery since Java man (*Homo erectus*), (see page 621).

Scientist and explorer A Hart Everett led expeditions to Niah Caves in 1873 and 1879, after which he pronounced that they justified no further work. Seventy-nine years later, Tom Harrisson, ethnologist, explorer and conservationist and curator of the Sarawak Museum, confirmed the most important archaeological find in Southeast Asia at Niah. He unearthed fragments of a 37,000-year-old human skull – the earliest evidence of *Homo sapiens* in the region – at the W mouth of the Niah Great Cave itself. The skull was buried under 2.4m of guano. His find debunked and prompted a radical reappraisal of popular theories about where modern man's ancestors had sprung from. A wide range of Palaeolithic and Neolithic tools, pottery, ornaments and beads were also found at the site. Anthropologists believe Niah's caves may have been permanently inhabited until around 1400 AD. Harrisson's excavation site, office and house have been left intact in the mouth of the Great Cave. A total of 166 burial sites have been excavated, 38 of which are Mesolithic (up to 20,000 years before present) and the remainder Neolithic (4,000 years before present). Some of the finds are now in the Sarawak Museum in Kuching.

Today, Niah National Park is one of the most popular tourist attractions in Sarawak and attracts more than 15,000 visitors every year. The caves were declared a national historic monument in 1958, but it was not until 1974 that the 3,000 ha of jungle surrounding the caves were turned into a national park to protect the area from logging.

To reach the caves, take a longboat across the river from Park Headquarters at Palangkalan Lubang to the start of the 4 km belian (ironwood) plankwalk to the entrance of the **Great Cave**. (Take the right fork 1 km from the entrance.) The remains of a small kampung, formerly inhabited by birds' nest collectors (see below) and guano collectors, is just before the entrance, in the shelter of overhanging rocks. It is known as **Traders' Cave**.

The **Painted Cave** is beyond the Great Cave, and can be reached via a plankwalk from the rear of the Great Cave. (It is possible to hire a guide to find the Painted Cave: local maps are very poor.) Prehistoric wall-paintings – the only ones in Borneo – stretch for about 32m along the cave wall. Most of the drawings are of dancing human figures and boats, thought to be associated with a death ritual. On the floor of the cave, several 'death-ships' were found with some Chinese stoneware, shell ornaments and ancient glass beads. These death-ships served as coffins and have been carbon-dated to between 1 and 780 AD. By around 700 AD there is thought to have been a flourishing community based in the caves,

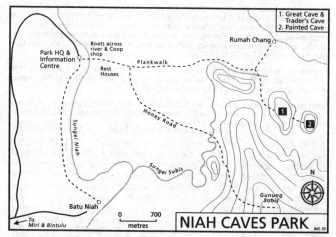

NIAH CAVES PARK

trading hornbill ivory and birds' nests with the Chinese in exchange for porcelain and beads. But then it seems the caves were suddenly deserted in about 1400. In Penan folklore there are references to 'the ancestors who lived in the big caves' and tribal elders are said to be able to recall funeral rites using death-boats similar to those found at Niah.

Flora and fauna The Niah National Park is primarily comprised of alluvial or peat swamp as well as some mixed dipterocarp forest. Long-tailed macaques, hornbills, squirrels, flying lizards and crocodiles have all been recorded in the park. There are also bat hawks which present an impressive spectacle when they home in on one of the millions of bats which pour out of the caves at dusk.

Treks A lowland trail called Jalan Madu (Honey Road), traverses the peat swamp forest and up Gunung Subis; it is not well marked. Return trips need a full day. The trail leads off the plankwalk to the right, about 1 km from Pangkalan Lubang. The left-fork on the plankwalk, before the gate to the caves, goes to an Iban longhouse, Rumah Chang (40 mins walk).

Park Headquarters at Pangkalan Lubang next to Sungei Subis.

Transport around the Park From Park HQ, longboats can be hired for upriver trips (M$40/day; 8 people max per boat). Crossing the river from HQ costs M$0.50.

Equipment Visitors are advised to bring a powerful torch for the caves. Walking boots are advisable during the wet season as the plankwalk can get very slippery.

Guides can be hired from Park HQ to Painted Cave (M$35 for groups of up to 20) and to Gunung Subis.

Park Information Centre At Park

Niah's guano collectors: scraping the bottom

Eight bat species live in the Niah Caves, some of them more common ones such as the horseshoe bat and fruit bats. Other more exotic varieties include the bearded tomb bat, Cantor's roundleaf horseshoe bat and the lesser bent-winged bat. The ammonia-stench of bat guano permeates the humid air. People began collecting guano in 1929 – it is used as a fertilizer and to prevent pepper vines from rotting. Guano collectors pay a licence fee of M$1 per day for the privilege of sweeping up *tahi sapu* (fresh guano) and digging up *tahi timbang* (mature guano) which they sell to the Bat Guano Cooperative at the end of the plankwalk.

Headquarters, has displays on birds' nests and flora and fauna. The exhibition includes the 37,000-year-old human skull which drew world attention to Niah in 1958. Also on display are 35,000-year-old oyster shells, as well as palaeolithic pig bones, monkey bones, turtle-shells and crabs which were found littering the cave floor. There are also burial vessels dating from 1600BC and carved seashell jewellery from around 400BC. Open: 0800-1230, 1400-1615 Mon-Fri; 0800-1245 Sat; 0800-1200 Sun.

Permits No permit is required for the Great Cave but it is necessary to acquire one in order to visit the Painted Cave. This can be picked up from the curator's office in the Sarawak Museum, Kuching or from Park Headquarters at Niah.

Accommodation can be booked at the National Parks office, Forest Department, Jln Gartak, Kuching, T 248988 or in Miri, at the Old Forestry Building, Jln Angkasa, T 36637. Both the

How to make a swift buck

The Malay name for Niah's Painted Cave is *Kain Hitam* – or 'black cloth' – because the profitable rights to the birds' nests were traditionally exchanged for bolts of black cloth. The Chinese have had a taste for swiftlets' nests for well over a thousand years, and the business of collecting them from 60 m up in the cavernous chamber of the Great Cave is as lucrative (and as hazardous) a profession now as it was then. The nests are used to prepare birds' nest soup – they are blended with chicken stock and rock salt – which is a famous Chinese delicacy, prized as an aphrodisiac and for its supposed remedial properties for asthma and rhumatism. Birds' nests are one of the most expensive foods in the world: they sell for up to US$400/kilo in Hong Kong, where about 100 tonnes of them (worth US$40 million) are consumed annually. The Chinese communities of North America import 30 tonnes of birds' nests a year. Locally, they fetch M$150-600/kg, depending on the grade.

Hundreds of thousands – possibly millions – of swiftlets (of the *Collocalia* swift family) live in the caves. Unlike other parts of Southeast Asia, where collectors use rotan ladders to reach the nests (see Gomontong Caves, Sabah, **page 331**), Niah's collectors scale belian (ironwood) poles to heights of more than 60 m. They use bamboo sticks with a scraper attached to one end (called *penyulok*) to pick the nests off the cave-roof. The nests are harvested 3 times each season (which run from Aug to Dec and Jan to Mar). On the first 2 occasions, the nests are removed before the eggs are laid and a third left until the nestlings are fledged. Nest collectors are now all supposed to have licences, but in reality, no one does. Although the birds nests are supposed to be protected by the National Park in the off-season, wardens turn a blind eye to illegal harvesting – the collectors also know many secret entrances to the caves. Officially, people caught harvesting out of season can be fined M$2,000 or sent to jail for a year, but no one's ever caught. Despite the fact that it is a dangerous operation (there are usually several fatal accidents at Niah each year), collecting has become such a popular pursuit that harvesters have to reserve their spot with a lamp. Nest collecting is run on a first-come, first-served basis.

Nests of the white nest swiftlets and the black nest swiftlets are collected – the nests of the mossy-nest and white-bellied swiftlets require too much effort to clean. The nests are built by the male swiftlets using a glutinous substance produced by the salivary glands under the tongue which is regurgitated in long threads; the saliva sets like cement producing a rounded cup which sticks to the cave wall. In the swifts' nest market, price is dictated by colour: the best are the white nests which are without any plant material or feathers. Most of the uncleaned nests are bought up by middlemen, agents of traders in Kuching, but locals at Batu Niah also do some of the cleaning. The nests are first soaked in water for about 3 hours, and when softened, feathers and dirt are laboriously removed with tweezers. The resulting 'cakes' of nests are left to dry over-night: if they are dried in the sun they turn yellow.

resthouse and the hostel have electricity and are equipped with mattresses, bedding, fans, showers, refrigerator and cooking facilities. *Resthouse (deluxe)*, M$60/house, M$30/room (4 beds/room); *Resthouse (standard)*, M$40/house, M$20/room; *New hostel*, M$72/house, M$18/room; *Old hostel* M$3/person (Students M$1). **Batu Niah** There are also 2 small hotels in Batu Niah (4 km from Park HQ): **D** *Hock Seng* and **D** *Niah Caves Hotel*.

Camping Tents can be hired from Park HQ (M$2).

Restaurants The Guano Collectors' Cooperative shop at the beginning of the plankwalk sells basic food and cold drinks.

Transport to & from Niah National Park 109 km from Miri to Batu Niah. **By bus**: regular connections from Miri, 2-3 hrs ($M10), Bintulu, 2-3 hrs (M$10) and Sibu via Bintulu. There are irregular buses running from the main road junction to Batu Niah. **By taxi**: from Miri (M$15) to Batu Niah from Batu Niah to national park (M$5). From Bintulu to Batu Niah (M$30). **By boat**: boats from Batu Niah (near the market) to Park Headquarters at Pengkalan Lubang, Niah National Park (M$2 per person) or 45 mins walk to Park Headquarters.

MIRI AND THE BARAM RIVER

Miri

Miri is the starting point for adventurous trips up the Barani River to Marudi, Bareo and the Kelabit Highlands. Also accessible from Miri and Marudi is the incomparable Gunung Mulu National Park with the biggest limestone cave system in the world and one of the richest assemblages of plants and animals.

The capital of Sarawak's 4th division is a busy, prosperous town; more than half its population is Chinese. In the latter years of the 19th century, a small trading company set up in Sarawak, to import kerosine and export polished shells and pepper. In 1910, when 'earth oil' was first struck on the hill overlooking Miri, the little trading company took the plunge and diversified into the new commodity. The company's name was Shell. Together with the Malaysian national oil company, Petronas, Shell has been responsible for discovering, producing and refining Sarawak's offshore oil deposits. Oil is a key contributor to Malaysia's export earnings and Miri has been a beneficiary of the boom. There is a big refinery at Lutong to the N, which is connected by pipeline with Seria in Brunei. Lutong is the next town on the Miri River and the main headquarters for Shell.

The oil boom in this area began on Canada Hill, behind the town. **Oil Well No 1** was built by Shell and was the first oil well in Malaysia, spudded on 10th Aug 1910. The well was still yielding oil 62 years later, but its productivity began to slump. It is estimated that a total of 600,000 barrels were extracted from Well No 1 during its operational life. It was shut off in 1972. There are now 624 oil wells in the Miri Field, producing 80 million barrels of oil a year.

Juxtaposed against Miri's modern boom-town image is **Tamu Muhiba** (the native jungle produce market, open 24 hrs), opposite the *Park Hotel* on the roundabout connecting Malay Street and Jalan Padang. Orang Ulu come downriver to sell their produce, and a walk round the market provides an illuminating lesson in jungle nutrition. Colourful characters run impromptu 'stalls' from rattan mats, selling yellow cucumbers that look like mangoes, mangoes that look like turnips, huge crimson durians, tiny loofah sponges, sackfulls of fragrant Bareo rice (brown and white), every shape, size and hue of banana, *tuak* (rice wine) in old Heineken bottles and a menagerie of jungle fauna – including mousedeer, falcons, pangolins and the apparently delicious long-snouted *tupai*, or jungle squirrel. There is a large selection of dried and fresh seafood – fish and *bubok* (tiny prawns), and big buckets boiling with catfish or stacked with turtles.

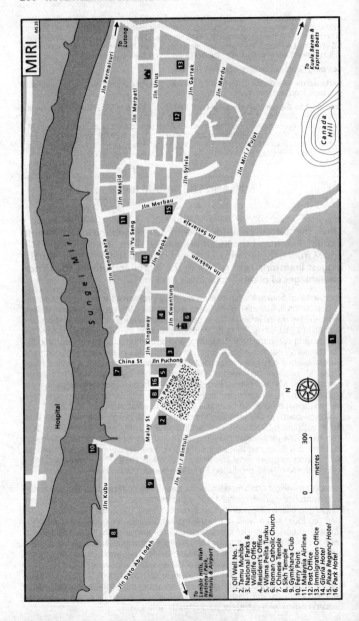

MIRI

MS.35

To Lutong

Jln Permaisuri

Jln Merpati

Jln Unus

Jln Gartak

Jln Merdu

13

12

Jln Masjid

Jln Sylvia

Jln Miri/Pujut

Sungei Miri

Jln Merbau

15

11

Jln Yu Seng

14

Jln Bendahara

Jln Brooke

Jln Setaraja

Jln Hokkien

Canada Hill

To Kuala Baram & Express Boats

Hospital

Jln Kwantung

4

6

Jln Kingsway

3

China St

Jln Puchong

7

B 16

5

Jln Padang

2

Malay St

N

Jln Kubu

9

Jln Miri/Bintulu

0   300

metres

8

Jln Dato Abg Indeh

To Lambir Hills, Niah
National Park,
Bintulu & Airport

10

1. Oil Well No. 1
2. Tamu Muhiba
3. National Parks &
   Wildlife Office
4. Resident's Office
5. Wisma Pelita Tunku
6. Roman Catholic Church
7. Chinese Temple
8. Sikh Temple
9. Gymkhana Club
10. Ferry Point
11. Malaysia Airlines
12. Immigration Office
13. Post Office
14. Gloria Hotel
15. Plaza Regency Hotel
16. Park Hotel

Miri is the main centre for organizing tours up the Baram River, to Mulu National Park.

Excursions
Permits are required to go upriver to Gunung Mulu and the interior. Apply at the Resident's office, Jalan Kwantung, T 33203. Permits are also available from Marudi. If travelling with a tour company it will take care of the bureaucracy.

Niah Caves & National Park, see page 276.

Gunung Mulu National Park, see page 285.

Lambir Hills The park mainly consists of a chain of sandstone hills bounded by rugged cliffs, 19 km S of Miri and just visible from the town. **Flora and fauna**: *Kerangas* (heath forest) covers the higher ridges and hills while the lowland areas are mixed dipterocarp forest. Bornean gibbons, bearded pigs, barking deer and over 100 species of bird have been recorded in the park. **Treks**: there is only one path across a rickety suspension bridge at present, but there are numerous waterfalls and tree towers for birdwatching. The park attracts hoardes of day-trippers from Miri at weekends. No overnight accommodation is available but there is an information centre and a canteen. The Park Headquarters is close to the Miri-Niah road. **Getting there**: from *Park Hotel* take Bintulu or Bakong bus (M$3).

Tours Although most tour companies specialize in trips up the Baram River to Mulu National Park, some are much better than others – in terms of facilities and services offered. The best agents are *Alo Doda* and *Tropical Adventure* which have private accommodation in the Park and run an interesting selection of more off-beat treks to remote destinations; they are also the most expensive. *Alo Doda*, for example, organizes treks to the Penan areas and Kenyah longhouses of Ulu Baram – on the upper stretches of the river. Every agency has a Mulu National Park itinerary covering the caves, pinnacles, and summits. It is also possible to trek to Bareo and Mount Murud, as well as to Limbang from Mulu. Most of the agencies employ experienced guides who will be able to advise on longer, more ambitious treks. The Mulu National Park is one destination where it is usually cheaper to go through a tour company than to try to do it independently. Costs vary considerably according to the number of people in a group: for the 3 day Mulu trip, a single tourist can expect to pay M$500; this drops to M$400 a head for a group of 4 and about M$350 each for a group of 10, all accommodation, food, travel and guide costs included. An 8-day tour of Ulu Baram longhouses, would cost M$1,800 for one person and M$1,200 per person in a group of 10. A 20-day trek will cost 2 people (minimum number) around M$2,000 each, and a group of 6-10, M$1,300 a head. For those who want to visit remote longhouses, tour companies present by far the best option. Tour fees cover 'gifts' and all payments to longhouse headmen for food, accommodation and entertainment.

Accommodation Most people going to Mulu will have to spend at least one night in Miri. The town has a reasonable selection of mid-to-upmarket hotels; many offer discounts of 30-40% off quoted prices as a matter of course. Many of the mid-range hotels are around Jln Yu Seng Selatan. But being an oil town, and close to Brunei, Miri has a booming prostitution industry. Many of the cheaper lodging houses, particularly those around Jln China, are sleezy brothels. The cheaper accommodation listed below represents the more respectable end of the market. **A** *Holiday Inn*, Taman Selera Beach (S of Miri), a/c, restaurant, pool, newly opened; **A** *Park*, Jln Kingsway, T 414555, a/c, restaurant, until the *Holiday Inn* opened, the *Park* was the best hotel in town, ranks as about a 3-star hotel, discounts offered; **A-B** *Rinwood*, Jln Yu Seng Utara, T 415888, F 415009, a/c, restaurant; **B** *Apollo*, 4 Jln Yu Seng Selatan, T 33077/415236, F 33749, a/c; **B** *Cosy Inn*, 545-547 Jln Yu Seng Selatan, T 415522, F 415155, a/c, restaurant; **B** *Gloria*, 27 Brooke Rd, T 416699, F 418866, a/c, restaurant; **B** *Plaza Regency*, Jln Brooke, T 413113, a/c, restaurant; **B** *River Inn*, Lot 653 Jln Nankoda Gampar, T 415507/8, a/c, clean, rec; **B** *Today Inn*, 571 Lee Tak St, T 414000/411531, F 413951, a/c, small rooms but spotlessly clean; **B** *Tropical Inn*, Jln Teo Chew, T 411376; **B-C** *Rasa Sayang*, 1st Flr, 566 Lee Tak St, T 413880, F 411366, a/c; **C** *Gaya Inn*, 1st Flr, Jln China, T 410022, a/c; **C** *Mulu Inn*, Lot 2453 Jln China, T 417168, F 417172, a/c, clean, small rooms, another branch on River Rd; **C** *New South East Asia Lodging House*, 1st Flr, Jln China, some a/c, not all have attached bathroom; **C** *Thai Foh*, 18-19 Jln China, T 418395, a/c; *Richmond*, Lot 243, Setia Raja Rd, T 413280, a/c, restaurant.

A land where money grows on trees

Ever since Sarawak's riverbanks were first settled, the Iban and Orang Ulu tribespeople have practiced shifting cultivation, growing crops in their clearings. Today, most of the clearing is done by commercial loggers and the cash-crop is the jungle itself. No one can travel up the Baram without feeling alarmed at the volume of logs, stockpiled like giant matchsticks, on either side of the river for mile after mile. In Jul 1991 members of 2 European environmental protest groups chained themselves to logs at Kuala Baram; they were promptly arrested and deported. In Mar 1992, James Barclay, author of *A Stroll Through Borneo*, a book about logging on the Baram, was also deported from Sarawak after a month in jail. The government says environmentalists are ill-informed and are presenting a false picture to the world. Sarawak's forests, it maintains, will be there in perpetuity.

The Borneo Company first tried logging on the Baram in the early 1900s, and built Sarawak's first timber mill at Kuala Baram in 1904 but early logging operations were not successful as the timber was attacked by pests. Commercial logging only really began in the 1950s with the arrival of the tractor and the chainsaw. Now, Sarawak's 130 million-year-old forests are being felled at the rate of 400,000 ha a year – an area 5 times the size of Singapore – and log exports earn the state more than US$1 billion a year. Log output doubled during the 1980s.

Who derives the benefits from the lucrative logging industry is a sensitive political issue – in Sarawak, politics is timber. Logging licences are tickets to get rich quick and the state's chief minister can award timber concessions to whom he wants. In 1987 a rival politician disclosed that the Chief Minister and his allies held about a $\frac{1}{3}$ of the state's logging concessions alone. The previous Chief Minister had held nearly as much. Sarawak's Minister for Tourism and the Environment, James Wong is himself a partner in a 180,000 ha logging concession in Limbang. Environmentalists say these politicians, together with Chinese timber tycoons, are amassing fortunes at the expense of forest tribes. The rush to extract what they can before environmental pressure puts them out of business has fuelled allegations of political manoeuvring, corruption and malpractice.

Although logging companies have provided jobs for upriver tribespeople (a total of 150,000 people are employed in Sarawak's timber industry), logging

Restaurants Malay: ♦*Nabila's*, 1st Flr, 441 DUBS Building, Jln Bendahara, also serves Indonesian and Oriental, curries, good rendang. **Chinese:** ♦♦♦*Kochee*, 1st Flr *Park Hotel*, Jln Kingsway; ♦♦*Maxim's Seafood Centre*, Lot 394 Jln Yu Seng Selatan, best seafood in Miri, no menu, just select snapper, pomfret or prawns for the barbeque, rec; ♦♦*Sea View Café*, Jln China. **International:** ♦♦*Bonzer Garden Steak House*, Jln Yu Seng Utara, local dishes much cheaper than burgers; *Cosy Garden*, pleasant restaurant, but the air-conditioning inhibits any cosiness, limited menu but reasonable prices, steak; ♦♦♦*Golden Steak Garden*, *Gloria Hotel*, 27 Jln Brooke, steak; ♦♦♦*Park View Restaurant* (coffee house of *Park Hotel*), Jln Kingsway, most sophisticated menu in town, jellyfish, good selection of seafood and grill; ♦*Sugar Bun*, Grd Flr, Wisma Pelita Tunku, burgers. **Bakeries:** *Appletree*, Grd Flr, Wisma Pelita Tunku. **Foodstalls:** *Tamu Muhiba* (Native Market), opposite *Park Hotel* on roundabout connecting Malay St and Jln Padang; *Tanjung Seafood stalls*, Tanjung Lobung (S of Miri).

Entertainment Miri has scores of karaoke lounges and discos, mostly along Jln Yu Seng.

Shopping Books: *Pelita Book Centre*, 1st Flr, Wisma Pelita Tunku. **Handicrafts:** *Longhouse Handicraft Centre*, 2nd Flr, Wisma Pelita Tunku; only handicraft shop in town. Roadside stalls at Nakat, 18 km down the southbound road to Niah (1 km before Lambir Hills National Park) also sell handicrafts. **Supermarket:** *Pelita*, Grd Flr, Wisma Pelita Tunku. Useful for upriver expeditions.

Sport Golf: *Miri Golf Club*, Jln Datuk Patinggi, by the sea, green fees: M$50.

Local transport Car hire: A & Z Motor, Lot 108 Jln Bendahara, T 412692, F 414145; **Mewah Bunga**, 81 Jln Permaisuri, T 655639.

has wreaked ecological havoc and impinged on tribal lands. The traditional lifestyles of the Penan hunter-gatherers and other Orang Ulu tribes have been threatened as loggers push deeper into the jungle. In the past, Kayan tribesmen would simply have decapitated anyone caught trespassing on their tribal lands; these days the Orang Ulu protest against the encroachment by blockading logging access roads. Many have been jailed for such protests. The government argues that the jungle tribes are a sideshow and says they have been hijacked by Western environmental groups in a bid to give their campaigns a human face. Environmentalist groups counter that the livelihoods of the forest tribes are as important in the sustainability stakes as the trees themselves.

Since the early 1980s, the water in Sarawak's main rivers has turned brown, due to the sediment which is washed into it from the timber camps upstream. Water supplies have been contaminated by chemical pollutants and fish stocks have been depleted – few can survive in the turgid waters. In Belaga, on the upper Rejang, the price of fish has risen 10-fold in a decade. In Orang Ulu longhouses, tribespeople complain that logging operations have chased their game away, turning hunting trips for wild boar into major expeditions.

The state government is eager to allay fears that it is logging without regard to the forest ecology and the indigenous tribes. But while the state's forestry policy looks good on paper, the Enforcement Division of the Forest Department cannot cope with the vast territory it has to police; it is now using satellites to detect areas where illegal logging has occurred. The government dismisses warnings that Sarawak's logging rates (which are the highest in the world) cannot be sustained as scaremongering. But in 1991, the Japan-based International Tropical Timber Organization said that if logging rates were not halved, the state could be 'logged-out' within the decade.

In the course of the next few years, Sarawak will be cutting its log production down to a level which it claims will make its forestry sustainable by the mid-1990s. But the state will always be dependent on timber as 90% of its oil and gas revenues – its only other major resources – are diverted to federal coffers. Without logging Sarawak would be left high and dry. To ensure the survival of the industry, wood-processing industries are being promoted, because furniture and sawn timber exports will yield more money from fewer logs.

Banks & money changers Standard Chartered, High St; **Bank Bumiputra** (among others) Jln Bendahara.

Useful addresses General **Post Office**: just off Jln Gartak. **National Parks Office**: Jln Puchong, T 36637. **Resident's Office**: Jln Kwantung, T 33203.

Airline offices Borneo Skyways, Miri, T 334242; **MAS**, 239 Beautiful Jade Garden, T 34407.

Tour companies & travel agents *Alo Doda*, 2 Jln Setia Raja, T 37408, F 415887, probably the best of the Mulu adventure specialists, private accommodation in Mulu Park, rec; *Borneo Adventure*, Unit 9.02, 9th Flr, Wisma Pelita Tunku, Jln Puchong, T 414935, rec; *Borneo Leisure*, Lot 227, Grd Flr, Jln Maju, Beautiful Jade Centre, T 413011; *Borneo Overland*, 37 Grd Flr, Bangunan Raghavan, Jln Brooke, T 302255, F 416424; *East-West*, Lot 688 Mini Arcade, SEDC Complex, Jln Melayu, T 410717; *Hornbill Travel*, G26 Park Arcade, Jln Raja, T 417385, F 412751; *JJM Tours & Travel*, Lot 3002, Grd Flr, Morsjaya Commercial Centre, 2.5 Miles, Miri-Bintulu Rd, T 416051, F 414390, young company with some very experienced guides, rec; *KKM Travel & Tours*, Lot 236, Beautiful Jade Centre, T 417899, F 414629; *Malang's Sister's Agency*, Lot 260 Beautiful Jade Centre, 1st Flr, T 38141/417770, F 417123; *Mulu Tutoh Travel Service*, T 55037, recommended by National Parks office; *Robert Ding*, Lot 556, 1st Flr, Royal Snooker Centre, Jln Permaisuri, T 416051, F 414390, recommended by National Parks Office; *Seridan Mulu*, Lot 140, Tingkat 2, Jln Bendahara, T 416066, private accommodation with park, recommended by National Parks Office; *Telang Usan*, Lot 166 Tingkat Bawah, Bangunan Baram Trading, Jln Permaisuri, T 38715, F 417588; *Travel & Tours*,

Grd Flr, Bangunan Pei, Lot 1180B Lorong 2, T 34250, F 514677; *Tropical Adventure*, 288 1st Flr, Beautiful Jade Centre, Jln Maju, T 414503, F 416452, private accommodation within Mulu Park, rec; *Vista Borneo*, Aras 3, Block G, Lot 13, Taman Sri Sarawak, Jln Borneo, T 417791, F 417781.

Transport to & from Miri By air: regular connections with Kuching (M$166), Sibu (M$63), Marudi (M$35), Bareo, via Marudi, (M$84), Bintulu (M$68), Labuan (M$68). Also connections with Kota Kinabalu (M$98). **By bus**: buses leave from next to *Park Hotel*. Regular connections with Batu Niah, 2-3 hrs (M$10), Bintulu (M$13-18) and Sibu (M$35).

To Kuala Baram & the express boat upriver Regular bus connections with Kuala Baram (M$2). Taxis to Kuala Baram for Marudi (M$4; chartered M$16). **By boat**: express boats, upriver to Marudi from Kuala Baram, 3 hrs (M$12). Roughly one boat every hour from 0715. Last boat 1430. This is the first leg of the journey to Mulu and the interior.

International connections with Brunei Regular connections (Miri-Belait Transport Company) with Kuala Belait, 2 hrs (M$10.50). From Kuala Belait regular connections with Seria, 1 hr (B$1.50) and from Seria regular connections with Bandar Seri Begawan, 1-2 hours (B$15). It takes best part of a day to reach BSB.

Marudi

Four major tribal groups – Iban, Kelabit, Kayan and Penan – come to Marudi to do business with the Chinese, Indian and Malay merchants. Marudi is the furthest upriver trading post on the Baram and services all the longhouses in the Tutoh, Tinjar and Baram river basins. Most tourists only stop long enough in Marudi to down a cold drink before catching the next express boat upriver – as the trip to Mulu National Park can now be done in a day, not many have to spend the night here. Because it is a major trading post, however, there are a lot of hotels, and the standards are reasonably good.

Fort Hose was built in 1901, when Marudi was still called Claudetown, and has good views of the river. It is named after the last of the Rajah's Residents, the anthropologist, geographer and natural historian Dr Charles Hose. The fort is now used as administrative offices. Also of note is the intricately carved **Thaw Peh Kong Chinese Temple** (diagonally opposite the express boat jetty), built in the early 1900s.

Excursions

Permits are necessary to go upriver from Marudi. Permits for Mulu and Bareo are issued by the district officer in Fort Hose.

Gunung Mulu National Park, see below.

Brunei The **Marudi-Kampung Teraja log walk** is normally done from the Brunei end, as the return trek, across the Sarawak/Brunei border takes a full day, dawn to dusk. It is, however, possible to reach an Iban longhouse inside Brunei without going the full distance to Kampung Teraja. The longhouse is on the Sungei Ridan, about 2½ hrs down the jungle trail. The trail starts 3 km from Marudi, on the airport road. A local Chinese man, who runs an unofficial taxi service to and from the trail head, may spot you before you find the trail (ask at the houses along the road). There is no customs post on the border; the trail is not an official route into Brunei. Trekkers are advised to take their passports in the unlikely event of being stopped by police, who will probably turn a blind eye. Kampung Teraja in Brunei is the furthest accessible point which can be reached by road (from Labi; see page 483).

Longhouses 3 longhouses, **Long Seleban**, **Long Moh** and **Leo Mato**, are accessible by road from Marudi.

Accommodation C *Zola*, Lot 14-15, T 75531-3, a/c, restaurant next door, clean, occasionally lacking in sheets; **C-D** *Alisan*, 63-5 Queen's Sq, T 755911, a/c, big rooms; **D** *Marudi*, 3 Queen's Sq, T 755141, a/c; **D-E** *Hup Chung*, 1 Queen St, T 755146/755387, some a/c.

Restaurants There are several coffee shops dotted around town. The ♦*Rose Garden*, opposite *Alisan Hotel* is an air-conditioned coffee shop serving mainly Chinese dishes.

Banks & money changers There are 2 local banks with foreign exchange facilities.

Useful addresses Post office and police station on Airport Road.

Transport to & from Marudi **By air**: the airport is 5 km from town. Connections with Miri (M$35) Bareo (M$66), Sibu (M$132). **By boat**: boats leave from opposite the Chinese temple. Connections with Kuala Baram; 8 boats a day from 0700-1430 (M$12), Tutoh (for longboats to Long Terawan and Mulu National Park) (M$8), Long Lama (for longboats to Bareo) one boat every hour 0730-1400 (M$12).

GUNUNG MULU NATIONAL PARK

Tucked in behind Brunei, the 52,866 ha Gunung Mulu National Park lays claim to Gunung Mulu (at 2,376m, the second highest mountain in Sarawak) and the biggest limestone cave system in the world. Its primary jungle contains astonishing biological diversity. In Robin Hanbury-Tenison's book *The Rain Forest*, he says of Mulu: "All sense of time and direction is lost." Every scientific expedition that has visited Mulu's forests has encountered plant and animal species unknown to science. In 1990, 5 years after it was officially opened to the public, Mulu National Park was handling an average 400 visitors a month.

In 1974, 3 years after Mulu was gazetted as a National Park, the first of a succession of joint expeditions led by the British Royal Geographical Society (RGS) and the Sarawak government began to make the discoveries that put Mulu on the map. In 1980 a cave passage over 50 km long was surveyed for the first time. Since then, a further 137 km of passages have been discovered. Altogether 27 major caves have now been found – speleologists believe they probably represent a tiny fraction of what is actually there. The world's biggest cave, the **Sarawak Chamber**, was not discovered until 1984.

   The first attempt on Gunung Mulu was made by Spencer St John, the British consul in Brunei, in 1856 (see also his attempts on Gunung Kinabalu, Sabah, **page 322**). His efforts were thwarted by "limestone cliffs, dense jungle and sharp pinnacles of rock." Dr Charles Hose, Resident of Marudi, led a 25-day expedition to Gunung Mulu in 1893, but also found his path blocked by 600m-high cliffs. Nearly half a century later, in 1932, a Berawan rhinoceros-hunter called Tama Nilong guided Edward Shackleton's Oxford University expedition to the summit. (One of the young Oxford undergraduates on that expedition was Tom Harrisson, who later made the Niah archaeological discoveries, **see page 276**.) Tama Nilong, the hunter from Long Terawan, had previously reached the main SW ridge of Mulu while tracking a rhinoceros.

   The limestone massifs of Gunung Api and Gunung Benarat were originally at the same elevation as Gunung Mulu, but their limestone outcrops were more prone to erosion than the Mulu's sandstone. The cliffs of the Melinau Gorge rise a sheer 600m, and are the highest limestone rockfaces between North Thailand and Papua New Guinea. NW of the gorge lies a large, undisturbed alluvial plain which is rich in flora and fauna. Penan tribespeople (**see page 255**) are allowed to maintain their lifestyle of fishing, hunting and gathering in the park. At no small expense, the Malaysian government has encouraged them to settle at a purpose-built longhouse at **Batu Bungan**, just a few minutes upriver from Park HQ – but its efforts have met with limited success. Penan shelters can often be found by river banks.

Flora and fauna In the 1960s and 70s, botanical expeditions were beginning to shed more light on the Mulu area's flora and fauna: 100 new plant species

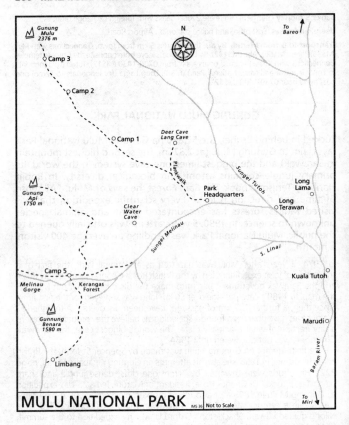

MULU NATIONAL PARK IMS 36 | Not to Scale

were discovered between 1960 and 1973 alone. Mulu park encompasses an area of diverse altitudes and soil types – it includes all the forest types found in Borneo except mangrove. About 20,000 animal species have been recorded in Mulu Park, as well as 3,500 plant species and 8,000 varieties of fungi (more than 100 of these are endemic to the Mulu area). Mulu's ecological statistics are astounding: it is home to 1,500 species of flowering plant, 170 species of orchid and 109 varieties of palm. More than 280 butterfly species have been recorded. Within the park boundaries, 262 species of birds (including all 8 varieties of hornbill), 67 mamalian species, 50 species of reptile and 75 amphibian species have been recorded.

Mulu's caves contain an unusual array of flora and fauna too. There are 3 species of swiftlet, 12 species of bat, and 9 species of fish, including the cave flying fish (*Nemaaramis everetti*) and blind catfish (*Silurus furnessi*). Cave scorpions (*Chaerilus chapmani*) – which are poisonous but not deadly – are not uncommon. Other subterranean species include albino crabs, huntsman spiders, cave crickets, centipedes and snakes (which dine on swiftlets and bats). These creatures have been described as "living fossils...[which are] isolated survivors of ancient groups long since disappeared from Southeast Asia."

Treks from Park Headquarters Trails around headquarters are well marked but it is illegal to go anywhere without hiring a guide.

Gunung Mulu The minimum time to allow for the climb is 4 days, 3 nights; tents are not required if you stay at Camps 1 and 2. The main summit route starts from the plankwalk at Park HQ heading towards Deer Cave. The Mulu walkway forks left after about 1 km. From Park HQ it is an easy 4-5 hr trek to Camp 1 at 150m, where there is a shelter, built by the RGS/Sarawak government expedition in 1978. The second day is a long uphill slog (8-10 hrs) to Camp 4 (1,800m), where there is also a shelter. Past Camp 3, the trail climbs steeply up Bukit Tumau, which affords good views over the park, and above which the last wild rhinoceros in Sarawak was shot in the mid-1940s. There are many pitcher plants (*Nepenthes lowii*) along this stretch of trail (**see page 57**). From Camp 4, known as 'The Summit Camp', the path passes the helicopter pad, from where there are magnificent views of Gunung Benarat, the Melinau Gorge and Gunung Api. The final haul to the summit is very steep; there are fixed ropes. Around the summit area, the *Nepenthes muluensis* pitcher plant is common – it is endemic to Mulu. From Camp 4 it takes 1½ hrs to reach the summit, and a further 7 hrs back down the mountain to Camp 1. The views from the summit are best during Apr and May.

Equipment Camp 1 has water, as does Camp 4 if it has been raining. (Water should be boiled before drinking). It is necessary to bring your own food; in the rainy season it is wise to bring a gas cooking stove. A sleeping bag and waterproofs are also necessary and spare clothes, wrapped in a plastic bag, are a good idea.

Mulu can also be climbed from the S ridge of Melinau Gorge (see below) – 3 hrs to Camp 1, 5 hrs to Camp 3, steep 4-5 hour climb to Camp 4, 2 hrs to the top. Forest changes from alluvial/swamp forest through mixed dipterocarp to mossy sub-montane and summit scrub.

Treks from Camp 5 (in the Melanau Gorge, facing Gunung Benarat, about 4-6 hrs upstream from Park HQ). From the camp it is possible to trek up the gorge as well as to the Pinnacles, on Gunung Api. **Getting there**: it is advisable to hire a longboat for the duration of your time at and around Camp 5. The boat has to be abandoned at Kuala Berar, at the confluence of the Melanau and Berar rivers: it is only used for the first and last hours of the trip, but in the event of an emergency, there are no trails leading back to HQ and there are grim stories of fever-stricken people being stranded in the jungle. For a 3-day trip, a longboat will cost M$450 to hire – as opposed to M$300 if you just arrange to be collected 3 days later. It takes 2-3 hrs, depending on the river level, from Park Headquarters to Kuala Berar; it is then a 2-3 hour trek (8 km) to Camp 5. Visitors to the Camp 5 area are also advised to plan their itinerary carefully as it is necessary to calculate how much food will be required and to carry it up there.

Accommodation at Camp 5 There is a basic shelter (built by the RGS/Sarawak government expedition in 1978), which can house about 30 people. The camp is next to the Melinau River; river water should be boiled before drinking.

Melinau Gorge Camp 5 nestles at the S end of the gorge, across a fast-flowing section of the Melinau River and opposite the unclimbed 1,580m Gunung Benarat's stark, sheer limestone cliffs. The steep limestone ridges, that lead eventually to Gunung Api, comprise the E wall of the gorge. Heading N from Camp 5, the trail fizzles out after a few minutes. It takes an arduous 2-3 hrs of endless river-crossings and scrambles to reach a narrow chute of white water, under which is a large, deep and clear jungle pool with a convenient sandbank and plenty of large boulders to perch on. Alfred Russel Wallace's *Troides brookiana* – the majestic Rajah Brooke's birdwing – is particularly common at this little oasis, deep in undisturbed jungle. The walk involves criss-crossing through waist-deep, fast-flowing water and over stones that have been smoothed to a high polish over centuries: strong shoes are recommended – as is a walking stick. Only occasionally in the walk upstream is it possible to glimpse the towering 600m cliffs.

The Pinnacles are a forest of sharp limestone needles three-quarters of the way up Gunung Api. Some of the pinnacles rise above tree-tops to heights of 45m. The trail leaves from Camp 5, at the base of the Melinau Gorge. It is a very steep climb all the way and takes about 6-7 hrs to reach the pinnacles (1200m) and 4-5 hrs to get down. There is no source of water *en route*. It is not possible to reach Gunung Api from the pinnacles. Is is strongly recommended that climbers wear gloves as well as long-sleeved shirts, trousers and strong boots to protect themselves against cuts from the razor-sharp rocks. Explorers on Spenser St John's expedition to Mulu in 1856 were cut to shreds on the pinnacles: "...3 of our men had already been sent back with severe wounds, whilst several of those left were much injured," he wrote, concluding that it was "the world's most nightmarish surface to travel over".

Gungung Api ('Fire Mountain') The vegetation is so dry at the summit that it is often set ablaze by lightning in the dry season. The story goes that the fires were so big that locals once thought the mountains were volcanoes. Some of the fires could be seen as far away as the Brunei coast. The summit trek takes a minimum of 3 days. At 1,710m, it is the tallest limestone outcrop in Borneo and, other than Gunung Benarat (on the other side of the gorge), is probably the most difficult mountain to climb in Borneo. Many attempts to climb it ended in failure; 2 Berawans from Long Terawan finally made it to the top in 1978, one of them the grandson of Tama Nilong, the rhinoceros-hunter who had climbed Gunung Mulu in 1932. It is impossible to proceed upwards beyond the Pinnacles.

Kerangas forest From Camp 5, cross the Melanau River and head down the Limbang trail towards Lubang Cina. Less than 30 mins down the trail, fork left along a new trail which leads along a ridge to the S of Gunung Benarat. Climbing higher, after about 40 mins, the trail passes into an area of leached sandy soils called *kerangas* (heath) forest. This little patch of thinner jungle is a tangle of many varieties of pitcher plants.

Limbang It is possible to trek from Camp 5 to Limbang, although it is easier to do it the other way. (See page 291.)

Caves In 1961 geologist Dr G Wilford first surveyed Deer Cave and parts of the Cave of the Winds. But Mulu's biggest subterranean secrets were not revealed until the 1980s.

Clearwater Cave (*Gua Ayer Jernih*): part of the Clearwater System, on a small tributary of the Melinau River, is the world's longest underground cavity. The cave passage – 75 km of which has been explored – links Clearwater Cave with the **Cave of the Winds** (*Lubang Angin*), to the S. It was discovered in 1988 and is the longest cave system in Southeast Asia. Clearwater is named after the jungle pool at the foot of the steps leading up to the cavemouth, where the longboats moor. Two species of monophytes – single-leafed plants – grow in the sunlight at the mouth of the cave. They only grow on limestone. A lighting system has been installed down the path to Young Lady's Cave, which ends in a 60m-deep pot hole.

On the cave walls are some helictites – coral-like lateral formations – and, even more dramatic, are the photokarsts, tiny needles of rock, all pointing towards the light. These are formed in much the same way as their monstrous cousins, the pinnacles (see above), by vegetation (in this case algae) eating into and eroding the softer rock, leaving sharp points of harder rock which 'grow' at about half a millimetre a year. Inside Clearwater it is possible to hire a rowing boat for M$10 – the river can be followed for about 1½ km upstream, although the current is strong. It is illegal to fish at Clearwater, although it is possible to fish anywhere else in park waters with a hook and line. *Getting there*: Clearwater can be reached by a 30 mins longboat ride from Park HQ. Individual travellers must charter a boat for M$100 (return). Tour agents build the cost of this trip into their package – which works out considerably cheaper.

Deer Cave is another of Mulu's record-breakers: it has the world's biggest cave mouth and the biggest cave passage, which is 2.2 km long and 220m high at its highest point. Before its inclusion in the Park, the cave had been a well known hunting ground for deer attracted to the pools of salty water running off the guano. The silhouettes of some of the cave's limestone formations have been creatively interpreted; notably the profile of Abraham Lincoln. Adam's and Eve's Showers, at the E end of the cave, are hollow stalactites; water pressure increases when it rains. This darker section at the E end of Deer Cave is the preferred habitat of the naked bat. Albino earwigs live on the bats' oily skin and regularly drop off. The cave's E entrance opens onto 'The Garden of Eden' – a luxuriant patch of jungle, which was once part of the cave system until the roof collapsed. This separated Deer Cave and Green Cave, which lies adjacent to the E mouth; it is open only to caving expeditions.

The W end of the cave is home to several million wrinkle-lipped, and horseshoe bats. Black, twisting ribbons of hundreds of thousands of these bats pour out of the cave at dusk. Bat hawks can often be seen swooping in for spectacular kills. The helipad, about 500m S of the cavemouth, and the specially constructed 'Batview Lodge', provide excellent vantage points. (VIPs' helicopters, arriving for the show, are said to have disturbed the bats in recent years.) From the analysis of the 3 tonnes of saline guano the bats excrete every day, scientists conclude that they make an 80 km dash to the coast for meals of insects washed down with seawater. Cave cockroaches eat the guano, ensuring that the cavern does not become choked with what locals call 'black snow'. **Getting there**: 1 hr trek along a plank walk from Park HQ.

Lang's Cave, which is part of the same hollow mountain as Deer Cave, is less well known but its formations are more beautiful, and contains impressive curtain stalactites and intricate coral-like helictites. The cave is well illuminated and protected by bus-stop-style plastic tunnels.

The Sarawak Chamber, the largest natural chamber in the world, was discovered in 1984 and is scheduled to open to the public in 1994. It is 600m long, 450m wide and 100m high – big enough, it is said, to accommodate 40 Jumbo Jets wing-tip to wing-tip and 8 nose-to-tail.

For cavers wishing to explore caves not open to the public, there are designated 'adventure caves' within an hour of park HQ. Experienced cave-guides can be organised from HQ. The most accessible of these is the 1 hr trek following the river course through Clearwater Cave. Cavers should bring their own equipment.

Rapids Just outside the national park boundary on the Tutoh River there are rapids which are possible to shoot; this can be arranged through tour agencies.

Transport around the park Independent travellers will find it more expensive arranging the trip on their own. Longboats can be chartered privately from Park HQ, if required; (maximum 10 persons per boat). Costs: M$10 per boat; M$1 per horse power for the engine (usual 15-25hp); driver plus front-man M$20 each; fuel: M$2/litre. How far these boats can actually get upriver depends on the season. They often have to be hauled over rapids, whatever the time of year.

Equipment Visitors have to bring their own provisions from Miri or Marudi. (There is only one small shop – itself just outside the Park boundary, at Long Pala.) A sleeping bag is essential for Gunung Mulu trips; other essential equipment includes good insect repellent and a powerful torch.

Guides No visitors are permitted to travel in the park without an authorized guide which can be arranged from park HQ or booked in advance from the National Parks office in Miri (see above). Most of the Mulu Park guides are very well-informed about flora and fauna, geology and tribal customs. Tour agencies organize guides as part of their fee. **Guide fees**: M$20 per cave (or per day) and an extra M$10 per night. Mulu summit trips: minimum of M$110 for 4 days, 3 nights; Melinau Gorge and Pinnacles: minimum M$80 (3 days, 2 nights). Ornithological guides cost an additional M$10 a day. Porterage: max 10 kg. M$15/day, M$10/night. M$1 for each extra kilo. Mulu summit: minimum M$90; Melanau Gorge (Camp 5): minimum M$65. It is usual to tip guides and porters.

Permits can be obtained from the National Parks and Wildlife Office, Old Forestry Building, Jalan Angkasa, Miri, T 36637/31975. It is necessary to book and pay a deposit for accommodation at the same time. Permits can also be picked up from the National Parks and Wildlife Office, Jalan Gartak, Kuching, T 248088; accommodation can be booked through Kuching too. It is also necessary to get a permit from the police and the Miri or Marudi Residents. In Marudi, both the resident's office (Fort Hose) and the police station are on the airport road. This bureaucratic mess can be avoided if travel arrangements are left to a Miri travel agent.

Accommodation in the park must be booked in advance at the National Parks and Wildlife Office Forest Department in Miri or Kuching. Booking fee is M$20 per party and the maximum party size is 10 people. Bookings must be confirmed 5 days before visit. 3 Miri-based travel agents have private accommodation in the park: *Tropical Adventure* (M$10/night); *Seridan Mulu Tour* (M$10/night); *Alo Doda* (M$15/night). **Park Headquarters**: *Government Resthouse*, Park HQ compound: *Old Rest House* (M$30/room accommodates 6); *New Rest House* (M$60/room accommodates 6) (VIP suites: M$150). **Long Pala**: 20 min (M$5) boat ride downstream from Park HQ. *2 hostels*, kitchen and bathrooms, crockery and bed linen provided. *Private guesthouses*, run by tour companies (M$10-15 plus meals). Tour agents offer private accommodation of a high standard, just outside the National Park boundary, M$5/person.

Camping within the national park is free (including permanent shelters at Camp 5 and Gunung Mulu).

Restaurants Small canteen at park headquarters. *Melinau Canteen*, just downriver from HQ. Small shop with basic supplies at Long Pala. All tour companies with their own accommodation offer food.

Transport to & from Gunung Mulu National Park Visitors are recommended to go through one of the Miri-based travel agents (see page 283). The average cost of a Mulu package (per person) is M$350-400 (4 days/3 nights) or M$500 (6 days/5 nights). **By air**: daily flights from Miri to Marudi, 15 mins ($35). A new airstrip has been constructed just downriver from Park

HQ and is now operating. Miri-Mulu (M$60 one way/M$138 return). Currently 3 flights/day; frequency expected to increase to 5 flights/day. **By bus/taxi and boat**: bus or taxi from Miri to Marudi express boat jetty near Kuala Baram at mouth of River Baram (**see page 284**). Regular express boats from Kuala Baram to Marudi, 3 hrs (M$12). One express boat per day (leaves around noon) from Marudi to Long Tarawan on the Tutoh River (tributary of the Baram), via Long Apoh (M$12). During the dry season express boats cannot reach Long Terawan and terminate at Long Panai, on the Tutoh River, where longboats continue to Long Terawan (M$10). Longboats leave Long Tarawan for Mulu Park HQ when the express boats from Marudi get in. Mulu Park HQ is 1½ hrs up the Melinau River (a tributary of the Tutoh), (M$35). As you approach the park from Long Tarawan the Tutoh River narrows and becomes shallower; there are 14 rapids before the Melinau River, which forms the park boundary. When the water is low, the trip can be very slow and involve pulling the boat over the shallows, this accounts for high charter rates. For a group of 9 or 10 it is cheaper to charter a boat (M$250 one way). The first jetty on the Melinau River is Long Pala, where most of the tour companies have accommodation. The Park HQ is another 15 mins upriver. Longboats returning to Long Terawan leave Park HQ at dawn each day, calling at jetties *en route*.

NB: it is best to avoid visiting Mulu National Park during school and public holidays. In Dec he park is closed to locals, but remains open to tourists.

BAREO AND THE KELABIT HIGHLANDS

Bareo lies in the Kelabit Highlands, a plateau, 1,000m above sea level (close to the Kalimantan border). The highlands are Sarawak's answer to the hill stations on the peninsula. The undulating Bareo valley is surrounded by mountains and fed by countless small streams which in turn feed into a maze of irrigation canals. The local Kelabits' skill in harnessing water has allowed them to practice wet rice cultivation rather than the more common slash-and-burn hill rice techniques. Fragrant Bareo rice is prized in Sarawak and commands a premium in the coastal markets. The Kelabit Highlands' more temperate climate also allows the cultivation of a wide range of fruit and vegetables.

The plateau's near-impregnable ring of mountains effectively cut the Kelabit off from the outside world: it is the only area in Borneo which was never penetrated by Islam. In 1911 the Resident of Baram mounted an expedition which ventured into the mountains to ask the Kelabit to stop raiding the Brooke Government's subjects. It took the expedition 17 days to cross the Tamu Abu mountain range, to the W of Bareo. The Kelabit were then brought under the control of the Sarawak government. The most impressive mountain in the Bareo area is the distinctive twin-peak of the sheer-faced 2,043m **Bukit Batu Lawi**, to the NW of Bareo itself. The Kelabit traditionally believed the mountain had an evil spirit and so never went near it. Today such superstitions are a thing of the past – locals are mostly evangelical Christians.

In 1945, the plateau was selected as the only possible parachute drop zone in N Borneo not captured by the Japanese. The Allied Special Forces which parachuted into Bareo were led by Tom Harrisson, who later became curator of the Sarawak Museum and made the famous archaeological discoveries at Niah Caves (**see page 276**). His expedition formed an irregular tribal army against the Japanese, which gained control over large areas of N Borneo in the following months.

Treks around Bareo Because of the rugged terrain surrounding the plateau, the area mainly attracts serious mountaineers. There are many trails to the longhouses around the plateau area, however. Treks to Bareo can be organized through travel agents in Miri (**see page 281**). Guides can also be hired in Bareo and surrounding longhouses for M$30-40/day. It is best to go through the Penghulu, Ngiap Ayu, the Kelabit chief. He goes round visiting many of the longhouses in the area once a month. It is recommended that visitors to Bareo come equipped with sleeping bags and camping equipment. There are no formal facilities for tourists and provisions should be brought from Miri or Marudi. The best time to visit Bareo is between Mar and Oct. **NB**: There are no banks or money-changers in Bareo.

Several of the surrounding mountains can be climbed from Bareo, but they are, without exception, difficult climbs. Even on walks just around the Bareo area, guides are essential as trails are poorly marked. The lower ('female') peak of **Bukit Batu Lawi** can be climbed without equipment, but the sheer sided 'male' peak requires proper rock-climbing equipment – it was first scaled in 1986. **Gunung Marudi** (2,423m) is the highest mountain in Sarawak; it is a very tough climb.

Permits It is necessary to have a permit to visit the Bareo area, obtainable from the Resident's offices in Miri or Marudi.

Accommodation *Bareo Lodging House*, above the shop, or with the Penghulu in his kampung house, at Bareo Bahru, 10 mins from the airstrip. Most visitors camp.

Transport to & from Bareo By air: Bareo's airstrip is very small and because of its position, flights are often cancelled because of mist and clouds. Connections with Miri (M$84), and Marudi (M$66). **By foot**: it is a 7-day trek from Marudi to Bareo; accommodation in longhouses *en route*. This trip should be organized through a Miri travel agent (**see page 281**). *Alo Doda* rec.

LIMBANG AND LAWAS

Limbang

Very few tourists reach Limbang or Lawas but they are good stopping-off points for more adventurous routes to Sabah and Brunei.

Limbang is the finger of Sarawak territory which splits Brunei in two. It is the administrative centre for the 5th Division, and was ceded to the Brooke government by the Sultan of Brunei in 1890. The Trusan Valley, to the E of the wedge of Brunei, had been ceded to Sarawak in 1884.

Limbang's **Old Fort** was built in 1897 (renovated 1966) and was used as the administrative centre. During the Brooke era half the ground floor was used as a jail. It is now a centre of religious instruction, *Majlis Islam*. Limbang is famous for its **Pasar Tamu** every Friday, where jungle and native produce is sold.

Excursions
Trek to Gunung Mulu National Park Take car S to Medamit; from there hire a longboat upriver to Mulu Madang, an Iban longhouse (3 hrs, depending on water level). Alternatively, go further upriver to Kuala Terikan (6-7 hrs at low-water, 4 hrs at high-water) where there is a simple zinc-roofed camp. From there take a longboat one hour up the Terikan River to Lubang China – which is the start of a 2-hour trek along a well-used trail to Camp 5. There is a park rangers' camp about 20 mins out of Kuala Terikan where it is possible to obtain permits and arrange for a guide to meet you at Camp 5. The longboats are cheaper to hire in the wet season.

Tours *Sitt Travel*, specializes in treks in this area.

Festivals May: *Buffalo Racing* (moveable) marks the end of the harvesting season.

Accommodation **B** *National Inn*, 62a Jln Buang Siol, T 22922/82; **B-C** *Muhibbah*, Lot T 790, Bank St, T 22488/22482; **C** *Bunga Raya*, 42 Main Bazaar, T 21181; **D** *South East Asia*, 27 Market St, T 21013.

Useful addresses Resident's Office: T 21960.

Transport to & from Limbang By air: flights every day except Mon and Fri from Kuching (M$163) and Miri (M$54). Also connections with Lawas (M$30). **By boat**: regular connections with Lawas, departs early in the morning (2 hrs, M$15).

To Brunei Regular connections with Bandar Seri Begawan, Brunei (1-2 hrs, M$15).

Lawas

Lawas District was ceded to Sarawak in 1905. The Limbang River, which cuts through the town, is the main transport route. Very few tourists visit Limbang or Lawas; they are however, on the route through to Sabah. It is possible to travel from Miri to Bandar Seri Begawan (Brunei) by road, then on to Limbang and Lawas. From Lawas there are direct buses to Kota Kinabalu in Sabah.

Accommodation A-B *Country Park Hotel*, Lot 235, Jln Trusan, T 85522, a/c, restaurant; **C** *Lawas Federal*, 8 Jln Masjid Baru, T 85115, a/c, restaurant.

Transport to & from Lawas By air: connections with Miri (M$71), Limbang (M$30), Kuching (M$234) and Kota Kinabalu (M$56). **By bus**: connections with Merapok on the Sarwak/Sabah border (M$3). From here there are connections to Beaufort in Sabah. Twice-daily connections with Kota Kinabalu, 4 hrs (M$20). **By boat**: regular connections to Limbang, 2 hrs (M$15).

SABAH

Introduction, 293; **Kota Kinabalu & Tunku Abdul Rahman NP**, 302; **South of Kota Kinabalu**, 312; **The North and Gunung Kinabalu NP**, 320; **The East Coast**, 327; **Sandakan**, 328; **Turtle Islands NP**, 334; **Sepilok Orang-Utan Rehabilitation Centre**, 336; **Lahad Datu**, 337; **Danum Valley Conservation Area**, 338; **Sipidan Island Marine Reserve**, 341.

Maps Sabah, 294; Kota Kinabalu, 304; Gunung Kinabalu National Park, 323; Sandakan, 330; Sandakan Bay, 332.

INTRODUCTION

Sabah occupies the NE corner of Borneo, and is shaped rather like a dog's head. Sabah covers 72,500 sq km – about the size of Ireland – and is the second largest of Malaysia's 13 states, after Sarawak. To the W, it faces the South China Sea and to the E, the Sulu and Celebes seas.

Malaysian Prime Minister Dr Mahathir Mohamad once called Sabah "the wild east". In the popular imagination of West Malaysians, Sabah is the land of the Bajau 'cowboys', gun-toting pirates, timber *towkays* and one-horse towns. The state does indeed have a frontier feel to it; jeeps and Land Cruisers are the only practical way of travelling long-distances overland and piracy is still rife along its E seaboard. It can be an expensive place to travel – particularly if you intend to hire a 4-wheel-drive vehicle. There is not yet a metalled road connecting the 2 biggest towns, Kota Kinabalu and Sandakan: the easiest way to get between them is by air.

The name 'Sabah' probably derives from the Arabic *Zir-e Bad*, meaning 'the land below the wind'. It is an appropriate name for the state as it lies just to the S of the typhoon belt. Officially, the territory has only been called Sabah since 1963, when it joined the Malay federation, but the name appears to have been in use long before that. When Baron Gustav Von Overbeck was awarded the cession rights to N Borneo by the Sultan of Brunei in 1877 (see page 295), one of the titles conferred on him was 'Maharajah of Sabah'. And in the *Handbook of British North Borneo*, published in 1890, it says: "In Darvel Bay there are the remnants of a tribe which seems to have been much more plentiful in bygone days – the Sabahans". From the founding of the Chartered Company until 1963, Sabah was known as British North Borneo.

Sabah has a population of about 1.4 million, about half of whom are illegal immigrants (**see page 298**). The inhabitants of Sabah can be divided into 4 main groups: the Muruts, the Kadazans, the Bajaus and the Chinese, as well as a small Malay population. These main groups are subdivided into several different tribes (**see page 296**). For information on geography, climate, flora and fauna, **see page 223**.

HISTORY

Prehistoric stone tools have been found in eastern Sabah, suggesting that people were living in limestone caves in the Madai area 17,000-20,000 years ago. The caves were periodically settled from then on; pottery dating from the late Neolithic period has been found, and by the early years of the first millennium AD, Madai's inhabitants were making iron spears and decorated pottery. The Madai and

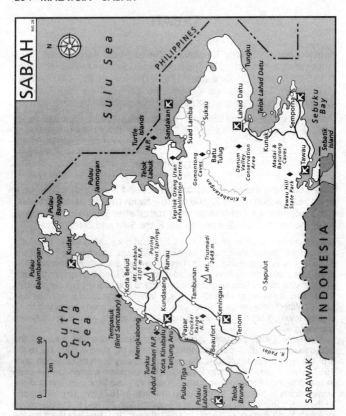

Baturong caves were lived in continuously until about the 16th century, and several carved stone coffins and burial jars have been discovered in the jungle caves (one of which is exhibited in the Sabah State Museum, **see page 303**). The caves were also known for their birds nests; Chinese traders were buying the nests from Borneo as far back as 700 AD.

There are very few archaeological records indicating Sabah's early history, although there is documentary evidence of links between a long-lost kingdom, based somewhere in the area of the Kinabatangan River, and the Sultanate of Brunei, whose suzerainty once extended over most of N Borneo. By the beginning of the 18th century, Brunei's power had begun to wane in the face of European expansionism. To counter the economic decline, the sultan is thought to have increased taxation – which led to civil unrest. In 1704 the Sultan of Brunei had to ask the Sultan of Sulu's help in putting down a rebellion in Sabah, and in return, the Sultan of Sulu received most of what is now Sabah.

The would-be white rajahs of Sabah
It was not until 1846 that the British entered into a treaty with the Sultan of Brunei and took possession of the island of Labuan (**see page 317**) – this was in part to

counter the growing influence of the Rajah of Sarawak, James Brooke. The British were also wary of the Americans – the US Navy signed a trade treaty with the Sultan of Brunei in 1845 and in 1860 Claude Lee Moses was appointed American Consul-General in Brunei Town. He was only interested in making a personal fortune and quickly persuaded the sultan to cede him land in Sabah. He sold these rights to two Hong Kong-based American businessmen who formed the American Trading Company of Borneo. They styled themselves as Rajahs and set up a base at Kimanis, just S of Papar. It was a disaster. One of them died of malaria, the Chinese labourers they imported from Hong Kong began to starve and the settlement was abandoned in 1866.

But the idea of a trading colony on the N Borneo coast interested the Austrian consul in Hong Kong, Baron Gustav von Overbeck, who, in turn, sold the concept to Alfred Dent, a wealthy English businessman also based in Hong Kong. With Dent's money, Overbeck bought the Americans' cession from the Sultan of Brunei, and extended the territory to cover most of modern-day Sabah. The deal was clinched on 29 Dec 1877, and Overbeck agreed to pay the sultan 15,000 Straits dollars a year. A few days later Overbeck discovered that the entire area had already been ceded to the Sultan of Sulu 173 years earlier, so he immediately sailed to Sulu and offered the sultan an annual payment of 5,000 Straits dollars for the territory. On his return, he dropped 3 Englishmen off along the coast to set up trading posts – one of them was William Pryer, who founded Sandakan (**see page 328**). Three years later, Queen Victoria granted Dent a royal charter and, to the chagrin of the Dutch, the Spanish and the Americans, the British North Borneo Company was formed. London insisted that it was to be a British-only enterprise however, and Overbeck was forced to sell out. The first managing director of the company was the Scottish adventurer and former gun-runner William C Cowie. He was in charge of the day-to-day running of the territory, while the British government supplied a governor.

The new chartered company, with its headquarters in the City of London, was given sovereignty over Sabah and a free hand to develop it. The British administrators soon began to collect taxes from local people and quickly clashed with members of the Brunei nobility. John Whitehead, a British administrator, wrote: "I must say, it seemed rather hard on these people that they should be allowed to surrender up their goods and chattels to swell even indirectly the revenue of the company". The administration levied poll-tax, boat tax, land tax, fishing tax, rice tax, *tapai* (rice wine) tax and a 10% tax on proceeds from the sale of birds' nests. Resentment against these taxes sparked the 6-year Mat Salleh rebellion (**see page 313**) and the Rundum Rebellion, which peaked in 1915, during which hundreds of Muruts were killed by the British.

Relations were not helped by colonial attitudes towards the local Malays and tribal people. One particularly arrogant district officer, Charles Bruce, wrote: "The mind of the average native is equivalent to that of a child of four... So long as one remembers that the native is essentially a child and treats him accordingly he is really tractable". Most recruits to the chartered company administration were fresh-faced graduates from British universities, mainly Oxford and Cambridge. For much of the time there were only 40-50 officials running the country. Besides the government officials, there were planters and businessmen: tobacco, rubber and timber became the most important exports. There were also Anglican and Roman Catholic missionaries. British North Borneo was never much of a money-spinner – the economy suffered badly whenever commodity prices slumped – but it managed to pay for itself for most of the time up until World War II.

The Japanese interregnum

Sabah became part of *Dai Nippon* – Greater Japan – on New Year's Day 1942, when the Japanese took Labuan. On the mainland, the Japanese Imperial Army and *Kempetai* (military police) were faced with the might of the North Borneo Armed Constabulary – about 650 men. Jesselton (Kota Kinabalu) was occupied on 9 Jan and Sandakan, 10 days later. All Europeans were interned and when Singapore fell in 1942, 2,740 prisoners of war were moved to Sandakan, most of whom were Australian, where they were forced to build an airstrip. On its completion, the POWs were ordered to march to Ranau – 240 km through the jungle. This became known as 'The Borneo Death March' and only six men survived (**see page 331**).

The Japanese were hated in Sabah and the Chinese mounted a resistance movement which was led by the Kuching-born Albert Kwok Hing Nam. He also recruited Bajaus and Sulus to join his guerrilla force which launched the 'Double Tenth Rebellion' (the attacks took place on 10 Oct 1943). The guerrillas took Tuaran, Jesselton and Kota Belud, killing many Japanese and sending others fleeing into the jungle. But the following day the Japanese bombed the towns and troops quickly retook the towns and captured the rebels. There followed a mass-execution in which 175 rebels were decapitated. On 10 Jun 1945 Australian forces landed at Labuan, under the command of American General MacArthur. Allied planes bombed the main towns and virtually obliterated Jesselton and Sandakan. Sabah was liberated on 9 Sept, and thousands of the remaining 21,000 Japanese troops were killed in retaliation – many by Muruts.

A British Military Administration governed Sabah in the immediate aftermath of the war, and the cash-strapped chartered company sold the territory to the British crown for £1.4 million in mid-1946. The new crown colony was modelled on the chartered company's administration and set about rebuilding the main towns and war-shattered infrastructure. In May 1961, following Malaysian independence, Prime Minister Tunku Abdul Rahman proposed the formation of a federation incorporating Malaysia, Singapore, Brunei, Sabah and Sarawak (**see page 69**). Later that same year, Tun Fuad Stephens, a timber magnate and newspaper publisher formed Sabah's first-ever political party, the United National Kadazan Association (UNKA). Two other parties were founded shortly afterwards – the Sabah Chinese Association and the United Sabah National Organization (USNO). The British were keen to leave the colony and the Sabahan parties thrashed out the pros and cons of joining the proposed federation. Elections were held in late-1962 – in which a UNKA-USNO alliance (the Sabah Alliance) swept to power – and the following August, Sabah became an independent country... for 16 days. Like Singapore and Sarawak, Sabah opted to join the federation, to the indignation of the Philippines and Indonesia which both had claims on the territory. Jakarta's objections resulted in the *konfrontasi* – an undeclared war with Malaysia (**see page 237**) which was not settled until 1966.

CULTURE AND LIFE

People

Sabah's main tribal communities are comprised of the Kadazan, who mostly live on the W coast, the Murut, who inhabit the interior, to the S, and the Bajau, who are mainly settled around Mount Kinabalu. There are more than 20 tribes and more than 50 different dialects are spoken. Sabah also has a large Chinese population and many illegal Filipino immigrants.

Kadazans

The Kadazans are the largest ethnic group in Sabah (comprising about a third of the population), and are a peaceful agrarian people with a strong cultural identity. Until

Sabah joined the Malaysian Federation in 1963, they were known as 'Dusuns', meaning 'peasants' or 'orchard people'. This name was given to them by outsiders, and picked up by the British. Most Kadazans call themselves after their tribal place names. They can be broken into several tribes including the Lotud of Tuaran, the Rungus of the Kudat and Bengkoka Peninsular, the Tempasuk, the Tambanuo, Kimarangan and the Sanayo. Minokok and Tengara Kadazans live in the upper Kinabatangan River basin while those living near other big rivers are just known as *Orang Sungei*, or 'river people'. Most Kadazans used to live in longhouses; these are virtually all gone now. The greatest likelihood of a visitor coming across a longhouse in Sabah is in the Rungus area of the Kudat Peninsula; even there, former longhouse residents are moving into detached, kampung-style houses.

All the Kadazan groups share a common language (although dialects vary) and all had similar customs and modes of dress (see below). Up to World War II, many Kadazan men wore the *chawat* loin cloth. The Kadazans used to hunt with blow-pipes, and in the 19th century, were still head-hunting. Today, however, they are known for their gentleness and honesty; their produce can often be seen sitting unattended at roadside stalls, and passing motorists are expected to pay what they think fair. The Kadazans traditionally traded their agricultural produce at large markets, held at meeting points, called *tamus* (see box). The Kadazan are farmers, and the main rice-producers of Sabah. They used to be animists, and were said to live in great fear of evil spirits; most of their ceremonies were rituals aimed at driving out these spirits. The job of communicating with the spirits of the dead, the *tombiivo*, was done by priestesses, called *bobohizan*. They are the only ones who can speak the ancient Kadazan language, using a completely different vocabulary from modern Kadazan. Most Kadazans converted to Christianity (mainly Roman Catholicism) during the 1930s, although there are also some Muslim Kadazan.

The big cultural event in the Kadazan year is the **Harvest Festival** which takes place on 10-11 May. Following ceremonies, Catholic, Muslim and animist Kadazans all come together to play traditional sports such as wrestling and buffalo racing. This is about the only occasion when visitors are likely to see Kadazans in their traditional costumes. In the Penampang area a woman's costume consists of a fitted, sleeveless tunic and ankle-length skirt of black velvet. Belts of silver coins (*himpogot*) and brass rings are worn round the waist; a colourful sash is also worn. Men dress in a black, long-sleeved jacket over black trousers; they also wear a *siga*, colourful woven head gear. These costumes have become more decorative in recent years, with colourful embroidery.

Bajaus

The Bajaus – the famous 'cowboys' of the 'wild east' – came from the S Philippines during the 18th and 19th centuries and settled in the coastal area around Kota Belud, Papar and Kudat, where they made a handsome living from piracy. The Bajaus who came to Sabah joined forces with the notorious Illanun and Balinini pirates. They are natural seafarers and were dubbed 'the sea gypsies'; today they form the second largest indigenous group in Sabah and are divided into subgroups, notably the Binadan, Suluk and Obian. They call themselves 'Samah' – it was the Brunei Malays who first called them Bajaus. They are strict Muslims and the famous Sabahan folk hero, Mat Salleh, who led a rebellion in the 1890s against British Chartered Company rule, was a Bajau (see page 313). Despite their seafaring credentials, they are also renowned horsemen and (very occasionally) still put in an appearance at Kota Belud's *tamu* (see page 320).

Muruts

The Muruts live around Tenom and Pensiangan in the lowland and hilly parts of the interior, in the SW of Sabah – and in the Trusan Valley of N Sarawak. Some

Tamus – Sabah's markets and trade fairs

In Sabah, an open trade fair is called a *tamu*. Locals gather to buy and sell jungle produce, handicrafts and traditional wares. *Tamu* literally means 'meeting place' and the biggest and most famous is held at Kota Belud, N of Kota Kinabalu in Bajau country (**see page 320**). Tamus were fostered by the pre-war British North Borneo Chartered Company, when district officers would encourage villagers from miles around to trade among themselves. It was also a convenient opportunity for officials to meet with village headmen. They used to be strictly Kadazan affairs, but today tamus are multiracial events. Sometimes public auction of water buffalo and cattle are held. Some of the biggest tamus around the state are:

Mon:	Tankdek
Tues:	Kiulu, Topokan
Wed:	Tamparuli
Thurs:	Keningau, Tambunan, Sipitang, Telipok, Simpangan
Fri:	Sinsuran, Weston
Sat:	Penanmpang, Beaufort, Sindumin, Matunggong, Kinarut
Sun:	Tambunan, Tenom, Kota Belud, Papar, Gaya St (KK).

of those living in more remote jungle areas, retain their traditional longhouse way of life – but many Muruts have now opted for detached kampung-style houses. *Murut* means 'hill people' and is not the term used by the people themselves. They refer to themselves by their individual tribal names. The Nabai, Bokan and Timogun Muruts live in the lowlands and are wet-rice farmers, while the Peluan, Bokan and Tagul Muruts live in the hills and are mainly shifting cultivators. They are thought to be related to Sarawak's Kelabit and Kalimantan's Lun Dayeh people, although some of the tribes in the S Philippines have similar characteristics. The Murut staples are rice and tapioca, they are known for their weaving and basketry and have a penchant for drinking *tapai* (rice wine – **see page 299**). They are also enthusiastic dancers and devised the *lansaran* – a sprung dance floor like a trapeze (**see page 316**). The Muruts are a mixture of animists, Christians and Muslims and were the last tribe in Sabah to give up head-hunting, a practice finally stopped by British North Borneo Chartered Company administrators.

Chinese

The Chinese accounted for nearly a third of Sabah's population in 1960; today they make up just a fifth. Unlike Sarawak, however, where the Chinese were a well-established community in the early 1800s, Sabah's Chinese came as a result of the British North Borneo Chartered Company's immigration policy, designed to ease a labour shortage. About 70% of Sabah's Chinese are Christian Hakkas, who first began arriving at the end of the 19th century, under the supervision of the Company. They were given free passage from China and most settled in the Jesselton and Kudat areas; today most Hakka are farmers. There are also large Teochew and Hokkien communities in Tawau, Kota Kinabalu and Labuan while Sandakan is mainly Cantonese – who originally came from Hong Kong.

Filipinos

Immigration from the Philippines started in the 1950s and refugees began flooding into Sabah when the separatist war erupted in Mindanao in the 1970s. Today there are believed to be between 500,000 and 700,000 illegal Filipino immigrants in Sabah (although their migration has been undocumented for so long that no one is certain), and the state government fears they could outnumber locals by early next century. There are many in Kota Kinabalu, the state capital and a large community – mainly women and children – in Labuan, but the bulk of the Filipino population is in Semporna, Lahad Datu, Tawau and Kunak (on the

Tapai – Sabah's rice wine

Tapai – the fiery Sabahan rice wine – is much loved by the Kadazans and the Muruts. It was even more popular before the 2 tribal groups' wholesale conversion to Christianity in the 1930s. Writer Hedda Morrison noted in 1957 that: "The squalor and wretchedness arising from [their] continual drunkenness made the Muruts a particularly useful object of missionary endeavour. In the thirties missionaries succeeded in converting nearly all the Muruts to Christianity. The Muruts grasped at this new faith much as the drowning man is said to grasp at a straw. From being the most drunken people in Borneo, they became the most sober." In the Sabah State Museum (**see page 303**) there is a recipe for tapai – also known as 'buffalos' blood', which was taken down by an administrator during chartered company days:

"Boil 12lbs of the best glutinous rice until well done. In a wide-mouthed jar, lay the rice in layers of no more than 2 fingers deep, and between layers, place a total of about 20 ½-oz yeast cakes. Add 2 cups of water, tinctured with the juice of 6 beetroots. Cover jar with muslin and leave to ferment. Each day, uncover it and remove dew which forms on the muslin. On the fifth day, stir the mixture vigorously and leave for four weeks. Store for one full year, after which it shall be full of virtue and potence and most smooth upon the palate."

Tapai is drunk from communal jars – which were also used as burial urns – through straws. The jar is filled nearly to its brim with tapai. Large leaves are placed on the top just under the lower edge of the rim. These leaves are pierced with straws for sucking up the liquid and the intervening space between the leaves and the top of the jar is filled with water. Etiquette demands that one drinks till the water has been drained off the leaves. They are then flooded again and the process is repeated. There is also the distilled form of tapai, called *montaku*, which is even more potent. When North Borneo became a British crown colony after World War II, the administration was concerned about the scourge of tapai drinking on 3 counts. First, it was said to consume a large portion of the natives' potential food crop, second, it usually caused a crime-wave whenever it was drunk, and thirdly, it was blamed for the high rate of infant mortality as mothers frequently gave their babies a suck at the straw.

Oscar Cook, a former district officer in the North Borneo Civil Service, noted in his 1923 book *Borneo: the stealer of hearts*, that tapai was not to everyone's fancy – and certainly not to his. "As an alternative occupation to head-hunting, the Murut possess a fondness for getting drunk, indulged in on every possible occasion. Tapai, or *pengasai*, as the Murut calls it, is not a nice drink. In fact, to my thinking it is the very reverse, for it is chiefly made from fermented rice... is very potent, and generally sour and possessed of a pungent and nauseating odour. Births, marriages, deaths, sowing, harvesting and any occasion that comes to mind is made the excuse for a debauch. It is customary for Muruts to show respect to the white man by producing their very best tapai, and pitting the oldest and ugliest women of the village against him in a drinking competition." Cook admits that all this proved too much for him and when he was transferred to Keningau, he had to employ an "official drinker". "The applicants to the post were many," he noted.

E coast) where they already outnumber locals 3:1. One Sabah government minister, referring to the long-running territorial dispute between Malaysia and the Philippines, was quoted as saying "We do not require a strong military presence at the border any more: the aliens have already landed."

Although the federal government has talked of its intention to deport illegal aliens, it is also mindful of the political reality: the majority of the Filipinos are Muslim, and making them legal Malaysian citizens could ruin Sabah's predominantly Christian, Kadazan-led state government. The Filipino community is also a thorn in Sabah's flesh because of the crime-wave associated with their arrival: the Sabah police claims 65% of all crimes in the state are committed by Filipinos. The police do not ask many questions when dealing with Filipino criminal suspects – about 40-50 are shot every year. Another local politician was quoted as saying: "the immigrants take away our jobs, cause political instability and pose a health hazard because of the appalling conditions in which some of them live".

There are 6 different Filipino groups in Sabah: the Visayas and Ilocano are Christian as are the Ilongo (Ilo Ilo), from Zamboanga. The Suluks are Muslim; they come from S Mindanao and have the advantage of speaking a dialect of Bahasa Malaysia. Many Filipinos were born in Sabah and all second generation immigrants are fluent in Bahasa. Migration first accelerated in the 1950s during the logging boom, and continued when the oil palm plantation economy took off – the biggest oil palm plantation is at Tengku, E of Lahad Datu. Many migrants have settled along the roadsides on the way to Danum Valley; it is easy to claim land – all they have to do is simply clear a plot and plant a few fruit trees.

Religion

For information on religion, **see page 229**.

Crafts

Compared with neighbouring Sarawak and Kalimantan, Sabah's handicraft industry is rather impoverished. Sabah's tribal groups were less protected from Western influences than Sarawak's, and traditional skills quickly began to die out as the state modernized and the economy grew. In Kota Kinabalu today, the markets are full of Filipino handicrafts and shell-products; local arts and crafts are largely confined to basketry, mats, hats, beadwork, musical instruments and pottery.

The elongated Kadazan backpack baskets (found around Mount Kinabalu National Park) are called **wakids** and are made from bamboo, rattan and bark. Woven food covers – or **tudong saji** – are often mistaken for hats, and are made by the Bajau of Kota Belud. **Hats**, made from nipah palm or rattan, and whose shape varies markedly from place to place, are decorated with traditional motifs. One of the most common motifs is the *nantuapan*, or 'meeting', which represents four people all drinking out of the same tapai (rice wine) jar. The Rungus people (from the Kudat peninsula) also make **linago basketware** from a strong wild grass; it is tightly woven and not decorated. At *tamus* – Sabah's big open-air markets (**see page 298**) – there are usually some handicrafts for sale. The Kota Belud tamu is the best place to find the Bajau horseman's embroidered turban, the **destar (see page 320)**. Traditionally, the Rungus people, who live on the Kudat Peninsula, were renowned as fine weavers, and detailed patterns were woven into their ceremonial skirts, or **tinugupan**. These patterns all had different names, but, like the ingredients of the traditional dyes, many have now been forgotten.

MODERN SABAH

Politics

Following Sabah's first state election in 1967, the Sabah Alliance ruled until 1975 when the newly formed multi-racial party, Berjaya, swept the polls. Berjaya had been set up with the financial backing of the United Malays National Organization (UMNO), the mainstay of the ruling Barisan Nasional (National Front) coalition on the peninsula. Ten years later, the Parti Bersatu Sabah (PBS) or United Sabah Party – led by the Christian Kadazan Datuk Joseph Pairin Kitingan – won a landslide victory and became the only state government in Malaysia that did not belong to the UMNO-led coalition. It became an obvious embarrassment to Prime Minister

Chips on the shoulder and chips on the table

The Kitingan family claims resource-rich Sabah is not getting its fair share of Malaysia's economic boom. The central government has done little to foster Sabah's allegiance and because many Sabahans feel short-changed, anti-federal feelings run high. The Parti Bersatu Sabah (United Sabah Party) maintains that it is unable to make its voice heard within the federation, but the Chief Minister denies that Sabah has any intention of secession. He maintains that ever since Sabah joined the federation, the state's constitutional rights – enshrined in a 20-point agreement – have been eroded. The main bone of contention has been Sabah's huge oil revenues – worth around US$852 million a year – of which 95% disappears into federal coffers. Kuala Lumpur has refused to entertain repeated Sabahan requests for an increased share of them. The state has increasingly resorted to the lucrative logging industry for funds.

The PBS has also complained that the federal government has not paid enough attention to Sabah's infrastructural development – there is not even a surfaced road between the two main towns, Kota Kinabalu and Sandakan. It says Islam has been made the official state religion, although there is not meant to be one; that Bahasa Malaysia has become the state language instead of English (as agreed) and that Sabah now requires federal approval to borrow funds, even though it was meant to control its own finances. Other grievances include everything from Sabah wanting its own television network to the deportation of the estimated 500,000 illegal Filipino and Indonesian immigrants.

The tense situation was aggravated in 1991 when the federal government curbed Sabah's timber exports – which are worth nearly US$1 billion a year. This was done on the pretext of bowing to environmentalist pressures – and a worrying World Bank report which said that Sabah's rainforest was disappearing too quickly. Malaysian primary industries minister denied the move was an act of political revenge, but Sabahans thought otherwise. Pairin says it infringes the terms of the 1963 agreement by which Sabah was given sole responsibility for the development of its timber industry. In 1991, Prime Minister, Dr Mahathir Mohamad's UMNO party set up in Sabah for the first time, and, within months, won a by-election victory in a predominantly Muslim constituency.

About half of the state's population is Muslim, although very few of them are Malays. The federal government has been fairly blatant in wooing their support, offering generous grants for the construction of mosques in villages with only a handful of Muslims. Mahathir's actions since the 1990 election show clearly that he wants to see Sabahan politics become divided along religious and racial lines. But in April 1993, it became apparent that these efforts had completely backfired when Sabah's main Muslim party hitched up with the Christian PBS. Many observers suspect that the federal government will continue to squeeze Sabah financially in the hope that economic hardship under Pairin's government will eventually prompt Sabahans to vote him out of power.

Dr Mahathir Mohamad to have a rebel Christian state in his predominantly Muslim federation. Nonetheless, the PBS eventually joined Mahathir's ruling coalition, believing its partnership would help iron things out. It did not.

Ever since PBS came to power, the federal government and Sabahan opposition parties openly courted Filipino and Indonesian immigrants in the state – almost all of whom are Muslim – and secured identity cards for them, enabling them to vote. Dr Mahathir has made no secret of his preference for a Muslim government, in Sabah. Nothing, however, has been able to dislodge the PBS, which was resoundingly returned to power in 1990. The federal government has long been suspicious of Sabahan politicians – particularly following the PBS defection from

Dr Mahathir's coalition in the days before the 1990 general election, bolstering the opposition alliance. Dr Mahathir described the move as "a stab in the back", but in the event, he won convincingly without PBS help, prompting political retaliation which many Sabahans now believe has turned into a personal vendetta.

Sabah has paid a heavy price for its 'disloyalty'; several prominent Sabahans have been arrested under Malaysia's draconian Internal Security Act, which provides for indefinite detention without trial. Among them were Joseph Pairin Kitingan (the Chief Minister) and his brother Jeffrey, head of the influential Yayasan Sabah, or Sabah Foundation (**see page 305**). Both were arrested on corruption charges although Jeffrey was also linked to an alleged secessionist conspiracy which was 'uncovered' in 1990. Kuala Lumpur has regularly voiced concern about Sabah's political fidelity within the federation, but the arrests only served to spotlight the venomous political feud between Pairin and Dr Mahathir. The 'persecution' of the Kitingan brothers, who come from Tambunan, has turned them into local folk heroes. The political jousting between Pairin and Mahathir has continued since 1990. In Jan 1993, Sabah decreed that Malaysians not resident in Sabah would have to carry passports when entering the state. In February, an incensed Mahathir said his government would be reviewing Sabah's special powers, to bring it into greater political union with Peninsular Malaysia.

Today, anti-federal feelings in Sabah are reckoned to have heightened further. Dr Mahathir suffered another humiliation in April 1993 when state assemblymen from the Muslim-based United Sabah National Organization (USNO) entered into a coalition with the Christian-dominated PBS. Mahathir had been banking on USNO joining forces with his own UMNO party to topple Pairin's government. Michael Vatikiotis, correspondent for the *Far Eastern Economic Review*, noted that the Prime Minister's efforts to impose an ethnic/religious split on Sabahan politics had backfired. Furthermore, the trial of Pairin, the Chief Minister, which has been rumbling slowly on in Sabah's High Court, has convinced Pairin's supporters that he is a political victim. Vatikiotis says there are fears that any unrest resulting from a conviction would give the federal government the chance to impose a state of emergency in Sabah, allowing it to be ruled from Kuala Lumpur.

If Sabah's internal politicking is fractious, the threat posed by six external claimants is deeply worrying. In what some commentators dismissed as scare-mongering, the former editor of the Far Eastern Economic Review, Philip Bowring, said Sabah was the nearest thing East Asia has to Bosnia. In an article in the *International Herald Tribune* in April 1993, he listed the claimants – Indonesia, the Philippines, the Sultans of Sulu, Brunei and Sabahan separatists – and concluded that "Bosnia is a warning to economically dynamic East Asia that such issues need constant and careful management".

KOTA KINABALU & TUNKU ABDUL RAHMAN NATIONAL PARK

Kota Kinabalu is a modern city and lacks the charm of neighbouring Kuching, but just off-shore are clear waters and coral reefs in Tunku Abdul Rahman National Park.

Kota Kinabalu

Kota Kinabalu started life as a trading post in 1881 – not on the mainland, but on Gaya Island, opposite the present town, where a Filipino shanty is today. On 9 Jul 1897 rebel leader Mat Salleh, who engaged in a series of hit-and-run raids against the North Borneo Chartered Company's administration, landed on Pulau Gaya. His men looted and sacked the settlement and Gaya township was abandoned.

Two years later the Europeans established another township but this time located on the mainland, opposite Pulau Gaya, adjacent to a Bajau stilt village. The kampung was called '*Api Api*' – meaning 'Fire! Fire!' – because it had been repeatedly torched by pirates over the years. After the Gaya experience, it was an inauspicious name. The Chartered Company rechristened it Jesselton, after Sir Charles Jessel, one of the company directors. But for years, only the Europeans called it Jesselton; locals preferred the old name, and even today Sabahans sometimes refer to their state capital as 'Api'.

Jesselton owed its raison d'être to a plan that back-fired. William C Cowie – formerly a gun-runner for the Sultan of Sulu – became managing director of the Chartered Company in 1894. He wanted to build a trans-Borneo railway (**see page 315**) and the narrow strip of land just N of Tanjung Aru and opposite Pulau Gaya, with its sheltered anchorage, was selected as a terminus.

Photographs in the Sabah State Museum chart the town's development from 1899, when work on the North Borneo Railway terminus began in earnest. By 1905, Jesselton was linked to Beaufort by a 92 km narrow-gauge track. By 1911 it had a population of 2,686, half of whom were Chinese and the remainder Kadazans and Dusuns; there were 33 European residents. Jesselton was of little importance in comparison to Sandakan, the capital of North Borneo.

When the Japanese Imperial Army invaded Borneo in 1942, Jesselton's harbour gave the town strategic significance and it was consequently completely flattened by the Allies during World War II. The modern town lacks the colonial charm of Sarawak's state capital Kuching. Only 3 buildings – the old **General Post Office** on Gaya Street, **Attkinson's Clock Tower** (built in 1905 and named after Jesselton's first district officer) and the old red-roofed **Lands and Surveys building** remain of the old town. The renovated post office now houses the Sabah Tourist Promotion Corporation. Jesselton followed Kudat and Sandakan as the administrative centre of North Borneo, at the end of World War II.

In Sept 1967 Jesselton was renamed Kota Kinabalu after the mountain – its name is usually shortened to KK. The modern city, which has a population of about 180,000, is strung out along the coast, with jungle-clad hills as a backdrop. Two-thirds of the town is built on land reclaimed from the shallow Gaya Bay – during the spring tides it is possible to walk across to the island. Only light fishing boats and passenger vessels can dock at KK's wharves – heavy cargo is unloaded at Likas Bay, to the N. Jalan Pantai, or Beach Road, is now in the centre of town. Successive land reclamation projects has meant that many of the original stilt villages, such as Kampung Ayer, have been cut off from the sea and some now stand in stinking, stagnant lagoons. The government plans to clean up and reclaim these areas in the next few years and the inhabitants of the water villages are being rehoused.

Places of interest

The golden dome of **Masjid Sabah**, on Jalan Tunku Abdul Rahman, is visible from most areas of town. Completed in 1975, it is the second biggest mosque in Malaysia and, like the Federal Mosque in Kuala Lumpur, is a fine example of contemporary Islamic architecture. It can accommodate 5,000 worshippers.

Perched on a small hill overlooking the mosque is the **Sabah State Museum** (and State Archives) on Jalan Mat Salleh/Bukit Istana Lama. The museum is designed to look like a longhouse. It has a fascinating ethnographic section which includes an excellent exhibition on the uses of bamboo. Tribal brassware, silverware, musical instruments, basketry and pottery are also on display. On the same floor is a collection of costumes and artifacts from Sabah tribes – the Kadazan/Dusun, Bajau, Murut and Runggus.

One of the most interesting items in this collection is a *sininggazanak* – a sort of totem pole. If a Kadazan man dies without an heir, it was the custom to erect a sininggazanak – a wooden

KOTA KINABALU

Not to Scale

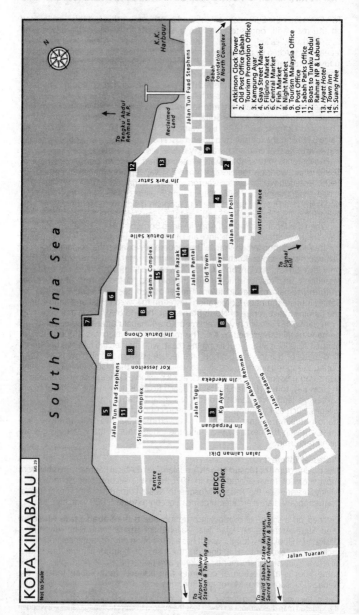

South China Sea

K.K. Harbour

To Tengku Abdul Rehman N.P.

Reclaimed Land

To Signal Hill

Jalan Tun Fuad Stephens

Jalan Park Satur

Jalan Datuk Salle

Jalan Balai Polis

Australia Place

Jalan Gaya

Old Town

Jalan Pantai

Jalan Tun Razak

Segama Complex

Jalan Datuk Chong

Kor Jesselton

Jalan Tun Fuad Stephens

Sinsuran Complex

Jalan Tugu

Jalan Perpaduan

Kg Ayer

Jalan Merdeka

Jalan Tengku Abdul Rehman

Jalan Padang

Jalan Laiman Diki

Centre Point

SEDCO Complex

To Airport, Railway Station & Tanjung Aru

To Masjid Sabah, State Museum, Sacred Heart Cathedral & South

Jalan Tuaran

1. Atkinson Clock Tower
2. Old Post Office (Sabah Tourism Promotion Office)
3. Kampung Ayer
4. Gaya Street Market
5. Filipino Market
6. Central Market
7. Fish Market
8. Night Market
9. Tourism Malaysia Office
10. Post Office
11. Sabah Parks Office
12. Boats to Tunku Abdul Rahman NP & Labuan
13. Hyatt Hotel
14. Town Inn
15. Suang Hee

To Sabah Foundation & North Complex

statue supposedly resembling the deceased – on his land. There is also a collection of human skulls – called a *bangkaran* – which before the tribe's wholesale conversion to Christianity, would have been suspended from the rafters of Kadazan longhouses. Every 5 years a *magang* feast was held to appease the spirits of the skulls.

The museum's archaeological section contains a magnificently carved coffin found in a limestone cave in the Madai area. Upstairs, the natural history section, provides a good introduction to Sabah's flora and fauna. Next door is a collection of jars, called *pusaka*, which are tribal heirlooms. They were originally exchanged by the Chinese for jungle produce, such as beeswax, camphor and bird's nests.

Next door is the **Science Museum**, containing an exhibition on Shell's offshore activities. The **Art Gallery & Multivision Theatre**, within the same complex, are also worth a browse. The art gallery is small and mainly exhibits works by local artists; among the more interesting works on display are those of Suzie Mojikol, a Kadazan artist, Bakri Dani, who adapts Bajau designs and Philip Biji who specializes in burning Murut designs onto chunks of wood with a soldering iron. The ethnobotanical gardens are on the hillside below the museum complex. There is a cafeteria at the base of the main building. Open: 1000-1800 Mon-Thur, 0900-1800 Sat & Sun.

Sabah has a large Christian population and the **Sacred Heart Cathedral** has a striking pyramidal roof which is clearly visible from the Sabah State Museum complex.

Further into town and nearer the coast are a series of water villages, including **Kampung Ayer**, although its size has shrunk in recent years. **Signal Hill** (Bukit Bendera), just SE of the central area, gives a panoramic view of the town and islands. In the past, the hill was used as a vantage point for signalling to ships approaching the harbour. There is an even better view of the coastline from the top of the **Sabah Foundation (Yayasan Sabah) Complex**, 4 km out of town, overlooking Likas Bay. This surreal glass sculpture has circular floors suspended on high-tensile steel rods and houses the Chief Minister's office. There is a revolving restaurant (**see page 307**) and helipad on top.

Gaya street market is held every Sunday (from 0800), selling a vast range of goods from jungle produce and handicrafts to pots and pans. The market almost opposite the main minibus station on Jalan Tun Fuad Stephens is known as the **Filipino market**, as most of the stalls are run by Filipino immigrants. A variety of Filipino and local handicrafts are sold in the hundreds of cramped stalls, along winding alleyways which are strung with low-slung curtains of shells, baskets and bags. The Filipino market is a good place to buy cultured pearls (about M$5 each)

The Sabah Foundation

The Sabah Foundation was set up in 1966 to help improve Sabahans' quality of life. The foundation has a 972,800 ha timber concession, which it claims to manage on a sustainable-yield basis. Two-thirds of this concession has already been logged. Profits from the timber go towards loans and scholarships for Sabahan students, funding the construction of hospitals and schools and supplying milk, textbooks and uniforms to school children. The Foundation also operates a 24-hour flying ambulance service to remote parts of the interior.

and has everything from fake gemstones to camagong-wood salad bowls, fibre shirts and traditional Indonesian medicines. Further into town, on the waterfront, is the **central market** selling mainly fish, fruit and vegetables. The daily fishing catch is unloaded on the wharf near the market.

Excursions

Hongkod Koisaan (KDCA Cultural Centre) is at Mile 4.5, Jalan Penampang. Each year in May, after the harvest, the Kadazan perform the *Magavau* ritual to nurse the spirit of the grain back to health in readiness for the next planting season. Traditionally the ritual is conducted in the paddy fields by a *bobhizan* – or high priestess. It is now carried out at the Kadazans' Honkod Koisaan or Unity Hall. The centre is worth visiting during the *Tadau Keamatan* harvest festival in May (**see page 354**). **Getting there**: red and white buses go to Penampang from in front of the MPKK building next to the State Library.

Penampang, a Kadazan village, is 13 km from KK. The old town was demolished in the early 1980s and the new township built in 1982. The population is mainly Kadazan or Sino-Kadazan and about 90% Christian. The oldest church in Sabah, **St Michael's** Roman Catholic church, is on a steep hill on the far side of the new town. It was originally built in 1897 but is not dramatic to look at and has been much renovated over the years. Services are conducted in Kadazan.

There are many megaliths in the Penampang area which are thought to be associated with property claims – particularly when a land-owner died without a direct heir. Some solitary stones, which can be seen standing in the middle of paddy fields, are more than 2m tall. The age of the megaliths has not been determined. Wooden figures, called *sininggazanak* can also be seen in the ricefields (**see page 303**).

There is an excellent Kadazan/Dusun restaurant in Penampang New Town: *Yun Chuan, Penampang New Town*, which specializes in Kadazan dishes, such as *hinava* – or raw fish, the Kadazan equivalent of sushi. Tapai chicken is a recommended dish and local vegetables include yams and *pakis* ferns, which are fried up with chilli, belacan and mushrooms. This dish is known as *sayur manis* (sweet vegetables). The best ferns are imported from Lahad Datu; they are often eaten raw, with a squeeze of lime, which 'cooks' it (*sayur pakis limau*). *Sup terjun* (jumping soup) is another Kadazan favourite; it is made with salted fish, mango and ginger. This is typical of many Kadazan dishes which tend to use a lot of mango and are on the sour side, M$4-6. **Getting there**: red and white buses go to Penampang from in front of the MPKK building next to the State Library.

House of Skulls is in Kampung Monsopiad (named after a fearsome Kadazan warrior-cum-headhunter – the so-called Hercules of Sabah) just outside Penampang. There are 42 human skulls in the collection, some of which are said to be 300 years old and possess spiritual powers. They are laced together with leaves of the hissad palm, which represents the hair of the victims. Dousia Mousing, who lives in the ordinary little kampung house, is a direct descendent of Monsopiad. He presides over his ancestor's dreaded sword, its handle decorated with human hair, sliced from Monsopiad's victims. A 3-day, 3-night-long feast is held at the house in May, in the run-up to the harvest festival.

Tanjung Aru Beach is the best beach, after those in Tunku Abdul Rahman National Park, and is close to Tanjung Aru resort, 5 km S of KK. It is particularly popular at weekends and there is a good hawker centre. **Getting there**: minibuses from the terminus in front of the market, Jalan Tun Fuad Stephens (M$1); red and white buses to Tanjung Aru leave from outside the MPKK building, next to the State Library.

Tampuruli, 32 km N of KK at the junction of the roads N and E, has a suspension bridge straddling the Tuaran River. It was built by the British Army in 1922. Popular stop for tour buses. **Getting there**: minibuses from the terminus in front of the market, Jalan Tun Fuad Stephens (M$1.50). Green buses leave for Tuaran from the padang at the foot of Signal Hill.

Mengkabong is a Bajau – or sea gypsy – fishing village within easy reach of KK. The village is particularly photogenic in the early morning, before Mount Kinabalu, which serves as a dramatic backdrop, is obscured by cloud. The Bajau build their atap houses on stilts over the water and these are interconnected by a network of narrow wooden planks. The price of a Bajau bride was traditionally assessed in stilts, shaped from the trunks of bakau mangrove trees. A father erected one under his house on the day a daughter was born and replaced it whenever it wore out. The longer the daughter remained at home, the more stilts he got through and the more water buffalo he demanded from a prospective husband. The Bajau first settled in Sabah in the 18th century and are fishermen *par excellence*. The men leave Mengkabong at high tide and arrive back with their catch at the next high tide. They use sampan canoes, hollowed out of a single tree-trunk, which are crafted in huts around the village. Bajau women are known for their brightly coloured basketry – *tudong saji*. Some of the waterways and fields around Menkabong are choked by water hyacinth, an ornamental plant that was originally introduced by Chinese farmers as pig-fodder from South America. Now no one can get rid of it. **Getting there**: minibus (M$1.50) to Tuaran, taxis to Menkabong.

Tunku Abdul Rahman National Park, see page 311.

Tours Most companies run city tours. Other tours that are widely available include: **Kota Belud tamu** (Sunday market), **Gunung Kinabalu National Park** (including Poring Hot Springs), **Sandakan's Sepilok Orang Utan Rehabilitation Centre**, train trips to **Tenom through the Padas Gorge** and tours of the islands in the **Tunku Abdul Rahman National Park**. Several companies specialize in scuba-diving tours, **see page 309**.

Accommodation A+ *Hyatt Kinabalu International*, Jln Datuk Salleh Sulong, T 221234, F 225972, a/c, restaurant; **A+** *Tanjung Aru Beach Resort*, Tanjung Aru, T 58711, F 217155, a/c, restaurant, pool, simply the best hotel in Sabah, the only thing it does not have is its own private beach: Tanjung Aru is a public beach, frequented by kite-flyers, swimmers, joggers, and lovers, the hotel is noticeably on the European honeymoon circuit, rec; **A** *Borneo Resthouse*, Mile 3.5 Jln Penampang, Taman Fraser, T 215342, F 222081, a/c, restaurant, pool, garden; **A** *Jesselton*, 69 Jln Gaya, T 55633, F 240401/225985, a/c, restaurant, good for price bracket; **A** *Palace*, 1 Jln Tingi, Karamunsing, T 211911, F 211600, a/c, restaurant, pool, proprietor James Sheng has a small resort, with chalets, on Pulau Gaya, at Maluham Bay, E of Police Bay, enquire at hotel; **A** *Shangri-La*, 75 Bandaran Berjaya, T 212800/223177, F 212078, a/c, restaurant, not up to usual Shangri-La standards, but the haunt of visiting businessmen; **B** *Ang's*, 28 Jln Bakau, T 54466/33, F 217867, a/c, basic; **B** *City Inn*, 41 Jln Pantai, T 218933, F 218937/235333, a/c, good for the price, often full; **B** *Town Inn*, 31 & 33 Jln Pantai, T 225823, F 217762, a/c, good for the price, rec; **B** *Winner*, 9 & 10 Jln Pasar Baru, Kampong Air, T 243222, F 215546, a/c, restaurant, pleasant hotel in a central location with friendly staff and a good restaurant; **C** *Asia*, 68 Jln Bandaran Berjaya, T 53533/53638, a/c, occasionally screens eyebrow-raising in-house videos; **C** *Bilal*, 2nd Flr, Block B, Lot 1 Segama Complex, T 56709, a/c, above the Indian Muslim restaurant of the same name, this hotel, although basic, is spotless and bright with friendly management, rec; **C** *Suang Hee*, Block F, 7 Segama Shopping Centre, T 56343, a/c, restaurant, clean Chinese hotel, reasonable value for money; **C-D** *Celia's Bed & Breakfast*, 413 Jln Saga, Kampung Likas, T 35733, out of town but recommended by all who stay there; **C-D** *Traveller's Resthouse*, Block L, 3rd Flr, Lot 5 & 6, Sinsuran Complex, Bangunan Pelancungan, T 240624, some a/c, no attached bath, some rooms don't have a window, friendly, lots of travel information; **D** *Government Sports Complex Hostel*, Likas (behind Signal Hill), facilities include running track, gym, swimming pool, tennis and badminton courts, takes 15 mins by Likas-bound minibus from town, or walk over Signal Hill, dorm (**E**), a/c (**C**); **D** *Segama*, 2nd/3rd Flr, Block D, Lot 1, 16 Jln Labuk, Segama, T 221327, a/c, clean, but rooms are dark.

Restaurants Malay: ♦♦*Copelia*, Jln Gaya, *nasi lemak* for breakfast, also does takeaway; ♦♦*Hot Chilli Café*, Grd Flr, Block BC, No 3, Sadong Jaya, T 239242, superb curry dishes and rendangs, also serves Indonesian and Chinese dishes, open until 0200; ♦♦♦*Sri Kayangan Revolving Restaurant*, 18th Flr Yayasan Sabah Bldg (Sabah Foundation), Likas Bay, serves local Malay and Chinese dishes and offers set dinners; ♦*Restoran Ali*, Segama Complex, opposite *Hyatt Hotel*, best in a string of coffee shops, all of which are good value for money.

Chinese: ♦♦*Avasi Cafeteria & Garden Restaurant*, EG 11 Kompleks Kuwasa, steamboat and seafood; ♦*Chuan Hin*, Jln Kolam (next to the Cottage Pub), excellent *ikan panggan* (barbecued fish); ♦*Friendly*, Tuaran Rd, Mile 2, Likas, cheap; ♦♦♦*Hyatt Poolside Hawker Centre*, Hyatt, Jln Datuk Salleh Sulong, steamboat (minimum 2 persons); *Nam Xing*, opposite the *Hyatt* and emporium, specializes in dim sum; ♦♦*Phoenix Court*, Hyatt, Jln Datuk Salleh Sulong, dim sum 0700-1400; ♦♦*Tioman*, Lot 56 Bandaran Berjaya, good claypot and lemon chicken.

Seafood: **NB**: seafood in KK is seasonally prone to red tide. Locals will know when it's prevalent. Avoid all shellfish if there is any suspicion. ♦*Port View*, Jln Haji Saman (opposite old customs wharf), huge selection of fresh seafood and delicious chilli crab, open until 0200 weekdays and 0300 on Sat, very popular with locals; *Golf View*, Jln Swamp (near Sabah Golf and Country Club), rec by locals; ***Garden Restaurant**, Tanjung Aru Beach Resort*, tables outside; ***Seafood Market & Supplies**, Tanjung Aru Beach, pick your own fresh seafood and get advice on how to have it cooked; ***Merdeka**, 11th Flr, Wisma Merdeka, reasonably good seafood, but the view is better in this restaurant which offers "karaoke at no extra charge".

Nonya: **Sri Melaka Restoran*, 9 Jln Laiman Diki, Kampung Air (Sedco Complex, near *Shiraz*).

Other Asian cuisine: *Bilal*, Block B, Lot 1 Segama Complex, Indian Muslim food, rotis, chapatis, curries, rec; ***Shiraz**, Lot 5, Block B, Sedco Square, Kampong Ayer, Indian, rec; *Sri Sakthi*, Mile 4.5 Jln Penampeng (opposite Towering Heights Industrial Estate), S Indian banana-leaf – good value; ***Jaws**, 4th Flr, Gaya Centre, Jln Tun Fuad Stephens, Thai/Chinese cuisine, such as tom yam steamboat; **Korean*, Jln Bandaran Berjaya, next to *Asia Hotel*, large selection, barbeques speciality; ***Azuma**, 3rd Flr, Wisma Merdeka, Japanese; ***Nishiki**, Gaya St (opposite Wing On Life Building), Japanese.

International: **Capital Coffee House*, Grd Flr, *Hotel Capital*, Jln Haji Saman, european breakfasts; *Fat Cat*, Jln Haji Saman, cheap slap-up breakfasts; ***Gardenia**, Jesselton Hotel*, 55 Jln Gaya; ***Peppino**, Tanjung Aru Beach Resort*, tasty but expensive, Italian, good Filipino cover band. **Coffee shops**: *Restoran Ali, Nam Seng Milkbar and Restaurant, Kedai Kopi Tung Meng* – all in the Segama Complex, across from the *Hyatt Hotel*.

Foodstalls ** Stalls above *central market*; **Sedco Square*, Kampong Ayer, large square filled with stalls, great atmosphere in the evenings, ubiquitous *ikan panggang* (spicy barbecued fish) and satay; *Tanjung Aru Beach*, mainly seafood – recommended for *ikan panggang* – and satay stalls: very busy at weekends, when the stalls do a brisk business, on weekdays, it is rather quiet, with only a few stalls to choose from. There are other foodstalls around the minibus station in KK, at the night market on Jln Tugu, on the waterfront at the Sinsuran Food Centre and at the Merdeka Food Stall Centre, Wisma Merdeka.

Bars *Tidbits Café*, Segama Complex, above Traffic Jam and opposite *Hyatt Hotel*,no food, but a pleasant spot for a cheap Tiger.

Entertainment **Cultural shows**: *Tanjung Aru Beach Hotel* on Wed & Sat, 2000; *Kadazan-Dusun Cultural Centre* (Hongkod Koisaan), KDCA Building, Mile 4.5, Jln Penampang, restaurant open year-round, but at the end of May, during the harvest festival, the cultural association comes into its own, with dances, feasts and shows and lots of *tapai* (M$15).

Discos *Heartbeat*, 22 Karamunsing Warehouse, Jln Sembulan Lama. KK's hot spot; *Tiffiny*, 9Blk A, Jln Karamunsing; *Sergeant Pepper's*, next to the old airport/flying club, Tanjung Aru, intimate club playing oldies and catering for the nostalgia brigade.

Sports The sports complex at Likas is open to the general public. To get there take a Likas-bound minibus from town or walk over Signal Hill. **Bowling**: *Merdeka Bowl*, 11th Flr Wisma Merdeka. **Diving**: snorkelling and scuba-diving in Tunku Abdul Rahman National Park. Tour operators specializing in dive trips also organize dives all over Sabah. **Golf**: courses at Tanjung Aru and the *Sabah Golf and Country Club* at Bukit Padang, an 18-hole championship course, which affords magnificent views of Mount Kinabalu on clear days. **Hash**: there are 3 hashes in KK. **1**: *K2 H4* (KK Hash House Harriers) – men only, T 428535. Mon, 1715. **2**: *K2 H2* (KK Hash House Bunnies) – women (but not exclusively), T 244333, ext. 389. **3**: *K2 H4* (KK Hash House Harriers and Harriets) – mixed, T 217541. Fri, 1715. **Sailing**: yacht club at Tanjung Aru, next to the hotel. **White water rafting**: Papar River (Grades I & II), Kadamaian River (Grades II & III), Padas River (Grade IV). Usually requires a minimum of 3 people. Main operators include *Api Tours, Borneo Expeditions* and *Discovery Tours* (**see page 307**). **Watersports**: *Tanjung Aru Marina* snorkelling M$10/day, water skiing M$120/hr, fishing M$12-25/day, sailing M$20-40/hr, water scooter M$60/hr.

Shopping **Antiques** good antiques shop at the bottom of the Chun Eng Bldg on Jln Tun Razak. It is necessary to have an export licence from the Sabah State Museum if you intend to export rare antiques. **Books**: *Rahmant Bookstore*, Hyatt Hotel, Jln Datuk Salleh Sulong; *Arena Book Centre*, Lot 2, Grd Flr, Block 1, Sinsuran Kompleks; *Arena Book Centre*, Block L, Sinsuran Kompleks. **Handicrafts**: mainly baskets, mats, tribal clothing, beadwork and pottery. *Borneo Gifts*, Grd Flr, Wisma Sabah; *Borneo Handicraft*, 1st Flr, Wisma Merdeka, local pottery and material made up into clothes; *Elegance Souvenir*, 1st Flr, Wisma Merdeka, lots of beads of local interest (another branch on Grd Flr of Centre Point); *Filipino Market*, Jln Tun Fuad Stephens (**see page 305**); *Kaandaman Handicraft Centre* below *Seafood Market Restaurant*, Tanjung Aru Beach; *Kampung Air Night Market*,mainly Filipino handicrafts; *Sabah Art and Handicraft Centre*, 1st Flr, Block B, Segama Complex (opposite

New Sabah Hotel); **Sabah Handicraft Centre**, Lot 49 Bandaran Berjaya (next to *Shangri-La*) good selection (also has branches at the museum and the airport). There are also several handicraft shops in the arcade at the *Tanjung Aru Beach Hotel* and one at the airport. *Api Tours*, Lot 49, Bandaran Berjaya also has a small selection of handicrafts. **Jewellery**: most shops in Wisma Merdeka. **Markets: see page 305**. **Shopping complexes**: *Sinsuran* and *Segama* on Jln Tun Fuad Stephens.

Local transport Car hire: not all roads in Sabah are paved and a 4-wheel-drive vehicle is advisable. However, car hire is expensive and start at around M$280/day. Rates often increase for use outside a 50 km radius of KK. All vehicles have to be returned to KK as there are no agency offices outside KK, although local car-hire is usually available. **Adaras Rent-a-Car**, Lot G03, Grd Flr, Wisma Sabah, T 222137/216010, F 232641; **Avis**, *Hyatt Kinabalu Hotel*, Jln Datuk Salleh Sullong, T 51577; **E & C Limousine Services**, Grd Flr, Wisma Sabah, T 57679, F 221466 and at Lot 2.74, 2nd Flr, Kompleks Karamunsing, T 57679; **Kinabalu Rent-a-Car**, Lot 3.61, 3rd Flr, Kompleks Karamunsing, T 232602; **Sintat**, Block L, Lots 4-6, Sinsuran Complex, T 57729; **Hertz**, Block B, Sedco Complex, T 221635. **City buses**: leave from area between Jln Tun Razak/Jln Tugu. Red and white buses go to Penampang and Tanjung Aru and leave from the bus station in front of the MPKK building, next to the state library. Green buses go to areas N of KK (Tuaran, Likas etc) and leave from the padang at the bottom of Signal Hill. **Minibuses**: most of the local minibuses to the airport and suburbs and kampungs such as Likas, Tanjung Aru leave from Lorong Jesselton/Jln Tun Fuad Stephens, just behind the General Post Office. All have their destinations on the windscreen, most rides in town are 20¢ and they will leave when full. You can get off wherever you like. **Taxis**: there are taxi stands outside most of the bigger hotels and outside the General Post Office, the Segama complex, the Sunsuran complex, next to the MPKK building, the Kojasa supermarket and the Capitol cinema. Fares from town: M$8 to *Tanjung Aru Beach Resort*, M$10 Sabah Foundation, M$5 to the museum, M$10 airport. **NB**: most taxis are not metered. Radio taxi numbers: T 52113, 56346, 52188, 52669.

Banks & money changers There are money changers in main shopping complexes. **Standard Chartered**, 20 Jln Haji Saman; **Hong Kong & Shanghai**, 56 Jln Gaya; **Sabah Bank**, Wisma Tun Fuad Stephens, Jln Tuaran.

Embassies & consulates **Indonesian Consulate**, Jln Karamunsing, T 54100; **Japanese Consulate**, Wisma Yakim, T 54169.

Useful addresses General Post Office: Jln Tun Razak, Segama Quarter (*poste restante* facilities). Telekom: Block C, Kompleks Kuwaus, Jln Tunku Abdul Rahman. International calls as well as local. Fax service. **Immigration**: 4th Flr Government Bldg, Jln Haji Yaakub. Visas can be renewed at this office, without having to leave the country. **Sabah National Park Headquarters**: Jln Tun Fuad Stephens, T 211585 for reservations for Kinabalu National Park or Poring Hot Springs. **Forestry Division**: Sabah Foundation, Sabah Foundation Building, Likas, T 354496. Reservations for Danum Valley Field Centre **(see page 338)** should be made here. **Business centres**: at the *Hyatt Hotel* and *Tanjung Aru Beach Hotel*. **Church services** (English): Sacred Heart (KK) Sun 0700; Stella Maris (Tanjung Aru) Sun 0715; St Michael's (Penampang – Kadazan only) Sun 0800.

Airline offices British Airways, Jln Haji Saman, T 52057/52292; **Cathay Pacific**, Grd Flr, Block C, Lot CG, Kompleks Kuwasa, 49 Jln Karamunsing, T 54733; **Garuda Airways**, Wisma Sabah; **MAS**, Karamunsing Kompleks, Jln Kemajuan, T 51455, also have an office at the airport; **Philippine Airlines**, Lot 3.48, Karamunsing Complex, Jln Kemajuan, T 218925; **Royal Brunei Airlines**, G13, Wisma Sabah, Jln Haji Saman, T 54830; **Sabah Air**, KK Airport, T 56733/51326; **Singapore Airlines**, 20 Jln Pantai Tempahan, T 55444/55333.

Tour companies & travel agents *Api Tours (Borneo)*, Lot 49, Bandaran Berjaya, T 221231, F 221230. Run by Albert Teo, the kingpin of Sabah's tourist industry, photographer and author of various guides. Offers a wide variety of tours, including some more unusual ones such as overnight stays in longhouses, rec. *Borneo Divers*, Lot 529, Mile 3.5 Tuaran Road, T 53074 and 401-404, 4th Flr, Wisma Sabah, T 222226, F 221550. (There is another branch in the *Tanjung Aru Beach Hotel*.) Operates exotic scuba diving trips and runs a dive station on Pulau Sipadan **(see page 341)**. *Borneo Divers* also runs an excellent dive store and operates 5-day training courses with classes tailored for beginners or advanced divers (M$875-575 depending on group size). The company also has an office in Labuan **(see page 317)** which organizes 2-day dives to shipwrecks off the island. Trips are seamlessly organized, but very expensive. *Borneo Expeditions*, Unit 306, 3rd Flr, Wisma Sabah, Jln Tun Razak, T 222721, F 222720. Specialists in mountain trekking and white water rafting – mainly on the Padas River; run by a former British outward-bound school instructor, Stephen Pinfield, whose forte is safari tours. A trek to Kampung Long Pa Sia, deep in Murut country, near the Sarawak and Kalimantan borders is highly rec. *Borneo Sea Adventures*, 1st Flr, 8a Karamunsing Warehouse, T 55390, F 221106 also conducts scuba diving courses and runs diving and fishing trips all around Sabah. It specializes in the 'Wall Dive' off Pulau Sipadan (see page 341). *Coral Island Cruises*, G19, Grd Flr, Wisma Sabah, Jln Tun Razak, T 223490, F 223404. Specializes in boat cruises, mostly around Tunku Abdul Rahman National Park, and offers night fishing trips. Coral Island Cruises has teamed up with the Labuan-based dive company Ocean Sports to run 6-day scuba-diving trips to Layang Layang, an atol in the disputed Spratly group, 6-9 day dive packages, costing M$1,000+, leave 2-3 times a month in peak season (Jun-Aug), rec. *Discovery Tours*, Lot 6 Shopping Arcade, *Tanjung Aru Beach Hotel*, T 216426-7/58711 or 122 Wisma Sabah, T 53787/221244, F 221600. Run by experienced tour-operator Albert Wong, rec. *Kosa World Tours*, 215-216, 2nd Flr, Wisma Sabah, Jln Tun Razak, T 221703-4, F 237975; *Kota Aquatics*, AG04 Wisma Merdeka, Jln Tun Razak, T/F 218710 runs diving courses, hires scuba and snorkelling equipment and organizes diving trips. Also runs fishing trips. *Sabah Air*, Sabah Air Bldg, Old Airport Rd, T 56733, F 235195. Sightseeing by helicopter. *Tanjung Aru Tours*, The Marina, *Tanjung Aru Beach Hotel*, T 214215/232721. Fishing & island tours – particularly to Tunku Abdul Rahman National Park. *Transworld*, Lot 4, 1st Flr, Fortuna Commercial Centre, Km 4, Penampang Rd, T 51021/50162 (also an office at Tanjung Aru Beach Resort). Glass-bottom boat trips to Tunku Abdul Rahman National Park. *White Water Adventures*, PO Box 13076 KK, T 231892.

Tourist offices Tourism Malaysia Sabah, Grd Flr, Wing On Life Building, Jln Sagunting, T 211698/211732; **Sarawak Tourist Promotion Corporation**, The Old Post Office, Jln Gaya, they also have a desk at KK airport; **Sabah Parks Office**, Block K, Sinsuran Kompleks, Jln Tun Fuad Stephens, T 211585/211652, necessary to book accommodation for the National Parks – particularly Mount Kinabalu National Park. Also has general information on the parks. The office has a good library with reports on wildlife in the parks and natural history surveys which can be used with the permission of the office. Open 0800-1600 Mon-Fri; 0830-1230 Sat.

Forestry Division, Sabah Foundation, Sabah Foundation Bldg, Likas, T 34596. Reservations for Danum Valley Field Centre should be made here.

Transport to & from Kota Kinabalu 77 km from Kota Belud, 128 km from Keningau, 386 km from Sandakan. **By air**: the airport is 6 km from town. *Transport into town*: Bus 12 and 13 go from the main road to the town centre (65¢). Minibus: regular minibus service (M$1.50). Taxi M$10 to town centre – coupon must be purchased in advance from the booths outside the arrivals hall. Connections with Singapore (M$566), Bandar Seri Begawan, Brunei (M$73), Hong Kong twice a week, Manila 5 times a week, Jakarta, Seoul and Taipei as well as domestic destinations. Regular domestic connections to KL (M$380) – cheaper flights if in a group of 3 or more, late-night flights, or book 14 days in advance. Bintulu (M$132), Kudat (M$60), Lahad Datu (M$106), Labuan (M$52), Miri (M$98), Sandakan (M$83), Tawau (M$96).

By train: the station is 5 km out of town in Tanjung Aru. Diesel trains run 3 times daily to Beaufort, 4 hrs (M$4.75) and on to Tenom, a further 3 hrs (M$2.75). Departure times are subject to change, T 52536/54611.

By bus: buses around the state are cheaper than minibuses but not as regular or efficient. The large buses go mainly to destinations in and around KK itself.

By minibus/taxi: there is no central bus station in KK. Taxis and minibuses bound N for Kota Belud, Tamparuli and Kudat and those going S to Papar, Beaufort, Keningau and Tenom leave from the corner of Australia Place/Jln Tunku Abdul Rahman. Taxis and minibuses going W to Kinabalu National Park, Ranau and Sandakan leave from Jln Tunku Abdul Rahman. Tamparuli, a few kilometres E of Tuaran, serves as a mini-terminus for minibuses heading to Kinabalu National Park. Minibuses to the airport, Penampang, Likas and Beaufort also leave from station between Lorong Jesselton/Jln Tun Fuad Stephens just behind the General Post Office. Minibuses leave when full and those for long-distance destinations leave in the early morning. Long-distance taxis also leave when full but are generally more expensive. Minibus fares from KK: Tuaran 45 mins (M$1.50), Kota Belud 2 hrs (M$5), Kudat 4-5 hrs (M$12), Beaufort 2-3 hrs (M$7), Keningau 2-3 hrs (M$10), Tenom 4 hrs (M$15), Kinabalu National Park 1½ hrs (M$10), Ranau 2 hrs (M$12), Sandakan 8-10 hrs (M$35).

By boat: an express boat leaves for Labuan (see page 317) at 0800 Mon-Sun, 2½ hrs (M$28). Boats leave from the jetty behind the *Hyatt Hotel*. Reservations can be made at *Rezeki Murmi Sdn Bhd*, Lot 3, 1st Flr, Block D, Segama Shopping Complex, T 236834/5. It is advisable to book ahead on weekends or public holidays. Return boats leave Labuan for KK at 1300.

Tunku Abdul Rahman National Park

The islands in Gaya Bay which make up Tunku Abdul Rahman National Park lie 3-8 km offshore. The 5 islands became Sabah's first national park in 1923 and were gazetted in an effort to protect their coral reefs and sandy beaches. Geologically, the islands are part of the Crocker Range formation, but as sea-levels rose after the last ice age, they became isolated from the massif. Coral reefs fringe all the islands in the park. The best reefs are between Pulau Sapi and Pulau Gaya, although there is also reasonable coral around Manukan, Mamutik and Sulug.

Flora & fauna Some of the only undisturbed coastal dipterocarp forest left in Sabah is on Pulau Gaya. On the other islands most of the original vegetation has been destroyed and established secondary vegetation predominates. Mangrove forests can be found at 2 locations on Pulau Gaya. Animal and bird life includes long-tailed macaques, bearded pig and pangolin (on Pulau Gaya), white-bellied sea eagle, pied hornbill, green heron, sandpipers, flycatchers and sunbirds.

There is a magnificent range of marine life because of the variety of the reefs surrounding the islands. The coral reefs are teaming with fish-tank exotica such as butterfly fish, Moorish idols, parrot fish, bat fish, razor fish, lion fish and stone fish – in stark contrast to the areas which have been depth-charged by Gaya's notorious dynamite fishermen.

Four of the 5 islands have excellent snorkelling and diving as well as jungle trails. The largest island, **Pulau Gaya**, was the site of the first British North Borneo Chartered Company settlement in the area in 1892. There is still a large settlement on the island on the promontory facing KK – but today it is a shanty town, populated mainly by Filipino immigrants (see page 298). On Pulau Gaya there are 20 km of marked trails including a plank-walk across a mangrove swamp. Police Bay has a beautiful shaded beach.

Pulau Sapi, the most popular of the island group for weekenders, also has good beaches and trails. It is connected to Pulau Gaya by a sandbar. **Pulau Mamutik** is the smallest island but closer to the mainland and has a well-preserved reef off the NE tip. **Pulau Manukan** is the site of the park headquarters and most of the park accommodation. It has good snorkelling to the S and E and a particularly good beach on the E tip; it is probably the nicest of all the islands. Marine sports facilities and a swimming pool are being built here. The best reefs are off **Pulau Sulang**, which is less developed being a little bit further away.

It is necessary to hire snorkel, mask and fins from boatmen at the KK jetty beforehand. Fishing with a hook and line is permitted but the use of spearguns and nets is prohibited.

Permits not necessary.

Park Headquarters on Pulau Manukan and ranger stations on Gaya, Sapi and Mamutik.

Accommodation Chalets and resthouses on Pulau Mamutik and Manukan or camp on any of the islands (it is necessary to obtain permission from the Sabah Parks Office in KK). Note they all tend to be cheaper during the week. **A** *Resthouse, Pulau Mamutik*, 3 bedrooms (can accommodate up to 8). **A** *Chalets, Pulau Manukan*, restaurant, facilities include tennis and squash courts and a restaurant. *Chalets at Maluham Bay*, E of Police Bay, Pulau Gaya. Enquire at *Palace Hotel*, KK.

Restaurants Restaurant on Pulau Manukan.

Transport to & from Tunku Abdul Rahman 3-8 km offshore. **By boat**: most boats leave from the jetty opposite the *Hyatt Hotel*. Regular ferry services at weekends, M$10-12 to one island, otherwise boats must be chartered from KK, most cost M$185 and take 12 passengers. It is possible to negotiate trips with local fishermen, M$50-70. Boats also leave from *Tanjung Aru Beach Hotel*.

SOUTH OF KOTA KINABALU

The suggested route goes south from KK and crosses the Crocher Range to Tambunan. Continuing south the road passes through the logging town of Keningan and on to Tenom, where it is possible to take the North Borneo railway, which snakes down the Padas Gorge to Beaufort. The Padas River is the best place to go white-water rafting in Sabah. Few towns are worth staying in for long on this route but it is a scenic journey.

Tambunan

The twisting mountain road that cuts across the **Crocker Range National Park** (see page 312) and over the Sinsuran Pass at 1,670m is very beautiful. The road itself, from KK to Tambunan, was the old bridle way that linked the W coast to the interior. It descends into the sprawling flood plain of Tambunan – which is a magnificent patchwork of greens in the height of the paddy season. The Tambunan area is largely Kadazan and the whole area explodes into life each May during the harvest festival.

Tambunan also lays claim to Sabah's modern folk-heroes – the Kitingan clan. Joseph Pairin Kitingan became the state's first Christian Chief Minister in 1986. His brother, Jeffrey, heads the Sabah Foundation. The family home is in Tambunan, and both men are regular visitors.

A modest plaque just outside Tambunan, among the ricefields and surrounded by peaceful kampung houses, commemorates the site of **Mat Salleh's fort**. Mat Salleh, now a nationalist folk-hero, led a rebellion for 6 years against the Chartered Company administration until he was killed in 1900. There is not much left of his fort for visitors to inspect.

Excursions

Crocker Range National Park incorporates 139,919 ha of hill and montane forest, which includes many species endemic to Borneo. It is the largest single totally protected area in Sabah. No visitors' facilities have yet been developed. But private development is taking place along the narrow strips of land each side of the KK-Tambunan road, which were unfortunately overlooked when the park was gazetted. A decrepit motel – complete with a horrifying menagerie – has sprung up at Sinsuran Pass and an outward bound school also has its headquarters here. **Getting there**: as for Tambunan.

Gunung Trusmadi, 70 km SE of KK, is the second highest mountain in Malaysia at 2,642m , but very few people climb it. There are 2 main routes to the top: the N route, which takes 4 days to the summit (and 3 days down) and the S route, which is harder but shorter – 2 days to the summit. Trusmadi is famous for its huge, and very rare, pitcher plant *Nepethes trusmadiensis*, which is only found on one spot on the summit ridge (see page 57). It is also known for its fantastic view N, towards Gunung Kinabalu, which rises above the Tambunan valley. There

Mat Salleh – fort-builder and folk hero

Mat Salleh was a Bajau, and son of a Sulu Chief, born in the court of the Sultan of Sulu. He was the only native leader to stand up against the increasingly autocratic whims of the North Borneo government as it sequestrated land traditionally belonging to tribal chiefs. Under the Chartered Company and the subsequent colonial administration, generations of school children were taught that Mat Salleh was a deplorable rabble-rouser and trouble-maker. Now Sabahans regard him as a nationalist hero.

In the British North Borneo Herald of 16 Feb 1899, it was reported that when he spoke, flames leapt from his mouth; lightening flashed with each stroke of his *parang* and when he scattered rice, the grains became wasps. He was said to have been endowed with 'special knowledge' by the spirits of his ancestors and was also reported to have been able to throw a buffalo by its horns.

In 1897 Mat Salleh raided and set fire to the first British settlement on Pulau Gaya (off modern-day Kota Kinabalu). For this, and other acts of sabotage, he was declared an outlaw by the Governor. A price tag of 700 Straits dollars was put on his head and an administrative officer, Raffles Flint, was assigned the unenviable task of tracking him down. Flint failed to catch him and Mat Salleh gained a reputation as a military genius.

Finally, the managing director of the Chartered Company, Scottish adventurer and former gun-runner William C Cowie, struck a deal with Mat Salleh and promised that his people would be allowed to settle peacefully in Tambunan – which at that time was not under Chartered Company control. After the negotiations Cowie wrote: "His manner and appearance made me aware that I was face to face with the Rob Roy of British North Borneo, the notorious Mat Salleh, whom I at once saluted with a *takek* [a greeting from an inferior]."

Half the North Borneo administration resigned as they considered Cowie's concessions outrageous. With it looking less and less likely that the terms of his agreement with Cowie would be respected, Mat Salleh retreated to Tambunan where he started building his fort; he had already gained a fearsome reputation for these stockades. West Coast Resident G Hewett described it as "the most extraordinary place and without [our] guns it would have been absolutely impregnable". Rifle fire could not penetrate it and Hewett blasted 200 shells into the fort with no noticeable effect. The stone walls were 2.5 m thick and were surrounded by 3 bamboo fences, the ground in front of which was studded with row upon row of sharpened bamboo spikes. Hewett wrote: "...had we been able to form any idea of the external strength of the place we should never have attempted to rush in as we did." His party retreated having suffered 4 dead and 9 wounded.

Mat Salleh had built similar forts all over Sabah, and the hearts of the protectorate's administrators must have sunk when they heard he was building one at Tambunan. A government expedition arrived in the Tambunan Valley on the last day of 1899. There was intensive fighting throughout Jan, with the government taking village after village, until at last, the North Borneo Constabulary came within 50 m of Mat Salleh's fort. Its water supply had been cut off and the fort had been shelled incessantly for 10 days. Mat Salleh was trapped. On 31 Jan 1900 he was killed by a stray bullet which hit him in the left temple.

is a wide variety of vegetation on the mountain as it rises from dipterocarp primary jungle through oak montane forest with mossy forest near the summit and heath-like vegetation on top. The best time to climb is in Mar and it is advisable to take guides and porters for the tough climb (ask the District Officer in Tambunan). An expedition to Trusmadi requires careful planning – it should not be undertaken casually. A more detailed account of the 2 routes can be found in *Mountains of Malaysia – a practical guide and manual*, by John Briggs.

Accommodation Both hotels are out of town. **C** *Tambunan Resort (TVRC)*, signposted off the main road before the town, a/c, restaurant, the 'resort' claims to stage the occasional cultural show and arranges for tourists to spend a day or 2 in the paddy fields, planting or harvesting rice and ploughing with water buffalo; **D** *Government Resthouse*, T 774339.

Transport to & from Tambunan 90 km from KK. **By minibus**: minibuses for Tambunan leave from the corner of Australia Place/Jln Tunku Abdul Rahman in KK. Those leaving Tambunan go from the centre of town by the mosque. Regular connections to KK, 1½ hrs (M$4) and Ranau (M$4).

Keningau

The Japanese built fortifications around their base in Keningau during World War II. It is now rather a depressing, shabby lumber town, smothered in smoke from the sawmills. The timber business in this area turned Keningau into a boom town in the 1980s and the population virtually doubled within a decade. The felling continues – but there is not much primary forest left these days. There are huge logging camps all around the town and the hills to the W. Logging roads lead into these hills off the Keningau-Tenom road which are accessible by 4-wheel-drive vehicles. It is just possible to drive across them to Papar, which is a magnificent route. **NB:** anyone attempting the drive should be warned to steer well clear of log-laden trucks as they make their way down the mountain.

Excursions
Murut villages Sapulut is deep in Murut country and is accessible from Keningau by a rough road via Kampung Nabawan. At Sapulut, follow the river of the same name E through Bigor and Kampung Labang to Kampung Batu Punggul at the confluence of Sungei Palangan. **Batu Punggul** is a limestone outcrop protruding 200m above the surrounding forest, a half hour walk from the kampung; it can be climbed without any equipment, but with care. Nearby is the recently discovered, but less impressive limestone outcrop, **Batu Tinahas**, which has huge caves with many unexplored passages. From Sapulut, it is a fairly painless exercise to cross the border into Kalimantan. A short stretch of road leads from Sapulut to Agis which is just a 4-hr boat ride from the border. There is even an immigration checkpoint at Pegalungan, a settlement en route. **Getting there**: it is possible to charter a minibus along the Nabawan road to Sapulut, where you can hire boats upriver. At Sapulut, ask for Lantir (the headman, or *kepala*). He will arrange the boat-trip upriver (which could take up to 2 days depending on the river) and accommodation in Murut longhouses, through the gloriously named *Sapulut Adventurism Tourism Travel Company*, run by Lantir and his mate. As in neighbouring Sarawak, these long upriver trips can be prohibitively expensive unless you are in a decent-sized group.

Accommodation A-B *Perkasa*, Jln Keningau, T 31044, a/c, restaurant, on the edge of town; **C** *Rai*, Jln Masak, T 333188, some a/c, walking distance from the bus stop; *Government Rest House*, T 31525.

Transport to & from Keningau 40 km from Tenom, 128 km from KK. **By air**: connections to KK (M$46). **By minibus**: minibuses leave from centre of town, by the market. Regular connections with KK (M$20) and Tenom (M$5).

Tenom

Tenom, at the end of the North Borneo Railway, is a hilly inland town, with a population of about 4,000 – predominantly Chinese. Although it was the centre of an administrative district under the Chartered Company from the turn of the century, most of the modern town was built during the Japanese occupation in World War II. It is in the heart of Murut country – but do not expect to see longhouses and Muruts in traditional costume. Many Muruts have moved into individual houses except in the remoter parts of the interior, and their modernized bamboo houses are often well equipped.

The surrounding area is very fertile and the main crops here are soya beans,

The railway which ran out of steam

In the last years of the 19th century, William Cowie, the managing director of the North Borneo Chartered Company, had a vision. With Governor Beaufort, he outlined his ambitious plans for a Trans-Borneo Railway, cutting through 200 km of dense jungle, from Brunei Bay to Sandakan, straight through the interior of North Borneo. Work started at Weston on Brunei Bay in 1896 and 2 years later, the stretch of line linking the new township and Beaufort triumphantly opened.

But A J West – the railway engineer who humbly named the new town after himself – somehow overlooked the fact that Weston was surrounded by an impenetrable mangrove swamp, not an ideal location for a railway terminus or port. Two alternative sites were toyed with before the stretch of narrow land opposite Pulau Gaya was finally selected as the site for the new terminus in 1899. It was thought to be a promising site for a town as it had a sheltered harbour. They called it Jesselton.

But Cowie's visionary railway project – and the innovative telegraph line that was to run alongside the track – was to be a costly undertaking. The administration, headed by Governor Beaufort, levied a new tax on rice to pay for it: a move which proved disastrously unpopular. Chinese retailers and tribal chiefs petitioned London to intervene – but to no avail. Historians believe the North Borneo Railway indirectly sparked the 6-year Mat Salleh rebellion (**see page 313**).

The 92 km line between Jesselton and Beaufort started operating in 1905. The track was pushed into the interior at the same time, and on 5 Apr 1905 the first train steamed into Tenom. The line went on to the railhead at Melalap, 16 km further up the valley. But that was as far as the 186 km 'trans-Borneo railway' ever got – it seems that after struggling up the Padas Gorge from Beaufort, the prospect of building another 200 km of track was too much to bear. The idea was abandoned. The towns of Papar, Beaufort and Tenom however, became totally dependent on the railway. The Chartered Company administration refused to build roads in an effort to force people to use it.

Oscar Cook, a former District Officer in the North Borneo Civil Service, served in Tenom in 1912, and recorded his journey from Beaufort in his 1923 book, *Borneo: the Stealer of Hearts*. "Normally the journey of about 30 miles took 3 hours, but one always considered it lucky to reach one's destination only an hour late... The route twisted and turned to such an extent, as the line followed its precarious course along the river bank, that... passengers in the front portion could almost put their hands out of the windows and shake those of passengers in the rear. On wet days up certain grades passengers have even been known to descend and help push the train over the most slippery and steepest gradients, while at one watering place chocks of wood were invariably put under the engine wheels to prevent the train from slowly slipping backwards!"

The train, now pulled by a diesel engine, still creeps along the 45 km narrow-gauge track, and the 2½ hour trip is well worth it.

maize and a variety of vegetables. Cocoa is also widely grown; the cocoa trees are often obscured under shade trees called *pokok belindujan*, which have bright pink flowers. The durians from Tenom (and Beaufort) are reckoned to be the best in Sabah.

Excursions

Murut villages There are many Murut villages surrounding Tenom all with their own churches. In some villages there is also an over-sized mosque or *surau*; the federal government has viewed the spread of Christianity in Sabah with some displeasure and there are financial incentives for anyone converting back to Islam.

The best local longhouses are along the Padas River towards Sarawak at Kampung Marais and Kampung Kalibatang where blowpipes are still made. At Kemabong, about 25 km S of Tenom, the Murut community has a *lansaran* dancing trampoline. The wooden platform is sprung with bamboo and can support about 10 Muruts doing a jig. **Getting there**: irregular minibuses.

Lagud Sebren Cocoa Research Station, 10 km out of Tenom, is in fact better known for its orchids, although it was originally a research centre for cocoa and rubber. Much of the work has been done by British botanist Tony Lamb who has turned the station into an important breeding centre for orchids. The flowering season is mainly between Oct and Feb. The centre also conducts research on tropical fruits. There is a resthouse about 5 km from the research centre: *Rumah Rehat Lagud Sebren* (Orchid Research Station resthouse), a/c. M$15. **Getting there**: minibus from main road (M$1.50); if driving, take the road over the railway tracks next to the station and head down the valley.

Batu Bunatikan Lumuyu (rock carvings), are at Kuala Tomani near Kampung Tomani, 40 km S of Tenom. A huge boulder, now protected from the elements by a corrugated tin roof, is carved with mysterious, distorted faces. Swirling lines, etched into the rock, depict various facial features as well as feet, a bird and a snake. The rock was discovered by villagers clearing land for agriculture around the River Lumuyu in Apr 1971. The Sabah State Museum in KK has no idea what the patterns represent or how old they are. The local explanation is an absurd story about 7 brothers, one of whom is killed; the other 6 doodle on a rock in their bereaved depression as they head into the mountains to bury him. Disappointing. **Getting there**: requires a 4-wheel drive vehicle: from Tenom, head S, crossing the Padas River at Tomani. After 2 km, turn right; follow this track for 20 km, through Kampung Kungkular to Kampung Ulu Tomani. Outside Kampung Ulu Tomani, turn right just before the river. Follow the track for 1½ km. At the point where a stream crosses the track, take the footpath to the rock carvings (20 mins).

Accommodation *Tenom Hotel* and *Sri Jaya Hotel* are both within walking distance of the bus stop. **B** *Perkasa*, top of the hill above the town (PO Box 225), T 735485, a/c, restaurant, this monster of a hotel was the brainchild of former Chief Minister and multi-millionaire Datuk Harris Salleh (now retired to his palace on Labuan), built to be a casino, the *Tenom Perkasa* (one of a chain of 3 – the others are at *Keningau* and *Kundasang*) failed to take off, was converted into a training hotel and it is now a rambling money-loser and rarely has more than 3 guests dotted around its 7 storeys, the staff are delightful however and will help arrange sightseeing on request; **D** *Tenom*, Jln Tun Datu Mustapha, T 736378, fan only, restaurant, no attached bath, roof terrace; **D** *Sri Jaya*, Main St, T 736689, a/c.

Restaurants ♦♦*Y&L (Young & Lovely) Food & Entertainment*, Jln Sapong (2 km out of town), noisy but easily the best restaurant in Tenom, it serves mainly Chinese food: freshwater fish (steamed *sun hok* – also known as *ikan hantu*) and venison, these can be washed down with the local version of *air limau* (or *kitchai*) which comes with dried plums, there is a giant screen which was shipped in to allow Tenomese to enjoy the 1990 Football World Cup, rec; ♦♦*Sapong*, Perkasa Hotel, local and Western; ♦♦*Jolly*, near the station, serves western food (including lamb chops) and karaoke; ♦♦*Restaurant Curry Emas*, which specializes in monitor lizard claypot curries, dog meat and wild cat. **Foodstalls**: *Gerai Makanan*, above the market.

Shopping Tamu on Sun.

Transport to & from Tenom 140 km from KK, 45 km from Beaufort. **By train**: leaves 4 times a day and takes about 3 hrs to Beaufort and another 2½ hrs to Tanjung Aru, KK (Tenom-Beaufort M$2.75-8.35). **By minibus**: minibuses leave from centre of town by the market. Regular connections with Keningau (M$5) and KK 4 hrs (M$15).

Beaufort

This small sleepy, but unexciting, town is named after British Governor P Beaufort of the North Borneo Company, who was a lawyer and was appointed to the post despite having no experience of the East or of administration. He was savaged by Sabahan historian K G Tregonning as "the most impotent Governor North

Borneo ever acquired and who, in the manner of nonentities, had a town named after him." Beaufort is a quaint town, with riverside houses built on stilts to escape the constant flooding of the Padas River.

Accommodation Both hotels are within walking distance from bus and train stations. **C** *Beaufort*, centre of town, T 211911, a/c; **C** *Padas*, riverfront by the bridge (opposite the fish market), T 211441, a/c, restaurant, not as nice as the Beaufort.

Restaurants ♦♦*Jin Jin Restaurant*, behind *Beaufort Hotel*, Chinese, popular with locals; *Beaufort Bakery*, behind *Beaufort Hotel*, "Freshness with every bite".

Shopping Tamu on Sat.

Banks & money changers Hongkong Bank & Standard Chartered in centre of town.

Useful addresses General Post Office & Telekom: next to Hongkong Bank. **Area code**: 087.

Transport to & from Beaufort 90 km from KK. **By train**: the KK-Tenom line passes through Beaufort: Tenom, 2½ hrs (M$2.75-835), KK, 3 hrs (M$4.75-1445). **By minibus**: minibuses meet the train, otherwise leave from centre of town. Regular connections with KK, 2 hrs (M$6).

To Sarawak Sipitang is S of Beaufort and the closest town in Sabah to the Sarawak border. It is possible to take minibuses from Beaufort to Sipitang and from there on to Merapok in Sarawak, 1 hr (M$2). There is an immigration checkpoint at Sipitang. From Sipitang there are also regular boats to Labuan (M$8).

Pulau Labuan

The Sultan of Brunei ceded the 92 sq km island to the British crown in 1846 (**see page 465**). The island had a superb deep water harbour. Labuan promised an excellent location from which the British could engage the pirates which were terrorizing the NW Borneo coast. Labuan also had coal, which could be used to service steamships. Sarawak's Rajah James Brooke became the island's first governor in 1846; 2 years later it was declared a free port. It also became a penal colony: long-sentence convicts from Hong Kong were put to work on the coal face and in the jungle – clearing roads. The island was little more than a malarial swamp and its inept colonial administration was perpetually plagued by fever and liver disorders. Its 9 drunken civil servants provided a gold mine of eccentricity for the novelists Joseph Conrad and Somerset Maugham.

By the 1880s ships were already by-passing the island, and the tiny colony began to disintegrate. In 1881 William Hood Treacher moved the capital of the new territory of British North Borneo from Labuan to Kudat. And 8 years later, the Chartered Company was asked to take over the administration of the island. In 1907 it became part of the Straits Settlements, along with Singapore, Malacca (Melaka) and Penang. In 1946 Labuan became a part of British North Borneo and was later incorporated into Sabah as part of the Federation of Malaysia in 1963.

Datuk Harris is thought to own half the island (including the *Hotel Labuan*). As Chief Minister, he offered the island as a gift to the federal government in 1984 in exchange for a government undertaking to bail out his industrial projects and build up the island's flagging economy. The election of a Christian government in Sabah in 1986 proved an embarrassment to Malaysian Prime Minister Dr Mahathir Mohamad: making it Malaysia's only non-Muslim-ruled state. As a result, Labuan has assumed strategic importance as a Federal Territory, wedged between Sabah and Sarawak. It is used as a staging post for large garrisons of the Malaysian army, navy and air force.

In declaring Labuan a tax haven, the Malaysian government wants to turn it into the Bermuda of the Asia-Pacific for the 21st century. A few offshore banks have set up in Labuan since 1991, but the standard trimmings of a cosmopolitan offshore financial centre are hundreds of millions of dollars away.

Today the island has a population of about 30,000 – not including 10,000 Filipino refugees, with about 21 different ethnic groups. The island is the centre of a booming 'barter' trade with the S Philippines – the island is home to a clutch of so-called string vest millionaires, who have grown rich on the trade. In Labuan, 'barter' is the name given to smuggling. The Filipino traders leaving the Philippines simply over-declare their exports (usually copra, hardwood, rotan and San Miguel beer) and under-declare the imports (Shogun jeeps, Japanese hi-fi and motorbikes) – all ordered through duty-free Labuan. With such valuable cargoes, the traders are at the mercy of pirates in the South China Sea. To get round this, they arm themselves with M-16s, bazookas and shoulder-launched missiles. This ammunition is confiscated on their arrival in Labuan, stored in a marine police warehouse, and given back to them for the return trip.

Away from the bustling barter jetty, Labuan Town (this name has largely superceded its name of Port Victoria) is a dozy, unremarkable Chinese-Malaysian mix of shophouses, coffee shops and karaoke bars. There is a new US$11 million mosque, and a manicured golf course. Illegal cockfights are staged every Sunday afternoon. There is an old brick coal chimney at Tunjung Kubong – or coal point – with a good view of the E coast. On the W coast there are pleasant beaches, mostly lined with kampungs. There is a large Japanese war memorial on the E coast and a vast, and well tended, Allied war cemetery between the town and the airport.

Excursions
Boat trips can be made to the small islands around Labuan, although only by chartering a fishing vessel. The main islands are Pulau Papan (a boring island between Labuan and the mainland), Pulau Kuraman, Pulau Rusukan Kecil (known locally as '*the floating lady*' for obvious reasons) and Pulau Rusukan Besar ('*floating man*'). The latter 3 have good beaches and coral reefs (see *Diving*, below) but none has any facilities.

Accommodation A *Labuan*, Jln Merdeka, T 412504, F 415355, a/c, restaurant, decaying and overpriced; **B** *Emas Labuan*, 27-30 Jln Muhibbah, T 43966, a/c, restaurant (*Golden Palace Restaurant* downstairs); **B-C** *Victoria*, 150 Jln Tanjong Kubang, T 412411, F 412550, a/c, rec; **C** *Kartika Sari*, Jln Bunga Tanjung, T 414591, a/c, restaurant, frequented by Filipino barter traders, but clean and reasonable; **C** *Kelab Golf*, Jln Tanjong Batu, a/c, restaurant, 6 simple but pleasant rooms in the clubhouse, 3 have a view down the manicured fairways; **C** *Pantai View*, Jln Bunga Tanjung, T 411339, F 412793, a/c, basic but clean and not much of a view of the pantai; **C** *Pertama*, Ujong Pasir, Jln OKK Awang Besar (next to fish market), T 413311, a/c.

Restaurants Malay: ♦♦*Restoran Zainab*, Jln Merdeka (opposite duty free shop), Indian/Muslim; **Chinese:** ♦*Café Imperial*, Chinese coffee shop behind *Federal Hotel*, better than average coffee shop fare; ♦♦♦*Golden Palace*, 27 Jln Muhibbah. **Seafood:** ♦♦♦*Sung Hwa Restaurant*, 2nd Flr, Ujong Pasir, Jln OKK Awang Besar (across from fish market and above Kedai Kopi South Sea, rec. **International:** ♦♦♦*Labuan Beach*, Jln Tanjong Batu, T 415611, International and local cuisine, popular spot with local businessmen; ♦♦*Labuan Island Club*, Jln Merdeka (at E end of town), T 41439, popular with oil rig brigade, slow service, rec. **Foodstalls:** above wet market and at the other end of town, along the beach next to the Island Club. There is an area of stalls on Jln Muhibbah opposite the end of Jln Bahasa, next to the cinema and there are a few hawker stalls behind *Hotel Labuan*.

Sports Diving: *Borneo Divers*, 359 Jln Tanjung Purun, T 415867, F 413454. Specialises in 2-day packages diving on shipwrecks off Labuan for certified scuba divers, M$200. *Ocean Sports*, 134 Jln OKK Awang Besar, T 415389, F 411911/415844. Offers 5-day full-time scuba courses for M$700 and reef dives on the nearby islands of Pulau Kuraman, Pulau Rusukan Kecil and Pulau Rusukan Besar. These islands have good beaches but no facilities. Diving around Pulau Papan is not very exciting and the water is often cloudy because of river silt. The reefs around Labuan suffer from the after-effects of the Allied bombing during World War II and from Filipino dynamite fishermen. *Ocean Sports*, in association with Coral Island Cruises in KK takes groups of divers 18 hrs into the South China Sea to Terumba Layang Layang, an atol on the edge of the disputed Spratley-reef, reputed to be "even better than Sipadan". A 6-day package (which includes a 4-day sojourn at a Malaysian naval station) costs around M$2,000/person. **Golf:** *Kelab Golf*, Jln Tanjong Batu. Magnificent 9-hole golf course. Visitors may be asked to see proof of handicap or a membership card from your own club. Non-members pay M$30 a round on weekdays, M$50 on weekends. There are also tennis courts at the golf club and a swimming pool which can be used by visitors for M$5.

Shopping *Labuan Duty Free*, Bangunan Terminal, Jln Merdeka, T 411573. 142 years after Rajah James Brooke first declared Labuan a free port, *Labuan Duty Free* opened in Oct 1990. The island's original duty free concession did not include alcohol or cigarettes, but the new shop was given special dispensation to sell them. Two months later the government extended the privilege to all shops on the island, which explains the absurd existence of a duty free shop on a duty free island. The shop claims to be the cheapest duty free in the world however. It can undercut most other outlets on the island due to the volume of merchandise it turns over: more than M$1-million a month.

The shop owes its success to Filipino 'barter traders' who place bulk purchase orders for VCRs or hundreds of thousands of dollars' worth of Champion cigarettes. These are smuggled back to Zamboanga and Jolo and find their way onto Manila's streets within a week. Brunei's alcohol-free citizens also keep the shop in business – they brought nearly M$2-million worth of liquor from Labuan into Brunei within the first 3 months of the shop opening. **NB**: if you plan to take duty-free goods into Sabah or Sarawak, you have to stay on Labuan for a minimum of 72 hrs. Behind Jln Merdeka and before the fish market, there is a congregation of corrugated tin-roofed shacks which houses a small *Filipino textile and handicraft market*.

Local transport **By bus**: local buses around the island leave from Jln Bunga Raya. **By taxi**: old Singapore NTUC cabs are not in abundant supply, but easy enough to get at the airport and from outside *Hotel Labuan*. It is impossible to get a taxi after 1900.

Banks & money changers Hongkong, Jln Merdeka; **Standard Chartered**, Jln Tanjong Kubang (next to *Victoria Hotel*).

Useful addresses General Post Office: Jln Merdeka. **Area code**: 087.

Transport to & from Labuan 7 km from the mainland. **By air**: 5 km from town. Regular connections with KK (M$52), Miri (M$68). The MAS office is in the *Federal Hotel* block, T 412263. **By boat**: from the Bangunan Terminal Feri Penumpang (T 411573) next to the duty free shop on Jln Merdeka. Regular connections with Memumbuk every 45 mins (M$5.30, M$15 with a car). Speedboats leave every few minutes (M$20). There are 2 speedboats every day to Limbang (Sarawak) (M$20); enquiries, T 22908. Express boats for KK leave daily at 1300, 2½ hrs.

International connections with Brunei On weekends and public holidays in Brunei the ferries are packed-out and it is a scramble to get a ticket. It is possible to reserve tickets to Brunei at 4 agents: *Victoria Agency House* (T 412332) (next to the *Federal Hotel* in Wisma Kee Chia), *Borneo Leisure Travel* (opposite Standard Chartered) and the booking office at the back of the Sports Toto on Jln Merdeka all deal with advanced bookings to Brunei. *Broadwin Agency*, also on Jln Merdeka, takes bookings for ferries to Malaysian destinations. Five express boats leave Labuan for Brunei (Bandar Seri Begawan). They depart at 0800, 1300, 1400, 1500 Mon-Sat, 0800, 1000 and 1200, Sun, 1½ hrs (M$22 or B$20).

Papar

Formerly a sleepy Kadazan village, about 40 km S of KK, Papar is developing fast. In *bandar lama* (the old town) there are several rows of quaint wooden shophouses, painted blue and laid out along spacious boulevards lined with travellers' palms. There is a large market in the centre of town. The Papar area is famous for its fruit and there is a good *tamu* every Sunday.

There is a scenic drive between Papar and KK, with paddy fields and jungle lining the roadside. The nearby beach at Pantai Manis is good for swimming and can be reached easily from Papar; it is also possible to make boat trips up the Papar River, which offers gentle rapids for less-energetic white-water-rafters. White-water rafting trips can be organized through tour agents in KK (**see page 307**).

Excursion

Pulau Tiga National Park is 48 km S of KK. Declared a Forest Reserve in 1933, the 15,864 ha park is made up of 3 islands, Pulau Tiga, Kalampunian Damit and Kalampunian Besar. Pulau Tiga's 3 low hills were all formed by mud volcanoes. The last big eruption was in 1941, which was heard 160 km away and covered the island in a layer of boiling mud. The dipterocarp forest on the islands is virtually untouched and they contain species not found on other W coast islands, such as a poisonous amphibious sea snake (*Laticauda colubrina*), which comes ashore on Pulau Kalampunian Damit to lay its eggs.

Park Headquarters on the S side of Pulau Tiga, is mainly used as a botanical and marine research centre and tourism is not vigorously promoted; as a result there are no special facilities for tourists. There is a resthouse, however, which can accommodate 6: it is also possible to camp. **Getting there**: boats from Kuala Penyu (at the tip of the Klias Peninsula), 45 mins (M$60 return).

Accommodation *Papar Lodging House*, Papar New Town; **B** *Seaside Travellers Inn*, H30 Gaya Park, Penampang Rd (near Kinarut), T 22399, some a/c, price includes breakfast, water sports, dorm (**D**); **C** *Seri Takis Lodging House*, Papar New Town, T 219173, a/c, very clean, friendly management.

Restaurants Several run-of-the-mill coffee shops and restaurants in the old town. *Sugar Buns Bakery*, old town. ♦*Seri Takis*, Papar New Town (below the lodging house), Padang food (see page 1020).

Transport to & from Papar 40 km S of KK. **By minibus**: leave from Bandar Lama area. Regular connections with KK, 1 hr (M$2.50) and Beaufort, 1 hr (M$2.50).

THE NORTH AND GUNUNG KINABALU NATIONAL PARK

From KK, the route heads N to the sleepy Bajau town of Kota Belud which wakes up on Sundays for its colourful *tamu* market. Near the northernmost tip of the state is Kudat, the former state capital. The region N of KK is a more interesting area with Gunung Kinabalu always in sight.

Kota Belud

The town is in a beautiful location, nestling in the foothills of Mount Kinabalu. It is the heart of Bajau country – the so-called 'cowboys of the east'. The first Bajau to migrate to Sabah were pushed into the interior, around Kota Belud. They were originally a seafaring people but then settled as farmers in this area. The famed Bajau horsemen wear jewelled costumes, carry spears and ride bareback on ceremonial occasions. The ceremonial headdresses worn by the horsemen – called *dastars* – are woven on backstrap looms by the womenfolk of Kota Belud. Each piece takes 4 to 6 weeks to complete. Traditionally, the points of the headdress were stiffened using wax – these days, strips of cardboard are inserted into the points.

The largest **tamu** (traditional open air market) in Sabah is held every Sunday in Kota Belud (behind the mosque), starting at 0800. Visitors are strongly recommended to get there early. A mix of nationalities – Bajau, Kadazan/Dusun, Rungus, Chinese, Indian and Malay – come to sell their goods and it is a social occasion as much as it is a market.

This is the account of a civil servant, posted to the KB district office in 1915:

> "The tamu itself is a babel and buzz of excitement; in little groups the natives sit and spread their wares out on the ground before them; bananas, langsats, pines and bread-fruit; and, in season, that much beloved but foul-smelling fruit the Durian. Mats and straw-hats and ropes; fowls, ducks, goats and buffaloes; pepper, *gambia sirih* and vegetables; rice (padi), sweet potatoes, *ubi kayu* and indian-corn; dastars and handkerchiefs, silver and brass-ware. In little booths, made of wood, with open sides and floors of split bamboos and roofs of atap (sago palm-leaf) squat the Chinese traders along one side of the Tamu. For cash or barter they will sell; and many a wrangle, haggle and bargain is driven and fought ere the goods change hands, or money parted with."

Every other day of the week, Kota Belud is a small, sleepy town. Kota Beludians observe an early bedtime: nearly all restaurants close at 1800.

Excursion

Tempasuk has a wide variety of migrating birds and is a proposed conservation area. More than 127 species of birds have been recorded along this area of the coastal plain and over half a million birds flock to the area every year, many migrating from N latitudes in winter. These include 300,000 swallows, 50,000 yellow longtails and 5,000 water birds. The best period for bird watching is from Oct to Mar.

Accommodation C *Kota Belud*, 21 Jln Francis (just off the central square), T 976576, a/c, noisy; **E** *Government Resthouse*, Jln Ranau (on hill N of town, signed from the main road), T 67532, some a/c, often full of officials.

Restaurants There are several Indian coffee shops around the main square. **♦♦***Bismillah Restoran*, 35 Jln Keruak (main square), excellent *roti telur*; *Indonesia Restoran*, next to the car park behind the *Kota Belud Hotel*.

Shopping Market in main square every day, fish market to the S of the main market. Large *tamu* every Sunday.

Transport to & from Kota Belud 77 km from KK. **By minibus**: leave from main square. Regular connections with KK (M$5), Kudat (M$10) and Ranau (M$12).

Kudat

The town, surrounded by coconut groves, is right on the NE tip of Sabah and home to the Runggus people, members of the Kadazan tribe. The Runggus have clung to their traditions more than other Sabahan tribes and some still live in longhouses, although many are now building their own houses. Runggus longhouses are built in a distinctive style with outward-leaning walls (the Sabah State Museum incorporates many of the design features of a Runggus longhouse). The Runggus used to wear coils of copper and brass round their arms and legs and today the older generation still dress in black. They are renowned for their fine beadwork and weaving. A handful of Runggus longhouses are dotted around the peninsula, away from Kudat town.

The East India Company first realized the potential of the Kudat Peninsula and set up a trading station on Balambanganan Island, to the N of Kudat. The settlement was finally abandoned after countless pirate raids. Kudat became the first administrative capital of Sabah in 1881. William Hood Fletcher, the protectorate's first governor, first tried to administer the territory from Labuan, which proved impossible, so he moved to the newly founded town of Kudat which was nothing more than a handful of atap houses built out into the sea on stilts. It was a promising location, however, situated on an inlet of Marudu Bay, and it had a good harbour. Kudat's glory-years were short-lived: it was displaced as the capital of North Borneo by Sandakan in 1883.

Today it is a busy town dominated by Chinese and Filipino traders (legal and illegal) on the coast, and prostitutes trading downtown. Kudat was one of the main centres of Chinese migration at the end of the 19th century. Most of the Chinese who came to Kudat were Christian Hakka vegetable farmers: 96 of them arrived in Apr 1883, and they were followed by others, given free passages by the Chartered Company.

Excursions
Beaches There are some beautiful unspoilt beaches N of town, the best known is **Bak-Bak**, 11 km from Kudat. This beach, however, can get crowded at weekends and there are plans to transform it into a resort. It is signposted off the Kota Belud-Kudat road. **Getting there**: minibus.

Sikuati is 23 km W of Kudat. Every Sunday (0800) the Runggus come to the tamu in this village, on the NW side of the Kudat peninsula. Local handicrafts are sold. **Getting there**: minibus (M$2).

Accommodation The *Sunrise* and *Oriental* hotels are within walking distance of the bus stop. **B-C** *Greenland*, Lot 9/10, Block E, Sedco Shophouse (new town), T 62211, a/c, standard rooms shared bath; **D** *Oriental*, Jln Lo Thien Chock, T 61677/61045, a/c, big, clean rooms, some shared bathrooms; **C** *Sunrise*, Jln Lo Thien Hock, T 61517/61568, a/c, restaurant (*Silver Inn*); **E** *Government Resthouse*, T 61304.

Restaurants Malay: *Cahaya Timur*, Jln Lo Thien Hock (next to *Kudat Hotel*); ♦*Restoran Rakyat*, Jln Lo Thien Hock. **Chinese:** ♦♦*Silver Inn*, Jln Lo Thien Hock (below *Sunrise*).

Banks & money changers Standard Chartered, Jln Lo Thien Hock.

Transport to & from Kudat 122 km N of KK. **By air:** connections with KK (M$60), Sandakan (M$65). **By minibus:** minibuses leave from Jln Lo Thien Hock. Regular connections with KK, 4 hrs (M$10).

Gunung Kinabalu National Park

Southeast Asia's highest mountain, is the pride of Sabah, the focal point of the national park and probably the most magnificent sight in Borneo. In the first written mention of the mountain, in 1769, Captain Alexander Dalrymple of the East India Company, observing the mountain from his ship in the South China Sea, wrote: "Though perhaps not the highest mountain in the world, it is of *immense* height." During World War II Kinabalu was used as a navigational aid by Allied bombers – one of whom was quoted as saying "That... thing... must be near as high as Mount Everest". It's not, but at 4101m, Gunung Kinabalu is the highest peak between the Himalayas and New Guinea.

Mount Kinabalu is still growing at the rate of 5 cm a year. Those reaching the summit in the 1990s are climbing a mountain more than a metre higher than it was when it was first conquered just over a century ago. Although it has foothills, Kinabalu's dramatic rockfaces, with cloud swirling around them, loom starkly out of the jungle. The view from the top is unsurpassed and on a clear day you can see the shadow of the mountain in the S China sea, over 50 km away.

There are a number of theories about the derivation of its name. The most convincing is the corruption of the Kadazan *Aki Nabulu* – 'the revered place of the spirits'. For the Kadazan, the mountain is sacred as they consider it to be the last resting place of the dead, and the summit was believed to be inhabited by their ghosts. In the past the Kadazan are said to have carried out human sacrifices on Mount Kinabalu, carrying their captives to the summit in bamboo cages, where they would be speared to death. The Kadazan guides still perform an annual sacrifice to appease the spirits – today they make do with chickens, eggs, cigars, betel nuts and rice – on the rock plateau below the Panar Laban Rockface.

The Chinese also lay claim to a theory. According to this legend, a Chinese prince arrived on the shores of N Borneo and went in search of a huge pearl on the top of the mountain, which was guarded by a dragon. He duly slew the dragon, grabbed the pearl and married a beautiful Kadazan girl. After a while he grew homesick, and took the boat back to China, promising his wife that he would return. She climbed the mountain every day for years on end to watch for her husband's boat. He never came and in desperation and depression, she lay down and died and was turned to stone. The mountain was then christened *China Balu* – or Chinaman's widow.

In 1851, Sir Hugh Low, the British colonial secretary in Labuan made the first unsuccessful attempt at the summit. Seven years later he returned with Spencer St John, the British Consul in Brunei. Low's feet were in bad shape after the long walk to the base of the mountain, so St John went on without him, with a handful of reluctant Kadazan porters. He made it to the top of the conical South Peak, but was "mortified to find that the most westerly [peak] and another to the E appeared higher than where I sat." He retreated, and returned 3 months later with Low, but again failed to reach the summit – now called Low's Peak. It remained unconquered for another 30 years. The first to reach the summit was John Whitehead, a zoologist, in 1888. Today the mountain lures around 200,000 visitors a year – although not all of them end up climbing it.

In plan, the top of the mountain is U-shaped, with bare rock plateaux. Several peaks stand proud of these plateaux, around the edge of the U; the space between the W and E arms is known as Low's Gully. No one has ever scaled its precipitous walls, nor has anyone climbed the Northern Ridge (an extension of the E arm) from the back of the mountain. From Low's Peak, the E peaks, just 1½ km away, look within easy reach. As John Briggs points out in his book *Mountains of Malaysia*, "It seems so close, yet it is one of the most difficult places to get to in the whole of Borneo."

The 754 sq km Gunung Kinabalu National Park was established in 1964 to protect the mountain and its remarkably diverse flora and fauna. Gunung Kinabalu is an important watershed: 8 major rivers originate on the mountain.

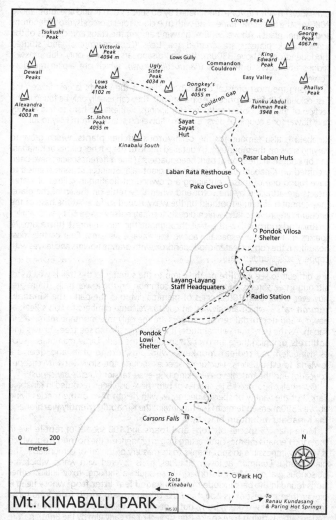

Mt. KINABALU PARK

Flora & fauna The range of climatic zones on the mountain has led to the incredible diversity of plant and animal life. Kinabalu Park is the meeting point of plants from Asia and Australasia and has one of the richest assemblages of flora in the world, with over 1,000 species of flowering plants. These represent more than half the families of flowering plants in the world. Within the space of 3 km, the vegetation changes from lowland tropical rainforest to alpine meadow and 'cloud' forest. The jungle reaches up to 1300m; above that, to a height of 1800m, is the lower montane zone, dominated by 60 species of oak and chestnut; above 2000m is the upper montane zone with true cloud forest, orchids, rhododendrons and pitcher plants. Above 2600m, growing among the crags and crevices of the summit rock plateau are gnarled tea trees (*Leptospermums*) and stunted rhododendrons. Above 3300m, the soil disappears, leaving only club mosses, sedges and Low's buttercups (*Ranunculus lowii*), which are alpine meadow flowers.

Among the most unusual of Kinabalu's flora is the world's largest flower, the rust-coloured **Rafflesia pricei** (see page 780). They can usually only be found in the section of the park closest to Poring Hot Springs. Rafflesia are hard to find as they only flower for a couple of days; the main flowering season is from May to Jul.

Kinabalu is also famous for the **carnivorous pitcher plants**, which grow to varying sizes on the mountain. (A detailed guide to the pitcher plants of Kinabalu can be bought in the shop at park headquarters.) Nine different species have been recorded on Kinabalu. The largest is the giant raja; Spencer St John claimed to have found one of these containing a drowned rat floating in 4 litres of water. Insects are attracted by the scent and when they settle on the lip of the plant, they cannot maintain a foothold on the waxy, ribbed surface. At the base of the pitcher is an enzymic fluid which digests the 'catch' (see page 57).

Rhododendrons line the trail throughout the mossy forest (there are 27 species in the park), especially above the Paka Cave area. One of the most beautiful is the copper leafed rhododendron, with orange flowers and leaves with coppery scales underneath.

It is difficult to see **wildlife** on the climb to the summit as the trail is well used, although tree shrews and squirrels are common on the lower trails. There are, however, more than 100 species of mammal living in the park. The **Kinabalu summit rats** – which are always on cue to welcome climbers to Low's Peak at dawn – and **nocturnal ferret badgers** are the only true montane mammals in Sabah. As the trees thin with altitude, it is often possible to see **tree-shrews** and **squirrels**, of which there are over 28 species in the park. Large mammals – such as flying **lemurs, redleaf monkeys, wild pigs, orang-utan and deer** are lowland forest dwellers. Nocturnal species include the **slow loris** (*Nycticebus coucang*) and the mischievous-looking bug-eyed **tarsier** (*Tarsius bancanus*).

Over half of Borneo's 518 species of birds have also been recorded in Kinabalu Park, but the variety of species decreases with height. Two of the species living above 2500m are endemic to the mountain: the **Kinabalu friendly warbler** and the **Kinabalu mountain blackbird**.

More than 75 species of **frogs and toads** and 100 species of **reptile** live in the park. Perhaps the most interesting frog in residence is the **horned frog**, which is virtually impossible to spot thanks to its mastery of the art of camouflage. The giant toad is common at lower altitudes; he is covered with warts, which are poisonous glands. When disturbed, these squirt a stinking, toxic liquid. Other frogs found in the park include the **big-headed leaf-litter frog**, whose head is bigger than the rest of its body, and the **green stream shrub frog**, who has a magnificent metallic green body, but is deadly if swallowed by any predator.

The famous **flying tree snake** (the subject of an early film by the British nature documentary-maker David Attenborough) has been seen in the park. It spreads its skin flaps, which act as a parachute when the snake leaps blindly from one tree to another.

There are nearly 30 species of **fish** in the park's rivers – including the unusual **Borneo sucker fish** (*Gastomyzon borneensis*), which attaches itself to rocks in fast-flowing streams. One Sabah Parks publication likens them to 'underwater cows', grazing on algae as they move slowly over the rocks.

Walkers and climbers are more likely to come across the park's abundant **insect** life than anything else. Examples include pill millipedes, rhinoceros beetles, the emerald green and turquoise jewel beetles, stick insects, 'flying peapods', cicadas, and a vast array of moths (including the giant atlas moth) and butterflies (including the magnificent emerald green and black Rajah Brooke's birdwing).

The climb Mount Kinabalu is a tough, steep climb but requires no special skills or equipment. The climb to the summit and back should take 2 days – 4-6 hrs to the overnight stop on the first day and then 3 hrs to the summit for dawn, returning to the park headquarters at around noon on the 2nd day. Gurkha soldiers and others have made it to the summit and back in well under 3 hrs.

A jeep for 12 people can take groups from headquarters to the power station at 1829m where the trail starts (M$10-20). A minibus also makes the 4 km run to the power station from park headquarters on a regular basis (M$2). It is a 25 mins walk from the **Power Station** to the first shelter, **Pondok Lowi**. The trail splits in 2 soon afterwards, the left goes to the radio station and the helipad and the right towards the summit. The next stop is **Layang Layang staff headquarters** (drinking water, cooking facilities, accommodation) – also known as **Carson's Camp** (2621m), named after the first warden of the park. There is one more shelter, **Ponkok Villosa** (2942m, and about 45 mins from Carson's Camp) before the stop at the path to **Paka Caves** – really an overhanging rock on the side of a stream. Paka is a 10 mins detour to the left, where Low and St John made their camps.

From the cave/5th shelter the vegetation thins out and it is a steep climb to **Panar Laban** huts – which includes the well equipped *Laban Rata Resthouse*, affording magnificent views at sunset and in the early morning. The name *Panar Laban* is derived from Kadazan words meaning 'place of sacrifice': early explorers had to make a sacrifice here to appease the spirits – this ritual is still performed by the Kadazan once a year. **Sayat Sayat** (3810m) hut – named after the ubiquitous shrubby tea tree – is an hour further on, above the Panar Laban Rockface. Most climbers reach Panar Laban (or the other huts) in the early afternoon in order to rest up for a 0300 start the next morning in order to reach the summit by sunrise. The first 2 hours after dawn are the most likely to be cloud-free. For enthusiasts interested in alternative routes to the summit, John Briggs's *Mountains of Malaysia* provides a detailed guide to the climb.

Equipment A thick jacket is useful, but at the very least you should have a light waterproof or wind-cheater to beat the windchill on the summit. Remarkably, no one appears to have set up rental facilities; contrary to rumour, it is not possible to hire jackets or windcheaters from park HQ. It is also necessary to bring a sweater or some thick shirts. Walking boots and a sleeping bag are recommended, but not essential. The latter can be hired from HQ. Many people climb the mountain in training shoes. Carry a bit of food and a few sweets as a precaution. Essential items include: torch, toilet paper, water bottle, plasters, headache tablets and sun tan lotion. A hat is also a good idea – as protection against the sun and the cold. Gloves can be bought in the *Perkasa Hotel* shop, if required. Lockers are available, free of charge, at the park headquarters reception office. It is possible to hire blankets, pillows, mattresses, rucksacks and sleeping bags, if arranged in advance. Rented sleeping bags (which can be picked up from the small hostel above Panar Laban), tend to be thin; it is better to hire 2 (M$4 each). The *Panar Laban Hostel* has welcome hot-water showers, but soap and towels are not provided. The hostel is well heated and bedding is provided.

Guides Hiring a guide is compulsory: M$25/day (1-3 people), M$28/day (4-6), M$30/day (7-8). Porter's available for M$25/day, maximum load 11 kg. Guides and porters should be reserved at least a day in advance at the park headquarters or at the parks office in KK.

Permits M$10/person to climb Gunung Kinabalu, no permit necessary if just visiting the park. It is necessary to obtain permission to visit the park by visiting the Sabah Parks Office in Kota Kinabalu (see page 310). It is possible to book accommodation at park headquarters and at Panar Laban from KK.

Treks There are other marked trails around the park, leading from headquarters. Guided trail walk 1115 Mon-Sun from park administration building.

Mountain Garden (behind park administration building) The landscaped garden has species from all over the mid-levels of the mountain, which have been planted in natural surroundings. Open: 0730-1630 Mon-Fri, 0800-1700 Sat, 0900-1600 Sun.

Museum At headquarters with information on local flora and fauna. Beetles "as large as Tom Jones' medallions" and foot-long stick insects. There is also a slide show introducing some of the park's flora and fauna.

Poring Hot Springs **Getting there**: take a minibus to Ranau and taxi from there to Poring (see page 327).

Park Headquarters A short walk from the main Ranau-KK road and all the accommodation and restaurants are within 15 mins' walk from the main compound. **Souvenir and bookshop**: next to the park headquarters has good books on the mountain and flora and fauna.

Accommodation (Also see Ranau and Kundasang below). **NB**: it is necessary to book in advance: either write to Park Warden, Kinabalu National Park, Sabah Parks Office, Jln Tun Fuad Stephens, PO Box 10626, KK, T 211585 or visit the office while in KK. Prices are generally lower on weekdays, except during holidays. **Park Headquarters**: electricity, piped water and firewood are provided free of charge. *Annex suite*, 4 people, M$160/night; *Basement room*, 2 people, M$80/night; *Double storey deluxe cabin*, 7 people, M$250/night; *Duplex chalet*, 6 people, M$200/night; *Kinabalu Lodge*, 8 people, M$360/night; *Nepenthes Villa*, 4 people, M$250/night; *New Hostel*, M$15/night; *Old Hostel*, M$10/night; *Single storey deluxe cabin*, 2 bedrooms, M$200/night; *Twin bed cabin*, 2 people, M$80/night.

Mount Kinabalu: *Laban Rata Rest House*, Panar Laban, dormitory rooms, canteen and shower facilities plus electricity and heated rooms, bedding provided. M$27/night/person. **Huts** All shared rooms with wooden bunks and mattresses, gas cylinder cooking stoves supplied and limited eating utensils; no heating. Climbers must bring their own food for cooking. *Gunting Lagandan Hut*; *Panar Laban Hut*; *Sayat Sayat Huts*; *Waras Hut*, all M$4.

Restaurants Park Headquarters: ✦✦*Club Canteen*, decent meals; ✦✦*Steak & Coffee House*. **Cooking facilities** at *Kinabalu Lodge, Double storey, Single storey, Duplex chalet, Nepenthes villa, New hostel, Old hostel*.

Best time to visit The average rainfall is 4,000m a year, with an average temperature of 20°C at park headquarters but at Panar Laban it drops to 1-2°C at night. With the wind chill factor on the summit, it feels very cold. The best time to climb Gunung Kinabalu is in the dry season between Mar and Apr when views are clearest. Avoid weekends, school and public holidays if at all possible.

Transport to & from Mount Kinabalu National Park 60 km NE of KK. **By minibus**: regular connections from KK to Ranau, ask to be dropped at the park, 2 hrs (M$13). Return minibus must be waved down from the main road. Chartered 28-seater minibus from the National Parks office: M$300. **By taxi**: at least M$80/taxi from KK.

Ranau and Kundasang

The Ranau plateau, surrounding the Kinabalu massif, is one of the richest farming areas in Sabah and much of the forest not in the park has now been devastated by market gardeners. Even within the national park's boundaries, on the lower slopes of Mount Kinabalu itself, shifting cultivators have clear-felled tracts of jungle and planted their patches. More than 1,000 ha are now planted out with spinach, cabbage, cauliflower, asparagus, broccoli and tomatoes.

Kundasang and Ranau are unremarkable towns a few kilometres apart; the latter is bigger. The **war memorial**, behind Kundasang, which unfortunately looks like Colditz, is in memory of those who died in the 'death march' in World War II (**see page 331**). In Sept 1944, the Japanese marched 2,400 Allied prisoners of war through the jungle from Sandakan to Kundasang. The march took 11 months and only 6 men survived to tell the tale. The walled gardens represent the national gardens of Borneo, Australia and Britain.

Excursions
Mentapok and Monkobo are SE of Ranau. Both are rarely climbed. Mentapok, 1581m, can be reached in 1½ days from Kampung Mireru, a village at the base of the mountain. A logging track provides easy access half way up the S side of the mountain. Monkobo is most easily climbed from the NW, a logging track from Telupid goes up to 900m and from here it is a 2 hr trek to the top. It is advisable to take guides, organized from Ranau or one of the near-by villages.

Accommodation Kundasang: **A** *Perkasa*, visible on the hill above Kundasang, T 79511/10881, a/c, restaurant, slightly run down but a good view of the mountain, organizes tours to Kinabalu National Park and surrounding area; **B-C** *Ranau*, on the bottom side of the square, nearest the main road, T 876176, some a/c; **D** *Mountain View Motel*, near the market, price includes breakfast. Ranau: **D** *Sapati*, top left side of the square, no attached bath; **E** *Government Rest House*, half a mile out on the Sandakan Rd, T 875229.

Restaurants Kundasang: ✦✦✦*Perkasa Hotel Restaurant*, local and Western dishes, service good and food excellent. Ranau: ✦*Sin Mui Mui*, top side of the square near the market. Chinese: ✦*Five Star Seafood Restaurant*, opposite the market.

Sports Golf: *Kundasang Golf Course*, 3 km behind Kundasang in the shadow of the mountain is one of the most beautiful courses in the region, 9-hole, increasing it to 18, club hire from the *Perkasa Hotel*, Kundasang, M$25/round.

Shopping Cheap sweaters and waterproofs for the climb from *Kedai Kien Hin*, Ranau. A *tamu* is held near Ranau on the first of each month.

Transport to & from Ranau 113 km from KK. **By minibus**: minibuses leave from the market place. Regular connections to park headquarters (M$4), to KK (M$12), to Sandakan 8 hrs (M$25).

Poring Hot Springs

Poring lies 43 km from Kinabalu Park Headquarters – and is actually part of the national park. The **hot sulphur baths** were installed during the Japanese occupation for the jungle-weary Japanese troops. There are individual concrete pools with taps, one for the hot spring mineral water and the other for cold. The springs are on the other side of the Mamut River, over a suspension bridge, from the entrance. They are a fantastic antidote to tiredness after a tough climb up Gunung Kinabalu. The Kadazans named the area Poring after the towering bamboos, of that name, nearby. (These big bamboos were traditionally used as water-carriers and examples can be seen in the museum in KK). Admission: M$1. The **canopy walk** at Poring is best in the early morning and evening.

If the weather is clear at Ranau, it is generally safe to assume that the canopy walk will also be clear. The warmer climate at lower altitudes means there is an abundance of wild fruit in the park, which attracts flying lemur, red leaf monkeys; even orang-utans have occasionally been seen here. Admission: 1030-1600: M$5/person; 1830-2230: M$10/person; 2230-1030: M$20/person if in group of 4 or more, otherwise M$60 for 1-3 persons.

Permits Not necessary.

Accommodation *Mamutik Resthouse*, 8 people, M$180/night; *Manukan Chalet*, 4 people, M$220/night; *Poring New Cabin*, 4 people, M$95/cabin/night; *Poring Old Cabin*, 6 people, M$115/cabin/night.

Camping M$3.50.

Restaurants Bring your own food, no canteen facilities. A restaurant is opening in late 1992.

Transport to & from Poring No minibuses to Poring. **Taxi**: M$5.

THE EAST COAST

From Ranau it is possible to reach Sandakan by road – although the road is not metalled and is a quagmire in the wet season. Several key sights are within reach of **Sandakan**: the **Turtle Islands National Park**, 40 km N in the Sulu Sea, **Sepilok Orang Utan Rehabilitation Centre**, and the **Kinabatangan Basin**, to the SE. From Sandakan, the route continues S to the wilds of Lahad Datu and Dunum Valley and onto Semporna, the jumping off point for Pulau Sipidan. This island has achieved legendary status among snorkellers and scuba divers in recent years.

Sandakan

Sandakan is at the neck of a bay on the NE coast of Sabah and looks out to the Sulu Sea. For the Sulu traders, the Sandakan area was an important source of beeswax and came under the sway of the Sultans of Sulu. William Clarke Cowie, a Scotsman with a carefully waxed handlebar moustache, who ran guns for the Sultan of Sulu (and was later to become the managing director of the North Borneo Chartered Company), first set up camp in Sandakan Bay in the early 1870s. He called his camp, which was on Pulau Timbang, 'Sandakan', which had been the Sulu name for the area for about 200 years – but it became known as Kampung German as there were several German traders living there. The power of the Sulu sultanate was already on the wane when Cowie set up.

The modern town of Sandakan was founded by an Englishman, William Pryer, in 1879. Baron von Overbeck – the Austrian consul from Hong Kong who founded the Chartered Company with businessman Alfred Dent – had signed a leasing agreement for the territory with the Sultan of Brunei, only to discover that large tracts on the E side of modern-day Sabah actually belonged to the Sultan of Sulu. Overbeck sailed to Sulu in Jan 1878 and on obtaining the cession rights from the Sultan, dropped William Pryer off at Kampung German to make the British presence felt. Pryer's wife Ada later described the scene: "He had with him a West Indian black named Anderson, a half-cast Hindoo named Abdul, a couple of China boys. For food they had a barrel of flour and 17 fowls and the artillery was half a dozen sinder rifles." Pryer set about organizing the 3 existing villages in the area, cultivating friendly relations with the local tribespeople and fending off pirates. He raised the Union Jack on 11 Feb 1878.

Cowie tried to do a deal with the Sultan of Sulu to wrest control of Sandakan back from Pryer, but Dent and Overbeck finally bought him off. A few months later Cowie's Kampung German burned to the ground, so Pryer went in search of a new site, which he found at Buli Sim Sim. He called his new settlement Elopura – meaning 'beautiful city' – but the name did not catch on, and by the mid-1880s it was re-called Sandakan and became the capital of North Borneo. In 1891 the town had 20 Chinese-run brothels and 71 Japanese prostitutes – according to the 1891 census there were 3 men for every one woman. The town quickly established itself as the source of birds' nests harvested from the caves at Gomontong (**see page 333**) and shipped directly to Hong Kong – as they are today.

Timber was first exported from this area in 1885 and was used to construct Beijing's Temple of Heaven. Sandakan was, until a few years ago, the main E coast port for timber and it became a very wealthy town. In its heyday, the town is said to have boasted one of the greatest concentrations of millionaires in the world. The timber-boom days are over; the primary jungle has gone, and so has the big money. The hinterland is now dominated by cocoa and oil palm plantations.

Following the Japanese invasion in 1942, Sandakan was devastated by Allied bombing. In 1946 North Borneo became a British colony and the new colonial government moved the capital to Jesselton (later to become Kota Kinabalu).

Sandakan is a post-war town, much of it rebuilt on reclaimed land. It is Malaysia's biggest fishing port – and even exports some of its catch to Singapore.

Sandakan is often dubbed 'mini Hong Kong' because of its Cantonese influence; its occupants are well-heeled and there are many prosperous businesses. It is now also home to a large Filipino community, mostly traders from Mindanao and the Sulu Islands. The Philippines only recently relaxed its posturing in its claim to Sabah – Sandakan is only 28 km from Philippines' territorial waters.

Places of interest

Sandakan is strung out along the coast but in the centre of town is the riotous

daily fish market, which is the biggest and best in Sabah.

The **Australian war memorial**, near the government building at Mile Seven on Labuk Road, between Sandakan and Sepilok, stands on the site of a Japanese prison camp. **Getting there**: Labuk bus service nos 19, 30 & 32 (60¢). The Japanese invaded North Borneo in 1942 and many Japanese also died in the area. In 1989 a new **Japanese war memorial** was built in the Japanese cemetery, on Red Hill (Bukit Berenda), financed by the families of the deceased soldiers.

St Michael's Anglican church is one of the very few stone churches in Sabah; it is an attractive building, designed by a New Zealander in 1893. Most of Sandakan's stone churches were levelled in the war. It is just off Singapore Road, on the hill at the S end of town. In 1988 a big new **mosque** was built for the burgeoning Muslim population at the mouth of Sandakan Bay. The main Filipino settlements are in this area of town. The mosque is outside Sandakan, on Jalan Buli Sim Sim, just after the jetty for Turtle Islands National Park and is an imposing landmark.

Pertubuhan Ugama Buddhist (Puu Jih Shih Buddhist temple), overlooks Tanah Merah town. The US$2 million temple was completed in 1987 and stands at the top of the hill, accessible by a twisting road which hairpins its way up the hillside. The temple is very gaudy, contains 3 large Buddha images and is nothing special, although the 34 teakwood supporting pillars, made in Macau, are quite a feature. There is a good view of Sandakan from the top, with Tanah Merah and the log ponds directly below, in Sandakan Bay. The names of local donors are inscribed on the walls of the walkway.

There are a couple of other notable Chinese temples in Sandakan. The oldest one, the **Goddess of Mercy Temple** is just off Singapore Road, on the hillside. Originally built in the early 1880s, it has been expanded over the years. The **Three Saints Temple**, further down the hill at the end of the padang, was completed in 1887. The 3 saints are Kwan Woon Cheung (a Kwan clan ancestor), the goddess Tin Hou (worshipped by seafarers) and the Min Cheong Emperor.

The only **Crocodile Farm** in Sabah is a commercial enterprise, set up in 1982 when the government made the crocodile a protected species. The farm, at Mile 8, Labuk Road, is open to the public and has about 200 residents. Admission: $2. Open: 0800-1700 Mon-Sun. Labuk Rd bus.

Excursions
Sepilok Orang-utan Sanctuary, see page 336.

Turtle Islands National Park, see page 334.

Agnes Keith's house

American authoress Agnes Keith lived with her English husband in Sandakan from 1934 to 1952. He was the Conservator of Forests in North Borneo and she wrote 3 books about her time in the colony. *The Land Below the Wind* relates tales of dinner parties and tiffins in pre-war days; *Three Came Home* is about her 3 years in a Japanese internment camp during the war (on Pulau Berhala, off Sandakan and in Kuching) and was made into a film. *White Man Returns* tells the story of their time in British North Borneo. The Keiths' rambling wooden house on the hill above the town was destroyed during the war but was rebuilt by the government to exactly the same design when Harry Keith returned to his job after the war. The house, near Sandakan Viewpoint and *Ramada Renaissance Hotel*, has been unoccupied for a number of years and its garden neglected.

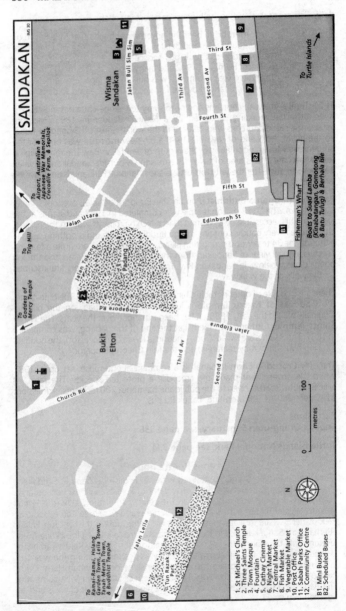

SANDAKAN

To Turtle Islands

Wisma Sandakan

To Airport, Australian & Japanese War Memorials, Crocodile Farm, & Sepilok

To Trig Hill

Jalan Utara

To Goddess of Mercy Temple

Bukit Elton

Jalan Totong

Padang

Singapore Rd

Jalan Elopura

Church Rd

To Ramai-Ramai, Hsiang Garden Town, Leila Town, Tanah Merah Town, & Buddhist Temple

Jalan Leila

Tun Razak Park

Jalan Buli Sim Sim

Third St

Third Av

Second Av

Fourth St

Fifth St

Edinburgh St

Fisherman's Wharf

Boats to Suad Lamba (Kinabatangan), Gomantong & Batu Tulug) & Berhala Isle

Third Av

Second Av

0   100
metres

N

1. St Michael's Church
2. Three Saints Temple
3. Town Mosque
4. Fountain
5. Cathay Cinema
6. Night Market
7. Central Market
8. Fish Market
9. Vegetable Market
10. Post Office
11. Sabah Parks Office
12. Community Centre

B1. Mini Buses
B2. Scheduled Buses

Gomontong Caves are 32 km S of Sandakan Bay, between the road to Sukau and the Kinabatangan River. They are in the 3,600 ha Gomontong Forest Reserve. There are sometimes orang-utan, many deer, mouse deer, wild boar and wild buffalo in the reserve, which was logged in the 1950s. The main limestone cave is called Simud Hitam – or the **Black Cave**. The smaller and more complex **White Cave** or (Simud Putih) is above. Over 2 million bats of 2 different species are thought to live in the caves: at sunset they swarm out to feed. Sixty-four species of bat have been recorded in Sabah – most in these caves are fruit bats whose guano is a breeding ground for cockroaches. The squirming larvae make the floor of the cave seethe. The guano can cause an itchy skin irritation. Niah Caves (**see page 276**) are on a larger scale and more interesting. **Getting there**: it is easiest on a tour (**see page 333**). The caves are accessible by an old logging road, which can be reached by bus from the main Sandakan-Sukau road. There are plans to upgrade the road to Gomontong. The timing of the bus is inconvenient for those wishing to visit the caves. It is much easier to take the 1100 boat from Sandakan's fish market to Suad Lamba, 1½ hrs (M$3). From there it is possible to take a minibus to Gomontong (M$10/head, if there are a reasonable number of passengers). Visitors can stay overnight in the resthouse at nearby Sukau (see below). There are plans afoot to build a chalet and restaurant at Gomontong. Minibuses will pick up passengers for the return trip to Suad Lamba by arrangement – the daily boat back to Sandakan leaves Suad Lamba at 0530.

Kinabatangan River is Sabah's longest. The lower basin is rich in wildlife: black hornbill, kingfisher, tree snake, storm stalk, monitor lizard, long tailed macaque, orang-utan and the proboscis monkey (*Nasalis larvatus*). It is the most accessible area in Borneo to see proboscis monkey. Rhinoceros have also been spotted in the area and herds of wild elephant often pass through. (For details on Borneo's flora and fauna, **see page 224**.)

Because of the diversity of its wildlife, the Kinabatangan riverine forest area has been proposed as a forest reserve. In addition, there is little disturbance from human settlements: the Kinabatangan basin has always been sparsely inhabited because of flooding and the threat posed by pirates. The best destination for a jungle river safari is not on the Kinabatangan itself, but on the narrow, winding Sungei Menanggol tributary, about 6 km from Sukau. The Kinabatangan estuary – largely mangrove – is also rich in wildlife, and is a haven for migratory birds. Boats can be chartered from Sandakan to Abai (at the mouth of the river).

A minimum of 2-3 days is recommended for the trip. *Wildlife Expeditions* has a well-equipped lodge on the Kinabatangan (see tours below) and plans to build a trail and treehouse for ornithological pursuits. *Uncle Tan* has a wildlife camp one hour upriver from Sukau (see below), near some ox-bow lakes. There is also a private resthouse in Sukau that

The Borneo death march

The 4 years of Japanese occupation ended when the Australian 9th division liberated British North Borneo. Sandakan was chosen by the Japanese as a regional centre for holding Allied prisoners. In 1942 the Japanese shipped 2,750 prisoners of war (2,000 of whom were Australian and 750 British) to Sandakan from Changi Prison, Singapore. A further 800 British and 500 Australian POWs arrived in 1944. They were ordered to build an airfield (on the site of the present airport) and were forced to work from dawn to dusk. Many died, but in Sept 1944 2,400 POWs were force-marched to Ranau – a 240 km trek through the jungle which only 6 Australians survived. This 'Death March', although not widely reported in World War II literature, claimed more Australian lives than any other single event during the war in Asia – including the notorious Burma-Siam railway.

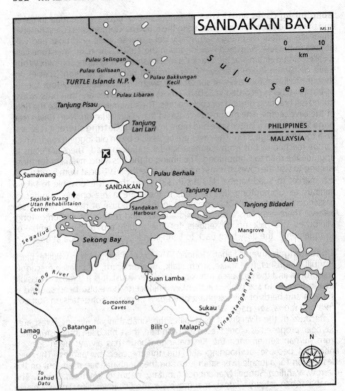

independent tourists can use – the caretaker will help organize river trips (see below). **Accommodation: E** *Sukau Resthouse*, Sukau. The resthouse is the cream and orange house, to the left at the village crossroads. It has 5 rooms. Karim, the caretaker can organize boat trips – with experienced local boatmen, who know many of the tributaries – from the village up to Sungei Menanggol for about M\$25-30/hour (capacity: 3 max). Guests are advised to bring fresh food from Sandakan (a stove is provided). **Getting there**: boat to Suad Lamba, on the far side of Sandakan Bay leaves from the rear of Sandakan's wet market at 1100 every day, 1½ hrs (M\$3). (The return boat leaves Suad Lamba at 0530.) It is also possible to charter a minibus to take you from Suad Lamba to Gomontong and on to Sukau. It will pick passengers up again at a set time, by arrangement (M\$70-100 return). A bus leaves from Sandakan to Sukau (via Gomontong turn-off) at 1400, 115 km 3½ hrs (M\$10). The return bus leaves Sukau for Sandakan at 0600.

Batu Tulug (also known as Batu Putih, or White Stone) on the Kinabatangan River (100 km upstream from Sukau), is a cave containing wooden coffins dating back several hundred years (some of the better examples have been removed to the Sabah State Museum in KK). The caves are about 1 km N of the Kinabatangan Bridge, on the E side of the Sandakan-Lahad Datu road. **Getting there**: take the Sukau bus from Sandakan, 1400.

Pulau Berhala is ideal for picnicking and swimming. It has 200m rust-coloured sandstone cliffs on the S end of the island, with a beach at the foot, within easy reach by boat. The island was used as a leper colony before World War II and as a prisoner of war camp by the Japanese. Agnes Keith (**see page 329**) was interned on the island during the war. **Getting there**: boats from the fish market (M$10).

Tours Most tour companies operate tours to Turtle Islands, Sepilok and the Kinabatangan River. See Tour companies and travel agents, **page 334**.

Accommodation A+ *Ramada Renaissance* (formerly *Sabah Hotel*), Mile 1, Jln Utara, T 213299, F 271271, a/c, restaurant, Sandakan's top hotel was refurbished to 5-star standard and reopened in 1991 with 120 rooms and 7 chefs, recruited in Hong Kong, to cater for the hotel's 4 restaurants; **B** *Hsiang Garden*, Jln Leila, Hsiang Garden Estate, T 273122, F 273127, a/c, restaurant, all facilities, good bar; **B** *Ramai*, Km 2, Jln Leila, T 273222, F 271884, a/c, restaurant, rec; **C** *En Khin*, Jln Tiga (next to Maybank), T 217300, a/c, clean, reasonable value; **B** *Hung Wing*, Jln Tiga, T 218855/218895, a/c, probably the best of the middle-bracket hotels; **B** *Malaysia*, 32 2nd Ave, T 218322/218340, clean and more spacious than Hung Wing, rooms have TVs; **C** *Mayfair*, 24 Jln Pryer, a/c, central location; **B** *Sabah*, T 218711, a/c, well kept; **D** *Uncle Tan's*, Mile 17.5 (Km 29), Labuk Rd (5 km beyond Sepilok junction), T 216227, F 271215, out of town but convenient for Sepilok, set in fruit plantation; bicycle hire M$3/day, all meals incl., tours arranged (see *Tour companies*, below), rec.

Restaurants Seafood: four Chinese seafood restaurants on Trig Hill overlooking the harbour. The seafood is fantastic. ♦♦♦*Golden Palace*, Trig Hill (2 km out of town), fresh seafood, specialises in drunken prawns, crab and lobster, rec; ♦♦♦*Regent Garden*, Hotel Hsiang Garden, Jln Leila, Hsiang Garden Estate, lobster and tiger prawns, good value and a popular local lunch venue; ♦♦♦*Sea View Garden*, just before community centre on left, on road to Ramai Ramai, superb Chinese-run fresh seafood restaurant which opens onto the sea, highly rec. by locals; *See Lok Yum*, next door to *Sea View Garden*, also very popular with locals.
   Malay: ♦♦*Perwira*, Hotel Ramai, Jln Leila, Malay and Indonesian, good value, rec; **Chinese:** ♦♦*Sandakan Recreation Club*, just off the Padang; **Indian:** ♦*Restoran Awalia*, Roti and curry.
   International: ♦♦*Seoul Garden*, Hsiang Garden Estate, Mile 1.5, Leila Rd, Korean. ♦*Apple Fast Food*, Lorong Edinburgh, good spot for breakfasts; ♦*Fat Cat*, 206 Wisma Sandakan, 18 Jln Haji Saman, several branches around town, breakfasts rec; ♦♦*Hawaii*, City View Hotel, Lot 1, Block 23, Third Ave, Western and local food, set lunch, rec; ♦♦♦*X. O. Steak House*, Lot 16, Hsiang Garden Estate, Mile 1.5, Jln Leila, T 42510, lobster and tiger prawns and a good choice of fresh fish as well as Australian steaks, buffet barbecue on Fri nights, rec. **Coffee Shops:** *New Bangsawan*, next to New Bangsawan cinema, just off Jln Leila, Tanah Merah, no great shakes, but best restaurant in Tanah Merah (where there are stacks of coffee shops). *Union Coffee Shop*, 2nd Flr Hakka Association Bldg, Third Ave, budget; *Silver*

Edible nests

The edible nests of black and white swiftlets are collected from the cave chambers, but the trade is now strictly controlled by Wildlife Department wardens. The white nests (of pure saliva) fetch more than US$400/kg in Hong Kong; black nests go for around US$40/kg. The nest-collectors pick about 250 kg a day in the lower chamber and about 50 kg a day in the upper chamber. They earn about M$25 a day. The collectors use 60 m-long rotan ladders. Heavy bundles of wood are lashed to the ladders to minimize swaying – but fatal accidents do occur. On average, a collector is killed once every 4 or 5 years in a fall. Bat guano is not collected from the floor of the cave so that it can act as a sponge mattress in the event of a serious fall.

The nests, which are relished as a delicacy by the Chinese (**see page 278**), are harvested for periods of 10 days, 3 times a year – in Feb, Jun and Sept. (Conservationists want the harvesting restricted to twice a year so the swiftlets have more time to breed.) Harvesting contracts are auctioned to wholesalers who export the nests to Hong Kong, where their impurities are taken out and they are sold at a huge mark-up. Of the profits, about half go to the state government, and more than a third to the contractor. Less than a fifth goes to the collectors. It is possible to buy the birds nests in Sandakan restaurants, although they are all re-imported from Hong Kong.

Star Ice Cream and Café, Third Ave, popular coffee shop with on-site satay stall in the evenings, particularly friendly and helpful management, rec. **Foodstalls**: Malay foodstalls next to minibus station, just before the community centre on the road to Ramai Ramai.

Entertainment *Cathay Cinema*, next to Wisma Sabah and town mosque. *Tiffany Discotheatre and Karaoke*, Block C, 7-10, Grd and 1st Flrs, Jln Leila, Bandar Ramai-Ramai. *Champion Bowl*, Jln Leila, Bandar Ramai Ramai.

Local transport Local minibuses from the back of the *Mayfair Hotel*, 24 Jln Pryer.

Sport Golf: *Sandakan Golf Club*, 10 km out of town.

Shopping Almost everything in Sandakan is imported. There are some inexpensive batik shops and some good tailors. *Wisma Sandakan*, next to the town mosque and the *Cathay*, is the trendiest place in town and offers 3-floors of a/c Singapore-style shopping.

Banks & money changers Most around Third Ave and Jln Pelabuhan. **Hong Kong & Shanghai**, Jln Pelabuhan/Lebuh Tiga; **Standard Chartered**, Jln Pelabuhan.

Embassies & consulates Indonesian Consulate, Jln Karamunsing, T 215170.

Useful addresses General Post Office: Jln Leila. **Immigration**: Federal Bldg, Jln Leila. **Area code**: 080. **Sabah Parks Office**: Room 906, 9th Flr, Wisma Khoo, Lebuh Tiga, T 273453. Bookings for Turtle Islands National Park (**see below**). **Wildlife Department**: 6th Flr, State Secretariat Bldg, Mile 7 (on road to the airport), T 666550. Permits for Gomontong caves and Sepilok. **Churches**: St Michael's (Anglican) and St Mary's (RC) are on the hill at the S end of Sandakan town.

Airline offices MAS, Ground Flr, Sabah Bldg, Lorong Edinburgh, T 273966; **Sabah Air**, Sandakan Airport, T 660527, F 660545.

Tour companies & travel agents *Alexander Ng*, Pejabat Pos Jln Utara, Batu 1.5, T 212225, caters for specialist interests and offers individually-tailored tours. *Uncle Tan's*, Mile 17.5 (Km 29), Labuk Rd (5 km beyond Sepilok junction), T 216227, F 271215. Inexpensive tours to his "Utan Wildlife Camp" on the Kinabatangan (max. 20 people). There are guides and a cook at the camp. Departures Tue & Fri only (M\$130 transport, M\$15/night – all meals incl.). Also runs reasonably priced tours to Turtle Islands and Gomontong Caves. Advance bookings can be addressed to P O Box 620, 90007 Sandakan, rec. *Unique Tours*, Lot 6, Block 1, Bandar Kim Fung, Batu 4, Jln Utara, T 212150. *Wildlife Expeditions*, Room 903, 9th Flr, Wisma Khoo Siak Chiew, 3rd Ave, Sim Sim Rd, T 219616/214570. The most expensive, but also the most efficient, with the best facilities and the best guides, rec.

Tourist offices National Parks Office, Jln Leila, T 42188.

Transport to & from Sandakan 386 km from KK. **By air**: the airport is 11 km from the town centre (M\$10-12 by taxi into town). Early morning flights from KK to Sandakan allow breath-taking close-up views of Mount Kinabalu as the sun rises. Connections with Lahad Datu (M\$48), Kudat (M\$65), Semporna (M\$60), Tawau (M\$73). **By minibus**: Sandakan's mud-splattered long distance minibuses leave from the footbridge over Lebuh Tiga or from the minibus station just before the community centre on the Ramai Ramai road. Regular connections from both stops with Kota Kinabalu (a bone-shaking journey on an unmetalled road to Ranau), 10 hrs, (M\$35), Ranau, 8 hrs (M\$25), Lahad Datu (M\$15), Tawau (M\$25).

Turtle Islands National Park

40 km N of Sandakan, the Turtle Islands are at the S entrance to Labuk Bay. The park is separated from the Philippine island of Bakkungan Kecil by a narrow stretch of water. The turtle sanctuary is made up of 3 tiny islands (Pulau Selingaan, Pulau Bakkungan Kecil and Pulau Gulisaan) and also encompasses the surrounding coral reefs and sea, covering 1,700 ha. On Pulau Bakkungan Kecil there is a small mud volcano.

The islands are famous for their green turtles (*Chelonia mydas*) – which account for about four fifths of the turtles in the park – and hawksbill turtles (*Eretmochelys imbricata*) – known locally as *sisik*. Most green turtles lay their eggs on Pulau Selingaan. The green turtles copulate about 50-200m off Pulau Selingaan and can often be seen during the day, their heads popping up like submarine periscopes. Hawksbills prefer to nest on Pulau Gulisan.

Both species come ashore, year-round, to lay their eggs, although the peak season is between Jul and Oct. Even during the off-season between 4 and 10 turtles come up the beach each night to lay their eggs. Pulau Bakkungan Kecil and Pulau Gulisaan can only be visited during the day but visitors can stay overnight on Pulau Selingaan to watch the green turtles.

The numbers of visitors are restricted to 20/night in an effort to protect the female turtles, which are easily alarmed by noise and light when laying. Visitors are asked not to build camp fires, shine bright torches or make noise at night on the beach. The turtles should be watched from a distance to avoid upsetting the nesting process. Only the females come ashore; the male waits in the sea nearby for his mate. The females cautiously come ashore to nest after 2000, or with the high tide. The nesting site is above the high tide mark and is cleared by the female's front and hind flippers to make a 'body pit', just under a metre deep. She then digs an egg chamber with her powerful rear flippers after which she proceeds to lay her eggs. The clutch size can be anything between 40 and 200 (batches of 50-80 are most common).

When all the eggs have been laid, they are covered with sand and the body pit laboriously filled to conceal the site of the nest, after which the exhausted turtle struggles back to the sea, leaving her Range Rover-like tracks in the sand. The egg-laying process can take about an hour or two to complete. Some say the temperature of the sand effects the sex of the young, if it is warm the batch will be mostly female and if cold, mostly male. After laying her eggs, a tag reading "If found, return to Turtle Island Park, Sabah, East Malaysia" is attached to each turtle by the rangers, who are stationed on each island. Over 27,000 have been tagged since 1970; the measurements of each turtle are recorded and the clutches of eggs are removed and transplanted to the hatchery where they are protected from natural predators – such as monitor lizards, birds and snakes.

The golf ball-sized eggs are placed by hand into 80 cm-deep pits, covered in sand and surrounded by wire. They take up to 60 days to hatch. The hatchlings mostly emerge at night when the temperature is cooler, breaking their shells with their one sharp tooth. There are hatcheries on all 3 islands and nearly every night a batch is released into the sea. More than 2.6 million hatchlings were released between 1977 and 1988. They are released at different points on the island to protect them from predators: they are a favoured snack for white-bellied gulls and only a fraction – about 3 to 5% – survive to become teenage turtles.

Permits are required by all visitors, M$30 from the Sabah Parks Office in Sandakan: Room 906, 9th Flr, Wisma Khoo, Lebuh Tiga (Third Ave), T 273453. It is necessary to acquire special permits to visit Pulau Bakkungan Kecil and Pulau Gulisaan. Unofficially, however, it is possible to make the 5-minute boat-trip to Pulau Bakkungan Kecil where there is some excellent coral.

Tours The average cost of a one-night tour is M$150-200. Most tour companies (**see page 333**) operate tours to Turtle Islands and have their own boats, which makes the trip a bit cheaper. An expedition to the islands needs to be well-planned; vagaries such as bad weather, which can prevent you from leaving the islands as planned, can mess up itineraries. Most visitors to the islands book their trips in advance. Rough journey during the rainy season, Oct to Feb.

Accommodation The number of visitors to the islands is restricted, even at peak season. There are 3 chalets on Pulau Selingaan (M$30/night). They accommodate a maximum of 20 people/night, so it is necessary to book in advance through the Sabah Parks office, Rm 906, 9th Flr, Wisma Khoo, Lebuh Tiga (Third Ave).

Restaurants Chalets are equipped with cooking facilities and visitors can bring their own food. A new restaurant in the information Centre building opened in 1992.

Best time to visit The driest months and the calmest seas are between Mar and Jul. The peak egg laying season is Jul-Oct. Seas are rough between Oct and Feb.

Transport to & from Turtle Islands 40 km NE of Sandakan. **By boat**: no regular transport to the islands. Boats for hire from Sandakan port: speedboat, 1 hr (M$500 return), slow boat, 2-3 hrs (M$400 return). Cheaper to go in groups. National Parks office in Sandakan recommend boats and tour companies.

Sepilok Orang-Utan Rehabilitation Centre

Sepilok, a reserve of 4,530 ha of lowland primary rainforest and mangrove was set up in 1964 to protect the orang-utan – 'the wild man of Borneo' – or *Pongo pygmaeus* – from extinction. It is one of only 3 orang-utan sanctuaries in the world and now receives around 40,000 visitors a year. Logging has seriously threatened Sabah's population of wild orang-utan, as has their capture for zoos and as pets. Wild ones can still be found in Sabah in the Kinabatangan basin region (see page 331) and Danum Valley Conservation Area (see page 338) and a few other isolated tracts of jungle.

Sepilok is an old forest reserve, where orphaned or captured orang-utans are rehabilitated and protected and eventually returned to the wild. The orang-utan (for details, see page 224) lives on the islands of Borneo and Sumatra and there are estimated to be only about 5,000 still in the wild. Since Sepilok's establishment,

The tough life of a turtle

Historically, green and hawksbill turtles have been hunted for their meat, shells and their edible eggs (a Chinese delicacy). They were a favourite food of British and Spanish mariners for centuries. Japanese soldiers slaughtered thousands of turtles for food during World War II. Dynamite fishermen are also thought to have killed off many turtles in both Malaysian and Philippines waters in recent years.

Malaysia, Japan, Hong Kong, Japan and the Philippines, where green turtle meat and eggs are much in demand, are all signatories of the Convention in International Trade in Endangered Species (CITES), and trading in sea turtles has been proscribed under Appendix 1 of the Convention since 1981. However, the eggs are still sold illegally in Sandakan's wet market and can be bought for about M$1 each.

In his book *Forest Life and Adventures in the Malay Archipelago*, the Swedish adventurer and wildlife enthusiast Eric Mjoberg documents turtle egg-hunting and shell collecting in Sabah and Sarawak in the 1920s. He tells of how the Bajaus would lie in wait for hawksbills, grab them and put them on the fire so their horny shields could be removed. "The poor beasts are put straight on the fire so that their shield may be more readily removed, and suffer, in the process, the tortures of the damned. They are then allowed to go alive, or perhaps half-dead into the sea, only to come back again after a few years and undergo the same cruel process." The Bajaus, he says, used an 'ingenious contrivance' to hunt their prey. They would press pieces of common glass against their eyes 'in a watertight fashion' and would lie face-down on a piece of floating wood, dipping their faces into the water, watching for hawksbills feeding on seaweed. They would then dive in, armed with a small harpoon, and catch them, knocking them out with a blow to the head.

The British North Borneo Company first introduced conservation measures in 1927 limiting the turtle hunting seasons. In 1964, 8 islands in the Selingaan area were constituted as turtle farms; the rights to collect turtle eggs were only granted to contractors, who bid for them at auction. In 1964, the highest bid was M$20,000, which gives some idea of the profitability of the egg-collecting industry. Egg collecting was a hazardous profession: the first (and last) egg collector on Pulau Selingaan was murdered by pirates in 1964. Even today staff at the government hatchery on Pulau Selingaan have to be periodically withdrawn because of the threat posed by pirates. Selingaan always had the richest harvest of about 285,000 eggs a year. Pulau Bakkungan Kechil yielded about 127,000 eggs a year and Pulau Bulisaan, 63,000.

In Aug 1966 the first turtle hatchery in Malaysia was set up on Pulau Selingaan and in 1971 the 3 islands now comprising the park were compulsorily acquired by the Sabah state government.

more than 100 orang-utans have been rehabilitated into the wild.

After an initial period of quarantine at Sepilok, newly arrived orang-utans are moved to **Platform A** and taught necessary survival skills by the rangers. At the age of 7 they are moved deeper into the forest to **Platform B** (about half an hour walk from Platform A). At Platform B, they are encouraged to forage for themselves.

Feeding times Platform A: 1000 and 1430, Platform B: 1100. Visitors are more likely to see orang-utans at feeding times at Platform A, as they depend on the food given to them. At Platform B food is only given to them as a dietary supplement. Orang-utans undergo training exercises on Mon, Tues & Fri at 0800-0900 and 1400-1500.

Sepilok also has a rare Sumatran rhinoceros (*Dicerorhinus sumatrensis*) – also known as the Asian 2-horned rhinoceros (**see page 806**). The rhino enclosure is open 0930-1030 and 1400-1500.

The information centre, next to park headquarters, runs a nature education exhibition with replicas of jungle mammals and educational videos. There are several well marked trails in the park, which get crowded on weekends and school holidays. Admission: free, but plans are afoot to charge M$5-10 once the new nature centre and restaurant open. Open: 0900-1600 Mon-Sun.

Transport to & from Sepilok 24 km from Sandakan. **By bus**: Labuk Bus Service (blue buses) 19,30 & 32. Buses leave from waterfront (W end of the fruit market) in Sandakan at 0920, 1120, 1315 and 1500 (M$1.25). Alternatively, take a minibus going to Sungei Api, Sungei Monyet or Ulu Susun. Sepilok is 1.9 km from the main road.

Lahad Datu

Lahad Datu is Malaysia's 'wild east' at its wildest, and its recent history testifies to its reputation as the capital of cowboy country. The population is an intriguing mixture of Filipinos, Sulu islanders, migrants from Kalimantan, Orang Bugis, Timorese – and a few Malays. Most came to work on the oil palm plantations. Nowadays there are so many migrants, few can find employment. There are reckoned to be more illegal Filipino immigrants in Lahad Datu than the whole official population put together. Piracy in the Sulu Sea and the offshore islands in Kennedy Bay is rife – local fishermen live in terror.

The town itself is grubby and uninteresting. During World War II, the Japanese made Lahad Datu their naval headquarters for E Borneo. After the war, the timber companies moved in: the British Kennedy Bay Timber Company built the Lahad Datu's first plywood mill in the early 1950s. Oil palm plantations grew up in the hinterland after the timber boom finished in the 1970s. As for the town, what it lacks in aesthetic appeal is made up for by its colourful recent history.

Kampung Panji is a water village with a small market at the end of Jalan Teratai, where many of the poorer immigrant families live.

Excursions
Beaches and islands The only good beaches are on the road to Tungku; Pantai Perkapi and Pantai Tungku. They can be reached by minibus from Lahad Datu or by boat from the old wharf. It is possible to get to the nearby islands from the old wharf behind the *Mido Hotel*, but at the moment it is too dangerous for tourists.

Danum Valley, see page 338.

Madai Caves are about 2 km off the Tawau-Lahad Datu road, near Kunak. The caves are an important archaeological site – there is evidence they were inhabited over 15,000 years ago. The birds' nests are harvested 3 times a year by local Idahan people whose lean-to kampung goes right up to the cave mouth. Another 15 km W of Madai is **Baturong**, another limestone massif and cave system in the middle of what was originally Tingkayu Lake. The route is not obvious, so it is advisable to take a local guide. Stone tools, wooden coffins and rock paintings have been found there. Take a torch. **Getting there**: minibus from Lahad Datu (M$10).

Gunung Silam, 18 km from Lahad Datu on the Tawau road, a track leads up the mountain to a Telekom station at 620m and from there, a jungle trail to the summit. There are good views over the bay and out to the islands beyond. It is advisable to take a guide. **Getting there**: minibus from Lahad Datu (M$10).

Accommodation Lahad Datu is not a popular tourist spot and accommodation is poor and expensive. The *Jago Kota Hotel* opened in 1992 and may prove to be a better option than the Mido. The *Perdana* and *Venus hotels* on Jln Seroja are worth avoiding. **A-B** *Mido*, 94 Jln Main, T 81800, a/c, restaurant, the façade (facing the Standard Chartered Bank) is pock-marked with M-16 bullet holes – the result of over-curious residents watching the 1986 pirate raid on the bank, the *Mido* comes with all the sleaze of 'the wild east' and fails miserably to live up to its reputation as the best hotel in town; **C** *Full Wah*, Jln Anggrek (opposite Chinese temple), T 83948, a/c, clean enough and probably a better bet than the Mido; **C** *Ocean*, Jln Teratai (just past the Esso Station), T 81700, a/c; *Government Resthouse*, T 81579.

Restaurants Seafood: **♦♦***Evergreen Snack Bar and Pub*, on 2nd Flr, Jln Teratai, opposite the Hap Seng Bldg, a/c, excellent fish and chips and best-known for its tuna steaks, rec; **♦♦***Golden Key*, on stilts over the sea opposite the end of Jln Teratai, it is really just a tumble-down wooden coffee shop, but is well known for its seafood; **♦♦♦***Melawar*, 2nd Flr, Block 47, off Jln Teratai (around the corner from the *Mido Hotel*), seafood restaurant, popular with locals; **♦♦♦***Ping Foong*, one mile out of Lahad Datu, on Sandakan Rd, open-air seafood restaurant, highly rec. by locals; **♦♦***Good View*, just over ¹/₂ km out of town on Tengku Rd, rec by locals; **♦♦***Seng Kee*, Block 39, opposite *Mido Hotel* and next to Standard Chartered Bank, cheap and good. *Restoran Ali*, opposite *Hotel New Sabah*, Indian, good roti. **Foodstalls**: **♦***Pasar Malam* behind *Mido Hotel* on Jln Kastam Lama. Spicy barbecued fish (*ikan panggang*) and skewered chicken wings rec.

Shopping There is a new *Central Market* on Jln Bungaraya and a spice market off Jln Teratai where Indonesian smugglers tout Gudang Garam cigarettes and itinerant dentists and bumohs draw large crowds.

Entertainment The *Lacin cinema* (which usually screens violent kung-fu movies) is next to the post office on Jalan Kenanga.

Banks & money changers Standard Chartered, in front of *Mido Hotel*.

Useful addresses Post Office: Jln Kenanga, next to the Lacin cinema. Sabah Foundation: 2nd Flr, Hap Seng Bldg, Jln Main, T 81092. Bookings for Danum Valley. Bookings can also be made at the Sabah Foundation headquarters in Kota Kinabalu (T 35496).

Airline offices MAS, Grd Flr, *Mido Hotel* building, Jln Main.

Transport to & from Lahad Datu By air: connections with Tawau (M$48), Sandakan (M$48). Connections with KK on Mon, Wed & Fri. By minibus: minibuses leave from the bus station on Jln Bunga Raya (behind Bangunan Hap Seng at the mosque end of Jln Teratai) and from opposite the Shell station. Regular connections with Tawau, 2¹/₂ hrs (M$8), Semporna (M$8), Sandakan (M$12), Madai (M$5). By boat: fishing boats take paying passengers from the old wharf (end of Jln Kastam Lama) to the Kennedy Bay islands, Tawau and Semporna, although time-wise (and, more to the point, safety-wise) it makes much more sense to go by road or air.

Danum Valley Conservation Area

Danum Valley's 438 sq km of virgin jungle is the largest expanse of undisturbed lowland dipterocarp forest in Sabah. The field centre, which is 85 km W of Lahad Datu – and 40 km from the nearest habitation – was set up by the Sabah Foundation in 1985 for forest research, nature education and recreation. The Segama River runs through the conservation area, and past the field centre. The Danum River is a tributary of the Segama joining it 9 km downstream of the Field Centre. Gunung Danum (1093m) is the highest peak, 13 km SW of the Field Centre. Within the area is a Yayasan Sabah timber concession, which is tightly controlled.

This area has never really been inhabited, although much of the forest on the road up to Danum Valley has been logged. There is evidence of some settlement

The Long John Silvers of Sabah's east coast

In Aug 1986 a group of pirates invaded Lahad Datu one Friday afternoon when the Muslims were at prayer. Twenty-two of them, dressed in army fatigues and led by a 'beautiful woman' landed at the wharf and made straight for the blue and white-painted wooden police station on the hill behind the town. They hit it with several mortar rounds. They then entered the Standard Chartered Bank firing wildly as they went. One civilian was killed and the bank's security guard was shot dead. They made off with M$80,000 in cash, crossed the road and raided the MAS office on the ground floor of the *Mido Hotel*, which yielded another M$8,000 in cash. They escaped in Miami-Vice-style speed boats to one of the outer islands in Kennedy Bay, close to Philippines' waters.

Malaysian police field forces, reinforced by Royal Malaysian Air Force fighter-bombers from Labuan took on the pirates outside Malaysian territorial waters. They bombed a fishing village on one island where the Lahad Datu raiders were suspected of taking refuge. The Malaysian government claimed that most of the pirates had been killed and the Philippines government stayed silent. Corpses of 7 of those killed were later brought back to Lahad Datu for identification.

The word on the local rumour mill was that the pirates would retaliate. A fortnight after the pirate attack, an enterprising robber pulled off a gold heist in town. He detonated a smoke bomb outside a goldsmith's and then calmly walked into the abandoned gold shop. No one raised an alarm. Instances of piracy are still common in the Lahad Datu area. In Jan 1993, a Malaysian marine police patrol sank a hijacked trawler and speedboat after a gun-battle with pirates. The Malaysian news agency reported: "Eight policemen sank the trawler with a canon shot. The pirates from the trawler jumped into the speedboat, and, when it too was sank, all jumped into the sea and were presumed to have escaped. The trawler skipper swam ashore and reported to police."

during the Japanese occupation – townspeople came upstream to escape from the Japanese troops. There is also growing evidence of pre-historic cave-dwellers in the Segama River area. Not far downstream from the field centre, in a riverside cave, 2 wooden coffins have been found, together with a copper bracelet and a tapai jar, all of uncertain date. The area was first recommended as a national park by the World Wide Fund for Nature's Malaysia Expedition in 1975 and designated a conservation area in 1981. The field centre was officially opened in 1986.

The main reason for this large conservation area is to undertake research into the impact of logging on flora and fauna and to try and improve forest management, to understand processes which maintain tropical rainforest and to provide wildlife management and training opportunities for Sabahans. Many are collaborative projects between Malaysian and foreign scientists.

Flora and fauna Because of its size and remoteness, Danum Valley is home to some of Sabah's rarest animals and plants. The conservation area is teeming with wildlife: Sumatran rhinoceroses have been recorded, as have elephants, clouded leopards, orang-utans, proboscis monkeys, sunbears and 220 species of bird. (For details on Borneo's flora and fauna, **see page 224**.) A species of monkey, which looks like an albino version of the red leaf monkey, was first seen on the road to Danum in 1988, and appears to be unique to this area.

There are over 30 km of marked trails in the conservation area, including a ½ km self-guided nature trail, with over 300 labelled trees. Trails vary from 0.7 km around the centre to an 18 km trek to Kuala Sabran, where there is a hut built by a visiting team from Operation Raleigh.

There are also 2 tree-top observation towers close to the centre. It is possible to shoot the Dismal Gorge rapids in a canoe, but only if organized beforehand as it involves a long trek upstream. At the Field Centre there is a visitor information centre and a small shop, which sells maps, leach socks, guides to the nature trails and drinks. It also rents out binoculars.

NB: it is important to inform the visitor information centre where you are going before setting off. People have been lost in the Danum Valley jungle for days.

Guides M$30/day, M$20 for half day.

Night drives The best way to see the wildlife at night is to persuade one of the Danum staff to go for a drive (for an agreed fee) in the hope of catching a few nocturnal exotica in the headlights. M$0.35 per km, driver M$2 per hour, M$5 per person per trip.

Admission M$2/person for day visitors (no more than 30 visitors on one day).

Accommodation The field centre is mainly for visiting scientists. Accommodation is available for visitors but must be booked in advance at the Sabah Foundation headquarters in KK, T 354496 or the Forestry Division in Lahad Datu, T 81092. Electricity from 1200-2300. *Resthouse*, 5 double rooms, often booked up with visiting scientists; *Hostel*, 30 beds; *Forest Cabin* (built by Operation Raleigh), 18 km from field centre.

Restaurants Resthouse guests are provided with full board for M$30 a day. Large groups must be prepared to cater for themselves in the kitchen attached to the dining hall.

Transport to & from Danum Valley 85 km W of Lahad Datu (left along the logging road at Km 15 on the Lahad Datu-Tawau road to Taliwas and then left again to field centre). The field centre is not on any public transport route. Field centre vehicles come into Lahad Datu on Mon, Wed and Fri and meet arrivals at the airport (M$30/person each way). If arriving at other times transport can be arranged through the Sabah Foundation Regional Office, 2nd Flr Hap Seng Bldg, Lahad Datu (M$130 one way).

Semporna

Semporna is a small fishing town at the end of the peninsula and is the main departure point for Sipidan Island (see below). Semporna has a lively and very photogenic market, spilling out onto piers over the water. It is a Bajau town and is known for its seafood. There are scores of small fishing boats, many with outriggers and square sails. The town is built on an old coral reef – said to be 35,000 years old – that was exposed by the uplift of the sea bed.

Excursions
Sipidan, see below.

Other islands The islands off Semporna stand along the edge of the continental shelf, which drops away to a depth of 200m to the S and E of Pulau Ligitan, the outermost island in the group. Darvel Bay, and the adjacent waters, are dotted with small, mainly volcanic islands all part of the 73,000 acre Semporna Marine Park. The bigger ones are Pulau Mabol, Pulau Kapalai, Pulau Si Amil, Pulau Danawan and Pulau Sipidan. The coral reefs surrounding these islands have around 70 genera of coral – placing them in terms of their diversity, on a par with Australia's Great Barrier Reef. More than 200 species of fish have also been recorded in these waters.

Locals live in traditional boats called *lipa-lipa* or in pilehouses at the water's edge and survive by fishing. In the shallow channels off Semporna, there are 3 fishing villages, built on stilts: Kampung Potok Satu, Kampung Potok Dua and Kampung Larus. There are many more islands than are marked on the map; most are hilly, uninhabited and have beautiful white sandy beaches.

Reefs in the 73,000 acre Semporna Marine Park include Bohey Dulang, Sibuan Ulaiga, Tetugan, Mantabuan Bodgaya, Sibuan, Maigu, Selakan and Sebangkat. Pulau Bohey Dulang is a volcanic island with a Japanese-run pearl culture station. Visitors can only visit it if there is a boat from the pearl culture station going out. The Kaya Pearl company leases part of the lagoon and Japanese pearl oysters are artificially implanted with a core material to induce the growth of pearls. The oysters are attached to rafts moored in the lagoon. The pearls are later harvested and exported directly to Japan. **Getting there**: the islands can be reached by local fishing boats from the main jetty by the market, Sibun (M$150 return), Sibankat (M$80 return), Myga (M$150 return), Selakan (M$100 return).

Accommodation B *Dragon Inn*, T 781088, hotel built on stilts over the sea, a/c, restaurant; **E** *Government Resthouse*, T 7718709.

Restaurants ◆*Floating Restoran dan Bar*, attached to *Dragon Inn*, pile house with good seafood at about M$5 a plate. There is an excellent Muslim restaurant at the top end of town, furthest from the market, and a number of coffee shops.

Shopping Cultured pearls are sold by traders in town.

Useful addresses General Post Office: next to minibus station.

Transport to & from Semporna 106 km N of Tawau. **By air**: regular connections with Sandakan (M$60). **By minibus**: minibus station in front of USNO headquarters. Regular connections with Tawau (M$5), Lahad Datu.

Sipidan Island Marine Reserve

The venerable French marine biologist Jacques Cousteau 'discovered' Sipidan in 1989 and after spending 3 months diving around the island from his research vessel *Calypso* had this to say: "I have seen other places like Sipidan 45 years ago, but now no more. Now we have found... an untouched piece of art." Since then Sipidan has become a sub-aqua Shangri-La for serious divers. In Sept 1990 Australia's *Sport Diving* magazine called the island "one of the most exciting dive spots imaginable... an absolutely bewildering underwater experience." The reef is without parallel in Malaysia. But Sipidan Island is not just for scuba divers: it is a magnificent tiny tropical island with pristine beaches and crystal clear water and its coral can be enjoyed by even the most amateur of snorkellers.

Pulau Sipidan is the only oceanic island in Malaysia – it is not attached to the continental shelf, and stands on a limestone and coral stalk, rising 200m from the bed of the Celebes Sea. The limestone pinnacle mushrooms out near the surface, but a few metres offshore drops off in a sheer underwater cliff to the seabed. The reef comes right into the island's small pier, allowing snorkellers to swim along the edge of the coral cliff, while remaining close to the coral-sand beach. The edge is much further out around the rest of the island. The tiny island has a cool forested interior and it is common to see flying foxes and monitor lizards. It is also a stop-over point for migratory birds, and was originally declared a bird sanctuary in 1933. It has been a marine reserve since 1981 and 3 Wildlife Department officials are permanently stationed on the island. The island is also a breeding ground for the green turtle; Aug and Sept are the main egg-laying months (**see page 336**).

Sipidan is known for its underwater overhangs and caverns, funnels and ledges, all covered in coral. Five metres down from the edge of the precipice there is a coral overhang known as the Hanging Gardens, where coral dangles from the underside of the reef. The cavern is located on the cliff right in front of the island's accommodation area. Its mouth is 24m wide and the cave, which has fine formations of stalactites and stalagmites, goes back almost 100m , sometimes less than 4m below the surface. Visibility blurs where fresh water mixes with sea water. Inside, there are catacombs of underwater passages.

The island is disputed between the Indonesian and Malaysian governments. Indonesia has asked Malaysia to stop developing marine tourism facilities on Sipidan. Malaysia's claim to the island rests on historical documents signed by the British and Dutch colonial administrations. A third party also contests ownership of Sipidan: a Malaysian who claims his grandfather, Abdul Hamid Haji, was given the island by the Sultan of Sulu. He has the customary rights to collect turtles eggs on the island – although the Malaysian government disputes this.

The island's tourist facilities are run by 2 tour companies, who control everything. They are required to restrict the number of visitors allowed on the island at any one time to about 40 and on arrival visitors have to sign a guarantee that they will do nothing to spoil the island.

Tours *Borneo Divers*, Rooms 401-404, 4th Flr, Wisma Sabah, Kota Kinabalu, T 222226, F 221550. Run monthly trips, 8-20 divers for any trip. Packages include transfers, transport, accommodation, food and diving: 5 days/4 nights US$700. *Pulau Sipidan Resort*, 2nd Flr, 188 Jln Bakau, Tawau, T 772689, F 763575, T (Semporna) 781336, T (Sipidin) 881800. Lodging and food M$150 first day, for more than 3 days M$130/day, over 1 week M$120/day. M$75/day for tent. Return boat trip from Semporna and snorkelling equipment (good quality fins and masks) included, diving instructor M$80/dive. The number of visitors is restricted by the facilities: there is a maximum of 22 at any one time at the resort.

Accommodation & restaurants Run by the 2 tour agents on the island. Both provide simple "A" frame and chalet accommodation and full board. The island's drinking water is brought in from Semporna.

Sports Deep sea fishing: for tuna, marlin, barracuda and bonito can be organized from Sipidan. Trawler operated by *Pulau Sipidan Resort* costs M$150/person for the first 2 hours and M$70 for every additional hour. Early mornings and evenings are best. Because the island and the reef are protected, line fishing from the shore is illegal.

Best time to visit Best diving season from mid-Feb to mid-Dec when visibility is greater (20-60m); mostly drift diving; night diving is said to be spectacular.

Transport to & from Sipidan 32 km from Semporna in the Celebes Sea. **By boat:** boats organized by the 2 tour companies from Semporna, included in price of trip. Also boats from Tawau once a week from the main dock (much rougher journey as have to go more on the open sea). **By hired speedboat:** 1½ hrs from Semporna (M$400 return).

Tawau

Tawau is a timber port in Sabah's SE corner. It is surrounded by plantations and smallholdings of rubber, copra, cocoa and palm oil. The local soils are volcanic and very fertile and cocoa is the main crop. Now that the Sandakan area has been almost completely logged, Tawau has taken over as the main logging centre on the E coast. The forest is disappearing fast but there are ongoing reafforestation programmes. At Kalabakan (W of Tawau) there is a large scale reafforestation project with experiments on fast-growing trees such as *Albizzia falcataria*, which is said to grow 30m in 5 years. Tawau is a busy commercial centre and the main channel for the entry of Indonesian workers into Sabah. Kalimantan is visible, just across the bay.

Excursions

Tawau Hill State Park protects Tawau's water catchment area. The Tawau river flows through the middle of the 27,972 ha park and forms a natural deepwater pool, at Table Waterfall, which is good for swimming. There is a trail from there to some hot water springs (3 hrs), and another to the top of Bombalai Hill, an extinct volcano. Most of the forest in the park below 500m has been logged. Only the forest on the central hills and ridges is untouched. The park is a popular away-day destination for locals at weekends. **Accommodation**: it is possible to camp – bring your own equipment. **Getting there**: access to the park is via a maze of rough roads through the Borneo Abaca Limited agricultural estates. Minibuses from Tawau.

Accommodation Hotels in Tawau are not great value for money. The cheaper lodging houses, around Jln Stephen Tan, Jln Chester and Jln Cole Adams should be avoided. **A** *Emas*, Jln Utara, T 773300, F 763569, a/c, restaurant; **A** *Marco Polo*, Jln Abaca/Jln Clinic, T 777988, F 763739, a/c, restaurant, best hotel in Tawau; **B** *Merdeka*, Jln Masjid, T 776655, F 761743, a/c, restaurant; **B** *Royal*, 177 Jln Bilian, T 773100/772856, a/c, restaurant; **C** *Tawau*, 72-3 Jln Chester, T 771100, value for money, cheaper rooms without attached bathroom.

Restaurants Malay: **♦♦**Asnur, 325B, Block 41 Fajar Complex, Thai and Malay, large choice; **♦♦**Venice Coffee House, Marco Polo Hotel, Jln Abaca/Jln Clinic, 'hawker centre' for late night eating, Malay & Chinese. **Chinese:** **♦♦**Dragon Court, 1st Flr, Lot 15, Block 37 Jln Haji Karim,

Chinese, popular with locals, lots of seafood. **Seafood:** *May Garden*, 1 km outside town on road to Semporna, outside seating; *Maxims*, Block 30, Lot 6 Jln Haji Karim. **International:** **Dreamland*, 541 Jln Haji Karim, also good local selection; **The Hut*, Block 29, Lot 5 Fajar Complex, Town Extension II, Western, Malay and Chinese, large menu; *Kublai*, Marco Polo Hotel, Jln Abaca/Jln Clinic. **Foodstalls:** stalls along the seafront.

Entertainment Cinema is on Jln Stephen Tan, next to central market.

Shopping General and fish market at the W end of Jln Dunlop, near the Custom's Wharf.

Embassies & consulates Indonesian Consulate, Jln Kuharsa.

Banks & money changers Standard Chartered, 518 Jln Habib Husein (behind Hongkong Bank); Hong Kong, 210 Jln Utara, opposite the padang; Bumiputra, Jln Nusantor, on seafront.

Useful addresses Post Office: off Jln Nusantor, behind the fish market. Immigration: Jln Stephen Tan. Area code: 089.

Airline offices MAS, Lot 1A, Wisma SASCO, Fajar Complex, Extension 211, T 772659; **Merdeka Travel**, 41 Jln Dunlop, T 772534/1, booking agents for Bouraq (Indonesian airline); Sabah Air, Tawau Airport, T 774005.

Travel agents *GSU*, T 772531. Booking agent for Kalimantan.

Transport to & from Tawau 110 km from Semporna. **By air:** the airport is 2 km from town centre. Regular connections with KK (M$96), Lahad Datu (M$48), Sandakan twice a week (M$73). **By bus:** station on Jln Wing Lock (W end of town). Minibus station on Jln Dunlop (centre of town). **By four-wheel-drive:** it is possible to drive from Sapulut (S of Keningau, see page 314) across the interior to Tawau on logging roads but a 4WD vehicle is required.

International connections with Indonesia The Indonesian town of Tarakan is not a visa-free entry point; it is necessary to obtain a one-month visa in advance (takes one day and costs M$15). There is an Indonesian consulate in Tawau and in KK. **By air:** it is possible to fly to Tarakan from Tawau: Indonesian Bouraq and MAS flights every Mon, 35 mins (M$180). **By boat:** boats leave Tawau's Customs Wharf for Tarakan (via Pulau Nunukan Timur) on Mon, Wed & Sat. Tickets for Tarakan (**see page 847**) can be purchased from Perkhidmatan Perjalanan Merdeka Sdn Bhd, 41 Dunlop St, Tawau. Boats run by Samidrah Indah company, T 776972: connections with Tarakan (M$50), Naunukan (M$30). Boats tend to run irregularly, check with shipping company in advance.

INFORMATION FOR VISITORS

DOCUMENTS

Visas

No visa is required for Commonwealth citizens (except Indians), British protected persons or citizens of the Republic of Ireland, Switzerland, the Netherlands, San Marino and Liechtenstein. Citizens of the USA, Germany, France, Italy, Norway, Sweden, Denmark, Belgium, Finland, Luxembourg and Iceland may stay for 3 months without a visa if they are not working. On arrival visitors normally receive a one-month visitor's permit (Commonwealth citizens get 2 months). If you intend to stay longer, permits can be extended to three months at immigration departments in Kuala Lumpur, Penang or Johor Bahru.

Citizens of ASEAN countries do not need visas for visits not exceeding a month – they are issued on arrival. Nationals of most other countries may stop over in Malaysia for up to 14 days without advance visas but it is preferable to have proof of outward bookings. The exception to this rule are citizens of Eastern European countries, the Commonwealth of Independent States, Cambodia, Laos and Vietnam. Applications for visas should be made well in advance to the nearest Malaysian diplomatic mission, or, in countries where there are no Malaysian representatives, to the British Consular Representative.

Visit passes issued for entry into Peninsular Malaysia are not automatically valid for entry into Sabah and Sarawak; visitors have to go through immigration even though the flight is an internal one. The East Malaysian states will issue their own permit – usually of one month – on entry; apply to the immigration offices in Kota Kinabalu and Kuching for an extension. There are certain areas where permits are necessary in East Malaysia, eg for upriver trips in Sarawak permits are obtained from the residents' offices (see appropriate sections). All national parks in Peninsular and East Malaysia require permits from the national or state parks offices.

Vaccinations

A certificate of vaccination for Yellow Fever is necessary for those coming from endemic zones.

Representation overseas

Australia, High Commission, 7 Perth Avenue, Yarralumla, Canberra, A.C.T. 2600, T (602) 731-543; **Austria**, Prinz Eugenstrasse 18, A-1040 Vienna, T 65-11-42; **Bangladesh**, High Commission, No. 4 Road No. 118, Gulshan Model Town, Dacca-12, T 600-291; **Brunei**, High Commission, Lot 12-15, 6th Flr Darussalam Complex, P.O. Box 2826, Bandar Seri Begawan, T 28410; **Belgium**, 414A, Avenue de Tervueran, 1150 Brussels, T 762-67-67; **Burma**, 82 Diplomatic Quarters, Pyidaundsu Yeikhta Road, Rangoon, T 20248; **Canada**, High Commission, 60 Boteler Street, Ottawa, Ontario KIN 8Y7, T (613) 237-5182; **China**, 13, Dong Zhi Menwai Dajie, San Li Tun, Beijing, T 522-531; **CIS**, Mosfilmovskaya Ulitsa 50, Moscow, T 147-1514; **France**, 2, Bis Rue Benouville, Paris, T 4553-1185; **Germany**, Mittelstr 43, 5300 Bonn 2, T (0228) 37-68-03-06; **Hong Kong**, 24th Flr, Malaysia Building, 50 Gloucester Road, Wanchai, Hong Kong, T 5-270921; **India**, High Commission, 50M Satya Marg, Chanakyapuri, New Delhi 110021, T 601291; No. 287, T.T.K. Road, Madras-600 018, T 453580; **Indonesia**, 17, Jalan Imam Bonjol, 10310 Jakarta Pusat, T 336438. Consulate: Medan T 25315; **Italy**, Via Nomentana 297, Rome T 06 855764; **Japan**, 20-16 Nampeidai Machi, Shibuya-ku, Tokyo, T (03) 770-9331; **Laos**, Route That Luang, Quartier Nong Bone, P.O. Box 789, Vientiane, T 2662; **Netherlands**, Rustenburgweg 2, 2517

KE The Hague, T 070-506506; **New Zealand**, High Commission, 10 Washington Avenue, Brooklyn, Wellington, T 852439; **Pakistan**, No. 224, Nazimuddin Road, F-7/4, Islamabad, T 820147; **Singapore**, 301, Jervois Road, Singapore 1024, T 2350111; **Spain**, Paseo de La Castellana 91-50, Centro 23, 28046 Madrid, T (91) 455.0684; **Sri Lanka**, High Commission, 87 Horton Place, Colombo 7, T 94837; **Sweden**, P.O. Box 260 53, 10041 Stockholm, T (08) 14 59 90; **Switzerland**, Laupenstrasse 37, 3008 Berne, T (031) 25 21 05; **Switzerland**, 43, Rue de Lausanne, 1201, Geneva, T (022) 32-83-40; **Thailand**, 35 South Sathorn Road, Bangkok 10500, T 286-1390; Consulate: Songkhla, T 331062; **UK**, High Commission, 45, Belgrave Square, London SW1X 8QT, T 071-235 8033; **USA**, 140 East 45th Street, 43rd Flr, New York, NY 10017, T (212) 371-6927; **USA**, 240, Massachusetts Avenue N.W., Washington, D.C. 20008, T (202) 328-2700. Consulate: Los Angeles T (212) 621-2991; **Vietnam**, Block A-3, Van Phuc, Hanoi, T 53371.

Specialist tour companies

In the UK: *High Places*, Globe Works, Penistone Rd, Sheffield S6 3AE, UK, T (0742) 822333, F (0742) 820016. Manager Simon Galpine specialises in pre-arranging tours to the Sandakan area. *Magic of the Orient*, 2 Kingsland Court, Crawley, Sussex RH10 1HL, UK, T (0293) 537700 can arrange visits to Malay kampungs through *Village Homestay*, a cultural exchange service.

TRANSPORT TO AND FROM MALAYSIA

By air

The main airport for Malaysia is Kuala Lumpur's Subang International Airport. (The construction of a new international airport has recently begun at Sepang, between KL and Seremban. It is scheduled for completion in 1997.) Some international flights also go direct to Penang, Kota Kinabalu and Kuching. Smaller airlines also run services between Singapore and island resorts such as Langkawi and Tioman. More than 25 international carriers serve Kuala Lumpur.

Non-Malaysian passport holders are eligible for the Discover Malaysia Pass, if they fly into the country on Malaysian Airlines (MAS). It offers huge savings on domestic air travel. The pass is valid for any 5 sectors within the peninsula, within Sabah or within Sarawak; the pass costs US$115. It must be purchased within 14 days of arrival and evidence of incoming international sector MAS ticket must be presented on purchase. In addition, pass holders receive an automatic 40% discount on all published fares between the peninsula and Sabah and Sarawak (including cheaper night flights) and for the sector between Sabah and Sarawak.

Singapore Airlines (SIA) and Malaysia Airlines (MAS) run regular joint shuttle services between KL and Singapore with planes nearly every hour (more during peak hours); Singapore-KL (S$135), KL-Singapore (M$135). **NB**: flights between Singapore and Malaysia cost the same dollar figure whether bought in Malaysia or Singapore; it saves money buying a return ticket in Malaysia. There are flights from KL to most Asian destinations.

From Europe Approx time from London to Kuala Lumpur (non-stop): 14 hrs. From **London** Heathrow British Airways have 3 flights a week and Malaysia Airlines fly out weekly. From **Amsterdam** Malaysia Airlines have 2 flights a week and KLM 1. From **Frankfurt** Malaysia Airlines depart 3 times a week and Lufthansa twice. You can fly from **Zurich** with Malaysia Airlines twice a week. From **Paris** Malaysia Airlines have 2 flights a week and UTA 1. From other cities a change of plane is often necessary en route.

Selected air fares

KL to:	M$		M$
Johor Bahru	92	Limbang	163
Ipoh	66	Lawas	234
Penang	96	Johor Bahru	169
Langkawi	134	Kota Kinabalu	237
Alor Setar	161	BSB, Brunei	192
Pulau Tioman	120	Singapore	170
Kuantan	84	KL	266
Kuala Terengganu	103		
Kota Bahru	103	**Kota Kinabalu to:**	
Kota Kinabalu	437	Kudat	60
Kuching	266	Lahad Dahtu	106
		Labuan	52
Kuching to:		Sandakan	83
Bintulu	116	Tawau	96
Miri	166	Bintulu	132
Sibu	72	Singapore	492
		BSB, Brunei	65

From the USA and Canada Approx time from LAX (Los Angeles): 22 hrs. Malaysia Airlines has flights leaving 6 times a week from LA. Go via Los Angeles from New York, San Francisco and Canada.

From Australasia You can fly direct from Sydney, Melbourne and Perth (flight times range between 3 and 5 hrs). Malaysia Airlines flights leave from Sydney and Melbourne 4 times a week and from Perth 3. Flights with Qantas from Sydney leave 3 times a week and British Airways depart from Perth once a week. From Auckland Malaysia Airlines flights depart twice a week and Air New Zealand once (approx 5 hrs).

From South Asia Malaysia Airlines and Air India fly from Delhi 3 times a week. From Colombo both Air Lanka and Malaysia Airlines have 2 flights a week and UTA 1. You can fly from Dhaka with Biman Bangladesh Airlines once a week. PIA and Malaysia Airlines fly twice a week from Karachi. Flights via other cities available from Male and Kathmandu.

From the Far East Malaysia Airlines and Japan Airlines have daily flights from Tokyo. From Hong Kong Malaysia Airlines, Cathay Pacific and Air China fly daily. From Manila Malaysia Airlines fly daily and Philippine Airlines twice a week.

From the Middle East You can fly from Bahrain with UTA once a week.

Airport information
Subang International Airport is 24 km south-west of Kuala Lumpur. There are banks in the departure and arrivals halls, a good selection of duty-free shops, a tourist information desk, hotel reservation service and car hire offices as well as an international telecoms office. Subang airport enquiries/flight confirmation: T7461235. For details of other international airports (Penang, Kota Kinabalu and Kuching), see relevant sections.

Airport tax
Airport departure tax is M$3 for domestic flights, M$5 for Singapore and Brunei and M$15 for all other countries.

Transport to town
By taxi: the price is fixed for taxi rides into KL and it is necessary to buy a coupon at the taxi booth in the airport (M$15-18). The coupon system was introduced to prevent tourists being overcharged. The drive into KL takes about 45 mins. **By**

bus: buses 47 and 343 connect the airport and central KL, (M$1.50). **Car hire**: major car hire firms have desks in the terminal. **Hotel pick-up service**: hotel transport must be arranged in advance or at the office just outside the terminal exit.

By train

Keretapi Tanah Melayu (KTM) runs 5 express trains daily between Singapore and the major cities on the west coast of Malaysia. There is a daily express train between Bangkok and Butterworth (M$38.70), which connects with Kuala Lumpur (M$28); KL-Singapore (M$28.30). Bangkok to Singapore via Malaysia (M$80.30). Another railway line runs from Gemas (half way between KL and Johor Bahru) to Kota Bahru, on the north-east coast.

From late 1992, *Orient-Express Hotels*, which operates the Venice Simplon Orient-Express, will run a luxury Eastern & Oriental Express train between Singapore, KL and Bangkok. The 2,000 km trip will take 41 hours (2 nights, one day) and fares will start from US$950 for the full trip. It will be possible to embark/disembark at KL or Butterworth (for Penang). Reservations can be made at *Orient-Express Hotels*, Sea Containers House, 20 Upper Ground, London SE1 9PF, UK T(071)9286000; Orient-Express Hotels also has agents in Kuala Lumpur, Singapore and Bangkok to handle reservations (contact through Tourism Malaysia).

Transport to town Taxis from KL's magnificent Moorish railway station also run on a fixed-price coupon system; coupons must be bought in advance from the booth next to the taxi rank.

By road

It is possible to travel to/from Malaysia by bus or collective taxi from Thailand and Singapore. Direct buses/taxis are much easier than the local alternatives which stop at the borders. Singapore is 6 hrs by taxi from KL (via Johor Bahru) and about 7 hrs by bus (**see page 114**). Taxi fares are approximately double bus fares.

There are direct buses and taxis to destinations in Thailand from most major towns in northern Malaysia (see relevant sections). The main routes are Penang/Butterworth to south Thailand via Grik and Keroh to Betong (**see page 220**) and from Kota Bahru to Rantau Panjang/Sungei Golok (**see page 213**). Local buses and taxis terminate at the border crossing points, but there are regular connections to towns and cities from each side.

By sea

Most passenger ships/cruise liners run between Port Klang, west of Kuala Lumpur, Georgetown (Penang), Singapore, Kuantan, Kuching and Kota Kinabalu. Feri Malaysia connects these Malaysian ports and Singapore. Economy fares: Port Klang-Singapore (M$99), Kuantan-Singapore (M$99), Kota Kinabalu-Singapore (M$310), Kuching-Singapore (M$200). Deluxe cabins are also available. Schedules change annually; contact Tourism Malaysia for bookings. There are also regular ferry services from Melaka to Dumai, Sumatra and Georgetown (Penang) to Medan, Sumatra (see relevant sections). Passenger boats connect Langkawi Island with Satun in South Thailand (**see page 146**). High-speed catamarans connect Singapore's Finger Pier with Pulau Tioman (off the East Coast of Peninsular Malaysia), $4\frac{1}{2}$ hrs (S$120 return). Small boats also run between Johor state and Singapore's Changi Point (**see page 415**).

Customs

Duty free allowance 200 cigarettes, 50 cigars or 250g of tobacco and 1 litre of liquor or wine. Cameras, watches, pens, lighters, cosmetics, perfumes, portable radio/cassette players are also duty-free in Malaysia. Visitors bringing in dutiable goods such as video equipment may have to pay a refundable deposit for temporary importation. It is advisable to carry receipt of purchases to avoid this problem.

Currency Visitors are allowed to import M$10,000 and export M$5,000. There is no limit imposed on other currencies or travellers' cheques.

Prohibited items *The trafficking of illegal drugs into Malaysia carries the death penalty* (see page 83).

Export restrictions Export permits are required for arms, ammunition, explosives, animals and plants, gold, platinum, precious stones and jewellery (except reasonable personal effects), poisons, drugs, motor vehicles. Unlike Singapore, export permits are also required for antiques (from the Director General of Museums, Muzium Negara, Kuala Lumpur).

INTERNAL TRAVEL

Transport around the East Malaysian states of Sabah and Sarawak is not as easy as it is on the peninsula – there are fewer roads and they are not in a good state of repair. There are excellent coastal and upriver express boat services in Sarawak and the national airline, MAS has an extensive network in both states; flying is relatively inexpensive.

Air

Malaysia Airlines (MAS) operates an extensive network to domestic destinations: Kuala Lumpur, Ipoh, Penang, Alor Setar, Langkawi, Kota Bahru, Kuala Terengganu, Kuantan, Johor Bahru, Singapore, Kota Kinabalu, Sandakan, Lahad Datu, Labuan, Kuching, Sibu, Bintulu and Miri (plus many more internal flights in Sabah and Sarawak). Local MAS offices are listed under each town; the head office is at Bangunan MAS (opposite Equatorial Hotel), Jalan Sultan Ismail, 50250, Kuala Lumpur.

Pelangi Air, a solely domestic airline, operates services to certain resorts and smaller towns from Kuala Lumpur, Ipoh and Penang: Sitiawan, Alor Setar, Langkawi, Melaka, Taman Negara, Tioman Island, Kuantan, Kerteh and Kuala Terengganu. See appropriate sections for fares (prices quoted are single fares). There are reductions for night flights, group and advance bookings. **NB**: flights get very booked up on public holidays.

Train

Malaysian Railways or Keretapi Tanah Melayu (KTM) is an economical and comfortable way to travel round the peninsula. There are two main lines. One runs up the west coast from Singapore, through KL, Ipoh and Butterworth, connecting with Thai railways at Padang Besar (where one half of the extra-long platform is managed by Malaysian officials and the other half by Thais). The Sumpitan Emas (Golden Blowpipe) 'express' runs on the other line, which branches off from the west coast line at Gemas (half way between KL and Singapore) and heads north-east to Kota Bahru. From Kota Bahru it is possible to take buses/taxis to Rantau Panjang/Sungei Golok for connections with Thai railways. The express service (Ekspres Rakyat or Ekspres Sinaran) only stops at major towns; the regular service stops at every station but is slightly cheaper. All 1st class and 2nd class coaches have sleeping berths on overnight trains and 1st class is air-conditioned. Reservations can be made for both classes. Fares quoted are for a/c, 2nd class. Visitors should note that the air-conditioning on Malaysian trains is very cold. 1st and 2nd class carriages are equipped with videos. In East Malaysia there is only one railway line, running from Kota Kinabalu to Tenom, via Beaufort (see page 310).

10-day and 30-day **rail passes** are available for every class and there are no restrictions (other than availability of seats). Passes are available from railway stations in Singapore, KL, Johor Bahru, Butterworth, Padang Besar, Rantau Panjang, Wakaf Bahru (Kota Bahru).

Bus

Peninsular Malaysia has an excellent bus system with a network of public express buses and several privately run services. A/c express buses connect the major towns, seats can be reserved and prices are reasonable. Prices quoted are for a/c buses (see relevant sections). (The air-conditioning on Malaysian buses is, like the trains, very cold.) There are also cheaper non-a/c buses that ply between the states and provide an intra-state service. Prices vary according to whether the bus is a/c or non a/c, express or regular and between companies. The largest bus company is MARA, the government service. In larger towns there may be a number of bus stops; some private companies may also operate directly from their own offices. Travelling up the east coast of the peninsular is often quicker as the roads are less congested; west coast travel is very slow but will be improved with the completion of the north-south highway.

Buses in East Malaysia are more unreliable because of the road conditions; in Sarawak, the Sibu-Bintulu and Bintulu-Miri roads are rough and often impassable in the wet season, as is the road connecting Kota Kinabalu and Sandakan in Sabah.

Boat

Local water transport comes into its own in Sarawak, where lack of roads makes coastal and river transport the only viable means of communication. On the larger rivers in Sarawak – such as the Rajang and the Baram – there are specially adapted express boats (**see page 265**). If there is no regular boat, it is nearly always possible to charter a local longboat, although this can be expensive. In the dry season the upper reaches of many rivers are unnavigable (except by smaller boats). In times of heavy rain, logs and branch debris can make rivers unsafe. Some river transport still operates on rivers on the peninsula's east coast.

Feri Malaysia runs 2 routes, both on a weekly schedule. 1) Port Klang – Singapore – Kuching – Kota Kinabalu – Singapore – Kuantan – Port Klang. 2) Kuantan – Kota Kinabalu – Kuching – Singapore – Port Klang. **Tourism Malaysia** offices have information on Feri Malaysia and can place bookings. (For price guidelines, **see page 199**.)

There are regular scheduled ferry services between the main islands – Pulau Pangkor, Penang and Pulau Langkawi – and the mainland. There are services from Mersing and Singapore to Pulau Tioman. There are passenger/car ferries between Butterworth and Georgetown (Penang) every 20 mins. For other offshore islands, mostly off the east coast, fishing boats (and sometimes regular boats) leave from the nearest fishing port.

Car and motorbike hire

Car hire companies are listed in individual towns under **Local Transport**. Visitors can hire a car provided they are in possession of an international driving licence, are over 23 and not older than 65. Car hire costs from M$99 to M$250/day (approximately) depending on the model. Cheaper weekly/monthly rates and special deals are available. Driving is on the left and within towns the speed limit is 50km/hr; seat belts are compulsory. Most road signs are international but *awas* means "caution". Road maps are on sale at most petrol stations; Petronas (the national oil company) produces an excellent atlas: *Touring Malaysia by Road*. During the monsoon season, heavy rains may make some east coast travel difficult and the west coast roads can be congested. In Sarawak the road network is extremely limited: air or water transport are the only option in many areas. In Sabah, four-wheel-drive vehicles are *de rigeur*; they are readily available, but expensive. On some islands, such as Penang, Langkawi and Pankgor, motorbikes are available for hire, for around M$20-25/day.

Other local transport

Taxi There are two types of taxi in Malaysia – local and 'out-station' – or long distance. The latter – usually Mercedes or Peugeot – connect all major towns and cities. They operate on a shared-cost basis – as soon as the full complement of 5 passengers turns up the taxis set off. Alternatively, it is possible to charter the whole taxi. Taxi stands are usually next-door to major bus stations. If shared, taxi fares usually cost about twice as much as bus fares, but they are much faster.

Local taxi fares in Malaysia are among the cheapest in Southeast Asia. Most local taxis in major towns are now metered and air-conditioned. The starting fare is M$1 and is M$0.50 for every additional kilometre; a/c costs an additional 20%. If there is no meter – or, as is more often the case, the meter is broken – fares should be negotiated in advance.

Hitch-hiking It is easy to hitch-hike in Malaysia; it is not advisable for single women to hitch-hike alone.

Trishaws In Kuala Lumpur it has long been too dangerous for trishaws, apart from around Chinatown and suburban areas. In towns such as Melaka, Georgetown and Kota Bahru, as well as in many other smaller towns, they remain one of the best – and certainly most pleasant – ways of getting around, particularly for sightseeing. It is necessary to negotiate fares in advance: approximately M$1/km.

ACCOMMODATION, FOOD AND DRINK

Accommodation

Malaysia offers a good selection of international class hotels as well as simpler hotels, rest houses and hostels. Many of the major international chains have hotels in Malaysia, such as Hilton, Regent, Holiday Inn and Hyatt plus local and regional chains such as Merlin, Ming Court and Shangri-La; most of these are on the west coast. Room rates in the big hotels – particularly in Kuala Lumpur – have risen steeply in recent years, however it is still possible to find bargains and by world standards, even the most expensive hotels are good value for money. It is also possible to rent condominiums in some cities – mainly KL and Georgetown.

There are Youth Hostels in KL, Georgetown (Penang), Port Dickson, Fraser's Hill, Cameron Highlands, Kuantan, Kota Bahru, Kota Kinabalu and Pulau Pangkor. There are also scores of government rest houses (*rumah rehat*) around the country; these often offer well-maintained, reasonably priced rooms, although they can become heavily booked, particularly during public holidays. On the east coast of Peninsular Malaysia, it is often possible to stay with families in Malay *kampungs* (villages). The most popular place to do this is at Kampung Cerating, north of Kuantan, although it has become increasingly touristy in recent years; it is also possible to stay in a kampung house in Merang. Along many of Malaysia's beaches and on islands, there are simple atap-roofed 'A'-frame bungalows. Room rates are subject to a 5% government tax and 10% service charge.

Accommodation in East Malaysia does not offer such value for money as hotels on the peninsula, although, again, there are some bargains. As on the peninsula, there are government rest houses in many of the main towns. For accommodation in National Parks, see relevant sections: it is necessary to book in advance. In Sarawak it is possible to stay in longhouses, where rates are at the discretion of the visitor (see page 260).

L : M$500+ **Luxury**: hotels in this bracket are few and far between. Kuala Lumpur's splendid *Carcosa Seri Negara* is one such hotel, most **A+** grade hotels have luxury presidential suites.

A+: M$250-500 **International class**: impeccable service, beautifully appointed offering a wide array of facilities and business services. Malaysia's **A+** grade hotels – most of which are grouped towards the bottom end of the price category – are regarded as among the best value in the region.

A: M$100-250 **First class**: good range of services and facilities. Very competitively priced, given the standards of service.

B: M$50-100 **Tourist class**: hotels in this category will have swimming pools; most provide just a basic range of services and facilities although all will have a/c.

C : M$30-50 **Economy**: while there are some excellent economy hotels in this category, few provide much in the way of services. Guests will usually have the option of a/c or fan-cooled rooms and a choice of attached/shared bathrooms. Government rest-houses (*rumah rehat*) offer the best value for money in this grade.

D: M$15-30 **Budget**: most hotels in the budget class are Chinese-run and located in town centres (they are therefore often noisy). At the upper end, rooms have a/c and attached bathrooms; cheaper rooms have fans and communal bathrooms (with *mandi*). Some fine old tumbledown colonial relics in this range offer good value for money. Youth hostels also fall into this price-range.

E: M$10-15 **Lodging house/guesthouse/hostel**: rooms are rarely a/c; shared *mandi* with squat toilet; few facilities. Lodging houses (*rumah tumpangan*) sometimes double as brothels. Tourist-oriented guesthouses usually offer better value and a better atmosphere; there are a few exceptionally good places in this category.

F: under M$10 there is little accommodation in this price bracket in Malaysia, although many guesthouses and hostels in the D and E categories provide the option of bottom-dollar, cramped dormitory accommodation. In some beach resort areas it is sometimes possible to find simple 'A'-frame accommodation in this range.

Food

Malaysians, like neighbouring Singaporeans, love their food, and the dishes of the 3 main communities – Malay, Chinese and Indian – comprise a hugely varied national menu. Even within each ethnic cuisine, there is a vast choice – every state has its own special Malay dishes and the different Chinese provincial specialities are well represented; in addition there is north Indian food, south Indian food and Indian Muslim food. Nonya cuisine is found in the old Straits Settlements of Penang and Melaka. Malaysia also has great seafood – which the Chinese do best – and in recent years a profusion of restaurants, representing other Asian and European cuisines, have set up, mainly in the big cities. In the East Malaysian states of Sabah and Sarawak, there are tribal specialities.

Restaurants range from smart hotel restaurants in the major towns to Chinese coffee shops (*kedi kopi*). **NB**: restaurants charge 15% service and tax on top of menu prices. As in Singapore, good food is not confined to restaurants – some of the best local dishes can be sampled at hawker centres, which are cheap and often stay open late into the night. There are few towns in Malaysia without at least a handful of stalls. In Malaysia, Chinese, Malay and Nonya cuisines use liberal quantities of *belacan* – a hot, fermented prawn paste – which generally tastes a lot better than it smells.

Prices:

◆◆◆◆	M$37.50+ (hotel restaurants and exclusive restaurants)
◆◆◆	M$12.50-37.50 (restaurants in tourist class hotels and more expensive local restaurants)
◆◆	M$5-12.50 (coffee shops and basic restaurants)
◆	under M$5 (hawker stalls)

Malay The Malay staple diet is rice and curry which is usually rich and creamy due to the use of coconut milk; it also uses many herbs and spices including chillis, ginger, turmeric, coriander, lemon grass, anise, cloves, cumin, caraway and cinnamon. One of the best ways to sample a Malay curry – which is traditionally served with lots of fresh vegetables and fruit – is *nasi campur*. This is a curry buffet with meat, fish and vegetable curries; *rendang* – a thick, coconut curry dish – is usually available at *campur* stalls. *Sambal*, a spicy paste of pounded chilli, onions and tamarind, is often served with dishes. *Satay* is Malaysia's ubiquitous national dish (although its origins are Middle Eastern) – you never have to walk far to find a satay stall. It is made with marinated cubes of chicken, mutton or beef which are skewered with bamboo and barbecued over a charcoal brazier. Satay sticks are served with a spicy peanut sauce and are usually accompanied with *ketupat* – cold, pressed rice dumplings wrapped in coconut leaves. Because all Malays are Muslim, pork is never used and Malay stalls and restaurants rarely serve alcohol.

A common – and invigorating – breakfast dish is *nasi lemak*: rice cooked in coconut milk and served with prawn sambal, *ikan bilis* (dried anchovies), a hard boiled egg, peanuts and cucumber. Dried fish is a Malay speciality and is even eaten where fresh fish is available. Other popular dishes include *soto ayam* (spicy chicken served with rice cubes and vegetables), *mee jawa* (noodles in a thick gravy served with prawns, potato slices and tofu, or beancurd), *mee rebus* (noodles with beef, chicken or prawn with soybean in spicy sauce), *longong* (vegetable curry made from rice cakes cooked in coconut, beans, cabbage and bamboo shoots), *udang belacon* (prawn paste cooked with spices) and the ubiquitous *nasi goreng* (rice, meat and vegetables fried with garlic, onions and sambal). *Rojak* is the Malaysian answer to Indonesia's *gado-gado* (mixed vegetable salad served in peanut sauce with ketupat), and is the closest thing to mixed salad. The best Malay food is usually found at stalls in hawker centres.

Nonya The Nonyas are the descendants of the earliest Chinese migrants, mainly Hokkien from south China, who first settled in Melaka, although communities also grew up in Penang and Singapore. Through inter-marriage with local Malays a unique culture evolved (**see page 168**), and with it, a cuisine that has grown out of a blend of the two races. Nonya food is spicier than Chinese food, and unlike Malay food, it uses pork. Nonya dishes in Penang have adopted flavours from neighbouring Thailand, whereas Melaka's Nonya food has Indonesian overtones. Typical dishes include chicken *kapitan* (chicken cooked in coconut milk) and *otak otak* (minced fish, coconut milk and spices, steamed in a banana leaf). *Laska* (rice noodles in spicy coconut-milk and prawn-flavoured gravy blended with spices and served with shellfish, chicken, beancurd and belacan) is a Nonya favourite and *assam laksa* is the specialized Penang version (rice noodles served in fish gravy with shredded cucumber, pineapple, raw onions and mint). In traditional Straits Chinese households, great emphasis was placed on presentation and the fine-chopping of ingredients.

Chinese Cantonese and Hainanese cooking are the most prevalent Chinese cuisines in Malaysia (for details on these and other Chinese cuisines found in Malaysia and Singapore, **see page 444**). Some of the more common Malaysian-Chinese dishes are Hainanese chicken rice (rice cooked in chicken stock and served with steamed or roast chicken), *char kway teow* (Teochew-style fried noodles, with eggs, cockles and chilli paste), *or luak* (Hokkien oyster omelette), *dim sum* (steamed dumplings and patties) and *yong tow foo* (beancurd and vegetables stuffed with fish). Good Chinese food is available in restaurants, coffee shops and from hawker stalls.

Indian Indian cooking can be divided into 3 schools: northern and southern (neither eat beef) and Muslim (no pork). Northern dishes tend to be more subtly spiced, use more meat and are served with breads. Southern dishes use fiery spices, emphasize vegetables and are served with rice. The best-known North Indian food are the *tandoori* dishes, which are served with delicious fresh *naan* breads, baked in ovens on-site. The best known South Indian dish is banana-leaf rice, served with hot vegetable curries (and sometimes meat curries) as well as *poppadom* and curd. Malaysia's famous *mamak*-men are Indian Muslims who are highly skilled in everything from *teh tarik* (see below) to rotis. *Nasi kandar* is the Mamaks' version of the Malay's *nasi campur* (curry buffet); other dishes include *roti canai* (pancakes served with lentils and curry), *murtabak* (a thick roti-pizza with minced meat, onion and egg) and *nasi biriyani* (rice cooked in ghee with spices and vegetable and served with beef or chicken).

Sabahan The Kadazans form the largest ethnic group in Sabah. Popular dishes here include *hinava* (marinated raw fish), *sup manuk on hiing* (chicken soup with rice wine) and *hinompula* (a dessert made from tapioca, sugar, coconut and the juice from screwpine leaves). *Tapai* chicken – which is cooked in local rice wine – is a popular dish as are *pakis* ferns, which are fried with mushrooms and belacan. Sometimes ferns are eaten raw, with a squeeze of lime.

Sarawakian *Ternbok* fish, either grilled or steamed, and *pan suh manok* (chicken pieces cooked in bamboo cup) and served with *bario* (Kelabit mountain rice) are dishes peculiar to Sarawak.

Drink

As in Singapore there is a wide variety of fresh fruit juices available as well as fizzy soft drinks, mineral water and Anchor and Tiger beer (M$6-10/bottle in coffee shops). Malaysian-brewed Guinness is also popular, mainly because Chinese believe it has medicinal qualities as it has been successfully sold on the "Guinness Stout is good for you" line. Malaysian tea is grown in the Cameron Highlands and is very good. One of the most interesting cultural refinements of the Indian Muslim community is the Mamak-man, who is famed for *teh tarik* (pulled tea), which is thrown across a distance of about a metre, from one cup to another, with no spillages. The idea is to cool it down for customers, but it has become an art form; mamak-men appear to cultivate the nonchalant look when pouring. Malaysian satirist Kit Leee says a tea-stall mamak "could 'pull' tea in free fall without spilling a drop – while balancing a *beedi* on his lower lip and making a statement on Economic Determinism". Most of the coffee comes from Indonesia, although some is locally produced. Malaysians like their coffee strong and unless you specify *kurang manis* (less sugar), *tak mahu manis* (don't want sugar) or *kopi kosong* (empty coffee – black, no sugar), it will come with lashings of sweet condensed milk.

PUBLIC HOLIDAYS AND NATIONAL FESTIVALS

Tourism Malaysia has dates of moveable holidays and festivals.

Jan: *New Year's Day* (1st: public holiday except Johor, Kedah, Kelantan, Perlis and Terengganu). *Thaipusam* (moveable: public holiday Negeri Sembilan, Perak, Penang and Selangor only) celebrated by many Hindus throughout Malaysia in honour of the Hindu deity Lord Subramanian (also known as Lord Muruga); he represents virtue, bravery, youth and power. Held during full moon in the month of Thai, it is a day of penance and thanksgiving. Devotees pay homage to Lord Subramanian by piercing their bodies, cheeks and tongues with sharp skewers (*vel*) and hooks weighted with oranges and carrying *kevadis* (steel structures bearing the image of Lord Muruga). There are strict rules the devotee must follow in order to purify himself before carrying the kevadi – he becomes a vegetarian and abstains from worldly pleasures. Women cannot carry kevadis as they are not allowed to bare their bodies in order to be pierced. Although a kevadi carrier can have as many as a hundred spears piercing his flesh he only loses a small amount of blood in his trance. Each participant tries to outdo the others in the severity of his torture. At certain temples fire-walking is also part of this ceremony. Many Hindus disapprove of the spectacle and believe that their bodies are a gift from Siva; they should serve as a temple for the soul and should not be abused. This festival is peculiar to Hindus in Malaysia, Singapore and Thailand and is a corruption of a Tamil ceremony from South India. The biggest gatherings are at Batu Caves just outside KL, when thousands of pilgrims from all over the country congregate in a carnival-like atmosphere (**see page 101**); there are also festivals held in Melaka, Penang and Singapore.

Feb: *Chinese New Year* (moveable: public holiday) a 15-day lunar festival celebrated in late Jan/early Feb (for more details, **see page 447**). Chinatown streets are crowded for weeks with shoppers buying traditional oranges which signify luck. Lion, unicorn or dragon dances welcome in the new year and, unlike in Singapore, thousands of fire crackers are let off to ward off evil spirits. *Chap Goh Mei* is the 15th day of the Chinese New Year and brings celebrations to a close; it is marked with a final dinner, another firecracker fest, prayers and offerings. The Chinese believe that in order to find good husbands, girls should throw oranges into the river/sea on this day. In Sarawak the festival is known as *Guan Hsiao Cheih* (Lantern Festival).

Mar: *Awal Ramadan* (moveable: public holiday Johor only) the first day of Ramadan, a month of fasting for all Muslims – and by implication, all Malays. During this month Muslims abstain from all food and drink (as well as smoking) from sunrise to sundown – if they are very strict, Muslims do not even swallow their own saliva during daylight hours. It is strictly adhered to in the conservative Islamic states of Kelantan and Terengganu. Every evening for 30 days before breaking of fast, stalls are set up which sell traditional Malay cakes and delicacies. The only people exempt from fasting are the elderly as well as women who are pregnant or are menstruating. *Easter* (moveable) celebrated in Melaka with candle-lit processions and special services (**see page 172**).

Apr: *Hari Raya Puasa* or *Aidil Fitri* (moveable: public holiday) marks the end of the Muslim fasting month of Ramadan and is a day of prayer and celebration. In order for Hari Raya to be declared, the new moon of *Syawal* has to be sighted; if it is not, fasting continues for another day. It is the most important time of the year for Muslim families to get together; Malays living in towns and cities *balek kampung* (return home to their village), where it is 'open house' for relatives and friends, and special Malay delicacies are served. Hari Raya is also enthusiastically celebrated by Indian Muslims.

May: *Labour Day* (1st: public holiday). *Kurah Aran* (1st) celebrated by the Bidayuh tribe in Sarawak (**see page 241**) after the paddy harvest is over. *Wesak Day* (moveable: public holiday except Labuan) the most important day in the Buddhist calendar, celebrates the Buddha's birth, death and enlightenment. Temples throughout the country are packed with devotees offering incense, joss-sticks and prayers. Lectures on Buddhism and special exhibitions are held. In Melaka there is a procession at night with decorated floats, bands, dancers and acrobatics.

June: *Birthday of His Majesty the King* (6th: public holiday) mainly celebrated in KL with processions. *Dragon Boat Festival* (moveable) honours the suicide of an ancient Chinese poet hero, Qu Yuan. He tried to press for political reform by drowning himself in the Mi Luo River as a protest against corruption. In an attempt to save him fishermen played drums and threw rice dumplings to try and distract vultures. His death is commemorated with dragon boat races and the enthusiastic consumption of rice dumplings; biggest celebrations are in Penang.

July: *Hari Raya Haji* (moveable: public holiday) celebrated by Muslims to mark the 10th day of Zulhijjah, the 12th month of the Islamic calendar when pilgrims celebrate their return from the Haj to Mecca. In the morning, prayers are offered and later, families hold 'open house'. Those who can afford it sacrifice goats or cows to be distributed to the poor. Many Malays have the title Haji in their name, meaning they have made the pilgrimage to Mecca; men who have been on the Haj wear a white skull-hat. The Haj is one of the five keystones of Islam. *Festival of the Hungry Ghosts* (moveable) on the seventh moon in the Chinese lunar calendar, souls in purgatory are believed to return to earth to feast. Food is offered to these wandering spirits. Altars are set up in the streets and candles with faces are burned on them (for more detail **see page 449**). *Maal Hijrah* (moveable: public holiday) marks the first day of the Muslim calendar, marking the Prophet Muhammad's journey from Mecca to Medina on the lunar equivalent of 16 July 622 AD. Religious discussions and lectures commemorate the day.

Aug: *Hari Kebangsaan* or *National Day* (31st: public holiday) commemorates Malaysian independence (*merdeka*) in 1957. Big celebration in KL with processions of floats representing all the states; best places to see it: on the Padang (Merdeka Square) or on TV. In Sarawak Hari Kebangsaan is celebrated in a different

Festivals in East Malaysia

Besides those celebrated throughout the country, Sabah and Sarawak have their own festivals. Exact dates can be procured from the tourist offices in the capitals. *Kadazan Harvest Festival* (moveable: public holiday Sabah and Labuan only) marks the end of the rice harvest in Sabah; celebrated in style with feasting, *tapai* (rice wine) drinking, dancing and general merry-making, particularly by the Kadazan. There are also agricultural shows, buffalo races, cultural performances and traditional games. The traditional *sumazal* dance is one of the highlights of the festivities.

Gawai (moveable: public holiday Sarawak only) this is the major festival of the year for the Iban of Sarawak; longhouses party continuously for a week. The Gawai celebrates the end of the rice harvest and welcomes the new planting season. The main ritual is called *magavau* and nurses the spirit of the grain back to health in advance of the new planting season. Like the Kadazan harvest festival in Sabah, visitors are welcome to join in, but in Sarawak, the harvest festival is much more traditional. On the first day of celebrations everyone dresses up in traditional costumes and sings and dances and drinks *tuak* rice wine until they drop.

Gawai Burung (Sarawak) biggest of all the gawais and honours the war god of the Ibans. *Gawai Kenyalang* is one stage of Gawai Burung and is celebrated only after a tribesman has been instructed to do so after a dream.

Gawai Antu (Sarawak) also known as *Gawai Nyunkup* or *Rugan*. Iban tribute to departed spirits. In simple terms a party to mark the end of mourning for anyone whose relative had died in the previous 6 months.

Gawai Batu (Sarawak) whetstone feast held by Iban farmers sometime in June.

Gawai Mpijog Jaran Rantau (Sarawak) celebrated by the Bidayuh before the cutting of grass in new paddy fields.

Gawai Bineh (Sarawak) Iban festival celebrated after harvest. Welcomes back all the spirits of the paddy from the fields.

Gawai Sawa (moveable) celebrated by the Bidayuh in Sarawak to offer thanksgiving for the last year and to make the next year a plentiful one.

---

divisional capital each year. *Mooncake* or *Lantern Festival* (moveable). This Chinese festival marks the overthrow of the Mongol dynasty in China; celebrated, as the name suggests, with the exchange and eating of mooncakes. According to Chinese legend secret messages of revolt were carried inside these cakes and led to the uprising. In the evening, children light festive lanterns while women pray to the Goddess of the Moon.

Oct: *Festival of the Nine Emperor Gods* or *Kiew Ong Yeah* (moveable) marks the return of the spirits of the 9 emperor gods to earth. The mediums whom they are to possess purify themselves by observing a vegetarian diet. The gods possess the mediums, who go into trance and are then carried on sedan chairs whose seats are comprised of razor-sharp blades or spikes. Devotees visit temples dedicated to the 9 gods. A strip of yellow cotton is often bought from the temple and worn on the right wrist as a sign of devotion. The ceremonies usually culminate with a fire walking ritual. *Birthday of the Prophet Muhammad* (moveable: public holiday) to commemorate Prophet Muhammad's birthday in 571 AD. Processions and Koran recitals in most big towns.

Nov: *Deepvali* (moveable: public holiday except Sabah, Sarawak and Labuan) the Hindu festival of lights commemorates the victory of light over darkness and good over evil: the triumphant return of Rama after his defeat of the evil Ravanna in the Hindu epic, the Ramayana. Every Hindu home is brightly lit and decorated for the occasion.

Dec: *Christmas Day* (25th: public holiday) Christmas in Malaysia is a commercial spectacle these days with fairy lights and decorations and tropical Santa Clauses – although it does not compare with celebrations in Singapore. Mostly celebrated on the west coast and ignored on the more Muslim east coast. Midnight mass is the main Christmas service held in churches throughout Malaysia.

State holidays Only sultans' and governors' birthday celebrations are marked with processions and festivities; state holidays can disrupt travel itineraries – particularly in east coast states where they may run for several days.

Jan: *Sultan of Kedah's birthday* (21st, Kedah).

Feb: *Federal Territory Day* (1st, KL and Labuan); *Hari Hol Sultan Ismail* (2nd, Johor); *Israk and Mikraj* (23rd, Kedah & Negri Sembilan).

Mar: *Sultan of Selangor's birthday* (8th, Selangor); *Installation of Sultan of Terengganu Day* (21st, Terengganu); *Sultan of Kelantan's birthday* (30th & 31st).

Apr: *Sultan of Johor's birthday* (8th, Johor); *Good Friday* (moveable: Sabah & Sarawak); *Sultan of Perak's birthday* (19th); *Sultan of Terengganu's birthday* (29th, Terengganu).

May: *Pahang Hol Day* (7th, Pahang).

Jul: *Governor of Penang's birthday* (16th, Penang); *Yang Di-Pertuan Besar of Negri Sembilan's birthday* (19th, Negri Sembilan); *Kelantan state holiday* (30th & 31st, Kelantan).

Aug: *Governor of Melaka's birthday* (15th, Melaka); *Rajah of Perlis' birthday* (23rd, Perlis).

Sep: *Governor of Sarawak's birthday* (16th, Sarawak); *Governor of Sabah's birthday* (16th, Sabah).

Oct: *Sultan of Pahang's birthday* (24th, Pahang).

OTHER ESSENTIAL INFORMATION

Conduct

Dress Malaysians dress smartly, particularly in cities; tourists in vests, shorts and flip-flops look out of place in modern cosmopolitan KL. Dress codes are important to observe from the point of view of Islamic sensitivities, particularly on the peninsula's East Coast. In some places such as Marang, bikinis are banned and wearing them will cause great offence. Topless bathing is completely taboo in Malaysia; this should be remembered even where tourists have started doing it, such as on Pulau Tioman. Dress modestly out of respect for Muslim tradition.

Malaysia's cross-cultural differences are most apparent on the streets: many Chinese girls think nothing of wearing brief mini-skirts and shorts, while their Malay counterparts are clad from head to toe. The *tudung* (or *telukung*) veil signifies adherence to the puritanical lifestyle of the fervently Islamic *dakwah* movement; during the 1980s, this almost became a fashion among women at universities as well as among blue-collar workers in factories. Some women began to dress in the full black purdah until it was forbidden by the government. Much of this was the result of peer pressure and reflected a revival of strict Islamic values in Malaysia during and after the 1970s.

Religion Remove shoes before entering mosques and Hindu and Buddhist temples; in mosques, women should cover their heads, shoulders and legs and men should wear long trousers.

Eating When picking up and passing food, do not use the left hand in Muslim company. It is worth remembering that Malays do not make pork satay and that Hindus do not make beef curries.

Malaysian manners – as learned from a princess

In modern, cosmopolitan Malaysia, traditional customs and cultural conventions are alive and well and rigorously adhered to. In Malaysia's multi-ethnic melting pot, Malays, Chinese, Indians, Eurasians and expatriates have discovered that cross-cultural etiquette and the art of obliging another's sense of decorum is the essence of racial harmony. The trouble is that for many visitors, commiting a Malaysian-style *faux pas* is one of life's inevitabilities. Or it was, until Datin Noor Aini Syed Amir published her practical handbook to Malaysian customs and etiquette in 1991. As a Malay princess, Datin Noor – Malaysia's Miss Manners – should know. "While the Malays are very generous and forgiving with foreigners who make Malay *faux pas*, those who do not make such blunders will be highly admired and respected," the Datin says.

Her catch-all advice to visitors is to utter "a profuse apology *in advance* to the person you may offend". For those who forget to absolve themselves before they slip up, her social observations cover every conceivable situation *mat sallehs* – the local nickname for foreigners – might find themselves in. When eating with chopsticks, warns Datin Noor, avoid crossing them and never stick them vertically into your ricebowl so they resemble joss sticks. Do not be offended by enthusiastic belches and slurps around the dinner table either: Malaysians live to eat and like to share their appreciation.

Visitors must also learn to distinguish between flabby handshakes and Malay *salams*. "Unlike the Western handshake, which is a rather vigorous up and down movement... the Malay handshake is a simple palm-to-palm touch", she writes. The most important part of the gesture is immediately touching your hand to your heart as a signal of sincerity. And, she adds, "never use your left hand in Malay company!" Datin Noor goes on to warn newcomers not to touch people's heads, when to take their shoes off and to think before they kiss a lady's cheek – in greeting. Dazzling, long-sleeved batik shirts are what you wear to formal dinners and black is taboo for happy occasions. She explains what Tunkus, Tuns, Datuks, Dato's and Datins are and notes that the King's title 'Yang Di-Pertuan Agong' means 'He Who is Made Supreme Lord'.

Malaysian Customs & Etiquette A Practical Handbook by Datin Noor Aini Syed Amir. Times Books International, 1991.

Private homes Remove shoes before entering a private home; it is usual to bring a small gift for the host.

General Everywhere in Southeast Asia, 'losing face' brings shame. You lose face if you lose your temper, and even in a situation like bargaining, using a loud voice or wild gesticulations will be taken to signify anger. By the same token, the person you shout at will also feel loss of face too, particularly if it happens in public. It should also be noted that in Muslim company it is impolite to touch others with the left hand and other objects – even loose change.

Visiting longhouses in Sarawak: see page 260.

Tipping Tipping is unusual in Malaysia as a service of 10% is added automatically to restaurant and hotel bills, plus a 5% government tax.

Shopping

Most big towns now have modern shopping complexes as well as shops and markets. Department stores are fixed-price, but nearly everywhere else it is possible – and necessary – to bargain. In most places, at least 30% can be knocked off the asking price; your first offer should be roughly half the first quote.

The islands of Langkawi (see page 152) and Labuan (see page 317) have duty-free shopping; the range of goods is poor, however. In addition to the duty-free shops, cameras, watches, pens, lighters, cosmetics, perfumes and portable radio/cassette players are all duty-free in Malaysia. Film and camera equipment are still cheaper in Singapore, which offers a wider selection of most products – especially electronics and computer products.

Kuala Lumpur and most of the state capitals have a Chinatown which usually has a few curio shops and nearly always a *pasar malam*. Indian quarters, which are invariably labelled 'Little India', are only found in bigger towns; they are the best places to buy *sarungs*, *longuis*, *dotis* and *saris* (mostly imported from India) as well as other textiles. Malay handicrafts are usually only found in markets or government craft centres.

Handicrafts The Malaysian arts and crafts industry used to enjoy much more royal patronage, but when craftsmen went in search of more lucrative jobs, the industry began to decline. The growth of tourism in recent years has helped to re-invigorate it – particularly in traditional handicraft-producing areas, such as the east coast states of Terengganu and Kelantan. The Malay Arts and Crafts Society has also been instrumental in preventing the decline of the industry. In 1981, Malaysian Handicraft and Souvenir Centres (*Karyaneka* centres), were set up to market Malaysian arts and crafts in KL and some state capitals. Typical Malaysian handicrafts which can be found on the peninsula include woodcarvings, batik, *songket* (cloth woven with gold and silver thread), pewterware, silverware, kites, tops and *wayang kulit* (shadow puppets). For more detail on Malaysian arts and crafts, **see page 80**.

Other than the peninsula's east coast states, Sarawak is the other place where the traditional handicraft industry is flourishing (**see page 245**). The state capital, Kuching, is full of handicraft and antique shops selling tribal pieces collected from upriver; those going upriver themselves can often find items being sold in towns and even longhouses *en route*. Typical Sarawakian handicrafts include woodcarvings, *pua kumbu* (rust-coloured tie-dye blankets), beadwork and basketry. Many handicraft shops on Peninsular Malaysia also sell Sarawakian handicrafts – particularly those in KL – although there is a considerable mark-up.

Safety

Normal precautions should be taken with passports and valuables such as cameras; many hotels have safes. Pickpocketing is a problem in some cities. Women – if not accompanied by men – usually attract unwarranted attention, particularly in more Islamic areas, such as the east coast. Mostly this is bravado, however, and there have been no serious incidents involving foreign tourists.

Health

Vaccinations: visiting the peninsula's west coast does not require any medical precautions other than some insect repellent. Those travelling to national parks, rural areas and to Sabah and Sarawak are advised to have vaccinations against cholera, typhoid and polio. **Malaria** is not a problem in main cities but it is advisable to take malaria pills if you are going to rural areas. Malaria is more prevalent in East Malaysia.

Food & water: water is clean and safe to drink in major cities on the peninsula but in other areas it should be boiled or sterilized. Mineral water can be bought fairly easily, although there was a scam in 1991 when several mineral water companies were discovered to be bottling tap water. With food, normal precautions should be taken with shellfish; ensure stall food is properly cooked and avoid unpeeled fruits.

Medical facilities: Malaysian health care is excellent and private clinics are found in most small towns and there are good government hospitals in major cities. All state capitals have general hospitals and every town has a district hospital. On the whole it is inexpensive to visit a private doctor (about M$20-40

Dr Watson solves the Malayan malaria mystery

The word 'malaria' was first used in the 18th century and comes from the Italian *mala aria* – or 'bad air' – because it was thought to be caused by unwholesome air in swampy districts. It was not until 1899 that Dr Ronald Ross, a medical officer in Panama during the construction of the canal, discovered that the real culprit was not the air, but the swamp inhabitants themselves – mosquitos. The following year a young Scotsman, Dr Malcolm Watson, was appointed as a government medical officer in Malaya, where malaria was the biggest killer. Dr Watson was posted to Klang where a malarial epidemic was wreaking havoc. In September 1901 nearby Port Swettenham (now Port Klang) opened for business; by Christmas 118 out of the 176 government employees had been struck down by the disease.

Armed with the knowledge of the recent Panama discovery, Dr Watson set about draining the coastal swamplands, spraying them and improving the water-flow in streams. It worked, and the doctor became known as the 'White Knight of Malaria Control'. Historian Mary Turnbull writes that "it was said of Watson that 'he could probably have claimed to have saved more lives than any other physician in history', and Ronald Ross described his work in Malaya as 'the greatest sanitary achievement ever accomplished in the British Empire'". The methods used in his battle against the *nyamuk* – the menacing and almost onomatopoeic Malay word for mosquito – became standard practice in the colony. Combined with the increased use of quinine, malaria was controlled, which is one of the reasons why colonial Malaya's plantation economy began to take off in the early 1900s. The planting of rubber estates in the coastal lowlands – greatly encouraged by the zealous director of Singapore's Botanic Gardens, 'Mad' Henry Ridley (see page 411) – would otherwise have been a much more hazardous occupation.

including medicine), and a sojourn in a government hospital is cheaper than most hotels (no a/c or pool). Big hotels have their own in-house doctors – who are extremely expensive. Other doctors are listed in the telephone directory. Pharmaceuticals are available from numerous outlets including shopping centres, supermarkets and hotels. Most pharmacists are open 0900-1800 Mon-Sat. A number of drugs that can only be obtained on prescription in Western countries can be bought over the counter in Malaysia. Traditional Chinese pharmacies – mostly found in Chinatowns – also dispense Chinese medicines, and will advise on traditional remedies for most ailments. Facilities in East Malaysia are not as good as those on the Peninsula.

Emergencies
Ambulance, police or fire, T 999.

Best time to visit
The rainy seasons should be borne in mind when planning itineraries in Malaysia; the best time to visit the **Peninsular's** east coast is between Mar and Sep. Trips along the east coast and interior jungles are not advisable between Nov and Feb, during the north-east monsoon. The east coast suffers flooding at this time of year, and it is inadvisable to take fishing boats to offshore islands such as Pulau Tioman as the sea can be very rough. Taman Negara (the National Park) is closed from Nov to the end of Jan. Other parts of Peninsular Malaysia can be visited year round as the rainy season is not torrential, although it is generally fairly wet during the north-east monsoon period. In **East Malaysia** March and June are the best times to visit the interior, the worst rains are usually from Nov to Feb and some roads are impassable in these months. Conversely, in the dry season, some rivers become unnavigable. In recent years the onset of the wet and dry seasons in both Sabah and Sarawak have become less predictable; environmentalists ascribe this to deforestation, although there is no scientifically proven link.

Clothing
Malaysians dress for the heat – clothes are light, cool and casual most of the time; but they

also dress fairly smartly. Some establishments – mainly exclusive restaurants – require a long sleeved shirt with tie (or local batik shirt) and do not allow shorts in the evening. Those visiting the Cameron Highlands or other upland areas are advised to bring a light sweater. For those planning to go on jungle treks, a waterproof is advisable, as are canvas jungle boots, which dry faster than leather.

Although many Malaysian business people have adopted the Western jacket and tie for formal occasions, the batik shirt, or *baju*, is the traditional formal wear for men, while women wear the graceful *sarung kebaya*. It is worth bearing Islamic conservatism in mind when visiting east coast states (see page 183).

Official time
8 hours ahead of GMT.

Hours of business
Government: 0800-1245, 1400-1615 Mon-Thur, 0800-1200, 1430-1615 Fri, 0800-1245 Sat. **Banks**: 1000-1500 Mon-Fri and 0930-1130 Sat. **NB**: for Kedah, Perlis, Kelantan and Terengganu banks are open 0930-1130 on Thurs and closed on Fri. **Shops**: generally open from 0930-1900 (department stores often later) and supermarkets and department stores from 1000-2200.

In the former Federated States, which were under the British (Selangor, Melaka, Penang, Perak, Pahang and Negri Sembilan), there is a half day holiday on Sat and full day holiday on Sun. The former Unfederated States of Kelantan and Terengganu retain the traditional half day holiday on Thurs and full day holiday on Fri. Sat and Sun are treated as weekdays. In the other former Unfederated States – Johor, Kedah and Perlis, the half day on Thurs is often observed, but most businesses now observe the Sat/Sun weekend.

Money
The Malaysian dollar (M$), is called the **ringgit**, and is divided into 100 **sen** (cents). Bank notes come in denominations of $1, 5, 10, 20, 50, 100, 500 and 1,000. Coins are issued in 1, 5, 10, 20 and 50 cent denominations. As a rough guideline, US$1=M$2.50 (July 1992). Travellers' cheques can be exchanged at banks and money-changers and in some big hotels (often guests-only). Money-changers often offer the best rates, but it is worth shopping around. Banks charge commission on travellers' cheques.

Credit cards: most of the bigger hotels, restaurants and shops accept international credit cards, including American Express, Bankamericard, Diners, Mastercard and Visa. Cash advances can be issued against credit cards in most banks, although some banks – notably Bank Bumiputra – limit the amount that can be drawn; passports are also required for such transactions.

Cost of living
While the average inflation rate is about 5%, the cost of living in the main cities – particularly KL – is rising much faster. This has affected the cost of not only consumer durables but also hotels and restaurants.

Weights & measures
Malaysia has gone metric although road distances are marked in both kilometres and miles.

Voltage
Malaysia's current is 220-240 volts, 50 cycle AC. Some hotels supply adaptors.

Postal services
Malaysia's post is cheap and reasonably reliable, although incoming and outgoing parcels should be registered. In May 1993 the Post Office was rather embarrassed when a letter posted by a doting grandmother to her grandson was delivered 16 years late.
International postal charges: start at M$0.40 for a letter (all postcards are M$0.40) and aerogrammes also cost M$0.40. **Post office opening hours**: 0800-1700 Mon-Fri, 0800-1200 Sat. **Fax and telex services**: available in most state capitals. **Poste Restante**: reliable services at general post offices in major cities.

Telephone services
Local: there are public telephone booths in most towns; telephones take M$0.10 and M$0.20 coins. Card phones are now widespread; cards, of various denominations, are available from post offices, hotels and some shops. On most public phones it is necessary to press the release button once the other person responds. **Operator**: for 'outstation' (trunk) calls T101; enquiries T102; directory T103; international IDD assistance and details on country codes T108. **Area codes**: Georgetown (and Penang) 04; Ipoh 05; Johor Bahru 07; Kota Kinabalu 088; Kuala Lumpur 03; Kuantan 06; Kuching 082; Melaka 06; Pahang 05; Perak 05; Sandakan 089; Taiping 05. **International**: there is an international telephone exchange in KL and calls can be booked to

USEFUL MALAYSIAN WORDS & PHRASES

Basic Malay grammar is very simple, and, like in Indonesian, there are no tenses, genders or articles and the structure of sentences is straight-forward. Plurals are also easy: one "man", for example is *laki*, "men" is *laki-laki*, often denoted as *laki²*. For basic guidelines to pronunciation, see the Indonesian language section, page 1028. Certain words differ in Malay and Indonesian, although the two are mutually intelligible. A brief, essential list of words and phrases is provided below. For those wanting to get a better grasp of the language, it is possible to take courses in Kuala Lumpur (enquire at Tourism Malaysia offices) and other big cities. The best way to take a crash-course in Malay is to buy a "teach-yourself" book; there are several on the market, but one of the best ones is *Malay in 3 Weeks*, by John Parry and Sahari bin Sulaiman (Times Books, 1989), which is widely available. A Malay/English dictionary or phrase book is a useful companion too; these are also readily available in bookshops.

Yes	*ia*
No	*tidak*
Thank you	*Terimah kaseh*
You're welcome	*Sama-sama*
Good morning	*Selamat pagi*
Good afternoon (early)	*Selamat tengahari*
Good afternoon (late)	*Selamat petang*
Good evening/night	*Selamat malam*
Welcome	*Selamat datang*
Goodbye (said by the person leaving)	*Selamat tinggal*
Goodbye (said by the person staying)	*Selamat jalan*
Excuse me / sorry	*Ma'af saya*
Where's the...?	*Dimana...*
How much is this...?	*Ini berapa?*
I [don't] understand	*Saya [tidak] mengerti*
I want...	*Saya mahu*
I don't want	*Saya tak mahu*

The hotel

How much is a room?	*Bilik berapa?*
Does the room have air-conditioning?	*Ada bilik yang ada air-con-kah?*
I want to see the room first please	*Saya mahu lihat bilik dulu*
Does the room have hot water?	*Ada bilik yang ada air panas?*
Does the room have a bathroom?	*Ada bilik yang ada mandi-kah?*

Travel

Where is the railway station?	*Stesen keretapi dimana?*
Where is the bus station?	*Stesen bas dimana?*
How much to go to...?	*Berapa harga ke...?*
I want to buy a ticket to...	*Saya mahu beli tiket ke...*
Is it far?	*Ada jauh?*
Turn left / turn right	*Belok kiri / belok kanan*
Go staight on!	*Turus turus!*

Time and days

Monday	*Hari Isnin (Hari Satu)*	Today	*Hari ini*
Tuesday	*Hari Selasa (Hari Dua)*	Tomorrow	*Esok*
Wednesday	*Hari Rabu (Hari Tiga)*	Week	*Minggu*
Thursday	*Hari Khamis (Hari Empat)*	Month	*Bulan*
Friday	*Hari Jumaat (Hari Lima)*	Year	*Tahun*
Saturday	*Hari Sabtu (Hari Enam)*		
Sunday	*Hari Minggu (Hari Ahad)*		

Numbers

1	satu	20	dua puluh
2	dua	21	dua puluh satu...etc
3	tiga	30	tiga puluh
4	empat	100	se-ratus
5	lima	101	se-ratus satu
6	enam	150	se-ratus limah puluh
7	tujuh	200	dua ratus...etc
8	lapan	1,000	se-ribu
9	sembilan	2,000	dua ribu...
10	sepuluh	100,000	se-ratus ribu
11	se-belas	1,000,000	se-juta
12	dua-belas...etc		

Basic vocabulary

all right/good	baik	island	pulau
and	dan	man	laki
bank	bank	market	pasar
bathroom	bilek mandi	medicine	ubat ubatan
beach	pantai	milk	susu
beautiful	cantik	more	lagi / lebeh
bed sheet	cadar	open	masuk
big	besar	please	sila
boat	perahu	police	polis
broken	tak makan / rosak	police station	pejabat polis
bus	bas	post office	pejabat pos
bus station	setsen bas	railway station	stesen keretapi / tren
buy	beli	restaurant	restoran / kedai
can	boleh		makanan
cannot	tak boleh	room	bilik
chemist	rumah ubat	sea	laut
cigarette	rokok	ship	kapal
clean	bersih	shop	kedai
closed	tutup	sick	sakit
coffee	kopi	small	kecil
cold	sejuk	stand	berdiri
crazy	gila	stop	berhenti
day	hari	sugar	gula
delicious	sedap	taxi	teksi
dentist	doktor gigi	tea	teh
dirty	kotor	they	mereka
doctor	doktor	that	itu
eat	makan	this	ini
excellent	bagus	ticket	tiket
expensive	mahal	toilet	tandas
fruit	buah	town	bandar
hospital	rumah sakit	very	sangat
hot (temperature)	panas	water	air
hot (chilli)	pedas	what	apa
I/me	saya	woman	perempuan
ice	air batuais	you	awak/anda

Learning the language – a practical alternative

Malaysian English – which has been dubbed "Manglish", as opposed to Singaporean English ("Singlish") – has evolved its own usages, abbreviations and expressions. Its very distinctive pronunciation can be almost unintelligible to visitors when they first arrive. The first thing many visitors notice is the use of the suffix "lah" which is attached to just about anything and means absolutely nothing. English has been spoken in the Malay world since the late 18th century, but over time, it has been mixed with local terms. The converse has also happened: English has corrupted Malay to such a degree that it is now quite common to hear the likes of "you *pergi-mana*?" for "where are you going?" In abbreviated Malaysian-Chinese English, "can" is a key word. "Can-ah?" (inflection) means "may I?"; "can-lah" means "yes"; "cannot" means "no way"; "also can" means "yes, but I'd prefer you not to" and "how can?" is an expression of disbelief.

The man who first applied the term Manglish to mangled Malaysian English was Chinese-Malaysian satirist Kit Leee, in his book *Adoi* (which means "ouch") which gives an uncannily accurate and very humorous pseudo-anthropological run-down on Malaysia's inhabitants. His section on Manglish, which should be pronounced exactly as it is written is introduced: "*Aitelyu-ah, nemmain wat debladigarmen say, mose Malaysians tok Manglish... Donkair you Malay or Chinese or Indian or everyting miksup... we Malaysians orways tok like dis wan-kain oni...*" Below are extracts from his glossary of common Manglish words and phrases (which will help decipher the above).

atoyu (wat) – gentle expression of triumph: "What did I tell you?"

baiwanfriwan – ploy used mainly by shop assistants to promote sales: "If you buy one you'll get one free".

betayudon – mild warning, as in "You'd better not do that".

debladigarmen – contraction of "the bloody government"; widely used scapegoat for all of life's disappointments, delays, denials, and prohibitions.

hauken – another flexible expression applicable in almost any situation, eg "That's not right!", "Impossible!" or "Don't tell me!".

izzenit – from "isn't it?" but applied very loosely at the end of any particular statement to elicit an immediate response, eg. "Yused you will spen me a beer, izzenit?"

kennonot – request or enquiry, contraction of "can or not": "May I?" or "Will you?" or "Is it possible?"

nola – a dilute negative, used as a device to interrupt, deny or cancel someone else's statement.

oridi – contraction of already.

sohau – polite interrogative, usually used as a greeting, as in "Well, how are things with you?"

tingwat – highly adaptable expression stemming from "What do you think?"

wan-kain – adjective denoting uniqueness... contraction of "one of a kind". Sometimes rendered as "*wan-kain oni*" ("only").

watudu – rhetorical question: "But what can we do?"

yala – non-committal agreement, liberally used when confronted with a bore.

yusobadwan – expression of mild reproach: "That's not very nice!"

(With thanks to Kit Leee and his co-etymologists: Rafique Rashid, Julian Mokhtar and Jeanne M C Donven. Leee, Kit (1989) *Adoi*, Times Books International: Singapore.)

most countries in the world. Calls may be booked in advance. Collect calls can be linked to destination countries without delay (the operator will call you back). Direct calls can be made from telephones with IDD (international direct dialling) facility (007 + country code + area code + number). Direct international calls can be made from most Kedai Telekom.

Media
Newspapers: the main English-language dailies are *The New Straits Times*, *Business Times*, *The Star* and *The Malay Mail* (afternoon). The main Sunday papers are *The New Sunday Times*, *The Sunday Mail* and *The Sunday Star*. The English-language dailies are government-owned and this is reflected in their content. *Aliran Monthly* is a high-brow but fascinating publication offering current affairs analysis from a non-government perspective. *The Rochet* is the Democratic Action Party's opposition newspaper, and also presents an alternative perspective. Both are available at news outlets. International editions of leading foreign newspapers and news magazines can be obtained at main news stands and book stalls, although some of these are not cleared through customs until mid-afternoon (notably *The Asian Wall Street Journal*). **Television**: RTM1 and RTM2 are operated by Radio Television Malaysia, the government-run broadcasting station. Apart from locally produced programmes, some American and British series are shown. A third channel, TV3 (TV Tiga), is run commercially. There is a broad mixture of content, from Chinese kung-fu movies to Tamil musicals and English-language blockbusters and series. On TV3, all programmes are liberally interspersed with advertising, most of it for cigarettes, and leading tobacco companies sponsor film shows. Programmes for all channels are listed in daily newspapers. Singapore Broadcasting Service programmes can be received as far north as Melaka and are often listed in Malaysian papers. The government has banned the use of satellite dishes, although CNN news is rebroadcast daily at 1900 on RTM1. **Radio**: there are 6 government radio stations which broadcast in various languages including English. Radio 1 broadcasts in Bahasa Melayu; Radio 2 is a music station; Radio 3 is mainly Bahasa but broadcasts a special programme for tourists every day at 1800; Radio 4 is in English; Radio 5, Chinese; Radio 6, Tamil. In KL you can tune into the Federal Capital's radio station and elsewhere in the country there are local stations. The BBC World Service can be picked up on FM in southern Johor, from the Singapore transmitter. Elsewhere it can be received on shortwave. The main frequencies are (in kHz): 11750, 9740, 6195 and 3915.

Language
Bahasa Melayu (the Malay language – normally just shortened to *bahasa*) is the national language; it is very similar to Bahasa Indonesia (**see page 504**) – which evolved from Malay – and can be understood in southern Thailand, throughout Borneo and as far afield as the Moro areas of the southern Philippines. All communities – Malay, Chinese and Indian, as well as tribal groups in Sabah and Sarawak – speak Malay as most are schooled in the Malay medium. Nearly everyone in Malaysia speaks some English – except in remoter rural areas – although the standard of English has declined markedly in the past 10 years. Realizing this, and because good English is essential for business, the government has sought to reverse the decline. The other main languages spoken in Malaysia include the Chinese dialects of Mandarin, Cantonese and Hokkien as well as Tamil and Punjabi.

Tourist information
Malaysia Tourism Promotion (Tourism Malaysia) (headquarters), 24-27 Flr, Menara Dato' Onn, Putra World Trade Centre, 45, Jln Tun Ismail, 50480 Kuala Lumpur T (03) 2935188. There is an information centre on Level 2 of the Putra World Trade Centre (in the convention centre). For practical advice, visitors are better advised to contact Malaysian Tourist Information Centre (MATIC), 109 Jln Ampang, Kuala Lumpur T2423929. There are several other tourist information bureaux in KL (**see page 114**) and regional tourism offices in state capitals, all of which are reasonably efficiently run.

Tourism Malaysia has tourist information bureaux in most large towns. Tourism Malaysia is very efficient and can supply further details on tourist sights, advise on itineraries, help place bookings for travel and cultural events and provide updated information on hotels, restaurants and air, road, rail, sea and river transport timetables and prices. If there is no Tourism Malaysia office in a town, travel agents are usually helpful.

Suggested reading
Novels: Burgess, Anthony *Malayan Trilogy*; Chapman, F Spencer *The Jungle is Neutral*; Conrad, Joseph *Victory*; O'Hanlon, Redmond *Into the Heart of Borneo*; Theroux, Paul *The Consul's File*.

General: Barber, Noel (1971) *The War of the Running Dogs – Malaya 1948-1960*, Arrow Books; Bock, Carl (1985) *The Headhunters of Borneo*, Singapore; Briggs, John (1988) *Mountains of Malaysia – a practical guide and manual*, Longman; Chay, Peter (1988) *The Land Below the Wind*, Foto Technik; Cranbrook, Earl of (1987) *Riches of the Wild: Land Mammals of South-East Asia*, OUP; Hanbury-Tenison, Robin (1980) *Mulu, the Rain Forest*; Endicott, K

M (1991) *An analysis of Malay Magic*, Oxford University Press: Singapore; Hansen, Eric (1988) *Stranger in the Forest: On foot across Borneo*, Century; Harrisson, Tom (1986) *World Within: A Borneo Story*, OUP; Hose, Charles (1985, first published 1929); *The Field Book of a Jungle-Wallah*, OUP; Leee, Kit (1989) *Adoi*, Times Books: Singapore (1988); Mjoberg, Eric *Forest Life & Adventures in the Malay Archipelago*, OUP; Payne, Junaidi, Francis, Charles & Philipps, Karen *Pocket Guide to Birds of Borneo*, World Wildlife Fund/Sabah Society; Turnbull, Mary C (1989) *A History of Malaysia, Singapore and Brunei*, Allen & Unwin; Tweedie, MWF and Harrison JL (1954 with regularly updated editions) *Malayan Animal Life*, Longman.

Lim Jee Yuan (1987) *The Malay House: rediscovering Malaysia's indigenous shelter system*, Institut Masyarakat: Penang. L Chin *Cultural Heritage of Sarawak*; H Clifford *Saleh A Prince of Malaya*; P Little *Penang*; M MacDonald *Borneo People*; H Miller *The Story of Malaysia*; J Mackinnon *Borneo*; E Ong *Pua Iban Weavings of Sarawak*; Sarawak Museum *Sarawak in the Museum*; W Skeat *Malay Magic*; D Tate *Rajah Brooke's Borneo*; Alfred Russel Wallace *The Malay Archipelago – The Land of the Orangutan and the Bird of Paradise*.

Maps & Guides: Malaysia Nelles Map; Shell Map of Malaysia (available from Shell stations in Malaysia).

Acknowledgements

Special thanks to Adrian Finn (UK), Matthew Geiger (USA), Mika Ostroff (USA), Joe Casey (Ireland), Hilary Bristow (UK), Lucy Simmonds (UK), Paul Blount (UK).

SINGAPORE

	Page		Page
Introduction	367	Arab Street	409
The colonial core	396	Around Singapore Island	411
The river and port	400	Singapore's islands	417
Orchard Road	403	Services	421
Chinatown	404	Information for Visitors	436
Little India	407		

Maps: Singapore, 368; Singapore General, 394-395; The Colonial Core, 397; Orchard Road, 402-403; Chinatown, 406; Little India, 408; Arab Street, 410; Singapore MRT, 439.

INTRODUCTION

Modern Singapore primarily owes its existence and its prosperity to two men, both of them forceful characters and visionaries: Sir Thomas Stamford Raffles (see page 372) and Lee Kuan Yew (see page 384). Beneath Raffles' statue in London's Westminster Abbey, there is an inscription, dated 1832, crediting him with 'founding an emporium at Singapore'. Little did his epitaph-writer know the truth of what he wrote. Singapore is not only one enormous retail outlet; it is the trade, transport, business and financial hub of the region. Raffles, being a great believer in free trade, would have been delighted by Singapore's economic success story; his little trading-post is now one of the richest countries in Asia and one of the most politically stable in the world. It is affluent and prosperous and unlike its neighbours, Singapore's political economy is not riddled with corruption.

But beneath its slick veneer of Westernized modernity, Singapore's heart and soul are Asian. Behind all the computers, hi-tech industries, marble, steel and smoked-glass tower blocks, highways and shopping centres is a society with an ingrained sense of conservative Confucian values. In 1992, an editorial in the pro-government *Straits Times* said: "Values are the software which makes the nation's social and economic hardware tick." Singapore still believes in extended families, filial piety, discipline and respect and most of all, it believes in the Asian work ethic. The man who has instilled and preserved these values is former Prime Minister Lee Kuan Yew. But, to some, his far-sighted vision has transformed his clockwork island into a regimented city-state. In this view of things, modern, automated Singapore has spawned a generation of angst-ridden, over-programmed people who have given their country the reputation of being the most crushingly dull in Asia. But now, all that is changing. The architect of

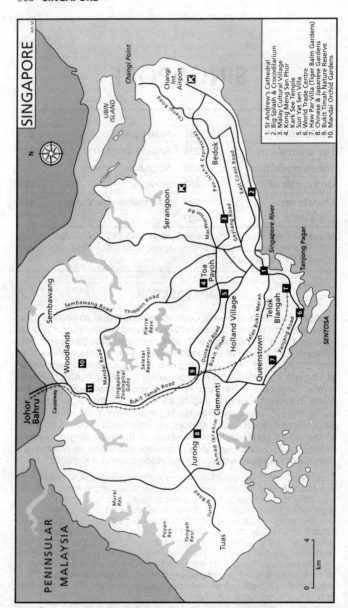

SINGAPORE

IMS 50

N

Changi Point

UBIN ISLAND

Changi Int. Airport ✈

PENINSULAR MALAYSIA

Johor Bahru

Causeway

Woodlands

Sembawang

Sembawang Road

Thomson Road

Mandai Road

Pierce Resv.

Seletar Reservoir

Singapore Zoological Gdns

Bukit Timah Road

Murai Res.

Poyan Res.

Tengah Resr.

Jurong

Jurong Road

Ahmad Ibrahim Road

Clementi

Tuas

Dunearn Road

Bukit Timah

Holland Village

Queensland

Jalan Bukit Merah

Telok Blangah

Panjang Road

Toa Payoh

Serangoon

✈

MacPherson Rd

Pan Island Expressway

Geylang Road

East Coast Road

Bedok

Changi Road

Singapore River

Tanjong Pagar

SENTOSA

km 0 4

1. St Andrew's Cathedral
2. Big Splash & Crocodiarium
3. Malay Cultural Village
4. Kong Meng San Phor Kark See Temple
5. Sun Yat Sen Villa
6. World Trade Centre
7. Haw Par Villa (Tiger Balm Gardens)
8. Chinese & Japanese Gardens
9. Bukit Timah Nature Reserve
10. Mandai Orchid Gardens

modern Singapore has allowed a new generation of Singaporeans to step up to the drawing board – although he finds it hard not to interfere with their plans.

When Stamford Raffles first set foot on Singapore in 1819, the island had a population of about 150 – mostly pirates and fishermen. By the time of the first census, 5 years later, the population was 10,683 and growing fast. It included 3,317 Chinese, 4,850 'Malays', 756 Indians (Muslim, Hindu and Sikh), 74 Europeans, 15 Arabs and 16 Americans; there were also Javanese, Bugis, Minangkabau, Filipinos and Terengganu and Kelantan Malays. The Bugis comprised one fifth of the population in the 1820s, but they gradually merged with the Malay and Javanese communities. By 1827, due to massive immigration (**see page 374**), half the population was Chinese; by 1860 this had risen to 65% and today they make up more than three-quarters of the population (**see page 379**). At the turn of the 19th century, Singapore was the most polyglot city in Asia.

The island now has a population of 2.7 million and one of the highest population densities in the world, with over 4,200 people per sq km. Because most people live in tower blocks, about 61% of the population lives on just 17% of the land area. About a third of Singaporeans are under 20 years of age, and 40% are under 40.

ENVIRONMENT

Land

Singapore is a small, roughly diamond-shaped island at the end of peninsular Malaysia and is not much bigger than Britain's Isle of Wight. It occupies a strategic position at the turning-point for shipping on the shortest sea-route between the Indian Ocean and the South China Sea. It is separated from Malaysia by the narrow Strait of Johor, but the 2 are linked by a 1.2 km-long causeway. To the S, Singapore is separated from the N islands of the Indonesian Riau Archipelago by the Strait of Singapore, which has been a favoured pirate haunt for centuries (**see page 233**). The country includes 58 other small islands, islets and reefs which lie a little over one degree (137 km) N of the equator. The biggest of Singapore's other islands are Pulau Tekong (18 sq km) and Pulau Ubin (10 sq km), both to the NE. Singapore island itself measures 22.9 km N to S and 41.8 km E to W and has an area of around 600 sq km, although this is increasing, thanks to ambitious land reclamation schemes. After 1961 large areas of land were reclaimed from mangrove swamps to provide the Jurong industrial estate. There has been further reclamation along the E coast and at Marina Bay.

Singapore's skyscrapers are mostly taller than the island's highest point, Bukit Timah Peak (Tin Hill), whose summit is 165 m. Most of the island is about 10 m above sea-level, although there are scattered undulating hillocks and ridges – such as the one ending at Mount Faber, where the cable car goes across to Sentosa. The hillier areas at the centre of the island are mainly made up of granite and other igneous rocks. The W of the island is composed of sedimentary shales and sandstones while alluvial deposits cover the E end. Singapore's foreshore provides a superb, sheltered deep-water anchorage, in the lee of 2 islands – Sentosa (formerly Pulau Blakang Mati) and Pulau Brani (now a naval base).

Climate

Singapore's climate is uniformly hot and sticky throughout the year, although the NE monsoon, which blows from Nov to Jan gives some respite. These 'winter' months are also the wettest. The average daily maximum temperature is 30.7°C which drops to an average minimum of 23°C. The hottest months are Mar to Jul; the highest temperature on record was 35.8°C in Apr 1983. The coolest month is Jan and the coldest temperature recorded this century was 19.4°C. Relative humidity peaks at over 96% (just before dawn), while the daily average is about 84%. Most Singaporeans prefer their air-conditioned microclimates to their balmy equatorial air and frequently catch colds from rushing between the two.

It rains throughout the year, but the NE monsoon, brings the most prolonged downpours. The average annual rainfall is 2,369 mm; the wettest month is Dec, with an average of 277 mm and the driest is Jul with 159 mm. The most rain ever recorded in a single day fell on 2 Dec 1978, when Singapore received 512 mm of rain. Sometimes it rains for several days continuously and on these occasions there is often serious flooding. Between monsoons, from Apr to Nov, there are regular pre-dawn thunderstorms which strike with frightening intensity 3 or 4 times a month; they are called Sumatras (**see page 56**). Dramatic thunderstorms are fairly common at other times of year too; Singapore has an average of 180 lightning days a year. The sunniest month is Feb and the cloudiest, Dec.

Flora and fauna

When Stamford Raffles first arrived, Singapore was blanketed in dense jungle and skirted by mangroves. An 1825 account of Bukit Timah (in the centre of the island), which appeared in the *Singapore Chronicle*, gives a graphic impression of what Singapore must have been like in those days. "Bukit Timah, although not above 7 or 8 miles from the town, has never been visited by a European, seldom by a native; and such is the character of the intervening country, that it would be almost as easy a task to make a voyage to Calcutta as to travel to it." Originally the island was 83% forested; but by the 1880s, about 90% of that had already been cleared. Today virtually all the jungle has disappeared and 49% of Singapore's land area is concreted over. Many endemic plant species have disappeared too, including more than 50 species of mangrove orchid. Bukit Timah Nature Reserve has 62 ha of mature rainforest however, and there is a total of 2,796 ha of forest reserve under management – including 15 sq km of mangrove along the N coastline.

Singapore is one of only 2 cities in the world to have genuine tropical rainforest – the other being Rio de Janeiro in Brazil. Although few tourists come to Singapore to see wildlife, the tourism board is promoting ecotourism at Bukit Timah Nature Reserve and at Kranji, MacRitchie, Seletar and the Upper and Lower Peirce reservoirs. All have areas of primary rainforest and contain more plant species than the whole of North America – a mere 45 minutes from the centre of the city. Modern Singapore is a big, carefully planned landscaped garden. About 80% of its trees and shrubs are imported however: even frangipani – with its fragrant white blossoms – was originally introduced from Mexico. Bougainvillaea was imported from South America and the travellers' palm, so often associated with old Singapore, is a native of Madagascar. It is related to the banana tree and was introduced to Singapore in the early 1900s.

Despite the name Singapura – 'Lion City' – there have been no reported sightings of lions since the 13th century, when, according to the *Sejara Melayu* (the 16th century Malay Annals), Sri Tri Buana, the ruler of Palembang (Sumatra) mistakenly thought he saw one while sheltering from a storm on the island. He named the

Flower power

The Vanda Miss Joaquim orchid was named after an Armenian woman, Agnes Joaquim, who found the orchid – a 'natural hybrid' – growing in her garden and presented it to the Botanic Gardens. In 1981 it was chosen as Singapore's national flower and then became the motif on Singapore's national costume – the flowery shirts sported by politicians. The purple and white orchid is on sale in all Singapore florists and can also be seen at the orchidarium in Singapore's botanic gardens (**see page 411**) and at Mandai Orchid Gardens (**see page 416**).

nearby settlement accordingly. Many of Singapore's bigger mammals and more exotic species have long-since disappeared, along with their habitat.

Man-eating tigers provoked a national emergency in 1855 and created a furore in the *Raffles Hotel* in 1902; but the last wild tiger was shot in Singapore by a Mr Ong Kim Hong in October 1930. Sambar deer, barking deer, wild boars and wild cats, which were once common, have all now gone. But flying lemurs (*Cynocephalus cariegatus*), flying squirrels (*Callosciurus notatus* and *Sandasciurus tenuis*), flying lizards and flying foxes still inhabit the protected forests where there are also small populations of mouse deer, porcupines and pangolins (scaly anteaters). Singapore also has many reptiles – the most common being lizards and snakes – but there are also crocodiles, whose fertilized eggs have been found in Seletar Reservoir. In 1989 a Thai construction worker was bitten by one while fishing. More than 300 bird species have been recorded in Singapore; the government has established a small bird sanctuary in mangrove swamps at Sungei Buloh (near Lim Chu Kang on the N coast) where there are many migratory birds.

HISTORY

Early records
Although Singapore has probably been inhabited for the past 2 millennia, there are few early records. In the 3rd century, Chinese sailors mention *Pu-luo-chung* – 'the island at the end of the peninsula' – and historians speculate that this may have been Singapore. Even its name, Singapura, from the Sanskrit for 'Lion City', is unexplained – other than by the legendary account in the *Sejara Melayu* (see page 370). It was originally called Temasek – or 'Sea Town' – and may have been a small seaport in the days of the Sumatran Srivijayan Empire. Following Srivijaya's decline at the end of the 13th century, however, Singapore emerged from the shadows.

Marco Polo, the Venetian adventurer, visited Sumatra in the late 1200s and referred to 'Chiamassie', which he says was a 'very large and noble city'. Historians believe this was probably Temasek. According to the 16th century *Sejara Melayu*, Temasek was a thriving entrepôt by the 14th century, when it changed its name to Singapura. Another contemporary account, however, by the Chinese traveller, Wang Ta-yuan, noted that the island was a dreaded pirate haunt. Whatever prosperity it may have had did not last. In the late 1300s, it was destroyed by invading Siamese and Javanese, for Singapura fell in the middle ground between the expanding Ayutthaya (Thai) and Majapahit (Indonesian) Empires. The ruler – called Parameswara, who was said to be a fugitive prince from Palembang in Sumatra – fled to Melaka, where he founded the powerful Malay sultanate in the 1390s (see page 161). Following Parameswara's hasty departure, Singapura was abandoned – other than for a few *Orang Laut* ('Sea People'), who made a living from fishing and piracy. While trade flourished elsewhere in the region, the port which today is the busiest in the world, was a jungled backwater and it remained that way for 4 centuries.

Raffles steps ashore
In the early 1800s, the British East India Company occupied Dutch colonies in the East to prevent them falling into French hands: Napoleon had occupied Holland and the Dutch East India Company had gone bankrupt. In Jan 1819 Sir Thomas Stamford Raffles arrived in Singapore with the hope that he could set up a trading post at the mouth of the Singapore River. He was relieved to hear that the Dutch had never been there and promptly struck a deal with the resident *temenggong* (Malay chief) of the Riau-Johor Empire. To seal this agreement he had to obtain official approval from the Sultan of Riau-Johor.

Due to a succession squabble following the previous sultan's death in 1812,

Thomas Stamford Raffles: architect of Singapore

"It is a pity to my mind that when Thomas Stamford Raffles... was knighted by his friend the Prince Regent in 1817, he chose to be dubbed Sir Stamford," writes Jan Morris in her introduction to Maurice Collis' biography of Singapore's founding father. "Tom Raffles was much more his style." He was the son of an undistinguished sea-captain, and was born in 1781 aboard his father's West Indian slaving ship somewhere in the mid-Atlantic. Raffles joined the East India Company as a clerk aged 14 when his father could no longer afford his school fees. Ten years later, in 1805, he was posted to Penang as an assistant secretary to the government, getting a 21-fold salary rise in the process. On the journey out, he learned Malay and because no other colonial official had bothered, he was an accepted expert within a few months.

In 1808, while working for the High Court in Penang, he took a holiday in Melaka and prevented the final destruction of the old Portuguese fortifications (see page 162). On a visit to Calcutta 2 years later, the Governor-General of India appointed him Governor of Java, a post he held from 1811-1816, while the British occupied Dutch colonies during the Napoleonic Wars in Europe. The old British Governor of India was impressed by him; he described Raffles as "a very clever, able, active and judicious man". In 1814 his wife, Olivia, died. Raffles was devastated by her death, but occupied himself researching *A History of Java*, which, was published in 1817, and is considered a landmark study of the island's history, culture and zoology.

As an administrator, Raffles was well-liked. He was known as a fair and reasonable man; he had a forceful character and opportunistic streak but few social pretentions. He was cheerful despite a succession of personal tragedies (he lost 3 of his children as well as his first wife). He battled to suppress piracy and slavery (he was a close friend of William Wilberforce, the social reformer, who forced the abolition of slavery in Britain). Raffles' aim was to bring prosperity to a region whose development had been hampered by the Dutch monopoly on trade in the Indonesian archipelago. He became convinced of the virtues of free trade, and later applied these principles to Singapore. Raffles was a great admirer of Napoleon (and actually met the exiled emperor on St Helena in 1823) but he never took part in any military campaign himself. He believed it was important for Britain to have a power base on the China trade route, at the S end of the Indo-Chinese land mass, and seems never to have questioned the forcible extension of the British Empire. In the words of Jan Morris, that would have happened anyway and "he was only the instrument of inexorable geo-political forces... [although] he believed in his country as the chief agent of human progress."

After 5 years in Java, Raffles returned to England, where, in 1817 he married an Irish woman, Sophia Hull, who he loved dearly but described as "affectionate and sensible, though not very handsome". He took her back to the East, where he was appointed Lieutenant-Governor of Bencoolen (Sumatra) in 1818. The

there were 2 claimants, one on Pulau Lingga (far to the S), who was recognized by the Dutch, and one on Pulau Bintan. Realizing that the Dutch would bar the Lingga sultan from sanctioning his settlement on Singapore, Raffles conveniently approached the other one, flattering him, offering him money and pronouncing him Sultan of Johor. He agreed to pay Sultan Hussein Mohamed Shah 5,000 Spanish dollars a year in rent and a further 3,000 Spanish dollars to the temenggong. The Union Jack was raised over Singapore on 6 Feb 1819 and Raffles set sail the next day – having been there less than a week – and left the former Resident of Melaka, Colonel William Farquhar, in charge.

The Dutch were enraged by Raffles' bold initiative and the British government was embarrassed. But after a protracted diplomatic frisson, the Treaty of London same year, while on a visit to Calcutta, Raffles persuaded the Governor-General of India, Lord Hastings, to sanction a mission to set up a trading post at the S tip of the Strait of Melaka, on the condition it did not bring the East India Company into conflict with the Dutch. Raffles had his eye on the Riau archipelago, but discovered that the Dutch had already re-established themselves on Riau's Pulau Bintan. On 28 Jan 1819, after casting around some other islands in the area, he headed for Singapore, anchoring off St John's Island (see page 419) before sailing up the Singapore River the next day.

After stepping ashore, he reportedly snacked on rambutans before visiting the *temenggong* (Malay chief) of the Riau-Johor Empire, to seek his permission to set up a trading post. Having formalized the agreement with the sultan, Raffles left the island and did not return to Singapore again until Sept 1822, by which time it was a booming port with 10,000 inhabitants. Raffles noted that in the first 2½ years, 2,839 vessels had entered and cleared the harbour; the total turnover was 8 million Spanish dollars. In 1822 itself, an even greater number of ships arrived and in that year alone, trade was worth 8.5 million Spanish dollars. It was an omen of things to come. Raffles allowed unrestricted immigration and free trade. During this second (and final) visit, Raffles quarrelled with Farquhar, took over the administration himself, wrote a constitution, drew up a street plan and 3 days before he left in 1823, he laid the foundation stone of what later became the Raffles Institution. Many prominent Singaporeans were educated at the college over the next 150 years, including the first Prime Minister Lee Kuan Yew. (The grand old building was demolished in 1984 to make way for Raffles City.)

Sir Stamford returned to England and having founded Singapore, he went on to found London Zoo. But he was far from well; for some time he had been suffering from terrible, unexplained headaches. He fell out with the East India Company over Farquhar's repeated claims to have founded Singapore himself and died the day before his 45th birthday in his home in Hendon, N London from a suspected brain tumour. His funeral was virtually ignored by London society and the local vicar refused permission for a plaque to be erected in his memory. Eight years later, his friends and admirers commissioned a marble statue of him which was placed in the N aisle of Westminster Abbey. There is another statue of Raffles, which still stands on the bank of the Singapore River, near where he landed in 1819. When Lee Kuan Yew first came to power in 1965, his Dutch economic adviser Dr Albert Winsemius told him to get rid of the Communists but to "let Raffles stand where he is today. Say publicly that you accept the heavy ties with the West because you will very much need them in your economic programme". Jan Morris writes that despite Raffles' short sojourn in Singapore, "he is honoured still in the Lion City as no other Western imperialist is honoured in the East".

was finally signed in 1824 and the Dutch withdrew their objection to the British presence on Singapore in exchange for the British withdrawal from Bencoolen (Benkulu) in Sumatra, where Raffles had served as governor. Seven years later, the trading post was tied with Penang (which had been in British hands since 1786 – see page 132) and Melaka (which the Dutch had swapped with Bencoolen). They became known as the Straits Settlements and attracted traders and settlers from all over Southeast Asia – and the world.

From fishing village to international port

Within 4 years of its founding, Singapore had overshadowed Penang in importance and grew from a fishing village to an international trading port. Thanks to its strategic location, it expanded quickly as an entrepôt, assuming the

Chinese immigration: Singapore's life-blood

Today, Singaporeans attach great social prestige to claims to be third or fourth generation Singaporeans. Immigrants flooded into Singapore from virtually the day it was founded and within months the local Malay Orang Laut population was outnumbered. The first junk arrived from Xiamen (Amoy) in Feb 1821. By 1827 the Chinese had become the biggest community on the island and by the turn of the century, they made up three-quarters of the population. The first Chinese immigrants came from the neighbouring Straits Settlement of Melaka. But most came from the S Chinese provinces of Guangdong, Fujian and later Hainan; the different dialect groups included Fukien, Cantonese, Teochew, Hakka and Hainanese. One observer in the 1820s listed the Chinese as being involved in 110 separate occupations, but mostly they were concentrated in trade and merchandising and agriculture (vegetable farming and pepper and gambier cultivation). They also worked as coolies.

Most immigrants were young men and a big prostitution industry sprang up to service them. As late as 1911 there were more than 240 men to every 100 women. That same year there were reported to be 48 races living in Singapore, speaking 54 languages. Despite China's Ch'ing government outlawing emigration, they continued to arrive, driven by overpopulation and civil war. The new immigrants were known as *sinkheh*. Most were illiterate and penniless; for their first year, while paying off the cost of their passage, they were not paid any wages. Immigrant groups from different countries settled in particular districts, and were administered by local community leaders, or *kapitans*. But in the Chinese community, real power was vested in the *hui*, or secret societies. The most powerful of these was the Triad – the Heaven and Earth Society – which had political roots in Fujian province. These societies remained legal in Singapore until the 1890s; only their membership and rituals were kept secret. They organized the division of labour – including prostitution

role Melaka had held in earlier centuries. But by 1833, the East India Company had lost its China trade monopoly and its interest in Singapore and the other Straits Settlements declined. Their status was downgraded and their administration trimmed. But while Penang and Melaka went downhill, Singapore boomed, having benefited from the abolition of the East India Company's monopoly. When the Dutch lifted trade restrictions in the 1840s, this boosted Singapore's economy again. New trade channels opened up with the Brooke government in Sarawak (**see page 232**) and with Thailand. The volume of trade increased fourfold between 1824 and 1868. However, the lack of restrictions and regulation developed into a state of commercial anarchy and in 1857 the merchants, who were dissatisfied with the administration, petitioned for Singapore to come under direct British rule.

Ten years later, the Colonial Office in London reluctantly made Singapore a crown colony. Then in 1869 the Suez Canal opened which meant that the Strait of Melaka was an even more obvious route for East-West shipping traffic than the Sunda Strait, which was controlled by the Dutch. Five years after that, Britain signed the first of its protection treaties with the Malay sultans on the peninsula (**see page 64**). The governor of Singapore immediately became the most senior authority for the Straits Settlements Colony, the Federated Malay States and the British protectorates of Sarawak, Brunei and North Borneo. In one stroke, Singapore had become the political capital of a small empire within an empire. As Malaysia's plantation economy grew (with the introduction of rubber at the end of the 19th century – **see page 411**) and with tin-mining also expanding rapidly, Singapore emerged as the financing and administrative centre and export outlet. By then Singapore was the uncontested commercial and transport centre

– and ran a crude judicial system; the societies were locked in competition.

The wealthiest of the Chinese immigrant communities were the Straits-born Chinese (the Peranakans – **see page 168**), many of whom came to Singapore from Melaka, where their extraordinary Chinese-Malay culture had taken root in the 15th century. Most spurned Chinese-vernacular education for English-language schooling, and many went on to university in Britain. They were set apart from the *sinkheh* immigrants because of their wealth. Although they were among the first to arrive in Singapore, they only accounted for about a tenth of the population by the turn of the century. But they continued to make money in the tin, timber and rubber trades and were unabashedly ostentatious with their wealth.

By the early 1900s the transitory nature of Singapore's population was beginning to change as immigrants married, settled and raised families. This encouraged the immigration of more women. Immigration peaked in 1927 when 360,000 Chinese landed in Singapore. Three years later the government began to impose restrictions following the onset of the Great Depression. In 1933 the Aliens Ordnance imposed a monthly quota for male immigrants, which was aimed at balancing the skewed sex ratio. Politically, Chinese immigrants were more attuned to what was happening in China. In the mid-1920s a local legislative councillor, Tan Cheng Lock, began to call for elected representation for the Straits-born population, on the governing council. Its local members were nominated by the governor – the first local nominee had been an immigrant Chinese merchant called Hoo Ah Kay (but nicknamed Whampoa, after his birthplace) who was appointed in 1869. Despite Tan's efforts to raise their political consciousness, the immigrant communities remained more interested in trade than politics until after World War II.

of Southeast Asia. Between 1873 and 1913 there was an eightfold increase in Singapore's trade. Joseph Conrad dubbed it 'the thoroughfare to the East'.

Historian Mary Turnbull writes: "Growing Western interests in South-East Asia and the expansion of international trade, the liberalizing of Dutch colonial policy in the Netherlands East Indies, the increasing use of steamships (which from the 1880s replaced sailing ships as the main carriers) and the development of telegraphs all put Singapore, with its fine natural sheltered harbour, at the hub of international trade in South-East Asia. It became a vital link in the chain of British ports which stretched from Gibraltar, through the Mediterranean Sea and the Indian Ocean to the Far East. The 60 years from the opening of the Suez Canal to the onset of the Great Depression in 1929 were a time of unbroken peace, steady economic expansion and population growth in Singapore, with little dramatic incident to ruffle the calm."

The Japanese occupation

World War I gave Singapore a measure of strategic significance and by 1938 the colony was bristling with guns; it became known as 'Fortress Singapore'. Unfortunately, the impregnable Fortress Singapore had anticipated that any attack would be from the sea and all its big guns were facing seawards. The Japanese entered through the back door. Japan attacked Malaya in Dec 1941 and having landed on the NE coast, they took the entire peninsular in a lightning campaign, arriving in Johor Bahru at the end of Jan 1942.

The Japanese invasion of Singapore was planned by General Tomoyuki Yamashita and was coordinated from the Sultan Ibrahim tower in Johor Bahru, which afforded a commanding view over the strait and N Singapore. Yamashita became known as the Tiger of Malaya for the speed with which the Japanese

25th Army over-ran the peninsula. The NE coast of Singapore was heavily protected but the NW was vulnerable and the Japanese attacked in a 3-pronged offensive by the 18th Division, 5th Division and the Imperial Guards. About 20,000 Japanese landed on the NE coast, surrounding the Australian 22nd Brigade and wiping them out. The 27th Australian Brigade fared much better and was beating back the Japanese at Kranji when orders were misunderstood and the Australians retreated, to the bemused delight of the Japanese. There were 3 main battlefronts at Sarimbum Point, Bukit Timah, Mandai and Pasir Panjang; in each case, the Allies were out-manoeuvred, out-numbered and out-gunned. Towards the end, the battle became increasingly desperate and degenerated into hand-to-hand combat. On 13 Feb 1942 the Japanese captured Kent Ridge and Alexandra Barracks on Alexandra Road. They entered the hospital where they bayoneted the wounded and executed doctors, surgeons and nurses. The Allies and the local people were left in little doubt as to what was in store.

With their water supplies from the peninsula cut off by the Japanese, and facing an epidemic because of thousands of rotting corpses, British Lieutenant-General Arthur Percival was forced to surrender in the Ford Motor Company boardroom on Bukit Timah Road at 1950 on 15 Feb 1942. The fall of Singapore, which was a crushing humiliation for the British, left 140,000 Australian, British and Indian troops killed, wounded or captured. Japan had taken the island in one week.

The Japanese ran a brutal regime and their occupation was characterized by terror, starvation and misery. They renamed Singapore 'Syonan' – meaning 'light of the south'. The intention was to retain Syonan as a permanent colony, and turn it into a military base and a centre in its 'Greater East Asia Co-Prosperity Sphere'. During the war Singapore became the base of the collaborationist Indian National Army and the Indian Independence League.

In the fortnight that followed the surrender, the Japanese required all Chinese males aged 18-50 to register. 'Undesirables' were herded into trucks and taken for interrogation and torture by the *Kempetai* military police to the old YMCA building on Stamford Road or were summarily bayoneted and shot. The purge was known as *sook ching* – or 'the purification campaign'. Thousands were killed (Singapore says 50,000, Japan says 6,000) and most of the executions took place on Changi Beach and Sentosa. The sand on Changi Beach is said to have turned red from the blood.

Allied prisoners-of-war were herded into prison camps, the conditions in which are accurately described in James Clavell's book *King Rat*; the author was himself a Changi POW. Many of the Allied troops who were not dispatched to work on the Burma railway or sent to Sandakan in North Borneo, where 2,400 died (**see page 331**), were imprisoned in Selarang Barracks on the NE side of the island. On the site of Changi Airport's Runway Number 1, 4 men, who attempted to escape were summarily executed. Three-and-a-half years later, a Japanese commander, Major General Shempei Fukuei was sentenced to death for ordering the killings and executed on the same site.

Following the dropping of atomic bombs on Hiroshima and Nagasaki, the Japanese surrendered on 12 Sept 1945. The Japanese 5th and 18th Divisions which had spear-headed the invasion of Singapore and had carried out the massacres of civilians were from the towns of Hiroshima and Nagasaki respectively. The bombs saved Singapore from an Allied invasion. Lord Louis Mountbatten, who took the surrender, described it as the greatest day of his life.

In the wake of the war, the Japanese partially atoned for their 'blood debt' by extending 'gifts' and 'special loans' to Singapore of US$50 million. But Japanese war crimes were neither forgiven nor forgotten. When the head of Sony, Morita Akio and Japanese parliamentarian Ishihara Shintaro wrote in their 1990 book

The Japan that can say 'No' that the countries that Japan occupied during the war had become the best performing economies in Asia, it caused outrage and old wounds were reopened. They wrote: "We have to admit that we have done some wrong there... but we cannot deny the positive influence we had". Older Singaporeans also noted with dismay and concern how Japan had re-written its historical text-books to gloss over its wartime atrocities and many Singaporeans harbour a deep-seated mistrust of the Japanese. Among the most outspoken of them is former Prime Minister Lee Kuan Yew. This mistrust remains despite former Japanese Prime Minister Toshiki Kaifu's public apology in 1991 for what his countrymen had done half a century before.

After the war

Following a few months under a British military administration, Singapore became a crown colony and was separated from the other Straits Settlements of Penang, Melaka and Labuan. The Malay sultanates on the peninsula were brought into the Malayan Union. The British decision to keep Singapore separate from the Malayan Union sparked protests on the island and resulted in the founding of its first political party, the Malayan Democratic Union (MDU), which wanted Singapore to be integrated into a socialist union. In Malaya, the Union was very unpopular too, and the British replaced it with the Federation of Malaya in 1948. Singapore was excluded again because Malaya's emergent Malay leaders did not want to upset the peninsula's already delicate ethnic balance by incorporating predominantly Chinese Singapore.

The same year, elections were held for Singapore's legislative council. The MDU, which had been heavily infiltrated by Communists, boycotted the election, allowing the Singapore Progressive Party (SPP) – dominated by an English-educated élite – to win a majority. The council was irrelevant to the majority of the population however and did nothing to combat poverty and unemployment and little to promote social services. When the Communist Emergency broke out on the peninsula later the same year (**see page 384**), the Malayan Communist Party of Malaya (CPM) was banned in Singapore and the MDU disbanded.

In 1955 a new constitution was introduced which aimed to jolt the island's apathetic electorate into political life. Two new parties were formed to contest the election – the Labour Front under lawyer David Marshall (descended from an Iraqi Jewish family) and the People's Action Party (PAP), headed by Lee Kuan Yew (**see page 384**). These 2 parties routed the conservative SPP and Marshall formed a minority government. His tenure as Chief Minister was marked by violence and by tempestuous exchanges in the Legislative Assembly with Lee. Marshall resigned in 1956 after failing to negotiate self-government for Singapore by his self-imposed deadline. His deputy, Lim Yew Hock (who later became a Muslim) took over as Chief Minister and more Communist-instigated violence followed.

The influence of the PAP grew rapidly, in league with the Communists and radical union leaders, through the trades unions and Chinese-language schools. For Lee, who hated Communism, it was a Machiavellian alliance of convenience. The Communists came to dominate the PAP central committee and managed to sideline Lee before their leaders were arrested by Marshall's government. At the same time, Singapore's administration was localized rapidly: the 4 main languages (Malay, Chinese, Tamil and English) were given parity within the education system and locals took over the civil service. In 1957, as Malaya secured independence from the British, Singapore negotiated terms for full self-government. In 1959 the PAP swept the polls, winning a clear majority, and Lee became Prime Minister, a post he was to hold for more than 3 decades.

The PAP government began a programme of rapid industrialization and social reform. Singapore also moved closer to Malaysia, which Lee considered a vital move, to guarantee free access to the Malaysian market and provide military security in the run-up to its own independence. But the PAP leaders were split over the wisdom of this move, and the extreme left wing, which had come to the forefront again, was becoming more vociferous in its opposition. Malaysia, for its part, felt threatened by Singapore's large Chinese population and by its increasingly Communist-orientated government. Tunku Abdul Rahman, independent Malaysia's first Prime Minister, voiced concerns that an independent Singapore could be 'a second Cuba', a Communist state on Malaysia's doorstep. Instead of letting the situation deteriorate, however, Tunku Abdul Rahman cleverly proposed Singapore's inclusion in the Federation of Malaysia.

He hoped the racial equilibrium of the federation would be balanced by the inclusion of Sarawak, Brunei and North Borneo. Lee liked the idea, but the radical left wing of the PAP were vehemently opposed to it, having no desire to see Singapore absorbed by a Malay-dominated, anti-Communist regime, and in Jul 1961 they tried to topple Lee's government. Their bid narrowly failed and resulted in the left-wing dissenters breaking away to form the Barisan Sosialis (BS), or Socialist Front. Despite continued opposition to the merger, a referendum showed that a majority of Singapore's population supported it. In Feb 1963, in *Operation Coldstore*, more than 100 Communist and pro-Communist politicians, trades unionists and student leaders were arrested, including half the BS Central Executive Committee.

On 31 Aug 1963, Singapore joined the Federation of Malaysia. The following month, during a delay in the implementation of the Federation while the wishes of the Borneo states were being ascertained, Singapore declared unilateral independence from Britain. The PAP also won another resounding victory in an election and secured a comfortable majority. Almost immediately, however, the new federation ran into trouble, due to Indonesian objections, and Jakarta launched its *Konfrontasi* – or Confrontation (see page 237). Indonesian saboteurs infiltrated Singapore and began a bombing spree which severely damaged Singapore's trade. In mid-1964 Singapore was wracked by communal riots which caused great concern in Kuala Lumpur, and Lee and Tunku Abdul Rahman clashed over what they considered undue interference in each others' internal affairs. Tensions rose still further when the PAP contested Malaysia's general election in 1964, and Lee attempted to unite all Malaysian opposition parties under the PAP banner. Finally, on 9 Aug 1965, Kuala Lumpur forced Singapore to agree to pull out of the Federation, and it became an independent state against the wishes of the government. At a press conference announcing Singapore's expulsion from the federation, Lee Kuan Yew wept.

ART AND ARCHITECTURE

Among the first things a visitor notices on arrival in Singapore are the towering modern high-rise buildings. Many of these are public Housing Development Board (HDB) blocks, but there are countless luxury condominium developments and, in the city, huge, office towers. The rush to modernise the city skyline and clear the urban slums resulted in what is now dubbed the 'architectural holocaust' of the 1960s and 1970s. When Singapore's older colonial buildings fell into disrepair, and the old shophouses had become squalid, decaying wrecks, they were demolished, instead of being gutted and restored. Other old buildings – perhaps most notably, the Raffles Institution – were torn down to make way for gleaming skyscrapers.

During the 1980s the government began to realize its mistake and the Urban Redevelopment Authority (URA) became the national conservation body. Since then, great effort has been put into restoring shophouses to their former glory – although their original residents have given way to advertising agencies and fancy restaurants. Other renovation efforts have notably lacked good taste. The Convent of the Holy Infant Jesus on Victoria Street is a classic example. The URA spotted its commercial potential and a developer intends to spend S$50 million turning the former convent into a shopping complex. Plans to turn the chapel into a disco were abandoned. The URA has however gazetted conservation areas such as Tanjong Pagar and Boat Quay and many old churches, temples, mosques, markets and even hotels (notably the *Raffles Hotel* – **see page 398** – and the *Goodwood Park Hotel*) were declared national monuments. Not that gazetting buildings as conservation areas solves all the problems, however. In March 1993, a contractor demolished a pre-war row of shophouses – earmarked by the URA for conservation – 'by mistake'. His defence was that because he could not read English, he could not understand the URA's plans or instructions. He was fined S$2,000.

In 1823, when the British administration decided to make Singapore a penal station, several hundred Indian convicts were shipped in to work as labourers. They built St Andrew's Cathedral, the Sri Mariamman Temple and the Istana. The British also imported indentured labourers – who were exclusively Tamils – to build roads, bridges, canals and wharves.

Among the more interesting architectural innovations at this time was *Madras chunam*, devised by Indian labourers to conceal deficiencies of building materials. The recipe for Madras chunam was egg white, egg shell, lime and a coarse sugar (called jaggery), mixed with coconut husks and water into a paste. Once the paste had hardened, it was polished to give a smooth surface, and moulded to give many of the buildings their ornate fronts.

The Chinese temple form is based on that of a traditional Chinese house or palace and is a grouping of pavilions around open courtyards – this method of constructing Chinese temples has changed little over the centuries. Chinese builders are also bound by the strict principles of Yin and Yang, and the complicated nuances of Chinese geomancy or *feng shui*. To do otherwise is to court catastrophe. Even in modern Singapore, feng shui plays an important role in architectural design. *Feng* means 'wind' and *shui* means 'water'. Chinese superstition dictates that the 'dragon' must be able to breathe life into any building and that doors, walls and furniture must be aligned according to the principles of geomancy to prevent good spirits, wealth and harmony flowing out. There must be running water near-by too. If a building in Singapore does not meet the feng shui criteria it is extremely rare for a Chinese to live there. All the big hotels and office blocks are designed with feng shui in mind; expensive alterations are made to buildings that do not have the required qualities. New buildings are also opened on auspicious days. The classic case of this was the towering OUB Centre in Raffles Place. Its construction was completed in 1986, but its official opening was delayed until 8 Aug 1988 (8-8-88), which translated into quadruple good luck.

CULTURE AND LIFE

People

Today, 78% of Singapore's population is of Chinese extraction; 15% are Malay and 6.5% Indian. There is also a small Eurasian population. The government has worked hard to stop Singaporeans thinking of themselves as Chinese, Malays or Indians; it wants them to think of themselves as Singaporeans. The republic's 'ambassador-at-large', Professor Tommy Koh (who also heads the government think-tank) wrote in 1991: "The primordial pull of race dominates... group

Population policies and designer genes

One of the government's key social programmes during the 1970s was an effort to slow the country's spiralling birth rate by family planning. The policy proved to be so successful, however, that declining fertility rates forced a policy U-turn in the mid-1980s. The government is concerned that in 40 years' time, one fifth of Singapore's population will be aged 65 or over. But racial concerns appear to have been an even greater motivating factor. Apparently driven by fears that the Malay population was growing faster than the Chinese population, the government scrapped the old slogan 'Stop at Two', and replaced it with 'Go for Three'. It offered generous tax incentives to induce Singaporeans to have more children. At the same time, Prime Minister Lee Kuan Yew instigated the selective 'breeding for brilliance' campaign, which sought to mobilize the latent talent in Singapore's limited gene-pool. He promoted procreation among the more prosperous and better-educated members of Singapore society. In 1983 he warned that if something was not done: "Levels of competence will decline, our economy will falter, the administration will suffer and society will decline." These were ominous portents of the future but Lee's genetic engineering policy was very unpopular and prompted mocking disbelief abroad. Once, when regaling Britain's Princess Royal on the virtues of eugenics, she reportedly retorted: "Very interesting Prime Minister, but I can tell you, it doesn't work with horses".

The policy was officially shelved in 1985, but this did not stop Lee continuing to propound it. Lee himself got a double first at Cambridge (with a distinction) and his wife got a first; together they have produced highly intelligent offspring. In his landmark national day speech before stepping down as Prime Minister in 1990 Lee noted with satisfaction that more male graduates had married female graduates during the 1980s. He remained concerned, however, that highly educated women were not having superior babies because of Singapore men's apparent "immature" preference for younger, less-well educated girls. He said that Singapore's female graduates face "the stark option of marrying downwards, marrying foreigners or staying unmarried." Despite the fact that

identity, but for most Singaporeans, especially the younger Singaporeans, their racial identity is weaker than their group identity as Singaporeans. The fact that this has been achieved in 25 years is a remarkable example of nation-building." As present Prime Minister Goh Chok Tong once pointed out, in the space of 25 years, Singaporeans have been British subjects, Japanese subjects, Malaysians and now Singaporeans.

Singapore likes to take Switzerland as its model, because Switzerland has a Swiss identity that supersedes the separate German, French and Italian ethnic and cultural influences. The difference is that Switzerland has been a confederation for 700 years. Critics of the Singapore government have voiced concern over the 'Sinification' of Singapore and fear that in the long term, resentment in minority communities could turn Singapore into a Sri Lanka instead. The spectre of ethnic unrest, however, is far from being a reality. Today, Singaporeans are affluent and their prosperity has largely distracted them from ethnic prejudices. Even the Malays (see below) are, on average, better off in Singapore than they are in Malaysia, and the Indians have no doubts. Goh Chok Tong said in 1991: "So long as the economy is growing, there is plenty for everybody, I don't think people will fight over small things. But if the pie is shrinking, that will be the real test of whether we are cohesive, solid or whether we are fragile".

Historian Mary Turnbull writes that "as a largely Chinese city state in an alien region [Singapore] could not afford to build up a cultural Sino-nationalism. Its salvation lay in a secular, multi-racial statehood, encouraging communities to take pride in their cultural roots and language but conforming to a common national the smart baby policy was officially withdrawn, the pairing-off of educated people has remained an unofficial objective on the government agenda.

Singapore's drive to reverse its declining birth rate has had its amusing moments. Senior government ministers regularly attend baby shows and talk of procreation as if it were an industry. Baby output is currently estimated to be about 50,000 units a year. Meanwhile, the local press has continued to sing the joys of parenthood and the Social Development Unit – the government funded computer match-making agency – is forever dreaming up new schemes for getting people (particularly, bright people) together. The head of the SDU – better known as 'Chief Cupid' – organizes discos, barbeques, computer courses and harbour cruises in the SDU 'love boat'. The SDU has 13,000 clients, of whom about 2,500 are 'active' at any one time. Each client is offered 90 computer dates over 5 years. In 1991, 1,643 pairs of college graduates married, up from 704 pairs in 1984. More than half of male graduates now marry fellow graduates, compared with 38% ten years ago. One of the hottest-selling books in 1993 has been the Ministry of Community Development's *Preparing for Marriage*. In June, a Chinese-language edition rolled off the presses, offering tips on how to woo in the vernacular. The government is behind the matrimonial rush in more ways than one. Women have to be 35 or over to qualify for their own Housing Development Board flats. Marriage therefore offers a means of escaping parental homes.

From time to time the SDU organizes mass-weddings, with young couples with 'O' level qualifications in one batch, and 'A' level couples in the next. These ceremonies involve the newly weds promenading down red carpets with dry ice billowing around them for that 'head-in-the-clouds' effect. Singapore Broadcasting has chipped in with a local version of *Blind Date*. Yet despite the substantial tax incentives on offer to parents who produce more babies, Singapore's population is only growing at about 1% a year.

character." The government's efforts at forging this national character have been professionally stage-managed. On National Day every year crowds of cheer-leaders repeatedly sing 'One people, one nation, one Singapore' as if trying to convince themselves that they do have a national identity. But as the older first-generation immigrants have died off, the proportion of Singapore-born Singaporeans has risen, which has helped towards building a sense of nationhood. More than 80% of the population is now Singapore-born. Today, national pride is not in question: Singaporeans rarely tire of boasting to visitors that they have the best airline in the world, the best airport in the world, the busiest port in the world and one of the fastest growing economies in the world.

The Malays in modern Singapore are considered a downtrodden minority, despite the government's stated efforts to build a multi-racial society. While Malay is still the country's official language, the Malays themselves have been subsumed by the dominant Chinese culture and they complain of feeling alienated in their own country. Malays have not taken to living in tower blocks – they are kampung people by nature – and within Singaporean society, they are regarded as under-achievers, particularly in business and finance, where the Chinese reign supreme. This becomes most obvious when an embarrassing fuss is made of Malays who succeed in the academic world or as professionals. Today Singapore's Malay community has a poorer academic record in school, a higher drug addiction rate and less economic muscle than any other community. Malay (and Indian) community leaders have criticised the government's 'Speak Mandarin' campaign as racially divisive.

Ironically, however, the roots of Malay nationalism, that led eventually to calls for independence from the British, were first planted in Singapore. In 1926 the *Kesatuan Melayu Singapura* (KMS), or Singapore Malay Union, was founded by the 'father of Malay journalism' Mohammed Eunos bin Abdullah. He was Singapore's first Malay legislative councillor and magistrate, having been educated at the élite English-language Raffles Institution. The KMS set up branches in the peninsula and was the forerunner of the United Malays National Organization (UMNO) which has been at the helm of the Malaysian government since independence.

Religion

Nearly 60% of Singapore's population professes to be Buddhist (mostly Mahayana) or Taoists. Taoists follow the teachings of Confucius, Mencius and Lao Zi and practice ancestor worship. Islam is practised by virtually all Malays as well as many Indians – in total, Muslims comprise 15% of the population. Singaporean Muslims are under the authority of the *Majlis Ugama Islam Singapura* (MUIS) – the Islamic Religious Council of Singapore – which advises the government on all matters Islamic. Christians account for nearly 13% of the population, about 60% of whom are Protestants. Christian missionaries arrived in Singapore within a year of Raffles founding the city. Hindus make up 4% of the population and the most important Hindu shrine is the Sri Mariamman Temple in South Bridge Road, which was built in 1827 (**see page 406**). There are also 9 Sikh *Gurdwara* (temples) in Singapore and 2 Jewish synagogues.

Following the government's allegations in 1988 that the Roman Catholic church had been infiltrated by Marxists (**see page 383**), the government introduced the Maintenance of Religious Harmony Act, which totally barred the mixing of politics and religion. It also introduced very strict rules regarding inter-religious proselytization. Evangelical Christians, for example, were banned – on pain of imprisonment – from any sort of missionary work in the Muslim community, which had been outraged by Christians passing Muslims tracts and leaflets on Christianity. The bill also banned the teaching of any religion in schools. The government is acutely aware of the need to remain a secular state and is extremely wary of anything it perceives as 'fundamentalist' and as a threat to ethnic harmony.

Language

There are 4 official languages in Singapore: Malay, English, Chinese and Tamil. Malay is still officially the national language. English is the language of administration and business. This means there are very few Singaporeans who do not speak it – although Singaporean English (commonly known as 'Singlish' is virtually a dialect in itself (**see page 453**). Since 1979, the government has enthusiastically promoted the use of Mandarin – probably in the hope that Singaporeans who are bilingual in Mandarin and English will provide a bridge between the West and China. Mandarin is increasingly being used instead of Chinese dialects. Although minority communities might regard the 'Speak Mandarin' campaign as evidence of Chinese cultural dominance, it is not uncommon to find even Tamil children in Singapore who are fluent in Mandarin. Today 46% of the population is literate in 2 or more languages. The main Chinese dialects still spoken in Singapore include Hokkien, Teochew, Cantonese, Hakka, Hainanese and Foochow. About 80% of Singapore's Indians are Tamil, but other Indian languages are spoken, including Punjabi, Malayalam, Telegu, Hindi and Bengali.

Dance, drama and music

The Ministry for Information and the Arts was created in 1990; it was immediately dubbed 'the ministry of fun' and is presided over by a senior cabinet minister. The intention is to make Singapore into a cultural and entertainment hub and no expense has been spared in bringing art exhibitions and top stage acts – theatre, dance and music – to the republic as well as promoting the arts within Singapore. The Singapore Symphony Orchestra gives regular performances – including many free open-air shows in the Botanic Gardens – and the National Theatre Trust promotes cultural dance performances and local theatre as well as inviting international dance and theatre groups to Singapore.

Traditional Chinese street operas (*wayang*) mostly take place during the 7th lunar month, following the Festival of the Hungry Ghosts (**see page 449**). Wayangs are regularly staged on makeshift wooden platforms which are erected in vacant lots all over the city. To the sound of clashing cymbals and drums, the wayang actors – adorned in ornate costumes and with faces painted – act out the roles of gods, goddesses, heroes, heroines, sages and villains from Chinese folklore. Many professional wayang troupes are freelancers who come from Malaysia and Hong Kong to perform.

MODERN SINGAPORE

Politics

In 1965, the newly independent Republic of Singapore committed itself to non-Communist, multi-racial, democratic socialist government and secured Malaysian cooperation in trade and defence. The new government faced what most observers considered impossible: forging a viable economy in a densely populated micro-state with no natural resources. At first Singapore hoped for readmission to the Malaysian Federation, but as Lee surprised everyone by presiding over one of the fastest-growing economies in the world, the republic soon realized that striking out alone was the best approach. Within a few years, independent Singapore was being hailed as an 'economic miracle'. But the government had to work hard to forge a sense of nationhood (**see page 381**). Because most Singaporeans were still more interested in wealth creation than in politics, the government became increasingly paternalistic, declaring that it knew what was best for the people, and because most people agreed, few raised any objections.

Singapore's foreign policy was built around regional cooperation and it was a vociferous founder member of the Association of South-East Asian Nations (ASEAN). Friendly international relations were considered of paramount importance for a state which relied so heavily on foreign trade. Although Singapore continued to trade with the former Communist states of Eastern Europe and the Soviet Union, Lee had a great fear and loathing of Communism. At home, 'Communists' became bogeymen; 'hard-core' subversives were imprisoned without trial, under emergency legislation enshrined in the Internal Security Act, a legacy of the British colonial administration.

Singapore's political stability since independence, which has helped attract foreign investors to the island, was tempered by the government's increasing tendency to stifle criticism. The media are state-owned and are so pro-government that they have become self-censoring. Foreign publications are summarily banned or their circulation restricted if they are deemed to be critical of Singapore's internal affairs. Probably because Lee Kuan Yew's People's Action Party (PAP) was so successful at bringing about the economic miracle, no credible political opposition emerged. Politicians who stood out bravely against Lee's benevolent but autocratic style of government, were effectively silenced as the government set about undermining their credibility in the eyes of the electorate. For 13 years, between 1968 and 1981, the PAP held every single seat in parliament. The London-based *Economist Intelligence Unit* says: "Opposition to the ruling party and its ideals of strength through economic achievement is welcomed in theory but not in practice. Those who criticise the government are, in such a small community, both visible and vulnerable."

Harry Lee Kuan Yew – the father of modern Singapore

British political scientist Michael Leifer once described Lee Kuan Yew – better known as 'Harry' or 'LKY' – as "a political superman of his time, albeit in charge of a metropolis". The father of modern Singapore, who finally stepped down after 31 years as Prime Minister in 1990, believed he knew what was best for his country. Partly because of the Confucian ethic of respect for one's elders, and partly because his policies worked wonders, Singaporeans, by and large, assigned their fate to Harry Lee's better judgement. To Western observers, Lee was variously cast as a miracle-worker, a classic benevolent dictator, and, in some quarters, as a tyrant. British newspaper columnist Bernard Levin (who writes for *The Times*, London) became one of Lee's most outspoken critics. Just a few months before his resignation, Levin wrote "Today, his rule is based on a frenzied determination to allow no one in his realm to defy him, from which it follows that those who dare to do so, even in the smallest particular, must be crushed and having been crushed must be indefinitely pursued with an implacable and crazed vindictiveness". To a point, what Levin wrote was true – Lee did not suffer his critics or political opponents gladly.

But by his own hand, Lee turned tiny Singapore into a by-word for excellence, efficiency and high-achievement. In his 3 decades in power, Lee built Singapore into a powerful economy, but his authoritarian style also turned Singaporeans into timid citizens. In 1991 London's *Financial Times* wrote that Lee's laudable achievements had been "at the cost of creating an antiseptic and dull society which leaves little room for individual creativity or imagination..." *The Economist* put it more succinctly, saying that "Lee ran Singapore like a well-managed nursery". He has been compared with a master-watchmaker who built the perfect timepiece, but could not resist the temptation of constantly taking it apart again and rebuilding it, to see if it could be improved. By the late 1980s, the electorate's swing against Lee's ruling People's Action Party and its controversial policies (such as the 'breeding for brilliance' campaign – **see page 380**) suggested that the people were sick of the constant re-tuning. They were ready for change.

Harry Lee Kuan Yew was born on 16 Sept 1923. While his family was of Hakka Chinese origin, his parents were Straits-born Peranakan Chinese (**see page 168**) who had lived in the Straits Settlements for several generations. At home he grew up speaking English, Malay and Cantonese. He was the eldest son and was accorded all the privileges of a male first-born. But despite ingraining Singaporeans with the Confucian ethic of filial piety, Lee Kuan Yew himself did not like his father. In 1936 he attended the prestigious Raffles Institution. Even as a schoolboy, Lee was known for his aggressive streak and his domineering personality, according to his unauthorized biographer, James Minchin, in *No Man is an Island*. Minchin wrote: "Since coming to office, Lee has tended to indulge his instinct to bully and demolish... Power mostly removes the humiliation of being bested. Within this dominant characteristic of aggression we may trace elements of rage, fear and self-aggrandisement".

The PAP has lost votes, however; its popularity has declined over the past decade and despite the party's strong majority in parliament, its percentage of the vote has fallen. In the 1984 election there was a 13% swing against the PAP, and support declined further in 1988 and 1991. As Lee Kuan Yew came to be regarded as one of the region's 'elder statesmen', questions were raised over his succession. The PAP's old guard gradually made way for young blood, but Lee clung on until Nov 1990. Three months after Singapore's extravagant 25th anniversary, he finally handed over to his first deputy prime minister Goh Chok Tong, in whom he quite obviously had little confidence. He remained chairman of the PAP and became

In World War II Lee worked as a functionary for the Japanese occupying forces, but by the end of it he had become determined that Singapore should never again be ruled by foreigners. After the war he went to London (which he hated), and soon abandoned an economics degree at the London School of Economics. He was then accepted by Cambridge University to study law – the same department as his future wife, Kwa Geok Choo. They both graduated in 1949 with first class honours, although Lee got a distinction. On returning to Singapore they married and set up a law firm, Lee and Lee. He became increasingly involved in politics and resigned as a partner in the firm when he became Prime Minister in 1959. His brother Denis took over and the company is still operating today. Lee proved to be a shrewd political operator, and quickly became known for his traits of honesty, efficiency, firmness and intolerance. As a political leader, he was able to inspire both confidence and fear.

Lee was known for his disciplined, austere lifestyle; he exercises regularly (ever since his days at Cambridge, he has enjoyed playing golf); he watches his diet carefully and steers clear of anyone with a cold. He has fetishes about cleanliness and health. His private residence on Oxley Rise is guarded by Gurkha soldiers. One of Lee's most telling speeches, which gives some insight into his personal philosophy was given in 1973. He said: "The greatest satisfaction in life comes from achievement. To achieve is to be happy. Singaporeans must be imbued with this spirit. We must never get into the vicious cycle of expecting more and more for less and less... Solid satisfaction comes out of achievement... It generates inner or spiritual strength, a strength which grows out of an inner discipline."

Despite stepping down as Prime Minister in 1990, Lee retains the post of Senior Minister in Prime Minister Goh Chok Tong's cabinet. He is now Southeast Asia's best-known elder statesman and Singapore is too small for him. There has been joking speculation that he wanted to be a mercenary prime minister somewhere else: what better for China than to have Lee Kuan Yew at the helm?

In the run up to his 'retirement', Lee pushed through a controversial constitutional amendment by which Singapore's next president will be popularly elected instead of appointed. The term of the current President Wee Kim Wee – a former journalist and diplomat – expires in Oct 1993 and his successor is expected to play a much more prominent role in national affairs. There was much speculation that Lee would stand as a candidate for the elected presidency – although he has said he will not. Whatever materializes in that respect, few Singaporeans expect Lee to disappear into the wings – he will remain Singapore's chief puppet master. In 1988, when speculation that he was going to stand was mounting, Lee said in his National Day speech: "Even from my sickbed, even if you are going to lower me into the grave and I feel that something is wrong, I'll get up". Singaporeans joked that with his new threat of resurrection, the old visionary had begun to cast himself in the messianic mould.

'senior minister without portfolio' in Goh's cabinet.

Although Singapore has been run as a meritocracy since independence, there are signs that a Gandhi-style dynasty may be in the making. Goh is widely assumed to be a seat-warmer for Lee Kuan Yew's eldest son, Brigadier-General Lee Hsien Loong, better known locally as 'B G Lee' or 'The Rising Son'. B G Lee is currently deputy prime minister and trade and industry minister – a key portfolio. B G Lee, like his father, got a first at Cambridge, returned to Singapore, joined the army as a platoon commander and within 8 years was a Brigadier-General in charge of the Joint Operations Planning Directorate. During that period he got a masters degree at Harvard and then in 1984, at the age of 32, was elected to parliament. The following year he became a cabinet minister.

When Lee senior stepped down, a new era began; it became known as 'The Next Lap' and the government-sponsored book of that title outlines the general directions of national development over the next 25 years. Goh promised to usher in a more open, 'people-oriented', consensus-style of government. Among his first acts was the creation of a new ministry for the arts and to underscore his faith in Singapore's maturity, he permitted the showing of blue movies, which proved very popular (**see page 429**). The rationale behind the new openness was to create a more cultured and less restrictive environment aimed at dissuading Singapore's brightest and best from emigrating due to boredom and concern about the country's authoritarian government. Goh's government has introduced a more relaxed atmosphere; he has moved towards a freer press (particularly in regard to foreign publications), released long-term political prisoners and has allowed ageing exiles to return home.

A kinder, but still sensitive Singapore

Coinciding with the introduction of Singapore's long-promised more relaxed style of government, a cartoon book appeared on bookshelves in late 1990 entitled *Hello Chok Tong, Goodbye Kuan Yew*. The new cabinet was portrayed as a football team with former Prime Minister Lee Kuan Yew as the goal-keeper, shouting things like 'Just try it!'. The cartoonist was reported as saying that Singapore's 'glasnost', a result of Goh's 'kinder, gentler Singapore', allowed him to get away with it. The former Prime Minister's son, Lee Hsien Loong, was portrayed as the would-be striker on the team's right wing. The script reads: 'Fans and opponents alike are watching carefully how quickly he matures in an attacking role... Tends to over-react under pressure. Would do a lot better if he relaxed.'

There have been other signs that Singapore is easing up – including the release of its erstwhile longest-serving political prisoner, Chia Thye Poh, who had to suffer two years of internal exile on Sentosa before being allowed back into society. But the government let itself down again in April 1993 when a university lecturer and opposition politician, Dr Chee Soon Juan, who stood against Goh in a by-election the previous December (see below) was unceremoniously sacked. Believing his dismissal was politically motivated, Chee went on hunger-strike. His crime had been to allegedly spend some of his research grant to courier his wife's thesis to the United States. More to the point, perhaps, was that he had challenged government policy on social welfare issues.

The results of a general election in Oct 1991, which was meant to provide an endorsement for Goh's more caring brand of government came as a bit of a shock to the PAP. Its share of the vote declined even further than it had done in the 1988 election and there are now an unprecedented 4 opposition members of parliament – up from just one in the previous parliament. Since 1980 there has been a 15% swing to the opposition. In the wake of what foreign newspaper reports called the PAP's 'stunning losses', Goh said that he could "be a little deaf" to the needs of people in opposition constituencies – Lee had, after all, assured the electorate that his successor would be "no softie". One of the successful opposition candidates said that while the PAP liked to treat the people like children, the opposition parties were offering a change, making people realize that "the relationship between government and the people is not a parent and child relationship, but a relationship of equals". Goh fought a by-election just before Christmas 1992 in the middle-class constituency of Marine Parade. It was an opportunity for him to garner more political legitimacy – but in the event, the PAP won 73% of the vote, down from the 77% in the 1991 general election. The opposition Singapore Democratic Party won 24% of the vote. Political minutiae maybe, but the concensus was that Goh had strengthened his hand by the inevitable landslide. But Goh's hopes of being much more than a seat-warmer for BG Lee – Lee Kuan Yew's son – were dashed by the announcement in May 1993 that Lee junior had made a recovery from cancer. In November 1992 he had been diagnosed as having lymphona. In a newspaper interview, his father said: "Singapore needs the best it can get. If Singapore can get a man who has never had cancer and who is better than (Lee Hsien) Loong, then that man is the answer. But if it can't, take the best man that is available." Goh Chok Tong said the younger Lee remained his choice for a successor.

Defence

Singapore spends more than US$2 billion a year on defence – over a third of government expenditure. It promotes the idea of 'total defence', meaning that everyone, plays some role in protecting the country, economically and militarily. Regular emergency exercises are conducted involving the civilian population, which is designed to instill preparedness. This policy is probably influenced by memories of Singapore's inglorious surrender to the Japanese in Feb 1942 (**see page 376**). Men have to serve a compulsory 24-30 months in the Singapore Defence Forces, followed by annual 40-day training exercises for reservists, who undergo twice-yearly physical fitness tests until they are 40 years old. Being a predominantly Chinese state in the middle of the Malay world, Singapore feels very vulnerable, and government ministers have expressed their fears of a 'Kuwait situation', despite Singapore's good relations with its Malaysian and Indonesian neighbours. The armed forces are known to be trained by Israelis. Singapore is also the biggest arms manufacturer in the region and is an entrepôt for the arms trade.

Economy

Singapore has natural advantages: its strategic location and an excellent harbour. It also owes a debt to its founding father, Stamford Raffles and to former Prime Minister Lee Kuan Yew. Raffles allowed unrestricted immigration and free trade, declaring Singapore a free port. In this respect, Singapore was the first place to adopt 18th century Scottish economist and philosopher Adam Smith's principle of *laissez-faire*. This policy was enshrined as the *modus operandi* of Singapore's flourishing merchant community and was the most important factor influencing the commercial growth of Raffles' trading centre. For more than a century-and-a-half, Singapore boomed as a regional trans-shipment centre.

For his part, Lee Kuan Yew gave Singapore political stability unrivalled in the region, making the island republic a magnet for multinational investment. His pragmatic and far-sighted government ploughed the profits of the booming economy into the island's physical and social infrastructure. It also concentrated on building Singapore up as a financial centre. Following independence, Singapore maintained its *laissez-faire* image only when it came to international trade; in every other sector of the economy the government has been interventionist.

The economy remained largely in the hands of the private sector but the government set up strategic public sector firms to direct and catalyse rapid industrialization. At the same time, the government subsidized public housing, health and education. It placed great emphasis on the latter, promoting bi-lingualism and vocational training, focused on the skills required by targeted industries. Singapore's public housing policies are now legendary. New high-rise towns have sprung up around the island and the government demolished village after village, moving people into tower blocks. Over four-fifths of the population lives in Housing Development Board flats, of which three-quarters are now owner-occupied. Singaporeans are encouraged to use their compulsory savings in the Central Provident Fund (CPF) to purchase their flats from the government. The government has been careful to keep these blocks racially mixed: if, for example, you are a Chinese and want to move out, you cannot sell to another Chinese.

When Singapore became an independent country in 1965 it had a per capita income of US$700 a year. It had virtually no natural resources and even had to import its water from Malaysia. To compound the problem, the British military withdrew from their bases in Singapore in 1971; they had contributed a fifth of Singapore's GDP and employed nearly a fifth of the labour force. Within 12 years of independence, however, per capita income had risen to US$2,500 and by the early 1980s Singapore had the third highest per capita income in Asia after Japan and Brunei. In 1990 Singapore's average per capita income was US$12,800, well ahead of many European nations including Ireland and Spain. After Japan, Singapore is now rated as the least-risky Asian country for foreign investment and the world's second best economic performer.

Singapore's economy has expanded by an average of 9% a year ever since independence in 1965. Government policies have resulted in high growth except for a 2-year hiccough in the mid-1980s when Singapore was hit by recession and low inflation; Singapore has no external debt and a healthy balance of trade surplus. In 1988 the United States removed Singapore from its list of preferential developing country trading partners, which was the first official sign that Singapore had ascended – in the eyes of the industrialized West – to the status of a Newly Industrialized Economy (NIE), along with the other 'Tiger Economies' of Hong Kong, Taiwan and South Korea. In 1991 Singapore was officially declared a 'developed country'.

In 1965, when the government was still reeling at separation from Malaysia, the top priority was job creation and basic industrialization. During the 1970s, when more sophisticated industries set up, the government focused on diversifying the economy and upgrading skills. Export promotion, aimed at finding new markets, coupled with the intensive campaign to attract foreign investment, meant that Singapore became less and less dependent on entrepôt trade. The services sector was expanded to build up financial services and the tourism industry. Great emphasis was placed on mechanizing and increasing productivity. By the end of the 1970s, Singapore's scarcity of labour was beginning to bite and the government began to switch from labour-intensive industries to capital-intensive and hi-tech industries, including aerospace, biotechnology, information technology and petrochemicals. Instead of assembling radios, production line workers began making disk drives. Corporations were given tax incentives to facilitate their use of Singapore as a regional headquarters and international purchasing centre. Within Singapore the buzzword was 'excellence'.

The recession which hit Singapore in 1985 and 1986 came as a shock to a country which had experienced fast and furious growth for 2 decades. But it allowed for a stock-taking exercise and the government carefully drew up a recovery strategy. By 1987 the economic growth rate was nearly 10% again and the following year it topped 11%. New effort was put into promoting Singapore as the financial hub of Asia; by the early 1990s, the financial services industry was growing by

The Central Providence Fund – saving for a rainy day

Thanks to Singapore's compulsory savings scheme, the country has the highest savings rate in the world. The Central Provident Fund (CPF) was set up in 1955 to provide pensions for workers, health care and to help people put down-payments and pay off mortgages on flats. It now covers insurance schemes and education as well. Employees below 55 years of age have to contribute 16.5% of their monthly income (older workers pay less) to the CPF and their employers contribute a further 23%. In 1991, CPF's two million members had S$40.6 billion (US$22.4 billion) under management. Members can withdraw their savings when they reach 55, but they have to leave S$8,000 in their Medisave account to cover any health care needs during retirement.

Singapore traffic – no more for the road

Singapore now has a highly efficient local and international transport network, with the Mass Rapid Transit railway, the splendid Changi Airport and an urban road system unrivalled in Asia. The latest addition has been the underground Central Expressway (CTE), which makes it possible to drive into the heart of the city without encountering a single red light. Above ground, Singapore is internationally renowned for its 'Restricted Zone' system, which controls traffic flows into the Central Business District at rush-hour. The average speed of vehicles during peak hours is 30 kph compared with 16 kph in Hong Kong, 15 kph in London and 5 kph in Bangkok. The island has a highly efficient public transport system, but no matter what it does, the government has been unable to stop Singaporeans buying cars.

Besides having one of the highest population densities in the world, Singapore also has one of the highest automobile densities in the world (81 km of roadway, against 43 in Japan and 27 in the US). Yet its ultra-efficient, visionary urban planners have avoided the gridlock typical of most other capitals in the region. Part of this is to do with the CBD restrictions, but more importantly, the government has ruled that the car population cannot grow any faster than the road network. Due to this policy, Singapore's cars are about the most expensive in the world. There is a 45% import tariff, a huge registration fee and an additional charge of 150% of the car's market value.

Because all this was still not deterring Singaporeans from buying cars, the government introduced a Certificate of Entitlement, which would-be car owners must obtain before they purchase a car. These are sold through a complex auction system. Prices of cars vary each month depending on how many people are bidding for them and how much they bid. The government sets the cut-off price for each model according to the bids, and anyone below that price does not get their car. In addition, all new cars are now legally required to have catalytic converters fitted, which increases the price still further. And because Singapore does not want its roads clogged with old bangers, owners of cars which are more than 10 years old have to pay a road tax surcharge of 10% which rises to 50% on a car's 14th birthday. The result, of course, is that only the republic's most affluent citizens can afford to buy a car.

more than 20% a year. Then, in 1990 the Gulf Crisis erupted and the US suffered an economic downturn. To the delight of the Singapore government however, its economy – although dented – did not slide into recession too. The *Economist Intelligence Unit* notes that "...this demonstrated that the Singaporean economy had finally come of age and was no longer vulnerable, in the classic newly industrialized country manner, to sharp slowdowns in world trade".

Foreign investors have continued to flock to Singapore because of its unrivalled infrastructure and international communications links. This is despite the fact that Singapore is no longer a cheap place to locate. Land is expensive and so is labour: employers have to contribute 23% of workers' salaries to their Central Provident Fund (the compulsory state savings scheme – **see page 388**) as well as paying a skills development tax. But while the costs of locating in Singapore have continued to rise markedly, there has not been a corresponding rise in productivity, which has made analysts question how long the investors will keep coming. Productivity in other 'tiger economies' is growing much faster. The government may be forced to lower some of the levies it charges employers for importing foreign workers.

Labour squeeze

With no mineral wealth, oil or timber, people are Singapore's only true resource and, despite the government's efforts, people are in short supply. The government says tight labour supply will continue to limit Singapore's economic growth, and that rising labour costs will curb its exports. Manufacturers report difficulty in recruiting production workers and there is a continuing exodus of professionals. Because of Singapore's race to industrialize, demand for labour has always exceeded supply. It got round this by importing labour from Malaysia, Indonesia, Thailand and the Philippines. There is virtually no unemployment in Singapore – everyone who wants to work can and because the labour market is so tight, skilled white collar workers have been able to demand higher and higher salaries. The government plans to raise the mandatory retirement age to 60 and to continue to fill the labour gap, to introduce more labour-saving technology and allow an even greater influx of migrant workers. In early 1993 the head of the International Manpower Policy section of the Economic Development Board announced that Singapore would be attempting to recruit researchers and scientists from the former Soviet Union in an effort to bolster its high-tech industries.

Today more than one in 10 of the republic's workforce is a non-Singaporean. There are around 200,000 unskilled and semi-skilled migrant workers, up 60% on 1980. Quota restrictions on the number allowed into each sector of the economy have been relaxed, but the government is alarmed that foreigners now represent nearly half the workforce in certain sectors. Singapore wants to avoid them settling on the island – it says it cannot absorb or accommodate too many unskilled workers. Because foreign workers have also begun to depress local wages, the government has increased levies on foreign labour paid by employers to try to dampen the demand. This has made Singapore's labour costs about 3 or 4 times those of neighbouring countries.

The drive to increase labour efficiency has been a major policy thrust in recent years. Industrial robots have helped trim the workforce in many manufacturing plants. Manufacturers who are unable to automate their operations have gone to cheaper locations in nearby Indonesia or Malaysia, which have both benefited from the overspill. Prime Minister Goh Chok Tong, appears to have found a solution of sorts in his proposed 'Growth Triangle', which includes the city state, Johor (the southernmost state on the Malaysian peninsula) and Pulau Batam (the northernmost island in Indonesia's Riau Archipelago). The idea is that all 3 should be promoted as a single unit.

Singapore remains the hub of the Growth Triangle, with its communications and financial infrastructure, while Johor and Batam offer cheaper land and labour. The proposal is now starting to bear fruit. Over recent years, scores of transnational investors have stampeded across the causeway to Johor, and investment in Batam is picking up. Singapore benefits enormously from its new found hinterland and unskilled foreign workers can be kept conveniently at arm's length so that they do not upset the flavour of the city-state's racial cocktail. Economically speaking, Singapore is a comfortable 10-15 years ahead of its neighbours and intends to stay ahead. The Economic Development Board is training people with a vengeance and has labelled them 'thinking workers'. Policy makers believe that once they are in place, no labour crisis will ever be insurmountable.

At the other end of the labour market, in the professional, white-collar sector, there have been problems too. The government has become particularly concerned about 'the emigration problem' in which thousands of highly skilled Singaporeans have been choosing to work and live abroad. Many are Malays and Indians, who claim their long-term opportunities are limited in Singapore. Emigration peaked in 1988 when nearly 5,000 families left Singapore, and this came as a double blow to a government already facing a serious labour shortage. To stem the 'brain drain' an aggressive overseas recruitment campaign was launched for white-collar workers and this was matched by the liberalization of immigration regulations for foreign professionals. In an effort to ensure that there is a continued supply of skilled labour, Singapore offered 25,000 skilled Hong Kong workers and their dependents – a total of around 100,000 – permanent residence status in 1989. It hoped to cash in on fears arising from the colony's reversion to Chinese rule in 1997. Singapore was secretly banking on poaching Hong Kong's brainiest emigres before they went to Canada or Australia. The government has been careful, however, to assure Singapore's other ethnic communities that should this distort the current racial mix, it will permit the immigration of Malays and Indians to maintain the balance.

Industry

Manufacturing has been the backbone of Singapore's post-independence economy. The sector has been entirely dependent on foreign investment and it now contributes nearly 30% of Singapore's GDP, compared with 18% in 1965. Despite the fact that Singapore has no oil of its own, it is the world's third largest oil refining centre. Oil refining constitutes a large portion of manufacturing output; the other key industries include petrochemicals and petroleum products, industrial chemicals, electronic and electrical products and components, transport equipment and, of course, food.

The services sector is booming, and its growth over the past 20 years has completely altered the structure of the economy. The contribution of trade has halved to just 17% since 1970, yet Singapore still has the busiest port in the world and the value of goods passing through Singapore is more than 3 times as much as Singapore's own GDP. The relative decline in Singapore's role as an entrepôt has been countered by the massive growth of services. The financial services sector has grown fastest: in 1970 it contributed about 14% of GDP – it now makes up

Singapore: fact file

Geographic		Social	
Land area	600 sq km	Population	2.8 million
Arable land as % of total	11%	Population growth rate (1960-90)	1.7%
Average annual rate of deforestation	n.a.	Adult literacy rate	88%
		Mean years of schooling	3.9 years
Highest point, Bukit Timah	165 m	Tertiary graduate as	
Average rainfall in Singapore	2,369 mm	% of age group	5.8%
		Population below poverty line	n.a.
Average temperature in Singapore	26.5°C	Rural population as % of total	0%
		Growth of urban population (1960-90)	1.7%/year
Economic		Urban population in	
GNP/person (1990)	US$11,200	largest city (%)	100%
Income/person (PPP*, 1989)	US$15,880	Televisions per 1,000 people	376
GNP growth (/capita, 1980-1990)	5.7%	**Health**	
GDP growth 1992	5.6%	Life expectancy at birth	74 years
GDP growth 1993	6.3% (est.)	Population with access to clean water	100%
% labour force in agriculture	0.5%	Calorie intake as % of requirements	136%
Total debt (% GNP)	n.a.	Malnourished children	
Debt service ratio (% exports)	n.a.	less than 5 years	0 million
Military expenditure (% GNP)	5.0%	Contraceptive prevalence rate†	74%

* PPP = Purchasing Power Parity (based on what it costs to buy a similar basket of goods and services in other countries)
† % of women of childbearing age using a form of modern contraception
Source: World Bank (1993) *Human development report 1993*, OUP: New York; and other sources.

a third. Other service industries include information technology (software development), conventions and exhibitions, agrotechnology, medical services (Singapore is now the region's top medical centre), consultancy and tourism.

The latter is now one of Singapore's most important industries; well over 5 million visitors pass through every year – more than double the island's population. Between them, they spend more than US$4 billion a year. Tourism contributes about 16% of Singapore's foreign exchange earnings: in 1990, total tourism earnings reached US$4.2 billion, accounting for 5.5% of GDP. The number of tourists has been growing at between 10% and 15% a year since 1987. The average length of stay is only 3.4 days. More than a quarter come from neighbouring ASEAN countries, another third from the rest of Asia. Nonetheless, nearly a million Japanese visit Singapore every year, about half-a-million Australasians, 300,000 Britons and just over a quarter of a million Americans.

SINGAPORE

PLACES OF INTEREST IN SINGAPORE CITY

Singapore is a neat, clean, green, prosperous place. The government wants it to be known as the Garden of the Orient and in the first few years of the 1990s is spending S$500 million beautifying the island. It is a city of futuristic skyscrapers, condominiums, hotels and tens of thousands of shops. It is also a city of joggers, hawkers, shoppers, bankers, businessmen and tourists. The number of tourists flooding in each year is now more than double the island's population. Singapore has a Western façade, but although much of the mystical East, about which Somerset Maugham and Joseph Conrad waxed lyrical, has been bulldozed and sanitized, the city state remains Asian to its core.

Singapore highlights

Museums and galleries *Empress Place* (see page 396), *National Museum* (page 399).

Temples *Sri Mariamman Temple* (see page 406), *Thian Hock Keng Temple* (page 405).

Historic areas of interest *Arab Street* (see page 409), *Serangoon Road* (page 407), *Chinatown* (page 404), *Padang area* (see below), *Raffles Hotel* (page 398), *river area* (page 400).

Gardens *Botanic Gardens* (see page 411), *Jurong Bird Park* (page 412).

Islands *St Johns* (see page 419), *Pulau Ubin* (page 419), *Underwater World, Sentosa* (see page 418).

Shopping *Orchard and Scotts roads* (see page 403).

Hawker centres *Newton Circus* (see page 428), *Adam Road* (page 427), *Cuppage Centre* (page 427).

To some, it has all the ambience of a supermarket checkout lane. It has even been described as "a Californian resort-town run by Mormons". It has frequently been dubbed sterile and dull: a report in *The Economist* in 1987 judged Singapore to be the most boring city in the world. For those who fail to venture beyond the plazas that line Orchard Road, or spend their 3½ days on coach-trips to the ersatz cultural extravaganzas, this is not surprising. But there is a cultural and architectural heritage in Singapore beyond the one which the government tries so hard to manufacture. Despite its brash consumerism and toytown mentality, it is not without its charm.

Singapore is transforming faster than guidebooks can be printed; the skyline changes every week, whole streets disappear overnight, and new ones are built. The island's tourist sights are being constantly upgraded and renovated. There are also many new recreational facilities to attract foreign tourists, such as Tang Dynasty City, the Japanese and Chinese Gardens, the Jurong Bird Park, the open zoo and Sentosa Island.

For those stopping over in Singapore for just a few days – en route, as most of the island's tourists are to somewhere else – there are a handful of key sights. But

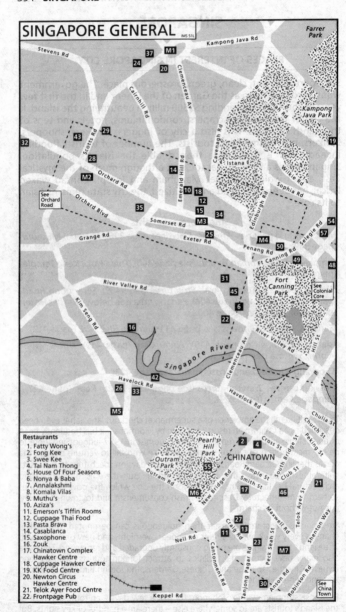

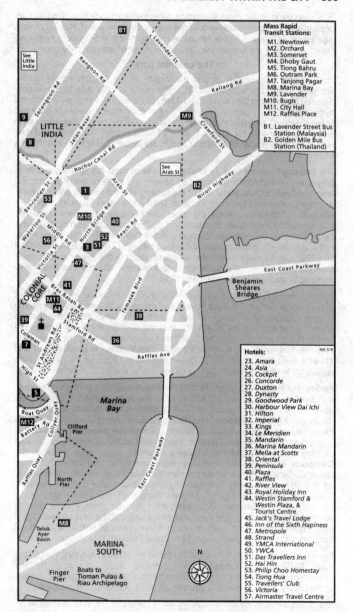

Mass Rapid
Transit Stations:

M1. Newtown
M2. Orchard
M3. Somerset
M4. Dhoby Gaut
M5. Tiong Bahru
M6. Outram Park
M7. Tanjong Pagar
M8. Marina Bay
M9. Lavender
M10. Bugis
M11. City Hall
M12. Raffles Place

B1. Lavender Street Bus
Station (Malaysia)
B2. Golden Mile Bus
Station (Thailand)

Hotels:

23. Amara
24. Asia
25. Cockpit
26. Concorde
27. Duxton
28. Dynasty
29. Goodwood Park
30. Harbour View Dai Ichi
31. Hilton
32. Imperial
33. Kings
34. Le Meridien
35. Mandarin
36. Marina Mandarin
37. Melia at Scotts
38. Oriental
39. Peninsula
40. Plaza
41. Raffles
42. River View
43. Royal Holiday Inn
44. Westin Stamford &
Westin Plaza, &
Tourist Centre
45. Jack's Travel Lodge
46. Inn of the Sixth Hapiness
47. Metropole
48. Strand
49. YMCA International
50. YWCA
51. Das Travellers Inn
52. Hai Hin
53. Philip Choo Homestay
54. Tiong Hua
55. Travellers' Club
56. Victoria
57. Airmaster Travel Centre

in Singapore it is far more important to enjoy the food: the island has an unparalleled variety of restaurants to suit every palate and wallet. Hawker centres (see page 427) are a highly recommended part of the Singapore epicurean experience – they are inexpensive, and many are open into the early hours.

The colonial core

The heart of Singapore is around the mouth of the Singapore River, where Stamford Raffles first set foot in 1817. The grand colonial architecture is now dwarfed by glass and steel skyscrapers. Many of the early buildings were designed by the Irish architect, George Coleman (the Armenian church, Cadwell House and Maxwell House). Singapore's other main architect of the period was Alfred John Bidwell – responsible for the main wing of *Raffles Hotel*, the *Goodwood Park Hotel*, Stamford House, St Joseph's Church, Singapore Cricket Club and Victoria Memorial Hall.

The **Padang** ('playing field' in Malay), the site of most big sporting events in Singapore – including the National Day parades – is at the centre of the colonial area. The **Cricket Club**, at the end of the Padang, was the focus of British activity. A sports pavilion was first constructed in 1850 and a larger Victorian clubhouse was built in 1884 with 2 levels, the upper level being the ladies' viewing gallery. It is flanked by the houses of justice and government – the domed **Supreme Court** (formerly the *Hôtel de l'Europe*) and the **City Hall**. The neo-classical City Hall was built with Indian convict labour for a trifling S$2 million and was finished in 1929. On 12 Sept 1945 the Japanese surrendered here to Lord Louis Mountbatten and on the same spot, former-Prime Minister Lee Kuan Yew declared Singapore's independence in 1959.

Between the High Street and Singapore River there are other architectural legacies of the colonial period: the **clock tower,** Parliament House (originally designed by George Coleman – although it was subsequently remodelled), the Victoria Memorial Hall and Victoria Theatre. It was in this area that the Temenggongs, the former Malay rulers of Singapore, built their kampung – the royal family was later persuaded to move out to Telok Blangah. The **Victoria Memorial Hall** and **Theatre** were built as tributes to Queen Victoria in 1905 and are still the main venues for Singapore's multi-cultural dance, drama and musical extravaganzas.

Parliament House was originally the private residence of a wealthy Singaporean merchant before being rebuilt, first in 1901 and again in 1953. It is the oldest government building in Singapore. The bronze elephant in front of Parliament House was a gift to Singapore from the King of Siam, Rama V, in 1872. **Empress Place**, nearby, on the river (for details on the river, see page 400), was one of Singapore's first conservation projects. Built as the East India Company courthouse in 1865, it later housed the legislative assembly. In its grounds stands the **Dalhousie Memorial**, an obelisk erected in honour of Lord James Dalhousie, Governor-General of India, who visited Singapore for 3 days in 1850. He is credited on the plaque as having "emphatically recognized the wisdom of liberating commerce from all restraints". Empress Place itself has been magnificently restored, and now accommodates up-market souvenir shops with restaurants downstairs (overlooking the river) and temporary cultural and archaeological exhibitions upstairs. There is an on-going 5 year series of historic and cultural exhibitions from China. Admission: S$6. Open: 0930-2100 Mon-Sun.

Beyond the Padang is the world's tallest hotel, the *Westin Stamford*, part of the huge **Raffles City Complex** on Stamford Road. Designed by the Chinese-American architect, I M Pei (most famous for the glass pyramid in front of the Louvre, Paris), it contains 2 hotels, an office and shopping complex.

Just down the road are the 4 tapering white towers of the **War Memorial** on

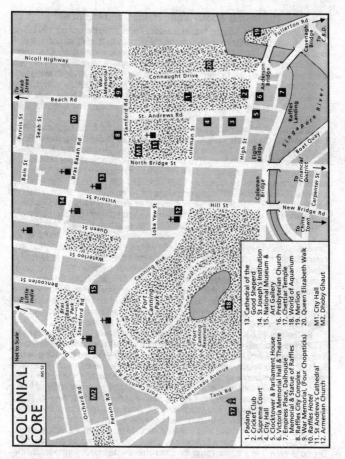

1. Padang
2. Cricket Club
3. Supreme Court
4. City Hall
5. Clocktower & Parliament House
6. Victoria Memorial Hall & Theatre
7. Empress Place, Dalhousie
   Memorial & Statue of Raffles
8. Raffles City Complex
9. War Memorial, (Four Chopsticks)
10. *Raffles Hotel*
11. St Andrew's Cathedral
12. Armenian Church
13. Cathedral of the
    Good Sheperd
14. St Joseph's Institution
15. National Museum &
    Art Gallery
16. Presbyterian Church
17. Chettiar Temple
18. World of Aquarium
19. Merlion
20. Queen Elizabeth Walk

M1. City Hall
M2. Dhoby Ghaut

Beach Road – better known as the 4 chopsticks – symbolizing the 4 cultures of Singapore: the Chinese, Malays, Indians and 'others'. It was built in memory of the 50,000-odd civilians who died during the Japanese occupation. A memorial service is held at the monument on 15 Feb each year.

The newly revamped ***Raffles Hotel***, with its 875 designer-uniformed staff (there is a ratio of 2½ staff to every guest) and 104 suites (each fitted with Persian carpets), 7 restaurants and 5 bars, playhouse and custom-built, leather-upholstered cabs, is the jewel in the crown of Singapore's tourist industry. In true Singapore-style it manages to boast a 5,000 sq m shopping arcade. There's even a museum of Rafflesian memorabilia. (Open: 1000-1900 Mon-Sun.)

The *Raffles Hotel's* original (but restored) billiard table still stands in the Billiard Room. Palm court – the old heart of the Raffles – is still there and so is the Tiffin

The *Raffles Hotel* – immortalized and sanitized

"Tiger shot in *Raffles Hotel*!" blazed a *Straits Times* headline in Aug 1902. The wild tiger was shot while cowering among the stilts under the Billiard Room. It was one more exotic claim to fame for an already legendary institution. The hotel's magnificent teak staircases, big verandahs, bars and palm courtyards had made it the haunt of the rich and famous. It had the first electric lights, lifts and ceiling fans on the island and a French chef, which at the turn of the century was quite a novelty. To use Somerset Maugham's oft-quoted cliché, the old hotel "stood for all the fables of the exotic East... immortalized by writers and patronized by everyone". Now it has been sanitized by developers.

The main building was completed in 1889, but the hotel began life as a bungalow on the beach front, belonging to an Arab trader (today Beach Road is a long way from the sea due to land reclamation). An Englishman, Captain Dare, established a tiffin house (tiffin is the Anglo-Indian term for a light lunch) there before he expanded it into a hotel. It was then bought by the Armenian hoteliers, the Sarkies brothers, in 1885 who had just set up the *Eastern and Oriental (E & O) Hotel* in Penang and went on to establish the *Strand Hotel* in Rangoon in 1892. Under the Sarkies' management, the Raffles and its sister hotels were the epitome of British colonialism – even though the brothers were refused entry to the Singapore Cricket Club because they weren't 'white'.

Today Raffles boasts of its former guests like a public school would list its famous sons. They include celebrities, writers, kings, sultans, politicians, comedians and what one local journalist called "the flotsam and jetsam of a newly-mobile world". The hotel's literary tradition became its trump card: Somerset Maugham, Rudyard Kipling, Joseph Conrad, Noel Coward and Herman Hesse all visited the hotel at one time or another. Not all were particularly impressed: Kipling said the rooms were bad and recommended that travellers go to the late great *Hôtel de l'Europe* on the Padang instead. But the Raffles was *the* social epicentre of Singapore – if not the region.

By the late 1920s, Arshak Sarkie – who had taken over the management of the Raffles and was known for his party-trick of waltzing around the Grand Ballroom with a whisky glass perched on his bald head – started gambling at the Turf Club. He got heavily into debt and at the same time launched into an expensive renovation programme at the hotel. By the turn of the decade, the bottom had fallen out of the Malayan rubber industry and the local economy collapsed into the Great Depression, taking the Raffles with it. Arshak Sarkies died in 1931, bankrupt and miserable. Two years later the hotel was taken over by a new company, but its golden years had died with the Sarkies'. During the war, the Japanese turned Palm Court into a drill ground. At the end of the war, patriotic British POWs gathered in the Ballroom to sing *"There'll always be an England"*. The hotel served as a transit camp for them after the Japanese surrender. By the mid-1980s the hotel had become a quaint, but crumbling colonial relic, which, like the back-packers who had taken to staying there, looked increasingly out of place in the brave new Singapore of glass and steel. The Raffles was rusting, peeling and mouldering. The Long Bar, the home of the Singapore Sling – first shaken in the Long Bar by bar-tender Ngiam Tong Boon in 1915 – became a tourist gimmick. The record for Sing-Sling-slinging was set by 5 Australian visitors in 1985. They downed 131 inside 2 hours. Then suddenly the government woke up to the fact that it had unwittingly bulldozed half its cultural heritage. The hotel's neighbour, the Raffles Institution, had been demolished to make way for Raffles City. To save the old hotel from going the same way, it was declared a protected monument in 1987. Its recognition as an architectural treasure immediately put Raffles on the shortlist for a facelift. The developers went out and spent S$160 million on consultants, white paint and fake Victorian trimmings.

Room, which still serves tiffins. The hotel is very bright and very, very white. Teams of restoration consultants undertook painstaking research into the original colours of paint, ornate plasterwork and fittings. A replica of the cast-iron portico, known as 'cad's alley' was built to the original 19th century specifications of a Glasgow foundry.

Although just about anyone who's anyone visiting Singapore still makes a pilgrimage to the hotel, *The Raffles* has, in the process of refurbishment, lost much of its atmosphere and appeal. It's been done well – architecturally it can hardly be faulted and lawns and courtyards are lush with foliage – but critics say they've tried a little too hard. The month after it re-opened (on former Prime Minister Lee Kuan Yew's birthday, 16 Sept 1991), *Newsweek* said that in trying to roll a luxury hotel, a shopping mall and national tourist attraction into one, "The result is synergy run amok... great if you need a Hermes scarf, sad if you'd like to imagine a tiger beneath the billiard table."

West from the Padang are St Andrew's Cathedral and the Armenian Church. **St Andrew's Cathedral** just off Coleman Street was designed by Colonel Ronald MacPherson and built in the 1850s by Indian convict labourers in early neo-gothic style. Its interior walls are coated with a plaster called 'Madras chunam', a mixture of shell, lime, egg whites and sugar. The cathedral is often packed out – 13% of Singapore's population is Christian – and there are several services a day in different languages.

Built in 1835, long before the American Embassy ruined the view, the **Armenian Church of St Gregory the Illuminator** on Hill Street is the island's oldest church, designed by Irish architect George Coleman. The church seats 50 people at a squeeze. The design is said to have been influenced by London's St Martin's-in-the-Fields and Cambridge's Round Church. Agnes Joaquim is buried here – she discovered what is now the national flower of Singapore, the Vanda Miss Joaquim orchid. One of George Coleman's pupils, Denis McSwiney, designed the Roman Catholic **Cathedral of the Good Shepherd**, on the junction of Queen Street and Bras Basah Road. It is a national monument. The former Catholic boys' school, **St Joseph's Institution**, next to it, is also a good example of colonial religious architecture. Built in 1867, it will be transformed into a gallery by 1994.

Not far away on Stamford Road is the **National Museum and Art Gallery**. The idea of setting up a museum was first mooted by Stamford Raffles in 1823; it was finally built in 1887 and was called the Raffles Museum. Renamed the National Museum, it has been magnificently refurbished and reopened, in late 1991.

The exhibits, while not extensive, make for an interesting browse. They include opium pipes, from Singapore's once-famed opium dens, a white jade mahjong set, and rickshaws – which were introduced to the island from China in the 1880s and remained popular through to the 1930s. Rickshaw-wallah manakins are kept cool by ancient electric fans. Other memorabilia of this virtually extinct side of old Singapore are extraordinary wooden clogs – wooden strapless flip-flops worn by *chakhree* washerwomen. Models depict marriage ceremonies from various ethnic communities and there is also a large collection of ceramics and jade, crystal, lapis lazuli and agate carvings from the Haw Par collection, donated to the museum by the Aw family (of Tiger Balm fame) in 1980. There are some excellent photographs of the city at various stages in its life, although, strangely, there are virtually no photographs or exhibits on the war years. Admission: S$1. Open: 0900-1630, Tues-Sun. Conducted tours from the information counter at 1100, Tues-Fri. Multi-slide shows (recommended) at 1015, 1215, 1445 and 1545 Mon-Sun in the AV Theatre.

The **National Art Gallery**, next to the museum, is disappointing, although from time to time there is a more invigorating visiting exhibition on show. The permanent collection contains mediocre works by Singaporean and Asian artists. Open: 0900-1730 Tues-Sun. The national library is on the other side of the museum.

Where Stamford Road meets Orchard Road, just up from the museum and next to the YMCA, is the **Presbyterian church**, built in 1878 and now a protected monument. The church's caretaker's house was the centre of the 1984 'Curry Murder Horror'. The Tamil caretaker was dismembered and his body disposed of by cooking it up with curry and rice. It was then discarded in rubbish bins around Singapore, masquerading as the remains of a hawker-stall takeaway. Six people, including a butcher and a mutton curry stall holder, were arrested in 1987, but later released for lack of evidence.

Behind the museum is **Fort Canning Park**. It is known as 'Forbidden Hill' by the Malays as this was the site of the ancient fortress of the Malay kings and reputedly contains the tomb of the last Malay ruler of the kingdom of Singapura, Sultan Iskandar Shah (**see page 371**). Also in the 20 ha park are the ruins of Fort Canning – the Gothic gateway, derelict guardhouse and earthworks are all that remain of a fort which once covered 3 ha – and an old Christian cemetery where the first settlers were buried. Not Stamford Raffles though – after an ignominious death and funeral in N London, he was reburied in Westminster Abbey. Archaeological digs in the area have discovered remains from the days of the Majapahit Empire (**see page 517**). Fort Canning Park has been restored and redeveloped. The Ministry of National Development intends to include a museum, underground bunkers and a house to tell the story of Sir Stamford Raffles.

On the other side of the park is the Hindu **Chettiar Temple** on Tank Road. The original temple on this site was built by wealthy Chettiar Indians (money lenders). It has been superseded by a modern version, finished in 1984, and is dedicated to Lord Subramaniam. The ceiling has 48 painted glass panels, angled to reflect sunset and sunrise. Many Hindu temples close in the heat of the day, so are best seen before 1100 and after 1500.

Returning towards the city centre is the **Word of Aquarium** (*sic*), T 3343762, (formerly Van Kleef Aquarium) on River Valley Road. It has recently been renovated and has a large variety of local fish, coral and sea creatures. Their feeding time is at 1200 daily. Admission: S$4 adults, $2 children. Open: 1000-1800 Mon-Sun.

The river and port

Singapore is strategically located at the S end of the Strait of Melaka, half way between China and India. It is a free port, open to all maritime nations. The **port**, largely sheltered from the city, has 7 gateways; the biggest – the container port – is the Tanjong Pagar terminal.

There are usually 700 or more ships in port at any one time – one arrives, on average, every 9 minutes: in 1990 45,000 vessels called at the port. Singapore is the world's second busiest port after Rotterdam and overtook Hong Kong in 1990 as the world's busiest container port; about 6-million containers pass through each year. The container handling system is computerized and fully automated and ships are unloaded using Artificial Intelligence. These so-called 'expert-systems', designed and built in Singapore, have reduced the processing time to about 30 seconds per container. The Port of Singapore Authority operates 5 terminals: Tanjong Pagar is the main terminal for handling containers, Keppel Wharves and Sembawang Wharves (on the N of the island) are for conventional cargoes, Jurong Port is for dry bulk cargoes, and there is a new billion-dollar container terminal at Pulau Brani, which will become fully operational in 1996.

To the W of Tanjong Pagar port, on Keppel Road, to the S is the **World Trade Centre**, which houses the Guinness World of Records exhibition. It was Singapore's tallest building until 1980. Its prominence symbolizes Singapore's dependence on international trade. Admission: S$4. Open: 1000-2100 Mon-Sun. Opposite the exhibition halls, lies the Telok Blangah **Johor State Mosque**, dating from the 1840s, which was the focal point of the pre-Raffles Malay royalty in Singapore. The tomb of the Temenggong Abdul Rahman – the *tanah kubor Rajah* – is nearby; he was partly responsible for negotiating Singapore's status as a

Bankers' rising aspirations

Singapore's big-four banks are obsessed with reaching for the sky. The city skyline is dominated by the banks' corporate pyramids. In the 1970s, the Oversea-Chinese Banking Corporation (OCBC) invited American-Chinese architect IM Pei to design its so-called 'vertical calculator'. DBS Bank occupies a drab building on Shenton Way, but in the 1980s funded the construction of Raffles City, which boasts the tallest hotel in the world at 220m – again built by Pei.

More recently, Overseas Union Bank (OUB) glossed its corporate image with a 280m-high aluminium triangle designed by distinguished Japanese architect Kanzo Tange. As Singapore's trivia kings never fail to remind visitors, it is the tallest building in the world, outside America. Not to be out-done, United Overseas Bank (UOB) also commissioned Kanzo Tange to dream up the S$500 million, 66-storey UOB Plaza which now presides over Boat Quay and Chinatown. UOB had long suffered a loss of face in the local financial community, thanks to its squat HQ on Bonham Street – a trifling 32 storeys. A picture of the new building appeared on a UOB Visa card as early as 1988, showing it towering over the nearby OUB building. But in fact, Singapore law states that 280m is the highest a building can go without becoming an aviation hazard and both buildings are exactly 280m high.

UOB's move to its new premises may prove too much for Singapore's vertical marathon runners: the Singapore Adventurers' Club organizes an annual race to the top of the old UOB building and down again, the marathon consisting of 6 round trips – or 4,692 steps. The record is just under 27 minutes.

trading post with Stamford Raffles. The Johor royal family lived at Telok Blangah until 1855 when the town of Iskandar Putri was founded on the other side of the straits; it was renamed Johor Bahru in 1866. **Getting there:** buses 65, 167 or 143 from Orchard Road; 61, 84, 143, 145, 166 and 167 from Chinatown.

East of Tanjong Pagar terminal is the **Singapore River**, which separates the high-rise, hi-tech financial district from the colonial, tourist and shopping districts. Standing guard at the mouth of the river (and best viewed from Queen Elizabeth Walk) is the mythical **Merlion**, half-lion, half-fish, the grotesque saturnine symbol of Singapore (sculpted by local artist Lim Nang Seng in 1972). It is inspired by the 2 ancient (Sanskrit) names for the island: *Singa Pura* meaning 'lion city', and *Temasek* meaning 'sea-town'. The confused creature is now emblazoned on every trinket and T-shirt.

Queen Elizabeth Walk, running from Raffles Avenue to the river-mouth, runs along the waterfront. Further upstream is a marble replica of the original **statue of Raffles**, founder of modern Singapore, on the spot where he is first believed to have stepped on to the swampy shore in 1819. The original, sculpted in bronze by Thomas Woolner in 1887, stands in front of the Victoria Theatre. Behind the statue is **Empress Place** and **Parliament House**. From here it is a short walk along Parliament Lane to the Padang (see above). Despite modernization, the waterfront area still bears some resemblance to pre-war Singapore. Cavenagh Bridge erected in 1869 still has its old sign that forbids bullock carts from crossing. Bumboats (or *tankangs*, a wooden lighter), barges and sampans once littered the river, but they were cleared out to Marina Bay, or destroyed and scuttled, as part of the government's river-cleaning programme over a period of 10 years. Singapore River is now 'pollution-free', but what it gained in cleanliness, it lost in aesthetics. Godowns along the river are being restored and turned into cafés, galleries, shops and clubs. Boat Quay, the picturesque stretch of riverbank on the south side, facing Empress Place, has had a major face-lift. The obsessive

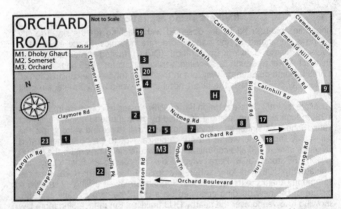

renovation projects have resulted in some very classy restaurants and bars, most of which cater for the suits working in the skyscrapers behind. Clarke Quay, further upriver, is being redeveloped too. It is best reached via River Valley Road (see page 407).

A good way of seeing the sights along Singapore River is on a bumboat cruise. A recorded commentary points out the godowns, shophouses, government buildings and skyscrapers lining the riverbank. The boats leave from Raffles Landing, just down from his statue near Parliament House and the Empress Place (see page 420).

Next to the Merlion is **Clifford Pier**, built in the 1930s. It is possible to hire boats to cruise up and down the river and around Marina Bay from the pier (see page 420). Marina Bay is dotted with small craft and ferries and framed by Benjamin Sheares Bridge. The Chinese tongkangs have eyes painted on them so they can see where they're going; traditionally they were used as lighters, to transport cargo from larger ships. Bumboats and junks also go to the S islands from Clifford Pier. Behind it (across the shopping arcade/footbridge) is **Change Alley** – once a crowded bazaar and the cheapest spot in Singapore. Appropriately, Change Alley has changed more than anywhere else in Singapore – it has been knocked down and anything that remains has disappeared into the void between two tower blocks.

Shenton Way (Singapore's equivalent of Wall Street), Raffles Place, Robinson Road and Cecil Street, all packed-tight with skyscrapers, form the **financial heart** of modern Singapore. These streets contain most of the buildings that give the city its distinctive skyline, which is best seen from the Benjamin Sheares Bridge or from the boat coming back from Batam island. The first foreign institutions to arrive on the island still occupy the prime sites – the Hong Kong and Shanghai Banking Corporation and Standard Chartered Bank. The Telok Ayer Food Centre (see page 427) on Robinson Road, was the first municipal market in Singapore; the Victorian cast-iron structure was shipped out from a foundry in Glasgow.

Marina South, directly S of the city proper, is a vast expanse of land reclaimed from the sea in the 1970s and 1980s as an overspill area for the envisaged spread of Singapore's financial district. To make something out of nothing, Marina Village was built, complete with restaurants, bars, concert venues, discos, a night bazaar, and a bowling alley. It was, however, a complete flop, and the ebullient Moroccan businessman who financed it has fled the country. The fate of the development remains uncertain: one proposal is to turn it into a honeymoon village.

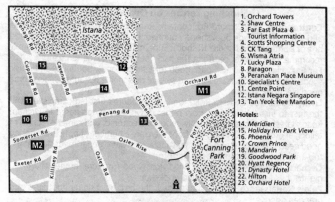

1. Orchard Towers
2. Shaw Centre
3. Far East Plaza & Tourist Information
4. Scotts Shopping Centre
5. CK Tang
6. Wisma Atria
7. Lucky Plaza
8. Paragon
9. Peranakan Place Museum
10. Specialist's Centre
11. Centre Point
12. Istana Negara Singapore
13. Tan Yeok Nee Mansion

Hotels:

14. Meridien
15. Holiday Inn Park View
16. Phoenix
17. Crown Prince
18. Mandarin
19. Goodwood Park
20. Hyatt Regency
21. Dynasty Hotel
22. Hilton
23. Orchard Hotel

Orchard Road

In the mid 1800s the Orchard Road area was one vast nutmeg plantation before being cleared for the construction of colonial mansions. Until the 1970s, Raffles' Place was the core of Singapore's shopping district. Choon Keng Tang, a rags-to-riches immigrant from Swatow who in the 1920s sold linen door-to-door from a rickshaw, bought a plot of land on Orchard Road in 1945 and built CK Tang's Oriental curio store, in Chinese imperial style. In 1982 the old shop was demolished and the new hotel and department store complex went up. The pagoda-style *Dynasty Hotel*, the adjunct to CK's shopping empire, is one of the most eye-catching buildings on the road. Today, for hundreds of metres on either side of Tangs, there are scores of multi-storey shopping complexes.

Orchard Road is now a shoppers' paradise and is said to have the highest density of shops in the world as well as being one of the world's most expensive shopping streets. Orchard Road is a mix of 20th century architectural styles. Peranakan Place, Cuppage Road and Emerald Hill have managed to escape demolition; they have been tarted up and the Peranakan (Straits Chinese) shophouses have been carefully restored to their original ornate condition. Most were constructed between 1918 and 1930 and combined European and Chinese designs. The area is an official conservation project.

Shoppers can browse along Orchard Road – and adjoining Scotts Road – to their hearts' content; the leading shopping centres are listed below. (For a guide to where to go for the best buys, **see page 404**.)

The **Peranakan Place Museum** on Emerald Hill gives some idea of what Straits Chinese townhouses were originally like inside, although this recreation is a poor example (there is a much better one in Melaka, **see page 168**). (For a detailed background on Peranakan culture, **see page 168**.) Admission: S$4. Open: 1000-1800 Mon-Sun. Other tourist attractions here include the *Keday Kopi Shop* and *Bibi's Theatre Pub*; touristy atmosphere and prices to match.

About three-quarters of the way down Orchard Road, towards Bras Basah Road, are the great gates that lead along a shady avenue to the **Istana Negara Singapura**, the residence of the former British governors of Singapore and now home to the President of the Republic. The Istana was built in 1869 by the colonial architect, Captain McNair, in Malay-style – with overhanging roofs and raised off the ground and blended with classical details. It has been much altered over the

Shopping centres on Orchard Road

Centrepoint, 175 Orchard Rd: contains Robinsons department store, Marks and Spencers, 2 huge bookshops, countless boutiques, electronics shops and one or 2 antique and handicraft shops. Supermarket in the basement and highly recommended hawker centre at the back (behind Cuppage Terrace).

Far East Plaza, 14 Scotts Road: good for leather goods, boutiques and music shops. Money-changers, tailors and several reasonable restaurants; also some good electronics shops.

Lucky Plaza, 304 Orchard Road: one of Singapore's first big complexes, and the first to install bullet lifts; now rather down-market compared to Orchard Road's latest offerings. Reasonably good for electronics and cameras, scores of tailors; at ground level, along the front there are a number of opticians offering good deals on Raybans and designer sunglasses. Metro department store at the top and copy-watch touts at the bottom.

Orchard Towers, 400 Orchard Road: rosewood furniture, money-changers, nightclubs, restaurants and a good bookshop.

Palais Renaissance, 390 Orchard Road: the best in designer-boutiques and branded goods.

Plaza Singapura, 68 Orchard Road: department store and several music shops – both for CDs and for instruments.

Scotts Shopping Centre, 6 Scotts Road: department store, "Picnic" food court in basement (mainly local fast food – Satay Anika rec.), boutiques and good electronics shops.

Shaw Centre, 1 Scotts Road: recently revamped, with new look and new shops; best for shoes and boutiques.

Specialists' Centre, 277 Orchard Road: just across from Centrepoint; department stores and chocolate chip cookies.

The Paragon, 290 Orchard Road: one of the best places for boutique browsers; branded names, but not that exclusive.

Wisma Atria, 435 Orchard Road: department store, boutiques and bookshops.

years and is not open to the public. **Dhoby Gaut**, the end of Orchard Road next to the Cathay cinema, got its name from the Bengali and Madrasi dhobies who used to wash the clothes of local residents in the stream which ran down the side of Orchard Road and dry them on the land now occupied by the YMCA.

On Tank Road is **Tan Yeok Nee Mansion**, one of the very few remaining traditionally designed Chinese houses, built in 1885 by a wealthy Teochew merchant. The building was badly damaged during the Japanese occupation but later restored by the Salvation Army. It is now a national monument and is open to the public Mon-Fri.

Chinatown

Immigrants from China settled in Singapore in the latter half of the 19th century, and recreated much of what they had left behind. Clan groups began migrating from the S provinces of China to the South Seas in successive waves from the 17th century on. The greatest numbers migrated in the 40 years after 1870. Separate streets were occupied by different Chinese groups. Clubs and clan houses – or *kongsi* – aided family or regional ties. The kongsi were often affiliated with secret societies – or *tongs* – which controlled the gambling and prostitution industries and the drug trade.

Smith Street, Temple Street, Pagoda Street, Trengganu and Sago streets still have their characteristic baroque-style shophouses with weathered shutters and ornamentation. The typical Straits Chinese house accommodated the family business on the ground floor; the second and third floors were family living quarters, sometimes accommodating 2 families. (A number of wealthy Chinese merchants – or *towkays* – built their houses according to traditional Chinese architectural design, such as Tan Yeok Nee's house on Tank Road.)

Today Chinatown is overshadowed by the 200 m-high skyscrapers of the financial area. High-rise developments have invaded Chinatown itself, and from time to time parts of it are demolished to make way for new complexes, like Chinatown Point, which opened in 1991. Organized indoor markets have replaced many street stalls and the night markets that made Chinatown the favoured tourist spot in days gone by. These night markets – known by their Malay name, *pasar malam* (pasar from the Arabic, bazaar) – still reappear in the run-up to Chinese New Year. Many of the small businesses dotted along the streets and sidewalks of Chinatown have been relocated to the modern Kereta Ayer complex, in the street of the same name, nearby. The traditional craftsmen and merchants are fast-disappearing and are being replaced by tourist trinket shops.

Chinatown was being knocked down at such a rate that by the time the authorities grasped that tourists actually wanted to see its crumbling buildings, it was almost too late. Chinatown had become a slum, which the government thought unbecoming of Singapore's otherwise germ-free environment. The area was sanitized, its markets cleared out, shops and stalls relocated, shophouses refurbished and the smells and noises of Chinatown banished to a world that only a few confused grandparents care to remember. Many residents have been moved out to new modern flats in the Housing Development Board estates scattered around the island. But parts of it retain something of the original atmosphere – side streets still house remnants of family businesses; there are a handful of good family-run coffee-shops and restaurants and shops selling the taste of Chinatown: barbecued pork.

In **Sago Street** (or 'death house alley', after its hostels for the dying) and **Temple Street**, there are shops making paper houses and cars, designed to improve the quality of the after-life for dead relatives. By burning the models after the funeral, it is believed that one's worldly wealth hurries after you into the next world. Chinese temple-carvers still live on **Club Street** – which also has a number of *kongsi* along it – and there are several coffee-shops on **Mosque Street** (where many of the buildings were originally stables). Chinese traditional medicine halls still do a roaring trade, despite the advantages of Medisave schemes and 21st century pharmaceuticals. The Hong Lim complex on **Upper Cross Street** has several such medicine halls. There are also a few skilled Chinese calligraphers still around Upper Cross Street.

In the heart of Chinatown (14b Trengganu Street), up a narrow staircase, is the **Chinaman Scholars Gallery**, a mini-museum of life in the merchants' and scholars' houses in the 1920s. The gallery is run by antique dealer Vincent Tan, and visitors can sip Chinese tea as they wander around the living areas and flick through photographs. Mr Tan gives musical interludes with demonstrations of instruments from China, such as the lute, *pipa* (mandolin) and *yang chin* (harp). Admission: S$4. Open: 0900-1600 Mon-Sun.

There are hundreds of Chinese temples listed in Singapore's Yellow Pages. The city's oldest Chinese temple, the Taoist **Thian Hock Keng Temple** or Temple of Heavenly Happiness is on Telok Ayer Street. It started life as a joss house, where newly arrived Hokkien immigrants would gather to thank Ma Cho Po, the goddess of the sea, for granting them a safe journey. Most of the beautifully carved building was brought from China in 1840, including the statue of the goddess, although the cast-iron railings came from Glasgow and the decorative tiles from Holland. Thian Hock Keng is built according to classical Chinese architectural traditions, with a grouping of pavilions around open courtyards, designed to comply with the dictates of geomancy (**see page 379**). The temple used to be on the waterfront before land reclamation projects in the 1880s moved the harbour several blocks E.

The **Al-Abrar Mosque**, also on Telok Ayer Street, was built from 1850-55 by Indian Muslims, who were also responsible for the fancy turrets of the **Nagore**

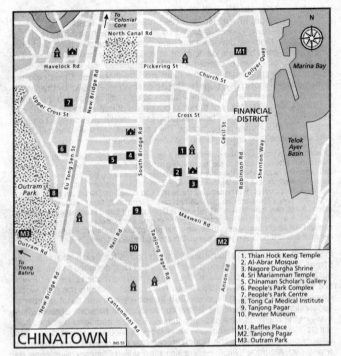

CHINATOWN

1. Thian Hock Keng Temple
2. Al-Abrar Mosque
3. Nagore Durgha Shrine
4. Sri Mariamman Temple
5. Chinaman Scholar's Gallery
6. People's Park Complex
7. People's Park Centre
8. Tong Cai Medical Institute
9. Tanjong Pagar
10. Pewter Museum

M1. Raffles Place
M2. Tanjong Pagar
M3. Outram Park

Durgha Shrine – a little further down the street – which was built in 1829.

As if to illustrate Singapore's reputation as a racial and religious melting-pot, the Hindu **Sri Mariamman Temple** is situated nearby on South Bridge Road. The temple shop is piled high with books on Hindu philosophy and cosmology and, unsurprisingly, is run by a Chinese family. Although recently renovated, this gaudy, Dravidian-style temple dates from 1823, when Stamford Raffles first granted the land to Narian Pillai, an Indian who arrived in Singapore at the same time as its founder and set up Singapore's first brickworks. The building, in its present form, opened in 1863 and is dedicated to Sri Mariamman, a manifestation of Siva's wife Parvati. The temple is the site of the annual Thimithi festival which takes place at the end of Oct or the beginning of Nov (see page 450).

On the edge of Chinatown are **People's Park Complex** (the first shopping centre of its kind in Southeast Asia) and **People's Park Centre**, both large shopping centres full of emporia, cheap textiles and electronic goods. The **Tong Chai Medical Institute** is another traditionally designed Chinese house, just a short walk from People's Park, on Eu Tong Sen Street. It was recently made a national monument and now houses a selection of antiques, Singapore souvenirs and trinkets.

Tanjong Pagar is a part of Chinatown, but on the other side of People's Park. It is bordered by Tanjong Pagar Road and Neil Road and contains some of the best examples of pre-war shophouse architecture on the island. In the 19th century this area was ruled by the Triads – or *tongs* – and packed full of brothels and opium dens, populated by prostitutes, pimps, merchants, Tamil coolies, Chinese rickshawmen and hawkers. The white building on the corner of Tanjong Pagar was known as the Jinriksha Building, which was built in 1913.

Tanjong Pagar has now been declared a conservation area, where traditional arts and crafts have been encouraged and today is populated only by those who can afford the ground-rents. The Urban Redevelopment Authority has refurbished several rows of shophouses – they all retain their original façades – and some have been leased out to 'traditional businesses'. It is all a bit ersatz and, although quite busy in the evenings, is still to get the buzz to make it into Singapore's equivalent of Covent Garden in London. That said, tea houses (see Chinese Tea House, **page 427**), mahjong-makers, reflexologists, calligraphers, lacquer-painters and mask-makers have set up among the advertising agencies and smart restaurants. There is even a night market. **The Pewter Museum**, at 49a Duxton Road, is located in 3 refurbished shophouses. The museum contains 19th and 20th century pewter household utensils and ceremonial pieces, crafted by Selangor Pewter. There is a tribute to the founder of Selangor Pewter, Yong Koon (1868-1951) and an exhibition containing lots of photographs but little by way of explanation. It is the only such museum in Southeast Asia and features demonstrations of hammering, casting and polishing. Open: 0900-1730, Mon-Sun.

On Sunday mornings many Chinese gather at the corner of Tiong Bahru and Seng Poh roads for traditional **bird singing competitions**, where row upon row of thrushes, merboks and sharmas singing their hearts out in antique bamboo cages with ivory and porcelain fittings. The birds are fed on a carefully designed diet to ensure the quality of their song. Owners place their younger birds next to more experienced songsters to try to improve their voices and pick up new tunes.

The middle section of **River Valley Road**, around the junction with Jalan Mohamed Sultan is worth stopping off at. There are several antique and junk shops on one side of the road (including Keng's breathtaking little shop – **see page 431**). The walk down Jalan Mohamed Sultan itself is rewarding as it is little-changed – there are many still-lived-in shophouses in this area. Walk down past *The Front Page* and *The Next Page* bars, following the road round, down to **Clarke Quay**, which is nearing completion as the Tourist Promotion Board's latest cultural attraction, having been completely renovated at a cost of S$240 million. This is godown country – in colonial days, the streets around the warehouses would have been bustling with coolies. (For location of this area, see Singapore General map, **page 394**, W and SW of Fort Canning Park.) **Getting there**: SBS buses 16, 65 and 92 from Orchard Rd/Orchard Boulevard.

Little India

The beginning of Serangoon Road (named after the Rongong stork which used to inhabit swampland in the area) and its colourful side streets make up the community of Little India. The area remained swampland until the 1920s when its brick kilns and lime pits attracted Indian (mainly Tamil) labourers to the area. The Indians introduced a traditional technique of external plasterwork, *Madras chunam* (**see page 379**), which gave Serangoon Road's shophouses their ornate fronts. The majority of Indians in this area are Chettiars – a money-lending caste from S India – but there are also Tamils, Bengalis and Sikhs, among other groups.

The fragrance of incense and freshly cut jasmine hangs over the area and with the sound-tracks of Tamil epic-musicals blaring from the video shops, the *pan* salesmen on the sidestreets and colourful milk-sweets behind the glass counters of *dosai* restaurants, Serangoon Road is India in microcosm. Every Indian product imaginable is for sale: lunggyis, dotis, saris and spices, sweetmeats, flower garlands, nostril studs, bidis and stalls with mounds of dried beans, rice and back-copies of *India Today*. Little India is also an excellent area to eat (**see page 424**).

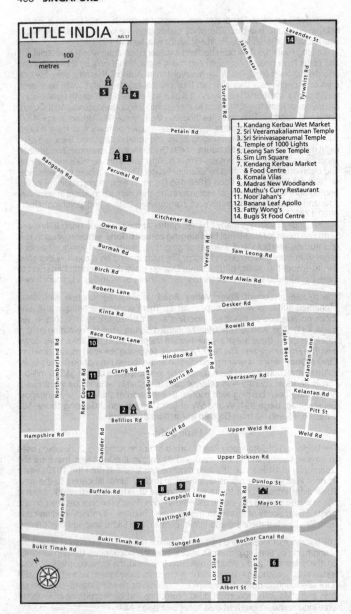

LITTLE INDIA

0 — 100
metres

1. Kandang Kerbau Wet Market
2. Sri Veeramakaliamman Temple
3. Sri Srinivasaperumal Temple
4. Temple of 1000 Lights
5. Leong San See Temple
6. Sim Lim Square
7. Kandang Kerbau Market & Food Centre
8. Komala Vilas
9. Madras New Woodlands
10. Muthu's Curry Restaurant
11. Noor Jahan's
12. Banana Leaf Apollo
13. Fatty Wong's
14. Bugis St Food Centre

The lively **Kandang Kerbau (KK) wet market** (or food market) on the corner of Buffalo and Serangoon roads is an entertaining spot to spend an hour or two. Spices can be ground to your own requirements. Upstairs there is a maze of shops and stalls; the wet market is downstairs and next to it the hawker centre. New legislation introduced in 1993, which ruled that no animals could be slaughtered on wet market premises, saw the end of the chicken-plucking machine. It used to do the job in 12.4 seconds. Kandang Kerbau – Malay for corral – was the centre of Singapore's cattle-rearing area in the 1870s. IR Belilios, a Venetian Jew who gave his name to a road nearby, was the top cattle trader. The roads around KK have names connected to the trade: Lembu (cow) Road and Buffalo Road.

The **Sri Veeramakaliamman Temple** on Belilios Road, just off Serangoon Road, was built by the Bengali community and is dedicated to Kali, a ferocious incarnation of Siva's wife. This small, gaudy temple with its polychromed gods was built by indentured Bengali workers in 1881. It is similar in composition to most other temples of its kind and has 3 main elements: a shrine for the gods, a hall for worship and a *goporum* (or tower), built so that pilgrims can identify the temple from far off. Further up Serangoon Road is another Indian temple, **Sri Perumal**, with its high goporum sculptured with 5 manifestations of Vishnu. This carving was finished in 1979 and was paid for by local philanthropist Govindasamy Pillai.

On Race Course Road (parallel to Serangoon Road) is the Buddhist **Sakayamuni Buddha Gaya Temple** or Temple of One Thousand Lights dominated by a 15m-high, 300 tonne, rather crude, statue of the Buddha surrounded by 987 lights. Devotees come here to worship the branch of the sacred Bodhi tree – under which the Buddha gained enlightenment – and the mother-of-pearl footprint of the Buddha. Open: 0900-1630 Mon-Sun. Across the road is the Chinese **Leong San See Temple**, Dragon Mountain Temple, with its carved entrance. It is dedicated to Kuan Yin (the goddess of mercy) who had 18 hands, which are said to symbolize her boundless mercy and compassion. There are many well preserved – but as yet, thankfully unrefurbished – shophouses in the area, especially along Petain Road and Jalan Besar.

Arab Street

Originally this area was a thriving Arab village known as Kampong Glam (Eucalyptus Village). The area got its name from the Gelam tribe of sea-gypsies who once lived there. Singapore's Arabs were among its earliest settlers, the first being a wealthy merchant called Syed Mohammed bin Harum Al-Junied who arrived in 1819, a couple of months after Stamford Raffles. The Alkaffs were another important local Arab family, who built their ostentatious mansion on Mount Faber. Arab merchants began settling in the area around Arab Street in the mid 19th century. Arab Street is still the main artery of Muslim Singapore, and is the name applied to the district between the Rochor Canal Road and Jalan Sultan.

The focal point is the Middle Eastern-looking **Sultan Mosque** with its golden towers on Muscat Street. Completed in 1928 and designed by colonial architects Swan and Maclaren, it is Singapore's largest mosque and attracts thousands of faithful every Friday. The original building, constructed in the 1820s, was part of a deal between the Temenggong of Johor and the East India Company in return for sovereignty over Singapore. Next door is the old **Kampong Glam Istana**, built in the early 1840s as the Temenggong Ali Iskander Shah's palace. Nearby at the junction of Jalan Sultan and Victoria Street is the **old royal cemetery**. The Urban Redevelopment Authority is currently giving Kampong Glam a S$12 million facelift.

Another popular mosque in the area is the **Hajjah Fatimah Mosque** on Java Road. It was financed by a wealthy Melakan Malay woman, Hajjah Fatimah (Hajjah is the female equivalent of Haji, meaning someone who has made the pilgrimage

ARAB STREET

1. Sultan Mosque
2. Hajjah Fatmah Mosque
3. Swee Kee
4. *Das Travelers' Inn*
5. *Raffles Hotel*
6. *Metropole Hotel*
7. Muslim Cemetery
8. Golden Cinema
9. Police Station

Not to Scale

MARINA CENTRE

to Mecca). It was designed by an unknown British architect and the work contracted to a French construction company. It was completed in 1846 and has, as a result of its cosmopolitan history, a distinctive flavour. Unfortunately, it is now dwarfed by surrounding Housing Development Board (HDB) blocks, but inside there are photographs of its HDB-less hinterland in 1959.

In the maze of side streets around the Sultan Mosque there is a colourful jumble of Malay, Indonesian and Middle Eastern merchandise: a good selection of batik (which is sold in sarong lengths of just over 2 m), silk and Indian textiles, wickerware, jewellery, perfumes and religious paraphernalia. In the weeks before Hari Raya Puasa, Bussorah Street is lined with stalls selling all kinds of traditional foods – after dark it is a favourite haunt of famished Muslims during Ramadan. Tombstone-makers are based along Pahang Street.

AROUND SINGAPORE ISLAND

See map of Singapore Island, page 368.

West of the Island

The West Coast is dominated by the industrial district of **Jurong**, where about two-thirds of the island's industrial workforce is employed. Jurong is the product of Singapore's first big state-supported industrialization programme in the 1960s and early 1970s. Since the late 1960s, the whole stretch of coast, from the Singapore River W, has been reclaimed from mangrove swampland and now makes up the busiest container port in the world (**see page 400**).

Botanic Gardens is on Cluny Road, not far from Tanglin and the top end of Orchard Road, the gardens contain almost half a million species of plants and trees from around the world in its 54 ha of landscaped parkland, primary jungle, lawns and lakes. The Botanic Gardens also houses an orchidarium where 250 hybrids and species of Singapore's favourite flower are lovingly cultivated. In 1963 former Prime Minister Lee Kuan Yew launched the successful Garden City campaign and most of the trees lining Singapore's highways were supplied by the Botanic Gardens.

The gardens now cater for the recreational needs of modern Singapore. Every evening and morning the park fills with joggers and Tai Chi fanatics. During the day, wedding parties pose for pictures among the foliage. Under the latest S$51 million development plan for the gardens, a 'reverse greenhouse', called the 'Cloud Forest' is being built in a giant glass pyramid. It will contain cold climate, high altitude flora and swirling mists (opens in 1994). The gardens are well worth a visit. Open: 0530-2300 Mon-Fri, 0530-2400 Sat and Sun. **Getting there:** buses 7, 14, 105, 106, 174 from Orchard Road to the junction of Cluny and Napier roads, next to Gleneagles Hospital.

Haw Par Villa (formerly **Tiger Balm Gardens**) 262 Pasir Panjang Road (on the way out to Jurong), and has just been renovated. Built by Aw Boon Haw and Aw Boon Par, brothers of Tiger Balm fame, it was their family home until they opened it to the public. It has now been transformed into a gaudy adventureland of

'Mad Ridley'- the rubber missionary

The Botanic Gardens were founded by an agri-horticultural society in 1859. In the early years they played an important role in fostering agricultural development in Singapore and Malaya by collecting, growing and distributing plants with economic potential, the most famous of which was rubber. Henry Ridley, director of the gardens from 1888-1912, pioneered the planting of the Brazilian para rubber tree (*Hevea brasiliensis*). In 1877, 11 seedlings brought from Kew Gardens in London were planted in the Singapore gardens. One rubber tree, an immediate descendant of one of the 11 originals is still alive in the Botanic Gardens today, near the main entrance. By the lake at the junction of Tyersall and Cluny roads there is a memorial to Ridley on the site where the original trees were planted. Ridley was known as 'Mad Ridley' because of the proselytizing zeal with which he lobbied Malaya's former coffee planters to take up rubber instead.

His first convert was Melakan planter Tan Chay Yan, who planted out 1,200 ha in 1896. Ridley devised a way of tapping the rubber trees for latex without hampering their growth. By 1920 the Botanic Gardens had distributed over 7 million seeds and the Malayan rubber industry was producing 210,000 tonnes of sheet rubber a year, accounting for half the world's rubber production. Only in 1990 did it lose its place as the world's largest producer.

The Tiger Balm story

In the latter years of the 19th century, a Chinese herbal doctor called Aw Chu Kin left China for Burma, where he hoped to make his fortune. In Rangoon he peddled his concoctions to ailing Burmese. Before his death in the early 1920s he invented a balm which he claimed was a miracle-cure for insect bites, stomach aches, colds, headaches, bronchial problems and muscle strain. Nobody believed him and when old Mr Aw died, his wife had to pawn all her jewellery to cover his funeral costs.

The only thing his sons Boon Haw (Haw means 'tiger') and Boon Par inherited was his secret recipe, but being entrepreneurs, they decided to market their birthright and rename it Tiger Balm. It became so well known in Rangoon that Boon Haw decided to try his luck in Singapore while Boon Par struck out for Hong Kong. Within years, the balm empire expanded to Malaysia, Hong Kong and China. In 1926 he built a magnificent villa on Nassim Road, Singapore, which the Urban Redevelopment Authority demolished in 1990. In 1931 he began work on Haw Par Villa, commissioning an artist from Swatow, China to landscape the gardens. The Japanese wrecked the place during the war and Boon Haw died in Honolulu in 1950 before it was restored to its lurid splendour. Tiger Balm, which is manufactured by the company Haw Par Brothers (despite the fact that the family no longer has any interests in it), now cures people all over the world. A small dab of it on a mosquito bite works wonders.

Chinese folklore – the biggest Chinese mythological theme park in the world. Boon Haw originally designed the gardens for his family's enjoyment. His gory sculptures have instilled a sense of traditional morality in generations of Singaporeans. Sequences depict wrongdoers being punished in creative ways: one is having his tongue cut out, another is galled by a spear, others are variously impaled on spikes, gnawed by dogs, boiled in oil, bitten by snakes, sliced in 2 or ground into paste by enormous millstones. The delightful estate was finally sequestrated by the Singapore government in 1985 and turned into the island's most revolting theme park.

Its 9-ha site is 5 times the size of the original villa and its grounds. There is a large section on ancient China, with pagoda-roofed buildings, arts and crafts shops and restaurants serving authentic cuisine as well as traditional theatre – in which lion dances and *wayangs* are performed. The 'Creation of the World theatre' tells classic tales from the Qin dynasty; in the 'Legends and Heroes theatre' a life-like robot is programmed to relate stories, and a video in the 'Spirit of the Orient theatre' explains Chinese folklore, customs, traditions and festivals. Two popular attractions are the 'Wrath of the water gods flume ride' and the gory 'Tales of China' boat ride. Admission: S$16. Open: 0900-1800 Mon-Fri; 0900-2100 weekends and public holidays. **NB:** do not even think about visiting Haw Par Villa over Chinese New Year – each year about 12,000 people saunter around it in the space of about 4 days. **Getting there:** MRT W-bound to Buona Vista, then bus 200; buses 10, 30, 51 and 143 along Pasir Panjang Rd.

Jurong Bird Park, on Jalan Ahmad Ibrahim, is a 20-ha haven for more than 4,500 birds from all over the world, including a large collection of Southeast Asian birds and 420 species from Africa, South America, Europe and Asia. The main attractions are the largest walk-in aviary in the world, complete with man-made waterfall and air-conditioned penguins. There is also an interesting nocturnal house with owls, herons, frogmouths and kiwis. Bird shows daily (the birds of prey show is particularly awe-inspiring) or breakfast with the birds from 0900-1100. There is a monorail service round the park for those who find the heat too much. Admission: S$9.50. Open: 0900-1800 Mon-Sun. **Getting there:** see Jurong Crocodile Paradise, below.

Jurong Crocodile Paradise – this S$10 million reptilian extravaganza is next-door to the bird park. Crocodiles and golden pythons are put through their paces and are stretched and wrestled before being fed. As Christopher Hawtree, visiting travel journalist, wrote: "… even more hideous than the accompanying disco music is the spectacle of a man leaping into a pool, grasping a crocodile from behind and cavorting with it: Tarzan did not have an assistant with a pole in case the brute took offence." You can watch the crocodiles swimming from an underwater observatory. They are at their most active in their 'cavern of darkness' – a simulated night-time environment in which their eyes glow – and at their least active in the Classique Paradise Leather Gift Shop. Admission: S$4.50. Open: 0900-1800 Mon-Sun. **Getting there:** MRT W-bound to Boon Lay; buses 250, 251 or 253 to both attractions from Boon Lay Interchange.

Tang Dynasty City, Jalan Ahmad Ibrahim/Yuan Ching Rd, Jurong, covers 12 ha and is the closest thing to an Oriental Disneyland. Developers have worked for 3 years to build this S$70 million theme park. The City includes 100 shophouses and a temple, with carvings by workmen from China and a 600 m-long, 10 m-high model of the Great Wall of China, built with bricks imported from Shenzhen. There is a 7-storey pagoda, housing the monkey god. Next door, is a cave, modelled after the legend of the monkey god, which simulates an earthquake. The theme park also includes an 'underground palace', with replicas of the 1,500 terracotta warriors found in the tomb of Shih Huang Ti in Xian, China. The City doubles as a huge movie studio (the Tang Dynasty Motion Picture company plans to make 3 feature films a year) and punters can star in their own videos, filmed on location. Real actors stage elaborate Tang Dynasty festivals and weddings. Admission: S$16 (approx).

Chinese and Japanese Gardens are on Yuan Ching Road, Jurong. The Chinese garden gives some idea of what an imperial Sung Dynasty garden would have been like, although the biggest attraction is the giant rocking horse. Yu-Hwa Yuan, as the gardens are known in Chinese, are actually a series of theme gardens, based on the classical style of Beijing's Summer Palace. The latest attraction is the Penjing Garden ('Yun Xin Yuan – or Garden of Beauty'), a large landscaped area costing S$6 million to develop and containing 3,000 miniature penjing (bonsai) trees, from all over Asia. Two of the Chinese ones are thought to be 200 years old. On the whole the gardens are colourful but disappointingly commercial. Just across the stream is the more peaceful Japanese garden, one of the largest outside Japan. Situated on a man-made island on Jurong Lake, it is designed to mirror the natural order (typical of Japanese tradition). The *Seiwaen* (or 'garden of tranquility') is based on Japanese landscaping techniques that were practised from the 14th to 17th centuries, characterized by sweeping lawns and gently flowing streams. Combined admission for both gardens: S$4. Open: 0900-1900 Mon-Fri, 0830-1900 Sat-Sun. **Getting there:** bus 171, 179 or 190 from Scotts Rd or Orchard Boulevard, change to 154 at Coronation Plaza on Bukit Timah Rd; bus 98 from Jurong Interchange or MRT to Chinese Gardens (much easier).

Science Centre, on Science Centre Road, Jurong, might be aimed more at children than adults – but there is plenty of fun for grown-ups too. The centre succeeds in its mission to make science come alive and with plenty of gadgets and hands-on exhibits. The museum is divided into 4 galleries covering social and life sciences. Admission: S$2. Open: 1000-1800 Tues-Sun. In the **Omni-theatre and Planetarium** (T 5603316/5641432) next door, the marvels of science, technology and the universe can be viewed in a 284-seat amphitheatre with a huge hemispherical (3-D) screen and a 20,000 watt sound system. Excellent films and very popular. Admission: S$9 for Omninax movies; $6 for Planetarium show. Open: 1000-2100 Tues-Sun. **Getting there:** bus 7 from Orchard Boulevard and change to 336 at Jurong East Interchange; 179 from Orchard Boulevard and change to 178 at Bukit Batok Central.

Ming Village, 32 Pandan Road (T 2657711) is one of the last factories in the world that faithfully reproduces Chinese porcelain antiques using traditional methods – from mould-making to hand-throwing – dating from Sung, Yuan, Ming and Qin Dynasties. Ring to book conducted tours around the factory premises by trained guides. Seeing the work that goes into the pots helps explain why the prices are so high in the showroom. The shop has an export department which will pack items for shipment. The Village also runs traditional pottery and painting classes for long-stay and short-stay visitors – telephone for details. Open: 0900-1730 Mon-Sun. **Getting there:** MRT to Clementi, then bus 78.

East coast

The E part of the island used to be dotted with small Malay fishing kampungs (most have now been demolished and replaced by Housing Development Board tower blocks). Great chunks of land have been reclaimed from the sea and carefully landscaped beaches now line the coast up to Changi. Just off the city end of the East Coast Parkway is the National Sports Stadium.

The suburbs of **Katong** and **Geylang Serai** are an enclave of Peranakan architecture; there are still streets of well-preserved shophouses and terraced houses in their original condition. Joo Chiat Road gives a good feel of old Singapore, sandwiched between the upmarket residential districts and government housing development projects. On Koon Seng Road, many of the houses have been carefully restored – and it is less touristy than Emerald Hill and Tanjong Pagar. Katong was also the haven for weekenders from the civil services: European and Straits Chinese mandarins had grand houses along the waterfront, a handful of which still stand today among the HDB blocks and condominiums. A little further away is Geylang Serai (on Geylang Road), considered the heart of Malay culture in Singapore; it was once an agricultural area but has been transformed into a modern industrial zone. Geylang market is well-stocked with Malay food.

Malay Cultural Village, Geylang Serai, is on a 1.7 ha site between Geylang Serai, Sims Avenue and Geylang Road. But the Malay answer to the new Tang Dynasty City, with its mock-kampung houses and Malay foodstalls, failed to draw many visitors. The irony of it is not lost on Singapore's Malay community, who have been resettled from their kampungs into HDB flats over the past 20 years. Malay cultural identity is better characterized in the stalls at Geylang market than in the cultural village. There is said to be only one remaining Malay kampung in Singapore, near Pasir Panjang. **Getting there:** by bus, SBS 2, 7; MRT to Paya Lebar, followed by 5 mins' walk.

East Coast Park is a popular recreation area with beaches and gardens as well as a tennis centre, driving range, sailing centre (**see page 429**) the now rather tacky **Big Splash** and a food centre. The sand along these beaches was imported from near-by Indonesian islands. **Getting there:** bus 16 goes direct from Orchard Road. The **Crocodilarium**, 730 East Coast Parkway, T 4473722, has over 1,200 inmates, bred in pens. The best time to visit is at feeding times (1100 Tues, Thur and Sat) – the Crocodilarium also stages crocodile-wrestling bouts; ring for times. Crocodile-skin goods are for sale. Admission: S$2. Open: 0900-1730 Mon-Sun. **Getting there:** buses 111, 118 from Orchard Road. The **Singapore Crocodile Farm**, 790 Upper Serangoon Road, is a similar set-up, where visitors can learn more about skinning techniques. This farm, with its population of about 800 crocodiles, has been on the same site since 1945, importing crocodiles from rivers in Sarawak. **Getting there:** buses 81, 83, 97, 111 from Serangoon Rd.

Changi Prison is on Upper Changi Road. The prison, as featured on the 'Go to Jail' square in the Singapore version of *Monopoly*, is where Singapore's hangman

Changi Airport: prisoner of war camp to international travel hub

Changi gets its name from *changi ular*, a climbing shrub. But Changi is mainly associated with the World War II POW camp based here, where 12,000 American, Australian and British servicemen were interned (**see page 376**). The name Changi, which for one generation meant misery and squalor, now stands for comfort and the ultimate in efficiency. International business and travel magazines regularly rate Singapore's Changi airport the world's best.

With its two rambling, marble-floored terminals, it was thought big enough to merit being called Airtropolis when Terminal Two opened in 1991. It was even mooted that it was about to be rechristened LKY Airport (after former Prime Minister Lee Kuan Yew, and Singapore's answer to New York's JFK). The spacious, uncluttered terminals are adorned with cool fountains, luxuriant plants and tropical fish tanks and boast an array of executive leisure facilities, including saunas and squash courts, to help jet-lagged executives unwind. The airport's stress-free terminals belie its status as one of the world's most hectic transit hubs.

Because of its strategic location, Singapore has long been a refuelling stop for trans-continental jetliners and today more than 40 international airlines have landing rights at Changi. Now that the island republic has also been successfully promoted as a 'shop-stop', well over 4 million passengers touch down at Changi every year. The new terminal has more than doubled the airport's capacity, allowing it to handle 20 million passengers a year. About 80% of Singapore's tourists arrive by air and it takes only 20 minutes from touch down to baggage claim – characteristically called accelerated passenger throughflow. True to form, Singapore's far-sighted government planners have already got a third terminal on the drawing board, which will cater for a further 10 million.

dispenses with drug traffickers – with gruesome regularity. It was originally built to house 600 prisoners; during the war, more than 3,500 civilians were incarcerated. In 1944, POWs were moved into the prison, and 12,000 American, Australian and British servicemen were interned in and around it. Many contracted ulcers, beriberi, dysentery and fevers. It is mostly visited by World War II veterans – there is a small museum with reproductions of WRM Haxworth's paintings and the then 17-year-old trooper George Aspinall's photographs, which record the misery of internment. A replica of the atap-roofed Changi Prison chapel stands in the prison yard. The memorial chapel's original altar cross, whose base was made from a Howitzer shell casing, was returned to the chapel in 1992. James Clavell's novel *King Rat* is more enlightening than a visit to Changi. Open: 0830-1230, 1400-1630 Mon-Fri, 0830-1230 Sat. Chapel holds a service on Sunday evening, 1730, T 5451411, presided over by Rev Henry Khoo, prison chaplain for the past 25 years. **Getting there**: bus 2 or 14 from Orchard Road.

Less than a generation ago, **Changi Village** was a sleepy backwater of Singapore, with a good beach and a few sailors' bars. Now it is dwarfed by its housing estate and has one of Asia's busiest airports in its back yard. The photo shop, *George Photo*, on Changi Village Road, is named after wartime photographer George Aspinall, who learned how to process film in the shop's darkroom in 1941. From **Changi Point**, bumboats leave for various destinations in Johor, just across the straits and an immigration and customs post. There are also boats to Singapore's NE islands (**see page 420**). **Getting there**: bus 2 or 14.

North of the island

The N of the island is Singapore's back garden: in between the sprawling new housing estates there are areas of jungly wilderness, mangroves, lakes and landscaped gardens. Immediately N of the city is the modern suburb of Toa Payoh with its Siong Lim temple. The Housing Development Board has built a string of new towns outside the central area: Queenstown and Toa Payoh in the 1960s, Ang Mo Kio and Bedok in the 70s and Hougang and Tampines in the 80s. (Ang Mo Kio – literally 'bridge of the red-haired foreign devil' – was named after John Turnbull Thomson, a government surveyor in the 19th century, who was responsible for extending Singapore's road network into the interior.)

Kong Meng San Phor Kark See Chinese Temple Complex (Bright Hill Drive) has, since its construction in 1989, grown into a sprawling, million dollar religious centre whose golden roofs spread over 7½ ha. The temple complex has been the backdrop for many kung-fu movies and is one of the largest such complexes in Southeast Asia. There are halls for prayer and meditation, a pool containing thousands of turtles, a Buddhist library, an old people's home (and, appropriately, a crematorium), as well as a 9 m-high marble statue of Kuan Yin, the 15-headed goddess of mercy, carved by Italian sculptors. Resident geriatrics spend their last days making paper cars and other worldly symbols which are torched after their deaths and, hopefully, follow them into the next world. **Getting there:** buses 4, 56, 74, 93, 104, 125, 130, 132, 143, 157, 163, 165, 166.

Singapore Zoological Gardens, 80 Mandai Lake Road, T 2693411, is one of the world's few open zoos (moats replace bars) with animals in environments vaguely reminiscent of their habitats. In its promotional brochure, the 20-ha zoo claims that its open-design concept has paid off: "Our reward is happy animals. The proof lies in the zoo's good breeding record: unhappy animals do not make love!" It contains over 170 species of animals (about 1,700 actual animals), some of them rare – like the dinosauric Komodo dragons and the golden lion tamarin – as well as many endangered species from Asia, such as the Sumatran tiger and the clouded leopard. Ring for times of feedings and animal shows. Most popular are elephants' bath time and tea with the orang utans. Animals are sponsored by companies – Tiger Beer, for example, sponsors the tigers and Qantas the kangaroos. Well-managed, informative and worth a visit. There are tram tours, recorded commentaries and restaurants. Animal showtimes: 1030 and 1430 daily (primates and reptiles); 1130 and 1530 daily (elephants and sealions). Elephant, camel and pony rides are on offer at various times each afternoon. The zoo has an excellent shop selling environmentally sound T-shirts and inexpensive cuddly toy animals. Video cameras can also be hired (S$10/hr). Admission: S$5. Open: 0830-1830 Mon-Sun. **Getting there:** the air-con Zoo Express provides guided tours on demand (contact Elpin, T 7322133). SBS bus 171 from Marina Centre or Orchard Boulevard (S$0.90), or catch it from Yishun interchange, near Yishun MRT station. Or SBS 137 from Toa Payoh Interchange (take MRT to Toa Payoh station). Taxis cost about S$10 to the zoo from the Orchard Rd area.

Singapore Orchids, Mandai Lake Road, is Singapore's largest commercial orchid farm, started life in 1960 as a hobby for orchidologists John Ede and John Laycock. The rare black orchid of Sumatra blossoms in Jul. Admission: S$1. Open: 0900-1730 Mon-Fri. **Getting there:** bus 171 from Scotts Road or Orchard Boulevard.

Bukit Timah Nature Reserve, on Hindhede Rd off Upper Bukit Timah Road, nestles in the centre of the island and has a resident population of wild monkeys, pythons and scorpions. The naturalist Alfred Russel Wallace collected beetles at Bukit Timah in 1854. Jungle trails go through the forested terrain (130 million-year-old tropical rainforest) that once covered the whole island. The artificial lakes supply the city with much of its water. Clearly marked paths in the 60-ha reserve lead to Singapore's highest point (165 m) for scenic views. A new visitor centre opened in 1992 which includes an informative exhibition on natural history (open 0830-1800). The nature reserve is at its quietest and best in the early mornings. It is a wonderful contrast to the bustle of modern Singapore. At **Bukit Batok**, there is what little remains of a Japanese Syonan Shrine, built by Australian and British POWs. All that remains are the 125 stone steps leading up to the shrine sight. The shrine's demise is attributed to the termites which the POWs reportedly placed in the materials they used to build it. From here you can walk to the rock formations known as Little Guilin. Entrance is at Bukit Batok on top of the hill at Larong Sesuan off Upper Bukit Timah Rd. **Getting there:** buses 171, 179, 182 from Orchard Boulevard or Scotts Rd.

MacRitchie and Seletar Reservoirs on Lornie and Mandai roads, are popular for weekend picnickers. Jungle paths surround the reservoirs. **Getting there:** MacRitchie, buses 104, 132, 167 from Scotts Rd or Orchard Boulevard. Also 171 outside *Holiday Inn*, Scotts Rd.

Kranji War Memorial and Cemetery, Woodlands Road, is where the Allied soldiers killed in Singapore in World War II are buried. In the heart of the cemetery is the War Memorial, bearing the names of 24,346 servicemen who died in the Asia-Pacific region during the war. The design of the memorial is symbolic, representing the 3 arms of the services – the army, navy and airforce. The upright section was designed to represent a conning tower, the lateral elements are wings, and the walls symbolize army lines. Flowers are not allowed to be placed on graves, in case tiger mosquitoes breed in the jars. **Getting there:** bus 182 goes direct from Orchard Boulevard or Scotts Road. Alternatively, take 171, 179, 190 from Scotts Road or 171, 174, 179, 190 from Orchard Boulevard and change to 170 on Bukit Timah Road after Farrer Road.

Singapore's islands

Singapore's islands are not all of the tropical dream variety, although no expense has been spared, in the case of **Sentosa**, trying to make it into a tropical paradise.

The harder-to-get-to islands are a welcome break from the city and offer a pleasing contrast to everything that modern Singapore stands for. There are around 40 neighbouring small islands, the largest of which is **Pulau Tekong**. The group of islands W of Sentosa – **Pulau Brani**, **Bukom** and **Sambol** – are industrial adjuncts of Singapore proper. You can get a scenic view of the oil refinery on Pulau Bukum from Sentosa's swimming lagoon. Ferries link the city with all its surrounding islands but for more obscure spots it's necessary to hire a boat from Clifford Pier. **NB**: avoid going to them on public holidays.

Sentosa

A British military base until 1970, Sentosa – formerly Pulau Belakang Mati – is now an elaborate 'pleasure' resort. The name chosen for the island is hardly appropriate: 'Sentosa' means 'peace and tranquility'. In 1990, Sentosa had a million visitors, about 45% of whom were foreign tourists. On weekends, Sentosa can be a nightmare, as crowds converge on the island's attractions. It is not the sort of island escape one would choose to 'get away from it all'. It is guaranteed, however, to provide plenty of entertainment for children, and adults may be pleasantly surprised with one or two attractions.

History World Pioneers of Singapore and the Surrender Chambers (monorail station 5): a well displayed history of Singapore and the World War II story, although the wax models are not up to Madame Tussaud's standard. Admission: S$3. Open: 0900-2100 Mon-Sun. **Fort Siloso** (monorail station 6): built to guard the narrow W entrance to Keppel Harbour. It is possible to explore the underground tunnels, artillery nests and bunkers. Also in the fort is a permanent exhibition, "*Behind Bars – Life as a Prisoner of War*", which features the work of wartime artist Stanley Warren, a model of a wartime Changi prison cell and a video of life in the internment camps. Admission: S$1. Open: 0900-1900

Mon-Sun. **Maritime Museum**: the history of Singapore as a port. Admission: S$1. Open: 0900-1900 Mon-Sun. There is also a **Ruined City** and a **Lost Civilization** on the waterfront.

Asian Village, a short walk from the ferry terminal, is Sentosa's latest attraction. It opened before it was fully completed in 1993, and understandably has had difficulty attracting patrons. The idea was to construct three theme villages – for East Asia, South Asia and Southeast Asia. They're pretty dismal, although some quality souvenirs are for sale. Adventure Asia – a rather half-hearted attempt at an all-Asian kiddies' funfair was added in for good measure, and an all-Asian restaurant in the middle should be open by late 1993, as should the village theatre, built up a hillside and capable of seating up to 800 people. Admission: S$4.

Nature World Butterfly Park and Insectarium (monorail station 5): a 1 ha park containing 2,500 butterflies through all stages of their life cycle. Admission: S$2.50. Open: 0930-1730 Mon-Fri, 0930-1830 Sat and Sun. **Coralarium**: display of live corals and shells; with nature ramble. Admission: S$1.50. Open: 0900-1900 Mon-Sun. **Rare Stone Museum**: 4,000 stones from China collected by one family over 5 generations. Admission: S$2. Open: 0900-1900 Mon-Sun. **Underwater World** (monorail station 7): this walk-through oceanarium is the largest in Asia. A 100m tunnel, with a moving conveyor, allows a glimpse of some of its 350 underwater species and 4,000 specimens. Feeding times are well-worth arriving for: 1130 & 1630. The Underwater World is a highly recommended visit. Admission: S$9. Open 0900-2100 Mon-Sun. **Musical fountains**: disco-lit fountains which gyrate to everything from *Joan Jett and the Blackhearts* to the *1812* courtesy of the engineers in the computer control room. Shows: 1930-2100 Mon-Sun, disco hour 2115 Sat.

Orchid Fantasy Singapore, very close to the ferry terminal, is planted out with a vast variety of orchids. Among the gardens is a restaurant and Ranwatei, a Japanese tea room. Open: 0930-1830 Mon-Sun. Admission: S$3.

Sun World Sunbathing or swimming at the lagoons and nearby 'beach'. You can hire pedal boats, windsurfers, canoes or aqua bikes. Siloso Beach, at the W end of the island has been redeveloped by the Sentosa Development Corporation. Tens of thousands of cubic metres of golden sand were shipped in, as were 300 mature coconut palms and over 100 ornamental shrubs and flowering trees.

Fun World Cycling, roller-skating or golf on the 18-hole course, also a maze and an 'enchanted grove'. There is a suitably sanitized hawker centre at Rasa Sentosa or there is the *Newfun Kelong Restaurant* at the end of the old jetty. There is also a rather staged night market.

Accommodation Contrary to first impressions, it is possible to escape from Sentosa's hoardes thanks to the construction of two new hotels. **A+** *Rasa Sentosa (Shangri-La)*, T 2750100, F 2750355, built in a curved, tapered wedge-shape behind Fort Siloso, this hotel opened mid-93, it has 1st class facilities (including good food and beverage outlets) and an unsurpassed view of the oil refinery just across the water, a pleasant enough alternative, though, to the city hotels, competitive weekend package deals available; **A+** *Beaufort*. **Sentosa Youth Hostel** (next to the lagoon), bookings at the World Trade Centre. The hostel is really meant for local youth groups and community groups, but an air conditioned room accommodating up to 12 costs S$80 a night during the week and S$100 on weekends. Non a/c rooms: S$5 per person. Tents can be hired by the day (4-man: S$12; 6-man: S$14.50; camp bed S$0.50).

Restaurants There are fast-food outlets at the ferry terminal. Rasa Sentosa is a squeaky-clean hawker centre, open 1100-2200 and there are other restaurants in Asian Village and at the two hotels. On the second floor of the World Trade Centre, a permanent Guinness World of Records Exhibition has been set up. NASA space suits, long, tall, short people and things and another reminder that *Raffles City* is the tallest hotel in the world. Admission: S$5. **Getting there**: easiest by taxi from Tanjong Pagar MRT station.

Getting around Bicycles, tandems and trishaws for hire from the ferry terminal or take the **free buses** (run from 0900-1900 Mon-Sun, every 10 mins). Service A goes to all the main attractions, service B, to the beach. The **monorail** links all the island's attractions (runs from 0900-2200 Mon-Sun).

Getting there Buses 65, 167 or 143 from Orchard Road to the World Trade Centre; 61, 84, 143, 145, 166 and 167 from Chinatown (the nearest MRT station is at Tanjong Pagar, from which buses 10, 97, 100 and 125 go to World Trade Centre). Sentosa bus service C goes across the new bridge to the island, which saves the ferry ride. There are various combinations of tickets to buy but it's worth taking the cable car up to **Mount Faber** (the highest point in Singapore, with scenic views and seafood restaurants) and across to Sentosa, S\$6. Cable car operates: 1000-2100 Mon-Sat, 0900-2100 Sun. **Getting there:** buses 124 or 143 from Orchard Rd; 61, 124 or 166 from Raffles City and 166, 97, 125 or 146 from Bencoolen St. Alternatively, take the ferry from the World Trade Centre; leaves every 15 mins from 0730-2245 (S\$3 including basic entrance to Sentosa). On Fridays and weekends, the last boat back leaves at 2300. Admission to Sentosa: S\$3.50 during the day, S\$3 in the evenings.

Sentosa Island Tour S\$28 from the following hotels: *Sheraton Towers, Mandarin, Boulevard, Shangri-La, Orchard, Hilton International*.

St John's and Kusu Island

Happily, developers have been less active on Singapore's other S islands, although they are popular city escapes. **St John's** is the larger with a few holiday camps and swimming lagoons. It used to be a quarantine station and an opium treatment centre. When Stamford Raffles first approached Singapore, his 6 ships anchored off St John's. The Malays called it Pulau Si-Kijang – barking deer island. The English sailors could not pronounce it, and corrupted it to St John's. **Accommodation**: a few holiday bungalows and camping is permitted; there is a cafeteria and shop; contact the World Trade Centre T 2707888 or 2707889.

It is possible to walk around **Kusu**, or Turtle Island, in a few minutes. Kusu has a Chinese temple and Malay shrine (see Festivals, **page 449**).

Getting there There is a regular ferry to both islands from the World Trade Centre, 30 mins to Kusu, 1 hr to St John's (S\$6 return). The last boat back from St John's leaves the jetty at 1445.

Other islands to the south

Pulau Hantu, **Sister's Island** (Subar Laut and Subar Darat) and **Lazarus Island**, like Pulau Biola near Raffles Lighthouse, are popular for snorkelling and fishing. **Pulau Seking** is slightly further away and village life here is still just about intact although the population of less than 50 inhabitants, living in a traditional fishing village on stilts, is rapidly dwindling.

Getting there There are no regular ferry services to these islands. Charter a boat or sampan from Jardine Steps or Clifford Pier (S\$30 an hour) and stock up on food and water before you go. Many tour operators have snorkelling equipment for hire.

Islands to the north-east

Off the E end of Singapore is **Pulau Tekong**. The main village, Kampung Salabin, has a run-down restaurant that serves first class seafood.

Getting there Ferries leave every hour between 0700 and 1830 Mon-Sat (there are infrequent boats on Sun) from Changi Point, Changi Village. It is also possible to get to and from Malaysia very cheaply via Changi Point (**see page 415**).

Pulau Ubin A great – but little-known – awayday from concrete and capitalism. This island is the source of granite for the causeway and Singapore's earlier buildings and skyscrapers. Its name derives from the Javanese word for 'squared stone'. Ubin village affords a taste of Singapore in bygone days, with dilapidated wooden shophouses, coffee-shops and community spirit. The island, with its beaten-up cars and old taxis, quarry pits, jungle tracks, hills and beaches, is a mountain-biker's paradise. A couple of astute Singaporean entrepreneurs have already cashed in on the idea, and it is possible to hire bicycles in the village. The best restaurant on the island – which doubles as one of the best restaurants in Singapore – is *Ubin Seafood*, on the NE shore at the end of a pot-holed jungle track (**see below**).

Accommodation C *Nature Traveller House*, 8Y Pulau Ubin, T 5426154 – ask for Thian, run by the owner of the biggest mountain-bike shop, fan-cooled only, kitchen facilities.
Restaurant: ◆◆◆*Ubin Seafood*, T 5458202/5426215 (ask for Liang) is on the NE shore of Pulau Ubin, at the end of a jungly track, and is one of the best seafood restaurants in Singapore. It is best to book – not because it is always crowded, but to ensure they have stocked up on all the crabs, fish, mussels and Tiger beer you need, rec.

Getting there From Changi Point it costs S$1 to go to Pulau Ubin; bumboats go when they're full. (For transport to and from Changi Village, **see page 415**.)

TOURS AND TOUR OPERATORS

For those constrained by time, there is a big choice of organized tours which cover everything from cultural heritage to island-hopping, eating and shopping. Most city and island tours take about 3½ hrs, and depending on admission fees to various sights, cost between S$20 and S$40.

Guides For private guided tours, call the Registered Guides Association, T 3383441; S$50 for a minimum of 4 hrs. Licenced tourist guides wear official badges and should produce ID on request.

Tour Operators Singapore's leading tour operators are: *Franco Asian Travel*, T 2938282; *Holiday Tours*, T 7382622; *Malaysia and Singapore Travelcentre*, T 7378877; *RMG Tours*, T 3377626; *Siakson Coach Tours*, T 3360288; *Singapore Sightseeing*, T 4736900 and *Tour East*, T 2355703.

Eco-tours *Eureka Travel*, 277A Holland Ave, Holland Village, T 4625077, F 4622853, organises local and regional tours with an environmental bias. It is the only such company in Singapore and guides are all highly qualified naturalists. Offers everything from ornithological tours of Singapore to trips to national parks in E and W Malaysia, rec.

City tours Most popular are the city tours which involve coach rides along Orchard Road, past the Istana, through Little India and visit Shenton Way, Raffles Place, Chinatown, Mount Faber and the Botanic Gardens. 3½ hrs (S$21) 0900 and 1400 Mon-Sun. Main operators: *Tour East, Jetset Tours, RMG, Siakson* and *Singapore Sightseeing*.

Round-the-island tours involve a coach ride along the W coast, stopping at Ming Village, then on to Changi Village, through orchid farms, and returning to town via selected housing estates. These tours usually include a bumboat ride in the Straits of Johor and a stop at Crocodile Paradise. Full day tour (S$60). Mon, Wed, Fri, 0900. Main operators: *Tour East* and *Jetset Tours*.

Singapore River Tours leave from 3 points – next to Parliament House, Liang Court and Clifford Pier. Most are half-hour or one-hour bumboat tours of the river with a commentary in English. **From Parliament House Landing Steps**: tours run at hourly intervals from 0900-1900 Mon-Sun; (S$6). The nearest MRT stop to the landing steps is Raffles Place (Standard Chartered Bank exit). For further information, call enquiries at *Singapore River Cruises and Leisure*, T 2279228 or *Lian Hup Choon Marine*, T 3366119. **From Liang Court Landing Steps and Clifford Pier**: one-hour bumboat tours of the river every 2 hours from 1000-1800 Mon-Sun, operated by *Eastwind Organization*, T 5333432, 30 mins (S$6), or 1 hr (S$15), concessionary rates for children. River trips are best at high tide. Bumboats can also be chartered privately for a more extensive tour.

Harbour A variety of harbour and island cruises are available from Clifford Pier – but not during Kusu festival. Craft vary from catamarans to imperial Chinese vessels (with modern facilities) and luxury cruise boats, prices range from S$20-60. Buffets and twilight or starlit dinners are served on some of the more elaborate tours for around S$35. The leading junk cruise operators are *Eastwind Organization*, T 5333432 and *Watertours*, T 5339811. All harbour and island cruises depart from Clifford Pier. Scheduled launch cruises also depart from Clifford Pier.

Longer Cruises For longer cruises and trips into Indonesian and Malaysian waters, the main operators are *Island Cruises*, T 2218333; *J and N Cruises*, T 2707100; *Watertours*, T 5339811; *Amaril Cruises*, T 2216969; *Beachcomber*, T 3361690; *Club Travel*

International, T 7333788; *Fantasy Cruises*, T 2840424; *Orient Charters*, T 2789397; *Phoenix Offshore*, T 5341868; *Waterfront Cruises*, T 5324497 and *Raffles Cruises*, T 7378778. Luxury motor launches can be hired for around S$140/person/day. For a detailed guide to the operators and the cruises they offer, refer to the Singapore Tourist Promotion Board's *Official Guide*, which is available free-of-charge at STPB offices and big hotels.

Other miscellaneous tours and theme tours (operators in brackets): Breakfast with Orang Utans tour (*Holiday Tours, Tour East*); Culinary tour (*Franco Asian Travel*); Cultural tour (*Singapore Sightseeing*); East Coast tour (*Tour East, RMG, Singapore Sightseeing, Holiday Tours*); Footsteps of Raffles tour (*Tour East*); Golf tour (*Franco Asian Travel*); Housing Development Board Estate tour (*Singapore Sightseeing*); Jurong Bird Park and Crocodile Paradise tour (*RMG, Siakson Coach Tours, Singapore Sightseeing*); Little India and Chinatown – walking tour (*Singapore Sightseeing*); Orchid and Orang Utan tour (*Singapore Sightseeing*); Raffles Experience (*Singapore Sightseeing*); Sentosa sunset (*Holiday Tours*); Sentosa tour (*Singapore Sightseeing, Tour East, Holiday Tours*); Singapore by Night (*Holiday Tours, Singapore Sightseeing, Holiday Tours*); Singapore Science Centre (*Singapore Sightseeing*); Trishaw tour (*Tour East, Holiday Tours*); World War II battlefield tours – specially tailored to WW II veterans (*Malaysia and Singapore Travelcentre, Singapore Sightseeing*).

Festivals See page 447.

SERVICES

Accommodation Because Singapore receives more than 5 million tourists a year, the number of hotels on the island is rather overwhelming. The vast majority are clean and well-appointed by Asian standards – although they are relatively expensive compared with prices in other Southeast Asian capitals (even the YMCA falls within the 'A' category in Singapore). Nearly all the top-end hotels offer a full range of amenities and for that reason, are fairly homogenous. The main differentiating factor is location – some hotels are more conveniently located for shopping areas, others for Chinatown or the Colonial core. L and A+ grade hotels offer various degrees of opulence – all have restaurants, swimming pools and other facilities, including health and fitness centres and business centres. As there are so many hotels in these categories, only a selection has been provided below. At the bottom end, there are a few cheap Chinese hotels (some of those in Geylang quote room rates by the hour) and crashpads where backpackers can still find dormitory accommodation, with no frills attached. The *STPB* publishes two accommodation guides, one covering luxury and 'tourist-class' hotels and another for budget hotels. These are available from *STPB* offices (**see page 453**). Visitors arriving by air who do not have hotel reservations can contact the hotel counter at Changi Airport; it is worth inquiring about any special rates that might be available.

L *Goodwood Park*, 22 Scotts Rd, T 7377411, a/c, restaurant, pool, began life in the 19th century as the German Club, *The Teutonia*, the Sultan of Brunei has a suite of rooms here, rec; **L** *Hyatt Regency*, 10-12 Scott's Rd, T 7321696, a/c, restaurant, pool; **L** *Mandarin*, 333 Orchard Rd, T 7374411, a/c, restaurant, pool, revolving restaurant on top, with good views up and down Orchard Road; **L** *Marina Mandarin*, Marina Sq, 6 Raffles Boulevard, T 3383388, a/c, restaurant, pool, built on reclaimed land next to Oriental and Pan-Pacific, ready access to large shopping centre; **L** *Oriental*, Marina Sq, 5 Raffles Av, T 3380066, a/c, restaurant, pool, on reclaimed land, next to Marina Mandarin and Pan Pacific; **L** *Pan-Pacific*, Marina Sq, 6 Raffles Boulevard, T 3368111, a/c, restaurant, pool; **L** *Raffles*, 1 Beach Rd, T 3378041, a/c, pool, re-opened after major refurbishment in Sept 1991 (**see page 398**), *Raffles Hotel* has all the 5-star facilities including 7 restaurants, 5 bars (see separate entries under *restaurants* and *bars*) and 70 shops, advance reservations can be made in the UK (T 0800 282124), Australia (T 02 9566144), Japan (T 0120 416220) and the USA (T 800 5447570), all calls are toll-free, tariffs for suites start at S$600 plus tax, to S$4,000 and beyond; **L** *Regent Singapore*, 1 Cuscaden Rd, T 7338888, a/c, restaurant, pool, beautiful hotel set back off Tanglin Rd near the top of Orchard Rd; **L** *Shangri-La*, 22 Orange Grove Rd, T 7373644, a/c, restaurant, pool, one of Singapore's finer hotels set in a park with golf course, spacious rooms with balconies, rec, winner of Singapore Tourism Promotion Board's tourism award for best hotel, year after year; **L-A+ Westin Stamford and Westin Plaza**, 2 Stamford Rd, T 3388585, a/c, restaurant, pool, caters mainly for business travellers, listed in the *Guinness Book of Records* as the tallest hotel in the world, the *Compass Rose* restaurant on top which affords excellent views over 3 countries – Singapore, Malaysia and Indonesia.

A+ Amara, 165 Tanjong Pagar Rd, T 2244488, a/c, restaurant, pool, conveniently located for Finger Pier, the Railway Station and Chinatown; **A+ ANA**, 16 Nassim Hill, T 7321222, a/c, restaurant, pool, formerly the Sheraton, on the hill behind Tanglin, a short walk from Orchard Rd; **A+ Boulevard**, 200 Orchard Boulevard, T 7372911, a/c, restaurant, pool; **A+ Cairnhill**, 19 Cairnhill Circle, T 7346622, a/c, restaurant, pool; **A+ Concorde** (formerly *Glass Hotel*), 317 Outram Rd, T 7330188, a/c, restaurant, pool, close to Chinatown and good night spots; **A+ Duxton**, 83 Duxton Rd, T 2277678, a/c restaurant (*L'Aigle d'Or*, **page 426**), pool, 50-room hotel in refurbished shophouses in Tanjong Pagar, price includes breakfast, can be booked in London through *Small Luxury Hotels of the World*, T 0800 282124, deluxe rooms are built in twin tiers, which are very nice, but none of the rooms are large, the hotel has arrangements with the nearby *Amara* hotel to use its pool, mainly frequented by business people as it's convenient for financial district, offers good discounts on published rates, rec; **A+ Dynasty**, 320 Orchard Rd, T 7349900, a/c, restaurant, pool, in the lobby of the pagoda-style hotel hang a series of 24 3-storey-high carved teak panels, made in Shanghai by 120 craftsmen, and portraying scenes from Chinese history and mythology; **A+ Furama**, 10 Eu Tong Sen St, T 5333888, a/c, restaurant, pool, in the heart of Chinatown; **A+ Harbour View Dai Ichi**, 81 Anson Rd, T 2241133, a/c, restaurant, pool, handy location for central business district and Tanjong Pagar; **A+ Hilton International**, 581 Orchard Rd, T 7372233, a/c, restaurant, pool, one of the first big hotels in the shopping hub; **A+ Imperial**, 1 Jalan Rumbia, Oxley Rise, T 7371666, a/c, restaurant, pool, near Lee Kuan Year's private residence and well located in quiet area between Orchard Road and Chinatown; **A+ Le Meridien**, 1 Netheravon Rd, off Upper Changi Rd, T 5427700, a/c, restaurant, pool, 5 mins from the airport, relaxed seaside feel, handy for Changi Village and Pulau Ubini, rec; **A+ Le Meridien**, 100 Orchard Rd, T 7338855, a/c, restaurant, pool; **A+ Melia at Scotts**, 45 Scotts Rd, T 7325885, a/c, restaurant, pool, only Spanish-run hotel in Singapore – with Spanish restaurant; **A+ New Otani**, 177A River Valley Rd, T 3383333, a/c, restaurant, pool, on the riverbank in godown country; **A+ Novotel Orchid Inn**, 214 Dunearn Rd, T 2503322, a/c, restaurant, pool, convenient for travel to Johor Bahru's Senai Airport as MAS buses terminate here; **A+ Omni Marco Polo**, 247 Tanglin Rd, T 4747141, a/c, restaurant, pool, a short hop from Orchard Rd shopping area and a short jog from the Botanic Gardens; **A+ Orchard Parade**, 11 Tanglin Rd, T 7371133, a/c, restaurant, pool; **A+ Peninsula**, 3 Coleman St, T 3372200, a/c, restaurant, pool, conveniently located for the colonial cove; **A+ Phoenix**, Orchard/Somerset rds, T 7278666, a/c, restaurant, pool; **A+ Plaza**, 7500a Beach Rd, T 2980011, a/c, restaurant, pool, within walking distance from Arab Street and the Muslim quarter; **A+ River View**, 382 Havelock Rd, T 7329922, a/c, restaurant, pool, run by Robert Pregarz, a former Italian sailor and ex-manager of the pre-theme park Raffles; **A+ Royal Holiday Inn**, Crowne Plaza, 25 Scotts Rd, T 7377966, a/c, restaurant, pool, owned by the Sultan of Brunei, for whom an entire floor of suites is permanently reserved; **A+ Sheraton Towers**, 39 Scotts Rd, T 7376888, a/c, restaurant, pool; **A+ York**, 21 Mount Elizabeth, T 7370511, a/c, restaurant, pool.

A Asia, 37 Scotts Rd, T 7378388, a/c, restaurant, pool, close to Newton Circus Hawker Centre; **A Bencoolen**, 47 Bencoolen St, T 3360822, a/c, restaurant, foreboding highrise from outside, but pleasantly surprising within, very clean, if boxy, rooms with good range of facilities, rooftop garden with restaurant, good central location for Orchard Rd and city; **A Cockpit**, 6/7 Oxley Rise, T 7379111, a/c, restaurant, pool, in the Orchard Road shopping belt; **A Dragon Cityview**, 18 Mosque St, T 2239228, F 2218198, a/c, restaurant, new hotel in refurbished shophouses smack in the heart of Chinatown, well-appointed rooms with Chinesey rosewood replica furnishings, sister hotel to the down-market *New Asia* (see below); **A Garden**, 14 Balmoral Rd, T 2353344, a/c, restaurant, pool; **A Inn of the Sixth Happiness**, 9-35 Erskine Rd, T 2233266, a/c, restaurant, in the 1860s the buildings housed rickshaw stables and later became a row of 40 shophouses, now after a S$3 million refurbishment they have been transformed into an original little hotel, unfortunately none of the standard rooms has any windows and the superior rooms upstairs, which do, have no view, it's a pleasant hotel with wood-beamed ceilings, tasteful interior decor – including replica Peranakan furniture made specially in Fujian province, China, good promotional rates and excellent discounts, there is a rather loud karaoke bar down the street; **A Jack's Travelodge**, 05-01/16 AA Centre, 336 River Valley Rd, T 7329222, a/c, restaurant, characterless rooms in characterless AA Building, clean and smart enough but big zero for everything else; **A Lloyds Inn**, 2 Lloyd Rd, T 7377309, a/c, restaurant, scrupulously clean, well-appointed rooms – if a little cramped, excellent location near River Valley Rd/Somerset MRT, up the road past Mario-ville; **A** *Metropolitan YMCA*, 60 Stevens Rd, T 7377755, a/c, comfortable but not the facilities of the Orchard Rd branch; **A** *Negara*, 15 Claymore Drive, T 7370811, a/c, restaurant, tucked in behind Orchard Rd's shopping centres; **A** *RELC International House*, 30 Orange Grove Rd, T 7379044, a/c, breakfast included; **A** *Sloane Court*, 17 Balmoral Rd, T 2353311, a/c, restaurant; **A** *Strand*, 25 Bencoolen St, T 3381866, rec; **A** *YMCA*, International House, 1 Orchard Rd, T 3373444, a/c, restaurant, pool, the old YMCA, which stood on Stamford Road, was used by the Japanese during the war as their dreaded interrogation and torture centre, the new one's facilities are well above the usual YMCA standard, rec.

B *Air View*, 10 Peck Seah St, T 2257788, a/c, very conveniently located for Tanjong Pagar MRT, Maxwell Rd hawker centre and Chinatown, rooms clean but tatty, big rooms better, shower in room, shared loo; **B** *Broadway*, 195 Serangoon Rd, T 2924661, F 2916414, a/c, restaurant, Indian-run, Indian-frequented hotel in downtown Little India with excellent Indian restaurant downstairs: 'we know the way to your heart is through your stomach' (see *Bombay Coffee House*), hotel very clean, friendly; **B** *Great Southern*, 36-42 a/b Eu Tong Sen St, T 5333223, a/c, cheaper fan-cooled rooms; **B** *Kam Leng*, 377 and 383 Jalan Besar, T 2929470, a/c, cheaper rooms with shared bathroom and fans; **B** *Kim San*, 40 Amber Rd, T 3457502, a/c, cheaper rooms with shared bathroom and fan; **B** *Mario-Ville Boarding House*, 64 Lloyd Rd, T 7345342, a/c, restaurant and dreadful darts bar, fantastic old towkay's mansion of pre-war vintage, and beautiful balcony upstairs, unfortunately rooms ruined by owners who didn't like high ceilings and covered everything in gypsum board, annex block outside not converted and quite nice, ballet academy practices upstairs; **B** *May Sing*, 23 Lorong 20, Geylang, T 7442973, a/c; **B** *Mayfair City*, 40-45 Armenian St, T 3375405, a/c, big rooms and well-kept, not bad value for money, good location just along from red-and-white MPH bookshop, ancient crank-handle lift; **B** *New Asia*, 2 Peck Seah St, T 2211861, a/c, very convenient for Tanjong Pagar/Chinatown, similar to Air View but dingier; **B** *Victoria*, 87 Victoria St, T 3382381, a/c, rec; **B** *Waterloo Hostel*, 4th Flr, 55 Waterloo St, T 3366555, a/c, centrally located, big rooms with TVs and telephones, complimentary tea/coffee, very pleasant, friendly atmosphere, rec; **B** *YWCA Hostel*, just up from International House, 6-8 Fort Canning Road, T 3363150; **B-D** *Peony Mansion Travellers' Lodge* (formerly *Beethoven Crash Pad*), 4th Flr, 46 Bencoolen St, (lift round back of building), T 3385638, reasonable value for money with rooms (some a/c) and dorms, breakfast included, cheap ticketing service; *Peony Mansion Latin House*, 3rd Flr, 46 Bencoolen St (lift round back of building), T 3396308, some a/c, rooms and dorms, complimentary tea/coffee, not particularly friendly, you get what you pay for.

C *Central (Allenby)*, 10a/b Allenby Rd, T 2984122, a/c; **C** *Hai Hin*, 97 Beach Rd, T 3363739, shared bathrooms, fan-cooled only; **C** *Mitre*, 145 Killiney Rd (up side lane, parallel to Lloyd Rd), T 7373811, a/c, restaurant, bar, colonial relic, full of character and characters, the only hotel in Singapore where room rates keep going down, may not be around much longer, rec; **C** *Shang Onn*, Purvis St, T 3384153, a/c, rec; **C** *Sin Wah*, 36 Bencoolen St, T 3362428, one of the very few remaining family-run Chinese hotels, more than 50 years old, run by old gentleman, Mr Chao Yoke San and his son, very clean, good atmosphere, rec; **C-E** *Das Travellers Inn*, 87 Beach Rd (opposite Shaw Tower), T 3387460, free breakfast, coffee and tea; **D-F** *Why Not Homestay*, 127 Bencoolen St, T 3388838, rooms the size of cupboards but incredibly popular with travellers, clean enough with good coffee shop and Muslim restaurant downstairs, very cramped dorms.

Backpack Guest House, 15a Mackenzie Rd, T 3369384, clean and friendly; **E** *Lee Travellers' Club*, 07-52 Peony Mansion, 46-52 Bencoolen St, T 3383149, calls itself 'the exclusive club for travellers' and is rated by backpackers, complimentary breakfast of sorts, pretty grotty, travel information service.

Camping Camping on Sentosa Island and Pulau Ubin, where there are pre-erected tents available (see page 417).

Restaurants

Chinese: ✦✦✦✦*Canton Garden*, Westin Stamford and Westin Plaza, 2 Stamford Rd, T 3388585, dim sum rec; ✦✦✦✦*Dragon City Sichuan*, Novotel, 214 Dunearn Rd, popular, renowned for its spicy seafood, rec; ✦✦✦✦*Imperial Herbal*, Metropole Hotel, 41 Seah St, an in-house herbalist takes your pulse and recommends a meal, food prepared using ancient Chinese remedies, pricey; ✦✦✦✦*Red Lantern Revolving Restaurant*, 60a, Change Alley Aerial Plaza, Collyer Quay, high-priced, low-rise revolver, with a view over the harbour; ✦✦✦*Grand City*, 7th Flr, Cathay Building, 11 Dhoby Gant, T 3383622, big Chinese restaurant convenient for cinemas, better value with bigger groups, good Szechuan (spicy) soup; ✦✦✦*Dynasty Hotel* (3rd Floor), Orchard Rd, first class dim sum until 1400; ✦✦✦*Kee Ling Garden Steamboat*, 60

Waterloo St; ♦♦♦*Prima Tower Revolving Restaurant*, 201 Keppel Rd, T 2728822, revolving restaurant atop a huge silo looks out over the harbour and city, Beijing cuisine, book in advance; ♦♦♦*Steamboat Garden*, 03-257 Selegie Complex, 257 Selegie Rd; ♦♦♦*Tai Seng Gourmet Corner*, 6-8 Murray St. Teochew restaurant that has been run by the same family for 3 generations, specializes in fresh crayfish and serves deep-fried pomegranate chicken on weekends; ♦♦*Fatty Wong's*, Albert St, excellent steamed garoupa, roast duck and pork, peeled chilli prawns and other Cantonese dishes, rec; ♦♦*Fong Kee*, New Market Rd, 01-1148 People's Park, Singapore's Tienjin meat dumpling king; rec; ♦♦*Hoi Seng*, B1-20 Sim Lim Square, Rochor Rd, in the food centre in the basement of Singapore's electronic epicentre, Mr Ho is best known for his roast duck; ♦♦*Inn of the Sixth Happiness*, 33-35 Erskine Rd, restaurant attached to hotel of same name, old-style repro marble-top tables, good local snack menu (a little pricey) and selection of 8 sorts of tea; ♦♦*Swee Kee*, 51 Middle Rd (towards Beach Rd), best Hainanese chicken and rice in Singapore; ♦♦*Xiang Ji Seafood*, 181 New Bridge Rd (opposite and down from People's Park), best known for its dim sum menu and its superb deals, food served all day every day but from 1430-1730, eat as much as you can manage for less than S$10, rec.

Seafood: several seafood restaurants on Mount Faber hill, with a good view – they are not that popular and the seafood is far from being the best in town, but it's a pleasant location. ♦♦♦*Beng Hiang*, 20 Murray St, Food Alley (off Maxwell Rd), Hokkien seafood menu; ♦♦♦*House of Four Seasons*, Empress Place Building, 01-03, 1 Empress Place, large indoor restaurant in the majestic Empress Place, but at night, spreads onto the outside terrace, next to the river, drunken prawns and steamboat specialities, rec; ♦♦♦ *Jumbo Restaurant*, E Coast Parkway Marina Seafood Centre, rec, especially their drunken prawns (open evenings only); ♦♦♦*Kim's Eating House*, 447/443a Changi Rd (Five-and-a-half mile), claypot pepper crabs are the speciality in Mr Tan's cheap and informal seafood restaurant, open to 0130 weekdays and 0230 on Sats; ♦♦♦*Long Beach Seafood*, 610 Bedok Rd, T 2410196, one of the island's most famous seafood restaurants, specializing in pepper and chilli-crabs and drunken prawns, formerly on the beach, this was one of a string of pre-reclamation seafood restaurants, most of which have now migrated to the East Coast Parkway Marina, rec; ♦♦♦*Loo Tien Seafood Centre*, 2 Purvis St, open to 0330, good choice and value for money; ♦♦*Choon Seng*, 892 Ponggol Rd, at Ponggol Point, fresh seafood, good stop off if you've been water-skiing, but always worth the trip anyway, superb pepper crabs, this row of restaurants is, however, under the developers' death sentence; *East Coast Parkway Marina Seafood Centre*, Block 1206 UDMC Seafood Centre, East Coast Parkway, sit out by the sea and enjoy fresh seafood (opens evenings only).

Nonya (Straits Chinese): ♦♦♦*Nonya and Baba*, 262/264 River Valley Rd, for those wanting a Peranakan theme to the evening, the Frontpage pub, in a refurbished shophouse, is nearby, rec; ♦♦*Bibi's*, 180 Orchard Rd/corner of Peranakan Place, rather-too-trendy, but the food is good; ♦♦*Ivins*, 19/21 Binjai Park, 6½ miles, Upper Bukit Timah Rd (next to Caltex garage and antique shops), T 4683060, this restaurant, which opened in 1993, leaves all other Peranakan joints standing still, extremely hectic, popular a/c restaurant serving all main Nonya dishes (and beer), no dish costs more than S$4.50, open 1100-1500, 1700-2100, rec.

Indian: ♦♦♦♦*Annalakshmi*, 02-10 Excelsior Hotel and Shopping Centre, 5 Coleman St, vegetarian cuisine, the Annalakshmi is run on the same basis as KL's Annapoorna, it is staffed by unpaid housewives and profits go to the Kalamandair Indian cultural group, the health drinks are excellent – especially Mango Tharang (mango juice, honey and ginger) and Annalakshmi Special (fruit juices, yoghurt, honey and ginger), Sun lunchtime buffet rec. S$25; daily lunchtime buffet $20, cultural show every full moon; the restaurant, which sprawls out onto the verandah overlooking the tennis courts, serves N and S Indian food, Samy's banana-leaf and fish-head curries are unrivalled, rec; ♦♦♦♦*Maharani*, 05-36 Far East Plaza, Scotts Rd, rated as one of the best for N Indian cuisine – tandoori chicken and kormas are specialities; ♦♦♦*Hazara*, 24 Lorong Mambong (behind the front row of shophouses, Holland Village), T 4674101, sister restaurant to *Kinara* (below), specializing in NW Frontier cuisine (tandooris etc), splendid decor with genuine frontier feel; ♦♦♦*Kinara*, 57 Boat Quay, T 5330412, sister restaurant to *Hazara* (above) serving coconutty seafood using N Indian spices, Kinara means 'riverbank', the food is bettered only by the decor – magnificent Rajastani-style with carved pillars and *jharoka* window niches, book for upper room with river view, rec; ♦♦♦*Moghul Mahal*, 01-11 Columbo Court, great food, shame about the decor, N Indian tandoori food, reasonably priced; ♦♦♦*Muthu's Curry*, 75/78 Race Course Rd, reckoned by connoisseurs to be among the best banana leaf restaurants in town, *Muthu's* fish-heads are famous, rec; ♦♦♦*Noor Jahan's*, Race Course Rd, N Indian cuisine – good value for money, rec; ♦♦♦*Orchard Maharajah*, 25 Cuppage Terrace, excellent N Indian food – tandoori and

Kashmiri, conveniently located next door to Saxophone (**see page 426**) in converted shophouse; ♦♦♦*Ramu's*, 246-F Upper Thomson Rd (opposite Thomson Post Office). Melakan-Indian specialities such as deep-fried yoghurt chicken, sizzling prawns, claypot fish-head, mutton Mysore and fish curries, rec by locals; ♦♦♦*Samy's*, Civil Service Club, Tanglin Club House, Dempsey Rd (off Napier Rd), diners are obliged to become temporary members of the Civil Service Club for $1... but Samy makes it worth your while, excellent banana leaf curries in relaxed atmosphere, rec; ♦♦*Bombay Coffee House*, Broadway Hotel, 195 Serangoon Rd, good, cheap vegetarian and non-vegetarian N Indian food in Little India; ♦♦*Hakim*, 91 Pasir Panjang Rd, (west of World Trade Centre), 24-hour Indian Muslim coffee shop serving rotis, murtabaks and curries of all descriptions, cheap and very friendly, rec; ♦♦*Komala Vilas*, 76-78 Serangoon Rd, thali and masala dosa, rec; ♦♦*Madras New Woodlands*, 14 Upper Dickson Rd (off Serangoon Rd), thalis, masala dosa and vegetarian curries, good and cheap; ♦♦*Naan*, 07-31 Funan Centre, 109 North Bridge Rd, specially to cater to the needs of curry-loving computer-shoppers, located in the food centre at the top of the Funan Centre; ♦♦*Royal Banana Leaf*, 238 River Valley Rd, among a string of antique shops and near the *Frontpage* and *Next Page* pubs, food good, service amateur; ♦♦*Sahib*, 129 Bencoolen St, Indian Muslim food (murtabaks, rotis etc), very popular with travellers from *Why Not Homestay*, next door, rec; ♦♦*The Prata Shop*, 126 Casuarina Rd, prata and murtabaks with chicken, mutton and fish curry, rec.

Malay: ♦♦♦*Aziza's*, 36 Emerald Hill Rd, popular restaurant which always lives up to its reputation; ♦♦♦*Sukmaindra*, 3rd Flr, *Royal Holiday Inn*, Crowne Plaza, 25 Scotts Rd, named after the handwoven Bruneian material which decorates its walls (the hotel is owned by the Sultan of Brunei), the Sukmaindra has great rendang, satay (prawn satay rec) and curries, at prices any old sultan could afford...; ♦♦*Bintang Timur*, 14 Scotts Rd, 02-08/13 Far East Plaza, excellent satays and curries, the ambience allows you to forget that you're in a shopping centre.

Indonesian: ♦♦♦♦+*Alkaff Mansion*, Mount Faber Ridge, 10 Telok Blangah Green, built in the 1920s, the huge house has undergone a S$3 million refurbishment and makes a magnificent restaurant, it's Indonesian chef has earned himself quite a reputation for his Rijstaffel, 6 main dishes S$32, set dinner S$52; ♦♦♦*House of Sundanese Food*, 218 East Coast Rd, T 3455020, typical Sundanese (from W Java) dishes include spicy salad (*keredok*), charcoal-grilled seafood (*ikan Sunda, ikan emas*) and curries, simply decorated non-a/c restaurant, with a real home-cooked taste; ♦♦♦*Rasa Rasa*, 61 Boat Quay, open-fronted café facing river with Indon-style restaurant upstairs, decor nothing special but food good and great view over river; ♦♦♦*Sanur*, 17/18, 4th Flr, Centrepoint, 176 Orchard Rd, cramped Malay/Indonesian restaurant ideally placed for shoppers, specialities include fish-head curries and spicy grilled chicken or fish; ♦♦*Jawa Timur*, 9th Flr, Chiat Hong Bldg, 110 Middle Rd, T 3375532, very reasonably priced Javanese food (incl rendang, gado gado and good satay, but not much by way of atmosphere; ♦♦*Pagisore Nasi Padang*, 20 Duxton Rd (Tanjong Pagar), tiny upmarket coffee shop serving excellent Padang food and real coffee, rec; ♦♦*Tambuah Emas*, 4th Flr, Tanglin Shopping Centre, a/c restaurant, very popular and cramped, what it lacks in ambience, it more than makes up for with the food.

Tiffin: an English word meaning afternoon meal. The word originated in India during the heyday of the East India Company. It came to refer to special containers in which lunch is packed and sent to work places by special couriers. ♦♦♦♦+*Tiffin Room*, Raffles Hotel, 1 Beach Rd, (main building, ground floor), tiffin curry buffet (plus à la carte menu) in pristine white, over-lit ersatz Victorian grandeur, it's good food, but at S$35 for the buffet, you're paying a lot more for the surroundings than for the curry; ♦♦♦*Alkaff Mansion*, Mount Faber Ridge, 10 Telok Blangah Green, tiffin curry lunches, rec; *Emerson's Tiffin Rooms*, 51 Neil Rd, open breakfast, lunch, dinner and supper, named after Charles Emerson who ran a famous restaurant for 40 years from 1866 at the spot where Cavenagh Bridge now stands.

Thai: ♦♦♦*Bangkok Garden*, Kecksing Towers, Cecil St, cultural show to whet the appetite (lunchtime only Mon, Wed, Fri); ♦♦♦*Chao Phaya*, 211 Holland Ave, 04-01 Holland Rd Shopping Centre, choice of over 200 dishes with selection of green, yellow and red curried fish and prawns and excellent chilli crabs, restaurant has seafood market where you can stalk your dinner; ♦♦♦*Cuppage Thai Food*, 49 Cuppage Terrace, popular Thai restaurant with outside tables... makes for a good evening if combined with a visit to Saxophone bar, just a few doors down, rec.

Vietnamese: ♦♦♦♦*Sai Gon*, Cairnhill Place, 15 Cairnhill Rd, superb food, with very helpful waiters to give advice, pan-fried beef rec and innovative and tasty dishes such as crab in beer; ♦♦*Pare'gu Vietnamese Seafood Restaurant*, 01-24/34 Orchard Plaza, 150 Orchard Rd. (Also has a branch in Marina Sq shopping centre: 6 Raffles Boulevard 03-140.

Japanese: ✦✦✦✦++*Inagiku*, Westin Stamford and Westin Plaza, 2 Stamford Rd, clientele include the Raffles City corporate dinner brigade, so pricey; ✦✦✦✦++*Suntory*, 06-01 Delfi Orchard, Orchard Rd, for sushi, tempura, teppanyaki and shabu-shabu-lovers with a serious yen (or two); ✦✦✦✦*Sushi Nogawa Kaiseki*, *Crown Prince Hotel*, 270 Orchard Rd, expensive little joint favoured by Japanese businesspeople; ✦✦✦✦*Izakaya Nijumaru*, 5 Koek Rd, 02-10/12 Cuppage Plaza, reasonably priced Japanese robatayaki restaurant; ✦✦✦*Kushi-Zen*, 3rd Flr, *Hotel Royal*, 36 Newton Rd, set menus are good value, lunch: $10-20, dinner: $15-25, kushi-katsu is Kushi-Zen's *pièce de résistance* – a Nipponese version of satay; ✦✦✦*Shabushin*, 4th Flr, Tanglin Shopping Centre, Tanglin Rd, popular restaurant offering set lunches and dinners at reasonable prices; ✦✦✦*Sushi Dokoro Yoshida*, 58 Boat Quay, another new riverfront restaurant specializing in *izakaya* (barbecued fish), upstairs, designed around sushi bar, branch in *Lucky Plaza*, Orchard Rd.

Korean: ✦✦✦*Ar-Li-Lang*, B1-09/20 United Sq, 101 Thomson Rd, barbecue sets; ✦✦✦*Korean Restaurant*, Specialists' Centre, Orchard Rd, this imaginatively-named restaurant is well known for its *bulgogi* meat barbecues.

Italian: ✦✦✦✦++*Ristorante Bologna*, *Marina Mandarin Hotel*, 6 Raffles Boulevard, Marina Square, award winning restaurant where jeans and T-shirts are banned and diners with bulging wallets are welcome; ✦✦✦*Da Paolo*, 66 Tanjong Pagar Rd, T 2247081, one of the two Italians in Tanjong Pagar in restored shophouse, popular with expats, home-made pasta, over-priced; ✦*Pasta Fresca da Salvatore*, 30 Boat Quay, very small but fresh and tasty; *Pasta Brava*, 11 Craig Rd, Tanjong Pagar, lean cuisine, but tastiest Italian in town in an equally tasty shophouse conversion, fairly expensive, rec.

Mexican: ✦✦✦*Chico's N Charlie's*, 05-01 Liat Towers, 541 Orchard Rd, an expat hang-out, good atmosphere, good hacienda food and good value; ✦✦✦*El Felipe's* (2 branches) – 360 Orchard Rd 02-09, International Building; 34 Lorong Mambong, Holland Village (behind front row of shophouses), *El Felipe's* frozen margaritas are even more delicious than the burittos, rec; ✦✦✦*Margarita's*, 108 Faber Drive, appropriately named after the Tequila cocktails it's best at.

International: ✦✦✦✦++*Maxim's de Paris*, *The Regent Singapore*, 1 Cuscaden Rd, French extravaganza; ✦✦✦✦*Alkaff Mansion*, Mount Faber Ridge, 10 Telok Blangah Green, splendid refurbished mansion, originally owned by Arab trader, offers a Western grill and barbecue, open for lunch, tea and dinner, the terrace is a very grand cocktail haunt; ✦✦✦✦*Casablanca*, 7 Emerald Hill Rd, Humphrey Bogart decor in refurbished Paranakan house, chef's recommendations are excellent – as are his escargots; ✦✦✦✦*Gordon Grill*, Lobby, *Goodwood Park Hotel*, 22 Scotts Rd, Singapore's only Scottish Restaurant with haggis on the menu... at 24 hours' advance notice; ✦✦✦✦*L'Aigle d'Or*, *Duxton Hotel*, 83 Duxton Rd, T 2274388, extensive, expensive menu with wine list to match, French, a few Oriental touches and a good vegetarian selection, sophisticated atmosphere; ✦✦✦✦*Raffles Grill*, *Raffles Hotel*, 1 Beach Rd (main building, first floor), serving breakfast, lunch and dinner, continental cuisine, French doors open onto Palm Court, Chippendale furniture; ✦✦✦✦*Truffles*, Level 2, *The Dynasty*, 320 Orchard Rd, continental menu – French chef, good buffet lunches; ✦✦✦✦*Zouk*, 19 Jiak Kim St, (off Kim Seng Rd), the Zouk restaurant menu caters for refined tastes, with fine wines to match, pleasant riverside canopied terrace outside with *Zouk* bars, café and disco; ✦✦✦*Bar and Billiard Room*, *Raffles Hotel*, 1 Beach Rd, (corner block), contains many of Raffles' original furnishings, serves business lunches; ✦✦✦*Fondue Café 81*, Block 44, Jalan Merah Saga 01-60, Chip Bee Garden, excellent fondues – although the chocolate one weighs heavy; ✦✦✦*Hot Stones*, 22 Lorong Mambong (behind front row of shophouses, Holland Village), speciality: cooking slabs of meat or seafood on baking-hot Serpentine rock – a German idea, so it tends to work, cooks at the table, the restaurant was built on what was, until 1992, the village's best coffee shop; ✦✦✦*Movenpick*, B1-01 Scotts Shopping Centre, 6 Scotts Rd, B1-01 6 Battery Rd, good value for money; ✦✦✦*Saxophone*, 23 Cuppage Terrace, Singapore's best live-music joint also has an excellent French restaurant: the menu is select, eat at the bar, on the terrace or upstairs in the restaurant, escargots and chocolate mousse rec; ✦✦✦*Singapore Polo Club*, 80 Mount Pleasant Rd, (just off Thomson Rd), if you're not put off by the polo set or visiting sultans, the Polo Club is a great place to dine on the verandah – especially on match days (Tues, Thurs and Sat) when there's plenty to look at, there is a snack menu (steak sandwich, fish and chips etc) on the verandah overlooking the turf ($8-15) and a smarter restaurant inside ($20-30), rec; ✦✦✦*Tradewinds*, Top Flr, *Hilton International*, 581 Orchard Rd, don't be put off by the fact it's in the *Hilton* – Tradewinds is a reasonably priced, poolside restaurant, with delicious food and serenading Spanish guitarists, the local dishes are particularly good, rec; ✦✦*Charlie's*, Block 2, 01-08, Changi Village, Charlie's folks, who were first generation immigrants from China, set up the *Changi Milk* Bar in the 1940s, then Charlie's

Corner became the favoured watering hole and makan stop for sailors and riggers for decades, his mum still fries up the chips that gave them the reputation as the best chippies E of London's Isle of Dogs, excellent chilli-dogs, spicy chicken wings and 70 beers to choose from, closed weekends, rec. **Getting there**: bus from Changi Point from Tampines MRT; ♦♦*Duxtons*, 21 Duxton Hill (Tanjong Pagar), bar and coffee house serving deli food, pleasant converted shophouse with terrace, connected to *China Inn*, next door; ♦♦*Empire Café*, Grd Flr, *Raffles Hotel*, 1 Beach Rd, not bad for pork chops and oxtail stew, prepared by Chinese cooks and served on marble-top tables, also serves chicken rice, burgers and ice-creams, open 24 hours, *Ah Teng's Bakery* joins on, it sells pricey pastries, pies and biscuits – mostly local favourites; ♦♦*Le Chalet*, 1 Ladyhill Rd, Swiss fondue house with a creative line in sauces for meat-eaters; *Hard Rock Café*, 02-01 HPL House, 50 Cuscaden Rd, one of the best bets for a decent steak, buffalo wings or a bacon cheeseburger, open until 0300.

Tea, cakes and snacks Afternoon tea, especially on Sundays, is the in-thing in Singapore. All top hotels offer competitive deals for less than S$15. Check the newspapers for special offers. ♦♦♦*Compass Rose Lounge*, *Westin Stamford Hotel*, 2 Stamford Rd, best views in Singapore, strict dress code; ♦♦♦*Goodwood Park Hotel*, Scotts Rd, sophisticated buffet tea, served on the lawn by the pool; ♦♦♦*Upstairs*, Tudor Court, 145a Tanglin Rd, cakes and pies and cream teas and Earl Grey; ♦♦*Chinese Tea House*, 1 Ann Siang Hill (Tanjong Pagar), T 2213986, traditional tea house in beautifully restored shophouse, shop selling exotic brews and blends downstairs and elegant tea room above, among other curative properties these Chinese teas are traditionally renowned for their ability to reduce blood cholesterol levels, cure diabetes, prevent cancer, strengthen the memory and alleviate giddiness; *Café Vienna*, *Royal Holiday Inn*, Crowne Plaza, Scotts Rd, tea and cakes served by prancing Mozarts; *Corner House*, 30 Cluny Rd, this colonial black and white bungalow, in the heart of colonial black and white country, is named after EJH Corner, assistant director of the Botanic Gardens from 1929-1945, it is being refurbished into tea rooms and an outdoor restaurant, there is also a verandah made for pre-dinner 'stengahs', it will be linked to the Botanic Gardens and will open in late 1993; *Ovenpride Cakes and English Teahouse*, 54 Tanjung Pagar Rd, located in refurbished shophouse selling everything from almond tarts to distinctly un-English durian puffs, also branch at Peranakan Place, 180 Orchard Rd, under Bibi's; *Polar Café*, B1-04 OUB Centre, Raffles Place (also branch in Lucky Plaza), the original home of the curry puff, first created at its former premises on Hill Street in 1926, S$0.70 each, rec; *Seah Street Deli*, Ground Level, *Raffles Hotel*, 1 Beach Rd, New York-style deli serving everything, from corned beef and smoked-salmon to cheese cakes and Turkish pastries.

Fast-food restaurants Despite Singapore's gourmet delights, fast-food outlets do a roaring trade in Singapore. Most of the big ones are represented – check *Yellow Pages* for branch addresses. They include: *A&W* (which in 1968 became the first fast-feeder in town), *Burger King, Denny's, KFC, McDonalds, Milano Pizza, Orange Julius, Pizza Hut, Shakey's Pizza* and one called *Fat Mama's*. The best, beyond doubt, is *Delifrance*, which is rapidly expanding in Singapore. There are Delifrance restaurants at: Clifford Centre, Marina Square, The Dynasty, Wisma Atria, The Promenade, Holland Village and Changi Airport.

Hawker Centres ♦♦*Telok Ayer Food Centre*, at the Raffles Quay end of Shenton Way in the old Victorian market. The old wet market was commissioned by Stamford Raffles in 1822 and rebuilt in cast-iron imported from Glasgow in 1894, as the last-remaining Victorian cast-iron structure in Southeast Asia, Telok Ayer (also known as *Lau Pa Sat* – or 'old market') was gazetted as a national monument in 1973, but had to be taken to pieces in 1985 as they built the MRT underneath it, all food is to be cooked off-site to avoid corrosion of the cast-iron. The revamped food centre suffers a bit from 'Raffles syndrome'. It is too brightly lit and rather dinky. Outside, though, on the street, there are some excellent and reasonably-priced stalls. Across the main road there is an even more popular genuine hawker centre, with Chinese and Muslim food stalls. ♦*Adam Road*, open all night, excellent Indian food – including one of the best roti stalls in Singapore, safest hawker centre in Singapore – adjacent to the police station; ♦*Chinatown Complex Hawker Centre*, Block 335, 1st Flr, Smith St, recommended stall: Ming Shan (No. 179), for its kambing (mutton) soup, famed for decades; ♦*Cuppage Centre*, behind Centrepoint shopping centre, undercover, hot and not as big as Newton Circus but much less touristy, one of Singapore's last remaining hand-made noodle-makers has a stall here; ♦*Farrer Park Food Centre*, Hampshire Rd, raided by police in 1988 after stall-holder Goh Choon Kwee began advertising 'Penis Soup', Goh was not charged under the obscene publication act on the condition he renamed his speciality, organ soup, made from goats' gonads, retails at S$2.50 a bowl; ♦*Kandang Kerbau (KK) Food Centre*, in the same complex as the wet market, on the corner of Buffalo and Serangoon rds, big range of dishes, and the best place for Indian Muslim food: curries, rotis, dosai and murtabak are hard to beat (beer can be bought from the Chinese stalls on the other side); *Maxwell Road Hawker Centre*, (corner of Maxwell and South Bridge roads), Tanjong Pagar, mainly Chinese, best known for its two chicken rice stalls; ♦*Newton Circus*, Scotts Rd, over 100 stalls, all types of Asian food, open until 0300, touristy, more expensive and quality and service not always up to scratch; ♦*Paradiz Centre Basement Food Centre*, 1 Selegie Rd, recommended stall: *Mr Boo's Teochew Mushroom Minced Meat Mee* (No. 34); ♦*Taman Serasi*, Cluny Rd, opposite entrance to Botanic Gardens, small centre but well known for Roti John and superb satay, mainly Malay stalls; excellent fruit juice stall. **NB**: the *Satay Club* on Queen Elizabeth Walk has now closed.

Bars NB: Drinkers should note that alcohol is overpriced in Singapore (see page 447). Coffee shops and hawker centres present a much cheaper option for beer-drinkers. *Alkaff Mansion*, Mount Faber Ridge, 10 Telok Blangah Green, perfect for sundowner 'stengahs' on the terrace with an excellent view of the harbour; *Anywhere*, 04-08 Tanglin Shopping Centre. Alvin, the transvestite, heads the bill; the bands mainly play cover numbers, but they are entertaining musicians and perform excellent renditions of rock classics, an interesting experience for those who think Singapore antiseptic; *Bar and Billiard Room*, Raffles Hotel, Beach Rd, (corner block), relocated from its original position, the bar is lavishly furnished with teak tables and oriental carpets; *Bibi's Theatre Pub*, Peranakan Place, 180 Orchard Rd, live bands every night, decorated in traditional Peranakan style; *Brannigan's* (underneath *Hyatt Regency*), 10/12 Scotts Rd, open until 0100, 0200 on Fri and Sat, American style, touristy bar with loud live music and video screens; *Canopy Bar*, Hyatt Hotel, 10/12 Scotts Rd, Singapore's only champagne bar for the more sophisticated *bon viveur*; *Casablanca Wine Bar*, 7 Emerald Hill Rd, one of the first bars to offer refurbished Peranakan style to Singapore's young and upwardly mobile, attached to the French restaurant of the same name; *Changi Sailing Club*, Changi Village, pleasant and, surprisingly, one of the cheapest places for a quiet beer, overlooking the Strait of Johor; *Charlie's*, Block 2, 01-08, Changi Village, Charlie Han describes his bar as 'the pulse of the point', tucked away behind the local hawker centre, he is a teetotaller but serves 70 brands of beer from all over the world, which you can sip as you watch the red-eyes touchdown on runway one, Charlie's is best known for its fish and chips (see *Restaurants*), rec; *Choon Huat Eating House*, 2 Desker Rd, a lot more drinking goes on here than eating, in the heart of the red-light district – echoes of old Bugis St – as police regularly chase hoards of screaming transvestites down the alley, lively outdoor bar with flashing neons, beer banners, cheap Tigers and an exclusively male clientele; *Frontpage Pub*, 9 Jln Mohamed Sultan, formerly a grocery shop, but converted to a bar by former *Straits Times* journalists in 1991, the Frontpage is a tastefully decorated shophouse, with original Peranakan fittings (including marble floors) and a beer garden conservatory at the back, local snacks – samosas, chicken wings etc – are also served, makes for a good evening if combined with a meal at the nearby Nonya and Baba restaurant on River Valley Road, rec; *Hard Rock Café*, Cuscaden Rd, complete with limo in suspended animation and queues to enter; *Harry's Quayside*, 28 Boat Quay, big bar with seating outside overlooking river, popular with City boys, serves food, pricey; *Jack's Place*, Yen San Building (opposite Mandarin), Orchard Rd, cellar bar with live music, squashed and not very sophisticated; *Next Page Pub*, 15 Jln Mohamed Sultan, like its sister pub, the *Front Page*, a converted shophouse, great decor – salon style with opium beds, cubby holes and cushions, rec; *Number 5 Emerald Hill*, 5 Emerald Hill, surprising mixture of decor, in this retro-chic restored shophouse bar and restaurant (upstairs), popular with young expats and Chuppies (Chinese yuppies), great music, rec; *Observation Lounge*, Mandarin Hotel, 333 Orchard Rd, circular cocktail bar on 38th floor; *Saxophone*, 23 Cuppage Terrace, probably Singapore's most popular bar – particularly with expats, offers the best live music in Singapore (usually rhythm and blues) and pleasant open-air terrace, rec; *Somerset's*, Westin Stamford, Raffles City, large pleasant bar with frieze of the padang in the days before Raffles City, live music; *The Long Bar*, Raffles Hotel, 1-3 Beach Rd, the home of the Singapore Sling, originally concocted by bar-tender Ngiam Tong Boon in 1915 (see page 398), now on two levels and extremely popular with tourists and locals alike, gratuitous tiny dancing mechanical punkawallahs sway out of sync to the cover band; *The Yard*, 294 River Valley Rd, the Singaporean version of a London pub complete with darts, dominos, fish 'n' chips and Newcastle Brown Ale; *Trader Vics*, 5th Flr, New Otani Hotel, River Valley Rd, Hawaii 5-0 decor and Chin-Ho's favourite cocktails – try a few goblets of Tikki Puka Puka for something violently different; *Woodstock*, Rooftop, 06-02 Far East Plaza, 14 Scotts Rd, take the bullet lift up the outside of the building, expect to meet long-hairs and hear hard rock, open until 0200; *Writers' Bar*, Raffles Hotel, 1 Beach Rd (just off the main lobby), in honour of the likes of Somerset Maugham, Rudyard Kipling, Joseph Conrad, Noel Coward and Herman Hesse who were said either to have wined, dined or stayed at the hotel, bar research indicates that other literary luminaries from James A Michener to Noel Barber and the great Arthur Hailey are said to have sipped Tigers at the bar – as the bookcases and mementoes suggest; *Zouk*, 17 Jiak Kim St (off Kim Seng Rd), pleasant streetside bar affording perfect opportunity to pose with a Sol, attached disco and restaurant, rec.

Entertainment Hotels and nightclubs are the main source of night time entertainment in Singapore. Refer to the *What's On* section in the *Straits Times* or the *New Paper* for details on concerts, dance and theatre. The tourist magazine *City Mag* also has details in its *This Week* section.

Music: there are live music bars all over Singapore (see bars above). The Singapore Cultural Theatre and the Victoria Hall host most of the classical shows – the Singapore Symphony Orchestra gives regular performances and there are often visiting orchestras, quartets and choirs. There are also plenty of **karaoke** lounges.

Discos/nightclubs: most big hotels have house discos – they all have a cover charge; usually S$25-30 (which normally includes a drink or two). Good hotel discos include: *Ridleys*, ANA Hotel, Nassim Hill, *Chinoiserie*, Hyatt Regency, *Scandals*, Westin Plaza Hotel, *Xanadu* Shangri-La Hotel, **The Reading Room**, Marina Mandarin Hotel, is smart, expensive and pretentious and attracts a younger crowd. Other non-hotel discos include: *Fabrice's World Music Bar*, Basement, *Dynasty Hotel*, 320 Orchard Rd, Singapore's latest hot-spot, run by Fabrice De Barcy, the Belgian long-hair of *Saxophone* fame, Arabesque decor with low tables, candles and Persian rugs, live music and dance tracks, open: 1700-0300 Mon-Sun, no cover before 2200, S$25 thereafter, rec; *Rumours*, Level 3, Forum Gallaria, 583 Orchard Rd, once it was the trendiest spot in town... now it has gone off the boil; *Top Ten Club*, Orchard Towers, 400 Orchard Rd, huge converted cinema; often has live black-American or Filipino disco bands, rec. Also in Orchard Towers: *Club 392* and *Caesars*; *The Warehouse*, 332 Havelock Rd, an old godown on the Singapore River, large dance hall mainly frequented by teenagers; *Zouk*, 21 Jiak Kim St (off Kim Seng Rd), the best of the warehouse venues but overtaken of late by *Fabrice's*, occasionally has one-off concerts, open until 0430, cover: $25.

Theatre/dance: most performances are held at *Victoria Hall* and are advertised in the newspapers. The latest offering on the thespian and artistic scene is *The Substation*, 45 Armenian St, set up in a former power station, which organizes drama, dance and batik workshops, art and photography exhibitions, lectures on the arts and produces plays. Stages a market every Sunday (1100-1700) selling bric-a-brac and arts and crafts. Call T 3377800 for details on what's on when.

Cabaret: *Lido Palace*, Concorde Hotel Shopping Centre, Outram Rd, Cantonese cuisine with variety of acts to eat to. *Neptune Theatre Restaurant*, Collyer Quay.

Chinese Street Operas (wayang): dramatizations of Chinese legends (the heroes wear red or green, the emperor, yellow and the villains, black). Staged throughout the year but more frequent from Aug-Sep during the *Festival of the Hungry Ghosts* (**see page 449**).

Cultural shows: *Mandarin Hotel*, 333 Orchard Rd, ASEAN Night, songs and dances from the Philippines, Malaysia, Thailand and Indonesia as well as Singapore, dinner at 1900, show starts 1945, admission: show (without dinner) S$18; show (including dinner) S$36; *Instant Asia Cultural Show*, Merlion Ballroom, Basement 1, *Cockpit Hotel*, Oxley Rise, featuring Chinese, Malay and Indian dances (including lion dance and snake charmer's act) at 1145, admission: S$2, also, evening shows with buffet dinner at 1900, show starts 2000, admission: show (including dinner) S$30; *Singa Inn Seafood Restaurant*, 920 East Coast Parkway, instant Asia Show, lion dance, Malay harvest dance and Indian snake charmers, 2000-2045 Mon-Fri (dinner from 1800); *Hyatt Regency*, 10-12 Scott's Rd, Malam Singapura, dinner and cultural show, dinner starts 1900, show at 2000, admission: show (without dinner) S$21, show (including dinner) S$42.

Cinema: with more than 50 cinemas, Singapore gets most of the blockbusters and they arrive quickly. These will be more entertaining now that the censors are easing up. Newspapers publish listings. When the *Cathay*, at the bottom of Orchard Rd, opened in 1939 and became the first air-conditioned public building in Singapore, local celebrities turned up in fur coats. Today, all the cinemas are severely air-conditioned, so prepare to freeze. The trendiest cinema in town, the *Picturehouse*, is next-door to the Cathay. It opened in 1991 and shows 'alternative' films which would otherwise not be shown in Singapore. The Isetan Scotts Lido Cineplex, with five cinemas inside, is to open by the end of 1993 after several years of redevelopment. It is part of the Shaw Centre at the corner of Scotts and Orchard rds.

Sports Bowling: most alleys charge from S$2.50-$3.50 a game; bowling after 1800 and on weekends is more expensive. *Jackie's Bowl*, 542B East Coast Rd; *Orchard Bowl*, 8 Grange Rd; *Kallang Bowl*, 5 Stadium Walk; *Kim Seng Bowl*, 04-01 Kim Seng Plaza; *Marina Bowl*, 7 Marina Grove; *ODS Bowl*, 269 Pasir Panjang Rd; *Plaza Bowl, Textile Centre*, Jalan Sultan; *Superbowl*, 15 Marina Grove, Marina South, open: 24 hrs.

Canoeing: *Canoe Centre*, East Coast Parkway (just along the beach from the Lagoon Food Centre). Also possible to hire canoes at the swimming lagoon on Sentosa Island.

Bicycling: *East Coast Bicycle Centre*, East Coast Parkway, rents bikes – including tandems – by the hour.

Golf: there is no shortage of courses; they are beautifully kept and non-members can play at most of the private club courses on weekdays. Green fees are expensive. *Keppel Club*, Bukit Chermin. 18-hole, par 72, green fees: S$90 Mon-Fri, S$150 weekends, caddy S$18-25; *Raffles Country Club*, Jalan Ahmad Ibrahim, Tengah Reservoir, two 18-holers, par 71 and 69, green fees S$100 weekdays, S$160 weekends; *Seletar Country Club*, Seletar Airbase, 9-hole, par 70, green fees, S$80 Tues-Fri only, caddy, S$15-20; *Sembawang Country Club*, Sembawang Rd, 18-hole, par 70, green fees S$60 Mon-Fri, S$100 weekends, caddy S$18-24; *Sentosa Golf Club*, Sentosa Island, 18-hole, par 72, green fees S$60 Mon-Fri, S$120 weekends; *Changi Golf Club*, Nethavon Rd, 9-hole, par 68, green fees S$50, Mon-Fri, caddy S$14-19; *Singapore Island Country Club*, Upper Thompson Rd, two 18-holers, both par 72, green fees S$130 Mon-Fri only, caddy S$18-21; *Warren Golf Club*, Folkstone Rd, 9-hole, par 70, green fees S$50 Mon-Fri only, caddies compulsory, S$18-25. Driving ranges *Marina Bay Golf and Country Club*, Marina South. Said, in true Singapore-style, to be 'the biggest driving range in the world'. True or not, it does have 150 mat-bays on 3 storeys, overlooking a 230m fairway. Restaurants and club facilities. S$9 for 100 balls; *Parkland*, East Coast Parkway. 60 bays; 200m fairway. S$6 for 95 balls (S$5 weekdays before 1530).

Ice-Skating: *Musical Skate*, 1 Selegie Rd, you have to buy woolly gloves on the way in. Soon to close down. **Roller Skating**: *Sentosa Roller Skating*, Jelly Rd, Sentosa Island; *Texas Roller Skating Discorama*, 165 Tanjong Pagar Rd.

Scuba Diving: *Sentosa Sports Centre*, Eastern Lagoon, rents out diving gear and snorkels. Equipment hire and open water scuba diving instruction: *Sentosa Water Sports Centre* (Scuba Schools International), World Trade Centre; *Dive Asia*, Lucky Plaza; *Adventure Sports*, Forum Galleria; *Aqua and Leisure Sports*, Marina Sq; *Exclusive Sport and Leisure*, 435 Orchard Rd; *C and N Diving Services*, 45 Gentle Rd.

Swimming: most of the big hotels have swimming pools, some of which are open to non-residents for a fee. *Big Splash*, East Coast Parkway, wave pool, current pool and the longest water-slides in Southeast Asia, open 1200-1745 Mon-Fri, 0900-1745 weekends; *CN West Leisure Park*, 9 Japanese Garden Rd, wave pool and 15m-long water-slide, admission: S$4, open: 1200-1800 Tue-Fri, 0930-1800 weekends. Singapore has 20 public swimming pools listed in the *Yellow Pages*.

Tennis: *Burghley Squash and Tennis Centre*, 43 Burghley Drive; *Clementi Recreation Centre*, 12 West Coast Walk; *Dover Tennis Centre*, Dover Rd; *Farrer Park Tennis Courts*, Rutland Rd; *Kallang Tennis Centre*, Stadium Rd; *Singapore Tennis Centre*, 1020 East Coast Parkway; *St Wilfrid Squash and Tennis Centre*, St Wilfrid Rd.

Water Skiing: *Seashore Boating Centre*, Track 24 Ponggol Rd, T 4820888/4822800 also rents fishing boats and cruisers, for water-skiing, it is necessary to telephone in advance to book a slot, S$50 an hou;. *William Water Sports*, Ponggol Point, T 2826879, skiing: S$60 an hour.

Sailing and windsurfing: *Changi Sailing Club*, Changi Village, for those interested in crewing yachts, the club has a noticeboard listing possibilities; *East Coast Sailing Centre*, East Coast Park Swimming Lagoon, 1210 East Coast Parkway, T 495118, 4455108. Two day courses in small craft: Lasers (S$270) and windsurfers (S$80), rental rates: Laser, S$40 for first 2 hours, then S$20 an hour; windsurfer, S$20 for first 2 hours, then S$10 an hour. Bar and barbecue restaurant.

Snooker: Singapore has several huge snooker halls, where dress code is casual-smart. Prices between S$5 and S$9 per hour. *King's Leisurium*, Marina Sq, T 3393811. *King's Snookerium*, Amara Hotel Shopping Complex; *Academy of Snooker*, Albert Complex, Albert Street, T 2862879.

Spectator sports: see newspapers for listings. Most games of any significance take place on the Padang or the National Stadium which seats up to 60,000 and regularly stages Malaysia Cup football matches and the occasional exhibition match with touring league sides from abroad (buses 14 and 16 go direct from Orchard Road). **Horse racing**: is at the *Bukit Turf Club*, on Bukit Timah Rd, where Malaysian racing is broadcast on huge 18x16m screens. No jeans, T-shirts, flip-flops etc. **Polo matches**: are held every Tue, Thur and Sat at the *Singapore Polo Club* on Thomson Rd.

Shopping Few visitors have any trouble spending money in Singapore – which in the eyes of many tourists must seem to be a nation of shop-keepers. There is an endless variety of consumer items and gimmicks – electronics is Singapore's forté. There is no import duty or sales tax on most items, which usually makes Singapore cheaper than other Asian capitals. The choice is incredible – but do not labour round the shopping centres thinking Singapore is cheap. For many things, it's not. Due to the recent volatility of some European exchange rates and the strength of the Singapore currency (which is pegged to the US dollar), it has become even more expensive for many visitors.

The best area for window shopping is the **Scotts** and **Orchard Road** area where many of the big complexes and department stores are located (**see page 404**). This area comes alive after dark and most shops stay open until late. Many of the shops in these areas sell designer goods at prices you would balk at back home. The towering Raffles City complex and Marina Square, close to the old *Raffles Hotel*, are the other main shopping centres. The East Coast shopping centres are not frequented by tourists. Serangoon Road (or Little India), Arab Street and Chinatown offer a more colourful shopping experience. For specific types of goods, certain places are better than others; there are some recommendations below.

Holland Village, which has long been the preferred shopping centre for Singapore's expatriate community, has a number of curio shops selling handicrafts, cloisonné ware, antique porcelain, framed silk tapestries and paper umbrellas (*Lims Arts and Crafts*, above Cold Storage is a good place to buy presents). Behind (and parallel) to the main road, there are a number of interesting shops; they range from Oriental curio shops to very up-market interior-decoration shops. On the corner, by the wet market, there is a furniture-maker that specializes in re-touching marble-top tables and other Peranakan furniture and re-stringing planters' chairs. *Joo Ann Foh*, a film-processing shop at the N end of the shophouse terrace is a particularly reliable and inexpensive shop. The village's old shophouses have been taken over by restaurants and up-market coffee shops.

Tanjong Pagar is on line to become the arty-crafty focal point for tourists and Singapore's young professionals who are rapidly acquiring refurbished shophouse studio flats. The area's once decrepit shophouses have been transformed into craft shops and galleries. The government is attempting to recreate the ambiance of the city's old *pasar malam* (night markets) and many of the trinket-wallahs from the old Singapore handicrafts centre (formerly on Tanglin Road, but now demolished) have been relocated here. Tanjong Pagar (**see page 406**) is just a short walk from Chinatown and People's Park. The new *Singapore Handicraft Centre* is located in Chinatown Point, the high-rise building that has recently appeared in the middle of Chinatown, opposite People's Park.

Touts Although, the government has come down hard on copy-watch touts, tourists can still be accosted (and ripped off) along Orchard Road – particularly outside *Lucky Plaza*.

Tips on buying It does not take long to get the feel of where you can bargain and where you cannot. Department stores are fixed-price, but most smaller outfits – even those in smart shopping complexes – can be talked into discounts. As ever, it is best not to buy at the first shop; compare prices; get an idea of what you should be paying from big department stores – *Tang's* department store is a good measuring rod, which you can nearly always undercut. In ordinary shops, 20-30% can be knocked off the original asking price – sometimes more. Keep smiling, joking and teasing when bargaining and never believe a shopkeeper who tells you he is giving you something at cost or is not making a profit. The golden rule is to keep a sense of humour. If you lose face, they've won.

❑ For big purchases, ask for an international guarantee (they are often extra), although sometimes you will have to be content with Singapore-only guarantees.
❑ Once goods are sold they are not returnable, unless faulty, make sure you keep your receipt.
❑ Deposits, not usually more than 50% of the value of the goods, are generally required when orders are placed for custom-made goods.
❑ Make sure electrical goods are compatible with the voltage back home.
❑ Complaints about retailers (who from time to time exhibit aggressive tendencies when selling merchandise to tourists) can be registered at the Consumers' Association of Singapore, T 2224165.

Best buys Singapore has all the latest electronic gadgetry and probably as wide a choice as you will find anywhere. It also has a big selection of antiques (although they tend to be over-priced), arts and crafts, jewellery, silks and batiks. Designer-label clothes from Japan and the West are widely available and locally designed clothes are fashionable and good value.

Antiques: Singapore's antique shops stock everything from opium beds, planters' chairs, gramophones, brass fans, porcelain, jade, Peranakan marble-top tables and 17th century maps to smuggled Burmese Buddhas, Sulawesian spirit statues and Dayak masks. There are few restrictions on bringing antiques into Singapore or exporting them. Many of the top antique shops are in the *Tanglin Shopping Centre* – including the old map shop, *Antiques of the Orient*, on the first floor. This is probably the best place to buy antique maps and prints in Southeast Asia. The most interesting place to go browsing is along River Valley Road, opposite the junction with Jln Mohamed Sultan. *Tong Mern Sern Antiques*, 226 River Valley Rd, (also called Keng's, after its inimitable owner), is a treasure trove. Keng's adage: "We buy junk and sell antiques; some fool buy and some fool sell". Other shops along the same stretch include: *China Trading Co* (used to be in the old *Raffles Hotel*); *Eng Tiang Huat* (specialist musical instruments, caligraphy to order), *Hua Shi Oriental Arts*, and *Terese Jade and Minerals*. For general antique shops, there are others dotted around **Cuppage Terrace** behind Centrepoint (upstairs, above *Saxophone*, there are several good shops, selling antique Melaka furniture, porcelain, and Peranakan pieces), **Holland Village** and the **Shaw Centre**. *Abanico*, selling antique and modern Asian pieces is on the 5th Flr of Centre Point shopping centre (it also has a warehouse showroom off River Valley Rd). There are also some good shops (selling antiques and restored/imitation items) at Binjai Park, off Upper Bukit Timah Rd. Among the best is the oxymoronic *Young Antique Co*. Geylang has a number of good antique junk shops where occasional treasures can be found. *Peter Wee's Katong Antique House* at 208 East Coast Road (half museum, half shop) has one of the best selections of Peranakan antiques. For furniture: *Roger's Carve Furniture*, 142 Kim Seng Rd. *A Guide to Buying Antiques, Arts and Crafts in Singapore* by Anne Jones is recommended, available in most bookshops.

Batik and silk: Malaysian and Indonesian batiks are sold by the metre or in sarong lengths. **Arab Street** is the best area for reasonably priced batik and silk – but you should bargain; big department stores usually have batik ready-mades. Ready-made Chinese silk garments can be found all over Singapore in Chinese emporia. Arab Street and the Serangoon Road area are the best for bargain hunters. If you want silk without the hassle, at reasonable prices, big department stores (such as Tangs) have good selections. The best known of the silk boutiques, with fine silks at high prices, is *China Silk House*, which has shops in Tanglin, Scotts, Centrepoint and Marina Square shopping centres. China Silk House designers come up with new collections every month. There is also a *Jim Thomson Thai Silk* shop on Tanglin Rd next to Tanglin Shopping Centre.

Books: there is a good selection of English language literature available in Singapore, including specialist books on the region. One or all of *Times*, *MPH* and *Wordshop* bookshops can be found in most shopping complexes. *Sogo* department store (Raffles City and Wisma Atria) also has a books section. There is a good selection of second-hand bookshops, the best is probably on the 2nd floor of the Holland Road Shopping Centre (above Cold Storage) – there is also one behind Cold Storage in the same block.

Camping gear: *Campers' Corner*, 1, Selegie Rd, 01-11 Paradiz Centre, T 3374743. Stocks good range of camping and trekking equipment for sale and hire. Also organizes trekking expeditions around Singapore and Malaysia.

Computers: the **Funan Centre** on North Bridge Road is computer city. (*Travelling Computers*, on the 6th floor, is particularly recommended for Laptops.) Even the Japanese come to Singapore to buy their computers in the Funan Centre. **Sim Lim Tower** (upper floors) and the nearby **Albert Complex**, both just off Bukit Timah on Rochor Canal Road, are also good places for computer shoppers.

Designer clothes/fashion: Singapore boasts all the international designer labels – the shops are strung out along **Orchard Road**. Designer fashion comes a bit cheaper in Singapore than other Southeast Asian capitals as no duty is levied. Locally-designed clothes keep up with the trends and are very reasonably priced; for exceptional value, very slightly damaged clothes – factory seconds – can be purchased from *Factory Outlet*, which has branches in several shopping centres. The best local designers with boutiques and outlets in department stores are: *Bibi & Baba* (casual fashion; Plaza Singapura, Thomson Plaza and Wisma Atria), *Bodynits Sports* (sportswear; most big department stores), *Indoko's* (casual fashion; 14 Raffles Link Rd; Marina Sq; 45 Duxton Rd and the Shangri-La), and *Thomas Wee* (mixture of Asian and Western themes; Luxe Boutique, Shaw Towers).

Electronic goods: Singapore has all the latest electronic equipment – from hi-fi compo-units to digital diaries and computers – hot from Japan at duty free prices. **Sim Lim Tower** (Rochor Canal Road), **Lucky Plaza** (Orchard Road) and **Far East Plaza** (Scotts Road) have a good selection of other electronic goods: hi-fi, cameras and videos. *Pertama* (in Wisma Atria on Orchard Road) and *Cost Plus* (Scotts Shopping Centre, Scotts Road and Holland Village) offer good value for money. *Tangs* has a good selection and serves as a rough price-guide if you intend to bargain elsewhere. The Changi Airport duty free is also very competitive and a lot less hassle.

Film: Singapore is cheaper for film than neighbouring Malaysia or Indonesia, so it is a good place to stock up. Developing film is reasonably priced and on the whole good quality in Singapore and many outlets offer anything down to a ½-hour service. Singapore is also the best place in Southeast Asia for getting slides converted to prints (S\$1 each). **Try Lucky** and **Far East plazas** or **Wisma Atria** for standard colour print processing. For quality enlargements and slide/print conversions, *Joo Ann Foh Colour Service*, 273 Holland Avenue, T 4662216 is recommended.

Handicrafts: for Chinese goods – opera masks, kites, silk dressing gowns etc – wander round Chinatown and Tanjong Pagar. There are trinkety-tourist handicraft shops in most shopping centres. **Chinese emporia** sell merchandise which is all made in China; it is cheap and prices are not negotiable. The biggest Chinese Emporia are in the *People's Park Complex* and *Katong Shopping Centre*, East Coast Road. The *Thong Chai Medical Institution* (built 1892) on Wayang Street, off New Bridge Road, has been converted into the Singapore handicraft centre – prices are reasonable as it's run by the STPB. The *Substation*, 45 Armenian St, runs a Sunday market where some arts and crafts are on sale.

Jewellery: gold (mostly Asian, 18, 22 or 24 carat), precious stones, pearls (freshwater and cultured) are all easily found in Singapore. Gold is a good buy. The Singapore Assay Office uses a merlion head as a hallmark. Most of the jewellery shops are in **South Bridge Road**; for Indian goldsmiths, go to **Serangoon Road**. A good haunt for unusual made-to-order jewellery is *Shangai Lee and Co* at 286 River Valley Road. Don't be taken in by shops along Orchard Rd advertising 'incredible reductions' – usually they're not. Bargaining is *de rigeur*, and it requires much shopping-around to gain an appreciation of what the true price should be.

Markets: the most accessible market of interest is **KK Market** on the corner of Bukit Timah and Serangoon Roads. It contains a vegetable market, wet market (you can be transfixed by the automatic chicken defeathering machines), and a spice-and-everything-else market upstairs. There is also a hawker centre in the complex. There's a colourful fruit, vegetable and flower market in the **Cuppage Centre** (behind Centrepoint on Orchard Road), which also boasts an excellent hawker centre on top. Another good place to buy orchids is in **Holland Village's** small wet market; this stall is much cheaper than the more touristy flower shops downtown and will pack them for shipment. The government closed down the last of Singapore's once-vibrant night markets (*pasar malam*) – in Chinatown – in 1990; what remains these days is what the STPB imagines tourists imagine night markets to be like. There are one or two good community **night markets** still around, the best being at Toa Payoh housing estate. The night market, which sets up between Housing Development Board blocks, migrates around the area throughout the week. On Mon nights it's on Lorong 7; Tues, Lorong 4 and Wed and Thurs, Lorong 1.

Optical goods: leading makes of sunglasses, hard and soft contact lenses and designer spectacles frames are all available in Singapore at reasonable prices. Unless you have stigmatic complications, contact lenses can usually be fitted on the spot and glasses should be ready within the day. Singapore is one of the cheapest places in the world to buy Rayban sunglasses.

Tailoring: quick, efficient and usually high-quality tailoring can be found in most shopping centres. The tailors in the main tourist shopping belt along Orchard and Scotts roads, notably **Far East** and **Lucky** plazas, are as good a bet as any. You can design virtually what you want for yourself, but it is worth shopping around for the best deal. For more upmarket tailoring, hotel tailors are recommended.

Watches: a huge range of watches are available at duty free prices in most shopping centres. Copy watches do not officially exist in Singapore, where most people prefer the real thing. No amount of fines or embarrassing newspaper reports have managed to clear the precincts of **Lucky Plaza** of fake watch touts who approach you as if they're peddling heroin.

Singapore knick-knacks: although considered rather twee by many, the most popular Singapore souvenirs have been ceramic models of shophouses in the 'Little Island Collection', which first came out in 1991. Five local artists make and paint each house and come out with 2 new designs a month. The miniatures cost from S$60-300 and can be bought from any of the big department stores or leading handicraft shops.

Indian/Southeast Asian goods: for **Indian** silks, sarees, gold jewellery and trinkets try Serangoon Road, otherwise known as **Little India**, but by far the best shop for Indian exotica is *Natraj's Arts & Crafts*, 03-202 Marina Sq shopping centre, which is in a row of Far Eastern handicraft shops. Natraj's specialities are the *papier mâché* Bharata Natayam dancing girl dolls which wobble and shake just like the real thing. For **Malay handicrafts** there's a handicraft centre in a reconstruction of a Malay kampung on Geylang Serai. The *Marina Square shopping centre*, next to the Marina Mandarin, also contains a large number of very good handicraft shops selling stuff from all over the region.

Banks & money changers Singapore has 13 local banks but the big 4 are DBS Bank, United Overseas Bank, Overseas-Chinese Banking Corporation and Overseas Union Bank.

Most leading foreign banks are well represented in Singapore, although some in the financial district are offshore branches only and may not provide services to the public. All local banks and the majority of big names have foreign exchange facilities and most have branches within easy access of main tourist areas. Check *Yellow Pages* for lists of branches. There are also licenced money-changers in all main shopping centres, many give better rates than the banks for travellers' cheques – but it's worth shopping around. Others: **Bank of Singapore**, Tong Eng Bldg, 101 Cecil St; **Chase Manhattan Bank NA**, Shell Tower, 50 Raffles Place; **Citibank NA**, 1 Shenton Way, Robina House; **DBS Bank**, DBS Bldg, 6 Shenton Way; **Deutsche Bank AG**, Treasury Building, 8 Shenton Way; **Far Eastern Bank**, 156 Cecil St; **Hong Kong and Shanghai Banking Corporation**, 10 Collyer Quay, Ocean Building; **Keppel Bank**, 60 Robinson Rd; **Overseas Chinese Banking Corporation**, OCBC Centre, 65 Chulia St; **Overseas Union Bank**, OUB Centre, 1 Raffles Place; **Standard Chartered Bank**, 6 Battery Rd; **United Overseas Bank**, UOB Bldg, 1 Bonham St.

Embassies & consulates **Australia**, 25 Napier Rd, T 7379311; **Austria**, Shaw Centre, 1 Scotts Rd, T 2354088; **Belgium**, International Plaza, 10 Anson Rd, T 2207677; **Britain**, Tanglin Rd, T 4739333; **Brunei**, 7a Tanglin Hill, T 4743393; **Burma**, 15 S, St Martin Drive, T 2358704; **Canada**, 15th Storey IBM Towers, 80 Anson Rd, T 2256363; **Denmark**, 13-01 Goldhill Sq, 101 Thompson Rd, T 2503383; **Finland**, 21-02 Goldhill Sq, 101 Thompson Rd, T 2544042; **France**, 5 Gallop Rd, T 4664866; **Germany**, 14-01 Far East, Shopping Centre, T 7371355; **Greece**, 11-15 Anson Centre, 51 Anson Rd, T 2208622; **Indonesia**, 7 Chatsworth Rd, T 7377422; **Ireland**, 08-02 Liat Towers, 541 Orchard Rd, T 7323430; **Italy**, 27-02 Goldhill Sq, 101 Thompson Rd, T 2506022; **Japan**, 16 Nassim Rd, T 2358855; **Malaysia**, 301 Jervois Rd, T 2350111; **Netherlands**, 13-01 Lia, T Towers, 541 Orchard Rd, T 7371155; **New Zealand**, 13 Nassim Rd, T 2359966; **Philippines**, 20 Nassim Rd, T 7373977; **Spain**, 27-00 CPF Building, 79 Robinson Rd, T 3205801; **Sweden**, 05-08 Pub Building, Devonshire Wing, 111 Somerset Rd, T 7342771; **Switzerland**, 1 Swiss Club Liak, T 4685788; **Thailand**, 370 Orchard Rd, T 7372644; **USA**, 30 Hill Street, T 3380251.

Useful addresses **General Post Office**: Fullerton Rd just off Collyer Quay & Battery Rd. **Churches**: for service times call telephone numbers provided. *St Andrew's Cathedral* (Anglican), Coleman St, T 3376104; *St George's* (Anglican), Minden Rd; *Cathedral of the Good Shepherd* (Roman Catholic), Queen St (City Hall MRT), T 3372036; *Wesley Methodist*, 5 Fort Canning Rd (Dhoby Gant MRT), T 3361433; *Orchard Road Presbyterian*, 3 Orchard Rd, T 3376681; *Prinsep St. Presbyterian*, 144 Prinsep Sep, T 3384571; *Queenstown Baptist*, 495 Margaret Drive; *Calvary Charismatic Centre*, 179 River Valley Rd, (5th Flr, former SISIR Bldg), T 3392955. **Hospitals**: *American Hospital of Singapore*, T 3447588; *Gleneagles Hospital*, T 4732222; *Mount Elizabeth Hospital*, T 7372666; *National University Hospital*, T 7725000; *Singapore General Hospital*, T 3214105. **Library**: *National Library*, Stamford Rd (next to the National Museum). **Comcentre**: main public telephone office, 31 Exeter Rd. 24-hour facilities.

Airline offices **Aeroflot Soviet Airlines**, 01-02 Tan Chong Tower, 15 Queen St, T 3361757; **Air Canada**, 02-43 Meridien Shopping Centre, 100 Orchard Rd, T 732855; **Air India**, 17-01 UIC Bldg, 5 Shenton Way, T 2259411; **Air Mauritius**, 01-00 LKN Bldg, 135 Cecil St, T 2223033; **Air New Zealand**, 24-08 Ocean Bldg, 10 Collyer Quay, T 5358266; **Air Lanka**, 02-00 PIL Bldg, 140 Cecil St, T 2236026; **ALIA – Royal Jordanian**, 03-11 Beach Centre, Beach Rd, T 3388188; **Alitalia**, 15-05 Wisma Atria, 435 Orchard Rd, T 7373166; **All Nipon Airways**, 01-01 Cecil House, 139 Cecil St, T 2248173; **American Airlines**, 11-02 Natwest Centre, 15 McCallum St, T 2216988; **Biman Airlines of Bangladesh**, 01-02 Natwest Centre, 15 McCallum St, T 2217155; **British Airways**, 02-16 Paragon, 290 Orchard Rd, T 2535922; **Cathay Pacific Airways**, 16-01 Ocean Bldg, 10 Collyer Quay, T 5331333; **China Airlines**, 08-02 Orchard Towers, 400 Orchard Rd, T 7372211; **Czechoslovak Airlines**, 06-00 Thong Sia Bldg, 30 Bideford Rd, T 7379844; **Emirates**, 19-06 Wisma Atria, 435 Orchard Rd, T 2351911; **El Al Israel Airlines**, 06-00 Thong Sia Bldg, 30 Bideford Rd, T 7338433; **Finnair**, 18-01 Liat Towers, 541 Orchard Rd, T 7333377; **Garuda Indonesia Airways**, 01-68 United Sq, 101 Thompson Rd, T 2502888; **Indian Airlines**, 01-03 Marina House, 70 Shenton Way, T 2254949; **Japan Airlines**, 01-01 Hong Leong Bldg, 16 Raffles Quay, T 2210522; **KLM Royal Dutch Airlines**, 01-02 Mandarin Hotel Arcade, 333 Orchard Rd, T 7377622; **Korean Air**, 07-08 Ocean Bldg, 10 Collyer Quay, T 5342111; **Kuwait Airways**, 06-09 Ocean Bldg, 10 Collyer Quay, T 2912730; **Lauda Air**, 08-03 PIL Bldg, 140 Cecil St, T 2261266; **Lufthansa German Airlines**, 05-07 Palais Renaissance, 390 Orchard Rd, T 7379222; **Malaysian Airline System**, 02-09 Singapore Shopping Centre, 190 Clemenceau Avenue, T 3366777; **Northwest Orient Airlines**, 20-01 Wisma Atria, 435 Orchard Rd, T 2357166; **Olympic Airways**, 08-21 Parkmall, 9 Penang Rd, T 3366061; **Pakistan International Airlines**, 01-01 United Sq, 101 Thomson Rd, T 2512322; **Philippine Airlines**, 01-022 Parklane Shopping Mall, 35 Selegie Rd, T 3361611; **Qantas Airways**, 04-02 The Promenade, 300 Orchard Rd,

T 7373744; **Royal Brunei Airlines**, 01-4a Royal Holiday Inn Shopping Centre, 25 Scotts Rd, T 2354672; **Royal Nepal Airlines**, 9th Storey SIA Bldg, 77 Robinson Rd, T 2257575; **Sabena World Airlines**, 06-03 Gateway East, 152 Beach Rd, T 2933112; **Saudi Arabian Airlines**, 10-318 The Plaza, 7500a Beach Rd, T 2917300; **Scandinavian Airlines System**, 23-01 Gateway East, T 2941611; **Singapore Airlines**, 77 Robinson Rd, T 2238888; *Mandarin Hotel*, Orchard Td, T 2297293; Raffles City Shopping Centre, T 2297274; **Swissair**, 18-01 Wisma Atria, 435 Orchard Rd, T 7378133; **Tarom Romanian Air Transport**, 03-01 Peninsula Shopping Complex, 3 Coleman Street, T 3881467; **Thai International**, 08-01 Keck Seng Towers, 133 Cecil Street, T 2249977; **Tradewinds**, SIA Bldg, 77 Robinson Rd, T 2212221; **Trans World Airlines (TWA)**, 09-324 The Plaza, 7500a Beach Rd, T 2989911; **Turkish Airlines**, 02-21 Far East Shopping Centre, 545 Orchard Rd, T 7324556; **United Airlines**, 01-03 Hong Leong Bldg, 16 Raffles Quay, T 2200711; **UTA French Airlines**, 14-05 Orchard Towers, 400 Orchard Rd, T 7376355; **Varig Brazilian Airlines**, 10-02 SIA Bldg, 77 Robinson Rd, T 2258233; **Yugoslav Airlines**, 19-02 Liat Towers, 541 Orchard Rd, T 2353017.

Tour companies & travel agents *Airmaster Travel*, 02-36 Princep St, T 3383942, budget flights worldwide, they have a travel notice board for Southeast Asia, recommending hotels, places to go etc from other travellers; *Aloha Travel and Tours*, 02-27 Orchard Towers T 7332266; *AT Travel*, 279 Balestier Rd, T 2554488, F 2502388; *Australasia Travel and Tours*, Hotel Royal, 36 Newton Rd, T 2503924; *Centre Wind Travel*, People's Park Complex, T 5327777; *Eureka Travel*, 277A Holland Ave, Holland Village, T 4625077, F 4622853, offers local and regional ecologically orientated tours; destinations include national parks in Peninsular Malaysia, Sabah and Sarawak, including Endau Rompin National Park on the E Coast (see page 191), rec.

INFORMATION FOR VISITORS

DOCUMENTS

Visas

No visa is required for citizens of the Commonwealth, USA or Western Europe. On arrival in Singapore by air, citizens of these countries are granted a month-long visitor's permit. Tourists entering Singapore via the causeway from Johor Bahru in Malaysia or by sea, are allowed to stay for 14 days. Nationals of most other countries (except India, China and the Commonwealth of Independent States) with confirmed onward reservations may stop over in Singapore for up to 14 days without a visa. It is necessary to keep the stub of your immigration card until you leave.

Visas can be extended (although it's a time-consuming process) at the **Immigration Department**, 7th floor, Pidemco Centre, 95 South Bridge Rd, Singapore 0105, T 5322877. Alternatively, it can be just as easy to nip across the causeway to Johor Bahru (in Malaysia) then re-enter Singapore on a two-week permit.

Vaccinations

A certificate of vaccination against cholera and yellow fever is necessary for those coming from endemic areas within the previous six days.

Representation overseas

Australia, High Commission, 17 Forster Crescent, Yarralumla, Canberra ACT 2600, T 6 273-3944; **Austria**, c/o Embassy in Bonn; Consulate: Raiffeisen Zentral Bank, Osterreich AG, Am Stadtpark 9, 1030 Vienna, T 222 71707-1229; **Belgium**, 198 Avenue Franklin Roosevelt, 1050 Brussels, T 2 660-30908; **Brunei**, High Commission, P O Box 2159, Negara Brunei Darussalam, Bandar Seri Begawan 192, T (2) 22-7583; **Canada**, Consulate, c/o Russell & Du Moulin 1075 West Georgia Street, Vancouver BC V6E 3G2, T (604) 224-7386; **China**, 4 Liangmahe Nanlu, Sanlitun, Beijing 100600, T (1) 432-3926; **CIS**, Per Voyevodina 5, Moscow, T 095 241-3702; **Denmark**, c/o High Commission in London; **Finland**, c/o Embassy in Moscow; **France**, 12 Square de l'Avenue Foch, 75116 Paris, T 4500-3361; **Germany**, Sudstrasse 133, 5300 Bonn 2, T 228 31-2007; **Greece**, Consulate, 10-12 Kifissias Avenue, 151 25 Maroussi, Athens, T 1 683-4875; **Hong Kong**, Units 901-2, Admiralty Centre Tower 1, 9th Floor, 18 Harcourt Road, Hong Kong, T 527-2212; **India**, High Commission, E-6 Chandragupta Marg, Chanakyapuri, New Delhi 110021, T 11 60-4162. Consulates: Bombay T 2 204-3205; Madras T 44 47-6637; **Indonesia**, Block X/4 KAV No. 2, Jalan HR Rasuna Said, Kuningan, Jakarta 12950, T 21 520-1489. Consulate: Medan, North Sumatra, T 61 51-3366; **Japan**, 14th Floor, Osaka, Kokusai Building, 3-13 Azuchimachi 2-Chome, Chuo-Ku, Tokyo T (6) 261-5131; **Japan**, 12-3 Roppongi, 5-Chome, Minato-ku, Tokyo 106, T 3 3586-9111; **Luxemburg**, c/o Embassy in Brussels; **Malaysia**, High Commission, 209 Jalan Tun Razak, Kuala Lumpur, 50400, T (03) 261-6277; **Maldives**, c/o High Commission, New Delhi; **Myanmar**, 287 Prome Road, Yangon, T 33200; **Nepal**, c/o High Commission in New Delhi; **Netherlands**, Grindweg 88, 3055 VD Rotterdam, T (10) 461-5899; **New Zealand**, High Commission, 17 Kabul Street, Khandallah, Wellington, T (4) 79-2076; **Norway**, c/o High Commission in London. Consulate: Oslo, T 47 2 485000; **Pakistan**, Consulate, Lakson Square Building, 2 Sarwar Shaheed Road, Karachi-1, T 21 52-6419; **Philippines**, 6th Floor ODC Bldg, International Plaza, 219 Salcedo Street, Legaspi Village, Makati,

Metro Manila, T (2) 816-1764; **Portugal**, Consulate: Lusograin, Rua dos Franqueiros 135-1, 1100 Lisbon, T (1) 87-8647; **Spain**, Consulate: Huertas 13, Madrid 28012, T 1 429-3193; **Sri Lanka**, High Commission, c/o High Commission in New Delhi; **Sweden**, c/o Embassy in Bonn. Consulate: Stockholm T 8 663-7488; **Switzerland**, c/o Embassy in Bonn; **Thailand**, 129 South Sathorn Road, Bangkok, T 2 286-2111; **UK**, High Commission, 9 Wilton Crescent, London SW1X 8SA, T 071-235 8315; **USA**, 1824 R Street NW, Washington DC 20009-1691, T (202) 667-7555. Consulates: Los Angeles T (714) 760-9400; Minneapolis T (612) 332-8063.

TRANSPORT TO AND FROM SINGAPORE

By air

As an international crossroads, Singapore is within easy reach of all key points in the region and there are flights from Changi to destinations throughout Southeast Asia. Approximate cost of one-way tickets from Singapore are: Bandar Seri Begawan, Brunei (M$320), Bali (S$500), Bangkok (S$200), Ho Chi Minh City (S$760), Jakarta (S$200), Medan (S$275), Penang (S$150). Because of the number of carriers serving Singapore, it is easy to buy a ticket out. Long-haul prices are not as competitive as London bucket shops, although they undercut some other Asian capitals. Tickets to Southeast Asian destinations are subject to minimum selling price restrictions imposed by a cartel of regional airlines. It is still possible to get special deals to selected destinations from the discount travel agents (**see page 453** and Singapore *Yellow Pages*) but tickets bought in Bangkok and Penang are now a bit cheaper.

The **Singapore-Kuala Lumpur** air shuttle (operated jointly by SIA and MAS) runs every 50 mins from Changi Terminal 1. Singapore-KL shuttle tickets can be bought on a first-come-first-served basis at Changi Airport for S$132. For timetables, call SIA on T 2238888 or MAS on T 3366777. For return flights to Kuala Lumpur, just buy a single ticket. It costs S$132, while the Kuala Lumpur-Singapore leg costs M$132. Agents do not differentiate between the two currencies.

Long haul flights from Kuala Lumpur, particularly on MAS, can be considerably cheaper than outbound flights from Singapore. It is also much cheaper when flying between Singapore and other points in Malaysia to use Johor Bahru's airport across the causeway. Johor Bahru is well connected to the Malaysian domestic network. Chartered express coaches ply between Singapore and JB airport; they leave Singapore from the *Novotel Orchid Inn* on Dunearn Road and cost S$10 one way. The courier ensures express clearance of Malaysian customs and immigration. Details from MAS office in Singapore: 190 Clemenceau Ave, T 3366777.

From Europe Approx time from London to Singapore (non-stop): 13 hours. From London Heathrow Singapore Airlines, British Airways and Qantas have daily flights. From Amsterdam Singapore Airlines and KLM flights leave daily and Garuda Indonesia have 3 flights a week. From Frankfurt Singapore Airlines flies daily, Lufthansa has 5 flights a week and Garuda Indonesia 2. You can fly from Zurich with Singapore Airlines 4 times a week, Swissair 3 and Garuda Indonesia once. From Paris Singapore Airlines flights leave 3 times a week and UTA 4. Singapore Airlines leaves Rome 3 times a week and from Athens twice a week. Olympic Airways also leave from Athens twice a week. From Moscow Saudia flies four times a week. Direct flights from other major European cities leave two or three times a week.

From the USA and Canada   Approx time from LAX (Los Angeles): 22 hrs. Singapore Airlines and United Airlines have flights leaving daily from Los Angeles and San Francisco. Travel via Los Angeles from New York. Singapore Airlines has 2 flights a week from Vancouver.

From Australasia   You can fly from Sydney, Perth and Melbourne (approx 4 hrs) daily with Qantas. Flights with Singapore Airlines, JAT and British Airways leave less frequently. From Auckland Air New Zealand leaves daily (approx 4 hrs), Singapore Airlines 4 times a week and Qantas 2.

From South Asia   Singapore Airlines fly from Delhi 3 times a week, and KLM, Aeroflot and Air India all have 2 flights a week. Both Air Lanka and Emirates have 3 flights a week from Colombo. You can fly from Dhaka with Biman Bangladesh Airlines (4 times a week) or Singapore Airlines (3 times a week). PIA flies 3 times a week from Karachi, Singapore Airlines 2 and KLM one. Singapore Airlines has 3 flights a week from Male, and one from Kathmandu. Royal Nepal Airlines also leave from Kathmandu twice a week.

From the Far East   Singapore Airlines, Japan Air Lines, VIASA and Northwest Airlines have daily flights from Tokyo, Japan Air System 4 times a week and Biman Bangladesh Airlines once a week. From Hong Kong Singapore Airlines, Cathay Pacific, Air China and United Airlines leave daily and Qantas has 3 flights a week. Singapore Airlines and Philippine Airlines fly daily from Manila.

From the Middle East   You can fly from Bahrain with Gulf Air twice a week, and Turkish Airlines once. Singapore Airlines flies from Cairo twice a week.

Airport information   The airport is at the extreme eastern tip of the island, about 20 km from town. Facilities are excellent and include banks, hotel reservation and Singapore Tourist Promotion Board desks, business centre, day rooms, restaurants, left-luggage facilities, mail and telecommunications desks, shopping arcades, supermarkets, sports facilities and accommodation which are all open from 0700-2300. Everything is clearly signposted in English and the two terminals are connected by a monorail. **Computerised flight information**, T 5424422 for all arrivals and departures.

Airport tax   Payable on departure – S$5 for flights to Brunei and Malaysia and S$12 to all other countries. A PSC (Passenger Service Charge) coupon can be purchased at most hotels, travel agencies and airline offices in town before departure, which will save time at the airport.

Transport to town   Hotels will only meet guests with a previous arrangement; some charge but others offer the service free. The car pick up area is outside the arrivals halls of both terminals. **By taxi**: taxis queue up outside the arrival halls. They are metered plus there is an airport surcharge of S$3. **By bus**: a number of buses run between the airport and nearby bus interchanges but the a/c 390 goes direct to Orchard Road (and the main hotel area) from the basement of terminal 1, stopping at terminal 2. The end of its loop is opposite Tanglin Shopping Centre, near the top of Orchard Road 1 hr (S$1.20); exact fare needed. **Car rental**: **Avis** and **Hertz** desks are in the arrivals hall (close 1800).

By train

The railway station is on Keppel Road, T 2225165. Singapore is the last port of call for the Malaysian railway system (Keretapi Tanah Melayu – KTM). The cavernous, domed station – apparently inspired by Helsinki's – opened in 1932 and was renovated in 1990, supposedly to make it a slightly more glamorous terminal for the Eastern & Oriental Express (see below). Malaysian immigration and customs clearance for inbound and outbound passengers is taken care of in the Singapore station (with the help of sniffer dogs). **Transport to town**: from the station, bus 20 goes to Beach Road and 148 to Serangoon Road.

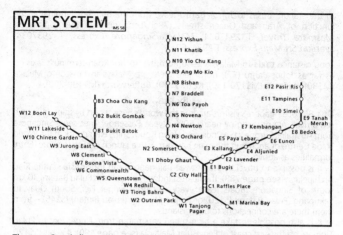

There are 2 main lines connecting Singapore and Malaysia: one up the West Coast to KL and Butterworth and on to Thailand and another line which goes through the centre of Peninsular Malaysia and on to Kota Bahru on the NE coast. Some travellers use the train to go to Johor Bahru to avoid the long wait going through customs at the border (S\$1.50). There are 5 express trains daily between Singapore and Malaysia: Kuala Lumpur, 6 hrs (S\$25-28), Butterworth, opposite Penang, 13 hrs (S\$47-50). Departure times: 0745, 0830, 1420, 2015 and 2200. The overnight sleeper arrives in Kuala Lumpur at 0655. There are also express trains 3 times a week to/from Bangkok crossing the Malaysian/Thai border at Padang Besar (S\$80) (**see page 151**). There are also cheaper, but slower, mail trains which stop at every station en route. Trains are clean and efficient and overnight trains have cabins in first class, sleeping berths in second class and restaurants.

Orient-Express Hotels, which operates the Venice Simplon Orient-Express plans to launch a new luxury *Eastern & Oriental Express* late January 1993, making one return trip a week between Singapore, Kuala Lumpur and Bangkok. The journey takes 41 hrs (2 nights, 1 day) to cover the 2,000 km one-way trip. Passengers will be able to disembark at Kuala Lumpur, Butterworth (Penang), Phuket and Hua Hin. A single fare from Singapore to Bangkok starts from US\$950 in a shared cabin; departs Singapore 1600 every Sun and arrives Bangkok 0930 Tues. Reservations can be made at Orient-Express Hotels, Sea Containers House, 20 Upper Ground, London SE1 9PF, UK T (071) 928 6000; *Orient-Express Hotels* also has agents in Singapore, Kuala Lumpur and Bangkok to handle reservations – in Singapore contact: 90 Cecil St 14-03, Carlton Building, T 2272068. For Kuala Lumpur and Bangkok agents, see relevant sections.

By road

Long distance **buses** to and from **Malaysia** operate out of the terminal at the junction of Lavender Street and Kallang Bahru. There are connections every few minutes to Johor Bahru. Bus 170 goes to Woodlands immigration point and across the causeway to Johor Bahru bus station; leaves every 15 mins from Queen Street (S\$1.50) or Bukit Timah Road (S\$0.80). Most travel agents sell bus tickets to Malaysia: KL (S\$16), Melaka (S\$11), Butterworth (S\$30), Mersing (S\$11), Kota Bahru (S\$30). **Buses to Thailand** leave from the Golden Mile Complex on Beach Road: Hat Yai (S\$24), Bangkok (S\$55). There are several agents selling tickets close to the station. Buses to **Johor Bahru** leave from the Ban San Terminal at the junction of Arab and Queen streets (79c). Long distance bus companies: *Masmara Travel*, T 2947034; *Malacca/Singapore Express*, T 2937034; *Syarikat Sri Maju Express*, T 2934160.

Long distance **taxis** to Malaysia leave from the Rochor Road terminus. Taxis go as far as Johor Bahru ($7), from here there are Malaysian taxis onto Melaka (M$80), Kuantan (M$120-150), KL (M$100), Butterworth (M$180-200).

By sea
Only 8% of Singapore's visitors arrive in the world's busiest port by ship – although sea arrivals are growing by nearly 50% a year. Passenger lines serve Singapore from Australia, Europe, USA, India and Hong Kong. Ships either dock at the World Trade Centre or anchor in the main harbour with a launch service to shore. Entry formalities as above.

It is possible to travel by sea between Singapore and **Indonesia** via the Riau Archipelago (**see page 788**); the nearest Indonesian island is Pulau Batam, 30 km south of Singapore. Boats leave every day from Finger Pier, South Quay to Sekupang (Pulau Batam) (S$20) or Tanjung Pinang (Pulau Bintan) (S$45) – from them there are connections to other islands.

It is also possible to take a high-speed catamaran from Finger Pier to Pulau Tioman, off the east coast of Peninsular Malaysia (**see page 190**), $4\frac{1}{2}$ hrs (S$120 return). Ferry operators have offices in the PSA Building, Finger Pier.

A timetable of all shipping arrivals and departures is published daily in the *Shipping Times* (a section of the *Business Times*). According to some travellers freighter operators are reasonably amenable to marine hitchers who want lifts to Vietnam (although it is difficult to enter Vietnam by sea), the Philippines or Indonesia. Some passenger-carrying cargo ships are booked-out well in advance, but fare-paying travellers can expect high standards, usually including comfortable single or double cabins. Passengers often eat at the Captain's table and the ships are usually well equipped with leisure facilities. Those who have travelled by freighter say the experience is unbeatable. The Australian publication *Slow Boats Freighter Travel News* (Sydney International Travel Centre, 8/F, 75 King Street, Sydney, NSW 2000, Australia) lists worldwide freighter-passenger services for subscribers. It is possible to enter Singapore from Malaysia by fishing boat from Johor Bahru (S$4), Tanjung Pengileh or Tanjung Surat (S$6) in southern Johor to Changi Point, on the northeast tip of Singapore – a nifty way of beating the bottleneck at the causeway. First boat 0700, last at 1600. Boats depart as soon as they have a full complement of 12 passengers.

Customs
Singapore is a free port.

Duty free allowance 1 litre of liquor.

Currency There is no limit to the amount of Singapore and foreign currency or travellers' cheques you can bring in or take out.

Export restrictions There is no export duty but export permits are required for arms, ammunition, explosives, animals, gold, platinum, precious stones and jewellery, poisons and drugs. No permit is needed for the export of antiques.

Prohibited items **Narcotics are strictly forbidden in Singapore** and, as in neighbouring Malaysia, trafficking is a capital offence which is rigorously enforced. Dawn hangings at Changi prison are regularly reported. Trafficking in more than 30 g of morphine and 15 g of heroin or cocaine is punishable by death. Anyone trafficking in more than 10 kg of cannabis faces 20-30 years in Changi and 15 strokes of the rotan, a punishment devised by the British colonial administration. Passengers arriving from Malaysia by rail have to march, single-file past sniffer dogs.

In 1992, the Singapore Government banned the importation and sale of chewing gum, after the MRT Corporation claimed the substance threatened the efficient running of its underground trains. Cleaners complained about gum stuck under seats, and drivers cited incidents of train doors being gummed up. Officially, therefore, any person travelling to Singapore is prohibited from bringing gum into the country, even if it is intended for personal use.

INTERNAL TRAVEL

In an unsuccessful attempt to discourage Singaporeans from clogging the roads with private cars, the island's public transport system was designed to be cheap and painless. Cars can now, however, cruise from the suburbs straight into the city on the underground expressway, the CTE, which opened in 1991. As yet, not many buses are air-conditioned, but they go almost everywhere, and the Mass Rapid Transit (MRT) underground railway provides an extremely efficient subterranean back-up. Smoking is strictly banned on all public transport – transgression is punishable by a large fine. In addition, Big Macs and durians are not allowed on the MRT.

NB: the **Singapore Council of Social Services** publishes *Access Singapore*, a guidebook especially for physically disabled visitors, which gives information on easily accessible tourist attractions and facilities for the disabled. Copies can be picked up from the SCSS offices at 11 Penang Lane.

Mass Rapid Transit (MRT)

Since Nov 1987 Singapore has had one of the most technologically advanced, user-friendly light railway systems in the world – about a third of the system is underground. The arty designer-stations of marble, glass and chrome are cool, spotless and suicide-free – thanks to the sealed-in, air-conditioned platforms. Nine of the underground stations serve as self-sufficient, blast-proof emergency bunkers for Singaporeans, should they ever need them.

The S$5 billion MRT is indeed a rapid way of transiting – it is electrically driven and trains reach 80 km/hr. Within minutes of leaving the bustle of Orchard Road passengers hear the honey-toned welcome to the Raffles City interchange in English, Mandarin, Malay and Tamil. The MRT's 66 fully automated trains operate every 3-8 mins, depending on the time of day, between 0600 and 2400. The 800,000-odd daily passenger trips made on the MRT could have been boosted enormously if the authorities had allowed the line to go out to the airport. However, the lobbying power of the NTUC taxi trade unionists put paid to that idea – but the two main lines run N-S and E-W and cover the main tourist belt. Fare stages are posted in station concourses, and tickets dispensed, with change, from the vending machines. Fares range from 50¢ to S$2. Stored value tickets, in various denominations, can be bought at all stations from ticket dispensing machines. (There are note changing machines nearby, which will change $1 bills into $1 coins.) It is also possible to buy combined MRT and bus farecards costing S$12 and S$22 (including a S$2 deposit) from the Transitlink offices in the MRT stations. Buses are armed with 'validator machines'.

Bus

SBS (Singapore Bus Service) is efficient, convenient and cheap. Routes for all the buses are listed (with a special section on buses to tourist spots) in an SBS guide (70¢) available at news outlets and bookshops as well as at many hotels. The Singapore Tourist Promotion Board's *Official Guide* (free-of-charge from STPB offices) also carries a tourist-friendly synopsis of the service. All buses are operated by a driver only, so it is necessary to have the exact fare to hand. Fares range from 50¢ to 90¢ and buses run from 0630 to 2330 Mon-Sun. There are buses to most destinations from Orchard Road.

One-day (S$5) or three-day (S$12) explorer tickets allow unlimited travel island-wide on SBS and TIBS (Trans-Island Bus Service); available at all major hotels, tour agencies, SBS travel centres and main bus interchanges.

Taxis

Taxis are the fastest and easiest way to get around in comfort. More than 12,000 taxis, all of them metered and air-conditioned, ply the island's roads. The taxis' bells are an alarm warning cabbies once they're over the 80 km/hr expressway speed limit. Fares start at S$2.20, for the first 1.5 km, and rise 10¢ for every subsequent 300m up to 10 km. If there are more than two passengers there is a 50¢ surcharge; luggage costs S$1 extra and there's a 50% 'midnight charge' from 2400 to 0600. There's also a S$3 surcharge for journeys starting from Changi International airport, a S$2 flat fee for calling a radio taxi, and S$1 extra for all trips going into or through the Central Business District (CBD) between 1600 and 1900 on weekdays and 1200-1500 on Saturdays. TIBS taxis now has a fleet of London cabs which cost an extra S$1, but have the advantage of accommodating 5 passengers.

The CBD area scheme restricts all cars and taxis from entering the area between 0730-1015 and 1630-1900 Mon-Fri, 0730-1015 Sat, unless they purchase an area licence (S$3 cars, $1 for motorbikes). Passengers entering the restricted zone are liable unless the taxi is already displaying a licence. Taxis are usually plentiful; there are stands outside most main shopping centres and hotels. Smoking is illegal in taxis. For 24-hour taxi services ring: T 4811211 (TIBS – which also has London cabs), T 2500700/1 (SABS), T 4669912, T 4815151, T 2825545/6/7, T 4747707, T 2614774, T 7624040, T 4672363, T 4525555, T 2827700, T 5339009, T 4686188, T 2686277, T 2738889, T 2542379, T 2541117. That may seem a lot of options, but when it rains and taxis are in heavy demand, it is difficult to find a number which is not permanently engaged.

Car hire

One of the most expensive ways to get around. It is not worth it unless travelling to Malaysia, as parking is expensive in Singapore (parking coupons can be bought in shops and daily licence booths). If travelling to Malaysia it is cheaper to hire a car in Johor Bahru. Rental agencies require a licence, passport and for the driver to be over 20 with a valid driver's licence (preferably international but national is usually sufficient) and passport. Car rental cost is anything from S$60 to S$350 per day, depending on size and comfort, plus mileage. Vans and pickups are much cheaper as they are classified as commercial vehicles and are taxed at a lower rate.

Driving is on the left, the speed limit 50 km/hr (80 km/hr on expressways) and wearing a seat-belt is compulsory. Remember that to drive into the restricted zone a licence must be purchased (S$3). Petrol is cheap, about S$1.20 per litre. In addition to car hire counters at the airport and booking offices in some top hotels, the Singapore *Yellow Pages* lists scores of local firms under 'Motorcar Renting and Leasing'. Some of the main companies are: **Avis**, 01-01 Liat Tower, T 7379477; **Budget**, Haw Par Centre, 154 Clemenceau Ave, T 3360606/ T 7345511; **City Car Rentals**, 02-20 *Hotel Miramar*, 401 Havelock Rd, T 7332145; **Hertz**, 01-20, 19 Tanglin Rd, T 7344646; **National**, 01-01 Tong Nam Building, 73 Bukit Timah Rd, T 3888444; **Orchard**, B1-02 Orchard Towers, T 2358775; **Sintat**, 1306, 1 Maritime Square, World Trade Centre, T 2732211; **Thrifty**, T 2732211.

Boat

Ferries to the southern islands – Sentosa, Kusu, St John's etc – leave from the World Trade Centre or it is possible to hire a **sampan** from Jardine Steps on Keppel Road or Clifford Pier. Boats for the northern islands go from Changi Point or Ponggol Point (**see page 415**).

Other local transport

Trishaw Trishaws, descendants of the rickshaw, have all but left the Singapore street-scene. A few genuine articles can still be found in the depths of Geylang or Chinatown, Serangoon Road or outside Raffles city, but most now cater for tourists and charge accordingly, making trishaws the most expensive form of public transport in town. As ever, agree a price before climbing in. Top hotels offer top dollar trishaw tours. Off-duty trishaw drivers hang out in a large pack at the bottom of Bras Basah Road, near St Joseph's Institution.

Hitch-hiking There is no law against hitch-hiking, but the idea is anathema to most Singaporeans and those trying are unlikely to have any success.

ACCOMMODATION, FOOD AND DRINK

The government has announced that from 1 April 1994, it will introduce a 3% Goods and Services Tax (GST) which will operate like a value-added tax on all products bought in shops, as well as hotel and restaurant bills and taxi fares.

Accommodation

Singapore has about 70 gazetted hotels (approved by STPB) with 23,700 rooms and scores more besides. There are many excellent international class hotels – mostly around the main shopping areas, Orchard and Scotts Roads, near Raffles City and the Marina complexes. They are all run to a very high standard and cost from S$150-S$300 a night – although discounts are often on offer. Enquire at the airport hotel desk, on arrival, whether there are any special offers. It is advisable to book in advance. After a room glut in the early 1980s, Singapore's hotel industry is suffering a room shortage and contractors are racing to catch up. In major hotels there is a 4% tax and a 10% service charge added to the bill.

In Singapore, hotels have been graded as follows:
L: S$320+; all the facilities of international class hotels with more sumptuous trimmings and unrivalled service.
A+: S$160-320; international class hotels offer all the usual five-star services like 24-hour service, minibars, swimming pools, white towelling dressing gowns, hairdryers and daily newspapers. Many also have their own shopping arcades, business facilities and fitness centres.
A: S$65-160; while facilities are good for hotels in this price range, those at the lower end of the category are not up to first class hotel standards, as they might be elsewhere in Southeast Asia.
B: S$30-65 economy; while deluxe and middle budget tourists are spoilt for choice, cheaper accommodation is less abundant. The budget mainly Chinese-run hotels, are concentrated around Bras Basah Road, Bencoolen Street, Beach Road and Middle Road with a few more out in Geylang. Rooms are usually basic but some have air-conditioning.
C: S$20-30; budget.
D: S$10-20; Singapore has hardly any accommodation in this range; most are half-way between budget and crashpad and facilities are basic.
E: less than S$10.

Food

Eating is the national pastime in Singapore and has acquired the status of a refined art. The island is a tropical paradise for epicureans of every persuasion and budget. While every country in the region boasts national dishes, none offers such a delectably wide variety as Singapore. Fish-head curry must surely qualify as *the* national dish but you can sample 10 Chinese cuisines, N and S Indian, Malay and Nonya (Straits Chinese) food, plus Indonesian, Vietnamese, Thai, Japanese, Korean, Continental, Russian, Mexican, Polynesian, and Scottish. There's a very respectable selection of Western food at the top end of the market, a few good places in the middle bracket and swelling ranks of cheaper fastfood restaurants. At the last count, Singapore had 32 *Kentucky Fried Chickens* and 32 *McDonalds'*, not to mention a smattering of *Burger Kings* and *A&Ws* and an explosion of pizza outlets. For young, trendy Singaporeans, there's more kudos being seen devouring a Big Mac than a plate of chicken rice.

Unlike in the West, where meals are usually sociable affairs, Asians tend to separate eating and talking. At business lunches, for example, the food comes first. Then the business.

There are so many excellent restaurants in Singapore that everyone has their own recommendations – there is rarely agreement on 'the best'. New restaurants open every other day and in this gourmet paradise chefs are eminently poachable. In recent years there has been a gluttonous trend towards value-for-money, where quantity rules and patrons are encouraged to cram their plates. Hotel buffets compete to offer the biggest and cheapest spread of sumptuous savouries, salads and sweets: ads in *The Straits Times* announce the latest offers and the tourist magazine, *City Mag* also notes all on-going food promotions in its *This Week* section. Typical 'teas' include everything from dim sum to Black Forest Gateaux and cost S$12-17 a head.

Do not be put off by characterless, brightly lit restaurants in Singapore: the food can be superb. Eating spots range from high-rise revolving restaurants to neon-lit pavement seafood extravaganzas. A delicious dinner can cost as little as S$3 or more than S$30. And in Singapore, because of its rigorously enforced hygiene standards, it is possible to eat just about anywhere. The *Secret Food Map* (available at most bookstores – S$5) is a good buy.

Prices:

Hawker centres (♦-♦♦)	S$2.50-6.00
Chinese coffee shops (♦♦-♦♦♦)	S$3.50-10.00
Basic restaurants (♦♦-♦♦♦)	S$8.00-15.00
Upmarket restaurants (♦♦♦-♦♦♦♦♦)	S$20.00+
Hotel restaurants & exclusive restaurants(♦♦♦♦♦)	S$30.00+

Durians One local favourite, is durian fruit (**see page 17**). During the Malaysian and S Thai *montong* durian seasons (Jun/Jul and Nov/Dec), fleets of trucks ferry durians over the causeway; about eight million are sold in Singapore each year. The roadside market on the junction of Albert and Waterloo streets is probably the best durian centre, but Smith Street (Chinatown), Lavender Street and Geylang Serai market are also well known by durian-lovers. An average-sized durian costs around S$10, big Thai ones command more than S$100, expect to bargain.

Hawker centres The government might have cleared hawkers off the streets, but there are plenty of hawker centres in modern Singapore. They provide the local equivalent of café culture and the human equivalent of grazing. Large numbers of stalls are packed together under one roof, although most are really open-air affairs. The seats and tableware may be basic (hygiene regulations demand plastic cutlery and polystyrene plates), but the food is always fresh and diners are spoilt for choice. Customers claim themselves a table, then graze their way down the rows of Chinese, Malay and Indian stalls. It is not necessary to eat from the stall you are sitting next to. Vendors will deliver to your table when the food's ready and payment is on receipt. The food is cheap (although more touristy hawker centres charge more touristy prices) and prices are non-negotiable. *The Guide to Singapore Hawker Food*, by James Hooi, is recommended reading.

Chinese cuisines Each province of China has its own distinct cuisine. A balanced meal should contain the 5 basic taste sensations: sweet, bitter, salty, spicy and acidic to balance the yin and yang.

Szechuan – very spicy (garlic and chilli are dominant) is widely considered the tastiest Chinese cuisine. Szechuan food includes heaps of hot red peppers – traditionally considered to be protection against cold and disease. Among the best Szechuan dishes are: smoked duck in tea leaves and camphor sawdust, minced pork with bean curd, steamed chicken in lotus leaves, fried eels in garlic sauce.

Peking (Beijing) – chefs at the imperial court in Peking had a repertoire of over 8,000 recipes. Dumplings, noodles and steamed buns predominate since wheat is the staple diet, but in Singapore, rice may accompany the meal. *Peking duck* (the skin is basted with syrup and cooked until crisp), *shi choy* (deep fried bamboo shoots), hot and sour soup are among the best Peking dishes. *Crispy Peking duck* is another typical dish; it is usually eaten in steamed buns or rolled into a pancake. Fish dishes are usually deep-fried and served with sweet and sour sauce.

Cantonese – dishes are often steamed with ginger and are not very spicy. Shark's fin and birds' nest soups, *dim sum* (mostly steamed delicacies trollied to your table, but only served until early afternoon) are Cantonese classics. Other typical dishes include fish steamed with soya sauce, ginger, chicken stock and wine, wan ton, blanched green vegetables in oyster sauce and suckling pig.

Hokkien – being one of Singapore's biggest dialect groups means Hokkien cuisine is prominent, particularly in hawker centres, although there are very few Hokkien restaurants. Hokkien Chinese invented the spring roll and their cooking uses lots of noodles and in one or two places you can still see them being made by hand (one noodle-maker has a stall in the food centre behind Cuppage Terrace and Centre Point). Hokkien cuisine is also characterized by clear soups and steamed seafood, eaten with soya sauce. *Hay cho* (deep fried balls of prawn) and *bee hoon* (rice vermicelli cooked with prawns, squid and beansprouts with lime and chillies) are specialities.

Shanghainese – seafood dominates this cuisine and many dishes are cooked in soya sauce. Braised fish-heads, braised abalone (a shellfish) in sesame sauce and crab and sweetcorn soup are typical dishes. Wine is often used in the preparation of meat dishes – hence drunken prawn and drunken crab.

Hainanese – simple cuisine from the southern island of Hainan; chicken rice with ginger and garlic is their tastiest contribution.

Hakka – uses plenty of sweet potato and dried shrimp and specializes in stewed pigs' trotters, *yong tau foo* (deep fried bean curd), and chillis and other vegetables stuffed with fish paste.

Hunanese – known for its glutinous rice, honeyed ham and pigeon soup.

Teochew – famous for its *muay* porridges – a light, clear broth consumed with side dishes of crayfish, salted eggs and vegetables.

Steamboat – the Chinese answer to fondue – is a popular dish in Singapore and can be found in numerous restaurants and at some hawker centres. Thinly sliced pieces of raw meat, fish, prawns, cuttlefish, fishballs and vegetables are gradually tossed into a bubbling cauldron in the centre of the table, then dunked into hot chilli and soya sauces. The resulting soup provides a flavoursome broth to wash it all down at the end.

Malay In Singapore Malay cooking is overshadowed by the Chinese gastronomic array, and because Malay curries take much longer to prepare, they do not lend themselves so easily to instant hawker food. But Malay hawkers' trump card is satay. Islam bans the use of pork (Chinese hawkers have a monopoly in pork satay) and Malay stalls and restaurants rarely serve alcohol. There are a handful of upmarket Malay restaurants but *makanan Melayu* is mostly found in hawker centres. *Roti John* (a French loaf, sliced open and fried with mutton, egg and onion) is the Malay interpretation of a European breakfast. For other Malay dishes, **see page 352**.

Nonya The cuisine of the Straits Chinese blends tastes from China and the Malay peninsula. *Poh piah* (savoury spring rolls filled with shredded turnip and bamboo shoots, beancurd, prawns and pork), and *otak-otak* (coconut milk with spices, prawns and fish, wrapped in strips of coconut leaves) are typical Nonya dishes.

Indian There is probably as wide a selection of Indian edibles in Singapore as there is on the entire Indian sub-continent – from scorching-hot Madrasi curries to the mild, creamy kormas of the north. There is also the Indian Muslim food that is special to Singapore and Malaysia – *prata kosong* (*roti prata*, the skillfully stretched Indian dough-bread, fried and served with a thin curry sauce) and fish-head curry (do not be put off by the idea: the tenderest, most succulent flesh is on and around the head) are both local specialities. Other typical Indian dishes include *murtabak* (*paratha* filled with meat, onion and egg), southern Indian vegetarian food such as *masala dosa* (Indian pancake) and *thali* (several curries eaten with rice and served on a banana leaf).

Seafood Singapore offers a vast variety of seafood. There are specialist seafood centres in which to sample fish from all cuisines. Chilli or pepper crabs, 'drunken' prawns (cooked in rice wine) and deep-fried squid (*sotong*) dishes are Singaporean favourites.

Drink

Every hawker centre has at least a couple of stalls selling fresh fruit juice – a more wholesome alternative to the ubiquitous bottles of fizzy drink. A big pineapple or papaya juice costs up to S$2. Four-in-one cocktails can be made on request; simple mixers, like orange and carrot, are also recommended. Freshly squeezed fruit juices are widely available at stalls and in restaurants. Fresh lime juice is served in most restaurants, and is a perfect complement to the banana-leaf curry, tandoori and dosai. Carbonated soft drinks, cartons of fruit juice and air-flown fresh milk can be found in supermarkets. For local flavour, the Malay favourite is *bandung* (a sickly-sweet, bright pink concoction of rose essence and condensed milk), found in most hawker centres, as well as the Chinese thirst quenchers, soya bean milk or chrysanthemum tea. *Red Bull* (*Krating Daeng*), the Thai tonic is also widely available – and is the toast of Singapore's army of Thai building site labourers.

Tiger and Anchor beer are the local brews and Tsingtao, the Chinese nectar, is also available. Tiger Beer was first brewed at the Malayan Breweries with imported Dutch hops and yeast on Alexandra Road in 1932 and was the product of a joint venture between Singapore's Fraser & Neave and Heineken. Recently Tiger Beer has produced two new brews: Tiger Classic is a strong bottled beer and Tiger Light, which is now available on draught in some bars. Anchor was the result of German brewers Beck's setting up the rival Archipelago Brewery. Because of its German roots, Archipelago was bought out by Malayan Breweries in 1941 and is today part of the same empire. Popular Western lager beers can also be found in supermarkets, bars and restaurants, and Guinness, brewed in Kuala Lumpur and popular with the Chinese (for medicinal purposes) is available everywhere. Some bars (such as Charlie's at Changi) specialize in imported beers but even local beer is expensive (around S$6 a bottle in hawker centres and S$8 a glass in bars and pubs). International selection of drinks at top bars but they're often pricey. Coffee houses, hawker centres and small bars or coffee shops around Serangoon Road, Jalan Besar and Chinatown have the cheapest beer. Expect to pay around S$8-10 for a half pint of beer in most smart bars. One of our correspondents, who went apoplectic at the price of a pint, pointed out some artful ploys. He noted that adjacent bars and hotels have different 'happy hours' allowing one "to gravitate from one to another". It is also possible to order several rounds of drinks before 'happy hour' expires. Once rung up on the till before the deadline, drinks can be consumed at any stage during the evening. There is no shortage of wine available in Singapore; Australian wines are generally a better deal than imported European ones. Supermarkets all have good wines and spirits sections; the best is probably at *Jason's*, behind Orchard Towers, 400 Orchard Road.

The **Singapore Sling** is the island's best known cocktail. It was invented in the Raffles Hotel in 1915 and contains a blend of gin, cherry brandy, sugar, lemon juice and angostura bitters. There are lounge bars in all main hotels and many pubs, bars and nightclubs. Coffee shops – traditionally in Chinese shophouses – serve as community bars, where locals talk business over bottles of stout.

PUBLIC HOLIDAYS AND NATIONAL FESTIVALS

Singapore's cultural diversity gives Singaporeans the excuse to celebrate plenty of festivals, most of which visitors can attend. The Singapore Tourist Promotion Board produces a brochure every year on festivals, with their precise dates. The *Monkey King* by Timothy Mo is very descriptive of Chinese customs and festivals, although it is set in Hong Kong.

Jan/Feb: *New Year's Day* (1st Jan: public holiday). *Chinese New Year* (moveable: public holiday) a 15-day lunar festival celebrated in late Jan or early Feb is the most important event in the entire Chinese calendar. Each new year is given the name of an animal in 12-year rotation and each has a special significance. The seasonal Mandarin catchphrase is *Gong Xi Fa Chai* (happy new year).

The new year celebration derives from a legend in which Chinese villagers were snatched by a monster who turned out to be terrified of noise, bright lights and the colour red. Little squares of red paper, decorated with good wishes in Chinese calligraphy, are plastered on to doors and walls. New Year's eve is a family occasion with a special reunion dinner. It is the time to exchange good wishes and *hong bao* – little red envelopes containing good luck money. Employees receive a hong bao at work – usually with a symbolic 10 cent-piece inside – and unmarried children get little treats too. Chinese New Year is not a good time to visit Singapore as the city is ominously quiet (most of the shops are closed) and tourist attractions are seething.

Traditionally, the celebrations should continue for 2 weeks but Chinese shops re-open after 4 or 5 days. Compared to the celebrations in other neighbouring countries, Singapore's are rather tame and a lot quieter. Fire-crackers were banned in Singapore because of the number of injuries and deaths resulting from their indiscriminate use. Lunar New Year is publicly celebrated with the *Chingay parade* – which has lion and dragon floats, acrobats, stiltwalkers, skateboarders and dancers. Chingay translates as 'the art of masquerading'. It is now more of a multi-racial affair and not particularly Chinese. The parade is colourful and entertaining and makes its way slowly down Orchard Road – see press for details of times.

Thaipusam (moveable – Jan/Feb in the Hindu month of *Thai*) in honour of the Hindu deity Lord Subramaniam – or Murgham. Penitents pierce their bodies, cheeks and tongues with sharp skewers and weighted hooks and in trance carry *kavadi* (steel structures decorated with flowers, fruits, peacock feathers, pots of milk and pious images) on their shoulders from the Sri Perumal Temple on Serangoon Road to the Chettiar Sri Thandayuthapani temple on Tank Road. Penitents are accompanied by chanting well-wishers. (**See page 354.**)

Jade Emperor's Birthday (moveable) crowds converge on the Giok Hong Tian Temple on Havelock Road to celebrate the Jade Emperor's birthday. A Chinese opera is performed in the courtyard of the temple and lanterns are lit in the doorways of houses. *T'se Tien Tai Seng's (the monkey god) Birthday* (moveable, but celebrated twice a year, in Feb and Oct). Participants go into trance and pierce their cheeks and tongues with skewers before handing out paper charms. Celebrated at the Monkey God Temple, Eng Hoon Street, near Seng Poh market.

March/Apr: *Kwan Yin's Birthday* (moveable) Chinese visit temples dedicated to the goddess of Mercy (like the one on Waterloo Road). Childless couples come to pray for fertility. *Qing Ming* (moveable – early Apr) is a Chinese ancestor-worship extravaganza in which family graves are spruced up and offerings of food and wine placed on tombs to appease their forebears' spirits. *Songkran* (moveable) this Buddhist water festival is celebrated in Thai Buddhist temples. To welcome the New Year, the image of the Buddha is bathed and celebrants are sprinkled – or doused – with water, as a sign of purification. Offerings of flowers, incense and candles are brought to the temples – the Anada Metyarama Temple on Silat Road is the best place to see this. *Hari Raya Puasa* or *Aidil Fitri* (moveable) marks the end of Ramadan, the month of fasting for Muslims and is a day of celebration. Once the Muftis have confirmed the new moon of *Syawal*, the 10th Islamic month, Muslims don traditional clothing and spend the day praying in the mosques and visiting friends and family. During Ramadan, Muslims gather to eat at stalls after dark; Geyland Serai and Bussorah Street (near Arab Street) are favourite makan stops. *Tamil New Year* (moveable – Apr-May) begins at the start of the Hindu month of *Chithirai*. *Pujas* are held at Singapore's main temples to honour *Surya*, the sun god. An almanac, containing the Hindu horoscope is published at this time. *Easter* (moveable – Good Friday is a public holiday) services are held in the island's churches. There is a candlelit procession in the grounds of St Joseph's Catholic Church, Victoria Street.

May: *Labour Day* (1st: public holiday). *Vesak Day* (moveable – usually in May, on the full moon of the fifth lunar month) commemorates the Buddha's birth, death and enlightenment and is celebrated in Buddhist temples everywhere (Kong Meng San Phor Kark See temple in Bright Hill Drive and the Temple of a Thousand Lights in Race Course Road are particularly lively). In Singapore celebrations begin before dawn: monks chant *sutras* (prayers) and lanterns and candles are lit to symbolize the Buddha's enlightenment. Statues of the Buddha are ritually bathed. Some temples also stage special exhibitions, conduct initiation ceremonies and present lectures on the Buddha's teachings. Buddhists release captive animals and fish, make offerings to monks and nuns and meditate. Vegetarian meals are served, Buddhists take part in a mass blood-donation exercise and cash and food are distributed to the poor and various charities.

Birthday of the Third Prince (moveable) festivities to mark the birthday of this child-god, who carries a magic bracelet in one hand and a spear in the other, while riding wheels of wind and fire. Chinese mediums go into trance, slashing themselves with swords and spikes.

Dragon Boat Festival (moveable) honours the suicide of an ancient Chinese poet-hero, Qu Yuan. He drowned himself in protest against corrupt government. In an attempt to save him, fishermen played drums and threw rice dumplings to try and distract predators. His death is commemorated with dragon boat races and the eating of rice dumplings.

Hari Raya Haji (moveable – falls on the 10th day of *Zulhijjah*, the 12th month of the Muslim calendar) to celebrate Moslems who have made the pilgrimage to Mecca (the men are known as *haji* – identifiable by their white skull caps – and the women as *hajjah*). The feast-day is marked by prayers at mosques and the sacrificial slaughter of goats and buffalo for distribution to the poor as a sign of gratitude to Allah.

Aug/Sept: *National Day* (9th Aug: public holiday) to celebrate the Republic's independence in 1965. The highlight of the day is the military parade, airforce fly-past and carnival procession on and around the Padang or National Stadium. It is necessary to have tickets to get into the Padang area, but the whole thing is televised live, and broadcast again on the weekend. Cheer leaders twirl to a 'Singapore we love you' chant. Political dignitaries and honoured guests look on from the courthouse steps.

Festival of the Hungry Ghosts (Yu Lan Jie): (moveable: runs for 30 days after the last day of the 6th moon). It is the second most important festival after the lunar new year. Banquets given by stallholders, lavish feasts are laid out on the streets, there are roving bands of Chinese street opera singers, puppet shows and lotteries. Then there is the ritual burning of huge incense sticks and paper 'hell money' to appease the spirits, who are believed to wander around on earth for a month after the annual opening of the gates of hell. The souls of the dead, who have been murdered or wronged or just bugged by their relatives, return to torment and haunt them. Because these spirits continue to wander around for several weeks, the 7th lunar month is known as 'the devil's month' – an inauspicious month to get married.

Another legend relates that the festival commemorates Buddha's suggestion to one of his disciples, Mu Lien, that in order to save his mother from hell, he must offer food to 'the ancestors of seven generations'. Whatever its derivation, the side streets and car parks in housing estates are the venue for the festivities, which have now degenerated into noisy auctions – the goods are believed to have been blessed by the gods. Bidders for items such as ceremonial charcoal (which, thanks to its supernatural powers can command up to S$20,000 a stick) do not have to pay up until the following year. It is extremely unusual that these creditors forget to pay – it is considered unlucky to do so. The festival affords the best opportunity to see *wayang* – street opera – and the best place to catch one is in Chinatown.

Mooncake or Lantern Festival (moveable – mid-way through the Chinese 8th moon). This Chinese festival commemorates the overthrow of the Mongul Dynasty in China. Children parade with elaborate candlelit lanterns and eat mooncakes filled with lotus seed paste. According to Chinese legend, secret messages of revolt were carried inside these cakes and led to the uprising which caused the overthrow of their oppressors. A gentler interpretation is that the round cakes represent the full moon, the end of the farming year and an abundant harvest – a bucolic symbolism that must be lost on most city-born Singaporeans. Lantern competitions are held and winning entries are exhibited at the Chinese Garden (see page 413).

Pilgrimage to Kusu Island (moveable) around 10,000 Taoist and Muslim pilgrims, over a month, crowd onto ferries to this sacred but ugly little island, $1/2$ an hour S of Singapore. There they make offerings at the Malay Kramat (shrine) or the Chinese temple dedicated to Tua Pekong. Kusu means turtle in Malay and according to legend, a giant turtle turned itself into an island in order to save 2 shipwrecked sailors, a Malay and a Chinese, who lived here peacefully until they died.

Navarathri Festival (moveable) 9 days of prayer, temple music and classical dance honour the consorts of Siva, Vishnu and Brahma (the Hindu trinity of Gods).

The festival is celebrated notably at the Chettiar Temple on Tank Road, ending with a procession on the 10th day along River Valley Road, Killiney Road, Orchard Road, Clemenceau Avenue and returning to the temple.

Oct/Nov: *Deepavali* (moveable – usually in Oct in the Hindu month of *Aipasi*) the Hindu festival of lights commemorates the victory of Lord Krishna over the demon king Narakasura, symbolizing the victory of light over darkness and good over evil. Indian mythology tells that as Narakasura lay dying he asked Krishna to grant him one last favour – to commemorate their battle as a day of fun for all the family. Every Hindu home is brightly lit and decorated for the occasion. Shrines are swamped with offerings and altars piled high with flowers. Row upon row of little earthen oil lamps are lit to guide the souls of departed relatives in their journey back to the next world, after their brief annual visit to earth during Deepavali.

Guru Nanak's Birthday (moveable) the first of the 10 gurus of the Sikh faith. The domed Gurdwara in Katong (Wilkinson Road) is buzzing on the Sikh holy day.

Thimithi Festival (moveable: around end Oct/beginning Nov, in the Hindu month of *Aipasi*) this Hindu festival often draws a big crowd to watch devotees fulfil their vows by walking over a 3 m long pit of burning coals in the courtyard of the Sri Mariamman Temple on South Bridge Road. Fire walking starts at around 1600 on the arrival of the procession from Perumal Temple on Serangoon Road. The priests walk the pit first, followed by devotees.

Dec: *Christmas Day* (25th: public holiday) Christmas in Singapore is a spectacle of dazzling lights, the best along Orchard Road, where the roadside trees are bejewelled with strings of fairy lights. Shopping centres and hotels compete to have the year's most extravagant or creative display. These seasonal exhibitions are often conveniently designed to last through Chinese New Year. It would not be untypical, for example, to find Santa riding on a man-eater in the year of the tiger. In shopping arcades, sweating tropical Santa Clauses dash through the fake snow. Choirs from Singapore's many churches line the sidewalks and Singaporeans go shopping.

OTHER ESSENTIAL INFORMATION

Conduct

Private homes Most Singaporeans remove their shoes at the door – more to keep their homes clean than out of any deep religious conviction. No host would insist his visitors do so, but it is the polite way to enter a home.

Eating Chinese meals are eaten with chopsticks and Malays and Indians traditionally eat with their right hands. It is just as acceptable, however, to eat with spoons and forks. In Malay and Indian company, do not use the left hand for eating.

Religion Make sure shoulders and legs are covered when entering a mosque and always take your shoes off. It is also necessary to remove shoes before entering Indian temples and many Chinese ones.

Prohibited in Singapore The old joke is that Singapore is a 'fine' place to live; you get a fine for smoking, spitting, breeding mosquitoes, not flushing the toilet and road hogging. From time to time Singapore, which is totally dependent for its water supplies from Malaysia, tries to 'conserve water'. At such times, stickers appear in toilets saying conserve water. These are plastered next to the stickers reading 'Penalty for not flushing $500'. Much worse is the fate awaiting people who urinate in lifts and are stupid enough to get caught: they have their pictures printed on the front of the next day's *Straits Times*. The latest prohibition was chewing gum in January 1991. *The Economist* noted: "The nanny of Southeast Asia has swooped again." Chewing gum was said to be a "perennial nuisance", jamming doors in the MRT and glueing pedestrians to the pavement. Wrigley's traffickers now face a year's jail or a fine of up to S$6,200. The fact that you can now buy T-shirts ridiculing all this might suggest that things have eased up a bit. But in Singapore, it is never wise to jump to hasty conclusions. In 1993, the government managed to shock many Singaporeans with a new, vindictive campaign which commentators compared with China's Cultural Revolution. Litterbugs were forced to wear fluorescent vests and pick up rubbish in the full glare of TV lights and in front of jeering onlookers. They had added humiliation heaped on them on the front page of *The Straits Times*, whose editor was unapologetic. Some of his journalists disagreed with him in the paper's pages, government MPs spoke out and concerned citizens phoned in complaints. The story has a two-pronged moral: (1) Singapore has still not outgrown its toytown mentality, and (2) unless you are a self-publicist, it is inadvisable to drop litter.

There are several rules and regulations visitors should note: **Drugs**: **see page 440** for details. **Smoking**: is discouraged and prohibited by law in many public places – such as buses, cinemas, theatres, libraries and department stores – and all air-conditioned restaurants. You can be fined up to S$500 for lighting up in prohibited places. **Litter**: Littering means a fine of up to S$1,000. **Jaywalking**: although less rigorously enforced than it used to be, crossing the road where you're not meant to – ie within 50m of a pedestrian crossing, bridge or underpass – could cost S$500.

Tipping Tipping is unusual in Singapore. Most international hotels and restaurants add 10% service charge and 4% government tax to bills. Only tip for special personal service such as porters.

Shopping

See page 430 for details.

Safety

Singapore is probably the safest big city in Southeast Asia – women travelling alone need have few worries. It is wise, however to take the normal precautions and not wander into lonely places after dark.

Health

Vaccinations: none required for Singapore. Vaccination services are available at the Government Vaccination Centre, Institute of Health, 226 Outram Road, T 2227711. **Malaria**: malarial mosquitoes have long been banished from the island – although there are regular outbreaks of dengue (transmitted by the Aedes, or tiger, mosquito). **Food and water**: the water in Singapore, most of which is pumped across the causeway from Johor, but is treated in Singapore, is clean and safe to drink straight from the tap.

   Medical facilities: Singapore's medical facilities are amongst the best in the world. See the *Yellow Pages* for listing of public and private hospitals. Medical insurance is recommended. Hospitals are experienced in dealing with obscure tropical diseases and serious cases are flown here from all over the region. Most big hotels have their own doctor on 24-hour call. Other doctors are listed under 'Medical Practitioners' in the *Yellow Pages*. Pharmaceuticals are readily available over the counter. The *Singapore Medical Centre*, on the 6th Floor of Tanglin Shopping Centre houses a large community of specialist doctors. Local **Chinese cures** can be found in traditional clinics in Chinatown where there are medical halls and acupuncture centres. Acupuncturists and herbalists are listed in the Yellow Pages.

Emergencies
Police: T 999. **Ambulance or fire brigade**: T 995.

Best time to visit
There is no best season to visit Singapore. It gets even hotter and stickier before the monsoon breaks in Nov, and wetter (but cooler) in Dec and Jan.

Clothing
Singapore is smart but casual dress-wise. It is rare to find places insisting on jacket and tie – although jeans and T-shirts are taboo at some nightclubs. Flip-flops, singlets and denim cut-offs look out of place in Singapore, where the locals treat Orchard Road like the national catwalk.

Official time
8 hrs ahead of GMT.

Hours of business
Banks: normal banking hours are from 1000-1500 Mon-Fri, 0930-1130 Sat. Most banks handle travellers' cheques and currency exchange. Some, however, do not offer foreign exchange dealings on Saturdays. **Shops**: most shops in the tourist belt open around 0930-2100. In the Orchard and Scotts road area, Sunday is a normal working day.

Money
Local currency is dollars and cents. Bank notes are available in denominations of S$1, 2, 5, 10, 20, 50, 100, 500, 1,000 and 10,000. Coins are in 1, 5, 10, 20 and 50 cent and 1 dollar denominations. Singapore is the first country in the world to have plastic notes. In July 1992, the Singapore dollar was valued at 1.62 to the US dollar. Brunei currency is interchangeable with Singapore currency; the Malaysian Ringgit is not.

It is possible to change money at banks, licenced money changers and hotels – although they sometimes add on a service charge. Licenced money-changers often give a better rates than banks, but it is worth shopping around. Passports are required for cashing travellers' cheques or getting cash-advances on credit cards. Singapore is one of the major banking centres of Southeast Asia so it is relatively easy to get money wired from home.

Credit cards: most of Singapore's hotels, shops, restaurants and banks accept the big international credit cards, and some down-town cash machines allow you to draw cash on Visa or Mastercard. After bargaining, expect to pay at least 3% for credit card transactions; most shops insist on this surcharge although you do not have to pay it. **Notification of credit card loss**: American Express, T 2358133; Diners Card, T 2944222; Master Card, T 5332888; Visa, T 2249033.

Weights and measures
Metric.

Voltage
220-240 volts, 50 cycle AC, most hotels can supply adaptors.

Postal services
Local postal charges: start at 20¢, aerograms, 35¢. **International postal charges**: 30¢ (postcard), 75¢ (letter, log). **Post office opening hours**: 0830-1700 Mon-Fri, 0830-1300 Sat. Orchard Point and Changi Airport, 0800-2000 Mon-Sun. **Fax and telex services**: all post offices have facilities for outgoing messages. To receive faxes, the sender must contact the fax bureau in your home country. Pages will then be faxed to the *Singapore Fax Bureau*, Crosby House, Robinson Road, T 2223600. The Singapore Post Office provides four sizes of sturdy carton, called Postpacs, for sending parcels abroad. These can be bought cheaply at all post offices. **Poste Restante**: Poste Restante Service, General Post Office, Fullerton Building, Singapore 0104. Correspondents should write the family name in capital letters and underline it to avoid confusion.

Telephone services
Local: in public phones the minimum charge is 10¢. Card phones are being installed – cards can be bought in all post offices and from the 24-hour telecom counters at the General Post Office in Fullerton Square and the Comms Centre in Exeter Road. **Directory enquiries**: T 103, and for operator-assisted and collect calls, T 104. **Calls to Malaysia**: T 109. Operators all speak English. **International**: in contrast to many other countries in the region, Singapore Telecom offers a very efficient service. Singapore's IDD code is 65. For long distance calls dial 162 for details on country codes. International calls can be made from public phones with the red 'Worldphone' sign; these phones take 50¢ and S$1 coins.

Media
Newspapers/Magazines: the press is privately owned and legally free but is carefully

monitored and strictly controlled. The Singapore press runs on Confucianist principles – respect for one's elders – which translates as unwavering support of the government. In the past, papers that were judged to have overstepped their mark, such as the former *Singapore Herald*, have been shut down. English language dailies are: *The Straits Times* (and *The Sunday Times*) which runs better foreign news pages than any other regional newspaper. *The Business Times* and *The New Paper* – Singapore's very own tabloid. In 1989 the *The Straits Times* banned the use of pseudonyms on its letters page, and all would-be correspondents are vetted for authenticity before their letters are published. This has proved an effective form of censorship although as Singaporeans have got braver, with the emergence of a more relaxed government, more letters, critical of the government, have appeared. Walter Woon, an outspoken law lecturer at the National University of Singapore, believes the Singapore media is now entering a new period of *glasnost*, although it is extremely unlikely that the government will allow a truly free press.

The international press is rigorously monitored and, due to its aversion to criticism, the government has traditionally kept foreign journalists on a short leash. Having watched correspondents being unceremoniously expelled and a number of legal battles go the government's way, some foreign publications have given up caring about their Singapore circulation. A rift between the government and the New York-based Dow Jones meant that *The Asian Wall Street Journal's* circulation was heavily restricted until 1991; and only a few officially pirated copies of the *Far Eastern Economic Review* are on sale in NTUC supermarkets. *Asiaweek* and *Time* have both had their circulations curtailed in the past, although the former kowtowed sufficiently to the government and was allowed unrestricted circulation of its English and Chinese-language editions. International editions of most leading foreign newspapers are available however. Most international news and business magazines can be found in bookshops and on news stands. Many other US, Australian and European general interest glossies are also on sale. Pornographic publications are strictly prohibited under Singapore's Obscene Publications Act.

Television: Channels 5, 8 and 12 show English, Chinese, Malay and Tamil programmes; most sets also receive Malaysian channels. Many large hotel TV sets are linked with the teletext system which has information on entertainment, sports, finance, aircraft arrivals and departures, and special events from 0700-2400. Programmes for all channels are listed in the daily newspapers. CNN international news is broadcast daily at 1900 on SBC 12. BBC World Service TV is also negotiating for some air-time on the SBC network.

Radio: daily services in English and Chinese from 0600-2400, in Malay from 0445-2400 and Tamil from 0500-2100. There are 5 local radio stations and 2 on nearby Batam Island which blast rock music across the Straits of Singapore. **The BBC World Service**: broadcasts 24 hours a day on FM 88.9 thanks to an old British forces transmitter. The 'London Calling' programme guide is available from bookshops.

Language

The official languages are Malay, Chinese (Mandarin), Tamil and English. Interestingly, Malay is the national language and English, the language of administration. Because of the republic's importance as an international trade centre, there is a high standard of English in business. Many dialects of Chinese are also spoken although the government's 'Speak Mandarin' campaign has begun to change this. Most Singaporeans speak their own version of English, which is dubbed 'Singlish', and is an English patois full of curious Chinese and Malay-inspired idiosyncracies and phonetic peculiarities.

As in neighbouring Malaysia, *'lah'* is a favourite suffix to just about any sentence. The words *'izzit'* and *'izzinit'* also figure prominently at the end of sentences – albeit for no particular reason. *'Wah!'* is a typical Singlish expression of surprise, horror, delight and disappointment. Singlish is generally spoken at high speed and incorporates numerous syntactical contortions, designed to make the language virtually unintelligible to the first-time visitor. The most commonly used words and phrases of Singapore's lingua-franca are linguistically related to 'Manglish', the mangled English dialect spoken across the causeway. Malaysian satirist Kit Leee has unravelled its complex vocabulary and phraseology in his book *Adoi* (**see page 364**).

Tourist information

The main **Singapore Tourist Promotion Board** (STPB) office is at: 36-04 Raffles City Tower, 250 North Bridge Road, T 3396622. There are also two STPB tourist information centres, one at Raffles City (01-19), T 3300431 (open 0830-1800), and the other in Scotts Shopping Centre (02-02/03), T 7383778, on Scotts Road (open 0930-2130). They are all very helpful, supplying brochures and maps. Complaints can also be registered at these offices. **Maps**: American Express/Singapore Tourist Board Map of Singapore and The Map of Singapore endorsed by the Singapore Hotel Association. Both available from the STPB office. **Guides**: *The Singapore*

Official Guide and the STPB's *Singapore Tour it Yourself* are available from STPB offices. STA Travel in the *Orchard Parade Hotel* on Tanglin Road, T 7345681, or at the Singapore Polytechnic, (next to Canteen 5), Dover Road, T 7742270, is Singapore's top student and youth (under 26) travel centre, offering student fares, discounted tours and budget accommodation. *Street Smart Singapore*, David Brazil.

Suggested reading
Novels/biography: Anderson, P *Snake Wine: A Singapore Episode*; Bloodworth, D *The Tiger and the Trojan Horse*; Clavell, James *King Rat*; Collis, M *Raffles*; Farrell, J G *The Singapore Grip*; Grenfell, R *Main Fleet to Singapore*; McCormac, C *You'll Die in Singapore*; Michin, J *No Man is an Island*; Swinstead, G *Singapore Stopover*; Theroux, P *Saint Jack*; Wise, M *Traveller's Tales of Old Singapore*; Barber, Noel *Tanamera*. **History:** Turnbull, C M *A History of Malaysia, Singapore and Brunei*. **Maps:** *Nelles Map of Singapore*, 1:22500; *Secret Map of Singapore*; *Secret Food Map of Singapore*.

Acknowledgements
Joe Casey, Ireland.

BRUNEI

	Page		Page
Introduction	457	Parks and Walks	483
Bandar Seri Begawan	475	Information for visitors	484
Around Brunei	481		

Maps: Country Map, 460; Bandar Seri Begawan, 477.

INTRODUCTION

The microscopic Sultanate of Brunei lays claim to one of the most dramatic rags-to-riches stories of all time. Its now-legendary oil-wealth rests on a stroke of geological luck. Had it not been for oil, the Sultan of Brunei would probably be struggling to make ends meet as a member of the Federation of Malaysia's minor nobility. In the early 1900s, the kingpin of Brunei's industrial economy was the Kampung Subok cutch (or gambier) factory, hidden in the mangrove swamps on the shores of Brunei Bay. This obscure dye produced at Subok – extracted from the bark of the *bakau* mangrove tree, and used in the tanning of leather – accounted for 90% of Brunei's exports. For the average Bruneian, life had changed little in centuries. The once-great trading empire, which in its heyday held sway over vast tracts of Borneo and beyond, had crumbled. For generations, the sultanate had been sandwiched, squeezed and bullied by marauding pirates and successive colonial and commercial adventurers.

Today, the citizens of this oil-rich sultanate are the wealthiest people in the Asia-Pacific region after the Japanese. The paternalistic government directly employs a third of the workforce, and ensures they are the best-paid bureaucrats in the world. Few Bruneian Malays want to work in the private sector and certainly none as manual labourers – but foreign migrants willingly flock to Southeast Asia's El Dorado to fill the gap.

Bruneians bask in the munificence of their autocratic monarch – whose personal fortune is estimated at US$25 billion – and his government, whose treasury is overflowing with the profits of Brunei Shell Petroleum. The sultanate has been dubbed a 'Shell-fare state': Bruneians do not pay income tax, enjoy free education, medical care and old-age pensions. And if one of the Faithful cannot afford the pilgrimage to Mecca, the government is happy to subsidize it.

Sultan Hassanal Bolkiah has kept the lid on political dissent – which has not erupted since an abortive revolt in 1962 – by, according to some commentators, buying the loyalty of his subjects. The hedonistic monarch (see profile, below) appears to have no trouble reconciling his extravagant, cosmopolitan lifestyle with

The Sultan of Brunei – living by the profit

When Hassanal Bolkiah was crowned the 29th Sultan of Brunei, in August 1968, at the age of 21, a barrel of oil cost US$1.33. As oil prices rocketed in the wake of the 1973 oil crisis, so did the Sultan's fortune. *Fortune* magazine and *The Guinness Book of Records* rate him the richest man in the world. His personal wealth was recently assessed at US$37 billion – 3 times that of Queen Elizabeth II. It is believed that he earns more than US$100 a second – or US$2 billion a year.

As befitting the man with the biggest bank account in the world, the biggest palace in the world, and head of the second oldest dynasty in the world (after Japan), Sultan Bolkiah also has a long name. The official version, even when condensed, is an alphabet soup of acronyms and honorifics:

> His Majesty Paduka Seri Baginda Sultan and Yang Di-Pertuan, Sultan Hassanal Bolkiah Mu'izzaddin Waddaulah Ibni Al-Marhum Sultan Haji Omar Ali Saifuddien Sa'adul Khairi Waddien, DKMB, DK, PSSUB, DPKG, DPKT, PSPNB, PSNB, PSLJ, SPMB, PANB, GCMG, DMN, DK (Kelantan), DK (Johor), DK (Negri Sembilan), Collar of the Supreme Order of the Chrysanthemum, Grand Order of the Mugunghwa, DK (Pahang), BRI, Collar of the Nile, the Order of Al-Hussein bin Ali, the Civil Order of Oman, DK (Selangor), DK (Perlis), PGAT, Sultan and Yang Di-Pertuan Negara Brunei Darussalam.

Sultan Hassanal Bolkiah was named after the fifth Sultan of Brunei, who presided over Brunei's golden age. He was sent to boarding school at Kuala Lumpur's Victoria Institution, which was modelled on the British public school. He was not academically inclined, and in 1965, on his return from Malaysia, married his cousin, Princess Saleha. A year later, he was dispatched to the Royal Military Academy at Sandhurst in England, but was unable to attend his own passing-out parade, due to his father's sudden abdication in October 1967. He was gazetted as a captain and returned, unwillingly, to Brunei to become Sultan. 5 years later, he was knighted by Queen Elizabeth II, and on independence in 1984, was awarded the rank of major-general.

The Sultan now has 2 wives – the most recent, Queen Mariam Bell, is a former airline hostess. She is quarter British, quarter Japanese and half Bruneian, and a commoner. To the chagrin of his father, Hassanal Bolkiah married her secretly in 1981. He has 2 sons and 4 daughters by his first wife, Queen Saleha, and a son and 2 daughters by Queen Mariam.

The Sultan insists that the assertions about his wealth are an exaggeration. But it is very difficult to separate his private fortune from that of the state. His unauthorized biographer James Bartholomew writes: "Brunei is a private country run like a private possession... The line between his personal wealth and that of the state is far from clear." A government committee determines the Sultan's salary – as Head of State, Prime Minister and Minister of Defence – which is separate from his family inheritance, private funds and investments. However, state funds were allegedly used to purchase London's Dorchester Hotel in 1985 for £88 million, and to fund the construction of the Sultan's palace, the Istana Nurul Iman in Bandar Seri Begawan.

the strictures of Islam – as ruler, he is the head of the Islamic faith. Good salaries and creature comforts have, however, politically lobotomized a people who might otherwise rebel against a monarchical system which appears to be out of step with the 20th century.

Brunei Darussalam – the country's official name – means 'Abode of Peace' and life is indeed very peaceful in the sultanate. In some diplomatic and governmental circles, the capital, Bandar Seri Begawan, is known as the 'Geneva of ASEAN', ostensibly because of its generous hospitality budget; but Brunei is also dull and expensive.

He developed a soft spot for fast cars and now owns about 350. He also has a personal fleet of aircraft – including a private Airbus, Gulfstream executive jet and a helicopter. Before he abandoned his polo-playing image, he used to hire freelance Argentinian polo stars to play in his polo teams in the same way he hires Gurkha 'mercenaries' from the British army to defend his sultanate. Sultan Hassanal Bolkiah also has a penchant for glitzy hotels, of which he has several around the world.

He has not been so successful in his forays onto the world stage. In 1986, at the request of former US President Ronald Reagan, the Sultan agreed to contribute 'humanitarian aid' of US$10 million to the right-wing Nicaraguan Contra rebels. The funds were wired to a Swiss bank account set up by Colonel Oliver North. The money was accidentally deposited in the wrong account; that of a Swiss businessman, who promptly moved his windfall to another bank. Because the Sultan forgot to notify Washington that the money had been sent, its loss went unnoticed for 3 months. It was finally returned to the embarrassed Sultan in mid-1987, amid much publicity.

Sultan Hassanal Bolkiah seems genuinely bemused by the attention accorded him by gossip columnists in the West who have consistently cast him as a spendthrift, polygamous, polo-playing Oriental potentate with dubious acquaintances – among them, Adnan Khashoggi, the Al-Fayed brothers (of Harrods fame) and an Indian swami. To counter their muck-raking tendencies, he hired Shandwick plc, a British public relations firm in 1987 to bolster Brunei's image abroad. He also commissioned Shandwick's director, Lord Alun Chalfont to write a hagiography: *By God's Will: a portrait of the Sultan of Brunei.* Chalfont writes: "He has had to put up with the routine distortions, and sometimes straight inventions, of Fleet Street gossip columnists and others who trawl the fashionable shopping areas of London collecting rumours and anecdotes."

Recently the Sultan has undergone a change of image – possibly orchestrated by Shandwick. The *Far Eastern Economic Review* says he has been moving to assert himself as a religiously inclined, caring monarch. He has even abandoned polo in favour of the less-elitist games of badminton and golf. Any softening might well be in response to fears about internal security: local broadcasters have been instructed to play down news reports about violent coups elsewhere in the world. Sultan Hassanal Bolkish celebrated 25 years on the throne in October 1992. He was pulled through the streets of BSB on a 23m-long chariot made of gilded teak to the strains of 'Colonel Bogey'. In the evening he hosted a banquet at his palace for 5,000 guests. In a speech to mark the occasion, he said Brunei "has proven that the system of monarchy, which we have practised all along, is strong and has been successful in bringing benefits to the people".

The Sultan's fiefdom has featured on seafarers' maps of Southeast Asia for over a millennium, the first documented mention of Brunei being a Chinese trader's account of P'o-ni (Brunei) in the 9th century. The name 'Brunei' is said to derive from the Sanskrit *Varunai*, meaning 'sea-people'. In the 19th century, when the White Rajahs of Sarawak had their eyes on the Sultan's territory, Brunei was known as 'Borneo Proper'. The name 'Borneo' itself may be a European cartographer's corruption of the word Brunei – although Iban folklore has it that 'Borneo' derives from the Malay *buah nyiur* – meaning coconut.

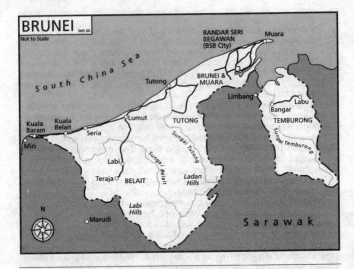

ENVIRONMENT

Brunei Darussalam lies about 400 km N of the equator, between 4° and 5° N, on the NW coast of Borneo. The sultanate has a 160 km-long coastline, facing the South China Sea. The country is divided into 4 districts: Brunei/Muara, Tutong, Belait and Temburong.

Land

Territorially, modern Brunei is the rump of what was once a sprawling empire. Today the sultanate has a land area of 5,769 sq km – a pinprick on the map, about twice the size of Luxembourg. In 1981 the government bought a cattle ranch at Willeroo, in Australia's Northern Territory, which is larger than the whole of Brunei. As a country, it is a geographical absurdity; its 2 wedges of territory are separated by Limbang, ceded to the expansionist Charles Brooke, Rajah of Sarawak in 1890. Bruneians commute between the Temburong district and Bandar Seri Begawan in speedboats nicknamed 'flying coffins'.

Most of Brunei occupies a low alluvial coastal plain. There are 4 main rivers, flowing N into the South China Sea. The coastal lowlands and river valleys are characterized by a flat or gently undulating landscape, rarely rising more than 15m above sea level. The coastline is mainly sandy except for a stretch of rocky headlands between Muara and Pekan Tutong. These cliffs rise to a height of about 30m, where the N coastal hills meet the South China Sea. Further W, the Andulau Hills stand at the N end of a watershed separating the Belait and Tutong drainage basins.

Towards the interior of W Brunei, along the border with Sarawak and in S Temburong district, it gets much hillier. In W Brunei there are 2 upland areas: the Ladan Hills run N to S between the Tutong and Limbang basins. Bukit Bedawan is the highest of these, at 529m. In Belait district, near the border with Sarawak, are the Labi Hills – the highest being Bukit Teraja at 417m. The S half of Temburong district is much more mountainous, with deep, narrow valleys and several hills of over 600m. The highest of these is Bukit Pagon at 1,850m, although the summit itself is actually outside Brunei.

Geology The Seria oilfield, the source of Brunei's liquidity, lies on a narrow anticline, a quarter of which is submerged by the sea. All the oil comes from a strip just 13 km long and 2.5 km wide. The oil is in fractured blocks of sandstone between 240m and 3,000m below the surface. Some of the oil under the sea is accessed by wells drilled from the shore which reach more than 1.5 km out to sea. The oil has a low sulphur content (**see page 472**).

Brunei's upland areas are comprised of sandstones and shale.

Climate

Brunei is only 5° N of the equator and so is characterized, like the rest of N and W Borneo, by consistently hot and sticky weather: uniform temperature, high humidity (average: 82%) and regular rainfall.

Daily temperatures average between 22°C and 28°C. Mid-day temperatures rarely exceed 35°C; at night it is unusual for the temperature to dip below 21°C. The average daily minimum temperature is 23°C, the maximum 32°C.

Rainfall is well distributed throughout the year but 2 seasons are distinguishable: there is less rainfall between Feb and Aug, and the rainy season sets in during September and runs through to the end of January. The NE monsoon peaks in Dec and Jan and is characterized by short-lived, violent downpours. Even during the monsoon season, though, there is a 50% chance of it not raining each day and a daily average of 7 hrs of sunshine. The annual average rainfall is over 2,500 mm a year, nearly 5 times that of London. The S interior region, including Temburong district, is wetter, with up to 4,060 mm a year. The W coast areas get between 2,540 and 3,300 mm of rainfall a year. In Bandar Seri Begawan, the average annual rainfall is 2,921 mm.

Flora and fauna

(For more detail on jungle flora and fauna, see Introduction to Borneo, **page 224**). Like much of the neighbouring Malaysian state of Sarawak, the low-lying areas of Brunei are characterized by peat swamp forest which is unsuited to agriculture. In parts the peat is up to 9m thick and cannot support permanent agriculture. Over three-quarters of Brunei is still covered in lush virgin jungle. If secondary forest – known as *belukar* – is included, about 85% of Brunei's land area is still forested.

Apart from the peat swamp forest, Brunei has areas of heath forest (*kerangas*) on sandy soils near the coast, and mangrove, which grows on the tidal mudflats around Brunei Bay and in the Belait and Tutong estuaries. The most common mangrove tree is the bakau, which grows to a height of about 9m and has stilt roots to trap sediment. The bakau was the source of cutch – a dye made from boiling its bark, and used in leather-tanning – which was produced at Brunei Bay until the 1950s. Bakau wood also made useful piles for stilt-houses in Bandar Seri Begawan's Kampung Ayer as it is resistant to rotting, and excellent charcoal. Also on the coast, between Kuala Belait and Muara, are stretches of casuarina forest.

Away from the coastal plain and the river valleys, the forest changes to lowland rainforest – or mixed dipterocarp forest – which supports at least 8 commercial hardwood species. The *Dipterocarpacae* family forms the jungle canopy, 30-50m above the ground. Timber from Brunei's jungle is used locally – none is exported. By 1990, logging firms were required to use sustainable management techniques and within a year, felling was cut to half the 1989 level. Forest reserves have been expanded and cover 320,000 ha.

Wildlife Brunei's jungle has been left largely intact – thanks to Brunei's oil wealth there is no need to exploit the forest. Loggers and shifting cultivators have been less active than they have in neighbouring territories and the forest fauna have been less disturbed. Their only disruptions come from a few upriver tribespeople, a handful of wandering Penan hunter-gatherers, the odd scientist and the occasional platoon of muddied soldiers enduring jungle warfare training exercises. Tourists rarely venture into Brunei's jungle as Sarawak's nearby national parks are much more accessible and better known. For those who have access to a car, however, there are several jungle trails on Brunei's doorstep (see Parks and walks, **page 483**).

Brunei boasts most of Borneo's jungle exotica. For oil explorers and their families in the early 1900s, some local residents proved more daunting than others. Up until the 1960s, encounters with large crocodiles were commonplace in Brunei, and in the oil town of Seria they posed a constant menace to the local community. In August 1959 Brunei Shell Petroleum was forced to recruit a professional crocodile-catcher. Mat Yassin bin Hussin claimed to have caught and destroyed more than 700 crocodiles in a career spanning 4 decades, the largest being a highly unlikely 8.5m long man-eater which had devoured 12 Ibans S of Kuala Belait.

Mat Yassin's technique was to sprinkle gold dust into the river as part of a magic ritual, then to dangle chickens over bridges on baited rattan hooks. According to G C Harper, a Seria oilfield historian, Mat Yassin would wait until a crocodile jumped for the bait and then he would "blow down its snout with the aid of a blowpipe to make the strong reptile weak. It could then be dragged up the river bank and its jaws tied before it was destroyed." Mat Yassin silenced cynics when he landed 2 maneaters in as many days and said he had come across an old white crocodile which was considered sacred; he refused to touch it because it "could never be destroyed either by bullets or by magic".

HISTORY

Brunei's early history is obscure – but although precise dates have been muddied by time, there is no doubt that the sultanate's early prosperity was rooted in trade. As far back as the 7th century, China was importing birds' nests from Brunei, and Arab, Indian, Chinese and other Southeast Asian traders were regularly passing through. Links with Chinese merchants were strongest: they traded silk, metals, stoneware and porcelain for Brunei's jungle produce: bezoar stones, hornbill-ivory, timber and birds' nests. Chinese coins dating from the 8th century have been unearthed at Kota Batu, 3 km from Bandar Seri Begawan. Large quantities of Chinese porcelain dating from the Tang, Sung and Ming dynasties have also been found. A Chinese trader mentioned P'o-ni – a Sinified transliteration of Brunei – in an account of his travels in the 9th century. The sultanate was on the main trade route between China and the western reaches of the Malayan archipelago and by the Chinese Sung Dynasty, in the 10th to 13th centuries, trade was booming. By the turn of the 15th century there was a sizeable Chinese population settled in Brunei.

With the decline of the Srivijayan Empire (based at Palembang, Sumatra) in the late 13th century, the Thai kingdom of Sukhothai and the Hindu empire of Majapahit, centred on E Java, were on the rise. Brunei and W Borneo became tributary states of the Majapahit empire in the 1300s. As the Brunei royal chronicles only list the names of rulers and not their dates, it is impossible to establish specific dates for the origin of the Sultanate. However, it is thought that some time around 1370 Sultan Mohammad became first Sultan.

In the mid-1400s, Sultan Awang Alak ber Tabar, married a Melakan princess and converted to Islam. Brunei already had substantial trade links with Melaka and exported camphor, rice, gold and sago in exchange for Indian textiles. But it was not until an Arab, Sharif Ali, married Sultan Awang Alak's niece, that Islam spread beyond the confines of the royal household. Sharif Ali – who is said to have descended from the Prophet Mohammad – became Sultan Berkat, and was responsible for consolidating Islam, converting the townspeople, building mosques and setting up a legal system based on Islamic Sharia law. Trade flourished and Brunei assumed the epithet 'Darussalam' – 'the abode of peace'. The oldest tombstone in Brunei dates from 1432 – or the Islamic Hijra equivalent – indicating that by then, Islam had already made its mark.

The golden years

The very first rajahs of Brunei are likely to have been Bisayas or Muruts. Bruneians only became known as 'Malays' as they converted to Islam – there is no evidence to suggest that Malays migrated to N Borneo from Sumatra. The coastal Melanaus quickly embraced the Muslim faith, but tribal groups in the interior were largely unaffected by the spread of Islam and retained their animist beliefs. As Islam spread along the coasts of N and W Borneo, the sultanate expanded its political and commercial sphere of influence. By the 16th century, communities all along the coasts of present-day Sabah and Sarawak were paying tribute to the Sultan. The sultanate became the centre of a minor empire whose influence stretched beyond the coasts of Borneo to many surrounding islands, including the Sulu archipelago and Mindanao in the Philippines. Even Manila had to pay tribute to the Sultan's court.

The first half of the 16th century, under Sultan Bolkiah and Sultan Hassan, was Brunei's golden age. The latter was the 9th sultan; he vigorously resisted European territorial encroachments. One of the ways he did this was by formalizing Brunei's political and hierarchical administrative system – based on the tenets of Islam – which lent the Sultanate internal cohesion. Sultan Hassan's system still forms the basis of Brunei's government.

On 8 July 1521 Antonio Pigafetta, an Italian historian on Portuguese explorer Ferdinand Magellan's expedition, visited the Sultanate of Brunei and described it as a rich, hospitable and powerful kingdom with an established Islamic monarchy and strong regional influence. Pigafetta published his experiences in his book, *The First Voyage Around the World*. He records the existence of a sophisticated royal court and the lavishly decorated Sultan's palace. Brunei Town was reported to be a large, wealthy city of 25,000 households. The townspeople lived in houses built on stilts over the water. Returning today, Pigafetta would find it little changed – apart from the Mercedes' and BMWs parked nose to tail along the riverfront.

When Melaka fell to the Portuguese in 1511, Muslim merchants turned to Brunei instead, although the Sultan was careful to maintain good relations with the Portuguese. In 1526 the Portuguese set up a trading post in Brunei, and from there conducted trade with the Moluccas – the famed Spice Islands – via Brunei. At the same time, more Chinese traders immigrated to Brunei, to service the booming trade between Melaka and Macau and to trade with Pattani on the S Thai isthmus.

But relations with the Spaniards were not so warm; the King of Spain and the Sultan of Brunei had mutually exclusive interests in the Philippines. In the 1570s Spaniards attacked several important Muslim centres and in March 1578, the captain-general of the Philippines, Francesco de Sande, led a naval expedition to Brunei, demanding the Sultan pay tribute to Spain and allow Roman Catholic missionaries to proselytize. The Sultan would have none of it and a battle ensued off Muara, which the Spaniards won. They captured the city, but within days the victors were stopped in their tracks by a cholera epidemic and had to withdraw. In 1579 they returned and once again did battle off Muara, but this time they were defeated.

The sun sets on an empire

Portugal came under Spanish rule in 1580, and Brunei lost a valuable European ally: the sultanate was raided by the Spanish again in 1588 and 1645. But by then

Brunei's golden age was history and the Sultan's grip on his further-flung dependencies had begun to slip. The Sultan of Sulu had asserted his independence and Brunei was even losing its influence over its Borneo territories. It was to go downhill for a further 2 centuries.

In the 1660s, civil war erupted in Brunei due to feuding between princes and together with additional external pressures of European expansionism, the once mighty sultanate all but collapsed. Only a handful of foreign merchants dealt with the sultanate and Chinese traders passed it by. Balanini pirates from Sulu and Illanun pirates from Mindanao posed a constant threat to the Sultan and any European traders or adventurers foolhardy enough to take them on (**see page 233**). In return for protection from these sea-borne terrorists, the Sultan offered the British East India Company a base on the island of Labuan in Brunei Bay in the late 1600s – although the trading post failed to take off.

For 150 years, Brunei languished in obscurity. By the early 1800s, Brunei's territory did not extend much beyond the town boundaries, although the Sarawak River, and the W coastal strip of N Borneo officially remained under the Sultan's sway. Historian Mary Turnbull writes: "Brunei town was little more than a centre for pirates' loot and slaves, a shrunken shadow of its former self." Within a period of 50 years, its population had been reduced by three-quarters: by the 1830s it was just 10,000, compared to Penang's 125,000.

James Brooke – the man who would be king

The collection of mini-river states that made up what was left of the Sultanate were ruled by the *pangiran*, the lesser nobles of the Brunei court. In the 1830s Brunei chiefs had gone to the Sarawak valley to organize the mining and trade in the high-grade antimony ore which had been discovered there in 1824. They recruited Dayaks as workers and founded Kuching. But, with the support of local Malay chiefs, the Dayaks rebelled against one of the Brunei noblemen, the corrupt, Pangiran Makota, one of the Rajah's 14 brothers. By all accounts, Makota was a nasty piece of work, known for his exquisite charm and diabolical cunning.

It was into this troubled riverine mini-state, in armed rebellion against Makota, that the English adventurer James Brooke sailed in 1839 (see box, **page 234**). Robert Payne, in his book *The White Rajahs of Sarawak*, describes Makota as a "princely racketeer" and "a man of satanic gifts, who practised crimes for pleasure". Makota confided to Brooke: "I was brought up to plunder the Dayaks, and it makes me laugh to think that I have fleeced a tribe down to its cooking-pots." With Brooke's arrival, Makota realized his days were numbered.

In 1837, the Sultan of Brunei, Omar Ali Saiffuddin, had dispatched his uncle, Pengiran Muda Hashim, to contain the rebellion. He failed, and turned to Brooke for help. In return for his services, Brooke demanded to be made Governor of Sarawak. After vacillating for several years, Hashim abdicated, ceding Sarawak and its dependencies to "the well-born James Brooke" in September 1841. The new Rajah promptly left for Brunei Town to have the transfer of power rubber stamped by the Sultan of Brunei, Omar Ali Saifuddin II, whom he mistook as a harmless lunatic. In reality, Sultan Omar was cool and cunning. This is how Robert Payne describes him:

> "Like Prince Makota, the Sultan was one of those men who appear to belong to legend rather than to history. He was the incarnation of murderous imbecility. He was over 50, a small, thin, bald man, who could neither read nor write; he had 3 thumbs, having an extra thumb, like a small claw, on his right hand. He suffered from cancer of the mouth, his arms and legs were painfully thin, and he wore an expression of permanent confusion. He was dressed in purple satin and cloth-of-gold, and wore a gold-headed kriss at his waist. James was fascinated by the monster, who talked continually, often joked, and was unable to concentrate on a serious matter for more than a few seconds. Given handsome presents, he kept asking for more."

After he had been formally installed in his new role by Sultan Omar, Brooke set about building his own empire. In 1848 he said: "I am going in these revolutionary times to get up a league and covenant between all the good rivers of the coast, to the purpose that they will not pay revenue or obey the government of Brunei..." Brooke exploited rivalries between various aristocratic factions of Brunei's royal court which climaxed in the murder of Pengiran Muda Hashim and his family.

No longer required in Sarawak, Hashim had returned to Brunei to become Chief Minister and heir apparent. He was murdered along with 11 other princes and their families, by Sultan Omar. The Sultan and his advisers had felt threatened by their presence, so they disposed of Hashim to prevent a coup. The massacre incensed Brooke. In June 1846, his British ally, Admiral Sir Thomas Cochrane bombarded Brunei Town, set it ablaze and chased the Sultan into the jungle.

Cochrane wanted to proclaim Brooke Sultan of Brunei, but decided, in the end, to offer Sultan Omar protection if he cleaned up his act and demonstrated his loyalty to Queen Victoria. After several weeks, the humiliated Sultan emerged from the jungle and swore undying loyalty to the Queen. As penance, Sultan Omar formally ceded the island of Labuan to the British crown on 18 December 1846. The brow-beaten Sultan pleaded proneness to sea sickness in an effort to avoid having to witness the hoisting of the Union Jack on Labuan Island. Although Brunei forfeited more territory in handing Labuan to the British, the Sultan calculated that he would benefit from a direct relationship with Whitehall. It seemed that London was becoming almost as concerned as he was about Brooke's expansionist instincts. A Treaty of Friendship and Commerce was signed between Britain and Brunei in 1847 in which the Sultan agreed not to cede any more territory to any power, except with the consent of the British government.

The Sultan's shrinking shadow
The treaty did not stop Brooke. His mission, since arriving in Sarawak, had been the destruction of the pirates who specialized in terrorising Borneo's coastal communities. Because he knew the Sultan of Brunei was powerless to contain them, he calculated that their liquidation would be his best bargaining chip with the Sultan, and would enable him to prise yet more territory from the Sultan's grasp. Over the years he engaged the dreaded Balanini and Illanun pirates from Sulu and Mindanao as well as the so-called Sea-Dayaks and Brunei Malays, who regularly attacked Chinese, Bugis and other Asian trading ships off the Borneo coast.

At the battle of Batang Maru in 1849, Brooke annihilated a Saribas Dayak pirate fleet, sinking 87 of their 98 boats and killing more than 1,500 pirates. As a result of this, Sultan Abdul Mumin of Brunei ceded to him the Saribas and Skrang districts, which became the Second Division of Sarawak in 1853. Eight years later, the Sultan was in trouble with the Illanun pirates, who were wreaking havoc with the profitable sago trade W of Bintulu. Brooke successfully persuaded the Sultan to hand the region over to him and it became the Third Division of Sarawak. The Illanun raided for the last time in 1862. From 1868, James Brooke's successor, Rajah Charles Brooke, attempted to further erode the Sultan's territory, but by this stage even the British were becoming wary of the White Rajahs' expansionism. London rejected Brooke's 1874 proposal that it should make the Sultanate a protectorate.

But by now the Sultan was as worried about territorial encroachment by the British as he was about the Brookes and as a counterweight to both, granted a 10-year concession to much of what is modern-day Sabah to the American consul in Brunei, Charles Lee Moses. This 72,500 sq km tract of N Borneo later became British North Borneo and is now the East Malaysian state of Sabah, **see page 295**.

With the emergence of British North Borneo, the British reneged on their agreement with the Sultan of Brunei again and the following year approved Brooke's annexation of the Baram river basin by Sarawak – which became its Fourth Division. The Sarawak frontier was advancing ever-northwards.

In 1884 a rebellion broke out in Limbang and Rajah Charles Brooke refused to help the Sultan restore order. Sultan Hashim Jalilul Alam Aqamaddin, who acceded to the throne in 1885, wrote to Queen Victoria complaining that the British had not kept their word. Sir Frederick Weld was dispatched to mediate; he sympathized with the Sultan, and his visit resulted in the Protectorate Agreement of 1888 between Brunei and Britain, which gave London full control of the Sultanate's external affairs. When Brooke annexed Limbang in 1890 and united it with the Trusan valley to form the Fifth Division of Sarawak, while the Queen's men looked on, the Sultan was reduced to a state of disbelief. His sultanate had now been completely surrounded by Brooke's Sarawak. Some years later the British labelled this a cession by default and recognized Limbang as part of Sarawak.

From sultanate to oilfield

In 1906 a British Resident was appointed to the Sultan's court to advise on all aspects of government except traditional customs and religion. In his book *By God's Will*, Lord Chalfont suggests that the British government's enthusiastic recommitment to the Sultanate through the treaty may have been motivated by Machiavellian desires. "More cynical observers have suggested that the new-found enthusiasm of the British Government may not have been entirely unconnected with the discovery of oil... around the turn of the century." Oil exploration started in 1899, although it was not until the discovery of the Seria oilfield in 1929 that it merited commercial exploitation. Historian Mary Turnbull notes the quirk of destiny that ensured the survival of the micro-sultanate: "It was ironic that the small area left unswallowed by Sarawak and North Borneo should prove to be the most richly endowed part of the old sultanate."

The Brunei oilfield fell to the Japanese on 18 Dec 1942. Allied bombing and Japanese sabotage prior to the sultanate's liberation caused considerable damage to oil and port installations and urban areas, necessitating a long period of reconstruction in the late 1940s and early 1950s. Australian forces landed at Muara Beach on 10 Jul 1945. A British Military Administration ruled the country for a year, before Sultan Sir Ahmad Tajuddin took over.

In 1948 the Governor of Sarawak, which was by then a British crown colony, was appointed High Commissioner for Brunei, but although never a colony itself, the Sultanate remained what one commentator describes as "a constitutional anachronism". In Sept 1959 the United Kingdom resolved this by withdrawing the Resident and signing an agreement with the Sultan giving Whitehall responsibility for Brunei's defence and foreign affairs.

Because of his post-war influence on the development of Brunei, Sultan Omar was variously referred to as the 'father' and 'architect' of modern Brunei. He shaped his sultanate into the anti-Communist, non-democratic state it is today and, being an Anglophile, held out against independence from Britain. By the early 1960s, Whitehall was enthusiastically promoting the idea of a North Borneo Federation, encompassing Sarawak, Brunei and British North Borneo. But Sultan Omar did not want anything to do with the neighbouring territories – he felt Brunei's interests were more in keeping with those of peninsular Malaysia. The proposed federation would have been heavily dependent on Brunei's oil wealth. Kuala Lumpur did not need much persuasion that Brunei's joining the Federation of Malaysia was an excellent idea – probably because Brunei's Malays presented a convenient ethnic counterweight to Singapore's Chinese.

Democrats versus autocrat

In Brunei's first-ever general election in 1962, the left-wing Brunei People's Party (known by its Malay acronym, PRB) swept the polls. The party's election ticket had been an end to the Sultan's autocratic rule, the formation of a democratic government and immediate independence. Aware that there was quite a lot at stake, the Sultan refused to let the PRB form a government. The Sultan's emergency powers, under which he banned the PRB, which were passed in 1962, remain in force, enabling him to rule by decree.

On 8 Dec 1962, the PRB, backed by the Communist North Kalimantan National Army – effectively its military wing – launched a revolt. The Sultan's insistence on British military protection paid off as the disorganized rebellion was quickly put down with the help of a Gurkha infantry brigade, and other British troops. Within 4 days the British troops had pushed the rebels into Limbang, where the hard core holed up. By 12 Dec, the revolt had been crushed and the vast majority of the rebels disappeared into the interior, pursued by the 7th Gurkha Rifles and Kelabit tribesmen.

Early in 1963, negotiations over Brunei joining the Malaysian Federation ran into trouble, to the disappointment of the British. The Malaysian Prime Minister, the late Tunku Abdul Rahman, wanted the Sultanate's oil and gas revenues to feed the federal treasury in Kuala Lumpur and made the mistake of making his intentions too obvious. The Tunku envisaged central government exercising absolute control over oil revenues – in the way it controls the oil wealth of Sabah and Sarawak today. Unhappy with this proposal and unwilling to become 'just another Malaysian sultan', Omar abandoned his intention to join the Federation.

Meanwhile, Indonesia's Sukarno was resolute in his objective of crushing the new Federation of Malaysia and launched his *Konfrontasi* between 1963 and 1966. Brunei offered itself as an operational base for the British army. But while Brunei supported Malaysia against Indonesia, relations between them became very strained following the declaration of the Federation in Sept 1963. Ten years later, Malaysian intelligence services allegedly supported the breakout, by 8 political detainees from the 1962 revolt, from Berakas internment camp. They were given asylum in Malaysia, and were allowed to broadcast anti-Brunei propaganda from Limbang. Libya's Colonel Gadaffi reportedly offered military training to PRB members.

In 1975 Kuala Lumpur sponsored the visit of a PRB delegation to the UN, to propose a resolution calling on Brunei to hold elections, abolish restrictions on political parties and allow political exiles to return. In 1976 Bruneian government supporters protested against Malaysian 'interference' in Bruneian affairs. Nonetheless, the resolution was adopted by the UN in November 1977, receiving 117 votes in favour and none against. The United Kingdom abstained. Relations with Malaysia warmed after the death of Prime Minister Tun Abdul Razak in 1976, leaving the PRB weak and isolated. The party still operates in exile, although it is a spent force. Throughout the difficult years, the Sultan had used his favourite sport to conduct what was dubbed 'polo diplomacy', fostering links with like-minded Malaysian royalty despite the tensions in official bilateral relations.

By 1967, Britain's Labour government was pushing Sultan Omar to introduce a democratic system of government. Instead, however, the Sultan opted to abdicate in favour of his 21-year-old son, Hassanal Bolkiah. In Nov 1971, a new treaty was signed with Britain. London retained its responsibility for Brunei's external affairs, but its advisory role applied only to defence. The Sultan was given full control of all internal matters. Under a separate agreement, a battalion of British Gurkhas was stationed in the Sultanate. As Bruneians grew richer, the likelihood of another revolt receded.

Independence

Britain was keen to disentangle itself from the 1971 agreement: maintaining the protectorate relationship was expensive and left London open to criticism that it was maintaining an anachronistic colonial relationship. Brunei did not particularly relish the prospect of independence as without British protection, it would be at the mercy of its more powerful neighbours. But in Jan 1979, having secured Malaysian and Indonesian assurances that they would respect its independence, the government signed another agreement with London, allowing for the Sultanate to become independent from midnight on 31 Dec 1983 after a century-and-a-half of close involvement with Britain and 96 years as a protectorate.

At a Commonwealth Heads of Government Meeting in 1985 Hassanal Bolkiah explained the sultanate's position:

> "There can be few instances in the history of a relationship between a protecting power and a protected state where the protector applied pressure on the protected to accept early independence, and this pressure was vigorously resisted by the latter. That was precisely what happened between Britain and Brunei."

The role of the 900-odd remaining Gurkhas is primarily to guard the oil and gas fields in the Seria district – for which Brunei pays £3 million a year.

Population

In the days of Charles Brooke, the sultanate had a population of about 20,000. A hundred years on, it was estimated to be 260,000 (1990). The city-state of Singapore has 10 times as many people. Today 60% of the country's population lives in towns; more than half is aged under 20, a third under 14. With the population growing at 2.5% a year, Brunei has one of the fastest-growing populations in the region; it also has the region's lowest death rate and second lowest infant mortality rate after Singapore. Bruneians' average life expectancy, at 71, is also second only to Singaporeans'. About 40% of the population is Malay, 30% Chinese and 29% indigenous tribal groups (see **Culture and life**, below); there are also 20,000 expatriate workers – both professionals and labourers. The average density of population is low: about 34 people per sq km; most are concentrated along the narrow coastal belt.

CULTURE AND LIFE

People

Brunei 'Malays', who make up 68% of the sultanate's population, are indigenous to N Borneo – most are Kedayans or Melanaus. There was no great migration of Malays from the peninsula. Similarly, few Iban migrated into what is modern Brunei, although in the 19th century, they pushed up to the middle-reaches of Sarawak's rivers, which in those days came under the sultanate's ambit. Ibans, Muruts, Kedayans, Dayaks and even Dusuns are, however, all represented in the 29% of the population labelled 'indigenous tribal groups' (for more detail on individual tribal groups, **see page 228**).

Today most Bruneian Malays are well off and well-educated; more than half of them have secure government jobs. They pay no tax and live in spacious villas with servants. The increase in car-ownership in Brunei is a telling indicator of Bruneians' growing affluence: the number of cars trebled in the decade to 1981. The standard of living is high by Southeast Asian standards although there are poorer communities living in Kampung Ayer and Kampung Kianggeh (near the open market). Many of these are recent immigrants – there is a high level of illegal immigration from the neighbouring states of Sabah and Sarawak as well as from Kalimantan.

The government policy of 'Bruneization' discriminates positively in favour of the Malays and against the Chinese, who make up 30% of the population. Most of the Chinese are fairly wealthy as they account for the vast majority of Brunei's private sector businessmen.

Unlike the Malays, the Chinese did not automatically become citizens of Brunei at independence – even if they could trace their ancestry back several generations. The question of citizenship is very important as only citizens of Brunei can enjoy the benefits of the welfare state – free education, health care, subsidized housing and government jobs.

Only about 6,000 Chinese presently have citizenship; the rest hold British 'protected person' passports – which, like the situation in Hong Kong, does not give them the right to live in the UK. At independence the Sultan decreed that it would only be possible for a Chinese to qualify for citizenship if he or she had lived in Brunei continuously for 25 years in the 30 years prior to the application. Candidates for citizenship are tested in their ability to speak Malay and in their cultural understanding of the country.

Brunei Shell Petroleum was forced to freeze the promotion of Chinese employees to allow Malays access to top jobs. Foreign businesses have trouble filling vacancies because of this so-called 'Bruneization' policy – there are simply not enough skilled Bruneian Malays. A leading international business intelligence publication reports that this policy is "sapping morale, with an adverse impact on output and efficiency." It adds that the policy "is a source of considerable resentment among non-Malays." The Chinese would think that an understatement: their emigration rate of about 3,000 a year suggests that they have begun to vote with their feet.

Religion

Brunei is a Sunni Muslim monarchy; the state motto is 'Always render service by God's guidance'. The sultan uses Islam as a form of social control. Islam appears to have been firmly established in the Sultanate by the mid 15th century. Today it is the official religion, and a religious council advises the Sultan, who is head of the Islamic faith in Brunei, on all Islamic matters. The minister of Religious Affairs, Yang Berhormat Pehin Orang Kaya Ratna Deraja Dato Seri Utama Dr Ustaz Haji Awang Mohammad Zain bin Haji Serudin, holds a cabinet post. Besides acting as the religious police, patrolling the streets for errant drinkers, kissers and adulterers, his ministry is in charge of maintaining Brunei's 60 mosques, paying religious teachers and subsidizing pilgrimages to Mecca. In 1992, the Religious Affairs ministry objected strongly to the tyres on imported Daihatsu jeeps and the company was ordered to supply every Daihatsu in Brunei with new ones. Their sin? A rubber-engraved squiggle on the tyres was branded as blasphemous – it apparently spelled the word 'Allah' in Arabic.

Crafts

Brassware brass casting is said to have been introduced into Brunei Darussalam at the end of the 15th century, when the Sultanate became particularly famous for its brass cannons. Italian historian Antonio Pigafetta – who visited Brunei in 1521 – describes "a fortress with 56 brass cannons and six of iron in front of the king's house". The cannons were also used to decorate boats and were prominently displayed in longhouses: brassware is a traditional symbol of wealth and power in Brunei. Cannons were used in battle and to convey messages from one village to another about deaths, births and festivities – such as the beginning and end of Ramadan. The collection of 500 cannons and guns in the Brunei Museum is largely of local manufacture. Brass cannons and gongs were items of currency and barter and often used in dowries, particularly among the tribal Belaits and Dusuns. Brassware is a prized family heirloom, and was the basis of fines in the traditional legal system.

In 1908 there were more than 200 brass workers in Brunei, but by the mid-1970s their numbers had reportedly fallen to fewer than 10. Today, traditional casting by the 'lost wax' technique is being revived.

Silverware Silversmiths have a good reputation for their intricate designs, betelnut boxes being a speciality. Brunei is a reasonable place to buy gold jewellery, mostly 22 and 24 carat.

Textiles The best known local fabric is *Kain Jong Sarat*, a cotton sarong, usually about 2m in length, woven with more than 1,000 gold threads on a handloom. Another textile is the *Sukma-Indera* which is distinguished by its multi-coloured floral patterns. Jong Sarat are said to have been brought to Brunei from Java by the consort of Sultan Bolkiah, Princess Laila Menchanai, who occupied herself on the voyage by weaving them; Jong Sarat means 'fully laden junk'. Today they are only used on ceremonial occasions. The *tenunan*, a special cloth woven with gold thread and worn by men round the waist on Hari Raya Aidil Adha can cost up to B$1,000.

MODERN BRUNEI

Politics

On independence in Jan 1984, Sultan Hassanal Bolkiah declared Brunei a 'democratic' monarchy. Three years later, he told his official biographer Lord Chalfont: "I do not believe that the time is ripe for elections and the revival of the legislature. What I would wish to see first is real evidence of an interest in politics by a responsible majority of the people... When I see some genuine interest among the citizenry, we may move towards elections." But his well-heeled subjects are not particularly interested in politics or elections.

Independence has changed nothing: absolute power is still vested in the Sultan, who mostly relies on his close family for advice. Two of his brothers hold the most sensitive cabinet portfolios: Prince Mohammed is foreign affairs minister and Prince Jefri heads the finance ministry. Following independence, the Sultan took up the offices of Prime Minister, Minister of Finance and Minister of Home Affairs. In 1986, he relinquished the latter 2, but appointed himself Minister of Defence.

In May 1985 the Brunei National Democratic Party (BNDP) was officially registered. Its aim was to introduce a parliamentary democracy under the Sultan. But just before the Malays-only party came into being, the government announced that government employees would not be allowed to join it – or any other political party. In one stroke, the BNDP's potential membership was halved. In early 1986, the Brunei United National Party – an offshoot of the BNDP – was formed. Unlike its parent, its manifesto was multi-racial. The Sultan allowed these parties to exist until 27 January 1988 when he proscribed all political parties and imprisoned, without trial, 2 of the BNDP's leaders.

In the early 1990s, the Sultan was reported to have become increasingly worried about internal security and about Brunei's image abroad. In 1992 he brought the security division of the Brunei police force under his direct control. The *Far Eastern Economic Review* also quoted sources as saying that the Brunei army is kept under the discreet surveillance of the Gurkha battalion personally employed by the sultan. Eight long-term political detainees, in prison since the abortive 1962 coup, were released in 1990 – the government says there are no more behind bars. The deputy leader of the Brunei People's Party (PRB), Zaini Ahmad, is said to have written to the Sultan from exile in Kuala Lumpur following the releases. He apparently apologized for the 1962 revolt and called for the democratically elected Legislative Council – as outlined in the 1959 constitution – to be reconvened. The exiled PRB has been greatly weakened and increasingly isolated since Brunei's relations with Malaysia became more cordial following the sultanate's accession to the Association of Southeast Asian Nations (ASEAN) in 1984.

Foreign relations

Brunei, according to the *Far Eastern Economic Review*, remains ASEAN's new-boy, having joined the six-nation organization on independence in 1984. Prince Mohammed, the foreign affairs minister, is said to be one of the brightest, more thoughtful members of the royal family, but in foreign policy, Brunei is 'timid' and goes quietly along with its ASEAN partners. Relations with Malaysia are greatly improved, but the sultanate's closest ties in the region, especially in fiscal and economic matters, are with Singapore. Their relationship was initially founded on their mutual distrust of the Malaysian Federation, which Brunei never joined and Singapore left 2 years after its inception in 1965. Singapore provides assistance in the training of Brunei's public servants and their currencies are linked.

As a member of ASEAN, on good terms with its neighbours, Brunei does not have many enemies to fear. But if its Scorpion tanks, Exocet rockets, Rapier ground-to-air missiles and helicopter gunships seem a little redundant, it is worth considering the recent experience of another oil-rich Islamic mini-state. As *The Economist* wrote, in October 1992, "substitute jungle for desert and Brunei is uncannily like Kuwait."

Economy

Whenever a world oil glut depresses petroleum prices, Brunei suffers – relatively speaking. Brunei is wealthy enough not to have to worry too much about fluctuating oil prices. Because Bruneians' incomes are directly dependent on oil, per capita incomes also tend to fluctuate. In 1980 Brunei's oil exports earned it US$6 billion; by 1988 they were worth US$1.6 billion. Even so, the average personal income level in 1990 was slightly less than Japan's, more than Australia's and double Singapore's.

Economic growth stagnated in the 1980s – for several years Brunei registered a negative growth rate. While the economy will continue to be dominated by the oil and natural gas industries for the foreseeable future, other sectors, such as services, have assumed greater importance in recent years – partly because the government has tried to diversify the economy. In 1979, hydrocarbons accounted for 83% of the GDP; in the late 1980s they accounted for less than half the sultanate's GDP. Increased oil revenues in the early 1990s, in the wake of the Gulf Crisis, have pushed the sector's contribution up again: it now accounts for about 60% of GDP.

Thanks to its unrivalled liquidity, Brunei is a huge international investor. Economists reckon that should the oil and gas run dry tomorrow, Brunei would have no trouble financing all its needs from the Brunei Investment Agency's foreign investment yields. Brunei's foreign reserves stand at about US$30 billion – well over 5 times those of Indonesia and more than the entire GDP of neighbouring Malaysia.

As oil-rich Brunei's per capita income exceeds Britain's or Italy's, it does not have to resort to **tourism** promotion to generate foreign exchange. Visiting Brunei can be quite expensive and because the country is not geared to tourism, it has successfully kept itself off the Southeast Asian tourist map. That said, the government has reportedly shown some interest in developing ecotourism, for, unlike the neighbouring Malaysian states of Sabah and Sarawak, Brunei has never had to resort to commercial logging either. Its ancient rainforest remains

Brunei's hydrocarbonated economy

Brunei's oil reserves were estimated in 1990 to be 1.4 billion barrels – enough to last until 2018 at the current rate of extraction. The sultanate also has 322 billion m^3 of natural gas, which at present extraction rates, should keep the economy ticking over until 2027. Given the probability of there being new finds, and the government's conservation policy, production should continue well into the 21st century. Brunei Shell Petroleum is now producing about 150,000 barrels per day (b/d), down from 243,000 b/d in the late 1970s.

In 1899 Brunei's first oil well was drilled at Ayer Bekunchi, near Brunei Town, at the site of a natural oil seepage. The bore went down 260m but amazingly failed to strike oil. By 1923 Shell had drilled 8 exploratory holes around Tutong and several other companies – including the British Borneo Petroleum Syndicate and others from Singapore and the Netherlands – had drilled wells. All were dry. Only Shell persevered, and with the aid of modern survey methods drilled a further 17 exploration wells before hitting the Seria field in 1929.

By the time the Japanese invaded in 1941, the Seria field was already producing 17,000 b/d. During their World War II occupation, the Japanese did everything they could to repair war-damaged oil installations and step up production at Seria. They managed to get 11.5 million barrels out before the Australian 9th Division liberated Seria on 21 June 1945. Threatened by the Allied advance however, the Japanese did exactly what Saddam Hussein did in Kuwait nearly half a century later: they torched 38 well-heads and dug defensive pits which they flooded with blazing oil. The fires took several months to extinguish.

It was not until the 1970s that Brunei hit the jackpot; oil prices rose ninefold through the '70s, and the price increases coincided with a series of new finds. By 1980, Brunei's oil and gas revenues were thirty-five times higher than they had been in 1970. Today, the government, which has a 50% stake in Brunei Shell Petroleum, taxes oil and gas revenue at 55%.

In 1973, the year oil prices increased fourfold, the liquified natural gas (LNG) plant at Lumut came on-stream. It is the gas that has given Brunei the licence to print money. Brunei is now the world's second largest exporter of LNG. It produces 3 million tonnes of liquified gas a year, which is sold exclusively to Japan: the 20-year contract comes up for renewal in 1993. The gas is taken by a tanker fleet directly to Tokyo: one of the partners in the Lumut plant is the Mitsubishi Corporation. About a third of Brunei's oil exports also go directly to Japan. The Sultanate uses only about 3% of its oil for domestic purposes.

After more than 50 years, Seria's 'nodding donkeys' are still pumping oil, although 80% of it now comes from the 5 offshore fields which began production in 1963. The oil is piped to Seria's terminal via the 84 km-long Champion underwater pipeline.

unscathed by the 20th century – except for the odd wandering band of heavily armed and camouflaged soldiers. The elite 22nd Special Air Service (SAS) regiment is one of the British army units which conducts its jungle warfare training exercises in Brunei. The Singapore defence force also has a jungle training school in Brunei.

Diversification drive   Aware of Brunei's over-dependence on oil and gas revenues, the Sultan has put increasing emphasis on economic diversification. Despite the stated aim of the government's Fifth National Development Plan (1986-90) to build up a more diversified economy, commentators have been sceptical, saying the policy has more to do with national pride than economic sense. One visiting foreign journalist was told: "It makes more sense to keep handing out cheques than setting up factories." Petroleum revenues still comprise 95% of Brunei's export earnings. The government has, however, identified pioneer industries which it wants to develop for the day the oil runs out. These include pharmaceuticals, cement, aluminium, steel, chemicals, ceramics and other hi-tech industries.

The fifth development plan, which ended in 1990 set expenditure at B$3.73 billion. It aimed to expand social and welfare services, such as housing, transport and communications. One third of the plan allocation was contingency – in case of project cost over-runs. Keeping within budgetary margins is not a necessity.

Five per cent of Brunei's land area is cultivated and agriculture accounts for about 1% of GDP. Most Bruneians consider themselves above working the land. Four-fifths of Brunei's rice requirements are imported. The government is trying to encourage local agricultural production but rice grown at the government rice project outside Bandar Seri Begawan costs 3 times as much to produce as rice imported from Thailand.

Rubber was introduced to Brunei in 1908. By the 1950s it was Brunei's chief export, but with the discovery of oil and natural gas, rubber planting declined rapidly. In 1980 the area under rubber was just 4,600 ha. Pepper was introduced in the 19th century – although, today there are only 30 ha under pepper cultivation – mainly by Chinese commercial farmers. The pepper is grown on terraced hillsides and the vines yield for about 15 years. The red berries are soaked in water to remove their pericarps (skins) and then dried in sun for 3 days to make white pepper. For black pepper, the berries are dried but not soaked.

Most of Brunei's meat comes from its huge state-owned farm in Australia which the sultanate bought in 1981. Recently, the government was reported to be negotiating the purchase of another farm in Queensland for rice cultivation. Even vegetables come from Australia, instead of neighbouring Sabah and Sarawak. A cargo plane arrives from Australia every Thursday with food requirements for the next week.

Employment In 1989, the working population was 90,000, of which about 40,000 were foreigners, for like nearly everything else in Brunei – except oil and gas – management expertise and manual labour has to be imported. Apart from contracted migrant workers, there are many illegal immigrant labourers: mainly from Indonesia and the Philippines. More than a third of the local workforce is employed by the government, and Brunei Shell Petroleum employs about another 8,000. The private sector is dominated by the Chinese. But because government jobs offered such attractive salaries and fringe benefits, private sector firms were having trouble tempting Malays into jobs. In 1989 the government became worried about rising unemployment – because people were becoming too choosy – and listed a range of jobs in which only Bruneians could be employed. The government hopes to create 40,000 private sector jobs for Bruneian Malays.

Brunei University opened in 1988, and about 500 students enrolled in 1990. One of the ideas behind the university was to discourage students from attending universities abroad – the government is wary of 'less-desirable Western habits' – one of the few commodities it does not want to import. In the past, students have been detained for several months on their return from studying overseas. The Sultan has vigorously promoted the concept of Melayu Islam Beraja (MIB – Malay tradition, Islam and the monarch) as a national ideology in an effort to stem social problems such as alcoholism and drug abuse – which have been attributed to these foreign influences and sparked off by rising unemployment. All students at the university are required to attend courses in MIB, which is styled to give the sultanate a sense of national identity.

Brunei: fact file

Geographic			
Land area	5,769 sq km		
Arable land as % of total	n.a.		
Average annual rate of deforestation	n.a.		
Highest mountain Bukit Pagon	1,850 m		
Average rainfall in BSB	2,921 mm		
Average temperature in BSB	27.5°C		
Economic			
GNP/person (1989)	US$15,390		
GDP/person (PPP*, 1990)	US$14,000		
GNP growth (/capita, 1980-1990)	n.a.		
% labour force in agriculture	n.a.		
Total debt (% GNP)	n.a.		
Debt service ratio (% exports)	n.a.		
Military expenditure (% GNP)	7.7%		
Social			
Population	0.3 million		

Population growth rate (1960-90)	n.a.
Adult literacy rate	86%
Mean years of schooling	5.0 years
Tertiary graduate as % of age group	n.a.
Population below poverty line	n.a.
Rural population as % of total	n.a.
Growth of urban population (1960-90)	n.a.
Urban population in largest city	n.a.
Televisions per 1,000 people	233
Health	
Life expectancy at birth	73.5 years
Population with access to clean water	n.a.
Calorie intake as % of requirements	n.a.
Malnourished children less than 5 years	n.a.
Contraceptive prevalence rate†	n.a.

* PPP = Purchasing Power Parity (based on what it costs to buy a similar basket of goods and services in different countries)
† % of women of childbearing age using a form of modern contraception
Source: World Bank (1993) *Human development report 1993*, OUP: New York; and other sources.

BANDAR SERI BEGAWAN

Bandar Seri Begawan, informally dubbed BSB or just Bandar – 'town' in Malay – is the capital of Brunei Darussalam and is sited on a natural inlet of Brunei Bay. It is a fraction of the size of neighbouring Asian capitals and has a population of only 80,000. It used to be called Brunei Town, but was renamed in 1970 in honour of the present Sultan's father, Sir Omar Ali Saifuddin III, who first started modernizing the town and was known as the architect of modern Brunei. Following his abdication in 1967, Sir Omar took the title Seri Begawan, which, roughly translated, means 'blessed teacher'. Built on the wide Brunei River, BSB used to be the sultanate's main port – the oldest parts of town run along the waterfront – but the port declined as ships got bigger and navigating the narrow channels became more hazardous.

BSB is a neat, modern city. Unlike other Southeast Asian cities, there is a noticeable absence of motorbikes, dogs, roadside stalls, brothels, bars, beggars and nightclubs. But in common with many of them, BSB still has a sprawling maze of wooden houses, built on stilts over the river. Healthy bank balances, and the trimmings of capitalism have not tempted Kampung Ayer's 30,000 residents to abandon their traditional lifestyles.

The river kampung lends an element of aesthetic curiosity to an otherwise unexciting, modern city: most of its buildings are low-slung and modern and government buildings stand out. BSB is split into 3 main areas: the **'old'** 1950s-built central area; the **Seri Complex** – a commercial area on the way out to the Sultan's palace near the river, which dates from the 1970s – and the light industrial district at **Gadong**. The latter stands on the site of an old rubber plantation from the days when the economy ran on latex rather than oil. Around the multi-storey carpark in the centre of modern BSB, there are several rows of shophouses dating back to the early 1900s.

PLACES OF INTEREST

Although the city is relatively spread out, the list of sights is short: it is easy to walk round them in a day.

The golden dome of **Omar Ali Saifuddin Mosque** on Jalan Pretty dominates BSB's skyline. Named after the current Sultan's father, a devout Muslim, it was designed by British architects and built in 1958 in classical Islamic style and cost US$5 million to complete. The mosque is impressive enough from the outside but rather unimaginative within. Its 44m minaret has a lift and the top affords a good view of the city. The floors are made of Italian marble, the stained glass windows and chandeliers were made in England, the carpets in Iran and Belgium and the granite imported from Hong Kong. Linked to the mosque and built in the middle of a lake is a concrete reconstruction of a 16th century royal barge. Open: 0800-1200, 1300-1530, 1630-1730 Sat-Wed, 1630-1730 Fri. Opening times apply to non-Muslims only.

The mosque overlooks the 400-year-old **Kampung Ayer**, once the centre of a trading empire and still the world's biggest stilt village. In 1521, Italian historian, Antonio Pigafetta, who was travelling with Ferdinand Magellan's expedition, described "a city that is entirely built in salt water". James Brooke, the Rajah of Sarawak, described Brunei's aquapolis as "a very Venice of hovels, fit only for frogs". Visitors to modern Brunei might consider that rather harsh – it is the sultanate's most picturesque tourist attraction. The government, however, is said to be aware of its health hazards and has been trying to lower its profile as a tourist destination. However, in 1987 it was declared a national monument and rates as the most interesting 'sight' in BSB.

Francesco de Sande, Spain's Captain-General in the Philippines in the 1770s, appears to have been the source of the 'Oriental Venice' cliché. Following his naval expedition to Brunei in 1578, he wrote to King Philip II of Spain that "the city was very large and rich and was built over a very broad and deep river that had the appearance of another Venice. The buildings were of wood, but the houses were excellently constructed of stonework and gilded, especially the king's palaces, which were of huge size. That city contained a very sumptuous mosque, a very large and interesting building, quite covered with half relief and gilded." It seems that little has changed.

Even though many families have been resettled on the mainland in recent years, the 40 separate kampungs – on the N and S banks of the river – which make up Kampung Ayer, probably house about 30,000 people – mostly Malays. In 1909, Sultan Muhammad Jamalul Alam II moved the Istana onto dry land. The most upmarket district is the area furthest upstream, overlooked by the palace. This is mainly due to the lack of a modern sewerage disposal system. Some families now have their sewerage collected daily and a piped waste disposal system may soon be introduced. But until then, the Thai and Filipino migrant workers who rent some of the less desirable downstream properties face health risks when bathing.

Kampung Ayer's houses are not short of other amenities however: most have electricity, air-conditioning and street lighting. Many are owned by prosperous families whose cars are parked bumper to bumper along Jalan Residency (on the way out to the museum). The 20th century has also influenced the construction of the houses. Stilt piles used to be made of mangrove wood: today houses are built on concrete columns and two-storey buildings are in vogue. This does not, however, make them fireproof: a lot of wood is still used in construction, especially on the rickety catwalks that snake around the village. Every so often a fire breaks out which demolishes a large section of the water village: in 1981 there was a big fire at Kampung Sultan Lama, and another broke out in 1990 in the area around the mosque.

Some traditional cottage industries such as weaving, silverware and brassware, are still practised in the maze of alleys. Each of the 40 kampungs was traditionally centred on one such cottage industry, although now they are in decline.

It is safe to walk around Kampung Ayer – although care should be taken on some of the older catwalks. Either go on foot to visit the section linked to dry land near the mosque (also accessible from the end of the customs wharf) or catch a water taxi out to the larger community in mid-stream (B$1). Boats can be hired from the creek which runs parallel to Jalan Sungai Kianggah: a 'tour' up to the Sultan's palace at the end of Kampung Ayer and then downriver costs B$10-20. Agree on the price before setting off. You can also hail boats, like taxis, from the waterfront along Jalan Residency.

The **Churchill Memorial Museum**, N of the mosque on Jalan Stoney, is a peculiar colonial throwback. It was built by the Anglophile Sultan Omar (the present Sultan's father), who held Sir Winston, the former British prime minister, in great esteem. It is full of Churchillian memorabilia – uniforms, books, pictures, photographs and displays. The collection has deteriorated since the Sultan died. Open: 0930-1700 Tue, Wed, Thur, Sat & Sun, 0930-1130, 1430-1700 Fri.

Next door, in the same complex, is the **Brunei History Museum**. This was opened in 1984 to mark Brunei's full independence. It was founded to undertake research into the history of Brunei. Exhibits go back to the arrival of James Brooke

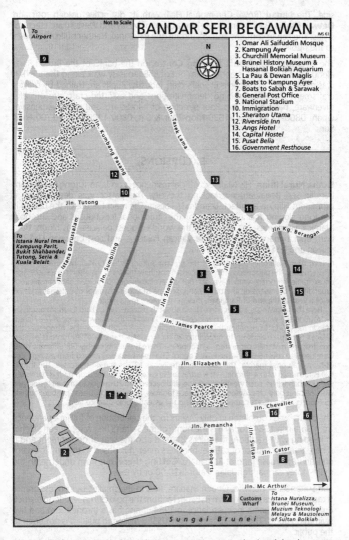

BANDAR SERI BEGAWAN
Not to Scale

N

1. Omar Ali Saifuddin Mosque
2. Kampung Ayer
3. Churchill Memorial Museum
4. Brunei History Museum &
   Hassanal Bolkiah Aquarium
5. La Pau & Dewan Maglis
6. Boats to Kampung Ayer
7. Boats to Sabah & Sarawak
8. General Post Office
9. National Stadium
10. Immigration
11. *Sheraton Utama*
12. *Riverside Inn*
13. *Angs Hotel*
14. *Capital Hostel*
15. *Pusat Belia*
16. *Government Resthouse*

To Airport

Jln. Haji Basir

Jln. Kumbang Pasang

Jln. Tasek Lama

Jln. Tutong

To
Istana Nural Iman,
Kampung Parit,
Bukit Shahbandar,
Tutong, Seria &
Kuala Belait

Jln. Istana Darussalam

Jln. Sumbiling

Jln. Stoney

Jln. Sultan

Jln. Bandahasa

Jln. Kg. Berangan

Jln. Sungai Kianggeh

Jln. James Pearce

Jln. Elizabeth II

Jln. Chevalier

Jln. Pemancha

Jln. Pretty

Jln. Roberts

Jln. Sultan

Jln. Cator

Jln. Mc Arthur

To
Istana Nuralizza,
Brunei Museum,
Muzium Teknologi
Melayu & Mausoleum
of Sultan Bolkiah

Customs
Wharf

Sungai Brunei

in 1839 but focus on episodes in the country's recent constitutional development.
Open: 0930-1730 Mon, Wed & Thur, 0930-1130, 1430-1700 Fri. Closed: Tue.
In the same complex is the **Hassanal Bolkiah Aquarium**, whose tanks are full
of fish found in Brunei waters. This includes a 4.5m Arapaima. Admission: B$0.30.
Open: 0900-1200, 1315-1900 Tue-Thur, Sat, Sun; 0900-1130, 1400-1900 Fri.

The nearby **Lapau and Dewan Majlis** on Jalan Sungai Kianggeh stand side by side. The **Lapau** (Royal Ceremonial Hall) with its distinctive golden roof and **Dewan Majlis** (Parliament House) are a blend of Malay and Western architectural styles. The Lapau contains Brunei's throne (the Patarana). Neither building is open to the public.

The **Arts and Handicraft Training Centre,** on the banks of the Brunei River along Jalan Residency is about 1 km out of BSB (an easy walk along the river). It was established to preserve Brunei's craft industry. Pupils are trained by master craftsmen. There are training demonstrations and assorted crafts are on sale: silverware, basketware etc. Poor selection of handicrafts and rather expensive. Open: 0800-1215, 1330-1630 Mon-Thur & Sat; 0800-1200, 1400-1700 Fri & Sun.

EXCURSIONS

Istana Nural Iman His Majesty's official residence is on Jalan Tutong (4 km from Bandar Seri Begawan) overlooking the city. The palace was designed by a prominent Filipino architect, Leandro V. Locsin. The main feature of the design is the long sloping roofs like those of the traditional longhouses and the gold Islamic-style domes. It is said to be the world's biggest palace – it is bigger than both Buckingham Palace and the Vatican Palace – and cost between US$350 million and US$600 million to build.

In Lord Alun Chalfont's biography of the present Sultan, *By God's Will*, he writes: "In the Western press the palace has attained a certain notoriety thanks to the efforts of a succession of excitable reporters who have set out to evoke images of vulgar and conspicuous expenditure. Bruneians on the other hand, see the Istana as a symbol of national pride..." Once a year, at the end of Ramadan, they get a chance to go inside.

Here the following is a collection of trivia about the Istana – which Lord Chalfont dismisses as "routine gee-whizzery" – which was collated by James Bartholomew, author of *The Richest Man in the World*. Illuminating the 1,780 rooms requires 51,490 light bulbs. Altogether, the palace's floorspace adds up to more than 20 ha – roughly the area of 30 football pitches. Construction materials came from 31 countries. There is enough marble (38 different kinds were used) to cover 5.6 ha – The Privy Council Chamber has a wall carved from a single slab of Moroccan onyx marble. The palace reportedly has 18 lifts and 44 staircases. The throne hall is furnished with 4 thrones – the extras are in case royal couples drop by. It is garnished with 12 chandeliers, each weighing a tonne, and backed by a 20 m-high Islamic arch, adorned with 22-carat gold tiles. Among other palace facilities, there is a 4,000-seat banqueting hall, 257 toilets and a sports complex – including the essential polo practice field.

The palace was completed in only 2 years for the celebration of full independence from Britain in 1984. Today it is the home of the Sultan's first wife, Queen Saleha. In keeping with tradition, the ruler's Istana is also the seat of government and it is here that the council of cabinet ministers meet. It is closed to the public except on Hari Raya Puasa (end of Ramadan). **Getting there**: bus from underneath the multi-storey car park on Jalan Cator (B$0.50 or by taxi).

The Sultan's second wife, Queen Mariam, lives in the smaller, but no less grand, **Istana Nurulizza**, 24 km from BSB, not far from the polo club in Jerudong district. Built to mark Brunei's independence in 1984, it also has a throne room and five swimming pools. The Nurulizza cost only US$60 million to build. It is not open to the public.

Brunei Museum Mile 3, Jalan Kota Batu (continuation of Jalan Residency), is located in Kota Batu, the original site of the capital, past the Arts and Crafts Training Centre, 5 km from the centre of BSB. It is a modern building, overlooking the Brunei River. The museum houses exhibits of life in Brunei, archaeology, history and natural history as well as a section on the oil industry, sponsored by Shell. No money has been spared collecting exhibits for the New Islamic Art gallery. Open:

0930-1700 Sat, Sun, Tue-Thur; 0900-1130, 1430-1700 Fri. **Getting there**: bus from underneath the multi-storey car park on Jalan Cator (B$1).

Muzium Teknologi Melayu (Malay Technology Museum) is about 1 km on up the road from the Brunei Museum and about 500m off Jalan Kota Batu below the Brunei Museum. (The two museums are connected by a path through the trees on the hillside.) Opened in 1988, the museum's 3 galleries focus on traditional house construction from 1850-1950. It contains models (virtually full-size) of the traditional Malay homes of Kampung Ayer, Kedayan and Dusun houses, and a Murut longhouse. The models are meticulous recreations, built by villagers with first-hand knowledge of age-old building skills. There are also exhibits of traditional technology, such as gold and silversmithing, iron-founding techniques, fishing and boat making.

The third gallery contains exhibits of Brunei's indigenous people showing how they lived as nomadic hunter-gatherers (as in the case of the Penan), as shifting cultivators or as settled agriculturalists like the Dusuns, Murut and Kedayan. Open: 0930-1700 Mon, Wed, Thur, Sat and Sun 0900-1130, 1400-1700 Fri; closed Tue. **Getting there**: bus from station below the car park on Jalan Cator (B$1), by taxi B$10, or 10 mins walk from Brunei Museum.

Mausoleum of Sultan Bolkiah is on the way to the museums along Jalan Kota Batu. He was fifth Sultan of the dynasty (1473-1521) and one of Brunei's most colourful rulers. The mausoleum is surrounded by a peaceful garden dotted with frangipani trees. The site of an old fort here is currently being excavated. The mausoleum is about 4 km from BSB, 1 km before Brunei Museum. **Getting there**: bus from station on Jalan Cator (B$1).

Kampung Parit (also known as Taman Mini Perayaan or Celebration Mini Park) is part of a new resort area 26 km from BSB. More than 20 traditional-style houses have been built on the site as part of an effort to preserve the country's traditional construction techniques. They range from rural villages, to a mini-water village with houses like those in Kampung Ayer, built as they would have been a century ago. There is a restaurant in the Kampung. **Getting there**: buses go to Kampung Parit from Tutong (B$2); taxi B$30 from Jalan Cator, BSB. It is situated just off the BSB-Seria road.

Bukit Shahbandar is a 70 ha park in kerangas forest with an observation tower. The park is between Pantai Tengku and Jerudong on the coast road. There are trails, picnic sites and a good view over BSB.

Tours Only one company offers city tours and tours around Brunei. There is also a trishaw tour of the city, a sunset cruise by water taxi and Bruneian cultural show which includes a recreation of a traditional Malay wedding ceremony. Tours outside BSB include the oil town of Seria and parks such as Sungei Liang near Tutong.

SERVICES

Accommodation If you want to avoid the high costs of staying in Brunei, Limbang or Miri in Sarawak are the nearest accessible towns with more reasonable accommodation: hotels in Brunei cost upwards of B$70/night. (For Transport to and from Sarawak, **see page 485**.)

A+ *Sheraton Utama,* Jln Bendahara, T 244272, F 221579, a/c, restaurant, pool, lucky guests are treated to a twice daily videotaped interview with the Sultan (he dismisses as "irresponsible" assertions in *Fortune* magazine that he is the world's richest man); **A** *Ang's,* Jln Bendahara, T 243553/4, F 227302, a/c, pool; **A** *Brunei Hotel,* 95 Jln Pemancha, T 242372-9, F 226196, a/c, restaurant (European & local cuisine), the hotel now boasts a health club and has been recently renovated, it is the favoured haunt of visiting business people as its communications are good and its prices undercut those of the *Sheraton*, rec;

B *Capital Hostel,* 7 Simpang 2, Jln Berangan (behind the Youth Centre), T 223561, F 228789, a/c, restaurant, cheapest hotel in town; **B** *National Inn,* Jln Tutong, T 221128, a/c, a bit further out of town but there is a shuttle service into the capital, B$70; **B** *Princess Inn* (formerly the National Inn), Seri Complex, Mile One, Jln Tutong (PO Box 109), T 241128, F 241138, a/c, restaurant; **E** *Pusat Belia* (Youth Centre), Jln Sungei Kianggeh, T 223936, a/c, restaurant, pool, proof of membership of some youth or student organization is usually required before you can register – although a passport listing occupation as student will suffice, swimming pool open to public 0900-2130, B$1 entrance, B$5S B$10D; **F** *Government Rest House,* Jln Cator, T 223571, a/c, you usually have to be linked to the civil service in some way to stay here, but a letter to the Municipal Chairman (Bandar Seri Begawan 2031) at least one week before your arrival, stating your purpose and intended length of stay can do the trick, if you're on a tight budget this is worth trying as the cheapest hotel is 20 times the price, rec.

Restaurants Malay: *Greenland Café,* Begawali Shopping Complex, Jln Gedong; ♦♦*Isma Jaya,* Jln Sultan, also Indian and Chinese dishes; *Mohammed's Coffee Shop,* Jln Sultan; *Rindurasa,* 3 Bangunan Hasbullah 4, Jln Gadong; *Rosanika,* Jln Roberts; *Seri Indah,* Jln McArthur; ♦♦*Wisma Bahru Dan Anak-Anak,* Jln Sultan (opposite Brunei Shell), Malay and Indian food.

Chinese: *Chin Lian,* 20 Grd Flr, Jln Sultan; *Hoover,* Jln Sungei Kianggeh; *Lucky,* 1st Flr, PAP Umi Kalthum Bldg, Mile 1, Jln Tutong; *New China,* Ang's Bldg, Jln Sultan Omar Ali; ♦♦♦♦*Phongmun,* 2nd Flr, Teck Guan Plaza, good seafood, also specializes in birds' nest, view over Kampung Ayer; *Rasa Sayang,* 5th Flr, Bangunan Guru Guru Melayu, Jln Sungai Kianggeh.

Indian: ♦♦*Tenaga,* 1st Flr, No. 6 Bangunan Hasbullah – 4, Jln Gadong, T 241685, rec; *Regents Rang Mahel,* Mile 1, Jln Tutong. Thai: *Chao Phaya,* Abdul Razak Bldg, Mile One, Jln Tutong. Indonesian: *Keri,* Seri Complex, Jln Tutong.

International: ♦♦*Coffee Shop,* Mabohai Shopping Complex, Jln Kebangsaan, real coffee, excellent home-made pizzas; ♦♦♦*Café Melati, Sheraton,* Jln Bendahara, also serves local food; ♦♦♦♦*Cempaka Café, Ang's,* Jln Pendahara, also serves local seafood, and steamboat, outside tables around the pool; *Grill Room,* 22 Jln Sultan; ♦♦♦♦ *Heritage Room, Sheraton,* Jln Bendahara, occasionally serves local dishes – everything else is overpriced; ♦*Makanan Cepat* (Fast Food), Jln Sultan/Cator, burgers and pizzas; ♦♦♦*Mawar Coffee Garden,* Brunei Hotel, 95 Jln Pemancha, buffet lunch; ♦♦♦*Maximillian's, Ang's Hotel,* Jln Pendahara, Chinese, grills and steaks. **Foodstalls:** at riverfront near bridge, where Jln McArthur/Jln Residency cross the creek, satay rec. At intersection of Jln Sungai Kianggeh and Jln Pemancha, on the other side of the creek, there is a night market and one of the few places where you can buy food from stalls. Excellent barbecued fish.

Bars Since Jan 1991, Brunei's bars have ceased to exist (see **Food and Drink**, page 487).

Entertainment BSB is not the place to come if you are after a wild nightlife. It is rather tame by Southeast Asian standards – alcohol is banned, entertainment is restricted and what night life there is shuts down by 2200. Islamic codes of conduct are rigorously adhered to. For a good night out, locals take the short boat ride to Labuan. **Cinemas:** Hasanal Bolkiah Theatre, Jln Kianggeh, sometimes shows films in English (T22176), B$3 for a deluxe seat.

Sports Main sports complex at the *National Stadium,* Berakas. Facilities for badminton, squash, football, table tennis, athletics and swimming. Also a public swimming pool nearby. **Bowling:** ten pin bowling (2 km out of BSB) Mile 1 Jln Tutong, next to Yaohan. **Golf:** courses in Mentiri, Jln Pengkalan Si-Babau, T 86208 (19 km from BSB) and one at Seria. **Swimming:** public swimming pool at the Youth Centre, Jln Sungai Kianngeh, open 0900-2130, Mon-Sun, (B$10). **Tennis:** *Brunei Tennis Club,* Jln Tapak Kuda, T 25344. **Sailing:** *Royal Brunei Yacht Club,* Pantai Serasa, Muara, T 72011.

Shopping Books: 3rd Flr, Teck Guan Plaza Bldg, Jln Sultan. Handicrafts: *Brunei Arts and Handicrafts Centre* on Jln Residency, a 1 km walk along the Brunei River, **see page 478**. Markets: open air market facing Jln Sungai Kianggeh is the closest thing you will get to a Southeast Asian market. Some open air food stalls. Worth a wander but not much to buy.

Local transport Bus: local buses leave infrequently from the terminal behind the *Brunei Hotel.* Hitchhiking: an easy way to get around, even on short trips, although women should never hitchhike alone. At the very least, women should hitch in pairs or in a group with a man. Car hire: *Avis,* 21st Flr, Bangunan Hasbollah 4, T 24921, they also have an office in the *Sheraton Utama*; *Ellis,* 3a 1st Flr, Bangunan Gadong Properties, T 27237; *Roseraya,* 1st Flr, Britannia House, Jln Sungai Kianggeh, T 41442; *Zisen Enterprise,* 7, Block C, Sufri Shopping Complex, Km 2 Jln Tutong, T 26228/44618. Taxis: T 26853/22214.

Banks & money changers Citibank, 147 Jln Pemanch, T 43983; **Hong Kong & Shanghai**

Bank, Jln Sultan/Jln Pemancha, T 42305; **International Bank of Brunei**, Bangunan IBB, 155 Jln Roberts, T 21692; **Standard Chartered**, 51-55 Jln Sultan, T 42386. Money changers don't officially exist, but some local shops will change money. Residents advise sticking to the banks.

Embassies & consulates Australia, 4th Flr, Teck Guan Plaza, Jln Sultan, T 29435; **France**, 5th Flr, UNF Bldg, Jln Sultan, T 20960; **Germany**, Lot 49-50, 6th Flr, UNF Bldg, Jln Sultan, T 25547; **Indonesia**, Simpang 528, Lot 4498, Jln Sungai Hanching Baru, Jln Muara, T 30108; **Japan**, LB16464 Kampong Mabohai, Jln Kebansaan, T 29265; **Malaysia**, 3rd Flr, Bangunan Darussalam, Jln Sultan, T 28515; **Netherlands**, Brunei Shell Petroleum Sdn Bhd, Seria, T 34892; **Philippines**, Room 1-2, 4th Flr, Badi'ah Complex, Mile 1, Jln Tutong, BSB, T 41465; **Singapore**, 5th Flr, RBA Plaza, T 27583; **UK**, 3rd Flr, Hong Kong & Shanghai Bank Bldg, T 22231; **USA**, 3rd Flr, Teck Guan Plaza, Jln Sultan, T 29670.

Useful addresses General Post Office: corner of Jln Elizabeth II and Jln Sultan. **Central Telegraph Office**: Jln Sultan. Telephone, telex and fax services here. **Churches:** *St Andrew's* (Anglican), Jln Kumbang Pasang, T 22768; *St George's* (Roman Catholic), Jln Kumbang Pasang, T 24458. **Hospital:** *Raja Isteri Pengiran Anak Saleha Hospital*, Jln Tutong, T 42424.

Airline offices British Airways (part of Jasra Harrisons), Jln Kianggeh, T 243911; **Cathay Pacific**, c/o Royal Brunei Airlines, RBA Plaza, Jln Sultan, T 42222; **Malaysia Airlines**, 144 Jln Pemancha, T 24141; **Philippine Airlines**, Suite B, 1st Flr, Wisma Hazzah Fatimah Bldg, Jln Sultan, T 22976; **Royal Brunei Airlines**, RBA Plaza, Jln Sultan, T 29438/42222; **Singapore Airlines**, 49-50 Jln Sultan, T 27253; **Thai International**, 4th Flr, Complex Jln Sultan, 51-52 Jln Sultan, T 42991. Agent for **Qantas, Royal Brunei and Cathay Pacific**, on the Grd Flr, Britannica House, Jln Cator.

Tour companies & travel agents *Antara Travel & Tours*, 102 Grd Flr, Bangunan Guru, Jln Kianggeh, T/F 2236608.

Tourist offices Tourist information desk at the airport. **Public Relations Office**, Tourist Section, Economic Development Board, Room 13, Customs Wharf, Jln McArthur.

Transport to & from BSB See Information for visitors, **page 485** and Around Brunei section below.

AROUND BRUNEI

Brunei only has a handful of towns, all situated on, or near the coast and easily accessible from BSB in a day. Public transport is slow and irregular and hiring a car is probably the best way to get around Brunei, particularly if you want to get off the beaten track.

Temburong District

Temburong district is isolated from the rest of Brunei and is surrounded by Sarawak-Limbang, the land in between, was ceded to Sarawak in 1884. It is the most mountainous area of Brunei. In the S are the inaccessible ridges of Bukit Pagan. Temburong can only be reached by boat or air. It is possible to take a boat through the mangrove swamps up to Bangar (48 km to the SE of BSB). **Bangar**, whose population just tops 1,000, is the main town and administrative centre for the Temburong district and is sited on the Temburong River, about 15 km upriver from Brunei Bay. It is comprised of a row of shophouses, a market, hospital, school and a collection of longhouses – all with cars and televisions bought with Brunei's oil wealth. There is a road going further upstream to **Batang Duri**, a 'resort' with a riverside picnic area. Along this reach of river are several Iban longhouses (the nearest is 13 km from Bangar). The new **Kuala Belalong Forestry Centre**, upriver from Bangar, is conducting research into forest flora and fauna and is open to tourists. **Limbang** (Sarawak) can be reached by road from Bangar.

Transport to & from Temburong By boat: it is possible to take either a slow ferry from the Customs Wharf in BSB or the faster and more dangerous 'Flying Coffins' from the jetty, just across the bridge over Sungei Kianggeh, on Jln Residency, also in BSB (B$7-12). From Temburong, the last boat back to BSB leaves at 1630. If you are forced to stay overnight you are obliged to report to the district officer.

Muara

This is another oil centre 25 km NE of BSB. **Serasa Beach**, which is popular with windsurfers, is awful. The good sandy beach at Muara is on the seaward side (as opposed to the harbour side), which is simply known as **Muara Beach**. It is inadvisable to swim in the sea between mid-Feb and Apr, when the jellyfish invade.

Transport to & from Muara 28 km E of BSB. **By bus:** regular connections with BSB (B$2).

Tutong

This agricultural area, 48 km SW of BSB, is the focus of government efforts to diversify the economy. For strategic reasons, it has invested heavily in commercial agricultural projects: Brunei imports most of its food supplies. There is a coffee plantation at Kampong Bukit Udal, tapioca and cinnamon are grown at Kampung Sinaut, and Birau Agricultural Station conducts research into cereals.

Tutong itself doesn't offer much more than a Standard Chartered Bank and a couple of sawmills. It is, however, a picturesque little place; the food in the open-fronted shops next to the river, is cheap and tasty.

Excursion

Tasek Merimbun is not a very large lake by international standards, but lies 27 km inland from Tutong. It is possible to take canoes onto the lake. There are also jungle trails in the area. **Tutong and Lumut** have good beaches. The best known is **Pantai Seri Kenangan**, meaning 'unforgettable beach', near Tutong. The Pantai Istana, one of the Sultan's old seaside retreats, is on the beach.

Transport to & from Tutong **By bus:** regular connections with BSB (B$2), Lumut (B$4). **By taxi:** BSB (B$60), and Lumut (B$80 full car).

Seria

Seria lies 64 km SW of BSB; it has a population of around 25,000 and is the economic heart of the country. The road to Seria from BSB is flanked by jungle and huge mansions with smoked glass windows. Panaga is a residential area between the two towns: it has large houses with gardens and tree-lined avenues. There is a forestry reserve and museum between BSB and Seria, about 2 km before Seria's first oil well. Seria is a Shell oil town and the source of much of the country's wealth. The town was originally called Padang Berawa – 'wild pigeon's field' – and apart from the beach was a virtually inaccessible mangrove swamp. Early accounts relate the terrible problems encountered by explorers – not least the fact that the brackish, muddy red water was undrinkable and turned cooked rice into sticky paste. Even the Dayaks could not stomach it; one report stated they would "drink the little rain water contained in the chalices of the Nepenthes leaves (pitcher plants) after fishing out the dead insects".

Anyone posted to Seria right up to the 1960s was almost guaranteed to contract malaria – in 1941 the hospital in Kuala Belait was treating 200 cases a month. It is now malaria-free and booming; set out on a grid pattern, it has a large expatriate community mostly involved with the oil industry (**see page 472**).

Seria is the second biggest metropolis in the country: it only takes about $3\frac{1}{2}$ minutes to circum navigate the commercial area. The town is built on a grid iron pattern of *lorongs* (lanes): the centre comprising lorongs 1-3, while lorongs 4-14 are lined with military bungalows – for the Brunei garrison and the Gurkhas – and oil workers' quarters. Further out, down the road to Kuala Belait, parallel to the beach, stands the BSP Club, or Peanaga Club, with its manicured golf course. The club is strictly private. To the E of town lies the industrial area with the refinery, oil storage tanks and power stations.

Accommodation C *Seria*, a/c.

Useful addresses General Post Office: Jln Sultan Omar Ali. Taxis: T (03)23255/22030.

Transport to & from Seria **By bus:** regular connections with BSB, roughly hourly until 1500

(B$4). Green Line bus from Jln Cator, under multi-storey car park. **By taxi**: from BSB (B$100 full car).

Kuala Belait

Kuala Belait is situated on the E bank of the Belait estuary and traffic still crosses by ferry. It is a small port with a population of around 20,000. Like neighbouring Seria, KB is laid out on a grid-iron pattern of shophouses, centred on Jalan Pretty, the central business district. From Kuala Belait there are boats up river to Kuala Balai.

Accommodation B *Seaview*, Lot 3678, Km 2.6 Jln Moulana, T 332651, F 331175, Avis car hire desk found here; **B** *Sentosa*, 92-3 Jln McKerron, T 334341, F 331129.

Useful addresses General Post Office: Jln Bendahara. **Churches**: *St John's Church* (Anglican), Jln Bunga Raya, T (03) 34546; *St James's Church*, Jln McKerron T (03) 34372. **Hospital**: *Suri Seri Begawan Hospital*, Jln Panglima, T (03) 35331. **Taxis**: T (03) 34581.

Transport to & from Kuala Belait By bus: regular connections via Seria (BSB-Seria B$4, Seria-Kuala Belait B$1). Buses to Miri: 5 connections daily, first 0730, last 1530 (B$9.50). **By taxi**: to/from BSB (B$100 full car).
For those travelling to Miri (**Sarawak**), an alternative to the bus is to take a sampan across the river from behind the market (B$1) and hitch from the other side. From the Sungei Tujoh immigration post, Miri is 35 km away.

PARKS AND WALKS

Rampayoh Waterfall, Labi (NB: there is no public transport to this area, so it is necessary to hire a car from BSB.) From Tutong drive to Labi (about 40 mins) – which is as far as it is possible to drive. After Labi, the road turns to laterite, and there are several walks from various points along this road, 2 of which are signposted. The first starts 300m after the end of the metalled road. A 2 hour walk brings you to a large waterfall, which has a picnic site. The second walk starts 10 mins further down the road from Labi: there is a waterfall and a rock pool for swimming. A third walk begins at Kampung Teraja, at the end of the road to Labi – about a half hour drive. At Teraja longhouse, follow the stream eastwards for about 45 mins to another waterfall. The Teraja villagers are usually delighted to help lost *orang putehs* to find the trail.

The Marudi Log Walk starts from Kampung Teraja, at the end of the Labi road (see above) and takes you across to Marudi, the trading town on the Baram River in Sarawak. It is best to set aside two days for the return trip, although one-way it's just a 4 to 6 hour walk. It is officially illegal to cross from Brunei into Malaysia as there is no customs post at the Sarawak border, which is not even marked in the jungle. It is essential to carry a passport, however, in the event of being stopped by police in Marudi.
The local Ibans have laid a log trail across the swampy sections of the trail. You pass an impressive Iban longhouse on Sungei Ridan, which is surrounded by paddy fields. If you are constrained by time, the log-trail to the longhouse (which takes between 1½-2 hours) is a pleasant jungle walk in itself. For those venturing across the border, the trail ends about 3 km from Marudi. A local Chinese has set up a Hyundai van 'taxi' service into and out of town for about M$1 each way. If you do not bump into him as you emerge from the jungle, stop at one of the houses next to the road and he will find you. It is best to stay overnight in Marudi (for accommodation, **see page 284**). The Hyundai man is happy to pick you up at your hotel the following morning to take you back to the trail head.

INFORMATION FOR VISITORS

DOCUMENTS

Visas

Citizens of the UK, Malaysia and Singapore can visit Brunei for up to 30 days without a visa, and citizens of Thailand, Indonesia, Philippines, Japan, Switzerland, Canada, South Korea and Germany do not need visas for visits of up to 14 days. All others, including British Overseas Citizens and British Dependent Territories Citizens, must have visas. In countries where there is no Brunei Darussalam diplomatic mission, visas can be obtained from British consulates or from the Immigration Department on arrival. Visa exemption is granted with a confirmed onward ticket, valid passport and sufficient funds. **NB**: visas cannot be obtained in the neighbouring Malaysian states of Sabah and Sarawak.

Vaccinations

Certificates of vaccination against yellow fever and cholera are necessary for those over one year of age coming from infected countries within the last 6 days.

Representation overseas

Australia, Diplomat International Corner, Canberra Ave and Heiv St. Griffith Act, PO Box 74, Manuka 2603, Canberra, T 62 396296, F 62 3964321; **Indonesia**, Bank Central Asia Bldg, 8th Flr Jln Jend. Sudirman, KAV 22-23 Jakarta, T 5782180, F (62) 5782205; **Japan**, 5-2 Kitashinagawa 6-Chome, Sinagaway-Ku, Tokyo 141, T 3-4477997, F (81) 3-4479260; **Malaysia**, High Commission, 16th Flr, Plaza MBF, Jln Ampang, 50450 Kuala Lumpur, T 2612828, F (60) 2612898; **Philippines**, 11th Flr, Bank of Philippines Islands Bldg, Ayala Ave, Cor Paseo De Roxas, Makati, Metro Manila, T 8162836, F (63) 8152872; **Singapore**, 7A Tanglin Hill, Singapore 1024, T 4743393, F (65) 4740844; **Switzerland**, Hotel Royal Geneva, Suite 718, 41, Rue De Lausanne-CH, 1202 Geneva, T 22-313600, F (41) 22-867085; **Thailand**, 14th Flr, Orakarn Bldg, 26/50 Soi Chitlom, Ploenchit Rd, Bangkok 10500, T 515766, F (66) 2535951; **UK**, High Commission, 49 Cromwell Rd, London SW7 2ED, T 071-5810521, F 0712359717; **USA**, Watergate Suite 300, 3rd Flr, 2600 Virginia Ave NW, Washington D.C. 20037, T (202) 342-0159, F (202) 342-0158 and 866 United Nations Plaza, New York, NY 10017, T (212) 838-1600, F (212) 980-6478.

TRANSPORT TO AND FROM BRUNEI

By air

There are regular connections with Singapore (B$640 return), Kuala Lumpur (B$744), Bangkok (B$600), Hong Kong (B$690), Jakarta (B$680), Manila (B$500), Dubai (B$2,000), Taipei (B$1050), Darwin (Australia), London (B$690) and Frankfurt (B$1,780). There are also daily flights from Kuching (Sarawak) one way x 2 (B$192), Kota Kinabalu (Sabah) (B$65). **Royal Brunei Airlines** is the national carrier (and one of the biggest employers in Brunei). It serves 11 destinations, including Darwin, Dubai, Bangkok, Hong Kong, Taipei and Jakarta. **British Airways**, **Singapore Airlines** and **Malaysia Airlines** also fly regularly to Bandar Seri Begawan.

Airport information Brunei International Airport is at Berakas, about 15 mins (11 km) N from Bandar Seri Begawan (BSB). The airport was given a facelift in 1987 by the Dutch firm that built Singapore's Changi Airport and has all the modern facilities including shops, offices, restaurants, banks and car rental desks. There is also a small tourist information desk at the airport. **Flight information**: T 331747.

Airport tax B$5 on flights to Malaysia and Singapore, B$12 for all other international destinations.

Transport to town **By bus**: ADBS (yellow and red) buses leave every half hour for the central bus station in BSB on Jalan Cator (B$1). **By taxi**: the ride into town costs around B$15-20, but bargain as taxis are not metered. **Car rental**: Avis and Hertz have desks at the airport.

By road

There are regular bus/ferry connections daily between Miri, Sarawak and Kuala Belait via the Baram and Belait rivers (B$11). Regular connections between Kuala Belait and BSB via Seria (Kuala Belait-Seria B$1, Seria-BSB B$4). There are no road connections between Brunei and Sabah. Overland travellers must use a combination of buses and boats.

By sea

The main port is Muara, NE of BSB. Buses to Muara leave from the main terminal on Jalan Cator, BSB (B$2). There are regular connections with Limbang in Sarawak (B$10). The Limbang ticket office is opposite the Plaza Sumber Mulia on the wharf. There are regular connections with Labuan in Sabah (B$20). Boats from Labuan to BSB leave twice daily (M$22, B$20). Alternatively, there are two ferries daily from Lawas (Sabah) to BSB (B$25). The agent for the Labuan ferry tickets is between two goldsmith shops opposite the Limbang ticket office: *Borneo Leisure Travel*, No. 63 Jln McArthur, T 224542. It is essential to book the day before you travel – otherwise you will not be allowed to board.

Customs

Duty free allowance 200 cigarettes, 50 cigars or 250 grammes of tobacco, 'any two bottles of any alcoholic beverage' (about a litre each) and perfume for personal use.

Currency The import of Indian and Indonesian currencies is prohibited but otherwise any amount of foreign currency or travellers' cheques is allowed.

Prohibited items The death penalty applies to anyone caught smuggling narcotics. Certain books are banned if they are regarded as offensive to Muslims or critical of Brunei – James Bartholomew's *The Richest Man in the World* is one such book. Any videos brought into the country will be confiscated.

INTERNAL TRAVEL

Bus

Most people have cars and so the public transport system is not highly developed – it is one of the only countries in Asia where the buses are not crowded. Buses run between the capital and other main centres but are infrequent. The central bus station – where all local and long-distance buses leave from – is underneath the multi-storey car park on Jalan Cator. Buses are not air-conditioned.

Boat

Boats are still the most common means of transport in Brunei; the largest waterways are Sungei Belait, Sungei Tutong and Sungei Brunei. There are regular boat services from BSB to Bangar, Limbang (Sarawak), Labuan and some towns in Sabah. **Water taxis** – open longboats with outboard engines – are fast and widely used. On longer routes, larger boats with covered cabins, accurately dubbed 'flying coffins', operate. **Ferries** leave from the Customs Wharf, BSB to Labuan, Tutong, Temburong and Limbang. There are also flying coffins to many of the above; they leave when full. It is also possible to take smaller river and coastal boats to destinations in Sabah and Sarawak.

Car hire

Cars can be rented by those aged between 23 and 60 who have an international driving licence. Hire cost is upwards of B$60/day. Driving is on the left and speed limits are 50 km/hr in town, 80 km/hr out of town. Seatbelts are compulsory. Brunei's roads are well maintained: there is a good network of sealed roads – although they are largely confined to coastal areas. A single main road runs the full 135 km length of the sultanate; there are just over 1,000 km of paved roads in the country. Car-ownership levels are high in Brunei: there are about 90,000 privately owned cars in a population of 260,000. A road map of BSB is available from the information office at the airport. Parking in BSB is difficult – although the multi-storey car park next to the Jalan Cator bus station always has spaces. Beware of black limousines while driving: never overtake one. An expatriate wife recently sped past one and an expulsion order was delivered to her home the same evening.

Taxi

Taxis charge B$2 per mile, with a minimum fare of B$4. Taxis are not metered so a price should be agreed before setting off. They are expensive by Southeast Asian standards and are also thin on the ground. There is a taxi rank next to the bus station, underneath the multi-storey car park on Jalan Cator. Many hotels have their own free car services to ferry guests into and around BSB. Long distance taxis are expensive: for example, it costs B$100 for the whole car from BSB to Seria.

Hitch-hiking

It is surprisingly easy to hitch in Brunei: local businessmen travelling south to Seria, Kuala Belait and Sarawak make sure you are not left standing for long.

ACCOMMODATION, FOOD AND DRINK

Accommodation

With a small population and no tourist industry to speak of, there are very few places to stay. Facilities for campers and low-budget travellers are virtually non-existent. There is a cheapish youth centre but no down-market Chinese-run hotels so expect to pay upwards of B$70 a night. In BSB it is advisable to book accommodation in advance.

A+: B$160-320; international-class hotel with usual 5-star services.

A: B$65-160; better value than **A+** category – particularly in the case of the *Brunei Hotel* in BSB.

B: B$30-65 economy; average and over-priced compared with similar accommodation elsewhere in the region.

C-F: B$30-under B$10; does not really exist in Brunei, other than the *Youth Hostel* and *Government Rest House* in BSB and some small hotels in district towns.

Food

Prices:

Hawker centres (♦-♦♦)	B$2.50-6.00
Chinese coffee shops (♦♦-♦♦♦)	B$3.50-10.00
Basic restaurants (♦♦-♦♦♦)	B$8.00-15.00
Upmarket restaurants (♦♦♦-♦♦♦♦♦)	S$20.00+
Hotel restaurants & exclusive restaurants(♦♦♦♦♦+)	B$30.00+

As in Malaysia, there is a plethora of Chinese, Malay and Indian restaurants and foodstalls to choose from. But the quality of food in Brunei is particularly high as most of it is imported from Australia. All its meat is imported from a government-owned cattle ranch in Australia which covers a larger area than the country.

Kalupi is peculiar to Brunei: individually packaged, steamed sweet cake made from rice or cassava. Other traditional dishes are *kueh koci* (rice flour dumplings with sweetened coconut filling wrapped in banana leaves) and *cucur ubi* (sweet potato fritters).

Fish is the Bruneians' biggest source of protein, although the sultanate imports 40% of its needs. The barbecued fish sold in food stalls by the river (off Jln Sungai Kianggeh) is excellent. The most common fish found there are mackerel (*rumahan* or *tenggiri*), red snapper (*ikan merah*), garoupa (*kerapu*) and pomfret *(duai puteh)*.

Drink

To the obvious regret of many Bruneians – particularly hoteliers, bar tenders and liquor-shop owners – the Sultanate dried up on New Year's Day 1991. Chinese restaurants can no longer sell their 'special tea'. Anchor draft hand pumps gather dust in the gloomy silence of *Ang's English Pub* and the once-busy *Sheraton bar* has been re-christened *The Executive Relaxation Lounge*, where the most popular pre-dinner drink is iced tea. In chic restaurants, wine buffs now sniff the bouquet of alcohol-free Californian Ariel Blanc and beer-drinkers have to content themselves with alcohol-free Swan and Lowenbrau.

Prohibition was introduced by the Department of Religious Affairs because of the increasing influence of radical Islam in Brunei. Bruneians regularly run the gauntlet of the Department of Religious Affairs and anyone guilty of giving or selling alcohol to a Malay, which is *haram*, or forbidden, risks a hefty fine or arrest. Alcohol flows in from Malaysia's strategically located duty-free island of Labuan, and non-Muslims can bring in bottles for personal consumption. It can also be procured discreetly on the black market – with a 500% mark up. For tourists however, this is an inadvisable pursuit. The authorities have recently stepped up their patrols in an effort to stamp out liquor-smuggling.

PUBLIC HOLIDAYS AND NATIONAL FESTIVALS

Jan: *New Year's Day* (1st: public holiday). *Chinese New Year* (moveable, late Jan/early Feb: public holiday) a 15 day lunar festival. See Malaysia, Information for visitors, **page 354**.

Feb: *Israk Mekraj (National Day)* (23rd: public holiday) processions in BSB, parades and firework displays.

Mar: *Nuzul Al-Quran (Anniversary of the Revelation of the Koran)* (moveable: public holiday). Includes various religious observances, climaxing in a Koran-reading competition. *Hari Raya Aidil Fitri (Puasa)* (moveable, two-day public holiday). Celebrates the end of Ramadan, the Islamic fasting month. Families keep themselves to themselves on the first day – on the second, they throw their doors open. Everyone dresses up in their Friday-best; men wear a length of *tenunan* around their waist, a cloth woven with gold thread.

May: *Armed Forces Day* (31st: public holiday), celebrated with the help of the Royal Brunei Armed Forces who parade their equipment around town.

Jul: *Sultan's Birthday* (15th: public holiday – but celebrations go on until the end of the second week in August). Birthday procession, with lanterns and fireworks and traditional boat race in BSB. *Hari Raya Haji* (moveable: public holiday), celebrated by Muslims to mark the 10th day of Zulhijgah, the 12th month of the Islamic calendar when pilgrims perform their Haj to Mecca. In the morning, prayers are offered and later families hold an 'open house'. Those who can afford it sacrifice goats or buffalo to be distributed to the poor. Unlike in neighbouring

Islamic states, the cost of a trip to Mecca is affordable by many in Brunei, so there is a large population of Hajis. Every year 4,000 Bruneians go on the Haj – the Sultan went in 1987. If any pilgrim has difficulty making ends meet, the Ministry of Religious Affairs provides a generous subsidy.

Aug: *Maal Hijrah* (moveable) is the day the Muslim calendar began, when the Prophet Mohammad journeyed from Mecca to Medina on 16th July 622AD (lunar based). Religious discussions and lectures commemorate the day.

Sept: *Maulud Nabi* (Prophet Mohammad's birthday), celebrated with public gatherings and coloured lights in BSB.

Dec: *Christmas Day* and *Boxing Day* (25th & 26th).

OTHER ESSENTIAL INFORMATION

Conduct

Religion   When visiting a mosque remove your shoes and avoid passing in front of someone who is praying. Bruneians adhere closely to the strictures of Islam. Muslims are forbidden to eat pork or drink alcohol, although the former is available in hotels and Chinese restaurants. During *Ramadan* it is an offence for Muslims to eat or smoke during daylight hours.

Forms of address   Shoes should be removed before entering private houses. Avoid showing the soles of feet when sitting. Only the right hand should be used when offering or receiving something. It is considered impolite for members of the opposite sex to shake hands and it is discourteous to refuse a drink, wear revealing clothing or to point the index finger.

Tipping is not necessary in Brunei – except in the case of porters at hotels. Some restaurants impose a service charge.

Shopping

There is almost nothing to buy in Brunei that you cannot get cheaper elsewhere. There is little or no duty on watches and electronic goods but prices are lower in Singapore. Almost everything is imported. Handicrafts are available from the **Arts and Handicrafts Centre** on the waterfront in BSB but stock tends to be modern and expensive. The main handicrafts are **brassware**, **silverware**, **weaving** and **basketry**.

Safety

BSB is a very safe city – but take the usual precautions.

Health

Vaccinations: the usual injections for this part of the world are unnecessary for those just visiting Brunei. Malaria was eliminated in 1970. **Food and water**: about 90% of Brunei's water supply is treated so there is no need to boil water or use sterilizing tablets, except in remote areas. That said, many residents do take the precaution of boiling drinking water. **Medical facilities**: there are 5 main hospitals in Brunei, several clinics and dispensaries and a flying doctor service for outlying areas. Emergency treatment (including emergency dental treatment) is available free at the casualty department of the *RIPAS General Hospital* in BSB. Treatment is also available at a low cost from private doctors. Pharmaceuticals are available from the main shopping complexes in BSB.

Emergencies
Police: T 22333/23901; Ambulance: T 23366; Fire brigade: T 22555.

Best time to visit
Brunei is hot and sticky all year round – but to avoid the rainy season do not visit between Nov and Mar.

Clothing
Dress in Brunei is informal – for big occasions, a long-sleeved batik shirt is appropriate. Yellow should be avoided on formal occasions if there is any possibility of a member of the royal family being present. Light cotton clothing is recommended, but bear in mind Islamic sensitivities to skimpiness (bikinis, for example, are out of the question). Women should keep their arms and legs covered; men should wear trousers except when playing sport or at the beach.

Official time
8 hours ahead of GMT.

Hours of business
Government offices: 0800-1200, 1300-1630 Mon-Thur and Sat. The working day is shortened during Ramadan. **Banks**: 0900-1500 Mon-Fri, 0900-1100 Sat. **Shops**: 0800-1900 Mon-Sat and some on Sun.

Money
The sultanate does not have a Central Bank – the money supply is managed by Singapore. **Currency**: the Brunei dollar (B$) is the official currency and is linked to the Singapore dollar. In Brunei, Singapore currency is interchangeable with the Brunei dollar. Dollar notes are available in denominations of B$1, 5, 10, 50, 100, 500 and 1000 and coins are in 1, 5, 20 and 50 cent denominations. (Singapore $2 notes are also legal tender.) Subject to fluctuation, US$1 is worth B$1.60. Foreign currencies and travellers' cheques can be exchanged at banks, licenced money changers, big hotels and department stores. **Credit cards**: most credit cards are accepted.

Weights and measures
Metric.

Voltage
230 volts, 50 cycles. Most plugs are 13 amp, 3 pin.

Postal services
Brunei's postal service is efficient and reliable. **Local postal charges**: B$0.20. **International postal charges**: B$0.90/10g, aerogrammes B$0.40. **Post office opening hours**: 0745-1630 Mon-Thur & Sat.

Telephone services
Local: free unless made from a telephone box, when they cost B$0.10. There are 4 area codes: 02 for Brunei/Muara district (including BSB), 03 for Belait district, 04 for Tutong district and 05 for Temburong district. **International**: IDD code: 673; dial 0124 for the operator. International calls can be made through the operator or using IDD country codes. International calls cannot be made from coin boxes except from the public telephones in the Central Telegraph Office, Jln Sultan, BSB, which operates 24 hrs a day. There is a telex & fax service here as well.

Media
Newspapers: the *Borneo Bulletin* is the only local English newspaper and comes out daily Mon to Sat. It is owned by royalty and avoids reporting any news that might be domestically sensitive. International newspapers and magazines can be purchased at hotel news stands. The *Straits Times* (Singapore), *Borneo Post* and *Borneo Mail* are relatively widely available. The *Daily Express* (Sabah) and *Sabah Times* are also on sale. **Television**: TV programmes in Malay and English, viewing starts at 1600 most days, earlier on Fri and Sun. There is an English-language news bulletin, covering local and foreign news, at 1900. 60% of the programmes are imported, mostly from ASEAN, the UK and USA. **Radio**: there are 2 radio networks, one in Malay and one in English (95.9 MHz) and Chinese.

Language
Malay (Bahasa Melayu) is the official language but English is widely spoken and taught in schools. Chinese is also spoken, mainly Hokkien but also Cantonese, Hakka and Mandarin.

Tourist information
There is a tourist information desk at the airport, but there is no real tourist office in Brunei. *The Tourism Section*, Economic Development Board, PO Box 2318, Jln James Pearce, BSB 2011, T 20243, is listed as the official tourist board but its *public relations office*, Room 13, 2nd Flr, Customs Wharf, Jln MacArthur/Jln Sungai Kianggeh is a (slightly) better bet. The office is not geared up for tourists although it does print brochures and pamphlets. These are hard to come by and are not particularly helpful.

Suggested reading
Bartholomew, J. *The World's Richest Man the Sultan of Brunei*, Viking: London.

INDONESIA

	Page		Page
Introduction	490	West Nusa Tenggara	903
Java	513	East Nusa Tenggara	929
Bali	666	Maluku	971
Sumatra	731	Irian Jaya	989
Kalimantan	821	Information for Visitors	1003
Sulawesi	857		

INTRODUCTION

Indonesia is the world's largest archipelago with 13,677 islands, stretching along the equator for 5,120 km (twice the distance from London to Moscow) – or, as Indonesians say, from 'Sebang to Merauke'. It has a population of 185 million – making it the fourth most populous country in the world – comprising 300 ethnic groups who speak an estimated 583 languages and dialects. Indonesia also has the world's largest Muslim population. Its geography is just as varied. There are glaciers in the central highlands of Irian Jaya, and vast expanses of tropical swamps in Kalimantan and Sumatra. Across the archipelago there are over 300 volcanoes, more than 200 of which have been active in historical times. From the floor of the Weber Deep in the Banda Sea, to the summit of Mount Jaya, Indonesia's highest mountain in Irian Jaya, it is 12,470 m.

No wonder Indonesia's motto is *Bhinneka Tunggal Ika*, officially – and rather loosely – translated as 'Unity in Diversity'. Indonesia's coat of arms is the Garuda, the eagle of ancient Indonesian mythology, symbolizing creative energy. With such a bewildering mosaic of cultures, landscapes and histories, it often makes more sense to break the country down into its constituent parts. With this in mind, each of the major regions of the country has been given a separate introduction: Java, Bali, Sumatra, Kalimantan, Sulawesi, Nusa Tenggara, Timor, Maluku and Irian Jaya. This general introduction is intended to provide an overview of Indonesia's geography, history, politics and economy.

ENVIRONMENT

The regions of Indonesia

With a country of such enormous size, how it is divided takes on great importance. Many people simply talk of the 'Inner' or 'Metropolitan' islands of Java, Bali and Madura, and the Outer Islands – the rest. This division is one of core and periphery, in a political, economic, cultural and historic sense. Jakarta and Java are the main centres of political and economic power, and Javanese culture has an over-riding effect upon the rest of the nation. As the anthropologist Clifford Geertz wrote in 1966: "If ever there was a tail which wagged a dog, Java is the tail, Indonesia the dog."

The country can also be broken down into the Greater and Lesser Sunda Islands. The Greater Sundas comprise Sumatra, Java, Kalimantan and Sulawesi; the Lesser Sundas, Bali, Timor and the myriad islands of Maluku and Nusa Tenggara. This division has a certain zoological and geological logic: plants and animals of the two broadly reflect their contrasting Asian and Australasian origins.

Officially however, the country is divided into 27 provinces or *propinsi* (including the disputed territory of East Timor), each administered by a governor (*gubernur*). The administrative unit beneath the province is the district or *kabupaten* (regency), of which there are 20-50 in each province; each of these is headed by a regent or *bupati*. Urban municipalities, which have the same administrative status as districts, are known as *kotamadya*. Kabupaten are in turn divided into sub-districts or *kecamatan*, and they into villages or *desa*. Each village is headed by a *kepala desa*, literally 'village head'.

In addition to this division, there are 3 special administrative units: the Special Territories or *Daerah Istimewa* of Aceh and Yogyakarta, and the Special Capital District or *Daerah Khusus Ibukota* (DKI) of Jakarta.

Land

In total, Indonesia covers a land area of 1,919,443 sq km – or 8 times the land area of Britain. The country also claims sovereignty over 3,272,160 sq km of sea,

The regions of Indonesia		
	Population (millions 1990 census)	**Land area (sq km)**
Java	107.6	132,187
Bali	2.8	5,561
Sumatra	36.6	473,606
Kalimantan	9.1	539,460
Nusa Tenggara*	7.5	82,927
Sulawesi	12.5	189,216
Maluku	1.9	74,505
Irian Jaya	1.6	421,981
INDONESIA	179.3†	1,919,443

* Nusa Tenggara = the islands of West and East Nusa Tenggara and East Timor.
† There is a rounding error in this figure.

stretching from Asia to Australasia. The political, historic and economic heart of the country are the islands of Java and Bali, which support 60% of the population but account for only 7% of the land area. On Java's N coast is the capital or 'mother city' (*ibu kota*) of Jakarta, formerly Batavia. Ranged around these so-called Inner Islands, are the Outer Islands: Sumatra, Kalimantan, Sulawesi, Timor and Irian Jaya, and the assorted islands of Maluku and Nusa Tenggara.

An active volcanic arc runs through Sumatra, Java and the islands of Nusa Tenggara, and then N through Maluku to Sulawesi. It marks the point where 2 tectonic plates plunge, one beneath the other. This is an area of intense volcanic activity – a 'ring of fire' – most dramatically illustrated when Krakatau erupted and then exploded in 1883 (**see page 564**). Off the coast of these islands is a deep sea trench, in places more than 7,000 m deep. Within the arc is the more stable Sunda Shelf with shallow seas and a less dramatic landscape.

Another division that has attracted considerable attention is a biological divide: between Indonesia's Asian and Australasian faunal realms. This 'line' runs between Bali and Lombok, and N to divide Kalimantan and Sulawesi. It is known as Wallace's Line after the great Victorian naturalist Alfred Russel Wallace who first observed the distinction in the 19th century (**see page 905**). To the SE of the line, animals tend to be Australasian in origin – for example, marsupials are found in the Kai Islands and in Sulawesi. By contrast, to the NW of Wallace's Line, no marsupials are found but there are many of the large Asian mammals, including tigers, elephants, orang utans and rhinoceros.

The 2 Indonesian landscapes that are most striking are the **terraced rice field** and the **tropical forest**. The terraced rice field, exemplified by those on Java and Bali are cut from the land, bunded by small embankments, irrigated, and can

support well over 1,000 people/sq km. They are managed, artificial ecosystems in which nature is re-worked and harnessed to Man's own ends. In contrast, the tropical forest is a natural ecosystem. Hunter, gatherers and shifting cultivators (**see page 32**) do not so much replace the forest, as work with and within it. Population densities rarely exceed 10 people/sq km, and their livelihoods are dependent on maintaining the forest resource. But although the tropical lowland rainforests contain a greater variety of species than any other terrestrial ecosystem, they are also one of the most sensitive. If the forest is cleared over large areas, then the land and soil suffer from erosion and degradation.

Indonesia's climate

REGION	SEASON		
	Dry	Wet	Rainfall
Java	Jun-Aug	Dec-Feb	West 2,360 mm
			Central 2,400 mm
			East 1,660 mm
Bali	May-Oct	Nov-Apr	Average 2,150 mm
Sumatra	Jun-Jul	Oct-Apr	West coast 4-6,000 mm
			Other areas 3,000 mm
Kalimantan	Jul-Sep	–	Average 3,810 mm
Sulawesi	Aug-Sep	Dec-Feb	Manado 3,352 mm
			Ujung Pandang 3,188 mm
			Palu 533 mm
Nusa Tenggara	Apr-Oct	–	E Flores & Sumba 8-900 mm
North Maluku	–	May-Oct	Ambon 3,450 mm
SE Maluku	Dec-Mar	–	Ceram 1,400 mm
Irian Jaya	–	–	North coast 2,500 mm
			Interior 5-8,000 mm
			Merauke 1,500 mm

NB: The distinction between the wet and dry seasons is least pronounced in Sumatra, Sulawesi, N Maluku and Irian Jaya; and most pronounced in Nusa Tenggara and SE Maluku.

Climate

Straddling the equator, and stretching over 5,000 km from E to W and almost 2,000 km from N to S, Indonesia encompasses several climatic zones. It is possible to fly from one region's wet season to another area's dry, and from towns with annual rainfall of nearly 5,000 mm, to places where it is less than 500 mm. The only constant – at least at sea-level – is the temperature, which averages about 26°C.

Much of Indonesia has what climatologists term an **'equatorial monsoon' climate**. This broad classification covers a multitude of climate types. Annual rainfall usually exceeds 2,000 mm, but can be more than twice that, or less than a quarter of it. Close to the equator rainfall is distributed evenly through the year, and there is no marked dry season. However, moving N and S from the equator, the dry season becomes more pronounced, and rainfall becomes concentrated in one or 2 seasonal peaks.

This pattern of rainfall is determined by 2 monsoons: the NE monsoon and the SW monsoon. The NE monsoon prevails from Nov/Dec to Feb/Mar and forms the wet season. The SW monsoon extends from Jun to Aug/Sep and brings dry conditions to the area. But, there are a large number of exceptions to disturb this general pattern. The effect of local wind systems and climates, and the shadowing effect of mountainous areas means rainfall can either be significantly higher than the 'norm', or lower. Palu in Sulawesi, for example, is on exactly the same latitude as Padang on the W coast of Sumatra, yet the former has an annual rainfall of only 530 mm, while the latter receives a drenching 4,500 mm.

Eastern Indonesia has a rather different climate from the rest of the country. It too is affected by 2 monsoons: the W monsoon from Dec to Mar, and the E monsoon from May to Sept. The W monsoon is a continuation of the Asian NE monsoon after it has changed direction on crossing the equator. However, by the time it has arrived, the monsoon has picked up moisture over the warm seas of the Indonesian archipelago. It therefore brings large quantities of rainfall to the area between the months of Dec and Mar. By May the NE monsoon has retreated and E Indonesia comes under the influence of the hot and dry South Pacific Trade-winds. This E monsoon generally extends from May to Sept, although the dry season (which is very dry) can be as much as 7 months long.

The climate of each of the regions of Indonesia is discussed in the relevant introductory section. The characteristics of each is summarized in the climate box above.

Flora and fauna

The greatest naturalist to have travelled through the islands of Indonesia was the Victorian, Alfred Russel Wallace (1823-1913). His book *The Malay Archipelago: the land of the Orang-utan and the Bird of Paradise* (1869), is a *tour de force*, dedicated, significantly, to the other great Victorian naturalist Charles Darwin "not only as a token of personal esteem and friendship but also to express my deep admiration for his genius and his works". Wallace was enchanted by the animals and people that he encountered during his 8 years away from England. He travelled 14,000 miles through the archipelago, made 60 or 70 separate journeys, and collected 125,600 specimens – which he shipped back to London and donated to the British Museum.

Straddling the equator and marking the interface between the Asian and Australasian worlds, Indonesia has the richest flora and fauna of any country in Southeast Asia. Although it accounts for only 1.3% of the earth's land area, Indonesia supports 10% of the world's flowering plants (25,000 species), 12% of mammal species (500), 16% of the world's amphibian and reptile species, 17% of bird species (1,600) and 25% of the world's species of fish (8,500). In total there are 816 endemic species of fauna – animals found no where else in the world except Indonesia – including 210 mammal species, 356 bird, and 150 reptile. Along with Australia, there are more endemic vertebrates in Indonesia than in any other country. Many of the large Asian mammals are represented: tigers, elephants, 2 species of rhinoceros, tapirs, buffaloes, gibbons and orang-utans (**see Borneo, page 224**). There are also oddities such as the bird of paradise (**page 992**), the maleo bird (**page 900**), the Komodo dragon (**page 932**) and the Rafflesia flower (**page 780**). The characteristic flora and fauna of each region are discussed in the relevant introductory section.

Sadly, not only has Indonesia got one of the richest flora and faunas in the world, it also suffers from rapid loss of habitat as forests are cleared for timber and human settlement. The Javan wattled lapwing (*Vanellus Macropterus*) and the caerulean paradise flycatcher (*Eutrichomyias rowleyi*) of the Sangihe Islands off North Sulawesi are both extinct, as are the small Balinese and Javan (probably) tigers, both subspecies of tiger. Other animals are represented by such small populations that they are probably unsustainable – the Javan gibbon, for example. As Tony and Jane Whitten remark in their book *Wild Indonesia*, the "term living dead' has been applied to such species". For more detail on Indonesia's regional flora and fauna see the relevant regional introduction.

National parks

As of early 1991, 24 **national parks** had been gazetted by the Indonesian government covering 6.9 million ha. Three of these have been adopted by the IUCN as World Heritage Sites: Ujung Kulon in West Java, Komodo in Nusa Tenggara, and Lore Lindu in Sulawesi. In general, Indonesian parks have limited tourist facilities when compared with parks in Malaysia and Thailand, although those in Java (e.g. Ujung Kulon) and Bali represent exceptions to this rule. The Indonesian government also recognizes separate categories of Recreational Forests, Grand Forest Parks and Hunting Parks. These areas are less rigorously protected. The fact that 1993 was heralded as Visit Indonesia Environment and Heritage Year possibly indicates that some people are beginning to accept that the environment is worth preserving on sound, pecuniary grounds.

But the task facing the Indonesian government is how to protect the country's plants, animals and wild areas when the population is growing at nearly 2% a year, and when economic pressures on resources are escalating at an even faster rate. About 10% of the country's land area is now protected. An environmental movement has also emerged in Indonesia, spurring the government to take greater notice of infractions of environmental laws. But in the Outer Islands it is difficult for farmers and settlers to appreciate that any environmental crisis exists. In Sumatra, Kalimantan, Sulawesi and Irian Jaya it is all too easy to believe that the forest is a limitless resource. When families have to be fed and clothed, and children sent to school, cutting-down trees to sell the timber and clear the land for agriculture, seems not just a reasonable response but often also the only response.

HISTORY

Prehistory

After Thailand and East Malaysia, Indonesia – and particularly Java – has probably revealed more of Southeast Asia's prehistory than any other country in the region. Most significant was the discovery of **hominid fossils** in Central Java in 1890, when Eugene Dubois uncovered the bones of so-called 'Java Man' near the village of Trinil. He named his ape-man *Pithecanthropus erectus*, since changed to *Homo erectus erectus*. These, and other discoveries – particularly at Sangiran, also in Central Java – indicate that Indonesia was inhabited by hominids perhaps as long as 800,000 years ago (the dating of the fossils remains disputed). Excavations in Central Java have also revealed other fossils of early Man – *Pithecanthropus soloensis* and *P. modjokertensis*. Among the skulls of *P. soloensis* a number has been found to have had their cranial bases removed, leading scientists to postulate that the species practised anthropophagy – less politely known as cannibalism – which involved gouging the brains out through the base. Alternatively, the surgery might have been part of a post mortem ritual.

Following the end of the last Ice Age 15,000 years ago, there began a movement of Mongoloid peoples from the Asian mainland, S and E, and into the Southeast Asian archipelago. As this occurred, the immigrants displaced the existing Austro-melanesian inhabitants, pushing them further E or into remote mountain areas.

The practice of **settled agriculture** seems to have filtered into the islands of Indonesia from mainland Southeast Asia about 2,500 BC, along with these Mongoloid migrants. Settled life is associated with the production of primitive earthenware pottery, examples of which have been found in Java, Sulawesi and Flores. Later, **ancestor cults** evolved, echoes of which are to be seen in the megaliths of Sumatra, Java, Sulawesi, Bali, Sumbawa and Sumba. These cultures

Major pre-colonial powers

Empire, kingdom or sultanate	Date (century)	Centre of power
Srivijaya	7th-14th	Palembang
Sailendra	8th-10th	Central Java
Sanjaya	8th-11th	Central & E Java
Kediri	11th-13th	Kediri, E Java
Banten	12th-17th	Banten, W Java
Singasari	13th	E Java
Majapahit	13th-15th	E Java
Gowa	16th-17th	Makassar, S Sulawesi
Mataram	16th-18th	Central Java
Aceh	16th-19th	Aceh, N Sumatra
Karangkasem	18th-19th	Bali & Lombok

reached their height about 500 BC. Among the various discoveries has been evidence of the mutilation of corpses – presumably to prevent the deceased from returning to the world of the living. In some cases, ritual elements of these megalithic cultures still exist – for example on the island of Sumba in Nusa Tenggara, among the inhabitants of Nias Island off West Sumatra, and among the Batak of North Sumatra.

The technology of **bronze casting** was also known to prehistoric Indonesians. Socketed axes have been discovered in Java, several islands of Nusa Tenggara (e.g. Roti) and in Sulawesi. But the finest bronze artefacts are the magnificent kettledrums of E Indonesia (**see page 706**). It is thought these were made in Vietnam, not in Indonesia, and arrived in the archipelago when traders used them as barter goods. Later, locally made equivalents such as the *moko* of Alor (**see page 948**) were produced, but they never achieved the refinement of the originals.

Pre-colonial history

Unlike the states of mainland Southeast Asia which did enjoy a certain geographical legitimacy prior to the colonial period, Indonesia was a fragmented assemblage of kingdoms, sultanates, principalities and villages. It is true that there was a far greater degree of communication and intercourse than many assume, so that no part of the archipelago can be treated in isolation but nonetheless, it is still difficult to talk of 'Indonesian' history prior to the 19th century.

The great empires of the pre-colonial period did range beyond their centres of power, but none came close to controlling all the area now encompassed by the modern Indonesian state. Among these empires, the most powerful were the Srivijayan Kingdom based at Palembang in south Sumatra; and the great Javanese Dynasties of Sailendra, Majapahit and Mataram. There was also a string of less powerful, but nonetheless influential, kingdoms: for example, the Sultanate of Aceh in N Sumatra, the Gowa Kingdom of south Sulawesi, the trading sultanates of the Spice Islands of Maluku, and the Hindu Kingdoms of Bali. The history of each of these powers is dealt with in the appropriate regional introduction.

Even after the European powers arrived in the archipelago, their influence was often superficial. They were concerned only with controlling the valuable spice trade, and were not inclined to feats of territorial expansion. To get around this lack of a common history, historians tend to talk instead in terms of common processes of change. The main ones affecting the archipelago were the 'Indianization' of the region from the first century AD and the introduction of Hinduism and Buddhism; the arrival of Islam in N Sumatra in the 13th century and then its spread E and S during the 15th century; and the contrast between inwardly-focused agricultural kingdoms and outwardly-orientated trading states.

Colonial history

Many accounts of Indonesian history treat the arrival of the Portuguese Admiral Alfonso de Albuquerque off Malacca (Melaka) in 1511 (**see page 162**), and the dispatch of a small fleet to the Spice Islands, as a watershed in Indonesian history. As the historian M.C. Ricklefs argues, this view is untenable, writing that "...in the early years of the Europeans' presence, their influence was sharply limited in both area and depth".

The Portuguese only made a significant impact in the Spice Islands, leaving their mark in a number of Indonesian words of Portuguese origin – for example, *sabun* (soap), *meja* (table) and *Minggu* (Sunday). They also introduced Christianity to E Indonesia and disrupted the islands' prime export – spices. But it was the Dutch, in the guise of the *Vereenigde Oost-Indische Compagnie* or VOC (the Dutch East India Company), who began the process of Western intrusion. They established a toehold in Java – which the Portuguese had never done – a precursor to later territorial expansion. But this was a slow process and it was not until the early 20th century – barely a generation before the Japanese occupation – that the Dutch could legitimately claim they held administrative authority over the whole country.

The idea of Indonesia, 1900-1942

The beginning of the 20th century marks a turning point in Indonesian history. As Raden Kartini, a young educated Javanese woman, wrote in a letter dated 12 Jan 1900: "Oh, it is splendid just to live in this age; the transition of the old into the new!". It was in 1899 that the Dutch lawyer C. Th. van Deventer published a ground-breaking paper entitled *Een eereschuld* or 'A debt of honour'. This article argued that having exploited the East Indies for so long, and having extracted so much wealth from the colony, it was time for the Dutch government to restructure their policies and focus instead on improving conditions for Indonesians. In 1901, the Ethical Policy – as it became known – was officially embraced. Van Deventer was commissioned to propose ways to further such a policy and suggested a formulation of "education, irrigation and emigration". The Ethical Policy represented a remarkable change in perspective, but scholars point out that it was very much a creation of the European mind and made little sense in Indonesian terms.

The Indonesian economy was also changing in character. The diffusion of the cash economy through the islands and the growing importance of export crops like rubber and coffee, and minerals such as tin and oil, were transforming the country. Christianity, too, became a powerful force for change, particularly in the islands beyond Muslim Java. There was large-scale conversion in central and N Sulawesi, Flores, among the Batak of Sumatra, in Kalimantan,

The expansion of Dutch influence and control	
	Date of Establishment of Control*
Maluku	1610
Java	1811
Kalimantan	1863
Lombok	1894
Sumatra	1903
Sulawesi	1905
Nusa Tenggara	1907
Bali	1908
Irian Jaya	1928

* marking the date when effective Dutch control over the bulk of the area had been established.

and Timor. In response to the inroads that Christianity was making in the Outer Islands, Islam in Java became more orthodox and reformist. The 'corrupt' *abangan* who adhered to what has become known as the 'Javanese religion' – a mixture of Muslim, Hindu, Buddhist and animist beliefs – were gradually displaced by the stricter *santris*.

At about the same time, there was an influx of *trekkers*, or Dutch expatriates, who came to the East Indies with their wives and Dutch cultural perspectives, with the intention of going 'home' after completing their contracts. They overwhelmed the older group of *blijvers* or 'stayers', and there emerged a more racist European culture, one that denigrated *Indische* culture and extolled the life-style of the Dutch. The Chinese community, like the Dutch, was also divided into 2 groups: the older immigrants or *peranakan* who had assimilated into Indies culture, and the more recent *totok* arrivals who zealously maintained their culture, clinging to their Chinese roots (see box, **page 509**).

So, the opening years of the 20th century presented a series of paradoxes. On the one hand, Dutch policy was more sensitive to the needs of the 'natives'; yet many Dutch were becoming less understanding of Indonesian culture and more bigoted. At the same time, while the Chinese and Dutch communities were drawing apart from the native Indonesians and into distinct communities based upon Chinese and European cultural norms; so the economy was becoming increasingly integrated and international. Perhaps inevitably, tensions arose and these began to mould the social and political landscape of confrontation between the colonialists and the natives.

A number of political parties and pressure groups emerged from this maelstrom of forces. In 1912, a Eurasian – one of those who found himself ostracized from European-colonial culture – E.F.E. Douwes Dekker founded the Indies Party. This was a revolutionary grouping with the slogan 'the Indies for those who make their home there'. In the same year, a batik merchant from Surakarta established the Sarekat Islam or 'Islamic Union', which quickly became a mass organization under the leadership of the charismatic orator H.O.S. Cokroaminoto. Seven years later it had over 2 million members. In 1914, a small group of *totok* Dutch immigrants founded the Indies Social-Democratic Association in Semarang. Finally, in 1920 the Perserikatan Komunis di India (PKI) or the Indies Communist Party was established.

In 1919, the Dutch colonial authorities decided to clamp down on all dissent. The flexibility that had characterised Dutch policy until then was abandoned in favour of an increasingly tough approach. But despite the rounding-up of large numbers of subversives, and the demise of the PKI and emasculation of the Sarekat Islam, it was at this time that the notion of 'Indonesia' first emerged. In Jul 1927, Sukarno founded the Partai Nasional Indonesia or PNI. In Oct 1928 a Congress of Indonesian Youth coined the phrase "one nation – Indonesia, one people – Indonesian, one language – Indonesian". At the same congress the Indonesian flag was designed and the Indonesian national anthem sung for the first time – *Indonesia Raya*. As John Smail writes in the book *In Search of Southeast Asia*:

> "The idea of Indonesia spread so easily, once launched, that it seemed to later historians as if it had always existed, if not actually explicitly then inchoate in the hearts of the people. But it was, in fact, a new creation, the product of a great and difficult leap of the imagination. The idea of Indonesia required the denial of the political meaning of the societies into which the first Indonesians had been born".

In spite of Dutch attempts to stifle the nationalist spirit, it spread through Indonesian, and particularly Javanese, society. By 1942 when the Japanese occupied the country, the idea of Indonesia as an independent nation was firmly rooted.

A stroll along jalan history

Many important figures in Indonesia's independence movement, as well as heroes from history, have lent their names to thoroughfares throughout the archipelago.

Abdul Muis – Sumatran independence writer.

Jend. A. Yani, Brig. Jend. Sutoyo, and Lets. Jend. Haryono, Panjaitan, S. Parman, and Suprapto – were the 6 generals (along with one captain) killed on 30 Sept 1965 in the attempted PKI coup (**see page 502**).

Cik di Tiro (1836-1891) – most famous of the *ulamas* or religious leaders who led the resistance against the Dutch in Aceh.

Cokroaminoto (1882-1934) – a leader of the Sareket Islam (Islamic Union), the first mass organization to be established in Indonesia in 1912. He was a forceful orator and highlighted numerous grievances against the Dutch.

Diponegoro, Prince (1785-1855) – led the Java War of 1825-1830 against the Dutch (**see page 596**), was captured in 1830 and then exiled to Manado and Ujung Pandang in Sulawesi where he died (**page 863**).

Gajah Mada – famous Prime Minister of the Majapahit Kingdom who served from 1331-1364 during the first 14 years of Hayam Wuruk's reign. Gajah Mada University in Yogya is one of the country's premier universities.

Haji Agus Salim – leader of the political Reform Islam movement, and right-hand man to Cokroaminoto.

Hang Tuah – naval hero who's exploits are immortalized and glorified in the *Sejarah Malayu* (Malay History), the literary masterpiece of the Malay world. Hang is an honorific equivalent to Sir.

Hasanuddin (r.1653-1669) – Sultan of Gowa in south Sulawesi who resisted the Dutch (**see page 862**).

Hayam Wuruk (r.1350-1389) – less well known as King Rajasanagara, he presided over Majapahit's golden age.

Imam Bonjol (1772-1864) – the most influential leader of the religious Padri movement in West Sumatra (**see page 773**). He was captured by the Dutch in 1837 and exiled to Priangan, then to Ambon and finally to Manado where he died in 1864 (**page 897**).

Jendral Sudirman (1915-1950) – Islamic teacher who became an officer in the Japanese volunteer army Peta (Pembela Tanah Air, Protectors of the Fatherland) and later a leading force in the revolution.

Kartini, Raden Ajeng (1879-1904) – the daughter of a noble bupati, educated at a European lower school in Jepara, Kartini is seen as an early Indonesian suffragette (**see page 636**). She tragically died in childbirth at the age of 25. Her moving letters have been published in Dutch (*Door duisternis tot licht* – 'Through darkness into light') and in English (*Letters of a Javanese princess*).

Majapahit – the Java-based empire (**see page 517**).

Pattimura (1783-1817) – a Christian Ambonese soldier who's proper name was Thomas Matulesia and who led a rebellion against the Dutch from Saparua, near Ambon in Maluku (**see page 974**).

Srivijaya – the Palembang-based empire (**see page 733**).

Teuku Umar – Acehnese leader who helped lead the *ulama* movement against the Dutch in the late 19th century (**see page 746**).

The Japanese occupation, 1942-1945

Although the Japanese occupation lasted less than 4 years, it fundamentally altered the forces driving the country towards independence. Prior to 1942, the Dutch faced no real challenge to their authority; after 1945 it was only a question of time before independence. The stunning victory of the Japanese in the Dutch

East Indies destroyed the image of colonial invincibility, undermined the prestige of the Dutch among many Indonesians, and – when the Dutch returned to power after 1945 – created an entirely new psychological relationship between rulers and ruled.

But the Japanese were not liberators. Their intention of creating a Greater East Asia Co-Prosperity Sphere did not include offering Indonesians independence. They wished to control Indonesia for their own interests. The Japanese did give a certain latitude to nationalist politicians in Java, but only as a means of mobilizing Indonesian support for their war effort. Sukarno and Muhammad Hatta were flown to Tokyo in Nov 1943 and decorated by Emperor Hirohito. For the Dutch and their allies, the war meant incarceration. There were 170,000 internees, including 60,000 women and children. About a quarter died in captivity.

One particularly sordid side of the occupation which has come to light in recent years is the role of 'comfort women'. This euphemism should be more accurately translated as 'sex slave' – women who were forced to satisfy the needs of Japanese soldiers to aid the war effort. For years the Japanese government denied such comfort stations existed, but documents unearthed in Japan have indicated beyond doubt that they were very much part of the war infrastructure. Much of the attention has focused upon comfort women from Korea, China and the Philippines, but there were also stations in Indonesia. These women, so long cowed and humiliated into silence, are now talking about their experiences to force the Japanese government to accept responsibility. Dutch-Australian Jan Ruff is one of these brave women. A young girl living in Java before the war, she was interned in Camp Ambarawa with her mother and two sisters. In February 1944 she was taken, along with nine other girls, to a brothel in Semarang for the sexual pleasure of Japanese officers. In her testimony at a public meeting in Tokyo in December 1992 she recounted: "During that time [at the brothel] the Japanese had abused me and humiliated me. They had ruined my young life. They had stripped me of everything, my self-esteem, my dignity, my freedom, my possessions, my family." Jan Ruff, and other comfort women, are still waiting for an official apology from Tokyo.

As the Japanese military lost ground in the Pacific to the advancing Americans, so their rule over Indonesia became increasingly harsh. Peasants were forcibly recruited as 'economic soldiers' to help the war effort – about 75,000 died – and the Japanese were even firmer in their suppression of dissent than the Dutch had been before them. But as the military situation deteriorated, the Japanese gradually came to realize the necessity of allowing nationalist sentiments greater rein. On 7 Sept 1944 Prime Minister Koiso promised independence, and in Mar 1945 the creation of an Investigating Committee for Preparatory Work for Indonesian Independence was announced. Among its members were Sukarno, Hatta and Muhammad Yamin. On 1 Jun Sukarno mapped out his philosophy of Pancasila or Five Principles which were to become central tenets of independent Indonesia. On 15 Aug, after the second atomic bomb was dropped on Nagasaki, the Japanese unconditionally surrendered. Sukarno, Hatta, and the other independence leaders now had to act quickly before the Allies helped the Dutch re-establish control. On 17 Aug 1945 Sukarno read out the Declaration of Independence, Indonesia's red and white flag was raised and a small group of onlookers sang the national anthem, Indonesia Raya.

The revolutionary struggle, 1945–1950

In Sept 1945, the first units of the British Army landed at Jakarta to re-impose Dutch rule. They arrived to find an Indonesian administration already in operation. Confrontation was inevitable. Young Indonesians responded by joining the revolutionary struggle, which became known as the Pemuda Movement (*pemuda* means youth). This reached its height between 1945 and mid-1946, and brought

Pancasila: Sukarno's five principles
❏ Belief in the One Supreme God
❏ Just and Civilized Humanity
❏ Unity of Indonesia
❏ Democracy guided by the inner wisdom of unanimity
❏ Social Justice for all the people of Indonesia

together young men and women of all classes, binding them together in a common cause. The older nationalists found themselves marginalized in this increasingly violent and fanatical response. Men like Sukarno and Hatta adopted a policy of *diplomasi* – negotiating with the Dutch. The supporters of the Pemuda Movement embraced *perjuangan* – the armed struggle. Not only the Dutch, were also minorities like the Chinese, Eurasians and Ambonese suffered from atrocities at the hands of the Pemuda supporters. The climax of the Pemuda Movement came in Nov 1945 with the battle for Surabaya (**see page 650**).

In 1947, the Dutch were militarily strong enough to re-gain control of Java, and E and S Sumatra. At the end of 1948, a second thrust of this 'Police Action', re-established control over much of the rest of the country. Ironically, these military successes played an important role in the final 'defeat' of the Dutch in Indonesia. They turned the United Nations against Holland, forcing the Dutch government to give way over negotiations. On 2 Nov the Hague Agreement was signed paving the way for full political independence of all former territories of the Dutch East Indies (with the exception of West Irian), on 27 Dec 1949.

From independence to Guided Democracy to coup 1950-1965

In 1950, Indonesia was an economic shambles and in political chaos. Initially, there was an attempt to create a political system based on the Western European model of parliamentary democracy. By 1952 the futility of expecting a relatively painless progression to this democratic ideal were becoming obvious, despite the holding of a parliamentary general election in 1955 with a voter turnout of over 90%. Conflicts between Communists, radical Muslims, traditional Muslims, regional groups and minorities led to a series of coups, rebel governments and violent confrontations. Indonesia was unravelling and in the middle of 1959, President Sukarno cancelled the provisional constitution and introduced his period of Guided Democracy.

This period of relative political stability rested on an alliance between the army, the Communist PKI, and Sukarno himself. It was characterized by extreme economic nationalism with assets controlled by Dutch, British and Indian companies and individuals being expropriated. The *Konfrontasi* with the Dutch over the 'recovery' of West Irian from 1960-1962, and with Malaysia over Borneo beginning in 1963 (**see page 237**), forced Sukarno to rely on Soviet arms shipments and Indonesia moved increasingly into the Soviet sphere of influence. Cracks between the odd alliance of PKI and the army widened and even Sukarno's popular support and force of character could not stop the dam from bursting. On 1 Oct 1965, 6 senior generals were assassinated by a group of middle-ranking officers, thus ending the period of Guided Democracy. M.C. Ricklefs writes:

> "...on that night the balance of hostile forces which underlay guided democracy came to an end. Many observers have seen tragedy in the period, especially in the tragedy of Sukarno, the man who outlived his time and used his popular support to maintain a regime of extravagant corruption and hypocrisy."

The coup was defeated by the quick-thinking of General Suharto whose forces overcame those of the coup's leaders. However, it undermined both Sukarno and the PKI as both were linked with the plot – the former by allowing the PKI to gain such influence, and the latter by allegedly master-minding the coup. Most Indonesians, although not all Western academics, see the coup as a Communist plot hatched by the PKI with the support of Mao Zedong and the People's Republic of China. It led to massacres on a huge scale as bands of youths set about exterminating those who were thought to be PKI supporters. This was supported, implicitly, by the army and there were news reports of 'streams choked with bodies'. The reaction was most extreme in Java and Bali, but there were murders across the archipelago. The number killed is not certain; estimates vary from 100,000 to one million and the true figure probably lies somewhere between the two. As it was an anti-Communist purge, and as China had been blamed for fermenting the coup, most of those killed were Chinese. Few doubt that the majority were innocent traders and middlemen, whose economic success and ethnic origin made them scapegoats. While these uncontrolled massacres were occurring, power was transferred to General Suharto (although he was not elected president until 1968). This marked the shift from what has become known as the Old Order, to the New Order.

Political and economic developments under the New Order, 1965-present
When Suharto took power in 1965 he had to deal with an economy in disarray. There was hyper-inflation, virtually no inward investment and declining productivity. To put the economy back on the rails he turned to a group of US-trained economists who have become known as the Berkeley Mafia. They recommended economic reform, the return of expropriated assets, and a more welcoming political and economic climate for foreign investment. In terms of international relations, Suharto abandoned the policy of support for China and the Soviet Union and moved towards the Western fold. Diplomatic relations with China were severed (and only renewed in 1990), and the policy of confrontation against Malaysia brought to an end.

The period since 1965 has been one of political stability. Suharto has now been president for more than a quarter of a century, and he has presided over a political system which in a number of respects has more in common with the Dutch era than with that of former President Sukarno. Suharto has eschewed ideology as a motivating force, kept a tight control of administration and attempted to justify his leadership by offering his people economic well-being. He is known as the 'Father of Development'.

ART AND ARCHITECTURE

Indonesia has one of the richest artistic inheritances in the world, embracing the sublime Buddhist and Hindu monuments of Central Java, including Borobudur and Prambanan; the elegant vernacular architecture of the Toraja of Sulawesi and the Batak of Sumatra; the skilled woodcarvings of the Asmat of Irian Jaya; the ikat cloth of Sumba and batiks of Java; the soaring-roofed palaces of the Minangkabau in West Sumatra; and the mountainside *puras* (temples) of Bali.

The problem is that given this enormously diverse heritage, it is not possible to talk of 'Indonesian' art and architectural style. The country's material culture is a diffuse collection of different regional inspirations, that occasionally overlap with one another but which scarcely comprise a unified 'national' output. For this reason, the distinctive regional arts and architectures of Indonesia are discussed in the relevant regional introductions of this book.

CULTURE AND LIFE

Religion – Islam in Indonesia
Indonesia has the largest population of Muslims in the world – about 80% of the country's 180 million inhabitants call themselves Muslims. Despite pressure from

Javanese Muslim leaders during the formative years of the independence movement, Sukarno resisted attempts to make the country an explicitly Islamic state. Indeed, a feature of both President Sukarno and President Suharto's rule has been their common dislike and fear of Islamic zealotry. When it has threatened stability, such movements have been vigorously suppressed. Significantly, Pancasila stipulates a belief in One Supreme God – this god being seen to be the same whether Muslim, Christian, Hindu or Buddhist – and despite the difficulty of nominating a single supreme Buddhist or Hindu god.

Over the centuries, the people of Indonesia have been influenced by a succession of religions. Each has left its imprint on aspects of Indonesian culture. Buddhism and Hinduism were introduced from India in about the 5th century, and made an impact in Sumatra and Java where they fused to become a composite Hindu-Buddhist religion. The Islamization of the Indonesian archipelago began in Sumatra, filtering SE to the N coast of Java, and from there to the Javanese interior during the 15th century (**see page 527** and also **page 39** for a summary of the practice of Islam). Christianity meanwhile, did not begin to make significant inroads in Eastern Indonesia until the 19th century.

Despite the overwhelming numerical dominance of Muslims today, many of them feel threatened by the advance of other religions, particularly Christianity. In 1933, 2.8% of the population was Christian; in 1971 this figure had risen to 7.4%. Meanwhile, some Muslims feel that their position is being eroded: over the period of the last generation, the proportion of the Indonesian population who are Muslim has fallen by over 5 percentage points – from 93% to 88%. The spread of Christianity, allied with an Islamic revival has led to greater religious tensions in a country where they have been expressly played-down in an effort to promote unity.

Muslim-Christian tensions came to a head at the end of 1992 when there were a series of attacks on churches in Java. Abdurrahman Wahid, the moderate Muslim leader of the Nahdlathul Ulama (NU), an Islamic group with 20 million members, wrote a letter to Suharto warning the president that Indonesia risked a religious conflagration if he did not act to prevent "warmongering against the Christians". Suharto pointedly ignored the missive while earlier supporting the establishment of the Organization of Indonesian Muslim Intellectuals (ICMI) in December 1990, headed by the president's great friend B.J. Habibie. There are worries that ICMI will mobilize, or at least focus, discontent as Muslims try to regain – as they see it – the initiative. There is a feeling that Christians have economic and political power that far outweighs their number. Christian, in Muslim eyes, is often equated with rich. They also point out that both of Indonesia's leading newspapers, *Kompas* and *Suara Pembaruan* are controlled by Christians while, at least until the recent reshuffle, the cabinet also had a surfeit of Christians. While Muslims continue to count Christian and Muslim heads it is likely that the issue of religion will remain prominent.

Language and literature

The Indonesian language – Bahasa Indonesia

There are more than 500 languages and dialects spoken across the archipelago, but it was Malay that was embraced as the national language – the language of unity – at the All Indonesia Youth Congress in 1928. Republicans had recognized for some time the important role that a common language might play in binding together the different religions and ethnic groups that comprised the East Indies. Malay had long been the *lingua franca* of traders in the archipelago, and, importantly, it was not identified with any particular group. Most importantly of all though, it was not a Javanese language. This muted any criticism that Java was imposing its culture on the rest of the country. Before long, Malay was being referred to as *Bahasa Indonesia* – the Indonesian language.

As visitors to Indonesia will quickly notice, the written language uses the Roman script. Through history, 3 scripts have been used in the country: 'Indian', Arabic and Roman. Indian-derived scripts include Old Javanese or Kawi, and Balinese. Arabic was associated with the spread of Islam and has tended to be confined to religious works. It proved to be particularly unsuited to use with Javanese. At the beginning of the 20th century, the Dutch assigned Ch. A. van Ophuysen to devise a system for Romanizing the Malay language. The Roman script gained popularity during the 1920s when the Indonesian nationalist movement associated its use with political change and modernity. In 1947 a number of spelling reforms were introduced of which the most important was the change from using 'oe' to 'u', so that 'Soekarno' and 'Soeharto' became, respectively, 'Sukarno' and 'Suharto'. Another series of spelling changes were introduced in 1972 to bring Bahasa Indonesia in line with Bahasa Melayu (Bahasa Malay). Nonetheless, as Bahasa Indonesia gained acceptance as a 'national' language, so it began to diverge from the Malay spoken in Malaysia. Today, although the 2 are mutually intelligible, there are noticeable differences between them in terms of both vocabulary and structure. The 2 countries' respective colonial legacy can be seen reflected in such loan words as *nomor*, from the Dutch for number in Indonesia, and *nombor* from the English in Malaysia.

The government has avidly promoted Bahasa Indonesia as the language of unity and it is now spoken in all but the most remote areas of the archipelago. Children are schooled in the national language, and television, radio and newspapers and magazines all help to propagate its use. But although most Indonesians are able to speak 'Bahasa', as it is known, they are likely to converse in their own language or dialect. Of the 500 other languages and dialects spoken in the country, the dominant ones are Sundanese, Javanese and Madurese (all 3 spoken on Java or Madura), Minang and Batak (on Sumatra), and Balinese.

Literature

Many of Indonesia's hundreds of languages have produced no written literature – although oral traditions do exist. However, the distinction between oral folk traditions and written literature is often blurred, as is the distinction between local traditions and imported literatures. For example, the series of popular stories which tell of the exploits of the *kancil* or mousedeer, who through guile and

The Ramayana and Mahabharata

Across much of Southeast Asia, the Indian epics of the Ramayana and Mahabharata have been translated and adapted for local consumption. The stories of the **Mahabharata** are the more popular. These centre on a long-standing feud between 2 family clans: the Pandawas and the Korawas. The feud culminates in an epic battle during which the 5 Pandawa brothers come face to face with their one hundred first cousins from the Korawa clan. After 18 days of fighting, the Pandawas emerge victorious and the eldest brother becomes king. The plays usually focus on one or other of the 5 Pandawa brothers, each of whom is a hero.

The **Ramayana** was written by the poet Valmiki about 2,000 years ago. It was translated from Sanskrit into Javanese during the early 10th century. The 48,000 line story tells of the abduction of the beautiful Sita by the evil king, Ravana. Sita's husband Rama, King of Ayodhia, sets out on an odyssey to retrieve his wife from Ravana's clutches, finally succeeding with the help of Hanuman the monkey god and his army of monkeys. Today it is rare to see the Ramayana performed; the orchestra needs to be large (and is therefore expensive), and in the case of *wayang* (see page 529) few puppet masters have a sufficiently large collection of puppets to cover all the characters.

cleverness is able to overcome far stronger beasts, are Indian in influence, as are some of the Batak and Dayak tales.

But Indian influence is clearest in Old Javanese literature (900-1500 AD) when the Ramayana and Mahabharata were translated from Sanskrit (see box). However, this was not merely a case of absorbing outside influences wholesale. Most notably, *Kakawin* literature – though derived from an Indian genre – is clearly a Javanese art form. *Kakawin* poetry was commissioned by noblemen and performed at court. They were regarded not merely as stories, but as spiritual works of worship – almost as a form of written yoga. Perhaps the finest of the *kakawin* is the 14th century *Nagarakertagama*, discovered in 1894.

With the fall of the Hindu Majapahit Empire and the rise of Islam, so 'modern' Javanese literature evolved, from around the beginning of the 18th century. This combined Indian and Muslim traditions and produced such works as the *Babad Tanah Jawi*, a historical text, and the *Hikayat Aceh*, a record of Sultan Iskander Muda of Aceh's reign (1607-1636). The greatest source of dispute among scholars is how far such texts can be regarded as historically accurate – some scholars use them as a template to recreate Javanese life of the time, while others maintain that they are fundamentally inaccurate. Among religious texts of this period, the most highly regarded – for example the 3,000 page *Serat Centhini* – were produced at the court in Aceh, where they took on an almost mystical tone.

With the arrival of the Dutch and the gradual extension of their control over the archipelago, so a modern literature emerged. Many of the finest novelists of the early years of the 20th century were from Sumatra – and particularly from Minangkabau (West Sumatra) – men such as Adbul Muis, Marah Rusli (who wrote the highly regarded *Sitti Nurbaya*) and Nur St. Iskander. The Japanese occupation of the country stifled publication, but following the 1945 revolution a group of idealists formed the *Angkatan 45* – the generation of 1945 – to support and develop Indonesian literature. Foremost among its members was Chairil Anwar. *Angkatan 45* became caught up in the political maelstrom of the 1960s, and

Art form	Centre of performance	Further information
Dance and drama		
Barong or kris	Bali	page 682
Kecak	Bali	page 681
Legong	Bali	page 683
Pencak silat	W Sumatra	page 776
Wayang kulit	Java	page 529
Wayang topeng	Java	page 529
Wayang wong	Java	page 533
Ramayana ballet	Java	page 533
Court dances	Java	page 533
Bambu gila	Maluku	page 978
Cakalele	Maluku	page 979
Music		
Angklung	Sundanese, Java	page 575
Gamelan	Java	page 534

following the attempted coup of 1965 many of its members were imprisoned. The years since have seen an emasculation of Indonesian literature, and the radicalism and invention of the 1950s and 1960s has still yet to be equalled.

Dance, drama and music

Like Indonesian art and architecture, the dance, drama and music of the archipelago also spans a large number of regional styles and forms. Many of these are discussed in the relevant regional sections. Nonetheless, the influence of Javanese drama and music has spread beyond Java to the Outer Islands – in a process of artistic imperialism. In so doing these art forms have begun to take on a 'national' character, and have become representative of the country as a whole. This applies, for example, to the gamelan orchestra and the wayang shadow puppet theatre.

MODERN INDONESIA

Politics

Since 1965, with few hiccups, Indonesia's political landscape has remained unchanged. President Suharto still holds power, and influence still lies with a loose grouping of businessmen, civilian politicians and the army. This military-bureaucratic élite has exercised popular power through Sekber Golkar, a political party based upon the armed forces or Abri.

Golkar is, in effect, the state's own party. All state employees are automatically members of Golkar, and during election campaigns, the state controls the activities of other parties. Not surprisingly therefore, Golkar has been able consistently to win over 60% of the votes cast in parliamentary elections, and controls the Parliament (DPR) and the People's Consultative Assembly. In the 1987 elections, Golkar won 73% of the vote. The most recent elections were held in Jun 1992 and Golkar once again achieved a convincing majority, winning 68% of the vote.

That said, at each election, 'opposition' parties claim that they are well set to eat into the Golkar majority. Both the Indonesian Democratic Party (PDI) and the United Development Party (PPP) (which represents a coalition of Muslim groups), were hoping for more success in 1992. Both recorded modest increases in their share of the popular vote: the PDI from 11% to 15%, and the PPP from 16% to 17%. But Golkar had reason to be satisfied with the result. The only area of concern was the loss of support in Java, the country's heartland. As the people of Java are the most politically aware, this may give an indication of things to come.

In the Indonesian context, 'opposition' is a relative term: there is really little to choose in matters of substance between the policies and perspectives of Golkar, the PDI and the PPP. Even should an opposition party win a majority, there is no chance that it would wield power. In the People's Consultative Assembly, only slightly over 400 out of 1,000 seats are up for election. Of the remaining 600, 500 are appointed directly by the President, and 100 are reserved for army members.

A rather more interesting question – and one which arouses some consternation among Indonesians – concerns the future of President Suharto. He has brought great stability to Indonesia, but he has now been in power for nearly a quarter of a century, and is 71 years old. Only such paragons of democracy as Kim Il Sung of North Korea and Ne Win of Burma have held power for so long. In Mar 1993 Suharto began his sixth consecutive 5-year term as president. Despite this remarkable political longevity – or perhaps because of it – there is the looming issue of succession. Mrs Suharto slyly commented before her husband's 71st birthday on 8 Jun 1992 that "a coconut has more juice the older it gets", but even President Suharto is not thought to have found the elixir of everlasting youth. In Mar 1993 some indication of a possible successor was provided by the election of Try Sutrisno, the retired armed forces commander, to the post of vice-president. Significantly, Sutrisno was the army's choice, and after their nomination Suharto had little choice but to follow Golkar's lead. There lingers the impression that the army is manoeuvring skilfully to be in a strong position to influence events when Suharto is expected to retire in 1998.

Although Suharto's 26 years in power has brought unparalleled political stability to Indonesia, there is increasing criticism of his family's economic power. Nepotism may be a way of life in Southeast Asia, but there are limits to what is deemed acceptable. The president's wife, Siti Hartinah, has long been nick-named Madame Ten Percent, but now Suharto's 6 children (3 sons and 3 daughters) have also built up considerable business empires. The two biggest non-Chinese conglomerates – Bimantara and Humpuss – are both run by sons of the president. They have managed to do this by drawing on their ties with the President to secure lucrative contracts and licences – even enjoying preferential rates of interest on loans from the central Bank of Indonesia. Perhaps the most infamous of recent deals, is the clove monopoly created by Suharto's youngest son Hutomo 'Tommy' Mandala Putra (**see page 635**). One Asian ambassador in Jakarta was quoted in the *Far Eastern Economic Review* in Apr 1992 as saying: "The central question is whether the avarice of the children will ultimately undermine 25 years of pretty good leadership". An *Economist* survey of the country in 1993 reflected similar sentiments, when – likening him to former Javanese kings – it described Suharto's as having: "A paternal style, a professed lack of interest in power, a circle of deferential courtiers and the ability to dispense seemingly unlimited patronage ...". Despite the obvious sensitivity of the subject, opposition leaders and academics are becoming less reticent in voicing their thoughts, believing that the system of nepotism could begin to undermine the country's economic progress.

Indonesia suffered a set-back to its international image in the wider world when the army killed at least 50 East Timorese in Nov 1991 (**see page 967**). Despite some evidence of a loosening of political control, the government treats all pressure groups – whether radical Muslim or secular human rights-orientated – with suspicion. Continuing difficulties in Aceh (**see page 746**) and Irian Jaya (**see page 993**) as well as in East Timor, ensures that the government will keep a tight rein on dissent. Nonetheless, as living standards grow and the economy is reformed, it is difficult not to see how pressure for greater political reform and openness will also continue to grow. Perhaps this is already occurring: at the end of 1992, the number of people on the government's immigration blacklist was reduced from 17,000 to 9,000.

Economy

Since 1965, the Indonesian economy has gradually recovered from the extreme mismanagement that characterized the period from independence in 1950. With the advice of the Berkeley Mafia – a group of reform-minded, US-trained economists – there has been an attempt to increase efficiency, reduce corruption and entice foreign investment. Like the other countries of the region, export-orientated development has become the name of the game. President Suharto is known as the 'Father of Development' – and sometimes as the '5 per cent President' (because his legitimacy is based on maintaining at least a 5% economic growth rate). Development has been based upon a series of 5-year plans known as *Repelitas* (standing for *Rencana Pembangunan Lima Tahun*), the first beginning in 1969. Today, Indonesia's GNP/person is US$600; in 1967 it was

The politics of envy: the Chinese in Indonesia

The Chinese make up about 5% of Indonesia's population and are still treated with suspicion. There are still 300,000 Chinese living in Indonesia who have yet to choose whether they are Indonesians by nationality, or Chinese. The community adopts a low profile – in Glodok (Jakarta's Chinatown), for example, there are few Chinese signs on the shopfronts. Indeed, until recently there was a ban on displaying Chinese characters. The so-called *masalah Cina* – or 'Chinese problem' – continues to be hotly discussed, much of the debate centering on whether the Chinese should be assimilated or integrated into Indonesian culture.

The animosity between the 'Indonesian' and Chinese communities is based upon the latter's economic success, and their role as middlemen, shopkeepers and moneylenders. Most of the country's largest firms are Chinese-owned – known as *cukong* – and the richest families are also Chinese. Such evident success has given rise to envy. Even President Suharto has publicly stated that the Chinese should be prepared to redistribute their wealth to prevent a 'social disturbance'. Some indigenous businessmen, known as *pribumi*, have called for the implementation of an explicit economic policy of positive discrimination in favour of native Indonesians modelled on the New Economic Policy in Malaysia (see page 86).

So far at least, President Suharto has scorned such an idea. Perhaps part of the reason is because influential indigenous politicians make considerable fortunes through their links with the *cukongs*. The politicians provide political protection, and they in turn are rewarded financially by the *cukong*. The Chinese still have codes on their ID cards which identify them as Chinese – although this may soon change – and there are numerous other ways in which they face discrimination. In 1990, President Suharto invited 30 of the country's top Chinese businessmen to his palace and was seen, on television, explaining to them that if inequalities were not reduced – implying the gap between the Chinese rich and the Indonesian poor – "social gap, social envy and even social disturbance will happen". This barely concealed warning of a possible repeat of the events of 1965 was not lost on the Chinese community.

only US$70. At that time, the average Indonesian – statistically – was twice as poor as the average Indian or Bangladeshi, so a great deal has been achieved. The World Bank projects that Indonesia will crack the US$1,000 mark in the year 2000.

Indonesia has benefited from its **oil wealth (see page 510)**. This has enabled the government to pursue ambitious programmes of social, agricultural and regional development. After the first oil price rise in 1973 following in the wake of the Arab-Israeli Yom Kippur War, when the cost of a barrel of oil quadrupled in less than a year, the government was awash with funds. These were used to build 6,000 primary schools a year, expand roads into the less accessible parts of the Outer Islands, and subsidize rice cultivation so that the country attained self-sufficiency by the 1980s. But the oil boom also promoted **corruption** on a scale that was remarkable even by Southeast Asian standards. It was said, for example, that importers were having to pay US$200 million a year in bribes to the notoriously corrupt Customs Department, and that even the lowliest coffee boy had to pass US$1,000 under the table to buy himself a job. This investment would, of course, be repaid in a few months, as the coffee boy's share of the bribes trickled down through the system. Such was the degree of corruption that in 1985 Suharto was forced to take the unprecedented step of calling in a Swiss firm, Société Générale de Surveillance, to oversee import procedures. They did much to clean up the Customs Department, but their contract was only temporary and in 1992 SGS began to hand back control to the Indonesian customs. Regrettably, the department does not seem to have been reformed. Corruption is on the increase again, and the *Economist* reported that "sadly, an unruly child seems to have matured into a delinquent adolescent".

The decline in oil prices since the early 1980s has forced the government to become rather more hard-headed in its approach to economic management. Growth in recent years has been rapid, and the value of **non-oil exports** has expanded particularly impressively – today, over 20% of Indonesia's GDP is produced by the manufacturing sector. Foreign investors have been attracted by Indonesia's low wage rates when compared with the region's other emergent economies, Malaysia and Thailand. Other than oil and gas, Indonesia's major exports – in order of importance – include wood products, rubber and coffee. This serves to illustrate the continued importance of **agriculture** and other primary products. Much of the glitz may be attached to prestige projects such as the aircraft manufacturer IPTN (**see page 572**), but agriculture remains the backbone of the economy employing nearly half the country's workforce.

Tourism is Indonesia's third largest foreign exchange earner: the sector generated US$3.2 billion in 1992. In that year, 3.1 million tourists visited the country – well over double the figure for 1988. Tourist arrival figures are, however, still low compared with Thailand, Singapore or Malaysia. In terms of tourists per sq km, Thailand had 10 tourists/year, Indonesia only a little over one per year. To more fully exploit the country's tourism potential, 1991 was declared Visit Indonesia Year by the government with the slogan 'Let's Go Archipelago'. Unfortunately, this promotion blitz happened to coincide with the Gulf War and recession in the West, so numbers were rather disappointing – about 2.5 million. It is also true that many areas have limited facilities. About one third of all tourists visit Bali, and beyond one or 2 other destinations like the Riau Islands, Jakarta and Yogya, travel is only for the more adventurous.

Despite impressive recent growth, foreign investors and local businessmen still highlight excessive corruption, a poor infrastructure, the lack of skilled workers, a cumbersome bureaucracy and high interest rates as the major constraints to growth. The liberalization programme also has its own risks, as exemplified in the collapse of Bank Summa, one of the country's largest private banks, in late 1992. Another issue that needs to be addressed are the glaring inequalities between the rich and the poor, and between different regions of the country.

There is also the deep-seated problem of political patronage. This means it is often more useful for a businessman to cultivate close connections with influential politicians, and thereby secure lucrative government contracts, than it is to produce the best product at the lowest price. This is particularly true of Chinese businessmen who often feel politically exposed in a country where there is ingrained mistrust of the Chinese community, founded partly on their economic success and partly on the perception that they do not show total allegiance to their adopted country. The two best examples of this approach to business are Liem Sioe Liong, who was Suharto's quartermaster in the 1960s, and Bob Hasan, who helped to finance the president's Central Java Command, also in the 1960s. They are both Chinese; they both have impeccable links with Suharto; and they are both highly successful and very rich. As the saying goes, this success has been based more on know-who, rather than know-how.

In March 1993 Suharto reshuffled his cabinet. Many Western commentators identified a shift in influence away from the so-called Berkeley Mafia – the technocrats who have been instrumental in Indonesia's economic liberalization – towards the economic nationalists led by B.J. Habibie. A number of Habibie's acolytes gained cabinet portfolios in the reshuffle and some observers are arguing

that Indonesia is on the verge of a highly significant change in economic policy –
towards what is known as 'Habibienomics'. This may be reading too much into
the cabinet moves: to an extent the changes are generational, and there is little
doubt that Suharto remains firmly in control. Who proves to be correct will clearly
depend on how policy evolves over the next year to 18 months.

Indonesia: fact file

Geographic

Land area	1,919,443 sq km
Arable land as % of total	9%
Average annual rate of deforestation	0.5%
Highest mountain, Mount Jaya	5,030 m
Average rainfall in Jakarta	1,766 mm
Average temperature in Jakarta	26°C

Economic

GNP/person (1990)	US$560
GDP/person (PPP*, 1990)	US$2,181
GNP growth (/capita, 1980-1990)	4.1%
GDP growth 1990	6.7%
GDP growth 1991	7%
GDP growth 1992	5.5%
GDP growth 1993	6% (est.)
% labour force in agriculture	54%
Total debt (% GNP)	66%
Debt service ratio (% exports)	31%
Military expenditure (% GNP)	1.6%

Social

Population	188 million
Population growth rate (1960-91)	2.2%

Adult literacy rate	82%
Mean years of schooling	3.9 years
Tertiary graduate as % of age group	0.6%
Population in absolute poverty	17%
Rural population as % of total	69%
Growth of urban population (1960-91)	4.7%/year
Urban population in largest city	23%
Televisions per 1,000 people	60

Health

Life expectancy at birth	62 years
Population with access to clean water	42%
Calorie intake as % of requirements	121%
Malnourished children less than 5 years old	9.4 million
Contraceptive prevalence rate‡	48%

*PPP = *Purchasing Power Parity* (based on what it costs to buy a similar
basket of goods and services in different countries).
‡ % of women of childbearing age using a form of contraception.
Source: World Bank (1993) *Human Development Report 1993*, OUP: New
York; and other sources.

JAVA

Introduction, 513; Jakarta, 537; West Java, 557; Central Java and Yogyakarta, 587; East Java, 638

Maps: Jakarta General, 538; Kota, 543; Jakarta Centre, 546; West Java, 559; Banten, 560; Bogor, 566; Bandung, 573; Cirebon, 580; Pangandaran, 585; Central Java, 588; Yogyakarta, 591; Kraton, 593; Around Yogyakarta, 597; Borobudur, 605; Prambanan, 613; Solo, 617; Dieng Plateau, 626; Semarang, 629; Kudus, 634; East Java, 639; Panataran Complex, 641; Malang, 643; Around Malang and Mt. Bromo, 645; Surabaya, 649; Trowulan, 652; Madura, 656.

INTRODUCTION

Java is the cultural and economic heart of Indonesia. Although the island covers only 6% of the country's land area, well over 100 million people live here – more than 60% of Indonesia's total population. This makes it one of the most densely populated islands on earth. Historically, Java has been home to Indonesia's most glorious kingdoms (an exception being Sumatra's Srivijayan Empire), and has produced the archipelago's finest art and architecture. Today, it is the centre of political and economic power, generating more than half of the country's GDP and dominating Indonesia to the extent that inhabitants in the Outer Islands decry the so-called 'Javanization' of their cultures.

The immense population of Java has not just been a concern of recent years. From the beginning of the 19th century, Dutch administrators and commentators had been talking of the island's 'overpopulation'. Nederburgh in 1802 wrote of Java as overcrowded and its population unemployed. In 1827, L.P.J. du Bus de Gisignies painted a picture of an island that before too long would be populated by millions of tenants living at the very margins of existence; even Stamford Raffles in his *History of Java*, published in 1817, believed there would have to be an emigration of surplus population from Java to other, less densely populated, islands. Yet, the predictions of the prophets of doom – who had forecast famines on a scale hitherto unimagined – have not been fulfilled. This is all the more remarkable when it is considered that in 1845, Java's population was just one tenth of today's figure. This astonishing feat has been achieved by continually increasing the output of wet rice or *sawah* (see box, **page 514**). A lesser, though still significant role has been played by the programme of 'transmigration' – the resettlement of Javanese in sites cleared from the forest in the Outer Islands (see box, **page 97**).

ENVIRONMENT

Land

Java stretches more than 1,000 km from E to W, but is only 81 km broad at its widest point, and covers an area of 132,187 sq km. The island lies over a volcanic arc that marks the boundary between 2 tectonic (continental) plates, making it one of the most volcanically active places on earth. There are 121 volcanoes on Java – more than any other country – of which between 27 and 35 are classified

---

Sawah: wet rice cultivation in Java

Every visitor to Java is struck by the immense patchwork of verdant rice paddys, often terraced down precipitous hillsides. Rice (*Oryza sativa* L.) cultivation seems to have been introduced into Java some time during the first millennium BC. But at that time the crop was grown in dry fields in the same way as other grains such as millet, wheat and corn. The cultivation of 'wet' rice – rice grown in flooded conditions (see box, **see page 34**) – probably did not begin until the early centuries of the first millennium. By the 8th century rice was being grown in irrigated fields in E Java, while the Chinese adventurer Ma Huan reported at the beginning of the 15th century that in N-E Java "the rice ripens twice in one year", indicating that double cropping was practiced. By the time European mariners began to arrive in Southeast Asia during the 16th century, Java had become the greatest rice exporter in the region. Central Java was sending 50-60 rice junks each year to Melaka on the Malay Peninsula, while the Dutch reported in 1615 that they could purchase 2,000 tonnes a year at the N coast town of Jepara.

The logic of cultivating rice in flooded conditions is that higher yields can be achieved. In Java today, there are areas where 3 crops are harvested every year, each crop producing up to 5 tonnes per hectare. Hectare for hectare, the wet rice system of cultivation in Java probably produces more calories than almost any other agricultural system. The lack of land and an exploding population – which has grown 10-fold over the space of less than 150 years – has forced rice farmers to search for new ways to increase yields. In response, terraces have been built up ever-steeper slopes, irrigation systems have been perfected to ensure year-round supplies of water, and the land has been cultivated ever-more assiduously and minutely.

By squeezing a few extra kilograms of grain from each minutely cultivated field, the Javanese farmer has managed to feed each extra mouth. But only just: in the mid-1980s, the government estimated that over ¾ of the rural population were living below the poverty line. Some scholars believe that the system of cultivation has perpetuated poverty, by preventing the accumulation of any surplus.

Historically, rules of harvesting guaranteed that everyone in a village had the right to harvest any piece of land – all they had to do was to turn up on the day. This *bawon* ('share') system of harvesting guaranteed that even people with no land could secure enough rice to feed themselves and their families. For land owners today this is not always a desirable tradition – there have been reports of up to 600 people harvesting a single hectare, leading to trampling of the crop and the loss of production. To get round this, land owners have taken to harvesting their land at night or very early in the morning, and not announcing the date of the harvest. Even so, the *bawon* system has now been replaced in many villages with the *tebasan* system, where the standing crop is sold to a middleman before it is harvested, thereby getting around such community obligations.

as active. This degree of vulcanicity has periodically led to catastrophe. Most famously, in 1883, the island of Krakatau just off Java's W coast exploded killing 36,000 people (**see page 564**). Further back in history, in 928 or 929AD, it is thought that Mount Merapi erupted leading to the mass migration of the court and people of Central Java eastwards (**see page 523**). More recently, in 1982, Mount Galunggung in East Java erupted causing 60,000 people to lose their homes and livelihoods.

But Java's volcanoes have not just been a source of misery and disruption; they are the reason why the island has some of the richest soils in the world. Fertile ash coats the land and volcanic rocks are slowly eroded to release more nutrients. Admittedly, not all the discharge is fertile – a distinction needs to be made between the good, neutral-basic volcanic soils, and the poor acidic volcanic soils of parts of East and West Java. Nonetheless, Java's fertility explains how agricultural populations, crowded at densities of up to 2,000 per sq km, can produce enough food to support themselves. It also explains why farmers continue to cultivate the land around volcanoes that are at constant risk of eruption. Thomas Stamford Raffles in 1830 wrote that "whoever has viewed the fertile plains of Java or beheld with astonishment the surprising efforts of human industry, which have carried cultivation to the summits of the most stupendous mountains, will be inclined to consider that nothing short of a permanent interest in the soil could have effected such a change in the face of the country...". In Raffles' view, it was Java's extraordinary natural fertility which allowed great civilisations to arise on the island.

Climate
The 'east monsoon' from Jun to Aug brings dry weather to Java while the 'west monsoon' from Dec to Feb corresponds with the wet season. During the transitional months between these 2 seasons, rainfall can be even heavier than during the wet season. In general it becomes drier from west to east, and while the western two thirds of the island receives rain throughout the year, the eastern third of Java has a pronounced dry season. Average annual rainfall in West Java is 2,360 mm, in Central Java, 2,400 mm, and in East Java, only 1,660 mm. Temperatures vary little through the year, averaging 26°C-27°C at sea-level.

THE HISTORY OF JAVA

Java's epic and convoluted history encompasses an array of kingdoms, empires, sultanates and dynasties. Although the history portrayed below might give the impression that one kingdom neatly followed another in dominating the island, there were always a number of powers vying for influence at any one time. It was only a case of which dominated, when.

Sailendra (Central Java, mid-8th-10th century)
The Sailendra Dynasty of Central Java, which lasted for only 2 centuries, was the greatest of all the Javanese kingdoms and produced architectural monuments of such grandeur and artistic brilliance that they are among the finest not just in Indonesia, but in the world.

In the middle of the 8th century a descendant of Funanese immigrants from S Vietnam established a kingdom called Sailendra, meaning 'King of the Mountain' – a name that associates it with the temple mountain-builders of Cambodia. At the height of its power, Sailendra's sphere of influence stretched as far as Champa on the Vietnamese coast and Angkor in Cambodia.

The kings of the Sailendra dynasty derived their wealth and power from agriculture, rather than trade which was the backbone of Sumatra's Srivijayan

Empire. Exploiting the year-round rains, tropical warmth, and fertile volcanic soils of Java, the farmers of Sailendra produced a substantial rice surplus. This allowed a large court, with its holy men, artisans and soldiers to be maintained, and a series of impressive monuments to be constructed. The Sailendras were Buddhists, and they attracted Buddhist scholars from all over Asia to their court. It also seems that the kings were linked through marriage with the rulers of Srivijaya.

Of all the monuments erected by the Sailendras, none is more imposing than **Borobudur** – possibly the single most magnificent temple in Southeast Asia. This enormous edifice, built between 778 and 824, represented the cosmological and spiritual centre of the kingdom. Along its terraces, row upon row of superbly executed reliefs, depict the Sailendra world order: the 9 previous lives of the Gautama Buddha, princes and carpenters, dancers and fishermen. Borobudur offered a religious justification for Sailendra rule, and at the same time gave the kings religious authority over Srivijaya. Johann Scheltema, a German traveller, on seeing Java's monuments wrote – rather pompously – at the beginning of this century that they were "...eloquent evidence of that innate consciousness which moves men to propitiate the principle of life by sacrifice in temples as gloriously divine as mortal hand can raise".

Sanjaya (Central and East Java, 8th-11th century)
At about the same time as the Sailendra kings were building Borobudur, another Central Javanese Kingdom was also engaged in an extensive monument-building programme: Sanjaya (sometimes known as Mataram). In this instance, Hinduism, rather than Buddhism, was the dominant religion, but no less energy was expended. Foremost among this kingdom's temples was **Prambanan**, the finest Hindu shrine on Java. The Sanjaya Kingdom derived its wealth from controlling the spice trade between Maluku (the Moluccas), China and the sultanates of the Arab world. The control of port facilities focused on the strategic Strait of Melaka (Malacca). This led Sanjaya into open conflict with the more powerful kingdom of Srivijaya based at Palembang, Sumatra. In 1006, Srivijaya defeated Sanjaya and sacked its capital, slaughtering many of its inhabitants. It was not until 1026 that Srivijaya's hold over the Strait of Melaka was relinquished following an expedition headed by a prince from South India.

Before the conflict between Sanjaya and Srivijaya, at the beginning of the 10th century, the kingdoms of Central Java mysteriously moved E to the area of the Brantas River. This move was associated with the reign of King Sindok, whose power is reflected in a multitude of inscriptions recording his successes and decrees. Various explanations have been proposed to explain the shift in focus from Central to East Java, including war, pestilence and the eruption of Mount Merapi. A century later, in 1020, a new figurehead emerged in the Sanjaya kingdom – Airlangga – the son of a Balinese prince and a Sanjaya princess. His reign was peaceful and he restored relations with Srivijaya by marrying a Srivijayan princess. Religious syncretism was at its height during Airlangga's reign and he pragmatically recognized both Buddhism and Hinduism, hoping to appeal to supporters of both faiths. He also eroded the strength of the Brahmin priests by appropriating their land. Towards the end of his life, Airlangga became a Buddhist monk, while at the same time styling himself as a re-incarnation of Vishnu (Hindu). His biggest mistake was to divide his kingdom just before his death in 1049. He had no direct heir and feared a dispute between 2 of his children, born of concubines. His fears were realised when – following his death – the empire was divided into 2 kingdoms – Kediri and Janggala.

Kediri & Janggala (1050-1222)
Kediri was centred in the Brantas River valley near the site of the modern day city of the same name; while it is thought that Janggala was focused S of Surabaya, near

Malang. Inscriptions indicate that Kediri became a locally powerful maritime kingdom, operating on the N coast of Java. It traded extensively in spices from Maluku with India, and was preferred as a port over Srivijaya because of its proximity to the source of those spices. Of Janggala, historians know almost nothing. However, in 1222, Ken Angrok of Kediri captured the lesser kingdom of Janggala and then went on to kill the ruler of Kediri and establish his new kingdom at Singasari.

Between 1486 and 1512, the capital was moved from Majapahit, SW to Kediri, perhaps to escape from the powerful Islamic incursion from the N coast. The move did nothing to prevent Demak from overpowering Kediri in 1527.

Singasari (1222-1292)
The short-lived Singasari Kingdom was founded in East Java by Ken Angrok in 1222 after the defeat of Kediri and Janggala. The kingdom's greatest king was its last, Kertanagara (1268-1292). His aggressively expansionist policies took Singasari's influence beyond the confines of East Java and in 1290 he defeated the once powerful empire of Srivijaya.

Although Singasari lasted just 70 years, a considerable temple-building programme was undertaken, which included the construction of Candi Kidal and Candi Jago, to house the funerary remains of the kings. In 1289 the Chinese Emperor Kublai Khan sent a diplomatic mission to Singasari, ordering Kertanagara to accept the suzerainty of the Middle Kingdom and pay tribute. Kertanagara ignored his demands and after torturing the members of the Chinese mission, sent a message back to Peking carved into the forehead of the Emperor's delegate. The enraged Kublai Khan responded to this diplomatic slap-in-the-face by dispatching a large army to attack Singasari. A rival prince from the old kingdom of Kediri took advantage of the disarray caused by the imminent arrival of the Chinese force and seized the kingdom of Singasari, killing Kertanagara in the process. Kertanagara's heir, Vijaya, promptly fled to Majapahit. The Chinese arrived to find a country in turmoil. Vijaya, sensing Chinese reluctance to return home without some recognition of suzerainty, promised to become a vassal of China if the Chinese fleet would assist him in overthrowing the rebel from Kediri. In such inauspicious circumstances, the great Majapahit dynasty was founded.

Majapahit (1292-1478)
The Majapahit – or 'Bitter Gourd' – empire was the last and most powerful of the Javanese kingdoms and at the height of its influence claimed suzerainty over parts of Sumatra, Malaya and Borneo. The capital of this far-flung empire was Trowulan, which at the time was one of the largest cities in Asia.

The flowering of the Majapahit Kingdom spanned the middle years of the 14th century and is associated with 2 brilliant men: **Gajah Mada** and **Hayam Wuruk**. Gajah Mada was a skilled general and consummate politician – and filled the post

The curse of the kris-maker
The Singasari king Ken Angrok fell in love with a Queen of Tumapel, called Ken Dedes. However, to marry her he first needed to murder her husband. This required the forging of a *kris*, or sword, (see page 548) endowed with supernatural powers. Unfortunately, the swordsmith engaged to make the weapon took so long to forge the *kris* that, in his impatience, Angrok stabbed the poor man to death. As he lay dying, he cursed the king and his descendants, claiming they would all die by the kris Angrok held in his hand. The curse did not take long to take effect; Angrok was murdered by his stepson Anusapati, having been betrayed by his new wife Ken Dedes. Anusapati, in his turn, and despite taking precautions such as building a moat around his bed, was also murdered by the same sword after ruling Singasari for twenty years (his memorial shrine is at Candi Kidal).

A summary of Javanese history 400-1870

400	First Hindu Kingdom of Tarumanegara is established

Central Javanese Period 600-929

	Sailendra Dynasty (mid 8th-10th century)
	Sanjaya Dynasty (8th-11th century)

East Javanese Period 929-1527

	King Sindok of Sanjaya (928-950)
1006	Srivijaya defeats Sanjaya Kingdom
	King Airlangga of Sanjaya (1020-1049)
1045	Partition of Sanjaya into Kediri and Janggala
	Kediri Dynasty (929-1222)
	Singasari Dynasty (1222-1292)
	King Ken Angrok (1222-1227)
1222	King Ken Angrok conquers Janggala
	King Kertanagara (1268-1292)
	Majapahit Dynasty (1292-1527)
	Chief Minister Gajah Mada (1331-1364)
1343	Javanese colony established on Bali
	King Hayam Wuruk (1350-1389)
1400	Decline of Majapahit

Islamic Period 1527-1757

1500	Sultanate of Demak
1527	Demak overpowers Kediri
	Wali Dynasty in W Java
	Foundation of Jakarta
1575	Islamic Kingdom of Mataram
	King Senopati (1575-1601)

Colonial Period 1513-1870

1513	Portuguese land at Sunda Kelapa; first European contact with Java
1522	Portuguese establish a godown at Sunda Kelapa
1602	VOC established
	Sultan Agung of Mataram (1613-1645)
1619	Batavia established by Jan Pieterszoon Coen
1628-29	Sultan Agung attacks Batavia, but fails to dislodge Dutch
1757	Dutch conquer Mataram and divide kingdom into 3 vassal sultanates
	Governor-General Daendels (1808-1810)
	British administration under Raffles (1811-1816)
	Java War (1825-1830)
	Culture System (1830-1870)

of Prime Minister from 1331 to 1364. Hayam Wuruk, the grandson of Majapahit's founder Vijaya, acceded to the throne after the death of Vijaya's widow in 1350 and reigned until 1389. His formal title was Rajasanagara and he was the greatest king of the Majapahit Period. During Hayam Wuruk's reign, and under the guidance of Gajah Mada, Java experienced what many regard as the island's golden years, during which there was a flowering of the arts. The kingdom of Majapahit had contacts as far afield as Burma, Thailand, Cambodia and Vietnam. Though ostensibly Buddhist, the king and his subjects also worshipped the Hindu gods Siva and Vishnu. All 3 were incarnate in the king, who was known as Siva-Buddha or Nirguna.

By 1402, Melaka (Malacca), on the Malay Peninsula, had been established as a trading-post and the importance of Java waned. At the same time as Majapahit was losing its economic *raison d'être*, the infiltration of Islam began to undermine the religious legitimacy of the kingdom. Majapahit finally fell to Demak, the Islamic state on Java's north coast, in 1478.

Java in disarray: 1400-1600

Following the decline and subsequent fall of Majapahit at the beginning of the 15th century, Java entered a 200-year period of in-fighting between numerous small kingdoms and sultanates. Along the N coast, trading sultanates (so-called *pasisir* states) drew their religious inspiration from Islam and their wealth from controlling the spice trade between Maluku and Melaka. Foremost among these trading states was **Demak** which reached the height of its power under Sultan Trenggono in the 16th century. At that time its influence, if not its power, spread through Central and East Java. Meanwhile, a group of weak agriculturally-oriented kingdoms dominated the interior. These maintained their links – religious and cultural – with the preceding Hindu-Buddhist empires. Hardly worthy successors to Sailendra and Majapahit, they maintained a tradition that was on the wane. It was not until the early part of the 17th century that Java was once again to come under the influence of a single dominant power: Mataram.

Mataram (16th century-1757)

The last of the great Javanese kingdoms was Mataram, focused on Central Java near Yogyakarta and Surakarta. Mataram's greatest king was Sultan Agung (r.1613-1645), a devout Muslim. With the help of the Dutch, he vanquished the coastal trading states and promoted Islam in Java's interior. At its peak, his kingdom encompassed Surabaya in the E and Cirebon in the N. He had every intention of uniting the whole of Java, but was prevented from achieving this aim by the presence of the Dutch in Batavia (Jakarta). His 2 attempts to dislodge the Dutch in 1628 and 1629 failed, with great loss of life.

Although Mataram's kings were not the god-kings of earlier empires they were still regarded as divine. Their names indicate as much: Hamengkubuwono means 'He who holds the World on his Lap', while Pakubuwono can be translated as 'Axis of the World'. The king and his capital – or *negara*, from the Sanskrit – lay at the centre, not just of the kingdom, but of the cosmos. To live close to a King was to bask in his reflected glory and power—a notion which links the rulers of Mataram with their Hindu-Buddhist predecessors. The kings of Mataram ruled through an assortment of hereditary lords and appointed officials. The officials were servants of the king and were called *bupati* or regents, a word which is still in use today. Through this network, the king was able to draw taxes in food and labour. There was no Majapahit money in circulation – although the Spanish silver dollar and Chinese copper coins were in use.

In a number of respects the Mataram kingdom was weak. It generated 'income' by extracting the small agricultural surplus that a peasant family produced each year. By doing this many thousands of times, the king accumulated considerable wealth. But the basis of this wealth was wholly different from the coastal or *pasisir* kingdoms, whose economic power was founded on trade. Historians argue that Mataram managed to unite Java as a political whole because there existed a common language and culture, and as John Smail says "a political myth that was universally accepted because it rested on common religious beliefs". Such an explanation is only partially convincing, and the Mataram empire was beginning to degenerate even as it reached the greatest extent of its power. Sultan Agung's son, Amangkurat I (r.1645-1677), faced a rebellion in 1672 after Mount Merapi erupted, and it was only with Dutch assistance and the crowning of a new king, Amangkurat

II, that the kingdom was pieced-back together. Ironically, the assistance afforded by the Dutch gave them a foothold and presaged their domination of Java by 1757.

Colonial expansion and control (1513-1870)

Colonial contact with Java dates back to 1513, when a Portuguese expedition arrived off Sunda Kelapa (Jakarta). But the Portuguese were in no position to make their presence felt. Instead, it was the Dutch who were to extend their control over the archipelago. This was a gradual affair (see box, **page 498**, and for the first 150 years, Dutch influence was restricted to the town of Batavia (Jakarta) and its environs. The history of this period is recounted in the introduction to Jakarta (**see page 539**).

The Dutch, in the guise of the **Vereenigte Ooste-Indische Compagnie (VOC)** or Dutch East India Company, only began to expand their influence inland as the Mataram Kingdom went into decline. They did this with little enthusiasm, merely filling a political vacuum that otherwise might have been occupied by another colonial power. On conquering Mataram in 1757, the VOC divided the kingdom into 3: the senior sultanates of Surakarta and Yogyakarta, and a junior sultanate also at Surakarta. Over the rest of the island, the VOC appointed *bupati* to rule in their name, effectively duplicating the traditional system and structure of control. An important difference however was that the focus of power was reversed. Under the VOC, it was the coast and particularly Batavia that was the centre; the *negara* of the former Mataram Kingdom had become unimportant backwaters.

Under the rule of the VOC there was a modicum of expansion in commercial activity in Java. Looking for a means to justify the expense of managing what was fast becoming a colonial empire, the Dutch forced the Priangan regents of West Java to deliver a fixed quota of coffee beans each year. The arabica coffee bush had been found to grow well in the highlands of Priangan in the early 18th century and it quickly became one of Java's most valuable exports. To produce the coffee to pay the Dutch, the Priangan regents in turn imposed a quota on their peasants. Road and river tolls, the 'leasing' of villages and other forms of taxation all generated wealth for local lords, Dutch officials, Chinese businessmen and for the Company. The cost, invariably, rested on the bony shoulders of the Javanese peasant who was, more often than not, mired in poverty.

In 1795 the French occupied the Netherlands and the Dutch King William V fled to Britain where he asked the British to take control of his colonies. But before the English were to make their mark on the island a new, reformist, governor-general was to arrive in Batavia: **Herman Daendels**, a Dutchman, but also a supporter of Napoleon. Daendel's period as governor-general spanned only 2 years, from 1808 to 1810. But it led to a revolutionary change in the way in which Java was administered. In place of the existing system of regencies, he introduced a far more structured, centralised and bureaucratic system of colonial rule. Like the Englishman Thomas Stamford Raffles who would follow him as governor-general, Daendels recognized the inequities of the existing system. He introduced courts based on *adat* or traditional law, rather than on Dutch law, and he successfully reduced corruption. But by doing this he alienated the Javanese aristocracy, whose powers had been diminished, and angered the Dutch administrators, for whom the possibilities of graft had been substantially reduced. Such was the discontent that he was recalled in 1810 – leaving with the title that had been informally bestowed on him, Tuwan Desar Guntur or Great Thundering Lord, ringing in his ears.

Although it took a few years, the English acted upon King William's request and the **English East India Company** occupied the Dutch East Indies between 1811 and 1816. Just as the VOC had expanded into Java with some trepidation, so the English were equally reluctant to commit men and resources to an enterprise which appeared to offer little financial return.

Thomas Stamford Raffles (see page 372) was to follow in Daendels' footsteps when he became governor-general at the age of 30 in 1811, after forces of the English East India Company landed on Java unopposed. There is some dispute over the extent of the reforms that Raffles wrought in Java. In the past both he and his actions have been, respectively, excessively idolised and idealised. But the recent tendency to denigrate his efforts are similarly unconvincing. There is little reason to doubt his libertarian outlook, and particularly his liberal economics. He introduced economic, political and social reforms and improved the lives of the local population. The great colonial economist J.S. Furnivall noted that the reforms removed most of the more iniquitous laws and ensured that the peasant retained some of the rewards of his labour. However, Raffles did not end the quota system of coffee cultivation in the Priangan Highlands, and some view the commercialisation of peasant life that the more liberal economic policies introduced as heralding a shift from village self-sufficiency to dependence. Raffles was also a keen botanist and helped to establish the **gardens at Bogor** (see **page 566**). His keen interest in the history and culture of Java led him to write the 2-volume *History of Java* in 1817, and to commission the first archaeological survey of Borobudur. With the defeat of France, the British – to Raffles' chagrin – returned Java and the Indies to Dutch rule.

Less than 10 years after Java was returned to Dutch rule, the **Java War** erupted in 1825. Several factors combined to spark the rebellion. First, the revolt's leader, **Prince Diponegoro** (see page 596), had been given short shrift by the Dutch who had overlooked his rights of succession to the Sultanate of Yogyakarta. He was able to gather support due to disaffection over the Dutch decision to allow Chinese to exact tolls at border crossings, and the ruling that forced landowners to repay rent to their tenants. To add insult to injury, the Dutch were building a road that passed through the site of a sacred Muslim tomb. Diponegoro called for a *jihad* – or holy war – against the Dutch, and this clarion call received widespread support. The war, focused on Central Java, lasted until 1830 when Diponegoro, his support dwindling, was forced to negotiate. His arrest and subsequent exile to the Celebes (Sulawesi) marked the end of the movement and resulted in a considerable loss of power in the Javanese court. During the war, 8,000 Europeans are thought to have died, along with 200,000 Javanese – mostly victims of the famine that accompanied the conflict.

The end of the Java War saw the introduction of possibly the most infamous of all Holland's economic policies in the Indies: the **Cultuurstelsel** or **Culture System**. Reverting to the pre-colonial system of taxation, the colonial government, under a new governor-general **Van den Bosch**, required that each peasant family deliver a certain quantity of produce for export – or the equivalent labour and land for its production. The latter was estimated at one-fifth of a farm's land area or 66 working days each year.

Export crops such as **sugar cane**, **indigo** and **coffee** were often cultivated on land that was previously reserved for subsistence crops, like rice. For some cultivators, the Culture System became an intolerable burden and some historians have directly blamed it for a series of famines. For the Dutch government, it brought great wealth, enabling Holland to pay off its public debt. In 1861, the English writer J.B. Money published a book extolling the virtues of the system, entitled *Java, or How to Manage a Colony*. Not everyone was so impressed, and from the 1850s liberals in Holland began to campaign for the Culture System's abolition. It was finally rescinded in 1870, although many elements of it continued to operate until the early years of the 20th century. The English merchant William d'Almeida in his visit to Java in the 1860s wrote:

"Nature has blessed Java with a healthy climate, genial temperature, and fertile soil, and the Dutch – notwithstanding their former arbitrary measures, modified of late years by a more liberal system of government – have made it what it is, a happy contented land, yielding a splendid revenue".

From the final decades of the 19th century, the history of Java becomes intertwined with the history of Indonesia (**see page 498**).

ART AND ARCHITECTURE

Of all the islands of Indonesia, none is more richly endowed with architectural monuments than Java. It is here that the former great empires of the country were centred, and their artistic achievements are still reflected in the temples and palaces that lie scattered across the mountains and plains of the central and E regions. Joseph Jukes, the British naturalist aboard the ship *HMS Fly*, who travelled through the Indonesian archipelago in the 1840s, wrote after seeing the temples of Java:

"The latest date that can be assigned to these ruins is in the time of our (King) Edwards; – making allowance for the difference of climate and race, was the civilization of England at that time more advanced than that of Java?"

There are 2 major periods of Javanese art and architecture, usually referred to as the **Central** and **East Javanese** periods. But this does not necessarily mean that all the monuments linked to these 2 periods are to be found in those 2 regions – it only indicates their respective centres of influence. Nonetheless, West Java has far fewer remains, possibly because Buddhism never spread to the W.

The art and architecture of both the Central and East Javanese periods is known as '**Classical**', because it was influenced by the art and architecture of India. The question which still preoccupies scholars is whether the Indian or the Indonesian element should be stressed. During the 5th to 7th centuries, Indian culture arrived in Southeast Asia along with Indian merchants (*vaisyas*) and religious men (*brahmanas*) – a period which is sometimes termed the 'Indianisation' of

The building sequence in Java (late 6th-late 15th century)		
The Central Javanese Period	**The East Javanese Period**	
The Early Javanese Style	**(11th-15th century)**	
(late 7th-9th century)	**The Early Classical Style**	
	(11th-12th century)	
Dieng Plateau c. end 7th century		
Candi Gunung Wukir 732	Gua Gajah (Bali) 1000	
Candi Badut (East Java) 760	Gunung Kawi (Bali) late 11th century	
Gedung Songo c. early 8th century	**The Later Classical Style**	
The Early Classical Style	**(1197-1470)**	
(late 8th-9th century)	Candi Panataran 1197	
Candi Borobudur 778-824	Candi Kidal 1247	
Candi Mendut 800	Candi Jago 1268	
Candi Pawon 800	Candi Jawi 1292	
Candi Ngawen ?	Candi Singasari early 13th century	
Candi Kalasan 778-810	Candi Tikus 1350	
Candi Sewu 782-792	Candi Jedong 1385	
Candi Sari 835	Candi Plumbangan 1390	
Candi Plaosan 835	Candi Sukuh 1430	
Candi Loro Jonggrang 835-856	Candi Ceto 1470	

NB: these dates are approximate; inscriptions do give exact dates, but they only refer to one period of construction. Many monuments were built, redesigned and then rebuilt on a number of occasions spanning a long period.

Southeast Asia (**see page 38**). In fact, before the term Southeast Asia was used to describe the region, it was called Further India or Greater India. The candi of Java appeared just at the time when Indian influence was strongest and there are stylistic links between the earliest candi of the Dieng Plateau and Gedung Songo and some N and S Indian structures. But, in the late 19th century, scholars began to question how far these buildings should be seen in terms of Indian influences, and how far in terms of local art and culture. In recent years, the tendancy has been to stress the 'local genius' rather than the imported Indian traditions.

The search for specifically Indonesian artistic styles was emphasised when Indonesia was searching for a wider national unity in the run up to independence. It is now argued that by the 8th and 9th centuries, Javanese artists had effectively created their own Javanese style of architecture and ornamentation. The Indonesian art historian Soekmono, for instance, writes that the candi is "an unquestionably Indonesian art form, based upon the Indian world of thought, nevertheless created and developed by Indonesians themselves in accordance with their own native potential and tradition".

Central Javanese Period (730 AD-929 AD)

The **Central Javanese Period** embraces one of the most extraordinary periods of monument-building anywhere in the world. This was associated with the advent of the Sailendra Dynasty and the arrival of Buddhism. The building boom spanned 2 centuries from 730, during which Candi Kalasan, Candi Prambanan and Candi Borobudur were all built, along with numerous smaller temples. The temples were built of andesite, a porous volcanic stone found in abundance across Central Java. The period came to a spectacular end in 928 or 929 when Mount Merapi is thought to have erupted. Not only would such an eruption have affected agricultural production by coating the land in a deep layer of ash and lava, but it would doubtless have been taken as a sign that the gods were displeased, thus necessitating a move on religious grounds as well. From 928 until the 15th century there are no epigraphic – or carved – records from Central Java. This gives some indication of the scale of the disaster.

From the 10th century, the magnificent monuments of Central Java were left to be ravaged by earthquakes and storms, and consumed by the forest. When the Dutchman, Ijzerman discovered Borobudur's base in 1885 he found only "pityful ruins, dismantled by bastardized descendants incapable of appreciation for the greatness of their ancestors". Central Javanese temples were coated with *vajiralepa*, literally 'plaster as indestructable as diamond'. This white plaster helped to prevent moisture from entering the porous building stone. The question that still has to be satisfactorily answered is whether the monuments were left bleached white like those in Burma, or whether they were subsequently painted.

East Javanese Period (929 AD-1527 AD)

The **East Javanese Period** is associated with the dramatic move of the palace of King Sindok, along with his subjects, E in 929 to the fertile lands of East Java and the Brantas River. It seems that this massive migration followed the catastrophic eruption of Mount Merapi. The East Javanese Period spans just over 6 centuries and is dominated by the dynasties of Kediri (929-1222), Singasari (1222-1292) and Majapahit (1293-1527).

During the East Javanese Period, the plan of the temple complex gradually changed, so that the primary shrine no longer sat in the middle of the complex but was to be found towards the rear of the enclosure. Panataran is the greatest achievement of this age (**see page 641**). The movement away from symmetry led to the inclusion of different kinds of building within the compound, for instance, assembly halls. The deeply carved reliefs of Central Javanese monuments also make way for a much flatter style of decoration, more akin to the form of the *wayang* puppet. In general, ornamentation moved away from the sculptural

Balinese door guardian or *karang sae*, closely related to the
kalamakara or *banaspati* of Java (adapted from Ramseyer, Urs
(1986) *The art and culture of Bali*, OUP: Singapore).

The Javanese candi

The *candis* of Java – the word has been variously translated as 'sepulchral monument' and 'ancient shrine' – are the equivalent of the cathedrals of Europe. They were places of worship or homage, and dedicated either to deified kings or to gods and spirits. An important difference though is that while cathedrals are designed to accommodate large numbers of the faithful, candis were exclusively the abodes of the gods. The gods descended to inhabit the monuments during special ceremonies attended by only a handful of priests. Drawing heavily upon Indian cosmology, candis were representations of the universe in microcosm, with Mount Meru, the cosmic mountain and abode of the gods, at the centre and surrounded by concentric circles of mountains, separated by oceans. The frequent presence of the lotus flower is linked to the belief that gods were born out of these flowers and then sat upon them.

A candi has 3 distinct elements: a square base, on which rests a single-celled, usually cuboid, shrine, and a stepped roof. This 3-fold division mirrors the symbolic 3-fold division of the universe into a lower Sphere of the Mortals (*bhurloka*) and an upper Sphere of the Gods (*swarloka*), between which is the Sphere of the Purified, where the objects of worship are placed (*bhuwarloka*). The base is larger than the shrine, so leaving room for the movement of people around the building. Under the shrine, a hole in the base contained the ashes of a dead king – perhaps explaining why they were called candis (=sepulchral monument).

The summit of the stepped roof is often surmounted with a stupa or *linga* shape. On the E side of the shrine, steps lead up to a portico which houses an icon. Numerous embellishments were added to this basic design: external niches, porticoes built out on all 4 walls, and steps added to the base to provide more wall space for decoration. Sculptural decoration also varied, but again there were common elements: for example the *kalamakara* and *kalanaga* motifs above doorways (known as *banaspati* in E Java), which acted as door guardians, warding-off evil spirits.

The names given to most candis in Java – a notable exception being Borobudur – are not original. They date from the late 19th or early 20th century and rarely indicate the king or deity to which a particular shrine is dedicated. The names are often linked to nearby towns or villages, and other geographical features.

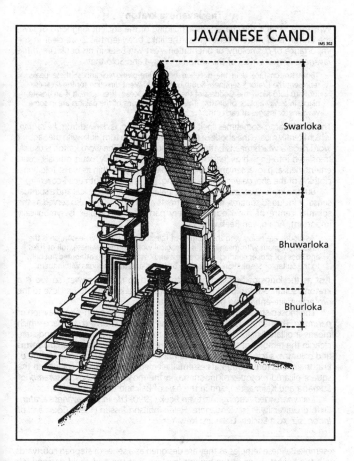

JAVANESE CANDI

IMS 302

Swarloka

Bhuwarloka

Bhurloka

order of Central Java, into extravagant fantasy. Many monuments were built at this time, but none on the scale or artistic magnificence of Borobudur or Prambanan. The most significant are Candi Kidal and Candi Singasari – more slender and steeper-roofed than their predecessors in Central Java. Candi Jago displays wayang-style reliefs while Candi Jawi shows the blend of Buddhism and Hinduism in having both Siva and Buddha displayed on the one shrine. It is often observed that although plastic arts suffered a decline during the East Javanese period, it represented the golden period of Javanese literature.

The last structures to be built during this period were the mountain-top candis of Sukuh and Ceto (**see page 620**), and a handful of lesser monuments on Mount Penanggungan, where the last inscription dates from 1512. These later candis

The Javanese kraton

While the candi is the characteristic building of the ancient kingdoms of Java, the kraton is of more recent times. The links between the 2 are clear in the importance of cosmology, or orientation. Aart van Beek in his book *Life in the Javanese Kraton* writes of the kraton of Yogya and Solo that:

> "Both Kraton face N in the direction of the life-giving volcanoes...these peaks represent the Kraton's sentinels. South is the ambivalent direction for the Javanese, for Ratu Loro Kidul, the Goddess of the Southern Ocean, lives there. It is an unsafe place, in a way a place of death... The N and S sections of the palaces are in some ways mirror images of each other".

The word *kraton*, sometimes spelt *keraton* or *karaton*, is derived from *ke-ratuan*, which literally means the abode of the monarch. This, in turn, links with the Sanskrit word *negara* which means both kingdom and capital. The word kraton is usually translated into English as 'palace'. The king and his family, court officials, court entertainers and royal servants – the *abdi dalem* – lived within its walls. Traditional clothing of the *abdi dalem* include a sarong, kris and *iket* (cloth head-covering).

But the kraton was more than just a 'palace' in both a physical and a spiritual sense. It included squares, mosques, streets and houses, and also served as the spiritual centre of the kingdom. Every part of the complex is symbolically important. Again, van Beek writes:

> "As clouds are heavy with the promise of rain towards the rainy season, so is the Kraton pregnant with meaning. It is a magical world to the Javanese, full of rules and codes of proper conduct. A sacredness and cosmic energy is attributed not only to the Sultan or Susuhunan but also the buildings and the weapons within them".

Just as the kings of Mataram were conceived to radiate power, so too is a kraton's sultan. And to be close to the walls of the kraton is to be close to the protective, life-enhancing powers of the sultan.

The most distinctive building within the kraton is the open-sided pavilion or *pendopo*. The name is probably derived from the Sanskrit word *mandapa* which means a pillared hall. The links between the pendopo and earlier candis are clear in the temples of the late East Javanese Period with their raised platforms and columns, such as those at Panataran. The pendopo is not just a feature of kraton architecture though; its essential elements can be seen repeated in the square pillared mosques of Indonesia, in the mosque pavilions or *surambi* of Sumatra and Kalimantan, and in the *bale* of Bali and Lombok.

Recommended reading: Aart van Beek (1990) *Life in the Javanese Kraton*, Oxford University Press: Singapore. Helen Ibbitson Jessup (1990) *Court arts of Indonesia*, Asia Society Galleries: New York.

resemble Balinese temples as they are designed as a series of stepped courtyards, with the holiest shrine at the highest level (so that the god could descend into the temple from his home on the mountain).

The Islamic Period (1527- present)

The end of the Indianized period of monument building in Java during the 15th and 16th centuries coincided with the arrival of **Islam** from W India via Sumatra. Temple-building stopped, and mosque construction began. But this did not mean the rejection of local styles for imported ones. The early mosques had square floor plans like Javanese candis, and tiered roofs like the *pura* of Bali. They also had courtyards and split gates. The brick-built minaret at Kudus for example, mirrors the *kulkul* tower of Bali and even displays the Hindu-Buddhist *kalamakara* motif.

CULTURE AND LIFE

People of Java

Although it is common to hear people talk of the 'Javanese', Java supports a number of different cultural and linguistic groups of which the Javanese are only one, albeit the most numerous. The **Javanese** occupy the island's geographical and cultural heart, encompassing such royal cities as Surakarta and Yogyakarta, along with the important trading ports of the north coast. A broad distinction can be drawn between the courtly, refined and reserved *Kejawen* of the interior, and the more extrovert, 'coarse' and religiously orthodox inhabitants of the coastal *pasisir* areas. The Javanese are wet rice farmers *par excellence*, although population growth has meant that land holdings are growing smaller by the year – today they average 400 sq m per family (0.035 ha) – and many farmers have become landless agricultural labourers. The Javanese often have only one name, the upper classes choosing their own family name. This invariably ends in an 'o'.

The **Sundanese** are concentrated in the Priangan Highlands of West Java and share many of the same traditions as the Javanese. However, the great court culture of Central Java never made a great impact here. The land is less fertile, and villages tended to be more isolated and self-sufficient. The Sundanese are therefore less encumbered with complex rules of etiquette and behaviour. Like the Javanese of the north coast, they are orthodox Muslims. Sundanese family names commonly end in an 'a'.

Among Java's patchwork of peoples are the **Madurese**, inhabitants of the island of Madura. During the Dutch period the Madurese made up a disproportionate share of the colonial army and have a reputation as fierce warriors. Also in East Java, the Hindu **Tenggerese** are thought to be descended from the Majapahit refugees who fled Central Java in the 10th century, following the eruption of Mount Merapi. Finally, the enigmatic **Badui** of West Java live in 35 isolated villages near Rangkasbitung. Outsiders are expressly excluded from the remote 'inner' Badui villages, although the 'outer' communities permit some limited contact.

Islam in Java

Java is a Muslim society, although in many cases Islam is intertwined with pre-Islamic religions and beliefs. Peacock writes of the Javanese world that it is "composed of spiritual energies contained in forms and images, such as magically potent swords, sacred shrines, spirits, deities, teachers and rulers; the Javanese syncretistic world is what Weber termed a 'garden of magic' – indeed, animist jungle". The roots of this mixture can be traced back to the reign of the great Majapahit King Agung (1613-1645), a devout Muslim. He had the Islamic title of sultan, but at the same time bore the Hindu-Javanese title of *susuhunan*. The calendar Agung introduced in 1633 numbered its years according to the Hindu Shaka Era (1 Shaka = 78 AD), but borrowed from the Islamic system adopting a lunar year, in place of the Hindu solar one.

Most Javanese Muslims maintain that the mysticism and spirituality so evident in Java – though a departure from the Prophet Mohammad's original teachings – are nonetheless derived from Islamic traditions. Orthodox Islam is based upon the *shariah* – Islamic law – together with the Koran and the Hadith (the sayings, practices and rites not contained in the Koran) (see page 39). A **Sufi** is a Muslim who follows the mystical path, or secret doctrine. Sufism aims to free the soul from earthly concerns, but the doctrine – which is believed to be the key to salvation – is kept secret from the masses because it is often in conflict with orthodox Islam and therefore should only be revealed to those able to appreciate its subtleties. Through history, the Sufis have been in periodic conflict with the scholars of orthodox Islam or *Ulama*. The former taught the path of mysticism, the latter the path of orthodoxy.

The introduction of Islam to Java and the nine Walis

One of the most significant processes in Indonesian history was the spread of Islam. When and how it occurred are not clear. Muslim traders had, presumably, been visiting Java and other islands in the archipelago from early in the second millennium and some had probably married local women and settled. When Marco Polo's expedition stopped in Sumatra in 1292 on its return from China, he recorded that the town of Perlak was Muslim. But it was not until the 14th century that Islam appears to have spread from Trengganu on the Malay Peninsula, to Sumatra and from there to Java. It is assumed that Islam first made an impact on the N coast, and then diffused to the interior, which was Hindu. The discovery of Muslim graves at Trowulan, dated 1368-1369, indicates that there were Muslims of considerable prestige living there, even when the Hindu Majapahit Empire was at its height. But Indonesians have their own accounts of the spread of Islam. They say Islam arrived by magic, not diffusion. In his history of Indonesia, Riklefs relates one such tale:

> "In this story, the Caliph of Mecca hears of the existence of Samudra and decides to send a ship there in fulfilment of a prophesy of the Prophet Muhammed that there would one day be a great city in the East called Samudra, which would produce many saints. The ship's captain, Shaikh Ismail, stops en route in India to pick up a Sultan who has stepped down from his throne to become a holy man. The ruler of Samudra, Merah Silau, has a dream in which the Prophet appears to him, magically transfers knowledge of Islam to him by spitting in his mouth, and gives him the title Sultan Malik as-Salih. Upon awakening, the new Sultan discovers that he can read the Qur'an although he has never been instructed and that he has been magically circumcised."

The influential manuscripts that comprise the *Babad Tanah Jawi* or 'History of the Land of Java' ascribe the conversion of Java to Islam to the work of 9 saints – or *wali sanga*. Unfortunately, the manuscripts are not agreed on who the 9 wali were, and whether there might not have been more. Usually, the 9 are listed as: Sunan Ngampel-Denta, Sunan Kudus, Sunan Murya, Sunan Bonang, Sunan Giri, Sunan Kalijaga, Sunan Sitijenar, Sunan Gunung Jati, and Sunan Walilanang. Sometimes a tenth wali, Sunan Bayat, is also listed. Today the graves of the 9

The nine Walis of Java

The title *wali* is an Arabic word meaning saint, while *Sunan* is a Javanese title, probably derived from the word *suhun* meaning 'honoured'. The 9 walis were of mixed origin. Some were clearly non-Javanese, while at least 3 (Sunan Giri, Sunan Bonang and Sunan Walilanang) are thought to have studied Islam in Melaka before arriving in Java. The *Babad Tanah Jawi* recounts numerous stories about the lives of the 9 wali and how they came to embrace Islam and arrive in Java. Many involve miraculous conversions. For example, Sunan Kalijaga - at that time named Said (an Arabic name) - is said to have lost at gambling while working for the Majapahit court and became a highway robber. One day he accosted another future wali named Sunan Bonang who convinced Said not to rob him but to wait for the next traveller who would appear wearing blue with a red hibiscus flower behind his ear. Three days later, a man dressed as Sunan Bonang described came along the path and Said duly pounced on him. The man in blue was, of course, really Sunan Bonang in disguise, who quickly turned himself into 4 people. Understandably, Said was taken aback by this turn of events, renounced his evil ways, embraced Islam and the life of an ascetic, became a wali, and married one of Sunan Gunung Jati's daughters.

You are
A STUDENT

You travel
THE WORLD

You want
TO SAVE MONEY

Here's
how

The International Student Identity Card

Entitles you to discounts and special services worldwide.

Little
Andaman
ANDAMAN

10°
Ten
Degree Channel
Car Nicobar

SEA

Katchall
Nicobàr
Little
Nicobar
Great
Nicobar
Islands
(India)

Banda Aceh⊙ Sigli
5°
Lhokseumawe
ACEH
Meulaboh
Langsa
Binjai
Leuser 3361▲
Tapaktuan⊙
Pematangsiantar
Sibolga⊙
Tarutung
Gunungsitoli⊙
Nias
Natal⊙
Pini⊙
Kep.
Banyak
Simeulue
0°   Equator
Kep.
Batu
Siberut
Kep.
Sipura⊙
Painan⊙
Mentawai
Pagai Utara
Pagai Selatan
Siloqui⊙

I N D I A N

5°

O C E A N

10°

Scale 1:15 000 000
100   200   300   400   500 Miles
200   400   600   800 Kms
Bonne Projection

Prachuap
Khiri Khan
Phnom Penh⊙ **CAMBODIA**
Kâmpóng
Chhnang   Kâmpóng
Cham
Prev
Din
Bang
Saphan
Gulf of
Kâmpôt
Saôm
Long Xuyen
Phu Quoc
Prey
My Tho
Ranong⊙⊙Chumphon   **Thailand**
Isthmus
of Kra   Ko Phangan
Ko Samui
Surat Thani
Rach Gia
Can
Quan
Long
Bac
Phangnga
Ko⊙
Phuket⊙ Krabi
Phuket
Nakhon Si Thammarat
Mui Ca Mau
Trang⊙
Thale
Luang
THAILAND
B. Hat Yai⊙⊙Songkhla
Langkawi
Kangar⊙Pattani
Alor Setar   Yala⊙ Narathiwat
Kota Baharu
George Town⊙   Butterworth   Pasir
P. Pinang   Puteh   **M A**
(Pinang)   Kuala Trengganu
Peureulak⊙   Taiping⊙   **PENINSULAR**
Medan   Ipoh⊙   **MALAYSIA**   Kuala Dungun
Tebingtinggi⊙   Teluk   Kuala
Intan⊙   Lipis⊙   Chukai
Kisaran⊙Tanjungbalai   Jerantut⊙   Kuantan
Rantauprapat   **Malacca**   Mentakab⊙
Danau   **Kuala Lumpur**
Toba   Kelang⊙   Seremban
Gemas⊙   P. Tioman
Padangsidempuan   Dumai⊙   Melaka⊙   Mersing   Anam
Muar⊙⊙   Keluang
Batu Pahat⊙
Sungaipakning   Johor   **SINGAPORE**
Pekanbaru   Baharu   **Singapore**
Bukittinggi⊙   Mendung⊙   **Kep. Riau**   Bintan
Padangpanjang   Kampar   **RIAU**   Lingga
Pariaman⊙   Marapi 2891▲   Indragiri⊙   Singkep
Padang⊙   Muara⊙   Rengat⊙   Kampa
Painan⊙   **SUMATERA**   Pa
BARAT   Kerinci▲   Hari   Ba
3805   **JAMBI**   Jambi⊙
Sungaipenuh   Tempino⊙
Sekayu⊙   **SUMATERA**
SELATAN   Talangbetutu
Ipuh⊙   Musi   **Palembang** To
Tebingtinggi   Perabumulih⊙
Bengkulu⊙   Lahat⊙   Baturaja⊙
Manna⊙   Kotabumi⊙
Enggano   Telukbetung⊙   **Tanjungka**
Kalianda⊙   Serang⊙
Selat Sunda   **Bogor**
Sukabu
JA
BA
J

Christmas I.
(Austl.)

SUMATERA UTARA
BARISAN

walis, to be found in towns along the N coast of Java, are important pilgrimage centres for Indonesians.

But these stories of the 9 wali do not explain why Islam suddenly took hold in Indonesia in the 14th century. The accepted view used to be that Islam, as an egalitarian and populist faith, was simply more attractive than the corrupt Hindu-Buddhist religion that existed at the time. But some historians maintain that Islam seems to have been imposed from above, and not embraced from below. Others believe Sufism was instrumental, as it, like Hindu-Buddhism, was a mystical faith and could compete on equal terms. That said, there is little evidence to support the notion that large numbers of Sufis were actively proselytising across the country at the time. Another possibility is that Muslim traders were responsible for introducing Islam, and spreading it through the island.

Dance, drama and music

The wayang: shadow puppet theatre

Wayang means 'shadow', and the art form is best translated as 'shadow theatre' or 'shadow play'. Some people believe that the wayang is Indian in origin, pointing to the fact that most of the characters are from Indian epic tales such as the Ramayana and Mahabharata. Others maintain that wayang was established before the Indianisation of Java and Sumatra and that the art form stems from ancient Malayo-Polynesian culture. They say the puppets represented ancestral spirits, who were summoned to solve the problems of the living. It was only later that the medium was used to teach Indian spiritual values through such Hindu epic stories as the Ramayana and Mahabharata (**see page 505**).

Wayang is possibly first hinted at in 2 royal charters dated 840 and 907 which mention officials who supervised musicians and performers, and talk of a play called *mawayang*. But historians are dubious whether the inscriptions refer to wayang at all. The first certain reference – by which time it was already a well established art form in Java – is in an 11th century poem, *The Meditation of Ardjuna*, composed by the court poet of King Airlangga (1020-1049):

"There are people who weep, are sad and aroused watching the puppets, though they know they are merely carved pieces of leather manipulated and made to speak. These people are like men, thirsting for sensual pleasures, who live in a world of illusion; they do not realise the magic hallucinations they see are not real".

An important development in wayang, was the introduction of articulated arms in 1630 at the court of Mataram, which in turn led to further changes in the plays themselves. Most of the classic repertoire, which puppet masters – or *dalang* – are expected to absorb dates from this period.

There are various forms of wayang, and not all are 'shadow' theatre in the true sense. *Wayang purwa* or *wayang kulit* is the original shadow play and is performed using flat puppets, chiselled out of leather, and is associated with the Javanese and Balinese. *Wayang golek* uses 3 dimensional cloth and wood puppets and is a Sundanese adaptation of wayang kulit. *Wayang berber* is enacted using painted paper or cloth scrolls which are unrolled while the narrator chants the story. *Wayang topeng* is performed by masked, live actors, while *wayang wong* or *wayang orang* uses maskless live actors.

The commonest and oldest form of wayang is the *purwa* or *kulit*. These are finely carved and painted leather, 2-dimensional puppets, jointed at the elbows and shoulders and manipulated using horn rods. In order to enact the entire repertoire of 179 plays, 200 puppets are needed. A single performance can last as long as 9 hours. The plays have various origins. Some are animistic, featuring, for example, the Rice Goddess, Dewi Sri. Others are adapted from the epic literature; these are known as *pondok* or 'trunk' tales and include the Ramayana. Others have been developed over the years by influential puppet masters. They feature heroic deeds, romantic encounters, court intrigues, bloody battles, and mystical observations, and are known as *carangan* or 'branch' tales.

The *gunungan* or 'Tree of Life', is an important element of wayang theatre. It represents all aspects of life, and is always the same in design: shaped like a stupa, the tree has painted red flames on one side and a complex design on the other (this is the side which faces the audience). At the base of the tree are a pair of closed doors, flanked by 2 fierce demons or *yaksas*. Above the demons are 2 garudas and within the branches of the tree there are monkeys, snakes and 2 animals – usually an ox and a tiger. The gunungan is placed in the middle of the screen at the beginning and end of the performance – and sometimes between major scene changes. During the performance it stands at one side, and flutters across the screen to indicate minor scene changes.

Traditionally, performances were requested by individuals to celebrate particular occasions – for example the seventh month of pregnancy (*tingkep*) – or to accompany village festivities. Admission was free, as the individual commissioning the performance would meet the costs. Of course, this has changed now and tourists invariably have to pay an entrance charge.

Javanese puppets are characteristically highly stylized, with long necks, very long arms and extended shoulders. To the wayang cognoscenti, every nuance of the puppet is significant. It tells, so to speak, a tale. There are 15 eye shapes, 11 mouths and 13 nose shapes for example. Heroes are required to conform to the Javanese physical ideal. They must be slender, with long, elegant noses, down cast eyes (denoting humility and restraint) and balanced proportions. Major characters like Arjuna in the Mahabharata have numerous – more than 10 – puppet shapes, deployed according to the scene being enacted.

Traditionally, the shadows of the puppets were reflected onto a white cotton cloth stretched across a wooden frame using the light from a bronze coconut oil lamp. Today, electric light is more common – a change which, in many people's minds, has meant the unfortunate substitution of the flickering, mysterious shadows of the oil lamp, with the constant harsh light of the electric bulb. There are both day and night wayang performances. The latter, for obvious reasons, are the most dramatic, although the former are regarded as artistically superior.

The audience sits on both sides of the screen. Those sitting with the puppet master see a puppet play; those on the far side, out of view of the puppet master

Making a wayang kulit puppet

Wayang kulit puppets are made of buffalo hide, preferably taken from a female animal of about 4 years of age. The skin is dried and scraped, and then left to mature for as long as 10 years to achieve the stiffness required for carving. After carving, the puppet is painted in traditional pigments. In carving the puppet, the artist is constrained by convention. The excellence of the puppet is judged according to the fineness of chisel-work and the subtlety of painting. If the puppet is well made it may have *guna* - a magical quality which is supposed to make the audience suspend its disbelief during the performance. Puppets accumulate *guna* with age; this is why old puppets are preferred to new ones.

Each major character has a particular iconography, and even the angle of the head and the slant of the eyes and mouth are important in determining the character. Some puppets may be called on to perform a number of minor parts, but in the main a knowledgeable wayang-goer will be able to recognise each character immediately.

The *cempurit* or rods used to manipulate the puppet are made of buffalo horn while the studs used to attach the limbs are made of metal, bone or bamboo. Court puppets might even be made of gold, studded with precious stones.

and the accompanying gamelan orchestra, see a shadow play. It is possible that in the past, the audience was segregated according to sex: men on the dalang's side of the screen, women on the shadow side.

The puppet master or *dalang*, is a consecrated priest. The word is said to be derived from *galang*, meaning bright or clear, the implication being that the dalang makes the sacred texts understandable. He sits on a plinth, an arm's length away from the cloth screen. From this position he manipulates the puppets, while also narrating the story. Although any male can become a dalang, it is usual for

Semar: the most sacred of all the puppets

Kresna: a King and spiritual guide of Ajuna (a warrior and hero in the Pandawa cycle of plays).

sons to follow their fathers into the profession. The dalang is the key to a successful performance: he must be multi-skilled, have strength and stamina, be able to manipulate numerous puppets simultaneously, narrate the story, and give the lead to the accompanying gamelan orchestra. No wonder that an adept dalang is a man with considerable status.

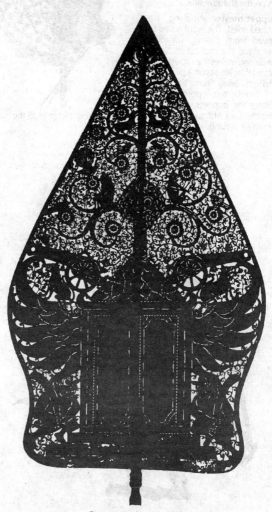

Gunungan: the tree of life

Wayang topeng: masked dance

The masked dance either evolved from initiation rites in which a masked man indicated the ideal human state, or from the story of the Hindu god, Vishnu. In this story, Vishnu on seeing the world to be an evil place descended from the heavens to dance and try to change it by a release of spiritual energy. To preserve his anonymity, Vishnu danced disguised by a mask. We know from Tomé Pires' account of his visit to Java in the early 16th century, that wayang topeng dances were already being performed on the N coast. This seems to indicate that far from being a court innovation of the interior – as previously believed – it was a popular coastal form of entertainment.

Nonetheless, the carving of topeng has always been regarded as a suitable way for royalty to occupy their time. Princes have become skilled artists as well as dancers. The kraton in Surakarta has a particularly fine collection of topeng masks (**see page 619**). Most wayang topeng performances are based on the *Ramayana* and *Mahabharata*. However, of the repertoire of dances, perhaps the most ritually important is the Panji dance based on *The Adventures of Prince Panji*, a tale which dates from the Majapahit period and which has produced – in the character of Prince Panji – the archetypal Javanese hero along with Arjuna in the *Mahabharata* and Rama in the *Ramayana*. The Panji dance consists of 4 parts, personifying the spirituality and worldliness of men. A well-performed Panji is regarded as being among the most graceful of dances. Unfortunately, full-length topeng performances are rare today, a fact which may well be linked to the spread of Islam.

Wayang wong and the Ramayana ballet

Wayang wong is the grandest form of dance drama performed on Java. It is thought to post-date wayang kulit, although it shares many of the shadow puppet theatre's characteristics. It draws its repertoire of stories primarily from the Indian epics, the play is accompanied by the music of the gamelan orchestra, and the aesthetic is essentially the same as that of wayang kulit. The principal difference is that actors, often masked, play the characters, not puppets – although the movements of the actors often imitate puppets.

Like many performing arts in Java, wayang wong was intimately linked to the kratons of Yogyakarta and Surakarta and reached its apogee during the 18th century. The costs of staging a performance were so great that only a sultan could raise the necessary funds, making it a strictly élite affair. In Yogya only men performed wayang wong; in Surakarta, though, women played the female roles. The movements are highly stylized; females dance slowly, in a restrained manner, rarely allowing their feet to leave the floor; men – especially those playing powerful figures – adopt an open-legged position and raise their legs high off the floor to indicate their strength and masculinity.

At the end of the 19th century, a variant of wayang wong known as **wayang orang**, emerged. This was an attempt to popularize the dance-drama and bring it to a wider audience. But perhaps the dance most likely to be seen by tourists is the **sendratari**, better known today as the **Ramayana ballet**. This dance was first performed in 1961 and is now staged most notably at Prambanan, outside Yogyakarta (**see page 616**). The open-air 'ballet' is held once a year and is mounted on an epic scale, with large numbers of actors playing four episodes of the Ramayana over four days: namely, the abduction of Sita, Hanuman's mission to Lanka, the conquest of Lanka, and the fall of Ravana.

Court dances

Various court dances evolved in the kratons of Java of which the most important are *bedhaya* and *serimpi*. Both are subdued dances performed by groups of women to the accompaniment of gamelan music and singing. Jukka Miettinen in her book *Classical dance and theatre in South-East Asia* describes the bedhaya as "extremely slow and solemn", writing that the "face is kept strictly expressionless, and the eyes look down, while the dancers undulate to the *gamelan* music in a continuous flow of movement like underwater plants". The serimpi dance is similarly slow and languid, but is performed by only 4 dancers who are presumed to represent both the four cardinal points and the four elements (fire, water, earth and air). Although some private dance academies teach these court dances, the best place to see them performed is at the kratons in Yogyakarta and Surakarta (Solo).

Music

The **angklung** is a traditional and ancient Javanese instrument used to accompany story-telling and marching. It probably originated in West Java, although it is used throughout Java and Bali (see box, **page 575**).

The **gamelan orchestra** is the most important assemblage of musical instruments in Indonesia. It is essential to the performance of wayang plays, accompanies celebrations at the royal kratons, and is inextricably bound-up in ceremonies at Balinese temples. The gamelan is a Javanese and Balinese musical form, although there are important differences between the music of the 2 islands.

Gamelan orchestras vary according to the context in which they are being played. However, it is usual to have large hanging gongs or *gong*, medium-sized hanging gongs or *kempul*, inverted bronze bowls – either single (*ketuk*) or grouped in fives (*kenong*) – bronze xylophones constructed of heavy bars (*saron*) or lighter hanging bars (*gender*), a wooden xylophone or *gambang*, finger drums or *kendang*, a zither or *celempung*, and a 2-stringed fiddle or *rebab*. Many of the instruments are made of bronze, and most are struck like percussion instruments. The only remaining workshops making these instruments are to be found in Bogor and Yogyakarta.

If there is more than one example of a particular instrument, then these are usually tuned to connecting or overlapping octaves, giving the orchestra a range of 6 or 7 octaves. Each octave is divided into either 5 (*slendro*) or 7 (*pelog*) notes. This means that instruments are usually designed for one or other scale. The most important members of a gamelan are the kendang drummer, who sets the tempo, and the lead gender player. The latter plays the *gender barung* and cues the other members of the orchestra.

Textiles

Batik

Batik is the characteristic textile patterning technique of Java and Madura, and to a lesser degree, Bali, Lombok and Central Sulawesi. It is also prominent on the Malay Peninsula. Like *ikat* (see page 721), it is a method of **resist-dyeing**. But in this instance, the resist – beeswax – is applied to the woven cloth rather than to the yarn. The word batik may be derived from the Malay word *tik*, meaning to 'drip'.

Traditionally, the **wax was painted onto the woven cloth** using a *canting* (pronounced 'janting'), a small copper cup with a spout, mounted on a bamboo handle. The cup is filled with melted wax, which flows from the spout like ink from a fountain pen – although the canting never touches the surface of the cloth. In areas such as the town of Pekalongan where batik is finely detailed, waxers are sometimes taught meditation and deep-breathing exercises to help soothe the mind. Batik artists have a number of canting with various widths of spout, some even with several spouts, to give varied thicknesses of line and differences of effect.

The canting was probably invented in Java in the 12th century, whereupon it replaced the crude painting stick, enabling far more complex designs to be produced. Inscriptions from this period refer to *tulis warna*, literally 'drawing in

A batik primer

There are 2 principal batik-producing areas in Java, each with its own distinctive designs: North coast and Central Java. However, within this crude division there are countless variations:

Central Java The batik of Central Java is characterized by the use of **repeated geometric motifs**, today invariably produced using a *cap* or stamp. Rouffaer counted 3,000 named motifs in the early 20th century. The introduction and spread of Islam from the 12th-16th centuries led to a change from portraying living creatures realistically, to their abstraction into geometric designs. By creating people and animals realistically, the artist was seen to be trying to compete with God. Brown, black and blue are the traditional colours and patterns are very dense with an absence of straight lines and empty areas. There are 3 principle designs: *ceplokkan* (inter-linking squares, diamonds and other shapes), *garis miring* (geometric shapes which run diagonally across the cloth) and *semen* (more flowing, with tendrils linking the design).

In Central Java, the art of batik is linked with the *priyayi* gentry class who have traditionally viewed it as one of the 'high' arts. Certain motifs were reserved for the sole use of sultans, and people of high rank. The garuda motif for example, was reserved for the crown prince and his consort. Today, no such restrictions exist.

North coast Because of the trading tradition of the N coast, this part of Java has tended to assimilate foreign cultural influences. From the 17th century, Chinese from Fukien province began to settle along the N coast, and by the late 19th century they had cornered the trade in cambric cloth and dominated the batik industry. As a result, batik produced along the N coast shows **Chinese influences**. It is also notable that whereas most batik designs in Central Java were court-inspired, those from the N coast – with the exception of Cirebon – were commercial in origin. In general, designs are less geometric and fussier than those of Central Java; colours are brighter and realistic designs more common. Centres include:

Indramayu: where the *luk cuan* bird – an adaptation of the Chinese phoenix – is a common motif, colours are dull, and the use of linking tendrils is widespread.

Cirebon: the **most distinctive designs** in Java originate from Cirebon, and many are Chinese in inspiration. Palaces, gardens, mountains and fantastic animals are drawn as if on a landscape, making the cloth suitable for wall hanging. The renowned cloud designs (*megamendung* and *wadasan*), produced for the court, died out some time ago but have now been resuscitated. Again, they are Chinese in inspiration (**see page 579**).

Pekalongan: more batik is produced here than anywhere else in Java. Chinese influence is clear in the use of the *luk cuan* and other motifs. Pekalongan batik also – and unusually – shows Dutch influence, for example in the floral bouquets. Fortunately, just at the time that imported printed cloth and stamped batik was pushing hand-drawn Pekalongan batik into extinction, a group of Dutch women began to promote and support this traditional industry. At this time batik artists also began to sign their works – again a European influence. **Very fine designs, minutely detailed**, often with a profusion of dots (known as *citcik*) are characteristic of Pekalongan cloth.

Batik from other parts of Indonesia

Toraja, Sulawesi: The Torajans produce simple batik known as *sarita*, using large motifs similar to those carved on Torajan houses and rice barns. Rarely produced today, sarita was worn as a headdress by Torajan warriors. The sarita is viewed as magical and can bring good fortune to its owner.

colour', which was probably some sort of resist dyeing technique similar, but ancestral, to batik. Cloth produced using a canting should be labelled *tulis* (literally, to write) and one sarong length can take from one to 6 months to complete. Reflecting the skill and artistry required to produce such batik, waxers used to be called *lukis* or painters. Drawing the design with a canting is a laborious process and has largely been replaced by stamping.

In the mid-19th century, **the 'modern' batik industry** was born with the invention of the *cap* (pronounced 'jap') – a copper, sometimes a wooden, stamp. This is dipped in wax, and then pressed onto the cloth. The cap revolutionised batik production. As Wanda Warming and Michael Gaworski say in their book *The world of Indonesian textiles* "...it took a small cottage industry, a fine art, an expression of Javanese sensibilities, and a hobby for aristocratic women, and turned it into a real commercial enterprise". With the invention of the cap, so there evolved a parallel cap-making industry. Old copper stamps have become collectors' pieces, and now are only produced in large numbers in the towns of Solo, Pekalongan and, to a lesser extent, in Yogyakarta. Not only did the cap speed-up production, it also took the artistry out of waxing: waxers merely stamp the design onto the cloth. Some designs are produced using both the canting and the cap – such cloth is called *combinasi*.

Two types of wax are often used in the batik process. *Klowong* is a light and brittle wax that is used for the first stamping only, on both sides of the cloth. *Tembok* is darker and more durable, and needs to survive numerous washings, re-waxings and dyeings. If it cracks, then dye will reach the cloth. The marbled effect that is often viewed by visitors as characteristic of batik is due to this cracking of the tembok – Javanese regard such work as inferior.

Unlike ikat where women perform all the stages of cloth production, in the case of batik they usually only draw the design, while men dye the waxed cloth. In recent years, male batik artists, many of whom are based around Yogya, have taken to both waxing and dyeing. At the same time, there has been a decline in home-produced batik and an expansion in the number of small workshops and factories. Like weaving in many societies, the ability to produce finely-worked batik was expected of well-bred Javanese girls. Far fewer women make their own batik today, but they still appreciate and recognize well-made and well-designed cloth, and batiks worn at weddings and other functions are carefully, though surreptitiously, scrutinised by the guests.

Distinguishing hand-drawn from stamped batik It can be hard differentiating drawn (*tulis*) and stamped (*cap*) batik, particularly in the case of the repetitious geometric designs of Central Java. Look for irregular lines and examine repetitive motifs like flowers carefully – stamped batik will show no variation. On poorly-executed stamped cloth, there may be a line at the point where 2 stamps have been imperfectly aligned. Note that there is also machine printed cloth with traditional batik designs: this can be identified by the clear design and colour on one side only; batik, whether drawn or printed, will have the design clearly revealed on both sides of the fabric.

Books on Textiles Hitchcock, Michael (1985) *Indonesian textile techniques*, Shire Ethnography: Aylesbury, UK. Hitchcock, Michael (1991) *Indonesian textiles*, British Museum Press: London. Warming, Wanda and Gaworski, Michael (1981) *The world of Indonesian textiles*, Serindia: London.

JAKARTA

INTRODUCTION

Jakarta is officially named the Special Capital Region of Jakarta or in Indonesian, *Dearah Khusus Ibukota*. Hence the prefix, DKI Jakarta. With a population of well over 8 million, it is the centre of commerce and communications, of manufacturing activity and consumption, of research and publishing. It has the highest per capita income and the greatest concentration of rupiah billionaires. The economist Lance Castles notes that, just as "cream rises to the top of the milk, surpluses from whatever industries are currently flourishing [in Indonesia] tend to gravitate to the metropolis".

Jakarta highlights

Museums and galleries: the *National Museum* (see page 545) is one of the most impressive museums in Southeast Asia. Other museums include the *Fatahillah Museum* (see page 542), the *Wayang Museum* (see page 543), the *Textile Museum* (see page 547) and the private *Adam Malik Museum* (see page 549).

Religious sights: the *Istiqlal Mosque* (see page 547) is the largest mosque in Southeast Asia.

Areas of historical interest: *Kota*, the core of old Batavia (see page 542), and the mosque and ruined fortress at *Banten*, 100 km west of Jakarta (see page 560).

Sights of natural interest: day excursions are possible to the beaches, swimming and snorkelling at *Pulau Seribu* (see page 558) and to the renowned *Bogor Botanical Gardens* (see page 566).

Shopping areas: *Jalan Surabaya flea market* for 'antiques' (see page 554) and *Blok M* for anything else (see page 554).

Culture & performance: the *Taman Mini-Indonesia* (see page 549) and the *Taman Ismail Marzuki* (see page 553).

DKI Jakarta is administered as a province, yet covers a meagre 656 sq km (about the same area as Singapore) – making it the smallest region in the country. During the last half century its population has grown spectacularly. In 1942 the city had 563,000 inhabitants; in the next 10 years this more than doubled and by the census of 1971 had reached 4,579,000. In the most recent census in 1990, a figure of 8,254,000 was recorded. In other words, over the space of just 48 years, the population of Jakarta has increased 15-fold – a far higher rate than the country as a whole. Its economic attractions have effectively sucked people in from other parts of Java and the Outer Islands. It is also worth noting that census figures considerably understate the actual numbers of people living and working in the city, as they do not account for so-called 'circular migrants' – those people who still 'live' in the countryside, but who spend most of the year based in the capital.

Over the years, Jakarta has grown from its original position at the mouth of the Ciliwung River, on the Java Sea, and sprawled inland. Jakarta has, in effect, outgrown its borders. The town of Bogor, for example, one hour's drive to the S, acts as a dormitory town for Jakarta. For this reason, planning agencies and economists now talk of Jabotabek – an area which encompasses Jakarta, along with the 3 West Java *kabupaten* (or regencies) of Bogor, Tangerang and Bekasi, and the municipality of Bogor.

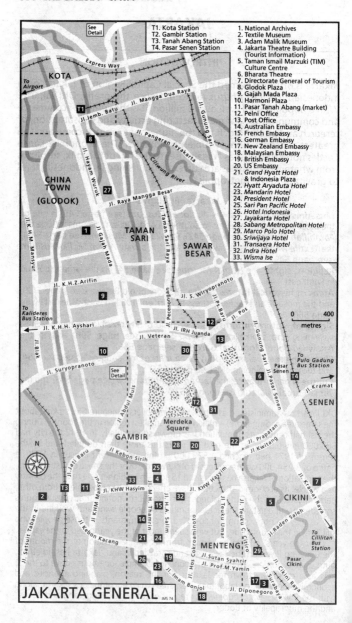

T1. Kota Station
T2. Gambir Station
T3. Tanah Abang Station
T4. Pasar Senen Station

1. National Archives
2. Textile Museum
3. Adam Malik Museum
4. Jakarta Theatre Building (Tourist Information)
5. Taman Ismail Marzuki (TIM) Culture Centre
6. Bharata Theatre
7. Directorate General of Tourism
8. Glodok Plaza
9. Gajah Mada Plaza
10. Harmoni Plaza
11. Pasar Tanah Abang (market)
12. Pelni Office
13. Post Office
14. Australian Embassy
15. French Embassy
16. German Embassy
17. New Zealand Embassy
18. Malaysian Embassy
19. British Embassy
20. US Embassy
21. *Grand Hyatt Hotel & Indonesia Plaza*
22. *Hyatt Aryaduta Hotel*
23. *Mandarin Hotel*
24. *President Hotel*
25. *Sari Pan Pacific Hotel*
26. *Hotel Indonesia*
27. *Jayakarta Hotel*
28. *Sabang Metropolitan Hotel*
29. *Marco Polo Hotel*
30. *Sriwijaya Hotel*
31. *Transaera Hotel*
32. *Indra Hotel*
33. *Wisma Ise*

JAKARTA GENERAL

A history of Jakarta

From trading post to Queen of the East, 16th-18th century

Evidence suggests that there was a Hindu settlement on the site of modern-day Jakarta as early as the 5th century. By the 12th century, Sunda Kelapa, the name of the old harbour of Jakarta, was already flourishing as a port serving the Sundanese Kingdom of Pajajaran, S of Bogor. In 1513, the first Portuguese mariners arrived from Melaka (in Malaysia) in search of spices. No trading-post was established during this first visit but a few years later, they returned, bearing gifts for the King of Sunda. In 1522 a Treaty of Friendship was concluded, and the Portuguese were given permission to erect a godown.

The proud and independent Hindu Sundanese probably agreed to such a treaty because they felt threatened by the encroaching Muslims from the powerful N coast sultanate of Demak. However, this alliance failed to deter the aggressive instincts of the Muslim leader, Fatahillah. He attacked and took Sunda Kelapa in 1527, making it a vassal state of Demak, and renamed the town **Jayakarta**, meaning 'Complete Victory'. The date of the victory – 21 June – is still celebrated annually as the anniversary of Jakarta's founding.

By the end of the 16th century, the Dutch had superseded the Portuguese in their race to dominate the lucrative trade in spices centred on the E Indonesian islands of the Moluccas or Maluku (**see page 971**). Appreciating the commercial attractions of the large harbour at Sunda Kelapa, the Dutch began to shift their operations from Banten (**see page 560**), and in 1610 they were given permission by Prince Fatahillah to build a godown on the E bank of the Ciliwung River. By 1618 they had abused their agreement by converting the godown into a fort. At the same time, the English were also busy jostling for position and Prince Fatahillah gave them permission to build a lodge, in the hope of keeping the increasingly powerful Dutch at bay. In spite of limited English support, it was all to no avail. In 1619, a Dutch fleet arrived led by Jan Pieterszoon Coen who led an attack on the town, and razed it to the ground. A new town, renamed **Batavia**, was built and became the property of the Dutch East India Company (or VOC), with Coen as its first governor-general. Under Dutch rule, Batavia became a thriving centre for trade and the most powerful city in the archipelago.

The Javanese kingdoms of Banten and Mataram (based near Yogyakarta and Surakarta) did try to dislodge the Dutch – unsuccessfully. Sultan Agung attacked the town in 1628, and again in 1629; each time the forces of the VOC prevailed. But it would be wrong to think of the Dutch 'ruling' Java during these early decades. The VOC was only interested in Batavia as a port and base from which to manage the spice trade. The city was a bustling centre of enterprise, but there was no attempt at territorial expansion. It was not until the end of the 17th century, as Mataram and the other sultanates went into terminal decline, that the VOC began to expand and annex these former kingdoms. By 1757, Banten, and the sultans of Mataram were vassals of the VOC based at Batavia, a city which had become known by then in Europe as the 'Queen of the East'.

From health hazard to capital city, 18th-20th century

During the 18th century, Batavia developed a reputation as the unhealthiest town in the East – a White Man's graveyard. When designing the city, the Dutch had made the mistake of attempting to recreate Holland, digging canals and ditches in an already swampy area surrounded by marshland and jungle. The effect was to create – to use a word popular at the time – a noxious 'miasma'. The canals were often stagnant and quickly became open sewers – there was scarcely a toilet in the city – choked with rotting carcasses, human 'ordure', slime and filth: perfect conditions for the spread of disease, notably cholera and malaria.

The mortality rate was stunningly high; in 1806 the English traveller Sir John

The Chinese of Java and Jakarta

From as early as the 17th century, the Chinese formed an indispensable element of Jakarta's population. But it was not until the middle of the 18th century that large numbers of Chinese began to arrive in the city, driven out of S China by famine and economic hardship.

Unfortunately, many of the immigrants failed to secure work and were seen as a nuisance by the VOC. The Dutch attempted to control the situation by deporting unemployed Chinese to Ceylon, but rumours spread that deportees were being dumped in the Java Sea. The Chinese formed gangs and attacked Dutch outposts, resulting in a government search for arms in all Chinese homes in 1740. When the search started, shots were heard, a fire broke out and bedlam ensued. Chinese were attacked, robbed and killed by Dutch citizens, soldiers and sailors. Five hundred who were being held prisoner in the City Hall were slaughtered after the bailiff gave the order for them all to be killed. It is estimated that in all between 5,000 and 10,000 Chinese were massacred. During the riot, much of the old city was destroyed. Batavia never really recovered from this incident, not so much because the fabric of the city had been destroyed, but because the economic heart – the Chinese – had been decimated.

This incident did not prevent the Chinese population of Jakarta achieving great economic power – although it did presage an even more horrific massacre of Chinese in 1965 (see box, **page 509**). By the 19th century, there were already the beginnings of a deep-seated antipathy towards the Chinese on the part of the indigenous Javanese population. But even then, the numbers of Chinese were hardly large: in 1870, Chinese in the Indies numbered only 250,000. These were known as *peranakan* – literally 'half-caste' – Chinese men intermarried and, to a large degree, assimilated into Javanese society. Many lost their ability to read, write, or even speak Chinese. Their position in society was often as middlemen, marketing rice, selling fertilizers, and providing credit to farmers. However, this gradual process of assimilation was not to last. The increasing nationalism of mainland China broke upon the shores of the Indonesian archipelago, making the *peranakan* conscious of their roots.

Peranakan families began to enrol their children into Chinese language schools, and to verse them in the culture and ideals of their homeland. But far more important than this change of heart, was the influx of large numbers of Chinese *totok* (full-blood Chinese) from the end of the 19th century, attracted to the Indies by the economic opportunities to be found there. Importantly, the men were also accompanied by large numbers of *totok* women, so that pure Chinese families could be formed. Peranakan Chinese found themselves alienated from Dutch, Javanese and Chinese society. As was said of one Peranakan, Kapitein Cina Tan Jin Sing of Yogya in 1813: *Cina wurung, Londa durung, Jawa Tanggung* or "No longer a Chinese, not yet a Dutchman, a half-baked Javanese." In the 1930s the Partai Tionghoa Indonesia (Chinese Indonesian Party) was formed to represent the interests of the Chinese in the country, who by that time numbered about 1,250,000, or 2% of the total population of Indonesia.

Barrows concluded, from studying a register of deaths, that *every* soldier sent out to Batavia had 'perished there'; a posting to the city was, in effect, a death sentence. The geographer Victor Savage in his book *Western impressions of nature and landscape in Southeast Asia* writes that Batavia was "in the Western sphere, the most notoriously insalubrious place in Southeast Asia, and possibly the world".

At the beginning of the 19th century, under the leadership of Governor-General Daendels (1808-1810), a clean-up operation was undertaken.

Canals were filled in, rivers were cleared and became free-flowing, and swamps were drained and brought under cultivation. Paddy fields close to the city were abandoned, and a new Batavia was built on a higher elevation, 4 km from the old city. These efforts did much to control disease and improve the health of the population.

When the Napoleonic Wars in Europe resulted in the annexation of Holland by the French, the British, led by Thomas Stamford Raffles, invaded Java in 1811 and took control of the island (see page 521). Raffles' administration only lasted until 1816, when he was forced to hand control back to the Dutch. He left Java to establish Singapore, which eventually eclipsed Batavia as the most important regional trading centre. From 1820 through to the early part of the 20th century, Batavia flourished and once again earned itself another glowing title – this time the 'Pearl of the Orient'.

Certainly, improved sanitation and the construction of wide boulevards and leafy parks leant it a more sophisticated air and by the early 20th century the city had a population of 300,000. However, the improvements to the physical infrastructure of Jakarta only served to disguise the dissatisfaction felt by the Indonesians, who continued to live in appalling conditions. The Dutch were also too slow to share any power with the indigenous population, and nationalist groups began to gain support and influence (see page 499). This was aided by the concomitant rise of a more orthodox Islam.

At the end of 1941, the Japanese began their whirlwind invasion of Southeast Asia, taking Batavia on 5 March 1942. They renamed the city **Jakarta**, a shortened version of Jayakarta. During the relatively short period of Japanese wartime occupation, Jakarta lost many of its colonial buildings – destroyed in civil disturbances or demolished to make way for new structures. With the imminent defeat of the Japanese, Indonesia proclaimed its independence on the 17 August 1945, under the leadership of Sukarno and Mohammad Hatta. However, the Dutch were not prepared to give up sovereignty so easily and in 1946, Jakarta again became the capital of a decidedly shaky colony. Over the next 3 years, nationalist groups throughout the country gained in influence and the Dutch came to realise that their colonial ambitions had reached the end of the road. In 1949, Sukarno returned to the capital in a blaze of glory to become the first President of the new Republic of Indonesia (see page 502).

Modern Jakarta

Today, Jakarta is a sprawling, cosmopolitan city, the centre of government, commerce and industry, with a population of well over 8 million – making it much the largest city in Indonesia. Growth has been extremely rapid. During the 1965 attempted coup for example, journalists holed-up in the *Hotel Indonesia* were at the S extremities of the city; today the hotel sits in the heart of a sprawling conurbation. Like Bangkok, Jakarta is perceived by the poorer rural Indonesians as a city paved with gold and they have flocked to the capital in their thousands. A survey in 1985 revealed that 40% of Jakarta's population had been born outside the city.

The central area is dominated by large office blocks, international hotels and wide, tree-lined roads. Off the main thoroughfares, the streets become smaller and more intimate, almost village-like. These are the densely inhabited *kampungs* where immigrants have tended to live – one-storey, tile-roofed houses crammed together and linked by a maze of narrow paths. Initially, kampungs developed their own identity, with people from particular language and ethnic groups, even from particular towns, congregating in the same place and maintaining their individual identities. Today those distinctions are less obvious but the names of the kampungs are a reminder of their origins: Kampung Bali, Kampung Aceh (N

Sumatra), and Kampung Makassar (Ujung Pandang) for example. The diverse mix of cultures is something Jakartans are particularly proud of; visitors to the capital are frequently reminded that the city is a 'melting pot' of the country's many ethnic groups (an example of Indonesia's motto 'Unity in Diversity').

It seems that Jakarta may be attempting to become another Singapore; first-class hotels have sprouted-up and there are any number of sophisticated shopping-malls, restaurants and night clubs. Jakarta is not often rated very highly as a tourist attraction but if visitors can tolerate the traffic, then it is possible to spend an enjoyable few days visiting the excellent museums, admiring the architectural heritage of the Dutch era, strolling through the old harbour or discovering some of the many antique or arts and crafts shops.

KOTA OR OLD BATAVIA

The city of Jakarta developed from the small area known as **Kota**, which stretches from the Pasar Ikan, or Fish Market, to Jalan Jembatan Batu, just S of Kota train station. North of Pasar Ikan was the old harbour town of **Sunda Kelapa** which thrived from the 12th century to 1527. *Sunda* refers to the region of West Java and *Kelapa* means coconut, and the port is still worth a visit today. Impressive, traditional Bugis or Makassar schooners dock here on their inter-island voyages and can be seen moored along the wharf (**see page 867**). Gradually, they are being supplanted by modern freighters, but for the time being at least it is possible to see these graceful ships being loaded and unloaded by wiry barefooted men, who cross precariously between the wharf and the boats along narrow planks. It is also sometimes possible to arrange a passage on one of the boats to Kalimantan and elsewhere in the archipelago – ask around. **Admission to harbour area**: 110Rp (800Rp for a car).

Much of the original town of Sunda Kelapa was demolished after the area was declared unhealthy in the 18th century. On its S edge and close to the Lookout Tower (see below) is the original, and still functioning, **Pasar Ikan** (Fish Market) which is now undergoing renovation. Close by is the **Bahari Museum** which was one of the original Dutch warehouses used for storing spices, coffee and tea. Today, it is home to a rather unimpressive maritime collection. The museum is worth a visit for the building rather than its contents. **Admission**: 250Rp. Open: 0900-1600 Tues-Thurs and Sun, 0900-1200 Fri and Sat. Other warehouses behind this museum were built between 1663 and 1669. The area around the Pasar Ikan is due to be developed further as a tourist attraction, recreating the atmosphere of the Dutch period by renovating and reconstructing the original buildings. Overlooking the fetid **Kali Besar** (Big Canal) is the **Lookout Tower** (or *Uitkijk*) built in 1839 on the walls of the Dutch fortress Bastion Culemborg (itself constructed in 1645). The tower was initially used to spy on (and signal to) incoming ships, and later as a meteorological post – a role it continued to fill until this century.

Less than 1 km to the S of Sunda Kelapa, down Jalan Cengkeh, is **Fatahillah Square**, or **Taman Fatahillah**. This was the heart of the old Dutch city and the site of public executions and punishments – hangings, death by impalement and public floggings. It was also a bustling market place. In the middle of the square is a small, domed building (rebuilt in 1972), the site of the old drinking fountain. The Dutch were unaware that the water from this fountain was infested, and it contributed to the city's high incidence of cholera and consequently high death-rate. On the S side of the square is the **Fatahillah Museum**, on the site of the first City Hall built in 1620. A second hall was constructed in 1627 and today's building was completed in 1710. A fine example of Dutch architecture (reminiscent of the old city hall of Amsterdam), it became a military headquarters

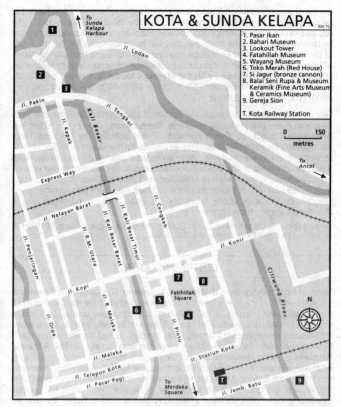

KOTA & SUNDA KELAPA
IMS 75

To Sunda Kelapa Harbour

1. Pasar Ikan
2. Bahari Museum
3. Lookout Tower
4. Fatahillah Museum
5. Wayang Museum
6. Toko Merah (Red House)
7. Si Jagur (bronze cannon)
8. Balai Seni Rupa & Museum Keramik (Fine Arts Museum & Ceramics Museum)
9. Gereja Sion

T. Kota Railway Station

0   150
metres

To Ancol

N

To Merdeka Square

after independence and finally the **Museum of the History of Jakarta** in 1974. It is a lovely building but, like so many Indonesian museums, the collection is poorly laid out. It contains Dutch furniture and VOC memorabilia (the museum is undergoing renovation). In the courtyard behind the museum, 2 *ondel-ondel* figures stand outside another room of rather down-at-heel exhibits. Below the main building are the prison cells. Admission: 250Rp. Open: 0900-1430 Tues-Thurs and Sun, 0900-1100 Fri, 0900-1300 Sat.

The **Wayang Museum**, previously called the Museum of Old Batavia, is on the W side of the square. All that remains of the original 1912 building is its façade. Until 1974 it housed the collection now in the Fatahillah Museum and today contains a good collection of wayang kulit and wayang golek puppets (**see page 529**). Admission: 250Rp. Open: 0900-1500 Tues-Thurs and Sun, 0900-1400 Fri, 0900-1230 Sat. Performances of wayang kulit or wayang golek are held here on Sundays at 1000 or 1100 (see entertainment). West from the Wayang Museum and over the Kali Besar is the **Toko Merah** or Red House. This was once the home of Governor-General Gustaaf van Imhoff. There are some other interesting 18th century Dutch buildings in the vicinity.

On the N side of Fatahillah Square is an old Portuguese bronze cannon called **Si Jagur**, brought to Batavia by the Dutch after the fall of Melaka in 1641. The design of a clenched fist is supposed to be a symbol of cohabitation and it is visited by childless women in the hope that they will be rendered fertile. On the E side of the square is the **Balai Seni Rupa** (the Fine Arts Museum), formerly the Palace of Justice. Built in the 1860's, it houses a poor exhibition of paintings by Indonesian artists. The building is shared with the **Museum Keramik**, a collection of badly displayed ceramics. Admission: 250Rp. Open: 0900-1400 Tues-Thurs and Sun, 0900-1100 Fri, 0900-1330 Sat.

East of Kota railway station on the corner of Jalan Jembatan Batu and Jalan Pangeran is the oldest church in Jakarta, **Gereja Sion**, also known as the 'old Portuguese Church' or 'Gereja Portugis'. It was built for the so-called 'Black Portuguese', Eurasian slaves brought to Batavia by the Dutch from Portuguese settlements in India and Ceylon. These slaves were promised freedom, provided that they converted to the Dutch Reformed Church. The freed men and women became a social group known as *Mardijkers* or 'Liberated Ones'. The church was built in 1693 and is a fine example of the Baroque style, with a handsome carved wooden pulpit, black ebony pews and an elaborately carved organ. The 4 chandeliers are of yellow copper.

Getting there: To get to Kota or the Old City from the centre of town, take bus P16 or P17 to Terminal Bis Kota (450Rp) or microlet M08 or M12.

CENTRAL JAKARTA

South of Fatahillah Square is **Glodok**, or **Chinatown**. This lay outside the original city walls and was the area where the Chinese settled after the massacre of 1740 (**see page 540**). Despite a national ban on the public display of Chinese characters, Glodok's warren of back streets still feels like a Chinatown: shophouses, enterprise and activity, and temples tucked behind shop fronts. Midway between Fatahillah Square and Merdeka Square is the **National Archives** or **Arsip Nasional**. This building (which no longer holds the National Archives) was erected in 1760 as a country house for Reiner de Klerk, a wealthy resident who subsequently became governor-general. After de Klerk's death, the house was bought by John Siberg, who likewise was later to become governor-general. But its most interesting owner was a Polish Jew named Leendert Miero. It is said that Leendert, a mere guard at the house, was given fifty strokes for falling asleep whilst on duty. From that day, he swore that he would one day own the building. He duly made his fortune as a goldsmith and purchased the house in 1818. Since 1925, it has been owned by the state and now houses an interesting collection of Dutch furniture.

The enormous **Medan Merdeka** or Liberty Square dominates the centre of Jakarta. It measures one sq km and is one of the largest city squares in the world. In 1818, it was renamed King's Square and since independence, following its enlargement by Sukarno, it has been known as Merdeka Square. In its centre is the **National Monument** (*Monas*), a 137 m-high pinnacle commissioned by President Sukarno in 1961 to celebrate Indonesia's independence. Construction of this monument entailed the bulldozing of a large squatter community to make way for the former President's monumental ambitions. It is known among residents of the city, rather irreverently, as Sukarno's Last Erection. Covered in Italian marble, it is topped by a bronze flame (representing the spirit of the revolutionaries), coated in 35 kg of gold leaf. Take the lift to the observation platform for magnificent views over the city. In the basement below the monument is a *museum* housing dioramas depicting the history of Indonesia's

Jakarta's heroic monuments

A particular feature of the city is the monumental heroic sculpture which dominates many busy intersections. Commissioned by Sukarno, these sculptures were conceived as one element in his remodelling of Jakarta as a great modern city. In the same vein as Communist heroic art, they also romanticise Indonesia's struggle for independence. Examples include the 2 waving figures of the **Welcome Monument** on the traffic circle between the *Hotel Indonesia* and the *Mandarin Hotel*. The so-called **Farmers' Monument** or *Patung Tani* depicts a couple bidding farewell, as the husband leaves to join the revolution. Sculpted by 2 Russians and with Communist overtones, it has not been the favourite monument of Jakartans in recent years; a group even lobbied for its removal. Other monuments include the muscular **Irian Jaya Freedom Monument** (also known as the Incredible Hulk) in the centre of Lapangan Banteng which shows a man symbolically breaking free from his chains; and the distinctly uninspired **Youth Monument**, to the S on Jalan Jend. Sudirman, known as Hot Plate Harry or The Pizza Man. Indonesians call this last monument *Adu, Panas* ('Ow, Hot') or Pertamina – a reference to the national oil company and the volatility of its product. Finally there is the **Dirgantara Monument** (or Pancoran), which can be seen from the highway to Bogor. It has various names: the Dutch in Jakarta call it Ard Schenk because the figure's arms are like those of a skater in motion; some Indonesians call it Truper (a corruption of Trooper), because the ragged clothes look like the remains of a parachute; while many English-speaking residents refer to it as the 7-Up Man because of the statue's pedestal. The latest addition to Jakarta's monuments is the figure of **Arjuna Wijaya** (Arjuna driving a chariot of galloping horses) near the National Museum on the corner of Jalan Thamrin, which looks as though it has been sculpted out of white chocolate.

independence. The entrance to the museum is N of the road immediately in front of the monument, where there is a statue of Diponegoro (a Javanese hero, **see page 596**) on horseback. Admission: 500Rp for museum, 2,000Rp to take the lift to the top, 300Rp for camera, 500Rp for video, 2,500Rp for booklet with English description of the dioramas. Open: 0830-1700 Mon-Fri, 0830-2100 Sat, Sun and holidays.

On the W side of the square is the neo-classical **National Museum**. Established in 1860 by the Batavian Fine Arts Society, it is an excellent museum and well worth a visit. Set around a courtyard, the collection consists of some fine stone sculpture (mostly of Hindu gods), a textile collection, and a collection of mainly Chinese ceramics found in Indonesia and bequeathed to the museum by a Dutchman, Orsoy de Flines, in the 1930s. Next to the ceramics is a display of bronzeware including Dongson drums (**see page 706**) and krisses (see box). The pre-history room is well laid out. Its collection includes the skull cap and thigh bone of Java Man, a rare example of *Homo erectus*, discovered by Eugene Dubois in 1890 (**see page 621**). The ethnographic collection has been reorganized recently and includes an excellent range of masks, puppets, household articles, musical instruments and some models of traditional buildings representing cultures from several of the main islands in the archipelago. Upstairs there is a display of archaeological finds including recently discovered gold treasures found in Klaten, Central Java. Outside the museum entrance is the bronze statue of an elephant presented by King Chulalongkorn of Thailand, in 1871. Admission: 300Rp. Open: 0830-1430 Tues-Thurs and Sun, 0830-1130 Fri, 0830-1330 Sat. Good volunteer guides available: English, German, French, Dutch and Japanese language tours available. See the Jakarta Post for details. There is a handicraft shop and a

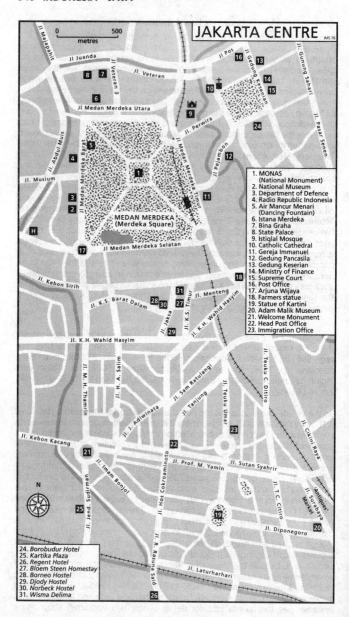

JAKARTA CENTRE

JMS 76

0   500
metres

Jl. Majapahit
Jl Juanda
Jl. Veteran 3
Jl. Veteran
Jl Medan Merdeka Utara
Jl. Abdul Muis
Jl. Musium
Jl Medan Merdeka Barat
Jl Medan Merdeka Timur
Jl Medan Merdeka Selatan
Jl. Kebon Sirih
Jl. K.S. Barat Dalam
Jl. Jaksa
Jl. Menteng
Jl. K.S. Timur
Jl. K.H. Wahid Hasyim
Jl. K.H. Wahid Hasyim
Jl. M. H. Thamrin
Jl. H. A. Salim
Jl. J. Adiwinata
Jl. Sam Ratulangi
Jl. Tanjung
Jl. Teuku Umar
Jl. Teuku C. Ditiro
Jl. CIkini Raya
Jl. Kebon Kacang
Jl. Jend. Sudirman
Jl. Imam Bonjol
Jl. Hos Cokroaminoto
Jl. Prof. M. Yamin
Jl. R. Rasuna Said
Jl. Sutan Syahrir
Jl. T.C. Citiro
Jl. Diponegoro
Jl. Laturharhari
Jl. Pos
Jl. Gedung Kesenian
Jl. Gunung Sahari
Jl. Pasar Senen
Jl. Perwira
Jl. Pejambon

MEDAN MERDEKA
(Merdeka Square)

Antiques Market
Jl. Surabaya

N

1. MONAS
   (National Monument)
2. National Museum
3. Department of Defence
4. Radio Republic Indonesia
5. Air Mancur Menari
   (Dancing Fountain)
6. Istana Merdeka
7. Bina Graha
8. State Palace
9. Istiqlal Mosque
10. Catholic Cathedral
11. Gereja Immanuel
12. Gedung Pancasila
13. Gedung Keserian
14. Ministry of Finance
15. Supreme Court
16. Post Office
17. Arjuna Wijaya
18. Farmers statue
19. Statue of Kartini
20. Adam Malik Museum
21. Welcome Monument
22. Head Post Office
23. Immigration Office

24. Borobudur Hotel
25. Kartika Plaza
26. Regent Hotel
27. Bloem Steen Homestay
28. Borneo Hostel
29. Djody Hostel
30. Norbeck Hostel
31. Wisma Delima

telecommunications centre here (visitors can make faxes, telexes and long distance phone calls), set up by a museum co-operative.

On the N side of the square, is the neo-classical Presidential Palace or **Istana Merdeka**, built in 1861 and set in immaculate gardens. Originally named **Koningsplein Paleis**, it was renamed after the independence ceremony was held in front of the building on 27 December, 1949. The large crowd that assembled for the ceremony is reputed to have shouted 'merdeka, merdeka' ('freedom, freedom') as the new red and white flag of the Republic of Indonesia was raised; this ceremony and episode is re-enacted each year on Independence Day. President Sukarno resided at the Istana Merdeka, but President Suharto moved to a more modest residence and the building is now only used for state occasions. Behind the palace is the older **State Palace**, next to the Bina Graha, the presidential office building. To get to the State Palace, walk down Jalan Veteran 3 and turn W on Jalan Veteran.

In the NE corner of Medan Merdeka is the impressive **Istiqlal Mosque**, built in 1978. It is the principal place of worship for Jakarta's Muslims and reputedly the largest mosque in Southeast Asia. Non-muslims can visit the mosque when prayers are not in progress (women should take a scarf to cover their heads, and dress modestly). Facing the mosque, in the NW corner of Lapangan Banteng (see below), is the strange neo-gothic **Catholic Cathedral**, built in 1901.

Due E of the mosque is **Lapangan Banteng**, or 'Buffalo Field', used by the Dutch military during the late 18th century. Daendels built a huge palace on this square in 1809; it is now the Department of Finance. Next door is the Supreme Court. In 1828, the Waterloo Memorial was erected in the centre of the Lapangan Banteng. Demolished by the Japanese during their wartime occupation, it has since been replaced by the **Irian Jaya Liberation Monument**. Positioned as it is in front of the Treasury, residents wryly joked that the figure's stance with raised, open hands was not one of freedom but represented the exclamation '*kosong*', or 'empty' (refering to the Treasury).

From the S corner of Lapangan Banteng, Jalan Pejambon runs S past **Gedung Pancasila**, the building where Sukarno gave his famous *proklamasi*, outlining the 5 principles of Pancasila (**see page 502**). At the S end of Jalan Pejambon, backing onto Merdeka Square, is the **Gereja Immanuel**, an attractive circular domed church, built by Dutch Protestants in the classical style in 1835.

OTHER PLACES OF INTEREST

Jakarta's kampungs, or villages, are home to the bulk of the city's population and one of the most memorable excursions is simply to wander through these effervescent, vivacious communities with their labyrinthine streets. (They are clearly seen on the approach to Jakarta airport – look out for the patchworks of ochre rooftiles). The kampungs still tend to be inhabited by migrants from particular parts of the archipelago, and are named accordingly: Aceh (North Sumatra), Bali and Ujung Pandang Makassar (Sulawesi) for example. They often have stalls and *warungs* (restaurants) which serve regional specialities and offer an insight into the lifestyle of ordinary Jakartans. Although crime is a minor problem, visitors are far more likely to suffer the indignity of getting lost.

West of the city centre

The **Textile Museum**, near the Tanah Abang Market (and railway station), Jalan Satsuit Tuban 4, is housed in an airy Dutch colonial house set back from the road W of the centre of town. It contains a good range of Indonesian textiles, both

The kris: martial and mystic masterpiece of the Malay world

The kris occupies an important place in Indonesian warfare, art and philosophy. It is a short sword – the Malay word *keris* means dagger – and the blade may be either straight or sinuous (there are over 100 blade shapes), sharpened on both edges. Such was the high reputation of these weapons that they were exported as far afield as India. Krisses are often attributed with peculiar powers – one was reputed to have rattled violently before a family feud. Another, kept at the museum in Taiping (Malaysia), has a particularly bloodthirsty reputation. It would sneak away after dark, kill someone, and then wipe itself clean before miraculously returning to its display cabinet. Because each kris has a power and spirit of its own, they must be compatible with their owners. Nor should they be purchased – a kris should be given or inherited. Ceremonial events often involve the ritual exchanging of krisses (Pakubuwono X gave the ruler of Gianyar a Surakarta kris).

The fact that so few kris blades have been unearthed has led some people to assume that the various kingdoms of Java were peaceful and adverse to war. The more likely explanation is that the pre-Muslim Javanese attributed such magical power to sword blades that they were only very rarely buried. The art historian Jan Fontein writes that "the process of forging the sword from clumps of iron ore and meteorite into a sharp blade of patterned steel is often seen as a parallel to the process of purification to which the soul is subjected after death by the gods".

The earliest confirmed date for a kris is the 14th century – they are depicted in the reliefs of Candi Panataran and possibly also at Candi Sukuh. However, in all likelihood they were introduced considerably earlier – possibly during the 10th century. A European visitor to Java in 1515 commented "Every man in Java, rich or poor, must have a kris in his house...no man between the ages of twelve and eighty may go out of doors without a kris in his belt". Even women sometimes wore krisses.

Krisses are forged by beating nickel or nickeliferous meteoritic material into iron in a complex series of laminations (iron from meteors is particularly prized because of its celestial origin). After forging, ceremonies are performed and offerings made before the blade is tempered. The *empu*, or swordsmith, was a respected member of society, who was felt to be imbued with mystical powers. After forging the blade, it is then patinated using a mixture of lime juice and arsenicum. Each part of the sword, even each curve of the blade, has a name and the best krisses are elaborately decorated. Inlaid with gold, the cross-pieces carved into floral patterns and animal motifs, grips made of ivory and studded with jewels, they are works of art.

But they were also tools of combat. In the Malay world, a central element of any battle was the amok. Taken from the Malay verb *mengamok*, the amok was a furious charge by men armed with krisses, designed to spread confusion among the enemy ranks. Amok warriors would be committed to dying in the charge and often dressed in white to indicate self-sacrifice. They were also often drugged with opium or cannabis. It was also a honourable way for a man to commit suicide. Alfred Russel Wallace in *The Malay Archipelago* (1869) writes: "He grasps his kris-handle, and the next moment draws out the weapon and stabs a man to the heart. He runs on, with the bloody kris in his hand, stabbing at everyone he meets. 'Amok! Amok!' then resounds through the streets. Spears, krisses, knives and guns are brought out against him. He rushes madly forward, kills all he can – men, women and children – and dies overwhelmed by numbers...". The English expression 'to run amok' is taken from this Malay word.

Recommended reading: Frey, Edward (1986) *The Kris: mystic weapon of the Malay world*, OUP: Singapore.

batik and ikat. Admission: 250Rp. Open: 0900-1500 Tues-Thurs and Sun, 0900-1100 Fri, 0900-1300 Sat. Get there on Bus S6 or S4. Close by, on Jalan Tanah Abang, is the **Taman Prasati Museum**, which was once a cemetery. Raffles' first wife was buried here.

South of the city centre
The **Adam Malik Museum** is on the N side of Jalan Diponegoro, W from the junction with Jalan Surabaya. This unique private collection was only opened to the public in 1985, one year after the death of Adam Malik. His widow still lives in the house. The quirky but excellent collection includes cameras, radios, walking sticks, watches, as well as Chinese ceramics and some interesting icons. Admission: 2,000Rp. Open: 0930-1500 Tues-Sat, 0930-1600 Sun. Get there by bus.

The **Satriamandala Museum**, or Armed Forces Museum lies to the S of the city on Jalan Gatot Subroto, opposite the Kastika Chandra Hotel. It was formerly the home of Dewi Sukarno, wife of the late President. Today it houses a display of armaments and a series of dioramas, showing steps towards Indonesia's independence. Open: 0900-1530 Tues-Sun.

A night-time drive, or perhaps even a walk, down **Jalan Latuharhary**, in Menteng reveals a seedier side of life in Jakarta. *Transvestites*, dressed up to the nines, and known as *banci* (meaning hermaphrodite or homosexual) or *waria*, hawk their wares. Foreign visitors may be astonished not only by the beauty of these 'imitation ladies', but also by the fact that this is countenanced in an otherwise relatively strict Muslim society. Transvestites have, in fact, a long and honourable tradition not just in Indonesia but throughout Southeast Asia.

The large, wholesale, **Pasar Cikini**, in the district of Menteng, is worth a visit to see the range of fruits, vegetables, fish and other fresh products trucked in from the surrounding countryside and the coast for sale in Jakarta. The second floor houses a Gold Market.

North of the city centre
The **Crocodile Park** (Taman Buaya) is at Jalan Badengan Utara 27, towards Pluit NW of Kota. It has 500 crocodiles and regular shows take themes from popular Indonesian folktales. Admission: 1,000Rp. Open: 0900-1700 Mon-Sun. Get there by bus.

EXCURSIONS

Taman Mini-Indonesia is a 120 hectare 'cultural park', 10 km SE of Jakarta. Completed in 1975, there are 27 houses, each representing one of Indonesia's provinces and built in the traditional style of that region. There is even a miniature Borobudur. All the houses are set around a lake with boats for hire. It is possible to drive around the park on weekdays, walk, take the mini train, cable car or horse and cart (small charges for these). The cable car takes passengers over the lake, upon which there is a replica of the whole archipelago. The **Keong Mas Theatre** (so-called because its shape resembles a golden snail) presents a superb not-to-be-missed film on Indonesia, projected on the world's largest imax screen (check in Jakarta Post for viewing times). Admission: 1,000Rp. The **Museum Indonesia**, a Balinese-style building, houses a good collection of arts and crafts and costumes from across the archipelago. Open: 0900-1500. The **Museum Komodo** is, as the name suggests, built in the form of the *Varanus komodiensis*, better known as the Komodo dragon (**see page 932**). It houses dioramas of Indonesian fauna and flora. Open: 0800-1500. Visit Taman Mini at the weekends for cultural performances but on weekdays to avoid the crowds. Admission to the park: 300Rp. Open: 0800-1700 Mon-Sun. **Getting there:** take bus 408 from Jalan Thamrin or a P11 bus from Cililitan terminal and from there a T55 to the park.

Taman Impian Jaya Ancol lies 10 km N of Merdeka Square, on the waterfront E of Sunda Kelapa. Built on reclaimed land, it is Southeast Asia's largest recreation park, with Disneyland-type rides, a 'fantasy land', drive-in cinema, sporting facilities (including a golf course) and the *Pasar Seni* art market. There is also an oceanarium and a swimming pool complex/waterworld. Accommodation, restaurants and foodstalls are all available. But the park can become very crowded at weekends. Admission at main gate: 850Rp; additional 6,000Rp for Fantasyland, and 5,000Rp for waterworld. Note that prices increase on Friday and over the weekend. Open: 1500-2200 Mon-Fri, 1000-2200 w/e and holidays. **Getting there**: by bus no 64 or 65 from the Kota station, or by minibus no M15.

Lubang Buaya (or 'Crocodile Hole') **Heroes Monument** is a memorial park that lies 15 km SE of town. It is dedicated to the 6 army generals and one officer slain in the abortive Communist-inspired coup d'état in 1965 (**see page 502**). The centrepiece is the *Pancasila Monument*, with statues of the 7 heroes standing near the well in which their bodies were thrown, after having been tortured and then executed by Communist militia squads. **Getting there:** by bus from Cililitan terminal SE of town.

Ragunan Zoo is in Ragunan, 15 km S of the city centre; see the famous Komodo dragon (**see page 932**) and other regional animals. Admission: 500Rp. Open: 0800-1800 Mon-Sun. **Getting there:** take a P19 bus from the centre of town.

Pulau Seribu or the 'Thousand Islands' are situated just off the coast, NW of Jakarta (**see page 558**). The closest thing to a tropical island paradise within easy reach of the capital. **Getting there:** by ferry, hydrofoil, helicopter or speedboat from Ancol Marina.

Banten is a historic town 100 km W of Jakarta on Java's N coast (**see page 560**). **Getting there:** Banten can be visited in a day from the capital, provided you hire a car or taxi.

Bogor is a hill resort 60 km S of Jakarta and famous for its *Botanical Gardens* (**see page 566**). Nearby is the *Safari Park* at Cisarua (**see page 567**) and the *Puncak Pass* (**see page 571**). **Getting there:** by bus from the Cililitan terminal 1-2½hrs (800-1,200Rp); by train from Gambir station 1-1½hrs (500-1,500Rp).

Bandung is one of Indonesia's largest cities, almost 200 km from Jakarta (**see page 572**). **Getting there**: by bus from the Cililitan terminal 5 hrs (8,000Rp), by train from the Gambir station 3 hrs (9,000-18,000Rp) or by minibus with Media, Jl. Johar 15 T 343643 (10,000Rp).

SERVICES

Tours outlined below can be organized by any of the travel agents or tour operators found in the major hotel complexes. City tours can include a visit to the National Museum, Old Batavia, Pasar Ikan and Sunda Kelapa, Taman Mini and a batik factory or the flea market on Jalan Surabaya. Evening tours can be arranged to Ancol Amusement Park and the Pasar Seni (an arts and crafts market within Ancol), with dinner included. Out-of-town tours can be arranged to Bogor and the Puncak Pass, the Safari Park at Cisarua, Bandung and the Tangkuban Perahu crater. One day tour by hovercraft to Pulau Seribu are organized on Sundays and holidays, 0700-1700, 1 hr 20 mins ride, T 325608 for more information. There are also day tours to the West, to visit the historic site of Banten and the beach at Anyer, on the W coast.

Cruise holidays starting from Tanjung Priok, Jakarta's port, are available with the *Island Explorer*, a luxury 18 cabin ship. From Dec to Mar it travels from Jakarta to Krakatau, the Ujung Kulon National Park and to Sumatra to see an elephant training centre. 7 day trip costs US$2,049. The rest of the year it cruises between Bali and Kupang (Timor) (see page 687) Jl. Let. Jen. S. Parman 78, Slipi, Jakarta Barat, T 593401, F 593403.

Festivals Apr: *Anniversary of Taman Mini* (20th), performances of traditional music and dance. Jun: *Anniversary of Jakarta* (22nd), commemorates the founding of Jakarta. Followed by the *Jakarta Fair* which lasts one month.

Accommodation L *Borobudur*, Jl. Lap. Banteng Selatan, T 370333, F 3809595, a/c, several restaurants, large pool, large hotel block set amidst extensive gardens, on the S side of the square; shopping arcade and airline offices all found here; **L** *Grand Hyatt*, 4th flr, Plaza Indonesia, Jl. Jend. M.H. Thamrin, PO Box 4546, T 3107400, F 334321, a/c, restaurant, pool. Very smart new block in central location next to Plaza Indonesia – an extensive new shopping mall. 5th floor facilities include landscaped garden with pool, tennis and squash courts and fitness centre.; **A+** *Hilton*, Jl. Jend. Gatot Subroto, T 587981, F 583091, a/c, several restaurants, large pool, considered by many to be the best hotel in town, it includes a penthouse with its own swimming pool, set in lovely gardens, with good sports and business facilities; **A+** *Hyatt Aryaduta*, Jl. Prapatan 44-46, T 376008, F 349836, a/c, restaurant, pool, recently renovated; **A+** *Mandarin Oriental*, Jl. M.H. Thamrin, PO Box 3392, T 321307, F 324669, a/c, several restaurants, pool, sandwiched in between Jl. Thamrin and Jl. Imam Bonjol, this hotel is immaculately maintained, with superb service and large rooms; **A+** *President*, Jl. M.H. Thamrin 59, T 320508, F 333631, Japanese owned and frequented almost entirely by Japanese businessmen and tourists; **A+** *Sari Pan Pacific*, Jl. M.H. Thamrin 6, T 323707, F 323650, a/c, several restaurants, pool, large tower block in central position, with good facilities including a health centre. **A+** *Horison*, Jl. Pantai Indah, Jaya Ancol, T 680008, F 684004, a/c, restaurant, pool, rather out of town, within the entertainment park on the beach; **A+** *Indonesia*, Jl. M.H. Thamrin, T 320008, F 321508, a/c, restaurant, pool, Jakarta's original premier hotel, built in the 1960s for the Asian Games, reputedly with war reparations from the Japanese, recently refurbished and still popular, although there is no way of getting rid of its ugly exterior; **A+** *Sahid Jaya*, Jl. Jend. Sudirman 86, T 587031, F 583168, a/c, restaurant, pool, recently renovated, popular with tour groups and Indonesian businessmen but still rather lacking in ambience.

A *Kartika Plaza*, Jl. M.H. Thamrin 10, T 321008, F 322547, a/c, restaurant, good pool, recently renovated, with central position in city and popular with businessmen, gym; **A** *Kemang*, Jl. Kemang Raya, T 7993208, a/c, restaurant, pool, inconvenient location S of the city; **A** *Menteng 1*, Jl. Gondangdia Lama 28, T 357635, a/c, restaurant, pool; **A** *Jayakarta Tower*, Jl. Hayam Wuruk 126, T 6294408, F 6295000, a/c, restaurant, pool, not a very convenient location; **A** *Kartika Chandra*, Jl. Jend. Gatot Subroto, T 511008, F 5204230, a/c, restaurant, pool, uninspired, plain decor but good sized rooms; **A** *Patra Jasa*, Jl. A. Yani 2, T 410608, F 5203092, a/c, restaurant; **A** *Sabang Metropolitan*, Jl. Agus Salim 11, T 354031, a/c, restaurant, pool. Good central location; **A** *Wisata*, Jl. M.H. Thamrin, T 320308, F 324597, a/c, restaurant. **A** *Cipta*, Jl. K.H. Wahid Hasyim 53, T 4214700, F 326531, good location, price includes breakfast; **A** *Grand Menteng*, Jl. Matraman Raya 21, T 882153, F 882398, a/c, restaurant, pool, fitness centre, central.

B *Cengkareng Transit*, Jl. Jurumudi, T 611964. 10 mins from the airport, only useful if in transit or catching early flight; **B** *Chitra*, Jl. Otoko Tiga Seberang 23, T 6291125; **B** *Garden*, Jl. Kemang Raya, T 7995808, F 7980763, a/c, restaurant, pool, quiet position S of the city, rec; **B** *Melati*, Jl. Hayam Waruk 1, T 377208, F 360526; **B** *Prapanca*, Jl. Prapanca Raya 30, T 712630, F 7395030, S of the city, good value; **B** *Sriwijaya*, Jl. Veteran 1, T 370409, good location; **B** *Surya Baru*, Jl. Batu Ceper 11A, T 368108; **B** *Transaera*, Jl. Merdeka Timur 16, T 357059. Old colonial hotel. **B-C** *Wisata Jaya*, Jl. Hayam Wuruk 123, T 6008437, a/c, hot water. Also in the **B** category are: *Asri*, Jl. Pintu I Senayan, T 584071; *Cikini Sofyan*, Jl. Cikini Raya 79, T 320695, good value; *Djakarta*, Jl. Hayam Wuruk 35, T 377709; *Fabiola*, Jl. Gajah Mada 27, T 6394008; *Hasta*, Jl. Asia Afrika Senayan, T 581559; *Metropole*, Jl. Pintu Besar Selatan 39, T 676921; *Paripurna*, Jl. Hayam Wuruk 25-26, T 376311; *Sabang Palace*, Jl. Setia Budi Raya 24, T 514640; **C** *Marco Polo*, Jl. Cik Ditiro, T 325409, F 3107138, a/c, restaurant, pool, good.

The area around Jl. Jaksa has quite a number of **budget hotels**. There are also a number of travel agents on this road as well as a post office, laundry services and several travellers' eating houses. Long-stay guesthouses are to be found on Jl. Leuku Umar. **E** *Bloem Steen*, Jl. Kebon Sirih Timur 1, small, popular and good value; **E** *Borneo*, Jl.Kebon Sirih Barat Dalam 35, T 320095, small rooms but popular, some with attached mandi; **B-C** *Djody*, Jl. Jaksa 35, T 346600, some a/c, attractive courtyard, reasonable rooms, some with attached mandi, rec; **B-C** *Indra*, Jl. Wahid Hasyim 63, T 337432, some a/c, unattractive, but good value; **E** *Kresna*, Jl. Kebon Sirih Timur 1 175, T 325403, clean, some rooms with attached bathroom, rec; **D** *Nirwana*, Jl. Otto Iskandardinata 14, T 8191708, a/c, attached mandi; **C** *Norbek*, Jl. Jaksa 14, a/c, popular, clean but small rooms, some with attached mandi, organize taxis to the airport (18,000Rp); **E** *Wisma Delima*, Jl. Jaksa 5, T 337026, restaurant, popular, but cramped and rather worn, some with attached mandi. **E** *Wisma ISE*, Jl. K.H.W. Hasyim 168, just W of Jl. M.H. Thamrin. Friendly owners, central location, good value.

Restaurants Jakarta is a good place to eat out, with a wide choice of Indonesian, other Asian and international cuisines.

Indonesian: ♦*Bami Gajah Mada*, Jl. Gajah Mada 92, and Studio 21 cinema, Jl. M.H. Thamrin, cheap noodlehouse, rec; ♦♦*Handayani*, chain of restaurants – Jl. Abdul Muis 36 and Jl. Kebon Sirih 31, rec; ♦♦♦♦*Oasis*, Jl. Raden Saleh 47, T 326397, also serves International food, Dutch governor's house built in 1928 the walls are adorned with Indonesian arts and crafts, rijstaffel served here, one of the best restaurants in town, local music performances, reservations necessary; ♦*Sari Kuring*, Jl. Silang Monas Timur, popular with locals, cheap and good; ♦*Sari Nusantara*, Jl. Silang Monas Tenggara (all regions of Indonesia); ♦ *Sate House Senayan*, Jl. Kebon Sirih 31A, sate and gado gado, rec. Several cheap restaurants in the Jl. Jaksa area.

Foodstalls: *Hotel Indonesia*, Jl. M.H. Thamrin, buffet of different Indonesian cuisines, a good place to survey the variety; *The basement of Pasar Raya*, Blok M has a variety of reliably good 'stalls' (not just Indonesian), the top floor of *Sogo*, in the Plaza Indonesia, has similar stalls; *Jl. Pecenongan* (also known as Jl. Used Cars) – warungs at night, used car workshops by day, particularly good seafood, rec. (BYOB); *Jl. H.A. Salim* has a great number of cheap regional restaurants, Western, Padang, Sundanese etc; *Jl. Mangga Besar* has night-time warungs, as does the car-park for Sarinah's Department Store on Jl. M.H. Thamrin.

Other Asian cuisine: ♦♦♦♦*Arirang*, Jl. Mahakam 1/28, Korean BBQ, rec; ♦♦♦♦*Chikuyo-Tei*, Summit Mas Tower, Jl. Jend. Sudirman, Japanese, rec; *Gang Gang Sulai*, Jl. Cideng Timur 65 and Jl. Kemang Raya 10; ♦♦*Kikugawa*, Jl. Cikini IV 13, Japanese, central location, good value; ♦♦♦♦*Korea Tower*, Bank Bumi Daya Bldg, 30th flr, Jl. Imam Bonjol 61, Korean, rec; ♦♦♦♦*Keyaki*, Sari Pacific Hotel, Jl. M.H. Thamrin 6, Japanese, rec; ♦♦♦♦*Nippon-Kan*, Hilton Hotel, Jl. Gatot Subroto, expensive but good value Japanese; *Phinisi floating restaurant*, Ancol, also serves seafood; ♦♦♦♦*Shima*, Hyatt Aryaduta Hotel, Jl. Prapatan 44, the best Japanese food in town; ♦♦♦♦*Spice Garden*, Mandarin Oriental Hotel, Jl. M.H. Thamrin. Sezhuan, rec; ♦♦♦*Summer Palace*, Tedja Buana Bldg, 8th flr, Jl. Menteng Raya 29, Sechuan, large but reliable restaurant, rec; ♦♦♦♦*Tokyo Garden*, Jl. Rasuna Said 10, Tapanyaki, rec; ♦♦♦*Yakiniku*, Jl. Mahakam 1/166, set price for all you can eat, buffet style.

Seafood: ♦♦♦*Kuningan*, Jl. H.O.S. Cokroaminoto 122; ♦♦*Nelayan*, Manggala Wanabakti Building, Jl. Gatot Subroto, T 5700248, also serves Chinese, large, very popular, reservations necessary, rec; ♦♦♦*Ratu Bahari*, Jl. Melawai V11/4 Blok M, Chinese style; ♦♦♦*Seafood Senayan*, Jl. Pakubuwono V1/6 and Jl. H.O.S. Cokroaminoto 78, fresh, Chinese style; ♦♦♦*Yun Nyan*, Jl. Batuceper 69 (off Jl. Hayam Wuruk) and Jl. Panglima Polim Raya 77 (in South Jakarta), closed Mon, rec.

International: ♦♦♦*A La Bastille*, Jl. Yusuf Adiwinata 30, traditional French, BYOB; ♦♦♦♦*Ambiente*, Hyatt Aryaduta Hotel, Jl. Prapatan, best Northern Italian in town, but overpriced, rec; *Amigos*, Setiabudi Bldg, Jl. H.R. Rasuna Said. Mexican food to accompaniment of live country and western music. *Casablanca*, Jl. R.H. Rasuna Said; ♦♦♦♦*Club Room*, Mandarin Oriental, Jl. M.H. Thamrin, exclusive French; ♦♦♦*Green Pub*, Jakarta Theatre Bldg, Jl. M.H. Thamrin 9, best Mexican; *Jaya Pub*, Jl. M.H. Thamrin, pub food; ♦♦♦♦*Jayakarta Grill*, Sari Pacific Hotel, Jl. M.H. Thamrin; *Kon Tiki*, 16th floor, Wisma Metropolitan II, Jl. Jend. Sudirman. Waikiki salad, seafood chowder, baked crab Honolulu. Good views of the city. ♦♦♦*La Rose*, Landmark Centre, Jl. Jend Sudirman 1, intimate and romantic; ♦♦♦♦*Le Bistro*, Jl. Wahid Hasyim 75. Jakarta's first French restaurant, established 15 yrs. ago. Classic French favourites such as bouillabaisse and Lamb Provençale. ♦♦♦♦*Maxis*, Plaza Indonesia, Jl. M.H. Thamrin. Small Italian café, classic Italian dishes, average quality. ♦♦♦*Memories*, Wisma Indocement Bldg, Jl. Jend. Sudirman, interior decorated with Dutch memorabilia, Dutch cuisine, rec; ♦♦♦*Ponderosa*, chain of standard steakhouses – carvery and salad, Lippo Bldg, Jl. Gatot Subroto 35, Jl. Jend. Sudirman 57; ♦♦♦*Pinocchio*, top floor Wisma Metropolitan I, Jl. Jend. Sudirman. Italian. Good place for families – birds and monkeys in cages near the dining area. Fixed price Sunday lunch and dinner. ♦♦♦*Pizzaria*, Hilton Hotel,

Jl. Gatot Subroto, outdoor, set in Balinese Garden, over-loud musical accompaniment;♦♦♦*Rugantino's*, Jl. Melawai Raya 28, indifferent Italian;♦♦♦♦+*Taman Sari*, *Hilton Hotel*, Jl. Gatot Subroto, rec;♦♦♦♦*Toba Rotisserie*, Borobudur Intercontinental Hotel, Jl. Lapangan Banteng, French, expensive but excellent. **Fast food:** ♦♦*Pizza Hut*, Jakarta Theatre Bldg, Jl. M.H. Thamrin. All-you-can-pile-on-your-plate salads and pizzas.

Bakeries popular (and good) in Jakarta. There are a number down Hayam Wuruk and in some hotels for example, *Hilton*, *Sari Pacific*, *Hyatt* and *Mandarin*. *Sakura Anpan* on Jl. H.A. Salim has been recommended.

Bars *Captain's Bar*, Mandarin Hotel, Jl. M.H. Thamrin, good for lunch, large-screen sports news; *George and Dragon*, Jl. Teluk Betung 32; *Green Pub*, Jakarta Theatre Bldg, Jl. M.H. Thamrin, Country and Western band; *Jaya Pub*, Jl. M.H. Thamrin, live music; *Kudus Bar*, Jakarta Hilton, Jl. Gatot Subroto; *Pendopo Bar*, Borobudur Hotel, Jl. Lap. Banteng Selatan, open 1100-0100, Mon-Fri; *Pink Qasbar*, Jl. Kemang Raya; *Sundance*, Jl. Pelatehan Blok K, Kebayoran, darts and pool; *Tavern*, Hyatt Aryaduta, Jl. Prapatan 44/48; *Top Gun*, Jl. Pelatehan 132, (Blok M) Kebayoran Baru. **Karaoke** bars abound.

Entertainment For a schedule of events, look in the 'Where to Go' section of the Jakarta Post, or buy Jakarta Program's 'What's On and Where', obtainable from most bookstores for up-to-date information on the city's entertainment.
   Cultural Shows: *Taman Ismail Marzuki* (or TIM) just off Jl. Cikini Raya is the focal point of cultural activities in the city with performances almost every night. The centre contains exhibition halls, 2 art galleries, theatres, cinema complex and a planetarium (admission: 1,000Rp, tours on Tues-Thurs, 0930, 1100 and 1330, Fri 1000, 1330, Sat 0930). Their monthly calendar of events is usually available at hotel-counters, or call T 322606 for information. *Gedung Kesenian*, Jl. Gedung Kesenian 1, organizes wayang orang performances, piano recitals, theatre and other cultural events. A modern art gallery is attached to the theatre. Hotels should provide information on their programme or phone, T 3808283. *The Indonesian/American Cultural Centre* on Jl. Pramuka Kav. 30 has exhibits, films and lectures on Indonesia. '*Ganesha*', a volunteer group interested in Indonesian culture, organize a Tuesday evening lecture series at the Erasmus Huis, Jl. H.R. Rasuna Said; check the Jakarta Post and hotels for details. *Pasar Raya Theatre*, 2000-2100 Fri. *Pondok Garminah*, Jl. Taman Kebon Sirih 11/6, T 335716 combine an evening meal with entertainment: Indonesian traditional dance and music 20,000Rp incl. dinner. 1900-2100 Sun and Wed. *Manari Theatre Restaurant*, Jl. Jend. Gatot Subroto 14, T 5204036.
   Gamelan: *National Museum*, 0930-1030 Sun. *Taman Mini*, Sun. *Miss Tjitjih's Theatre*: Sundanese folk drama, Jl. Kabel Pendek, 1900 and 2100 Mon-Sun.
   Traditional dance: *Taman Mini*, Sun and hols 1000-1400. *Bharata Theatre*, Jl. Pasar Senen 15 has nightly performances of wayang orang and Ketoprak from 2015-2400 (except Sat).
   Wayang: *Wayang Museum* has alternate wayang kulit and wayang golek performances 1000-1200 Sun (200Rp). Alternate wayang kulit and wayang golek shows at the National Museum 2000 Sun (entrance included in museum entry ticket).
   Cinemas: *Jakarta Theatre Building*, Jl. M.H. Thamrin; *Taman Ismail Marzuki* (TIM) has a cinema complex (see above for address); *Studio 21* on Jl. Hayam Wuruk; *Eldorado Complex* on E side of Merdeka.
   Jakarta Fair: Annual event from 15 Jun-13 Jul, now at a new site, the old Kemayoran Airport N.E. of the city centre. Entertainment, art market etc. Admission: 1,000Rp. Open: 1700-2300.
   Music: Jazz at the *Captain's Bar*, Mandarin Hotel; *Borobudur Kintamani Garden*, Borobudur Hotel. Country and Western music at the *Green Pub*, Jakarta Theatre Bldg, Jl. M.H. Thamrin.
   Disco: *Ebony*, Kuningan Plaza, Jl. Rasuna Said; *Manhattan Disco*, Jl. Pantai Indah; *Hollywood East*, Harmoni Plaza Blok B; *Music Room*, Borobudur Hotel; *Pitstop*, Sari Pacific Hotel, Jl. M.H. Thamrin; *Stardust*, Jayakarta Tower Hotel, Jl. Hayam Wuruk; *Tanamur*, Jl. Tanah Abang Timur 14.

Sports **Bowling:** at Ancol, Monas and Kebayoran Bowling Centres. **Fitness centres:** many of the big hotels have these. **Golf:** There are several courses around town: Jakarta Golf Club, Jl. Rawamungun Muka Raya, T 4891208; Padang Golf Jaya Ancol, Jl. Lodan Timur Ancol, T 681121 and Kebayoran Golf Course, Jl. Asia Afrika Senayan, T 582508. **Swimming:** all the major hotels have pools, some will allow non-residents to use their pools for a small charge. Other pools are at Ancol Waterworld and Taman Mini. **Waterskiing:** at Ancol. **Spectator sports:** *jai alai* (similar to pelota)—said to be the fastest ball game in the world—can be seen at Ancol, 2100 Mon-Sun.

Shopping Fixed priced stores are becoming more common in Jakarta but bargaining is still the norm. When buying 'antiques' and handicrafts, bargain down to 30%-40% of the original asking price, especially on Jl. Surabaya. Guaranteed quality can only be found in stores such as the *Sarinah Department store group*.

Shopping centres: there is now a glut of these in town. *Blok M*, S of town in Kebayoran Baru is still the largest; it includes *Pasar Raya* (which had its top 5 storeys gutted by fire recently, most of which were offices), *Matahari* and *Melawai Plaza*. *Glodok Plaza* is N of town on Jl. Hayam Wuruk and is another large shopping complex. *Pasar Baru* is N of Merdeka Square.

Markets For more information on the markets of Jakarta, buy *A Jakarta market* by Kaarin Wall, published by the American Women's Association (5,000Rp).

'Antiques': Jl. Kebon Sirih Timur supports a row of antique shops said to be among the best in town – the goods on sale here are more likely to be genuine that anywhere else. Jl. Palatehan 1 (near *Blok M*) S of town in Kebayoran has several shops selling antiques and Indonesian handicrafts. The mass of stalls which line the famous Jl. Surabaya is a great place to browse for smaller objects but there is little genuine for sale here – men sit by the side of the road openly 'distressing' newly-made objects. Jl. Majapahit, NW of Merdeka Square, houses a number of shops with genuine antiques. Jl. Ciputat Raya is quite a distance S of town, with better quality antiques and good furniture.

Bangka tin: locally mined pewter from *Pigura*, Palatehan 1/41. Also at *Pasar Raya*, *Sarinah* and hotel boutiques.

Batik: One floor of *Pasar Raya*, Blok M, is devoted to batik; *Batik Keris*, Danar Hadi, Jl. Raden Saleh 1A; *Government Batik Cooperative (GKBI)*, Jl. Jend. Sudirman 28; *Batik Semar*, Jl. Tomang Raya 54; *Iwan Tirta*, Jl. Panarukan 25 or *Hotel Borobudur*; *Srikandi*, Jl. Melawai VI/6A; *Pasar Tanar Abang*, a market W of Merdeka Square has good modern textiles – batik and ikat by the metre; a batik factory at Jl. Bendungan Hilir 2, in Senayan, is open to visitors.

Bookshops: *Gunung Agung Bookstore* on Jl. Kwitang 6 for English books; *Gramedia*, Jl. Gajah Mada 109; the new *Plaza Indonesia* has a couple of bookshops, as do the major hotels.

Clothes: childrens clothes are good value at *Pasar Raya* (Blok M). Adult fashions are improving and also are good value. *Sarinah Department Store* for international designs at reasonable prices and rack upon rack of ethnic clothing (such as batik shirts, dresses and jackets). Some of the large chain batik shops now supply ready-made batik, hand-painted silk and ikat in modern designs.

Furniture: Jakarta is a good place to buy Indonesian specialities such as Palembang chests, painted Madura chests, Javanese chairs, planters' chairs, cupboards and boxes. Jl. Kemang Raya and Jl. Ciputat Raya (the latter is rather out of town, SW) both contain a number of furniture shops and are good places to start.

Gold: gold market on the second floor of *Pasar Cikini*, off Jl. Pegangasaan Timur (an extension of Jl. Cikini Raya), Menteng. Other suppliers can be found in Blok M.

Handicrafts: found at *Pasar Raya* and the *Sarinah Department Store*, in Blok M and Jl. *Palatehan 1* (Pigura at 41, Djenta at 37). *Pasar Seni* in Ancol. *Indonesian Bazaar*, Hilton Hotel. *Jl. Pasar Baru* for Balinese woodcarving, silver workshops etc. Another *Sarinah Department Store* is on Jl. M.H. Thamrin.

Jewellery: *Pasar Raya*, Blok M; *Sogo*, Plaza Indonesia, Jl. Kemang Raya. For precious stones, try the *Indonesian Bazaar*, Hilton Hotel or *Pasar Uler* NE of town in Tanjung Priok. For 'cheap' jewellery, the prices are higher than in Yogya or Bali.

Paintings: *Oet's Gallery*, Jl. Palatehan 1/33; *Harris Art Gallery*, Jl. Cipete 41; *Duta Fine Arts Foundation*, Jl. Bangka 1/55A; *Hadiprana Galleries*, Jl. Palatehan 1/38; *Pasar Seni* (art market) at Ancol.

Supermarket: for all Westerners' deli cravings, visit *Kemchicks*, Jl. Kemang Raya 3, S of town.

Local transport Bus: up to 500Rp around town. Crowded, beware of pickpockets. Express buses (marked 'P') are smaller and less crowded, 450Rp. **Metropolitan Electric Train (KRL)**: Jakarta's elevated railway is under construction, and has been for years, the proposed date of completion is now sometime in 1993. *Bajaj* (orange motorized 3-wheelers, Indian made, pronounced *bajai*): the cheapest way to get around other than by bus, negotiate price before boarding. A short journey should cost 500-1,000Rp. *Helicak*: strange looking motorized bubbles, now rather rare. Taxi: the most comfortable and convenient way to get around the city. All are metered. Drivers often have limited knowledge of the city and its roads – they are usually migrants from out of town – so it is useful to keep track on a map. 800Rp flagfall and 250Rp for each additional kilometre. **Microlets**: similar to colts; blue vans with set routes, 250-300Rp. **Car hire**: most international companies strongly recommend a driver and local expats believe it is pure madness to attempt tackling the streets of Jakarta oneself. Cars with driver can be hired by the day for about US$50. **Avis**, Jl. Diponegoro, T 341964; **Bluebird**, Hilton Hotel, Jl. Jend. Gatot Subroto, T 325607; **Hertz**, Plaza Podium, 7th floor, Jl. Jend. Sudirman; **National**, Kartika Plaza Hotel, Jl. M.H. Thamrin 10, T 332006; **Toyota Rentacar**, Jl. Sudirman 5, T 5703327.

Banks & money changers Most of the larger hotels will have money changing facilities, and banks and money changers can be found throughout the city centre, particularly, for example, in shopping centres. Below is a list of the head offices of the main local banks, and international banks only. **Local banks Bumi Daya**, Jl. Imam Bonjol 61; **Central Asia**, Jl. Asemka 27-30; **Dagang Negara**, Jl. M.H. Thamrin 5; **Duta**, Jl. Kebon Sirih 12; **Ekspor Impor**, Jl. Lapangan Stasiun; **Indonesia**, Jl. M.H. Thamrin 2; **Negara Indonesia**, Jl. Jend. Sudirman 1; **Niaga**, Jl. Gajah Mada 18; **Rakyat Indonesia**, Jl. Jend. Sudirman 44-46. **Foreign banks American Express**, Jl. Jend. Sudirman; **Bank of America**, Wisma Antara, Jl. Merdeka Selatan 17; **Bangkok Bank**, Jl. M.H. Thamrin 3; **Banque Nationale de Paris**, Skyline Bldg, Jl. M.H. Thamrin 9; **Barclays Bank**, Wisma Metropolitan 1, Jl. Jend. Sudirman Kav-29; **Citibank**, Jl. M.H. Thamrin 55; **Chartered Bank**, Jl. M.H. Thamrin; **Chase Manhattan**, Jl. Merdeka Barat 6; **Deutsche Bank**, Gedung Eurasbank, Jl. Imam Bonjol 80; **Hongkong and Shanghai Bank**, Jl. Hayam Wuruk 8; **Westpac**, Summitmas Tower Bldg, Jl. Jend. Sudirman.

Embassies & consulates Australia, Jl. M.H. Thamrin 15, T 323109; **Austria**, Jl. Diponegoro 44, T 338090; **Belgium**, Jl. Cicurug 4, T 348719; **Brunei**, Central Plaza, Jl. Jend. Sudirman, T 510638; **Burma**, JL. H. Agus Salim 109, T 327204; **Canada**, Jl. Jend. Sudirman Kav. 29, T 510709; **Czechoslovakia**, Jl. Prof. M. Yamin SH 29, T 344944; **Denmark**, Jl. H.R. Rasuna Said Kav.10, T 5204350; **Finland**, Jl. H.R. Rasuna Said Kav.10, T 516980; **France**, Jl. M.H. Thamrin 20, T 332807; **Germany**, Jl. M.H. Thamrin 1, T 323908; **Greece**, Jl. Kebon Sirih 16, T 347016; **Hungary**, Jl. H.R. Rasuna Said Kav.10, T 587521; **Italy**, Jl. Diponegoro 45, T 337430; **Malaysia**, Jl. Imam Bonjol 17, T 332864; **Netherlands**, Jl. H.R. Rasuna Said Kav.S-3, T 511515; **New Zealand**, Jl. Diponegoro 41, T 330680; **Norway**, Bina Mulia Bldg, Jl. H.R. Rasuna Said Kav.10, T 511990; **Philippines**, Jl. Imam Bonjol 6-8, T 3848917; **Singapore**, Jl. H.R. Rasuna Said Block X, Kav2/4, T 5201489; **Spain**, Jl. H. Agus Salim 61, T 335937; **Sweden**, Jl. H.R. Rasuna Said Kav 10, T 5201551; **Switzerland**, Jl. H.R. Rasuna Said Block X, 3/2, T 516061; **Thailand**, Jl. Imam Bonjol 74, T 3904225; **UK**, Jl. M.H. Thamrin 75, T 330904; **USA**, Jl. Medan Merdeka Selatan 5, T 360360; **Vietnam**, Jl. Teuku Umar 25, T 3100359.

Useful addresses General **Post Office**: Jl. Pos Utara 2, Pasar Baru (or access from Jl. Lapangan Banteng); other **Post Offices** on Jl. Gajah Mada, Jl. Fatahillah 3 (Kota), Jl. Sumenep 9 (Menteng), Jl. Cikini Raya. **Telegraph office**: Jl. Merdeka Selatan 12. **Area code**: 021. **American Express**: T 5703310. **Hospitals**: Cipto Mangunkusumo, Jl. Diponegoro 71, T 332029; Pondok Indah, Jl. Metro Duta 1, T 767525; St. Carolus, Jl. Salemba Raya 41, T 8580091; **Red Cross**, Jl. Kramat Raya 47. **Private clinics with English speaking doctors**: Medical Scheme, Setia Budi Bldg, Kuningan; SOS Medika, Jl. Puri Sakti 10/10, T 7393014. **24 hour emergency ambulance service**: T 334030.

Police: Jl. Jend. Sudirman 45, T 587771. **Immigration**: Jl. Warung Buncit Raya 207, T 796334.The **PHPA office** provides permits for Java's National Parks, Jl. Merdeka a Selatan 8-9 Blok G. **Libraries**: British Council library, Wijoyo Centre, Jl. Jend. Sudirman 56, open: 0900-1300 (visitors must join to use the library). **British Council**: Wijoyo Centre, Jl. Jend. Sudirman 71, T 587411, F 586181 (visitors must join to use the facilities). **Church Services**: Jemaat Anugerah (Methodist), Jl. Daan Mogot 100, every Sun, 0800; St. Canisiut (Catholic), Jl. Menteng Raya; All Saints (Anglican), Jl. Prapatan, opp. Hyatt Aryaduta Hotel; St Patrick's Cathedral (see Jakarta Post for times of services).

Airline offices International airline offices: **Air India**, Sari Pacific Hotel, Jl. M.H. Thamrin, T 325534; **British Airways**, Wisma Metropolitan 1, Jl. Jend. Sudirman, T 5782460; **Cathay Pacific**, Borobudur Hotel, Jl. Lap. Banteng, T 3806664; **China Airlines**, Duta Merlin, Jl. Gajah Mada, T 354448; **Czechoslovak Airlines**, Wisata International Hotel, Jl. M.H. Thamrin, T 325530; **Japan Airlines**, Mid Plaza, Jl. Jend. Sudirman, T 582758; **KLM**, Plaza Indonesia, Jl. M.H. Thamrin, T 320708; **Korean Air**, Wisma Met. ll, Jl. Jend. Sudirman, T 5780236; **Lufthansa**, Panin Centre Bldg, Jl. Jend. Sudirman, T 710247; **Malaysian Airlines System**, Hotel Indonesia, Jl. M.H. Thamrin, T 320909; **Philippine Airlines**, Borobudur Hotel, Jl. Lap. Banteng, T 370108; **Qantas**, BDN Bldg, Jl. M.H. Thamrin, T 327707; **Royal Brunei Airlines**, Hotel Indonesia, Jl. M.H. Thamrin, T 321214; **Sabena Airlines**, Borobudur Hotel, Jl. Lap. Banteng, T 372039; **Scandinavian Airlines System**, S. Wijoyo Bldg, Jl. Jend. Sudirman, T 584110; **Saudi Arabian Airlines**, Bumiputera Bldg, Jl. M.H. Thamrin, T 5780628; **Singapore Airlines**, Chase Bldg, Jl. Jend. Sudirman, T 584021; **Swissair**, Borobudur Hotel, Jl. Lap. Banteng, T 373608; **Thai International**, BDN Bldg, Jl. M.H. Thamrin, T 320607; **Trans World**

Airlines, Ayuberga, PP Bldg, Jl. M.H. Thamrin, T 321979.

 Domestic airlines offices **Bouraq**, Jl. Angkasa 1-3, T 6295150; **Garuda**, Jl. Jend. Sudirman 31, T 588797; also ticket sales offices at *Hotel Indonesia*, T 3100568, *Borobudur Hotel*, T 360048 and in the BDN Building, Jl. M.H. Thamrin 5, T 334425; **Mandala**, Jl. Garuda 36 T413480; **Merpati**, Jl. Angkasa 2 T417404; **Sempati**, Jl. Merdeka Timur 7, T 348760.

Tour companies & travel agents Most of the larger hotels have travel agents. The list of tour firms below is not comprehensive but includes many of the larger firms. Most will arrange city tours, out-of-town day tours and also longer tours throughout the Indonesian archipelago: *Atlantictour*, B-15, Harmoni Plaza Bldg., Jl. Suryopranoto 2, T 46609; *Continental*, Komplek Duta Merlin Blok A/22, Jl. Gajah Mada 3-5, T 3803442; *Kalpataru Adventure*, Jl. Galur Sari II/54, T 882150, organize wildlife tours to Krakatau and Ujung Kulon as well as further afield to Komodo, Kalimantan and Flores; *Kaltim Adventure Tour*, Jl. Tanah Abang 11/23, T 361950, F 3802678, specializes in trekking tours to East Kalimantan; *Musi Holiday Travel Agency*, Jl Cikini Raya 30, T 322709, F 377031; *Natrabu*, Kartika Plaza, Jl. M.H. Thamrin, T 322978; *Pacto*, Jl. Surabaya 8, T 320390, F 347415; *Puri Tour*, Duta Merlin Complex Blok C 56-57, Jl. Gajah Mada 3-5, T 3844646; *Satriavi*, Jl. Prapatan 32, T 3803944, F 3806556; *Setia Tour*, Glodok Plaza, Jl. Pinangsia Raya, T 336183; *Tomaco*, Jakarta Theatre Building, Jl. M.H. Thamrin 9, T 317435; *Universal Tour*, Jl. Pintu Besar Selatan 82C, T 6901669; *Vayatour*, Jl. Batutulis 38, T 365008; *Citra Wisata*, Hotel Indonesia, Jl. M.H. Thamrin, T 321220; *Chandragama Muda*, Hotel Kartika Plaza, Jl. Jend. Sudirman, T 321008; *Panorama*, Jl. Balikpapan 22B, T 350438; *Pantravel*, Kartika Plaza, Jl. M.H. Thamrin 10, T 320908; *Sona Topas*, Panin Bank Bldg, Jl. Jend. Sudirman 1, T 710636, *Borobudur Hotel*, 3rd Flr, T 361738 and *Hotel Indonesia*, T 3107567; *Robertur Kencana*, Jl. Jaksa 20B, T 332926. Can organize visa extension (50,000Rp for 2 weeks) or cheap trips to Singapore to renew visa; *Seabreeze*, Jl. Jaksa.

Tourist offices Directorate General of Tourism, Jl. Kramat Raya 81, T 3103117. Good range of handouts on all regions of the country; the **Jakarta Tourist Office** is in the Jakarta Theatre Bldg, Jl. M.H. Thamrin 9, T 354094, they supply maps and information on sights in the city. There is a tourist information desk at the airport.

Transport to & from Jakarta **By Air**: Jakarta's **Soekarno-Hatta Airport** lies 35 km NW of the city, and connects Jakarta with all other major cities and towns in the country, as well as regional and global destinations (**see pages 1006-1007** for route maps). State-owned Garuda and Merpati Airlines operate out of Terminal A, all other international airlines from Terminal B (for airport facilities, **see page 1005**). Terminal C is used by domestic airlines other than Garuda and Merpati – namely, Bouraq, Sempati and Mandala. *Transport to town*: there is a city 'air terminal' at Plaza Indonesia, Jl. M.H. Thamrin 28-30. They will organize reconfirmation of flights, airport transfer and baggage check-in, all for 40,000Rp. Limousine service, 80,000Rp, metered taxis, 20,000Rp (plus a toll fee of about 5,900Rp). Airport a/c buses are available from: Gambir Railway Station; Blok M, Jl. Bulungan; and Kemayoran (former domestic airport). Buses leave from Gambir on the hour from 0500 (3,000Rp). Many of the first class hotels lay on transport.

 By train: the main station is **Gambir**, on the E side of Merdeka Square (Jl. Merdeka Timur). Regular connections with Bogor 1 hr and Bandung 3 hrs, and connections with Yogya 10 hrs, Solo and Surabaya 14½ hrs. **Kota** station, in the old town also services Bandung and Yogya, and Surabaya (via Semarang and Cirebon). Night trains tend to depart from Kota. **Tanah Abang** station connects towns in West Java with Jakarta, including the port of Merak 4 hrs – the ferry departure point to Sumatra. **Pasar Senen** connects the north coast towns of Cirebon, Semarang and Surabaya (see timetable on **page 1012**).

 By bus: there are 3 city bus terminals. **Kalideres Terminal**, T 592274, on the W edge of the city, serves the W coast, including Merak and connections on to Sumatra. **Cililitan Terminal** SE of the city, T 884554 serves Bogor 30 mins, Bandung 4½ hrs and other points S. **Pulo Gadung Terminal**, T 881763, E of the centre at the junction of Jl. Bekasi Timur Raya and Jl. Perintis Kemerdekaan, serves the Central and East Java towns of Cirebon 5 hrs, Yogya 12 hrs and Surabaya 15 hrs, Malang 18 hrs. All terminals are connected to the city centre by local buses. Private bus companies have their offices at these terminals. Alternatively, purchase tickets from a travel agent.

 By boat: the state-owned shipping company PELNI has its head office at Jl. Angkasa 18, T 416262. The Jakarta Tourist Board, Jakarta Theatre Bldg, has information on sailing schedules (**see page 1008**).

WEST JAVA

Introduction, 557; The Western Route: Jakarta to Ujung Kulon and Krakatau, 558; The Eastern Route: Jakarta to Bogor and Pelabuhanratu, 565; The Eastern Route: Bogor to Bandung via the Puncak Pass, 571; The Northern Route: Bandung to Cirebon, 579; The Eastern Route: Bandung to Pangandaran via Garut, 583.

Maps: West Java, 559; Banten, 560; Bogor, 566; Bandung, 573; Cirebon, 580; Pangandaran, 585.

INTRODUCTION

The province of West Java accounts for much of the W third of the island of Java, bar the Special Territory of Greater Jakarta which is a province in its own right. Long regarded as the most prosperous of the provinces of Java (excepting Jakarta), West Java supports the greatest concentration of people and the most prestigious universities in Indonesia, as well as two of the country's most important industrial enterprises: the Krakatau Steelworks and the aircraft manufacturer, IPTN. The province covers 46,300 sq km and has a population of 35 million – giving it a population density of over 750 people per sq km. The capital of West Java is the hill city of Bandung with a population in excess of 2 million.

West Java consists of 3 regions. First, the narrow, poor and undeveloped **South and West Coast**. An absence of good agricultural land, poor natural harbours, and the difficulties of overland communication, makes this the poorest region in West Java. For the visitor, the S coast offers the beach resorts of Pangandaran and Pelabuhanratu, while the W coast has those of Carita and Anyer, as well as the famous Ujung Kulon National Park.

The second region, is the **Central Highlands**. As the name hints, this is an area of spectacular scenery, with a series of impressive volcanoes. During the colonial era, the highlands were developed as an area of plantation agriculture, with stands of coffee, tea, cinchona (the bark of which is used to produce quinine) and other crops. The 2 hill towns of Bogor and Bandung were also developed by the Dutch, although as the plantation economy has declined, so they have lost out to other more dynamic Javanese cities. In place of plantation crops, farmers now grow so-called *palawija* (non-rice food) crops – cassava, maize, groundnuts, sweet potatoes and various beans. It is this region which holds the greatest attractions for the visitor: the cool, hill resorts of Bogor and those in the vicinity of the Puncak Pass; the university city of Bandung, and hiking in the highlands around towns such as Garut.

The third region is the **Northern Coastal Plain**, an area of intensive rice production. At the very NW corner of this region, an industrial centre has developed around the town of Cilegon, exploiting the improved communications which link Jakarta with Sumatra via the port of Merak. Other than Jakarta, the largest town on the N coast is Cirebon, at the E edge of the province and famous for its distinctive style of batik.

THE WESTERN ROUTE: Jakarta to Ujung Kulon and Krakatau

From Jakarta, an expressway or 'Jalan Toll' runs 67 km W to the dirty town of Serang. From here, *angkutans* ferry passengers 10 km N to the historic port of Banten. It is another 31 km W from Serang, on a busy road, to Merak, the ferry port for Sumatra. The expressway is due to be extended so that it runs all the way from Jakarta to Merak. En route to Merak at Cilegon, the road passes the enormous Krakatau Steelworks. Here the road divides: the main branch continues on the final 14 km to Merak, while the second branch turns S to follow the W coast of Java. On this coast, Anyer (12 km), Carita and Labuan (another 41 km) offer mediocre beaches and are popular with Jakartans at weekends. They can also be used as bases from which to visit the Krakatau Islands and the Ujung Kulon National Park which encompasses the SW 'leg' of Java.

Pulau Seribu

Pulau Seribu, or 'Thousand Islands', is in fact an archipelago that consists of just 112 small islands in the Java Sea. They are situated off Java's N coast, just to the W of Jakarta, and are becoming an increasingly popular tourist destination. The Dutch VOC had a presence on the islands from the 17th century, building forts, churches and shipyards.

Pulau Onrust is one of the closest islands to the mainland. It was used by the Dutch from the early 17th century and became an important ship repair centre; by 1775 as many as 2,000 people were living on the island. But in the 1800's the British sacked and burnt the small settlement, so that today only ruins remain. **Pulau Bidadari** has ruins of a fort and leper hospital built by the VOC. **Pulau Laki** is one of the inner islands situated 3 km offshore from Tanjung Kait W of Jakarta.

Venturing further N into the Java Sea, there are a succession of privately-owned resorts including **Pulau Ayer, Pulau Putri, Pulau Pelangi, Pulau Kotok** and **Pulau Panjang**, in that order. They have beautiful beaches and offer snorkeling, scuba diving, jet skiing, and windsurfing.

Accommodation Pulau Bidadari **A-B** Cottage accommodation and restaurant, managed by *Marina Ancol*, Taman Impian Jaya Ancol, T 680048.
Pulau Ayer **A** Cottages available, some built over the sea, pool, tennis, jetski, fishing, snorkeling facilities, contact *Sarotama Prima Perkasa*, Jl. Ir. H. Juanda 111/6, T 342031, F 358142.
Pulau Putri, Pulau Pelangi, Pulau Perak, Pulau Melintang and Pulau Petonden. **A+-A** Cottage-style accommodation managed by *Pulau Seribu Paradise*, Jl. Wahid Hasyim 69, T 348533, F 344039, a/c, restaurants, diving and sailing facilities.
Pulau Kotok **A** Wooden bungalow accommodation (a/c and non a/c) and restaurant, together with a full range of watersports facilities including diving; contact *Kotok Island Resort*, Duta Merlin Shopping Arcade 3rd flr, Jl. Gajah Mada, T 362948, F 362499.
Pulau Laki **A** Cottages with pool, tennis, jetski, windsurfing, scuba, fishing etc, contact *Fadent Gema Scorpio*, Jl. H.O.S Cokroaminoto 116, T 44353.
Pulau Macan Besar **L-A+** *Matahari Island Resort*, cottage accommodation on 6 ha island with bathrooms and TV, swimming pool, price includes all meals and transfer from Ancol Marina, contact Matahari Impian Indah, Jl. Pangeran, T 6281234, F 6296652.

Transport to & from Pulau Seribu By air: There is an airstrip on Pulau Panjang. The trip takes 25 mins from Jakarta. Boat transfers to other islands. **By boat:** a regular ferry service leaves from the Marina Jaya at Ancol at 0700, returning from the islands at 1430. The trip takes 2-4 hrs to the outer islands, 30 mins-1 hr to Onrust and Bidadari. **By hydrofoil:** Hover

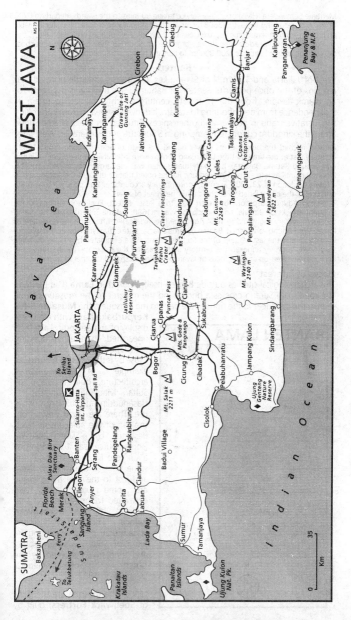

WEST JAVA

Maritime Semandera (HMS) operate a service taking 90 mins to the islands, departing 0700 from Ancol, returning 1500, T 325608 for more information. **By helicopter**: transfer available on request from Fadent Gema Scorpio (see above), who have cottages on Pulau Laki.

Pulau Seribu Paradise (see above): organize transport to their islands by speedboat (80,000Rp), or small airplane (200,000Rp) to Panjang Island and speedboat on.

Banten

West of Jakarta and 10 km N of Serang lies a rather scruffy little port; all that remains of the once powerful Banten (or Bantam). This town was the centre of an Islamic Empire from the 12th-15th century which managed to retain its independence from neighbouring Mataram. It derived its wealth from controlling the lucrative trade in pepper and other spices. Situated on the strategic Sunda Strait, the kingdom conquered Lampung in S Sumatra and Pajajaran in West Java.

Banten reached the height of its power during the reign of Sultan Agung (1651-1683), ironically just at the time that the Dutch and English were intensifying their presence in the area around Batavia (Jakarta). It is likely that Banten was the largest city in Java (possibly Indonesia) until as late as the 19th century; Raffles noted that he thought the sultanate had a total population of 232,000. Even so, contemporary accounts tell that people living on the outskirts of the city still had to contend with the threat of tigers.

Sultan Agung, suspicious of Dutch and, to a lesser extent, English intentions, made frequent attacks on Batavia, finally declaring war in 1680. But the Sultanate was no match for Dutch military might and by 1684 Agung had been defeated, after suffering considerable losses. With Agung vanquished, Banten became a vassal state of Batavia. However, it was not until 1832 that the last vestiges of the Sultans' power were eliminated by the Dutch when they finally formally annexed the territory and abolished the sultanate. By that time, the harbour had silted-up and the focus of Javanese trade had shifted to other locations.

Places of interest

The archaeological site lies outside Banten itself, at **Banten Lama** (Old Banten). The road from Serang crosses a bridge and the minaret of the mosque can be seen in the distance. To the right of the path to the mosque is the **Museum Situs**

Kerpurbakalaan, with a modest display of archaeological artefacts unearthed in the surrounding area. Open: 0900-1600 Tues-Sun. Close by is the **Mesjid Agung**, an example of Hindu-Islamic architecture, built in 1556 by Sultan Maulana Jusuf, son of Hasanuddin, and still very much in use. There are good views from the top of the adjacent minaret, designed by a Dutch Muslim (some sources say it was built by a *Chinese* Muslim) at about the same time as the mosque. Near and just to the S of the mosque are some ruined walls and excavated foundations – all that remains of the **Surosowan Palace**, built by Sultan Hasanuddin, destroyed during the reign of Sultan Agung, rebuilt, and then finally levelled by the Dutch Governor-General Daendels in 1832.

NW of the mosque are the ruins of **Spellwijck Fortress,** built by the Dutch in 1682 (and subsequently extended), in an attempt to keep Sultan Agung at bay. Near the fort are tombs of Europeans who died in the battle for Banten. West of the fort is a large 200-year-old renovated Chinese temple, **Klenteng**, which is still in use today. Just outside the town, back on the road to Serang and just before the bridge over the river, are the ruins of the **Istana Kaibon**, the palace of Queen Aisyah, mother of Banten's last sultan. It was destroyed by the Dutch in 1832, at the same time that Banten lost its final struggle with Batavia for even a small morsel of independence. The Dutch used the bricks to construct their own buildings.

Excursions
Pulau Dua is a low-lying island off the coast from Banten and an ornithologist's dream, being Indonesia's (and one of the world's) major **bird sanctuaries**. The island is best visited between Mar and Jul when migratory birds arrive on the island to breed. There are good, though sometimes poorly maintained, observation towers for viewing nesting sites. The island has no accommodation, but guides are available to point out birdlife. **Getting there:** from Karanghantu Harbour, 1 km from Banten. The boat ride takes 30 mins and a 2 hr tour costs 50,000Rp. It can also be reached by land, along a recently made causeway.

Accommodation None available in Banten. The nearest town with accommodation is Serang, 10 km S of Banten where there are **E** *Abadi*, Jl. Jend. Sudirman 36, T 81641; and **E** *Serang*, Jl. Jend. A. Yani 38.

Restaurants Foodstalls surround the car-park by the mesjid.

Transport to & from Banten 10 km from Serang, 100 km from Jakarta. **By bus:** from Jakarta's Kalideres station to Serang (1,000Rp). From Serang, catch an angkutan to Banten from the minibus station at Pasar Lama (100Rp). **By train:** slow local trains run from Tanah Abang Station in Jakarta to Serang. **By taxi:** from Jakarta, 2½-3hrs (100,000Rp).

Merak

Merak is the point of departure and arrival for **Sumatra** and is one of the dirtiest and noisiest towns in Java.

Excursions
The massive **Krakatau Steelworks** are 14 km outside Merak on the road to Jakarta, is near the town of Cilegon. P.T. Krakatau Steel is one of the 2 largest state enterprises in the country (the other being P.T. Nusantara at Bandung). Built by the state oil company Pertamina during the period of booming oil prices between 1973 and 1982, it received investments totalling nearly US$4 billion. Undoubtedly, an impressive monument to the oil boom, although corruption was on a scale unheard of even in Indonesia and many people believe the money could have been more productively spent in some other way. In short, it was a prestige project which gained a momentum of its own. Tours can be taken around the steelworks.

Florida Beach is a few km N of Merak and has good sand, but is too close to Merak to be attractive to most visitors.

Accommodation in Merak is over-priced and poor; only people waiting for a ferry stay here. **B** *Merak Beach*, Jl. Raya Merak, T 3106440, a/c, most comfortable hotel in town, but only recommended as a stopover while waiting for the ferry; 2 km from the ferry squashed between the road and the sea; **E** *Hotel Anda*, Jl. Florida 4, close to the ferry; **E** *Nirmala*, Jl. Pelabuhan Merak 30; **E** *Sulawesi I*, Jl. Pelabuhan 8; **E** *Sulawesi II*, Jl. Pelabuhan 8; **E** *Hotel Robinson*, Jl. Florida 7, close to the ferry.

Transport to & from Merak 140 km from Jakarta. The fast Jalan Toll road is partially complete and is due to be finished all the way from Jakarta to Merak, 'soon'; in the meantime, the road is busy and progress can be slow. **By train:** the station is close to the ferry. Connections with Jakarta's Tanah Abang station 0600 and 1700 3½-4 hrs (1,500Rp). **By bus:** the station is close to the ferry dock. Regular connections with Jakarta's Kalideres station, 2½ hrs (2,000Rp). **By boat:** regular car ferries link Merak with Bakauheni on the S tip of Sumatra. Times of departure vary through the year, but normally there are about 15 crossings/day, 1½ hrs (21,300Rp/car, 1,100-2,200Rp/person).

Anyer

South of Cilegon and Merak is the small town of Anyer, once an important Dutch port. Much of the town was destroyed by the tidal wave which followed the eruption of Krakatau in 1883. The most notable feature of the town is the elegant white **lighthouse**, built by Queen Wilhelmina of the Netherlands in 1886, following the Krakatau disaster.

Anyer is more popular with Jakarta residents than with foreign visitors, and there are innumerable holiday bungalows along the coast S from Merak.

Excursions
Pulau Sangiang is a jungle-clothed island in the Sunda Straits. The waters around the island offer good diving and snorkeling (both coral and World War II wrecks). There is no accommodation on the island. **Getting there**: chartered traditional wooden boats take about $1\frac{1}{2}$ hrs from Anyer Kidul, a speedboat takes about half the time.

Krakatau (see page 564) and **Ujung Kulon (see page 562)** can both be reached from Anyer.

Accommodation Weekday rates are often less than those at weekends. Accommodation is strung out along the coast. **A+-A** *Mambruk Beach Resort*, Jl. Raya Karang Bolong, T 81601, F 81723, J 716318, a/c, restaurant, pool, tennis courts, diving and fishing, expensive, but professionally run and highly recommended by those who stay here; **A** *Anyer Beach Hometel & Resort*, Jl. Raya Karang Bolong Km 17/153, T 6492492, F 6295000, a/c, pool, large, clean bungalows; **A** *Anyer Seaside Cottages*, Jl. Raya Karang Bolong Km 35; **A** *Ancott*, Jl. Raya Anyer Km 21, J 7994809; **A** *Villa Ryugu*, T 91894, a/c, 2 bedroom 'units'; **A** *Patra Jasa (Anyer Beach Hotel)*, Jl. Raya Karang Bolong, T 81376, F 81872, J 510503, a/c, built in 1973 by Pertamina, comfortable enough.

Transport to & from Anyer 119 km from Jakarta, 12 km from Cilegon, 26 km from Merak, 41 km from Labuan. **By bus**: regular connections with Jakarta's Kalideres station, Merak and Cilegon.

Labuan/Carita Beach

Labuan is the main point of departure for the Ujung Kulon National Park (**see page 562**) and for Krakatau (**page 564**). There are holiday bungalows all along the coast, as well as some hotels. Like Anyer, Carita is a resort for tired Jakartans rather than foreign visitors. There is an attractive 3 km-long sandy beach here with reasonable surf (best in the afternoon).

Accommodation A selection of hotels and losmen along these two beaches includes: **Carita Beach**: **A** *Mutiara Carita Cottages*, J 514737, F 5207191, pool, new development offering wooden cottages with attached kitchens, beach is only average here; **A-C** *Desiana*, T 21010, J 593316, a/c, restaurant, boat trips, the beach here is poor and rather dirty, although the hotel is homely and friendly; **B-D** *Carita Krakatau Beach*, T 81206, J 320252, most popular base from which to visit Krakatau and Ujung Kulon, good information with excellent beach front position, a one-time favourite among budget travellers – now rather too expensive, although also offers cheaper hostel accommodation, showing its age (**B-C** at weekends); **E** *Rakata Hostel*, linked to *Carita Krakatau Beach Hotel*, popular base for those on lower budget.

Labuan Town and Carita Village: **E** *Caringin*, Jl. Caringin 20 (Carita side of Labuan town); **E** *Losman Sunset*, Carita Village, simple but well kept rooms, friendly, away from beach, good budget accommodation.

Transport to & from Labuan 158 km from Jakarta, 41 km from Anyer, 67 km from Merak. **By bus**: regular connections with Jakarta's Kalideres station and with Merak and Cilegon. To reach Carita Beach, take one of the frequent colts from Labuan.

Ujung Kulon National Park

This peaceful wilderness occupies 162,000 ha of land and sea on the SW tip of Java, and contains some of the last stands of tropical lowland rainforest on densely populated Java. It is a little-visited haven for people wishing to escape the crowds

The Javan rhinoceros (*Rhinoceros sondaicus*): the rarest mammal on earth?

The Javan (also known as the lesser, or Javan one-horned) rhinoceros was once distributed from Upper Burma S to Java but is now thought to be restricted to a small population in the Ujung Kulon National Park, West Java (but see below). When Europeans first arrived in Southeast Asia, the Javan rhinoceros was still to be found in Sumatra, Malaya, Thailand, Burma and Vietnam. Their disappearance was due to over-hunting. A. Hoogerwerf notes that the Belgian big game hunter, Baron Robert de Charcourt, killed 300 rhinoceros in his lifetime (mostly in Africa). He met his end in Sumatra when, appropriately, he was killed by one of the wounded beasts that he had been terrorizing for so many years. A British newspaper, recording his fate, reported: "Shortly before he died, de Charcourt opened his eyes once more and said with a loud, clear voice to his head boy: 'Mark him down, Latiki. He is number 300...'". As A. Hoogerwerf notes "it is only to be regretted that such 'heroes' lived so long".

In 1930, various estimates of the numbers of *sondaicus* left ranged from 5 to 100. By 1970, there was thought to be only a single herd of 28 animals, giving it the dubious honour of being the rarest mammal in the world. However, with the protection against poaching now given by the guards of the Ujung Kulon National Park, the numbers have increased to approximately 60 animals. In 1990 Vietnamese naturalists discovered to their, and the world's, amazement, another small herd in Vietnam.

The Javan rhinoceros' distinctive 'armour plated' appearance is due to the folds of skin which delineate the neck and legs from the body. With an average shoulder height of 1.6 m, they carry a single horn, and inhabit dense lowland forest. They particularly enjoy wallowing in mud and water and are rarely found far from water. Their small stature (for a rhino) and tendency to inhabit thick forest, rather than the open savannas and grasslands like their African cousins, makes them difficult to spot.

As with other rhinos, the value of the powdered horn as a universal medicine to the Chinese led to widespread hunting and its extermination throughout Southeast Asia bar these two small, relict populations. The female only gives birth once every 3-4 years so rebuilding the population will be a long, perhaps a fruitless, process. The supposed effectiveness of rhino horn as a cure-all was noted by George Rumphius in his *Amboinese rariteitenkamer* written during his long stay in the East Indies from 1654-1702 as a VOC official. He claimed it cured snakebite, could indicate the presence of poison in drink (the drink will foam if drunk from a horn cup) and, of course, was an aphrodisiac. But it is not just the horn (*say kak*) that is prized. Hooves (*sie kok sze*), 'salt' from the hide (*say goe phwee*), '2 blunt teeth lying between the canine teeth', and even the undigested contents of the stomach, are believed to have medicinal powers. Gee (1964) notes that the horn placed under the bed of pregnant mothers would alleviate the pain of birth, writing: "Persons owning a horn would rent it out to expectant mothers for the equivalent of 30 pounds each time!". He goes on: "Yet another absurd belief was that a rhino horn left to soak in a filled bucket turned the water into a sort of elixir of life, of which members of a family would sip a spoonful every day!". The outcome of these unfounded beliefs was not a happy one for the Javan, as well as other, rhinoceros.

and enjoy some walking on the cool trails through the forest. The park comprises several islands (including Panaitan, Peucang and Handeuleum), and the surrounding sea. The eruption of Krakatau in 1883, and the subsequent tidal wave, destroyed some of the lowland tropical rainforest here; trees fossilized by volcanic dust bear witness to the event. The area was declared a Nature Reserve in 1958, and was upgraded to National Park status in 1980. It has recently been given World Heritage status – one of only two natural World Heritage sites in Indonesia (the other being Komodo Island).

The Park's main claim to fame is its population of Javan Rhinoceros (see box) – although these are very rarely seen by visitors to the park. Other, more accessible, wildlife include wild pig, barking deer (*muntjak*), wild buffalo (*banteng*), leopard, the rare leaf-eating monkey, crab-eating macaques and civets. Nine of the mammals to be found at Ujung Kulon are on the Red List of threatened mammals, and there are over 50 species of rare plants. The park also supports a diverse community of birdlife – about half of the known species of bird to be found on Java are present in the park, including hornbills. There are a number of established trails through the park's forests, the most popular being the 3-day hike from Tamanjaya to Peucang Island. Marine life is good around Peucang Island and off the northern coast. In contrast to the calm waters of the north coast, the south is rugged and wave-swept and in consequence is becoming increasingly popular with surfers.

Handeleum Island's attractions include an area where banteng (wild buffalo) can be seen grazing, canoe trips up the Cigenter River, a 2 hr walk to the Curung Waterfall through an area frequented by rhino, and motorboat trips up the Cikabeumbeum River through mangrove forest.

Best time to visit From Apr-Nov.

Permits and guides The PHPA office (park office) recommends that visitors hiking through the park employ a guide (7,500-10,000Rp/day); porters and cooks are also available. Enquire at the PHPA office in Labuan. Admission: a permit must be obtained, available from the PHPA office in Labuan at Jl. Perintis Kemerdekaan 43. 2,000Rp/person, plus 1,500Rp/person insurance (for search and rescue), for a period of 7 days. Office hours: 0730-1400 Mon-Thurs & Sat, 0730-1100 Fri.

Accommodation Guesthouses are managed by Wanawisata Alam Hayati, Gedung Manggala Wanabakti, Blok 4, Jl. Jend. Gatot Subroto, Senayan, Jakarta T 5700238. Bookings can be made through them or at the Labuan PHPA office (see address above). **Peucang Island**: **A** *Peucang Lodges* (opened 1991) has 16 bedrooms and holds a max. of 32 people, a/c, restaurant, hot water, tv, all meals provided; **B** *Peucang Guesthouse* (the original guesthouse in the park) holds a max. of 12 people in 5 double/triple rooms, with attached bathrooms for 3 rooms, price includes breakfast. **Handeuleum Island**: **C** Attractive Swiss-style cottages, with 4 bedrooms, sleeping a max. of 10 people, shared bathroom. **Tamanjaya (mainland village)**: **C** *Wanawisata Lodges*, 2 lodges recently renovated, each with 3 bedrooms and shared bathroom. US$15.

Camping Camping sites are available throughout the park, but no facilities are provided.

Restaurants Visitors should take their own food and water. Restaurants are available at the accommodation site on Peucang Island. For campers, take all your food and drink with you.

Transport to & from Ujung Kulon By bus: regular connections with Jakarta's Kalideres station to Labuan. From there, take a bus to Sumur, and then an *ojek* to Tamanjaya. 4-wheel drive vehicles can also negotiate the road to Tamanjaya. Alternatively, go by boat from Labuan (see below). By boat: available from Labuan. The Wanawisata Alamhayati company provides a boat every Mon and Fri at 0800 for trips to Peucang Island, via Tamanjaya and Handeuleum Island. The boat returns to Labuan every Thurs and Sun; for further information contact the PHPA office. Boats also run from Tamanjaya to the islands. Approximate cost is 60,000Rp from Labuan or Tamanjaya to Peucang Island. Faster launches can be chartered to the park from Anyer, Merak and Carita.

Krakatau

Krakatau is the site of the largest volcanic eruption ever recorded. The explosion occurred on the morning of the 27 Aug 1883, had a force equivalent to 2,000 Hiroshima bombs, and resulted in the death of 36,000 people. Tidal waves (*tsunami*) 40m high, radiating outwards at speeds, reportedly, of over 500 km per hour destroyed coastal towns and villages. The explosion was heard from Sri Lanka to Perth (Australia) and the resulting waves led to a noticeable surge in the English Channel. The explosion was such that the 400m-high cone was replaced by a marine trench 300m deep.

Rupert Furneau writes in his book *Krakatoa* (1965):-

> "At ten o'clock plus two minutes, three-quarters of Krakatoa Island, eleven square miles of its surface, an area not much less than Manhattan, a mass of rock and earth one and one-eighth cubic miles in extent, collapsed into a chasm beneath. Nineteen hours of continuous eruption had drained the magma from the chamber faster than it could be replenished from below. Their support removed, thousands of tons of roof rock crashed into the void below. Krakatoa's three cones caved in. The sea bed reared and opened in upheaval. The sea rushed into the gaping hole. From the raging cauldron of seething rocks, frothing magma and hissing sea, spewed an immense quantity of water......From the volcano roared a mighty blast, Krakatoa's death cry, the greatest volume of sound recorded in human history".

In 1927, further volcanic activity caused a new island to rise above the sea – Anak Krakatau (child of Krakatau). Today this island stands 200m above sea-level and visitors may walk from the E side of the island upon the warm, devastated landscape through deep ash, to the main crater. It remains desolate and uninhabited, though the other surrounding islands have been extensively recolonized (a process carefully recorded by naturalists; the first visitor after the 1883 explosion noted a spider vainly spinning a web). Check that the volcano is safe to visit and take thick-soled walking shoes. There is good snorkeling and diving in the water around the cliffs; the undersea thermal springs cause abundant marine plant growth and this in turn attracts a wealth of sea creatures, big and small.

Best time to visit The sea crossing is calmest and the weather best Apr-Jun and Sept-Oct.

Transport to & from Krakatau By boat: boats can be chartered from Anyer, Carita and Labuan. Locals have gained a reputation for overcharging and then providing un-seaworthy boats (it is said that 2 Californian women spent 3 weeks drifting in the Sunda Strait, living on sea-water and toothpaste, before being washed ashore near Bengkulu, W Sumatra). The *Mambruk Beach Resort* at Anyer has a fast launch for hire to Krakatau (2 hrs) while the *Carita Krakatau Beach Hotel* has 2 boats, one costing 300,000Rp to charter, taking 4 hrs each way, the other costing 750,000Rp and taking 2 hrs (they also have a waiting list for single travellers). If chartering a local boat from Carita, Labuan or Anyer, make certain that there is sufficient petrol for the 2 way journey and that it is understood at what time you wish to return to the mainland – visitors have been stranded on Krakatau, no doubt with visions of a repeat of the 1883 event. Prices vary according to the size and condition of the vessel, but expect to pay 250-300,000Rp.

THE EASTERN ROUTE: Jakarta to Bogor and Pelabuhanratu

From Jakarta, an expressway makes for a quick – though unexciting – 60 km journey to the hill town of Bogor, famous for its excellent Botanical Gardens and refreshing climate. Bogor is a popular weekend retreat for Jakartans and lies within the capital's commuter belt. From Bogor, a road winds its way S for 90 km around and between volcanoes, to the beach resort of Pelabuhanratu. En route there are good views over plantations and forested slopes to paddy fields below. The town of Cicurug and the surrounding area is a centre for small-scale brick production.

Bogor

Bogor is best known as the site of one of the finest Botanical Gardens in Southeast Asia. But the town's history pre-dates the Gardens. It seems that during the 5th century the Hindu Kingdom of Tarumanegara had its capital in the vicinity of Bogor. Rather later, a second Hindu Kingdom, Pajajaran, was focused here from the 12th-16th century. Little remains of this period save for the Batutulis monolith

BOGOR

Legend:

1. Kebun Raya (Botanical Gardens)
2. Gates to Botanical Gardens
3. Istana Bogor
4. Zoological Museum
5. Herbarium
6. Gong Foundry
7. Post Office

8. Tourist Office
9. Telecommunications Office
10. Wisma Permata
11. Quality Hotel Salak
12. Bogor Inn
13. Hotel Pangrango
14. Abu Pensione
15. Puri Bali
16. Firman Pensione
17. Sempur Kencana Guesthouse

which records the reign of King Surawisesa who ascended to the throne of Pajajaran in 1533 (see below).

The town lies 290m above sea-level in an upland valley, surrounded by Mounts Salak, Pangrango and Gede. Average temperatures are a pleasant 26°C, significantly cooler than Jakarta, but rainfall is the highest in Java at 3,000-4,000 mm/year. The Dutch, quite literally sick to death of the heat, humidity and the swampy conditions of Jakarta, developed Bogor as a hill retreat.

In 1745, Governor-General Imhoff built a palace here which he named 'Buitenzorg' ('Without a Care'), modelling it on Blenheim Palace in Oxfordshire, England. The palace later burnt down, but was rebuilt and became the official residence of successive governor-generals from 1870-1942. Stamford Raffles, governor-general of Java during the Napoleonic Wars, stayed here, so it was not just the Dutch who found the town enticing. A memorial to Raffles' first wife stands in the Botanical Gardens.

Bogor is centred on the lush botanical gardens, with views over red-tiled roofs, stacked one on top of the other, and toppling down to the Ciliwung River which runs through the middle of the town and gardens. It has a large community of Christians, and a surprising number of Western fastfood outlets and department stores. These serve the large population of wealthy Indonesians who live here and commute to Jakarta. A scattering of old colonial buildings is still to be found around town – for instance, set back from the road on Jalan Suryakencana.

Places of interest
The superb **Botanical Gardens (Kebun Raya)** dominate the centre of the city,

covering an immense 87 ha. The gardens are usually thought to have been established under the instructions of Sir Stamford Raffles. Certainly, Raffles was a keen botanist – borne out in his numerous publications. However, it was the Dutch Governor-General Van de Capellan who commissioned the transformation of the gardens into arguably the finest in Asia. The botanist Professor Reinhardt from Kew Gardens in England, assisted by James Hooper and William Rent, also from Kew, undertook the major portion of the work in 1817. As early as 1822 the Gardens contained 912 recorded plant species, and today there are said to be 2,735. The gardens became world renowned for their research into the cash crops of the region (tea, rubber, coffee, tobacco and chinchona – from the bark of which quinine is derived). The giant water lily, as well as a huge variety of orchids, palms and bamboos can be seen here. It used to be possible to see the giant Rafflesia flower as well (**see page 780**), although it is reported that the specimen has now died. Admission: 1,100Rp, Mon-Sat, 650Rp Sun. Open: 0800-1600 Mon-Sun.

Deer graze in front of the imposing **Presidential Palace** or **Istana Bogor**, which lies within the Gardens, directly N of the main gates (there is also an entrance on Jalan Ir. H. Juanda). The building is not the original 'Buitenzorg' of Governor-General Imhoff. That building was destroyed by fire, rebuilt by Governor-Generals Daendels and Raffles and again destroyed in 1834 after an earthquake, triggered by the eruption of Mount Salak. It was not until 1850 that reconstruction commenced, and the present one-storey building was designed to be able to withstand violent earth tremors. The Palace was a particular favourite of President Sukarno and contains a large collection of his paintings, sculpture and ceramics (he had a passion for the female nude). Sukarno lived here under 'house arrest' from 1967 until his death in 1970. Today, it is used as a guesthouse for important visitors (for instance, the King of Thailand and former President Sadat of Egypt both stayed here) and for high-level meetings (the Cambodian talks of 1990 were held at the palace). Only open to visitors after permission has been obtained from the Secretary of State.

The **Zoological Museum** is on the left of the entrance to the Botanical Gardens and was founded in 1894. It contains an extensive collection of stuffed, dried and otherwise preserved fauna (over 15,000 species) of which only a small proportion is on show at any one time. The museum also has a library. Admission: 400Rp. Open: 0800-1600 Mon-Sun, except Fri when it is closed between 1100 and 1300. There is also a **Herbarium** associated with the Botanical Gardens, on Jalan Ir. H. Juanda, across the road from the W gate to the Gardens. It is said to have a collection of 2 million specimens, which seems suspiciously inflated.

Jalan Otista (also known as Otto Iskandardinata) is a road running along the S edge of the Botanical Gardens. The street is lined with stalls selling fruit, rabbits (not to eat), some batik, children's clothes and unneccessary plastic objects.

The **gong foundry** at Jalan Pancasan 17, SE of the Gardens, is one of the few foundries left in Indonesia – on one side of the street is the foundry, and on the other the gong stands are carved from wood. Visitors can watch metalsmiths making gongs in the traditional manner – a process which takes between 1 and 3 days per gong.

A **batutulis** (meaning 'inscribed stone') dating from the 16th century and erected by one of the sons of a Pajajaran king is housed in a building 2km S of town on Jalan Batutulis (which runs off Jalan Bondongon). Admission: by donation.

Excursions

Taman Safari 2½ km off the main road just before Cisarua is an open-air safari park. It also houses a mini zoo and offers amusement rides, elephant and horse riding, various animal shows throughout the day, a waterfall, swimming pool, restaurant and camping facilities. Admission: 3,000Rp for car. Open: 0900-1700 Mon-Fri, 0800-1700 Sat, Sun & holidays. **Accommodation**: the *Safari Garden Hotel* is on the main road, Jl. Raya Puncak 601, T (0251) 4747, F 4111, J 7695482, restaurant, pool and sports facilities. **Getting there**: take a bus heading for Cisarua and ask to be let off at the turning to the park. Motorbike taxis ply the route from the main road to the park gates.

Accommodation **A+** *Wisma Permata*, Jl. Raya Pajajaran 35, T 323402, F 311082, a/c, hot water, price includes breakfast, immaculate, small rooms, friendly and professional, rec; **A-C** *Quality Hotel Salak*, Jl. Ir. H. Juanda 8, T 322092, F 322093, some a/c, price includes breakfast, formerly run-down and rather decrepit (it was built in 1906 and was called *Hotel Binnenhof*), the hotel has been renamed and a new wing opened in 1993, however it is doubtful whether the original rooms have seen any improvements; **B** *Abu Pensione*, Jl. Mayor Oking 7, T 322893, some a/c, poor restaurant, friendly, overlooking river, very popular, fan and bathroom, overpriced, dormitory **F**; **B** *Bogor Inn*, Jl. Kumbang 12A, T 328134, most a/c, hot water, Imelda Marcos could have been commissioned to do the interior decorating for this hotel, charming owner called Mary, with good English; **B** *Pakuan Palace*, Jl. Pakuan 5, T 323062, F 311207, a/c, best range of business facilities, clean, comfortable; **B** *Wisma Mirah II*, Jl. Mandalawangi 3, T 312385, some a/c, price includes breakfast, peaceful and welcoming; **B-C** *Wisma Mirah I*, Jl. R.E. Martadinata 17, T 323520, some a/c, price includes breakfast, out of town, friendly; **C** *KWIK (International Youth Hostel)*, Desa Tonjong Km 36, T 31523, pool, new, not really a hostel, with tennis and conference facilities, outside Bogor at Km 36; **C** *New Mirah*, Jl. Megamendung 2, T 328044, a/c, pool, clean and kitsch, price includes breakfast; **C** *Pangrango*, Jl. Pangrango 23, T 328670, F 314060, a/c, pool, price includes breakfast; **C** *Puri Bali*, Jl. Pledang 30, T 322307, big rooms and friendly, but running to seed, price includes breakfast, discount for longer stay; **D** *Elsana Transit*, Jl. Sawojajar 36, T 22552, rooms are rather small, set around a courtyard; **D** *Firman Pensione*, Jl. Pledang 48, T 323246, small rooms, friendly, popular, some bathrooms, price includes breakfast; **D** *Sempur Kencana*, Jl. Sempur 4, T 328347, restaurant.

Restaurants Indonesian: ♦*Dewi Sri*, Jl. Raya Pajajaran, near bus station, simple Indonesian food; ♦*Ponyo*, Jl. Raya Pajajaran, specializes in Sundanese food; *Simpang Raya*, Jl. Pajajaran 7, near the bus station, Padang food; *Trio*, Jl. Ir.H. Juanda 38, Jl. Pajajaran, near the bus station; *Ramayana*, Jl. Dewi Sartika 34, also serves Chinese and International; ♦*Jongko Ibu*, Jl. Ir. H. Juanda 44, simple Indonesian food, rec. Western: *Bogor Permai*, Jl. Jend Sudirman 23A, also serves Chinese and Indonesian food; *Kentucky Fried Chicken*, Jl. Raya Pajajaran, near the bus station; *Lautan*, Jl. Jend Sudirman 15, also serves Chinese food; *Pizza Hut*, Internusa Bldg, Jl. Raya Pajajaran. Bakeries: *Jumbo Modern bakery*, Jl. Raya Pajajaran 3F; *Singapore*, Jl. Suryakencana. **Foodstalls**: on Jl. Dewi Sartika and Pasar Bogor and along Jl. Suryakencana; *Taman Jajar* 'food court' on Jl. Mayor Oking.

Entertainment Sundanese dance, gamelan and Wayang golek: Mekah Galuh Pakuan, Jl. Layung Sari Rt 6/XIV, S of town, just off Jl. Pahlawan, performances once a month on 4th Sat, (5,000Rp). **Cinema**: Jl. Merdeka.

Shopping Batik: *Batik Semar*, Jl. Capten Muslihat 7. **Books**: *Gunung Agung*, Jl. Raya Pajajaran (Internusa Shopping Centre); *Toko Buku Bookstore*, Jl. Otto Iskandardinata 80 (near intersection with Jl. Raya Pajajaran). **Handicrafts**: *Pasar Bogor* on Jl. Suryakencana; *Kenari Indah*, Jl. Pahlawan. **Market**: *Kebon Kembang* on Jl. Dewi Sartika. **Shopping centres**: *Internusa Bldg*, Jl. Raya Pajajaran; Dewi Sartika Plaza, Jl. Dewi Sartika. **Wayang golek**: Lebak Kantin Rt 2/VI.

Sports Golf: Jl. Dr. Semeru, T 322891. **Swimming pool**: Villa Duta Real Estate, Jl. Pakuan (4,000Rp).

Local transport There are **becaks**, **bajajs** and **taxis**. **Colts**: omnipresent green machines; seem to be more of them than there are passengers. Fixed fare of 250Rp around town, destinations marked on the front. **Delman (horse-drawn carts)**: from outside the bus station or the entrance to the Botanical Gardens, 500-1,000Rp. **Bicycle hire**: from Abu Pensione, 3,500Rp/day. Taxis: *Omega Motor*, Jl. Pajajaran 217, T 311242; *Tropical Wind*, Jl. Sempur 30, T 320272.

Banks & money changers A number on Jl. Ir. H. Juanda and Jl. Capten Muslihat, eg: **Central Asia**, Jl. Ir. H. Juanda 24; **BNI 46**, Jl. Ir.H. Juanda 42. **Pembangunan Daeran**, Jl. Capten Muslihat 13. There is a money changer at Jl. Siliwangi 40E.

Useful addresses Post Office: Jl. Ir. H. Juanda 3, almost opposite Tourist Information Centre. **Telephone Exchange**: Jl. Pengadilan 8 for international calls, fax, telex; 50% discount between 2100 and 0600. **Area code**: 0251. **Police**: Jl. Capten Muslihat 16. **Chemist**: Jl. Raya Pajajaran, near bus station. **Doctor**: Jl. Ir. H. Juanda 40. **Hospital**: Jl. Pajajaran 80, T 24080. **Immigration**: Jl. Jend. A. Yani 65, T 22870.

Tour companies & travel agents *Arcana Tours*, Jl. Jend. Sudirman 23A. *Finisa Jasa Lestari*, Jl. Jend. Sudirman 14A; *Tropical Wind*, Jl. Sempur 30, T 320272; *Travel agent*, Jl. Mayor Oking (opposite Pensione Abu), rec.

Tourist offices Jl. Ir. H. Juanda 39. **PHPA**, Jl. Ir. H. Juanda 9 (for permits to visit National Parks).

Transport to & from Bogor 60 km S of Jakarta. **By train**: the station (a colonial building) is NW of the Botanical Gardens on Jl. Rajapermas, also known as Jl. Stasiun. Regular connections with Jakarta 1-1½ hrs (500-1500Rp); no trains on to Bandung. **By bus**: the station is just off Jl. Raya Pajajaran, S from the Botanical Gardens and opposite the intersection with the toll road from Jakarta. Frequent connections with Jakarta's Cililitan terminal 1½ hrs, or by express bus 30-45 mins. Green bemos from here to the centre of town cost 200Rp. Regular connections with Bandung, via the Puncak Pass 3 hrs (1750Rp), Yogya and Surabaya.

Pelabuhanratu

Pelabuhanratu is a small beach resort, more popular with Jakartans than with foreign visitors, with kilometre after kilometre of rather dirty-coloured sand beaches. The surf is generally moderate although Cimaja (see excursions) has a reputation of sorts as a surfing beach. Local folklore has it that the waters off Pelabuhanratu are home to a mythical goddess, **Nyi Loro Kidul**, the Queen of the South Seas. In the large *Samudra Beach Hotel*, a room is kept permanently empty for her. The goddess is said to claim anyone who ventures into the sea wearing green, especially men, whisking them away to her watery lair. Why she has a penchant for green has never been adequately explained.

There is not much to Pelabuhanratu and the better hotels are all E of town on the road to Cisolok. At the end of Jalan Siliwangi, right on the beach and next to the petrol station, is the **Pasar Ikan** or fish market, with a good array of denizens of the deep, and a smell which permeates the whole town. Fish auctions are held at 1000 and 1800. There are a number of good seafood restaurants in town. Close to the Pasar Ikan, fishing boats – among them large outriggers – are pulled up onto the beach, and boats are still being built here.

Excursions

Fishing expeditions can be arranged from Pelabuhanratu, but it's quite expensive at 200,000-300,000Rp for the day, including tackle. Ask at the hotels or near the fish market in town.

Pantai Citepus is the most popular beach, about 3 km from town on the road to Cisolok. The beach is lined with official stalls, restaurants and tank traps (presumably put there by the Japanese to thwart an American landing). The beach is wide and sandy and paddy fields descend from the hills to within yards of the beach. It's an attractive spot. **Getting there**: take any colt heading for Cisolok.

Cimaja beach, popular with surfers, is about 9 km W from town and 100m walk off the road. **NB**: currents here can be vicious and swimming dangerous – possibly explaining the legend of Nyi Loro Kidul. **Getting there**: take any colt heading for Cisolok.

Karanghawu 'cliff' beach is W of Cimaja and 12 km from town. The beach is popular, but the 'cliff' is really just a finger of rock jutting into the sea. **Getting there**: take any colt heading for Cisolok.

Cisolok Hot Springs can be found 16 km from Pelabuhanratu and about a 20-30 minute walk from Cisolok. The springs are set in a verdant valley. **Getting there**: take a bemo from Pelabuhanratu to Cisolok and walk.

Festivals Apr: *Pesta Nelayan*, (moveable) a thanksgiving to Nyi Loro Kidul, the Goddess of the South Seas. Flowers are scattered on the sea from a decorated boat and a buffalo is

The legend of Nyi Loro Kidul, the Queen of the South Seas

Nyi Loro Kidul, the Queen of the South Seas, is mentioned in the ancient history of Java the *Babad Tanah Jawi*, as well as a number of other manuscripts. She was born a princess in the ancient West Javanese kingdom of Pajajaran, but her thirst for power forced her father to place a curse upon her head. He said that she would, indeed, have greater power than he but that she would wield it only over the Southern Seas. Re-incarnated as the extraordinarily beautiful Nyi Loro Kidul – more powerful than all the spirits – the Goddess has been closely associated with kingship. Even during the coronation of Hamengkubuwono X of Yogyakarta in 1989, some of the participants said that she was present wearing a transparent green *kabaya*.

One of the nine walis (Muslim saints, see page 528), Sunan Senopati, is said to have found her sleeping – naked, fat, and snoring, with huge breasts. Nonetheless, in the *Babad Tanah Jawi*, Senopati is recorded as having asked, with about as much subtlety as a latterday Casanova: "Dear, I would like to see how your bedroom is arranged". He was whisked off to her watery palace where he became her lover. After three days of bliss he was allowed to return home. Sultan Hamengkubuwono IX of Yogyakarta also claimed he was visited by the temptress on many occasions, and that she gave him strength in times of difficulty.

Throughout Java there are places linked with the legend of Nyi Loro Kidul – Mount Merapi, Mount Lawu, Parangtritis, the Kraton in Yogya, Solo and Tawangmangu. Even today, male swimmers in the sea off Java's south coast are advised not to wear green. If they do, they too are at risk of being taken by the goddess to her abode beneath the sea.

sacrificed. Various events – competitions and cultural shows – are held on the previous evening.

Accommodation Cheap accommodation can be found in town, but most of the better hotels are on the road running W from Pelabuhanratu towards Cisolok.

Pelabuhanratu town: D *Wisma Karang Naya*, Jl. Siliwangi 82, T 88, best of a poor bunch, the opulence of the lobby is not reflected in the rooms, some bathrooms; **E** *Penginapan Laut Kidaul*, Jl. Siliwangi 148, T 41, rather run down but friendly management; **E** *Wisma Putra*, Jl. Siliwangi 86, T 35, rooms are rather dark, some with mandi.

Hotels on the coast (in order from town W towards Cisolok): **A** *Samudra Beach*, Jl. Cisolok (6 km from town), T 23, J 340601, a/c, good pool, large international-style hotel, tennis, right on the beach, special deals on weekdays; **B** *Pondok Dewata*, Jl. Cisolok (1 km from town), T 22, a/c, small pool, individual cottages on the beach, clean, fishing trips arranged; **B-D** *Karang Sari*, Jl. Cisolok, T 78, some a/c, above the beach, cheaper rooms are very average and rather dark, more expensive bungalows are good with views over the bay; **C** *Cleopatra*, Jl. Raya Citepus 114, T 41185, some a/c, small pool, friendly and clean; **D** *Bayu Amrta*, Jl. Cisolok, T 31, has a rather unfinished feel, but rooms are fine, above beach with views back to the town, fishing trips arranged; **E** *Penginapan Simpang Raya*, Jl. Cisolok (Km 3).

Restaurants Good seafood restaurants: *Sederhana*, Jl. Kidang Kencana, also serves Indonesian; *Maya Sari*, Jl. Siliwangi 19, also serves Chinese, Indonesian; *Wantilan*, Cisolok road 1 km from town just past Pondok Dewata; *Nelayan*, Jl. Raya Citepus (Km 3 – at E end of Citepus Beach), Sundanese, Chinese, Western.

Local transport Becaks, horse-drawn carts, colts. Regular colts run from near the bus terminal in town to Cisolok passing all the hotels and beaches en route.

Banks & money changers Bank Central Asia, Jl. Siliwangi 109.

Transport to & from Pelabuhanratu 90 km from Bogor. By bus: the station is near the centre of town, just inland from the Fish Market. Regular connections with Bogor, 2½ hrs and Bandung. There are no direct buses from Jakarta – catch a bus to Bogor and get a connection onward, or a bus to Sukabumi getting off at Cibadak (17 km before Sukabumi) where there are numerous colts to Pelabuhanratu. By train: from Bogor to Cibadak, and then take a colt.

THE EASTERN ROUTE: Bogor to Bandung via the Puncak Pass

The journey from Bogor to Bandung via the Puncak Pass includes one of the most spectacular stretches of road in Indonesia. From Bogor, Route 2 climbs from 300m to the Puncak Pass at 2,900 m, passing rice terraces and tea plantations, and with magnificent views (on a clear day) over the surrounding landscape. The invigorating climate led to the creation of a number of hill resorts in the vicinity of the pass including Cisarua and Cipanas. The Gede-Pangrango National Park offers fine hiking. From the Puncak Pass, the road descends to the town of Cianjur, and from there runs 68 km to the capital of West Java, the university city of Bandung. This hill town began life as a quiet, Dutch-built, centre. It now has a population of at least 2 million. Good facilities, excursions to surrounding hot springs and volcanoes, and the best collection of Art Deco architecture in Asia makes it a good base.

Puncak Pass and Cisarua

The road from Bogor to Bandung winds through immaculately kept tea plantations, rice terraces and bamboo forest, climbing steadily to the **Puncak Pass** at 2,900 m. On the road up to the pass, **Cisarua** nestles in the foothills; a place to stop for walks and a visit to a **Gunung Mas Tea Factory and Estate** (open to visitors on Sundays). The hills are often shrouded in mist but on clear days it is said that it is possible to see all the way to Jakarta. There are a surprising number of places to stay (and eat) along this road, catering largely to Indonesian tourists attempting to escape from the heat of the plain.

Accommodation A *Puncak Pass Hotel*, Jl. Raya Puncak, T 512503, F 512180, restaurant, pool, tennis, just over the pass itself, in a spectacular position, dating from the colonial period, it is still the best hotel in the area; **C** *Kopo Hostels and Bungalows*, Jl. Raya Puncak 557 (next to the petrol station in Cisarua), T 4296, private rooms and dormitory accommodation.

Restaurants *Rindu Alam*, on the summit, surprisingly good food to go with the position.

Useful addresses Area code: 0255.

Transport to & from Puncak Pass and Cisarua 20 km from Cisarua to Bogor, 98 km from Cisarua to Bandung, 9 km from Cisarua to Puncak Pass. **By bus:** regular connections from Jakarta's Cililitan terminal to Cianjur or Bandung via the Puncak Pass; ask to be let off, the buses don't officially stop here. Also regular bus connections with Bogor.

Cibodas and Cipanas

10 km beyond Puncak Pass and 1.5 km before Cipanas town there is a turning to the right (easily missed – look out for a sign to the Cibodas Youth Hostel – Pondok Pemuda Cibodas) leading to the **Cibodas Botanical Gardens** which cover 60 ha. The 3½ km drive or walk up to the gardens from the turn-off is through a spectacular array of flowering shrubs and other plants; 'nurseries' line the route. The beautifully maintained Gardens were created in 1889 and are an extension of the Gardens in Bogor but for temperate and high altitude species. The Gardens were established 170 years ago and have been an important research centre. Admission: 1,000Rp.

The Gardens are also the starting point for climbs up Mount Gede (2,958 m) and Mount Pangrango (3,019 m), through the **Gede-Pangrango National Park**. The Park was established in 1862 and is the oldest in Indonesia. The climb to the summit of either of the 2 peaks takes a full day – 6-8 hrs. It is possible to camp on the slopes, but warm clothing and sleeping bags are essential. There are also other, shorter, hikes for the less ambitious. Permits must be obtained from the PHPA office (just before the entrance to the gardens) which can take 2 days to 'process' and permission is not always granted. The best time of year for climbing is from May-Oct and guides are recommended for those who have not climbed the routes before. **Getting to the gardens**: catch a colt from Cipanas to Ranahan or charter one.

1½ km on down the road towards Bandung from the turn-off for the Cibodas Gardens is the spa town of **Cipanas**. Here hot sulphur baths are fed by springs that issue from the slopes of Mount Guntur which last erupted in 1889. The mountain resort is centred on the Istana Cipanas – looking rather like an elegant cream hunting lodge – where former President Sukarno would come, so it is said, to write his more inspired speeches. The palace even has its own private hot spring and spa. Like Cisarua, this is primarily an Indonesian resort town, although it makes a good stopping place on the road to Bandung.

Accommodation There is a profusion of hotels and holiday homes in the area. **C** *New Puri Meru*, Jl. Singdanglaya 184, T 512415; **C** *Santosa*, Jl. Raya Cipanas 87, T 512612, price includes breakfast; **D** *Botanical Gardens Guesthouse*, in the Gardens, restaurant, recommended for its position; **E** *Pondok Pemuda Cibodas*, attractive position (near PHPA office).

Transport to & from Cibodas and Cipanas 32 km from Cipanas to Bogor, 86 km from Cipanas to the town, 12 km from Cipanas to Puncak Pass. **By bus**: regular connections from Jakarta's Cililitan terminal to Cianjur or Bandung via the Puncak Pass; ask to be let off, the buses don't officially stop here. Also regular bus connections with Bogor.

Bandung

Known as Kota Kembang (the flower city), Bandung was established by the Dutch in the late 19th century as a cool retreat from the sweltering plains of Jakarta. In 1811, Governor-General Daendels encouraged the regent, Dalem Wiranatajusumah II, to move his capital 10 km to the N, so that the town would link up with the new 1,000 km long Great Post Road which was under construction. By the end of the century, the town had become the headquarters for the Dutch army and the centre of the plantation industry.

Set in a huge volcanic basin, at an altitude of 700m and surrounded by mountains, Bandung has one of the most pleasant climates in Java with temperatures averaging 22°C. It is also the third largest city in Indonesia and is the capital of the province of West Java. Bandung has a population of over 2 million, with a further 3 million living in the surrounding area, making this one of the most densely populated areas of Java. The farmland around the town, though hilly, is relatively fertile – though the volcanic soils are not as fertile as those of Central and East Java.

Bandung is regarded as the intellectual heart of Java, with over 50 universities and colleges in and around the city. It is no accident that the Minister for Science and Technology, Dr. Habibie, decided to establish Indonesia's first aircraft industry – IPTN or P.T. Nurtanio – just outside the city in 1976. The company is one of the largest state operations in Indonesia, and employs over 2,000 university graduates. The factory assembles helicopters and aeroplanes under licence from CASA of Spain, Messerschmitt of Germany, Bell of the USA and Aerospatiale of France; it also makes parts for Boeing.

In the early part of the century, Bandung was a centre of the fledgling independence movement. It was here in 1928 that the historic 'Youth Pledge' committed students to serve only one Indonesia and speak one language – Bahasa Indonesia. A remarkable pledge considering that at the time the Dutch still had complete control over the country, and the islands were divided into sultanates and a heterogenous patchwork of ethnic, cultural, religious and linguistic groups. Rather later, Bandung was the site of the inaugural meeting of the Non-Aligned Movement in 1955. 29 countries attended the conference, which showed

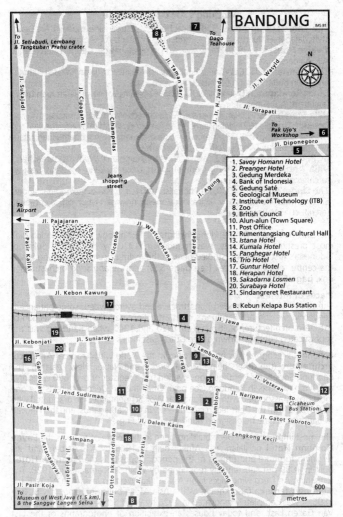

BANDUNG IMS 81

1. Savoy Homann Hotel
2. Preanger Hotel
3. Gedung Merdeka
4. Bank of Indonesia
5. Gedung Saté
6. Geological Museum
7. Institute of Technology (ITB)
8. Zoo
9. British Council
10. Alun-alun (Town Square)
11. Post Office
12. Rumentangsiang Cultural Hall
13. Istana Hotel
14. Kumala Hotel
15. Panghegar Hotel
16. Trio Hotel
17. Guntur Hotel
18. Herapan Hotel
19. Sakadarna Losmen
20. Surabaya Hotel
21. Sindangreret Restaurant

B. Kebun Kelapa Bus Station

Sukarno and Indonesia leading the developing world for the first time. Jalan Asia-Afrika is named after the event. In 1992, Indonesia hosted the NAM conference for a second time; on this occasion though, Indonesia was very much less revolutionary, its leaders radiating moderation and pragmatism.

The Institut Pasteur (now called the Bio Farma) became famous as a centre for research and production of the smallpox vaccine as well as a serum against rabies. Before the war, Bandung produced 90% of the world's quinine (from the bark of

Bandung's Art Deco heritage

The Three Locomotives: 3 identical houses in streamline modern Art Deco style, Jalan Ir. H. Juanda 113, 115 and 117 (architect: A.F. Aalbers).

Twelve Houses: 1939, in Prairie style Art Deco, Jalan Pager Ceunung (architect: A.F. Aalbers).

Tiga Warna: 1938, Curvilinear Functionalism Art Deco, Jalan Dr. Haji Juanda and Jalan Sultan Agung (architect: A.F. Aalbers).

Dinas Rendapatan Daerah: 1930-1935, Early Functionalism, Jalan Juanda 37 (architect: A.F. Aalbers).

Villa Merah: 1922, Jalan Tamansari 78 (architect: Wolff Schoemacher).

Boekkit Tinggi: 1925, Jalan Taman Sari (architect: Wolff Schoemacher).

Mesjid Cipaganti: 1933, the only mosque designed by Schoemacher, Jalan Cipaganti 85 (architect: Wolff Schoemacher).

St. Peter's Cathedral: 1932, Jalan Merdeka 10 (architect: Wolff Schoemacher).

Villa Ang Eng Kan: 1930, Geometric Art Deco building of great beauty (architect: F.W. Brinkman).

The Singer Building: 1930, functionalist Art Deco, this was the original Singer Sewing Machine Company Office in Indonesia, now part of an office complex (architect: F.W. Brinkman).

the cinchona tree). The Bandung Institute of Technology, arguably Indonesia's most prestigious university, was founded in 1920 by the Dutch. Sukarno, Indonesia's first president, studied here. In the realm of culture, Bandung is also the centre for *wayang golek* (**see page 529**) and the *angklung* orchestra (see box, **page 575**).

Places of interest
The centre of town is modern, unattractive and overcrowded; some patience is needed in seeking out Bandung's main attraction: namely, its fine collection of Art Deco architecture, built between 1920 and 1940 when Bandung was *the* sophisticated European town of the Dutch East Indies.

Bandung is recognized as one of 3 cities in the world with **'tropical Art Deco' architecture** (the others being Miami, Florida and Napier, New Zealand). The Bandung Society for Heritage Conservation has a register of over 600 category I and II monuments in Bandung (see box). Of all the Art Deco architects the one most closely associated with Bandung was Wolf Schoemacher. He graduated with Ed Cuypers from the Delft Technical University in the Netherlands, and then moved to Bandung where he designed hundreds of buildings.

The most impressive Art Deco building, lying in the centre of town, is the **Savoy Homann Hotel** on Jalan Asia Afrika, built in 1938 by A.F. Aalbers and still retaining furniture and fittings of the period. Opposite is the **Preanger Hotel**, built in 1889 but substantially redesigned by Wolff Schoemacher in 1928. The remaining Art Deco wing faces Jalan Asia Afrika. West on Jalan Asia Afrika is the **Gedung Merdeka** (also known as the Asia Afrika building). Originally built in 1895, it was completely renovated in 1926 by Wolff Schoemacher, Aalbers and Van Gallen Last, and today houses an exhibition of photographs of the first Non-Aligned Movement conference held here in 1955 (hence the name of the street). **Jalan Braga** is often said to be Bandung's colonial heart. Sadly though, most of the original façades have been disfigured or entirely replaced. North of the railway line also on Jalan Braga is the **Bank of Indonesia** designed by Ed Cuypers in the 1920s. Either side are church buildings designed by Schoemacher. Additional notable Art Deco buildings in Bandung are listed in the box on **page 574**. For visitors interested in learning more about Bandung's architectural heritage, a visit to the Bandung Society for Heritage Conservation (Bandung

The Angklung

The *angklung* is an ancient Sundanese instrument used to accompany story-telling and marching. It consists of a number of different length open bamboo tubes; in Bali these are sometimes assembled into an orchestra or *gamelan angklung* for certain ceremonies. The angklung is thought to have originated in West Java. It is still used by the Badui tribe in a number of their rituals, including the dance that precedes rice planting. In the past it probably accompanied the Badui into battle – hence its association with marching.

The antiquity of the angklung is indicated by the fact that its scale has only 4 notes (pentatonic). The name is thought to be onomatopoeic – the word imitates the sound of the instrument, *klung...klung...klung*. Along with the gamelan (**see page 534**), the angklung is peculiar to Indonesia – although there is a similar instrument in North Thailand – and in 1968 the Department of Education declared that it should be taught throughout the archipelago as a national instrument.

Paguyuban Pelestarian Budaya), *Hotel Savoy Homann*, Jalan Asia Afrika 112 is worthwhile. Their offices are open Mon-Sat 0900-1700, and they welcome interested travellers as well as professional researchers.

The N suburbs of Bandung are the most attractive part of the city, leafy and green – this is university land. **Gedung Sate** on Jalan Diponegoro was built in the 1920s and is one of Bandung's more imposing public buildings, with strong geometric lines and a formal garden. Almost opposite is the **Geological Museum** at no. 57 (reputed to be the largest in Southeast Asia). It houses skeletons of prehistoric elephants, rhinos, fossilized trees and a meteor weighing 156 kg which fell on Java in 1884; most notably, it is also home to the skull of 'Java Man' (**see page 496**). Open: 0900-1400 Mon-Thurs, 0900-1100 Fri, 0900-1300 Sat. Also N of the city centre on Jalan Taman Sari, the **Bandung Institute of Technology** or **ITB** was built by Maclaine Pont in 1918 and represents another good example of the architecture of the Art Deco era. Off Jalan Taman Sari, just before the ITB travelling N is the **Kebun Bintang**, Bandung's **zoo**. Admission: 500Rp. Open: 0900-1700 Mon-Sun.

South of town, the **Museum of West Java** (Negeri Propinsi Jawa Barat) is on the corner of Jalan Otto Iskandardinata and the ring road. It houses artefacts tracing the development and history of West Java. Admission: 200Rp. Open: 0800-1600 Tues-Sun.

On the north side of town, the rather bizarre **'Jean Street'** is worth a visit; shopkeepers vie for the most elaborate shopfront in an attempt to lure trade. Further north still is the **Dago Teahouse**, to be found behind the Pajajaran University housing complex. It was renovated in 1991, and provides a cultural hall and open-air theatre for evening Sundanese dance performances. Good views of the city from here. **Getting there**: catch a Dago colt up Jalan Ir. H. Juanda.

Excursions
Most visitors who venture out of the city travel N into the volcanic Priangan Highlands that surround Bandung, to see neat tea plantations, colossal craters and natural hotsprings.

Villa Isola lies on the route N on Jl. Setiabudi, 6 km from the city centre, and is yet another fine Art Deco building, set on a hill overlooking the city. **Getting there**: regular minibuses ply this route out of Bandung.

Lembang, 16 km N of Bandung, is a popular resort town on an upland plateau with restaurants and hotels. Garden nurseries line the road into Lembang and the town also supports the internationally respected **Bosscha Observatory** (visits must be prearranged). **Accommodation: B** (for new wing), **C** (in old building) *Grand Hotel*, Jl. Raya Lembang 228, T 82393, is the best place to stay in Lembang, an old hotel with swimming pool and tennis courts renovated by Aalbers of Savoy Homann fame. **Getting there:** regular minibuses connect Lembang with Bandung.

Tangkuban Prahu Crater (the capsized boat crater) is one of the most popular tourist sights in the vicinity of Bandung and possibly the most accessible volcanic Crater in Indonesia. The route up to the volcano from Lembang passes through rich agricultural land, with terraces of market garden crops clawing their way up the hillsides, chincona trees (the bark is used to produce quinine), teak and wild ginger. Nine km from Lembang is the entrance to the 'park' and 2 km from the gate is the lower carpark (with restaurant and tourist stalls). From here the road continues upwards for another 1 km to the rim of the impressive Ratu Crater. Alternatively, there is a footpath from the lower carpark to the Ratu Crater (1.5 km), and another from there to the smaller Domas Crater (1 km). Another path links the Domas and Ratu Craters (1.2 km). It is also possible to walk all the way round the Ratu Crater. Though visited by numerous tour buses and inhabited by large numbers of souvenir sellers, the natural splendour of the volcano makes the trip worthwhile. Ratu rises to an altitude of 1,830m, and the crater drops precipitously down from the rim. Bursts of steam and the smell of sulphur bear witness to the volcanic activity latent beneath the surface.

The curious shape of the summit of Tangkuban Prahu has given rise to the Sundanese *Legend of the Prince Sangkuriang* who unknowingly fell in love with his mother, Dayang Sumbi. She tried to prevent their marriage, insisting that her betrothed create a lake and canoe before sun-rise on their wedding day. Sangkuriang seemed to be endowed with magical powers and he nearly achieved this impossible task when Dayang Sumbi called upon the gods to hasten the sun to rise, in order to prevent their forbidden union. Sangkuriang was so angry, that he kicked his nearly finished canoe, which landed upside down on the horizon, thus creating this silhouette – all a little far fetched. Admission: 750Rp, 3,000Rp for car. Guides are available for off-path treks (inadvisable without a guide because of the emissions of sulphuric gases) and the wildlife in the surrounding forest includes a small population of native gibbons. At the summit hawkers sell anklungs to bemused tourists while tapping out *Auld Lang Syne*, and assorted lurid clothes. **Getting there:** bus or colt heading for Subang – and ask to be dropped off at the entrance to the crater. Hitch or walk (3.5 km) from here. At the week-end there are colts which go all the way up to the summit.

Ciater Hot Springs are 6.5 km on from Tangkuban Prahu, the road following the mountain side and winding through tea plantations. There are brilliantly clear hot water pools and waterfalls here situated on the side of a hill; unfortunately, the complex is rather seedy and run down. Admission: 1,000Rp, car 1,250Rp, and another 1,500Rp to bathe. **Accommodation: B** *Sari Ater Hotel*, on site, T 21319, F 21772. **Getting there:** take a colt or bus to Subang, asking to be let off at *Air Panas Ciater*; the hotel and springs are 150m off the main road.

Mount Papandayan is 74 km from Bandung and a full day's trip (see page 584).

Candi Cangkuang is an 8th century Hindu monument and can be visited in a day from Bandung (see page 583). The temple is 48 km from the city on the road to Garut. **Getting there:** catch a bus from Bandung's Cicaheum terminal on Jl. Jend. A. Yani travelling E towards Tasikmalaya and Banjar; get off 2 km after Kadungura, in the village of Leles.

Tours The tourist office on Jl. Asia Afrika will organize tours in and around town, as will many of the travel agents. Typical tours visit the Tangkuban Prahu crater and Ciater hotsprings (5 hrs, 64,000Rp/person), architecturally interesting buildings around town (3 hrs, 30,000Rp/person) and an angklung music performance, plus traditional Sundanese dancing (3 hrs, 24,000Rp/person).

Accommodation **A** *Abadi Gardens*, Jl. Dr. Setiabudi 287, T 210987, a/c, restaurant, pool, good sports facilities (including tennis courts) but 5 km N of town; **A** *Grand Preanger*, Jl. Asia Afrika 81, T 431631, F 430034, a/c, restaurant, pool, original art deco wing (1928), refurbished to a high standard, now 'complemented' by a 10-storey modern addition, central location, fitness centre; **A** *Istana*, Jl. Lembong 21-44, T 433025, F 432737, a/c, good restaurant, pool; **A** *Kumala*, Jl. Asia Afrika 140, T 52142, F 438852, a/c, restaurant, pool, a rather featureless hotel, but comfortable enough, Sundanese dance and music every Wed and Sat evening; **A** *Panghegar*, Jl. Merdeka 2, T 438695, F 431583, a/c, restaurant, pool, health club; **A** *Papandayan*, Jl. Jend. Gatot Subroto 83, T 430788, F 430988, J 587303, a/c, pool; **A** *Savoy Homann*, Jl. Asia Afrika 112, T 432244, F 431583, a/c, restaurant, superb art deco building, renovated but retaining original furnishings, central location – the most interesting place to stay in town; **A** *Sheraton*, 3 km N at Jl. Ir. H. Juanda 390, T 210303, F 210301, a/c, restaurant, pool, international standard hotel with good facilities (fitness centre); **A-B** *Trio*, Jl . Gardujati 56, T 615055, a/c. Clean, well-managed. Price includes breakfast; **B** *Mutiara*, Jl. Kebon Kawung 60-62, T 56356, a/c; **B** *Perdana Wisata*, Jl. Jend. Sudirman 66-68, T 438238, a/c, restaurant, centrally located but a modern, ugly block; **B** *Selekta Permai*, Jl. Pasir Kaliki 68-88, T 432279; **B** *Utari*, Jl. Ir. H. Juanda 50, T 56810, some a/c, nice area, professional, but slightly out of town. **B-C** *Braga*, Jl. Braga 8, T 51308, some a/c, old and rather scruffy; **B-C** *Famili*, Jl. Pasir Kaliki 96, T 50181; **C** *Guntur*, Jl. Otto Iskandarinata 20, T 50763, modern, set around courtyard, hot water; **C** *Herapan*, Jl. Kepatihan 14-16, T 51212; **D** *Melati 2 Kenangan*, Jl. Kb. Sirih 4, T 432239, friendly, but not very central.

Budget accommodation can be found around the railway station on Jl. Kebonjati and Jl. Pasir Kaliki. **E** *Cianjur*, Jl. Abdul Muis 169, T 56834, attractive guesthouse, rec; **E** *Mawar*, Jl. Pangarang 14, T 51934, central with clean rooms, popular with Indonesian travelling salesmen; **E** *Sakadarna*, Jl. Kebonjati 34, T 439897,restaurant, much nicer than the other Sakadarna at No. 50 and closer to the railway station, small rooms but clean; **E** *Surabaya*, Jl. Kebonjati 71, T 51133, Victorian railway hotel with interesting features but rather shabby, with grubby rooms.

Restaurants Indonesian: ♦♦♦*Savoy Homann Hotel*, Jl. Asia Afrika 112, traditional Rijstaffle dinner served nightly; ♦♦*Handayani*, Jl. Sukajadi 153, best Javanese restaurant in Bandung; ♦*Sate Ponorogo*, Jl. Jend. Gatot Subroto 38. Very good value open-air saté restaurant. Sundanese:♦♦*Babakan Siliwangi*, Jl. Siliwangi 7, near the zoo, open-air restaurant with large menu, rec; ♦♦*Ponyo*, Jl. Malabar 60, recommended by locals for its Sundanese specialities. Popular. Foodstalls: ♦*Night market*: Jl. Cikapundung Barat, good range of cheap Indonesian stall food; good foodstalls along Jl. Dalem Kaum, W of the alun alun. Chinese:♦♦*Queen*, Jl Dalem Laum 79, large menu, popular restaurant; ♦♦*Tjoan Kie*, Jl. Jend Sudirman 46, popular Cantonese restaurant; International:♦♦♦*Braga Permai*, Jl. Braga 58, also serves Chinese and Indonesian, one of the smartest restaurants in Bandung; ♦♦*Sukarasa*, Jl. Tamblong 52, T 438638, steaks and omelettes; ♦*Eliza Garden*, Jl. Kepatihan 21, attractive courtyard, simple food. Bakeries: *French Bakery*, Jl. Braga; *Sumber Hidangau*, Jl. Braga.

Entertainment Wayang golek: performances at *Sindangreret restaurant*, Jl. Nirapan 7-9 (near Jl. Braga) on Saturdays from 0700-2300 or an epic 8-hour performance every 2nd Saturday of the month at the *Rumentangsiang Cultural Hall*, near the Kosambi market on Jl. Jend. A. Yani.

Ketuk Tilu dance: a traditional social dance accompanied by gamelan music at the *Sanggar Langen Selna*, Jl. Otto Iskandarinata 541A. Professional dancers encourage you to join them in a dance (for which you pay). Nightly from 2100, show becomes more lively later on, cover charge 3,000Rp.

Jaipongan dance: another traditonal Sundanese dance form, performances at *Museum of West Java*, Jl. Otto Java, Wed. 1400.

Sundanese dance and gamelan recitals: at *Hotel Panghegar* on Jl. Merdeka on Wed and Sats at 1930, no charge but the audience is expected to eat or drink. Angklung (hand-held bamboo chimes): performances at *Pak Ujo's workshop*, Jl. Padasuka 118 (8 km NE of the town centre), when there are 20 or more people, T 71714. Admission: 3,000Rp, beginning 1530.

Cultural show: martial arts, dances etc. every Sun morning at the *zoo*, 0900-1300. Admission: entrance fee to zoo. *Museum of West Java* on Jl. Otto stages a cultural performance every Sun. **Adu Domba (ram fights)**: every other Sun at *Ranca Buni*, near Ledeng N of town on Jl. Setiabudi.

Art galleries: Bandung is a centre of modern art, possibly because of ITB's excellent fine art faculty. Galleries include Kertun, Jl. Pakar Wetan Dago Atas; Sri Hadi, Jl. Ciumbuleuit 173; and Surnaryo Jl. Bukit Pakar Dago Timur 25.

Cinema: opposite *Hotel Braga* on Jl. Braga. *Sartika 21* near intersection of Jl. Aceh and Jl. Merdeka. *Vanda*, Jl. Merdeka, near Jl. Jawa and the City Hall.

Discos: *Studio East*, 2nd flr, Premier Bldg, Jl. Cihampelas 129 (2100-0200). *La Dream Palace*, Jl. Asia Afrika, Plaza Lt 2 (2100-0200). *Lipstick Discoskate*, Gedung Palaguna Lt IV (1200-2100 for discoskating, 2130-0200 for standard standing disco).

Night Clubs: number on Jl. Jend Sudirman, e.g. *Panama* at no. 72, *Oriental* at no. 134. *Paramount* at no. 291 (all 2000-0200).

Shopping Angklung instruments: Jl. Madurasa. **Antiques**: Tasin Art, Jl. Braga 28. **Bookshops**: all over town, but especially N of the centre around the university. **Handicrafts**: next to *Sarinah department store* on Jl. Braga. Opposite is the *Indonesian National Crafts Council* (No.15). **Rubber stamp production**: a street of stalls and shops carving out stamps, Jl. Cikapundung Barat. **Jeans**: Jl. Pasar Celatan, off Jl. Otto Iskandardinata, for whacky shop fronts and cheap jeans, also Jl. Cihampelas for more weird shop fronts and bargain clothing. **Leather**: Jl. Braga 113, Jl. A. Yani 618. **Shoes**: good buy here, Jl. Cibaduyut (S of town on Jl. Kopo) for a wide variety. **Shopping centres**: an abundance, e.g. *Plaza Bandung Indah*, Jl. Merdeka 56, *Sarinah Dept Store*, Jl. Braga 10; **Wayang Golek**: *Pa. Aming*, Jl. M. Ramdhan 4 and *Pa. Ruchiyat*, Jl. Pangharang (behind No.20 in the alleyway). Both are workshops where you can also buy. Shops along Jl. Braga sell puppets.

Sports Golf: Dago Golf course, top end of Jl. Ir. H. Juanda.

Local transport Most roads in the centre of town are one way. This, coupled with the dense traffic, makes it quite a struggle getting around town. Bandung must have more orange-suited traffic wardens than any other town on Java, ready to dangerously direct traffic (and collect their 200Rp *parkir*). **Bus**: city buses go N-S or E-W; W on Jl. Asia Afrika, E on Jl. Kebonjati, S on Jl. Otto Iskandardinata, N on Jl. Astanaanyar. 150Rp. **Becaks** (very colourfully painted), **Delmans. Car rental**: National Car Rental at *Istana Hotel*, Jl. Lembong 21. **Colts**: 200Rp around town. Station on Jl. Kebonjati. **Taxi**: 3 or 4 companies run metered taxi services. Taxis can also be chartered for 5,000Rp/hr, minimum 2 hrs.

Embassies & consulates Austria, Jl. Prabu Dimuntur 2A, T 439505. France, Jl. Purnawarman 32, T 52864. **Netherlands**, Jl. Diponegoro 25, T 431419.

Banks & money changers Arta Mulia, Jl. Jend Sudirman 51. BPD, Jl. Braga. Djasa Arta, corner of Jl. Suniaraja and Jl. Otto Iskandarinata. Dwipa Mulia, Jl. Asia Afrika 148. Golden Money Changer, Jl. Otto Iskandardinata 127. Interstate Investment, Jl. Naripan 28. Metro Jasa, Jl. Jend. Gatot Subroto 21. Sejahtera Bagian Utama, Jl. Suniaraja 55.

Useful addresses Post Office: Jl. Asia Afrika 49, corner of Jl. Asia Afrika and Jl. Banceuy. Also Jl. Pahlawan 87. **Area code**: 022. **Hospital**: Jl. Cihampelas 161, T 82091. **American Express**: T 51983. **Immigration (local office)**: Jl. Surapati 82, T 72081. **British Council**: Jl. Lembong, nr. *Hotel Panghegar*.

Airline offices Garuda/Merpati, Jl. Asia Afrika 73-75, T 56986, opposite *Hotel Savoy Homann*. **Bouraq**, *Grand Hotel Preanger*, Jl. Asia Afrika 81, T 58061. **Sempati**, at *Hotel Panghegar*, Jl. Merdeka 2.

Tour companies & travel agents There are about 25 travel agents in town; most are branches of Jakarta-based companies. *Interlink*, Jl. Wastukencana 5. *Nitour*, Jl. Tamblong 2. *Satriavi*, *Grand Preanger Hotel*, Jl. Asia Afrika 81, T 50677 or at *Hotel Panghegar*, Jl. Merdeka 2, T 440192; *Natrabu*, *Hotel Papandayan*, Jl. Jend. Gatot Subroto 83, T 411866.

Tourist offices In his office at the NE corner of the city square on Jl. Asia Afrika, 'Yoga' can tell you anything you want to know about Bandung and the surrounding area. The office organizes 'designer' tours, custom made to suit each visitor's interests. For example, an architectural tour of the town, a pre-historic tour, a trip to the volcanoes, or a tour to Sundanese tribes and a Dragon village. **West Javan Regional Tourist Office** is on Jl. Cipaganti 153. **PHPA**: Jl. Jend A. Yani 276.

Transport to & from Bandung 187 km SE of Jakarta, 400 km W of Yogya. **By air**: Bandung's airport is 4 km from the city, T 614100. Regular connections on Garuda/Merpati and Bouraq with other destinations in Java, Sumatra, Kalimantan, Sulawesi, Bali, Lombok, Nusa Tenggara, Maluku and Irian Jaya (see page 1008 for route map). **By train**: the station is in the centre of town behind the bemo station, on Jl. Stasion Barat, T 50367. Regular connections with

Jakarta's 3 train stations 3-4 hrs. The journey between Jakarta and Bandung is spectacular, and highly recommended. There are 2 trains daily to Surabaya 13 hrs and 3 to Yogya. **By bus:** Bandung has 2 long-distance bus terminals: Kebun Kelapa on Jl. Dewi Sartika for all traffic W, and Cicaheum on Jl. Jend. A. Yani for traffic E. Tickets for a/c night buses can be bought on Jl. Kebonjati, near the *Hotel Surabaya*. Regular connections with Jakarta's Cililitan terminal 5 hrs, Bogor 3½ hrs, Pelabuhanratu 4 hrs, Cirebon, 3½ hrs, Yogya 12 hrs. **By minibus:** 2 companies from Jakarta – 4848, Jl. Kramet Raya 23, T 357656, and Media, Jl. Johar 15, T 343643, run minibuses to Bandung 4 hrs (10,000Rp). **By taxi:** share taxis for 6 cost about the same as the train.

THE NORTHERN ROUTE: Bandung to Cirebon

18 km E of Bandung, the road divides, turning NE along the Great Post Road, constructed under the direction of Governor-General Daendels between 1808 and 1810 for the defence of the island against the English. An engineering feat which required unprecedented numbers of *corvée* labourers, stretches of the road are carved through steep gorges and along narrow river valleys, and cost many lives. The route ends at the coastal city of Cirebon, a total of 130 km from Bandung. From Cirebon, Route 25 follows the coast for 117 km E to Pekalongan (see page 636).

Cirebon

At the end of the 15th century, the Kingdom of Cirebon reached its golden age under Sunan Gunung Jati, an ardent Muslim and one of the first *wali* – Muslim missionaries, now regarded as saints – to bring Islam to Java. He built the Pakungwati Kraton here in 1529. In 1677, the court was split into the Kasepuhan (elder) and Kanoman (younger) kratons. Unlike the kratons of Yogya and Solo, the kratons at Cirebon were not centres for the arts. Work was produced in nearby villages by guild-like organizations.

Today Cirebon is a busy port and one of the N coast's industrial centres, with a population of 250,000. The city is famous for its distinctive batik, heavily influenced by Chinese designs (see box, **page 579**). The area around Cirebon is a centre of chilli, mung bean and sugar cultivation.

Cirebon rock & cloud designs

The distinctive rock and cloud formations found not only on the batik of Cirebon but also in carvings on the carriages at the kratons, in the gates of the Kasepuhan kraton, and in decoration at the strange water garden Sunyaragi, are known as megamendung and wadasan. They are assumed to be derived from Chinese designs, probably adopted by local artisans after seeing ceramics and paintings brought by Chinese traders to the port. Each of the 4 courts developed their own particular styles, but all the designs featured clouds, rocks, gardens and heraldic animals.

Places of interest

Cirebon's main attractions are its **kratons**, of which there are 4, all still inhabited by their powerless sultans. The most interesting is the large **Kraton Kasepuhan**, which was built on the site of the earlier Hindu Pakungwati Kraton of 1529 (the home of Sunan Gunung Jati's queen, Pakungwati). It is the oldest palace, built in 1677 – although since much re-modelled (the last extensive renovation was in 1928). It is set on the S side of a square, and is approached along Jalan Kasepuhan through red brick split gates (*candi bentar*) – similar to Balinese temple gates. In front of the kraton is the **Siti Inggil** – a very attractive brick enclosure, with split gates and small wooden, tiled pendopos. Plates, brought

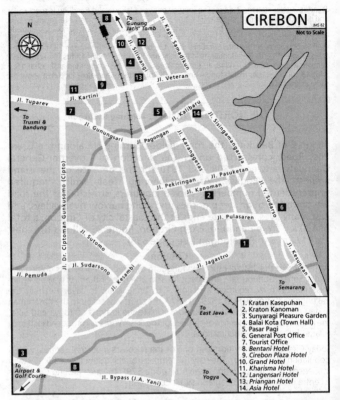

1. Kratan Kasepuhan
2. Kraton Kanoman
3. Sunyaragi Pleasure Garden
4. Balai Kota (Town Hall)
5. Pasar Pagi
6. General Post Office
7. Tourist Office
8. Bentani Hotel
9. Cirebon Plaza Hotel
10. Grand Hotel
11. Kharisma Hotel
12. Langensari Hotel
13. Priangan Hotel
14. Asia Hotel

here by Chinese traders, are set into the brick – it is regarded as the finest Siti Inggil in Java.

In the first of the kraton's white washed walled courtyards is a rather down-at-heel museum, with a badly displayed collection of gamelan sets, rice harvesting knives (*ani ani*), European glass, Indian chests and Portuguese armour. Towards the back of the compound, through some weathered wooden doors, are the Palace's 3 main rooms. They are wonderfully cool and airy, painted in soft greens, with Delft tiles and Chinese plates set into the walls. The painted ceiling of the first room is original (although the rattan roof is new), as is the second pillared room. The beautiful pendopo *Langgar Alit*, with its unusual 4-branched central pillar, was part of the earlier Hindu Pakungwati Kraton and was used for private worship by the Sultan's family.

Back in the main courtyard, visitors should not leave the kraton without asking to see the main attraction: the **Singa Barong Carriage**. It is housed in a stable opposite the museum and is an extraordinary amalgam of Hindu, Buddhist and Islamic elements. Built in 1548 in the shape of a fantastic animal, the carriage would have been yoked to 4 white buffalo. It has the body and trunk of an elephant, the head of a naga, and the wings of a garuda, and when the carriage moved, the wings flapped. In its trunk the beast holds a 3-pronged spear (symbolising the 3 religions). On the back of the carriage is the distinctive Cirebon cloud and rock design carved in wood. It was used by former sultans on ceremonial occasions, although it is said that the carriage has not left the stable since it was installed there in the 1940s. Behind the carriage are 3 palanquins, the central one, constructed in 1777, was used for circumcision ceremonies and has a garuda head and fish tail. The one on the left was for carrying the sultan's children, the one on the right for his wife. Admission: 500Rp, camera 1,000Rp, video 5,000Rp. Open: 0800-1700 Mon-Sun.

Next to the kraton, facing the square is the **Mesjid Agung** on Jalan Jagasatru. Built in 1480 it is one of the oldest (and most revered) mosques in Indonesia, with the characteristic 2-tiered roof found along the N coast of Java. Like other mosques in Demak and Kudus, the design shows links with pre-Islamic Hindu-Buddhist structures (see page 503).

Kraton Kanoman is reached by walking from Jalan Kanoman through **Pasar Kanoman** and across a rough piece of ground grazed by sheep. Less attractive than Kasepuhan and less well cared for, the walls at the entrance are of red plaster, again with Chinese plates set into them. It was probably built in the 17th century, but has been substantially re-modelled since then. Ask to see the 'museum' on the left-hand side of the compound with an even more motley collection than the Kasepuhan Museum. Noteworthy are 2 more carriages, dating from the period of the 16th century Pakungwati Kraton. The *Jempana Setia* may have been a litter used to carry the senior wife, or it may have been used to transport princes to the circumcision ceremony. It is of ornately carved wood in the Cirebon *megamendung-wadasan* style. The *Paksinagaliman* carriage is in the shape of a fantastic animal (an inferior version of the carriage at the Kraton Kasepuhan, see above) – a garuda, elephant and naga rolled into one ungainly beast.

Sunyaragi is a rather ugly 'grotto', built as a large pleasure garden (connected to the Kasepuhan Kraton) in 1740. It was constructed on 2 levels, the upper area being an ornamental lake, with a small island only accessible by boat. Since then, it has been extensively altered, many would say ruined, and is now a maze of concrete caves built for midgets and is remarkably unattractive. Locals promenade and picnic here on weekends and holidays. Admission: by donation. Open: 0700-1800, Mon-Sun. Sunyaragi is 3 km SW of town; take an angkutan 'G2' down Jalan Kesambi and get off at the intersection with Jalan Bypass (also known as Jalan Jend. A. Yani); the grotto is 500m N (right) on Jalan Bypass. Ask for *Gua* (cave) *Sunyaragi*.

Exploring the town on foot can be rewarding as there are some attractive old buildings and a number of Chinese temples. The **Balai Kota** (town hall) was built in the 1920s and is a good example of Art Deco design. At the time, Cirebon was known as Kota Udang (City of Shrimps) and to celebrate this title the hall has moulds of shrimps climbing up the towers. Cirebon supports a number of markets: among the most accessible is **Pasar Kanoman** on Jalan Kanoman; the 'morning' market or **Pasar Pagi** on Jalan Siliwangi is also worth a wander.

Excursions
The Tomb of Sunan Gunung Jati, one of Java's 9 'Walis', is 5 km N of town, 100m off the road to Karangampel and Indramayu (it is signposted 'Makam (grave) Gunung Jati'). This 15th century mosque and cemetery, this is a popular pilgrimage site for devout Muslims (see page 528). The whitewashed walls, like those of Cirebon's kratons, are inlaid with Chinese and Dutch plates and tiles. Gunung Jati's tomb is through wooden doors and is not open to visitors (the doors are sometimes opened on special occasions); the tomb in the open pavilion is that

of Sultan Sulaeman. Also buried here is the Wali's Chinese wife Ong Tien who fell in love with Sunan Jati while he was on a mission to China and implored her father to allow her to follow him to Java. She converted to Islam, but died 3 years after arriving in Cirebon. Admission: free, officially, but donations include parking a car, entering the cemetery, leaving shoes, and entering the tomb site. **Getting there:** take an angkutan 'GG' which runs down Jalan Siliwangi/ Raya Klayan, and ask to be let off at *Makam Gunung Jati*.

Trusmi is a village 6 km W of town, and is the best known of the various *batik villages* in the vicinity of Cirebon. Linked to the courts of the Sultans for many years, the small workshops produce high quality batik tulis (hand drawn designs) (**see page 536**). Prices start at 15,000Rp and go as high as 165,000Rp for the very best quality cloth. **Getting there:** by blue angkutan 'GP', which runs from Jalan Gunungsari, down Jalan Tuparev to Plered. In the village of Plered (really a suburb of Cirebon), turn right and walk down a becak-choked lane to Trusmi and its workshops (signposted).

Accommodation Most hotels are to be found along Jl. Siliwangi. **A-B** *Park Cirebon*, Jl. Siliwangi 107, T 27097; **A-B** *Patra Jasa*, Jl. Tuparev 11 (2 km out of town on the road to Bandung), T 29402, F 27696, a/c, pool, tennis, good facilities; **B** *Bentani*, Jl. Siliwangi 69, T 24269, F 27527, a/c, restaurant, pool, efficient new hotel with some style; **B** *Cirebon Plaza*, Jl. R.A. Kartini 54, T 2061, a/c, restaurant, modern; **B** *Grand*, Siliwangi 98, T 25457, a/c, impressive exterior, recently renovated interior, large suite rooms with the biggest doors in Cirebon; **B** *Kharisma*, Jl. R.A. Kartini 60, T 22295, F 22295, not much charisma, but quite adequate and comfortable; **C-D** *Nooraini*, Jl. Jend. A. Yani 55, T 21352, clean, next to the bus station; **D** *Asia*, Jl. Kalibaru 15-17, T 22193, old building, popular and clean with courtyard, on quiet street; **D** *Priangan*, Jl. Siliwangi 106, T 22929, a/c, good mid-range, clean; **E** *Islam*, Jl. Siliwangi 116, T 23403; **E** *Famili*, Jl. Siliwangi 76, T 27935, basic rooms, but clean; **E** *Langensari*, Jl. Siliwangi 127, T 24449, a/c, some with own bathrooms, friendly management; **E** *Losmen Semarang*, Jl. Siliwangi 124. Clean rooms, old building, good management.

Restaurants Local specialities include *nasi jamblang* (rice served in dried teak leaves), *mie kocok*, *sate kalong* and *nasi tengko*. Cirebon has a reputation for producing some of the best seafood in Java.
    Indonesian: *Baraya*, Jl. Yos Sudarso 45; *Jogja*, Jl. Siliwangi 162; ♦♦ *Maxim's*, Jl. Bahagia 45-47, also serves Chinese and seafood, large, popular with locals, rec; ♦ *Meja Panas Jumbo*, Jl. Siliwangi 191, good seafood, also serves Chinese. **Chinese:** ♦♦ *Canton*, Jl. Bahagia 18B. **Foodstalls:** *Pasar Kasepuhan*, on the square near Kraton Kasepuhan; **Bakeries:** *La Palma Bakery*, Jl. Siliwangi (near the Balai Kota); *Orchid German Bakery*, Jl. Karanggetas 122.

Entertainment Dance: *Topeng* (masked dance), at the Kraton Kasepuhan, 0800-1000 Sun ('usually'). **Theatre:** open air theatre at Sunyaragi. **Cinemas:** Mandala, Jl. Siliwangi; Matahari Dept Store (Balong Indah Plaza), Jl. Pekiringan. **Amusement Park:** Ade Irma Suryana Nasution Taman Rekreasi. Admission: 1,000Rp. Open: 0900-2100 Mon-Sun. **Disco and Karaoke:** big in Cirebon; the *Blue Diamond* at Jl. Yos Sudarso 1 is open 1900-0200/0300.

Sports Golf: Ciperna Golf Course, owned by the state oil company Pertamina, is 6 km SW of town and open to visitors. Angkutan 'GC' runs there.

Shopping Best buys here are batik, rattan, topeng masks, wayang kulit and wayang golek puppets. **Batik:** the Cirebon area produces its own style of very distinctive batik (see box above). The town contains many batik shops; a good number can be found on the ground floor of the *Indah Plaza*, on Jl. Pekiringan; other good shops include *Batik Permana*, Jl. Karanggetas 16; *Batik Keris*, Jl. Pasuketan 81; and *Batik Semar*, Jl. Bahagia 36B.

Banks & money changers Djasa Valasmas Artha, Jl. Yos Sudarso 56. Bank International Indonesia, Jl. Siliwangi 49. Bumi Daya, Jl. Siliwangi 127.

Useful addresses General Post Office: Jl. Yos Sudarso 7. Area code: 0231.

Tour companies & travel agents *Nenggala Tour*, Jl. Pasuketan 41, T 26421. *Sanggar Caruban*, Jl. Pemuda 11A, T 27196.

Tourist offices Cirebon Information Office (Dinas Pariwisata Daerah), Jl. Cipto 1 (at intersection with Jl. Kartini). Open: 0800-1400 Mon-Thurs, 0800-1100 Fri, 0800-1300 Sat. Not particularly helpful, but they have maps.

Transport to & from Cirebon 248 km from Jakarta, 317 km from Yogya, 237 km from Semarang. **By air**: Lapangan Airport is 5 km SW of the city, T 27085; angkutan 'GC' go past the airport. Daily connections by Garuda/Merpati with Jakarta, Bengkulu, Bandar Lampung, Balikpapan and Banjarmasin (**see page 1006** for route map). **By train**: the station is at the N end of Jl. Siliwangi, set back from the road (T 22400). Cirebon connects with the southern line, which arrives at Gambir station in Jakarta and links up with Yogyakarta, and the northern coastal line, which departs from Kota or Pasar Senen stations in Jakarta and links up with Semerang and Surabaya. Regular connections with Jakarta 3¼-4 hrs, Yogyakarta 6¾ hrs, or along the coast to Semarang (**see page 1012** for timetable). **By minibus**: minibus connections with Bandung, Yogyakarta and Semarang. The minibus office is at Jl Karanggetas 7. **By bus**: the station is 2 km S of town, on Jl. Bypass, also known as Jl. Jend. A. Yani. All long distance buses leave from here and express and a/c companies have their offices at the station. Regular connections with Jakarta 5 hrs, Semerang 5 hrs, Yogya 7 hrs and Bandung 3½ hrs.

THE EASTERN ROUTE: Bandung to Pangandaran via Garut

Travelling E, 18 km outside Bandung, the road divides: N to Cirebon (112 km), and E to Garut (46 km). Garut is a beautifully positioned, smallish hill town, 64 km from Bandung. It can be used as a base to visit the candi and lake at Cangkuang and to go hiking among the surrounding volcanoes. From Garut, the road continues E to Tasikmalaya (57 km), a centre of handicraft production, following the beautiful valley of the Wulan River. Continuing E from Tasikmalaya, it is 24 km to Ciamis where the road divides: N to Cirebon and E into Central Java. Travelling E, another 25 km from Ciamis is the small transport node of Banjar. Trains and buses from Jakarta stop here, and passengers are then bussed S to Pangandaran, arguably Java's finest beach resort. The journey S cuts down through narrow river valleys. From Pangandaran's 'port' of Kalipucang, ferries take passengers across the Anakan Lagoon to Cilacap, Central Java.

Garut

Garut lies 65 km SE of Bandung and was once a Dutch hill station, magnificently set at an altitude of over 700m amidst towering volcanoes. The area is renowned for its orchards and tobacco, and in the 1920's was a popular hill resort for wealthy residents of Batavia. It is a good point from which to visit Candi Cangkuang, volcanoes (e.g. Mount Papandayan), hot springs and lakes (see below). Few foreign tourists stop here, although the town is large enough to provide basic amenities. The surrounding area is also known for its batik.

Excursions

Candi Cangkuang is a small 8th century temple set on an island in the middle of a peaceful, water lily-covered lake. The **Candi** was first listed in a report of the Dutch Archaeological Service in 1914. It was then 're-discovered' in 1966, and restored in 1976. The temple is simple in design, square, only 8.5m high and built of andesite. It is one of the only Hindu temples to have been found in West Java and is thought, because of the absence of architectural ornamentation and the primitive building techniques, to predate Borobudur and the candis of the Dieng Plateau. It is believed to date from the 8th century, although some authorities consider it to be even older. Within the candi there is a statue of Siva riding upon his vehicle, the bull Nandi. Compared with other monuments in Java it is quite plain, although the position could hardly be more beautiful. At the foot of the temple, is the **Tomb of Arief Mohammad**, a 17th century warrior who is said to have been a very holy man who resisted the Dutch in Batavia. Surprisingly, when the tomb was excavated, no human remains were found. His descendants live in a **hamlet** 150m W of the temple, where one of the traditional houses has been restored. There are several taboos connected with this strange village: the houses cannot be altered, pilgrims are not permitted to pay homage at the tomb on Wed, 4 legged animals cannot be kept within the village compound, and musical instruments are forbidden during festivals. There is a small **museum** 50m NW of the candi. Admission to area: 200Rp, 300Rp for a car; admission to candi: 200Rp. **Getting there:** take a regular bus or colt travelling out of town on the Bandung road and ask to be let off at the turning for the lake and candi. This narrow road off to the right is easy to miss – there is only a small sign. The turning is 13 km N of Garut in the village of Leles (also known as Cangkuang). Travelling from Bandung, the turning is 2 km S of Kadungura (48 km from Bandung). Horse-drawn carts wait at the turning to transport visitors the 3 km from the main highway, through beautiful countryside, to Lake Cangkuang (about 4,000Rp). To reach the candi, take one of the (modified for tourists) bamboo rafts across the lake to the island (approx. 2,000Rp/raft). It is also possible to walk the 2 km around the edge of the lake.

The turning for the **Cipanas hot springs** is at the Km 4 mark travelling N from Garut towards Bandung. The waters are supposed to have healing properties. The springs are 2 km above Cipanas town, an easy and attractive walk. **Accommodation: B** *Tirtagangga*,restaurant, pool. Bungalows with hot spring water, and sports facilities. **Getting there:** regular bemos (No 04) from the bemo terminal to Cipanas town.

Mount Papandayan is an active volcano (2,622 m) with remarkable bubbling sulphur pools and crater, 36 km SW of town. **Getting there:** catch a bus to Arjuna and hike, 2-3 hrs.

Tasikmalaya is 53 km E of Garut, and the surrounding area is a centre for rattan, embroidery and batik cottage industries. **Accommodation: C-E** *Widuri*, Jl. Martadinata 51, some a/c, colonial era hotel, now rather seedy. **Getting there:** regular minibus connections from town.

Accommodation C *Kota Indah*, Jl. Otto Iskandardinata 236, T 61033, some rooms with hot water, clean, price includes breakfast; **C-E** *Paseban*, Jl. Otto Iskandardinata 260, T 81127, restaurant, some rooms with hot water, average, bungalows set amongst gardens, older rooms a little shabby, newer ones better, with hot water, price includes breakfast.

Local transport The bemo station is near the intersection of Jl. Jend. A. Yani and Jl. Cikuray; bemos from here to local towns.

Banks & money changers BNI 1946, Jl. Jend. A. Yani 56.

Useful addresses Post Office: Jl. Jend. A. Yani 40.

Transport to & from Garut 65 km from Bandung. **By bus:** Garut's Guntur terminal is on the N edge of town. Regular connections with Bandung, Tasikmalaya, Yogya and Banjar.

Pangandaran

Pangandaran is situated on the neck of a narrow isthmus and offers the best beaches on the S coast of Java – which is not saying a great deal. Originally a fishing village, many of the local people now derive their livelihoods from tourism. At weekends during peak season the town is crowded with Indonesian tourists; out of season on weekdays it is like a ghost town and hotel and losmen prices can be bargained down accordingly. The high season runs between Jun and Sept, the low season from Oct to Mar. Admission to the isthmus: 500Rp.

The best beach is on the W side of the isthmus and is named **West Beach** (Pantai Barat). Swimming is best at its S end; to the N, currents are vicious and swimming should be avoided. Souvenir shops line the beach front and it is here that most accommodation is concentrated. The E side of the isthmus (**East Beach** or Pantai Timur) is less developed; the water is often rough and swimming is poor,

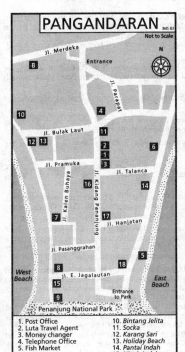

PANGANDARAN IMS 83
Not to Scale

1. Post Office
2. Luta Travel Agent
3. Money changer
4. Telephone Office
5. Fish Market
Hotels:
6. Bumi Pananjung
7. Bumi Nusantara
8. Mangkubumi
9. Pangandaran Beach
10. Bintang Jelita
11. Socka
12. Karang Sari
13. Holiday Beach
14. Pantai Indah
15. Niyuh Indah
Restaurants:
16. Bamboe
17. Cilacap
18. Gatul's

sometimes dangerous. Fishermen cast their nets from this shore and land their catches along the beach.

The promontory of the isthmus is a park – the **Penanjung National Park**. On both the E and W sides of the promontory are white sand beaches. It is possible to walk the 10 km around the shoreline of the peninsula, or hike through the jungle which is said to support small populations of buffalo, deer, tapirs, civet cats, porcupines and hornbills, although how they tolerate the herds of tourists is a mystery. The Rafflesia flower can, it is claimed, be seen here in season (**see page 780**). The park also has some limestone caves. Admission to the park: 300Rp.

Excursions
Parigi Bay is W of Pangandaran, and offers better and quieter beaches than the isthmus, namely Batu Hiu, Batu Karas and Parigi, and good water for surfing. **Getting there:** regular buses run from Pangandaran bus station on Jl. Merdeka (360Rp).

Boat trip: a worthwhile alternative to the bus trip back to Banjar is the much more enjoyable ferry journey from Kalipucang to Cilacap (see Transport to & from Pangandaran, below).

Tours Tour agencies (see Travel Agents) organize jungle, boat (fishing, snorkeling), home industry, village and other tours. Prices range from 5,500-23,000Rp/person.

Accommodation is concentrated on the W side of the isthmus. Rates can be bargained down during the low season (Oct-Mar). At Christmas, prices rise steeply, when Indonesian tourists flock here. Many of the hotels and guesthouses rent out family rooms – usually consisting of 2 double rooms and a living area.
East Beach (Pantai Timur): B *Bumi Pananjung*, a/c, rather dark; **B** *Pantai Indah Timur*, Jl. Talanca 153, T 39004, F 39327, a/c, hot water, clean, new, rather bare but good room facilities.
West Beach (Pantai Barat): B *Pangandaran Beach*, S end T 62, some a/c, clean, large rooms; **B** *Pondok Putri Duyung*, N end, a/c, attractively built, 2 double rooms, living area, more luxurious than most, hot water, rec; **B** *Susan's*, inland from the beach, large bungalows with 4 rooms, rec; **B** *Sunset*, N end, a/c, clean, bit dark, living room with 2 double bedrooms, bathrooms attached; **C** *Bumi Nusantara*, central section, some a/c, very clean, well designed and efficiently run, friendly, rec; **C** *Mangkubumi*, third of the way N, T 17, a/c; **C** *Niyur Indah*, S end, a/c, clean, friendly, price variation for old and new rooms, rec; **C** *Karang Sari*, N end, living room with 2 double bedrooms, bathrooms attached; **C** *Bintang Jelita*, N end, clean, with living area and 2 double bedrooms, well-run and popular, rec; **C** *Pondok Wisata Pantai Sari*, Jl. Bulak Laut, inland from beach, N end, some a/c, restaurant; **D** *Bulak Laut*, N end, chalet style with sitting-room and unusual bathroom; **E** *Holiday Beach*, inland from beach at the N end, popular, squat loo; **E** *Mutiara Selatan*, inland from beach at the N end, small rooms.

Restaurants *Bamboe*, Jl. Kidang Pananjung, just S of Luta Travel Agent; *Cilacap*, Jl. Kidang

Pananjung 187, a travellers' haven; *Gatul's*, East Beach, near the fish market, excellent seafood; *Mumbo's*, West Beach, next to Mangkubumi, seafood, Chinese, Indonesian; *Pantai Timur*, Jl. E. Jaga Lautan, East Beach, seafood, Chinese, Indonesian and International; *Scandinavian*, West Beach, just N of *Karang Sari Hotel*; *Sari Harum*, Jl. Pasanggrahan 2. Sundanese.

Entertainment Nanjung Cinema: Jl. Kidang Pananjung, N of Post Office. Disco: the 'Cultural Centre' on the West Beach Rd is no longer very cultural; it didn't make enough money and is now a disco.

Sports Swimming: the *Socka Hotel* on Jl. Kidang Pananjung, N of the cinema, opens its pool to non-residents.

Shopping Stalls on the beach and some shops on the central isthmus road, Jl. Kidang Pananjung (for instance Luta at 107) – shell jewellery, shells, clothing, knick-knacks.

Banks & money changers Bank Rakyat Indonesia, Jl. Kidang Pananjung 133 (near the intersection with Jl. Talanca).

Local transport Becaks and Bicycles: for rent along the beach and from guesthouses, approximately 2,500Rp/day. **Motorbikes**: *Luta*, Jl. Kidang Pananjung 107 rents motorbikes for 9,000Rp/day.

Useful addresses Post Office: Jl. Kidang Pananjung 111 (Poste restante available here). **Telephone office**: Jl. Kidang Pananjung (N end). **Area code**: 0265. **PHPA Office**: on the borders of the park at the S end of the isthmus, near the East Beach.

Tour companies & travel agents *Luta*, Jl. Kidang Pananjang 107, T 39294, organizes local tours and transport to & from Pangandaran; *Mumbo's*, West Beach (next to *Mangkubumi Hotel*) will organize buses to Jakarta, Yogya and Bandung. They also arrange the backwater boat trip from Kalipucang to Cilacap with connecting minibus to Yogya (13,500Rp).

Transport to & from Pangandaran 400 km from Jakarta, 129 km from Bandung, 66 km from Banjar and 312 km from Yogya. **NB**: there are no direct buses or trains linking Pangandaran with Jakarta, Yogya, Bandung, or Solo. Whether travelling by bus or train it is necessary to change in **Banjar**, a small town on the Bandung-Yogya road, and 66 km from Pangandaran. There are a number of cheap losmen over the railway bridge from the rail and bus stations in Banjar for those who arrive too late to make a connection. The train and bus stations are 500 m apart; becaks wait to take travellers between the two.

By train: regular connections with Jakarta 10 hrs, Bandung 5 hrs, Yogya 6-8 hrs and Surabaya to Banjar. Regular buses link Banjar with Pangandaran. By bus: station is on Jl. Merdeka, a 15 min walk N of most of the hotels and guesthouses (outside the main gates). Regular buses link Pangandaran with Banjar (960Rp) from where there are frequent buses onward to Jakarta 7-10 hrs, Bogor (via Ciawi), Bandung, Yogya and Solo, and less frequent buses to Wonogiri and Madiun. Jakarta-Banjar buses leave Jakarta's Cililitan station every hour. There are 2 direct Jakarta-Pangandaran buses a day, 8 hrs. Connections with Ciamis 2½ hrs and Tasikmalaya 3 hrs. By boat: An alternative to the bus or train is to take the boat between **Kalipucang** (Pangandaran's 'port') to **Cilacap** through the Anakan Lagoon, an 'inland' sea. A worthwhile journey and a gentle form of transport, the boat sails down the mangrove-clothed Tanduy River, stopping-off in various fishing villages on the way, before crossing the Anakan Lagoon. The boat docks at Sleko, outside Cilacap. Kalipucang is 15 km from Pangandaran; take a local bus there. **NB**: to catch a bus connection in Cilacap get either the 0700 or 0800 from Kalipucang, 4 hrs (1100Rp) (there are also 2 afternoon departures at 1200 and 1300). From Cilacap the boats leave from Sleko harbour, 4 departures a day (0700, 0800, 1200 and 1300).

CENTRAL JAVA and YOGYAKARTA

Introduction, 587; The Eastern Route: Cilacap to Yogyakarta, 587; Yogya to Magelang, via Borobudur, 604; Yogya to Surakarta via Prambanan, 612; Magelang to Dieng Plateau, via Wonosobo, 624; Magelang to Semarang via Ambarawa and Gedung Songo, 627; East from Semarang to Demak and Kudus, 633; West from Semarang to Pekalongan, 636.

Maps: Central Java, 588; Yogyakarta, 591; Yogya Kraton, 593; Yogya Surroundings, 597; Borobudur, 605; Prambanan, 613; Solo, 617; Dieng Plateau, 626; Semarang, 629; Kudus, 634.

INTRODUCTION

The central portion of Java comprises the province of Central Java and the Special Territory of Yogyakarta – the latter being one of only 2 such regions in Indonesia (the other is Aceh at the N tip of Sumatra). Although this part of Java contains some of the most magnificent monuments in the world, it is at the same time one of the poorest areas of Indonesia. Part of the explanation lies in the incredibly high population densities: combined, Central Java and Yogyakarta had a population of nearly 32 million in 1990, and in places farmers are crammed on to the land at a density of 2,000 per sq km.

In the 1960s, commentators were generally pessimistic about the ability of the region to escape the effects of what seemed to be such an intolerable burden of people. They highlighted the high incidence of malnutrition, the depths of poverty that existed, and could see little that might off-set a forthcoming 'Malthusian' catastrophe. Although conditions are still poor, the crisis has not materialized. Industrial growth – mostly small-scale, cottage industries – has been encouraging, while agriculture with the aid of the technology of the 'Green Revolution' – has managed, in the main, to keep production growing faster than population.

This central portion of Java lacks a city on the scale of Bandung in West Java or Surabaya in East Java. The largest towns are the historic towns of Yogyakarta and Surakarta (Solo). Central Java was the focus of the magnificent Buddhist Sailendra and Hindu Sanjaya dynasties which built, respectively, Borobudur and the temples on the Prambanan Plain. It was also the focus of the later Mataram Kingdom, and the sultanates of Yogyakarta and Surakarta. It is to visit these archaeological and historical sites, and to stay in what has become one of the most popular tourist towns in Indonesia – namely Yogyakarta – that visitors make their way here in droves. A general introduction to the art and history of Central Java can be found beginning on page 515.

THE EASTERN ROUTE: Cilacap to Yogyakarta

Cilacap is the port for the ferry which runs 4 times daily to Pangandaran. The E-W route 2 skirts Cilacap, running across the coastal plain at the foot of the Serayu Mountains towards Yogyakarta. Yogyakarta is a total of 415 km from Bandung, 351 km from Garut and 216 km from Cilacap.

CENTRAL JAVA IMS 84

0   35
Km

Java Sea

Indian Ocean

To Karimunjawa Islands

To Cirebon

Cilacap

This coastal town has little to offer the tourist, but it is near the port of Sleko where the daily ferry from the beach resort of Pangandaran (**see page 584**) docks. Because the bus journey to Pangandaran is a circuitous 163 km from Cilacap, it makes sense to take the far more relaxing ferry, a journey of 4 hrs. There are hotels in Cilacap for visitors who arrive too late to catch the ferry to Pangandaran or a bus on to Yogya, and it can also be used as a base for visits to the Jatijajar Caves (see Excursions).

Excursion
Jatijajar caves consist of gardens, pools and concrete figures arranged within and around a cave complex (**see page 599**). **Getting there:** take a bus N to Route 2 and then another one E towards Kebumen and Yogya.

Nusa Kambangan is a narrow island and nature reserve just off the coast and is worth a visit if you have time to kill in Cilacap. **Getting there:** regular car and passenger ferries from Sleko pier.

Accommodation A-B *Intan*, Jl. Jend. Gatot Subroto 136, T 22545, F 22547, a/c, restaurant, pool, part of a chain of hotels, good facilities; **A-B** *Wijaya Kusuma*, Jl. Jend. A. Yani 12A T 22871; **B-C** *Grand*, Jl. Dr. Wahidin 5-15, T 21332; **C** *Cilacap Inn*, Jl. Jend. Sudirman 1, T 41823; *Delima*, 5 Jl. Jend. Sudirman, T 21410.

Transport to & from Cilacap 216 km W of Yogya, 50 km S of Purwokerto. **By boat:** the ferry to/from Kalipucang, Pangandaran's 'port', docks at Sleko harbour, just outside Cilacap (**see page 586** for details on the journey). The ferry leaves for Pangandaran at 0700, 0800, 1200 and 1300 and takes 4 hrs. To catch a bus onwards from Pangandaran, take a morning ferry from Cilacap. **By bus:** minibuses leave for Yogya from the Sleko pier, and for Wonosobo (and Dieng), 6 hrs.

Yogyakarta

Yogyakarta – usually shortened to Yogya and pronounced 'Jogja' – is probably the most popular tourist destination in Java. It is a convenient base from which to visit the greatest Buddhist monument in the world – Borobudur – and the equally impressive Hindu temples on the Prambanan Plain. The town itself also has a number of worthwhile attractions: the large walled area of the kraton, with the Sultan's palace, the ruined water gardens or 'Taman Sari', and a colourful bird market. Yogya is arguably the cultural capital of Java and the ISI (Indonesian Art Institute) is based here, with faculties of Fine Art, Dance and Music. The town is the best place to see wayang performances and traditional dance (**see page 602**). In recent years it has become a popular town for Indonesian artists to base themselves. On the northern edge of the city is Indonesia's oldest, and one of its most prestigious, universities: Gadjah Mada University or UGM. It was 'founded' in Dec 1949 when Sultan Hamengkubuwono IX allowed students and their teachers to use the Siti Inggil within the precincts of the kraton. For the tourist, it is also one of the best centres for shopping and offers a good range of tourist services from excellent middle range accommodation to well-run tour companies.

Yogya is situated at the foot of the volcano Mount Merapi, which rises to a height of 2,911 m, to the N of the city. This peak is viewed as life-giving, and is set in opposition to the sea which is life-taking and situated to the S. The importance of orientation vis à vis Mount Merapi and the ocean is seen most clearly in the structure of the kraton, or Sultan's palace (see below).

History
The name Yogyakarta, or Yogya, is derived from the Sanskrit 'Ayodya' – the capital city of Rama in the Hindu epic, the Ramayana. The city was officially founded in 1755, although there were a succession of earlier settlements near the site, most notably the capital of the great Mataram Kingdom in the early 17th century (**see page 519**).

The Hamengkubuwono sultans of Yogyakarta
(1749 to the present day)

Hamengkubuwono I or Mangkubumi (1749-92)
Established the Sultanate and the City of Yogyakarta after fighting against the Dutch for almost a decade. Built the Kraton and the water gardens.

Hamengkubuwono II (1792-1810, 1811-12, 1826-28)
Not a man to match his father in stature, his undiplomatic behaviour made him unpopular with the Dutch. He was deposed 3 times by the Dutch and English, had 2 queens, 31 concubines and 80 children.

Hamengkubuwono III (1810-11, 1812-14)
Popular with the colonial powers and, as a result, unpopular with the Javanese aristocracy. It was during his reign, and that of his father, that the Sultanate lost all effective power.

Hamengkubuwono IV (1814-22)
Ascended to the throne at the age of thirteen and died under mysterious circumstances 8 years later.

Hamengkubuwono V (1822-26, 1828-55)
Ascended to the throne at the age of 3, under the tutelage of a Dutch-appointed committee. It was at this time that Prince Diponegoro (Hamenkubuwono V's uncle) stirred up rebellion and led the Java War from 1825-1830.

Hamengkubuwono VI

Hamengkubuwono VII

Hamengkubuwono VIII (1921-39)
His great love was *wayang* theatre, and his reign saw a revival of this and other Javanese arts.

Hamengkubuwono IX (1940-1989)
Reigned through the difficult periods of the Japanese Occupation and then the formation of the Republic. He gave support to the fledgling independence movement, and allowed the kraton to become a focus of resistance. Died in 1989, highly respected and loved by his people.

Hamengkubuwono X (1989-)
Said to be both an astute politician and businessman.

In the 1670s, the Mataram kingdom based near Yogyakarta, under Amangkurat I, began to decline. At the same time, the Dutch East India Company (VOC) based at Batavia – present-day Jakarta – was growing in military might and commercial influence. By the mid-18th century, the VOC – whose leaders up until then had been loathe to expand territorially – were forced to make their move. Worried that the power vacuum left by the crumbling Mataram Kingdom might be filled by competing colonial powers, the VOC sent a force to Mataram. In 1755, the Treaty of Giyanti partitioned the Kingdom into 3 sultanates: the 2 senior houses of Pakubuwono (meaning 'Nail of the Universe') of Surakarta, and Hamengkubuwono (meaning, 'He who holds the World on his Lap') of Yogyakarta, and the junior house of Mangkunegara, also of Surakarta. These 3 sultanates retained considerable independence but ultimate power from that point rested with the Dutch. Pangeran Mangkubumi, the brother of Susuhunan Pakubuwono II of Surakarta (see page 619) became Sultan of Yogyakarta, and was known as Hamengkubuwono I. He reigned until his death in 1792 at the age of eighty, during which time he had built up a powerful and prosperous state, which his son and successor Hamengkubuwono II was unable to maintain. Hamengkubuwono II was contemptuous of the Dutch, who were creating ill-feeling with their oppressive policies. Tension between the new French-backed Governor-General Daendels and the Javanese resulted in a rebellion led by Raden Ronggo. Daendels sent a force to Yogya in 1810, which succeeded in killing Ronggo and forcing the Sultan to step down in favour of his son, Hamengkubuwono III.

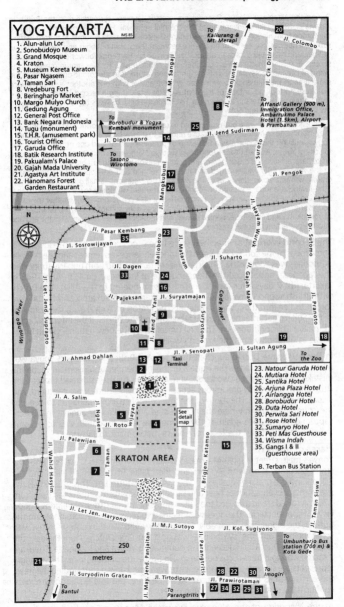

YOGYAKARTA
IMS 85

1. Alun-alun Lor
2. Sonobudoyo Museum
3. Grand Mosque
4. Kraton
5. Museum Kereta Karaton
6. Pasar Ngasem
7. Taman Sari
8. Vredeburg Fort
9. Beringharjo Market
10. Margo Mulyo Church
11. Gedung Agung
12. General Post Office
13. Bank Negara Indonesia
14. Tugu (monument)
15. T.H.R. (amusement park)
16. Tourist Office
17. Garuda Office
18. Batik Research Institute
19. Pakualam's Palace
20. Gajah Mada University
21. Agastya Art Institute
22. Hanomans Forest Garden Restaurant

23. Natour Garuda Hotel
24. Mutiara Hotel
25. Santika Hotel
26. Arjuna Plaza Hotel
27. Airlangga Hotel
28. Borobudur Hotel
29. Duta Hotel
30. Perwita Sari Hotel
31. Rose Hotel
32. Sumaryo Hotel
33. Peti Mas Guesthouse
34. Wisma Indah
35. Gangs I & II (guesthouse area)

B. Terban Bus Station

To Kaliurang & Mt. Merapi

Jl. Colombo

Jl. A.M. Sangaji

Jl. Simanjuntak

Jl. Cik Ditiro

To Affandi Gallery (900 m), Immigration Office, Ambarrukmo Palace Hotel (1.5km), Airport & Prambanan

Jl. Suroto

Jl. Pengok

To Borobudur & Yogya Kembali monument

Jl. Jend Sudirman

Jl. Diponegoro

To Sasono Wirotomo

Jl. Mangkubumi

Jl. Hayam Wuruk

Jl. Dr. Sutomo

N

Jl. Let. Jend Supratno

Winongo River

Jl. Pasar Kembang

Jl. Sosrowijayan

Jl. Malioboro

Jl. Mataram

Jl. Suharto

Code River

Jl. Gajah Mada

Jl. Pranoto

Jl. Dagen

Jl. Pajeksan

Jl. A. Yani

Jl. Suryatmajan

Jl. Suryotomo

Jl. Ahmad Dahlan

Jl. Jend A. Yani

Jl. P. Senopati

Taxi Terminal

Jl. Sultan Agung

To the Zoo

Jl. A. Salim

Jl. Ngasem

Jl. Roto Wijayan

See detail map

Jl. Taman

Jl. Palawijan

KRATON AREA

Jl. Brigjen. Katamso

Jl. Wahid Hasyim

Jl. Let. Jen. Haryono

Jl. M.J. Sutoyo

Jl. Kol. Sugiyono

Jl. Taman Siswa

To Umbunharjo Bus Station (700 m) & Kota Gede

Jl. May. Jend. Panjaitan

Jl. Parangtritis

Jl. Tirtodipuran

Jl. Prawirotaman

To Imogiri

0   250
metres

Jl. Suryodinin Gratan

To Bantul

To Parangtritis

During the Napoleonic Wars, Daendels's successor Janssens surrendered to the British in Batavia in 1811. Taking advantage of this colonial upheaval, Hamengkubuwono II regained the throne from his son. The British Lieutenant-General in Batavia, Thomas Stamford Raffles, subsequently became aware of an alliance between the Sultan of Yogya and the Susuhunan of Solo, and mounted a force to attack the city in 1812. Hamengkubuwono II, never a great success in military matters, was again defeated and deposed. He was sent into exile on the island of Penang (Malaysia), and his pro-British son returned to the throne once more. At the same time as the Hamengkubuwono family were at war with one another, a certain Prince Notokusomo took advantage of the confusion by establishing a second kraton in the city, naming himself Pangeran Pakualam I in 1813. For the next 16 years there were 4 princes in the 2 cities of Yogya and Solo.

Daendels and Raffles were both committed to ruling Java, not just controlling the island, and they introduced numerous administrative reforms that effectively emasculated the sultans of Yogyakarta. Yet this period saw a flowering of Javanese culture, and one of the centres was the city of Yogya. As the historian John Smail writes a "large new court literature grew up...the art of *batik* achieved its classical form and colours (indigo blue and rust brown), the repertoire of the *wayang kulit* was enlarged and its music refined and developed, and a new dance drama, *wayang orang*, grew out of the *wayang kulit* tradition". Smail goes on to note how "the Javanese language was polished into an instrument of superb social precision, so that Javanese came to speak what were almost different dialects, according to whether they were addressing social superiors, inferiors or equals". It is as if the sultans and *priyayi* or aristocracy of Yogyakarta and elsewhere, denied power, had re-directed their energies into the arts and into the perfection of social custom.

The **Second World War** effectively ended the Dutch colonial period in Indonesia, and a focus of the conflict between the independence movement and the colonial authorities was Yogyakarta. Sukarno and Hatta, who had both publicly announced the independence of Indonesia on 17th Aug 1945 in Jakarta, just 2 days after the Japanese had surrendered to the Allies. The Dutch, with British support, managed to re-take Jakarta, and Sukarno and Hatta were forced to flee into the Javanese interior. The kraton of Yogyakarta, the residence of the Sultan, became the centre of rebellion and the city itself the informal capital of the Republic of Indonesia. The first university of the new nation – Gajah Mada – was established within the kraton's walls.

In Dec 1948, the Dutch launched their **second Police Action** and Yogya was taken without a struggle. The leaders of the independence movement made the mistake of believing that world opinion would be on their side and prevent the Dutch from taking any precipitous action. Sukarno and Hatta were captured, and dispatched into exile. The rump of the independence army managed to flee into the countryside, from where they conducted a guerrilla war against the Dutch, capturing Yogya once again in 1949. One year later, Indonesia was to become truly independent and the focus of politics moved back to Jakarta.

Places of interest

Yogya's main street is Jalan Malioboro which runs from N to S. At its S end, the street becomes Jalan Jend. A. Yani and then Jalan Trikora, which leads into the kraton and the grassed square known as the **Alun-alun Lor**. This square was the site of major events such as tiger and buffalo fights, which were staged here from 1769. A raised stand afforded the sultan and any visiting Dutch dignitaries a good view of the spectacle. The tiger was deemed to represent the foreigner and the buffalo, the Indonesian. Invariably, the buffalo would win the contest – often with some help – but the symbolism was lost on the Dutch. Nonetheless, the unperceptive Dutch still succeeded in dominating Yogya and Indonesia. There are 2 sacred *waringin* trees (*Ficus benjamina*) in the centre of the square. The *waringin* represents the sky and the square fence or *waringin kurung* surrounding the trees, the earth with its four quarters. At the same time, the tree is said to symbolize chaotic nature, and the fence human order.

At the NW edge of the Alun-alun Lor is the **Museum Sonobudoyo**. It was

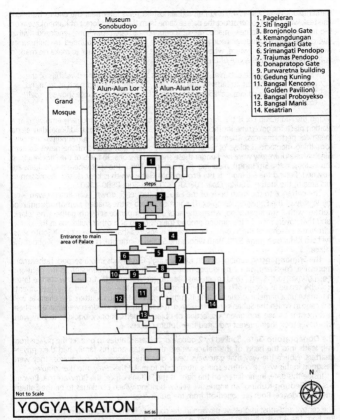

1. Pageleran
2. Siti Inggil
3. Bronjonolo Gate
4. Kemangdungan
5. Srimangati Gate
6. Srimangati Pendopo
7. Trajumas Pendopo
8. Donapratopo Gate
9. Purwaretna building
10. Gedung Kuning
11. Bangsal Kencono (Golden Pavilion)
12. Bangsal Proboyekso
13. Bangsal Manis
14. Kesatrian

YOGYA KRATON

established in 1935 as a centre for Javanese culture, and the collection is housed, appropriately, within a traditional Javanese building. It contains a good selection of Indonesian art, largely Javanese, including a collection of wayang puppets, but also some Balinese woodcarvings. Admission: 300Rp. Open: 0800-1330 Tues-Thurs, 0800-11.15 Fri, 0800-1200 Sat & Sun (see Entertainment, **page 602**). On the SW side of the Alun-alun Lor is the **Grand Mosque**, built in Javanese style, with a wooden frame and a tiled roof.

The Kraton of Yogyakarta

The **Kraton** or *Keraton* (see page 526) of Yogyakarta was one of 3 such palaces that came into existence when the Kingdom of Mataram was partitioned after the Treaty of Giyanti was signed with the VOC in 1755. It has been described as a city within a city; it not only houses the Sultan's Palace but also a maze of shops, markets and private homes supporting many thousands of people. This section only deals with the inner palace; the kraton actually extends far further, 'beginning' one km N at the far end of Jalan Malioboro.

The kraton was started in 1756 by the first Sultan, Mangkubumi (who became

Hamengkubuwono I in 1749) and finished almost 40 years later near the end of his reign. The teak wood used to construct the palace came from the sacred forest of Karangkasem on Mount Kidul. It is largely made up of *pendopo* or open pavilions, enclosed within interconnecting rectangular courtyards. The entire complex is surrounded by high white washed walls. John Crawfurd, who was an assistant to Raffles and later to make his mark in both Siam and Burma, wrote of the kraton in 1811:

> "...The actual palace occupies the centre and is surrounded by the dwellings of the princes, and those of attendants and retainers...The principal approach..is from the N, and through a square..called the *alun-alun*..it is here that the prince shows himself to his subjects..."

Facing the Alun-alun Lor is the **Pageleran**, a large open *pendopo*, originally employed as a waiting place for government officials. Today, this pendopo is used for traditional dance and theatrical performances. There are a number of further *pendopo* surrounding this one, containing mediocre displays of regal clothing. The very first classes of the newly-created Gajah Mada University were held under these shaded pavilions. To the S of the Pageleran, up some steps, is the **Siti Inggil**, meaning 'high ground'. This is the spot where new sultans are crowned. Behind the Siti Inggil is the **Bronjonolo Gate**, which is kept closed. Admission to this area of the kraton: 300Rp. Open: 0800-1300 Mon-Sun, 0800-1100 Fri.

The entrance to the main body of the Palace is further S, down Jalan Rotowijayan – on the W side of the Pageleran complex. The first courtyard is the shaded **Kemangdungan** or **Keben**, with 2 small pendopo, where the *abdi dalem* or palace servants gather. The 'black' sand that covers most of the ground around the pendopo and other buildings in the kraton is from the beaches of the S coast. In this way, it is ensured that the Queen of the South Seas, Nyi Loro Kidul (**see page 570**), with whom the Sultan is intimate, is present throughout the palace.

The **Srimanganti** (meaning 'to wait for the king') **Gate** leads into a second, rather more impressive, courtyard with 2 *pendopos* facing each other; the *Srimanganti* to the right and the *Trajumas* to the left. The former was used to receive important guests while the latter probably served as a court of law. The Srimanganti now contains gongs and other instruments that make up a gamelan orchestra. The Trajumas houses palanquins, litters and chairs as well as a cage in which the Sultan's children played. It is said that the children were placed in here at 8 months of age and given a selection of objects – pens, money, books – to play with; whichever took their interest indicated their future careers.

The **Donapratopo Gate**, flanked by 2 *gupala* or *raksasa* statues to protect the palace from evil, leads into the heart of the palace where the Sultan and his family had their private quarters. Notice the way that gateways never give direct access to courtyards; they were designed in this way to confuse spirits attempting to make their way into the complex.

Inside this gate, immediately on the right, is the Sultan's office, the **Purwaretna**. Beyond it is the **Gedung Kuning**, an impressive yellow building which continues to be the Sultan's private residence. Both are roped-off from the public.

The central and most impressive pavilion in the complex is the **Bangsal Kencono** or Golden Pavilion. The 4 teak pillars in the centre represent the 4 elements. On each is symbolized the 3 religions of Java: Hinduism (a red motif on the top of the columns), Buddhism (a golden design based on the lotus leaf) and Islam (black and gold letters of the Koran). Unfortunately, because the pavilion is roped-off it is difficult to see the pillars clearly. Behind the Golden Pavilion to the W is the **Bangsal Proboyekso** (which contains the armoury) and the **Gedung Keputrian**, the residence of the Sultan's wives and children, both closed to the public. Immediately to the S of the Golden Pavilion is the **Bangsal Manis**, the dining room. **Kemakanan**, a pendopo to the S reached through a set of gates, is used for wayang performances at the end of Ramadan. To the E, through another gate (to the side of which is a large drum made from the wood of the jackfruit tree) there is another courtyard, the **Kesatrian**. The Sultan's sons lived here. In the central pendopo of this courtyard there is another gamelan orchestra on display. Performances are held every Mon and Wed, 1030-1200 (the performance is included in the price of the entrance). At the E side of this courtyard is a collection of paintings, the best being by Raden Saleh, a 19th century court painter who gained a reputation of sorts (and whose grave can be found in Bogor). The photographs of the sultans and their wives are more interesting. North of the Kesatrian is the **Gedung Kopo**, originally the hospital and now a museum housing gifts to the sultans. There are also a pair of rooms given over to memorabilia of Hamengkubuwono IX, who died in 1989. Admission to complex: 1,000Rp. Open: 0830-1300 Mon-Sat, 0830-1400 Sun. Guide obligatory.

Close to the Palace, on Jalan Rotowijayan, is the **Museum Kereta Karaton**, which houses the royal carriages. Admission: 300Rp. Open: 0800-1600 Mon-Sun.

From the Palace it is a 5-10 mins walk to the Taman Sari. Walk S along Jalan Rotowijayan and turn left at the Dewi Srikandi Art Gallery. A number of batik painting galleries are down this road which leads into Jalan Ngasem and then onto the **Pasar Ngasem** or bird market, a fascinating place to wander. Song birds, and particularly turtle doves (Genus *Streptopelia*), are highly-prized by the Javanese. It is sometimes said that wives take second place to a man's **song bird** and that they can cost as much as US$15,000, although this seems hard to believe. Popular are the spotted-necked dove (*Streptopelia chinensis*), the Javan turtle dove (*Streptopelia bitorquata*) and the zebra dove (*Geopelia striata*).

By picking your way through the Pasar Ngasem it is possible to reach the **Taman Sari** or Fragrant Garden, which was known to the Dutch as the Water Castle. This is a maze of underground passageways, ruins and pools built as a pleasure garden by the first Sultan, Mangkubumi, in 1765 at the same time as the Kraton. Surrounded by high walls, it was the sultan's hideaway. He constructed 3 bathing pools – for his children, his *putri* (girls) and himself. A tower allowed the Sultan to watch his 'girls' bathing and to summon them to his company. In addition, there were a series of underwater corridors and even a partly underwater mosque. By climbing the stairs over the entrance gate it is possible to look over the surrounding kampung: this was originally an artificial lake, with a large colonnaded pavilion in the middle. Unfortunately, the gardens were damaged during the British attack on Yogya in 1812 and restoration programmes have been rather unsympathetic. It is difficult to imagine the gardens as they were – as a place of contemplation. Most visitors enter the water gardens from Jalan Taman, through the E gate, which leads into the bathing pool area. This small section is the most complete area of the gardens, having been reconstructed in 1971. Unfortunately, the pools are stagnant and filled with rubbish. The gardens fell into disrepair following the death of Hamengkubuwono III, a process which was accelerated by a devastating earthquake in 1865.

To the SE of the kraton and Taman Sari on Jalan Kol. Sugiyono is the small **Museum Perjuangan** or the struggle for Independence Museum. As the name suggests, this commemorates Indonesia's Declaration of Independence on 17 August 1945 and has a less than inspiring collection of historical artefacts relating to the episode.

The **Vredeburg Fort** lies to the N of the kraton on the E side of Jalan Jend. A. Yani, near the intersection with Jalan P. Senopati. It was built in 1765 by the Dutch as a military barracks. Restored in the late 1980s, the fort has lost what character it may have had, and today looks rather like an American shopping arcade (piped music adds to the effect). Now a museum, the fortress houses a series of dioramas depicting the history of Yogyakarta. Admission: 300Rp. Open: 0830-1330 Tues-Thurs, 0830-1100 Fri, 0830-1200 Sat & Sun. Close by is the **March 1st Monument** which commemorates the taking of Yogya from the Dutch in 1949 by a band of guerillas led by (then) Colonel Suharto. The **Beringharjo Market** is set back from Jalan Jend. A. Yani on the same side of the street and just N of the Vredeburg Fort. A dimly-lit mixed market, it is an interesting and colourful place to wander with fruit, vegetables, fish and meat, batik and household goods – all jumbled together and seemingly fighting for air. Locals warn that numerous pickpockets operate here. On the other side of Jalan Jend. A. Yani is **Margo Mulyo Church**, which dates from 1830.

Across the road from the fort is the **Gedung Agung** built initially in 1823 and then rebuilt in 1869 after the devastating earthquake of 1865. It was the former home of the Dutch Resident in Yogya and is now a state guesthouse. Queen

Diponegoro: prince and early freedom fighter

Prince Diponegoro (1785-1855) was the son of Sultan Hamengkubuwono III. He was both a learned and a devout man, dedicating much of his life to the study of the Islamic scriptures and to prayer. But he was also a man with a mission. He fervently hoped to return Java to its religious roots – by which he meant Islam, not Hinduism or Buddhism – and to cast off the infidel European yoke. Yet, even though he was a devout Muslim he also believed in the power of the Southern Ocean Goddess, Nyi Loro Kidul (see page 570) and he visited the ancient sites of the Mataram Kingdom, hoping that their past power might somehow invigorate him. Prince Diponegoro still remains a symbol of the nationalist movement in Indonesia, and virtually every town in the country has a road named after him.

In 1825, Prince Diponegoro led a rebellion against the colonial powers based in Batavia (Jakarta). This heralded 5 years of war – the Java Wars – during which time half the population of Yogya either fled the sultanate, were killed, or died of starvation. With the defeat of Diponegoro and his supporters in 1830, the Dutch were in a position to exercise yet firmer control. From that moment on, the Javanese courts never regained their authority in the country and became merely centres of the arts and of etiquette. Power in Yogya was from then on in the hands of the Dutch resident.

Elizabeth II of Great Britain, former Prime Minister Nehru of India and Queen Sirikit of Thailand have all stayed here. Between 1946 and 1949 President Sukarno lived in the Gedung Agung, while Yogya was the capital of an emerging independent Indonesia. South of the fort, on Jalan P. Senopati, are 3 impressive **colonial buildings**, the General Post Office (1910), Bank Indonesia and the Bank Negara Indonesia (1923).

North from the Vredeburg Fort, Jalan Jend. A. Yani becomes **Jalan Malioboro**. The origin of the name is shrouded in mystery; there has been a tendency in recent years to associate it with the English Duke of Marlborough, and also with a certain brand of cigarettes. Both explanations are highly unlikely. Whatever the origin of the name, this is the tourist heart of Yogya with shops, restaurants and a number of hotels. The town has the largest student population in Indonesia, and in the evenings they congregate along Jalan Malioboro for intellectual discussions, eating and music, staying there till 4 or 5 o'clock in the morning; it has become known as the 'Malioboro culture'. At its N extension, Jalan Malioboro becomes Jalan Mangkubumi. To the W of Jalan Mangkubumi in Tegalrejo is **Sasono Wirotomo**, or the Diponegoro Museum, a house built on the site of Prince Diponegoro's residence, which was levelled by the Dutch in 1825. The museum contains the princes' memorabilia including a collection of weapons. Open: 0730-1600 Mon-Sun. At the end of Jalan Malioboro is an **obelisk** or *tugu* which marks the N limit of the kraton. The original tugu was erected in 1755, but collapsed; the present structure dates from 1889. Aart van Beek in his book *Life in the Javanese Kraton* explains that this was "the focal point for the Sultan who would sit at an elevated place near the entrance of the palace and meditate by aligning his eyes with the *tugu* and the 3,000 m high Merapi volcano behind, in the distance".

To the E of the town centre on Jalan Sultan Agung, is **Paku Alam's Palace**. A small part of the palace in the East Wing is a museum. Admission: 500Rp. Open: Tues-Sun. Further E still, on Jalan Kusumanegara is the **Gembira Loka Zoo and Amusement Park**. It contains a reasonable range of Indonesian animals including the Komodo dragon, orang utan, tiger and rhinoceros. Open: 0800-1800 Mon-Sun.

Kota Gede, also known as Sar Gede, lies 5 km to the SE of Yogya and was the capital of the 16th century Mataram Kingdom. Nothing remains except for the

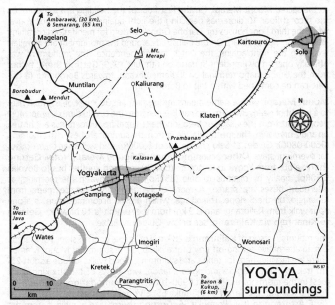

YOGYA surroundings

tombs of the rulers of Mataram. In particular, Panembahan Senopati, the founder of the kingdom and his son Krapyak (the father of the famous Sultan Agung). Senopati's son-in-law, Ki Ageng Mangir is also buried here, his tomb protruding into common ground as he was Senopati's foe. About 100m from the cemetery is the Watu Gilang, a stone on which Senopati killed Ki Ageng Mangir by smashing his head against it. Walled gardens and ponds with fish and a yellow turtle with claimed magical powers ('several hundred years old') add to the atmosphere. Like the tombs of Imogiri (see Excursions, below) visitors must wear traditional Javanese dress which can be hired at the entrance (500Rp). Admission: voluntary contribution. Open: 1030-1200 Mon, 1330-1600 Fri for the actual cemetery but the other areas are open daily. Kota Gede is better known for its **silver workshops** which date back to the 17th century rule of Sultan Agung. Both traditional silver and black (oxydized) silverwork can be purchased. Get to the tombs and workshops by taxi or by town bus (bis kota) no. 8 from Jl. Jend. Sudirman, no. 11 from Umbunharjo terminal and no. 14 from Jl. Prawirotaman.

Excursions

Hindu and Buddhist Monuments including the largest Buddhist monument in the world, **Borobudur** (see page 604), the magnificent Hindu temples at **Prambanan** (see page 612) and the small Hindu temples on the **Dieng Plateau** (see page 625) can all be visited on day trips from Yogya.

The **Yogya Kembali Monument** is situated to the N of the city, on Yogya's ring road, about 7 km from the centre. It is visited more by Indonesian than by foreign tourists, and commemorates the proclamation of Yogya as the capital of the newly-'independent' Indonesia on 6th July, 1945. The monument is a 31m-high cone, symbolizing Mount Meru, and is positioned on an axis that runs N from the kraton, through the Tugu monument, then to the Kembali Monument, and finally to the sacred Mount Merapi. On the first floor of the building is a museum, on the second floor 10 dioramas depicting the fight against the Dutch for Yogya, while the third floor houses the Garbha Graha – a room for meditation containing little but the national flag. On the balustrade around the monument are 40 reliefs recording the fight against the Dutch for independence. The monument was officially opened by President Suharto on 6th July, 1989. **Getting there**: by bus from the Umbunharjo terminal on Jl. Kemerdekaan, towards Borobudur (a visit here can be combined with a trip to Borobudur).

Mount Merapi, whose name means 'giving fire', lies 30 km N of Yogya. It rises to a height of nearly 3,000 m and can be seen from the city. To climb Merapi most people start from the village of **Selo** (on the N slope) from where it is a 3 hr trek up and 2 hrs down. The spectacular views from the summit are best in the morning (0600-0800). Guides at Selo charge about 5,000Rp and will offer their houses for overnight stays. **Other accommodation**: C *Agung Merapi Hotel*. **Getting there**: a bus from Yogya to Kartosuro (600Rp) and then another bus to Boyolali (250Rp), finally by minibus to Selo (350Rp); leave Yogya in the morning, as afternoon buses are scarce. A more challenging climb can be made from Kinahrejo, on the S slope. The village, which has no accommodation, is a one hour walk from Kaliurang, and is 9 km from the summit (a 10 hr walk). **Getting to Kinahrejo via Kaliurang**: see below. Guides available.

The mountain resort of **Kaliurang** is 28 km N of Yogya, on the S slopes of Merapi. It is an alternative setting-off point for a climb to the summit of Mount Merapi. There are facilities here for tennis and swimming. Good walks include a short 2.5 km trek to *Plawangan Seismological Station*, with views of the smoking giant (best in the morning, until about 0900-1000). **Accommodation**: C *Kinasih*, Jl. Boyong Kaliurang; E *Safari*, Jl. Pramuka 55; E *Vogel's Homestay*, Jl. Astomulyo 76; F *Astorenggo II*, Jl. Pramuka 56. **Getting there**: take a minibus from the Terban station on Jl. C. Simanjuntak, ¾ hr (500Rp), or a bus from the Umbulharjo terminal (450Rp).

Imogiri 17 km to the S of Yogya, is the site of the **tombs of the Mataram sultans** as well as the rulers of the Surakarta Kingdom. Perhaps the greatest Mataram king, Sultan Agung (reigned 1613-1646), is buried here. He built the cemetery in 1645, preparing a suitably magnificent site for his grave, on a hillside to the S of his court at Kartasura. It is said that he chose this site so that he had a view of the Queen of the South (the sea goddess Nyi Loro Kidul). To reach his tomb (directly in front at the top of the stairway), and those of 23 other royal personages (Surakarta susuhunans to the left, Yogya sultans to the right) the visitor must stagger up 345 steps. Walk behind the tombs to the top of the hill for fine views of the surrounding countryside. Javanese dress, which can be hired at the site, is required to enter the mausoleums. The Yogyakartan equivalent of Chelsea Pensioners, with turbans and krisses, make sure correct behaviour is observed at all times. Admission: by donation. Open: Agung's tomb is only open 1030-1200 Mon and 1330-1600 Fri, although it is possible to climb up to the site at any time. Some of the tombs are said to be open 1000-1330 Sun. *Festival*: a traditional ceremony to thank God for water involving the filling of 4 bronze water containers – known as 'enceh' – is held every Suro (in Jul), the first month of the Javanese year. **Getting there**: by bus or colt (buses continue on to Parangtritis from here – see below) (300Rp); it is a 1 km walk E to the foot of the stairs from Imogiri town (ask for the *makam* or cemetery). The bus journey is lovely, along a peaceful country road past paddy fields.

Parangtritis is a small seaside resort 28 km S of Yogya and 20 km from Imogiri. It caters largely to Indonesian weekend day-trippers. Warungs line the black sand beach and the bay is enclosed at its E end by cliffs. Horse-drawn carts take tourists on trips along the beach, and the resort has a wonderfully dated and innocent air. An attractive avenue houses warungs and most of the losmen. The beach is a centre for the worship of the South Sea Goddess Nyi Loro Kidul; offerings to her from the Sultan (consisting of food, clothes, the Sultan's hair and cuttings from his nails) are made at the annual *Labuhan* ceremony (see page 599). **NB:** the currents and undertow at the resort are vicious, and swimmers should exercise extreme caution. Inland from Parangtritis are **fresh water swimming pools** fed by natural springs, and to the W are the **Parang Wedang hot springs** (*air panas*), said to cure skin infections (which might keep people from even considering swimming there). Caves can be found to the E of town, most notably **Langse Cave** which is at sea-level and can only be reached along rickety bamboo ladders. The cave is a meditation spot. **Accommodation** (rates on Fri and Sat tend to be higher): **D** *Rang Do*, 300m on from main avenue, popular; **E** *Agung Gardens*, mandi and fan, quite good, on main avenue; **E** *Budi*, small, with mandi, friendly, on main avenue; **E** *Yenny Homestay*, on main avenue; **F** *Widodo*, with mandi and fan, on main avenue. Both *Yennys* and *Agung Gardens* have restaurants selling travellers' food. The latter rents out motorbikes (8,000Rp/day). Entrance to resort area: 300Rp, 1,500Rp for car. **Getting there:** buses to Parangtritis go via Kretek along the main road and over the Opak River (500Rp), or via Imogiri (see above). The longer, rougher, trip via Imogiri passes through beautiful rural scenery.

There are some less frequented **beaches** to the E of Parangtritis, not far from the town of Kemadang – Baron, Kukup and Krakal. Snorkeling is reported to be reasonable at **Krakal**, a white sand beach stretching for 5 km (which developers have their eye on). Swimming is relatively safe at **Baron** – it is protected from the sea and currents by coral ridges. **Kukup** is a white sand beach with strong currents.

Jatijajar Caves are to be found in the side of a strange ridge of jagged hills, SW of the small town of Gombong and 157 km from Yogya. Outside the entrance is a large concrete dinosaur which acts as a spout for the underground spring (bathing pools here). Inside, there are stalactites and stalagmites, springs and theatrical statues of human beings and animals which apparently recount the history of the kingdom of Pahaharan. Admission: 450Rp. **Getting there:** 7 km W of Gombong, turn to the left, 13 km off the main road. Minibus from Kebumen (50 km).

Karang Bolong Beach near to the Jatijajar Caves, is known as a site for collecting bird's nests for the soup of the same name (see page 333).

Tours For visitors without their own transport, the best way to see the sights around Yogya is to join a tour – travelling on public transport can be a hassle and is only recommended for those without any time restrictions. Yogya has more than its fair share of companies offering tours to the sights in and around the city. Listed below are a selection on offer; visit the tourist office for the latest information.
Tours include: **city tours** to the Kraton, Taman Sari, batik factories, wayang performances and Kota Gede silver workshops. **Out of town tours** to Prambanan, Borobudur, the Dieng Plateau, Kaliurang, Parangtritis and Mount Merapi. The least expensive companies charge 10,000Rp/day.

Festivals Being an ancient kingdom and a sultanate, Yogya is host to a number of colourful festivals. Apr: *Grebeg Syawal* (moveable – end of Ramadan). The day before is *Lebaran Day*, when the festivities begin with children parading through the streets. The next day, the military do likewise around the town and then a tall tower of groceries is carried through the streets, the provisions being distributed to the waiting people.
Apr/May: *Labuhan* (moveable – 26th day of 4th Javanese month Bakdomulud) (also held in Feb and Jul). Offerings made to the South Sea Goddess Nyi Loro Kidul. Especially colourful ceremony at Parangtritis, where offerings are floated on a bamboo palanquin and floated on the sea. Similar rituals are held on Mounts Merapi and Lawu.

Courtship Javanese-style – the *Lamaran*

Many elements of traditional Javanese life are disappearing in the wake of Western-style commercialization. **Lamaran** – the formal request by the parents of the groom to the bride's parents – is one such traditional ceremony. Like the Javanese language, it is laden with hidden meanings and metaphors.

Initially, the groom's family visits the bride's to broach the subject of marriage. But this must be done according to elaborate rules, and there should be no direct reference to the purpose of the visit. The father of the prospective groom might explain, opaquely, that 'frost in the morning means rain in the evening', implying that he has come to discuss a 'cool' matter, which should not stir up strong emotions. The bride's father might reply by exclaiming that his daughter is a 'good for nothing', a spoilt girl and not yet an adult.

2 or 3 visits later, the matter is finally settled and a meeting is arranged at the prospective bride's house. This occasion is known as the *nontoni* (the 'looking over'). Again governed by tradition and formality, the girl serves her husband-to-be a cup of tea, avoiding any eye-contact. In the past, this would have been the young man's – or probably a boy's – first opportunity of stealing a sideways glance at his bride. The marriage itself is called the *panggihan* and is held at the bride's home.

Jun: *Tamplak Wajik* (moveable) ritual preparing of 'gunungan' or rice mounds in the Kraton, to the accompaniment of rhythmic gamelan and chanting to ward off evil spirits. *Grebeg Besar* (moveable) a ceremony to celebrate the Muslim offering feast of Idul Adha. At 2000 the 'gunungan' mound of decorated rice is processed from the inner court of the Kraton to the Grand Mosque, where it is blessed and then distributed to the people.

Jul: *Siraman Pusaka* (moveable – first month of the Javanese year) ritual cleansing ceremony, when the sultan's heirlooms are cleaned. The water used is said to have magical powers. *Anniversary of Bantul* (20th) celebrated with a procession of sacred heirlooms in Paseban Square, Bantul, S Yogyakarta.

Aug: *Kraton Festival* (moveable), range of events including ancient ritual ceremonies, cultural shows, craft stalls. *Turtle dove singing contest* (2nd week) a national contest for the Hamengkubuwono X trophy, held in the S alun-alun from 0700. *Saparan Gamping* (moveable), held in Ambarketawang Gamping village, 5 km W of Yogya. This ancient festival is held to ensure the safety of the village. Sacrifices are made of life-sized statues of a bride and groom, made of glutinous rice and filled with brown sugar syrup, symbolizing human blood.

Sept: *Rebo Wekawan* (2nd), held at the crossing of the Opak and the Gajah Wong rivers, where Sultan Agung is alleged to have met the Goddess Nyi Loro Kidul. *Sekaten* (moveable – the 5th day of the Javanese month Mulud) a week long festival honouring the Prophet Mohammad's birthday. The festival starts with a mid-night procession of the royal servants (abdi dalem), carrying two sets of gamelan instruments from the kraton to the Grand Mosque. Here they are placed in opposite ends of the building, and played simultaneously. A fair is held before and during Sekatan in the Alun-alun Lor. *Tamplak Wajik* (5th day of Sekaten). Ritual preparation of 'gunungan' or mounds of rice, decorated with vegetables, eggs and cakes at the palace, to the accompaniment of a gamelan orchestra and chanting to ward off evil spirits. *Grebeg Mulud*, religious festival celebrating the birthday of Mohammad, and the climax of Sekatan. It is held on the last day of the festival (12th day of Mulud) and features a parade of the palace guard in the early morning from the Kemandungan (in the kraton) to the Alun-alun Lor.

Accommodation A+ *Natour Garuda*, Jl. Malioboro 60, T 86353, F 63074, a/c, restaurant, pool, large hotel block, with new addition and good facilities, central location; **A+-A** *Sriwedari*, Jl. Adisucipto, T 88288, a/c, restaurant, E of town; **A** *Ambarrukmo Palace*, Jl. Adisucipto, T 88488, F 63283, a/c, several restaurants, large pool, large, ugly block, one of the first international hotels to be built in Yogya in the 60s and it shows in clumsy design and decoration, inconvenient location out of town on the road to Borobudur; **A** *Mutiara* (new wing), Jl. Malioboro 18, T 4531, F 61201, a/c, overpriced restaurant, pool, rooms and food overpriced, but central position; **A** *Puri Artha*, Jl.Cendrawasih 38, T 5934, a/c, restaurant, pool, Javanese-style hotel with rooms set around a courtyard; **A** *Santika*, Jl. Jend. Sudirman 19, T 63036, F 62047, a/c, restaurant, good pool, new and plush with reasonable rates; **A**

Yogya International, Jl. Adisucipto 38, T 64750, F 64171, a/c, restaurant, pool, E of town.

A good selection of middle range accommodation is to be found on Jl. Prawirotaman, S of the Kraton. The hotels are the best of their kind in Yogya. The area's single disadvantage is that it is not very central but the street provides several restaurants, shops, travel agents and cultural shows. **B** *Airlangga*, Jl. Prawirotaman 6-8, T 63344, F 71427, a/c, restaurant, pool, hot water, good value with friendly atmosphere, price includes breakfast, rec; **B** *Arjuna Plaza*, Jl. P. Mangkubumi 48, T 3063, a/c, pool, rooms are small and rather dark; **B** *Mutiara* (old wing), Jl. Malioboro 18, T 4531, F 61201, a/c, small restaurant, access to pool (at new wing), rather tatty and overrun by mice but with a central location; **B** *New Batik Palace*, Jl. Mangkubumi 46, T 2229, a/c, restaurant, pool, rather grim, price includes breakfast; **B** *Sahid Garden*, Jl. Babarsari, off Jl. Adisucipto, T 3697, a/c, restaurant, pool, E of town with range of accommodation; **B-C** *Duta*, Jl. Prawirotaman 20/26, T 5064, some a/c, small pool, friendly atmosphere, price includes breakfast, rec; **C** *Hotel Asia Afrika*, Jl. Pasar Kembang 21, T 4489, a/c, restaurant, pool, small rooms set around an attractive courtyard, price includes breakfast; **C** *Old Batik Palace*, Jl. Pasar Kembang 29, T 2149, a/c, price includes breakfast, attached mandi, attractive courtyard, rec; **C** *Perwita Sari*, Jl. Prawirotaman 23, some a/c, good pool; **C** *Rose*, Jl. Prawirotaman 22, T 87991, a/c, big pool, hot water, set around a courtyard, scruffy rooms, but with pleasant atmosphere, price includes breakfast, free pick-up from airport, tours arranged, rec; **C** *Sumaryo*, Jl. Prawirotaman 22, T 2852, pool, price includes breakfast, large rooms, clean and friendly, attached mandi; **C-D** *Kenchana*, Jl. Pasar Kembang 15, T 3352, some a/c, modern, clean and comfortable, attached shower; **C-D** *Sri Timor*, Jl. Parangtritis 51, some a/c, price includes breakfast; **C-D** *Wisma Indah*, Jl. Prawirotaman, T 88021, F 88021, some a/c, pool, price includes breakfast. Other middle range accommodation on Jl. Pasar Kembang includes: **D** *Asia Afrika Guesthouse*, Jl. Pasar Kembang 9, T 87654, some a/c, central courtyard, attached showers; **D** *Borobudur*, Jl. Prawirotaman 5, T 63977, F 63203, central courtyard, popular; **D** *El Ratna*, Jl. Pasar Kembang 17A, T 61851, big rooms, with sitting area, fan and mandi; **D** *Peti Mas*, Jl. Dagen 39, T 4038, some a/c, restaurant (slow service), pool, central and good value, rec.

Budget accommodation is to be found near the train station around Jl. Pasar Kembang and Jl. Sosrowijayan. **D** *Oryza*, Jl. Sosrowijayan 49, T 2605, price includes breakfast; **E** *Aziatic*, Jl. Sosrowijayan 6, price includes breakfast, all rooms off a central hallway, friendly management, tours arranged here, rec; **E** *Indonesia*, Jl. Sosrowijayan 9, average rooms, some with attached mandi; **E** *Kartika*, Jl. Sosrowijayan 10, T 62016, some with attached mandi; **F** *Rama*, Gang 1/32A, small dark rooms.

Restaurants Central Javanese cooking uses a lot of sugar, tapped from the *aren* palm which produces 'red' sugar. Typical dishes include *tape* (a sweet dish made from fermented cassava), and *ketan* (sticky rice). Yogya specialities include *ayam goreng* (fried chicken) and *gudeg* (rice, jackfruit, chicken and an egg cooked in a spicy coconut sauce).

Indonesian: *Bu Citro*, Jl. Adisucipto Km 9, opposite the entrance to the airport, serves an excellent *gudeg*, the Yogya speciality; *Happy*, Jl. Jend. A. Yani 95, speciality *ayam goreng*; ♦♦*Hanoman's Forest Garden*, Jl. Prawirotaman 9, includes entertainment (see below); ♦*Shinta*, Jl. Malioboro 5, also serves Chinese food; *Sina Budi*, Jl. Mangkubumi 41, popular for Padang food; *Suharti*, Jl. Adisucipto 208, excellent *ayam goreng*; ♦*Tante Lies*, corner of Jl. Prawirotaman, excellent cheap Indonesian food and popular meeting place for travellers (mostly Dutch), cheap tours organized from here.

Foodstalls: on the E side of Jl. Mangkubumi, along Jl. Malioboro (best after 0900) and outside Pasar Beringharjo (excellent *martabak*), also along NE corner of the alun-alun.

Other Asian: ♦♦*Gita Buana*, Jl. Diponegoro 52B, small a/c restaurant serving Chinese and International food; *Sintawang*, Jl. Magelang 9, excellent Chinese and seafood; *Yashinoki*, Jl. Adisucipto 6, Japanese and some Indonesian.

International: ♦♦*Gita Buana*, Jl. Adisucipto 169 and Jl. Diponegoro 52A. A/c restaurant serving steaks and salads; ♦♦*Griya Bujana*, Jl. Prawirotaman, range of Indonesian, Chinese and International food; *Kentucky Fried Chicken*, Jl. Malioboro 133; ♦♦*Palm House*, Jl. Prawirotaman, range of Indonesian, Chinese and International food, rec; *Prambanan*, Jl. Prawirotaman; ♦♦*Legian*, Jl. Perwakilan 9, roof-top restaurant overlooking Jl. Malioboro, slow service but worth waiting for, good-value food (plus cocktails); ♦*Lima*, Jl. Sosrowijayan Gang 1, good value.

Travellers' food: ♦*Ana's*, Jl. Sosrowijayan Gang 2, good pancakes, yoghurts etc.; ♦*Busis Garden*, Gang 1; *Capuccino*, Jl. Pasar Kembang 17, restaurant and bar; ♦*Mamas*, Jl. Pasar Kembang 71, long-established and still popular; ♦*Manna*, Jl. Dagen 60; ♦*Superman New and Old*, Jl. Sosriwijayan, Gang 1, good breakfasts. rec; *Eko French Grill*, Jl. Sosrowijayan Gang 1; ♦*Foodstall* at the N end of Gang 1, rec.

Entertainment Information on shows can be obtained from the tourist office, travel agents or from hotels. There is a wide choice of performances and venues, with something happening somewhere every night. Details given below may have changed since going to press.

Gamelan: performances at the Kraton 1030-1200 Mon and Wed; *Ambarrukmo Palace Hotel* lobby 1030-1230 and 1600-1800 Mon-Sun.

Wayang kulit: performances held at the *French Grill*, Arjuna Plaza Hotel, Jl. Mangkubumi 48, 1900-2100 Tues (3,000Rp); *Agastya Art Institute*, Jl. Gedongkiwo,1500-1700 Sun-Fri (1,800Rp); *Ambarrukmo Palace Hotel*, Jl. Adisucipto 2000-2100 Thurs; *Hanoman's Forest Garden*, Jl. Prawirotaman, 2030-2130 Wed and Fri; *Museum Sonobudoyo*, Alun-alun Lor, 2000-2200 Tues-Sun; *Ambarbudaya* (Yogya's Craft Centre), Jl. Adisucipto, across from Ambarrukmo Palace Hotel, 2130-2230 Mon, Wed and Sat; *Auditorium Radio Republic Indonesia*, Jl. Gejayan, every second Sat of the month, 2100-0530; *Kraton* (South Palace Square-Alun-alun Selaton), every second Sat of the month, 2100-0530.

Wayang golek: performances held at the *French Grill*, Arjuna Plaza Hotel, Jl. Mangkubumi 48, 1900-2100 Sat (3,000Rp); *Ambarrukmo Palace Hotel*, Jl. Adisucipto, 2000-2100 Mon; *Hanoman's Forest Garden*, Jl. Prawirotoman, 1930-2130 Mon and Thurs (2,000Rp); *Nitour Travel Agency*, Jl. Ahmad Dahlan 71, 1100-1300 Mon-Sat (1,800Rp); *Agastya Art Institute*, Jl. Gedongkiwo, 1500-1700 Sat (1,800Rp).

Wayang orang: at the Kraton every Sun 1030-1200 (1,000Rp), nightly performances at the T.H.R. (the People's Amusement Park), Jl. Brig Jen. Katamso (1,000Rp); *French Grill*, Arjuna Plaza Hotel, Jl. Mangkubumi 48, 1900-2100 Thurs; *Hanoman's Forest Garden*, Jl. Prawirotaman, 98, 1930-2100 Tues and Sat; *Ambarrukmo Palace Hotel*, Jl. Adisucipto, 2000-2100 Tues, Fri and Sun.

Ramayana: *Arjuna Plaza Hotel*, Jl. Mangkubumi, 1900-2100 Thurs; *Ambarrukmo Palace Hotel*, Jl. Adisucipto, Mon, Wed, Sat 2000. Open-air performances at **Prambanan**, held during full moon, starting at 1900 and year-round at the Trimurti covered Theatre, also at Prambanan, on Tues, Wed and Thurs, 1930-2130. (**see page 616**). There are also regular performances at *Dalem Pujokusuman*, Jl. Katamso, Mon, Wed and Fri, 2000-2200; and at the *Purawisata Open Theatre*, Jl. Katamso, Mon-Sun 2000-2100.

Modern Javanese dance: *Hanoman's Forest Garden*, Jl. Prawirotaman, Sat.

Ketoprak: traditional Javanese drama at the auditorium of RRI Studio Nusantara 2, Jl. Gejayan 2030, twice a month (see Tourist Board for details).

Batik lessons: at the *Batik Research Centre* on Jl. Kusumanegara 2, plus a good exhibition. *Lucy Batik* on Jl. Sosrowijayan Gang 1. *Gapura Batik*, Jl. Taman KP 3/177, 3 or 5 day courses (near main entrance to Taman Sari).

Batik art galleries: 3 batik painters from Yogya have achieved an international reputation – Affandi, Amri Yahya and Sapto Hudoyo. The *Affandi Gallery* is at Jl. Adisucipto 167 (town bus 8) on the banks of the Gajah Wong River. It lies next to the home of the Indonesian expressionist painter Affandi (1907-1990). The gallery displays work by Affandi and his daughter Kartika. Open: 0900-1600 Mon-Sun. The *Amri Gallery* is at Jl. Gampingan 67 and *Sapto Hudoyo* has a studio on Jl. Adisucipto.

Modern art gallery: *Cemeti*, Jl. Ngadisuryan 7A (near the Taman Sari) has changing exhibits of good contemporary Indonesian and Western artists.

Samba music: *Slomoth*, Jl. Parangtritis 109, 2000-2230 Wed and Sat.

Cinemas: Ratih, Jl. P. Mangkubumi 26; Indra, Jl. Jend. A. Yani 13A.

Sports **Golf**: Adisucipto Golf Course (9 holes), T 3647, 9 km out of town on Prambanan road. **Swimming**: hotels allow non-guests to use their pools, e.g. *Ambarrukmo Palace*, Jl. Adisucipto (3,500Rp); *Colombo*, Jl. Gejayan (700Rp); *New Batik Palace*, Jl. Mangkubumi (750Rp); *Sri Wedari*, Jl. Adisucipto (1,250Rp). **Panahan:** traditional archery, performed to celebrate the birth of Sultan Hamengkubuwono X.

Shopping Yogya offers an enormous variety of Indonesian handicrafts, usually cheaper than can be found in Jakarta. Avoid using a guide or becak driver to take you to a shop as you will be charged more – their cut. The main shopping street, Jl. Malioboro also attracts more than its fair share of 'tricksters' who maintain, for example, that their exhibition of batik paintings is from Jakarta and is in its last day, so prices are good...don't believe a word of it. The W side of Jl. Malioboro is lined with stalls selling batik, wayang, topeng, woven bags... Note that the quality of some of the merchandise can be very poor – for example the batik shirts – something that may be difficult to see at night.

'**Antiques**': several shops along Jl. Tirtodipuran and Jl. Prawirotaman (S of the Kraton) and Jl. Malioboro sell a range of curios.

Batik: Yogya is a centre for both batik *tulis* and batik *cap* (**see page 536**) and it is widely available in lengths (which can be made up into garments) or as ready-made clothes. There are a number of shops along Jl. Malioboro. Contemporary 'European' fashions can be found in a couple of shops on Jl. Sosrowijayan Gang 1. Batik factories are to be found on Jl. Tirtodipuran S of the Kraton, where visitors can watch the cloth being produced. Batik paintings are on sale everywhere, with some of the cheapest available within the Kraton walls. There are some more shops down Jl. Prawirotaman and off Jl. Malioboro.

Bookshops: *Sari Ilmu*, Jl. Malioboro 117-119 for maps and guidebooks; *Prawirotaman International bookstore*, Jl. Prawirotaman 30. **Book exchange:** Jl. Sosrowijayan, opposite Gang 2.

Handicrafts: Government crafts centre – *Desa Kerajinan* on Jl. Adisucipto (Jl. Solo) and some shops along Jl. Prawirotaman, as well as the stalls lining Jl. Malioboro. **Ikat:** Jadin Workshop, Jl. Modang 70B. **Leatherware:** bags, suitcases, sandals and belts. All made from buffalo, cow or goat. Jl. Malioboro has a selection of roadside stalls as well as several shops specializing in leather goods. **Pottery:** earthenware is produced in a number of specialist villages around Yogya. Best known is Kasongan, 7 km S of the city, which produces pots, vases and assorted kitchen utensils. Get there by bus towards Bantul; the village is 700 m off the main road.

Silverware: in Kota Gede, to the SE of the city (most shops are to be found along Jl. Kemesan). Two major workshops – *M.D. Silver* and *Tom's Silver*. Two shops on Jl. Prawirotaman. **Topeng masks:** widely available from stalls along Jl. Malioboro and near the Taman Sari. **Wayang kulit** and **wayang golek:** widely available from roadside stalls along Jl. Malioboro.

Local transport **Andong** (horse-drawn carriage): traditional carriages with 4 wheels, the 2 in front being smaller, drawn by either 1 or 2 horses. They wait outside the railway station, the Kraton and next to the Bird Market. **Becak:** probably the best way to get around. Agree a price before boarding: approximately 500Rp/km – or charter one for the day, approximately 1,000Rp/hr. Beware of the drivers who seem to offer a very good price; they will almost certainly take you to batik or silverware shops. **Bemos and colts:** can be rented from Jl. Pasar Kembang 85. **Bicycle hire:** along Jl. Pasar Kembang or Gang 1 or 2, approximately 2,000Rp/day. **Bus:** Yogya town buses (*bis kota*) travel 17 routes criss-crossing the town; the tourist office sometimes has bus maps available (150Rp). Minibuses leave from the Terban station on Jl. C. Simanjuntak, NE of the train station. **Car hire:** self-drive from **Fortuna**, Jl, Jlagran 20-21 and on Jl. Pasar Kembang. **National Car Rental** from *Sahid Garden Hotel*; **Bali Car Rental**, by the airport. 50,000-70,000Rp/day. A driver will cost an extra 20,000Rp/day. **Motorbike hire:** along Jl. Pasar Kembang and at **Fortuna**, Jl. Jlagran 20-21; approximately 10,000Rp/day. **Taxi:** there are a few metered taxis, or taxis can be rented (from Jl. Pasar Kembang 85, or from Jl. Senopati, near the Post Office) for trips around town (7,000Rp/hour) or for longer trips to Borobudur, Prambanan etc. (30,000-50,000Rp/day).

Banks & money changers Artamas Buana Jati, Jl. P. Mangkubumi 4; **BNI**, near General Post Office, on Jl. Senopati; **Bumi Daya**, Jl. Sudirman 42; **CV Intan Biru Laut**, Jl. Malioboro 18; **Dagang Negara**, Jl. Sudirman 67; **Intrabilex**, Adisucipto Airport; **Niaga**, Jl. Jend. Sudirman 13; **Summa**, Jl. Laksda Adisucipto 63. Money changer next to the *Hotel Asia Afrika*, Jl. Pasar Kembang 17. Two money changers on Jl. Prawirotaman.

Embassies & consulates France, Jl. Sagan 1.

Useful addresses **General Post Office:** Jl. Senopati 2; **Post Office:** Jl. Pasar Kembang 37 (for international phone calls and faxes). **Telephone office:** Jl. Yos Sudarso 9. **Area code:** 0274. **Hospital:** Bethesda, Jl. Sudirman 81, T 81774. **Immigration Office:** Jl. Adisucipto Km 10, T 4948 (out of town on the road to the airport). **Police:** Jl. Pisang I, T 88234. **Tourist police:** Tourist Information, Jl. Malioboro.

Airline offices Bouraq, Jl. Mataram 60, T 62664; **Garuda**, Jl. P. Mangkubumi 56, T 4400; **Merpati**, Jl. Jend. Sudirman 9-11, T 4272; **Sempati**, Natour Garuda Hotel, Jl. Malioboro.

Tour companies & travel agents *Intan Pelangi*, Jl. Malioboro 18, T 62985; *Jaya*, Jl. Sosrowijayan 23; *Natrabu*, Ambarrukmo Palace Hotel, Jl. Adisucipto, T 88488; *Nitour*, Jl. KHA Dahlan 71, T 3165; *Pacto*, Ambarrukmo Palace, Jl. Adisucipto, T 62906; *Sahid*, Hotel Sahid Garden, Jl. Babarsari, T 87078; *Satriavi*, Ambarrukmo Palace Hotel, Jl. Adisucipto, T 88488; *Setia*, Jl. Adisucipto 169, T 62836; *Tante Lies*, Jl. Prawirotaman, 'Heri' in this restaurant organizes inexpensive tours around Java; *Vayatour*, Ambarrukmo Palace Hotel, Jl. Adisucipto, T 88488; *Vista Express*, Natour Garuda Hotel, Jl. Malioboro, T 61353. There are a number of companies around Jl. Sosrowijayan and Jl. Pasar Kembang as well as Jl. Prawirotaman who will organize onward travel by *bis malam* and train. Many of the hotels offer similar services.

Tourist offices Tourist Information office, Jl. Malioboro 16, T 2812 ext 30. Free maps of the town and environs, information on cultural events, bus routes etc. One of the most helpful tourist offices in Indonesia. Open: 0800-2100 Mon-Sat.

Transport to & from Yogyakarta 565 km from Jakarta, 327 km from Surabaya. **By air**: Adisucipto Airport is 8 km E of town, along Jl. Adisucipto (aka Jl. Solo). *Transport to town*: minibuses from the Terban station on Jl. Simanjuntak travelling to Prambanan pass the airport (400Rp), a taxi costs 7,500Rp. Regular connections on Garuda/Merpati, Sempati and Bouraq with other destinations in Java, Sumatra, Kalimantan, Sulawesi, Bali, Lombok, Nusa Tenggara, Maluku and Irian Jaya (**see page 1006** for route map). **By train**: the railway station is on Jl. Pasar Kembang. Regular connections with Jakarta 12 hrs (the night train leaves at 1930 and arrives at 0630), Bandung 9 hrs, Solo 1 hr, and with Surabaya 8 hrs (**see page 1012** for timetable). **Warning**: thieves are notorious on the overnight train between Jakarta and Surabaya via Yogya. **By bus**: the Umbunharjo bus station is 4 km SE of the city centre, at the intersection of Jl. Veteran and Jl. Kemerdekaan. Fastest services are at night (*bis malam*). Check times at the bus station or at the tourist office on Jl. Malioboro. Regular connections with Jakarta 9 hrs and Bandung 6 hrs. To get to Solo, 1½-2 hrs, or N to Semarang, 3½ hrs, it is better to take a local bus, which can be hailed on the main roads. A/c buses from various agents along Jl. Sosrowijayan (board bus here too) or from Jl. Mangkubumi to Jakarta, Bandung, Surabaya and Denpasar. **By colt**: private company colt offices are on Jl. Diponegoro, to the W of the Tugu Monument. Seats are bookable and pick-up from hotels can be arranged. Regular connections with Solo and Semarang (5,000Rp).

YOGYA TO MAGELANG, via Borobudur

Travelling N from Yogya, the road passes to the W of Mount Merapi before reaching, after 41 km, the town of Magelang. Surrounded on all sides by towering volcanoes – Mounts Merapi, Sumbing and Merbabu – Magelang is the nearest urban centre of any size to the Buddhist monument of Borobudur. The turn-off for Borobudur is S of Magelang and just N of the country town of Muntilan. The monument is 40 km from Yogya.

Borobudur

The travel business is only too ready to attach a superlative to the most mundane of sights. However, even travellers of a less jaundiced and world-weary age had little doubt after they set their eyes on this feast of stone that they were witnessing one of the wonders of the world. The German traveller Johan Scheltema in his 1912 book *Monumental Java* wrote that he felt the "fructifying touch of heaven; when tranquil love descends in waves of contentment, unspeakable satisfaction".

Borobudur was built when the Sailendra Dynasty of Central Java was at the height of its military and artistic powers. Construction of the monument is said to have taken about 75 years, spanning 4 or 5 periods from the end of the 8th century to the middle of the 9th century. Consisting of a 9-tiered 'mountain' rising to 34.5 metres, Borobudur is decorated with 5 km of superbly executed reliefs – some 1,500 in all – ornamented with 500 statues of the Buddha, and constructed of 1,600,000 andesite stones.

The choice of site on the densely populated and fertile valleys of the Progo and Elo rivers seems to have been partially dictated by the need for a massive labour force. Every farmer owed the kings of Sailendra a certain number of days labour each year – a labour tax – in return for the physical and spiritual protection of the ruler. Inscriptions from the 9th and 10th centuries indicate that there were several hundred villages in the vicinity of Borobudur. So, after the rice harvest, a massive labour force of farmers, slaves and others could be assembled to work on the monument. It is unlikely that they would have been resistant to working on the edifice – by so doing they would be accumulating merit and accelerating their progress towards nirvana.

Art historians have also made the point that the location of Borobudur at the confluence of the Elo and Progo rivers was probably meant to evoke, as Dumarçay says, "the most sacred confluence of all, that of the Ganga (Ganges) and the Yumna (Jumna)", in India. Finally, the monument is also close to a hill, just N of Magelang, called Tidar. Although hardly on the scale of the volcanoes that ring the Kedu Plain, this hill – known as the 'Nail of Java' – lies at the geographic centre of Java and has legendary significance. It is said that it was only after Java, which was floating on the sea, had been nailed to the centre of the earth that it became inhabitable.

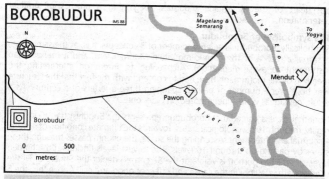

Borobudur: what's in a name?

The origin and meaning of the name Borobudur has been a source of dispute for many years. Some experts have maintained that it is derived from the Sanskrit words *Vihara Buddha Uhr*, meaning 'Buddhist Monastery on the Hill', and certainly it is situated on a slight rise above the surrounding plain. Other authorities reject this explanation, believing that *boro* is derived from the word *biara*, which means *vihara* or monastery, while *budur* is a place name, giving the monument the title 'Monastery of Budur'. De Casparis meanwhile, who uncovered a stone dated to the year 842 with the inscription *Bhumisambharabhudara* carved upon it, plumps for yet another explanation. The inscription means the 'Mountain of Virtues of the Ten Stages of the Bodhisattva', and he believes that the name is taken from the last part, *Bharabhudara*.

The temple is made of grey andesite – a volcanic rock – which was not quarried but 'mined' from river beds. Huge boulders are washed down volcano slopes during flood surges and these were cut to size and transported to the building site. The blocks were linked by double dovetail clamps – no mortar was used in construction. It is thought that the sculpture was done *in situ*, after the building work had been completed. The stone was then covered in stucco and probably painted.

The large base platform was added at a later date and remains something of an enigma. It actually hides a panel of reliefs, known as the 'hidden foot'. Some authorities believe that this series of reliefs was always meant to be hidden, because they depict earthly desires (this was true of a similar series of panels at Angkor Wat in Cambodia). Other art historians maintain that this is simply too elaborate an explanation and that the base was added as a buttress. Inherent design faults meant that even during initial construction, subsidence was probably already setting in. In 1885 these subterranean panels were uncovered by Yzerman to be photographed, only then to be covered up again to ensure the stability of the monument.

Aspects of Borobudur's design were brilliant: the removal of rain-water, for example, was achieved by the use of gargoyles placed on the diagonals of the monument, transferring water down each level to the base, where it was collected in a gutter before being soaked up by the earth. Despite annual rainfall of 1800 mm/year, this system would have coped admirably. Unfortunately, the latent instability of the overall structure led to subsidence, which in turn caused cracks to appear between the closely-laid stones, and this permitted water to seep into the heart of the man-made mountain, beginning a process of gradual deterioration.

The symbolism of Borobudur
Symbolically, Borobudur is an embodiment of 3 concepts. It is, at the same time, a *stupa*, a replica of the cosmic mountain *Mount Meru*, and a *mandala* (an instrument to assist meditation). Archaeologists, intent on interpreting the meaning of the monument, have had to contend with the fact that the structure was built over a number of periods spanning three-quarters of a century. As a result, new ideas were superimposed on older ones.

Nonetheless, it is agreed that Borobudur represents the Buddhist transition from reality, through 10 psychological states, towards the ultimate condition of *nirvana* – spiritual enlightenment. Ascending the stupa, the pilgrim passes through these states by passing up through 10 levels. The lowest levels (including the hidden layer, of which a portion is visible at the SE corner) depict the Sphere of Desire (*Kamadhatu*), describing the cause and effect of good and evil. Above this, the 5 lower quadrangular galleries with their multitude of reliefs (put end to end they would measure 2.5 km), represent the Sphere of Form (*Rupadhatu*). These are in stark contrast to the bare upper circular terraces with their half-hidden Buddhas within perforated stupas, representing the Sphere of Formlessness (*Arupadhatu*) – nothingness or nirvana.

The monument was planned so that the pilgrim would approach it from the E, along a path which started at Candi Mendut (see below). Architecturally, it is horizontal in conception, and in this sense contrasts with the strong verticality of Prambanan. However, architectural values were of less importance than the sculpture, and in a sense the monument was just an easel for the reliefs. Consideration had to be made for the movement of people, and the width of the galleries was dictated by the size of the panel, which had to be seen at a glance. It is evident that some of the reliefs were conceived as narrative 'padding', ensuring that continuity of story line was achieved. To 'read' the panels, start from the E stairway, keeping the monument on your right. This clockwise circumambulation is known as *pradaksina*. It means that while the balustrade or outer reliefs are read from left to right, those on the main, inner wall are viewed from right to left. The reliefs were carved in such a way that they are visually more effective when observed in this way.

The reliefs and the statues of the Buddha
The inner (or retaining) wall of the first gallery is $3\frac{1}{2}$ m high and contains 2 series of reliefs, one above the other, each of 120 panels. The upper panels relate events in the historic Buddha's life – the *Lalitavistara* – from his birth to the sermon at Benares, while the lower depict his former lives, as told in the *Jataka* tales. The upper and lower reliefs on the balustrades (or outer wall) also relate Jataka stories as well as *Avadanas* – another Buddhist text, relating previous lives of the Bodhisattvas – in the NE corner. After viewing this first series of reliefs, climb the E stairway – which was only used for ascending – to the next level. The retaining wall of the second gallery holds 128 panels in a single row 3 m high. This, along with the panels on the retaining walls and (some of the) balustrades of the third gallery, tells the story of Sudhana in search of the Highest Wisdom – one of the most important Buddhist texts, otherwise known as *Gandawyuha*. Finally, the retaining wall of the fourth terrace has 72 panels depicting the *Bhadratjari* – a drawn out conclusion to the story of Sudhana, during which he vows to follow in the footsteps of Bodhisattva Samantabhadra. In total there are a bewildering 2,700 panels – a prodigious artistic feat, not only in terms of numbers, but also the consistently high quality of the carvings and their composition.

From these enclosed galleries, the monument suddenly opens out onto a series

DETAILS of BOROBUDUR RELIEFS

Adapted from: John Miksic (1990) *Borobudur: golden tales of the Buddha*, Bemboo & Periplus: London & Singapore

IMS 68

Fourth Gallery, Main Wall
Gandawyuha

Third Gallery, Main Wall
Gandawyuha

Second Gallery, Main Wall
Gandawyuha

First Gallery, Main Wall (Lower)
Manohara, Other Avadanas

First Gallery, Main Wall (Upper)
Lalitavistara

Fourth Gallery, Balustrade Wall
Gandawyuha

Third Gallery, Balustrade Wall
Gandawyuha

Second Gallery, Balustrade Wall
Jatakas, Avadanas

First Gallery, Balustrade Wall (Lower)
Jatakamala, Other Jatakas

First Gallery, Balustrade Wall (Upper)
Jatakas

First Level, Outer Balustrade
Guardian Figures

Hidden Foot
Mahakarmavibhangga

Mudras and the Buddha Image

An artist producing an image of the Buddha does not try to create an original piece of art; he is trying to be faithful to a tradition which can be traced back over centuries. The Buddha can be represented either sitting, lying (indicating *paranirvana*), or standing, and (in Thailand) occasionally walking. Each image will be represented in a particular *mudra* or 'attitude', of which there are 40. The most common are:

Abhayamudra – dispelling fear or giving protection; right hand (sometimes both hands) raised, palm outwards, usually with the Buddha in a standing position.

Varamudra – giving blessing or charity; the right hand pointing downwards, the palm facing outwards, with the Buddha either seated or standing.

Vitarkamudra – preaching mudra; the ends of the thumb and index finger of the right hand touch to form a circle, symbolizing the Wheel of Law. The Buddha can either be seated or standing.

Dharmacakramudra – 'spinning the Wheel of Law'; a preaching mudra symbolizing the teaching of the first sermon. The hands are held in front of the chest, thumbs and index fingers of both joined, one facing inwards and one outwards.

Bhumisparcamudra – 'calling the earth goddess to witness' or 'touching the earth'; the right hand rests on the right knee with the tips of the fingers 'touching ground', thus calling the earth goddess Dharani/Thoranee to witness his enlightenment and victory over Mara, the king of demons. The Buddha is always seated.

Dhyanamudra – meditation; both hands resting open, palms upwards, in the lap, right over left.

Other points of note:

Vajrasana – yogic posture of meditation; cross-legged, both soles of the feet visible.

Virasana – yogic posture of meditation; cross-legged, but with the right leg on top of the left, covering the left foot (also known as *paryankasana*).

Buddha under Naga – a common image in Khmer art; the Buddha is shown seated in an attitude of meditation with a cobra rearing up over his head. This refers to an episode in the Buddha's life when he was meditating; a rain storm broke and Nagaraja, the king of the nagas (snakes), curled up under the Buddha (7 coils) and then used his 7-headed hood to protect the Holy One from the falling rain.

Buddha calling for rain – a common image in Laos; the Buddha is depicted standing, both arms held stiffly at the side of the body, fingers pointing downwards.

of bare, unadorned, circular terraces. On each are a number of small stupas, diminishing in size upwards from the first to third terrace, and pierced with lozenge-shaped openings. In total there are 72 such stupas, each containing a statue of the Buddha.

Including the Buddhas to be found in the niches opening outwards from the balustrades of the square terraces, there are a staggering 504 Buddha images. All are sculpted out of single blocks of stone. They are not representations of earthly beings who have reached nirvana, but transcendental saviours. The figures are strikingly simple, with a line delineating the edge of the robe, tightly-curled locks of hair, a top knot or *usnisa*, and an *urna* – the dot on the forehead. These last 2 features are distinctive bodily marks of the Buddha. On the square terraces, the symbolic gesture or mudra of the Buddha is different at each of the 4 compass points: the east-facing Buddhas are 'calling the earth to witness' or *bhumisparcamudra* (with right hand pointing down towards the earth), to the W,

Bhumisparcamudra – calling the earth goddess to witness. Sukhothai period, 13th-14th century.

Dhyanamudra – meditation. Sukhothai period, 13th-14th century.

Vitarkamudra – preaching, "spinning the Wheel of Law". Dvaravati Buddha, 7th-8th century, seated in the "European" manner.

Abhayamudra – dispelling fear or giving protection. Lopburi Buddha, Khmer style 12th century.

Abhayamudra – dispelling fear or giving protection; subduing Mara position. Lopburi Buddha, Khmer style 13th century.

they are in an attitude of meditation or *dhyanamudra* (hands together in the lap, with palms facing upwards), to the S, they express charity or *varamudra*, (right hand resting on the knee) and to the N, the Buddhas express dispelling fear or *abhayamudra* (with the right hand raised). On the upper circular terraces, all the Buddhas are in the same mudra. Each Buddha is slightly different, yet all retain a remarkable serenity.

The main central stupa on the summit contains 2 chambers which are empty. There has been some dispute as to whether they ever contained representations of the Buddha. Those who believe that they did not, argue that because this uppermost level denotes nirvana – nothingness – it would have been symbolically correct to have left them empty. For the pilgrim, these spacious top levels were also designed to afford a chance to rest before beginning the descent to the world of men. Any of the stairways, except the E one, could be used to descend.

The decline, fall and restoration of Borobudur

With the shift in power from Central to East Java in the 10th century (**see page 523**), Borobudur was abandoned and its ruin hastened by earthquakes. In 1814, Thomas Stamford Raffles appointed H.C. Cornelis to undertake investigations into the condition of the monument. Minor restoration was undertaken intermittantly over the next 80 years, but it was not until 1907 that a major reconstruction programme commenced. This was placed under the leadership of Theo Van Erp and under his guidance much of the top of the monument was dismantled and then rebuilt. Unfortunately, within 15 years the monument was deteriorating once again, and the combined effects of the world depression in the 1930s, the Japanese occupation in World War II, and then the trauma of independence, meant that it was not until the early 1970s that a team of international archaeologists were able to investigate the state of Borobudur once more. To their horror, they discovered that the condition of the foundations had deteriorated so much that the entire monument was in danger of caving inwards. In response, UNESCO began a 10-year restoration programme. This comprised dismantling all the square terraces – involving the removal of approximately one million pieces of stone. These were then cleaned, while a new concrete foundation was built, incorporating new water channels. The work was finally completed in 1983 and the monument re-opened by President Suharto.

There is a **museum** close to the monument which houses an exhibition showing the restoration process undertaken by UNESCO. Admission: 300Rp. Open: 0600-1800 Mon-Sun.

Best time to visit Early morning before the coaches arrive. Consider staying the night in Borobudur, to see the sun rise over the monument. Admission to complex: 550Rp (plus 500Rp for camera). Guides charge a fixed price of 2,500Rp/group. Open: 0600-1730 (ticket office closes at 1700) Mon-Sun.

Candis around Borobudur

Candi Pawon was probably built at the same time as Borobudur and is laid out with the same E-W orientation. It may have acted as an ante-room to Borobudur, catering to the worldly interests of pilgrims. Another theory is that it acted as a crematorium. *Candi Pawon* is also known as *Candi Dapur*, and both words mean kitchen. The unusually small windows may have been this size because they were designed as smoke outlets. The shrine was dedicated to Kuvera, the God of Fortune. The temple sits on a square base and contains an empty chamber. The exterior has some fine reliefs of female figures within pillared frames – reminiscent of Indian carvings – while the roof bears tiers of stupas. Among the reliefs are *kalpataru* or wish-granting trees, their branches dripping with jewels, and surrounded by pots of money. Bearded dwarfs over the entrance pour out jewels from sacks. Insensitive and poorly informed restoration of Candi Pawon at the beginning of the 20th century has made architectural interpretation rather difficult.

Candi Mendut lies further E still and 3 km from Borobudur. It was built by King Indra in 800. It is believed the candi was linked to Borobudur by a paved walkway; pilgrims may have congregated at Mendut, rested or meditated at Pawon, and then proceeded to Borobudur. The building was rediscovered in 1836, when the site was being cleared for a coffee plantation. The main body of the building was restored by Van Erp at the beginning of this century but the roof was left incomplete (it was probably a large stupa). The temple is raised on a high rectangular plinth and consists of a square cella containing 3 statues. The shrine is approached up a staircase, its balustrade decorated with reliefs depicting scenes from the jataka stories. The exterior is elaborately carved with a series of large relief panels of Bodhisattvas. One wall shows the **4-armed Tara** or **Cunda**, flanked by devotees, while another depicts **Hariti**, once a child-eating demon but here shown after her conversion to Buddhism, with children all around her. **Atavaka**, a flesh-eating ogre is shown in this panel holding a child's hand and sitting on pots of gold. The standing male figure, may be the **Bodhisattva Avalokitesvara**, whose consort is Cunda. There are also illustrations of classical Indian morality tales – look out for the fable of the tortoise and the 2 ducks on the left-hand side – and scenes from Buddhist literature. The interior is very impressive. There were originally 7 huge stone icons in the niches; 3 remain. These 3 were carved from single blocks of stone which may explain why they have survived. The central Buddha is seated in the unusual European fashion and is flanked by his 2 reincarnations (Avalokitesvara and Vajrapani). Notice how the feet of both the attendant statues are black from constant touching by devotees. The images are seated on elaborate thrones backed against the walls but conceived in the round (similar in style to cave-paintings found in Western Deccan, India). Admission: 100Rp. Open: 0615-1715 Sun-Mon.

There are no architectural remains of another, Sivaite, monument called **Candi Banon**, which was once situated near Candi Pawon. Five large sculptures, all fine examples of the Central Javanese Period, recovered from the site can be seen in the National Museum in Jakarta.

Festivals May: *Waicak* (moveable, usually during full moon). Celebrates the birth and death of the historic Buddha. The procession starts at Candi Mendut and converges on Borobudur at about 0400, all the monks and nuns carry candles – an impressive sight.

Accommodation Most people visit Borobudur as a day trip from Yogya. The nearest good hotels are in Magelang, 17 km to the N (**see page 611**). Limited accommodation at the sight includes: **B** *Taman Borobudur Guesthouse*, Borobudur Complex, T 3131, a/c; **C** *Tingal Youth Hostel*, Jl. Balaputradewa (about 2 km from the temple towards Yogya), T 4545, opened 1991, traditional-style wooden building set around courtyard, clean rooms with bathroom and character, includes breakfast; **E** *Losmen Borobudur*, Jl. Pramudawardani 1, clean, small rooms with mandi; **E** *Losmen Borokah*, Jl. Pramudawardani 2; **E** *Losmen Citra Rasa*, with mandi; **E** *Losmen Saraswati*, intersection of Jl. Pramudawardani and Jl. Balaputradewa.

Restaurants There are 2 restaurants within the complex, and a number around the stall and carpark area, and in Borobudur Village. The *Saraswati* has a reasonable restaurant.

Transport to & from Borobudur 42 km NW of Yogya, 90 km SW of Semarang, 17 km S of Magelang. **By bus:** Regular connections from Yogya's Umbunharjo terminal on Jl. Kemerdekaan to Muntilan (400Rp), and then catch a second bus from Muntilan to Borobudur (300Rp). The time needed to reach the monument means it is not possible to arrive early enough to miss the crowds – staying the night or booking a tour (**see below**) is the only answer. **By tour bus:** most visitors reach Borobudur on a tour from Yogya; it is by far the easiest way to reach the monument and costs about 13,500Rp (**see page 599** for list of tour companies).

By hire car or motorcycle: travel N on the road to Magelang. After 32 km, turn left shortly after the town of Muntilan; 5.5 km down this road is Candi Mendut, and after another 3 km, Borobudur. It is well signposted.

Magelang

Magelang, although a sizeable town, is really only used by tourists as a base from which to visit **Borobudur**, which lies 17 km to the S. It is also within reach of the **Dieng Plateau** (**see page 625**) which lies 90 km to the NW. On the town square there are a number of colonial era buildings: for example the offices of the former Dutch resident, built in 1810, and what is now the Prince Diponegoro Museum dating from 1920.

Accommodation Most of the town's hotels are to be found along Jalan Jend. A. Yani. **B** *Borobudur Indah*, Jl. Jend. A. Yani 492, T 4502; **B** *Plaza Panghegar*, Jl. Jend. A. Yani 4, T 4481; **C** *City*, Jl. Daha 23, T 3347.

Transport to & from Magelang 43 km N of Yogya. **By bus:** regular connections with Yogya and other regional centres.

YOGYA TO SURAKARTA via Prambanan

Route 2 runs NE from Yogya, skirting around the S apron of Mount Merapi, and across the Prambanan Plain. Prambanan village is 17 km from Yogya and is the site of the magnificent Candi Prambanan, as well as a number of other temples. Another 43 km NE from here, Route 2 reaches the second royal city of Central Java: Surakarta, better known as Solo. From Solo, a road winds up Mount Lawu towards the hill resort of Tawangmangu, 53 km E of the city. Near here are the last monuments of the Majapahit Kingdom, the stunningly positioned and enigmatic Candi Sukuh and Candi Ceto.

Prambanan

The Prambanan Plain was the centre of the powerful 10th century Mataram Kingdom which vanquished the Sailendra Dynasty – the builders of Borobudur. At the height of its influence, Mataram encompassed both Central and East Java together with Bali, Lombok, SW Borneo and S Sulawesi (see page 519 for more history). The magnificent temples that lie scattered over the Prambanan Plain – second only to Borobudur in size and artistic accomplishment – bear testament to the past glories of the kingdom. The village of Prambanan is little more than a way station with a handful of warungs, a market, and a bus stop.

Places of interest

After Borobudur, Candi Prambanan is probably the best-known archaeological sight in Indonesia. But, in addition to Prambanan, there are another 6 major candis on the Prambanan Plain, each with its own artistic character, and all well worth visiting. The account below describes the temples from E to W, travelling from Prambanan village towards Yogya (see map). From Yogya, the monuments are approached in reverse order.

Candi Prambanan or **Candi Loro Jonggrang** as it is also known, stands on open ground and can be clearly seen from the road in Prambanan village. This is the principal temple on the Prambanan Plain, and the greatest **Hindu** monument in Java. In scale, it is similar to Borobudur, the central tower rising, almost vertically, over 45m. Built between 900 and 930AD, Prambanan was the last great monument of the Central Javanese Period and – again like Borobudur – the architects were attempting to symbolically re-create the cosmic Mount Meru.

Originally, there were 232 temples at this site. The plan was focused on a square court, with 4 gates and 8 principal temples. The 3 largest candis are dedicated to Brahma (to the S), Vishnu (to the N) and, the central and tallest tower, to Siva. They are sometimes known as Candi Siva, Candi Brahma and Candi Vishnu. Facing each is a smaller shrine, dedicated to each of these gods' 'mounts'.

Candi Siva was restored by the Dutch, after an earthquake in the 16th century had left much of the temple in ruins. Like other Central Javanese candis, it was conceived as a square cell, with portico projections on each face, the porticos being an integral part of the structure. The tower was constructed as 6 diminishing storeys, each ringed with small stupas, and the whole surmounted by a larger stupa. The tower stands on a plinth with 4 approach stairways, the largest to the

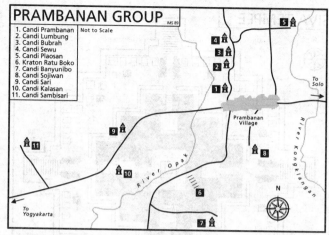

PRAMBANAN GROUP

IMS 89

Not to Scale

1. Candi Prambanan
2. Candi Lumbung
3. Candi Bubrah
4. Candi Sewu
5. Candi Plaosan
6. Kraton Ratu Boko
7. Candi Banyunibo
8. Candi Sojiwan
9. Candi Sari
10. Candi Kalasan
11. Candi Sambisari

To Solo

Prambanan Village

River Opak

River Kongklangan

N

To Yogyakarta

E, each with gate-towers imitating the main shrine and edged with similar shaped stupas. At the first level is an open gallery, with fine reliefs on the inside wall depicting the Javanese interpretation of the Hindu epic, the Ramayana (see plan **page 505**). The story begins to the left of the E stairway and is read by walking clockwise – known as *pradaksina*. Look out for the *kalpataru*, or wishing trees, with parrots above them and guardians in the shape of rabbits, monkeys and geese or *kinaras*. The story continues on the balustrade of Candi Brahma. Each stairway at Candi Siva leads up into 4 separate rooms. In the E room is a statue of Siva, to the S is the sage Agastya, behind him – to the W – is his son Ganesh and to the N is his wife Durga. Durga is also sometimes known as Loro Jonggrang, or Slender Maiden, and hence the alternative name for the Prambanan complex – Candi Loro Jonggrang.

The 2 neighbouring candis dedicated to Vishnu and Brahma are smaller. They have only one room each and one staircase on the E side, but have equally fine reliefs running round the galleries. On **Candi Vishnu**, the reliefs tell the stories of Krishna, while those on the balustrade of **Candi Brahma** are a continuation of the Ramayana epic which begins on Candi Siva. On the exterior walls of all three shrines can be seen voluptuous *apsaris*. These heavenly nymphs try to seduce gods, ascetics and mortal men; they encourage ascetics to break their vows of chastity and are skilled in the arts – poetry, dancing and painting.

Opposite these 3 shrines are the ruins of **3 smaller temples**, presently undergoing restoration. Each is dedicated to the mount of a Hindu god: facing Candi Siva is Nandi the bull – Siva's mount; facing Candi Vishnu is Garuda, the mythical bird; and facing Candi Brahma, Hamsa the goose. The magnificent statue of Nandi is the only mount which still survives.

This inner court is contained within a gated outer court. Between the walls are 224 smaller shrines – all miniature and simplified versions of the large central shrine – and further enclosed by a courtyard. They are in a poor state of repair. Admission: 550Rp, 500Rp for camera, 2,500Rp for video, 600Rp for parking. Open: 0600-1800 Mon-Sun. Guidebook, with descriptions of reliefs available from tourist information, 8,000Rp. Guides will show you around the complex, pointing out the various stories on the reliefs for 5,000-10,000Rp.

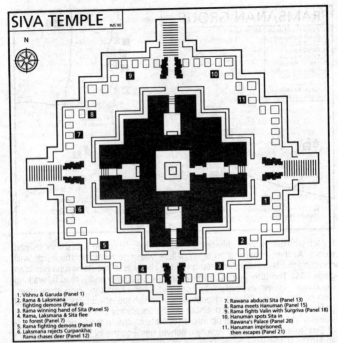

SIVA TEMPLE IMS 90

N

1. Vishnu & Garuda (Panel 1)
2. Rama & Laksmana
   fighting demons (Panel 4)
3. Rama winning hand of Sita (Panel 5)
4. Rama, Laksmana & Sita flee
   to forest (Panel 7)
5. Rama fighting demons (Panel 10)
6. Laksmana rejects Curpankha;
   Rama chases deer (Panel 12)

7. Rawana abducts Sita (Panel 13)
8. Rama meets Hanuman (Panel 15)
9. Rama fights Valin with Surgriva (Panel 18)
10. Hanuman spots Sita in
    Rawana's Palace (Panel 20)
11. Hanuman imprisoned;
    then escapes (Panel 21)

Other candis near Candi Prambanan

From Candi Prambanan, it is possible to walk N to the ruined **Candi Lumbung**, currently under restoration, as well as **Candi Bubrah**. Together with **Candi Sewu** (see below), they form a loose complex of 3 temples.

Candi Sewu – meaning 'a thousand temples' – lies 1 km to the N of Candi Prambanan and was constructed over 3 periods spanning the years 778-810. To begin with, the building was probably a simple square cella, surrounded by 4 smaller temples, unconnected to the main shrine. Later, they were incorporated into the current cruciform plan, and the surrounding 4 rows of 240 smaller shrines were also built. These smaller shrines are all square in plan, with a portico in front. The central temple probably contained a bronze statue of the Buddha. The candi is currently undergoing renovation. The complex is guarded by *raksasa* guardians brandishing clubs, placed here to protect the temple from evil spirits.

Two km to the NE of Candi Prambanan is **Candi Plaosan** built, probably, about 835, to celebrate the marriage of a princess of the Buddhist Sailendra Dynasty to a member of the court of the Hindu Sanjaya Dynasty. Candi Plaosan consists of 2 central sanctuaries surrounded by 116 stupas and 58 smaller shrines – presently ruined. Like Candi Sari, the 2 central shrines were built on 2 levels with 6 cellas. Each of the lower cellas may have housed a central bronze Buddha image, flanked by 2 stone Bodhisattvas (similar to Candi Mendut, **page 610**). Again, the shrines are guarded by raksasa. The monument is currently undergoing restoration.

The ruins of the late 9th century **Kraton Ratu Boko** occupy a superb position on a plateau 200m above the Prambanan Plain. Because this was probably a palace (hence the use of the word kraton in its name), it is thought that the site was chosen for its strong natural defensive position. The hill may also have been spiritually important. Little is known of the 'palace'; it may have been a religious or a secular royal site – or perhaps both. Inscriptions found in the area celebrate the victory of a ruler and may be related to the supremacy of the (Hindu) Sanjaya dynasty, over the Buddhist Sailendras.

For the visitor, it is difficult to make sense of the ruins – it is a large site, spread out over the hillside and needs some exploring. From the carpark area, walk up some steps and then for about 1 km through rice fields. The dominant restored triple ceremonial porch gives an idea of how impressive the palace must have been. To the N of the porch are the foundations of 2 buildings, one of which may have been a temple. Turn S and then E to reach the major part of the site. Many of the ruins here were probably Hindu shrines, and the stone bases held wooden pillars which supported large pendopo, or open-sided pavilions. Beyond the palace were a series of pools. To get to Kraton Ratu Boko: take the road S before crossing the Opak River, towards Piyungan, for about 5 km. On the road, just over a bridge on the left-hand side, are steep stone stairs which climb 100m to the summit of the plateau and to the kraton. Alternatively, it is possible to drive to the top; further on along the main road, a turning to the left leads to **Candi Banyunibo**, a small, attractive, restored Buddhist shrine dating from the 9th century. It is set in a well-kept garden and surrounded by cultivated land. Just before the candi, a narrow winding road, negotiable by car and motorbike, leads up to the plateau and Ratu Boko.

Two km to the S of Prambanan village is **Candi Sojiwan**, another Buddhist temple, undergoing restoration.

Candis on the road W to Yogya

About 3 km W of Candi Prambanan and Prambanan village, on the N side of the main road towards Yogya, is **Candi Sari**. This square temple, built around 825, is one of the most unusual in the area, consisting of 2-storeys and with the appearance of a third. With 3 cellas on each of the 2 levels and porticos almost like 'windows', it strongly resembles a house. Interestingly, reliefs at both Borobudur and Prambanan depict buildings – probably built of wood rather than stone – of similar design. Some art historians think that the inspiration for the design is derived from engravings on bronze Dongson drums **(see page 706)**. These were introduced into Indonesia from N Vietnam and date from between the 2nd and 5th century BC. There is an example of just such a drum in the National Museum in Jakarta. It is thought that both the lower and the upper level cellas of the candi were used for worship, the latter being reached by a wooden stairway. The exterior is decorated with particularly accomplished carvings of goddesses, Bodhisattvas playing musical instruments, the female Buddhist deity Tara, and male naga-kings. Like Candi Kalasan, the stupas on the roof bear some resemblance to those at Borobudur. Inside, there are 3 shrines, which would originally have housed Buddha images. Nothing remains of the outer buildings or surrounding walls, but it would have been of similar design to Candi Plaosan. The candi was restored by the Dutch in 1929 and like Candi Kalasan, is surrounded by trees and houses.

A short distance further W, and on the opposite side of the road from Candi Sari, is **Candi Kalasan** – situated just off the road in the midst of rice fields. The temple dates from 778, making it one of the oldest candis on Java. It is a Buddhist temple dedicated to the Goddess Tara and is thought to have been built either to honour the marriage of a princess of the Sailendra Dynasty, or as the sepulchre for a Sailendra prince's consort. The monument is strongly vertical and built in the form of a Greek cross – contrasting sharply with the squat and square Candi Sambisari. In fact, the plan of the temple was probably altered 12 years after construction. Of the elaborately carved kalamakaras on the porticos projecting from each face, only the S example remains intact. They would have originally been carved roughly in stone, and then coated with 2 layers of stucco, the second of which remained pliable just long enough for artists to carve the intricate designs. The 4 largest of the external niches are empty. The style of the reliefs is similar to SE Indian work of the same period. The roof was originally surmounted by a high circular stupa, mounted on an octagonal drum. Above the porticos are smaller stupas, rather similar in design to those at Borobudur. The only remaining Buddha images are to be found in niches towards the top of the structure. The building contains a mixture of Buddhist and Hindu cosmology – once again evidence of Java's religious syncretism. The main cella almost certainly contained a large bronze figure, as the pedestal has been found to have traces of metallic oxide. The side shrines would also have had statues in them, probably figures of the Buddha.

Another 5 km SW from Candi Kalasan towards Yogya is the turn-off for **Candi Sambisari** – the temple is 2 km N of the main road. If travelling from Yogya, turn left at the Km 12.5 marker – about 9.5 km out of town. Candi Sambisari, named after the village nearby, sits 6.5m below ground level, surrounded by a 2 m-high volcanic tuff wall. It has only recently been excavated from under layers of volcanic ash, having being discovered by a farmer in the mid-1960s. It is believed to have been buried by an eruption of Mount Merapi during the 14th century and as a result, is well preserved. The candi was probably built in the early 9th century, and if this is so, then it was one of the last temples to be built during the Mataram period. A central, rather squat, square shrine still contains its original linga, indicating that this was a Hindu temple dedicated to Siva. There are also smaller boundary lingams surrounding the temple. On the raised gallery, in niches, there are fine carvings of Durga (N), Ganesh (E) and Agastya (S). Pillar-bases on the terrace indicate that the entire candi was once covered by a wooden pavilion. In front (and to the W) of the main temple are 3 smaller shrines in rather poorer condition.

Accommodation **A** *Prambanan Village*, Klurak, Taman Martani, Kalasan, T 62674, a/c, restaurant, pool, overlooking Prambanan; **E** *Losmen Muharti*, opposite entrance to Prambanan.

Entertainment **Ramayana ballet (see page 533)**: at the open-air theatre at Candi Prambanan, 1900-2100, for 4 days every month over the full moon from May to Oct, 12,500-15,000Rp. Tickets available from tourist information at Candi Prambanan or from travel agents in Yogya. There are also performances year-round at the Trimurti Covered Theatre, 1930-2130.

Local transport In order to see the outlying candis, it is best to have some form of transport. If on a tour, enquire which candis are to be visited, or hire a taxi, minibus or motorbike from Yogya. Horse-drawn carts and minibuses wait at the bus station; they can be persuaded to drive visitors around. Alternatively, take a bus to Prambanan and work back, W or work E, ending at Prambanan.

Transport to & from Prambanan 17 km E of Yogya, 46 km W of Solo. **By bus:** regular connections with Yogya's bus station, or by minibus from the main roads in Yogya, 30 minutes. Connections with Solo, 1½ hrs.

Solo or Surakarta

Surakarta, better known simply as Solo, is Central Java's second royal city. It is situated between 3 of Java's highest volcanoes: Mount Merapi (2,911 m) and Mount Merbabu (3,142 m) to the W, and Mount Lawu (3,265 m) to the E. The kraton, or palace, of the great ancient kingdom of Mataram was moved to Surakarta in the 1670s. The town remained the *negara* or capital of the kingdom until 1755 when the VOC divided Mataram into 3 sultanates – 2 in Solo and one in Yogya. Although foreigners usually regard Yogya as Java's cultural heart, the

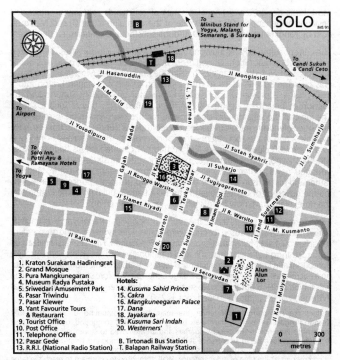

SOLO IMS 91

To
Minibus Stand for
Yogya, Malang,
Semarang, & Surabaya

To
Candi Sukuh
& Candi Ceto

To
Airport

To
Solo Inn &
Putri Ayu &
Ramayana Hotels

To
Yogya

Jl Hasanuddin

Jl Monginsidi

Jl R. M. Said

Jl Yosodipuro

Jl Sutan Syahrir

Jl Suharjo

Jl Sugiyopranoto

Jl Ronggo Warsito

Jl Slamet Riyadi

Jl Teuku Umar

Jl Imam Bonjol

Jl R. Warsito

Jl Jend. Sudirman

Jl. M. Kusmanto

Jl Rajiman

Jl G. Subroto

Jl Yos Sudarso

Jl Secoyudan

Jl Kapt. Mulyadi

Jl U. Sumoharjo

Jl L. S. Parman

Jl R. M. Said

Jl Gajah Mada

Jl Kartini

Alun
Alun
Lor

0   300
metres

1. Kraton Surakarta Hadiningrat
2. Grand Mosque
3. Pura Mangkunegaran
4. Museum Radya Pustaka
5. Sriwedari Amusement Park
6. Pasar Triwindu
7. Pasar Klewer
8. Yant Favourite Tours
   & Restaurant
9. Tourist Office
10. Post Office
11. Telephone Office
12. Pasar Gede
13. R.R.I. (National Radio Station)

Hotels:
14. Kusuma Sahid Prince
15. Cakra
16. Mangkuneegaran Palace
17. Dana
18. Jayakarta
19. Kusuma Sari Indah
20. Westerners'

B. Tirtonadi Bus Station
T. Balapan Railway Station

Javanese usually attach the sobriquet to Surakarta. Solo's motto is 'Berseri', which is an acronym for Bersih, Sehat, Rapi, Indah (clean, healthy, neat, beautiful). It has won several awards for being the cleanest city in Indonesia.

Solo is quieter, smaller and more relaxed than Yogya – even though its population is more than half a million – and has pleasant wide tree-lined streets. It is also less touristy than Yogya. Solo is one of the few towns in Indonesia which has bicycle lanes (on the main E-W road – Jalan Slamet Riyadi) and they are almost as busy as the main roads. Even the mountain bike is making its presence felt here. The city has gained a reputation as a good place to shop; not only is it a centre for the sale of batik – with a large market specializing in nothing else – but there is also an 'antiques' market which is worth visiting (see places of interest).

As the courts of Solo were denied administrative powers during the 2 centuries of colonial rule from 1757, the sultans devoted much of their energy to the promotion of Javanese arts and culture. This is reflected today in the presence in Solo of a cultural centre (Pusat Kebudayaan), an academy of music (Konservatori Karawitan) and an academy of art (STSI).

Places of interest
The **Kraton Surakarta Hadiningrat**, better known as the **Kasunanan Palace** is the senior of the city's 2 kratons (**see page 526**) and the more impressive. It lies S of the main E-W road, Jalan Slamet Riyadi. Like the kraton in Yogya, the Kasunanan Palace faces N onto a square – the Alun-Alun Lor – and follows the

same basic design, consisting of a series of courtyards containing open-sided pavilions or pendopos. On the W side of the alun alun is the **Grand Mosque**, built by Pangkubuwono III in 1750, though substantially embellished since then.

The current sultan is Pagkubuwono XII, a 68-year-old with six wives, 35 children and a playboy reputation. During 1992 and 1993 he was embroiled in a public relations war with the sultan's 25th child, the princess Koes Moertiyah. The battle was over the Sultan's plans to turn a portion of the Kasunanan Kraton into a luxury hotel, a project which had the imprimatur of President Suharto and the support of Bimantara, a company controlled by Bambang, one of Suharto's sons. The logic of the scheme was clear: the Sultan has seen his kraton dissolve from glorious splendour into ramshackle decrepitude as funds for its upkeep have dwindled, and as the *abdi dalem* – the court servants – have declined from 3,000 to a mere 600 elderly retainers. But he had not counted on his daughter Koes Moertiyah who, alarmed at the prospect of uncouth tourists degrading the palace, arranged news conferences, encouraged demonstrations and confronted her father and his plans in a manner almost unheard of from a princess. Her actions led the governor of Central Java to impose a ban on building in the kraton and the hotel plans have now been shelved – for the time being.

Entering the Kasunanan Palace, the first pendopo – the **Pagelaran** – is original, dating from 1745 and is used for public ceremonies. This is where visiting government officials would wait for an audience with the Susuhunan. From here, stairs lead up to the **Siti Inggil** or High Place, the area traditionally used for enthronements. Like Borobudur and Prambanan, the Siti Inggil represents the cosmic mountain Meru, but on a micro-scale. On the Siti Inggil is a large pendopo. The fore section of this pavilion was rebuilt in 1915 but the square section towards the rear (known as the **Bangsal Witana**), with its umbrella-shaped roof, is 250 years old.

Visitors are not permitted to enter the main palace compound through the large **Kemandungan Gates**. They must walk back out of the first compound, over a road, past the private entrance to the prince's quarters and an area used to store the royal carriages, through a second gate, to an entrance at the E of the main compound. Near the second gate is a school; this was originally a private school for the royal children but was opened to children of commoners at the time of independence. Walk through one courtyard to reach the large central courtyard, known as the *Plataran*. This shaded area, with its floor of black sand from the S coast, contains the main palace buildings. Much of the prince's private residence was destroyed in a disastrous fire in 1985, but has subsequently been restored. An electrical fault was the alleged cause of the fire, although local people believe that the Susuhunan neglected his duties and provoked the anger of the Goddess Nyi Loro Kidul (see page 570). Restoration was followed by extensive ceremonies to appease the goddess.

The 3 **pendopo** on the left are original, and are used for gamelan performances. Behind them, along the walls of the courtyard, are palanquins which were once used for transporting princesses around the city. An octagonal tower, the **Panggung Songgobuwono**, survived the fire and was supposedly used by the Susuhunan to communicate with the Goddess Nyi Loro Kidul. Songgobuwono means 'Support of the Universe'.

The main pendopo, the **Sasana Sewaka**, is not original – it was restored in 1987 – although the Dutch iron pillars which support it, are. Strictly speaking, if members of the public are to have an audience with the Sultan, they have to walk upon their knees across the pendopo; look out for the cleaners, who crouch to sweep the floor. It is used for 4 ceremonies a year and sacred dances are held here once a year. Behind this pendopo is the private residence of the prince, with the **kasatrian** (the sons' quarters) to the right and the **keputren** (the daughters' quarters) to the left. A concrete area to the left was the site of the Dining Hall, which also burnt to the ground in the fire of 1985, and which is awaiting restoration, once funds allow.

The guide leads visitors back to the first courtyard, where 2 sides of the square are a museum, containing an interesting collection of enthronement chairs, small bronze Hindu sculptures and 3 fine Dutch carriages which are 200-350 years old. Admission: 1,000Rp, 1,000Rp for camera. Open: 0830-1400 Sat-Thurs. All visitors are asked to wear a *samir* – a gold and red ribbon – as a mark of respect. Guide obligatory (they are the *abdi dalem* or palace servants).

A short history of the Susuhunan of Surakarta

In 1745 Pakubuwono II (his name means 'Nail of the Universe'), inheritor of the older Mataram Kingdom, decided to move his capital from Kartasura to Solo – the former capital had been all but destroyed by East Javanese and VOC attacks. Three locations were carefully chosen as potential sites for a new kraton and after much prevarication and argument, Solo was selected. It seems that the architects were unhappy with the choice because of Solo's position on swampy ground, but they were over-ruled by the all-important seers or wise men who believed that by moving the capital here, the Javanese kingdom would again prosper and war would come to an end.

Despite the move, the royal family was still riven by dissent, with 4 princes in conflict with one another and with the Susuhunan, Pakubuwono II. Among the 4, Prince Mangkubumi and Prince Mas Said were the most powerful. This dissent, coupled with the Susuhunan's agreement with the Dutch to lease the N coast of Central Java to the VOC for a nominal fee, led to the Third Javanese War of Succession (1746-57). Pakubuwono II did not live to see the end of this war and his heir was appointed the new Susuhunan, becoming Pakubuwono III. Prince Mangkubumi meanwhile, failing in his own attempt to become Susuhunan, established a second kraton, in Yogya, where he had developed a power base (**see page 590**). The only other person left to be placated was Prince Mas Said who became sultan of a third kraton (and the second in Solo) in 1757. From 1757-1795 he ruled his kraton as Mangkunegoro I and lived in harmony alongside Pakubuwono III.

The less impressive kraton, **Pura Mangkunegaran** at the N end of Jalan Diponegoro, is still lived in by the princely family who built it. In 1757, the rebel prince Mas Said established a new royal house here, crowning himself Mangkunegoro I. But his power was never as great as the Susuhunan, and Mangkunegoro's deference to him is evident in the design of his palace, which faces S, towards the Susuhunan's kraton. Much of the original structure has been restored. Built in traditional style, the layout is like other kratons, centred around a pendopo.

This central pendopo is the **Pendopo Agung**, built in 1810 and one of the largest and most majestic in Java. Note how the ceiling is painted with cosmic symbols. Mangkunegoro VII (1916-44), a scholar and patron of Indonesian performing and plastic arts, commissioned an addition to the kraton – the *pracimusono*. This octagonal pavilion was designed by a Dutch architect whose knowledge of Indonesian architectural traditions led to a sympathetic and innovative design. Behind the central pendopo is a large room – the **Paringgitan** – which houses, amongst other things, a good collection of antique jewellery and coins of the Majapahit and Mataram periods. In a corridor behind this room are a large number of topeng masks. Voyeurists can peer through the windows into the private rooms of the present prince. Beautiful cool gardens and verandahs give his quarters an air of a Victorian hunting lodge. Next to the ticket office are 3 fine carriages from London and Holland. Admission: 1,000Rp. Open: 0900-1400 Mon-Sat, 0900-1300 Sun. Guide obligatory. Gamelan performances are held here (see entertainment).

The small **Museum Radya Pustaka** housed in an attractive building on the main road, Jalan Slamet Riyadi, next door to the Tourist Office. It contains a collection of wayang kulit, topeng, gamelan instruments, royal barge figureheads and some Hindu sculpture. Admission: 300Rp. Open: 0800-1200 Tues-Thurs, Sat & Sun, 0800-1100 Fri.

Next door to the museum is **Sriwedari**, an amusement park. It is also the home of one of the most famous Javanese classical dancing troupes, specializing in wayang orang, who perform here in the evenings. Open: 0800-2200 Mon-Sun.

There are several markets in Solo worth visiting. The antiques market **Pasar**

Triwindu, is situated off Jalan Diponegoro, on the right-hand side, walking towards the Pura Mangkunegaran. This is the only authentic flea market in Central Java and is a wonderful place to browse through the piles of goods. There are some antiques to be found but time is needed to search them out. Bargaining is essential. **Pasar Klewer**, situated just beyond the W gate of the Alun-alun Lor near the kraton, is a batik-lover's paradise. It is filled with cloth, mostly locally produced batik – a dazzling array of both *cap* and *tulis* **(see page 536)**. Prices are cheaper than the chainstores, but the market is very busy and first time visitors may be bemused into paying more than they should. It's best to go in the mornings, as it starts to wind down after lunch. Again, bargain hard. It is worth taking a becak to explore the streets of Solo to find some of the interesting colonial houses.

Excursions

Candi Sukuh and **Candi Ceto**, 2 of the most unusual and stunningly positioned temples in Indonesia, lie to the E of Solo, on the W slopes of Mount Lawu.

Candi Sukuh stands at 910 m above sea-level and was probably built between 1434 and 1449 by the last king of the Majapahit Kingdom, Suhita. The enigmatic Candi Sukuh is situated in an area which had long been sacred and dedicated to ancestor-worship. The style is unlike any other temple in Java and has a close resemblance to South American Maya pyramid temples (which led archaeologists to believe, wrongly, that it was of an earlier date). It is built of laterite on 3 terraces, facing W. A path, between narrow stone gates, leads up from one terrace to the next, and steep stairs through the body of the main 'pyramid' to a flat summit. Good views over terraced fields down to the plain below.

The first terrace is approached through a gate from the W, which would have been guarded by dvarapalas **(see page 644)**. The relief carvings on the gate are *candra sangkala* – the elements that make up the picture signify numbers which, in this instance, represent a date (1359=1437AD). On the path of the first terrace is a relief of a phallus and vulva: it is said that if a woman's clothes tear on passing this relief, it signifies excessive promiscuity and she must purify herself. The gate to the second terrace is guarded by 2 more dvarapalas. On the terrace are a number of carved stones, including a depiction of 2 blacksmiths, one standing – probably Ganesh – the other squatting, in front of which is a selection of the weapons they have forged. The third, and most sacred, terrace is approached through a third gate. There are a number of relief carvings scattered over the terrace. The figures of many are carved in wayang form with long arms, and the principal relief depicts the Sudamala story. This story is performed in places where bodies are cremated, in order to ward off curses or to expel evil spirits. Also on the third terrace are standing winged figures (Garuda), giant turtles representing the underworld (strangely similar to the turtle stelae of pagodas in N Vietnam), and carvings of Bima and Kalantaka.

The 'topless' pyramid itself has little decoration on it. It is thought that originally it must have been topped-off with a wooden structure. A carved phallus was found at the summit; it is now in the National Museum, Jakarta. Although Candi Sukuh is often called Java's 'erotic' temple, the erotic elements are not very prominent; a couple of oversized penises, little else. Admission: by donation (visitors are sometimes asked for a 100Rp fee at Ngolrok). Open: 0615-1715 Mon-Sun. **Getting there**: take a bus from Solo's Tirtonadi station on Jl. Jend. A. Yani to Karangpandan (41 km). From Karangpandan take a minibus the 5.5 km to the village of Ngolrok; some minibuses continue right on up the steep road to the site of Candi Sukuh from the village – if not, it is an exhausting 1.6 km walk past women bringing wood down from the mountains. From Candi Sukuh there is a well-worn stone path to the mountain resort of **Tawangmangu** (see below), an easy 1½-2 hr hike.

Candi Ceto lies 7 km to the N of Sukuh, but is considerably higher at over 1,500 m. It was built in 1470 and is the last temple to have been constructed during the Majapahit era. Candi Ceto shows close architectural affinities with the pura of Bali, where the Hindu traditions of Majapahit escaped the intrusion of Islam. Getting to the temple is an adventure in itself (although tours do run from Solo and Tawangmangu); the road passes tea estates, incredibly steeply terraced fields, and towards the end of the journey climbs seemingly almost vertically up the mountainside – the road ends at the temple.

Candi Ceto is one of the most stunningly positioned temples in Southeast Asia. It has recently been restored and is set on 12 levels. Nine would originally have had narrow open gateways (like those at Sukuh) but only 7 of these remain. Pairs of reconstructed wooden pavilions on stone platforms lie to each side of the pathway on the final series of terraces. There is some sculpture (occasionally phallic) and strange stone decorations are set into the ground – again, very reminiscent of Mayan reliefs. Admission: by donation. Open: open access. **Getting there:** is not easy. From Karangpandan via Ngolrok there are minibuses to the village of Kadipekso; from Kadipekso it may be possible to hitch, or catch a motorcycle taxi, the final 2.6 km to the site. Alternatively walk, which is exhausting at this altitude. Or, take a tour, see below.

Tawangmangu is a hill resort town set at 1,200m, 12 km on from Kawangpandan and a total of 53 km from Solo (**see page 624**). **Getting there:** buses leave regularly from Solo's Tirtonadi station.

Sangiran, 18 km N from Solo, is one of Java's most important archaeological sites. In 1891, Eugene Dubois found the skullcap and upper jaw molar of what he took to be an ape. But 11 months later in Aug 1892 Dubois unearthed a femur which indicated that the 'ape' walked erect – he named this early hominid *Pithecantropus erectus* – popularly known as 'Java Man'. This 'ape-man' was far more advanced than Dubois presumed and is now classified as a subspecies of *Homo erectus* – namely *Homo erectus erectus*. Since then, excavations at Sangiran have revealed a wealth of fossil hominid remains, along with a hoard of other fossils dated 0.15-1.7 million years BP. The small Trinil Museum (opened 1989) in the nearby village of Krikilan has a display including stegadon tusks, buffalo skulls, assorted fossils and, of course, examples of Java Man (craniums). Visitors are assaulted by locals selling fossils. Some (for example, the fish) are clearly of late 20th century origin. **Getting there:** take a tour or catch a bus from Solo's Tirtonadi station towards Purwodadi; just beyond the 14 km mark (in the village of Kalijambe) there is a road to the right signposted to Sangiran. The museum is 4 km along the road; take an ojek, hitch or walk.

Miri is further N from Sangiran on the road to Purwodadi. This archaeological site and associated museum is less well known and not as well displayed as Sangiran. **Getting there:** turn left past the 21 km marker; the museum is some 2 km off the main road. Take a bus towards Purwodadi from Solo's Tirtonadi station and walk.

The hill village of **Selo** is accessible from Solo and from here **Mount Merapi** can be climbed (**see page 598**).

Pacitan is a small seaside resort 119 km S of Solo. **Getting there:** there are a few direct buses from Solo's Tirtonadi station; alternatively get a bus to Wonogiri, from where there are regular connections to Pacitan.

Tours *Yant Favourite Tours* run cycling tours of Solo, trips to the Kraton, batik and gamelan factories, arak distillers, Prambanan, Sangiran, Candi Sukuh and Candi Ceto (see Travel Agents).

Festivals Mar/Apr: Month-long fair held in the Sriwedari Amusement Park, with stalls selling handicrafts. Jul: *Kirab Pusaka Kraton* (moveable), a traditional ceremony held by the 2 kratons to celebrate the Javanese New Year. A procession of heirlooms starts at the Pura Mangkunegaran at 1900 and ends at the Kasunanan Palace at 2400. Sept: *Sekaten* or *Gunungan* (moveable), a 2 week long festival prior to Mohammad's birthday. The celebrations begin at midnight with the procession of 2 sets of ancient and sacred gamelan instruments from the kraton to the Grand Mosque. A performance is given on these instruments and at the end of the 2 weeks they are processed back to the kraton. A fair is held on the alun-alun in front of the mosque. The closing ceremony is known as *Grebeg Maulud*.

Accommodation A+-B *Kusuma Sahid Prince*, Jl. Sugiyopranoto 20, T 46356, F 44788, a/c, restaurant, pool, best in Solo, rather run-down old colonial building, some cottage-style accommodation, rec; **A+-C** *Cakra*, Jl. Brigjen. Slamet Riyadi 201, T 45847, F 48334, a/c, restaurant, garden, range of rooms available, price includes breakfast; **A** *Riyadhi Palace*, Jl. Slamet Riyadi 297/335, T 33300, a/c, overpriced and rather pretentious, price includes breakfast; **B** *Gatti*, Jl. Wetani, clean; **B** *Sahid*, Jl. Gajah Mada 82, T 35889; **B-C** *Mangkunegaran Palace*, Jl. Mangkunegaran, T 35683, pool, set within the palace grounds, lovely gardens, rooms have seen better days, price includes breakfast; **B-C** *Solo Inn*, Jl. Slamet Riyadi 366, T 36075, a/c, restaurant, varied rooms but rather overpriced; **C** *Putri Ayu*, Jl. Slamet Riyadi 293, T 36154, some a/c, set around a courtyard, good value, price includes breakfast; **C-D** *Dana*, Jl. Slamet Riyadi 286, T 33890, some a/c, some private bathrooms, colonial building with charm and a lovely garden; **C-D** *Pondok Persada Bengawan*, Jl. Kentingan, T 48616, a/c, tennis, on the banks of the Solo River, 4 km from town centre, large garden; **C-D** *Ramayana*, Jl. Dr. Wahidin 22, T 32814, some a/c, attractive 1-storey, rooms set around courtyard, friendly, popular, price includes breakfast, rec; **C-D** *Sanashtri*, Jl. Sutowijoyo 45, T 45807, some a/c, small, clean rooms, friendly management; **D-E** *Jayakarta*, Jl. Monginsidi 122 (near train station), T 3 (or 4)2813, some a/c in the new building, the cheaper rooms are in the old wing, set around a courtyard; **E** *Kemuning*, Jl. KH. Hasyim Asyari 7, central but rooms are squalid and dark; **E** *Kota*, Jl. Slamet Riyadi 113, T 32841, around courtyard, reasonable rooms, clean, TV, some with attached mandi, good location and price; **E** *Kusuma Sari Indah*, Kp. Kestalan Rt4/III (just off Jl. Monginsidi opposite railway station), T 42574, clean, with attached mandi, rec; **E** *Marga Jaya*, down alley off Jl. Monginsidi (near train station), next to *Jayakarta Hotel*; **E** *San Francisco*, down alley off Jl. Monginsidi (near train station), next to *Jayakarta Hotel*, clean, basic; **E** *Sinar Dhady*, down alley off Jl. Monginsidi (near train station), next to *Jayakarta Hotel*; **F** *Bebas*, Jl. Monginsidi 90A (near train station), T 32810, some private bathrooms; **F** *Moro Seneng*, Jl. Ahmad Dahlan 49, average; **F** *Nirwana*, Jl. Ronggo Warsito 59, T 2843; **F** *Timur*, Jl. Keprabon Wetani I/5 (off Jl. Ahmad Dahlan); **F** *Westerners* (Pak Mawardi's Homestay), Kampung Kemlayan Kidul (right off Jl. Yos Sudarso, from Jl. Slamet Riyadi), set in the old part of the city, this popular guesthouse is difficult to find but worth the effort, good source of information, rec.

Restaurants Solo is renowned as a good place to eat, particularly local specialities; there is certainly no shortage of restaurants and warungs to choose from. Solo specialities include *nasi gudeg* (egg, beans, rice, vegetables and coconut sauce), *nasi liwet* (rice cooked in coconut milk and served with a vegetable) and *timlo* (embellished chicken broth). The Yogyanese speciality *gudeg* is also popular here. **Indonesian:** ✦*Bakso Triwindu*, Jl. Diponegoro, good vegetarian food; ✦*Bu Mari's*, Jl. Jend. Gatot Subroto, recommended *gudeg*, open late; ✦*Denai*, Jl. Musium, near Radya Pustaka Museum, good Padang food; ✦*Malioboro*, N end of Jl. Diponegoro, for excellent *ayam bakar* (barbecued chicken); ✦✦*Pondok Bambu*, Adisucipto 183 (out of town on way to airport), open restaurant with fish specialities; ✦✦*Pondok Segaran*, Sriwedari amusement park, good Javanese food; ✦✦*Pringgon Dani*, Jl. Bhayangkara, good food and a pleasant atmosphere, rec; ✦✦*Sari*, Jl. Slamet Riyadi 421, best Javanese restaurant in town; ✦*Sumber Rejeki*, Jl. Balong 66 for delicious *jajan* (snacks); ✦✦*Timlo Sastro*, Jl. Balong 28, locals maintain this serves the best *timlo* in town, open till after lunch; ✦✦*Tio Ciu*, N side of Jl. Slamet Riyadi, near the shopping plaza, fresh seafood; ✦*Warung Baru*, Jl. Ahmad Dahlan 8, travellers' food; ✦*Yant's Favourite*, Jl. Ahmad Dahlan 22. Popular, travellers' food.

Indonesian foodstalls: There are many warungs and food carts to be found around Solo, which vary enormously in quality; 3rd flr of Matahari Dept. Store at Singosaren Plaza offers a variety of Indonesian food; **night market** at Pujasari (Sriwedari Park) next to the Radya Pustaka Museum on Jl. Slamet Riyadi; **Carts** set-up along the N side of Jl. Slamet Riyadi in the afternoon and evening and sell delicious snacks (*jajan* in Javanese). On the S side of town, near **Nonongan**, saté stalls set-up in the evenings; stalls near the **train station** on Jl. Monginsidi.

Other Asian cuisine: ✦✦*Centrum*, Jl. Kratonan 151, a/c, best Chinese in town; ✦✦*Orient*, Jl. Slamet Riyadi, a/c, good Chinese, good seafood, rec; ✦*Populer*, Jl. Slamet Riyadi. Chinese noodles; ✦*Laris*, Jl. Slamet Riyadi. Chinese noodles.

International: There is little to offer the Westerner who does not have the stomach for Indonesian or Javanese food. Listed under Indonesian are a couple of places serving travellers' food. The better hotels will serve a limited number of Western dishes; **Kentucky Fried Chicken**, Jl. Slamet Riyadi; **Kusuma Sari**, Jl. Slamet Riyadi 111, icecreams; **La Tansa**, Jl. Imam Bonjol 31, bakery; **New Holland**, Jl. Slamet Riyadi, recommended bakery; **Svensen's**, Jl. Slamet Riyadi, icecreams.

Entertainment Solo has a cultural centre (Pusat Kebudayan), a Musical Academy and an Art Academy (STSI), with departments for dance, music, handicrafts and 'dalang' (the narrator of wayang kulit performances). The R.R.I. (National Radio Station) Auditorium at Jl. Marconi

51 organizes cultural performances. **Gamelan**: at the Pura Mangkunegaran on Sat 1000-1200 and accompanied by dance on Wed at 0900. Admission: entrance fee to palace. Also at *Kusuma Sahid Prince Hotel* 1800 Mon-Sun. **Ketoprak**: traditional folk drama performances at the R.R.I. every 4th Tues of the month 2000-2400. **Wayang Kulit**: R.R.I., every 3rd Sat of the month from 0900-0500 the next morning. **Wayang Orang**: at the Sriwedari Amusement Park on Jl. Slamet Riyadi 2000-2300 Mon-Sat and at the R.R.I. every 2nd Tues of the month 2000-2400. **Dance practices**: Javanese classical dance at Pura Mangkunegaran every Wed 1000-1200.

Sports **Golf**: Panasan Course, NW of town, near airport, T 42245, 80,000Rp. **Swimming**: at *Kusuma Sahid Prince Hotel* (2,500Rp), and at the *Mankunegaran Palace Hotel*.

Shopping Solo has much to offer the shopper, particularly batik and 'antique' curios. **Antique bric a brac**: *Pasar Triwindu*, off Jl. Diponegoro (see sights). Much of the merchandise is poor quality, 'antique' bric-à-brac, but the odd genuine bargain also turns up. Bargaining is essential. **Batik**: classical and modern designs, both *tulis* and *cap*, can be found at the Pasar Klewer, situated just beyond the W gate of the Alun-alun Lor, near the kraton (see sights). Prices are cheaper than the chainstores, but the market is very busy and bargaining is essential. It is best to go in the mornings, as the market starts to wind down after lunch. *Batik Keris*, Jl. Yos Sudarso 37; *Batik Danar Hadi*, Jl. Dr. Rajiman 164; *Ce Pe*, Jl. Ahmad Dahlan 4; *Batik Semar*, Jl. Dr. Rajiman 164.

Handicrafts: *Sriwedari Amusement Park*, Jl. Slamet Riyadi; *Usaha Pelajar*, Jl. Majapahit 6-10. **Bookstore**: *Toko Sekawan*, Jl. Kartini, not much in English. **Ceramics**: *PKK Artshops*, Jl. Alun-alun. **Pasar Besar**: is on Jl. Urip Sumoharjo and is the main market in Solo. **Department store**: *Matahari*, intersection of Jl. Jend. Gatot Subroto and Jl. Dr. Rajiman.

Banks & money changers Bumi Daya, Jl. Slamet Riyadi 16; **Central Asia**, Jl. Slamet Riyadi 7; **Pan Indonesia**, Jl. Major Kusmanto 7; **P.T.Grakarta** (money changer), Jl. Slamet Riyadi 20.

Useful addresses **General Post Office**: Jl. Jend. Sudirman 7. **Area code**: 0271. **Telephone Office**: Jl. Mayor Kusmanto 1 (24 hrs). **Immigration Office**: Jl. Adisucipto (out of town on way to airport) T 48479. **Hospital Kasih Ibu**: Jl. Slamet Riyadi 404 (T 44422). **Police Station**: Jl. Adisucipto, T 34500.

Airline offices Garuda, *Kusuma Sahid Prince Hotel*, Jl. Sugiyopranoto 22, T 36846. **Bouraq**, Jl Gajah Mada 86, T 34376. **Sempati Air**, *Solo Inn*, Jl. Slamet Riyadi 366, T 46240.

Local transport **Angkutan**: this is the local name for colts, which ply fixed routes around town, 150Rp. The station is close to the intercity bus terminal at Gilingan. **Becaks**: about 500Rp for a short trip in town, bargain hard. **Bicycles**: can be rented from the tourist information office on Jl. Slamet Riyadi 275, 1,000Rp/day. **Double-decker town bus**: 125-150Rp. **Horse-drawn carts**. **Taxis**: a few metered ones in town.

Tour companies & travel agents Natratour, Jl. Gajah Mada 86; **Nusantara**, Jl. Urip Sumoharjo 65; **Rosalia 121 Solo Indah Tour**, Jl. Slamet Riyadi 380, T 41916; **Sahid Gema Wisata**, Jl. Slamet Riyadi 332; **Sahid Tours and Travel**, Jl. Slamet Riyadi 332, T 42105; *Yant Favourite*, Jl. Ahmad Dahlan 22, T 34378.

Tourist office Jl. Slamet Riyadi 275, T 46501, can supply town maps and some information on cultural events. Open: 0800-1700 Mon-Sat. There are also tourist information centres at the bus station and at the airport.

Transport to & from Solo 585 km from Jakarta, 63 km NE of Yogya, 262 km from Surabaya. **By air**: Solo's Adisumarmo Airport is 10 km NW of the city. Taxis are available for the trip into town. Regular connections on Garuda/Merpati and Sempati with other destinations in Java, Sumatra, Kalimantan, Sulawesi, Bali, Lombok, Nusa Tenggara, Muluku and Irian Jaya (**see page 1008** for route map). **By train**: Solo's Balapan station is on Jl. Monginsidi (T 32228), a short distance N of the city centre. A/c connection with Jakarta 8-12 hrs, arrives Solo 0300, non-a/c arrives 0530 and on to Surabaya, 7 hrs. Crowded local train daily from Yogya 1 hr 20 mins (**see page 1012** timetable). **By bus**: the Tirtonadi station (T 35097) is on Jl. Jend. A. Yani, 2 km N of the city centre. Most bus companies have their offices on Jl. Sutan Syahrir or Jl. Urip Sumoharjo. Regular connections with most cities including Jakarta, Bogor, Bandung 12 hrs, Malang 9 hrs, Surabaya 6 hrs, Semarang 2½ hrs, Denpasar. Local buses regularly leave Yogya for Solo 2 hrs. **By minibus**: regular connections with Yogya, 2 hrs. **By taxi**: connections with Yogya cost about 34,000Rp.

Tawangmangu

Tawangmangu is a hill resort at 1,200 m set on the W slopes of Mount Sewu. Good walks, fresh air and pony 'trekking'. A short walk away is **Grojogan Sewu Waterfall** and up towards the top of town is the **Balekambang swimming pool** for cold dips. At the bottom of town, opposite the bus station, is a quaintly squalid **market**.

Excursions

Candi Sukuh (see page 620) can be reached on foot; it is a 1½-2 hr hike along the mountainside. Alternatively catch a bus down the mountain to Karangpandan. **Candi Ceto** can be reached from Sukuh or via Karangpandan (see page 620).

Sarangan is another hill resort 14 km to the E of Tawangmangu, and just into the neighbouring province of East Java. The town is centred around a lake (where there are facilities for fishing and rowing) and offers beautiful views of the surrounding countryside. Accommodation at Sarangan is more expensive than at Tawangmangu. **Getting there:** by colt from Tawangmangu.

Tours Tours to Candi Sukuh and Ceto are arranged by *Komajaya Komaratih Hotel*.

Accommodation A good range of hotels and losmen; the better hotels are cheaper than Solo for the same standard of accommodation, making it a good 'alternative' hill resort. **B** *Komajaya Komaratih*, Jl. Lawu Kav. 150-151, T 105, restaurant, pool, 'best' in town, good rooms, hot water, price includes breakfast, **A** for a family room for 4; **C** *Pondok Sari*, Jl. Timur Balekambang (to left of main road going up), T 112, pool, clean, hot water, good value, price includes breakfast; **D** *Pondok Sari I*, Jl. Utara Balekambang (100 m from Pondok Sari), hot water and separate sitting-room; **E** *Pak Amat*, Jl. Lawu Kav (50 m from bus station up hill), bungalows set around garden, rooms a little musty but clean; **E** *Losmen Mekar Indah*, Jl. Lawu Tawangmangu, reasonable rooms with own mandi; **E** *Losmen Ngesti Sariro*, Jl. Lawu Tawangmangu, reasonable.

Restaurants *Pondok Makan Lesehan*, Jl. Lawu Tawangmangu, Indonesian, Chinese and Western in attractive open pavilion; *Sapto Argo*, Jl. Lawu Tawangmangu; *Pak Amat*, Jl. Lawu Kav, for cheap burgers, Wienerschnitzel and Indonesian dishes.

Local transport Horses: are available for rent for about 6,000Rp/hr.

Transport to & from Tawangmangu 40 km from Solo. **By bus**: regular connections with Solo's Tirtonadi station. **By chartered minibus**: from the Balapan railway station in Solo. **By taxi**: from Solo, 1 hr (about 50,000Rp/day).

MAGELANG TO DIENG PLATEAU, via Wonosobo

Travelling N from the town of Magelang, the road divides after 10 km, one fork turning W to make a wide semi-circle around the foot of Mount Sumbing (3,371 m). In so doing, it passes through the town of Temanggung before turning S to climb towards Wonosobo, the route working its way between the looming Mount Sumbing to the SE and Mount Sundoro (3,136 m) to the NW. In total, the hill town of Wonosobo is around 66 km by road from Magelang, 107 km from Yogya; it is also the closest town of any size to the Dieng Plateau. From Wonosobo, the road climbs steeply N through spectacular scenery. Every square inch of land is cultivated, almost to the top of some of the mountains, and often on precipitous slopes. On a clear morning, there are stunning views back down to the valley. Eventually, at 1,800 m and after 26 kms the road reaches the Dieng Plateau.

Wonosobo

A small mountain town with a cool climate, Wonosobo is the best base from which to visit the **Dieng Plateau** and its temples (see below). There is a **market** running between Jalan Jend. A. Yani (the main road) and Jalan Resimen, at the N end of town.

Excursions
Dieng Plateau see below.

Tours Angkutans can be chartered for tours to Dieng, from Jl. Angkutan 45, T 21880 (30,000--35,000Rp).

Accommodation C *Nirwana*, Jl. Resimen 18/36, T 21066, hot water, bath, clean, best in town, price includes breakfast, rec; **C-D** *Bhima*, Jl. Jend. A. Yani 4, T 21233, hot water, bath, adequate accommodation, price includes breakfast; **D** *Famili*, Jl. Sumbing 6, T 396, nice building, average rooms, with outside mandi, a little overpriced; **D** *Parama*, Jl. Jend. A. Yani 96, T 21789, hot water, bath, clean; **E** *Sindoro*, Jl. Sumbing 5, T 179, clean, rec; **E-F** *Petra*, Jl. Jend. A. Yani 97, T 21152; **F** *Surya*, Jl. Jend. A. Yani 4, T 272.

Restaurants ✦✦*Asia*, Jl. Kawedanan 35, good Indonesian/Chinese, rec;✦*Banyumas*, Jl. Sumbing (near intersection with Jl. Jend. A. Yani); *Dieng*, Jl. Kawedanan.

Shopping Batik: Busaka Dewi, Jl. Jend. A. Yani, plus a number of shops around the market.

Banks & money changers Rakyat, Jl. Jend. A. Yani, top end, on corner of Jl. Kartini.

Useful addresses Post Office: Jl. Pemuda, top of town on main square. **Area code**: 0286.

Tourist office Jl. Pemuda 2. Open: 0800-1400 Mon-Sat.

Local transport Horse carts or *dokar*: 5,000Rp for a tour of the town. **Local bus**: including those for Dieng, leave from Jl. Resimen near the market, just up the road from the colt station, 800Rp. **Colt**: the station is in the market on Jl. Resimen.

Transport to & from Wonosobo 107 km NW of Yogya, 134 km SE of Pekalongan, 119 km SW of Semarang. **By bus**: the long-distance bus terminal is at the S end of Jl. Jend. A. Yani, 1 km up hill from the town centre. Regular connections with Magelang 2 hrs and on to Yogya 40 mins, Semarang (via Ambarawa) 4 hrs; minibuses also leave for Cilacap 6 hrs.

Dieng Plateau

The Dieng Plateau presents an extraordinary landscape; a rich volcanic basin of sulphur springs, lakes and the oldest Hindu temples on Java. Visitors sometimes report great disappointment on arriving at Dieng, having heard in advance of the stunning journey up to the plateau. This is often because most people do not get here until after midday when it can be misty and grey. It is undoubtedly best to travel to Dieng and explore the plateau in the clear highland mornings – this can only be achieved by staying in Wonosobo (26 km S) or in Dieng itself.

Places of interest

The Dieng Plateau (Dieng comes from the Sanskrit word *Di-hyang*, meaning the 'Abode of the Gods') was occupied from the end of the 7th century to the 13th century. Eight temples remain, out of a possible 200, all of which were on a small scale and dedicated to Siva, the Hindu god of destruction. Little is known of the history of these temples, but the volatile volcanic landscape probably had something to do with the construction of so many candis here – the area was almost certainly considered an ideal place to communicate with the ancestors. Beginning at the end of the 7th century and ending in the late 8th or possibly early 9th centuries, these candis are some of the oldest on Java. Their construction was probably linked to the Central Javanese Sanjaya Dynasty. The names that the various candi have been given are not original, and give no indication of their dedication. Built on swampy ground, evidence remains of a vast, intricate underground drainage system, some of which still functions today.

Archaeologists believe that there were 2 building periods at Dieng. Candi Arjuna, Semar, Srikandi and Gatokaca all date from between the late 7th century to about 730, while Candi Puntadewa, Sembadra, Bima and Dvaravati were built between 730 and 780. The latter group

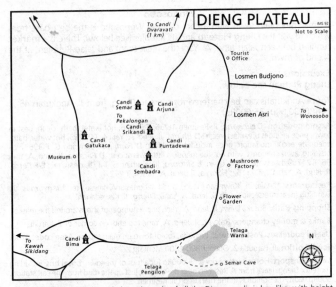

DIENG PLATEAU IMS 92

Not to Scale

To Candi
Dvaravati
(1 km)

Tourist
Office

Losmen Budjono

Losmen Asri

To
Wonosobo

Candi
Semar   Candi
Arjuna

To
Pekalongan   Candi
Srikandi

Candi
Puntadewa

Candi
Gatukaca

Museum

Candi
Sembadra

Mushroom
Factory

Flower
Garden

To
Kawah
Sikidang

Candi
Bima

Telaga
Warna

Semar Cave

N

Telaga
Pengilon

were more elaborate. Nonetheless, the style of all the Dieng candis is box-like, with height and width of similar proportions, and little ornamentation. Outlined below is a circular route from Dieng village, which takes about 3 hours to walk. It takes in most of the shrines, a couple of sulphur springs and a sulphur lake.

On arrival from Wonosobo, the major group of shrines can be seen, looking rather small, in the middle of the plateau. From the minibus/taxi stand next to the *Losmen Budjono*, walk along the main road (towards Pekalongan) for 300m. There is a small track on the right that leads up to **Candi Dvaravati** which dates from the middle of the 8th century. Returning to the main road, and walking 100m back towards the bus stop, is a road on the right leading to the main group of shrines.

Five small shrines remain amidst the foundations of a much larger group of buildings. They lack the ornamentation of candis on the lowlands, but their proportions are pleasing. The first temple to be reached by the footpath is **Candi Arjuna**. This and Candi Semar, which lies opposite, were probably the first temples to be built on Dieng. Arjuna originally housed a linga, which would have been ritually bathed each day. This necessitated the construction of a gutter through the N wall, which ends in an impressive gargoyle in the shape of a makara head. **Candi Semar**, is squat and rectangular in shape, and would originally have housed a statue of Nandi the bull – Siva's vehicle. It and Candi Arjuna were built as a unit, dedicated to the cult of Siva. The roofless **Candi Srikandi** is the squarest and possibly the most beautiful of the candis on Dieng. It retains some fine carving on its exterior walls with Vishnu on the N, Siva on the E and Brahma on the S wall – an unusual placement of these Hindu gods. Dumarçay postulates that at the early date that these shrines were built, the placement conventions evident in later temples were not yet established. **Candi Puntadewa** is the tallest and most elegant in this group, resting on a large plinth, with a stairway leading up to the shrine. It has the characteristic door frame ornamentation of the monster kala vomiting out foliage. **Candi Sembadra** is the smallest shrine here, with narrow niches, and a kala motif above the entrance. Open: 0615-1715.

From this group of candis, walk over the grazing land to **Candi Gatukaca**, set apart from the main group. It is believed that the base of this candi was extended in the middle of the 9th century in order to house another shrine. In so doing, the foundations were weakened and its ruin hastened. Close by on the other side of the road is a rather unimpressive museum; more like a storehouse for sculptures of Hindu gods and lingam found on the plateau.

A 1 km walk S along this road leads to **Candi Bima**, built in a very different style, and unique in Java. The tower is a tall pyramid, with small heads in some of the niches on each layer. It shows strong stylistic links with the Orissan temples of E central India. It is thought that the architects must have had a plan of the Indian prototype, which they followed. The scale is very different however, presumably because the builders had no way of knowing the proportions of the original. It has been vandalized with graffiti, but remains one of the most impressive monuments on the plateau, being considerably more elaborate than the others.

From Candi Bima, turn W and after another 1½-2 km the path arrives at **Kawah Sikidang**, bubbling mud pools, sulphurous odours and a scarred landscape. The **thermal springs** here are used to produce power, the geothermal station being just a short distance on from the springs. From Kawah Sikidang, walk back past Candi Bima, and turn left at the 'T' junction, 50 m on from the temple. Less than a kilometre along this road is **Telaga Warna**, an emerald green **sulphur lake**. From here there is a path skirting the lake and leading to further sulphur lakes and the **Semar Cave** (ask for *Gua Semar*), among others. Close to Telaga Warna is a terraced flower garden with such temperate plants as pansies, roses, marigolds and hydrangea. The garden is private. On past the mushroom factory, the road leads back to Losmen Budjono. Admission to area: 300Rp/person, 550Rp/car. Guide to temples: 7,500Rp.

Accommodation If intending to stay overnight on the plateau, be sure to have some warm clothing as it gets very cold. One visitor reported the losmen here have the coldest mandi water in Indonesia. **E** *Losmen Asri*, left from T-junction into the village from Wonosobo; **E** *Losmen Budjono*, Jl. Raya, basic facilities but friendly management; **E** *Losmen Gunung Mas*, Jl. Raya, opposite road to main temples.

Restaurants *Losmen Budjono*, Jl. Raya, at intersection to Wonosobo road, simple Indonesian dishes, friendly atmosphere.

Tourist office Dieng Tourist Information, Jl. Raya (near the bus stop). Not particularly helpful.

Transport to & from Dieng 26 km from Wonosobo. **By bus:** the bus stop is near the *Losmen Budjono*. Regular connections with Wonosobo 1 hr and Yogya. It is also possible to reach Pekalongan, with difficulty, from Dieng – a trip of 105 km and 3-4 hrs. The Wonosobo-Dieng bus continues on to Batur. From there, there are minibuses to Kalibening, where it is possible to pick up another minibus to Pekalongan.

MAGELANG TO SEMARANG via Ambarawa and Gedung Songo

Travelling N from the town of Magelang, the road divides after 10 km, the E fork continuing for another 24 km to Ambarawa, noted for its railway museum. At Ambarawa, a road climbs 6 km to the hill resort of Bandungan at 1,000 m, which is situated 7 km E of the 8th century Hindu temples of Gedung Songo. The main road from Ambarawa continues N for another 37 km before reaching the N Java coast at Semarang – the largest city in Central Java.

Bandungan

Bandungan – yet another Javanese hill resort with a selection of wisma, losmen and one good hotel – is situated 1,000 m above sea-level on the slopes of Mount Ungaran (which rises to 2,050 m). It is the most convenient place to stay when visiting the temples at Gedung Songo (see below) and is a good alternative base.

Excursions

The Hindu temples of **Gedung Songo** are to be found 7 km W of Bandungan. The road to the site passes through an area of highland agriculture, with a great diversity of crops being cultivated – including such strange tropical sights as roses intercropped with cabbages. Set on the S slopes of Mount Ungaran, the temples of Gedung Songo – meaning '9 buildings' in Javanese – are all Hindu and were probably built between 730 and 780. The area has a number of volcanic vents which would have made it a revered site and probably explains the presence of these small candi, scattered over an area of several sq km. They occupy one of the most spectacular positions of any group of temples in Java. The temperature is wonderfully cool after the plains, with mist characteristically hanging over the mountains behind.

The shrines are numbered from 1 to 9, starting at the bottom. The main shrine in each group was dedicated to Siva. These temples became the prototype for subsequent Javanese Hindu temples. The sixth group is an excellent example; a square base is cut through by a stairway leading up to a portico on the W side of the building, which opens into a small square cella. The other 3 sides of the building are decorated by pilasters and a central niche which housed a statue. Three false storeys rise up above the central cella, decreasing in size and thus giving a deceptive impression of verticality. None of the shrines are particularly elaborate, although some display carvings of kala-makara heads and nagas. Some of the temples have been restored. Admission: 350Rp. Open: 0700-1700, Mon-Sun. It is possible to walk around all the temples in 2-3 hrs, but it is exhausting at this altitude. An easier way of getting around is on horseback, 1½ hrs. Expect to pay about 2,500-3,000Rp for these old animals. **Getting there:** catch a minibus towards Sumowono and get off after 3½ km at the junction where a minor road runs steeply up the mountainside (it is signposted). The entrance is 2½ km up this road and ojeks wait at the bottom. If coming from Ambarawa, catch a minibus to Bandungan or through Bandungan to Sumowono.

Ambarawa Railway Museum is 6 km from Bandungan (**see page 631**). **Getting there:** catch one of the regular buses or minibuses (200Rp).

Accommodation B *Rawa Pening*, Jl. Pandanaran 33, T (313)338, restaurant, good pool, tennis courts, friendly, rec; **C** *Kusuma Madya*, Jl. Jend Sudirman 219, T 23162, a/c, hot water, tennis, average; **E** *Wina Prawatya*, off Jl. Pandanaran, mostly for families, good value, rec.

Transport to & from Bandungan 6 km from Ambarawa, 35 km from Semarang. **By minibus**: regular connections with Ambarawa (200Rp); from Semarang or Yogya catch a bus or minibus to Ambarawa (500Rp), then change.

Semarang

Semarang is one of the oldest cities in Indonesia, and was the seat of the Dutch Governor of the North-East Provinces. It is situated between the shore and a small ridge of mountains and consequently is very hot. The city was ceded to the Dutch VOC in 1677 by the Mataram king Amangkurat I, in lieu of debts. A base was established along the coast at Jepara (which was already a trading centre), with additional trading-posts at Semarang as well as at Surabaya, Rembang, Demak and Tegal. However, it was not until 1705 that the VOC finally brought Semarang firmly under its control. Only then did the Dutch move their headquarters here, and the town gradually grew in commercial influence.

Semarang's usefulness as a port waned with the gradual silting up of the harbour, and by the 19th century the city had been eclipsed as Java's premier port by Surabaya. Even so, Semarang remains the largest city in Central Java. It is an important commercial centre with a population of over a million, a third of whom are thought to be of Chinese extraction. In 1741, the Chinese of Semarang responded to the murder of their kinsmen in Batavia (**see page 540**) by, in their

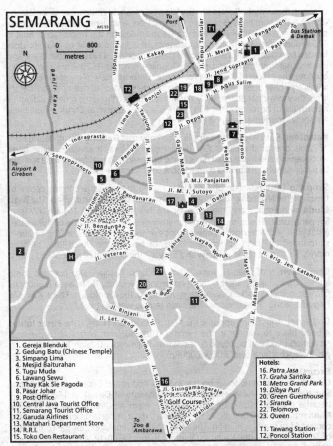

SEMARANG

IMS 93

0 800 metres

Banjir Kanal

To Port

To Bus Station & Demak

To Airport & Cirebon

To Zoo & Ambarawa

Golf Course

1. Gereja Blenduk
2. Gedung Batu (Chinese Temple)
3. Simpang Lima
4. Mesjid Baiturahan
5. Tugu Muda
6. Lawang Sewu
7. Thay Kak Sie Pagoda
8. Pasar Johar
9. Post Office
10. Central Java Tourist Office
11. Semarang Tourist Office
12. Garuda Airlines
13. Matahari Department Store
14. R.R.I.
15. Toko Oen Restaurant

Hotels:
16. Patra Jasa
17. Graha Santika
18. Metro Grand Park
19. Dibya Puri
20. Green Guesthouse
21. Siranda
22. Telomoyo
23. Queen

T1. Tawang Station
T2. Poncol Station

turn, attacking the Dutch of Semarang. This turned out to be a misjudgement. The VOC, with the help of Cakraningrat IV of Madura, defeated the Chinese and slaughtered all those they could lay their hands on.

Semarang is divided into 2 parts: the coastal lowland where most of businesses and industrial activities are to be found; and an inland, hilly, residential area.

Places of interest
Even though Semarang seems to be taking the shopping plaza route to urban development, Islamic, Chinese and European influences are still in evidence and there are numerous **beautiful buildings** dotted among the streets. Indeed, in parts at least, it is one of Java's most attractive cities. The best area to explore is N and E from the Post Office on Jalan Pemuda (itself a notable building). Roads with interesting buildings include Jalan Jend. Suprapto, Jalan Kepodang, Jalan Garuda, Jalan Suari and Jalan Merak, and the maze of streets cutting across and

between these roads. **Gereja Blenduk** (*gereja* meaning church, *blenduk* meaning dome) – the Immanuel Protestant Church – on Jalan Jend. Suprapto 32 is the oldest church in Central Java, and the second oldest on the whole island. Built in 1753, and rather Wren-like in appearance, it is in the shape of a Greek cross fronted by 4 pillars. It has a handsome classical portico, a faded copper dome and inside a Baroque organ and pulpit. Opposite is a fine 1920s-style commercial building, the offices of Jiwasraya Assurance. Unfortunately, many of the buildings in this area have been abandoned, and most are in a state of deterioration. Before long, they may disappear entirely. For architectural enthusiasts, other buildings of interest are to be found in the hills to the S, an area known as **Candi**, where there are some wonderful decaying villas.

Kelenteng Sam Poo Kong Temple (also known as **Gedung Batu**), dating from 1772, is one of the oldest Chinese temples in Java. It contains some good woodcarving and many ritual objects and brassware. To get there, take a minibus to Banjir Kanal (150Rp) and then a becak to the temple (500Rp).

Simpang Lima (junction of 5 roads) is the huge main square in the centre of town. On the NW side of the square is the modern **Mesjid Baiturahan**. The **Tugu Muda** monument marks the centre of another square, about 1½ km NW from Simpang Lima. The monument commemorates the 5-day battle of Indonesian republican youth against Japanese troops at the end of the war. The square is surrounded by grand government buildings built by the Dutch (they planned more), the largest being the **Lawang Sewu** – the building of a thousand doors.

Chinatown, S of Jalan H. Agus Salim, off Jalan Pekojan, also contains some interesting buildings, notably those bordering the canal. There are a number of Chinese temples tucked away here, including the Confucian **Thay Kak Sie Pagoda**, along Gang Lombok. The main temple was built in 1772.

On Jalan H. Agus Salim, opposite the *Metro Grand Park Hotel*, is the **Pasar Johar**, a good place to wander in the evening. The **zoo** (with botanical garden and recreation park) can be found S of town in Tinjimoyo, off Jalan Teuku Umar. To get there, charter a colt (3,000-5,000Rp).

Excursions
Demak is an historic town on the road to Kudus and Surabaya, 25 km from Semarang. Raden Patah established the Sultanate of Demak in 1500, when it became the first Islamic kingdom on Java. Islam was introduced via India by Muslim traders and Demak, as one of Java's most important ports, was rapidly converted to the new religion. The town gained a reputation for the community of scholars or *pesantren* who established themselves here, and pilgrims would travel from all over Java and beyond to be taught by these holy men. Demak remained powerful until the end of the 16th century when power shifted S to Mataram, near Yogyakarta. The oldest mosque in Central Java can be found in the town square, on the Semarang side of the centre. Founded by the 9 *walis* (the first Muslim evangelists in Java, **see page 528**) in 1478, the **Agung Demak Mosque** has the characteristic 3-tiered roof of N Java. In the N part of the mosque is a graveyard of the family of Sultan Demak and the **tomb** of one of the 9 walis is to be found here: Sunan Kalijaga. The minaret looks uncannily like a World War II air raid tower, but does in fact echo earlier Hindu, Majapahit architectural styles. The mosque is an important pilgrimage spot and souvenir stalls line the outside walls, where posters of the 9 walis can be bought. The main street leading from the square N towards Kudus, **Jalan Sultan Patah**, is lined by houses with graceful, sweeping tiled roofs. The **market** is also on this street. **Getting there:** by bus from Semarang's Terboyo station on Jl. Patah; the Demak station is on the Semarang side of town, a short walk from the main square.

Kudus, 19 km on from Demak and 50 km in total from Semarang, is another historically interesting town – (**see page 633**). Another 30 km NW from Kudus is the **woodcarving port of Jepara** (**see page 634**) where it is possible to catch boats to the **Karimunjawa Islands** (**see page 635**).

Grobogan is an **active mud volcano** which lies about 85 km E of Semarang and 15 km E of Purwodadi. It makes rather a long detour from Semarang but is of interest to budding volcanologists and has a certain novelty value. Visitors can walk across spongy dried earth to within about 10m of the bubbling mud. Admission: 150Rp. Open: Mon-Sun. **Getting there:** catch a bus travelling E through Purwodadi towards Surabaya and get off at the crossroads in the village of Wirasari. From there catch a minibus going S (right), or take an ojek. The volcano lies 6 km along this road – ask for *berapi lumpur*.

Ambarawa town and its **Railway Museum** (*kereta api*) are 32 km from Semarang and 4 km off the main Semarang-Solo road. The Railway Museum is through the town, past the road to Bandungan, and about 1 km off Jalan Pemuda. It is a charming, well kept museum set around the old railway station and has a large collection of locomotives, the oldest dating from 1891. It is possible to charter the single working cog locomotive for 500,000Rp and ride into the mountains to Bedono, 18 km away. The train seats 90 people and lunch is provided on the day-long outing. One day's notice required (write to: PJKA Wilayah Usaha Jawa, Jl. M.H. Thamrin 3, Semarang, Jawa Tengah, Indonesia or contact one of the main railway stations). Admission: 200Rp. Open: 0700-2000 Mon-Sun. **Getting there:** 'medium' sized buses travel to the town, or catch a Semarang/Yogya bus, which pass through Ambarawa (45 mins from Semarang). It is a 1½ km walk from the centre of town to the museum. The road from Semarang to Ambarawa is notable for a row of trees just outside Semarang which are home to thousands of white ibis.

The Hindu temples of **Gedung Songo** (**see page 628**) lie 13 km from Ambarawa, past the hill resort of **Bandungan**. **Getting there:** by bus from Semarang to Ambarawa, ¾ hr (500Rp) and then one of the regular minibuses that climb up to Bandungan (200Rp).

Tours Tour companies in Semarang run day tours around the sights of the city, as well as to Borobudur, the Dieng Plateau, Kudus and Demak, Gedung Songo, Solo, and cultural tours to, for example, Jepara (a woodcarving village). 'Teak plantation tours' to Cepu, 160 km E of Semarang: travelling in a steam locomotive, the tourist visits teak plantations in different stages of development. Contact Perum Perhutani, Jl. Pehlawan 151, Semarang, T 311611.

Festivals Feb: *Dugderan Festival*, marks the start of the month-long Muslim fast, held in front of Grand Mosque. July: *Jaran Sam Po*, Chinese ceremony, procession to Thay Kak Sie Pagoda. Aug: *Semarang Fair*, month-long festivities on Jl. Sriwijaya every evening. Oct: *Pertempuran Lima Hari* (14th), held around the Tugu Muda to commemorate the 5 day battle of Indonesian youth against the Japanese in 1945.

Accommodation A+ *Graha Santika*, Jl. Pandanaran 116-120, T 318850, F 413113, a/c, restaurant, pool, new hotel, facilities include a fitness centre, rec; **A+-C** *Metro Grand Park*, Jl. H. Agus Salim 2-4, T 27371, a/c, restaurant, faceless hotel, rather down-at-heel; **A** *Patrajasa*, Jl. Sisingamangaraja, PO Box 8, T 314441, F 314448, a/c, restaurant, pool, good views, good facilities, sophisticated; **B-C** *Siranda*, Jl. Diponegoro 1, T 313271, a/c, early 70s-style hotel built on the hill overlooking Semarang, good views and reasonable value, price includes breakfast; **B-D** *Candi Baru*, Jl. Rinjani 21, T 315272, a/c, old hotel with character; **B-D** *Dibya Puri*, Jl. Pemuda 11, T 27821, a/c, colonial hotel which has seen better days, rather scruffy, price includes breakfast; **C** *Bukit Asri*, Jl. Setiabudi 5, T 315743, a/c, 4 km from town on road to Ambarawa, clean rooms; **B-D** *Telomoyo*, Jl. Gajah Mada 138, T 25436, some a/c, modern, clean and comfortable; **C-D** *Green Guesthouse*, Jl. Kesambi 7, Candi Baru, T 312642, some a/c, attractive old-style hotel with good rooms and fine views looking S from Semarang, out of town in Candi Baru, price includes breakfast, rec; **C-D** *Queen*, Jl. Gajah Mada 44-52, T 27063, a/c, large rooms, hot water, clean; **E** *Losmen Singapore*, Jl. Imam

Bonjol 12, T 23757, rooms set attractively around a courtyard, atmospheric, unfortunately the rooms themselves are rather grubby, shared bathroom; **E** *Losmen Tanjung*, Jl. Tanjung 9-11, old Dutch era house, friendly management.

Restaurants Semarang has, seemingly, more restaurants per sq inch than any other town in Java. Jl. Gajah Mada and Jl. H.M. Thamrin, which run parallel to one another N-S, in particular have restaurants serving virtually every variety of Asian food (particularly Chinese). For foodstalls in the evenings, try the *Pasar Johor Yaik* opposite the *Metro Hotel* at the NE end of Jl. Pemuda, or the S end of Jl. Gajah Mada, leading into the square dominated by the Matahari Department store. The Semarang speciality is *bandeng* – a smoked fish.

Indonesian: ♦*Nglaras Roso*, Jl. Haryono 701, rec; ♦*Timlo Lontong Solo*, Jl. Jend. A. Yani 182, Javanese; ♦♦*Toko Oen*, Jl. Pemuda 52 (N from intersection with Jl. Gajah Mada), excellent Indonesian food, good variety of ice-creams, some European food, all served in moth eaten colonial splendour; ♦♦*Tan Goei*, Jl. Tanjung 25, also serves Chinese food and ice-creams, popular. Foodstalls: Pasar Johar, Jl. H.A. Salim.

Other Asian Cuisine: ♦♦♦*Istana*, Jl. Haryono 836, Chinese and International food; ♦♦*Pringgading*, Jl. Pringgading 54 off Jl. L.J. Haryono, excellent Chinese seafood; *Seoul Palace*, Jl. Gajah Mada 99B, Korean. International: ♦♦*Ritzeky pub*, Jl. Sinabung Buntu, popular place for international food; ♦♦*Sukarasa*, Jl. Ungaran, French food. Bakeries: *Wijaya Bakery*, Jl. Pemuda 38.

Bars: Karaoke: Jl. K.H. Wahid Hasyim 121.

Entertainment Ketoprak and wayang orang: the Ngesti Pandowo, Jl. Pemuda 116, Mon and Thurs 2015. Wayang kulit: the RRI (Radio station) on Jl. Jend. A. Yani organize performances on the first Sat of every month. Cinemas: *Manggala*, Jl. Gajah Mada 119. Disco: *Xanadu*, Metro Hotel, Jl. H.A. Salim.

Sports Golf: *Semarang Golf Club*, Jl. Sisingamangaraja 14, T 312582, close to the *Patrajasa Hotel*. Swimming: *Patrajasa Hotel* has a pool open to the public.

Shopping Batik: *GKBI*, Jl. Pemuda 48; *Batik Keris*, Gajah Mada Plaza; *Kerta Niaga*, Stadion 1A and Jl. Gajah Mada; *Batik Pekalongan*, Jl. Pemuda 66. Woodcarving: *Kerta Niaga*. Handicrafts: *Wijaya*, Jl. Gajah Mada 2; *Toko Panjang*, Jl. Widoharjo 31.

Night market: *Pasar Johar*, Jl. A. Salim, good place to wander, vast range of goods on sale. Shopping Plazas: *Simpang Lima*, on Simpang Lima, at the corner of Jl. A. Dahlan and Jl. Jend. A. Yani; *Semarang Plaza*, Jl. H. Agus Salim (E of the market).

Local transport Bus: fixed price city buses (200Rp). Taxi: metered taxis, or rent them by the hour or the day. Colts and becaks ply the streets, although becaks are outlawed on the main streets.

Banks & money changers Ekspor Impor, Jl. M. Tantular 19; BNI Jl. L.M.T. Haryono 16; Bumi Daya, Jl. Kepodeng 34.

Airline offices Garuda, Jl. Gajah Mada 11, T 20178. Merpati, Jl. Gajah Mada 58, T 23027. Bouraq, Jl. Gajah Mada 61, T 23065. Mandala, Jl. Pemuda 40.

Tour companies & travel agents Electra Duta Wisata, Jl. Gajah Mada 1, T 288444; Nitour, Jl. Indraprasta 97; Nusantara, Simpang Lima Shopping Centre Blok C6; Satura, Simpang Lima Shopping Centre Blok I,II,III; Tedjo Express, Jl. Haryono 786.

Tourist offices Central Java Tourist Office (Dinas Pariwisata), Jl. Imam Bonjol 209, T 511773. In an old building on the square with Tugu Muda. Very helpful staff. Open 0700-1400 Mon-Thurs, 0700-1100 Fri, 0700-1230 Sat. Semarang Municipal Tourist Office (Dinas Pariwisata Kodia Semarang) Jl. Srivijaya 29, T 311220 (at the old site of the zoo; colts drive down Jl. Srivijaya).

Useful addresses General Post Office: Jl. Pemuda 4. Area code: 024. Hospital: William Booth, Jl. Letjen. S. Parman 5.

Transport to & from Semarang 120 km N of Yogya, 485 km E of Jakarta, 308 km W of Surabaya. By air: Ahmad Yani airport is 5 km W of town off Jl. Siliwangi. *Transport to town*: No.2 town bus goes from Jl. Pemuda as far as the roundabout, but it is a 1 km walk down Jl. Kalibanteng to the airport itself. Take a becak from here or a taxi from town. Regular connections on Garuda/Merpati, Sempati, Mandala and Bouraq with other destinations in Java, Sumatra, Kalimantan, Sulawesi, Bali, Lombok, Nusa Tenggara, Maluku and Irian Jaya (see page 1006 for route map). By train: there are 2 train stations; Poncol is on Jl. Imam Bonjol but is only for freight; passenger trains run from Tawang station on Jl. Merak. Regular connections with Jakarta on the Mutiara Utara and via Surabaya on the Mutiara Timur. Connections with Jakarta on the Mutiara Utara night express 7 hrs which continues on to Surabaya 8-10 hrs. The Senja Utama from Jakarta is non a/c night train 8-10 hrs, connections with Pekalongan 4 hrs (see page 1012 for timetable). By bus: Terminal Terboyo is on the E side of town, 200m N of the road towards Demak. Town buses travelling along Jl. Pemuda travel out to the terminal. To buy tickets for onward journeys, plenty of bus companies have their offices here. Taxi rank for journeys into town. Regular connections with Kudus 1 hr, Yogya 3½ hrs, Solo 2½ hrs, Cirebon 6 hrs, Pekalongan 3 hrs and Jakarta 9 hrs. **By minibus**: minibuses leave from the corner of Jl. H.A. Salim and Jl. M.T. Haryono. Regular connections with Solo, Yogya, Cirebon and Jakarta.

EAST FROM SEMARANG TO DEMAK AND KUDUS

From Semarang, the road E passes through the historic town of Demak (26 km) and continues on to the Islamic, *kretek*-producing centre of Kudus, a total of 51 km from Semarang. A road runs 30 km NW from Kudus to the ancient port and woodcarving centre of Jepara. Continuing E from Kudus, the road passes through the port of Rembang after 47 km and then 57 km further on still, crosses into the province of East Java. From here it is another 138 km, following the coast, to Surabaya via Tuban and Gresik.

Kudus

Founded by the Muslim saint Sunan Kudus, Ja'far Shodik, Kudus developed as an important Islamic holy city and is still a pilgrimage centre today. Its name is taken from the Arabic *al-Quds*, which means 'holy', and it is the only town in Java which has retained an Arabic name. Kudus and the surrounding countryside is still one of the most orthodox Muslim areas on Java. It is also relatively prosperous, enjoying the fruits of being a major kretek-producing town (see box).

Places of interest
Less than 1 km off the main road into town from Semarang is a **kretek museum** on Jalan Jetas Pejaten – only Indonesia could have a museum in praise of the cigarette. Models, machinery, dioramas, photo portraits and a collection of kretek packets make up the display. In front of the museum, there is a statue of a family group with the man smoking an enormous kretek while remaining protective towards his wife and children. A traditional Kudus house (*rumah adat Kudus*) stands next to the museum (see below). Admission: by donation. Open: 0900-1400, Mon-Thurs, 0900-1300 Sat., 0800-1400 Sun.

Down an alleyway off Jalan Sunan Kudus, the main road to Jepara, is the **Al-Manar** or **Al-Aqsa Mosque** (on Jalan Menara). Built in 1549 by Sunan Kudus on the site of a Hindu-Javanese temple, its name is the same as the mosque at Jerusalem. It is an important place of pilgrimage for Muslims and interesting for non-Muslims, with its attractive red brick **Kudus Menara** or **Clock Tower**. The tower was built in 1685, and shows clear architectural links with the Hindu Majapahit kingdom and with similar towers in Bali, notably the Kulkul towers found in temple compounds. It is possible to climb the steep stairs and then a wooden ladder to the top, where there are magnificent views of the town over a sea of tiled roofs. Behind the mosque, to the left of the main entrance, are a series of charming brick courtyards separated by weathered wooden doors. Each courtyard contains gravestones leading, eventually, to the revered **tomb of Sunan Kudus**. His mausoleum of finely carved stone is draped with a curtain of lace.

In town, on Jalan Jend. A. Yani, is the large **Djarum kretek factory**, Kudus' major employer. Free tours of the factory are run on work days from 0800. Not far S from the factory, and facing onto the large new Kudus Plaza shopping centre, is a **Chinese Pagoda**.

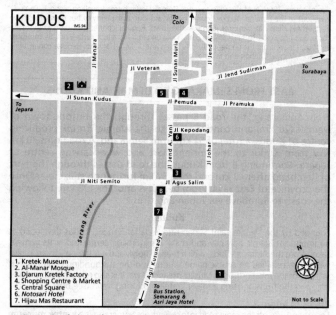

KUDUS IMS 94

To Colo

Jl Menara

Jl Veteran

Jl Sunan Muria

Jl Jend A. Yani

Jl Jend Sudirman

To Surabaya

Jl Sunan Kudus

To Jepara

5   **4**

Jl Pemuda

Jl Pramuka

Jl Kepodang

6

Jl Jend A. Yani

Jl Johar

3

Jl Niti Semito

Jl Agus Salim

B

7

Jl Agil Kusumadya

Serang River

2

1. Kretek Museum
2. Al-Manar Mosque
3. Djarum Kretek Factory
4. Shopping Centre & Market
5. Central Square
6. *Notosari Hotel*
7. *Hijau Mas Restaurant*

To Bus Station, Semarang & Asri Jaya Hotel

1

N

Not to Scale

Kudus is also famous for its **traditional houses** or *rumah adat Kudus*. It was here, and at the nearby port of Jepara, that woodcarving was developed to its highest degree of refinement and houses were decorated with elaborately carved internal and external screens. Abdul Syukur owns a traditional Kudus teak house on Jalan Veteran, with just such intricately carved woodwork. To visit the house, contact the tourist office in Kudus and they will accompany you there.

Excursions

Rembang lies 60 km E of Kudus, on the N coast, and is associated with the short life and works of Raden Ajeng Kartini, a woman who devoted her life to the education and emancipation of women (see box). In the Regent's office in Rembang is a room containing some of Kartini's possessions and a collection of her writings. She was born in the nearby town of Jepara where she was instrumental in developing the woodcarving industry (see below). **Getting there:** regular connections from Kudus bus terminal.

The historic town of **Demak** is 19 km S of Kudus (see page 633). **Getting there:** regular connections by colt and bus.

Jepara is an ancient port situated 30 km NW of Kudus. When the Dutch first began exploring the route to the Spice Islands they recorded that Jepara was a significant trading centre supplying, among other products, rice, palm sugar and cattle. It reached the height of its maritime power at the end of the 16th century, under the rule of the famous queen Kali-nyamat. Even at this time Jepara was highly regarded for its woodcarving and furniture and the traditional and elaborately carved houses here are some of the finest in Java. The tourist office still touts Jepara as the 'world renowned' centre for woodcarving. Furniture, figures, and other products are all for sale. Accommodation: **C** *Kalingga Star*

The life-blood of the Indonesian male: the clove or 'kretek' cigarette

One of the most important upland crops in East Java is *cengkeh* or cloves. These are grown for a single purpose: to supply the massive *kretek* or clove cigarette industry. It is difficult to go anywhere in Indonesia where there is not the lingering scent of the spice. The centre of the industry is East Java where it employs about 100,000 workers. The giant Gudang Garam factory at Kediri alone has over 40,000 employees, while Bentoel in Malang employs another 20,000. In Central Java, the centre of kretek production is the Djarum factory in Kudus. Over the course of the 1980s and 90s the traditional hand-made kretek has been displaced by the machine-made variety. At the same time, the kretek has been eating into the market share of so-called 'white' cigarettes.

In late 1990, Suharto's youngest son, Hutomo 'Tommy' Mandala Putra, used his impeccable contacts to set up a clove monopoly, known as BPCC. He managed to convince his father that the best way to help 500,000 poor clove farmers was to create such a monopoly, enabling him to buy the spice from farmers at 7,000Rp/kg – double the prevailing market price – and then selling it on to the captive kretek manufacturers for 12,700-15,000Rp/kg. The powerful manufacturers resisted the move by paying less to tobacco farmers. Tommy, in turn, secured US$325 million in subsidized credits from the central Bank Indonesia and began to buy huge quantities of cloves, but mostly from powerful Chinese traders rather than from farmers. The monopoly seemed to be flying in the face of the government's attempts to de-regulate industry. By the beginning of 1992, BPCC was effectively bankrupt: it had no funds left to buy cloves, had built up a 2-year stock of the spice, and Tommy suggested – amidst much recrimination – that farmers burn half their crop to restore demand. BPCC became a semi-public monopoly with farmers receiving only 4,000Rp/kg for their crop, while kretek manufacturers were still required to buy their stocks from BPCC. In mid 1993, Tommy admitted that his company was no longer able to service its loan from Bank Indonesia, and suggested that he borrow money from a commercial - but state-owned - bank to repay the central bank.

Hotel, Jl. Dr. Sutomo 16, T 54 and some losmen. **Getting there:** catch a colt from the colt station on Jl. Jend. A. Yani.

The 27 **Karimunjawa Islands** lie 150 km off-shore, and have been designated a National Marine Park. Two of the islands are protected areas, where eagles nest and where there is some rare red coral. Several islands are protected in order to preserve forest plants. Best time to visit: Apr to Nov. Authorization is needed from the Office of Native Conservation (KSDA), Jl. Menteri Supeno 1/2, T 414750, Semarang. Four of the islands are inhabited and Sanbangan Island has guesthouses for the few tourists who make it out here, approx. 40,000Rp. There are white sand beaches and good coral for snorkeling, although there are not, as yet, any diving facilities. **Getting there**: twice a week connections by ferry boat on Mon. and Thurs. 6-7 hrs (5,000Rp) or charter a boat for about 45,000Rp/day.

Accommodation B-C *Asri Jaya*, Jl. Agil Kusumadya, T 22449, a/c, restaurant, pool, hot water, best accommodation here, 2.8 km from centre of town; **C** *Notosari*, Jl. Kepodang 12, T 21245, restaurant, clean, central; **E** *Losmen Kepodang Asri*, Jl. Kepodang 17, central, popular.

Restaurants *Hijau Mas*, Jl. Jend. A. Yani 1; *Pondok Gizi*, Jl. Agil Kusumadya 59 (road into town from Semarang); *Sederhana*, Jl. Agil Kusumadya 59B, excellent Indonesian, seafood specialities, rec; *Soto Ayam Pak Denuh*, Jl. Agil Kusumadya. *Night stalls* at Pasar Bitingan near the bus station.

Sport *Swimming*: *The Asri Jaya Hotel* has a pool open to the public for 1,000Rp, 1,250Rp at weekends.

Raden Kartini

Raden Ajeng Kartini was born in 1880, daughter of the Regent or *bupati* of Jepara. She was fortunate in having a father who did not entirely disagree with the idea of female education, and he sent her to the European lower school in Jepara. Here, the distinctly revolutionary belief that women should be educated and emancipated, took hold. At the very end of the 19th century, the East Indies, like Europe, was caught up in the idea that with the dawn of the 20th century a new era would begin, one of enlightenment. Kartini was thrilled to be part of this change. She wrote to a friend on 12 Jan 1900 "Oh, it is splendid just to live in this age; the transition of the old into the new!".

Unfortunately, her dreams were not allowed time to unfold. She died at the tragically young age of 24 on 17 Sept 1904, while giving birth to her first child. Nonetheless, in her short life Kartini established a reputation for herself as a budding suffragette: she founded a school for the daughters of Javanese officials, and promoted the rights of Javanese women. For her rôle, Kartini is immortalised on a banknote. However, there are rumours of dissent emanating from some quarters. The fact that Kartini was so European in outlook, and apparently pro-Dutch in a number of respects, means that her nationalist credentials are slightly sullied. Her burial place, and that of her sons (at Desa Bulu, 20 km S of Rembang), has become a pilgrimage spot for Indonesian women nonetheless, and crowds travel here particularly on 21 Apr known as Kartini Day.

Tourist office Jl. Sunan Muria 3, T 21555.

Useful addresses Area code: 0291.

Transport to & from Kudus 51 km from Semarang. **By bus:** the station is on the Semarang side of town, 4 km from the centre. Regular connections with Semarang 1 hr and Solo 2 hrs. **By colt:** the station is on Jl. Jend. A. Yani, opposite the *Kudus Plaza*, connections with Rembang and Jepara.

WEST FROM SEMARANG TO PEKALONGAN

The road W from Semarang, route 25, passes through a number of small N coast towns before reaching the batik-producing centre of Pekalongan after 101 km. Continuing W from here, the road passes, in turn, Pemalang (34 km), Tegal (23 km) and Brebes (13 km) before crossing into West Java and reaching the major N coast city of Cirebon (59 km).

Pekalongan

Pekalongan is best known for the distinctive **batik** that is produced here. Pastel shades, fine designs, and floral and animal motifs are all characteristic of the area's work (**see page 535**). There is a **Batik Museum** at Jalan Majapahit 10 with a small display of characteristic designs from various areas of Java, along with a few tools. The museum is on the outskirts of town, tucked away along with government offices. Get there by becak. If the building is closed, ask the caretaker to unlock it.

The **town square** is off the main road, a short distance along Jalan H.M. Wahid Hasim. The local mosque – a strange amalgam of lighthouse (the minaret), castle (the crenellated gateway) and Javanese (the tiered roof) – is situated on the W side of the square. Pekalongan is also said to have the biggest **fish auction** in Java. Few tourists venture here, but because it is on the main N route between Surabaya and Jakarta, it has a good selection of losmen and restaurants.

Excursions

Kedungwuni, a town 9 km to the S of town, is a centre of *batik* production and sale where the production process can be observed. **Getting there:** regular colts from town.

Accommodation **B-C** *Istana*, Jl. Gajah Mada 23-25, T 61581, some a/c, popular with Indonesian business travellers; **B-C** *Nirwana*, Jl. Dr. Wahidin 11 (E side of town), T 41691, some a/c, restaurant, large pool, most luxurious in town, price includes breakfast; **C-D** *Hayam Wuruk*, Jl. Hayam Wuruk 152-158, T 81322, some a/c, clean rooms, central location, good value, rec; **D** *Losmen Sari Dewi*, Jl. Hayam Wuruk 1, some a/c, friendly, rec; **E** *Asia Losmen*, Jl. K.H. Wahid Hasyim 49, T 41125; **E** *Gajah Mada*, Jl. Gajah Mada 11A, T 41185; **E** *Losmen Cempaka*, Jl. Cempaka 53 (20 m off the main road, E of the bridge), T 21555, nothing special; **E** *Pekalongan*, Jl. Hayam Wuruk 158, T 21021, old building with some character, reasonable rooms.

Restaurants **♦♦***Maduroso*, Jl. Merdeka, Indonesian; *Purimas Bakery*, intersection of Jl. Hayam Wuruk and Jl. K.H. Wahid Hasim; *Remaja*, Jl. Dr. Cipto 17, serves Indonesian, International and Chinese (Chinese food rec.).

Sports Swimming: non-residents can swim at the *Nirwana Hotel*, Jl. Dr. Wahidin 11.

Shopping Batik: Pekalongan is famous as a centre of batik production and sale. The style is very different from that of Solo and Yogya; designs are fine, with intricate representations of flowers and birds. Colours tend to be softer, using pastel shades. There are many shops along the main road, Jl. Hayam Wuruk; *B.L. Batik* at Jl. K.H.M. Mansyer 87 sells good quality made-up garments and lengths of cloth.

Banks & money changers Expor Inspor Indonesia, Jl. Hayam Wuruk 5.

Useful addresses General Post Office: Jl. Cendrawasih 1. **Area code:** 0285.

Tour companies & travel agents *Amatama*, Jl. Mansyer 25, T 81121.

Tourist offices Dinas Pariwisata, Jl. K.H. Wahid Hasyim 1. Open: 0700-1330, Mon-Sat.

Transport to & from Pekalongan 384 km from Jakarta, 101 km from Semarang and 409 km from Surabaya. **By train:** the train station is just to the W of the centre of town at Jl. Gajah Mada 10. Regular connections with Jakarta and Surabaya on slow daytime trains. **By bus:** the intercity bus terminal is to the SE of the town centre, near the intersection of Jl. Dr. Wahidin and Jl. Dr. Sutomo. Connections with Semarang 2 hrs, Bandung, Cirebon 4 hrs and Jakarta.

EAST JAVA

Introduction, 638; Blitar to Surabaya via Malang, 640; Madura Island, 655; Madura: Bangkalan to Sumenep, 658; Eastern Java: from Surabaya to Banyuwangi and Bali via Mount Bromo, 660.

Maps: East Java 639; Panataran 641; Malang 643; Malang surroundings, 645; Surabaya 649; Trowulan, 652; Madura Island, 656.

INTRODUCTION

East Java covers an area of 47,922 sq km and includes not only the east portion of Java, but also the island of Madura. The province is drained by two principal rivers – the Brantas and the Bengawan Solo. Two-thirds of East Java is mountainous, the highest peak – Mount Semeru – reaching 3,676m. The population of 32.5 million is made up largely of Javanese, Madurese and Tenggerese. The *ayam bekisar*, a cross-breed between a chicken and a green woodcock (and visible in most hotel lobbies), is East Java's symbol and so too is the *sedap malam*, a white flower.

For the visitor, the principal attractions of East Java are likely to lie in the magnificent volcanic scenery, the elegant candis and other architectural remains, and in the persistence – despite rapid economic change – of many facets of traditional life.

Like Central Java, East Java is rich in archaeological sites. The East Javanese Period of art and architecture began in 929 when King Sindok was forced to move his court to the rich Brantas River area following the eruption of Mount Merapi in 928 (**see page 523**). The East Javanese Period spanned 6 centuries and included the kingdoms of Kediri (929-1222), Singasari (1222-1292) and Majapahit (1292-1527). Among the various monuments, Candi Panataran is the greatest, although the elegant Candi Kidal and Candi Singasari, as well as Candi Jawi, are also significant.

In rural areas, traditional forms of dress are much in evidence, with women tending to carry loads on their heads, rather than tied with a sarong on their backs as in Central and West Java. Buffalo-drawn wagons, horse-pulled carts and carriages, and an abundance of bicycles show that the internal combustion engine is still facing a stiff challenge from less frenetic modes of transport.

Not only is East Java one of the country's most densely populated provinces, it is also one of the richest. An industrial 'golden triangle' (in fact a diamond) is centred on the port of Surabaya – the second largest city in Indonesia. Along with Surabaya, this golden triangle incorporates the towns of Malang, Jombang and Pasuruan. More people are engaged in industrial activities and live in urban areas in East Java than in any other province in the country, bar the capital Jakarta. These industries are dominated by *kretek* (clove cigarette) manufacturing – with the mammoth Gudang Garam factory at Kediri – sugar milling and weaving.

But this picture of East Java as a vibrant, modern province obscures great inequalities and continuing poverty in some of the more remote areas. In particular, Madura and the SW districts such as Pacitan have not benefited from East Java's recent economic growth. Although it has been the province's expanding industries which have generated much of the economic growth in recent years, East Java still has a larger area under plantations – sugar cane, coffee, cloves and tobacco – than any other province except North Sumatra. Other crops

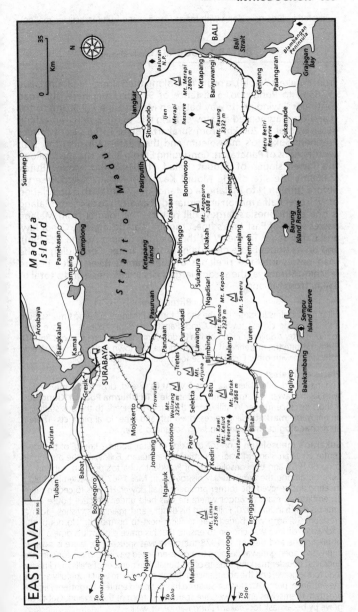

EAST JAVA

cultivated include rice, along with maize, cassava and fruit (particularly mango).

BLITAR TO SURABAYA via Malang

From Surakarta (Solo), a route runs along the S slopes of Mount Lawu (3,265m) to Ponorogo, a distance of 97 km. From here, the road continues E winding its way between Mount Liman (2,563m) to the N and the fragmented and lower-lying hills to the S, before reaching Blitar, a total of 200 km from Surakarta. Blitar is the site of former President Sukarno's mausoleum and the nearest town to the 14th century ruins of Panataran. Continuing E from Blitar, the road follows the lower slopes of Mount Kelud (1,731m) and Mount Butak (2,868m), the site of the Mount Kawi and Mount Kelud Reserve, before turning N to Malang, a distance of 77 km. With a population of well over half a million and situated at an altitude of 450m, Malang is one of Indonesia's largest hill resorts. The road N from Malang passes some of East Java's finest candis – Candi Singasari, Candi Jawi and Candi Jago. To the W of the road lies Mount Arjuna (3,339m), and on its slopes is the mountain resort of Tretes. Continuing N, the road passes into the ricelands of the Brantas River valley before reaching Surabaya, the second largest city in Indonesia and a total of 85 km from Malang.

Blitar

Blitar has 2 claims to fame: it is the site of former President Sukarno's mausoleum and is also the closest town to Candi Panataran. Blitar appears to have been founded after a Sailendra king built a Buddhist monastery here in about 860AD. Today, despite the presence of Sukarno's grave, the town is a quiet backwater in comparison with other East Javanese towns such as Malang or Solo.

Places of interest

The main road, Jalan Merdeka, runs E-W. At its W end, close to the intersection with Jalan Mawar, is a small **Chinese temple – Tri Dharma Poo An Kiong**. Just a short distance further W still, along the street that leads to the bus station, is an enjoyable **market** selling spices, dried fish and other local products. There is an **archaeological museum** on Jalan Sodancho Supriyadi.

Sukarno's mausoleum is on the outskirts of Blitar, about 2 km NE of the town centre on Jalan Slamet Riyadi, the road to Panataran. Following the attempted coup of 1965 and the consolidation of President Suharto's position, support for Sukarno among the army quickly dissipated. In Mar 1967 the Assembly held a meeting and relieved the former president of all power. He was forced to retire, an embittered man, to Bogor where he was held under effective house arrest until his death in Jun 1970. Following his death – and against his wishes – former President Sukarno was buried here in Blitar next to his mother. No doubt this backwater of Java was chosen to ensure that his grave did not become a focus of pilgrimage and dissent. In 1978 the grave was spruced-up; there is now an impressive open gateway, leading to a glass-enclosed pavilion which contains the engraved boulder marking the site of his burial. The number of stalls that line the road to the grave, and the abundance of becak drivers who wait hopefully around the entrance, demonstrate that Sukarno has not been entirely forgotten. Pilgrims prostrate themselves and flowers are scattered in front of the pavilion. Get to the grave by becak (ask for *makam Bung Karno*), or walk.

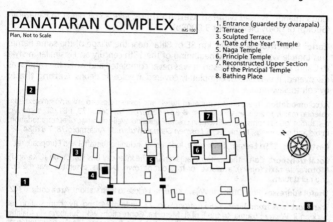

PANATARAN COMPLEX IMS 100
Plan, Not to Scale

1. Entrance (guarded by dvarapala)
2. Terrace
3. Sculpted Terrace
4. 'Date of the Year' Temple
5. Naga Temple
6. Principle Temple
7. Reconstructed Upper Section of the Principal Temple
8. Bathing Place

Excursions

Candi Panataran is 10 km N of Blitar and was built from 1320-1370 during the Majapahit Period, although work may have started during the Singasari era (1222-1292). It is the largest and most important candi of the East Javanese Period and anticipates the design of later Balinese temples. Asymmetrical in layout, it consists of 3 stepped courtyards surrounded by a wall. The visitor approaches the temple from the lowest level to the W, past a pair of *raksasa* or *dvarapala* (**see page 644**). The first courtyard originally contained 2 wooden buildings which would have been used as assembly rooms. All that remains is the base of a *terrace*, with fine bas-reliefs encircling it. These relate tales of the *kidungs*, with figures carved in the wayang-like stylization which is characteristic of East Javanese reliefs: flat, with no illusion of depth and with faces portrayed in profile. The N face of the terrace is the least weathered. Also in this courtyard is a small square building of vertical design, the so-called *'Date of the year temple'*, built in 1369 (since restored) and a good example of East Javanese candi architecture (it is similar in appearance to Candi Kidal, **see page 646**).

The second court contains the larger *Naga Temple*, which has lost its top section (originally of wood and similar to a Balinese *meru*, **see page 724**) but what remains is of very fine workmanship. It is identifiable by the 4 naga which wind around the top of the temple, supported by 9 beautiful figures in royal attire. *Dvarapala* guard the entrance to the shrine, but the kala head above the door is now missing – although *tumpal* motifs can be seen at the front of each flight of steps. The building was used as a repository for sacred possessions.

The highest and most E court contains the *principal shrine*, which was originally surrounded by 4 smaller structures, remnants of which remain. The main shrine stands to the rear of the complex, nearest to the mountains, enabling the gods to descend into the temple. The base is decorated with relief carvings representing the Ramayana, interspersed with carved animal motif medallions. Four guardian figures patrol the steps upwards, rather disturbingly standing on bands of skulls (behind one of them the artist has carved a lizard, perhaps his signature). The steps lead up to a second level where there are carved winged creatures. To the left of the temple is its reconstructed upper section.

Down some stairs behind and to the right of the principal shrine is a clear pool, lined with stone and carved with animals. The pool, which would have been the king's 'mandi', is filled with fish. **Getting there:** take a colt direct to Panataran (500Rp) or go by ojek (about 3,000Rp).

Candi Sawentar lies a few km SE of Blitar near the village of the same name. This temple was built at the beginning of the 13th century and is similar in style to Candi Kidal. For some reason, it was never completed and when the candi was discovered, it was almost completely covered in volcanic debris. **Getting there:** by colt to Sawentar.

Accommodation There are a number of hotels and losmen close to Sukarno's mausoleum catering mainly to Indonesian 'pilgrims'. **B-E** *Sri Lestari*, Jl. Merdeka 173, T 81766, some a/c, restaurant, good rooms, attractive main colonial building, well-run range of accommodation, in old and new wings, highly rec; **E** *Losmen Damar Wulan*, Jl. Anjasmoro 78, T 81884.

Restaurants ♦♦*Sri Lestari*, Jl. Merdeka, Indonesian including Rijstaffel and European, rec.

Local transport Colts: the station is adjacent to the inter-city bus station on Jl. Kerantil. **Motorcycle taxis (ojeks):** available for trips out of town. **Dokars:** assemble near the bus and rail stations.

Useful addresses Post Office: Jl. Wijaya Kusuma 1 (close to train station). **Area code:** 0342.

Transport to & from Blitar 225 km from Solo, 77 km from Malang. **By train:** station set back on Jl. Wijaya Kusuma, to the S of Jl. Merdeka. Connections with Surabaya via Malang 5 hrs (see timetable, **page 1012**). **By bus:** the station is on Jl. Kerantil, the W continuation of Jl. Merdeka. Connections with Solo 6 hrs, Malang 3 hrs, Surabaya 4 hrs and Jakarta.

Malang

Surrounded by volcanoes – Mount Butak (2,868m) to the W, Mount Arjuna (3,339m) to the N, and Mounts Kepolo (3,035m) and Bromo (2,329m) to the E – Malang is one of the most beautifully situated cities in Java. Lying at 450m, it is arguably Indonesia's largest hill resort with a population of 650,000 (Bandung residents might also, rather optimistically, call their city a hill resort too). During the colonial period, Malang was a small, quaint town where Dutch planters and civil servants could escape the heat of the lowlands. The elegant villas are still in evidence, even if it has grown considerably in size since independence. Fortunately, the climate has not changed and it is still a good deal cooler than the plains. Malang is a friendly town, free from mass tourism and although it is not noted for its sights, there are a number of places of interest within easy reach of the city, making it a good base or stopping-off point en route to or from Mount Bromo or Bali. The largest single industry in Malang is Bentoel's *kretek* factory which employs over 20,000 people (see box, **page 635**).

At the end of the Third Javanese War of Succession (1746-1757), Malang became a haven for the defeated rebels of the Hindu King, Surapati. They retreated here because of its inaccessibility. It was not until 1771 that the last of the Surapati line was finally captured. By then the area had been virtually de-populated such had been the turmoil caused by successive campaigns. Interestingly, because the VOC were worried about the Hindu Balinese coming to the rescue of Surapati's supporters, this was the only part of Java where the Company positively supported the spread of Islam.

Places of interest

The city is divided into 2 by the Brantas River which flows within a deep cutting. Tiled houses, some of colonial vintage, picturesquely – at least from a distance – tumble down the steep banks. In the E half of the city is Jalan Tugu, with the uninspired **independence monument** as its centrepiece, facing which is the old Dutch town hall, renovated and renamed the **Balai Kota Malang**.

On the W bank of the Brantas, at the intersection of Jalan Gatot Subroto/Laks Martadinata and Jalan Zainal Zacse is the large **Eng An Kiong Chinese Pagoda**. Nearby is the **Pasar Besar**, on Jalan Pasar Besar and Jalan Gatot Subroto, a large

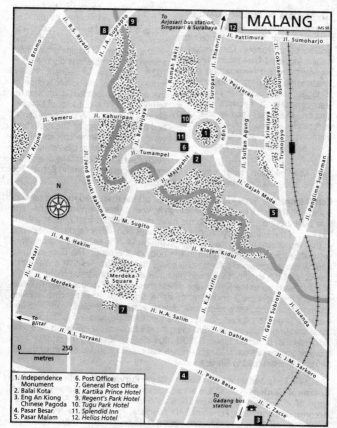

MALANG IMS 98

To Arjosari bus station, Singasari & Surabaya

Jl. Pattimura

Jl. Sumoharjo

Jl. Bromo

Jl. B.S. Riyadi

Jl. J.A. Suprapto

Jl. Rumah Sakit

Jl. Suropati

Jl. Thamrin

Jl. Pejajaran

Jl. Cokroaminoto

Jl. Semeru

Jl. Kahuripan

Jl. Brawijaya

Jl. Tugu

Jl. Sultan Agung

Jl. Sriwijaya

Jl. Trunojoyo

Jl. Arjuna

Jl. Jend Basuki Rakhmat

Jl. Tumampel

Jl. Malapahit

Jl. Gajah Mada

Jl. Panglima Sudirman

N

Jl. M. Sugito

Jl. Klojen Kidul

Jl. A.R. Hakim

Jl. H. Asari

Jl. K. Merdeka

Merdeka Square

Jl. H.A. Salim

Jl. K.Z. Arifin

Jl. A. Dahlan

Jl. Gatot Subroto

Jl. Juanda

To Blitar

Jl. A.I. Suryani

0   250
metres

Jl. J.M. Sarkoro

Jl. Pasar Besar

To Gadang bus station

Jl. Z. Zacse

1. Independence Monument
2. Balai Kota
3. Eng An Kiong Chinese Pagoda
4. Pasar Besar
5. Pasar Malam
6. Post Office
7. General Post Office
8. Kartika Prince Hotel
9. Regent's Park Hotel
10. Tugu Park Hotel
11. Splendid Inn
12. Helios Hotel

and very colourful market selling everything from fruit, to live animals to batik. Other markets include the flower market, **Pasar Bunga**, and the nearby **Pasar Senggol**, a night market on Jalan Brawijaya. The military **Museum Brawijaya** is at Jalan Besar Ijen 25A.

Excursions

NB: Candi Singasari, the Purwodadi Gardens and Candi Jawi are all on or just off the main road between Surabaya and Malang. It is easy to visit them en route between the 2 towns; simply hop-off one bus (there are many) and onto another.

Candi Badut this plain candi is thought to be the oldest surviving Hindu (Sivaite) temple in East Java, probably dating from 760 and built in honour of King Gajayana of the Kanjuruhan Kingdom (the earliest recorded kingdom in E Java). The word *badut* is derived from a Sanskrit word meaning 'joker', or 'a man who is fond of making jokes'. The candi is similar in design to the temples of Gedung Songo, but on a larger scale. It seems that the building was altered in the 13th

Dvarapala or Temple guardians

Dvarapala are the terrifying temple guardians that flank and protect the entrances to candis. The demon is usually depicted kneeling on his right leg, with the left hand resting on his raised knee. In the right hand he holds a dagger, while his jewellery consists of ear pendants, a necklace, bracelets around the wrists and ankles, and armbands around the upper arms. Particularly fine dvarapala can be seen close to Singasari, in East Java.

century, which caused it to become unstable and so hastened its ruin. The niches are framed by kalamakaras and some still contain Hindu gods. The central cella would originally have held a linga. The temple was discovered in 1923 and has subsequently been renovated up to the lower section of the roof. It is located in an area of scrubland, on the outskirts of Malang, about 4 km to the NW of the city centre and past the university. The route here winds through narrow suburban lanes and quite suddenly passes into rice fields. **Getting there:** take one of the 'Jalur M-K' microlets, which travel between Madyupuro and Karang Besuki. The candi is 100 m on from the end of the route.

Candi Singasari lies 9 km N of Malang just off the main road running towards Surabaya. The candi is East Javanese in style, with its heavy pyramidal roofs, and was built around 1300 as one of the funerary sanctuaries for Kertanagara, the last king of the Singasari Dynasty. Its design varies from other candis of the period in that the square base is much larger than normal. The cellas are – unusually – set within this base, rather than in the body of the candi. The body contains narrow niches, crowned by *banaspati* heads. Its shape implies that it was either a symbol of the *linga* or that it was meant as a replica of Mount Meru. A flight of stairs leads up to the first terrace where there are 5 chambers. About 150 m on from the candi are 2 enclosures on either side of the street each containing an enormous, corpulent and demonic *dvarapala* statue with skull headbands and earrings, large staring eyes, sharp canine teeth and clasping a club. Traditionally these giant figures were placed at the gateway to ward off evil spirits (see box). Admission: by donation. Open: 0700-1700 Mon-Sun. **Getting there:** take a bus towards Surabaya from Malang's Arjosari station. The candi is 600 m to the left (W) off the main road in Singasari town.

The well kept and attractive **Kebun Raya Purwodadi** – the **Purwodadi Botanical Gardens** – lie 12 km N of Singasari (21 km from Malang), at the N edge of Purwodadi town. Admission: 800Rp. Open: 0730-1600 Mon-Sun. **Accommodation** near Purwodadi: **D** *Niagara*, in Lawang, a few km S of Purwodadi; on the main road, stylish but run-down. **Getting there:** take a bus towards Surabaya from Malang's Arjosari station.

Candi Jawi is a 13th century candi 49 km N of Malang, just off the road running to Surabaya. The monument was built as a commemorative shrine to the last king of the Singasari Dynasty, King Kertanagara (1268-1292). It is one of the most complete candis in East Java, and still shows the remains of the surrounding double enclosure as well as a brick-lined moat. Jawi is also perhaps the most graceful of all East Javanese shrines with its tall, tapering tower, rising to 17 m. When the British naturalist Joseph Jukes saw Candi Jawi and the other temples around Malang in the 1840s, he wrote:

"The imagination became busy in restoring their former glories, in picturing large cities, adorned with temples and palaces, seated on the plain, and in recalling the departed power, wealth and state of the native kingdom that once flourished in a land so noble, so beautiful, and so well adapted for its growth and its security".

The architecture of the monument shows elements of both Sivaism, in its foundations, and Buddhism, in its stupa-like finial. It also originally housed both

a statue of Siva and the Buddha Aksobhya, so revealing the King's belief in the unity of Sivaism and Buddhism. Weathered reliefs of stories as yet undeciphered decorate the base. The upper door frame holds kala heads and there are a pair of makaras at the end of the stairs. Up these stairs is a small chamber containing a stone block. The candi was redesigned in the 14th century and restored in 1938 and again in 1970. Close to Candi Jawi is the open air theatre Taman Chandra Wilwatika (see below). **Getting there:** the candi lies 49 km N of Malang, off the road to Surabaya. In the roadside town of **Pandaan** there is a turn-off for the hill resort of Tretes (**see page 647**), and 2 km up this road is Candi Jawi. Take a bus from Malang towards Surabaya and ask to be let off at Pandaan; walk the final 2 km or take a minibus heading for Tretes.

Taman Chandra Wilwatika this open air theatre, only 1 km from Candi Jawi and 48 km from Malang, stages performances of classical ballet on the 2nd and 4th Saturday nights of each month from June to Nov, 1930-2300. **Getting there:** the theatre lies 1 km downhill (and closer to the main road) from Candi Jawi (see above). Take a bus from Malang towards Surabaya and ask to be let off at Pandaan, walk the final kilometre or take a minibus heading for Tretes.

Candi Jago (also named Jajaghu) can be found down a side street (and before the minibus station) off the main road in the town of Tumpang, 22 km E of Malang. The candi feels rather enclosed, as it is squashed into a small space and surrounded by houses. This Buddhist shrine was probably built around 1270-1280 as a funerary monument to King Vishnuvardhana of the Singasari Dynasty. Today, the upper part of the cell and the tower are missing – it is thought that they were made of wood and palm, in the multi-tiered design characteristic of the Balinese meru. The candi is unusual in that the cella was placed at the back edge of a 3-tiered base and is approached up a steep stairway. The finely carved friezes on all 3 levels of the base are important as they appear to establish the existence of buildings with tiered roofs in the 13th century. The meaning of the friezes has not been firmly ascertained, although they seem to recount Hindu, Buddhist and local legends. However, on the basis of the reliefs, some commentators have argued that the temple dates from the later Majapahit Period. The 4 statues that were originally in the now ruined upper chamber are to be found in the National Museum, Jakarta (King Vishnuvardhana was portrayed in the form of a Buddhist god). **Getting there:** catch a minibus from Malang's Arjosari station to Tumpang and walk from the minibus station.

Candi Kidal is 7 km further on from Tumpang travelling SW, and was built in the mid-13th century as a memorial shrine to King Anusapati who died in 1248. Built of andesite, the shrine consists of a square cell with projecting porticos, set within low walls on a large plinth. The tower – now in ruins – would originally have been about 15 m high and made up of 3 false storeys of diminishing height. However, its elegant proportions made it susceptible to earthquake damage and the structure has not survived the 750 years since it was built. Facing W, the stairway leads up to a chamber above which is a fearsome kala head. The icon within the inner chamber may have been the Siva statue which is in the collection of a museum in Amsterdam, or it may have been a post-mortem image of King Anusapati, or both – often shrines of this kind housed an image of a god whom the departed king was believed to have represented on earth. Around the base are some fine carvings of garuda, depicting the story of garuda liberating his mother Winata from the tyranny of the dragon Kadru. Admission: by donation. **Getting there:** catch a minibus from Malang's Arjosari station to Tumpang, and then a colt or ojek from Tumpang station. The route to the site passes through Tumpang for 1 km before coming to a 'T' junction; turn right, the temple is on the left another 6 km along the road. It is set back from the street, so is easily missed.

Selekta and Batu are 2 hill resorts 4 km apart on the S face of Mount Arjuna and Mount Welirang, 23 km from Malang. **Candi Songgoriti** dated to 732 can be reached from either resort. There are hot springs and pools, waterfalls and hiking trails around this beautiful scenery, sometimes referred to as Java's 'little Switzerland'. **Accommodation:** in both towns, including the luxurious **A-B Kartika Wijaya Hotel**, Jl. P. Sudirman 127, T 92008, F 91004 in Batu (with restaurant, swimming pool, miniature zoo and sports facilities). **Getting there:** buses leave from Malang's Dinoyo station on Jl. M. Haryono.

Mount Bromo and Ngadas lie to the E of Malang. Most people visit Mount Bromo from Probolinggo (**see page 660**), although it is possible to climb the mountain from the village of Ngadas, on Bromo's S face. From Ngadas there are 2 trekking trails; one leads to the village of Ranupani, the highest community in Java, the other to Bromo's summit (12.5 km). The trekking here is more demanding than from Probolinggo, although the route is well worn and a guide is not required. Villagers may offer their homes as guesthouses. **Getting to Ngadas:** catch a minibus from Malang's Arjosari station to Tumpang (22 km); from Tumpang catch a minibus to Gubuk Klakah and from there a 4-wheel drive vehicle (or hitch) up to Ngadas (another 22 km from Tumpang).

Ngliyep and Balekambang are 2 beach resorts, 67 km and 57 km S of Malang respectively. Both have accommodation. **Getting there:** by bus from Malang's Gadang station. For Balekambang take a bus to Turen and then change. For Ngliyep take a bus to Kepanjen and change, or take a colt to Bantur and change.

Festivals Nov: *Anniversary of Malang Regency* (28th), commemorated with traditional art performances and other shows.

Accommodation For a city which is not on the tourist trail, Malang has a good selection of hotels. **A** *Regent's Park*, Jl. Jaksa Agung Suprapto 12-16, T 63388, F 61408, a/c, poor restaurant, pool, Western-style 'luxury' hotel; **A** *Tugu Park*, Jl. Tugu 3, T 63891, F 62747, a/c, restaurant, pool, stylish new hotel (1990) by the independence monument, best in Malang, with well-appointed rooms, rec; **A-B** *Kartika Prince*, Jl. Jaksa Agung Suprapto 17, T 61900, F 61911, a/c, restaurant, pool, 'Chinese' style luxury hotel, on main road; **B-C** *Splendid Inn*, Jl. Majapahit 4, PO Box 142, T 66860, some a/c, villa with wonderful 50s decor next to Balai Kota, rec; **C-D** *Menara*, Jl. Pejajaran 5 (walking distance from train station), T 62871, rather characterless, price includes breakfast; **D** *Pajajaran*, Jl. Pejajaran 17 (walking distance from train station), T 25306, set in quiet street but rooms are rather shabby; **D** *Aloha*, Jl. Gajah Mada, wacky Hawaiian-style hotel like a seedy fair ground show, rooms are less than average; **D-F** *Helios*, Jl. Pattimura 37 (walking distance from train station), T 62741, set around courtyard, the rooms in the new wing are immaculate and more expensive, the old rooms are quite serviceable, rec.

Restaurants *Dirga Surya*, Jl. Jend. Gatot Subroto 81, good Chinese; **✦✦*Toko Oen*, Jl. Basuki Rakhmat 5, an old colonial favourite; **✦✦*Minang Jaya*, Jl. Jend. Basuki Rakhmat 111, good Padang food; **✦✦*New Hong Kong*, Jl. A.R. Hakim, best Chinese in town. **Foodstalls** in the Gajah Mada Plaza, Jl. H. Agus Salimor or at the night market at the S end of Jl. Majapahit.

Useful addresses General Post Office: Jl. Merdeka Selatan. **Area code**: 0341. **Immigration Office**: Jl. Raden Panji Suroso 4, T 4039. **PHPA office**: Jl. Raden Intan 6, T 65100.

Local transport Becaks. Colts/Microlets: are the main form of public transport (there are no town buses). They run between the 3 bus stations, through the centre of town. Letters on the front indicate the route – A-D is Arjosari to Dinoyo, G-A is Gadang to Arjosari and D-G, Dinoyo to Gadang. (300Rp).

Airline offices *Merpati*, Jl. Jaksa Agung Suprapto 50, T 27962.

Tour companies & travel agents *Mujur Surya*, 33A Jl. Bromo, T 27955; *Tanjung Permai*, Jl. Basuki Rakhmat 41, T 66924; *Penghela Swedesi*, Jl. Basuki Rakhmat, T 62564.

Tourist offices Dinas Pariwisata, Jl. Kawi 41, T 68473, helpful and knowledgeable staff, and Govt. Tourist Information at Jl. Semeru 2, T 61632.

Transport to & from Malang 882 km from Jakarta, 89 km from Surabaya. **By train:** the central station is at the E end of Jl. Kerta Negara. Trains leave here for Jakarta via Surabaya; the fastest service. There is another station to the S of the city, the Kota Lama Station. Trains leave here for Jakarta via Blitar. Trains coming in to Malang from the S continue on to the more convenient new central station. Regular connections with Surabaya 3 hrs and Jakarta 12½ hrs (see timetable **page 1012**). **By bus:** Malang has 3 bus stations. The largest is Arjosari on Jl. R. Intan to the N of town which serves Jakarta, Surabaya 2½ hrs, Probolinggo, Bandung and Bogor. For Yogya and Solo, change in Surabaya. The Gadang station on Jl. Kol. Sugiono, to the S of the city centre and serves Blitar (from where there are connections by the S route for Solo and Yogya) and Kediri. The Dinoyo station on Jl. M. Haryono to the NW serves Kediri, Batu, Selekta and Jombang.

Tretes

Tretes is yet another Javanese hill resort, set at 700m above sea-level on the NE slopes of the twin peaks of Mount Arjuna (at 3,339m, one of the highest volcanoes on Java) and Mount Welirang (3,156m). The town is an attractive little place, cool at night, and with good views to the plain below and mountains above. Perhaps because it is a weekend retreat for wealthy Surabayans, accommodation is over-priced compared with Java's other hill resorts.

The **Kakek Bodo Waterfall** is a short walk S from town; walking uphill, take the road to the right before the river. The path begins before the *Dirga Hayu Hotel* and leads to the waterfall. There are numerous other **hiking trails** from Tretes; ask at hotels for information. The area around Tretes is said to produce some of the best fruit in Indonesia – particularly durians (see **page 17**). There is a **fruit market** towards the bottom of town near the intersection of Jalan Ke Trawas and Jalan Palembon.

Excursions
Candi Jawi is about 5 km down the mountain from Tretes (see **page 644**). **Getting there:** catch a minibus towards Pandaan.

The **Botanical Gardens at Purwodadi** are 22 km from Tretes (see **page 644**). **Getting there:** catch a minibus to Pandaan, and from there, one of the many south-bound buses which run between Surabaya and Malang. The gardens are about 15 km S of Pandaan.

Trowulan, the former capital of the Majapahit Kingdom, can be reached from Tretes. A beautiful mountain road winds for about an hour round the lower slopes of Mount Arjuna, past holiday homes for the Surabaya rich and famous, to the site of the city (see **page 651**). **Getting there:** no regular colts or buses take this route; hire a car and driver for the journey.

Accommodation NB: there is additional accommodation a few km down the mountain at Prigen. **A** *Natour*, Jl. Pesanggrahan 2, T 81776, F 81101, restaurant, pool, tennis, particularly good position on the edge of a gully, but rather spartan rooms and generally overpriced; **A** *Surya*, Jl. Taman Wisata, T 81002, F 81058, pool, tennis, most luxurious hotel in town, lacking in hill resort character, recently extended; **B** *Tanjung Plaza*, Jl. Wilis 7, T 81102, rather scruffy; **D** *Sri Katon*, Jl. Taman Wisata.

Camping There is a camping ground at the Kakek Bodo Waterfall.

Sports Horse riding: in the hills around. Men loiter outside hotels with their mangy looking animals, in the hope of luring some custom.

Banks & money changers There are no banks in Tretes although hotels will change money.

Transport to & from Tretes 55 km from Malang, 60 km from Surabaya. **By bus:** buses between Surabaya and Malang will drop passengers off at Pandaan. From here minibuses travel up the mountain to Tretes.

Surabaya

Surabaya is Indonesia's second largest city with a population of over 3 million – 10 times the figure for 1940. In 1900 it was the largest town in the Dutch East Indies, exceeding even Batavia in the size of its population. It was also the colony's most important port, and was only superceded by Jakarta's Tanjung Priok, in terms of tonnage handled, in the 1950s. Surabaya remains an important manufacturing centre, and the city lies at the heart of one of the fastest growing industrial regions in Indonesia.

Surabaya is not a popular tourist destination. It has no sights to compare with those around Yogyakarta, and lies to the N of the overland route between Bali, Yogya and Jakarta. However, it is an important port for vessels sailing to Sulawesi, Maluku, Kalimantan and Nusa Tenggara, and is frequently a port of call for local and foreign businessmen.

History

Surabaya emerged as an important port during the 16th century, although it was not until the 17th century that it became an influential power. By 1622, Surabaya exercised control over Gresik on the N coast, over parts of SW Kalimantan, and over the rich ricelands of the Brantas River valley. Ships from Surabaya were frequent visitors to Melaka, the ports of Ambon and Ternate in Maluku (the Moluccas), and other regional trading centres. However, as it expanded, the kingdom came into conflict with Mataram over control of East and Central Java.

The son of King Senopati of Mataram, Panembahan Sedaing Krapyak, began the war against Surabaya in 1610 and for the next 3 years he sent an army to devastate the surrounding ricelands on which the city's economy depended. Krapyak died in 1613, to be succeeded by his great warrior son, Agung. Like Krapyak, Sultan Agung harrassed the towns and villages of East Java that were loyal to Surabaya. It was not until 1620 that he turned his attention to the city itself. He besieged Surabaya with 80,000 troops – one of the largest armies ever assembled in pre-colonial Java – burning crops and killing livestock. Then he ordered the damming of the River Brantas and the poisoning of the city's water supply. By 1625, Surabaya had been starved into submission. The *Dagh-Register* records that "in Surabaya not more than 500 of its 50 to 60,000 people were left, the rest having died or gone away because of misery and famine".

Despite this drawn-out and debilitating war with Mataram, Surabaya quickly regained its position as one of Java's premier ports. By the latter part of the 17th century the city was again a conduit for the export of rice, salt, sugar, bronze and other products and the Dutch had established a trading post in the city.

By the beginning of the 18th century, the heavy-handed actions of the Dutch had served to alienate the rulers of Surabaya. In 1717 the city rebelled, calling for the Balinese to help their cause. There followed 6 years of vicious conflict which ultimately led to complete defeat, and the death or imprisonment of the rulers

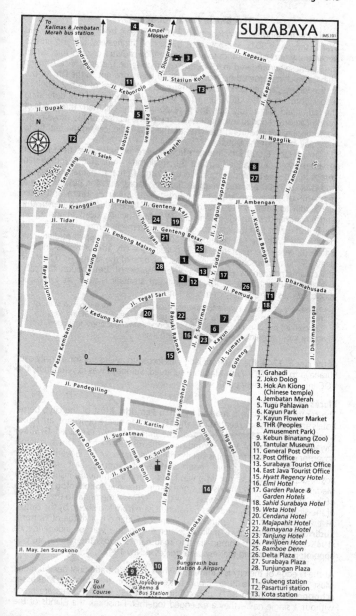

SURABAYA
IMS.101

1. Grahadi
2. Joko Dolog
3. Hok An Kiong (Chinese temple)
4. Jembatan Merah
5. Tugu Pahlawan
6. Kayun Park
7. Kayun Flower Market
8. THR (Peoples Amusement Park)
9. Kebun Binatang (Zoo)
10. Tantular Museum
11. General Post Office
12. Post Office
13. Surabaya Tourist Office
14. East Java Tourist Office
15. Hyatt Regency Hotel
16. Elmi Hotel
17. Garden Palace & Garden Hotels
18. Sahid Surabaya Hotel
19. Weta Hotel
20. Cendana Hotel
21. Majapahit Hotel
22. Ramayana Hotel
23. Tanjung Hotel
24. Paviljoen Hotel
25. Bamboe Denn
26. Delta Plaza
27. Surabaya Plaza
28. Tunjungan Plaza

T1. Gubeng station
T2. Pasarturi station
T3. Kota station

The Battle for Surabaya, 1945

The battle for Indonesia's independence lasted 5 years from the end of World War II (**see page 501**). Surabaya was the site of the heaviest fighting and so became a symbol of resistance to the re-imposition of Dutch colonial rule. When the Japanese surrendered in 1945, the commander in the area, Vice-Admiral Shibata Yaichiro, ordered his men to give-up their arms not to the Dutch, but to the Indonesian resistance. Soon afterwards, at the end of Oct, 2 religious associations – the Nahdatul Ulama and Masyumi – announced that defending the fatherland was a Holy War, and in response to the call many thousands of young Muslims flooded into Surabaya. One of the leaders of the movement, Soetomo, broadcast stirring speeches on the local radio, calling the faithful to resist any return of the Dutch.

On 25 Oct, 6,000 British Indian troops were landed to evacuate former Japanese internees. Ranged against this small force were 20,000 Indonesian troops in a newly-formed People's Security Army (Tentara Keamanan Rakyat), and over 100,000 assorted irregular fighters. Faced with the possibility of a massacre of their own troops, the British flew Sukarno, Hatta and Amir Sjarifuddin to Surabaya to arrange a ceasefire. When this broke down, the British commander, Brigadier-General A.W.S. Mallaby was killed. In retribution the British – who had by now brought in reinforcements – mounted an assault on the city. With the use of airpower and their better equipped soldiers, the British defeated the resistance, finally quelling the city after 3 weeks and the death of many thousands of Indonesians. The date of the assault – 10 Nov – is still commemorated as Heroes' Day (*Hari Pahlawan*). But though tactically defeated, the resistance scored a significant strategic victory. As Professor Ricklefs writes in his history of modern Indonesia:

> "The battle of Surabaya was a turning-point for the Dutch... for it shocked many of them into facing reality. Many had quite genuinely believed that the Republic represented only a gang of [Japanese] collaborators without popular support. No longer could any serious observer defend such a view".

of the city. In 1743, the Mataram king was forced to award full sovereignty over Surabaya to the VOC. With Mataram subdued, Surabaya was developed by the VOC into Java's premier port.

Places of interest

The centre of Surabaya is marked by **Jalan Pemuda**. Most of the city's better hotels and the shopping centres for which it seems to have a penchant, are found within walking distance of this road. The immaculately maintained **Grahadi** towards the W end of Jalan Pemuda was the residence of the Dutch colonial governor of East Java; today it is still the official residence of the Governor of East Java. Opposite is a rather poor **statue of Soerjo**, East Java's first post-independence governor who was killed during a communist insurrection in Madiun in 1948. Behind him is the stone statue known as **Joko Dolog** (guardian of the young teak forest). This was carved in 1326 as a memorial to the last king of the Singasari Dynasty, and was transferred here from Mojokerto by the Dutch. At the junction of Jalan Pemuda and Jalan Yos Sudarso is a statue of **General Sudirman** (Soedirman), a military leader during the war of independence (1945-1949) and now immortalized in road names across the nation. He was appointed to command the resistance forces in Nov 1945.

At the N edge of the city is **Kalimas**, a wharf at which traditional *perahu* moor. Most vessels here are Bugis *pinisi*, better known in the West as **Makassar schooners** (see page 867). It is claimed that these elegant boats are made without a single nail – they are pegged together. Pinisi link the islands of the archipelago, carrying mixed cargoes of lumber, barbed wire, glass, tinned goods, house tiles...just about anything that is relatively water resistant. Although modern cargo vessels are becoming more common, the versatility of the pinisi mean that they remain popular and profitable, and indeed represent one of the largest sailing fleets still operating in the world today. The wharf is on Jalan Kalimas Baru, in the Tanjung Perak Port area. Strictly-speaking, photographs can only be taken with permission from the harbour master. Ask at the police post.

South of the port, to the E of the Surabaya River, is **Kampung Arab** or the Kasbah Quarter. This is the heart of the old city and contains the **Ampel Mosque**, the oldest mosque in East Java, built by Sunan Ampel, one of the 9 walis (see page 528). Sunan Ampel died in Surabaya in 1481 and his grave lies within the mosque compound. The site is a popular pilgrimage spot for Indonesians.

South of the Arab quarter is the **Jembatan Merah** or Red Bridge, a strategic site in the Battle of Surabaya waged during Nov 1945 (see box). Close to the bridge, on Jalan Slompretan is the Chinese temple **Hok An Kiong**. South of here is the **Tugu Pahlawan** or Heroes Monument, which stands in the centre of the rather unexciting main city square, opposite the Governor's office on Jalan Pahlawan. It commemorates the thousands of young Muslims who poured into the city and died fighting against British forces during the Battle of Surabaya (see box).

The **Kayun Flower Market** is situated on Jalan Kayun, while the **People's Amusement Park** (known as THR) is E of the river on Jalan Kusuma Bangsa. Open:1800-2300 Mon-Sun.

The **Kebun Binatang** (or Zoo) is within walking distance of the Joyoboyo bemo station on Jalan Setail, but about 3 km from the centre of the city. It is one of the best zoos in Southeast Asia, with a good collection of local and regional animals. Most bemos run to Joyoboyo. Admission: 1,000Rp (additional 400Rp for aquarium). Open: 0700-1800 Mon-Sun. Opposite the zoo on Jalan Raya Diponegoro is the **Tantular Museum**, an ethnographic and archaeological museum. Open: 0800-1400 Tues-Sun.

Excursions

Trowulan lies 52 km SW of Surabaya on the Surabaya-Solo road not far from Mojokerto. This was the site of the capital of the powerful Majapahit Kingdom which reached its zenith in the 14th century. The remains of temples, bathing pools and an artificial lake can be found spread over a wide area and only the major buildings are described below. The ruins, most of which have undergone restoration, are built of red brick, making them quite distinctive from other Javanese temple complexes.

A good place to start is the excellent **Museum**, which lies 1 km off the main road to the left, through a red-brick split gate. It houses a wealth of archaeological finds from the area, the majority dating from the Majapahit Period. Fine metalwork and sculpture, well displayed and labelled, give an indication of the sophistication of the society. Admission: 200Rp. Open: 0700-1600 Tues-Sun. Opposite the museum is the restored **Kolam Segaran**, a large artificial lake, measuring 375 m by 175 m. Contemporary accounts record that the lake was used as a banquet spot for the entertainment of foreign envoys. At the end of a repast, the precious plates and other tableware would be tossed nonchalantly into the lake to indicate the wealth that the kingdom had at its disposal.

From the lake and museum, continue S for ½ km to a crossroads; turn left and a further 2 km along this road is **Bajang Ratu**, a tall slender gateway, with a pyramidal roof. It was built at the beginning of the 14th century and is believed to have been the entrance to a sacred building which has now disappeared. There is some ornamentation on the stepped upper levels. By the Majapahit Period, the

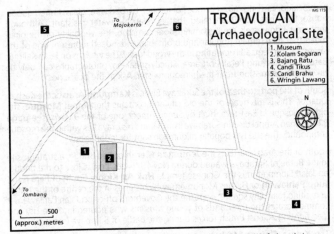

TROWULAN
Archaeological Site

IMS 173

1. Museum
2. Kolam Segaran
3. Bajang Ratu
4. Candi Tikus
5. Candi Brahu
6. Wringin Lawang

To Mojokerto

To Jombang

0   500
(approx.) metres

N

entrance doorway had become the most important feature of the shrine – a feature which is duplicated in the pura of Bali. Bajang Ratu is the most complete of these gateways, although one of the smaller ones.

A further 1 km on is the unornamented **Candi Tikus**, situated on the left-hand side of the road. The shrine lies below ground level, and is believed to have been a ritual bathing place. The small pavilion set in the middle of the pool represented Mount Penanggungan (the East Javanese equivalent of Mount Meru), while the surrounding water evoked the sea. The candi was only discovered in 1914 when a plague of rats were found to be nesting in a mound. Upon excavation of the mound, the locals were surprised to discover a temple buried beneath the earth along with the rats; this may be why it became known as Candi Tikus, 'tikus' meaning rat.

Leading off the main road is a narrow lane which runs to **Candi Brahu**, a rectangular temple with cellas projecting from each of its four sides. No decoration remains, and it is at present undergoing restoration. Returning to the main road, and 1.2 km back towards Mojokerto, is a turning on the right to **Wringin Lawang** (so called because a banyen tree – 'wringin' – was found near the gate – 'lawang'). The site is about 200m off the main road and is also known as Candi Bentar because it resembles a temple cut in two, vertically. **Getting there:** take a bus from Surabaya's Bungurasih terminal travelling towards Jombang (there are many) and ask to be let off in Trowulan. Some of the sights can be reached on foot, although hiring a becak for a couple of hours is much easier; becak drivers wait for custom on the main road.

Kenjeran is a rather unexciting beach E of Surabaya. **Getting there:** take a bemo, either line (lyn) 'S' (from Joyoboyo) or 'R1' (from Jembatan Merah).

Madura can be visited as a day excursion – best during the *bull racing* season from Aug-Oct (**see page 655**).

Gresik lies 14 km N of Surabaya and is an ugly industrial satellite town, with one saving grace: it is the site of the grave of Sunan Giri, one of the 9 imam (or walis) who are credited with having first brought Islam to Java (**see page 528**). A staircase leads up past graves of other holy men to the imam's resting place, which is housed inside an attractive double chamber of heavily carved wood. To the left of the imam's grave are the graves of his children. **Festival**: *Khol Sunan Giri* (30 Sept), commemorates the death of Sunan Giri. **Getting there**: microlets travel from Surabaya to Gresik, through an unattractive industrial landscape. Get off at a marked turning to the left, on Jl. Sunan Giri (ask for *makam Sunan Giri*); horse-drawn carts and ojeks wait at the end of the road to transport visitors and pilgrims the 1½ km to the tomb.

Paciran lies on Java's north coast, 60 km NW of Surabaya. Near here, on a hill top, is the intricately carved gateway of **Sendang Duwur**, named after the Muslim saint Sunan Sendang who was buried here in 1585. It is interesting for its combination of styles – the carving includes Arabic calligraphy alongside Hindu designs. **Getting there**: from the Bungurasih bus terminal, S of town.

Tuban lies 100 km NW of Surabaya on Java's north coast. Today it is a sleepy little fishing town, but 400 years ago Tuban was an important port servicing the spice trade between the islands of Maluku and India, the Middle East and Europe. Visitors to the Majapahit Kingdom arrived at Tuban, and Kublai Khan's envoy in the 13th century landed here. The former wealth of this town is reflected in the fine Chinese ceramics which have been found in the vicinity (there was a large community of Chinese merchants), and in the pageantry of the jousts that were held on the alun-alun (or square) which are recorded in European accounts of the period. Another of Java's nine walis is buried here (**see page 528**), behind the Persian style **Jami'q Mosque**. To the W of town is E Java's largest Chinese temple – **Klenteng Kwan Sing Bio**. The area is also a centre of batik production, using coarse cloth and deep indigo dyes. **Getting there**: buses from Bungurasih terminal S of town.

Mount Bromo lies 145 km SE of Surabaya (**see page 661**).

Tours Local travel agents offer city tours (about 24,000Rp), trips to Mt. Bromo (80,000Rp for day trip), Trowulan and the ancient sites of the Majapahit Kingdom (80,000Rp), as well as to Malang, Madura, Selecta and Batu. *P.T. Wisata Bahari Mas Permai*, Jl. Tanjung Priok 11 (T 291633) provide 'traditional' day-long cruises on their *perahu* (schooner). **The East Java Regional Tourism Office**, in association with the provincial agricultural department (Jl. Gayung Kebonsari 173, Wonocolo, (S of centre), T 811879), are pushing 'agrotourism': they organize tours of coffee estates, tobacco farms, coconut plantations, sugarcane mills and other similar 'sights'. There are also trips to a teak plantation, 150 km W of Surabaya (**see page 631**).

Festivals May: *Anniversary of THR* (Peoples' Amusement Park) (19th), cultural performances and stalls at THR Surabaya Hall. *Anniversary of founding of the city* (3rd) held at Taman Surya, cultural performances and other ceremonies.
Nov: *Heroes Day* (10th), centred around the Heroes Monument, commemorates those who died in the Battle of Surabaya in Nov 1945. Parades and various festivities.

Accommodation Reflecting the status of the city as a business centre, not a tourist destination, there are a good number of mid and upper range hotels, but woefully few decent losmen and homestays. **A+** *Hyatt Regency*, Jl. Basuki Rakhmat 124-128, T 511234, F 470508, a/c, restaurant, pool, best in town, all facilities; **A** *Altea*, Jl. Raya Darmo 68-76, T 69501, F 69204, a/c, restaurant; **A** *Elmi*, Jl. Panglima Sudirman 42-44, T 471571, F 525625, a/c, restaurant, large pool, modern and characterless; **A** *Garden*, Jl. Pemuda 21, T 521001, F 516111, a/c, restaurant, access to pool, the older version of the *Garden Palace*, price includes breakfast; **A** *Garden Palace*, Jl. Yos Sudarso 11, T 470001, a/c, restaurant, rooftop pool, under renovation, price includes breakfast; **A** *Natour Simpang*, Jl. Pemuda 1-3, T 42151, F 510156, a/c, restaurant, central location; **A** *Sahid Surabaya*, Jl. Sumatra 1, T 522711, F 516292, a/c, restaurant; **B** *Cendana*, Jl. KBP M. Duryat, T 42251, F 514367; **B** *Jane's House*, Jl. Dinoyo 100-102, T 67722, price includes breakfast; **B** *Majapahit*, Jl. Tunjungan 65, T 43351, F 43599, a/c, attractive old building, centrally located, recently undergone limited renovation, cheaper rooms are cramped; **B** *Ramayana*, 67-69 Jl. Basuki Rakhmat, T 46321; **B** *Tanjung*, Jl. Panglima Sudirman 43-45, T 42431, F 512290, rather dirty, price includes breakfast; **B** *Weta*, 3-11 Jl. Genteng Kali, T 519494, a/c, restaurant, new and efficient, glitzy

Western-style hotel; **D** *Ganesha*, Jl. Prapen Indah 41B, T 818705, price includes breakfast; **D** *Hamanda*, Jl. Cokroaminoto 2, T 67325, a/c; **C-D** *Colonial Villa*, rather run down, good location, friendly management; **E** *Bamboe Denn*, Jl. Ketabang Kali 6A, the best-known travellers' losmen in Surabaya, linked to a language school; small rooms but central and clean; **E** *Stasiun*, Jl. Stasiun Kota 1, T 20630, next to the Surabaya Kota train station; *Paviljoen*, Jl. Genteng Besar 94-98, T 43449, some a/c, old hotel in need of renovation, dark and musty.

Restaurants The *Tunjungan Plaza*, on Jl. Tunjungan houses a large selection of restaurants, serving Chinese, Javanese, Japanese and seafood. **Indonesian:** ♦♦*Antika*, Jl. Raya Darmo 1, good Padang food; *Dewi Sri*, Jl. Tunjungan 96-98; ♦*Mie Ayam*, Jl. Genteng Kali 119, good, cheap food; ♦*Mie Tunjungan*, Jl. Genteng Kali 127 (near intersection with Jl. Tunjungan), good, cheap food; ♦*Puri Garden*, Jl. Pemuda 33-37 (in the *Delta Plaza*), huge Indonesian menu; ♦*Soto Ambengan*, Jl. Ambengan 3, locally renowned for its excellent soto, rec; *Coffee House*, Jl. Praban 2 (near intersection with Jl. Tunjungan). **Foodstalls:** *Kayun Park*, along Jl. Kedung Doro and Jl. Pasar Genteng. **Chinese:** *Phoenix*, Jl. Mayjen. Sungkono. **International:** limited choice of restaurants although the big hotels serve international food, *Café Venezia*, Jl. Ambengan 16; *Granada Bakery*, intersection of Jl. Pemuda and Jl. Panglima Sudirman; *Pizza Hut*, Delta Plaza – the best salad bar in town; *Texas Fried Chicken*, Jl. Basuki Rakhmat 16.

Entertainment Classical Javanese dance performances and music: *Taman Budaya*, Jl. Genteng Kali 85, lessons in these arts are also available here; *The People's Amusement Park* or *THR*, E of the river on Jalan Kusuma Bangsa, stages performances of wayang, ketoprak, and other dances and drama (open:1800-2300 Mon-Sun); *French Culture Centre*, Jl. Darmokali 10-12, T 68639; *Goethe Institute*, Jl. Taman Ade Irma Suryani, T 40368. **Cinemas:** *Mitra*, Jl. Pemuda 15; *Studio 1-4*, Tunjungan Plaza, Jl. Basuki Rakhmat (N end).

Sports Bowling: *Wijaya Bowling Centre*, Jl. Bubutan 1-7 (3rd floor). Golf: *Yani Golf Club*, Jl. Gunungsari (next to *Patra Jasa Motel*, 5 km from city), T 40834. Swimming: a number of the hotels allow visitors to use their pools, e.g. *Garden Palace*, Jl. Yos Sudarso, 3,000Rp. The *Delta Plaza* on Jl. Pemuda (at the back) has a large, usually empty, pool for serious swimmers, 2,500Rp (no shade available). The *Margorejo Indah Sports Centre*, Jl. Margorejo (S of town), has a water world.

Shopping Antiques and handicrafts: Jl. Basuki Rakhmat; *Sarinah Craft and Batik Centre*, Jl. Tunjungan 7. Batik: *Batik Keris*, Jl. Tunjungan 12; *Batik Danar Hadi*, Jl. Diponegoro 184. Books: *Toko Buku Nasional*, Tunjungan Plaza, Jl. Basuki Rakhmat. Shopping malls: Surabaya has an abundance of these. The *Delta Plaza* on Jl. Pemuda is said to be the biggest in Southeast Asia; *Surabaya Mall* on Jl. Kusuma Bangsa, just S of the THR, *Tunjungan Plaza* (N end of Jl. Basuki Rakhmat), *Apollo Plaza*, *Indo Plaza*.

Local transport Town bus: some town maps mark bus routes, 200-300Rp. Bemo: there are innumerable bemo routes, again some maps mark their routes. There is a flat rate fare of 300Rp. Taxi: metered, with flagfall at 800Rp (300Rp for non-a/c). Becak: banned from much of the city centre.

Banks & money changers Swadesi, Jl. Tunjungan 32. Niaga, Jl. Tunjungan; BNI, Jl. Pemuda.

Embassies & consulates Belgium, Jl. Raya Kupang Indah 28, T 67698. France, Jl. Darmokali 10, T 68639. Japan, Jl. Sumatra 93, T 44677. Netherlands, Jl. Sumatra 79, T 45202. CIS, Jl. Sumatra 116, T 46290. UK, Jl. Jemur Sari (S of town) PO Box 310. USA, Jl. Raya Dr. Sutomo 33, T 692827.

Useful addresses General Post Office: Jl. Kebonrojo and Jl. Taman Apsari (off Jl. Pemuda, near Joko Dolog). Area code: 031. Immigration Office : Jl. Jend. S. Parman 58A, T 818070.

Airline offices Bouraq, Jl. Jend. Sudirman 70-72, T 470621; British Airways, Jl. Panglima Sudirman 70-72, T 470621; Cathay Pacific, Jl. Basuki Rakhmat 124-128, T 45052; Garuda, Jl. Tunjungan 29, T 40480; KLM, Jl. Yos Sudarso 11, T 479251; Mandala, Jl. Raya Diponegoro 49, T 66473; Merpati, Jl. Urip Sumoharjo 68, T 40773; Thai, Jl. Panglima Sudirman 72, T 40681.

Tour companies & travel agents Haryono, Jl. Pang. Sudirman 93, T 41006; Natrabu, Jl. Dinoyo 40, T 68513; Orient Express, Jl. Basuki Rakhmat 78, T 43315; Pacto, Altea Miramar Hotel, Jl. Raya Darmo 68-76, T 69501; Prima Vijaya Indah Tours, Delta Plaza, Jl. Pemuda 31, T 514399; Suman Tours, Jl. Yos Sudarso 17, T 510417; Wiedas Karya Gemilang, Jl. Pucang Rinenggo 1, T 60110.

Tourist offices East Java Tourism Office, Jl. Darmokali 35, T 575448. Good range of pamphlets, maps and other information on East Java. Surabaya Municipal Tourist Development Board, Jl. Yos Sudarso 22, T 46174. Only moderately helpful, some maps. Open: 0700-1500 Mon-Sat. Tourist Information Centre, Jl. Pemuda 113.

Transport to & from Surabaya 793 km from Jakarta, 327 km from Yogya, 89 km from Malang. **By air:** Juanda Airport is 18 km S of Surabaya. *Transport to town:* irregular town buses into town; taxis cost about 10,000Rp depending on destination. Regular connections on Garuda/Merpati, Sempati and Bouraq with other destinations in Java, Sumatra, Kalimantan, Sulawesi, Bali, Lombok, Nusa Tenggara, Muluku and Irian Jaya (**see page 1008** for route map). **By train:** Surabaya has 3 main railway stations. Gubeng, at the end of Jl. Pemuda on Jl. Gubeng Masjid, serves Jakarta, Solo, Yogya, Blitar, Malang and Banyuwangi. Some of these trains also stop at Kota station. Pasarturi station on Jl. Semarang serves Jakarta via Semarang and other towns on the N route (see timetable, **page 1012**). It is possible to buy a 'combination' ticket – train, ferry, bus – through to Denpasar, Bali 15 hrs. Regular connections with Banyuwangi 7 hrs, Malang 2 hrs, Blitar 5 hrs, Semarang 6½ hrs, Solo 4½ hrs, Bandung 14 hrs and Jakarta 15 hrs. **By bus:** the new Bungurasih station – the largest, so it is said, in Indonesia – was opened 6 km to the S of the city in 1991. It is at the intersection of Jl. Jend. A. Yani and Jl. Let. Jen. Sutoyo and both town buses and bemos (often via Joyoboyo bus station) link it with the city centre. Regular connections with most destinations in Java; also buses to Denpasar (Bali), Mataram (Lombok), and Sumbawa Besar and Bima (Sumbawa). Local buses run between the Jembatan Merah terminal, in the N of town, and the Bratang terminal in Wonokromo, in the S (250Rp). Night bus companies can be found at Bungurasih Station or on Jl. Arjuno and Jl. Tidar. **By boat:** Surabaya is an important port of call for Pelni ships sailing to towns in Sulawesi, Kalimantan and the islands of Maluku and Nusa Tenggara. (**See page 1008** for route map.) The Pelni ticket office is on Jl. Pahlawan 20, T 21041. There are also numerous unscheduled local cargo vessels sailing to destinations throughout the archipelago – ask the harbour master or simply wander around the Tanjung Perak port for the latest departures. For ferries to Madura see below.

MADURA ISLAND

Separated from the mainland by a 3 km-wide strait, Madura is a world apart from Java. The island – 160 km long and 30 km wide – lies off the NW coast and although it is administered as part of the province of East Java, its people regard

Kerapan sapi (bull racing)

Most tourists come to Madura to see the kerapan sapi (bull races) which are staged between Aug and Oct. Bull racing is said to have originated as a simple ploughing contest which, through time, has become institutionalized as an annual festival. The fastest bulls go to stud, on the theory that fast bulls also plough fast.

Like most rural festivals in Southeast Asia, Madura's bull racing occurs after the rice harvest, when farmers – free from the rigours of cultivation – have time to celebrate. However, the demands of tourism mean that today races are staged throughout the year. Associated with the races are parades, dancing and the music of the gamelan orchestra. The bulls are harnessed in pairs and race down a 120 m course – taking about 10 seconds to cover the distance. The winner is the bull whose legs cross the line first.

Villages and districts compete against one another in knock-out competitions, culminating in the major contest – the Kerapan Besar or Grand Island Championship – which is held in Pamekasan in Sept and preceded by a week of celebrations and ceremonies. Leading up to the big race, bulls are fed up to 50 eggs a day and are dosed up with herbs and various potions of doubtful provenance. It is said they are even given massages and are sung to sleep.

There are bull racing stadiums in Bangkalan, Pamekasan and Sumenep. *Panorama*, the East Java tourist newspaper (Apr 1991), describes the Kerapan Sapi in these terms:

"A folk and home grown enthusiasm which came to existence long ago though lacking the rattle and scarf crew English soccer or the baton twirling beauties of college football as far as the crowd is concerned, its races, district against district, regency against regency even village against village are superbly colorful."

themselves as Madurese rather than Javanese. Ardent Muslims, and proud of a history of forceful independence, they speak a distinct language and have been partially insulated from the commercialization so evident in Java. Towns are slow-moving and low-key, the landscape is dry, and the people poor by the standards of Java. However, Madura is transformed during the kerapan sapi – or bull racing season (see box, **page 655**) – when large numbers of tourists are drawn to this backwater of East Java.

Madura is predominantly flat, with a ridge of hills running along the N coast. Most of its 3 million population secure their livelihoods through farming (including growing tobacco), cattle breeding and fishing. Historically there was little of economic value to interest the Dutch. Madura became regarded as a source of fine soldiers and also from the late 19th century as a source of salt, in which the colonial authorities maintained a lucrative monopoly. But more than anything else, Madura is famous for its bulls – and certainly they appear healthier-looking than in any other part of Java. Out of the racing season they are put to good use on the land, toning-up their muscles for the big event.

There are 3 principal towns on Madura: Bangkalan on the W coast and closest to Kamal (the port for Surabaya); Pamekasan, the island's capital in the south-central portion; and Sumenep to the E which offers the greatest concentration of historical sights. The road between the 3 towns follows the S coast and is relatively quiet and well maintained, passing through small fishing villages notable for their colourful traditional boats moored along the shore.

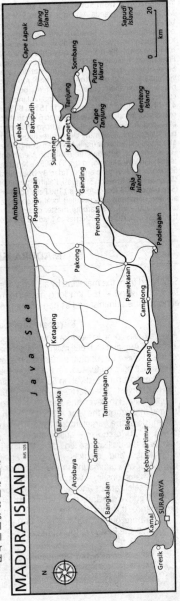

MADURA ISLAND JMS 105

Traditional boats of Madura

Madura is noted for the range and style of its traditional sailing vessels. Particular characteristics of Madurese boats is the boomed triangular sail – the so-called protolateen rig.

The **prahu jaring** (literally, 'fishing net boat') is a heavily-built, single-masted fishing boat with slightly up-turned bow and stern, a triangular sail, and a crew of 3. Each village will produce slightly different versions of the boat and they are used for in-shore fishing and the carrying of local cargoes.

The **golekan** is a squat, stubby sea-going boat with twin masts and triangular sails, displacing about 20 tonnes. The name is derived from the Malay word *kolek*, meaning small boat. Today it is rare to see golekan, although they can sometimes be viewed at Bangkalan. In the 1920s the boats were frequent visitors to Singapore, Penang and other regional ports.

The **lis-alis** is a small river or coastal boat ranging from 5 to 10 metres in length, narrow and elegant, and used for fishing and carrying light general cargoes. Like other Madurese vessels it has a triangular sail, with paired stem- and stern-posts, a projecting keel, and flattened bow and stern.

The **leti leti** is a stubby, sea-going cargo vessel with a short, pointed stem post and a single mast with lateen sail. They were important in serving the trade routes between the islands of Maluku, Nusa Tenggara and Java carrying cattle, salt, rice and simple manufactures.

The **janggolan** was one of the most common of Madurese boats and the word simply means 'transport'. Today they are rarely seen and it is thought that no more are being built – they have been superceded by the smaller lis-alis. Large, sea-going examples exceeded 100 tonnes. They are identifiable by their extended keel, protolateen triangular sail, and decorated flat face between the stern-posts.

Source: Adrian Horridge (1981) *The Prahu: traditional sailing boat of Indonesia*, Oxford University Press: Kuala Lumpur.

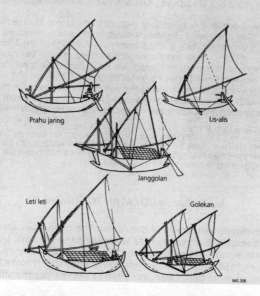

Prahu jaring

Lis-alis

Janggolan

Leti leti

Golekan

IMS 308

History

Before the 17th century, Madura was a Java in miniature. A number of royal courts or *dalem* controlled the local economy, and these were at the same time the spiritual, cultural and artistic focus of the island. Although today Madura is regarded as being one of the more ardent Muslim areas of Indonesia, the people of the island were not converted to Islam until the 16th century. When Tomé Pires visited Madura in 1512 for example, it was still Hindu, and although local tradition maintains that the conversion of the inhabitants occurred in 1528 when the Prince of Arsobaya embraced Islam, this is likely to have been restricted to the local élite.

Madura was incorporated into the empire of the great Mataram king Sultan Agung during the seige of Surabaya (**see page 648**) from 1620-1625. By all accounts the campaign for Madura was long and arduous and Agung's army suffered considerable losses. He was forced to devastate the ricelands of the island and also to fight the island's women who joined their menfolk to wage war against the invading army. On finally vanquishing the local forces in 1624, he set about unifying the island, placing it under the control of a single prince with a capital at Sampang. In less than 50 years however, the empire that Sultan Agung had created – and of which Madura was a part – began to fragment.

In 1670 Prince Trunojoyo, buoyed-up by a prophesy that maintained he would be a great hero and that Mataram would fall, travelled to Madura to prepare for revolution. He defeated the local prince and his Javanese soldiers and established a base at Pamekasan on the S coast. By 1671 he had control over the whole island and assembled an impressive army, exploiting the dislike that the local population felt over domination from Java. In 1675, Prince Trunojoyo sailed with his army to the mainland and took Surabaya. By 1677 the rebellion against Mataram was at its height and much of East Java was under rebel control. But with the support of the European troops of the VOC, who sided against Prince Trunojoyo, the rebellion ultimately failed in 1677. Three years later the island was divided into 2 – West and East Madura and placed under the control of 2 royal lineages. Later, Mataram ceded East Madura (in 1705), and then West Madura (in 1743) to the Dutch.

But the defeat of Prince Trunojoyo was not to mean that Madura had been pacified. Over the next 7 decades Madurese lords would periodically mount campaigns and attack Java. It is this history which has given the Madurese a reputation of being a brave and warlike people. Indeed, many of the troops in the Dutch colonial army came from Madura. The Dutch divided the administration of Madura between 3 royal houses – based at Bangkalan, Pamekasan and Sumenep. These local lords maintained considerable power until the administrative reforms of 1816. By 1887, their influence had been eroded further still until they were reduced to the same status as *bupatis* in Java – mere aristocratic regency figureheads.

Transport to & from Madura By boat: car ferries leave every 30 mins, 24 hrs a day from N of Surabaya on Jl. Kalimas Baru (see Surabaya map), docking at Kamal, on the SW coast of Madura, 45 mins later (400Rp/person, 4,500Rp/car). Minibuses wait at the Kamal dockside to transport passengers to Bangkalan and onward. A daily ferry leaves Sumenep at 0700 for Jangkar (120 km NW of Banyuwangi) 4 hrs (2,500Rp).

MADURA: BANGKALAN TO SUMENEP

Two principal roads traverse the island. The main road across the island begins in Bangkalan, runs SE to Sampang (61 km), and then follows the coast to Pamekasan (another 29 km) and Sumenep, a total distance of 154 km. The longer, less well maintained, N route follows the N coast from Bangkalan and after 11 km reaches the village of

Arosbaya. Continuing along the N coast for about another 40 km, Pasongsongan offers a good beach and swimming.

Bangkalan

Bangkalan is focused on a large central square or *alun-alun*. There is a **small museum** near the square with characteristic Madurese architecture housing ethnographic and historical artefacts including agricultural tools and palm-leaf manuscripts. The bull racing stadium, the centre of activity during **kerapan sapi**, is 1 km out of town on the road S to Kamal.

Excursions

Arosbaya is a small village 11 km NE of town. Nearby, at Air Mata is the royal cemetery of the Cakraningrat family, the lords of Sumenep, who dominated the island during the 17th and 18th centuries. **Getting there:** by minibus from Bangkalan station on the central square.

Festivals Aug to Oct: *Kerapan Sapi*, traditional bull racing festival (see box, **page 655**).

Accommodation A-D *Ningrat*, Jl. H. Moh Cholil 113, T 338, some a/c, best hotel in town, well run, with attractive rooms and bathrooms, rec; **E** *Purnama*, Jl. Kartini 19.

Useful addresses Post Office: Jl. Trunojoyo 2.

Transport to & from Bangkalan 16 km N of Kamal, 90 km from Pamekasan. **By minibus:** the station is on the town square. Regular connections with Kamal, Pamekasan and Sumenep.

Pamekasan

Pamekasan is the capital of Madura island, but is still a low key, sleepy town of single-storeyed houses with yellow shutters and attractive white-washed walled alleys. Like Bangkalan, Pamekasan is focused upon a central square in the middle of which is an enigmatic Indonesian monument, in this case looking rather like waving seaweed. Also on the square (Jalan Mesjid), is the central **mosque** with its characteristic tiered Javanese roof.

Excursions

Camplong is a beach resort 29 km W of town. It offers visitors a mini amusement park as well as a beach, of sorts; the water here is rather muddy. Traditional boats are picturesquely moored along the shore. **Getting there:** by minibus.

Accommodation D-E *Purnama*, Jl. Ponorogo 10A, T 81375; **D-E** *Trunojoyo*, Jl. Trunojoyo 28, T 81181, some a/c; **E** *Garuda*, Jl. Masigit 1, T 81589, good location right on the square, attractive old house in need of upkeep.

Shopping Batik: Jl. Diponegoro 96.

Useful addresses Post Office: Jl. Masigit 3A. **Area code**: 0234.

Transport to & from Pamekasan 90 km from Bangkalan, 64 km from Sumenep. **By minibus:** regular connections with Sumenep, Bangkalan and Kamal.

Sumenep

Sumenep is the most frequently visited town on Madura, as it offers the most sights of historical interest. These are focused upon the large central square. On the N side of the square is the 18th century **Mesjid Jamik Mosque** with tiered roof, and fronted by a white and yellow washed Madurese gateway. On the opposite side of the square is the street leading to the kraton, Jalan Dr. Sutomo. On the right-hand side of this street is the badly maintained **Museum Daerah**, with a poorly displayed collection of mainly European pieces, including a carriage. Admission: 200Rp. Open: Mon-Sun. Opposite, is the 18th century **kraton** built by Panembahan Sumolo, where some of the rooms are open to the public and display a motley collection of Chinese ceramics, krisses, swords, topeng masks, and wayang puppets. Next to the palace is a small water garden or **Taman Sari**. Enclosed by white-washed walls, it contains a clear bathing pool filled with fish. It is said that bathing in the pool will ensure eternal youth.

Excursions

Asta Tinggi The graves of the sultan's family lie $1\frac{1}{2}$ km W of the town.

Pasongsongan Swimming is possible at this mediocre beach NW of Sumenep, home to traditional shipbuilders. **Getting there:** by minibus.

Accommodation D *Safari Jaya*, Jl. Trunojoyo 90 (2 km S of town on road to Pamekasan), T 21989, some a/c; **D-E** *Wijaya I*, Jl. Wahid Hasyim 1, T 21532, some a/c, clean rooms and efficiently run; **D-E** *Wijaya II*, Jl. Trunojoyo 45-47, T 21433, some a/c, similar standard to sister losmen, Wijaya I.

Restaurants ✦✦*Bimba*, Jl. Trunojoyo 41, Padang food; *Mawar*, Jl. Diponegoro, Chinese; *Wijaya II*, Jl. Trunojoyo 45-47, Indonesian.

Entertainment Bull racing: out of kerapan sapi season, ask the officials at the kraton or museum about staging a bull race.

Shopping Batik: the Madurese have a distinctive form of batik, made up of flower patterns of red, purple and blue. Available from *Toko Mashur* (Koleksi Batik Madura), Jl. Trunojoyo. Furniture: several shops in Sumenep sell both antique and new furniture.

Useful addresses Area code: 0328.

Transport to & from Sumenep 64 km from Pamekasan, 154 km from Bangkalan. **By minibus**: the station is on Jl. Trunojoyo, at the S side of town. Regular connections with Bangkalan, Pamekasan and Kamal. **By boat**: see Transport to & from Madura (**page 658**). A **daily ferry** leaves Sumenep at 0700 for Jangkar (60 km N of Banyuwangi) 4 hrs.

EASTERN JAVA: From Surabaya to Banyuwangi and Bali via Mount Bromo

---

From Surabaya travelling S and then E it is 97 km to Probolinggo on Java's N coast. Probolinggo is the most popular jumping-off point for trips up the volcano Mount Bromo (2,329m), one of the most spectacular natural sights on Java. From Probolinggo, the road follows the coast E to Situbondo. Bondowoso, famous for its bull fights, lies 30 km inland, wedged between Mount Bromo and Mount Raung. After Situbondo, the road turns S, skirting around Mount Raung (3,332m) and passing between the Baluran and Ijen-Merapi National Parks. This E extremity of Java, like the far W, is one of the few areas of the island where wild animals are resisting the encroachment of people. Finally, 196 km from Probolinggo, the road reaches the E coast port of Banyuwangi, near the ferry dock for Bali.

Probolinggo

A Javanese holiday resort inhabited by a mixture of Javanese and Madurese, and notable only as the major stopping-off point for trips to Mount Bromo.

Excursions

Candi Jabung lies E of Probolinggo, about 10 km on from the small coastal town of Kraksaan. It was completed in 1354 and – unusually – is circular in plan (although the inner cella is square). It was a Buddhist shrine, built as a funerary temple for a Majapahit princess. The finial is now ruined but was probably in the form of a stupa.

The tiny island **Gili Ketapang** lies 20 mins offshore by boat from Probolinggo.

Accommodation D *Bromo Permai*, Jl. Sudirman 237, T 41256, some a/c, good location for catching the bus to Bromo, clean rooms, helpful management; **D** *Ratna*, Jl. Sudirman 16, T 21597, some a/c, best available in town, good value; *Victoria*, Jl. Suroyo 1-3, T 21461.

Useful addresses Area code: 0335.

Transport to & from Probolinggo 99 km from Surabaya, 190 km from Banyuwangi. **By**

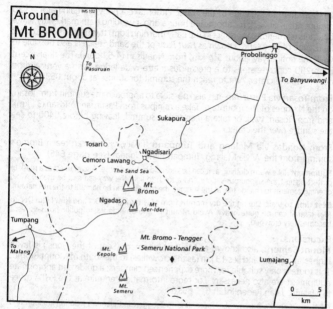

train: regular connections on the Mutiara Timur train with Surabaya and on to Yogyakarta and Banyuwangi via Jember 9 hrs. By bus: regular connections with Surabaya 3 hrs, Malang 3 hrs and Banyuwangi 4 hrs. Night buses to Denpasar (Bali) 8 hrs.

Mount Bromo

This active volcano stands at 2,329m and is one of the most popular natural sights on Java, lying within the **Bromo-Tengger-Semeru National Park**. The park consists of a range of volcanic mountains, the highest of which (and Java's highest) is Mount Semeru at 3,676m. Wildlife in the park includes wild pig (*Sus scrofa*), Timor deer (*Cervus timorensis*), barking deer and leopard (*Pantera pardus*) as well as an abundance of flying squirrels. The local inhabitants of this area are the Tenggerese people, believed to be descended from the refugees of the Majapahit Kingdom, who fled their lands in 928 following the eruption of Mount Merapi. They embrace the Hindu religion and are the only group of Hindus left on Java today.

Reaching the crater

From Ngadisari via Probolinggo and Sukapura: the easiest access to the park is from the N coast town of Probolinggo, via Sukapura and Ngadisari and then to Cemoro Lawang on the edge of the caldera. On arrival in Ngadisari, it is important to obtain a ticket from the 'tourist information' booth in order to visit the crater's edge. The trip to the caldera is usually undertaken in the early morning in order to watch the sunrise over the volcanic lakes. To reach the summit for dawn, an early start from nearby Ngadisari is essential, leaving no later than 0330. It is easiest to travel to Cemoro Lawang (from Ngadisari) on one of the 6-seater jeeps, organized by guesthouses in Ngadisari. Independent travel to Cemoro Lawang is not advisable, as the road is circuitous and busy with traffic. It takes twenty minutes from Ngadisari to the outer crater at Cemoro Lawang, and is another 3 km from here to the edge of the crater. Either take a pony (bargain hard) – a 30 minute ride – or walk for about one hour along a winding path marked by white boulders (sometimes indistinct in the early morning light) through a strange crater landscape of grey sand, known as *Laut Pasir* or the Sand Sea. It is also possible to walk the entire way, about 5$\frac{1}{2}$ km, from Ngadisari (4-5 hours). The final ascent is up 250 concrete steps to a precarious metre-wide ledge, with a vertical drop down into the crater. Aim to reach the summit for sunrise at about 0530.

From Tosari via Pasuruan: it is also possible to approach the summit from Tosari, on the N slopes of the mountain. Take a minibus from Pasuruan to Tosari (31 km), and from Tosari, walk or take a jeep to the summit, leaving before 0400 to see the sunrise over the crater.

From Ngadas via Malang and Tumpang: finally, visitors can reach Bromo's summit from the W via Malang, Tumpang and Ngadas (see page 646).

Equipment Take warm clothing as it can be very cold before sunrise. A scarf to act as a mask to protect against the sulphurous vapour and a torch to light the way can also be useful. Avoid opening cameras to change film at the summit; the thin dust can be harmful to the mechanism.

Best time to visit During the dry months from May through to Oct and Nov. From Dec to Mar rainfall can be quite heavy. Avoid Mount Bromo on Indonesian public holidays, as it becomes very crowded.

Excursions
Mount Semeru, also known as Mount Mahameru ('seat of the Gods') is Java's highest mountain and lies 13 km (as the crow flies) to the south of Mount Bromo. This route is only suitable for more experienced climbers; a guide and appropriate equipment are also necessary. For more information, enquire at the PHPA office in Malang, Jalan Raden Intan 6, T 65100.

Festivals Feb: *Karo* (moveable, according to Tenggerese Calendar) held in Ngadisari and Wonokitri to commemorate the creation of Man by Sang Hyang Widi. Tenggerese men perform dances to celebrate the event. Dec: *Kasodo* (moveable, according to Tenggerese Calendar). This ceremony is linked to a legend which relates how a princess and her husband pleaded with the gods of the mountain to give them children. Their request was heeded on the condition that their youngest child should be sacrificed to the mountain. The couple then had 25 children, but were understandably reluctant to meet their side of the bargain. The mountain continued to erupt periodically to remind the couple of their vow. They finally conceded to the gods' wishes and when the child was thrown into the abyss her voice could be heard chiding the parents for not offering her sooner and requesting that on the night of the full moon in the month of Kasado, offerings should be made to the mountain. The ceremony reaches a climax with a midnight pilgrimage to the crater to make offerings to the gods. Ritual sacrifices of animals, and offerings of vegetables and fruit, are thrown into the crater to appease the gods.

Accommodation at Sukapura **A** *Grand Bromo*, T (031) 711802, restaurant, tennis courts, **E** for dorm beds, 9 km for crater, ostentatious and unsuitable position for visits to Mt. Bromo. At Ngadisari **D-E** *Yoschi's*, Jl. Wonokerto 1, 2 km before Ngadisari, run by a Dutch woman, married to a Javanese, who speaks good English and is an excellent source of information on the mountain, the restaurant serves huge portions of very good Javanese food, rec; **E** *Sukapura Permai*, clean and basic. At Cemoro Lawang **C** *Bromo Permai*, book at Bromo Permai in Probolinggo (Jl. Sudirman 237, T 41256), restaurant, small rooms perched on the edge of the crater, magnificent views, popular, **F** for dorm beds. At Tosari **A** *Bromo Cottages*, T (031) 515253, F 511811, restaurant, hot water, tennis courts, great views. At Wonokitri **C** *Pendopo Agung*, hot water; **D** *Bromo Surya Indah Homestay*, T 332411, restaurant.

Transport to & from Mt Bromo 2 hrs drive E of the city of Malang, 3 hrs S of Surabaya and 30 km SW of Probolinggo. **By bus/minibus from Probolinggo**: regular connections with Sukapura and Ngadisari 1$\frac{1}{2}$ hrs (connections on to Surabaya or Maleng). **Minibus charter from Probolinggo**: for about 60,000Rp, ask at any of the local hotels. **By minibus from Pasuruan** (1$\frac{1}{2}$ hrs from Malang and Surabaya): regular minibuses to Tosari (3,000Rp). **By minibus from Malang**: take a bus to Tumpang and change onto a (rather irregular) minibus for the climb up to Ngadas (see page 646).

Pasir Putih

Coastal resort with what is rather optimistically called a "white" sand beach. Snorkeling, diving and boats for rent (6,000Rp/hr).

Festivals Nov: *Sapp sapp* – traditional chicken race; chickens are released from boats on the water and they try to fly to the shore. The winner is the one that flies the furthest. Animal rights activists might have something to say about it.

Accommodation C-E *Pasir Putih Inn*, attractive surroundings and reasonable rooms; **E** *Oriental*, own mandi, good value; **E** *Sidho Muncul*, some a/c, best on the beach.

Transport to & from Pasir Putih 105 km from Banyuwangi. **By bus:** buses travelling along the N coast all stop in Pasir Putih – regular connections with Banyuwangi.

Bondowoso

This tidy little town lies 34 km inland from Situbondo and the N coast and is squeezed into the narrow valley of the Sampean River between Mount Argopuro (3,088m) to the W and Mount Raung (3,332m) to the E. The town is locally famous for its bull fighting, which takes place throughout the year. The aim of the fight is to improve the quality of the breeding stock (**see page 655**).

Excursions

Jember lies 33 km S of Bondowoso. A company called Perkebunan XXVI organize enterprising tours to coconut, coffee, rubber and sugar plantations. They can be found at Jl. Gajah Mada 249, T 21061. **Getting there**: by regular bus.

Accommodation A-C *Palm*, Jl. A. Yani 32, a/c, pool, breakfast included; **E** *Anugerah*, Jl. Mayjen Sutoyo 12, T 21870, clean rooms.

Useful addresses Area code: 0332.

Transport to & from Bondowoso By bus: from Pasih Putih (200Rp).

Banyuwangi

Banyuwangi, on Java's E coast, is not noted either for its sights or its beauty, but many tourists are forced to pass through the town as it is near the ferry port for Bali. The **Mesjid Baiturrachman** in the centre of town is worth visiting if visitors have time to kill.

Mount Merapi and the Ijen Crater are both accessible from Banyuwangi. It is best to hire a guide for the walk to the summit, which takes about 6 hrs each way (34 km round trip). Ask at the tourist board for a recommendation. A third of the path is steep but cobbled; it was constructed by the Japanese during World War II, who needed sulphur for their munitions. Wildlife within the park includes leopard, pig, civet, peafowl and silver leaf-monkey. After a jungle walk, the landscape opens up and the climb is less steep to the crater's edge. The walk down the crater wall to the 175m deep blue-green sulphur lake is precipitous. Sulphur is extracted from the spring here, where the orange liquid quickly solidifies and is broken off, to be carried in baskets on men's shoulders down the mountainside (60 kg at a time). **Getting there:** accessible from Banyuwangi, 18 km away (minibus to Jambu), or from the W side via Bondowoso and Sempol.

Grajagan Bay is situated within the South Banyuwangi reserve, faces W and is renowned for its surfing. The beach is reputed to have one of the longest left breaks in the world, and is a pilgrimage spot for Australian surfers. The reserve itself contains the **alas purwo** (or 'ancient forest') – a collection of rare trees as well as wildlife including leopard, banteng and wild boar. A permit is needed to enter the park, obtainable from the park office near Tegaldlimo or from the PHPA office in Banyuwangi. Accommodation: basic huts (**D**) are available in Grajagan Bay. **Getting there:** by bus from Banyuwangi to Benculuk (1,000Rp), then by minibus to Grajagan (500Rp).

Meru Betiri Reserve is the last home of the small Javanese tiger, which was common throughout Java until the 1800s and early 1900s, when it was hunted to the point of extinction. **Getting there:** by bus to Genteng or Jajag and then by bemo to Pasanggaran. From there, hitch a lift.

Sukamade is a 3 km stretch of beach on the S coast, within the Meru Betiri Reserve, and about 50 km from Banyuwangi. It is protected as a nesting ground for turtles. **Getting there:** as above.

Baluran Reserve is 40 km N of Banyuwangi, on the E coast. The reserve supports small populations of monkeys, deer, wild buffalo and banteng (wild oxen). Good walks, beaches and snorkelling. Guesthouses here can be booked through the PHPA in Banyuwangi or c/o Taman Baluran, T 68453. **Getting there:** take a bus from Banyuwangi heading along the coast and ask to be dropped off at the park entrance. Ojeks wait there to take visitors to the coast (3,000Rp).

Accommodation A-B *Manyar*, on Ketapang road, T 41741, a/c, hot water, restaurant, best hotel around; **C** *Blambangan*, Jl. Dr. Wahidin 4, T 21598, some a/c; **D** *Slamet*, Jl. Wahid Hasyim 96, some a/c, own mandis; **E** *Baru*, Jl. Pattimura 82-84, T 21369, own mandi, price includes breakfast, large clean rooms, friendly management, popular; **F** *Baru Raya*, Jl. Dr. Sutomo 26, own mandi.

Restaurants *Samudra*, Jl. Jend. Sudirman 171; *Wina*, by Blambangan bus terminal.

Useful addresses Area code: 0333. **PHPA office**, Jl. Jend. A. Yani 108, T 41118.

Tourist office Head office is at the dock, where ferries arrive from Bali. Branch office, Jl. Diponegoro 2, T 41282.

Transport to & from Banyuwangi 288 km from Surabaya, 194 km from Probolinggo. **By train:** day and night connections with Surabaya's Kota terminal 7 hrs (3,000Rp). Combined bus-train tickets to Denpasar (Bali) cost an extra 3,500Rp (**see page 1012**). **By bus:** Banyuwangi has 2 bus terminals. The Blambangan terminal is at the N edge of town and serves Ketapang (for ferries to Bali) and stops along the coast to Surabaya and Malang including Probolinggo. On the S edge of town is the Banjarsari terminal for destinations S of town. **By boat:** passenger and car ferries to & from Gilimanuk on Bali dock at Ketapang, 8 km N of town. They depart regularly from early morning until about 2100, 30 mins (500Rp). **NB:** If driving to Bali, note that it is not easy to obtain fuel between the ferry terminal at Gilimanuk and Denpasar, so fill up before leaving Java. To get to Ketapang, catch a regular minibus from the Blambangan terminal on the N edge of town.

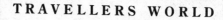

BALI

Introduction, 666; Information for Visitors, 685; Denpasar, 689; The Southern resorts, 692; The Bukit Peninsula, 699; North from Denpasar to Ubud, 702; North of Ubud, 711; North of Denpasar, 712; Pura Besakih and Mount Agung, 715; The East, 718; North to Lake Bratan, 723; Lake Bratan to the North Coast, 726; The West, 729. **Maps:** Bali, 669; Denpasar, 691; South Bali, 693; Uluwatu, 701; Around Ubud, 703; Goa Gajah, 705; Gunung Kawi, 711; North & East Bali, 714.

INTRODUCTION

More tourists visit the island of Bali than any other place in Indonesia, and many visitors believe they are actually in a separate country, called Bali. The island has gained a reputation as the exotic tropical island paradise *par excellence* – a reputation which dates from the early years of this century when artists began to visit the island and record its breath-taking beauty. With its majestic volcanoes, spectacular terraced rice fields, golden beaches, and a rich and colourful culture, Bali is the jewel in the crown of Indonesia's tourism industry. When the author and Bali-lover Miguel Covarrubias and his wife arrived off Bali's N coast on a steamer in 1930, he wrote: "We had our first unforgettable glimpse of Bali at dawn when the little K.P.M. steamer approached Buleleng – a high dark peak reflected on a sea as smooth as polished steel, with the summit of the cone hidden in dark metallic clouds".

But Bali suffers from the curse of being too popular – intrepid explorers feel that visiting such an island is beneath their dignity. Yet somehow Bali has retained its beauty and charm, and no one should spurn the island just because of its image as an over-popular tropical sun trap. As far back as the 1930s, insightful commentators were predicting what lay in store for Bali. Miguel Covarrubias, for one, in his seminal book, *Island of Bali* (1937) wrote:

> "Undoubtedly Bali will soon enough be 'spoiled' for those fastidious travellers who abhor all that which they bring with them. No longer will the curious Balinese of the remote mountain villages, still unaccustomed to the sight of whites, crowd around their cars to stare silently at the 'exotic' long-nosed, yellow-haired foreigners in their midst. But even when all the Balinese will have learned to wear shirts, to beg, lie, steal, and prostitute themselves to satisfy new needs, the tourists will continue to come to Bali to see the sights, snapping pictures frantically, dashing from temple to temple, back to hotel for meals, and on to watch rites and dances staged for them."

ENVIRONMENT

Land

Bali is the westernmost island of the chain that make up the Lesser Sundas, and is one of Indonesia's smallest provinces. It covers 5,561 sq km and has a population

Bali highlights

Temples The most important and impressively situated temple is *Besakih* on Mount Agung (**page 715**). *Uluwatu* is perched on a cliff-top on the Bukit Peninsula (**page 700**), while the coastal temple *Tanah Lot* (**page 724**) is the most photographed sight on Bali. Other notable temples include *Taman Ayun* at Mengwi (**page 724**) and *Kehen* at Bangli (**page 713**).

Other Historical Sights Within easy reach of **Ubud** are *Goa Gajah* or Elephant Cave (**page 705**), the ancient stone carvings at *Yeh Pulu* (**page 706**), the mysterious monumental burial chambers of *Gunung Kawi* (**page 711**), and the holy springs at *Tirta Empul* (**page 712**). The royal bathing pools of *Tirtagangga* are in the E (**page 723**). The *Museum Bali* in Denpasar (**page 689**) has a good collection of ethnographic and archaeological exhibits.

Beaches The main beach resort areas are *Kuta* (**page 692**), *Sanur* (**page 696**) and *Nusa Dua* (see **page 701**); *Candi Dasa* (**page 719**) and *Lovina Beach* (**page 727**) are smaller and less developed.

Shopping Bali is a shoppers paradise (**see page 688**); *fashions* in Kuta (**page 695**), *craft villages* N of Sanur (**page 702**), *paintings and crafts* in Ubud (**page 703**).

Natural sights Among the most notable, is the extraordinary volcanic landscape of *Mount Batur* (**page 713**); the upland, almost alpine, area centred on *Lake Bratan* (**page 725**) of the S and E and the countryside around **Ubud** (**page 704**); and the *Bali Barat National Park* (**page 729**).

Sports *Surfing* (see **page 688**), *white water rafting* (**page 708**), *snorkeling* (**page 688**), *golf* (**pages 702 and 726**) and *diving* (**page 688**) are the most notable.

Culture & Performance *Balinese dancing* in and around Ubud (**page 710**), and the traditional *Bali Aga village of Tenganan* (**page 719**).

of 3 million. Like the other islands of the Lesser Sundas, it rises from the deep sea as a series of spectacular volcanic peaks, the highest of which – Mount Agung – exceeds 3,000 m.

Separating Bali from Java is the narrow Bali Strait. It is 40-50 m deep, and during the last Ice Age when sea-levels were considerably lower than today, Bali would have been connected to the mainland by a land bridge, allowing animals to move freely between the two. To the E, Bali is separated from the next of the Lesser Sunda Islands, Lombok, by the far deeper Lombok Strait. At its deepest, the water depth exceeds 1,300 m – and even during the Pleistocene Ice Age the strait would have remained submerged. Wallace's Line, the division between the Asian and Australasian faunal realms, first identified by the great Victorian naturalist Alfred Russel Wallace, passes between the two islands (**see page 905**). Because of the depth of the water here, the strait is an important passage for nuclear submarines making the trip between the Indian and Pacific oceans.

A feature of life on an island that lies over the spot where 2 tectonic plates overlap, is great geological instability. One of the most serious earthquakes this century occurred in 1917. During Jan and Feb of that year, a series of tremors hit the E and S regions of the island, followed by the eruption of Mount Batur. When this activity came to an end on 20 Feb, a total of 2,431 temples had been badly damaged – including Pura Besakih on Mount Agung – 64,000 homes had been wrecked, and 1,500 people had died. The inference was clear to every Balinese: the gods were angry. It is partly for this reason that the Balinese have felt it necessary to build temples in great numbers to appease the spirits and therefore help prevent natural catastrophe. In the case of Mount Batur's 1917 eruption,

The gift of water: rice and water in Bali

Among anthropologists, agronomists and geographers, Bali is famous for its system of irrigation. It is a three-fold fascination, bringing together impressive feats of engineering, elaborate social structures, and the guiding hand of religion. (For general background to wet rice cultivation see page 514 and page 34.)

Most of the 162 large streams and rivers which flow from Bali's mountainous interior have cut deep channels into the soft volcanic rock. This has made it impossible for farmers to dam and channel water for irrigation in the usual way. Instead, they have taken to cutting tunnels through the rock, and constructing elaborate aquaducts and bamboo piping systems to carry the water to the top of a series of terraced rice fields. From here it can flow, with gravity, from paddy field (or sawah) to paddy field.

The Balinese have been digging irrigation tunnels in this way for over a thousand years. One tunnel has an inscription recording that it was cut in 944AD. They are dug by professional tunnellers whose main difficulty is not cutting through the soft volcanic rock, but making sure they emerge in the correct place - some are over a kilometre long.

But, these feats of engineering are only half the story. The water then needs to be managed, and the tunnels, weirs and aquaducts, maintained. As American anthropologist Stephen Lansing writes in his book *Priests and Programmers*, "virtually every farmer depends on an irrigation system that originates several kilometres upstream and flows in fragile channels through the lands of many neighbours...". He notes that even a brief interruption of flow will destroy a farmers' crop. To prevent this, every rice farmer is a member of a *subak* or irrigation society. The subak brings together all the farmers who receive water from a common source, and this may include farmers from more than one village. The subak is designed to ensure the equitable distribution of water. Each subak is headed by a *kliang subak* or *penyarikan subak* who can call on his members to police canals, mend dykes and wiers, and generally maintain the system.

Nor does the story of rice and water end with the subak. The subaks, in turn, look to the regional water temple or *pura*, and the head of the pura sets the schedule of planting and harvesting. Subaks are not self-reliant; water control among the farmers of one subak is usually dependent upon those of another. The head of Pura Er Jeruk explained the system to Stephen Lansing in these terms:

> There are fourteen... subaks all of which meet together as one here. They meet at the Temple Er Jeruk. Every decision, every rule concerning planting seasons and so forth, is always discussed here. Then after the meeting here, decisions are carried down to each subak. The subaks each call all their members together: 'In accord with the meeting we held at the Temple Er Jeruk, we must fix our planting dates, beginning on day one through day ten'. For example, first subak Sango plants, then subak Somi, beginning from day ten through day twenty. Thus it is arranged in accordance with water and Pandewasan...".

though the lava engulfed the village of Batur, it stopped at the gates to the temple. The villagers took this as a good omen and refused to move, rebuilding their village at the same site. Nine years later, the volcano erupted again, this time swamping the temple and leading to one death, an old woman, who died of fright. Nonetheless, the villagers still rebuilt their village on the rim of the volcano – albeit in a safer location – courting possible future disaster.

Despite the devastating effects of periodic earthquakes and volcanic eruptions, Bali has also been blessed by nature in its rich and fertile soils and abundant rainfall. Farmers have exploited this natural wealth by creating terraces on the hillsides, cutting tunnels through the rock to carry irrigation water, and cultivating rice throughout the year (see box).

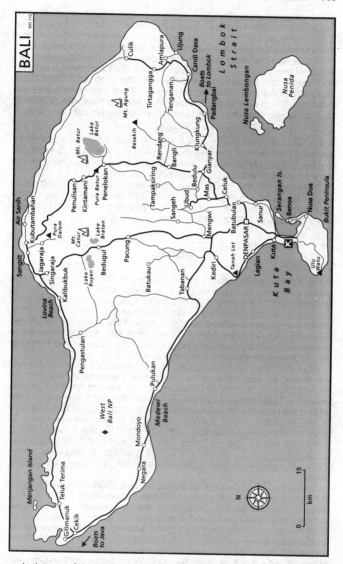

At the core of the island is a central mountain range consisting of 6 peaks all exceeding 2,000 m. These trap rain clouds and ensure that perennial rivers water the lower slopes. The main expanse of lowland lies to the S of this mountainous interior, and most of the rivers flow S. It is here, on the S slopes and plain, that

Bali's famous terraced rice fields are concentrated. Most of the villages or *banjars* are perched on the edge of ridges, surrounded by ricefields. To the N, the lowland fringe is much narrower and the absence of rivers makes the land drier and less suited to intensive rice cultivation. The W peninsula, with its poor soils, is yet more arid still.

Despite Bali's unquestioned natural fecundity, the island has begun to feel the effects of over-population. In the 1950s, about 3,000 people were leaving Bali each year to take up places on transmigration settlements in the Outer Islands (see page 732); by the 1960s this had risen to 5,000. It has only been the boom in tourism since the 1970s that has prevented this stream becoming a flood, as tourism has offered young Balinese alternative opportunities outside agriculture.

Climate

Bali is hot and humid, but this is alleviated by ocean breezes. Annual rainfall averages 2,150 mm, the driest months being Aug and Sept and the wettest, Dec and Jan. Temperatures at sea-level average 26°C and vary only marginally through the year; in highland areas it is considerably cooler, about 20°C.

There are 2 seasons: the dry season from May-Oct; and the wet season from Nov to Apr. But this should not deter visitors. Rain tends to fall throughout the year, but it usually comes in short, sharp showers during the afternoon and early evening (see page 689 for best time to visit).

HISTORY

Balinese recorded history begins in the 10th century with the marriage of King Udayana and the East Javanese princess Mahendradatta. In 991 their union resulted in the birth of a son, named Airlangga. He was sent to Java to rule a principality of his father-in-law King Dharmawangsa of Sanjaya. When Dharmawangsa was murdered, Airlangga assumed the throne and for the next 30 years ruled his empire with great skill (see page 516). As a Balinese prince he forged strong links between his island of origin and Java, and in so doing began the pattern of Javanese cultural influence over Bali.

After 1049 when, on Airlangga's death, the kingdom of Sanjaya (or Mataram) was divided, Bali became independent once more. It remained self-governing for the next 235 years until King Kertanagara of the East Javanese dynasty of Singasari invaded in 1284. Kertanagara's domination over Bali was to last only 8 years, when it was invaded by the stronger Majapahit Kingdom of Central Java. Relieved of their Singasari overlords, the Balinese were left to themselves for another 50 years. In 1343, General Gajah Mada, under the flag of Majapahit, conquered Bali, making the island a Javanese colony. Though the various Balinese principalities revolted time and again against Majapahit overlordship, they were neither individually strong enough nor sufficiently united to resist the weight of Javanese power.

During the 15th century, as Islam filtered into Java, Majapahit began to decline in influence. The last Hindu prince of Majapahit crossed the Bali Strait in 1478, escaping from the Muslim onslaught to the Hindu haven of Bali. He was accompanied by priests, artists and other courtesans – as well as by large numbers of ordinary East Javanese. The prince declared himself King of Bali (his descendants are the rajas of Klungkung) and promptly divided the island up between his various supporters. These later Javanese immigrants are still referred to as *Wong Majapahit* and a shrine for *Batara Majapahit*, or the teachers of Majapahit, can be found in nearly every temple. Some commentators argue that it was because of this wholesale migration of the cream of Javanese artists and craftsmen, that Balinese art today is so strong and prolific. It was on Bali that Java's pre-Islamic artistic accomplishments were preserved.

The Dutch arrival

The Dutch first made contact with Bali in 1597, when a fleet led by Cornelius Houtman landed on the island. His men enjoyed a long sojourn, falling in love with the people and the place. When the expedition returned to Holland, such was the wonder at the stories that the sailors told that another fleet was dispatched, in 1601, with gifts for the hospitable king. The king received these gifts with dignity, and in return presented the captain with a beautiful Balinese girl.

But this initial friendly encounter was not to be the pattern of future contacts. In 1815 Tambora Volcano erupted on Sumbawa (**see page 925**), and more than 10,000 people on Bali perished in the subsequent famine and plague. This was seen by the Balinese as a taste of things to come. In 1817 a Dutch ship arrived laden with goods to be traded, and in 1826, a trade agreement was signed and the first permanent Dutch representative settled in Kuta. But by then, relations between the Balinese, and what they perceived to be the arrogant, crude and ill-behaved Dutch, were already strained. In 1841, a Dutch ship ran aground and the King of Bali accepted it as a gift. This was the excuse the Dutch needed for intervention.

Five years later, the Dutch sent a large, punitive expeditionary force to conquer N Bali. The attempt failed, but the Dutch, persistent as ever, followed it with another in 1848, and yet a third in 1849. Jagaraga, the capital of the N Balinese kingdom of Buleleng, was eventually vanquished, but not without considerable losses on both sides. The fact that Bali was divided into various different competing principalities made the Dutch campaign all the easier. Even so, an attack on S Bali at the same time led to the death of the Dutch general, and the Europeans were forced to accept a treaty which left S Bali under Balinese control. This was not the initial intention, and for the next 40 years the Dutch searched for a means of extending their influence from N Bali over the rest of the island.

To do this, the Dutch attacked Lombok in 1894, which was under the control of the E Balinese kingdom of Karangkasem (**see page 677**). When Lombok fell, so too did Karangkasem, and then Bangli and Gianyar also accepted Dutch rule. But it was not until the first decade of the 20th century that the final 3 stubborn, recalcitrant kingdoms of Badung, Tabanan and Klungkung fell to the might of the Dutch.

This last campaign was associated with the arrival in 1904 of a new governor-general, J.B. van Heutz. He was determined to complete the campaign for Bali, the new Resident of Bali and Lombok recalling that when he first met van Heutz, the governor-general had run "his hand across the principalities of South Bali [saying] no more than 'this all has to be changed'". An expeditionary force sailed from Surabaya in 1906 and, anchoring off the coast of S Bali, began to shell Denpasar's royal palace. The kings remained defiant and the Dutch force had to land in order to subdue the Balinese.

The Balinese king of Denpasar quickly realized that his cause was lost. He announced that anyone who wished could accompany him in a *puputan*, or 'fight to the end'. Most men, and many women as well, heeded their King's call. They dressed in their best clothes (the women wearing men's clothes) and wore their finest gold krisses. The following extract is from Miguel Covarrubias' 1937 book *Island of Bali*:

> "At nine in the morning the fantastic procession left the palace, with the Radja at the head, carried on the shoulders of his men, protected by his gold umbrellas of state, staring intently at the road in front of him, and clutching in his right hand his kris of gold and diamonds. He was followed by silent men and entranced women, and even boys joined the procession, armed with spears and krisses. They marched on through what is today the main avenue of Denpasar towards Kesiman, and when they turned the corner, the Dutch regiment was only 300 yards away. The

commander, astonished at the sight of the strange procession, gave orders to halt; Balinese interpreters from Buleleng spoke to the Radja and his followers, begging them anxiously to stop, but they only walked faster. They came within 100 feet, then 70 feet, then made a mad rush at the soldiers, waving their krisses and spears. The soldiers fired the first volley and a few fell, the Radja among them. Frenzied men and women continued to attack, and the soldiers, to avoid being killed, were obliged to fire continually. Someone went among the fallen people with a kris killing the wounded. He was shot down, but immediately another man took his place; he was shot, but an old woman took the kris and continued the bloody task. The wives of the Radja stabbed themselves over his body, which lay buried under the corpses of the princes and princesses who had dragged them over to die upon the body of their king. When the horrified soldiers stopped firing, the women threw handfuls of gold coins, yelling that it was payment for killing them...".

In the battle, the entire court of the King of Denpasar – bar a few wounded women – died. The king himself is said to have adopted the position of *semadi* meditation before falling under a hail of bullets. Following this battle, the same sequence of events was to be repeated at other palaces across Bali. For many Dutch soldiers, what was an overwhelming military victory had the sour taste of moral defeat.

The King of Tabanan to the W, rather than sacrificing his army, came to negotiate with the Dutch. As a symbol of his intentions, he was shielded by a green umbrella rather than the usual gold one. When they took him prisoner, the king cut his own throat with a blunt *sirih* (betel) knife, and the crown prince took an overdose of opium. The last palace to fall was that of Klungkung on 28 April 1908. Again the king chose to die rather than surrender, together with his wives and many members of the court, he was killed in yet another *puputan*. Bali was finally subdued; although the Dutch army remained on the island until 1914.

The problem for the Dutch was how to make the island profitable. The answer was through revenue collected from the opium monopoly, the use of which was actively promoted. Opium did even more damage to Bali's population than the preceding wars. Van Kol argued strenuously for the ending of the monopoly, writing: "The loss of opium monies will be recompensated by the increasing prosperity of the population whose productive force will no longer be paralysed, and the enormous amounts presently spent on this juice will be used for the purchase of necessities which will increase tax income. Moreover, this will be income to which no tears are attached".

After the Dutch had gained full control of Bali, they set about reorganizing the island so that they could administer it efficiently, with the minimum of fuss. They sent those few members of Bali's royal houses who had survived the various *puputan* into exile and moulded the younger princes into their colonially designated roles. Perhaps even more significantly in the longer term, the Dutch asked the senior priests to simplify the caste system. This was then frozen, removing the flexibility and mobility inherent in the original system. The years of Dutch rule were not happy ones for many Balinese. There was a devastating earthquake in 1917, followed by a plague which decimated the island's rice crop, then an influenza epidemic, and finally the population had to contend with the economic effects of the Depression. As Adrian Vickers says in his book *Bali: a paradise created* "Bali from 1908 to 1942...was an island of social tensions and conflicts for the Balinese".

The Japanese occupation of World War II did not provide a respite from oppression. Although initially welcomed as liberators, this quickly changed as the Japanese began to target Bali's elite – who were identified with the Dutch – with considerable brutality. The end of the War shifted the conflict to one between the Dutch and the republicans among the island's population. But these periods of confrontation were comparatively mild when compared with the murderous months from Oct 1965 to Feb 1966.

The Communist puputan

During the course of the late 1950s and early 1960s, Bali became one of the strongholds of the Indonesian Communist Party – the PKI. With the failure of the attempted coup in Jakarta at the end of Sept 1965, a wave of violence erupted across the country (**see page 502**). Nowhere was it more devastating than on Bali. Adrian Vickers in his book *Bali: a paradise created* describes the progress of the massacre:

> "They began in the north and west, where the Left was strongest, but by the end of this period the whole of Bali was a landscape of blackened areas where entire villages had beeen burnt to the ground, and the graveyards could not cope with the numbers of corpses. ... The military distanced themselves from the killings. They simply went into each village and produced a list of Communists to be killed, which was given to the head of the village to organise. ... After the initial struggle the killing took on a dispassionate tone. Those identified as PKI dressed in white and were led to graveyards to be executed *puputan*-style."

The numbers killed in this orgy of violence will never be known. One estimate puts the figure at an astonishing 100,000. Rivers were reported to be choked with bodies and the graveyards overflowing with corpses. Today, few on the island will talk about this dark episode, and none with relish.

ART AND ARCHITECTURE

The American anthropologist Margaret Mead, like many other observers of Balinese life, observed that "everyone in Bali is an artist". This extends from painting and carving, through to the dramatic arts, and into ceremony and ritual. Sometimes the sheer density of artistic endeavour can seem overwhelming. As Noel Coward wrote to Charlie Chaplin in a poem:

> As I said this morning to Charlie
> There is *far* too much music in Bali,
> And although as a place it's entrancing,
> There is also a *thought* too much dancing.
> It appears that each Balinese native,
> From the womb to the tomb is creative,
> And although the results are quite clever,
> There is too much artistic endeavour.

Most of Bali's art and architecture is linked to the 'Javanization' of the island that began in the 10th century with a marriage between 2 royal houses of Java and Bali (**see page 516**). However, it was the fall of the Majapahit Empire in the 15th century and the escape of the remnants of the Majapahit court, together with many skilled artisans, that led to the greatest infusion of East Javanese art and architecture. While Java was undergoing a process of Islamization, Bali effectively preserved the Indo-Javanese cultural traditions, though adapting them to accord with existing Balinese traditions.

The Balinese pura

In Bali there are over 20,000 temples – or *pura* – and most villages should have at least 3. The *pura puseh*, literally 'navel temple', is the village-origin temple where the village ancestors are worshipped. The *pura dalem* – or 'temple of the dead' – is usually found near the cremation ground. The *pura bale agung* is the temple of the great assembly hall and is used for meetings of the village. There are also irrigation temples, temples at particular geographical sites, and the 6 great temples or *sadkahyangan*. Finally, there is the mother temple, Pura Besakih.

Balinese pura are places where the gods rule supreme, and evil spirits are rendered harmless. But the gods must be appeased and courted if they are to protect people, so offerings are brought to the site. The buildings that constitute a temple are not as important as the ground, which is consecrated.

The temple complex consists of 3 courts (2 in N Bali), each separated by walls; the front court, or *jaba*, the central court, or *jaba tengah*, and the inner court, or *jeroan*. The innermost court is the most sacred and is thought to represent heaven; the outermost, the underworld; and the central court, an intermediate place. The generalized description of the pura given below accords most closely with newer temples. Old temples, and particularly those on the N coast, tend to show differences in their configuration. **NB:** colonies of longtail macaques inhabit some temple sites; they should not be teased or fed, and certainly not purchased – as has been occurring. Macaques are social animals that suffer if removed from their family group.

The outer court or *jaba* The entrance to the jaba is usually through a *candi bentar*, literally 'split temple' gate. The visual symbolism is clear – if the 2 halves of the gate are pushed together, closing the entranceway, they would form the shape of a complete candi (**see page 524**). The split gates may represent the symbolic splitting of the material world, so that the physical body can enter the realm of the spirits. Other art historians maintain that the gates represent duality: male to the right, female to the left.

Within the jaba are a number of structures. In one corner is the *bale kulkul* (*bale* = pavilion, *kulkul* = wooden gong), a pavilion in which hangs a large hollow, wooden, gong or drum. The kulkul is beaten during temple ceremonies and also in times of emergency or disaster – during an earthquake for example. The bale and the kulkul are often decorated. Also within the jaba, it is uncommon to find a *jineng* – a small barn used to store rice produced from the temple's own fields (*laba pura*).

The central court or *jaba tengah* The entrance leading to the central court is through the *candi kurung*. Like the split gate, and as the name implies, this is also in the form of a candi, but in this case a wooden doorway allows visitors to pass through. In a village pura, the centre of the jaba tengah will be dominated by an open pavilion with a roof of grass or reed. This is the *bale agung* or village conference hall. There is also often a *bale* for pilgrims who wish to stay overnight in the temple.

The inner court or *jeroan* The entrance to the inner court is through a second, larger, candi kurung called the *paduraksa*. The entrance way is usually guarded by a demon's head and rises up in the form of a pyramid. In larger temples, there may be 3 gateways, the central one of which is only opened during ceremonies. Along the back wall of the jeroan are the most sacred of the shrines. These may have multiple roofs – as many as eleven. The greater the number of roofs, the more important the god. Also on the back wall, there is a stone pillar or *tugu*. It is at the tugu that offerings are left for the *taksu*, the god who's job it is to protect the temple and through whom the wishes of the gods are transmitted to the dancer during a trance dance. In the centre of the jeroan is the *parungan* or *pepelik* – the seat of all the gods, where they assemble during temple ceremonies. Finally, along the right-hand wall of the inner courtyard, are 2 *sanggahs* – *Ngurah Gde* and *Ngurah Alit*. These are the 'secretaries' of the gods; they ensure that temple offerings are properly prepared. (Condensed from: E. Utrecht and B. Hering (1986) *The temples of Bali*.)

Bali's artistic renaissance

During the early decades of the 20th century, Bali became famous as the haunt of a small community of Western artists. They 'discovered' Balinese art and laid the foundations for a significant artistic flowering. Up until that point, art had been produced for the pleasure of the gods and, in some cases, for aristocratic families. Among these early Western artists, the most famous were Walter Spies, the son of a German diplomat, and the Dutchman Rudolf Bonnet. Spies, who had first worked for the Sultan of Yogya, arrived in Bali on a short visit and was so taken with the island that he decided to stay. He was also a homosexual, and there seems little doubt that he found Bali less suffocating than Europe. Homosexual activity was accepted as a pursuit among unmarried young men, and the great anthropologist Margaret Mead defended him in these terms when he was tried for homosexuality in 1939. Over the years, Spies recorded Balinese music, collected its art, contributed to academic journals, and established the Bali Museum. He also painted a handful of rich paintings recording in minute detail Bali's natural and cultural wealth. However, Spies was not keen to teach the

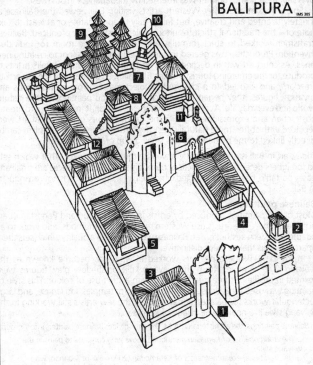

BALI PURA
IMS 305

1 Candi Bentar (split gate)
2 Kulkul (drum tower)
3 Paon (kitchen)
4 Bale Gong
  (shed for gamelan orchestra)
5 Bale (resthouse for pilgrims)
6 Paduraksa

7 Jeroan (inner court)
8 Parungan or Pepelik
9 Meru (shrines of the gods)
10 Padmasana (stone throne for
   sun god Surya)
11 Sanggahs
   (secretaries of the gods)
12 Bale Piasan (sheds for offerings)

Balinese.

In contrast, Rudolf Bonnet was more than happy to train and advise Balinese artists in Western techniques and to transmit the European aesthetic. In 1936, Bonnet and Spies established the first artists' cooperative – the *Pita Maha* (meaning Great or Noble Aspiration) at Ubud. Balinese artists would bring works to the cooperative and Bonnet and Spies would select those they felt were good enough for sale and exhibition. This naturally led to a trend towards Western tastes and Bonnet, particularly, would offer advice to artists as to why their work had been rejected. As the art historian Djelantik writes, in "those years when the prestige of the white man was at its height, Bonnet's word was law and readily accepted". Both Spies and Bonnet remained on Bali until the Japanese occupation from 1941-45. Spies was killed when the ship carrying him to Ceylon was sunk by a Japanese bomb; Bonnet was interned by the Japanese in Sulawesi.

Spies, Bonnet and other Western artists visiting Bali viewed the Balinese as innately talented and creative, but failed fully to appreciate – or at least to take note of – the traditional strictures under which most art was produced. Balinese craftsmen worked to strict formulas and there was little room for individual invention. Production was geared to copying existing works, not to creating new ones. As court art was in decline, Spies and Bonnet encouraged Bali's artists to produce for the emerging tourist market. This allowed the Balinese greater artistic freedom, and also led to a change in subject matter; from carving gods and mythical figures, they began to produce carvings and paintings of the natural world and everyday life. At the same time, there was a shift from realism to greater abstraction and expressionism, while the gaudy colours of traditional art were replaced with softer, more natural hues. The birth of Balinese modernism can be directly linked to the influence of this small group of Western artists.

Today, art in Bali is predominantly driven by the tourist market. That which sells to foreigners determines production: output is standardized, pieces are small and easily portable, designs are selected which sell well...in short, art is now an industry in Bali.

Balinese painting

Most of the paintings produced by artists in Ubud, Batuan and Penestanan are not 'traditional'. The artists use Western materials and methods, and work to an adapted Western aesthetic. Yet, Balinese works do have a quality which sets them apart and thus makes them distinctive.

In the past, Balinese painters worked in what has become known as the *wayang* style. Adapted from the wayang kulit or shadow play, figures were painted in profile or three-quarters view, with a strict use of colour. This style of painting was used for Balinese calendars, scrolls for temples and *langse*, and large rectangular works for palaces. Today, most of the few artists still working in the wayang style live near the SE village of Kamasan.

In *Balinese paintings*, the art historian A.A.M. Djelantik divides Balinese painters into 7 groups:

❏ The *Traditionalists of Kamasan* mentioned above who continue to paint in the wayang style.
❏ The *Traditional experimentalists of Kerambitan* (20 km SW of Tabanan) who produce wayang-style paintings but use additional colours (like blue and green) and a bolder, stronger style.
❏ The *Pita Maha painters of Ubud* concentrate on realistically reproducing the natural world – fish, birds, frogs, tropical flora – in fresh and vibrant colours.
❏ The *Pita Maha painters of Batuan* produce eclectic paintings; detailed scenes from Buddhist mythology, lively and innovative wayang-style images, and naive-style works – almost caricatures – that depict modern life with humour.
❏ The *Young artists of Penestanan* make up a group initially inspired by the Dutch painter Arie Smit who arrived in Bali in 1956; he took farm boys, and trained them, but also allowed their innate talent to emerge. The resulting works are bold and bright, naive in form, and depict everyday scenes.
❏ The *Academicians* are artists who have received training at Western-style art schools in Java. Although the works sometimes employ Balinese or Javanese motifs and even techniques (for example, painting on batik), they are Western in inspiration and sometimes abstract.
❏ The *Adventurers* are untrained Balinese artists who have broken away from Balinese tradition, experimenting with new styles and techniques. Their work is diverse and cannot be simply characterised.

CULTURE AND LIFE

People

The original inhabitants of Bali are the Bali Aga, who still live in a handful of communities in the E of the island (**see page 720**). Since the intrusion of Javanese Hindu-Buddhist people and culture from the 10th century, the Bali Aga have been gradually relegated to a subordinate position. For most visitors today, the culture of Bali means that of the dominant Hindu population.

Despite population growth and considerable modernization, most Balinese still live in villages or *banjar* ranging in size from 200 to several thousand inhabitants. Family compounds or *kuren* are enclosed by high walls and are clustered around a central village courtyard. A kuren will support several families, all eating food from the same kitchen and worshipping at the same family altar. The family gods are paternal ancestors, and descent is patrilineal. The central courtyard is the place where villagers congregate for group activities; for wayang performances, village meetings, and periodic markets. In the past, each village would have been headed by a hereditary prince.

Balinese social structure is stratified in 2 ways. First, every individual belongs to a ranked descent group or *wangsa* ('peoples'). This system of ordering people is akin to the Indian caste system and was adopted after Javanese rule was established on the island. The nobility are divided into 3 castes – the *brahmanas* or priests, *satriyas* or ruling nobles, and *wesyas* or warriors. Members of these 3 castes are said to be the descendants of aristocrats from the Majapahit Kingdom who settled here towards the end of the 15th century. But 90% of the population, belong to the *sudras* or *jaba*; literally, the outsiders of the court. In addition to belonging to a caste, a Balinese will also belong to a far more egalitarian class structure based upon where a person lives. The *banjar* system of associations is the epitome of this (**see page 677**).

As dictated by Balinese tradition, a child is not placed on the floor until the 105th day of its life; he or she will be carried until able to stand and walk – never being allowed to crawl, as the Balinese believe this is animalistic. At 210 days (one Balinese year) the child is given its name. A ceremony occurs to celebrate puberty;

The banjar

Every Balinese male is a member of a *banjar*, the basic unit of organization and local government. After marriage, a man is invited to join the banjar. This invitation is in reality a compulsion; if after the third summons, the man has not joined, he is declared 'dead' and loses most of his village rights - even the right to be cremated on the village cremation ground. The members of the banjar democratically elect one of their group to act as head (*klian banjar*). He enjoys the status and prestige of being head, and some other minor advantages such as additional rice during group festivities, but no cash payment for his work.

Members of the banjar are bound to assist one another in a variety of tasks. It is, in effect, a cooperative society. In any village there are likely to be a number of banjars, each drawing its members from a geographical neighbourhood. They sometimes own ricefields communally, the production going towards group festivities. Today, money owned through tourist activities - such as staging dances - also goes to the banjar, the society then redistributing it among its members. As Miguel Covarrubias wrote in 1937 (while ignoring the position of women): "Everyone enjoys absolute equality and all are compelled to help one another with labour and materials, often assisting a member to build his house, to prepare his son's wedding, or to cremate a relative".

first menstruation is followed by a tooth-filing ceremony (often occurring at the same time as the marriage ceremony). From the time of the tooth-filing ceremony, daughters are no longer the father's responsibility. Sons have their marriages financed for them by their fathers. Marriages are still sometimes pre-arranged among aristocratic families, although increasingly men want to choose their spouses (and *vice versa*) and mixed-caste relationships are occurring.

Religion

Except for small numbers of people in East Java, the Balinese are the only Indonesians who still embrace Hinduism – or at least a variant form of the Indian religion. While across Java and Sumatra, Islam replaced Hinduism, on Bali it managed to persist. Today, 95% of Balinese are still Hindu.

Known as *Hindu Dharma* or *Agama Hindu*, the Balinese religion is an unique blend of Buddhism, Hinduism and pre-Hindu animist beliefs. So, along with the worship of the Hindu trinity of Vishnu, Brahma and Siva, the Balinese also worship deified ancestors or *leluhur*, as well as deities of fertility, of the elements and of the natural world. The whole is suffused with a belief in a transcendental spiritual unity known as *Sang Hyang Widi*.

Reflecting the diverse roots of Balinese Hinduism, there is a corresponding variety of priests and other religious practitioners. There are high-ranking Brahmana priests of both Sivaite and Buddhist persuasions (Buddha is regarded as Siva's younger brother), lower order village priests or *jero mangku*, exorcists, herbal healers, and puppet masters or *dalang*.

The aim of Balinese Hinduism is to reach 'peace of spirit and harmony in the material life' by achieving a balance between philosophy, morals and ritual. The principles of their philosophy or *tattwa* are belief in:

- the existence of one God
- the soul and the spirit
- reincarnation
- the law of reciprocal actions
- the possibility of unity with the divine.

The 3 moral rules – or *susila* – of the religion are reasonable enough:

- think good thoughts
- talk honestly
- do good deeds.

Their ritual – or *upacara* – is divided into 5 areas of sacrifice; ritual for the gods, the higher spirits, the Hindu prophets, for and on behalf of humans, and sacrifices for neutralizing the negative influences of the natural and supernatural worlds. Praying is also important, for which the devotee requires flowers, incense and *tirta* or holy water. Men sit on the floor with their legs crossed and their hands held together, either at the level of their foreheads (if they are praying to the

Janur

Visitors to Bali cannot fail to notice the tall, elegant bamboo poles which bend over the roads, signifying some celebration or festival. Hanging from the slender poles are decorations made out of the yellow leaf of the coconut, known as *janur*. Their design varies enormously, according to the festival and to the place where they are made. So many festivals take place on Bali that there are always janur to be seen in varying states of decay. Travelling around Bali, visitors may notice arches of palms over the gateway to a house, with janur and banana leaves on either side; this usually signifies a wedding ceremony. Fruit and flowers are placed on (or within) the janur, as offerings to the gods. Janurs are not unique to Bali, and can also be found in parts of Java and North Sulawesi. Reliefs depicting janur on the 9th century Hindu temple of Prambanan, in Central Java, indicate that they have been made for many centuries.

The Balinese calendars: *saka* and *wuku*

The Balinese use 2 traditional calendars, and now have had to add a third, the Gregorian calendar. The Hindu *saka* year is solar and lasts between 354 and 356 days, and is divided into 12 lunar months. But the saka year is 80 years 'behind' the Christian year, so that 1992 AD is saka 1912.

The Balinese also use the Hindu-Javanese 210-day lunar *wuku* year, which operates in parallel with the saka year. But to make things very complicated, the wuku calendar is divided into weeks of 10 days, 10 of which run together so that every day has 10 names according to each of the 10 weeks that it is measured against. Most festivals on Bali are calculated on the basis of the wuku calendar, although some are timed according to the saka year.

Supreme God), or at the level of their lips (when praying to Sang Hyang Kala) or resting on their chests (if praying to a dead family member). In Balinese, praying is referred to as *muspa* or *mbakti*. The former means to show respect with flowers, the latter means to worship by means of devotion.

Festivals and ceremonies

There can be few places of comparable size that have more ceremonies and festivals than Bali. The most common are temple anniversary celebrations. Every temple on the island holds an *odalan* once every 210 days, one complete cycle according to the Balinese *wuku* calendar. With more than 20,000 temples, every day is a festival day, somewhere.

The major ceremonies are those of marriage and cremation, both of which are traditionally costly affairs. Also important is tooth-filing. Along with these ceremonies associated with a person's progression through his or her life-cycle, are a vast range of other rites, festivals and ceremonies.

Sesajen
This is not a ceremony, so much as a ritual, but it is so commonplace that it is in some respects the most important religious activity on the island. Three times a day before meals, small woven coconut trays filled with glutinous rice, flowers and salt are sprinkled with holy water and are offered to the gods. They can be seen placed outside the front door of every house.

Eka Dasa Rudra
This is the most important of Bali's festivals and is held, in theory, only once every hundred years at the 'Mother Temple' – Besakih – on Mount Agung. In 1963, the volcano erupted during the festival, killing 2,000 people. As a result, another had to be organized. It took place in 1979 and this time no catastrophe occurred (**see page 715** for more details).

Panca Walikrama
This festival is meant to take place once a decade at Besakih temple. However, in practice this has not happened, with only 4 festivals taking place this century, the last one in 1989.

Odalan
The *odalan* festival celebrates the anniversary of a temple's consecration and is held over about 3 days, every 210 days. This is the festival that visitors to Bali are most likely to see and it includes a great feast to which all the villagers are invited. The villagers prepare for odalan for many days beforehand by cleaning the temple, building altars and awnings, erecting flag poles, and preparing offerings. On the first day of the celebration, women dress in their finest clothes – sarongs, sashes and head-dresses – and walk in procession to the temple. On their heads they carry their colourful offerings of fruit and rice cakes, arranged in beautiful and carefully balanced pyramids. The offerings remain at the temple for 3 days during which time they are sprinkled daily with holy water. At the end of this period, the food is taken home again and eaten.

During odalan, the men sit around the compound proudly wearing their krisses tucked into their sarongs. Over the 3 days the temple buzzes with activity; around the entrance locals set up stalls selling food and trinkets, medicine men market cure-alls, cockfights are staged, a gamelan orchestra plays, and in the evenings dance and wayang kulit performances take place. The inner courtyards are reserved for the sacred offerings and here the *pemangku* – or officiating priest – prays in front of the altars.

Marriage

In contrast with Western marriages, the traditional Balinese marriage is preceded by the honeymoon – or *ngrorod*. The prospective couple secretly prepare for their honeymoon and, on the day they select, arrange for the abduction of the bride with the complicity of a few close friends. The girl is expected to put up a good fight, but the event is staged. When the parents discover that their daughter has been kidnapped, they send a search party to look for her; again this is for show. During their time in hiding, the couple are expected to consummate their marriage before it happens – an event which is witnessed by the gods. The marriage itself is supposed to occur within 42 days of the abduction, but not before a substantial bride-price has been paid to the parents of the girl. From this point on, the girl becomes part of her future husband's family and relinquishes her own family affiliations. She adopts the groom's ancestral gods to symbolize this. Among aristocratic families marriages were usually pre-arranged (*mapadik*).

The marriage, or *masakapan*, is held on an auspicious day selected by the priest. Invitations are sent out asking guests to bring certain types and amounts of food. The bride and groom used to have their teeth filed during the ceremony if this had not already been done (see below). While the bride is being prepared for the marriage rite, men – arranged according to status – sit, eat and chew betel nut while being entertained by professional story tellers. The rite varies from area to area, but usually the bride and groom offer food and drink to one another, and then eat together in public; an important symbolic act because in the past only married men and women were allowed to be seen eating food together. In the afternoon, the priest performs a ritual purification and blesses the couple.

Cremation

Cremation is the most important ceremony in the Balinese life-cycle. It is a time for celebration, not sorrow, and is wonderfully colourful. It is also an extremely costly affair, and people will begin to save for their cremation from middle age. Even the poorest family will need to spend about one million rupiah, whilst wealthy families have been known to lavish hundreds of millions of rupiah. If there is not enough money saved, families may have to wait years – sometimes more than a decade – before they can hold the cremation of a loved one, thus releasing his or her soul. To avoid the wait, poorer people may be helped out by other members of the village, or they may share in a big ceremony when a number of bodies are cremated together. Another option is to be cremated with an aristocrat who needs a retinue to accompany him to the next life. Towards the end of 1992, the Rajah of Gianyar, 71-year-old Ide Anak Agung Gede Agung, staged an elaborate cremation for his former wife, two stepmothers and two of his late father's concubines: rumour had it that the total cost to the royal house – the richest on Bali – was as much as US$1 million.

Rich people may be cremated soon after they have died, in which case the corpse simply lies in state in the family compound. If there is going to be a considerable time period before cremation, then the body is either buried or mummified first. When enough money has been accumulated, an auspicious day is chosen by a priest for the cremation. The body is disinterred (if buried), the bones collected up, arranged in human form, and draped with a new white cloth. The corpse is carried back to the family compound and placed in a bamboo and paper tower, richly painted and decorated. Here it is adorned with jewellery and cloths decorated with magic symbols. Various rites are performed before the ceremony to awaken and satisfy the soul. An *adegan*, a dual effigy, is carved in palmleaf and sandalwood. On the day before the cremation the effigy is taken in a grand procession to a high priest, accompanied by the dead person's relatives dressed in their finest clothes.

For the cremation itself, a large bamboo tower is built; its size and shape is dictated by the caste of the dead person. A wooden life-size bull (for men) or cow (for women) is sometimes carved. On the morning of the cremation, friends and relatives are entertained by the family of the deceased and then the body is placed inside the bamboo tower. The village *kulkul* – or gong – is struck, and the construction is carried in a noisy procession (designed to confuse the soul of the departed so that it cannot return to the family home) to the cremation ground by other members of the dead person's *banjar* or village association. The body is roughly handled as it is placed in the tower. At the cremation site, the wooden bull or cow and the corpse are set alight. After the incineration, the ashes are carried off in another raucous procession, to the nearest water, where they are thrown into the wind. The cremation is the most impressive of the Balinese ceremonies, but it is not one where any respect is shown for the corpse. The body is treated like an unclean container; it is the soul that is paramount. To illustrate the point, bodies are poked with sticks to help them burn, and are shown none of the respect evident in the funeral ceremonies of other religions.

Tooth-filing

The practice of tooth-filing was once common across island Southeast Asia. Savages, wild

Self-immolation and human sacrifice in a Dutch account of 1633

In 1633 a Dutch expedition visited Gelgel on Bali, and its members witnessed 2 cremations, one of a queen and another of 2 princes. In both cases, a number of female slaves and other courtiers also died. The English historian John Crawfurd, quoted the account of the visit and spectacle at some length in his book *The Malay Archipelago* (1820). In the case of the female slaves, each was poignarded:

"Some of the most courageous demanded the poignard themselves, which they received with their right hand, passing it to the left, after respectfully kissing the weapon. They wounded their right arms, sucked the blood which flowed from the wound, and stained their lips with it, making a bloody mark on the forehead with the point of the finger. Then returning the dagger to their executioners, they received a first stab between the false ribs, and a second under the shoulder blade, the weapon being thrust up to the hilt towards the heart. As soon as the horrors of death were visible in the countenance, without a complaint escaping them, they were permitted to fall to the ground...".

In the case of the courtiers and princesses who were cremated with the bodies of the princes, they would not allow anyone of lower status to touch them, and so had to kill themselves:

"For this purpose, a kind of bridge is erected over a burning pile, which they mount, holding a paper close to their foreheads, and having their robe tucked under their arm. As soon as they feel the heat, they precipitate themselves into the burning pile... In case firmness should abandon them... a brother, or another near relative, is at hand to push them in, and render them, out of affection, that cruel office...".

animals and demons have long, white teeth, so filing them down at puberty was necessary to ensure that at death a person would not be mistaken for a wild creature. In some areas of Sumatra this is taken to extremes and every tooth is filed flat; in Bali it is only the front teeth that are filed, although the rationale is the same.

In the past, not only were the front teeth filed, but they were also blackened. In theory, tooth-filing should occur at puberty, but because of the cost of staging the ceremony, it is often delayed until later in life. It is said that filing is necessary to control the 6 evil characteristics of the human condition, known as *sad ripu* – passion, greed, anger, confusion, jealousy and earthly intoxication. If someone dies without having had their teeth filed, the priest will often file the teeth of the corpse before cremation. Miguel Covarrubias describes a tooth-filing ceremony he witnessed in the 1930s:

"The operation is performed by a specialist, generally a Brahmana, who knows formulas by which his tools – files and whetstones – are blessed 'to take the poison out of them', to make the operation painless. The patient is laid on a *bale* among offerings, the head resting on a pillow which is covered with a protective scarf, *gringsing wayang wangsul*, one of the magic cloths woven in Tenganan, the warp of which is left uncut. The body is wrapped in a new white cloth and assistants hold down the victim by the hands and feet. The tooth-filer stands at the head of the *bale* and inscribes magic syllables (*aksara*) on the teeth about to be filed with a ruby set in a gold ring. The filing then proceeds, taking from fifteen minutes to a half-hour, endured stoically with clenched hands and goose-flesh but without even a noise from the patient..."

Dance, drama and music

Dance

The Balinese are consummate dancers. Everyone dances, and dancing forms an essential element of private and public life accompanying, as Beryl de Zoete and Walter Spies wrote in 1938, "every stage of a man's life from infancy to the grave". Of the various dances, those most often staged for tourists are the masked dance or *topeng*, the monkey dance or *kecak*, and the dance between the witch Rangda and the mythical lion, known as the *barong*. A brief description of the various dances is given below; tourists are normally provided with a printed sheet with information on the dance(s) when they attend a performance.

Kecak – or monkey dance, originates from a trance dance (or *sanghyang*), when a central

The evil witch *Rangda*, enemy of the mythical lion *Barong* in the Barong dance from a Balinese manuscript (reproduced in Miguel Covarrubin's *Island of Bali*, 1937)

person in a state of trance communicates with a god or ancestor. The surrounding chorus of men rhythmically chant *kecak kecak kecak*, which encourages the state of trance and gives the dance its name. The dance itself tells the story of the Ramayana when Sita is abducted by Ravana and subsequently rescued by an army of monkeys (see page 505). The dance is a relatively new creation, having been invented in the 20th century by Walter Spies who combined an ancient dance chorus tradition with an episode from the Ramayana.

Barong or kris dance – is also a trance dance and the epitome of the battle between good and evil. Good, in the shape of the mythical lion *Barong*, fights the evil witch *Rangda*. The witch's spell turns the krisses of the Barong's accomplices against themselves. Inside the barong costume are two men who coordinate their movements much like a Chinese lion dance; indeed, it is thought that the barong dance is derived from the Chinese New Year lion dance. The masks themselves are believed to be infused with magic power, and they are often kept in village temples where they act as patron spirits. Rangda, the personification of evil, has bulging eyes and tusks and is linked to the Indian goddess Durga. Like the barong (the word refers to both the dance and the mask), the mask of Rangda is also revered.

Sanghyang dedari – the Dance of the Holy Angels – is the best known, and possibly the most beautiful of a type of trance dance known as *Sang* [Lord] *Hyong* [God]. Young girls perform this religious dance of exorcism, designed to rid a community of evil spirits, while a chorus of men and women provide accompaniment. The dancers are often relatives of temple servants and usually have no professional training. They are believed to be possessed by celestial nymphs, and at the end of the performance – traditionally – would walk on hot coals before being brought back to consciousness.

Legong – a Balinese dance for girls from 8 to early teens (although today many tourist dances employ adult performers) which was created at the beginning of the 18th century. This is not a trance dance, but rigorous physical training is needed to perform the movements. Three dancers perform the most popular version, the *legong kraton*, a story taken from the East Javanese classic tale of Prince Panji. In this story, a bird warns the king of the futility of war, which he ignores, and is killed in battle. The dance is regarded as the finest, and most feminine, of Balinese dances and the girls dress in fine silks and wear elaborate headdresses decorated with frangipani and other flowers. The dancers do not speak or sing – the lines of the story are recounted by singers accompanied by a gamelan orchestra. Because of the demands of the dance, girls must be taught – literally physically manipulated – from an early age, so that 'the dance enters their innermost being'.

Topeng – the wayang topeng is a masked dance which, in Bali, recounts stories of former kings and princes. In its purest form, it is performed in silence by a single actor who portrays a series of characters changing his mask each time. Today, he is more likely to be accompanied by a narrator (**see page 531**).

Ramayana ballet – a portrayal of the great Hindu epic (**see page 533** and **page 519**).

Wayang kulit – the famous shadow theatre of Java and Bali in which two-dimensional leather puppets are manipulated, their forms reflected onto a white cloth (**see page 533**). In Bali, wayang kulit accords, it is thought, more closely with the original Majapahit form than does the Javanese equivalent. This can be seen in the puppets with their elaborate headdresses and costumes, and in the carving of the faces which is similar in style to the low relief carvings on Majapahit temples in East Java.

Music

Beryl de Zoete and Walter Spies, early foreign residents of Bali, wrote of its music in their paper of 1938 *Dance and Drama in Bali*: "Music permeates their life to a degree which we can hardly imagine; a music of incomparable subtlety and intricacy, yet as simple as breathing. Like every other expression of Balinese life, it is easily accessible and at the same time inexhaustible in its interest and variety." It was Walter Spies, an American composer who was captivated when he first heard a recording of Balinese music in the late 1920s in New York, who played a crucial role in detailing and preserving the music of the island. He acted as a patron, wrote a brilliant, seminal book entitled *Music in Bali* (1966), and spread the gospel around the capitals of the world. He even wrote an orchestral work – *Tabuh-Tabuhan* – based on Balinese musical formulas, for which he won a Pulitzer prize in 1936. Such was his love of Bali and its music that what began as a short jaunt to the island turned into a life-long love affair.

Like Java, the basis of Balinese music is the gamelan orchestra (**see page 534**). Sets of gamelan instruments – of which the gongs are regarded as the most important – are usually owned corporately, by the village or *banjar*. Making music is a tightly structured event; the notion of 'jamming' is simply not the Balinese way. Musicians learn their parts and the aim is for an orchestra to produce a perfect rendition of a composed piece. Reflecting this approach, the brilliance of Balinese music is in the whole, which is greater that its constituent parts. There are few superstars; it is the orchestra as a perfectly coordinated unit that determines success.

Experiencing Balinese music, dance and theatre: most visitors to Bali hear Balinese music or see local dances in the context of their hotels. Although people often assume that such performances cannot be 'authentic', all gamelan and dance groups are regulated by LISTIBIYA, the government arts council. This means that the quality is invariably high, and although pieces are usually condensed to make them more 'acceptable' to tourist audiences, the quality of the performance is rarely affected. However, for a more authentic environment, it is necessary to visit a temple anniversary festival or *odalan* (**see page 679**). Performances usually begin in the late afternoon or early evening with a gamelan recital and then continue after dark with dances and shadow plays. Note that visitors should dress and behave appropriately (see Temple etiquette, **page 688**). The two main music academies are STSI (Werdi Budaya Art Centre) on Jalan Nusa Indah in Denpasar; and KOKAR/SMKI in Batubulan. There is also an annual Bali Arts Festival held from mid-June to mid-July in Denpasar.

MODERN BALI

Economy and tourism

Visitors to Bali may leave with the impression that the island's economy is founded on tourism. Certainly, tourism is a crucial element in Bali's economic growth and well-being. Yet over three-quarters of Bali's population still lives in rural areas, and the bulk of the inhabitants depend upon agriculture for their livelihoods. Since the mid-1960s, farmers have turned to the cultivation of high yielding varieties of rice and the use of large quantities of chemical fertilizers. Three-quarters of Bali's riceland now produces two or more crops of rice each year. There has also been a diversification of agricultural production into vegetables and fruit, cloves, vanilla, and livestock.

Outside agriculture, tourism is the next most important industry. The first tourists began to arrive just 6 years after the Klungkung *puputan* (**see page 671**). In 1914 the Dutch steamship line KPM was publishing brochures with lines like: "You leave this island with a sigh of regret and as long as you live you can never forget this Garden of Eden." Today about 300,000 tourists arrive each year by air, the same number again by sea from Java and Lombok. With a population of 3 million, this means a considerable influx of outsiders – both international and domestic. Given that approaching one half of visitors to Indonesia visit Bali alone, the significance of the island – which accounts for a mere 0.3% of the country's land area – in Indonesia's overall tourist industry is immense.

To serve this influx of visitors, a major building boom has been underway. By 1984, there were already over 9,000 hotel rooms on the island, and the boom continued through the 1980s so that now there are 20,000. The government has tried to restrict development to buildings no taller than a coconut palm, and has encouraged construction in Balinese 'style'. Although there are not the crude, ungainly high-rise hotels of some other Asian resorts (the only such hotel is the *Bali Beach* on Sanur, constructed before the regulations came into force), the designs do rather stretch the notion of "traditional" style (particularly those in Nusa Dua and Kuta).

At present, resorts are largely restricted to the S coast, but the government has plans to develop other parts of the island. A projected new road around the island and tourist information centres in each of the island's districts are expected to help the dispersal of tourism to other areas. There is also a plan to develop 'special interest tourism' (or ecotourism), focusing on the island's marine and other natural resources. But although tourism has generated income, jobs and opportunities for Bali's inhabitants, there are those who point to the 'downside' of the industry: cultural erosion, environmental degradation, the undermining of traditional activities, inflation, the growth of crime and drug abuse. To combat such trends, the residents of Ubud have set up the Tourism Guidance and Counseling Service to encourage visitors to respect the island and its culture and history. But perceptive visitors have been worrying about the impacts of tourism for over half a century. Miguel Covarrubias, who lived on Bali in the early 1930s, wrote that the absence of beggars "is now threatened by tourists who lure boys and girls with dimes to take their pictures, and lately, in places frequented by tourists, people are beginning to ask for money as a return for a service".

Suggested reading Belo, Jane (edit.) (1970) *Traditional Balinese culture*, Columbia University Press: New York. Collection of academic papers, most focusing upon dance, music and drama. Covarrubias, Miguel (1937) *Island of Bali*, Cassell: London (reprinted, OUP: Singapore, 1987). The original treatment of Bali's culture; despite being over 50 years old it is still an excellent background to the island and is highly entertaining. Djelantik, A.A.M. (1990) *Balinese paintings*, OUP: Singapore. Concise history of Balinese painting also covering the major contemporary schools of art. Eiseman, Fred and Eiseman, Margaret (1988) *Woodcarvings of Bali*, Periplus: Berkeley. Hobart, Angela (1987) *Dancing shadows of Bali: theatre and myth*, KPI: London. Academic book examining the wayang theatre in Bali. Kempers, A.J. Bernet (1991) *Monumental Bali: introduction to Balinese archaeology and guide to the monuments*, Periplus: Berkeley and Singapore. New edition of Kempers's 1977 book, with photos and additional 'guide' section; best available. Lansing, J. Stephen (1991) *Priests and Programmers: technologies of power in the engineered landscape of Bali*, Princeton University Press: Princeton. An anthropological account of Bali's irrigation system; interesting for rice enthusiasts. Stuart Fox, David (1982) *Once a century: Pura Besakih and the Eka Dasa Rudra Festival*, Penerbit Citra Indonesia: Jakarta. Tenzer, Michael (1991) *Balinese music*, Periplus: Berkeley and Singapore. Illustrated summary of Balinese music, drawing heavily on Spies's work, best introduction available. Utrecht, E. and Hering, B. (1987) 'The temples of Bali', *Kabar Seberang Sulating Maphilindo* 18: 161-74. Vickers, Adrian (1989) *Bali: a paradise created*, Periplus: Berkeley and Singapore. Excellent account of the evolution of Bali as a tourist paradise; good historical and cultural background, informed without being turgid.

INFORMATION FOR VISITORS

Transport to and from Bali

By air Denpasar's Ngurah Rai International Airport is at the S end of the island, just S of Kuta. It is one of Indonesia's 'gateway' cities, with international connections with Australia, Hong Kong, Europe, Singapore, Japan and North America. **From Europe** From London Heathrow, Singapore Airlines fly via Singapore 4 times a week and Garuda Indonesia via Singapore 5 times a week. From Amsterdam, KLM and Garuda Indonesia fly direct once a week. From Frankfurt, Lufthansa and Garuda Indonesia fly direct once a week. You can fly from Zurich via Singapore with Singapore Airlines twice a week or Garuda Indonesia and Swissair 4 times a week. From Paris there are weekly flights with UTA (direct), Singapore Airlines and Garuda Indonesia via Singapore, and Lufthansa via Frankfurt.

Regular domestic connections with Java, Sumatra, Maluku, Sulawesi, Lombok, Nusa Tenggara and Irian Jaya (**see page 1006** for route map). Note that although flights are often 'full' no shows are common and it is worth waiting to see if a seat becomes available. *Airport facilities*: 24 hr airport information, T 51011 ext. 2131. A tourist office with a well-run hotel booking counter offers comprehensive details and prices of accommodation on Bali. Other facilities include bars, restaurant, shops and taxi counter. *Transport to town* there are fixed-price taxis from the airport: 6,500Rp to Kuta; 6,500Rp to Legian (12,000Rp to Oberoi); 12,000Rp to Sanur; 9,000Rp to Denpasar.

By train From Jakarta, take the train to Surabaya, a bus to Banyuwangi, and then the ferry to Bali. Alternatively, take the train all the way to Banyuwangi and catch a bus onwards from there. 'All in' train and bus tickets are available in Jakarta.

By bus Most long distance bus companies have their offices on Jl. Diponegoro and Jl. Hasannudin in Denpasar. Regular overnight connections with most destinations in Java, for example to Surabaya, Malang, Yogyakarta, Bandung, Bogor and Jakarta. Examples of prices: a/c buses to Jakarta 30,800Rp; to Yogya 19,600Rp; to Surabaya 10,650Rp. If you are arriving from Java and wish to stay on the N coast, get-off the bus at Gilimanuk (where the ferry docks) and take a bemo to Lovina beach (the price of the bemo is sometimes included in bus/ferry ticket).

By boat Car ferries every 20 minutes from Ketapang, just N of Banyuwangi on Java's E coast, to Gilimanuk on the W tip of Bali 30 mins (500Rp). Regular ferries every 2 hrs from Padangbai, near Candi Dasa, to Lembar, Lombok 4 hrs (4,000Rp); a new high-speed boat service to Bangsal, on Lombok (for the Gilis) has also started operating; buses to Padangbai leave from Denpasar's Batubulan terminal. Cruise liners dock at Benoa Port on the Bukit Peninsula and occasionally at Padangbai. The Pelni ship *Kelimutu* docks at Padangbai on its 2-week circuit (see route map **page 1008**). The Pelni office is at Benoa, T 28962. For Lombok, the ferry leaves from Padangbai.

Internal travel

Bemo Bemos are the cheapest way to get around Bali, although it usually means a trip to Denpasar, the bemo 'node' for most destinations. So, to travel from, say, Kuta to Ubud means getting a bemo from Kuta to Denpasar's Tegal terminal, transferring to Kereneng and then, taking a cross-town trip to the Batubulan terminal, followed by another bemo from there to Ubud. This makes for slow travelling and it can be almost as cheap and a lot quicker to charter a bemo (see below). It is also worth noting that bemo services are less frequent in the afternoons, and out of the tourist centres are almost non-existent after nightfall. Approx. cost of travel is 25Rp/km, with a minimum charge of 100Rp.

The **different terminals** are as follows (note that terminals serve other terminals as well as out of town destinations):
Ubung, N of town on Jl. Cokroaminoto for trips to N and W Bali including Gilimanuk and Singaraja, Mengwi, Tanah Lot, Bedugul, Negara and Java (see Transport to & from Bali).
Tegal, W of town, near the intersection of Jl. Imam Bonjol and Jl. G. Wilis, for journeys to S Bali including Kuta, Legian, Sanur, Ngurah Rai Airport, Jimbaran, Nusa Dua and Uluwatu (in the morning).
Suci, near the intersection of Jl. Diponegoro and Jl. Hasanuddin for Benoa Port.
Batubulan, 6 km NE of town just before the village of Batubulan on the road to Gianyar, for buses running E to Gianyar, Klungkung, Padangbai, Candi Dasa, Amlapura and Tirtagangga, and N to Ubud, Tampaksiring, Bangli, Penelokan and Kintamani.
Kereneng, at the E edge of town off Jl. Kamboja (Jl. Hayam Wuruk) has now been replaced as the station for central and E Bali by Batubulan; but bemos do still run from here to the other terminals.

Chartered bemo 'You want transport' is a much used expression on Bali. Chartering a bemo is easy and often the best way to travel around the island. Expect to pay about 4,000-5,000Rp/hr, 50,000Rp for a full day. **NB**: drivers may try to take you to a craft village as part of the deal.

Car/motorbike/bicycle hire Available at each resort. **Cars** for approx 45,000Rp/day from local firms, US$45/day from international companies (for example, Avis). Note that hire cars cannot be taken off the island and an international driving licence is officially required (local firms often do not bother with this). **Motorbike** hire costs from 7,000Rp/day. Strictly-speaking, those without an international motorbike licence, should obtain a temporary licence from the Police Station in Denpasar. Applicants need their passport, 3 photographs and their national driving licence; they will also need to undertake a short police driving test (NB: few people bother with this). **Bicycles** can be hired for about 3,000Rp/day.

Taxis There are some metered taxis; but more are unmetered cars available for charter.

Accommodation

Bali has the best range of accommodation in Indonesia from luxury hotels of the highest standard to comfortable homestays. The degree of competition means that rooms are often very moderately priced. Rates are usually reduced after the peak season; ask for a discount. Peak season is Christmas/New Year and July/August – hotels can get very full at these times. Accommodation is geared to foreign tastes with, for example, Western toilets in even the cheapest homestays.

Tours

At the last count, the tourist office listed 136 tour companies, usually with little to choose between them. Most provide the same range of tours at competitive prices, although it is worth shopping around before booking. Check the numbers on the tour, whether the guide speaks good English, if entrance fees and meals are included, and whether the car/bus is air-conditioned. Most tour companies are concentrated in the principal tourist centres. Average prices for standard tours are as follows: **Lake Batur, volcano and Ubud**, US$8-14; **Denpasar City**, US$8; **Singaraja and Lake Bratan**, US$14-20; **Besakih Temple**, US$8-US$12; **Amlapura (Karangasem) and the East Coast**, US$14-18; **Uluwatu and Kuta Beach**, US$10; **Mengwi and Tanah Lot**, US$8-12; **Dance evenings** (kecak, legong, sanghyang, barong, Ramayana ballet, wayang), US$7-12; **Nature Trek**, US$17; **Shopping Tour**, US$10; **Turtle Island and Snorkelling**, US$7.

There are also a number of 'speciality' tours: **Adventure rafting**, down the Ayung River near Ubud (ask at hotel or T 88796), US$45-60. Both prices are for a day trip including hotel pick-up, all equipment, insurance and lunch. **Adventure Tours** are organized by *Ja's Tours and Travel*, Jl. Nusa Indah 62, Denpasar, T 34930, F 31009. They try to show visitors the 'real' Bali, also organize sailing, diving and trekking tours and a 3 day/2 night trip to Lombok. **Cruises**

Bali Hai, luxurious catamaran; day trips to Nusa Penida island for snorkeling and lunch, US$60; dinner cruise US$30; T 34331. *Golden Hawk*, old gaff-rigged ketch (tall ship) for day trips, fishing, snorkeling, lunch and alcoholic drinks, US$68; Jl. Sri Kesari 19, Sanur, T 88860. *Bali Yacht Charter*, one day (US$59) and 2 days/one night (US$99) on a 47-foot yacht to Nusa Penida, T 52628. *Puri Tour* organize 10-day pinisi boat cruises from Bali to Flores for US$150/day, all inclusive (Jl. Padang Galak 7A, Sanur, T (361) 88788, F (361) 87269.

Specialist tours: *P & O Spice Island Cruises*, Jl. Let. Jen S. Parmen 78, Slipi, Jakarta Barat, T 5673401, F 5673403, organize luxury island-hopping cruises between Bali and Kupang (Timor), 2 week round-trip, calling at Komodo, Sumbawa, Flores and Sumba. One way trip, about US$2,289, round trip US$4,180. They also organize a 7 day trip from Jakarta to Krakatau, up the east coast of Sumatra and S to the Ujung Kulon National Park US$8,869.

Festivals

Bali is the festival capital of Southeast Asia; there is a festival every day of the year. With 20,000 temples, each celebrating its anniversary or *odalan* every 210 days (according to the Balinese *wuku* calendar), it is easy to see why (**see page 679** for a fuller background to the main ceremonies).

The tourist office supplies a booklet cataloguing the year's festivals, while the *Bali News* (often found in hotel lobbys) lists current events. Both sources of information are extremely useful, as the Balinese calendar, in fact 2 calendars, is complex. The *wuku* calendar which governs most, but not all, festivals is lunar and runs, as noted above, over only 210 days. As a result, festival dates vary dramatically from year to year and a particular festival may be held twice in any one (365-day) year. Locals do not object to tourists being present at most of their ceremonies but they do ask that visitors dress appropriately, with sarong and sash, and behave discreetly (see Temple Etiquette, below).

Wuku Year Festivals (210-day calendar)

Day 1: *Galungan*, the most important holiday of the Balinese year. It is a 10-day festival marking the Balinese *wuku* 'New Year' (in fact it comes mid-way through the year, but is usually translated as New Year). It also commemorates the creation of the world by the Supreme God and symbolizes the victory of good over evil. Women make *banten* (offerings of sweets, fruits and flowers) while men make *lawar* (a food made of vegetables and meat). Both are presented as thanksgiving offerings. *Penjors* (a variant of the *janur*, **see page 678**) are the long bamboo poles which can be seen on the right-hand side of every house entrance, with offerings such as fruit, cakes and flowers hanging from them as symbols of gratitude for the god's gift of life and prosperity. It is said that the offerings are hung on these tall poles so that the gods can see them from their mountain abodes. *Barong* and other dances are traditionally held at this time.

Day 10: *Kuningan* held 10 days after Galungan and marking the end of the holiday period. It is believed to be the day when the Gods ascend back to Heaven and is a time for honouring the souls of ancestors and saints who have lived their lives in accordance with the customs of their religion. Temple compounds are decorated with flowers and offerings are made.

Day 137: *Saraswati*, commemorates the Goddess of Learning and Knowledge, Batari Dewi Saraswati. All books are given to the Goddess to be blessed and no reading or writing is allowed.

Day 142: *Pangerwesi*, the word means 'iron fence', and the ceremony is dedicated to Shanghyang Pramesti Guru. It is particularly popular in the N.

Day 210: *Penampahan Galungan*, the day prior to Galungan when every Balinese prepares for the big day, slaughtering pigs and chickens and preparing offerings and food. It marks the end of the wuku year.

Recurrent Wuku Festivals In addition to the above wuku festivals, there are also a number of recurrent festival days which are regarded as propitious for making offerings. *Kadjeng-klion* is held every 15 days; *Tumpak*, every 35 days; *Budda-klion*, every 42 days; *Anggara-kasih*, every 35 days; and *Budda-wage*, every 35 days.

Saka Year Festivals (354 to 356-day calendar)

March: *Pengerupuk* (moveable), the last day of the Balinese year. Purification sacrifices and offerings are made, while priests chant mantras to exorcize the demons of the old year. At night, gongs and cymbals are struck and torchlit processions with *ogoh-ogoh* (large monsters) parade through the streets in order to exorcize the spirits. The spectacle is best in Denpasar, where thousands gather in Puputan Square before the start of the march.

Nyepi (moveable) celebrates the *saka*, solar New Year. It is a day of silence when everything closes down and no activity is allowed. It is hoped that the evil spirits roused by the previous night's activities will find Bali to be a barren land and will leave the island. People stay indoors to meditate and pray, visitors are advised to stay within their hotel compound.

Other essential information

Conduct

Temple etiquette Visitors are permitted to visit most temples and to attend ceremonies. However, traditional (*adat*) dress is required – a sash around the waist (at some temples a sarong is also required); these are available for hire at the more popular temples, or can be bought for about 1,200Rp (7,000Rp for a sarong). Modest and tidy dress is also required when visiting temples; women should not enter wearing short dresses or with bare shoulders. Do not use flash-guns during ceremonies. Women menstruating are requested not to enter temples. Avoid walking or placing oneself in front of a person praying.

General etiquette As in other countries of Southeast Asia, open displays of emotion – whether anger or affection – should be avoided. Dress modestly and tidily, especially when visiting someone's house or a temple (see above). Try not to point the soles of your feet (the lowest part of the body) at another person, and when gesturing do not point and crook the finger; point the hand and fingers downwards and then motion inwards. The head should not be touched (the holiest part of the body), and the left hand should not be used to give or receive (it is unclean). Although the Balinese have become used to tourists' transgressions, it is polite to adhere to the above rules of conduct.

Tipping The Balinese authorities are trying to prevent the infiltration of tipping, so avoid doing so.

Shopping

Bali has a wide range of goods for sale targeted at the tourist market: a good choice of clothing – ikat, batik and some quality 'fashion' clothes as well as countless T-shirts, shorts and beachware; brightly-coloured, carved wooden fruit, mobiles, trays and birds; silver jewellery and a scattering of 'antiques'. Carved wooden doors are in plentiful supply and can be dismantled for shipping (packers/shippers can be found in each tourist centre). Ubud and its surrounding craft villages are good places to buy locally-produced handicrafts, while Kuta has the biggest selection of clothing. Always bargain; expect to pay 30%-50% of the asking price except, of course, in fixed-price stores.

Inevitably, much on sale is second-rate and ersatz. This is not a recent development. Miguel Covarrubias when he arrived in Denpasar in 1930 observed that "there are always pretty Balinese girls who sell curios, plainly junk. ...[They] have discovered that the tourists generally prefer hideous statuettes made by beginners or the gaudy weaving dyed with [chemical] anilines to the fine old pieces of wood-carving or to the sumptuous ancient textiles that now rarely find their way into the curio market".

Sports

Diving Diving around Bali is not the best in Indonesia, but the island does have the greatest concentration of dive shops and diving expertise. It is a good place to learn how to dive, but those who have experienced other spots in Southeast Asia or the Pacific may be disappointed. Dive spots include the **Menjangan Marine Park**, an island off the NW tip of Bali, 30 minutes by boat (depth 3-50 m); **Tulamben**, the submerged wreck of a US Liberty ship, sunk during World War II off the NE coast, and a haven for fish (beach dive 10-30 m); **Padangbai**, near Candi Dasa, for 3-20 m dives; **Tepekong Island** (depth 15-30 m), on the E coast; **Lembongan** and **Nusa Penida Islands**, 2 hrs by boat (depth 3-40 m); **Amed**, off the NE coast (depth 3-40 m); and the reefs off Sanur and Nusa Dua beaches. With reputable companies expect to pay US$30 for one dive, US$80 for an introductory one-day course, US$250 for a 4-day diving certificate. Most of the larger hotels have dive desks; see relevant sections for addresses of dive shops.

Golf The **Handara Country Club** is in a beautiful position just N of Lake Bratan (**see page 726**). A new Golf and Country Club has opened near Nusa Dua – ask at the Tourist Information Centre in Denpasar for details.

Surfing Kuta Beach was the location upon which Bali's reputation as a surfer's paradise was based. However, there are other, better locations. Below is a very brief summary of conditions; far more information can be gleaned from surf shops and places where surfers hang out. Some of the best surfing in Bali is on the Bukit Peninsula. **Uluwatu**, with a 'world famous' left break; the Peak is a high tide break, Race Track a mid-tide, and Outside Corner a low tide wave. If the current is too strong to reach the cave or onto the reef in front of the cave, make for the beach. **Padang Padang** is close to Uluwatu and can be reached along a track or by car/motorbike. The very hollow left is dangerous because of the cliff; very dangerous below mid-tide. Down from Padang Padang is **Bingin**; hollow left best at low to medium tides; often crowded. **Nyang Nyang**, accessible by track; both left and right. **Suluban**, not far from Jimbaran; the Annual Surf Championships are held here. Minibuses (C1) travel from Kuta to Uluwatu; tracks to the surfing beaches are reasonably well-marked along the road. Other surfing beaches include **Canggu**, near the village of Kerobokan, N on the Legian road (both left and right); and **Madewi** about 75 km W of Denpasar, best above mid-tide. Boards can be hired for about 5,000-10,000Rp/day; repair and other services are also available – see relevant sections for surf shops. **Best time to surf**: reasonable throughout the year, although surf is best between June and August.

Best time to visit is the dry season between May and Oct when it is slightly cooler and there is less chance of rain. The wet season runs from Nov-Apr. Accommodation is priciest over Christmas and New Year and several weeks either side, which corresponds with the main holiday period in Australia; July and August, the northern hemisphere's holiday period, are also busy. Out of these months accommodation is often cheaper.

Banks and money changers As an international tourist destination, it is easier to change money – either cash or travellers' cheques in all major currencies – in Bali than any other spot in Indonesia. All the tourist centres offer money changing facilities at competitive rates.

Useful addresses Area code: 0361. **Credit Card Representatives: Amex**, *Bali Beach Hotel*, Sanur, T 88449; **Visa and Mastercharge**, Bank Duta, Jl. Hayam Wuruk 165, Denpasar, T 26578; **Diners Club**, Jl. Veteran 5, Denpasar, T 27138; **Ambulance**: T 118; **Police**: T 110.

Media The free English language *Bali News* is published once a fortnight and can be found at many hotel desks.

DENPASAR

Originally called Badung, Denpasar is Bali's capital and has grown in the past 10 to 15 years from a sleepy village to a bustling city. It is situated in the S of the island, about 5 km from the coast. Today, the town has a population of over 300,000 and is Bali's main trade and transport hub, with its central business area centred around Jalan Gajah Mada.

Denpasar was once the royal capital of the princely kingdom of Badung, but there is little evidence of its past. **Puputan Square** pays homage to the tragic end of the Rajah and his court in 1906; it is named after the 'battle to the death' – or *puputan* – against a force of Dutch soldiers on the morning of the 20th Sept (**see page 671**). A monument in the square commemorates the event.

Places of interest

Denpasar is not a particularly attractive town and it contains limited sights of interest for the visitor. The major tourist attraction is easily found, in the centre of town. The **Museum Bali** was established in 1931 and is situated on the E side of Puputan Square. The museum mirrors the architecture of Balinese temples, consisting of a series of attractive courtyards which contain the museum's buildings. The impressive collection of prehistoric artefacts, sculpture, masks, textiles, weaponry and contemporary arts and crafts was assembled with the help of Walter Spies, the German artist who made Bali his home. The artefacts on display are apparently only a small proportion of the museum's collection. Labelling could be better and there is no guide to the museum to help the inquisitive visitor. Nevertheless, it gives an impression of the breadth of the island's culture. Admission: 250Rp. Open: 0800-1700 Tues-Thurs, Sat and Sun, 0800-1530 Fri.

Next door to the museum is the new **Pura Jaganatha**, a temple dedicated to the Supreme God *Sang Hyang Widi Wasa*. The statue of a turtle and 2 nagas signify the foundation of the world. The complex is dominated by the *Padma Sana* or lotus throne, upon which the gods sit. The central courtyard is surrounded by a lily-filled moat with the most enormous carp.

The most important temple in Denpasar from an archaeological perspective is **Pura Masopahit**, down a side street off the W end of Jalan Tabanan (the main gateway to the pura faces the main street, but the entrance is down a side road). The temple is one of the oldest in Bali, probably dating from the introduction of Javanese civilization from Majapahit in the 15th century, after which it is named. It was badly damaged during the 1917 earthquake, but has since been partly restored. Note the fine, reconstructed, split gate with its massive figures of a giant and a garuda. Unfortunately, this temple is not open to the public.

The **Werdi Budaya Art Centre** on Jalan Nusa Indah was established in 1973 to promote Balinese visual and performing arts. The centre contains an open-air auditorium, along with 3 art galleries. Arts and crafts are also sold here. Activity peaks during the annual Bali Festival of Art held from mid-Jun for a month. Admission: 250Rp. Open: 0800-1600 Mon-Sun, closed on holidays.

Excursions

As Denpasar is the transport hub of the island, it is easy to get to most of the main towns, beaches and sights from here.

Festivals Mid Jun-mid Jul: the Werdi Budaya presents an *Annual Arts Festival*, with demonstrations of local music, dance and performance. Hotels or the tourist office will supply a calendar of events.

Accommodation Until the 1950s, Denpasar was the place where most tourists stayed; today it is largely frequented by domestic tourists – foreign visitors either head for the beaches or inland to Ubud. Nonetheless, there is an adequate range of accommodation. **A** *Natour Bali*, Jl. Veteran 3, T 35344, F 35347, a/c, restaurant, pool, central location, built in the 1930s, it was the first hotel on Bali, rather frayed now but it does retain some charm; **B-C** *Chandra Garden*, Jl. Diponegoro 114, T 26425, some a/c, popular with Indonesians, price includes breakfast; **B-C** *Pemecutan Palace*, Jl. Thamrin 2, T 23491, some a/c, a reconstruction of a palace which was destroyed here by the Dutch in 1906, rooms are shabby; **C-D** *Pura Alit*, Jl. Sutomo 26, T 28831, F 88766, some a/c; **D** *Dewi*, Jl. Diponegoro 112, T 26720; **D-E** *Dharmawisata*, Jl. Imam Bonjol 89, T 22186, pool, clean rooms with own mandi.

Restaurants *Atoom Baru*, Jl. Gajah Mada 106-108., Chinese, popular with the locals; **✦✦***Hong Kong*, Jl. Gajah Mada 85, a/c, a tour group stop, so rather overpriced; *Kakman*, Jl. Teuku Umar (half way to Kuta), excellent Indonesian. Nusa Indah: *Warung Wardani* for cheap, genuine Balinese food, rec; Several *warungs* are to be found within the Kumbasari market.

Entertainment Cinema: *Wisata Complex*, Jl. Thamrin. Dance: KOKAR (recently renamed SMKI) is based in Batubulan, it is a conservatory of dance – students perform many different styles of traditional dance, accompanied by a gamelan orchestra. The *Werdi Budaya* Art Centre gives Kecak dance performances every day from 1830-1930.

Shopping Handicrafts: the *Sanggraha Kriya Asta*, 7 Km E of the centre of town, is a government handicrafts shop, selling batik, jewellery, paintings and woodcarvings. The prices are set and quality is controlled. They will organize free transport to the shop from your hotel if telephoned (T 22942). There are also a number of handicraft shops on Jl. Thamrin, and on the third floor of the Kumbasari Market (see Markets, below). **Textiles**: a large selection of textiles is to be found in the shops along Jl. Sulawesi. **Department stores**: *Duta Plaza*, Jl. Dewi Sartika and *Matahari* both have a range of goods, including reasonably priced children's clothes and some handicrafts. **Markets**: the biggest market in town (and the biggest on Bali) is the Kumbasari Market, off Jl. Dr. Wahidin, on the banks of the Badung River. It is a great place to browse, with a range of goods including textiles and handicrafts.

Local transport Bemos: the original, rickety and under-powered 3-wheeler bemos travel between the main bemo terminals (300Rp), criss-crossing town. It is also possible to charter

DENPASAR

IMS 111

To Ubung bus station, & Tanah Lot
Jl. Pattimura
Jl. Supratman
To Glanyar →
Jl. Kartini
Jl. Veteran
Jl. Kepundung
Jl. Melati
Jl. Kamboja
Jl. Palawa
Jl. Nusa Indah
Jl. Dr. Wahidin
Jl. Gajah Mada
Jl. Surapati
Jl. Hayam Wuruk
Jl. Thamrin
Jl. Hassanuddin
Jl. M.J. Sutoyo
Jl. Diponegoro
Jl. Sudirman
Jl. Teuku Umar
Jl. D. Sartika
Jl. Raya Puputan
Jl. Niti Mandala
To Tegal bus station & Kuta
To Airport & Kuta
To Sanur

1. Puputan Square
2. Museum Bali & Pura Jaganatha
3. Werdi Budaya Art Centre
4. Kumbasari Market
5. Post Office
6. Telephone Exchange
7. Paket Pos.
8. Garuda & Merpati offices
9. Immigration office
10. Tourist office
11. Tourist office (more helpful)
12. *Natour Bali Hotel*
13. *Pemecutan Palace Hotel*

B1. Kereneng Bus terminal
B2. Suci Bus terminal (for Bemos)

N

these bemos for trips around town. From the terminals – of which there are several – bemos travel to all of Bali's main towns: The **Ubung** terminal, N of town on Jl. Cokroaminoto, for trips to W Bali, N Bali and Java; **Tegal**, W of town, near the intersection of Jl. Imam Bonjol and Jl. G. Wilis, for journeys to S Bali; **Suci**, near the intersection of Jl. Diponegoro and Jl. Hasanuddin, for Benoa Port; **Kereneng**, at the E edge of town off Jl. Kamboja (Jl. Hayam Wuruk) for destinations around town and for Sanur; while **Batubulan**, E of town just before the village of Batubulan on the road to Gianyar, for buses running E and N (**see page 686** for more details). Taxis: there are numerous un-metered cars that can be chartered by the hour or day, or which can be hired for specific journeys. Bargain hard. There are also some metered taxis. Dokars: pony-drawn carriages, now on the verge of extinction and/or asphyxiation. Ojeks: motorcycle taxis, and the fastest way around town; ojek riders can be identified by their red jackets (500-1000Rp).

Banks & money changers Bank Negara Indonesia, Jl.Gajah Mada 20. **Bank Bumi Daya**, Jl.Veteran 2. **Bank Dagang Negara**, Jl.Gajah Mada 2.

Useful addresses Post Office: Jl. Raya Puputan. Open 0800-1400 Mon-Thurs, 0800-1200 Fri, 0800-1300 Sat. *Poste Restante* available here. **Paket Pos** (packing service and parcel post): Jl. Diponegoro 146. **Telecommunications centre**: Jl. Teuku Umar 6. **Immigration office**: Jl. Panjaitan, off Jl. Puputan Raya, T 27828. **Police**: Jl. Diponegoro, T 110.

Hospitals: Jl. Kesehatan Selatan 1, T 27911; Jl. Kartini, T 22141. **Emergency dental clinic**: Jl. Pattimura 19, T 22445. **Churches**: Catholic church of St. Joseph on Jl. Kepundung (1730, Sat, 0830, 1730, Sun). Evangelical church, Jl. Melati. Protestant Church, Jl. Surapati.

Embassies & consulates Australia, Jl. Muhammad Yamin 51, T 35092. **Japan**, Jl. Muhammad Yamin 9, T 31308. **France**, Jl.Rayan Sesectan 46, T 33555.

Airline offices Bouraq, Jl. Sudirman 19A, T 24656. **Garuda**, Jl. Melati 61, T 22028. **Merpati**, Jl. Melati 57, T 22864. **UTA**, Jl. Bypass Ngurah Rai, T 33341.

Tourist offices Dinas Parawisata, Jl. Raya Puputan, T 22387. Map of the island and a calendar of events available. **Badung Government Tourist Office**, Jl.Surapati 7, T 23602.

Open: 0700-1400 Mon-Thurs, Sat; 0700-1100 Fri. Free map, calendar of events and Bali brochure.

Transport to & from Denpasar By air: see page 685 for details. **By bus:** bus connections with Java from the Ubung terminal, just N of Denpasar on Jl. Cokroaminoto. Express and night bus offices are concentrated near the intersection of Jl. Diponegoro and Jl. Hasanuddin, for example, Chandra Ticketing, Jl. Diponegoro 114, T 26425. Journey time and departure times for night and express buses are as follows: Jakarta 30 hrs (0630-0700), Surabaya 11 hrs (0700 and 1700-2000), Malang (1800-1930), Yogya/Solo 16 hrs (1500-1600), Semarang (1600), Bandung (0700), Bogor (0700), Blitar (1900), Sape (Flores) (0400).

   By bemo: these provide transportation from Denpasar's five terminals to most places on the island (**see page 686**). Small, 3-wheeled bemos run between the various terminals.

KUTA, LEGIAN, SANUR, NUSA PENIDA & NUSA LAMBONGAN

Most visitors to Bali stay in one of the resorts at the S end of the island. Most famous is Kuta, the original backpackers' haven, together with its N extension, Legian. Less frenetic than Kuta, Sanur is on Bali's E coast and offers largely middle to upper-range accommodation. Serangan, or Turtle, Island is a short distance offshore. Rather further off the E coast, in the Lombok Strait, are the 2 islands of Nusa Penida and Nusa Lembongan, offering some accommodation but also accessible on a day trip.

Kuta and Legian

The first pub was opened in Kuta in 1930 by an American, Ketut Tantri; in the same decade another American couple opened the first hotel on the beach. Nonetheless, the author and Bali-phile Miguel Covarrubias wrote in 1937 that Kuta and Sanur were "small settlements of fishermen who brave the malarial coasts". It was not until the 1960s that large numbers of Western travellers 'discovered' Kuta. Since then, it has grown into a highly developed beach resort with a mind-boggling array of hotels, restaurants and shops. It is no longer a backpackers' haven; most of the cheap losmen have either closed down or moved up-market. There is however, a plentiful supply of good middle to high range accommodation here.

Traffic in Kuta frequently comes to a standstill, despite the one-way system. The main drag, containing most of Kuta's shops, is Jalan Legian, which runs N-S (traffic travels one way S). Jalan Pantai meets Jalan Legian at the notorious 'Bemo Corner' and is the main E-W road to the S end of the beach (with traffic going one way W). The beach road is northbound only.

Kuta Beach is rather unattractive and clinical, offering no shade from trees and fenced off from the road (admission: 200Rp). It is because of its accessibility that it is popular with surfers, although better waves can be found elsewhere. The surf seldom exceeds 2 m, but it is an excellent spot for beginners and recreational surfers. Boards can be hired on the beach and there are usually locals who will offer their insider's knowledge of surf conditions. Strong and irregular currents can make swimming a little hazardous – look out for the warning notices. The sand is white to the S, but grey further N. Hoards of locals sell trinkets and offer hair-plaiting and massage services. The beach faces W, so is popular at sunset.

Legian Beach is narrower than Kuta, with grey sand and, like Kuta, an abundance of hawkers providing manicures, massage and hair-braiding services.

Accommodation It is advisable to book accommodation during the peak periods of Jul/Aug and at Christmas and New Year, as hotels are often full. There are countless places to stay on Kuta and Legian, the list below is not comprehensive; look around when you arrive, or go on recommendations. The large 4- and 5-star hotels are concentrated at the S end of Kuta or to

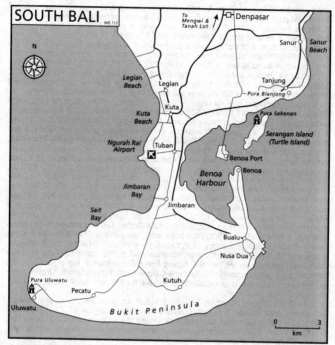

the N of Legian, while the middle range and smaller cottage-style accommodation is situated nearer the centre of town.

L *Puri Ratih*, Jl. Puri Ratih, PO Box 1114, T 51546, F 51549, N of Legian, a/c, restaurant, pool, all suites, with own kitchen, living-room and garden, excellent facilities; **A+** *Bali Imperial*, Jl. Dhyanapura, Legian, T 54545, F 51545, a/c, restaurant, pools, tennis, Japanese-owned hotel on a beachfront plot, opened 1992 with 121 luxurious rooms and perhaps the most inviting swimming pool on South Bali; **A+** *Bintang Bali*, Jl. Kartika Plaza, PO Box 1068, T 53292, F 53288, S end of beach, a/c, restaurant, pool, large, ugly hotel with all amenities; **A+** *Oberoi*, Jl. Kayu Aya, PO Box 351, T 51061, F 52791, N end of Legian, one of the 2 best hotels on Bali, a/c, restaurant, pool, private beach, cottages and villas (which include their own pools), sports facilities include tennis, health centre, highly rec; **A+** *Pertamina Cottages*, Jl. Kuta Beach, T 51161, the southernmost hotel on Kuta, close to the airport, a/c, restaurant, pool, good sports facilities, suites available.

A *Bali Anggrek Inn*, Jl. Pantai, PO Box 435, T 51265, F 51766, a/c, restaurant, large pool, facing the beach, average rooms; **A** *Bali Dynasty*, Jl. Kartika Plaza, T 53955, F 87738, S end of Kuta, a/c, restaurant, pool, large and ugly, extensive facilities; **A** *Bali Garden*, Jl. Kartika Plaza, PO Box 1101, T 52725, F 53851, S end of Kuta, a/c, restaurant, pool, extensive facilities; **A** *Indah*, Poppies Lane II, T 53327, F 52787, pool, central location for shopping, price includes breakfast; **A** *Intan Beach Village*, PO Box 1089, Batubelig Beach, N of Kuta, T 52191, F 52193, a/c, several restaurants, 2 pools, extensive sports facilities, large central block, with some bungalow accommodation; **A** *Kartika Plaza*, Jl. Kartika Plaza, PO Box 84, T 51067, F 52475, S end of beach, a/c, 5 restaurants, large pool, part of the *Aerowisata* chain, facilities include squash courts, tennis, fitness centre, huge, ugly reception, some cottage-style accommodation; **A** *Kuta Palace*, Jl. Pura Bagus Teruna, N end of Legian, PO Box 244, T 51433, F 52074, a/c, 5 restaurants, 2 pools, tennis, fitness centre, all facilities, facing the beach, large hotel with 2-storey blocks of accommodation and some family bungalows; **A** *Kulkul*, Jl. Pantai, PO Box 97, T 52520, F 52519, a/c, restaurant, pool, on the beach road, well designed hotel with attractive rooms, rec; **A** *Legian Garden Cottages*, Jl. Legian Cottage, Legian, T 51876, a/c, pool, quiet, except when the *Double Six* disco is operating; **A** *Mandira Cottages*, Jl. Padma, Legian, T 51381, F 52377, a/c, restaurant, large pool, close to sea, free airport pick-up, rec; **A** *Pesona Bali*, Jl. Kayu Aya, T 53914, F 53915, N of Legian, a/c, restaurant, pool, quiet location, with cottage-style accommodation; **A** *Poppies I*, Poppies Lane, PO Box 378, T 51059, F 52364, a/c, pool, lovely garden, well-run hotel with cottage accommodation, very popular; **A** *Rama Palace*, Jl. Pantai, PO Box 293, T 52063, F 53078, on the beach road, a/c, restaurant, pool, standard accommodation; **A** *Sahid Bali*, Jl. Pantai, PO Box 1102, T 53855, F 52019, a/c, restaurant, biggest pool in Kuta, large hotel on the beachfront; **A-B** *Mutiara*, Poppies Lane I, T 52091, some a/c, attractive pool, nice garden, clean rooms.

B *Agung Cottages*, Jl. Raya Legian, T 51147, some a/c, restaurant, good pool, rec; **B** *Aneka Beach*, Jl. Pantai, T 52067, F 52892, a/c, pool, on the beach road, 3-storey hotel plus some thatched bungalows, attractive grounds; **B** *Bakungsari*, Jl. Bakungsari, PO Box 1044, T 35396, F 52704, a/c, pool, built around a central swimming pool, clean rooms; **B** *Bali Bungalows*, PO Box 371, T 35285, F 51899, a/c, pool, near *Rama Palace* on the beach road, nice grounds; **B** *Bruna Beach*, PO Box 116, T 51565, F 53201, a/c, on beachfront road, average rooms, price includes breakfast; **B** *Five One Cottages*, behind Poppies Lane I, a/c, small pool, hot water; **B** *Flora Beach*, Jl. Bakungsari 13A, PO Box 1040, T 51870, F 31034, a/c, pool, new hotel with attractive pool and clean, well-designed rooms, one of the better of the mid-range hotels, rec; **B** *Garden View*, Jl. Padma, Legian, T 51559, F 53265, a/c, pool, quiet location, a walk to the beach; **B** *Kuta Cottages*, Jl. Bakungsari, PO Box 300, T 51101, pool, small hotel; **B** *Legian Village*, Jl. Padma, Legian, T 51182, some a/c, pool, popular; **B** *Melasti*, Jl. Kartika, PO Box 295, T 51335, F 51563, a/c, pool, on the beach, may be rather overpriced and living on its reputation, end of Kuta; **B** *Orchid Garden Cottage*, Jl. Pura Bagus Taruna 525, PO Box 379, T 51802, small hotel, attractive gardens, clean; **B** *Satriya*, Poppies Lane II, T 52741, pool, hot water, clean rooms, price includes breakfast, rec; **B** *Willy*, Jl. Tegalwangi 18, T 51281, F 52641, small, attractive pool, central location in Kuta, attractive rooms, built around a garden, rec; **B-C** *Agung Beach Bungalows*, Jl. Bakungsari, T 51263, some a/c, pool, good location S of Jl. Pantai; **B-C** *Dewi Ratih*, Poppies Lane II, T 51694, some a/c, small pool, hot water, price includes breakfast; **B-C** *R.J.'s*, Jl. Rum Jungle, Legian, T 51922, pool, good value, good food.

C *Barong Cottages*, Jl. Legian, T 51488, F 51804, a/c, pool, 3-storey accommodation, nice garden, price includes breakfast; **C** *Jesen's Inn III*, Jl. Bakungsari 19, T 51561, off the main road in a large palm-filled courtyard, rooms in the new wing are best; **C** *Lumbung Sari*, Jl. Three Brothers, T 52009, rather squashed in between other developments, cottage with kitchen, (**D**) no fan; **C** *Mandara Cottages*, Jl. Kartika Plaza, T 51775, small pool, open air bathrooms, rec; **C-D** *Dharma Yudha*, Jl. Bakungsari, T 51685, some a/c, friendly, but rooms are rather dark; **C-D** *Lasi Erawati*, Poppies Lane I, T 51665, fan, clean, nice garden, rec; **D** *Bamboo Inn*, Gang Kresek 1, Jl. Bakungsari, T 51935, friendly, clean, but not very close to the beach, price includes breakfast; **D** *Kuta Suci*, just off Poppies Lane II, T 52617, small but clean rooms; **D** *Legian Beach Bungalow*, Jl. Padma, Legian, T 51087, good discount for longer stay; **D** *Masa Inn*, Poppies Lane I, T 52606, fan, clean (motorbike hire – 10,000Rp/day); **D** *Oka*, Jl. Padma, Legian, T 51085, small, clean, but hemmed in by other buildings; **D** *Puri Damai Cottage I*, Jl. Padma, Legian, T 51965, popular; **D** *Puri Mangga Cottages*, Jl. Legian Cottages 23, Legian, T 51447, F 53007, long stay (90,000Rp/week), good value, nice garden; **D** *Sareg*, Jl. Pantai Kuta, basic, Western toilets, clean, rec; **D** *Sari Yasa Beach Inn I*, Jl. Rum Jungle, Legian, T 52836, basic but O.K. rooms; **E** *Bali Indah Beach Inn*, just N of Poppies Lane II, big clean rooms, own shower, very friendly management, price includes breakfast, rec; **E** *Komala Indah*, Poppies Lane I (opposite *Poppies*).

Restaurants Most of the restaurants in Kuta and Legian offer a range of food, including Indonesian and International. For this reason, the listing below is not split into cuisine. *Bennys*, Jl. Pura Bagus Taruna, Legian, great range of coffee; ♦*Bobbies*, towards Legian, to left of Jl. Legian, excellent value food, particularly the pizzas, rec; *Burger King*, Jl. Legian; *Do Drop Inn*, steakhouse bar and restaurant, Jl. Legian; ♦*Golden Palace International*, Poppies Lane II, good lasagnes, opposite here is a small, popular and cheap restaurant (♦), with pizza, fried rice etc and cheap beer; *Il Pirata*, Jl. Legian, 24 hour pizzaria; *Koko's Warung*, Jl. Pura Bagus Taruna, Legian, Indian; *Locanda Fat Yogi*, Poppies Lane I, bakery and Italian restaurant with good pizzas, rec; ♦*Made's Warung*, Jl. Pantai, the oldest eating establishment on Kuta, serving Asian and travellers' food and still very popular, rec; *Mini's*, Jl. Legian, popular Chinese restaurant, with good seafood; ♦♦*Poppies*, Poppies Lane I, attractive garden, good food (mostly international), popular, rec; ♦♦*S.C.*, Jl. Legian, seafood, Chinese; ♦♦*T.J.'s*, Poppies Lane I, good Mexican food; ♦*Tree House*, Poppies Lane I, travellers' food; ♦♦*Un's*, Poppies Lane I,

Indonesian, travellers' food, seafood, both only average quality; ♦*Yunna*, Poppies Lane II, travellers' food, popular.

Bars Most of the bars are to be found on the main road – Jl. Legian. *Club Bruna*, Jl. Pantai (beach road). *Do Drop Inn*, Jl. Legian. *Sari Club*, Jl. Legian. *The Bounty*, Jl. Legian, popular Australian drinking-hole, with jugs of Marguerites and videos. Every Tues and Sat a pub crawl leaves *Peanuts*, on Jl. Legian at 1830. Arrives at *Casablancas* (Jl. Buni Sari – just S of Bemo Corner) at about 2200.

Entertainment Balinese performing arts: kecak, legong, Ramayana dance and Balinese music; performances take place at many of the major hotels. **Discos**: *Peanut's* (4,000Rp entry fee), *Warehouse* (next door to *Peanuts*), free entry, *Spotlights* and *Cheater's*, all on Jl. Legian; open-air discos at *Gado-Gado* and *Double Six* (both N of Legian, off Jl. Dhyanapura and Jl. Legian Cottage).

Sports Diving: Bali Dolphin Divers at *Bali Garden Hotel*, Jl. Kartika Plaza, T 52725. They also provide fishing, parasailing, jetskiing and waterskiing facilities. **Surfing**: Kuta is famous for its surfing, although the cognoscenti would now rather go elsewhere (**see page 688**). Surfboards are available for rent on the beach. Surf equipment is available from *The Surf Shop*, Jl. Legian, *Amphibia Surf Shop*, Jl. Legian and *Ulu's Shop*, Jl. Bakungsari. They will all provide information on currents, tides and latest surfing reports. **Massage**: numerous masseurs – with little professional training – roam the beach; more skilled masseurs can be found at hotels or specialist clinics around Kuta.

Shopping Best buys: Kuta is undoubtedly the best place on Bali to shop for clothing; the quality is reasonable (sometimes good), and designs are close to the latest Western fashions, with a strong Australian bias for bright colours and bold designs. There is a good range of children's clothes shops. Silver jewellery is also a good buy (although some of it is of rather inferior quality). In addition, Kuta has a vast selection of 'tourist' trinkets and curios: leather goods, woodcarvings, mobiles, batik. Quality is poor to average. **Children's clothes shops**: *Kuta Kidz*, Bemo Corner; *Hop on Pop*, Jl. Pantai 45; *Outrageous*, Jl. Legian Kaja 460. **Handicrafts**: a range of 'antiques' and Indonesian fabrics can be found towards the N end of Jl. Legian. **Jewellery**: several shops on Jl. Legian and Jl. Pantai. **Men's fashions**: shirts at *Aladdin's Cave*, Jl. Legian and in several shops around Bemo Corner. **Swimwear and sportswear**: Jl. Pantai, and from the surfing shops on Jl. Legian and Jl. Bakungsari; several shops in Legian on (and down the gangs off) Jl. Legian. **T-shirts**: a multitude of shops along Jl. Legian; good designs from *Tony's* on Jl. Bakungsari. **Women's clothes shops**: mostly along Jl. Legian and Jl. Pantai. Lots of lycra, available from *Coconut Tree*, Jl. Legian. Outrageous sequined garments from *Dallas*, Jl. Legian 496. Batik jump-suits and jackets from *Aladdin's Cave*, Jl. Legian. **Tapes**: beware – dodgy cassette tapes sold.

Local transport Bemos: bemos run from Bemo Corner up Jl. Pantai to Legian (200Rp); and from just E of Bemo Corner, to Denpasar's Tegal terminal. Bemos for charter also hang around Bemo Corner. **Car hire**: arrange through hotels, approximately 40,000Rp/day; there are also private cars (with drivers) that can be chartered by the hour or day, or for specific journeys. Bargain hard, expect to pay about 50,000Rp/day. Drivers can be found around Bemo Corner. **Motorbike hire**: arranged through travel agents, hotels or from operations on the street, from 7,000Rp/day. **Bicycle hire**: 3,000Rp/day.

Banks & money changers Plenty of money changers on Jl. Legian. Branches of **Lippo Bank** and **Danamon** in Galael Plaza (on road into Kuta from Denpasar).

Useful addresses Post Office: Jl. Raya Tuban, S of Jl. Bakungsari. **Postal Agent**: Jl. Legian; *poste restante* service. **Telecommunications Centre**: Jl. Legian. **Police Station**: Jl. Raya Kuta, T 51598. **Immigration**: S of town on the road to the airport. **Clinic**: Jl. Raya Kuta 100, T 53268, 24 hrs on call.

Consulates & embassies Netherlands, Jl. Imam Bonjol 599, T 51094. Switzerland, c/o Swiss restaurant, Jl. Pura Bagus Taruna, Legian, T 51735.

Airline offices Garuda, *Kuta Beach Hotel*, Jl. Pantai, T 24664.

Travel agents Genta Jaya, Jl. Padma. *Perama*, Jl. Legian.

Tourist office Jl. Bakungsari, T 51419.

Transport to & from Kuta 11 km from Denpasar, 4 km from the airport. **By bemo**: to Tegal terminal in Denpasar and from there, change to other terminals for next destination (see Local transport **page 686**). **By shuttle bus**: to most tourist destinations on the island; shop around for best price. **By taxi**: 6,500Rp to the airport.

Sanur

Like Kuta, Sanur was also a malaria-infested swamp which local people, bar a few intrepid fishermen, tended to avoid. In the past, the villages around Sanur had a reputation for producing some of the best dancers and story-tellers, as well as some of the most effective priests and shamans.

In May 1904 the Chinese steamer *Sri Koemala* was wrecked off Sanur and looted by the local Balinese. The Dutch used the failure (and subsequent outright refusal) of the King of Badung to offer compensation for this 'outrage' as justification for blockading the principality. On the 15 Sept 1906, there followed an armed invasion by the Dutch on the beaches of Sanur, which was unopposed by the peaceful local Brahmanas (the priestly caste). However, an army arrived from Denpasar to confront the Dutch the following morning. Fighting lasted for much of the day, resulting in the death of a handful of Dutchmen and hundreds of Balinese. After the skirmish, the Dutch remained at Sanur for a few days – apparently giving concerts for the local inhabitants – before setting out for Denpasar and the King of Badung's palace. The rest, as they say, is history (see page 671).

Barely 2 decades after the Dutch military invasion of Sanur, the beginning of another invasion took root: tourism. Hotels sprang up along the beachfront and intrepid travellers from the West began to arrive, enticed by tales of a tropical paradise. Bali's first, and ugliest, international hotel was built here (the *Bali Beach*) but despite considerable development, Sanur remains quieter and more low-key than Kuta, with the most attractive beach on the island and a village atmosphere. The road parallel to the beach is lined with money changers, tourist shops (selling clothing and jewellery), tour companies, car rental outlets and shipping agents.

Places of interest

The **Le Mayeur Museum** is just to the N of the *Bali Beach Hotel* and is named after the famous Belgian artist Adrien Yean Le Mayeur, who arrived in Bali in 1932. He was immediately captivated by the culture and beauty of the island, made Sanur his home and married a local beauty, Ni Polok, in 1935. He died in 1958. The museum contains his collection of local artefacts and some of Le Mayeur's work. The interior is dark and rather dilapidated, making the pieces difficult to view – a great shame because Le Mayeur's impressionistic works are full of tropical sunlight and colour. Le Mayeur's paintings made a great impression on a number of Balinese artists, including the highly regarded I Gusti Nyoman Nodya. Admission: 200Rp. Open: 0800-1400 Tues-Thurs and Sun, 0800-1100 Fri, 0800-1200 Sat.

To the S of Sanur, on the route to the main road, is the **Pura Blanjong** (on the left-hand side of the road). It houses the **Blanjong Inscription,** an inscribed cylindrical stone pillar, discovered in 1932 and believed to date from 914. The inscription is written in 2 languages, Sanskrit and Old Balinese, and was carved during the reign of King Kesari, a Buddhist King of the Sailendra Dynasty (who may also have founded the Besakih temple). It supports the view that there was an Indianized principality on Bali at a very early date. The inscription itself, though difficult to decipher, refers to a military expedition.

Excursions

Serangan Island or Turtle Island is, as the name suggests, famous for its turtles which are caught in the surrounding sea, raised in pens, and then slaughtered for their meat – which explains why they are becoming rarer by the year. The formerly common green turtle is now said to be virtually extinct in the area. The beaches on the E coast of the island are best, with offshore coral providing good snorkeling. One of Bali's most important coastal temples is the **Pura Sakenan** in Sakenan village, at the N end of the island. The temple was founded at the end of the 15th century and contains a rare prasada *(prasat)* or stepped stone tower. Stylistically this is a combination of the Javanese candi and pre-Hindu megalithic stone altar. Like Uluwatu on the Bukit Peninsula, it is constructed of hard coral.

Pura Sakenan's *odalan* or anniversary festival, held at Kuningan (the 210th day of the Balinese calendar) is thought by many to be one of the best on Bali. **Getting there**: boats can be chartered from Sanur or from Nusa Dua and Benoa. Usually visitors leave from a jetty just S of Kampung Mesigit and 2 km SW of Sanur. From here there are regular public boats to Serangan Island (600Rp); the problem is that tourists are often forced to charter a boat for far more; share if possible and bargain furiously. It is easier, and often just as cheap, to go on a tour. It is also possible to wade out to the island at low tide.

Nusa Lembongan (see page 698) lies just off the coast. Boats leave every morning for the island from close to the *Bali Beach Hotel*, 1 hr (17,000Rp).

Tours The major hotels on the beach all have tour companies which organize the usual range of tours: for example to Lake Bratan (where waterskiing can be arranged); to Karangasem and Tenganan, to visit a traditional Aga village; to Ubud; white-water rafting on the Agung River; to the temples of Tanah Lot and Mengwi; to the Bali Barat National Park; and to Besakih Temple. *Santa Bali Tours*, Bali Beach Hotel Arcade, T 88056.

Accommodation Accommodation on Sanur is largely mid- to high-range, with 2 large-scale luxury developments – the *Bali Hyatt* and *Bali Beach*. There is very little low-budget accommodation here. **L** *Tanjung Sari*, Jl. Tanjung Sari, PO Box 25, Denpasar, T 88441, F 87930, a/c, restaurant, pool, built in the 1960s, 29 bungalows with own sitting-room and outside pavilion, tastefully decorated, although some rooms are becoming threadbare, rather overpriced, and seems to be living off its reputation; **A+** *Bali Beach*, PO Box 275 Denpasar, T 88511, F 87917, J 320107, N end of the beach, a/c, restaurant, 3 pools, 9-hole golf course, 10-pin bowling, tennis, the original international hotel in Bali, built in the 1960s as a showpiece, with the backing of President Sukarno, an ugly high-rise block rather out-of-place now that low-rise designs employing Balinese motifs are all the rage, the more recently built bungalows, to the S, are more attractive, good facilities (the hotel suffered a serious fire in late 1992 but is said to have been repaired); **A+** *Bali Hyatt*, entrance on Jl. Tanjung Sari, PO Box 392, T 88271, F 87693, a/c, several restaurants, lovely pool, one of the oldest but still one of the best hotels on the beach, extensive and immaculate grounds, range of sports activities and recently renovated, rec; **A+** *Sanur Beach*, PO Box 279, T 88011, F 87566, S end of beach, a/c, several restaurants (fish restaurant rec), lovely pool, sports facilities include fitness centre, attractively decorated rooms in 3-storey block; **A+** *Sindhu Beach*, Jl. Danau Tondano 14, PO Box 181, T 88351, bungalow-style rooms. **A** *Bali Sanur Bungalows* (includes 5 separate developments in Sanur – *Paneeda View, Besakih Beach, Irama Bungalows, Respati Beach* and *Sanur Village Club*), Jl. Tanjung Sari, PO Box 306, T 88421, F 88426, a/c, restaurant, pool, all have well-kept gardens, small pools, standard bungalow rooms; **A** *Bumi Ayu*, Jl. Bumi Ayu, PO Box 1077, T 89101, F 87517, a/c, restaurant (of sorts), pool, inconveniently away from the beach, but attractive gardens and pool, and well-run, rec; **A** *La Taverna*, Jl. Tanjung Sari, PO Box 40, T 88497, F 87126, restaurant (rec.), pool, rooms are quite dark but are well decorated with traditional furnishings, attractive gardens. **A** *Natour Sindhu Beach*, Jl. Danau Tandano 14, PO Box 181, T 88351, a/c, pool, bungalow rooms on the beach; **A** *New Santrian*, Jl. Tanjung Sari, T 88181, F 88185, a/c, good restaurant, pool, bungalow accommodation, tennis courts; **A** *Palm Garden*, Jl. Kesuma Sari, T 88299, F 88299, S end of beach, a/c, restaurant, pool; **A** *Santrian*, T 88184, F 88185, a/c, restaurant, pool, watersports facilities, traditional style accommodation, amidst large garden; **A** *Sativa*, Jl. D. Tamblingan, T 87276, a/c, attractive pool, attractively designed with thatched cottage accommodation; **A** *Surya Beach*, Jl. Mertasari, T 88833, F 87303, J 5706421, S end of beach, a/c, restaurant, pool, sports facilities, large hotel with 2 storey cottage-style accommodation; **A-B** *Gazebo Cottages*, Jl. Tanjung Sari 45, T 88300, F 88300, a/c, restaurant, pool, attractive gardens, strip of private beach.

B *Alit's Beach Bungalows*, Jl. Hang Tuah 45, T 88560, F 88766, N end of beach, a/c, pool, large complex of traditional Balinese design, with attractive gardens; **B** *Ramayana*, Jl. Danau Tamblingan 130, T 88429, a/c, small, family-run hotel, away from the beach but good value; **B-C** *Abian Srama*, Jl. Bypass, T 88415, F 88673, some a/c, small pool, bad location, away from the beach, but well-run; **B-C** *Kalpatharu*, Jl. D. Tamblingan, T 88457, some a/c, restaurant, small hotel, rooms are rather hemmed-in, lacking character; **C** *Watering Hole*, Jl. Hangtuah 35, T 88289, some a/c, average; **C-D** *Made's Homestay*, Jl. D. Tamblingan 74, T 88152; **D** *Rani's*, Jl. Segara, T 88578, next to the Indah, away from the beach, clean rooms; **E** *Indah*, Jl. Segara, T 88568, away from the beach.

Restaurants Many of the best restaurants on Sanur are concentrated at the S end of the beach, on Jl. Bali Hyatt. The 3 big hotels, namely the *Hyatt*, the *Bali Beach* and the *Sanur Beach* all have several good restaurants although prices tend be higher.

♦♦♦*Bali Moon*, Jl. Tamblingan 19. Italian, attractive setting in an open-air pavilion, good food; **♦*Jawa Barat*,** S end of Jl. Bali Hyatt, Indonesian; **♦♦♦*Made's Bar and restaurant*,** Jl. Tanjung Sari 51, seafood, Italian, Indonesian, generous portions, good food and atmosphere, rec; **♦♦*Mina Garden*,** Jl. Tanjung Sari. Balinese, Indonesian, Italian and international, Balinese dance, rec; **♦♦♦♦*Kita*,** Jl. Danau Tamblingan 104, average Japanese food; **♦♦♦*Paon*,** Jl. Danau Tamblingan (not far from *Bali Hyatt*), seafood and steaks; **♦♦♦*Tanjung Sari Hotel*,** Jl. Tanjung Sari, Indonesian and International food (French cook) served in elegant, peaceful surroundings, drinks at candlelit tables on the beach provide a romantic atmosphere; **♦♦♦*Telaga Naga*,** near *Hyatt*, romantic setting in building on stilts overlooking lily pond, classy Szechuan and Chinese food; *Terrazza Martini*, on the beach at the S end, small restaurant serving good Italian food; *Trattoria Da Marco*, on the beach at the S end, Italian, rec.

Supermarket: *Galaels* is on the By Pass road and has a good range of food and wine, as well as an ice-cream parlour and a *Kentucky Fried Chicken* next door.

Entertainment **Dance:** the *Sanur Beach Hotel* offers a buffet dinner with Legong (Mon), Ramayana Ballet (Wed), Genggong/frog dance (Sun) all at 1930. The *Tanjung Sari Hotel* has legong dance and gamelan performances on Saturday nights. The *Penjor* restaurant (near the Bali Hyatt Hotel) stages legong dance performances on Tues, Thurs and Sun 1930-2100, frog dance every Mon 2015, joged dance every Wed 2015 and janger dance every Fri 2015.
Massage: on the beach, or at *Sehatku*, Jl. D. Tamblingan 23, T 87880, 10,000Rp for a traditional massage. **Sauna/Spa:** *Sehatku*, Jl. D. Tamblingan 23, T 87880, 40,000Rp.

Sports **Diving:** *Baruna* Watersports at the *Bali Beach Hotel*, T 88511, *Sanur Beach*, T 88011 and *Bali Hyatt*, T 88271; **Oceana Dive Centre**, Jl. Bypass Let Kol. 1 Gusti, T 88652, F 88652. **Golf:** 9-hole courses at the *Bali Beach Hotel*, Green fee US$25, club hire US$11.50/US$16.50, caddy US$1.50. **10-Pin Bowling:** at the *Bali Beach Hotel*, 3,500Rp/person/game. **Watersports:** equipment available from the bigger hotels or on the beach.

Shopping **Clothing:** *Pisces*, Jl. Sanur Beach (near the *Bali Hyatt*) has good designs. **Ikat:** *Nogo*, Jl. Tamblingan 98. High quality ikat made in Gianyar and sold for 14,000Rp/metre for plain colours and 16,000Rp/metre for designs, plus ready-made clothing. They also sell batik. **Jewellery:** *Bali Sun Sri*, Jl. Bypass Ngurah Rai (out of town) has a wide selection of silver jewellery and good designs. *Pisces*, Jl. Sanur Beach (near *Bali Hyatt*) sells a limited range of contemporary silver jewellery. **Leather and rattan bags:** *The Hanging Tree*, Jl. Tamblingan. **Tourist trinkets:** T-shirts, bags, batik, at the N end of Jl. Tanjung Sari.

Local transport **Car hire:** larger national and international firms tend to be based at the bigger hotels; there are also many smaller outfits along the main road. Big companies charge about 90,000Rp/day, smaller ones about 45,000Rp/day. Note that cars cannot be taken off the island. *Avis*, Bali Hyatt Hotel, T 88271 ext 85023; *Bali Car Rental*, Jl. Ngurah Rai 17, T 88550; *National*, Bali Beach Hotel, T 88511 ext 1304.
Bicycle hire: the *Bali Hyatt Hotel* has mountain bikes for hire.

Banks & money changers There are several along the main street.

Embassies & consulates **France**, Jl. Sekar Waru 3, T 88090. **Germany**, Jl. Pantai Karang 17, T 88826. **US**, Jl. Segara Ayu 5, T 88478.

Useful addresses **Postal Agent:** Jl. Tamblingan 66 (opposite *Taverna Bali Hotel*); including poste restante. **Perumtel telephone service:** on the corner of Jl. Tanjung Sari and Jl. Sindu. **Church Service (Catholic):** *Bali Beach Hotel*, 1800 Sun and *Bali Hyatt Hotel* 1900 Sun (times may vary). **Doctor**, *Bali Beach Hotel* from 0800-1200 daily.

Airline offices **Air France**, *Bali Beach Hotel*.

Transport to & from Sanur 6 km from Denpasar. **By bemo:** regular connections on green bemos with Denpasar's Kreneng terminal (400-500Rp); also regular connections with the Batubulan terminal, N of Sanur (600Rp).

Nusa Penida and Nusa Lembongan

These 2 islands off Bali's SE coast in the Lombok Strait are relatively isolated from the 'mainland' and have not experienced the same degree of tourist development. **Nusa Lembongan** is the smaller of the 2, with beautiful white sand beaches and good surfing along the N shore. Surrounded by reefs, the diving and snorkeling off the island is among the best within easy reach of Bali. These attractions have already caught the attention of both developers and tourists looking for somewhere new. A number of losmen have sprung up around the N coast village of Jungut Batu. Nonetheless, for the time being it seems that the harvesting of seaweed for export – primarily to Hong Kong for the cosmetics industry – will remain the island's main source of income.

The far larger sister island of **Nusa Penida** is rugged and barren, with steep cliffs along its S shore and sandy beaches to the N. It has a reputation among the Balinese as a cursed place and criminals and outcasts used to be sent here to live out their days. Perhaps because of its reputation, Nusa Penida has not yet been caught up in the tourist mêlée and there is no formal accommodation available. Most visitors come for the day only, although it might be possible to persuade a local to take you in. Ask the *kepala desa* (headman).

Accommodation on Nusa Lembongan C *Nusa Lembongan Bungalows* (booking office on Kuta at Jl. Pantai Legian, T 53071), price includes breakfast, attractive, clean and spacious rooms. **E** *Agung*, good restaurant, thatched-roof bungalows, some with private mandi.

Shopping Textiles: distinctive weft ikat cotton cloth is produced on Nusa Penida; usually in the form of a red *kamben*.

Transport to & from Nusa Penida and Nusa Lembongan By boat: regular connections to Nusa Penida from either Padangbai or Kesamba, docking near Sampalan at (respectively) Buyuk or Toyapakeh (the boats from Kesamba are small junks), 1 hr (3,000Rp). For Nusa Lembongan they leave every morning from near the *Bali Beach Hotel* (Sanur Beach) and dock at Jungut Batu.

THE BUKIT PENINSULA AND NUSA DUA

The Bukit Peninsula extends to the S of Kuta, with just a narrow isthmus connecting it to the mainland. On the W side of the isthmus is Jimbaran Beach, and on the E side, Benoa. The purpose-built resort area of Nusa Dua, created from a barren landscape into a landscaped park of large, international-style hotels lies on the E side, to the south of Benoa. The Bukit Peninsula is a barren, arid, limestone tableland – the Dutch called it Tafelhoek – which rises to 200 m. There is a big contrast between the barren landscape here and the lushness of the rest of the S of the island. The soils are sandy and infertile, rainfall is less abundant and highly seasonal, and it was considered such an unpleasant place to live that criminals were once banished here.

In 1969 the Indonesian government commissioned a French consultancy firm to draw up a report on the future development of Bali. The resulting report became the master plan for the island's tourist industry. The plan envisaged that tourist development would be confined to designated resort areas, thus preventing tourists from intruding too much on daily life. Central to this strategy was the creation of **Nusa Dua**: an extraordinary area of large 4- and 5-star hotels and immaculately kept gardens on the E coast of the Bukit Peninsula. Deep bore holes were sunk to provide ample supplies of fresh water, the area was landscaped and replanted, and a highway was built from the airport – the most expensive road ever to have been built on Bali. Although there can be little doubt that the development has isolated the tourists from the locals – a good thing some might maintain – it has also meant that only larger hotels and businesses have benefitted from the tourist dollars. The only way that a Balinese businessman of limited means can set-up in the 'amenity core' of Nusa Dua is by hiring a stall from the Tourist Authority. Even the bulk of the food is imported.

The only 'sight' on the Bukit Peninsula is the **Uluwatu Temple** (see page 700), magnificently positioned on a cliff top overlooking the sea at the SW extremity of the peninsula. Much of the W coast has remained relatively undeveloped because of the steep cliffs. But the excellent surf for which this area is renowned draws large numbers of surfers to the W coast. At the neck of the peninsula is the sandy **Jimbaran Bay**, which is set to become the next target for tourist development.

Jimbaran

Fifteen minutes drive S of Kuta is the sandy beach of Jimbaran Bay. At present, it is a quiet, unspoilt bay, with a relaxed, village atmosphere. Unfortunately, developers have their eyes on it and it may not be long before it is transformed into another bustling resort. 2 hotels have already been built and the *Intercontinental Group* plan to complete another hotel in 1993. At the end of the road down to the bay, on the W road to Uluwatu, is an attractive temple, the **Ulun Siwi Temple**, dating from the 17th century.

Accommodation *Intercontinental*, opening 1993; **A+** *Pansea Jimbaran*, T (20) 52227, F 52220, a/c, restaurants, pool, first class facilities; **A** *Keraton Bali*, very attractive traditional bungalows; **B** *Jimbaran Beach Club*, T (20) 80361; **C** *Puri Indra Prasta*, Jl. Uluwatu 28A, restaurant, pool, prices include breakfast.

Transport to & from Jimbaran By bemo: connections with Denpasar's Tegal terminal.

Benoa

Benoa consists of a small fishing village called Tanjung Benoa, at the tip of a finger of land extending N from Nusa Dua. Close by is Benoa port, built by the Dutch in 1906 and the main port of call for cruise ships and yachts – this is the place to come for anyone hoping to sign on as crew. The area around Benoa, particularly between Tanjung Benoa and Nusa Dua, is becoming increasingly popular for tourists who want to escape from the excesses of Kuta and Sanur. Benoa has gained a reputation for the quality of its watersports, including diving.

Tours *Tour Devco* (T 31592) organize trips on a tall ship to Nusa Lembongan; price includes lunch and watersports equipment. *The Bali International Yacht Club*, T 88391, also organizes yacht and fishing trips to the islands.

Accommodation **A** *Puri Joma Bungalows*, pool; **A** *Sorga Nusa Dua*, T (20) 71604, F 71143, a/c; **B** *Chez Agung*; **C** *Rasa Dua*, T 71751; **D** *Asa*, cheapest in the area, clean rooms.

Restaurants There are several on the beachfront opposite the hotels, rather overpriced.

Transport to & from Benoa By bemo: connections with Denpasar's Suci terminal.

Uluwatu Temple

Pura Uluwatu, also known as Pura Ulu Atu, is considered one of Bali's *sadkahyangan* – the 6 most important temples on the island. Its full name, *Pura Luhur Uluwatu* literally means 'high headland', an apt name as the temple is spectacularly situated on the S tip of the Bukit Peninsula, perched on a cliff 70 m above the sea. The area used to be closed to visitors, and was jealously guarded by The Prince of Badung. The pura's inhospitable location also kept the curious away. Today it is easily accessible.

Pura Uluwatu may have been constructed during the 11th century, although it was substantially rebuilt in the 16th century – and as a result is rather difficult to date. The temple was owned by the Prince of Badung (today's Denpasar) and he alone was allowed to visit it. Once a year the Prince travelled to Uluwatu to make his offerings, a journey that he made until his death at the hands of the Dutch in 1906 (see page 671). It is said that part of the temple fell into the sea 18 months before the massacre at Denpasar – an event which was therefore prophesied.

Uluwatu has several unusual features; it is built of hard grey coral, which means that the temple's decoration has survived the centuries of weathering remarkably well. Secondly, the *candi bentar* or split gate is shaped in the form of a stylized *garuda* (mythical bird) rather than with smooth sides, as is usual. Also unusually, 2 statues of Ganesh flank the inner gateway. It was at Uluwatu that the famous Hindu saint, Danghyang Nirartha, is reputed to have achieved *moksa*, or oneness with the godhead.

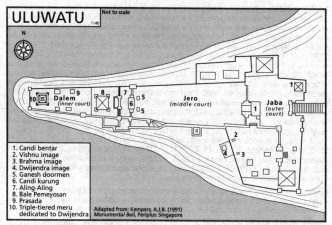

ULUWATU

Not to scale

N

10 Dalem (inner court) 9   8 7   5
                              6 5
Jero (middle court)

Jaba (outer court)

1

2

4   3

1. Candi bentar
2. Vishnu image
3. Brahma image
4. Dwijendra image
5. Ganesh doormen
6. Candi kurung
7. Aling-Aling
8. Bale Pemeyosan
9. Prasada
10. Triple-tiered meru dedicated to Dwijendra

Adapted from: Kempers, A.J.B. (1991)
Monumental Bali, Periplus: Singapore

There are several good **surfing beaches** near Uluwatu, including Bingin, Nyang Nyang (on the S coast) and Padang Padang (just S of Jimbaran Bay) (**see page 688**).

Accommodation A+ *Bali Cliffs Resort*, on cliff to S of Uluwatu, a/c, restaurant, 2 large pools, large hotel perched on a cliff overlooking the Indian Ocean, rather isolated and sterile but all facilities; **D** *Gobleg Inn*, off the track to the beach.

Transport to & from Uluwatu 20 km from Kuta. **By minibus**: minibuses (C1) leave from Kuta for Uluwatu; connections with Denpasar's Tegal terminal.

Nusa Dua

Nusa Dua is a 'planned resort', developed with assistance from the World Bank and funds from private developers. The first hotels opened here in 1983. The barren landscape of the Bukit Peninsula has been transformed into a tropical haven: 5-star hotels, beautiful gardens, tennis courts, horse riding and a golf course. The intention was to build a resort which would be isolated from the 'real' Bali and, in so doing, protect the locals from the excesses of international tourism. To make way for the resort, the few farmers who scratched a living from the reluctant soil were unceremoniously turfed out and an enclave created.

The entrance to the resort area is through huge split gates, and the hotels have been designed in keeping with Balinese traditions (rather loosely interpreted). There are no ugly high-rise blocks here, although the sheer scale of the development can be rather forbidding. Within the resort precinct are travel agencies, airline offices, banks, a post office, restaurants, art shops, a supermarket, performing arts shows – in short, everything that a Western tourist could want. Or at least that is what the consultants thought. What Nusa Dua does not provide is any insight, indeed any sense, of what life in Bali is like. Tourists are sheltered and pampered, but if you wish for more, it is necessary to venture beyond the Bukit Peninsula to Bali proper. On the beach, the surf is gentle along the N shore, but bigger to the S.

Accommodation The hotels below provide a wide variety of sports facilities – waterskiing, windsurfing, scuba diving, fishing, parasailing, horse riding, tennis.
   L *Amanusa*, PO Box 33, T 72333, F 72335, a/c, restaurant, pool, tennis, latest hotel in the luxurious Aman chain of resorts, 35 suite-rooms with own patios and sunken baths, but first reports indicate it is not up to the standard of its sister hotels; **A+** *Bali Tropic*, Jl. Pratama 34A, T 72130, F 72131, to the N of Nusa Dua, a/c, restaurant, pool; **A+** *Grand Hyatt*, PO

Box 53, T 71188, F 71084, a/c, restaurant, 5 pools, opened Apr 1991, large and very plush, with extensive and elaborate grounds; **A+** *Nusa Indah*, PO Box 36, T 71565, F 71908, a/c, 4 restaurants, pool, a recent addition to the Nusa Dua scene, consisting of a large 'U'-shaped block overlooking the beach, huge convention centre attached, gardens in formative stages, rather too large to be in any sense personal; **A+** *Melia Bali Sol*, PO Box 1048, T 71410, F 71360, a/c, several restaurants (rec.), large pool, owned by a Spanish chain of hotels, a fact reflected in the design which is rather Mediterranean, good sports facilities; **A+** *Nusa Dua Beach*, PO Box 1028, T 71210, F 71229, a/c, 4 restaurants, pool, part of the *Aerowisata* chain of hotels, the lavish entrance is through split gates into an echoing lobby with fountains, lush gardens and painstakingly recreated traditional Balinese buildings, good sports facilities, but rather featureless accommodation; **A+** *Putri Bali*, PO Box 1, T 71020, F 71139, J 320107, a/c, restaurant, pool, set in attractive landscaped grounds, all facilities, and some cottage-style accommodation; **A+** *Sheraton Lagoon*, PO Box 2044, T 71327, F 71326, attractive development with perhaps the largest pool in Bali; **A** *Club Med*, PO Box 7, T 71521, F 71831, a/c, 2 restaurants, pool, excellent sports facilities and cultural activities, and also caters well for children; **A** *Mirage*, PO Box 43, T 72147, F 72148, a/c, restaurant, pool; **B** *Bali Resort Palace*, Jl. Pratama, Tanjung Benoa, T 72026, F 72237, to the N of Nusa Dua, a/c, restaurant, pool; **B** *Club Bualu*, PO Box 6, T 71310, F 71313, a/c, restaurant, pool, away from the beach, but the most peaceful of the hotels in the area.

Restaurants All the hotels have a range of restaurants serving Indonesian, Balinese, other Asian cuisines and International food. Quality is generally good but prices are far higher than anywhere else in Bali – presumably because the management feel they have a captive clientele.

Sports Diving: Baruna Watersports at the *Melia Bali Sol*, T 71350, *Nusa Dua Beach*, T 71210, *Mirage*, T 72147 and *Nusa Indah*, T 71566; *Bali Marine Sports*, Club Bualu, T 71310. **Golf**: 18-hole Bali Golf Course (opened 1991, designed by Nelson and Wright), green fee US$65, club hire US$20, cart US$24, T 71791, F 71797.

Local transport Taxi: taxis and hotel cars will take guests into Kuta and elsewhere; prices are high. Car hire: *Avis*, Nusa Dua Beach Hotel, T 71220 ext 739 and *Club Med*, T 71521.

Useful addresses Interdenominational church service at the Nusa Dua Beach Hotel, Sun 1730.

Transport to & from Nusa Dua 27 km from Denpasar, 9 km from airport. **By bemo**: from Jl. Pantai in Kuta to Nusa Dua; and regular connections from Denpasar's Tegal terminal.

NORTH FROM DENPASAR TO UBUD

NE from Denpasar, the road passes through a series of craft villages specializing in the production of wood and stone carvings, and gold and silver jewellery. After 22 km through picturesque paddy fields and past steep-sided ravines, the road arrives at the hill resort and artists' colony of Ubud.

Craft villages on the road from Denpasar to Ubud

A number of craft villages, each specializing in a different craft, line the road N from Denpasar to Ubud. Most have been centres of production for many years – Miguel Covarrubias in his book *Island of Bali* notes that they had a reputation for the quality of their work in the 1930s. Since then the demands of the tourist industry have caused the mass production of second-rate pieces to become common. Nonetheless there are still some fine works to be found.

Batubulan, 8 km from Denpasar, is a ribbon-like village, stretched out for about 2 km along the road. It is renowned for its stone carving, although the production of carved wooden Balinese screens and doors is very much in evidence. In addition, there is a sizeable pottery industry here. Barong, kecak (fire dance) and kris dances are performed every day (times vary, 0900-1030, 1800-1930) at the N end of the village. One of Bali's principal performing arts academies – KOKAR/SMKI – is based in Batubulan. **Celuk**, 4 km on from Batubulan and 12 km from Denpasar, supports large numbers of gold and silversmiths who sell their jewellery from countless

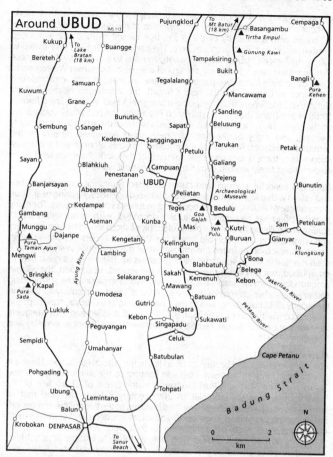

shops and showrooms along the road. Much of the work is inferior, although there are some shops selling slightly better quality jewellery; for example, *Runa* and *Banjar Telabah*. Another 4 km N from Celuk is another woodcarving village, **Batuan**. A range of products are on sale although the artists have a particular reputation for the quality of their carved wood panels. Finally, **Mas**, 20 km from Denpasar and 2 km S of Ubud, is a woodcarving village. In the mid-1980s this was the centre of woodcarving in Bali; now the industry is far more dispersed. Nevertheless, some of the finest (unpainted) works are still produced here and it is possible to watch the artists at work.

Ubud

Ubud was one of the more powerful of the principalities that controlled Bali before the Dutch extended their control over the whole island at the beginning of this century. Though primarily an upland rice-growing area it also gained an early reputation for the skill of its artists, particularly for the intricacy of their work. Perhaps it was the latent artistic temperament of the people of Ubud, coupled no doubt with the beauty of the place, that caused many of the entranced Western artists to base themselves here. The painter Walter Spies was invited to Bali by the Prince of Ubud, Raka Sukawati, and was so entranced with the place that he settled here – becoming the first of a series of bohemian Westerners to make Ubud their home (**see page 674**). These residents, in turn, attracted such luminaries as Charlie Chaplin, Noel Coward, the Woolworth heiress Barbara Hutton, and the American anthropologist Margaret Mead. In 1936, Spies, Bonnet (another artist) and the Prince established *Pita Maha*, the first artists' cooperative on the island. Since then Ubud has remained a centre of the arts in Bali, particularly painting, and many of the finest Balinese artists are based here or in the surrounding villages. Because of the influence of Spies, Bonnet and the artists' cooperative, there is a distinct style to much of the work. Paintings tend to be colourful and finely-worked depictions of the natural world.

Ubud is a peaceful, tranquil, and rather dispersed community, spread over hills and valleys with deep forested ravines and terraced rice fields. A spring near Ubud is the source of *AQUA*, the most popular of Indonesia's bottled waters. For many tourists, Ubud has become the cultural heart of Bali, with its numerous artist's studios and galleries as well as a plentiful supply of shops selling clothes, jewellery and woodcarving. Although old-timers feel that the numbers of people staying here has irrevocably changed the atmosphere of the area, once away from the 2 main roads, it is still a wonderful place to retreat to. There is not a great deal to do in Ubud, but it is a relaxing place to potter around. In addition, the villages around Ubud remain unspoilt and it is well worth exploring the surrounding countryside, either on foot or by bicycle. Around Ubud, particularly to the N in the vicinity of Tampaksiring, and to the E near Pejeng and Gianyar, is perhaps the greatest concentration of temples in Bali. The most detailed and accurate guide to these pura is A.J. Bernet Kempers's *Monumental Bali* (Periplus: Berkeley and Singapore, 1991).

Places of interest

Much of the charm and beauty of Ubud lies in the natural landscape. There are few official 'sights' in the town itself – in contrast to the surrounding area (see Excursions). The **Museum Puri Lukisan** is in the centre of Ubud. Two of the buildings here contain examples of 20th century Balinese art (and that of Europeans who have lived here). The third building, to the back of the compound, has a changing exhibition, organized by an artists' cooperative. 50 artists exhibit one or two pieces each; it is a showcase for their work. All work is for sale, but visitors are advised just to look at work here and then to visit the artist's studio, where they will be offered a wider range of work, at discounted prices. Admission: 500Rp. Open: 0800-1600.

Antonio Blanco, a Western artist who settled in Ubud has turned his home into a gallery. The house is in a stunning position, perched on the side of a hill, but the collection is disappointing and includes an array of his 'erotic art', where the frames are more interesting than the actual pictures. Blanco – unlike Spies and Bonnet – has had no influence on the style of local artists. Most people visit his house to meet the man, rather than to see his work. He is an eccentric character who is interesting to talk to about Balinese life. He may try to interest you in his recently published autobiography. Admission: 500Rp. To get there, walk W on the main road and over a ravine – the house is immediately on the left-hand side of the road.

The **Museum Neka**, 1½ km from town, on past Blanco's house, contains a good collection of traditional and contemporary Indonesian painting. Admission: 500Rp. Open: 0900-1700, Mon-Sun. There is a good art bookshop here.

GOA GAJAH IMS 114a

Not to Scale

To Ubud

To Gianyar →

stalls

Hariti pavilion

Main Cave

Meditation Niche

N

Rock cut candi remains

Buddha statues

Adapted from: Kempers, A.J.B. (1991) *Monumental Bali*, Periplus: Singapore

At the S end of Jalan Monkey Forest is the forest itself, which is overrun with monkeys. An attractive walk through the forest leads to the **Pura Dalem Agung Padangtegal**, a Temple of the Dead. Admission to forest: 500Rp. **NB**: Do NOT enter the forest with food – these monkeys have been known to bite and victims will only have 48 hours to get to Jakarta for a rabies injection. Some tourists have also taken to teasing the animals; it is cruel and dangerous. Back in town on Jalan Raya Ubud, opposite Jalan Monkey Forest, is the **Puri Saren**, with richly carved gateways and courtyards. West of here is the **Pura Saraswati**, behind the Lotus Café.

Excursions

Sangeh and the **Pura Bukit Sari** are two temples about 25 km W of Ubud, but easier to reach via Mengwi (**see page 724**).

Craft villages line the route to Batubulan and Denpasar (**see page 702**).

Goa Gajah or 'Elephant Cave', lies about 4 km E of Ubud, via Peliatan, on the right-hand side of the road and just before Bedulu. The caves are hard to miss as there is a large car park, with an imposing line of stallholders. The complex is on the side of a hill overlooking the Petanu River, down some steep steps.

Hewn out of the rock, the entrance to the **cave** has been carved to resemble the mouth of a demon and is surrounded by additional carvings of animals, plants, rocks and monsters. The name of the complex is thought to have been given by the first visitors who mistakenly thought that the demon was an elephant. The small 'T'-shaped cave is man-made and contains 15 niches carved out of the rock. Those on the main passageway are long enough to lead archaeologists to speculate that they were sleeping chambers. At the end of one of the arms of the 'T' is a 4-armed statue of Ganesh, and at the end of the other, a collection of lingams.

The **bathing pools** next to the caves are more interesting. These were only discovered in the mid-1950s by the Dutch archaeologist J.C. Krijgsman, who excavated the area in front of the cave on information provided by local people. He discovered stone steps and eventually uncovered 2 bathing pools (probably one for men and the other for women). Stone carvings of the legs of 3 figures were uncovered in each of the 2 pools. These seemed to have been cut from the rock at the same time that the pools were dug. It was realized that the heads and torsos of 3 buxom nymphs which had been placed in front of the cave entrance belonged with the legs, and the 2 halves were happily re-united. Originally, the figures were connected to a water system and acted as waterspouts.

Stairs lead down from the cave and pool area to some meditation niches, with 2 small statues of the Buddha in an attitude of meditation. The remains of an

706 INDONESIA – BALI

Bronze kettledrums of Vietnam

One of the most remarkable and intriguing of metal objects found in Southeast Asia is the bronze kettledrum. These were first produced in Northern Vietnam and southern China in the 4th century BC and were associated with the Dongson culture. However, they have also been discovered widely distributed across island Southeast Asia – as far east as the island of Alor in Nusa Tenggara and Irian Jaya. In total, 26 kettledrums have been found in Indonesia. Some of the examples discovered were probably traded from Vietnam; others may have been made in situ. Whatever the case, they are skilfully produced, wonderfully decorated, and were clearly objects of considerable value and prestige.

Strictly-speaking they are not drums at all but percussion instruments, as they have no membrane. In Indonesia they are known as *nekara*. They consist of a hollow body, open at the bottom, and covered at the top with a metal tympan. In size, they range from 0.4 m-1.3 m in diameter, and 0.4 m-1.0 m in height. The top is often highly decorated with birds, houses, canoes carrying the dead to the afterlife, dancers and drummers. They are also often surmounted by three-dimensional figures of frogs symbolizing rain. Hence their other name: rain drums. There is a fine collection of drums in the National Museum, Jakarta (see page 532).

enormous relief were also found in 1931 (by Conrad Spies, the painter and Walter Spies's cousin), depicting several stupas. To get there, walk down from the cave and bathing pools, through fields, and over a bridge. The complex is thought to date from the 11th century. Admission: 500Rp. Dress: sarong. **Getting there**: by bemo from Ubud or from the Batubulan terminal outside Denpasar; alternatively, join a tour.

Yeh Pulu is 2 km E of Goa Gajah, beautifully set amongst terraced rice fields, and a short walk from the end of the road. It also happens to be the location of the local laundrette, which has resulted in a profusion of plastic 'Rinso' bags littering the stream. Yeh Pulu is one of the oldest holy places in Bali, dating from the 14th or 15th century. Cut into the rock are 25 m of vigorous carvings depicting village life intermingled with Hindu and Balinese gods: figures carrying poles, men on horseback, Krishna saluting, wild animals and vegetation. Originally these would have been plastered over – and perhaps painted – although almost all of the plaster has since weathered away. A small cell cut into the rock at the S end of the reliefs is thought to have been the abode of a hermit – who probably helped to maintain the carvings. The site was 'discovered' by the artist Nieuwenkamp in 1925 when he was sketching nearby. Until 1937 when the site was renovated, water from the overhanging paddy fields washed over the carvings causing significant erosion. There is also a small bathing pool here.

Bernet Kempers, in his book *Monumental Bali*, interprets the sequence of carvings as follows, beginning at the top. There is an opening piece, followed by five 'scenes':

Opening: A standing man with his arm raised opens the yarn. This is probably Krishna, who as a young shepherd protected his friends from an irate Indra by using Mount Govardhana as an umbrella.

Scene I: A man carries two vessels (probably of palm wine) on a pole over his shoulders and is led by a woman of high status towards a hut where an old woman waits at a pair of double doors.

Scene II: Here, an old woman rests in a cave while a man, to her left, approaches with a hoe over his shoulder. Behind him sits an ascetic dwarf with a turban. On the far right is a demon with fangs and a large sacrificial ladel.

Scene III: Surrounded by trees, a man on a horse gallops towards two figures, with weapons raised, who are attacking a bear (?) while a fourth man advances from behind. In the lower right corner a frog with a sword fights for his life against a large snake.

Scene IV: Two men, their hunting trip completed and successful, carry a pair of dead bears on a pole.

DONGSON DRUM

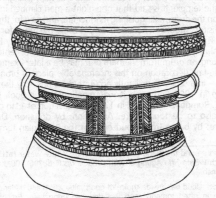

Dongson drum and mantle, bronze (79cm in width, 63cm high).
Unearthed, Northern Vietnam 1893–94.

Scene V: A woman holds a horse's tail while two monkeys play on her back. She is either trying to restrain the horse and rider, or they are helping to pull her up a hill.

Admission: 550Rp. **Dress:** sarong. **Open:** it is probably possible to visit this site at any time, as there are no 'entrance gates'. At the beginning of the path there is a restaurant, and close by is the *Lantur Homestay* (**E**). **Getting there:** Yeh Pulu is 350 m off the main Ubud-Gianyar road just S of the Tampaksiring turning, and is signposted to Bendung Bedaulu. Bemos from Ubud will drop passengers at the turning; it is an easy walk from there to the site.

The road north from Bedulu

400m N of Bedulu, is the small, poorly labelled, **Purbakala Archaeological Museum**, consisting largely of a collection of sarcophagi. About 200 m further N still is the **Pura Kebo Edan** or 'Mad Bull Temple', a rather ramshackle and ill-kept temple. Among the monumental weathered stone figures in the courtyard is a 4 m-high statue of Bima dancing on a corpse, its eyes open, protected under a wooden pavilion. The figure – sometimes known as the 'Pejeng Giant' – is renowned for its 'miraculous' penis, pierced with a peg or pin (used to stimulate women during intercourse, a feature of sexual relations across the region; **see page 41**). Snakes curl around the figure's wrists and ankles, and his face is covered by a mask, attached with ribbons around the back of the head. Although the figure was thought to be an image of Bima – and it is in all likelihood demonic – it is probably more accurately interpreted as an incarnation of Siva. Admission: by donation. Dress: sarong. **Pura Pusering Jagat** (the 'Navel of the World' Temple), is 50 m off the main road, a short distance N from Kebo Edan. **Pura Panataran Sasih** lies another 250 m N in Pejeng and is thought to date from the 9th or 10th century. This temple was the original navel pura of the old Pejeng Kingdom. The entrance is flanked by a pair of fine stone elephants. Walk through impressive split gates to see the **'Moon of Pejeng'** (*sasih* means 'moon'). It is housed in a raised pavilion towards the back of the compound and is supposedly the largest bronze kettledrum in the world (see box). In Balinese folklore, the drum is supposed to have been one of the wheels of the chariot that carries the moon across the night sky. The wheel fell to earth and was kept (still glowing with an inner fire) in the temple. It is said that one night a man climbed into the tower and urinated on the drum, extinguishing its inner fire, and paid for the desecration with his life. Visitors should on no account try to climb the tower for a better look at the drum. The drum is believed to date from the 3rd century BC, although no-one is absolutely sure – certainly, it has been housed here for centuries though. It may be a Dongson drum from Vietnam or it may be a later example produced elsewhere. The fine decoration on this incomparable piece of bronze work was first recorded – in a series of brilliantly accurate drawings – by the artist W.O.J. Nieuwenkamp in 1906 (although it was mentioned in a book by the blind chronicler G.E. Rumphius published in 1705). A collection of 11th century stone carvings are also to be found here. Admission: by donation. Dress: sarong. **Getting there**: by bemo from Ubud or from the Batubulan terminal outside Denpasar.

Tours Day tours around the island (10,000-30,000Rp). **White-water rafting**: down the Ayung River with *Wisata Tirta Agung* or with *Sobek Tours* (T 88796) 100,000Rp, for a 3-4 hour trip and lunch.

Accommodation Ubud has a wide choice of good value, clean and generally high quality accommodation in often romantic and well-designed bungalows. Except in the more expensive hotels, breakfast is included in the rates.
    L *Amandari*, Kedewatan, T 95333, F 95335, (NW of town), restaurant, pool, the ultimate hotel, set above the Agung River, among paddy fields, excellent service (personal staff for each of the 29 bungalow-suites), beautiful rooms, magnificently positioned pool and excellent food, one honeymooner called it 'Heaven on Earth', rec; **L** *Kupu Kupu Barong*, Kedewatan, F 95079, (NW of town), restaurant, pool, stunning position overlooking the Ayung River, superb service and rooms. No children under 12 years old.
    A *Cahaya Dewata*, Kedewatan, in between the *Amandari* and *Kupu Kupu Barong*, (out of town), excellent restaurant, pool, rec; **A** *Dewi Sri*, Jl. Hanoman, Padangtegal (near the intersection with Jl. Monkey Forest), T 95300, F 95005, pool, 2-storeyed thatched bungalows amid the rice fields, well-run, rec; **A** *Padma Indah Cottages*, Campuan, T 95719, F 95091, a/c, restaurant, pool, cottages could sleep 4, attractive cottages but badly managed. **A** *Siti Bungalows*, Jl. Kajeng 3, T 95699, F 95643, restaurant rec, very peaceful, 4 poster beds; **A**

Tjampuhan, PO Box 15, Denpasar, T 95368, F 95137, at W end of Jl. Raya Ubud, over the river and up the hill, this hotel was originally the artist Walter Spies' home, restaurant rec, small pool, stunning setting on the side of a ravine, lovely gardens, bungalows built in layers up the ravine, romantic rooms with old wooden beds and pleasant sitting areas, rec; **A** *Ulun Ubud*, Sanggingan, T 95024, F 95524, restaurant, pool, traditional Balinese style, attractive position on hillside facing the Campuan River.

B *Fibra Inn*, Jl. Monkey Forest, T 95451, F 95125, pool, good rooms and open-air bathrooms, hot water, rec; **B** *Oka Kartini*, Jl. Raya Ubud, T 95193, F 95759, pool, small hotel with friendly staff, rooms are a little over-elaborate but thoughtfully designed, rec; **B** *Pertiwi Bungalows*, Jl. Monkey Forest, T 95236, F 95559, restaurant, pool, lovely rooms, open-air bathroom, rec; **B** *Pringga Juwita*, off Jl. Raya Ubud (by *Miro's restaurant*), T 95451, F 95125, pool, fan, hot water, lovely grounds, well designed rooms, price includes breakfast, rec, **A** for a cottage with open-air bathroom, kitchen and sitting-room; **B** *Sehati*, Jl. Jembawan 7, T 95460, lovely cool rooms overlooking a leafy ravine, rec; **B-E** *Matahari Cottages*, Jl. Jembawan, T 95459, more expensive rooms are well-designed and secluded, some hot water, rec; **C** *Kori Agung*, Penestanan-Campuan, T 95166, a little out of town, off the main road, but lovely rooms with verandah, cold water showers only, rec; **C** *Kubu Ku*, Jl. Monkey Forest, at the end of the road, set in the middle of paddy fields with lovely rooms; **C** *Mandia*, 30 m off Jl. Monkey Forest, T 80571, lovely garden atmosphere, rec; **C** *Penestanan Bungalows*, Campuan, T 95604, F 95603, small pool, a little out of town, set scenically on a hill overlooking paddy fields, good rooms, hot water; **C** *Puri Garden*, Jl. Monkey Forest, T 95395, lovely water garden, good rooms, fan, rec; **C** *Siddhartha's Shelter*, Penestanan Kaja (Campuan), T 95748, W of town, set among paddy fields; **C** *Wisata Cottages*, Campuan, nr Neka Museum, T 95017, pool, lovely position with views over paddy fields.

D *Agungs*, off Jl. Raya Ubud (by *Nomad's restaurant*), friendly owner, but rooms are a little overpriced; **D** *Dewangga*, off Jl. Monkey Forest (by the football field), attractive setting, nice garden, good rooms, open-air bathroom, rec; **D-E** *Ibu Arsa*, Peliatan, (E of town), older rooms are rather dark, the newer rooms are characterful with attractive open bathrooms, friendly, rec; **D** *Ibunda Inn*, Jl. Monkey Forest, T 80571, 2-storeyed thatched houses with baths, hot water; **D** *Kajeng*, Jl. Kajeng 29, T 95018, rooms with verandahs overlooking a ravine and duck pond, clean with attractive open-air mandis; **D** *Karyawan*, Jl. Monkey Forest, lovely gardens, clean, rec; **D** *Paddy Fields*, off Jl. Monkey Forest (opposite Café Wayan), attractive position overlooking rice paddy, good breakfast, friendly owners, rec; **D** *Sama's*, off Jl. Raya Ubud (by *Miro's restaurant*), wonderful position among paddy fields, 3 rooms, clean, charming owner, rec; **D** *Shanti Homestay*, Jl. Kajeng 5, new homestay, friendly; **D** *Sri*, Jl. Monkey Forest, T 95394, very clean, rec; **D** *Ubud Terrace Bungalows*, Jl. Monkey Forest, situated in a quiet grove, friendly management; **D-E** *Suarsena House*, Jl. Monkey Forest (side street), clean, more expensive rooms with large bathrooms.

E *Alit's*, Jl. Monkey Forest, nice garden, clean rooms, friendly; **E** *Anom*, Jl. Monkey Forest (side street), only 3 rooms, but good; **E** *Arjana*, Jl. Kajeng 6, T 98233, quiet, clean rooms, good bathrooms, rec; **E** *Budi*, off Jl. Monkey Forest (by the football field), 3 rooms, clean, fan, good value, rec; **E** *Kubu Roda*, off Jl. Raya Ubud (by *Miro's restaurant*). 3 rooms, fan, friendly owners; **E** *Pandawa Homestay*, Jl. Monkey Forest, good value, big rooms; **E** *Pande Homestay*, Peliatan, (E of town), friendly, clean; **E** *Pujitwo*, Jl. Arjuna (off Jl. Monkey Forest), mosquito nets, large breakfast included, basic but the cheapest around; **E** *Puri Muwa*, Jl. Monkey Forest, T 95046, well-decorated rooms; **E** *Raka House* (off Jl. Meluti – near the football field), 3 or 4 rooms, rec; **E** *Roja's*, Jl. Kajeng 1, attractive bungalows, well kept garden, rec; **E** *Sukerti*, Jl. Bima, Banjar Kalah (near intersection with Jl. Raya Ubud), opened 1991, clean and very friendly; **E** *Wayan Sara*, off Jl. Monkey Forest (next to *Okawati's restaurant*), mandi, verandah and large breakfast, good value, rec.

Restaurants Food in Ubud is good, particularly international food. Most restaurants serve a mixture of Balinese, Indonesian and international dishes. ♦♦*Ary's Warung*, Jl. Raya Ubud (opposite the temple complex), international and Indonesian food served in relaxed, occasionally bohemian atmosphere, with musical accompaniment, frequented by the Ubud cognoscente, rec; *Bagus Café*, Jl. Raya Ubud, Peliatan (SE of the centre), Balinese specialities; ♦♦*Café Bali*, Jl. Monkey Forest (bottom end of football field), international, attractive setting, rec; ♦♦*Café Lotus*, Jl. Raya Ubud, overlooks lotus ponds of Puri Suraswati Palace, international (particularly Italian), overpriced; ♦♦♦*Café Wayan*, Jl. Monkey Forest, international, some seafood, very popular, delicious desserts, Balinese buffet on Sun evenings, rec; ♦♦*Gayatri's*, Jl. Monkey Forest, rec; *Griya's*, Jl. Raya Ubud, barbecued chicken is rec; ♦♦*Ibu Rai*, Jl. Monkey Forest (next to the football field), Balinese and international, rec; *Kura Kura*, Jl. Monkey Forest (at the end, near Jl. Padangtegal), Mexican; *Lilies*, Jl. Monkey Forest, rec; *Lotus Garden*, Jl.

Raya Ubud, attractive setting but a little run down, starts to close at about 2100; *Miro's*, Jl. Raya Ubud, in garden off Jl. Raya Ubud, excellent service, generous helpings, good food at very reasonable price, rec; ♦♦*Mumbul's Garden Terrace*, Jl. Raya Ubud (not far from the *Puri Lukisan Art Museum*) for excellent salads, international and Balinese food, rec; *Murni's Warung*, overlooking ravine at W end of Jl. Raya Ubud, Indonesian and international (mostly American), an old-time favourite; ♦♦*Nomad*, Jl. Raya Ubud, T 95131, international and Balinese including Balinese duck and suckling pig, good guacamole; *Pizzeria*, Jl. Monkey Forest, rec; ♦♦*Pondok Tjampuhan*, next to *Blanco's House*, pizza, Indonesian, Chinese, good position overlooking ravine; ♦♦♦*Tjampuhan Hotel restaurant*, W end of Jl. Raya Ubud, Indonesian and international, rec; ♦♦*Ubud Raya*, Jl. Raya Ubud (E end), Javanese, Japanese and international, rec; ♦*Night market*, Jl. Raya, very cheap but good food and a popular place, rec.

Bars *Beggars Bush*, English pub; *Miros*, Jl. Raya Ubud, cocktails.

Entertainment Artists colonies: Ubud has perhaps the greatest concentration of artists in Indonesia, exceeding even Yogya. Many will allow visitors to watch them at work in the hope that they will then buy their work. The *Pengosekan Community of Artists* is on Jl. Bima. **Dance**: there are numerous performances every day of the week; most begin at between 1900 and 2000 and cost 5,000Rp. A board at the *Bina Wisata Tourist Centre*, Jl. Raya Ubud (opposite the palace) lists the various dances, with time, location and cost. There are almost nightly performances at the *Puri Saren* at the junction of Jl. Raya Ubud and Jl. Monkey Forest. Performances include legong, Mahabharata, barong, kecak, Ramayana ballet and wayang kulit (5,000Rp). **Videos**: There is a very popular Video Bar on the far side of the football field on Jl. Monkey Forest. 2 shows a night of Western films.

Sport Swimming: some hotel pools are open to non-residents; the *Andong Inn*, Jl. Andong 26A; *Champlong Sari Hotel*, 3,000Rp; *Okawatis restaurant*, Jl. Monkey Forest, 2,500Rp; *Ubud Village*, Jl. Monkey Forest, 3,000Rp (for the day; you can come and go as you like).

Shopping Ubud offers a good range of crafts for sale. **Painting**: Ubud painters have a distinctive style, using bright colours and the depiction of natural and village scenes (**see page 676**). There is a large selection of paintings to be found in the town and galleries to be concentrated along the E section of Jl. Raya Ubud. It is possible to visit the artists in their homes; enquire at the galleries. **Batik and ikat**: *Ibu Rai travel agent* near *Lilies restaurant* on Jl. Monkey Forest; *Lotus Studio*, Jl. Raya Ubud; *Kunang Kunang*, Jl. Raya Ubud. **Books**: *Ubud Bookshop*, Jl. Raya Ubud (next to Ary's Warung) for a good range of English language books on the region.

   Clothing: *Bali Rosa*, on Jl. Raya Ubud, towards Campuan, for accessories (bags, belts, beaded pumps) rec; *Balika*, Jl. Monkey Forest for fashion clothing. *Hare Om*, Jl. Monkey Forest for well-designed but expensive hand-painted silk scarves and shirts; *Lotus Studio* for unusual designs and great hats; the market on the corner of Jl. Raya Ubud and Jl. Monkey Forest offers a range of 'travellers' clothes – T-shirts, batik etc.

   Jewellery: there are a number of shops along Jl. Raya Ubud. Good designs but the quality is not always very high– it looks better than it feels. **Pottery**: near the Post Office, just off Jl. Raya Ubud. **Shoes**: *Hare Om* for a range of individually designed suede shoes. *Bali Rosa*, Jl. Raya Ubud, for 'pumps'. **Woodcarving**: concentrated on the Peliatan road out of town. The so-called 'duck man' of Ubud (Ngurah Umum) is to be found on the road to Goa Gajah, with a selection of wooden fruits and birds. Recommended shop near the *Bamboo restaurant*, off Jl. Monkey Forest, facing the football field. **Wind chimes**: shop specializing in wind chimes at the end of Jl. Monkey Forest in the paddy fields – worth a visit.

Local transport Bicycle hire: bicycles are the best way to get about (apart from walking); there are several hire places on Jl. Monkey Forest, 3,000Rp/day. **Motorbike hire**: several outfits on Jl. Monkey Forest, from 7,000Rp/day. **Car hire**: hire shops on Jl. Monkey Forest. 40,000Rp/day.

Banks & money changers Numerous money changers will change cash and travellers' cheques and offer rates similar to banks.

Useful addresses Post Office: Jl. Jembawan 1 (road running S off Jl. Raya Ubud, opposite Neka Gallery); poste restante. **Postal Agents**: *Nominasi*, Jl. Monkey Forest 67 and Jl. Raya Ubud. **Perumtel**: for fax, telex and international telephone, Jl. Andong (close to intersection with Jl. Raya Ubud) and Jl. Raya Ubud (near *Nomad Bar and restaurant*), or on the road to Petulu, at the E end of Jl. Raya Ubud. **Police**: on the road to Petulu, E end of Jl. Raya Ubud.

Tour companies & travel agents Double check airline tickets bought here; there have been complaints that despite assurances that flights are confirmed, on reaching the airport, visitors have found they are not. *Ibu Rai*, Jl. Monkey Forest 72, T 95066, rec; *Cahaya Sakti Utama*, Jl. Raya Ubud, T 95131, F 95115; *Kurnia*, Jl. Raya Ubud, T 95020 for buses to Lombok and around Bali, tours and car rental; *Nominasi*, Jl. Monkey Forest 67-71, T 95065.

Tourist offices Bina Wisata, Jl. Raya Ubud (opposite the Puri Saren). Good for information on daily performances but otherwise not very helpful.

Transport to & from Ubud By bus: there are 'shuttle' (in fact not as regular as the name implies) buses to Kuta, the Ngurah Rai Airport (4,000Rp), Candi Dasa, Padangbai, Sanur, Denpasar. Details are available at the travel or tour agents. **By bemo:** bemos leave from the Pasar Ubud in the centre of town, at the junction of Jl. Monkey Forest and Jl. Raya Ubud; regular connections with Denpasars' Batubulan terminal (700Rp). **By taxi:** taxis congregate at the Pasar Ubud in the centre of town.

NORTH OF UBUD: GUNUNG KAWI & TIRTA EMPUL

4 km E of Ubud is the small town of Bedulu, close to which are the sights of Goa Gajah and Yeh Pulu (see page 705). 10 km N of Bedulu, on the road to Lake Batur, shortly after the village of Tampaksiring, are 2 popular tourist destinations: the temples of Gunung Kawi and Tirta Empul. By continuing N from here, the road runs up a steep-sided valley to Mount Batur and the town of Penelokan.

Gunung Kawi

Gunung Kawi, literally the 'Mountain of the Poets', is one of the most impressive, and unusual, temples in Bali. A steep rock stairway, with high sides leads down to the bottom of a humid, tree-filled, ravine. At the bottom lies the temple. The whole complex was literally hewn out of the rock during the 11th century, when it was thought to have been created as the burial temple for King Anak Wungsu and his wives, who probably threw themselves on his funeral pyre. Visitors descend 315 steps to a massive rock archway, and from there to the 9 tombs which face each other on either side of the Pakerisan River. These 2 rows of candis, 4 on the S side and 5 on the N, were cut out of the rock. It is believed that the 5 on the N bank of the river were for the King and his 4 wives, whilst the 4 on the

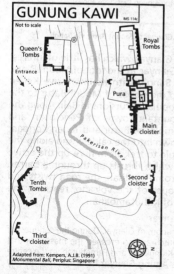

S bank may have been for 4 concubines. They resemble temples and are the earliest traces of a style of architecture which became popular in Java in the following centuries. As such they may represent the precursor to the Balinese *meru* (**see page 724**). Balinese mythology maintains that Empu Kuturan, a royal prince, carved these shrines with his fingernails. Over the years there has been disagreement over the function of the candis. The art historian C. Lekkerkerker in 1920 postulated that the corpses were left in the cells to be eaten by wild animals, picked-over by birds, and to putrify and degenerate. Rather later, Bernet Kempers argued that they were not tombs at all, but merely symbols of death.

East of the 5 candis on the far side of the river is a cloister of various courtyards and rooms, also carved out of the rock. They were created for the Buddhist priests who lived here (perhaps reflecting its Buddhist origins, visitors are asked to remove their shoes before entering). Still farther away, on the other side of the river, is the so-called 'tenth tomb'. The local people call this tomb 'the priest's house' and it was not discovered by Western archaeology until 1949 when Krijgsman revealed the site. The tenth tomb is, in all likelihood, a monastery and consists of a courtyard encircled by niches. To get to the tenth tomb take the path across the paddy fields that runs from the rock-hewn gateway that leads down into the gorge; it is about a 1 km walk. Admission: 550Rp. Dress: sash or sarong required. There is accommodation close by in Tampaksiring e.g. *Gusti Homestay*. Tampaksiring also has a number of good jewellery workshops.

Transport to & from Gunung Kawi By bemo: connections with Denpasar's Batubulan terminal or from Ubud to Tampaksiring. It is about a 3 km walk from here, passing Tirta Empul (see below), although bemos also make the journey to the temple site.

Tirta Empul

Tirta Empul is 2 km N of Tampaksiring, 1 km on from Gunung Kawi. The temple is one of the holiest sights on Bali and is a popular pilgrimage stop, evident by the maze of trinket stalls that has to be negotiated on the way out of the complex.

Tirta Empul is built on the site of a holy spring which is said to have magical healing powers. In the past, barong masks were bathed here to infuse them with supernatural powers during the dance. Originally constructed in 960, during the reign of Raja Candra Bayasingha, the temple is divided into 3 courtyards, and has been extensively restored and little of the original structure remains – bar a few stone fragments. The outer courtyard contains 2 long rectangular pools fed by 30 or more water spouts, each of which has a particular function – for example, there is one for spiritual purification. The holy springs bubble up in the inner courtyard. During the Galungan Festival (see page 687), sacred *barong* dance masks are brought here to be bathed in holy water. Admission: 550Rp.

Transport to & from Tirta Empul By bemo: take a bemo from Denpasar's Batubulan terminal or Ubud towards Tampaksiring. The temple is 2 km N of the town centre; either walk or catch a bemo. From here it is a 1 km walk to Gunung Kawi (see above).

NORTH OF DENPASAR: Gianyar to Mount Batur via Bangli

East of Ubud is the royal town of Gianyar, which has little of interest to attract the tourist. 15 km N of Gianyar, at the foot of Mount Batur, is another former royal capital, Bangli, with its impressive Kehen Temple. A further 20 km leads up the slopes of Mount Batur to the crater's edge – one of the most popular excursions in Bali. Along the rim of the caldera are the mountain towns of Penelokan and Kintamani, and the important temples of Batur and Tegen Koripan. From Kintamani, a road winds down into the caldera and along the W edge of Lake Batur. It is possible to trek from here up the active cone of Mount Batur (1,717 m), which thrusts up through a barren landscape of lava flows. North from Penulisan, the road twists and turns for 36 km down the N slopes of the volcano, reaching the narrow coastal strip at the town of Kubutambahan.

Gianyar

Gianyar is the former capital of the Kingdom of Gianyar. During the conquest of Bali, this principality sided with the Dutch and so escaped the massacres that accompanied the defeat of Denpasar, Klungkung and Pemetjutan. In the centre of Gianyar, on Jalan Ngurah Rai, is the **Agung Gianyar Palace**, surrounded by attractive red-brick walls. It is not normally open to the public, but the owner, Ide Anak Agung Gede Agung, a former politician and the rajah of Gianyar, does let visitors look around his house if asked. The bemo station is 5 mins walk to the W of the palace, also on Jalan Ngurah Rai. Traditionally regarded as Bali's weaving centre, there is only a limited amount of cloth on sale these days. Gianyar's other claim to fame is that it is said to have the best *babi guling* (roast suckling pig) on the island.

Accommodation B *Agung Gianyar Palace Guesthouse*, within the Palace walls.

Entertainment Dance: at 1900, every Mon and Thurs, a cultural show including dinner is staged at the Agung Gianyar Palace, T 93943/51654.

Tourist offices Gianyar Tourist Office (Dinas Pariwisata), Jl. Ngurah Rai 21, T 93401. The office provides visitors with pamphlets on sights in the regency.

Transport to & from Gianyar 27 km from Denpasar. **By bemo**: regular connections with Denpasar's Batubulan terminal.

Bangli

Bangli is a peaceful, rather beautiful town and the former capital of a mountain principality. Never the strongest of Balinese kingdoms, it capitulated to the Dutch in the middle of the 19th century. Bangli's principal claim to fame is the **Pura Kehen**, probably founded in the 13th century. There is some dispute over the true origin of the temple as inscriptions within the compound have been dated to the 9th century. Nonetheless, Pura Kehen is one of Bali's more impressive temples. It is the second largest on Bali and is built on the side of a wooded slope. Elephants flank the imposing entrance, leading up to 3 terraced courtyards, through finely carved and ornamented gateways decorated with myriad demons. The lower courtyard is dominated by a wonderful *waringin* tree (*Ficus benjamina*). It is here that performances are held to honour the gods. The middle courtyard houses the offertory shrines, while the top-most courtyard contains an eleven-tiered *meru* with a carved wood and stone base. Admission: by donation. The temple is about 1 km N of town on the back road to Besakih and Penelokan.

Accommodation *Jaya Giri Homestay*, by the Pura Kehen.

Transport to & from Bangli By bemo: from Denpasar's Batubulan terminal.

Mount Batur

The spectacular landscape of Mount Batur is one of the most visited inland areas on Bali. Despite the hawkers, bustle and general commercialization, it still makes a worthwhile trip. The huge crater – 20 km in diameter – contains within it Lake Batur and the active Mount Batur (1,717 m), with buckled lava flows on its slopes. The original **Mount Batur**, which first erupted centuries ago, must have been immense. In 1917, an eruption killed over 1,000 people and destroyed 65,000 homes and more than 2,000 temples. The lava flow stopped at the foot of the village of Batur's temple, which the local people took as a good omen and continued to live there. In 1926, the village of Batur, and its temple, were completely destroyed by another eruption. This time the village moved to a safer site.

Lake Batur in the centre of the caldera is considered sacred, as it is thought to be the fountain-head of the water that flows into Bali's rice fields. A local legend recounts that the Goddess of the Crater Lake, Dewi Danu and her male counterpart, the God of Mount Agung, rose from the depths of the lake and extended their power over the lands and waters of Bali. Dewi Danu and the God of Mount Agung are complementary; female and male, and occupy the 2 highest peaks on the island, Agung and Batur.

A steep road winds down the crater side and then through the lava boulders and along the W shore of Lake Batur. There are hot springs here and paths up the

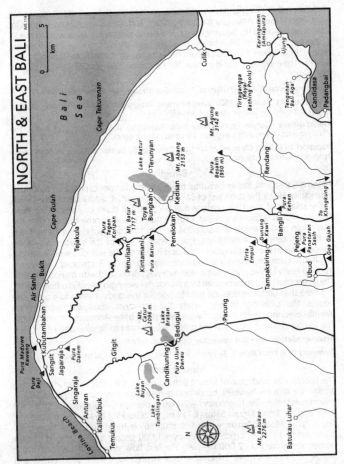

sides of Mount Batur, through the area's extraordinary landscape. **Treks** begin either from Purajati or Toya Bungkah (a 4 and 6 hour round trip respectively), or around the lake (guides are available from Ged's, see below). Boats can be hired from the village of Kedisan, on the S shore of Lake Batur, or from Toya Bungkah, to visit the traditional Bali Aga village of Trunyan and its cemetery, on the E side of the lake (see page 720).

On the W rim of the crater are 2 villages, Kintamani and Penelokan. Large-scale restaurants here cater for the tour group hoards. The area is also overrun with hawkers selling batik and woodcarvings. **Penelokan**, is perched on the edge of the crater and its name means 'place to look'. About 5 km N of here, following the crater rim, is the rather drab town of **Kintamani**, which is a centre of orange and passionfruit cultivation. The town's superb position overlooking the crater makes up for its drabness. Ged's trekking is based here; they can advise on the best walks in the area and provide a guide for the more dangerous routes up to the crater rim.

Just S of Kintamani is **Pura Batur**, spectacularly positioned on the side of the crater. This is the new temple built as a replacement for the original Pura Batur which was engulfed by lava in 1926. Although the temple is new and therefore not of great historical significance, it is in fact the second most important temple in Bali after Pura Besakih. As Stephen Lansing explains in his book *Priests and programmers* (1991), the Goddess of the Crater Lake is honoured here and symbolically the temple controls water for all the island's irrigation systems (**see page 668**). Ultimately therefore, it controls the livelihoods of the majority of the population. A 9-tiered meru honours the goddess and unlike other temples it is open 24 hours a day. A virgin priestess still selects 24 boys as priests who remain tied as servants of the temple for the rest of their lives. The most senior is regarded as the earthly representative of the goddess, with whom he is magically linked.

Excursions

Pura Tegen Koripan is on the main road 200 m N of Penulisan, a town on the N edge of the crater rim. Steep stairs lead up to the temple which stands at a height of over 1,700 m above sea-level. The temple was first visited by a European at a relatively early date – a scientist, Dr. J. Jacobs, climbed up to the temple in 1885. However, after that first visit, the local population forcibly kept foreigners away from the temple and it was only in 1918 that the archaeologist Nieuwenkamp managed to gain admission and become its second western visitor. The temple contains a number of highly weathered statues, thought to be portraits of royalty. They are dated between 1011 and 1335. Artistically they are surprising because they seem to anticipate later Majapahit works. Admission: 500Rp. Open: Mon-Sun. **Getting there**: catch a bemo running N and get off at Penulisan.

Accommodation On Lake Batur: **C-D** *Under the Volcano*, good restaurant, clean rooms, friendly management; **D** *The Art Centre*, (or *Balai Seni*), Toya Bungkah, quite old but still a good place to stay; **D** *Segara Bungalow*; **D** *Surya Homestay*, great position; **F** *Mountain View*. Penelokan: **B-D** *Lake View Homestay*, basic but good views over the lake; **C-D** *Gunawan Losmen*, clean, private bathroom, fantastic position. Kintamani: **C** *Puri Astina*, large clean rooms; *Losmen Sasaka*, stunning views over the crater and lake.

Transport to & from Lake Batur By bus: regular coach services from Denpasar (2-3 hrs); By bemo: from Denpasar's Batubulan terminal to Bangli and then another to Penelokan. Some bemos drive down into the crater to Kedisan and Toya Bungkah.

PURA BESAKIH AND MOUNT AGUNG

The holiest and most important temple on Bali is Pura Besakih, situated on the slopes of Bali's sacred Mount Agung. Twinned with Mount Batur to the NW, Agung is the highest mountain on the island, rising to 3,142 m. It is easiest to approach Besakih by taking the road N from Klungkung, a distance of 22 km. However, there are also 2 E-W roads, linking the Klungkung route to Besakih with Bangli in the W and Amlapura in the E. Although little public transport uses these routes, they are among the most beautiful drives in Bali, through verdant terraced rice paddys.

Besakih

Pura Besakih is not one temple, but a complex of 22 puras that lie scattered over the S slopes of Mount Agung at an altitude of about 1,000 m. Of these, the

The 1979 festival of Eka Dasa Rudra at Pura Besakih

The once-a-century Eka Dasa Rudra is the most important Hindu festival in Indonesia. It is held when, according to the Hindu *saka* calendar (see page 679), the year ends in 2 zeros. However, it can also be held when natural, political or economic calamity or disturbance is such that one needs to be called. Such was the case in 1963 (saka 1884), when it was deemed necessary to hold the festival following the events of the Indonesian revolution (1945-1949). An Eka Dasa Rudra had not been held for several centuries, and it was widely felt that one was due. Indeed, so many years had elapsed that the Balinese had forgotten, in large part, how to hold the festival and had to re-invent the celebration. However, shortly before the great sacrifice, scheduled for 8 March, Mount Agung began to erupt, leading to extensive death and destruction. Perhaps it was fortunate that saka 1900 (1979AD) was to fall only 16 years later, allowing the Balinese to atone for any wrongs that might have been committed.

Eka Dasa Rudra is not just one festival, but a series of many. The most important is the purification sacrifice, or *Taur Eka Dasa Rudra*, which occurs on the last day of a saka century – saka 1900 fell, for example, on 28 Mar 1979. The magnificence of the Eka Dasa Rudra can be imagined by magnifying immeasurably the colourful every-day festivals held in Bali's smaller temples; offerings on a massive scale, flowers in great piles, and janurs and colourful banners fluttering from the temple's shrines. During the course of the festival large numbers of animals were brought up to Besakih for sacrifice – about 60 species in all. It was not a reassuring sight for conservationists, as among the creatures were tiger cubs and rare eagles. President Suharto made an appearance at the ceremony and, unlike 1963, it ended with no incident or eruption. D.S. Fox writes at the back of his book about the festival *Once a century: Pura Besakih and the Eka Dasa Rudra Festival* (1982):

> "It is impossible to imagine the Balinese world in another 100 years able to support an Eka Dasa Rudra as extravagant as the 1980 [sic] festival: Will there still be baby tigers and eagles for the animal sacrifices? Will the Balinese still be willing to spend millions of man-hours weaving a spectacle of such scale? Will the tenacity of Balinese culture survive the severe pressures of 21st century life?"

central, largest and most important is the Pura Penataran Agung, the Mother Temple of all Bali. It is here that every Balinese, whatever his or her clan or class, can come to worship – although in the past it was reserved for the royal families of Klungkung, Karangkasem and Bangli. The other 21 temples that sprawl across the slopes of Mount Agung surrounding the Mother Temple are linked to particular clans. Mount Agung is an active volcano, and last erupted in 1963 killing 2,000 people. The traditional *lontar* manuscripts (see page 726) sometimes name the mountain *To Langkir* meaning Uppermost Man, or 'The Abode of the Gods' and the area has been a sacred spot for several centuries.

The **Pura Penataran Agung**, which most visitors refer to as Pura Besakih, is dedicated to Siva and was probably a pre-Indic terraced sanctuary. An indication that the pura is of great antiquity and pre-dates the arrival of Hinduism in Bali is the use of Old Indonesian and Old Balinese to name some of the gods that are worshipped here. Since then, it has seen many changes. It seems that the temple was enlarged during the reign of King Dharmavangsa (1022-1026). But the most significant changes occurred after 1343 when Gajah Mada of the Majapahit Kingdom of Java, sent a force to subdue the 'infamous and odious' ruler of Bali. With the victory of the Majapahit army, viceroys were sent from Java to rule the island. A descendant of one of these men established himself as the Prince of Gelgel, and this royal family became closely associated with Besakih, making it their ancestral *pura*. The *merus* were probably added at this time.

Temple layout

From the entrance gate, it is a 10 min walk up to the temple, past a long row of souvenir stalls. Although it is possible to walk up and around the sides of the temple, the courtyards themselves are only open to worshippers. It is the spectacular position of this pura, rather than the quality of its workmanship, which makes it special: there are views over fields to the waters of the Lombok Strait.

Pura Besakih consists of 3 distinct sections (for general background to Balinese temple layout **see page 673**). The entrance to the forecourt is through a *candi bentar* or split gate, immediately in front of which – unusually for Bali – is a *bale pegat*, which symbolizes the cutting of the material from the heavenly worlds. Also here is the *bale kulkul*, a pavilion for the wooden split gongs. At the far end of this first courtyard, are 2 *bale mundar-mandir* or *bale ongkara*, their roofs supported by single pillars.

Entering the central courtyard, almost directly in front of the gateway, is the *bale pewerdayan*. This is the spot where the priests recite the sacred texts. On the left-hand wall is the *pegongan*, a pavilion where a gamelan orchestra plays during ceremonies. Along the opposite (right-hand) side of the courtyard is the large *bale agung*, where meetings of Besakih village are held. The small *panggungan* or altar in front and at the near end of the bale agung is used to present offerings to the gods. The similar *bale pepelik* at the far end is the altar used to present offerings to the the Hindu trinity – Vishnu, Brahma and Siva. These gods descend and assemble in the larger *sanggar agung* which lies in front of the bale pepelik.

From the central courtyard, a steep stone stairway leads to the upper section, which is arranged into 4 terraces. The first of these terraces in the inner courtyard, is split into an E (right) and W (left) half. To the right are 2 large *merus*; the meru with the 7-tiered roof is dedicated to the locally venerated god Ratu Geng, while the 11-tiered meru is dedicated to Ratu Mas. The 3-tiered *kehen* meru is used to store the temple treasures. On the left-hand side is a row of 4 merus and 2 stone altars. The tallest meru, with 7-tiers, is dedicated to Ida Batara Tulus Sadewa. Up some steps, on the second terrace is another 11-tiered *meru*, this one dedicated to Ratu Sunar ing Jagat or Lord Light of the World. There are also a number of bale here; the bale in a separate enclosure to the left is dedicated to Sira Empu, the patron god of blacksmiths. Up some more stairs, to the third terrace is yet a further 11-tiered meru, dedicated in this instance to Batara Wisesa. On the final terrace are 2 *gedongs* – covered buildings enclosed on all 4 sides – both dedicated to the god of Mount Agung.

At the back of the complex there is a path leading to 3 other major puras: **Gelap** (200 m), **Pengubengan** (2.5 km) and **Tirta** (2 km). There are over 20 temples on these terraced slopes, dedicated to every Hindu god in the pantheon. Guides available (about 2,000Rp). Best time to visit: early morning, before the tour groups. Admission: by donation (ignore the vast sums that are claimed to have been donated). Open: from 0800, Mon-Sun.

Festivals There are a total of 70 festivals held in and around Pura Besakih each year, with every shrine having its own festival. The 2 most important festivals are occasional ceremonies: The *Panca Wali Krama* is held every 10 years, while the *Eka Dasa Rudra* is held only once every 100 years and lasts for 2 months. In fact, two Eka Dasa Rudra festivals have been held this century (see box above for explanation).

Jan: New moon of 7th lunar month.

Mar/Apr: *Nyepi* (moveable, full moon of 10th lunar month), the Balinese Saka new year, a month-long festival, which is attended by thousands of people from all over Bali, centering on the triple lotus throne (**see page 687**).

Transport to & from Besakih 22 km from Klungkung, 60 km from Denpasar. **By bemo/minibus:** regular minibuses from Klungkung; from Denpasar catch a bemo from the Batubulan terminal to Klungkung and then get a connection on to Besakih. But bemos are irregular and it makes more sense to charter a bemo for the entire trip or rent a car or motorbike.

The greatest of the former principalities of Bali is Klungkung and its capital still has a number of sights which hint at its former glory. East of here is the beach resort of Candi Dasa and 3 km outside Candi Dasa, the ancient Bali Aga village of Tenganan. The road then cuts inland and runs NE to Amlapura (Karangkasem), with its royal palace (40 km from Klungkung). 7 km inland and N from Karangkasem are the royal bathing pools of Tirtagangga. From here the road continues N following the coast all the way to Singaraja (almost 100 km from Amlapura). Few tourists make the drive, which is peaceful and very beautiful, passing black sand beaches, paddy fields and coconut groves.

Klungkung

Klungkung was the centre of another of the numerous principalities that made up Bali before the Dutch conquest of the island. It was also the oldest and most powerful, and the last to fall to the Dutch. It was not until 1908 that Dewa Agung of Klungkung had a force sent against him – in this case, under the pretext that he had been 'insolent'. Like the kings of Denpasar and Pemetjutan, the Dewa Agung opted to fight and die rather than surrender. Another *puputan* or 'fight to the death' took place (**see page 671**) in the main street in Klungkung, and the King and his entire family were killed by the Dutch forces.

The **Puri Smarapura** was once the symbolic heart of the Kingdom of Klungkung. All that remains of this palace on Jalan Untung Surapati are the gardens and 2 buildings; the rest was destroyed in 1908 by the Dutch during their advance on the capital and the ensuing *puputan*. The **Kherta Ghosa** or Hall of Justice, built in the 18th century by Ida Dewa Agung Jambe, was formerly the supreme court of the Kingdom of Klungkung. It is famous for its ceiling murals painted in traditional, wayang style, with vivid illustrations of heaven (towards the top) and hell (on the lower panels). As a court, the paintings represent the punishment that awaits a criminal in the afterlife. The murals have been repainted several times this century. Miguel Covarrubias describes the nature of traditional justice in Bali in the following terms:

> "A trial must be conducted with the greatest dignity and restraint. There are rules for the language employed, the behaviour of the participants, and the payment of trial expenses. It is interesting that the court procedure resembles that of cockfights in its rules and terminology. On the appointed day the plaintiff and the defendant must appear properly dressed, with their witnesses and their cases and declarations carefully written down. ... When the case has been thoroughly stated, the witnesses have testified and the evidence has been produced, the judges study the statements and go into deliberation among themselves until they reach a decision. ... Besides the witnesses and the material evidence, special attention is paid to the physical reaction of the participants during the trial, such as nervousness, change of colour in the face, or hard breathing."

The Kherta Ghosa was transformed into a Western court by the Dutch in 1908, when they added the carved seats, as they found sitting on mats too uncomfortable. It is said – although the story sounds rather dubious – that one of the Rajahs of Klungkung used the Kherta Ghosa as a watch tower. He would look over the town and when his eyes alighted on a particularly attractive woman going to the temple to make offerings, he would order his guards to fetch her and add the unsuspecting maid to his collection of wives.

Adjoining the Kherta Ghosa is the **Bale Kembang** (or Floating Pavilion), originally built in the 18th century, but extensively restored since then. Like the Kherta Ghosa, the ceiling is painted with murals; these date from 1942.

Further along the same road, just past a school, is the attractive **Taman Gili** also built in the 18th century. This consists of a series of open courtyards with finely carved stonework, in the centre of which is a floating pavilion surrounded by a lotus-filled moat. Admission: 600Rp. To the E of the main crossroads in the centre of town – behind the shopfronts – is a bustling **market**, held here every 3 days.

Excursions

Goa Lawah or 'bat cave', is one of the state temples of Klungkung. There are tunnels here which are reputed to lead as far as Pura Besakih. As the name suggests, the temple is overrun by bats and corresponding smells. **Getting there**: take a bemo heading for Padangbai or Candi Dasa.

Nusa Penida and **Nusa Lembongan**: boats leave for these 2 islands from Pandangbai (**see page 699**).

Accommodation E *Ramayana Palace*, Jl. Diponegoro (E edge of the town on road to Candi Dasa), T 21044, restaurant.

Shopping Textiles: although good examples are not easy to find, Klungkung is the centre of the production of royal *songket* cloth, traditionally woven with silk but today more often from synthetics. The cloth is worn for ceremonial occasions and characteristically features abstracted floral designs, geometric patterns, wayang figures and animals. It takes 2 months to weave a good piece.

Useful addresses Post Office: to the W of the Kherta Ghosa. **Area code**: 0366.

Transport to & from Klungkung By bemo: regular connections with Denpasar's Batubulan terminal and points E – Besakih, Amlapura, Candi Dasa (500Rp).

Padangbai

This is the port for ferries to Lombok and boats to Nusa Penida and Nusa Lembongan (**see page 698**). It is situated in a crescent-shaped bay and when there are no ships calling, is quiet and relaxed. There are beaches on either side of the town. Walking S from the pier and bus station along the coast, the road leads to Pantai Kecil or Little Beach, usually quiet and secluded.

Accommodation Several losmen in town including **E** *Homestay Dharma*, clean, homely and well-managed. Quieter places to the N along Jl. Silayukti which runs along the N sweep of the bay, e.g. **D** *Topi*, E side of bay, restaurant, isolated position, clean and comfortable but creaky floors and thin walls makes for little privacy; **E** *Rai Beach Inn*, cottage accommodation; **E** *Sedani Kerthi Beach Bungalows*, cottages and plain rooms on the beach front.

Restaurants *Pantai Ayu*, Jl. Silayukti, on the beach, great seafood, moneychanger.

Transport to & from Pandangbai By bemo: Padangbai is 2½ km off the main coastal road; connections with Denpasar's Batubulan terminal. The bemo and bus station is in the centre of the village next to the pier and the ferry ticket office for Lombok. By boat: ferries for Lembar on Lombok leave daily at 0800, 1100, 1400 and 1700, 4 hrs (4,000Rp). A new high-speed daily boat service to Bangsal on Lombok (for the Gilis) has started operating from Padangbai. Boats also depart for Nusa Penida and Nusa Lembongan (3,000Rp).

Candi Dasa

Candi Dasa is another fast-growing beach resort; until the 1980s it was only visited by the most adventurous of travellers, willing to stay in very basic bungalows. There are now up-market hotels with air-conditioning and swimming pools, and more are being built. Even so, it is far quieter and more relaxed than the resorts of the S, but also lacks the range of entertainment to be found there. It is an excellent place to stay for those wanting to explore the sights of east Bali.

The grey sand beach is interrupted by rather unsightly concrete groynes and piers, which have had to be constructed to prevent the beach eroding away. There is no surf, so swimming is safe. **Candi Dasa temple** is on the opposite side of the road from the lagoon.

Excursions

Tenganan 3 km N of Candi Dasa, the village of Tenganan is reputed to be the

The Bali Aga: the original Balinese

In pre-history, Bali was populated by animists whose descendants today are represented by the Bali Aga, literally 'Original Balinese'. The Aga are now restricted to a few relic communities in N and E Java, particularly in the regency of Karangkasem. Most have been extensively assimilated into the Hindu-Balinese mainstream. Miguel Covarrubias visited the Aga village of Tenganan in the 1930s, a village which even then was extraordinary in the extent to which it was resisting the pressures of change. He wrote:

"The people of Tenganan are tall, slender and aristocratic in a rather ghostly, decadent way, with light skins and refined manners. ...They are proud and look down even on the Hindu-Balinese nobility, who respect them and leave them alone. They live in a strange communistic... system in which individual ownership of property is not recognized and in which even the plans and measurements of the houses are set and alike for everybody".

Even today, a distinction is still made between the Bali Aga and the *Wong Majapahit*. The latter arrived from Java following the fall of the Majapahit Kingdom at the end of the 15th century.

In former years, the Aga were probably cannibalistic. It has been said that Aga corpses used to be washed with water which was allowed to drip onto a bundle of unhusked rice. This was then dried and threshed, cooked, moulded into the shape of a human being, and served to the relatives of the deceased. The eating of the rice figure is said to symbolize the ritual eating of the corpse, so imbibing its powers.

oldest on Bali – and is a village of the Bali Aga, the island's original inhabitants before the Hindu invasion almost 1,000 years ago (see box). The walled community consists of a number of longhouses, rice barns, shrines, pavilions and a large village meeting hall, all arranged in accordance with traditional beliefs. Membership of the village is exclusive and until recently visitors were actively discouraged. The inhabitants have to have been born here and then to marry within the village; anyone who violates the rules is banished to a neighbouring community. Despite the studied maintenance of a traditional way of life, the inhabitants of Tenganan have taken the decision to embrace the tourist industry. It is in fact a very wealthy village, deriving income not only from tourism but also from a large area of communally owned and worked rice paddys and dryland fields.

Tenganan is one of the last villages to produce the unusual double ikat or *geringsing*, where both the warp and the weft are tie-dyed and great skill is needed to align and then weave the 2 into the desired pattern (see box). The cloth is woven on body-tension (back-strap) looms with a continuous warp; colours used are dark rust, brown and purple, although newer pieces suffer from fading due to the use of inferior dyes. Motifs are floral and geometric, and designs are constrained to about 20 traditional forms. It is said that one piece of cloth takes about 5 years to complete and only 6 families still understand the process. Note that much of the cloth for sale in the village does not originate from Tenganan. **Getting there**: it is possible to walk the 3 km to Tenganan; take the road heading N, 1 km to the W of Candi Dasa – it ends at the village. Alternatively, walk or catch a bemo heading W towards Klungkung, get off at the turning 1 km W of Candi Dasa and catch an *ojek* up to the village. Tours to Tenganan are also arranged by the bigger hotels and the tour agents on the main road. Bemos run past the turn-off for the village from Denpasar's Batubulan terminal.

About 13 km SW of Candi Dasa is the temple and cave of **Goa Lawah** (see page 719). **Getting there**: regular bemos run along the coast.

Boats leave for **Nusa Penida** from Padangbai (see page 719).

Cloth as art: ikat in Southeast Asia

Ikat is a technique of patterning cloth characteristic of Southeast Asia and is produced from the hills of Burma to the islands of Eastern Indonesia. The word comes from the Malay word *mengikat* which means to bind or tie. Very simply, either the warp or the weft, and in one case both, are tied with material or fibre so that they resist the action of the dye. Hence the technique's name – resist dyeing. By dyeing, retieing and dyeing again through a number of cycles it is possible to build up complex patterns. Ikat is distinguishable by the bleeding of the dye which inevitably occurs no matter how carefully the threads are tied; this gives the finished cloth a blurred finish. The earliest ikats so far found date from the 14th-15th centuries.

To prepare the cloth for dyeing, the warp or weft is strung taut on a frame. Individual threads, or groups of threads are then tied tight with fibre and leaves. In some areas wax is then smeared on top to help in the resist process. The main colour is usually dyed first, secondary colours later. With complex patterns (which are done from memory, plans are only required for new designs) and using natural dyes, it may take up to 6 months to produce a piece of cloth. Prices are correspondingly high – in eastern Indonesia for example, top grade cloths can easily exceed 1,000,000Rp ($500), and ritual cloths considerably more still. Today, the pressures of the market place mean that it is more likely that cloth is produced using chemical dyes (which need only one short soaking, not multiple long ones as with some natural dyes), and design motifs have generally become larger and less complex. Traditionally, warp ikat used cotton (rarely silk) and weft ikat, silk. Silk in many areas has given way to cotton, and cotton sometimes to synthetic yarns. Double ikat, where incredibly both the warp *and* the weft are tie-dyed, is produced in only one spot in Southeast Asia: the village of Tenganan in eastern Bali.

Warp ikat:
Sumatra (Bataks)
Kalimantan (Dayaks)
Sulawesi (Toraja)
East Nusa Tenggara (Savu, Flores,
    Sumba, Roti)

Double ikat:
East Bali

Weft ikat:
Sulawesi (Bugis)
North-east Java
East Sumatra
Bali
Burma (Shans)
Thailand
Laos
Cambodia

The royal bathing pools of **Tirtagangga (see page 723)** and the town and palace of **Amlapura (see page 722)** are both within easy reach of Candi Dasa.

Three small islands with coral reefs are to be found: 30 mins by boat from Candi Dasa. They make a good day trip for snorkelling or diving. **Getting there:** most hotels and losmen will arrange a boat for the day.

Accommodation Most accommodation is concentrated along the seaward side of the main drag. There is a collection of quieter losmen and hotels off the main road to the N of the lagoon. Most include breakfast in their rates. **L** *Amankila* (outside Candi Dasa), T 71267, F 71266, 'soft' opened in mid-1992, one of the Aman group of hotels, highly luxurious with 35 guest pavilions overlooking the Lombok Strait, swimming pool on 3 levels, library, private beach and impeccable service, hard to beat but prices to match; **A+** *Puri Bagus* (E of lagoon), T 51223, F 52779, a/c, restaurant, pool, good rooms and attractive open-air bathrooms, but overpriced, shadeless pool area; **A** *Candi Beach Cottages*, T 51711, F 52652, a/c, pool, tennis, 2 km W of town so quieter with better beach, but inconvenient for restaurants, bars and Candi Dasa's other facilities, but good rooms; **A** *Rama Ocean View*, T 51864, F 51866, a/c, restaurant, pool, on the road into Candi Dasa about 1 km from the town 'centre', tennis and fitness centre, well designed hotel, good pool; **B** *Candi Dasa Beach Bungalows II*, T 35536, F 35537, a/c, 2 restaurants, pool, 2 storey blocks, food rec; **B** *Samudra Indah*, T

35542, F 35542, a/c, pool, on the S edge of town, nice pool, comfortable but featureless rooms with hot water; **B** *Water Garden*, PO Box 39, T 35540, restaurant, pool, individual cottages, set on the hillside in lovely gardens, each cottage has its own verandah overlooking a private lily pond, simple rooms (with hot water) but very attractively laid out, rec; **B-D** *Sindhu Brata* (E of lagoon), T 21032, some a/c, good mid-range rooms.

C-E *Puri Pudak* (E of lagoon), T 33978, well-designed, clean bungalows, friendly, rec; **D** *Ayodya*; **D** *Bunga Putri* (E of lagoon), at the N end of the bay, past the fishing boats, peaceful, good rooms, rec; **D** *Genggong* (E of lagoon), peaceful, appealing; *Nani Beach Inn*, T 25844, very average; **D** *Puri Amarta Beach Inn*, clean, average; **D** *Puri Oka*, T 24798, pool, hot water, clean, rec; **D** *Puri Pandan*, rooms average, bathrooms better than average with hot water; **D** *Satria* (E of lagoon), quiet, immaculate rooms, nice bathrooms, good value, rec; **D** *Srikandi* (E of lagoon), T 53125, clean rooms, rec; **E** *Pandawa Homestay* (E of lagoon), characterful, quiet, clean bungalows with hot water, rec.

Restaurants There are a variety of well-priced restaurants dotted along the main road with similar menus; seafood is the best bet. ♦♦*Kubu Bali*, good seafood and Chinese and Indonesian specialities; *Legend Rock Café*, Western and Indonesian; *Pandan*, on the beach, daily Balinese buffet; *Raja's Restaurant and Cocktail Bar*; ♦*T.J.'s Café*, Mexican, good food, friendly, rec.

Entertainment Dance: Balinese dance performances staged nightly at 2100 at the **Pandan Harum** near the centre of town.

Sports Diving: Stingray Dive Centre, *Puri Bali Homestay*; Baruna Watersports, *Puri Bagus Hotel*. **Snorkeling**: Rent snorkels from hotels and charter a boat to go out to a reef.

Shopping Crafts: *Geringsing*, on the main road, sells double ikat cloth from Tenganan and other Balinese arts and crafts.

Local transport Bicycle, motorbike and car hire from hotels, losmen and from shops along the main road.

Banks & money changers There are several money changers offering reasonable rates.

Useful addresses Postal Agent: opposite the Candi Dasa Beach Bungalows.

Tour companies & travel agents Several travel agents book tours, reconfirm tickets and sell bus tickets to major destinations in Java.

Transport to & from Candi Dasa By bemo: regular connections with Denpasar's Batubulan terminal (2,000Rp), Amlapura (500Rp) and Klungkung (500Rp). **By shuttle bus**: more expensive, but quicker, shuttle buses link Candi Dasa with Denpasar, Ubud, Kuta, Lovina and Kintamani (4,000-10,000Rp).

Amlapura (Karangasem)

At one time Amlapura, traditionally known as Karangasem, was among the most powerful of states in Bali. Today, this may be hard to believe – it is a quiet and attractive town, where little happens. Several palaces are to be found in Karangasem, the most accessible being the **Puri Agung**, or Puri Kanginan, to the E of the main N-S road, Jalan Gajah Mada. The last king of Karangasem was born at the Puri Agung. Entrance to the palace is through tall gateways. To the S are a cluster of buildings, which would have been offices and artist's workshops. Another gateway takes the visitor out of this first compound and a door to the S leads into the major part of the palace. A pillared building faces S onto a *bale Kembang* or floating pavilion. The buildings are all rather run-down, and are eclectic architecturally with European, Balinese and Chinese elements and motifs. There are interesting photographs from the early part of this century and some rather tatty furniture. Admission: 200Rp. Open: 0800-1700 Mon-Sun. There is a **market** to the S of the palace.

Excursions

The ruined water palace of **Ujung** is very beautiful in its romantic decrepitude. It lies 8 km S of town towards the coast and was built by the last King of Karangasem. The hills of Lombok can be seen from the site. Most of the complex was destroyed during an earthquake in 1963 so there is little to see. This is more than compensated for by the beautiful position. There are plans to have the palace restored. **Getting there**: bemos leave from the station near the market (S of the palace).

Tirtagangga These royal bathing pools are 7 km N of town (see below). **Getting there**: regular bemo connections from the station by the market.

Accommodation E *Homestay Sidha Karya*, Jl. Hasannudin; **E** *Lahar Mas Inn*, Jl. Gatot Subroto 1, T 145, small, friendly people.

Banks & money changers Bank Rakyat Indonesia, Jl. Gajah Mada.

Useful addresses Post Office: Jl. Gatot Subroto 25.

Transport to & from Amlapura By bemo/minibus: the bemo terminal is on Jl. Kesatrian. Regular connections with Denpasar's Batubulan terminal and to Manggis, Culik, Padangbai, Klungkung, Tirtagangga and Singaraja.

Tirtagangga

7 km NW of Amlapura is the site of the royal bathing pools of Tirtagangga. Built in 1947 by the last king of Amlapura, they were badly damaged by the earthquake of 1963 but have since been restored. The pools occupy a stunning position on the side of a hill, overlooking terraced ricefields. The complex consists of various pools (2 of which visitors can swim in), fed by mountain streams with water spouting from fountains and stone animals. It is popular with local people and is a peaceful place to retreat to. Admission: 200Rp, plus 700Rp to swim in the upper pool, 500Rp in the lower pool. Open: Mon-Sun.

Accommodation C *Kusuma Jaya Inn*, brilliant position on the steep hill overlooking Tirtagangga, the best place to stay, price includes breakfast; **D** *Rijasa*, attractive thatched bungalows, rec; **D** *Tirta Ayu Homestay*, within the water garden itself, rather overpriced for unexciting rooms, but a great position; **E** *Dhangin Taman Inn*, just outside the water gardens, rooms rather bunched together, but good views over ricefields and friendly management.

Restaurants ♦♦*Tirta Ayu restaurant*, an open-air restaurant within the water garden, with a fabulous position overlooking the pools and the terraced paddy fields beyond.

Transport to & from Tirtagangga By minibus/bemo: connections with Amlapura, Culik, Kubu, Singaraja. From Denpasar's Batubulan terminal catch a bemo to Amlapura and get off at the intersection just before Amlapura to catch a connection up the hill to Tirtagangga.

NORTH FROM DENPASAR TO LAKE BRATAN

15 km NW of Denpasar is the town of Kapal. Shortly after Kapal, in the village of Bringkit, the road branches; W for Tanah Lot and Gilimanuk, and N for Lake Bratan, Singaraja and Lovina Beach. The coastal temple of Tanah Lot is 10 km off the main road and is a popular tourist attraction. The other arm of the fork runs N for 2 km to Mengwi (with its impressive temple complex). Continuing N, the road climbs through breathtaking terraced paddy fields to Lake Bratan, one of 3 crater lakes that fill part of a massive caldera. Mount Catur lies to the N of the lake and is the highest peak in the area at 2,096m.

Kapal

The meru-making town of Kapal is best-known for its red-brick **Pura Sada** which lies just S of the main road, past the bend near the market place (it is signposted). The pura is an important shrine of the former dynasty of the kingdom of Mengwi. Inside the enclosure is an unusual 16 m-high *prasada* or *prasat* (possibly explaining its name 'Pura Sada'), similar in style to Javanese candis, and dedicated to the king's ancestors. An earthquake in 1917 all but destroyed the prasada and the *candi bentar* or split gate. In 1949, it was carefully restored by local craftsmen. The sculptures that decorate the prasada were all carved after 1950.

Transport to & from Kapal 15 km from Denpasar. By bemo: regular bemos from the Ubung terminal, just NW of Denpasar.

The Balinese pagoda: the meru

Perhaps the most characteristic feature of Balinese architecture is the *meru*. These are multi-tiered (but always odd in number) pagoda-like towers made of wood and coir thatch. As the name suggests, they symbolize the cosmic Hindu-Buddhist mountain, Mount Meru (as do candis and prasada/prasats). The underworld is represented by the lower section, the world of men by the middle section, and the heavens by the towering, tapering roofs. There are clear stylistic links between merus and the brick candis of Java, as well as with similar buildings in Nepal. Whether the idea of making the upper portions from perishable materials was introduced from Java is not clear. Certainly, there are structures today in Java which consist only of a base, indicating that there may have been an upper portion of wood or thatch.

Tanah Lot

The coastal temple of **Tanah Lot**, perched on a rock at the edge of the shore-line and 30 km NW of Denpasar, is probably the most photographed sight in Bali. The temple is one of the *sadkahyangan* – the 6 holiest shrines – and is said to have been built after the Hindu saint Danghyang Nirartha spent a night here and subsequently suggested that a temple be constructed on the spot.

The temple itself is small, and hardly remarkable artistically, with 2 tiered merus and several other pavilions. What makes it special, and so popular, is its incomparable position. Built on a rock outcrop just off the coast, it can only be reached at low tide. The surrounding rocks are said to be inhabited by sea-snakes but this does nothing to deter the hoards of visitors who clamber over the rocks and stroll along the beach. The profusion of trinket stalls, warungs and hawkers can be over-powering, detracting from the overall ambience of the location, but it is still well worth the visit, particularly in the late afternoon, when the sun sets behind the temple (and photographers line-up to catch the moment). There are good coastline walks S from Tanah Lot. Admission: by donation. Facilities here include a money changer, restaurant and post office.

Accommodation C *Dewi Sinta*, some a/c, restaurant, hot water, attractive position overlooking rice fields, close to the walkway to Tanah Lot.

Transport to & from Tanah Lot 30 km from Denpasar. **By bemo:** connections with Denpasar's Ubung terminal, N of town to Kediri (500Rp) and then another from Kediri to Tanah Lot (300Rp); be sure to leave Tanah Lot by 1400 in order to catch a connecting bemo from Kediri back to town. The turning for the temple is 20 km NW of Denpasar on the road to Negara and Gilimanuk. From here it is a 10 km drive down a lovely road through paddy fields to the sea.

Mengwi

Mengwi is an unremarkable market town, save for the **Pura Taman Ayun**; take the turning to the right opposite the colt station to get there. This impressive temple was built for the founder of the Mengwi Kingdom in 1634. Surrounded by a moat, it consists, characteristically, of a series of 3 courtyards. The tallest gate leads into the back courtyard, where there are two rows of *palinggih-palinggih* or shrines for visiting deities on the N and E sides, each with ornate pillars and beautifully carved doors. On the W side are a number of *bales* or pavilions. The courtyard also contains a stone altar (*paibon*) with reasonable relief carvings. To the left of the main entrance there is a poor 'Museum of Complete Cremation' (admission by donation).

Excursions

Sangeh nutmeg forest is 15 km N of Mengwi (it is also known as 'monkey forest' because of the many monkeys found here) and is the sight of the **Pura Bukit Sari**. The temple was built at the beginning of the 17th century by the son of the

King of Mengwi as a meditation temple. Today it is a *subak* (or irrigation) temple. **Getting there**: although the forest and temple are closest to Mengwi it is difficult to get there on public transport except by returning to Denpasar's Ubung terminal and taking another bemo N (600Rp) – which means a total journey of nearly 40km. With private transport, it is easy to take the road E towards Kedampat.

Pura Luhur is an isolated mountain temple situated on the slopes of Mount Batukau (or 'shell' mountain), amidst tropical forest. **Getting there**: it is not easy to reach by public transport – it is best to charter a bemo from Denpasar or Mengwi, turning N at Tabanan. The final climb is steep. On the way, visit the **hot springs** at **Penatahan**.

Pura Yeh Gangga is an attractive temple 15 km from Mengwi off the road N to Lake Bratan. Unusually, the base of the merus are constructed of stone, rather than wood, with porcelain set into the walls. A stone inscription discovered within the compound can be dated to 1334. **Getting there**: take a bemo running N towards Lake Bratan from Mengwi or Denpasar's Ubung terminal and ask to be let off just after the village of Bereteh (and before Kukup). Take the turning to the left and walk through the village of Paang to Perean, where the pura can be found (a walk of about 1½ km).

Transport to & from Mengwi 18 km from Denpasar. **By bus**: connections with Denpasar's Ubung terminal; buses turn off the main road to Gilimanuk at Bringkit, and fork N. Alternatively, big buses travel the main road from Denpasar to Gilimanuk from Denpasar's Ubung terminal; ask to be let off at the turning to Mengwi and Bedugul (in the village of Bringkit); bemos wait at this junction and run N.

Lake Bratan and Lake Buyan

The beautiful, almost alpine, Lake Bratan is surrounded by the crater walls of the now extinct volcano, Mount Catur. There are attractive walks around the lake and boats can be hired from in front of the Lila Graha Hotel (6,000Rp/hour) or from the Bedugul Hotel. On its W shore is the stunningly positioned and mystical, **Pura Ulun Danau Bratan**, which seems to almost float on the water (indeed, in the 1970s it was at risk of sinking beneath the rising waters of the lake). The temple was built in 1633 by the King of Mengwi to honour the Goddess of the Lake who provides water for irrigation. Along with the temple at Lake Batur (**see page 713**), the Pura Ulun Danau Bratan, is the most important of the various irrigation temples on Bali. Outside the walls of this Hindu temple is a stupa with seated Buddha images in its niches, revealing Bali's Buddhist roots. Admission: 500Rp. Open: 0800-1600 Mon-Sun. There is a **flower and spice market** held each Sunday at Candikuning, 500m N from the temple.

South of Candikuning, on the S lip of the crater is the small town of **Bedugul**. Near Bedugul, at an altitude of 1,240 m, the road passes the **Bali Botanical Gardens**. North from Lake Bratan, the road crosses the floor of the crater and as the road climbs up over its N walls, **Lake Buyan** comes into sight. This is another lake of great natural beauty and is the proposed site of a national park. Again, there are beautiful walks around the lake. Just 2 km N of Lake Bratan is the site of the Handara Kosaido Country Club and golf course, voted one of the world's 50 most beautiful courses (see below for details).

Excursions

Air Terjun Gitgit lies about 15 km N of Lake Bratan, near the village of Gitgit. A path leads to this waterfall which is quite impressive during the wet season. Admission on main road: 500Rp, 15 minute walk to the falls. **Getting there**: take a bemo heading for Singaraja.

Accommodation near Lake Bratan **A** *Handara Country Club Pancasari*, T 28866/88944, some bungalows, tennis, fitness centre, golf course, beautiful location, but rather overpriced; **A** *Pacung Mountain Hotel*, Pacung, T 21039, F 37638, a/c, restaurant, pool, stunning position with panoramic views over paddy fields, rec; **A** *Pancasari Inn*, just N of *Handara Country Club*, T 53142, tennis; **B** *Bukit Mungsu Indah* (before Bedugul, at Baturiti), price includes breakfast; **B** *Lake Buyan Cottages*, N of Lake Bratan, tennis; **B-C** *Bedugul* (overlooking the lake), T 29593, good watersports facilities; **C** *Ashram Guesthouse*, superb position overlooking Lake Bratan, rec; **C** *Lila Graha*, Candikuning, overlooking the lake (and the road).

Sports Golf: *Handara Country Club*, 18 holes, designed by the Australian golfer Peter Thomson; green fees 90,000Rp, clubs for hire, T 28866. **Watersports**: the *Bedugul Hotel* offers jetskiing, waterskiing, parasailing, fishing and motorboats for hire.

Transport to & from Lake Bratan 53 km from Denpasar, 35 km from Mengwi. **By bemo:** regular 'express' bemos leave from Denpasar's Ubung terminal for Singaraja (see below), passing through Bedugul and Lake Bratan *en route*.

LAKE BRATAN TO THE NORTH COAST

The road descends from Lake Bratan through clove and coffee plantations to the much drier landscape of the N coast. There are fewer rivers watering this side of the island and rainfall is less; as a result the lushness of the S is replaced by savanna forest. Singaraja, the former Dutch capital of Bali and Nusa Tenggara, remains an important local town but has little to entice the visitor. 11 km W from here is the resort of Lovina Beach. The road continues W following the N coast all the way to Gilimanuk (and the ferry for Java). The road E from Singaraja passes a number of important temples built in distinctive N Balinese style. Although few people take the road along the N coast eastwards and then S to Amlapura, the drive is very beautiful and peaceful, passing black sand beaches, paddy fields and coconut groves. The distance from Singaraja to Amlapura is almost 100 km.

Singaraja

Singaraja is the capital of the regency of Buleleng and was the original Dutch capital of Bali and the other islands of Nusa Tenggara. During this period, it was a relatively important harbour and trading post, but has since declined in significance.

On Jalan Veteran, next door to the tourist office, is the **Gedong Kirtya**, a manuscript library founded by the Dutch in 1928 when it was named the Kirtya Liefrinck van der Tuuk. It contains Bali's best collection of palm leaf illustrated books or *lontars* which record local myths, magic formulas, literature and dances. Many were taken from the palace in Lombok during the Dutch campaign at the beginning of this century. Some of the Lombok manuscripts originated in Java, from where they were rescued during the disintegration of the Majapahit Empire. The palm leaves are cut into lengths of about 50 cm and then incised with a sharp blade and the incisions filled with a mixture of soot and oil to accentuate the marks. They are then bound together using lengths of cord and protected between 2 wooden boards.

Excursions

Singaraja is the most convenient base for visiting the sights of the N coast, E of town. Accommodation however is limited and most visitors base themselves elsewhere (e.g. Lovina Beach). The temples of the N are interesting for their distinct N style of architecture; in general they are artistically 'busier', exhibiting much more elaborate and dense carving.

Pura Beji is situated just N of the main coastal road 8 km E of Singaraja, near the village of Sangsit. The temple is dedicated to the rice goddess Dewi Sri and belongs to the local *subak* or irrigation society which is served with the task of managing and allocating water resources among its members (**see page 668**). The association of rice, water and religion reflects the dependence of rice cultivation upon an adequate and constant supply of water, and of people upon rice for their survival. Visitors are likely to be mobbed by the local children. **Getting there**: take a bemo from Singaraja's Kampung Tinggi terminal.

Jagaraga village is 13 km SE from Singaraja, and 4 km inland from the coast road. The village has 2 claims to fame. In 1849 the Dutch wiped out virtually the entire settlement in what has come to be known as the **Puputan** (or 'battle to the death') **Jagaraga**. Also in the village is the **Pura Dalem** – a Temple of the Dead – which has reliefs depicting, for example, Model 'T' Ford motorcars being held up by bandits, Dutchmen being eaten by crocodiles, and aeroplane dogfights. Admission: suggested donation comparatively overpriced at 1,000Rp. **Getting there**: if travelling independently, turn right off the main coast road 1 km beyond Sangsit, and then travel S for 4 km to the village of Jagaraga. Getting to the village is more difficult by public transport; take a bemo E from Singaraja's Kampung Tinggi terminal and get off 1 km past Sangsit – from there either walk the 4 km or wait and hope for a lift.

Pura Maduwe Karang is situated in the village of Kubutambahan, 12 km E of Singaraja and on the main coast road. Like Pura Beji, the temple of Maduwe Karang is dedicated to ensuring a bountiful harvest, though not of irrigated rice, but of dry land crops. An interesting relief here is of an official (some people maintain that the cyclist is the artist W.O.J. Nieuwenkamp (1874-1950) who played such an important role recording Bali's artistic heritage) riding a bicycle, found in the base of the temple wall. The image is reproduced on the cover of this book. **Getting there**: by bemo from Singaraja's Kampung Tinggi terminal.

Air Sanih lies 17 km E of Singaraja and has become quite a popular tourist stop, because of its spring-fed swimming-pool. There are also empty beaches of glistening black sand and an attractive garden – marred by tourist stalls. Accommodation at the Purih Sanih Bungalows (**E**), and a handful of other losmen. **Getting there**: by bemo from Singaraja's Kampung Tinggi terminal.

Accommodation **E** *Gelarsari*, Jl. Jend. A. Yani, T 21495; *Garuda*, Jl. Jend. A. Yani 76; *Sakabindu*, Jl. Jend. A. Yani, T 21791

Shopping Textiles: Singaraja is known for its finely detailed ikat cotton and silk weft ikat; there are 2 factories in town producing the cloth.

Useful addresses General Post Office: Jl. Gajah Mada 158; poste restante service. **General Hospital**: Jl. Ngurah Rai, T 41046. **Area code**: 0362.

Airline offices Garuda, Jl. Jend. A. Yani (next to *Hotel Duta Karya*), T 41691.

Tour companies & travel agents *Nitour*, Jl. Jend. A. Yani.

Tourist offices Tourist Office, Jl. Veteran 23 T61141. Brochures and local map. Open: 0700-1400 Mon-Sat.

Transport to & from Singaraja 78 km from Denpasar, 11 km from Lovina Beach. **By bus**: Singaraja has 2 bus stations, Kampung Tinggi at the E edge of the town on Jl. Surapati for destinations to the E (Kubu, Amlapura and Kintamani); and Banyuasri on the W edge at the intersection of Jl. Jend. Sudirman and Jl. Jend. A. Yani for destinations S and W of the town (Denpasar, Lovina, Gilimanuk and Bedugul). Bemos link the 2 terminals. Night buses leave from the Banyuasri terminal at 1700 for Surabaya (bus companies have their offices at Taman Lila, Jl. Jend. A. Yani 2).

Lovina Beach

Lovina Beach, an 8 km stretch of grey sand, is the name given to 3 beaches which merge into one another. From E to W, they are Anturan, Kalibukbuk and Temukus. Lovina has been the latest section of Bali's coastline to be developed for tourism

728 INDONESIA – BALI

and it has already become a mini-resort. The beach itself is quite narrow, with calm but rather murky waters close in to the shore, and reasonable snorkelling on the reef just off-shore. The most popular outing is an early morning boat trip to see the **dolphins** cavorting off the coast (8,000Rp, with coffee and snack).

At present, Lovina remains largely a backpackers' resort, although there are a handful of mid-range hotels with a/c and swimming pools and yet more are under construction. But there are no large-scale hotels. The general standard of accommodation is good and prices are competitive.

Excursions
Along the N coast E of Singaraja are a number of northern-style temples and other sights (**see page 726**). Air Terjun Gigit is a waterfall 11 km S of Singaraja, worth visiting in the wet season (**see page 725**). **Getting there**: catch a bemo to Singaraja and then one heading towards Lake Bratan.

Accommodation Most hotels are situated on the central beach area of Kalibukbuk and rates include breakfast and tax. **NB: mosquitoes** are bad at night; not all bungalows provide nets. Telephone numbers are within the Singaraja area code. **Anturan Beach** : **D** *Baruna Beach*, T 41252, private mandi, some rooms overlook beach.

Kalibukbuk Beach: A-B *Bali Lovina Beach Cottages*, T 41385 or T 33386 (Denpasar), some a/c, pool, bungalows, hot water, rather overpriced, rates include breakfast; **B-E** *Angsoka*, T 41841, some a/c, restaurant, pool, attractive and clean; **C-D** *Permata*, T 41653, good value; **D** *Rini*, clean, big room, fan, own mandi, rec; **D-E** *Manggala Homestay*, basic, fan; **E** *Astina*, reasonable accommodation but no mosquito protection, some private mandis; **E** *Dayana*, clean, fan; **E** *Nirwana*, clean but no mosquito protection, rather over-priced; **E** *Toto*, 4 or 5 rooms, noisy bungalows near the road, better ones on the beach, good value; **F** *Arjuna*, small basic rooms with fan; **F** *Purnama Homestay*, small, friendly, average rooms.

Temukus Beach: B-D *Aditya*, PO Box 134, T 41059, some a/c, pool, clean, hot water and baths; **C-D** *Puri Tasik Madu*, towards Temukus, T 21585, dark but characterful with 4-poster beds and a good restaurant; **D** *Krisna*, clean, big rooms, good value; **D** *Pulestis*, gaudy but big clean rooms; **D** *Samudra*, PO Box 15, some a/c, hot water; **F** *Susila Beach Inn*, T 61565, price includes breakfast, friendly people but basic accommodation.

Restaurants Many of the restaurants at Lovina serve good, and reasonably priced, seafood. *Wina restaurant*, excellent Chinese and Indonesian food, rec; *Bali Pub*, good fresh fish, rec.

Entertainment Live music: at *Wina's* and *Malibu*. Videos: evening showings at *Malibu* and *Wina's*, both popular.

Sports Boat tours: organized by the *Bali Lovina Beach Cottages*. Diving: *Spice Dive*, Kaliasem, US$45-60 for 2 dives all inclusive; introductory training and one dive US$45; 5 day certification course US$230. *Spice Dive* also arrange offshore snorkeling trips (25,000Rp). *Lovina Marine Resort* and *Bali Lovina Beach Cottages* organize diving expeditions. Fishing: most hotels and losmen offer fishing trips (7,000Rp). Sailing: boats available for hire. Snorkelling: average snorkelling just off the beach (5,000Rp); better marine life at Menjangan Island (25,000Rp for a day trip with *Spice Dive*). Equipment available from the *Bali Lovina Beach Cottages*. Swimming: at the *Bali Lovina Beach Cottages*, 5,000Rp to non-residents.

Local transport Car/motorbike/bicycle hire from several of the hotels; for example *Rambutan* have motorbikes for hire.

Money changers On the main road.

Useful addresses Postal Agent on main road.

Tourist office The police station doubles as a tourist information office; they supply a map but little else.

Transport to & from Lovina 11 km from Singaraja. **By bus:** from Denpasar's Ubung terminal catch an express bus to Singaraja, 1½-2 hrs. The bus stops at Singaraja's Banyuasri terminal, from where there are regular buses to Lovina. There are also regular buses and minibuses from Gilimanuk, taking the N coast route, 1½ hrs (buses from Java will drop passengers off at Gilimanuk to catch a connection to Lovina – sometimes included in the cost of the ferry and bus ticket). **By shuttle bus:** range of prices, 9,000Rp to Kuta.

THE WEST: Gilimanuk and the Bali Barat National Park

The west of Bali is the least visited part of the island; most visitors merely pass through en route between the E of Bali and Java. In a number of respects the west is atypical: the area is far less rich agriculturally, it remains the least populated part of Bali, there are no historic sights to match those of the E, and there is a strong Muslim representation with settlers from Madura, Java and Sulawesi. At the W tip and 134 km from Denpasar is Gilimanuk, the ferry port for Java. Completely encompassing the port and much of the W is the Bali Barat National Park.

Gilimanuk

Gilimanuk is the departure and arrival point for the ferry that runs between Bali and Java. There is no reason to stay here unless forced to; it is only a transit point. 3 km S of Gilimanuk is **Cekik** and the headquarters of the Bali Barat National Park. For archaeologists, Gilimanuk is important as the site of a bronze/iron age burial ground excavated in the 1960s and 1970s, thus providing evidence of prehistoric settlement on Bali.

Excursions
The **Bali Barat** (or West Bali) **National Park** was established as recently as 1984, and covers over 75,000 ha straddling both the dry N coast and the forested, tropical S. The Bali white mynah or *jalak putih Bali* (*Leucopsar rothschildi*), one of the rarest birds in the world, is found here, mostly confined to Menjangan Island. It is a small white bird, with black tips to its wings and tail, and a streak of blue around its eye (easily confused with the black-winged starling, which has wholly black wings and tail). Only 50 still exist in the wild although there are thousands in captivity. A programme to re-introduce captive birds back into the wild has begun, although trapping is still a problem. One captive bird recently released promptly reappeared for sale at the Jakarta bird market. The wild Javan buffalo (*Bos javanicus*) is also present in small numbers. Other less rare animals include monkeys, leopard, civets and the rusa, barking and mouse deers. The PHPA office for the Bali Barat National Park is in Cekik. Permits and information on trails can be obtained from the office (permits are also available from the Forestry Department, Jalan Suwung, Denpasar, and from Labuan Lalang). **NB** guides are obligatory. Accommodation is available in the park but it is very basic.

Accommodation E *Kartika Candra*.

Transport to & from Gilimanuk 134 km from Denpasar, 88 km from Singaraja. **By bus:** regular connections with Denpasar's Ubung terminal. Connections with Singaraja via Lovina Beach. **By ferry**: regular connections throughout the day with Ketapang on Java, ferries leaving every 15-30 mins during the day and less regularly at night, 25 mins. **NB** during Indonesian holidays and at weekends there may be a long wait for a boat.

Labuan Lalang (Teluk Terima)

Labuan Lalang, also known as Teluk Terima, is the most convenient base for visits to Menjangan Island (see below, Excursions).

Accommodation Basic losmen accommodation.

Excursions
Pulau Menjangan lies just off Bali's N coast and is part of the Bali Barat National Park. It offers the best diving to be found around Bali and boats can be chartered to the island from Labuan Lalang. Fins and masks are available but diving equipment must be hired from a dive shop at one of the major beach resorts. The island, fringed with mangroves, is very beautiful and home to the rare Java deer

and Bali white mynah. There are no losmen on the island and camping is not permitted.

Transport to & from Labuan Lalang By bemo: connections with Gilimanuk/Cekik. Take a bus from Denpasar's Ubung terminal to Gilimanuk and then catch a connection on. From Singaraja, take a bemo from the Banyuasri terminal, running W towards Gilimanuk.

Negara

Negara is the main town of the regency of Jembrana and is best known for the *mekepung* or **bullock races** which are held here between Jul and Oct. The sport was introduced by migrants from the island of Madura where the *kerapan sapi* (bull races) are the main form of entertainment (**see page 655**). Information on Negara's bull races can be obtained from the Bali Tourist Office on Jalan S. Parman in Denpasar. Races normally take place after the rice harvest.

Excursions
Medewi Beach is situated 15 km E of Negara, near the village of Pulukan. Medewi is a black sand beach and is good for surfing. Some accommodation here. **Getting there**: take a bus running E towards Denpasar and ask to be let off at *Pantai Medewi*.

Accommodation E *Ana*, Jl. Ngurah Rai 75, T 65; **E** *Indraloka*, Jl. Nakula 13.

Transport to & from Negara 100 km from Denpasar, 34 km from Gilimanuk. **By bus:** regular connections with Gilimanuk and Denpasar's Ubung terminal.

SUMATRA

Introduction, 731; Information for visitors, 735. **Northern Sumatra** Introduction, 738; Medan, 738; The route north: Medan to Bukit Lawang and Banda Aceh, 744; The Gayo Highlands: Takengon, 751; The route south: Medan to Lake Toba via Brastagi, 751; Samosir Island, 759; Lake Toba south to Padangsidempuan, 765; Nias Island, 766. **Southern Sumatra** introduction, 772; The Minang Homeland: Bukittinggi and Padang, 776; The Riau Archipelago, 784; Batam Island, 786; Bintan Island, 788; The Riau islands to Pekanbaru and Bukittinggi, 793; The West Coast: Bukittinggi to Padang and Sungai Penuh, 797; The Mentawi islands, 801; Padang to Jambi and Palembang via Bangka and Belitung islands, 805; Palembang to Bengkulu via Pagaralam, 813; Muaraenim to Bandar Lampung, Bakauheni and Java, 818.

Maps: Northern Sumatra, 739; Medan, 740; Banda Aceh, 747; Weh Island, 750; Samosir Island, 760; Nias Island, 767; Southern Sumatra, 774-775; Bukittinggi, 777; Around Bukittinggi, 779; Riau Archipelago, 785; Batam Island, 786; Bintan Island, 789; Tanjung Pinang, 790; Pekanbaru, 795; Padang, 798; Siberut Island (Mentawi), 802; Palembang, 808; Bangka Island, 811; Bengkulu, 815.

The island of Sumatra straddles the Indian Ocean and the Java Sea. It stretches from the town of Banda Aceh in the NE, over 1,750 km S to Bakauheni at its S extremity. The name Sumatra is thought to derive from one of the 13th century trading ports on the island's NE coast – Samudra, Sanskrit for 'ocean'.

INTRODUCTION

Sumatra has a surface area of nearly 475,000 sq km, making it the fourth largest island in the world. To put Sumatra's size into perspective: it is twice the size of Britain, or one third larger than Japan. It is also relatively sparsely settled, with 37 million inhabitants. Population densities here are less than one tenth those on neighbouring Java, although some areas – such as Lampung province – are beginning to suffer the effects of overcrowding.

Although Sumatra does not have the historical and archaeological sights that distinguish Java, it does offer magnificent natural landscapes. There are over a dozen ethnic groups who speak some 20 different dialects. Among these are the peripatetic Minangkabau of West Sumatra (see page 772), the Christian Bataks of North Sumatra (see page 756) the Ferrant Muslins of Aceh, and the tribal peoples of the islands of Nias (see page 767) and Mentawi (page 802). The forests, mountains, rivers and coasts of Sumatra provide trekking and rafting opportunities and pristine beaches.

Transmigration: 'A matter of life and death'

Transmigration is the government sponsored movement and resettlement of people from Java and Bali to the Outer Islands. President Sukarno said in the 1950s that transmigration was a 'matter of life and death for the Indonesian nation'. In believing this, he was emulating the Dutch who thought that the only way to solve what they saw to be Java's chronic overpopulation problem and resultant poverty, was by moving surplus people from Java to the Outer Islands. Since 1950, this process of resettlement has been known as 'transmigration', and the scheme has become one of the largest social engineering projects in the world. In total, over 6 million people have been plucked from Java and Bali and deposited in newly-built villages across the archipelago – in Sumatra, Kalimantan, Sulawesi, Nusa Tenggara and Irian Jaya.

Of these transmigrants, over 60% have been settled in Sumatra, and most of these in Lampung province. Lampung was chosen by the Dutch as the site for the first of the country's transmigration settlements (at that time called *kolonisasi*) in 1905, when 155 families were moved to Gedong Tataan District. Since then, hundreds of thousands have followed. For the Indonesian government, the transmigration scheme has had multiple objectives: to ease population pressure on Java, improve the standard of living of those being settled, promote regional development in the Outer Islands, raise agricultural output, and secure sensitive frontier areas.

But the scheme has also drawn severe criticism from environmentalists and human rights activists. They claim that it has led to massive deforestation and has displaced indigenous people from land that is rightfully theirs. The fact that the indigenous inhabitants of Irian Jaya and Kalimantan are ethnically, religiously and linguistically distinct from the settlers has led to accusations of 'Javanization' and 'ethnocide'. The construction of settlements in politically volatile areas such as East Timor and along the Irian Jaya-Papua New Guinea border lends some support to the notion that transmigration is being used as a political and military tool to unify the country.

It is also true that some of the settlements appear to have transferred the problems of Java to the Outer Islands. Lampung province now has a population of over 6 million, and during the 1970s and 1980s population growth averaged over 4% a year. As a result, deforestation and erosion have become severe problems and the province itself has now been designated a source area for transmigrants. The problem has come full circle.

Sumatra is also crucial to the Indonesian economy. It was in North Sumatra that Indonesia's first commercial oil well was sunk in 1871, and over 60% of the country's total production comes from the island and the waters around it. Sumatra also acts as a 'safety valve' for Java's 'excess' population. About 60% of Indonesia's transmigrants – 4 million people – have been resettled on Sumatra, mostly in the S (see box).

ENVIRONMENT

Land

A range of mountains – the Bukit Barisan – forms a spine running down Sumatra's W edge. Many of the 93 peaks exceed 2,000 m, the highest point being Mount Kerinci at 3,805 m. Like Java, Sumatra also has a string of active volcanoes, and the bowl that forms Lake Toba in North Sumatra was formed after a massive volcanic eruption. This occurred 100,000 years ago, and was probably the greatest explosion in geological history – causing over 1,500 km³ of rock to be blown into the sky.

To the W of the Bukit Barisan is a narrow ribbon of lowland – rarely more than 20 km wide – on which towns such as Padang and Sibolga cling tenaciously. Offshore, to the W, are the ethnologically fascinating Nias and Mentawi islands. To the E there is a wide expanse of mostly swampy lowland. Sumatra's largest rivers – such as the Musi, Hari and Rokan – cut through this lowland, carrying large quantities of silt and sediment to the coast, which is advancing at rates as high as 90 m a year. As it advances, so Sumatra is enveloping the inshore islands that constitute the Riau archipelago.

In general, the soils of Sumatra are poorer than those of Java and agriculture is correspondingly less productive. The lowlands of the E suffer from extensive waterlogging, and development is difficult. In the foothills, farmers have to contend with soils that are heavily leached and although the land may support thick forest, fertility quickly declines when it is cleared for agriculture. Tree crops have fared relatively well on these former forest lands and Sumatra is a significant exporter of natural rubber and palm oil. However, the area of Sumatra with the greatest agricultural potential is in the vicinity of the city of Medan. There, the volcanic soils are fertile and the Dutch colonial administration successfully promoted the cultivation of such estate crops as tea, tobacco, coffee and sisal.

Climate

Sumatra is bisected by the equator which runs through the island, just N of Bukittinggi. Temperatures vary little through the year – the annual range is only 1.4°C at sea-level. Far more important is rainfall in determining the seasons. The wettest part of the island is the narrow W coast plain and the W foothills of the Bukit Barisan. Here rainfall averages about 4,000 mm/year, but rises to 6,000 mm/year in the town of Bengkulu, as rain-filled clouds blown in over the Indian Ocean release their load before being forced up and over the Bukit Barisan. In central, E and N Sumatra rainfall is lower, ranging from 2,500 mm to 3,000 mm/year. To put these figures into perspective, average rainfall in Padang – some 4,500 mm – is 7 times higher than the figure for London.

There is rain throughout the year in Sumatra, but it is heaviest N of the equator between Oct and Apr, and S of the equator from Oct to Jan. The 'dry' season – a relative concept in this part of the world – is during Jun and Jul.

HISTORY

Pre-Colonial kingdoms: Srivijaya, Melayu and Aceh Sumatra does not have as rich a history as Java, but one great empire did evolve here – Srivijaya, or 'Glorious Victory'. **Srivijaya** was possibly the greatest of all Southeast Asia's maritime empires. Founded during the 7th century, it aggressively expanded its influence so that by the 9th century Srivijaya controlled all Sumatra, W Java, the E portion of Borneo and the Malay Peninsula as far N as S Thailand. In total, Srivijaya was the dominant power in the area for 350 years, from 670-1025, finally dissolving in the 14th century. With its capital at Palembang on the Musi River in SE Sumatra, Srivijaya was in a strategic position to control trade through the 2 most important straits in Southeast Asia: the Melaka Strait between the Malay Peninsula and Sumatra, and the Sunda Strait between Sumatra and Java. Palembang offered exhausted seafarers an excellent harbour and repair facilities, and an ample selection of recreational activities. In this last respect, the city acted in a manner not unlike latter-day Bangkok during the Vietnam War.

In order to exploit its position, the rulers of Srivijaya built up an impressive fleet with which they suppressed piracy in the Strait of Melaka. This gave traders the confidence to forego the more arduous – but safer – overland route across the Kra Isthmus. In a rather less humanitarian fashion, the fleet also forced all shipping passing through the strait to pay exorbitant taxes – an element of Srivijayan foreign policy which infuriated seafarers. With their stranglehold on trade that flowed through the region, Srivijaya's wealth and power expanded.

The Arab geographers Ibn Khurdadhbih (writing in 846) and Abu Zaid (writing in 916) record the custom of Srivijaya Maharajas 'communicating with the sea'. Each day, the Maharaja would propitiate the ocean by throwing a gold bar into the water, saying "Look, there lies my treasure" – and in so doing demonstrating his debt to the waters. When the Maharaja died, the gold bars would be dredged from the river bed and distributed to the royal family, military commanders, and to the ruler's other subjects. Foreign accounts of Srivijaya – and these are the only records that historians have to draw on – paint a picture of a kingdom of almost mythical wealth.

However, for an empire of such apparent size and wealth, there was – until very recently – surprisingly little physical evidence of its existence. Few temples, inscriptions, or fine art survives. Why this should be so has concentrated scholars' minds ever since the French archaeologist George Coedès identified Palembang as the capital of the empire in 1918. Some have argued that the lack of physical evidence is an indication that Srivijaya was, in fact, a kingdom of little consequence. However, most historians and archaeologists find this hard to believe. It may be that the politico-religious amalgam of indigenous symbols and Hindu-Buddhist legitimacy required few physical monuments; or because this portion of Sumatra is so swampy and unstable, much of the evidence has simply been lost or merely overlooked. Buildings were constructed of wood, and most edicts were probably recorded on *lontar* palm paper – neither would have survived the intervening years in such a hot and humid environment. Recent work in Palembang has, however, helped to shed some light on the problem. Indonesian and French archaeologists have uncovered several tonnes of artefacts from multiple sites in the city and demonstrated that Palembang was, indeed, the capital of Srivijaya. They argue that the conundrum is not hard to solve: the archaeology of Sumatra has simply been ignored.

The beginning of the end for Srivijaya's Empire came in 1025 when an Indian fleet set sail and sacked the ports along the E Sumatran coastline, including the capital. The motivation for the action has been linked to Srivijaya's exploitation of merchants – of which those of south India's Chola Kingdom were among the more numerous. By the 14th century, this former great empire had vanished from the historical landscape.

Following the destruction of Srivijaya, the rival **Melayu** Kingdom based not far from Jambi in South Sumatra came to prominence. Archaeological remains uncovered at Muara Jambi (**see page 806**) indicate that Melayu was influential from the late 11th to the late 13th centuries, but dated back to the 7th century. In 1278, the East Javanese Singasari Dynasty (**see page 517**) launched an expedition against Melayu and kidnapped a royal princess. She was married to a Singasari prince, and their son Adityavarman returned to his mother's homeland to become ruler. But, in the mid-14th century, Adityavarman decided to move his capital from the lowlands of South Sumatra into the Minang highlands of West Sumatra. It is presumed that Adityavarman made this move to insulate his kingdom from the attentions of the more powerful Javanese empires with whom relations were deteriorating.

By the 14th century a number of Muslim trading states had also arisen along the coastline facing the Strait of Melaka. Within 200 years, Islam had spread all the way down the coast and was beginning to make an impact on the N coast of Java. Of these sultanates, the greatest was Aceh, which reached the zenith of its influence during the reign of Sultan Iskandar Muda (**see page 745**). But, just at the time that Aceh seemed set to become a great empire, the European powers began to exert their influence over Sumatra.

The colonial period in Sumatra The European powers first established footholds on Sumatra in the 17th century. The Dutch built a fort at Padang on the W coast in 1663, and the British at Bengkulu in 1685. But these were far from secure and hardly substantive. Both the Dutch and the British were periodically expelled by local raiders as well as by one another and by a third European power, the French.

It was Sumatra's wealth in pepper, tin, gambier and, rather later, in coffee, which attracted settlers and traders to the island. With no significant indigenous power to offer a bulwark against outside intervention, it became an international free-for-all. The British, Americans, Dutch and the French were all pressing various claims to the island and its wealth. However, it was the Dutch who emerged as the dominant influence. In 1824, the British renounced their various claims to Sumatra in return for the Dutch doing the same in Malaya, and Bengkulu and Melaka were effectively 'swapped'.

But striking an accord with the British did not mean that Sumatra was under Dutch control. Much of the interior had yet even to be explored, let alone brought under effective administration. To do this, the Dutch had to wage a succession of wars during the 19th and into the 20th century. Among these, the most bitterly fought were the 'Padri' Wars of the early 19th century, focused on West Sumatra (**see page 773**), and the Acehnese resistance which dates from 1873, and continues – in another form – today (**see page 746**). It was not until 1910 that the Dutch could claim to have brought all Sumatra under their authority.

INFORMATION FOR VISITORS

Transport to and from Sumatra

The usual 'route' through Sumatra begins (or ends) at Medan, and takes in Lake Toba, Bukittinggi and Padang. From Padang, most travellers then catch the ferry or a plane to Jakarta. The more adventurous can proceed overland to the S tip of Sumatra where there are ferries from Panjang or Bakauheni, across the Sunda Strait, to Merak on Java, 3 hours from Jakarta. The other main entry/exit point is via Pekanbaru and the Riau Islands.

By air Most visitors arrive at Medan, on the W coast of Sumatra which offers international connections with Penang, Singapore, and Kuala Lumpur. It is increasingly popular to fly to Batam (Riau Islands) which is just a ½ hr ferry ride away from Singapore (**see page 788**). There are also international connections between Singapore and Pekanbaru, and domestic connections with Jakarta from all Sumatran provincial capitals.

By boat There is a twice weekly 'international' ferry linking Penang (Malaysia) with Belawan (Medan's port), 14 hrs. Hydrofoils and high-speed catamarans also make the crossing, daily. An alternative route into or out of Indonesia is to catch a regular ferry or hydrofoil from Singapore's Finger Pier to Batam or Bintan islands in the Riau archipelago. The most common domestic seaborne entry/exit point is Bakauheni on Sumatra's S tip; hourly ferries link Bakauheni with Merak, West Java. The Pelni ship *Rinjani* docks at ports on Sumatra's E coast every fortnight, while the *Kerinci* does the same on the W coast. From Tanjung Pinang on Bintan Island, there are regular ferries to Pekanbaru (**see page 793**).

Internal travel

Air Merpati, Garuda, Mandala and SMAC all operate in Sumatra. All provincial capitals and other major towns are served by these carriers (see route map, **page 1006**).

Train There is a limited rail network in S Sumatra, although some routes are only for freight. The only regular passenger service used by travellers is that linking Bandar Lampung, Palembang and Lubuklinggau.

Bus Bus transport is the main mode of long-distance travel. It is often a cultural experience in itself. Buses are crammed with people, animals and their belongings. Space is limited, seats are designed with small bottoms and narrow hips in mind – except in the VIP coaches – and

Sumatra: good buys

Bandar Aceh: Achenese daggers (*rencong*) and jewellery.
Bandar Lampung: traditional textiles including 'ship cloths'.
Bukittinggi: silver and gold jewellery.
Lake Toba, Brastagi and Bukittinggi: Batak handicrafts, including Batak calenders, carved spirit figures, traditional textiles, carved buffalo horn, and basketry.
Medan: for antiques and textiles from all over Sumatra.
Nias & Mentawi islands: ethnographic pieces, mostly woodcarvings.
Padang: hand woven *songket* cloth, embroidery, jewellery including fine silverwork and 'primitive' art from Mentawi Islands.
Palembang: lacquerware and traditional Palembang textiles.

delays and breakdowns are common. In the rainy season, the problems and delays become even more severe. But, steady improvements to the 2,500 km Trans-Sumatran 'Highway' (a misnomer – over large sections it is more like a village road, one and a half lanes wide) which runs down the entire island from Banda Aceh in the N to Bakauheni in the S, is making road travel much faster and more comfortable. It used to take 20 hrs from Prapat to Bukittinggi, now it takes 13 hrs. 'Coach travel stories' are becoming a thing of the past and there are 'full' a/c, VIP or express buses plying all the major routes. Roads off the Trans-Sumatran Highway are still generally poor, and in the rainy season delays of 2 days are not unknown while floodwaters subside. The most highly regarded private bus companies are **ALS** and **ANS**.

Taxi An alternative way to travel between towns is by chartered long-distance taxi. Shared taxis can be similar in price to buses. See town entries for addresses.

Accommodation, food and drink

In parts of Sumatra, such as the Riau Islands, the term *losmen* to describe a guesthouse is not used – *penginapan* is employed instead. During the 'off' season – Nov to May – hotels often have low occupancy rates and prices can be bargained down.

The town of Padang in West Sumatra is the home of Padang food – *makan padang* – now available just about everywhere in Indonesia but best sampled in its place of origin. A large selection of usually hot and spicy food is brought to the table and customers pay for whatever they eat (see page 776).

Other essential information

Conduct Sumatra is home to a number of ethnic, religious and cultural groups. Being polite and unruffled works wonders at all times. In the N, the province of Aceh is one of the most strictly Islamic in Indonesia and the same is also true of Padang. Particular care should be taken to dress conservatively (women should wear bras, long skirts/trousers and shirts with sleeves) and to respect Islamic laws. In West Sumatra, there are also some additional rules of conduct that should be observed (see page 776).

Shopping Local and regional handicrafts, textiles, jewellery and other works of art are the best and most distinctive buys in Sumatra (see box). Genuine antiques are rare: if a salesperson tries to sell a 'very old and very rare' work of art it is probably a fake.

Health Parts of Sumatra – the Riau and Mentawi islands particularly – have a serious malaria problem. Take adequate precautions to protect against malaria (note that chloroquine-resistant strains are now common), and also avoid insect bites in general (see page 25).

Best time to visit The rainy season extends from Oct to Apr, to the N of the Equator and from Oct to Jan to the S. Road travel during the dry season is quicker and easier, but overland travel in the wet season is fine on the (largely) all-weather Trans-Sumatran Highway. The most comfortable time to travel is during the onset of the rains (Sept-Oct) when temperatures have cooled but showers have not become torrential. Most tourists visit between Jun and Oct, so travelling out of those months is relatively quiet and hotel rates can often be bargained down.

Money Changing money in Sumatra is more difficult than in Java. Banks will occasionally look at travellers' cheques with incredulity. In some towns there are no banks at all, and hotels provide unattractive rates of exchange. Travellers leaving for Samosir Island in the middle of Lake Toba, for example, are advised to change money in either Medan or Prapat. For those going to the Nias or Mentawi islands, sufficient money should be changed in Sibolga or Padang respectively.

Tourist information There are tourist information offices in major tourist centres, and regional offices (*Dinas Pariwisata*) in the regional capitals. In the main, the offices are poorly organized in comparison with Java and the staff are not very helpful.

Suggested reading Loeb, Edwin M (1972) *Sumatra: its history and people*, Oxford University Press: Kuala Lumpur (first published 1935). Carle, Rainer (edit) (1981) *Cultures and societies of North Sumatra*, Dietrich Rimmer Verlag: Berlin. Barlow, Colin and Thee Kian Wie (1988) *The North Sumatran regional economy: growth with unbalanced development*, Asian Economic Research Unit, Occasional paper No. 82, Institute of Southeast Asian Studies: Singapore.

NORTHERN SUMATRA

INTRODUCTION

For this guidebook, Sumatra has been split into 2: Northern and Southern Sumatra. The division does not correspond with any administrative division. Northern Sumatra consists of only 2 provinces: Aceh and North Sumatra. North Sumatra is the most populous province on the island with over 10 million inhabitants. The city of Medan is the 'gateway' to Sumatra. The Special Territory of Aceh encompasses the far N portion of the island. The 3½ million Acehnese are ardent Muslims and the area is still plagued by insurrection. Few visitors take the road N; most head SW to the Batak highlands and Lake Toba, both in North Sumatra. Nias Island is also administered as part of North Sumatra.

MEDAN

Medan, on the E of Sumatra, is the island's largest city with well over 2 million inhabitants. It is big, hot, noisy, congested and dirty with only a few havens of greenery – for example, Merdeka Square. Yet, travellers entering Indonesia from Malaysia will have to pass through Medan.

It is the third most important entry point after Jakarta and Bali. Most visitors try to keep their stay as short as possible. But the accommodation has improved in range and quality over the years, and there is a good selection of reasonable restaurants. Some visitors even profess to liking Medan.

Medan was established in 1682 as a trading centre and there is still some evidence of a graceful and rather less frenetic past. In 1886 the Dutch made it their regional capital, but even as recently as 1942 it had a fairly modest population of less than 100,000. During the period of Dutch rule, economic development was more marked in North Sumatra than in any other region outside Java. The volcanic soils of the surrounding area are rich and the land was rapidly cleared for plantation agriculture. Medan developed from little more than a village to become the administrative hub of an agriculturally-based export economy, and large quantities of tea, rubber, coffee and tobacco were funnelled through Belawan – Medan's port – to the Strait of Melaka and from there to markets in Europe. To fuel this economic growth, the Dutch used immigrant Chinese labourers, and even today Medan has one of the largest Chinese populations in Indonesia.

Medan remains the most important commercial centre in Sumatra, handling many of North Sumatra's natural resource exports. Among the most important are rubber, palm oil and, of course, petroleum. As in so many other towns in Southeast Asia, a disproportionate share of the wealth of Medan is controlled by an entrepreneurial Chinese community. The inequalities between the ostentaciously wealthy and the depressingly poor are all too obvious.

Places of interest
The greatest concentration of **colonial buildings** is to be found along Jalan Jend. A. Yani (which becomes Jalan Balai Kota) and around Merdeka Square. Few still perform their original functions as the headquarters of plantation companies, European clubs, and stately hotels. At Jalan Jend. A. Yani 105, to the S of Merdeka Square, there is a rather run-down and romantically decrepit **quasi-colonial/quasi-Chinese mansion** with a peacock-topped entrance arch;

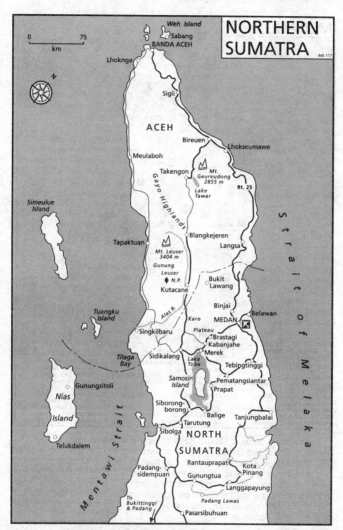

NORTHERN SUMATRA

IMS 117

this was built by a wealthy Chinese businessman named Tjong A. Fie. Other notable buildings include the **Bank of Indonesia** (formerly the De Javaamsche Bank), the **Balai Kota**, **Jakarta Lloyd** and the offices of the **British Council** (once the headquarters of the English plantation company Harrisons and Crosfield). The central **Post Office**, built in 1911 and unchanged since then, is at Jalan Bukit Barisan 1, overlooking Merdeka Square. Another road with historical buildings is the garden-like Jalan Jend. Sudirman (Polonia quarter), SW of the town square.

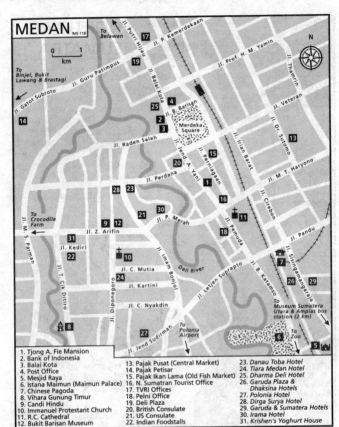

MEDAN IMS 118

1. Tjong A. Fie Mansion
2. Bank of Indonesia
3. Balai Kota
4. Post Office
5. Mesjid Raya
6. Istana Maimun (Maimun Palace)
7. Chinese Pagoda
8. Vihara Gunung Timur
9. Candi Hindu
10. Immanuel Protestant Church
11. R.C. Cathedral
12. Bukit Barisan Museum
13. Pajak Pusat (Central Market)
14. Pajak Petisar
15. Pajak Ikan Lama (Old Fish Market)
16. N. Sumatran Tourist Office
17. TVRI Offices
18. Pelni Office
19. Deli Plaza
20. British Consulate
21. US Consulate
22. Indian Foodstalls
23. Danau Toba Hotel
24. Tiara Medan Hotel
25. Dharma Deli Hotel
26. Garuda Plaza & Dhaksina Hotels
27. Polonia Hotel
28. Dirga Surya Hotel
29. Garuda & Sumatera Hotels
30. Irama Hotel
31. Krishen's Yoghurt House

The attractively decayed **Mesjid Raya** or **Grand Mosque**, with its fine black domes and turquoise tiles can be found at the corner of Jalan Sisingamangaraja and Jalan Mesjid Raya. The mosque was built in 1906 in 'Moroccan' style by Sultan Makmun Al-Rasyid, and designed by a Dutch architect. The marble came from Italy, the chandelier from Amsterdam, and the stained-glass from China. In the grounds is a small enclosed plot containing the tombs of the sultans of the Istana Maimun Palace (see below), and a fairy-tale style minaret. Admission: by donation.

To the W of the mosque, set back from the road on Jalan Brig. Jen. Katamso, is the **Istana Maimun** – also known as the **Istana Sultan Deli**. This impressive building was designed by a Dutchman (some say an Italian) and constructed in 1888 as one element in a complex that included the Grand Mosque. It is eclectic architecturally, embracing Italian, Arab, and Oriental styles. Inside are photographs of the various sultans and their wives, and a poor oil painting of the Sultan Deli himself who built the palace. The interior includes a few pieces of

Dutch furniture and the Sultan's throne. His descendants continue to live in one wing of the Palace. Admission: by donation. Open: daytime.

Scattered throughout the city are a large number of shrines, churches, temples, pagodas and mosques. The plain **Chinese pagoda**, just off Jalan Pandu, not far from the railway line (near No. 2), contains a jumbled array of Buddhas, Chinese deities and ancestor tablets, and is permeated with the smell of burning incense. At the SW edge of the city is the **Vihara Gunung Timur**, at Jalan Hang Tuah 16, just W of Jalan Cik Ditiro. This building is the largest Chinese pagoda in Medan. Set in a peaceful area, the entrance is flanked by 2 guardian lions. Filled with lanterns, incense and demons, the temple is a rewarding retreat from the bustle of the city. **NB:** no photography is allowed in the pagoda and remove shoes before entering the inner sanctuary with its Buddha statues. **Candi Hindu** at Jalan H. Zainul Arifin 130, is an Indian temple serving Medan's large South Asian community and has been recently renovated and expanded. The **Immanuel Protestant Church**, built in 1921 in Art-Deco style, can be found at Jalan Diponegoro 25, while the **Roman Catholic Cathedral of the Immaculate Conception** at Jalan Pemuda 1 was constructed in 1929. Strangely, the entrance is flanked by military mines and shells.

The **Museum Sumatera Utara**, on Jalan H.M. Joni, is an extensive building with an equally extensive – though of variable quality – collection of artefacts. Not surprisingly, it specializes in those of North Sumatran origin and upstairs has some fine wood and stone-carvings from the Nias Islands. Unfortunately it is ill-lit and poorly maintained, with little useful explanatory detail. Admission: 200Rp. Open: 0900-1700 Tues-Sun. The **Bukit Barisan Museum** at Jalan H. Zainul Arifin 8, displays a decaying selection of Sumatran tribal houses and arts and crafts as well as military paraphernalia. Open: 0800-1300 Mon-Thurs & Sat. Rather further out of downtown Medan, travelling S towards Prapat is the **Taman Margasatwa Zoo** (Kebun Binatang) on Jalan Katamso. It imprisons a miserable selection of poorly kept regional wildlife in a small park. Admission: 500Rp, 750Rp Sun and hols. Open: Mon-Sun.

One of the greatest attractions of Medan are its markets, known locally as *pajak*. The huge **Central Market** or *Pajak Pusat* (Pajak Sentral) – in fact an agglomeration of various markets selling just about everything – is located close to Jalan Dr. Sutomo. It is renowned for its pickpockets. Safer is the **Pajak Petisar**, on Jalan Rasak Baru, just off Jalan Gatot Subroto. It is a fruit and vegetable market in the morning (0600), that later develops into a general market, selling clothes, food, and general merchandise. The **Pajak Ikan Lama** (Old Fish Market) is a good place to buy cheap batik, other types of cloth, and assorted garments. It is on Jalan Perniagaan, close to Jalan Jend. A. Yani. Visitors may see live fruit bats strung up for sale – lucky ones could have the chance to eat them too.

Excursions

Asam Kumbang Crocodile Farm is 5 km from the city, off Jalan Kampung Lalang, at Asam Kumbang Village. It is the largest crocodile farm in Indonesia, with over 2,000 of the beasts. The crocodiles are hatched, reared and made into bags. **Getting there:** by town bus (*bis damri*) from Jalan Balai Kota. Ask for *Asam Kumbang* and take a becak the final few kilometres.

Binjei, Brastagi and the Orang Utan Rehabilitation Centre at Bukit Lawang are all accessible as day trips from Medan. 22 km W of Medan on route 25 is **Binjei**, famed for its fruit – and especially its rambutans and durians. The best time to visit is when they are in season, Jul-Aug. It is possible to reach **Brastagi (see page 752)** and the **Orang Utan Rehabilitation Centre** at Bukit Lawang **(page 744)** from here (about 3 hrs). **Getting there:** regular buses and minibuses travel down Jalan Gatot Subroto, which becomes Jalan Binjei, leaving from the Central Market, ¾hr (500Rp). Bukit Lawang can be visited as a long day trip.

Bandar Baru, on the road to Brastagi, is Medan's red light district – in fact a red light town. Bandar Baru is a vast collection of hotels and brothels, serving the city's male population, who can be seen driving out in convoy, in their darkened windowed cars on a Sat night. **N.B.** Indonesia does have AIDS.

Tours Tour companies have offices in most of the larger hotels and organize half day city tours, and day tours to Brastagi and to the orang utans at Bukit Lawang. Longer overnight tours to Lake Toba and to the Nias Islands are also offered by most tour agents. *Pacto Tours* run raft adventures down the Alas River from Medan (5 days, US$499; 13 days, US$1,299) **(see page 754)**. *Edelweiss* also organize rafting and trekking tours.

Festivals *Apr* (moveable): *Idul Fitri* (Islamic holy day), Muslims descend on the Maimun Palace in traditional dress to mark the end of the fasting month of Ramadan – very colourful. *Mar-May: Medan Fair* is held between Mar and May each year at the Taman Ria Amusement Park on Jalan Gatot Subroto. There are also permanent cultural exhibits at the park.

Accommodation **A+-A** *Danau Toba*, Jl. Imam Bonjol 17, T 327000, F 27020, a/c, several restaurants, good pool, good range of facilities, too large to be personal and some recent visitors have reported that the management is none too helpful; **A** *Dirga Surya*, Jl. Imam Bonjol 6, T 321555, F 513387, a/c, restaurant, modern, but with a Chinese ambiance; **A** *Tiara Medan*, Jl. Cut Mutia, T 516000, F 510176, a/c, restaurant, pool, tennis, squash, new and lavish, most stylish hotel in town, rec; **A-B** *Dharma Deli*, Jl. Balai Kota 2, T 327011, F 327153, a/c, restaurant, pool, colonial-style hotel in centre of town, reasonable rooms and service, attractive gardens and some original decor, rec; **A-B** *Garuda Plaza*, Jl. Sisingamangaraja 18, T 326255, F 517565, a/c, restaurant, small pool, health club, large, modern hotel, close to Maimun Palace and the mosque; **B** *Pardede*, Jl. Ir. H. Juanda 14, T 323866, a/c, restaurant, small pool; **B** *Polonia*, Jl. Jend. Sudirman 14, T 325300, F 519553, a/c, restaurant, pool, not very central but near the airport and recently renovated, good sports facilities; **B-C** *Angkasa*, Jl. Sutomo 1, T 322555, a/c, restaurant, pool, featureless hotel, average rooms; **C** *Dhaksina*, Jl. Sisingamangaraja 20, T 324561, some a/c, own bathroom, clean; **C** *Kenanga*, Jl. Sisingamangaraja 82, T 712426, F 716399, some a/c, dorm (**F**); **C-D** *Garuda*, Jl. Sisingamangaraja 27, T 324453, some a/c, recently renovated, clean, near mosque; **C-D** *Sumatera*, Jl. Sisingamangaraja 35, T 24973, some a/c, price includes breakfast, clean, good value, rec; **D** *Legundri*, Jl. Kirana 22 (near Medan Plaza), T 521924, some a/c, clean, but for shared bathroom rather expensive; **E** *Melati*, Jl. Amaluin 6, T 516021, some a/c, musty rooms with shared bathrooms; **F** *Irama*, Jl. Palang Merah 112-S, T 326416, good base for travellers just arriving in Indonesia, with information on destinations in Sumatra including Nias Island, friendly; **F** *Krishen's Yoghurt House* (formerly *Jacky's*), Jl. Kediri 96, T 516864, Jacky is an excellent source of information, friendly, some cheaper dorm beds, but beware, he has a bad reputation with Western women, rec; **F** *Losmen Berlin Baru*, Jl. Hindu 3, gloomy, dark, dingy, only as the very last of resorts; **F** *Sarah Guesthouse*, Jl. Pertama 10, friendly, with good information, 10 mins from bus station, rec.

Restaurants Medan is better served with decent and reasonable restaurants than it is with hotels. **Indonesian:** ◆◆*Ambassador*, Jl. Pemuda 2, specializes in Minang and Melayu food, rec.; ◆◆*Angelo's Café*, Jl. Jend. A. Yani 29; ◆◆*Garuda IV*, Jl. Gajah Mada; ◆◆*Famili*, Jl. Sisingamangaraja 21B, specializes in Padang food; ◆◆*Jumbo*, Jl. Putri Hijau 8, seafood. **Other Asian cuisines:** ◆◆◆*Angkasa Hotel*, Jl. Sutomo 1, good Chinese food; ◆*Krishen's Yoghurt House* (formerly *Jacky's*), Jl. Kediri 96, Indian, travellers' haven, good food; ◆*Kohinoor*, Jl. Mesjid 21, N Indian; ◆◆◆*Polonia Hotel*, Jl. Jend Sudirman 14, excellent Chinese; ◆◆◆*Yokohama*, Jl. Nibung Raya 58, best Japanese in town; ◆◆◆*Danau Toba Hotel*, Jl. Imam Bonjol 17, Japanese. **Foodstalls:** *Selat Panjang* behind Jl. Pandu has stalls selling Chinese (and seafood) and Indonesian favourites. Jl. Semarang off Jl. Pandu also has foodstalls. ◆*Surya Food Centre*, Jl. Imam Bonjol 6, lots of open-air stalls open till late, seafood, rec. The new shopping plazas, such as **Deli Plaza** and **Thamrin Plaza** have good, cheap 'food centres'. Indian food can be found at the foodstalls on Jl. Jenggala, Jl. Cik Ditiro and Jl. Pagaruyung. **International:** ◆◆*Kentucky Fried Chicken*, 5 of these scattered around town, mostly in the shopping complexes; ◆◆*Lyn's*, Jl. Jend. A. Yani 98A, steaks; ◆◆*Pizza Hut*, Jl. Jend. Sudirman; ◆◆*Tip Top*, Jl. Jend. A. Yani 92, an old favourite, with some tables outside, it also serves Chinese and Indonesian food and icecream.

Bars *Lyn's Bar*, Jl. Jend. A. Yani 98A.

Entertainment **Cultural performances:** are held twice a week at the *Bina Budaya* on Jl.

Perintis Kemerdekaan. **Discos**: the *Xanadu* at the *Dirga Surya Hotel*, Jl. Imam Bonjol 6; *Le Cartier*, Jl. Ir. H. Juanda 14; *Dynasty* at *Danau Toba Hotel*, Jl. Imam Bonjol. **Night Clubs**: the *Bali Plaza*, Jl. Kumango 1A.

Sports Golf: *Nicotiana*, Jl. Karya, 9 holes. *Polonia*, near the airport, 9 holes. *Tuntungan*, 30 minutes towards Brastagi, excellent 18 hole course. **Health clubs**: *Danau Toba Hotel*, *Polonia Hotel* and *Tiara Hotel*. **Swimming**: *Dharma Deli Hotel*, Jl. Balai Kota 2. **Tennis**: *Danau Toba Hotel*, Jl. Imam Bonjol 17, *Tiara Hotel*, Jl. Cut Mutia. **Ten-pin Bowling**: *Marati Bowling*, Jl. Gatot Subroto 32.

Shopping Antiques: Jl. Jend. A. Yani is the main shopping area, with the largest concentration of 'antique' shops. Beware of fakes: old Batak artefacts are cunningly mass produced. There are few real antiques for sale these days. Shops include *Borobudur Art Shop*, at No. 32; *ABC Art Gallery*, No. 50; *Rufindo*, No. 56; *Toko Bali*, No. 68. **Plazas**: *Sinar Plaza* and *Deli Plaza*, both on the corner of Jl. Putri Hijau and Jl. Guru Patimpus; *Thamrin Plaza* on Jl. Thamrin. **Textiles**: Jl. Jend. A. Yani III, which runs off Jl. Jend. A. Yani has a number of textile outlets. Browsing through the markets can be rewarding – either the massive Central Market or the Old Fish Market; the latter is the best place to buy batik (see Places of interest, above). Both *Batik Semar* and *Batik Keris* are to be found on Jl. Z. Arifin.

Local transport By becak, sudaco, mesin becak (motorized becak), bis damri (150Rp), metered taxi and kijang – if it moves, it can be hired. It is amazing how some of the mesin becaks keep going. **Car hire**: National Car Rental (*Dharma Deli Hotel*), Jl. Balai Kota 2, T 327011. **Taxis**: can be rented by the day; ask at your hotel or T 524659, T 520952.

Banks & money changers Bank Central Asia, Jl. Bukit Barisan 3; **Bank Dagang Negara**, Jl. Jend. A. Yani 109; **Ekspor Impor**, Jl. Balai Kota 8; **Bank Negara Indonesia**, Jl. Pemuda 12; **Bank Duta**, Jl. Pemuda 9.

Embassies & consulates Belgium, Jl. Pattimura 459, T 520559; **Denmark**, Jl. Hang Jebat 2, T 323020; **Germany**, Jl. Let. Jend. Parman 217, T 520908; **Japan**, Jl. Suryo 12, T 510533; **Malaysia**, Jl. Diponegoro 11, T 511567; **Netherlands**, Jl. Rivai 22, T 519025; **Norway**, Jl. Zainul Arifin 55, T 510158; **Singapore**, Jl. T. Daud 3, T 513366; **Sweden**, Jl. Hang Jebat 2, T 511017; **UK**, Jl. Jend. A. Yani 2, T 323564; **USA**, Jl. Imam Bonjol 13, T 322200.

Useful addresses General Post Office: Jl. Bukit Barisan 1 (on Merdeka Square). **Area code**: 061. **Perumtel**: Jl. Putri Hijau 1 (near GPO) for fax, telex, telegraph and international telephone. **Immigration office**: Jl. Jend. A. Yani 74. **Hospitals**: Herna Hospital, Jl. Majapahit 118A, T 515397; *St. Elizabeth's Hospital*, Jl. Haji Misbah 7, T 512455. **Clinic**: Bunda (24 hours), Jl. Sisingamangaraja. **Police station**: Jl. Durian, T 520453. **PHPA**: Jl. Sisingamangaraja Km 5.5, T 23658.

Airline offices Cathay Pacific, *Tiara Hotel*, Jl. Cut Mutia, T 526088; **Garuda**, *Dharma Deli Hotel*, Jl. Balai Kota 2, T 516066; and Jl. Suprapto 2, T 516680; **KLM**, *Dharma Deli Hotel*, Jl. Balai Kota 2, T 515266; **Mandala**, Jl. Brig. Jend. Katamso 37E, T 513309; **Malaysian Airlines (MAS)**, *Danau Toba Hotel*, Jl. Imam Bonjol 17, T 519333; **Merpati**, Jl. Brig. Jend. Katamso 41, T 28801; **Sempati**, *Tiara Hotel*, Jl. Cut Mutia, T 512444; **Singapore Airlines**, *Polonia Hotel*, Jl. Jend. Sudirman 14, T 518100; **SMAC**, Jl. Imam Bonjol 59, T 515934.

Tour companies & travel agents Concentration on Jl. Brig. Jend. Katamso. *Asri Nusantara*, Jl. Jend. S. Siswomiharjo 50B, T 325754; *Edelweiss*, Jl. Irian Barat 47, T 517297; *Mutiara*, *Danau Toba Hotel*, Jl. Imam Bonjol 17, T 327000; *Natrabu*, *Tiara Hotel*, Jl. Cut Mutia, T 516000; *Nitour Inc*, Jl. Prof. H.M. Yamin 21E, T 23191; *Pacto*, Jl. Brig. Jend. Katamso 35D, T 513669; *Trophy*, Jl. Brig. Jend. Katamso 33D, T 514888.

Tourist offices Medan Tourist Office (Kanwil Pariwisata), Jl. Alpalah 22, T 322838. Unhelpful and out of town. **North Sumatran Tourist Office** (Dinas Pariwisata), Jl. Jend. A. Yani 107, T 511101. Helpful; maps and other information. Open: 0800-1400 Mon-Thurs, 0800-1300 Sat. **Jacky**, at Krishen's Yoghurt House, Jl. Kediri 96, is also an informal information centre – a good place for travellers to obtain up-to-date information.

Transport to & from Medan 66 km from Brastagi, 176 km from Prapat/Lake Toba, 349 km from Sibolga, 728 km from Bukittinggi, 819 km from Padang, 594 km from Banda Aceh.

By air: Medan's international Polonia Airport is 3 km S of the town. A taxi to the city centre costs 4,500Rp. Regular connections on Mandala, Garuda/Merpati and Sempati with most Sumatran destinations including Padang, Banda Aceh, Batam, Pekanbaru and Nias; several flights a day to Jakarta and other Indonesian towns beyond Sumatra (**see route map, page 1006**). Passengers should ensure they have a confirmed seat.

By bus: Medan has two new, main bus terminals: Amplas and Pinang Baris. Amplas terminal is on Jl. Medan Tenggara VII and serves Bukittinggi, Prapat and Lake Toba (4 hrs),

Jakarta, Jambi, Pekanbaru, Palembang and Sibolga. Get there by oplet (250Rp). The Pinang Baris terminal is on Jl. Pinang Baris and serves Banda Aceh and other destinations N of Medan; buses to Brastagi 2 hrs, also leave from the Pinang Baris terminal.

Blue Timur 'taxis' (in fact minibuses) for Binjei leave regularly from Jl. Kumango which is parallel to Jl. Perniagaan, N of the tourist office (500Rp). For Bohorok and Bukit Lawang, **see page 745**.

By boat: Medan's port, Belawan, is 26 km N of the city. Town buses for Belawan leave from the intersection of Jl. Balai Kota and Jl. Guru Patimpus, near the TVRI offices. Pelni have connections with Jakarta once a week, 36 hrs (**see page 1006** for route map). Pelni's office is at Jl. Kol Sugiono 5, T 518899.

By train: the station is on Jl. Prof. M. Yamin. There is a limited rail network around Medan but few use it.

By taxi: most of the taxi companies are located at Jl. Sisingamangaraja 60-107.

International connections By air: with Penang and Singapore. Garuda runs weekly direct flights from Amsterdam and Vienna. **By boat**: ferry connections with Penang (Malaysia), the *Selasa Express*, a high speed catamaran, leaves Belawan (Medan's port) for Penang every Tues, Thurs, Fri and Sun at 1330, 4-5 hrs (80,000Rp). *Selasa's* office in Medan is at Jl. Brig. Jend. Katamso 35C, T 514888. Free transfer to port. *GSA* operate a hydrofoil between Belawan and Penang, every Tues, Thurs and Sun 0900, 4½ hrs (68,350Rp). Tickets from *Sukma Travel*, Jl. Brig. Jend. Katamso 62A, T 516045. Free transfer to port. *GSA* are considering adding Langkawi (Malaysia) to their destinations.

THE ROUTE NORTH: Medan to Bukit Lawang and Banda Aceh

The Trans-Sumatran Highway runs W from Medan to Binjei, a distance of 22 km. At Binjei, a minor road continues NW to Bukit Lawang and the Orang Utan Rehabilitation Centre, while the main highway turns N for the fast 600 km journey along the E coast past plantations, rice fields and swamps, to Banda Aceh. Stops could include the important natural gas town of Lhokseumawe, Bireuen – a provincial market town – or Sigli, famed for its strict adherence to Islam. All 3 towns have a reasonable selection of losmen, but little else. From Bireuen, a road cuts S and inland to Takengon and Lake Tawar, and from there into the Gunung Leuser National Park, before linking up with the Medan-Lake Toba road.

Bukit Lawang

Bukit Lawang is a small community on the edge of the **Gunung Leuser Reserve** (see page 754), an area of stunningly beautiful countryside. Just outside the village is the famous **Orang Utan Rehabilitation Centre**, established in 1973. The orang utan (*Pongo pygmaeus*) is on the verge of extinction throughout its limited range across island Southeast Asia, and the centre has been established by the World Wide Fund for Nature to rehabilitate domesticated orang utan's for life in the wild (**see page 224** for more information on these apes).

Seeing the orang utans The entrance to the reserve is a 30 minute walk from the village following the Bohorok River, which then has to be crossed by boat. Visitors can see the apes during feeding times (0800-0900 and 1500-1600), although these do sometimes change, so check at the PHPA office in Bukit Lawang. All visitors must obtain a 3-day permit from the PHPA office (3,000Rp) before entering the park. The office is open: 0700-1500 Mon-Sun. **NB:** passport must be shown before a permit is issued. Leave Bukit Lawang 45 minutes before feeding for the walk and river crossing. Afternoons are more crowded, especially at weekends; it is best to stay the night and watch a morning, weekday, feed if possible. Next door to the PHPA office is a Visitors Information Centre, with an informative slide show in English on Mon, Wed and Fri at 2000, a display, and small collection of relevant literature.

Excursions

Hiking is the best way to experience the forest and see the wildlife. The visitors centre has handouts and maps of hiking trails. Hikes, with obligatory guide, range from one day to one week and cost 15,000Rp/person for a 1 day hike, 20,000Rp/person/day for a 2 day hike, and 25,000Rp/person/day for a 3-5 days hike. Minimum 3 people, all inclusive. It is possible to hike to Brastagi in 3 days. Some people have marvellous treks, followed by friendly orang utans which allow themselves to be petted (hardly aiding their rehabilitation); others see nothing.

There are a number of **caves** in the vicinity of Bukit Lawang, along with **rubber processing plants** – ask at the visitors centre for a handout and map.

Floating down the Bohorok River on an inner tube has become a popular excursion. Tubes can be hired (1,000Rp/day) in the village for the 12 km (2-3 hrs) journey for 12 km (2-3 hrs) to the first bridge. There is public transport from the bridge back to Bukit Lawang. There have been reports of near drownings – take care.

Accommodation A number of losmen line the Bohorok River up to the crossing-point for the reserve. **E** *Wisma Bukit Lawang*; **E-F** *Wisma Leuser Sibayak*, T 20774, good swimming point, popular but not terribly clean; **F** *Yusman Guesthouse*, clean, shared bathroom, friendly, rec; **F** *Bukit Lawang Indah*, shared bathroom, clean; **F** *Selayang Indah* (10 mins from PHPA office), friendly, good food, rec; **F** *Eden Inn* (15 mins walk from PHPA office); **F** *Green Paradise Inn* (20 mins walk from PHPA office); **F** *Jungle Inn* (25 mins walk from PHPA office).

Camping Free camping ground about a 15 minute walk upriver towards the crossing-point for the reserve.

Restaurants Travellers' food at losmen; good at *Selayang Indah*, *Leuser Sibayak* and *Yusman*. Handful of warungs.

Banks & money changers Losmen will change money, but rates are poor so it is best to bring sufficient cash.

Tourist offices Visitors Information Centre (near the minibus stop), free maps and advice on hiking. Open: 0900-1500 Mon-Sat, 1000-1500 Sun.

Transport to & from Bukit Lawang 87 km from Medan. **By bus**: from Medan; first catch one of the many buses or minibuses that run down Jl. Jend. Gatot Subroto (which becomes Jl. Binjei) a busy 22 km to Binjei, 45 mins (200Rp by town bus, 500Rp by Timur 'taxi' minibus). From Binjei, Timur taxis leave every 20 mins for Bohorok and Bukit Lawang, 0800-1800, 2¼ hrs (1,750Rp). There are also occasional buses (1,100Rp). From Brastagi, catch a bus to Medan and get off when it reaches route 25; from here, catch a regular bus to Binjei; and from Binjei a minibus to Bukit Lawang (see above). There is one direct bus each day from Brastagi to Bukit Lawang via Medan; the bus doing the return trip leaves Bukit Lawang at 0530. The road deteriorates over the final 10 km to Bukit Lawang. **By taxi**: for hire in Medan, 2 hrs.

Banda Aceh

Banda Aceh, at the N extremity of Sumatra, has a population of 75,000 and is the capital of the Special Region or *Daerah Istimewa* of Aceh (the only other is Yogyakarta). It has been plagued by political turmoil ever since the Dutch began to exert their influence over the area in the late 19th century. The discovery of large reserves of natural gas in the 1960s has helped to make the province one of the richest in Indonesia, but the failure to unite the population behind the central government means the fruits have often not filtered down to the average man or woman. The bulk of the population are still farmers and even though much of the province is mountainous and inaccessible, Aceh maintains a healthy rice surplus.

Aceh grew to prominence as an Islamic trading centre during the 16th century. The sultanate's wealth was based upon the pepper trade and several expeditions were sent to Melaka to try and dislodge the competing – and infidel – Portuguese. They failed in each instance. Aceh reached the height of its power during the reign of the brilliant Sultan Iskandar Muda (1607-1636) when the city became a cultural and economic centre, controlling the entire W coast of Sumatra as well as a substantial proportion of the E coast and parts of the Malay

The Aceh War (1873-1878)

The Dutch found quelling the sultanate of Aceh to be their most difficult military task on Sumatra – something which in a sense they never achieved. In 1873 the Dutch mounted an expeditionary force of 3,000 men to confront the sultan and his army. Within weeks the force had retreated, its commander killed in the shadows of the city's mosque. The Dutch reacted to this humiliation by collecting together a force of 10,000 men, supported by 4,300 servants and coolies. They captured the city within 2 months, although not before losing several thousand men – mainly from cholera. The Dutch announced the abolition of the sultanate and the annexation of Aceh. But the resistance was far from subdued and the Dutch military were forced to continue to wage a low intensity war against the rebels until 1903.

Peninsula. Iskandar Muda enthusiastically promoted Islam in his kingdom (first introduced by Arab traders during the 9th or 10th centuries) and it is said that when 2 drunken Acehnese were brought to him he had them executed by pouring molten lead down their throats. His military forces included a regiment of cavalry mounted on Persian horses, an elephant corps, and a navy of heavy galleys. Iskandar was constantly worried about his successor and even had his own son killed because he could not trust him. Following Iskandar's death, and with a fall in pepper prices and the growing power of the Europeans, Aceh gradually declined in influence.

Although by all accounts Iskandar Muda was absolutely ruthless, his reign saw a flowering of Acehnese arts. For example, a tradition of goldsmithing was established as a result of the discovery of mines to the W and the city became famous for the quality of its gold jewellery and dagger hilts. Today, gold ornamentation is still highly valued; brides wear cloths known as *songket* (**see page 810**), which have gold woven into them, and belts of gold called *simplaih*.

The Acehnese have displayed a long-standing penchant for resisting externally imposed authority. This thirst for autonomy means that Aceh feels almost like a nation apart. The Dutch lost large numbers of soldiers during the Aceh War (1873-1878) which never succeeded in completely quelling local resistance (see box). Even since independence, Aceh has continued to demonstrate its distaste for central control. In 1953 there arose a vigorous rebellion over the role of Islam, and this rumbled on until 1962. There remains the impression that the authorities have only a tenuous hold over this diverse and fiercely independent province.

In the summer of 1990 there were widespread reports of increased activity by the rebel Aceh Merdeka (Free Aceh) guerrillas, and accusations of a heavy-handed military response, with summary arrest of suspects, torching of villages, and beatings. It should be stressed that few of these reports have been confirmed, although there is little doubt that Aceh remains a 'problem' area for the government and Amnesty International in 1993 estimated that 2,000 civilians have been unlawfully killed – some in public executions – since 1989. Few visitors will see any evidence of rebel activity, although buses are sometimes stopped at military roadblocks on the main road N (particularly at night). Tourists should remember that Aceh is possibly the most staunchly Muslim region in Indonesia.

Places of interest

Much of Banda Aceh's glorious past was destroyed when the Dutch invaded the town in 1874, including the Sultan's Palace and the Great Mosque. Banda Aceh is a small provincial capital and can be explored on foot, with most of the sights of interest found S of the centre of town.

A good place to start a tour of the sights is the **Mesjid Raya Baiturrahman**, or Great Mosque, at the intersection of Jalan Perdagangan and Jalan Balai Kota. The mosque was built by the Dutch in 1879 to replace the one that they had destroyed during the assault on 14 Apr 1873. The commander of the Dutch forces, J.H.R.

BANDA ACEH

IMS 119
Not to Scale

1. Mesjid Raya Baiturrahman
2. Market
3. Aceh Museum
4. Gunungan
5. Kher Khoff
6. Seulawah (a Dakota DC3)
7. Pasar Ikan
8. Post Office
9. Tourist Office
10. Immigration Office
11. Tropicana Restaurant
12. Kuala Tripa Hotel
13. Sultan Hotel
14. Losmen Yusry
15. Aceh Hotel
16. Losmen International
17. Losmen Palembang
18. Prapat Hotel
19. Wisma Lading

B. Bemo, short distance
   bus station

Kohler was killed in the attack and a plaque marks the spot where he fell. The black-domed and white-walled mosque, with its gardens and ponds, is an island of peace in the city. Open to non-Muslims: 0700-1100, 1330-1600 Mon-Sun. Remove shoes, women should be veiled, dress appropriately. Behind the mosque and to the W is the **Chinese quarter** and the **market** with jewellery and handicrafts for sale.

SE of the mosque, down Jalan Alauddin Mahmudsyah, is the **Aceh Museum** which displays a range of local artefacts, but unfortunately there is little explanatory information. Open: 0830-1330, 1430-1800 Tues-Thurs, 0830-1200 Fri & Sat. In the same compound as the museum is a black-stained **rumah Aceh**, a model of a traditional Acehnese aristocrat's house. Here too are the graves of a number of 18th century sultans of Aceh. Right next to the museum, in the grounds of part of the University Iskandar Muda, is the **tomb of Sultan Iskandar Muda** himself (1607-1636).

Further S still on Jalan T. Umar, is the site of **Gunungan**, a palace and enclosed pleasure garden built during the 17th century – possibly by Sultan Iskandar Muda. It is said to have been built by the Sultan for one of his queens who wished to be able to take an evening stroll – forbidden at that time. The grounds also contain a cake-like, white structure with stairs running up the side. There have been a number of theories as to the use and symbolism of this weird artificial mountain. Some argue that it was an observatory; others, a topographic map of the queen's homeland to make her feel less homesick; still others, the cosmic mountain, Mount Meru; or perhaps even an altar to Agni, the Hindu god of fire. The art historian Jacques Dumarçay believes all these to be wrong and argues that it is a phallic symbol – he notes that the name of the park, Ghairah, means ardour, love or passion, and believes the rest to be self-explanatory.

On the other side of the road is the immaculately kept **Kher Khoff**, which contains the graves of 2,200 Dutch soldiers killed fighting the Acehnese between the late 19th century and early 20th century. Among them is the grave of J.H.R. Kohler, killed while storming the Mesjid Raya. Admission: free (although the graveyard keeper may expect a 'donation'). Open: 0800-1200, 1400-1700 Mon-Sun.

The park on the other side of Jalan Sultan Iskandar Muda contains **Seulawah** – 'Golden Mountain' (RI-001) – a **Dakota DC3**, belonging to Indonesian Airways. Bought in 1948, it was Indonesian Airways' first plane, purchased with donations from people in Aceh Province and was intended to break the Dutch blockade. Facing onto the park are a number of fine examples of Dutch colonial architecture.

The **Pasar Ikan** (Fish Market) is worth a visit in the morning. It is at the N end of Jalan Jend. A. Yani, at the intersection with Jalan Supratman by the bridge crossing the Kreung Aceh.

Excursions

There are a number of beautiful **beaches** to the W of Banda Aceh. Travelling SW from town, **Lampuuk** beach is 13 km away and **Lhoknga** 18.5 km. There is good surf here, but beware of the dangerous currents. Swim only in modest swimsuits. There is snorkeling off-shore, for which you will have to hire a boat. Further on still is the beautiful beach area of **Lho'seuda**. **Getting there:** by bemo from Jl. Diponegoro.

Cut Nyak Dhien Museum is 33 km E of Banda Aceh in the town of Krueng Raya. The building is a replica of Cut Nyak Dhien's house, an Acehnese heroine who fought bravely in the Aceh War. The original house was burnt down by the Dutch. **Getting there:** by bemo from Jl. Diponegoro.

Sabang on the **Island of Weh** can be reached from Pelabuhan Malahayatia (Krueng Raya), a port 33 km E of the city (see page 749). **Getting there:** by bemo from Jl. Diponegoro.

Tours Tours to sights in the surrounding countryside and to Sabang (see page 749) are arranged by *Krueng Wayla* and by *Tripa Wisata*.

Accommodation Many of the budget-priced hotels are on Jl. Jend. A. Yani. **B** *Kuala Tripa*, Jl. Mesjid Raya 24, T 21455, F 21790, a/c, restaurant, pool, best in town, good value, all modern facilities; **B-C** *Rasa Sayang Ayu*, Jl. Tk. Umar 439, S of the centre, near the bus station, T 21983, a/c, restaurant, big clean rooms; **C** *Sultan*, Jl. Panglima Polim 127, T 22581, F 31770, a/c, clean and comfortable; **D** *Losmen Yusry*, Jl. Mohd. Jam 1, T 23160, attached mandis and reasonably clean; **E** *Aceh*, Jl. Mohd. Jam 1, T 21354, some a/c, colonial and rather decrepit, but excellent position facing the mosque; **E** *Losmen International*, Jl. Jend. A. Yani 19, T 22159, popular, with small but reasonable rooms; **E** *Losmen Palembang*, Jl. Khairil Anwar 51, T 22044, some private mandis; **E** *Prapat*, Jl. Jend. A. Yani 17, T 22159, some a/c, clean; **E** *Wisma Lading*, Jl. Cut Mutia 9, T 21359, private mandi; **F** *Losmen Rasasayang*, Jl. Cut Mutia 26, T 22124.

Restaurants Indonesian: ♦♦*Garuda Baru*, Jl. Jend. A. Yani 30-41; ♦*Minang Surya*, Jl. Safiatuddin, good Padang food; ♦*Satyva*, Jl. Khairil Anwar 3, bakery, good for breakfast; ♦*Sinar Surya*, Jl. Jend. A. Yani (by the night market), Minang food; ♦*Tropicana*, Jl. Jend. A. Yani 90-92, also serves Chinese and ice-cream, rec; ♦♦*Ujong Batee*, Jl. Krueng Raya, out of town, wide array of Acehnese and seafood, rec; ♦*Warung Surabaya*, Jl. Khairil Anwar 32. Satay. International: ♦♦♦*Kuala Tripa*, Jl. Mesjid Raya 2, also serves Chinese and seafood.

Foodstalls: there are a number of cheap warungs along Jl. Cik. Ditiro; also try the stalls in Penayong, Chinatown. There is a night market on the junction of Jl. Jend. A. Yani and Jl. Khairil Anwar, where good, cheap Indonesian and Chinese food can be found.

Entertainment Very little nightlife because of strict adherence to Islam. The stadium sometimes stages bullfights. **Disco**: *Kuala Tripa*, Jl. Mesjid Raya 24.

Shopping Antiques: Dutch, Acehnese and Chinese antiques to be found on Jl. Perdagangan. **Handicrafts**: there is a government handicraft shop at Jl. S. R. Safiatuddin 54. The Pasar Aceh (market) near the mosque is a good place to browse. **Jewellery**: shops line Jl. Perdagangan, and they will copy most things.

Local transport Bus: the Stasiun Kota (short-distance bus station) is by the mosque. Frequent service around town; just hail one from the side of the road. *Becak mesin*: (motorbikes with sidecarts). **Bemos**: leave from Jl. Diponegoro for the beaches at Lhoknga, Lampuuk and for the ferry to Sabang. *Labi-labi*: (minibuses) for short distances. 200Rp around town. **Taxis**: metered.

Banks & money changers Bank Negara Indonesia 1946, Jl. A.H.K. Dahlan; **Bank Dagang Negara**, Jl. Diponegoro; **Bank Bumi Daya**, Jl. Cut Mutia.

Useful addresses General Post Office: Jl. T. Angkasa. **Telephone office**: Jl. T. Nyak Arief. **Area code**: 0651. **Hospital**: Jl. T. Nyak Arief, T 22616. **Police**: Jl. T. Nyak Arief, T 21125. **Immigration Office**: Jl. T. Nyak Arief 82, T 23784.

Tour companies & travel agents *Kreung Wayla*, Jl. Safiatuddin 26, T 22066; *Nustra Agung*, Jl. Diponegoro, T 22026; *Sastra*, Jl. Jend. A. Yani, T 22207; *Tripa Wisata*, Kuala Tripa Hotel, Jl. Mesjid Raya 24, T 21455.

Airline offices Garuda Merpati, *Rasa Sayang Ayu Hotel*, Jl. Tk. Umar 439A, T 21983.

Tourist office Aceh regional tourist office, Jl. T. Nyak Arief 92, T 22697. Good for maps and other information; surprisingly well organized. Open: 0730-1430, Mon-Thurs, 0700-1100 Fri and 0730-1100 Sat.

Transport to & from Banda Aceh 594 km N of Medan, 112 km from Sigli, 218 km from Bireuen. **By air**: the airport is nearly 20 km from town (10,000Rp by taxi). Four connections a week on Merpati with Medan, and from there to other destinations in and beyond Sumatra (see route map, **page 1006**). **By bus**: the bus terminal is SW of town on Jl. Tk. Umar. Regular a/c and non-a/c bus connections with Medan. The road is fast and good, 12 hrs. The major bus companies (*ATS, Kurnia, Melati* and *ARS*) have their offices on Jl. Mohd. Jam.

Sabang and the Island of Weh

Under Dutch rule, this small island of 150 sq km – inhabited at that time only by fishermen – was developed into an important bunkering depot. Steamships and liners from around the world docked here to replenish their stocks of coal and fresh water. Indeed, up until World War II, Sabang was a more important port than Singapore. However, as diesel replaced steam, so the island became redundant. During World War II, the Japanese took over the island and reminders of the $3\frac{1}{2}$ year occupation can still be seen in the gun emplacements that dot the island's cliffs.

In 1970, **Sabang** – the main town on Weh with 25,000 inhabitants – was declared a duty-free port and it seemed that it would once again become a centre of commercial activity. These plans came to nothing when the port's duty-free status was abruptly terminated in 1986. Since then, the Island of Weh has developed into a modest beach resort, the population hopeful that great times may come again.

Places of interest

The best reason to visit Weh is for the **snorkelling, diving, swimming** and palm-lined **beaches** – and for the peace and quiet. The best beach is generally considered to be **Patai Sumur Tiga** (Three Wells Beach) on the NW coast, with good sand, swimming and snorkelling.

The **Rubiah Sea Garden**, a 2,600 ha marine reserve, provides excellent visibility and a wealth of sea life, although the coral is being gradually destroyed by

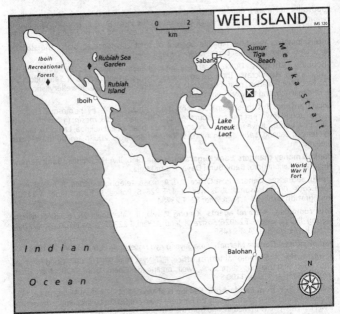

fishermen, illegally using dynamite. The marine reserve is centred on Pulau Rubiah, on the W of Sabang Bay, and is accessible from the village of Iboih, on the W of the island and 23 km from Sabang. Just outside Iboih is the small **Iboih Recreational Forest** (1,300 ha), a tropical forest reserve with good walks and a smattering of wildlife (for example, wild boar). Also accessible from Iboih is **Mount Merapi**, a small semi-active volcano with hot springs on its slopes. Boats can be chartered to explore the **caves** along the coast of the W peninsula.

The island is dotted with abandoned World War II **guns and fortifications** and there is also a Chinese temple – **Tua Peh Kong Bio** – the most northerly in Indonesia.

Accommodation There are a handful of losmen in Sabang; it is also possible to stay in surrounding villages. **D-E** *Holiday*, Jl. Perdagangan Belakang 1, T 21131, quiet and more relaxing than other losmen in town; **E** *Irma*, Jl. Seulawah 3, T 21235; **E** *Pulau Jaya*, Jl. Tk. Umar 17, T 21344, the largest of the losmen with clean rooms; **E-F** *Sabang Marouke*, Jl. Seulawah 1, T 21139.

Sports Snorkelling and diving: equipment is hired out by the *Stingray Dive Centre* at the Losmen Pulau Jaya, in town.

Local transport By taxi, bemo and motorbike. Fishing boats can be chartered for trips to the smaller islands for snorkelling and fishing.

Useful addresses Post Office: Jl. Cut Mutia. Area code: 0651. Police Station: Jl. Perdagangan, T 21306. Immigration Office: Jl. Seulawah, T 21343.

Transport to & from Sabang **By air**: there are daily flights by SMAC from Banda Aceh. **By boat**: a daily ferry leaves from Krueng Raya (Pelabuhan Malahayati), about 33 km E of Banda Aceh, at about 1500 each day 2½ hrs (3,400-5,400Rp). To get to Krueng Raya, take a bemo from Jl. Diponegoro in Banda Aceh 45 mins (1,200Rp). The ferry docks at Balohan, on the S coast of Weh, from where there are minibuses and taxis to take passengers the 10 km N to Sabang town. In Banda Aceh, the ferry office (PASDP) is at Jl. Gabus (Lam Prit), T 21377.

The west coast: Aceh To Sidikalang

For adventurous travellers there is now the possibility of continuing on from Banda Aceh S down the W coast of Sumatra to Sidikalang, and from there to Lake Toba. The road is much improved and the journey takes about 24 hrs by bus. There are isolated and rarely visited beaches along the coast, which bear the full brunt of the surf rolling in off the Indian Ocean. Accommodation is available in the coastal towns of **Meulaboh** and **Tapaktuan**, and also in **Sidikalang**.

THE GAYO HIGHLANDS: TAKENGON

The upland areas of Aceh Province are difficult to reach and rarely visited by tourists. The most accessible town is Takengon, situated on Lake Tawar at 1,000 m above sea-level, and 100 km S of the E coast town of Bireuen. There is a road which continues S from here, but it is slow, and sometimes closed to traffic between Takengon and Blangkejeren. From Blangkejeren, an all weather road follows the Alas River valley to Kutacane, where the headquarters of the huge Gunung Leuser National Park (see page 754) is located. From here the road continues S to Sidikalang and, finally, to the N shore of Lake Toba.

Takengon

Takengon is the most important town in the Gayo Highlands. It is beautifully situated at 1,000 m in the Bukit Barisan, on the shores of Lake Tawar. It is a new, rather unattractive, town with a mixed population of indigenous Gayo and immigrants from other parts of Sumatra and beyond.

The hills and valleys surrounding Takengon offer a number of attractive **hiking trails**. A road also circles Lake Tawar (50 km in total) and it is possible to hire a boat to explore the creeks and bays. Ask at your hotel for further information.

Accommodation B *Renggali*, Jl. Bintang, 2 km S of town, T 21630, best hotel in town with average rooms and good services; **C-E** *Triarga Inn*, Jl. Pasar Inpres, T 21073; **D** *Danau Tawar*, Jl. Leber Kader 35, T 21066, good value; **E** *Batang Ruang*, Jl. Mahkama 5, T 21524, clean rooms with friendly, helpful management.

Useful addresses Post Office: Jl. Lebe Kader. Area code: 0643.

Transport to & from Takengon 96 km from Bireuen. **By bus**: connections with Bireuen 3½ hrs, Banda Aceh 8 hrs, and Medan; buses running S to Kutacane and Lake Toba tend to run only during the dry season although as the road is improved a year round service should be possible.

THE ROUTE SOUTH: MEDAN TO LAKE TOBA Via Brastagi

From Medan there are 2 routes S. The Trans-Sumatran Highway runs S and then begins to climb into Sumatra's mountainous spine. The road winds its way upwards through a succession of hairpin bends, bus conductors clambering onto the roofs of their vehicles to spy out the competition: if there is a bus in front they will drive like the wind to overtake and catch any fares; if there is no other bus in sight they will dawdle to maximize their pick-up rate. After 68 km the road reaches the hill resort of Brastagi, established by the Dutch in the Karo Batak Highlands. The alternative route S passes through Tebingtinggi

Karo Batak architecture

The Karo Batak build the greatest variety of traditional or *adat* houses of all the Batak groups. Houses are always aligned according to religious criteria, and are usually divided by roof type and by differences in the body of the structure. Most distinctive and common is the gabled hipped roof, where the high-peaked, (traditionally thatched) roof – surmounted by buffalo horns – slopes steeply down below the projecting gable. The houses are either built on massive wooden pillars sunk into the ground (*rumah pasuk*), or resting on stone blocks (*rumah sangka manuk*) – to resist rotting (like the Toba Batak houses).

Extending from the front and the rear are bamboo platforms where food is prepared and provisions stored. Young couples also meet here in the evening. As many as 8 families may live in a single house, and there are no interior divides to ensure privacy. Two families will share a cooking hearth so that houses commonly have 4 hearths. The roof area is used to store tools and fuelwood.

Rectangular rice barns or *sapo page* are always built at right angles to the main dwelling house. They rest on stone blocks to protect against damp and are entered from above. Today traditional rice barns are rarely built. Peculiar to the Karo Batak are skull houses or ossuaries (*geriten*) used to store the bones of dead ancestors. These buildings are usually square in plan, and like the main dwelling usually feature a gabled hipped roof. Poorer families unable to afford the cost of building a dedicated skull house, keep the bones of their ancestors in the roof area of the main house. Traditional houses are no longer being built in the Karo area, and as older houses are replaced, so these wonderful *rumah adat* are becoming rarer.

(76 km from Medan) to Pemangtangsiantar (another 52 km). From Brastagi, the N route passes through the Karo Batak market town of Kabanjahe before linking up with the S route and arriving at Lake Toba.

Brastagi (Berestagi)

Brastagi, or Berestagi, is a hill resort town, lying 1,300 m above sea-level on the Karo Plateau among the traditional lands of the Karo Batak people. It was established by the Dutch in the early 20th century as a retreat from the heat and humidity of the lowlands and was frequented by Dutch planters from Sumatra's E coast, and by planters, businessmen and officials from British Malaya. The surrounding area is dotted with tea and coffee plantations and market gardens, growing temperate fruit and vegetables.

Places of interest

The town does not have many specific sights of interest, but its position, surrounded by active volcanoes, is memorable. Unfortunately, Brastagi has a rather uncared for feel, and it is dirty and featureless. There are plans afoot to revive the resort as a tourist destination; cleaning it up would be a good way to start. Nonetheless, Brastagi is a good place to cool off after the heat and bustle of Medan, and play a little golf, hike, or go riding.

For those without the time to visit the **Batak villages** outside Kabanjahe (see Excursions), there is a Batak village of sorts – **Paceren** – just outside town on the road to Medan, 100 m past the *Rose Garden Hotel*. Run down and interspersed with modern houses, it is in some respects more authentic than those which have been preserved, showing how living communities are adapting to the changing world. There is no admission fee, although the children will shout 'rupiah, rupiah'. There is a fresh fruit and vegetable **market** opposite the monument at the N end of Jalan Veteran.

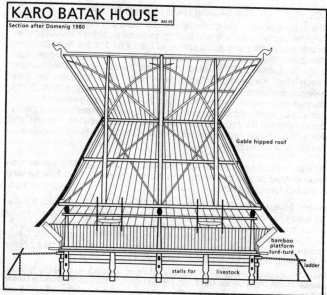

KARO BATAK HOUSE IMS 65
Section after Domenig 1980

Gable hipped roof

bamboo platform turé-turé

stalls for   livestock

ladder

Excursions

Kabanjahe meaning 'Ginger garden', is 12 km S of Brastagi and easily accessible by bus. It is a local market town of some size and is especially worth visiting on Mondays – market day. From here it is possible to walk to traditional villages of the *Karo Batak* people (see below). **Getting there**: regular buses from the station on Jl. Veteran.

Karo Batak villages are to be found dotted all over the hills around Brastagi. But note that the more traditional villages are not accessible by road and must be reached on foot; to visit these communities it is recommended to hire a guide (ask at your hotel or the tourist centre). Two villages which can be visited with relative ease from Kabanjahe are Lingga and Barusjahe – both can be reached by microlite from Kabanjahe. This ease of access has inevitably resulted in rather 'touristy' villages. **Lingga** is about 4 km NW of Kabanjahe and is a community of about 30 Batak longhouses. Be prepared to be pestered. **Barusjahe** is slightly more difficult to get to and as a result is marginally more 'traditional', but can still be reached by microlite from Kabanjahe. Some of the wooden houses are over 2 centuries old and the soaring roofs are particularly impressive. **Getting there**: for Lingga and Barusjahe, catch a bus from the bus station on Jl. Veteran to Kabanjahe, and from there a microlite or bemo onwards; if hoping to visit more remote villages hire a guide in town (ask at your hotel or the tourist centre). It can make sense to charter a bemo for the day – a great deal more ground can be covered.

It is possible to **hike** through spectacular countryside all the way to Bukit Lawang from Brastagi in 3 days. However, the government is anxious about visitors disturbing this culturally sensitive area and trekkers should take the time and care to organize trips properly. Ask in town at the *Sibayak Guesthouse* or at the

The Gunung Leuser Nature Reserve

The Gunung Leuser is one of the oldest and largest parks in Indonesia (850,000 ha), and supports populations of tiger, rhino, gibbon, elephant and orang utan, 500 species of bird, and 3,500 species of plant including the Rafflesia flower (**see page 780**). The park encompasses a number of ecological zones, with alpine flora above 3,000 m. Most visitors visit the park via the Bukit Lawang Orang Utan Rehabilitation Centre (**see page 744**), although the park headquarters are in Kutacane, about 150 km NW of Brastagi. Permits to visit the park are available from the PHPA office in Kutacane, and guides and porters can also be hired. One of the most exhilarating ways to experience the park is by rafting down the Alas River. Tour companies in Medan can arrange this (**see page 742**), and in Brastagi (see below). Information on trekking is available in Brastagi and Bukit Lawang.

Rafflesia Tourist Information Service, Jl. Veteran 84 for up-to-date information on trekking. Most people trek this route in the other direction, from Bukit Lawang to Brastagi (**see page 745**).

Mount Sibayak lies NW of Brastagi at 2,095 m and can be climbed in a day, but leave early for the best views. Take the trail from behind Gundaling Hill, asking at your hotel for directions before setting-out. Guides can be easily found (again, ask at your hotel) and it is advisable to wear good walking shoes and take a sweater as it can be chilly. About 4 hrs to the summit, quicker if you take a bemo to Semangat Gunung, in the Daulu valley.

Tours The volcanic landscape around Brastagi is stunning, and can be experienced by taking a **canoe or raft trip** along the **Alas River**. The journey passes through the **Gunung Leuser Nature Reserve** with traditional villages and tropical rainforest. A 5 day trip should cost about 125,000Rp, all inclusive. Alternatively, take a jungle trek (with a guide) through the reserve – a 3 day trek costing about 63,000Rp. Ask for details at the *Sibayak Guesthouse*. More expensive 4-6 day White Water Rafting trips are organized by *Pacto Tours* (in association with *Sobek Expeditions*, USA). Contact *Pacto*, Jl. Surabaya 8, T 3848634.

Accommodation **A** *International Sibayak*, Jl. Merdeka, T 20928, a/c, restaurant, pool, comfortable, well-appointed rooms and good sports facilities; **B** *Brastagi Cottages*, Jl. Gundaling, a/c, restaurant, large rooms, big garden, hot water, great views; **B** *Danau Toba*, Jl. Gundaling, T 20946, a/c, pool; **B** *Rose Garden*, Jl. Picaran, T 20099, a/c, pool, hot water; **C** *Bukit Kubu*, Jl. Sempurna 2, T 20832, restaurant, colonial-style grandeur, old wing has the best rooms, hot water, fabulous views, golf and tennis facilities, rec; **C** *Kolam Renang*, Jl. Kolam Renang, restaurant, large garden; **D** *Rudang*, Jl. Picaran, T 20921, restaurant, pool, bungalow-style accommodation near the *Bukit Kubu Hotel*, attractive setting; **E** *Ginsata*, Jl. Veteran 79, restaurant, mandi, friendly management; **F** *Anda*, Jl. Trimurti 72-77; **F** *Dieng*, Jl. Udara 27, colonial house with rather run-down rooms, but friendly management and good information, rec; **F** *Sibayak*, Jl. Veteran 119, T 20953, popular, good source of information, average rooms, rec.

Restaurants Some of the hotels have quite decent restaurants. ♦*Irfan*, Jl. Veteran 79, Padang food; ♦♦*Eropa*, Jl. Veteran 48G, International and Chinese. **Foodstalls**: there are many open-air warungs serving good, fresh food, using the temperate fruit and vegetables grown in the surrounding countryside; *Jalan Veteran* has the best selection. The market near the monument just off Jl. Veteran sells fresh fruit and vegetables.

Sports Golf: 9 hole course (very short) at the *Bukit Kubu Hotel*, Jl. Sempurna 2. Clubs for hire. **Horse riding**: ask the men and boys, who are to be found with their horses waiting for custom around the more expensive hotels. **Pool/snooker**: pool hall at Jl. Veteran 52. **Swimming**: public pool on Jl. Sempurna, opposite the *Bukit Kubu Hotel*. **Tennis**: *Bukit Kubu Hotel*, Jl. Sempurna 2.

Shopping Antiques and handicrafts: sold in several shops along Jl. Veteran.

Useful addresses Post Office: Jl. Veteran (by the monument at the top of the road). **Area code**: 0628. Health centre: Jl. Veteran 30.

Local transport Car hire: from *Rafflesia Tourist Information Service* at Jl. Veteran 84.

Banks & money changers Money can be changed at the bigger hotels or at the *Sibayak Guesthouse*, Jl. Veteran 119.

Tourist offices (unofficial) *Sibayak Guesthouse*, Jl. Veteran 119, is a good source of travellers' information. There is also the **Rafflesia Tourist Information Service** at Jl. Veteran 84, in the middle of the road.

Transport to & from Brastagi 68 km from Medan, 147 km from Prapat. **By bus**: the bus station is to the S of Jl. Veteran. Regular connections with Medan 2 hrs, Prapat – changing at Kabanjahe – 3½ hrs, Bukit Lawang 6 hrs and Sibolga 9 hrs. Alternative route to Samosir Island: catch a bus to Kabanjahe, then to Simpang Haranggaol and from there to Haranggaol, on the N side of Lake Toba. Ferries leave from Haranggaol for Tuk Tuk and Ambarita on Samosir every Mon and Thurs at 1300 and 1500. **By taxi**: share taxis sometimes run to Medan; ask at the *Sibayak Guesthouse*, or at the *Rafflesia Tourist Information Service*.

Pemangtangsiantar

Pemangtangsiantar, better known simply as **Siantar**, is the second largest city in North Sumatra and has built its wealth on the tea, tobacco, rubber and oil palm cultivated in the surrounding countryside. Most visitors simply pass it by on the route from Medan to Lake Toba. The **Museum Simalungun** is at Jalan Sudirman 20 and has a reasonable ethnographic collection of Simalungun Batak artefacts, which are poorly displayed and explained. There are also some colonial exhibits. Admission: small donation. Open: 0800-1200, 1400-1700 Mon-Sat. The **Central Market** on Jalan Merdeka is rather gloomy but large and bustling, while the **Siantar Zoo** has a poorly kept collection of Sumatran wildlife.

Accommodation **C** *Siantar*, Jl. W.R. Supratman 3, T 21091, colonial hotel with garden, good rooms, hot water, friendly, rec; **E** *Garuda*, Jl. Merdeka 33, shared mandi and dirty; **F** *Delima*, Jl. Thamrin 131.

Shopping Batak handicrafts, including *ikat* cloth, are on sale at the central market.

Banks & money changers Bank Rakyat Indonesia, on the corner of Jl. Sudirman and Jl. Merdeka.

Useful addresses Post Office: Jl. Sutomo 2.

Tour companies & travel agents *C.V. Titipan Kilat*, Jl. Merdeka 24.

Transport to & from Pemangtangsiantar 128 km from Medan, 103 km from Brastagi, 48 km from Prapat. **By bus**: there are 2 bus stations. Stasiun Sentral for Medan. Stasiun Parlusan for Prapat 1¼ hrs, Sibolga, Bukittinggi, Kabanjahe and Brastagi (changing at Kabanjahe) 3 hrs.

LAKE TOBA

Lake Toba and the surrounding countryside is among the most beautiful in Southeast Asia. This vast inland lake lies 160 km S of Medan and forms the core of Batakland in both a legendary and a geographical sense. 87 km long and 31 km across at its widest point, the lake covers a total of 1,707 sq km and is the largest inland body of water in Southeast Asia. From the lakeshore town of Prapat, ferries leave for the island of Samosir, one of Sumatra's most popular destinations.

Lake Toba was formed after a massive volcanic explosion 75,000 years ago, not dissimilar – although far more violent – to the one that vaporized Krakatau in the late 19th century. The eruption of Toba is thought to have been the most powerful eruption in the last million years. Michael Rampino and Stephen Self of New York University and the University of Hawaii respectively believe that it could have triggered the onset of the last ice age by lowering northern hemisphere temperatures by 3-5 °C for a year. This would have allowed snow to lie year-round in many areas, so reflecting light and lowering temperatures still further, turning a 'volcanic winter' into an ice age. It is not only one of the highest lakes in the world at 900 m above sea-level, but also one of the deepest at 529 m. The area

The Bataks of North Sumatra

The Bataks of North Sumatra inhabit the highland areas centred on Lake Toba, and most villages are situated at about 1,000 m above sea-level. There are 6 Batak groups: the *Toba Batak* in the centre, the *Karo* and *Simalungan* in the N and NE, the *Pakpak* or *Dairi* in the NW, and the *Angkola* and *Mandailing* in the S. Each group lives in a particular part of the highlands, and although they are distinct in linguistic and ritual terms, they share many common values and traditions. The word Batak is a derogatory Muslim term meaning 'pig-eater'.

The 2 Batak groups visitors are most likely to come into contact with are the *Toba Batak* - concentrated on Samosir Island and to the S of Lake Toba - and the *Karo Batak*, who live in the vicinity of Brastagi and Kabanjahe. The *Toba Batak* are considered to be more 'aggressive' and demonstrative and number about one million. The much 'younger' *Karo Batak* are more gentle, hospitable, and traditional and number around 250,000. In total there are about 3 million Batak in this part of Sumatra.

Because the Batak homeland is in such a moutainous and inaccessible area, the people were largely insulated from Western contact until the late 19th century.

The 'discovery' of the Batak The first European to mention the Batak was the Venetian trader Nicolo di Conti in the early 15th century who wrote that the 'Batech' ate human flesh, kept heads as valuable property and used skulls as coinage. The first detailed account of the Batak was provided by the Englishman William Marsden in his *History of Sumatra* published in 1783. He described a people who, to the great surprise of the 'civilized' world, possessed a sophisticated culture and a system of writing. His account also fleshed-out the stories of Batak cannibalism, titillating dinner party guests all over Europe. But it was not until the early 19th century that Batakland began to be explored in a comprehensive manner. Lake Toba was not discovered until 1853.

Although the Batak remained isolated from Western scrutiny until the 19th century, their culture and language shows distinct outside influences. For example, over 150 words in the *Karo Batak* language are Tamil in origin, while various rituals and some elements of Batak art also appear to show links with the Indian sub-continent. With the opening up of Batakland to Dutch and German missionaries, many converted to a mystical form of Christianity. Only the *Karo Bataks* have maintained their traditional animist beliefs in anything close to their original form.

Batak architecture and economy The most immediately distinctive element of Batak life are their traditional houses or *rumah adat*. The *Karo Batak* build houses with 'hipped' gabled roofs (see box, **page 752**), while the better known dwellings of the *Toba Batak* have 'saddleback' roofs with dramatic projecting gables (see box, **see page 762**). An average village rarely contains more than 10 houses, built close together. For the inhabitants, their community is regarded as the 'navel' of the world. In areas where inter-tribal warfare was prevalent,

is now volcanically dormant, the only indication of latent activity being the hotsprings on the hill overlooking Pangururan (**see page 764**). One problem that the authorities are having to face is a mysterious drop in the lake's water level. Between 1984 and 1986 it dropped by between 0.6 and 1.4 metres – if it drops much further, then there will not be a sufficient head of water to run the 2 hydropower plants downstream on the Asahan River, and this in turn will compromise the operation of the massive aluminium smelter at Kuala Tanjung.

The cool climate, pine-clothed mountain slopes, the lake, and the sprinkling of church spires gives the area an almost alpine flavour. After Medan or Padang, it is a welcome relief from the bustle, heat and humidity of the lowlands. Lodged stone fortifications are also sometimes present (for example in Simanindo, **see page 764**).

Economically, the Batak traditionally pursued a diverse subsistence system, growing dry and wet rice, maize, taro, potatoes and a wide range of other crops. They also raised cattle and pigs, while Batak horses were very highly regarded for their speed and endurance (although the Batak themselves did not ride). Hunting and gathering contributed a further important element to their diets.

Cannibalism among the Batak More than anything else, the reputation of the Batak in the West was coloured by their cannabalism, which continued among the Toba and Pakpak into the 20th century. However, cannibalism was not common, only occurring during warfare and as a punishment for certain crimes. The German geographer and physician Franz Junghuhn, who lived among the Toba Batak for 18 months between 1840-1841, witnessed only 3 cases. His 2 volume account of the Bataks is one of the best and most thoughtful descriptions of Batak life and society. He describes cannibalism as follows:

> "When an enemy is captured the day is set upon which he should be eaten. Then messengers are sent to all allied chiefs and their subjects inviting them to be present at the feast. ... The captive is now bound to a stake in an upright position. ... Then the chief of the village in which the ceremony takes place draws his knife, steps forward and addresses the people. ... It is explained that the victim is an utter scoundrel, and in fact not a human being at all...At this address the people water at the mouth and feel an irresistible impulse to have a piece of the criminal in their stomachs...All draw their knives. The radja [chief] cuts off the first piece...He holds up the flesh and drinks with gusto some of the blood streaming from it. ... Now all the remaining men fall upon the bloody sacrifice, tear the flesh off the bones and roast and eat it. ... The cries of the victim do not spoil their appetites. It is usually 8 or 10 minutes before the wounded man becomes unconscious, and a quarter of an hour before he dies."

Bataks and the modern world With the intrusion of the modern world into Batakland, so Batak society and economy has been encouraged to adapt to new pressures and incentives. Cash crops such as coffee and vegetables are grown for the market, many Batak have entered higher education and have attained important posts in the Indonesian army, while tourism has also brought the Batak in contact with the wider world. Given these pressures, it is surprising how far Batak traditional society and life has managed to survive. Traditional rules (*adat*) of land ownership are still usually maintained, the clan (*marga*) system appears as strong as ever, and Batak arts are still vigorously pursued if, in part, only for the tourist trade.

Recommended reading Sibeth, Achim (1991) *Living with Ancestors - the Batak, peoples of the Island of Sumatra*, Thames & Hudson: London.

in the centre of the lake is Samosir Island – a long-time haven for backpackers.

Prapat (Parapat)

Prapat, also known as Parapat, is a small resort on the E shores of Lake Toba frequented by the Medan wealthy, and increasing numbers of Asian tourists from beyond Indonesia. It was established by the Dutch in the 1930s, although today most Western visitors merely breeze through *en route* to Samosir Island. There are stunning views over the lake, but unfortunately, and like so many tourist success stories in Southeast Asia, uncontrolled development has diminished the attractiveness of the town.

There are few sights in Prapat. The best **beaches** are a little way out of town – but easily walkable – like those at Ajibata village, about 1 km S of Prapat. Saturday is market day when Bataks selling local handicrafts and 'antiques' converge on the town and particularly on the market area at **Pekan Tigaraja**, close to the ferry dock for Samosir. A smaller market is also held here on Thursdays. The bright, rust-red roofed church above the town sits in well cared for gardens, with views over the lake. On Sundays, services have as many as 8 to 10 hymns.

Excursions

Samosir Island with its Batak stone chairs and tables and *rumah adat*, is only a 30 minute boat trip from Prapat. **Getting there**: regular ferries (**see page 759**); or charter a speedboat to visit the sights (40,000-80,000Rp).

Festivals Jun/Jul: *Danau Toba Festival* (moveable), held over a week. Hardly traditional, but there are various cultural performances and canoe races on the lake.

Accommodation Most of the more expensive hotels are on the lakefront. Cheaper accommodation is concentrated along Jalan Sisingamangaraja. For those on a lower budget, the accommodation on Samosir Island is without doubt better and cheaper; there are no 'luxury' hotels on Samosir. **NB** During Indonesian public holidays and sometimes at weekends, it is a good idea to book ahead. **B** *Danau Toba International*, Jl. P. Samosir 17, T 41583, set on the side of the hill, overlooking the lake, modern and plush; **B** *Danau Toba International Cottages*, Jl. Nelson Purba, T 41172, on the lake, with good watersports facilities and comfortable rooms; **B** *Natour Prapat*, Jl. Marihat 1, T 41012, F 41019, a/c, restaurant, Dutch-built pre-war hotel in attractive position overlooking the lake, with its own beach; **B** *Niagara*, Jl. Pembangunan 1, T 41068, F 41233, a/c, restaurant, pool, golf and tennis, new hotel on hillside above the lake, well appointed rooms and excellent sports facilities; **B** *Patra Jasa*, Jl. Siuhan, T 41796, a/c, restaurant, pool, 4 km N of town overlooking the lake, with own golf course and lovely grounds; **B** *Tarabunga Sibigo*, Jl. Sibigo 1, T 41700; **C** *Astari*, Jl. P. Samosir 9, T 41219; **C** *Toba*, Jl. P. Samosir 10, T 41073; **C** *Wisma Danau Toba*, Jl. P. Samosir 3-6, T 41302; **D** *Budi Mulya*, Jl. P.Samosir 17, T 41216, clean rooms and well-run; **E** *Motel Samosir*, Jl. Balige 1; **E** *Saudara*, Jl. Balige 15; **E** *Sinar Baru*, Jl. Josep 45, rec; **E** *Singgalang*, Jl. Balige 20; **E** *Soloh Jaya*, Jl. Haranggoal 12, new hotel with good views, the more expensive rooms are large and good value; **F** *Pago Pago Inn*, Jl. Tigaraja 2, clean rooms, popular, shared mandi.

Camping There is a free camping ground on Jalan Bangun Dolok, off Jalan Sisingamangaraja, but it is a long walk up a steep hill.

Restaurants There are many cheap restaurants along Jalan Sisingamangaraja. ◆*Istina*, Jl. Sisinggamangaraja 68, Indonesian; ◆◆*Brastagi*, Jl. Sisingamangaraja 55, Indonesian; ◆◆*Hong Kong*, Jl. Haranggoal 1, good, cheap Chinese and Indonesian, rec.

Entertainment Batak cultural shows: held on Tues & Sat nights at the *Batak Cultural Centre*, Jl. Josep 19, at 2100 (2,000Rp). The more expensive hotels (e.g. *Natour Prapat*) also sometimes organize cultural shows. Disco: *Danau Toba International*, Jl. P. Samosir 17.

Sports Golf: there is a course 2 km out of town off the road to Balige, with clubs for hire. There is also a 9-hole course at the *Patra Jasa Hotel*, 4 km N of town, on Jl. Siuhan. **Riding**: enquire at better hotels. **Water-skiing**: on Lake Toba, surely one of the most dramatic places in the world to ski. Enquire at the more expensive hotels. **Watersports**: water-scooters and pedal boats can be hired on the waterfront.

Shopping Batak handicrafts, batik and woodcarvings: try the shops along Jl. Siantar and Jl. Sisingamangaraja. Jl. Haranggoal also has an array of rather tacky souvenir shops. There is a market at Pekan Tigaraja near the ferry jetty, held on Sat and a smaller one on Thurs. A good place to buy batik and Batak handicrafts.

Local transport Bemo and various forms of water transport.

Banks & money changers Bank Rakyat Indonesia.

Useful addresses Post Office: Jl. Sisingamangaraja 90. **Area code**: 0625. **Police Station**: Jl. Sisingamangaraja. **Hospital**: Jl. P. Samosir.

Tour companies & travel agents *Dolok Silao*, Jl. Sisingamangaraja 113; *Goraharaja*, Jl. Sisingamangaraja 87; *PT Andilo Nancy* (opposite bus terminal); *Dolok* and *Goraharaja* also have offices at the ferry dock for Samosir Island.

Tourist offices Pusat Informasi (tourist centre), Jl. P. Samosir, under the archway that welcomes visitors to the town. Little information available. **Batak Cultural Centre**, Jl. Josep 19 (for information on Batak cultural events).

Transport to & from Prapat 147 km from Brastagi, 176 km from Medan, 509 km from Bukittinggi. **By bus**: most people arrive in Prapat from Medan; there are regular connections via Tebingtinggi 4 hrs. There are also buses to Brastagi (some go via Kabanjahe), Bukittinggi 13 hrs, Padang 15 hrs, Palembang, Jambi, Pekanbaru and even Jakarta. **By car**: several companies in Medan will transport passengers to Prapat; contact one of the major hotels in Medan. **By boat**: Prapat is the main 'port' for Samosir Island and ferries leave the town from the jetty on Jl. Haranggaol for Samosir every hour or so 30 mins (800Rp).

Samosir Island

Samosir Island, 40 km long and 20 km wide, is not really an island at all, but a peninsula. It is attached to the mainland at Pangururan, although a canal dug by the Dutch cuts through the slender isthmus. An eruption 75,000 years ago thrust Samosir up from the lake bed and the peak contains lake sediments on its summit. The island's highest point at 1,657 m above sea-level is 750 m above the surface of the lake, or more than 1,250 m above the lake bed.

In all, Samosir covers 640 sq km. With a large number of traditional Batak villages, fine examples of *rumah adat* or traditional houses (see box, **page 762**), cemeteries, churches, enigmatic stone carvings, good swimming, hiking, cheap accommodation, and few cars, it has proved a favourite destination for travellers. Surrounded by the lake and mist-cloaked mountains, it is one of the most naturally beautiful and romantic spots in Southeast Asia.

But, Samosir is not the out-of-the-way, laid-back place that it once was. The locals have grown accustomed to tourists and sometimes treat them with disdain. A building boom is underway and this will no-doubt further reduce the mystery of the island. However, it is still a memorable place.

Staying on Samosir Accommodation is concentrated on the Tuk Tuk peninsula, and at Tomok and Ambarita, although there are basic guesthouses scattered right across the island. The cheaper losmen are in the E-F range, more expensive losmen and hotels, C-E. Camping is also easy on Samosir. It is a good idea to change money before landing, as exchange rates are even worse on Samosir than in Prapat. Money can be exchanged at some travel agents and hotels, and there is a money changer in Ambarita. Food on the island is good and cheap and there are a number of warungs in Tomok, Ambarita and on the Tuk Tuk Peninsula. Note that flight reservations cannot be confirmed on Samosir – it is necessary to visit Prapat.

Local transport A road in a reasonable state of repair follows the coast, running anti-clockwise from Tomok to Pangururan. There is also a road which runs around the S portion of the island, but it is rougher and is currently being improved. **Bus**: a minibus service runs about every 20 minutes in the morning between Tomok and Ambarita, and then on to Pangururan; the service runs less frequently in the afternoons. Note that the bus does not take the route that skirts around the lakeshore on the Tuk Tuk peninsula – it cuts straight across the neck of the peninsula. From Pangururan, a less frequent service operates to the interior village of Roonggurni Huta. There is no service operating in the S part of the island. **Car**: the more expensive hotels have kijangs for charter. **Boat**: there is a cruise around the N portion of the island on Wed, Fri and Sun which leaves from Tuk Tuk and Ambarita. It includes a visit to the hot springs on Mount Belirang (6,000Rp) (**see page 764**). Boats also carry passengers up and down the island during daylight hours – simply wait at a dock for the first vessel, state your destination, and make sure the fare is agreed in advance. **Motorcycle hire**: from Tuk Tuk, or from men found around the hotels or guesthouses. A driving licence is not required. Expect to pay about 20,000Rp/day. This is a recommended way to see the island. **Bicycle hire**: from guesthouses and hotels in Tuk Tuk, 5,000Rp/day. **Foot**: this is one of the most enjoyable ways to see Samosir. Walking across the island takes 2 days, with an overnight stop at Roonggurni Huta in the highland interior (see box, **page 761**). There are also other hiking trails across the island; ask at your hotel or losmen.

Useful addresses Area code: 0645.

Transport to & from Samosir **By bus**: buses arrive at Pangururan on the W side of the island from Medan, Brastagi, Sibolga and Sidikalang. **NB** There have been a number of reports of travellers having to pay an extra 'commission' when booking onward bus tickets through agents on Samosir. **By boat**: most visitors get to Samosir by ferry from Prapat. The ferry leaves

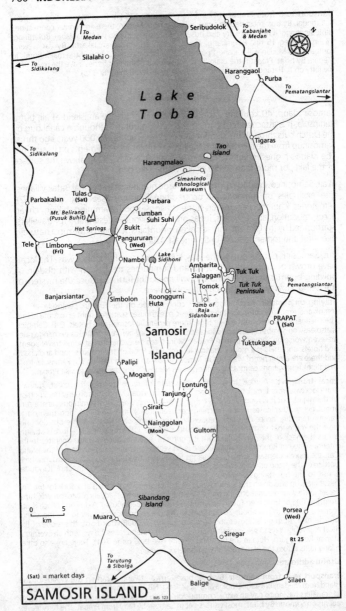

SAMOSIR ISLAND

Lake Toba

To Medan

Seribudolok

To Kabanjahe & Medan

To Sidikalang

Silalahi

Harranggaol

Purba

To Pematangsiantar

Tigaras

Tao Island

To Sidikalang

Harangmalao

Simanindo Ethnological Museum

Parbakalan

Tulas (Sat)

Parbara

Mt. Belirang (Pusuk Buhit)

Lumban Suhi Suhi

Hot Springs

Bukit

Tele

Limbong (Fri)

Pangururan (Wed)

Nambe

Lake Sidihoni

Ambarita

Sialaggan

Tuk Tuk

Banjarsiantar

Simbolon

Roonggurni Huta

Tomok

Tuk Tuk Peninsula

To Pematangsiantar

Tomb of Raja Sidanbutar

PRAPAT (Sat)

Samosir Island

Tuktukgaga

Palipi

Mogang

Lontung

Tanjung

Sirait

Nainggolan (Mon)

Gultom

0   5
km

Sibandang Island

Porsea (Wed)

Muara

Siregar

Rt 25

To Tarutung & Sibolga

(Sat) = market days

Balige

Silaen

IMS 123

Hiking across the Central Highlands

Hiking across Samosir's central highlands is one of the most rewarding ways to see the island. The distance from E to W is only about 20 km as the crow flies, but the route is a steep and circuitous climb of 750 m, making the real walking distance about 45 km. It is just possible to walk the route in a long day if tackling the hike from W to E (i.e. from Pangururan to Tomok), but it is best to stay overnight at the interior village of Roonggurni Huta to recuperate from the climb. There are a number of homestays here which charge about 5,000 Rp for a bed.

The hike from Roonggurni Huta to Tomok or *vice versa* is about 29 km: 10 hrs if walking uphill, 6 hrs down. There are also trails to Ambarita and (longer still) to Tuk Tuk, although these are less well marked. From Roonggurni Huta to Pangururan it is a less steep 17 km, about 3 hrs walking. There is also a bus service for the terminally exhausted between Pangururan and Roonggurni Huta. It is probably best to climb from W to E as this misses out the steep climb up to Roonggurni Huta from Tomok. Catch a bus to Pangururan and set off from there.

about every hour, 30 mins (800Rp). It stops at Tomok and Tuk Tuk and also at Ambarita. The first ferry from Prapat leaves at 0830, from Samosir at 0700. It is also possible to charter a 'special' boat for rather more (1,500-2,000Rp). Ferries also link Tuk Tuk and Ambarita with Haranggaol on Lake Toba's N shore, but these only run on Mon and Thurs. They leave Haranggaol for Samosir at 1300 and 1500; check in your hotel for the time of journeys in the other direction. To/from Haranggaol, there are buses to Simpang Haranggaol, then to Kabanjahe and finally to Brastagi and Medan.

Tomok

Positioned just to the S of the Tuk Tuk Peninsula, this was a traditional Batak village and remains the main landing point for visitors from Prapat. It contains some fine high prowed **Batak houses** and **carved stone coffins, elephants** and **chairs**. Walking from the jetty inland, there is a path lined with souvenir stalls which winds up a small hill. Half way up is the **Museum of King Soribunto Sidabutar**, housed in a traditional Batak house, containing a small number of Batak implements and photographs of the family. Admission: by donation.

Walking a little further up the hill, there is a carved stone coffin, protected by what remains of a large but dying *hariam* tree, which contains the body of Raja Sidabutar, the chief of the first tribe to migrate to the area. Surrounded by souvenir stalls, the sight has lost much of its mystery. The **church services** at the town and elsewhere on Samosir, are worthwhile for the enthusiasm of the congregations.

Accommodation B *Toba Beach*, S of Tomok, T 41275, good rooms, quiet position on the lakeside, but expensive for Samosir; **F** *Roy's* (in a Batak village, just outside town), good information and friendly management; **F** *Silalahi*, friendly.

Restaurants There are a number of warung in and around the village, e.g. *Islam* and *Roy's*. *Toba Beach Hotel* has a good restaurant serving Indonesian and international dishes.

Shopping This is the main landing point for day-trippers from Prapat, so there are a large number of souvenir stalls selling Batak handicrafts and 'antiques'.

Tourist offices Roy's Tourist Information.

Transport to & from Tomok By bus: in theory, every 20 mins to Pangururan and all stops along the route. By boat: ferry connections with Prapat about every hour (800Rp). By foot: 1 hr to Tuk Tuk, 1½ hrs to Ambarita.

Tuk Tuk Peninsula

Tuk Tuk is located almost at the tip of the Tuk Tuk Peninsula about 5 km from Tomok. This is really just a haven for tourists: there is nothing of cultural interest here. There are hotels and losmen scattered right across the Tuk Tuk peninsula, lining the road that skirts the lake shore. But in spite of rapid development it is still a peaceful spot, with good swimming.

Toba Batak architecture

The traditional soaring roofed houses of the *Toba Batak* are among the most characteristic sights in Indonesia. These *rumah adat* or *jabu* are rectangular buildings raised-up on piles which rest on stone bases to prevent rotting. The houses are entered through a trap door which can be locked.

Typical of the *Toba Batak* houses are the enormous saddleback roofs, sloping dramatically towards the centre, and surmounted at either end with buffalo horns (the horns are real, but the head is carved from *ijuk* wood). The gables extend much further at the front of the house than they do at the back, and the gable at the front is richly decorated with carvings of animals, birds and mythical creatures. The rear gable is left unadorned. Originally covered in thatch, corrugated iron has become increasingly common in recent years. The roof area is used for storage while that beneath the house is used to corral livestock. The houses are built of wood and rope, and are held together with wooden pegs – no nails are used in construction.

Of the Batak groups, the *Toba Batak* decorate their houses most profusely. Carvings are concentrated on the 2 side walls, but particularly on the front gable. Only the colours white, black and red are used; these symbolize the 3 kinship groups, the 3 realms of the Batak cosmos, and the 3 hearthstones. Black is obtained from charcoal, white from lime, and red from red earth. Formerly, the blood from killed enemies was also mixed with the red earth. At the ends of the side beams of many Toba Batak houses are large carvings of animal heads called *singa*, from the Sanskrit word for lion. These mythological creatures, tongues extended, serve a protective function.

A number of families – up to 12 – will live in each *jabu*, and traditionally each would have its own hearth at the front of the main living area. European influence means that today most cooking is done in extensions added onto the back of the building. Many traditional rice barns or *sopo* have been converted in recent years into dwellings – they can be identified by the working area mid-way between the ground and the main dwelling area.

Excursions
Cross-island hike to Pangururan (see box, see page 761).

Tours Every Wed, Fri and Sun a cruise sets out to tour the N part of Samosir including a stop at the hot springs on Mt Belirang (see page 764). Ask at your hotel or losmen for information.

Accommodation The more expensive accommodation is in the **C-D** range. Cheap losmen/huts are available in our **F** range. Hotels and losmen will commonly offer a wide range of rooms, in terms of size, location (view of lake) and facilities (hot water). Prices vary accordingly. In order from the S to the N around the peninsula, the following are recommended: **B** *Toledo Inn*, N tip of peninsula, T 41181, large restaurant, one of the oldest hotels on the island on the lakeshore; **B-C** *Slintong's* in the centre of the peninsula, T 41345, restaurant; **B-E** *Carolina's*, S end, T 41520, average restaurant, very popular, with a range of rooms, some with lovely views over the lake, rather impersonal service and a 'Youth Hostel' feel to the place; **D** *Duma Sari*, S end; **E** *Matahari* in the centre, popular place with an established reputation; **E** *Romlan*, S end, on the lakeshore; **E** *Smiley's* on the S neck of the peninsula; **F** *Abadi*, N end, basic; **F** *Christina's*, N section of isthmus; **F** *Tony's*, N end; *Murni*, N end.

Restaurants Most visitors tend to eat at their hotels. *Carolina's* has the best restaurant with the biggest menu; there are a number of other warungs serving basic Indonesian and travellers' food.

Shopping Books: *Gokhon Bookshop*. Crafts: there are a number of craft shops on Tuk Tuk, but they are expensive; there is a better, cheaper selection in Tomok.

Tour companies & travel agents *PT Andilo Nancy*, *Goraha Tour* and *Bukit Santai Travel and Tours*.

Transport to & from Tuk Tuk By bus: walk to the main road to catch one of the buses

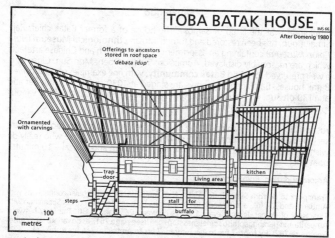

TOBA BATAK HOUSE
IMS 66
After Domenig 1980

Offerings to ancestors
stored in roof space
'debata idup'

Ornamented
with carvings

trap-
door

Living area

kitchen

steps

stall for
buffalo

0   100
metres

running between Tomok and Pangururan, in theory every 20 mins. **By boat:** ferry connections
with Prapat about every ½ hr (800Rp). **By foot:** 1 hr to Tomok and Ambarita.

Ambarita

The pretty town of Ambarita is an hour's walk from Tuk Tuk along the lake shore
travelling N. It has more to offer in the way of sights than Tuk Tuk, but a less
extensive range of accommodation. As the number of losmen grows, so Ambarita
is losing its former quiet and peaceful image.

There are several **megalithic complexes** in the vicinity of town which also has
a hospital (of sorts), a market, and a post office. The most important of the
megalithic complexes is near the jetty at **Siallagan village**. It consists of a group
of 300 year old stone chairs and a table where village disputes were settled. A
stone figure mysteriously occupies one of the seats. Facing the complex is a row
of well preserved **Batak houses**. Also here is the **tomb of Laga Siallagan**, the
first chief of Ambarita. There is another group of stone chairs close by where
criminals and other unfortunates were killed and then eaten. The last such
occurrence was at the beginning of this century. Tour guides delight in recounting
the gory details.

Tours Every Wed, Fri and Sun a cruise sets out to tour the N part of Samosir including a stop
at the hot springs on Mt. Belirang (see page 764). Ask at your hotel or losmen for details.

Accommodation C *Sopo Toba*, T 41616, 2 km N of the town, quiet position out of town,
with own beach; **E-F** *Gordon's*, 4 km N of the town; **F** *Barbara's*, T 41230, 4 km N of the
town; **F** *Le Shangri-La*, 7 km N of the town, very secluded, with clean, spacious bungalows,
good value; **F** *Rohandy's*, on the lakeshore in town, well-run and popular with good food.

Shopping There is a concentration of craft shops and stalls in the vicinity of Siallagan village.

Banks & money changers Bank Lainggolan, Bank Rakyat Indonesia.

Useful addresses Post Office: Jl. Besar 39. Clinic and Police station: in town.

Tourist offices *Golden Tourist Information Centre*.

Transport to & from Ambarita By bus: in theory, regular connections every 20 mins with
Tomok and all stops to Pangururan. By boat: a number of ferries from Prapat dock each day,
both scheduled and chartered. By foot: 1 hr to Tuk Tuk, 7 hrs to Simanindo at the N tip of
the island.

Simanindo

Simanindo is at the N tip of Samosir. The house of a former Batak chief, Raja Simalungun, has been restored and turned into an **Ethnological Museum** (*Huta Bolon Museum*) containing an assortment of Batak, Dutch and Chinese artefacts which are reasonably displayed. Admission: 500Rp. Open: Mon-Sun. Close by is a well preserved **fortified Batak community**, with fine examples of richly carved Batak houses. Batak dancing shows are staged at 1030 and 1130, Mon-Sat and at 1130 on Sun. Admission: 2,500Rp. This is the best maintained of the various 'preserved' communities on Samosir.

Just offshore from Simanindo is the small 'honeymoon' island of **Tao**. There are secluded and rather expensive bungalows on the island for those who really do wish to be alone. Day trippers can visit Tao for a swim and a meal – 10 minutes boat ride.

Accommodation *Boloboloni's*.

Transport to & from Simanindo 15 km N of Ambarita. **By bus**: regular connections with Ambarita and Tuk Tuk, and onwards to Pangururan. **By boat**: ferries connect Simanindo with Tigaras, N of Prapat, leaving every 1½ hrs between 0630 and 1430. The ferry between Ambarita and Haranggaol also sometimes stops here (see page 761), as do various lake cruises (see page 762). **By foot**: 7 hrs to Pangururan, 7 hrs to Ambarita, 7¾ hrs to Tuk Tuk.

Pangururan

Pangururan, the capital of Samosir, is on the W coast, close to the point where the island is attached to the mainland by a small bridge. There is not much in town. Most people visit the town on the way to the **hot springs** on Mount Belirang.

Excursions
The **Mt Belirang hot springs** or *air panas* are one hour's walk from town (2½ km). The sulphurous gases and water have killed the vegetation on the hillside, leaving a white residue which can be seen from Samosir. Cross the stone bridge and turn right (N). They are about a third of the way up Mount Belirang (also known as Mount Pusuk Buhit). It is too hot to bathe at the point where the spring issues from the ground, but lower down there are pools where visitors can soak in the healing sulphurous waters. It is said that bathing here 3 times will cure scabies. There are separate bathing pools for men and women and some warungs nearby for refreshments. There is even accommodation (for those with severe scabies). Views of the lake are spoilt by uncontrolled, unattractive development.

Cross-island hike to Tomok Pangururan is probably the best place from which to set out to hike across the island (see page 761).

Simarmata village lies between Pangururan and Siminindo and is one of the best preserved working communities in the N part of the island. It contains fine Batak houses, save for the corrugated iron roofs, and a large monument to the deceased King and Queen of Simarmata.

Accommodation **D** *Wisata*, Jl. Kejaksan 42; **F** *Barat Guesthouse*, popular.

Transport to & from Pangururan **By bus**: buses leave Pangururan for Medan, Brastagi, Sidikalang and Sibolga in the morning (0700-0900). Regular connections with Simanindo, Ambarita, Tuk Tuk and Tomok. Buses can also be caught, infrequently, to Ronggurni Huta. **By boat**: no boats leave from Pangururan for Prapat. **By foot**: 7 hrs to Simanindo; 10-12 hrs across the island to Tomok.

LAKE TOBA SOUTH TO PADANGSIDEMPUAN

Travelling SW from Lake Toba, the road reaches the administrative and marketing centre of Tarutung, 107 km from Prapat. Here the road divides; the Trans-Sumatran Highway continues S along the Bukit Barisan towards Bukittinggi, while another road turns W towards the coast and the port of Sibolga. The road descends spectacularly from the Bukit Barisan to the narrow coastal plain, a total distance of 173 km from Prapat. Sibolga is the main departure point for the 'Stone Age' Nias Island with its megalithic culture and some of the best surfing in Southeast Asia. 88 km S of Sibolga and 215 km from Prapat is Padangsidempuan, an important local town and the best base from which to visit the archaeological site of Padang Lawas.

Sibolga

Sibolga is not a town to linger in. Most visitors stay here merely *en route* to Prapat and Lake Toba from Bukittinggi, or as the transit point for Nias Island. The route into town on the Trans-Sumatran Highway is spectacular – descending steeply from the Bukit Barisan range of mountains to the narrow coastal strip.

Excursions

Pandan Beach is 10 km S of Sibolga. It is sandy and palm-fringed, with a refreshing un-commercialised air. **Getting there:** regular bus connections from the terminal on Jl. Sisingamangaraja.

Accommodation Hotels in Sibolga have a reputation for being dirty and uncomfortable. There are an assortment on Jl. Jend. A. Yani and Jl. Mesjid, including: **C** *Taman Nauli*, best hotel, but out of town to the N, near the immigration office, a/c, quiet, colonial-style with balconies; **D-E** *Indah Sari*, Jl. Jend. A. Yani 27-29, some a/c, better-managed and maintained than most hotels; **F** *Sudimampir*, Jl. Mesjid 98, small rooms, slightly squalid.

Local transport Becak: 300Rp around town.

Banks & money changers Bank Dagang Negara, Jl. Jend. A. Yani.

Useful addresses Post Office: Jl. Dr F.L. Tobing.

Tour companies & travel agents *P.T. Idapola*, Jl. S. Parman 34, T 21646; *P.T. Perlani*, Jl. Letjen 57.

Transport to & from Sibolga 173 km from Prapat, 381 km from Bukittinggi. **By bus:** the bus station is on Jl. Sisingamangaraja. Regular connections with Medan 8 hrs, Bukittinggi 10 hrs, Padang 12 hrs and Prapat 4 hrs. Local buses leave from the same terminal for Padangsidempuan, Barus and elsewhere. **By boat:** Sibolga is the main departure point for Nias. Boats leave every day except Sundays; details can be obtained from the travel agents listed above. The *Kerinci* also docks at Sibolga every other Sunday morning, and returns a few hours later to Padang and from there to Tanjung Priok (Jakarta's port). Pelni office is at Jl. Patuan Anggi, T 22291.

Padangsidempuan

Padangsidempuan is situated in the Bukit Barisan and lies on the Trans-Sumatran Highway at an important crossroads: highways run N to Lake Toba, NW to Sibolga, S to Bukittinggi and Padang, and E to the lowlands, Tebingtinggi and, eventually, Medan. Usually known simply as Sidempuan, the town is the best base from which to visit the 10th-14th century ruins at **Padang Lawas** (see below).

Excursions

Padang Lawas – meaning Great Plain – lies over 70 km east of Padangsidempuan. To archaeologists, the ruins here are the most interesting in Sumatra. So far, 26 temples scattered over 1,500 sq km along the course of the Barumun River have been discovered. Archaeological work did not begin until

The main temples at Padang Lawas

Biaro Si Pamutung The largest and most important of the shrines, near the confluence of the Panai and Barumun rivers. The temples are constructed of brick and are similar in style to 9th-10th century Central Javanese shrines. The staircase on the main tower, which faces E, is flanked by 2 crocodiles with human features.

Biaro Bahal I Located in the village of Bahal, near Portibi, this is regarded as the most beautiful of the Padang Lawas ruins. The 13 m-high brick built tower rises from a lotus cushion and is surmounted with a garland. Yakshas and makaras in relief are still in evidence, although the original life size figures which flanked the doorway have disappeared.

Biaro Pulo Situated on a hill, but only the ruins of the main tower remain. Five highly unusual reliefs of dancing figures were found here in a good state of repair, and are now on display in the National Museum, Jakarta.

after World War II, and the area has still to be properly researched. The monuments date from the 10th to 14th century, and are probably linked to an ancient Hindu-Buddhist kingdom called Panai.

The main concentration of ruins is at the village of Portibi, near Gunungtua. The surrounding area is a dry, almost treeless landscape, carpeted with *alang alang* grass and whipped by a dry wind. The temples are known as *biaros*, or sanctuaries, and only a few are easily accessible: Biaro Bahal I, II, III, Pulo, Bara, Si Topayan and Si Pamutung. Each is surrounded by a wall, the inner courtyard containing the principal shrine, surrounding minor shrines, and stupas. Statuary is limited, and generally in poor condition, while reliefs are also few in number. Given that rudimentary excavations have revealed no evidence of large-scale habitation, it would seem that the biaros were funerary/ceremonial in function. A day at least is needed to explore the area, and because of the heat it is worth taking water along. **Getting there:** take a bus from the large regional centre of Padangsidempuan to the market town of Gunungtua, 72 km to the E. From there, catch an oplet or a mesin becak to the turnoff to the temple site, 15 km in all.

Accommodation *Samudra*, Jl. T. Umar 60A.

Transport to & from Padangsidempuan 88 km from Sibolga, 215 km from Prapat, 293 km from Bukittinggi. **By bus:** regular connections with Sibolga, Prapat and Bukittinggi. Connections with Gunungtua (for the Padang Lawas ruins).

NIAS ISLAND

Nias Island is part of the series of submarine peaks which run down the W coast of Sumatra and which include the Mentawai, Batu and Simeulue islands. Nias is 125 km long and about 40 km wide, with a land area of 4,772 sq km. It is separated from the Sumatran mainland by 110 km of occasionally rough sea. The W coast is rocky and inhospitable, while the E coast is more accessible, with natural harbours and a more gently shelving shoreline. The interior of the island remains thickly forested.

The population of Nias is now about 500,000 and the capital of the district is Gunungsitoli, in the N. The island is usually divided into 3 regions: North, Central and South Nias. These divisions reflect important differences in language, culture, and art and architecture. There are 2 main reasons to visit Nias: for surfers, to

Cape Dowi
Sifahandra
Lahewa
Tubengbeluwa
Mt. Mazlaya
Muara Indah
Olora Beach
Gunungsitoli
Laraga Beach
Fulolo
Muzai River
Indian
Ocean
Oyo River
Hiliweto
Onolimbu
Sirombu
Tetehosi
Madsingo
Mt. Lolomatua
Lolowau
N
Gomo
Moale Beach
Bawoluo
Lahusa
Hilisimaetano
Bawamataluo
0   20
km
Telukdalam
Lagundi
Bay
Ferries to
Sibolga
Ferries to
Sibolga

NIAS ISLAND IMS 124

experience the waves at Lagundi Bay; and for non-surfers, to see its unique culture which has evolved over several thousand years, apparently in isolation from developments elsewhere in Southeast Asia.

Nias was first mentioned in Arab and Persian geographies of the 9th century, and over a long period the island was raided for slaves by stronger Sumatran states. Europeans began marking the island on their charts in the 16th century, and the Dutch established a trading post here in the 17th century as part of their efforts to control the spice trade. In the 18th century the British established a toehold in the N part of the island. The presence of Europeans led to the spread of Christianity, and now the majority of the population are Christian, although there are significant numbers of Muslims in the port towns.

Culture
The Nias culture presents something of a conundrum to anthropologists. There are clear links in linguistic and cultural terms with the Bataks of the mainland, and yet the Niha – as the inhabitants of Nias are known – do not have a tradition of writing nor of cannibalism (although headhunting was prevalent). There are also distinct differences between the Niha of the Southern, Central and Northern regions of the island. Niha society is divided into 3 groups: nobles or *si'ulu*, who were viewed as descendants of supernatural beings, commoners or *sato*, and slaves or *sawuyu*. The financing or sponsoring of feasts and the commissioning of sculptures and jewellery were – and still are to an extent – crucial in determining a person's status. By erecting a stone monument, a noble legitimated his position and made him eligible to join his deified ancestors in the upper world. With the

The earthquake-proof houses of Nias

The houses of the 3 cultural regions of Nias share certain common features: they are raised off the ground, they are wooden, and all have high 2-sided roofs. To defend against attack, the house support posts were 2 to 3 metres high, and entry was up a moveable ladder and through a trapdoor. A family's heirlooms were kept in a windowless room, situated in the heart of the house.

The houses of Nias are also uniquely designed to withstand the constant earthquakes that affect the area: the support posts are aligned both vertically and obliquely, and rest on stone slabs. This gives houses the flexibility and strength to resist earth tremors. The size of a house is determined by the number of posts (*ehomo*) wide it is: a commoner's house is usually 4 posts wide; a chief's house, 6.

There are significant differences between houses in the North, Centre and South. In the North, houses are – almost uniquely in Southeast Asia – oval in form, and are wider than they are long. In the Centre and South, they are rectangular, and longer than they are wide. In the South, the villages are encircled by defensive walls, protecting them from attack from rival villages; these were usually absent in the Centre and North. Within the house, a distinction is drawn between a communal front section and private rear quarters. Livestock are kept beneath the house.

The oval houses of the North are no longer built and modern, Malay-style houses are the norm. In the South, traditional houses of an adapted form are still constructed but they are gradually being replaced by Malay-style dwellings. It is in the Centre that the tradition of house construction is strongest.

spread of Christianity, so traditional beliefs and rituals have disappeared – the last traditional funeral for example occurred in 1914.

Niha settlements in the S are the most impressive and also the most visited. Villages consist of 2 rows of raised houses or *omo*, facing a paved stone courtyard which may be several hundred metres long. Formerly villages were surrounded by a palisade, and within that a sharpened stake-filled ditch. Now that internecine warfare has been eradicated, the fortifications have been allowed to fall into disrepair. The central street which separates the 2 rows of houses is known as the *ewali* and it is equally divided into 2 by a central stone pavement or *iri*. The centre of the village contains the chief's house (*omo sebua*), a meeting house (*bale*), and an assembly square (*gorahua newali*). The latter should be beautifully paved and surrounded by stone benches and other megaliths. It is here that village rituals, dances and other activities are held. The 2 metre-high stone pyramid used for stone-jumping (see below) is erected near the square.

Villages show that although the culture of Nias may popularly be considered 'primitive' or 'Stone Age', the inhabitants had a genius for design. There are village baths or *hele* with running water, sometimes even private baths for noblewomen. The houses of chiefs are particularly impressive, being richly decorated with polished wood panelling called *hagu laso*, recording the possessions of the present and former occupants of the house.

The Niha people are most famous for their **megalithic culture**. Formerly, archaeologists believed that this indicated close links with India, and particularly with the Naga of Assam. Latterly, there has been a tendency to play down possible outside influences and stress local origins. In every village there are stone benches or *daro daro* (erected as seats for the dead), beneath which human skulls are sometimes kept. Benches are also found by bathing places, and in the forests and hills. They are not just resting places of the dead; they are also for the living, and are starkly unadorned, bar a few symbolic shapes such as the rosette. Memorial stones are also widespread, as are idols (often phallic) made of wood, stone and clay. An idol was made whenever someone died, except when that person left no male descendants.

Woodcarving is a widespread traditional art form in Nias. In fact, the carvings of Central Nias are regarded as among the finest in Southeast Asia. Christianity however has had a marked effect on production. Ancestor or *adu* figures for example are rarely seen or made; missionaries discouraged production and most were either destroyed or taken off the island and placed in museums before World War II.

The Niah are not only renowned for their megalithic material culture, but also for their **dances**, and particularly for their '**stone-jumping**' – *fahombe*. A stone pedastal or *batu hombo* in the middle of the square that separates the 2 rows of houses in a Nias village was vaulted by acrobatic warriors, often with a sword in their hand, in preparation for battle. Warriors would spring from a smaller launching stone. The columns are 2-2.5 m high and 0.5 m wide – in the past they were also topped-off with pointed sticks to galvanize the competitors. Today, stone-jumping is enacted for tourists and important guests.

Economy
The economy of the Niha is based upon the cultivation of wet and dry rice (although this was only introduced in the late Dutch period), sago, maize and a wide variety of other crops and vegetables. Meat is eaten rarely, except during festivals, when large quantities of pork are consumed. Pigs are slaughtered in front of the house of the feast-giver; they are stabbed, their skin singed, and they are then cut up for distribution. The parts of the pig are allocated according to strict rules; the head goes to the foremost chief. In addition to livestock and crops, forest products also represent an important element in the Niha diet. Apes, civets, birds and turtles, tubers and wild fruits, insects and snakes are all consumed. Mice, however, are avoided because they are said to contain the souls of the ancestors, while women are forbidden to eat monkeys because a Niha legend recounts how a woman once turned herself into a monkey.

Today the economy of Nias is based upon the export of natural products such as rubber, pigs and *nilam* (pachouli) and – increasingly – upon tourism. Cash earned through the integration of Nias into the wider Indonesian economy is used to acquire prestige consumer goods and also to send children to the 'mainland' for higher education.

Where to go
For the visitor, S Nias is probably the more rewarding part of the island to visit. The N was raided by the Acehnese for slaves, and much of their material culture was destroyed in the process. The S has the greater cultural integrity, and more 'traditional' villages. It is also the S where the island's best surfing beaches are to be found. The isolated central portion of the island also contains a number of abandoned villages with monumental stone sculptures.

Banks & money changers Exchange rates are poor in Gunungsitoli, it is better to change money before leaving the mainland.

Recommended reading Feldman et al. (1990) *Nias, tribal treasures: cosmic reflections in stone, wood and gold*, Volkenkundig Museum Nusantara: Delft.

Conduct The inhabitants of Nias are even more sensitive to 'inappropriate' dress than most Indonesians. Except at the beach resorts of Lagundi and Jamborai, women should wear long skirts/trousers, a bra and shirt, and men should wear shirts.

Warning Malaria is a problem on Nias as some chloroquine-resistant strains have appeared. It is also recommended that visitors have a cholera inoculation. Nias has an unfortunate reputation for being a haven for tricksters and thieves. Be wary, but always be polite.

Local transport There is a fairly extensive road network on the island; the problem is that it is in a poor state of repair. There are buses, bemos and jeeps as well as the odd motorcyclist who might offer a ride. Bicycles can be hired in tourist destinations.

Transport to & from Nias By air: there are flights from Medan to Gunungsitoli by SMAC (210,000Rp return). **By boat**: there are boats from Sibolga to Gunungsitoli every day except Sun, leaving at 1100 and 2000, 7-9 hrs (12,500Rp). The return boat leaves at 0700, but again not on Sun. There are also ferries to Telukdalam twice a week at 2100. Ferries to Gunungsitoli leave from Pelabuhan Baru (New Harbour), those for Telukdalam from Pelabuhan Lama (Old Harbour) (8,500-22,500Rp). *P.T. Perlani*, Jl. Letjen 57 and *P.T. Pelni*, Jl. S. Parman 34, both in Sibolga have information on departures. In addition there are usually several cargo ships which leave for the island each week – cheaper, but can be uncomfortable.

Gunungsitoli

Gunungsitoli, on Nias' E coast, is the capital of the island, and much like any other Indonesian town. There is not much to see and the town has a poor selection of hotels. From the town there are many paths and attractive walks, and oval-shaped northern-style houses can be seen in the vicinity of the town. Ask at the tourist office for information.

Accommodation D-E *Gomo*, Jl. Sirao 8, T 21926, some a/c, the cheap rooms are dirty and dark; **E** *Wisata*, Jl. Sirao 2, T 21858, restaurant, all that can be said is that the rooms are relatively clean; **E** *Wisma Soliga*, 4 km out of town, Chinese restaurant, clean rooms and helpful management, best place to stay; **F** *Ketilang*.

Banks & money changers Bank 1946; Bank Negara Indonesia, Jl. Pattimura.

Tourist offices Tourist Information Office, near the dock.

Transport to & from Gunungsitoli 80 km from Telukdalam. **By air**: the airport is 19 km out of town. Flights from Medan on Merpati and SMAC. **By bus**: daily connections with Telukdalam 4-10 hrs depending on the state of the road and weather. **By boat**: daily ferry connections (except Sun) with Sibolga (see page 770). The ferry company, *P.T. Idapola*, has an office at Jl. Sirao 8.

Telukdalam

This is the second biggest town on Nias, and the entry point for those wishing to visit the S. There is nothing in town except for a church. Surfers head W for 12 km to Lagundi Bay (see below). Visitors wishing to see the traditional South Nias villages could use Telukdalam as a base.

Excursions

Bawamataluo (Sunhill) is a traditional village about 14 km NW of Telukdalam. Approached up a 480-step flight of stone stairs, the village contains impressive soaring-roofed houses, megaliths, funerary tables, woodcarvings, and a magnificent chief's 'palace'. The village was built in 1888 as a defensive measure against the Dutch who had attacked and sacked the previous village. The main *omo sebua* or chief's house is said to be the oldest in Nias, although it was built barely a century ago. The house is richly decorated with woodcarvings, depicting family heirlooms, ritual feasts – even a Dutch steamship. These carvings are designed to link the present with the past, and thereby assure the living a link with their deified ancestors. The position of each carving is tightly prescribed. Images of the village founders – *adu* figures – used to occupy the 2 carved chairs outside the house; like most *adu* figures, missionaries had these destroyed. Though still inhabited, the house has been turned into a museum. Admission: by donation. Bawamataluo is the most accessible of the traditional villages, so is fairly touristy. Nonetheless, for the budding anthropologist, it is a definite 'must'. **Getting there:** by minibus from Telukdalam.

Hilisimaetano is another traditional village, although it is considerably 'newer' than Bawamataluo. It lies 16 km from Telukdalam. Again, there is a fine collection of 140 *rumah adat* (traditional houses), megalithic stone benches, chairs and other stone and woodcarvings. *Fahombe* (stone-jumping) is performed on Saturdays (see page 769). **Accommodation: E** *Losmen Mawan*. **Getting there:** by minibus from Telukdalam.

Treks For the more intrepid, it is possible to trek to other, less visited, villages.

Most have megalithic complexes and, as always, the more remote the village the friendlier the villagers. **Getting there:** on foot, but hire a guide in town (ask at your hotel).

Accommodation D *Ampera*, Jl. Pasar, clean rooms; **D** *Effendi*, best in town; **E** *Sebar Menanti*; **E** *Wisma Jamburae*, clean rooms.

Transport to & from Telukdalam By bus: there is a bus each day linking Telukdalam with Gunungsitoli, 4-10 hrs. **By boat:** daily ferry connections with Sibolga (except Sun) (**see page 770**); also daily boat connections with Gunungsitoli (again, except Sun).

Lagundi Bay

Lying 12 km from Telukdalam, Lagundi Bay was an important port until Krakatau exploded and destroyed it in 1883. Now there are just 2 villages here – Lagundi and Jamborai. Since the late 1970s, the area has taken on a new life and become a surfer's paradise.

Surfing enthusiasts maintain that Lagundi has the most perfect reef right-hander on earth – although the surf can be inconsistent. The waves at Lagundi Bay are powerful and the coral is close to the surface, so it is not recommended for beginners. There are boards for hire on the beach. Other than surfing and swimming, there is not much to do here, except walking and visiting surrounding villages (see below).

Excursions
It is possible to visit the **traditional Nias villages** of **Hilisimaetano** (20 km N) or **Bawamataluo** (17 km) from Lagundi (see above).

Accommodation Losmen are concentrated at Jamburai village. They are basic and charge similar rates – our **F** range. Some losmen owners insist that their guests also eat all their meals at the losmen too (if room rates are very cheap this is usually the reason). It is best to look at a number before making a decision as standards change very fast. Among the more popular, at the last count, were *Ama Soni, Yanti, Jamburai* and *Friendly*. But try and obtain a personal recommendation from a recent visitor in Sibolga or Telukdalam.

Restaurants There are a handful of warungs serving basic Indonesian and travellers' food and, sometimes, superb seafood. Most people eat at their losmen.

Transport to & from Lagundi 12 km from Telukdalam. **By bus & ojek:** Lagundi is 6 km off the road from Telukdalam. It can be reached by bus or oplet (both irregular), or by hitching a lift on the back of a motorcycle.

SOUTHERN SUMATRA

INTRODUCTION

For this guidebook, Sumatra has been split into 2: Southern and Northern Sumatra. This division does not correspond with any administrative division. Southern Sumatra consists of 6 provinces: West Sumatra, Riau, Jambi, Bengkulu, South Sumatra and Lampung. West Sumatra with a population of 4 million is the home of the Minang people. The hill town of Bukittinggi and the provincial coastal capital of Padang are the province's best known settlements; the 'Stone Age' Mentawai Islands lie offshore. Riau Province with 3.4 million inhabitants is situated to the E of West Sumatra, and includes the islands of the Riau archipelago. The oil town of Pekanbaru on the Siak River is the provincial capital. South of Riau is another resource-rich but rarely visited province, Jambi, and S of here the province of South Sumatra with its capital, Palembang, situated on the Musi River. Bangka and Belitung islands off South Sumatra's E coast are being developed into tourist resorts. Far more imposing scenically is small Bengkulu province which encompasses the Bukit Barisan and a narrow coastal strip of lowland; the capital, also named Bengkulu, is one of the most attractive towns in Sumatra. Finally, densely settled Lampung province is the gateway to Java, its capital of Bandar Lampung overlooking the Sunda Strait.

The Minangkabau of West Sumatra

The Minangkabau people are concentrated in the upland areas of West Sumatra province and number about 4 million. They are known throughout Indonesia for their business acumen and peripatetic habits: there are Minangs, as the Minangkabau are usually known, scattered right across the Indonesian archipelago from Aceh to Irian Jaya, and every town has its Minang or Padang restaurant run by a Minang family. They are also beloved by anthropologists for their unique matrilineal society. One Minang poem dating at least from the early 19th century, even exhorts mothers to teach their daughters "to judge the rise and fall of prices". Important Minang towns include the hill towns of Bukittinggi, Payamkumpuh and Batusangkar, which lie near the centre of the Minang homeland or *darek*, and the coastal provincial capital, Padang.

History

The origins of the Minang Kingdom are hazy, although Adityavarman (r.1356-1375), who had links with Majapahit (**see page 517**), seems to have been influential in unifying the state. Power was based upon gold which was mined in the Minang highlands. During the 14th and 15th centuries when Minangkabau power was at its height, the kingdom's influence extended over much of central Sumatra.

Early European explorers searched unsuccessfully for the ancient city of 'Menangkabu', thought to be the source of the wealth and gold of Malesia – the mythical and unimaginably rich Golden Khersonese. When Stamford Raffles visited the area at the beginning of the 19th century, he was immensely impressed by the Minangkabau Kingdom, believing the technology of agriculture and the level of civilization to be superior to that of Java. However by the time the Dutch

Islam versus tradition: the Padri Wars (1803-1838)

By the beginning of the 19th century, fundamentalist Muslims, or *Padris* – named after the Acehnese port of Pedir where pilgrims left for the journey to Mecca – were impatient for the Minangkabau to abandon their traditional beliefs and embrace the true, and pure, Islamic path. This probably stemmed from the return of 3 *hajis* – or pilgrims – from Mecca, where they had witnessed the violent overthrow of the holy city by the puritanical Wahhabi in 1803. Among the aspects of Minang culture which they most opposed were gambling, drinking, the taking of betel and opium, and the continued influence of matriarchal customs. The most influential of the Padris was Imam Bonjol (1772-1864), immortalized today in road names across the country.

To impose their beliefs, the Padris resorted to force, killing and imprisoning those who resisted their religious reform movement. By 1815, they had killed most of the Minangkabau royal family and imposed their will over the Minang homeland. They were even beginning to convert the Batak. However, their religious war was not won: in 1821 the few remaining members of the Minang royal house signed a treaty and surrendered their kingdom to the Dutch. This marked the beginning of the Padri War which lasted until 1838. The Dutch saw the contest as a battle between *adat* or traditional law and Islamic law, and between traditional Minang leaders and the new breed of Muslim leaders.

The traditional Minangkabau *adat* chiefs joined forces with the Dutch to fight their common enemy, the Padris. The Dutch had to virtually blockade West Sumatra before they were victorious – capturing the leader Imam Bonjol in 1837. Today, although the Minang are ardent Muslims – a legacy of the Wars – traditional pre-Islamic beliefs still exert a strong influence. In particular, the Minangkabau have stubbornly clung to the matrilineal *adat* organization of their society.

began to establish a presence in the 18th century, Minangkabau was already in decline. The gold mines had been worked out by the 1780s, and the old royal order was being undermined by new sources of wealth: coffee, gambier and pepper. A Hindu kingdom between the 12th and 14th centuries, the Minang turned increasingly to Islam as the religion's influence gradually filtered S from Aceh, in the N. This culminated in the Padri Wars between 1820 and 1837 which pitted the traditionalists against a new breed of Muslim fundamentalists (see box).

Minangkabau matrilineal society

Each Minangkabau *sa-buah-parui* or clan, the smallest unit of traditional 'government', traces its lineage from a common female ancestor. Titles, wealth and family names are all passed down through the female line. Men are given the responsibility of looking after the family's heirlooms, but it is the women who keep the keys. It is felt by many that the tendency for Minang men to leave the village and go *merantau* – or walkabout – is because of the dominant role that women play. Many Minang feel that it is improper, for example, for young men to stay in their mother's house. E.M. Loeb, in his 1935 book *Sumatra: its history and people*, describes a system that might warm the heart of many a Western woman:

"According to Minangkabau adat, a man neither gains possession of a woman by marriage nor a woman a man. By the payment of a certain price the woman rents the services of her husband at night. The husband then can sleep with his wife in her bilik, the small sleeping room of the family house, or else with the men in the men's house. ... The Minangkabau man has no rights over his wife other than demanding that she remains faithful to him. He cannot ask her to make clothes for him... The woman on the other hand, can always demand that her husband come to visit her from time to time and fulfil his marital obligations".

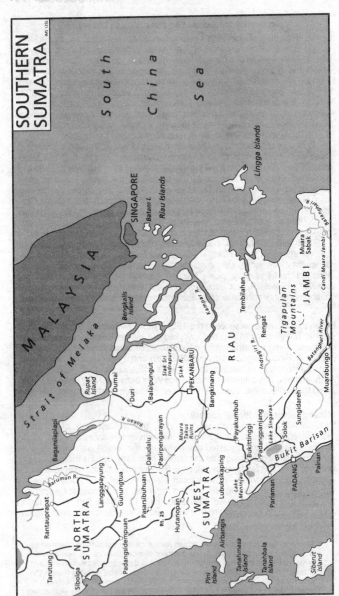

SOUTHERN
SUMATRA

IMS 1251

South

China

Sea

MALAYSIA

SINGAPORE

Strait of Melaka

Lingga Islands

Batam I.
Riau Islands

Bengkalis
Island

Rupat
Island

Kampar R.

Muara
Sabak

Batanghari R.

Candi Muara Jambi

JAMBI

Dumai

Duri

Siak Sri
Indrapura

Siak R.

PEKANBARU

Bangkinang

Tembilahan

Rengat

RIAU

Indragiri R.

Tigapulan
Mountains

Batanghari River

Balaipungut

Rokan R.

Bagansiapiapi

Pasirpengarayan

Muara
Takus
Ruins

Daludalu

Payakumbuh

Bukittinggi

Padangpanjang

Muarabungo

Sungidareh

Solok

Lake
Singarak

Barumun R.

Rantauprapat

Langgapayung

Gunungtua

Pasarsibuhuan

Rt. 25

Hutanopan

Lubuksikaping

WEST
SUMATRA

Lake
Maninjau

Bukit Barisan

Pariaman

PADANG

Painan

Tarutung

Sibolga

Padangsidempuan

NORTH
SUMATRA

Airbangis

Pini
Island

Tanahmasa
Island

Tanahbala
Island

Siberut
Island

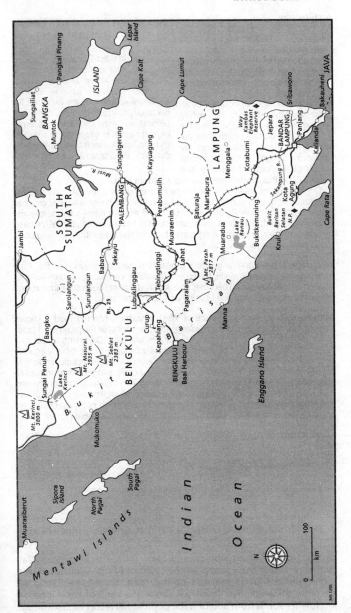

Architecture

To the visitor, the most obviously distinctive element of the Minangkabau is their magnificent architecture. The traditional wooden house or *rumah adat* – literally, 'customary house', also known as *rumah gadang* or 'big house' – is raised off the ground and surmounted by an impressive curved roof, the gables soaring upwards at either end like the horns of the buffalo which they are said to represent. These houses are similar in design to the traditional houses of the Toraja of Sulawesi (**see page 877**), although they are now, sadly, seldom built.

One side of the interior of the house is taken up by a row of small sleeping cubicles, in front of which is a large meeting room. The house is flanked by a pair of rice barns. Traditionally, both the house and the rice barns were deeply and colourfully carved. In a village, each compound of houses will usually be inhabited by one matrilineal line, with a separate structure (*surau*) for the men and boys, along with one or more rice barns.

Language The Minang language is similar to Bahasa Indonesia, and the 2 are mutually intelligible. However, the vowels 'a' and 'e' commonly become an 'o' in Minang so that *apa* (what) becomes *apo*, *kemana* (where) becomes *kamano*, and the numbers *dua* (2) and *tiga* (3), *duo* and *tigo* respectively.

Minang cuisine Another feature of West Sumatra is Minang food – known throughout Indonesia as *Makan Padang*, after the capital of the province. It tends to be chilli hot, although some of the dishes are mild. On taking a seat in a restaurant, an assortment of bowls of food are brought to the table – and the customer only pays for what he or she eats. Distinctive dishes include *rendang* (a dry beef curry cooked in coconut milk, spices and chilli), *pangek ikan* (fish cooked in coconut milk with chilli and spices), *panggang ikan* (fish roasted over an open fire), *kalio* (beef or chicken rendang where some of the juice remains), and cassava leaves in coconut milk (somewhat like spinach). Although not characteristically Minang, sweet fresh West Sumatran coffee (*kopi manis*) is also delicious.

Conduct amongst the Minangkabau Like most Indonesians, the majority of Minang people are Muslims – and staunchly so. It is also regarded as polite to offer food to neighbours – even in a restaurant and sitting next to complete strangers. The offer will invariably be refused. Further, it is considered rude to stand with hands on hips, to point a finger at an adult, or to sit with legs crossed. And finally, it is regarded as extremely impolite to touch a person's head.

Pencak silat: martial art of West Sumatra

Pencak silat is a martial art that originated in West Sumatra and is now practiced in various forms throughout Indonesia and also in Malaysia. Using the feet as well as the hands, Minanagkabau males are expected to become proficient in this deadly art before they can be said to have become men. It has been adapted into a dance form and can be seen along with other dances in Bukittinggi and Padang.

THE MINANG HOMELAND: BUKITTINGGI AND SURROUNDS

On the route S from Sibolga and Lake Toba, the Trans-Sumatran Highway crosses the Equator at the town of Bonjol – indicated by a globe and a sign at the side of the road. From here Batakland becomes Minangkabau country – about 450 km S of Lake Toba. 50 km further south from Bonjol is the popular hill resort of Bukittinggi.

Bukittinggi

Bukittinggi – meaning High Hill – is one of the most attractive towns in Sumatra and has many places of interest in the immediate vicinity. The town is situated at 1,000 m, encircled by volcanoes, and the climate is cool and invigorating. Like the Minang people in general, the inhabitants of Bukittinggi are relaxed and welcoming, making it a very popular place to stay.

Bukittinggi is the cultural centre of the Minangkabau people. It supports a university, zoo, museum, a good market, and yet is small and accessible. Many travellers arrive here, and after the trials of the road and such towns as Sibolga, seem very reluctant to leave. Compared with some other resort towns, it is clean (by Sumatran standards) and reasonably well organized. The core of the town is Jalan Jend. A. Yani, marked at one end by a clock tower and the other by a statue of a turbaned man mounted on a rearing horse – the Padri hero, Imam Bonjol (**see page 773**). Along this road are concentrated many restaurants and tour and

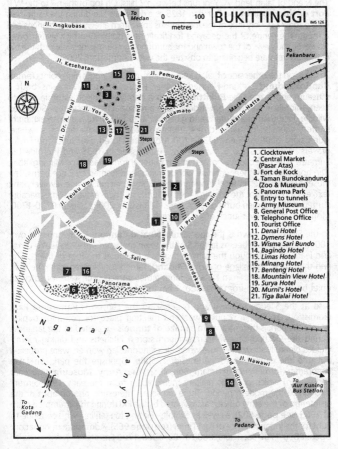

BUKITTINGGI

To Medan

To Pekanbaru

Jl. Angkubasa

Jl. Veteran

Jl. Kesehatan

Jl. Pemuda

Jl. Jend. A. Yani

Jl. Yos Sudarso

Canduamato

Jl. Sukarno-Hatta

Market

Steps

Steps

Jl. Dr. A. Rival

Jl. Teuku Umar

Jl. A. Karim

Jl. Minangkabu

Jl. Prof. A. Yamin

Jl. Setiabudi

Jl. A. Salim

Jl. Imam Bonjol

Jl. Panorama

Jl. Kemerdekaan

N g a r a i

C a n y o n

Jl. Nawawi

Jl. Jend Sudirman

To Kota Gadang

To Aur Kuning Bus Station

To Padang

0   100
metres

1. Clocktower
2. Central Market (Pasar Atas)
3. Fort de Kock
4. Taman Bundokandung (Zoo & Museum)
5. Panorama Park
6. Entry to tunnels
7. Army Museum
8. General Post Office
9. Telephone Office
10. Tourist Office
11. *Denai Hotel*
12. *Dymens Hotel*
13. *Wisma Sari Bundo*
14. *Bagindo Hotel*
15. *Limas Hotel*
16. *Minang Hotel*
17. *Benteng Hotel*
18. *Mountain View Hotel*
19. *Surya Hotel*
20. *Murni's Hotel*
21. *Tiga Balai Hotel*

travel companies, as well as the cheaper travellers' hotels.

Places of interest
The geographic and functional centre of Bukittinggi is marked by a strange-looking **clock tower** at the S end of Jalan Jend. A. Yani, the town's main thoroughfare. The Jam Gadang or 'Great Clock' as it is known, was built by the Dutch in 1827. It is a veritable Sumatran 'Big Ben' and has a Minangkabau-style roof perched uneasily on the top. The **central market** is close to the clock tower. Although there is a market every day of the week, market day is on Wed and Sat (0800-1700) when hoards of Minangkabau men and women descend on Bukittinggi. The market – in fact there are 2 markets, the Upper Market (*Pasar Atas*) and Lower Market (*Pasar Bawah*) – covers an enormous area and sells virtually everything. Good for souvenirs, handicrafts, jewellery, fruit, spices and weird foods.

The N end of Jalan Jend. A. Yani runs between 2 hills. On top of the hill to the W is **Fort de Kock**, built by the Dutch in 1825 as a defensive site during the Padri Wars (**see page 773**). Very little of the fort remains apart from a few rusting cannons and a moat. The centre of the decaying fortifications is dominated by a water tower. However, the views of the town and the surrounding countryside are worth the trip (although trees are beginning to obscure the view). Admission: 200Rp.

To the E, on the other side of Jalan Jend. A. Yani, is Bukittinggi's high point, **Taman Bundokandung** – 'Kind-Hearted Mother Park'. The park contains both a museum and a zoo. The **Bukittinggi zoo** is hardly an object lesson in how to keep animals in captivity, but it does have a reasonable collection of Sumatran wildlife, including orang utans and gibbons. Strangely, there is also an exhibit of stuffed animals (perhaps former inmates?) and the skeleton of a whale. Admission: 600Rp. Open: 0730-1700 Mon-Sun, closed over lunch on Fri for prayers. Within the zoo is a **museum** – established in 1935 and the oldest in Sumatra. The collection is housed in a traditional *rumah adat*, or Minangkabau clan house, embellished with fine woodcarvings and fronted by 2 rice barns. The museum specializes in local ethnographic exhibits, including fine jewellery and textiles, and is one of the best arranged in Sumatra. There are also some macabre stuffed and deformed buffalo calves here. Admission: 200Rp. Open: 0730-1700, Mon-Sun, closed over lunch on Fri for prayers.

To the SW of the town is the spectacular **Ngarai Canyon**, 4 km long and over 100 m deep. A path begins to the S of the town at the end of Jalan Teuku Umar, and leads down through the canyon, across a bridge at the foot of the chasm, and then on to the village of **Kota Gadang**, famed for its silverwork. The walk takes about an hour. From Kota Gadang, either retrace your steps, or catch an oplet back into town from Koto Tuo, 1 km to the S of the village.

Also at the S edge of town and overlooking the canyon is **Panorama Park** (admission: 100Rp), a popular weekend meeting place for courting couples. Within the park is the entrance to a **maze of tunnels** excavated by the Japanese during the Occupation, with ammunition stores, kitchens and dining rooms. Guides gleefully show the chute where dead Indonesian workers were propelled out into the canyon to rot. Admission: 250Rp. Opposite the park, on Jalan Panorama (formerly Jalan Imam Bonjol), is the **Army Museum** (*Museum Perjuangan*) which contains military memorabilia from the early 19th century through to the modern period. There are some interesting photographs of the disintering of the army officers assassinated by the PKI during the attempted coup of 1965 (**see page 502**), as well as exhibits relating to Fretilin – who continue to fight for the independence of East Timor (**see page 965**). Admission: by donation. Open: 0800-1700 Sat-Thurs, 0800-1100, 1300-1700 Fri.

IMS 115
Around BUKITTINGGI

To Padangsidempuan · Bonjol · To Pekanbaru · Rafflesia Reserve · Harau Valley · Harau Canyon · Lamaksari · Lawang · Ladan Gpanjang · Payakumbuh · Matur · Bayur · Bukittinggi · Mt. Malintang · Lake Maninjau · Mt. Singgalang 2880 m · Mt. Merapi 2890 m · Padang Pajang · Batusangkar · Pagaruyung · Batipuh · Balimbing · Pariaman · Lake Singkarak · To Padang · km (approx) · To Solok

1. Maninjau Village
2. Muko Muko
3. Alamada Hot Springs
4. Puncak Lawang
5. Kota Baru
6. Pandai Sikat
7. Pariangan

Excursions

One of the attractions of Bukittinggi is the wide array of sights in the surrounding area. Below are the main excursions, although there are also additional hikes, waterfalls, traditional villages, lakes and centres of craft production. Tour companies will be able to provide information on these other sights. Note that sights around the nearby town of Batusangkar are listed in the box on **page 781**.

Lake Maninjau lies about 35 km to the W of town and is one of the most beautiful natural sights in Sumatra, rivalling Lake Toba: it is a huge, flooded volcanic crater with 600 m-high walls. Maninjau village lies on the E shore of the lake. The area supports a fair amount of wildlife, and the lake is good for swimming, fishing and waterskiing. There are also hiking trails through the surrounding countryside. From Maninjau village, a worthwhile walk is around the N edge of the lake to the village of **Muko Muko**, 16 km in all (buses also ply the route). Just before Muko Muko there are the **Alamada Hotsprings**, an excellent fish restaurant, and a hydropower station. **Accommodation and restaurant** in Maninjau village: **C** *Maninjau Indah*, T 18, a/c, pool, rec.; **B-C** *Pasir Panjang Permai*, 1 km from the village on the lakeside, restaurant, tennis, rec.; **E** *Beach Guesthouse*, friendly and on the lake; **F** *Amai Guesthouse*, in the village. There are several warungs and restaurants. **Getting there:** for the modestly energetic, take a bus from Bukittinggi's *stasiun bis* to Lawang. From Lawang walk the 4 km to Puncak Lawang (Lawang Top) at the lip of the crater and 1,400 m up – a spectacular view. The walk down to the lake starts at Lawang, a stunning descent of 1,000 m which should take about 2 hrs, and ends up at the hamlet of Bayur, 4 km N of Maninjau village. Alternatively, catch a bus straight to Maninjau village

Rafflesia arnoldi: the largest flower in the world

The rafflesia (*Rafflesia arnoldi*), named after Stamford Raffles, is the largest flower in the world. The Swedish naturalist Eric Mjoberg wrote in 1930 on seeing the flower: "The whole phenomenon seems so amazing, so unfamiliar, so fantastic, that we are tempted to explain: such flowers cannot be real!". Stamford Raffles, who discovered the flower for Western science one hundred years earlier during his first sojourn at Bengkulu, noted that it was "a full yard across, weighs fifteen pounds, and contains in the nectary no less than 8 pints [of nectar]...". The problem is that the rafflesia does not flower for very long – only for a couple of weeks, usually between Aug and Dec. Out of these months there is usually nothing to see. The plant is in fact parasitic, so appropriately its scent is more akin to rotting meat than any perfume. Its natural habitat is moist, shaded areas.

Almost as monstrous, but far less well known, is the massive *Amorphophallus titanum* (a giant aroid lily) discovered for Western science by the Italian explorer Odoardo Beccari in 1879 in West Sumatra. When he reported that this flower was 2m tall no-one believed him; he had to wait until a tuber of the plant, a full 2m in circumference, bloomed at Kew Gardens, London in 1889. *A. titanum's* close relative *A. decus-silvae* has a stalk almost 4.5m tall and makes Sumatra truly the island of giant flowers.

on the lake shore, navigating 44 hairpin bends on the way down. The last bus leaves Maninjau village for Bukittinggi at between 1600 and 1700, later on market days.

Batang Palupuh, situated 12 km N of town, is a reserve for the monstrous *rafflesia* flower (see box). **Getting there**: catch a bus to Batang Palupuh on the Trans-Sumatran Highway, or take an oplet and then walk to the reserve (30 minutes). A guide from the village will point the flower out for a small fee.

Kota Baru is a rather unattractive town 10 km south of town on the main road to Padang, redeemed only by the fact that it has a good **market**. The villages surrounding Kota Baru often hold **bullfights** (in fact buffalo fights) on Tues and Sat at 1700 – for example, at Panin Jauan (22 km, Tues 1700) and Batagak (8 km, Sat 1700). The bulls fight one another rather than a matador, and the ring is formed by the spectators rather than by a protective fence. The buffaloes are believed to be possessed by the spirit of their owners, so that it is they who are in combat, not their animals. **Getting there**: by bus from Aur Kuning terminal.

Pandai Sikat is one of a number of villages specializing in traditional craft production. It is situated 13 km S of town at the foot of Mount Singgalang, just off the road to Padang Panjang, and is a cloth and woodcarving centre. The carvings tend to use natural motifs (trees, animals, flowers etc.), as does the famous *songket* cloth (**see page 810**) that is produced here. About 1,000 women weave richly patterned cloth. Note that the warp may be rayon, imported from Japan, and only the weft, cotton or silk. **Getting there**: by bus to Kota Baru from Aur Kuning terminal and then walk the final 2 km (or take a bemo). Other craft villages include **Desa Sunga**, 17 km S of town, which specializes in brasswork; and **Sungaipua**, on the slopes of Mount Merapi, which specializes in metalwork (knives, swords).

Mount Merapi is an active volcano to the SE of town which stands at a height of 2,891 m and last erupted in 1979. It is possible to make the difficult climb to the summit in 4-6 hrs, but start very early as mist envelopes the mountain by 1100. The route is sometimes indistinct – register at the Police Station in Kota Baru before ascending, and ask for directions – preferably taking a guide. Wear warm clothes: it is cold on the summit. The ground around the crater is loose and hikers should keep away from the lip. On Saturday nights, locals from Bukittinggi

Places of interest around Batusangkar: the Minang *darek*

The Minang highlands around Bukittinggi constitute the *darek*, or the core of the Minang Homeland. Many of the most interesting sights lie to the SE of town, in the area around the cultural centre of Batusangkar. Seeing these sights is easiest on a tour from Bukittinggi (see Tours, page 782). Travelling by local transport is time-consuming and often cramped, although it is not difficult: take a bus to Batusangkar and then catch a bemo from the station close to the market in Batusangkar.

The road to Batusangkar, after the turn-off at Padang Panjang (which has some fine examples of *rumah adat* along the main street), is breathtaking. Like Bukittinggi, **Batusangkar** is located on an upland plateau, surrounded by terraced rice fields and mountains. The town of Batusangkar, although it is regarded as one of the 3 centres of Minang culture, is not particularly attractive. It has a mediocre market and an array of souvenir shops. However, there is much to see in the vicinity (see below). **Getting there:** take a bus to Padang Panjang and then another local bus to Batusangkar.

Pagaruyung lies 5 km E of Batusangkar, and is the site of a Minangkabau **sultan's palace** – in effect a very large traditional Minang house – now a museum. In 1815 during the Padri War (**see page 773**), Muslim radicals slaughtered nearly all the sultan's family. Unfortunately, the original palace was destroyed during World War II, and this is a reconstruction. Beneath the wooden cladding it is made of concrete, and the dimensions and lay-out of the original palace have been altered to accord with its new function as a museum. Admission: 300Rp. Close by are some ancient stone slabs inscribed in Sanskrit. **Getting there:** by bus to Batusangkar and then a bemo from the station near the market in Batusangkar (250Rp).

Balimbiang is situated 10 km S of Batusangkar. It is a 'traditional' village, where some of the 300 year old *rumah adat* – built without nails – have been opened-up to visitors (the owners, very sensibly, making sure they make a profit). **Getting there:** by bus to Batusangkar and then a bemo from the station near the market in Batusangkar.

Pariangan is a less visited, and more peaceful, traditional Minang village. It nestles in a small valley on the slopes of Mount Merapi at an altitude of 850 m, surrounded by ricefields. It is thought to be one of the original Minang villages – inscriptions found here certainly date it to the 14th century reign of King Adityavarman – and it is one of the few villages where *surau* quarters for men and boys are still in use (**see page 776**). It is one of the most beautiful and friendly villages in the Minang highlands. **Getting there:** by bus towards Batusangkar and ask to be let off at the track for Pariangan, about 7 km E of Batipuh; the track leads uphill to the villages.

Lake Singkarak is a 20 km-long lake to the SW of Batusangkar and about 30 km S of Bukittinggi. It does not compare with the beauty of Lake Maninjau, but the swimming is refreshing and there are several hotels for those who wish to stay longer. **Accommodation: B** *Sumpur*, on the N shore, T 82529, a/c, restaurant, pool, sports facilities, best on the lake; 2 hotels on the E shore (**D**) are not good value, but are cheaper. **Getting there:** by bus from Bukittinggi, or by bemo from Batusangkar and Balimbiang.

make the ascent to be at the top for the sunrise; following them is easy. **Getting there:** catch a bus to Kota Baru from the Aur Kuning terminal (first departure 0500), and then hike. **NB** Sometimes the mountain is closed because of volcanic activity; check at your hotel before leaving.

Mount Singgalang to the SW of Bukittinggi stands at a height of 2,878 m, and offers a less arduous climb than Mount Merapi. The trail starts at the village of Pandai Sikat, and the climb takes about 4-5 hrs. Start early, as mist often descends over the mountain later in the day. **Getting there:** take a bus to Kota Baru from the Aur Kuning terminal and then walk the 2 km to Pandai Sikat (or take a bemo).

Kamanga Cave is an impressive cave 15 km E of Bukittinggi. It is said to have been used as a haven from which rebels fighting against the Dutch during the 19th century carried out their raids. A number of stone statues commemorate the heroes of the movement. The cave is 1,500 m deep, with the usual array of stalacmites and stalactites. **Getting there:** by bemo to the village of Kamanga and then walk.

Harau Canyon is a nature reserve of 300 ha encircled by 100 m-high canyon walls, 47 km NE of Bukittinggi. Dense tropical forest, waterfalls and a wide selection of bird and animal life – even, it is said, tigers and leopards – make the canyon a good place to trek. Admission: small charge. **Getting there:** the entrance to the reserve lies only 3 km off the main Bukittinggi-Pekanbaru road; take a bus from the Aur Kuning terminal running NE, through the market town of Payakumbuh (33 km), and get off at the village of Lamaksari (another 11 km); it is a 3 km walk from here.

Tours There are a range of tours organized to Lake Maninjau, Batusangkar, Lake Singkarak and other sights around Bukittinggi. Tours tend to take one of 3 routes: the so-called Pagaruyung line (including Batusangkar, Pagaruyung, and Lake Singkarak), the Maninjau line (including Kota Gadang and Lake Maninjau), and the Harau Valley line (including Mount Merapi and the Harau Valley). Most tour/travel agents organize these day-long tours for about 12,000Rp. **NB:** tour operators also organize tours further afield – for example, 10-day trips to the Mentawi Islands for US$100 (**see page 801**).

Accommodation Most of the travellers' hotels and guesthouses are concentrated along the N end of Jl. Jend. A. Yani. Quieter, smaller and often cleaner homestays are located on the hills either side of Jl. Jend. A. Yani. **A** *Hotel Pusako*, Jl. Sukarno-Hatta 7, T 22111, F 21017, a/c, restaurant, pool, new hotel with 185 rooms and all facilities, low rise block modelled – very approximately – on traditional lines, best in town and part of the Aerowisata chain; **B** *Denai*, Jl. Rivai 26, T 21524, restaurant, best in town, well-run and quiet, some separate bungalows, popular, but undergoing renovation at present; **B** *Dymens*, Jl. Nawawi 3, T 21015, F 21613, a/c, restaurant, comfortable, but on the S edge of town near the bus station, inconvenient; **B** *Wisma Sari Bundo*, Jl. Yos Sudarso 7A, T 22953, well-run, with small but comfortable rooms, rooms above parking space can be noisy, rec; **C** *Bagindo*, Jl. Sudirman, T 21279, S of town not far from the bus station, clean but inconvenient location; **C** *Lima's*, Jl. Kesehatan 34, T 22641, clean and popular; **C** *Marmy's Homestay*, Jl. Kesehatan 30, friendly, up-market homestay; **C** *Minang*, Jl. Panorama 20, T 21120, great views over the canyon; **D-E** *Benteng*, Jl. Benteng 1, T 22596, restaurant, peaceful hotel overlooking the centre of town, well-managed and popular with some ambience; rec; **D-E** *Mountain View*, Jl. Yos Sudarso 3, T 21621, good views, friendly management, peaceful, rec.

All the guesthouses listed below are of similar price and quality, with little to choose between them. **E** *Gangga*, Jl. Jend. A. Yani 70, T 22967, some with attached mandi, popular; **E** *Murni's*, Jl. Jend. A. Yani 115, popular, clean rooms; **E** *Nirwana*, Jl. Jend. A. Yani 113, T 21292; **E** *Surya*, Jl. Teuku Umar 7, T 22587, off the main road and quieter than other guesthouses; **F** *Pelita*, Jl. Jend. A. Yani 17, T 22883; **F** *Singgalang*, Jl. Jend. A. Yani 130, T 21576; **F** *Tiga Balai*, Jl. Jend. A. Yani 100, T 21824, one of the better of the cheap places to stay, rec.

Restaurants Bukittinggi is renowned for the quality of its food. The town has many excellent foodstalls selling sate, gulai soup and other specialities. Like the guesthouses, most of the restaurants are concentrated along Jl. Jend. A. Yani, particularly the popular travellers' restaurants. **Indonesian:** ◆*Simpang Raya*, Jl. Lantai 2, near Pasar Atas, popular Padang restaurant, part of the chain, good views; ◆◆*Famili*, Jl. Benteng 1, near the *Benteng Hotel*, perched on the hillside with good views and excellent food with friendly management, rec; ◆*Roda*, Pasar Atas (Upper Market), Blok C-155, Padang food; ◆*Selamat*, Jl. Jend. A. Yani 19, good Padang food. **Other Asian cuisine:** ◆◆ *Golden Leaf*, Jl. Jend. A. Yani, good Chinese; *Selecta*, Jl. Jend. A. Yani 3, Chinese; ◆*Asean*, Jl. A. Karim 6A, good Chinese. **International:**

♦♦Coffee Shop, Jl. Jend. A. Yani 105, very popular with travellers for breakfast (and evening meals), tables on street, usual range of travellers' dishes; **♦♦♦Dymens Hotel**, Jl. Nawawi 3, Indonesian, Chinese, Japanese, International; **♦♦Mexico**, Jl. Jend. A. Yani 134, good place for steaks and beer, rec; **♦Three Tables Coffee House**, Jl. Jend. A. Yani 142, popular with budget travellers, serving travellers' food and good standard Indonesian food. **Foodstalls**: the best foodstalls are found in and around the market area; sate, fruit, Padang dishes etc.

Entertainment Minangkabau dances: including *Pencak silat* (**see page 776**), a traditional form of self-defence, can be seen performed at Medan Nan Balindung, Jl. Khatib Suleiman 1, at 2030 every day except Thurs (admission 5,000Rp). Another venue is the Hoya Kota Wisata, Pasar Banto Building, where shows are also held at 2030 but on Thurs and Sat only.

Shopping Bukittinggi has a good selection of shops selling handicrafts and antiques, and has a particular reputation for its silver and gold jewellery. The shops are concentrated on Jl. Minangkabau (close to the Central Market) and along Jl. Jend. A. Yani. The most enjoyable way to shop is in the Central Market on Wed or Sat (see above, Places of interest). If interested in buying jewellery, it is worth visiting the Kota Gadang silversmithing village (see above, Places of interest), which specializes in producing silver filigree.

Local transport Bukittinggi is a small enough (and cool enough) town to wander around on foot. However, there are **bemos** and **bendis** – romantic 2-wheeled horse-drawn carts – for longer trips. **Oplets**: from the bus station at Aur Kuning, 3 km SE of town, for excursions. **Motorbike hire**: from most tour/travel companies for about 17,500Rp/day. **Mountain bike hire**: ask at your hotel or losmen.

Banks & money changers Bank Negara Indonesia 1946, 3rd fl, Pasar Atas; **Bank Rakyat Indonesia**, Jl. Jend. A. Yani 3 (in the shadow of the clock tower); **P.T. Enzet Corindo Perkasa**, Jl. Minangkabau 51 (moneychanger). Many of the tour and travel companies will change money.

Airline offices Garuda and Merpati, *Dymens Hotel*, Jl. Nawawi 3.

Useful addresses General Post Office: Jl. Jend. Sudirman (opposite *Dymens Hotel*), on the S edge of town. **Area code**: 0752. **Telephone office**: Jl. Jend. Sudirman (just N of General Post Office). **Hospital**: *Dokter Achmad Mochtar Hospital*, Jl. Rivai (opposite the *Denai Hotel*).

Tour companies & travel agents Concentrated along Jl. Jend. A. Yani. They include: *Maju Indosari Travel Bureau*, Jl. Muka Jam Gadang 17; *Parindo Tourist Service*, Jl. Jend. A. Yani 99; *Gangga Tours and Travel*, Jl. Jend. A. Yani 70; *Nintrabu*, Jl. Jend. A. Yani 100; *Batours*, Jl. Jend. A. Yani 105; *P.T. Travina Inti*, Jl. Jend. A. Yani 107.

Tourist office *Bukittinggi Tourist Office*, Jl. Byekh Bantam 1, T 22403. Provides some information but is not well organized considering Bukittinggi is a major tourist destination. Open: 0800-1400 Mon-Thurs, 0800-1100 Fri, 0800-1230 Sat.

Transport to & from Bukittinggi 108 km from Padang, 381 km from Sibolga, 508 km from Prapat, 174 km from Pekanbaru. **By bus**: the station is at Aur Kuning, 3 km SE of town. Regular connections with Padang 2-3 hrs, Sibolga 11 hrs, Prapat 14 hrs, Medan 20 hrs, Pekanbaru 6 hrs and Jambi 22 hrs. Most of the bus companies have their offices here including *ANS*. Tickets are also available from travel agents (see above) but beware of buying tickets from touts roaming hotels and guesthouse; the bus is unlikely to be 'air-conditioned, express and very, very comfortable'. Early morning buses to Padang leave from the clock tower. **Transport to town**: travellers arriving at Aur Kuning are sometimes encouraged to take a 'taxi' into town; there are constant regular oplets plying the route between Aur Kuning and town for a fraction of the price. **By chartered minibus**: for comfort, a minibus to Prapat (for Samosir Island) is an attractive option, 12 hrs (200,000Rp for whole bus). **By taxi**: taxis can be hired, even as far as Medan. Ask at one of the tour offices (see above).

THE RIAU ARCHIPELAGO

Insular Riau – or *Kepulauan Riau* – is made up of more than 3,000 islands, scattered in a belt stretching 700 km from the Sumatran mainland, NE to the Natuna and Anambas islands. A third of the Riau islands are uninhabited and many do not even have names. The other two-thirds have a total population of just over 400,000 and include Batam – which is fast turning into Singapore's industrial back yard – and Bintan, the biggest in the group. Bintan played a pivotal role in Malay history with the founding of the Riau-Johor Empire there in the 16th century. Many of the Riau islands have beautiful deserted beaches, although Batam is a far cry from the palm-fringed paradise it is sold as.

People

The Riau islands were first settled in the second millennium BC by proto-Malays who were later displaced by successive streams of Malay migrants. The *Orang Laut* (Sea Gypsies) were among the islands' earliest inhabitants, but the Malays are the ethnic majority in insular Riau, followed by descendants of Bugis seafarers (originally from S Sulawesi, **see page 864**). There are also many Chinese (mainly in the towns), Bataks (from the Sumatran mainland) and Minangkabaus (from W Sumatra). One Riau island serves as a Vietnamese refugee camp. The islands are predominantly Islamic, but Buddhism and Christianity are also practised. The traditional games of Riau reflect the dominant Malay culture: they include *gasing* (spinning tops), flying kites, and the martial art *pencak silat* (**see page 776**).

History

The Riau islands are strategically located on the shortest sea route between China and India at the S end of the Straits of Melaka. From the beginning of the first millennium AD, important seafaring kingdoms grew up in the area, exploiting the islands' location; Riau's rajahs controlled regional trade in gold, silk, spices and porcelain. Bintan was even important enough to merit a visit from Marco Polo in 1202. By the 15th century, with the rise of the Melakan sultanate, the Straits had become the trading crossroads of the Orient. But to the Chinese and Arab traders, insular Riau was one sprawling navigational nightmare. Many boats sank on Riau's reefs (**see box, page 164**) and the hundreds of scattered islets made perfect pirates' dens. Today it is possible to wander along beaches and pick up fragments of Ming dynasty porcelain, which are still being washed ashore from wrecked Chinese junks which sank over 400 years ago.

When the Portuguese took Melaka and forced the sultan to flee S he re-established his kingdom in Johor (**see page 175**) and when the Portuguese destroyed the Johor capital in 1526, it was uprooted again and moved to Bintan. Throughout the 16th and 17th centuries, the sultanate's capitals alternated between Johor, Bintan and Lingga, to the S. In the 18th century the Buginese, displaced by the Dutch from their homelands in S Sulawesi, arrived in Riau and soon came to dominate the Malay court. The 2 main centres of power were Penyenget Island (off Bintan) and Lingga Island. Dutch influence increased after the defeat of the Portuguese in Melaka in 1641 and the sultans gradually lost their hold on trade and then their independence.

The Riau-Johor Empire was already disintegrating when the British ousted the Dutch from both Melaka and Riau and in 1812, following a succession crisis prompted by the death of Sultan Mahmud, the kingdom split in two. Mahmud's eldest son, who was recognized by the British, went to Singapore to become the

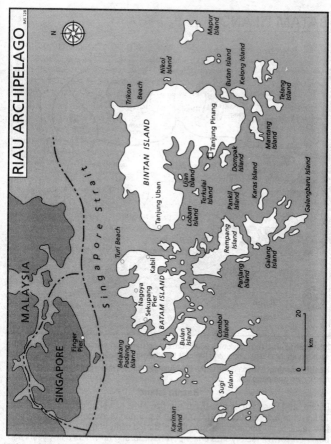

Sultan of Johor. His younger son, supported by the Buginese and the Dutch, became the Sultan of Lingga-Riau. This division of the Riau-Johor Empire was formalized with the signing of the Treaty of London between the Dutch and the British in 1824.

Modern Riau

The islands of Batam and Bintan have had their fortunes revived by Singapore's decision to transfer the republic's cumbersome land and labour-intensive industries to Riau. At the same time, both islands are being turned into resort islands catering for the Singapore market. Despite sometimes environmentally savage redevelopment, there are still long stretches of deserted beaches on Bintan. It is also possible to get away to tiny, untouched islands, with good beaches and coral. The Riau islands are a great escape from Singapore – Bintan's beaches and Tanjung Pinang's rickety backstreets could not be a greater contrast to ultra-modern Singapore, just 2 hours away. They are also a good stepping stone between Singapore and Sumatra.

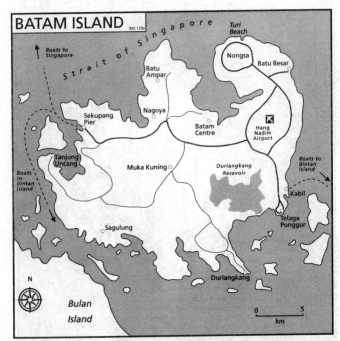

Best time to visit The monsoon season from Oct-Feb brings an average of 250 mm of rainfall each month. Mar-Sept is drier and the best time to visit the islands.

Health warning Malaria is rife in the Riau Archipelago. It is important to take preventative medication (**see page 25**).

Batam Island

Batam, at 415 sq km, is two-thirds the size of its rich N neighbour, Singapore. Today it has a population of 100,000 but is planned to increase 20-fold within a few years. Since Singaporean speculators started venturing across the Strait (see box) new towns, factory sites and a port have sprung up where a few years ago there was only jungle. Batam is no longer a beautiful island; most tourists pass through quickly, *en route* to Singapore or other islands in the archipelago and Sumatra. But Batam is a popular getaway from Singapore, and there are a number of beach resorts, designed for weekenders, which are fairly quiet during the week.

The main town, **Nagoya** (formerly Lubuk Baja) has nothing to offer visitors other than a few hotels, restaurants, shops and banks.

Tours For an island bereft of sights, there are a remarkable number of travel agencies offering round-the-island tours. One typical itinerary reads: "You will visit a modern Chinese temple in Nagoya, eat a delicious seafood lunch, proceed to Smiling Hill where you can have a panoramic view of the Singapore skyline and Batu Ampar Industrial Estate. You are then at leisure to explore the Duty Free Shop."

Accommodation Top-end beach-side accommodation is over-subscribed and over-priced during weekends – big discounts are on offer during the week. Singaporeans and expatriates comprise the majority of the clientele. **NB** hotels are priced in Singapore dollars, although rupiah are acceptable.

Batam – Singapore's industrial zone and holiday playground

Until 1990, most Singaporeans had only heard of Batam because of Radio ZOO, a rock music station operating from Riau. Now it has become their latest holiday playground. Batam is also the buzzword on the lips of Singapore industrialists and the pace of developments on the island in the early 1990s has had transnational investors scrambling for their atlases. In the course of a few months, Singapore's private sector achieved more than Batam's inert bureaucracy managed to achieve in decades.

The surge of speculative money that flooded into Batam in the early 1990s was spearheaded by the huge Batam Industrial Park, a Singapore-Indonesian joint venture. BIP provides foreign investors with the industrial equivalent of a package tour. The park's management takes care of everything, from immigration clearance to the supply of cheap labour – at wage-rates 4 times cheaper than in Singapore. Foreign companies using Batam as an export base can even retain 100% ownership for 5 years – something they are not allowed to do anywhere else in Indonesia.

On a clear day in Batam, Singapore's skyscrapers shimmer on the horizon, 20 km to the NW across the Strait of Singapore. The tourist literature, which is designed with the lucrative Singapore market in mind, describes Batam as "a microcosm of Indonesia's rich cultural heritage" – in reality you learn a lot more about Singapore and Singaporeans on Batam than you learn about Indonesians.

When the Singapore government joined hands with Jakarta and the state government of Johor (Malaysia's southernmost state) to form the so-called 'Growth Triangle', the Singapore press called it a 'vision of mutual gain' (see page 177). While Batam and Johor get investors' dollars and development, the claustrophobic island republic gets a hinterland with cheap land and labour. By the time Indonesia has shipped in workers from over-populated Java and pumped water across from nearby Bintan Island, Singapore will have 2-million workers on its doorstep, living in model industrial towns in a duty-free export processing zone. Batam will also be plugging directly into Singapore's power network and telecommunications system. In short, the island is becoming the ultimate insurance policy for Singapore's future industrial growth.

Nagoya: A *Holiday*, Jl. Imam Bonjol Blok B, No. 1, T 458616, a/c, restaurant, clean, popular with Singaporeans; **A** *Horisona*, Complek Lumbung Rezeki Blok E, T 457111, F 57123, a/c, restaurant, recently refurbished, central, popular karaoke bar, ticketing service for ferries to Singapore and Tanjung Pinang; **B** *Batam Jaya*, Jl. Raya Ali Haji, T 458707, F 58057, a/c, restaurant, pool, large, ugly hotel, but well-equipped, disco, massage centre and in-house travel agent.

Around the island: A+ *Batam Fantasy Resort*, Tanjung Pinggir, Sekupang, T 22850, a/c, restaurant, pool, well designed (the rooms actually face the sea), good range of sports facilities; **A** *Batam Island Country Club*, Tanjung Pinggir, Sekupang, T 22825 (Bookable in Singapore, T 2256819), a/c, restaurant, pool, view over the straits towards Singapore, one of Batam's first hotels on an ugly private beach, duty-free shop, tennis courts and a golf driving range, chalets; **A** *Batam View*, Jl. Hang Lekir, Nongsa, T 322281, F 22735, a/c restaurant, pool, luxurious, but characterless, on a hill overlooking a featureless beach (with no waves), full range of facilities including a golf driving range, quiet during the week; **A** *Hill Top*, Jl. Ir. Sutami 8, Sekupang, T 22391, F 22211, a/c, restaurant, pool, 5 mins from the ferry terminal, recently upgraded; **A** *Turi Beach Resort*, Nongsa, T 321543 (bookable in Singapore, T 7322577, F 7333740), a/c, restaurant, pool, well-equipped rooms, full range of facilities (including golf course), timber-built traditional-style chalets and the best beach on Batam, rec; **A** *Wisma Persero Batam*, Jl. Kuda Laut, Batu Ampar, T 58281, a/c, restaurant, pool, full range of facilities, pleasant garden; **D** *Setia Budi Chalets*, Nongsa Beach (between *Batam View Beach Resort* and *Turi Beach Resort*), restaurant (see below), simple beachside chalet accommodation – one of the very few places catering for budget travellers, organizes excursions to islands and fishing trips.

Restaurants The Riau seafood speciality is the *gong-gong* shellfish, which lives in a twisting, tapered shell, is served with a sweet chilli sauce and which is said by locals to have aphrodisiacal properties. Riau is also known for its *ikan bilis*, or anchovies.

Nagoya: ♦♦*Pagi Sore*, Block B, Jl. Imam Bonjol, 2, Padang food, rec; ♦♦*Palapa*, Pulat Perbelanjaan, Blok 1, Komplex Bumi Indah, No 8, upmarket coffee shop, Muslim food; ♦♦*Tunas Baru*, 3rd Fl, Blok E (blue block), Jl. Nagoya 42, seafood, the oldest established restaurant in town.

Around the island: *Batam Punggur*, Pantai Telaga Punggur (4 km from Kabil), another *klong*-style seafood restaurant which is also not at its best at low tide, its seafood is said to be the best on the island; ♦♦*Rejeki*, Pantai Batu Besar, near Nongsa, *klong*-style jetty with open-sided dining areas, seafood, chilli crabs and deep-fried crispy sotong, particularly pleasant at high tide, muddy at low tide, rec; ♦♦*Setia Budi Seafood*, Nongsa Beach, fresh seafood in pleasant open-sided restaurant overlooking the beach. **Foodstalls:** *Batama Food Centre*, Blok C, Nagoya; *Shangri-La Food Centre*, 2 km from Sekupang on road to Nagoya, good selection of Malay/Indonesian and Chinese stalls.

Entertainment Karaoke is popular, mainly for the benefit of visiting Singaporeans. Almost every big hotel has a disco. *Studio 21*, in Nagoya, is a cinema complex (4 theatres) with the latest Hollywood releases.

Shopping Handicrafts/batik: *Aloha Souvenirs*, 1 Blok B, Jl. Imam Bonjol, Nagoya; *Batik Danar Hadi Solo*, Pusat Pembelanjaan, Sekupang; *Duty-free shop*, Sikupang ferry terminal; *House of Bata Fiesta*, 12 Blok H, Jl. Sultan Aburrachman, Nagoya; *Utami Souvenir and Batik Shop*, Sekupang ferry terminal. **Duty-free goods** are also available from hotel shops around the island. For Singapore duty-free allowances, **see page 440**.

Sport Golf: **Turi Golf Club** at Nongsa has 18-hole and 9-hole courses.

Local transport Car hire: **Turi Travel**, *Turi Beach Resort*, T 21543, big range of vehicles for hire including limousines, jeeps and even Austin Princess London taxis, from S$12.50/hr. **Pinang Jaya**, 14 Block H, Jl. Sultan Abdurachman, Nagoya, T 58585, self-drive from S$12.50/hr. **Taxis:** from Sekupang port around the island. Taxis can be chartered for about 15,000Rp/hr.

Banks & money changers Nagoya: **Bank Bumi Daya, Bank Dagang Negara, Bank Rakyat Indonesia, Bank Duta** and **Bank Lippo.** There are money-changing facilities at Sekupang ferry terminal, in Nagoya and at major hotels. Singapore currency is widely used.

Useful addresses Area code: 0778.

Airline offices Garuda, 2nd Flr, Persero Bldg, Jl. Kuda Laut, Batu Ampar, T 58510; **Merpati**, Pertokoan Pribumi, Jl. Teuku Umar 6, Batu Ampar, T 58963.

Tour companies & travel agents *Hanita Wisatama*, Sekupang ferry terminal, T 321429, reservations and ticketing; *Natrabu*, Batam Jaya Hotel, Jl. Raja Ali Haji, Nagoya, T 58787; *Persero Baram*, Wisma Persero Batam, Jl. Kuda Laut, Batu Ampar, T 58281; *Pinang Jaya*, 14 Blok H, Jl. Sultan Abdurachman, Nagoya, T 458585; ticketing and tours around Riau islands; *Turi*, Turi Beach Resort, Nongsa, T 321323.

Tourist offices Tourist Information Centre at Sekupang ferry terminal.

Transport to & from Batam **By air:** Hang Nadim Airport is on the E side of the island. Regular connections on Garuda/Mexpati with Medan, Pekanbaru, Padang, Palembang, Banda Aceh, Bandung, Pontianak and Jakarta. **By sea:** Regular connections with Singapore; contact Singapore shipping companies for schedules: *Dino*, T 2214916; *Yang Passenger Ferry Service*, T 2239902; *Inasco Enterprises*, T 2240698; *Sinba Shipping*, T 2240901; *Indo-Falcon Shipping*, T 2203251. Also regular connections with Bintan Island from Sekupang, the main port on the NW of the island, and from Kabil, on the E side of the island. A/c high-speed passenger ferries run between Sekupang and Singapore's Finger Pier 30 mins (S$20) and there is a twice-daily service to Johor. Services run in daylight hours. There are regular boats from Sekupang to Bintan (19,000Rp). There are regular speedboat services (and fishing boats) from Kabil to Bintan 30-75 mins (8,800-12,500Rp). (For those travelling between Bintan and Singapore, there is a direct service, bypassing Batam, **see page 793**).

Bintan Island

Bintan Island is about 2$\frac{1}{2}$ times the size of Singapore and was once the capital of the Malay sultanate of Riau-Johor. A few disappointing archaeological relics of the old sultanate remain on Penyenget Island, just offshore from Bintan's modern capital, Tanjung Pinang, which is a busy and interesting little town. Within 45 mins drive of Tanjung Pinang, it is possible to reach long stretches of secluded beach, where there is a range of accommodation. But if Bintan is a remote

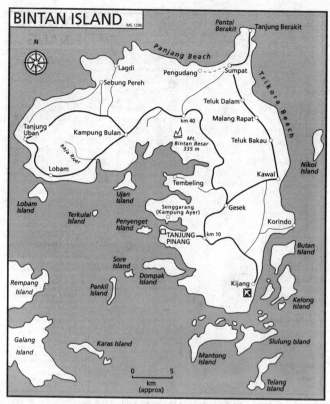

backwater in comparison to Batam, the Indonesian government intends to change things soon. In the course of the next few years, it plans to attract industrial investment to the island and expand its tourism industry. There are also proposals to set up oil refineries and oil-related industries as well as an aluminium smelting plant – Bintan is rich in bauxite. Upmarket holiday resorts, complete with marinas, villas, a shopping centre and golf courses – will take shape on the tranquil N shore. Most travellers entering Indonesia via Bintan stay just as long as it takes to catch a boat to Sumatra proper. For those with more time, it makes a good base from which to explore the Riau Islands.

Tanjung Pinang
The seaward side of insular Riau's capital is built out on stilts over what, at low tide, is a rat and mosquito-infested mudflat. But above the mud, the narrow piers – or *pelantar* – teem with life and have a maze of alleyways leading off on each side to residential pile houses. The older part of town is found around the piers; this is the interesting area to explore. The night's catch is carried down the old pier (Pejantan II) to the **fish market** on Jl. Pasar Ikan every morning. There are stalls and coffee shops lining the piers, which are good places to sit and watch

life go by; there is a hectic bazaar at the town end of the piers.

The **pasar malam** (night market) around *Hotel Tanjung Pinang* on Jalan Pos is also a lively spot in the early evening.

Excursions

Sungei Ular (Snake River) is on the other side of the harbour from Tanjung Pinang. The narrow river winds its way through mangroves to *Jodoh Temple* – the oldest Chinese temple in Riau, built as a refuge by Buddhist monks in the late 18th century. Murals on the walls depict unpleasant visions of hell. *Senggarang* is the old Bugis stilt village Tanjung Pinang's *kampung ayer* – which today is predominantly Chinese. *Bayan Island,* in the middle of the harbour, has been earmarked for an ambitious marina and hotel project. **Getting there**: boats leave from the end of either jetty.

Penyenget Island – covering only 2½ sq km – is just offshore, facing Tanjung Pinang. Once the centre of the Riau-Johor sultanate, the island is littered with relics, most of them in the NW corner. The island can be walked around in 1-2 hours. From the jetty, turn right and the road runs past most of the sights of interest. The unusual and beautifully kept yellow mosque, the *Mesjid Raya Sultan Riau* – which houses a library of antique Islamic texts – was built in 1818, and is said to be cemented together with egg-white mortar. There are a few ruins of an old fort, and further round is the ruined *Kerjaan Melayu Palace*, also built at the beginning of the 19th century in a blend of Javanese and Dutch styles, but abandoned in the early 1900s. In the centre of the island, on the way back to the jetty, are the *tombs* of Rajah Ali Jaji, who wrote the first Malay grammar and compiled a dictionary (classical Malay is still spoken on Penyenget), and Engku Peteri Permaisuri, a Bugis princess who received the island of Penyenget as her dowry from Sultan Mahmud. She ruled until her death in 1844. The descendants of the Riau-Johor royal family still live in pile houses on the S side of the island; most are fishermen. **Getting there**: regular sampans to the island leave from the end of the old pier (Pejantan II) (500Rp).

The **Riau Kandil Museum** is 2 km E of town on Jalan Bakarbatu. The museum contains an eccentric but impressive array of historical artefacts – ceramics, manuscripts, *kris*, and guns. Nothing is catalogued, and the curator's explanations are delightfully confusing. Open: on demand. **Getting there**: ojek (300Rp).

The **Regional Houses of Parliament** are in a traditional Riau-style house (*rumah lipat kijang*) at Batu Lima (5th Mile). It is decorated with symbolic carvings of flowers (prosperity), bees (mutual understanding) and various other emblems.

Trikora Beach is a long stretch of palm-fringed beach, 45 km NE of town on the quiet E side of the island. The beach is safe for swimming and the water is clear, although most of the coral on the nearby reefs is dead. The road to Trikora passes through the picturesque fishing kampung of *Teluk Kawal*. Offshore are Mapor, Nikoi and Merapas, islands which can be reached by hired boat (either from the kampung or from the resort). The beach itself is a little way off the road. The road, which follows the beach, leads N to *Tanjung Berakit,* where there are more good beaches. **Getting there**: the best way to explore the beach is to hire a motorbike in town (see Local transport). Taxi 2,500Rp/person; mini-buses can be chartered for 60,000Rp/day. Yasin (see Accommodation) leaves the *pasar malam* in Tanjung Pinang for Trikora every morning at 1100 (4,000Rp). **Accommodation: B** *Trikora Country Club*, Km 37 Teluk Bakau, (bookable in Singapore, T 2216421, private transport to Trikora can be arranged through *Wisma Kartika*, Tanjung Pinang), a/c, restaurant, pool, pleasant, low-key resort on a steep hill overlooking the sea, with private beach and shady coconut palms, tennis court and boat for snorkeling expeditions, best value resort in Riau, but prices go up on the weekends, rec; **E** *Yasin Guesthouse*, all food included, beach-side kampung-style chalets, very friendly on a pleasant stretch of beach, seasonally invaded by sandflies – from Jul-Oct, there is a sea breeze which keeps them away, rec; *Riau Beach Resort*, Teluk Bakau, 175 atap-roofed chalets opened late 1992. **Restaurants**: ♦♦*Rumah Makan Pantai Trikora*, Km 39, Jl. Teluk Bakau, fresh seafood on a genuine bamboo fishing *klong*, a little further out from the Country Club, rec. On Sundays there are stalls selling sate and grilled fish along one stretch of beach.

Panjang Beach is on the N coast. There is some reasonably good coral offshore. The beach has been earmarked for resort development. **Getting there**: can only be reached by chartered taxi, minibus or hired motorbike.

Mount Bintan Besar is Bintan's highest (335 m) peak and can be climbed in about 3 hours. From the top there are good views over Bintan and the surrounding islands of the archipelago. **Getting there**: it is not easy to reach Kampung Sekuning at the foot of the hill. It is 60 km from town and buses do not go directly to the village. Take an ojek from town (see Local transport, below).

Other islands Tanjung Pinang can be used as the jumping-off point for visits to other islands in the archipelago, although there are no regular boat services. They include **Singkep Island** (capital: **Dabo** – with good beaches, markets and walking

Business milestones

The 2 villages of Batu Duabelas (12th Kilometre) and Batu Enambelas (16th Kilometre), on the road to Kijang, are Tanjung Pinang's red light districts. Most of the 800 prostitutes come from W Java and have earned themselves a reputation in Singapore. When Singaporeans first heard of the risk of catching AIDS in Thailand (Hat Yai was – and still is – their favourite haunt), many made a bee-line for Tanjung Pinang's brothels. They calculated that because the island's womenfolk had not been exploited by Western tourists, sex would carry fewer risks. The 2 villages have been booming with the patronage ever since.

– can also be reached by air), **Penuba Island** (said to have beautiful beaches and good coral) and **Lingga Island** (home of the last Riau sultanate). Each has cheap and basic accommodation. Ask at the tourist information kiosk at the harbour or at Infotravel (on Jl. Samudra) about boats. The nearest deserted islands from Bintan are **Terkulai Island** (W of Tanjung Pinang; 20 mins by speedboat) and **Sore Island** (SW of Tanjung Pinang; 20 mins by speedboat). Both have good beaches and, like Penyenget, are littered with shards of Ming dynasty porcelain.

Accommodation Cheapest homestays are concentrated in the alleyways enclosed by Jl. Merdeka, Jl. Samudra and Jl. Yusup Kahar. On arrival at the harbour, expect to be bombarded with suggestions about where to stay.

A *Sampurna Inn* (formerly *Sampurna Jaya International*), Jl. Yusuf Kahar 15, T 21555, a/c, restaurant, biggest – and supposedly smartest – hotel in Tanjung Pinang, 3-star facilities (including "the mini beautifully garden for your relaxes"); **B** *Bintan Island Indah*, Jl. Bakar Batu 22, T 21946, a/c, restaurant, almost next door to *Sri Santai Seafood*, very clean and new – the best value in town; **B** *Pinang Island Cottages*, 133 Komplek Rimba Jaya, T 21307, F 22099, a/c, restaurant, pleasant newish complex on the outskirts of town; **B** *Riau Holiday Inn*, Jl. Pelantar II 53, T 22644, a/c, restaurant (bookable in Singapore, T 7375735, F 7330163), organizes marine sports (including water-skiing, *Apocalypse Now*-style, through the mangroves up Snake River) and trips around the island, built out on stilts off Jl. Pelantar II (the old pier), beer garden, interesting location, but attracts big tour groups from Singapore; **B** *Shangri La Hotel and Island Resort*, Jl. Gudang Minyak, T 23164 (bookable in Singapore, T 2925889, F 2983978), a/c, restaurant, good location on the seaward side of town, in-house videos in all rooms, breakfast included; **B** *Wisma Asean*, Jl. Gudang Minyak, T 22161, F 21162, breakfast included and big discounts during the week; **B** *Wisma Kartika*, 3.5 Km Jl. MT Haryono, T 22446, a/c, restaurant, sister hotel to the *Trikora Country Club* (above), pleasant, well managed; **B** *Wisma Riau*, Jl. Yusuf Kahar 8, T 21023, a/c, restaurant, reasonable hotel opposite *Sampurna Inn*, on the hill, sometimes smells a bit like a hospital, expect to be woken for prayer regularly – the town mosque is on the opposite corner, breakfast included; **C** *Tanjung Pinang*, Jl. Pos 692, T 21236, a/c, all rooms have attached bathrooms, reasonable value for money, central location, next to the Kabil pier; **D** *Surya*, Jl. Bintan, T 21811, a/c, restaurant, clean, good coffee house attached; **F** *Bong's Homestay*, Lorong Bintan II 20 (behind Jl. Merdeka), cheap and friendly, very similar to *Johnny's*, next door, dormitory or rooms; **F** *Jaafar's Guesthouse*, Lorong Bintan II, near *Bong's*, similar set-up; **F** *Johnny's Guesthouse*, Lorong Bintan II 22 (behind Jl. Merdeka), probably the most popular of the budget places, clean and friendly, breakfast included; popular getaway for Singaporeans, mountain bike hire.

Restaurants Food is neither cheap nor particularly good in Tanjung Pinang, nor is it that good. There are a few Chinese coffee shops where the coffee is wonderful, but the food very average. **♦♦***Teluk Keriting Seafood Centre*, Jl. Usman Harun 16. (Getting there: ojek from Jl. Merdeka, 400Rp.) rec. **Foodstalls**: *Pasar Malam*, around the *Tanjung Pinang Hotel*, has a number of stalls in the evening selling seafood (mud crabs, *sotong* (squid), prawns etc.) and satay. Also on sale: *gong-gong* – Riau's aphrodisiacal shellfish. Night stalls at the bus station compound off Jl. Teuku Umar; during the day there are pavement cafés next to the market on the corner of Jl. Teuku Umar and Jl. Terat I.

Festivals 5th month of the lunar calendar: *Bak Chang* (Meat Dumpling Festival) (moveable) celebrated with dragon boat races between different Hakka Chinese clans around Tanjung Pinang.

Shopping Handicrafts: *Lasmin Art Shop*, Jl Tugu Pahlawan 12, Kampung Kolam; *Toko*

Batik Gloria, Jl. Temiang; *Batik Prima*, Jl. Mawar. There are souvenir shops in the market area next to the cinema (and indoor stadium) on the corner of Jl. Teuku Umar and Jl. Terat I. There is also a souvenir shop opposite the travel agents on Jl. Samudra, next to the harbour.

Local transport The bus station is on Jl. Teuku Umar. **Taxis**: Bintan's taxis verge on the vintage, with 1950s Fords and Chevrolets and a number of ex-NTUC Singapore taxis. They can be chartered for around 40,000Rp/day. **Ojek**: the easiest way to get around is by ojek (public motorcycle), 200Rp around town. Motorbike hire: check at hotels, or rent an ojek (without the driver) along Jl. Merdeka for 20,000-25,000Rp/day.

Banks & money changers Bank Dagang Negara, Jl. Teuku Umar, next to the bus station; Bank Rakyat Indonesia, Jl. Teuku Umar, on the other side of the bus station. Money changers on Jl. Merdeka, where some shops also change money.

Useful addresses General Post Office: Jl. Hang Tuah (extension of Jl. Merdeka). **Area code**: 0771. **Immigration Office**: ferry jetty.

Airline offices Garuda, Jl. Bakar 44-46, T 21225.

Tour companies & travel agents *Bintan Panorama*, 50A Jl. Bakar Batu, T 21894, F 22572, services *Bintan Island Resort*; watersports and fishing; *Infotravel*, Jl. Samudra 12, next to the harbour-master's office, between the jetty and Jl. Merdeka, mainly a ticketing agency, schedules for ferries to Java/Sumatra and advice on how to get to other islands; *Toko New Oriental*, Jl. Merdeka 61, T 21614, ferry tickets to Batam and Singapore; *Netra Service* (Jaya Travel Bureau) Jl. Samudra 8, T 21882; *Pinang Jaya*, Jl. Bintan 44, T 21267; *Zura Abadi Travel Bureau*, Jl. Samudra 6.

Tourist offices Tourist Information Office on the main jetty, next to the immigration point.

Transport to & from Bintan Island By air: Kijang airport is 15 km SE of Tanjung Pinang. Regular connections on Merpati and Sempati with Jakarta and Pekanbaru and less regular flights to Medan, Dabo and Palembang. *Transport to town*: by bus (800Rp) by taxi (1,500Rp). **By boat**: Regular connections with Singapore, direct or via Kabil/Sekupang on Batam Island (Kabil 10,000Rp, Sekupang 19,000Rp). **Speedboats** to Kabil leave hourly (0700-1600) from the jetty off Jl. Pos/Pasar Ikan next to the *Tanjung Pinang Hotel* (8,800-10,000Rp). There are many ticket agents along the pier. There are also regular **direct ferries** between Bintan Island and Singapore's Finger Pier every day 2 hrs (S$50-60). In Singapore, contact shipping companies for schedules: *Dino*, T 2214916; *Yang Passenger Ferry Service*, T 2239902; *Inasco Enterprises*, T 2240698; *Sinba Shipping*, T 2240901; *Indo-Falcon Shipping*, T 2203251. There are daily boats from Tanjung Pinang to Pekanbaru (15,000-20,000Rp). The trip can take 2 days, with long stops at island ports along the way. Passengers are advised to take food (**see page 797**). There are less regular connections with Jakarta, Jambi, Medan, Pontianak and many other destinations elsewhere in Indonesia. Schedules from Pelni office, Jl. Ketapang/Temiang, T 21513 or from *Infotravel* (see Tour companies & travel agents, above).

THE RIAU ISLANDS TO PEKANBARU AND BUKITTINGGI

An alternative route into Sumatra is by ship from the Riau Islands, up the Siak River, to the wealthy oil town of Pekanbaru, 160 km from the coast. From Pekanbaru, a road runs W through the humid and swampy Riau lowlands to the foot of the Bukit Barisan. About 70 km from Pekanbaru the road passes the turn-off for the Srivijayan ruins at Muara Takus, before beginning the climb upwards, passing through Payakumbuh before reaching the popular hill resort of Bukittinggi, a total of 174 km from Pekanbaru.

Pekanbaru

Pekanbaru is the regional capital of Riau province, and was founded in 1784. Located on the Siak River, 160 km from the coast, it is the administrative centre of the oil industry in the area. Oil was discovered just prior to World War II, although the Japanese were the first to exploit the resource (see box). Over 85% of Riau province's GDP is generated by petroleum and natural gas production, an industry which is dominated by Caltex Pacific Indonesia Company (CPI). CPI has

Black gold: Indonesia's oil industry

Indonesia is the only Asian member of the Organization of Petroleum Exporting Countries (OPEC), and production averages about 0.5 billion barrels/year. In the peak years of the early 1980s when oil prices were over US$35/barrel, exports of oil and gas were generating US$20 billion/year in foreign exchange earnings.

Acehnese chronicles of the 17th century record that oil naturally bubbled to the surface at Perlak in N Sumatra. People at the time saw this as evidence of God's special blessing on the area. James Bontius, a scientist and one of the first Europeans to write about the diseases of the East Indies in 1629, thought oil to be an excellent cure for *beri beri* and was appalled that it should be wasted as lighting oil. But the commercial exploitation of oil had to wait another 250 years until 1871, when the first well was sunk in North Sumatra. By the outbreak of World War II, production was 55 million barrels/year.

Indonesia's breakthrough into the big league of producers came with the discovery of the huge Central Sumatran Minas field by Caltex just before World War II. Oilmen say that the initial productive well (now a tourist sight) was drilled by a Japanese army corporal. Between 1938 and 1969, production of oil rose five-fold, doubling again between 1969 and 1977. More importantly, the value of exports rose by a factor of nearly 45 between 1969 and 1981 – from US$0.4 billion to US$18.2 billion.

Some of the revenue generated by the oil boom was pumped back into the economy. After the first oil price rise of 1973, teachers' pay was quadrupled and civil servants' salaries doubled. More important in the longer term, over 6,000 schools were built each year, roads were extended into the more remote areas of the country, and fertilizer prices were subsidized, allowing Javanese farmers to become self-sufficient in rice production. But large sums were also lost through increased corruption and investment in what some economists view as prestige 'white elephants' such as the Krakatau steel works (see page 561) and the aircraft manufacturer, IPTN (page 572).

Despite the expansion of oil and gas production and exploration to other parts of Indonesia, Sumatra – and particularly Riau province – remains the biggest producer, yielding over 60% of total output. The problem for the Indonesian government is that with prices weak and exports declining in volume as domestic needs increase, it is unlikely that oil will ever play such a significant role again.

helped to build the Riau University, sports facilities, 52 schools, the Pekanbaru airport and roads to Dumai and Duri.

Much of the area surrounding Pekanbaru remains a wilderness of forest and swamp. Although criss-crossed by pipelines and dotted with oil rigs, the activity of oil exploration and production has not, seemingly, adversely affected the wildlife. Indeed, the companies are so worried about the effects that roads might have on access to the forest by spontaneous settlers that they helicopter in the equipment, creating an isolated island of activity in the jungle. This is one of the few areas with reasonable numbers of Sumatran rhinoceros, tigers and other rare Sumatran animals. More of a threat than the oil industry is the settlement of transmigrants (see page 732). During the government's third 5 year plan (1980-1984), over 100,000 transmigrants arrived on settlements in Riau province.

Riau exhibits many of the features of a 'dual' economy: on the one hand there is the high technology, capital intensive oil sector; and on the other traditional, low technology, agriculture. The 2 seldom interact, and animist tribes such as the Sakai and Kubu (perhaps 10,000 individuals) have only marginally benefited from all the wealth that has been generated.

PEKANBARU

To Siak Sri Indrapura
To Siak, Duri & Dumai
Siak River
Ferries to Batam / Tanjung Pinang
Jl. Juanda   Jl. S. Budi
Jl. Riau
Jl. S.S. Qasyim
Jl. Dr. Sutomo
Jl. T. Umar
Jl. Gatot Subroto
Jl. Melati
Jl. Teratai
Jl. Jend A. Yani
Jl. Sisingamangaraja
Jl. H. Tuah
Jl. Jend Sudirman
Jl. Diponegoro
N
Jl. Pepaya
Jl. Pelajar
Jl. Pattimura
To Bukittinggi & Muaro Tukus
Jl. Nangka
0   250
metres
To Airport & Museum
IMS-127

1. Mesjid An Nur
2. Markets
3. Tourist Office
4. General Post Office
5. Telephone Office
6. Indrapura Hotel
7. Mutiara Panghegar Hotel
8. Sri Indrayani Hotel
9. Anom Hotel
10. Riau Hotel
11. Linda Hotel

Places of interest

Pekanbaru is a featureless town with little charm or colour. Well-maintained and wide streets, impressive government buildings and opulent commercial offices bear testimony to the wealth generated by the oil industry. Few tourists visit here except in transit. Boats arrive and depart from the river dock for the Riau archipelago, an alternative route into or out of Sumatra from Singapore.

Although there are a number of worthwhile excursions from Pekanbaru, sights in the city itself are few and far between. The **Mesjid An Nur** is a large, rather uninspired, mosque off Jalan Jend. Sudirman, while the older and more attractive **Grand Mosque** and the **Marhum Bukit Cemetery** are to be found near the river, off Jalan Riau. The latter mosque was built in the 18th century and is said to have a 'magic' well. In the centre of town is the large **Pasar Pusat** on and among the streets lining Jalan Jend. A. Yani and Jalan Jend. Sudirman. 4½ km S of town on Jalan Jend. Sudirman is the **Museum Negeri**, on the road to the airport.

Excursions

Muara Takus is an archaeological site 2½ km outside a village of the same name and about 80 km W of Pekanbaru. These Buddhist Srivijayan ruins, were probably built between the 9th and 11th centuries. Four buildings have been uncovered: *Candi Tua, Candi Bungsu, Candi Pelangka* and the *Mahligai Stupa*. **Getting there:** the ruins are off the inter-provincial bus routes and can only be reached easily by taxi, private car, or on a tour (US$40/person, see below).

Siak Sri Indrapura is an historic town downstream on the Siak River, 125 km by road NE of Pekanbaru. The sultanate of Siak Sri Indrapura was founded in 1723 and there have been 12 sultans, the last surrendering his position in 1949. The stark white, gothic-style *Asseriyah Hasyimlah Palace* was built in 1889 and contains various pieces of royal regalia. Also notable is the *Royal Graveyard* (Makam Kota Tinggi) and the *Mesjid Raya*. There is basic accommodation at the *Peningapan Harmonis* (**E**), although the town is easily visited on a day trip. **Getting there:** by regular minibus from Pekanbaru's Pasar Lima Puluh terminal at the N end of Jl. Sultan S Hasyim 2½ hrs, or charter a taxi (40,000Rp), take a tour (US$40), go by speedboat down the river 2 hrs (15,000Rp), or take a ferry.

The **Sabanga Elephant Training Camp** is 135 km from Pekanbaru, 19 km from Duri. **Getting there:** by charter taxi or on a tour; buses go to Duri from the Loket terminal on Jl. Nangka.

A **boat trip along the Siak River to the Riau Islands** might be viewed as an (overnight) excursion – it certainly can be an adventure. The number of logs being floated down the river makes it clear that considerable deforestation is occurring – with or without official consent. There are also a number of settlements along the route, established by pioneer agriculturalists who have used the river as an artery of access and have cut small plots out of the forest for cultivation (see Transport to & from Pekanbaru for further details).

Tours Local companies offer day tours around the 'sights' of the city (US$15), to Siak Sri Indrapura (US$40), Muara Takus (US$40) and to the elephant training camp at Sabanga (US$40). See Excursions for background and Travel agents (below) for addresses.

Accommodation A-B *Indrapura*, Jl. Dr. Sutomo 86, T 36233, F 56337, a/c, good restaurant, pool; **A-B** *Mutiara Panghegar*, Jl. Yos Sudarso 12A, T 23102, F 23380, a/c, good restaurant, pool, tennis, best hotel in Pekanbaru, professionally managed with well appointed rooms, near the Siak River and slightly out of town; **A-B** *Sri Indrayani*, Jl. Dr. Sam Ratulangi 2, T 31870, F 21509, a/c, tennis; **B** *Tasai Ratu*, Jl. K.H. Hasyim Ashari 10 (off Jl. Jend. Sudirman), T 33225, F 25912, a/c, central, average rooms for the price; **C** *Badarussamsi*, Jl. Sisingamangaraja 71, T 22475, a/c, restaurant; **C** *Riau*, Jl. Diponegoro 34, T 22986, restaurant; **C-D** *Anom*, Jl. J. Gatot Subroto 3, T 22636, a/c, restaurant, popular with Chinese visitors, central, good value; **C-D** *Yani*, Jl. Pepaya 17 (near bus station), T 23647, some a/c, price includes breakfast, private mandi, pleasant atmosphere. **C-E** *Linda*, Jl. Nangka 133 (opp. bus station), T 22375, some a/c, cheaper upstairs rooms are clean, convenient for buses, rec.

Restaurants The cheap restaurants and foodstalls are on Jl. Jend. Sudirman, near the central market, and along the market's inner streets. **Indonesian:** ♦♦♦*Indrapura Hotel*, Jl. Dr. Sutomo, good hotel restaurant serving Indonesian, Chinese and international dishes; ♦*Mitra Sari*, Jl. Sisingamangaraja, tasty Padang food; ♦♦♦*Mutiara Panghegar*, Jl. Yos. Sudarso 12A, some locals maintain this hotel restaurant is the best in town, also serves International and Chinese food; ♦♦*Sari Bunda 88*, Jl. Gatot Subroto, Padang food. **Other Asian cuisines:** ♦♦*Gelas Mas*, Jl. H. Sulaiman, Chinese and International; ♦♦*Jumbo*, Jl. Juanda. Chinese, particularly good seafood; ♦♦*Medan*, Jl. Juanda, large menu of Szechuan, Mandarin and International food, rec. **International food:** ♦♦*Kota Piring*, Jl. Sisingamangaraja, some cheaper Indonesian food; ♦♦*Ky-Ky*, Jl. Jend. Sudirman, steaks and Indonesian food. **Bakeries:** *Big M*, Jl. Jend. Sudirman 143; *New Holland*, Jl. Jend. Sudirman 155.

Entertainment Cinema: *Dewi Santika*, Jl. Jend. Sudirman 306, a/c, modern, comfortable.

Shopping Antiques: *Rezki Utama*, Jl. Sisingamangaraja 12, carvings from the Nias Islands, Chinese porcelain, krisses, wayang puppets.

Local transport No becaks. Oplets/microlets: the station is next to the long-distance bus terminal on Jl. Nangka, in front of the Pasar Cik Puan (125 Rp). Unmetered **taxis**.

Banks & money changers Bank Bumi Daya, Jl. Jend. Sudirman. **Bank Central Asia**, Jl. Jend. Sudirman; **Ekspor Impor**, Jl. Jend. A. Yani.

Tourist offices *Riau Provincial Tourist Office* (Dinas Pariwisata Propinsi Riau), Jl. Gajah Mada 200 (unmarked, in new white government building). Some useful pamphlets.

Useful addresses General Post Office: Jl. Jend. Sudirman 229. **Area code:** 0761. **Warparpostel:** Jl. Jend. Sudirman 306A (next to the Dewi Santika Cinema) for fax, international telephone and telex/telegraph services. **General Hospital:** Jl. Diponegoro 2.

Airline offices Merpati, Jl. H.O.S. Cokroaminoto 18, T 23558; **Sempati**, Jl. Sisingamangaraja 2; **Garuda**, Jl. Jend. Sudirman 343, T 21026.

Tour companies & travel agents *Alindo*, Jl. Jend. Sudirman 211, T 22107; *Inti Angkasa*, Jl. W.R. Monginsidi 1, T 21074; *Kotapiring Kencana*, Jl. Sisingamangaraja 3, T 21382; *P.T. Cendrawasih Kencana*, Jl. Imam Bonjol 32, T 21915.

Transport to & from Pekanbaru 174 km from Bukittinggi, 158 km from Dumai. **By air:** Simpangtiga Airport is 8½ km S of town. Merpati, Sempati, Garuda and Pelangi Air all fly out of Pekanbaru. International connections with Singapore, Melaka and Kuala Lumpur. Domestic connections with Batam, Jakarta, Medan, Tanjung Pinang and Palembang. *Transport to town*: taxis to the town centre cost 7,000Rp, there is no public transport. *Airport facilities:* Post Office, money changer and a souvenir shop in the departure lounge selling stuffed frogs and what look like badly baked baguettes.

    By bus: the long-distance Mayang Terurai terminal is at Jl. Nangka 92 on the S edge of town, next to the Pasar Cik Puan. Microlets go there from the city centre (ask for 'Loket').

Regular connections with Bukittinggi 6 hrs, Padang, Bandung, Yogya, Aceh, Palembang, Jakarta 34 hrs, Medan and other destinations. Bus companies such as *ANS* (T 22065) have their offices at the terminal. Local and intra-provincial buses go from the Pasar Lima Puluh terminal at the N end of Jl. Sultan Syarit Hasyim. **By minibus**: regular connections with Bukittinggi and Padang 7 hrs. **By boat**: Pekanbaru 'port' is at the end of Jl. Saleh Abbas, the northward continuation of Jl. Jend. A. Yani. Microlets from the centre of town are marked 'Boom Baru' although it is an easy walk. Numerous companies have desks and sell tickets along Jl. Saleh Abbas. Regular connections with Tanjung Pinang, Batam Island and other stops in the Riau archipelago (including Selat Panjang, Moro, Tanjung Batu and Tanjung Balai). The boats thread their way along the Siak River and between the Riau islands. Most are Conradian cowboy operations, with overloaded boats, smuggling of goods, drunk captains and frequent groundings. Take food along. Slow boats take 36-48 hrs (16,000-21,000Rp), fast boats 24 hrs (38,000-43,000Rp).

International connections By air: with Singapore, Melaka and Kuala Lumpur.

THE WEST COAST: Bukittinggi to Padang and Sungai Penuh

The Trans-Sumatran Highway continues S from Bukittinggi through the town of Padang Panjang (19 km), before descending steeply to the narrow coastal plain and the provincial capital of Padang, a total distance of 108 km. Off the W coast are the undeveloped and thickly forested Mentawi Islands, anthropologically interesting and offering good trekking. Travelling S from Padang – along the coastal lowlands for much of the way – it is 236 km to the small district capital of Sungai Penuh, lodged in the centre of the Kerinci-Seblat National Park. After climbing into the Bukit Barisan and before reaching Sungai Penuh, the road passes Mount Kerinci, the highest peak in Sumatra (3,805 m). From Sungai Penuh, buses run E to Bangko through the narrow Batang Merankin Valley, and from there to Jambi (410 km). There are also buses which continue S along a poor road to Muko Muko and Bengkulu.

Padang

Padang, with a population of 400,000, is the capital of the small province of West Sumatra (Sumatera Barat) and the largest town on Sumatra's W coast. Lying on the narrow plain between the Bukit Barisan and the Indian Ocean, it supports a university (Universitas Andalas), an impressive array of regional government and private offices, and an enormous cement plant with an annual capacity of nearly 5 million tonnes. The romantic mist which hangs over the hills is in fact dust and smoke from the plant.

The town is also hot and very, very wet – with annual rainfall of 4,500 mm (seven times greater than London's annual rainfall, four times more than New York). Moisture-laden clouds blow in from the Indian Ocean and are forced to deposit rain on the coastal lowlands – and on Padang – as they rise over the peaks of the Bukit Barisan.

The black, red and yellow flag – similar to the German flag – which can be seen flying from offices and along roads throughout the city, is the Minangkabau or West Sumatran provincial flag. It is said that when civic dignitaries from the German town twinned with Padang arrived on an official visit, they were overcome by the effort to welcome them. No one was brave enough to tell the truth.

NB: Padang is a very Muslim and conservative town. Women should dress modestly.

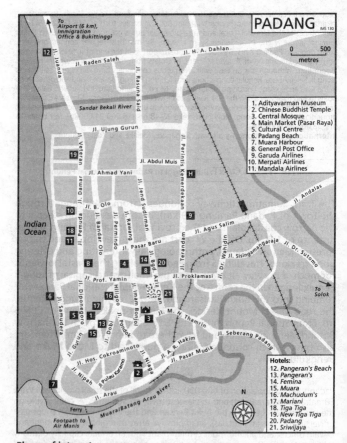

PADANG
IMS 130

1. Adityavarman Museum
2. Chinese Buddhist Temple
3. Central Mosque
4. Main Market (Pasar Raya)
5. Cultural Centre
6. Padang Beach
7. Muara Harbour
8. General Post Office
9. Garuda Airlines
10. Merpati Airlines
11. Mandala Airlines

Hotels:
12. Pangeran's Beach
13. Pangeran's
14. Femina
15. Muara
16. Machudum's
17. Mariani
18. Tiga Tiga
19. New Tiga Tiga
20. Padang
21. Sriwijaya

Places of interest
The **Adityavarman Museum** is at Jalan Diponegoro 10. Housed in a large traditional Minangkabau house and flanked by 2 rice barns, the museum has a limited display of cultural objects (textiles, tools and antiques), poorly arranged and catalogued. Admission: 200Rp. Open: 0800-1800 Tues-Thurs, Sat and Sun, 0800-1100 Fri.

Padang has some **Dutch colonial buildings** in the Padang Baru area, and a **Chinese Buddhist temple** in Chinatown or Kampung Cina. Chinatown, which lies between Jalan Dobi, Jalan Pondok and Jalan Cokroaminoto, also contains a number of older colonial buildings as well as traditional Chinese herbalists. It is one of the more interesting areas of Padang to wander around. The modern and rather drab **central mosque** is at Jalan Imam Bonjol 1.

The **main market** or Pasar Raya covers a large area between Jalan Pasar Baru and Jalan M. Yamin. It is certainly worth walking through, especially if looking for traditional textiles.

Padang beach is rather dirty and has a strong undercurrent – not recommended for swimming (see Excursions, below, for other beaches). Foodstalls line the seafront and it receives an on-shore breeze in the evening, making it a good place to sit and watch the sunset.

Excursions
Air Manis is a fishing village, 5 km to the S of town. The beach here is popular with locals and crowded at the weekend; the surf can be strong and swimming dangerous. A local legend tells of an unfaithful son, Malin Kundang, who left his family to seek his fortune. When he returned to Air Manis by sea a rich man, he was so ashamed by the shabby appearance of his mother he refused to greet her. Falling to her knees, she prayed that God punish her son; a wind rose and the boat carrying Malin sank drowning all on board. **Getting there:** walk, or catch a bemo, to the coast at the mouth of the Batang Arau River and then take the ferry boat to the other side. From there it is a 45 min walk to Air Manis, through a Chinese cemetery overlooking the sea. Alternatively, catch a bemo straight to the beach. From Air Manis it is possible to walk further S to **Padang Port** and **Teluk Bayur**; from there, regular bemos run back into town.

Bungus Beach lies 22 km S of Padang. At one time this was the most romantic beach in the area; it has now been disfigured by the construction of a wood processing enterprise. The plant is a joint South Korean/Indonesian venture and uses timber from the Mentawi Islands, contributing to the islands' rapid deforestation. There is an attractive 7 km walk from Bungus, S, to the – at present – isolated and peaceful **Telur Sei Pisang Beach**. The Japanese International Cooperation Agency and the Indonesian government are thinking of developing the area as a tourist destination. Offshore from Bungus Beach are a number of small, uninhabited, **palm-fringed coral islands**, including **Sirandah** – peaceful, with excellent snorkeling and sandy beaches. To visit the islands, hire a boat for the day (ask at one of the hotels). **Accommodation: C** *Carolina Beach Resort*, rec; **E** *Carlos Hotel*; **E** *Bungus Beach Hotel*. **Getting there:** by bemo, 1 hr.

Off-shore Islands Idyllic palm-fringed tropical islands including Pisang Besar Island, Padang Island and Bintangur Island lie offshore from Padang. All have good snorkeling, and are very peaceful. Pisang Besar Island is the closest – 15 mins by outrigger from Muara Harbour at the mouth of the Batang Arau River. Further information on how to reach the islands is available from the Tourist Information Office. **Getting there:** by chartered boat from Muara Harbour, 15-30 mins (10,000-15,000Rp).

The **Kerinci-Seblat Nature Reserve** lies S of Padang, and stretches nearly 350 km down to the tip of Sumatra (**see page 804**).

Bukittinggi and the surrounding sights are only 108 km away (**see page 777**). **Getting there:** regular bus connections from the city terminal, 2 hrs.

The **Taman Hutan Raya Bung Hatta** is a botanical gardens situated in the mountains on the road to Solok, 20 km from Padang. The reserve covers 70,000 ha of the Bukit Barisan; among its flora is the rafflesia flower (**see page 780**). Good views of the coast 700 m below. **Getting there:** by bus from the city terminal, heading E towards Solok.

Festivals Jul: *Tabut* (moveable), Islamic festival commemorating the martyrdom of Mohammad's 2 grandchildren Hasan and Husain. Symbolic coffins and models of *Bouraq*, the mythical winged horse who carried them into paradise, are paraded through the streets to the accompaniment of music and dancing and are then cast into the sea.
Aug: *Independence Day* (17th: public holiday). A carnival, parades and exciting boat races on the Batang Arau River are held on Independence Day; events extend one week either side of the 17th.

Accommodation A *Pangeran's Beach*, Jl. Ir. H. Juanda 79 (out of town on the road to the airport), T 31333, F 31613, a/c, restaurant, pool, the smartest hotel in town, well-managed, with good rooms, its location on the beach means it is quiet but suffers from an inconvenient location; **A-C** *Pangeran's*, Jl. Dobi 3-5, T 32133, F 27189, a/c, popular hotel and best in the city centre; **B** *Femina*, Jl. Bgd. Aziz Chan 15, T 21950, a/c, small hotel, centrally located with friendly and efficient management and good rooms, rec; **B** *Muara*, Jl. Gereja 34, T 25600, F 21613, a/c, restaurant, pool, new hotel, international 'style' but really only provincial standard, popular for office parties; **B-C** *Wisma Mayangsari*, Jl. Jend Sudirman 19, T 22647, a/c, price includes breakfast, clean and convenient for the airport, rec; **C** *Machudum's*, Jl. Hiligoo 45, T 32283, some a/c, colonial hotel, centrally located, now rather down-at-heel, friendly management and ambience still make it one of the more attractive places to stay, rec; **C** *Mariani*, Jl. Bundo Kandung 35, T 25466, F 25410, a/c, restaurant, unattractive decor but efficiently-run, rec; **C-D** *New Tiga Tiga*, Jl. Veteran 33, T 22173, some a/c, N of town and out of city centre, quiet; **C-D** *Padang*, Jl. Bgd. Aziz Chan 28, T 22653, some a/c, set in gardens with range of rooms some with a/c and attached bathrooms; **D** *Candrawasih*, Jl. Pemuda 27, T 22894, rather grubby; **D** *Hang Tuah*, Jl. Pemuda 1, T 26556, some a/c, unattractive 'new' hotel near bus station, rooms are adequate; **D** *Immanuel*, Jl. Tanah Beroyo 1, T 23917, quiet location S of town, reasonable rooms; **D** *Jakarta*, Jl. Bgd. Olo 55, T 23331, close to the bus terminal; **D** *Tiga Tiga*, Jl. Pemuda 31, T 22633, opposite the bus terminal, a favourite with backpackers, rooms are bare but clean, some with attached mandis, rec; **E** *Sriwijaya*, Jl. Alanglawas 1/15, T 23577, quiet location away from main road, clean.

Restaurants Padang is the place to sample Padang food (**see page 776**); there are a number to choose from on Jl. Pasar Raya. A large assortment of bowls are brought to the table, and the bill is calculated according to the quantity eaten. Hot and spicy beef *rendang* is probably the most characteristic Padang dish. Try, if you dare, Sate Padang – made with boiled cow's intestines, skewered and grilled, served with a curry sauce. **Padang:** ◆◆◆*Bak Haji*, Jl. Permindo 61A, rec.; ◆◆*Kartini*, Jl. Pasar Baru 24; ◆◆*Purnama*, Jl. Pasar Raya 111-117; ◆◆*Roda Baru*, Jl. Pasar Raya 6; ◆◆*Serba Nikmat*, Jl. Dobi 12, rec.; ◆◆*Simpang Pauk*, Jl. Pasar Baru 34F; ◆◆*Simpang Raya*, Jl. Bgd. Aziz Chan 24; ◆◆*Simpang Raya*, Jl. Bundo Kandung 3-5; ◆◆*Simpang Raya*, Jl. Pasar Baru 34; ◆◆*Surya*, Jl. Pasar Baru 38; ◆◆*Tanpa Nama*, Jl. Rohana Kudus 87, rec. **Indonesian:** ◆◆*Mariani*, Jl. Bundo Kandung 35, also serves Chinese and International food; *Taman Sari*, Jl. Jend. A. Yani 23. Javanese food, rec. **Chinese:** Several noodle houses along Jl. Niaga. ◆◆◆*Apollo*, Jl. Hos. Cokroaminoto 36, locals maintain this is the best Chinese in town. **Seafood:** ◆◆*Nelayan*, Jl. Hos. Cokroaminoto 34; ◆◆*Sari*, Jl. Thamrin 79. **International:** ◆◆*3M*, Jl. Damar 69, breakfasts, sandwiches, omelettes, pasta. **Bakeries:** *Aromey*, Jl. Miaga 275; *Indonesian*, Jl. Nipa; *Tulip's*, Jl. Pondok 139. **Ice-cream:** *Chan's*, Jl. Pondok 94, Chinese and International food, live music.

Entertainment Cultural Centre (Taman Budaya) on Jl. Diponegoro. Dances, plays and exhibitions are regularly held here. Open: 0900-1400. **Cinema:** *New Raya* (film) *Theatre*, Jl. Pasar Baru (near the market), a/c, comfortable, films with English soundtrack and Indonesian subtitles.

Sports Pool: Pool Hall, Jl. Pondok 151. **Swimming:** non-residents can use *Pangeran's Beach Hotel* at Jl. Ir. H. Juanda 79 (5,000Rp).

Shopping Antiques: *Sartika*, Jl. Jend. Sudirman 5, specializes in Sumatran and Mentawai ethnographic pieces, both souvenirs and antiques. **Basketry:** Jl. Pasar Raya and Jl. Imam Bonjol. **Books:** *Budi Daya*, Jl. Prof. M. Yamin, Blok D II/4; *Lari Anggrek*, Jl. Permindo. **Textiles:** cheap cloth is sold in the central market, at the corner of Jl. Pasar Raya and Jl. Prof. M. Yamin; several specialist textile shops along Jl. Imam Bonjol – some sell *kain songket* (**see page 810**). **Jewellery:** shops on Jl. Prof. M. Yamin and Jl. Pasar Baru. **Woodcarving:** several shops along Jl. Pasar Raya and Jl. Imam Bonjol.

Local transport Buses (*bis kota*) and bemos: travel along fixed routes, setting off from the oplet terminal on Jl. Prof. M. Yamin, next to the central market. **Dokars**, also known as *bendis*: horse-drawn carts; rows of them are to be found at the central market. **Taxis:** new taxis with meters; some unmetered for charter. **Oplets:** run from the oplet terminal on Jl. Prof. M. Yamin, between Jl. Pemuda and Jl. Olo. **Motorcycle hire:** check with your hotel or at the Information Office (see below).

Banks & money changers Bank Negara Indonesia 1946, Jl. Dobi 2; Bank Dagang Negara, Jl. Bgd. Aziz Chan 21; Bank Bumi Daya, Jl. Jend. Sudirman; T. Citra Setia Prima (money changer), Jl. Diponegoro 5.

Useful addresses General Post Office: Jl. Bgd. Aziz Chan 7 (near clock tower). **Area code:** 0751. **Immigration Office:** Jl. Khatib Sulaiman, T 25113 (for visa extension). **Telephone**

Office: Jl. Veteran 47. **Police**: Jl. Prof. M. Yamin. **General Hospital**: Jl. Perintis Kemerdekaan, T 22355. **Nature Conservation Office (PHPA)**: Jl. Raden Saleh, T 24136. **Protestant Church**: Jl. Bgd. Aziz Chan. **Catholic Church**: *St. Joseph's*, Jl. Gereja 43.

Airline offices Garuda, Jl. Jend. Sudirman 2, T 23823; *Merpati*, Jl. Pemuda 51B, T 31303; *Mandala*, Jl. Pemuda 29A, T 21979; *Sempati*, Jl. Pemuda 29B, T 25366.

Tour companies & travel agents A number are located opposite the long-distance bus terminal: *Desa Air*, Jl. Pemuda 1, T 23022; *Nitour*, Jl. Pemuda 20, T 22175; *Tunas Indonesia*, Jl. Pondok 86C, T 31661; *Pacto*, Jl. Pemuda 1, T 22780; *Natrabu*, Jl. Pemuda 23B, T 25366.

Tourist offices *Tourist Information Office*, Jl. Khatib Sulaiman (the N extension of Jl. Jend. Sudirman), T 23231, open: 0700-1400 Mon-Thurs, 0700-1100 Fri and 0700-1230 Sat (**NB**: it is about 3 km N of the town centre). *Regional Tourist Office*, Jl. Jend. Sudirman 46, T 21389.

Transport to & from Padang 108 km from Bukittinggi, 246 km from Sungai Penuh. **By air**: Tabing Airport is 7 km N of town. International connections on Garuda with Singapore, and on Sempati with Kuala Lumpur. Daily domestic connections on Merpati and Mandala with Jakarta, and on Merpati with Medan, Palembang and Pekanbaru; and 3 connections a week with Batam. *Transport to town*: hire a taxi (5,000Rp) or go out onto the main road and catch an orange *bis kota* (town bus) – it runs to the market area, close to a number of hotels. Taxis are expensive and unmetered from the airport; apparently the air force who run the airport have an 'arrangement' with the taxi drivers and do not allow the new, cheaper metered taxis to pick up passengers – although they can be dropped off. **By bus**: the station, *Lintas Andalas*, is on Jl. Pemuda close to the junction with Jl. Prof. M. Yamin. Regular connections with Bukittinggi 3 hrs, Sibolga, Pekanbaru 6 hrs, Bengkulu 14 hrs, Prapat 16 hrs, Medan 20 hrs, Palembang 24 hrs, and Jakarta 48 hrs. *ANS* has an office at the bus terminal and at Jl. Khatib Sulaiman, T 26689. **By boat**: the modern and comfortable Pelni ship *Kerinci* runs on a 2-week circuit between Jakarta and Padang 27 hrs. There are 5 classes (including deck class). It docks at Padang's port, Teluk Bayur, which is 7 km S of town. Book tickets at travel agencies or at Pelni's office at Teluk Bayur, Jl. Tanjung Priok 32, T 22109. The ship also docks at Surabaya, Ujung Padang, Balikpapan, Pantoloan, Toli Toli, Tarakan and Sibolga (**see route map, page 1006**). **By taxi**: chartered taxis are available just N of *Machudum's Hotel* on Jl. Hiligoo.

International connections By air: with Singapore and Kuala Lumpur.

THE MENTAWI ISLANDS

The Mentawi group of islands lie about 100 km off the W coast of Sumatra and are part of the same chain as Nias to the N. The name *Mentawi* is derived from the local word *si manteu* which means a 'man' or 'male'. The group consists of 4 islands – **Siberut, Sipora, Pagai Utara** (North Pagai) and **Pagai Selatan** (South Pagai). All the islands are inhabited but only Siberut is visited by significant numbers of tourists. The primary reason to visit Mentawi is to see a culture and people who have remained relatively unscathed by the 20th century.

A few years ago, visiting the Mentawi Islands was an adventure; now there are tours from Padang and Bukittinggi – 10 days for US$100. Even so, the number of visitors is still relatively small: the West Sumatran Regional Tourist Office in Padang estimated that in 1989, only 1,000 tourists visited these islands.

Fauna

For the same reason that the inhabitants of the Mentawi Islands are unique among the peoples of Indonesia, so too is some of the fauna. The archipelago was separated from the mainland about 500,000 years ago, an event which isolated the islands and allowed the wildlife to evolve independently. As a result there are a surprising number of endemic species. In 1980 the then World Wildlife Fund reported that 60% of mammal species were endemic and 15% of plant species including 4 species of primate: the black gibbon (*Hylobates klossii*), the Mentawi macaque, the long-tailed *joja* (*Presbytis potenziani*) and the pig-tailed langur

SIBERUT ISLAND (MENTAWI)

IMS 131

(Simias concolor). Appreciating the supreme importance of the islands' flora and fauna, UNESCO formally recognized Siberut Island as a National Biosphere Reserve in 1981. Sadly, the Indonesian government has only gazetted two protected areas of 90,000 ha in total, and logging and development is fast eroding the archipelago's environment.

History

The indigenous inhabitants of the Mentawi Islands are Austronesians, descendants of the original inhabitants of Southeast Asia. As the islands lie off the main trading routes, they were cocooned from the wider world until after World War II. Not even the influx of Hindu civilization and, later, that of Islam, broke upon the shores of these islands. The Dutch claimed the Mentawi group in 1864 and established a limited presence in 1904, but did little to integrate the population into the wider cash economy. Large-scale conversion to Christianity only began with increased missionary activity in the 1950s. As many as 60% of the population are now nominal Christians, although animism still plays an important role in their lives.

Economy and culture

There are several different tribes in Mentawi, among them the Sakkudei, Sarareiket and Simatalu. The Sakkudei live in the most remote and inaccessible regions, and a few still cling tenaciously to their traditional life-styles. These beautiful people tattoo their bodies, and wear loin cloths and elaborate head-dresses. They hunt with bows and poisoned arrows and live in communal long houses or *uma*, sheltering 5-10 families. The chief of the community is the *rimata*, and his right-hand man the shaman or *sikerei*. Transport through the thick forest is by dug-out canoe along rivers.

Traditionally, their subsistence needs were met through hunting and gathering in the rich forests which even today – and despite considerable deforestation – make-up the majority of the islands' land area. The pressures of modern day life have led to a decline in hunting and gathering and a corresponding rise in agricultural activities: rice, sago, taro, fruit trees and other crops are all cultivated. But to supplement their diet, the inhabitants still eat such diverse natural products as wild boar, deer, monkey, beetle larvae and fish.

As tourists and mainland Indonesians increase their presence on the islands, it is inevitable that traditional ways of life will disappear. Most alarmingly for those who would wish to preserve the Mentawi way of life, the islands have now been designated as a transmigration site for landless Javanese (**see page 732**) and settlement was scheduled to begin in 1992. Tourists should be aware that most of the guides come from Bukittinggi and have little understanding of Mentawi language and customs. An organization has been established to press for the better protection of Siberut's people and environment. For more information write to SOS Siberut, 36 Matlock Court, 46 Kensington Park Road, London W11 3BS, UK (T 071-727-4118).

Orientation
Most boats from Sumatra land at the town of Muarasiberut, at the S end of Siberut Island's E coast. There is one losmen here, and a restaurant. The other main town on Siberut is Sikabaluan, which lies to the N of Muarasiberut, also on the E coast. There is no accommodation at Sikabaluan, although homestays are available.

Trekking
There are a number of traditional villages within hiking distance (1-8 km) of Muarasiberut. More remote villages can only be reached by first taking a chartered longboat inland; ask on arrival. Note that living conditions are very basic.

Tours
Tours to the Mentawi Islands can be arranged through tour companies in Bukittinggi (see Travel agents, Bukittinggi) and Padang. Organizing an expedition independently is difficult and time-consuming. In Padang, tour agents include *P.T. Desa Air*, Jl. Pemuda 23B, T 23022, F 33335 and *Pacto*, Jl. Pemuda 1, T 27780. Tours vary a great deal in price, from US$100 to US$330, depending on what is provided. They should include trekking and canoe trips, and take the visitor through virgin forest and to what are rather condescendingly referred to as 'primitive' villages.

Travelling independently
Independent travel is not advised for those without some Indonesian language. In the past it was necessary to register first at the police station in Padang before leaving, to obtain a permit or *surat jalan*. Recent information maintains that this is no longer required. However, check first at the Regional Tourist Office in Padang – they also provide a list of recommended guides and other useful information. On arrival in Muarasiberut, tourists should register at the police station there. Porters can be hired in Muarasiberut. Visitors should expect to spend a week on Mentawi to get a good taste of local life.

What to take:
❑ trekking equipment (good walking shoes, waterproof, warm clothing).
❑ waterproof bags.
❑ toiletries.
❑ mosquito repellent and a net (malaria pills are essential).
❑ food and cooking equipment.
❑ barter goods (cigarettes, tobacco and pens).
❑ rupiah notes in small denominations sufficient for stay; about US$150
   for a week (there are no money changing facilities).

Accommodation The only losmen is at Muarasiberut (**F**), although doubtless more will shortly appear. Trekking accommodation is in the homes of missionaries or with local headmen. Gifts of pens and tobacco are essential.

Local transport This is expensive as there is no public transport and **private boats** must be chartered.

Transport to & from Mentawi By boat: boats leave for Muarasiberut (the capital of Siberut Island) from Teluk Bayur (Padang's port) twice a week on Mon and Thurs. They usually leave at 1900 and arrive at 0600 the next morning. One of the services stops at Sikabaluan, also on Siberut, but 60 km N. The return boat leaves at about 1900 on Tues and Fri, again via Sikabaluan. The services are run by *P.T. Simeulue*, Jl. Batang Arau 79, T 26179 and *P.T. Rusco Lines*, Jl. Batang Arau 31, T 21941. Tickets can be booked through travel agents (7,000-10,500Rp). It is also possible, though expensive, to charter a boat. **NB:** during the rainy season (Oct-Jan) seas can be rough and departures may be delayed.

Sungai Penuh

Sungai Penuh is a small, dirty and rather unexciting district capital, 236 km S of Padang. Cinnamon trees are cultivated in the valleys and foothills around the town. When mature, the trees are cut down and the bark stripped off and then dried in the sun before being sold. Few tourists stop here, but those interested in Sumatran wildlife can use Sungai Penuh as a base to explore the large **Kerinci-Seblat Nature Reserve** which surrounds the town (see below). In Pondok Tinggi, the old part of town, is the **Mesjid Agung**, a mosque built in 1874, in pagoda-style and decorated with Dutch tiles and carved doors and columns. Across the street is one of the town's few remaining **rumah panjang** – traditional wooden longhouses up to 200 m in length which were occupied by members of a single clan or *marga*. Most residents have moved into Javanese-style houses which are regarded as a sign of modernity.

Excursions
Lake Kerinci is situated about 5 km to the SE of town in a beautiful upland valley nearly 750 m above sea-level and surrounded by 2,000 m peaks. **Getting there:** bus to Sanggaranagung or by hired motorbike or bicycle.

Mount Kerinci lies to the N of town and at 3,805 m, is the highest peak in Sumatra. It can be climbed in 2 days, with one night spent at a hut part way up at 3,000 m. The trail to the summit is about 16 km. The best base from which to climb the mountain is the small town of **Kersik Tuo** where accommodation is available in homestays (**E**). The Eco-Rural cooperative on Jalan Raya, to which all homestays and guides belong, can provide guide services for climbing the mountain. Another popular trek is to the 10 km² mountain lake of Gunung Tuju (Seven Mountain Lake), said to be the highest freshwater lake in Southeast Asia at 1,996 m. It is also one of the least disturbed. The Eco-rural Coop charges about 30,000Rp/person/day for its tours. **Getting there**: regular buses and bemos run from the station in the market area in Sungai Penuh. Visit the Nature Conservation Office (PHPA) in Sungai Penuh on Jl. Arga Selebar Daun 11 for a permit, advice and information.

Kerinci-Seblat Nature Reserve is named after 2 of the highest mountains in Sumatra: Mount Kerinci (3,805 m) and Mount Seblat (2,385 m). The reserve stretches almost 350 km from Padang S to Bengkulu and covers almost 15,000 sq km in 4 provinces – making it the largest park in Sumatra. It accounts for a large segment of the mountainous spine of Sumatra, the Bukit Barisan, and supports a wide variety of wildlife including tigers, tapirs, elephants, Sumatran rhinoceros, sun bears, clouded leopards, semiang, five species of hornbill and the endemic short-eared rabbit (*Nesolagus netscheri*). There are no orang utans, but there have been many reported sightings of the *orang pendek* (a hairy 1½m tall and immensely strong hominid), the *cigau* (half lion, half tiger) and *kuda liar* (wild horses). The vegetation is primarily lowland, hill and montane tropical forest, with alpine vegetation on the higher slopes. Guides can be hired in Sungai Penuh and in Kersik Tuo (see Mount Kerinci excursion). Visit the Nature Conservation Office (PHPA) in town for permits, advice and information, or the PHPA offices in Padang or Bengkulu. **Best time to visit**: Jan-Mar and May-Nov, when it is driest in the valley enclave around Sungai Penuh; road travel out of these months may be difficult. Note that the mountainous areas of the reserve are wet year-round.

Accommodation D *Busana*, Jl. Martadinata, T 122, attached bathrooms with mandi, hot water brought to rooms, friendly and popular with tour groups, best in town; **D-E** *Mata Han*, good source of information; **F** *Jaya*, basic.

Local transport   Mr Bukari, owner of the *Busana Hotel*, will arrange car charter for 50,000Rp/day.

Useful addresses   Area code: 0748. PHPA office, Jl. Argo Selebar Daun 11.

Transport to & from Sungai Penuh   236 km from Padang, 410 km from Jambi. **By air**: occasional SMAC connections with Jambi. **By bus**: the bus station is in the market area. Bus connections with Jambi via Bangko 24 hrs, and Padang 10-12 hrs. There are also buses running S to Bengkulu via Muko Muko about 24 hrs; note that the road is poor.

PADANG TO JAMBI and PALEMBANG via Bangka and Belitung Islands

From Padang, the Trans-Sumatran Highway turns inland and climbs into the Bukit Barisan. The drive is beautiful, passing through the town of Solok after 59 km, and gradually descending to the humid plain. The road then turns SE into the province of Jambi, before arriving at Muarabungo, 295 km from Padang. This small, nondescript roadside town lies at an important junction. The Trans-Sumatran Highway continues S, while another main road cuts E for the 212 km trip to the provincial capital of Jambi, a gruelling 507 km from Padang. Travelling S from Jambi across marshy terrain, the road passes into the province of South Sumatra before reaching the important city of Palembang, about 260 km from Jambi. To the NE of Palembang are the islands of Bangka and Belitung, formerly important tin mining areas and now emerging as tourist centres.

Jambi

Jambi, with a population of about 300,000, is the capital of the province of the same name. It is a featureless town and the city centre occupies a relatively small area on the Batanghari River, near the port. There are a few old shophouses on Jalan Sam Ratulangi. Boats sail from here for Batam Island, Tanjung Pinang (on Bintan Island) and, occasionally, Jakarta and Singapore, negotiating the river for over 150 km to the sea (see below). Modest freighters can navigate as far inland as Jambi.

The **Museum Negeri Jambi** is on Jalan Prof. Dr. Sro. Soedewi Masjahun Sofwan and has a small collection of ethnographic and archaeological pieces from the surrounding area. There is a sprawling **street market** on Jalan Ir. Sutami, Jalan

Small and hairy: the Sumatran rhinoceros

Although not as rare as its Javan brother (**see page 563**), the Sumatran, or lesser two-horned rhino (*Didermoceros sumatrensis*) is severely endangered. It was once widespread through mainland and island Southeast Asia but has now been hunted to the point of extinction; there are probably less than 1,000 in the wild, mostly in Sumatra but with small populations in Borneo, Peninsular Malaysia and Vietnam. Only on Sumatra does it have a chance of surviving. The situation has become so serious that naturalists have established a captive breeding programme as a precaution against extinction in the wild. The species has suffered from the destruction of its natural habitat, and the price placed on its head by the value that the Chinese attach to its grated horn as a cure-all. Should the Sumatran rhino disappear so too, it is thought, will a number of plants whose seeds will only germinate after passing through the animal's intestines.

The Sumatran rhino is the smallest of all the family, and is a shy, retiring creature, inhabiting thick forest. Tracks have been discovered as high as 3,300m in the Mount Leuser National Park. It lacks the 'armoured' skin of other species and has a soft, hairy hide. It also has an acute sense of smell and hearing, but poor eyesight.

Wahid Hasyim and Jalan Supratman. **Speedboats** can be hired from close to the bridge on Jalan Sultan Taha, at the intersection with Jalan Ir. Sutami, for trips along the river.

Excursions

Candi Muara Jambi is a complex of partly restored ruins that lie 25 km E of the city, on the banks of the Batanghari River (downstream). They are part of the largest archaeological site in Sumatra and are believed to date from the 7th-13th centuries and to be associated with the Melayu Kingdom (**see page 734**), a rival of Srivijaya. They were first researched by Captain S.C. Cook in 1810. The chronicles record 35 structures here, although so far only 8 have been excavated and restored stretching over nearly 2 km, E to W. They have little decorative detail, consisting of stupas and shrines surrounded by brick walls with steps leading up into plain, square cellas. The best of the artefacts have been carted-off to the National Museum in Jakarta. Open: 0800-1600 Mon-Sun (including small site museum with a small collection of ceramics and incomplete statuary). **Getting there:** by speedboat from close to the bridge on Jl. Sultan Taha, 1hr; or by waterbus bound for Muara Sabak.

Accommodation No budget accommodation, because few travellers visit Jambi. However, there is a reasonable selection of mid-range hotels serving local businessmen. The *Jambi River View Resort*, a four star hotel, is due to open in mid-1993 and will be the best hotel in town. **B-C** *Abadi*, Jl. Jend. Gatot Subroto 92-98, T 24054, F 23065, a/c, restaurant, 'best' in town, rooms in the old wing are musty and dark, better in the new extension, service is enthusiastic rather than slick; **B-C** *Surya*, Jl. Husni Thamrin 48, T 25399, a/c, like a multi-storey carpark, hotel on 1st floor; rooms in the new wing are slightly better; **C-D** *Kartika Jaya*, Jl. Dr. Sutomo 32, T 22690, a/c, dark rooms, but better than expected given hotel's run-down appearance; **C-D** *Makmur*, Jl. Cut Nyak Dien 14, T 22324, some a/c, friendly, darkish rooms, rather out of centre of town; **C-D** *Pamalayu*, Jl. Jend. Gatot Subroto 100, T 22588, a/c; **C-D** *Pinang*, Jl. Dr. Sutomo 9, T 23969, some a/c, unfriendly, basic accommodation for the price; **C-D** *Sederhana*, Jl. Dr. Sutomo 46A, T 22786, some a/c, central location, clean rooms but a little musty and windowless rooms.

Restaurants Padang food: several restaurants in the town centre, near the market. Indonesian: *Ayam Yogya*, Jl. Abdul Muis 58, good chicken dishes; *Safari*, Jl. Dr. Wahidin. Chinese: *Aneka Rasa*, Jl. Empu Gandring; *Terkenal*, Jl. M. Asa'at 124, large menu, rec. Bakery: *French Modern Bakery*, Jl. Husni Thamrin 46.

Sports Swimming: large public swimming pool (*Kolam Renang Tepian Ratu*), Jl. Slamat

Riyadi (3 km from town centre). Open: 0800-1700 Mon-Sun.

Shopping Antiques: *Pasar Cintra Mata*, Jl. Pinang Masak 14. **Books and Maps**: *Media Agung Bookshop*, Jl. Jend. Gatot Subroto Blok A No. 1 (near *Abadi Hotel*). **Handicrafts**: handicraft centre at *Sanggar Batik dan Kerajinan*, Jl. Prof. Dr. Sri Soedewi Masjchun, 4 km from the centre of town; also outlet at Jl. Jend. Sudirman 32A.

Local transport No becaks. **Colts** (150-200Rp), **dokars, taxis, oplets**. **Speedboats**: can be hired near the bridge on Jl. Sultan Taha, near the intersection with Jl. Ir. Sutami (upstream from the Port Administration Office).

Banks & money changers **Bank Danamon**, Jl. Dr. Sutomo 21; **Bank Dagang Negara**, Jl. K.H. Wahid Hasyim 8-12.

Useful addresses **General Post Office**: Jl. Sultan Taha Syaifuddin 5. **Area code**: 0741. **Immigration Office**: Jl. Dr. Sam Ratulangi 2. **General Hospital**: Jl. Jend. Suprapto, T 22364.

Airline offices **Merpati**, Jl. Damar 83, T 22184. **Garuda**, Jl. Dr. Wahidin 95, T 22041.

Tour companies & travel agents *Mayang*, Jl. Hayam Wuruk 7, T 25450; *Jambora Kencana*, Jl. Jend. Gatot Subroto, T 23926.

Tourist offices *Provincial Tourist Office*, Jl. Basuki Rachmat 11 (about 5 km S of town), T 25330. Get there by oplet (150Rp) or taxi. Little English spoken, some brochures.

Transport to & from Jambi 507 km from Padang, 260 km from Palembang. **By air**: Sultan Taha Airport is 6 km S of town, off Jl. Jend. Sudirman. Taxis to the centre of Jambi cost 4,500Rp; oplets also go past the airport (200Rp). Regular daily connections on Merpati with Jakarta, Palembang and Pangkalpinang. SMAC operate flights to Sungai Penuh. **By bus**: the Simpang Karwat long-distance bus terminal is 3½ km SW of town, at the intersection of Jl. Hos. Cokroaminoto and Jl. Prof. M. Yamin. Colts run there from the city centre (150Rp), a/c express bus companies have their offices on Jl. Mr. Assa'ad (*ACC* at no. 60 and *Jaya Bersama* and *ALS* at no. 64), which runs off Jl. Jend. Gatot Subroto, not far from the *Abadi Hotel*. Buses to major Sumatran towns and to Jakarta 30 hrs, Bali, Bandung and Sungai Penuh. **By boat**: boats leave from the docks on the river near the centre of town, Boom Batu and Boom Rakit. Daily boats to Kuala Tungka; slow ferry 12 hrs (4,000-6,000Rp), speedboat 4 hrs (15,000Rp). Also ships/boats to Batam Island and Tanjung Pinang (Bintan Island); journey time varies but averages 48 hrs (25,000Rp). Occasional departures for Singapore and Jakarta. The best source of information about departures is the Kantor Administrator Pelabuhan (Port Administration Office) at Jl. Sultan Taha 4, on the river front, or ask around the various offices at Jl. Sultan Taha 2 (Pelabuhan Jambi). *Pelni* have an office at Jl. Sultan Taha 17, T 23649.

Palembang

For years there has been debate in archaeological circles about Palembang's status. Was it really the capital of Srivijaya, the greatest maritime empire in Southeast Asian history, as George Coedès postulated in 1918? If so, why did the city reveal so little in the way of artefacts to indicate as much? Some scholars maintained that Coedès was wrong all along; others that the low lying, swampy land, had simply enveloped what remained. The conundrum is now, it seems, solved. Work by Indonesian archaeologists in collaboration with the French scholar Pierre-Yves Manguin have uncovered a wealth of evidence in and around the city. As Manguin writes, it was due "to an amazing neglect for Sumatran archeology" that these sites had been left un-excavated for so long. It seems that Coedès, prescient as ever, was correct all the time and Palembang was the former capital of magnificent Srivijaya (**see page 733**).

The Dutch developed Palembang as an administrative centre serving the tin mines of Bangka Island and the plantations of the surrounding area. In more recent years, the city has emerged as the administrative oil export hub of South Sumatra and has a population of about 750,000. Palembang sprawls across both banks of the Musi River, about 80 km from the sea, the 2 halves of the town linked by the Ampera Bridge. Palembang's commercial core, central shopping district and most of the sights are on the N bank, in Seberang Ilir.

Places of interest

The heart of the city is marked by the 1960s built **Ampera Bridge** which spans

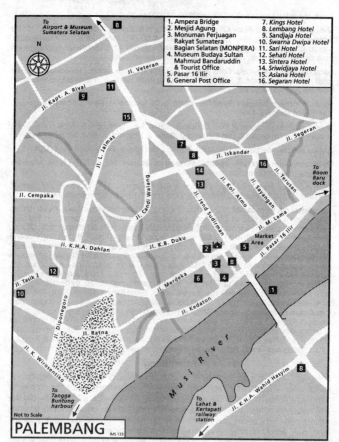

1. Ampera Bridge
2. Mesjid Agung
3. Monumen Perjuagan Rakyat Sumatera Bagian Selatan (MONPERA)
4. Museum Budaya Sultan Mahmud Bandaruddin & Tourist Office
5. Pasar 16 Ilir
6. General Post Office
7. Kings Hotel
8. Lembang Hotel
9. Sandjaja Hotel
10. Swarna Dwipa Hotel
11. Sari Hotel
12. Sehati Hotel
13. Sintera Hotel
14. Sriwidjaya Hotel
15. Asiana Hotel
16. Segaran Hotel

PALEMBANG IMS 133

the Musi River and links Palembang's 2 halves: Seberang Ulu (upstream, S) and Seberang Ilir (downstream, N). The river is 500 m wide at this point, and in total is about 600 km long. There are good views of the city from the bridge.

Within sight of the bridge, on its N side, down Jalan Jend. Sudirman, is the elegant **Mesjid Agung** or **Grand Mosque**, with its fine minaret. The mosque was built in 1738 by Sultan Mahmud Bandaruddin I, and has recently been restored. Across Jalan Merdeka is the ugly **Monumen Perjuagan Rakyat Sumatera Bagian Selatan** (sensibly known as MONPERA) which commemorates the 1947 'Battle of Five Days and Nights' when the Dutch succeeded in wrenching control of the oil and coal fields around Palembang away from republican rebels. Behind this, on Jalan Sultan Mahmud Bandaruddin II and almost on the river is the **Museum Budaya Sultan Mahmud Bandaruddin**. The museum was renovated in 1991 (the building dates from 1826) and contains a small collection of local and European pieces (the provincial museum is better, see Excursions). In the grounds is a fine stone Srivijayan Buddha, along with a new arts and crafts market. The grounds of the museum are an important excavation site: 55,000 artefacts have been uncovered dating back to the Srivijaya period. Open: 0800-1230, 1330-1600 Mon-Thurs and Sat; 0800-1100, 1330-1600 Fri. The city's tourist office occupies the ground floor of the museum.

Immediately to the E of the Ampera Bridge, on the N bank of the Musi, is the **Pasar 16 Ilir**, a maze of streets, stalls and houses reaching down to, and over, the river (see Shopping). This is Palembang's **Chinatown** and among the streets are some Chinese temples (e.g. **Klenteng Kwa Sam Yo** on Jalan Sungai Lapangan Hatal and the river). Another attractive and interesting area to explore is N of the river and W of Jalan Jend. Sudirman. Here, among the winding streets are numerous **rumah limas** – traditional Palembang houses – with their distinctive roof decoration, far more attractive than the sterile example at the Provincial Museum (see below). Jalan Datuk M. Akib is a particularly good place to view them.

Excursions

Museum Negeri Propensi Sumatera Selatan is a large museum, 5½ km N of town at Jalan Srivijaya 1. It has rooms exhibiting traditional houses, ceremonies, technology, and arts and crafts of South Sumatra. At the back are 2 traditional **limas houses**, said to be 300 years old. They have been rebuilt 4 times and although originally held together with bamboo pegs are now nailed in place and incorporate much new material. Most interesting is a collection of megaliths from Lahat District and 2 Srivijayan stone Buddhas, under a protective awning outside the museum. Of the megaliths (**see page 814**), note the wonderfully rounded elephant with a rider and a Dongson drum (*batu purbakala*) on its back (**see page 706**). Admission: 200Rp. Open: 0800-1200, 1330-1600 Tues-Thurs and Sat; 0800-1200 Mon; 0800-1100, 1330-1600 Fri. **Getting there:** take a kijang or town bus travelling N on Jalan Jend. Sudirman (which becomes Jalan Kol. H. Barlian) towards 'Km 12'; ask for 'Museum' and alight just past Jalan Srivijaya – the museum is a ½ km walk off the main road.

Hutan Wisata Puntikayu are public gardens opened in 1991, 7 km from the city centre continuing N from the turn-off for the museum along Jalan Kol. H. Barlian. **Getting there:** by kijang or town bus running towards 'Km 12'.

Boats can be hired close to the Ampera Bridge to explore the **Musi River**. The usual trip passes houseboats, takes in the Pasar 16 Ilir, and then proceeds into the countryside. Expect to pay about 5,000Rp/hour. The city tourist office recommend that visitors contact them beforehand.

The **Megaliths in Lahat District** are an overnight excursion from Palembang; it takes a day to reach the plateau and at least a day to view the sculptures and megaliths. The megaliths are scattered over the highland Pasemah Plateau about 260 km W of Palembang (**see page 814**). **Getting there:** really only possible by chartered car; by public transport, take a bus heading for Bengkulu and get off at Lahat, then catch another to Pagaralam; some of the megaliths are within walking distance from the town.

Festivals Aug: *Independence Day* (17th), *Bidar* (boat) races on the Musi in the morning, each boat carrying as many as 40 oarsmen. Commercial firms sponsor boats and village teams compete.

Accommodation A *King's*, Jl. Kol. Atmo 623, T 310033, F 310937, a/c, restaurant, central location, comfortable rooms, but over-priced; **A-B** *Lembang*, Jl. Kol. Atmo 16, T 313476, F 22472, a/c, restaurant, new, large, centrally located hotel with no character; **A-B** *Sanjaya*, Jl. Kapt. A. Rivai 6193, T 310675, F 313693, a/c, restaurant, pool, central location, good facilities but cheaper rooms are poor for the price; **B** *Swarna Dwipa*, Jl. Tasik 2, T 313322, F 28999, a/c, restaurant, pool, hotel on the W edge of town; quiet location in gardens with average rooms but friendly management, rec; **C** *Sari*, Jl. Jend. Sudirman 1301, T 353319, a/c, restaurant, average rooms, popular with Indonesians, price includes breakfast; **C-D** *Sehati*,

Cloths of gold and silver: *kain songket*

The characteristic cloth of coastal Sumatra is *songket*. This covers a wide range of types but perhaps most immediately recognizable is *kain songket* (literally, songket cloth), where supplementary gold and silver yarns are woven into plain cloth. Among the centres of production are Padang, Palembang and the towns around Bukittinggi. Floral motifs are most common, and the metallic yarn is usually woven into a cloth made from a mix of cotton and silk. In the past, 14-carat gold thread was used to embellish the cloth; today, new supplies of such thread are no longer available. Instead, weavers resort to removing the yarn from old pieces of cloth, using threads thinly coated in metal, or even weaving the patterns with plaited copper wire.

Fine pieces of kain songket were regarded as family heirlooms. They were indicative of wealth and envoys to the court of Aceh were presented with ornately wrought sarongs, headcloths and scarves. Wearing the richest examples – known as *songket lupus* – clearly marked a person's position in society. In some pieces, for example those made in the villages around Bukittinggi where they are also known as *kain balapak*, the metallic yarn is so thickly interwoven that the underlying silk or cotton cloth is barely visible. Kain songket were an essential part of the bride price, and were also exchanged on the birth of a child or during circumcision ceremonies.

Jl. Dr. Wahidin 1, T 350338, some a/c, large rooms with separate sitting area, rather musty; **C-D** *Sintera*, Jl. Jend. Sudirman 38, T 24618, some a/c, a little run down, but central, not far from Ampera Bridge; **C-D** *Sriwidjaya*, Jl. Let. Kol. Iskandar 31, T 24193, some a/c, central, rooms are poorly maintained and dark, price includes breakfast; **E** *Asiana*, Jl. Jend. Sudirman 45, popular, simple but clean rooms; best of a poor bunch; **E** *Segaran*, Jl. Segaran 207C, popular, rooms are grubby.

Restaurants **Indonesian**: *Pagi Sore*, Jl. Jend. Sudirman, Padang food; ♦*Sari Mulia*, Jl. Jend. Sudirman 589, excellent soup 'kitchen'; ♦♦*Sudi Mampir*, Jl. Merdeka, one of the best places to sample Palembang food which is served like Padang food – you only pay for what you eat. ♦*Suwito*, Jl. Demang Lebar Daun, good sate. **Chinese**: ♦♦*Kings Hotel*, Jl. Kol. Atmo 623, rather characterless restaurant, but serves good Chinese; ♦♦*Selatan Indah*, Jl. Let. Iskandar, locals maintain this is the best Chinese restaurant in Palembang. **Other Asian cuisine**: *Har*, Jl. Tustam Effendi, Indian Muslim food. **Foodstalls**: on Jl. Jend. Sudirman, W side, N from the Pasar Cinde. Cheap restaurants concentrated here as well.

Sports **Golf**: Palembang Gold Club is on Jl. AKBP Cek Agus, T 22952, N of the city centre, run by the state oil company Pertamina. Green fee for non-members: 15,000Rp, 25,000Rp on Fri, Sun and public holidays. Caddy fee: 3,000Rp. Clubs for hire. **Swimming**: large public pool, *Lumban Tirta*, on Jl. Kapt. A. Rivai ('kampus'). Admission: 1,250Rp, 1,750Rp Sun and public holidays. Open: 0800-1930 Mon-Sun.

Shopping **Jewellery**: traditional designs available at the Pasar 16 Ilir. **Lacquerware**: Palembang has a reputation for its lacquerware, a technique which was introduced by Chinese craftsmen. Shops include *Mekar Jaya*, Jl. Slamet Riyadi. **Textiles**: Palembang is a centre of songket weaving (see box); *jumputan pelangi* is a tie-dyed cloth unique to Palembang. Shops include: *Songket Palace*, Megaria Shopping Centre, Pasar 16 Ilir; *Shopping Centre*, Jl. Kol. Atmo 623; *Taras*, Jl. Merdeka; and in the Pasar 16 Ilir.

Local transport **Becaks**. Town buses travel fixed routes (150Rp). **Kijangs/oplets** (150Rp). Unmetered **taxis**. **Ferry boats** cross the river from Tangga Buntung Dock (200Rp).

Banks & money changers Bank Central Asia, Jl. Mesjid Lama 27-29; **Ekspor-Impor**, Jl. Rustan Effendi 81.

Useful addresses **General Post Office**: Jl. Merdeka 5; **Post Office**: Jl. Kapt. A. Rivai 63. **Area code**: 0711. **Hospital** Caritas: Jl. Jend. Sudirman (at intersection with Jl. Kapt. A. Rivai).

Airline offices Garuda, Jl. Kapt. Ravai 20, T 22029; **Merpati**, Jl. Kapt. Rivai 6193, T 21604; Deraya, T 21040 (for Pangkal Pinang, Bangka Island).

Tour companies & travel agents *Ista Travel*, Jl. Jend. Sudirman 53F, T 350800, Santra, Jl. Kapt. A. Rivai 6193, T 310675.

Tourist offices *Palembang City Tourist Office*, Jl. Sultan Mahmud Badaruddin II (ground floor of the Museum Budaya), T 28450, some useful maps and information; *South Sumatra Tourist Office*, Jl. Bay Salim 200, T 24981, not very helpful; *Parpostel Tourist Office*, Jl. Rajawali 22, unhelpful.

Transport to & from Palembang 260 km from Jambi, 247 km from Bengkulu, 202 km from Lahat. **By air**: Sultan Mahmud Badaruddin II Airport is 12 km N of town. *Transport to town*: unmetered taxis for 9,000Rp or walk onto the main road, 2 km away, to catch a minibus (300Rp). Palembang is a Sumatran travel hub, with regular connections with Jakarta (several daily), Bandar Lampung, Batam, Bengkulu, Jambi, Padang, Medan, and Pangkal Pinang; also connections with Dumai. **By train**: Kertapati station is 4 km SW of town, close to the Musi River. From the station, take an oplet going to Warna Kuning (150Rp) – they cross the river and then run along Jl. Merdeka and Jl. Sudirman to the centre of the city. Daily trains to Tanjungkarang, 10 hrs (11,000-20,000Rp); buses leave from here for Bakauheni and Jakarta. Connections with Lubuklinggau (7,000Rp), where there are bus connections to Padang and Lampung 9 hrs (12,000-20,000Rp). **By bus**: buses to Jambi leave from the terminal on Jl. Jend. Sudirman to the north of the city centre; buses running south depart from the terminal on Jl. Kl Ronggo Wirosentiko, not far from the southern end of the Ampera Bridge. There is also a terminal--the Tujuluh terminal--on Jl. Iskandar, in the centre of the city. Express and a/c bus offices are scattered over the city; there are a number on Jl. Kol. Atmo, a short distance N from the *King's Hotel*; *C.V. Manila* on Jl. Kapt. Cek Syeh 200 (off Jl. Jend. Sudirman); *Putra Remeja* at Jl. Veteran 6887F (just off road near intersection with Jl. Jend. Sudirman); *ALS* also on Jl. Veteran, T 20640. Regular connections with Medan, Jambi 4 hrs, Jakarta 24 hrs, Padang, Bukittinggi, Pekanbaru, Medan, Aceh, Bogor, Bali, Yogya and Solo. **By boat**: *Wisin Tour*, Jl. Veteran 173C, T 21811 run daily fast boats from Boom Baru Dock to Muntok on Bangka Island, 3 hrs (20,000Rp). Depart 0830; depart Muntok for return trip 1300. A slower ferry leaves daily from Tangga Buntung Harbour for Muntok, 13 hrs (6,000Rp).

Bangka Island

Bangka Island – shaped rather like a seahorse – lies to the NE of Palembang and is separated from the mainland by the 20 km-wide Bangka Strait. It covers an area of about 11,500 sq km and has a population of ½ million. The capital is Pangkal Pinang on the E coast; its most important port, Muntuk, is on the NW coast. Formerly Bangka's wealth was founded on tin; today, as tin declines in importance, the island is turning to tourism. But Bangka is not on the travel itinerary of most Western visitors – it remains a holiday resort catering mainly to Asian tourists.

The attraction of Bangka to visitors today are the island's sublime white-sand **beaches**, concentrated on the NE coast. Among the most popular are Hakok Beach and Matras Beach, both about 35 km N of Pangkal Pinang, past the town of Sungailiat.

The capital, Pangkal Pinang, has a population of about 100,000, and in the town there are a few remnants of Dutch colonial architecture to serve as reminders of the past. But sights are few and far between. There is a small **mining museum** at the intersection of Jalan Jend. A. Yani and Jalan Depati Amir, and a **Chinese temple**, built in the 1830s, on Jalan M. H. Muhidir.

The town of Muntok, on the W coast of Bangka and 125 km from Pangkal Pinang was the original capital of the island (until 1913) and is the main ferry point for boats to Sumatra. The **lighthouse** and **fort** in the harbour area were built at the beginning of the 19th century, while in town there is a 150 year-old **mosque** and an early 19th century **Chinese temple**.

Accommodation In Pangkal Pinang: **C** *Jaya II*, Jl. Mangkol 10, T 21656; **D** *Menumbing*, Jl. Gereja 5, T 22991, best in town; **E** *Bukit Shofa*, Jl. Mesjid Jamik 43, T 21062. On the beaches: **A** *Parai*, bookable from Jakarta T (021) 356025, F 356383, a/c, restaurant, pool, bungalow accommodation; **B** *Romodong*, on the N tip, bookable from Jakarta T (021) 560415, F 594469, a/c, restaurant (with good seafood), attractive gardens and cottage accommodation.

Restaurants Excellent seafood (several restaurants in Pangkal Pinang) and a large selection of Chinese stall food.

Bangka's tin mines

Bangka is part of a series of tin deposits which run from the lower hills of Burma, through Thailand and Peninsular Malaysia, to the islands of Belitung and Bangka. Between them, these deposits account for the bulk of world tin production. However, tin was not mined in Bangka until 1709 and today the rich alluvial deposits which attracted the Dutch have been nearly exhausted. The tin content of the ore has declined from 70% to 20%, or less.

The Dutch East India Company reached an agreement with the Sultan of Palembang over the exploitation of the tin ores of Bangka in 1755, and by the 19th century it had become one of the Dutch colonial government's most lucrative sources of revenue. However, the locals proved both unproductive and unwilling workers, and the mining firms – like those in British Malaya – began to employ Chinese indentured labourers. Conditions on the 'coolie' ships that brought these men from the over-populated and famine afflicted provinces of S China were sometimes little better than the vessels that took black slaves to the Caribbean. The death rate occasionally exceeded 50% just on the journey from Guangdong (Canton). The miners then had to endure hazardous and appalling working and living conditions.

At the beginning of the 20th century, the steam tin dredger revolutionised production and led to a dramatic improvement in working conditions. It also had the effect of putting the smaller (often Chinese-run) operations out of business, leading to the concentration of mining activity among a handful of large companies.

Local transport Infrequent bus services around the island, and between Pangkal Pinang and Muntok. Cars can be chartered.

Useful addresses Post Office: Jl. Jend. Sudirman. **Area code**: 0717. **Immigration office**: Jl. Taman Ican Saleh 2, T 21774.

Airline offices Sempati, Jl. Kapt. Sulaiman Arif 41, T 21796; Merpati, Jl. Jend. Sudirman 31, T 22077.

Tour companies & travel agents *Duta Bangka Sarana (DBS)*, Jl. Jend. Sudirman 10, Pangkal Pinang, T 21698, F 22300.

Transport to & from Bangka **By air**: the airport lies 6 km S of Pangkal Pinang. Taxis available to town (6,000Rp) or to the beaches (16,000Rp). Regular daily connections on Merpati with Jakarta and Palembang; Sempati have 2 connections a week with Batam, and Singkep. Deraya offers connections with Belitung Island, Singkep and Batam. *DBS* at Jl. Jend. Sudirman 10 will book tickets on Merpati and Deraya.

By boat: twice daily ferry connections with Palembang's Tangga Buntung Harbour leave from Mentok on the W coast (and 125 km from Pangkal Pinang) 13 hrs (6,000Rp). Jetfoils also run between Muntok and Palembang, leaving Muntok daily at 1300, 3 hrs (20,000Rp). There are some ferries which go to Kayu Arang, on the N coast and only an hour from Pangkal Pinang (and closer to the best beaches). A Pelni ship visits Muntok every 2 weeks on its circuit between Jakarta and Medan via Batam.

Belitung Island

This is Bangka's smaller sister island, 80 km off Bangka's SE coast. Belitung covers an area of 4,000 sq km and has a population of about 175,000. Like Bangka, its wealth was founded on tin, and it is now turning to tourism as an alternative source of revenue as the tin mining industry declines. The capital of Belitung is Tanjung Pandan.

The best beaches are found to the N of the capital. Tanjung Kelayang, 25 km N, is probably the best. **Getting there**: by bus from Tanjung Pandan to Tanjung Binga; and then change for Tanjung Kelayang.

Accommodation **A** *Biliton Beach Hotel*, Belitung's first international hotel is opening in early 1993, with 300 rooms, a beach front location, large pool and tennis, T 788011 or F 88106 for details, part of the Aerowisata chain of hotels. In Tanjung Pandan: **B-C** *Martani*, Jl. Yos Sudarso, T 432, some a/c, clean rooms, well-run; **D** *Wisma Dewi*, Jl. Srivijaya, some a/c, old house with ambience, clean rooms and friendly. At Kelayan Beach: **D** *Kelayang Beach*.

Transport to & from Belitung **By air**: daily connections on Merpati with Jakarta; 2 connections a week with Palembang and Bandar Lampung. Deraya fly to Pangkal Pinang. **By boat**: 2 ferry connections a week travel with Pangkal Pinang, 10 hrs (14,000Rp).

PALEMBANG TO BENGKULU via Pagaralam

The road W from Palembang crosses the swampy plain and meets up with the Trans-Sumatran Highway at Muaraenim, 159 km away. From here it is only 43 km to Lahat where a minor road leads to Pagaralam and the megaliths of the Pasemah Plateau. Continuing NW from Lahat for 158 km, the Trans-Sumatran Highway reaches the junction town of Lubuklinggau. From here the Highway continues N towards Padang, while another road runs W. It crosses the Bukit Barisan and descends to the peaceful, and relatively unspoilt, town of Bengkulu – the capital of Bengkulu Province – and 268 km from Lahat. About 100 km offshore from Bengkulu is the remote and untouched island of Enggano.

Pagaralam

Pagaralam is a small market town about 60 km SW of Lahat, set in the middle of the upland Pasemah Plateau. Its single claim to fame are the megaliths that lie scattered over the surrounding countryside. They include obelisks, massive enigmatic carved figures of warriors, some carrying Dongson drums (see page 706), others riding on elephants or struggling with buffalo and some with helmets and swords. It is thought they were carved during the first centuries AD, although archaeologists' knowledge of their origins and meaning remains limited. There is a good example of one of the megaliths in the Provincial Museum in Palembang (see page 809). A number of these massive stone carvings can be seen, literally, in among the houses of Pagaralam. Simply ask for directions. Better examples lie outside the town (see Excursions).

Excursions
Megaliths The best concentrations of the finest megaliths are to be found in the vicinity of the villages of Muara Pinang (7 km from town) and Tegur Wangi (15 km from town). **Getting there:** easiest by chartered bemo.

Accommodation D *Dharmakarya*, garden atmosphere; **D** *Losmen Mirasa*, friendly and helpful management with knowledge of surrounding area and megaliths, good rooms and food.

Transport to & from Pagaralam 260 km from Palembang, 60 km from Lahat, 328 km from Bengkulu. **By bus:** Pagaralam lies off the Trans-Sumatran Highway; to get there it is usually necessary to change at the district capital of Lahat; there are buses to Lahat from Bengkulu and Palembang. From Lahat, there are local buses to Pagaralam, 2 hrs. There are also direct bus connections between Pagaralam and Bengkulu via Manna, but the road is poor.

Bengkulu

Bengkulu is the capital of Bengkulu province, the smallest province in Sumatra with 1.2 million inhabitants. Although few tourists visit the town, it is one of the most attractive in Sumatra. Bengkulu retains a large proportion of its colonial architectural inheritance and has not (yet) been scarred by insensitive redevelopment. Attractive wooden houses with raised porches, verandahs and elaborate fretwork still grace much of the town.

Bengkulu was originally known as *Bencoolen*. The English East India Company established a trading post here in 1685, building York Fort near Muara Air to protect their claim (of which nothing remains). For nearly 150 years, Bengkulu remained Britain's only colony in Southeast Asia. By the 18th century – and despite the population being periodically decimated by malaria – the port had become an important centre for the pepper trade. However, with the downturn in the pepper market in the 19th century, the town lost its economic *raison d'être*, and became a backwater. Perhaps because of the undemanding nature of administration in Bengkulu, the British Residents dispatched to the colony turned their attention to the surrounding countryside instead. Both Sir William Marsden (1771-1779) and Sir Stamford Raffles (1817-1824) were Residents of Bengkulu and both contributed significantly to contemporary knowledge of Sumatra. In 1824 the British and Dutch signed the Treaty of London, exchanging Bengkulu for Melaka and rationalizing their spheres of influence in the region.

In contemporary Indonesia, Bengkulu has acquired a degree of fame in being the town where Sukarno was placed under house arrest between 1933 and 1942, the Dutch no doubt believing that being such a quiet and inaccessible town it was the perfect place to 'lose' him.

Places of interest
Overlooking the sea on Jalan Benteng is **Fort Marlborough** or Benteng Marlborough. Dating from 1715 and approached through massive walls, it is an impressive and well-maintained piece of history – reputedly the strongest fort

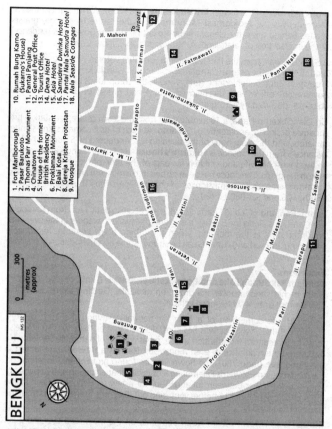

1. Fort Marlborough
2. Pasar Barukoto
3. Thomas Parr Monument
4. Chinatown
5. House of the former
   British Residency
6. Prokamasi Monument
7. Balai Kota
8. Gereja Kristen Protestan
9. Mosque
10. Rumah Bung Karno
    (Sukarno's House)
11. Pantai Panjang
12. General Post Office
13. Tourist Office
14. Dena Hotel
15. Asia Hotel
16. Samudera Dwinka Hotel
17. Pantai Nala Samudra Hotel
18. Nala Seaside Cottages

BENGKULU

constructed by the British in the East after George Fort in Madras. Graves of British soldiers can be found here and there are reasonable views from the ramparts. Sukarno was incarcerated in Fort Marlborough when he was banished into internal exile by the Dutch in 1933; his bare quarters are marked. Despite the size of the fort's defences, it was twice overwhelmed, in 1719 by local rebels and in 1760 by the French. Malaria also took its toll and few soldiers or administrators made it back to Britain. Admission: by donation. Open: 0800-1400 Mon-Thurs, 0900-1100 Fri, 0800-1200 Sat (**NB:** it is also often open out of these official hours).

Just up the hill from the fort is the **Pasar Barukoto**, a large covered market. It faces onto a **classical British monument** built by Stamford Raffles – who was Resident from 1817-1824 – to a previous Resident, Thomas Parr. Parr was stabbed to death and then decapitated by disatisfied Bugis officers in 1807. The monument and market overlook **Chinatown** or *Kampung Cina*, which includes many of the town's older colonial buildings, among them the overgrown, though protected, ruins of the former **British Residency** (1760). Within sight of the Parr Monument is the **Proklamasi Monument**, in the centre of a large, grassed square. Behind this is the elegant **Balai Kota** (the current Governor's residence), at the intersection of Jalan Jend. A. Yani and Jalan Ir. Indra Caya.

A 5 minute walk from the Parr Monument, on Jalan Veteran which runs off Jalan Jend. A. Yani, is the orange corrugated iron-roofed **Gereja Kristen Protestan** or Protestant Church. Behind the church and in the compounds of the surrounding government offices, are the unloved tombs and graves of British and Dutch colonists, distorted by earthquakes.

On Jalan Sukarno-Hatta, a 10 minute walk from the town centre, is a stark-white **mosque** designed, apparently, by Sukarno. At each of its 4 corners stand slender minarets, and the main body of the building is surmounted by 5 domes. A short distance S from the mosque is **Sukarno's house** – or Rumah Bung Karno – where he lived with his wife and children for part of the time of his period of internal exile in Bengkulu. The house has been turned into a museum and displays assorted Sukarno memorabilia. Admission: small charge. Open: Tues-Thurs 0800-1400, Fri 0800-1100 and Sat 0800-1200.

Pantai Panjang or 'Long Beach' (7 km in all) begins about 1 km from Kampung Cina, and runs along the S coast. It is a romantic place to wander in the evenings, and interesting in the morning, when the fishing boats come in. Reasonable swimming, but surf and currents can be strong. Some accommodation is available (see below).

Excursions
Dendam Tak Sudah Lake and Botanical Gardens lie 8 km E of town. The rare water orchid *Vanda hookeriana* grows on its banks. **Getting there:** accessible only on foot or by 4 wheel-drive vehicle.

Bengkulu was something of a base for naturalists during the 19th century. Stamford Raffles, while he was Resident, decided that as there was so little else to do he would turn his attention to the 'great volume of nature' in Sumatra. He discovered the magnificent, even monstrous, **Rafflesia flower** – the largest in the world (**see page 780**). The flower can be found growing in 2 locations off the road running E towards Palembang – outside Tabapenanjung and Kepahiang. They usually flower between Jul and Aug, for a few weeks only. Check at the PHPA Office, Jl. Mahoni 11 before venturing out. **Getting there:** by bus from the Terminal Panorama.

Curup is a hill town 63 km NE of Bengkulu on the main road over the Bukit Barisan to Palembang. About 19 km E of Curup town is the active Mount Raba. Rising to a height of 1,937 m, its 12 craters smoulder menacingly. A road runs from the foot of the mountain. **Getting there:** bus towards Palembang.

The **megaliths of Pagaralam** are to be found near the small market town of Pagaralam about 60 km SW of Lahat, over the Bukit Barisan, and 328 km from Bengkulu. In and around the town are numerous megaliths (**see page 814**). Accommodation available. **Getting there:** the trip really requires an overnight stay in Pagaralam; catch a bus to Lahat and then a connecting bus to Pagaralam (there are also direct buses via Manna, but the road is poor and travel slow); taxis from Bengkulu to Pagaralam cost 90,000Rp one way.

Festivals Jul: *Tabot* (moveable): extends over 10 days and celebrates the martyrdom of Hussin and Hassan, 2 of Mohammad's grandsons. Effigies of Bouraq, a winged horse, are carried in procession with music and dancing. One of the most colourful and extravagant festivals in Sumatra.

Accommodation In town: **B** *Dena*, Jl. Fatmawati 29, T 21981, a/c, comfortable, but slightly out of town and overpriced; **B** *Garden Inn*, Jl. Kartini 25, T 21952, a/c, pool, best hotel in town, friendly management, attractive situation, central, rec; **C** *Asia*, Jl. Jend. A. Yani 922B, T 31901, a/c; restaurant, large rooms, central location; **C-D** *Samudera Dwinka*, Jl. Jend. Sudirman 246, T 21604, some a/c, friendly and central, price includes breakfast, rec; **D** *Bumi Endah*, Jl. Fatmawati 29, T 31665, a/c, out of town centre, average rooms; **D** *Wisma Pemuda*, Jl. Veteran 1, T 20562, a/c, peaceful location, good value, price includes breakfast; **E** *Losmen Hayani*, Jl. S. Parman 5, T 20718, out of town near General Post Office, attractive colonial house, average rooms; **E** *Surya*, Jl. K.Z. Abidin 26 (Chinatown), T 31341; **E** *Wisma Kenanga*, Jl. Let. Kol. Santoso, T 31709, attractive colonial house with only average rooms; **F** *Damai*, Jl. K.Z. Abidin 18 (Chinatown), T 31439, some rooms with attached mandi; **F** *Losmen Samudera*, Jl. Benteng 213, T 31231, in the shadow of Fort Marlborough, dirty rooms.

On the beach (4 km from town): **A-B** *Pantai Nala Samudra*, Jl. Pantai Nala 142, T 31722, a/c, pool, best available beach accommodation but rather characterless; **C** *Nala Seaside Cottages*, Jl. Pantai Nala 133, T 31855, restaurant, bungalows on the beach, attractive but basic amenities for the price.

Restaurants There are a number of restaurants along Jl. Jend. Sudirman (which becomes Jl. Suprapto), including *Pak Liha* at no. 215 and *Simpang Raya* at 380A (serving Padang food). There are many foodstalls on the same road, some with excellent and cheap seafood. The *Citra*, also on Jl. Jend. Sudirman, serves Chinese and Javanese food. There is a **bakery** (the *New Holland*) at Jl. Suprapto 85.

Entertainment Cinemas: 2 a/c cinemas on Jl. Jend. Sudirman.

Sports Golf: *Lampangan Golf Course* on Jl. Rustandi, SE of town, open to non-members.

Shopping Handicrafts: rattan products and the local batik *besurek*. There is a handicraft shop between the Nala Seaside Cottages and Pantai Nala Samudra.

Local transport The inter-provincial and local **bus** station is Terminal Panorama, about 7 km from town; get there by **bemo** from the central market. Bemos run fixed routes around town (150Rp), or they can be chartered.

Banks & money changers Bumi Daya, Jl. Indra Caya; Ekspor Impor, Jl. Suprapto.

Useful addresses General Post Office: Jl. S. Parman 111 (S edge of town); Post Office: Jl. Jend. A. Yani 38 (facing the Parr Monument). **Area code**: 0736. **Perumtel**: Jl. Suprapto 155 for long distance telephone calls. **General Hospital**: Jl. Padang Harapan, T 31919. **Immigration Office**: Jl. Padang Harapan. PHPA: Jl. Mahoni 11 (for permits to local National Park).

Airline offices Garuda, Jl. Jend. A. Yani 922B, T 31119; **Merpati**, Jl. S. Parman 178.

Tour companies & travel agents *Citra Rafflesia*, Jl. M.T. Haryono 12; *Indah*, Jl. M.T. Haryono 14; *Swadaya*, Jl. J. Suprapto 67, T 31331.

Tourist offices *Bengkulu Tourist Office*, Jl. Sukarno-Hatta, T 31272, out of town; not really geared to tourists.

Transport to & from Bengkulu 560 km from Padang, 460 km from Palembang. **By air**: Kemiling Airport is 14 km E of town. Regular connections by Merpati with Jakarta, Bandar Lampung, Batam, Palembang, Jambi, Medan, and Padang. *Transport to town*: by taxi, 7,500Rp; or walk out onto the road and catch a bus or bemo. **By bus**: the Terminal Panorama is 7 km E of town; regular bemos link it with the central market. *Citra Rafflesia*, Jl. M.T. Haryono 12 operate a/c and non-a/c buses to Jakarta 22 hrs, Padang 18 hrs, Palembang 16 hrs and other destinations in Java and Sumatra. *Indah Tour and Travel*, Jl. M.T. Haryono 14 also arrange bus transport. **By boat**: there are weekly boats to Enggano Island from Baai Harbour about 15 km S of town.

Enggano Island

Enggano Island is about 100 km off the W coast of Sumatra, and is one of the least visited spots in Indonesia. There is excellent snorkeling, peaceful villages and jungle walks. It is said the name *Enggano* is derived from the Portuguese for 'disappointment'; they had hoped it would be clothed in valuable clove trees – it was not.

Accommodation None; locals will allow visitors to stay in their homes – ask the *kepala desa* (village headman) on arrival.

Transport to & from Enggano By boat: irregular connections with Bengkulu; about one a week from Bengkulu's Baai Harbour about 15 km south of town.

MUARAENIM TO BANDAR LAMPUNG, BAKAUHENI AND JAVA

Muaraenim is an important crossroads, linking Palembang, Bengkulu, Bandar Lampung and destinations to the N. From Muaraenim the Trans-Sumatran Highway runs S through monotonous countryside into Lampung province and the provincial capital of Bandar Lampung, almost 400 km away. Another 90 km S of here is Bakauheni, the port where ferries cross the Sunda Strait – passing Krakatau – to Merak in West Java.

Bandar Lampung

Tanjungkarang, a hillside administrative centre and **Telukbetung**, the port 5 km to the S, are the twin cities of Lampung province and have recently been amalgamated and renamed **Bandar Lampung**. Telukbetung was almost entirely destroyed by the tidal wave which followed the eruption of Krakatau. Bandar Lampung is the main bus and train terminus for travellers arriving from, or leaving for, the N of Sumatra. The train and bus stations are both in Tanjungkarang.

Today Lampung is one of the poorest provinces in Indonesia, a consequence – in part – of the numbers of transmigrants who have been settled here from Java (see box, **page 732**). Annual population growth was over 5% in the 1970s, and now the province has more than 6 million inhabitants, a degraded environment, and severe poverty. It is claimed only one in ten of Lampung's inhabitants were born in the province.

Places of interest

As a major transit point, there is a good range of accommodation, but few sights. The **Provincial Museum** is situated on Jalan Teuku Umar, and has a small collection of local *kain tapis* – or 'ship cloths' (see box below) – and archaeological and ethnographic pieces. Open: 0800-1230, 1330-1600 Mon-Thurs and Sat; 0800-1100, 1330-1600 Fri.

Excursions

Pasir Putih is the closest good beach to the city, situated 16 km S on the road to Bakauheni. Rather further afield is **Merak Belantung**, 43 km S of town; this is a beautiful sandy beach, good for swimming, with facilities for windsurfing. Accommodation available. **Getting there**: bus to Panjang and then on towards Bakauheni.

Mount Rajabasa lies about 80 km S of Bandar Lampung and close to Bakauheni. A scenic road runs around the S slopes of this dormant volcano. The route to Mount Rajabasa passes through **Canti**, where it is possible to take the ferry to the small islands of **Sebuku** and **Sebesi**, or to charter a boat to **Krakatau** (3 hrs) (see page 564).

Pugung Raharja Archaeological Park is situated about 40 km NE of town. This fortified town is thought to date from the 12th to the 17th century, and among the remains are megaliths and stepped temples. It was discovered in the 1950s by transmigrants who had moved to the area. There is a small museum 1 km from the site. **Getting there**: the site is about $2^{1}/_{2}$ km N (left) off the main road; catch a bus running towards Sribawono and alight after the road crosses the Sekampung River; then walk.

Way Kambas Elephant Reserve occupies an expanse of low-lying land bordering the Sunda Strait and Java Sea. The park was established in 1937 and is one of the oldest in Indonesia. It is best known for its large population of

Ship cloths and *tapis*: textiles of Lampung

Some of the finest examples of weaving Indonesia has ever produced are the 'ship cloths' of Lampung. Sadly, fine pieces are no longer woven, and can only be seen in museums and private collections. The principal motif is usually a ship, or a pair of ships, geometrically interpreted and symbolizing death and the afterlife. This motif is complemented by animals, houses, umbrellas, banners and other designs. The pattern is produced using a supplementary coloured weft woven into a plain, unbleached, cotton ground.

Usually, 2 types of ship cloth are identified. The *palepai* was produced by the aristocratic Kroe families of Lake Ranau, and are more often called *kain kroe*. These were traditionally used during important transitional ceremonies such as birth, death and circumcision, and were hung on the wall of the wife's side of the house. In this instance, the ship symbolizes not just death, but more generally the progress from one stage of life to the next. As the function of these pieces as ceremonial objects has declined, so too has their quality. Many of the pieces on sale today are second-rate. The second type of ship cloth is the *tampan*. These were produced more widely across Lampung and were not associated solely with higher class families. They were commonly exchanged as gifts, and motifs and designs are less constrained by convention.

However, the most ostentatious Lampung textiles were the glorious gold and silver embroidered *tapis* sarongs worn as ceremonial cloths by women. Tapis began to be made after Chinese technology of sericulture and embroidery were introduced by traders in the 14th century. The gold and silver thread is a cotton or silk yarn, wrapped around with gold or silver leaf; it must be embroidered using couching stitches because the process of sewing would damage it. Fine pieces might take a year to make and weigh 5 kg. It is still possible to buy *tapis*, although decoration tends to be simpler and the work less fine.

elephants – about 250-300 – and its elephant training school. Fauna also includes a number of primates including macaques and gibbons. The park office is at Tridatu, about 10 km N of Jepara; permits are issued here. The Elephant Training Camp is the most popular tourist attraction and is situated at Kadangsari. **Getting there:** easiest on a tour, including a visit to the Pugung Raharja Archaeological Park. Alternatively, charter a bemo from Bandar Lampung (2 hrs).

Bukit Barisan Selatan National Park straddles the southernmost section of the Barisan range of mountains and includes 120 km of coast. A road runs W from Bandar Lampung to the town of Kota Agung (about 80 km), on the edge of the park. Fauna include Sumatran tigers, elephants, honey bear, rhinoceros, pigs, pheasant as well as some rare flora including the famous rafflesia flower (**see page 780**). **Getting there:** the easiest entry point into the park is via Kota Agung (accommodation available); regular buses from Bandar Lampung, 2½ hrs.

Tours Tours can be arranged to most of the sights around Bandar Lampung (see Travel agents).

Accommodation Most of the top and mid-range accommodation is in what was formerly Telukbetung, on Lampung Bay; while lower-range losmen are concentrated in Tanjungkarang, 5 km to the N. Regular bemos link the two towns. In Telukbetung: **A** *Indra Palace*, Jl. W. Monginsidi 70, T 62766, F 62399, a/c, rooms are well appointed, situated outside the town on a hill with good views but inconvenient; **A** *Sheraton*, Jl. W. Monginsidi 175, T 63960, F 63960, a/c, restaurant, pool, good sports facilities including tennis and fitness centre, top class, low-rise hotel set around a swimming pool- best in town; **B** *Marcopolo*, Jl. Dr. Susilo 4, T 62511, F 54419, a/c, restaurant, large pool, set on the hill with good views and friendly management, best of the mid-range hotels; **B** *Sahid Krakatau*, Jl. Yos Sudarso 294, T 44022, F 63589, a/c, restaurant, pool, on the beach; **C-D** *Andalas*, Jl. Raden Intan 89, T 63432, some a/c, comfortable but characterless; **C-D** *Kurnia City*, Jl. Raden Intan 114, T 62030, some a/c, restaurant, pool, tennis courts, rather noisy location but central with good range of facilities;

D *Kurnia Dua*, Jl. Raden Intan 75, T 52906; **E** *Losmen Bahagia Raya*, Jl. Bawal 72, small rooms, rather dark and dirty. In **Tanjungkarang**: Numerous, generally poor quality accommodation, on Jl. Kota Raja; **D-E** *Hotel Ria*, Jl. Kartini, T 53974, some a/c; **E** *Losmen Gunungsari*, Jl. Kota Raja 21; **E** *Penginapan Berkah*, Jl. Kota Raja 19.

Restaurants An abundance of Padang food restaurants here – even more than usual – but also some excellent Chinese, seafood and European food too – the Sheraton and Sahid Krakatau both have good, but expensive, restaurants. **Padang**: *Begadang II*, Jl. Diponegoro, also serves other Indonesian food, rec; **♦♦***Simpang Raya*, Jl. Diponegoro 18, rec. **International**: **♦***Cookies Corner*, Jl. Kartini 29, good burgers and salads, as well as Chinese and Indonesian food. **Foodstalls**: **♦**Jl. Yos Sudarso in the evenings; **♦***Pasar Mambo*, S end of Jl. W. Monginsidi, evening stalls selling excellent seafood and Chinese food.

Shopping Textiles: Lampung is best known for its fine traditional textiles (see box). Good examples are harder and harder to find though; try the *Lampung Art Shop*, Jl. Kartini 12 (Tanjungkarang).

Local transport By **bus, minibus** and **bemos** (200Rp around town): buses and bemos run between Telukbetung, Tanjungkarang and the main Rajabasa bus terminal, N of town. Both intra and inter-provincial buses leave from Rajabasa. Bemos can also be chartered (about 8,000Rp/hr). Taxis hang around the more expensive hotels. Car rental: Avis at the *Sheraton Hotel*.

Airline offices Garuda, *Marcopolo Hotel*, Jl. Dr. Susilo 4; **Merpati**, Jl. Simba 20, T 42325.

Tour companies & travel agents *Femmy*, Jl. W. Monginsidi 143, T 44911; *Sahid Gema Wisata*, Sahid Krakatau Hotel, Jl. Yos Sudarso 294, T 62167.

Tourist offices *Telukbetung Tourist Office*, Jl. Selat Gaspar 39.

Useful addresses Area code: 0721.

Transport to & from Bandar Lampung 90 km from Bakauheni. **By air**: the airport is at Branti, 24 km N of the city. Taxis run passengers into town. Regular connections on Merpati with Jakarta, Palembang, Jambi and Padang. **By train**: the station is on the N side of town. Two trains a day leave for Palembang at 0800 and 2030, 9 hrs. From Palembang there are trains to Lubuklinggau, or buses to various other Sumatran destinations (see Palembang). If intending to travel straight on by train to Lubuklinggau, get off at Prabumulih – the Lubuklinggau train stops here. 2**By bus**: the Rajabasa terminal lies 10 km N of town. Constant minibuses run there from town. Bus companies have their offices at the terminal and a/c and non-a/c buses leave for Palembang, Jambi 30 hrs, Padang 36 hrs, Bukittinggi 38 hrs, Sibolga 48 hrs, Medan 60 hrs, Banda Aceh 72 hrs and Jakarta – via the ferry at Bakauheni 8 hrs.

Bakauheni

Bakauheni, situated at Sumatra's SE tip, is the ferry port for Java. Ferries ply the 27 km-wide Sunda Strait to Merak every hour or so, within sight of Krakatau (**see page 564**). There is little here, although the 90 km trip N to Bandar Lampung passes through attractive scenery.

Transport to & from Bakauheni 90 km from Bandar Lampung. **By boat**: regular car ferries link Bakauheni with Merak, West Java. Times of departure vary through the year, but normally there are about 15 crossings/day, 1½ hrs (21,300Rp/car, 1,100-2,200Rp/person). **By bus**: from the terminal to Bandar Lampung 2 hrs.

KALIMANTAN

Introduction, 821; **South Kalimantan**, 825; **Central Kalimantan**, 833; **East Kalimantan**, 835; **West Kalimantan**, 848.

Maps Kalimantan, 822; Selatan, 826; Banjarmasin, 828; Around Banjarmasin, 830; Balikpapan, 837; Samarinda, 841; Mahakam River, 845; Pontianak, 850.

Kalimantan is a huge, thinly populated territory of swamps, jungle, mountains and rivers. Its 549,000 sq km (nearly 30% of Indonesia's total land area) has just 5% of the country's population (about 9.5 million), most of which is concentrated in a handful of coastal cities. The interior is populated by various Dayak tribes, whose villages are scattered along the riverbanks.

INTRODUCTION

Kalimantan is divided into 4 provinces. South Kalimantan (or Kalimantan Selatan) is ubiquitously referred to as **Kalsel** and is the smallest of the 4; it is the most accessible from Java and is also the highlight of most tourists' visits to Kalimantan. To the W is Central Kalimantan (Kalimantan Tenggah) which is known as **Kalteng**. It is a vast province with a very small population; few foreign tourists venture here – its only real tourist attraction is a remote orang utan rehabilitation centre near the swampy S coast. East Kalimantan (Kalimantan Timur) is known as **Kaltim** and is the richest of the 4 provinces because of its timber, oil and gas resources. Its main attraction is the Mahakam River which penetrates deep into the interior from the provincial capital, Samarinda. West Kalimantan (Kalimantan Barat) – or **Kalbar** – is, like neighbouring Kalteng, visited by few tourists. It is cut off from the rest of Kalimantan by the mountainous, jungled interior and can only be reached by air – although some E coast tour operators offer 2-week trans-Borneo treks. The longest river in Indonesia, the 1,243 km-long Kapuas, reaches far into the interior from Kalbar's capital, Pontianak.

Tourists usually come to Kalimantan in search of 2 things: jungle and jungle culture – the Dayak forest tribes. It sometimes comes as a shock that loggers have beaten them into the jungle, particularly in the more accessible areas along the coasts and rivers. For quite long distances on either side of the riverbanks, the primary forest has all been 'harvested'. Kalimantan's powerful rivers (the Kapuas, Mahakam and Berito) have been the arteries of commerce and 'civilization'; the riverbanks are lined with towns and villages as far as they are navigable. Missionaries and traders have also beaten tourists into the tribal interior. Many Dayak tribes have been converted to Christianity and most have completely abandoned their cultures, traditions and animist religion. The majority of upriver people – apart from those in the remoter parts of the Apo Kayan in Kaltim – prefer to wear jeans and T-shirts and many have relatively well-payed jobs in the timber industry.

In the neighbouring Malaysian state of Sarawak (which can now be reached overland from Pontianak), tribal culture is much more intact and more readily accessible. Despite Sarawak's notorious logging industry, its national parks are better geared to cater for 'ecotourists' than Kalimantan's and the state's tourism infrastructure is more developed. That said, it is still possible to visit traditional longhouses in Kalimantan (in the hills of Kalsel and the upper reaches of the Mahakam and Kenyah rivers in Kaltim) – and trek through tracts of virgin rainforest. But trips to these areas take time and cost money. There are several experienced adventure tourism companies in Kalimantan – mostly based in Balikpapan and Samarinda. They categorize their tours into 'comfortable', 'safari' and 'adventure'. There are also a number of tour operators and travel agents around the world dealing with adventure tours to Kalimantan. Most have direct dealings with tour companies in Banjarmasin, Balikpapan and Samarinda. For a general introduction to the island of Borneo, **see page 227**.

CULTURE AND LIFE

People

The coasts of Kalimantan are dominated by Malays – a broad term which includes Muslim Dayaks – and the Malays make up about three-quarters of the population. Many originally migrated to Kalimantan from the Malay peninsula, the Riau islands and from Sumatra and they embraced Islam in the 15th century, following the conversion of the ruler of Banjarmasin.

The Kalimantan Dayaks can be broadly grouped by region. Kalsel (South Kalimantan) and Kalteng (Central Kalimantan) groups are collectively known as the **Barito River Dayaks** and include the '**Hill Dayaks**' of the Meratus mountains, NE of Banjarmasin. The **Ngaju** live in Kalteng; they were the first Dayak group in Kalimantan to assert their political rights, by lobbying (and fighting) for the creation of Kalteng in the 1950s. The province was later separated from Kalsel, which was dominated by the strictly Islamic Banjarese. Other Dayak groups in Kalteng include the **Ma'anyan** and the **Ot Danum**, who live along the rivers on either side of the Schwaner Range.

The main groups living in East Kalimantan are the **Kayan** and **Kenyah** (see page 242) who live in the Apo Kayan region, almost all of whom have converted to Christianity (most are Protestant). The **Bahau**, who are related to the Kayan, live in the upper Mahakam region, upriver from Long Iram; the majority are Roman Catholics. The other groups living in the upper Mahakam area include the **Modang** (they are mainly Catholic and are a subgroup of the Kenyah who migrated S), the **Bentian** and the **Penihing**. **Tanjung** Dayaks live in the middle reaches of the Mahakam; some remain animist although large numbers have converted to Christianity (both Roman Catholic and Protestant). The other main group on the middle Mahakam are the **Benuaq** – Tanjung Isuy (see page 844) is a Benuaq village, for example. They are also Roman Catholic. In addition, there are a few **Murut** groups (the **Tidung** and the **Bulungan**) to the NE (see page 297). Also in the far NE, there are the **Lun Dayeh** and **Lun Bawang**, who are closely related to Sarawak's Kelabits (see page 243). Deep in the forested interior of all the provinces, but mostly around the Apo Kayan, there is a very small population of nomadic **Penan** (see page 242), who are related to the Punan, Bukat, Bukit, Bekatan and Ot, most of whom are now settled agriculturalists.

Dayak communities in Kalbar (West Kalimantan) include the **Iban** (see page 240), who live to the N of the upper Kapuas River – although there are only a few thousand on the S side of the border. This is the area where Sarawak's Iban originated. Groups related to the Iban include the **Seberuang**, **Kantuq** and **Mualang**. There are also several '**Land Dayak**' groups in Kalbar, related to the Bidayuh of Sarawak (see page 241).

Another of the groups which lives along Kalimantan's coasts are the **Bugis** ('Sea Gypsy') people, originally from S Sulawesi (see page 864). They are famous shipbuilders and their schooners are still made in Kalsel (South Kalimantan) (see page 827).

Crafts

Textiles The Benuaq Dayaks of the Mahakam are known for their *ikat* weaving, producing colourful pieces of varied designs. They are woven with thread produced from pineapple leaves. While traditional costumes are disappearing fast, it is still possible to find the *sholang*, colourful appliqué skirts, which have black human figures and dragon-dogs (*aso/asok*) sewn on top. The traditional sarong

Traditional Banjarese architecture – high ridged roofs

Before the demise of the Banjar sultanate in 1860, the big houses, called *bubungan tinggi*, with their characteristic high, sharply pointed roofs (*bunbungan* means 'the ridge of the roof' and *tinggi* means 'tall'), were the homes of royalty, the high aristocracy and important state officials. All the older Banjar houses, dating back to the time of the sultanate, have disappeared, although there are several, scattered around the province, dating to the early 1900s. The nearest to Banjarmasin are at Kampung Melayu Laut and in Teluk Selong village. Increasingly, the traditional Banjar house-style is being adopted and readapted by modern architects - in Banjarmasin, the governor's official residence and the Mahligai Pancasila (Palace of the Five Principles) next door, being good examples. They are on Jalan Jend. Sudirman, facing the river - as all good Banjar houses should be.

Traditional (and modern) *bubungan tinggi* houses are known for their decorative woodwork, all carved in belian, or ironwood - better known in Kalimantan as *kayu ulin*. The most distinctive decorative features are the 'wings', which continue the line of the eaves upwards, crossing at the ridgeline. Typically, these wings were carved with stylized hornbill figures, a design which originates in pre-Islamic times. According to ancient Dayak belief, the hornbill embodies the gods of the upper world. Other common decorative themes include floral and geometric designs on the woodwork in and around the house as well as Arabic calligraphy. Many other patterns were also used including pineapples (representing success in life), mangosteens (whose pure white soul is enclosed in a dark and scruffy shell), bamboo shoots (symbolic of perceptiveness) and twisted rope (representing the family bonding of those who live inside). Today traditional woodcarving skills are still practised, although it is a dying art.

worn by Dayak women is called a *ta-ah*, which is a short, colourful, patchwork-style material.

Beadwork Like the Orang Ulu of Sarawak, the upriver tribes in Kalimantan are known for their beadwork, which decorates everything from betelnut containers to baby-carriers. Kenyah beadwork is mostly black against a yellow background. Beads are family heirlooms and antique ones are highly valued.

Woodcarving Small carved statues, or *hampatong*, are commonly found in handicraft shops. They are figures of humans, animals or mythical creatures and traditionally have ritual functions. They are often kept in Dayak homes to bring good luck, good health or good harvests. They are divided according to the Dayak cosmology: male figures (human and animal) are associated with the upper world, female figures (human and animal), with the lower world while hermaphrodite figures symbolize the middle world. Large hampatong are associated either with death or headhunting, while others, usually placed as a totem outside a village, will serve as its protector. Another group of large hampatong are the *sapundu*, to which sacrificial victims were tied before being put to death – the victims used to be slaves; no buffalo are used.

Hats Kalimantan's Dayak hats are called *seraung* and are made from biru leaves; they are conical and often have colourful *ta-ah* patchwork cloth sewn onto them, or they might be decorated with beads. The Kenyah – like their relations across the Sarawak border – wear distinctive grass-plaited caps called *tapung*.

Weapons The traditional Dayak head-hunting knife is called a *mandau*. It is a multi-purpose knife with practical and ritualistic uses. The different tribes have different-shaped mandau blades, which are made of steel; their handles are carved in the shape of a hornbill's head from bone. Human hair was traditionally attached to the end of the handle. Other Dayak weapons include the *tombak* hunting spear, made from ironwood, with a steel tip. The *sumpit*, or blowpipe, was used for hunting, but now plays a largely ceremonial rôle during rituals and festivals. The Dayak battle shield (*kelbit*) is made from cork, and is shaped like an elongated diamond.

Basketry There are four main types of back-pack baskets: the *anjat* (which is finely woven and has two shoulder straps), the *kiang* (which is a rougher weave and much stronger), the *lanjung* (a big basket, used for carrying rice) and the *bakul* (which is worn when harvesting rice, so that the panicles drop in). The *bening aban* is the famous baby-carrier; it is woven in fine rattan, has a wooden seat and is colourfully decorated with intricate beadwork.

SOUTH KALIMANTAN (Kalimantan Selatan – Kalsel)

South Kalimantan or Kalsel is the smallest and most densely populated of the 4 provinces in Indonesian Borneo: it has a population of 2.6 million. The population density is about 60/sq km – low by Javanese standards, but high in comparison with Kalimantan's other sparsely populated provinces. Kalsel used to include all of Central Kalimantan (Kalteng), until the latter's predominantly Dayak population won administrative autonomy from the Muslim Banjarese. The Banjarese are descended from a mixture of Dayak, Sumatran Malay, Javanese and Buginese stock – although their dialect is close to classical Malay.

The timber industry is an important source of revenue for Kalsel, although it is not as important as in East Kalimantan. Much of the logging has been along the coast and on either side of the main road to Balikpapan. There has been increasing concern voiced over the pace of deforestation and about the frequent and damaging forest fires; however, about 50% of the province's 3.7 million ha is still officially forested. The area between the road and the coast, the *Pegunungan Meratus* (the Range of 100 Mountains), which forms the backbone of the state, is still covered in primary forest – it is too remote even for loggers.

To the W of this range is the Barito River which has its headwaters deep in the interior. The coastal area is low lying and swampy: the name of the provincial capital, Banjarmasin, derives from the Javanese term 'saline garden'. Kalsel's coasts are dominated by riceland – where high yielding varieties have been successfully introduced (**see page 239**). The hybrid strains have been named after Kalsel's main rivers, the Barito and Negara. Over the past 50 years most of these ricefields have been reclaimed from the tidal swamps. Paddy seedlings are planted in the swamps during the dry season, and in the wet season they flood to a depth of 2-3m. This *padi air dalam* (deep water paddy) is harvested from boats. These swamplands are also home to another oddity: the swimming buffalo of South Kalimantan. Herds of water buffalo paddle from one grazing area to another, sometimes swimming long distances. Farmers build log platforms (called *kalang*) as resting places for their buffalo (which are known as *kalang* buffalo). In recent years the unchecked spread of water hyacinth has begun to threaten their grazing grounds.

The best time to visit Kalsel is during the dry season from Jun to Sept.

History

Legend has it that a kingdom centred on the SE corner of Borneo was founded by Ampu-jatmika, the son of a merchant from India's Coromandel coast who

settled in the area in the 12th century. He called it Negara-dipa. It became a vassal state of Java's Hindu kingdom of Majapahit in the 13th century and from then on, the city retained close cultural and trade links with Java, which led to its conversion to Islam in the 1540s. The city of Banjarmasin was founded by the Hindu ruler Pangeran Samudera (The Prince from the Sea) in 1526; it was he who first embraced Islam, changing his name to Pangeran Suriansyah in the process.

The Banjarese sultanate – which continued through a succession of 22 rulers – was the most important in Borneo (other than Brunei, on the N coast) and its tributary states included all the smaller sultanates on the W and E coasts of the island. However, in 1860, after several years of political turmoil, the Dutch abolished the sultanate altogether, and installed its administrative headquarters for all of what is now Kalimantan, in Banjarmasin. This sparked the 4 year Banjarmasin War against the Dutch occupiers; long after the uprising was put down, the Dutch presence was deeply resented. The hero of the guerrilla struggle against the Dutch was Pangeran Antasari (his name immortalized in many Kalimantan street names), who was born in the nearby city of Martapura. He unified the Banjarese, the Dayaks and the Buginese against the Dutch and had a 100,000 guilder price on his head. He died in 1862, having evaded capture, and 106 years later was proclaimed an Indonesian national hero.

Banjarmasin

Like several other cities in Asia, Banjarmasin has been dubbed 'The Venice of the Orient'. It might be an over-worked cliché, but if there is one city that deserves the epithet, it is Banjarmasin, the capital of Kalsel. The number of tourists visiting Banjarmasin is growing fast; an estimated 30,000 every year, mostly from Java and Bali. There is plenty to see in Banjarmasin, and much of the sightseeing can be done from a *klotok* (a motorized gondola): a Banjar proverb goes *'Sekali jukung didayuh, haram balabuh'* – 'once you start paddling, don't dock'.

The city grew up at the confluence of the Barito and Martapura rivers – at a point where the Barito is over 1 km wide – about 22 km upstream from the sea. Banjarmasin is dominated by its waterways: most of its population lives in pile houses and floating houses (*lanting*) on the sides of the Martapura, Barito, Kuin and Andai rivers along and around which the city is built. These rivers – and the canals which link them – are the focus of day-to-day life in Banjarmasin. The waterways are alive with people bathing, swimming, fishing and washing their clothes; they clean their teeth in them, squat over them and shop on them.

Places of interest

The imposing **Sabila Muhtadin Mosque** (Grand Mosque), built in 1980, dominates the city's waterfront. Every Friday 15,000 Muslims gather for prayer in its cool marbled interior; about 98% of Banjarmasin's population is Muslim. The Banjarese became Muslims when the local prince, Pangeran Samudera, converted to Islam around 1540, after which he became known as Pangeran Suriansyah. The city has more mosques per head of population than anywhere else in Indonesia – about one for every 40 families. Mosques, and their smaller equivalent *surau*, line the city's waterways – their domes and minarets, standing out among the parabola satellite dishes and television aerials on the skyline.

NB Muslim sensitivities should be observed in Banjarmasin – women should dress modestly and should avoid smoking in public.

The highlight of most peoples' visit to Banjarmasin is the **Pasar Terapung** (floating market) which lies on the W outskirts of town on the Barito River. Unlike floating markets elsewhere in the region – notably Bangkok's – this is far from being a tourist-showpiece. The market is big and very lively – perhaps because sellers can actively pursue buyers, paddling after them in their sampans and canoes (*jukung*) or chasing them in their *klotoks*. The market includes a floating clinic (*posyandu*) and floating pharmacy; as well as jukung-vendors selling rice, fish, fruit and vegetables, there are floating boutique shops, hardware shops, supermarkets, petrol stations and soup stalls. There is even a floating parking attendant, taking 50Rp from each of the stall-holders. There are also delightful floating tea shops; these little covered sampans have their front sections covered in plates of sticky rice, doughnuts, cakes and delicacies which customers draw up alongside and spear with a long harpoon-rod handed over by the tea-man. When the sun comes up, the *tanggui* – the famous wide-brimmed Banjar hat – comes into its own as marketeers shelter from the heat under its lofty rim.

The floating market starts early (0400) and finishes early (0900-1000) – but there is little point getting there much before 0700. By 0600 it is just light enough to see, so the river trip down the canals to the market, as Banjarmasin is awakening, is fantastic.

En route to the floating market, from town, in Kuin village, is the **Grave of Pangeran Samudera** (see page 141). Next to the floating market and along the canals there are *pengger gajian* – small family-run **sawmills** – making sawn timber for the construction industry and for construction of Bugis schooners (**see page 142**). The main schooner-building yards – in riverside dry docks called *alalak* – are just upstream from the floating market at the confluence of the Barito and

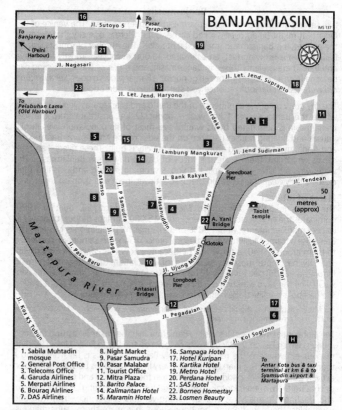

BANJARMASIN

1. Sabila Muhtadin mosque	8. Night Market
2. General Post Office	9. Pasar Samudra
3. Telecoms Office	10. Pasar Malabar
4. Garuda Airlines	11. Tourist Office
5. Merpati Airlines	12. Mitra Plaza
6. Bouraq Airlines	13. *Barito Palace*
7. DAS Airlines	14. *Kalimantan Hotel*
	15. *Maramin Hotel*

16. *Sampaga Hotel*
17. *Hotel Kuripan*
18. *Kartika Hotel*
19. *Metro Hotel*
20. *Perdana Hotel*
21. *SAS Hotel*
22. *Borneo Homestay*
23. *Losmen Beauty*

Andai rivers. But the best place to see the schooners is at the **Pelabuhan Lama** (Old Harbour) on the Martapura River, not far from the town centre. The Orang Bugis, who still build their beautiful sailing ships in the traditional manner, live in little pockets along the Kalsel coast (there is another boat-building yard at Batu Licin on the coast, 225 km east of Banjarmasin). The schooners, with their sweeping bows and tall masts are known as *perahu layar* – sailing boats. These days, most of them have powerful engines too, so they are commonly known as PLMs (*parahu layar motor*). At the 1989 World Expo' in Vancouver, Canada, a Bugis schooner sailed over from Banjarmasin carrying skilled boatbuilders and the materials to build another one. It was completed within the year and was one of the stars of the show. When the boatbuilders came home to Indonesia, they were welcomed as national heroes and received medals from President Suharto. The schooners are still in frequent use as trading vessels and most have a crew of about 30, living in quarters at the stern. On the opposite bank of the Barito River to the floating market there are several large plywood factories, one of which belongs to President Suharto's daughter, Batuti.

Pulau Kembang (Flower Island, but better known as 'Monkey Island' because of the troops of monkeys found here) is just downriver from the floating market, in the middle of the Barito. Do not touch the big male long-tailed macaques: these 'rajahs' can be vicious. The island gets rather overcrowded on weekends; donation on arrival (around 500Rp). **Getting there:** often included at the end of a tour to the floating market; alternatively take a klotok from under A. Yani Bridge. About 12 km further down the Barito River is **Pulau Kaget**, also in the middle of the river. The river around the island is one of the best places to observe the proboscis monkey (*Nasalis larvatus* – **see page 225**) which are active on the shoreline at dawn and dusk. The local name for these is the *kera Belanda* – the monkey that looks like a Dutchman. The trip takes 1¹/₂-2 hrs return.

Excursions
Martapura and the Cempaka Diamond Fields are the focus of Kalsel's gemstone-mining industry, about 40 km SE of Banjarmasin. The diamond fields are near the village of Cempaka, 10 km from Martapura. There, labourers dig 5 m-deep shafts using techniques little changed in over a century, extending tunnels from the bottom of the shafts. The stoney mud is handed to the top in bamboo baskets and then sifted and swilled in flowing water in the hope of striking lucky. If other precious stones are found in the pan, it is taken as an indication that a diamond is nearby. Many large diamonds have been unearthed at Cempaka over the past 150 years; the biggest was the 167.5-carat *Intan Trisakti* diamond, found in 1965. In 1990 a 48-carat diamond was found and was named *Intan Galuh Pampung*.

Diamonds are traditionally believed to be benevolent spirits with characters like virtuous virgins and are treated by the miners with similar respect; they refer to them as *Galuh*, or 'Princess'. A rigorously observed code of social conduct is in force in the diamond field so that nothing is done to frighten or offend 'her' in case 'she' refuses to appear. This includes the barring of sour-tasting food (said to be craved for by pregnant women), the banning of whistling (a vulgar means of attracting a girl's attention) and smoking is also taboo in case it offends Galuh. Other precious metals and stones mined at the site include gold as well as sapphires and amethysts. Cempaka is one of at least six diamond-mining villages in the area.

Around 30,000 people are employed in the gemstone industry, both in the mines and at Martapura. The latter is the gemstone cutting and polishing centre and there are many shops selling stones of all qualities. The best of Martapura's jewellery shops is *Kayu Tangi*, Jl. Sukaramail 4/J; it is the only one where stones are guaranteed. They have a good selection of precious and semi-precious stones, from diamonds to rough-cut lapis lazuli, but it is still important to bargain. Although this is the best shop in Kalsel for stones, they are not well finished and will probably require recutting and repolishing. There is a **polishing factory** next door (closed Fri) and many stalls selling semi-precious stones, beads and jewellery – including *manik manik* stone necklaces – in the **Pasar Niaga** market (some shops close Fri).

There is a vast and very colourful vegetable market next to Pasar Niaga (Mon-Sun, but the Friday market is the biggest). Behind the vegetable market is a building with shops where silversmiths make rings. **Getting there**: see below.

NB When to visit: Martapura's Diamond Fields are shut on Fridays, as are the stone-cutting and polishing workshops; most jewellery shops do, however, stay open on Fridays. Friday is also the best day to see the Martapura market in full swing.

Lambung Mangkurat State Museum, housed in a dubious modern interpretation of a traditional Banjar-style building at Banjarbaru, near Martapura, has historical and cultural displays on Kalsel. On the ground floor there is a life-size, ulin-wood (belian/ironwood) *tambangan* boat (the traditional Banjar river boat, in use from the 17th century to the 1950s). Admission: 200Rp. Open: 0830-1400

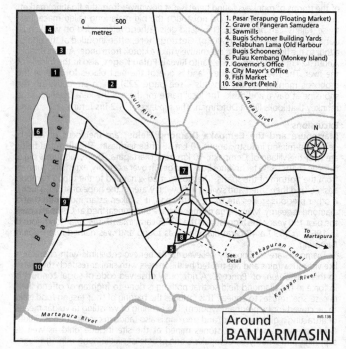

1. Pasar Terapung (Floating Market)
2. Grave of Pangeran Samudera
3. Sawmills
4. Bugis Schooner Building Yards
5. Pelabuhan Lama (Old Harbour Bugis Schooners)
6. Pulau Kembang (Monkey Island)
7. Governor's Office
8. City Mayor's Office
9. Fish Market
10. Sea Port (Pelni)

Around **BANJARMASIN**

IMS 138

Tues-Sun; closes early on Fri (1100) and Sat (1300).

Getting there: taxi (30,000Rp round trip), minibus (1,200Rp) or bus (800Rp), both from the intercity bus terminal or speedboat (10,000Rp) from the Dermaga Pier in front of the Grand Mosque. Cempaka can be reached from the bemo terminal in Martapura (take green minibuses to the Diamond Fields).

Jungle trekking and white-water rafting The best area for trekking is in the Meratus Dayak – or Hill Dayak – country around Loksado (on the Amandit River) and Mt. Besar (1,892 m), 190 km NE of Banjarmasin in the *Pegunungan Muratus* range. From Loksado, it is possible to run the rapids on the Amandit by bamboo raft – there are many stretches of white water, of different grades of difficulty. There are more than 30 longhouses – or *balai* – in and around Loksado, where trekkers can stay overnight. There are also caves in the area. The Kalsel tourism office produces a detailed list of treks between villages, with distances and approximate timings. To the SE of Banjarmasin, at the S end of the range, there are jungle trails around Lake Riamkanan, accessible from Martapura/Awang Bankal. It is necessary to take guides to both these areas (see *Tours*, below); few people speak English. **Essential equipment**: mosquito repellent, a torch and a sleeping bag (temperatures drop sharply at night).

Tours Prices listed below are those of Johan Yasin; he undercuts bigger tour operators' prices substantially. **Banjarmasin waterways**: 1½ hrs, 7,500Rp/person. **Floating Market**: 3 hrs, 12,500Rp (for groups of 2 or more). **Kaget Island**: 5 hrs, 20,000Rp (for groups of 2 or more). **Martapura and Cempaka**: 15,000Rp. **Tanjung Puteh Orang Utan Sanctuary** (Central Kalimantan): 3-4 days, 650,000Rp/person. (Cost includes flight to Pankalanbun, SW

The Hill Dayaks of Kalsel –a fragile culture

The Hill Dayak tribal areas of the Pegunungan Muratus have a fragile culture which is being eroded as groups of trekkers venture further into remote areas. Tour operators stress that Westerners should be particularly sensitive to cultural traditions and respect tribal customs. (Although there are many differences between the Muratus Dayak people and the tribal groups in Sarawak, visitors may wish to refer to the basic ground rules of longhouse etiquette, see *House rules*, **page 260**). Johan Yasin, the most experienced tour operator in Banjarmasin (see below) tells of tourists on trekking expeditions who have swapped T-shirts for tribal handicrafts and heirlooms. On another occasion, a European doctor began handing out Western medicines liberally; while drugs are in short supply and are much needed, it seems he was too generous and managed not only to put the local *balian* (shaman) out of business, but completely undermined his authority and social standing in the community.

Kalimantan). **Trekking tours**: typical 5-day trek to Loksado and Mt. Besar areas NE of Banjarmasin, involves rafting and trekking through Hill Dayak areas, staying overnight in longhouses (*balai*), (roughly 200,000Rp). Shorter 1-2 day jungle tours to Lake Riamkanan (nestled into the S end of the Pegunungan Muratus range, 100 km SE of Banjarmasin), 75,000Rp/day. Johan Yasin and Pujo Santoso are actually highly rec operations. More expensive but good tours can be organized through the travel agents *Adi Angkasa* and *Arjuna*.

Festivals Traditional Banjarese wedding ceremonies take place on Sundays, in the auspicious month before Ramadan. Tourists are always welcome at these celebrations and do not require invitations. Traditional dances (such as the *hadrah* and *rudat*, which have Middle Eastern origins) are performed during wedding festivities.
Mar/Apr: *Mappanre Tassi Buginese Fishermens' Festival* (moveable, but usually around mid-month): 7 day festival on Pagatan beach (S of Batu Licin on the SE coast, 240 km E of Banjarmasin) in which local Buginese fishermen sacrifice chickens, food and flour to the sea. Dancing and traditional songs, boat races and tug-of-war competitions. The festival climaxes on the last day. It is possible to stay overnight in the village where there are several losmen; enquire at tourist office or with tour operators as to how best to get to Pagatan. *Ramadan* (moveable) throughout the Islamic fasting month, when Banjaris break *puasa* after sundown, they indulge in local delicacies. Every day from 1400-1800, in front of the Grand Mosque, the Ramadan Cake Fair is held, where people come to sell cakes for the evening feast. Traditional Banjari cakes are made from rice flour, glutinous rice, cassava and sago. Most are colourful, sweet and sticky.
Aug/Sept: *Aruh Ganal* – the 'big feast' (moveable) is the Hill Dayak harvest festival. (Another smaller harvest festival, *Aruh Halus*, is held in Jun, to celebrate the first of the twice-yearly rice crop). Dancing all night from around 2000-0800; celebrated in the Hill Dayak longhouses in the Loksado and South Hulu Sungai districts. Boat races (17 Aug). Teams compete in traditional *tanabangan* rowing boats on the river in front of the mosque – the course is from the government office to the Grand Mosque.

Accommodation A *Barito Palace*, Jl. Haryono MT 16-20, T 67301, F 2240, a/c, restaurant, pool, best hotel in town, smart, with spacious lobby, a full range of facilities and well-appointed, spotless rooms, big discounts are often on offer, rec; **A** *Kalimantan*, Jl. Lambung Mangkurat, T 66818, F 67345, a/c, restaurant, pool, very smart, new hotel in central location, standard rooms are small but well appointed, rec; **B** *Maramin*, Jl. Lambung Mangkurat 32, T 8944, F 3350, a/c, restaurant, mid-market hotel in central location, avoid rooms on the top floor as they are close to the noisy *Matt's Disco and Karaoke*; **B** *Nabilla Palace* (formerly *Fabiola*), Km 3.5 Jl. Jend. A. Yani, T 2707, a/c, restaurant, out of town, on the airport road, good range of facilities including tennis courts; **B** *Sampaga*, Jl. May. Jend. Sutoyo S 128, T 2480 (on the N outskirts of town, but plenty of *becaks* available), a/c, restaurant, very clean rooms with big windows looking out onto a long verandah, rec; **C** *Kartika*, Jl. Pulau Laut 1, T 2325, a/c, restaurant, clean enough rooms, but the bathrooms leave a bit to be desired; **C** *Kuripan*, Jl. Jend. A. Yani 3313, a/c, very smart looking new hotel with interesting architecture and sculptured front desk, but rooms average, difficult to get transport into town because it is on a one-way street; **C** *Metro*, Jl. May. Jend. Sutoyo S 26, T 2427, some a/c; **C** *Perdana*, Jl. Brig. Jend. Katamso 3, T 3276, a/c, restaurant, airy, bright and clean, good range of rooms, rec; **C** *Sabrina*, Jl. Bank Rakyat (Jl. Samudra end) 21, T 4442, a/c, restaurant, clean, but some rooms a bit dark and pokey, some triple rooms; **C**

SAS, Jl. Kacapiring 2, T 3054, some a/c, restaurant, traditional Banjari house in quiet location, but rooms a bit dark, breakfast included, rec; **D** *Rahmat*, Jl. Jend. A. Yani 9, T 4322, fan-cooled rooms only (economy rooms do not even have a fan); **F** *Beauty*, Jl. Haryono MT 174, T 4493, a/c, does not live up to its name, but it is cheap and clean; **F** *Borneo Homestay*, Jl. Pos, T 66545 123, F 66418, run by Johan and Lina Yasin, very simple accommodation right next to the river (adjacent to A. Yani Bridge), the friendliest homestay/hotel in Borneo, rec.

Restaurants One of the best known Banjar foods is *soto banjar*, a duck egg soup; roast duck also appears frequently on Banjarmasin menus. This is thanks to the celebrated Alabio duck, which is thought to be related to the Peking Duck, discovered at the village of Alabio in 1927. Kalimantan is the biggest producer of ducks and duck eggs in Indonesia. Alcohol in Kalsel has a 40% tax imposed upon it; this is an attempt to cut down the problem of alcoholism amongst the young in Banjarmasin.

 Indonesian: ◆*Cendrawasih*, Jl. P. Samudra 65, simple but excellent Padang food, good selection of seafood including spicy roast fish and turtle eggs; ◆*Corner Garden*, Jl. Hasanuddin 1, T 2488, seafood speciality is fried lobster in butter sauce, good crab curries, rec.; ◆*Kaganangan Depot Makan*, Jl. P. Samudra 16, seafood, freshwater fish and sate (300Rp/stick). **Other Asian cuisine:** ◆◆*Golden Lotus*, Jl. Veteran 61, (near the 150-year-old Tempat Ibadai Tri Dharma Suci-Nurani Taoist temple), big Chinese restaurant – popular for big Chinese functions for the Chinese community, big menu, speciality: sapo with sticky sauce; ◆◆*Hakone*, Arjuna Plaza, Jl. Lambung Mangkurat 62, Japanese restaurant, upstairs from *Rama Steak House* (see below), private rooms and a huge menu; ◆◆*Lezat Baru*, Jl. Pang. Samudra 22, part of a small chain of restaurants, with branches in Samarinda and Balikpapan, huge Chinese menu with a good choice of seafood, specials include oysters done 10 different ways; ◆◆*Shinta*, 3rd Floor, Arjuna Plaza, Jl. Lambung Mangkurat 62, Chinese restaurant attached to a nightclub and disco, private rooms, open until 0200. **International:** ◆◆◆*Rama Steak Corner*, Arjuna Plaza, Jl. Lambung Mangkurat 62, very cosy restaurant with soft lighting, imported Australian steaks double cost of local ones. **Bakery:** *Minseng Bakery*, near corner of Jl. Pasar Baru and Jl. Samudra, good selection of cakes and ice creams. **Food centre:** *Grand Palace* is an upmarket, air-conditioned food centre in Mitra Plaza, on the S side of Antisari Bridge; good views over the river. There are several good buffet-style restaurants including: ◆*Japanese Corner*; ◆*Hero Fast Food* (cheap, high quality local dishes – curries etc.); *Home Bakery* (pastries, cakes). **Warungs:** in night market, off Jl. Lambung Mangkurat. Open to 0100.

Entertainment **Cinemas:** *Studio 21* (3 screens), Mitra Plaza, S side of Antisari Bridge. There are several other cinemas around town including: *Banjarmasin*, *President* and *Ria* theatres.

Shopping **Antiques:** Jl. Kacapiring II 10, T 4386. The home of Mr Ilmiyanto is an antiques supermarket without parallel in Kalimantan. It is a real treasure trove, anything purchased there can be professionally exported to your home country. The contents of the house – in a quiet suburban area of Banjarmasin – include ancient Chinese ceramics, rare, beaded Dayak baby-carriers (which sell for up to 400,000Rp), Dayak statuettes, masks, blowpipes, spears, knives, drums, basketware and canoe paddles as well as coins and precious and semi-precious stones, rec.

 Handicrafts: Hill Dayak handicrafts, basketware and semi-precious stones from the Martapura mines. Many of the shops have good selections of Dayak knives (*mandau*) from Central Kalimantan; in South Kalimantan, these knives are just called *parang*. One of the more unusual items on sale are the Dayak war canoes/death ships, intricately carved from rubber. There are several art shops on Simpang Sudimampir and Pasar Malabar (near Antisari Bridge); bargain. **Jewellery/precious stones:** *Toko Banjar Baru*, Jl. Sudimanpir 61. *Gloria Jewellery*, Junjung Buig Plaza, Lt. I/48. For those who do not have time to go to Martapura; expensive selection. Streetside jewellers around Pasar Malabar can be seen cutting and polishing agate and amethyst (among other stones); the stones are rarely of high quality.

 Markets: *Pasar Malabar* is next to Antasari Bridge (on the opposite side of the river from Mitra Plaza), handicraft stalls and jewellers; *Pasar Samudra* on Jl. Samudra/Jl. Pangeran, mainly textiles: good for sarungs and mosquito nets.

 Shopping Centres: *Mitra Plaza*, on the S side of Antisari Bridge is a modern shopping centre with a supermarket which is the best place to stock up on provisions before treks and upriver expeditions; *Jujung Buik Plaza* (under *Kalimantan Hotel*), more expensive jewellery shops and boutiques; *Svensons* and supermarket.

 Textiles/Batik: *Toko Citra*, Km 3.5 Jl. Jerend. A. Yani (towards the airport, near *Nabilla Palace hotel*), best place in town for Sasiragan tie-dyes (see below); *Batik Semar*, Jl. Hasanuddin 90, mainly imported Javanese batiks.

Local transport **Boat:** for travelling on the waterways, the best place to hire a klotok is from under A. Yani Bridge or Kuin Cerucuk (also known as Kuin Pertamina), to the NW side of town on the Kuin River. Motorized klotoks (which can hold up to 8 or 10 passengers) cost about 5,000Rp/hr; paddle-powered ones cost around 3,000Rp/hr. Speedboats or hired for around 30,000Rp/hr and leave from the Dermaga speedboat pier near the Grand Mosque. **Ojeks and becaks**: congregate around Mitra Plaza. **Bemos**: yellow bemos leave from in front of the Minseng Bakery near the corner of Jl. Pasar Baru and Jl. Samudra. They follow fixed routes, but go all over town (250Rp to any destination). Bemos can also be found on the corner of Jl. Bank Rakyat and Jl. Hasanuddin, in front of the Corner Steak House. **Bajaj**: congregate around Pasar Malabar (off Jl. Samudra); 1,000-1,500Rp, to anywhere in town; or chartered for 3,000Rp/hr. **Taxis**: the city taxi terminal is on Jl. Antisari, next to the main market.

Banks & money changers Bumi Daya, Dagang Negara and Negara are along Jl. Lambung Mangkurat. **Rakyat** is on Jl. P. Samudra. **Money-changer** in the back of *Adi Angkasa Travel*, Jl. Hasanuddin 27.

Useful addresses Post Office: on the corner of Jl. Lambung Mangkurat and Jl. Samudra. **Area code**: 0511. **Hospital**: *Suaka Insan*, Jl. Pembangunan (on the N side of town), best in Banjarmasin, with wards and private rooms.

Airline offices Garuda, Jl. Hasanuddin 11A, T 4203; **Merpati**, Jl. Let. Jen. Haryono, T 4433; **Bouraq**, Jl. Lambung Mangkurat 50, T 2445; **DAS**, Jl. Hasanuddin 6, T 2902.

Tour companies & travel agents *Johan Yasin, Borneo Homestay*, Jl. Pos 123, T 66545, F 66418; *Pujo Santoso*, Jl. Nagasari 80, T 3023; *Adi Angkasa*, Jl. Hasanuddin 27, T 3131, F 66200; *Arjuna*, Grd. flr, Arjuna Plaza, Jl. Lambung Mangkurat 62, T 65235, F 4444.

Tourist offices The Kalsel provincial tourist office is the best organized in Kalimantan; it produces some reasonably informative literature. **Dinas Pariwisata Kalimantan Selatan**, Jl. Panjaitan 23, T 2982.

Transport to & from Banjarmasin By air: Syamsudin Noor Airport is 27 km E of town. Regular connections on Garuda, Merpati, Sempati, Bouraq, Asahi and DAS with most major Indonesian cities including Jakarta, Surabaya, Balikpapan, Palangkaraya, Yogyakarta and Semarang. *Transport to town*: 7,000Rp by taxi, 1,000Rp by minibus to the intercity bus terminal.

By bus: Intercity buses leave from the Terminal Taksi Antar Kota at Km 6. Overnight buses (a/c and non-a/c) to Balikpapan leave at 1600-1700, 12 hrs. Overnight buses direct to Samarinda leave at the same time, 15 hrs. **By taxi**: taxis around Kalsel leave from the Terminal Taksi Antar Kota at Km 6.

By boat: Passenger boats leave for destinations upriver from Bajaraya Pier, at the far W end of Jl. Sutoyo. The boats are double-deckers which, for trips beyond Palangkaraya, are equipped with beds (which can be rented for 1,000Rp) and even warungs. Behind the warungs there is a small prayer room and toilets and mandi. Those travelling long distances upriver should reserve beds the day before. Boats have signs next to them indicating their departure times. Most leave in the morning around 1100; ticket office open 0800-1400. Getting to Bajaraya pier: bemos (250Rp) or bajaj (2,500Rp) from Pasar Malabar. Palangkaraya, 24 hrs (5,100Rp), Muara Teweh, 48 hrs (12,000Rp) and Puruk Cahu, 60 hrs (13,000Rp). In the dry season big passenger boats cannot make it to Muara Teweh and Puruk Cahu; it is necessary to disembark at Pendang and take speedboats and motorized klotoks further upriver, 3 hrs (10,000Rp to Muara Teweh and 8 hrs, 6,000Rp to Puruk Cahu. Pelni passenger ferries leave Banjarmasin's Trisakti terminal (on the Barito River) for other destinations in Indonesia. The *Karakatau* leaves for Pangkalanbun (for Orang Utan Sanctuary – **see page 834**) every fortnight, 18 hrs. The *Kelimutu*, also sails once a fortnight to Surabaya, Padangbai (Bali), Ujung Pandang and other ports in Java, Bali and the E end of the archipelago. See route map, page 1008. Pelni office, Jl. Laks E Martadinata 192, T 3171. **By speedboat**: regular connections with Palangkaraya (and other upriver destinations) from the Dermaga pier in front of the Grand Mosque. Most leave from 0900-1100, 5 hrs (20,000Rp). **By Bugis schooner**: to Java, enquire at *Kantor Syahbandar Pelabuhan I*, Jl. Barito Hilir at Trisakti dock.

CENTRAL KALIMANTAN (Kalimantan Tengah – Kalteng)

The vast province of Kalteng is most easily reached from Banjarmasin, but few tourists go there; it is the domain of Dayaks and loggers. It is Borneo's Dayak heartland, and the province was created in the late 1950s when the Dayak tribes sought autonomy from the Muslims of

Sasirangan tie-dyes - from the shaman to the shop shelves

The bright Banjar cloth is called *sasirangan* and was traditionally believed to hold magical powers capable of driving out evil spirits and curing illnesses. The cloth could be made only by shamans - it was *pamali* (taboo) for common people to make it - and was designed to cure specific medical problems, from headaches to malaria. It was tailor-made by the shaman for specific customers and was known as *kain pamintan*, or 'the cloth that is made to order'. Patterns had particular significance to the spirit world, and dragons, bamboo shoots, rocks and waves, lotus and sun motifs were prescribed like drugs at a pharmacy. Colours were also important: the most common ones were yellow, green, red and purple. The afflicted person's medical prescription was then worn as a headcloth (*laung*) by men and a scarf (*serudung*) by women, who would also wear sasirangan blouses. Babies swung in sasirangan hammocks and children wore sasirangan sarungs to protect them from disease.

When pharmaceuticals arrived in Banjarmasin, the shamans began to go out of business and with their demise, the sasirangan faded into obscurity. Realising that the art form had all but disappeared, local women enthusiastically began to revive the dying art in the 1980s. Within a few years, hundreds of tiny cottage industries had sprung up across the town and in a bid to popularize the material, sasirangan shirts and blouses were presented to celebrities. The cloth was traditionally coloured with natural dyes: yellow came from turmeric root, brown from the areca nut and red from the *karabintang* fruit; today chemical dyes are used. Sasirangan is made by a lengthy tie-dye procedure, involving several dyeing stages, interspersed with intricate tying and stitching sessions. A simple sasirangan with basic motifs can take up to 4 days to produce, while complex ones are said to take several months.

Banjarmasin. It covers nearly 154,000 sq km and has a population of 1.4 million. The N part of Kalteng is particularly remote, and is fringed by the mountains of the Schwaner and Muller ranges. The S part of the state is nearly all marshland with virtually impenetrable mangrove swamps which reach inland as far as 100 km.

Palangkaraya

This provincial capital was built virtually from scratch in 1957, and has little to offer the tourist. There is a small state **museum**, containing some Dayak heirlooms; mostly brass and ceramic jars. The only real tourist attraction here is the Tanjung Puting Orang Utan Rehabilitation Centre (see below).

Accommodation C *Dandang Matingang*, Jl. Yos Sudarso 11, T 21805, a/c, restaurant, best in town.

Transport to & from Palangkaraya The town can be reached by river from Banjarmasin; canals, cut by the Dutch in the late 19th century, connect the Barito, Kapuas and Kahayan river systems.

Tanjung Puting National Park and Orang Utan Rehabilitation Centre

The 3,000 ha Tanjung Puting National Park was founded by Dr Birute Galdikas in the early 1970s in an area with a wild population of orang utans, see page 224). The park straddles several forest types, including swamp forest, heath forest and lowland dipterocarp rainforest. The orang utan centre is smaller and less touristy than Sepilok in Sabah, Malaysia (see page 336) and Bukit Lawang in Sumatra (see page 744) but has the same mission: to look after and rehabilitate orang utans orphaned by logging or rescued from captivity. In addition to the orang utans, there is a large population of other fauna in Tanjung Puting, including proboscis monkeys (**see page 225**), crab-eating macaques, crocodiles and monitor lizards. There are 2 main stations in the park; **Camp Leakey** is the main research centre; **Tanjung Harapan** was set up in the late 1980s as an overflow centre – it is the one visited by most tourists. At Camp Leakey, orang utans are fed at 1500, 1600 and 1700.

Permits A police permit must be obtained in Pangkalanbun before making the 25 km road trip to Kumai where visitors should obtain a park permit (no charge) from the Conservation Office (PHPA Office). (A photocopy of the police letter and a photocopy of the first page of your passport is required to secure the park permit). Most people stay overnight in Pangkalanbun (9,500Rp by taxi from airport). **Accommodation**: *Andika Hotel* or *Blue Kecubung Hotel* (both **B-C** with a/c). Minibus from Pangkalanbun to Kumai (7,500Rp).

NB: anyone who is sick is strictly barred from entering the centre. Visitors should also note that malaria is rife in this region and that anti-malarial drugs are essential.

Tours Tours to the park are organized from Banjarmasin (**see page 830**).

Accommodation C *Hotel Rimba* (near Tanjung Harapan), restaurant, most visitors stay on the klotok houseboats, hired from Kumai.

Transport to & from Tanjung Puting By air: regular Bouraq and DAS flights from Banjarmasin to Pangkalanbun 2 hrs (100,000Rp). DAS also flies to Pangkalanbun from Palangkaraya (100,000Rp) and Pontianak (100,000Rp). Merpati flies daily to Pangkalanbun from Semarang and Bandung. **By boat**: it is also possible to take a Pelni passenger boat from Banjarmasin to Pangkalanbun; the boat leaves twice a month. Tanjung Puting is 4 hours up the Sekonyer River from Kumai. Klotoks can be hired at Kumai from around 50,000Rp/day. The boats *Garuda I & II* - the best-fitted of the Kumai klotoks - can be chartered for 60,000-70,000Rp/day and sleep 6 and 10 people respectively. The boatman running the Garuda boats is called Ha Baso and can be contacted at Jl. H M Idris 6, Kumai Hulu. It is necessary to bring food and water upriver unless you stay at *Hotel Rimba*. River water must be thoroughly boiled before drinking.

EAST KALIMANTAN (Kalimantan Timur – Kaltim)

With its economy founded on timber (it produces 70% of Indonesia's sawn timber exports), oil, gas and coal, Kaltim is the wealthiest province in Kalimantan. Its capital is Samarinda, the launch-pad for trips up the Mahakam River. Balikpapan is bigger than Samarinda and is the provincial transport hub; it is an ugly oil town. The province covers an area of 211,400 sq km – more than 6 times the size of The Netherlands – and has a population of 1.9 million. It is the second largest province in Indonesia after Irian Jaya.

Archaeological digs on the E Kalimantan coast have uncovered stone 'yupa' poles with Sanskrit inscriptions, suggesting Indian cultural influence possibly dating back to the 5th century or even earlier. The province's first substantial settlement was founded by refugees from Java in the 13th century, who fled from the Majapahits. They founded the kingdom of Kertanegara ('the lawful nation' – which later became known as Kutai). This kingdom is believed to have been an important centre on the trade route between Java and China. The word 'Kutai' is thought to have been the term used by Chinese traders, who knew it as 'the great land'. The imaginative Chinese traders also gave the Mahakam River its name; *Mahakam* means 'big river'.

Following Banjarmasin's conversion to Islam, Kutai also embraced the faith in 1565 and became an Islamic sultanate. It came into conflict with neighbouring kingdoms – most notably the Hindu kingdom of Martapura, on the Mahakam River. Their disputes were settled by a royal marriage which forged an alliance between the upriver kingdom and the Islamic sultanate. In the 17th century, hostilities broke out again and Kutai defeated and then absorbed the kingdom of Martapura. The first Buginese settlers arrived from Sulawesi in 1701. As piracy in the Sulu Sea grew worse in the 18th century, Kutai's capital was moved inland and was finally transferred to Tenggarong on the Mahakam in 1781. Kutai remained intact as a sultanate until 1960.

Balikpapan

At night, from the dirty beach along Balikpapan's sea front, the clouds are periodically lit up by the orange glow of flares from the offshore rigs in the Makassar Strait. There are several big offshore fields and the town is the administrative headquarters for Kaltim's oil and gas industry. The support staff of Pertamina, the Indonesian national oil company, live mainly on Gunung Dubb, in Dutch colonial villas dating from the 1920s and overlooking the refinery. Unocal and Total, US oil companies, have their residential complexes on the opposite hill, on Pasir Ridge, overlooking the town.

The foreign oil workers live like kings in Balikpapan which is a soulless town: it is strung out untidily along several kilometres of road. Some attempt has been made in recent years to create a business district and this has begun to bear fruit around the bottom of Jalan Jend. A Yani, next to the smart *Altea Benakutai Hotel*. The new shopping centre at the T-junction at the end of Jalan Jend. A Yani will help towards the creation of a commercial centre. Apart from some excellent arts and crafts shops and some good restaurants and hotels, Balikpapan has little to offer

---

Balikpapan's streetnames - selamat jalan-jalan

The Kota Madya (Municipal Office) in Balikpapan has a lot to answer for. In late 1991 it unilaterally declared that more than half the streets in town were to be renamed. But it went one step further than just changing the names: it swapped them round too. Balikpapan's hoteliers, restaurateurs and businessmen all had to print new cards, tourists (and guidebook writers) became hopelessly lost and even Kijang taxi drivers where unable to tell people where they were. To compound the problem, the municipal office failed to print a new town map.

The most important changes concerned the T-junction at the S end of town. Jalan P. Antisari, Jalan May. Jend. Sutayo and Jalan May. Jend. D. L. Panjaitan were all changed to just one road name: Jalan Jend. A. Yani. The fact that there was already an important road called Jalan Jend. A. Yani did not bother the municipal office: its name was changed to Jalan Jend. Sudirman - which now stretches along the coast from W to E, also encompassing the old Jalan Gajah Mada. To confuse matters further, Jalan Dondang, which cuts between the old Jalan Jend. A. Yani and the new Jalan Jend. A. Yani, was renamed Jalan Gajah Mada - for what town could be without one? The road further to the E, towards the airport, which used to be called Jalan K. S. Tubun, is now Jalan Sukarno Hatta.

The nightmare of Balikpapan's urban nomenclature does not end there. Because the locals are so confused, they have taken to using both names. This will ease in time, but until then, a typical conversation between a lost tourist and a bewildered local might go something like this:

"Excuse me, where is the *Benakutai Hotel*?"
"It's over there on Jalan Jend. A. Yani."
"But I thought that was Jalan Antisari."
"Yes, it is."

The only comforting irony was that the municipal office managed to embroil itself in the mess. Those wishing to complain should contact the municipal officer on Jalan Jend. Sudirman - formerly Jalan Jend. A. Yani.

NB For more detail on Indonesia's street names, see page 500.

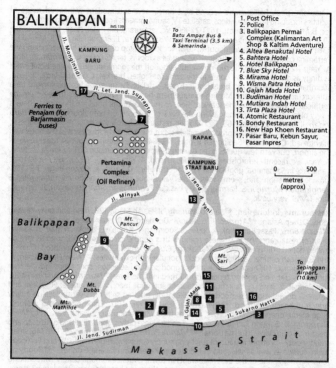

BALIKPAPAN IMS 139

1. Post Office
2. Police
3. Balikpapan Permai Complex (Kalimantan Art Shop & Kaltim Adventure)
4. Altea Benakutai Hotel
5. Bahtera Hotel
6. Hotel Balikpapan
7. Blue Sky Hotel
8. Mirama Hotel
9. Wisma Patra Hotel
10. Gajah Mada Hotel
11. Budiman Hotel
12. Mutiara Indah Hotel
13. Tirta Plaza Hotel
14. Atomic Restaurant
15. Bondy Restaurant
16. New Hap Khoen Restaurant
17. Pasar Baru, Kebun Sayur, Pasar Inpres

tourists; it is a transit camp for visits to Samarinda and the Mahakam River or for Banjarmasin, to the S.

Excursions

The best **beaches** are to the N of Balikpapan at Tanah Merah and Manggar (3 km from town). These tend to become crowded at weekends.

Tours There are 3 big agents (*Tomaco*, *Kaltim Adventure* and *Musi Holidays*) which operate tours, mainly up the Mahakam River (see page 843) as well as more unusual treks around the Apo Kayan (see page 846) and trans-Borneo treks to Putussibau and Pontianak in Kalbar. On the whole these agents are more expensive than the smaller (but often equally efficient) companies at Samarinda. *Kaltim Adventure Tour* has 2 houseboats at Samarinda for Mahakam trips as well as 5 full-time guides and cooks. Tours include: 3-15 day Mahakam trips; Long Apung/Apo Kayan tours; Kutai Game Reserve and overland 15-day treks from Balikpapan to Pontianak, rec; *Musi Holidays*, variety of package tours, mainly up the Mahakam River, rec; *Tomaco*, biggest, most professional and most expensive tour agent in town. Has a new houseboat in Samarinda with a/c cabins to accommodate 12; also several other smaller boats. Tour prices 15% off published rates for walk-in tourists, rec. See page 550 for Jakarta head offices.

Accommodation A *Altea Benakutai*, Jl. Jend. A. Yani, T 31896, F 31823, a/c, restaurant, pool, very smart, international-class hotel, mainly used by oil industry workers, good service and wide range of facilities, helpful representative office at airport; **B** *Bahtera*, Jl. Jend. Sudirman 2, T 22603, F 31889, a/c, restaurant, nothing special, but adequate; **B** *Balikpapan*, Jl. Erry Suparjan 2, T 21491, a/c, restaurant, clean hotel and reasonable value, satellite TV, disco, sauna and massage parlour; **B** *Blue Sky*, Jl. Let. Jend. Suprapto 1, T 22267, a/c, restaurant, pool, Balikpapan's second-best hotel, new and modern with good range of facilities including in-house videos, satellite TV, sauna, billiards and Japanese Shiatsu massage, rec; **B** *Mirama*, Jl. A. P. Pranoto 16, T 22960, a/c, restaurant, big hotel, clean, be wary of the lift which periodically jams between floors; **B** *Wisma Patra*, Jl. Prabumulih (off Jl. Minyak), T 33011, a/c, restaurant, pleasant out-of-town location on top of the steep hill overlooking the Pertamina complex, detached bungalows as well as rooms, tennis court; **C** *Budiman*, Jl. Jend. A. Yani, T 22583, a/c, a little run-down but although the rooms are grubby, the hotel is not as dingy as many other local hotels in the same (or higher) bracket; **C** *Gajah Mada*, Jl. Jend. Sudirman 14, T 23019, a/c, breakfast included, satellite TV, unmarried couples might be a little circumspect here, the Muslim management has been known to ask to see marriage certificates! The rooms on the seaward side, at the back of the hotel are the nicest, there is a very pleasant balcony running along the back of the hotel on both floors, rec; **C** *Mutiara Indah*, Jl. May. Jend. Sutoyo 65, T 22925, a/c, restaurant, hardly the 'pearl' its name suggests, its 'cottages' look more like prison complexes, but the rooms are spotless and the hotel well maintained; **C** *Piersa*, Jl. Sepinggan Bypass, T 23048, a/c, restaurant, out of town towards the airport, but with few guests it is a quiet retreat; clean and empty; **C** *Tirta Plaza*, Jl. Jend. A. Yani, a/c, recently refurbished; **C-D** *Aida*, Jl. Jend. A. Yani 1/12, T 76123, sister hotel to its namesake in Samarinda, popular with budget travellers; **D** *Surya*, Jl. Karang Bugis, T 21580, a/c, clean enough and seems reasonable value, but offers a half-hourly room rate; **E** *Penginapan Murni*, Jl. S. Parman 1, very basic; **E** *Penginapan Sinar Lumayan*, Jl. Jend. A. Yani 1A/49, very basic.

Restaurants Indonesian: **♦♦**<i>Salero Minang</i>, Jl. Gajah Mada 12B, fresh and tasty Padang food. Other Asian: **♦♦**<i>Atomic</i>, Jl. Sutoyo/Jl. Dondang 3/10, mainly seafood and Chinese; **♦♦**<i>Lezat Baru</i>, Pasar Baru Blok A, Jl. Jend. Sudirman 1, Komplek Pertokoan, part of a small chain of restaurants, huge Chinese menu with a good choice of seafood, specials include oysters done 10 different ways; **♦♦**<i>Mahakam</i>, Blue Sky Hotel, Jl. Let. Jend. Suprapto 1, Chinese and European cuisine, seafood and steaks, popular with expatriates; **♦♦**<i>New Hap Khoen</i>, Jl. Jend. Sudirman 19, huge Chinese menu, good seafood selection, specialities include crab curry, chilli crab and *goreng tepung* (squid fried in batter), rec; **♦♦**<i>Paradise</i>, Komplek Pantai Mas Permai. Jl. Jend. A. Yani, huge restaurant and huge menu with Chinese, European and Japanese dishes, mostly seafood, fish grill outside, built on stilts out over the sea on a dirty stretch of beach. Seafood: **♦♦**<i>Dynasty</i>, Jl. Jend. A. Yani 10/7, Chinese food and seafood, huge menu, deep-fried crab claws, prawns fried with rambutan, shellfish, sate, rec; **♦**<i>New Shangrila</i>, Jl. Gunung Sari Ilir 29, seafood and Chinese dishes, speciality *kangkung asap* and deep-fried crab claws. International: **♦♦♦**<i>Banua Patra</i>, Jl. Jend. Sudirman 39, T 23746, smart – and snooty – seafront restaurant run by rig supply company, imported steaks and European *haute cuisine* as well as selection of Indonesian, Korean and Japanese dishes; **♦♦♦**<i>Bondy</i>, Jl. Jend. A. Yani 7, one of the best restaurants in town, entrance through bakery with enticing smell of fresh pastries, past the fast-food area, to the rear where it opens into a large 2-storey open-air restaurant, built around an open courtyard, European and local food, mixed grill very good and local and imported steaks, vast selection of sundaes and ice creams, very popular with locals, rec; **♦♦**<i>Modern Holland</i>, Jl. Jend. A. Yani 2, bakery with small restaurant attached serving local and imported steaks, good ice creams; **♦♦**<i>Sampan</i>, Altea Benakutai Hotel, Jl. Jend. A. Yani, coffee shop with Chinese, Indonesian and international selection, rec; **♦♦♦**<i>Tenggarong Grill</i>, Altea Benakutai Hotel, Jl. Jend. A. Yani, international, steaks and seafood, popular with expatriates. **Foodstalls**: there are stalls in the new Balikpapan Permai complex on the road to the airport, more at the vegetable market (Kebun Sayur) – the Chinatown of Balikpapan.

Entertainment Cinemas: there are 3 big cinemas, all showing recent Hollywood releases; the biggest and best is on Jalan Sudirman. Discos: the best known nightclub in town is the *Altea Benakutai Hotel's Black Orchid Disco* (known locally as 'The B O'); nearby is the *Sabatini; The Club*, near the airport also has a disco.

Shopping Balikpapan has a vast array of arts and crafts shops and is probably the best place in Kalimantan to buy Dayak handicrafts; 'antiques' may not, however, be as old as they first appear. A new shopping centre (to be opened by mid-1993) has been built right on the seafront at the bottom of Jl. Jend. A. Yani. **Arts and crafts**: *Bahati Jaya Art Shop*, Jl. May. Jen. Sutoyo 9, good range of tribal arts and crafts and antiques; *Borneo Art Shop*, Jl. Jend. A. Yani 34/03, one of the best selections in handicrafts, Dayak antiques, ceramics, gemstones and coins; *Kalimantan Art Shop*, Blok A1, Damai Balikpapan Permai, Jl. Jend. Sudirman 7, the undisputed king of Balikpapan's antiques, and Dayak arts and crafts shops; textiles, beads, porcelain etc, proprietor Eddy Amran is friendly and knowledgeable; *Susila Art Shop*, Jl. Jend. A. Yani 11 (near *Dynasty Restaurant*), small, but good selection of Dayak pieces and ceramics; *Syahda Mestika*, Jl. Jend. A. Yani 147, vast selection of tribal arts and crafts, Chinese porcelain

Deforestation in Kalimantan – the chainsaw massacre

At Balikpapan's Sepinggang airport, on the road leading into town, there is a huge billboard saying 'Welcome to Balikpapan'; the words superimposed on a picture showing caterpillars clearing logs out of the jungle. It might be intended to signify development and progress, but it leaves a graphic, striking – and, as it turns out, accurate – first impression of East Kalimantan. From Balikpapan, the road to Samarinda winds through hills affording panoramic views over the denuded landscape: virtually the whole area has been deforested, leaving only scrubland and secondary forest. Few trees are higher than 10 m tall, other than the occasional towering *Kompassia*, whose wood is too brittle for commercial use, and scattered palms. The sky is often hazy from smoke as shifting cultivators clear the remaining vegetation for their *ladangs* (farms).

Originally East Kalimantan had 17.3 million ha of forest. Most of this has been divided up; 3.6 million ha is protected forest, 2 million ha is classed as forest reserve and 10.3 million ha is classed as 'productive forest'. East Kalimantan is Indonesia's biggest timber-producing province; most of which goes to supply the thriving downstream wood processing industries. Round-log exports were banned in 1985 in an effort to increase the value of wood exports, but this did little to slow the rate of felling. Logging directly employs around 10,000 people in the province, and downstream industries another 40,000.

Sawmills manufacture plywood, chipboard, furniture and veneer. About 40% of the wood products produced in East Kalimantan go to supply the domestic market. But plywood exports alone earn the province US$250 million a year. For every cubic metre of Meranti hardwood bought by the wood processing industry, the buyer is legally required to pay a premium of US$10 which is put towards replanting projects. Whether this actually happens or not is another matter – although the government has reportedly come down hard on timber companies shirking their environmental responsibilities. However, distances in Kaltim are so huge that the Forestry Department cannot hope to police the timber industry adequately, either to collect premiums or to prevent illegal logging. The other problem is that most silviculturists believe it is impossible to replant a rainforest. This has not stopped scientists from trying: 36 km from Balikpapan, just off the Samarinda Road, is the Tropen Bosch/Wana Riset Forest Research Institute, which has had some measure of success in trying to propagate dipterocarps.

Forest fires have been almost as destructive as the logging industry. In 1991, fires in E and central Kalimantan contributed to a thick white smoke haze that blanketed a large area for several weeks. As far away as Singapore and Peninsular Malaysia, people were complaining of eye problems and breathing difficulties and air traffic and shipping were disrupted. Some fires flare up when rice farmers burn the stubble and the flames rage out of control. But many are thought to take hold in areas where indiscriminate logging has taken place. The blazes reach temperatures of 600°C, roasting the subsoil and killing root systems and micro-organisms to depths of more than 2 m. Experts believe some of the worst fires have coincided with areas where there are underground coal deposits, suggesting that some of these may have been set alight; the coal smoulders for years and is virtually impossible to extinguish. In 1982/83 fires destroyed more than 29,000 sq km of Kalimantan's forests.

and antiques. There are also a large number of arts and crafts shops above the vegetable market (Kebun Sayur/Pasar Inpres) on Jl. Let. Jend. Suprapto at the N end of town. Many stalls also sell stones from Martapura (including *manik manik* stone necklaces) and antique jewellery. **Batik**: *Iwan Suharto Batik Gallery*, *Hotel Benakutai*, Jl. Jend. A. Yani, T 31896; excellent selection of very original batik paintings (traditional and modern); much of it is by batik artists on Java, but includes some interesting batiks with Dayak designs. **Newspapers**:

a good selection of national and international English-language publications are on sale in the *Altea Benakutai Hotel* shop, including the *Jakarta Post*, the *Singapore Straits Times, USA Today, The International Herald Tribune*. Elsewhere in Kaltim, English-language newspapers are hard to come by.

Local transport Taxis: in Balikpapan the old yellow Toyota minibuses/Kijangs – which look like Russian-designed moon vehicles – are all called 'taxis'. 250Rp around town. Most do a circuit around Jl. Jend. A. Yani, Jl. Jend. Sudirman and past the Pertamina complex on Jl. Minyak. They can be hailed at any point; shout 'STOP!' when you want to alight. **Ojeks**: short trips cost 300-500Rp; or charter for 2,000-3,000Rp/hr.

Banks & money changers Bank Duta, Jl. Jend. Sudirman 26 (near *Altea Benakutai Hotel*, probably the best place for foreign exchange); **Bank Dagang Negara**, Jl. Jend. A. Yani; **Bank Negara Indonesia**, Jl. Jend. Sudirman 30; **Bank Rakyat**, Jl. May. Jend. Sutoyo.

Useful addresses Post Office: Jl. Jend. Sudirman. **Area code**: 0542. **Hospital**: *Pertamina*.

Airline offices Garuda, Jl. Jend. A. Yani 19, T 22300; **Merpati**, Jl. Jend. Sudirman 29, T 22380; **Bouraq**, Jl. Jend. A. Yani, T 23117 4; **Sempati**, *Altea Benakutai Hotel*, Jl. Jend. A. Yani, T 31896; **Asahi**, Jl. Jend. A. Yani 41, T 22044.

Tour companies & travel agents *Kaltim Adventure Tour*, Blok C-1/1 Komplex Balikpapan Permai, Jl. Jend. Sudirman, T 31158, F 33408; *Musi*, Jl. Dondang (Antasari) 5A, T 24272, F 24984; *Natrabu*, Jl. Jend. A. Yani 58, T 22443; *Tomaco*, Hotel Benakutai, Jl. Jend. A. Yani, T 22747.

Tourist offices Tourist Information Office, Seppinggang Airport, T 21605, unpredictable opening hours, but *Altea Benakutai Hotel* representative office is usually staffed and can help with immediate queries.

Transport to & from Balikpapan **By air**: Sepinggang Airport is 10 km from Balikpapan. *Airport facilities*: a post office, souvenir shop, money-changer and restaurant and an international telephone which takes major credit cards. *Transport to town*: fixed price taxis (7,500Rp); or direct to Samarinda (55,000Rp). Regular connections on Garuda, Merpati, Sempati, Bouraq and Asahi airlines with most major cities in Indonesia such as Samarinda, Banjarmasin, Pontianak, Jakarta, Semarang, Tarakan, Ujung Pandang, Yogyakarta, Pangkalanbun as well as Singapore (via Pontianak).

By bus: Regular long-distance bus connections with Samarinda and Banjarmasin. *C V Gelora* express buses to Samarinda leave every 30 mins from 0530-2000 from Batu Ampar terminal at Km 3.5 on Samarinda road, 2 hrs. Buses to Banjarmasin also leave from the Batu Ampar terminal or from Penajam, on the other side of the bay. Boats cross to Penajam from Pasar Baru at the N end of town on Jl. Monginsidi (2,000Rp). **Getting to Batu Ampar terminal**: take a Kijang taxi to Rapak, the junction with the Samarinda Rd. (300Rp). From Rapak, taxis leave for Batu Ampar when full (300Rp); alternatively an ojek costs 500-700Rp.

By taxi: Saloon taxis also go to Samarinda from Batu Ampar bus terminal; one car takes up to 7 people (5,000-6,000Rp/person). It is also possible to charter an a/c taxi to Samarinda (60,000Rp), T 35555.

By boat: the Pelni ships *Tidar, Kerinci* and *Kambuna* dock at the harbour to the W of the city centre, off Jl. Yos Sudarso, and call at Tarakan, Toli-Toli, Ujung Pandang, Surabaya and Tanjung Priok (Jakarta) – among other ports – on their two-week circuits (see route map, **page 1008**). The Pelni office is at Jl. Pelabuhan (off Jl. Yos Sudarso), T 22187.

Samarinda

Kaltim's capital, 120 km N of Balikpapan, is one of Kalimantan's main tourism centres – it is the gateway to the interior, up the Mahakam River and to the remote Dayak areas of the Apo Kayan, near the border with Sarawak. The town, however, is short on tourist attractions: the only real 'sight' is the Mahakam River itself Samarinda is a bustling modern town and has grown rich from the proceeds of the timber industry (see box). The town was founded by Buginese seafarers from S Sulawesi in the early 1700s and is 40 km from the coast at the head of the splayed Mahakam estuary. The river is navigable by large ships right up to the town – only the recently-built bridge across the Mahakam prevents them going further upriver.

Places of interest
It is well worth chartering a boat to cruise around the **Mahakam River** for an

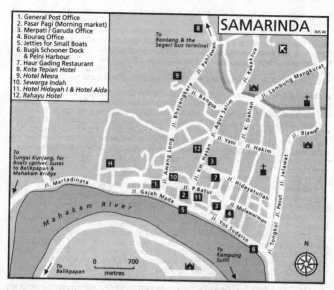

1. General Post Office
2. Pasar Pagi (Morning market)
3. Merpati / Garuda Office
4. Bouraq Office
5. Jetties for Small Boats
6. Bugis Schooner Dock
   & Pelni Harbour
7. Haur Gading Restaurant
8. Kota Tepian Hotel
9. Hotel Mesra
10. Sewarga Indah
11. Hotel Hidayah I & Hotel Aida
12. Rahayu Hotel

SAMARINDA

hour. On the left bank, at the E end of town, is the harbour, where the elegant Bugis schooners dock (**see page 866**). Kampung Sulili, further downriver from Samarinda is built out over the river on stilts and backed by a steep hillside; there are lively scenes all along the riverbank. Small boats can be hired from any of the countless jetties behind the Pasar Pagi (Morning Market) for around 5,000Rp/hr.

Excursions
Mahakam River, see page 843.

Kutai National Park, 120 km N of Samarinda is a 200,000 ha area of primary forest. The World Wide Fund for Nature (WWF) believes it contains at least 239 species of bird. It is also home to a population of wild orang utans (around Teluk Kaba) and proboscis monkeys. Kutai park is reached via **Bontang**, which lies on the equator. Bontang is the site of a large liquified natural gas plant. Nearby, at Kuala Bontang, there is a Bajau fishing kampung built out on stilts over the water. **Accommodation in Bontang: C** *Equator Hotel*, PT Pupuk Kaltim (Persero Complex), Loktuan, Bontang Utara (owned by Pupuk Kaltim fertilizer company) T J3845286, a/c, restaurant. **Accommodation in the park**: there are a number of rangers' posts in the park with basic accommodation and food. There is one on Teluk Kaba and others along the Sengata River (5,000Rp/night; 3,000Rp/meal). **Permits/guides**: it is necessary to acquire a permit from the Conservation Office (PHPA Office) in Bontang (no charge). The office can advise independent travellers on their itinerary and organize boat trips to the park; it will also provide guides (10,000Rp/day) and help charter boats. **Getting there**: most people visit the park on an organized tour (see below). Regular buses, 3 hrs (3,000Rp) and passenger boats (10,000Rp) from Samarinda to Bontang. Tour agencies sometimes fly tourists into Bontang (45 mins flight from Balikpapan). From Bontang (Lok Tuan or Tanjung Limau harbours) the park can be reached by speedboat in 30 mins. Hiring boats can be expensive for the independent traveller.

Tours About 15,000 tourists travel up the Mahakam River annually. The vast majority go on organized tours which can be tailored to suit all budgets. Most tours are prohibitively expensive for groups smaller than two; the costs fall dramatically the more people there are. Tour agents usually require a deposit of 50% upon booking. There are some excellent tour companies in Samarinda and three major ones in Balikpapan (see page 830) offering similar deals. There are also more adventurous trekking trips to the Apo Kayan (see page 846) and 3-4 day package deals to the Kutai National Park, north of Samarinda (see above) for about 450,000-500,000Rp for groups of 4-6 people (including full board and travel).

Unlike neighbouring Sarawak, upriver tours on the Mahakam of less than a week's duration will not get far enough upstream to reach traditional longhouses. 3-4 day tours cost about US$300/head for 4-6 people and travel to Lake Jempang and Tanjung Isuy. 5-9 day tours continue upriver to Tunjung, Bahau and Kenyah Dayak villages west of Long Iram, they cost from US$400-800/head for 4-6 people. A 14 day tour reaches Long Baun or beyond. **Apo Kayan Tours** All tours to the Apo Kayan area include the return flight from Samarinda to Long Ampung. Few are shorter than 6 days, most are about 9-10 days. Most tours involve a mixture of trekking and river trips by longboat and canoe, visiting Long Nawang and nearby longhouses and waterfalls. Some even throw in a day's hunting with local Dayaks. Tours cost around US$700-900 for groups of 4-6.
Cisma Angkasa is an experienced tour agent specializing in adventure tourism along Mahakam River and Apo Kayan. The company owns 4 well fitted double-decker river boats (a/c cabins) and supplies mosquito nets. Can arrange tours to destinations well off the beaten track (including trans-Borneo treks) and caters for all budgets (cheaper tours use public transport), rec. *Ayus Wisata* is an adventure tourism specialist (Jakarta, T 749155, F 7491560). Has good boats with a/c cabins and bunks as well as experienced guides to go upriver. Some are good, others terrible: it is advisable to stick to those with tourist guide licences. (When planning a trip with a freelance guide, ask them to trace the intended route on a map; it soon becomes apparent whether they know what they are talking about). Many of the good guides in Samarinda contract out their services to tour companies. An average daily rate for a freelance guide should be about 30,000Rp. Suriyadi is a recommended freelance guide who can be contacted through the *Hidaya Hotel* or through *Anggrek Hitam* tour company.

Accommodation B *Kota Tepian*, Jl. Pahlawan 4, T 32513, a/c, restaurant, good facilities; B *Mesra*, Jl. Pahlawan 1, T 21011, F 21017, a/c, restaurant, pool, Samarinda's top hotel – at the top of a hill, golf course and tennis, good bar, rooms, suites and cottages, rec; B *Sewarga Indah*, Jl. Jend. Sudirman 11, T 22066, F 23662, a/c, restaurant, clean and reasonable, souvenir shop downstairs; C *Djakarta*, Jl. Jend. Sudirman 57, a/c, average; C *Hidayah I*, Jl. K. H. Mas Temenggung, T 31408, a/c, restaurant, next to the morning market and the *Aida*, friendly staff, average rooms, pleasant balcony overlooking the street; C *Hidayah II*, Jl. K. H. Halid 25, T 21712, some a/c; D *Aida*, Jl. K. H. Mas Temenggung, a/c, next to morning market and *Hidayah I*, popular with budget travellers; D *Andhira*, Jl. H. Agus Salim 37, T 22358, some a/c, clean enough; D *Rahayu*, Jl. K. H. Abul Hasan 17, T 22622, clean and best of the budget options, shared bathroom; D *Sukarni*, Jl. Panglima Batur 154, T 21134, some a/c, very basic.

Restaurants Indonesian: ♦*Depot Handayani*, Jl. K. H. Abul Hasan 11, curries, Padang style; ♦*Gumarang*, Jl. Jend. Sudirman 30, extraordinary menu which includes cow brain gravy, cow foot gravy, cow lung gravy, sliced lung, raw leaves and potatoes, spicy *tongkol* fish wrapped in banana leaf rec; ♦♦*Haur Gading*, Jl. Pulau Sulawesi 4, T 22456, beautifully decorated with ikats, baskets and Dayak handicrafts, soft lighting, does not fill up until after 2000, freshwater fish (*ikan mas*) and saltwater – *ikan bawal*, *terkulu*, *bandeng* and kakap, also Mahakam River prawns, rec; ♦*Lembur Kuring*, Jl. Bhayangkara (next to cinema), small, basic but tasty selection of curry dishes; ♦*Mirasa*, Jl. H. Agus Salim 18/2 (opposite *Andhika Hotel*), good *nasi campur* curries, specializes in grilled fish and chicken; ♦*Prambanan*, Jl. H. Agus Salim 16, grilled fish and chicken; ♦*Rumah Makan Banjar*, Jl. K. H. Abul Hasan 19, cheap and cheerful restaurant with simple menu, curries; ♦*Sari Bundo*, Jl. K. H. M. Halid 42, simple but tasty Padang food. Other Asian: ♦♦*Lezat Baru*, Jl. Mulawarman 56, part of a small chain of restaurants, huge Chinese menu with a good choice of seafood; specials include oysters done 10 different ways, rec; ♦♦*Sari Rasa*, Jl. H. Agus Salim 26, offers Chinese, Japanese and European dishes with a good line in seafood, pleasant ambience but rather empty.

Entertainment Disco: *Tepian Mahakam*, Jl. Untung Suropati, T 34204, floating discotheque – which plays a mixture of chart hits and traditional Indonesian love songs – is in the bowels of a barge moored next to the bridge on the Mahakam, restaurant on top, rec, cover charge 5,000Rp (weekdays), 7,500Rp (weekends); *Blue Pacific Disco*, Kaltim Bldg, Citra

Niaga, there are 5 discotheques in the building, and this is the best, lively music, good atmosphere and no cover charge.

Shopping The Pasar Pagi (morning market) is in the middle of town and is busy most of the day; the area around the modern Citra Niaga shopping complex, between Jl. Yos Sudarso and Jl. P. Batur is particularly lively in the evenings with musicians, fortune-tellers and quack doctors and dentists. Samarinda has many small arts and crafts shops, mostly selling Dayak bits and pieces; there are one or 2 good ones, but the selection is not as good as Balikpapan. Always bargain and be suspicious of 'antiques'. *Dewi Art Shop*, Jl. Awang Long 19, T 21482, antiques and tribal arts and crafts; especially good selection of statues and sculptures; *Fatmawati*, Jl. Kesuma Bangsa 2, good selection of semi-precious stones and rings. Other art shops are located along Jl. Martadinata (*Berhati Jaya*, *Sutra Borneo Art Shop* and *Kings of Dayak Primitive Art Shop*); Jl. K. H. Agus Salim (*Permata Sinar*, *Dan Daman Art Shop* and *Armarta Art Shop*); Jl. P. Batur (*Hollywood* and *Syachran*).

Local transport Minibuses: like in Balikpapan, these are called taxis. Red ones go anywhere in town and congregate around Mesra Indah Komplex, 300Rp. Green ones go to Sungai Kunjang (for upriver trips and express buses to Balikpapan), 400-500Rp. **Ojeks**: congregate around the Pasar Pagi (Morning Market); 300-400Rp around town (can be chartered for 2,000-3,000Rp/hr).

Banks & money changers Bank Dagang Negara, Jl. Mulawarman 66; **Bank Bumi Daya**, Jl. Irian 160; **Bank Negara Indonesia**, Jl. Pulau Sebatik 1 (corner with Jl. Batur); **Bank Rakyat**, Jl. Gajah Mada 1 (across from the post office).

Useful addresses Post Office: Jl. Awang Long/Jl. Gajah Mada. **Area code:** 0541. **Pelni office**, Jl. Yos Sudarso 40/56.

Airline offices Garuda, Jl. Jend. Sudirman 57, T 22624; **Merpati**, Jl. Imam Bonjol, T 23928; **Bouraq**, Jl. Mulawarman 24, T 21105; **Sempati**, Masnun Anindya, T 22624; **Asahi**, Jl. Imam Bonjol 4, T 23928; **MAF**, Jl. Ruhui Rahayu, T 23628.

Tour companies & travel agents *Cisma Angkasa*, Jl. Imam Bonjol 10/27, T 21572, F 22700; *Anggrek Hitam*, Jl. Yos Sudarso 21, T 22132, F 23161; *Dayakindo*, Jl. Bhayangkara; *Ayus Wisata*, Jl. H. Agus Salim 13B, T 22644, F 32080.

Tourist offices Kantor Pariwisata, Jl. Ade Irma Suryani 1 (off Jl. Kesuma Bangsa), T 21669, poorly organized and badly informed: visitors are best advised to get their information from travel agents.

Transport to & from Samarinda By air: the airport is on the NE outskirts of town. Regular connections on Bouraq, Merpati, Sempati, Garuda and Asahi airlines with Balikpapan, Banjarmasin, Berau, Tarakan, Surabaya, Jakarta, Yogyakarta, Semarang. Other less regular connections include Bandung and Ujung Pandang. Asahi also flies to Datah Dawai on the upper Mahakam and both Asahi and Merpati fly to Long Ampung in the Apo Kayan (see page 847). **By bus**: to Balikpapan 2 hrs and Tenggarong 1 hr leave from Seberang on the outskirts of town on the S bank of the river. The terminal can be reached by green taxis (see above) or by boat – a pleasant trip from the Pasar Pagi; the station is immediately behind the ferry terminal. Buses to Bontang leave from the Segeri bus terminal on the N side of town. **By taxi**: to Balikpapan leave from Sungai Kunjang (5,000-6,000Rp/person). Taxis to Bontang leave from Terminal Segeri (7,000Rp/person). **By boat**: Sapulidi speedboat from end of Jl. Gajah Mada (near the Post Office), T 23821. Terminal Feri, Jl. Sungai Kunjang: is the launch-pad for Mahakam River tours.

The Mahakam River

The 920 km-long muddy Mahakam is the biggest of Kaltim's 14 large rivers; it is navigable for 523 km. There are 3 main stretches. The lower Mahakam runs from Samarinda, through Tenggarong to Muara Muntai and the 3 lakes; these lower reaches are most frequently visited by tourists. The middle Mahakam stretches to the W from Kuara Muntai, through Long Iram to Long Bagun – where public river-boat services terminate. The upper Mahakam, past the long stretch of rapids, runs from Long Gelat into the Muller Range: only a few adventure tours go this far. Most tours reach the upper Mahakam by plane (Asahi Airways flies to Data Dawai airstrip at Long Lunuk). The Mahakam's riverbanks have been extensively logged, or turned over to cultivation. Visitors wishing to reach less touristed destinations along the river should have plenty of time on their hands, and if on organized tours (see above), they should also have plenty of funds at their disposal.

Many tourists just enjoy relaxing on the decks of the boats as they wind their way slowly upriver: one of the most important pieces of equipment for a Mahakam trip is a good long book.

When they are taking time out from their cultural performances for tourists, the Mahakam's Dayaks are not the noble savages, dressed in loin cloths and hornbill feathers, that some of the tourist literature might paint them as. Longhouses are quite commercialized; tourists are likely to be asked for money for photographs. Most villages on the lower and middle reaches of the river have been drawn – economically and socially – into the modern world over the past century. Although the traditional Kaharingan religion is still practised in some areas (see page 229), many upriver Dayak groups have been converted to Christianity. This is all in marked contrast to neighbouring Sarawak, where the upriver tribespeople maintain their traditional lifestyles to a much greater degree.

The reason for this can be traced back to the policy of Sarawak's successive Brooke governments – the White Rajahs of Sarawak (see page 234) who attempted to protect the Orang Ulu (the upriver tribes) from the warring Ibans and Chinese traders. Other than attempting to stamp out 'social vices' such as head-hunting, they were largely left undisturbed. In Kalimantan, the Dutch colonial government did nothing to discourage the activities of Muslim and Christian missionaries, traders and administrators.

Best time to visit Sept-Oct, before the rainy season starts; this coincides with rice-planting rituals and the Erau festival (see below). Harvesting festivals are held Feb-Mar. During the dry season (Jul-Sept), many of the smaller tributaries and shallow lakes are unnavigable except by small canoes; during the height of the wet season (Nov-Jan), many rivers are in flood and currents are often too strong for upriver trips.

The Lower Mahakam: Samarinda to Muara Muntai

Tenggarong, the last capital of the Sultanate of Kutai, is the first major town (40 km) upriver from Samarinda. The highlight of a visit to the town is the **Mulawarman Museum**. It is housed in the Dutch-built former sultan's palace – his old wooden one, which was exquisitely furnished, burned to the ground in the mid-1930s. The museum contains a recreation of the opulent royal bed chamber, a selection of the sultan's *krisses* (see page 548), clothes and other bits and pieces of royal regalia as well as his collection of Chinese ceramics. There are also replicas of the stone stelae bearing Sanskrit inscriptions dating from the 4th or 5th centuries. There is a poor display of Dayak arts and crafts, although there are some woodcarvings in the grounds – notably the tall Dayak *belawang* pole (with a carved hornbill on top) in front of the museum. Open: Tues-Sun 1000-1400. **NB**: a Dayak cultural show is often staged in the museum on Sundays.

Near the museum is the **royal cemetery**, containing graves of the founder of Tenggarong, Sultan Muslidhuddin and his descendants. There are some cheap losmen in town, a few simple restaurants and a good arts and crafts shop – the *Karya Indah Art Shop* on Jl. Diponegoro. (Tenggarong can also be reached by road from Samarinda, see below).

Upriver tours pass through the villages of Muara Kaman and Kota Bangun before reaching **Muara Muntai**, a village built out over the riverbank on ironwood stilts. The lakes of **Semayang**, **Melintang** and **Jempang** lie to the W and SW of Kota Bangun, about 6-7 hrs upriver from Tenggarong. The lakes are known for their freshwater dolphins and other wildlife in the area include proboscis monkeys. The Dayak village of **Tanjung Isuy** is on the Mancong River, which feeds into Lake Jempang, the most southerly of the 3 main lakes; it takes about 2$\frac{1}{2}$ hrs to reach the village from Muara Muntai. Tanjung Isuy is quite touristy. It is, however, the best place on the Mahakam to witness traditional dance performances in full costume; these are included in most tour packages. **NB:** it is necessary to report to the police post on arrival. **Accommodation**: most visitors stay at the longhouse which the villagers have rejected in favour of detached kampung houses, strung out along the riverbank. It is possible to visit the **Mancong longhouse**, about 10 km from Tanjung Isuy; 3 hrs walk (one-way); 2$\frac{1}{2}$ hrs canoe (one way); 15,000Rp (return) by hired motorcycle.

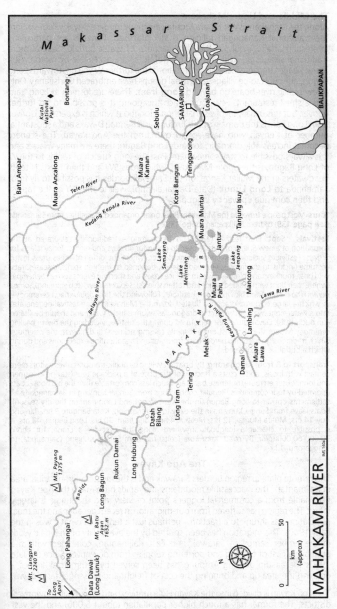

MAHAKAM RIVER

The Middle and Upper Mahakam

Along the Mahakam, W of Muara Muntai, are many modern Dayak villages where the traditional Kaharingan religion is still practised. Funerals are particularly interesting affairs, involving the ritual sacrifice of water buffalo. Several more traditional villages are within reach of **Melak** (all are accessible by motorcycle). These villages become increasingly traditional the further W you go, towards Long Bagun, although some villages and tribal groups have embraced Christianity. Only a few public river-boats go beyond **Long Iram**. There are losmen in Long Iram and a small restaurant. Few tours reach this point; it is possible to go further upriver, but this usually involves chartering a longboat which is expensive. Upriver from Long Iram is the domain of the Tunjung and Benuaq Dayaks and a substantial number of Kenyah who have spilled over from the Apo Kayan. The scenery becomes increasingly dramatic, towards Long Bagun; there are many villages and it is always possible to stay somewhere. Past the long stretch of rapids to the W of Long Bagun, is the upper Mahakam, which runs SW and then twists N to its headwaters in the Muller Range, on the Sarawak border. It is possible to fly from Samarinda to **Long Lunuk** (Data Dawai airstrip), well to the SW of the rapids, and then continue upriver by longboat.

Tours Most people travel up the Mahakam River on an organized tour, either from Samarinda (see page 139) or from Balikpapan (page 139).

Festivals Sept: *Erau festival* (23-28) in Tenggarong – traditionally celebrated at the coronation of a new Sultan of Kutai – used to go on for 40 days and nights. Today it lasts for 5 days. Festivities include traditional Dayak dances, where the different tribes dress in full costume (including the impressive Hudoq dance, designed to frighten spirits, diseases, rats, wild boar, monkeys and birds away from the rice crops) and sporting events such as *behempas* (where men fight with braided whips and rattan shields), *sepak takraw*, (top spinning), *lomba perahu* (boat races) and blowpipe competitions. Following the final *ngulur naga* ceremony – in which a large colourful dragon is floated down the Mahakam – the festival degenerates into a water-fight (water in which the dragon has swum is lucky water and should be shared – in bucketfuls). Dayak rituals are performed during the festival, including the *belian* healing ceremony (where shamans cast out evil spirits causing sickness) and *mamat*, the ceremony which traditionally welcomed heroes back from war and headhunting expeditions and during which a buffalo is slaughtered.

Transport to & from Tenggarong By boat: travelling by public transport gives visitors more contact with locals, and it costs a fraction of the price of a package tour (staying in losmen and longhouses en route) but these boats are much less comfortable than the big houseboats operated by tour companies. Regular connections from Sungai Kunjang in Samarinda to all settlements upriver to Long Bagun (in the wet season) and Long Iram (in the dry season). Boats leave from Sungai Kunjang in the early to mid-morning, Kota Bangun, 9 hrs, Tanjung Isuy, 14 hrs, Muara Muntai, 12 hrs, Melak, 24 hrs, Long Iram, 30 hrs, Long Bagun, 40 hrs. It is possible to charter a longboat anywhere along the river for a cruise; for about 30,000-60,000Rp/hr. By road: *taksi kota* (colts) run from Sungai Kunjang (Samarinda) to Tenggarong, 1 hr.

The Apo Kayan

This remote plateau region borders Sarawak and is the most traditional tribal area in Kalimantan. The inaccessible mountains and rapids have made the Apo Kayan non-viable from a commercial logger's point of view, and the jungle is largely intact. The region has suffered from out-migration in recent decades and the tribal population has shrunk to a fraction – perhaps just a tenth – of what it was in the early 1900s. This migration has been spurred by the availability of well-paid work in the timber camps of Sarawak and East Kalimantan, combined with the prohibitive cost of ferrying and portering supplies from downriver. Since the late 1980s the airstrip at Long Ampung has been served by commercial airlines – opening the area up and bringing the cost of freight and passenger fares down.

The Apo Kayan is divided into the Kayan Hulu (upriver) and Kayan Hilir (downriver) districts. The former has a much higher population (about 5,000) and the vast majority are Kayan (**see page 242**), most originally from Sarawak, driven upriver by Iban raids. Nearly all of them have converted to Christianity – most are Protestant. Until the 1920s the Kayan were the sworn enemies of Sarawak's Iban: in 1924 the Sarawak Brooke government convened a peace conference in Kapit (on the Rejang River) which was attended by Dayak groups from both sides of the border. This formally put a stop to upriver and cross-border headhunting raids.

During World War II, many Europeans in the coastal towns of E Kalimantan made their way upriver to what they considered the relative safety of Long Nawang, deep in the Apo Kayan, in the face of Japanese occupation. The Japanese troops followed them upriver and many were killed, having been forced to dig their own graves. Among those shot was a group of women and children – refugees from Kapit in Sarawak (**see page 27294_903**).

Most tours to the Apo Kayan involve trekking and canoe trips from Long Ampung to Long Nawang and visits to longhouses in the area such as Nawang Baru and Long Betoah and W of Long Ampung, along the Boh River, to Long Uro, Lidung Panau and Long Sungai Barang. **Accommodation**: it is possible to stay in these longhouses but it is important to bring gifts (see box, **page 260**). Independent travellers should pay around 6,000Rp/night to the longhouse headman. Visitors should bring a sleeping bag (it gets cold at night) and essential equipment includes insect repellent and a torch.

Transport to & from the Apo Kayan By air: the only realistic way of getting to the Apo Kayan is by air. Connections (on Wed and Sun) to Long Ampung from Samarinda on Merpati and Asahi 1½ hrs (100,000Rp). Flights into Long Ampung can carry 21 passengers, but on departure they can only carry 10 passengers, due to a short airstrip. Organized package tours to the Apo Kayan with big tour companies are more expensive, but your flight out is guaranteed. *Kaltim Adventure* (based in Balikpapan) undertakes to charter a helicopter if its tourists cannot get onto a flight. *Missionary Aviation Fellowship (MAF)* also flies Cessna aircraft to longhouses in the interior, including Long Ampung. But MAF is not a commercial airline and should not be treated as one. It does not have a concession from the government to operate on a commercial basis and also has an agreement with Merpati that it will not poach passengers. It is a religious, non-profitmaking organization servicing remote communities; it will only agree to fly tourists out of Long Ampung in the case of emergencies or in the unlikely event of planes being empty. Once in Long Ampung, MAF may consider requests for flights further into the interior; prices vary depending on whether they are scheduled or non-scheduled flights. Write in advance to: MAF, Box No. 82, Samarinda with details of where and when you intend to go. MAF flies to about five airstrips in the remote parts of the Apo Kayan.

Tarakan

The oil-island of Tarakan has little to offer the tourist, besides being a hopping-off point to neighbouring Sabah.

Accommodation B *Tarakan Plaza*, Jl. Yos Sudarso, T 2187, a/c, restaurant; **D** *Bahetra*, Jl. Sulawesi, T 21821, a/c.

Tour companies & travel agents *Aruis*, Jl. Sudarjo V/19, T 21240; *Angkasa*, Jl. Sebengkok 33, T21130; *Nusantara Raya Sari*, Jl. R. E. Martadinata; *Tam Jaya*, Jl. Yos Sudarso, T 21250.

Useful addresses Area code: 0551.

Airline offices Garuda, Jl. Sebengkok 33, T 21130; **Merpati**, Jl. Yos Sudarso 8, T 21875; **Bouraq**, Jl. Yos Sudarso 8, T 21248; **Sempati**, Jl. Yos Sudarso 8, T 21871; **Asahi**, *Hotel Tarakan Plaza*, Jl. Yos Sudarso, T 21871.

Transport to & from Tarakan By air: regular connections on Bouraq, Merpati and Asahi with Balikpapan and Samarinda. By boat: regular passenger boat connections with Samarinda and Balikpapan. **International connections with Malaysia** By air: regular connections on Bouraq and MAS every Mon with Tawau in Sabah 35 mins. By boat: regular passenger boat connections with Tawau in Sabah. The Pelni ship *Kerinci* calls here; the Pelni office is at the port (see route map, **page 890**).

WEST KALIMANTAN (Kalimantan Barat – Kalbar)

Because it is cut off from Kalimantan's other provinces, Kalbar attracts few tourists. It occupies about a fifth of Kalimantan's land area (146,800 sq km), most of which is very flat. The **Kapuas River** is Indonesia's longest at 1,243 km and runs through the middle of the province, E to W. Its headwaters, deep in the interior, are in the Muller range, which fringes the NE and E borders of Kalbar.

The Kapuas River is navigable for most of its length, which – as with the Mahakam River in East Kalimantan – has allowed the penetration of the interior by merchants and missionaries over the past century. There are small towns all along the river, and the surrounding forest has been heavily logged. For tourists, the Kapuas is less interesting to travel up than the Mahakam River, and pales in comparison with the rivers in neighbouring Sarawak. Because few foreign visitors make the trip however, the Kapuas River is certainly not 'touristy'. To the N, the province borders Sarawak, and the E end of this frontier runs along the remote Kapuas Hulu mountain range. The SE border with Central Kalimantan province, follows the Schwaner Range. About ⅔ of West Kalimantan's jungle (a total of about 9.5 million ha) is classed as 'production forest'; most of the remaining 3 million ha is protected, but it is such a large area that it is impossible to guard against illegal loggers. The timber industry is the province's economic backbone, but Kalbar is also a major rubber producer.

People
West Kalimantan's 3.9 million inhabitants are concentrated along the coasts and rivers. Malay Muslims make up about 40% of the inhabitants, Dayaks account for another 40%, Chinese 11% and the remainder include Buginese (originally from Sulawesi) and Minangkabau (originally from Sumatra). West Kalimantan has also received large numbers of transmigrants (**see page 732**) from Java. Most were originally resettled at Rasau Jaya, to the S of Pontianak, but many have come to the metropolis to find work as labourers – others have simply resorted to begging. Tribal people also come to Pontianak from settlements upriver on the Kapuas; they have usually fared better than the transmigrants and a number hold important jobs in the provincial administration.

Tourism
In 1986 only 5,000 foreign tourists arrived in Kalbar; by 1990 this had quadrupled and, following the opening of the Entikong border crossing on the Sarawak frontier, the number of tourists rose again by around 50%. The vast majority of these tourists were curious Malaysians; Westerners account for less than a tenth of Pontianak's tourist arrivals – according to provincial government statistics, a maximum of around 2,000 pass through a year. The main reason for this is that the province is rather lacking in 'tourist objects' and receives little attention in the national tourism promotion literature. True, Kalbar has jungle and rivers and Dayaks and offshore islands – but these can also be found in countless other more accessible places in Indonesia.

English is not widely spoken in Kalbar: visitors are advised to learn some basic Bahasa – particularly those heading upriver. The tourist literature produced by the provincial tourism office waxes lyrical about Kalbar's many beautiful islands just offshore and the national parks. But besides being written in rather opaque English, it also fails to mention that few of these have any facilities for tourists and most are extremely difficult to get to. Visitors who want to immerse themselves in Dayak culture and visit traditional longhouses will not find much of interest in Kalbar; only a few tribal groups still live in longhouses on the uppermost reaches of the Kapuas River and its tributaries.

History

At about the time Java's Hindu Majapahit Empire was disintegrating in the mid-1300s, a number of small Malay sultanates grew up along the coast of West Kalimantan. These controlled upriver trade and exploited the Dayaks of the interior. When Abdul Rahman, an Arab seafarer-cum-pirate decided to set up a small trading settlement at Pontianak in 1770, he crossed the paths of some of these sultans. This prompted the first Dutch intervention in the affairs of West Kalimantan, but they did not stay long, and for the next 150 years, their presence there was minimal: Borneo's W coast ranked low on the colonial administration's agenda. A gold rush in the 1780s brought Hakka Chinese immigrants flooding into the Sambas area. Their descendants – after several generations of intermarriage with Dayaks – make up more than 10% of West Kalimantan's population today, most living in Pontianak. In the 19th century, the Dutch were worried about the intentions of Rajah James Brooke of Sarawak (**see page 234**) as he occupied successive chunks of the Sultanate of Brunei. In response, the Dutch increased their presence but any threat that Brooke posed to Dutch territory never materialized. During World War II, the people of Kalbar suffered terribly at the hands of the Japanese Imperial Army, who massacred more than 21,000 people in the province, many at Mandor in Jun 1944.

Pontianak

Living in Pontianak is like a European living in a city called 'Dracula' – the name literally translates as 'the vampire ghost of a woman who dies in childbirth'. Apparently, hunters who first came to this area heard terrible screams in the jungle at night and were so scared by them that they dubbed the area 'the place that sounds like a *pontianak*'. But modern Pontianak is no ghost town. It is a thriving, prosperous town with a population of about 450,000 – a third of whom are Chinese – and a 'parabola' on almost every rooftop. These satellite dishes pick up television stations from around the region as well as blue movie channels from the United States and are no small investment: 3m-diameter dishes cost about 1.5 million rupiahs (US$750) while the big 4m ones cost up to 3 million rupiahs.

The confluence of the Kapuas and Landak rivers, where the Arab adventurer Abdul Rahman founded the original settlement in 1770, is a strongly Malay part of town. This area, which encompasses several older kampungs, is known as Kampung Bugis. The commercial heart of Pontianak, is on the left bank of the Kapuas, around the old Chinese quarter. The other side of the river is called Siantan and is distinguished only by its bus terminal, a few rubber-smoking factories (whose choking smell permeates the air) and the pride of Pontianak: the equator monument.

Places of interest

The **Musium Negeri** – the state museum – at the southern end of Jalan Jend. A. Yani, contains good models of longhouses and a comprehensive display of Dayak household implements including a collection of tattoo blocks, weapons from blowpipes to blunderbusts, one sad-looking skull, masks, fishtraps and musical instruments. There are examples of Dayak textiles, ikat (**see page 721**) and songket (**see page 118**) and basketry. There is also a model of a Malay house and a collection of typical household implements. The Dayak and Malay communities are represented in the huge relief-sculptures on the front of the museum. But there is absolutely nothing on or in it acknowledging the presence of the large Chinese population – other than some Chinese ceramics. Nor, unfortunately, are any of the objects labelled in English. Open: 0900-1600 Mon-Sun, 0900-1100 Fri. **Getting there:** oplet from Kapuas Indah Covered Market (400Rp). Just past the museum is the huge whitewashed West Kalimantan governor's office. There

PONTIANAK IMS 136

1. Musium Negeri (State Museum)
2. Kadriyah Palace
3. Mesjid Jami (Mosque)
4. Chinese temple
5. Kapuas Indah (market)
6. Garuda Office
7. Bugis Schooner Dock
8. Immigration Office
9. Post Office
10. St. Yosef Kathedral
11. Hotel Mahkota
12. Pontianak City Hotel
13. Hotel Dharma

14. Wijata Kusuma
15. Wisma Patria
16. Hotel Kartika
17. Kapuas Palace
18. Nusa Indah Shopping Centre

B1. Sintan bus terminal
B2. Bemo bus terminal

is a replica Dayak longhouse near the museum, off Jalan Jend. A. Yani, built in 1985 to stage a Koran-reading contest.

The ironwood *istana* or *kraton* – **Kadriyah Palace** – was built at the confluence of the Landak and Kapuas rivers by the town's Arab founding father, Abdul Rahman, shortly after he established the trading settlement. The palace was home to 7 sultans; Sharif Yusof, son of the the 7th, looks after it today. His uncle married a Dutch woman whose marble bust is one of the eccentric collection of items which decorate the palace museum. Among the fascinating array of odds and ends are two 5 m-tall decorated French mirrors, made in 1923; these face each other across the room and Sharif's party trick is to hold a lighter up to create an endless corridor of reflected flames. There is also a selection of past sultans' *bajus* and *songkoks*, a jumble of royal regalia, including 2 thrones and tables of Italian marble and a photograph of the 6th sultan and his heir, who were murdered by the Japanese in a mass killing during World War II. Admission by donation, about 500Rp. Open: 0900-1730.

The **Mesjid Jami** (mosque) – which is next to the palace – was built shortly after the founding of the city in the late 1700s, although it has been renovated and reconstructed over the years. It is a beautiful building with tiered roofs, standing at the confluence of the 2 rivers, with its lime-green turret-like minarets and its bell-shaped upper roof. The Kapuas riverbank next to the mosque is a pleasant place to sit and watch life on the river – the elegant Bugis schooners berth at the docks on the opposite bank. The sky over the mosque and palace is alive with kites flown by the children in Kampung Bugis.

Over the Landak Bridge and past the stinking Siantan rubber smokehouses, which line the right bank of the Kapuas, is the **Tugu Khatulistiwa** (Equator Monument), standing at exactly 109 degrees, 20 minutes E of Greenwich. During the Mar and Sept equinoxes, the column's shadow disappears, which is an excuse for a party in Pontianak. In 1991, the old belian (ironwood) equator column was encased in a new architectural wonder, a sort of concrete mausoleum where it is intelligently hidden from the sun. There is a new 6 m-high column on top.

The heart of the city, around **Kapuas Indah** indoor market, is an interesting and lively part of town. There are a number of *pekong* (Taoist temples) around the market area; the oldest, **Sa Seng Keng**, contains a huge array of gods. The **Dwi Dharma Bhakti Chinese Temple** on Jalan Tanjungpura is notable for its location in the middle of the main street.

> ### Pontianak's red-light district – forlorn hopes
>
> As if cinemas, amusement arcades, discos, karaoke lounges and blue movies on satellite television were not enough to keep them occupied, Pontianak's male population also has recourse to a village full of 300 prostitutes. This village is known – rather sadly – as *Harapan Kita*, or 'Our Hope' and is to the right immediately after the bridge over Sungai Landak. Locally, it is euphemistically dubbed 'Kampung Brunei' and came into existence following the government clamp-down on prostitution; prostitutes were taken off the streets and moved into one huge, self-contained brothel.

The **Pasar Ikan** (Fish Market), downriver from town, on Jalan Pak Kasih, is a great place to wander in the early morning; the stallholders are just as interesting as the incredible variety of fish they sell.

Excursions

Tourist facilities are limited outside Pontianak – and so are tourist sights. Some areas along the NW coast – including offshore islands – can be visited in day-long excursions from Pontianak, and these have been listed under the separate sections below. Package excursions are operated by the 2 main travel agents in Pontianak (see below).

Tours Pontianak's 2 main tour operators offer city tours and short package tours along the W coast to Singkawang and Sambas regencies as well as offshore islands. Longer upriver trips on the Kapuas can be arranged, as can adventure tours with jungle trekking and white-water rafting. *Insan* offers one particularly adventurous white-water rafting trip to rapids on the Pinoh River.

Festivals Jan: *West Kalimantan anniversary* (1st), commemorating its accession to the status of an autonomous province in 1957. Folk art exhibitions and dance. **Sept**: *Naik Dango* (21st) (rice storage) festival, when the sun is directly overhead at noon. **Nov**: *Trans-Equator marathon*; in the past this has been a full 42 km event; from 1992 it has become a quarter marathon (10 km).

Accommodation B *Kapuas Palace* (formerly *Kapuas Permai*), Jl. Imam Bonjol, T 36122, a/c, restaurant, large pool, modern low-rise hotel in spacious grounds with good range of facilities, located quite a long way from the market area, rooms and cottages; **B** *Kartika*, Jl. Rohadi Usman, T 34401, F 38457, a/c, good location on the river, next to the docks and the market area, rooms facing the river rec; **B** *Mahkota*, Jl. Sidas 8, T 36022, F 36200, a/c, restaurant, pool, newest, smartest best hotel in Pontianak, with full range of facilities including tennis courts, a billiard room and a good bar, rooms small but well appointed, rec; **B** *Pontianak City*, Jl. Pak Kasih, T 32495, a/c; **C** *Dharma*, Jl. Imam Bonjol, T 34759, a/c, restaurant, once Pontianak's top hotel, now a bit run down, the top floor has recently turned into a brothel; **D** *Wijata Kusuma*, Jl. Kapten Marsan 51-53, T 32547, some a/c, restaurant, on the grimy side, but passable, good location on the riverfront, opposite Kapuas Indah Indoor Market and the warungs, popular with budget travellers; **D** *Wisma Patria*, Jl. Hos Cokroaminoto 497 (Jl. Merdeka Timur), T 6063, a/c, restaurant, sprawling overgrown home-stay, without much charm, rooms average but popular with tourists and friendly staff, automatic 'teh/kopi' wake-up call at 0630.

Restaurants Indonesian: ◆*Beringin*, Jl. Diponegoro 115, Padang food, rec; ◆*Sahara*, Jl. Imam Bonjol. Padang food; ◆*Satria Wangi*, Jl. Nusa Indah II 11A, Indonesian cuisine and some Chinese food, rec. by locals. Other Asian: ◆◆*Gajah Mada*, Jl. Gajah Mada 202, big Chinese-run restaurant, with a landscaped interior offering very high quality food, particularly seafood and freshwater fish, specialities include: *jelawat* (West Kalimantan river fish), *hekeng* (chopped, deep-fried shrimp), *kailan ca thik pow* (thinly sliced salted fish), crab *fu yung* and sautéed frog, rec; ◆*Hawaii*, Jl. Satria 79-80 (across the road from Nusa Indah Plaza), also branch at Jl. Gajah Mada 24, a/c restaurant serving Chinese dishes and seafood, specialities: *puyung hai* (crab or prawn omelette with spicy peanut sauce) and chicken steaks, rec; ◆◆*Nikisa*, Jl. Sisingamangaraja 108. Sophisticated Japanese restaurant, the most upmarket in Pontianak, shabu-shabu buffet, sukiyaki, teriyaki burgers and an international selection – mainly imported steaks, set lunch/dinner, rec. by locals; ◆◆*Pinang Merah Restoran*, Disko dan Singing House, Jl. Kapten Marsan 51-53 (behind Kapuas Indah), down the alleyway past the *Wijaya Kusuma Hotel*, very cool and pleasant place for a drink in the early evening, on wooden walkway next to the river; seafood and Chinese dishes. Seafood: ◆*Corina*, Jl. Tanjungpura 124, simple seafood menu. Foodstalls: *Bobo Indah*, opposite the *Wijaya Kusuma Hotel* next to the colourful cinema hoardings. There are also some stalls next to the river. In the mornings there are hawker stalls selling breakfast fishballs and *mee kepitang* (noodles and crab) along Jl. Nusa Indah II. In the evenings, on the S side of Jl. Diponegoro there are lots of hawker stalls selling cheap Chinese, Padang and Batawi (Jakarta) food. **Fruit market**: at the top of Jl. Nusah Indah next to St Yosef Katholik Kathedral, excellent selection, including jeruk oranges from around Tebas, W of Singkawang. Their greeny-yellow appearance makes them look rather unappetizing but they are very sweet. Good durians when in season in July and August. Out of town: ◆◆*Sea Food Garden*, Kakap, about 30 mins drive W of Pontianak, on the coast, in a village famous for its seafood, local farm crabs, lobsters, shrimps and fish, rec. by locals.

Bars *Corner Bar*, round the corner from Pontianak Theatre and next to *Bandung Indah* fastfood restaurant. Bamboo and brick open-sided bar with good atmosphere.

Entertainment Cinemas: several in town, most of them screening the latest Hollywood releases with a few kung-fu movies. They are owned by a Jakarta businessman who has virtually put the old Pontianak Theatre out of business. Top Floor, Kapuas Indah Indoor Market; 4 cinema halls. Nusa Indah Plaza, Jl. Nusa Indah; 7 cinema halls.

Sport Golf: course at Siantan Hulu and a driving range at Jl. Haryono.

Shopping Due mainly to its large Chinese population, Pontianak is full of gold shops. There are a number of art and craft shops selling Dayak handicrafts, porcelain, textiles (including *ikat* and *songket*) and antiques, but the selection is limited in comparison with Balikpapan and Samarinda. *Koperasi Kerta*, Jl. Adisucipto 187; *Fariz Art Shop*, 3 Blok C, Pasar Nusa Indah I, good selection of old ikats; *Borneo Art Shop*, Blok VII, Jl. Nusa Indah I 27; *Leny Art Shop*, Jl. Khattulistiwa (at the roundabout opposite the equator monument), interesting collection of antique Dayak pieces – including stone axes, medicine boxes, knives, ikat, basketware and Chinese ceramics – and not forgetting a few model equator monuments (also branch at 1A Blok D, Jl. Nusa Indah III). Batik: good batik shop in Nusa Indah Plaza. **Markets**: *Piska Centre* (Kapuas Indah Indoor Market) opposite *Wijaya Kusuma Hotel*, uninteresting selection of cheap clothes and goods. **Maps**: *Juanda Baru Toko Buku*, Jl. Hos Cokroaminoto 232.

Local transport Bus (*bis kota*): around the Pontianak area leave from Sintian terminal on the N side of the river (regular ferries cross the river from Jl. Bardan to the terminal, 200Rp). **Oplets**: leave from Jl. Kapten Marsan in front of the Kapuas Indah Indoor Market, next to the warungs; special demarcated routes to most destinations around town. Also oplet stations on Jl. Sisingamangaraja and Jl. Teuku Cik Ditiro. **Ojeks**: good way to see the sights. The easiest place to pick up an ojek is along Jl. Tanjungpura; short trips cost 300-400Rp or chartered for 3,000Rp. **Taxis** (saloons): congregate around *Dharma Hotel* on Jl. Tanjungpura, 6,500Rp/hr.

Banks & money changers There are several banks along Jl. Tanjungpura (including **Bank Duta** and **Bank Dagang Negara**). **Safari Money-changer**, Jl. Tanjungpura 12 (and Jl. Nusa Indah III 57).

Useful addresses Post Office: Jl. Rahadi Usman 1. **Area code**: 0561. **Hospitals**: *Dr. Sudarso Hospital*, Jl. Adisucipto; *Sei Jawi Hospital Centre*, Jl. Merdeka Barat.

Airline offices Garuda/Merpati, Jl. Rohadi Usman 8A, T 34142; **Sempati/Deraya**, Jl. Sisingamangaraja 145, T 34840; **Bouraq**, Jl. Tanjungpura 253, T 32371; **DAS**, Jl. Gajah Mada 67, T 34383.

Tour companies & travel agents *Ateng*, Jl. Gajah Mada 201, T 32683, F 36620, rec; *Insan*

Worldwide Tours & Travel (ITT) Jl. Tanjungpura 149; *Jambore Express Tour*, Jl. Diponegoro 64, T 34604.

Tourist offices Tourist Promotion Office (Kalbar), Jl. Achmad Sood 25, T 36712; **Tourist Information Office** at the airport (and at Entikong border crossing). The Department of Posts and Telecommunications (Parpostel), Jl. Sutan Syahril 17, T 39444 has information on travelling around Kalbar; not much English spoken.

Transport to & from Pontianak **By air:** Supadio Airport is 20 km from town. Taxis from airport into town cost 10,000Rp. Regular connections on Garuda, Merpati, Sempati and Bouraq with most major destinations in Indonesia such as Jakarta, Medan, Balikpapan, Ketapang, Sintang, Putu Siban and Pangkalanbur.

By bus: Long-distance buses (*Kirana, Sago & SJS* bus companies) leave from Batu Layang terminal at Km 8 on the Sambas road. Tickets can be bought at the bus station. Regular buses to Singkawang 3½ hrs, Sambas, Sintang (on the Kapuas River) 10 hrs, Meliau, Tayan, Sekadan and Ngabang. **Getting to Batu Layang:** *bis kota* (city bus) from Sintian terminal (200Rp) or oplet (200Rp).

By boat: a/c express launches bought from Sibu in Sarawak leave for Ketapang (S of Pontianak) daily at 0900. Tickets for Malindo and Kita express boats sold at *Insan Worldwide Tour & Travel. Bandong*, Kalbar's ungainly big river cargo barges, go from Pontianak to Putusibau (4 days, 3 nights) from Sept to Apr when the water level is high. Pelni's *K M Lawit* leaves Pontianak for Semarang on the last Sat of every month (see route map, **page 1008**). The *Tanjung Priok* leaves for Jakarta and Semarang on the first and third Mon of every month and the *Belawan* leaves once a month for Medan in Sumatra. There are also regular connections with Montok, Kijang, Dumai and Mahayati. Pelni office: Jl. Pelabuhan 2, T 34133.

International connections **By air:** with Kuching (Sarawak) on MAS (Mon, Thur) and Singapore (Tue, Thur, Sat); although it is much cheaper to fly to Batam Island and then take the half-hour boat trip to Singapore from Sekupang (**see page 127**). **By bus:** the border is open 0600-1800 West Indonesian time (0500-1700 Malaysian time). Public buses (*SJS Bus Co.*) leave Pontianak (Batu Layang) for Entikong at 0600 daily 9 hrs. Passengers cross the border on foot and change to a Malaysian bus to Kuching (**see page 259**). Tickets from *Insan Worldwide Tour & Travel.* A new government-run Damri bus company is believed to have started running direct buses to Kuching.

The Northwest Coast
Singkawang

Singkawang was originally settled by Hakka Chinese in the early 1800s and was the main town servicing the nearby gold rush shanty at Mantrado. It is now an important farming area and is named after a local turnip.

Excursions

About 7 km S of Singkawang there is a **pottery** village where replicas of antique Chinese ceramics are fired in a big kiln. **Pasir Panjang** beach is 17 km S of Singkawang. **Accommodation: C** cottage-style beach-side hotel, a/c, restaurant, pool, facilities include tennis court and watersports.

Pulau Randayan is a 12 ha island with good coral; facilities are being developed on the island and it is possible to stay overnight. Trips to the island are organized by Mr Sukartadji, owner of the *Palapa Hotel* in Singkawang. **Getting there:** 2 hrs by boat from Pasir Panjang.

Pulau Temajo is 60 km S of Singkawang (off the coast from the village of Sungai Kunyit), an island with white sand beaches and good coral. There is some accommodation available on the island. *Ateng Tours & Travel* in Pontianak (**see page 852**) can advise on the best way to get there; the company also runs one-day package tours to the island costing 25,000Rp, including transport, food and skin-diving equipment.

Accommodation B *Mahkota*, Jl. Diponegoro 1, a/c, restaurant, pool, sister hotel to *Mahkota* in Pontianak with equally good range of facilities; **C** *Palapa*, Jl. Ismael Tahir 152, T 21449, a/c, restaurant; **D** *Kalbar*, Jl. Kepol, T 21404, a/c.

Restaurants *Diponegoro*, Jl. Diponegoro (Padang food) and 2 Chinese restaurants, *A Hin and A Sun*, next door to each other on Jl. Diponegoro.

Transport to & from Singkawang 143 km N of Pontianak. **By colt:** regular connections with Pontianak's Sintian terminal, 3½ hrs.

The Kapuas River

The first European to venture up the 1,243 km-long Kapuas River was a Dutchman, Major George Muller, who reached the site of present-day Putussibau in 1822 and who lent his name to the mountains to the E. Four years later, while attempting to cross these mountains, from the upper Mahakam to the Kapuas, he had his head taken by Dayaks. The Dayaks of the upper Kapuas were themselves terrorized by Iban headhunters, mostly from the Batang Lupar in Sarawak (**see page 67**) – although some Iban settled in the area to the N of the Kapuas. Few Dayak communities – except those in more remote areas – live in traditional longhouses or observe tribal rituals today. Those who did not turn to Islam – under the influence of the coastal Malays – converted to Christianity: there is a large number of Roman Catholic and Protestant evangelists working throughout the Kapuas basin. Christians (mainly Catholics) make up about 28% of Kalbar's population.

There is still a lot of gold-panning along the Kapuas – using *palong dulang* pans – and larger operations have turned some areas of jungle into a moonscape. Many Dayaks are also employed in the logging industry. Although it is possible to take a *bandung* barge all the way up the river from Pontianak (4-5 days to Putussibau, 40,000Rp), most tourists opt to travel to Sintang by road, which branches off the coast road from Sungai Pinyuh, 50 km NW of Pontianak. A road is being built between Sintang and Putussibau.

Entikong's fiscal advantages

For thousands of years tribal people have travelled freely across the ill-defined Kalimantan/Sarawak jungle frontier on the so-called *jalan tikus* – 'mouse trails'. Finally, 25 years after the *Konfrontasi* ended – the 2 year war between Indonesia and Malaysia – the first official border crossing point between the 2 countries opened. The steel barrier at the Entikong frontier post was dismantled in 1991, and the 400 km road between Kuching and Pontianak declared open. While many Malaysians have visited Pontianak for the first time, most of the traffic has been in the other direction. This was thanks to the strange decision to make Entikong the only exit point in Indonesia where Indonesians should not have to pay any *fiskal* – the exit tax of 250,000Rp. This has been a welcome boon to Pontianak's tour companies who have attracted huge business since 1991 – not just from the city's wealthy Chinese population, but from Java and Sumatra too. They now route all their international tours through Kuching instead of Jakarta. It makes sense for families on pilgrimage to Singapore, Hong Kong or China: a family of 4, for example would save 1 million Rp. Pontianak travel agents say shopping tours to Singapore have become big sellers.

Pah Auman, between Pontianak and Ngabang (120 km from Pontianak, *en route* to Entikong) is the nearest village to Kamung Saham Pinyuh (12 km by road). This 30-door Kendayang (or Kenatyan) longhouse is one of the most traditional longhouses remaining in Kalbar, despite the fact that it is not particularly remote. Tourists are under the impression that the further they go into the interior, the further they will get from civilization – but in that, Kalbar is not like neighbouring Sarawak. **Accommodation:** it is possible to ask the Kepala's (headman's) permission to stay overnight in the Kendayang longhouse. **Getting there:** any E-bound bus from Pontianak's Batu Layang bus station (3,500Rp).

The area N of the Kapuas River was a focus of the *Konfrontasi* – the brief war between Indonesia and Malaysia between 1963 and 1965 (**see page 237**). The West Kalimantan Communist Party was also very active in the area in the late 1960s, before being crushed. While tourists heading into remoter areas upriver are no longer shadowed by soldiers, it is still necessary to report to the local police station on arrival.

Sintang (245 km, 8 hrs E of Pontianak) is at the confluence of the Kapuas and Melawi rivers. About 18 km from town is Mount Kelam – 'Dark Mountain' – which at 900 m affords good views of the surrounding plains and rivers. Guides can be hired in Sintang (2 hrs walk to the summit). Sintang is a mainly Chinese town, founded by traders dealing with the Dayaks of the interior. On the upper reaches of the Melawi – and its tributary, the Pinoh – there are some traditional Ot Danum (upriver) Dayak groups (the equivalent of Sarawak's Orang Ulu), notably the Dohoi on the upper Melawi. The 2 rivers begin in the Schwaner Range. **Accommodation: C** *Sasean Hotel*, Jl. Brigjend. Katamso on the river. **Getting there:** Regular buses from Pontianak's Batu Layang bus station (9,000Rp). There are regular passenger boats leaving Sintang for Putussibau (35,000Rp). Deraya also flies from Sintang to Putussibau (62,000Rp).

From **Semitau** – half way between Sintang and Putussibau – it is possible to visit Sentarum, Luar and Sumpa lakes. The lake area is predominantly settled by Ibans, who originally came upriver from the Batang Lupar in Sarawak; other tribal groups include the Maloh Dayaks (famed for their skill as silversmiths and goldsmiths) and the Kantuq.

Putussibau is the last noteworthy settlement on the Kapuas before the Muller range, which divides the watersheds of the Kapuas and Mahakam (in East Kalimantan). In the 1800s, when Chinese traders first visited the upper Kapuas, the settlement was frequently raided by Iban headhunters from the Batang Lupar in Sarawak. The Malays along the upper Kapuas are mainly Dayaks who converted to Islam. Despite Putussibau's remoteness, few Dayaks in the area live in traditional longhouses, the exception being the Taman Kapuas Dayaks. Two Taman Kapuas longhouses are accessible from Putussibau: Melapi I and Semangkok, the latter being more traditional; it is possible to stay overnight at both (see *House Rules,* **page 138**). Longboats for expeditions further upriver are prohibitively expensive to charter (roughly 60,000Rp/hr; 100,000Rp/hr with rapids); regular passenger boats connect main towns. **Accommodation:** *Harapan Kita Bersama Losmen, Marisa Hotel* (both **E**).

South of Pontianak

There are few tourist attractions in the southern **Ketapang** regency, except for the 90,000 ha **Mount Palung Wildlife Reserve**, which encompasses most forest types and contains a wealth of flora and fauna, including orang utans and proboscis monkeys. It is difficult – and expensive – to get to and is mainly a scientific research centre; there are, however, basic facilities at 9 camps within the park. Permits must be obtained from the Conservation Office (PHPA) in Pontianak (at Jl. Abdurrahman Saleh 33). Tourists wishing to visit the reserve should contact Mr Tan Yong Seng, director of *Ateng Tours & Travel*, whose company can organize the tortuous travel arrangements.

SULAWESI

Introduction, 857; Information for Visitors, 862; Ujung Pandang, 863; Ujung Pandang to Toraja via Pare Pare, 870; Toraja, 873; Southeast Sulawesi: Kendari, Kolaka and the Buton and Muna Islands, 886; Pendolo to Palu via Lake Poso and the Lore Lindu National Park, 888; Palu to Manado via Gorontalo, 893.

Maps: Sulawesi, 858-859; Ujung Pandang, 865; South Sulawesi, 871; Tana Toraja, 881; Central Sulawesi, 887; Palu, 891; Manado, 896; Around Manado, 898.

Formerly known as the Celebes, Sulawesi is the third largest of the so-called Greater Sundas, with a land area of 189,216 sq km and a population of 13 million. The first use of the name by a European was by the Portuguese apothecary, secretary and accountant Tomé Pires who, in his journals written at the beginning of the 16th century, referred to the N tip of the island as **Punta de Celebres.** The origins of the word, though, are the subject of dispute. Some people have argued it is derived from the Bugis word *selihe* meaning 'sea current', some that it is an amalgamation of *sula* ('island') and *besi* ('iron'), and still others that it is taken from *si-lebih* ('the one with more islands'). The modern name's origin is not disputed: it means 'Island of Iron' (*Sula-besi*), referring to the rich deposits of nickel-iron ore in the centre of the island. This ore furnished the iron – it was called Luwu iron – for the laminated krisses of Majapahit, famous across the region for their strength.

INTRODUCTION

A glance at any map of Sulawesi immediately highlights the island's strangest attribute: its shape. Variously described as looking like an orchid, a deformed spider, giant crab and mutant starfish, the island's 4 'arms' radiate from a mountainous core. Despite covering an area nearly as great as Britain, no place is more than about 40 km from the sea.

Sulawesi is divided into 4 provinces: North, South, Central and Southeast. Combined, they have a population of nearly 13 million. Most people visit the island to see the Toraja of South Sulawesi; their funeral ceremonies, cliff burial sites and soaring-roofed houses make this culture one of the most fascinating in the world. Ujung Pandang, Sulawesi's largest city and unofficial capital, is the usual port of entry. Manado on the N tip of the island offers some of the best diving in the country and is also becoming increasingly popular. However, with improving transport, other places are becoming more accessible.

Land
Sulawesi's strange shape is linked to its geological evolution. Studies have shown

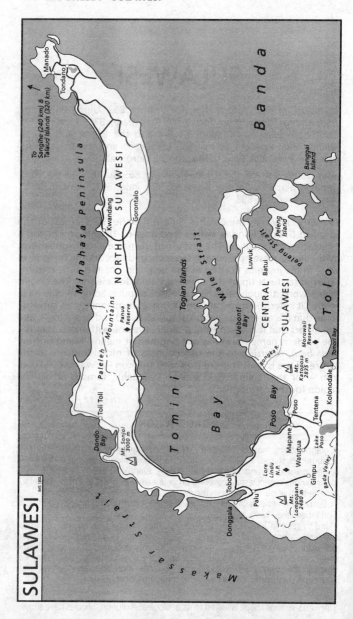

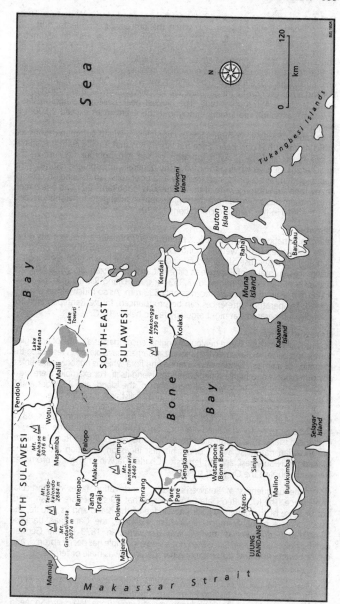

that the island is composed of 2 distinct halves – an E and a W portion. These only collided 15 million years ago when the process of continental drift – or tectonics – caused them to be thrust together. Like Java, Bali and Sumatra, Sulawesi is geologically unstable – altogether, the island has 11 active volcanoes, concentrated in the Minahasa area and N of Toli Toli.

But despite these complicated geological origins, Sulawesi is characteristically an island of uplands cut through by deep rift valleys with short, fast-flowing rivers. Beyond a narrow coastal fringe, there are few areas of lowland and most of the island is above 450m in altitude. The highest peak is Mount Sonjol in the S (3,225m), although mountains throughout the 4 provinces exceed 2,500m in height.

Because of Sulawesi's mountainous character, overland communications are difficult, and it has only been since the late 1980s that an all-weather road has linked the N and the S. Even transport by sea is dangerous because of the treacherous reefs which ring the island. The generally inhospitable nature of the island, and in particular its inaccessibility and poor soils, led the English colonial envoy John Crawfurd to write of the indigenous inhabitants that "no one nation among them has emerged from the savage state to subjugate its neighbours, and take the lead in the march to civilization" (1820).

Climate
Seasonal variations in rainfall are less pronounced in Sulawesi than in many other parts of Indonesia. The wettest months are from Dec to Feb, and the driest are Aug and Sept. Because of the mountainous landscape however, there are great differences in total rainfall between different areas. For example, while Manado in the far N has annual rainfall of 3,352 mm and Ujung Pandang in the far S, 3,188 mm; Palu in the centre receives only 533 mm. As so much of the island is upland, temperature differences can be pronounced. In the Rantepao area for example, temperatures at night regularly fall to below 10°C.

Flora and fauna
Because Sulawesi has diverse geological origins, encompasses a range of ecological zones, and because of the role that mountain barriers have played in restricting the migration of animals, the island has a fauna and flora which is not only quite unlike any other, but is also highly varied within the island itself. For example, there are 7 species of macaques occupying different parts of the island, and 2 species and 9 sub-species of carpenter bee. It is, in short, a naturalist's dream come true.

Of the 127 mammal species, an incredible 79 (62%) are endemic (i.e. found nowhere else); if bats are excluded, this rises to 98%. Even among birds, 88 of the 328 species so far identified are endemic to the island. The same degree of endemism is also true of amphibians, reptiles and insects. Alfred Russel Wallace, the Victorian naturalist, wrote down his first ideas on evolution after visiting Manado in N Sulawesi, and his letters to Charles Darwin in England prompted Darwin to publish the *Origin of species*.

Given the uniqueness of Sulawesi's fauna, conservation takes on particular importance. The IUCN Red Data Books record that 19 species are endangered; but because of the generally poor knowledge of the island and its wildlife, the true figure is probably much higher. For example, the Caerulean paradise fly-catcher (*Eutrichomyias rowleyi*) was discovered in 1873 by the German ornithologist A.B. Meyer. Since then not a single example has been captured, and it is not even known whether the original specimen was male or female.

History
The pre-colonial history of Sulawesi was focused upon the coastal regions of the S. Among a number of trading kingdoms which developed between the 13th and 15th century were the Bugis kingdoms of Luwu, Bone, Wajo and Soppeng

A Noah's Ark: endemic animals of Sulawesi

Curly-tusked babirusa (*Babyrousa babyrussa*): as the name suggests – it means 'pig-deer' – naturalists have found this animal hard to classify. Described first by Piso in 1658, they are usually grouped with pigs but have no near common ancestor because they have evolved in isolation for 30 million years. Most distinctively, the upper canines grow through the animal's lips and curl upwards towards the head. Confused early naturalists thought these tusks were used to hook onto trees when the animal was exhausted; now the received wisdom is that they are used as sparring weapons when males fight during the breeding season.

Anoa (*Bubalus depressicornis* and *B. quarlesi*): these are both dwarf buffalo – about the size of a large dog – but are the largest indigenous mammals on Sulawesi. They are renowned for their ferocity and have not been tamed for captivity despite attempts by the Torajans and others.

Bear cuscus (*Phalanger ursinus* and *P. celebensis*): these animals look rather like sloths and are related to the possums of Australia. They are arboreal and use their prehensile tails as a fifth limb.

Black-crested macaques (*Macaca nigra*): there are 4 species of macaque found in Sulawesi, but only *M. nigra* has been studied by scientists. They are arboreal, foraging in the upper canopy, and live in groups of up to about 50.

Large-eyed jumping tarsier (*Tarsius spectrum*): this is one of the world's smallest primates, with a body length of not more than 10 cm and a weight of 100 g. They are nocturnal and form long-standing monogamous relationships.

Maleo (*Macrocephalon maleo*): perhaps Sulawesi's most famous animal, this bird incubates its eggs in holes dug in the sun-baked ground (**see page 900**).

Red-knobbed hornbill (*Rhyticeros cassadix*): like other hornbills, the red-knobbed hornbill incubates its eggs in hollow trees (see box, **page 226**). They are solitary, monogamous birds and are only rarely seen in flocks.

Source: Whitten, A.J. *et al.* (1988) *The ecology of Sulawesi*, Gajah Mada University Press: Yogyakarta. Whitten, Tony and Whitten, Jane (1992) *Wild Indonesia*, New Holland: London.

and, most importantly, the Makassarese kingdom of Gowa. Both the Bugis and the Makassarese had a reputation across the archipelago for fearlessness in battle.

At the beginning of the 16th century, Gowa, in alliance with the Bajau or sea nomads (not to be muddled with the Bugis – see box), began to emerge as the dominant power in the area. They extended their influence over the neighbouring Bugis kingdoms and the commercial capital, Makassar, became an important trading centre. By the 17th century there were Dutch, English, Arab, Malay, Chinese and Indian seafarers striding the streets of Makassar and doing business in spices, slaves, birds' nests, Dammar resin, sandalwood and products of the sea such as trepang (edible sea cucumbers), pearls, shark's fin and ambergris (a waxy substance secreted by whales and used in perfumes).

Gowa was the last of the great kingdoms of Indonesia to accept Islam (at about the same time that European traders were beginning to establish godowns and factories there). In 1605 the King of Gowa accepted Islam, and when the subordinate kings of the Bugis states failed to follow suit, he staged a number of religiously-inspired military campaigns (1608-1611). By the second decade of the 17th century, Gowa was at the head of the greatest Muslim trading empire in Southeast Asia.

Although the Dutch had established a trading post in south Sulawesi as early as 1609, they were never satisfied with the Gowa sultanate's tendency to allow the smuggling of spices from the Moluccas. By 1615, the VOC had closed down their trading post and limited military action had begun. Despite peace agreements in 1637, 1655 and 1660, conditions were brewing towards a major confrontation between Gowa and the Dutch.

Appreciating the military power of Gowa, the Dutch forged an alliance with the Bugis prince Arung Palakka of Bone. Like other Bugis leaders, Arung Palakka resented the domination of Gowa. In 1660 the Dutch attacked Gowa with the support of Arung Palakka and his men and forced Sultan Hasanuddin to sign a peace treaty. Sultan Hasanuddin chose to ignore the treaty, and in 1666 the VOC mounted a second expedition of 21 ships with Arung Palakka again in support. As the Dutch had hoped, the vassal Bugis kingdoms of Bone and Soppeng joined in the campaign against the Makassarese and after a year of hard fighting on both land and sea, Sultan Hasanuddin was forced to capitulate and sign the Treaty of Bungaya on 18 Nov 1667. Again, Hasanuddin chose to ignore the treaty, forcing the Dutch to mount a third, and final, campaign against the duplicitous Sultan in Apr 1668. By Jun 1669, the Sultan of Gowa and his armies were finally vanquished. The great days of Makassarese trading power were at an end.

Following the Dutch victory, Arung Palakka – upon whom the Dutch had depended for their success – became the *de facto* king of South Sulawesi. By all accounts, his rule was authoritarian and heavy-handed, depending more on military might than consultation and conciliation. The historian of Indonesia, R.C. Ricklefs maintains that Arung Palakka's rule led to large numbers of Bugis and Makassarese fleeing Sulawesi. He writes: "They took to their ships like marauding Vikings in search of honour, wealth and new homes. They intervened in the affairs of Lombok, Sumbawa, Kalimantan, Java, Sumatra, the Malay Peninsula and even Siam". Arung Palakka finally died in 1696.

Minahasa in N Sulawesi was first visited by Europeans in 1524 when Magellan's fleet anchored there. Shortly afterwards in the 1560s, Portuguese missionaries were successful in converting the population to Christianity and in 1568, Indonesia's oldest church – the Evangelical Church of Minahasa – was founded. The Spanish, from their colony in the Philippines, exerted control over Minahasa until 1643 when their attempt to place a half Spanish king on the throne led to the Minahasans turning to the Dutch for support.

In the interior, contact between the European powers and the various local groups was virtually non-existent. The Torajans, for example, were not brought under Dutch administrative control until the 20th century. After World War II, Dutch attempts to cling onto the East Indies led to greater bloodshed in Sulawesi than anywhere else in the archipelago. Even after independence in 1950, there were strong movements in the S and N for greater regional and religious autonomy. By 1958, only the larger towns of the S remained under government control, and between 1958 and 1961 there was a regional rebellion in Minahasa (see page 895).

INFORMATION FOR VISITORS

Internal travel Road: not long ago, Sulawesi enjoyed a reputation for having some of the worst roads in Indonesia, particularly in Central Sulawesi between Palopo and Palu. The roads in the area are still poor and long journeys can be extremely arduous, particularly in the wet season. However, the Indonesian government has allocated considerable funds to improving and upgrading the 2,500 km-long Trans-Sulawesi Highway and conditions are now much improved.

Boat: because of the poor state of much of Sulawesi's road system, the traditional mode of transport was boat. *Pinisi* schooners (**see page 867**) still link much of the island and travel by ship and boat can be an alternative, more comfortable, and sometimes quicker, means of getting from A to B.

UJUNG PANDANG

Ujung Pandang, lying on the W coast of Sulawesi's S peninsula, is the hot and rather ramshackle capital of the province of South Sulawesi, and the *de facto* capital of the island. It was formerly called Makassar, after the people who live in the area – the Makassarese.

Makassar was the port and commercial hub of the powerful trading sultanate of Gowa which dominated the area between the 13th and 15th centuries. The skilled sailors who operated out of Makassar – the Bajau 'sea nomads' – were instrumental in enabling the sultanate to control the lucrative trade in spices from the Moluccas. Makassar became one of the great entrepôts of Southeast Asia and traders from India, China and Europe would gather here to buy produce. The kings of Gowa did not accept Islam until 1605, and a Dutch visitor of 1607 remarked on the continued use of penis balls (**see page 41**) and the tendency for lower class women to roam the city with bare breasts. Less than 40 years later when the French priest Alexandre de Rhodes published his account of the Orient, he noted that women in Makassar were clothed from head to foot so that "not even their faces can be seen".

Gowa's position as the most powerful trading kingdom in eastern Indonesia finally came to an end in 1669 when Sultan Hasanuddin signed a peace treaty with the Dutch after 60 years of intermittent warfare (**see page 862**). The Sultan was forced to give up control of the fort of Ujung Pandang, which became the core of a new, colonial, city.

As Sulawesi's main port of entry and exit, Ujung Pandang is visited by considerable numbers of tourists. But there is not a great deal to see in this characterless city, and most visitors merely pass through *en route* to Tana Toraja and elsewhere. Accommodation for budget travellers is poor, a situation partially rectified by the presence of some excellent seafood restaurants.

Places of interest
Benteng (fort) Ujung Pandang was built in 1545 during the reign of Tuni Pallanga, the 10th Sultan of Gowa, overlooking the sea. When the city was captured by the Dutch in 1667 it was renamed Fort Rotterdam by the victorious Dutch admiral Speelman. The Indonesian independence hero **Prince Diponegoro**, now immortalized in virtually every town, was incarcerated here for 27 years. His cell in the SW corner of the fort is unmarked, although a statue of the 19th century independence hero on horseback stands outside the fort (his grave is on Jalan Diponegoro – see below). Admission: 500Rp. Open: 0800-1600 Tues-Sun.

Within the precincts of the substantially remodelled fort are 13 buildings; 11 built by the Dutch and the remaining 2 by the Japanese. Among them is the **Ujung Pandang State Museum**. One half contains a diverse collection of coins, photographs and ceramics; the other, ethnographic artefacts, models of Torajan houses and elaborate Dutch and local sailing vessels. The collection continues upstairs, with agricultural implements, weaving technology, and examples of traditional textiles and dress. Admission: 200Rp. Open: 0800-1330 Tues-Thurs, 0800-1030 Fri, 0800-1230 Sat-Sun. Also found here is the **Conservatory of Dance and Music**, the **National Archives**, and the **Historical and Archaeological Institute**. The town bus No. 6 which runs between the Central

The original bogeymen – the Bugis of South Sulawesi

The Bugis were, and remain, coastal adventurers from S Sulawesi. They became renowned throughout the region for their sailing skills and fearlessness. Often likened to the Vikings, the appearance of an elegant Bugis schooner (**see page 867**) offshore would strike fear into coastal communities. Reports of fleets of Buginese boats plundering the islands around Java date back to the beginning of the 16th century, and when the Portuguese captured Melaka in 1511, a large Bugis fleet is said to have been sent to ward off the impertinent newcomers. Bugis wealth was not just founded on violence however; they were also skilled businessmen and controlled much of the trade between the islands of the Malay world.

Such was the Bugis' success in imposing their will across Southeast Asia, that by the early 18th century they controlled the sultanates of Johor, Kedah and Perak on the Malay Peninsula, and had established their own kingdom or *negeri* at Selangor near present day Kuala Lumpur. Their success inevitably brought the Bugis into conflict with the colonial powers, and by the late 18th century the Dutch and English between them had ejected the Bugis from Malaya. Befitting their role as the scourge of the archipelago, the English word bogey, or bogeyman, is derived from bugis (**see page 866**).

Market and Perumnas, along Jalan Rajawali, stops by the fort.

NE of Fort Rotterdam, on Jalan Diponegoro is the **Tomb of Prince Diponegoro** (**see page 596**) along with his genealogy chart. He challenged the Dutch in Java for 5 years during the early part of the 19th century, finally being arrested in 1830 and exiled to Manado; from there he was transferred to Ujung Pandang where he spent the remaining 27 years of his life in Fort Rotterdam.

North of the fort, are a number of **Chinese temples** on (or near) Jalan Sulawesi, the earliest of which dates from the early 18th century. Just W of here, off Jalan Martadinata is one of the three harbours where boats are loaded and unloaded with every conceivable merchandise. Further N still, at the edge of the city and 3 km from the centre, is **Paotere Harbour**. *Pinisi* schooners, a smaller version of the famous island-linking bugis schooners, can be seen berthed here (**see page 867**). Wiry men laden with sacks and timber climb the narrow planks to load the boats with cargo. Get there by bemo from the Central Market, or by becak.

Running S from Fort Rotterdam is the seafront road, **Jalan Penghibur**. During the cooler evening hours, scores of *soto* carts and other stalls set-up along the road S from the *Makassar Golden Hotel* to sell cheap food to promenading locals. Not far away at Jalan Mochtar Lofti 15, is the residence of Clara Bundt. An avid collector of marine life, her house is now a museum displaying a collection of **seashells and corals**. Many of the beautiful shells are also for sale. Behind the house, the garden is filled with orchids and roses (best time to visit Mar-Sept). **NB**: the rather run-down house looks locked; walk through the garage to reach the shell collection and garden. Open: Mon-Sun.

The **Sutera Alam Silk Factory** at Jalan Onta 47 is one of the best places to watch women laboriously spinning and weaving silk in a range of vibrant colours. This goes on upstairs, while the ground floor is a shop, selling a good range of silks, both plain and patterned, by the metre. Dyeing is done in the central courtyard. The **Pasar Sentral** (Central Market) is a huge market, up Jalan Cokroaminoto and just to the N of Jalan Ramli.

Excursions

Old Gowa lies S of town and was the administrative centre of the once powerful Sultanate of Gowa (see history, **page 860**). Sights of interest here include a

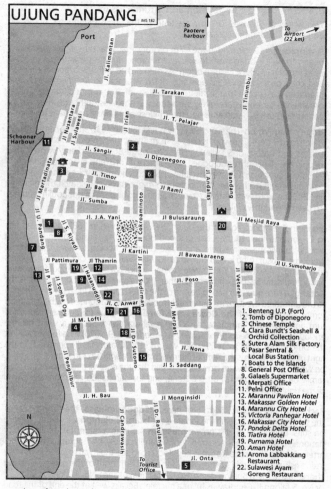

UJUNG PANDANG IMS 182

To Paotere harbour

To Airport (22 km)

Port

Jl. Kalimantan

Jl. Tarakan

Jl. Nusantara

Jl. Sulawesi

Jl. Irian

Jl. T. Pelajar

Schooner Harbour

11

Jl. Sangir

2

Jl Diponegoro

Jl. Martadjpata

3

Jl. Timor

6

Jl. Bandang

Jl. Andalas

Jl. Bali

Jl Ramli

Jl. Sumba

Jl. J.A. Yani

Jl Bulusaraung

Jl Mesjid Raya

Jl. U. Pandang

Jl Cokroaminoto

20

1

8

Jl S. Riyadi

Jl Kartini

Jl Bawakaraeng

7

Jl Pattimura

Jl Thamrin

10

Jl U. Sumoharjo

13

Jl P. Ikan

19

Jl Hasanuddin

12

Jl Jend Sudirman

Jl. Poso

Jl Latimo Jong

Jl Veteran

9

14

Jl Somba Opu

22

Jl. Merpati

17

21

16

Jl. C. Anwar

4

Jl. M. Lofti

18

Jl. Dr. Sutomo

Jl. Nona

15

Jl Penghibur

Jl S. Saddang

Jl. H. Bau

Jl Monginsidi

Jl Candrawasih

Jl Dr. Ratulangi

N

To Tourist Office

Jl. Onta

5

1. Benteng U.P. (Fort)
2. Tomb of Diponegoro
3. Chinese Temple
4. Clara Bundt's Seashell & Orchid Collection
5. Sutera Alam Silk Factory
6. Pasar Sentral & Local Bus Station
7. Boats to the islands
8. General Post Office
9. Galaels Supermarket
10. Merpati Office
11. Pelni Office
12. *Marannu Pavilion Hotel*
13. *Makassar Golden Hotel*
14. *Marannu City Hotel*
15. *Victoria Panhegar Hotel*
16. *Makassar City Hotel*
17. *Pondok Delta Hotel*
18. *Tiatira Hotel*
19. *Purnama Hotel*
20. *Aman Hotel*
21. *Aroma Labbakkang Restaurant*
22. *Sulawesi Ayam Goreng Restaurant*

number of tombs and a 'palace', spread over several square kilometres; they are not particularly exciting architecturally but are historically significant. About 8 km S of Ujung Pandang, just before the archway welcoming visitors to Sungguminasa, a road to the left leads to Old Gowa and its sights. The **Syech Yusuf Mosque** is a short distance off the main road. Next to the mosque are some tombs and graves; the grave of *Syech Yusuf* (1626-1694) is sacred to Muslims and an important pilgrimage spot. Yusuf was a 17th century religious scholar who left Gowa on a pilgrimage to Mecca in 1644 and never returned to Sulawesi alive. Instead he settled in Banten, West Java in 1671 where, with the support of a force of fierce Makassarese soldiers, he was instrumental in

Bogeymen and antimacassars

Two words of Sulawesi origin have entered the English language: bogey or bogeyman, and antimacassar.

Antimacassar Beginning in the 17th century, macassar oil – a hair dressing – began to be exported from Makassar to Europe. It later became the generic term for all hair oils of Eastern origin. As men slicked with the oil, greased sofas and chair backs all over Europe and North America, so antimacassars were produced to soothe the ruffled sensibilities of house-proud wives. These ornamental coverings are rarely seen today in the West although they are in widespread use in aeroplanes and the Chinese also have a penchant for them.

Bogey, Bogeymen The word bogey was first used in 1836 and is a semi-proper name for the devil. The word is derived from Bugis, the name given to the feared pirates and traders of S Sulawesi (see box, **page 864**). Thackeray wrote "The people are all naughty and bogey carries them all off" and even today, parents in Europe and North America still invoke the bogeyman at bedtime, warning that if children misbehave the bogeyman might come and snatch them away. In 1865 the word was bastardized once again into bugbear, a hobgoblin reputed to devour naughty children.

organizing resistance against the Dutch. He was captured in 1682, and exiled first to Ceylon and then to the Cape of Good Hope. To the consternation of Muslim purists, supplicants come here and make offerings hoping to have their wishes granted by Yusuf, who is also known as Tuanta Salamaka or 'Our Lord who grants us blessings'. Also here is Yusuf's wife's tomb – which is a pilgrimage spot for women having difficulty bearing children. Another 1 km along this road, on a bend, is the **Katangka Mosque**, claimed to be one of the oldest mosques in Sulawesi (although to the untutored eye it seems remarkably modern). It is surrounded by the pyramidal tombs and **graves of the Gowa royal family**. Continue for another 100m and turn right to reach **Tamalate**, a second royal graveyard. Set on a slight hill, the enclosure includes the *tomb of Sultan Hasanuddin* (1629-1670) who fought against the Dutch from 1666 to 1669 when weight of VOC arms finally prevailed. To the right of the enclosure is the *Tempat* (literally 'place') *Pelantikan* or Inauguration Stone, on which the Sultans were crowned. It is said that the original ancestors of the royal family descended to earth on the stone, and the coronation ceremony bestowed divine right of kingship.

Back on the main road, 3 km S of here, is **Sungguminasa**, the former seat of the sultans of Gowa. Facing the square is the **Istana Ballampoa**, a wooden palace on stilts, built in 1936. It is now a **museum**, housing a rather tatty collection of national costumes, a backstrap loom, family trees, photographs and other artefacts. The **Treasure Room** is kept locked; to see the royal regalia (or *pusaka*) inside ask at the bupati's office, across the square in front of the palace. **Getting there:** take a town bus (*bis damri*) No. 2 (via Panakukang), No. 4 (along Jl. Veteran) or No. 5 (along Jl. Candrawasih), or a microlet. Becaks wait at the end of the road to take visitors to the tombs.

The **hill resort of Malino** lies 70 km E of Ujung Pandang, past Sungguminasa, at an altitude of 1,050m, on the slopes of Mount Bawakaraeng (also known as Mount Lompobatang). The best day to visit is Sunday – market day – when traders from the surrounding hills bring produce to sell here. There are good walks through the surrounding forests. *Takkapala Waterfall* is 4 km S of town, with swimming pools. **Accommodation:** in basic hotels/losmen. Guides are available in town for longer treks and to climb Mount Bawakaraeng which rises to 2,876m. **Getting there:** take a bus running towards Sinjai or charter a car.

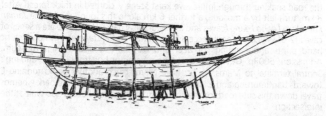

Source: Horridge

The *Pinisi* schooner of Sulawesi

One of the most evocative sights in Indonesia is that of a *bugis* or *pinisi* schooner. In the past, these boats carried cargo to all the main ports of the region. But the elegant boats that can be seen today docked at Ujung Pandang, Surabaya, Balikpapan, Sunda Kelapa (Jakarta) and other ports across Indonesia are in fact modelled on Western schooners of the 19th century. The design of the boat has continually changed as advances have been incorporated – *pinisi* only refers to the current design. They weigh from 120-200 tonnes, have a ketch rig of 7 sails, and twin rudders. When fully loaded – usually with water resistant cargoes such as timber – the decks are virtually awash.

Today, many *pinisi* are also fitted with a 10-cylinder Mercedes engine – which costs almost as much as the boat itself – and which gives the vessels an average speed of 8-12 knots. But, despite these advances in design, the schooners are still built without plans, using handsaws and traditional tools. Instead of metal nails and bolts, 30 cm-long pegs of ironwood (*belian* or *kayu ulin*) are used to bind the *pajala* hull together below the waterline. The problem for shipyards in Southern Sulawesi is that there is almost no ironwood left – forcing shipwrights to use inferior alternative woods. The best boats are said to be made in Banjarmasin (**see page 828**) where ironwood is still plentiful. Despite competition from alternative forms of marine transport, Indonesia's *pinisi* fleet remains one of the largest surviving fleets of sailing craft in the world.

Offshore Islands There are a number of beautiful islands off Ujung Pandang, easily accessible as day trips from the city. **Lae Lae Island** is 3 km offshore and is populated by Makassarese fishermen. Tiny **Samalona Island** is a 45 min boat ride across the harbour and is one of the best places to go on a day trip from Ujung Pandang. It is a popular local resort with swimming, snorkelling, fishing and waterskiing (admission to the island: 2,000Rp). Snorkelling equipment is available for hire on the island. **Accommodation: C** (more at weekends), *Pulau Samalona* have house boats and chalets, T 22417, F 312838 for reservations. **Barrang Lompo Island** is rather further afield and offers excellent snorkelling; many of the shells on sale at Clara Bundt's museum in Ujung Pandang are pillaged from the reefs around Barrang Lompo. Simple accommodation available. **Getting to the islands**: boats for all 3 of these islands leave from the dock just N of the Makassar Golden Hotel on Jl. Pasar Ikan, or from opposite the Fort. Regular ferries leave daily at 0900, returning at 1400 and 1600 with 2 extra outward services on Sat and Sun at 1400 and 1600. Private boats can be chartered, approx. 25,000Rp for a half day.

Caves at Taman Purbakala Leang Leang are 42 km NE of Ujung Pandang, and 14 km from Maros. **Maros** is a riverside town 28 km N of Ujung Pandang. Great rafts of bamboo can be seen being floated down the Maros River, which flows through the town. In Maros, a turning to the right is signposted to Bantimurung, the road snaking through impressive karst scenery, clothed in thick forest. After 8 km, turn left by a mosque; a further 6 km along this rough road is the *Taman Purbakala Leang Leang* (caves and archaeological park). Here there are a series of caves (2 of which are easily accessible – *Pettae* and *Pettakere*), with prehistoric hand prints and paintings of deer and ox. There is also a small museum. Admission: 500Rp. **Getting there:** take a bemo or bus from Ujung Pandang's Sentral terminal to Maros, ³/₄ hr; from Maros catch another bemo running E towards Bantimurung and alight after 8 km at the turn-off for the park – bemos travel down this side road for the final 6 km to the caves; becaks also wait at the intersection.

Bantimurung Falls lie 41 km NE of Ujung Pandang on the road to Bone and are hard to miss – the entrance is marked by a monstrous archway in the form of a concrete monkey. The impressive falls cascade over a smooth rock surface, and a spectacular number of butterflies fill the air over the plunge pool. Alfred Russel Wallace came here in 1856 and was astounded by the myriad of butterflies. However, the numbers are dwindling as local boys use nets to catch protected species to sell to unscrupulous tourists. The whole area is rather ruined by an over-enthusiastic use of concrete, with grottos, bridges and concrete animals disfiguring the area. There is a swimming pool and restaurant. About 1 km above the falls is *Gua Mimpi* or Dream Cave. **Accommodation: D-E** *Wisma Bantimurung*. Admission: 900Rp to the falls area; 200Rp to the top of the falls; 200Rp to enter the associated caves. **Getting there:** take a bemo from Ujung Pandang's Sentral terminal to Maros ³/₄ hr and then another from Maros to Bantimurung ¹/₂ hr. Alternatively, charter a taxi (25,000Rp), or book a tour (60,000Rp).

Tours Most tour companies run city tours, day trips to Bantimurung (60,000Rp), Malino (80,000Rp) and to the off-shore islands. Overnight tours are also available to Toraja (about US$200 for 4 days/3 nights), and to the megaliths of Central Sulawesi (US$400 for 8 days/7 nights).

Accommodation Ujung Pandang has a good range of mid- and upper-bracket accommodation. Losmen for budget travellers are thin on the ground and often dirty. **A** *Makassar Golden*, Jl. Pasar Ikan 50, T 314408, F 317999, a/c, restaurant, pool, best hotel in town, with great position on the seafront, attractive pool, the deluxe rooms are in separate bungalows (rec) on the waterfront, the standard rooms are windowless and grim; **A** *Marannu City*, Jl. Selatan Hasanuddin 3-5, T 21470, F 21821, a/c, restaurant, pool, ugly hotel block in city centre, with very dirty pool; **A** *Victoria Panhegar*, Jl. Jend. Sudirman 24, T 311556, F 312468, a/c, restaurant, pool, central and comfortable, well managed, rec; **B** *Delia Orchid Park*, Jl. Urip Sumaharjo Km 6, T 24111, a/c, out of town, in garden compound with orchids and birds; **B** *Losari Beach*, Jl. Penghibur 3, T 23609, F 319611, a/c, excellent position on the seafront close to Fort Rotterdam, ugly furnishings but comfortable enough rooms; **B** *Makassar City*, Jl. Chairil Anwar 28, T 317055, F 311818, a/c, restaurant, central location with good amenities, but characterless; **B** *Marannu Garden*, Jl. Baji Gau 52, T 852244, T 21821, a/c, restaurant, large pool with no shade, inconvenient location S of the city, bungalows have little character, tennis; **B** *Marannu Pavilion*, Jl. M.H. Thamrin 2, T 22234, F 21821, a/c, uninspired concrete block but central position; **B** *Pondok Delta*, Jl. Hasanuddin 25A, T 22553, F 312655, a/c, small hotel, large rooms, friendly, rec; **B** *Venus Golden*, Jl. Botolempangan 17, T 24995, a/c, medium-sized new hotel, very clean; **B-C** *Wisata Inn*, Jl. Sultan Hasanuddin 36-38, T 24344, F 312783, some a/c, immaculate, medium-sized hotel with rooms set around courtyard; **C** *Losari Beach Inn*, Jl. Pasar Ikan 10, T 24363, F 6303, a/c, attractive position overlooking the sea, rooms could be cleaner; **C** *Oriental*, Jl. W.R. Monginsidi 38A, T 83558, some a/c, ramshackle and grubby, but cheap a/c rooms; **C** *Tiatira*, Jl. Dr. Sutomo 25, T 311301, a/c, hot water, friendly, price includes breakfast; **C** *Widhana*, Jl. Botolempangan 53, T 22499, some a/c, hot water; **C** *Wisma Amala*, Jl. Arif Rate 6, T 854709, small hotel, clean, price includes breakfast; **D** *Marannu*, Jl. Bulukunyi 19, T 81919, some a/c; **D** *Purnama*, Jl. Pattimura 3-3A, T 23830, central location and good value; **D** *Sentral*, Jl. Bulusaraung 7, noisy and dirty; **F** *Aman*, Jl. Mesjid Raya, opposite the mosque, popular, but small rooms and unpleasant bathrooms.

Restaurants One of the saving graces of Ujung Pandang is its delicious, inexpensive seafood. The local speciality is *ikan bakar* – barbecue grilled fish.

Indonesian: ♦♦*Aroma Labbakkang*, Jl. Chairil Anwar 25, excellent seafood restaurant with ugly grotto exterior, frequented by the Ujung Pandang Chinese community, rec; ♦♦*Asia Baru*, Jl. Salahutu 2, good seafood and Indonesian (delicious jackfruit stew); ♦♦*Empang*, Jl. Siau 7, seafood and Indonesian, popular; ♦♦*Sulawesi Ayam Goreng*, on corner of Jl. Hasanuddin and Jl. Ince Nurdin, popular, with some tables outside, amongst the barbecue smells, chicken and fish; ♦♦*Surya*, Jl. Nusakembangan 16, crab is their speciality, but they also serve prawns, squid and fish and other Chinese dishes; above *Galeal's supermarket*, on Jl. Hasanuddin there is a cheap ♦*self-service* restaurant serving a range of good Indonesian dishes.

International: there is little to offer in the way of W food although the large hotels have coffee shops and restaurants serving international cuisine. There are several bakeries/pastry shops and ice-cream parlours (the one in front of the *Golden Makassar Hotel* is recommended) and a *Kentucky Fried Chicken* above Galael's supermarket on Jl. Hasanuddin.

Foodstalls: the best place to eat cheaply in the evening is along the waterfront, where hundreds of stalls set up to serve the local community.

Entertainment Cinema: **Studio 21**, Jl. Dr. Ratulangi (near intersection with Jl. Lanto Dg. Pasewang), a/c cinema showing occasional Western films; **Benteng Theatre**, Jl. Ujung Pandang. Karaoke bars: **Irani**, S end of Jl. Somba Opu.

Sport Golf: **Makassar Golf Club**, 14 km N of town off the road to the airport; open to non-members, clubs for hire. Swimming: the *Victoria Panhegar* and *Marannu City* hotels both allow non-residents to use their pools, 2,500Rp (although neither are very good), as does the inconveniently located *Marannu Garden*, S of town, where there is a large, often empty, pool.

Shopping Antiques: shops along Jl. Somba Opu and Jl. Pasar Ikan. Good antique buys are still to be had in Ujung Pandang, but these are outnumbered by the fakes on sale. **Baskets**: Jl. Tinumbu. Shops along Jl. Nusantara and Jl. Kakatua sell rattan and bamboo. **Ceramics**: N end of Jl. Somba Opu. **Gold and silver**: several shops along Jl. Somba Opu. **Silk**: **Sutera Alam**, Jl. Onta 47 (**see page 864**), 18,000Rp/m (plain), 27,500Rp/m (patterned). **Market**: Jl. Sultan Alauddin, good local baskets.

Banks & money changers **Bumi Daya**, Jl. Nusantara 70-72; **Rakyat Indonesia**, Jl. Slamet Riyadi; **5,BNI**, Jl. Sudirman; **Bank Dagang Negara**, Jl. Nusantara 147-149.

Local transport Bemos: locally known as *pete pete*, 200Rp around town; the main terminal is by the central market, appropriately named 'Sentral'. Bemos from here to most local destinations. **Becaks**: known as *tiga roda*, they are available all over town. **Metered taxis**: flagfall 800Rp, or hired for the day through your hotel for about 80,000Rp.

Town buses (bis damri): run set routes, most setting off from the Sentral terminal (200Rp): No. 1 to Daya, No. 2 to Sungguminasa via Jl. Panakukand, No. 3 to Batangase and the airport via the toll road, No. 5 to Sungguminasa via Jl. Cendrawasih, No. 6 to Perumnas via Jl. Rajawali. Bus No. 4 leaves from the Pannampu Market along Jl. Veteran to Sungguminasa.

Useful addresses General Post Office: Jl. Andi Pangerang Petta Rani, E of town. Post Office: Jl. Slamet Riyadi 10. Area code: 0411. Immigration Office: Jl. Sultan Alauddin 34A, T 83153. Wartel: Jl. Bawakaraeng 84 (for fax, telegrams and telephone).

Airline offices **Bouraq**, Jl. Veteran Selatan 1, T 83039; **Garuda**, Jl. Slamet Riyadi 6, T 22543; **Mandala**, Jl. Irian 2A, T 317965; **Merpati**, Jl. G. Bawakaraeng 109, T 4114; **Sempati**, Jl. Cendrawasih 178, T 81270.

Tour companies & travel agents *Ceria Nugraha*, Jl. Usman Jafar 9, T 22482, F 311848; *Libra Golden Star*, Victoria Panhegar Hotel, Jl. Sudirman 26, T 312841, F 312468; *Mattappa*, Jl. Pattimura 16-18, T 3932; *Pacto*, Jl. Jend. Sudirman 56, T 32208; *Nitour*, Jl. Lamaddukelleng 2, T 217723; *P.T. Aksa Utama Tour and Travel*, Artis Bldg, Jl. G. Lompobattang 3, T 22417, F 312838.

Tourist offices *Dinas Pariwisata*, Jl. Selatan Alauddin 105B (travelling E, turn left off Jl. Alauddin just after the Wisma Diklat Dep. Agama – it is 75m down a rough road), T 83897, inconveniently located some distance SE of the city centre, free maps and brochure, open: 0700-1400 Mon-Thurs, 0700-1100 Fri, 0800-1300 Sat; *Kanwil Pariwisata*, Jl. Andi Pangerang Petta Rani, T 317128, inconveniently located E of the city centre, some handouts, open: 0800-1400 Mon-Thurs, 0800-1100 Fri, 0800-1300 Sat.

Transport to & from Ujung Pandang 70 km from Malino, 155 km from Pare Pare, 180 km from Bone (Watampone), 328 km from Rantepao.

By air: Ujung Pandang's Hasanuddin Airport is 23 km N of the city centre (30 mins drive). Regular connections by Merpati/Garuda, Sempati and Bouraq with numerous destinations including daily direct flights to Ambon, Balikpapan, Biak, Denpasar, Jakarta and Surabaya. Within Sulawesi, there are connections with Gorontalo, Kendari, Manado, Palu, Maumere and Tana Toraja (for Rantepao). *Transport to town:* Taxis to the city centre cost 13,000Rp; city bus (bis damri) No. 3 goes past the airport from the Central Market (on the toll road) – it is a 1 km walk to the airport buildings. *Airport facilities:* a money changer, information desk (poor) and hotel booking counters.

By bus: the Panaikang Terminal for long-distance buses is at the E edge of town on Jl. Urip Sumoharjo just past Ujung Pandang University. Regular bemos run between the terminal and the Sentral bemo station in the city centre. Regular connections with Tana Toraja 10 hrs, Bone Bone 4 hrs, Pare Pare, Senkang 5 hrs, Soppeng 4 hrs, Bulukumba, Selayar, Palopo and other major destinations in South Sulawesi. No direct buses to destinations further N except Poso. There are also buses to Bajoe, where nightly ferries depart for Kolako in Southeast Sulawesi (10,000Rp). *Liman Express*, Jl. Laiya 25 and *Litha*, Jl. G. Merapi 160 run buses to Toraja via Pare Pare; *PIPOSS*, Jl. Buru 10A operates buses to Palopo; while *Cahaya Bone*, Jl. Andalas 33 have a service to Bone.

By boat: Ujung Pandang is a major port and a good place to catch a ship or boat; 8 Pelni ships stop here – there are 4 ships a fortnight to Jakarta and 6 to Surabaya (see route map, **page 1008**). The Pelni Office is at Jl. Laks. E. Martadinata 38, T 317965. Kalla Lines run a ship which follows a 2 week loop stopping at Jakarta, Surabaya, Balikpapan, Tarakan, Pantoloan and Ternate. The Kalla Lines office is at Jl. Jend. Sudirman 78, T 82464. Ships leave from the Pelabuhan Sukarno to the N of town. Pinisi schooners also run regularly between Ujung Pandang's Paotere harbour and most other ports in Sulawesi and beyond; simply ask around.

UJUNG PANDANG TO TORAJA via Pare Pare

The road from Ujung Pandang runs N for 28 km to the riverside town of Maros. Here it divides, one route running NE through Bantimurung to the capital of the former Bugis kingdom of Bone – Watampone – 180 km from Ujung. Continuing N from Watampone, the road passes through the attractive silk weaving town of Sengkang and then follows the coast N to Palopo. The more usual route runs N from Maros up the coast, usually out of sight of the sea, but on occasions passing through small fishing villages with attractive clapboard houses on stilts, before reaching the port of Pare Pare, 155 km from Ujung Pandang. From here, the road turns inland and threads its way upwards between limestone crags and past ricefields – scenically stunning, but exhausting by bus. 156 km from Pare Pare the road reaches the district capital of Makale and, 17 km N from Makale, the town of Rantepao – in the heartland of the Toraja. From Rantepao, the road turns E and descends spectacularly to the coastal town of Palopo, a distance of 62 km, where it meets up with the road from Sengkang.

Pare Pare

Pare Pare is South Sulawesi's second city with a population of 100,000 – although it feels more like a market town. The 'city' runs eel-like up the coast and for much of its length is only 2 or 3 streets wide. The centre is marked by the **Monumen Rakyat Pejuan**; a statue of a man, staff in hand, pointing into the distance and standing on a map of Indonesia.

Primarily a trans-shipment point for inter-island cargoes, Pare Pare is a quiet town. Visitors usually only come here as a stopping-off point between Ujung Pandang and Rantepao, in Tana Toraja; it is also a good port to catch a passage to Kalimantan (see below). The small **La Bangenge Museum** is 2 km S of town in Bacukiki sub-district; it has a small collection of local enthnographic pieces. Get there by becak. There is an attractive, provincial, multi-domed **mosque** on Jalan Hasanuddin.

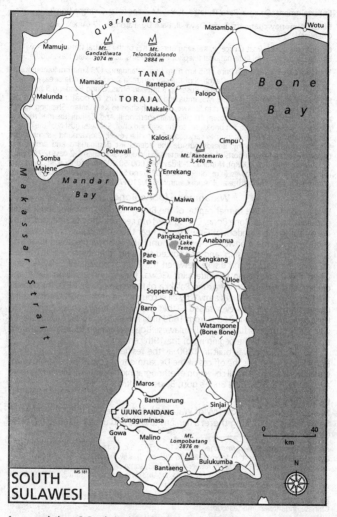

Accommodation; **C** *Gandaria*, Jl. Bau Massepe 171, T 21093, some a/c, clean, though small, rooms, pleasant courtyard and open-air restaurant; **D** *Tanty*, Jl. Hasanuddin, T 21378, rather over-priced, but rooms are clean enough; **E** *Siswa*, Jl. Baso Dg. Patompo 3, T 21374, attractive colonial façade, dirty rooms, not rec.

Restaurants Good, fresh, grilled seafood – particularly the excellent *ikan bakar* – is one reason to visit Pare Pare. The food is grilled in front of the restaurants, and there are a number just N of the central statue on Jl. Baso Dg. Patompo: **♦♦***Asia*, Jl. Baso Dg. Patompo 25, also serves Chinese food; **♦***Monas*, Jl. Baso Dg. Patompo 33; **♦***Sedap*, Jl. Baso Dg. Patompo 21, good fish; **♦***Sempurna*, Jl. Bau Massepe, good Indonesian and Chinese food.

Entertainment Cinema: **Pare Theatre**, Jl. Bau Massepe (near *Gandaria Hotel*).

Banks & money changers **Bumi Daya**, Jl. Baso Dg. Patompo 17 (Amex, US$, Travellers' Cheques).

Useful addresses Post Office: Jl. Karaeng Burane 1 (S of the central statue, corner with Jl. Bau Massepe). **Wartel** (international telephone, telegrams, fax): Jl. Sultan Hasanuddin 53.

Transport to & from Pare Pare 155 km from Ujung Pandang, 173 km from Rantepao. **By bus**: the bus terminal is on Jl. Delma, S of the city centre (a short becak ride or easy walk to the centre), just off Jl. Bau Massepe. Buses to Rantepao 6 hrs, Ujung Pandang 3 hrs, Bone Bone, Soppeng, Majene, Palopo, Masamba and Sengkang 3 hrs. **By boat**: regular ships call at Pare Pare and it is the best port in Sulawesi to catch ships to Kalimantan. Shipping agents are concentrated in 2 areas of town, 10 mins walk apart: on Jl. Andi Cammi (the road running parallel to Jl. Bau Massepe but one closer to the sea) and on Jl. Sulawesi (just N of the central statue). Rates and length of journey vary according to the vessel; shop around – some of the ships are barely seaworthy. Boards outside the agents list destinations and arrival and departure dates. Regular ports of call in Kalimantan include Balikpapan 1-2 days (20,000Rp), Samarinda 2 days (20,000Rp), Nunukan 2-3 days (40,000-50,000Rp) and Tarakan. Ships also call at other ports in Sulawesi (e.g. Toli Toli, 40,000Rp) and Surabaya, Kupang and Dili among others. Pelni have their office at Jl. Andi Cammi 96, T 21017.

Watampone (Bone Bone)

Watampone was the former capital of the Bugis kingdom of Bone, and it is still popularly known as Bone Bone. During the 16th century, the city emerged as the main rival to the Kingdom of Gowa based near Ujung Pandang, and it was not subdued by its more powerful neighbour until 1611. Gowa pressured Bone into a subordinate relationship, and also forced the king to embrace Islam. This left an enduring distrust and dislike between the 2 great powers of Sulawesi, and when the Dutch began to undermine Gowa, they found a willing ally in the brilliant and ruthless Prince Arung Palakka of Bone (**see page 862**). It was with the help of Arung Palakka's army – by all accounts one of the most fearsome any Indonesian power has ever raised – that the Dutch finally conquered Sultan Hasanuddin of Gowa in 1669. From 1669 until his death in 1696, Arung Palakka was the most powerful man in all Sulawesi. Bone continued to be an important trading centre until the beginning of the 19th century.

The **Bola Soba** was built in 1890 as the residence of Baso Pagiling Abdul Hamid; it now houses the offices of the Department of Education. The **Museum Lapawawoi**, with a small collection of ethnographic pieces, is on the main square and is worth a visit. Bone Bone's port, Bajoe, is 4 km E of town.

Excursions

Mampu caves lie 34 km NW of Watampone, and are said to be the largest in South Sulawesi. **Getting there**: a minibus to Uloe and then a bemo to the caves (ask for *Gua Mampu*).

Accommodation **B** *Watampone*, Jl. Biru 14, T 362, a/c, restaurant, pool, modern, clean but featureless, the 'best' in town; **C** *Mario Pulana*, Jl. Kawerang 16, T 98, some a/c, price includes breakfast; **C** *Rio Rita*, Jl. Kawerang 4, T 53, some a/c, attached mandi, small hotel, attractive and quiet, price includes breakfast; **D** *Amarah*, Jl. Jend. A. Yani 2A, T 569, small, noisy, but clean rooms, price includes breakfast.

Restaurants Several restaurants along Jl. Mesjid. **♦♦***Pondok Selera*, Jl. Biru 28, best in town, Chinese, Indonesian and seafood.

Local transport Bemo: around town for 150Rp.

Transport to & from Watampone 180 km NE of Ujung Pandang. **By bus**: connections with Ujung Pandang 6 hrs, Pare Pare, Sengkang and Rantepao 8 hrs. **By boat**: there are nightly ferries departing 2000 from Bajoe, Bone Bone's port, to Kolaka in Southeast Sulawesi, 8 hrs (10,000Rp). Bemos run regularly between the town and the port, 4 km to the E.

Sengkang

Sengkang is a Bugis town and the capital of Wajo district with one of the most attractive settings in Sulawesi, overlooking Lake Tempe. The town is a good base

Buginese textiles of Sengkang

It is said that 4,700 women weave nearly 500,000 sarongs a year on back-strap looms in the Sengkang area. This is the only place in Indonesia where silk is produced in large quantities. Imported yarn tends to be used for the warp, and local yarn for the weft. Chemical, aniline dyes have replaced natural dyes to a large extent but traditional Buginese designs are still much in evidence. These include plaids, checks and stripes. The distinctive zig-zag pattern – known as *bombang* or wave pattern – is produced using a warp ikat technique. Also popular are floral designs picked out using a supplementary metallic weft.

to explore the surrounding countryside – there are some excellent walks. Sengkang and nearby villages are also highly regarded for their silk weaving (see box).

Accommodation **D** *Apada*, Jl. Durian, restaurant, the house of a Buginese aristocrat transformed into a hotel with traditional atmosphere, the rooms are clean; **E** *Ayuni*, Jl. Puang Ri Maggalatung, colonial house with spacious, clean rooms and attached mandi, rec; **F** *Wisma Pondok Eka*, Jl. Maluku, traditional wooden house, welcoming owners.

Restaurants Several small restaurants, with good food at very reasonable prices. ♦*Melati*, Jl. Kartini; ♦♦*Romantis*, Jl. Petta Rani, excellent Indonesian; ♦♦*Tomudi*, Jl. Andi Oddang, chicken a speciality.

Shopping Silk: Sengkang is a centre of silk production, (see box). Hand-woven silk is becoming harder to find, but there is plenty of machine-made cloth; try the factory, *Mustaquiem*, on Jl. A. Panggaru.

Transport to & from Sengkang By bus: the terminal is in the town centre; regular connections with Ujung Pandang, Watampone, Palopo, Rantepao 6-7 hrs and Pare Pare.

TORAJA

The mountainous N region of South Sulawesi is inhabited by the Toraja. The name is probably taken from the Buginese words, *to ri aja* – meaning 'those people in the highlands upstream'. The Sa'dan Toraja live in the basin of the Sa'dan River at an altitude of 900-1,200m, in the administrative district of Tana Toraja (often known by its acronym Tator). They number about 320,000. The capital and largest town in the area is Makale, although Rantepao, a local market town about 17 km to the N, has developed into the main tourist base. It is to visit Toraja that most visitors venture to Sulawesi.

It is not hard to understand why this remote area should have become such a tourist attraction: cool and refreshing weather; breathtaking scenery of limestone cliffs sharply contrasting with lush valleys and terraced rice fields; and a people who live in extraordinary boat-shaped houses, spend their savings on elaborate funeral ceremonies, and place their dead in holes carved into the limestone cliffs. All this contributes to make Toraja one of the highlights of any trip to Indonesia.

History

Local mythology maintains that the Toraja originated from the island of Pongko'. It is said that 8 boats set sail from Pongko' and were driven by a storm onto the shores of S Sulawesi. Following the Sa'dan River upstream, the original ancestors arrived after a long and eventful journey in the area now known as Toraja.

Whatever the true origins of the Torajans, they remained isolated from the outside world for considerably longer than the Buginese and Makassarese of the coast. They experienced an unhappy period of occupation during the 17th century, when fierce Buginese warriors – aided and abetted by the Dutch East

The buffalo: symbol of wealth & power

Buffalo are the most highly prized animals in Torajan society. Wealth is measured in terms of buffalo – it is often said of a rich or important man "He has a lot of buffalo". Buffalo are also associated with men, while pigs are linked with women. Even today, riceland is not valued in terms of its yield but according to the buffalo standard – in other words, how many buffalo were sacrificed at the funeral of the field's previous owner. As Toby Alice Volkman writes in her book *Feasts of honour*: "Buffalo, in short, are symbols of the person, his land and ancestors, and his wealth and power".

Buffalo come with different colourings, hair swirls, horn shapes and eyes, and each of these factors is taken into account in the valuation of an animal. A buffalo with the right colour configuration can command a very high price. The most valuable are piebalds – but with white heads and black bodies – pink spots and blue eyes, known as *bonga*. They can be sold for as much as 6-7 million rupiahs (US$3,000-3,500). A standard slate grey buffalo, in contrast, sells for only 1-2 million rupiahs, while an all white animal is only worth 200,000 rupiahs (US$100). Also prized are long legs and horns. Buffaloes with black bodies are thought to be very strong and good for fighting.

The buffalo and their horns are status symbols; a buffalo is given as a bride price, as well as gifts at funerals. They are rarely put to work in the fields but are cosseted and pampered, bathed and polished, even their genitals rubbed, until it is time to present them for a sacrifice. Generally, a woman's funeral warrants the slaughtering of an additional animal – in payment for the milk she has provided for her children. Depictions of buffalo are prominent on Torajan houses and rice barns. Buffalo heads adorn the *tulak somba*, whilst stylized low relief images are often carved on doors of rice barns, on interior doors within the homes, or on the shutters of graves. They act as guardians, to ward off evil spirits.

Indies Company – invaded their land and ransacked their sacred burial sites. Naturally, the Toraja were incensed by this desecration and after a period of 7 years, they rebelled, slaughtered the interlopers and regained control of the area. Little information leaked out of their inaccessible highland home until the 20th century. The French Jesuit priest, Nicolas Gervaise, mentions the Toraja at the end of the 17th century, and the White Raja James Brooke also wrote of the 'Turajah' in the mid-19th century – but both were second-hand reports.

Two Swiss scientist-explorers, the Sarasins, together with a Dutchman, Van Rijn, were the first Europeans to cross the lands of the Toraja from coast to coast in 1902. However, even they failed to discover the Torajan heartland. It was not until 1905 that the Dutch finally decided it was time to extend their control into the highlands and to subdue these 'primitive' people. Among the Torajan leaders, only Pong Tiku resisted the Dutch for long. Fighting a guerrilla campaign, he and his men frustrated the Dutch for 2 years, finally succumbing to their enemy's far greater firepower in Oct 1906. An old woman, Ne'Bulaan, remembers when she first saw the Dutch: "I was just a girl, and then they came, thorns on their feet and smoke pouring from their mouths! Waduuh, I was scared". Pong Tiku was awarded with the title 'National Hero' in 1960.

On achieving supremacy in the highlands, the Dutch abolished slavery and, in 1913, sent the first missionaries of the Dutch Reformed Church into the area. But conversions were few: by 1930, only 1,700 Torajans had been converted to Christianity (1% of the population), and in 1950 when Indonesia attained independence, the figure had risen to just 10%. Today however, over 80% are nominal Christians – mostly Protestants – although traditional beliefs and practices still exert a pervasive influence, most clearly evident in their elaborate funeral ceremonies. This rapid spread of Christianity since independence is said to have been driven by the Torajan's fear of *to sallang* – Muslims.

Economy

In the past, the Toraja economy was founded on the cultivation of wet rice (**see page 514**) in the upland valleys that dissect the area. Rice is still the pre-eminent subsistence and ritual crop, although other activities are taking on increasing importance. The rice cycle lasts 6 months and in addition to white rice, black rice (*nasi hitam*) and red rice (mixed with coconut milk for sweets) are also cultivated. Other crops include maize, cassava and vegetables, while the raising of livestock, both for sale and ritual purposes, is also important.

Since the late 1970s, tourism has played an increasing role in the local economy. As ever, there are those who view this with concern, maintaining it is undermining local customs, and those who welcome it as a healthy diversification of economic activity. Many younger Torajans have moved away to Ujung Pandang, partly because of the lack of agricultural land and partly because they no longer want to farm. Paradoxically, this exodus has probably helped to keep Torajan traditions alive – the migrants send money home to finance funeral ceremonies and return for important ceremonies. When a migrant dies away from home, he will often be transported back to be buried with his ancestors.

Traditional society and religion

The Toraja world consisted of 3 classes of people: nobles or *to parengnge'* (literally, 'to carry a heavy load'), commoners or *makaka*, and – formerly – slaves, or *kaunan*. Slavery was common until the beginning of this century and there are numerous accounts of women being plucked from their fields and houses and sold into slavery. Even visiting the market demanded a protective escort, and many villages were surrounded by earthern and stone ramparts, and connected to neighbouring villages by underground passageways. People even sold their own brothers "like buffalo or vegetables".

The traditional 'religion' of the Toraja is called *Aluk to Dolo*, meaning Ceremonies of the Ancestors. It is based around the complementary elements of life and death, E and W, sunrise and sunset, morning and afternoon, and right and left (known to anthropologists as 'complementary binary opposition'). These contrasting elements are reflected in house architecture and the timing of rituals. Rituals associated with rice, and therefore life, are held in the mornings, people will face east and wear light clothes; while funerals are held after noon, people will face west and wear black. 'Rituals of the East' are known as *rambu tuka'*, which means 'smoke ascending', and are concerned with life-giving events. They include rice rituals, rituals of exorcism to heal the sick, birth rituals, the first haircut, circumcision, teeth-filing, body decoration, weddings – even growth, prosperity and the rising of the sun. 'Rituals of the West' or *rambu solo*, which means 'smoke descending' are concerned with death, decrease and the setting sun.

Village and house

Among the many notable features of Torajan culture and life are their stunning peaked houses. Many are anything from one to 3 centuries old, although the bamboo roofs are changed every 50 years or so. Houses are known as *banua*, or, if the house is the 'ancestral seat' of an important family, as *tongkonan* – a name derived from the word *tongkon*, which means 'to sit'.

The village Torajan villages or *tondok* have changed since the Dutch pacified the highlands at the beginning of this century. Before then, villages were built on ridges or at the top of hills to provide protection against attack. The Dutch encouraged communities to relocate in the valleys, and few of these newer villages have the defensive ramparts that were such a feature of earlier settlements. A village will often consist of a line of houses, facing a line of rice barns. The residence or *tongkonan* is the 'mother' house, while the rice barn or *alang* is the 'father' house. The latter is a miniature copy of the former. Tradition requires that the roof-lines of

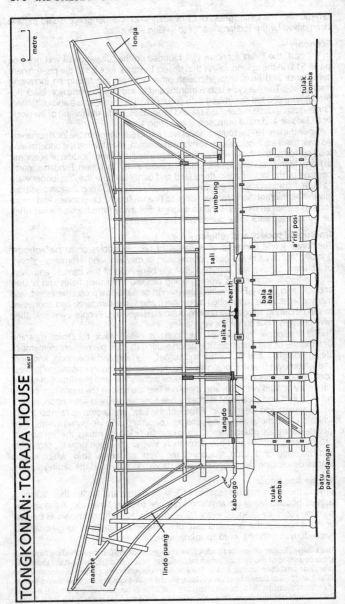

TONGKONAN: TORAJA HOUSE

0 — 1 metre

longa

tulak somba

sumbung

sali

hearth

lalikan

a'riri posi

bala bala

tangdo

kabongo

lindo puang

manete

tulak somba

batu parandangan

both are aligned N-S, a requirement which gives Torajan villages a certain orderliness.

Another important division is between the 2 ritual grounds that every village must have: to the W is an area reserved for burial rites and associated with death; to the E is an area associated with life, crops, livestock and the general well-being of the community. Villages should also have a rock face burial ground – although given the shortage of such sites, this may be shared with another village.

The house The Torajan house bears some resemblance to the houses of the Batak (see page 762), the Niha of the Nias Islands (page 766), and the Minangkabau (page 772). The shape resembles a boat, and this is said to symbolize the boats that brought the original inhabitants to Sulawesi (see above).

Torajan houses are raised off the ground on sturdy piles. The area between the piles, below the living quarters, is known as the *bala bala* and was originally used to stable buffalo. Today it is more commonly used for the storage of farm implements. A steep staircase leads from the E side of the house into the home. There are 3 rooms. The back room or *sumbung* is the sleeping quarters of the head of the household and his wife and small children. Valuables and important heirlooms are also stored here. Unmarried girls sleep in the front room or *tangdo'* (sometimes *sondong*). While the central room or *sali* is the main living and eating area, and is also used as the sleeping area for young, unmarried men. The hearth is positioned on the East side of the *sali* – the E, and food, both being associated with life. The Torajans never sleep with their feet pointing towards the W, as this is the direction of death.

The N gable of the house – facing the rice barn – is one of the most sacred parts of the house, particularly the triangular upper part, which is sometimes called the *lindo puang* or 'face of the lords'. The Torajans believe that this is where the gods enter the house and it is here that heirlooms are hung during important rituals. In the case of *tongkonan*, the lindo puang is protected by the overhang of the roof, which is known as the *longa*. The *tulak somba* are the posts at either end of the more important houses, which support the roof ends, and are often elaborately decorated with geometric patterns, buffalo horns, carved images of buffalo heads (known as *kabongo*) and images of the *katik* bird.

The rice barn or *alang* faces the home. It is like a house in miniature, but all the directions are reversed. This is because the rice barn neither belongs to one binary element, nor the other (see note on complementary binary opposition, page 875). It contains both the rice seed for the next year's crop and traditionally, human skulls. The rice barn is therefore a mediator, where life and death meet, and so its orientation is inverted. In Western culture the classic mediator is New Year's Eve – neither one year nor the next – when, for example, officers serve their men, reversing roles. In Thailand and Laos, New Year – or Pimai – usually falls in mid-April, but again it represents a period when people can take liberties, dousing one another with water. The impressive piles supporting the structure are round, unlike those of the house which are rectangular. The wood of these piles is polished, to prevent mice from climbing up into the granary. The platform below the storage area is used for sitting and socializing as well as for sleeping during festivals. The inner walls of the barn and the ceiling of the sitting area are traditionally decorated with geometric patterns and scenes from everyday life. The area of ground between the house and the rice barn is known as the *parampa* and is used to dry rice or coffee, as a space for children to play, men to stage cock-fights and women to work (for instance, at weaving).

The house represents a microcosm of the Torajan world. Like the houses of the Batak and Minangkabau, it can be divided into 3 sections: the roof and gables represent the Upper World of gods and spirits; the central living area, the Middle World of men and earthly concerns; while the *bala bala* represents the Under World. A central post, known as the *a'riri posi'* (or navel post) connects the whole structure with the earth.

The Torajan death ritual

The Toraja people are probably best known in the West for their elaborate death or funeral ritual – the *aluk rambe matampu'* – which transports the soul of the deceased to the next life. This elaborate ceremony is the major event in the life cycle of a Torajan and the costs of mounting an *aluk rambe matampu'* can be financially crippling for the family concerned. Rituals vary according to the rank and wealth of the dead person: for a noble, an elaborate ceremony is required, lasting up to 7 days; for a commoner, a more modest event, extending over only one or 2 days. Unless the deceased is given an appropriate funeral, he or she is unable to become an active ancestor and watch over the rice and the family group.

Torajan mortuary effigies (*tau tau*)

Tau tau means 'little person' and refers to the wooden, life-sized, effigies of the deceased, which are to be found on stone galleries carved out of the cliffs, or on wooden hanging galleries, positioned close to burial vaults. Tau tau images are only commissioned following the death of wealthy people or nobles. Some (lesser) tau tau – known as *tau tau lampa* – are made out of bamboo and cloth, but they are rare. Full tau tau are carved from the durable wood of the jackfruit tree (*nangka*) and are repaired every 25 years or so. An event known as *Ma'nene* is performed sometime between Jul and Sept, when the tau tau's clothing is replaced.

A living jackfruit tree is cut to provide the wood for the carving. The lemon-yellow wood is treated with coconut oil over several weeks to stain it to the colour of the Torajan skin, and then a specialist sculptor ritually carves the image. The body is made of several pieces which are moveable – rather like a puppet – and during the funeral ceremony the figure may be manipulated. As the tau tau is a 'living' representation of the deceased, great attention is paid to detail. Traditionally, the head was carved with almond-shaped eyes and finely formed features. Under the sarong, sexual organs are carefully carved – the male penis always erect. The clothing also helps to establish the identity of the deceased. In modern images, the figure is almost an exact representation of the deceased.

A problem that has arisen in recent years is the stealing of tau tau images. As demand for these aesthetically pleasing carvings has increased in the West, so the incentive to raid cliff face galleries has likewise increased. The spread of Christianity may also have played a role, reducing the traditional fear of these spirit-imbued figures. Today many are duplicates – the originals having disappeared during the night, doubtless to be sold to collectors.

The Torajans accept the ephemeral nature of life:

> "We are as the phantoms of this world,
> the apparitions of this region,
> as the wind that blows along the house."

The *aluk rambe matampu'* consists of 3 stages, which are adhered to whatever the status of the deceased: first the wrapping of the corpse and lamentation, then the funeral ritual and the associated slaughter of animals, and last the entombment of the corpse in a rock grave.

The wrapping and lamentation After a person dies, they are dressed in ceremonial clothes and placed on a chair in the southern-most room of the house. Several days later, the corpse is cacooned in multiple layers of funeral shroud and a kapok blanket and then transferred to the W side of the central room. The body remains in the house until the second phase. This may involve a wait of anything from 6 months to 6 years – indeed, in 1985, it was reported that there was one dead person still waiting to be buried who had died during the Japanese occupation. During this period of waiting, the death is not acknowledged; the deceased is referred to simply as the 'sick one'.

Over the subsequent months and years, considerable sums of money have to be amassed, relatives informed, a site chosen for the construction of the temporary houses needed to stage the ritual, and agreement reached on suitable contributions of buffalo. In addition, the rice has to have been harvested before the ceremony can commence. The following description of the second phase of the ceremony only applies to the *Diripai* – the most elaborate of the ceremonies. It should also be noted that because most Torajans are now nominal Christians, the traditional ceremony is becoming increasingly rare.

The funeral and ritual slaughter The houses for the funeral ceremony are constructed to form a square around the *rante* (the place chosen for the funeral rites). Older *rante* may have megaliths standing in them. In the centre of the rante stands the *lakkean* or 'corpse tower'. The tower is several storeys high and is surmounted with a roof similar in style to that of the Torajan house. A bier – or *sarigan* – is also constructed in the shape of a miniature house.

The second phase is heralded by the transferring of the body from the house to the floor of the rice barn. At this stage, a buffalo is sacrificed – preferably one with a white head and black body. The *tau tau* – a representation or portrait of the deceased (see box) – is held by the sculptor, who manipulates it, and precedes the body in procession to the rice barn.

After 2 days, the corpse is transferred to the bier and a colourful procession – known as the *mapalao* – moves off in the direction of the *rante* or funeral field. Upon arrival, the body is paraded around the central *lakkean* 3 times and is then transferred to a platform, where other family members sit.

From this point, the festivities get into full swing. Buffalo fights, dances, parades and kick fights (*sisepak*) take place (although kick fights have been officially banned). Funerals are important social events. As Torajans explain, "if there were no funerals, none of us would ever get married". The next day, the guests (dressed in black) are formally received and the slaughtering of the animals begins. Buffalo are slaughtered in a central area on the ceremonial field in front of the guests. This is not for the faint-hearted; the entire central area becomes awash with blood and gore, staring buffalo heads, bones, hooves, entrails and dung. The pigs are often slaughtered out of sight, and are then carried in for dismemberment, after having been singed over an open fire. In the past, the crowd would attack the animal alive and dismember it – this practice was banned by the Dutch. Each animal, as it is slaughtered, is registered in a notebook and a value placed against the gift. After offerings to the ancestors, the meat is shared out among the guests, palm wine (*tuak*) contained in bamboo is passed around, more dancing takes place and buffalo - and cock-fights (also banned) – are organized.

The entombment Several days later, after all the sacrifices have taken place and debts recorded, the guests start to leave, carrying their meat with them strung onto bamboo poles. A small procession of close family then accompanies the corpse to its final resting place with its ancestors (this stage is known as *mapeliang*). These resting places are traditionally burial vaults carved out of the limestone cliffs. Family members climb bamboo ladders and clear out a place in the vault to make room for the corpse. The body is placed in the tomb head first, with its feet towards the door; thus easing the passage of the soul to the next world (the *Tondok Bombo*, or Land of the Souls). Then the tau tau of the deceased is placed with the other mortuary effigies in a gallery on the cliff face. At this point a black chicken is released at the burial site, symbolizing the release of the soul.

Visiting a funeral ceremony

It is not difficult to find out where and when ceremonies are due to occur; local guides make it their business to discover where they are taking place and hotel staff are also often well informed. Jul and Aug are the most active funeral period as this coincides with the long Indonesian holiday and is the period when Torajans living away from home can return to their villages. If you are visiting a ceremony and are invited into the guests' enclosure, it is usual to bring a small gift – several packets of cigarettes for example. Visitors are generally welcomed at such events, but they should dress modestly and be sensitive to the occasion.

The burial chamber

There are 4 kinds of burial place in Tana Toraja. The oldest burial places are the *erong*, which date back about 500 years. These are beautifully carved wooden sarcophagi, which were placed at the base of cliffs. They were made in the shape of boats, houses or animals; possibly signifying different ranks of the deceased. Heirlooms and other valued possessions were placed in the erong along with the corpse. In the 17th century, marauding Buginese working for the Dutch East India Company invaded Tana Toraja and plundered these sacred burial sites (**see page 873**). When, after 7 years of occupation, the Buginese were ejected, the Toraja abandoned the erong system of burial as too vulnerable.

Instead, they began to cut tombs – known as *keborang batu* – high-up in inaccessible limestone cliff faces. This new form of burial was made possible due to the metal-working skills the Torajans had acquired during the Buginese occupation, enabling them to make iron chisels and other metal tools. They now placed their dead, along with their valuables, in these catacombs, safely sealed behind wooden doors. Only by climbing high up the vertical cliff face could these graves be plundered.

The most recent burial method to emerge is the **burial 'house'**. These are associated with the pacification of the area in the 20th century and, also, a simple lack of cliff space. An example of these ground-level tombs can be seen at Ke'te Kesu' (**see page 882**).

Finally, there are the *'tree graves'* of babies who die before their first tooth is cut. The corpse is taken to an *antolong* tree (also known as *kayu mate*, literally 'dead wood'), and placed in a cavity hollowed out of the trunk. The hole is covered with fibres from the sugar palm, a dog and pig slaughtered, and the tree allowed to grow around the baby's body (see Kembira excursion, **page 882**).

Further reading Crystal, Eric (1985) "The soul that is seen: the tau tau as shadow of death", in: Jerome Feldman (edit) *The eloquent dead: ancestral sculpture of Indonesia and Southeast Asia*, UCLA: Los Angeles. Well illustrated article. Kis-Jovak, J.I. *et al.* (1988) *Banua Toraja: changing patterns in architecture and symbolism among the Sa'dan Toraja, Sulawesi*, Royal Tropical Institute: Amsterdam. Wonderful black & white photo-essay with informative text. Nooy-Palm, Netty (1986) *The Sa'dan Toraja: a study of their social life and religion – rituals of the east and west*, Foris: Dordrecht. Dense but informative anthropological work. Volkman, Toby A. (1985) *Feasts of honour: ritual and change in the Toraja highlands*, University of Illinois Press: Urbana. Readable account – part academic, part personal – of an anthropologist's stay in Toraja.

Makale

Makale is the largest town in the Toraja region and the administrative capital of the district of Tana Toraja. Most tourists choose to stay in Rantepao, 17 km to the N, which has a much more extensive tourist infrastructure. However, there are a number of hotels and losmen in Makale. The heart of the town is arranged around a large – and sometimes empty – artificial lake. The **Pasar Umum** (General Market) is at the end of Jalan Pasar Baru.

Excursions Most of the sights in the area are equally accessible from Makale and Rantepao, and some are considerably closer to Makale (see Excursions Rantepao).

Accommodation A *Marannu City*, Jl. Pongtiku 116-118 (1 km N of town), T 22028, restaurant, pool, tennis courts, best hotel in Makale with good facilities but little character; **E** *Batupapan*, Jl. Pongtiku (2 km N of town); **E** *Wisma Bungin*, Jl. Nusantara 35, T 22255, central, near the lake, clean rooms with bathrooms, rec; **E** *Wisma Puri Artha*, Jl. Pongtiku, T 22047, N of town, basic; **F** *Losmen Merry*, Jl. Muh. Yamin 168, T 22013, rudimentary rooms, near bus offices. The main road has changed its name from Jl. Pongtiku to Jl. Nusantara – most of the hotels have yet to acknowledge the change.

Useful addresses Area code: 0423. Perumtel (international telephone, telegram and fax): Jl. Pongtiku 8 (N of town). **Hospital:** *Fatima*, Jl. Pongtiku 103.

Transport to & from Makale 17 km from Rantepao, 79 km from Palopo, 156 km from Pare Pare, 333 km from Ujung Pandang. **By air:** see Transport to & from Rantepao, **page 885**. **By bus:** regular connections with Rantepao 40 mins, Pare Pare and Ujung Pandang. Also buses to Poso and Palu 36 hrs, Tator, Watampone, Polmas and Pinrang. Most of the bus companies have their offices on Jl. Ikhwan, off the central square.

Rantepao

This rather ramshackle market town is utterly overshadowed by the beautiful countryside and villages which surround it. It has become a 'tourist centre' because it is undoubtedly the best base from which to explore the surrounding area. The 4 roads into town meet at a roundabout, where there is a miniature tongkonan (Torajan house). The central market has some handicrafts, textiles and 'antiques' for sale (see shopping).

Excursions

Getting around the sites of Toraja Because the sites of interest around Rantepao are scattered over a wide area, it is easiest to charter a car or bemo for the day (see Local transport). Public bemos do travel along most roads, but it is often a time-consuming business getting from one sight to the next. It is also possible to hire motorbikes and bicycles in town (see Local transport). However, many visitors find that the best way to see the sights, and experience the

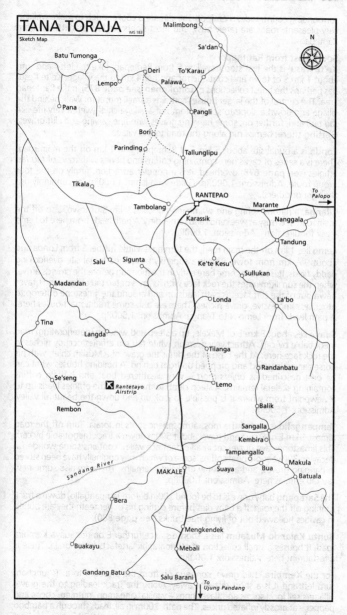

TANA TORAJA
Sketch Map
IMS 183

N

Malimbong
Sa'dan
Batu Tumonga
Deri
To'Karau
Lempo
Palawa
Pana
Pangli
Bori
Parinding
Tallunglipu
Tikala
Tambolang
RANTEPAO
To Palopo
Marante
Karassik
Nanggala
Salu
Sigunta
Ke'te Kesu'
Tandung
Madandan
Sullukan
Tina
Londa
La'bo
Langda
Tilanga
Se'seng
Lemo
Randanbatu
Rantetayo
Airstrip
Rembon
Balik
Sangalla
Kembira
Tampangallo
Makula
MAKALE
Suaya
Bua
Batuala
Sandang River
Bera
Mengkendek
Buakayu
Mebali
Gandang Batu
Salu Barani
To Ujung Pandang

surrounding countryside, is on foot. The climate is cool enough to make walking very pleasant, roads are rarely busy, and most sights are less than 10 km from Rantepao.

South-east from Rantepao

Ke'te Kesu' is the first stop travelling S from Rantepao; take the left-hand turn about 1 km S of town and continue for another 4 km to the village. Ke'te Kesu' has perhaps the finest collections of **tongkonan (see page 875)** in the Rantepao area. The central of the larger houses contains a small museum. Walk behind the village and down a slope to see the tomb of a village chief (with a very life-like *tau tau*) and, further on, some hanging graves with fine carving and cliff graves. **Getting there:** bemos run along the road to this village.

Londa is a burial site about 5 km S of Rantepao, and 1 km off the main road. There is a series of caves here containing coffins and bones with rows of *tau tau* effigies **(see page 878)** overhead. It is a popular attraction, firmly on the tour group route. Admission: 1,000Rp. Guide with lamp: 1,000Rp (or cunningly use the light of others).

Tilanga, a natural spring and swimming-pool, lies 9 km S of town, also off the main road. It is busy at weekends and rather dirty. A path leads from here to Lemo – ask for directions. Admission: 1,000Rp.

Lemo lies 1 km off the main road, the turning is a little further S from Londa and about 9½ km from town. This is a superbly positioned burial site overlooking paddy fields. It is best to come here early in the morning before the crowds arrive, when the sun illuminates the rock face with its rows of *tau tau* effigies and graves hewn out of the cliff face. A path leads up and around the limestone outcrop to other, less impressive, grave niches. There are also some more traditional houses here. A path leads from Lemo N to Tilanga. Admission: 1,500Rp.

Suaya lies about 8 km E of Makale, up a steep and winding (deteriorating) road (negotiable by car). Attractively decrepit white *tau tau* effigies occupy niches in the rock face here. At the base of the cliff is the grave of a Muslim chief, with his horse carved in wood and propped up from behind. A building houses what can be best described as *objets mort* – very weathered boat and buffalo coffins containing skeletal remains. A steep climb to the right of the effigies leads up to a viewpoint from where it is possible to look up and down the beautiful valley. Admission: 1,500Rp.

Tampangallo is one of the most atmospheric spots in Toraja. Turn off the road almost 1 km E of Suaya and travel about 500m down a track (negotiable by car). This limestone cave grave, set in a verdant rice valley, contains some wonderful decaying 300 year-old boat coffins, some of which may originally have been stored in hanging graves, and a quantity of skeletal remains. There are also some new *tau tau* effigies here. Admission: 1,000Rp.

The **Sarapang** baby grave is to be found 200m before Tampangallo, down a track running off the road. If a baby dies before cutting his or her teeth they are buried in cavities hollowed out of living tree trunks **(see page 880)**.

Buntu Kalando Museum lies a short distance further E on the Suaya-Kembira road. It houses a small collection of ethnographic artefacts from Toraja. There is a restaurant here. Admission: 1,000Rp.

For the **Kembira** child grave, continue on from the museum to a 'T' junction; turn left and it is a short distance away. Along the track leading to the grave, villagers sell local spices and flavourings – vanilla, cinnamon, nutmeg, cocoa and pepper – at grossly inflated prices. The path, 200m in all, leads through a bamboo

Trekking around Rantepao

One of the best ways to see and experience the Torajan highlands is to go on an organized trek for several days. There are a number of local guides in Rantepao who will arrange and lead trekking expeditions. There are few losmen outside the main towns, the exception being the village of Batu Tumonga, to the NW of Rantepao, where there are 5, and Mamasa. Outside these 2 villages, expect to stay with the *kepala desa* (headman), the local teacher, or with another family. Note that it is usual to bring small gifts for your host (soap, cigarettes etc.). Horses can sometimes be hired to carry baggage (10,000 Rp/day). Most treks explore the hills, valleys and villages to the W of Rantepao. Expect to pay US$60/day for 2, all inclusive (local guides hired independently of tour companies will be cheaper). The best time to trek is between Mar and Nov. Treks, with approximate length, include:

Rantepao–Sesean–Rantepao: 2 days/1 night
Rantepao–Sesean–Dende–Rantepao: 3 days/2 nights
Bittuang–Mamasa: 3 days/4 nights
Ulusalu–Pangala–Rantepao: 4 days/3 nights
Mamasa–Ulusalu–Rantepao: 5 days/4 nights

Trekking companies *Eskell*, Jl. Pongtiku, T 21344, F 21500, and *Ramayana Satrya*, Jl. Pongtiku, T 21336, F 21485 are both recommended. There are also many private guides who can be hired for about $25/day. Ask at your hotel.

Suggested equipment: Good walking shoes, hat, sweater for the nights, sleeping roll, sleeping bag, food for lunches, water (or a means of boiling, or sterilizing it), mosquito repellent, gifts for your hosts.

grove to a buttressed tree in which families have hewn-out niches for their dead children. These are then pegged over with a fibre curtain and the tree is allowed to grow around the corpse (**see page 880**). Admission: 1,000Rp.

Getting to the sights SE of Rentapao: most of these sights lie within walking distance of the main Rantepao-Makale road; bemos run constantly along the road. Bemos also run E from Makale to Kembira and then N to the market town of Sangalla before looping westwards back to the main road, coming out opposite the hospital N of Makale (9 km from Kembira).

North-east from Rantepao
Marante is 5 km E from Rantepao and 500m off the main road, set in a beautiful valley. There are some rather untidy cliff and cave graves here and some heavily carved *tongkonan*. Follow the path past the cliff graves and the bridge to a small group of traditional houses. From here, the path returns quickly to the main road. Admission: 900Rp. **Getting there:** regular bemos run along this road.

The turn-off for **Nanggala** is 7 km further E (12 km in all from Rantepao). The village is 1.8 km along the rough road, which makes for a pleasant walk. This village contains a great swathe of beautifully carved rice barns facing 2 houses, one said to be 500 years old. Admission: 1,500Rp. **Getting there:** regular bemos from Rantepao pass the turn-off for Nanggala.

North and north-west from Rantepao
Pangli, 8 km due N from Rantepao, contains a house grave and *tau tau* effigies. At this point the road forks; one route runs NW, while the main road continues due N. An alternative to taking the main road N is to trek along the path from **Tallunglipu**, just N of Rantepao, to **Bori** (where there are some huge *rante* stones), 6 km in all from Rantepao, and from there to the road running E-W, which is only 1½ km from Pangli.

Palawa is a hamlet 2 km N from Pangli on the main road, and ½ km off the road

Torajan ikat blankets

Distinctive warp ikat blankets with bold, geometric designs in black, red and blue are important ritual objects in Toraja. At funerals, they are used to decorate ceremonial buildings and sometimes to wrap the corpse. They were traditionally made from home-grown and spun cotton, and took several months to make. Such originals are expensive and difficult to find today.

However, similar blankets made from imported yarn and coloured with chemical dyes are now made around Rantepao to supply the tourist market. One important weaving centre is Sa'dan, N of Rantepao. Motifs used for these textiles include representations of buffalo and tongkonan houses.

(9½ km in all from Rantepao). Palawa consists of a wonderful double row of *tongkonan* and rice barns, with stacks of buffalo horns, dense carving and carved life-size buffalo heads. Although many of the families have set up small souvenir stalls selling cloth, woodcarvings and jewellery, few tourists make it out here and the primary source of income is still agriculture. Admission: 500Rp. On the track to Palawa, about 200m before the village, is a group of neglected **megaliths**.

To'karau is a village another 1 km on the 'main' road N. A periodic market is held here.

Sa'dan is a market centre a further 4 km N. The town is an important ritual centre and has emerged in recent years as a centre of weaving. The cloths are made for the tourist market using imported yarn and chemical dyes, but maintaining traditional designs and motifs (see shopping, below).

Taking the W fork at Pangli the road leads to **Deri** where it deteriorates into little more than a track. Many treks start here. At the last count there were 5 homestays in **Batu Tumonga**.

Getting to the sights N and NW from Rantepao: bemos run from Rantepao through Pangli and on to Palawa, To'karau and Sa'dan with the road threading its way along a beautiful rice valley.

Tours Marthen Madoi at Wisma Tanabua on Jalan Diponegoro organizes 7 day tours to North Sulawesi. For **treks** in the surrounding countryside, see box, **page 883**.

Accommodation A large new hotel, the *Sahid Toraja* (A), has recently opened in Rantepao. **A** *Misiliana*, PO Box 01 (3 km S of town), T 21212, F 21512, restaurant, pool, large, new hotel with good amenities, comfortable rooms; **A** *Toraja Cottages*, Desa Bolu, Paku (3 km E of town), T 21089, F 21369, restaurant, pool, quiet location out of town, set on the side of a hill in attractive gardens; **A** *Toraja Prince* (3 km E of town), T 21089, F 21369, pool, new hotel with well appointed rooms; **B** *Hebron Inn*, Jl. Pembangunan, T 21519, rec; **B** *Indra City*, Jl. Dr. Ratulangi 28, T 21442, rooms set around a courtyard; **B** *Pondok Torsina* (50m off main road, ½ km S of town), T 21293, restaurant, pool, hot water, set among rice fields, large, clean rooms; **B** *Rantepao Lodge*, Jl. Pao Rura (1.5 km S of town), T 21248, restaurant; **C** *Indra I*, Jl. Landorundun 63, T 21163, restaurant, hot water, clean and comfortable, with an attempt at 'traditional' decor; **C** *Maria II*, Jl. Pongtiku (S of town), popular; **C** *Pison*, Jl. Pongtiku 8, T 21344 (just off main road, S edge of town), restaurant, very popular, good food, clean rooms with hot water and own balcony, rec; **C** *Pondok Wisata*, Jl. Pembangunan, new hotel, large clean rooms; **C-D** *Tanabua*, Jl. Diponegoro 43, T 21072, restaurant, clean, but the rooms are dark.

   D *Irama*, Jl. U. Abdul Gani 2, T 21371, restaurant, basic but clean; **D** *Maria I*, Jl. Dr. Ratulangi 23, T 21165, some hot water, quiet, friendly, simple rooms, nice garden, rec; **D** *Pia's Poppies*, Jl. Pongtiku (just off main road S edge of town), T 21121, restaurant, hot water, strange grotto-like bathrooms, the hotel has character and is friendly, price includes breakfast, rec; **E** *Flora*, Jl. Sesan 25, T 21210, small losmen near the mosque, rooms are clean but noisy; **E** *Rosa*, Jl. Pahlawan, T 21075, on the outskirts of town on the road to Sa'dan, quiet rooms with mandis in garden surroundings, rec; **E** *Sarla*, Jl. Mappanyuki 83; **F** *Marlin*, Jl. Mappanyuki 75, restaurant, basic but clean, motorbike hire; **F** *Palawa*, Jl. Mappanyuki 81.

Restaurants Most hotels have their own restaurants. Local specialities include black rice (*nasi hitam*), fish and chicken cooked in bamboo (*piong*), and palm wine (*tuak*). *Central Market*, for cheap warung food, Indonesian and Torajan; ✦*Dodeng*, Jl. Pembangunan 30 (on the market square), good Indonesian/Chinese menu and food; ♦♦*Indra I*, Jl. Landorundun 63, good hotel restaurant, rec; ♦♦*Pia's Poppies*, Jl. Pongtiku, unbelievably slow service and overambitious menu; ♦♦*Pison*, Jl. Pongtiku 8, good Indonesian/Chinese food, with Torajan specialities, rec; *Rachmat*, Jl. Achmad Yani, large and central, geared to tour groups, Indonesian/Chinese; ♦*Satria Desa*, Jl. Diponegoro 15, basic Indonesian dishes; ♦♦♦*Tamu Pub & Restaurant*, Jl. Mappanyuki, for Torajan specialities order 2 hrs ahead.

Sport Swimming: the small pool at the *Toraja Cottages* is open to non-residents (3,000Rp).

Shopping Rantepao has a selection of shops selling crafts and some antiques. Most are concentrated in the town centre on Jl. Achmad Yani, and on the ground floor of the central market. Crafts include hats, basketry, carved wooden statues, model tongkonan, and bamboo containers. Antiques include weavings and carved house panels.

Banks & money changers Raya Eka Abadi, Jl. Achmad Yani 102; **Danamon**, Jl. Achmad Yani (next to Post Office); **Rakyat Indonesia**, Jl. Achmad Yani.

Local transport Bemos: the 'station' is behind the central market. **Chartered bemos**: can be picked up anywhere and cost about 10,000Rp/hr. **Car hire**: from 45,000Rp/day. **Motorbike hire**: about 10,000Rp/day. **Bicycle hire**: about 3,000-5,000Rp/day. To hire cars, motorbikes or bicycles ask at your hotel.

Useful addresses Post Office: Jl. Achmad Yani 111. Poste Restante available. **Area code**: 0423. **Perumtel**: Jl. Achmad Yani (next door to Post Office).

Airline offices Merpati, Rantepao Lodge, Jl. Pongtiku (S of town).

Tour companies & travel agents *Ramayana Satrya*, Jl. Pongtiku, T 21615, F 21485.

Tourist offices *Rantepao Tourist Office*, Jl. Achmad Yani, T 21277, free maps but little else, open: 0730-1400 Mon-Sun.

Transport to & from Rantepao 17 km from Makale, 62 km from Palopo, 173 km from Pare Pare, 350 km from Ujung Pandang. **By air**: Pongtiku airport is just N of Makale and 21 km S of Rantepao. It is spectacularly built along a mountain ridge. Daily flights to Ujung Pandang. *Transport to town*: minibuses wait for the daily flight to take passengers to Rantepao (5,000Rp). Merpati have their office in the *Rantepao Lodge*, S of town. **NB**: fog is a problem at Pongtiku airport and it is not uncommon for planes to be unable to land, and the return flight to be cancelled. In addition, the flights are regularly over-booked in the tourist season, particularly the return flight to Ujung Pandang – the shortness of the runway and the altitude means that only 8 seats are filled on the flight and it must be one of the few airports where both the passengers as well as their luggage are weighed-in. The office also sometimes fails to register reservations made through other Merpati offices (it is not on-line). It is best to allow for a day extra in Ujung Pandang, if connecting with an onward flight. **By bus**: buses leave from outside the bus offices N of and around the market on Jl. Mappanyuki. Regular connections with Palopo 2 hrs, Ujung Pandang 9 hrs, Pare Pare 6 hrs, Watampone, Pendolo 10 hrs, Poso 12½ hrs, Tentena 11½ hrs and Palu 18-24 hrs. For the windy journey S to Pare Pare and Ujung Pandang, try to get a seat on one of the larger buses, not on the cramped and uncomfortable minibuses. Bus offices are concentrated along Jl. Mappanyuki and include *Litha* at No. 18.

Palopo (Luwu)

Palopo is a quiet coastal town, sandwiched on a narrow slice of lowland between Bone Bay and the South Sulawesi Highlands. It is useful as a stopping-off point on the arduous journey between Central Sulawesi and Toraja. There is a **museum** on Jalan Andi Jemma, which was formerly a palace. It contains a modest, but interesting collection of local ethnographic artefacts and some Asian ceramics. Admission: 2,000Rp. Fishing boats, ferries and *pinisi* schooners dock at the long pier reaching out into the bay.

Accommodation D *Buana*, Jl. K.H. Ahmad Dahlan, T 664, some a/c, clean; **D** *Kumdah Indah*, Jl. Opu Tosapaille, some a/c, best hotel in town, clean, pleasant and well-run; **D-E** *Adifati*, T 467, some a/c, new.

Transport to & from Palopo **By bus**: buses to Rantepao 3-4 hrs, Ujung Pandang 8 hrs and N to Tentena, Poso and Palu. **By boat**: regular connections with Malili and Kolaka (Southeast Sulawesi).

SOUTHEAST SULAWESI: Kendari, Kolaka and the Buton & Muna Islands

The province of Southeast Sulawesi, with a population of 1.4 million, is very rarely visited by tourists and has only limited facilities for the traveller. The provincial capital is Kendari on the E coast; Kolaka, on the W coast, is the ferry port for South Sulawesi. Off Southeast Sulawesi's S tip are the large and formerly influential island kingdoms of Buton and Muna. The province is relatively rich in natural resources with nickel mines, asphalt and timber. It is also an important transmigration settlement area (see page 732).

Kolaka

A minor port and transit point for South Sulawesi. Ferries from Bajoe, Watampone's port, dock here and there is accommodation for those forced to stay overnight.

Accommodation **E** *Alkaosar*, Jl. Jend. Sudirman 20; **E** *Rahmat*, Jl. Kadue 6, own mandi; **F** *Pelita*, Jl. Repelita 56.

Transport to & from Kolaka   173 km from Kendari. **By bus**: regular buses to Kendari, 3½ hrs. **By boat**: nightly ferries to Bajoe (Watampone's port) 10 hrs.

Kendari

Kendari lies on the E coast of Southeast Sulawesi and is the capital of the province. It was developed by the Japanese as a military base during their occupation of Indonesia when the capital was moved from Baubau on Buton Island to Kendari. As the provincial capital, it is endowed with all the usual paraphernalia of government and has a population of over 100,000. The town is strung-out, ribbon-like, over several kilometres.

Excursions

Moramo Waterfall which cascades down 7 terraces, is 50 km S of town. The pools at each level make for pleasant swimming. **Getting there:** by bus (1¾ hrs) from the Madonga terminal.

Tours *Alam Jaya*, Jl. Konggoasa 50, T 21729, organizes 5-7 day trips around Southeast Sulawesi; *BPU*, Jl. Konggoasa 48 will organize boat and car trips around the area.

Accommodation At present, accommodation is rather expensive, with few cheap places for travellers to stay. **A** *Kendari Beach*, Jl. Hasanuddin 44, T 21988, a/c, restaurant, out of town and expensive, but the only upmarket place in town, attractively positioned overlooking the bay, with tennis courts; **C-D** *Armins*, Jl. Diponegoro 55 and Jl. Diponegoro 75, some a/c; **E** *Cendrawasih*, Jl. Diponegoro, best place for budget travellers.

Banks & money changers It is advisable to change Travellers' Cheques before travelling to Southeast Sulawesi.

Useful addresses Post Office Jl. S. Ratulangi 79. **Area code**: 0401.

Airline offices Merpati, Jl. Konggoasa 29, T 21729.

Tourist office on the hill behind the harbour, T 21764.

Transport to & from Kendari 173 km from Kolaka. **By air**: the airport is 35 km N of town. *Transport to town*: minibus 30 mins (4,000Rp), or share a taxi service for 5,000Rp/person. Regular connections on Merpati with Ujung Pandang. **By bus**: regular connections with Kolaka 3½ hrs from the Wawotobi terminal, 7 km from town (regular bemos into town for 150Rp). From Kolaka, there are ferries to Ujung Pandang (see above). **By boat**: a daily ferry leaves for Muna and Buton Islands (see below). A ship making a fortnightly circuit between Ujung Pandang and Surabaya also docks here.

Buton and Muna Islands

Buton and Muna islands lie side by side, off the SE tip of Southeast Sulawesi, separated from one another by the narrow Buton Strait. Buton is the larger and

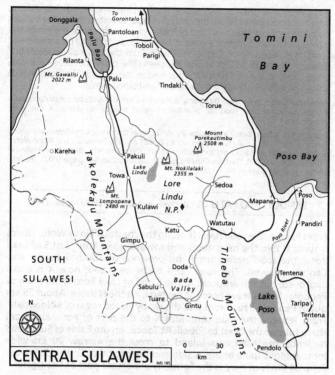

Donggala
To
Gorontalo
Pantoloan
Palu Bay
Toboli
Rilanta
Parigi
Mt. Gawalisi
2022 m
Palu
Tindaki
T o m i n i

B a y
Torue
Mount
Porekautimbu
2508 m
Kareha
Pakuli
Poso Bay
Towa
Lake
Lindu
Mt. Nokilalaki
2355 m
Sedoa
Takolekaju Mountains
Mt.
Lompopana
2480 m
Kulawi
*Lore
Lindu
N.P.*
Mapane
Poso
Poso River
Pandiri
Katu
Watutau
Gimpu
Pendolo
SOUTH
SULAWESI
Doda
*Bada
Valley*
Tineba Mountains
Sabulu
Tuare
Gintu
*Lake
Poso*
Taripa
Tentena
Tentena
N
0   30
km
CENTRAL SULAWESI IMS 185

more important of the 2 covering nearly 6,500 sq km with a population of over
400,000, while Muna has a land area of 4,900 sq km and over 200,000
inhabitants. They are administered as separate districts. The largest town is
Baubau, at the SW corner of Buton Island, and overlooking the straits to Muna,
with a population of about 50,000.

During the 16th and 17th centuries, Buton was a powerful local sultanate, making
vassal states of several neighbouring islands, including Muna. The Dutch made
contact with Buton in 1690, and were on friendly terms with the sultanate during
the VOC's confrontation with Gowa. It was off Buton in 1666 that the Dutch admiral
Speelman devastated the Makassarese fleet, leading to the downfall of Gowa.

Places of interest

In **Baubau**, the new **Wolio Kraton**, and a 16th century **mosque** within it are
worth visiting. The kraton contains an eclectic collection of local and colonial
artefacts. The hilltop **fort** was built by the Dutch in the early part of the 17th
century. About 10 km outside Baubau is **Nirwana Beach** with good swimming;
popular at weekends.

Raha is the capital of Muna Island. The main attractions here are
horse-fighting – a practice which seems to have been part of an ancient local
ritual – and the **caves** near Bolo (9 km from Raha), which contain prehistoric
paintings. Horse-fighting is best seen at the village of Latugo (24 km from Raha),

and can be arranged at a day's notice. The fight involves two riderless stallions, who are shown mares before the contest in order to agitate them. The stallions do battle until one loses heart and gallops away, at which point another animal is brought forward to fight the victor. If the fight gets vicious, the horses are prised apart. It is necessary to acquire permission from the National Archaeological Research Centre in Jakarta to visit the caves. The caves themselves are quite inaccessible, as they are high up – it is best to take a guide. Paintings include images of sailboats, hunters, the sun, deer and other animals.

Accommodation In Baubau: **D** *Liliyana*, Jl. Kartini. In Raha: **D** *Andalas*, comfortable, price includes breakfast, other food can be arranged, bemo available for charter; **E** *Tani*, price includes breakfast.

Transport to & from Buton and Muna By air: 2 connections a week on Merpati with Ujung Pandang. By boat: a daily ferry leaves from Kendari at 1400 for Buton and Muna islands docking, in order, at Raha 7 hrs and Baubau 15 hrs. The return ferry leaves from Baubau at 1300 and Raha at 2300. The Pelni ship *Rinjani* also calls at Baubau (**see page 1008**). The Pelni office is at Jl. Yos Sudarso 19, T 188.

PENDOLO TO PALU via Lake Poso and the Lore Lindu National Park

From Palopo, the road runs NE along the coastal plain to Wotu, where it turns N into the mountains and towards Lake Poso. Just S of Lake Poso, the road passes from the province of South Sulawesi into Central Sulawesi. This road used to be very bad; now it is much improved, but still arduous. At the S end of Lake Poso is the town of Pendolo; ferries leave here for Tentena, on the N shore. About 25 km out of Pendolo a road runs E to the rarely visited town of Kolonodale. From Tentena the road continues N to the port of Poso, and from there follows the coast to Toboli. At Toboli, on the E side of Sulawesi's N 'limb', the road cuts inland to cross the narrow 20 km-wide mountainous spine to the W side and the capital of Central Sulawesi, Palu. 34 km N of here is the formerly important port of Donggala.

Pendolo

Pendolo is a small town on the S shores of Lake Poso. There are regular boats from here N to Tentena – following an ancient trade route between Central Sulawesi and Toraja. This is the most relaxing way to make the journey N.

Accommodation Most people choose to stay in the more attractive town of Tentena, on Lake Poso's N shores, rather than in Pendolo. There is basic accommodation available however; the losmen are near, or on, the lake. **E** *Danau Poso*, Jl. Pelabuhan; **E** *Sederhana*, Jl. Pelabuhan; **F** *Masamba*, Jl. Pelabuhan, some private bathrooms.

Transport to & from Pendolo By bus: buses ply (very slowly) N to Tentena 6 hrs, and S to Palopo. The journey to Rantepao takes about 10 hrs. **NB**: although the road is being continually improved, during the wet season buses may be delayed. By boat: boats run between Pendolo and Tentena at the N end of Lake Poso, departing daily at 0800, 4 hrs. Strong winds whip across the lake later in the day.

Kolonodale

This small town on the rarely visited E coast of Central Sulawesi is the best base for trips into the magnificent **Morowali Nature Reserve** (see Excursions, below). It also provides easy access to **Tomori Bay**. The town has few facilities for tourists and is only for those who really want to be off the traveller's trail.

Excursions

The Morowali Nature Reserve covers over 160,000 ha of Central Sulawesi to

Lake Poso

This ancient, upland lake, at 600 m above sea-level, covers over 32,000 ha and is the third largest lake in Indonesia (after Toba and Towuti, the latter also in Sulawesi). Lake Poso is famed for its clear waters and for its rare fauna. 67% of species so far identified in Lake Poso are endemic – they are found nowhere else – and some are already thought to have become extinct. Early travellers to the lake reported seeing estuarine crocodiles (*Crocodylus porosus*) – some exceeding 5 m in length – although they now seem to have been hunted to extinction.

the N of Kolonodale, including extensive stands of virgin tropical rainforest, pristine coastline, and islands in Tomori Bay. Originally tagged as a potential site for transmigration settlements, the untouched environment and rich flora and fauna fortunately drove the government to gazette it as a national park in the 1980s. The park's fauna include the pig-deer or babirusa, the anoa (**see page 861**) and the maleo bird (**see page 900**); the black orchid is also found in Morowali. **Accommodation**: none available as yet but the coastal Bajo people and the interior Wana tribe do sometimes offer homestays; it is best to book a tour in Palu (**see page 892**), Tentena or Poso or hire a guide in Kolonodale – ask at your hotel. **Best time to visit**: during the dry season, October to February. **Getting there**: on a tour or by boat (1½ hrs); there are also MAF flights to Tokala Atas and Beteleme, both outside the park's NE boundary.

Accommodation E *Cahaya Mori Ata*, Jl. Trans Sulawesi; E *Sederhana*, Jl. Yos Sudarso 13.

Transport to & from Kolonodale By air: MAF flies irregularly from Tentena to Kolonodale. By bus: buses leave daily from Pendolo 4 hrs, Tentena 6-7 hrs and Poso 10 hrs.

Tentena

Tentena is a small town situated on the N shores of **Lake Poso**. It has a cool and invigorating climate and a reasonable range of simple accommodation, making it the best stopping-off point between Palu and Toraja. A **210m wooden bridge** crosses the lake at this, its northern-most and narrowest extremity. Eels – which migrate as elvers from the sea 50 km away – and carp are trapped below the bridge. The largest eel caught measured 1.8m and carp weighing as much as 20 kg are also netted. Tentena was a centre of missionary activity in the area when 2 Dutch priests, Dr. A.C. Kruyt and Dr. Adriani, set up operations here in 1895. It still supports the oldest **Protestant church** in the province.

Excursions

Lore Lindu National Park Tentena is one of the best spots to organize **treks** into the Lore Lindu National Park to see the **megaliths** of the **Bada Valley** (**see page 890**). Ask at the *Pamona Indah* for information.

Caves The limestone hills around Tentena, and along the shores of Lake Poso, are rich in caves, most of which are not as exciting as the tourist literature tries to make out. Most famous – in relative terms – is **Pamona Cave** near the Theological School, a series of caves running deep into the mountainside (it is said that no one has yet reached the end, or at least has returned to tell the story). Closer to town, near the offices of the Protestant church, are a number of caves with skulls and crude coffins.

Lake trips It is possible to charter boats in Tentena to venture out onto the lake (15,000Rp/hr), or to travel to Bancea and the **Bancea Orchid Reserve** on the W shore, where there are 50 species of orchid.

Accommodation Most hotels are on, or overlooking, Lake Poso. D *Pamona Indah*, a/c, on the lakeshore, with good, clean rooms, tours of lake arranged from here, rec; E *Panorama*, out of town, with good views over the lake; E *Wasantara*, some rooms with good views; F

Wisata Remaja, Government guesthouse.

Transport to & from Tentena 57 km S of Poso. **By air**: MAF (Missionary Aviation Fellowship) operates an irregular service to Palu, Gintu (twice a week) – in the Bada Valley – Kolonodale and other, even more remote, destinations in Sulawesi. Note that MAF is not a commercial airline and may decline to take passengers. **By bus**: connections N to Poso 2 hrs, Palu 10 hrs and S to Pendolo 6 hrs, Rantepao and Ujung Pandang; also buses E to Kolonodale. **By boat**: to Pendolo, on the S shores of the lake (the best way to travel S); departs at 1600, 6 hrs (2,000Rp).

Poso

Poso is the largest town in the area and the capital of the district of Poso. The people of the area are largely Christian, converted at the beginning of this century by a very patient member of the Dutch Reformed Church. The town is scattered with churches and administrative buildings, with a central market on the W side of town and the few hotels and restaurants on the E side.

Accommodation **D** *Bambu Jaya*, Jl. Agus Salim 105, T 21570, some a/c, clean and comfortable; **E** *Kalimantan*, Jl. Agus Salim 14, T 21420, old hotel with big, light rooms; **E** *Nels*, Jl. Yos Sudarso 9, T 21013, private mandi, friendly and clean; **F** *Beringin*, Jl. P. Sumatra 11; **F** *Sulawesi*, Jl. Agus Salim, T 21294, small, dark rooms but helpful owners.

Banks & money changers Negara Indonesia 1946, Jl. Yos Sudarso.

Airline offices Merpati, Jl. Sumatra 69A, T 94619.

Tour companies & travel agents *Aksa Utama*, Jl. Yos Sudarso 10, T 386.

Transport to & from Poso 57 km N of Tentena. **By air**: the airport is out of town – ask at the Merpati office to arrange transport. Merpati has 4 flights a week to Palu and Luwuk. **By bus**: regular connections N to Palu 7 hrs and S to Tentena (for example, with the bus company *Alugoro* on Jl. P. Sumatra 20). **By boat**: boats leave Poso harbour for Gorontalo, stopping along the way. Irregular boats to Ujung Pandang and Bitung (for Manado).

Lore Lindu National Park

The Lore Lindu National Park covers 229,000 ha of upland in Central Sulawesi between Palu and Lake Poso. Ranging between 300m and 2,610m above sea-level, the park is mainly composed of montane forest, with the upland Lake Lindu in the NW corner. The area is renowned for the massive and enigmatic **megalithic statues** and **'cisterns'** that lie scattered over the Bada, Besoa and Napu valleys (copies stand outside the Central Sulawesi Museum in Palu), and for its wonderful **birds**. 19 species of waterfowl have been identified on Lake Lindu including the spotted tree duck (*Dendrocygna guttata*) and the little pied cormorant (*Phalacrocorax melanoleuca*), and in the montane forests that characterize the national park there are flocks of such insectivorous birds as the Sulawesi leaf warbler (*Phylloscopus sarasinorum*), the mountain white-eye (*Zosterops montana*) and citrine flycatcher (*Culicicapa helianthea*).

The strange megaliths were erected by a people who have long-since disappeared and possibly date from the first millennium AD – archaeologists are still unsure. They are found in a number of spots in Central Sulawesi, but are most numerous in and around Lore Lindu. They are 'worked' stones, in the form of giant urns, menhirs, vats, stone blocks, statues and mortars. These are decorated with faces, lizards, figures and monkeys. What use they were put to is not certain although it has been postulated that they were burial chambers. They show a remarkable resemblance to the 'jars' of the Plain of Jars in Laos, although no connection between the 2 cultures has been identified. The greatest concentration of megaliths is near Gintu, at the S edge of the park.

Organizing a trip to Lore Lindu Few, though increasing, numbers of visitors make it to this remote spot and it is easiest to venture here on a tour (see below). Those intending to visit the park independently are recommended by the Tourist Office in Palu to first check-in at the PHPA Office also in Palu on Jl. Moh. Yamin for advice, although this is not strictly necessary. Guides can be found in Gimpu and Tentena and treks of 6 days or more link the 2 towns. Horses can also be hired, either to carry bags or to ride. The megaliths are in the vicinity of

1. Museum of Central Sulawesi
2. Pasar Bambaru
3. Pasar Masomba
4. Pasar Inpres
5. Post Office
6. Tourist Office
7. Immigration Office
8. Pelni Office
9. Golden Bakery
10. New Oriental Restaurant
11. Night Market foodstalls
12. Palu Golden Hotel
13. Pattimura Hotel
14. Central & Buana Hotels
15. Pasifik Hotel
16. Purnama Raya Hotel

B1. Inpres Bus Station
B2. Masomba Bus Station

Gintu (for instance, on the Sepe Plateau), and an additional, local guide needs to be employed here as the the statues are difficult to find.

Tours Palu is the main base for specialist tours to Lore Lindu; *Katriall Utama*, in Palu, is a specialist operator. Treks can also be mounted from Tentena; for instance, from the *Pamona Indah Hotel*, on the lakeshore.

Accommodation There are homestays/losmen in Gintu, Gimpu and Tentena, and it is sometimes possible to stay in locals' homes in Tuare. But outside these towns it is necessary to sleep in the open – often on covered bridges along with villagers away from home.

Best time to visit At the driest time of year from Jun to Aug.

Transport to & from Lore Lindu By air: MAF (Missionary Aviation Fellowship) flies to Gintu and Tentena from Palu. Note that MAF is not a commercial airline and may decline to take passengers. **By bus**: from Palu's Masomba terminal to Gimpu, 8 hrs (poor road); there are also regular buses from Tentena to Masomba.

Palu

Palu, with a population of 150,000, is the capital of the province of Central Sulawesi. Located on the S shores of Palu Bay, it is sandwiched between 2 ranges of mountains running N-S. Because it lies in the rain shadow, rainfall here is very low – only 600 mm – making the Palu valley one of the driest spots in Indonesia.

Palu is usually only visited as a rest stop on the arduous overland route N to Gorontalo and Manado, and S to Rantepao and Ujung Pandang. The Palu River neatly divides this dispersed town into 2.

Places of interest

The **Museum of Central Sulawesi** is at Jalan Sapiri 23. It houses a reasonable display of model traditional houses and assorted local ethnographic artefacts. Outside the museum stand replicas of the megaliths of Lore Lindu (**see page 890**).

Admission: 200Rp. Open: 0900-1600 Tues-Thurs, 0900-1530 Fri & Sat, 0900-1200 Sun. The central market, **Pasar Bambaru**, is N of Jalan Imam Bonjol, between Jalan Teuku Umar and Jalan Hr. Dg. Pawindu. It is a rather characterless, modern, concrete affair. More interesting are the **alleys** running E off Jalan Teuku Umar. The sprawling **Pasar Masomba** is SE of town, off Jalan Monginsidi.

Excursions

Donggala lies 34 km N of Palu and is a small, formerly important, port which has fallen on hard times since being eclipsed by other ports in Central Sulawesi. The road to Donggala runs along the W shoreline of Palu Bay past fishing villages and mangroves. With the hills rising up on either side it could almost be a loch in the Scottish highlands. Donggala is quiet and peaceful, the port picturesque, with cloves drying on the pavements. Boats can be caught from the dock in Donggala for other destinations in Sulawesi (see Transport to & from Palu). **Accommodation** here includes: **E** Bhakti, Jl. Hi. Samauna 9 and **Rame**, Jl. Pettalolo 51. 5 km N of Donggala is **Tanjung Karang Beach** with reasonable swimming. **Getting there:** take a kijang from the Inpres terminal at the SW corner of the Inpres market, just S of Jl. Kunduri, 40 mins (1,000Rp). Share taxis also travel between the 2 towns (1,250Rp), leaving from Jl. Imam Bonjol, not far from the intersection with Jl. Teuku Umar. Donggala station is S of the port; walk or catch a dokar into town.

Tours Palu is the base for specialist tours to the **Lore Lindu** and **Morowali National Parks** (see page 890). Recommended are the well-organized tours of *Katriall Utama*. A 5-day all-inclusive tour costs US$400-$450 (1-4 people). Treks to visit the hilltribes of Central Sulawesi are organized by the *Milano Restaurant*, Jl. Hasanuddin 2.

Accommodation A *Palu Golden*, Jl. Raden Saleh 1, T 21126, a/c, pool (usually empty), the characterful though run-down Palu Beach has been demolished and replaced by this nondescript structure, 'best' in town with comfortable rooms, tour groups stay here, discounts are often available; **B** *Wisata*, Jl. S. Parman 39, T 21175, F 22427, a/c, clean, well-run hotel, even has a fitness centre – of sorts; **C** *Pattimura*, Jl. Pattimura 18, T 21775, restaurant; **C-D** *Central*, Jl. R.A. Kartini 6 (behind Warpostel office), T 22418, a/c, immaculate new hotel run by Warpostel, price includes breakfast, rec; **D** *Buana*, Jl. R.A. Kartini 8, T 21475, some a/c, clean, pleasant atmosphere, walking distance from Masomba bus terminal, rec; **D** *New Dely*, Jl. Tadulako 17, T 21037; **E** *Kemajuan*, Jl. Cokroaminoto 57 (near the Pasar Baru), T 21479, basic; **E** *Pasifik*, Jl. Gaja Mada 99, T 22675, good clean rooms, best on airy top floor, rec; **E** *Penginapan Karsam*, Jl. Dr. Suharso 50, T 21776, rather dirty, attached mandis; **E** *Purnama Raya*, Jl. Dr. Wahidin 4, T 23646, with mandis, basic, but clean, rec; **E** *Taurus*, Jl. Hasanuddin, rooms and mandis could be cleaner.

Restaurants ♦*Andalas*, Jl. Raden Saleh 50, good Padang food; ♦*Golden Bakery*, intersection Jl. Hasanuddin and Jl. Dr. Wahidin, good cakes; ♦*Meranu Setiabudi*, Jl. Setia Budi 44, excellent Chinese/Indonesian and seafood; ♦*New Oriental*, Jl. Hasanuddin II, great Chinese food. **Foodstalls**: one of the most pleasant places to eat or drink is at the stalls which setup on the seafront, just W of the *Palu Golden Hotel* on Jl. Raja Moili. With the onshore breeze, view and wicker chairs it is very civilized and cheap.

Banks & money changers Concentrated on Jl. Jend. Sudirman, Jl. Imam Bonjol and Jl. Hasanuddin. Ekspor Impor, Jl. Hasanuddin.

Local transport Microlets: 250Rp around town.

Useful addresses General Post Office: Jl. Jend. Sudirman 15-17. **Area code**: 0451. **Warpostel**: Jl. R.A. Kartini 6. International telephone, telegram and fax. **Hospital**: Jl. Dr. Suharso 33, T 21270. **Immigration Office**: Jl. R.A. Kartini, T 21433. **PHPA Office**: Jl. Moh. Yamin.

Airline offices Garuda and Merpati, Jl. Hasanuddin 71, T 21172; **Bouraq**, Jl. Juanda 87, T 22995.

Tour companies & travel agents *Aksa Utama*, Jl. Hasanuddin 33, T 21295; *Bemagy Travel*, Jl. Raden Saleh 22, T 21126; *Katriall Utama*, Jl. Hasanuddin 10, T 23236, F 23017; *Rajawali*, Jl. S.I.S Aldjufri 12B, T 21095.

Tourist offices *Central Sulawesi Tourist Office*, Jl. Cik Ditiro 32, T 2175, open: 0800-1400

Mon-Thurs, 0800-1100 Fri, 0800-1300 Sat, handouts available and they will also help with organizing treks to Lore Lindu National Park and the Bada Valley (**see page 890**).

Transport to & from Palu **By air:** Palu's Mutiara airport is 7 km SE of town. Regular daily connections on Merpati or Bouraq with Ujung Pandang, Gorontalo, Manado Toli Toli and Luwuk, and 4 flights a week to Poso. There is an information and hotel booking counter at the airport. Taxis to town, 4,000Rp. **By bus:** the long-distance Masomba terminal is between Jl. Monginsidi and Jl. TG. Pagimpuan. Regular connections with Gorontalo 24 hrs, Manado 36 hrs, Rantepao 24 hrs, Ujung Pandang, Soppeng, Watampone, Sengkang, Palopo, Pare Pare, and Poso 8 hrs. Bus companies have their offices at Masomba terminal and bemos travel constantly between the terminal and the town centre. In addition, *Bina Wisata Sulteng*, Jl. S.I.S. Aldjufri 12B, run buses S to Ujung Pandang and Rantepao. Minibuses to Rantepao are operated by *Modern* on Jl. Pramuka (near intersection with Jl. Jend. Sudirman) 18 hrs. Regular connections with Poso 7 hrs and Tentena from bus offices on Jl. Raden Saleh (e.g. *Alugoro* at No. 48) and Jl. S. Parman (e.g. *Jawa Indah* at No. 5). Buses from these offices also travel along the E 'leg' of Sulawesi to such rarely visited towns as Bunta, Luwuk and Ampana. The roads N to Gorontalo and Manado and S towards Palopo are slow, although much improved in recent years and being further upgraded.

   By boat: boats leave from Donggala – 34 km N of town – irregularly, for Pare Pare and other destinations. Enquire at the harbour office on Jl. Mutiara in Donggala (see excursions for transport details to Donggala). Larger vessels, including the Pelni ships *Kambuna* and *Kerinci*, dock at Pantoloan on the E shores of Palu Bay (see route map, **page 1008**). Pelni office is at Jl. Gaja Mada 86, T 21696. Get to Pantoloan by bus from the Masomba terminal.

PALU TO MANADO via Gorontalo

From Palu, the road crosses Sulawesi's N limb to the E shore at Toboli and then follows the coast N to the attractive town of Gorontalo. Before Gorontalo, a road crosses the mountainous spine of the island to the small, out-of-the-way port of Toli-Toli. From Gorontalo, the road cuts across to the N coast and runs E to the provincial capital of Manado. The coral reefs off Manado offer some of the finest diving in Southeast Asia, and there are a large number of worthwhile excursions from the city. It is also a transport hub for air and sea connections with Maluku and Irian Jaya. Off Sulawesi's N coast are the rarely visited Sangihe and Talaud islands.

Toli-Toli

This small town on the N coast of Sulawesi's northern 'leg' is a locally important port but because it lies off the main trans-Sulawesi highway is not on the itineraries of most visitors. The mountainous spine further serves to isolate the town from the rest of the island and when the first five-year development plan, *Repelita I*, was introduced in 1969 the town was still inaccessible by land.

Excursions

Batu Bangga Beach offers the best swimming in the area; it lies 12 km N of town. **Getting there:** bemos runs north along the coast.

Lutungan Island lies only 1 km off the coast and is said to be the site of the tomb of one of the former kings of Toli-Toli. The surrounding waters offer reasonable snorkelling and swimming. **Getting there:** boats can be chartered from town; ask at your hotel.

Accommodation *Anda*, Jl. H. Mansyur 27; *Nirmala*, Jl. Jend Sudirman; *Salamae*, Jl. Jend. A. Yani.

Tour companies & travel agents *Alia Dirgantara Travel Service*, Jl. Suprapto 69.

Transport to & from Toli-Toli **By air:** Merpati operate one return flight a day to Palu. **By bus:** buses link Toli-Toli with Palu, Gorontalo and Manado; the trip is arduous. **By boat:** the

Pelni ship *Kerinci* calls at Toli-Toli on its fortnightly circuit (**see page 1008**). The Pelni office is on Jl. Yos Sudarso. Smaller ferries also operate between Toli-Toli and Donggala (Palu), Manado and Bitung.

Gorontalo

A peaceful, low-rise, low-key and friendly town with bendis, houses with verandahs, fretwork and wicker chairs. Few 'sights' as such, but a perfect place to rest-up on the overland route between Palu and Manado. Unlike so many other towns in Indonesia it has not yet suffered the scourge of the Redevelopment and Shopping Centre Disease. There are some wonderful examples of **Dutch provincial architecture** – the hospital on Jalan Jend. A. Yani and the Mitra Cinema at Jalan S. Parman 45 (Art Deco) for example. The **Pasar Satya Pradja** is at the intersection of Jalan S. Parman and Jalan M.T. Haryono. More interesting is the **Pasar Sentral** with its narrow alleys, at the intersection of Jalan Pattimura and Jalan Dr. Sam Ratulangi. Gorontalo has 2 small harbours – bigger ships dock at Kwandang, 45 km NW. To get to the smaller and closer **Pelabuhan Kota** (literally 'Town Port') take a bemo from the Pasar Sentral.

Excursions

Kwandang is a port 45 km NW of Gorontalo. Shortly before the town there are 2 **forts**, a short walk from the main road. **Getting there:** by bus from the Andalas terminal.

Panua Reserve lies about 100 km W of Gorontalo, on the coast near Marisa. This is one of the spots where the rare and extraordinary maleo bird (*Macrocephalon maleo*) nests – although uncontrolled egg collection has substantially reduced the number of nesting adults (**see page 900**). **Getting there:** by bus from the Andalas terminal.

Accommodation B *Saronde*, Jl. Walanda Maramis 17, T 21735, some a/c, biggest hotel in town, charming owner with good English, set around courtyard, range of rooms, rec; **C** *Indah Ria*, Jl. Jend. A. Yani 20, T 21296, some a/c, central, friendly, clean, price includes all meals, rec; **C-D** *Wisata*, Jl. 23 Januari 19, T 21736, some a/c, range of rooms, rec; **E** *Penginapan Sinar Utama*, Jl. Dr. Sam Ratulangi 33B, near market and bemo station, thin walls, dark but clean and homely; **E** *Teluk Kau*, Jl. S. Parman 42, T 21785, rather shabby and down-at-heel; **E** *Wisma Budi Utomo*, Jl. Budi Utomo 24, T 21564, clean and well run, rec; **F** *Penginapan Teluk Kau*, Jl. S. Parman 44, wonderful wooden villa, but rooms are dark and dirty, they will not always take foreigners.

Restaurants ◆*Foodstalls*, cheap and good, set up on Jl. Pertiwi in the evenings. ◆*Brantas*, Jl. Hasanuddin 5, bakery and reasonable Indonesian dishes.

Shopping Basketware: local baskets can be bought at the Pasar Sentral. *Krawang* embroidery: a speciality of the area. Shops along Jl. Jend. Suprapto.

Banks & money changers BNI, Bank Dagang Negara and Bank Rakyat Indonesia all on Jl. Jend. A. Yani near the intersection with Jl. M.T. Haryono.

Local transport Bemos: the main terminal is at the Pasar Sentral, at the N end of Jl. Dr. Sam Ratulangi, near the intersection with Jl. Pattimura. Frequent departures for the long-distance Andalas bus terminal. 200Rp around town. **Horse-drawn bendis:** 2,000Rp/hr for touring around town. **Microlets:** can be chartered for approximately 4,000Rp/hr for touring around town and the harbour.

Useful addresses General Post Office: Jl. Jend. A. Yani 14. **Area code:** 0435. **Perumtel:** Jl. 23 Januari 35.

Airline offices Merpati, *Hotel Wisata*, Jl. 23 Januari 19, T 21736; **Bouraq,** Jl. Jend. A. Yani 34, T 21070.

Transport to & from Gorontalo By air: Jalaluddin airport is 32 km NW of town. Regular daily connections by Merpati or Bouraq with Palu, Manado, Ujung Pandang and to Ternate and Ambon in Maluku. Minibuses wait to take passengers to town, 45 mins (3,500Rp). The road between Gorontalo and the airport passes through the charming town of Limboto 30 mins (4,000Rp). **By bus:** the long-distance Andalas terminal is on the outskirts of town; get there by regular bemo from the Pasar Sentral. Regular connections with Manado 12 hrs and

Palu 24 hrs. **By boat**: the main port is at Kwandang, 45 km NW of town, on the N shores of this 'leg' of Sulawesi. The Pelni ship *Umsini* stops here (see route map **page 1008**). Pelni office, Jl. 23 Januari 31, T 20419. There are regular buses to Kwandang from the Andalas terminal.

Manado

Looking out from the 'beach' front over Manado Bay, it is easy to understand why travellers such as Alfred Russel Wallace thought the area so beautiful: the 2 peninsulas curling around like crab claws, and Bunaken Island, the volcanic cone of Manado Tua, and the other islands, shimmering in the distance. However, for people arriving here after travelling through the quiet towns of Central and North Sulawesi, Manado is something of a culture shock – the city centre is brash, noisy and fast-paced. It is as if the influence of the nearby Philippines has filtered in across the Celebes Sea to transform the city.

Manado has a population of 275,000 and is the capital of the province of North Sulawesi. The area around Manado is known as Minahasa, and was a separate province until 1964, when it was combined with Gorontalo to form North Sumatra. Although rather featureless, it is – by Indonesian standards – visibly wealthy. This wealth is built primarily on cloves, but also on coconuts, nutmeg and coffee. The area is now being targeted for rapid tourist growth; the airport runway is being lengthened to take wide-bodied jets, and the big hotel chains are moving-in.

History

In the 16th century, Minahasa consisted of a number of small, independent states including Gorontalo, Limboto and the Talaud and Sangihe islands. The Spanish and Portuguese were already calling at ports in the area in the 1500s, and by the middle of the 16th century missionaries were having considerable success converting the population to Christianity. The Dutch concluded a treaty with the chiefs of Minahasa in 1679, heralding nearly 300 years of close association between the Christians of the area and the colonial government. Among the various peoples of the East Indies, the Dutch felt a greater affinity for the Minahasans than with almost any other group. This led to a proportionately greater role in the Dutch civil service and army, a rapid development spread of education and health facilities – in which Church schools were at the forefront – and a more pervasive 'Westernization' of culture.

It was this close association which played a part in encouraging rebels in North Sulawesi to join with the PRRI – the Revolutionary Government of the Indonesian Republic – in the Permesta rebellion of 1958 and challenge the authority of President Sukarno and his associates. The 2 centres of this rebellion against Jakarta were West Sumatra and North Sulawesi. Sukarno demanded harsh reprisals against the rebels, and in Feb 1958 the Indonesian airforce bombed Manado. By mid-May the army had overwhelmed the rebels in Gorontalo and in late-June recaptured Manado. The U.S., anxious about Sukarno's association with the Indonesian Communist Party even considered sending troops to assist the rebels; in the end they decided not to, but sent arms instead. The rebellion stuttered on until 1961 when the rebels were finally defeated.

Places of interest

There are few places of interest in Manado – most people come here for the incomparable diving and snorkelling, and for the sights outside the city (see below, Excursions). The **North Sulawesi Provincial Museum** is on Jalan W.R. Supratman (S of town) and has a moderate collection. Open: 0800-1330 Tues-Thurs, 0800-1030 Fri, 0800-1230 Sat and Sun. The **Ban Hing Kiong Chinese temple** is at the end of Jalan Panjaitan, in the centre of town. It was originally built in the early part of the 19th century, but has since been renovated. The temple is neither impressive nor unusual, with the requisite array of Chinese temple paraphernalia – incense, a predominance of gold, red and black, and

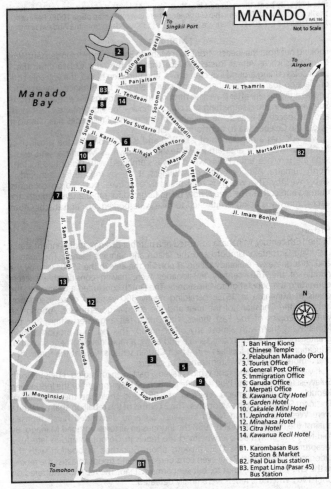

MANADO IMS 186
Not to Scale

Manado Bay

1. Ban Hing Kiong Chinese Temple
2. Pelabuhan Manado (Port)
3. Tourist Office
4. General Post Office
5. Immigration Office
6. Garuda Office
7. Merpati Office
8. *Kawanua City Hotel*
9. *Garden Hotel*
10. *Cakalele Mini Hotel*
11. *Jepindra Hotel*
12. *Minahasa Hotel*
13. *Citra Hotel*
14. *Kawanua Kecil Hotel*

B1. Karombasan Bus Station & Market
B2. Paal Dua bus station
B3. Empat Lima (Pasar 45) Bus Station

lanterns. **Pelabuhan Manado**, off Jalan Suprapto, also in the town centre, might be of interest to ship and port lovers.

Excursions

Bunaken Sea Garden is Manado's greatest attraction. It is a magnificent underwater park covering 808 ha with crystal clear waters, named after Bunaken Island which lies 8 km offshore. The North Sulawesi tourist handbook describes – with minor amendments – the garden as follows: "The coral reef formation begins with a flat reef to about 5m, then slopes down forming underwater valleys, or drops-off vertically several hundred metres. These fantastic underwater greatwalls are cut through with crevices, caves and hanging corals. On these unique coral reefs a tremendous assortment of marine life thrives...". **Accommodation**: there are several losmen on Bunaken. *Daniel's Homestay* (near Bunaken village) is recommended. **Getting there**: contact one of the dive clubs at Molas (see accommodation), or book a tour (see tours). Tour companies will also arrange dive packages over 3 days or more.

Excursions S from Manado

Tomb of the nationalist leader Imam Bonjol is to be found 8 km S of Manado. Just before the town of Pineleng, there is a small paved road to the left which winds uphill for 2 km to this tomb of a native of West Sumatra, who was exiled here by the Dutch after his capture during the Padri Wars (**see page 773**). He died in Pineleng on 6 Nov 1864. The tomb does not begin to match the stature of the man. Admission: by donation. **Getting there**: by minibus from the Karombasan terminal either to Kali (which passes the tomb) or the more frequent service towards Tomohon, walking the last 2 km up the hill from the main road (ask for *makam Imam Bonjol*).

Continuing S from Pineleng, the road winds upwards (there are said to be 135 corners) between 2 volcanoes – Mount Lokon (1,589m) and Mount Mahawu (1,311m) towards the hill village of **Kinilow**. On a clear day, there are stunning views back over the city, with Bunaken and the other islands in the distance. 12 km on from the turn-off for Imam Bonjol's tomb and 20 km from Manado the road reaches Kinilow. **Accommodation**: **D** *Indraloka*, T 64, pool, rather down-at-heel. **Getting there**: regular departures from Manado's Karombasan terminal.

Kakas Kasen is another hill town which almost merges with Kinilow and is a more attractive, horticultural centre. Villages on this upland plateau – known as Minahasa – are almost 100% Christian and small communities have not one, but 3 to 5 churches of different denominations. On Sunday mornings, streams of smartly dressed Minahasans file to worship. **Accommodation**: **B** *Lokon Resting Resort*, T 203, new, clean and peaceful, discounts available. Paths lead from Kakas Kasen up **Mt. Lokon**. Unfortunately the volcano has been recently active and climbing it may still be forbidden; the same is also true of **Mt. Mahawu**. Check at the tourist office in town for the latest news. Climbing the volcano from Kakas Kasen should not take more than half a day. **Getting to Kakas Kasen**: regular departures from Manado's Karombasan terminal.

Tomohon is 25 km from Manado and 700m above sea-level. It is rather a shabby town notable as the centre of missionary activity in the area and for perhaps the finest bendi horses in Indonesia. **Getting there**: regular departures from Manado's Karombasan terminal.

Lake Linau lies almost 1 km off the road from the village of *Lahendong* and 32 km S of Manado. Sulphurous odours tell the story: steam roars out of vents in the ground and muddy water bubbles noisily – it is not very spectacular, and is spoilt by discarded rubbish. **Getting there**: regular departures from Manado's Karombasan terminal to Lahendong, and then walk the final 1 km.

Continuing S, some 37 km from Manado, is **Sonder** – the centre of clove production in the area. Clove trees can be seen growing at the side of the road (sparsely leaved, and rather like eucalypts): the smell of the spice drying permeates the air. **Getting there**: regular departures from Manado's Karombasan terminal.

Kawangkoan cave complex – one of a series – lies just N of Kawangkoan, over a bridge (there is another just S of Tanggari). They were dug on the orders of the Japanese to store and protect supplies and ammunition from Allied bombing. For

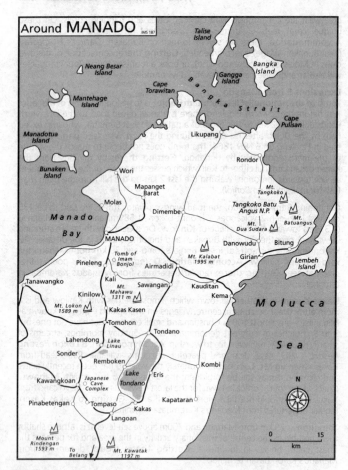

a small gratuity someone in the restaurant opposite will provide a torch (to illuminate the bats). This is only interesting for those who dream of being on the set of a Harrison Ford film. **Getting there:** regular departures from Manado's Karombasan terminal.

Watu Pinabetengan is a large boulder which lies 3 km beyond the village of Pinabetengan, on the lower slopes of Mount Rindengan. On it are as yet undeciphered pictographic carvings. It was at this spot that the 17 chiefs of the Minahasa tribes met to discuss important matters. During the full moon, ceremonies and sacrifices are still held. It is disappointing – graffiti obscures the dim carvings and the stone itself has been set in concrete and an ugly pavilion built over it. **Getting there:** catch a bus to Kawangkoan from Manado's Karombasan terminal, and from there a bemo to Pinabetengan village. It is a pleasant 2½ km walk uphill to the site. A path behind the stone leads down into a ravine to some **hot springs**.

The town of **Langoan** lies S on the main road from Kawangkoan, some 54 km from Manado. From here bemos run N to **Kakas** on the S shores of **Lake Tondano**, and from there link the various communities that line the beautiful W shores of the lake. From Tondano at the N extremity of the lake there are bemos to Airmadidi (see Excursions SE from Manado, below), and from there back to Manado's Paal II terminal.

Excursions SE from Manado

Airmadidi lies 19 km SE of Manado. It is proudly touted as the **kenari nut** capital of Indonesia (kenari nuts are tropical almonds from which the oil is usually extracted; they are also used as shade trees in the cultivation of nutmeg (**see page 974**). There is a big copra factory in Airmadidi, and some examples of *waruga* (see below). Tourists usually stop here to visit the **Taman Anggrek** or **orchid garden**, which has a reasonable collection of orchids (disappointing out of season). Admission: by donation. The garden is on the Manado side of Airmadidi, just past the 6 km marker. **Getting there:** by bemo from the Paal II terminal.

Mt. Kalabat is a 1,995m-high volcano NE of Airmadidi. It can be climbed in 4-6 hrs. Popular with university students from Manado who climb during the night and watch the sun rise. **Getting there:** take a bemo to Airmadidi from the Paal II terminal.

Taman Purbakala Waruga is a cemetery in **Sawangan**, 24 km from Manado, and 50m off the main road. It contains 144 upright megalithic sarcophagi or *waruga*, with prism-shaped lids, each of which would have been used by one family. They were assembled here from surrounding villages in 1817 and the oldest is believed to date from the 10th century. The ancient Minahasans 'buried' their dead above ground to stop the smell of the rotting corpses reaching the earth god Makawalang – an event which would have led to earthquakes. It is speculated that corpses were placed upright in the *waruga* because this is the way the foetus was thought to form in the womb and so this is the way a dead person should enter the afterlife. The massive stone chambers and lids are decorated with crude carvings – some depicting 17th century figures in frock coats. Just outside the cemetery is a small museum containing artefacts retrieved from the sarcophagi – bronze bracelets, ceramics from China and spear heads. Admission: by donation. **Getting there:** take a bemo to Airmadidi from the Paal II terminal, and then another from Airmadidi to Sawangan.

Tondano lies S from Sawangan, 36 km from Manado, on the N shores of **Lake Tondano**. The area is still volcanically active and many villages on the lake shore have hot springs and public baths. Hot water is even piped through bores sunk 75m into Lake Tondano's bed. In Tondano town, a number of hotels/losmen offer thermal hot water (e.g. *Asri*, *Kanopasu* and the *Tamaska Hijau Homestay*). The Minahasa tourism office is out of town on the road to Tomohon. **Getting there:** bus from Manado's Paal II terminal to Airmadidi and then an onward bemo to Tondano.

Remboken is situated on the W shore of Lake Tondano, almost 50 km S of Manado. From Tondano, bemos run down both shores of the lake, linking the various lakeside communities. The W shore is particularly attractive. Just N of Remboken (49 km from Manado) is a lakeside **Taman Wisata** (tourist garden) with accommodation (**C**), hot swimming baths and restaurant. Very popular with locals at the weekend. Continuing S from Remboken, the road leads to **Kakas** on the S edge of the lake. From here bemos run to **Langoan**, and from there N back to Manado's Karombasan terminal (see Excursions S from Manado, above). **Getting there:** by bemo from Manado's Paal II terminal to Airmadidi and then an onward bemo to Remboken.

The extraordinary maleo bird

The maleo (*Macrocephalon maleo*) is a member of the small Megapode family of birds which build mounds to incubate their eggs. It is only found in Sulawesi. The bird is about the size of a domestic hen, with striking black and white plumage, and a bald skull. It has been argued that this is to keep its brain cool when it is on hot, exposed beaches. The Megapodes are the only birds – other than the Egyptian plover – which do not incubate their eggs with their bodies. Instead the maleo uses hot beaches, or land near hot springs or volcanic vents. The maleo digs a hole in the ground and buries its enormous – relative to its body weight – eggs in the sand to incubate. They also dig false pits to confuse predators. After 3 months the single egg hatches and then the chick struggles upwards, through the sand, for 2 to 3 days. The large size of the egg enables the chick to fly immediately upon emerging from the sand. Unfortunately for the maleo, their eggs are a delicacy and as a result their numbers have diminished. The national parks service have begun to hatch the eggs themselves to maintain the population – a strategy which has had some success.

Excursions east of Manado

Tangkoko Batu Angus National Park covers 3,196 ha on the lower slopes of Mount Dua Sudara, N of the port of Bitung and about 65 km E of Manado. Wildlife includes the endemic Large-eyed jumping tarsier (*Tarsius spectrum*), and the extraordinary and endangered maleo bird (see box, above). Trails into the park lead from Danowudu, where there is also a campsite. **Accommodation**: simple accommodation in the park at Tangkoko. Obtain a permit to visit the park from the PHPA office in Manado and check availability of guesthouses. Tour companies in Manado also run tours here. **Getting to Danowudu**: take a bus from Manado's Paal II terminal towards Bitung and get off at Girian; from here, buses run N to Danowudu.

Tours A number of tour companies in Manado offer roughly the same range of tours (all prices are for a group of 3-4 people). **City tours** (US$12, half day); **highland/Minahasa tour** to Tomohon, Kawangkoan, Remboken, Sawangan (US$32); **Tangkoko Batu Angus National Park** (US$45); **Bunaken sea garden** (US$35 snorkelling, US$65 diving).

Festivals Jul: *Bunaken Festival*, assorted cultural and sporting festivities; not a traditional event but created by and for the tourist industry.

Accommodation Manado has a lack of cheap accommodation, but some good mid-range hotels. **A** *Kawanua City*, Jl. Sam Ratulangi 1, T 52222, F 65220, a/c, restaurant, pool, ugly brown hotel, pretensions of grandeur largely unfulfilled; **A** *Manado Beach*, Jl. Raya Trans Sulawesi, Tasik Ria, T 62260, F 62260, opened mid-1991, the most expensive and luxurious hotel in the area, S of town; **A-B** *New Garden*, Jl. Babe Palar, T 52688, a/c, restaurant, clean, bright rooms; **A-B** *Sahid Manado*, Jl. Babe Palar 1, T 51688, F 63326, a/c, inconvenient location S of city centre, rather ugly hotel; **B** *Manado Plaza*, Jl. Walanda Maramis 1, T 63382, F 62940, a/c, fitness centre; **B** *Tulip Airport Hotel*, 1½ km from airport, a/c, only worth considering if flying next day; **B-D** *Cakalele Mini*, Jl. Korengkeng 40, T 52942, rooms are small but clean, rather over-priced; **C** *Jepindra*, Jl. Sam Ratulangi 33, T 64049, central, rooms OK but a little shabby, price includes breakfast; **C** *Minahasa*, Jl. Sam Ratulangi 199, T 62059, some a/c, restaurant, old villa with view to the sea over rooftops, friendly with good service, rec; **C-D** *Malinda*, Jl. Garuda 29, T 52918, some a/c; **C-D** *Wisma Charlotte*, Jl. Yos Sudarso 56, T 62265, F 65100, well-run, N of town centre, price includes breakfast; **D** *Citra*, Jl. Sam Ratulangi XVIII 12, T 63812, new wisma set off the road, clean with garden atmosphere, friendly and peaceful, rec; **D** *Kawanua Kecil*, Jl. Jend. Sudirman II 40, T 63842, some a/c, open-air restaurant, central, but set off the main road, bare, clean rooms – a/c are better value, rec; **F** *Jakarta Jaya*, Jl. Hasanuddin 25, T 64330, small rooms, but cheap, price includes breakfast; **F** *Keluarga*, Jl. Jembatan Singkil, small rooms, thin walls, noisy, basic – and cheap.

Diving accommodation **B** *Barracuda Diving Resort*, Molas Beach (office Jl. Sam Ratulangi 61, T 62033, F 64848), 8 km N of town, hill side bungalows; **B** *Murex*, S of town (office Jl. Jend. Sudirman 28, T 52116), attractive bungalows in garden environment; **B-D** *Nusantara Diving Centre (NDC)*, Molas Beach, T 63988, F 60368, 7 km N of town, this was the first diving centre in North Sulawesi (established 1975) and is widely recognized for professionalism, attractive bungalow accommodation.

Restaurants Minahasan food is spicy hot. Specialities include *rintek wuuk* or *RW* – pronounced 'air way' (dog), *paniki* (fruit bat), field rat, *bubur manado* (a local congee) and *kenari* (coconut crab). There are a range of restaurants stretched out along Jl. Sam Ratulangi from the centre of town: ♦♦*Cakalang* (in *Kawanua City Hotel*), Jl. Sam Ratulangi 1, Indonesian, Chinese and International; ♦♦♦*Fiesta Ria*, Jl. Sam Ratulangi, Chinese and International; ♦♦*Klabat Indah*, Jl. Sam Ratulangi 211, good seafood; ♦*Singgalang Sago*, Jl. Sam Ratulangi 164, Padang food; ♦*Solo*, Jl. Sam Ratulangi 192, open air, sate and chicken specialities; ♦♦*Tinoor Jaya*, Jl. Sam Ratulangi, Minahasan food; ♦♦*Turin Italian Ice Cream and Restaurant*, Jl. Sam Ratulangi 155.

Jl. Sudirman also has a number of good, cheap and very popular **warungs** – e.g. those just N from the *Kawanua Kecil Hotel*; stalls set up in the evenings on Jl. Sudirman near the intersection with Jl. Sam Ratulangi. On the same stretch of road is the ♦♦*Sate House*, seafood, sate and squeaky clean; *Kentucky Fried Chicken/Svensen's Ice Cream*, Jl. Sudirman 73; ♦*Dua Raya*, Jl. Piere Tendean 84, good Chinese. There are also good moderate priced places on Jl. Dr. Sutomo, e.g. *Kios 18, Andalas Fast Food, Kios Nasi Kuning Sederhana*.

Entertainment Cinemas: *Benteng*, Jl. Sam Ratulangi (opposite the *Kawanua City Hotel*); *President*, President Complex, Jl. Piere Tendean. Discos: in the *New Garden Hotel* and the Manado Plaza.

Shopping Manado's shopping district is crammed into a small area delineated by Jl. Sudirman, Jl. Dr. Sutomo and Jl. Sam Ratulangi. Within this quarter there are tailors, opticians and shopping complexes. **Clothing**: *Ramayana* and *Makmur* department stores on Jl. Walanda Maramis, cheap, reasonable quality. **Krawang embroidery**: a Gorontalo speciality, available at *Krawang*, Jl. Walanda Maramis and *UD Kawanua*, Jl. Balai Kota 1/30 (a private house). **Supermarkets**: *Galael's*, Jl. Sudirman 73; *Jumbo*, Jl. Suprapto 1. **Tailoring services**: fast and cheap, many available throughout the city. **Textiles**: shops along Jl. Dotulolong Lasut.

Sport Golf: Kayuwatu course is NE of town on the way to the airport. Open to non-members, clubs for hire. Get there by bus from the Paal II terminal. **Swimming**: *Kawanua City Hotel* open to non-residents (3,500Rp).

Banks & money changers Ekspor Impor, Jl. Sudirman 47; **Rakyat Indonesia**, Jl. Sudirman; **Bumi Daya**, Jl. Dotulolong Lasut 9; **Central Asia**, Jl. Dotulolong Lasut 6; **Indra Arta Money Changer**, Jl. Sam Ratulangi 1 (in the *Kawanua City Hotel*).

Local transport Bemos/buses: there are no fewer than 4 bemo/minibus terminals serving different local towns (see map for locations of terminals). The central Pasar 45 terminal (Terminal Empat Lima) serves Molas and also has constant bemos travelling to the other 3 terminals; the Karombasan terminal serves Pineleng, Tomohon, Sonder, Kawangkoan, Langoan, and Tondano; the Paal II (Paal Dua) is the terminal for Airmadidi, Bitung and the airport (from Airmadidi there are buses to Tondano); and the Malalayang terminal for Tanawangko (from here there are buses to Tomohon). **Bendis**: horse-drawn carts – about 300Rp for 2 people, or they can be chartered for about 5,000Rp/hr. **Mikrolets**: 200-250Rp around town. **Oplets**: 200Rp around town, or chartered for about 3,000Rp/hr. **Taxi**: some are metered (white, marked cars). 600Rp flagfall and 300Rp/km. For unmetered taxis, agree price before boarding. Taxis can be chartered for about 6,000Rp/hr (T 52033 for taxi service).

Useful addresses General Post Office: Jl. Sam Ratulangi 23. **Area code**: 0431. **Perumtel**: Jl. Sam Ratulangi 4. **Warpostel**: Jl. Walanda Maramis 81. **Immigration Office**: Jl. 17 Augustus, T 3491. **PHPA**: Jl. Babe Palar 68, T 62688.

Airline offices Garuda, Jl. Diponegoro 15, T 51544; **Merpati**, Jl. Sam Ratulangi 138; **Bouraq**, Jl. Serapung 27B, T 62757.

Tour companies & travel agents *Pandu Express*, Jl. Sam Ratulangi 190, T 65188, F 51487; *Pola Polita*, Jl. Sam Ratulangi 113, T 52231, F 64520; *Metropole*, Jl. Sudirman 135, T 51333, F 66445.

Tourist offices *North Sulawesi Tourist Office*, Jl. 17 Augustus, T 64299, open: 0800-1400 Mon-Thurs, 0800-1100 Fri, 0800-1300 Sat, rather out of town; catch a bemo going to Jl. 17 Augustus and get out at the large new Governor's office (ask for the Dinas Pariwisata), it is off the road (signposted), down towards the sea, very helpful, worth the effort; *Parpostel Tourist Office*, Jl. Diponegoro 111, T 51723; easier to get to, but not as useful.

Transport to & from Manado By air: Manado's Sam Ratulangi Airport is 13 km NE of town. Regular daily connections on Merpati or Bouraq with Ujung Pandang, Gorontalo, Palu, Ternate and Ambon. Less regular flights to Biak, Jayapura, Luwuk, Poso and Sorong. *Transport to town:* metered taxis for 4,000-5,000Rp. Bemos to/from the Paal II terminal stop 100m from the airport buildings at Lepangan. Useful visitors information counter at airport.

By bus: the new long-distance Malalayang terminal is on the S edge of town. Buses from here to Gorontalo 12 hrs, Palu 36 hrs, Rantepao 60 hrs and Ujung Pandang. Bus companies tend to have their offices at the terminal. Get there by bemo from the Pasar 45 or Karombasan terminals.

By boat: Manado's main port is Bitung on the other side of this leg of Sulawesi and 55 km E of the city. The Pelni ship *Umsini* docks here (see route map, **page 1008**). The Pelni Office is at Jl. Sam Ratulangi 7, T 2844. *Kalla Lines* run a ship which also follows a 2 week loop stopping at Jakarta, Surabaya, Ujung Pandang, Balikpapan, Tarakan, Pantoloan and Ternate. The Kalla Lines office is at Jl. Sam Ratulangi 100. For further information on unscheduled ship departures from Bitung visit the AGAPE/TERATAI at Bitung port. There are also 2 smaller ports in Manado itself. Close to the Pasar 45 terminal, off Jl. Suprapto, and in the heart of town is Manado Port (Pelabuhan Manado). Ship offices line Jl. Rumambi which leads to the port. Ships/boats leave from here for Palu, Toli Toli, Ternate, Sangir, Talaud, Pare Pare, Ambon and elsewhere. Finally, Singkil port is 1 km N of the city centre; boats from here go to Sangihe and Talaud. Get to the port by bemo from Pasar 45 terminal.

The Sangihe and Talaud Islands

These are 2 of 77 islands that comprise the district of Sangihe Talaud, which has a total population of over 250,000. **Tahuna**, on Sangihe Besar, is the capital. The economic mainstays of the area are farming and fishing, with the primary crops being coconut, nutmeg and cloves. The principal attraction of the islands are its **white sand beaches** and magnificent **sea gardens**.

Accommodation *Nasional*, Jl. Makaampo 58; *Tagaroa*, Jl. Malahasa 1; *Veronica*, Jl. Raramenusa 16, T 79.

Transport to & from Sangihe/Talaud **By air:** daily flights from Manado to Naha Airport, 21 km from Tahuna. **By boat:** boats leave from Pelabuhan Manado and also from Pelabuhan Singkil, about 1 km N of Manado's city centre (take a bemo from Pasar 45).

WEST NUSA TENGGARA: LOMBOK and SUMBAWA

West Nusa Tenggara Introduction, 903; **Lombok** Introduction, 904; **Information for visitors**, 908; Ampenan – Mataram – Cakranegara, 910; The West Coast: Senggigi Beach and the Gilis, 914; The Gilis, 915; The NW Coast and Mount Rinjani, 917; Central Lombok and the West, 918; South Lombok and the south coast, 920; **Sumbawa** Introduction, 922; Sumbawa Besar, 924; Sumbawa Besar to Bima-Raba, 926.

Maps: Lombok, 907; Mataram, 912-913; Sumbawa, 923.

The islands of Lombok and Sumbawa make up the province of West Nusa Tenggara, or *Nusa Tenggara Barat*. Until recently, these islands, along with the rest of E Indonesia, were isolated and under-developed. Roads were poor, and travel slow and difficult. Since the 1980s this has changed, and it is now possible to travel through West Nusa Tenggara with relative ease. Lombok is by far the better known of the two islands, and contains the provincial capital, Mataram. Accessible by ferry or by air from Bali, it has become a popular tourist destination.

INTRODUCTION

Travelling E from Bali into West Nusa Tenggara, rainfall lessens and the dry season becomes markedly longer. This transition continues all the way along the island arc of the Lesser Sundas, but it is travelling from Bali, through Lombok, and into Sumbawa, that the change in climate and landscape are most pronounced. From a biogeographical perspective, it is on Sumbawa that Alfred Russel Wallace's observation that Nusa Tenggara marked the division between the Asian and Australasian faunal realms becomes most obvious (**see page 905**).

Lombok, though drier than Bali, is nonetheless rich agriculturally – particularly on the central plain where irrigated rice is cultivated. The island supports three-quarters of West Nusa Tenggara's population of 3.4 million, yet covers only one quarter of the province's land area. Sumbawa, in contrast, is far less well developed. It is dry and infertile and supports just $3/4$ million people.

What is surprising about West Nusa Tenggara is that although it enjoys better communications and a higher income than East Nusa Tenggara, infant mortality rates and levels of literacy are lower in the W. It is a sensitive issue because it addresses differences between religions: some commentators put this variation down to the differing influences of Islam and Christianity. They highlight the role of Church schools and hospitals in the E, and also the liberating influence of Christianity for women.

LOMBOK

The almost circular island of Lombok stretches 80 km from N to S and 70 km from E to W, making it only slightly smaller than its more illustrious neighbour, Bali. However, although there has been a tendency to view Lombok as 'Bali twenty years ago' – or Bali 'before the fall' – there are in fact major differences between the two islands embracing geography, climate, culture and religion. Lombok is drier, it is predominantly Muslim, and it is artistically less rich; the Hindu temples are mediocre imitations of those on Bali, even the textiles are unremarkable in comparison. What Lombok does have to offer is a unique culture, a beautiful landscape, the magnificent Mount Rinjani and a far less frenetic, pressured atmosphere than its better-known sister.

Lombok highlights

Temples The *Mayura Water Palace and Gardens* (page 911) is the largest temple complex on Bali; other significant historical sights include *Taman Narmada* (page 918) and *Suranadi* (page 919).

Beaches The main beach resort area is *Senggigi* (page 914), while the *Gilis* (page 915) and *Kuta* (page 921) cater largely to budget travellers.

Natural sights *Mount Rinjani* dominates the island and can be climbed in 3-4 days (page 917).

Culture and performance *Traditional villages* in the centre (page 918) and S (page 920).

Sports *Diving and snorkelling* off the Gilis (page 915).

Shopping Traditional *ikat textiles* from Pringgasela (page 920) and from workshops in Mataram (page 911) and *basketry* from Kota Raja (page 919).

Nonetheless, Lombok has been earmarked for tourist development over the next decade, on the pretext that it is in a position to emulate Bali's success. For the time being however, it remains a relatively quiet alternative. Although there are a number of first-class hotels along the beaches (and several more under construction), away from these tourist areas, Lombok is still 'traditional' and foreigners a novelty. It is also a poor island; the famines of the Dutch period and the 1960s remain very much in the collective consciousness (see below).

Most visitors to Lombok stay on Senggigi Beach, on the W coast and just N of the capital Mataram, or on the 'Gilis', a small group of islands N of Senggigi. The S coast, around Kuta, is more dramatic with beautiful sandy bays set between rocky outcrops. At present the road to Kuta is poor and accommodation consists of basic bungalows. However, plans are afoot to make Kuta a focus of future tourist development (see below). There are also a handful of towns inland with accommodation.

INTRODUCTION

Land

The name Lombok is Javanese for 'chilli pepper'. The island is divided into 3 *kabupaten* or districts – West, East and Central. The capital Mataram has become fused with the former royal city of Cakranegara, forming a rather sprawling town

Wallace's Line

In his book *The Malay Archipelago*, published in 1869, the great Victorian naturalist Alfred Russel Wallace wrote: "If we look at a map of the Archipelago, nothing seems more unlikely than that the closely related chain of islands from Java to Timor should differ materially in their natural productions". During his travels he noted the "remarkable change...which occurs at the Straits of Lombock, separating the island of that name from Bali; and which is at once so large in amount and of so fundamental a character, as to form an important feature in the zoological geography of our globe". Wallace was struck by the change in the faunal composition of Bali and Lombok – two islands separated by a strait only a few kilometres wide. The former was dominated by animals of Asian origin, and the latter of Australasian – Wallace's Indo-Malayan and Austro-Malayan regions respectively.

The first reference to Wallace's 'line', as it became known, is contained in a letter he wrote to Henry Bates who had just returned to London from his South American travels, in January 1858. Since then, numerous zoogeographers and naturalists have offered their own interpretations, all highlighting the change in fauna but postulating various different 'lines'. Even Wallace changed his mind: his original line had Sulawesi in the Austro-Malayan region, by 1880 had decided the island to be anomalous, and then in 1910 he drew his line to the east of Sulawesi, placing it in the Indo-Malayan region. The other lines proposed include Weber's line (1894), Lydekker's line (1896) and an updated Weber's line (1904), of which the last has received the greatest recognition.

The validity of Wallace's line rests on the distribution of animals through the island arc of the Lesser Sundas. Botanists have found little to lead them to similar conclusions. For example, the majority of East Asian mammals – like the elephant and rhinoceros – do not extend beyond Bali. Likewise, over 80% of reptiles, amphibians and butterflies in Sulawesi are of western origin. But some naturalists have stressed the importance of ecology in determining the faunal composition of the islands of the Lesser Sundas. The Oxford zoologist W. George has summed up this view by writing that Wallace's line "marks the division between a rich continental fauna associated with high rainfall, forests and varied habitats and an impoverished fauna associated with low rainfall, thorn scrub and restricted habitats".

However, perhaps most remarkably, Wallace 'predicted' the theory of plate tectonics and continental drift when he wrote that the distribution of animals "can only be explained by a bold acceptance of vast changes in the surface of the earth".

along the main E-W road. In 1991 the population of Lombok was 2.5 million, the majority of whom are Muslim Sasaks.

Covering 4,700 sq km, Lombok is dominated by the magnificent volcano Mount Rinjani which rises to 3,726m – making it the highest peak in Indonesia outside Irian Jaya. A hard, 3 day climb to the crater can be organized (see Tours). The island's main crop is rice, which is primarily cultivated in irrigated paddy fields on the fertile central plain. Like Bali, irrigation is regulated through a supra-village organization, the *subak* (**see page 668**). Other crops include cassava, cotton, tobacco, soyabean, areca nuts, chilli peppers, cinnamon, cloves, vanilla and coffee. Lombok is also an important exporter of frogs' legs. Because of the rapid increase in the population of Lombok, there has been an associated increase in the pressure on the environment. Forests are now reduced to degraded secondary growth, over-grazing is commonplace, and erosion serious. To try to offset the decline in the fortunes of agriculture, there has been some attempt to diversify the economy. The island's main export is now pumice, although seaweed and sea cucumber are harvested for the Asian market and tourism is rapidly becoming a major source of revenue.

Climate

Lombok is drier than Bali, but wetter than the islands to the E, and receives an annual rainfall of 1,500-2,000 mm. The dry season spans the months from May to Jul, the hot rainy season from Nov to Mar. The W is considerably wetter than the rest of the island, receiving rain even during the dry season. The E, N and S are noticeably more arid.

A brief history of Lombok

It seems that the Sasak population of Lombok converted to Islam during the 16th century when either Sunan Giri or possibly Senopati, 2 of the 9 Muslim saints (**see page 528**), arrived from Java. Local legend has it that epidemics only began to afflict Lombok after the introduction of Islam and that it was by turning to Islam Waktu Telu that further epidemics were prevented. At this time – although the history is sketchy to say the least – it seems that Lombok was ruled by a series of Sasak princes who spent their time fending off successive invasions from Sumbawanese, Makassarese and Balinese attackers.

In the 17th century, the Balinese king of Karangasem invaded West Lombok and attempted to annex the island. He failed, and it was not until 1740 that the Balinese established a stronghold in the W. Even then, the independently-minded Sasaks of the E managed to maintain their autonomy until the 19th century. Nonetheless, the Balinese – as the dominant group – imposed their culture on the Sasaks. They became the ruling caste, occupied all the positions of authority, and stipulated for example, that while a Balinese man could marry a Sasak woman, a Balinese woman was prohibited from marrying a Sasak man. The Balinese overlords also attempted to control the economy of the island: if a Sasak man died without leaving any male children, all his lands were automatically confiscated. Given the harshness with which the Sasaks were treated by their rulers, it is no wonder that they rebelled on a number of occasions, and when the chance offered itself, asked the Dutch to come to their rescue.

The Dutch In 1894, the Dutch resident of North Bali succeeded in persuading his superiors in Batavia to mount an invasion of Lombok as a prelude to an invasion of south Bali. The pretext for the invasion was that the local Sasaks had requested Dutch assistance in ridding themselves of their Balinese overlords. General Vetter was put in charge of the invasion force and he landed his troops on the S coast. Negotiations with the Balinese and the Sasaks broke down, and the former attacked the bivouacked Dutch. General Van Ham, the second in command, along with 100 other soldiers were killed and the Dutch withdrew to the coast where they built further fortifications. Reinforcements were sent to bolster Vetter's force, which in the Dutch view had been a victim of 'sinister treachery' on the part of the Balinese. With their Sasak allies, the Dutch set about attacking and looting every town and village in S Lombok. Mataram was taken apart, literally stone by stone – even the trees were cut down. On the 18 November 1894 Vetter shelled and destroyed the palace at Cakranegara. The Crown Prince Ktut and several thousand Balinese defenders were killed in the attack, while the Dutch lost only 460 men – 246 of whom died of disease. As was later to be the case during the Dutch campaigns in Bali, rather than surrender, the Balinese chose to die in a *puputan* or 'fight to the death' (**see page 671**). The King of Cakranegara was sent into exile, where he died 6 months later, and when the treasure house of the palace was opened it yielded, to the delight of the Dutch, 230 kg of gold, 7,299 kg of silver and 3 caskets of jewels.

For the Sasaks and the remnant Balinese population of Lombok, the years of Dutch rule from 1900 to 1940 were not happy ones. Indeed, the Dutch period on Lombok represents, in the eyes of many historians, an object lesson in the excesses and inequities of colonial rule. The Dutch taxed everyone heavily, not just the peasants, but also the landlords and the aristocracy. The latter passed the costs of their taxation on to their tenants, who therefore had a double burden to bear. It has been estimated that over a quarter of a farmer's rice harvest – which was already barely sufficient to ensure subsistence – was forfeited in taxes. There was a consequent sharp deterioration in conditions in the countryside and by the 1920s a class of marginalized paupers had been created where previously there was none. Meat and rice consumption fell, malnutrition became widespread, and when harvests failed, famine ensued. Farmers were forced to eat their seed grain and an island which should have produced a surplus of food was afflicted with endemic famine. Historians believe Lombok's condition was rooted in the nature of the colonial system itself.

Even after the Dutch had withdrawn and Indonesia had achieved independence, life on Lombok remained difficult. Famines became almost a way of life, and in 1966 many thousands died of starvation after a particularly poor harvest. The inhabitants of Lombok, and of the other islands of Nusa Tenggara, talk of *lapar biasa*, literally 'normal hunger' (akin to the 'hungry season' in Africa). Even the introduction of new rice technology in the early 1970s helped little – the rice was devastated by the brown plant hopper (known by entomologists as the BPH). To try and ease these pressures, the government has been settling people elsewhere in the archipelago as part of the transmigration scheme (**see page 732**) – 42,000 were moved between 1973 and 1983. But, this out-migration of Lombok's inhabitants has not stemmed the growth of the island's population. Unlike many other areas of Indonesia, the country's family planning programme has had only a marginal effect on Lombok. Analysts maintain that the strong Muslim beliefs of the majority of Sasaks has prevented the adoption of family planning methods, and fertility rates remain high, as does infant mortality.

People
The largest ethnic group are the Muslim Sasaks, the original inhabitants of Lombok, who maintain their unique language, dress and customs. There is also a significant population of Hindu Balinese who survived the Dutch invasion of 1894 (see below), along with smaller groups of Chinese, Sumbawanese, Buginese and Makassarese. Most of the Balinese and the other 'immigrant' groups are concentrated in the W, and it is in this area that Balinese *pura* are interspersed with Islamic mosques.

The Sasaks embrace 2 forms of Islam: the traditional – and now virtually 'extinct' – Islam Waktu Telu (see below) and the more orthodox, and more popular, *Islam Waktu Lima*.

Arts and crafts
In comparison to neighbouring Bali, Lombok is not nearly as rich in terms of artistic achievement. Distinctive ikat cloth is still produced on the island, although even this is suffering from a decline in quality as weavers turn out material at an ever-faster rate to satisfy burgeoning tourist demand. Traditionally, Sasak women were expected to weave a trousseau of about 40 pieces of cloth. Some of these are believed to be imbued with magical powers and they are important in ceremonies during the life cycle, for example during circumcision and tooth-filing. Such *kain umbak* are unremarkable, coarse weave cloths, often striped. Lombok's basketwork is also highly regarded, and finely worked baskets are probably one of the best, and most distinctive, products of the island.

Tourist development: the next decade
Since the late 1980s, Lombok has undergone considerable change and it is likely to see much more in the next few years. The Indonesian government views Lombok as a nascent Bali, and the Lombok Tourism Development Corporation has been established to oversee an expansion in hotels and other facilities. Virtually all the planned developments are along the coast, particularly on the W side of the island. A large proportion of the coastline from Senggigi to Bangsal has already been bought by speculators or hotel groups and has been fenced-off.

One constraint to these plans is Lombok's limited infrastructure. Rural roads are generally poor, the airport can only accommodate small planes, and telecommunications capacity is limited. Nonetheless, *Sheraton* opened a large luxury hotel on Senggigi in late 1991 and is interested in a second property and *Heritage* completed a development on the W coast in 1992. *Griyawisata* is planning a 200-room hotel near Lembar, while *Hotel Indonesia International* and the *Hilton* and *Ramada* groups have also expressed an interest in building on the island. Kuta, on the S coast, is also the focus of plans that will change this quiet stretch of coastline into a large international resort with marinas, golf courses and several luxury hotels. Old Lombok hands view the changes with horror and trepidation.

INFORMATION FOR VISITORS

Transport to & from Lombok
By air: Selaparang Mataram Airport lies N of Mataram and 20 minutes S of Senggigi Beach. Multiple daily connections on Merpati with Denpasar. Regular connections (on Merpati) with destinations in Java, Sumatra and most towns in Nusa Tenggara, including Sumbawa Besar, Bima, Labuan Bajo, Bajawa, Ende, Maumere, Waingapu, Waikabubak and Kupang. *Airport facilities*: a money

changer (for US$ travellers' cheques only and cash), information office, and hotel booking counter. *Transport to town*: Fixed-fare taxis to Senggigi Beach (7,500Rp). **By bus**: Shuttle buses from Bali, and buses to major destinations in Java, and also E to Sumbawa. *Damai Indah,* Jl. Hasanuddin 17, Cakranegara (for Bali and Surabaya); *Karya Baru,* Jl. Pejanggik, Mataram (for Surabaya, Bandung and Jakarta). A/c buses travel from Mataram to Bima (on Sumbawa) via Sumbawa Besar. Companies that operate this route include *Tirta Sari, Langsung Jaya* and *Mawar Indah,* all with offices on Jl. Pejanggik. From Mataram to Sumbawa Besar, 6½ hrs (9,000Rp), to Bima (9,000-10,000Rp). Most buses leave from the Sweta terminal in Cakranegara. **By hydrofoil**: Nuwala Hydrofoil daily from Benoa (Bali) at 0845 and 1530 to Lembar, 1½ hrs (32,000Rp); **NB**: 10 kg weight allowance. Return trip from Lembar (see below) starts at 1045 and 1530. Office at Jl. Langko 11A, T 21655, Mataram and on Senggigi Beach (opposite turning to *Senggigi Beach Hotel*). Bemos link Lembar with the Sweta bus terminal and with Mataram and Ampenan. **By ferry**: 3 ferries/day link Lembar (22 km S of Mataram on the W coast) with Padangbai, near Candi Dasa on Bali 4 hrs (4,000-5,000Rp). From Lembar, bemos run to Mataram, Ampenan and the Sweta bus terminal, E of Mataram (for onward connections); for other destinations, it is easier to charter a bemo (for example, a large proportion of the people arriving at Lembar head straight for Bangsal, to catch a boat to the Gilis; a chartered bemo to Bangsal costs about 20,000Rp). A new daily high-speed boat service links Padangbai (Bali) with Bangsal on Lombok's W coast, where there are regular boats to the Gilis. There are 3 ferry crossings each way every day between Labuhan Lombok on Lombok's E coast and Poto Tano on Sumbawa's NW coast, 1 hr 50 min (2,500Rp). The Pelni ship *Kelimutu* docks at Lembar on its circuit between Semarang and Kupang via Banjarmasin, Surabaya, Padangbai (Bali), Lembar, Ujung Pandang (Sulawesi), Bima (Sumbawa), Waingapu and Ende (see route map, **page 1008**). The Pelni office is in Ampenan, Jl. Kapitan 1, T 21604.

Local transport
Lombok's main artery is the road running E from Mataram to Labuhan Lombok. There is now a paved road to Lembar and Praya, and to Bangsal in the N. However, many of Lombok's roads remain unpaved, rough tracks and car travel can be slow and uncomfortable. This is likely to change over the next few years as tourism expands.

Bus/colt Minibuses (called bemos here) and colts are the main forms of inter-town and village transport. It is a good cheap way to get around the island and, unlike Bali, frequent changes of bemo are not necessary to get from A to B. However, they can be crowded and beware of being overcharged - check with other travellers before boarding. The transport hub of Lombok is the Sweta terminal, 2 km E of Cakranegara **(see page 913)**.
Cidomos These are the Lombok equivalent of the *dokar*, a 2-wheeled horse-drawn cart. The word is said to be an amalgamation of *cikar* (a horse cart), dokar and automobile (because they now have pneumatic tyres). In the W cidomos are gradually being replaced by bemos, but in the less developed E they remain the main mode of local transport and are more elaborate, with brightly coloured carts and ponies decked out with pompoms and bells.

Transport hire Greatest selection and availability at Senggigi Beach. **Cars** from 35,000-60,000Rp/day; **Motorbikes** 7,000-10,000Rp/day; **Bicycles** 5,000Rp/day.

Useful addresses Area code: 0364.

Accommodation
Unlike Bali, it is unusual for losmen and bungalows to include breakfast in their room rates. In general, accommodation is less good value than Bali and bungalows have not been as attractively designed.

Tours
Most tour companies have their offices in Mataram, although there are also some at Senggigi. They tend to run variations on the tours described below:

Islam Waktu Telu

On Lombok, it is thought that there are still a handful of adherents of Islam Waktu Telu. A figure of one percent of the population (25,000 people) is quoted, but this seems unlikely. Waktu Telu is a mixture of Islam and ancestor and spirit worship. Because the religion is not considered one of the 5 'official' religions of Indonesia (they are Islam, Hinduism, Buddhism, Catholicism and Protestantism), the adherents of Islam Waktu Telu have been ignored and – at times – even persecuted. In 1919-1920 the Waktu Telu rebelled against what they saw to be an unholy coalition between the Dutch and members of the rival religion, Islam Waktu Lima. Orthodox Muslims regard Waktu Telu as a travesty of the teachings of the Prophet and between 1927 and 1933 one fervant Islam Waktu Lima missionary travelled the island breaking-up idols and converting the population to orthodox Islam. Now that many Sasaks are almost embarrassed to admit they are believers of Waktu Telu, it is likely that before the century is out, the religion will have been consigned to the history books. This is not just because the religion is unpopular, but also because while it is possible for a Sasak to convert to orthodox Islam, a Sasak is only a Waktu Telu by birth, and cannot convert from orthodox Islam to Waktu Telu. Like the giant panda, Islam Waktu Telu is on an evolutionary dead-end.

The ceremonies and festivals of the religion focus upon the stages of a person's life, and upon the natural world – particularly that connected with agricultural production. Adherents to Waktu Telu only obey the central tenets of Islam – namely, belief in Allah and Mohammad as his prophet.

Southern tour To Sukarara (weaving village), Penujak (pottery village), Kuta Beach, Sengkol and Rambitan ('traditional' Sasak villages), Narmada (summer palace) and the Lingsar Temple, 30,000-50,000Rp/person.
Northern tour Landang Bajur Market, Bali Kuku temple, Pusuk, Sendang Gile and Senaru ('traditional' Sasak village), 40,000-50,000Rp/person.
Gili Air tour To a Chinese cemetery, Bangsal Beach and Ledang Bajur Market, Gili Air (for snorkelling), and Batubolong, 40,000-60,000Rp/person.
Tetebatu tour To Narmada, Loyok (rattan village) and Tetebatu, 27,500Rp/person.
Mt. Rinjani Trek up Mt. Rinjani (1-3 nights), approximately 250,000Rp/person.
Komodo Island 3/4 days, 750,000Rp (all inclusive).

Alternative tours Environmental Forum, Jl. Pejanggik 10B, Cakranegara. This agency specializes in arranging stays in traditional Sasak villages so that visitors can experience village life and customs at first hand.

Sports

A variety of **watersports** are available on Senggigi Beach (**see page 915**). Day trips can be made to the 'Gilis', for the best snorkelling and diving. Several diving companies are listed in the Mataram section. Golf: *Golong Golf Course* (E of Narmada), 9 holes, charmingly informal. Green fee: 10,000Rp. Office: Jl. Langko 27, Mataram, T 22017.

AMPENAN – MATARAM – CAKRANEGARA

The Mataram 'conurbation' is not the most attractive town in Indonesia, sprawling from Ampenan on the W coast, inland to Mataram and then to the former royal capital of Cakranegara. The 3 towns have a combined population of about 250,000. They have a rather drab and bedraggled feel, and the few remaining Dutch-era buildings in the Ampenan port area are ramshackle and unloved. Cakranegara was the site of the battle between the Balinese king of

Lombok and the Dutch in 1894, during which the palace was badly shelled (see below and page 911). As the capital of the province of Nusa Tenggara Barat, Mataram has a large number of grand government buildings – rather out-of-place in a town of this size.

Places of interest
Most of the conurbation's few sights are in Cakranegara, in the E of town. The description below runs from W to E.

The **West Nusa Tenggara Provincial Museum** is in Ampenan on Jalan Banjar Tilar Negara, at the W end of town. It houses a collection of assorted regional textiles and krisses. Admission: 200Rp. Open: 0800-1400 Tues-Thurs, 0800-1100 Fri, 0800-1300 Sat-Sun. Travelling E into Mataram, there are a number of **weaving factories** producing ikat cloth, although rarely in traditional designs. *Rinjani Hand Woven* on Jalan Pejanggik was established in 1948 and tends to produce cotton textiles for the Balinese market, using motifs from Sulawesi, Bali and the other islands of Nusa Tenggara as well as Lombok. Behind the shop is a large weaving operation where the various processes can be seen. There are also a number of other factories in this area of town: *Slamet Riyadi Weaving* (which produces Balinese-style cloth) is on Jalan Tenun, a narrow back street near the Mayura Water Palace (see below), while the well-known *Sari Kusuma* is at Jalan Selaparang 45, in Cakranegara.

To the E, the **Mayura Water Palace and Gardens** and associated Pura Mayura just N of Jalan Selaparang were built in 1744 by the Balinese king of Lombok. The Gardens contain a water lily-filled lake, with a floating pavilion – the *Bale Kembang* – set in the centre. The king would conduct audiences here, and originally there were tiers of wooden benches for officials of different grades. These were destroyed in 1894 during the Dutch assault on Cakranegara and have not been replaced, the *Bales Wedas* within the Palace was used to store weapons. Admission: 500Rp. Open: 0700-1700. Across the road to the E of the Gardens is the Balinese **Pura Mayura**, also known as the **Pura Meru**. This temple was built in 1720 and is dedicated to the Hindu trinity – Siva, Vishnu and Brahma. It is composed of 3 courtyards, the innermost of which contains 3 symbolic Mount Merus, aligned N-S. The 11-tiered meru is dedicated to Siva, and the 9-tiered merus to the S and N, Brahma and Vishnu respectively. Admission: by donation. Open: Mon-Sun.

Right at the E edge of the town is Lombok's main **market** (see shopping), next to the Sweta bus terminal on Jalan Selaparang. Also here is the Cakranegara **bird market**. **Horse racing** takes place at the Selakalas track, on Jalan Gora, N of the Water Palace, twice a week on Thurs and Sun from 0800-1200 and at festivals. The ponies are ridden bare-back by young boys.

Excursions
Mount Pengsong lies about 6 km S of Mataram. There is a small shrine at the summit and, on clear days, good views over to Bali and Mount Agung and to Mount Rinjani. **Getting there:** by chartered bemo.

Tours For the range of tours on offer, **see page 909**, Information for visitors.

Festivals **Apr:** *Anniversary of Mataram* (16th) is marked by parades and performances. **June:** *Pura Meru festival*. **Aug:** *Independence Day* (17th). **Oct:** *War memorial* (5th).
   Nov/Dec: *Pujawali* (15th day of the 4th month of the Balinese lunar calendar), held at Pura Meru in Cakranegara, at Pura Kalasa (Narmada) and at Pura Lingsar (N of Cakra). The Pujawali ceremony is followed 3 days later by the *ketupat war*, when participants throw *ketupat* (steamed rice wrapped in palm leaves) at one another. **Dec:** *Anniversary of West Nusa Tenggara* (17th) is celebrated with dance and wayang kulit performances.

Accommodation Ampenan: B *Nitour* (*Wisma Melati*), Jl. Yos Sudarso 4, T 202364, a/c,

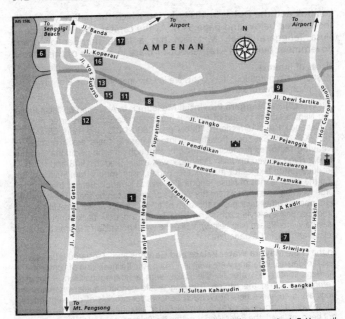

comfortable rooms, small garden, breakfast on verandah, rather overpriced; **E** *Horas*, Jl. Koperasi 65, T 2021695, very clean. **Mataram**: There are several cheap losmen on Jl. Pancawarga. **D** *Wisma Giri Putri*, Jl. Pancawarga 29, T 2023222, some a/c, attractive house, clean rooms; **E** *Triguna*, Jl. Koperasi, restaurant, good source of information on trekking. **Cakranegara**: **B** *Granada*, Jl. Bung Karno, T 2022275, F 2023856, a/c, restaurant, pool, best hotel in the area, attractive tropical gardens and aviary, good rooms with adequate services; **D** *Handika*, Jl. Panca Usaha 3, T 2023578, some a/c, price includes breakfast, rooms are standard but clean, the hotel organizes car rental and tours; **C** *Mataram*, Jl. Pejanggik 105, T 2023411, some a/c, price includes breakfast; **D** *Selaparang*, Jl. Pejanggik 40-42, T 2022670, some a/c, clean, reasonable rooms; **E** *Shanti Puri*, Jl. Maktalis, T 2022649, restaurant, best of the budget places.

Restaurants ◆*Cirebon*, Jl. Yos Sudarso 113, Ampenan. Chinese and seafood, very popular; ◆*Flamboyant*, Jl. Pejanggik 101, seafood, with attractive ambience; *Kentucky Fried Chicken*, Cakra Plaza, Jl. Pejanggik; ◆*Sekawan*, Jl. Pejanggik 59, seafood and Chinese, good portions, tasty; *Selaparang*, Jl. Pejanggik, next to Rinjani's Weaving. There are several warungs along Jl. Yos Sudarso, in Ampenan.

Sports Diving companies: *Corona*, Jl. Dr. W. Rambige, Mataram; *Rinjani*, Jl. Banteng 9, Mataram, T 21402; *Satriavi*, Jl. Pejanggik 17, Mataram, T 21788.

Shopping 'Antiques': there are a number of shops in Ampenan on the road N towards Senggigi, most with rather poor quality merchandise. Despite the layer of authentic dust, virtually none of the pieces on sale is antique. The original shop on this strip was *Sudirman*, Jl. Yos Sudarso 88; close by is *Hary Antiques*, Jl. Saleh Sungkar Gg. Tengiri 2. **Baskets**: the market next to the Sweta bus terminal (E of town) on Jl. Selaparang sells local products, including baskets. **Handicrafts**: *Pandawa*, Jl. Ismail Marzuki; *Sidhu Putra*, Jl. Gora 36, Cakranegara; *Lombok Asli*, Jl. Gunung Kerinci 36 (near the University). **Supermarket**: *Galael's*, Cakra Plaza Blok B, Jl. Pejanggik. **Textiles**: *Rinjani Hand Woven*, Jl. Pejanggik 46. Good value cotton (15,000Rp/m) and silk (40,000-60,000Rp/m) ikat. Other weaving shops include *Slamet Riyadi*, Jl. Tenun and *Sari Kusuma*, Jl. Separang 45.

Local transport There is a one-way road system linking the 3 towns of the 'conurbation';

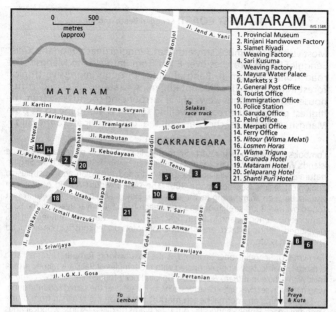

bemos run across the city, travelling E down Jl. Langko/Pejanggik and Selaparang to the Sweta bus terminal and W down Jl. Pancawarga/Pendidikan and Jl. Yos Sudarso (200Rp) to Ampenan. **Dokars**: for short journeys around town; should cost about 250Rp/person.

Banks & money changers Bank Central Asia, Jl. Yos Sudarso 16C, Ampenan and Jl. Pejanggik 67, Mataram. **Bank Negara Indonesia**, Jl. Langko. Money changers on road into Ampenan from Senggigi.

Useful addresses General Post Office: Jl. Majapahit Taman, Mataram. **Post Office**: Jl. Langko 21, Ampenan. **Perumtel telephone exchange**: Jl. Pejanggik; **telephone office**: Jl. Langko. **Area code**: 0364. **General Hospital**: Jl. Pejanggik 6, Mataram. **Immigration Office**: Jl. Udayana 2, T 22520.

Airline offices Merpati, Jl. Pejanggik 40-42, T 22226 (next to the *Selaparang Hotel*); there is also a Merpati office at Jl. Yos Sudarso 4 (next to the *Nitour Hotel*).

Tour companies & travel agents *Bidy Tours*, Jl. Ragigenep 17, T 2022127; *Environmental Forum*, Jl. Pejanggik 10B; *Mavista*, Jl. Pejanggik Complek, Mataram, T 22314; *Nominasi*, Jl. Dr Wahidin 3, T 21034; *Perama*, Jl. Pejanggik 66, T 22764; *Satriavi*, Jl. Pejanggik 17, T 21788; *Setia*, Jl. Pejanggik; *Putri Mandalika*, Jl. Pejanggik 49, T 2022240; *Sakatours*, Jl. Langko 60, T 2023114; *Wisma Triguna*, Jl. Adisucipto 76, Ampenan, T 2021705 for 3 or 4 day hikes to the summit of Mount Rinjani.

Tourist office Regional tourist office for West Nusa Tenggara: Jl. Langko 70, T 21866, maps and brochures available, open: 0700-1400 Mon-Thurs, 0700-1100 Fri, 0700-1200 Sat.

Transport to & from Ampenan-Mataram-Cakranegara By bemo/bus: the Terminal Induk Sweta, Lombok's transport hub, is on Jl. Selaparang at the E edge of Cakranegara (2 km E of Mataram). Regular buses and bemos from here to Labuhan Lombok (and on to Sumbawa), Bangsal (for the Gilis), Tanjung, Keruak and Bayan. Bemos wait on Jl. Salah Singkar to pick up passengers for Senggigi Beach (see local transport for bemo routes in town).

THE WEST COAST: Senggigi Beach and the Gilis

Most visitors to Lombok stay either at Senggigi Beach or on the 'Gilis'. Senggigi Beach stretches over 8 km from Batulayar to Mangsit. The road from Mataram to Bangsal winds through impressive tropical forest in the foothills of Mount Rinjani. A strategically placed 'coffee house' offers fabulous views of the surrounding countryside from the highest point on the road. Travelling further N along the coast from Mangsit, the road reaches Bangsal, the 'port' for boats to the Gilis.

Senggigi

Lombok's principle beach resort, **Senggigi**, lies 12 km N of Mataram on the island's W coast. The beach overlooks the famous Lombok Strait which the English naturalist Alfred Russel Wallace postulated divided the Asian and Australasian zoological realms (see box, **page 905**). The sacred Mount Agung on Bali can usually be seen shimmering in the distance. Hotels and bungalows are in fact found over an 8 km stretch of road and beach from Batulayar Beach in the S, to Batubolong, Senggigi, and Mangsit beaches, to the N. Mangsit is quieter and less developed, although there are a number of hotels under construction and land speculation is rife.

Two km S of Senggigi, on a headland, is the **Batubolong Temple**. Unremarkable artistically (particularly when compared with the temples of Bali), it is named after a rock with a hole in it (*Batu Bolong* or 'Hollow Rock') found here. Tourists come to watch the sun set over Bali – devotees, to watch it set over the sacred Mount Agung.

Each evening an informal **beach market** sets-up on the beach in front of the Senggigi Beach Hotel; vendors lay out their wares (textiles, T-shirts, woodcarvings and 'antiques'); heavy bargaining is required.

Tours Day trips to the Gilis; for example, on the *Studio 22 - Anthea Wisata* catamaran (US$20/head), Jl. Lazoardi. *Nazareth Tours* and *Satriavi* both organize treks up Mount Rinjani (see page 917).

Accommodation The accommodation on Senggigi is spread out for several kilometres along the main beach road and is easily accessible by bemo from Mataram. **A+ *Lombok Intan Laguna***, PO Box 50, T 2023659, a/c, restaurant, attractive pool, most exclusive hotel on Senggigi until being recently displaced by the Sheraton, good sports facilities; **A+ *Sheraton***, Jl. Raya Senggigi Km 8, PO Box 155, T 2027721, F 2027730, a/c, restaurant, free-form pool, largest and newest addition to Senggigi. Facilities include tennis courts, fitness centre and jacuzzi set into an attractive pool on beach-front; **A *Graha***, T 2025331, a/c, restaurant, watersports available, hot water, price includes breakfast; **A *Ida Beach Cottages***, PO Box 51, T 2021013, F 2021286, a/c, restaurant, pool, situated above the beach, ornate rooms set on the side of the hill overlooking the sea, hot water; **A *Senggigi Beach***, PO Box 2, T 2023430, F 2031200, a/c, restaurant, pool, large, well-run hotel, in prime position, with extensive grounds, greater competition should improve it, overpriced; **B *Bunga Beach Cottages***, Jl. Senggigi, Pemenang (N of the main beach area), T 2021462, F 2021462, a/c, restaurant, pool, attractive new hotel (opened 1991) with spacious, well-furnished rooms, the manager, Anna, is charming, rec; **B *Mascot Berugaq Elen Cottages***, PO Box 100, T 2023865, a/c, restaurant, large but rather dark rooms with hot water; **B *Pacific Beach Cottages***, PO Box 36 (N of Senggigi), T 2026006, F 2026027, a/c, restaurant, shadeless pool, a bit tatty; **B *Windy Beach Cottages***, Mangsit, T 2022550, quiet location, attractive cottages, rec; **C *Asri Beach Cottages***, Jl. Senggigi, the rooms in the new block are reasonable, those in the older 2-storeyed bungalows are dirty and in poor condition; **C *Batu Bolong Cottages***, restaurant, large, clean rooms but nothing special, rooms on the beach are more expensive; *Berbintang* (5 km N of Senggigi Beach), new development; **C *Pondok Senggigi***, restaurant, traditional huts in garden compound, good value; **D *Atithi Sanggraha***, Jl. Senggigi, average; **D *Melati Dua***, Jl. Raya Senggigi Km 13, T 2024488, clean, popular; **E *Pondok Shinta***, Senggigi, T 2025012, friendly, good value, rec, new wing more expensive; *Seaside Cottage* (5 km N of Senggigi Beach), new development.

Restaurants There are not many independent restaurants on Senggigi – most eating places are attached to hotels. However, with the recent and continuing rapid expansion in accommodation there should be an accompanying increase in the number of restaurants. **♦♦Dynasty**, large open-air restaurant, overlooking the sea on the road to Senggigi, Indonesian and International; **♦Gossip**, Jl. Lazoardi (near Senggigi Beach Hotel), live music, good food (particularly seafood) although limited menu, rec.

Sports The *Sasak Gardens* is the centre for watersports, with parasailing, waterskiing, windsurfing, sailing. **Diving**: *Baruna Watersports*, Senggigi Beach Hotel, T 23430; *Rinjani* have a branch at the *Intan Laguna Hotel*. **Snorkelling**: around Senggigi beach, masks for hire (2-3,000Rp/day).

Local transport Various forms of transport can be hired from travel agents along the main road. **Car hire**: 35,000-60,000Rp/day, both self-drive and with driver. **Motorbike hire**: 10,000Rp/day. **Bicycle hire**: 5,000Rp/day.

Useful addresses Police: opposite *Ida Cottages* (N end of beach).

Tour companies & travel agents *Anthea Wisata*, Jl. Lazoardi, T 21572; *Mavista*, at *Mascot Cottages*, T 23865; *Nazareth Tours*, T 21705 (in Ampenan); *Satriavi*, Senggigi Beach Hotel.

Transport to & from Senggigi 12 km from Mataram. **By bemo**: bemos wait on Jl. Salah Singkar in Ampenan to pick-up fares for Senggigi Beach and N to Mangsit. There are regular bemos linking Ampenan with Mataram, Cakranegara and the main Cakra bemo terminal.

Bangsal

Bangsal is just off the main road from Pemenang, and is little more than a tiny fishing village. However, as it is also the departure point for the Gilis, there are a couple of restaurants here which double up as tourist information centres, a ferry booking office, a money changer and a diving company.

Accommodation E *Kontiki Bangsal Beach Inn*, traditional cottages near beach.

Tourist information *Perama Tourist Service* (near the beach) provides bus and ferry connections with the Gilis, Senggigi and Lembar, and all towns on Bali. They also organize tours on Lombok (US$8-US$14) as well as an excellent 7-day boat tour from Bangsal to Labuanbajo (Flores) via Moyo Island (Sumbawa) and Komodo; 200,000Rp all inclusive. This tour then returns to Bangsal from Labuanbajo along the same route. A worthwhile alternative to travelling overland; 8 people maximum. *Kontiki Coffee Shop*, is an informal information centre with a particularly helpful man who will advise on boat crossings.

Transport to & from Bangsal **By bus**: regular connections with Lembar with *Perama Tour*, who have an office by the pier and sell all-in bus/ferry tickets to most destinations in Bali (Kuta, Sanur, Ubud, Lovina, Candi Dasa). **By bemo**: regular connections from Mataram or the Sweta terminal in Cakranegara; take a bemo heading for Tanjung or Bayan. Bemos stop at the junction at Pemenang, take a dokar the last 1 km to the coast (about 200Rp/person). From Pelabuhan Lombok there are no direct bemos; either charter one (20,000Rp) or catch a bemo to the Sweta Terminal in Cakranegara and then another travelling to Bayan/Tanjung. From the port of Lembar, it is easiest to club together with other passengers and charter a bemo to Bangsal (20,000Rp). **By boat**: a new high speed boat service with Padangbai on Bali has recently started operating, which saves on the overland bemo trip from Lembar to Bangsal. Regular ferries and boats to the Gilis (see Transport to & from Gilis).

THE GILIS: Gili Trewangan, Gili Meno and Gili Air

These 3 tropical island idylls lie off Lombok's NW coast, 20-45 minutes by boat from Bangsal. Known as the Gilis or the Gili Islands by many travellers, this only means 'the Islands' or 'the Island Islands' in Sasak. Most locals have accepted this Western adaptation and will understand where you want to go.

With the development of Bali into an international tourist resort, many backpackers have moved E and the Gilis are the most popular of the various alternatives. This is already straining the islands' limited sewerage and water infrastructures. During the peak months between Jun and Aug Gili Trewangan becomes particularly crowded.

The attraction of the Gilis resides in their golden sand beaches and the best snorkelling and diving on Lombok – for the amateur the experience is breath-taking. However, the coral does not compare with locations such as Flores, Maluku and N Sulawesi: large sections are dead or damaged (perhaps because of dynamite fishing). The islands are flat and quite featureless; there is little to do except sunbathe, swim, snorkel or dive, or perhaps go for a walk. Nonetheless, one visitor remained here for 8 weeks and professed to having a 'wild time'. **NB**: be careful swimming away from the shore as there are strong currents between the islands.

The largest of the 3 islands – and the furthest W from Bangsal – is **Gili Trewangan**. Originally a penal colony, it now supports the greatest number of tourist bungalows. These are concentrated along its E coast, as are a number of restaurants (serving excellent seafood) and bars. Snorkelling is good off the E shore, particularly at the point where the shelf drops away and at the N end of the beach (near Pasir Putih).

Gili Meno, between Trewangan and Air, is the smallest of the islands, and also the quietest and least developed. The snorkelling off Gili Meno – especially off the NE coast – is better than Trewangan, with growths of rare blue coral.

Gili Air is the eastern-most island, lying closest to Bangsal. It has the largest local population, with a village in the centre of the island, and the tourist accommodation is concentrated around the S coast. Despite the number of bungalows, it remains a peaceful place to stay. Snorkelling is quite good off the island.

Sport Diving: *Rinjani* operates from Gili Meno, *Boronang* from Gili Air and *Albatross* from Gili Trawangan. The latter is the longest established and is recommended. **Snorkelling**: masks and fins are for hire from many of the losmen (2,000Rp/day for each). **Massage**: sometimes available at *Rudi's*, a restaurant set back from the beach, near where the ferry docks.

Accommodation There is little to choose between the basic bungalows on the Gilis – they all tend to charge the same rates, and the huts are similar in design and size, mostly raised on stilts. There is no electricity and mosquitoes can be a problem at certain times of year. Rates tends to be 12,000/15,000Rp attached/outside mandi with breakfast, 17,500/20,000Rp with all meals. Friendliness and the cleanliness of the mandis tends to be the deciding factor. Note that during the peak months between Jun and Aug it can be difficult to get a room, so arrive early in the day. There are only 2 upmarket hotels, both on Gili Meno. **NB:** there are rumours that some losmen have been forced to close.

Gili Trawangan (25 bungalows, all along the E coast): **D** *Creative*, outside mandi; **D** *Danau Hujau*, N of the ferry stop, quiet, well-spaced, rec; **D** *Halim*, on beach, nice bungalows, friendly, rec; **D** *Losmen Pak Majid*, on beach, close to ferry stop, friendly, rec; **D** *Pasir Putih*, just N of Danau Hujau, quiet, popular, price includes all meals, rec; **D** *Santigi Bungalows*, on beach, outside mandi; **D-E** *Rudy's Bungalows*, off beach, some attached mandis; **D** *Trawangan Beach Cottages*, on beach, outside mandi, noisy; **D** *Wisma Mountain View*, on beach, attached mandi; **E** *Simple Bungalows*, off beach, simple.

Gili Meno (11 bungalows): **A** *Gazebo Resort*, Office: Jl. Majapahit 1, Mataram (booking: Bali T 88212, F 88300), a/c, classiest hotel in the Gilis, lovely bungalows with wooden floors and attractively decorated, rec; **B** *Indra Cemana*; **D** *Janur Indah Bungalows*; **D** *Kontiki*, southern end of bungalows, with mandi and meals; **D** *Malia's Child*, nice bungalows, rec; **D** *Matahari Bungalows*.

Gili Air (22 bungalows): *Bupati's Place*; *Gili Beach Inn*, E coast; *Gita Gili Beach*, just N of *Gili Beach Inn*; *Gili Indah*, the southernmost losmen; *Hans Bungalows*, to the N of the island, disco at least once a week, rec; *Nusa Tiga Bungalows*, inland from the E coast, excellent buffet style food, large helpings.

Restaurants A number of restaurants serving excellent seafood, particularly fish; other dishes are only average.

Banks & money changers It is best to change money before leaving the 'mainland', although the *Wisma Mountain View* on Trewangan will change travellers' cheques ($US, $A, Sterling, DM, $HK) and cash at not far off the best rates on Lombok.

Transport to & from the Gilis By boat: regular boats from Bangsal to the Gilis wait until about 20 people have congregated for the trip to the islands, 1 hr (2,000Rp). Chartering a boat costs 12,000Rp one way. **Gili Air** boats are blue, **Gili Meno** are yellow, and **Gili Trewangan** are red and white. *Rinjani Tours* at the *Trewangan Beach Cottages* book seats on the hydrofoil from Lembar to Padangbai (Bali). There is also a new daily high-speed boat service direct from Padangbai (Bali) to Bangsal.

THE NORTH-WEST COAST AND MOUNT RINJANI

Following the coast N from Pemenang and Bangsal, the road passes the turn-off for Sire Beach (about 2 km N of Pemenang) which has been earmarked for tourist development. This NW coast is little touched by tourism and there are several 'traditional villages' where the more adventurous tour companies take visitors. The best-known of these is Bayan at the foot of Mount Rinjani and about 50 km from Pemenang. Mount Rinjani at 3,726m dominates N Lombok.

Bayan

This is a traditional Sasak village and the birthplace of Lombok's unique Muslim 'schism' – *Islam Waktu Telu* (**see page 910**). There is a mosque here which is believed to be 300 years old. Some authorities postulate that when the Muslim 'saint' Sunan Giri (or possibly Senopati) arrived on Lombok he landed here, and so Bayan was the first village to be converted to Islam. The village is the jumping-off point for climbs up Mount Rinjani (see below). No accommodation.

Transport to & from Bayan 50 km from Pemenang. **By bemo**: from the Sweta terminal in Cakranegara to Anyer. Hitch a lift or charter a bemo from here to Bayan, a distance of 5 km.

Mount Rinjani

Visitors who have made the effort invariably say that the highlight of their stay on Lombok was climbing Mount Rinjani. It is certainly the most memorable thing to do on the island. The problem is that the ascent requires 3 (although some keen climbers try to do it in 2) days and few tourists are willing to sacrifice so much time. There is the additional problem that not only is the summit often wreathed in cloud, but views down to the blue-green lake within the caldera are also often obscured by a layer of cloud which lies trapped in the enormous crater.

Mount Rinjani is the third highest mountain in Indonesia – and the highest outside Irian Jaya – rising to an altitude of 3,726m. The land surrounding the peak is a national park. Mount Rinjani is believed by locals to be the seat of the gods, in particular Batara, and although Lombok is ostensibly Islamic, each year during the *Pakelem* ceremony gold offerings are carried up to the mountain and tossed into the lake. There are also regular pilgrimages of local Sasak (Waktu Telu) priests to the summit each full moon.

The climb There are 2 routes up Mount Rinjani. The easiest and more convenient begins about 2 km to the W of the village of Bayan, on the way to Anyer. The track leads upwards from the road to the small settlement of **Batu Koq** and from there to another village, **Senaru**. Tents, equipment and guides or porters can be hired in either of these 2 settlements (ask at the losmen); accommodation is available (see below). It is recommended that trekkers check in at the conservation office in Senaru before beginning the ascent. A guide is not essential as the trail is well-marked from Senaru to the crater rim; however, suitable climbing gear is required (see below). From Senaru, the trek to the summit takes about 2 days, or 10 hours solid climbing. On the trek up, the path passes through stands of teak and mahogany, then passing into pine forest and lichin. There are stunning views from the lip of the crater down to the beautiful blue-green and mineral rich lake, **Segara Anak** (Child of the Sea), below. A third day is needed to walk down into the caldera. The caldera is 8 km long by 5 km wide.

On the E side of the lake is **Mount Baru** (New Mountain), an active cone within a cone that rose out of the lake in 1942. It can be reached by boat and the climb to Mount Baru's summit, through a wasteland of volcanic debris, is rewarded with a view into this secondary crater. Along the base of the main crater are numerous hot springs – like **Goa Susu** (Milk Cave – so called because of its colour) – which are reputed to have spectacular healing powers; bathing in them is a good way to round-off a tiring descent.

An alternative and more difficult route up the mountain is via **Sembalun Lawang**, **Sembalun Bumbung** or **Sapit** on the mountain's eastern slopes. There is accommodation here and guides are also available but, as yet, there is no equipment for hire. To get to Sembalun Bumbung, take a bus from Labuhan Lombok. For details on Sapit, **see page 920**. The climb to the crater takes about 12 hrs. For ambitious climbers who intend to reach the true summit of Mount Rinjani – rather than just the caldera – this is the better of the 2 routes. Note that this alternative route is less well marked.

Best time to climb From May to Nov, during the dry season when it is less likely to be cloudy. **Recommended equipment**: water, sweater and coat, foam camping roll, sleeping bag, tough walking shoes, food/supplies. **Guides:** cost about 7,500Rp/day.

NB: the climb, though not technically difficult, is arduous and climbers should be in reasonable physical condition.

Tours The most convenient way to climb Rinjani is by booking a place on a 'tour'. Several tour operators in Mataram (**see page 911**) and Senggigi (**page 914**) organize climbs, about 250,000Rp/person.

Festivals Dec: *Pakelem* (2nd week), offering feast on Segara Anak to ask for God's blessings.

Accommodation It is possible to stay at Batu Koq and Senaru, as well as at Sembalun Lawang if making the climb from the E. Senaru has the best selection of (basic, all **E**) losmen: *Pondok Senaru, Rinjani; Guru Bakti, Segara Anak Homestay* (**E**) at Batu Koq has been recommended. Price includes breakfast and supper. On the SE slopes of Rinjani at the village of Sapit is the **Hati Suci Homestay (D-F)**, peaceful and highly rec; a good base for climbing the mountain.

Camping There are trekkers' camp-sites at various positions up the mountain – the corrugated shelters are rather dilapidated and the litter is bad.

Transport to & from Mount Rinjani By bemo: for the more usual N route, take a bemo from the Sweta terminal to Bayan, and then a second bemo from Bayan to Senaru. Alternatively, walk from Bayan. For the E route, take a bemo from Labuhan Lombok to Sembalun Bumbung; for transport to Sapit, **see page 920**.

CENTRAL LOMBOK & THE WEST: Traditional Villages and Hill Resorts

Lombok's main road runs for 74 km, E to W; from Mataram to Labuhan Lombok – the small port where ferries leave for Sumbawa. Most of these places can be visited on a day trip from Senggigi Beach; there is little accommodation available. East of Mataram (and 10 km from Cakranegara) is the town of Narmada with its rather down-at-heel 'pleasure garden'. A little way NE of here is Lingsar, the site of the Waktu Telu Temple. 7 km to the N of Narmada is the cool hill town of Suranadi set at 400m above sea-level (where there is a hotel). About 25 km E of Narmada, a road to the N (just after Sikur) leads up the lower slopes of Mount Rinjani, through Kota Raja, to a second hill resort, Tetebatu.

Narmada

The **Taman Narmada**, or terraced 'pleasure garden' opposite the bemo station, was built in 1805. There are various spring-fed pools here, one of which is open to the public for swimming (admission to pool: 300Rp). The gardens are supposed to be a scale model of the upper slopes of Mount Rinjani, including a replica of the holy crater lake, *Segara Anak*. The whole ensemble was laid out by King Anak Gede Karangasem of Mataram when he was too old to climb the real thing. A Hindu Balinese temple is situated above the bathing pools. The gardens are a popular picnic spot for Indonesians, but sadly are poorly maintained and rather dirty. Dance performances are held here (1,500Rp). Admission to garden: 200Rp. Open: 0700-1800 Mon-Sun.

Festival Nov/Dec: *Pujawali*, an annual festival held in conjunction with the *Pekalem* festival on Mount Rinjani, when pieces of gold are thrown into the crater lake.

Transport to & from Narmada 11 km E of Mataram. **By bemo:** regular connections with the Sweta terminal in Cakranegara.

Lingsar

The **Waktu Telu Temple**, also known as the Lingsar Temple, was originally built in 1714, and then rebuilt in 1878. Both Hindu Balinese and Muslim Sasaks come to worship here, and there are compounds dedicated to each religion. It is particularly favoured by adherents of Lombok's unique Islam Waktu Telu religion – although their numbers are rapidly dwindling (**see page 910**). A lake here is said to contain holy fish, but seems rather too dirty to sustain any kind of marine life. Admission: 1,000Rp. Open: 0700 - 1800. Dress: modest, sash required.

Festival Nov/Dec: *Pujawali*. A 7-day festival, culminating in the 2 religions, the Muslims and Hindus, staging mock battles in the lower courtyard where they throw rice cakes (or *ketupat*) at one another.

Transport to & from Lingsar By bemo: take a bemo from the Sweta terminal in Cakranegara to Narmada, and change here for Lingsar. If driving oneself, there is a more direct back route along a minor road from Cakranegara to Lingsar.

Suranadi

Set at an altitude of 400m, this is the site of one of Lombok's holiest temples – **Pura Suranadi**. The site was chosen by a Hindu saint who led settlers here while in a trance. Suranadi is the name of a celestial river in Hindu mythology and the temple is situated at the source of a mountain spring. Ornate Balinese carvings decorate the shrine. In the courtyards of the temple are several holy springs; the fish living in the pools fed by the springs are sacred and catching them is forbidden.

Accommodation B-C *Suranadi*, Jl. Raya Suranadi, PO Box 10, T 23686, a/c, restaurant, tennis, hot water, Lombok's original colonial hotel, now rather worn, although the rooms in the new wing are fine, friendly, with a slightly murky, spring-fed, swimming pool.

Transport to & from Suranadi 7 km N of Narmada, 18 km from Mataram. **By bemo:** from the Sweta terminal in Cakranegara to Narmada, and then change to another travelling N to Suranadi (500Rp).

Tetebatu

Tetebatu is a tiny village on the slopes of Mount Rinjani. There is very little to do here, except enjoy the beautiful scenery and visit the surrounding villages. The presence of the *Wisma Soedjono* here at the end of the road has made Tetebatu into something of a mountain 'retreat' for westerners.

Excursions
Kota Raja is a market town 7 km S of Tetebatu noted for its handicrafts, particularly basketwork. **Loyok**, just off the road to Tetebatu, is known for its bamboo crafts and palm leaf boxes while **Pringgasela**, E of Kota Raja, is a centre for ikat weaving (see below). **Lendang Nangka** is a traditional Sasak village 7 km E of Kota Raja; while **Masbagik**, on the main road just to the E of the turn-off for Kota Raja and Tetebatu is a pottery-making town. There are other craft villages in the central highlands area. **Getting there**: the best way to explore these villages is by hire car or motorcycle.

Accommodation C-D *Wisma Soedjono*, some a/c, good restaurant (cheap-medium), large pool, occupies a lovely position looking out over paddy and pineapple fields and the S slopes of Mount Rinjani, the owners speak English and hire out motorbikes for visiting the surrounding countryside. There is a variety of accommodation, including some 'traditional' Sasak houses along the side of the hill; **E** *Wisma Dewi Enjeni*, 2 km S of Tetebatu, lovely views, price includes breakfast.

Transport to & from Tetebatu 11 km N of the main road linking Mataram with Labuhan Lombok. **By bemo**: from the Sweta terminal in Cakranegara to Paok Motong and then another bemo to Tetebatu (1,500Rp).

Pringgasela

East of Kota Raja is this small weaving village, where traditional back-strap looms have not yet been displaced by more advanced technology, and where natural rather than artificial (chemical aniline) dyes are still in use. As there is accommodation available in Pringgasela, this is an excellent place to experience the 'real' Lombok.

Accommodation Both delightful, family-run homestays set amidst beautiful scenery. Suhaidi (better known as 'Eddie') can arrange tours and trekking. **D** *Sasah House Homestay*, friendly, all meals included in price, shared mandi, highly rec. **E** *Rainbow Bungalows*, with restaurant and attached mandis, price includes breakfast.

Transport to & from Pringgasela By bemo: from the Sweta terminal in Cakranegara to Rempung (1,000Rp) and then a dokar to Pringgasela (300Rp) or from Labuhan Lombok (600Rp).

Sapit

Sapit is a small Sasak village on the SE slopes of Mount Rinjani, with views W towards the mountain and E over the sea to Sumbawa. Set amidst rice paddies, it is one of the most relaxing places to unwind and also makes a good base for climbing Mount Rinjani (see Excursions, below).

Excursions
Mount Rinjani is a 3-5 day excursion from Sapit (**see page 917**); guides are available in the village and charge about 10,000Rp/day.

Accommodation D-F *Hati Suci Homestay*, bungalow and dormitory accommodation, clean and professionally run, stunning views, peaceful, breakfast included, highly rec.

Transport to & from Sapit By bus: regular buses from the Sweta terminal in Cakranegara to Masbaggik (1,000Rp); from Masbaggik catch a bemo to Sapit (1,000Rp). Total journey time 2½-3 hrs.

Labuhan Lombok

Labuhan Lombok is the small ferry port for Sumbawa. It is little more than a fishing village and most tourists are only too happy to catch the first ferry out.

Accommodation E *Losmen Muanawar*, basic.

Transport to & from Labuhan Lombok 74 km from Mataram. **By bemo**: from the Sweta terminal in Cakranegara. **By boat**: there is a ferry linking Labuhan Lombok, with Poto Tano on Sumbawa's W coast, 6 departures each day, each way (0700-1730), 1½ hrs (1,700-4,000Rp).

SOUTH LOMBOK AND THE SOUTH COAST

From Cakranegara, a good road runs 26 km SE to the market town of Praya. Three kilometres before Praya is the small village of Puyung, and 2 km S of here the popular weaving village of Sukarara. Turning S from Praya, the road reaches the pottery-making village of Penujak after 5 km and continues S to Sengkol. This area is one of the centres of Sasak culture with a number of traditional villages. The road ends at the quiet beach resort of Kuta, 32 km from Praya and 58 km from Mataram.

Sukarara

Sukarara is a small **weaving village** SE of Mataram. The weavers here still use traditional backstrap looms but the workshops along the main road are now geared to tourists and the quality is indifferent, with artificial dyes in widespread use. Traditional Lombok designs are still produced – in particular cloth inter-woven with gold and silver thread – but it is becoming increasingly difficult to find finely-worked, quality cloth.

Transport to & from Sukarara 25 km from Mataram. **By bemo**: from the Sweta terminal in Cakranegara bound for Praya; get off at Puyung, 3 km N of Praya. From here either walk or hire a dokar for the 2 km ride to the village.

Penujak

Penujak is a **pottery-making village** 5 km S of Praya on the road to Kuta. The New Zealand government has been providing aid to support and develop the craft since 1988, in particular through improving design, technology and marketing. Both traditional pottery forms such as the *gentong* (storage jar), *kaling* (water jar) and *periuk* (cooking vessel) along with designs produced purely for the tourist market are on sale. A major problem the industry has faced is adapting to a market where size/weight and fragility are both serious impediments to increased sales. Other important pottery-making villages include **Rungkang** and **Masbaggik** in East Lombok, and **Banyumulek** to the S of Mataram. The latter two villages also receive support from the New Zealand project.

Transport to & from Penujak **By bemo**: from the Sweta terminal in Cakranegara to Praya; change in Praya and catch another travelling S to Penujak (900Rp).

Sade

The area S of the town of Sengkol to Kuta Beach is one of the centres of Sasak culture and there are a number of 'traditional' Sasak villages here. The best known is Sade where women, realizing their potential as a tourist attraction, still wear traditional Sasak dress. Also here, there are some of the few remaining examples of Sasak architecture, including the tall-roofed, thatched, *lumbungs* (rice barns). But, Sade is firmly on the tour bus circuit and although the villagers have made a conscious effort to maintain 'tradition' for the foreign visitors, the economy is geared as much to tourism as to agriculture. Women frantically sell textiles while the children hustle.

Transport to & from Sade **By bemo**: from the Sweta terminal in Cakranegara to Praya; change here and catch another travelling S towards Kuta.

Kuta Beach

Kuta Beach is situated amongst the most spectacular coastal scenery on Lombok; rocky outcrops and cliff faces give way to sheltered sandy bays, ideal for swimming and surfing.

Kuta itself is a 5 km stretch of beautiful white sand on Lombok's S coast, consisting of 3 beaches: **Putri Nyale**, **Seger** and **Tanjung Aan**. Beaches to the W of Kuta are good for surfing and windsurfing. After Tanjung Aan, the coastline curves round, ending at Grupuk (or Desert Point).

The beach is the focal point of a strange annual festival, called the *Bau Nyale* (see Sumba, **page 955** for similar event), when thousands of seaworms come to the surface of the sea. Local people flock here to witness the event, and it is becoming quite a popular tourist attraction. See below for details.

Still a quiet resort, with basic accommodation and a poor road linking it with Mataram, Kuta has been earmarked for future development. A plan for a 'Putri Nyale Resort' has been published, envisaging the construction of multiple luxury hotels, 2 golf courses, lagoons, craft villages and an international size airport... Whether it will come to anything is another matter, but the Lombok Tourism

Development Corporation has big ideas for Kuta. Much of the coast has been bought up by speculators as a result.

Festivals Feb/Mar (on the 19th day of the 10th month of the Sasak lunar calendar): *Nyale ceremony:* thousands of mysterious sea worms called Nyale fish (*Eunice viridis*), 'hatch' on the reef and rise to the surface of the sea off Kuta. According to the legend of Putri Nyale, the episode is linked to the beautiful Princess Nyale who drowned herself here after failing to choose between a bevy of eligible men. The worms are supposed to represent her hair, and celebrations are held each year to mark her death. Traditionally, this was a time for young people to find a partner for marriage and it is still an occasion when the usual strictures controlling contact between the sexes are eased. The worms are scooped from the sea and eaten.

Accommodation Bungalows are all of similar standard and mostly in our **D** range: *Anda; Kocattoo Cottages; Mandalika Seaview Cottages; Maria Homestay; Mascot Cottages; Pondok Sekar Kuning; Tanjung Aan Hotel.*

Transport to & from Kuta 32 km from Praya, 54 km from Mataram. **By bemo:** from the Sweta terminal to Praya and then a second from Praya to Kuta (1,500Rp).

SUMBAWA

Sumbawa is a harsh, dry landscape with rugged, boulder-strewn hills, scrubby vegetation and a bright searing light. When the mist hangs over the land in the early mornings, the island looks almost like a moonscape. There are a handful of oases of cultivation – for example, around Dompu, to the E of the island – but generally Sumbawa is infertile and population densities here are markedly lower than the richer islands of Lombok and Bali to the W.

The island runs E-W for 280 km but varies in width from as little as 15 km, to 90 km at its widest point. Even though Sumbawa covers nearly 16,000 sq km its population remains less than one million. The island is divided into 3 districts: Sumbawa, Dompu and Bima.

Like the rest of Nusa Tenggara, Sumbawa is volcanic in origin, most clearly illustrated when Mount Tambora erupted in 1815 to devastating effect, killing an estimated 12,000 people (**see page 925**). In a number of respects, Sumbawa is 2 islands, joined by a thin isthmus. The W section is known as Sumbawa Besar and the E as Bima. Sumbawa Besar has been influenced by its neighbours to the W, with a language reminiscent of Sasak, whilst Bima looks to the E, with a language more akin to that spoken in Flores.

Islam was introduced to Sumbawa in the early 17th century when the King of Bima became a Muslim, and thus a Sultan. The Dutch did not exercise control over the island until the early part of the 20th century, and this lasted barely a single generation before the Japanese invaded. Today, the royal court of Bima still survives, but in an impoverished state. The 2 main towns on Sumbawa are Sumbawa Besar, to the W, and Bima-Raba in the E.

Transport in Sumbawa The Trans-Sumbawa highway is excellent, and made-up all the way from Poto Tano (the port on the W coast, serving Lombok) to Sape (on the E coast, serving Komodo and Flores). There are 'direct' buses from Mataram (Lombok) via Sumbawa Besar and Dompu to Bima-Raba (**see page 913**). *Jawa Baru* run direct buses all the way from Surabaya to Bima-Raba, a crippling 2 night/1 day journey (42,000-46,000Rp).

Alas

Alas was once the main port for Lombok; now ferries leave from Poto Tano, 22 km to the S and 10 km off the main road. There is little reason to stay here, but there are losmen available if travellers get stranded (Poto Tano has no accommodation).

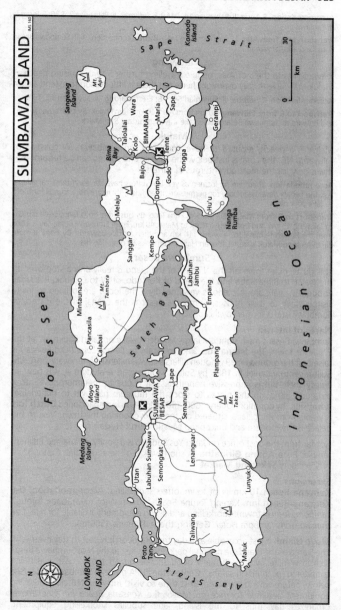

Accommodation E *Anda*, Jl. Pahlawan 14, T 169; **E** *Selamat*, Jl. Pahlawan 7, T 26; **E** *Telaga*, Jl. Pahlawan.

Transport to & from Alas 22 km from Poto Tano. **By bus**: connections with Sumbawa Besar, Poto Tano and Taliwang.

Taliwang

Taliwang lies to the S of Alas; people travelling further S to the surfing beach at Maluk may have to stay overnight here, but there is little reason to extend a stay.

Accommodation E *Hamba*, Jl. Sudirman 64, T 8; **E-F** *Tubalong*, Jl. Sudirman 11, T 18.

Transport to & from Taliwang 40 km from Alas, 40 km from Maluk. **By bus**: buses to Alas and onward to Sumbawa Besar; trucks take travellers further S to Maluk.

Maluk

Maluk is a beach, reputed to have good surf, on Sumbawa's W coast, S of Taliwang. **NB**: the coral is just below the surface and surfing can be hazardous – this is only for the most adventurous of surfers.

Accommodation There are no losmen as yet, but visitors have stayed in the local village. Ask the *kepala desa* (headman) for permission. In addition, there are no warungs for food, so take your own.

Transport to & from Maluk 95 km S of Poto Tano. **By bus**: from Poto Tano, catch a bus S to Taliwang 45 km, and from here a truck to Maluk 40 km. From Sumbawa Besar, catch a bus from the Bawah terminal to Taliwang 114 km and then a truck onwards. **By boat**: a more direct route to Maluk is from Labuhan Haji on Lombok's E coast, 1½ hrs.

Sumbawa Besar

This dusty, quiet town on the N coast of the island is really only a stop-over on the way E to Bima-Raba and the island of Komodo, or W to Lombok. It is small enough to walk around, and is very friendly – the locals are inclined to invite visitors back to their houses. Sumbawa Besar is the capital of the district of Sumbawa and a former royal capital.

Places of interest

Sumbawa Besar's main sight is a large wooden palace on Jalan Sudirman, at the E side of town. The **Istana Tua**, known locally as *Dalam Loka* ('Old Palace') is raised off the ground on 99 wooden pillars and was extensively renovated in 1985. Built a century earlier in 1885 by Sultan Mohammad Jalaluddin III, it is now an empty shell, but is impressive nonetheless. It is due to metamorphose into a museum, although the pieces to stock the museum have yet to materialize. Admission: by donation. Open: 0600-1800 Mon-Sun. An abandoned **Dutch fort** is visible from the palace, situated on the hill overlooking the town. Next to the palace is the modern and uninspired **Mesjid Nurul Huda**.

Not far from the post office on Jalan Yos Sudarso is a poorly maintained Balinese temple, **Pura Agung Girinatha**. A short walk E of here, on Jalan Cipto, is the very ordinary **Seketeng Market**.

Excursions

Kencana Beach 10 km W of town, offers snorkelling. **Accommodation: D-E Kencana Beach Inn**, Karang Teruna Beach, 10 km W of town (book through *Tambora Hotel* in town). Snorkelling and diving equipment available for hire, free transfer from *Tambora Hotel*. **Getting there**: by bemo (500Rp).

Moyo Island is just accessible as a day trip, although it is best to stay overnight. The S area of the island is a national park and lies just to the N of Sumbawa Besar. Rich in wildlife, with particularly good snorkelling off the S coast, it is being considered for 'hunting safaris'. Contact the PHPA office in Sumbawa Besar (see below) before visiting the island. **Best time to visit**: Jun-Aug. **NB**: no snorkelling equipment available for hire on Moyo, the *Kencana Beach Inn* (see above) organizes day trips to the island, and supplies snorkelling equipment.

Accommodation available in PHPA bungalows, **F**. **Getting there**: there are 3 ways to reach the island. From Labuhan Sumbawa, sailing boats can be chartered for the 3-4 hr journey (75,000Rp each way). Alternatively, go to Labuhan Sawo, much closer to Moyo, and charter a local boat for 10,000-15,000Rp. Get to both Labuhan Sawo and Sumbawa by bemo (200Rp) from the Seketeng market in Sumbawa Besar. It is also possible to reach Moyo from Kencana Beach, 10 km W of Sumbawa Besar. The *Kencana Beach Inn* has a speedboat which can be chartered, 1½ hrs (200,000Rp) and a slower launch, 3 hrs (80,000Rp). Bemos run to Kencana Beach from Sumbawa Besar (500Rp).

Mount Tambora is 2,800m high and is best known for the eruption of 5-15 July 1815, which directly killed 12,000 people and indirectly a further 44,000 from starvation during the famine brought on by the devastation. Such was the amount of sulphur ejected into the air that the following year temperatures fell sharply in the northern hemisphere and 1816 became renowned as the 'year without summer', bringing June frosts to New England and the latest wine harvest in Europe on record, dating back over 500 years. There are 2 coloured lakes in the caldera. To climb the mountain really requires a 2-3 day excursion. A guide is essential – they can be hired at Pancasila; the police also recommend that trekkers register at their station in Calabai before setting out. The track is often difficult to follow, through thick forest. Wear trousers and long-sleeved shirts (to avoid leeches) and a sturdy pair of walking boots. There are freshwater streams en route, but they are not always easy to find, so take a supply of water and some food. Thick vegetation gives way to pine forest and then a volcanic landscape on the approach to the rim of the volcano. Cloud cover is often bad, making for disappointing views from the summit. It is possible to climb down a precipitous slope into the caldera, where there is a lake. **Getting there**: charter an early morning boat from the harbour in Sumbawa Besar to Calabai (60,000Rp), where there is accommodation; then take an ojek or dokar the 15 km to Pancasila; this is the start of the climb.

Tours Tours can be organized to surrounding villages for buffalo races, to off-shore islands (including Moyo), and to trek to the summit of Mount Tambora (2,820m) (see above). The *Tambora Hotel* will organize 3-day treks to the summit of Mount Tambora, and Abdul Muis and Stephen Annas are recommended as guides (both contactable through the hotel). The *Kencana Beach Inn* (see excursions) organize trips to Moyo.

Accommodation B-E *Tambora*, Jl. Kebayan 2, T 21555, F 21624, some a/c, best hotel in town, less than 1 km from airport, well-run, clean rooms, quiet, price includes breakfast, rec; **E *Losmen Saudara***, Jl. Hasanuddin 50, T 21528, rather dark rooms, attached mandi; **E *Suci***, Jl. Hasanuddin 57, T 21589, restaurant, courtyard with open air restaurant, some rooms rather dirty, friendly staff; **F *Losmen Indra***, Jl. Diponegoro 48A, T 278, basic, attached mandi.

Restaurants Stalls and warungs around the Bawah bus terminal on Jl. Diponegoro and at the Pasar Seketeng on Jl. Dr. Cipto. Restaurants on Jl. Hasanuddin and Jl. Kartini; nothing of culinary excellence. ♦*Usfa Warna*, Jl. Kartini 16, Chinese and seafood; ♦*Rukun Jaya*, Jl. Hasanuddin 53, Indonesian; ♦♦*Tambora Restaurant* (at hotel of same name), Jl. Kebayan 2.

Sports Diving & snorkelling: snorkelling equipment available from the *Kencana Beach Inn*; they also claim to have diving equipment for hire now, but check at the sister *Tambora Hotel* in town for availability beforehand.

Local transport Bemos: the station is in front of the Seketeng Market on Jl. Dr. Cipto. **Dokars** (known as *cidomos*): 200Rp.

Banks & money changers BNI, Jl. Kartini 10. US$ cash only.

Useful addresses General Post Office: Jl. Yos Sudarso 6A. **Area code**: 0371. **Perumtel** (international telephone, telex, telegram and fax): Jl. Yos Sudarso (opposite Post Office). **General Hospital**: Jl. Garuda (W edge of town). PHPA Office: Jl. Candrawasih 1A, T 21446 (W, just past the General Hospital).

Airline offices Merpati, Jl. Garuda 2, T 21416.

Tour companies & travel agents *Tarindo Wisata*, Jl. Hasanuddin 80, T 21026; *Tirta Martan*, Jl. Garuda 88.

Transport to & from Sumbawa Besar 70 km from Alas, 92 km from Poto Tano, 250 km from Bima-Raba. **By air:** the airport is only 2 km W of the town centre. There are 'taxis', but it is easy to walk, or catch a bemo. Regular connections on Garuda/Merpati with Denpasar, Jakarta, Mataram, Surabaya, Ujung Pandang and Yogyakarta.

By bus: there are 2 bus stations. In the heart of town on Jl. Diponegoro is **Terminal Bawah**. Connections from here W to Utan, Alas, Taliwang and to Poto Tano port (for Lombok). There are direct buses from Mataram (Lombok) to Sumbawa Besar and onward to Bima-Raba. For Bima-Raba, Dompu and other destinations E of Sumbawa Besar, buses leave from **Terminal Brangbara** on Jl. Sultan Kaharuddin on the E edge of town. Buses to Bima-Raba leave roughly hourly, 0600-1200; there is also a night bus at 2130, 7-8 hrs (5,000Rp). **NB:** buying a ticket from the touts who visit the hotels will cost an extra 1,000Rp; the advantage is that you will be picked up from your hotel.

By boat: there is a ferry linking Labuhan Lombok, on Lombok's E coast, with Poto Tano on Sumbawa's W coast, 6 departures each day, each way (0700-1730), 1½ hrs (1,700-4,000Rp). There are regular buses from Poto Tano to Alas, and then onward to Sumbawa Besar and Bima-Raba.

SUMBAWA BESAR TO BIMA-RABA

The road E from Sumbawa Besar runs through a boulder-strewn, arid landscape and after just over 100 km reaches the coast, passing the picturesque fishing village of Labuhan Jambu. Wood and tile houses are elevated on stilts, with traditional boats hauled up on the beach or moored along the shore. Tour parties sometimes stop here; the regular bus will stop, but it won't wait. From here the road follows the coast before cutting inland to Dompu. The surfing beach of Hu'u lies 40 km to the S of Dompu. From Dompu the road continues E to Sumbawa's main town, Bima-Raba.

Dompu

Dompu is the capital of Dompu district and en route between Sumbawa's 2 principal towns, Sumbawa Besar and Bima-Raba. Surfers making their way S to the beach at Hu'u (see below) may have to change buses here and possibly stop-over for the night.

Accommodation E *Anda*, Jl. Jend A. Yani, T195; **E** *Karijawa*, Jl. Sudirman T230; **E** *Losmen Ati*; **E** *Manura Kupang*, attractive garden location; **E** *Wisma Praja*, Jl. Jend. A. Yani 9, T 211.

Transport to & from Dompu 40 km from Hu'u. **By bus:** regular connections with Bima-Raba and Sumbawa Besar. Onward buses to Hu'u.

Hu'u

A surfing beach popular with Australians since the late 1980s who come here on 'package tours' and stay in surf camps. The surf is best in Apr, although the resort is most crowded during Jul and Aug.

Accommodation D *Bobby's Surf Camp*; **D** *Mona Lisa*, some with attached mandi; **E** *Lestari*, some with attached mandi.

Transport to & from Hu'u 40 km from Dompu. **By bus:** direct morning buses to Hu'u from Terminal Bima in Bima (4,500Rp). Otherwise catch a bus from either Bima or Sumbawa Besar to Dompu, and from here a connection S to Hu'u.

Bima-Raba

Bima-Raba, also known as Raba-Bima, are twin towns separated by about 3 km. Most of the activity is centred on Bima. This is where the hotels and losmen are to be found, where the port is located, and from where buses leave for Sumbawa Besar and Lombok/Bali. The bus terminal for Sape (and from there to Flores) is in Raba, as well as the central post office. Constant bemos link the 2 towns. *Dokars* here are called *ben hurs* - and it really is due to the film (it must have made quite an impact on the population of Bima-Raba). The half-starved, large dog-sized animals that masquerade as horses would not have passed muster in Roman days. On the *ben hurs* 'don't eat too much' is often written in the Sumbawa language, reflecting the desolate nature of the island, the formerly frequent famines and the concern of its inhabitants for food security.

Places of interest

Bima's principal sight is the **Sultan's Palace** which faces onto the main square, at the E edge of the town centre. Built in 1927, it has been converted into a museum and houses a dismal collection of weapons, baskets, farm implements and other assorted paraphernalia. Admission: by donation. Open: 0700-1800 Mon-Sun. The **central market** is in the heart of town between Jalan Sultan Kharuddin and Jalan Sulawesi. Stall food is available here. Climb up the hills behind the Terminal Bima, or to the S of Jalan Soekarno-Hatta for views over the town and bay. One of the Sultans has his grave here (ask for *makam sultan*).

Excursions

Lawata Beach 3 km S of town on the road to Dompu and Sumbawa Besar, hardly deserves to be called a beach. Locals come here for the sunsets. **Getting there**: by *ben hur* or walk.

Kolo on Bima Bay to the N of town is visited for its snorkelling. **Getting there**: boats can be chartered from Bima port, or cadge a lift on one of the regular boats, 1 hr (1,000Rp).

Maria lies 30 mins outside Bima-Raba, on the road to Sape and is notable for its traditional wood and tile rice barns (*lengge*) massed on the overlooking hill. **Getting there**: by bus from Kumbe terminal in Raba.

Climbing Mount Tambora to the NW of Bima-Raba is a 3-day excursion (**see page 925**). **Getting there**: there is usually one bus a day to Calabai from the Bima station.

Tours *Grand Komodo* run recommended tours from Bali to Komodo (**see page 931**), but it is possible to sign on in Bima-Raba. They also arrange tours to sights around the town. Their office in Bima is at Jl. Soekarno-Hatta, T 2812, F 2018. **Komodo Tours**, as well as the *Parewa Hotel* (which also has a boat for charter to Komodo) have minibuses for charter to explore the surrounding countryside.

Accommodation B *Sangyang Bima*, Jl. Sultan Hasanuddin 6, T 2788, F 2017, a/c, pool in new extension, well-run, but rooms only average for the price; **C-D** *Lila Graha*, Jl. Lombok 20, T 2645, some a/c, central, friendly, a/c rooms rather overpriced, price includes breakfast; **C-D** *Parewa*, Jl. Soekarno-Hatta 40, T 2652, some a/c, this building was to be a cinema but the owner couldn't get the licence, and it shows – there are no outside windows, but well run and clean, good for a stop-over, price includes breakfast; **D** *Sonco Tengge Beach Hotel*, Jl. Sultan Salahuddin, T 2987. 1½ km from town on road to Dompu, alternative to being in town, rooms are clean, beach is nothing to speak of, get there by *ben hur*; **E** *Losmen Kartini*, Jl. Pasar 11, T 2072, shared mandi, upstairs rooms are more airy, a little grubby, central, near market; **E** *Losmen Komodo*, Jl. Sultan Ibrahim (next to Sultan's Palace), T 2070, shared mandi, simple but fine, rec; **E** *Putera Sari*, Jl. Soekarno-Hatta 7 (near intersection with Jl. Sultan Hasanuddin), T 2825, acceptable rooms, shared mandi; **E** *Viva*, Jl. Soekarno-Hatta (near intersection with Jl. Sultan Hasanuddin), T 2411, reasonable rooms, shared mandi.

Restaurants *Ariana*, Jl. Martadinata (on road to harbour); ◆◆*Lila Graha*, Jl. Lombok 20. Chinese, Indonesian, seafood; *Parewa Modern Bakery and Ice Cream*, Jl. Lombok.

Local transport Bemos run between the 2 bus terminals and through both Bima and Raba (150Rp).

Banks & money changers BNI, Jl. Sultan Hasanuddin. US$ cash only.

Useful addresses General Post Office: Raba (get there by minibus from Bima, 150Rp). Area code: 0374.

Airline offices *Merpati*, Jl. Soekarno-Hatta 60, T 2697.

Transport to & from Bima-Raba 250 km from Sumbawa Besar, 45 km from Bima-Raba. **By air**: Mohammad Salahuddin airport is 20 km S of town, outside Tente and on the Trans-Sumbawa highway. Regular connections by Garuda/Merpati with Bali, Lombok and other destinations in Nusa Tenggara. Bemo taxis into town cost 8,500Rp, although it is easy to walk out onto the main road and wait for a bus. **By bus**: Bima-Raba has 2 bus stations. Terminal Bima is at the SW edge of Bima town on Jl. Terminal Baru. Buses from here for all points W – Dompu, Hu'u, Sumbawa Besar, Lombok, Bali and Surabaya. The Kumbe terminal for Sape (the port for Komodo and Flores) is in Raba town, 5 km from Bima. Regular minibuses to Sape. Bemos run constantly between the 2 terminals through Bima and Raba. Bus companies such as *Jawa Baru*, *Bima Indah* and *Surya Kencana* have their offices on or near Jl. Kharuddin, between the market and Terminal Bima. **By boat**: Bima's harbour is walking distance from Bima town. The Pelni ship *Kelimutu* docks here on its 2-week circuit from Java and through Nusa Tenggara (see route map, **page 1008**). The Pelni office is at Jl. Martadinata (also known as Jl. Pelabuhan) 103, near the docks.

Sape

Sape is the usual place to stay, while waiting for the ferry to Komodo Island and Flores. The port itself – Labuhan Sape – is about 4 km from Sape town. Nothing happens in Sape, but staying here does make it easier catching the 0800 ferry. The accommodation is some of the poorest in Indonesia.

Excursions

Labuhan Sape (Sape Port) is 4 km from town and can be reached on foot or by *ben hur*. There is boat building along the road, fishing boats landing their catch in the morning, and a mosque with a lighthouse-style minaret.

Accommodation Basic and of uniformly poor quality, losmen are all found on Jl. Pelabuhan, on the seaward side of town. Because it is usually necessary to stay the night in Sape to catch the ferry, the town is a 'choke point' and accommodation is sometimes in short supply between the peak months from Jul to Sept. An alternative is to stay in Bima and catch an early bus to Sape. **F** *Friendship*, dirty, small rooms, dark with uncomfortable beds; **F** *Give*, dirty; **F** *Ratnasari*, new, cleanish (for Sape), the best of a very bad bunch. **NB**: a new losmen, the **E-F** *Mutiara*, should have opened in Labuan Sape, right by the dock and is said to be good. The competition might help the others to improve and there are signs that other losmen will open soon.

Restaurants *Hovita*, Jl. Pelabuhan, friendly, cold beer, good fish (if asked in advance), rec; *Surabaya*, next to *Losmen Give*.

Useful addresses Post Office: Jl. Pelabuhan 34. **Wartel**: Jl. Pelabuhan (between *Losmens Give* and *Ratnasari*).

Tourist offices *Komodo Tourist Centre*, between Labuhan Sape and Sape town, only marginally useful, but some information on Komodo.

Transport to & from Sape 45 km from Bima-Raba. **By bus**: the station is on the seaward side of town, although buses will drop passengers off near the losmen. Regular connections with Raba's Kumbe terminal, 1½ hrs. From Kumbe, bemos run to Bima town and then on to the Bima terminal for buses W (**see page 928**). **By boat**: the ferry for Komodo 6½ hrs and Labuanbajo 10 hrs leaves from the port 4 km E of town at 0800 each Mon, Wed and Sat. *Ben hurs* wisk passengers from Sape town to the port for 150Rp (inflated on morning of ferry departure). The ferry also takes motorcycles, cars (63,200Rp), goats (2,000Rp) and buffalo (4,000Rp); buying tickets the night before means you miss the scrum on the morning of departure. The ferry returns on Tues, Thurs and Fri. The boat ride between Sape and Komodo is uneventful; but between Komodo and Labuanbajo the ferry weaves between barren, mangrove wreathed islands.

EAST NUSA TENGGARA & EAST TIMOR

East Nusa Tenggara: Introduction, 929; **Komodo:** The National Park, 931. **Flores**: Introduction, 933; Labuanbajo to Ende via Bajawa, 936; Ende to Larantuka via Kelimutu and Maumere, 942. **Alor**: 948. **Sumba**: Introduction, 949; Waingapu, 950; Waikabubak, 954; **Timor**: Introduction, 956. West Timor, 957. **East Timor**, 963; Dili, 966; East from Dili to Los Palos, 969; South from Dili to Maubessi, 970.

Maps: East Nusa Tenggara and East Timor, 930; Komodo National Park, 932; Flores, 934; Ende, 940; Around Ende, 942; Sumba, 950; West Timor, 957; Kupang, 958; East Timor, 963; Dili, 968

INTRODUCTION

East Nusa Tenggara (Nusa Tenggara Timur or NTT) is also known, unattractively, as FLOBAMORA, designating the 4 major islands that make up the province: Flores, Sumba, Timor and Alor. There are an additional 562 smaller islands, 320 of which are so small that they are not even named. In total, the province covers an area of almost 250,000 sq km, and has a population of 3.3 million, with its capital at Kupang in West Timor. It spans over 600 km from Komodo and Sumba in the W to Timor and Alor in the E. The eastern half of Timor, together with the small coastal enclave of Ambeno, are designated a separate, and Indonesia's newest, province: East Timor or Timor Timur. East Timor was not incorporated into the nation until 1975 when Indonesia invaded, and then annexed, the former Portuguese territory (see page 964).

Until recently, East Nusa Tenggara was, in Indonesian terms, at the very edge of the world. Overland communications were slow, and occasionally impossible, and few visitors had the time, or the inclination, to brave the system. As recently as 1974, 2 Indonesian economists, Makaliwe and Partadireja found they were able to write that East Nusa Tenggara was "...a society rather remote from the nation's centre, where small farmers work their plots according to their traditions... Most of the adult population will seldom or never hear a radio, see a film, send or receive letters, or read daily newspapers...". This has all changed. Improvements in the road system and the spread of commercial life has brought most of the population of these islands in touch with the centre.

East Nusa Tenggara and East Timor are considerably drier than the islands to the W, and the further E, the more arid it becomes. Compared with other areas of

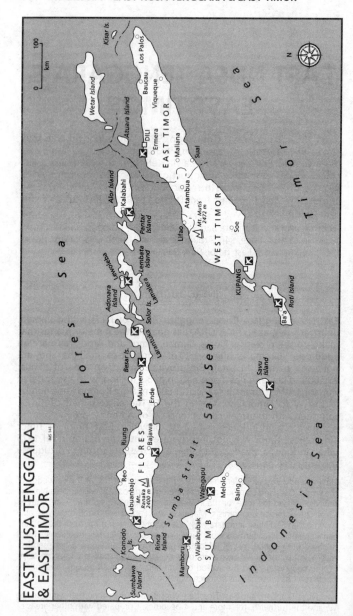

EAST NUSA TENGGARA & EAST TIMOR

Indonesia, it is dry and barren, more like Australia than the jungle-clad tropics. Rainfall averages only 800-900 mm in E Flores, Alor and E Sumba, and the dry season stretches over 7 months, from Apr to Oct. The lack of rain is compounded by the geography of the islands. They are long and thin, and rivers tend to be short and fast-flowing. This makes it difficult to utilize the water for agriculture. East Nusa Tenggara is not one of Indonesia's industrial powerhouses. The province's main exports are coffee, fish and sandalwood.

Christianity has made greater inroads into the provinces of Nusa Tenggara and East Timor than anywhere else in Indonesia. Islam had scarcely penetrated these remote islands before the Portuguese arrived in the 16th century, and the population were therefore more amenable to conversion. Today, 90% of the population is Christian, and Christianity is one of the few forces which binds together a geographically dispersed population, made up of no less than 37 ethnic groups with different histories and cultural traditions.

Transport in East Nusa Tenggara

Travelling through the islands of East Nusa Tenggara and East Timor, particularly Flores (**see page 935** for more information), used to be difficult enough to deter all but the most adventurous visitor. Now the islands are readily accessible, and surfaced all-weather roads link the main towns of the province. This has meant that in the peak tourist months from Jul to Sept, accommodation may become very stretched. There is essentially only one road through Flores, so visitors travel along a very tightly defined route; choke points include Labuanbajo (the port for the ferry to Komodo and Sumbawa) and Bajawa, both on Flores.

Language

Bahasa Indonesia is useful in Nusa Tenggara and East Timor, but not essential if travellers stick to the main route through the islands.

KOMODO

THE NATIONAL PARK

The principal reason people come to Komodo is to see the illustrious Komodo dragon (**see page 932**). But there is more to Komodo than giant lizards – there is also good trekking, swimming and snorkelling. The island is a national park and visitors must register and pay an entrance fee of 1,000Rp on arrival at the village of Loh Liang. The park covers 170,000 ha, and is made up not just of Komodo Island, but also Rinca and a number of other surrounding islets. The highest peak on this barren and rugged spot is Mount Satalibo (735m).

Despite the other attractions of Komodo, it is the dragons which steal the show. Feeding and goat purchase are now organized by the wardens. The cost of the goat is split between the audience – during the peak season up to 150 people may witness the ritual slaughter and feeding. The goat is killed and then thrown into a natural amphitheatre where numerous beasts of various sizes slither up to the corpse and devour it. Surprisingly, there is little noise or commotion.

NB: Komodo is busiest between Jul and Sept when feeding time is rather like feeding time at the zoo. Visitors are only allowed to walk alone along marked trails. Those wishing to hike off the trails must hire a guide. This is not just to generate income for the wardens: there have been fatalities (see box).

Excursions

Rinca Island can be reached from Komodo. There are dragons here too, as well as wild horses and good snorkelling. PHPA accommodation available. **Getting there**: by chartered boat from Loh Liang, about 60,000-100,000Rp for the day.

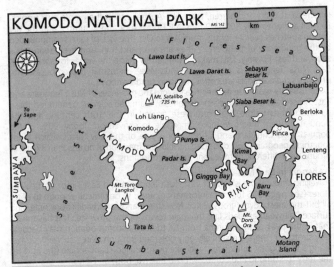

KOMODO NATIONAL PARK IMS 142

Indonesia's living dinosaur: the Komodo dragon

The Komodo dragon (*Varanus komodoensis*), a massive monitor lizard, is the largest lizard in the world and can grow to 3 m and weigh over 150 kg. They are locally called *ora* and were not discovered by the West until 1911. In total there are estimated to be about 3,000-4,000 of them. About 2,000 live on Komodo Island, with significant numbers also on Rinca (750) and on Flores. Of all the large carnivore species, the *ora* has the most restricted range – and the fossil evidence so far does not indicate that they lived anywhere beyond this small area of Nusa Tenggara Timur. They are strictly protected and cannot be exported live to zoos or, for that matter, dead to museums.

Like other animals, the size of the Komodo dragon has been grossly exaggerated. Major P.A. Ouwens, the curator of the Botanical Gardens at Buitenzorg (Bogor), Java, who first scientifically described the animal and collected the type specimen in 1912, was informed by the Governor of Flores that specimens of over 7 m existed; these were almost certainly over-estimates or mis-identified estuarine crocodiles. Even the celebrated British television zoologist David Attenborough, during his 1957 visit to the island succumbed to exaggeration, claiming to have seen a dragon "a full twelve feet" in length. The largest accurately measured dragon was one exhibited at the St. Louis Zoological Gardens in 1937 reported as measuring 10ft 2ins and weighing 365lbs. The extreme size of the Komodo dragon is thought to be due to it having evolved on these isolated islands, insulated from competition by other carnivores. The same is true of other reptiles – for example, the Galapagos iguana.

Young lizards, less than 4 years old, are remarkably fast moving, and are said to be able to outrun a dog over short distances. The reptiles live on carrion of goat, deer and even eat carcasses of their own kind. Although primarily carrion eaters, they will also prey on deer and pigs and have even been known to kill water buffalo. They are also voracious feeders, consuming 80% of their body weight in a single day. They have also been known to kill and eat people: a Swiss baron – admittedly a frail 80-year old – was killed in 1979 and there has been another reported fatality since. Flesh is torn from the carcass with teeth and claws and swallowed whole. The female lays parchment-shelled eggs of 10 cm in length.

Accommodation   The only accommodation is in the **(E) PHPA bungalows** at Loh Liang. Rooms are often dirty and poorly maintained, and there is a rat problem. During peak months (Jul-Sept), rooms are often unavailable and visitors must resort to sleeping in the dining-room.

Camping   There is a camp ground at Loh Liang.

Sports   Snorkelling: good snorkelling, but no equipment for hire.

Transport to & from Komodo   By air: Merpati flies to both Labuanbajo (**see page 937**) and to Bima (**page 928**); the former is closer to Komodo. From either town it is then necessary to catch the ferry (see below). The rich and famous arrive direct by helicopter. **By boat**: the ferry which runs between Sape and Labuanbajo stops to drop people off at Komodo. It leaves for Komodo from Sape on Mon, Wed and Sat at 0800, 6½ hrs; and from Labuanbajo for Komodo on Tues, Thur and Sun, also at 0800, 3½ hrs. The ferry cannot dock at Komodo; small boats come alongside to take passengers to the PHPA office to register. It is possible to charter a boat for a 2 day trip to Komodo from Sape (about 400,000Rp). But some of the boats are said to be unreliable and currents in the Sape Strait are strong. Locals recommend going through one of the tour companies in Bima for safety's sake (**see page 927**). It is cheaper to hire a boat from the nearer port of Labuanbajo, a one day trip should cost 75,000Rp. Before chartering a boat, visit the Komodo Park offices in Sape or Labuanbajo for advice.

FLORES

INTRODUCTION

Flores stretches over 350 km from E to W, but at most only 70 km from N to S. It is one of the most beautiful islands in the Lesser Sundas. Mountainous, with steep-sided valleys cut through by fast-flowing rivers, dense forests and open savanna landscapes, Flores embraces a wide range of ecological zones. One of the local names for the island is *Nusa Nipa* or 'Serpent Island', because of its shape.

On 12 December 1992 at 1330 an **earthquake** measuring 7.2 on the Richter scale struck eastern Flores. Over 1,500 people were killed by the quake and associated *tsunami*, many in the districts of Sikka, Ende and East Flores and their respective capitals of Maumere, Ende and Larantuka. Islands off the N coast where the wave struck were devastated – particularly Pulau Babi where 700 out of a total population of 1,000, died. One fisherman was quoted as saying: "The second [tidal] wave was as high as a coconut tree. The waves were hot, like lava." Low-lying islands were literally swamped as the *tsunami* washed over them, destroying everything in their paths. In Maumere it is thought that over 40% of the town was destroyed by the quake and similar levels of devastation have been reported for Ende. However, reconstruction is now well under way and most hotels in the two district capitals have survived relatively unscathed. Check the relevant sections below for more details on problems in particular areas and ask other travellers for up-to-the-minute information.

Land
Unlike neighbouring Sumbawa, the deep volcanic soils here are fertile; the problem is that in most areas the unreliable and highly seasonal rainfall makes agriculture difficult. Strangely, the area of the island with the highest density of population is also among the driest: the district of Sikka (Maumere). Here population densities can exceed 600 people/sq km, and even the 1930 census recorded a population of over 100,000. Because of the population pressure, farmers have cleared forested slopes right up to the watersheds, causing severe problems of erosion and land degradation. Conservation measures such as terracing were introduced by the Dutch, but in general these have proved ineffective. It has only been when farmers have owned their land that they have seen the economic sense of investing time and money protecting the land and soil.

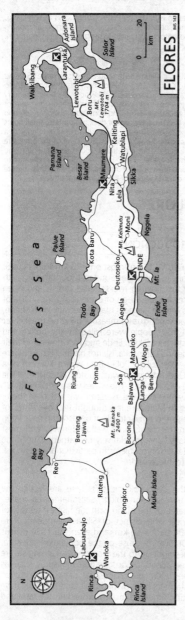

History

Flores' history is sketchy. It appears that Chinese mariners first made contact with the island – perhaps as early as the 12th century – to trade in sandalwood. As Flores lay on the trading route to Timor (sandalwood) and the Moluccas (spices), Portuguese chroniclers also noted the existence of the island in the 16th century. Dominican missionaries built a stone fort and church on Solor, just off Flores' E coast, in 1561, and later one at Larantuka. So enthusiastic were the Dominican friars in their proselytizing that by 1599 there were thought to be 100,000 Roman Catholics in E Flores, laying the foundations for Flores' Roman Catholic complexion. The sandalwood traders from Melaka and Macao who based themselves here also began inter-marrying with local women, creating a group of *mestizos* (half castes).

By the time the Portuguese were in decline as a power in the archipelago at the beginning of the 17th century, they had established settlements at Solor, Ende and Sikka. The Dutch, seeing little of value on Flores, concentrated their attentions elsewhere. As a result, although they established a mission at Ende in 1670, Portuguese religious influence over Flores continued to remain strong (see box, page 946). It was not until 1859 that Portugal officially ceded all its claims to Flores to the Dutch. And this was only agreed on the understanding that Flores would remain Roman Catholic.

People

In total, the island covers an area of 14,300 sq km, and supports a population of 1.5 million. The majority of the population is Roman Catholic, but pre-Christian animist beliefs still exert a considerable influence even among those who are nominally

The textiles of Flores

Because Flores' geography has made contact between the island's peoples difficult, a number of distinct textile traditions have evolved. Three broad types stand out: the textiles of Manggarai to the W, those of Ngada in the centre, and the cloths of Ende, Sikka, Lio and Larantuka to the E.

Manggarai textiles show stylistic links with both Bima (Sumbawa) and south Sulawesi. Predominant colours are red, blue and green, and designs may be either bold and simple, or complex and minutely worked. Geometric motifs are the norm, and it is unusual for these to be interlinked. The best cloths have a tapestry weave border design along the edge. Unlike other areas of Flores, the designs of Manggarai are produced by weaving, not by dyeing the warp (*ikat*).

Ngada textiles from central Flores can be found on sale at the market in Bajawa. Women's sarongs and men's shawls are made from rough home-grown and home-spun cotton, dyed red and blue, with an elementary ikat design. The more expensive and harder to find weft ikat *kain kudu* have horse motifs and are traditionally part of a woman's dowry.

The textiles of the E are the richest and show a range of influences, from Sumba, Solor, and even Europe and India. They are made using the warp ikat technique (**see page 721**) and feature geometric, animal and floral motifs. If weavers are Muslim, the animal designs have been reduced to geometric shapes. Cloths from **Lio** villages (e.g. Nggela and Jopu, **see page 943 and 943**) are finely patterned, with yellowish-brown designs on a dark red or blue ground. The motifs, often floral, are contained within parallel bands. It is also possible today to find cloth decorated with aeroplanes, cars, ships, and even teapots. The warp ikat from **Sikka** (**see page 944**) is probably the most immediately attractive of Flores' textiles to the Westerner. Cloth is made from thick, handspun cotton, and the ikat designs are bolder. Sikka ikat is a grey weave on a dark blue, almost black, background, although reddish hues are also common. Motifs are usually natural – flowers, chickens, crabs.

Across the island, it is increasingly difficult to find quality cloth made using natural dyes and handspun cotton. It is more usual to see cloth coloured using synthetic dyes and made from commercially-spun cotton.

Christian. There are 5 major ethnic groups on the island: the Manggarai, Ngada, Sikka, Ende and Larantuka. In general, while the inhabitants in E and central Flores are Papuan-Melanesian, those in the W are Malay. The mountainous terrain and the difficulties of communication have effectively isolated these various groups from one another until fairly recently.

Conduct on Flores
Flores is a conservative island – short skirts and vests are not appropriate; dressing in such a manner is considered impolite.

Accommodation
There is a shortage of accommodation and people travelling alone may find it hard to find single rooms; they may be encouraged to share, particularly in Moni, Riung and Bajawa. Late arrivals may be offered floor space. Blankets are also at a premium (essential if you have no sleeping bag). **NB:** an earthquake in Dec 1992 caused serious damage in Maumere and Ende, and in surrounding towns and villages. Reconstruction is progressing, but hotel space in some smaller towns may still be in short supply during 1993 and into 1994 (**see page 933**).

Transport in Flores
Travelling by road in Flores was, until fairly recently, a nightmare. However the Trans-Flores Highway is now almost complete and though hardly comfortable,

travel is quite bearable. The road twists and turns, and rises and falls, through hill, mountain and valley. It is these contortions that the road must endure to cross Flores' rugged landscape which makes travel slow – expect to average 25-30 km/hr, less in the wet season. The Highway is made up about 80% of the way from Labuanbajo in the E to Larantuka in the W and the scenery is beautiful, at times breath-taking. But despite the improvements in communications, overland travel is still exhausting and it is best to stay overnight in at least 3 towns on the journey across the island. Buses travel along the main routes, while open trucks with seats (known as *bis kayu*) ply the secondary roads. In most towns, buses will pick-up and drop-off passengers from their losmen/hotels. It is best to book your seat the day before travel with a bus agency or through your losmen (who may take a commission). This ensures you get a seat and avoid the very uncomfortable back seat. Be prepared for a 2 hour drive around town, whilst the driver picks up passengers.

LABUANBAJO TO ENDE via Ruteng and Bajawa

Labuanbajo at the western tip of Flores is the ferry port for Komodo Island and Sape (Sumbawa). From here the Trans-Flores Highway works its way eastwards through a fragmented and mountainous landscape to the hill town of Ruteng, 125 km away. Nearly 40 km N of Ruteng is the small port of Reo. Continuing on the Trans-Flores Highway from Ruteng, the road runs E and then turns S towards the coast, before climbing again to another hill town – Bajawa – a distance of 130 km. The district of Bajawa is best known for the strange thatched cult 'houses' which can be found in the surrounding villages. With a good range of accommodation, Bajawa is one of the best places to stop-off on a journey through Flores. From Bajawa, the road deteriorates, although it is in the process of being improved. The route passes through a rock-strewn, almost African savanna-like landscape, before reaching the coast after about 100 km, which the road follows for the final 30 km to the port of Ende.

Labuanbajo

Labuanbajo, or Bajo, is really just an overgrown fishing village. Like Sape on Sumbawa, the town is little more than a transit point for catching or disembarking from the ferry. But there the comparison ends. There is good accommodation here, some excellent restaurants, and reasonable beaches, with offshore snorkelling. The town is stretched out along one road which runs from the dock, along the seashore, and then S towards Ruteng. **Pramuka Hill**, behind the town, offers good views over the bay, especially at sunset.

Excursions
Waicicu Beach lies 15 mins by boat N of town. It offers good snorkelling and diving (snorkel equipment is for hire from the *Bajo Beach Hotel*). Accommodation: **E** *Waicicu*, relaxed atmosphere, all meals included in price, difficult to get a single room – 2 or 3 to a room, popular place; **E** *Waerama Beach Resort*, P.O. Box 3, T 86554, approachable by road or boat, a kiosk in town organizes free transport, the *Waerama* lies between Labuanbajo and Waicicu.

Komodo It is possible to charter a boat for the day to see the dragons; expect to pay about 75,000Rp (see Rinca, below for details).

Rinca Island is part of the Komodo National Park and even closer to Labuanbajo.

It also has a small population of Komodo dragons. PHPA accommodation available. **Getting there**: boat charter, 60,000Rp for a day trip (1½ hrs each way). Ask at the Komodo Park office in town about boat charter; the *Bajo Beach* and *Mutiara Beach Hotels* both have vessels for charter.

Tours *Perama Tours* run an excellent 7-day boat tour from Labuanbajo to Bangsal (Lombok) stopping at Komodo and Moyo Island (Sumbawa) en route, 200,000Rp all inclusive. The tour then returns from Bangsal to Labuanbajo along the same route. A worthwhile alternative to overland travel; 8 people maximum. For snorkelling trips, 'Eddy' at *Sanjei's* is very helpful. *Waicicu Beach Hotel* and 'Eddy' both organize a 2 day boat trip to Sape, via Rinca Island and Komodo (with snorkelling stops) and a visit to 'Flying Fox Island'. Average 8 people per boat, good service and food, 25,000Rp, or 35,000Rp if stopping at Sape.

Accommodation Hotels and losmen stretch out along the main street running S (to the right as the ferry docks from Sape). **C** *Pede Beach*, 2 km S of town; **D** *Wisata*, past bridge on road to Ruteng, excellent restaurant, own shower, rec; **E** *Bajo Beach*, central, clean, well run, car, boat and snorkelling equipment (2,500Rp/day) for hire, price includes breakfast, rec; **E** *Mutiara Beach* (opposite *Bajo Beach*), attached mandi; **E** *Sony and Chez Felix*, friendly homestays on hill overlooking bay, 15-20 mins walk from the dock – walk through the town, past the bank and turn left, another 150m; **F** *Sanjei*, clean, new, rec.

Restaurants ♦*Bajo Beach Hotel*, good food, friendly; *Banyuwangi*, past the bank, Indonesian; ♦*New Tenck Nikmat* (on the main road, between Post Office and *Bajo Beach Hotel*), attractive, with friendly ambience, good fish, rec.

Local transport The *Bajo Beach* and *Mutiara Beach Hotels* both have vehicles for hire to explore the surrounding countryside.

Banks & money changers BNI, main road (150m towards Ruteng from *Bajo Beach Hotel*), will change US$ cash and travellers' cheques.

Useful addresses Post Office: main road, next to *Sanjei Losmen*.

Airline offices Merpati, E of town, towards airport.

Tour companies & travel agents *Varanus*, *Waerana Beach Resort*.

Transport to & from Labuanbajo 125 km from Ruteng, 255 km from Bajawa, 380 km from Ende, 528 km from Maumere. **By air**: the airport is 2 km from town. Daily connections on Merpati with Denpasar, Kupang and other destinations in Nusa Tenggara. **NB**: flights are often booked well ahead during the peak season (Jul-Sept). **By bus**: there is no bus station; buses cruise the hotels and losmen picking up passengers. Connections with Ruteng, 4 hrs and Bajawa, 11-12 hrs. *Sinar 99* run a packed, but relatively efficient service; *Komodo* run buses to Ruteng. As yet, no through buses to Ende. **By boat**: the ferry from Labuanbajo to Sape via Komodo leaves on Tues, Thurs and Sun at 0800. To Komodo 3½ hrs, to Sape 10 hrs. It returns from Sape to Labuanbajo on Mon, Wed and Sat. Buses meet the ferry from Sape/Komodo and take passengers straight on to Ruteng.

Ruteng

Ruteng is a market town at the head of a fertile valley. It is a peaceful, pleasant spot to stop en route through Flores. This upland area is a centre of coffee cultivation and it gets chilly at night. Despite being predominantly Catholic, the practice of **whip fighting** or *caci* is still practiced, particularly during wedding festivities. Opponents flail each other, the scars being regarded as honourable and, apparently, beautiful by local women. Most weddings are held during the peak tourist months from Jun to Sept; ask at hotels and losmen for information on weddings. **NB**: try to be invited; turning-up unannounced and uninvited is bad manners and not recommended.

Excursions

Pongkor, 45 km SW of Ruteng and **Lambaleda**, 50 km to the NW are two traditional villages worth visiting. Lambaleda is a weaving centre. **Getting there**: trucks (*bis kayu*) run from Ruteng to Pongkor (2 hrs) and to Lambaleda via Benteng Jawa. Alternatively, explore the route N to **Reo** – regular trucks make the journey, through spectacular scenery (see below).

Accommodation **C-E** *Dahlia*, just off Jl. Motang Rua (main road), T 377, restaurant, most

Traditional architecture: *ngadhu* and bhaga

Much of the art of the Lesser Sundas is based upon maintaining balance between opposites: between male and female, old and young, living and dead, white and black. This concern for harmony is reflected in the cult altars of Bajawa where *ngadhu* represent the male ancestors of the clan, and *bhaga* the female ancestors. The former consists of a carved wooden post surmounted by a thatched roof; while the latter is like a miniature house, again with a thatched roof and usually a raised platform. They are built in pairs, and are usually constructed outside the residence of a prominent household after a sign has been received from the ancestors. The male post is carved from the wood of a *sebu* tree, which is dug from the ground, roots and all. Only when the ngadhu post has been planted in the earth, can the construction of the bhaga begin.

sophisticated losmen in town, clean and efficiently-run; **D-E** *Agung II*, Jl. Motang Rua in centre of town; **E** *Agung I*, T 80, N of town on road to Reo, quiet and popular, big rooms, rec.

Restaurants Ruteng is not renowned for the quality of its food. There are several warung in the bus station and market area, and losmen also serve meals. Dog, known as 'RW', is available in some places.

Useful addresses Post Office: Jl. Baruk (S side of town).

Transport to & from Ruteng 125 km from Labuanbajo, 130 km from Bajawa, 255 km from Ende. **By air**: the airport is on the outskirts of town; bemos meet flights. Daily connections on Merpati with Denpasar, Kupang and other destinations in Nusa Tenggara. **By bus**: the station is on the W side of town, a short walk downhill from the centre. Regular connections with Labuanbajo 4 hrs, Bajawa 6 hrs, Ende 12 hrs and N to Reo 2 hrs. Also buses to other local destinations. *Komodo Bus* and *Nusa Indah* (for Labuanbajo) both have their offices on Jl. Amenhung; *Agogo* (for buses to Ende) is at Jl. Yos Sudarso 4.

Reo

A small town on the N coast, is off the Trans-Flores Highway and therefore rarely visited by tourists.

Accommodation E *Losmen Nisang Nai*, Jl. Pelabuhan, outskirts of town, towards Kedindi; **F** *Telukbayar*, Jl. Mesjit 8, bit grim.

Transport to & from Reo 38 km from Ruteng. **By bus**: regular connections with Ruteng; the road is reasonable. **By boat**: there are said to be infrequent boats from Reo to Labuanbajo. It might be possible to hitch a lift to other ports in Flores, and mixed cargo boats bound for Surabaya also sometimes stop here.

Bajawa

This hill town is the capital of the Ngada District and has a pleasant climate, with fresh days and chilly nights. It is a predominantly Christian area but is best known for its thatched cult altars known as *ngadhu* and *bhaga* (see Excursions and box). Bajawa town makes a pleasant and logical stop on the Trans-Flores route. The **Inpres market** sells traditional textiles – blankets from Bajawa and ikat from Ende and Kelimutu.

Excursions

The surrounding villages are interesting to visit to see their cult houses. **Langa** has a fine collection of *ngadhu* and *bhaga* (see box). **Getting there**: the village lies 2½ km off the main Trans-Flores road towards Ende (east); bemos are sometimes available for the short trip from the turnoff. It is also possible to walk from Bajawa to Langa (about 5 km).

Bena is a village S of town, past the turn off to Langa and en route to Monas. It is the ceremonial centre of the area. **Getting there**: buses leave from the market in Bajawa, 1hr (1,000Rp).

Wogo lies E of Langa and Bena and has a collection of rather neglected megaliths just beyond the village. **Accommodation**: there is a Christian mission at nearby

Mataloko which will provide accommodation for visitors. **Getting there**: take a bus from the market in Bajawa to Mataloko which is on the main road to Ende ($^3/_4$ hr) and then walk the final 100m or so to Wogo.

Accommodation NB: during peak months between Jul and Sept, losmen may be full, although space will be found somehow and somewhere. All prices below include a simple breakfast. **D** *Kambang*, Jl. Diponegoro 18, T 72, featureless building, but good large rooms and mandis, rec; **E** *Dagalos*, Jl. A. Yani 70, with mandi, excellent food but dingy rooms, friendly family; **E** *Dam*, Jl. Gereja, T 45, on quiet street near church, mostly frequented by Indonesians; **E** *Kambera*, Jl. Eltari 9, T 166, popular, friendly and helpful, if a little (and charmingly) disorganized, rec; **E** *Korina*, Jl. A. Yani; **E** *Losmen Anggrek*, Jl. Let. Jend. Haryono 9, T 172, clean, with attached mandi, good value; **E** *Losmen Johny*, Jl. Gajah Mada, T 79, rather grubby, attached mandi; **E** *Melati Virgo*, Jl. May. Jend. D.1. Panjaitan, T 621, good value, rec; **E** *Sunflower*, off Jl. Basuki Rahmat; **F** *Kencana*, Jl. Palapa 7, T 155, on quiet track not far from the market and bus station, attached mandi.

Restaurants ♦*Losmen Kambera* has a popular, though disorganized, restaurant serving good food. Also try the *Kasih Bahagia* and the *Rumah Makan Wisata*, both near the entrance to the market.

Shopping Textiles: Bajawa blankets and ikat from Ende and Kelimutu are available from the Inpres market (see box, **page 935**).

Banks & money changers BNI, Jl. Boulevard (aka Jl. Soekarno-Hatta), will change travellers' cheques and cash in most major currencies.

Useful addresses General Post Office: Jl. Boulevard (aka Jl. Soekarno-Hatta). **Perumtel** (telephone and telegraph): Jl. Boulevard/Soekarno-Hatta (near Bank Rakyat Indonesia).

Airline offices Merpati, Jl. Budi Utomo/Pasar Rahmat (by market).

Transport to & from Bajawa 130 km from Ruteng, 255 km from Labuanbajo, 125 km from Ende. **By air**: the airport lies 30 km N of town, near Soa. Minibuses bring passengers into Bajawa. Connections on Merpati with Denpasar, Kupang and other destinations in Nusa Tenggara. **By bus**: the terminal is in the heart of town, near the market. Regular connections with Ruteng 6 hrs; also to Labuanbajo 11 hrs, Ende 5 hrs and Riung. Buses cruise the losmen looking for passengers. *Sinar 99* operates buses to Labuanbajo via Ruteng and has its office at Jl. Martadinata 8. No direct buses to Maumere (yet), but by catching a morning bus to Ende it is possible to get the 1700 connection from there to Maumere. **By truck**: (*bis kayu*) to Bena, Langa, Mataloko (see excursions) and other surrounding towns leave from the terminal next to the market.

Ende

Ende is the largest town on Flores with 66,000 inhabitants, and is the capital of the district of Ende. The town is sited in a spectacular position on the neck of a peninsula, surrounded by mountains. To the S is the distinctive Mount Meja (Table Mountain), and on the other side of town is Mount Ia, a dormant volcano that last erupted in 1969. The Portuguese had established a settlement here as early as the 17th century. In Dec 1992 the town was devastated by an earthquake, with an estimated 40% of buildings destroyed (**see page 933**).

Places of interest

Ende is best known in Indonesia as the spot to which Sukarno was exiled by the Dutch between 1934 and 1938. **Sukarno's house** and **museum**, is on Jalan Perwira. It has a poor collection of photographs, and little else. The museum is only likely to be of interest to Sukarno acolytes and students of modern Indonesian history. Open: mornings (but variable).

In town, the **Mbongawani market** on Jalan Pelabuhan is colourful with traditional healers selling local cures, and a good range of textiles also on sale (see Shopping, below). There is a night market, **Pasar Potulando**, on Jalan Kelimutu. For good views of the town and bay, climb **Mount Meja**, about a $1^1/_2$ hr walk, starting from the market; walk S on Jalan Gajah Mada and turn left towards Waniwona village.

Excursions

Mount Ia To climb to the crater of this dormant volcano takes about 2 hrs, and

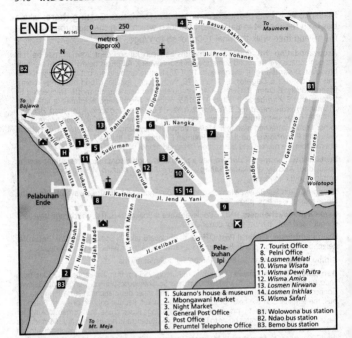

ENDE IMS 145

To Maumere

To Bajawa

To Wolotopo

Pelabuhan Ende

Pelabuhan Ipi

To Mt. Meja

Jl. Basuki Rakhmat
Jl. Sam Ratulangi
Jl. Prof. Yohanes
Jl. Eltari
Jl. Diponegoro
Jl. Pahlawan
Jl. Nangka
Jl. Banteng
Jl. Perwira
Jl. Mesjid
Jl. Mahoni
Jl. Sudirman
Jl. Hatta
Jl. Sukarno
Jl. Garuda
Jl. Kelimutu
Jl. Melati
Jl. Anggrek
Jl. Gatot Subroto
Jl. Flores
Jl. Kathedral
Jl. Kemak Muran
Jl. Jend A. Yani
Jl. Gajah Mada
Jl. Nusantara
Jl. Pelabuhan
Jl. Kelibara
Jl. I.H. Doko

7. Tourist Office
8. Pelni Office
9. Losmen Melati
10. Wisma Wisata
11. Wisma Dewi Putra
12. Wisma Amica
13. Losmen Nirwana
14. Losmen Inkhlas
15. Wisma Safari

1. Sukarno's house & museum
2. Mbongawani Market
3. Night Market
4. General Post Office
5. Post Office
6. Perumtel Telephone Office

B1. Wolowona bus station
B2. Ndao bus station
B3. Bemo bus station

affords good views of the town and bay. **Getting there**: catch a bemo to Rate village from the central market and ask for directions.

Mount Kelimutu is too far to reach in a single day except by chartered vehicle; it is better to spend the night in Moni (**see page 942**). However, the *Wisata* and *Dewi Putra* hotels both have vehicles for charter (60,000Rp and 75,000Rp respectively) for a day trip to Kelimutu with a *very* early departure.

Nangalala Beach lies 13 km W of Ende. The beach has reasonable swimming and is popular at weekends with locals. **Getting there**: catch a bemo from the central market bound for Nangapanda or Nangaroro and get off at the Km 13 marker.

Nuabosi, 9 km NW of Ende, offers wonderful views of the town; there is also a *rumah adat* (traditional clan house) here. **Getting there**: catch a bemo from the central market.

There is a **pleasant walk** along the coast from the Wolowona bus terminal on the edge of town (constant bemos travel there from the town centre) E to **Wolotopo**, about 6 km. Wolotopo has some *rumah adat* (traditional houses) and weaving. It is beautifully positioned.

Ngalupolo is a village a further 7 km E of Wolotopo (see above). It has some *rumah adat*, ikat weaving, ivory tusks and gold jewellery on show (donation required for display). **Getting there**: there *should* be a daily boat at 0700 (except Fri) from Pelabuhan Ipi in Ende to Ngalupolo, which then returns in the afternoon. It is possible to walk from town to the port, or catch a bemo heading E.

Nggela is a coastal weaving village is E of Ende (**see page 943**). **Getting there**:

4-5 hrs from Ende by *bis kayu* (truck) from the Wolowona terminal (one departure/day). There *should* also be a daily 0700 boat (except Fri) from Pelabuhan Ipi in Ende to Nggela (2½ hrs). From Nggela it is possible to return to Ende by *bis kayu* via Wolowaru and Moni, making a long day's excursion.

Tours   There are as yet no good tour agents in Ende, but the *Dewi Putra* and *Wisata* hotels have cars for charter to Kelimutu, and surrounding villages.

Accommodation   All losmen and hotels include a simple breakfast in the room rate; most are out of the centre of town. **NB**: the Dec 1992 earthquake caused extensive damage; hotel rooms may be scarce. **C-D *Dewi Putra***, Jl. Yos Sudarso, T 21465, some a/c, noisy downstairs, quieter upstairs, clean, and unlike all other losmen it is central, rec; **C-E *Nirwana***, Jl. Pahlawan 29, T 21199, some a/c, on hill above town but still quite central, rooms are rather run-down; **C-E *Wisata***, Jl. Kelimutu 68, T 21368, some a/c, clean, attached mandi; **E *Amica***, Jl. Garuda, T 21683, quiet street, rather dark, attached mandi; **E *Inkhlas***, Jl. Jend. A. Yani, T 21695, good restaurant, small rooms, some rather dark, but popular with travellers and well-run; some with attached mandi; **E *Safari***, Jl. Jend. A. Yani, T 21499, villa with large clean rooms and attractive garden and restaurant area, rec; **F *Melati***, Jl. Gatot Subroto, T 311, reasonably clean with attached mandi, and a raised area for sipping tea and coffee.

Restaurants   ♦*Adi Putra*, Jl. Kemakmuran 30, good Indonesian food in attractive shuttered house, near mosque; ♦*Depot Ende*, Jl. Jend. Sudirman 6, good cheap Indonesian and Chinese; ♦*Merlyn*, Jl. Jend. A. Yani 6 (E of *Inkhlas Losmen*), Indonesian, good, simple food; *Minang Baru*, Jl. Souekarno (near Cathedral), excellent Padang food, also sells textiles; ♦*Saiyo*, Jl. Benteng 7, very good Padang food; ♦♦*Terminal Restaurant*, Jl. Hatta 70 (by the old terminal kota), good fish and lobsters plus Indonesian favourites. **Bakeries and coffee shops**: Jl. Kemakmuran (near Flores Theatre).

Entertainment   Cinema: **Flores Theatre**, Jl. Kemakmuran 1 – occasionally shows Western movies.

Shopping   Books: *Toko Nusa Indah*, Jl. Kathedral 5 (just up the hill from the Cathedral). **Tailors**: for making-up new clothes and mending, Jl. Sukarno, near Cathedral. **Textiles**: Ende is a good place to buy local ikat from Ende, Kelimutu, Moni and elsewhere (see box, **page 935**). Salesmen and women visit the losmen, and congregate at the end of Jl. Pelabuhan (near Jl. Hatta and the port). For a sarong, expect to pay 15,000-30,000Rp, depending on quality. There is also a good range on sale at the *Minang Baru Restaurant*, including Sumba blankets.

Local transport   Bemos ply the main roads, routes are marked over the roof (200Rp). Most link the town bus terminals, Ndao and Wolowona. The bemo terminal is by the Pasar Mbongawani, near the centre of town.

Banks & money changers   BNI, Jl. Jend. Sudirman (up hill from Depot Ende Restaurant), will change cash and travellers' cheques in major currencies.

Useful addresses   General Post Office: Jl. Sam Ratulangi (inconvenient, out of town); Post Office: Jl. Yos Sudarso 4. Perumtel: Jl. Kelimutu 5 (international telephone, telegraph and fax.). Hospital: Jl. Mesjid.

Airline offices   Merpati, Jl. Nangka, T 355.

Tourist offices   Tourist 'desk', *Kantor Bupati*, Jl. Eltari (near intersection with Jl. Nangka), very helpful man running the desk; useful pamphlet and map on sights around Ende and practicalities.

Transport to & from Ende   54 km from Moni, 147 km from Maumere, 284 km from Larantuka, 125 km from Bajawa, 255 km from Ruteng. **NB**: the road to Maumere was badly damaged during the Dec 1992 earthquake; it is now open but in poor condition; expect delays during the rainy season. **By air**: Ende's Ipi airport is on the SE edge of town; bemos to the centre cost about 1,500Rp, although it's only a 50m walk to the main road where there are frequent public bemos for 200Rp. It is a 5-10 min walk from the airport to the closest of the losmen. Daily connections on Merpati with Denpasar, Kupang and other destinations in Nusa Tenggara. **By bus**: Ende has 2 bus terminals. Ndao terminal is for Bajawa 5 hrs, Ruteng 10 hrs and other destinations to the W. It is situated on the NW side of town, off Jl. Imam Bonjol and 1 km from the centre. Wolowona terminal is for buses to Wolowaru 2¼ hrs, Moni/Kelimutu 2¾ hrs, Maumere 6 hrs, Larantuka 10 hrs, and other destinations to the E and is at the end of Jl. Gatot Subroto, away from the town centre. Constant bemos link both terminals and the town centre. Buses from Bajawa and Maumere drop passengers off at losmen if requested. *Agogo* bus company runs a service to Ruteng and Maumere and has its offices at Jl. Pelabuhan 28. **By boat**: the Pelni ship *Kelimutu* docks at Ende twice on its 2-week circuit between Semarang and Dili (see route map, **page 1008**). The Pelni office is at Jl.

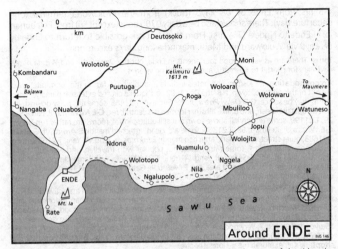

Around **ENDE**

Kathedral 2, T 21043. **NB**: at different times, depending upon the state of the tides, the *Kelimutu* docks at either of Ende's 2 ports – Pelabuhan Ende at Jl. Hatta 1 in the heart of town, or the new Pelabuhan Ipi to the south-east. Check at the Pelni office. There is also a weekly ferry on Wed to Kupang, and it is sometimes possible to hitch a lift on a freighter.

ENDE TO LARANTUKA via Kelimutu and Maumere

For the first 45 mins out of Ende the road rises spectacularly up through a limestone gorge, with worryingly precipitous drops. After 50 km the road reaches the town of Moni, the logical base for trips to the stunning crater lakes of Mount Kelimutu. From Moni the road descends to the coast and the town of Maumere, a distance of 93 km. The coral gardens near Maumere offer some of the best snorkelling and diving in Indonesia. Continuing E from Maumere, the last leg of the Trans-Flores Highway runs 137 km to the port of Larantuka. This was one of the centres of Portuguese missionary activity in Flores, and remains among the most obviously Christian towns on the island.

Kelimutu and Moni

Mount Kelimutu, with its three-coloured crater lakes, is one of the highlights of Flores. The first foreigners to climb the volcano were the Dutchmen Le Roux and Van Suchtelen in 1915. The lakes are at 1,640m and their colours have changed over the years, as the chemicals and minerals in the waters have reacted. In the 1970s they were red, white and blue; now they are, rather less spectacularly, maroon (almost black), iridescent green, and yellow-green. Local villagers believe that the lakes are the resting places for souls called by Mutu (Kelimutu): young people are destined for one lake, old for another, while witches and evil people go to the third. On a clear morning, the view of the crater lakes and the surrounding mountains is simply unforgettable.

The nearby village of **Moni** has become the main tourist base from which to visit

Mount Kelimutu. **Getting to Kelimutu**: reaching the summit used to require an early morning/late night trek of 8 km; today there is a truck which takes people up to the summit at about 0400, in time for the sunrise, 1 hr (2,500Rp). Ask at your losmen to check on departure time and make it known that you wish to be picked-up. The truck will also take passengers down again, although the 8 km walk is easy enough and very worthwhile (the road to the summit is 12 km, but the well marked path – Jalan Potong (Jalan Shortcut) – only 8 km). *Ojeks* (motorcycle taxis) will also take people to the top (5,000Rp). Having reached the viewing spot on the summit, everyone waits for the dawn and hopes that it will be clear. The road to the summit was closed following the Dec 1992 earthquake, but is now open once more. **NB**: it is very cold, both at the summit and on the open truck; take a sweater/blanket – the really well prepared also have a flask of coffee. Also note that it is often cloudy and it may be necessary to wait a few days for a clear morning. Moni is a friendly village with beautiful walks in the surrounding area and excursions to local villages (see below).

In Moni, the **market** on Tuesday mornings on the playing field is worth seeing. There are also **hot springs** and a waterfall just off the road to Ende.

Excursions

Wolowaru is situated on the main Ende-Maumere road, 11 km from Moni. This is a bigger town than Moni but has not developed into such a tourist base for climbing Mount Kelimutu. It is worth visiting on market days (Mon, Wed and Sat) when there is a reasonable range of ikat on sale (**see page 935**). **Accommodation** includes: **D Losmen Kelimutu**, T 20, clean, some attached mandis. The **Jawa Timur** is a popular restaurant stop for buses travelling through the town; it has good food. **Getting there**: by *bis kayu* from Moni, or on a bus from Ende or Maumere.

Jopu is a weaving village 4 km from Wolowaru, producing weft ikat (**see page 935**). The various processes involved in producing ikat are on view to visitors (**see page 721**). **Getting there**: take a *bis kayu* to Wolowaru and then a bemo to Jopu.

Nggela 15 km from Wolowaru on the same road as Jopu, this weaving village has become over-touristed. However ikat is on sale and production processes are on view (**see page 721**). The locals employ rather pushy sales tactics. There are hotsprings and a couple of homestays here. **Getting there**: take a *bis kayu* to Wolowaru, and a bemo to Nggela; there is also a daily boat (except Fri) to Ende from the beach, which is a steep 2 km descent from Nggela, 2½ hrs, only recommended for the hardy, as it is easy to fall out of the small canoe, which transports you from shore to boat.

Accommodation in Moni Accommodation is quite poor in Moni, and the Dec 1992 earthquake compounded this by causing extensive damage. Note that although rebuilding is continuing apace, there may be a shortage of rooms during 1993 and into 1994. **D** *Bungalow Hotel* (10 mins walk from Moni village on road to Ende), clean and attractive, rec; **E** *Wisma Kelimutu*; **F** *Amina Moe*, friendly with excellent food, must book in restaurant, if you are not staying there, rec; **F** *Daniel*, cold water, shared mandi, friendly and popular; **F** *Friendly*, best of the low price range.

Restaurants *Kelimutu* (next to the *Bungalow Hotel*), 10 min walk from the village towards Ende, usual Indonesian dishes, rec.

Transport to & from Moni 11 km from Wolowaru, 54 km from Ende, 93 km from Maumere. **NB**: it can be difficult to get out of Moni in the high season; you may have to hitch a lift on a truck travelling to Nggela on market day. **By bus**: regular connections with Ende 2¼ hrs, Wolowaru 2¾ hrs and Maumere, 3½ hrs. Getting out of Moni can sometimes be difficult as the buses passing through the town are often full; it may be necessary to catch a *bis kayu* to Wolowaru and wait for the bus there.

Maumere

Maumere, with a population of about 50,000, is a rather featureless, disorganized town: as if a small town suddenly had pretensions of being large and was not sure how to cope. Most people come here to dive and snorkel in some of the best sea gardens in Indonesia, and to explore the sights around the town.

It is possible to walk around Maumere in a morning. The central **market** is just that – central – with a good selection of ikat cloth on sale (see Shopping). The **port** (Pelabuhan Maumere), usually quiet, is 5 mins walk to the NW; on the way there the road passes **Maumere Cathedral**. **NB**: in Dec 1992 Maumere was devastated by earthquake and reconstruction is still underway (**see page 933**).

Excursions

Waiara and Sao Wisata Beaches lie 12-13 km E of Maumere. There is good swimming and the sea off the coast is a marine park and offers superb snorkelling and diving – or at least it did until the Dec 1992 earthquake. The coral has been badly damaged, especially off Sao Wisata Beach. The most seriously affected coral gardens are those in shallow waters. Experts are currently surveying the damage but preliminary indications are that some of the deeper dive sites still offer excellent diving. Two dive clubs are based here and run dive boats out to the reefs (see Accommodation and Sports). It is easiest to reach the reef by booking a place on one of these dive boats (US$25 – see Sports). **Getting to the beaches**: by bemo from the Terminal Timur (500Rp). It is also possible to reach the marine park by chartering a boat from Keliting (9 km E, take a bemo from Terminal Timur) for about 50,000Rp/day. There are regular boats crossing between the islands out on the reef and Keliting on market days (Wed and Fri). Homestays available on Permaan Island, and local guides (but little English) 10,000Rp/day.

Ladalero houses the only museum on Flores, the **Blikan Blewut Museum**. It is situated 9 km from town, on the road to Ende. A cluttered, mixed, yet interesting display of ethnographic exhibits, textiles and ceramics assembled by the local Seminary (Societas Verbi Divini). The Seminary suffered heavy damage during the earthquake, but the museum is still open to visitors. Admission: by donation. Open: 0730-1400 Mon-Sat, 1000-1400 Sun. **Getting there**: take a bus from Terminal Barat (250Rp).

Nita is about 2 km from Ladalero and 11 km from Maumere. The 'Rajah' here has a collection of old elephant tusks and other memorabilia. **Getting there**: take a bus from Terminal Barat (500Rp).

Sikka is a weaving village 25 km south of town. It is possible to buy ikat here at reasonable prices (check at *Harapan Jaya* for comparison – see Shopping) and see some of the multiple stages of the ikat process – something like 35 in all (**see page 721**). If on a tour, all the stages may be demonstrated. There is also an attractive **Portuguese church** at Sikka, white with green fretwork, built in 1800. **Getting there**: take a bus from Terminal Barat.

Watublapi is another, less frequently visited, weaving village, 11 km S from Geliting (which lies just E of Maumere, on the main trans-Flores road). Nearby is Bliran Sina Hill from where there are views N to the Flores Sea and S to the Sawu Sea. **Getting there**: take a bus from Terminal Timur.

Tours Day tours from Maumere to Sikka weaving village, the Ladalero museum and Nita; or to Geliting Market and Watublapi weaving village. Some hotels and shops have cars and drivers for charter. *Hotel Maiwali*, minibus to Wairara Beach (8,000Rp), Sikka weaving village (25,000Rp), Ladalero (8,000Rp), Kelimutu (75,000Rp one day leaving at 0300; 125,000Rp 2 days with one night in Moni). *Harapan Jaya*, a textile shop on Jl. Moa Toda has a car for hire (50,000Rp/day around town, 100,000Rp to Kelimutu). *Wina Ria Hotel* can arrange boats for snorkelling (60,000Rp). *Sea World* at Wairara Beach also organise tours to Sikka, Kelimutu and elsewhere (see accommodation).

Accommodation NB: the Dec 1992 earthquake caused extensive damage; however rooms are still available and most hotels are open. **B-D** *Maiwali*, Jl. Raja Don Tomas, T 180, some a/c, comfortable, but rather overpriced, karaoke bar, noisy at weekends, damaged during the earthquake but now largely repaired; **D** *Benggoan III*, Jl. K.S. Tubun, T 284, some a/c, featureless hollow building, but rooms are fine, price includes breakfast; **D** *Flora Jaya*, Jl. Raja Don Tomas, homely atmosphere, small rooms, price includes breakfast, damaged during the Dec 1992 earthquake but now largely repaired; **D-E** *Gardena*, Jl. Pattirangga 5, T 489, some a/c, 5 mins from town centre on quiet side street, popular with Indonesian officials; **E** *Benggoan I*, Jl. Moa Toda, T 41, some attached mandis, dirty and overpriced; **E** *Losmen Benggoan II*, Jl. Raya Centis (by market), T 283, dirty, overpriced; **E** *Losmen Bogor II*, Jl. Slamet Riyadi 4, T 271, thin walls, shared mandi, lacklustre management, edge of town; **E** *Wina Ria*, Jl. Gajah Mada, T 388 (about 5-10 mins walk out of town on road to Ende), shared mandi but large rooms, very clean, garden, rec; **F** *Homestay Varanus*, Jl. Nong Meak, friendly, nice garden, good value, rec; **F** *Losmen Bogor I*, Jl. Slamet Riyadi, rather dirty, shared mandi.

Dive Clubs at Waiara, 12 km from town: **B** *Flores Sao Wisata*, Wairara Beach, T 555, J 370333, F 3809595, better of the 2 dive centres, good equipment, **A** per day if diving; **B-C** *Sea World*, Jl. Nai Noha, Km 13, PO Box 3, T 570, some a/c, attractive cottages, price includes breakfast.

Restaurants Concentrated near the market on Jl. Raya Centis (aka Jl. Pasar Baru). ♦*Andika*, Jl. Raya Centis, simple Indonesian bakso, soto etc; *Saiyo*, Jl. Raya Centis, Padang; ♦♦*Sarinah*, Jl. Raya Centis, Chinese, excellent seafood, rec; ♦♦*Stevani Pub and Restaurant*, Jl. Raya Centis (near intersection with Jl. Raja Don Tomas), seafood, open air pavilions in garden; *Surya Indah II*, Jl. Raya Centis.

Entertainment Karaoke: *Maiwali Hotel*, Jl. Raja Don Tomas.

Sports Diving: excellent diving, approx. US$70/day; best to stay at one of the dive clubs (see accommodation). **Snorkelling**: it is possible to book a place on *Sao Wisata's* dive boat, US$25 with equipment, lunch and drinks provided.

Shopping Textiles: excellent range of ikat from all over Nusa Tenggara on sale at *Harapan Jaya*, Jl. Moa Toda (market area, opposite *Losmen Benggoan I*). Reasonable prices (but not bargains): ikat from Roti and Sabu, Ende (50,000Rp), Sumba (250,000Rp), Larantuka and Lembata (100-200,000Rp), Manggarai (near Ruteng) (50,000Rp), West Timor (150,000Rp), Sikka (25,000Rp). Also textiles next door at Subur Jaya.

Local transport Bemos: The bemo station is by the market on Jl. Jend. A. Yani in the centre of town. Bemos criss-cross the town linking the 2 bus terminals, Barat and Timur (200Rp).

Banks & money changers BNI, Jl. Soekarno-Hatta (behind and to the side of the Kantor Bupati), will change travellers' cheques and cash in major currencies.

Useful addresses General Post Office: Jl. Pos 2 (on the square near the Kantor Bupati). **Perumtel**: Jl. Soekarno-Hatta (200m from Jl. Jend. A. Yani) (international telephone and telegram). **Immigration Office**: Jl. Kom. A. Sucipto, T 151 (slip road to airport). **General Hospital**: Jl. Kesehatan, T 118. **Police**: Jl. Jend. A. Yani, T 110.

Airline offices Merpati, Jl. Raja Don Tomas, T 347; **Bouraq**, Jl. Nong Meak, T 467 (also agent on Jl. Moa Toda, next to *Benggoan I losmen*).

Tour companies & travel agents *Astura*, Jl. Yos Sudarso, T 498; *Floressa Wisata*, Jl. Jend. A. Yani, T 242; *Sikka Permai*, Jl. Pasar Lama, T 236.

Tourist offices Kantor Pariwisata, Jl. Wairklau, T 562, to get there, walk along Jl. Gajah Mada towards Ende, turn right after the Perusahaan Umum Listrik, and walk 400m – the office is just past the Kantor Statistik, 10-15 min in total from town centre, useful booklet, little English spoken.

Transport to & from Maumere 82 km from Wolowaru, 93 km from Moni, 147 km from Ende, 137 km from Larantuka. **NB**: the road to Ende was badly damaged during the Dec 1992 earthquake; it is now open but in poor condition; expect delays during the rainy season. **By air**: Maumere's Waioti Airport is 2 km E of the town centre, off the road towards Larantuka. Taxis to the town centre (3,000Rp) or walk the 750m to the main road and catch a bemo (200Rp). Regular connections by Merpati and Bouraq with Jakarta, Denpasar, Bima and Kupang, and towns in Kalimantan and Sulawesi. **By bus**: Maumere has 2 bus terminals; Terminal Barat on Jl. Gajah Mada for destinations to the W, including Wolowaru 3 hrs, Moni 3½ hrs and Ende 6 hrs; and Terminal Timur E of town on Jl. Larantuka for eastern destinations including Larantuka 4 hrs. Buses link the 2 terminals and the town centre (200Rp). Buses arriving in Maumere drop passengers off at their losmen/hotels. *Agogo* (for Ende, Moni and Wolowaru) has its offices on Jl. Jend. A. Yani; *Sinar Remaja* on Jl. Pattirangga, and *Sinar Agung* (for Larantuka and Ende) on Jl. Gajah Mada by the Terminal Barat. Losmen/hotels will also usually book tickets.

By boat: the Pelabuhan Maumere is a 5-10 min walk NW from the town centre. The Pelni ship *Tatamailu* docks here on its two week circuit between Surabaya, Sulawesi, Maluku and Irian Jaya (see route map, **page 1008**). The Pelni office is next to *Losmen Bogor II* on Jl. I. S. Pranoto (aka Jl. Slamet Riyadi), just over the bridge on the road to the port. Irregular mixed cargo vessels leave here for Ende, Reo, Kupang, Larantuka and Surabaya.

Larantuka

The small town of Larantuka is the district capital of East Flores, with a population of 25,000. It is strongly Christian, with a remarkable Easter celebration showing Portuguese origins (16th century). Particular devotion is shown to the Virgin Mary, a statue of whom is reportedly miraculously washed-up on the shore here. On 8 Sept 1887, Don Lorenzo Diaz Viera de Godinho II consecrated the entire town to the Virgin. The town's name means 'on the way', and its strategic position made it a locally important port – Magellan's chronicler Francesco Antonio Pigafetta records passing here in 1522 on the expedition's voyage home from the Spice Islands (Maluku).

The **Chapel of the Virgin Mary**, in the centre of town, houses the sacred statue of the Virgin (see Festivals). On Saturdays, the Mama Muji pray in ancient Latin and Portuguese, distorted to such a degree that it is unintelligible even to students of the language (see box). There are also prayers said each evening. There are a number of other churches in town including the century-old **Cathedral of Larantuka** and the **Chapel of Christ** (Tuan Ana Chapel). The old **docks** are also worth visiting. Larantuka was fortunate to survive the earthquake, which devastated much of eastern Flores, relatively unscathed.

Festivals Easter (moveable): the sacred statue of the Virgin is washed and dressed on Easter Thursday (the water, in the process, becoming Holy Water with healing powers). In the afternoon the statue is kissed (the *Cio Tuan* ceremony) by the townspeople and other pilgrims, while the streets are cleaned and prepared for Good Friday. On the afternoon of Good Friday, the statue is taken to the Cathedral, where a statue of Jesus from the Chapel of Christ joins it. Following the service at about 1900, the statues are paraded through the town in a candle-lit procession. There are numerous other festivities during Holy Week.

The old Catholics of Larantuka

In 1613 a Dutch ship, the *Half Moon*, anchored off Solor and bombarded the Portuguese fort there, forcing the 1,000 strong population to surrender. Two of the Dominican friars – Caspar de Spiritu Santo and Augustino de Magdalena – asked that rather than withdraw to Melaka with the rest of the population, they be landed at Larantuka. Here they set about building another mission and by 1618 they had established more than 20 missions in the area. However, as the Portuguese lost influence so the Roman Catholics of Larantuka became isolated. The raja of the area took the title 'Servant of the Queen of the Rosary' and the church's devotional objects – chalice, cross, statues and so on – became part of local *adat* or tradition. Christianity became fossilized: the few Dutch Protestant ministers were sent smartly packing when they unsatisfactorily answered questions about Mary, Mother of Jesus, and visits by Portuguese Roman Catholic priests were few and far between.

Even so, the Roman Catholic rites and beliefs inculcated by the original Dominican friars were handed down through the generations. Devotees were taught to say their prayers in Latin and old Portuguese, and to wear robes like those of 17th century *penitentes*, with pointed hoods. When the Roman Catholics of Larantuka were finally 're-discovered' by the Dutch priest, Father C. de Hesselle in 1853 he was amazed to see the population keeping to a tradition over two centuries old. The most remarkable of these ceremonies is the Easter parade, replete with a rudely-hewn cross carried in procession (see Festivals).

Accommodation **D** *Fortuna*, Jl. Diponegoro 171, T 190, 2 km NE of town, private bathroom; **D** *Tresna*, Jl. Liker, T 140, best hotel in town; **D-E** *Rulis*, Jl. Yos Sudarso 36, T 198, rather scruffy, popular.

Transport to & from Larantuka 137 km from Maumere. **By air**: Gewayan Tana airport is 12 km N of town. 2 flights/week on Merpati from Kupang and on to Lewoleba and Lembata. **By bus**: regular connections with Maumere's Terminal Timur, 4 hrs. **By boat**: a ferry leaves Larantuka port (5 km from town on road to Maumere) on Tues and Sat nights for Kupang. It is usually packed, although the captain sometimes allows tourists to sleep behind the wheelhouse or on the roof; making for a wonderful panorama of the stars and far more comfortable than on deck. Return ferry from Kupang departs Thur and Sun.

LEMBATA

Lembata is a small island to the E of Flores, famous for its traditional whaling communities. The largest town on the island is **Lewoleba**, situated on the W coast. There is a spectacular **weekly market** held in Lewoleba each Mon; Lembata ikat is available.

The traditional **whaling village of Lamalera** is on Lembata's S coast. The population trace their origins to Lapan Batan, an island between Lembata and Pantar. Unlike many of the other villages on Lembata which are land-based and rely on maize, rice and sweet potatoes, the population of Lamalera relies on fishing, and particularly whaling (see box). Until the late 1980s, Lamalera was so far off the beaten-track that virtually no one ventured there; the village has now become part of the travellers' itinerary. Even the tour company *Natrabu* runs a tour to Lamalera from Kupang.

Accommodation In Lewoleba: **D** *Losmen Rejeki I & II*, helpful owners, excellent food, shared mandi.

Shopping Textiles: Lembata ikat (**see page 935**) is produced in villages across the island; available from Lewoleba market.

Banks & money changers The *Losmen Rejeki I & II* will change US$ cash.

Transport to & from Lembata **By air**: Lewoleba airport is 3 km from town. Merpati has 2 flights/week from Kupang to Lewoleba via Larantuka, returning the same day to Kupang. **By boat**: 2 ferries/day from Larantuka to Lewoleba, 4 hrs. There are also irregular boats from Larantuka to Lamalera, 9 hrs. The Kupang-Larantuka ferry calls at Lewoleba on Mon and Fri, returning to Larantuka before continuing on to Kupang on Tues and Sat.

Lamalera's whaling

The whaling season runs from Apr to Sept when the great whales migrate through the area to the rich southern oceans, and the villagers set out in man-powered boats in search of sperm whales (*ikan paus* – 'pope fish'), sharks, manta rays and other large denizens of the deep. The boats belong to village clans, or sections of clans, and have been constantly repaired and rebuilt over the centuries. They are said to be modelled on the ships that brought the original inhabitants from Lapan Batar.

The animals are killed using hand-thrown harpoons, the harpooner literally launching himself off the boat to plunge the iron as deeply as possible into the whale. Because, like Eskimos and a handful of other people, the hunters of Lamalera are traditional, they have been exempted from the world-wide ban on whaling. It is thought the two villages who still hunt whales only kill 20-30 a year; hardly a threat to the population. The meat is divided traditionally among families in the village, and the women then barter a portion for agricultural products and other goods. Only the teeth of the sperm whales are traded beyond the island.

Sadly, but perhaps predictably, insensitive tourists seem to have already made an impact: there have been reports that whalers have stopped rowing mid-ocean and demanded additional payment.

ALOR

The rugged island of Alor is E of Lembata and is 100 km long and 35 km wide at its widest point. The capital, **Kalabahi**, is on the W coast and the island has a population of about 150,000. The various tribes of the island – Nedebang, Dieng, Kaka and Mauta – practice shifting cultivation (see page 32), although as land becomes scarcer, so they are being forced to become settled agriculturalists. Most of the population are Christian.

Alor illustrates, in microcosm, the enormous diversity of Indonesia's people. There are 7 major language groups spoken on the island, representing some 50 languages in all – or one language for every 3,000 inhabitants.

Accommodation in Kalabahi D-E *Adi Dharma*, on the waterfront, owner speaks English and is a good source of information; **D-E** *Melati*, on the waterfront.

Shopping Textiles: Alor ikat.

Transport to & from Alor By air: Alor's Mali airport is 28 km from Kalabahi. Connections on Merpati with Kupang, Larantuka, Lewoleba, Rote and Denpasar. **By boat:** one ferry/week from Kupang to Kalabahi, leaving Kupang on Mon and returning from Kalabahi on Tues (12,000Rp).

The *Moko* drum currency debacle

Before the 19th century, bronze *moko* drums were traded and used as bride price. They are related to the Dongson drums of northern Vietnam (**see page 706**), although no exact equivalent has ever been found there. The older examples of *moko* also show similar decoration to their presumed Vietnamese prototypes, although newer examples have Chinese and Indian inspired floral motifs. How these drums came to Alor is not known, but they have also been discovered elsewhere in the Indonesian archipelago (see Bali, **page 708**).

Around 1900, imitation brass *moko* began to be made in large quantities in Gresik, Java and exported to Alor. They created chaos in a monetary system which owed its stability to there always being a limited number of *moko* in circulation. In 1914, in an attempt to stabilize the *moko*, the Dutch introduced coinage and forbad all use of the drums in transactions, except in tax payments. This exemption was designed to take *moko* out of circulation; some 1,660 drums were acquired, and then melted down.

Bride price in Alor is still sometimes paid using *moko*. The cheapest drum, and thus presumably the cheapest wife, is said to cost about 150,000-200,000 Rp. The oldest drums are the most valuable, and through time and their association with powerful people, drums are thought to acquire powers of their own. Such drums are rarely traded, but remain within the family.

SUMBA

INTRODUCTION

The oval island of Sumba is noted for its megalithic tombs (mainly in the E), fine ikat cloth (mainly in the W) and horseback-fighting festivals. It is divided into 2 administrative districts covering a land area of 11,052 sq km: the regencies of East and West Sumba. Their capitals are Waingapu and Waikabubak respectively. The island lies outside the volcanic arc that runs through Java and the other islands of Nusa Tenggara. The generally subdued relief presents a startling contrast to Java, Bali and Flores.

Though Sumba is only 300 km long and 80 km wide, the 2 regencies of East and West Sumba are environmentally very different. While the E of the island is generally dry (annual rainfall 674 mm) and barren, the W is considerably wetter (1,826 mm), and consequently much greener. The dry season stretches over 7 to 8 months from Apr to Oct. During these months, the rolling landscape is dry and desolate; but during the rainy season the green grasslands of the W are not unlike those of Ireland. Rice can be cultivated only in the valleys where perennial rivers flow, and in the dry season these – like the Lewa Valley, mid-way between Waingapu and Waikabubak – are small oases of green in an otherwise parched landscape. Most of the rest of the island is fit only for extensive cattle grazing and horse raising. The island's population is about 425,000: 280,000 in the agriculturally richer west, the remainder in the east.

Historically, Sumba was known as a source of horses, slaves and sandalwood, but lying as it does to the S of the island arc of Nusa Tenggara, it managed to escape the successive streams of Hindu, Muslim and Christian interlopers who influenced the area. Although the island did come under the influence of the Majapahit Kingdom of Java from the 5th century, and rather later from the Sultanate of Bima in Flores, it was never directly ruled from the outside. The first Europeans to note the existence of the island were the crew of the Portuguese vessel the *Victoria* in

The Sumbanese slave trade

Sumba's role as a source of slaves dates from as early as historical accounts exist. The Sultan of Bima on Sumbawa, and the sultans and kings of S Sulawesi, Flores, Lombok and Bali all obtained slaves from the island. At Ende, in Flores, it was said by the Dutch visitor Goronvius in 1855 that "there is hardly a man to be found, of moderate or even limited means, who is not the owner of some twenty slaves, all of them from Sumba". Dutch interest in Sumba as a source of slaves dates from the mid-18th century, and the island quickly became the major supplier to the colonial power.

Why Sumba should have filled this role is linked to the nature of society and the absence of a strong, central power. The structure of Sumbanese society was rigidly divided into an aristocratic (*maramba*) class, and a slave (*ata*) class. The latter could be freely bought and sold, and even denied the right to marry, own property or to have a funeral – the essential qualities of human existence. When the first colonial administrator was dispatched to Sumba in 1866, he reported the island to be lawless and politically fragmented. By this time, the NW coast was effectively depopulated, such were the numbers of slaves plucked from the island by raiders. The trade was officially abolished in 1860, but continued until the early 20th century. The first Resident was even given a slave girl as a welcome gift when he first arrived on the island.

the 16th century, part of Magellan's expedition. Although marked on maps following this original sighting, it was not until the Dutch arrived in the 17th century that Western contact intensified.

Today, it is thought that over 50% of the population, predominantly in the W, still adhere to the traditional, animist, Merapu beliefs. Another 35% are Protestant and the remainder, Catholic, Muslim, Hindu and Buddhist.

WAINGAPU

Waingapu is the capital of the regency of East Sumba, and the island's largest town with a population of 25,000. In reality, it is little more than an overgrown village. It is a quiet place to read and rest-up, and a base from which to explore the far more interesting surrounding countryside.

The **Old Docks** area (*Pelabuhan Lama*) can be entertaining: fishing boats, and the occasional inter-island mixed cargo boat, dock here. Near by, just off Jalan Yos Sudarso, is a small **market**, with a larger market next to the bus station on the outskirts of town. Neither is particularly notable.

Excursions
Although Waingapu and East Sumba do not have the megaliths of West Sumba, it is the centre of fine ikat production (**see page 952**) and there are a number of weaving villages within easy reach of the town.

Prailiu is an ikat weaving village only 2 km SE of town. Stages in the ikat weaving process can usually be seen and there is cloth for sale – it is even sometimes possible to buy good, finely-worked ikat here. The village has a small number of inferior 'megalithic' tombs, both modern and traditional in design. **Getting there**: walk or take one of the constant bemos that run from the bemo stop near the bus terminal (200Rp).

Kawangu is another weaving village, 11 km E of Waingapu. Like Prailiu, stages in the ikat process can often be witnessed and there is cloth for sale. **Getting there**: regular bemos run from the bemo stop next to the bus station (300Rp).

Villages, houses and tombs of Sumba

The layout of a *paraingu* – or village – in Sumba should conform to traditional rules. The village symbolizes a ship, with a bow (*tunda kambata*), deck (*kani padua*) and stern (*kiku kemudi*). The houses are arranged around the ancestors' burial place.

The striking, traditional, thatched houses – low-sided, yet high-peaked – are built around a fireplace which is positioned between the 4 main pillars. There are 2 doors: a front door for men, and a rear entrance for women. Due to poor ventilation, the smoke from the open fire tends to fill the houses, making them dirty and suffocating. Each consists of 3 'floors': cattle are kept at ground level and most weaving takes place here. The first floor is the main living area, with various rooms for sleeping (divided according to sex, age and rank), grain storage, cooking and eating. The upper section, known as the *uma deta* or *hindi merapu*, is for the spirits; here, sacred objects are stored. In West Sumba, some of the finest traditional houses can be seen at Anakalang, Tarung and Prai Goli; in East Sumba, at Prailiu and Pau. The only difference between the dwellings is that those in West Sumba tend to have higher roofs.

At the centre of the village are the megalithic tombs for which Sumba is famous. These fall into 4 broad types: the first is a simple dolmen, with 4 stone pillars supporting a rectangular stone slab. The second, is similar to the first, but carved and ornamented. The third has stone walls enclosing the 4 pillars. And the fourth, the added feature of stone stairs leading up to the covering slab.

Melolo is a lovely, overgrown (with vegetation), little town 60 km SE of Waingapu and one of the most rewarding of excursions. From here there is local transport to the traditional village and weaving centre of Rende, 7 km on along the road S to Baing. Rende not only produces good *ikat*, but also has some of the most impressive *megalithic tombs* in East Sumba, surrounded by high-peaked *traditional houses* (**see page 951**). Unfortunately, because Rende is firmly on the tour group itinerary, prices of cloth are high and rising. Good pieces made with home-grown cotton and using natural dyes are around 1,000,000Rp. The best weaver in the village sells cloth from the house close to the *kepala desa's* (headman's) residence. From Melolo, there is a pleasant walk past rice paddys to another traditional village: **Pau**. There are more megalithic tombs, peaked traditional houses and ikat at the village of *Umabara*, about 5 km W of Melolo. **Accommodation**: there is a **losmen** in Melolo and a **homestay** in Rende (at the *kepala desa's*). **Getting to Melolo**: several buses each day from the bus terminal, 2 hrs (1,500Rp).

Kaliuda is an ikat weaving village, 50 km past Melolo and 110 km from Waingapu, just off the road to Baing. The ikat produced here features, predominantly, chicken and horse motifs. Weavers from other villages make fun of the local artists saying – 'Oh, all they can do are chickens and horses'. Much of the ikat is unfinished (that is, without the border strip) and clearly, therefore, for tourist rather than local consumption. **Accommodation**: the *kepala desa* takes in visitors, but the rooms are very basic and rather dirty. **Getting there**: 2-3 buses each day from the bus terminal.

Tours The *Elim* and *Sandle Wood Hotels* can arrange cars and guides to take tourists around the main sights. *Zaid Bachmid* (with some English) at the Tourist Office is also willing to guide tourists.

Accommodation Most of Waingapu's hotels and losmen are found around the bus station, about 1½ km S of the town centre. **C-D** *Elim*, Jl. Jend. A. Yani 73, T 323, some a/c, friendly, good rooms and source of information, this is where the local intelligentsia meet – the Sumbanese equivalent of the left bank of the Seine; **C-D** *Lima Saudara*, Jl. Wanggameti 2, T 282, rooms rather dirty, attached bathrooms, average, price includes breakfast; **C-D** *Sandle*

The ikat *hinggi* blankets of Sumba

Sumba produces perhaps the most distinctive warp ikat in Indonesia. Traditionally, the weaving of cloth was the preserve of aristocratic women who, free from agricultural and household chores, had the time to produce finely woven cloth. Ikat is still woven on backstrap looms, although natural indigo and red morinda dyes are being replaced by chemical substitutes. The most commonly produced cloth is the *hinggi*, a large blanket worn by men. Characteristic motifs include animals such as horses, dogs, snakes, monkeys, crocodiles, fish and lizards. Each has its own symbolism – dogs with warriors, snakes with rebirth and long life, crocodiles with the afterlife. Another common motif is the skull tree or *andung*, which draws upon the former practice of hanging the heads of vanquished enemies from a tree in the centre of a village to scare away evil spirits.

The quality of Sumba ikat is declining, and most lengths of cloth can only be described as 'tourist' material: large and simple motifs, often without the important border strip or *kabakil*, woven with machine spun yarn, coloured with chemical dyes, and showing 'bleeding' of dye across the borders between design elements. First-class cloth is almost exclusively reserved for burial, and no local, quite literally, would be seen dead in the blankets sold to visitors. Wrapping the body in fine ikat ensures that the spirit of the dead man or woman will reach *Parai Merapu* – Merapu heaven. The transition from the physical world to that of the spirits is critical, and the various elements of the death rite must be strictly adhered to.

Some people maintain that it is cheaper to buy cloth in Bali where shop owners purchase in bulk from villages with which they have special relations. Tour groups visiting villages like Rende have pushed prices up considerably. To buy a good piece of cloth expect to have to pay 300,000Rp or more.

Wood, Jl. D.I. Panjaitan, T 119, some a/c, behind the bus station, large, clean rooms, some attached mandis, rec; **D** *Losmen Surabaya*, Jl. El Tari 2, T 125, opposite the bus station, average, noisy, some attached mandis; **E** *Kaliuda*, Jl. D.I. Panjaitan, behind bus station, clean; **E** *Losmen Permata*, Jl. Kartini 10, overlooking the old docks near the centre of town, large, clean rooms with mandis, nice position on grassed square, excellent value, price includes breakfast, rec.

Restaurants ♦*Rajawali*, Jl. Sutomo 96, good Chinese, seafood, pleasant atmosphere, rec; *Sumbawa*, Jl. Palapa (behind the bus station); ♦*Surabaya*, Jl. El Tari 2, Chinese, seafood.

Shopping Textiles: ikat is the obvious thing to buy in Sumba, and East Sumba produces the best. Men peddle cloth around hotels and on the street; or try one of the cloth-making villages outside Waingapu (see excursions). Most hotels have a selection of cloth for sale, particularly the *Sandle Wood Hotel*. **NB**: Sumba blankets vary a great deal in quality and a reasonable piece cannot be bought for less than 150,000Rp; good lengths are 300,000Rp or more.

Local transport Bemos: ply the main routes around town (200Rp); the central bemo stop is near the bus terminal. **Motorcycle hire**: from the *Losmen Surabaya* (1,500Rp/hr). **Car/minibus hire**: from the *Losmen Surabaya* (6,000Rp/hr); or the *Sandle Wood Hotel* (5,000Rp/hr); for longer journeys, charges are 50,000Rp return to Melolo, 60,000Rp to Paun and Rende, and 100,000Rp to Waikabubak and Baing.

Banks & money changers Bank Rakyat Indonesia, Jl. Jend. A. Yani 36, changes cash and travellers' cheques.

Useful addresses General Post Office: Jl. Sutomo 21. **Perumtel**: Jl. Cut Nyak Din 19 (international telephone, telex and fax). **General Hospital**: Jl. Adam Malik, Hambala.

Airline offices Merpati, Jl. Jend. A. Yani 73 (at the *Elim Hotel*), T 323; **Bouraq**, Jl. Yos Sudarso 57, T 363.

Tour companies & travel agents *Eben Haezer*, Jl. Jend. A. Yani 73, T 323.

Tourist offices *Kantor Cabang Dinas Pariwisata*, Jl. Suharto T791, no useful maps or pamphlets, but helpful staff.

Transport to & from Waingapu 173 km from Waikabubak, 178 km from Melolo, 185 km from

Sumba Ikat motifs

A design based on the mamuli, a gold ear ornament and traditional marriage gift.

Man with skull tree (andung), and cockatoos.

Cockatoos

Roosters

Horses

Rende, 220 km from Baing. **By air**: Waingapu's Mau Hau Airport is 6 km SE of town. *Transport to town*: a share minibus takes passengers to their hotels (2,000Rp) or catch one of the regular bemos that run along the road just outside the terminal to the bus station in town (200Rp). The Merpati minibus takes passengers from the Merpati Office (*Hotel Elim*) to the airport. Daily flights by Merpati to Kupang; 3 flights/week to Denpasar via Tambolaka (Waikabubak), Bima and Mataram. Bouraq fly 3 times/week to Kupang and Denpasar. **By bus**: the station is 1½ km S of town, near most of the hotels, on Jl. El Tari. Regular bemos link it with town. Several buses each day to Waikabubak, 5-6 hrs (with over an hour cruising for fares). Also several departures each day to Melolo (for Rende) 2 hrs, Lewa 2 hrs and Baing. Buses will pick passengers up from hotels and losmen with advance warning. **By taxi**: for groups of 4 or more it can make sense to hire a car; public transport, though cheap, is slow (see Local transport). **By boat**: larger vessels, including the Pelni ship *Kelimutu* and Pelni pioneer vessels (*Perintis*), dock at the new harbour – Pelabuhan Baru. Though only 200m from the old harbour by water, it is a circuitous 7 km ride by bemo. The *Kelimutu* docks once a fortnight on its circuit through Nusa Tenggara (see route map page 1008). Example of fares: Ende (13,500-34,070Rp); Padangbai, Bali (42,600-129,570Rp); Banjarmasin (73,600-231,570Rp); Semarang, Java (93,600-192,570Rp). *Pelni* ships sail to Ende and Kupang via Sawu and Roti; ask at the Pelni office for details. The Pelni office is close to the old harbour at Jl. Pelabuhan 2 T27, near the centre of town.

WAIKABUBAK

Waikabubak is the largest town on Sumba and the capital of West Sumba. Even so, it is really little more than a village, with a population of only 15,000. Situated at 800m above sea-level, the town is cooler than Waingapu and during the coldest months of Jun and Jul can be chilly at night. West Sumba has the greatest concentration, and the finest, megalithic tombs on the island. Between Feb and Mar, it is possible to see the spectacular *Pasola* festival in some of the surrounding districts (see Festivals, below).

The village of **Tarung** is only ½ km W of town, set on a small hill. Being so close to Waikabubak, it has inevitably been influenced by the large number of tourists who walk up here. Nevertheless, it has several – rather plain – tombs and 33 traditional, thatched houses (see box, page 951). Tarung is also an important ceremonial centre. Admission to village: by donation. Another village that can be reached on foot from Waikabubak is **Bondomaroto**. This is an ikat-producing village with some rather inferior tombs. Admission to village: by donation.

Excursions
Anakalang is a district 20 km E of Waikabubak and, conveniently, close to the main road to Waingapu. This district has the greatest concentration of megalithic tombs to be found in Sumba: at **Pasunga**, on the main road, there is one of the largest tombs in Sumba. The nearby village of **Kabunduk** also has some well-carved graves, while **Lai Tarung** – walking distance from Kabunduk and set on a hill – is regarded as an important ceremonial and spiritual centre. There are 10 carved stone pillars on which sits a 'traditional' house. From Kabunduk, it is a

Sumba death rites
The transition from the physical world to the world of the spirits is critical to the Sumbanese and is ensured by strict adherence to the burial rite. Following a person's death, a close relative calls his or her name 4 times; should there be no answer, he or she is pronounced dead. The body is bathed, coated in coconut oil, and dressed in ikat sarongs. The number, and quality, of the sarongs is indicative of status. The arms and legs of the body are broken, and the dead person placed in the foetal position, either in a wooden coffin, or wrapped in buffalo hide. The body, except if the dead person was of lowly status, is guarded by 4 men. During this period, the spirit of the deceased is still regarded as roaming the village.

The second stage of the burial ceremony involves the preparation of the tomb. A stone is dragged into the village by large numbers of people. Relatives bring cattle, horses or pigs to be sacrificed, the size of the sacrificial gift being dictated by the status and closeness of relationship with the deceased. The corpse is then taken to the tomb and buried. In the past, if the person was of royal blood, a slave was buried alive along with the corpse.

20 mins walk to **Matakakeri**, where there is what is touted as being the heaviest megalith in Sumba – weighing 70 tonnes – and erected in 1939 following the death of the King of Anakalang. It is said (these figures are often quoted, but have not been substantiated) that 2,000 men were required to quarry the stone and then move it here, and that 3 people died in the process. 250 buffalo were slaughtered and 10 tonnes of rice consumed during the burial ritual. **Getting there**: take a bus heading for Lewa/Waingapu or for Anakalang.

Wanokaka lies 18 km S of Waikabubak. This is one of the districts where the spectacular annual *Pasola festival* is held (see below). Nearby, the village of **Prai Goli** or Paigoli has one of the finest, and best carved, tombs in Sumba. **Getting there**: by hire car or motorcycle (see Local transport).

Pantai Rua and Pantai Morossi are two beaches S of Waikabubak. Pantai Rua is good for surfing and has the new *Sumba Reefs Hotel*. The surfing at Pantai Morossi is reputed to be even better; the S coastline of Sumba is exposed to the onslaught of the Southern Seas. There are no losmen at Morossi, although it is possible to stay in surrounding villages. **Getting there**: it is easiest to hire a motorcycle, 1-2 hrs (see Local transport).

Festivals Feb/Mar: *Pasola* (moveable) – Sumba's most exciting festival is the annual pasola, held over 8 days following the full moon. This fertility rite involves a battle between massed ranks of horsemen representing 2 villages. They use (blunted) spears, and the battle can last from morning until nightfall. It not unusually results in serious injury, even death. The battle is preceded by other traditional pursuits and ceremonies – traditional boxing (*pajura*), purification rituals, and the nyale ceremony (see below). The pasola is particularly popular in the districts of Wanokaka (18 km S of town), Lamboya and Kodi. It is also linked with the appearance of the nyale worms – multi-coloured seaworms that mass along the coast at a certain time of year (**see page 921**). The *wua nyali* are believed to foretell the state of the harvest – the larger the number, the more abundant the crop.

Nov: *Wula Podhu* (moveable), a period of fasting, and a festival, held in the village of Tarung just outside Waikabubak. Traditional dances, musical celebrations and sacrifices, ending with an extravagant night of dance and song.

Accommodation C *Mona Lisa*, Jl. Adiaksa (2 km NW out of town towards Waikelo), no food, poor location; D *Losmen Mona Lisa*, Jl. Gajah Mada, T 24, has moved up-market, but is still a good source of information; D *Manandang*, Jl. Pemuda 4, T 197, good, clean rooms, friendly, with the best losmen food in town, rec; D *Rakuta*, Jl. Veteran, T 75, shared mandi, rather run down, all meals included; E *Pelita*, Jl. Jend. A. Yani 2, T 104, dirty.

Restaurants Most visitors eat in their hotels or losmen; the *Manandang* has the best food in town. Alternatively, there are a selection of cheap warungs on Jl. Jend. A. Yani.

Local transport Public transport is irregular. Hiring a car to visit out-of-town sights makes good sense for groups of 4 or more. Most losmen and hotels have vehicles for charter. Examples of return rates are: 15,000Rp to Waikelosawa; 35,000Rp to Wanokaka; 50,000Rp to Lamboya/Sodan and Waitabuta; 60,000Rp to Waikelo; 75,000Rp to Memboro; 85,000Rp to Kodi. A cheaper and equally flexible way to get around is by motorcycle taxi; alternatively, some losmen/hotels are willing to rent out motorbikes by the day (10,000-15,000Rp).

Banks & money changers Bank Rakyat Indonesia, Jl. Gajah Mada.

Useful addresses Post Office: corner Jl. Jend. A. Yani and Jl. Sudirman.

Airline offices Merpati, corner Jl. Malada and Jl. Jend. A. Yani.

Transport to & from Waikabubak 137 km from Waingapu, 47 km from Waikelo. **By air**: the airport is 42 km NW of town at Tambolaka. Merpati operate 3 flights/week to Kupang via Waingapu, and to Denpasar via Bima and Mataram. There are share minibuses into town. **By bus**: the terminal is on the SW edge of town, off Jl. Jend. A. Yani. 3 morning departures daily for Waingapu, the first at about 0700, 5-6 hrs. Connections with regional market towns. From Waingapu, passengers are dropped-off at their losmen or hotel; those travelling to Waingapu will be picked-up at their hotel or losmen if given advance warning. **By boat**: no passenger ships operate out of Waikelo harbour, 60 km from Waikabubak on Sumba's N coast and near the airport. However, it is sometimes possible to hitch a ride on one of the inter-island mixed cargo boats that stop here.

TIMOR

INTRODUCTION

Timor is one of the driest islands in the Indonesian Archipelago. The terrain is beautiful but often bleak: rock strewn hills, isolated communities, and poor soils. In the West it is probably most often associated with the Indonesian invasion and annexation of the former Portuguese colony of East Timor in 1975 (**see page 964**).

Administratively, Timor Island is slightly confusing. **West Timor** or **Timor Barat** consists of 3 districts which constitute part of the province of East Nusa Tenggara: Kupang (centred on the city of Kupang which is also the capital of East Nusa Tenggara), Timor Tengah Selatan and Timor Tengah Utara. The E section of Timor, and a small coastal enclave in W Timor known as Ambeno, is a province in its own right: **East Timor** or **Timor Timur**, formerly Portuguese East Timor.

The districts of West Timor cover a total of 16,500 sq km and have a population of 1.25 million. East Timor covers 14,500 sq km and has a population of about 750,000. The long dry season on both halves of the island stretches from Apr to Oct, with annual rainfall of 1,200 mm – 2,000 mm being concentrated in the months from Nov to Mar. Soils are generally thin and unproductive. Most of the population is concentrated in the slightly wetter interior where cattle raising is the principal occupation. Because of the Portuguese and Dutch influences, the bulk of the population is Christian: 58% are classified as Protestant, 35% Roman Catholic.

History

Timor became a focus of European interest because of the valuable aromatic sandalwood that grows here. Formerly an important export of Sumba and Solor as well as Timor, the earliest reference to trade in perfumed sandalwood is contained in the chronicles of the Chanyu Kua Dynasty, written in 1225. The Chinese, sometimes using Javanese intermediaries, probably began buying the wood in the 10th century, perhaps even as early as the 3rd century. Their accounts describe Timor as being covered with sandalwood trees – something that is difficult to believe today.

European contact with the island dates from the early 16th century. The Portuguese may have sighted Timor in 1512 when an expedition was sent from Melaka to seek the famed and fabulously wealthy Spice Islands (**see page 973**). However, the earliest confirmed European reference to the island is contained in a letter from the Commander of Melaka, dated 6 Jan 1514. Physical contact with the island dates from 1561 when a Portuguese settlement was established on neighbouring Solor and Dominican friars began to evangelize on Timor. Though much of their time was spent on missionary activity, they also became involved in the sandalwood trade. Other important exports of the period were horses and slaves. It was at this time that the inter-marriage between Portuguese sailors, soldiers and traders from Melaka and Macao with local women laid the foundations for Timor's influential *mestizos* community – locally known as the *Topasses*, from the Dravidian word *tupassi*, meaning 'interpreter'.

The Portuguese began to lose influence to the Dutch at the beginning of the 17th century and the important harbour of Kupang was wrested from the Portuguese in 1637. However, the Dutch showed only a marginal interest in securing this distant colonial possession and the day-to-day administration of the island was left to 62 petty kingdoms, ruled by Catholic princes. Indeed, it was not until 1859 that a treaty was finally ratified determining the boundary between the Dutch and Portuguese territories. Even this agreement was unsatisfactory as it left the status of the Portuguese enclave of Ocussi (now Ambeno), ambiguous. This was not to be resolved until 1905. The friction between the Dutch and the Portuguese provided the basis for the later conflict between Indonesia and East Timor (**see page 964**).

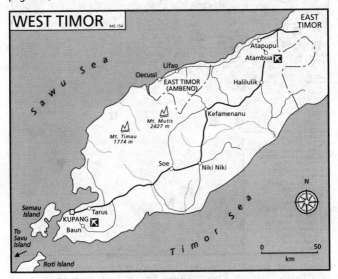

WEST TIMOR

Kupang

The origins of Kupang are not known, although the name is Timorese for 'Lord', probably referring to the ruler of the area. The Dutch first landed here in 1613, and received a warm welcome from the Kupang. He apparently even expressed an interest in being converted to Christianity. This was not pursued by the Dutch who left, not to return for another 40 years. In 1647 the Portuguese began construction of a fort, which was abandoned before it was completed. Six years later, the headquarters of the Dutch in Solor were damaged by an earthquake, and they moved their operations to Kupang, building upon the fortifications left by the Portuguese. Kupang was to remain the centre of Dutch influence in the area until independence.

The town was initially focused on Jalan Siliwangi, but quickly spread inland from the coast. Today, the city is the capital of the province of East Nusa Tenggara with a population of 120,000, most of them Protestants, and a university (the University of Nusa Cendana, 12 km outside town).

Places of interest

Kupang is not well-endowed with sights. Despite its history, there are virtually no pre-World War II buildings. Jalan Siliwangi, the seafront road (although the sea is usually out of sight), is the bustling heart of the city, as it has been since the Dutch settled here in 1637. Street salesmen and women market traditional herbal and

KUPANG IMS 149
Not to Scale

To Airport
Jl. Tim Tim
Jl. Garuda
Jl. Sumatra
Jl. Sumba
Jl. Cendrawasih
Jl. G. Mutis
Jl. J.A. Yani
Jl. U. Sumoharjo
Jl. Soekarno
Jl. Tompelo
Jl. Nangka
To Tenau harbour
Jl. M. Hatta
Jl. Yohanes
Jl. C. Doko
To Museum & Walikota long distance bus station
Jl. Pemuda
Jl. W.J. Lalamentik
Jl. Palapa
Jl. Jend Sudirman
Jl. Raya E. Tari
Jl. Surapati
Jl. Soeharto
Market
To Baun
N

1. Fort Concordia
2. Dutch Church & Tourist
   Information (next door)
3. General Post Office
4. Bouraq Office
5. Merpati Office
6. Market
7. Cendana Hotel
8. Astiti Hotel
9. Eden Hotel
10. Backpackers
11. Flobamor II Hotel
12. Marina Hotel
13. Fatuleu Homestay
14. Laguna Inn
    & Adian Hotel
15. Losmen Susi
16. Maya Hotel

spiritual cures, and there is a **market** at the E end of the street (where it becomes Jalan Garuda). To the W of Jalan Siliwangi, the coast road crosses **Air Mata**. This is the small river where Captain Bligh landed after his extraordinary 7,000 km, 41-day voyage in an open boat from the spot near Tonga in the Pacific where the mutineers on his ship *H.M.S. Bounty* set him and his supporters adrift. Walking further W along the road, past the army barracks and church, are good views of the coast and the islands beyond. This was the site of the Dutch **Fort Concordia** built in 1653. Back in town and close to the Kota Kupang bemo terminal at Jalan Soekarno 23, is a fine and well-maintained **Dutch church**, originally constructed in 1873. It is simple and pure in conception, barring the ornate porchway.

About 4 km out of town, 300m from the long-distance bus terminal, is the **Museum of Nusa Tenggara Timur**. The exhibits are well displayed, but less well explained. The collection includes textiles, ceramics, traditional weapons and ethnographic pieces. Notable is the fine bronze Dongson (Vietnamese) drum (**see page 706**), collected on Alor, with its frogs symbolizing and promoting rain, along with the bronze *moko* dowry vessels, also from Alor (see box, **page 948**). The ikat process is illustrated with the use of a series of models and sets. Admission: by donation. Open: 0800-1600 Mon-Thur & Sat. **Getting there**: take a bemo from the city centre to Walikota (200Rp).

Excursions
Lasiana Beach lies 12 km east of Kupang, and is quiet during weekdays. At weekends it becomes popular as a picnic spot for locals. **Getting there**: take a bemo heading for Tarus (200Rp).

Baun lies 30 km from Kupang and is a weaving town; the processes of ikat can be seen, although the quality of the work produced is variable. Visitors have recommended *Ibu Raja* as producing the best cloth. There is a **market** in Baun on Sat (from 0700). **Getting there**: take a bus from the Walikota terminal (600Rp) or a bemo from the Kota Kupang terminal in town.

Semau Island is good for swimming and snorkelling but is best reached on a tour (see Tours) as there are no regular ferries. There is talk of running game-fishing boats (marlin) from the island, the season stretching from Mar-Sept. **Accommodation: C Uiasa Beach Cottages**, attached mandi, price includes 3 meals; and **Flobamor II Cottages** (book through *Flobamor II Hotel* in Kupang, see below). **Getting there**: if not on a tour, catch a bemo bound for Bolok or Tenau (200Rp) from the Kota Kupang terminal and get off at Pantai (Beach) Namosain, SW of town. Boats can sometimes be hired from here for the trip to Semau (¾ hr).

Sandalwood factory is open to visitors, lies 3 km N of town at Bakunase. **Getting there**: direct bemos to Bakunase from Terminal Kota (200Rp).

Tours There are a number of well-organized tour and travel companies in Kupang. They offer city tours (US$17/person), tours to the weaving village of Baun (US$22/person), Lesiana Beach tours (US$15/person) and a number of other day trips (all these are prices for 3 people). They also arrange longer tours to destinations on Timor and the other islands of East Nusa Tenggara (Flores, Alor, Komodo, Sumba etc). *Teddy's Bar and Restaurant*, also run a less formal tour service, with day snorkelling tours to Semau Island (17,000Rp) departing 1000, Rote Island surfing safaris, city tours, fishing and camping expeditions.

Accommodation A *Sasando*, Jl. Perintis Kemerdekaan 1, T 22224, a/c, restaurant, pool, tennis, good views, but out of town near bus terminal; **B** *Flobamor II*, Jl. Jend. Sudirman 21, T 21346, a/c, hot water, comfortable but over-priced; **B-D** *Marina*, Jl. Jend. A. Yani 79, T 22566, some a/c, small, friendly, clean, central, price includes breakfast, rec; **C** *Astiti*, Jl. Jend. Sudirman 96, T 21810, a/c, good mid-range hotel, well-run, expansion underway, rooms at front noisy, 3 km from town centre; **C-D** *Cendana*, Jl. Raya El Tari 23, T 21541, some a/c, some distance out of town near the Kantor Gubernor, but regular bemos into city centre, nice garden atmosphere, popular, price includes breakfast, rec; **C-D** *Laguna*, Jl. Gunung Kelimutu 36, T 21559, some a/c, painted entirely in a wonderful green, on a quiet side street but central, clean with good bathrooms, rec; **C-D** *Maya*, Jl. Sumatra 31, T 22697, some a/c, good rooms and good value, garden, on sea front but still central, price includes breakfast, rec; **C-D** *Susi*, Jl. Sumatra 37, T 22172, some a/c, on seafront but still central, undergoing expansion; **C-D** *Timor Beach*, Jl. Sumatra, T 31651, some a/c, on seafront but still central; **D** *Adian*, Jl; Kelimutu 40, T 21913, popular with Indonesians, good position; **D** *Fatuleu Homestay*, Jl. Fatuleu 1, T 31374, quiet street in garden atmosphere, clean, and central, rec; **E** *Losmen Safariah*, Jl. Moh. Hatta 34, T 21595, rooms only average, attached mandi, reasonable location; **F** *Backpackers*, Jl. Kancil 37B, Airnona, T 31291, clean, very popular, quiet and peaceful, good for information, about 4½ km from town centre but there are regular bemos, price includes breakfast, rec; **F** *Eden*, Jl. Kancil, Airnona, T 21921, thatched bungalows in peaceful location, spring-fed bathing pool, wonderful trees, but rooms shabby and poorly maintained, 4½ km from town centre, regular bemos, price includes breakfast; **F** *Losmen Isabella*, Jl. Gunung Mutis 21, T 21407, central (just off Jl. Siliwangi), but dirty.

Restaurants Local specialities include *daging s'ei* (smoked beef); ♦*Bundo Kanduang*, Jl. Jend. Sudirman 49, Padang; ♦*Depot Makan*, Jl. Moh. Hatta 54, *Hemaliki*, Jl. Soekarno good, cheap Chinese and seafood; ♦♦*Hemaliki*, Jl. Soekarno, attractive garden and restaurant serving Indonesian, Chinese, seafood and Japanese; ♦*Ibu Soekardjo*, Jl. Moh. Hatta 23, Indonesian; ♦♦*5 Jaya Raya*, Jl. Soekarno 15, Chinese, crab specialities; ♦♦*Mandarin*, Jl. Jend. Sudirman 148 (next to *Astiti Hotel* and intersection with Jl. Harimau), good, simple, Chinese, rec; ♦♦*Teddy's Bar & Restaurant*, Jl. Ikan Tongkol 1-3, Western, seafood, lobsters, steak, live music; ♦♦*Timor Beach*, Jl. Sumatra. Seafood, overlooking beach.

Bars *Teddy's Bar*, Jl. Ikan Tongkol 1-3, live music.

Shopping Books: *Istana Beta Bookshop* on Jl. Jend. A. Yani 58 (past the *Marina Hotel*) has town maps. **Crafts**: *Loka Binkra Crafts Centre* is on the road to the airport, just before the 8 Km marker. Catch a bemo bound for Tarus or Penfui (200Rp). **Textiles**: Kupang is a centre for the sale of Nusa Tenggara Timur ikat, but it is highly variable in quality. For *tenunan asli* (cloth woven from home-grown and spun cotton and coloured with natural dyes) expect to pay 150,000Rp upwards. Wrap-around sarong blankets or *selimut* worn by men are decorated with bright, bold geometric and stylized animal and bird motifs. Try: *Toko Dharma Bakti*, Jl. Sumba, or the house (21D) on the side street off Jl. Soekarno near the *5 Jaya Raya Restaurant*.

Local transport Bemos: there are a huge number of bemos, which must be among the noisiest and most ostentatious in Indonesia with names like James Bond and Givenchy (200Rp). Routes are marked over the roof, and most ply between the city bemo terminal (Terminal Kota Kupang) at the end of Jl. Soekarno near the intersection with Jl. Siliwangi, and the out-of-town bus terminal, Walikota. A board at Terminal Kota Kupang gives all routes and fares.

Banks & money changers Danamon, Jl. Jend. Sudirman 21, only Citibank and Amex travellers' cheques in US$, plus most major currencies cash; **Bank Rakyat Indonesia**, Jl. Soekarno, change most travellers' cheques in US$ and A$, plus major currencies cash; **Bank Dagang Negara**, Jl. Soekarno 10.

Useful addresses General Post Office: Jl. Palapa (out of centre). **Post Office**: Jl. Soekarno 29 (more convenient). **Area code**: 0391. **Perumtel**: Jl. Palapa. **General Hospital**: Jl. Moh. Hatta. **Immigration Office**: Jl. Soekarno 16, T 21077.

Airline offices Garuda/Merpati, Jl. Kosasih 13, T 21205; **Bouraq**, Jl. Jend. Sudirman 20A, T 21421.

Tour companies & travel agents *Natrabu*, Jl. Gunung Mutis 18, T 21095; *Pitoby Tours*, Jl. Jend. Sudirman 118, T 21443, F 31044, branch at Jl. Siliwangi 75, T 21222; *Varanus*, Jl. Perintis Kemerdekaan.

Tourist offices *Provincial Tourist Office*, Jl. Basuki Rakhmat 1, T 21540. 5 km from town off Jl. Soeharto. Catch a bemo travelling towards Baun and ask for Kantor Gubernor Lama; the turning is just past the Pentecostal Chapel. Some useful handouts. Open: 0700-1400 Mon-Thur, 0700-1100 Fri, 0700-1230 Sat. *Kantor Pariwisata Parpostel*, Jl. Soekarno 29 (next to Post Office). Central location but next to useless. *Tourist Information Desk*, Jl. Soekarno 25 (next to church). Helpful and convenient source of information, especially for independent travellers.

Transport to & from Kupang 110 km from Soe, 283 km from Atambua. **By air**: Kupang's El Tari international airport is 14 km NE of town. *Transport to town*: taxis into the centre of town (6,500Rp). **NB**: taxi drivers encourage tourists to go to hotels of their choice, saying others are full – they receive a commission. Bemos running between Penfui/Baumata and town (250Rp) pass the airport turn off – it is a 1½ km walk from the airport buildings to this spot. Connections by Merpati and Bouraq with Jakarta, Dili and Bali, and other destination in Java, Sulawesi, Nusa Tenggara, Irian Jaya and Kalimantan.

By bus: the long-distance Oebobo bus terminal, better known as Walikota, is some way E of town. Regular bemos run between it, along different routes, and the central bemo terminal at the end of Jl. Siliwangi. Buses from Oebobo to Baun, Bolok, Baumata, Tarus Kejamenanu 5 hrs, Soe 2 hrs, Niki Niki 3 hrs, Atambua 7 hrs and Dili 10 hrs, with change of bus at Atambua). *Natrans*, who run buses to Dili via Atambua have a counter at the terminal; *Tunas Mekar*, who run night buses to Dili sell tickets at Jl. Siliwangi 94 (near the Terminal Kota bemo station).

By boat: Kupang's Tenau harbour is SW of town. Catch a bemo bound for Tenau or Bolok. The Pelni ship *Kelimutu* visits Kupang on its two week circuit (**see route map page 1008**). The Pelni office is at Jl. Pahlawan 3, T 21944 (5 mins walk W of Jl. Siliwangi; a new building off, but visible from, the road). There are also a number of ferries serving surrounding ports and islands; these leave from the Bolok ferry terminal, a few kms further on from Tenau. Catch a bemo bound for Bolok (500Rp). The ferry office (Perum Angkutan Sungai, Danau dan Penyeberangan) is at Jl. Cak Doko 20, T 21140. Ferry services are as follows: Kupang-Ba'a (Rote) 0900 (3,700Rp) Mon, Wed, Fri & Sat (returning same day); Kupang-Ende (Flores) 1300 Tues (returning Wed); Kupang-Larantuka (Flores) 1500 (10,000Rp) Sun & Thur (returning Tues & Sat); Kupang-Sabu 1600 (10,000Rp) Wed (returning Thur); Kupang-Kalabahi (Alor) 1400 (12,000Rp) Mon (returning Tues).

International connections By air: with Darwin, Australia on Garuda.

Soe

Soe is the cool capital of the regency of Timor Tengah Selatan, lying 800m above sea-level. During the coldest months of Jun and Jul it can be chilly and a sweater is needed during the day – it is always cool at night. The town is best-known for the large regional market held here every day of the week.

Accommodation C-D *Bahagia*, Jl. Diponegoro 72, good restaurant, some rooms have their own mandi; **D** *Mahkota Plaza*, Jl. Suharto 11 (near the bus station), restaurant, new and reasonably comfortable, private bathrooms; **E** *Sejati*, Jl. Gajah Mada 18, T 101; **F** *Anda*, Jl. Kartini 5, very friendly.

Transport to & from Soe 111 km from Kupang, 86 km from Kefamenanu, 172 km from Atambua. **By bus**: regular connections with Kupang 2½ hrs, Kefamenanu 2 hrs, Atambua 3½ hrs, and Dili.

Kefamenanu

Kefamenanu is the capital of the regency of Timor Tengah Utara. Like Soe, this is a highland town, at an altitude of 600m, with chilly nights. During Jun and Jul, the coldest months, a sweater may be needed throughout the day. The town has simple accommodation and can be used as a base to explore the surrounding countryside.

Excursions
The area around Kefamenanu is rarely visited by tourists. There are numerous **traditional villages** and towns including **Maslete** (4 km S) and **Nilulat** (at 1300m).

Accommodation C-D *Cendana*, Jl. Sonbay, T 168, some a/c, breakfast included, new losmen; **E** *Ariesta*, Jl. Basuki Rakhmat 29, T 7, restaurant, large rooms; **E** *Sederhana*, Jl. Pattimura; **E** *Sokowindu*, Jl. Kartini, T 122, breakfast included, friendly, rec; **E** *Victory*, Jl. Kartini.

Transport to & from Kefamenanu 197 km from Kupang, 86 km from Soe, 86 km from Atambua. **By bus**: regular connections with Soe 2 hrs, Kupang 4½ hrs, Atambua 1½ hrs, and Dili.

Atambua

The small town of Atambua is set an altitude of 500m and is the last large settlement before crossing from West Timor into the province of East Timor. Atambua's port of Atapupu is 24 km N of town. Travellers going by bus between Kupang and Dili have to change here.

Accommodation D *Kalpataru*, Jl. Jend. Subroto 3, T 351; **D** *Nusantara*, Jl. Sukarno 4, T 117, own bathroom, breakfast included, best in town; **E** *Klaben*, Jl. Dubosinanaet 4, T 79; **E** *Liurai*, Jl. Satsuitubun 12, T 84; **E** *Sahabat*, Jl. Merdeka 7; **F** *Minang*, Jl. Sukarno 12A, T 135, clean and central.

Transport to & from Atambua 283 km from Kupang, 173 km from Soe, 86 km from Kefamenanu. **By air**: Merpati run one flight/week from Atambua to Kupang and Dili. **By bus**: regular connections with Kupang 6 hrs, Soe 3½ hrs, Kefamenanu 1½ hrs, and Dili. **By boat**: Pelni operate a ship which circuits between Kupang and Dili via Atapupu (Atambua's port).

ROTI

Roti Island, just off the SW tip of Timor, is administered as part of the regency of Kupang. It covers 1,214 sq km and has a population of nearly 100,000. The capital is the town of **Ba'a**, on the N coast.

   Like Savu, the lontar palm is the traditional subsistence crop here (**see page 962**), although rice is increasingly cultivated. The tradition of making working clothes from the fibres of the lontar palm has now died out, but some people still continue to make shrouds for the dead from the fibres. At birth, each Rotinese baby is given, when it cries, a drop of Roti sugar – presumably indicating the former importance of the lontar palm to the islanders' collective livelihoods.

Namberala (or Dela) village, on the W coast, about 35 km from Ba'a, is close to the main surfing beach and there are a handful of homestays here for the really adventurous surfer. The best months for surfing are reputed to be from Apr to Sept. The villages both NE and SW from Ba'a are worth visiting for their markets and traditional architecture. **Getting around**: bemos and buses run along the main roads, or hire a car or motorcycle for the day. **Oeseli Beach**, 58 km SW from Ba'a is good for swimming.

Accommodation At Ba'a: **D** *Ricky's*, near the mosque, some a/c. There are a number of other cheaper losmen. At Namberala: **D-E** *Homestays*.

Shopping Textiles: the Rotinese produce a distinctive ikat, which is strongly influenced by *patola* cloth – Gujarati cloth from India which was imported in large quantities from the 16th century. Patola motifs – floral designs, diagonal crosses – were incorporated into the traditional textiles of the island, as they were through much of Nusa Tenggara. Cloth is often decorated with flower motifs using red, white, brown and black hues. Unfortunately, there are few weavers left on Roti now – many of the local people have left the island, seeking work in Kupang – and it is becoming hard to find good cloth.

Local transport Bemos and buses ply the main roads. It is best, though, to hire a motorcycle, bemo or car for the day (ask at losmen).

Transport to & from Roti **By air:** 2 flights/week on Merpati from Kupang; the service is unreliable. **By boat:** the ferry dock is at Pante Baru, about 30 km NE of Ba'a; bemos wait to take passengers up to the capital. Pelni Perintis vessels leave Kupang at 0900 on Mon, Wed, Fri & Sat, returning the same day, 3 hrs (3,700Rp).

SAVU

Savu Island, over 250 km west of Kupang, is still part of the regency of Kupang. The island covers 460 sq km and supports a population of about 50,000 people, predominantly Protestants. The 'capital' of the island is the town of **Seba**, which has an airport and a dock. The dry season here extends over 7 months (Apr-Oct), sometimes longer, and the rains are intermittant. It is a dry, barren and unproductive island.

Traditionally, the slow-growing lontar palm (*Borassus sundaicus*) has met the subsistence needs of the population. The sap from this tree, known as *tuak*, is both drunk fresh and boiled into a sugary syrup (*gula air*). The fruit of the tree is eaten, and its wood and leaves are used for thatching and, in the past, for cloth and paper.

The women of Savu produce a distinct warp ikat cloth. It is said that about 300 years ago the people of Savu were divided into 2 distinct clans – the Greater Blossoms (*Hubi'Ae*) and the Lesser Blossoms (*Hubi'Ike*) – based on female blood lines. Within each clan there were several sub-groups called Seeds (*Wini*). Each group wove distinctive motifs on their cloth and even today, local people can recognize cloth and its origin by its clan motif.

Accommodation Basic accommodation in Seba. **E** *Makarim Homestay*; **E** *Ongko Da'i Homestay*; **E** *Petykuswan Homestay*.

Shopping Textiles: a distinctive warp ikat cloth is hand-woven on Savu, in bands of floral and geometric designs, set against a dark indigo and rust ground. The Savunese sarung is known as the *si hawu*, while the *higi huri* is a blanket. Men's clothing has tended to keep more faithfully to traditional designs, while women have been happy to incorporate Western-inspired motifs such as vases of flowers, birds and rampant lions.

Transport to & from Savu **By air:** 2 flights/week on Merpati from Kupang to Seba town; the service is unreliable. **By boat:** boats dock at Seba on the N coast. There is a weekly Pelni Perintis vessel from Kupang leaving on Wed at 1600 and returning to Kupang on Thurs, 8 hrs. There are also other, irregular, departures from Kupang's Tenau harbour.

EAST TIMOR

INTRODUCTION

The former Portuguese colony of East Timor was invaded by Indonesian forces in December 1975, and annexed in 1976 – to become the country's 27th province. It is this event for which East Timor is best remembered in the West. In Nov 1991, a British camera crew coincidentally captured a massacre of East Timorese demonstrators at the cemetery of Santa Cruz on film, rekindling the West's interest in this remote territory (see page 967).

East Timor is known locally as *Tim-Tim*, the shortened version of the Indonesian name for the province: Timor Timur. It covers a total of 14,500 sq km and has a population of about 750,000. By a quirk of colonial history, the province encompasses not only the E half of Timor Island but also a small coastal enclave in the W, known as Ambeno (formerly Oecussi). The province is divided into 13 districts, 2 of which are in the W.

History
The Colonial Period (1701-1975) East Timor became an official colony of Portugal in 1701 when a governor was appointed and placed under the control

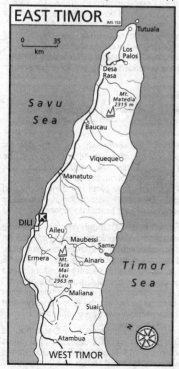

of the Viceroy of Goa, over 6,000 km away on the W coast of India. Before that date, Dominican friars were busy converting the East Timorese to Roman Catholicism, while making fortunes from the sandalwood trade. Most historians rate the moral rectitude of these priests as very low. Even after the appointment of a governor, control over East Timor was lax. In 1750 there were just 8 white Portuguese in the territory, and control really lay with the local chiefs, the Dominican friars, and the so-called 'Black Portuguese' – the descendants of Portuguese soldiers, merchants and sailors who had had children by local women.

During the early years of Portuguese 'rule', the capital of East Timor was the port of Lifao, in the enclave of Ambeno. It was only moved to Dili in 1769 when rebels took Lifao forcing the governor and his supporters to flee N. The boundaries between Dutch and Portuguese Timor were not finally demarcated until 1914. Foreign visitors who bothered to venture to East Timor during the early decades of this century invariably either derided Portuguese colonial rule or treated the administration with amused disdain. Officialdom was languid and ineffective, and the country was the most underdeveloped and primitive colony in all Southeast Asia. Incredibly, on the eve of World War II, East Timor's capital – Dili – had no electricity, no water supply, no paved roads, and no telephones.

In Feb 1942 the Japanese Imperial Army landed an army of 20,000 men in Dili and occupied the colony. A small force of 300 Australians of the 2/2nd and 2/4th Independent Companies fought a remarkably successful guerrilla campaign killing 1,500 Japanese and losing only 40 men themselves before withdrawing in Jan 1943. It is acknowledged as one of the finest episodes of the Allied war in Southeast Asia. But the battle for East Timor caused considerable suffering among the East Timorese. After the Australians were evacuated, the Japanese exacted a terrible revenge on the many locals who had provided support. The population of the territory declined from 472,000 in 1930 to 403,000 by 1946.

After the capitulation of the Japanese at Kupang in Sept 1945, East Timor returned to Portuguese control. The most that can be said of the Portuguese stewardship of East Timor is that they converted about half of the population to Roman Catholicism (or nominal Roman Catholicism), and introduced some elements of Portuguese cuisine and culture. Otherwise, the authorities in Lisbon effectively ignored what was to them an insignificant colonial backwater.

Indonesia's independence leaders differed over East Timor's status. The radical politician Mohammad Yamin in May 1945 stated that like North Borneo, East Timor should "come within the control and complete unity of the State of Indonesia", noting that they were "not only physically part of us but have been inhabited by Indonesian people since history began, forming part of our motherland". In contrast, Mohammad Hatta, who was later to become Vice-President, was actively opposed to any incorporation. Overall, most Indonesian leaders did not support expansionism and the incorporation of East Timor.

The 1975 invasion and annexation

> "50,000 people or perhaps 80,000 people might have been killed during the war in East Timor... It was war... Then what is the big fuss?" (Adam Malik, Foreign Minister of Indonesia, 30 March 1977).

In 1974 the rightist dictatorship in Lisbon was overthrown, paving the way for East Timor's decolonization. Three political groups emerged in the colony: the Social-Democratic Association of East Timor or ASDT, which was middle-of-the-road and supported a decolonization period of 5 years; the Timorese Democratic Union or UDT, a conservative party favouring continued Portuguese stewardship; and the Popular Democratic Association of Timorese or Apodeti which supported the incorporation of East Timor into Indonesia.

The third party was by far the weakest. In late 1974, Gough Whitlam, the Prime Minister of Australia, appeared to indicate that he would not oppose annexation – or at least this is the way the Indonesian military chose to interpret his comments. The US administration also seemed reconciled to Indonesian intervention. US Ambassador Newsom was reported as saying that his country hoped Indonesia should preferably do so "effectively, quickly and not use our [military] equipment". At the same time, the UDT changed its stance to one of independence from Portugal, while the ASDT changed its name to Fretilin, the Revolutionary Front for an Independent East Timor, and became more overtly revolutionary.

By late 1974, fears of an Indonesian invasion were growing while the authorities in Jakarta fermented stories of a 'reign of terror' in Dili. Independent journalists found no evidence to support such claims. On 11 August 1975 the UDT staged a coup in Dili. Fighting erupted between the UDT and Fretilin and thousands of

East Timorese fled into West Timor. By Sept, Fretilin had emerged as victors in the civil war which had caused the death of 1,500-3,000 people. Their cause lost, the leaders of the UDT fled into Indonesian territory, whereupon the Indonesian government claimed they were pro-integrationist.

On the 7 Dec 1975, Indonesian forces invaded Dili, although the official Indonesian view is still that they were 'invited' in. The brutality of the invasion and its aftermath was verified by most journalists who witnessed it, and by independent scholars. Indonesian troops quickly gained control of the capital. In Apr, the UN Security Council passed a resolution re-affirming East Timor's right to self-determination. But at the time, the West was preoccupied with the American withdrawal from Vietnam and the US, the countries of Western Europe and Japan abstained in the vote. South Vietnam had just fallen to the North Vietnamese Communists, as too had Cambodia. America found its geo-political interests to be at odds with supporting a revolutionary party like Fretilin, especially as Indonesia was gradually becoming more pro-Western. Even Portugal was in no state to offer support to its former colony, having just experienced political upheaval itself. In turn, the Indonesian government claimed that it could not live with a revolutionary state on its doorstep, noting that just a decade earlier they had had to contend with their own Communist-inspired coup. The fact that East Timor's population was 200 times smaller than Indonesia's seemed to make no difference.

East Timor: Indonesia's youngest province 1976-1990 From 1975 until 1990, East Timor was sealed to the outside world, while the Indonesian army quashed the secessionist threat. Despite East Timor's small population, Fretilin has managed to sustain a long-term insurgency. Since the annexation, an estimated 100,000-200,000 East Timorese have died – either from violence or neglect – out of a population of only 750,000. At its worst, more than a quarter of the population may have been killed – a figure which puts East Timor on a par with Cambodia during the terrible Pol Pot years. During the period of 'occupation' (the UN has still not recognized Indonesia's annexation of East Timor and marks it as a separate country on maps), an estimated 60,000 soldiers, policemen and informants have tried to keep the peace: one for every 10 East Timorese. But despite this (relatively) massive military presence, few foreign observers dispute that East Timor's pro-independence movement is far from dead. The reluctance of the Indonesian government to countenance any sort of plebiscite illustrates that they must have a good idea how most people would vote. The resistance may have dwindled to a handful of guerrillas – and the government scored a considerable coup with the capture of Fretilin leader Xanana Gusmao in Nov 1992 – but passive resistance, if anything, is becoming stronger as overt resistance crumbles.

Gusmao was tried in Dili in May, and on the 21st the High Court judge presiding found the resistance leader guilty of a series of charges ranging from disrupting national stability to possession of fire arms and pronounced a sentence of life imprisonment. Amnesty International said the trial was a "travesty of justice", adding that "In view of the fact that Indonesia's sovereignty over East Timor has not been recognised by the UN, the competence of Indonesian courts to try Xanana Gusmao ... is open to question." To repair the damage done to Indonesia's image abroad, a public relations firm was hired to promote Jakarta's view of events, and of history. In this they have – so far – been only partially successful.

Economy
Since integration in 1976, Indonesia has allocated considerable investment to East Timor, on the theory – presumably – that it is possible to 'buy' allegiance. Since 1976, the population of East Timor has received more central government money

– on a per capita basis – than any other province in the country. But the territory is still poor and undeveloped, and barely viable as an economic unit – which would pose problems for an independent East Timor. It is decades behind much of the country, with poorly developed schools, roads, hospitals and other physical and social infrastructure. Efforts to promote agricultural and industrial development have constantly been frustrated by security considerations, and much of the economic growth that has occurred has been linked to government activity. Manufacturing only accounts for 1% of the province's economy, and 90% of families depend on agriculture for their living. Despite this, the province has to import food. Among the cash crops cultivated, coffee is the most important.

Accommodation in East Timor The province welcomes fewer tourists than any other in Indonesia and tourist facilities are limited. Dili is relatively well-provided with hotels – built to serve visiting officials – but in the countryside there is a dearth of accommodation.

Travelling to East Timor East Timor was a closed province until 1990 when it was opened to visitors for the first time since 1975. Following the events at Santa Cruz at the end of 1991, the government became more suspicious of foreign visitors and the province was closed for most of 1992. **NB**: check entry regulations beforehand in Kupang.

Books on East Timor Budiardjo, Carmel and Liem Soei Liong (1984) *The war against East Timor*, Zed Books: London; Hiorth, F. (1985) *Timor past and present*, James Cook University of Queensland: Townsville; Jolliffe, Jill (1978) *East Timor: nationalism and colonialism*, University of Queensland Press: St. Lucia; Retbold, Torben (ed.) (1984) *East Timor: the struggle continues*, IWGIA: Copenhagen; Kohen, E.T. and Taylor, John (1979) *An act of genocide: Indonesia's invasion of East Timor*, Tapol: London; Taylor, John G. (1991) *Indonesia's forgotten war: the hidden history of East Timor*, Zed Books: London.

DILI

Dili, the capital of East Timor, is situated in the heart of a bay, surrounded by dry, scrub-covered, hills. It is a shell of a city. There are few cars on the roads, shops seem more often to be shut than open, and there is little of the bustle and confusion so evident in other Indonesian towns. People appear generally glum and reserved – except for the children. It is difficult not to assume that this must be linked to the Indonesian invasion and annexation of this former Portuguese territory in 1975. With the enormous scale of human suffering over the intervening years, it is small wonder that people are not filled with zest for life.

Dili became the capital of the former Portuguese colony in 1769. Due to colonial mismanagement and the dislocations and ferment caused by the war since 1975, the city has failed to prosper. The population of the district of Dili – which also includes surrounding settlements and countryside – was only 81,000 in 1985. There are numerous examples of Indonesian investment in Dili – impressive municipal buildings for example – but these seem out of place in such a quiet town.

Places of interest
Dili has numerous architectural reminders of the Portuguese period, but few are noteworthy. On the seafront, just W of the port, is Dili's oldest church, **Motael Church**. It is rather too heavy to be elegant and is fronted by a hideous concrete statue of Joseph, Mary and the infant Jesus, perched on top of a globe and hand. In the evenings, the seafront on the W side of the bay is a pleasant area to walk. Food carts set up near the lighthouse, not far from the Motael Church, and there is usually a cooling on-shore breeze. Also in the W of the town is the new **Cathedral of the Immaculate Conception**, said to be the largest in Southeast Asia. It was inaugurated by President Suharto in 1988 and blessed by Pope Paul

The massacre at Santa Cruz, November 1991

Although the Indonesian government had some reason to believe that Fretilin was on the verge of defeat and the desire of the population of East Timor for independence almost extinguished, recent events have underscored the degree to which East Timorese still hanker for self-rule. In Nov 1991, during the funeral of a man allegedly killed by Indonesian forces, the army opened fire on mourners at Santa Cruz Cemetery in Dili. Not surprisingly, accounts are greatly at odds. Locals and Fretilin sympathizers, supported by 8 foreign journalists who were also present at the cemetery, claim that the army opened fire without warning on a peaceful demonstration of 2,000-3,000 East Timorese, resulting in the death of between 50 and 100 mourners. One journalist, Amy Goodman of Pacific Radio Network, was reported as saying: "The Timorese didn't do anything to the troops. They just chanted *Viva Timor L'este*. These were truly defenceless people". The commander-in-chief of the Indonesian army General Try Sutrisno, by contrast, claimed that the army opened fire only after his men had been attacked, and that they seized many grenades, guns and knives. They also claim that only a handful of demonstrators were killed.

The film of the massacre was shown across the world and provoked international condemnation. The Indonesian government responded by setting-up an independent commission which published its findings in December 1991, confirming that 50 demonstrators had, indeed, been killed. The commission also placed blame on the army for excessive use of force. President Suharto sacked the 2 most senior commanders with operational control in the province, and ordered a military commission to investigate the matter. This commission published its results in Mar 1992, disciplining 6 officers and calling for the court martial of 8 other soldiers. Although many observers believed that the 2 reports failed to uncover the whole truth, they were unprecedented in Indonesian political history. They also did just enough to deflect international criticism – for the time being at least. With the Cold War at an end, the Western powers have been less restrained in their criticism of human rights abuses in pro-Western countries. Significantly, however, in June 1992, it was reported by the human rights group Asia Watch that several of the demonstrators at Santa Cruz had been jailed for 10 years or more. In contrast Indonesian soldiers who fired on, and killed, the demonstrators have received sentences of 20 months, or less. At the end of 1992, General Syajei, who took over the East Timor command after the massacre, bragged that had he been in charge many more would have been killed. A strange way to win hearts and minds.

in October 1989. During the Pope's visit, over 250,000 people assembled to hear him preach. Not far away to the N is the government **craft centre** with a reproduction traditional **Timorese house** in its compound. Across the road is the appalling **Integration Monument** showing a muscle-bound wild man breaking-off the shackles of colonialism. Locals must view it as a wry joke.

In the centre of town, facing the seafront, is the **Kantor Gubernor** or Governor's Office, a long, arched and slightly Mediterranean-style building which was once surrounded by trees. The Indonesian assault is still starkly in evidence in the rusting **landing craft** that lie haphazardly on the beach in front of the *Dili Hotel*. It is peculiar that the authorities have not removed these obvious signs of the invasion. Perhaps they are designed to act as a reminder of Indonesia's military might to deter any erstwhile Fretilin supporters. Further E on the seafront, between the *Dili* and *Turismo hotels*, is a statue of the **Virgin Mary**, said to be carved from marble shipped from Portugal. Inland from the seafront, near the Perumtel Office at the intersection of Jalan Kaikolo and Jalan Bispo Medeiros, is the **Mercado Municipal Dili** – Dili's abandoned municipal market, now only used for festivals.

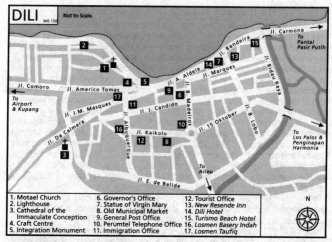

1. Motael Church	6. Governor's Office	12. Tourist Office
2. Lighthouse	7. Statue of Virgin Mary	13. New Resende Inn
3. Cathedral of the	8. Old Municipal Market	14. Dili Hotel
Immaculate Conception	9. General Post Office	15. Turismo Beach Hotel
4. Craft Centre	10. Perumtel Telephone Office	16. Losmen Basery Indah
5. Integration Monument	11. Immigration Office	17. Losmen Taufiq

Excursions

Pantai Pasir Putih or 'White Sand Beach', lies 6 km E of town, on the far E side of Dili Bay. There is reasonable snorkelling here and it is becoming popular at weekends. The Indonesians claim that before 1975 it was a segregated 'whites only' beach, although foreign residents of the time maintain that in fact it provided ample evidence of the lack of colour consciousness within the Portuguese colonial administration: there would be blacks, Goans, *mestizos*, East Timorese and Portuguese whites all crowded onto the sand. **Getting there**: buses only run to the beach on Sun and public holidays (bus 'D'); on other days catch a taxi and arrange a pick-up time (or walk back).

Manatuto is a pottery-making centre 64 km E of Dili and one of the driest places on an already arid island. **Getting there**: regular buses from 'Terminal'.

Aileu is a major interior town 47 km S of Dili with an impressive Portuguese church. **Getting there**: by bus from 'Terminal'.

Tours Day tours to Maubessi, Baucau and Los Palos. *Natrabu*, Jl. 15 Oktober 10, T 21080. It is best to book Natrabu tours from Kupang; the office in Dili is only a branch office and is often closed.

Accommodation Few tourists make it to Dili; hotels are thin on the ground and expensive. There are no travellers' losmen. **B** *Mahkota Timor*, Jl. Gov. Alves Aideia (opposite the port), T 21283, F 21063, a/c, restaurant, a barn of a new hotel, totally lacking in character, though the rooms are comfortable; **B** *New Resende*, Jl. Av. Bispo Medeiros, T 22094, a/c, restaurant, the best equipped hotel in Dili, central with good service and clean rooms – popular with Indonesian officials, so often full, price includes breakfast; **B-D** *Turismo Beach*, Jl. Av. Marechal Carmona, T 22029, F 22284, about 1 km from town centre, villa on seafront, some a/c, restaurant, rooms are clean and fan rooms are a good deal; **C** *Dili*, Jl. A. Sade Bandeira, T 21871, some a/c, quaintly decrepit, rooms have sitting area, some character, with 1950s furnishings and bathroom fittings from Scotland, on seafront; **C** *Wisma Cendana*, Jl. Americo Tomas (not far from the port), T 21141, a/c, looks nicer than it is, rooms have been allowed to deteriorate; **D** *Losmen Basery Indah*, Jl. Estrade de Balide, T 2731, dark rooms, shared mandi, rather grubby, grossly over-priced; **D** *Losmen Taufiq*, Jl. A. Thomas, T 22152; **E** *Penginapan Harmonia*, 4 km E of town, T 22065, restaurant, friendly management (English speaking).

Restaurants Timorese coffee is very good in Dili. There is a kilometre-long stretch of cheap warungs along one side of Jl. Bidau Raya; some serve excellent *ikan bakar* (fresh barbecued fish) e.g. *Parai Katte* near the intersection with Jl. Barros Gomes. ♦♦*Beringin Jaya*, Jl. Ameriko Tomas, Padang food, excellent; ♦♦*Djakarta*, Jl. Kolmera 125, good, Chinese and steaks; ♦♦*Turismo Beach Hotel*, Jl. Av. Marechal Carmona, Indonesian and Chinese, good selection of Portuguese dishes and wine; *Aru Bakery*, Jl. M. Alburqueque; *Golden Bakery*, Jl. Jose Maria Marques 24.

Entertainment Cinema: on the seafront, W past the Post Office.

Shopping The main shopping street is Jl. Jose Maria Marques. Shops shut in the afternoon for siesta. **Crafts**: the *Toko Dili*, Jl. Bispo Medeiros 11; *Pusat Pengembangan Kerajinan Rakyat* (Craft Centre), Jl. Americo Tomas (near the Integration Monument). Crafts are generally poor quality. Street sellers hawk textiles (usually made from machine-spun cotton and chemically dyed) near the larger hotels (e.g. *New Resende*).

Local transport Town buses run fixed routes (200Rp). Ancient, un-metered taxis can be easily hailed. The *New Resende Hotel* has a car for charter for day excursions out of town.

Banks & money changers Bank Summa, Jl. Bispo Medeiros, US$ cash and some travellers' cheques; **Bank Dagang Negara**, Jl. Bispo Medeiros, most major travellers' cheques; **Danamon**, Jl. Bispo Medeiros, US$ cash, no travellers' cheques.

Useful addresses General Post Office: Jl. Inf. D. Hendrique (next to *Kantor Gubernor*, on seafront). **Perumtel**: Jl. Bispo Medeiros (near intersection with Jl. Kaikolo). **Immigration Office**: Jl. Kolmera, T 21862. **General Hospital**: Jl. Toko Baru Bidau.

Airline offices Merpati, Jl. Bispo Medeiros 5, T 21880 (next to the *New Resende Hotel*).

Tour companies & travel agents *Multi Perona Maya*, Jl. Jose Maria Marques 23.

Tourist offices *Dinas Pariwisata*, Jl. Kaikolio Baru, T 21350, large new offices but, as yet, little information to offer, however a helpful lady works here – Lourdes – who speaks some English.

Transport to & from Dili By air: Dili's Komoro Airport is on the coast 6 km W of town. Ancient taxis run into Dili (3,500Rp), or walk ½ km to the main road and catch a bus ('AB') (200Rp). Regular twice daily connections by Merpati with Kupang; one flight/week to Atambua. **By bus**: Dili has no central bus terminal; buses leave from the roundabout near the Perumtel Office (intersection of Jl. Kaikolo and Jl. Bispo Medeiros), a spot known as 'Terminal'. Buses to Kupang travel via Atambua where passengers change, 10 hrs. *Tunas Mekar* run daily buses to Kupang; agents all over town sell tickets e.g. *Abundo Kanduang Padang Restaurant*, Jl. 15 Oktober 29A; *Losmen Basmery Indah*, Jl. Estrade de Balide. Also buses to Suai via Atambua, to Same via Aileu and Maubessi (departing at 0600 and at other hours), and regular departures for Manatuto, Baucau and Los Palos. **NB**: buses for Same sometimes leave from the Gereja Balide 1½ km S of town on Jl. Bispo Medeiros; check at 'Terminal' beforehand. **By boat**: Pelabuhan Dili is close to the town centre, to the E of the Motael Church. The Pelni ship *Kelimutu* docks here on its two week circuit through Nusa Tenggara (see route map, **page 1008**). The Pelni Office is at Jl. Sebastiao da Costa 1, T 21415 (next to the *Djakarta Restaurant*). Mixed cargo/passenger ships to other destinations also call at Pelabuhan Dili; check with the harbour master.

EAST FROM DILI TO LOS PALOS

The route east from Dili along the coast has only recently opened to tourists and facilities are few. After passing through the pottery-making town of Manatuto, the road continues to Baucau and Los Palos. Before Los Palos, the village of Desa Rasa contains some of the few remaining examples of traditional Timorese architecture.

Baucau

Baucau is situated on the edge of a high plain and is an important agricultural area. It is best known for its impressive Portuguese market – the **Mercado Municipal** – which is now rather dilapidated. Baucau is an important local centre with roads leading E to Los Palos and S to Viqueque.

Accommodation C-D *Flamboyant*, elegant colonial structure, which has seen better days; **E** *Wisma Goya Lida*.

Transport to & from Baucau 130 km from Dili. **By bus**: the station is near the Mercado Municipal. Connections with Dili and Los Palos, and S to Viqueque.

Los Palos

This is the most important town in the E, situated at an altitude of 500 metres. It is a busy town but unattractive; there are ruins of a Portuguese fort here.

Excursions

Rasa Village is 10 km N of town and has some of the finest examples of traditional Timorese architecture – tall-roofed, elegant, wooden structures, raised off the ground on pillars (there is a poor imitation at the craft centre in Dili). Ikat cloth is also woven here. **Getting there**: by bus from Los Palos, or get off en route from Dili.

Accommodation A guesthouse is reported to have opened; check at the Tourist Office in Dili before leaving.

Transport to & from Los Palos By bus: connections with Baucau and Dili.

SOUTH FROM DILI TO MAUBESSI

The route S from Dili climbs into the rugged interior highlands. Aileu, 47 km from Dili, has a beautiful church, while the highland town of Maubessi, formerly a minor colonial resort, offers a bracing climate, mountain walks and good views. At Maubessi the road divides; S to Same and SW to Ainaro.

Maubessi

A beautiful highland town, 800m above sea-level, with fine views over the ocean. Maubessi is a centre of traditional arts, and good ikat cloth is still produced here. The hills that surround the town are good for walking. It gets cold at night, particularly during Jul and Aug, so take warm clothing.

Excursions

Same is an attractive hill town to the S of Maubessi. There is some accommodation here. **Getting there**: by bus.

Accommodation Attractive colonial guesthouse.

Transport to & from Maubessi By bus: connections with Dili, via Aileu.

MALUKU

Introduction, 971; Ambon, 974; The Lease Islands, 980; Seram, 981; Banda Islands, 981; Ternate and Tidore, 983; Halmahera, 987; Morotai, 987; South East Maluku, 988.

Maps: Maluku, 972; Ambon, 975; Ambon Town, 976; Ternate & Tidore, 984.

Maluku, formerly known as the Moluccas, is not so much a province as an archipelago: it sprawls across 851,000 sq km, of which only one tenth is land, and consists of over 1,000 islands. Their total population is 1.9 million. The sea in this area is very deep – reaching 4,971m in the Bacan Basin, SE of Halmahera. The highest mountain is Mount Binaiya on Seram, at 3,000m. The largest islands are Seram, Halmahera and Buru, although the most important economically are Ambon, tiny Ternate and the Bandas. Recent economic attention has focused upon the expansion of the fishing industry, especially tuna and shellfish, and on forestry. Other important crops include the sago palm (see page 973), coffee and coconut.

INTRODUCTION

Although the islands are very much at the edge of the Indonesian world, both geographically and economically, it was the spices of Maluku which initially attracted the European powers to Asia and to the E isles (see page 17 and below). They became known as the **Spice Islands**, or Spiceries. It was only here that cloves and nutmeg were cultivated and the early history of Southeast Asia was moulded and driven by the fabulous wealth that the Spice Islands had to offer the adventurous explorer.

Now that spices no longer generate the wealth that they once did, Maluku has been forced to find an alternative *raison d'être*. Not only are the islands more than 2,000 km from Jakarta, but they are very geographically dispersed: Morotai in the N is over 1,000 km from Tanimbar in the S.

Climate
Maluku's climate is complex because it straddles the equator and covers such a vast area. In **north and central Maluku** there is rain throughout the year, but it is concentrated between May and Oct – the period of the east monsoon. In Ambon for example, the wettest month is Jul (590 mm), and the driest, Nov (104 mm). Total annual rainfall in Ambon is a very wet 3,450 mm.

In **SE Maluku**, S of the equator, the climate is very different and more akin to that of Nusa Tenggara. The islands here experience a long dry season between Dec and Mar corresponding with the west monsoon and annual rainfall is 1,400 mm. As a result, while the islands to the N are clothed in forest, Seram in the south has savanna vegetation.

MALUKU ISLANDS IMS 165

History

Maluku was important as a source of spices long before the first Europeans discovered the islands. Arab, Chinese, Malay and other seafarers traded here, and indeed the first Europeans had to employ the services of local pilots in Melaka to help them find the fabled Spiceries. The name *Maluku* is said to be derived from the words *Jaziratul Jabal Maluk* – meaning the 'Land of Many Kings', and the islands of *Miliku* are mentioned in 7th century T'ang Chinese documents.

Multi-purpose tree par excellence: the sago palm

Sago, not rice, is the traditional staple of Maluku as well as parts of Nusa Tenggara. The sago palm (*Metroxylon sago*) grows to a height of 5-10 m, and flowers once, after about 15 years. Shortly before the flowers open, the tree is cut down and the pith scooped out. This is then washed, removing the starchy flesh from the inedible fibrous material. After being sieved, this flesh, rich in carbohydrate – though of poor quality – is dried and becomes what is commercially known as 'pearl sugar'. Eaten with fish and fruit, it provides a balanced diet. The sago tree not only provides nutrition, but does so with virtually no toil whatsoever; it grows without cultivation, needs no maintenance and a man and a boy, leisurely working for half a day, can process a mature palm and produce sufficient pulp to feed a family of 5 for over a month. The palm also provides fibre for rope, matting and cloth, the leaves can be used for thatch, and the sap ferments into a liquor. It is the multi-purpose tree *par excellence*.

The first reference to sago appears in Antonio Pigafetta's account of his journey around the world with the Portuguese explorer Ferdinand Magellan at the beginning of the 16th century. Always an acute observer, he wrote: "They eat wooden bread made from a tree resembling the palm, which is made as follows. They take a piece of that soft wood from which they take certain long black thorns. Then they pound the wood, and so make the bread. They use that bread, which they call saghu, almost as their sole food at sea".

Many Europeans commented on the abundance of sago in island Southeast Asia, Arthur Russel Wallace and Stamford Raffles among them. Wallace thought the tree a curse because it induced extreme laziness. He explained in 1862 that the "habit of industry not being acquired by stern necessity, all labour is distasteful, and the sago-eaters have, as a general rule, the most miserable of huts and the scantiest of clothing".

The spices of Maluku

It was spices that initially enticed European mariners to Southeast Asia. The expedition of the Portuguese general Alfonso d'Albuquerque was the first to make landfall on the legendary Banda Islands in 1512. The General himself did not accompany the small fleet (he was resting in Melaka), but Ferdinand Magellan, then a lowly junior officer, probably did. The great attraction of the Spice Islands lay in the value of the spices that they seemed to produce in prodigious quantities, and the universal European belief that cloves (*Eugenia aromatica*), nutmeg (*Myristica fragrans)* and mace (another product of the nutmeg tree) could be grown nowhere else on earth. Nutmegs were known as the golden fruit, and it is easy to see why. Jan Huygen van Linschoten, a Dutchman who sailed with d'Albuquerque's expedition, wrote of the benefits of nutmeg: "The nutmeg comforts the brain, sharpens the memory, warms and strengthens the Maw, drives wind out of the body, makes a sweet breath, drives down Urine, stops the Laske, and to conclude, is good against all cold diseases in the head, in the brain, the Maw, the Lice and the Matrice". Cloves were similarly regarded; German naturalist George Rumphius viewed the clove tree as "the most beautiful, the most elegant, and the most precious of all known trees".

Having displaced the Portuguese from the Moluccas, the Dutch were intent on maintaining a monopoly of the spice trade and proceeded to extirpate every tree not under their control – they literally sent expeditions to neighbouring islands to uproot and destroy any potential competitor plants. They did this so successfully that it was 200 years before people began to question whether nutmeg and cloves could be grown beyond the Spice Islands.

Cloves and nutmeg proved to be very sensitive to transportation – a fact that helped perpetuate the myth. The clove is not a seed or fruit at all, but a dried flower and most trees were grown from so-called volunteer seedlings, not from seeds. The nutmeg tree requires similar careful management. Sensitive to sunlight, it was grown under the protective shadow of huge *kenari* shade trees, which also provided an edible nut and hulls for dug-out canoes. Nutmeg is the dried kernel within the nutmeg nut, while mace is processed from the dried fibre which surrounds the pit of the nut.

The English and French spent much of the 18th century trying to break the Dutch spice monopoly but were not successful until 1770 when French missionary and naturalist Pierre Poivre (1719-1786) smuggled out nutmeg and clove seedlings and managed to propagate them in Mauritius. With the British soon following suit, the wealth of the Moluccas was effectively undermined. From this date, these distant eastern isles were relegated to obscurity and economic insignificance. But the importance of spices remains enshrined in the popular nursery rhyme 'I had a little nut-tree':

> I had a little nut tree, nothing would it bare
> But a silver nut-meg and a golden pear;
> The King of Spain's daughter came to visit me,
> And all for the sake of my little nut-tree.

AMBON

Ambon, or Amboina as it was known during the colonial period, is the capital of the province of Maluku and has a population of 250,000. The island goes by the same name and covers a total of 780 sq km. The origin of the name, which was in use before the arrival of the Dutch, is not certain; it could be derived from the word *Ambwan* meaning 'dew', or *Nusa Ombong*, 'dawn'.

The city is rather featureless, the allies having bombed it extensively during raids against the Japanese occupiers in August 1944. However, it is a bright and breezy city, with a distinct island atmosphere, and manageable on foot (or by one of the countless *bejaks*).

Places of interest

Ambon has more than its fair share of second-rate **heroic monuments**. The most interesting is that of **Saint Francis Xavier** outside the Catholic Cathedral of St. Francis Xavier at Jalan Raya Pattimura 1. The Spanish saint and co-founder of the Jesuit Order stands, bible in hand, on the shore while a crab offers him a crucifix. He visited the Moluccas between 1546 and 1547 and was struck by the volcanic violence of these islands, believing it to be the work of God. He wrote in his journal:

> "It would seem that as these men have no one to warn them about the punishment of the wicked, God has been pleased as it were to open to them the abode of hell, and give them some pictures of the fires in which sinners are to be forever tormented, so that they may be admonished by that awful sight, and come to understand what punishments will await them unless they abandon their abominable vices and crimes".

Overlooking the stadium and running track is the **statue of Thomas Matulessy** – better known as the liberation hero **Kapitan Thomas Pattimura**. He rather like a cartoon pirate in cut-off jeans, wielding an enormous cutlass. He led a group of rebels who besieged and over-ran Fort Duurstede, on the island of Saparua in 1817, killing the Dutch Resident and his family, bar a baby boy. Pattimura was captured by the Dutch and hanged where his statue now stands. Also facing onto the stadium is an army base, housed within the walls of **Fort**

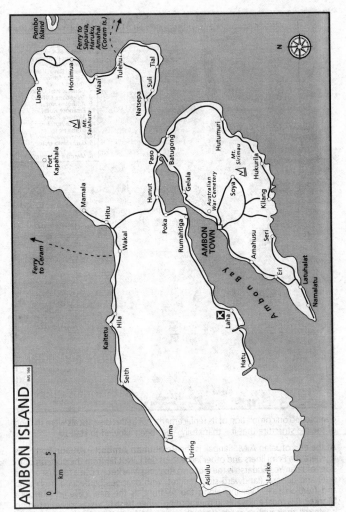

AMBON ISLAND IMS 166

0 — 5 km

Pombo Island

Ferry to Saparua, Haruku, Amahai (Coram I.)

Liang
Honimua
Waai
Tulehu
Suli
Tial
Natsepa

Mt. Salahutu

Fort Kapahala

Mamala
Hitu
Paso
Batugong
Hutumuri

Hunut
Gelala
Australian War Cemetery
Mt. Sirimau
Soya
Hukurila
Kilang

Ferry to Ceram
Wakal
Poka
Rumahtiga
AMBON TOWN
Amahusu
Seri
Eri
Latuhalat
Namalatu

Kaitetu
Hila
Ambon Bay
Laha
Hatu

Seith

Lima
Uring

Asilulu
Larike

Victoria, the first of over 40 forts built on Ambon and constructed by the Portuguese in 1575 (when it was known as *Nossa Seinhora da Annonciada*). The guards will only allow visitors to see the gateway to the old fort (which originally stood on the sea front), with its faded crests and fine plaster ships over the apex, and may allow photographs to be taken on request (officially prohibited).

The lovely green-roofed and walled **Jame Mosque**, with its silver dome, is at the NW edge of town on Jalan A.J. Patty. Next door is the newer, bigger, and rather less attractive **Mesjid Raya**. Ordinarily, the old mosque would have been

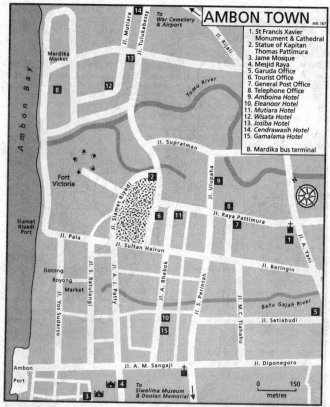

AMBON TOWN IMS 167

1. St Francis Xavier Monument & Cathedral
2. Statue of Kapitan Thomas Pattimura
3. Jame Mosque
4. Mesjid Raya
5. Garuda Office
6. Tourist Office
7. General Post Office
8. Telephone Office
9. *Amboina Hotel*
10. *Eleanoor Hotel*
11. *Mutiara Hotel*
12. *Wisata Hotel*
13. *Josiba Hotel*
14. *Cendrawasih Hotel*
15. *Gamalama Hotel*

B. Mardika bus terminal

demolished on completion of its replacement, but in this case, locals were so fond of the old structure that it – thankfully – has been allowed to stand.

At the end of Jalan A.M. Sangaji is the **Pelabuhan Ambon** – Ambon Port. This is where the Pelni liners and other large ships dock. Not far from the port, on both sides of Jalan Yos Sudarso is the **Gotong Royong Market** – both a food (seaward side) and general (landward side) market, with delicious barbecued fresh tuna and fruit on sale. Walking along the seafront, is the new covered **Mardika Market**. It is most enjoyable in the morning, when fresh fish is on sale and fishing boats sell their night's catch along the promenade. This is also the central bus terminal.

The **Siwalima Museum** is 2½ km SW of town at Taman Makmur. Established in 1973, it is primarily an ethnographic collection with carved boats, ancestor figures, musical instruments and textiles. Open: 0800-1400 Tues-Thurs, 0800-1100 Fri, 0800-1300 Sat-Sun. **Getting there**: bus from the Mardika terminal for Amahusu (ask for 'musium').

About 2 km NE of the town centre, on **Karang Panjang Hill**, is the statue of

19-year-old **Marta Tiahahu**, a Christian Ambonese who gazes, spear in hand, over Ambon city and bay. When her father, who was leading a rebellion against the Dutch, was captured and imprisoned she took up the fight on Nusa Laut. Eventually captured herself, Marta was told of her father's execution while she was being taken to Java and starved herself to death. She was buried at sea on 2 Jan 1818. Get there by bus (150 Rp), or on foot. The **Doolan Memorial**, is on Jalan Dr. Kayadou in Kudamati (just past the Rehoboth Church) at the SW edge of town. This simple monument commemorates an Australian soldier who provided covering fire for retreating comrades. He was only killed by the Japanese after tenacious resistance, and his body was spirited away by local Ambonese and buried beneath a gandaria tree on this spot.

Excursions
The Australian War Cemetery lies 5 km NE of town. Immaculately maintained, 2,000 Australian, British, Canadian, Dutch and US servicemen who fought and died during the Second World War are buried here. **Getting there**: bus to Tantui (150Rp).

Ambon's beaches are not the best. Most of the reefs have been destroyed or seriously degraded by dynamite fishing or killed by pollution, and the more accessible are busy at weekends. **Natsepa Beach** at Baguala Bay is 14 km NE of town, and one of the most popular. Losmen accommodation available. **Getting there**: bus from the Mardika terminal bound for Suli (450Rp). **Amahusu Beach** is 7 km SW of town. The reef here is depressingly degraded. This spot is the finish line for the annual Darwin-Ambon yacht race. Hotel accommodation available. **Getting there**: bus from the Mardika terminal (250Rp). Finally, **Namalatu Beach** is 15 km from town, SW from Amahusu, at the tip of this arm of Ambon Island. Snorkelling is reasonable here. **Accommodation**: B *Lelisa Beach*, a/c, and some losmen. **Getting there**: by bus bound for Latuhalat from the Mardika terminal.

Pombo Island is situated just off Ambon's NE coast (10 minutes by boat). The surrounding waters are said by locals to offer the best snorkelling and swimming. The island is a national park and there are PHPA bungalows which visitors can use with prior booking (see Useful addresses for PHPA Office address). **Getting there**: boats to Pombo can be chartered from Tulehu, Waai, Honimua and Liang. Expect to pay 75,000 Rp for a day's charter. Buses to all 4 towns leave from the Mardika terminal.

The holy eels of Waai 31 km NE of town, past Tulehu, are one of the strangest sights on Ambon: these 1½ m eels live in a pool, fed from a 50m waterfall. They are summoned by the sound of splashing and are fed eggs by the keeper. **Getting there**: by bus from the Mardika terminal.

Tours *Daya Patal Tours & Travel* operate a range of tours around the island (US$50-60/day). *Natrabu* also run tours.

Festivals Jul: *Darwin-Ambon yacht race*. First contested in 1976, the race is over a distance of more than 1,000 km.

Accommodation There are no cheap losmen, or first class hotels in Ambon, but a reasonable range of mid-range accommodation. Note that during the Darwin-Ambon yacht race (Jul) hotels are booked-up. **A** *Manise*, Jl. W.R. Supratman 1, T 42905, F 41054, a/c, standard rooms are windowless, superior rooms are OK; **B** *Amboina*, Jl. Kapt. Ulupaha 5A, T 41725, F 3354, a/c; **B** *Cendrawasih*, Jl. Tulukabessy 39, T 52487, F 53373, a/c, hot water, on edge of town, comfortable; **B** *Mutiara*, Jl. Raya Pattimura 90, T 97124, a/c, well-run, clean and modern rooms; **B-C** *Josiba*, Jl. Tulukabessy 27, T 41280, on the edge of town, rooms rather shabby and overpriced; **B-C** *Wisata*, Jl. Mutiara SK 1/3-15 no. 67, T 53293, F 53592, a/c, hot water, on edge of town in a quiet alley, friendly, rooms rather like ships' cabins with hotch-potch of furniture and fittings; **C** *Eleanoor*, Jl. Anthone Rhebok 30, T 2834, some a/c, on quiet side street, friendly, with balconies, price includes breakfast, rec; **C** *Penginapan Simponi*, Jl. Tulukabessy 46, T 54305, some a/c, on edge of town, clean but no windows; **C**

Butchery in the Bandas: the curse of the spice trade

The Banda Islands' experience of colonialism is a case study in the excesses, inequities, inadequacies and inefficiencies of Dutch rule in Indonesia. The tiny size of the Bandas belies their former economic significance. These were the famous Spiceries of the E, on which Europeans depended for nutmeg and mace to flavour an otherwise monotonous diet. The first Europeans to arrive here were the Portuguese, under the captainship of Antonio de Abreu who landed on Banda in early 1512. The first Dutch vessel did not arrive until 1599, and the English landed in 1601.

The arrival of the Dutch coincided with increased activity from the volcano Mount Api, a portent – and taken as such by the Bandanese – of what was to follow. The Dutch established trading posts (known as *logies*) and proceeded to buy nutmeg and mace. Profits were vast: the spices were purchased at $1/320$th of the price they realized in Amsterdam. From 1602, the Dutch presence in the Bandas was financed and administered by the VOC (Vereenigde Oost-indische Compagnie) or the United East India Company.

The appalling Dutch treatment of the local population can be traced back to 1609 when Admiral Verhoeven attempted to negotiate without a sufficiently large guard; he and 26 other Dutchmen were slaughtered by the Bandanese. This 'treachery' was not to be forgotten. In 1621 the new VOC governor-general Jan Pieterszoon Coen sailed for Banda with a large force to deal, once and for all, with the duplicitous locals. He forced a one-sided treaty upon the *Orang Kaya* (the rich men or chiefs) and when they failed to keep their side of the agreement proceeded to depopulate the islands. Many Bandanese were captured and shipped to Batavia to be sold into slavery, others committed suicide by throwing themselves from cliffs. Of a population of 15,000, only 1,000 remained – and most of these on the English controlled islands of Pulau Ai and Pulau Run. The 44 Orang Kaya faced a particularly vile fate, which even Dutchmen in Holland felt was beyond the realms of acceptable, civilized behaviour. The historian Willard Hanna quotes an eyewitness, Naval Lieutenant Nicolas van Waert:

> The condemned victims being brought within the [Fort Nassau] enclosure, 6 Japanese [mercenary] soldiers were also ordered inside, and with their sharp swords they beheaded and quartered the eight chief orang kaya and then beheaded and quartered the thirty-six others. Their execution was awful to see. ... All of us, as professing Christians, were filled with dismay at the way the affair was brought to a conclusion, and we took no pleasure in such dealings.

Having disposed of the Bandanese, Coen had to find a way to maintain spice production. He chose to colonize the islands with *Perkeniers* – licensed planters

Wisma Carlo, Jl. Philip Latumahina 24A, T 42220, some a/c, small, friendly and clean, set around courtyard, with narrow beds, price includes breakfast, rec; **C-D** *Rezfanny*, Jl. Wim. Reawaru, T 42300, some a/c, a little shabby, price includes breakfast; **D** *Beta Guesthouse*, Jl. Wim. Reawaru 114, T 3463, clean, central, attached mandi, price includes breakfast; **D** *Gamalama*, Jl. Anthone Rhebok 11, T 53724, bare rooms, attached mandi; **D** *Wisma Game*, Jl. Jend. A. Yani, T 53525, small rooms, rather musty, attached mandi, price includes breakfast.

Restaurants Cheap warungs on Jl. Said Perintah e.g. *Roda Baru* (Padang food) at No. 42, *Sonata* at No. 92, and near the mosque on Jl. Sultan Babullah. *Amboina*, Jl. A.J. Patty 63, bakery and ice cream; **◆◆***Asri*, Jl. W.R. Supratman (next to *Manise Hotel*), Indonesian food in spotless restaurant; *Halim*, Jl. Sultan Hairun, seafood specialities; *Kakatoe*, Jl. Said Perintha 20, Belgian chef produces Western and Indonesian food with, it is claimed, no additives, served in an old house in the centre of the city; *Tip Top*, Jl. Sultan Hairun, Chinese and Indonesian; *Utama*, Jl. Setiabudi 58, good seafood, Chinese, dog sometimes served.

Entertainment *Dance*: there are a number of dances characteristic of Maluku; unfortunately it is rare to find them being performed in 'authentic' surroundings. The oddest is the *Bambu Gila* or Crazy Bamboo dance. The Maluku tourist office provides an enlightening description who, for the most part, were 'free burghers' who had completed their contracts of service with the VOC. They leased the land from the VOC and had to sell all their production to the company at a fixed price. For their part, the VOC provided slaves, supplies and protection.

Life, even for the Perkeniers, was harsh and short. Mortality from disease was high, and earthquakes, eruptions, tidal waves and hurricanes periodically decimated the settlement of Banda Neira. Even company rule was unforgiving. A German resident between 1633 and 1638 recorded 25 executions: 2 buried alive, 1 broken on the wheel, 9 hanged, 9 decapitated, 3 garotted, and 1 arquebussed (shot with an early form of portable gun, supported on a tripod). Less fatal punishments were equally gruesome – one woman who had blasphemed had her tongue pierced by a red hot needle. Even the executioner was executed.

Despite the high mortality, the costs of maintaining a garrison, and the extensive smuggling and cheating on the part of the Perkeniers (for instance, substitution of inferior long nutmegs for Bandas' product), profits for the VOC remained high, and the Bandas were regarded as the jewel in the VOC crown. The Perkeniers, though usually in debt, lived in extravagant style.

The end of the Banda's monopoly position in nutmeg production is linked to the British period of control during the Napoleonic Wars. The British controlled the islands over 2 periods, between 1796 and 1803, and 1810 to 1817. During these years, nutmeg seedlings were taken to Bengkulu (Sumatra), Ceylon and Penang (Malaysia) for cultivation, while the French – a few years earlier in 1770 – had also obtained seedlings and planted them in Mauritius, Zanzibar and Madagascar (see page 974). Their monopoly in production lost, the VOC was never again in a position to set the price of nutmeg. As production elsewhere increased, so competition grew and prices fell, and the Banda Islands languished into obscurity. There was a brief period of excitement between 1936 and 1942 when 2 leaders of the fledgling Indonesian nationalist movement, Mohammad Hatta (to become Vice President) and Sutan Sjahrir (to become Prime Minister) were exiled here. But, other than this short period, the Bandas became just another group of breathtakingly beautiful islands in the eastern seas.

For an entertaining account of the Bandas see: Hanna, Willard A. (1991) *Indonesian Banda: colonialism and its aftermath in the nutmeg islands*, Yayasan Warisan dan Budaya: Banda Neira. Available at the museum and the Hotel Laguna in Banda, or from the *Dian Pertiwi* bookshop in Ambon (see page 979).

of the dance: '...it is a performance using a bamboo-pole, held by 7 young strong men. In using supernatural powers, the bamboo begin to move, while still held, and at a sudden moment, it throw down the men'. More interesting is the Cakalele (Chakalaylee), a war dance which features dancers wearing headgear inspired by the helmets of Portuguese soldiers.

Sports Diving: not very well developed around Ambon (compared to, say, Manado). In Ambon Bay spots include Eri, Silale and Tanjung Setan (Ghost Cape – good drop-offs here); around Saparua Island (E of Ambon) at Itawaka and Kulor (off Nusa Laut), and at Tiga Island. At present, only one company arranges diving trips: *Daya Patal* on Jl. Said Perintah 27A, T 3529, F 44709, they can provide all equipment except regulators and BCDs; divers must bring their own, rates are approximately US$200 for 3 days, US$675 for 7 days.

Shopping The main shopping street is Jl. A.J. Patty. There are a number of souvenir shops here selling pearls, silver, shell collages, shell lamps, jewellery and tortoise shell. Bargain hard. **Books:** *Dian Pertiwi*, Jl. Diponegoro 25 – for 2 books on the histories of Banda and Ternate/Tidore by Willard Hanna, shop closes at 1500, re-opens 1700.

Local transport Bemos & buses: link most places on Ambon Island with the capital. The central Mardika terminal is next to the market of the same name, on the seafront, 1 km NE of town. In town, bemos take one of 5 routes or 'lines', all beginning and ending at the Mardika terminal (150Rp). **Taxis**: unmetered, can be hired for specific trips or by the hour (about 5,000Rp/hr, 25,000Rp half day). Taxi 'ranks' at the intersection of Jl. Setiabudi and Jl. Said Perintah, and near the Gotong Royong market on Jl. Pala/Slamet Riyadi (at the end of Jl. Dr. Sam Ratulangi). Taxis also wait outside the bigger hotels. **Bejaks**: there are so many that different colours denote those which are allowed to operate on certain days; yellow (Wed, Sat), red (Tues, Fri), and white (Mon, Thurs).

Banks & money changers Ekspor Impor, Jl. Raya Pattimura 14; **Bank Central Asia**, Jl. Sultan Hairun 24; **BNI**, Jl. Said Perintah; **Danamon**, Jl. Diponegoro; **Bank Dagang Negara**, Jl. Raya Pattimura.

Useful addresses General Post Office: Jl. Raya Pattimura 20. **Area code**: 0911. **Perumtel**: Jl. Raya Pattimura 11. **Immigration Office**: Jl. Dr. Kayadoe 48A, T 3066. **PHPA**: Jl. Tantui (near the Australian War Cemetery outside town), T 41189.

Airline offices Merpati/Garuda, Jl. Jend. A. Yani, T 52481; **Mandala**, Jl. A.J. Patty 29, T 42551 (for Ujung Pandang, Jakarta and Surabaya); **Indoavia**, Jl. Anthone Rhebok 29 (for Banda).

Tour companies & travel agents *Natrabu*, Jl. Rijali 53, T 2593, F 3537; *Daya Patal*, Jl. Said Perintah 27A, T 3529, F 44709 (they also organize tours); *Netral Jaya*, Jl. Diponegoro 76.

Tourist offices *Maluku Tourist Office*, Jl. Raya Pattimura 1 (in the large offices of the Gubernor Kepala Daerah Tingkat Maluku – ask for the Dinas Pariwisata), open: 0830-1430 Mon-Thurs, 0830-1130 Fri, 0830-1300 Sat, useful maps and other handouts.

Transport to & from Ambon By air: Ambon's Pattimura airport is only a few kms NW of town as the crow flies, but 36 km by road. *Transport to town*: Ancient taxis cost 15,000Rp. A much cheaper alternative is to catch a bus from just outside the airport to Poka, 14 km (250Rp); from here, there are ferries across Ambon Bay to Gelala (150Rp), where bemos wait to whisk passengers the final 5 km into town (150Rp). Going from town to the airport, catch a bemo to Gelala, take the ferry, and then one from Poka, bound for Laha. *Airport facilities*: include a tourist information desk which is not always open. Ambon is Maluku's air transport hub with daily connections with Biak, Ternate, Ujung Pandang, Sorong, Langgur, Manado and Jayapura. Indoavia have services to less visited islands – Amahai (1/week), Banda (3/week), Labuha (3/week), Langgur (7/week), Mangole (2/week), Namlea (2/week), Sanana (3/week), Saumlaki (3/week) and Ternate (3/week). Examples of fares: Ambon-Banda 62,000Rp; Ambon-Ternate 146,000Rp. **By bus**: see Local transport. **By boat**: larger ships dock at the Pelabuhan Ambon, near the centre of town, at the intersection of Jl. Yos Sudarso and Jl. A.M. Sangaji. Pelni and other shipping companies have their offices in the port complex. The Pelni ships *Rinjani* and *Tidar* leave for other destinations in Maluku; and for Sulawesi, Java and Irian Jaya (see route map **page 1008**). Smaller vessels use the Pelabuhan Slamet Riyadi at the end of Jl. Pala near the Gotong Royong market, and leave for Banda (1 night), Seram Utara (Wahai – 18 hrs), Seram Timur, Irian Jaya and other ports. Boats also leave daily for Seram, Saparua and Haruku from Hurnala Port, Tulehu, on Ambon's E coast. **Getting there**: bus from the Mardika terminal.

THE LEASE ISLANDS

To the E of Ambon are a collection of other, less frequently visited islands – Saparua, Haruku and Nusa Laut – collectively known as the Lease Islands. **Saparua**, with a population of 50,000 and a fairly well developed infrastructure offers good beaches, snorkelling and diving. This was the island where Kapitan Pattimura led his rebellion against the Dutch (see page 974). There are also clove and nutmeg plantations and the recently restored **Fort Duurstede**, which can be found at the edge of Saparua town.

Haruku and **Nusa Laut** both offer wonderful beaches and good snorkelling. On Nusa Laut are the remains of **Fort Beverwijk**.

Accommodation Saparua: **B** *Maha Village Resort*, N coast, attractive bungalows with fans, diving and fishing equipment available, all meals included; **Losmen** at Siri Sori, Mahu (e.g. *Mahu Cottages*) and Saparua. **Nusa Laut and Haruku**: no accommodation, but some homestays.

Transport to & from the Lease Islands By boat: boats to Haria on Saparua (2 hrs) leave daily from Liang on Ambon's NE coast (get there by bus from the Mardika terminal). The dock at Haria is 5 km from Saparua town. Boats for Pelauw, on Haruku, also leave from Liang. There are boats from Haria to Nusa Laut.

SERAM

Seram, is the largest island in Maluku, with a land area of 18,400 sq km. It supports a mixed population of ethnic groups numbering about 300,000. The island lies to the NE of Ambon and, in size at least, dominates its smaller neighbour. The capital, **Masohi** – also known as Amahai – is situated on the S coast, and the island's second town, **Wahai** is on the N coast. Transportation between the two is not good.

Mount Binaiya – also known as Mount Manusela – is the highest peak in Maluku at 3,019m. There are several other mountains that exceed 2,000m on the island. Spectacular waterfalls, rivers big enough to raft down, and dense tropical forest are all features of the island. Beyond the settled coastline, the land is only thinly populated. The Naulu and Bati tribes maintain their traditional lifestyles here, although fortunately head-hunting is no longer practiced.

Manusela National Park, covering a 1,890 km^2 swathe of forest from Seram's N coast to S coast and including Mount Manusela, is Maluku's most important protected area. The park supports a remarkably varied flora and fauna which is relatively well recorded as the park was selected as a research site for an Operation Raleigh expedition. Visitors are recommended to take a guide, and to obtain a permit and/or advice from the PHPA office at Air Besar, 2 km E of Wahai, or from the PHPA office in Ambon. There is no accommodation in the park, except as guests of village heads (*Bapak Raja*). Routes are hard going and usually unmarked.

Accommodation There are no good hotels on Seram, but a number of adequate losmen. Most are found in the capital, Masohi. Most are in our **C-E** range. **Masohi**: **C** *Lelemuku*, Jl. Tiahahu 12, T 129; **D** *Nusa Ina*, Jl. Banda 9, T 221; **D** *Nusantara*, Jl. Abd. Soulisa 15, T 119; **D** *Sri Lestari*, Jl. Abd. Soulisa 5, T 178. **Wahai**: **D** *Sinar Indah*; **D** *Taman Baru*. Tehoru: **D** *Susi*.

Transport to & from Seram By air: one flight/week by Indoavia to Amahai (Masohi). By boat: numerous boats leave for various destinations on Seram from various points on Ambon. For Amahai/Masohi there are daily boats from Hurnala Port in Tulehu, Ambon 3½ hrs. There are less regular boats from Pelabuhan Slamet Riyadi in Ambon town to both Amahai and Wahai 18 hrs. A ferry makes a daily run from Liang (N coast of Ambon) to Kairatu 2 hrs, another from Hitu (also on Ambon's N coast) to Piru 4 hrs, and there are also said to be boat connections from Ambon's Honimua Beach to Seram.

BANDA ISLANDS

The 6 tiny and beautiful islands that constitute the Banda archipelago lie SE of Ambon and cover a combined area of only 60 sq km. The capital Bandaneira is on the island of the same name (but spelt as 2 words, Banda Neira), separated from the active volcano Mount Api by a strait just a few hundred metres across. The largest island in the group is Banda Besar (literally 'Big Banda') or Lontar, situated to the S of Banda Neira, while the smaller islands of Pulau Ai and Run to the W, and Pulau Rozengain to the E, make up this microscopic archipelago.

The Bandas were 'discovered' by the Portuguese in 1512 in their search for spices, and as they were the only source of nutmeg and mace, brought vast profits to those able to control production and trade (see box). Thrust into obscurity with the fall in nutmeg prices in the early 19th century, the Bandas are now beginning to benefit from a new industry: tourism. With excellent game fishing, superb snorkelling and diving, and a rich history the islands have considerable potential. It is hoped that the development of tourism and fishing can arrest the slow depopulation of the islands – between 1971 and 1980 the population declined from 13,368 to 12,635.

Banda is almost run by Des Alwi who owns the *Maulana Inn* – the best hotel – and has a monopoly on diving. He is the self-appointed guardian of the archipelago and has big plans to develop it as a centre for eco-tourism. Des Alwi is currently having talks with the Amanresort group – who build possibly the most luxurious hotels in the world – to construct a 20-room hotel on Banda (although it will probably be a 'down market' version).

Places of interest

The core of the archipelago, both geographically and economically, is the island of **Banda Neira**. It is here that most of the 15,000 strong population live and where the capital Bandaneira is to be found. The town is peaceful and attractive, and still contains a good array of Dutch mansions – gradually crumbling, due to lack of upkeep.

Fort Belgica, built in 1611, stands above Bandaneira and has recently been restored; below it are the crumbling remains of **Fort Nassau** (built in 1609). Also to be found on Banda Neira are the **former residences** of the nationalist leaders Hatta and Sutan Sjahrir who were exiled to the Bandas by the Dutch. The **Museum Rumah Buaya** is an old colonial villa with a collection of unremarkable colonial memorabilia and some ethnographic exhibits. The residence of the infamous governor-general Jan Pieterszoon Coen (built 1611) is also in Bandaneira.

Across a narrow strait and overlooking Banda Neira is the volcano **Mount Api** (650m) which last erupted in 1988. It can be climbed in half a day; for the best views, set off before 0600. A guide is recommended.

Nutmeg, the Bandas' most famous export, is still cultivated and the nuts are reputed to still be among the best in the world. The best groves are on **Lontar Island**, which also contains the remains of **Fort Hollandia**, built by the Dutch in 1621 and then destroyed by an earthquake over a century later. **Getting there**: by boat from the market in Bandaneira.

Accommodation Des Alwi and the Amanresort are planning a new, luxury hotel. **B** *Laguna Inn*, Jl. Pelabuhan, a/c, same ownership as *Maulana* (Des Alwi), also well-run; **B** *Maulana Inn*, Jl. Pelabuhan, on the seafront, 55 rooms, relaxed and graceful service, friendly, owned and managed by Des Alwi, uncrowned King of Banda, recently voted one of the best hotels in the world by a British Sunday paper which, frankly, probably says more about the beauty of the island than the brilliance of the hotel, rec; **D** *Delfica*, Jl. Nusantara, old Dutch house, friendly management, attractive garden; **D** *Rumah Budaya*, Jl. Nusantara; **D** *Selecta*, Jl. Nusantara.

Restaurants *Nusantara*, Jl. Pelabuhan, good fish.

Sports Diving: some of the best diving in Indonesia; *Maulana* and *Laguna* hotels rent out equipment and charter boats. **Fishing**: excellent game fishing (tuna, swordfish); hotels hire out tackle. **Snorkelling**: superb snorkelling in the shallow waters of Banda Bay, and off Lontar and Api. **Waterskiing and windsurfing**: both available in Banda Bay.

Banks & money changers There are no banks on the islands; bring sufficient Indonesian currency.

Transport to & from Banda By air: the airport is a short distance from town; walkable with limited luggage. There are 3 flights/week from Ambon by Indoavia (**see page 980** for address) to Bandaneira (62,000Rp). They are often overbooked, and it is not unknown for confirmed seats to 'disappear'. **By boat**: Pelni and Perintis ships, along with other mixed cargo vessels dock at Bandaneira.

TERNATE & TIDORE

The tiny, twin, circular islands of Ternate and Tidore, separated from one another by a narrow strait, lie just to the W of the far larger island of Halmahera. Neither Ternate nor Tidore measure much more than 10 km in diameter and both are dominated by volcanos: the former by the active Mount Gamalama (1,720m), and the latter by Mount Kiemtabu (1,740m). The largest town is Ternate, on the E coast of the island with a population of about 50,000. Tidore is more sparsely settled with 40,000 inhabitants. Taken together, the islands have a population of about 120,000.

Like the Bandas, these 2 pinpricks were once of enormous economic and hence strategic value. Many saw this as a curse rather than as a blessing, the Portuguese soldier and poet Luis Camões writing in the mid 16th century:

> Tidore and Ternate, whence on high
> From his hot crest and waves of fire are thrown.
> There trees of burning cloves you may descry,
> Portuguese blood has purchased for our own
> (Camões, book 10, stanza 132)

History
Ternate, a sultanate rich in spices, was first visited by Europeans on 6 Nov 1521 when the expedition of Ferdinand Magellan dropped anchor off Tidore. Financed by King Charles of Spain, Magellan's devastated fleet arrived after 27 months at sea, having lost 3 ships as well as its illustrious leader in a skirmish in the Philippines. The remaining 2 vessels were worm-eaten, waterlogged and rotten. But the emaciated crew managed to fill the holds with spices and returned to Spain to sell their spoiled cargo for 5,100 pounds, 300 pounds more than it cost King Charles to fit out the expedition. Only 17 of the original crew returned and a joyous procession through the city and a Mass in the cathedral marked their ragged arrival.

Though the crew did not return to Ternate, amazingly, Magellan's reconditioned flagship the *Victoria* did, in early 1527. The historian Willard Hanna writes:

> It arrived...in even more woeful state than before, the rigging reduced to mere rudiments, the bottom barnacled and worm-eaten, the crew famished and exhausted. ...Don Garcias [the Portuguese captain of the island] exchanged grandiloquent messages of felicitation and abuse with the Spanish captain...engaged the ship in brief combat, discreetly retiring when its cannon proved still to be functional, and watched with gratification as it proceeded to sink of sheer decrepitude' (1990:39).

Like Banda to the S (**see page 981**), Ternate and Tidore have had a remarkably colourful history. One uprising against the Portuguese in 1529 occurred after a pig escaped from their castle. The local Muslims, unsurprisingly, had it killed, whereupon the Portuguese Captain Menesez imprisoned the chief *ulama*. The locals rebelled and had their priest released, but not before his face had been daubed in pig fat. The apoplectic *ulama* called a holy war and the Portuguese garrison was effectively blockaded. Without supplies, Menesez captured 3 elders and demanded food before he would release them. These demands were ignored, and so 2 of the 3 captives had their ears sliced off, while the third was thrown to

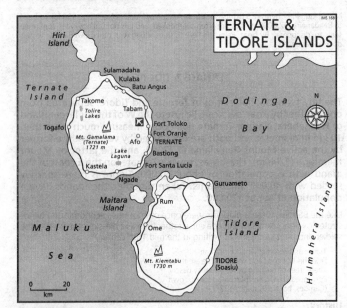

a mastiff who drove him into the sea. Seizing one of the dog's ears between his teeth, this third elder dragged both himself and the beast beneath the waves to their respective deaths.

A succession of Captains followed Menesez, all with instructions to increase trade and profits and mete out justice. In all areas they were generally unsuccessful. The only Governor to leave with any semblance of a good reputation was 'Good Governor Galvao' who arrived in 1536. As Hanna writes: "In the chronicles of the Moluccas during the 16th century, Galvao's is the only Portuguese name other than that of Francis Xavier to which, four centuries later, any very bright luster still adheres" (1990:68). The Portuguese left the island on 15 Jul 1575 after 60 years of ineptitude.

Other visitors to Ternate included the English explorer Francis Drake who moored here in the *Golden Hind* in 1579, after ravaging the Spanish on the Main. He appears to have got on famously with the rogue of a Sultan who ruled at the time, Sultan Baab. The Dutch, who replaced the Portuguese as the dominant power (though harassed by the British), continued the tradition of blundering and provided their own cast of tragi-comedy characters to play next to a succession of colourful sultans. The terrible de Vlaming allowed his men to cut Prince Saidi up alive and throw morsels of his flesh over a cliff (1655), while Sultan Sibori had to cut the throat of the husband of a beautiful and seductive Chinese woman and then drown her mother-in-law in a bath before he was able to marry the cursed female.

For visitors interested in the history of Ternate and its sister island Tidore, Willard Hanna's history is highly recommended – *Turbulent times past in Ternate and Tidore*, Yayasan Warisan dan Budaya: Banda Neira 1990. It can be bought from the Tourist Office in Ternate at a rather inflated price or from the *Dian Pertiwi Bookshop* in Ambon (**see page 979**).

Places of interest

Ternate is a small, quiet town, where the bemos are driven at a refreshingly sedate pace and people stop to talk to visitors. Although the town is spread, ribbon-like, over 3 km or 4 km, and sandwiched between the lower slopes of Gamalama Volcano and the sea, it is manageable on foot. The main street is Jalan Pahlawan Revolusi on which are found the major hotels, banks, shops and the **Gama Lama Market**. The **Pasar Sayur** ('Vegetable Market') is at the N edge of the town centre; the main bemo terminal is also here.

In Ternate town, **Fort Oranje** is on Jalan Babullah, opposite the bemo station and Pasar Sayur. Built in 1607, it is the best preserved and largest fort on the island. Now the quarters for the local army garrison, it nevertheless has a rather abandoned, decayed and in some respects attractive, air about it. About 1 km N is the **Mesjid Sultan Ternate** dating from the 13th century. This mosque has a layered red-orange roof above high yellow-wash walls. Inside, the absence of decoration and the bare soaring roof give it a satisfying purity. About 500m further N from the mosque, on a rise, is the **Kedaton Sultan Ternate**, the Sultan's Palace, but looking rather like a modest European hunting lodge. There was a palace on this site during the 13th century, although the present structure dates from the 19th century. It is now a small **museum**, displaying gifts presented to previous Sultans – armour, swords – along with basketry and some local costumes. The prize exhibit is, unfortunately, rarely on show. This is Sultan Awal's crown, still plastered with some of his hair (which is said to grow – see below, festivals), and kept locked away. Persistence and a modest payment (5,000-10,000Rp) may entice the officials to allow a peep. Good views from the verandah of the kedaton, back over the town. Admission: by donation (ignore the vast sums stated in the visitor's book). Open: 0800-1400 Mon-Thurs, 0800-1100 Fri, 0800-1400 Sat.

Excursions

Circumnavigating the island is a good way to spend a day. It is easiest by chartered bemo, but is also possible by regular public bemo.

Sights travelling anti-clockwise from town: **Benteng (Fort) Toloko** is 2 km from town, and was built by Alfonso d'Alburqueque in 1512. Little remains, except the vegetation-covered walls. **Batu Angus** lies just before the village of Kulaba, and is the crumpled lava flow from Mount Gamalama's eruption of 1737. There is also a **Japanese war memorial** here. **Sulamadaha** is a village 16 km from town; close by are good black sand beaches. Finally, the **Tolire Lakes** lie almost diagonally opposite Ternate town about 25 km away, on the other side of the island and the mountain. There are 2 peaceful lakes here, Tolire Besar ('Big Tolire') and Tolire Kecil ('Little Tolire').

Sights travelling clockwise from town: **Fort Santa Lucia**, also known as Fort Kayu Merah (Red Wood) or Fort Kalamata, is just past Bastiong port and about 3 km from town. It was built by the English in 1518 right on the coast; only the walls of this small fortress remain. Good views over to Tidore. Admission: by donation. **Lake Laguna** is inland from the village of Ngade, 7 km from town. Climb up above the lake for good views. Further on along the coast road, **Fort Kastella** has been almost weathered out of existence.

Mount Gamalama which is in effect Ternate, rises to 1,721m. It erupted in 1737 and again in 1987 and 1990 and can be climbed (just) in a day. Ask at the tourist office for further information.

Afo clove tree is claimed to be the oldest clove tree in the world. It lies inland from Fort Oranje, 4 km from town. Known as Afo or 'Giant', it is 400 years old and still produces 600 kg of cloves each harvest. The path to the tree begins behind the town and branches off before the TVRI mast. Ask for 'Cekih Afo' along the way.

Tidore is Ternate's neighbouring and less developed twin island and can be visited in a day trip. There is a fort at Rum, where the ferry docks. Soasiu, the main town, is on the easternmost side of the island; good markets are held here on Tuesdays and Fridays. There is a losmen at Soasiu. **Getting there**: take a ferry from Bastiong, 20 mins (500Rp). They run during daytime at fairly frequent intervals.

Festivals *Cutting the Hair of the Sultan's Crown*. This is said to be performed once a year, although there is no fixed date for the ceremony. The crown is believed to hold supernatural powers, one manifestation of which is the alleged continued growth of the Sultan Awal's hair.

Accommodation B-C *Neraca*, Jl. Pahlawan Revolusi 30, T 21668, a/c, hot water, new, clean, rather stark, in town centre; **B-D** *Elshinta*, Jl. Pahlawan Revolusi 426, T 21059, some a/c, OK, with cars parked in lobby, all meals included; **C** *Chrysant*, Jl. Jend. A. Yani 131, T 21580, a/c, friendly and quiet, rooms are reasonable but rather overpriced; **C-D** *Nirwana* (and fitness studio), Jl. Pahlawan Revolusi 58, T 21787, F 21487, some a/c, hot water, in centre of town, noisy, good rooms, price includes breakfast; **D** *Sejahtera*, Jl. Salim Fabanyo 21, T 21139, dark, windowless rooms with shared mandi, all meals included; **E** *Penginapan Yamin*, Jl. Pelabuhan Revolusi (by port), average rooms, verandah, shared mandi; **F** *Penginapan Sentosa*, Jl. Pahlawan Revolusi, T 21857, basic but friendly and popular, shared mandi.

Restaurants No excellent restaurants, but a number of mid-range establishments selling reasonable Indonesian and Chinese dishes. Most are found on Jl. Pahlawan Revolusi – e.g. *Gama Lama* at No. 248 (Chinese), *Garuda* (Indonesian), and *Roda Baru* (Padang food). Stalls set up at night opposite and N from the local government offices (Kantor Bupati Kapala Daerah). For local specialities, try the cakes and bread which use the kenari nut (from the huge shade tree that protects nutmeg groves) as an ingredient: *roti kenari* and *bagea kenari*.

Shopping Spices: nutmegs, cloves, etc are very cheap. Not always the best quality but this, after all, is where it all began, so they have a certain romantic appeal.

Local transport Bemos: the main terminal is opposite the Pasar Sayur at the N edge of the town centre. Give the destination, and the appropriate vehicle will be pointed out. Although there are routes, these are loosely adhered to – most passengers are dropped right outside their house, hotel or wherever. Note that although regular bemos travel both clockwise and anticlockwise, they rarely circle the island completely. Destinations at the far side of Ternate are more difficult to get to, and to get back from. Fares are 200Rp for short trips, up to 500Rp for longer journeys. For the more remote spots (or if in a group) it is best to charter a bemo; expect to pay 3,500Rp/hr. **Ferries**: regular ferries to Tidore leave from Bastiang, 20 mins (500Rp). Take a bemo the 3 km from town to the ferry dock.

Banks & money changers Ekspor Impor, Jl. Pahlawan Revolusi (near corner with Jl. Tenang); BNI, Jl. Pahlawan Revolusi; Bank Rakyat Indonesia, Jl. Pahlawan Revolusi 234.

Useful addresses General Post Office: Jl. Pahlawan Revolusi 420. **Area code**: 0921. **Perumtel**: Jl. Pahlawan Revolusi (next to *Elshinta Hotel*), telephone and telegram. **General Hospital**: Jl. Tanah Tinggi.

Airline offices *Merpati/Garuda*, Jl. Basoiri 81, T 314; *Bouraq*, Jl. Sultan Babullah 96, T 21042.

Tour companies & travel agents *Indo Gama*, Jl. Pahlawan Revolusi 17, T 21681; *Noname*, Jl. Jend. A. Yani 129 (next door to *Chrysant Hotel*).

Tourist offices North Maluku Tourist Office, Jl. Pahlawan Revolusi (in the Kantor Bupati Kepala Daerah), open: 0800-1400 Mon-Thurs, 0800-1100 Fri, 0800-1200 Sat, limited information.

Transport to & from Ternate By air: Ternate's tiny airport is 5 km N of the town centre; planes brush the palm trees on landing. Regular connections by Merpati with Ambon and Manado; less regular flights to Galela and Kao on Halmahera, and to Gebe and Morotai. Bouraq also run 4 flights/week to Manado, Indoavia fly 3 times a week between Ternate and Ambon (146,000Rp). Taxis to town cost 3,000Rp. There is a tourist information counter at the airport, but it is usually unattended. To see the island on landing sit on the right-hand side of the aircraft. By boat: Ternate's main port is conveniently located just S of the town centre at the end of Jl. Pahlawan Revolusi. Shipping companies, including Pelni, have their offices in the town centre. Arrivals and departures are posted on boards outside the offices. The Pelni ships *Umsini* and *Tidar* call here (see route map **page 1008**), as does the Kalla Lines vessel (**page 902**). Other vessels of various sizes and states of seaworthiness call at Morotai and Halmahera, Bitung, Laiwui, Madapolo, Babang, Mangoli, Sanana and Ambon, among other destinations.

HALMAHERA

The weirdly shaped island of Halmahera, something like a miniature version of Sulawesi, is the second largest in Maluku with a land area of 18,000 sq km. It is one of the least visited islands in the archipelago. Like the relationship between Ambon and Seram, Halmahera is overshadowed in historical and economic terms by its far smaller neighbour, Ternate.

Much of Halmahera remains forested and transport is distinctly limited. Tribal groups inhabit the interior and it is thought that there are some for whom life has only changed marginally over the last century. The establishment of transmigration settlements on the island for Javanese settlers (**see page 706**), and the financial attractions offered by Halmahera's primary forests may mean that this beautiful island will not remain isolated and beautiful for very much longer. Trekking in the forests and mountains of Halmahera may become an important alternative source of income, although even this will have its cultural costs. It was here, in February 1858, that Alfred Russel Wallace, the great Victorian naturalist, wrote his famous paper 'On the tendency of varieties to depart indefinitely, from the original type', which laid out his ideas on the principle on natural selection. Although the paper (published in the *Proceedings of the Linnean Society*) drew upon his observations in Borneo, South America and in other areas of Indonesia, perhaps it was the wonder of Halmahera which cemented his thoughts into this seminal paper.

At the N end of Halmahera, the largest settlement is the town of **Tobelo** with about 15,000 inhabitants. On the coast near the centre of the island, **Kao** is the biggest town with a population of less than 5,000. Kao was an important Japanese air base during World War II. There is a road linking Kao with Tobelo. There are flights to Kao and Galela (see below) and ferries link Ternate with Tobelo and Jailolo.

Accommodation Tobelo: **C-D** *President*; **D** *Karunia*, Jl. Makmuran; **D** *Megaria*, Jl. Bayankara; **D** *Pantai Indah*, Jl. Lorong Pantai Indah, T 108. Kao: **D** *Dirgahayu*; **D** *Sejahtera*.

Local transport Minibuses provide a reasonable service between Kao, Galela and Tobelo, and more limited links with other towns.

Airline offices *Merpati*, Cabang PT Eterna Galela, Jl. Kampung Soasiu, Galela.

Transport to & from Halmahera By air: there are connections between Kao and Ternate and Galela (2/week); and between Galela (60 km from Tobelo, take a shared taxi) and Ternate and Kao (2/week), and Morotai (1/week). By boat: daily ferries from Ternate to Tobelo via Morotai (18-20 hrs); there is also an infrequent service from Ternate to Kao.

MOROTAI

Morotai was an important airforce base for the allies as they advanced across the Pacific and there is a good deal of war scrap still lying about as evidence. Covering an area of over 1,800 sq km, the Japanese Private Nakamura holed-up here until 1973 when he emerged from the forest to surrender after nearly 30 years. **Daruba**, the capital, has a population of about 5,000 and the diving and snorkelling is reputed to be excellent. The population of the island is about 50,000.

Accommodation Daruba: **D** *Tonggak*.

Sports Diving: it is reported that some shopkeepers in Daruba are willing to hire out diving equipment; maintenance may be poor.

Transport to & from Morotai **By air**: Merpati flies a once weekly loop between Ternate, Galela and Morotai. **By boat**: daily ferry connections with Ternate 12½ hrs and Tobelo on Halmahera 3½ hrs.

SOUTH EAST MALUKU

The *Kabupaten*, or district, of South East Maluku is the remotest and least visited part of the province (or at least of that part which can be visited). The largest and most important islands are the Kei, Aru, Tanimbar, Babar, Wetar and Kisar Islands. The district covers almost 25,000 sq km and has a population of about 275,000. These islands were never important in the spice trade with Europe and they were largely insulated from the events that were so fundamentally altering life elsewhere in the archipelago. However, there were local trading links with the N Moluccas and South Sulawesi, and forest products were exchanged for metal implements.

Lying S of the equator, these islands are drier than those to the N and the people subsist primarily on yams, maize, millet, coconut and sago, rather than rice. Missionaries have converted most of the population to nominal Christianity, although traditional ancestor worship is still important.

Places of interest

The 3 **Kei Islands** (population 100,000) have magnificent beaches and wonderful snorkelling – but this is a long way to come for a beach holiday. The capital **Tual** is surprisingly busy for an area, seemingly, at the edge of the world. The locals are renowned for their boat building skills, and the **Laut Cave** on Kei Kecil contains enigmatic ideograms indicating a long period of human settlement.

The densely forested **Tanimbar Islands** (over 60 in all, population 75,000) are similarly endowed with beaches and sea gardens. The 'largest' towns are **Larat**, on the island of the same name, and **Saumlaki** on Yamdena. The Christian inhabitants of Tanimbar have been influenced by Hinduism from distant India (evident in textile design), and by Polynesian and Micronesian cultures (for instance, the tradition of cooking food wrapped in banana leaves over hot stones). On the E coast of Yamdena, at the village of **Sanglia Dol** are **megalithic carvings** which visitors have reported to be well worth visiting.

Accommodation Tual (Kei): **D** *Rosemgen I*, Jl. K. Sadsuitubun, T 45, top of the range for Kei; **E** *Nini Gerhana*, Jl. Pattimura; *Mira*, Jl. Sapta Marga, T 172. Langgur (Kei): **D** *Ramah Indah*, Jl. Baru Watdek, T 232; *Rosemgen II*, Jl. Watdek. Saumlaki (Tanimbar): **D** *Harapan Indah*, Jl. Pelabuhan; **D** *Kellybait*, Jl. Bhinneka, T 67; **E** *Ratulel*, Jl. Bhinneka, T 14.

Banks & money changers It is possible to change US$ cash in some shops, but it is best to take enough for your stay.

Airline offices *Merpati*, Rahmat Jaya, Jl. Pattimura, T 376, Langgur (Kei) and Jl. Bhineka, Saumlaki (Tanimbar).

Transport to & from South East Maluku By air: daily connections on Merpati between Langgur (Kei) and Ambon; 3 flights/week between Saumlaki (Tanimbar) and Ambon. **By boat**: Perintis ships leave Ambon every 2 weeks or so and call at the major ports of South East Maluku. There are 2 routes – one links Ambon with the Near South East or Tenggara Dekat (calling at harbours in the Kei and Tanimbar Islands); the other linking Ambon with the Far South East or Tenggara Jauh (calling at harbours in the Babar and Kisar Islands).

IRIAN JAYA

Introduction, 989; Information for Visitors, 995; Biak, 996; Jayapura, 997; The Baliem Valley, 998.

Maps: Irian Jaya, 990; The Baliem Valley, 999.

Irian Jaya, known before 1973 as Irian Barat or West Irian, comprises the W half of the island of New Guinea – the world's second largest island after Greenland. It is Indonesia's largest, most remote, and least populated province. Large areas have yet to be explored, and this is one of the few parts of the world where maps can still legitimately be marked: 'Here be Dragons'.

INTRODUCTION

Irian Jaya has a population of only 1.7 million, scattered over an expanse nearly twice the size of Great Britain – about 4 people per sq km. The province is also one of the country's newest: Indonesian forces *de facto* occupied Irian Jaya in 1962, but *de jure* only annexed the province in 1969. The word *irian* is derived from a Biak word meaning 'pretty' or 'light'. *Jaya* is an Indonesian word meaning 'glorious'. The shape of the island of New Guinea is often likened to a bird. The inhabitants sometimes talk of Pulau Cassoway – or Cassoway Island – and the Dutch named the NW corner Vogelkop or 'Bird's Head' (now Kepala Burung, also meaning Bird's Head).

Land
Irian Jaya was once part of a land bridge that linked Australia and Southeast Asia. The main geological feature of the province is a central range of mountains that runs from NW to SE. Near the border with Papua New Guinea (PNG) is the Jayawijaya Range, separated from the W Sudirman Range by the fertile Grand Baliem Valley. The highest peak – and also the highest in Indonesia – is Mount Jaya at 5,030m. There are 10 other mountains which exceed 4,800m, making this the consistently highest part of Southeast Asia, and the only area with glaciers.

North of this impressive, central spine of mountains are a small range known as the Coastal Range or Van Rees Mountains. The highest peak here is 2,272m. To the S, the central mountains descend steeply to a vast, swampy, lowland plain.

As well as the W half of New Guinea, Irian Jaya also comprises a number of islands. The main ones are Japen, Biak-Supiori and Numfor to the N, and the Raja Amphat group – including Waigeo, Batanta, Salawat and Misool – to the NW.

Climate
Irian Jaya is hot, wet and humid. Rainfall tends to be heavy throughout the year, with only minor seasonal variations. On the N coast rainfall is about 2,500 mm/year; in the mountains it can exceed 8,000 mm/year, making this one of the wettest spots on earth. It is also one of the cloudiest (which poses a major problem for air transport). However, there are areas where rainfall is markedly less. Merauke in the SE, for example, receives less than 1,500 mm; also drier are

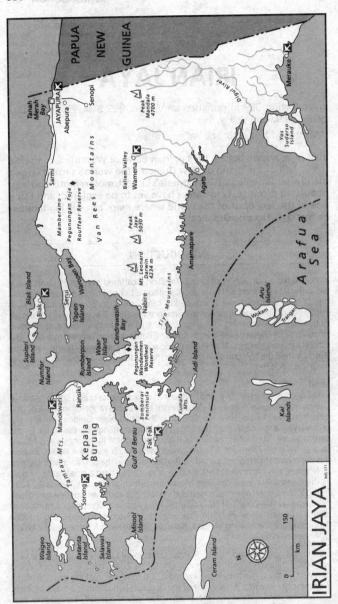

IRIAN JAYA

sections of the NW and the N (e.g. Jayapura). Temperatures, except at altitude, average a fairly constant 29°C-32°C.

Fauna and flora

Irian Jaya's flora and fauna are complex and diverse. In total, 'Papuasia' – as the whole region is known – has over 20,000 species of plant, 200 mammal, 725 bird, 253 reptile and 80,000-100,000 species of insect. In the Arfak Nature Reserve alone, which covers only 70 km² outside Manokwari, 800 species of spider and 5,000 species of butterflies and moths have been recorded. Not only does the province cover a wide variety of ecological zones from coastal mangrove swamp, to lowland rainforest, montane forest, up to alpine grasslands; but it also lies at a biogeographical crossroads: the animals and plants are both Asian and Australasian in origin. In the mountains, for example, there are N latitude oaks from China such as *Quercus junghunii* growing alongside 'Antarctic' beeches (*Nothofagus*). Among the large number of fascinating plants are insectivorous pitcher plants (*Nepenthes*) (**see page 57**) and the weird and wonderful giant anthouse plant (*Myrmecodia brasii*), an epiphyte over 2 km in length with a bulbous, honeycombed stem inhabited by large numbers of ants.

Like Irian's flora, its fauna shows clear links with both Asia and Australasia. There are 2 species of primitive monotremes, the short-beaked (*Tachyglossus aculeatus*) and long-beaked (*Zaglossus bruijni*) echidna, marsupial mice (Dasyuridae), tree kangaroos (*Dendrolagus*) and the rare sea mammal, the dugong (*Dugong dugon*). Among its 725 species of bird, the best known are the 26 species of birds of paradise (see box). Other notable birds include 9 species of bower bird (*Ptilonorhynchidae*), the large, flightless cassowary (*Casuarius*) and the orange and black *pitohui*. In 1992, the pitohui became the first bird to be proved poisonous. The feathers, skin and flesh of the pitohui contain homobatrachotoxin, powerful enough to kill a mouse in minutes. It explains why snakes and hawks – the birds' natural enemies – steer well clear of the 3 species of pitohui and why it is known locally as the 'rubbish bird'.

History

The first sighting of New Guinea by a European was by d'Abreu in 1512. Long before this date however, Chinese and Arab traders and seafarers from the Spice Islands of Maluku were trading with the coastal communities of Irian Jaya, exchanging manufactured goods for forest products. In 1526, de Menses, the first governor of the Spice Islands, was forced to take shelter in a cove on Bird's Head (Kepala Burung) during a storm and named the land Ilhas dos Papuas or Islands of the Papuans. He took the word Papuas from the Malay *papuah* – for orang papuah, or 'frizzy-haired men'.

From the 16th century mariners continued to sail along and map the coasts, but there was no attempt at interior exploration or settlement. The first colony was established in 1793 by the English East India Company near Manokwari; it was abandoned after only 2 years. The Dutch did not establish a presence until 1828 when they built a fortress at Fort du Bus, in Triton Bay; it was abandoned less than 10 years later. They re-established a presence at the end of the 19th century, building forts at Manokwari, on the N coast of the Bird's Head, and at Fak-Fak, on the W peninsular, declaring all the land to the W of the 141st meridian as Dutch territory. In 1902 a settlement was established at Merauke in the SE and at Humboldt Bay (near present day Jayapura), on the N coast. However, the Dutch presence was restricted to the coastal regions; forays into the harsh, inpenetrable interior were intermittant and generally unsuccessful.

Coordinated exploration of the interior did not begin until the second decade of the 20th century. And it was only in 1938 that the American Richard Archbold, leader of the Archbold Expeditions, discovered the Grand Baliem Valley. The

The bird of paradise: legless bird of God

When Ferdinand Magellan's ship the *Victoria* docked at Seville after her monumental circumnavigation of the globe, the hold contained, along with spices, five skins of the bird of paradise (*Paradisaeidae*) which had been given to the crew as a gift when they landed at Tidore in the Moluccas. Although the name was coined by a Dutchman, Jan van Linschoten in 1590, they had long been viewed as Birds of God or Golden Birds from 'a land of departed souls'.

'Paradise' referred not just to their spectacular plumage, but also to the fact that the birds were thought to be legless. The skins arrived in Europe with no legs, and sometimes no wings, and it was thought the birds were naturally this way and fed, bred and reared their young on the wing – only falling to earth when they died. Thomas Pennant, an 18th century British naturalist, went so far as to claim that "they lived on the dew of Heaven, and had no evacuation like other mortal birds". It was presumed that the female incubated her egg in a shallow depression on the male's back. Getting it there must have entailed some skilled aerobatics. Why they were transported legless is not certain. The British naval captain Thomas Forrest, who visited New Guinea between 1774 and 1776, maintained that it was for 2 reasons: because they could be more easily preserved that way, and because the Moors wanted to "put them in mock flight, on their helmets, as ornaments".

In all, there are 26 species of bird of paradise, of which the most valuable – because they have the most spectacular plumage – are those of the genus *Paradisae*, in particular the much sought-after Greater (*Paradisaeidae apoda*) and Lesser (*P. minor*) bird of paradise. Naturalists point to these birds as an example of evolution run wild in the absence of predators. The wonderful plumage is necessary to attract a mate, so an ever larger, more magnificent, and less efficient plumage, tends to evolve, locking them into an evolutionary dead end.

Although it was demand for their feathers (in the West) which really threatened the bird, the magnificent plumage was in demand in the courts and among noblemen and women in Southeast Asia, China, India and Persia. The European fashion for hats decorated with feathers of the bird of paradise dates from the late 19th century, and between 1884 and 1889 50,000 skins were exported to Europe. Today, they are protected, but sadly it is still possible to buy birds of paradise skins, and their valuable plumage, in places like the market in Biak for only US$20. In the countryside around Biak, many of the churches – tragically and rather ironically – have been built on the back of the trade in the skins of these Birds of God.

Japanese occupied New Guinea in 1942, and some of the bitterest fighting in the Pacific Theatre took place here. Legacies of the war include the large numbers of airfields built by the Allies and the Japanese, and topographic maps which are still in use today. The Japanese were defeated in 1945 and the territory was returned to the Dutch.

In 1962, the Dutch gave up control of West Papua to a United Nations Temporary Executive Authority (UNTEA). A year later, in May 1963, the territory was handed over to Indonesia to administer on the condition that within 6 years there would be an Act of Free Choice – a plebiscite – to ascertain whether the population wished to become a part of Indonesia. It is at this point that opinions – like those on East Timor (see page 965) – differ. According to the Indonesian government, in 1969 the people of Irian were given a choice of whether to become an independent country, or part of the Republic of Indonesia; they freely, chose the latter. Critics like the Anti-Slavery Society maintain that: "The Act was stage-managed by the Indonesians, who used a combination of bribery and brute force to persuade 1,025 local 'delegates' to approve the continued Indonesian occupation of West Papua" (1990:6). Despite a highly critical report by the UN observer Fernando Ortiz Sanz, the UN voted to endorse the Indonesian annexation of the territory in Nov 1969. Since that date, the Operasi Papua Merdeka (OPM) or Free Papua Movement have been fighting a largely ignored guerrilla war of independence in Irian Jaya.

People

There are 3 ecological regions in Irian Jaya: the coast, the interior lowlands, and the highlands. Because travel is so difficult through the harsh terrain, the people of these different zones remained largely isolated from one another. Even today, the only feasible way to get around the province is by air. This inaccessibility is reflected in a huge diversity of languages; about 250 different dialects are thought to be spoken in Irian Jaya. About 30% of the population live in agricultural communities in the cool, temperate valleys of the Baliem Valley, Paniai Lakes and Anggi Lakes. In recent years however, there has been a dramatic increase in the urban population of such centres as Jayapura, Biak and Merauke. Most of this increase has been through an influx of immigrants from other regions of Indonesia, rather than a shift in population from rural areas in Irian Jaya. As the last great frontier zone in Indonesia, the province has also been targeted as a major destination for transmigrant settlers (see page 732).

The coasts The coastal people cultivate sago, taro and coconuts, raise pigs, and fish. Sago is their dietary staple (see page 973). Traditionally, they lived in large houses built on stilts, which could hold up to 100 people, with a central communal area for cooking and socializing and separate rooms for each family; this tradition has died out and most families now have their own homes. The people of the coasts grew rich on maritime trade; they were able to sell local products such as sea cucumber (trepang), rare woods, animal skins and exotic birds in exchange for foreign goods such as metals, textiles, glass beads and porcelain. In their turn, and despite the difficulties of communication, the coastal people would trade these imported goods to the inhabitants of the interior, where they became an important part of a bride's trousseau.

The lowland and highland interior Like the coastal people, the interior lowlanders also grow sago and taro, but hunting and gathering play a more important role in their livelihoods. They 'farm' the larvae of the capricorn beetle by cultivating fallen, rotting trees where the insects breed. The highlanders cultivate sweet potatoes and taro in a rotational field system, and also raise pigs for ceremonial and ritual events.

Arts and crafts

The inhabitants of Irian Jaya produce fine woodcarvings – those of the Asmat are particularly highly regarded (see box). On the N coast, elaborately carved spatulas for serving food are the most distinctive art form. Food was traditionally served on carved plates, and large ceremonial platters were reserved for feasts and kept by the headman.

Betel nut holders – used to carry the lime powder that is a part of the betel nut preparation (see page 35) – are also common. These are made from gourds and are incised with patterns. Men's gourds are long and thin, whilst women's are short and fat. The incisions on a woman's gourd are also rubbed with lime. Spatulas with pointed ends were carved as stoppers for the gourds, sometimes with figures on the top.

There is no tradition of weaving in Irian Jaya. The inhabitants traditionally adorned their bodies with necklaces, armbands and head-dresses, and the women sometimes wore barkcloth skirts.

Master craftsmen: the Asmat of Irian Jaya

The woodcarvings of the Asmat of SE Irian Jaya are regarded as some of the finest examples of 'primitive' art in the world. They now command high prices on the international art market. The Asmat are primarily hunter-gatherers who live on the banks of rivers and subsist on fish, sago and game. Their homeland is the area around the town of Agats. Formerly, the Asmat were headhunters and cannibals. The motivation was on the one hand revenge, and on the other the acquisition of prestige. Heads also became important objects in initiation ceremonies. Cannibalism was a product of headhunting: it gave the victor the strength of the vanquished.

The Asmat believe carving to be an almost religious experience. Ancestral spirits or *ndet* could not be released from the world of the living until an enemy had been killed by a close relative. Until then, the spirit of the ancestor would persecute the living, and carving ritual objects named after particular ancestors was one way of minimizing this. Although there is no word in Asmat for either art or artist – the latter is simply known as a *tsjestsju ipitsj* or 'clever man' – skilled artists were accorded the same prestige as successful warriors. Asmat art varies a great deal. Among more common works are:

❑ ancestor poles or *bis* made from mangrove wood, and sometimes as much as 5-6 m high and carved with an ancestor figure and various motifs and symbols (one root of the mangrove tree is left attached to become the *tjemen* or penis).

❑ carved sago worm containers; carved drums with lizard skin drumheads; crocodile poles from the Casuarina coast area.

❑ carved paddles with handles over 2 m long sometimes decorated with human heads or hornbills (symbols of head-hunting).

❑ 'soul' ships or *wuramon* (made only by the inland Asmat) in the form of dug-out canoes.

❑ incised war shields, carved from the trunks of mangrove trees and painted in red, black and white.

Pottery is unknown, and the area that the Asmat inhabit is almost devoid of stone, so wood and wood products are virtually the only materials used to produce 'art'.

The finest collection of Asmat art in the world is displayed at the **Asmat Museum of Culture and Progress** in Agats. The collection was assembled by the Crosier Mission under Bishop Alphonse Sowada and Father F. Trenkenschug. They began buying Asmat art in the early 1960s, and when the Indonesian government ordered the destruction of carvings to stop headhunting and cannibalism in 1962, they frantically assembled as much as their limited funds allowed. The museum was opened in 1973.

Although evaluating the 'artistic', and hence commercial, value of Asmat art is difficult, fine pieces now command high prices on the international art market. It is said that there are only 40 master carvers still at work in Irian Jaya and well-produced ancestor poles sell for well over US$1,000; war shields for over US$500. **NB**: formerly, most Asmat art was carved from soft woods which deteriorate in the cold and dry climates of the N hemisphere. Now, with the introduction of metal tools, many carvings are made from far more durable ironwood (*belian*). Nevertheless, many cheaper pieces are still carved from softwood.

Economic change

The development of Irian Jaya by the Indonesian government has taken 3 main directions. On the one hand the government has allotted considerable sums to upgrading the province's infrastructure. This is partly for security reasons – the secessionist OPM (see above) is still active and there is continued political disaffection. Another important motivation however, is that the government sees Irian Jaya as a major source of primary resources. Already, oil and copper represent over 90% of the value of the province's exports and any expansion in exploitation is partly contingent upon improving the physical infrastructure. Finally, with a population density of only 4 people/sq km, Irian Jaya is seen as a vast un-tapped source of agricultural land to satisfy the land hunger of the poor in Java and Bali. It has therefore been targeted as a major destination area for transmigrants (**see page 732**).

The need to develop the province has led to considerable investment by the government. It has also encouraged the immigration of large numbers of Indonesians from outside Irian Jaya – primarily Javanese, Makassarese and people from Maluku. This process is most obvious in the cities where nearly 90% of the population are non-Irian born. This has led to criticisms that the Irianese are failing to derive any benefit from the exploitation of the province and accusations that the central government is trying to 'Javanize' the area by swamping the locals with immigrants. Today, over 20% of the population are non-Irian born, and with only 1.7 million inhabitants in total, it may not be long before immigrants outnumber the indigenous inhabitants.

For the moment however, Irian Jaya remains one of the few true frontier areas left on earth. Vast expanses remain largely unexplored and traditional customs exert a dominant influence. On 19 Mar 1992, the Jakarta-based Indonesian daily newspaper *Kompas* reported that a tribesman had killed his wife when he hit her over the head with a bottle during an argument. He was fined 11 cows and ordered to part with his treasured collection of stones and seeds.

INFORMATION FOR VISITORS

Permits

A transit visa is required to visit Irian Jaya; and a *surat jalan* (literally 'travel letter') for all parts of the province outside the major towns of Jayapura, Sorong and Biak – for example, the Baliem Valley. *Surat jalan* can be obtained from the central police stations in Jayapura, Sorong and Biak (4 passport photographs – sometimes fewer – are required, along with your passport, or photocopies of the first page, the photo page, the date of issue and expiry page and the immigration entry stamp page). Most hotels will organize *surat jalan* for a small fee (about 1,500Rp). There are some parts of the province which are off-limits to all visitors, even with a *surat jalan*. Check at the local police station.

Internal travel

An ambitious road building programme is underway in Irian Jaya, but because of the size of the task, most of the country can still only be reached by air, sea, or on foot. For most visitors, the only feasible way to get around the country is by air. At last count, there were over 250 airstrips scattered over the province, most built by Christian missionary groups. Merpati operates services to the larger towns, and 2 missionary airlines – MAF (Missionary Aviation Fellowship) and AMA (Associated Missions Aviation) – to smaller settlements, as well as the main towns. **NB**: the missionary airlines do take passengers but it should be stressed they are not commercial airlines and are under no compunction to carry fare-paying passengers.

Money

It is difficult to change money in Irian Jaya. Banks in Jayapura, Biak and Wamena (Baliem Valley) are the only places where travellers' cheques can be changed.

Tours The *Tropical Princess* cruises from Biak Island for 5-10 day scuba-diving trips. The boat can also be chartered. Contact: *Tropical Princess Cruises*, P.T. Prima Marindo Paradise, 3rd flr., East Wing, Shop 36, *Borobudur Intercontinental Hotel*, Jl. Lapangan Banteng Selatan 1, Jakarta, T 371108, F 370477.

BIAK

Biak is the capital of Biak Island, which covers less than 2,000 sq km off the mainland's N coast. The town has a population of about 25,000. It is a one road town – all the main hotels, restaurants and government offices are strung out along Jalan Jend. A. Yani, with the harbour at the W end of town (where the road becomes Jalan Sudirman) and the airport at the E (where the road becomes Jalan Prof. Moh. Yamin).

There are no sights as such in the town, although the **markets** are colourful. The central **Pasar Panir** is on Jalan Selat Makassar and sells, among other things, animal skins and live birds. At the W edge of town is the **Pasar Inpres**, next to the taxi terminal, which is mainly a food market. In the morning a **fish market** sets up just off the W end of Jalan Sudirman near the harbour.

Excursions
There are a number of **idyllic beaches** within 2 hours or so of Biak by public transport. To the E, in the vicinity of the market town of **Bosnik** (18 km from town), are white-sand beaches with good snorkelling.

Padaido Islands lie off Biak Island to the SE. These paradisical islands offer superb snorkelling and beaches. **Getting there:** charter a boat from town or from Bosnik, or go on a tour. Expect to pay about US$50-80 for the day, but bargain hard.

Korem is a market town about 50 km N of Biak on the island's N coast. A good market is staged here on Wed and Sats. **Getting there:** by bemo from town.

Tours *Sentonsa Tosiga*, organize tours around town and to such spots as the Padaido Islands.

Accommodation B *Irian*, Jl. Prof Moh. Yamin, T 21139 (2 km E of town near the airport), some a/c, good restaurant, colonial feel (like something out of a Hemingway novel) and comfortable rooms, set in gardens and overlooking the sea; **B** *Titawaka*, Jl. Selat Makassar 3, T 21835, a/c, quiet and comfortable, rather expensive; **B-C** *Mapia*, Jl. Jend. A. Yani, T 31383, some a/c, large, pleasant rooms with attached mandi, friendly and clean; **D** *Maju*, Jl. Imam Bonjol 45, T 21218, small, but clean rooms with attached mandi; **D** *Solo*, Jl. Monginsidi 4, T 21397, best of the 'budget' accommodation, near the market.

Restaurants There are cheap warungs on Jl. Monginsidi and stalls on Jl. Jend. A. Yani near the centre of town. **♦♦***Cleopatra*, Jl. Jend. A. Yani, fish and chicken specialities and tables outside; **♦♦***Jakarta*, Jl. Imam Bonjol, Indonesian and Chinese, good seafood.

Shopping Crafts: available from the markets and from shops like the *Pusaka Art Shop* at the Pasar Lama. **NB:** skins of the bird of paradise are available for US$20 – they are a protected species and their trade should not be encouraged.

Local transport Minibuses/colts run to most local destinations. The terminal is off Jl. Airlangga at the W edge of town, near the Inpres Market. **Taxis** can be chartered for about 8,000Rp/hr.

Banks & money changers Ekspor Impor, Jl. Jend. A. Yani (near intersection with Jl. Imam Bonjol), will change most major travellers' cheques and cash; **Bank Rakyat Indonesia**, Jl. Sudirman, will change most major travellers' cheques and cash.

Useful addresses General Post Office Jl. Prof. M. Yamin (at the edge of town on the road to the airport). **Area code:** 0961. **Immigration Office:** Jl. Jend. Sudirman 1, T 21109 (corner of Jl. Sudirman and Jl. Imam Bonjol). **Central Police Station:** Jl. Selat Makassar (for *surat jalan*, see page 995). **General Hospital:** Jl. Sriwijaya Ridge 1.

Airline offices Garuda, Jl. Sudirman 3, T 21416; **Merpati**, Jl. Prof. Moh. Yamin 1, T 21213.

Tour companies & travel agents *Granda Irja*, Jl. Imam Bonjol 16, T 21616; *Sentosa Tosiga*, Jl. Jend. A. Yani 36, T 21398.

Transport to & from Biak By air: the airport is on the outskirts of town, about 2 km E of the centre. *Transport to town*: minibus or taxi (about 5,000Rp), or catch a public bemo, or it is possible to walk. Regular daily connections on Merpati with Jayapura, Ujung Pandang, Denpasar, Nabire and Serui; less regular connections with Ambon, Sorong and Timika. **International connections**: on Garuda with Los Angeles, via Honolulu and on to Denpasar. **By boat**: the harbour is at the W edge of town. Pelni boats make the trip to Jayapura about every week (deck passage only). The Pelni office is at Jl. Sudirman 27.

JAYAPURA

Formerly the Dutch city of Hollandia, Jayapura is the capital of Irian Jaya province and has a population of about 100,000. As most of the inhabitants – like those in other urban areas in Irian Jaya – are immigrants from other parts of Indonesia, it lacks any distinctive 'Papuan' atmosphere. The Irianese here are outnumbered by Javanese, Makassarese and others.

Jayapura is one of Indonesia's more featureless towns, and most visitors only use it as a base before venturing inland. It is a ribbon development stretching inland from the coast, with most commercial buildings on Jl. Jend. A. Yani.

Excursions

Hamadi is a coastal suburb about 4 km NE of town. This was the spot where the Americans landed in Apr 1944 to wrest control of New Guinea from the Japanese. On the beach, a few rusting landing-craft and tanks half-buried in the sand bear testament to the event. After gaining control of the area, General Douglas McArthur made Jayapura – or Hollandia as it was then – into one of the major forward staging posts for the advance N. The beach is attractive; walk through the Indonesian military base to get there. The town also has an interesting central market and a number of shops and stalls selling souvenirs. **Accommodation** here includes: **D** *Hamadi Jaya*, clean rooms, noisy, but probably the best of the 'budget' accommodation (both here and in Jayapura); **C** *Asia*, T 22277, clean but expensive. **Getting there:** by colt from Jl. Jend. A. Yani.

Base G is a beach 6 km W of town named after the U.S. base established here at the end of the war. Swimming is moderate, but currents can be strong. Very popular at the weekend. **Getting there:** colts only run out to Base G on weekends; on weekdays, charter a colt for the journey.

Candrawasih University Museum is located at Abepura, about 25 km S of town. It displays a reasonable collection of ethnographic pieces and is worth a visit before venturing into the interior. Open: 0800-1300 Mon-Fri. **Getting there:** by colt from the station or from Jl. Jend. A. Yani.

Museum Negeri is situated just outside Adepura and has a collection of natural history exhibits as well as ethnographic pieces. Open: 0800-1300 Mon-Fri. **Getting there:** by colt from the station or from Jl. Jend. A. Yani to Adepura.

Tanah Merah Bay is about 55 km W of the city and offers some of the best swimming in the area, as well as reasonable snorkelling. **Getting there:** by colt to Depapre from the bus station.

Tours There are a number of tour agents in town running tours outside the city and to more distant destinations in Irian Jaya.

Accommodation Accommodation in Jayapura is some of the most expensive in Indonesia. Sentani lies 37 km from town and only 3 km from the airport. It is recommended as a more attractive place to stay than Jayapura, where there is little to do. **B** *Mantoa*, Jl. Jend. A. Yani

14, T 22336, a/c, hot water, best hotel in town, comfortable rooms with good facilities; **B** *Triton*, Jl. Jend. A. Yani 2, T 21218, a/c, one notch down from the Mantoa, but comfortable and well run; **C** *Dafonsoro*, Jl. Percetakan Negara 20-24, T 21870, a/c; **C-D** *Ratna*, Jl. Raya Sentani 7, T 91435, some a/c, own bathroom, good location 5 mins from airport, clean new rooms, rec; **C-D** *Sederhana*, Jl. Halmahera 2, T 21291, some a/c, range of rooms with attached mandi; **C-E** *Kartini*, Jl. Perintis 2, T 22371, some attached mandi, central and clean; **D** *Sentani Inn*, Jl. Raya Sentani, T 91440, some a/c, price includes breakfast, basic accommodation with attached mandi, very helpful staff with good English.

Restaurants The better restaurants are strung out along Jl. Percetakan. Cheaper warungs can be found near the mosque on Jl. Jend. A. Yani. There is a night market by the Pelni office with good Indonesian stall food; for cheap seafood try the stalls on Jl. Halmahera. ♦♦♦*Jaya Grill*, Jl. Koti 5, seafood and steaks served on the waterfront, expensive; ♦♦*Nirwana*, Jl. Jend. A. Yani 40, good Padang food.

Shopping Tribal art: is sold at Hamadi 4 km from town (see above, Excursions). It is mass produced, and usually ersatz, although good pieces do sometimes crop up. For better pieces, try the *Madinah Art Shop*, Jl. Perikanan.

Local transport Colts: the terminal is on Jl. Percetakan, close to the waterfront.

Banks & money changers Ekspor-Impor, Jl. Jend. A. Yani, will change travellers' cheques and cash.

Useful addresses General Post Office: Jl. Sam Ratulangi (on the waterfront). **Area code**: 0967. **Immigration Office**: Jl. Percetakan 15, T 22147. **Central Police Station**: Jl. Jend. A. Yani (for *surat jalan* permits for the interior, **see page 995**). **General Hospital**: Jl. Kesehatan 1.

Airline offices Merpati, Jl. Jend. A. Yani 15, T 21327. **MAF**, Sentani airport. **AMA**, Sentani airport.

Tour companies & travel agents *Natrabu*, Jl. Jend. A. Yani 72; *Indonesia Safari*, Jl. Kemiri, T 94; *Bawa Makmur*, Jl. Koti 72, T 22180; *Duta Baliem*, Jl. Nindya Karya, T 21416; *Limbunan*, Jl. Tugu 11, T 31633, F 31437.

Transport to & from Jayapura By air: Sentani airport is 35 km from town. Minibuses take passengers into town, or walk out onto the main road and catch a public colt to town via Abepura. Regular connections on Merpati/Garuda with Biak, Wamena, and Ujung Pandang; less regular connections with Sorong, Nabire, Sarmi, Senggeh, Serui, Manokwari and Merauke. MAF and AMA fly to even less prominent destinations in Irian. By boat: the Pelni ship *Umsini* docks at Jayapura every fortnight on its circuit between here and Jakarta (see route map, page 1008). The Pelni office is at Jl. Halmahera 1, T 21270, on the waterfront.

THE BALIEM VALLEY

The Grand Valley of the Baliem was one of the most remarkable finds of this century. In 1938, the American explorer Richard Archbold flew his seaplane over the Snow Mountain Range (now called the Sudirman Range), and peered out of the cockpit to see an extensive and lush, cultivated valley where he and everyone else expected to find only forest. The network of gardens and canals brought to mind the great civilizations of Asia and the Middle East – nothing like it was expected in New Guinea, let alone in this isolated spot. The expedition named the valley *Shrangrala*.

Today it is known as the **Baliem Valley**, a verdant and fertile upland valley set at an altitude of over 1,500m and encircled by mountain peaks. It is drained by the Baliem River and is about 55 km long and 15 km wide. The population of the area is 60,000, making this the most densely populated rural area in Irian Jaya. The inhabitants make up Irian Jaya's largest, and probably most famous, tribe: the **Dani**.

Despite conversion to Christianity and the intrusion of all the paraphernalia of Indonesian

BALIEM VALLEY

IMS 172

To Mulia

Kelila

Jugwa

Wolo

Bugi

Waga Waga

Jiwika

Akima

Pyramid

Kimbin

Hom Hom

Wamena

Pugima

North Baliem R.

Hepoba

Hetegima

Sugokmo

Kurima

Mt Trikora
4730 m

Holuwan

0   10
km

N

administration, the Dani continue to wear their traditional penis sheaths and to farm in the traditional manner. The economy is based upon a sophisticated system of gardens, allied with the raising of pigs. On the valley floors, canals help to control flooding in the wet season, and provide irrigation water during the dry. Fields located on the hillsides even have erosion control structures, giving lie to the notion that the inhabitants of New Guinea practised only an unsophisticated agriculture before the arrival of Europeans. Pigs, the other side of the Dani agricultural coin, are raised by the women and are only eaten in ritual or ceremonial situations. Among the tribes of Irian Jaya, the Dani have been among the most resistant to change. They do not seem to be attracted by the trappings of a 'Western' lifestyle, and have clung to their traditions.

Wamena

Wamena is the largest town in the Baliem Valley and most visitors use it as a base to explore the surrounding countryside. The settlement was established by the Dutch in 1958, at about the same time that missionaries began working in the valley. It is really just a small group of administrative buildings, hotels, tour companies and restaurants.

Excursions

There are a number of Dani villages and other sights within easy reach of Wamena. Not surprisingly, these are relatively heavily touristed. It is much more rewarding to go on an overnight(s) trek.

South-east and east of Wamena

Pugima is the closest Dani village to Wamena, about 1 hour's walk E of town. Walk through **Wesaput** and then cross the Baliem River to reach the village. There are some traditional houses here, but being so close to Wamena it is changing fast. **Getting there:** on foot, 1 hr.

Kurima is a district capital about 30 km SE of Wamena. A market is held here on Tues and it can be used as a base for treks into the surrounding hills, particularly S through the **Baliem River Gorge**. **Accommodation:** basic accommodation available. **Getting there:** public bemos venture 15 km SE from Wamena to Hepoba; sometimes the drivers can be persuaded to continue to Hetegima or

Sugokmo (another 5 km) for an additional charge. From these towns it is an easy hike to Kurima.

North and north-west of Wamena
Akima is famous for its blackened, **mummified warrior**. In former times, powerful or important men were not cremated but preserved through desiccation so that their influence could continue to benefit the village. The hunched figure is dressed in the regalia of a Dani warrior. To see the mummy, haggle with the keeper – expect to pay 5,000-10,000Rp depending on your bargaining skills. There is a market in Akima on Sundays. **Getting there**: take the NW road out of town towards Hom Hom; at Hom Hom cross the Baliem River on the suspension bridge and then follow the track; the village is just off the road. In all, about 2 hrs walk. Bemos also run past Akima.

Jiwika is a district capital about 18 km NW of Wamena and the largest village in the area. Like Akima, there is a mummy here. Expect to pay about 5,000Rp to see the wizened figure. **Accommodation**: **E** *Losmen Lauk*, very basic, shared mandi, fleas. **Getting there**: bemos run to Jiwika from Wamena, or walk.

Waga Waga is a small community on the track running N from Jiwika. The unexciting Kontilolo Cave attracts some visitors. Admission: 2,000Rp. **Getting there**: by bemo, or walk.

Kimbin is a district capital NW of Wamena. **Accommodation**: homestay available. About 5 km further N still is the missionary centre of **Pyramid**, an oasis of civilization at the end of the road running N out of town. **Getting there**: public bemos run to Kimbin and sometimes on to Pyramid. To walk to Kimbin should take about 6 hrs, Pyramid 7 hrs.

Organizing your own 'tour': it is essential for anyone intending to trek in the Baliem Valley – and who is not fluent in Dani – to hire a guide. Even Indonesian is not widely spoken. Given the necessity to have a guide, it is not surprising that there are always independent guides offering their services. Hotels will also have their own suggestions. These private guides will charge from 10,000-30,000Rp/day depending on their experience; you will be expected to meet all their costs. If staying in a village – usually in a teacher's or nurse/doctor's house – expect to pay 3,000-6,000Rp/night. There are likely to be additional costs incurred: photographing a person usually costs 100Rp or a cigarette; a Dani warrior might expect 1,000Rp for the privilege; while being present at a funeral might mean an outlay of 25,000Rp or more. The Dani are well aware that their traditions have a market value. For a 5-day tour with a guide, porter and cook, inclusive of accommodation in villages and food, expect to pay about 250,000Rp for 2 people.

Organized tours Far less bother is to book a tour through one of the established tour companies who offer a variety of treks and expeditions from 3 nights to 2 weeks. It is best to have a day just to judge the competition and get an idea of prices. The prices of tours obviously vary depending on the itinerary, but expect to pay about US$60-120/day/person. At last count there were only 3 local companies: *Chandra Tours*, Jl. Trikora; *Insatra*; and *Insos Moon*.

When booking a tour, bear in mind the following:
  ❏ Does the guide speak good English, as he is your link with the Dani.
  ❏ How many people will be going on the trek?
  ❏ What is the mode of transport?
  ❏ What does the cost of the trek include?
  ❏ What is the route and destinations (more adventurous treks venture beyond the Baliem Valley)?

What to take
  ❏ good walking boots
  ❏ insect repellent
  ❏ sleeping bag
  ❏ toiletries
  ❏ medical kit
  ❏ candles/matches and a torch (there is no electricity and it is dark by 1800)
  ❏ light day clothes

❏ warm clothing for the night
❏ raincoat and/or collapsible umbrella
❏ food for trip; only vegetables and fruit are easily available outside Wamena.
Taking high energy food is a good idea
❏ barter goods and gifts like cigarettes
❏ sun hat and sun cream
❏ ample small change

Accommodation   Accommodation is some of the most expensive in Indonesia – understandably, as Baliem is only connected by air (or foot) with the outside world. **B** *Baliem Cottages*, Jl. Thamrin, T 31370, 'traditional' thatched cottages, rather down-at-heel; **C** *Anggrek*, Jl. Ambon, T 31242, clean and well-run, some attached mandis; **C** *Jayawijaya*, 3 km out of town, inconvenient location, expensive; used only by tour groups; **C** *Nayak*, Jl. Gatot Subroto 1, T 31067, good rooms, quiet, near the airport, with attached bathrooms, Ricardo speaks some English, very accommodating; **C** *Sri Lestari*, Jl. Trikora, Pasar Sentral, T 31221.

Restaurants   Most visitors choose to eat in their hotels. There are a few warung in the market area but the quality is poor. *Sinta Prima*, Jl. Panjaitan, best restaurant in Wamena with local crayfish and Chinese dishes.

Shopping   Tribal art: the Dani do not have a rich material culture, but hawkers sell what there is in town: penis gourds, well-made stone axes and adzes, spears, and bows and arrows. Try the souvenir shop near the market first to get an idea of price.

Local transport   Public bemos run to local centres within about a 20 km radius of Wamena. Bemos can also be chartered to venture a little further off the beaten track – about 10,000Rp/hr.

Useful addresses   Post Office: Jl. Timor.

Banks & money changers   Bank Rakyat Indonesia, will change most major travellers' cheques and cash.

Airline offices   Merpati, Jl. Trikora 41. **MAF**, Airport building; **AMA**, far end of airfield.

Transport to & from Wamena   By air: the airstrip is virtually in the town. Multiple daily connections on Merpati with Jayapura. **NB**: bad weather and over-booking are a perennial problem. MAF and AMA fly to numerous destinations in surrounding area, but only intermittantly.

Merauke

Merauke, near the SE border with Papua New Guinea, is as far from Jakarta as it is possible to get – and still stay a night in a hotel room. The area is an important transmigration settlement zone although the numbers targeted for settlement during Repelita IV (1985-89) – some 50,000 for the Merauke district – were not attained. Immigrants from South Sulawesi and from Java are also prominent in the town and in local trade, and many locals feel marginalized.

In 1990, only 50 foreign tourists made it to this distant outpost. However, the tourist office has big plans – almost all of them tied to the perceived potential of eco-tourism and the attractions of the Wasur National Park (see Excursions, below). The town itself is unremarkable, but during the cool, dry season (June-Sept) walking in the surrounding countryside is wonderful and sending a postcard from Merauke (bring them with you) has a certain cuedos. Note that basics such as soap are expensive in Merauke because of the high transportation costs.

Excursions
Wasur National Park is one of Indonesia's newest reserves and abuts Papua New Guinea's Tonda Reserve, creating a huge protected area. It occupies 400,000 ha of flat, wet land with mangroves, lakes and a network of rivers. The dominant forest formation is open eucalyptus forest. It is richest in birdlife, with nearly 400 recorded species including cranes, storks, ibis, spoonbills and other waterbirds. Mammals include the agile wallaby (*Macropus agilis*), the spotted cuscus (*Spilocuscus maculatus*) and the short-beaked echidna (*Tachyglossus aculeatus*). The park is partially occupied by two tribal groups – the Marind and Kanum – and

there has been no attempt (yet) to relocate them outside the park's boundaries. **Accommodation**: there are plans to accommodate visitors in tribal villages where facilities are likely to be basic to non-existent. **Best time to visit**: June-Sept during the Southern Hemisphere winter when temperatures are cool enough for trekking. **Getting there**: the park is 30 mins by car from town, and despite Merauke's remote location is easily accessible because the Trans-Irian highway dissects the park, E to W.

Accommodation C *Asmat*; **D-E** *Abadi*; **E** *Wisma Praja*.

Useful addresses Area code: 971. **Hospital**: *General Hospital*, Jl. Sukarjowiryopranoto.

Airline offices Garuda, Jl. Raya Mandala, T 21084; *Merpati*, Jl. Raya Mandala 163, T 21242.

Transport to & from Merauke By air: daily connections with Jayapura on Merpati.

INFORMATION FOR VISITORS

DOCUMENTS

Passports

All visitors to Indonesia must possess passports valid for at least 6 months from their date of arrival in Indonesia and, in theory, they should have proof of onward travel. Many visitors find that immigration officials are happy with some indication that sufficient funds (e.g. travellers' cheques) are available to purchase a return flight.

Visas

Visas are not required for nationals of ASEAN countries, Australia, Austria, Belgium, Canada, Denmark, Finland, France, Germany, Greece, Iceland, Ireland, Italy, Japan, Liechtenstein, Luxembourg, Malta, the Netherlands, New Zealand, Norway, South Korea, Spain, Sweden, Switzerland, Turkey, the UK, and the USA. Tourists may stay for a maximum of 2 months (non-extendable). Entry or exit must be through one of the so-called 'Gateway' cities, namely Jakarta, Bali, Medan, Manado, Biak, Ambon, Batam, Kupang, Pontianak, Balikpapan, Surabaya, and Pekanbaru airports, and the seaports of Jakarta, Bali, Semarang, Medan, Ambon, Manado, Riau, Surabaya and Batam. If entering the country through any other city, a visa is required. These can be obtained from any Indonesian Embassy or Consulate, are only valid for one month, but can be extended (apply at an immigration office).

For nationals of countries other than those listed above, visas can be obtained from any Indonesian Embassy or Consulate, but are valid for one month only (extension possible). Two passport photographs and a small fee are required, plus a confirmed onward flight.

Business visas People intending to work in Indonesia need to take their passport, 2 photos and a covering letter from their company to an Indonesian Embassy or Consulate. The application takes 24 hours to process and costs between £10-22, maximum stay 5 weeks.

Visa extension Jl. Teuku Umar I, Jakarta, T 349811.

Vaccinations

None required unless visitors have been in a cholera, yellow fever or smallpox infected area in the 6 days prior to arrival.

Representation overseas

Australia, 8 Darwin Avenue, Yarralumla, Canberra ACT 2600, T 73 3222. Consulates: Adelaide T 223 6535, Darwin T 819352, Melbourne T 690 7811, Perth T 219 8212, Sydney T 344 9933; *Austria*, Gustav Tschenmakgasse 5-7, 1180 Vienna, T 0222 342533; *Bangladesh*, Gulshan Avenue 75, Gulshan Model Town, Dhaka 12, T 6003131; *Belgium*, 294 Avenue de Turvueren, 1150 Brussels, T 771 2014. Consulates: Antwerp T 031 322130, Charleroi T 071 310050; *Brunei*, EDR 4303 Lot 4498 KG, Sungai Hanching Baru, Simpang 528, Jl. Muara, PO Box 3013, Bandar Seri Begawan, T 30180; *Canada*, 287 Maclaren Street, Ottawa, Ontario K2P 0L9, T 613 236 7403. Consulates: Toronto T 416 591 6462, Vancouver T 604 682 8855; *Denmark*, Orehoj Alle 1, 2900 Hellerup, Copenhagen, T 01 624539; *Finland*, 37 Berikinkatu, 00810 Helsinki 18, T 694 7744; *France*, 47-49 Rue Contambert, 75116 Paris, T 45030760. Consulate: Marseilles, T 91713435; *Germany*, Bernkasteler Strasse 2, 5300 Bonn 2, T 0228 328990. Consulates: Berlin, T 030 8315076, Bremen T 0421 3322224, Dusseldorf T 0211 353081, Frankfurt/Main, T 06105 76003, Hamburg T 040 512071, Hannover T 511 103 2150, Kiel T 0431 603425, Munich T 089 294609, Stuttgart

T 711 223729; *Greece*, Consulate: 11-13 Shyrou Street, Athens 811, T 9914082; *Hong Kong*, Consulate: 127-129 Leighton Road, Causeway Bay, Hong Kong, T 890 4421; *India*, 50A Chanakyapuri, New Delhi 110021, T 602353, Consulates: Bombay T 368678, Calcutta T 460297; *Italy*, 53 Via Campania, 00187 Rome, T 475 9251. Consulates: Genoa T 268322, Napoli T 400143, Trieste T 765601; *Japan*, 2-9 Higashi Gotanda 5 Chome, Shinagawa - Ku, Tokyo, T 441 4201. Consulates: Fukuoka T 092 761 3031, Kobe T 078 321 1656, Sapporo T 011 251 6002; *Laos*, Route Phone Keng, Boita Postale 277, Vientiane, T 2372; *Luxemburg*, Consulate: Gote d'Eich 15, Luxemburg, T 0352 471591; *Malaysia*, Jl. Tun Razak No. 233, P.O. Box. 10889, 50400 Kuala Lumpur, T 9842011. Consulates: Kota Kinabalu T 54100, Penang Island, T 25162; *Myanmar (Burma)*, 100 Pyidaungsu Yeiktha Road, P.O. Box 1401, Rangoon, T 81174; *Netherlands*, 8 Tobias Asserlaan, 5517, s'-Gravenhage, T 070 469796; *New Zealand*, 70 Glen Road, Kelburn, Wellington, T 758695; *Norway*, Gt 8 Inkognito, 0258 Oslo 2, T 441121; *Pakistan*, Diplomatic Enclave Ramna 5/4, P.O. Box 1019, Islamabad, T 820266. Consulate: Karachi T 531938; *Philippines*, 185 Salcedo Street, Lagaspi Village P.O. Box 372 MCC, Makati, Metro Manila, T 855061; *Russia*, 12 Novokuznetskaya Ulitsa, Moscow, T 2319549; *Singapore*, 7 Chatsworth Road, Singapore 1024, T 737 7422; *Spain*, 65 Calle de Agestia, Madrid 28043, T 413 0294. Consulate: Barcelona T 317 1900; *Sri Lanka*, 1 Police Park, Colombo 5, T 580113; *Sweden*, 47/ V Strandvagen 11456, Stockholm, T 6635470; *Switzerland*, 51 Elfenauweg, P.O. Box 270, 3006 Bern, T 440983; *Thailand*, 600-602 Phetburi Road, Bangkok, T 252 3135; *UK*, 157 Edgware Road, London W2 2HR, T 071 499 7661; *USA*, 2020 Massachusetts Avenue N.W., Washington DC 20036, T 202 775 5200. Consulates: Chicago T 312 938 0101, Houston T 713 785 1691, Honolulu T 808 524 4300, Los Angeles T 213 383 5126, New York T 212 879 0600, San Francisco T 415 474 9571; *Vietnam*, 50 Pho Ngo Quyen, Hanoi, T 56316.

TRANSPORT TO AND FROM INDONESIA

By air

The 4 main gateways into Indonesia are Jakarta, Bali, Medan and Kupang. Garuda, the national flag carrier, flies daily between Jakarta and Europe and Australia. However, most visitors fly to Jakarta via Singapore. British Airways, Singapore Airlines, Qantas and Air Canada all fly from London to Singapore. There are also flights via Bangkok, Kuala Lumpur and Hong Kong. Garuda and Singapore Airlines operate 5-8 flights daily from Singapore. Garuda operates flights direct between Jakarta and London (3 each week).

From Europe There are direct flights from London, Amsterdam, Frankfurt, Zurich, Paris, Rome, Vienna, Brussels, Prague and Moscow. From London, British Airways flies twice a week from Heathrow. From Gatwick, Garuda has 3 flights a week. From Amsterdam, KLM flights leave daily and Garuda has 5 flights a week. From Frankfurt, Lufthansa and Garuda depart 4 times a week. You can fly from Zurich with Garuda once a week. From Paris, Garuda have 2 flights a week and UTA, 3. Garuda leave Rome once a week. Weekly direct flights also from Brussels (Garuda and Sabena), Vienna (Garuda), Prague and Moscow.

From the USA and Canada From Los Angeles Garuda fly direct 4 times a week.

From Australasia From Sydney, Garuda fly daily, UTA has 3 flights a week and Qantas, 2. From Melbourne, Garuda has 5 flights a week and Qantas, 2. Garuda fly from Perth 4 times a week. From Auckland, Garuda have 2 direct flights a week.

From South Asia Flights are via Singapore, Bangkok or Kuala Lumpur.

From the Far East Japan Airlines, and Garuda have daily flights from Tokyo. From Hong Kong, Cathay Pacific and Garuda leave daily. From Manila, fly via Hong Kong, Singapore or Brunei.

From the Middle East There are flights from Bahrain with UTA via Hong Kong once a week. Garuda has a weekly flight from Cairo, via Saudi Arabia and Singapore.

Jakarta airport Jakarta's **Soekarno-Hatta International Airport** lies 30 km NW of the city. It is Indonesia's main international gateway and has 2 separate terminal complexes 5 km apart: one for domestic connections (terminals A to D) and the other for international flights (E to H). The only exception is the national flag carrier, Garuda, which operates out of the international terminal (see route map, page 1006). **Facilities** at the airport include car rental (Hertz, Avis and Blue Bird Limo), currency exchange booths, the *Transit Hotel* (**see page 551**), the Transit Restaurant, *Dunkin Donuts*, a Post Office for 24 hr long-distance calls, fax, telex and postal facilities.

Airport tax 15,000Rp on international flights, 3,500Rp on domestic flights.

Transport to town Metered taxis to the city centre cost about 20,000Rp plus a surcharge of 2,300Rp and a 3,600Rp toll for the airport toll road. There is also a city toll road, which is the quickest route to take, which costs another 2,000Rp. A/c buses run every 20 mins from the airport to 5 points in the city centre including Gambir train station (3,000Rp).

Other International Airports Denpasar's (Bali) **Ngurah Rai Airport** has direct flights from Singapore, Kuala Lumpur, Hong Kong, Japan and Amsterdam (**see page 685** for details). **Medan's Polonia Airport** has direct flights from Singapore, Penang and Kuala Lumpur on Garuda, Singapore Airlines and MAS (**see page 743** for details). **Kupang's El Tari Airport** has flights from Darwin, Australia (**see page 943**), while there are flights from Los Angeles, via Honolulu, to **Biak**, Irian Jaya (**see page 935**). **Pontianak's Supadio Airport** has connections with Kuching (East Malaysia) and Singapore (**see page 935**), as does **Balikpapan's Sepinggang Airport**, (**see page 706**). From **Pekanbaru's Simpangtiga Airport**, there are flights to Melaka and Kuala Lumpur (Malaysia) and to Singapore (**see page 964**).

By sea

Visitors can enter Indonesia by sea without a visa at the gateway ports of Jakarta, Bali, Semarang, Pontianak, Balikpapan, Tanjung Pinang, Surabaya, Medan and Batam. There are regular ferries from Singapore to Batam (**see page 788**), and from Penang to Medan's Belawan Port (**see page 744**); there is also a ferry service from Melaka to the non-gateway city of Dumai (Sumatra). Otherwise visitors will have to take a freighter or some other form of irregular sea transport.

Customs

Duty free allowance: 2 litres of alcohol, 200 cigarettes or 50 cigars or 100 grammes of tobacco along with a reasonable amount of perfume. **Currency**: a limit of 50,000Rp can be carried in or out of the country. There are no restrictions on the import or export of foreign currency, either cash or travellers' cheques.

Prohibited items Narcotics, arms and ammunition, TV sets, radio/cassette recorders, pornographic objects or printed matter, printed matter in Chinese characters and Chinese medicines. In theory, approval should also be sought for carrying transceivers, movie film and video cassettes.

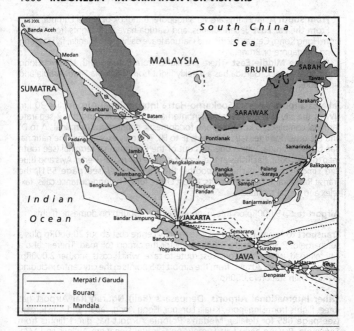

INTERNAL TRAVEL

Air

This is the most convenient and comfortable way to travel around Indonesia. **Garuda** and **Merpati**, now sister-companies, service all the main provincial cities. Merpati tends to operate the short-hop services to smaller towns and cities, particularly in Eastern Indonesia (see route map). Garuda/Merpati offers a **Visit Indonesia Decade Pass**. The basic pass is for 3 'stretches' (legs) and costs US$300. Each additional stretch costs a further US$100, up to a maximum of 10. The pass is valid for 2 months, with a minimum stay of 5 days, and can be used on all Garuda/Merpati routes except 'pioneer' services (perintis). These passes are obtainable by non-Indonesian citizens outside Indonesia in Japan, Hong Kong, Australia, New Zealand, Europe and US. They are also available in Indonesia, if purchased within 14 days of arrival. The other main domestic airlines are **Bouraq**, **Mandala** and **Sempati** (see route map, **page 948**). Bouraq's network is concentrated in Kalimantan and eastern Indonesia (Sulawesi and Nusa Tenggara); Sempati's in Kalimantan, Sumatra, Java and Sulawesi; while Mandala has the most restricted network, serving only a handful of cities in Java, Sumatra, Sulawesi and Maluku. On some routes, Bouraq, Mandala and Sempati offer fares that are marginally cheaper than Garuda/Merpati. There are also non-commercial air services such as the **Missionary Aviation Fellowship** (MAF) and **Associated Missions Aviation** (AMA) which offer non-scheduled flights in Irian Jaya, Kalimantan and Sulawesi to more out of the way spots. **NB**: these are not commercial airlines and can refuse passage.

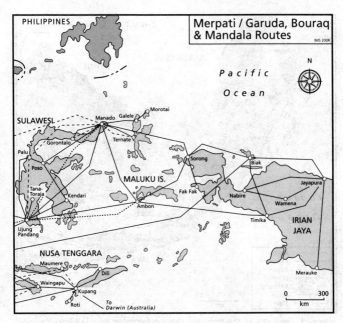

Train

Passenger train services are limited to Java and certain areas of Sumatra, including a route in Lampung and South Sumatra, and in North Sumatra. Trains are usually slow and often delayed. Single track connects many major cities. First class is a/c with a dining car. There are two main trunk routes on Java: Jakarta – Cirebon – Semarang – Surabaya and Jakarta – Bandung – Yogyakarta – Surakarta (Solo) – Surabaya. The principal services are identified by name, e.g. the **Bima** is the a/c night-express from Jakarta via Yogya and Solo, to Surabaya (16 hrs); the **Mutiara Utara** is the northern route train to Surabaya via Semarang; the **Senja Utama Solo** is the express train to Yogya and Solo; while the **Senja Utama Semarang** is the express train to Cirebon and Semarang. Reservations should be made well in advance; it is often easier through a travel agent in the town where you are staying.

Bus

Road transport in Indonesia has improved greatly in recent years, and main roads on most of the islands are generally in reasonably good condition. The single major exception is Irian Jaya, where air transport is the only sensible way to get around. It should be noted that in many areas in Indonesia during the rainy season and after severe storms, even main roads may be impassable. For details on road transport and conditions in a specific area, see the relevant regional introduction.

Most Indonesians, as well as many visitors, get around by bus. The network is vast – there are buses from Bali to Banda Aceh, a distance of 2,618 km – and although it is not always quick or comfortable, buses are the cheapest way to travel. Buses – and particularly non-a/c buses – are often overfilled and seats are designed for Indonesian, rather than Western bodies. A/c buses are generally less

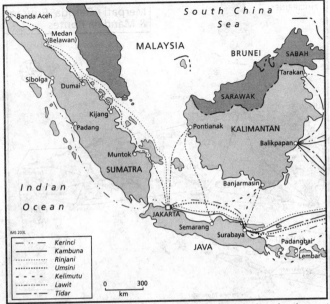

Kerinci
Kambuna
Rinjani
Umsini
Kelimutu
Lawit
Tidar

0   300
km

cramped. The seats at the front are the most comfortable, but also the most dangerous (crash-wise). In May 1993, it was reported that the police had asked bus drivers to pray before setting off – presumably hoping that divine intervention might reduce the number of accidents. Some people recommend booking two seats for comfort, although on non a/c buses it is difficult to lounge over two seats free from guilt when the vehicle is packed. Roads are often windy and rough, and buses are badly sprung (or totally un-sprung). Despite harrowingly fast speeds at times, do not expect to average much more than 40km/hour (particularly on Flores and Sulawesi) except on the best highways. Overnight buses (*bis malam*) are usually faster and recommended for longer journeys. However, a/c *bis malam* can be very cold and a sarong or blanket is useful. Their other disadvantages are that the scenery passes in the darkness and they invariably arrive at anti-social, inconvenient times of day (or night). **NB**: watch out for pickpockets.

The key word when travelling by bus is: patience. On non-a/c buses be prepared for a tedious 'trawl' around town (for up to an hour) collecting passengers, until the bus is full to overflowing. Buses stop regularly for refreshments at dubious looking roadside restaurants, hawkers cram the aisle, selling hot sate, fruit, sweets, sunglasses, magazines, even pornographic playing cards. Loud music and violent videos keep the passengers either in heaven or purgatory. As most Indonesians have still to be convinced that smoking is bad for your health ("that's only true with Western cigarettes, *kreteks* [Indonesian clove cigarettes] are good for you") or that some people might find it distasteful, buses – and especially a/c buses – are also often fogged with cigarette smoke. The buses themselves are usually plastered with perplexing names such as 'No Problem – Banana on the Road', 'Sweet Memory' and 'Khasoggi'. But, despite the drawbacks, buses are not only the cheapest and often the only way to get about, they are also one of the best ways to see the scenery and to meet Indonesians.

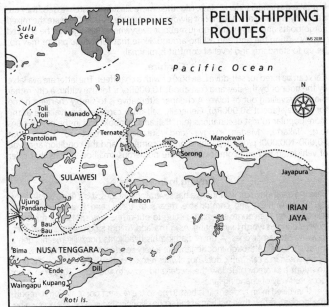

PELNI SHIPPING ROUTES

In many towns, bus companies have their offices at the bus terminal. However, this is not always true, and some long-distance buses may depart directly from a bus company's office located in another part of town to the terminal. Larger towns may also have several bus terminals, serving different points of the compass. These are often out of town, with regular bemos linking the various terminals with one another and with the town centre. In smaller towns, buses will sometimes pick up passengers from outside their losmen or hotel (although occasionally passengers may be asked for a surcharge). They may also drop passengers outside a losmen at the other end of the journey.

Tickets can be obtained from bus company offices or through travel agents; shop around for the best fare, bargaining is possible. Estimated journey times are often wildly inaccurate. During Ramadan all forms of public transport are packed.

Boat

The national shipping company is **PELNI**, standing for Pelayaran Nasional Indonesia. Its head office is at Jl. Gajah Mada 14, Jakarta, T 343307, F 3810341. For ticket offices, see relevant town entries. Pelni operates 7 modern passenger ships which ply fortnightly circuits throughout the archipelago (see route map). The ships are well maintained and run, have an excellent safety record, and are a comfortable and leisurely way to travel. Each accommodates 1,000-1,500 passengers in five classes, has central air-conditioning, a bar, restaurant and cafeteria. First class cabins have attached bathrooms and TV sets. Fares include meals, and classes I-IV are cabin classes, while class V is 'deck' class (in fact, in a large a/c room). Booking ahead is advisable.

In addition to these ships, Pelni also operates a so-called 'pioneer' service – *Pelayaran Perintis* – serving smaller, more out-of-the-way ports. Perintis vessels are important means of travel in Maluku for example. These ships have no cabins but take passengers 'deck' class. Like their more illustrious sister vessels, they are generally well-run and safe, if not always comfortable. Finally, there are the mixed cargo boats and ships which go just about everywhere. Passage can be secured just by visiting the port and asking around. Note that safety equipment may not be up to standard, and level of comfort is minimal.

Car hire

Cars can be hired for self-drive (see box) or with a chauffeur. The latter are available by the hour or by the day, and cost about 10,000Rp/hr for use within a city, rather more if travelling out of town. A cheaper alternative is to simply charter a bemo for the day (about 50,000Rp). Generally, self-drive cars are only available at the more popular tourist destinations (e.g. Bali and Lombok) and in the bigger cities (e.g. Jakarta, Medan, Yogya and Surabaya); expect to pay about 50,000-100,000Rp/day depending on the company, and the condition and type of vehicle. In Bali and Lombok, there are numerous small operations that offer

Driving in Indonesia

Renting a self-drive car in Indonesia has several advantages: it is a flexible, relatively quick, convenient and comfortable means of travel, and is a good way of experiencing the countryside and getting to out-of-the-way spots. But there are several dangers worth highlighting. As in Thailand, 'might is right' – smaller vehicles give way to larger ones. A driver flashing his headlights normally means 'don't mess with me'. Although Indonesians are a very courteous people, this does not apply when in a car. Traffic does not always remain in the allotted lanes – it is best to adopt a strategy of follow-the-leader and go with the flow. Cutting in is an accepted way of changing lanes.

If involved in an accident, it is best to go to the nearest police station to report the incident, rather than waiting at the scene. Signposting is generally poor, so be sure to get a good map. Many towns have complicated one-way systems, which take a bit of negotiating. Every town has its army of semi-official traffic wardens – often dressed in orange jumpsuits – waiting with whistle poised to usher motorists into a parking spot. All 'parkir' must be paid for – 200 Rp, or 300 Rp in Jakarta. Petrol is cheap and Pertamina stations are found on all main highways.

cars and jeeps for hire. For car rental offices, see appropriate town entry.

Other local transport

Bis kayu Trucks converted into buses with bench seats down each side. They are now only in use on minor roads on some islands in Nusa Tenggara, such as Flores. Slow and uncomfortable, they often ply unsealed roads.

Becaks Becaks or bicycle rickshaws are one of the cheapest, and most important, forms of short-distance transport in Indonesia. Literally hundreds of thousands of poor people make a living driving becaks. However, they are now illegal in central Jakarta and often officially barred from main thoroughfares in other large cities. They are a good – and sedate – way to explore the backstreets and alleys of a city and can be chartered by the hour or for a particular journey. Bargain hard and agree a fare before boarding. Minimum fare 200Rp.

Bemos These are small buses or adapted pick-ups which operate fixed routes. The name originates from 'motorized becak'. They carry 4-6 passengers and are found in Jakarta, Bandung, Semarang, Surabaya and Surakarta (Solo). The bemo is gradually being replaced by the larger oplet. They can be chartered by the hour or day (bargain hard, about 50,000Rp/day).

Selected Garuda/Merpati air fares (local prices quoted*)

To \ From	Jakarta	Surabaya	Denpasar	Medan	Ujung Pandang	Balik Papan	Manado
Ambon	422,900	365,700	-	293,900	204,200	-	221,600
Banda Aceh	399,800	-	-	113,450	-	-	-
Bandung	56,600	133,250	194,850	-	-	-	-
Banjarmasin	220,500	133,250	-	-	188,800	88,700	297,700
Balikpapan	282,100	-	198,150	-	475,250	-	367,000
Batam	209,500	-	-	353,250	-	173,950	-
Bengkulu	147,900	-	-	-	-	-	-
Biak	604,400	542,450	475,350	-	-	-	-
Cirebon	77,500	-	-	-	-	-	-
Denpasar	200,700	83,750	-	413,750	140,400	-	338,400
Dumai	208,400	-	-	-	107,950	-	-
Dili	448,200	-	331,250	250,950	-	-	-
Gorontalo	-	-	-	-	153,500	178,900	83,200
Jambi	157,800	-	-	-	180,550	-	-
Jayapura	668,200	-	659,050	580,950	-	483,600	-
Kendari	378,900	256,450	-	-	-	-	-
Kupang	398,700	271,850	204,750	-	170,100	-	-
Malang	165,500	-	-	-	-	-	-
Manado	492,200	374,150	338,950	-	218,500	236,100	-
Mataram	228,200	98,050	48,550	-	-	-	-
Maumere	-	236,650	-	-	-	-	-
Medan	305,200	-	413,750	-	570,500	-	-
Merauke	799,100	-	-	-	-	-	-
Padang	220,500	-	-	136,550	-	-	-
Pekanbaru	223,800	-	-	124,450	-	433,000	-
Palembang	122,600	242,150	-	232,250	-	-	-
Pangkal Pinang	124,800	-	-	-	-	-	-
Pontianak	179,800	-	-	-	-	-	205,300
Palu	424,000	276,250	-	-	-	-	101,900
Semarang	105,000	63,950	143,150	329,050	-	-	205,300
Solo	118,200	54,050	-	-	-	-	-
Surabaya	166,600	-	83,750	-	-	-	37,360
Samarinda	-	-	-	200,350	-	49,100	-
Tanjung Pinang	200,700	-	-	200,350	-	-	-
Ternate	-	-	-	-	-	-	87,600
Ujung Pandang	298,600	188,250	140,950	571,050	-	-	-
Yogyakarta	117,100	58,450	109,050	-	-	-	-

* 1993 prices quoted, approx 2,000Rp = US$1. NB: internal flights purchased outside Indonesia are quoted in US$ and are up to 50% more expensive than tickets bought locally in rupiahs.

Selected train timetable: Java

Jakarta to/from Surabaya via Solo & Semarang
Daily night trains:

Bima:	Jakarta (Kota) – Solo – Surabaya (Gubeng)
Mutiara Utara:	Jakarta (Kota) – Semarang (Tawang) – Surabaya (Pasar Turi)
Gaya Baru Malam Utara:	Jakarta (Pasar Senen) – Solo – Surabaya (Kota)
Gaya Baru Malam Selatan:	Jakarta (Gambir) – Solo – Surabaya (Kota)

Jakarta to/from Semarang
Daily night trains:

Bangun Karta:	Jakarta (Gambir) – Semarang (Tawang) – Jombang
Matamarja:	Jakarta (Gambir) – Semarang (Tawang) – Malang
Senja Utama / Semarang	Jakarta (Pasar Senen) – Semarang (Tawang)

Daily day trains:

Cepat Siang:	Jakarta (Pasar Senen) – Semarang (Tawang)

Jakarta to/from Yogya and Solo
Daily night trains:

Senja Utama / Solo	Jakarta (Gambir) – Cirebon – Yogya – Solo

Daily day trains:

Fajar Utama:	Jakarta (Gambir) – Purwokerto – Yogya
Sawunggalih:	Jakarta (Pasar Senen) – Purwokerto – Kutoarjo
Cepat Solo:	Jakarta (Senen/Tanjung Priok) – Yogya – Solo

Jakarta to/from Cirebon
Daily day trains:

Cirebon Express:	Jakarta (Kota) – Cirebon
Gunung Jati:	Jakarta (Kota) – Cirebon
Tegal Arum:	Jakarta (Kota) – Cirebon – Tegal

Jakarta to/from Bandung
Daily day trains:

Parahyangan (5 daily):	Jakarta (Kota) – Bandung
Parahyangan (3 daily):	Jakarta (Gambir) – Bandung

Trains to/from Surabaya
Day trains:

Argopuro:	Surabaya (Kota) – Banyuwangi
Mutiara Timur Daylight:	Surabaya (Kota) – Banyuwangi
Penataran:	Surabaya (Kota) – Malang – Blitar
Express Siang:	Surabaya (Kota) – Solo – Bandung
Tumapel:	Surabaya (Kota) – Malang
Dhoho:	Surabaya (Kota) – Kertosono – Blitar
Tumapel Utama:	Surabaya (Kota) – Blitar
Purboyo:	Surabaya (Kota) – Purwokerto

Night trains:

Mutiara Timur Night:	Surabaya (Kota) – Banyuwangi
Mutiara Selatan:	Surabaya (Kota) – Solo – Bandung

Selected train timetables: Java

JAKARTA-CIREBON-SURABAYA

Train	Route	Dep	Arr	Fare in Rupiah			
				Spec.	Exc.A	Exc. B	Business
BIMA	Jakarta (Kota):	1555					
	Cirebon		1918	50,000	46,000	35,000	-
	Purwokerto		2138	50,000	46,000	35,000	-
	Yogyakarta		0027	55,000	52,000	40,000	-
	Solo		0147	55,000	52,000	40,000	-
	Madiun (Gobeng)		0310	55,000	52,000	40,000	-
	Surabaya (Gobeng)		0540	55,000	52,000	40,000	-
MUTIARA UTARA	Jakarta (Kota):	1625					
	Cirebon		1948	50,000	46,000	35,000	-
	Tegal		2130	50,000	46,000	35,000	-
	Pekalongan		2205	50,000	46,000	35,000	-
	Semarang		2345	50,000	46,000	35,000	-
	Cepu		0200	55,000	52,000	40,000	-
	Surabaya (Pasar Turi)		0455	55,000	52,000	40,000	-

JAKARTA-YOGYAKARTA-SOLO

Train	Route	Dep	Arr	Fare in Rupiah			
				Spec.	Exc.A	Exc. B	Business
SENJA UTAMA SOLO	Jakarta (Gambir):	1800					
	Cirebon		2151	-	38,000	28,000	18,000
	Purwokerto		0100	-	38,000	28,000	18,000
	Yogyakarta		0357	-	38,000	28,000	19,000
	Solo		0517	-	40,000	30,000	120,000
SENJA UTAMA SEMARANG	Jakarta (Pensar Senen):	1920					
	Cirebon		2249	-	33,000	25,000	14,000
	Tegal		0026	-	33,000	25,000	14,000
	Pekalongan		0123	-	33,000	25,000	14,000
	Semarang (Tawang)		0250	-	33,000	25,000	14,000

Selected bus fares (Rp)*

Route		Distance (km)	Fares (RS = reclining seat)		
			Economy	A/c	A/c + RS + Toilet
SUMATRA					
Medan to	Banda Aceh	839	12,450	19,800	30,400
	Bukittinggi	736	11,100	17,600	27,050
	Bakauheni	1,817	28,750	45,800	70,350
	Jambi	1,701	25,550	40,700	62,450
	Padang	985	14,800	23,550	36,150
	Pekanbaru	783	11,750	18,750	28,750
	Palembang	1,614	24,200	38,600	59,200
	Takengon	492	7,400	11,750	18,100
Padang to	Bengkulu	820	12,300	19,600	30,100
	Jambi	775	11,650	18,550	28,450
	Pekanbaru	308	4,650	7,400	11,300
	Palembang	1,092	16,400	25,000	40,100
	Sungai Penuh	276	4,150	6,600	10,150
JAVA-SUMATRA					
Jakarta to	Bengkulu	897	13,450	21,450	32,900
	Bandar Lampung	214	3,200	5,100	7,850
	Bukittinggi	1,514	22,700	36,200	55,550
	Banda Aceh	2,851	42,800	68,150	104,650
	Jambi	1,054	15,800	25,200	38,650
	Medan	2,244	33,650	53,650	82,350
	Palembang	774	11,600	18,500	28,400
	Pekanbaru	1,441	21,650	34,450	52,900
	Padang	1,507	22,600	36,000	55,300
JAVA-BALI					
Jakarta to	Anyer	116	1,750	2,000	4,300
	Bogor (via Jalan Tol)	47	700	1,150	1,750
	Bandung (via Jalan Tol)	147	2,600	4,150	6,400
	Bandung (via Sukabumi)	191	2,900	4,600	7,100
	Cirebon	255	3,850	6,100	9,350
	Cilacap	468	7,050	11,200	17,200
	Denpasar	1,432	21,500	34,250	52,550
	Jepara	542	8,150	13,000	19,900
	Merak	116	2,000	2,800	4,300
	Surabaya	816	12,250	19,500	29,950
	Solo	554	8,300	13,250	20,350

	Route	Distance (km)	Fares (RS = reclining seat)		
			Economy	A/c	A/c + RS + Toilet
	Tasikmalaya	273	4,100	6,550	10,100
	Yogyakarta (via Semarang)	660	10,000	15,200	24,250
	Yogyakarta (via Yogyakarta)	635	9,950	15,200	23,300
Bandung to	Cilacap	390	5,850	9,350	14,500
	Denpasar	1,268	19,100	30,300	46,550
	Semarang	395	5,950	9,500	14,500
	Solo	626	9,500	15,000	23,000
	Surabaya	691	10,400	16,550	25,500
	Tegal	204	3,100	5,000	7,500
	Yogyakarta	562	8,450	13,450	20,650
Yogyakarta to	Banyuwangi	779	11,700	18,600	28,600
	Denpasar	789	11,850	18,850	28,950
	Malang	388	5,850	9,300	14,250
	Mataram	826	12,400	19,750	30,350
	Solo	74	1,750	2,700	2,700
	Surabaya	341	5,150	8,150	12,550
	Tawangmangu	119	1,800	2,850	4,350
Surabaya to	Magelang	386	5,800	9,250	14,200
	Semarang	378	5,700	9,100	13,900
KALIMANTAN					
Banjarmasin to	Samarinda	620	9,300	14,850	22,750
SULAWESI					
Manado to	Palu	1,033	22,750	31,950	45,150
Ujung Pandang to	Kendari	355	7,800	10,950	15,500

* 1993 prices quoted.

Oplets Larger versions of bemos carrying 10-12 passengers. They have a bewildering number of other names – *Daihatsu* in Semarang, *Angkuta* in Solo, *Microlets* in Malang and Jakarta, while in rural areas they tend to be called *Colts*. In cities they operate on fixed routes at fixed fares (about 150-200Rp). In the countryside, routes can vary and so do fares; be prepared to bargain. Oplets can also be chartered by the hour or day (bargain hard).

Bajaj Small 3-wheeled motor scooters similar to the Thai *tuk-tuk*. They are probably the cheapest form of 'taxi' after the becak, but are only available in big cities – in Jakarta, they are orange and usually rather scruffy.

Taxis Taxis are metered in the major cities. 500Rp for the first kilometre and 250Rp for each additional kilometre; for a/c taxis, 800Rp for first kilometre and 400Rp for each additional kilometre. Unmetered taxis can be shared for longe journeys. Note that drivers cannot usually change large bills. All registered ta minibuses and rental cars have yellow number plates; black number plates ar private vehicles, and red are for government-owned vehicles. Pirate taxi black number plates) tend to operate at airports, supermarkets and in city

Selected Pelni fares (Rp)*

	I	II	III	IV	Economy
Jakarta to:					
Ambon	320,000	233,000	171,000	132,500	84,500
Balikpapan	224,500	165,000	123,000	97,000	63,500
Belawan/Medan	208,500	153,000	112,000	87,000	51,500
Banjarmasin	351,500	235,000	-	-	82,000
Biak	928,000	618,500	-	-	216,000
Jayapura	531,000	389,500	286,000	222,000	141,500
Kawandang	341,500	252,000	184,500	143,500	88,500
Muntok	83,000	56,000	-	-	22,500
Pontianak	128,500	91,500	-	-	33,500
Padang	120,000	92,000	67,500	52,000	34,500
Pantoloan	256,000	186,000	136,000	104,500	66,000
Sibolga	166,000	127,500	93,500	72,500	48,000
Surabaya	84,500	65,000	42,500	37,000	24,500
Semarang	213,500	156,000	-	-	54,000
Toli Toli	274,000	200,500	147,000	113,500	73,000
Tarakan	375,500	276,000	203,500	160,000	79,000
Ternate	396,000	292,000	215,000	168,000	103,000
Ujung Pandang	205,000	150,000	111,000	86,000	51,500

* 1993 prices quoted.
I-IV = 1st-4th class; Economy = deck class.
Infants 1-2 years old travel at 25% of full fare; less than 1 year olds at 10%.

Inter-city taxis/share taxis Share taxis make particular sense for a party of 4 or 5. Inter-city 'share taxis' are more expensive than buses, but are usually a quicker and cheaper alternative to going by air or private taxi. They are not available in all towns and only tend to run the busier routes, like Jakarta to Bandung. They depart when all five seats are taken.

Ojeks These are motorcycle taxis – a form of transport which is becoming increasingly popular. Ojek riders, often wearing coloured jackets, congregate at junctions, taking passengers pillion to their destination. Agree a price before boarding and bargain hard.

Horsecarts These come in various shapes and sizes. *Dokars* are two-wheeled pony carts carrying 2-3 passengers found, for example, in Padang, West Sumatra. In Lombok dokars are known as *cidomos*, while in Bima-Raba (Sumbawa) they are proudly named *Ben Hurs*. *Andongs* are larger 4-wheeled horse-drawn ~ons, carrying up to 6 people. These are found mainly in Yogya, Surakarta and ~rent version in Bogor. Horse-drawn transport is still very common in the ~side, and 'stands' of carts can be seen arrayed at most markets.

~ **hire** Available at many beach resorts. Rates per day vary according to ~dition of the machine, but range from 5,000-15,000Rp. It is illegal to ~ helmet, although this can just be a construction worker's hard hat. ~s are poorly maintained, so check brakes and lights before paying.

ACCOMMODATION, FOOD AND DRINK

Tourist and business centres usually have a good range of accommodation for all budgets. Bali, for example, has some of the finest hotels in the world – at a corresponding price – along with excellent middle and lower-range accommodation. However, visitors venturing off the beaten track may find hotels restricted to dingy 'Chinese' establishments and over-priced places catering for local businessmen and officials. The best run and most competitively priced budget accommodation is found in popular tourist spots – like Bali and Yogya.

Terminology can be confusing: a *losmen* is a lower price range hotel; in parts of Sumatra and in some other areas, losmen are known as *penginapan*; a *wisma* is a guesthouse, but these can range in price from cheap to moderately expensive; finally, a *hotel* is a hotel, but can range from the cheap and squalid up to a Hilton.

Accommodation

Hotels Hotels are listed under 7 categories, according to the *average* price of a double/twin room for one night. It should be noted that many hotels will have a range of rooms, some with air-conditioning and attached bathroom facilities, others with just a fan and shared facilities. Prices can therefore vary a great deal. If a hotel entry lists 'some a/c', then these rooms are likely to be in the upper part of the range, perhaps even in the next category. Hotels in the middle and lower price categories often provide breakfast in the room rate. In the more expensive hotels, service charge (10%) and government tax (11%) are added onto the bill; they are usually excluded from the quoted room rate. More expensive hotels tend to quote their prices in US$. **NB**: during the off-season, hotels in tourist destinations may halve their room rates, so it is always worthwhile bargaining or asking whether there is a 'special' price.

Peculiarities of Indonesian hotels include the tendency to build rooms without windows and, more appealingly, to design middle and lower range hotels around a courtyard. Baths and showers are not a feature of many cheaper losmen. Instead a *mandi* – a tub and ladel – is used to wash.

L: *US$200+ (400,000Rp+)* **Luxury**: hotels in this bracket number a handful and are to be found only in Jakarta and Bali. All facilities, combined with sumptuous rooms and excellent service.

A+: *US$100-200 (200,000-400,000Rp)* **International class**: only to be found in a few cities and tourist destinations. They should provide the entire range of business services (fax, translation, seminar rooms etc), sports facilities (gym, swimming pool etc), Asian and Western restaurants, bars, and discotheques.

A: *US$40-100 (80,000-200,000Rp)* **First class**: will usually offer good business, sports and recreational facilities, with a range of restaurants and bars.

B: *40,000-80,000Rp* **Tourist class**: in tourist destinations, these will probably have a swimming pool and all rooms will have air-conditioning and an attached bathroom. Other services include one or more restaurants and 24-hour coffee shop/room service. Most will have televisions in the rooms.

C: *24,000-40,000Rp* **Economy**: rooms should be air-conditioned and have attached bathrooms with hot water. A restaurant and room service will probably be available but little else.

D: *12,000-24,000Rp* **Budget**: rooms are unlikely to be air-conditioned although they should have an attached bathroom or mandi. Toilets may be either Western-style or of the 'squat' Asian variety, depending on whether the town is on the tourist route. Toilet paper may not be provided. Many in this price range, out of tourist areas, are 'Chinese' hotels. Bed linen and towels are usually provided, and there may be a restaurant.

E: *6,000-12,000Rp* **Guesthouse**: fan-cooled rooms, often with shared mandi and 'squat' toilet. Toilet paper and towels are unlikely to be provided, although bed linen Guesthouses on the tourist route have better facilities and are sometimes excellent of information, offering cheap tours and services such as bicycle and motorcycle

An Indonesian food glossary

asam	tamarind; sold in a solid block, or still in the brown pod	jeruk	generic term in Java and Bali for citrus fruit
ayam	chicken	jeruk bali	pomelo
ayam goreng	fried chicken	jeruk manis	orange
babek	duck	jeruk nipis	lime
babi	pork	kacang	generic term for bean or nut
bakar	roast		
bakmi	rice flour noodles	kacang	peanut sauce
bakso	meat balls	kacang buncis	french bean
belimbing	star fruit	kacang kedele	soybean
bifstik	beef steak	kacang tanah	peanut
cabe	chilli	kambing	lamb/goat
cumi cumi	squid	kangkung	'greens' grown in water – sometimes known as water spinach
dadar	omelette/pancake		
daging	beef/meat		
durian	durian	kayu manis	cinnamon
es	ice	kecap asin	salt-soy sauce
es krim	ice cream	kelengkeng	lychee
garam	salt	kemiri	macadamia nut
goreng	stir fry	kenari	a shade tree which produces a nut similar to an almond
gula	sugar		
gulai	curry soup		
ikan	fish	kepiting	crab
istemiwa	'special' – nasi goreng istemiwa has a fried egg and other additions	ketimun	cucumber
		kodok	frog
		kopi	coffee

in this category vary a great deal, and can change very rapidly. Other travellers are the best source of up-to-the-minute reviews.

F: *under 6,000Rp* **Guesthouse:** fan-cooled rooms, shared mandi and 'squat' toilet. Rooms can be tiny, dark and dingy, with wafer-thin walls. There are also some real bargains in this bracket. Standards change very fast and other travellers are the best source of information.

Food

Although Indonesia is made-up of a bewildering array of ethnic groups dispersed over 5 million sq km of land and sea, the main staple across the archipelago is rice. Today, alternatives such as corn, sweet potatoes and sago, which are grown primarily in the dry islands of the east, are regarded as 'poor man's food', and rice is the preferred staple.

Indonesians will eat rice – or *nasi* (milled, cooked rice) – at least 3 times a day. Breakfast often consists of left-over rice, stir-fried and served up as *nasi goreng*. Mid-morning snacks are often sticky rice cakes or *pisang goreng* (fried bananas). Rice is the staple for lunch, served up with 2 or 3 meat and vegetable dishes and followed by fresh fruit. The main meal is supper, which is served quite early and again consists of rice, this time accompanied by as many as 5 or 6 other dishes. *e/satay* (grilled skewers of meat), *soto* (a nourishing soup) or *bakmie* (noodles, h of Chinese origin) may be served first.

y towns (particularly in Java), sate, soto or bakmi vendors roam the streets containing charcoal braziers, ringing a bell or hitting a block (the noise of th what he or she is selling), looking for customers in the early evenings. are known as *kaki lima* – literally '5 legs' – named after the 3 'legs' s the 2 of the vendor. Larger foodstalls where there is too much to

kopi bubuk	ground coffee (with grounds)	pisang	banana
		rambutan	rambutan
kopi saring	filtered coffee	rebus	boil
krupuk	deep-fried tapioca crackers	roti	bread
		salak	brown, pear shaped fruit, with a shiny, snake-like skin. The flesh is white, segmented and dry. Balinese salak are considered to be the sweetest
kuah	gravy		
kue	cake		
kunyit	turmeric		
lombok	chilli		
lontong	compressed rice, usually served with sate		
madu	honey	sambal	chilli paste
mangga	mango	santen	coconut milk
manggis	mangosteen	sawi	Chinese cabbage
manis	sweet	sayur	vegetables
merica	black pepper	semangka air	watermelon
mie	noodles	sereh	lemon grass
nangka	jackfruit, eaten ripe as a fruit or unripe cooked as a vegetable	serundeng	grated coconut roasted with peanuts
		sop	soup
nasi	rice	tahu	soybean curd
nasi putih	plain white rice	telur	egg
nenas	pineapple	tempe	fermented soybean cake (see box)
pala	nutmeg		
panggang	grill	udang	shrimp
papaya (kates)	papaya	udang karang	lobster

*For information on Indonesia's more exotic fruits, **see page 17**.

cart around tend to set up in the same place every evening in a central position in town. These **warungs**, as they are known, may be temporary structures or more permanent buildings, with simple tables and benches. In the larger cities, there may be an area of warungs, all under one roof. Often a particular street will become known as the best place to find particular dishes like *martabak* (savoury meat pancakes) or *gado gado* (vegetable salad served with peanut sauce). More formalised restaurants are known simply as *rumah makan*, literally 'eating houses'. A good place to look for cheap stall food is in and around the market or *pasar* (from the Arabic *bazaar*); night markets or *pasar malam* are usually better for eating than day markets.

Feast days, such as Lebaran marking the end of Ramadan, are a cause for great celebration and traditional dishes are served. *Lontong* or *ketupat* are made at this time (they are both versions of boiled rice – simmered in a small container or bag, so that as it cooks, the rice is compressed to make a solid block). This may be accompanied by *sambal goreng daging* (fried beef in a coconut sauce) in Java or *rendang* (curried beef) in Sumatra. *Nasi kuning* (yellow rice) is traditionally served at a *selamatan* (a Javanese celebration marking a birth, the collection of the rice harvest or the completion of a new house).

In addition to rice, there are a number of other common ingredients used across the country. Coconut milk, ginger, chilli peppers and peanuts are used nationas, while dried salted fish and soybeans are important sources of protein. In coast 80% fish and seafood tend to be more important than meat. As Indonesia is ̃e it. Muslim, pork is not widely eaten, although Chinese restaurants usually ̃

Regional cuisines Although Indonesia is becoming more homogeneous as

Tempe: soybean cake

Tempe has recently become a popular health food in the West, but its origins are Indonesian. It is believed to have originated in Java about 100 years ago, with the establishment of the soybean trade with China. In Indonesia, it is used as a meat-substitute by poorer communities, providing a cheap meal, rich in protein. During World War II, tempe became familiar to prisoners in Japanese prison camps. It is an easily digestible nutritious food, because it is fermented before being eaten. It contains no cholesterol or saturated fats, but does contain the vitamin B12. It is made by injecting cooked soybean with a fungal spore. The soybean is packed in banana leaves (now, more usually, plastic bags) and left to ferment. A solid white cake is formed, looking rather like a cheese, which is then cut into slices and may be deep fried (*tempe goreng*) or simmered in spicy coconut milk (*pechel tempe* – an East Javan speciality). Visitors to Indonesia are most likely to come across tempe in *gado-gado*, where it is served, along with a hard-boiled egg, on top of vegetables.

Javanese culture spreads to the Outer Islands, there are still distinctive regional cuisines. The food of **Java** itself embraces a number of regional forms, of which the most distinctive is **Sundanese**. *Lalap*, a Sundanese dish, consists of raw vegetables and is said to be the only Indonesian dish where vegetables are eaten uncooked. Characteristic ingredients of Javanese dishes are soybeans, beef, chicken and vegetables; characteristic flavours are an interplay of sweetness and spicyness. Probably the most famous regional cuisine however is **Padang** or **Minang** food, which has its origins in West Sumatra province. Padang food has 'colonized' the rest of the country and there are Padang restaurants in every town, no matter how small. Dishes tend to be hot and spicy (**see page 776**), using quantities of chilli and turmeric, and include *rendang* (dry beef curry), *kalo ayam* (creamy chicken curry) and *dendeng balado* (fried seasoned sun-dried meat with a spicy coating). In **eastern Indonesia**, seafood and fish are important elements in the diet, with fish grilled over an open brazier (*ikan panggang* or *ikan bakar*) and served with spices and rice being a delicious common dish. The **Toraja** of Sulawesi eat large amounts of pork and specialities include black rice (*nasi hitam*), and fish or chicken cooked in bamboo (*piong*). There are large numbers of Chinese people scattered across the archipelago and, like other countries of the region, **Chinese** restaurants are widespread.

Popular Indonesian dishes

Bubur – rice porridge. *Bubur hitam* is black glutinous rice boiled with sugar, garnished with coconut milk and served warm.

Cap cai – mixed, stir-fried vegetables, with various additions – such as pork and squid – and served with rice (Chinese).

Gado-gado – steamed vegetable salad, hard-boiled egg, krupuk and tempe, served with a peanut sauce and sometimes rice.

Ketupat – compressed, boiled rice; usually served with satay.

Lumpia – spring rolls; fried egg pancake stuffed with chicken, shrimps and vegetables (Chinese).

Martabak – pancake, either sweet or savoury, the latter usually in Java when stuffed with mutton, eggs and onions; served crispy with a curry sauce.

N goreng – the same as nasi goreng, but the rice is replaced by noodles.

Nasi campur – a rice platter, similar to *nasi rames*; often cold, usually of bean curd, chicken, beans and rice; campur means 'to mix'.

Nasi goreng – fried rice, served with shrimps, small pieces of meat, onion, garlic and cucumber.

Nasi gudeg – rice, chicken and jackfruit, cooked in coconut milk (Javanese).

Nasi kuning – yellow rice, usually a festival dish, cooked with turmeric and coconut milk; sometimes served with beef.

Nasi lemak – rice cooked with coconut milk and garnished with *ikan bilis* (fried anchovies), egg and cucumber.

Nasi liwet – rice and chicken cooked in coconut milk (Javanese).

Nasi rames – rice with meat and vegetables on top, accompanied by *serundeng* and *krupuk* (Padang).

Nasi uduk – rice cooked in coconut milk with spices.

Opor ayam – chicken cooked in a mild creamy coconut sauce.

Pisang goreng – banana fritters; coated in batter and deep fried.

Rendang – hot, dry beef curry (Padang) cooked in coriander, laos powder and tumeric; a West Sumatra speciality.

Rijstaffel – literally, 'rice table', rice served with as many as 16 other dishes (Dutch-Indonesian).

Sate – perhaps the Malay world's most famous dish: slivers of skewered meat, marinated, cooked over a charcoal fire and served with a peanut sauce and *lontong* (compressed rice).

Sayur lodeh – mixed vegetables in coconut milk (Javanese).

Serabi – scotch pancakes, made from rice flour, *santen* (coconut milk) and sugar (Javanese – Cirebon).

Soto – a soup of clear chicken stock, flavoured with lemon grass, to which is added glass noodles, hard-boiled eggs, chopped shallots, beansprouts, sambal and/or shredded chicken.

Drink

Unboiled **water** may not be safe to drink. Hotels and most restaurants, as a matter of course, should boil the water they offer customers. Ask for *air minum*, literally 'drinking water'. But in cheaper establishments it is probably best to play safe and ask for bottled water. Over the last few years **'mineral water'** – of which the most famous is *Aqua* ('aqua' has become the generic word for mineral water) – has become increasingly popular. It is now available from Aceh to Irian Jaya in all but the smallest and most remote towns. There have been some reports of empty mineral water bottles being re-filled with tap water: check the seal before accepting a bottle.

Western **bottled and canned drinks** like Sprite, Coca-cola, 7-Up and Fanta are widely available in Indonesia and are comparatively cheap. Alternatively many restaurants will serve *air jeruk* – citrus **fruit juices** – with or without ice (*es*). Ice in many places is fine, but in cheaper restaurants and away from tourist areas many people recommend taking drinks without ice. Javanese, Sumatran, Sulawesi or Timorese **coffee** (*kopi*), fresh and strong, is an excellent morning pick-you-up. It is usually served sweet (*kopi manis*) and black; if you want to have it without sugar ask for *kopi tidak ada gula*. **Milk** (*susu*) is available in tourist areas and large towns, but it may be sweetened condensed milk. **Tea** (*teh*) is obtainable almost everywhere.

Jamu: herbal drink

Jamu is the generic word used for traditional herbal medicines, which have been used throughout the archipelago for hundreds of years. The Indonesian people put great faith in the healing powers of jamu (secret recipes of herbs, roots, flowers, bark and nuts), which are believed to be able to cure anything from 'flu to cancer. These herbs are usually taken in the form of muddy-brown elixirs, which usually claim to restore not only your health but also your youthfulness and sexual vigour. Jamu sellers wander the streets of every town, selling their own secret concoction. They are recognizable by the heavy baskets they carry slung over their backs, full of bottles of murky brown liquid.

Although Indonesia is a predominantly Muslim country, alcoholic drinks are widely available. The 2 most popular **beers** – light lagers – are the locally brewed Anker and Bintang brands. Imported **spirits** like whisky and gin are usually only sold in the more expensive restaurants and hotels. They are comparatively expensive. There are, however, a number of local brews including *brem* (rice wine), *arak* (rice whisky) and *tuak* (palm wine).

PUBLIC HOLIDAYS AND NATIONAL FESTIVALS

Jan: *Tahun Baru*, New Year's Day (1st: public holiday). New Year's Eve is celebrated with street carnivals, shows, fireworks and all-night festivities. In Christian areas, festivities are more exuberant, with people visiting each other on New Year's Day and attending church services.

Jan/Feb: *Al Miraj* (moveable: public holiday). The Prophet Mohammad is led through the 7 heavens by the archangel. He speaks with God and returns to earth the same night, with instructions which include the 5 daily prayers.

Feb: *Imlek*, Chinese New Year (moveable). It is not an official holiday, but many shops and businesses will close for at least 2 days. Within the Chinese community, younger people visit their relatives, children are given *hong bao* (lucky money), new clothes are bought and any unfinished business is cleared up before the New Year (**see page 447**).

Mar: *Nyepi* (moveable: public holiday). Balinex Saka New Year (1993-1915), **see page 664**.

Mar/Apr: *Idul Fitri* or *Lebaran* (moveable: public holiday). A 2 day celebration which marks the end of the month-long period of Ramadan, when Muslims observe *puasa* and fast from dawn to dusk. Mass prayers are held in mosques and squares. Muslims go to each others homes to ask forgiveness and there is a general air of celebration.

Mar/Apr: *Good Friday* (moveable: public holiday).

Apr: *Kartini Day* (21st). A ceremony held by women to mark the birthday of Raden Ajeng Kartini, born in 1879 and proclaimed as a pioneer of women's emancipation (**see page 636**). The festival is rather like mothers' day, in that women are supposed to be pampered by their husbands and children, although it is women's organizations like the Dharma Wanita who get most excited. Women dress in national dress.

May: *Waisak Day* (moveable: public holiday). Marks the birth and death of the historic Buddha; at Candi Mendut outside Yogyakarta a procession of monks carrying flowers, candles, holy fire and images of the Buddha walk to Borobudur. *Ascension Day* (moveable: public holiday).

Jun: *Idhul Adha* (moveable: public holiday). This is the 'festival of the sacrifice' and is the time when burial graves are cleaned, and an animal is sacrificed to commemorate the willingness of Abraham to sacrifice his son.

Jun/Jul: *Muharram*, Muslim New Year (moveable: public holiday).

Aug: *Independence Day* (17th: public holiday). This is the most important national holiday, celebrated with processions, dancing and other merry-making.

Aug/Sept: *Garebeg Maulad (birthday of the Prophet Mohammad)* (moveable: public holiday). Celebrations begin a week before the actual day and last a month, with *selamatans* in homes, mosques and schools.

Oct: *Hari Pancasila* (1st). This commemorates the Five Basic Principles of Pancasila (**see page 502**). *Armed Forces Day* (5th). The anniversary of the founding of the Indonesian Armed Forces, with military parades and demonstrations.

Dec: *Christmas Day* (25th: public holiday). Celebrated by Christians – the Bataks of Sumatra, the Toraja and Minahasans of Sulawesi and in some of the islands of Nusa Tenggara, and Irian Jaya.

The Indonesian day

Indonesians divide the day into 4 periods:
pagi is from midnight to 1100.
siang is from 1100 to 1500.
sore is from 1500 to dusk.
malam is from dusk to midnight.
People greet one another accordingly – *selamat siang* (good afternoon), *selamat malam* (good evening).

OTHER ESSENTIAL INFORMATION

Conduct

As a rule, Indonesians are courteous and understanding. Visitors should be the same. As foreigners, visitors are often given the benefit of the doubt when norms are transgressed. However, it is best to have a grasp of at least the basics of accepted behaviour. In tourist areas and large cities, Westerners and their habits are better understood; but in remote areas be more aware of local sensibilities. There are also some areas – such as Aceh in North Sumatra – that are more fervently Muslim than other parts of the country. With such a diverse array of cultures and religions, accepted conduct varies. Specific cultural notes are given in the appropriate introductory sections.

Heads, hands and feet The head is considered sacred and should never be touched (especially those of children). Handshaking is common among both men and women, but the use of the left hand to give or receive is taboo. When eating with fingers, use the right hand only. Pointing with your finger is considered impolite; use your thumb to point, beckon buses (or any person) with a flapping motion of your right hand down by your side. When sitting with others, do not cross your legs; it is considered disrespectful. In addition, do not point with your feet and keep them off tables. Shoes are often not worn in the house and should be removed on entering.

Open affection Public displays of affection between men and women is considered objectionable.

Dress Indonesia is largely a Muslim country and women should be particularly careful not to offend. Dress modestly and avoid shorts, short skirts and sleeveless dresses or shirts (except at the beach). Public nudity and topless bathing are not acceptable.

Calmness Like other countries of Southeast Asia, a calm attitude is highly admired, especially if things are going wrong. Keep calm and cool when bargaining, or waiting for a delayed bus or appointment.

Jam karet or 'rubber time' is a peculiarly Indonesian phenomenon. Patience and a cool head are very important; appointments are rarely at the time arranged.

Face People should not be forced to lose face in public; especially in front of colleagues. Putting someone in a position of *malu* or social shame, should be avoided.

Gifts If you are invited to somebody's home, it is customary to take a gift. This is not opened until after the visitor has left.

For a more comprehensive background to do's and don'ts in Indonesia see: Draine, Cathy and Hall, Barbara (1986) *Culture shock! Indonesia*, Times Books: Singapore.

Religion Indonesia is the largest Muslim country in the world. In Java, Islam is a synthesis of Islam, Buddhism, Hinduism and animism – although the extent to which it is 'syncretic' is vigorously debated (**see page 527**). Orthodox Islam is strongest in northern Sumatra (Aceh), but is also present in parts of Sulawesi, Kalimantan and West Java. For a brief background to Islam **see page 503**.

Mosques are sacred houses of prayer; non-Muslims can enter a mosque, so long as they observe the appropriate customs: remove shoes before entering, dress appropriately (neatly and fully covered, avoiding singlets, shorts or short skirts), do not disturb the peace, and do not walk too close to or in front of somebody who is praying. During the fasting month of Ramadan, do not eat, drink or smoke in the presence of Muslims.

Bali has remained a Hindu island (**see page 678**), and remnants of Hinduism are also evident in parts of Central and East Java. To enter a temple or *pura* on Bali it is often necessary to wear a sash. Christianity is a growing religion in

Sulawesi (**see page 874**) and in East Nusa Tenggara (**page 931**). Although not a religion, **Pancasila** is the Indonesian state ideology and should not be slighted (**see page 502**).

Tipping Tipping is not usual in Indonesia. A 10% service charge is added to bills at more expensive hotels (in addition to tax of 11%). Porters expect to be tipped about 500Rp a bag. In more expensive restaurants where no service is charged, a tip of 5-10% is sometimes appropriate. Taxi drivers (in larger towns) appreciate a small tip (200-300Rp). *Parkirs* always expect payment for 'watching' your car – 200Rp, or 300Rp in Jakarta.

Shopping

Indonesia offers a wealth of distinctive handicrafts and other products. Best buys include textiles (batik and ikat), silverwork, woodcarving, puppets, paintings and ceramics. Bali has the greatest choice of handicrafts. It is not necessarily the case that you will find the best buys in the area where a particular product is made; the larger cities, especially Jakarta, sell a wide range of handicrafts and antiques from across the archipelago at competitive prices.

Tips on buying Early morning sales may well be cheaper, as salespeople often believe the first sale augers well for the rest of the day. **Bargaining**: except in the larger fixed price stores, bargaining (with good humour) is expected; start bargaining at 50-60% lower than the asking price. Do not expect to achieve instant results; if you walk away from the shop, you will almost certainly be followed, with a lower offer. If the salesperson agrees to your price, you should really feel obliged to purchase – it is considered very ill mannered to agree on a price and then not buy the article.

Antiques There are some good antique shops in Jakarta and a handful of other regional centres, but bargains usually need to be 'rooted out' by visiting little out-of-the-way shops. Antiques include Dutch memorabilia and Chinese ceramics (Indonesia was on the trade route between China and India), as well as local products like Javanese carvings and Sulawesi metalwork. **NB**: there are also a huge number of fakes on the market – you only have to walk down Jalan Surabaya (Jakarta's most popular flea market) to see men openly 'distressing' work, then to be sold as 150-year-old heirlooms.

Batik Centres of batik-making are focused on Java. Yogyakarta and Solo (Surakarta) probably offer the widest choice, although Cirebon and Pekalongan (both on the N coast), offer their own distinctive styles. There is also a good range of batik on sale in Jakarta. The traditional hand-drawn batiks (*batik tulis*) are naturally more expensive than the modern printed batiks. For more information on batik **see page 535**.

Clothing Very reasonably priced Western-style clothes can be found in most of the bigger cities. Large department stores and markets are the best places to browse. Children's clothes are also very good value (although dyes may run). Bali offers the best fashion clothing.

Ikat This dyed and woven cloth is found on the islands of Bali, Lombok and Nusa Tenggara (Sumba, Flores, Timor), although it is not cheap and is sometimes of rather dubious quality. For more information **see page 721**.

Jewellery Gems mined in Indonesia include diamonds and black opals from Kalimantan and pearls from Maluku. Contemporary-style jewellery is made in Bali (although some is of poor quality). There are several good jewellery shops in Jakarta, mostly found in 5-star hotels. West Sumatra and Aceh are both known for their silverwork.

Metalwork The traditional Malay sword, the **kris** is the most popular buy. Both antique and modern examples are available. For more information **see page 548**.

Painting Yogyakarta is a centre of painting, with several workshops of artists who have achieved world-wide acclaim. Work includes oil and batik painting. Ubud (Bali) has, since the 1930's, been a centre for local artists and is a good place to buy tropical-style paintings (**see page 676**).

Wayang puppets Wayang is a Javanese and Balinese art form and puppets are most widely available on these two islands, particularly in Yogyakarta and Jakarta. For more information **see page 530**.

Weaving Baskets of all shapes and sizes are made for practical, everyday use, out of rattan, bamboo, sisal and nipah and lontar palm. The intricate baskets of Lombok are particularly attractive.

Woodcarving This ranges from the clearly ersatz and tourist oriented (Bali), to fine classical pieces (Java), to 'primitive' (Irian Jaya). The greatest concentration of woodcarvers work in Bali producing skilful modern designs as well as more traditional pieces.

Safety

Indonesia is a safe country and violence is rare. However, single women should take care – it is unusual for women to travel alone and those who do will find Indonesians concerned for their safety. There is a notion held by too many Indonesians that Western women, by definition, are loose, so pestering males may be a problem. Be firm, but be polite. Older women travelling alone will not be faced with such problems and will be treated with great respect.

Far more of a problem is theft and deception. It is advisable for travellers to carry all valuables in a moneybelt. Avoid carrying large amounts of cash; travellers' cheques can be changed in most major towns. Pickpockets frequent the public transport systems. Reports of robbery on the overnight trains through Java are common. Take great care of your belongings on these longer journeys on public transport. Do not leave valuables in hotel rooms; most of the more expensive hotels will have safety deposit boxes.

Beware of the confidence tricksters who are widespread in tourist areas. Sudden reports of unbeatable bargains or closing down sales are usual ploys.

Health

For general health information **see page 21**. Long-term residents of Indonesia, even doctors, often offer differing advice on how to stay healthy. In many hotels in Bali, none of the tips listed below will apply; in more remote areas it would be wise to observe them all. In general:

❑ Malaria tablets are essential and mosquito repellent is an advisable addition to your luggage.
❑ Avoid drinking water unless you are sure that it has been boiled (mineral water is widely available).
❑ Do not accept drinks with ice in them, except in more expensive hotels and restaurants.
❑ Fresh fruit and vegetables should be limited to those that you can peel yourself.
❑ Salads should be avoided, as many vegetables are fertilized with human excrement and the organisms remain even after washing.
❑ Avoid eating food (particularly meat) at sidestalls where it has been left standing in the open.
❑ Avoid ice-creams.

Best time to visit
Indonesia spans several climatic zones and the 'best time to visit' varies across the country. The dry season for much of the archipelago, including Java and Bali, spans the months from May to Sept. For details on seasons elsewhere in Indonesia (**see page 494**) and the relevant regional introductions.

Clothing
Light clothing is suitable all the year round, except at night in the mountains. Shorts, miniskirts and singlets should be limited to beachwear only. Proper decorum should be observed when visiting places of worship; shorts are not permitted in mosques, shoulders and arms should

be covered, and women must cover their heads. Formal dress for men normally consists of a batik shirt and trousers; suits are rarely worn. Local dress is *batik* for men and *kebaya* for women.

Official time

There are 3 time zones in Indonesia. *Western Indonesia* (Sumatra, Java, West and Central Kalimantan) GMT + 7; *Central Indonesia* (Bali, South and East Kalimantan, Sulawesi, Nusa Tenggara) GMT + 8; and *East Indonesia* (Irian Jaya and the Maluku islands) GMT + 9.

Hours of business

Hours of business are highly variable; there are not even standard opening hours for government offices. The listing below is a rule of thumb: **Government offices**: 0800-1500 Mon-Thurs, 0800-1130 Fri and 0800-1400 Sat. **Banks**: foreign banks 0800-1200 Mon-Fri and 0800-1100 Sat; local banks 0800-1300, 1330-1600 Mon-Sat. Banks in hotels may stay open longer. Most **businesses** open 0800/0900-1200, 1300-1600/1700 Mon-Fri. **Museums**: 0830 or 0900-1400 Tues-Thurs, 0900-1100 Fri, 0900-1300 Sat and 0900-1500 Sun, closed Mon. **Shops**: 0900-2000 Mon-Fri, 0900-1300 Sat, sometimes on Sun. In smaller towns shops may close for a siesta between 1300 and 1700.

Money

One rupiah equals 100 sen. Note denominations are 100Rp, 500Rp, 1,000Rp, 5,000Rp and 10,000Rp. Coins are minted in 25Rp, 50Rp and 100Rp denominations.

Travellers' cheques can usually be changed in larger towns and tourist destinations. In smaller towns and more out of the way spots it may not be possible to change travellers' cheques. The US$ is the most readily acceptable currency, both for travellers' cheques and cash. Money changers often give better rates than banks. Hotels will sometimes change travellers' cheques (usually in popular tourist destinations), but rates vary a great deal from competitive to appalling, so it is worth checking. Note that banks will usually only change certain types of travellers' cheques, and not all branches of a particular bank will have travellers' cheque changing facilities. *Amex*: Dagang Negara, Danamon, Bumi Daya, Nasional Indonesia. *Thomas Cook*: Dagang Negara, Expor-Impor, Bank Central Asia, Nasional Indonesia, Bumi Daya. *Visa*: Expor-Impor, Bumi Daya. *Citicorp*: Bumi Daya, Dagang Negara.

Major credit cards are accepted in larger hotels, airline offices, department stores and some restaurants. If you are visiting very remote areas for a long period, it can make sense to obtain Indonesian Post Office travellers' cheques in one of the big cities. These are then easily changed into rupiahs in any post office in the country. For lost American Express cards and travellers' cheques T (021) 5703310.

Cost of living

Visitors staying in first class hotels and eating in hotel restaurants will probably spend about 150,000Rp/day (US$75/day). Tourists staying in cheaper air-conditioned accommodation, and eating in local restaurants will probably spend about 75,000-120,000Rp/day (US$37-60). A backpacker, staying in fan-cooled guesthouses and eating cheaply, might expect to be able to live on 20,000Rp/day (US$10/day).

Weights and measures

Metric, although local units are still in use in some areas.

Voltage

220 volts, 50 cycles in the big cities; 110 volts in some areas. Plugs are usually rounded and two pronged. Power surges are not common and well protected electrical equipment such as lap-top computers can be used.

Postal services

Post offices open from 0800-1600 Mon-Fri, 0800-1300 Sat. The postal service is not particularly reliable; important mail should be registered. Faxes and telexes can be sent from major hotels and Perumtel and Wartel offices, found in most major towns. Post and telex/fax offices are listed under Useful addresses in each town entry.

Telephone services

International Direct Dialling (IDD) is available from the major cities. All long distance calls within Indonesia can be dialled directly but lines are in limited supply and it is often extremely difficult to connect. Calls can be made (and faxes often sent) from Perumtel and Wartel offices to be found in most middle and large-sized towns. **International enquiries**: 102. **Operator**: 101. **Local enquiries**: 106, in Jakarta: 108. All telephone numbers marked in the text with a prefix 'J' mean that they are Jakarta numbers.

Media

Newspapers: English language newspapers are the *Indonesia Times*, *Jakarta Post* and *Indonesia Observer/Sunday Observer*. Of the international newspapers available in Indonesia, the *Asian Wall Street Journal* and the *International Herald Tribune* can be purchased in Jakarta and some other major cities and tourist destinations; so too can the Singapore *Straits Times*. Among English language magazines, the most widely available are the *Economist*, *Time*, *Newsweek* and the Hong Kong-based *Far Eastern Economic Review*. The latter provides the most comprehensive regional coverage and is well-informed, but can be rather heavy going.

Television: Many hotels now boast enormous 'parabola' – satellite dishes that receive TV signals from the Philippines, Singapore, Thailand and Malaysia. Large hotels may also offer CNN News.

Radio: Radio Republik Indonesia (RRI) broadcasts throughout the country. News and commentary in English is broadcast for about an hour a day. Shortwave radios will pick up Voice of America, the BBC World Service and Australian Broadcasting. **See page 19** for BBC and VoA frequencies.

Language

The national language is *Bahasa Indonesia*, which is written in Roman script (**see page 504**). There are 250 regional languages and dialects, of which Sundanese (the language of West Java and Jakarta) is the most widespread. The Bataks of North Sumatra have a number of mutually intelligible languages which are, in essence, forms of primitive *Bahasa*. In Padang and elsewhere in West Sumatra, the population speak *Minang* – which is also similar to 'Bahasa'. Despite the bewildering array of regional languages, most of the younger generation will be able to speak Bahasa – about 70% of the population. English is the most common foreign language, although there are Dutch speakers amongst the older generation and some Portuguese is still spoken in East Timor.

Bahasa Indonesia is a relatively easy language to learn, and visitors may have a small but functional vocabulary after just a few weeks. Unlike Thai, it is not tonal and is grammatically very straight forward. However this does not mean it is an easy language to speak well. A small number of useful words and phrases are listed in the box below.

Tourist information

The Directorate General of Tourism is to be found in Jakarta. Administratively, it is under the Department of Tourism, Post and Telecommunications, which has offices throughout the country. These offices are known as *Kanwil Depparpostel*. Each of the 27 provinces also have their own tourist offices, known as *Departa* or *Dinas Pariwisata*. The head office of the Directorate General of Tourism, with information on the whole country, is at Jl. Kramat Raya 81, Jakarta. The Dinas Pariwisata Jakarta is at Jl. Abdul Rohim 2, T 511073. For other offices, see relevant town entry.

Indonesian Tourist Promotion offices overseas are: **Europe**: Wiessenhuttenplatz 17, Frankfurt am Main, Germany, T (069) 2336778; **UK**: 3-4 Hanover St, London W1R 9HH, T (071) 4930030, F (071) 4931747; **USA**: 3457 Wilshire Boulevard, Los Angeles, California 90010, T (213) 3872078, F (213) 3804876; **Australia**: PR agency, Garuda Indonesia office, 4 Bligh St, PO Box 3836, Sydney 2000, T 2326044, F 2332828; **Asean and Hong Kong**: 10, Collyer Quay, 15-07 Ocean Bldg, Singapore 0104, T 5342837, F 5334287; **Japan**: Asia Trans Co, 2nd floor Sankaido Bldg, 1-9-13 Akasaka, Minato-ku, Tokyo, T 5853588.

Specialist tour companies

USA: *Sobek Expeditions Inc*, Angelo Camp, California 95222, T (209) 7364574, F 7362646; adventure tours to Kalimantan and elsewhere in Indonesia; *Kingfisher Asian Tours* (Friends in America Inc.), P O Box 281, Hawthorne, New Jersey 07506, T (201) 4274551, F 4232775; *Natrabu Tours & Travel*, 8th Flr 352, 27th Ave, New York, NY10001, T (212) 5641939/(800) 6287228 (toll-free) and at 433 California St, San Fransisco, CA 94104, T (800) 6546900 (toll-free); *Forum International*, 91 Gregory Lane, 21 Pleasant Hill, Calif 94523, T (510) 671-2900, F (510) 946-1500, eco-tours to Indonesia, interesting and well-planned.

Europe: *Gala International*, Franz-Joseph Str. 19, 8000 München 40, Schwabing, Germany, T (089) 335767, F 335774; *Windrose*, D-1000 Berlin 15, Germany, T (030) 8813059, adventure and safari tour specialist; *Airtours International*, Adalbertstrasse 44-48, D-6000 Frankfurt 90, Germany, T (069) 79280, F 7928502; *Feria Internationale Reisen*, Frankfurter Ring 243, 8000 München 40, Germany, T (089) 323790, F 323792; *Cross Country*, Postbus 164, 2180 AD Hillegom, The Netherlands, T (02520) 77677, F 23670, trekking specialist dealing with Kalimantan; *Sea Trek*, Heren Gracht 4/6, 1017 B2 Amsterdam, The Netherlands, T 0206244656, F 6247965; *Mistral Tour Internazionale*, 24 Via Leonardo Da Vinci, 10126 Torino, Italy, T (011) 638444, F 633969; *Nayak Travel and Expeditions*,

Useful Indonesian words & phrases

In Indonesian, there are no tenses, genders or articles and sentence structure is relatively simple. Pronunciation is not difficult as there is a close relationship between the letter as it is written and the sound. Stress is usually placed on the second syllable of a word. For example, *restoran* (restaurant) is pronounced res-TO-ran.

Vowels

a is pronounced as *ah* in an open syllable, or as in *but* for a closed syllable; *e* is pronounced as in *open* or *bed*; *i* is pronounced as in *feel*; *o* is pronounced as in *all*; *u* is pronounced as in *foot*.

The letter *c* is pronounced as *ch* as in *change* or *chat*; the *r*'s are rolled; plural is indicated by repetition, e.g. bapak-bapak.

Learning Indonesian

The list of words and phrases below is very rudimentary. For anyone serious about learning Indonesian it is best to buy a dedicated Indonesian language textbook or to enrol on an Indonesian course. In Indonesia, there are courses on offer in Jakarta, Bali and Yogyakarta.

Yes/no	*Ya/tidak*
Thank you [very much]	*Terima kasih [banyak]*
Good morning (until 1100)	*Selamat pagi*
Good day (until 1500)	*Selamat siang*
Good afternoon (until dusk)	*Selamat sore*
Good evening	*Selarnat malam*
Welcome	*Selamat datang*
Goodbye (said by the person leaving)	*Selamat tinggal*
Goodbye (said by the person staying)	*Selamat jalan*
Excuse me, sorry!	*ma'af*
Where's the...?	*...dimana?*
How much is...?	*...berapa harganya?*
You're welcome, don't mention it	*kembali*
I [don't] understand	*Saya [tidak] mengerti*

The Hotel

How much is a room?	*kamar berapa harga?*
Does the room have air-conditioning?	*Ada kamar yang ada AC-nya?*
I want to see the room first please	*Saya mau lihat kamar dulu*
Does the room have hot water?	*Ada kamar yang ada air panas?*
Does the room have a bathroom?	*Ada kamar yang ada kamar mandi?*

Travel

Where is the train station?	*Dimana stasiun kereta api?*
Where is the bus station?	*Dimana stasiun bis?*
How much to go to...?	*Berapa harga ke...?*
I want to go to...	*Saya mau pergi ke...*
I want to buy a ticket to...	*Saya mau beli karcis ke...*
Is it far?	*ada jauh?*
Turn left/turn right	*belok kiri/belok kanan*
Go straight on	*terus saja*

Days

Monday	*Hari Senin*	Saturday	*Hari Sabtu*
Tuesday	*Hari Selasa*	Sunday	*Hari Minggu*
Wednesday	*Hari Rabu*	today	*hari ini*
Thursday	*Hari Kamis*	tomorrow	*hari besok*
Friday	*Hari Jumat*	yesterday	*hari kemarin*

Numbers

1	*satu*	12-	*dua-belas...etc*
2	*dua*	20	*dua puluh*
3	*tiga*	21-	*dua puluh satu...etc*
4	*empat*	100	*se-ratus*
5	*lima*	101	*se-ratus satu*
6	*enam*	150	*se-ratus lima puluh*
7	*tujuh*	200-	*dua ratus...etc*
8	*delapan*	1,000	*se-ribu*
9	*sembilan*	2,000	*dua ribu*
10	*sepuluh*	100,000	*se-ratus ribu*
11	*se-belas*	1,000,000	*se-juta*

Basic Vocabulary

bank	*bank*	toilet	*WC ("way say")*
bathroom	*kamar mandi /kamar kecil*	ticket	*karcis*
big	*besar*	train station	*stasiun kereta api*
boat	*perahu*	water	*air*
bus	*bis*	all right/good	*baik*
bus station	*stasiun bis*	beach	*pantai*
chemist	*apotek*	beautiful	*cantik*
day	*hari*	buy	*beli*
delicious	*enak*	can	*boleh*
doctor	*doktor*	clean	*bersih*
expensive	*mahal*	closed	*tutup*
food	*makan*	dirty	*kotor*
fruit	*buah*	eat	*makan*
hospital	*rumah sakit*	excellent	*bagus*
hotel	*hotel/losmen/ penginapan/ wisma*	hot (temperature)	*panas*
		hot (spicy)	*pedas*
		I/me	*saya*
immigration office	*kantor imigrasi*	island	*pulau*
		open	*masuk*
market	*pasar*	shop	*toko*
medicine	*obat*	sick	*sakit*
police	*polisi*	stop	*berhenti*
police station	*stasiun polisi*	taxi	*taksi*
post office	*kantor pos*	that	*itu*
restaurant	*rumah makan*	this	*ini*
room	*kamar*	town	*kota*
small	*kecil*	very	*sekali*
		what	*apa*

Steinengraben 42, CH-4001 Switzerland, T (061) 224343, F 224383, specialists in adventure tourism in Kalimantan; *Natrabu Tours & Travel*, 129 Van Leyenberghlaan, 1028, Amsterdam, the Netherlands, T (020) 443429, F 423325; *Noble Caledonia*, 11 Charles St, London W1X 7HB, T (071) 491-4752, F (071) 409-0834, specialist cruise company with cruises to more remote areas of Indonesia, well run with resident experts.

Asia and Australia: *Natrabu Tours & Travel*, 16 Westlane Carpark, Darwin NT-5794, Australia, T 813695; *Natrabu Tours & Travel*, 6th Flr, Asabudai Bldg, 2-1, 2-Chome, Asabudai, Minato-ku, Tokyo, Japan, T (03) 5856209, F 5824479; *Setia Tours & Travel*, 100 Beach Rd 22-11, T 2986888, F 2922343.

Suggested reading

Other books relating to particular regions, towns and monuments are listed in the relevant sections of the text.
General Donner, Wolf (1987) *Land use and environment in Indonesia*, Hurst: London. Rather laboured but detailed summary of Indonesia's environmental problems and prospects. Draine, Cathie and Hall, Barbara (1986) *Culture shock! Indonesia*, Times Books: Singapore. A good summary of do's and don't's with some useful cultural background. Jessup, Helen I. (1990) *Court arts of Indonesia*, Asia Society Galleries: New York. Lavishly illustrated book produced for the Festival of Indonesia exhibition; good background on the pieces displayed. Horridge, Adrian (1986) *Sailing craft of Indonesia*, OUP: Singapore. Illustrated with concise, useful text. Geertz, Clifford (1963) *Agricultural involution: the process of ecological change in Indonesia*, University of California Press: Berkeley. Classic book by perhaps the foremost anthropologist of Indonesia; looks at rice and shifting cultivation and conditions in 19th and 20th century Java; some of his views have been vigorously attacked in recent years. Ricklefs, M.C. (1981) *A history of modern Indonesia, c.1300 to the present*, Macmillan: London. Dense but informative, and probably the best modern history of Indonesia. Wallace, Alfred Russel (1869) *The Malay Archipelago: the land of the orang-utan and the bird of paradise; a narrative of travel with studies of man and nature*, Macmillan: London. A classic natural history, recounting Wallace's 8 years in the archipelago and now re-printed. Warming, Wanda and Gaworski, Michael (1981) *The world of Indonesian textiles*, Serindia Publications: London. Summarizes all the processes of production and provides an outline of the major regional styles; illustrated. Whitten, Tony and Whitten, Jane (1992) *Wild Indonesia*, New Holland: London. Illustrated large format book with good text and background to major national parks and characteristic species and forest formations.
Java Abeyasekere, S. (1989) *Jakarta: a history*, OUP: Jakarta. A skilful and comprehensive history of Jakarta; the best available. Anderson, B. (1972) *Java in a time of revolution: occupation and resistance 1944-1946*. The best study of the period by one of the world's leading political scientists. Beek, Aart van (1990) *Life in the Javanese Kraton*, OUP: Singapore. Useful and interesting short history to the kraton or palace. Dumarçay, Jacques (1978) *Borobudur*, OUP: Singapore. Dumarçay, Jacques (1986) *The Temples of Java*, OUP: Singapore. Short art history of Java's main temples; rather dry. Forster, Harold (1989) *Flowering lotus: a view of Java in the 1950s*, OUP: Singapore. Forster recounts his life as an English lecturer at Gajah Mada University in Yogya in the 1950s; closely observed and informative of the period just after independence. Heuken, Adolf (1982) *Historical sites of Jakarta*, Cipta Loka Caraka: Jakarta. Best background available. Holmes, Derek and Nash, Stephen (1989) *The birds of Java and Bali*, OUP: Singapore. Manageable book with good colour illustrations. Koch, C.J. (1978) *The year of living dangerously*. Average novel transformed into a well-received film; romance based in Java during the 1965 attempted coup. Miksic, John (1990) *Borobudur: golden tales of the Buddha*, Bamboo and Periplus: London and Singapore. Well illustrated with better text than most coffee table books. Raffles, Thomas (1817) *The history of Java*, OUP: Singapore. The first history of Java, fascinating for Raffles' observations, sections have still yet to be bettered; available as a reprint, but large and expensive. Smithies, Michael (1986) *Yogyakarta, cultural heart of Indonesia*, OUP: Singapore. Good background to the city and its culture. Times Travel Library (1987) *Jakarta*, Times Editions: Singapore. Photographic guide to Jakarta with reasonable background text.
Bali Belo, Jane (edit.) (1970) *Traditional Balinese culture*, Columbia University Press: New York. Collection of academic papers most focusing upon dance, music and drama. Covarrubias, Miguel (1937) *Island of Bali*, Cassell: London (reprinted, OUP: Singapore, 1987). The original, full treatment of Bali's culture; despite being over 50 years old it is still an excellent background to the island and is highly entertaining. Djelantik, A.A.M. (1990) *Balinese paintings*, OUP: Singapore. Concise history of Balinese painting also covering the major contemporary schools of art. Eiseman, Fred and Eiseman, Margaret (1988) *Woodcarvings of Bali*, Periplus: Berkeley. Lansing, J. Stephen (1991) *Priests and programmers: technologies of power in the engineered landscape of Bali*, Princeton University Press: Princeton. An

anthropological account of Bali's irrigation system; interesting for rice fans. Stuart Fox, David (1982) *Once a century: Pura Besakih and the Eka Dasa Rudra Festival*, Penerbit Citra Indonesia: Jakarta.

Sumatra Loeb, Edwin M. (1972) *Sumatra: its history and people*, OUP: Kuala Lumpur (first published 1935). Despite being over 50 years old this book is still worthwhile reading, and the best of its type. Carle, Rainer (edit) (1981) *Cultures and societies of North Sumatra*, Dietrich Rimmer Verlag: Berlin. Whitten, Anthony et al. (1984) *The ecology of Sumatra*, Gajah Mada University Press: Yogya. Like its sister book on Sulawesi, a dense but informative and authoritative account of the island's ecology. Marsden, William (1783, 1811) *The history of Sumatra*, OUP: Singapore. Like Raffles' study of Java, a book by a polymath who believed history was also geography, anthropology and natural history; now available as an expensive reprint.

Sulawesi Barley, Nigel (1988) *Not a hazardous sport*, Penguin: London. Anthropologist Barley, in this humorous and entertaining book head off to Toraja and convinces a team of builders to travel to London to construct a traditional house for the Museum of Mankind. Kis-Jovak, J.I. et al. (1988) *Banua Toraja: changing patterns in architecture and symbolism among the Sa'dan Toraja*, Sulawesi, Royal Tropical Institute: Amsterdam. Wonderful black & white photo-essay with informative text. Nooy-Palm, Netty (1986) *The Sa'dan Toraja: a study of their social life and religion – rituals of the east and west*, Foris: Dordrecht. Dense but informative anthropological work. Volkman, Toby A. (1985) *Feasts of honour: ritual and change in the Toraja highlands*, University of Illinois Press: Urbana. Readable account – part academic, part personal – of an anthropologist's stay in Toraja. Whitten, A.J. et al. (1988) *The ecology of Sulawesi*, Gajah Mada University Press: Yogyakarta. Dense, comprehensive study of Sulawesi ecology. Wilcox, Harry (1989) *Six moons over Sulawesi*, OUP: Singapore. First published in 1949, it recounts the 6 month sojourn of Harry Wilcox in Toraja who went to there to recover from the horrors of the War.

Irian Jaya Anti-Slavery Society (1990) *West Papua: plunder in paradise*, Anti-Slavery Society: London. Records the people of Irian Jaya's fight for independence. Petocz, Ronald G. (1989) *Conservation and development in Irian Jaya*, E.J. Brill: Leiden. Schneebaum, Tobias (1990) *Embodied spirits: ritual carvings of the Asmat*, Peabody Museum: Salem, Mass.

Indonesian literature Lubis, Mochtar (1957) *Twilight in Djakarta*. One of the finest works of modern Indonesian fiction; tells of the poverty and destitution in 1950s Jakarta; journalist Lubis was imprisoned for his writings. Toer, Pramoedya Ananta (1979) *This earth of Mankind*, Penguin: Ringwood, Australia. Along with the other three books in this series – *Child of all nations*, *Footsteps*, and *Glass House*, this represents some of the finest of modern Indonesian writing; it tells the story of the writer Minke caught between the Dutch and modernity, and his own people and tradition. Toer was imprisoned on Buru Island between 1965-1979 and his books remain banned in Indonesia.

Acknowledgements

D. Bruce, Kuala Lumpur. Alastair Boyd, Burford, UK. Jenny Barry, London. A. G. M. van Elzakker and M. van der Plas, Netherlands. Abdul Manan, Department of Tourism, Post and Telecommunication, Medan. H. Mansyur Andi Sulthan, Dinas Pariwisata, South Sulawesi, Ujung Pandang. Frances, B. Affandy, Bandung Society for Heritage Conservation, Bandung. Tropical Wind Tour & Travel Service, Bogor. Meredith F. Small, Ithaca, New York. Mal Clarbrough, Ujung Kulon National Park. Lara Poland, London, UK. Paul Blount, Glasgow, UK. Kathryn Campbell, Mataram, Lombok. Theo Polii, Director, Indonesian Tourist Promotion Office, Frankfurt. Anak Agung Gde Ariawan, Ary's Warung, Ubud, Bali. Drs. Krt. Sosrohadiningrat, Director, Dinas Pariwisata, Yogyakarta. Maria Hooper, Maumere.

GLOSSARY

A

Abdi dalem	court servants of Java (I)
Adat	custom or tradition
Alang	Torajan rice barn (I)
Amitabha	the Buddha of the Past (see Avalokitsvara)
Andesite	volcanic building stone
Andong	horse-drawn carriage (I)
Angklung	traditional Javanese bamboo musical instrument (see page 575) (I)
Arhat	statues of former Buddhist monks
Atavaka	flesh-eating ogre
Avadana	Buddhist narrative, telling of the deeds of saintly souls
Avalokitsvara	also known as Amitabha and Lokeshvara, the name literally means "World Lord"; he is the compassionate male Bodhisattva, the saviour of Mahayana Buddhism and represents the central force of creation in the universe; usually portrayed with a lotus and water flask

B

Bahasa	language, as in Bahasa Malaysia and Bahasa Indonesia (I and M)
Bajaj	three-wheeled motorized taxi (I)
Banaspati	East Javan term for kala makara (see kala)
Banjar	Balinese village organization (see page 677) (I)
Banua	Torajan house (see page 875) (I)
Barisan Nasional	National Front, Malaysia's ruling coalition comprising UMNO, MCA and MIC along with seven other parties (M)
Batik	a form of resist dyeing common in Malay areas (see page 534)
Becak	three-wheeled bicycle rickshaw
Bendi	2-wheeled, horse-drawn cart (I)
Bhaga	cult altar of Flores (see page 938) (I)
Bodhi	the tree under which the Buddha achieved enlightenment (*Ficus religiosa*)
Bodhisattva	a future Buddha. In Mahayana Buddhism, someone who has attained enlightenment, but who postpones nirvana in order to help others reach the same state
Brahma	the Creator, one of the gods of the Hindu trinity, usually represented with four faces, and often mounted on a hamsa
Brahmin	a Hindu priest
Budaya	cultural (as in Muzium Budaya)
Bumiputra	literally, 'sons of the soil'; Malays as opposed to other races in Malaysia (see page 86) (M)
Bupati	regent (I)

C

Candi	sepulchral monument (see page 524) (I)
Candi bentar	split gate, characteristic of Balinese pura (see page 971) (I)
Cap	batik stamp (see page 536)

Chedi	from the Sanskrit *cetiya* (Pali, *caitya*) meaning memorial. Usually a religious monument (often bell-shaped) containing relics of the Buddha or other holy remains. Used interchangeably with stupa
Cidomo	Lombok's two-wheeled, pony carts (see page 909) (I)
Cukong	Chinese-owned corporations (I)
Cultuurstelsel	the Dutch 'culture system' introduced in Java in the 19th century (see page 521) (I)
Cunda	see Tara
Cutch	see Gambier

D

Dalang	wayang puppet master
DAP	Democratic Action Party, Malaysia's predominantly Chinese opposition party (M)
Dayak/Dyak	collective term for the tribal peoples of Borneo
Delman	horse-drawn carriage (I)
Dharma	the Buddhist law
Dipterocarp	family of trees (Dipterocarpaceae) characteristic of Southeast Asia's forests
Dokar	horse-drawn carriage (I)
Durga	the female goddess who slays the demon Mahisa, from an Indian epic story
Dvarapala	temple door guardian (see page 644) (I)

E

| Epiphyte | plant which grows on another plant (but usually not parasitic) |

F

| Fahombe | stone-jumping of Nias Island (see page 769) (I) |
| Feng shui | the Chinese art of geomancy |

G

Gambier	also known as cutch, a dye derived from the bark of the bakau mangrove and used in leather tanning
Gamelan	Javanese and Balinese orchestra of percussion instruments (see page 534)
Ganesh	elephant-headed son of Siva
Garuda	mythical divine bird, with predatory beak and claws, and human body; the king of birds, enemy of naga and mount of Vishnu.
Gautama	the historic Buddha
Golkar	ruling party in Indonesia (see page 507) (I)
Gopura	crowned or covered gate; entrance to a religious area
Gunung	mountain

H

Hamsa	sacred goose, Brahma's mount; in Buddhism it represents the flight of the doctrine
Hariti	child-eating demon who is converted to Buddhism
Hinayana	'Lesser Vehicle', major Buddhist sect in Southeast Asia, usually termed Theravada Buddhism (see page 40)

1034

I

Ikat	tie-dyeing method of patterning cloth (see page 721)
Indra	the Vedic god of the heavens, weather and war; usually mounted on a 3 headed elephant
Islam Waktu Telu	Islam of Lombok (see page 910) (I)

J

Jaba	front court of Balinese temple (see page 674) (I)
Jaba tengah	central court of Balinese temple (see page 674) (I)
Janur	Balinese bamboo 'pennants' (see page 678) (I)
Jataka(s)	birth stories of the Buddha, of which there are 547; the last ten are the most important
Jeroan	back court of Balinese temple (see page 674) (I)

K

Kabupaten	regency, Indonesian unit of administration (see page 491) (I)
Kala (makara)	literally, 'death' or 'black'; a demon ordered to consume itself; often sculpted over entranceways to act as a door guardian, also known as kirtamukha
Kalanaga	same as the kalamakara but incorporating the mythical naga (serpent)
Kepala desa	village headman (I)
Kerangas	from an Iban word meaning 'land on which rice will not grow' (M and I)
Kerapan sapi	bull races of East Java and Madura (see page 655) (I)
Keraton	see kraton
Kinaree	half-human, half-bird, usually depicted as a heavenly musician
Kirtamukha	see kala
Klotok	motorized gondolas of Banjarmasin (I)
Kraton	Javanese royal palace (see page 526) (I)
Kris	traditional Malay sword (see page 548)
Krishna	an incarnation of Vishnu
Kulkul	Balinese drum (I)
Kuti	living quarters of Buddhist monks

L

Lapar biasa	'normal hunger' (see page 907) (I)
Laterite	bright red tropical soil/stone sometimes used as a building material
Linga	phallic symbol and one of the forms of Siva. Embedded in a pedestal shaped to allow drainage of lustral water poured over it, the linga typically has a succession of cross sections: from square at the base through octagonal to round. These symbolize, in order, the trinity of Brahma, Vishnu and Siva
Lintel	a load-bearing stone spanning a doorway; often heavily carved
Lokeshvara	see Avalokitsvara
Lontar	multi-purpose palm tree (see page 962); the fronds were used for manuscript sheets (see page 726)
Losmen	guesthouse

M

Mahabharata	a Hindu epic text written about 2,000 years ago (see page 505)
Mahayana	'Greater Vehicle', major Buddhist sect (see page 40)
Mandi	Indonesian/Malay bathroom with water tub and dipper
Maitreya	the future Buddha
Makara	a mythological aquatic reptile, somewhat like a crocodile and sometimes with an elephant's trunk; often found, along with the kala, framing doorways
Mandala	a focus for meditation; a representation of the cosmos
MCA	Malaysian Chinese Association (M)
Meru	name given to the tapered shrines of Bali (see page 724) (I)
Meru	the mountain residence of the gods; the centre of the universe, the cosmic mountain
MIC	Malaysian Indian Congress (M)
Moko	bronze dowry 'drums' of Nusa Tenggara (see page 948) (I)
Mudra	symbolic gesture of the hands of the Buddha (see page 608)

N

Naga	benevolent mythical water serpent, enemy of Garuda
Naga makara	fusion of naga and makara
Nalagiri	the elephant let loose to attack the Buddha, who calmed him
Nandi/Nandin	bull, mount of Siva
NDP	New Development Policy (see page 87) (M)
Negara	kingdom and capital, from the Sanskrit
Negeri	also negri, state
NEP	New Economic Policy (see page 86) (M)
Ngadhu	cult altar of Flores (see page 938) (I)
Nirvana	'enlightenment', the Buddhist ideal
Nyi Loro Kidul	Goddess of the South Seas (see page 570) (I)

O

Odalan	festival celebrating a Balinese temple's anniversary (see page 671) (I)
Ojek	motorcycle 'taxi'
Ondel-ondel	paired human figures given to newly-weds in Java (I)
Orang Asli	indigenous people of Malaysia (M)

P

Paddy/padi	unhulled rice
Padmasana	stone throne (I)
Padu-raksa	ceremonial gate (I)
Paliwijaya/Palawija	a second crop, planted after rice
Pamedal Agung	main gate (I)
Pancasila	Sukarno's five guiding principles (see page 502) (I)
Pantai	beach
Pasar	market, from the Arabic 'bazaar'
Pasisir	Javanese coastal trading states (I)
Pelni	Indonesian state shipping line (I)
Pemuda	literally 'youth', but historically refers to the Pemuda Movement against the Dutch (see page 501) (I)
Pendopo	open-sided pavilion of Java (I)
Perahu/prau	boat

Peranakan	'half caste', usually applied to part Chinese and part Malay people
Perintis	'pioneer' ships which ply minor routes between Indonesia's islands (I)
PKI	Perserikatan Komunis di Indonesia, the Indonesian Communist Party (I)
Pradaksina	pilgrims' clockwise circumambulation of a holy structure
Prajnaparamita	the goddess of transcendental wisdom
Prang	form of stupa built in the Khmer style, shaped rather like a corncob
Prasada	see prasat
Prasat	residence of a king or of the gods (sanctuary tower), from the Indian prasada
Pribumi	indigenous (as opposed to Chinese) businessmen
Priyayi	Javanese aristocracy (I)
Pulau	island
Puputan	'fight to the death' (see page 671) (I)
Pura	Balinese temple (see page 673) (I)
Pusaka	heirloom

R

Raja/rajah	ruler
Raksasa	temple guardian statues
Ramayana	the Indian epic tale (see page 505)
Ruai	common gallery of an Iban longhouse, Sarawak (M)
Rumah adat	customary or traditional house

S

Sago	multi-purpose palm (see page 973)
Sal	the Indian sal tree (*Shorea robusta*), under which the historic Buddha was born
Saka	Hindu calendar used in Bali (see page 679) (I)
Sakyamuni	the historic Buddha
Sawah	wet rice (see page 514) (I)
Silat	or bersilat, traditional Malay martial art
Singha	mythical guardian lion
Siti Inggil	literally 'High Place' in a kraton; used for enthronements (I)
Siva	one of the Hindu triumvirate, the god of destruction and rebirth
Songket	Malay textile interwoven with supplementary gold and silver yarn (see page 810)
Sravasti	the miracle at Sravasti when the Buddha subdues the heretics in front of a mango tree
Sri Laksmi	the goddess of good fortune and Vishnu's wife
Stele	inscribed stone panel or slab
Stucco	plaster, often heavily moulded
Stupa	see chedi
Subak	Balinese irrigation society (see page 668) (I)
Susuhunan	Hindu king or sultan (I)

T

Tanju	open gallery of an Iban longhouse, Sarawak (M)
Tara	also known as Cunda; the four-armed consort of the Bodhisattva Avalokitsvara
Tau tau	Torajan effigies of the deceased (see page 878) (I)
Tavatimsa	heaven of the 33 gods at the summit of Mount Meru

Theravada	'Way of the Elders'; major Buddhism sect also known as Hinayana Buddhism ('Lesser Vehicle') (see page 40)
Timang	Iban sacred chants, Sarawak (M)
Tirta	holy water (I)
Tongkonan	Torajan ancestral house (see page 875) (I)
Totok	'full blooded'; usually applied to Chinese of pure blood
Transmigration	the Indonesian government sponsored resettlement of people from the Inner Islands to the Outer Islands (see page 732) (I)
Tunku	also Tuanku and Tengku, prince (M)

U

Ulama	Muslim priest
Ulu	jungle
UMNO	United Malays National Organization (M)
Urna	the dot or curl on the Buddha's forehead, one of the distinctive physical marks of the Enlightened One
Usnisa	the Buddha's top knot or 'wisdom bump', one of the physical marks of the Enlightened One

V

| Vishnu | the Protector, one of the gods of the Hindu trinity, generally with four arms holding the disc, the conch shell, the ball and the club |
| VOC | the Dutch East India Company or Vereenigde Oost-Indische Compagnie (I) |

W

Wali	the nine Muslim saints of Java (see page 528) (I)
Wallace's Line	division between the Asian and Australasian zoological realms (see page 905)
Waringin	banyan tree
Warung	foodstall or small restaurant
Wayang	traditional Malay shadow plays (see page 529)
Wayang Topeng	masked dance of Java (see page 533) (I)
Wuku	Hindu-Javanese calendar, now primarily in use only in Bali (see page 679) (I)

INDEX

A

Adam Malik Museum, Jakarta   549
Agung, Mount   715
Aileu   968
Air Sanih   727
Airmadidi   899
Al-Abrar Mosque, Singapore   405
Al-Aqsa Mosque, Kudus   633
Al-Manar Mosque, Kudus   633
Alas   922
ALOR   948
Alor Setar   149
Ambarawa   631
Ambarawa Railway Museum   628
Ambarita   763
Ambon   974
Amlapura   722
Ampenan   910
Anakalang   954
Angklung   575
Anyer   562
Apo Kayan   846
Arab Street, Singapore   409
Armenian Church, Singapore   399
Art & Architecture
    Bali   673
    Java   522
    Malaysia   70
    Singapore   378
Asmat Art   994
Astana, Kuching   251
Atambua   961
Ayer Itam Dam   141
Ayer Keroh   171

B

Ba'a   961
Baba-Nonya Heritage Museum, Melaka   167
Babas   168
Babi Besar, Pulau   190
Bada Valley   890
Badut, Candi, Malang   643
Bahari Museum, Jakarta   542
Bajaus, Sabah   297
Bajawa   938
Bakauheni   820
Bako National Park   259
BALI   666-730
Bali Barat National Park   729
Baliem Valley   998
Balikpapan   836
Balimbiang   781

Balinese pura   673
Baluran Reserve   664
Banda Aceh   745
Banda Islands   981
Banda Neira   982
Bandar Lampung   818
Bandar Seri Begawan   475
Bandar Sri Aman   262
Bandung   572
Bandungan   628
Bangka Island   812
Bangkalan   659
Bangli   713
Bangsal   915
banjar   677
Banjarmasin   827
Banten   560
Bantimurung Falls   868
Banyuwangi   663
Bareo & The Kelabit Highlands   290
Batak Architecture   762
Bataks   756
Batam Island   786
Batang Palupuh   780
Batik   534
Batu   646
Batu Caves   101
Batu Feringghi   146
Batu Tulug   332
Batuan   703
Batubulan   702
Batur, Mount   713
Batur, Pura, Bali   715
Baturong caves   337
Batusangkar   781
Baucau   969
Baun   959
Bawamataluo   770
Bayan   917
Beaufort   316
Beji, Pura, Bali   726
Belaga   270
Belitung Island   813
Bengkulu   814
Benoa   700
Beremban, Gunung   120
Besakih, Pura, Bali   715
Besar, Pulau   172
Beserah   196
Betel Nut   35
Biak   996
Bidayuh, Sarawak   241
Big Splash, Singapore   414
Bima-Raba   926
Bintan Island   788

Bintulu 273
Bird of Paradise 992
Blitar 640
Bogor 565
Bohorok River 745
Bondowoso 663
Bone Bone
   See Watampone
Bontang 841
Borobudur 604
Botanical Gardens, Singapore 411
Botanical Gardens, Bogor 566
Botanical Gardens, Penang 140
Brastagi 752
Bratan, Lake 725
Brinchang 122
Brinchang, Gunung 120
Bromo, Mount 661
Bromo-Tengger-Semeru National Park
   661
Brooke, Charles 235
Brooke, Charles Vyner 236
Brooke, James 234, 464
BRUNEI 457-489
Buddhism 36
Bugis 864
Bukit Barisan Selatan National Park 819
Bukit Cina, Melaka 170
Bukit Fraser 116
Bukit Larut 131
Bukit Lawang 744
Bukit Peninsula 699
Bukit Timah Nature Reserve, Singapore
   416
Bukittinggi 777
Bunaken Sea Garden, Manado 896
Buton 886
Butterworth 131
Buyan, Lake 725

C
Cakranegara 910
Cameron Highlands 118
Candi 524
Cangkuang, Candi 583
Carah Caves 196
Celuk 702
Cempaka 829
Cenering 209
Central Market, KL 97
Ceto, Candi 620
Chan See Shu Yuen Temple, KL 98
Changi Point, Singapore 415
Changi Prison, Singapore 414
Changi Village, Singapore 415
Cheng Hoon Teng Temple, Melaka 168
Chinatown, Singapore 404
Chinese and Japanese Gardens, Singapore
   413

Chinese, Indonesia 509
Chinese, Sabah 298
Chinese, Sarawak 239
Christ Church, Melaka 166
Cibodas 571
Cilacap 589
Cipanas 571
Cipanas hot springs 584
Cirebon 579
Cisarua 571
City Hall, Singapore 396
Clan Piers, Penang 139
Clifford Pier, Singapore 402
Climate
   Bali 670
   Indonesia 494
   Irian Jaya 989
   Malaysia 55
   Maluku 971
   Regional 30
   Singapore 369
   Sulawesi 860
   Sumatra 733
Colonial Core, Singapore 396
Crafts
   Irian Jaya 993
   Kalimantan 823
   Lombok 908
   Malaysia 80
   Sabah 300
   Sarawak 245
Crafts, Brunei 469
Crocker Range National Park 312
Culture & Life
   Bali 677
   Borneo 228
   Brunei 468
   Java 527
   Kalimantan 823
   Malaysia 72
   Sabah 296
   Singapore 379
Culture System 521

D
Damai Beach, Sarawak 256
Dance
   Bali 681
   Malaysia 78
Dance, drama and music
   Indonesia 507
   Java 529
   Malaysia 78
   Sarawak 244
   Singapore 382
Dani, Irian Jaya 998
Danum Valley, Sabah 338
Daruba 987
Dasa, Candi 719

Dayabumi Complex, KL   98
Dayang, Pulau   154
Demak   630
Desaru   178
Diarrhoea   24
Dieng Plateau   625
Dili   966
Diponegoro   596
Dompu   926
Donggala   892
Dua, Pulau   561
Duyung Besar, Pulau   209

E

East Coast Park, Singapore   414
EAST NUSA TENGGARA   929-970
EAST TIMOR   963-970
Economy
    Bali   684
    Brunei   471
    East Timor   965
    Indonesia   508
    Irian Jaya   994
    Malaysia   85
    Singapore   387
Elephant   225
Empress Place, Singapore   396
Endau Rompin National Park   191
Ende   939
Enggano Island   817
Environment
    Bali   666
    Borneo   223
    Brunei   460
    Indonesia   491
    Java   514
    Malaysia   54
    Singapore   369
    Sumatra   732

F

Fatahillah Square, Jakarta   542
Fauna and flora
    Irian Jaya   991
Filipinos, Sabah   298
Flora & Fauna
    Borneo   224
    Singapore   370
Flora and fauna
    Indonesia   495
    Malaysia   56
    Sulawesi   860
Flora and fauna, Brunei   461
FLORES   933-947
Fort Canning Park, Singapore   400
Fort Cornwallis, Penang   137
Fort Margherita, Kuching   251
Fort St John, Melaka   170

Fraser's Hill   116

G

Gamelan orchestra   534
Garut   583
Gede-Pangrango National Park   571
Gedung Songo   628
Genting Highlands   115
Georgetown   135
Geylang Serai, Singapore   414
Gianyar   712
Gili Air   916
Gili Meno   916
Gili Trewangan   916
Gilimanuk   729
Gilis, The   915
Glodok, Jakarta   544
Goa Gajah, Bali   705
Goddess of Mercy Temple, Penang   138
Golkar   507
Gomontong Caves   331
Gorontalo   894
Grajagan Bay   663
Grobogan   631
Gua Tambun   126
Gunung Gading National Park   254
Gunung Kinabalu National Park   322
Gunung Leuser Nature Reserve   754
Gunung Mulu National Park   285
Gunung Tapis Park   196
Gunungan, Banda Aceh   747
Gunungsitoli   770

H

Hajjah Fatimah Mosque, Singapore   409
Halmahera   987
Hamadi   997
Hantu, Pulau, Singapore   419
Harau Canyon   782
Haw Par Villa, Singapore   411
Head-hunting   243
Health   21
Hilisimaetano   770
History
    Bali   670
    Borneo   227
    Brunei   462
    East Timor   963
    Flores   934
    Indonesia   496
    Irian Jaya   991
    Jakarta   539
    Java   515
    Lombok   906
    Malaysia   61
    Maluku   972
    Sabah   293
    Sarawak   232

Singapore 371
Sulawesi 860
Sumatra 733
Ternate 983
Timor 956
Hornbill 227
Hornbill Festival 226
Hu'u 926

I

Ibans, Sarawak 240
Ijen Crater 663
Imogiri 598
Indianization 38
INDONESIA 490-1041
Ipoh 125
IRIAN JAYA 989-1002
Islam 39
Islam, Java 527
Istana Nural Iman, Brunei 478
Istiqlal Mosque, Jakarta 547

J

Jagaraga 727
Jago, Candi, Malang 645
JAKARTA 537-556
Jalan Ampang, KL 97
Jalan Tun Tan Cheng Lock, Melaka 167
Jambi 805
Janggala 516
Janur 678
Jasar, Gunung 121
Jatijajar Caves 599
JAVA 513-664
Jawi, Candi, Malang 644
Jayapura 997
Jepara 634
Jimbaran 700
Johor Bahru 175
Johor Lama 177
Jonkers Street, Melaka 167
Jopu 943
Jurong Bird Park, Singapore 412
Jurong Crocodile Paradise, Singapore 412
Jurong, Singapore 411

K

Kabanjahe 753
Kadazans, Sabah 296
Kakas Kasen 897
Kalasan, Candi, Prambanan 615
Kalbar 848
KALIMANTAN 821-855
Kaliuda 951
Kalsel 825
Kalteng 833

Kaltim 835
Kampung Ayer, 475
Kampung Cerating 202
Kampung Pulau Rusa 209
Kandang Kerbau (KK) wet market, Singapore 409
Kangar 151
Kanoman, Kraton, Cirebon 581
Kapal 723
Kapit 266
Kapitan Kling Mosque, Penang 139
Kapuas River 854
Karangasem 722
Karimunjawa Islands 635
Karo Batak 752
Karyaneka Handicraft Centre, KL 100
Kasepuhan, Kraton, Cirebon 579
Kasunanan Palace, Solo 617
Katong, Singapore 414
Kawangu 950
Kawi, Gunung 711
Kediri 516
Kefamenanu 961
Kehen, Pura 713
Kei Islands 988
Kek Lok Si Temple, Ayer Itam 141
Kelabits, Sarawak 243
Kelimutu 942
Kellie's Castle 125
Kendari 886
Keningau 314
Kenyahs and Kayans, Sarawak 242
Kenyir Lake 209
Kerapan Sapi 655
Kerinci-Seblat Nature Reserve 804
Ketam, Pulau 103
Khoo Kongsi, Penang 139
Kidal, Candi, Malang 646
Kinabatangan River 331
Kinilow 897
Kintamani 714
Klang 103
Klungkung 718
Kolaka 886
Kolonodale 888
KOMODO 931-933
Konfrontasi 237
Kong Meng San Phor Kark See Chinese Temple Complex, Singapore 416
Kota 542
Kota Bahru 213
Kota Belud 320
Kota Gede, Yogya 596
Kota Kinabalu 302
Kota Tinggi 177
Krakatau 564
Kranji War Memorial and Cemetery, Singapore 417
Kraton 526
Kraton of Yogyakarta 593

Kraton Ratu Boko, Prambanan   614
Kuala Belait, Brunei   483
Kuala Kangsar   127
Kuala Kedah   151
Kuala Lumpur   91
Kuala Perlis   151
Kuala Selangor   103
Kuala Selangor Nature Park   103
Kuala Terengganu   208
Kuantan   193
Kubah National Park   254
Kuching   248
Kudat   321
Kudus   633
Kukup   177
Kupang   957
Kusu, Singapore   419
Kuta   692
Kuta Beach, Lombok   921
Kutai National Park   841

L

Labuan Lalang   729
Labuan, Pulau   317
Labuan/Carita Beach, Java   562
Labuanbajo   936
Labuhan Lombok   920
Ladalero   944
Lagud Sebren Cocoa Research Station,
  Sabah   316
Lagundi Bay   771
Lahad Datu   337
Lake Gardens, KL   99
Lambir Hills   281
Lampung Textiles   819
Land
    Bali   666
    Brunei   460
    Flores   933
    Indonesia   491
    Irian Jaya   989
    Java   514
    Lombok   904
    Malaysia   54
    Singapore   369
    Sulawesi   857
    Sumatra   732
Langkawi   152
Langoan   899
Language
    East Nusa Tenggara   931
    Indonesia   504
    Singapore   382
Language & Literature
    Malaysia   77
Larantuka   946
Lawas   292
Lazarus Island, Singapore   419
Lease Islands   980

Ledang, Gunung   172
Legian   692
Lembata   947
Leong San See Temple, Singapore   409
Limbang   291
Lingsar, Lombok   919
Little India, Singapore   407
LOMBOK   904-922
Lombong   177
Long Iram   846
Long Lunuk   846
Lore Lindu National Park   890
Loro Jonggrang, Candi, Prambanan   612
Los Palos   970
Lovina Beach   727
Luhur, Pura   725
Lumut   128
Lundu   254
Lutungan Island   893
Luwu, See Palopo

M

Madai Caves   337
Madura Island   655
Maduwe Karang, Pura   727
Magelang   611
Mahabharata   505
Mahakam River   843
Mahayana Buddhism   40
Majapahit   517
Makale   880
Malang   642
Malaria   25
Malay Cultural Village, Singapore   414
Malays, Sarawak   239
MALAYSIA   51-366
Malaysian Armed Forces Museum, KL
  104
Maleo bird   900
Maluk   924
MALUKU   971-988
Manado   895
Manatuto   968
Maninjau, Lake   779
Marang   206
Martapura   829
Marudi   284
Mas   703
Masjid Jame, KL   96
Masjid Kampung Laut   218
Masjid Negara, KL   99
Mat Salleh   313
Mataram   519, 910
Maubessi   970
Maumere   944
Maxwell Hill   131
Mayura Water Palace and Gardens,
  Cakranegara   911
Medan   738

Medan Merdeka, Jakarta   544
Melak   846
Melaka   161
Melanaus, Sarawak   240
Melolo   951
Mendut, Candi, Borobudur   610
Mengkabong, Sabah   306
Mengwi, Bali   724
Menjangan, Pulau   729
Mentawi Islands   801
Merak   561
Merang   212
Merapi, Mount   598, 663, 780
Merauke   1001
Merdeka Stadium, KL   98
Merlion, Singapore   401
Mersing   184
meru   724
Meru Betiri Reserve   663
Mesjid Raya Baiturrahman, Banda Aceh   746
Meulaboh   751
Minangkabau   772
Ming Village, Singapore   414
Miri   279
Moko Drum   948
Monas, Jakarta   544
Moni   942
Moon of Pejeng, Bali   708
Morotai   987
Morowali Nature Reserve   888
Moyo Island   924
Muara Jambi   806
Muara Muntai   844
Muara Takus   795
Muara, Brunei   482
Mudras   608
Muna   886
Muruts, Sabah   297
Museum Bali, Denpasar   689
Museum of the History of Jakarta   543
Music
    Bali   683
    Malaysia   78
    Sarawak   244
Muzium Budaya, Melaka   167
Muzium Negara, KL   99

N

Namberala   961
Narmada   918
National Art Gallery, KL   96
National Monument, KL   99
National Museum and Art Gallery, Singapore   399
National Museum, Jakarta   545
National parks, Indonesia   496
National Zoo & Aquarium, Malaysia   104
Negara   730

Ngadas   646
Nggela   943
Niah National Park   276
Nias Island   766
Nonyas   168
Nusa Dua   701
Nusa Lembongan   698
Nusa Penida   698

O

Odalan   679
Oil Industry   794
Old Gowa   864
Ophir, Mount   172
Orang Asli Museum, KL   102
Orang Asli, Malaysia   75
Orang Ulu, Sarawak   241
Orang utan   224
Orchard Road, Singapore   403

P

Padaido Islands   996
Padang   797
Padang Besar   151
Padang Lawas   765
Padangbai   719
Padangsidempuan   765
Padri Wars   773
Pagaralam   814
Pagaruyung   781
Pah Auman   854
Palang   241
Palangkaraya   834
Palembang   807
Palopo   885
Palu   891
Pamekasan   659
Panataran, Candi, Blitar   641
Pancasila   502
Pangandaran   584
Pangkor Laut   129
Pangkor, Pulau   129
Pangururan   764
Pantai Cinta Berahi   217
Pantai Kundor   171
Papar   319
Parangtritis   598
Pare Pare   870
Pariangan   781
Parliament House, Singapore   396
Pasar Terapung, Banjarmasin   827
Pasir Putih   663
Pawon, Candi, Borobudur   610
Pekalongan   636
Pekan   192
Pekanbaru   793
Pelabuhanratu   569
Pemangtangsiantar   755

Penampang, KK   306
Penan, Sarawak   255
Penang   132
Penang Bridge   139
Penang Hill   140
Penang Museum & Art Gallery   138
Penanjung National Park   585
Penans, Sarawak   242
Pencak silat   776
Pendolo   888
Penelokan   714
Penrissen, Gunung   254
Penujak   921
Penyenget Island   790
People
    Flores   934
    Irian Jaya   993
    Kalimantan   823
    Malaysia   72
Perak Tong   126
Peranakan Place Museum, Singapore
    403
Peranakans   168
Perhentian, Pulau   213
Petaling Jaya, KL   102
Pinang, Pulau   132
Piracy   233
Plaosan, Candi, Prambanan   614
Politics
    Brunei   470
    Indonesia   507
    Malaysia   82
    Sabah   300
    Sarawak   247
    Singapore   383
Pombo Island   977
Pontianak   849
Poring Hot Springs   327
Port Dickson   160
Port Klang   103
Port, Singapore   400
Porta de Santiago, Melaka   166
Portuguese Settlement, Melaka   170
Poso   890
Poso, Lake   889
Prailiu   950
Prambanan   612
Prambanan, Candi   612
Prapat   757
Pre-colonial History   36
President Suharto   507
Pringgasela   920
Probolinggo   660
Proboscis monkey   225
Pua kumbu   245
Pugung Raharja Archaeological Park   818
Pulau Berhala   332
Pulau Tiga National Park   319
Puncak Pass   571
Pura Mangkunegaran, Solo   619

Purwodadi Botanical Gardens, Malang
    644
Putra World Trade Centre, KL   98

Q

Queen Elizabeth Walk, Singapore   401

R

Raden Kartini   636
Raffles City Complex, Singapore   396
Raffles Hotel, Singapore   398
Raffles, Thomas Stamford   372
Rafflesia flower   780
Railway Station, KL   96
Ramayana   505
Ranau & Kundasang   326
Rantepao   880
Rasa Village   970
Rawa, Pulau   190
Redang, Pulau   212
Rejang River   263
Religion
    Bali   678
    Borneo   229
    Brunei   469
    Indonesia   503
    Java   527
    Malaysia   76
    Singapore   382
Rembang   634
Remboken   899
Rende   951
Reo   938
Rhinoceros   227
Rhinoceros, Javan   563
Rhinoceros, Sumatran   806
Riau Archipelago   784
Ridley, Henry 'Mad'   411
Rinca Island   931
Ringlet   121
Rinjani, Mount   917
ROTI   961
Ruteng   937

S

SABAH   293-343
Sabah State Museum   303
Sabang   749
Sade   921
sago palm   973
Sago Street, Singapore   405
Sailendra   515
Sakayamuni Buddha Gaya Temple,
    Singapore   409
Sakenan, Pura   696
Sam Poh Tong   125
Samarinda   840

Sambisari, Candi, Prambanan   616
Same   970
Samosir Island   759
Sandakan   328
Sangeh   724
Sangihe   902
Sangiran   621
Sanjaya   516
Santa Cruz   967
Santubong, Gunung   256
Sanur   696
Sao Wisata   944
Saparua   980
Sape   928
Sapit   920
SARAWAK   230-292
Sarawak Cultural Village   254
Sarawak Museum   250
Sari, Candi, Prambanan   615
Sasirangan   834
Savu Island   962
Sawah   514
Sawangan   899
Sawentar, Candi, Blitar   642
Science Centre, Singapore   413
Seba   962
Second World War   46
Seking, Pulau, Singapore   419
Selangor Pewter Factory   104
Selekta   646
Semarang   628
Sematan   254
Semeru, Mount   662
Semonggoh Orang Utan Sanctuary   253
Semporna   340
Senggigi   914
Sengkang   872
Sentosa   417
Sepilok Orang Utan Rehabilitation Centre
   336
Seram   981
Serangan Island   696
Seremban   157
Seri Taman, KL   99
Seria, Brunei   482
Seribu, Pulau   558
Sewu, Candi, Prambanan   614
Shah Alam   102
Shifting cultivation   32
Shifting cultivation, Sarawak   239
Short Wave Radio Guide   19
Siak Sri Indrapura   795
Siallagan village   763
Sibayak, Mount   754
Sibolga   765
Sibu   263
Sibu, Pulau   190
Sidikalang   751
Sikka   944
Silam, Gunung   338

Simanindo   764
Similajau National Park   275
SINGAPORE   367-454
Singapore River   401
Singapore Zoological Gardens   416
Singaraja   726
Singasari   517
Singasari, Candi, Malang   644
Singkarak, Lake   781
Singkawang   853
Sintang   855
Sipidan Island Marine Reserve   341
Sister's Island, Singapore   419
Siva, Candi, Prambanan   612
Skrang   262
Snake Temple, Penang   142
Soe   960
Solo   616
Sonder   897
Songket   810
South East Maluku   988
spices of Maluku   973
Sri Mahamariamman Temple, KL   97
Sri Mariamann Temple, Penang   138
Sri Mariamman Temple, Singapore   406
Sri Menanti   159
Sri Perumal, Singapore   409
Sri Veeramakaliamman Temple, Singapore
   409
Srivijaya   733
St Andrew's Cathedral, Singapore   399
St George's Cathedral, Penang   138
St John's, Singapore   419
St Paul's Church, Melaka   166
St Paul's Hill, Melaka   166
St Peter's Church, Melaka   170
Stadthuys, Melaka   166
Straits Chinese   168
Sukarara   921
Sukuh, Candi   620
SULAWESI   857-902
Sultan Mosque, Singapore   409
Sultan of Brunei   458
SUMATRA   731-820
SUMBA   949-955
SUMBAWA   922-928
Sumbawa Besar   924
Sumenep   659
Sunburn   25
Sunda Kelapa, Jakarta   542
Sungai Penuh   804
Sungguminasa   866
Supreme Court, Singapore   396
Surabaya   648
Surakarta   616
Suranadi   919
Sze Ya Temple, KL   98

T

Taiping 130
Takengon 751
Talaud Islands 902
Taliwang 924
Taman Ayun, Pura 724
Taman Impian Jaya Ancol, Jakarta 550
Taman Mini-Indonesia, Jakarta 549
Taman Negara (National Park) 199
Taman Purbakala Waruga 899
Taman Sari 595
Taman Tasek Perdana Walk-in Aviary, KL 99
Tambora, Mount 925
Tambun Hot Springs 127
Tambunan 312
Tampuruli, Sabah 306
Tamus 298
Tanah Lot 724
Tanah Rata 122
Tang Dynasty City, Singapore 413
Tangkoko Batu Angus National Park 900
Tangkuban Prahu 576
Tanimbar Islands 988
Tanjung Pagar, Singapore 406
Tanjung Aru Beach, Sabah 306
Tanjung Bidara 171
Tanjung Kling 171
Tanjung Pinang 789
Tanjung Puting National Park 834
Tao 764
Tapai 299
Tapaktuan 751
Tarakan 847
Tasek Bera 196
Tasek Cini, Kuantan 195
Tasikmalaya 584
Tattoos 238
Tawangmangu 624
Tegen Koripan, Pura 715
Tekong, Pulau, Singapore 419
Teluk Bahang 147
Teluk Cempedak, Kuantan 193
Telukdalam 770
Temburong, Brunei 481
Tempasuk 320
Temple of the Goddess of Heaven, KL 100
Temple Street, Singapore 405
Templer Park, KL 101
Tengah Pulau 190
Tenganan 719
Tenggarong 844
Tenom 314
Tentena 889
Ternate & Tidore 983
Tetebatu 919
Textile Museum, Jakarta 547

Textiles, Sarawak 245
Theatre, Singapore 396
Theravada Buddhism 40
Thian Hock Keng Temple, Singapore 405
Tiger Balm Gardens, Singapore 411
Tiger Balm Story, Singapore 412
TIMOR 956-970
Tinggi, Pulau 190
Tioman, Pulau 186
Tirta Empul 712
Tirtagangga 723
Toba, Lake 755
Toli-Toli 893
Tomohon 897
Tomok 761
Tondano 899
Tondano, Lake 899
Toraja 873
Transmigration 732
Travelling with Children & Babies 14
Tretes 647
Trikora Beach 791
Trowulan 651
Trusmadi, Gunung 312
Trusmi 582
Tuban 653
Tuk Tuk 761
Tumpat 218
Tunku Abdul Rahman National Park 311
Turtle Islands National Park 334
Tutong, Brunei 482

U

Ubin, Pulau, Singapore 419
Ubud 703
Ujung Kulon National Park 562
Ujung Pandang 863
Ulun Danau Bratan, Pura 725
Uluwatu Temple 700

V

Vereenigte Ooste-Indische Compagnie 520
Victoria Memorial Hall, Singapore 396
VOC 520

W

Wah Aik Shoemaker Shop, Melaka 167
Waiara 944
Waikabubak 954
Waingapu 950
Walis 528
Wamena 999
Wasur National Park 1001
Watampone 872
Way Kambas Elephant Reserve 818
wayang 529

Wayang Museum, Jakarta 543
Wayang topeng 533
Weh 749
WEST NUSA TENGGARA 903-928
WEST TIMOR 957-962
wet rice cultivation 33-34
White Rajah, The 234
Wisma Loke, KL 100
Wolowaru 943
Women travelling alone 16

Wonosobo 625
World Trade Centre, Singapore 400

Y

Yeh Gangga, Pura 725
Yeh Pulu 706
Yogyakarta 589

TOWN AND REGIONAL MAPS

MALAYSIA

Bintulu   274
Cameron Highlands   119
East Coast Malaysia   182
Georgetown   136-137
Ipoh   126
Johor Bahru   176
Kapit   267
Kota Bahru   215
Kota Kinabalu   304
Kuala Lumpur environs   101
Kuala Lumpur Main Streets   92-93
Kuala Terengganu   208
Kuantan   194
Kuching   249
Langkawi   153
Malaysia   52
Malaysian Railways   349
Melaka   163
Miri   280
Mount Kinabalu National Park   323
Mulu National Park   286
Niah Caves National Park   277
North of Kuala Lumpur   117
Pulau Pangkor   129
Pulau Pinang   133
Pulau Tioman   187
Sabah   294
Sandakan Bay   332
Sandakan   330
Sarawak   231
Sibu   264
South of Kuala Lumpur   158
Taman Negara   199
Upper Rejang   271

SINGAPORE

Arab Street   410
Chinatown   406
Colonial core   397
Little India   408
Orchard Road   402-403
Singapore General   394-395
Singapore MRT   439
Singapore   368

BRUNEI

Brunei   460
Bandar Seri Begawan   477

INDONESIA

Ambon Island   975
Ambon Town   976
Around Banjarmasin   830
Bali   669
Baliem Valley   999
Balikpapan   837
Banda Aceh   747
Bandung   573
Bangka Island   811
Banjarmasin   828
Batam, Pulau   786
Banten   560
Bintan, Pulau   789
Bengkulu   815
Bogor   566
Borobudur Environs   605
Bukittinggi   777
Bukittinggi Environs   779
Candi Siwu   614
Central Java   588
Central Sulawesi   887
Cirebon   580
Denpasar   691
Dieng Plateau   626
Dili   968
East Java   639
East Timor   963
Ende   940
Ende Environs   942
Flores Island   934
Goa Gajah   705
Gunung Kawi   711
Indonesia   492-493
Irian Jaya   990
Jakarta Centre   546
Jakarta General   538
Kalimantan   822
Kalimantan Selalan   826
Komodo National Park   932
Kota & Sunda Kelapa   543
Kraton Palace   593
Kudus   634
Kupang   958
Lombok Island   907
Madura Island   656
Mahakam River   845
Malang   643
Malang Environs and Mt Bromo   645
Maluku   972
Manado Environs   898
Manado   896

Mataram   912-913
Medan   740
Merpati/Garuda, Bouraq
 & Mandala Routes   1006-1007
Mount Bromo   661
Nias Island   767
North & East Bali   714
Northern Sumatra   739
Nusa Tenggara   930
Padang   798
Palembang   808
Palu   891
Panataran Complex   641
Pangandaran   585
Pelni Shipping Routes   1008-1009
Pekanbaru   795
Pontianak   850
Prambanan Group   613
Riau Archipelago   785
Sabang Island   750
Samarinda   841
Samosir Island   760
Selatan   826
Semarang   629
Siberut Island (Mentawai)   802
Solo   617
South Bali   693
South Sulawesi   871
Southern Sumatra   774-775
Sulawesi   858-859
Sumba Island   950
Sumbawa Island   923
Surabaya   649
Tana Toraja   881

Tanjung Pinang   790
Ternate & Tidore Islands   984
Trowulan   652
Ubud Environs   703
Ujung Pandang   865
Uluwatu   701
Weh Island   750
West Java   559
West Timor   957
Yogyakarta   591
Yogya Environs   597

ILLUSTRATIONS

Bali pura   675
Borobudur reliefs   607
Candi (Java)   525
dongson drum   582
Iban hornbill   226
Karang sae   524
Karo Batak House end   753
Madura boats   582
Mudras   609
Pinisi schooner   867
Rangda   682
Sumba blankets   953
Toba Batak cross section   763
Toraja House   876
Wayang gunungan   532
Wayang kresna   531
Wayang semar   531

INDEX OF TINTED BOXES

INTRODUCTION

Travelling with children & babies in Southeast Asia   14
Distinctive fruits of Southeast Asia   17
Short wave radio guide   19
Maps of mainland Southeast Asia   20
Diarrhoea – diagnosis and treatment   24
Health: children & babies   26
Heat & lust: colonial impressions   30
Fields in the forest – shifting cultivation   32
The cycle of wet rice cultivation   34
The universal stimulant – the betel nut   35
In Siddhartha's footsteps: a short history of Buddhism   36
The practice of Islam: living by the Prophet   39
Penis balls and sexual roles in historical Southeast Asia   41

MALAYSIA

Putting Malaya on the map   53
Climatic variations: yes, we have no monsoons   55
Nepenthes – the jungle's poisoned chalice   57
Fireflies – flashers in the forest   60
Malaysia's monarchs – the public swings against the sultans   62
The Malay Istana – royals on the riverside   71
Malay magic and the spirits behind the prophet   77
Drugs trafficking – stiff punishment   83
Mahathir Mohamad – the doctor's prescription   84
The New Economic Policy – Malaysia's recipe for racial harmony   86
Environment – mud-slinging in the greenhouse   88
Malaysia: fact file   89
Kuala Lumpur highlights   91
The only legal hash in Malaysia   98
Kuala Lumpur's Golden Triangle   100
Proton Saga: driving the flag   104
Jungle walks: Cameron Highlands   120
Perak: the silver state that grew rich on tin   127
Penang highlights   132
Brand-name satay from the source   159
Minangkabau – the 'buffalo-horn' people from across the water   160
Sunken treasure and the mystery of the Flor de la Mar   164
The Nonyas and the Babas   168
Modern Johor: riding on the merlion's tail   177
Islam on the East Coast: fundamental pointers   183
Pahang: the land of the sacred tree   193
Dateline Kuantan: Churchill's Malayan nightmare   195

The Giant leatherback turtle (*Dermochelys coriacea*) **203**
The Crown-of-Thorns – the terminator on the reef **210**
Cementing neighbourly relations **214**
The Iban hornbill festival **226**
Piracy: the resurgence of an ancient scourge **233**
James Brooke: the white knight errant **234**
Konfrontasi **237**
Tribal tattoos **238**
Shifting cultivation – how to grow hill rice **239**
The palang – the stimulant that makes a vas diferens **241**
Skulls in the longhouse: heads you win **243**
A town called Cat **250**
A ceramic inheritance **253**
The Penan – museum pieces for the 21st century? **255**
Visiting longhouses: house rules **260**
Sarawak's river express boats – smoke on the water **265**
The Rajahs' fortresses – war and peace on the Rejang **268**
The longhouse – prime-site apartments with river view **269**
The massacre at Long Nawang **272**
Niah's guano collectors: scraping the bottom **277**
How to make a swift buck **278**
A land where money grows on trees **282**
Tamus – Sabah's markets and trade fairs **298**
Tapai – Sabah's rice wine **299**
Chips on the shoulder and chips on the table **301**
The Saba Foundation **305**
Mat Salleh – fort-builder and folk hero **313**
The railway which ran out of steam **315**
Agnes Keith's house **329**
The Borneo death march **331**
Edible nests **333**
The tough life of a turtle **336**
The long John Silvers of Sabah's east coast **339**
Selected air fares **346**
Festivals in East Malaysia **356**
Malaysian manners – as learned from a princess **358**
Dr Watson solves the Malayan malaria mystery **360**
Learning the language – a practical alternative **364**
Useful Malaysian words and phrases **365**

SINGAPORE

Flower power **370**
Thomas Stamford Raffles: architect of Singapore **372**
Chinese immigration: Singapore's life-blood **374**
Population policies and designer genes **380**
Harry Lee Kuan Yew – father of modern Singapore **384**
The Central Providence Fund – saving for a rainy day **388**
Singapore traffic – no more for the road **389**
Singapore: fact file **391**

Singapore highlights   393
The *Raffles Hotel* – immortalised and sanitized   398
Bankers' rising aspirations   401
Shopping centres on Orchard Road   404
'Mad Ridley' – the rubber missionary   411
The Tiger Balm story   412
Changi Airport: prisoner of war camp to international travel hub   415

BRUNEI

Brunei's hydrocarbonated economy   458
The Sultan of Brunei – living by the profit   472
Brunei: fact file   474

INDONESIA

The regions of Indonesia   491
Indonesia's climate   494
Major pre-colonial powers   497
The expansion of Dutch influence and control   498
A stroll along Jalan history   500
Pancasila: Sukarno's five principles   502
The Ramayana and Mahabharata   505
Art forms and where to find them   506
The politics of envy: the Chinese in Indonesia   509
Indonesia: fact file   511

JAVA

Sawah : wet rice cultivation in Java   514
The Curse of the Kris-maker   517
A summary of Javanese history 400–1870   518
The building sequence in Java (late 6th – late 15th century)   522
The Javanese candi   524
The Javanese kraton   526
The nine Walis of Java   528
Making a wayang kulit puppet   530
A batik primer   535
Jakarta highlights   537
The Chinese of Java & Jakarta   540
Jakarta's heroic monuments   545
The kris: martial and mystic masterpiece of the Malay world   548
The Javan rhinoceros (*Rhinoceros sondaicus*): the rarest mammal on earth?   563
The legend of Nyi Loro Kidul, the Queen of the South Seas   570
Bandung's Art Deco heritage   574
The Angklung   575
Cirebon rock & cloud designs   579
The Hamengkubuwono sultans of Yogyakarta (1749 to the present day)   590
Diponegoro: prince and early freedom fighter   596

Courtship Javanese style – the *lamaran*   600
Borobudur: what's in a name?   605
Mudras and the Buddha Image   608
A short history of the Susuhunan of Surakarta   619
The life-blood of the Indonesian male: the clove or 'kretek' cigarette   635
Raden Kartini   636
Dvarapala or Temple guardians   644
The Battle for Surabaya   650
Kerapan sapi (bull racing)   655
Traditional boats of Madura   657

BALI

Bali highlights   667
The gift of water: rice and water in Bali   668
The banjar   677
Janur   678
The Balinese calendars: *saka* and *wuku*   679
Self-immolation and human sacrifice in a Dutch account of 1633   681
Bronze kettledrums of Vietnam   706
The 1979 festival of Eka Dasa Rudra at Pura Besakih   716
The Bali Aga: the original Balinese   720
Cloth as art: ikat in Southeast Asia   721
The Balinese pagoda: the meru   724

SUMATRA

Transmigration: 'A matter of life and death'   732
Sumatra: good buys   736
The Aceh War (1873-1878)   746
Karo Batak architecture   752
The Gunung Leuser Nature Reserve   754
The Bataks of North Sumatra   756
Hiking across the Central Highlands   761
Toba Batak architecture   762
The main temples at Padang Lawas   766
The earthquake-proof houses of Nias   768
Islam versus tradition: the Padri Wars   773
Pencak silat: martial art of West Sumatra   776
Rafflesia arnoldi: the largest flower in the world   780
Places of interest around Batusangkar: the Minang *darek*   781
Batam: Singapore's industrial zone and holiday playground   787
Business milestones   792
Black gold – Indonesia's oil industry   794
Small and hairy: the Sumatran Rhinoceros   806
Cloths of gold and silver: *kain songket*   810
Bangka's tin mines   812
Ship cloths and *tapis*: textiles of Lampung   819

KALIMANTAN

Traditional Banjarese architecture – high ridged roofs   824
The Hill Dayaks of Kalsel – a fragile culture   831
Sasirangan tie-dyes – from the shaman to the shop shelves   834
Balikpapan's streetnames – selamat jalan-jalan   836
Deforestation in Kalimantan – the chainsaw massacre   839
Pontianak's red-light district – forlorn hopes   851
Entikong's fiscal advantages   854

SULAWESI

A Noah's Ark: endemic animals of Sulawesi   861
The original bogeymen – the Bugis of South Sulawesi   864
Bogeymen and antimaccasars   866
The *Pinisi* schooner of Sulawesi   867
Buginese textiles of Sengkang   873
The buffalo: symbol of wealth & power   874
Torajan mortuary effigies (*Tau Tau*)   878
Trekking around Rantepao   883
Torajan ikat blankets   884
Lake Poso   889
The extraordinary maleo bird   900

WEST NUSA TENGGARA, LOMBOK AND SUMBAWA

Lombok highlights   904
Wallace's Line   905
Islam Waktu Telu   910

EAST NUSA TENGGARA AND EAST TIMOR

Indonesia's living dinosaur: the Komodo Dragon   932
The textiles of Flores   935
Traditional architecture: *ngadhu* and *bhaga*   938
The old Catholics of Larantuka   946
Lamalera's whaling   947
The *Moko* drum currency debacle   948
The Sumbanese slave trade   949
Villages, houses & tombs of Sumba   951
The ikat *hinggi* blankets of Sumba   952
Sumba death rites   954
The Massacre at Santa Cruz, November 1991   967

MALUKU

Multi-purpose tree par excellence: the Sago Palm   973
Butchery in the Bandas: the curse of the spice trade   978

IRIAN JAYA

The bird of paradise: legless bird of God   992
Master craftsmen: the Asmat of Irian Jaya   994

INFORMATION FOR VISITORS (INDONESIA)

Selected Garuda and Merpati air fares   1011
Selected train timetable and fares: Java   1012-1013
Selected bus fares   1014-1015
Driving in Indonesia   1010
Selected Pelni fares   1016
An Indonesian food glossary   1018
Tempe: soybean cake   1020
Jamu: herbal drink   1021
The Indonesian day   1022
Useful Indonesian words and phrases   1028

INDEX OF ADVERTISERS

Bradt Publications, UK   13
Explore Worldwide, UK   Endpaper "a"
Forum Travel, USA   493
International Student Identity Card   map section
Kosa Travel Agency, Sabah   310
School of Oriental and African Studies, University of London   Endpaper "f"
STA Travel, London   Endpaper "b"
Travelling Light, UK   50